W0007694

Britains Leading Yachting Group

Boatbuilding, Repair & Maintenance

The Berthon Boat Company has been building top quality ocean going yachts for over 150 years. We provide full expertise for the construction, refit & repair of motor and sailing yachts up to 100' in wood, steel, aluminium, GRP and all other composite materials.

From our Lymington yard we have launched a wide variety of craft including blue water sailing yachts, tough R.N.L.I. lifeboats and world cruising motor yachts such as the Berthon 80.

Berthon craftsmen & engineers are equally at home installing modern electronic navigational & communications equipment or working with teak laid decks. The yard offers full rigging facilities and in its under-cover heated workshop – spray painting, osmosis treatment, engine overhauls and all other yacht maintenance.

Dry Sailing

The Berthon Boat Company offers a truly competitive annual Dry Sailing programme which includes 22 lifts/launches, high pressure fresh water rinse and free ashore storage.

The annual rate is based on overall length.

Contact: Steve Mehlmann
Berthon Boat Company
Tel: 0590 673312
Fax: 0590 676353

Berthon 80

Berthon's Lymington Marina

250 permanent berths and 100 visitors' berths, all with full facilities, near to the centre of Lymington town. Berthon's Marina, less than 5 miles from the Needles is the ideal port-of-call for crossings to and from France and perfectly situated for victualling and servicing.

Contact: Peter Crook
Berthon's
Lymington Marina
Tel: 0590 673312
Fax: 0590 679811

Berthon International

The UK's leading yacht brokerage house with over 1,500 listings of cruising, racing and motor yachts world-wide. With offices in the U.K. and the Mediterranean, in an increasingly international market our reputation as professional, experienced and dependable brokers has given us unparalleled success.

Contact: Robin Campbell
Berthon International
Tel: 0590 679222
Fax: 0590 679811

Berthon Boat Company, The Shipyard, Lymington, Hampshire SO41 9YL Tel: 0590 673312 Fax: 0590 676353

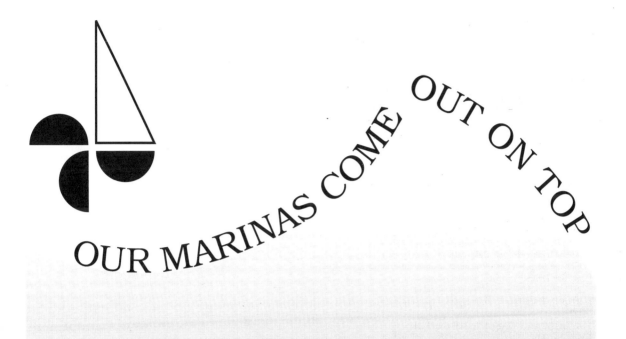

OUR MARINAS COME OUT ON TOP

At Yacht Havens Ltd we have established ourselves at the forefront of UK marina development and management. **Lymington Yacht Haven** paved the way in the early seventies, providing a superb base in the Solent for the cruising and the racing yachtsman.

Our experience has stretched further afield to **Swansea Yacht Haven** where our marina forms the focal point of the city's multi-million pound Maritime Quarter.

In Scotland we have created **Largs Yacht Haven,** perfectly located in the sheltered waters of the magnificent Clyde estuary, providing access to some of the world's finest cruising grounds.

All our yachting centres operate with the same high standards of efficiency and helpfulness, combined with all the modern facilities that today's discerning yachtsman requires.

Let us take care of your yacht this year and you will enjoy the benefits of berthing with Britain's leading marina operator.

LARGS YACHT HAVEN	**LYMINGTON YACHT HAVEN**	**SWANSEA YACHT HAVEN**
Tel: 0475 675333	Tel: 0590 677071	Tel: 0792 470310
Fax: 0475 672245	Fax: 0590 678186	Fax: 0792 463948

YACHT HAVENS LTD, King's Saltern Road, Lymington, Hampshire, SO41 9XY

First published 1980
This edition published 1991 by Macmillan Press Ltd
a division of MACMILLAN PUBLISHERS LTD
London and Basingstoke

This book is sold under the standard conditions of the Net Book Agreement.

British Cataloguing In Publication Data
A CIP catalogue record for this book is available for this book from the British Library.

ISBN 0–333–52381–4

MACMILLAN CONSULTANT EDITOR
Klaus Boehm

IMPORTANT NOTE
Whilst every care has been taken in compiling the information contained in this Almanac, the Publishers and Editors accept no responsibility for any errors or omissions, or for any accidents or mishaps which may arise from its use.

CORRESPONDENCE
Letters on editorial matters should be addressed to:
The Editors, the Macmillan & Silk Cut Nautical Almanac, St Olaf's, Wonston, Winchester, Hampshire, SO21 3LP, or 41 Arbor Lane, Winnersh, Wokingham, Berks RG11 5JE

Enquiries about despatch, invoicing or commercial matters should be addressed to:

Customer Services Department,
Macmillan Press Ltd, Houndmills, Basingstoke,
Hampshire RG21 2XS

Enquiries about advertising space should be addressed to:
Communications Management International,
Chiltern House, 120 Eskdale Avenue, Chesham,
Buckinghamshire HP5 3BD

Chapters 1–9   Page preparation by
                Wyvern Typesetting Limited, Bristol
Chapter 10   Cartography and page preparation by
                Lovell Johns Ltd, Oxford
Colour artwork by Dick Vine
Editorial colour separations by Excel Photolit Ltd, Slough

Printed and bound in Hong Kong

THE MACMILLAN & SILK CUT NAUTICAL ALMANAC

1991

EDITORS   Wing Commander B.D'Oliveira OBE, FRIN

Rear Admiral I.J. Lees-Spalding CB

CONSULTANT   Commander R.L. Hewitt LVO, RN
EDITORS   MIMechE, MRINA, FRIN

M.W. Richey MBE, Hon MRIN

W. Nicholson BSc, FRAS

K.E. Best

MACMILLAN

Our support team is the best in the business

With an Autohelm, you've invested in an autopilot that's designed and built to give years of outstanding service.

However, should it ever need attention we want you to know that there is a network of Service Centres to get you back in action quickly – if you're on a holiday cruise that's a really important point.

Each Service Centre has factory trained staff and comprehensive stocks of parts. Service Centres are located conveniently in every major sailing area and each one is a leading marine electronics specialist.

As part of the best team in the business they are ready to give you their help – when you need it – wherever you sail.

Autohelm Service Centres – U.K., Eire & Channel Islands

Factory Service
Nautech Ltd, Portsmouth
(0705) 693611

Hampshire
Emsworth
Greenham Marine
0243 378314
Lymington
Greenham Marine
0590 75771
Hamble
Greenham Marine
0489 575166
Hamble
Hudson Marine Electronics
0703 455129
Hamble
Hudson Marine Electronics
0703 454618
Hamble
Maricom
0703 454263
Isle of Wight
Regis Marine
0983 293996
Southampton
Regis Marine
0703 636555
Lymington
Regis Marine
0202 679251

Dorset
Poole
Danlea Electronics
0202 673880
Poole
Greenham Marine
0202 676363
Broadstone
Tolley Marine
0202 690028

Devon
Salcombe
Burwin Marine
054 884 3321
Dartmouth
Burwin Marine
080 43 5417
Brixham
T.D.S. Electrics
08045 58885
Plymouth
Ocean Marine Services
0752 223922
Plymouth
Sutton Marine
0752 662129
Plymouth
Tolley Marine
0752 222530

Berkshire
Thames Valley
Amberley Marine
0628 826104

Cornwall
Falmouth
Mylor Marine Electronics
0326 74001
Cornwall
Seacom
0326 76565

N.Devon
Marine Electronic Systems
080 52 2870

Avon & Gloucestershire
Bristol
A N D Electrics
0272 821441

Wales
Dyfed
Dale Sailing Co Ltd
0646 601636
Gwynedd
Rowlands Marine
0758 613193
Fleetwood
Jon N Jones
039 17 5241
Liverpool
Robbins Marine Radio
051 709 5431

Scotland
Ayrshire
Boat Electrics & Electronics
0290 315355
Ayrshire
Yacht Electrics & Electronics
0475 686463
Lothian
Forth Area Marine
031 331 4343
Shetland Isles
H Williamson & Sons Ltd
059 588 645
Aberdeen
Land & Sea Electronics Ltd
0224593281

Humberside
Hull
Electronics Marine
0482 25163

Norfolk
Norwich
R & J Marine
0603 897855

Suffolk
Lowestoft
Navtronics
0502 589159
Ipswich
R & J Marine
047 388 737

Essex
Maldon
Mansbrite Marine
0621 853003
Harwich
R & J Marine
0255 502849

Kent
Herne Bay
Heron Marine
0227 361255

Sussex
Brighton Marina
FAM Enterprises
0273 684 385
Itchenor
Regis Marine
0243 511070
Peacehaven
L D Electronics
0273 586179

Isle of Man & Eire
Ramsey
Bevan Ltd
0624 812583

Eire
Dublin 11
Eddie Brunker
0001 342590
Co Cork
Rider Services
010 353 3184 1176

Channel Islands
St Peter Port
Boatworks +
0481 26071
St Helier
Jersey Marine Electronics
0543 21603
Alderney
Mainbrayce Ltd
0481 82 2772

Autohelm Service Centres – France

Main Distributor

S.D. Marine Electronique
Tel: (010 33) 1 3914 6833
Tlx: 007 42 698347 SDMELEC
Fax: (010 33) 1 3913 3022

Local Service Centres

Grand Fort Philippe
Dieppe
Baude Electronique
28 23 10 92
Dunkerque
E.G.E.F.
28 59 34 56
Boulogne
Ocel
21 31 75 92
Lille
Chantier Naval du Nord
20 04 94 60/20 55 17 29
Saint Valery sur Somme
Latitude 50
22 26 82 06
Port en Bessin
L.K.E.
31 21 93 79
Carentan
Gam Marine
33 71 17 02
Saint Vaast La Hougue
Marelec
33 54 63 82

Cherbourg
Ergelin
Granville
Nautilec
33 50 04 96
Port du Herel
33 50 20 34
Saint Malo
S.E.E.
99 81 92 60
Saint Guenole
St Gue Electronique
98 58 74 98
Le Guilvinec
Cariou
98 58 12 90
Loctudy
E.B.S.
98 87 91 33
Concarneau
St Gue Electronique
98 97 50 86
C.E.S.
98 50 51 09
Lorient
Navelec
97 82 46 17
La Trinite sur Mer
S.E.E.M.A.
97 55 78 06
Les Sables d'Olonne
Masson
51 32 01 07
La Rochelle
Pochon
46 41 30 53
E.E.M.
35 84 54 24
Le Havre
Electronic Equipment
35 48 64 02
Honfleur
Labarriere
31 89 05 17
Deauville
Electronic Eqpmt
Top Marine
31 88 65 55

Ouistreham
Nauti Plaisance
31 97 03 08
Saint Brieuc
L'Habitat et la Mer
96 33 71 68
Paimpol
Le Lionnais Marine
96 20 85 18
M.E.E.
96 20 74 47
Brest
S.E.N
98 42 10 35
Morlaix
S.E.N.
98 88 42 42
Camaret
Celtic
97 83 06 07
Douarnenez
Poenot
98 92 02 98
Vannes
Marine'tronic
97 42 58 75
Quiberon
Marinelec
97 30 48 55
Arzal
Erelec
97 45 05 92
La Turballe
Hudault
40 23 30 77
Pornichet
Electro Nautic
40 61 25 01
Saint Nazaire
Emtec
40 66 42 10 Nazaire
St Gilles Croix de Vie
Force 5
51 55 83 57

Head straight for the best
Autohelm™

Contents

PERSONAL INDEX OF IMPORTANT PAGES

ATTENTION

SILK CUT NAUTICAL AWARDS

Now dubbed the 'Oscars of the sailing world', this highly respected Awards scheme seeks to recognise and reward acts of bravery and seamanship as well as outstanding nautical achievement.

The scheme is divided into five categories:- Seamanship, Rescue, Design, Club and Yachting Service and Yacht Racing. Nominations are judged by a distinguished judging committee, chaired by Chay Blyth. Prestigious nautical institutions are also represented – the RNLI, RYA Seamanship Foundation, H.M. Coastguard, The Royal Ocean Racing Club and The British Marine Industries Federation.

Over 4,000 nominations have been considered since the scheme's inception in 1983 and each year winners receive unique gold and glass plaques at a presentation in a top London hotel.

Candidates will be considered via press, radio and TV monitoring, the organisations represented by the judging committee and nominations from the public.

If you require further information or wish to put in a nomination please contact the Awards Secretary, Silk Cut Nautical Awards, 11a West Halkin Street, London SW1X 8JL. Tel. 071-235 7040.

SILK CUT HALL

As part of its continuing commitment to yachting, Silk Cut sponsor the Silk Cut Hall at the Southampton Boat Show in September which, since its introduction in 1985, has been visited by thousands of people each year. The hall houses a variety of exhibitors offering a wide range of maritime equipment and accessories. It also provides a large lounge bar area where visitors can relax away from the crowds.

ALL MARINERS

SILK CUT 'N' SAIL CHALLENGE

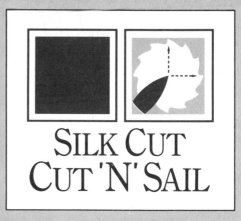

SILK CUT CUT 'N' SAIL

After the tremendous success of this event last year, entries are once again being invited from aspiring boat designers. This is the ultimate challenge in the design and fast construction of boats. Held at the Southampton Boat Show, competitors are challenged to build a boat from a very limited supply of materials provided in the fastest time possible. On the last day of the Show the resulting 'cruisers' will take to the water for the Great Race around a sheltered course. Prizes will be awarded for fast building, elegance, performance as well as originality of design! Sink or swim, this event is strictly for the adventurous! Aspiring designers should write for entry forms to Silk Cut 'N' Sail, 11a West Halkin Street, London SW1X 8JL. Tel. 071-235 7040.

MACMILLAN AND SILK CUT NAUTICAL ALMANAC AND YACHTSMAN'S HANDBOOK

These two authoritative nautical publications are essential reading for all yachtsmen.

Packed full of navigational data and information, the Almanac is now celebrating ten highly successful years and continues to go from strength to strength. With its comprehensive and meticulously researched chapters it is ideal for both armchair saling and the real thing! This is one item you cannot afford to leave ashore.

Its companion, the best-selling Yachtsman's Handbook contains carefully written and informative chapters covering such things as communications, navigation, weather forecasting, safety and boat handling. With its full colour illustrations and detailed indexing it ensures that information is easy to understand and always at your fingertips.

Be sure that your Almanac and Handbook are always on-board and sail safely with Silk Cut.

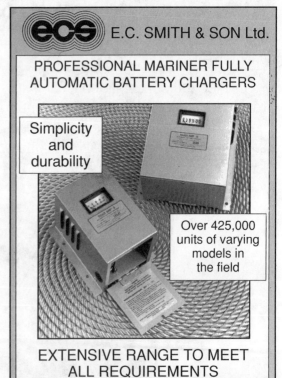

Quick Reference Marine Products and Services Guide

The following guide gives readers a quick reference to companies and organisations currently offering supplies or services to boat owners and the boating industry. Where possible, each entry carries a concise description and while every care is taken to ensure accuracy, the publisher does not necessarily endorse the information supplied.

BOAT BUILDERS
    & REPAIRS
BOOKS & CHARTS
CHANDLERS
CLOTHING
COMMUNICATIONS
    EQUIPMENT
ELECTRONIC EQUIPMENT
ELECTRONIC &
    ELECTRICAL ENGINEERS
ENGINES
FLAGS & PENNANTS
GENERAL MARINE
    EQUIPMENT & MACHINERY
HOLIDAYS
INSTRUMENTATION
    & POSITION FIXING
LIFERAFT HIRE & SERVICES
MAIL ORDER
MARINAS
MARINE ENGINEERS
MARINE INSURANCE
MARINE TRANSPORT
    & YACHT DELIVERIES
PAINT
REPAIR MATERIALS
SAFETY EQUIPMENT
SAILING SCHOOLS
SAILS
SPARS & RIGGING
YACHT BROKERS

BOAT BUILDERS & REPAIRS

BERTHON BOAT COMPANY
The Shipyard, Lymington,
Hampshire SO41 9YL
Tel: (0590) 673312
Fax: (0590) 676353
Provide full expertise for the construction, refit and repair of yachts in wood, steel, aluminium, GRP and all other composite materials, plus full rigging facilities, spray painting, osmosis treatment, engine overhauls and all other yacht maintenance.

BOATWORKS + LTD
Castle Emplacement,
St Peter Port, Guernsey
Tel: (0481) 26071
Fax: (0481) 714224
Boatworks+ provides a comprehensive range of services including electronics, chandlery, boatbuilding and repairs, engine sales and services, yacht brokerage, clothing and fuel supplies.

CAMBRIAN & WESTFLEET
The Boatyard,
Portway Village Marina,
Penarth, South Glamorgan
Tel: (0222) 709983
Boatbuilders and repairers, marine engineers, riggers, marine clothing specialists, chart agents, nautical booksellers, and yacht chandlers.

CAMUS MARINE SERVICES
Craobh Haven, Craignish,
By Lochgilphead, Argyll
Tel: (08525) 225/622/222
Fax: (08525) 252
Telex: 779828 Camus G
200 marina berths. Water. Electricity. Diesel fuel. Gas. Yacht repairs, fitting-out and engineering. Storage ashore. Chandlery. Brokerage. Insurance. Nearby facilities include: pub, shops, sailing school, dive centre, launderette, riding centre, hotels and guest houses, self catering accommodation. Electronic & electric installation & service. Agents for Yanmar, Bukl, L/P diesels, Honda & Mariner outboards.

CRINAN BOATS LTD
Crinan, By Lochgilphead,
Argyll PA31 8SP
Tel: (054 683) 232
Boatbuilders, chandlers, engineers, slipping, repairs, charts, electricians, pontoon.

DALE SAILING CO LTD
Brunel Quay, Neyland,
Milford Haven, Dyfed
Tel: (0646) 601636

Hull and engine repair and servicing, hauling out and storage, fuel, international interspray centre, comprehensive chandlery, main dealers for: Volvo Penta inboards, Mercury outboards, Dell Quay Dory, Furlex, Autohelm.

EVERSON AND SONS LTD
Phoenix Works, Riverside,
Woodbridge, Suffolk
Tel: (03943) 4358
Boatbuilding and marine engineers; chandlers and riggers; insurance and brokerage arranged. Full yard facilities.

FALMOUTH BOAT
CONSTRUCTION LTD
Little Falmouth Yacht Yard,
Flushing, Falmouth, Cornwall
TR11 5TJ
Tel: (0326) 74309
Fax: (0326) 77679
Repairs, refits, storage undercover and quayside, osmosis treatment specialists, resprays. Slipways to 100 ton. Commercial craft repairs. Specialist one-off builds. Full engineering shop for all diesel and petrol engines.

MITCHELL
MOULDINGS LTD
Unit 10, Essex Marina,
Wallasea Island, Canewdon,
Essex SS4 2HG
Tel: (0702) 258112
Mitchell Mouldings Ltd boatbuilders and repairers, produce 3 versions of the Mitchell 31ft, suitable for Workboat, Patrol Boat, Passenger Launch, Leisure Boat, and a 23 Fast Fisherman (FF700). We also produce contract mouldings, at present the Coaster 33, Duellist 32 and Sapphire Launch.

A H MOODY & SON LTD
Swanwick Shore Road,
Swanwick,
Southampton SO3 7ZL
Tel: (0489) 885000
Fax: (0489) 885509
Sail and motor new boat sales. New construction. Brokerage. Major refits, repair facilities. Winter lay-up, marina. Chandlery, bunkering, valeting. Insurance.

PADSTOW HARBOUR
Padstow Harbour
Commissioners,
Harbour Office,
West Quay, Padstow PL28 8AQ
Tel: (0841) 532239
Small West Country port having a vigorous
fishing fleet and enjoying an excellent repu-
tation for waterborne recreation. General
cargo capability extends up to vessels 1500/
2000 GRT.

BOOKS & CHARTS

CAMBRIAN & WESTFLEET
The Boatyard,
Portway Village Marina,
Penarth, South Glamorgan
Tel: (0222) 709983
Boatbuilders and repairers, marine engi-
neers, riggers, marine clothing specialists,
chart agents, nautical booksellers, and yacht
chandlers.

**CAMBRIAN SMALL BOATS
& CHANDLERY LTD**
14 Cambrian Place,
South Dock,
Swansea, West Glamorgan
Tel: (0792) 467263
Yacht chandlers, riggers, marine clothing
specialists, nautical booksellers and THE
ONLY ADMIRALTY 'A' CLASS CHART
AGENT IN WALES.

**DUBOIS PHILLIPS
& McCALLUM LTD**
Oriel Chambers, Covent
Garden,
Liverpool L2 8UD
Tel: 051- 236 2776
Fax: 051- 236 4577
Admiralty chart agents and nautical book-
sellers. Chart correction service. Worldwide
mail order service.

KELVIN HUGHES
Charts & Maritime Supplies
New North Road
Hainault, Ilford
Essex IG6 2UR
Tel: 081-500 6166
Kelvin Hughes is the world's largest supplier
of navigational charts and one of the UK's
leading nautical booksellers. They have re-
tail outlets in the City of London, Southamp-
ton, Glasgow and Aberdeen and offer a
worldwide mail order service.

HYDROGRAPHIC OFFICE
MOD Taunton,
Somerset TA1 2DN
Tel: (0823) 337900
Admiralty charts and hydrographic publica-
tions - worldwide coverage corrected to date
of issue. Available from appointed admiralty
agents together with notices to mariners.

LEIMA MARINE
Medway Bridge Marina,
Manor Lane,
Rochester, Kent ME1 3HS
Tel: (0634) 830061
Based at Medway Bridge Marina near Rochester, Leima Marine offers a full marina
chandlery service; stocking ropes, paints,
electric and electronic equipment and repair
and maintenance materials. Open seven days
a week.

**WARSASH NAUTICAL
BOOKSHOP**
31 Newtown Road,
Warsash, Southampton
Tel: (0489) 572384
Fax: (0489) 885756
Nautical bookseller and chart agent. Callers
and mail order. New and secondhand books.
Free lists. Credit cards taken. Publishers of
the bibliography of nautical books.

CHANDLERS

ABINGDON BOAT CENTRE
The Bridge, Abingdon,
Oxon OX14 3HX
Tel: (0235) 21125
The main chandlery on Upper Thames, sup-
plying a large range of equipment and cloth-
ing for offshore and inland cruising and sail-
ing. Admiralty chart agents. Talurit and Roll
Swage rigging. Trailers, inflatables.

**AXMINSTER POWER
TOOLS CHANDLERY**
George Street,
Axminster, Devon EX13 5PS
Tel: (0297) 33980
A large chandlery catering for all aspects of
boating from dinghies to round the world
cruisers. See our advertisements in P.B.O
and Yachting Monthly for a small selection
of our comprehensive stock and compare
prices!

BOATWORKS + LTD
Castle Emplacement,
St Peter Port, Guernsey
Tel: (0481) 26071
Fax: (0481) 714224
Boatworks+ provides a comprehensive range
of services including electronics, chandlery,
boatbuilding and repairs, engine sales and

services, yacht brokerage, clothing and fuel
supplies.

**BRENTFORD MARINE
SERVICES**
The Boathouse,
Brentford Dock Marina,
Justin Close, Brentford,
Middlesex TW8 8QA
Tel: 081-568 0287
Well stocked chandlery.

**BRIXHAM YACHT
SUPPLIES LTD**
72 Middle Street,
Brixham, Devon
Tel: (0803) 882290
We stock a complete range of sailing and
leisure clothing. English and continental pure
wool traditional knitwear. Admiralty charts.
Camping accessories.

CALEY MARINA
Canal Road, Inverness,
Scotland
Tel: (0463) 236539
Fax: (0463) 238323
Open : 08.30 - 17.30. Berths: 50 Pontoon
(visitors available). Facilities: Fuel, water,
provisions (nearby shops), repair, cranage,
storage afloat and ashore. Comprehensive
chandlery, showers, workshop. Situated at
eastern end of Caledonian canal above
Muirtown Locks. Access via sea locks four
hours either side of high water.

CAMBRIAN & WESTFLEET
The Boatyard,
Portway Village Marina,
Penarth, South Glamorgan
Tel: (0222) 709983
Boatbuilders and repairers, marine engi-
neers, riggers, marine clothing specialists,
chart agents, nautical booksellers, and yacht
chandlers.

**CAMBRIAN SMALL BOATS
& CHANDLERY LTD**
14 Cambrian Place,
South Dock, Swansea,
West Glamorgan
Tel: (0792) 467263
Yacht chandlers, riggers, marine clothing
specialists, nautical booksellers and THE
ONLY ADMIRALTY 'A' CLASS CHART
AGENT IN WALES.

CRINAN BOATS LTD
Crinan, By Lochgilphead,
Argyll PA31 8SP
Tel: (054 683) 232
Boatbuilders, chandlers, engineers, slipping,
repairs, charts, electricians, pontoon.

COMPASS POINT CHANDLERY
The Quay, Hamble
Southampton S03 5HA
TEL: (0703) 452388
FAX: (0703) 456942

Compass Point is adjacent to the new quay at Hamble. It stocks an attractive selection of leisure clothing and foulweather gear as well as a wide range of chandlery including British Seagull spares and Calor gas.

DALE SAILING CO LTD
Brunel Quay, Neyland,
Milford Haven, Dyfed
Tel: (0646) 601636

Hull and engine repair and servicing, hauling out and storage, fuel, international interspray centre, comprehensive chandlery, main dealers for: Volvo Penta inboards, Mercury outboards, Dell Quay Dory, Furlex, Autohelm.

THE DINGHY STORE AND WHITSTABLE MARINE
Sea Wall, Whitstable,
Kent CT5 1BX
Tel: (0227) 274168/262525
Fax: (0227) 770938

Chandlers - wet suits, buoyancy, clothing, paint, boots, electrical, books. Main agents for Johnson Outboards. Full workshop facilities, Orkney fishing boats, Narwhal inflatables. Main agents for Fletchers. Main dealer for Mercury. All outboards serviced.

EVERSON AND SONS LTD
Phoenix Works, Riverside,
Woodbridge, Suffolk
Tel: (03943) 4358

Boatbuilding and marine engineers; chandlers and riggers; insurance and brokerage arranged. Full yard facilities.

LEIMA MARINE
Medway Bridge Marina,
Manor Lane, Rochester,
Kent ME1 3HS
Tel: (0634) 830061

Based at Medway Bridge Marina near Rochester, Leima Marine offers a full marina chandlery service; stocking ropes, paints, electric and electronic equipment and repair and maintenance materials. Open seven days a week.

MARQUAND BROS LTD
North Quay, Guernsey
Tel: (0481) 20962
Fax: (0481) 713974.

Yacht chandlers, stockists of a comprehensive range of marine products.

MAYFLOWER INTERNATIONAL MARINA (SAILPORT) PLC
Ocean Quay, Richmond Walk,
Plymouth PL1 4LS
Tel: (0752) 556633

Marina operators with boat hoist (25-ton) facility. Restaurant, clubroom, launderette, fuel, chandlery, shop and off-licence. Winter storage. Owned by berth holders and operated to a very high standard.

L H MORGAN & SONS (MARINE) LTD
The Boat Centre,
32-42 Waterside, Brightlingsea,
Essex
Tel: (020630) 2003/4569

Marine engineers, chandlers, boat and engine repairers. Yacht brokers, marine insurance, tools and hardware, sailing and fashion clothing.

PADSTOW HARBOUR
Padstow Harbour
Commissioners,
Harbour Office, West Quay,
Padstow PL28 8AQ
Tel: (0841) 532239

Small West Country port having a vigorous fishing fleet and enjoying an excellent reputation for waterborne recreation. General cargo capability extends up to vessels 1500/2000 GRT.

SOLENT TRADING CO
Mercury Yacht Harbour,
Satchell Lane,
Hamble SO3 5HQ
Tel: (0703) 454849 (& FAX)

Chandlery charts and books, clothing, oilskins - boots and shoes. Avon agent. Liferaft sales, hire and service safety equipment. Paint, varnish and anti-fouling. Groceries and off licence sales.

WYATTS CHANDLERY
110 & 128 Coast Road,
West Mersea,
Nr Colchester, Essex
Tel: (0206) 384745
Fax: (0206) 384455

Wyatts Chandlery, well stocked and competitively priced.

CAMBRIAN SMALL BOATS & CHANDLERY LTD
14 Cambrian Place,
South Dock, Swansea,
West Glamorgan
Tel: (0792) 467263

Yacht chandlers, riggers, marine clothing specialists, nautical booksellers and THE ONLY ADMIRALTY 'A' CLASS CHART AGENT IN WALES.

COMMUNICATION AERIALS LTD
Woodland Industrial Estate,
Eden Vale Road,
Westbury, Wiltshire BA13 3QS
Tel: (0373) 822835

We have a wide range to suit every kind of vessel. Good performance does not end with a good aerial, you need good cable and connectors. Again we offer a wide choice. Ask to see the complete range of our VHF aerials together with the new 4 in 1 receiving aerial and 24v-12v convertor.

ROWLANDS MARINE ELECTRONICS LTD
The Outer Harbour,
Pwllheli, Gwynedd LL53 5HD
Tel: (0758) 613193

Marine Electronic Trade Association member, dealer for Autohelm, Brookes and Gatehouse, Cetrek, ICOM, Kelvin Hughes, Marconi, Nasa, Navico, Navstar, Neco, Seafarer, Shipmate, Stowe, Racal-Decca, V-Tronix, Ampro, Walker. Equipment supplied installed and serviced.

W & H CHINA
Howley Properties Ltd,
Howley Tannery, Howley Lane,
Warrington,
Cheshire WA1 2DN
Tel: (0925) 34621
Telex: 94013565 Chin G

Manufacturers of China chart dividers. Agents for LINEX navigational aids, slide rules etc.

KELVIN HUGHES
(Boat Electronics)
New North Road
Hainault, Ilford
Essex IG6 2UR
Tel: 081-500 1020

A supplier of electronic equipment to the leisure and fishing industries, Kelvin Hughes Boat electronics can provide radar systems, echo sounders, fish finders, plotters, navigators and radio systems to suit all budgets.

NAVICO LTD
**Star Lane,
Margate CT9 4NP
Tel: (0843) 290290
Fax: +44 843 290471**

Navico Limited manufacture a complete range of high quality marine electronics for sailing and powerboating: The world's most advanced cockpit autopilots for tiller and wheel steered yachts; high performance Powerboat Autopilot; stylish and reliable instruments including for sailing, echosounder, wind direction and speed, log, compass, close hauled, VMG; and instruments for power, echosounder, compass and log; and quality marine VHF radios.

REGIS ELECTRONICS LIMITED
**Regis House, Quay Hill,
Lymington, Hants SO41 9AR
Tel: (0590) 679251**

(Also at Southampton/Chichester/Cowes.) Sales, installation and service of marine electronic equipment. Leading south coast distributor for Furuno, Raytheon, Navstar, Cetreck, Autohelm, Kelvin Hughes, Robertson and other manufacturers of quality marine electronic equipment. Competitive quotations forwarded by return of post, including owner familiarisation and sea trials, on all equipment installed.

ROWLANDS MARINE ELECTRONICS LTD
**The Outer Harbour,
Pwllheli, Gwynedd LL53 5HD
Tel: (0758) 613193**

Marine Electronic Trade Association member, dealer for Autohelm, Brookes and Gatehouse, Cetrek, ICOM, Kelvin Hughes, Marconi, Nasa, Navico, Navstar, Neco, Seafarer, Shipmate, Stowe, Racal-Decca, V-Tronix, Ampro, Walker. Equipment supplied installed and serviced.

TAME TECHNOLOGY
**34 High Street,
Northfleet, Kent
Tel: (0474) 334414**

Supply and fitting of all marine electronics. Specialising in radar, autopilots and navigators. 24 hour call out service.

TOLLEY MARINE ELECTRONIC COMPANY
**Unit 5, Blackhill Road,
Holton Heath Trading Park,
Poole, Dorset BH16 6LS
Tel: (0202) 632644
Fax: (0202) 632622**

(Also at: 13 Commercial Road, Coxside, Plymouth, Devon) Tel: (0752) 222530. Agents of sales and service for Autohelm, Brookes & Gatehouse, Cetrek, Furuno, Icom, Kelvin Hughes, Lo-Kata, Navstar, Neco, Robertson, Sailor Shipmate.

ELECTRONIC & ELECTRICAL ENGINEERS

FALMOUTH BOAT CONSTRUCTION LTD
**Little Falmouth Yacht Yard,
Flushing, Falmouth,
Cornwall TR11 5TJ
Tel: (0326) 74309
Fax: (0326) 77679**

Repairs, refits, storage undercover and quayside, osmosis treatment specialists, resprays. Slipways to 100 ton. Commercial craft repairs. Specialist one-off builds. Full engineering shop for all diesel and petrol engines.

ENGINES

CAMBRIAN & WESTFLEET
**The Boatyard,
Portway Village Marina,
Penarth, South Glamorgan
Tel: (0222) 709983**

Boatbuilders and repairers, marine engineers, riggers, marine clothing specialists, chart agents, nautical booksellers, and yacht chandlers.

PETER HUMPHRIES MARINE ENGINEERING
**Val Wyatt Marina
Willow Lane, Wargrave
Berkshire RG10 8DY
Tel: (0734) 404419
Fax: (0734) 404890**

Importer of Fischer/BMW 07-050 engines. Supplier of service, parts and accessories for all BMW marine engines and sterndrives. Supplier of service, parts and accessories for all Mercruiser marine engines and sterndrives. Bennett Trimplane stockist.

VOLVO PENTA UK LTD
**Otterspool Way,
Watford WD2 8HW
Tel: (0923) 28544**

Volvo Penta's leading marine power - petrol and diesel for leisure craft and workboats - is supported by an extensive network of parts and service dealers.

FLAGS & PENNANTS

LOVELL LOGOS LTD
**Ringcroft Farm,
Cranfield Road, North Crawley,
Bucks MK16 9HP
Tel: (0234) 750735
Fax: (0234) 751369**

We manufacture flags/pennants of all sizes.

They can be personalised with your boat name, family crest, company logo etc. We supply Sweatshirts Tee-Shirts. Rugby Shirts, Jogging Suits, Yachting Scarves also personalised.

GENERAL MARINE EQUIPMENT & MACHINERY

AQUA-MARINE MANUFACTURING (UK) LTD
**216 Fair Oak Road,
Bishopstoke, Eastleigh,
Hants SO5 6NJ
Tel: (0703) 694949
Fax: (0703) 601381**

Manufacturers and distributors of chandlery, incl: Engel refrigeration; Dutton-Lainson and Muir winches; Anchor fenders; Rule pumps; Aquaflow water systems; Sierra engine spares; TX, Flexatrol and Detmar controls; Ritchie compasses; RWO, IYE and Holt fittings; Danforth anchors; Aqua-Signal lights.

BOATWORKS + LTD
**Castle Emplacement,
St Peter Port, Guernsey
Tel: (0481) 26071
Fax: (0481) 714224**

Boatworks+ provides a comprehensive range of services including electronics, chandlery, boatbuilding and repairs, engine sales and services, yacht brokerage, clothing and fuel supplies.

BROOKES & ADAMS LTD
**Shady Lane,
Kingstanding,
Birmingham B44 9DX
Tel: 021 360 1588**

Manufacturers of bronze and brass deck and interior fittings, rigging screws, shackles, snap shackles, berthlights and many other articles. Suppliers to the marine industry, the admiralty and other government departments.

FALMOUTH BOAT CONSTRUCTION LTD
**Little Falmouth Yacht Yard,
Flushing, Falmouth,
Cornwall TR11 5TJ
Tel: (0326) 74309
Fax: (0326) 77679**

Repairs, refits, storage undercover and quayside, osmosis treatment specialists, resprays. Slipways to 100 ton. Commercial craft repairs. Specialist one-off builds. Full engineering shop for all diesel and petrol engines.

GLASPLIES
2 Crowland Street, Southport,
Lancashire PR9 7RL
Tel: (0704) 40626
Every fibreglass requirement stocked at lowest prices in Europe.

GREENHAM MARINE LTD
King's Saltern Road,
Lymington, Hampshire
Tel: (0590) 671144
Fax: (0590) 679517
Greenham Marine can offer yachtsmen one of the most comprehensive selections of marine electronic equipment currently available.

PADSTOW HARBOUR
Padstow Harbour
Commissioners,
Harbour Office, West Quay,
Padstow PL28 8AQ
Tel: (0841) 532239
Small West Country port having a vigorous fishing fleet and enjoying an excellent reputation for waterborne recreation. General cargo capability extends up to vessels 1500/2000 GRT.

**E C SMITH & SONS
(MARINE FACTORS) LTD**
Units H & J
Kingsway Industrial Estate,
Luton, Beds LU1 1LP
Tel: (0582) 29721
Fax: (0582) 458893
Telex: 825473 ECSLTN G
Manufacturers and distributors: Lofrans Windlasses. Professional Mariner battery chargers, sealants, ECS ventilators, toilets, hardware, Quartz/other lighting, Firemaster fire extinguishers, table/seat pedestals, skin fittings, Shurflo water pumps, teak mouldings and general chandlery.

SOLENT LEISURE SUPPLIES
59 Stubbington Lane,
Stubbington, Fareham,
Hampshire PO14 2PG
Tel: (0329) 663237
Fax: (0329) 668602
Manufacturers and wholesalers of yacht chandlery and sail accessories, including 'fluorescent sail tell-tales'. Agents for: Bray Fenda-sox, Sheraton cabinet teak fittings. Safestrip non-slip mats, Super-flat hoses, Planaship prints, Safetycall charts.

SOLENT TRADING CO
Mercury Yacht Harbour,
Satchell Lane,
Hamble SO3 5HQ
Tel: (0703) 454849 (& FAX)

Chandlery charts and books, clothing, oil-skins - boots and shoes. Avon agent. Liferaft sales, hire and service safety equipment. Paint, varnish and anti-fouling. Groceries and off licence sales.

SOUTH WESTERN MARINE FACTORS LTD
P O Box 4, 43 Pottery Road,
Poole, Dorset BH14 8RE
Tel: (0202) 745414
Fax: Company (0202) 743931
Chandlery (0202) 731598
The Sowester group offers the most comprehensive range of marine equipment, engines, steering and control systems in the UK, distributing Mercury outboards, MerCruiser sterndrives and inboard engines, Morse-controls, Achilles inflatables, Maxwell winches, Bruce anchors, and many other well known products.

HOLIDAYS

**HAMBLE SCHOOL
OF YACHTING**
5 Mymms Drive,
Brookmans Park,
Hatfield, Herts AL9 7AE
Tel: (0707) 54367
Theory and practical RYA courses, complete beginner to yachtmaster. 36 ft Sigmas/HB 31 cruiser/racer, Feeling 326, 1090. Weekend, 5, 7, 12, 14 day courses. South coast England and North French coast.

**SOLENT COASTAL &
OFFSHORE SAILING
SCHOOL**
Archipelagoes,
South Mundham, Chichester,
Sussex PO20 6NA
Tel: (0243) 262724
We are an RYA recognised sailing school, based on the river Hamble. We offer a wide range of courses. All shorebased theory courses. Families, groups, couples and singles welcome. Ladies only - 5 day courses with lady instructor. Please write or telephone Philip or Julie Hawes for brochure or to discuss your requirements.

**INSTRUMENTATION
& POSITION FIXING**

AUTOHELM Nautech Ltd,
Anchorage Park,
Portsmouth, Hants PO3 5TD
Tel: (0705) 693611
Fax: (0705) 694642
Telex: 86384 Nautec G

Manufacturers of the Autohelm range of instruments, compasses and autopilots for power and sail craft from 22' to 125'. Manufacturer of the Autohelm personal compass.

BANAIR
31-32 Enterprise Road,
Horndean,
Portsmouth
Tel: (0705) 599404
Fax: (0705) 594241
Manufacturers of digital electronic barograph. Accessories include temperature and humidity sensors and NMEA interface.

CETREK LTD
Factory Road,
Upton,
Poole, Dorset BH16 5SJ
Tel: (0202) 632116
World leader in autopilot and electronic compass systems. Very large supplier of hydraulic and mechanical steering systems, battery chargers and trim tabs.

GREENHAM MARINE LTD
King's Saltern Road,
Lymington, Hampshire
Tel: (0590) 671144
Fax: (0590) 679517
Greenham Marine can offer yachtsmen one of the most comprehensive selections of marine electronic equipment currently available.

MARITEK LTD
B5 D2
Templeton Business Centre,
Glasgow G40 1DA,
Scotland
Tel: 041-554 2492
       041-942 0430
Computer programs for coastal/celestial navigation/tidal height prediction, using Psion organiser pocket computer. Yacht race management systems. Large computer systems and projects using 4th generation languages.

RIGEL COMPASSES LTD
1 Factory Road
Upton,
Poole, Dorset BH16 5SJ
Tel: (0202) 632116
Manufacturers and suppliers of a comprehensive range of magnetic and electronic compasses for both power and sail application. Rigel Chartnav and chart plotter, clocks, barometers and chartroom instruments.

ROWLANDS MARINE ELECTRONICS LTD
The Outer Harbour, Pwllheli, Gwynedd LL53 5HD
Tel: (0758) 613193
Marine Electronic Trade Association member, dealer for Autohelm, Brookes and Gatehouse, Cetrek, ICOM, Kelvin Hughes, Marconi, Nasa, Navico, Navstar, Neco, Seafarer, Shipmate, Stowe, Racal-Decca, V-Tronix, Ampro, Walker. Equipment supplied installed and serviced.

SOLENT TRADING CO
Mercury Yacht Harbour, Satchell Lane, Hamble SO3 5HQ
Tel: (0703) 454849 (& FAX)
Chandlery charts and books, clothing, oilskins - boots and shoes. Avon agent. Liferaft sales, hire and service safety equipment. Paint, varnish and anti-fouling. Groceries and off licence sales.

DUBOIS PHILLIPS & McCALLUM LTD
Oriel Chambers, Covent Garden, Liverpool L2 8UD
Tel: 051- 236 2776
Fax: 051- 236 4577
Admiralty chart agents and nautical booksellers. Chart correction service. Worldwide mail order service.

SHIPSIDES MARINE LTD
5 New Hall Lane, Preston, Lancashire
Tel: (0772) 797079
Yacht and dinghy chandlery store close to M6 motorway. Also worldwide mail order service (catalogue £1.00). Chart agents. International yacht paint centre. Lifecraft hire. Yacht clothing department.

ARDFERN YACHT CENTRE LTD
Ardfern By Lochgilphead, Argyll, Scotland PA31 8QN
Tel: (08525) 247/636
Fax: (08525) 624

Boatyard with full repair and maintenance facilities. Timber and GRP repairs, painting and engineering. Sheltered moorings and pontoon berthing. Winter storage, chandlery, showers, fuel calor, brokerage. Hotel, bars and restaurant.

ARDORAN MARINE
Lerags, By Oban, Argyll PA34 4SE
Tel: (0631) 66123
Fax: (0631) 66611
Swinging moorings, pontoons, diesel, gas, water, toilets, hot showers, slip and cranage for winter storage, engine sales and repairs, Suzuki/mariner outboards, Zodiac inflatables, Orkney boats, chain/shackles in stock.

BERTHON'S LYMINGTON MARINA
The Shipyard, Lymington, Hampshire SO41 9YL
Tel: (0590) 673312
Fax: (0590) 679811
250 permanent berths and 100 visitors' berths, all with full facilities, near to the centre of Lymington town. Rates: Annual £72 per foot, Daily 50p per foot, Weekly £2.30 per foot.

THE BRIGHTON MARINA COMPANY LTD
Brighton Marina Village, Brighton BN2 5UF
Tel: (0273) 693636
Britain's largest marina (1800 pontoon berths) with marina village under development. NYHA five gold anchors. Full boatyard and shore facilities. Brokerage and boat sales. Club racing throughout the year. Group visits, rallies welcome.

CALEY MARINA
Canal Road, Inverness, Scotland
Tel: (0463) 236539
Fax: (0463) 238323
Open 08.30 - 17.30. Berths: 50 Pontoon (visitors available). Facilities: Fuel, water, provisions (nearby shops), repair, cranage, storage afloat and ashore. Comprehensive chandlery, showers, workshop. Situated at eastern end of Caledonian canal above Muirtown Locks. Access via sea locks four hours either side of high water.

CAMUS MARINE SERVICES
Craobh Haven, Craignish, By Lochgilphead, Argyll
Tel: (08525) 225/622/222
Fax: (08525) 252
Telex: 779828 Camus G
200 marina berths. Water. Electricity. Diesel

fuel. Gas. Yacht repairs, fitting-out and engineering. Storage ashore. Chandlery. Brokerage. Insurance. Nearby facilities include: pub, shops, sailing school, dive centre, launderette, riding centre, hotels and guest houses, self catering accommodation. Electronic & electric installation & service. Agents for Yanmar, Bukl, L/P diesels, Honda & Mariner outboards.

CARRICKFERGUS MARINA
Rodger's Quay, Carrickfergus, Northern Ireland BT38 8BU
Tel: (09603) 66666
300 fully serviced pontoon berths with full on shore facilities (half a mile from town centre). Steeped in a wealth of historical legend, Carrickfergus has excellent restaurants, hotels, pubs, shops and a host of recreational leisure facilities.

CLARKE & CARTER BOATYARD
110 & 128 Coast Road, West Mersea, Nr Colchester, Essex
Tel: (0206) 382244
Fax: (0206) 384455
The Clarke & Carter boatyard is a division of West Mersea Marine Ltd. The yard is situated on the main waterfront at West Mersea. The anchorage, which has retained its traditional character, offers both swinging and post moorings for vessels up to about 50ft LOA. Access is at all states of the tide to the River Blackwater. There are also some edge moorings available.

DAN WEBB & FEESEY
Shipways, North Street, Maldon, Essex CM9 7HN
Tel: (0621) 54280 & 56829
(Also Marine Parade, Maylandsea, Essex CM3 6AN Tel: (0621) 740264/741267) On the river Blackwater, 600 moorings, excellent shore-based facilities. Shipwright repairs and GRP. Chandlery. Rigging.

DARTHAVEN MARINA
Kingswear Quay, Kingswear, Dartmouth, Devon
Tel: (080 425) 545/242
All services at Darthaven Marina and J W & A Upham Ltd: engineer, electricians, chandlery, brokerage, boat repairs, 30-ton travel hoist.

ESSEX MARINA LTD
Wallasea Island, Nr Rochford, Essex SS4 2HG
Tel: (0702) 258531
Fax: (0702) 258227
Yacht marina. Pontoon and offshore moorings. Fuel sales. Brokerage. Night security. Hauling and launching. Engineering and

shipwrights. Bars and restaurant. One hour from London.

FALMOUTH YACHT MARINA
North Parade, Falmouth, Cornwall TR11 2TD
Tel: (0326) 316620
The most westerly marina in England, strategically placed for transatlantic departures and arrivals. Fully serviced permanent and visitor berths. Diesel fuel. Chandlery, 30-ton hoist. Famous friendly service.

GRANARY YACHT HARBOUR LTD
Dock Lane,
Melton,
Woodbridge, Suffolk IP12 1PE
Tel:(03943) 6327
Pontoon berths (long or short term) laying-up facilities. Slipping and cranage. Craft maintenance/repairs and engineering. Chandlery.

HOO MARINA MEDWAY LTD
Vicarage Lane, Hoo,
Rochester, Kent ME3 9LE
Tel: (0634) 250311
Pontoon berthing afloat at all states of the tide. All facilities available. Visitors welcome.

HULL MARINA LTD
Warehouse 13, Kingston Street,
Hull HU1 2DQ
Tel: (0482) 25048
Situated 5 minutes from the centre of Hull and all national and international transport systems. First class leisure, boatyard and brokerage facilities, 4 star hotel and quayside restaurants.

KILMELFORD YACHT HAVEN
Kilmelford, Oban,
Argyll PA34 4XD
Tel: (08522) 248/279
Fax: (08522) 343
Yacht repairs. Fitting out. Engineering. Moorings. Storage ashore. Painting. Osmosis treatment. Rigging. Chandlery.

LANGSTONE MARINA PLC
Fort Cumberland Road,
Eastney, Portsmouth,
Hants PO4 9RJ
Tel: (0705) 822719
Langstone Marina is a 300 berth marina on the western side of the entrance to Langstone Harbour. Facilities include: hoist, brokerage, showers, toilets, chandlery, hard stand-

ing. Access over the sill is available approximately 3 hours either side of high water.

LARGS YACHT HAVEN LTD
Irvine Road, Largs,
Ayrshire KA30 8EZ
Tel: (0475) 675333
Perfectly situated in the Firth of Clyde for the best cruising grounds in Britain. 500 berths with first class shore facilities. 45-ton hoist. Regular racing off the marina. Visitors always welcome. Excellent shore facilities including pub.

LITTLEHAMPTON MARINA LTD
Ferry Road, Littlehampton,
Sussex
Tel: (0903) 713553
Marina and boatyard with storing ashore for all types of craft. Full marina amenities on site. Compressed air for diving cylinders with large slipway for visitors.

LYMINGTON YACHT HAVEN LTD
King's Saltern Road,
Lymington, Hants SO4 9XY
Tel: (0590) 677071
Established 700 berth marina with all the boatyard and shore facilities required by visiting yachtsmen. 50-ton hoist and emergency call out engineer.

MARINA DEVELOPMENTS
Shamrock Quay,
William Street,
Southampton SO1 1QL
Tel: (0703) 229461
The UK's leading marina developers and operators, owning 17 marinas and marina villages around the south coast of England.

MAYFLOWER INTERNATIONAL MARINA (SAILPORT) PLC
Ocean Quay, Richmond Walk,
Plymouth PL1 4LS
Tel: (0752) 556633
Marina operators with boat-hoist (25-ton) facility. Restaurant, clubroom, launderette, fuel, chandlery, shop and off-licence. Winter storage. Owned by berth holders and operated to a very high standard.

NEWHAVEN MARINA LTD
The Yacht Harbour, Newhaven,
East Sussex BN9 9BY
Tel: (0273) 513881
Fax: (0273) 517990
Awarded National Yacht Harbour Association FOUR GOLD ANCHORS for comprehensive facilities including boat yard, boat hoist, superb yacht club with accommoda-

tion and restaurant. Visiting craft always welcome.

PORT FLAIR LTD
Bradwell Marina, Waterside,
Bradwell-on-Sea,
Essex CM0 7RB
Tel: (0621) 76235/76391
300 pontoon berths with water and electricity, petrol and diesel, chandlery, marine slip/hoistage to 20 ton; repairs, winter lay-ups, licensed club, yacht brokerage.

PORT SOLENT LTD
The Port House, Port Solent,
Portsmouth, Hants PO6 4TH
Tel: (0705) 210765
Fax: (0705) 324241
Port Solent is a developing community of houses, apartments, restaurants and retail encompassing 900 berths. This includes 500 public berths with facilities for visitors, including travel hoist and yacht club.

PORT DINORWIC YACHT HARBOUR
Port Dinorwic,
Gwynedd LL56 4JN
Tel: (0248) 671252/671114
Fax: (0248) 670441
250 berths; 20 visitors berths; 30 moorings; yacht club and restaurant; all facilities available.

SALTERNS MARINA
40 Salterns Way, Lilliput,
Poole, Dorset BH14 8JR
Tel: (0202) 707321
Marina berths, swinging moorings, 5 ton hoist. Boatyard with 40 tonne hoist, full services, engineers, shipwrights. Engine sales. Brokerage. Fairline and Draco agents. Poole Harbour Yacht Club and Salterns Hotel with bar and excellent restaurant.

SEAWARD MARINE ENTERPRISES
Southdown Quay,
Millbrook, Torpoint
Cornwall Pl10 1EZ
Tel: (0752) 823084
We are opposite Plymouth in a quiet secluded location, in an area of outstanding natural beauty. We can offer a 32 berth marina with facilities for boats up to 150ft long, 12 ft draught, quayside moorings, good security. Electricity and water supplied. Winter lay-up facilities.

THE MARINA AT SOUTH DOCK
South Lock Office, Rope Street,
Plough Way,
London SE16 1AA
Tel: 071-252 2244

London's newest and largest marina with full boatyard facility and liftout to 20 tonnes. Welcomes visitors.

SWANSEA YACHT HAVEN LTD
**Lockside,
Maritime Quarter, Swansea,
West Glamorgan SA1 1WN
Tel: (0792) 470310**

Centre piece of a multi-million development. Locked marina with 360 berths and good facilities. Tidal access HW+/- 3 hrs. Excellent motorway/rail communications. Ideal for day-sailing cruising, racing.

WOOLVERSTONE MARINE MDL (MARINAS) LTD
**Woolverstone, Ipswich, Suffolk
Tel: (047384) 206/354**

Pontoon berths accessible any time, moorings, VHF channel 80 & 37, the 'Schooner' club/restaurant, chandlery, workshops, pantry, launderette, brokerage. Visitors welcome. NYHA 4 Gold Anchors.

MARINE ENGINEERS

WEST MERSEA MARINE ENGINEERING
**110 & 128 Coast Road,
West Mersea,
Nr Colchester, Essex
Tel: (0206) 384350
Fax: (0206) 384455**

Providing full marine engineering facilities. There are also undercover facilities for those vessels being worked on by our staff. Shipwrights, GRP specialists, painters and riggers are also available. There is a sailmaker and an outboard repair and service workshop nearby, and liferaft hire, sales and service together with inflatable dinghy repairs and service are also available locally.

MARINE INSURANCE

CAMUS MARINE SERVICES
**Craobh Haven, Craignish,
By Lochgilphead, Argyll
Tel: (08525) 225/622/222
Fax: (08525) 252
Telex: 779828 Camus G**

200 marina berths. Water. Electricity. Diesel fuel. Gas. Yacht repairs, fitting-out and engineering. Storage ashore. Chandlery. Brokerage. Insurance. Nearby facilities include: pub, shops, sailing school, dive centre, launderette, riding centre, hotels and guest houses, self catering accommodation. Electronic & electric installation & service. Agents for Yanmar, Bukl, L/P diesels, Honda & Mariner outboards.

CRAVEN HODGSON ASSOCIATES
**Suite 15, 30-38 Dock Street,
Leeds LS10 1JF
Tel: (0532) 438443**

Independent insurance and investment consultants and intermediaries. We recommend and advise in relation to all major experienced marine insurers.

MARINE TRANSPORT & YACHT DELIVERIES

DALE SAILING CO LTD
**Brunel Quay, Neyland,
Milford Haven, Dyfed
Tel: (0646) 601636**

Hull and engine repair and servicing, hauling out and storage, fuel, international interspray centre, comprehensive chandlery, main dealers for: Volvo Penta inboards, Mercury outboards, Dell Quay Dory, Furlex, Autohelm. Marine Transport.

PETER HAWARD (SEA FERRIES) LTD
**6 Shore Road, Warsash,
Southampton SO3 9GQ
Tel: (0489) 575222 Fax: (0489) 575220 and at (0424) 722414**

Yacht and small vessel deliveries. Sail, power, commercial. Established 1947. Skipper/ navigators for passage making, cruising, refits, emergencies. Brochure on request. Phone us to discuss your requirements.

PADSTOW HARBOUR
**Padstow Harbour Commissioners,
Harbour Office, West Quay,
Padstow PL28 8AQ
Tel: (0841) 532239**

Small West Country port having a vigorous fishing fleet and enjoying an excellent reputation for waterborne recreation. General cargo capability extends up to vessels 1500/ 2000 GRT.

PAINT

EXTENSOR AB
**24-30 Canute Road,
Southampton SO9 3AS
Tel: (0703) 226722
Fax: (0703) 335975**

Extensor provides a comprehensive range of yacht paint products designed for first class boat maintenance. This range includes the well known antifoulings, VC17M and VC-offshore (with Teflon) and a range of epoxies, fillers, boat care and accessory products.

INTERNATIONAL YACHT PAINTS
**24-30 Canute Road,
Southampton SO9 3AS
Tel: (0703) 226722
Fax: (0703) 335975**

Yachtpaint and antifouling manufacturers.

LEIMA MARINE
**Medway Bridge Marina,
Manor Lane, Rochester,
Kent ME1 3HS
Tel: (0634) 830061**

Based at Medway Bridge Marina near Rochester, Leima Marine offers a full marina chandlery service; stocking ropes, paints, electric and electronic equipment and repair and maintenance materials. Open seven days a week.

SHIPWRIGHT MARINE & INDUSTRIAL SUPPLIES LTD
**31 Chapel Road,
Southampton SO1 1GL
Tel: (0703) 333505**

Shipwright Marine & Industrial Supplies is a company specialising in a range of products for the leisure and maritime industry which includes paints, anti-fouling, plywood, adhesive sealants. Deckfast (teak plydeck) and batteries. A selective portfolio for the manufacturing sector.

REPAIR MATERIALS

LEIMA MARINE
**Medway Bridge Marina,
Manor Lane, Rochester,
Kent ME1 3HS
Tel: (0634) 830061**

Based at Medway Bridge Marina near Rochester, Leima Marine offers a full marina chandlery service; stocking ropes, paints, electric and electronic equipment and repair and maintenance materials. Open seven days a week.

STRUCTURAL POLYMER SYSTEMS LTD
**Love Lane, Cowes,
Isle of Wight PO31 7EU
Tel: (0983) 298451
Fax: (0983) 298453**

*Epoxy resins for laminating, bonding, coating, filling. Usable with wood, GRP, concrete. * GRP/FRP materials including glass, carbon and Kevlar fibres. * Structural engineering of GRP and composite materials. Technical advice service.

SAFETY EQUIPMENT

**ANGLO DUTCH
ENGINEERING CO LTD**
**4 Masons Avenue,
Croydon,
Surrey CR0 1EH
Tel: 081-686 9717**
Approved liferaft service station for South
East UK. Additionally we hire and sell new
rafts and sell a complete range of safety
equipment for yachts including pyrotech-
nics/fire extinguishers/lifejackets/buoys and
a buoyancy bag system.

CREWSAVER LTD
**Mumby Road,
Gosport,
Hampshire PO12 1AQ
Tel: (0705) 528621**
Crewsaver - leading UK manufacturers of
lifejackets, buoyancy aids and personal safety
equipment. Crewsaver is able to offer a
complete range designed to meet your indi-
vidual water sport needs.

LOKATA LTD
**Falmouth, Cornwall TR10 8AE
Tel: (0326) 73636
Fax: (0326) 73941**
Manufacturer of type approved 406 MHZ
epirbs including automatic float-free and
personal models for rapid detection and loca-
tion by rescue services. In addition:
NAVTEX; RDF; marine receiver, radar
detector.

SAILING SCHOOLS

**THE BRIGHTON MARINA
COMPANY LTD**
**Brighton Marina Village,
Brighton BN2 5UF
Tel: (0273) 693636**
Britain's largest marina (1800 pontoon
berths) with marina village under development. NYHA five gold anchors. Full boatyard
and shore facilities. Brokerage and boat
sales. Club racing throughout the year. Group
visits, rallies welcome.

DEVON OFFSHORE
**Newton Ferrers,
Plymouth PL8 1BL
Tel: (0752) 872908**
Instruction at all RYA levels sailing to Chan-
nel Islands, Brittany and West Country.
Specials include: cruising on traditional gaff
yawl; Yachtmaster intensive courses; ladies
only sailing.

**FOWEY CRUISING SCHOOL
(MALTA & UK)**
**32 Fore Street,
Fowey,
Cornwall PL23 1AQ
Tel: (0726) 832129**
All RYA cruising courses and shorebased
exam courses; plus skippered charters and
cruises available in the West Country. Skippered charters, bareboat charters, luxury
cruises and RYA Competent Crew or Keel-
boat courses all year round in Malta.

**HAMBLE SCHOOL
OF YACHTING**
**5 Mymms Drive,
Brookmans Park,
Hatfield, Herts AL9 7AE
Tel: (0707) 54367**
Theory and practical RYA courses - com-
plete beginner to yachtmaster. 36 ft Sigmas/
HB 31 cruiser/racer, Feeling 326, 1090.
Weekend, 5, 7, 12, 14 day courses. South
coast England and North French coast.

**JERSEY YACHT
MANAGEMENT**
**P O Box 531, Caledonia House,
Caledonia Place
St Helier, Jersey, CI
Tel: (0534) 78522
Fax: (0534) 71032
Telex: 4192243**
JERSEY YACHT MANAGEMENT and as-
sociate company JERSEY CRUISING
SCHOOL AND YACHT CHARTERS offer
a comprehensive range of specialised yacht-
ing services including sea school and charter,
yacht management, corporate ownership and
British registration.

PADSTOW HARBOUR
**Padstow Harbour
Commissioners,
Harbour Office, West Quay,
Padstow PL28 8AQ
Tel: (0841) 532239**
Small West Country port having a vigorous
fishing fleet and enjoying an excellent repu-
tation for waterborne recreation. General
cargo capability extends up to vessels 1500/
2000 GRT.

**SOLENT COASTAL &
OFFSHORE SAILING
SCHOOL**
**Archipelagoes, South
Mundham,
Chichester, Sussex PO20 6NA
Tel: (0243) 262724**
We are an RYA recognised sailing school,
based on the river Hamble. We offer a wide

range of courses. All shorebased theory
courses. Families, groups, couples and singles
welcome. Ladies only - 5 day courses with
lady instructor. Please write or telephone
Philip or Julie Hawes for brochure or to discuss your requirements.

**THE WHEELHOUSE
SCHOOL
OF NAVIGATION**
**Forest Gate,
Denmead,
Portsmouth, Hants PO7 6EX
Tel: (0705) 255901**
RYA shorebased certificate courses by cor-
respondence for day skipper. Yachtmaster
offshore and Yachtmaster ocean.

SAILS

BANKS SAILS
**Bruce Banks Sails Ltd
372 Brook Lane, Sarisbury,
Nr Southampton,
Hampshire SO3 6ZA
Tel: (0489) 582444
Fax: (0489) 589789**
Manufacturers of all types of sails, racing,
cruising, one design, plus accessories and
covers. Specialist repair and servicing de-
partment. Ideally positioned close to the
Hamble river and 10 minutes from South-
ampton and Portsmouth.

COPP SAILS & COVERS
**Brunel Quay,
Neyland,
Milford Haven,
Dyfed SA73 1PH
Tel: (0646) 601561
Fax: (0646) 601562**
'A complete made to measure sewing serv-
ice for the yachtsman.' Manufacture and
repair of sails, covers, upholstery, etc. Agents
for Rotostay, Harken and Easyreef reefing
systems.

SPARS & RIGGING

DALE SAILING CO LTD
**Brunel Quay, Neyland, Milford
Haven, Dyfed
Tel: (0646) 601636**
Hull and engine repair and servicing, hauling
out and storage, fuel, international interspray
centre, comprehensive chandlery, main dealers for: Volvo Penta inboards, Mercury
outboards, Dell Quay Dory, Furlex, Autohelm.

FALMOUTH BOAT CONSTRUCTION LTD
**Little Falmouth Yacht Yard,
Flushing, Falmouth,
Cornwall TR11 5TJ
Tel: (0326) 74309
Fax: (0326) 77679**

Repairs, refits, storage undercover and quayside, osmosis treatment specialists, resprays. Slipways to 100 ton. Commercial craft repairs. Specialist one-off builds. Full engineering shop for all diesel and petrol engines.

S S SPARS (1982) LTD
**Unit 4,
Parsons Hall Industrial Estate,
High Street, Irchester,
Northants NN9 7AB
Tel: (0933) 317143
Fax: (0933) 58643**

Manufacturers of alloy yacht masts, alloy toe-rails, stanchions, stanchion bases, fairleads and ancillary equipment.

YACHT BROKERS

BERTHON INTERNATIONAL
**The Shipyard, Lymington,
Hampshire SO41 9YL
Tel: (0590) 679222
Fax: (0590) 679811**

The UK's leading yacht brokerage house with 1,500 listings of cruising, racing and motor yachts world-wide. Offices in the U.K. and the Mediterranean.

BOATWORKS + LTD
**Castle Emplacement,
St Peter Port,
Guernsey
Tel: (0481) 26071
Fax: (0481) 714224**

Boatworks+ provides a comprehensive range of services including electronics, chandlery, boatbuilding and repairs, engine sales and services, yacht brokerage, clothing and fuel supplies.

BRENTFORD MARINE SERVICES
**The Boathouse,
Brentford Dock Marina,
Justin Close,
Brentford,
Middlesex TW8 8QA
Tel: 081 568 0287**

Yacht brokers and well stocked chandlery.

CAMUS MARINE SERVICES
**Craobh Haven, Craignish,
By Lochgilphead, Argyll
Tel: (08525) 225/622/222
Fax: (08525) 252
Telex: 779828 Camus G**

200 marina berths. Water. Electricity. Diesel fuel. Gas. Yacht repairs, fitting-out and engineering. Storage ashore. Chandlery. Brokerage. Insurance. Nearby facilities include: pub, shops, sailing school, dive centre, launderette, riding centre, hotels and guest houses, self catering accommodation. Electronic & electric installation & service. Agents for Yanmar, Bukl, L/P diesels, Honda & Mariner outboards.

ESSEX MARINA LTD
**Wallasea Island,
Nr Rochford, Essex SS4 2HG
Tel: (0702) 258531
Fax: (0702) 258227**

Yacht marina. Pontoon and offshore moorings. Fuel sales. Yacht brokerage. Night security. Hauling and launching. Engineering and shipwrights. Bars and restaurant. One hour from London.

L H MORGAN & SONS (MARINE) LTD
**The Boat Centre,
32-42 Waterside,
Brightlingsea, Essex
Tel: (020630) 2003/4569**

Marine engineers, chandlers, boat and engine repairers. Yacht brokers, marine insurance, tools and hardware, sailing and fashion clothing.

POWER ON THE WATER

Chapter 1

About this Almanac

Contents

Explanation

The 1991 edition of *The Macmillan & Silk Cut Nautical Almanac* follows the pattern established in 1985, when much of the standing information which does not alter from year to year was transferred to a new companion volume — *The Macmillan & Silk Cut Yachtsman's Handbook*. This will not be republished on an annual basis. A new and revised edition was published in 1988.

The 1991 *Almanac* contains the essential navigational data needed by yachtsmen for the waters round the United Kingdom, Ireland, and the coast of Europe from the border of Spain and France on the Atlantic coast to the North Sea border of Germany and Denmark.

Chapters 2–9 of the *Almanac* deal with the same subjects as Chapters 2–9 of the *Handbook*. Matters which are not likely to change, or which are of a permanent nature, are in the *Handbook*; things which are liable to alter from year to year (or which change completely, such as the tide tables and the ephemeris) are in this *Almanac*. Chapters 2–9 of the *Almanac* and the *Handbook* are cross-referenced where this is helpful to the user.

Chapter 10 — the bulk of the *Almanac* — contains harbour, coastal and tidal information, arranged area by area. A map of the twenty areas is shown on page 185.

1.1   INTRODUCTION

1.1.1   Numbering system

There are ten chapters. For ease of reference each chapter is divided into numbered sections, prefaced by the number of the chapter. Thus the sections in Chapter 7, for example, are numbered 7.1, 7.2 etc.

Within each section the key paragraphs are numbered. Thus in section 7.2 (say) the main paragraphs are numbered 7.2.1, 7.2.2, 7.2.3 etc.

Diagrams carry the chapter number and a figure in brackets, thus: Fig. 7(1), Fig. 7(2), Fig. 7(3) etc.

Tables carry the chapter number and a figure in brackets, thus Table 3(1), Table 3(2) etc.

1.1.2   Index

The main paragraph headings and the page number of each section are listed on the contents page at the start of each chapter. At the back of the book is a full page index, while at the front is a quick reference and personal index for important items.

1.1.3   General acknowledgments

The Editors wish to record their thanks to the many individuals and official bodies who have assisted by providing essential information and much advice in the preparation of this almanac. They include the Hydrographic Department of the Ministry of Defence (Navy) at Taunton, the Proudman Oceanographic Laboratory at Bidston, HM Nautical Almanac Office, HM Stationery Office, HM Customs, the Meteorological Office, HM Coastguard, British Telecom, Trinity House, the National Maritime Museum, the BBC and IBA, the Department of Transport, the Royal National Lifeboat Institution, the Port of London Authority, Associated British Ports, countless Harbour Masters, and our many individual agents.

Chartlets, tidal stream diagrams and tidal curves are produced from British Admiralty Charts and from Hydrographic Publications with the permission of the Controller of HM Stationery Office and of the Hydrographer of the Navy, and from French publications by permission of the Service Hydrographique et Océanographique de la Marine.

Information from the *Admiralty Lists of Lights*, *Admiralty Sailing Directions* and from the *Admiralty List of Radio Signals* is reproduced with the sanction of the Controller HM Stationery Office, and of the Hydrographer of the Navy.

Extracts from the following are published by permission of the Controller of HM Stationery Office: *International Code of Signals, 1969*; *Meteorological Office Weather Services for Shipping*.

Astronomical data is derived from the current edition of *The Nautical Almanac*, and is included by permission of HM Nautical Almanac Office and of the Science and Engineering Research Council.

Material from the *Handbook for Radio Operators* is by permission of British Telecom.

1.1.4   Acknowledgments — tidal information

Tidal predictions for Southampton, Dover, Sheerness, London Bridge, Harwich, Lowestoft, Immingham, River Tees, Leith, Aberdeen, Liverpool, Holyhead, Milford Haven, Avonmouth, Shoreham, Galway, Cobh, Belfast and St Helier are computed by the Proudman Oceanographic Laboratory, copyright reserved. Predictions for Dublin are prepared by the Proudman Oceanographic Laboratory for the Dublin Port and Docks Board, copyright reserved. Phases of the Moon are supplied by the Science and Engineering Research Council.

Tidal predictions for Devonport, Dartmouth, Poole, Portsmouth, Lerwick, Ullapool, Oban and Greenock are Crown Copyright and are supplied by permission of the Controller of HM Stationery Office, and the Hydrographer of the Navy.

Acknowledgment is made to the following authorities for permission to use the tidal predictions stated. Service Hydrographique et Océanographique de la Marine, France: Pointe de Grave, Brest, St Malo, Cherbourg, Le Havre and Dieppe. Department van Waterstaat, Netherlands: Flushing and Hook of Holland. Deutsches Hydrographisches Institut: Helgoland.

1.1.5   Standard terms

All bearings given in this Almanac are 'True', from seaward. For example, the sector of a light shown as G (Green) from 090°–180° is visible over an arc of 90° from the moment that the observer is due west of the light until he is due north of it.

Dimensions, in general, are stated in metric terms, the Imperial equivalent being included where appropriate. Distances, unless otherwise stated, are in International nautical (sea) miles, abbreviated as nm or M. All depths and heights are shown in metres (m) unless otherwise indicated.

Times are given in UT (GMT), unless stated otherwise (e.g. LT or local time), and are reckoned from 0000 (midnight) to 2400. DST refers to Daylight Saving Time (e.g. BST — British Summer Time). For BST and for standard time (in winter) in France, Belgium, Netherlands and West Germany — add one hour to UT (GMT). For Daylight Saving (DST) from last Sunday in March to last Saturday in September in France, Belgium, Netherlands and West Germany — add two hours to UT (GMT). Tidal predictions are given in UT (GMT) for the United Kingdom, and Zone −0100 for the Continent. (See 9.1.2.)

VHF frequencies are identified throughout by their International Maritime VHF series channel (Ch) designator. Frequencies used for calling and working may be separated thus Ch 16; 12.

1.1.6   Abbreviations

The following abbreviations are in general use, while others are explained where they appear in the Almanac. Abbreviations which appear on charts are shown in 3.1.4 on page 32, while those which refer to harbour facilities, lights, fog signals etc are given in 10.0.2, 10.0.3 and 10.0.4 at the start of Chapter 10.

Abbreviations for harbour facilities are also shown on the Dover tide table bookmark.

Alt	Altitude
anch	Anchor, anchorage
App	Apparent
approx	Approximate
Az	Azimuth
B	Bay
Bcst	Broadcast
Bn	Beacon
BFO	Beat frequency oscillator
brg	Bearing
BS	British Standard
BST	British Summer Time
°C	Degrees Celsius (Centigrade)
ca	Cable
CG	Coastguard
Ch	Channel (VHF)
chan	Channel (navigational)
conspic	Conspicuous
cont	Continuous
Corr	Correction
CS	Calibration Station
Dec	Declination
DF	Direction finding
DST	Daylight Saving Time
DW	Deep Water Route
E	East
ext	Extension
°F	Degrees Fahrenheit
Fcst	Forecast
Freq	Frequency
GHA	Greenwich Hour Angle
GMT	Greenwich Mean Time
h	Hours
H + ..	Commencing .. minutes past hour
H24	Continuous
harb	Harbour
Hd	Head
HF	High Frequency
HMSO	Her Majesty's Stationery Office
ht	Height
HW	High water
Hz	Hertz
I	Island
IALA	International Association of Lighthouse Authorities
Ident	Identification signal
in	Inch
inop	Inoperative
ITZ	Inshore traffic zone
kHz	Kilohertz

km	Kilometres
kn	Knot(s)
kW	Kilowatts
Lat	Latitude
LAT	Lowest Astronomical Tide
LANBY	Large Navigational Buoy
Ldg	Leading
LHA	Local Hour Angle
Long	Longitude
LT	Local time
Lt	Light
LtB	Light buoy
Lt F	Light float
Lt Ho	Lighthouse
Lt V	Light-vessel
LW	Low water
MF	Medium Frequency
MHWN	Mean High Water Neaps
MHWS	Mean High Water Springs
MHz	Megahertz
ML	Mean Level
MLWN	Mean Low Water Neaps
MLWS	Mean Low Water Springs
MRCC	Maritime Rescue Co-ordination Centre
MRSC	Maritime Rescue Sub-Centre
N	North
n mile	International nautical mile
np	Neaps
Occas	Occasional
(P)	Provisional
PA	Position approximate
Pt	Point
RC	Non-directional Radiobeacon
RD	Directional Radiobeacon
RG	Radio Direction Finding Station
rk(s)	Rock(s)
rky	Rocky
RT	Radio telephony
RNLI	Royal National Lifeboat Institution
S	South
sec, s	Seconds
Seq	Sequence
SHA	Sidereal Hour Angle
Sig	Signal
sp	Springs
SSB	Single sideband
Stn	Station
(T)	Temporary
Tel	Telephone
temp inop	Temporarily inoperative
Tr	Tower
TSS	Traffic Separation Scheme
Twi	Twilight
ufn	Until further notice
UT	Universal Time
VHF	Very High Frequency
W	West (longitude), White
wef	With effect from
WPT	Waypoint
WT	Radio telegraphy

1.2   IMPROVING IT

1.2.1   Suggestions for improvements

The Editors would be particularly grateful for suggestions for improving the content of the Almanac. Ideas based on experience with its practical use afloat would be specially welcome. It is not always feasible to implement suggestions received, but all will be carefully considered. Even minor ideas are welcome. Please send any ideas or comments to:

For Chapters 1 to 9 inclusive: The Editor, *The Macmillan & Silk Cut Nautical Almanac*, 41, Arbor Lane, Winnersh, Wokingham, Berkshire RG11 5JE.

For Chapter 10, Area 1 to 20 inclusive: The Editor, *The Macmillan & Silk Cut Nautical Almanac*, St Olaf's, Wonston, Winchester Hampshire, SO21 3LP.

1.2.2   Notification of errors

Although very great care has been taken in compiling all the information from innumerable sources, it is recognised that in a publication of this nature some errors may occur. The Editors would be extremely grateful if their attention could be called to any such lapses, by writing to them at the address in 1.2.1 above.

1.3   KEEPING IT UP TO DATE

1.3.1   Late corrections

Late corrections are at the back of the Almanac, in front of the index.

1.3.2   Sources of amendments

It is most important that charts and other navigational publications — such as this Almanac — are kept up to date. Corrections to Admiralty charts and publications are issued weekly in *Admiralty Notices to Mariners*. These are obtainable from Admiralty Chart Agents (by post if required), or they can be sighted at Customs Houses or Mercantile Marine Offices.

An alternative, but less frequent, service is given by the *Admiralty Notices to Mariners, Small Craft Edition*. This contains reprinted Notices for the British Isles and the European coast from the Gironde to the Elbe. Notices concerning depths greater in general than 7 metres (23ft), or which do not affect small craft for some other reason, are not included. They are available from Admiralty Chart Agents, or through the Royal Yachting Association.

1.3.3   Our free supplements

Important navigational information in this Almanac is corrected up to and including Admiralty Notices to Mariners, Weekly Edition No. 15 of 1990. Late amendments are at the back of the almanac, before the index. Inserted into the Almanac is a postcard application for two free supplements.

The first, to be published in January 1991, will contain corrections up to November 1990. The second to be published in May 1991, will contain corrections up to March 1991.

Please enter your name and address clearly in block capitals where indicated on the postcard. Affix a stamp and return it to: The Editors, *The Macmillan & Silk Cut Nautical Almanac*, 2 Church Farm Cottages, Barton Stacey, Winchester, Hampshire SO21 3RR.

The supplements will then be posted to you in due course, as they are published. Postage for the supplements will be paid by the publishers.

The Editors are grateful for any comments or suggestions. If you have any comments, please write them on the postcard in the space provided.

Supplements also include important corrections to *The Macmillan & Silk Cut Yachtsman's Handbook*.

1.3.4   Record of amendments

The amendment sheet below is intended to assist you in keeping the Almanac up to date, although it can also be used to record corrections to charts or other publications. Tick where indicated when the appropriate amendments have been made.

Weekly Notices to Mariners		Small Craft Editions
1	27	1 May 1990 ....
2	28	
3	29	1 July 1990 ....
4	30	
5	31	1 Sept 1990 ....
6	32	
7	33	1 Feb 1991 ....
8	34	
9	35	1 Mar 1991 ....
10	36	
11	37	1 May 1991 ....
12	38	
13	39	1 July 1991 ....
14	40	
15	41	1 Sept 1991 ....
16	42	
17	43	**Late corrections**
18	44	(see back of
19	45	Almanac, before
20	46	index)
21	47	
22	48	**Macmillan Supplements**
23	49	First ....
24	50	(Jan 1991)
25	51	Second ....
26	52	(May 1991)

For the connoisseur

Keep up to date with top international yacht racing
action, colourful waterborne adventure, and the
latest news from the high-society world of the
Superyachts with a subscription to
BOAT INTERNATIONAL
the world's best presented yachting magazine.

Subscribe to *Boat International*

SUBSCRIPTION RATES: UK £22.00 · EUROPE & EIRE (AIRMAIL) £35.00 · REST OF WORLD (AIRSPEEDED) £40.00

I would like a one-year (12 issue) subscription to *Boat International* commencing with the _____ (month) issue.

Pleae charge my Visa/Access/American Express/Mastercharge/Diners Club No _____

Credit Card expiry date _____ Signature _____

I enclose cheque/money order value £ _____   Please send a proforma invoice ☐

Cheques must be in sterling drawn on a UK bank and made payable to SF Publications Ltd.

Name _____ Address_____

Boat International Subs Dept.   Sterling House 5-7 Kingston Hill Kingston-upon-Thames Surrey KT2 7PW

The magazine with more Boats and Planes for sale than any other

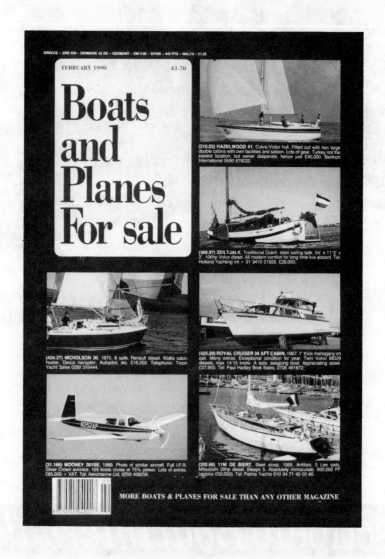

FIND IT FAST: If you're buying a boat you'll be sure to find it fast amongst over 1700 for sale (most with photographs) every month in **"Boats & Planes For Sale"**.

And the range of power and sailing boats is enormous, from £500 runabouts to luxury craft at over £1,000,000.

SELL IT FAST: Your boat will sell fast and cost you less in **"Boats & Planes For Sale"**.

Your advertisement will appear with a large photograph, black & white or colour, at a price to beat all other boating magazines.

And your advertisement appears in two consecutive monthly issues.

AVAILABLE AT ALL LEADING NEWSAGENTS, ON THE THIRD THURSDAY OF EVERY MONTH

For further details contact:
Freedom House Publishing Co. Ltd,
PO Box 93, Chichester, West Sussex, PO19 1HF
Tel: 0243 533394 Fax 0243 532025

Chapter 2

General Information

Contents

General information — introduction

The following subjects are described in detail in Chapter 2 of *The Macmillan & Silk Cut Yachtsman's Handbook*:

Limits and dangers — e.g. territorial waters; fishing limits; measured distances; hovercraft; warships on exercises; practice and exercise areas; submarines; minefields; wrecks; offshore oil and gas fields; power cables; traffic schemes. HM Customs — notice of departure; immigration; full and quick reports. Customs regulations in European countries. Yacht tonnage measurement — Net and Gross Tonnages; Lloyd's Register Tonnage; Deadweight Tonnage; One Ton Cup etc. Units and conversions. Glossaries of nautical terms. Yachting organisations — Royal Yachting Association; Seamanship Foundation; British Marine Industries Federation; Trinity House; useful addresses.

Here in the Almanac are given brief notes on the *International Regulations for Preventing Collisions at Sea*, traffic separation schemes, useful conversion factors, a summary of documentation and Customs procedures, and some useful addresses. For further details of these items, and of the subjects listed above, reference should be made to *The Macmillan & Silk Cut Yachtsman's Handbook*.

2.1   INTERNATIONAL REGULATIONS FOR PREVENTING COLLISIONS AT SEA

2.1.1   General

The regulations are stated in full, with diagrams and explanatory notes, in *The Macmillan & Silk Cut Yachtsman's Handbook* (2.1). The following are notes on provisions of special concern to yachtsmen. The numbers of the rules quoted are given for reference.

The rules must be interpreted in a seamanlike way if collisions are to be avoided (Rule 2). A vessel does not have right of way over another regardless of special factors — such as other vessels under way or at anchor, shallow water or other hazards, poor visibility, traffic schemes, fishing boats etc — or the handling characteristics of the vessels concerned in the prevailing conditions. Sometimes vessels must depart from the rules to avoid a collision. See Plate 4 on page 116.

A sailing vessel is so defined (Rule 3) when she is under sail only. When under power she must show the lights for a power-driven vessel, and when under sail and power a cone point down forward (Rule 25).

Keep a good lookout, using eyes and ears, particularly at night or in poor visibility (Rule 5).

Safe speed is dictated by visibility, traffic, depth of water, navigational dangers, and the manoeuvrability of the boat (Rule 6). Excess speed gives less time to appreciate the situation, less time to take avoiding action, and produces a worse collision if such action fails.

Risk of collision must be assessed by all available means (Rule 7). A yacht should take a series of compass bearings of a converging ship. Unless the bearings change appreciably, there is risk of collision. Take special care with large ships.

Take early and positive action to avoid collision (Rule 8). Large alterations of course and/or speed are more evident to the other skipper, particularly at night or on radar. Do not hesitate to slow down, stop (or even go astern, under power). While keeping clear of one vessel, watch out for others.

In narrow channels, keep to starboard whether under power or sail (Rule 9). A yacht under 20m in length must not impede larger vessels confined to a channel.

2.1.2   Traffic separation schemes

Yachts, like other vessels, must conform to traffic schemes (Rule 10). Traffic schemes are essential for the safety of larger vessels and, while inconvenient for yachtsmen, must be accepted as another element of passage planning, and be avoided where possible. They are shown on charts, and those around the British Isles are summarised in Figs 2(1)–2(8) on pages 7–13.

Proceed in the correct lane, and in the general direction of traffic. Normally join or leave a lane at its extremity, but when joining or leaving at the side, do so at as small an angle as possible. Boats under 20m in length, and any sailing yacht, may use inshore traffic zones — often the most sensible action for a yacht. If essential to cross a traffic lane, do so heading at as near right angles as possible to the lane, and do not impede vessels using the lane. If under sail, start the engine if speed falls below about three knots or if a reasonable course cannot be maintained.

Rule 10 does not modify the Collision Regulations when two vessels meet or converge in a traffic scheme and are in risk of collision. Some traffic schemes are under surveillance by radar, aircraft or patrol vessels. There are heavy penalties for breaking the rules. 'YG' in the International Code means 'You appear not to be complying with the traffic separation scheme'. See Plates 6 and 7 on pages 118 and 119.

2.1.3   Vessels in sight of each other

When two sailing vessels are in risk of collision and on opposite tacks, the port tack one keeps clear. If on the same tack, the windward one keeps clear (Rule 12).

Any overtaking vessel, whether power or sail, keeps clear of a vessel she is overtaking (Rule 13). Overtaking means approaching the other vessel from a direction more than $22\frac{1}{2}°$ abaft her beam (in the sector of her sternlight by night). An overtaken vessel must not hamper one overtaking: always look astern before altering course.

When two power-driven vessels approach head-on, each must alter course to starboard, to pass port to port (Rule 14). A substantial alteration may be needed, with the appropriate sound signal (see page 15 and Rule 34), to make intentions clear.

When two power-driven vessels are crossing and in risk of collision, the one with the other on her starboard side must keep clear and, if possible, avoid passing ahead of the other (Rule 15). The give-way vessel should normally alter to starboard; exceptionally, an alteration to port may be justified, in which case a large alteration may be needed to avoid crossing ahead of the other.

When one vessel has to keep clear, the other shall hold her course and speed. But if she realises that the give-way vessel is failing to keep clear, she must take independent action to avoid collision (Rule 17).

Under Rule 18, except where Rules 9 (Narrow Channels), 10 (Traffic Schemes) and 13 (Overtaking) otherwise require:

continued on page 14

Fig. 2(1) *TRAFFIC LANES — Ushant, Casquets*

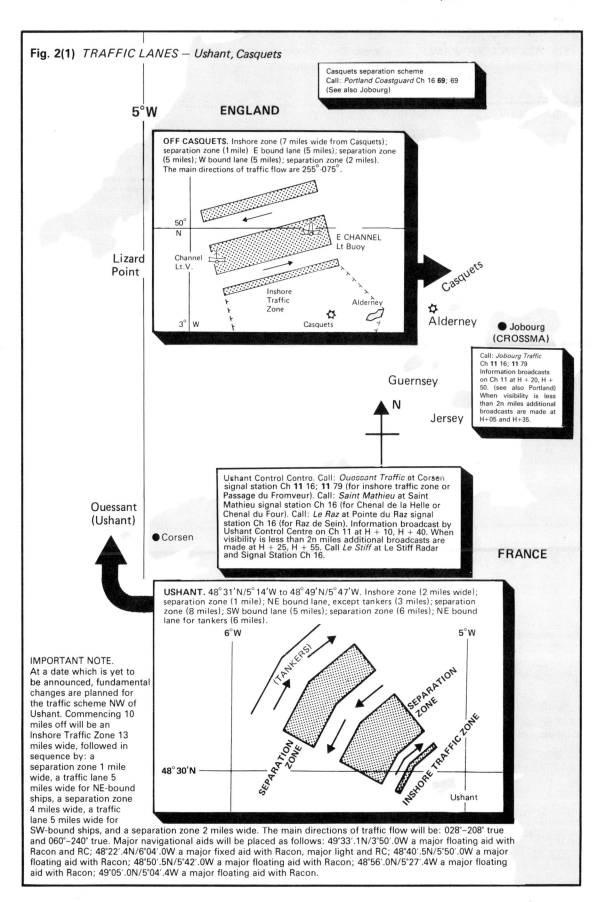

Casquets separation scheme
Call: *Portland Coastguard* Ch 16 **69**; 69
(See also Jobourg)

5°W   ENGLAND

OFF CASQUETS. Inshore zone (7 miles wide from Casquets); separation zone (1 mile) E bound lane (5 miles); separation zone (5 miles); W bound lane (5 miles); separation zone (2 miles). The main directions of traffic flow are 255°-075°.

50°N

Lizard Point

Channel Lt.V.

E CHANNEL Lt Buoy

Inshore Traffic Zone

3°W   Casquets

Casquets

Alderney

Alderney

● Jobourg (CROSSMA)

Call: *Jobourg Traffic* Ch **11** 16; **11** 79 Information broadcasts on Ch 11 at H + 20, H + 50. (see also Portland) When visibility is less than 2n miles additional broadcasts are made at H+05 and H+35.

Guernsey

N

Jersey

Ushant Control Contro. Call: *Ouessant Traffic* at Corsen signal station Ch **11** 16; **11** 79 (for inshore traffic zone or Passage du Fromveur). Call: *Saint Mathieu* at Saint Mathieu signal station Ch 16 (for Chenal de la Helle or Chenal du Four). Call: *Le Raz* at Pointe du Raz signal station Ch 16 (for Raz de Sein). Information broadcast by Ushant Control Centre on Ch 11 at H + 10, H + 40. When visibility is less than 2n miles additional broadcasts are made at H + 25, H + 55. Call *Le Stiff* at Le Stiff Radar and Signal Station Ch 16.

Ouessant (Ushant)

● Corsen

FRANCE

USHANT. 48°31'N/5°14'W to 48°49'N/5°47'W. Inshore zone (2 miles wide); separation zone (1 mile); NE bound lane, except tankers (3 miles); separation zone (8 miles); SW bound lane (5 miles); separation zone (6 miles); NE bound lane for tankers (6 miles).

6°W   5°W

(TANKERS)

SEPARATION ZONE

SEPARATION ZONE

48°30'N

SEPARATION ZONE

INSHORE TRAFFIC ZONE

Ushant

IMPORTANT NOTE. At a date which is yet to be announced, fundamental changes are planned for the traffic scheme NW of Ushant. Commencing 10 miles off will be an Inshore Traffic Zone 13 miles wide, followed in sequence by: a separation zone 1 mile wide, a traffic lane 5 miles wide for NE-bound ships, a separation zone 4 miles wide, a traffic lane 5 miles wide for SW-bound ships, and a separation zone 2 miles wide. The main directions of traffic flow will be: 028°-208° true and 060°-240° true. Major navigational aids will be placed as follows: 49°33'.1N/3°50'.0W a major floating aid with Racon and RC; 48°22'.4N/6°04'.0W a major fixed aid with Racon, major light and RC; 48°40'.5N/5°50'.0W a major floating aid with Racon; 48°50'.5N/5°42'.0W a major floating aid with Racon; 48°56'.0N/5°27'.4W a major floating aid with Racon; 49°05'.0N/5°04'.4W a major floating aid with Racon.

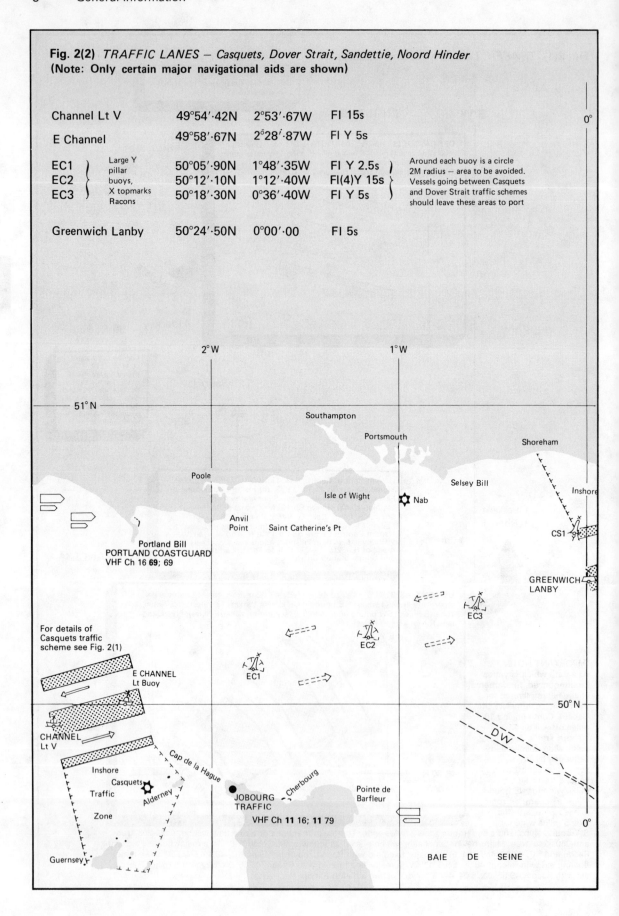

Fig. 2(2) *TRAFFIC LANES – Casquets, Dover Strait, Sandettie, Noord Hinder*
(Note: Only certain major navigational aids are shown)

Channel Lt V	49°54'·42N	2°53'·67W	Fl 15s
E Channel	49°58'·67N	2°28'·87W	Fl Y 5s
EC1	50°05'·90N	1°48'·35W	Fl Y 2.5s
EC2	50°12'·10N	1°12'·40W	Fl(4)Y 15s
EC3	50°18'·30N	0°36'·40W	Fl Y 5s
Greenwich Lanby	50°24'·50N	0°00'·00	Fl 5s

EC1, EC2, EC3: Large Y pillar buoys, X topmarks Racons

Around each buoy is a circle 2M radius — area to be avoided. Vessels going between Casquets and Dover Strait traffic schemes should leave these areas to port

0°

2° W

1° W

51° N

Southampton

Portsmouth

Shoreham

Poole

Selsey Bill

Inshore

Isle of Wight   Nab

Anvil Point   Saint Catherine's Pt

CS1

Portland Bill
PORTLAND COASTGUARD
VHF Ch 16 **69**; 69

GREENWICH LANBY

EC3

For details of Casquets traffic scheme see Fig. 2(1)

EC2

E CHANNEL Lt Buoy

EC1

50° N

CHANNEL Lt V

DW

Inshore

Cap de la Hague

Casquets

Cherbourg

Traffic

Alderney

Pointe de Barfleur

Zone

JOBOURG TRAFFIC
VHF Ch **11** 16; **11** 79

0°

Guernsey

BAIE   DE   SEINE

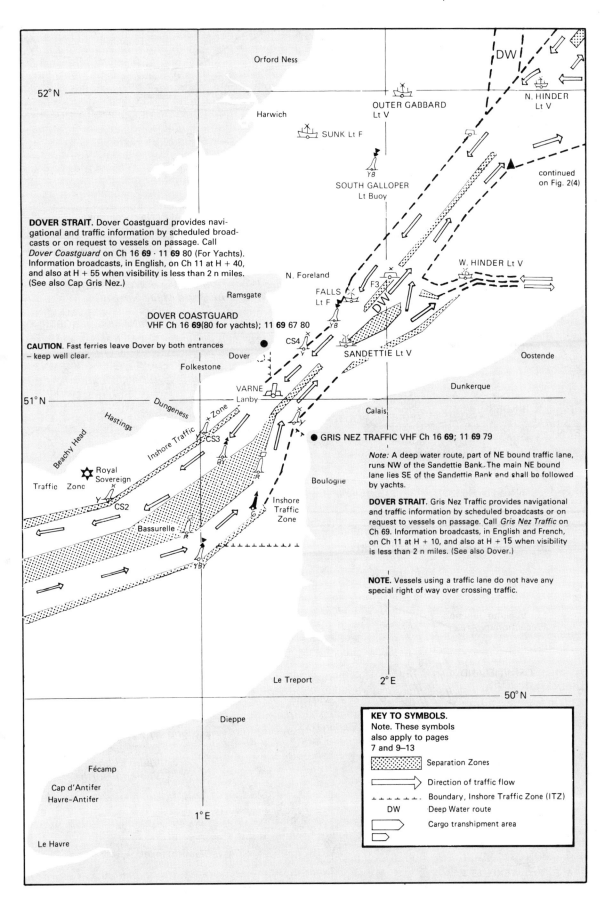

DOVER STRAIT. Dover Coastguard provides navigational and traffic information by scheduled broadcasts or on request to vessels on passage. Call *Dover Coastguard* on Ch 16 **69** · 11 **69** 80 (For Yachts). Information broadcasts, in English, on Ch 11 at H + 40, and also at H + 55 when visibility is less than 2 n miles. (See also Cap Gris Nez.)

DOVER COASTGUARD
VHF Ch 16 **69**(80 for yachts); 11 **69** 67 80

CAUTION. Fast ferries leave Dover by both entrances – keep well clear.

● GRIS NEZ TRAFFIC VHF Ch 16 **69**; 11 **69** 79

Note: A deep water route, part of NE bound traffic lane, runs NW of the Sandettie Bank.. The main NE bound lane lies SE of the Sandettie Bank and shall be followed by yachts.

DOVER STRAIT. Gris Nez Traffic provides navigational and traffic information by scheduled broadcasts or on request to vessels on passage. Call *Gris Nez Traffic* on Ch 69. Information broadcasts, in English and French, on Ch 11 at H + 10, and also at H + 15 when visibility is less than 2 n miles. (See also Dover.)

NOTE. Vessels using a traffic lane do not have any special right of way over crossing traffic.

KEY TO SYMBOLS.
Note. These symbols also apply to pages 7 and 9–13

Separation Zones
Direction of traffic flow
Boundary, Inshore Traffic Zone (ITZ)
DW Deep Water route
Cargo transhipment area

Fig. 2(3) *TRAFFIC LANES – Westerschelde*

Fig. 2(4) *TRAFFIC SCHEMES – Noord Hinder North, Maas West Outer, Maas West Inner, and Maas North*

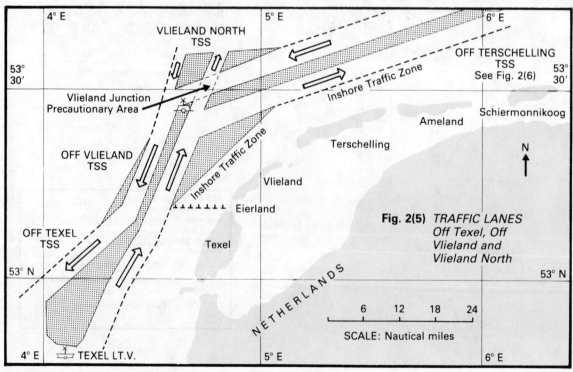

Fig. 2(5) *TRAFFIC LANES Off Texel, Off Vlieland and Vlieland North*

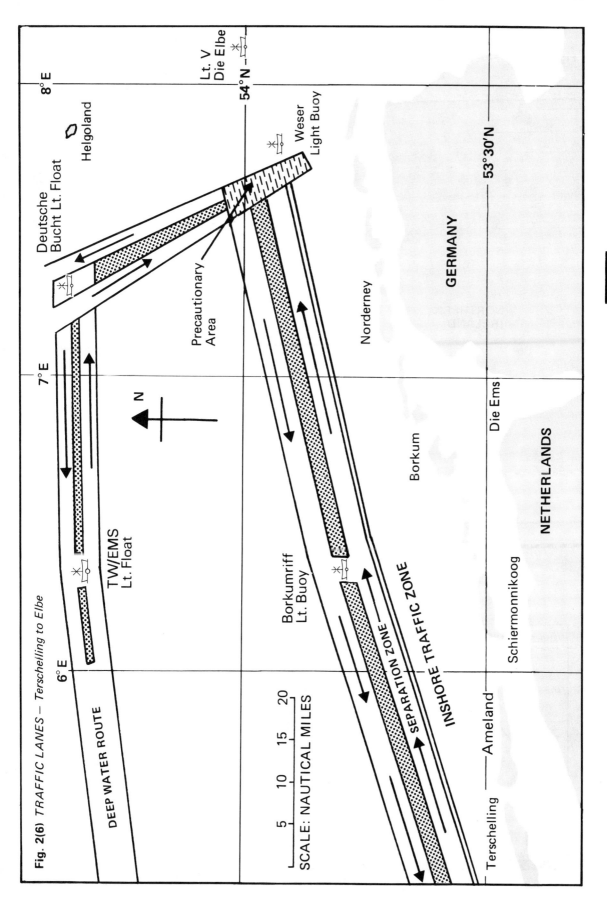

Fig. 2(6) *TRAFFIC LANES – Terschelling to Elbe*

DEEP WATER ROUTE

TW/EMS Lt. Float

Deutsche Bucht Lt. Float

Helgoland

Lt. V Die Elbe

Weser Light Buoy

Precautionary Area

N

Borkumriff Lt. Buoy

SEPARATION ZONE

INSHORE TRAFFIC ZONE

Norderney

Borkum

Die Ems

GERMANY

NETHERLANDS

Schiermonnikoog

Ameland

Terschelling

8° E

7° E

6° E

54° N

53° 30'N

SCALE: NAUTICAL MILES

5   10   15   20

2

Fig. 2(7) *TRAFFIC LANES – Irish Sea (Northern Part)*

NORTH CHANNEL. 55° 21′N/6°02′W. Lanes and separation zone all 2 miles wide. Inshore zones 2·5 miles wide.

6°W

55°
20′N

Kintyre

Mull ✪

Rathlin Is.

Sanda Is.

Altacarry Hd.

Ship Rock ✪

Fair Head

NORTH CHANNEL

NORTHERN
IRELAND

ISLE OF MAN

N

IRISH SEA

ANGLESEY

ANGLESEY. 58° 23′N/4°W to 53° 32′N/4° 32′W. Inshore zone (3·5 miles wide); NE bound lane (2 miles); separation zone (2 miles); SW bound lane (2 miles).

53°
30′N

Skerries ✪

✪

South
Stack ✪

Anglesey

5°W

WALES

Fig. 2(8) *TRAFFIC LANES – Irish Sea (Southern Part) and Scilly Isles*

TUSKAR ROCK. 52°08·5N/6°04′W. Inshore zone (2 miles wide); S bound lane (3 miles); separation zone (2 miles); N bound lane (3 miles).

Tuskar Rock

6°W

52°N

IRELAND

IRISH SEA

TUSKAR ROCK

ST DAVID'S HEAD

WALES

FASTNET. 51° 19′N/9° 31′. Inshore zone (2 miles wide); W going lane (2 miles); separation zone (2 miles); E going lane (2 miles).

Cape Clear

Fastnet Rock

51° 23′N

9° 30′W

SMALLS. 51° 45′N/N5°49 W. Inshore zone (4 miles) wide); N bound lane (3 miles); separation zone (2 miles); S bound lane (3 miles).

6°W

South Bishop

51° 50′N

Smalls

Skomer I.

Barrels

St Anns Hd

SCILLY ISLES. All lanes 3 miles and separation zones between them 2 miles wide. Inshore zones to S and W of Bishop Rock – 6 miles wide. Between Scillies and Lands End, S bound lane starts 0·5M eastward from Seven Stones Lt V; No bound lane starts 4 miles off Longships.

Seven Stones Lt.V.

ITZ

Longships

50° N

Round Island

ITZ

ITZ

50° N

St Marys

Wolf Rock

LANDS END

SCILLY ISLES

Bishop Rk

ITZ

ITZ

N

ENGLISH CHANNEL

6° W

(a) A power-driven vessel underway keeps clear of:
 (i) a vessel not under command;
 (ii) a vessel restricted in manoeuvrability;
 (iii) a vessel engaged in fishing;
 (iv) a sailing vessel.
(b) A sailing vessel underway keeps clear of: (i), (ii) and (iii) in (a) above.
(c) A vessel engaged in fishing, underway, keeps clear of: (i) and (ii) in (a) above.
(d) (i) Any vessel, except one not under command or one not restricted in her ability to manoeuvre, shall if possible avoid impeding a vessel constrained by her draught, showing the signals prescribed in Rule 28 (see page 116).
   (ii) A vessel constrained by her draught shall navigate with particular caution.

2.1.4   Restricted visibility
In poor visibility vessels must proceed at a safe speed (Rule 19). On hearing a fog signal ahead of the beam, be prepared to reduce speed or stop. If a vessel is detected by radar, take early action to avoid collision: if the other vessel is ahead of the beam avoid altering course to port, unless the other vessel is being overtaken: if the other vessel is abaft the beam, do not alter course towards. Sound the appropriate fog signal; keep a good lookout; have an efficient radar reflector; keep clear of shipping lanes; and be ready to take avoiding action. In thick fog it is best to anchor in shallow water, out of the shipping channels.

2.1.5   Lights and shapes
The required lights must be shown from sunset to sunrise, and by day in restricted visibility. The required shapes must be shown by day (Rule 20). See Plate 4 on page 116.

The types of navigation light are defined in Rule 21, and are shown in Plate 1 on page 113, together with illustrations of the lights to be shown by power-driven vessels and sailing vessels underway. A summary of the lights and shapes to be shown by various classes of vessel is given in Plate 4 on page 116.

A yacht, even with sails set, which is under engine must show the lights of a power-driven vessel. By day, a boat which is motor-sailing must show a cone, point down, forward.

In a sailing yacht up to 20m in length, the sidelights and sternlight may be combined in one tricolour lantern at the masthead. This gives excellent visibility for the lights, and maximum brightness for minimum battery drain, but must not be used when under power.

A sailing vessel underway may, in addition to her normal sidelights and sternlight, show near the masthead two all-round lights in a vertical line, red over green. But these lights must not be shown in conjunction with the tricolour lantern described in the previous paragraph (Rule 25).

Lights required for vessels towing and being towed (Rule 24) include a special yellow towing light above the sternlight of the towing vessel. But this is not required by a yacht or other small craft not normally used for towing.

The rules for vessels not under command, or restricted in their ability to manoeuvre (Rule 27) do not apply to vessels under 12m in length, except for showing flag 'A' International Code when engaged in diving operations. See Plates 6–7 on pages 118 and 119.

A power-driven vessel under 12m in length may combine her masthead light and sternlight in one all-round white light (Rule 23).

A yacht less than 7m in length is not required to show an anchor light or ball when she is not anchored in or near a narrow channel, fairway or anchorage, or where other vessels normally navigate (Rule 30). A vessel under 12m in length is not required to show the lights or shapes prescribed by that rule when she is aground.

2.1.6   Distress signals
Distress signals are listed below. See Plates 6 and 7 on pages 118 and 119. Those applicable to yachts are described in more detail in Chapter 8 (8.1.4). A DISTRESS SIGNAL MUST ONLY BE USED WHEN A VESSEL OR PERSON IS IN SERIOUS AND IMMEDIATE DANGER AND URGENT HELP IS NEEDED. For lesser emergencies use 'V' International Code — 'I require assistance'. See 6.1.5 for other signals of an emergency nature.

1. The following, together or separately, indicate distress and need of help:
(a) a gun or other explosive signal fired at intervals of about a minute;
(b) a continuous sounding with any fog-signalling apparatus;
(c) rockets or shells, throwing red stars fired one at a time at short intervals;
(d) a signal made by radiotelegraphy or by any other signalling method consisting of the group ··· ――― ··· (SOS) in the Morse Code;
(e) a signal sent by radiotelephony consisting of the spoken word 'Mayday';
(f) the International Code Signal of distress indicated by N.C.; see Plate 6 and 7 on pages 118 and 119.
(g) a signal consisting of a square flag having above or below it a ball or anything resembling a ball;
(h) flames on the vessel (as from a burning tar barrel, oil barrel, etc.);
(i) a rocket parachute flare or a hand flare showing a red light;

(j) a smoke signal giving off orange-coloured smoke;

(k) slowly and repeatedly raising and lowering arms outstretched to each side;

(l) the radiotelegraph alarm signal;

(m) the radiotelephone alarm signal;

(n) signals transmitted by emergency position-indicating radio beacons.

2. The use or exhibition of any of the foregoing signals except for the purpose of indicating distress and need of assistance and the use of other signals which may be confused with any of the above signals is prohibited.

3. Attention is drawn to the relevant sections of the *International Code of Signals,* the *Merchant Ship Search and Rescue Manual* and the following signals:

(a) a piece of orange-coloured canvas with either a black square and circle or other appropriate symbol (for identification from the air);

(b) a dye marker.

2.1.7 Sound signals

Sound signals required (by Rules 34 and 35) are summarised in the table below. Vessels over 12m in length must be provided with a whistle (foghorn) and a bell. A boat under 12m is not obliged to carry these sound signalling appliances, but must have some means of making an efficient sound signal. The effectiveness of a yacht's sound signal should be judged against its audibility from the bridge of a large ship, with conflicting noises from other sources.

Note that a short blast is about one second, and a prolonged blast four to six seconds in duration. A sailing vessel underway in fog sounds one prolonged blast, followed by two short blasts ('D'). The maximum intervals between sound signals for vessels underway in restricted visibility is two minutes, but they should be sounded more frequently if other craft are near.

2

Summary of important sound signals — Rules 34 and 35

Note: •   indicates a short blast of foghorn, of about one second's duration.

— indicates a prolonged blast of foghorn, of four to six seconds' duration.

Vessels in sight of each other (Rule 34)

•	I am altering course to starboard (power-driven vessel)
••	I am altering course to port (power-driven vessel)
•••	I am operating astern propulsion (power-driven vessel)
——•	(In a narrow channel) I intend to overtake you on your starboard side
——••	(In a narrow channel) I intend to overtake you on your port side
—•—•	Agreement with the overtaking signal above
•••••	I fail to understand your intentions or actions/I doubt if you are taking sufficient action to avoid collision
—	Warning signal by vessel(s) approaching a bend in channel

Sound signals in restricted visibility (Rule 35)

—	Power-driven vessel making way through the water
——	Power-driven vessel under way, but stopped and not making way through the water
—••	Vessel not under command, or restricted in her ability to manoeuvre, or constrained by her draught, or engaged in fishing, or towing or pushing, or a sailing vessel
—•••	Vessel being towed, or if more than one vessel is towed the last vessel in the tow
••••	Pilot vessel engaged on pilotage duties
Bell rung rapidly for about 5 seconds, every minute	Vessel at anchor
Gong rung rapidly for about 5 seconds following above signal, every minute	Vessel of 100 metres or more in length at anchor: the bell being sounded in the fore part of the vessel and the gong aft
•—•	Vessel at anchor (optional additional signal)
Bell rung rapidly for about 5 seconds, with three separate and distinct strokes before and after	Vessel aground

2.2.1   Conversion factors

To convert	Multiply by	To convert	Multiply by
sq in to sq mm	645.16	sq mm to sq in	0.00155
sq ft to sq m	0.0929	sq m to sq ft	10.76
lb/hp/hr to		gram/hp/hr to	
gram/hp/hr	447.4	lb/hp/hr	0.0022
in to mm	25.40	mm to in	0.0394
ft to m	0.3048	m to ft	3.2808
fathoms to m	1.8288	m to fathoms	0.5468
naut miles to statute	1.1515	statute miles to naut	0.8684
lbf to N	4.4482	N to lbf	0.2248
kgf to N	9.8066	N to kgf	0.101972
lb to kg	0.4536	kg to lb	2.205
tons to tonnes		tonnes to tons	
(1000 kg)	1.016	(2240 lb)	0.9842
horsepower to kW	0.7457	kW to hp	1.341
hp to metric hp	1.014	metric hp to hp	0.9862
metric hp to kW	0.735	kW to metric hp	1.359
lb/sq in to kg/sq cm	0.0703	kg/sq cm to lb/sq in	14.22
lb/sq in to ft of water	2.31	ft of water to lb/sq in	0.433
lb/sq in to atmospheres	0.0680	atmospheres to lb/sq in	14.7
ft/sec to m/sec	0.3048	m/sec to ft/sec	3.281
ft/sec to miles/hr	0.682	miles/hr to ft/sec	1.467
ft/min to m/sec	0.0051	m/sec to ft/min	196.8
knots to miles/hr	1.1515	miles/hr to knots	0.868
knots to km/hr	1.8520	km/hr to knots	0.5400
lbf ft to Nm	1.3558	Nm to lbf ft	0.7376
kgf m to Nm	9.8066	Nm to kgf m	0.1020
lbf ft to kgf m	0.1383	kgf m to lbf ft	7.2330
cu ft to galls	6.25	galls to cu ft	0.16
cu ft to litres	28.33	litres to cu ft	0.035
pints to litres	0.568	litres to pints	1.76
galls to litres	4.546	litres to galls	0.22
Imp galls to US galls	1.2	US galls to Imp galls	0.833

2.2.2   Feet to metres, metres to feet

Explanation: The central columns of figures in bold type can be referred in either direction. To the left to convert metres into feet, or to the right to convert feet into metres. For example, five lines down: 5 feet = 1.52 metres, and 5 metres = 16.40 feet.

Feet		Metres	Feet		Metres	Feet		Metres	Feet		Metres
3.28	**1**	0.30	45.93	**14**	4.27	88.58	**27**	8.23	131.23	**40**	12.19
6.56	**2**	0.61	49.21	**15**	4.57	91.86	**28**	8.53	134.51	**41**	12.50
9.84	**3**	0.91	52.49	**16**	4.88	95.14	**29**	8.84	137.80	**42**	12.80
13.12	**4**	1.22	55.77	**17**	5.18	98.43	**30**	9.14	141.08	**43**	13.11
16.40	**5**	1.52	59.06	**18**	5.49	101.71	**31**	9.45	144.36	**44**	13.41
19.69	**6**	1.83	62.34	**19**	5.79	104.99	**32**	9.75	147.64	**45**	13.72
22.97	**7**	2.13	65.62	**20**	6.10	108.27	**33**	10.06	150.92	**46**	14.02
26.25	**8**	2.44	68.90	**21**	6.40	111.55	**34**	10.36	154.20	**47**	14.33
29.53	**9**	2.74	72.18	**22**	6.71	114.83	**35**	10.67	157.48	**48**	14.63
32.81	**10**	3.05	75.46	**23**	7.01	118.11	**36**	10.97	160.76	**49**	14.94
36.09	**11**	3.55	78.74	**24**	7.32	121.39	**37**	11.28	164.04	**50**	15.24
39.37	**12**	3.66	82.02	**25**	7.62	124.67	**38**	11.58			
42.65	**13**	3.96	85.30	**26**	7.92	127.95	**39**	11.89			

2.3   DOCUMENTATION

2.3.1   Registration

Two forms of registration are available for British owned yachts. Both are described more fully in section 1.5 of *The Macmillan & Silk Cut Yachtsman's Handbook*.

Full registration, under the Merchant Shipping Act of 1894, is a relatively complex and expensive business since a yacht has to follow the same procedure as a large merchant vessel. It does however have the advantage of establishing title (ownership), and is also required for recording a marine mortgage. The procedure is described in Customs Notice No. 382, obtainable from any Registrar of British Ships, who can normally be located at the Custom House in major ports.

The Small Ships Register, established in 1983, is sufficient for most purposes. It satisfies the law that a British yacht proceeding abroad must be registered, and it also meets the registration requirement for a privileged ensign. The cost is only £10 for a five year period, and measurement is a simple matter of taking the overall length of the boat — well described in the instructions which accompany the application form, obtainable from the Royal Yachting Association, RYA House, Romsey Road, Easleigh, Hants SO5 4YA.

2.3.2   International Certificate for Pleasure Navigation

With the introduction of the Small Ships Register, this certificate has no relevance for yachts owned by UK or Commonwealth citizens resident in the UK. It is however available for other persons.

2.3.3   Helmsman's (Overseas) Certificate of Competence

Some countries require a skipper to have a certificate of competence. If a suitable RYA Certificate (e.g. Yachtmaster Offshore) is not held, the above certificate can be issued by the RYA to UK residents on receipt of the appropriate application form, endorsed by the secretary or flag officer of an RYA club or the principal of an RYA recognised teaching establishment.

2.3.4   Licences

A licence is required to operate a boat on most inland waterways (e.g. the River Thames above Teddington Lock, the Norfolk Broads, Yorkshire Ouse above Naburn Lock, and canals or rivers controlled by the British Waterways Board).

2.3.5   Insurance

Any cruising boat represents a large capital investment, which should be protected against possible loss or damage by adequate insurance. It is also essential to insure against third-party risks, and cover for at least £500,000 is recommended.

The value for which a boat is insured should be the replacement cost of the boat and all equipment. Read the proposal form carefully, and fill in the details required as accurately as possible. Take care to abide by the nominated period in commission and cruising area. Note the various warranties which are implied or expressed in the policy. For example, the owner is required to keep the boat in good, seaworthy condition; insurance does not cover charter, unless specially arranged; prompt notice must be given of any claim; a reduction may be made for fair wear and tear for items such as outboards, sails and rigging; theft is only covered if forcible entry or removal can be shown; engines and other mechanical items are only covered in exceptional circumstances; personal effects are not covered, unless specially arranged; and motor boats with speeds of 17 knots or more are subject to special clauses and often to extra premiums.

2.3.6   Classification

Lloyd's Register of Shipping provides an advisory and consultancy service to owners, builders, moulders and designers, and publishes rules for the construction of yachts in various materials. Experienced surveyors approve drawings, supervise moulding, inspect fitting out, check the machinery, and certify the completed yacht. To remain 'in class' a yacht must be subjected to periodical surveys.

As an alternative to full classification, Lloyd's Register Building Certificate is provided to newly-built yachts which have been constructed of any approved material in accordance with the Society's rules, and under the supervision of its surveyors, without the requirement for periodical survey.

2.3.7   Cruising formalities

Before, or while cruising abroad, certain formalities are necessary, as summarised below:
(1) Conform to HM Customs regulations, see 2.4.
(2) The yacht must be registered, see 2.3.1.
(3) Take valid passports for all the crew, and conform to health regulations (e.g. by reporting any infectious disease): exceptionally vaccination certificates may be needed.
(4) Conform to Customs regulations in countries visited. Brief notes are given in section 2.5, but if in doubt about specific items or procedures, ask. All

countries are sensitive to the importation (including carriage on board) of illegal quantities of alcohol and tobacco, and drugs of any kind.

(5) Make sure the yacht is covered by insurance for the intended cruising area, including third party cover.

(6) It is wise for the skipper to carry a Certificate of Competence or similar document (e.g. Yacht-master Certificate).

(7) The yacht should wear the Red Ensign (or a Special Ensign, if so authorised), and fly a courtesy ensign of the country concerned at starboard crosstree. Flag 'Q' must be carried to comply with Customs procedures.

(8) In most countries it is illegal to use a visiting cruising yacht for any commercial purpose (e.g. charter).

2.4   HM CUSTOMS

2.4.1   General information

Yachts arriving in or departing from the UK from or to places abroad must conform to the regulations in Customs Notice No. 8 summarised below. This notice, the forms mentioned, and further information may be obtained from any Customs and Excise office or from HM Customs and Excise, CDE 1, Dorset House, Stamford Street, London SE1 9PS (Tel: 071-620 1313). Foreign yachts are subject to Customs Notice No. 8A.

Yachtsmen are warned that a boat may be searched at any time; everything obtained abroad must be declared; nothing must be landed or transferred to another vessel until permission is given or the reporting formalities completed; all animals or birds must be securely confined below and out of contact with any other animals, and not landed except when licensed by an officer representing the Ministry of Agriculture, Fisheries and Food; the penalties for smuggling are severe and may include forfeiture of the boat.

2.4.2   Notice of departure

Each intended departure from the UK must be notified to HM Customs on Part I of Form C1328, copies of which are available at Customs offices and from most yacht clubs etc. The form is in three parts. When completed Part I should be delivered to the Customs office nearest the place of departure, so as to arrive before departure. It is valid for up to 48 hours after the stated time of departure. Should the voyage be abandoned, Parts II and III should be posted or delivered to the same office marked 'voyage abandoned'. Failure to give notice of departure may result in delay and inconvenience on return, and possible prosecution.

2.4.3   Stores

In general there is no restriction on reasonable quantities of food, fuel and other stores on which all duties and VAT have been paid. Duty free stores are normally restricted to vessels of 40 tons net register or more, but may be allowed for smaller yachts proceeding south of Brest or north of the Eider — details can be obtained from any Customs office. No other goods may be shipped unless all customs and export procedures are met.

2.4.4   Immigration

The skipper must ensure that the presence of any non-patrials (people not having the right to live in the UK) is reported to the immigration authorities, usually represented by the Customs officer, unless only bound for the Channel Islands, Isle of Man, or Republic of Ireland.

2.4.5   Arrivals

On arrival from abroad (including the Channel Islands and the Republic of Ireland) yachts are subject to Customs control from the 12 mile limit, and the skipper must make a written report on Form C1328 (C1239 for foreign yachts). The skipper must also conform to public and animal health and immigration requirements. Health regulations are stated in Form Port 38, Appendix A to Customs Notice No. 8, whereby any death, illness, disease, animal, bird etc on board must be reported. The signal 'QQ' means 'I require health clearance'.

Entering UK waters flag 'Q' must be flown from the 12 mile limit (illuminated at night), until formalities are completed.

2.4.6   Full report

The full report procedure is applicable if duty and/or VAT is payable on the vessel; or if the vessel has goods on which duty and/or VAT is payable; or has had repairs/modifications done abroad; or has on board any animal or bird, or goods which are prohibited or restricted; or non-patrials or patrial without a passport (except from Channel Isles or Ireland); or the vessel left the UK more than one year previously; or was not cleared outwards on Part I of Form C1328, notifying the nearest Customs office by telephone or RT and awaiting the arrival of a Customs Officer; or has any death or notifiable illness on board. Under the above circumstances the skipper must make a full report by completing Parts II and III of Form C1328 and awaiting the arrival of a Customs Officer.

2.4.7   Quick report

When none of the conditions in the previous paragraph apply, and animal and health clearance is not required, the skipper is to complete Parts II and III of Form C1328. If the yacht is not visited by a Customs officer, deliver Part II to the Customs office concerned (or post it in a Customs post box) and retain Part III for reference. The crew may then proceed ashore. This procedure is not available to foreign yachts.

2.4.8   Customs offices — telephone numbers

The telephone number of the appropriate Customs office (HMC) is given under the heading 'Telephone' for each British harbour in Chapter 10.

2.5   FOREIGN CUSTOMS PROCEDURES

2.5.1   General

It is the skipper's responsibility to find out and to observe the Customs formalities which vary from country to country. In some cases it is obligatory to fly flag 'Q' on arrival, but in others only when carrying dutiable stores above the normal 'tourist' allowances. It is useful to have duplicated lists of those people on board, with their passport numbers.

2.5.2   Irish Republic

It is preferable for yachts to clear Customs at a harbour where there are Customs facilities – Dublin, Dun Laoghaire, Dunmore East, Waterford, New Ross, Dungarvan, Cobh, Cork, Kinsale, Baltimore (summer only), Crookhaven, Bantry, Castletownbere, Cahirciveen, Fenit, Kilrush, Foynes, Limerick, Galway, Westport, Sligo or Killybegs. But yachts may arrive at any port, and if the correct procedure is followed may report to the Civil Guard if there is no Customs officer present.

On arrival therefore, all yachts from abroad (whether carrying dutiable stores or not) must fly flag 'Q' by day, or show a red light over a white light by night, and report to the local Customs (or Civil Guard). Dutiable, prohibited or restricted goods must be declared. United Kingdom citizens do not require passports or visas.

2.5.3   France

Provided that a boat which is on a temporary visit from Great Britain, Northern Ireland or the Channel Islands is only carrying effects of the crew, authorised goods intended for personal use which are within duty-free allowances (and not for commercial purposes) and foreign currency which does not exceed 5000 French francs, there are no Customs formalities on arriving in French waters.

If, for whatever reason, it is required to clear Customs, a yacht should berth in a port which has Customs facilities (*Douanes*), and must fly flag 'Q' by day, or show a red light over a white light by night. It is a requirement that a boat is registered, either under the full registration procedure or on the Small Ships Register (see 2.3.1), or equivalent documentation for the Channel Islands.

A private owner taking his yacht to France qualifies for six months *Importation en Franchise Temporaire* (IFT), with no duty payable. To qualify for IFT the yacht should normally be skippered by the owner: while in France the boat must not be chartered, or even lent to somebody else, and the owner and crew must not pursue any paid activity. There should not be a change of skipper. Nor should the crew contribute to running expenses, which might be construed by the authorities as a charter operation.

The six month period may be unbroken, or it may be split into two or more visits within one year. After that, the boat becomes liable to TVA (French VAT) and to an annual tax called *Droit de Passeport*. Details should be obtained from the French Customs. Special regulations apply to yachts chartered from outside France, and to yacht deliveries in and out of the country.

2.5.4   Belgium

Foreign yachts are temporarily admitted duty-free, and there are no arduous formalities unless a stay of more than two months is contemplated, in which case it is necessary to apply for a *plaque d'immatriculation*.

In normal circumstances, fly flag 'Q' at the port of entry, where the yacht will be boarded by Customs officers (in light blue uniform) and possibly by marine police (in blue uniform) for immigration control.

2.5.5   Netherlands

On arrival the skipper must report to Customs with documentation of the yacht and the passports of the crew, to obtain an entry certificate which is then valid for 12 months. Flag 'Q' need only be flown if dutiable stores are carried. Yachts are expected to carry, and to obey, the *Binnenvaart Politie Reglement* contained in part 1 of the Almanaak voor Watertoerisme (collision regulations etc.), and also, where applicable, the special regulations which apply to the Rivers Rhine, Lek and Waal. It is possible that on these rivers and other inland waterways a Certificate of Competence or equivalent documentation may have to be produced.

2.5.6   Federal Republic of Germany

On arrival it is necessary to clear Customs at one of the main ports of entry — Borkum, Norderney, Norddeich, Wilhelmshaven, Bremerhaven or Cuxhaven. It is not possible to clear Customs at Helgoland. Yachts arriving from EEC or Scandinavian harbours need not fly flag 'Q'. If the yacht is not boarded by Customs officers, go ashore and report to the Customs office (*Zoll*).

There are special arrangements for yachts arriving in the Elbe and which only intend to transit the Kiel Canal: they are not required to clear Customs, but should fly the Third Substitute flag. Special regulations governing the canal and giving details of signals etc are available at the locks.

It is probable that a Certificate of Competence or equivalent document will have to be produced for navigation on the rivers and inland waterways.

2.6   SOME USEFUL ADDRESSES

Amateur Yacht Research Society, 10 Boringdon Terrace, Turnchapel, Plymouth PL9 9TQ. Tel: Plymouth (0752) 592646.

Association of Brokers and Yacht Agents, The Wheelhouse, 5 Station Road, Liphook, Hants GU30 7DW. Tel: Liphook (0428) 722322.

British Marine Industries Federation, Boating Industry House, Vale Road, Oatlants, Weybridge, Surrey. Tel: Weybridge (0932) 54511.

British Sub-Aqua Club, 16 Upper Woburn Place, London WC1H 0QW. Tel: 071-387 9302.

British Telecom Maritime Radio Services, 43 Bartholomew Close, London. Tel: 071-583 9416.

British Waterways Board, Melbury House, Melbury Terrace, London NW1 6JX. Tel: 071-262 6711.

Clyde Cruise Club, S.V. *Carrick*, Clyde Street, Glasgow G1 4LN. Tel: 041–552 2183.

Cowes Combined Clubs, Secretary, 18/119 Bath Road, Cowes, I.O.W. Tel: Cowes (0983) 295744.

Cruising Association, Ivory House, St Katharine's Dock, World Trade Centre, London E1 9AT. Tel: 071-481 0881.

HM Customs and Excise, Dorset House, Stamford Street, London SE1 9PS. Tel: 071-620 1313.

International Maritime Organization, 4 Albert Embankment, London SE1. Tel: 071-735 7611.

Junior Offshore Group, 59 Queen's Road, Cowes, I.O.W. Tel: Cowes (0983) 291572.

Little Ship Club, at The Naval Club, 38 Hill Street, London W1X 8DP. Tel: 071-236 7729.

Lloyd's Register of Shipping, Yacht and Small Craft Services, 69 Oxford Street, Southampton, Hants SO1 1DL. Tel: Southampton (0703) 220353.

Maritime Trust, 16 Ebury Street, London SW1H 0LH. Tel: 071-730 0096.

Meteorological Office, London Road, Bracknell, Berkshire RG12 2SZ. Tel: Bracknell (0344) 420242.

Royal Cruising Club, 42 Half Moon Street, London W1. Tel: 071-499 2103.

Royal Institute of Navigation, 1 Kensington Gore, London SW7 2AT. Tel: 071-589 5021.

Royal National Lifeboat Institution, West Quay Road, Poole, Dorset BH15 1HZ. Tel: Poole (0213) 71133.

Royal Naval Sailing Association, c/o Royal Naval Club, Pembroke Road, Portsmouth, Hants PO1 2NT. Tel: Portsmouth (0705) 23524.

Royal Ocean Racing Club, 20 St James Place, London SW1A 1NN. Tel: 071-493 5252.

Royal Thames Yacht Club, 60 Knightsbridge, London SW1A 7LF. Tel: 071-235 2121.

Royal Yachting Association, RYA House, Romsey Road, Eastleigh, Hants SO5 4YA. Tel: Eastleigh (0703) 629962.

Royal Yaching Association (Scotland), Caledonia House, South Gyle, Edinburgh EH12 9DQ. Tel: 031-317 7388.

Solent Cruising and Racing Association, 18/19 Bath Road, Cowes, I.O.W. Tel: Cowes (0983) 295744.

Sports Council, 70 Brompton Road, London SW3 1HE. Tel: 071-589 3411.

Trinity House, Corporation of, Trinity House, 4th Floor, Lloyd's Chambers, 1 Portsoken St., London E1 8BT. Tel: 071-480 6601.

UK Civil Satnav Group (UK CSG), c/o The Royal Institute of Navigation, at the Royal Geographical Society, 1 Kensington Gore, London SW7 2AT. Tel: 071-589 5021. Fax: 071-823 8671.

UK Offshore Boating Association, Burn's House, 144 Holdenburst Road, Bournemouth BH8 8AS. Tel: Bournemouth (0202) 298555.

Yacht Brokers, Designers and Surveyors Association, Wheel House, Petersfield Road, Whitehill, Bordon, Hants GU35 8BU. Tel: Bordon (04203) 3862.

RABIES
PREVENTION

NEVER SAIL ABROAD WITH ANIMALS ON BOARD

Sailing overseas? If you're travelling to any place outside territorial waters, always leave pets at home and never bring back any animals. The reason, in a word, is rabies.

A horrifying disease, rabies is invariably fatal in humans, once symptoms develop. It is usually caused by the bite of a pet that has been infected by a wild or stray animal. With the sea as a natural barrier, Britain has been free of the disease for over 60 years. But this situation can only be maintained by the observance of strict animal import and quarantine controls. In other words, the care and common-sense of us all.

Any animal shipped overseas is automatically liable to quarantine regulations, whether or not it has stepped ashore. So you should consider, before deciding to take pets abroad, the expense and separation of six-months quarantine on return.

Moreover, the penalties for evading regulations are severe. So-called 'pet-lovers' attempting to break the rules face an unlimited fine or up to a year's imprisonment. In addition, the animal may be destroyed, and at best will have to undergo the full six-months quarantine.

Just one infected animal would endanger humans and animals throughout Britain.

IT'S JUST NOT WORTH THE RISK.

MAFF Ministry of Agriculture Fisheries and Food

Contents

Coastal Navigation

3

Coastal navigation — introduction

The following subjects are described in detail in Chapter 3 of *The Macmillan & Silk Cut Yachtsman's Handbook*:

The terms and definitions used in coastal navigation; magnetic variation and deviation; compass checks; compass adjusting and compass swinging; charts and their symbols; lights and fog signals; methods of laying off courses and position fixing; time, speed and distance; measured mile table; pilotage; IALA buoyage system; passage planning; the use of calculators; practical passage making; sailing directions.

Here in the Almanac is provided basic information, in the form of tables and other data, needed for coastal navigation. Some brief descriptions on how to use the tables etc are included, but for a fuller explanation of these matters or of the subjects listed above, reference should be made to Chapter 3 of *The Macmillan & Silk Cut Yachtsman's Handbook*.

3.1.1 Compass variation and deviation

The compass is the most vital navigational instrument in a cruising boat. It is affected by variation (the amount magnetic North is displaced from True North, and which varies from place to place) and by deviation (caused by the boat's local magnetic field). Variation, which alters slightly from year to year, is shown on the chart — normally at the compass rose. Deviation varies according to the boat's heading: it should be shown, for different headings, on a deviation card — produced as a result of adjusting and swinging the compass. With a properly adjusted compass, deviation should not be more than about 2° on any heading — in which case it can often be ignored except on long passages.

When converting a True course or a True bearing to Magnetic: add Westerly variation or deviation and subtract Easterly.

When converting a Magnetic course or bearing to True: subtract Westerly variation or deviation, and add Easterly.

Bearings given on charts and in Sailing Directions are normally True bearings, from seaward.

3.1.2 Tables — explanations

The tables listed below are given on pages 23–30. Here are brief explanations of their use. For greater detail see Chapter 3 of *The Macmillan & Silk Cut Yachtsman's Handbook.*

Table 3(1) — True bearing of Sun at sunrise and sunset

Enter with approximate latitude and with declination (extracted from the ephemeris in Chapter 5). The tabulated figure is the True bearing, measured from North if declination is North or from South if declination is South, towards the East if rising or towards the West if setting. Having extracted the True bearing, apply variation before comparing with compass to determine deviation on course steered. The bearing of the Sun should be taken when its lower limb is a little over half a diameter above the horizon.

Table 3(2) — Distance off by Vertical Sextant Angle

Enter with the height of the body (in metres or feet) and read across the page until the required sextant angle (corrected for index error) is met. Take out the distance of the object (in nautical miles) at the head of the column. Caution is needed when the base of the object (e.g. a lighthouse) is below the horizon. For precise ranges the distance that sea level is below MHWS must be added to the height of the object (above MHWS) before entering the table.

Table 3(3) — Distance of horizon for various heights of eye

Enter with height of eye (in metres or feet), and extract distance of horizon (in nautical miles). The actual distance may be affected by abnormal refraction.

Table 3(4) — Lights — distance off when rising or dipping

This table combines selected heights of eye with selected heights of lights, to give the range at which a light dips below or rises above the horizon.

Table 3(5) — Time, speed and distance table

Enter with time (in decimals of an hour, or in minutes) and speed (in knots) to determine distance run (in nautical miles).

Table 3(6) — Measured mile table

Enter with time (in minutes at the head of columns, and in seconds down the side of the table) to extract speed (in knots).

3.1.3 Navigation by electronic calculator

Speed, time and distance

$$\text{Speed (in knots)} = \frac{\text{Distance (n miles)} \times 60}{\text{Time (mins)}}$$

$$\text{Time (in mins)} = \frac{\text{Distance (n miles)} \times 60}{\text{Speed (knots)}}$$

Distance (in n miles) =

$$\frac{\text{Speed (knots)} \times \text{Time (mins)}}{60}$$

Distances and speed

Distance of horizon (in n miles) =

$$1.144 \times \sqrt{\text{Ht of eye (in ft)}}$$

or

$$2.072 \times \sqrt{\text{Ht of eye (in m)}}$$

Distance a light is visible (in n miles) =

$$1.144 \times (\sqrt{h_o} + \sqrt{h_e})$$

where h_o and h_e are heights of light and eye (ft)

or

$$= 2.072 \times (\sqrt{h_o} + \sqrt{h_e})$$

where heights are in metres.

Distance of mountains etc beyond horizon, in n miles $= \sqrt{1.13(h_o - h_e) + (a - .972 \times \sqrt{h_e})^2} - (a - .972 \times \sqrt{h_e})$ where h_o is height of mountain (ft), h_e is height of eye (ft), and a is the sextant angle in minutes; or $= \sqrt{3.71(h_o - h_e) + (a - 1.76 \times \sqrt{h_e})^2} - (a - 1.76 \times \sqrt{h_e})$ where the heights are in metres.

(Continued on page 31)

TABLE 3(1) True bearing of sun at sunrise and sunset.

LAT	0°	1°	2°	3°	4°	5°	6°	7°	8°	9°	10°	11°	LAT
	°	°	°	°	°	°	°	°	°	°	°	°	
30°	90	88.8	87.7	86.5	85.4	84.2	83.1	81.9	80.7	79.6	78.4	77.3	30°
31°	90	88.8	87.7	86.5	85.3	84.2	83.0	81.9	80.6	79.5	78.3	77.1	31°
32°	90	88.8	87.6	86.5	85.3	84.1	82.9	81.7	80.5	79.4	78.2	77.0	32°
33°	90	88.8	87.6	86.4	85.2	84.0	82.8	81.6	80.4	79.2	78.0	76.8	33°
34°	90	88.8	87.6	86.4	85.2	84.0	82.7	81.5	80.3	79.1	77.9	76.7	34°
35°	90	88.8	87.5	86.3	85.1	83.9	82.7	81.4	80.2	79.0	77.8	76.5	35°
36°	90	88.8	87.5	86.3	85.0	83.8	82.6	81.3	80.1	78.8	77.6	76.3	36°
37°	90	88.7	87.5	86.2	85.0	83.7	82.5	81.2	80.0	78.7	77.4	76.2	37°
38°	90	88.7	87.5	86.2	84.9	83.6	82.4	81.1	79.8	78.5	77.3	76.0	38°
39°	90	88.7	87.4	86.1	84.8	83.6	82.3	81.0	79.7	78.4	77.1	75.8	39°
40°	90	88.7	87.4	86.1	84.8	83.5	82.1	80.8	79.5	78.2	76.9	75.6	40°
41°	90	88.7	87.3	86.0	84.7	83.4	82.0	80.7	79.4	78.0	76.7	75.3	41°
42°	90	88.6	87.3	86.0	84.6	83.3	81.9	80.6	79.2	77.8	76.5	75.1	42°
43°	90	88.6	87.3	85.9	84.5	83.1	81.8	80.4	79.0	77.6	76.3	74.9	43°
44°	90	88.6	87.2	85.8	84.4	83.0	81.6	80.2	78.8	77.4	76.0	74.6	44°
45°	90	88.6	87.2	85.7	84.3	82.9	81.5	80.1	78.6	77.2	75.8	74.3	45°
46°	90	88.6	87.1	85.7	84.2	82.8	81.3	79.9	78.4	77.0	75.5	74.0	46°
47°	90	88.5	87.1	85.6	84.1	82.6	81.2	79.7	78.2	76.7	75.2	73.7	47°
48°	90	88.5	87.0	85.5	84.0	82.5	81.0	79.5	78.0	76.5	75.0	73.4	48°
49°	90	88.5	86.9	85.4	83.9	82.4	80.8	79.3	77.7	76.2	74.6	73.1	49°
50°	90	88.4	86.9	85.3	83.8	82.2	80.6	79.1	77.5	75.9	74.3	72.7	50°
51°	90	88.4	86.8	85.2	83.6	82.0	80.4	78.8	77.2	75.6	74.0	72.4	51°
52°	90	88.4	86.7	85.1	83.5	81.9	80.2	78.6	76.9	75.3	73.6	71.9	52°
53°	90	88.3	86.7	85.0	83.3	81.7	80.0	78.3	76.6	74.9	73.2	71.5	53°
54°	90	88.3	86.6	84.9	83.2	81.5	79.8	78.0	76.3	74.6	72.8	71.1	54°
55°	90	88.2	86.5	84.8	83.0	81.3	79.5	77.7	76.0	74.2	72.4	70.6	55°
56°	90	88.2	86.4	84.6	82.8	81.0	79.2	77.4	75.6	73.8	71.9	70.0	56°
57°	90	88.2	86.3	84.5	82.6	80.8	78.9	77.0	75.2	73.3	71.4	69.5	57°
58°	90	88.1	86.2	84.3	82.4	80.5	78.6	76.7	74.8	72.8	70.9	68.9	58°
59°	90	88.1	86.1	84.2	82.2	80.3	78.3	76.3	74.3	72.3	70.3	68.3	59°
60°	90	88.0	86.0	84.0	82.0	80.0	77.9	75.9	73.8	71.8	69.7	67.6	60°

DECLINATION

LAT	12°	13°	14°	15°	16°	17°	18°	19°	20°	21°	22°	23°	LAT
	°	°	°	°	°	°	°	°	°	°	°	°	
30°	76.1	74.9	73.8	72.6	71.4	70.3	69.1	67.9	66.7	65.5	64.4	63.2	30°
31°	76.0	74.8	73.6	72.4	71.2	70.0	68.9	67.7	66.5	65.3	64.1	62.9	31°
32°	75.8	74.6	73.4	72.2	71.0	69.8	68.6	67.4	66.2	65.0	63.8	62.6	32°
33°	75.6	74.4	73.2	72.1	70.8	69.6	68.4	67.1	65.9	64.7	63.5	62.2	33°
34°	75.5	74.2	73.0	71.8	70.6	69.3	68.1	66.9	65.6	64.4	63.1	61.9	34°
35°	75.3	74.1	72.8	71.6	70.3	69.1	67.8	66.6	65.3	64.1	62.8	61.5	35°
36°	75.1	73.8	72.6	71.3	70.1	68.8	67.5	66.3	65.0	63.7	62.4	61.1	36°
37°	74.9	73.6	72.4	71.1	69.8	68.5	67.2	65.9	64.6	63.3	62.0	60.7	37°
38°	74.7	73.4	72.0	70.8	69.5	68.2	66.9	65.6	64.3	62.9	61.6	60.3	38°
39°	74.5	73.2	71.9	70.5	69.2	67.9	66.6	65.2	63.9	62.5	61.2	59.8	39°
40°	74.2	72.9	71.6	70.2	68.9	67.6	66.2	64.8	63.5	62.1	60.7	59.3	40°
41°	74.0	72.7	71.3	69.9	68.6	67.2	65.8	64.4	63.0	61.6	60.2	58.8	41°
42°	73.7	72.4	71.0	69.6	68.2	66.8	65.4	64.0	62.6	61.2	59.7	58.3	42°
43°	73.5	72.1	70.7	69.3	67.9	66.4	65.0	63.6	62.1	60.7	59.2	57.7	43°
44°	73.2	71.8	70.3	68.9	67.5	66.0	64.6	63.1	61.6	60.1	58.6	57.1	44°
45°	72.9	71.4	70.0	68.5	67.0	65.6	64.1	62.6	61.1	59.5	58.0	56.4	45°
46°	72.6	71.1	69.6	68.1	66.6	65.1	63.6	62.0	60.5	58.9	57.4	55.8	46°
47°	72.2	70.7	69.2	67.7	66.2	64.6	63.1	61.5	59.9	58.3	56.7	55.0	47°
48°	71.9	70.3	68.8	67.2	65.7	64.1	62.5	60.9	59.3	57.6	55.9	54.3	48°
49°	71.5	69.9	68.4	66.8	65.1	63.5	61.9	60.2	58.6	56.9	55.2	53.4	49°
50°	71.1	69.5	67.9	66.2	64.6	62.9	61.3	59.6	57.8	56.1	54.3	52.6	50°
51°	70.7	69.1	67.4	65.7	64.0	62.3	60.6	58.8	57.1	55.3	53.5	51.6	51°
52°	70.3	68.6	66.9	65.1	63.4	61.6	59.9	58.1	56.3	54.4	52.5	50.6	52°
53°	69.8	68.1	66.3	64.5	62.7	60.9	59.1	57.3	55.4	53.5	51.5	49.5	53°
54°	69.3	67.5	65.7	63.9	62.0	60.2	58.3	56.4	54.4	52.4	50.4	48.3	54°
55°	68.7	66.9	65.1	63.2	61.3	59.4	57.4	55.4	53.4	51.3	49.2	47.1	55°
56°	68.2	66.3	64.4	62.4	60.5	58.5	56.5	54.4	52.3	50.1	47.9	45.7	56°
57°	67.6	65.6	63.6	61.6	59.6	57.5	55.4	53.3	51.1	48.9	46.5	44.2	57°
58°	66.9	64.9	62.8	60.8	58.7	56.5	54.3	52.1	49.8	47.4	45.0	42.5	58°
59°	66.2	64.1	62.0	59.8	57.6	55.4	53.1	50.8	48.4	45.9	43.3	40.7	59°
60°	65.4	63.3	61.1	58.8	56.5	54.2	51.8	49.4	46.8	44.2	41.5	38.6	60°

3

TABLE 3(2)   Distance off by Vertical Sextant Angle

Height of object ft	m	Distance of object (nautical miles)															Height of object m	ft
		0.1	0.2	0.3	0.4	0.5	0.6	0.7	0.8	0.9	1.0	1.1	1.2	1.3	1.4	1.5		
33	10	3 05	1 33	1 02	0 46	0 37	0 31	0 27	0 23	0 21	0 19	0 17	0 15	0 14	0 13	0 12	10	33
39	12	3 42	1 51	1 14	0 56	0 45	0 37	0 32	0 28	0 25	0 22	0 20	0 19	0 17	0 16	0 15	12	39
46	14	4 19	2 10	1 27	1 05	0 52	0 43	0 37	0 32	0 29	0 26	0 24	0 22	0 20	0 19	0 17	14	46
53	16	4 56	2 28	1 39	1 14	0 59	0 49	0 42	0 37	0 33	0 30	0 27	0 25	0 23	0 21	0 20	16	53
59	18	5 33	2 47	1 51	1 24	1 07	0 56	0 48	0 42	0 37	0 33	0 30	0 28	0 26	0 24	0 22	18	59
66	20	6 10	3 05	2 04	1 33	1 14	1 02	0 53	0 46	0 41	0 37	0 34	0 31	0 29	0 27	0 25	20	66
72	22	6 46	3 24	2 16	1 42	1 22	1 08	0 58	0 51	0 45	0 41	0 37	0 34	0 31	0 29	0 27	22	72
79	24	7 23	3 42	2 28	1 51	1 29	1 14	1 04	0 56	0 49	0 45	0 40	0 37	0 34	0 32	0 30	24	79
85	26	7 59	4 01	2 41	2 01	1 36	1 20	1 09	1 00	0 54	0 48	0 44	0 40	0 37	0 34	0 32	26	85
92	28	8 36	4 19	2 53	2 10	1 44	1 27	1 14	1 05	0 58	0 52	0 47	0 43	0 40	0 37	0 35	28	92
98	30	9 12	4 38	3 05	2 19	1 51	1 33	1 20	1 10	1 02	0 56	0 51	0 46	0 43	0 40	0 37	30	98
105	32	9 48	4 56	3 18	2 28	1 58	1 39	1 25	1 14	1 06	0 59	0 54	0 49	0 46	0 42	0 40	32	105
112	34	10 24	5 15	3 30	2 38	2 06	1 45	1 30	1 19	1 10	1 03	0 57	0 53	0 49	0 45	0 42	34	112
118	36	11 00	5 33	3 42	2 47	2 14	1 51	1 35	1 24	1 14	1 07	1 01	0 56	0 51	0 48	0 45	36	118
125	38	11 36	5 41	3 55	2 56	2 21	1 58	1 41	1 28	1 18	1 11	1 04	0 59	0 54	0 50	0 47	38	125
131	40	12 11	6 10	4 07	3 05	2 28	2 04	1 46	1 33	1 22	1 14	1 07	1 02	0 57	0 53	0 49	40	131
138	42	12 47	6 28	4 19	3 15	2 36	2 10	1 51	1 37	1 27	1 18	1 11	1 05	1 00	0 56	0 52	42	138
144	44	13 22	6 46	4 32	3 24	2 43	2 16	1 57	1 42	1 31	1 22	1 14	1 08	1 03	0 58	0 54	44	144
151	46	13 57	7 05	4 44	3 33	2 51	2 22	2 02	1 47	1 35	1 25	1 18	1 11	1 06	1 01	0 57	46	151
157	48	14 32	7 23	4 56	3 42	2 58	2 28	2 07	1 51	1 39	1 29	1 21	1 14	1 09	1 04	0 59	48	157
164	50	15 07	7 41	5 09	3 52	3 05	2 35	2 13	1 56	1 43	1 33	1 24	1 17	1 11	1 06	1 02	50	164
171	52	15 41	7 59	5 21	4 01	3 13	2 41	2 18	2 01	1 47	1 36	1 28	1 20	1 14	1 09	1 04	52	171
177	54	16 15	8 18	5 33	4 10	3 20	2 47	2 23	2 05	1 51	1 40	1 31	1 23	1 17	1 12	1 07	54	177
184	56	16 49	8 36	5 45	4 19	3 28	2 53	2 28	2 10	1 55	1 44	1 34	1 27	1 20	1 14	1 09	56	184
190	58	17 23	8 54	5 58	4 29	3 35	2 59	2 34	2 15	2 00	1 48	1 38	1 30	1 23	1 17	1 12	58	190
197	60	17 57	9 12	6 10	4 38	3 42	3 05	2 39	2 19	2 04	1 51	1 41	1 33	1 26	1 20	1 14	60	197
203	62	18 31	9 30	6 22	4 47	3 50	3 12	2 44	2 24	2 08	1 55	1 45	1 36	1 29	1 22	1 17	62	203
210	64	19 04	9 48	6 34	4 56	3 57	3 18	2 50	2 28	2 12	1 59	1 48	1 39	1 31	1 25	1 19	64	210
217	66	19 37	10 06	6 46	5 05	4 05	3 24	2 53	2 33	2 16	2 02	1 51	1 42	1 34	1 27	1 22	66	217
223	68	20 10	10 24	6 59	5 15	4 12	3 30	3 00	2 38	2 20	2 06	1 55	1 45	1 37	1 30	1 24	68	223
230	70	20 42	10 42	7 11	5 24	4 19	3 36	3 05	2 42	2 24	2 09	1 58	1 48	1 40	1 33	1 27	70	230
236	72	21 15	11 00	7 23	5 33	4 27	3 42	3 11	2 47	2 31	2 14	2 01	1 51	1 43	1 35	1 29	72	236
246	75	22 03	11 27	7 41	5 47	4 38	3 52	3 19	2 54	2 35	2 19	2 07	1 56	1 47	1 39	1 33	75	246
256	78	22 50	11 54	7 59	6 01	4 49	4 01	3 27	3 01	2 41	2 24	2 12	2 01	1 51	1 43	1 36	78	256
266	81	23 37	12 20	8 18	6 14	5 00	4 10	3 35	3 08	2 47	2 30	2 17	2 05	1 56	1 47	1 40	81	266
276	84	24 24	12 47	8 36	6 28	5 11	4 19	3 42	3 15	2 53	2 36	2 22	2 10	2 00	1 51	1 44	84	276
289	88	25 25	13 22	9 00	6 46	5 26	4 32	3 53	3 24	3 01	2 43	2 28	2 16	2 06	1 57	1 49	88	289
302	92	26 25	13 57	9 24	7 05	5 40	4 44	4 04	3 33	3 10	2 51	2 35	2 22	2 11	2 02	1 54	92	302
315	96	27 24	14 32	9 48	7 23	5 55	4 56	4 14	3 42	3 18	2 58	2 42	2 28	2 17	2 07	1 59	96	315
328	100	28 22	15 07	10 12	7 41	6 10	5 09	4 25	3 52	3 26	3 05	2 49	2 35	2 23	2 13	2 04	100	328
341	104	29 19	15 41	10 36	7 59	6 24	5 21	4 35	4 01	3 34	3 13	2 55	2 41	2 28	2 18	2 09	104	341
358	109	30 29	16 24	11 06	8 22	6 43	5 36	4 48	4 12	3 44	3 22	3 04	2 48	2 36	2 24	2 15	109	358
374	114	31 37	17 06	11 36	8 45	7 01	5 51	5 02	4 24	3 55	3 31	3 12	2 56	2 43	2 31	2 21	114	374
394	120	32 56	17 57	12 11	9 12	7 23	6 10	5 17	4 38	4 07	3 42	3 22	3 05	2 51	2 39	2 28	120	394
427	130	35 04	19 20	13 10	9 57	8 00	6 40	5 44	5 01	4 28	4 01	3 39	3 21	3 05	2 52	2 41	130	427
459	140	37 05	20 42	14 09	10 42	8 36	7 11	6 10	5 24	4 48	4 19	3 56	3 36	3 20	3 05	2 53	140	459
492	150	39 00	22 03	15 07	11 27	9 12	7 41	6 36	5 47	5 09	4 38	4 13	3 52	3 34	3 19	3 05	150	492
574	175		25 17	17 29	13 17	10 42	8 57	7 41	6 44	6 00	5 24	4 55	4 30	4 09	3 52	3 36	175	574
656	200		28 22	19 48	15 07	12 11	10 12	8 46	7 41	6 51	6 10	5 36	5 09	4 45	4 25	4 07	200	656
738	225			22 03	16 54	13 39	11 27	9 51	8 38	7 41	6 56	6 18	5 47	5 20	4 58	4 38	225	738
820	250			24 14	18 39	15 07	12 41	10 55	9 35	8 32	7 41	7 00	6 25	5 56	5 30	5 09	250	820
902	275			26 20	20 22	16 32	13 54	11 59	10 31	9 22	8 27	7 41	7 03	6 31	6 03	5 39	275	902
984	300				22 03	17 57	15 07	13 02	11 27	10 12	9 12	8 23	7 41	7 06	6 36	6 10	300	984
1148	350					20 42	17 29	15 07	13 17	11 51	10 42	9 45	8 57	8 16	7 41	7 11	350	1148
1312	400						19 48	17 09	15 07	13 30	12 11	11 07	10 12	9 26	8 46	8 12	400	1312
ft m Height of object		0.1	0.2	0.3	0.4	0.5	0.6	0.7	0.8	0.9	1.0	1.1	1.2	1.3	1.4	1.5	m ft Height of object	
							Distance of object (nautical miles)											

TABLE 3(2) Distance off by Vertical Sextant Angle (continued)

Height of object ft	m	1.6	1.7	1.8	1.9	2.0	2.1	2.2	2.3	2.4	2.5	2.6	2.7	2.8	2.9	3.0	m	ft
		° ′	° ′	° ′	° ′	° ′	° ′	° ′	° ′	° ′	° ′	° ′	° ′	° ′	° ′	° ′		
33	10	0 12	0 11	0 10	0 10												10	33
39	12	0 14	0 13	0 12	0 12	0 11	0 11	0 10	0 10	0 10							12	39
46	14	0 16	0 15	0 14	0 14	0 13	0 12	0 12	0 11	0 11	0 10	0 10	0 10				14	46
53	16	0 19	0 17	0 16	0 16	0 15	0 14	0 13	0 13	0 12	0 12	0 11	0 11	0 11	0 10	0 10	16	53
59	18	0 21	0 20	0 19	0 18	0 17	0 16	0 15	0 15	0 14	0 13	0 13	0 12	0 12	0 12	0 11	18	59
66	20	0 23	0 22	0 21	0 20	0 19	0 18	0 17	0 16	0 15	0 15	0 14	0 14	0 13	0 13	0 12	20	66
72	22	0 26	0 24	0 23	0 21	0 20	0 19	0 19	0 18	0 17	0 16	0 16	0 15	0 15	0 14	0 14	22	72
79	24	0 28	0 26	0 25	0 23	0 22	0 21	0 20	0 19	0 19	0 18	0 17	0 16	0 16	0 15	0 15	24	79
85	26	0 30	0 28	0 27	0 25	0 24	0 23	0 22	0 21	0 20	0 19	0 19	0 18	0 17	0 17	0 16	26	85
92	28	0 32	0 31	0 29	0 27	0 26	0 25	0 24	0 23	0 22	0 21	0 20	0 19	0 19	0 18	0 17	28	92
98	30	0 35	0 33	0 31	0 29	0 28	0 27	0 25	0 24	0 23	0 22	0 21	0 21	0 20	0 19	0 19	30	98
105	32	0 37	0 35	0 33	0 31	0 30	0 28	0 27	0 26	0 25	0 24	0 23	0 22	0 21	0 20	0 20	32	105
112	34	0 39	0 37	0 35	0 33	0 31	0 30	0 29	0 27	0 26	0 25	0 24	0 23	0 23	0 22	0 21	34	112
118	36	0 42	0 39	0 37	0 35	0 33	0 32	0 30	0 29	0 28	0 27	0 26	0 25	0 24	0 23	0 22	36	118
125	38	0 44	0 41	0 39	0 37	0 35	0 34	0 32	0 31	0 29	0 28	0 27	0 26	0 25	0 24	0 24	38	125
131	40	0 46	0 44	0 41	0 39	0 37	0 35	0 34	0 32	0 31	0 30	0 29	0 27	0 27	0 26	0 25	40	131
138	42	0 49	0 46	0 43	0 41	0 40	0 37	0 35	0 34	0 32	0 31	0 30	0 29	0 28	0 27	0 26	42	138
144	44	0 51	0 48	0 45	0 43	0 41	0 39	0 37	0 36	0 34	0 33	0 31	0 30	0 29	0 28	0 27	44	144
151	46	0 53	0 50	0 47	0 45	0 43	0 41	0 39	0 37	0 36	0 34	0 33	0 32	0 30	0 29	0 28	46	151
157	48	0 56	0 52	0 49	0 47	0 45	0 42	0 40	0 39	0 37	0 36	0 34	0 33	0 32	0 31	0 30	48	157
164	50	0 58	0 55	0 52	0 49	0 46	0 44	0 42	0 40	0 39	0 37	0 36	0 34	0 33	0 32	0 31	50	164
171	52	1 00	0 57	0 54	0 51	0 48	0 46	0 44	0 42	0 40	0 39	0 37	0 36	0 34	0 33	0 32	52	171
177	54	1 03	0 59	0 56	0 53	0 50	0 48	0 46	0 44	0 42	0 40	0 39	0 37	0 36	0 35	0 33	54	177
184	56	1 05	1 01	0 58	0 55	0 52	0 49	0 47	0 45	0 43	0 42	0 40	0 38	0 37	0 36	0 35	56	184
190	58	1 07	1 03	1 00	0 57	0 54	0 51	0 49	0 47	0 45	0 43	0 41	0 40	0 38	0 37	0 36	58	190
197	60	1 10	1 06	1 02	0 59	0 56	0 53	0 51	0 48	0 46	0 45	0 43	0 41	0 40	0 38	0 37	60	197
203	62	1 12	1 08	1 04	1 01	0 58	0 55	0 52	0 50	0 48	0 46	0 44	0 43	0 41	0 40	0 38	62	203
210	64	1 14	1 10	1 06	1 03	0 59	0 57	0 54	0 52	0 49	0 48	0 46	0 44	0 42	0 41	0 40	64	210
217	66	1 17	1 12	1 08	1 05	1 01	0 58	0 56	0 53	0 51	0 49	0 47	0 45	0 44	0 42	0 41	66	217
223	68	1 19	1 14	1 10	1 06	1 03	1 00	0 57	0 55	0 53	0 50	0 49	0 47	0 45	0 44	0 42	68	223
230	70	1 21	1 16	1 12	1 08	1 05	1 02	0 59	0 56	0 54	0 52	0 50	0 48	0 46	0 45	0 43	70	230
236	72	1 24	1 19	1 14	1 10	1 07	1 04	1 01	0 58	0 56	0 53	0 51	0 49	0 48	0 46	0 45	72	236
246	75	1 27	1 22	1 17	1 13	1 10	1 06	1 03	1 01	0 58	0 56	0 54	0 51	0 50	0 48	0 46	75	246
256	78	1 30	1 25	1 20	1 16	1 12	1 09	1 06	1 03	1 00	0 58	0 56	0 54	0 52	0 50	0 48	78	256
266	81	1 34	1 28	1 23	1 19	1 15	1 12	1 08	1 05	1 03	1 00	0 58	0 56	0 54	0 52	0 50	81	266
276	84	1 37	1 32	1 27	1 22	1 18	1 14	1 11	1 08	1 05	1 02	1 00	0 58	0 56	0 54	0 52	84	276
289	88	1 42	1 36	1 31	1 26	1 22	1 18	1 14	1 11	1 08	1 05	1 03	1 00	0 58	0 56	0 54	88	289
302	92	1 47	1 40	1 35	1 30	1 25	1 21	1 18	1 14	1 11	1 08	1 06	1 03	1 01	0 59	0 57	92	302
315	96	1 51	1 45	1 39	1 34	1 29	1 25	1 21	1 17	1 14	1 11	1 09	1 06	1 04	1 01	0 59	96	315
328	100	1 56	1 49	1 43	1 38	1 33	1 28	1 24	1 21	1 17	1 14	1 11	1 09	1 06	1 04	1 02	100	328
341	104	2 01	1 54	1 47	1 42	1 36	1 32	1 28	1 24	1 20	1 17	1 14	1 11	1 09	1 07	1 04	104	341
358	109	2 06	1 59	1 52	1 46	1 41	1 36	1 32	1 28	1 24	1 21	1 18	1 15	1 12	1 10	1 07	109	358
374	114	2 12	2 04	1 58	1 51	1 46	1 41	1 36	1 32	1 28	1 25	1 21	1 18	1 16	1 13	1 11	114	374
394	120	2 19	2 11	2 04	1 57	1 51	1 46	1 41	1 37	1 33	1 29	1 26	1 22	1 20	1 17	1 14	120	394
427	130	2 31	2 22	2 14	2 07	2 01	1 55	1 50	1 45	1 41	1 36	1 33	1 29	1 26	1 23	1 20	130	427
459	140	2 42	2 33	2 24	2 17	2 10	2 04	1 58	1 53	1 48	1 44	1 40	1 36	1 33	1 30	1 27	140	459
492	150	2 54	2 44	2 35	2 26	2 19	2 13	2 07	2 01	1 56	1 51	1 47	1 43	1 39	1 36	1 33	150	492
574	175	3 23	3 11	3 00	2 51	2 42	2 35	2 28	2 21	2 15	2 10	2 05	2 00	1 56	1 52	1 48	175	574
656	200	3 52	3 38	3 26	3 15	3 05	2 57	2 49	2 41	2 35	2 28	2 23	2 17	2 13	2 08	2 04	200	656
738	225	4 21	4 05	3 52	3 40	3 29	3 19	3 10	3 01	2 54	2 47	2 41	2 36	2 29	2 24	2 19	225	738
820	250	4 49	4 32	4 17	4 04	3 52	3 41	3 31	3 22	3 13	3 05	2 58	2 52	2 46	2 40	2 35	250	820
902	275	5 18	5 00	4 43	4 28	4 15	4 03	3 52	3 42	3 32	3 24	3 16	3 09	3 02	2 56	2 50	275	902
984	300	5 47	5 27	5 09	4 52	4 38	4 25	4 13	4 02	3 52	3 42	3 34	3 26	3 19	3 12	3 05	300	984
1148	350	6 44	6 21	6 00	5 41	5 24	5 09	4 55	4 42	4 30	4 19	4 09	4 00	3 52	3 44	3 36	350	1148
1312	400	7 41	7 14	6 51	6 29	6 10	5 52	5 36	5 22	5 09	4 56	4 45	4 34	4 25	4 16	4 07	400	1312
ft m		1.6	1.7	1.8	1.9	2.0	2.1	2.2	2.3	2.4	2.5	2.6	2.7	2.8	2.9	3.0	m ft	
Height of object					Distance of object (nautical miles)												Height of object	

3

TABLE 3(2)   Distance off by Vertical Sextant Angle (continued)

Height of object ft	m	3.1	3.2	3.3	3.4	3.5	3.6	3.7	3.8	3.9	4.0	4.2	4.4	4.6	4.8	5.0	m	ft
		° ′	° ′	° ′	° ′	° ′	° ′	° ′	° ′	° ′	° ′	° ′	° ′	° ′	° ′	° ′		
33	10																10	33
39	12																12	39
46	14																14	46
53	16	0 10															16	53
59	18	0 11	0 10	0 10	0 10	0 10											18	59
66	20	0 12	0 12	0 11	0 11	0 11	0 10	0 10	0 10	0 10							20	66
72	22	0 13	0 13	0 12	0 12	0 12	0 11	0 11	0 11	0 10	0 10						22	72
79	24	0 14	0 14	0 13	0 13	0 13	0 12	0 12	0 12	0 11	0 11	0 11	0 10				24	79
85	26	0 16	0 15	0 15	0 14	0 14	0 13	0 13	0 13	0 12	0 12	0 11	0 11	0 10	0 10		26	85
92	28	0 17	0 16	0 16	0 15	0 15	0 14	0 14	0 14	0 13	0 13	0 12	0 12	0 11	0 11	0 10	28	92
98	30	0 18	0 17	0 17	0 16	0 16	0 15	0 15	0 15	0 14	0 14	0 13	0 13	0 12	0 12	0 11	30	98
105	32	0 19	0 19	0 18	0 17	0 17	0 16	0 16	0 16	0 15	0 15	0 14	0 13	0 13	0 12	0 12	32	105
112	34	0 20	0 20	0 19	0 19	0 18	0 17	0 17	0 17	0 16	0 16	0 15	0 14	0 14	0 13	0 13	34	112
118	36	0 22	0 21	0 20	0 20	0 19	0 19	0 18	0 18	0 17	0 17	0 16	0 15	0 14	0 14	0 13	36	118
125	38	0 23	0 22	0 21	0 21	0 20	0 20	0 19	0 19	0 18	0 18	0 17	0 16	0 15	0 15	0 14	38	125
131	40	0 24	0 23	0 22	0 22	0 21	0 21	0 20	0 20	0 19	0 19	0 18	0 17	0 16	0 15	0 15	40	131
138	42	0 25	0 24	0 24	0 23	0 22	0 22	0 21	0 21	0 20	0 19	0 19	0 18	0 17	0 16	0 16	42	138
144	44	0 26	0 25	0 25	0 24	0 23	0 23	0 22	0 22	0 21	0 20	0 19	0 19	0 18	0 17	0 16	44	144
151	46	0 28	0 27	0 26	0 25	0 24	0 24	0 23	0 22	0 22	0 21	0 20	0 19	0 19	0 18	0 17	46	151
157	48	0 29	0 28	0 27	0 26	0 25	0 25	0 24	0 23	0 23	0 22	0 21	0 20	0 19	0 19	0 18	48	157
164	50	0 30	0 29	0 28	0 27	0 27	0 26	0 25	0 24	0 24	0 23	0 22	0 21	0 20	0 19	0 19	50	164
171	52	0 31	0 30	0 29	0 28	0 28	0 27	0 26	0 25	0 25	0 24	0 23	0 22	0 21	0 20	0 19	52	171
177	54	0 32	0 31	0 30	0 29	0 29	0 28	0 27	0 26	0 26	0 25	0 24	0 23	0 22	0 21	0 20	54	177
184	56	0 34	0 32	0 31	0 31	0 30	0 29	0 28	0 27	0 27	0 26	0 25	0 24	0 23	0 22	0 21	56	184
190	58	0 35	0 34	0 33	0 32	0 31	0 30	0 29	0 28	0 28	0 27	0 26	0 24	0 23	0 22	0 21	58	190
197	60	0 36	0 35	0 34	0 33	0 32	0 31	0 30	0 29	0 29	0 28	0 26	0 25	0 24	0 23	0 22	60	197
203	62	0 37	0 36	0 35	0 34	0 33	0 32	0 31	0 30	0 30	0 29	0 27	0 26	0 25	0 24	0 23	62	203
210	64	0 38	0 37	0 36	0 35	0 34	0 33	0 32	0 31	0 30	0 30	0 28	0 27	0 26	0 25	0 24	64	210
217	66	0 40	0 38	0 37	0 36	0 35	0 34	0 33	0 32	0 31	0 31	0 29	0 28	0 27	0 26	0 25	66	217
223	68	0 41	0 39	0 38	0 37	0 36	0 35	0 34	0 33	0 32	0 32	0 30	0 29	0 27	0 26	0 25	68	223
230	70	0 42	0 41	0 39	0 38	0 37	0 36	0 35	0 34	0 33	0 32	0 31	0 29	0 28	0 27	0 26	70	230
236	72	0 43	0 42	0 40	0 39	0 38	0 37	0 36	0 35	0 34	0 33	0 32	0 30	0 29	0 28	0 27	72	236
246	75	0 45	0 44	0 42	0 41	0 40	0 39	0 38	0 37	0 36	0 35	0 33	0 32	0 30	0 29	0 28	75	246
256	78	0 47	0 45	0 44	0 43	0 41	0 40	0 39	0 38	0 37	0 36	0 34	0 33	0 31	0 30	0 29	78	256
266	81	0 48	0 47	0 46	0 44	0 43	0 42	0 41	0 40	0 39	0 38	0 36	0 34	0 33	0 31	0 30	81	266
276	84	0 50	0 49	0 47	0 46	0 45	0 43	0 42	0 41	0 40	0 39	0 37	0 35	0 34	0 32	0 31	84	276
289	88	0 53	0 51	0 49	0 48	0 47	0 45	0 44	0 43	0 42	0 41	0 39	0 37	0 36	0 34	0 33	88	289
302	92	0 55	0 53	0 52	0 50	0 49	0 47	0 46	0 45	0 44	0 43	0 41	0 39	0 37	0 36	0 34	92	302
315	96	0 57	0 56	0 54	0 52	0 51	0 49	0 48	0 47	0 46	0 45	0 42	0 41	0 39	0 37	0 36	96	315
328	100	1 00	0 58	0 56	0 55	0 53	0 52	0 50	0 49	0 48	0 46	0 44	0 42	0 40	0 39	0 37	100	328
341	104	1 02	1 00	0 58	0 57	0 55	0 54	0 52	0 51	0 49	0 48	0 46	0 44	0 42	0 40	0 39	104	341
358	109	1 05	1 03	1 01	1 00	0 58	0 56	0 55	0 53	0 52	0 51	0 48	0 46	0 44	0 42	0 40	109	358
374	114	1 08	1 06	1 04	1 02	1 00	0 59	0 57	0 56	0 54	0 53	0 50	0 48	0 46	0 44	0 42	114	374
394	120	1 12	1 10	1 07	1 06	1 04	1 02	1 00	0 59	0 57	0 56	0 53	0 51	0 48	0 46	0 45	120	394
427	130	1 18	1 15	1 13	1 11	1 09	1 07	1 05	1 03	1 02	1 00	0 57	0 55	0 52	0 50	0 48	130	427
459	140	1 24	1 21	1 19	1 16	1 14	1 12	1 10	1 08	1 07	1 05	1 02	0 59	0 56	0 54	0 52	140	459
492	150	1 30	1 27	1 24	1 22	1 20	1 17	1 15	1 13	1 11	1 10	1 06	1 03	1 01	0 58	0 56	150	492
574	175	1 45	1 41	1 38	1 36	1 33	1 30	1 28	1 25	1 23	1 21	1 17	1 14	1 11	1 08	1 05	175	574
656	200	2 00	1 56	1 52	1 49	1 46	1 43	1 40	1 38	1 35	1 33	1 28	1 24	1 21	1 17	1 14	200	656
738	225	2 15	2 10	2 06	2 03	1 59	1 56	1 53	1 50	1 47	1 44	1 39	1 35	1 31	1 27	1 24	225	738
820	250	2 30	2 25	2 20	2 16	2 13	2 09	2 05	2 02	1 59	1 56	1 50	1 45	1 41	1 37	1 33	250	820
902	275	2 45	2 39	2 34	2 30	2 26	2 22	2 18	2 14	2 11	2 08	2 01	1 56	1 51	1 46	1 42	275	902
984	300	2 59	2 54	2 48	2 44	2 39	2 35	2 30	2 26	2 23	2 19	2 13	2 07	2 01	1 56	1 51	300	984
1148	350	3 29	3 23	3 16	3 11	3 05	3 00	2 55	2 51	2 46	2 42	2 35	2 28	2 21	2 15	2 10	350	1148
1312	400	3 59	3 52	3 44	3 38	3 32	3 26	3 20	3 15	3 10	3 05	2 57	2 49	2 41	2 35	2 28	400	1312
ft m Height of object		3.1	3.2	3.3	3.4	3.5	3.6	3.7	3.8	3.9	4.0	4.2	4.4	4.6	4.8	5.0	m ft Height of object	

Distance of object (nautical miles)

TABLE 3(3)   Distance of horizon for various heights of eye

Height of eye		Horizon distance	Height of eye		Horizon distance	Height of eye		Horizon distance
metres	feet	n. miles	metres	feet	n. miles	metres	feet	n. miles
1	3.3	2.1	21	68.9	9.5	41	134.5	13.3
2	6.6	2.9	22	72.2	9.8	42	137.8	13.5
3	9.8	3.6	23	75.5	10.0	43	141.1	13.7
4	13.1	4.1	24	78.7	10.2	44	144.4	13.8
5	16.4	4.7	25	82.0	10.4	45	147.6	14.0
6	19.7	5.1	26	85.3	10.6	46	150.9	14.1
7	23.0	5.5	27	88.6	10.8	47	154.2	14.3
8	26.2	5.9	28	91.9	11.0	48	157.5	14.4
9	29.6	6.2	29	95.1	11.2	49	160.8	14.6
10	32.8	6.6	30	98.4	11.4	50	164.0	14.7
11	36.1	6.9	31	101.7	11.6	51	167.3	14.9
12	39.4	7.2	32	105.0	11.8	52	170.6	15.0
13	42.7	7.5	33	108.3	12.0	53	173.9	15.2
14	45.9	7.8	34	111.6	12.1	54	177.2	15.3
15	49.2	8.1	35	114.8	12.3	55	180.4	15.4
16	52.5	8.3	36	118.1	12.5	56	183.7	15.6
17	55.8	8.6	37	121.4	12.7	57	187.0	15.7
18	59.1	8.8	38	124.7	12.8	58	190.3	15.9
19	62.3	9.1	39	128.0	13.0	59	193.6	16.0
20	65.6	9.3	40	131.2	13.2	60	196.9	16.1

3

TABLE 3 (4)   Lights — distance off when rising or dipping (n. miles)

Height of light			Height of eye									
		metres	1	2	3	4	5	6	7	8	9	10
metres	feet	feet	3	7	10	13	16	20	23	26	30	33
10	33		8.7	9.5	10.2	10.8	11.3	11.7	12.1	12.5	12.8	13.2
12	39		9.3	10.1	10.8	11.4	11.9	12.3	12.7	13.1	13.4	13.8
14	46		9.9	10.7	11.4	12.0	12.5	12.9	13.3	13.7	14.0	14.4
16	53		10.4	11.2	11.9	12.5	13.0	13.4	13.8	14.2	14.5	14.9
18	59		10.9	11.7	12.4	13.0	13.5	13.9	14.3	14.7	15.0	15.4
20	66		11.4	12.2	12.9	13.5	14.0	14.4	14.8	15.2	15.5	15.9
22	72		11.9	12.7	13.4	14.0	14.5	14.9	15.3	15.7	16.0	16.4
24	79		12.3	13.1	13.8	14.4	14.9	15.3	15.7	16.1	16.4	17.0
26	85		12.7	13.5	14.2	14.8	15.3	15.7	16.1	16.5	16.8	17.2
28	92		13.1	13.9	14.6	15.2	15.7	16.1	16.5	16.9	17.2	17.6
30	98		13.5	14.3	15.0	15.6	16.1	16.5	16.9	17.3	17.6	18.0
32	105		13.9	14.7	15.4	16.0	16.5	16.9	17.3	17.7	18.0	18.4
34	112		14.2	15.0	15.7	16.3	16.8	17.2	17.6	18.0	18.3	18.7
36	118		14.6	15.4	16.1	16.7	17.2	17.6	18.0	18.4	18.7	19.1
38	125		14.9	15.7	16.4	17.0	17.5	17.9	18.3	18.7	19.0	19.4
40	131		15.3	16.1	16.8	17.4	17.9	18.3	18.7	19.1	19.4	19.8
42	138		15.6	16.4	17.1	17.7	18.2	18.6	19.0	19.4	19.7	20.1
44	144		15.9	16.7	17.4	18.0	18.5	18.9	19.3	19.7	20.0	20.4
46	151		16.2	17.0	17.7	18.3	18.8	19.2	19.6	20.0	20.3	20.7
48	157		16.5	17.3	18.0	18.6	19.1	19.5	19.9	20.3	20.6	21.0
50	164		16.8	17.6	18.3	18.9	19.4	19.8	20.2	20.6	20.9	21.3
55	180		17.5	18.3	19.0	19.6	20.1	20.5	20.9	21.3	21.6	22.0
60	197		18.2	19.0	19.7	20.3	20.8	21.2	21.6	22.0	22.3	22.7
65	213		18.9	19.7	20.4	21.0	21.5	21.9	22.3	22.7	23.0	23.4
70	230		19.5	20.3	21.0	21.6	22.1	22.5	22.9	23.2	23.6	24.0
75	246		20.1	20.9	21.6	22.2	22.7	23.1	23.5	23.9	24.2	24.6
80	262		20.7	21.5	22.2	22.8	23.3	23.7	24.1	24.5	24.8	25.2
85	279		21.3	22.1	22.8	23.4	23.9	24.3	24.7	25.1	25.4	25.8
90	295		21.8	22.6	23.3	23.9	24.4	24.8	25.2	25.6	25.9	26.3
95	312		22.4	23.2	23.9	24.5	25.0	25.4	25.8	26.2	26.5	26.9
metres	feet	metres	1	2	3	4	5	6	7	8	9	10
Height of light		feet	3	7	10	13	16	20	23	26	30	33
							Height of eye					

TABLE 3(5)   Time, Speed and Distance Table

Time Decimal of hr.	Mins	2.5	3	3.5	4	4.5	5	5.5	6	6.5	7	7.5	8	8.5	9	9.5	10	Mins	Time Decimal of hr.
.0167	1				0.1	0.1	0.1	0.1	0.1	0.1	0.1	0.1	0.1	0.1	0.2	0.2	0.2	1	.0167
.0333	2	0.1	0.1	0.1	0.1	0.1	0.2	0.2	0.2	0.2	0.2	0.2	0.3	0.3	0.3	0.3	0.3	2	.0333
.0500	3	0.1	0.1	0.2	0.2	0.2	0.2	0.3	0.3	0.3	0.3	0.4	0.4	0.4	0.4	0.5	0.5	3	.0500
.0667	4	0.1	0.2	0.2	0.3	0.3	0.3	0.4	0.4	0.4	0.5	0.5	0.5	0.6	0.6	0.6	0.7	4	.0667
.0833	5	0.2	0.2	0.3	0.3	0.4	0.4	0.5	0.5	0.5	0.6	0.6	0.7	0.7	0.7	0.8	0.8	5	.0833
.1000	6	0.2	0.3	0.3	0.4	0.4	0.5	0.5	0.6	0.6	0.7	0.7	0.8	0.8	0.9	0.9	1.0	6	.1000
.1167	7	0.3	0.4	0.4	0.5	0.5	0.6	0.6	0.7	0.8	0.8	0.9	0.9	1.0	1.1	1.1	1.2	7	.1167
.1333	8	0.3	0.4	0.5	0.5	0.6	0.7	0.7	0.8	0.9	0.9	1.0	1.1	1.1	1.2	1.3	1.3	8	.1333
.1500	9	0.4	0.4	0.5	0.6	0.7	0.7	0.8	0.9	1.0	1.0	1.1	1.2	1.3	1.3	1.4	1.5	9	.1500
.1667	10	0.4	0.5	0.6	0.7	0.8	0.8	0.9	1.0	1.1	1.2	1.3	1.3	1.4	1.5	1.6	1.7	10	.1667
.1833	11	0.5	0.5	0.6	0.7	0.8	0.9	1.0	1.1	1.2	1.3	1.4	1.5	1.6	1.6	1.7	1.8	11	.1833
.2000	12	0.5	0.6	0.7	0.8	0.9	1.0	1.1	1.2	1.3	1.4	1.5	1.6	1.7	1.8	1.9	2.0	12	.2000
.2167	13	0.5	0.6	0.8	0.9	1.0	1.1	1.2	1.3	1.4	1.5	1.6	1.7	1.8	2.0	2.0	2.2	13	.2167
.2333	14	0.6	0.7	0.8	0.9	1.0	1.2	1.3	1.4	1.5	1.6	1.7	1.9	2.0	2.1	2.2	2.3	14	.2333
.2500	15	0.6	0.7	0.9	1.0	1.1	1.2	1.4	1.5	1.6	1.8	1.9	2.0	2.1	2.2	2.4	2.5	15	.2500
.2667	16	0.7	0.8	0.9	1.1	1.2	1.3	1.5	1.6	1.7	1.9	2.0	2.1	2.3	2.4	2.5	2.7	16	.2667
.2833	17	0.7	0.8	1.0	1.1	1.3	1.4	1.6	1.7	1.8	2.0	2.1	2.3	2.4	2.5	2.7	2.8	17	.2833
.3000	18	0.7	0.9	1.0	1.2	1.3	1.5	1.6	1.8	1.9	2.1	2.2	2.4	2.5	2.7	2.8	3.0	18	.3000
.3167	19	0.8	1.0	1.1	1.3	1.4	1.6	1.7	1.9	2.1	2.1	2.4	2.5	2.7	2.9	3.0	3.2	19	.3167
.3333	20	0.8	1.0	1.2	1.3	1.5	1.7	1.8	2.0	2.2	2.3	2.5	2.7	2.8	3.0	3.2	3.3	20	.3333
.3500	21	0.9	1.0	1.2	1.4	1.6	1.7	1.9	2.1	2.3	2.4	2.6	2.8	3.0	3.1	3.3	3.5	21	.3500
.3667	22	0.9	1.1	1.3	1.5	1.7	1.8	2.1	2.2	2.4	2.6	2.8	2.9	3.1	3.3	3.5	3.7	22	.3667
.3833	23	1.0	1.1	1.3	1.5	1.7	1.9	2.1	2.3	2.5	2.7	2.9	3.1	3.3	3.4	3.6	3.8	23	.3833
.4000	24	1.0	1.2	1.4	1.6	1.8	2.0	2.2	2.4	2.6	2.8	3.0	3.2	3.4	3.6	3.8	4.0	24	.4000
.4167	25	1.0	1.3	1.5	1.7	1.9	2.1	2.3	2.5	2.7	2.9	3.1	3.3	3.5	3.8	4.0	4.2	25	.4167
.4333	26	1.1	1.3	1.5	1.7	1.9	2.2	2.4	2.6	2.8	3.0	3.2	3.5	3.7	3.9	4.1	4.3	26	.4333
.4500	27	1.1	1.3	1.6	1.8	2.0	2.2	2.5	2.7	2.9	3.1	3.4	3.6	3.8	4.0	4.3	4.5	27	.4500
.4667	28	1.2	1.4	1.6	1.9	2.1	2.3	2.6	2.8	3.0	3.3	3.5	3.7	4.0	4.2	4.4	4.7	28	.4667
.4833	29	1.2	1.5	1.7	1.9	2.2	2.4	2.7	2.9	3.1	3.4	3.6	3.9	4.1	4.3	4.6	4.8	29	.4833
.5000	30	1.2	1.5	1.7	2.0	2.2	2.5	2.7	3.0	3.2	3.5	3.7	4.0	4.2	4.5	4.7	5.0	30	.5000
.5167	31	1.3	1.6	1.8	2.1	2.3	2.6	2.8	3.1	3.4	3.6	3.9	4.1	4.4	4.7	4.9	5.2	31	.5167
.5333	32	1.3	1.6	1.9	2.1	2.4	2.7	2.9	3.2	3.5	3.7	4.0	4.3	4.5	4.8	5.1	5.3	32	.5333
.5500	33	1.4	1.6	1.9	2.2	2.5	2.7	3.0	3.3	3.6	3.8	4.1	4.4	4.7	4.9	5.2	5.5	33	.5500
.5667	34	1.4	1.7	2.0	2.3	2.6	2.8	3.1	3.4	3.7	4.0	4.3	4.5	4.8	5.1	5.4	5.7	34	.5667
.5833	35	1.5	1.7	2.0	2.3	2.6	2.9	3.2	3.5	3.8	4.1	4.4	4.7	5.0	5.2	5.5	5.8	35	.5833
.6000	36	1.5	1.8	2.1	2.4	2.7	3.0	3.3	3.6	3.9	4.2	4.5	4.8	5.1	5.4	5.7	6.0	36	.6000
.6117	37	1.6	1.8	2.1	2.4	2.8	3.1	3.4	3.7	4.0	4.3	4.6	4.9	5.2	5.5	5.8	6.1	37	.6117
.6333	38	1.6	1.9	2.2	2.5	2.8	3.2	3.5	3.8	4.1	4.4	4.7	5.1	5.4	5.7	6.0	6.3	38	.6333
.6500	39	1.6	1.9	2.3	2.6	2.9	3.2	3.6	3.9	4.2	4.5	4.9	5.2	5.5	5.8	6.2	6.5	39	.6500
.6667	40	1.7	2.0	2.3	2.7	3.0	3.3	3.7	4.0	4.3	4.7	5.0	5.3	5.7	6.0	6.3	6.7	40	.6667
.6833	41	1.7	2.0	2.4	2.7	3.1	3.4	3.8	4.1	4.4	4.8	5.1	5.5	5.8	6.1	6.5	6.8	41	.6833
.7000	42	1.7	2.1	2.4	2.8	3.1	3.5	3.8	4.2	4.5	4.9	5.2	5.6	5.9	6.3	6.6	7.0	42	.7000
.7167	43	1.8	2.2	2.5	2.9	3.2	3.6	3.9	4.3	4.7	5.0	5.4	5.7	6.1	6.5	6.8	7.2	43	.7167
.7333	44	1.8	2.2	2.6	2.9	3.3	3.7	4.0	4.4	4.8	5.1	5.5	5.9	6.2	6.6	7.0	7.3	44	.7333
.7500	45	1.9	2.2	2.6	3.0	3.4	3.7	4.1	4.5	4.9	5.2	5.6	6.0	6.4	6.7	7.1	7.5	45	.7500
.7667	46	1.9	2.3	2.7	3.1	3.5	3.8	4.2	4.6	5.0	5.4	5.8	6.1	6.5	6.9	7.3	7.7	46	.7667
.7833	47	2.0	2.3	2.7	3.1	3.5	3.9	4.3	4.7	5.1	5.5	5.9	6.3	6.7	7.0	7.4	7.8	47	.7833
.8000	48	2.0	2.4	2.8	3.2	3.6	4.0	4.4	4.8	5.2	5.6	6.0	6.4	6.8	7.2	7.6	8.0	48	.8000
.8167	49	2.0	2.5	2.9	3.3	3.7	4.1	4.5	4.9	5.3	5.7	6.1	6.5	6.9	7.4	7.8	8.2	49	.8167
.8333	50	2.1	2.5	2.9	3.3	3.7	4.2	4.6	5.0	5.4	5.8	6.2	6.7	7.1	7.5	7.9	8.3	50	.8333
.8500	51	2.1	2.5	3.0	3.4	3.8	4.2	4.7	5.1	5.5	5.9	6.4	6.8	7.2	7.6	8.1	8.5	51	.8500
.8667	52	2.2	2.6	3.0	3.5	3.9	4.3	4.8	5.2	5.6	6.1	6.5	6.9	7.4	7.8	8.2	8.7	52	.8667
.8833	53	2.2	2.6	3.1	3.5	4.0	4.4	4.9	5.3	5.7	6.2	6.6	7.1	7.5	7.9	8.4	8.8	53	.8833
.9000	54	2.2	2.7	3.1	3.6	4.0	4.5	4.9	5.4	5.8	6.3	6.7	7.2	7.6	8.1	8.5	9.0	54	.9000
.9167	55	2.3	2.8	3.2	3.7	4.1	4.6	5.0	5.5	6.0	6.4	6.9	7.3	7.8	8.3	8.7	9.2	55	.9167
.9333	56	2.3	2.8	3.3	3.7	4.2	4.7	5.1	5.6	6.1	6.5	7.0	7.5	7.9	8.4	8.9	9.3	56	.9333
.9500	57	2.4	2.8	3.3	3.8	4.3	4.7	5.2	5.7	6.2	6.6	7.1	7.6	8.1	8.5	9.0	9.5	57	.9500
.9667	58	2.4	2.9	3.4	3.9	4.4	4.8	5.3	5.8	6.3	6.8	7.3	7.7	8.2	8.7	9.2	9.7	58	.9667
.9833	59	2.5	2.9	3.4	3.9	4.4	4.9	5.4	5.9	6.4	6.9	7.4	7.9	8.4	8.8	9.3	9.8	59	.9833
1.0000	60	2.5	3.0	3.5	4.0	4.5	5.0	5.5	6.0	6.5	7.0	7.5	8.0	8.5	9.0	9.5	10.0	60	1.0000
Decimal of hr. Mins. Time		2.5	3	3.5	4	4.5	5	5.5	6	6.5	7	7.5	8	8.5	9	9.5	10	Mins.	Decimal of hr. Time

Speed in knots

TABLE 3(5) Time, Speed and Distance Table (continued)

Time Decimal of hr.	Mins	10.5	11.0	11.5	12.0	12.5	13.0	13.5	14.0	14.5	15.0	15.5	16.0	17.0	18.0	19.0	20.0	Mins	Decimal of hr.
								Speed in knots											
.0167	1	0.2	0.2	0.2	0.2	0.2	0.2	0.2	0.2	0.2	0.3	0.3	0.3	0.3	0.3	0.3	0.3	1	.0167
.0333	2	0.3	0.4	0.4	0.4	0.4	0.4	0.4	0.5	0.5	0.5	0.5	0.5	0.6	0.6	0.6	0.7	2	.0333
.0500	3	0.5	0.5	0.6	0.6	0.6	0.6	0.7	0.7	0.7	0.7	0.8	0.8	0.8	0.8	0.9	1.0	3	.0500
.0667	4	0.7	0.7	0.8	0.8	0.8	0.9	0.9	0.9	1.0	1.0	1.0	1.1	1.1	1.2	1.3	1.3	4	.0667
.0833	5	0.9	0.9	1.0	1.0	1.0	1.1	1.1	1.2	1.2	1.2	1.3	1.3	1.4	1.5	1.6	1.7	5	.0833
.1000	6	1.0	1.1	1.1	1.2	1.2	1.3	1.3	1.4	1.4	1.5	1.5	1.6	1.7	1.8	1.9	2.0	6	.1000
.1167	7	1.2	1.3	1.3	1.4	1.5	1.5	1.6	1.6	1.7	1.8	1.8	1.9	2.0	2.1	2.2	2.3	7	.1167
.1333	8	1.4	1.5	1.5	1.6	1.7	1.7	1.8	1.9	1.9	2.0	2.1	2.1	2.3	2.4	2.5	2.7	8	.1333
.1500	9	1.6	1.6	1.7	1.8	1.9	1.9	2.0	2.1	2.1	2.2	2.3	2.4	2.5	2.7	2.8	3.0	9	.1500
.1667	10	1.8	1.8	1.9	2.0	2.1	2.2	2.3	2.3	2.4	2.5	2.6	2.7	2.8	3.0	3.2	3.3	10	.1667
.1833	11	1.9	2.0	2.1	2.2	2.3	2.4	2.5	2.6	2.7	2.7	2.8	2.9	3.1	3.3	3.5	3.7	11	.1833
.2000	12	2.1	2.2	2.3	2.4	2.5	2.6	2.7	2.8	2.9	3.0	3.1	3.2	3.4	3.6	3.8	4.0	12	2000
.2167	13	2.3	2.4	2.5	2.6	2.7	2.8	2.9	3.0	3.1	3.2	3.3	3.5	3.7	3.9	4.1	4.3	13	.2167
.2333	14	2.4	2.6	2.7	2.8	2.9	3.0	3.1	3.3	3.4	3.5	3.6	3.7	4.0	4.2	4.4	4.7	14	.2333
.2500	15	2.6	2.7	2.9	3.0	3.1	3.2	3.4	3.5	3.6	3.7	3.9	4.0	4.2	4.5	4.7	5.0	15	.2500
.2667	16	2.8	2.9	3.1	3.2	3.3	3.5	3.6	3.7	3.9	4.0	4.1	4.3	4.5	4.8	5.1	5.3	16	.2667
.2833	17	3.0	3.1	3.3	3.4	3.5	3.7	3.8	4.0	4.1	4.2	4.4	4.5	4.8	5.1	5.4	5.7	17	.2833
.3000	18	3.1	3.3	3.4	3.6	3.7	3.9	4.0	4.2	4.3	4.5	4.6	4.8	5.1	5.4	5.7	6.0	18	.3000
.3167	19	3.3	3.5	3.6	3.8	4.0	4.1	4.3	4.4	4.6	4.8	4.9	5.1	5.4	5.7	6.0	6.3	19	.3167
.3333	20	3.5	3.7	3.8	4.0	4.2	4.3	4.5	4.7	4.8	5.0	5.2	5.3	5.7	6.0	6.3	6.7	20	.3333
.3500	21	3.7	3.8	4.0	4.2	4.4	4.5	4.7	4.9	5.1	5.2	5.4	5.6	5.9	6.3	6.6	7.0	21	.3500
.3667	22	3.9	4.0	4.2	4.4	4.6	4.8	5.0	5.1	5.3	5.5	5.7	5.9	6.2	6.6	7.0	7.3	22	.3667
.3833	23	4.0	4.2	4.4	4.6	4.8	5.0	5.2	5.4	5.6	5.7	5.9	6.1	6.5	6.9	7.3	7.7	23	.3833
.4000	24	4.2	4.4	4.6	4.8	5.0	5.2	5.4	5.6	5.8	6.0	6.2	6.4	6.8	7.2	7.6	8.0	24	.4000
.4167	25	4.4	4.6	4.8	5.0	5.2	5.4	5.6	5.8	6.0	6.3	6.5	6.7	7.1	7.5	7.9	8.3	25	.4167
.4333	26	4.5	4.8	5.0	5.2	5.4	5.6	5.8	6.1	6.3	6.5	6.7	6.9	7.4	7.8	8.2	8.7	26	.4333
.4500	27	4.7	4.9	5.2	5.4	5.6	5.8	6.1	6.3	6.5	6.7	7.0	7.2	7.6	8.1	8.5	9.0	27	.4500
.4667	28	4.9	5.1	5.4	5.6	5.8	6.1	6.3	6.5	6.8	7.0	7.2	7.5	7.9	8.4	8.9	9.3	28	.4667
.4833	29	5.1	5.3	5.6	5.8	6.0	6.3	6.5	6.8	7.0	7.2	7.5	7.7	8.2	8.7	9.2	9.7	29	.4833
.5000	30	5.2	5.5	5.7	6.0	6.2	6.5	6.7	7.0	7.2	7.5	7.7	8.0	8.5	9.0	9.5	10.0	30	.5000
.5167	31	5.4	5.7	5.9	6.2	6.5	6.7	7.0	7.2	7.5	7.8	8.0	8.3	8.8	9.3	9.8	10.3	31	.5167
.5333	32	5.6	5.9	6.1	6.4	6.7	6.9	7.2	7.5	7.7	8.0	8.3	8.5	9.1	9.6	10.1	10.7	32	.5333
.5500	33	5.8	6.0	6.3	6.6	6.9	7.1	7.4	7.7	8.0	8.2	8.5	8.8	9.3	9.9	10.4	11.0	33	.5500
.5667	34	6.0	6.2	6.5	6.8	7.1	7.4	7.7	7.9	8.2	8.5	8.8	9.1	9.6	10.2	10.8	11.3	34	.5667
.5833	35	6.1	6.4	6.7	7.0	7.3	7.6	7.9	8.2	8.5	8.7	9.0	9.3	9.9	10.5	11.1	11.7	35	.5833
.6000	36	6.3	6.6	6.9	7.2	7.5	7.8	8.1	8.4	8.7	9.0	9.3	9.6	10.2	10.8	11.4	12.0	36	.6000
.6117	37	6.4	6.7	7.0	7.3	7.6	8.0	8.3	8.6	8.9	9.2	9.5	9.8	10.4	11.0	11.6	12.2	37	.6117
.6333	38	6.6	7.0	7.3	7.6	7.9	8.2	8.5	8.9	9.2	9.5	9.8	10.1	10.8	11.4	12.0	12.7	38	.6333
.6500	39	6.8	7.1	7.5	7.8	8.1	8.4	8.8	9.1	9.4	9.7	10.1	10.4	11.0	11.7	12.3	13.0	39	.6500
.6667	40	7.0	7.3	7.7	8.0	8.3	8.7	9.0	9.3	9.7	10.0	10.3	10.7	11.3	12.0	12.7	13.3	40	.6667
.6833	41	7.2	7.5	7.9	8.2	8.5	8.9	9.2	9.6	9.9	10.2	10.6	10.9	11.6	12.3	13.0	13.7	41	.6833
.7000	42	7.3	7.7	8.0	8.4	8.7	9.1	9.4	9.8	10.1	10.5	10.8	11.2	11.9	12.6	13.3	14.0	42	.7000
.7167	43	7.5	7.9	8.2	8.6	9.0	9.3	9.7	10.0	10.4	10.8	11.1	11.5	12.2	12.9	13.6	14.3	43	.7167
.7333	44	7.7	8.1	8.4	8.8	9.2	9.5	10.0	10.3	10.6	11.0	11.4	11.7	12.5	13.2	13.9	14.7	44	.7333
.7500	45	7.9	8.2	8.6	9.0	9.4	9.7	10.1	10.5	10.9	11.2	11.6	12.0	12.7	13.5	14.2	15.0	45	.7500
.7667	46	8.1	8.4	8.8	9.2	9.6	10.0	10.4	10.7	11.1	11.5	11.9	12.3	13.0	13.8	14.6	15.3	46	.7667
.7833	47	8.2	8.6	9.0	9.4	9.8	10.2	10.6	11.0	11.4	11.7	12.1	12.5	13.3	14.1	14.9	15.7	47	.7833
.8000	48	8.4	8.8	9.2	9.6	10.0	10.4	10.8	11.2	11.6	12.0	12.4	12.8	13.6	14.4	15.2	16.0	48	.8000
.8167	49	8.6	9.0	9.4	9.8	10.2	10.6	11.0	11.4	11.8	12.2	12.7	13.1	13.9	14.7	15.5	16.3	49	.8167
.8333	50	8.7	9.2	9.6	10.0	10.4	10.8	11.2	11.7	12.1	12.5	12.9	13.3	14.2	15.0	15.8	16.7	50	.8333
.8500	51	8.9	9.3	9.8	10.2	10.6	11.0	11.5	11.9	12.3	12.7	13.2	13.6	14.4	15.3	16.1	17.0	51	.8500
.8667	52	9.1	9.5	10.0	10.4	10.8	11.3	11.7	12.1	12.6	13.0	13.4	13.9	14.7	15.6	16.5	17.3	52	.8667
.8833	53	9.3	9.7	10.2	10.6	11.0	11.5	11.9	12.4	12.8	13.2	13.7	14.1	15.0	15.9	16.8	17.7	53	.8833
.9000	54	9.4	9.9	10.3	10.8	11.2	11.7	12.1	12.6	13.0	13.5	13.9	14.4	15.3	16.2	17.1	18.0	54	.9000
.9167	55	9.6	10.1	10.5	11.0	11.5	11.9	12.4	12.8	13.3	13.8	14.2	14.7	15.6	16.5	17.4	18.3	55	.9167
.9333	56	9.8	10.3	10.7	11.2	11.7	12.1	12.6	13.1	13.5	14.0	14.5	14.9	15.9	16.8	17.7	18.7	56	.9333
.9500	57	10.0	10.4	10.9	11.4	11.9	12.3	12.8	13.3	13.8	14.2	14.7	15.2	16.1	17.1	18.0	19.0	57	.9500
.9667	58	10.2	10.6	11.1	11.6	12.1	12.6	13.1	13.5	14.0	14.5	15.0	15.5	16.4	17.4	18.4	19.3	58	.9667
.9833	59	10.3	10.8	11.3	11.8	12.3	12.8	13.3	13.8	14.3	14.7	15.2	15.7	16.7	17.7	18.7	19.7	59	.9833
1.0000	60	10.5	11.0	11.5	12.0	12.5	13.0	13.5	14.0	14.5	15.0	15.5	16.0	17.0	18.0	19.0	20.0	60	1.0000
Decimal of hr. Mins Time		10.5	11.0	11.5	12.0	12.5	13.0	13.5	14.0	14.5	15.0	15.5	16.0	17.0	18.0	19.0	20.0	Mins	Decimal of hr. Time

Speed in knots

3

TABLE 3(6)   Measured Mile Table — Knots related to time over one nautical mile

Secs	1 min	2 min	3 min	4 min	5 min	6 min	7 min	8 min	9 min	10 min	11 min
0	60.00	30.00	20.00	15.00	12.00	10.00	8.57	7.50	6.67	6.00	5.45
1	59.02	29.75	19.89	14.94	11.96	9.97	8.55	7.48	6.66	5.99	5.45
2	58.06	29.51	19.78	14.88	11.92	9.94	8.53	7.47	6.64	5.98	5.44
3	57.14	29.27	19.67	14.81	11.88	9.92	8.51	7.45	6.63	5.97	5.43
4	56.25	29.03	19.57	14.75	11.84	9.89	8.49	7.44	6.62	5.96	5.42
5	55.38	28.80	19.46	14.69	11.80	9.86	8.47	7.42	6.61	5.95	5.41
6	54.55	28.57	19.35	14.63	11.76	9.84	8.45	7.41	6.59	5.94	5.41
7	53.73	28.35	19.25	14.57	11.73	9.81	8.43	7.39	6.58	5.93	5.40
8	52.94	28.12	19.15	14.52	11.69	9.78	8.41	7.38	6.57	5.92	5.39
9	52.17	27.91	19.05	14.46	11.65	9.76	8.39	7.36	6.56	5.91	5.38
10	51.43	27.69	18.95	14.40	11.61	9.73	8.37	7.35	6.55	5.90	5.37
11	50.70	27.48	18.85	14.34	11.58	9.70	8.35	7.33	6.53	5.89	5.37
12	50.00	27.27	18.75	14.29	11.54	9.68	8.33	7.32	6.52	5.88	5.36
13	49.32	27.07	18.65	14.23	11.50	9.65	8.31	7.30	6.51	5.87	5.35
14	48.65	26.87	18.56	14.17	11.46	9.63	8.29	7.29	6.50	5.86	5.34
15	48.00	26.67	18.46	14.12	11.43	9.60	8.28	7.27	6.49	5.85	5.33
16	47.37	26.47	18.37	14.06	11.39	9.58	8.26	7.26	6.47	5.84	5.33
17	46.75	26.28	18.27	14.01	11.36	9.55	8.24	7.24	6.46	5.83	5.32
18	46.15	26.09	18.18	13.95	11.32	9.52	8.22	7.23	6.45	5.83	5.31
19	45.57	25.90	18.09	13.90	11.29	9.50	8.20	7.21	6.44	5.82	5.30
20	45.00	25.71	18.00	13.85	11.25	9.47	8.18	7.20	6.43	5.81	5.29
21	44.44	25.53	17.91	13.79	11.21	9.45	8.16	7.19	6.42	5.80	5.29
22	43.90	25.35	17.82	13.74	11.18	9.42	8.14	7.17	6.41	5.79	5.28
23	43.37	25.17	17.73	13.69	11.15	9.40	8.13	7.16	6.39	5.78	5.27
24	42.86	25.00	17.65	13.64	11.11	9.37	8.11	7.14	6.38	5.77	5.26
25	42.35	24.83	17.56	13.58	11.08	9.35	8.09	7.13	6.37	5.76	5.26
26	41.86	24.66	17.48	13.53	11.04	9.33	8.07	7.11	6.36	5.75	5.25
27	41.38	24.49	17.39	13.48	11.01	9.30	8.05	7.10	6.35	5.74	5.24
28	40.91	24.32	17.31	13.43	10.98	9.28	8.04	7.09	6.34	5.73	5.23
29	40.45	24.16	17.22	13.38	10.94	9.25	8.02	7.07	6.33	5.72	5.22
30	40.00	24.00	17.14	13.33	10.91	9.23	8.00	7.06	6.32	5.71	5.22
31	39.56	23.84	17.06	13.28	10.88	9.21	7.98	7.04	6.30	5.71	5.21
32	39.13	23.68	16.98	13.24	10.84	9.18	7.96	7.03	6.29	5.70	5.20
33	38.71	23.53	16.90	13.19	10.81	9.16	7.95	7.02	6.28	5.69	5.19
34	38.30	23.38	16.82	13.14	10.78	9.14	7.93	7.00	6.27	5.68	5.19
35	37.89	23.23	16.74	13.09	10.75	9.11	7.91	6.99	6.26	5.67	5.18
36	37.50	23.08	16.67	13.04	10.71	9.09	7.89	6.98	6.25	5.66	5.17
37	37.11	22.93	16.59	13.00	10.68	9.07	7.88	6.96	6.24	5.65	5.16
38	36.73	22.78	16.51	12.95	10.65	9.05	7.86	6.95	6.23	5.64	5.16
39	36.36	22.64	16.44	12.90	10.62	9.02	7.84	6.94	6.22	5.63	5.15
40	36.00	22.50	16.36	12.86	10.59	9.00	7.83	6.92	6.21	5.62	5.14
41	35.64	22.36	16.29	12.81	10.56	8.98	7.81	6.91	6.20	5.62	5.13
42	35.29	22.22	16.22	12.77	10.53	8.96	7.79	6.90	6.19	5.61	5.13
43	34.95	22.09	16.14	12.72	10.50	8.93	7.78	6.89	6.17	5.60	5.12
44	34.62	21.95	16.07	12.68	10.47	8.91	7.76	6.87	6.16	5.59	5.11
45	34.29	21.82	16.00	12.63	10.43	8.89	7.74	6.86	6.15	5.58	5.10
46	33.96	21.69	15.93	12.59	10.40	8.87	7.72	6.84	6.14	5.57	5.10
47	33.64	21.56	15.86	12.54	10.37	8.85	7.71	6.83	6.13	5.56	5.09
48	33.33	21.43	15.79	12.50	10.34	8.82	7.69	6.82	6.12	5.56	5.08
49	33.03	21.30	15.72	12.46	10.32	8.80	7.68	6.80	6.11	5.55	5.08
50	32.73	21.18	15.65	12.41	10.29	8.78	7.66	6.79	6.10	5.54	5.07
51	32.43	21.05	15.58	12.37	10.26	8.76	7.64	6.78	6.09	5.53	5.06
52	32.14	20.93	15.52	12.33	10.23	8.74	7.63	6.77	6.08	5.52	5.06
53	31.86	20.81	15.45	12.29	10.20	8.72	7.61	6.75	6.07	5.51	5.05
54	31.58	20.69	15.38	12.24	19.17	8.70	7.59	6.74	6.06	5.50	5.04
55	31.30	20.57	15.32	12.20	10.14	8.67	7.58	6.73	6.05	5.50	5.04
56	31.03	20.45	15.25	12.16	10.11	8.65	7.56	6.72	6.04	5.49	5.03
57	30.77	20.34	15.19	12.12	10.08	8.63	7.55	6.70	6.03	5.48	5.02
58	30.51	20.22	15.13	12.08	10.06	8.61	7.53	6.69	6.02	5.47	5.01
59	30.25	20.11	15.06	12.04	10.03	8.59	7.52	6.68	6.01	5.46	5.00
Secs	1 min	2 min	3 min	4 min	5 min	6 min	7 min	8 min	9 min	10 min	11 min

(Continued from page 22)

Distance to radar horizon (in n miles) =

$$1.22 \times \sqrt{\text{Ht of scanner}} \text{ (in ft)},$$

or $\qquad 2.21 \times \sqrt{\text{Ht of scanner}}$ (in m)

Boat speed over measured distance of 1 n mile =

$$\frac{3600}{\text{time in seconds}} \text{ (knots)}$$

Horizontal sextant angle
Radius of position circle (in n miles) =

$$\frac{D}{2 \times \sin A}$$

where D is distance between objects in n miles, and A is the angle between them in degrees.

Vertical sextant angles

$$\frac{\text{Distance off}}{\text{(in n miles)}} = \frac{\text{Ht of object (above MHWS, in ft)}}{6076 \times \tan \text{ (sextant angle)}}$$

or $\qquad = \dfrac{\text{Ht of object (above MHWS, in m)}}{1852 \times \tan \text{ (sextant angle)}}$

Note: sextant angle above is in degrees and minutes, and must be corrected for index error.

An approximate distance off, in n miles, adequate for most purposes is given by:

$$\frac{\text{Distance}}{\text{(n miles)}} = \frac{\text{Ht of object (in feet)} \times 0.565}{\text{Sextant angle (in minutes)}}$$

or $\qquad = \dfrac{\text{Ht of object (in metres)} \times 1.854}{\text{Sextant angle (in minutes)}}$

Coastal navigation
To find the DR/EP, as bearing and distance from start position; example using TI.57. Key in:

1st distance run	5.2	x⇄t
1st course (°T)	230	→R STO 0 x⇄t STO 6
2nd distance run	1.9	x⇄t
2nd course (°T)	255	→R SUM 0 x⇄t SUM 6

Repeat for each subsequent Co(°T) and distance. For EP, treat Set/Drift as for Co(°T) and distance.

To display bearing and distance from start:
RCL 6 x⇄t RCL 0 → P $\boxed{236.6}$ (°T)
x⇄t $\boxed{6.97}$ (nm)
Note: To find EP, treat Set/Drift as for Co(°T) and distance run.
Example: Using RPN calculator. Key in:

1st course (°T)	230	ENTER
1st distance run	5.2	→R Σ+
2nd course (°T)	255	ENTER
2nd distance run	1.9	→R Σ+

Repeat for each subsequent Co (°T) and distance.

To display distance and bearing from start:
RCL 13[1]   RCL 11[1]   → P $\boxed{6.97}$ nm
x⇄y $\boxed{236.6^{[2]}}$ (°T)
Notes: (1) Check the actual stores used for vector summation in your calculator.
(2) If display negative (−), add 360
To find EP, treat Set/Drift as for Co(°T) and distance run.

Distance (D, in n miles) of object at second bearing

$$= \frac{R \times \sin A}{\sin (B - A)}$$

Predicted distance (in n miles) object will be off when abeam = D × sin B, where R is distance run (nm) between two relative bearings of an object, first A degrees and then B degrees.

Course to steer and speed made good
Co(°T) = Tr(°T) − sin⁻¹ (Drift ÷ Speed) × sin (Set − Track)
SMG = Speed × cos (Co.T − Track) + Drift × cos (Set − Track)
Note: The Drift must be less than yacht's speed.

Conversion angle (half convergency)
Radio bearings follow great circles, and become curved lines when plotted on a Mercator chart, see 4.1.10. A correction may be needed for bearings of beacons more than about 60 n miles away, and can be calculated from the formula:
Conversion angle = ½ d.Long × sin mid Latitude
A great circle always lies on the polar side of the rhumb line, and conversion angle is applied towards the equator.

Short distance sailing
(Note: These formulae should not be used for distances over 600 n miles).

Departure	= Distance × sin Course
	= d.Long × cos Mean Latitude
	= tan Course × d.Lat
d.Lat	= Distance × cos Course
d.Long	= Departure ÷ cos Mean Latitude
Distance	= Departure ÷ sin Course
	= d.Lat × sec Course
sin Course	= Departure ÷ Distance
cos Course	= d.Lat ÷ Distance
tan Course	= Departure ÷ d.Lat

Further explanation of the use of calculators, and formulae for the calculation of tracks and distances for distances over 600 n miles are contained in Chapter 3 of *The Macmillan & Silk Cut Yachtsman's Handbook.*

3.1.4 Chart abbreviations. (For symbols see Plates 2 and 3, pages 114–115)

Coastal Features

G.	Gulf
B.	Bay
L.	Loch, Lough, Lake
Cr.	Creek
Str.	Strait
Sd.	Sound
Pass.	Passage
Chan.	Channel
Appr.	Approaches
Ent.	Entrance
R.	River
Est.	Estuary
Mth.	Mouth
Rds.	Roads, Roadstead
Anch.	Anchorage
Hr.	Harbour
Hn.	Haven
P.	Port
I.	Island
It	Islet
C.	Cape
Prom.	Promontory
Pt.	Point
Mt.	Mountain, Mount
Lndg.	Landing place
Rk.	Rock

Units

m	Metre(s)
dm	Decimetre(s)
cm	Centimetre(s)
mm	Millimetre(s)
km	Kilometre(s)
ft	Foot, feet
M	Sea Mile(s)
kn	knot(s)
Lat	Latitude
Long	Longitude
Ht	Height
No	Number

Adjectives etc

Gt Grt	Great
Lit	Little
Mid	Middle
Anct	Ancient
S St	Saint
conspic	Conspicuous
dest	Destroyed
proj	Projected
dist	Distant
abt	About
illum	Illuminated
Aero	Aeronautical
Hr	Higher
Lr	Lower
exper	Experimental

discont	Discontinued
prohib	Prohibited
explos	Explosive
priv	Private
prom	Prominent
subm	Submerged
approx	Approximate
NM	Notices to Mariners
(P)	Preliminary (NM)
(T)	Temporary (NM)
SD	Sailing Directions
LL	List of Lights

Buildings etc

Cas	Castle
Ho	House
Va	Villa
Fm	Farm
Ch	Church, Chapel
Cath	Cathedral
Cemy	Cemetery
Ft	Fort
Baty	Battery
St	Street
Ave	Avenue
Tel	Telegraph
PO	Post Office
Hosp	Hospital
Mon	Monument, Memorial
Cup	Cupola
Ru	Ruin
Tr	Tower
Chy	Chimney
Sch	School
Bldg	Building
Tel	Telephone
Col	Column, Obelisk
Sta	Station
CG	Coastguard
LB	Lifeboat
SS	Signal Station
Sem	Semaphore
SS (Storm)	Storm signal station
FS	Flagstaff
Sig	Signal
Obsy	Observatory
Off	Office
NB	Notice Board

Dangers

Bk.	Bank
Sh.	Shoal
Rf.	Reef
Le.	Ledge
Obstn	Obstruction
Wk	Wreck
dr	Dries
cov	Covers

uncov	Uncovers
PA	Position approximate
PD	Position doubtful
ED	Existence doubtful
pos	Position.
unexam	Unexamined
Rep	Reported

Quality of the Bottom

Gd	Ground
S	Sand
M	Mud
Oz	Ooze
Ml	Marl
Cy	Clay
G	Gravel
Sn	Shingle
P	Pebbles
St	Stones
R	Rock
Bo	Boulders
Ck	Chalk
Qz	Quartz
Sh	Shells
Oy	Oysters
Ms	Mussels
Wd	Weed
f	Fine
c	Coarse
so	Soft
h	Hard
sf	Stiff
sm	Small
l	Large
sy	Sticky
bk	Broken
ga	Glacial

Tides and Currents

HW/LW	High Water/Low Water
ML	Mean Level
MTL	Mean Tide Level
MSL	Mean Sea Level
Sp/Np	Spring Tides/Neap Tides
MHWS	Mean High Water Springs
MHWN	Mean High Water Neaps
MLWS	Mean Low Water Springs
MLWN	Mean Low Water Neaps
HAT	Highest Astronomical Tide
LAT	Lowest Astronomical Tide
Vel	Velocity
kn	Knots
Dir	Direction
OD	Ordnance Datum

Compass

Mag	Magnetic
Var	Variation
annly	Annually

3.1.5   LIGHT CHARACTERS (Fathoms and Metric Charts)

Reproduced by kind permission of H.M. Stationery Office and the Hydrographer of the Navy

CLASS OF LIGHT		International abbreviations	Older form (where different)	Illustration Period shown ⊢——————⊣
Fixed *(steady light)*		F		
Occulting *(total duration of light more than dark)*				
Single-occulting		Oc	Occ	
Group-occulting	e.g.	Oc(2)	Gp Occ(2)	
Composite group-occulting	e.g.	Oc(2+3)	Gp Occ(2+3)	
Isophase *(light and dark equal)*		Iso		
Flashing *(total duration of light less than dark)*				
Single-flashing		Fl		
Long-flashing *(flash 2s or longer)*		L Fl		
Group-flashing	e.g.	Fl(3)	Gp Fl(3)	
Composite group-flashing	e.g.	Fl(2+1)	Gp Fl(2+1)	
Quick *(50 to 79—usually either 50 or 60—flashes per minute)*				
Continuous quick		Q	Qk Fl	
Group quick	e.g.	Q(3)	Qk Fl(3)	
Interrupted quick		IQ	Int Qk Fl	
Very Quick *(80 to 159—usually either 100 or 120—flashes per minute)*				
Continuous very quick		V Q	V Qk Fl	
Group very quick	e.g.	V Q(3)	V Qk Fl(3)	
Interrupted very quick		IV Q	Int V Qk Fl	
Ultra Quick *(100 or more—usually 240 to 300—flashes per minute)*				
Continuous ultra quick		UQ		
Interrupted ultra quick		IUQ		
Morse Code	e.g.	Mo(K)		
Fixed and Flashing		F Fl		
Alternating	e.g.	Al.WR	Alt.WR	

COLOUR	International abbreviations	Older form (where different)	RANGE in sea miles		International abbreviations	Older form
White	W *(may be omitted)*		Single range	e.g.	15M	
Red	R					
Green	G		2 ranges	e.g.	14/12M	14.12M
Yellow	Y					
Orange	Y	Or	3 or more ranges	e.g.	22–18M	22,20,18M
Blue	Bu	Bl				
Violet	Vi					
ELEVATION is given in metres (m) or feet (ft)			PERIOD in seconds *e.g.*		5s	5sec

3.1.6   IALA Buoyage System (Region A)

(See also Plate 5 on page 117.)

International buoyage is harmonized into a single system which, applied to Regions A and B, differs only in the use of red and green lateral marks. In Region A (which includes all Europe) lateral marks are red on the port hand, and in Region B red on the starboard hand, related to direction of buoyage. Five types of marks are used, as illustrated in Plate 5, on page 117.

(1) *Lateral marks* are used in conjunction with a direction of buoyage, shown by a special arrow on the chart. In and around the British Isles its general direction is from SW to NE in open waters, but from seaward when approaching a harbour, river or estuary. Where port or starboard lateral marks do not rely on can or conical buoy shapes for identification they carry, where practicable, the appropriate topmarks. Any numbering or lettering follows the direction of buoyage.

In Region A, port hand marks are coloured red, and port hand buoys are can or spar shaped. Any topmark fitted is a single red can. Any light fitted is red, any rhythm. Starboard hand marks are coloured green, and starboard hand buoys are conical or spar shaped. Any topmark fitted is a single green cone, point up. Any light fitted is green, any rhythm. In exceptional cases starboard hand marks may be coloured black.

At a division, the preferred channel may be shown by lateral marks with red or green stripes:

Preferred channel	Indicated by	Light (if any)
To starboard	Port lateral mark with green stripe	Flashing red (2 + 1)
To port	Starboard lateral mark with red stripe	Flashing green (2 + 1)

(2) *Cardinal marks* are used in conjunction with a compass to show where dangers exist or where the mariner may find navigable water. They are named after the quadrant in which the mark is placed, in relation to the danger or point indicated. The four quadrants (North, East, South and West) are bounded by the true bearings NW−NE, NE−SE, SE−SW and SW−NW, taken from the point of interest. The name of a cardinal mark indicates that it should be passed on the named side.

A cardinal mark may indicate the safe side on which to pass a danger, or that the deepest water is on the named side of the mark, or it may draw attention to a feature in a channel such as a bend, junction or fork, or the end of a shoal.

Cardinal marks are pillar or spar shaped, painted black and yellow, and always carry black double cone topmarks, one cone above the other. Their lights are white, either very quick flashing (VQ or VQkFl) 120 to 100 flashes per minute, or quick flashing (Q or QkFl) 60 to 50 flashes per minute. A long flash is one of not less than two seconds duration.

North cardinal mark

Two black cones	— Points up
Colour	— Black above yellow
Light (if fitted)	— White; VQ or Q

East cardinal mark

Two black cones —	Base to base
Colour	— Black, with horizontal yellow band
Light (if fitted)	— White; VQ(3) 5 sec or Q(3) 10 sec

South cardinal mark

Two black cones —	Points down
Colour	— Yellow above black
Light (if fitted) —	White; VQ(6) plus long flash 10 sec or Q(6) plus long flash 15 sec

West cardinal mark

Two black cones —	Point to point
Colour	— Yellow, with horizontal black band
Light (if fitted)	— White; VQ(9) 10 sec or Q(9) 15 sec

(3) *Isolated danger marks* are placed on or above an isolated danger such as a rock or a wreck which has navigable water all around it. The marks are black, with one or more broad horizontal red bands. Buoys are pillar or spar shaped. Any light is white, flashing (2). Topmark — two black spheres.

(4) *Safe water marks* indicate that there is navigable water all round the mark, and are used for mid-channel or landfall marks. Buoys are spherical, pillar, with spherical topmark or spar, and are coloured with red and white vertical stripes. Any topmark fitted is a single red sphere. Any light fitted is white — either isophase, occulting or long flash every 10 seconds.

(5) *Special marks* do not primarily assist navigation, but indicate a special area or feature (e.g. spoil grounds, exercise areas, water ski areas, cable or pipeline marks, outfalls, Ocean Data Acquisition Systems (ODAS), or traffic separation marks where conventional channel marks may cause confusion). Special marks are yellow, and any shape not conflicting with lateral or safe water marks. If can, spherical or conical are used they indicate the side on which to pass. Any topmark fitted is a yellow X. Any light fitted is yellow, and may have any rhythm not used for white lights.

New dangers (which may be natural obstructions such as a sandbank, or a wreck for example) are marked in accordance with the rules above, and lit accordingly. For a very grave danger one of the marks may be duplicated.

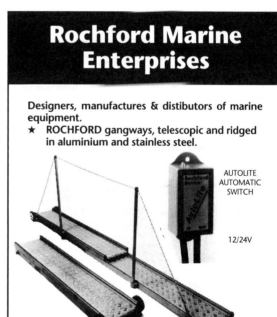

WILL IT? WON'T IT?

451
464
THURSO
INVERNESS
ULLAPOOL
DUNDEE
452
OBAN
EDINBURGH
453
GLASGOW
NEWCASTLE
AYR
462
SCARBOROUGH
454
BELFAST
461
CLEETHORPES
465
LIVERPOOL
BANGOR
GT. YARMOUTH
455
460
ABERYSTWYTH
SOUTHEND
SWANSEA
BRISTOL
LONDON
BRIGHTON
459
PORTSMOUTH
456
BOURNEMOUTH
458
PLYMOUTH
457

MARINECALL
0898 • 500 •
PLUS AREA NUMBER

Accurate information on weather conditions is essential for all sea-going activities. By telephoning Marinecall you can take advantage of a unique service available 24 hours a day, 7 days a week. Marinecall gives you detailed weather forecasts for 15 different coastal regions, for up to 5 days ahead.

Provided in association with:
HM Coastguard
RYA
British Marine
Industries Federation

**5 DAY
NATIONAL FORECAST
0898 • 500 • 450**

Marinecall Members Club offers regular users far greater convenience in accessing the service from payphones in the UK or abroad.
- pre-paid units
- access via 071(London) numbers
- easy use from payphones
- use when abroad

For further information telephone 071 236 3500

YOUR WEATHER.

WHEREVER. WHENEVER.

TELEPHONE INFORMATION SERVICES plc

24 – 30 West Smithfield, London, EC1A 9DL. Calls charged at 25p per minute cheap rate, 38p per minute at other times (inc. vat).

Chapter 4

Radio Navigational Aids

Contents

4

Radio navigational aids – introduction
The following subjects are described in detail in Chapter 4 of *The Macmillan & Silk Cut Yachtsman's Handbook*:
> Marine radiobeacons; DF receiving sets; grouping and sequence of beacons; directional radiobeacons; beacons incorporating distance finding; Aero radiobeacons; types of emissions; operating procedures; errors in radio bearings; calibration; QTG service from Coast Radio Stations; VHF emergency direction finding service; half convergency; Consol; Decca Navigator; Loran-C; Omega; satellite navigation; radar; radar beacons (Racons).

Here in the Almanac is provided the necessary detail about individual radiobeacons and Racons for navigational use, but for information on procedures and possible errors, together with the other subjects listed above, reference should be made to Chapter 4 of *The Macmillan & Silk Cut Yachtsman's Handbook*.

4.1   RADIOBEACONS

4.1.1   Marine radiobeacons — general

This widely-used system of direction finding allows a yachtsman to obtain a bearing from a non-directional radiobeacon, using a receiving set with an aerial which has directional qualities. This is useful in poor visibility, or when out of sight of land, but the effective range is limited, and few beacons give bearings of reasonable accuracy at distances of more than 50 miles.

Details of marine and aero radiobeacons in the area covered by this Almanac are given in Table 4(2), commencing on page 41. Often up to six marine beacons are grouped together to share the same frequency, and these groupings are also listed and shown diagrammatically in Table 4(2).

On Admiralty charts, marine radiobeacons are shown by a magenta circle with the letters 'RC'.

To obtain a bearing from a beacon, the yachtsman must tune his receiver to the frequency listed for that beacon in Table 4(2), positively identify its Morse callsign and then rotate the receiver aerial until a minimum, or null, signal is obtained.

4.1.2   DF receiving sets

Most sets have ferrite rod aerials, which give a minimum signal when in line with the direction of the beacon. Often the aerial incorporates a small compass, so that the operator can read the bearing at the moment that he identifies the null in his earphones. Such compasses are just as liable to error as any other magnetic compass, and must not be held close to magnetic objects.

With some sets the receiver itself is fixed, and the aerial rotates against a graduated scale, which shows the bearing relative to the ship's head. In this case it is necessary to record the course steered at the same moment as the null and the relative bearing.

An Automatic Direction Finding (ADF) set is tuned to the required frequency, and will then lock on to any transmission automatically, indicating the bearing. If there is a sequence of beacons on one frequency it will point to each in turn. Some sets even assess the reliability of individual bearings taken.

A quartz clock may be incorporated, to allow beacons to be identified by their time sequence, but this should only be considered an aid. A beacon should always be positively identified by its call (ident) sign in order to avoid possible errors.

4.1.3   Grouping and sequence of beacons

Where two or more beacons share a common frequency, they transmit on a strict time schedule, for one minute in turn. The minutes past each hour at which a beacon transmits, depending on its sequence number, is shown in the table at the foot of each relevant page of Table 4(2).

4.1.4   Beacons incorporating distance finding

A few beacons allow radio and sound signals to be synchronised for distance finding. The two signals are synchronised at an easily identifiable point in the cycle, e.g. at the start or end of a long dash. Using a stop watch, the difference between the two times in seconds, multiplied by 0·18, gives the distance in nautical miles.

Another system involves the transmission of a number of measuring signals, started when the fog signal is sounded. The number of measuring signals received before the fog signal is heard indicates the distance. An interval of 5·5 seconds between measuring signals is equivalent to a unit distance of one nautical mile.

4.1.5   Aero Radiobeacons

Although intended for aircraft, some of those near the coast are useful to yachtsmen. They are shown on a chart by a small magenta circle, and the letters 'Aero RC'. These beacons transmit continuously during operational hours. They must be used with care, because the land effect (see 4.1.7) is unpredictable. Details of those beacons which may be of use to yachtsmen, in the area covered by this Almanac, are included in Table 4(2).

4.1.6   Types of emission (Modes)

There are several different types of radio emission from radiobeacons, and these are identified under the heading of 'Mode' in Table 4(2). If the receiver on board is fitted with a separate Beat Frequency Oscillator (BFO), this control should be adjusted as follows when taking radio bearings:

Mode		BFO setting	
Old style	New style	For DF use	For ident.
A1	A1A	ON	ON
AOA1	NON A1A	ON	ON
AOA2	NON A2A	ON	OFF[2]
A2 ⎫ A2* ⎬ A3 ⎭	A2A	⎧ ON or OFF[1] ⎨ ON or OFF[1] ⎩ ON or OFF[1]	OFF[2] OFF[2] OFF[2]

Notes: (1) For best performance consult the maker's handbook.

(2) If BFO cannot be switched off, it may be difficult to hear the Morse identification.

4.1.7   Errors in radio bearings

The various errors to which radio bearings are subject are described in Chapter 4 of *The Macmillan & Silk Cut Yachtsman's Handbook* (4.2.9). They fall into two categories — signal errors (caused by distance from the beacon, night or sky-wave effect particularly near sunset and sunrise, land effect or coastal refraction where the beam passes over high ground or along the coast, and synchronised transmissions of two beacons), and errors on board the boat (caused by quadrantal error due to magnetic objects re-radiating the incoming signal, compass error, the possibility of inadvertently taking a reciprocal bearing, and operating error due to inexperience or bad weather). Do not rely on radio bearings exclusively, unless three or more give an acceptable cocked hat.

4.1.8   Radiobeacons — calibration

A DF set can be calibrated for quadrantal error by taking simultaneous radio and visual bearings of a beacon on different headings. Alternatively radio bearings may be taken from a known position, and the bearing of the beacon taken from the chart. To save time it is helpful if the beacon transmits continuously. Beacons which provide a calibration service are shown in Table 4(3).

4.1.9   Half convergency

Half convergency is a correction to be applied to a radio bearing — which always follows a great circle path — to enable it to be plotted as a straight line on a Mercator chart. The correction does not become significant until the difference in longitude between the radio station and the yacht is 3 degrees or more. Half convergency is therefore unlikely to be of concern to most yachtsmen.

In North latitudes, for bearings taken from a yacht — if the yacht is East of the station, half convergency must be subtracted; if West of the station it must be added. For bearings provided by a DF station — if the yacht is East of the station, half convergency must be added; if West of the station, it must be subtracted. The opposite applies in the Southern hemisphere.

For practical purposes the values of half convergency given in Table 4(1) can be used for distances up to 1000 n miles.

4.2   POSITION FIXING SYSTEMS

4.2.1   Types of systems

Five systems are available for yachtsmen: Decca, Loran-C and Omega (all hyperbolic systems) and satellite navigation from the American Transit and

4

TABLE 4(1)   Half convergency

Enter with difference in longitude between the station and the boat (along the top), and mid latitude between the station and the boat (down the side). The figures extracted are half convergency, in degrees.

Mid Lat	Difference in longitude (degrees)									
	3°	6°	9°	12°	15°	18°	21°	24°	27°	30°
5°	0.1	0.3	0.4	0.5	0.7	0.8	0.9	1.0	1.2	1.3
10°	0.3	0.5	0.8	1.0	1.3	1.6	1.8	2.1	2.3	2.6
15°	0.4	0.8	1.2	1.6	1.9	2.3	2.7	3.1	3.5	3.9
20°	0.5	1.0	1.5	2.1	2.6	3.1	3.6	4.1	4.6	5.1
25°	0.6	1.3	1.9	2.5	3.2	3.8	4.4	5.1	5.7	6.3
30°	0.7	1.5	2.2	3.0	3.7	4.5	5.2	6.0	6.7	7.5
35°	0.9	1.7	2.6	3.4	4.3	5.2	6.0	6.9	7.7	8.6
40°	1.0	1.9	2.9	3.9	4.8	5.8	6.7	7.7	8.7	9.6
45°	1.1	2.1	3.2	4.2	5.3	6.4	7.4	8.5	9.5	10.6
50°	1.1	2.3	3.4	4.6	5.7	6.9	8.0	9.2	10.3	11.5
55°	1.2	2.5	3.7	4.9	6.1	7.4	8.6	9.8	11.0	12.3
60°	1.3	2.6	3.9	5.2	6.5	7.8	9.1	10.4	11.7	13.0

Example. A yacht in DR position 42°N, 2°W obtains a radio bearing from a powerful station in position 58°N, 7°E. The difference in longitude between the two positions is 9°. The mid latitude is 50°. From inspection, the half convergency is 3·4°. Because the yacht is to the west of the station, this figure should be added to the bearing taken before it is plotted on the chart.

GPS satellites. Each has its merits for particular applications, and they are described in *The Macmillan & Silk Cut Yachtsman's Handbook* (4.5).

The Decca Yacht Navigator uses the established chains of Decca Navigator transmitting stations, and provides good coverage in NW Europe and in some other parts of the world (but not the Mediterranean). Loran-C covers the United States and much of the Northern hemisphere, but coverage of European waters is poor. Omega gives extensive global coverage, but the accuracy is not so good as Decca or Loran-C. Transit satellites give world-wide coverage, but a fix can only be obtained when there is a suitable satellite pass – about every 1½ hours in British waters. Navstar GPS gives better coverage and accuracy.

4.2.2   Waypoints
For use with position fixing systems, over 2100 waypoints are given in Chapter 10 — for individual harbours (under the heading of 'Navigation' in each area), in section 4 of each Area (where they are underlined in the lists of 'Lights, Fog Signals and Waypoints'), for the Solent area (10.2.10), for cross-Channel passages (10.1.7), SE England (10.3.8), S North Sea (10.4.6) and for the Clyde (10.9.7).

Latitudes and longitudes are normally stated to one-hundredth of a minute, as taken from a large scale chart. But it should be realised that a chart using a different datum or based on another survey may give a slightly different position. Charts may contain small errors, just like the read-out from an electronic instrument.

Electronic systems are only aids to navigation and are subject to fixed and variable errors – or sometimes total failure. It is essential to maintain a DR plot, not only as a stand-by but to make sure that the boat's track is well clear of all dangers. Take great care when using waypoints on shore.

4.3   RADIO DIRECTION FINDING AND RADIO LIGHTHOUSES

4.3.1   Principle of operation — radio direction finding
Radio direction finding stations are shown on charts by the letters 'RG', and are equipped with apparatus to determine the direction of signals transmitted by a vessel. The vessel calls the station, and is requested to transmit a series of long dashes, followed by her callsign. There are no stations in the United Kingdom except as shown in 4.3.2, where the procedure is modified.

4.3.2   VHF emergency DF service
The stations below operate a VHF DF service for emergency use only. See Fig. 4(1). They are controlled by a Coastguard MRCC or MRSC as shown in brackets. On request from a yacht in distress, the station transmits her bearing *from the DF site*. Watch is kept on Ch 16. A yacht should transmit on Ch 16 (Distress Only) or on Ch 67 (Ch 67 or 82 for Jersey, and Ch 11 for French stations) to allow the station to obtain the bearing, which is transmitted on the same frequency.

St Mary's	(Falmouth)	49°55'.7N	06°18'.2W
Pendeen	(Falmouth)	50°08'.1N	05°38'.2W
Pendennis	(Falmouth)	50°08'.7N	05°02'.7W
Rame Head	(Brixham)	50°19'.0N	04°13'.1W
East Prawle	(Brixham)	50°13'.1N	03°42'.5W
Berry Head	(Brixham)	50°23'.9N	03°29'.0W
Grove Point	(Portland)	50°32'.9N	02°25'.2W
Hengistbury Head	(Portland)	50°42'.9N	01°45'.6W
Stenbury Down	(Solent)	50°36'.8N	01°14'.5W
Selsey Bill	(Solent)	50°43'.8N	00°48'.1W
Newhaven	(Solent)	50°46'.9N	00°03'.1E
Fairlight	(Dover)	50°52'.2N	00°38'.8E
Dover	(Dover)	51°07'.9N	01°20'.7E
North Foreland	(Dover)	51°22'.5N	01°26'.8E
Bawdsey	(Thames)	51°59'.5N	01°24'.6E
Trimingham	(Yarmouth)	52°54'.5N	01°20'.7E
Easington	(Humber)	53°39'.1N	00°05'.9E
Flamborough	(Humber)	54°07'.0N	00°05'.0W
Whitby	(Humber)	54°29'.4N	00°36'.2W
Newton-by-the-Sea	(Tyne Tees)	55°31'.0N	01°37'.1W
Tynemouth	(Tyne Tees)	55°01'.1N	01°24'.9W
St Abb's Head	(Forth)	55°54'.5N	02°12'.2W
Fife Ness	(Forth)	56°16'.7N	02°35'.2W
Inverbervie	(Aberdeen)	56°51'.1N	02°15'.7W
Windyheads Hill	(Aberdeen)	57°38'.9N	02°14'.5W
Compass Head	(Shetland)	59°52'.0N	01°16'.3W
Thrumster	(Pentland)	58°23'.5N	03°07'.2W
Dunnett Head	(Pentland)	58°40'.3N	03°22'.5W
Wideford Hill	(Pentland)	58°59'.3N	03°01'.4W
Sandwick	(Stornoway)	58°12'.6N	06°21'.2W
Rodel	(Stornoway)	57°44'.9N	06°57'.5W
Tiree	(Oban)	56°30'.3N	06°57'.8W
Kilchiaran	(Clyde)	56°46'.0N	06°27'.1W
Snaefell	(Liverpool)	54°15'.8N	04°27'.6W
Walney Island	(Liverpool)	54°06'.6N	03°15'.9W
Great Ormes Head	(Holyhead)	53°20'.0N	03°51'.2W
Mynydd Rhiw	(Holyhead)	52°50'.0N	04°37'.7W
St Anns Head	(Milford Haven)	51°41'.0N	05°10'.5W
Hartland	(Swansea)	51°01'.1N	04°31'.3W
Trevose Head	(Falmouth)	50°32'.9N	05°01'.9W
Orlock Point	(Belfast)	54°40'.4N	05°35'.0W
West Torr	(Belfast)	55°11'.9N	06°05'.6W
Guernsey	—	49°26'.3N	02°35'.8W
Jersey	—	49°10'.8N	02°14'.3W
Etel	(CROSS)	47°39'.8N	03°12'.0W
Créac'h	(CROSS)	48°27'.6N	05°07'.7W
Roches Douvres	(CROSS)	49°06'.5N	02°48'.8W
Jobourg	(CROSS)	49°41'.1N	01°54'.6W
Griz-Nez	(CROSS)	50°52'.1N	01°35'.0E

For 4.3.3, details of VHF Radio Lighthouses, see pp. 60–61.

FIG. 4(1) VHF EMERGENCY DF SERVICE

VHF EMERGENCY DF SERVICE	
United Kingdom	Ch 16 (Distress only) Ch 67
Jersey	Ch 67 or 82
France	Ch 11

FIG. 4(2) DECCA CHAINS — WESTERN EUROPE

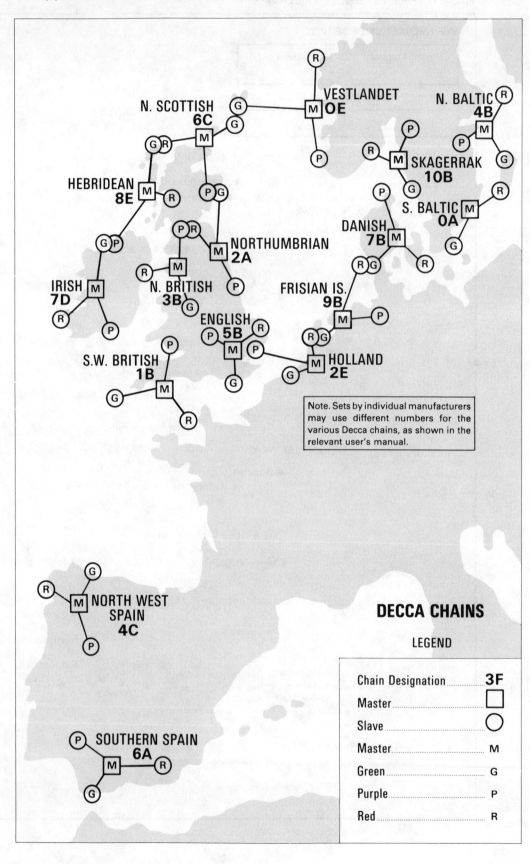

Note. Sets by individual manufacturers may use different numbers for the various Decca chains, as shown in the relevant user's manual.

DECCA CHAINS

LEGEND

Chain Designation	**3F**
Master	□
Slave	○
Master	M
Green	G
Purple	P
Red	R

TABLE 4(2) MARINE AND AERONAUTICAL RADIOBEACONS

Note: Beacon numbers prefixed with A are Aeronautical Radiobeacons

ENGLAND — SOUTH COAST

No	Name	Lat/Long	Ident		Freq	Mode	Range	Notes
1	Round Island Lt (grouped with 181)	49°58'.7N 06°19'.3W	RR	•—• •—•	308	A2A	200/100 M	
A1	St Mary's, Scilly	49°54'.8N 06°17'.4W	STM	••• — ——	321	NonA2A	15 M	Day service
A2	Penzance Heliport	50°07'.7N 05°31'.0W	PH	•—— • ••••	333	Non A2A	15 M	Day service: Mon–Sat
5	Lizard Lt (grouped with 9)	49°57'.6N 05°12'.1W	LZ	•—•• ——••	298.8	A2A	70 M	
9	Penlee Point	50°19'.1N 04°11'.3W	PE	•——• •	298.8	A2A	50 M	

No	Name	Ident		Range	Seq	Mode	Fog	Clear
9	Penlee Point	PE	•——• •	50	1	A2A	Cont	Cont
13	Start Point	SP	••• •—•—•	70	2	A2A	Cont	Cont
255	Casquets	QS	——•— •••	50	3	A2A	Cont	Cont
635	Roches Douvres	RD	•—• —••	70	4	A2A	Cont	Cont
623	Ile Vierge	VG	•••— ——•	70	5	A2A	Cont	Cont
5	Lizard	LZ	•—•• ——••	70	6	A2A	Cont	Cont

No	Name	Lat/Long	Ident		Freq	Mode	Range	Notes
A6	Plymouth	50°25'4N 04°06'.7W	PY	•——• —•—•	396.5	Non A2A	20 M	
13	Start Point Lt. (grouped with 9)	50°13'.3N 03°38'.5W	SP	••• •—•—•	298.8	A2A	70 M	
A10	Berry Head	50°23'.9N 03°29'.6W	BHD	—••• •••• —••	318	NonA2A	25 M	
A14	Exeter	50°45'.1N 03°17'.6W	EX	• —••—	337	NonA2A	15 M	Day service
17	Portland Bill	50°30'.8N 02°27'.3W	PB	•——• —•••	291.9	A2A	50 M	

No	Name	Ident		Range	Seq	Mode	Fog	Clear
17	Portland Bill	PB	•——• —•••	50	1	A2A	Cont	Cont
25	St Catherine's Pt	CP	—•—• •——•	50	2	A2A	Cont	Cont
667	C d'Antifer	TI	— ••	50	3	A2A	Cont	Cont
663	Le Havre Lanby	I H	•—•• ••••	30	4	A2A	Cont	Cont
659	P de Ver	ÉR	•••—••• •—•	20	5	A2A	Cont	Cont
651	P de Barfleur	FG	••—• ——••	70	6	A2A	Cont	Cont

No	Name	Lat/Long	Ident		Freq	Mode	Range	Notes
21	Poole Harbour (grouped with 29)	50°40'.9N 01°56'.7W	PO	•——• ———	303.4	A2A	10 M	
A18	Bournemouth/Hurn	50°48'.0N 01°43'.7W	HRN	•••• •—• —•	394	NonA2A	35 M	
25	St Catherine's Pt Lt (grouped with 17)	50°34'.5N 01°17'.8W	CP	—•—• •——•	291.9	A2A	50 M	
A26	Bembridge	50°40'.6N 01°05'.9W	IW	•• •——	276.5	Non A2A	15 M	
A30	Lee-on-Solent	50°52'.9N 01°06'.7W	LS	•—•• •••	323	Non A2A	10 M	
29	Chichester Bar Bn	50°45'.9N 00°56'.3W	CH	—•—• ••••	303.4	A2A	10 M	Coded wind info as below

CH 4 times: 4s dash: up to 8 dashes (direction; 1 dash = NE, 8 dashes = N): 4s dash: up to 8 dots (speed: Beaufort 1–8): 12s dash: CH twice: 5s silence.

No	Name	Ident		Range	Seq	Mode	Fog	Clear
29	Chichester	CH	—•—• ••••	10	1,4	A2A	Cont	Cont
37	Brighton	BM	—••• ——	10	2,5	A2A	Cont	Cont
41	Newhaven	NH	—• ••••	10	3,6	A2A	Cont	Cont
21	Poole	PO	•——• ———	10	3,6	A2A	Cont	Cont

4

No	Name	Lat/Long	Ident		Freq	Mode	Range	Notes
33	Nab Tower Lt	50°40′.0N 00°57′.1W	NB	— • — • • •	312.6	A2A	10 M	

No	Name	Ident		Range	Seq	Mode	Fog	Clear
33	Nab	NB	— • — • • •	10	1,3,5	A2A	Cont	Cont
647	Cherbourg	RB	• — • — • • •	20	2,4,6	A2A	Cont	Cont

No	Name	Lat/Long	Ident		Freq	Mode	Range	Notes
A38	Shoreham	50°49′.9N 00°17′.6W	SHM	• • • • • • • — —	332	Non A2A	10 M	Day service
37	Brighton Marina (grouped with 29)	50°48′.7N 00°05′.9W	BM	— • • • — —	303.4	A2A	10 M	
41	Newhaven (grouped with 29)	50°46′.9N 00°03′.5E	NH	— • • • • •	303.4	A2A	10 M	
45	Royal Sovereign Lt (grouped with 679)	50°43′.4N 00°26′.1E	RY	• — • — • — • •	310.3	A2A	50 M	
A42	Lydd	50°58′.2N 00°57′.3E	LYX	• — • • — • • — — — — • • —	397	Non A2A	15 M	
49	Dungeness Lt (grouped with 679)	50°54′.8N 00°58′.7E	DU	— • • • • —	310.3	A2A	30 M	
57	North Foreland Lt	51°22′.5N 01°26′.8E	NF	— • • • — •	301.1	A2A	50 M	
61	Falls Lt V	51°18′.1N 01°48′.5E	FS	• • — • • • •	305.7	A2A	50 M	

No	Name	Ident		Range	Seq	Mode	Fog	Clear
61	Falls Lt V	FS	• • — • • • •	50	1	A2A	Cont	Cont
701	W Hinder Lt V	WH	• — — • • • •	20	3	A2A	Cont	Cont
713	Oostende	OE	— — — • — •	30	4	A2A	Cont	Cont
691	Calais Main Lt	CS	— • — • • • •	20	5	A2A	Cont	Cont

ENGLAND — EAST COAST

No	Name	Lat/Long	Ident		Freq	Mode	Range	Notes
A46	Southend	51°34′.5N 00°42′.1E	SND	• • • — — • — • •	362.5	Non A2A	20 M	
69	Sunk Lt F	51°51′.0N 01°35′.0E	UK	• • — — — • —	312.6	A2A	10 M	
73	Outer Gabbard Lt V (grouped with 77)	51°59′.4N 02°04′.6E	GA	— — • • —	287.3	A2A	50 M	
77	Smith's Knoll Lt V	52°43′.5N 02°18′.0E	SK	• • • — • —	287.3	A2A	50 M	

No	Name	Ident		Range	Seq	Mode	Fog	Clear
77	Smith's Knoll Lt V	SK	• • • — • —	50	1	A2A	Cont	Cont
721	Goeree Lt	GR	— — • • — •	50	2	A2A	Cont	Cont
85	Dudgeon Lt V	LV	• — • • • • • —	50	3	A2A	Cont	Cont
73	Outer Gabbard Lt V	GA	— — • • —	50	4	A2A	Cont	Cont
81	Cromer	CM	— • — • — —	50	5	A2A	Cont	Cont
709	N Hinder Lt V	NR	— • • — •	50	6	A2A	Cont	Cont

BEACON SEQUENCE NUMBERS Commence transmission at the following minutes past the hour:

1 00 06 12 18 24 30 36 42 48 54	**2** 01 07 13 19 25 31 37 43 49 55	**3** 02 08 14 20 26 32 38 44 50 56
4 03 09 15 21 27 33 39 45 51 57	**5** 04 10 16 22 28 34 40 46 52 58	**6** 05 11 17 23 29 35 41 47 53 59

Fig. 4(3) *Marine and Aero Radiobeacons — Southern England, South Wales, North Coast of France, Belgium and South Holland*

Note: This plan is diagrammatic, to indicate the likely availability of beacons in different areas. Positions are only approximate. Calibration stations are excluded.

(Numbers prefixed with the letter A are Aero Radiobeacons.)

Local beacons at Poole (21), Chichester (29), Brighton Marina (37) and Newhaven (41).

See Fig. 4(3)

See Fig. 4(4)

See Fig. 4(4)

4

No	Name	Lat/Long	Ident		Freq	Mode	Range	Notes
A50	Great Yarmouth/North Denes	52°38'.2N 01°43'.5E	ND	— · — · ·	397	Non A2A	15 M	
81	Cromer Lt (grouped with 77)	52°55'.5N 01°19'.1E	CM	— · — · — —	287.3	A2A	50 M	
85	Dudgeon Lt V (grouped with 77)	53°16'.6N 01°17'.0E	LV	· — · · · · · —	287.3	A2A	50 M	
A54	Ottringham	53°41'.9N 00°06'.1W	OTR	— — — — · — ·	335	Non A2A	50 M	
97	Flamborough Head Lt (grouped with 109)	54°07'.0N 00°04'.9W	FB	· · — · — · · ·	303.4	A2A	70 M	
A58	Teeside	54°33'.6N 01°20'.0W	TD	— — · ·	347.5	Non A2A	25 M	
109	Souter Lt	54°58'.2N 01°21'.8W	SJ	· · · · — — —	303.4	A2A	70 M	
	Calibration station		PT	· — — · —	312.6	A2A	5 M	Cont from 1 hour after sunrise to 1 hr before sunset

No	Name	Ident		Range	Seq	Mode	Fog	Clear
109	Souter Lt	SJ	· · · · — — —	70	1,4	A2A	Cont	Cont
97	Flamborough Hd	FB	· · — · — · · ·	70	2	A2A	Cont	Cont
113	Longstone	LT	· — · · —	20	5	A2A	Cont	Cont
125	Fife Ness	FP	· · — · · — — ·	100/70	6	A2A	Cont	Cont

No	Name	Lat/Long	Ident		Freq	Mode	Range	Notes
113	Longstone Lt (Farne I) (grouped with 109)	55°38'.6N 01°36'.5W	LT	· — · · —	303.4	A2A	20 M	

SCOTLAND — EAST COAST

No	Name	Lat/Long	Ident		Freq	Mode	Range	Notes
A70	Edinburgh	55°58'.7N 03°17'.0W	EDN	· — · · — ·	341	Non A2A	35 M	
117	Inchkeith Lt	56°02'.0N 03°08'.1W	NK	— · — · —	296.5	A2A	10 M	
119	Fidra Lt	56°04'.4N 02°47'.0W	FD	· · — · — · ·	289.6	A2A	10 M	
125	Fife Ness (grouped with 109)	56°16'.7N 02°35'.1W	FP	· · — · · — — ·	303.4	A2A	100 M	
A74	Leuchars	56°22'.3N 02°51'.4W	LU	· — · · · · —	330	Non A2A	100 M	Subject to night interference
A78	Dundee	56°27'.3N 03°06'.6W	DND	— · · — · — · ·	394	Non A2A	25 M	
133	Girdle Ness Lt	57°08'.3N 02°02'.8W	GD	— — · — · ·	310.3	A2A	50 M	

BEACON SEQUENCE NUMBERS   Commence transmission at the following minutes past the hour:

1	00	06	12	18	24	30	36	42	48	54
2	01	07	13	19	25	31	37	43	49	55
3	02	08	14	20	26	32	38	44	50	56
4	03	09	15	21	27	33	39	45	51	57
5	04	10	16	22	28	34	40	46	52	58
6	05	11	17	23	29	35	41	47	53	59

No	Name	Lat/Long	Ident	Freq	Mode	Range	Notes
A82	Aberdeen	57°16'.1N 02°14'.7W	AOS ·— ——— ···	377	Non A2A	50 M	
A86	Scotstown Head	57°33'.6N 01°48'.9W	SHD ··· ···· —··	383	Non A2A	80 M	
137	Kinnairds Head	57°41'.9N 02°00'.1W	KD —·— —··	291.9	A2A	100/70 M	

No	Name	Ident		Range	Seq	Mode	Fog	Clear
137	Kinnairds Hd	KD	—·— —··	100/70	1,4	A2A	Cont	Cont
145	N Ronaldsay	NR	—· ·—·	100/70	2	A2A	Cont	Cont
141	Stroma (Swilkie Pt)	OM	——— ——	50	3,6	A2A	Cont	Cont
149	Sumburgh Hd	SB	··· —···	70	5	A2A	Cont	Cont

No	Name	Lat/Long	Ident	Freq	Mode	Range	Notes
A90	Kinloss	57°39'.0N 03°35'.0W	KS —·— ···	370	Non A2A	50 M	
A94	Wick	58°26'.8N 03°03'.7W	WIK ·—— ·· —·—	344	Non A2A	40 M	
141	Stroma, Swilkie Pt Lt (grouped with 137)	58°41'.8N 03°06'.9W	OM ——— ——	291.9	A2A	50 M	
A98	Kirkwall, Orkney	58°57'.6N 02°54'.6W	KW —·— ·——	395	Non A2A	30 M	
145	North Ronaldsay Lt (grouped with 137)	59°23'.4N 02°22'.8W	NR —· ·—·	291.9	A2A	100/70 M	
A102	Sumburgh	59°52'.1N 01°16'.3W	SUM ··· ··— ——	351	Non A2A	75 M	
149	Sumburgh Hd Lt (grouped with 137)	59°51'.3N 01°16'.4W	SB ··· —···	291.9	A2A	70 M	
153	Bressay Lt, Shetland I	60°07'.2N 01°07'.2W	BY —··· —·——	287.3	A2A	30 M	
A106	Lerwick/Tingwall	60°11'.3N 01°14'.7W	TL — ·—··	376	Non A2A	25 M	
A110	Scatsa	60°27'.7N 01°12'.8W	SS ··· ···	315.5	Non A2A	25 M	
A114	Unst	60°44'.3N 00°49'.2W	UT ··— —	325	Non A2A	20 M	
157	Muckle Flugga (N Unst Lt) (grouped with 165)	60°51'.3N 00°53'.0W	MF —— ··—·	298.8	A2A	150/70 M	
161	Sule Skerry Lt (grouped with 165)	59°05'.1N 04°24'.3W	LK ·—·· —·—	298.8	A2A	100/70 M	

SCOTLAND — WEST COAST

No	Name	Lat/Long	Ident	Freq	Mode	Range	Notes
A118	Dounreay/Thurso	58°34'.9N 03°43'.6W	DO —·· ———	364.5	Non A2A	15 M	
165	Cape Wrath Lt	58°37'.5N 04°59'.9W	CW —·—· ·——	298.8	A2A	50 M	

No	Name	Ident		Range	Seq	Mode	Fog	Clear
165	Cape Wrath	CW	—·—· ·——	50	1	A2A	Cont	Cont
169	Butt of Lewis	BL	—··· ·—··	150	2,5	A2A	Cont	Cont
157	Muckle Flugga	MF	—— ··—·	150/70	3,6	A2A	Cont	Cont
161	Sule Skerry	LK	·—·· —·—	100/70	4	A2A	Cont	Cont

4

No	Name	Lat/Long	Ident		Freq	Mode	Range	Notes
169	Butt of Lewis Lt (grouped with 165)	58°30'.9N 06°15'.7W	BL	— ··· · — ··	299.8	A2A	150 M	
A120	Stornoway	58°17'.2N 06°20'.6W	SWY	··· · — — — · — · —	669.5	Non A2A	60 M	
173	Eilean Glas Lt (grouped with 189)	57°51'.4N 06°38'.4W	LG	· — ·· — — ·	294.2	A2A	50 M	
177	Hyskeir Lt, Oigh Sgeir (grouped with 189)	56°58'.1N 06°40'.8W	OR	— — — · — ·	294.2	A2A	50 M	
A122	St Kilda	57°49'.0N 08°35'.0W	KL	— · — · — ··	338	A2A	30 M	
A124	Barra	57°01'.4N 07°26'.4W	BRR	— ···· · — · · — ·	316	Non A2A	20 M	Occas
181	Barra Head Lt, Berneray	56°47'.1N 07°39'.2W	BD	— ··· — ··	308	A2A	200/70 M	

No	Name	Ident		Range	Seq	Mode	Fog	Clear
181	Barra Hd	BD	— ··· — ··	200/70	1	A2A	Cont	Cont
337	Tory I	TY	— · — · —	100/70	2	A2A	Cont	Cont
341	Eagle I	GL	— — · · — ··	200/100	3	A2A	Cont	Cont
301	Mizen Hd	MZ	— — ·· — —	200/100	4	A2A	Cont	Cont
1	Round I	RR	· — · · — ·	200/100	5	A2A	Cont	Cont
615	Pte de Créac'h	CA	— · — · · —	100	6	A2A	Cont	Cont

No	Name	Lat/Long	Ident		Freq	Mode	Range	Notes
A126	Connel/Oban	56°28'.0N 05°24'.0W	CNL	— · — · — · — ··	404	Non A2A	15 M	
185	Rhinns of Islay Lt (grouped with 189)	55°40'.4N 06°30'.7W	RN	· — · — ·	294.2	A2A	70 M	
A128	Islay/Port Ellen	55°41'.0N 06°14'.9N	LAY	· — ·· · — —	395	A2A	30 M	Day service
189	Pladda Lt, Arran I	55°25'.5N 05°07'.1W	DA	— ·· · —	294.2	A2A	30 M	

No	Name	Ident		Range	Seq	Mode	Fog	Clear
189	Pladda	DA	— ·· · —	30	1	A2A	Cont	Cont
329	Mew I	MW	— — · — —	50	2	A2A	Cont	Cont
333	Altacarry Hd	AH	· — ····	50	3	A2A	Cont	Cont
185	Rhinns of Islay	RN	· — · — ·	70	4	A2A	Cont	Cont
177	Hyskeir	OR	— — — · — ·	50	5	A2A	Cont	Cont
173	Eilean Glas	LG	· — ·· — — ·	50	6	A2A	Cont	Cont

No	Name	Lat/Long	Ident		Freq	Mode	Range	Notes
193	Cloch Pt Lt (calibration station)	55°56'.5N 04°52'.7W	CL	— · — · · — ·	308		8 M	On request Tel: (0475) 26221 (6 hrs notice)
A138	Turnberry	55°18'.8N 04°47'.0W	TRN	— · — · — ·	355	Non A2A	25 M	
A142	New Galloway	55°10'.6N 04°10'.0W	NGY	— · — — · — · — —	399	Non A2A	35 M	

ENGLAND (WEST COAST), ISLE OF MAN, WALES

No	Name	Lat/Long	Ident		Freq	Mode	Range	Notes
197	Point of Ayre High Light (grouped with 217)	54°24'.9N 04°22'.0W	PY	· — — · — · — —	301.1	A2A	50 M	
201	Douglas, Victoria Pier Lt (grouped with 209)	54°08'.8N 04°28'.0W	DG	— ·· — — ·	287.3	A2A	50 M	

BEACON SEQUENCE NUMBERS Commence transmission at the following minutes past the hour:

1	00 06 12 18 24 30 36 42 48 54	2	01 07 13 19 25 31 37 43 49 55	3	02 08 14 20 26 32 38 44 50 56
4	03 09 15 21 27 33 39 45 51 57	5	04 10 16 22 28 34 40 46 52 58	6	05 11 17 23 29 35 41 47 53 59

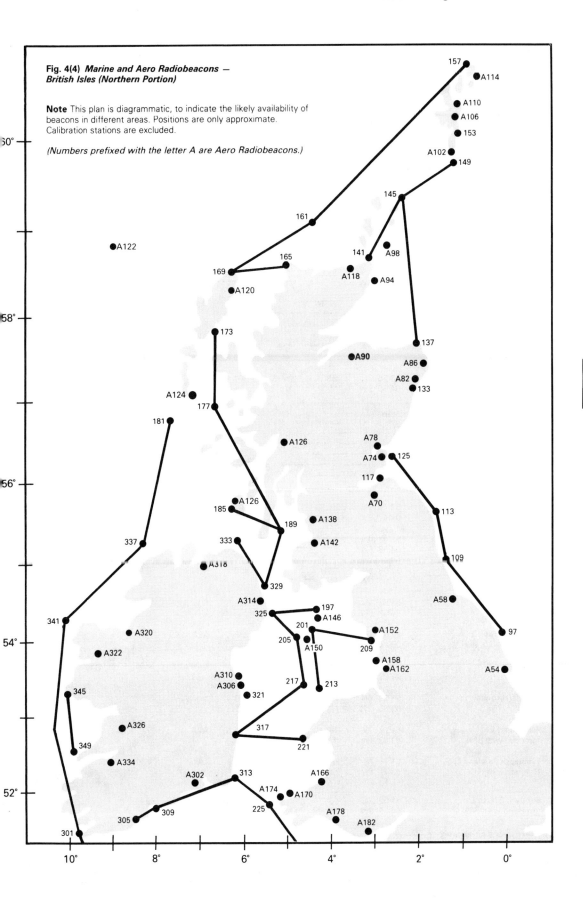

Fig. 4(4) *Marine and Aero Radiobeacons —*
British Isles (Northern Portion)

Note This plan is diagrammatic, to indicate the likely availability of
beacons in different areas. Positions are only approximate.
Calibration stations are excluded.

(Numbers prefixed with the letter A are Aero Radiobeacons.)

No	Name	Lat/Long	Ident		Freq	Mode	Range	Notes
A146	Carnane	54°08′.5N 04°29′.4W	CAR	—·—· ·— ·—·	366.5	Non A2A	25 M	
A150	IOM/Ronaldsway	54°05′.1N 04°36′.4W	RWY	·—· ·—— —·——	359	Non A2A	20 M	Day service
205	Cregneish, IOM (grouped with 217)	54°03′.9N 04°45′.9W	CN	—·—· —·	301.1	A2A	50 M	
209	Walney Island Lt	54°02′.9N 03°10′.5W	FN	··—· —·	287.3	A2A	30 M	

No	Name	Ident		Range	Seq	Mode	Fog	Clear
209	Walney I	FN	··—· —·	30	1,4	A2A	Cont	Cont
213	Point Lynas	PS	·——· ···	40	2,5	A2A	Cont	Cont
201	Douglas	DG	—·· ——·	50	3,6	A2A	Cont	Cont

No	Name	Lat/Long	Ident		Freq	Mode	Range	Notes
A152	Walney Island	54°07′.6N 03°15′.8W	WL	·—— ·—··	385	A2A	15 M	Day service
A158	Blackpool	53°46′.2N 02°59′.3W	BPL	—··· ·——· ·—··	276.5	Non A2A	15 M	Day service
A162	Warton	53°45′.1N 02°51′.1W	WTN	·—— — —·	337	A2A	15 M	Day service
213	Point Lynas Lt (grouped with 209) Calibration station	53°25′.0N 04°17′.3W	PS	·——· ···	287.3 / 310.3	A2A / A2A	40 M / 5 M	/ H24
217	Skerries Lt	53°25′.3N 04°36′.5W	SR	··· ·—·	301.1	A2A	50 M	

No	Name	Ident		Range	Seq	Mode	Fog	Clear
217	Skerries	SR	··· ·—·	50	1	A2A	Cont	Cont
221	Bardsey Lt	IB	·· —···	30	2	A2A	Cont	Cont
317	Wicklow Hd	WK	·—— —·—	70	3	A2A	Cont	Cont
205	Cregneish	CN	—·—· —·	50	4	A2A	Cont	Cont
197	Point of Ayre	PY	·——· —·——	50	5	A2A	Cont	Cont
325	South Rock Lt F	SU	··· ··—	50	6	A2A	Cont	Cont

No	Name	Lat/Long	Ident		Freq	Mode	Range	Notes
221	Bardsey Lt (grouped with 217)	52°45′.0N 04°47′.9W	IB	·· —···	301.1	A2A	30 M	
A166	Aberporth	52°07′.0N 04°33′.6W	AP	·— ·——·	370.5	Non A2A	20 M	
A170	Strumble	52°00′.5N 05°01′.0W	STU	··· — ··—	400	Non A2A	40 M	
A174	Brawdy	51°53′.4N 05°07′.3W	BY	—··· —·——	414.5	Non A2A	30 M	
225	South Bishop Lt (grouped with 309)	51°51′.1N 05°24′.6W	SB	··· —···	296.5	A2A	50 M	
A178	Swansea	51°36′.1N 04°03′.9W	SWN	··· ·—— —·	320.5	Non A2A	15 M	Day service
A182	Cardiff/Rhoose	51°23′.6N 03°20′.2W	CDF	—·—· —·· ·—··	363.5	Non A2A	20 M	
233	Nash Point Lt (grouped with 309)	51°24′.0N 03°33′.1W	NP	—· ·——·	296.5	A2A	50 M	
235	Lynmouth Foreland Lt Calibration station	51°14′.7N 03°47′.1W	FP	··—· ·——·	312.6	A2A	5 M	Cont from 1 hr after sunrise to 1 hr before sunset
237	Lundy I, South Lt (grouped with 309)	51°09′.7N 04°39′.3W	LS	·—·· ···	296.5	A2A	50 M	Reliable 234°–216°

BEACON SEQUENCE NUMBERS Commence transmission at the following minutes past the hour:

1	00 06 12 18 24 30 36 42 48 54	**2**	01 07 13 19 25 31 37 43 49 55	**3**	02 08 14 20 26 32 38 44 50 56
4	03 09 15 21 27 33 39 45 51 57	**5**	04 10 16 22 28 34 40 46 52 58	**6**	05 11 17 23 29 35 41 47 53 59

No	Name	Lat/Long	Ident		Freq	Mode	Range	Notes
A190	St Mawgan	50°26'.8N 04°59'.6W	**SM** ••• ━ ━		356.5	Non A2A	50 M	

CHANNEL ISLANDS

No	Name	Lat/Long	Ident		Freq	Mode	Range	Notes
251	Channel Lt V	49°54'.4N 02°53'.7W	**CR** ━•━• •━••		287.3	A2A	10 M	
255	Casquets Lt (grouped with 9)	49°43'.4N 02°22'.5W	**QS** ━━•━ •••		298.8	A2A	50 M	
A252	Alderney	49°42'.6N 02°11'.9W	**ALD** •━ •━•• ━••		383	Non A2A	50 M	Day service
259	Castle Breakwater, St Peter Port[1]	49°27'.4N 02°31'.4W	**GY** ━━•• ━•━━		285	A2A	10 M	

[1] Synchronised with horn for distance finding. Horn begins simultaneously with 27 sec long dash after the four GY ident signals. Time in secs from start of long dash until horn is heard, multiplied by 0.18, gives distance in nm

No	Name	Lat/Long	Ident		Freq	Mode	Range	Notes
A256	Guernsey	49°26'.1N 02°38'.3W	**GUR** ━━• ••━ •━•		361	Non A2A	30 M	Day service
263	La Corbière[1,2] (grouped with 639)	49°10'.9N 02°14'.9W	**CB** ━•━• ━•••		305.7	A2A	20 M	

[1] For details of coded wind information see 7.2.13. [2] Synchronised for distance finding. Horn blast (Morse 'C') begins with end of 18 sec long dash. Each pip heard before the blast corresponds to a distance of 335m from the light.

No	Name	Lat/Long	Ident		Freq	Mode	Range	Notes
267	St Helier Harbour	49°10'.6N 02°07'.5W	**EC** • ━•━•		287.3	A2A	10 M	
A260	Jersey East	49°13'.2N 02°02'.1W	**JEY** •━━━ • ━•━━		367	Non A2A	75 M	
A264	Jersey West	49°12'.4N 02°13'.3W	**JW** •━━━ •━━		329	Non A2A	25 M	

IRELAND — SOUTH AND EAST COASTS

No	Name	Lat/Long	Ident		Freq	Mode	Range	Notes
301	Mizen Head Lt (grouped with 181)	51°27'.0N 09°48'.8W	**MZ** ━━ ━━••		308	A2A	200/100 M	070° 475m from Lt.
305	Old Head of Kinsale Lt (grouped with 309)	51°36'.3N 08°32'.0W	**OH** ━━ ••••		296.5	A2A	50 M	
309	Ballycotton Lt	51°49'.5N 07°59'.0W	**BN** ━••• ━•		296.5	A2A	50 M	
	Calibration station		**BC** ━••• ━•━•		312.6	A2A	5 M	On request

No	Name	Ident		Range	Seq	Mode	Fog	Clear
309	Ballycotton Lt	BN ━••• ━•		50	1	A2A	Cont	Cont
305	Kinsale	OH ━━ ••••		50	2	A2A	Cont	Cont
237	Lundy	LS •━•• •••		50	3	A2A	Cont	Cont
233	Nash Point	NP ━• •━ ━•		50	4	A2A	Cont	Cont
225	South Bishop	SB ••• ━•••		50	5	A2A	Cont	Cont
313	Tuskar Rock	TR ━ •━•		50	6	A2A	Cont	Cont

No	Name	Lat/Long	Ident		Freq	Mode	Range	Notes
A302	Waterford	52°11'.8N 07°05'.3W	**WTD** •━━ ━ ━••		368	Non A2A	25 M	
313	Tuskar Rock Lt (grouped with 309)	52°12'.1N 06°12'.4W	**TR** ━ •━•		296.5	A2A	50 M	
317	Wicklow Hd Lt (grouped with 217)	52°57'.9N 05°59'.8W	**WK** •━━ ━•━		301.1	A2A	70 M	
A306	Killiney	53°16'.2N 06°06'.3W	**KLY** ━•━ •━•• ━•━━		378	Non A2A	50 M	
A310	Dublin/Rush	53°30'.7N 06°06'.6W	**RSH** •━• ••• ••••		326	Non A2A	30 M	
321	Kish Bank Lt	53°18'.7N 05°55'.4W	**KH** ━•━ ••••		312.6	A2A	20 M	
	Calibration station		**KH** ━•━ ••••		312.6	A2A	5 M	On request

No	Name	Lat/Long	Ident		Freq	Mode	Range	Notes
325	South Rock Lt F (grouped with 217)	54°24'.5N 05°21'.9W	SU	••• ••—	301.1	A2A	50 M	
A314	Belfast Harbour	54°37'.0N 05°52'.9W	HB	•••• —•••	275	Non A2A	15 M	
329	Mew Island Lt (grouped with 189)	54°41'.9N 05°30'.7W	MW	—— •——	294.2	A2A	50 M	
	Calibration station		MC	—— —•—•	312.6	A2A	5 M	On request
333	Altacarry Head Lt (grouped with 189)	55°18'.1N 06°10'.2W	AH	•— ••••	294.2	A2A	50 M	

IRELAND — WEST COAST

No	Name	Lat/Long	Ident		Freq	Mode	Range	Notes
A318	Eglinton/Londonderry	55°02'.7N 07°09'.2W	EGT	• ——• —	328.5	Non A2A	25 M	Occasional
337	Tory Island Lt (grouped with 181)	55°16'.3N 08°14'.9W	TY	— —•——	308	A2A	100/70 M	
341	Eagle Island Lt (grouped with 181)	54°17'.0N 10°05'.5W	GL	——• •—••	308	A2A	200/100 M	
A320	Sligo	54°16'.5N 08°36'.0W	SL	••• •—••	384	Non A2A	25 M	
345	Slyne Head Lt	53°24'.0N 10°14'.0W	SN	••• —•	289.6	A2A	50 M	

No	Name	Ident		Range	Seq	Mode	Fog	Clear
345	Slyne Head	SN	••• —•	50	1,3,5	A2A	Cont	Cont
349	Loop Head	LP	•—•• •—••	50	2,4,6	A2A	Cont	Cont

No	Name	Lat/Long	Ident		Freq	Mode	Range	Notes
A322	Carnmore/Galway	53°18'.0N 08°57'.0W	CRN	—•—• •—• —•	321	Non A2A	——	
A326	Ennis	52°54'.3N 08°55'.6W	ENS	•— —• •••	352	Non A2A	80 M	
A334	Foynes	52°34'.0N 09°11'.7W	FOY	••—• ——— —•——	395	Non A2A	50 M	
349	Loop Head Lt (grouped with 345)	52°33'.6N 09°55'.9W	LP	•—•• •—••	289.6	A2A	50 M	

SPAIN — NORTH COAST

No	Name	Lat/Long	Ident		Freq	Mode	Range	Notes
543	Cabo Mayor Lt (grouped with 551)	43°29'.5N 03°47'.4W	MY	—— —•——	296.5	A2A	50 M	
A548	Bilbao	43°19'.4N 02°58'.4W	BLO	—••• •—•• ———	370	Non A2A	70 M	
547	Cabo Machichaco Lt (grouped with 551)	43°27'.4N 02°45'.1W	MA	—— •—	296.5	A2A	100 M	Reliable sector 110°–220°
A552	San Sebastian	43°23'.3N 01°47'.7W	HIG	•••• •• ——•	328	Non A2A	50 M	

BEACON SEQUENCE NUMBERS Commence transmission at the following minutes past the hour:

1 00 06 12 18 24 30 36 42 48 54	**2** 01 07 13 19 25 31 37 43 49 55	**3** 02 08 14 20 26 32 38 44 50 56
4 03 09 15 21 27 33 39 45 51 57	**5** 04 10 16 22 28 34 40 46 52 58	**6** 05 11 17 23 29 35 41 47 53 59

FRANCE

No	Name	Lat/Long	Ident	Freq	Mode	Range	Notes
A556	Biarritz	43°28'.2N 01°24'.2W	BZ —··· —·—··	341	A1A	35 M	
A560	Cazaux	44°33'.1N 01°07'.1W	CAA —·—· ·— ·—	382	A1A	80 M	
551	Cap Ferret Lt	44°38'.8N 01°15'.0W	FT ··—· —	296.5	A2A	100 M	

No	Name	Ident		Range	Seq	Mode	Fog	Clear
551	Cap Ferret	FT	··—· —	100	1,2	A2A	Cont	Cont
547	Cabo Machichaco	MA	—— ·—	100	3,4	A2A	Cont	Cont
543	Cabo Mayor	MY	—— —·——	50	5,6	A2A	Cont	Cont

No	Name	Lat/Long	Ident	Freq	Mode	Range	Notes
A564	Bordeaux/Merignac	44°55'.9N 00°33'.9W	BD —··· —··	393	A1A	30 M	
A568	Cognac/Chateaubernard	45°40'.1N 00°18'.5W	CGC —·—· ——· —·—·	354	A1A	75 M	
559	Pointe de la Coubre (grouped with 607)	45°41'.9N 01°13'.9W	LK ·—·· —·—	303.4	A2A	100 M	
563	La Rochelle, Tour Richelieu Lt	46°09'.0N 1°10'.3W	RE ·—· ·	291.9	A1A	5 M	
571	Les Baleines Lt (Ile de Ré) (grouped with 607)	46°14'.7N 01°33'6W	BN —··· —·	303.4	A2A	50 M	
575	Les Sables d'Olonne Tour de la Chaume Lt	46°29'.6N 01°47'.8W	SO ··· ———	291.9	A2A	5 M	Temp inop (Aug 1988)
579	Ile d'Yeu Main Lt	46°43'.1N 02°22'.9W	YE —·—— ·	312.6	A2A	70 M	Sequence 3
583	Ile du Pilier Lt	47°02'.6N 02°21'.5W	PR ·——· ·—·	298.8	A2A	10 M	Temp inop (Aug 1988)
587	St Nazaire, Pointe de St Gildas Lt	47°08'.1N 02°14'.7W	NZ —· ——··	298.8	A1A	10 M	
A572	St Nazaire/Montoir	47°20'.0N 02°02'.6W	MT —— —	398	A1A	50 M	
A576	Vannes/Meucon	47°46'.2N 02°39'.6W	VA ···— ·—	342.5	A1A	25 M	
A580	Lorient/Lann-Bihoué	47°45'.7N 03°26'.4W	LOR ·—·· ——— ·—·	294.2	A1A	80 M	

4

BEACON SEQUENCE NUMBERS Commence transmission at the following minutes past the hour:

1 00 06 12 18 24 30 36 42 48 54	**2** 01 07 13 19 25 31 37 43 49 55	**3** 02 08 14 20 26 32 38 44 50 56
4 03 09 15 21 27 33 39 45 51 57	**5** 04 10 16 22 28 34 40 46 52 58	**6** 05 11 17 23 29 35 41 47 53 59

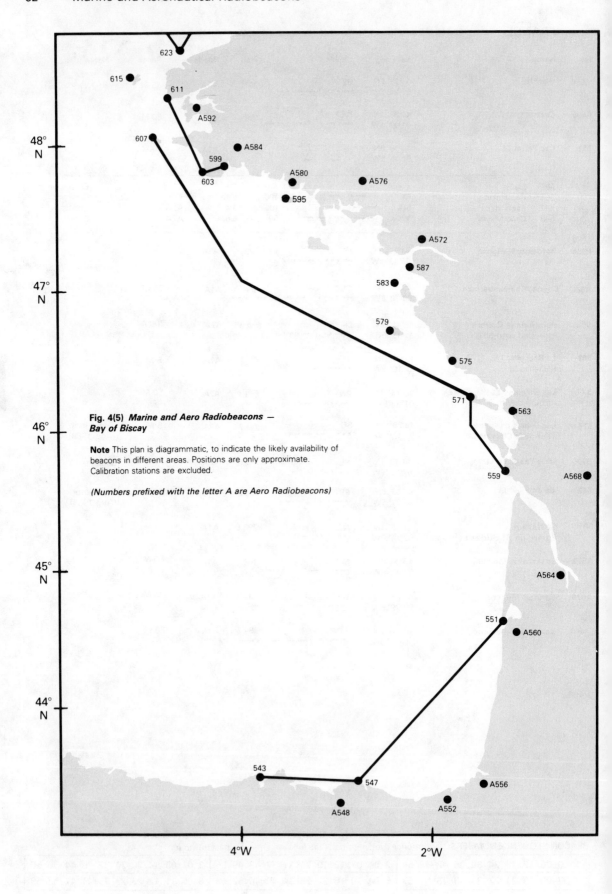

Fig. 4(5) *Marine and Aero Radiobeacons —*
Bay of Biscay

Note This plan is diagrammatic, to indicate the likely availability of
beacons in different areas. Positions are only approximate.
Calibration stations are excluded.

(Numbers prefixed with the letter A are Aero Radiobeacons)

No	Name	Lat/Long	Ident		Freq	Mode	Range	Notes
595	Pen Men Lt, Ile de Groix	47°38′.9N 03°30′.5W	GX	— — · — · · —	301.1	A1A	10 M	
A584	Quimper/Pluguffan	47°58′.1N 03°59′.8W	QR	— — · — · — ·	380	A1A		
599	Pointe de Combrit Lt (grouped with 603)	47°51′.9N 04°06′.7W	CT	— · — · —	289.6	A2A	20 M	
603	Eckmühl Lt, Pointe de Penmarc'h	47°47′.9N 04°22′.4W	ÜH	· · — — · · · ·	289.6	A2A	50 M	

No	Name	Ident		Range	Seq	Mode	Fog	Clear
603	Eckmühl	ÜH	· · — — · · · ·	50	1	A2A	Cont	Cont
611	Pte St Mathieu	SM	· · · — —	20	3	A2A	Cont	Cont
599	Pte de Combrit	CT	— · — · —	20	4	A2A	Cont	Cont

No	Name	Lat/Long	Ident		Freq	Mode	Range	Notes
607	Ile de Sein NW Lt	48°02′.7N 04°52′.0W	SN	· · · — ·	303.4	A2A	70 M	

No	Name	Ident		Range	Seq	Mode	Fog	Clear
607	Ile de Sein	SN	· · · — ·	100	3	A2A	Cont	Cont
559	Pte de la Coubre	LK	· — · · — · —	100	4	A2A	Cont	Cont
571	Les Baleines	BN	— · · · — ·	50	6	A2A	Cont	Cont

No	Name	Lat/Long	Ident		Freq	Mode	Range	Notes
A592	Lanvéoc, Poulmic	48°17′.1N 04°26′.0W	BST	— · · · · · · —	316	A1A	80 M	
611	Pte St Mathieu Lt (grouped with 603)	48°19′.8N 04°46′.2W	SM	· · · — —	289.6	A2A	20 M	
615	Pte de Créac'h Lt (grouped with 181)	48°27′.6N 05°07′.6W	CA	— · — · · —	308	A2A	100 M	
619	Ouessant SW Lanby	48°31′.7N 05°49′.1W	SW	· · · · — —	294.2	A2A	10 M	
623	Ile Vierge Lt (grouped with 9)	48°38′.4N 04°34′.0W	VG	· · · — — — ·	298.8	A2A	70 M	
A596	Landivisiau	48°32′.8N 04°08′.2W	LDV	· — · · — · · · · · —	324	A1A	60 M	
627	Roscoff-Bloscon Jetty Lt	48°43′.3N 03°57′.6W	BC	— · · · — · — ·	287.3	A2A	10 M	
A600	Lannion	48°43′.3N 03°18′.4W	LN	· — · · — ·	345.5	A1A	50 M	
631	Rosédo Lt, Ile Bréhat	48°51′.5N 03°00′.3W	DO	— · · — — —	294.2	A2A	10 M	

No	Name	Ident		Range	Seq	Mode	Fog	Clear
631	Rosédo	DO	— · · — — —	10	1,5	A2A	Cont	Cont
643	Le Grand Jardin	GJ	— — · · — — —	10	2,6	A2A	Cont	Cont

No	Name	Lat/Long	Ident		Freq	Mode	Range	Notes
635	Roches-Douvres Lt (grouped with 9)	49°06′.5N 02°48′.8W	RD	· — · — · ·	298.8	A2A	70 M	
A604	St Brieuc	48°34′.1N 02°46′.9W	SB	· · · — · · · ·	353	A1A	25 M	
639	Cap Fréhel Lt	48°41′.1N 02°19′.1W	FÉ	· · — · · · — · ·	305.7	A2A	20 M	

No	Name	Lat/Long	Ident		Freq	Mode	Range	Notes

No	Name	Ident		Range	Seq	Mode	Fog	Clear
639	Cap Fréhel	FÉ	··—· ··—··	20	1,3,5	A2A	Cont	Cont
263	La Corbière	CB	—·—· —···	20	2,4,6	A2A	Cont	Cont

No	Name	Lat/Long	Ident	Morse	Freq	Mode	Range	Notes
643	Le Grand Jardin Lt (grouped with 631)	48°40'.3N 02°04'.9W	GJ	——· ·———	294.2	A2A	10 M	
A608	Granville	48°55'.1N 01°28'.9W	GV	——· ···—	321	A1A	25 M	
647	Cherbourg W Fort Lt (grouped with 33)	49°40'.5N 01°38'.9W	RB	·—· —···	312.6	A2A	20 M	
651	Pte de Barfleur Lt (grouped with 17)	49°41'.9N 01°15'.9W	FG	··—· ——·	291.9	A2A	70 M	
655	Port en Bessin Rear Lt	49°21'.0N 00°45'.6W	BS	—··· ···	313.5	A2A	5 M	
A612	Cherbourg	49°38'.3N 01°22'.3W	MP	—— ·——·	373	A1A	— —	
659	Pte de Ver Lt (grouped with 17)	49°20'.5N 00°31'.1W	ÉR	··—·· ·—·	291.9	A2A	20 M	
663	Le Havre Lanby (grouped with 17)	49°31'.7N 00°09'.8W	LH	·—·· ····	291.9	A2A	30 M	
A616	Le Havre/Octeville	49°35'.7N 00°11'.0E	LHO	·—·· ···· ———	346	A2A	15 M	
667	Cap d'Antifer Lt (grouped with 17)	49°41'.1N 00°10'.0E	TI	— ··	291.9	A2A	50 M	
671	Pte d'Ailly Lt (grouped with 679)	49°55'.0N 00°57'.6E	AL	·— ·—··	310.3	A2A	50 M	
A624	Le Touquet/Paris Plage	50°32'.2N 01°35'.4E	LT	·—·· —	358	A2A	20 M	
679	Cap d'Alprech Lt	50°41'.95N 01°33'.83E	PH	·——· ····	310.3	A2A	20 M	

No	Name	Ident		Range	Seq	Mode	Fog	Clear
679	Cap d'Alprech	PH	·——· ····	20	1,3,5	A2A	Cont	Cont
45	Royal Sovereign	RY	·—· —·——	50	2	A2A	Cont	Cont
671	Pointe d'Ailly	AL	·— ·—··	50	4	A2A	Cont	Cont
49	Dungeness	DU	—·· ··—	30	6	A2A	Cont	Cont

No	Name	Lat/Long	Ident	Morse	Freq	Mode	Range	Notes
691	Calais Main Lt (grouped with 61)	50°57'.7N 01°51'.3E	CS	—·—· ···	305.7	A2A	20 M	
A628	Saint Inglevert	50°53'.0N 01°44'.6E	ING	·· —· ——·	387.5	A1A	50 M	
695	Dunkerque Lanby	51°03'.1N 01°51'.8E	DK	—·· —·—	294.2	A2A	10 M	Temp inop (Mar 1989)
A632	Calais/Dunkerque	50°59'.8N 02°03'.3E	MK	—— —·—	275	A1A	15 M	

BEACON SEQUENCE NUMBERS Commence transmission at the following minutes past the hour:

1 00 06 12 18 24 30 36 42 48 54	**2** 01 07 13 19 25 31 37 43 49 55	**3** 02 08 14 20 26 32 38 44 50 56
4 03 09 15 21 27 33 39 45 51 57	**5** 04 10 16 22 28 34 40 46 52 58	**6** 05 11 17 23 29 35 41 47 53 59

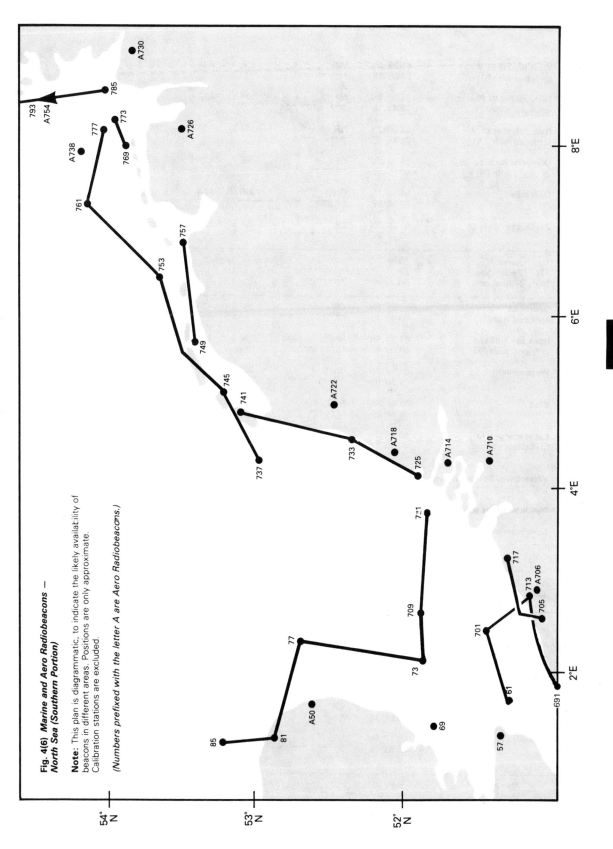

Fig. 4(6) *Marine and Aero Radiobeacons —*
North Sea (Southern Portion)

Note: This plan is diagrammatic, to indicate the likely availability of
beacons in different areas. Positions are only approximate.
Calibration stations are excluded.

(Numbers prefixed with the letter A are Aero Radiobeacons.)

4

BELGIUM, NETHERLANDS AND FEDERAL REPUBLIC OF GERMANY

No	Name	Lat/Long	Ident	Freq	Mode	Range	Notes
701	West Hinder Lt V (grouped with 61)	51°23'.0N 20°26'.3E	WH ·— ····	305.7	A2A	20 M	
705	Nieuwpoort W Pier Lt (grouped with 717)	51°09'.4N 02°43'.1E	NP —·· ·—·—··	296.5	A2A	5 M	
709	Noord Hinder Lt V (grouped with 77)	52°00'.2N 02°51'.2E	NR —·· ·—·	287.3	A2A	50 M	
713	Oostende Rear Lt (grouped with 61)	51°14'.2N 02°55'.9E	OE ——— ·	305.7	A2A	30 M	
A706	Oostende	51°13'.1N 02°59'.9E	ONO ——— —·· ———	399.5	A2A	50 M	
717	Zeebrugge Mole Lt	51°20'.9N 03°12'.2E	ZB ——·· —···	296.5	A2A	5 M	

No	Name	Ident		Range	Seq	Mode	Fog	Clear
717	Zeebrugge	ZB	——·· —···	5	1,2	A2A	Cont	Cont
705	Nieuwpoort	NP	—·· ·—·—··	5	4,5	A2A	Cont	Cont

No	Name	Lat/Long	Ident	Freq	Mode	Range	Notes
721	Goeree Lt (grouped with 77)	51°55'.5N 03°40'.2E	GR ——·· ·—·	287.3	A2A	50 M	
725	Hoek van Holland (grouped with 733)	51°58'.9N 04°06'.8E	HH ···· ····	294.2	A2A	20 M	
A710	Woensdrecht	51°26'.4N 04°20'.9E	WDT ·—— —·· —	345	Non A2A	25 M	
A714	Stad	51°44'.5N 04°14'.6E	STD ··· — —··	386	Non A2A	15 M	
729	Scheveningen Lt Calibration station	52°06'.3N 04°16'.2E	HO ···· ———	312.6	A2A		On request Tel: 01747 4840 or call Centralepost van DGSM on VHF Ch 01
A718	Valkenberg/Scheveningen	52°05'.6N 04°15'.2E	GV ——·· ···——	364	Non A2A	25 M	
733	IJmuiden Front Lt	52°27'.8N 04°34'.6E	YM —·—— ——	294.2	A2A	20 M	On request VHF Ch 12 Tel: 02550 19027 or call Scheveningen
	Calibration station		YC —·—· ——··	314.5	A2A	5 M	

No	Name	Ident		Range	Seq	Mode	Fog	Clear
733	IJmuiden	YM	—·—— ——	20	1,4	A2A	Cont	Cont
725	Hoek van Holland	HH	···· ····	20	2,5	A2A	Cont	Cont
741	Eierland	ER	· ·—··	20	3,6	A2A	Cont	Nil

No	Name	Lat/Long	Ident	Freq	Mode	Range	Notes
A722	Amsterdam/Spijkerboor	52°32'.5N 04°50'.5E	SPY ··· ·——·· —·——	381	Non A2A	75 M	
737	Texel Lt V (grouped with 745)	52°47'.1N 04°06'.6E	HK ···· —·—	308	A2A	50 M	
741	Eierland Lt (grouped with 733)	53°11'.0N 04°51'.4E	ER · ·—··	294.2	A2A	20 M	
745	Vlieland Lt	53°17'.8N 05°03'.6E	VL ···— ·—··	308	A2A	70 M	

No	Name	Ident		Range	Seq	Mode	Fog	Clear
745	Vlieland	VL	···— ·—··	70	1	A2A	Cont	Cont
761	Deutsche Bucht Lt F	DB	—·· —···	50	4	A2A	Cont	Cont
737	Texel Lt V	HK	···· —·—	50	5	A2A	Cont	Cont
777	Elbe No 1 Lt F	EL	· ·—··	50	6	A2A	Cont	Cont

No	Name	Lat/Long	Ident		Freq	Mode	Range	Notes
749	Ameland Lt	53°27'.0N 05°37'.6E	AD	•— —••	298.8	A2A	20 M	

No	Name	Ident		Range	Seq	Mode	Fog	Clear
749	Ameland	AD	•— —••	20	1,3,5	A2A	Cont	Nil
757	Borkum Little	BE	—••• •	20	2,4,6	A2A	Cont	Cont

No	Name	Lat/Long	Ident		Freq	Mode	Range	Notes
757	Borkum Little Lt (grouped with 749)	53°34'.8N 06°40'.1E	BE	—••• •	298.8	A2A	20 M	
761	Deutsche Bucht Lt F (grouped with 745)	54°10'.7N 07°26'.1E	DB	—•• —•••	308	A2A	50 M	
769	Wangerooge Lt	53°47'.4N 07°51'.5E	WE	•— — •	291.9	A2A	30 M	

No	Name	Ident		Range	Seq	Mode	Fog	Clear
769	Wangerooge	WE	•— — •	30	1,3,5	A2A	Cont	Cont
773	Alte Weser	AR	•— •—•	10	2,4,6	A2A	Cont	Cont

No	Name	Lat/Long	Ident		Freq	Mode	Range	Notes
773	Alte Weser Lt (grouped with 769)	53°51'.9N 08°07'.7E	AR	•— •—•	291.9	A2A	10 M	
777	Elbe No 1 Lt Float (grouped with 745)	54°00'.0N 08°06'.6E	EL	• •—••	308	A2A	50 M	
A726	Jever	53°31'.2N 08°00'.9E	JEV	•— — ••••	390	Non A2A	50 M	
779	Wilhelmshaven Calibration station	53°31'.0N 08°08'.8E	JB	•— — —•••	312.6	A2A		On request, call Jade Revier Ch 16 20
781	Bremerhaven Calibration station	53°32'.4N 08°34'.9E	GB	—•— —•••	312.6	A2A		On request, call West Revier Ch 05 07
785	Grosser Vogelsand Lt (grouped with 793)	53°59'.8N 08°28'.7E	VS	•••— •••	301.1	A2A	10 M	
A730	Nordholz	53°47'.2N 08°48'.5E	NDO	—• —•• ——	372	Non A2A	30 M	
789	Hollerwettern Lt Calibration station	53°50'.4N 09°21'.3E	HB	•••• —•••	313.5	A2A		On request, Tel 04852 8011–16
791	Krautsand Calibration station	53°45'.6N 09°22'.6E	KB	—•— —•••	312.6	A2A		On request, Tel 04852 8400
A734	Glukstadt	53°51'.1N 09°27'.3E	GLX	—•— •—•• —••—	365	Non A2A	30 M	
A738	Helgoland Lt	54°11'.0N 07°53'.0E	DHE	—•• •••• •	397.2	A1A	100 M	Aeromarine beacon
	Calibration station		NB	—• —•••	313.5	A2A		On request, Eider Lock Radio Ch 14
A754	Westerland/Sylt	54°51'.4N 08°24'.7E	SLT	••• •—•• —	286	Non A2A	25 M	
793	Kampen/Rote Kliff Lt, Sylt	54°56'.9N 08°20'.5E	RF	•—• ••—•	301.1	A2A	20 M	

No	Name	Ident		Range	Seq	Mode	Fog	Clear
793	Kampen	RF	•—• ••—•	20	1,3,5	A2A	Cont	Cont
785	Gr Vogelsand	VS	•••— •••	10	2,4,6	A2A	Cont	Cont

BEACON SEQUENCE NUMBERS   Commence transmission at the following minutes past the hour:

1	00 06 12 18 24 30 36 42 48 54	**2**	01 07 13 19 25 31 37 43 49 55	**3**	02 08 14 20 26 32 38 44 50 56
4	03 09 15 21 27 33 39 45 51 57	**5**	04 10 16 22 28 34 40 46 52 58	**6**	05 11 17 23 29 35 41 47 53 59

RADIOBEACONS —
CALL SIGNS AND STATION NUMBERS
(Numbers prefixed with the letter A are Aero Radiobeacons)
(CS) = Calibration Station

Call Sign	Station	No	Call Sign	Station	No
AD	Ameland Lt	749	DND	Dundee	A78
AH	Altacarry Hd Lt	333	DO	Rosédo Lt (Brehat)	631
AL	Pte d'Ailly Lt	671	DO	Dounreay	A118
ALD	Alderney	A252	DU	Dungeness Lt	49
AOS	Aberdeen	A82			
AP	Aberporth	A166	EC	St Helier	267
AR	Alte Weser Lt	773	EDN	Edinburgh	A70
			EGT	Eglington	A318
BC	Bloscon	627	EL	Elbe No 1 Lt V	777
BC	Ballycotton (CS)	309	ENS	Ennis	A326
BD	Barra Hd Lt	181	ER	Eierland Lt	741
BD	Bordeaux/Merignac	A564	ÉR	Pte der Ver Lt	659
BE	Borkum Little	757	EX	Exeter	A14
BHD	Berry Hd	A10			
BL	Butt of Lewis Lt	169	FB	Flamborough Hd	97
BLO	Bilbao	A548	FD	Fidra Lt	119
BM	Brighton Marina	37	FÉ	Cap Fréhel	639
BN	Ballycotton Lt	309	FG	Pte de Barfleur Lt	651
BN	Les Baleines Lt	571	FN	Walney Island Lt	209
BPL	Blackpool	A158	FOY	Foynes	A334
BRR	Barra	A124	FP	Fife Ness Lt	125
BS	Port en Bessin	655	FS	Falls Lt V	61
BST	Lanvéoc/Poulmic	A592	FT	Cap Ferret Lt	551
BY	Bressay Lt	153			
BY	Brawdy	A174	GA	Outer Gabbard Lt V	73
BZ	Biarritz	A556	GB	Bremerhaven (CS)	781
			GD	Girdle Ness Lt	133
CA	Pte de Creac'h Lt	615	GJ	Grand Jardin Lt	643
CAA	Cazaux	A560	GL	Eagle Island Lt	341
CAR	Isle of Man/Carnane	A146	GLX	Gluckstadt	A734
CB	La Corbière	263	GN	Cap Gris Nez Lt	687
CDF	Cardiff/Rhoose	A182	GR	Goeree Lt	721
CGC	Cognac/Chateaubernard	A568	GUR	Guernsey	A256
CH	Chichester Bar	29	GV	Granville	A608
CL	Cloch Pt Lt (CS)	193	GV	Valkenburg	A718
CM	Cromer Lt	81	GX	Ile de Groix, Pen Men	595
CN	Cregneish, IOM	205	GY	St Peter Port	259
CNL	Connel/Oban	A126			
CP	St Catherine's Pt Lt	25	HB	Hollerwettern (CS)	789
CR	Channel Lt V	251	HB	Belfast Harbour	A314
CRN	Carnmore	A322	HH	Hoek van Holland	725
CS	Calais Main Lt	691	HIG	San Sebastian	A552
CT	Pte de Combrit Lt	599	HK	Texel Lt V	737
CW	Cape Wrath Lt	165	HO	Scheveningen (CS)	729
			HRN	Hurn	A18
DA	Pladda Lt	189			
DB	Deutsche Bucht Lt V	761	IB	Bardsey Lt	221
DG	Douglas	201	ING	St Inglevert	A628
DHE	Helgoland	A738	IW	Bembridge	A26
DK	Dunkerque Lt Buoy	695			

(Numbers prefixed with the letter A are Aero Radiobeacons)
(CS) = Calibration Station

Call Sign	Station	No
JB	Wilhelmshaven (CS)	779
JEV	Jever	A726
JEY	Jersey East	A260
JW	Jersey West	A264
KB	Krautsand (CS)	791
KD	Kinnairds Hd	137
KH	Kish Bank Lt	321
KL	St Kilda	A122
KLY	Killiney	A306
KS	Kinloss	A90
KW	Kirkwall	A98
LAY	Islay/Port Ellen	A128
LDV	Landivisiau	A596
LG	Eilean Glas Lt	173
LH	Le Havre Lanby	663
LHO	Le Havre/Octeville	A616
LK	Sule Skerry Lt	161
LK	Pointe de la Coubre	559
LM	Isle of May	121
LN	Lannion	A600
LOR	Lorient/Lann-Bihoué	A580
LP	Loop Head Lt	349
LS	Lundy Island, S Lt	237
LS	Lee-on-Solent	A30
LT	Longstone Lt	113
LT	Le Touquet	A624
LU	Leuchars	A74
LV	Dudgeon Lt V	85
LYX	Lydd	A42
LZ	Lizard Lt	5
MA	Cabo Machichaco Lt	547
MC	Mew Island (CS)	329
MF	Muckle Flugga	157
MK	Calais/Dunkerque	A632
MP	Cherbourg	A612
MT	St Nazaire/Montoir	A572
MW	Mew Island Lt	329
MY	Cabo Mayor Lt	543
MZ	Mizen Head Lt	301
NB	Nab Tower Lt	33
NB	Helgoland Lt (CS)	A738
ND	Gt Yarmouth	A50
NDO	Nordholz	A730
NF	N Foreland Lt	57
NGY	New Galloway	A142
NH	Newhaven	41
NK	Inchkeith Lt	117

Call Sign	Station	No
NP	Nash Point Lt	233
NP	Nieuwpoort	705
NR	N Ronaldsay	145
NR	Noord Hinder Lt V	709
NZ	St Nazaire	587
OE	Oostende Rear Lt	713
OH	Kinsale	305
OM	Stroma	141
ONO	Oostende	A706
OR	Hyskeir Lt	177
OTR	Ottringham	A54
PB	Portland Bill	17
PE	Penlee Point	9
PH	Penzance	A2
PH	Cap d'Alprech Lt	679
PO	Poole Harbour	21
PR	Ile du Pilier Lt	583
PS	Point Lynas Lt	213
PT	Souter Lt (CS)	109
PY	Point of Ayre	197
PY	Plymouth	A6
QR	Quimper/Pluguffan	A584
QS	Casquets Lt	255
RB	Cherbourg	647
RD	Roches Douvres Lt	635
RE	La Rochelle	563
RF	Kampen/Rote Kliff Lt	793
RN	Rhinns of Islay Lt	185
RR	Round Island Lt	1
RSH	Dublin (Rush)	A310
RWY	Ronaldsway, IOM	A150
RY	Royal Sovereign Lt	45
SB	Sumburgh Hd Lt	149
SB	South Bishop Lt	225
SHD	Scotstown Hd	A86
SHM	Shoreham	A38
SJ	Souter Lt	109
SK	Smiths Knoll Lt V	77
SL	Sligo	A320
SLT	Westerland/Sylt	A754
SM	St Mawgan	A190
SM	Pt de St Mathieu Lt	611
SN	Slyne Head Lt	345
SN	Ile de Sein	607
SND	Southend	A46
SO	Les Sables d'Olonne	575
SP	Start Point Lt	13
SPY	Amsterdam	A722

(Numbers prefixed with the letter A are Aero Radiobeacons)
(CS) = Calibration Station

Call Sign	Station	No	Call Sign	Station	No
SR	Skerries Lt	217	VA	Vannes/Meucon	A576
SS	Scatsa	A110	VG	Ile Vierge Lt	623
STD	Stad	A714	VL	Vlieland Lt	745
STM	St Mary's Scilly	A1	VS	Gr Vogelsand Lt	785
STN	Stornoway	A122			
STU	Strumble	A170	WDT	Woensdrecht	A710
SU	South Rock Lt F	325	WE	Wangerooge Lt	769
SUM	Sumburgh	A102	WH	West Hinder Lt V	701
SW	Ouessant SW Lanby	619	WIK	Wick	A94
SWN	Swansea	A178	WK	Wicklow Head Lt	317
			WL	Walney Is	A152
TD	Teeside	A58	WTD	Waterford	A302
TI	Cap d'Antifer Lt	667	WTN	Warton	A162
TL	Lerwick	A106			
TR	Tuskar Rock Lt	313	YC	IJmuiden (CS)	733
TRN	Turnberry	A138	YE	Ile d'Yeu Main Lt	579
TY	Tory Island Lt	337	YM	IJmuiden	733
ÜH	Eckmühl Lt, Penmarc'h	603	ZB	Zeebrugge Mole Lt	717
UK	Sunk Lt F	69			
UT	Unst	A114			

4.3.3   VHF Radio Lighthouse

This is a beacon which transmits a rotating directional signal that can be received by a VHF set capable of receiving frequency modulated signals. The signals are modulated with an audio tone varying between a maximum and a null. The 'null radial' rotates at a uniform speed of 4° per second, and the bearing of the beacon is determined by measuring the time that the null radial takes to reach the observer from a known starting point. To measure the time interval, the tone is broken into a number of half-second beats, each beat being the equivalent of 2° of bearing. The observer simply counts the number of beats from the start of each transmission, until the tone disappears, and then refers to Table 4(3).

The signal composition is as follows: Pause 0.1s; Morse ident. 3.2s; Pause 1.0s; Digital data 0.3s; Pause 1.0s; 70 Nav. beats 35.0s; Pause 1.0s; Morse ident. 3.2s; Pause 1.0s; Digital data 0.1s; Pause 12.1s; Static gap 2.0s. Total 60.0s.

The digital data is of no navigational significance, and is transmitted for the use of test equipment.

Beat numbers 10, 20, 30, 40, 50 and 60 are marked by a change in audio tone frequency.

All the VHF Radio Lighthouses currently in service transmit on VHF Ch 88 (162.025 MHz). The mode of emission used is designated as FXX, in which the main carrier is frequency modulated.

In the event of a transmitting equipment fault, a warbling tone will be transmitted, rendering the preceding beats invalid.

In the absence of a table, the bearing can be found from the formula:

$$\text{Bearing} = A + 2(N - 7)$$

where N is the number of beats counted, and A is the start bearing for 7 beats.

Alternatively, the time (T) in seconds can be taken with a stopwatch between beat 7 and the null. Then:

$$\text{Bearing} = A + 4T$$

The overall bearing accuracy is estimated as $\pm 2°$ (root mean square error) or better.

The stations are experimental, and transmissions may be altered or discontinued without warning.

TABLE 4(3)   VHF RADIO LIGHTHOUSES

ANVIL POINT LT 50°35′.47N 01°57′.52W	Count of beats	Bearing of Lt Ho from seaward (degrees)									
		0	1	2	3	4	5	6	7	8	9
Morse ident: **AL** · — · — · ·	0	—	—	—	—	—	—	—	247	249	251
Frequency: Ch 88 (162.025 MHz)	10	253	255	257	259	261	263	265	267	269	271
Range: 14 n miles	20	273	275	277	279	281	283	285	287	289	291
Times: H24 (transmits	30	293	295	297	299	301	303	305	307	309	311
alternately with	40	313	315	317	319	321	323	325	327	329	331
Scratchell's Bay)	50	333	335	337	339	341	343	345	347	349	351
	60	353	355	357	359	001	003	005	007	—	—

HIGH DOWN (Scratchell's Bay) 50°39′.70N 01°34′.60W	Count of beats	Bearing of Lt Ho from seaward (degrees)									
		0	1	2	3	4	5	6	7	8	9
Morse ident: **HD** · · · · — · ·	0	—	—	—	—	—	—	—	337	339	341
Frequency: Ch 88 (162.025 MHz)	10	343	345	347	349	351	353	355	357	359	001
Range: 30 n miles	20	003	005	007	009	011	013	015	017	019	021
Times: H24 (transmits	30	023	025	027	029	031	033	035	037	039	041
alternately with	40	043	045	047	049	051	053	055	057	059	061
Anvil Point Lt)	50	063	065	067	069	071	073	075	077	079	081
	60	083	085	087	089	091	093	095	097	—	—

CALAIS MAIN LT 50°57′.73N 01°51′.30E	Count of beats	Bearing of Lt Ho from seaward (degrees)									
		0	1	2	3	4	5	6	7	8	9
Morse ident: **CL** — · — · · — · ·	0	—	—	—	—	—	—	—	090	092	094
Frequency: Ch 88 (162.025 MHz)	10	096	098	100	102	104	106	108	110	112	114
Range: 20 n miles	20	116	118	120	122	124	126	128	130	132	134
Times: H24	30	136	138	140	142	144	146	148	160	152	154
	40	156	158	160	162	164	166	168	170	172	174
	50	176	178	180	182	184	186	188	190	192	194
	60	196	198	200	202	204	206	208	210	—	—

4

4.4   RADAR

4.4.1   Radar in yachts

Radar is useful both for navigation and for collision avoidance, but to take full advantage of it and to use it in safety demands a proper understanding of its operation and of its limitations. Read the instruction book carefully, and practise using and adjusting the set so as to get optimum performance in different conditions. It is important to learn how to interpret what is actually seen on the display.

Radar beams do not discriminate so well in bearing as they do in range — so an accurate fix is sometimes best obtained by a radar range and a visual bearing of the same object.

The effective range of radar is approximately line of sight, but this can be decreased or increased by abnormal conditions. It is necessary to be aware that radar will not detect a low-lying coastline which is over the radar horizon.

The details of radar, and its use in yachts, are described in *The Macmillan & Silk Cut Yachtsman's Handbook* (4.6).

4.4.2   Radar for collision avoidance

Yacht radars invariably have a "ship's head up display", with the boat at the centre, apparently stationary. If a target is moving in the same direction and at the same speed, it is stationary relative to own ship, and its echo should be sharp and well defined. If it is on a reciprocal course, it paints an echo with a long tail.

If an echo is on a steady bearing, and the range is decreasing, there is risk of collision. But to determine the proper action to take it is necessary to plot an approaching echo three or four times, in order to determine her actual course and speed, and how close she will actually approach.

4.4.3   Radar as a navigation aid

Radar cannot see behind other objects, or round corners; it may not pick up small objects, or differentiate between two targets that are close together. As already stated, radar ranges are more accurate than radar bearings. Objects with sharp features such as buildings give a better reflection than those with curved or sloping surfaces. High cliffs make a good target, but low coastlines should be approached with extreme caution as the first thing to show on radar may be hills some distance inland.

4.4.4   Radar beacons (Racons)

A Racon is a transponder beacon which, when triggered by a transmission from a vessel's radar, sends back a distinctive signal which appears on the vessel's radar display. Racons are fitted to some light-vessels, buoys and lighthouses, and are marked on charts by a magenta circle and the word Racon.

In most cases the Racon flash on the display is a line extending radially outwards from a point slightly beyond the actual position of the Racon, due to the slight delay in the response of the beacon apparatus. Thus the distance to the mark of the Racon flash is a little more than the vessel's real distance from the Racon. Some Racons give a flash composed of a Morse identification signal, often with a tail to it, the length of the tail depending on the number of Morse characters.

The maximum range of a radar beacon is usually about 10 nautical miles, but may be more. In practice, picking up a Racon at greater distances depends also on the effective range of the boat's radar. With abnormal radio propagation, a spurious Racon flash may be seen at much greater distances than the beacon's normal range, appearing at any random position along the correct bearing on the display. Only rely on a Racon flash if its appearance is consistent, and the boat is believed to be within its range. At short range a Racon sometimes causes unwelcome interference on the radar display, and this may be reduced by adjusting the rain clutter control on the set.

The characteristics of Radar beacons around the coasts of Great Britain are given in Table 4(4). Details are arranged in the following columns:

(1) Reference number.
(2) The type of Radar beacon. Unless otherwise stated, all radar beacons sweep the frequency range of marine 3cm (X-band) radar emissions. The older type of radar beacon (swept frequency Racons) take 30 to 90 seconds to sweep the band and the period of sweep is adjusted during installation to suit the individual location. The newer type of radar beacon (agile frequency Racon) responds immediately to radar interrogations. However, in order that wanted echoes should not be obscured by the racon signal, the agile response is switched 'on' and 'off' at a pre-determined rate to suit the installation. Where indicated (marked by an asterisk), radar beacons respond to both 10cm (S-band) and 3cm (X-band) emissions and are usually agile frequency Racons.
(3) Name of the station.
(4) Latitude and longitude.
(5) The sector within which signals may be received, bearings being towards the beacon, clockwise from 000° to 359°. 360° indicates all round operation.
(6) Approximate range, in nautical miles. This also depends on the range of the yacht's radar set.
(7) The form of the beacon's flash on the radar display. Morse signals are shown alphabetically, and are often followed by a "tail". Racons coded 'D' are used to mark new dangers.

Table 4(4) LIST OF RADAR BEACONS
(For heading details see 4.4.4)

(1) No.	(2) Type	(3) Name	(4) Lat	Long	(5) Sector	(6) Approx range	(7) Form of flash
GREAT BRITAIN							
1	3 & 10 cm*	Bishop Rock Lt				18 M	T
3	3 & 10 cm*	Seven Stones Lt V	50°03'.6N	6°04'.3W	360°	15 M	O
5	3 & 10 cm*	Wolf Rock Lt	49°56'.7N	5°48'.5W	360°	10 M	T
7	3 & 10 cm	Eddystone Lt	50°10'.8N	4°15'.9W	360°	10 M	T
9	3 cm	West Bramble Lt Buoy	50°47'.2N	1°18'.6W	360°	3 M	T
11	3 cm	Nab Tower Lt	50°40'.1N	0°57'.1W	360°	10 M	T
13	3 & 10 cm*	Greenwich Lanby	50°24'.5N	0°00'.0	360°	15 M	T
15	3 & 10 cm*	Varne Lanby	51°01'.2N	1°24'.0E	360°	10 M	T
17	3 & 10 cm*	East Goodwin Lt F	51°13'.0N	1°36'.3E	360°	10 M	T
19	3 & 10 cm	Falls Lt V	51°18'.1N	1°48'.5E	360°	10 M	O
21	3 & 10 cm*	NE Goodwin Lt Buoy	51°20'.3N	1°34'.3E	360°	10 M	G
23	3 & 10 cm*	Dover Strait TSS, F3 Lanby	51°23'.8N	2°00'.6E	360°	10 M	T
25	3 cm	Sea Reach Lt Buoy No 1	51°29'.4N	0°52'.7E	360°	10 M	T
27	3 cm	Sea Reach Lt Buoy No 7	51°30'.1N	0°37'.1E	360°	10 M	T
29	3 & 10 cm*	Outer tongue Lt Buoy	51°30'.8N	1°26'.5E	360°	10 M	T
31	3 & 10 cm*	Barrow No 3 Lt Buoy	51°42'.0N	1°19'.9E	360°	10 M	B
33	3 & 10 cm	S Galloper Lt Buoy	51°43'.9N	1°56'.5E	360°	10 M	T
35	3 cm	Sunk Lt V	51°51'.0N	1°35'.0E	360°	10 M	T
37	3 & 10 cm*	Harwich Channel Lt Buoy No 1	51°55'.9N	1°27'.3E	360°	10 M	T
39	3 & 10 cm*	Outer Gabbard Lt V	51°59'.4N	2°04'.6E	360°	10 M	T
40		Orfordness Lt	52°05'.0N	1°34'.6E	360°	10 M	T
41	3 cm	Cross Sand Lt Buoy	52°37'.0N	1°59'.2E	360°	10 M	T
43	3 cm	Winterton Old Lighthouse	52°42'.8N	1°41'.8E	360°	10 M	T
45	3 & 10 cm*	Smiths Knoll Lt V	52°43'.5N	2°18'.0E	360°	10 M	T
47	3 & 10 cm	Newarp Lt V	52°48'.4N	1°55'.8E	360°	10 M	O
49	3 & 10 cm	Cromer Lt	52°55'.4N	1°19'.1E	360°	25 M	C
51	3 & 10 cm	North Haisbro Lt Buoy	53°00'.2N	1°32'.4E	360°	10 M	T
53	3 cm	North Well Lt Buoy	53°03'.0N	0°28'.0E	360°	10 M	T
55	3 9 10 cm*	Dudgeon Lt V	53°16'.6N	1°17'.0E	360°	10 M	O
57	3 & 10 cm*	Inner Dowsing Lt	53°19'.7N	0°34'.0E	360°	25 M	T
59	3 & 10 cm	Spurn Lt F	53°33'.5N	0°14'.3E	360°	5M	S
60		Dowsing Lt V	53°34'.0N	0°50'.2W	360°	10 M	T
61	3 & 10 cm	Humber Lt Buoy	53°36'.7N	0°21'.6E	360°	7 M	T
63	3 cm	Tees Fairway Buoy	54°40'.9N	1°06'.4W	360°		B
65	3 cm	St Abbs' Head Lt	55°55'.0N	2°03'.2W	360°	18 M	T
67	3 cm	Inchkeith Fairway Buoy	56°03'.5N	3°00'.0W	360°	5 M	T
69	3 cm	Forth North Channel Lt Buoy 7	56°02'.8N	3°10'.9W	360°	5 M	T
71	3 & 10 cm	Bell Rock Lt	56°26'.0N	2°23'.1W	360°	18 M	M
73	3 cm	Abertay Lt Buoy	56°27'.4N	2°40'.6W	360°	8 M	T
75	3 cm	Scurdie Ness Lt	56°42'.1N	2°26'.1W	360°	15 M	T
77	3 & 10 cm	Girdle Ness Lt	57°08'.3N	2°02'.8W	165°–055°[1]	25 M	G
	[1] Reduced coverage within sector 055°–165°						
79	3 cm	Aberdeen Fairway Buoy	57°09'.3N	2°01'.8W	360°	7 M	T
81	3 cm	Buchan Ness Lt	57°28'.2N	1°46'.4W	155°–045°[1]	25 M	O
	[1] Reduced coverage within sector 045°–155°						
83	3 cm	Cromarty Firth Fairway Buoy	57°40'.0N	3°54'.1W	360°	5 M	M
85	3 cm	Tarbat Ness Lt	57°51'.9N	3°46'.5W	360°	12 M	T
87	3 cm	Duncansby Head Lt	58°38'.7N	3°01'.4W	360°	20 M	T
89	3 cm	Lother Rock Lt	58°43'.8N	2°58'.6W	360°	10 M	M
91	3 cm	North Ronaldsay Lt	59°23'.4N	2°22'.8W	360°	10 M	T
93	3 cm	Rumble Rock Bn	60°28'.2N	1°07'.1W	360°	10 M	O
95	3 cm	Gruney Island Lt	60°39'.2N	1°18'.0W	360°	18 M	T

4

(1) No.	(2) Type	(3) Name	(4) Lat	Long	(5) Sector	(6) Approx range	(7) Form of flash
97	3 cm	Ve Skerries Lt	60°22'.4N	1°48'.7W	360°	15 M	T
99	3 cm	Sule Skerry Lt	59°05'.1N	4°24'.3W	360°	25 M	T
101	3 cm	Eilean Glas Lt	57°51'.4N	6°38'.5W	360°	12 M	T
103	3 cm	Castlebay South Buoy	56°56'.1N	7°27'.2W	360°	7 M	T
105	3 cm	Monach Lt Ho	57°31'.5N	7°41'.6W	360°	16 M	T
109	3 cm	Kyleakin Lt	57°16'.7N	5°44'.5W	360°	16 M	T
111	3 cm	Skerryvore Lt	56°19'.4N	7°06'.7W	360°	25 M	M
113	3 cm	Sanda Lt	56°16'.5N	5°34'.9W	360°	20 M	T
115	3 cm	Point of Ayre Lt	54°24'.9N	4°22'.0W	360°	15 M	M
117	3 & 10 cm*	Lune Deep Lt Buoy	53°55'.8N	3°11'.0W	360°	10 M	T
119	3 cm	Bar Lanby	53°32'.0N	3°20'.9W	360°	10 M	T
121	3 & 10 cm*	Skerries Lt	53°25'.3N	4°36'.4W	360°	25 M	T
123	3 & 10 cm*	The Smalls Lt	51°43'.2N	5°40'.1W	360°	25 M	T
125	3 & 10 cm*	St Gowan Lt V	51°30'.5N	4°59'.8W	360°	15 M	T
127	3 & 10 cm*	W Helwick Lt Buoy	51°31'.4N	4°23'.6W	360°	10 M	T
129	3 & 10 cm*	W Scar Lt Buoy	51°28'.3N	3°55'.5W	360°	10 M	T
131	3 & 10 cm*	English and Welsh Grounds Lt Buoy	51°26'.9N	3°00'.1W	360°	10 M	O
133	3 & 10 cm*	Breaksea Lt Float	51°19'.9N	3°19'.0W	360°	10 M	T

CHANNEL/CHANNEL ISLANDS (see also No 13)

(1) No.	(2) Type	(3) Name	(4) Lat	Long	(5) Sector	(6) Approx range	(7) Form of flash
151	3 cm	Lt Buoy EC1	50°05'.9N	1°48'.3W	360°	10 M	T
153	3 cm	Lt Buoy EC2	50°12'.1N	1°12'.4W	360°	10 M	T
155	3 cm	Lt Buoy EC3	50°18'.3N	0°36'.1W	360°	10 M	T
157	3 cm	East Channel Lt Buoy	49°58'.7N	2°28'.9W	360°	10 M	T
159	3 & 10 cm*	Channel Lt V	49°54'.4N	2°53'.7W	360°	15 M	O
161	3 & 10 cm*	Casquets Lt	49°43'.4N	2°22'.5W	360°	25 M	T
163	3 cm	Platte Fougère Lt	49°30'.9N	2°29'0W			P
165	3 cm	St Helier — Demie de Pas Lt	49°09'.1N	2°06'.0W	360°	10 M	T
167	3 cm	St Helier — Mount Ubé Lt	49°10'.3N	2°03'.5W	360°	14 M	T

IRELAND

(1) No.	(2) Type	(3) Name	(4) Lat	Long	(5) Sector	(6) Approx range	(7) Form of flash
201	3 cm	Mizzen Head Lt	51°27'.0N	9°49'.2W	360°	24 M	T
203	3 cm	Cork Lt Buoy	51°42'.9N	8°15'.5W	360°	7 M	T
205	3 & 10 cm	Hook Head Lt	52°07'.4N	6°55'.7W	237°–177°	10 M	K
207	3 cm	Coningbeg Lt F	52°02'.4N	6°39'.4W	360°	13 M	M
209	3 cm	Tuskar Rock Lt	52°12'.2N	6°12'.4W	360°	18 M	T
211	3 cm	Arklow Lanby	52°39'.5N	5°58'.1W	360°	10 M	O
213	3 cm	Codling Lanby	53°03'.0N	5°40'.7W	360°	10 M	G
215	3 cm	Kish Bank Lt	53°18'.7N	5°55'.4W	360°	15 M	T
217	3 cm	South Rock Lt F	54°24'.5N	5°21'.9W	360°	13 M	T
219	3 & 10 cm*	Inishtrahull Lt	55°25'.9N	7°14'.6W	060°–310°[1]	24 M	T

[1] Reduced or no signal 310°–060°

FRANCE

(1) No.	(2) Type	(3) Name	(4) Lat	Long	(5) Sector	(6) Approx range	(7) Form of flash
301	3 cm	BXA Lanby	45°37'.6N	1°28'.6W	360°		B
303	3 cm	San Nazaire Lt Buoy No 10	47°13'.7N	2°16'.1W	360°	3–5 M	See [1] T
305	3 cm	San Nazaire Lt Buoy SN1	47°00'.0N	2°39'.9W	360°	3–8 M	Z
307	3 cm	Chausée de Sein Lt Buoy	48°03'.8N	5°07'.7W	360°	10 M	O
309	3 cm	Pointe de Créac'h Lt	48°27'.6N	5°07'.6W	030°–248°	20 M	C

[1] Signals appears as a series of dots, the distance between each dot corresponding to 0.2 nm

(1) No.	(2) Type	(3) Name	(4) Lat	Long	(5) Sector	(6) Approx range	(7) Form of flash
311	3 & 10 cm	Ouessant SW Lanby	48°31'.7N	5°49'.1W	360°	20 M	M
313	3 cm	Ouessant NE Lt Buoy	48°45'.9N	5°11'.6W	360°	20 M	B
315	3 & 10 cm	Le Havre Lanby	49°31'.7N	0°09'.8W	360°	8–10 M	See [1]

[1] Signal appears as a series of 8 dots or 8 groups of dots, the distance between each dot or groups of dots corresponding to 0.3 nm.

317	3 cm	Antifer Approach Lt Buoy A5	49°45'.9N	0°17'.4W	360°		K
319	3 cm	Bassurelle Lt Buoy	50°32'.7N	0°57'.8E	360°	6–10 M	B
321	3 & 10 cm	Vergoyer Lt Buoy N	50°39'.7N	1°22'.3E	360°	5–8 M	C
323	3 cm	Sangatte	50°57'.2N	1°46'.6E	360°	11 M	See [1]

[1] Signal appears as 3 successions of 3 dots, the distance between each dot corresponding to 0.3 nm.

325	3 cm	Dunkerque Lt Buoy	51°03'.1N	1°51'.8E	360°		See [1]

[1] The signal appears as a succession of 8 dots, the distance between each dot corresponding to 0.3 M.

327	3 & 10 cm	Sandettié Lt V	51°09'.4N	1°47'.2E	360°	4–10 M	T

BELGIUM AND NETHERLANDS

375	3 & 10 cm	Wandelaar Lt MOW 0	51°23'.7N	3°02'.8E	360°	10 M	W
377	3 & 10 cm	Bol Van Heist Lt MOW 3	51°23'.4N	3°12'.0E	360°	10 M	H
399	3 & 10 cm	Zuid Vlije Lt Buoy ZV15/SRK28	51°38'.2N	4°14'.5E	360°		K
401	3 cm	Noord Hinder Buoy NHR-SE	51°45'.5N	2°40'.0E	360°	10 M	N
403	3 & 10 cm	Noord Hinder Lt V	52°00'.2N	2°51'.2E	360°	10 M	T
405	3 cm	Noord Hinder Lt Buoy NHR-N	52°13'.3N	2°59'.5E	360°	10 M	K
407	3 cm	Schouwenbank Lt Buoy	51°45'.0N	3°14'.4E	360°	10 M	O
409	3 & 10 cm	Goeree Lt	51°55'.5N	3°40'.2E	360°	10 M	T
411	3 cm	Maas Center Lt Buoy MC	52°01'.2N	3°53'.6E	360°	10 M	M
413	3 & 10 cm	Rijn Field Platform P15-B	52°18'.5N	3°46'.7E	30°–270°	10 M	B
415	3 cm	IJmuiden Lt Buoy	52°28'.7N	4°23'.9E	360°	10 M	Y
417	3 & 10 cm	Texel Lt V	52°47'.1N	4°06'.6E	360°	10 M	T
419	3 & 10 cm	Logger Platform	53°00'.9N	4°13'.0E	060°–270°	10 M	X
421	3 & 10 cm	Vlieland Lanby VL-CENTER	53°27'.0N	4°40'.0E	360°	10 M	C
423	3 & 10 cm	Terschelling Bank, Platform L8-G	53°34'.9N	4°36'.3E	000°–160°	12–15 M	G
425	3 & 10 cm	Petroland Field Platform L4-B	53°40'.6N	4°00.2E	360°	10 M	R
427	3 cm	DW Lt Buoy	54°02'.4N	4°44'.3E	360°	6–10 M	M

FEDERAL REPUBLIC OF GERMANY (North Sea Coast)

503	3 cm	Westerems Lt Buoy	53°37'.1N	6°19'.5E	360°	8 M	G
505	3 cm	TW/EMS Lt Float	54°10'.0N	6°20'.8E	360°	6–10 M	T
507	3 cm	Deutsche Bucht Lt F	54°10'.7N	7°26'.1E	360°	8 M	T
509	3 cm	DB/Weser Lt Buoy	54°02'.4N	7°43'.0E	360°	6 M	K
511	3 cm	Weser Lt Buoy	53°54'.2N	7°50'.0E	360°	7 M	T
513	3 cm	Elbe No 1 Lt Float	54°00'.0N	8°06'.6E	360°	6–8 M	T

Admiralty Charts and Hydrographic Publications

ADMIRALTY CHARTS A range of over 3,000 charts provides world-wide coverage. Many coastal and harbour charts of the British Isles now incorporate additional symbols showing the location of facilities of interest to small craft users.

Ⓐ	*Visitors' mooring*	↘	*Public Telephone*	Ⓟ	*Public car park*
Ⓥ	*Visitors' berth*	▯	*Post box*	⯒	*Parking for boats/trailers*
⟋	*Slipway*	⬛	*Public house or inn*	Ⓛ	*Laundrette*
☎	*Public landing*	✕	*Restaurant*	⯍	*Caravan site*
⚓	*Water tap*	►	*Yacht or sailing club*	△	*Camping site*
⛽	*Fuel*	▭	*Public toilets*	♨	*Nature reserve*

HYDROGRAPHIC PUBLICATIONS An extensive range, including:

- **SAILING DIRECTIONS (PILOTS)**
  Fully updated with supplements
- **RADIO PUBLICATIONS**
- **OCEAN PASSAGES FOR THE WORLD**

- **ADMIRALTY NOTICES TO MARINERS**
  small craft edition
- **LIST OF LIGHTS & FOG SIGNALS**
- **MARINER'S HANDBOOK** **NEW EDITION**

- **TIDAL INFORMATION** *Admiralty Tide Tables, Tidal Stream Atlases,*
  COMPUTERISED **TIDAL PREDICTION** *by the Simplified Harmonic Method*

Admiralty Charts and Hydrographic Publications including the WORLD CATALOGUE and the *FREE* HOME WATERS CATALOGUE are obtainable through an extensive network of Admiralty Chart Agents in the British Isles and overseas.

HYDROGRAPHIC OFFICE
Taunton, Somerset
Tel: Taunton (0823) 337900
Fax: (0823) 284077

Chapter 5

Astro-Navigation

Contents

5

Astro-Navigation — introduction

The following subjects are described in detail in Chapter 5 of *The Macmillan & Silk Cut Yachtsman's Handbook*

A general introduction to astro-navigation; the sextant; sextant errors and adjustments; sextant handling. The principles of nautical astronomy — angular and geographical distances; time and hour angle; glossary of terms. Altitude corrections — dip; refraction; semi-diameter; parallax. Theory into practice — the astronomical triangle; sight reduction methods. Practical sight taking — notes on observation; the accuracy of sights; Sun sights; Moon sights; star sights. Sight reduction — tables; latitude by meridian altitude; latitude by Polaris; plotting the Sun's geographical position; equal altitudes. The use of calculators — dip; refraction; amplitudes; sight reduction. The position line — the use of a single position line; angle of cut; rate of change of bearing and altitude. Plotting and evaluating the sight. Sight reduction table — description; notation, method, equations and rules; instructions and illustrative examples; table. Bibliography.

Here in the Almanac are given the necessary astronomical data for determining position at sea — the Greenwich Hour Angle of the first point of Aries, the Greenwich Hour Angle and the Declination of the Sun, Moon, planets and selected stars for any instant of Greenwich Mean Time, together with auxiliary data comprising corrections to observed altitude, times of rising and setting of the Sun and Moon, times of twilight, planning data, star diagrams and azimuth diagrams.

5.1   THE USE OF CALCULATORS

5.1.1   General
For sight reduction either a 'dedicated' calculator (designed for the purpose) or a calculator offering program capability, and adequate memory storage together with polar-rectangular conversion and statistical functions should be used. Further information on this subject, and on the formulae below, is given in Chapter 5 (section 5.7) of *The Macmillan & Silk Cut Yachtsman's Handbook*.

5.1.2   Dip
Dip corrections to the observed altitude are always negative (−), and may be calculated from:

$$\text{Dip (in mins)} = 1'\cdot76 \times \sqrt{\text{HE}} \text{ (in metres)}$$
$$\text{or} \qquad\qquad = 0'\cdot97 \times \sqrt{\text{HE}} \text{ (in feet)}$$

where HE is height of eye above sea level.

5.1.3   Refraction
The correction for refraction is always subtractive (−), and may be calculated from the formula:

$$R_M = \left(\frac{74}{h + 2} \right) - 0\cdot7$$

where R_M is mean refraction in minutes of arc
$\quad$ h $\quad$ is observed altitude in degrees at sea level air temperature 10°C and atmospheric pressure 1010 millibars

5.1.4   Amplitudes
Amplitude is the bearing of a body measured from true east or west when it is on the horizon (i.e. rising or setting), and is useful for checking the accuracy of the compass.

$$\sin \text{Amplitude} = \frac{\sin \text{Declination}}{\cos \text{Latitude}}$$

Amplitudes should not be used in high latitudes.

5.1.5   Sight reduction
Several different methods can be used for the reduction of sights. The following are two basic formulae upon which most of these are based.

$$\sin \text{Alt} = (\sin \text{Lat} \times \sin \text{Dec}) +$$
$$(\cos \text{Lat} \times \cos \text{Dec} \times \cos \text{LHA})$$

where: Dec is positive if the SAME name as Lat, and negative if CONTRARY name.

For the Azimuth Angle (Z): tan Z =

$$\frac{\sin \text{LHA}}{(\cos \text{Lat} \times \tan \text{Dec}) - (\sin \text{Lat} \times \cos \text{LHA})}$$

where the sign conventions are:

(a) If Lat or Dec are SOUTH change their sign to minus (−).

(b) If Z and sin LHA have the same sign, Zn = Z + 180°; if Z is minus (−) and LHA is less than 180°, Zn = Z + 360°; if Z is plus (+) and LHA is greater than 180°, Zn = Z.

5.2   ASTRONOMICAL DATA (EPHEMERIS) — EXPLANATION

5.2.1   Summary of contents
The object of this Almanac is to provide, in a condensed form, the data needed to determine position at sea to an accuracy of one or two minutes of arc. It is designed for European waters between latitudes N.30° and N.60°.

The presentation of the daily ephemerides has been changed from decimals of a degree to the more usual degrees and minutes of arc.

The ephemerides are derived from data supplied by Her Majesty's Nautical Almanac Office, but if comparisons are made with their publication, '*The Nautical Almanac*', it will be seen that there are occasional differences in the tabulated values—this is because the end figures in this almanac have been adjusted to allow linear interpolation to be used with a minimum of error.

For the Sun and planets this adjustment is rarely significant, with a maximum value (for Venus) of $0'\cdot1$. However, for the Moon it is more significant, with a maximum value of $0'\cdot8$. Such large adjustments then become inconsistent with end-figures of $0'\cdot1$ and hence the tabulation for the Moon has been reduced to 1'.

The main contents consist of data from which the *Greenwich Hour Angle* (GHA) and the *Declination* (Dec) of the Sun, Moon and planets (Venus, Mars, Jupiter and Saturn) can be determined for any instant of *Universal Time* (UT), or *Greenwich Mean*

Time (GMT). The *Local Hour Angle* (LHA) can then be obtained from:

$$LHA = GHA \quad \begin{array}{l} -\text{west} \\ +\text{east} \end{array} \quad \text{longitude}$$

Auxiliary data consist of: corrections to observed altitude, calendarial data, times of rising and setting of the Sun and Moon, times of twilight, planning data, star diagrams and azimuth diagrams.

For the Sun and planets, the GHA and Dec are tabulated directly for 00^h of each day throughout the year. For the Moon the tabulations are for 00^h, 08^h and 16^h each day. For the stars the *Sidereal Hour Angle* (SHA) is given, and the GHA is obtained from:

$$GHA\ Star = GHA\ Aries + SHA\ Star$$

The SHA and Dec of the stars change slowly but, to the accuracy required, mean values are adequate and are given for use throughout the year. The errors in the tabulated coordinates can rise to $\pm0'\cdot6$ in SHA and $\pm0'\cdot4$ in Dec. GHA Aries, or the Greenwich Hour Angle of the first point of Aries, is tabulated for 00^h each day. Permanent tables give the increments and corrections to the tabulated daily values of GHA and Dec for hours, minutes and seconds of UT.

The tabular accuracy of GHA and Dec of the Sun and planets, GHA Aries and of the SHA and Dec of the stars is $0'\cdot1$; for the Moon the tabular accuracy has been reduced to $1'$.

The ephemeral data for two months are given on an opening of two pages; the left-hand page contains data for Aries and the planets and the right-hand page data for the Sun and Moon. Separate tabulations give Local Mean Times (LMT), for every third day, of Morning Nautical Twilight, Sunrise, Sunset and Evening Civil Twilight for latitude N.50°, together with variations (*v*) which, with the aid of auxiliary tables, enable the LMT for other latitudes in the range N.30° to N.60° to be found. Tabulations for Moonrise and Moonset for each day for latitude N.50° are given together with variations (*v*) which, with the auxiliary tables, enable the LMT of Moonrise and Moonset to be found for latitudes N.30° to N.60°.

5.2.2   Main data

Monthly pages. These give on each left-hand page the GHA of Aries and the GHA and Dec of the four navigational planets at 00^h UT each day. On the right-hand page, the GHA and Dec of the Sun are given each day for 00^h UT, and the mean semi-diameter (SD) is shown each month; for the Moon the GHA and Dec are given each day for 00^h, 08^h

and 16^h UT, and horizontal parallax (HP) for 12^h. Values of the variations (*v*) in GHA and (*d*) in Declination allow the GHA and Dec of Sun, Moon or planets to be found at any instant of UT. South declinations are treated as negative.

Stars. The SHA and Dec of 48 selected stars are tabulated in numerical order in 5.3.3 on page 77 and are intended for use throughout the year; an alphabetical list of star names and numbers is also given.

Interpolation tables. These tables provide the increments for hours, minutes and seconds to be applied to the tabular values of GHA and Dec; the tables for Aries, Sun and planets comprise six pages, and those for the Moon four pages. The increment for GHA Aries is taken out in two parts, the first with argument UT in units of 12 minutes and the second part, with argument the remainder, in minutes and seconds, is given on the left-hand side of the opening. For the GHA of the Sun and planets the increment is found in three parts: the first with argument UT in units of 12 minutes, the second is for the remainder in minutes and seconds, given on the right hand side of the opening and the third with vertical argument UT (in units of 12 minutes) and horizontal argument *v*. The increments for Dec are found with vertical argument UT (in units of 12 minutes) and horizontal argument *d*.

For the Moon, the increment of GHA is found in three parts. First with argument UT in units of 4 minutes, second with argument the remainder of UT in minutes and seconds, and third with vertical argument UT (in units of 4 minutes) and horizontal argument *v*. The increments for Dec are found with vertical argument UT (in units of 4 minutes) and horizontal argument *d*.

The increments are based on the following adopted hourly rates of increase: Aries $15°\cdot0411$; Sun and planets $15°$ precisely; Moon $14°\cdot25$. The values of *v* are the differences (in minutes of arc) of the actual changes in GHA minus the adopted changes over the tabular interval, i.e. for the Sun and planets *v* is the daily change minus 360° and can be either positive or negative; for the Moon *v* is the change over eight hours minus 114° and is always positive. The values of *d* are the changes in Dec over the tabular interval. For the Sun and planets the full values (to $0'\cdot1$) of *v* and *d* should be obtained by inspection before using the interpolation tables.

The errors introduced by using the tables may amount to $0'\cdot15$ for Aries, $0'\cdot2$ for the Sun and planets, and $1'\cdot5$ for the Moon. If direct interpolation is used (see page 74) these errors can be reduced slightly, to $0'\cdot1$ for Aries, Sun and planets, and $1'\cdot0$ for the Moon.

5.2.3   Rising and setting phenomena

These tabulations give for every third day of the year, Local Mean Times (LMT) of Morning Nautical Twilight, Sunrise, Sunset and Evening Civil Twilight for latitude N.50°, together with variations (v) which, with the aid of auxiliary tables, enable the LMT for other latitudes (in the range N.30° to N.60°) to be found. The tabulations for Moonrise and Moonset are given for each day for latitude N.50°, together with variations (v) which, together with the auxiliary tables, enable the LMT to be found for latitudes N.30° to N.60°. The tabular values are for the Greenwich Meridian, but are approximately the Local Mean Times of the corresponding phenomena for the other meridians; only for the Moon phenomena need a correction for longitude be applied and a note of this correction is given in 5.3.7 on page 83. The UT of a phenomenon is obtained from the LMT by

$$UT = LMT \quad {}^{+\text{west}}_{-\text{east}} \quad \text{longitude}$$

in which the longitude must first be converted to time by the table in 5.3.12 on page 112.

At Sunrise and Sunset 16′ is allowed for semi-diameter and 34′ for horizontal refraction, so that at the times given the Sun's upper limb is on the visible horizon; all times refer to phenomena as seen from sea level with a clear horizon.

At the times given for the beginning and end of twilight, the Sun's zenith distance is 96° for Civil, and 102° for Nautical Twilight. The degree of illumination at the times given for Civil Twilight (in good conditions and in the absence of other illumination) is such that the brightest stars are visible and the horizon is clearly defined. At the times given for Nautical Twilight the horizon is in general not visible, and it is too dark for observation with a marine sextant.

At Moonrise and Moonset allowance is made for semi-diameter, parallax and refraction (34′), so that at the times given the Moon's upper limb is on the visible horizon as seen from sea level.

5.2.4   Altitude correction tables

Tables for the correction of dip of the horizon, due to height of eye above sea level, are given in 5.3.2 on page 76; this correction should be applied to the sextant altitude to give apparent altitude, which is the correct argument for the other tables.

The dip table is arranged as a critical table, where an interval of height of eye corresponds to a single value of dip. No interpolation is required. At a 'critical' entry the upper of the two possible values of the correction is to be used.

Separate tables for refraction are given for the Sun, stars and planets, and Moon. With the Sun and Moon, to allow for semi-diameter, separate correc-tions are given for the lower and upper limbs. For the Moon, corrections are also given for parallax.

The altitude correction tables are given to one decimal of a minute of arc so that the addition of several corrections does not lead to any significant error.

5.2.5   Polaris table

The table in 5.3.4 on page 77 provides means by which the latitude can be deduced from an observed altitude of *Polaris*; the azimuth of *Polaris* is also given. The correction Q, to be applied to the apparent altitude, corrected for refraction, is given corresponding to an argument of LHA Aries (LHA♈).

5.2.6   Auxiliary and planning data

Pages 78 and 79 (5.3.5) give the times of meridian passage (mer pass) of the Sun; symbols, approximate SHA and Dec, magnitude (mag) and meridian passage of the planets; an explanation of the symbols used and planet notes are given on page 79. Phases of the Moon, with brief eclipse notes, are also given on page 79.

Star diagrams. Star diagrams are given on pages 106–108; these have been drawn for latitude N.45° and show the approximate positions in altitude and azimuth, of stars in the Selected list for each range of 15° of LHA Aries; indications are also given of the horizons for latitude N.30° (shown as ··· ···) and N.60° (shown as ·—·—); these will enable the user to estimate the approximate altitude and azimuth of any particular star and will indicate stars suitable for observation at a given value of LHA Aries.

Symbols indicate the magnitude of the stars as follows:

·	Mag 2·1–3·1	
○	Mag 1·1–2·0	note that the larger symbols
●	Mag 0·0–1·0	indicate greater brilliance
⊙	Mag −1·6	

The symbol for any star indicates its position at the beginning of the range of LHA Aries and the arrow point the end of the range.

Azimuth diagrams are given on pages 109–111; they are used as follows: a point is plotted on the diagrams corresponding to the LHA and Dec of the object observed; the plotted point is then moved horizontally to the *left* corresponding to the co-latitude (90° − latitude) of the observer; the background graticule and the scale along the top of the diagram will assist in this movement; at the new position the corresponding value of LHA is read and is converted to azimuth according to the rules given below the diagrams.

5.2.7   Illustrations

Example (a) Required the GHA and Dec of the Sun on 1991 January 22 at UT 15^h 47^m 13^s.

		GHA	v	Dec	d
Monthly page,	Jan 22	177 09·5	−4	S.19 50·4	+14
Interpolation	UT 15^h 36^m	234			
Tables	UT 11^m 13^s	2 48·2			
Page 97	UT 15^h 47^m 13^s ($v = − 4·1$ $d = + 13·7$)	− 2·7		+ 9·0	
		413 55·0		S.19 41·4	
		−360			
		53 55·0			

Note that, in this case, the declination is south (i.e. negative) and the correction for d is positive, so that the correction must be subtracted.

Example (b) Required the GHA and Dec of the Moon on 1991 January 4 at UT 15^h 47^m 13^s.

			GHA	v	Dec	d
Monthly page,	Jan 4	8^h-16^h	70 43	128	N.08 06	−118
Interpolation	UT 7^h 44^m		110 12			
Tables	UT 3^m 13^s		0 46			
Page 105	UT 7^h 47^m 13^s ($v = 128$ $d = −118$)		2 05		− 1 55	
			183 46		N.06 11	

Note that the corrections for v and d are taken from the interpolation tables as +125 and −115 respectively.

Example (c) Required the LHA and Dec of Venus on 1991 December 26 at UT 07^h 47^m 13^s in longitude E.5°15′.

		GHA	v	Dec	d
Monthly page,	Dec 26	222 34·3	−13	S.16 23·6	−19
Interpolation	UT 07^h 36^m	114			
Tables	UT 11^m 13^s	2 48·2			
Pages 98, 99	UT 07^h 47^m 13^s ($v = −13·2$ $d = −18·7$)	−0 04·3		− 6.1	
		339 18·2		S.16 29·7	
Longitude East		+ 5 15·0			
	LHA	344 33·2			

The first correction for the GHA of the planets is taken from the column headed Sun/Planet.

Here, the declination is south (i.e. negative) and the correction for d is negative, so that the correction must be added.

Example (d) Required the GHA and Dec of *Aldebaran* on 1991 January 22 at UT $15^h 55^m 13^s$.

		° ′	° ′
Page 77,	SHA and Dec	291 08·1	N.16 29·6
Monthly page,	GHA Aries	120 50·8	
Interpolation ⌠	UT $15^h 48^m$	237 38·9	
Tables ⌡	UT $7^m 13^s$	1 48·5	
Pages 96, 97		———	
		651 26·3	
		−360	
		———	
		291 26·3	

Example (e) Required the UT of the beginning of nautical twilight and sunrise on 1991 January 22 for latitude N.30°50′, longitude W.7°25′.

		Naut Twi	*v*	Sunrise	*v*
		h m		h m	
Page 80,	Jan 22	06 31	+30	07 47	+52
Page 81,	Corrections for N.30°50′	−29		−50	
		———		———	
	LMT	06 02		06 57	
Page 112,	Long. equivalent in time	+30		+30	
		———		———	
	UT	06 32		07 27	

Example (f) Required the UT of sunset and evening civil twilight on 1991 January 22 for latitude N.36°07′, longitude E.18°20′.

		Sunset	*v*	Civil Twi	*v*
		h m		h m	
Page 80,	Jan 22	16 37	−52	17 13	−41
Page 81,	Corrections for N.36°07′	+39		+31	
		———		———	
	LMT	17 16		17 44	
Page 112,	Long. equivalent in time	−1 13		−1 13	
		———		———	
	UT	16 03		16 31	

Example (g) Required the UT of moonrise and moonset on 1991 January 11 for latitude N.36°07′, longitude W.6°30′.

		Moonrise	*v*	Moonset	*v*
		h m		h m	
Page 82,	Feb 7	04 29	+72	12 19	−75
Page 83,	Corrections for N.36°07′	−55		+57	
		———		———	
	LMT	03 34		13 16	
Page 112,	Long. equivalent in time	+26		+ 26	
		———		———	
	UT	04 00		13 42	

These times can be increased by $+1^m$ to allow for the effect of longitude on the LMT of the phenomena (see page 83).

Example (h) Required the correction to an observed altitude of *Polaris*, made on 1991 January 22 at UT 16^h 45^m in DR longitude E.18°20′ the sextant angle being 37°05′·5, height of eye 15ft.

Monthly page,	Jan 22	GHA Aries	120° 50′·8
Page 97,	Correction for 16^h 36^m		249 40·9
Page 96,	Correction for 9^m		2 15·4
			372 47·1
	Correction for Long E.18°20′		+ 18 20·0
			391 07·1
			−360
	LHA Aries		31 07·1

Sextant altitude			37° 05′·5
Page 76,	Dip, for 15ft		− 3·8
	Apparent altitude		37 01·7
Page 76,	Refraction, stars		− 1·3
	Corrected observed altitude		37 00·4
Page 77	Q for LHA Aries 31°		− 46
	Latitude		36 14

From page 77 azimuth of *Polaris* at LHA Aries of 31° is seen to be 0°.

The following examples illustrate the use of the altitude correction tables on page 76. The sextant altitudes are assumed to be taken on 1991 January 29 with a marine sextant at height 5·4 metres (18ft).

	SUN lower limb	SUN upper limb	MOON lower limb	MOON upper limb	Venus	*Polaris*
	° ′	° ′	° ′	° ′	° ′	° ′
Sextant altitude	21 19·7	3 20·2	33 27·6	26 06·7	4 32·6	49 36·5
Dip, height 5.4 metres (18ft)	− 4·1	− 4·1	− 4·1	− 4·1	− 4·1	− 4·1
Apparent altitude	21 15·6	3 16·1	33 23·5	26 02·6	4 28·5	49 32·4
Main correction	+13·7	−29·4	+58·5	+31·7	−10·8	− 0·8
Parallax correction for Moon (HP = 60′·4, from page 85)			+ 7·0	+ 3·9		
Corrected sextant altitude	21 29·3	2 46·7	34 29·0	26 38·2	4 17·7	49 31·6

The following example illustrates the use of the Star Diagrams: on 1991 January 22 an observer in an approximate position of latitude N.51°, longitude W.7° wishes to determine which stars are suitable for observation at about UT 7^h 20^m, and determines LHA Aries as follows.

Monthly page,	Jan 22	GHA Aries	120° 50′·8
Interpolation	UT	7^h 12^m	108 17·7
Tables,	UT	8^m	2 00·3
Page 96			
GHA Aries at	UT	7^h 20^m	231 08·8
			− 7 00·0
	LHA Aries		224 08·8

Inspection of the Star Diagram for LHA Aries 210° to 225° indicates that stars 53, 49, and 46 are visible towards the east, 39, 37 and 33 are towards the south, 28 and 26 are westerly and 3 (rather low) and 40 (rather high) are northerly; *Polaris* will also be available. The names of the stars corresponding to the numbers, can be found on page 77 and at the foot of the second star diagram.

5.2.8   The use of a calculator for interpolation

When using a calculator the tabular values of GHA, v, Dec and d should be extracted from the monthly pages for the date of observation (and in the case of the Moon, the nearest 8^h before the UT of observation). <u>The UT must be converted to hours and decimals</u>, i.e. hours + (minutes ÷ 60) + (seconds ÷ 3600). <u>The GHA and Dec should also be converted to decimal units</u>, i.e. degrees + (minutes ÷ 60), then the required values are found as follows. Southern declinations are treated as negative.

Stars

$$\text{GHA star} = \text{Tabular GHA Aries} + (15°{\cdot}0411 \times \text{UT}) + \text{SHA star}$$
$$\text{Dec star} = \text{Tabular Dec (from Star list)}$$

Sun

$$\text{GHA Sun} = \text{Tabular GHA Sun} + (15° + (v \div 1440)) \times \text{UT}$$
$$\text{Dec Sun} = \text{Tabular Dec Sun} + (d \div 1440) \times \text{UT}$$

Planets

$$\text{GHA Planet} = \text{Tabular GHA Planet} + (15° + (v \div 1440)) \times \text{UT}$$
$$\text{Dec Planet} = \text{Tabular Dec Planet} + (d \div 1440) \times \text{UT}$$

Moon

$$\text{GHA Moon} = \text{Tabular GHA Moon} + (14{\cdot}25 + (v \div 480)) \times \text{UT}^*$$
$$\text{Dec Moon} = \text{Tabular Dec Moon} + (d \div 480) \times \text{UT}^*$$

* For the Moon, multiples of 8 hours must be subtracted from the UT.

5.2.9   Standard Times

List 1 — Places fast on UT

The times given below should be { *added* to UT to give Standard Time / *subtracted* from Standard Time to give UT

	h		h		h
Albania*	01	France*	01	Monaco*	01
Algeria	01	Germany, East*	01	Netherlands, The*	01
Austria*	01	Germany, West[2]*	01	Norway*	01
Balearic Islands*	01	Gibraltar*	01	Poland*	01
Belgium*	01	Greece*	02	Romania*	02
Bulgaria*	02	Hungary*	01	Sardinia*	01
Corsica*	01	Israel*	02	Sicily*	01
Crete*	02	Italy*	01	Spain*	01
Cyprus, Ercan*	02	Latvia	03	Sweden*	01
Cyprus, Larnaca*	02	Lebanon*	02	Switzerland*	01
Czechoslovakia*	01	Libya*	01	Syria*	02
Denmark*	01	Liechtenstein*	01	Tunisia*	01
Egypt	02	Lithuania	03	Turkey*	02
Estonia	03	Luxembourg*	01	USSR west of 40°E*	03
Finland*	02	Malta*	01	Yugoslavia*	01

List 2 — Places normally keeping UT

Canary Islands*	Great Britain[1]	Irish Republic*
Channel Islands[1]	Iceland	Morocco*
Faeroes, The*	Ireland, Northern[1]	Portugal*

* Summer time may be kept in these countries.

[1] Summer time, one hour in advance of UT, is kept from March 31 01^h to October 27 01^hUT (1991).

[2] Including West Berlin.

5.3.1   CALENDAR, 1991

DAYS OF THE WEEK AND DAYS OF THE YEAR

DAY	JAN	FEB	MAR	APR	MAY	JUN	JUL	AUG	SEP	OCT	NOV	DEC
1	Tu 1	F 32	F 60	M 91	W 121	S 152	M 182	Th 213	Su 244	Tu 274	F 305	Su 335
2	W 2	S 33	S 61	Tu 92	Th 122	Su 153	Tu 183	F 214	M 245	W 275	S 306	M 336
3	Th 3	Su 34	Su 62	W 93	F 123	M 154	W 184	S 215	Tu 246	Th 276	Su 307	Tu 337
4	F 4	M 35	M 63	Th 94	S 124	Tu 155	Th 185	Su 216	W 247	F 277	M 308	W 338
5	S 5	Tu 36	Tu 64	F 95	Su 125	W 156	F 186	M 217	Th 248	S 278	Tu 309	Th 339
6	Su 6	W 37	W 65	S 96	M 126	Th 157	S 187	Tu 218	F 249	Su 279	W 310	F 340
7	M 7	Th 38	Th 66	Su 97	Tu 127	F 158	Su 188	W 219	S 250	M 280	Th 311	S 341
8	Tu 8	F 39	F 67	M 98	W 128	S 159	M 189	Th 220	Su 251	Tu 281	F 312	Su 342
9	W 9	S 40	S 68	Tu 99	Th 129	Su 160	Tu 190	F 221	M 252	W 282	S 313	M 343
10	Th 10	Su 41	Su 69	W 100	F 130	M 161	W 191	S 222	Tu 253	Th 283	Su 314	Tu 344
11	F 11	M 42	M 70	Th 101	S 131	Tu 162	Th 192	Su 223	W 254	F 284	M 315	W 345
12	S 12	Tu 43	Tu 71	F 102	Su 132	W 163	F 193	M 224	Th 255	S 285	Tu 316	Th 346
13	Su 13	W 44	W 72	S 103	M 133	Th 164	S 194	Tu 225	F 256	Su 286	W 317	F 347
14	M 14	Th 45	Th 73	Su 104	Tu 134	F 165	Su 195	W 226	S 257	M 287	Th 318	S 348
15	Tu 15	F 46	F 74	M 105	W 135	S 166	M 196	Th 227	Su 258	Tu 288	F 319	Su 349
16	W 16	S 47	S 75	Tu 106	Th 136	Su 167	Tu 197	F 228	M 259	W 289	S 320	M 350
17	Th 17	Su 48	Su 76	W 107	F 137	M 168	W 198	S 229	Tu 260	Th 290	Su 321	Tu 351
18	F 18	M 49	M 77	Th 108	S 138	Tu 169	Th 199	Su 230	W 261	F 291	M 322	W 352
19	S 19	Tu 50	Tu 78	F 109	Su 139	W 170	F 200	M 231	Th 262	S 292	Tu 323	Th 353
20	Su 20	W 51	W 79	S 110	M 140	Th 171	S 201	Tu 232	F 263	Su 293	W 324	F 354
21	M 21	Th 52	Th 80	Su 111	Tu 141	F 172	Su 202	W 233	S 264	M 294	Th 325	S 355
22	Tu 22	F 53	F 81	M 112	W 142	S 173	M 203	Th 234	Su 265	Tu 295	F 326	Su 356
23	W 23	S 54	S 82	Tu 113	Th 143	Su 174	Tu 204	F 235	M 266	W 296	S 327	M 357
24	Th 24	Su 55	Su 83	W 114	F 144	M 175	W 205	S 236	Tu 267	F 297	Su 328	Tu 358
25	F 25	M 56	M 84	Th 115	S 145	Tu 176	Th 206	Su 237	W 268	S 298	M 329	W 359
26	S 26	Tu 57	Tu 85	F 116	Su 146	W 177	F 207	M 238	Th 269	S 299	Tu 330	Th 360
27	Su 27	W 58	W 86	S 117	M 147	Th 178	S 208	Tu 239	F 270	Su 300	W 331	F 361
28	M 28	Th 59	Th 87	Su 118	Tu 148	F 179	Su 209	W 240	S 271	M 301	Th 332	S 362
29	Tu 29		F 88	M 119	W 149	S 180	M 210	Th 241	Su 272	Tu 302	F 333	Su 363
30	W 30		S 89	Tu 120	Th 150	Su 181	Tu 211	F 242	M 273	W 303	S 334	M 364
31	Th 31		Su 90		F 151		W 212	S 243		Th 304		Tu 365

RELIGIOUS CALENDARS

Epiphany	Jan 6	Low Sunday	Apr 7
Septuagesima Sunday	Jan 27	Ascension Day	May 9
Ash Wednesday	Feb 13	Whit Sunday	May 19
Good Friday	Mar 20	Christmas Day	Dec 25
Easter Day	Mar 31		
Jewish New Year (5752)	Sep 9	Islamic New Year (1412)	Jul 13

CIVIL CALENDAR

Accession of the Queen	Feb 6	Coronation Day	Jun 2
St David (Wales)	Mar 1	The Queen's Official Birthday	Jun 8
Commonwealth Day	Mar 11	Birthday of Prince Philip	Jun 10
St Patrick (Ireland)	Mar 17	Remembrance Sunday	Nov 10
Birthday of the Queen	Apr 21	Birthday of the Prince of Wales	Nov 14
St George (England)	Apr 23	St Andrew (Scotland)	Nov 30

BANK HOLIDAYS

ENGLAND & WALES
Jan 1, Apr 1, May 6, May 27, Aug 26, Dec 26

NORTHERN IRELAND
Jan 1, Mar 18, Apr 1, May 6, May 27, July 12, Aug 26, Dec 26

SCOTLAND
Jan 1, Jan 2, Mar 29, May 6, May 27, Aug 5, Dec 25, Dec 26

5

5.3.2 — ALTITUDE CORRECTION TABLES

DIP

Ht of eye (m)	Corr	Ht of eye (ft)
1.6	−2.3	5.3
1.7	−2.4	5.8
1.9	−2.5	6.3
2.1	−2.6	6.9
2.2	−2.7	7.4
2.4	−2.8	8.0
2.6	−2.9	8.6
2.8	−3.0	9.2
3.0	−3.1	9.8
3.2	−3.2	10.5
3.4	−3.3	11.2
3.6	−3.4	11.9
3.8	−3.5	12.6
4.0	−3.6	13.3
4.3	−3.7	14.1
4.5	−3.8	14.9
4.7	−3.9	15.7
5.0	−4.0	16.5
5.2	−4.1	17.4
5.5	−4.2	18.3
5.8	−4.3	19.1
6.1	−4.4	20.1
6.3	−4.5	21.0
6.6	−4.6	22.0
6.9	−4.7	22.9
7.2	−4.8	23.9
7.5	−4.9	24.9
7.9	−5.0	26.0
8.2	−5.1	27.1
8.5	−5.2	28.1
8.8	−5.3	29.2
9.2	−5.4	30.4
9.5	−5.5	31.5
9.9	−5.6	32.7
10.3	−5.7	33.9
10.6	−5.8	35.1
11.0	−5.9	36.3
11.4	−6.0	37.6
11.8	−6.1	38.9
12.2	−6.2	40.1
12.6	−6.3	41.5
13.0	−6.4	42.8
13.4	−6.5	44.2
13.8	−6.6	45.5
14.2	−6.7	46.9
14.7	−6.8	48.4
15.1	−6.9	49.8
15.5	−7.0	51.3
16.0	−7.1	52.8
16.5	−7.2	54.3
16.9	−7.3	55.8
17.4	−7.4	57.4
17.9	−7.5	58.9
18.4	−7.6	60.5
18.8		62.1

SUN / STARS and PLANETS

App Alt (°)	Sun Lower limb	Sun Upper limb	Stars and Planets
2.5	+ 0.1	−32.0	−16.1
3.0	1.8	30.2	14.4
3.5	3.2	28.8	13.0
4.0	4.4	27.7	11.8
4.5	5.4	26.6	10.7
5	+ 6.3	−25.8	− 9.9
6	7.7	24.3	8.5
7	8.7	23.3	7.4
8	9.6	22.4	6.6
9	10.3	21.8	5.9
10	+ 10.8	−21.2	− 5.3
12	11.7	20.4	4.5
14	12.4	19.7	3.8
16	12.8	19.2	3.3
18	13.2	18.8	3.0
20	+ 13.5	−18.5	− 2.6
25	14.1	18.0	2.1
30	14.5	17.6	1.7
35	14.8	17.3	1.4
40	15.0	17.0	1.2
45	+ 15.2	−16.9	− 1.0
50	15.3	16.8	0.8
55	15.5	16.6	0.7
60	15.6	16.5	0.6
70	15.7	16.3	0.4
80	+ 15.8	−16.1	− 0.2

MOON

App Alt (°)	Lower limb	Upper limb	App Alt (°)	Lower limb	Upper limb
2.5	+ 52.5	+ 23.1	40	+ 55.1	+ 25.3
3.0	54.2	24.8	42	53.9	24.2
3.5	55.7	26.2	44	52.7	23.0
4.0	56.8	27.4	46	51.5	21.7
4.5	57.8	28.4	48	50.2	20.4
5	+ 58.6	+ 29.2	50	+ 48.8	+ 19.0
6	60.0	30.5	52	47.4	17.6
7	60.9	31.5	54	46.0	16.1
8	61.7	32.2	56	44.5	14.6
9	62.2	32.7	58	42.9	13.1
10	+ 62.6	+ 33.1	60	+ 41.4	+ 11.5
12	63.1	33.6	62	39.8	9.9
14	63.3	33.8	64	38.1	8.3
16	63.3	33.7	66	36.5	6.6
18	63.2	33.6	68	34.8	4.9
20	+ 62.9	+ 33.3	70	+ 33.1	+ 3.2
22	62.5	32.9	71	32.2	+ 2.3
24	62.0	32.3	72	31.3	+ 1.4
26	61.4	31.7	73	30.4	+ 0.5
28	60.7	31.0	74	29.6	− 0.3
30	+ 59.9	+ 30.3	75	+ 28.7	− 1.2
32	59.1	29.4	76	27.8	− 2.1
34	58.2	28.5	77	26.9	− 3.0
36	57.2	27.5	78	26.0	− 3.9
38	56.2	26.4	79	25.1	− 4.8
40	+ 55.1	+ 25.3	80	+ 24.2	− 5.7

CORRECTION FOR MOON'S PARALLAX

App Alt HP	0° L	0° U	20° L	20° U	40° L	40° U	50° L	50° U	60° L	60° U	70° L	70° U	80° L	80° U
	+	+	+	+	+	+	+	+	+	+	+	+	+	
54.0	0.0	0.0	0.0	0.0	0.0	0.0	0.0	0.0	0.0	0.0	0.0	0.0	0.0	0.0
54.5	0.6	0.4	0.6	0.3	0.5	0.2	0.4	0.2	0.4	0.1	0.3	0.0	0.2	0.0
55.0	1.3	0.7	1.2	0.7	1.0	0.5	0.9	0.4	0.8	0.2	0.6	0.0	0.4	−0.1
55.5	1.9	1.1	1.8	1.0	1.5	0.7	1.3	0.6	1.1	0.3	0.9	0.1	0.6	−0.1
56.0	2.5	1.5	2.4	1.3	2.1	1.0	1.8	0.7	1.5	0.5	1.2	0.1	0.9	−0.2
56.5	3.1	1.8	3.0	1.7	2.6	1.2	2.2	0.9	1.9	0.6	1.5	0.2	1.1	−0.2
57.0	3.8	2.2	3.6	2.0	3.1	1.5	2.7	1.1	2.3	0.7	1.8	0.2	1.3	−0.3
57.5	4.5	2.5	4.2	2.3	3.6	1.7	3.2	1.3	2.7	0.8	2.1	0.2	1.5	−0.3
58.0	5.1	2.9	4.8	2.7	4.1	2.0	3.6	1.5	3.1	1.0	2.4	0.3	1.8	−0.4
58.5	5.7	3.3	5.4	3.0	4.7	2.2	4.1	1.7	3.4	1.1	2.8	0.3	2.0	−0.4
59.0	6.3	3.6	6.0	3.3	5.2	2.5	4.6	1.8	3.8	1.2	3.1	0.3	2.3	−0.5
59.5	7.0	4.0	6.6	3.7	5.7	2.7	5.0	2.0	4.2	1.3	3.4	0.4	2.5	−0.5
60.0	7.6	4.4	7.2	4.0	6.2	3.0	5.5	2.2	4.6	1.4	3.7	0.4	2.7	−0.6
60.5	8.2	4.8	7.8	4.3	6.7	3.2	6.0	2.4	4.9	1.5	4.0	0.4	2.9	−0.6
61.0	8.9	5.1	8.4	4.7	7.2	3.5	6.4	2.6	5.2	1.6	4.3	0.5	3.1	−0.7
61.5	9.5	5.5	9.0	5.0	7.7	3.7	6.8	2.7	5.5	1.7	4.6	0.5	3.4	−0.7

ALTITUDE CORRECTION TABLES

App Alt = Apparent altitude
= Sextant altitude corrected for index error and dip.

The correction for the Sun's lower or upper limbs can be taken out directly as also can the corrections for the stars and planets.

The correction for the Moon is in two parts; the first correction is taken from the upper table with argument apparent altitude, and the second correction from the lower table with arguments apparent altitude and HP.

Separate corrections are given for lower (L) and upper (U) limbs.

5.3.3
SELECTED STARS, 1991

No	Name	Mag	SHA	Dec	Name	No
			° ′	° ′		
1	Alpheratz	2.2	358 00.6	N29 02.8	Acamar	7
2	Ankaa	2.4	353 31.7	S42 21.1	Adhara	19
3	Schedar	2.5	349 59.5	N56 29.6	Aldebaran	10
4	Diphda	2.2	349 12.3	S18 01.9	Alioth	32
6	Hamal	2.2	328 19.3	N23 25.5	Alkaid	34
7	Acamar	3.1	315 30.7	S40 20.2	Al Na'ir	55
8	Menkar	2.8	314 32.2	N 4 03.5	Alnilam	15
9	Mirfak	1.9	309 03.9	N49 50.0	Alphard	25
10	Aldebaran	1.1	291 08.1	N16 29.6	Alphecca	41
11	Rigel	0.3	281 27.8	S 8 12.6	Alpheratz	1
12	Capella	0.2	280 58.6	N45 59.5	Altair	51
13	Bellatrix	1.7	278 49.5	N 6 20.6	Ankaa	2
14	Elnath	1.8	278 33.3	N28 36.1	Antares	42
15	Alnilam	1.8	276 02.9	S 1 12.4	Arcturus	37
16	Betelgeuse	*	271 18.9	N 7 24.4	Bellatrix	13
17	Canopus	-0.9	264 03.4	S52 41.4	Betelgeuse	16
18	Sirius	-1.6	258 48.0	S16 42.2	Canopus	17
19	Adhara	1.6	255 25.3	S28 57.5	Capella	12
20	Procyon	0.5	245 16.7	N 5 14.8	Deneb	53
21	Pollux	1.2	243 47.6	N28 02.8	Denebola	28
23	Suhail	2.2	223 04.6	S43 23.9	Diphda	4
25	Alphard	2.2	218 12.1	S 8 37.3	Dubhe	27
26	Regulus	1.3	208 00.8	N12 00.5	Elnath	14
27	Dubhe	2.0	194 11.5	N61 47.7	Eltanin	47
28	Denebola	2.2	182 50.3	N14 37.0	Enif	54
29	Gienah	2.8	176 09.3	S17 29.8	Fomalhaut	56
32	Alioth	1.7	166 34.8	N56 00.2	Gienah	29
33	Spica	1.2	158 48.7	S11 07.1	Hamal	6
34	Alkaid	1.9	153 11.7	N49 21.2	Kaus Aust	48
36	Menkent	2.3	148 27.2	S 36 19.8	Kochab	40
37	Arcturus	0.2	146 10.7	N19 13.4	Markab	57
39	Zuben'ubi	2.9	137 23.7	S16 00.5	Menkar	8
40	Kochab	2.2	137 19.1	N74 11.3	Menkent	36
41	Alphecca	2.3	126 24.9	N26 44.5	Mirfak	9
42	Antares	1.2	112 46.6	S26 24.9	Nunki	50
44	Sabik	2.6	102 31.5	S15 43.0	Pollux	21
45	Shaula	1.7	96 44.4	S37 06.0	Procyon	20
46	Rasalhague	2.1	96 21.8	N12 33.9	Rasalhague	46
47	Eltanin	2.4	90 53.8	N51 29.3	Regulus	26
48	Kaus Aust	2.0	84 05.7	S34 23.4	Rigel	11
49	Vega	0.1	80 50.2	N38 46.5	Sabik	44
50	Nunki	2.1	76 18.8	S26 18.5	Schedar	3
51	Altair	0.9	62 24.3	N 8 50.7	Shaula	45
53	Deneb	1.3	49 42.8	N45 15.0	Sirius	18
54	Enif	2.5	34 03.3	N 9 50.2	Spica	33
55	Al Na'ir	2.2	28 04.2	S47 00.1	Suhail	23
56	Fomalhaut	1.3	15 42.0	S29 40.0	Vega	49
57	Markab	2.6	13 54.7	N15 09.6	Zuben'ubi	39

* Variable 0.1 — 1.2

5.3.4
POLARIS TABLE, 1991

LHA ♈	Q	LHA ♈	Q	LHA ♈	Q
°	′	°	′		′
0	-37	120	- 4	240	+42
3	39	123	- 2	243	41
6	40	126	+ 1	246	40
9	41	129	3	249	39
12	42	132	5	252	37
15	-43	135	+ 8	255	+36
18	44	138	10	258	34
21	45	141	13	261	33
24	45	144	15	264	31
27	46	147	17	267	29
30	-46	150	+19	270	+27
33	46	153	22	273	25
36	46	156	24	276	23
39	46	159	26	279	21
42	46	162	28	282	19
45	-46	165	+30	285	+17
48	45	168	31	288	14
51	45	171	33	291	12
54	44	174	35	294	10
57	43	177	36	297	7
60	-42	180	+38	300	+ 5
63	41	183	39	303	+ 3
66	40	186	40	306	0
69	39	189	41	309	- 2
72	37	192	42	312	5
75	-36	195	+43	315	- 7
78	34	198	44	318	9
81	32	201	45	321	12
84	31	204	45	324	14
87	29	207	46	327	16
90	-27	210	+46	330	-19
93	25	213	46	333	21
96	23	216	46	336	23
99	21	219	46	339	25
102	18	222	46	342	27
105	-16	225	+46	345	-29
108	14	228	45	348	31
111	11	231	45	351	33
114	9	234	44	354	34
117	7	237	43	357	36
120	- 4	240	+42	360	-37

Azimuth of Polaris

LHA ♈	0°		11°	60°		190°
Az		1°		0°	359°	

LHA ♈	190°		240°	360°
Az		0°	1°	

Latitude = Apparent altitude (corrected for refraction)+Q

5.3.5 PLANET PLANNING DATA, 1991

Date	SUN Mer Pass	VENUS Symbol	S H A	Dec	Mag	Mer Pass	MARS Symbol	S H A	Dec	Mag	Mer Pass	JUPITER Symbol	S H A	Dec	Mag	Mer Pass	SATURN Symbol	S H A	Dec	Mag	Mer Pass
	h m		°	°		h m		°	°		h m		°	°		h m		°	°		h m
Jan 1	12 03	Wa	63	S22	−3.9	13 08	EA	305	N22	−1.0	20 56	WB	225	N18	−2.5	02 18	Wa	62	S21	+0.6	13 08
6	12 06		56	21	3.9	13 15	EA	305	22	0.8	20 37	V	226	18	2.6	01 56	☉	62	21	0.6	12 51
11	12 08		50	20	3.9	13 21	MA	305	22	0.7	20 19		226	18	2.6	01 34		61	21	0.5	12 34
16	12 10		44	18	3.9	13 27		304	22	0.5	20 03		227	18	2.6	01 12		60	21	0.5	12 17
21	12 11		37	16	3.9	13 32		303	22	0.4	19 47		228	19	2.6	00 50		60	21	0.5	11 59
26	12 12	Wa	31	S14	−3.9	13 37	MA	301	N23	−0.2	19 33	V	228	N19	−2.6	00 27	☉	59	S21	+0.6	11 42
31	12 13		25	12	3.9	13 41		300	23	−0.1	19 19		229	19	2.6	00 05	☉	59	20	0.6	11 25
Feb 5	12 14		19	10	3.9	13 44		298	23	0.0	19 06		230	19	2.6	23 38	Eb	58	20	0.6	11 08
10	12 14		14	7	3.9	13 48	MA	296	24	+0.1	18 54		230	19	2.6	23 16		57	20	0.6	10 51
15	12 14		8	5	3.9	13 51	WA	294	24	0.3	18 43		231	19	2.6	22 54		57	20	0.6	10 33
20	12 14	Wa	2	S 2	−3.9	13 54	WA	292	N24	+0.4	18 32	V	232	N20	−2.5	22 32	Eb	56	S20	+0.7	10 16
25	12 13		357	0	4.0	13 56		290	24	0.5	18 21	EA	232	20	2.5	22 10	Eb	56	20	0.7	09 58
Mar 2	12 12		351	N 3	4.0	13 59		287	25	0.6	18 11		233	20	2.5	21 48	EB	55	20	0.7	09 41
7	12 11		346	6	4.0	14 01		285	25	0.7	18 02		233	20	2.5	21 27		55	20	0.7	09 23
12	12 10		340	8	4.0	14 04		282	25	0.8	17 53		233	20	2.4	21 06		54	20	0.7	09 06
17	12 08	Wa	334	N11	−4.0	14 07	WA	280	N25	+0.8	17 44	EA	234	N20	−2.4	20 46	EB	54	S19	+0.7	08 48
22	12 07		329	13	4.0	14 10		277	25	0.9	17 35	MA	234	20	2.4	20 25		53	19	0.7	08 30
27	12 06		323	15	4.0	14 14		274	25	1.0	17 27		234	20	2.3	20 05		53	19	0.7	08 12
Apr 1	12 04		317	17	4.0	14 17		271	25	1.1	17 19		234	20	2.3	19 46		52	19	0.7	07 54
6	12 03		311	19	4.0	14 21		268	25	1.1	17 11		234	20	2.3	19 26		52	19	0.7	07 35
11	12 01	Wa	305	N21	−4.0	14 26	WA	265	N25	+1.2	17 03	MA	234	N20	−2.2	19 07	EB	52	S19	+0.7	07 17
16	12 00	WA	299	22	4.0	14 31		262	25	1.2	16 55		234	20	2.2	18 48		51	19	0.7	06 58
21	11 59		293	24	4.1	14 36		259	25	1.3	16 48	MA	233	20	2.2	18 30		51	19	0.7	06 40
26	11 58		286	25	4.1	14 41		256	25	1.3	16 40	WA	233	20	2.1	18 12		51	19	0.6	06 21
May 1	11 57		280	25	4.1	14 47		253	24	1.4	16 33		232	20	2.1	17 54	EB	51	19	0.6	06 02
6	11 57	WA	274	N26	−4.1	14 52	WA	250	N24	+1.4	16 25	WA	232	N20	−2.1	17 36	MB	51	S19	+0.6	05 43
11	11 56		268	26	4.1	14 57		247	23	1.5	16 18		231	19	2.0	17 19		51	19	0.6	05 23
16	11 56		261	26	4.1	15 02		244	23	1.5	16 10		231	19	2.0	17 02		51	19	0.6	05 04
21	11 57		255	25	4.2	15 06		241	22	1.6	16 03		230	19	2.0	16 45		51	19	0.5	04 44
26	11 57		250	25	4.2	15 10		238	22	1.6	15 56		229	19	1.9	16 28		51	19	0.5	04 24
31	11 58	WA	244	N24	−4.2	15 13	WA	235	N21	+1.6	15 48	WA	229	N19	−1.9	16 12	MB	51	S19	+0.5	04 04
Jun 5	11 58		238	23	4.2	15 15		232	20	1.6	15 41		228	19	1.9	15 55	WB	51	19	0.5	03 44
10	11 59		233	22	4.3	15 16		229	19	1.7	15 33		227	18	1.9	15 39		51	19	0.4	03 24
15	12 00		228	20	4.3	15 16		226	19	1.7	15 25		226	18	1.8	15 23		51	19	0.4	03 03
20	12 01		224	19	4.3	15 15		223	18	1.7	15 18		225	18	1.8	15 07		52	19	0.4	02 42
25	12 02	WA	219	N17	−4.4	15 12	WA	220	N17	+1.7	15 10	WA	224	N18	−1.8	14 51	WB	52	S19	+0.3	02 22
30	12 04		215	15	4.4	15 08	WA	217	16	1.7	15 02	WA	223	17	1.8	14 35	V	52	19	0.3	02 01
Jul 5	12 04		212	13	4.4	15 02		214	15	1.8	14 54	Wa	222	17	1.8	14 20		52	19	0.3	01 40
10	12 05		209	11	4.5	14 54		211	14	1.8	14 46		221	17	1.8	14 04		53	20	0.2	01 19
15	12 06	WA	206	10	4.5	14 44	WA	208	13	1.8	14 38		220	16	1.8	13 48		53	20	0.2	00 58
20	12 06	Wa	204	N 8	−4.5	14 32	Wa	205	N11	+1.8	14 30	Wa	219	N16	−1.8	13 33	V	54	S20	+0.2	00 37
25	12 06		203	7	4.5	14 17		202	10	1.8	14 22		218	16	1.7	13 17		54	20	0.1	00 15
30	12 06		203	5	4.4	13 59		199	9	1.8	14 14	Wa	217	15	1.7	13 02		54	20	0.1	23 50
Aug 4	12 06		203	4	4.4	13 37		196	8	1.8	14 06	☉	216	15	1.7	12 47		55	20	0.2	23 29
9	12 06	Wa	204	4	4.3	13 12		193	7	1.8	13 58		215	15	1.7	12 31		55	20	0.2	23 08
14	12 05	☉	206	N 3	−4.2	12 43	Wa	190	N 5	+1.8	13 50	☉	214	N14	−1.7	12 16	V	55	S20	+0.2	22 47
19	12 04		209	4	4.0	12 13		187	4	1.8	13 42		213	14	1.7	12 00		56	20	0.2	22 26
24	12 02	☉	212	4	4.0	11 41		185	3	1.8	13 34		212	14	1.7	11 45	V	56	20	0.3	22 05
29	12 01	Eb	215	5	4.1	11 10		182	N 2	1.8	13 26		211	13	1.7	11 29	EA	56	20	0.3	21 44
Sep 3	11 59		217	6	4.2	10 42		179	0	1.8	13 18	☉	210	13	1.7	11 14		57	20	0.3	21 23
8	11 58	Eb	218	N 7	−4.4	10 18	Wa	176	S 1	+1.8	13 10	Eb	208	N13	−1.7	10 58	EA	57	S20	+0.3	21 03
13	11 56		219	8	4.5	09 57		173	2	1.7	13 02		207	12	1.7	10 43	EA	57	21	0.4	20 42
18	11 54		218	9	4.5	09 40		170	4	1.7	12 54		206	12	1.7	10 27	MA	57	21	0.4	20 22
23	11 53	Eb	217	9	4.5	09 27	Wa	167	5	1.7	12 47		205	11	1.8	10 11		57	21	0.4	20 02
28	11 51	EB	214	9	4.6	09 17	☉	164	6	1.7	12 39		204	11	1.8	09 56		57	21	0.4	19 42
Oct 3	11 49	EB	212	N 9	−4.5	09 09	☉	161	S 8	+1.7	12 32	Eb	204	N11	−1.8	09 40	MA	57	S21	+0.5	19 22

PLANET PLANNING DATA — PHASES OF THE MOON, 1991

Date	SUN Mer Pass		VENUS					MARS					JUPITER					SATURN			
		Sym bol	SHA	Dec	Mag	Mer Pass	Sym bol	SHA	Dec	Mag	Mer Pass	Sym bol	SHA	Dec	Mag	Mer Pass	Sym bol	SHA	Dec	Mag	Mer Pass
	h m		°	°		h m		°	°		h m		°	°		h m		°	°		h m
Oct 3	11 49	EB	212	N 9	−4.5	09 09	⊙	161	S 8	+1.7	12 32	Eb	204	N11	−1.8	09 40	MA	57	S21	+0.5	19 22
8	11 48		208	9	4.5	09 02		158	9	1.6	12 24	Eb	203	10	1.8	09 24		57	21	0.5	19 02
13	11 46		204	8	4.5	08 58		154	10	1.6	12 17	EB	202	10	1.8	09 08		57	21	0.5	18 43
18	11 45		200	7	4.5	08 55		151	11	1.6	12 11		201	10	1.8	08 51	MA	57	21	0.5	18 24
23	11 44		196	6	4.5	08 52		148	13	1.6	12 04		200	9	1.8	08 35	WA	57	21	0.6	18 05
28	11 44	EB	191	N 5	−4.4	08 51	⊙	145	S14	+1.5	11 57	EB	199	N 9	−1.9	08 19	WA	57	S21	+0.6	17 46
Nov 2	11 44		187	3	4.4	08 50		141	15	1.5	11 51		198	9	1.9	08 02		57	21	0.6	17 27
7	11 44		182	N 2	4.4	08 50		138	16	1.5	11 45		198	9	1.9	07 45		57	20	0.6	17 08
12	11 44		177	0	4.3	08 50		134	17	1.5	11 39		197	8	1.9	07 28		56	20	0.6	16 50
17	11 45		172	S 2	4.3	08 51		131	18	1.5	11 33		196	8	2.0	07 11		56	20	0.6	16 32
22	11 46	EB	167	S 4	−4.3	08 52	⊙	127	S19	+1.5	11 28	EB	196	N 8	−2.0	06 53	WA	56	S20	+0.6	16 13
27	11 47		161	6	4.3	08 53		124	20	1.5	11 23		195	8	2.0	06 36		55	20	0.6	15 55
Dec 2	11 49		156	8	4.2	08 55		120	21	1.5	11 18		195	8	2.0	06 18		55	20	0.7	15 37
7	11 51		151	10	4.2	08 57		116	21	1.5	11 13	EB	195	7	2.1	06 00		54	20	0.7	15 20
12	11 54		145	12	4.2	09 00	⊙	113	22	1.5	11 09	MB	194	7	2.1	05 41		54	20	0.7	15 02
17	11 56	EB	139	S13	−4.2	09 03	Eb	109	S23	+1.5	11 05	MB	194	N 7	−2.1	05 23	WA	53	S20	+0.7	14 44
22	11 58		133	15	4.1	09 07		105	23	1.4	11 00		194	7	2.2	05 04	Wa	53	20	0.7	14 27
27	12 01		127	17	4.1	09 11		101	23	1.4	10 57		194	7	2.2	04 44		52	20	0.7	14 09
32	12 03	EB	121	S18	−4.1	09 16	Eb	97	S24	+1.4	10 53	MB	194	N 7	−2.2	04 25	Wa	52	S19	+0.7	13 52

The symbols indicate the position of the planet as follows:

⊙ Too close to the Sun for observation.
Eb Low in the east before sunrise.
EB Well placed in the east before sunrise.
MB Well placed near the meridian before sunrise.
WB Well placed in the west before sunrise.
V Visible all night or most of the night, in the east after sunset or in the west before sunrise.

Wa Low in the west after sunset.
WA Well placed in the west after sunset.
MA Well placed near the meridian after sunset.
EA Well placed in the east after sunset.

PLANET NOTES 1991

The approximate SHA and Dec of the planets as tabulated above can be used for plotting the positions of the planets on a star chart, or for determining their positions amongst the stars in a star list.

Venus, the most brilliant of the planets, is an evening object until mid-August when it becomes too close to the Sun for observation, and thereafter is in the morning sky for the remainder of the year. Conjunction with Mars on June 23 and July 22, with Jupiter on June 17 and October 17, with Saturn on January 1 and with Mercury on August 7 and 29.

Mars is an evening object until the end of September when it becomes too close to the Sun for observation, reappearing as a morning object in late December. Conjunction with Venus on June 23 and July 22 and with Jupiter on June 14.

Jupiter is initially visible for most of the night, coming to opposition on January 29, and is thereafter an evening object until early August when it becomes too close to the Sun for observation, reappearing at the beginning of September as a morning object for the remainder of the year. Conjunction with Venus on June 17 and October 17, with Mars on June 14, and with Mercury on July 15 and September 10.

Saturn is too close to the Sun for observation until it appears as a morning object in early February, moving to opposition on July 27 when it is visible all night, and is thereafter an evening object. Conjunction with Venus on January 1 and with Mercury on February 5.

Do not confuse — Mercury with Saturn around the end of the first week of February when Mercury is the brighter.
Venus with Saturn on January 1, with Mars in June and July, with Jupiter towards the end of June and mid-October, with Mercury in early August; on all occasions Venus is the brighter object.
Jupiter with Mars in June and with Mercury in mid-July and early September; on all occasions Jupiter is the brighter object.

PHASES OF THE MOON

New Moon				First Quarter				Full Moon				Last Quarter			
	d	h	m		d	h	m		d	h	m		d	h	m
												Jan	7	18	35
Jan	15	23	50	Jan	23	14	21	Jan	30	06	10	Feb	6	13	52
Feb	14	17	32	Feb	21	22	58	Feb	28	18	25	Mar	8	10	32
Mar	16	08	10	Mar	23	06	03	Mar	30	07	17	Apr	7	06	45
Apr	14	19	38	Apr	21	12	39	Apr	28	20	58	May	7	00	46
May	14	04	36	May	20	19	46	May	28	11	37	Jun	5	15	30
Jun	12	12	06	Jun	19	04	19	Jun	27	02	58	Jul	5	02	50
Jul	11	19	06	Jul	18	15	11	Jul	26	18	24	Aug	3	11	25
Aug	10	02	28	Aug	17	05	01	Aug	25	09	07	Sep	1	18	16
Sep	8	11	01	Sep	15	22	01	Sep	23	22	40	Oct	1	00	30
Oct	7	21	39	Oct	15	17	33	Oct	23	11	08	Oct	30	07	10
Nov	6	11	11	Nov	14	14	02	Nov	21	22	56	Nov	28	15	21
Dec	6	03	56	Dec	14	09	32	Dec	21	10	23	Dec	28	01	55

ECLIPSES

1. Annular eclipse of the Sun, January 15–16. Not visible in Europe.

2. Total eclipse of the Sun, July 11. Not visible in Europe.

3. Partial eclipse of the Moon, December 21. In Europe, northern Scandinavia only.

5

5.3.6   SUNRISE, SUNSET AND TWILIGHT — 1991

Date	Naut Twi	ν	Sun-rise	ν	Sun-set	Civil Twi	ν	Date	Naut Twi	ν	Sun-rise	ν	Sun-set	Civil Twi	ν
	h m		h m		h m	h m			h m		h m		m	h m	
Jan 1	06 39	+39	07 59	+63−	16 08	16 47	−50	Jul 3	02 08	−114	03 56	−67+	20 12	20 56	+83
4	06 39	38	07 58	62	16 12	16 50	49	6	02 11	113	03 58	66	20 11	20 54	82
7	06 39	38	07 57	61	16 15	16 53	49	9	02 16	110	04 01	65	20 09	20 52	81
10	06 38	37	07 56	59	16 19	16 56	48	12	02 20	107	04 04	63	20 07	20 49	78
13	06 37	35	07 54	57	16 23	17 00	46	15	02 25	104	04 07	62	20 04	20 46	76
16	06 35	+33	07 52	+55−	16 27	17 04	−45	18	02 31	−100	04 10	−60+	20 01	20 43	+75
19	06 33	32	07 50	54	16 32	17 08	43	21	02 36	97	04 14	58	19 58	20 39	72
22	06 31	30	07 47	52	16 37	17 13	41	24	02 42	94	04 18	56	19 55	20 35	70
25	06 28	28	07 43	49	16 42	17 17	39	27	02 48	90	04 22	54	19 51	20 30	67
28	06 25	26	07 40	47	16 47	17 22	37	30	02 54	86	04 26	52	19 46	20 25	64
31	06 22	+25	07 36	+44−	16 52	17 27	−34	Aug 2	03 00	−82	04 30	−49+	19 42	20 20	+61
Feb 3	06 18	22	07 31	42	16 57	17 31	32	5	03 06	78	04 34	47	19 37	20 15	59
6	06 14	20	07 27	39	17 02	17 36	30	8	03 13	74	04 38	44	19 32	20 09	55
9	06 10	18	07 22	37	17 07	17 41	27	11	03 19	70	04 43	42	19 27	20 03	52
12	06 05	15	07 17	34	17 12	17 46	25	14	03 25	66	04 47	39	19 21	19 57	49
15	06 00	+12	07 12	+31−	17 17	17 51	−22	17	03 31	−62	04 52	−36+	19 16	19 51	+46
18	05 55	10	07 06	28	17 23	17 56	19	20	03 36	59	04 56	33	19 10	19 45	44
21	05 50	7	07 00	25	17 28	18 01	16	23	03 42	55	05 01	31	19 04	19 39	41
24	05 44	4	06 55	22	17 33	18 06	13	26	03 48	52	05 05	28	18 58	19 32	37
27	05 39	+2	06 49	20	17 38	18 10	11	29	03 53	49	05 10	25	18 52	19 25	34
Mar 2	05 33	−1	06 42	+17−	17 43	18 15	−8	Sep 1	03 59	−44	05 14	−22+	18 45	19 19	+31
5	05 27	4	06 36	14	17 48	18 20	5	4	04 04	41	05 18	19	18 39	19 12	28
8	05 20	7	06 30	11	17 53	18 25	−2	7	04 10	37	05 23	17	18 32	19 05	25
11	05 14	10	06 24	8	17 58	18 30	+1	10	04 15	34	05 27	14	18 26	18 59	23
14	05 07	13	06 17	5	18 02	18 35	4	13	04 20	31	05 32	11	18 19	18 52	19
17	05 01	−16	06 11	+2−	18 07	18 39	+6	16	04 25	−28	05 36	−8+	18 13	18 45	+16
20	04 54	19	06 04	−1+	18 12	18 44	9	19	04 30	24	05 41	5	18 06	18 38	13
23	04 47	22	05 58	4	18 17	18 49	12	22	04 35	21	05 45	−2+	17 59	18 32	11
26	04 40	26	05 51	7	18 22	18 54	15	25	04 40	18	05 50	0	17 53	18 25	8
29	04 33	29	05 45	9	18 26	18 59	18	28	04 44	16	05 54	+3−	17 46	18 18	4
Apr 1	04 26	−32	05 38	−12+	18 31	19 04	+22	Oct 1	04 49	−12	05 59	+6−	17 40	18 12	+2
4	04 19	35	05 32	15	18 36	19 09	25	4	04 54	9	06 04	9	17 33	18 05	−1
7	04 12	38	05 25	18	18 40	19 14	28	7	04 59	6	06 08	12	17 27	17 59	4
10	04 05	42	05 19	21	18 45	19 19	31	10	05 03	−4	06 13	15	17 20	17 53	6
13	03 57	46	05 13	24	18 50	19 24	34	13	05 08	0	06 18	18	17 14	17 47	9
16	03 50	−49	05 06	−27+	18 54	19 29	+37	16	05 12	+2	06 23	+21−	17 08	17 41	−12
19	03 43	53	05 00	30	18 59	19 34	40	19	05 17	5	06 27	23	17 02	17 35	15
22	03 36	56	04 54	32	19 04	19 39	43	22	05 22	8	06 32	26	16 56	17 29	18
25	03 29	60	04 49	35	19 09	19 44	46	25	05 26	10	06 37	29	16 50	17 24	20
28	03 21	64	04 43	38	19 13	19 49	49	28	05 31	13	06 42	32	16 45	17 18	23
May 1	03 14	−68	04 37	−41+	19 18	19 54	+52	31	05 35	+15	06 47	+35−	16 40	17 13	−26
4	03 08	71	04 32	43	19 22	20 00	56	Nov 3	05 40	18	06 52	37	16 34	17 09	28
7	03 01	75	04 27	46	19 27	20 05	58	6	05 44	20	06 57	40	16 30	17 04	31
10	02 54	80	04 22	48	19 31	20 10	61	9	05 48	22	07 02	42	16 25	17 00	33
13	02 48	83	04 18	51	19 36	20 15	64	12	05 53	25	07 07	45	16 21	16 56	35
16	02 41	−88	04 14	−53+	19 40	20 20	+67	15	05 57	+27	07 12	+47−	16 17	16 52	−38
19	02 35	92	04 10	55	19 44	20 24	69	18	06 01	28	07 17	50	16 13	16 49	39
22	02 30	95	04 06	57	19 48	20 29	72	21	06 05	30	07 21	52	16 10	16 46	41
25	02 24	99	04 03	59	19 52	20 33	74	24	06 09	32	07 26	54	16 07	16 43	44
28	02 19	102	04 00	61	19 55	20 38	77	27	06 13	34	07 30	56	16 04	16 41	45
31	02 15	−105	03 57	−63+	19 59	20 41	+78	30	06 17	+35	07 35	+58−	16 02	16 39	−47
Jun 3	02 11	108	03 55	64	20 02	20 45	81	Dec 3	06 20	36	07 39	59	16 00	16 38	48
6	02 07	111	03 53	66	20 05	20 48	82	6	06 23	37	07 42	61	15 59	16 37	49
9	02 04	114	03 52	67	20 07	20 51	84	9	06 26	38	07 46	62	15 58	16 36	51
12	02 02	116	03 51	68	20 09	20 53	84	12	06 29	39	07 49	63	15 58	16 36	51
15	02 01	−117	03 50	−68+	20 11	20 55	+85	15	06 32	+40	07 52	+64−	15 58	16 36	−52
18	02 00	118	03 50	69	20 12	20 57	86	18	06 34	40	07 54	64	15 59	16 37	52
21	02 00	118	03 50	69	20 13	20 58	86	21	06 36	41	07 56	64	16 00	16 39	52
24	02 01	118	03 51	69	20 13	20 58	86	24	06 37	40	07 57	64	16 02	16 40	52
27	02 03	117	03 52	68	20 13	20 58	86	27	06 38	40	07 58	64	16 04	16 42	52
30	02 05	−116	03 54	−68+	20 13	20 57	+84	30	06 39	+40	07 59	+63−	16 06	16 45	−51
Jul 3	02 08	−114	03 56	−67+	20 12	20 56	+83	Jan 2	06 39	+39	07 59	+63−	16 09	16 47	−51

SUNRISE, SUNSET AND TWILIGHT — 1991

Corrections to Sunrise or Sunset

N.Lat	30°	35°	40°	45°	50°	52°	54°	56°	58°	60°
v	m	m	m	m	m	m	m	m	m	m
0	0	0	0	0	0	0	0	0	0	0
2	− 2	− 1	− 1	0	0	+ 1	+ 1	+ 1	+ 2	+ 2
4	4	3	2	− 1	0	1	1	1	2	3
6	6	5	3	2	0	1	2	3	4	5
8	8	6	5	2	0	1	2	3	5	6
10	−10	− 8	− 6	− 3	0	+ 1	+ 3	+ 4	+ 6	+ 8
12	12	10	7	4	0	2	4	6	8	10
14	14	11	8	5	0	2	4	6	9	12
16	16	13	9	5	0	2	5	8	11	14
18	18	14	10	6	0	2	5	9	12	16
20	−20	−16	−11	− 6	0	+ 3	+ 6	+10	+14	+18
22	22	17	12	7	0	3	7	11	15	20
24	24	19	14	8	0	3	7	12	16	22
26	26	21	15	8	0	4	8	13	18	24
28	28	22	16	9	0	4	9	14	19	26
30	−30	−24	−17	− 9	0	+ 5	+10	+15	+21	+28
32	32	26	19	10	0	5	10	16	22	30
34	34	27	20	10	0	5	11	17	24	32
36	36	29	21	11	0	5	11	17	25	33
38	38	31	22	12	0	5	11	18	26	35
40	−40	−32	−23	−13	0	+ 6	+12	+20	+28	+37
42	42	34	24	13	0	6	13	21	30	40
44	44	36	26	14	0	6	13	22	31	42
46	46	37	27	15	0	7	14	23	33	44
48	48	39	28	15	0	7	15	25	35	46
50	−50	−40	−29	−16	0	+ 7	+16	+26	+36	+48
52	52	42	30	16	0	8	17	27	38	51
54	54	43	31	17	0	8	17	27	39	53
56	56	45	33	18	0	8	17	28	40	55
58	58	47	34	19	0	9	18	30	42	57
60	−60	−48	−35	−20	0	+ 9	+19	+31	+45	+61
62	62	50	37	21	0	9	20	32	47	64
64	64	52	38	21	0	10	21	34	49	67
66	66	53	39	21	0	11	22	35	51	70
68	68	55	41	22	0	11	23	37	54	73
70	−70	−57	−42	−23	0	+11	+24	+38	+56	+76

Corrections to Nautical Twilight

N. Lat	30°	35°	40°	45°	50°	52°	54°	56°	58°	60°
v	m	m	m	m	m	m	m	m	m	m
+ 40	−40	−31	−22	−12	0	+ 5	+11	+17	+23	+30
30	30	23	16	9	0	3	7	12	16	21
20	20	15	10	6	0	2	4	7	10	13
+ 10	−10	− 7	− 5	− 2	0	+ 1	+ 2	+ 3	+ 4	+ 5
0	0	+ 1	+ 1	0	0	0	− 1	− 2	− 3	− 5
− 10	+10	+ 8	+ 6	+ 4	0	− 2	− 4	− 6	− 9	−13
20	20	17	13	7	0	3	7	12	17	23
30	30	25	19	11	0	4	10	16	24	32
40	40	33	24	14	0	6	14	22	32	44
50	50	41	30	17	0	9	18	29	42	58
− 60	+60	+49	+37	+21	0	−11	−22	−36	−53	−74
70	70	58	43	24	0	13	27	45	67	96
80	80	66	50	29	0	14	32	53	83	−134
90	90	75	56	32	0	18	39	68	−118	TAN
100	100	84	63	37	0	20	46	−87	TAN	TAN
−110	+110	+92	+70	+41	0	−25	−60	TAN	TAN	TAN
−120	+120	+100	+78	+46	0	−29	−83	TAN	TAN	TAN

Corrections to Civil Twilight

N. Lat	30°	35°	40°	45°	50°	52°	54°	56°	58°	60°
v	m	m	m	m	m	m	m	m	m	m
−50	+50	+40	+29	+16	0	− 7	−15	−23	−33	−44
40	40	32	22	12	0	6	12	19	26	35
30	30	24	17	10	0	4	8	13	18	24
20	20	16	11	7	0	3	6	9	12	16
−10	+10	+ 8	+ 5	+ 3	0	− 1	− 3	− 4	− 5	− 7
0	0	0	0	0	0	0	0	+ 1	+ 1	+ 2
+10	−10	− 8	− 6	− 4	0	+ 1	+ 3	5	8	11
20	20	16	12	7	0	3	7	11	15	20
30	30	24	18	10	0	5	10	16	22	30
40	40	32	24	13	0	6	13	21	30	41
+50	−50	−41	−30	−16	0	+ 8	+17	+27	+39	+53
60	60	49	36	20	0	9	20	33	47	65
70	70	57	42	23	0	12	25	41	60	85
80	80	65	48	27	0	14	30	50	75	111
83	83	68	50	28	0	15	32	52	80	121
+86	−86	−71	−52	−30	0	+15	+33	+55	+85	+135

The times given on the opposite page are the local mean times (LMT) of nautical twilight, sunrise, sunset and civil twilight for latitude N.50°, together with variations v. The variations are the differences in time between the times for latitude N.50° and those for latitude N.30°. The sign on the left-hand side of v (between sunrise and sunset) applies to sunrise, and the right-hand sign applies to sunset. The LMT for any latitude from N.30° to N.60° can be found by applying corrections, taken from the tables above, to the tabulated times.

To determine the LMT of sunrise or sunset, take out the tabulated time and v corresponding to the required date and, using v and latitude as arguments in the table of "Corrections to Sunrise or Sunset", extract the correction and apply it to the tabulated time as follows. If v is positive, apply the correction with the sign as tabulated. If v is negative, apply the correction with the opposite sign to that which is tabulated.

To determine LMT of nautical twilight the correction to the tabulated time must be taken from the table of "Corrections to Nautical Twilight" using as argument latitude and v; in entering the correction table the correct sign of v must be used, and in applying the correction to the tabulated time its sign must be used as given in the table. When TAN (Twilight All Night) is given, the Sun does not reach a zenith distance of 102°.

The corrections to civil twilight must be found in the same manner as those for nautical twilight.

LMT can be converted to UT by adding the longitude (in time) if west or subtracting if east.

Examples of the use of these tables are given on page 72.

5.3.7 — MOONRISE AND MOONSET — 1991

Date	JANUARY Rise	v	JANUARY Set	v	MARCH Rise	v	MARCH Set	v	MAY Rise	v	MAY Set	v	JULY Rise	v	JULY Set	v
	h m		h m		h m		h m		h m		h m		h m		h m	
1	17 08	−63	08 40	+67	19 02	+4	06 38	+4	22 38	+78	05 28	−75	22 09	+18	08 20	−27
2	18 36	46	09 13	52	20 18	20	06 54	−12	23 28	77	06 13	78	22 25	+5	09 29	−13
3	20 01	28	09 37	35	21 33	35	07 11	26	24 07	71	07 07	77	22 41	−8	10 39	+2
4	21 21	−12	09 57	19	22 47	50	07 30	41	00 07	71	08 09	69	22 58	23	11 50	16
5	22 37	+4	10 14	+4	23 59	64	07 52	54	00 39	62	09 15	59	23 18	37	13 05	31
6	23 50	+19	10 29	−11	25 06	+74	08 19	−66	01 03	+49	10 24	−45	23 43	−51	14 24	+48
7	25 02	34	10 45	25	01 06	74	08 53	75	01 24	37	11 34	32	24 15	66	15 45	62
8	01 02	34	11 03	39	02 06	79	09 36	80	01 42	23	12 45	17			17 04	73
9	02 13	49	11 23	52	02 58	80	10 28	79	01 58	+9	13 57	−2	01 01	75	18 17	78
10	03 22	61	11 48	64	03 39	74	11 29	73	02 15	−5	15 12	+13	02 02	78	19 16	74
11	04 29	+72	12 19	−75	04 12	+65	12 36	−62	02 32	−20	16 31	+29	03 18	−72	20 01	+63
12	05 31	80	13 00	80	04 39	54	13 47	49	02 53	35	17 54	46	04 44	59	20 35	48
13	06 24	81	13 50	80	05 00	40	14 59	35	03 19	50	19 19	61	06 13	42	21 00	31
14	07 08	77	14 50	75	05 18	25	16 12	20	03 52	65	20 42	74	07 39	25	21 21	+15
15	07 43	69	15 56	65	05 35	+11	17 27	−4	04 38	76	21 55	78	09 01	−8	21 39	−1
16	08 10	+56	17 07	−52	05 51	−4	18 43	+12	05 39	−78	22 54	+74	10 20	+8	21 57	−15
17	08 32	43	18 18	38	06 08	19	20 02	28	06 54	72	23 38	64	11 36	24	22 15	30
18	08 50	29	19 30	24	06 28	34	21 23	45	08 16	60	24 10	49	12 50	39	22 35	44
19	09 06	+15	20 43	−8	06 51	50	22 45	60	09 40	44	00 10	49	14 02	52	22 59	57
20	09 21	0	21 56	+7	07 21	64	24 05	72	11 01	28	00 34	34	15 12	64	23 28	68
21	09 37	−14	23 11	+23	08 02	−75	00 05	+72	12 19	−12	00 54	+19	16 17	+73	24 05	−75
22	09 54	30	24 29	39	08 56	79	01 18	79	13 34	+4	01 12	+4	17 15	78	00 05	75
23	10 15	45	00 29	39	10 03	76	02 18	78	14 47	18	01 28	−11	18 04	77	00 51	78
24	10 42	59	01 50	55	11 20	66	03 03	69	15 59	33	01 45	25	18 43	71	01 45	76
25	11 18	72	03 12	69	12 42	51	03 38	57	17 11	47	02 04	38	19 14	61	02 47	68
26	12 08	−80	04 30	+79	14 03	−36	04 04	+42	18 22	+60	02 26	−51	19 39	+49	03 53	−58
27	13 14	80	05 37	80	15 23	19	04 24	25	19 29	70	02 53	63	19 59	36	05 02	45
28	14 34	70	06 29	73	16 41	−3	04 43	+11	20 30	76	03 27	72	20 17	23	06 11	31
29	16 01	55	07 08	60	17 57	+13	04 59	−5	21 23	78	04 09	77	20 33	+9	07 20	17
30	17 27	39	07 36	44	19 12	28	05 16	20	22 06	74	05 00	77	20 49	−4	08 29	−3
31	18 51	−21	07 59	+28	20 26	+43	05 34	−34	22 40	+65	06 00	−71	21 05	−18	09 40	+12

Date	FEBRUARY Rise	v	FEBRUARY Set	v	APRIL Rise	v	APRIL Set	v	JUNE Rise	v	JUNE Set	v	AUGUST Rise	v	AUGUST Set	v
1	20 11	−4	08 17	+12	21 39	+57	05 55	−48	23 06	+53	07 05	−61	21 23	−33	10 53	+27
2	21 28	+12	08 34	−4	22 49	69	06 20	61	23 28	41	08 12	50	21 46	46	12 08	41
3	22 43	28	08 50	19	23 53	77	06 51	71	23 46	28	09 21	36	22 14	60	13 26	56
4	23 56	43	09 07	33	24 48	79	07 31	77	24 03	14	10 30	22	22 52	72	14 44	69
5	25 07	56	09 26	48	00 48	79	08 19	79	00 03	14	11 40	−8	23 44	78	15 58	76
6	01 07	+56	09 50	−60	01 34	+77	09 17	−75	00 19	+1	12 52	+7	24 52	−75	17 02	+77
7	02 16	68	10 19	71	02 10	69	10 21	66	00 35	−14	14 07	22	00 52	75	17 52	69
8	03 20	77	10 56	78	02 39	58	11 29	54	00 54	28	15 25	38	02 12	66	18 30	55
9	04 17	81	11 42	81	03 02	45	12 40	40	01 16	44	16 48	54	03 39	51	19 00	40
10	05 05	79	12 39	77	03 21	31	13 52	26	01 45	58	18 12	68	05 07	34	19 23	24
11	05 43	+72	13 43	−69	03 39	+18	15 05	−11	02 25	−70	19 31	+77	06 32	−17	19 43	+8
12	06 13	61	14 52	58	03 55	+3	16 20	+5	03 18	78	20 38	77	07 54	0	20 01	−8
13	06 36	48	16 04	44	04 12	−12	17 38	21	04 28	76	21 30	69	09 13	+16	20 20	23
14	06 56	34	17 17	29	04 31	27	18 59	37	05 50	66	22 08	56	10 31	33	20 39	38
15	07 13	20	18 31	−13	04 53	43	20 23	53	07 17	51	22 36	40	11 46	47	21 02	52
16	07 29	+5	19 45	+3	05 22	−58	21 47	+68	08 42	−34	22 58	+24	12 58	+60	21 30	−63
17	07 45	−9	21 00	18	05 59	71	23 05	77	10 04	17	23 17	+8	14 06	70	22 04	72
18	08 02	24	22 18	34	06 50	78	24 11	79	11 22	−1	23 35	−6	15 07	76	22 46	78
19	08 22	39	23 38	50	07 55	77	00 11	79	12 37	+14	23 52	20	16 00	78	23 38	77
20	08 46	55	24 59	65	09 10	69	01 01	71	13 50	29	24 10	34	16 42	73	24 37	71
21	09 18	−69	00 59	+65	10 31	−56	01 39	+59	15 02	+43	00 10	−34	17 16	+64	00 37	−71
22	10 02	78	02 17	76	11 53	39	02 07	44	16 13	56	00 31	48	17 43	53	01 42	62
23	11 00	81	03 26	81	13 12	23	02 30	30	17 21	68	00 56	60	18 05	41	02 50	50
24	12 12	75	04 22	77	14 28	−8	02 48	+14	18 24	75	01 27	70	18 24	28	03 59	36
25	13 34	62	05 04	66	15 43	+8	03 05	0	19 19	78	02 06	77	18 41	14	05 09	22
26	14 59	−46	05 36	+51	16 57	+23	03 22	−14	20 05	+75	02 55	−78	18 57	+1	06 19	−8
27	16 22	30	06 00	35	18 10	38	03 39	29	20 42	68	03 52	74	19 13	−14	07 30	+7
28	17 43	−13	06 20	+19	19 23	52	03 59	42	21 10	57	04 56	65	19 31	28	08 43	22
29					20 33	64	04 22	56	21 33	45	06 03	53	19 52	42	09 57	36
30					21 39	+73	04 51	−67	21 53	+32	07 11	−41	20 18	56	11 14	51
31													20 52	−68	12 31	+64

MOONRISE AND MOONSET — 1991

Date	SEPTEMBER Rise	v	Set	v	NOVEMBER Rise	v	Set	v
	h m		h m		h m		h m	
1	21 38	−75	13 46	+75	00 50	−20	14 13	+11
2	22 38	76	14 51	77	02 08	− 4	14 31	− 4
3	23 51	70	15 45	72	03 25	+12	14 50	18
4	25 12	58	16 27	62	04 41	27	15 10	32
5	01 12	58	16 59	47	05 56	41	15 33	46
6	02 38	−41	17 24	+31	07 10	+55	16 00	−59
7	04 03	25	17 45	+15	08 21	66	16 34	69
8	05 25	− 9	18 04	− 1	09 25	73	17 17	74
9	06 46	+ 8	18 23	16	10 21	75	18 07	75
10	08 05	24	18 43	30	11 06	71	19 06	70
11	09 23	+40	19 05	−44	11 42	+64	20 09	−62
12	10 38	54	19 31	57	12 10	53	21 15	50
13	11 49	65	20 03	68	12 33	41	22 23	37
14	12 55	74	20 42	75	12 53	29	23 30	24
15	13 51	77	21 31	76	13 10	16	24 38	11
16	14 38	+75	22 27	−73	13 27	+ 3	00 38	−11
17	15 15	67	23 30	65	13 44	−10	01 48	+ 4
18	15 45	58	24 37	53	14 02	25	03 00	18
19	16 09	46	00 37	53	14 24	39	04 15	33
20	16 29	33	01 45	41	14 51	53	05 34	48
21	16 46	+19	02 55	−27	15 27	−65	06 55	+62
22	17 03	+ 6	04 05	−13	16 15	73	08 13	72
23	17 20	− 8	05 16	+ 2	17 18	74	09 22	75
24	17 37	23	06 29	17	18 32	68	10 18	70
25	17 58	37	07 44	31	19 54	56	11 00	59
26	18 23	−51	09 01	+46	21 18	−40	11 32	+45
27	18 55	64	10 20	61	22 39	24	11 57	30
28	19 37	73	11 35	71	23 58	− 8	12 19	+16
29	20 33	76	12 44	76	25 15	+ 8	12 37	0
30	21 40	−72	13 41	+74	01 15	+ 8	12 56	−14

Date	OCTOBER Rise	v	Set	v	DECEMBER Rise	v	Set	v
1	22 58	−61	14 25	+65	02 30	+23	13 15	−28
2	24 19	48	14 59	51	03 44	37	13 37	41
3	00 19	48	15 26	37	04 57	50	14 02	54
4	01 42	31	15 48	21	06 08	62	14 33	65
5	03 03	−15	16 08	+ 7	07 14	70	15 12	77
6	04 23	+ 2	16 27	− 8	08 13	+75	16 00	−75
7	05 41	17	16 46	23	09 02	73	16 56	72
8	06 59	33	17 07	38	09 41	67	17 58	64
9	08 15	47	17 31	52	10 12	59	19 03	54
10	09 29	60	18 01	63	10 37	46	20 10	42
11	10 38	+70	18 38	−72	10 57	+34	21 17	−29
12	11 39	75	19 23	76	11 15	21	22 23	16
13	12 30	75	20 17	74	11 31	+ 8	23 31	− 2
14	13 11	70	21 17	68	11 48	− 4	24 40	+12
15	13 44	61	22 22	58	12 05	18	00 40	12
16	14 10	+50	23 30	−45	12 24	−32	01 52	+27
17	14 31	37	24 38	33	12 48	46	03 07	41
18	14 50	24	00 38	33	13 18	59	04 25	55
19	15 07	+11	01 47	19	14 00	69	05 44	67
20	15 24	− 2	02 57	− 5	14 55	74	06 58	74
21	15 41	−17	04 09	+10	16 05	−72	08 02	+73
22	16 01	31	05 24	25	17 27	62	08 52	65
23	16 25	45	06 41	40	18 54	46	09 30	51
24	16 55	59	08 01	55	20 20	30	09 59	36
25	17 35	70	09 20	67	21 43	−13	10 23	21
26	18 27	−75	10 33	+74	23 02	+ 2	10 43	+ 5
27	19 33	73	11 35	74	24 19	18	11 02	− 9
28	20 48	64	12 24	67	00 19	18	11 21	24
29	22 09	51	13 01	55	01 34	32	11 42	38
30	23 30	36	13 30	41	02 48	47	12 06	51
31	24 50	−20	13 53	+26	03 59	+59	12 35	−62

Corrections to Moonrise or Moonset

N Lat / v	30°	35°	40°	45°	50°	52°	54°	56°	58°	60°
	m	m	m	m	m	m	m	m	m	m
0	0	0	0	0	0	0	0	0	0	0
2	− 2	− 1	− 1	0	0	0	+ 1	+ 1	+ 2	+ 2
4	4	3	2	− 1	0	0	1	2	3	3
6	6	5	3	2	0	+ 1	2	3	4	5
8	8	6	5	2	0	1	2	3	5	6
10	−10	− 8	− 6	− 3	0	+ 1	+ 3	+ 4	+ 6	+ 8
12	12	10	7	4	0	2	4	5	8	10
14	14	11	8	5	0	2	4	6	9	12
16	16	13	9	5	0	2	5	8	11	14
18	18	14	10	6	0	2	5	9	12	16
20	−20	−16	−11	− 6	0	+ 3	+ 6	+10	+14	+18
22	22	17	12	7	0	3	7	11	15	20
24	24	19	14	8	0	3	7	12	16	22
26	26	21	15	8	0	4	8	13	18	24
28	28	22	16	9	0	4	9	14	19	26
30	−30	−24	−17	− 9	0	+ 5	+10	+15	+21	+28
32	32	26	19	10	0	5	10	16	22	30
34	34	27	20	10	0	5	11	17	24	32
36	36	29	21	11	0	5	11	17	25	33
38	38	31	22	12	0	5	11	18	26	35
40	−40	−32	−23	−13	0	+ 6	+12	+20	+28	+37
42	42	34	24	13	0	6	13	21	30	40
44	44	36	26	14	0	6	13	22	31	42
46	46	37	27	15	0	7	14	23	33	44
48	48	39	28	15	0	7	15	25	35	46
50	−50	−40	−29	−16	0	+ 7	+16	+26	+36	+48
52	52	42	30	16	0	8	17	27	38	51
54	54	43	31	17	0	8	17	27	39	53
56	56	45	33	18	0	8	17	28	40	55
58	58	47	34	19	0	9	18	30	42	57
60	−60	−48	−35	−20	0	+ 9	+19	+31	+45	+61
62	62	50	37	21	0	9	20	32	47	64
64	64	52	38	21	0	10	21	34	49	67
66	66	53	39	21	0	11	22	35	51	70
68	68	55	41	22	0	11	23	37	54	73
70	−70	−57	−42	−23	0	+11	+24	+38	+56	+76
72	72	58	43	24	0	12	25	40	58	80
74	74	60	44	24	0	12	26	41	60	84
76	76	62	45	25	0	12	27	43	62	87
78	78	63	46	26	0	12	27	44	64	90
80	−80	−65	−48	−27	0	+12	+27	+45	+67	+94
82	82	67	49	28	0	13	28	47	70	100
84	84	68	50	28	0	14	30	49	73	106
86	86	70	51	29	0	14	31	50	76	112
88	88	72	53	30	0	15	32	52	80	119
90	−90	−73	−54	−30	0	+16	+33	+55	+84	+127

The times given on the opposite page and alongside are the Local Mean Times (LMT) of moonrise and moonset for latitude N.50° and their variations v from the times for N.30°.

To find the times for any latitude between N.30° and N.60°, enter the table with arguments latitude and v, and apply the correction found to the tabulated time, *using the tabulated sign of the correction if v is positive, and the opposite sign of the correction if v is negative.* A very small extra correction due to the daily difference of the times has a mean value of +3ᵐ in longitude W.20° and −3ᵐ in longitude E.20°.

The LMT can be converted to UT by adding the longitude (in time) if west or subtracting if east.

Examples of the use of this table are given on page 72.

5.3.8 — 1991 JANUARY, FEBRUARY — ARIES AND PLANETS

0ʰ UT	ARIES GHA	VENUS GHA	v	Dec	d	MARS GHA	v	Dec	d	JUPITER GHA	v	Dec	d	SATURN GHA	v	Dec	d
Jan								**JANUARY**									
1	100 08.9	163 15.2	−21	S22 26.9	+13	45 13.7	+59	N21 56.3	+ 1	325 30.3	+65	N17 51.3	+ 2	162 28.8	+52	S21 09.2	+ 1
2	101 08.0	162 54.0	21	22 14.4	13	46 13.1	58	21 56.8	1	326 35.3	65	17 53.1	2	163 20.6	52	21 08.0	1
3	102 07.2	162 33.3	21	22 01.2	14	47 11.5	58	21 57.4	1	327 40.5	65	17 55.0	2	164 12.3	52	21 06.7	1
4	103 06.4	162 12.7	20	21 47.4	14	48 09.2	57	21 58.1	1	328 45.8	65	17 56.9	2	165 04.1	52	21 05.5	1
5	104 05.5	161 52.4	20	21 33.0	15	49 06.0	56	21 58.9	1	329 51.2	66	17 58.9	2	165 55.8	52	21 04.3	1
6	105 04.6	161 32.4	−20	S21 17.9	+16	50 02.1	+55	N21 59.9	+ 1	330 56.9	+66	N18 00.8	+ 2	166 47.5	+52	S21 03.0	+ 1
7	106 03.8	161 12.8	19	21 02.2	16	50 57.4	55	22 01.0	1	332 02.6	66	18 02.8	2	167 39.2	52	21 01.7	1
8	107 02.9	160 53.4	19	20 45.9	17	51 51.9	54	22 02.3	1	333 08.3	66	18 04.8	2	168 30.9	52	21 00.4	1
9	108 02.0	160 34.2	19	20 29.0	18	52 45.7	53	22 03.7	2	334 14.4	66	18 06.9	2	169 22.6	52	20 59.2	1
10	109 01.2	160 15.5	19	20 11.4	18	53 38.7	52	22 05.2	2	335 20.5	66	18 08.9	2	170 14.2	52	20 57.9	1
11	110 00.3	159 57.0	−18	S19 53.3	+19	54 31.0	+52	N22 06.8	+ 2	336 26.7	+66	N18 11.0	+ 2	171 05.9	+52	S20 56.6	+ 1
12	110 59.5	159 38.9	18	19 34.6	19	55 22.6	51	22 08.5	2	337 33.0	66	18 13.2	2	171 57.5	52	20 55.3	1
13	111 58.6	159 21.0	18	19 15.3	20	56 13.4	50	22 10.4	·2	338 39.4	67	18 15.3	2	172 49.2	52	20 54.0	1
14	112 57.7	159 03.5	17	18 55.5	20	57 03.6	50	22 12.4	2	339 45.9	67	18 17.5	2	173 40.9	52	20 52.7	1
15	113 56.9	158 46.3	17	18 35.1	21	57 53.1	49	22 14.4	2	340 52.5	67	18 19.7	2	174 32.5	52	20 51.4	1
16	114 56.0	158 29.4	−17	S18 14.3	+21	58 41.9	+48	N22 16.6	+ 2	341 59.2	+67	N18 21.8	+ 2	175 24.1	+52	S20 50.0	+ 1
17	115 55.1	158 12.9	16	17 52.9	22	59 30.0	48	22 18.8	2	343 06.0	67	18 24.1	2	176 15.8	52	20 48.7	1
18	116 54.3	157 56.7	16	17 31.0	22	60 17.5	47	22 21.2	3	344 12.8	67	18 26.3	2	177 07.4	52	20 47.3	1
19	117 53.4	157 40.9	16	17 08.6	23	61 04.4	46	22 23.7	3	345 19.7	67	18 28.5	2	177 59.0	52	20 46.0	1
20	118 52.6	157 25.4	15	16 45.7	23	61 50.6	46	22 26.3	3	346 26.7	67	18 30.7	2	178 50.6	52	20 44.6	1
21	119 51.7	157 10.2	−15	S16 22.4	+24	62 36.2	+45	N22 28.9	+ 3	347 33.7	+67	N18 32.9	+ 2	179 42.3	+52	S20 43.3	+ 1
22	120 50.8	156 55.3	15	15 58.6	24	63 21.2	45	22 31.7	3	348 40.9	67	18 35.2	2	180 34.0	52	20 41.9	1
23	121 50.0	156 40.7	14	15 34.5	25	64 05.7	44	22 34.4	3	349 47.9	67	18 37.4	2	181 25.6	52	20 40.6	1
24	122 49.1	156 26.5	14	15 09.8	25	64 49.5	43	22 37.3	3	350 55.1	67	18 39.7	2	182 17.3	52	20 39.2	1
25	123 48.2	156 12.6	14	14 44.8	26	65 32.8	43	22 40.3	3	352 02.3	67	18 41.9	2	183 08.9	52	20 37.9	1
26	124 47.4	155 59.0	−13	S14 19.3	+26	66 15.6	+42	N22 43.3	+ 3	353 09.6	+67	N18 44.2	+ 2	184 00.7	+52	S20 36.5	+ 1
27	125 46.6	155 45.7	13	13 53.5	26	66 57.8	42	22 46.4	3	354 16.9	67	18 46.4	2	184 52.3	52	20 35.1	1
28	126 45.7	155 32.7	13	13 27.3	27	67 39.5	41	22 49.6	3	355 24.1	67	18 48.7	2	185 44.0	52	20 33.7	1
29	127 44.8	155 20.0	12	13 00.7	27	68 20.7	41	22 52.7	3	356 31.4	67	18 50.9	2	186 35.8	52	20 32.3	1
30	128 44.0	155 07.7	12	12 33.9	27	69 01.4	40	22 56.0	3	357 38.7	67	18 53.0	2	187 27.5	52	20 31.0	1
31	129 43.1	154 55.5	−12	S12 06.6	+28	69 41.7	+40	N22 59.2	+ 3	358 46.0	+67	N18 55.3	+ 2	188 19.3	+52	S20 29.6	+ 1
Feb								**FEBRUARY**									
1	130 42.2	154 43.7	−12	S11 39.1	+28	70 21.4	+39	N23 02.6	+ 3	359 53.2	+67	N18 57.5	+ 2	189 11.0	+52	S20 28.2	+ 1
2	131 41.4	154 32.1	11	11 11.2	28	71 00.7	39	23 05.9	3	1 00.5	67	18 59.6	2	190 02.8	52	20 26.8	1
3	132 40.5	154 20.8	11	10 43.1	28	71 39.5	38	23 09.3	3	2 07.7	67	19 01.8	2	190 54.6	52	20 25.4	1
4	133 39.7	154 09.8	11	10 14.7	29	72 17.9	38	23 12.7	3	3 14.9	67	19 04.0	2	191 46.4	52	20 24.0	1
5	134 38.8	153 59.0	11	9 46.0	29	72 55.9	38	23 16.2	3	4 22.1	67	19 06.1	2	192 38.3	52	20 22.6	1
6	135 37.9	153 48.4	−10	S 9 17.1	+29	73 33.4	+37	N23 19.6	+ 4	5 29.3	+67	N19 08.2	+ 2	193 30.2	+52	S20 21.2	+ 1
7	136 37.1	153 38.1	10	8 47.8	29	74 10.5	37	23 23.1	4	6 36.4	67	19 10.3	2	194 22.1	52	20 19.9	1
8	137 36.2	153 27.9	10	8 18.4	30	74 47.2	36	23 26.6	4	7 43.4	67	19 12.3	2	195 14.0	52	20 18.4	1
9	138 35.3	153 18.0	10	7 48.8	30	75 23.5	36	23 30.1	4	8 50.4	67	19 14.3	2	196 05.9	52	20 17.0	1
10	139 34.5	153 08.3	10	7 19.0	30	75 59.4	36	23 33.6	4	9 57.4	67	19 16.4	2	196 57.9	52	20 15.7	1
11	140 33.6	152 58.8	− 9	S 6 49.0	+30	76 34.9	+35	N23 37.1	+ 4	11 04.2	+67	N19 18.4	+ 2	197 49.9	+52	S20 14.3	+ 1
12	141 32.8	152 49.5	9	6 18.7	30	77 10.1	35	23 40.6	4	12 11.0	67	19 20.3	2	198 41.9	52	20.12.9	1
13	142 31.9	152 40.4	9	5 48.4	31	77 44.9	34	23 44.1	4	13 17.7	67	19 22.3	2	199 34.0	52	20 11.5	1
14	143 31.0	152 31.4	9	5 17.9	31	78 19.3	34	23 47.6	4	14 24.4	66	19 24.1	2	200 26.1	52	20 10.1	1
15	144 30.2	152 22.6	9	4 47.2	31	78 53.4	34	23 51.1	3	15 30.8	66	19 26.0	2	201 18.2	52	20 08.7	1
16	145 29.3	152 13.9	− 9	S 4 16.4	+31	79 27.1	+33	N23 54.5	+ 3	16 37.3	+66	N19 27.8	+ 2	202 10.4	+52	S20 07.3	+ 1
17	146 28.4	152 05.3	8	3 45.5	31	80 00.4	33	23 57.9	3	17 43.6	66	19 29.6	2	203 02.6	52	20 06.0	1
18	147 27.6	151 56.9	8	3 14.6	31	80 33.5	33	24 01.3	3	18 49.9	66	19 31.4	2	203 54.9	52	20 04.6	1
19	148 26.8	151 48.6	8	2 43.5	31	81 06.2	32	24 04.7	3	19 56.0	66	19 33.2	2	204 47.2	52	20 03.2	1
20	149 25.9	151 40.4	8	2 12.4	31	81 38.6	32	24 08.0	3	21 02.0	66	19 34.9	2	205 39.5	52	20 01.9	1
21	150 25.0	151 32.3	− 8	S 1 41.1	+31	82 10.6	+32	N24 11.3	+ 3	22 07.9	+66	N19 36.5	+ 2	206 31.9	+52	S20.00.5	+ 1
22	151 24.2	151 24.2	8	1 09.8	31	82 42.4	32	24 14.6	3	23 13.6	66	19 38.2	2	207 24.2	53	19 59.2	1
23	152 23.3	151 16.3	8	0 38.5	31	83 13.9	31	24 17.8	3	24 19.3	65	19 39.7	2	208 16.7	53	19 57.8	1
24	153 22.4	151 08.5	8	S 0 07.2	31	83 45.1	31	24 20.9	3	25 24.7	65	19 41.3	2	209 09.2	53	19 56.5	1
25	154 21.6	151 00.6	8	N 0 24.1	31	84 16.0	31	24 24.1	3	26 30.1	65	19 42.8	1	210 01.7	53	19 55.1	1
26	155 20.7	150 52.9	− 8	N 0 55.5	+31	84 46.6	+30	N24 27.2	+ 3	27 35.3	+65	N19 44.2	+ 1	210 54.3	+53	S19 53.8	+ 1
27	156 19.9	150 45.1	8	1 26.8	31	85 17.0	30	24 30.2	3	28 40.4	65	19 45.7	1	211 46.9	53	19 52.4	1
28	157 19.0	150 37.4	− 8	N 1 58.1	+31	85 47.1	+30	N24 33.1	+ 3	29 45.3	+65	N19 47.0	+ 1	212 39.6	+53	S19 51.1	+ 1

1991 JANUARY, FEBRUARY — SUN AND MOON

0ʰ UT	SUN GHA	v	Dec	d	MOON 0ʰ–8ʰ GHA	v	Dec	d	8ʰ–16ʰ GHA	v	Dec	d	16ʰ–24ʰ GHA	v	Dec	d	HP
Jan	(SD 16'.3)						JANUARY										
1	179 12.6	– 7	S23 03.7	+ 5	355 37	57	N24 08	– 62	110 34	64	N23 06	– 73	225 38	71	N21 53	– 82	60.9
2	179 05.5	7	22 58.8	5	340 49	79	20 31	91	96 08	87	19 00	97	211 35	96	17 23	104	60.3
3	178 58.6	7	22 53.6	6	327 11	102	15 39	108	82 53	110	13 51	112	198 43	117	11 59	116	59.5
4	178 51.7	7	22 47.8	6	314 40	123	10 03	117	70 43	128	8 06	118	186 51	133	6 08	120	58.5
5	178 44.8	7	22 41.5	7	303 04	137	N 4 08	118	59 21	140	N 2 10	119	175 41	144	N 0 11	117	57.5
6	178 38.1	– 7	S22 34.9	+ 7	292 05	145	S 1 46	–115	48 30	147	S 3 41	–112	164 57	148	S 5 33	–111	56.6
7	178 31.5	7	22 27.8	8	281 25	149	7 24	107	37 54	148	9 11	103	154 22	148	10 54	100	55.8
8	178 25.0	6	22 20.2	8	270 50	146	12 34	96	27 16	145	14 10	91	143 41	144	15 41	87	55.1
9	178 18.6	6	22 12.2	8	260 05	141	17 08	81	16 26	138	18 29	76	132 44	136	19 45	70	54.6
10	178 12.4	6	22 03.8	9	249 00	134	20 55	64	5 14	130	21 59	58	121 24	128	22 57	51	54.3
11	178 06.2	– 6	S21 54.9	+ 9	237 32	125	S23 48	– 44	353 37	123	S24 32	– 37	109 40	120	S25 09	– 29	54.1
12	178 00.3	6	21 45.6	10	225 40	119	25 38	– 22	341 39	117	26 00	– 14	97 36	116	26 14	– 6	54.0
13	177 54.4	6	21 36.0	10	213 32	115	26 20	+ 3	329 27	116	26 17	+ 10	85 23	116	26 07	+ 18	54.1
14	177 48.8	6	21 25.8	11	201 19	117	25 49	27	317 16	118	25 22	34	73 14	121	24 48	42	54.2
15	177 43.3	5	21 15.3	11	189 15	122	24 06	49	305 17	125	23 17	56	61 22	128	22 21	63	54.5
16	177 37.9	– 5	S21 04.3	+11	177 30	130	S21 18	+ 69	293 40	134	S20 09	+ 76	49 54	136	S18 53	+ 81	54.8
17	177 32.7	5	20 52.9	12	166 10	138	17 32	87	282 28	142	16 05	91	38 50	143	14 34	96	55.2
18	177 27.7	5	20 41.2	12	155 13	146	12 58	99	271 39	147	11 19	104	28 06	149	9 35	106	55.6
19	177 22.8	5	20 29.1	13	144 35	149	7 49	109	261 04	150	6 00	111	17 34	149	S 4 09	113	56.1
20	177 18.2	4	20 16.5	13	134 03	149	S 2 16	114	250 32	148	S 0 22	115	7 00	146	N 1 33	115	56.6
21	177 13.8	– 4	S20 03.6	+13	123 26	143	N 3 28	+115	239 49	140	N 5 23	+113	356 09	137	N 7 16	+113	57.2
22	177 09.5	4	19 50.4	14	112 26	133	9 09	111	228 39	128	11 00	108	344 47	122	12 48	104	57.8
23	177 05.4	4	19 36.7	14	100 49	116	14 32	101	216 45	110	16 13	96	332 35	104	17 49	90	58.4
24	177 01.5	4	19 22.7	14	88 19	96	19 19	84	203 55	89	20 43	76	319 24	82	21 59	68	59.1
25	176 57.9	4	19 08.3	15	74 46	75	23 07	60	190 01	69	24 07	49	305 10	62	24 56	38	59.7
26	176 54.4	– 3	S18 53.6	+15	60 12	58	N25 34	+ 27	175 10	55	N26 01	+ 16	290 05	51	N26 17	+ 3	60.2
27	176 51.1	3	18 38.5	15	44 56	51	26 20	– 10	159 47	51	26 10	– 22	274 38	53	25 48	– 34	60.5
28	176 48.0	3	18 23.1	16	29 31	57	25 14	46	144 28	60	24 28	58	259 28	65	23 30	68	60.6
29	176 45.2	3	18 07.3	16	14 33	72	22 22	78	129 45	78	21 04	87	245 03	84	19 37	95	60.4
30	176 42.5	2	17 51.3	16	0 27	92	18 02	101	115 59	98	16 21	107	231 37	104	14 34	112	60.0
31	176 40.1	– 2	S17 34.9	+17	347 21	111	N12 42	–116	103 12	116	N10 46	–119	219 08	121	N 8 47	–120	59.3
Feb	(SD 16'.2)						FEBRUARY										
1	176 37.8	– 2	S17 18.2	+17	335 09	126	N 6 47	–122	91 15	130	N 4 45	–122	207 25	133	N 2 43	–121	58.5
2	176 35.8	2	17 01.2	17	323 38	137	N 0 42	121	79 55	138	S 1 19	118	196 13	140	S 3 17	117	57.7
3	176 33.9	2	16 43.9	18	312 33	142	S 5 14	114	68 55	141	7 08	110	185 16	142	8 58	107	56.8
4	176 32.3	1	16 26.3	18	301 38	142	10 45	102	58 00	141	12 27	99	174 21	140	14 06	93	56.0
5	176 30.9	1	16 08.4	18	290 41	138	15 39	88	46 59	137	17 07	83	163 16	134	18 30	77	55.3
6	176 29.6	– 1	S15 50.2	+18	279 30	133	S19 47	– 71	35 43	130	S20 58	– 64	151 53	128	S22 02	– 58	54.7
7	176 28.5	1	15 31.8	19	268 01	126	23 00	51	24 07	123	23 51	43	140 10	122	24 34	37	54.4
8	176 27.7	1	15 13.1	19	256 12	119	25 11	28	12 11	118	25 39	– 21	128 09	117	26 00	– 13	54.2
9	176 27.1	– 1	14 54.2	19	244 06	117	26 13	– 5	0 03	116	26 18	+ 3	115 59	116	26 15	+ 11	54.1
10	176 26.6	0	14 34.9	19	231 55	116	26 04	+ 19	347 51	118	25 45	27	103 49	119	25 18	34	54.3
11	176 26.3	0	S14 15.5	+20	219 48	120	S24 44	+ 42	335 48	123	S24 02	+ 50	91 51	125	S23 12	+ 57	54.5
12	176 26.3	0	13 55.8	20	207 56	127	22 15	64	324 03	129	21 11	70	80 12	132	20 01	76	54.9
13	176 26.4	0	13 35.9	20	196 24	135	18 45	83	312 39	136	17 23	88	68 55	140	15 55	93	55.3
14	176 26.7	+ 1	13 15.7	20	185 15	140	14 22	97	301 35	143	12 45	101	57 58	144	11 04	105	55.8
15	176 27.2	1	12 55.4	21	174 22	145	9 19	108	290 47	146	7 31	111	47 13	146	S 5 40	113	56.3
16	176 27.8	+ 1	S12 34.8	+21	163 39	145	S 3 47	+115	280 04	145	S 1 52	+116	36 29	143	N 0 04	+116	56.8
17	176 28.7	1	12 14.1	21	152 52	142	N 2 00	117	269 14	140	N 3 57	115	25 34	136	5 52	115	57.3
18	176 29.8	1	11 53.1	21	141 50	133	7 47	113	258 03	130	9 40	110	14 13	125	11 30	107	57.7
19	176 30.9	1	11 31.9	21	130 18	120	13 17	104	246 18	115	15 01	99	2 13	109	16 40	93	58.2
20	176 32.3	2	11 10.6	22	118 02	103	18 13	87	233 45	98	19 40	81	349 23	91	21 01	73	58.6
21	176 33.8	+ 2	S10 49.1	+22	104 54	85	N22 14	+ 64	220 19	80	N23 18	+ 56	335 39	75	N24 14	+ 45	58.9
22	176 35.6	2	10 27.4	22	90 54	70	24 59	36	206 04	67	25 35	+ 24	321 11	64	25 59	+ 13	59.2
23	176 37.4	2	10 05.6	22	76 15	62	26 12	+ 2	191 17	62	26 14	– 10	306 19	62	26 04	– 22	59.5
24	176 39.5	2	9 43.6	22	61 21	64	25 42	– 33	176 25	67	25 09	44	291 32	71	24 25	55	59.6
25	176 41.6	2	9 21.4	22	46 43	75	23 30	65	161 58	80	22 25	74	277 18	86	21 11	83	59.6
26	176 44.0	+ 3	S 8 59.2	+23	32 44	91	N19 48	– 90	148 15	97	N18 18	– 98	263 52	102	N16 40	–103	59.5
27	176 46.5	3	8 36.7	23	19 34	108	14 57	109	135 22	113	13 08	113	251 15	117	11 15	116	59.2
28	176 49.1	+ 3	S 8 14.2	+23	7 12	122	N 9 19	–118	123 14	126	N 7 21	–121	239 20	129	N 5 20	–121	58.7

1991 MARCH, APRIL — ARIES AND PLANETS

0h UT	ARIES GHA	VENUS GHA	v	Dec	d	MARS GHA	v	Dec	d	JUPITER GHA	v	Dec	d	SATURN GHA	v	Dec	d
Mar									**MARCH**								
1	158 18.1	150 29.7	8	N 2 29.4	+31	86 16.9	+30	N24 36.0	+ 3	30 50.0	+65	N19 48.4	+ 1	213 32.3	+53	S19 49.8	+ 1
2	159 17.3	150 22.0	8	3 00.6	31	86 46.5	29	24 38.9	3	31 54.7	64	19 49.7	1	214 25.1	53	19 48.5	1
3	160 16.4	150 14.3	8	3 31.8	31	87 15.9	29	24 41.6	3	32 59.1	64	19 50.9	1	215 17.9	53	19 47.2	1
4	161 15.5	150 06.6	8	4 02.9	31	87 45.0	29	24 44.3	3	34 03.4	64	19 52.1	1	216 10.8	53	19 45.9	1
5	162 14.7	149 58.9	8	4 33.9	31	88 13.9	29	24 47.0	3	35 07.4	64	19 53.3	1	217 03.7	53	19 44.6	1
6	163 13.8	149 51.1	8	N 5 04.8	+31	88 42.6	+29	N24 49.5	+ 3	36 11.4	+64	N19 54.4	+ 1	217 56.7	+53	S19 43.3	+ 1
7	164 13.0	149 43.3	8	5 35.6	31	89 11.1	28	24 52.0	2	37 15.2	64	19 55.5	1	218 49.7	53	19 42.1	1
8	165 12.1	149 35.4	8	6 06.3	31	89 39.3	28	24 54.4	2	38 18.8	63	19 56.5	1	219 42.8	53	19 40.8	1
9	166 11.2	149 27.4	8	6 36.8	31	90 07.3	28	24 56.7	2	39 22.1	63	19 57.5	1	220 36.0	53	19 39.5	1
10	167 10.4	149 19.4	8	7 07.3	30	90 35.1	28	24 58.9	2	40 25.4	63	19 58.4	1	221 29.2	53	19 38.3	1
11	168 09.5	149 11.3	8	N 7 37.5	+30	91 02.7	+27	N25 01.1	+ 2	41 28.5	+63	N19 59.3	+ 1	222 22.4	+53	S19 37.1	+ 1
12	169 08.6	149 03.1	8	8 07.6	30	91 30.1	27	25 03.1	2	42 31.3	63	20 00.2	1	223 15.8	53	19 35.9	1
13	170 07.8	148 54.8	9	8 37.5	30	91 57.3	27	25 05.1	2	43 34.0	63	20 01.0	1	224 09.2	53	19 34.6	1
14	171 07.0	148 46.3	9	9 07.3	30	92 24.3	27	25 07.0	2	44 36.6	62	20 01.7	1	225 02.6	54	19 33.4	1
15	172 06.1	148 37.8	9	9 36.8	29	92 51.1	27	25 08.7	2	45 38.8	62	20 02.5	1	225 56.2	54	19 32.3	1
16	173 05.2	148 29.1	9	N10 06.1	+29	93 17.8	+26	N25 10.4	+ 2	46 40.9	+62	N20 03.1	+ 1	226 49.7	+54	S19 31.1	+ 1
17	174 04.4	148 20.3	9	10 35.2	29	93 44.2	26	25 11.9	2	47 42.9	62	20 03.7	1	227 43.4	54	19 29.9	1
18	175 03.5	148 11.4	9	11 04.0	29	94 10.5	26	25 13.4	1	48 44.6	62	20 04.3	1	228 37.1	54	19 28.8	1
19	176 02.6	148 02.2	9	11 32.5	28	94 36.6	26	25 14.8	1	49 46.2	61	20 04.8	+ 1	229 30.9	54	19 27.7	1
20	177 01.7	147 52.9	10	12 00.9	28	95 02.5	26	25 16.1	1	50 47.5	61	20 05.3	0	230 24.7	54	19 26.5	1
21	178 00.9	147 43.4	10	N12 28.9	+28	95 28.3	+26	N25 17.2	+ 1	51 48.7	+61	N20 05.7	0	231 18.7	+54	S19 25.4	+ 1
22	179 00.1	147 33.9	10	12 56.7	27	95 53.9	26	25 18.2	1	52 49.6	61	20 06.1	0	232 12.7	54	19 24.4	1
23	179 59.2	147 24.1	10	13 24.1	27	96 19.4	25	25 19.2	1	53 50.4	61	20 06.4	0	233 06.7	54	19 23.3	1
24	180 58.3	147 14.1	10	13 51.2	27	96 44.7	25	25 20.0	1	54 50.9	60	20 06.7	0	234 00.8	54	19 22.2	1
25	181 57.5	147 04.0	10	14 18.0	27	97 09.9	25	25 20.7	1	55 51.2	60	20 07.0	0	234 55.1	54	19 21.1	1
26	182 56.6	146 53.6	11	N14 44.5	+26	97 34.9	+25	N25 21.2	+ 1	56 51.4	+60	N20 07.1	0	235 49.3	+54	S19 20.1	+ 1
27	183 55.7	146 43.1	11	15 10.6	26	97 59.9	25	25 21.7	0	57 51.3	60	20 07.3	0	236 43.7	54	19 19.1	1
28	184 54.9	146 32.4	11	15 36.3	25	98 24.7	25	25 22.1	0	58 51.1	60	20 07.4	0	237 38.2	54	19 18.1	1
29	185 54.0	146 21.4	11	16 01.7	25	98 49.3	25	25 22.3	0	59 50.6	59	20 07.4	0	238 32.6	55	19 17.1	1
30	186 53.2	146 10.3	11	16 26.7	25	99 13.9	24	25 22.4	0	60 50.0	59	20 07.4	0	239 27.2	55	19 16.1	1
31	187 52.3	145 58.9	12	N16 51.3	+24	99 38.3	+24	N25 22.4	0	61 49.2	+59	N20 07.4	0	240 21.9	+55	S19 15.2	+ 1
Apr									**APRIL**								
1	188 51.4	145 47.3	12	N17 15.4	+24	100 02.6	+24	N25 22.3	0	62 48.1	+59	N20 07.3	0	241 16.6	+55	S19 14.3	+ 1
2	189 50.6	145 35.5	12	17 39.2	23	100 26.8	24	25 22.0	0	63 46.9	59	20 07.2	0	242 11.5	55	19 13.4	1
3	190 49.7	145 23.5	12	18 02.5	23	100 50.9	24	25 21.5	0	64 45.4	58	20 07.0	0	243 06.4	55	19 12.5	1
4	191 48.8	145 11.3	13	18 25.4	22	101 14.9	24	25 21.1	– 1	65 43.8	58	20 06.8	0	244 01.4	55	19 11.6	1
5	192 48.0	144 58.8	13	18 47.8	22	101 38.8	24	25 20.4	1	66 42.0	58	20 06.5	0	244 56.5	55	19 10.7	1
6	193 47.1	144 46.2	13	N19 09.8	+21	102 02.6	+24	N25 19.6	– 1	67 40.0	+58	N20 06.2	0	245 51.6	+55	S19 09.9	+ 1
7	194 46.3	144 33.3	13	19 31.2	21	102 26.3	24	25 18.7	1	68 37.8	58	20 05.9	0	246 46.8	55	19 09.1	1
8	195 45.4	144 20.1	13	19 52.2	21	102 49.9	24	25 17.6	1	69 35.4	57	20 05.5	0	247 42.1	56	19 08.2	1
9	196 44.5	144 06.8	14	20 12.8	20	103 13.4	24	25 16.4	1	70 32.8	57	20 05.0	0	248 37.6	56	19 07.4	1
10	197 43.7	143 53.2	14	20 32.7	20	103 36.9	23	25 15.1	2	71 30.0	57	20 04.6	0	249 33.1	56	19 06.7	1
11	198 42.8	143 39.5	14	N20 52.2	+19	104 00.2	+23	N25 13.6	– 2	72 27.0	+57	N20 04.1	– 1	250 28.6	+56	S19 05.9	+ 1
12	199 41.9	143 25.5	14	21 11.1	19	104 23.5	23	25 12.0	2	73 23.8	57	20 03.5	1	251 24.3	56	19 05.2	1
13	200 41.1	143 11.4	14	21 29.6	18	104 46.7	23	25 10.3	2	74 20.5	56	20 02.9	1	252 20.0	56	19 04.5	1
14	201 40.3	142 57.0	15	21 47.4	17	105 09.8	23	25 08.4	2	75 16.9	56	20 02.2	1	253 15.9	56	19 03.8	1
15	202 39.4	142 42.4	15	22 04.7	17	105 32.9	23	25 06.4	2	76 13.2	56	20 01.5	1	254 11.8	56	19 03.1	1
16	203 38.5	142 27.6	15	N22 21.4	+16	105 55.9	+23	N25 04.3	– 2	77 09.2	+56	N20 00.8	– 1	255 07.9	+56	S19 02.5	+ 1
17	204 37.7	142 12.7	15	22 37.5	16	106 18.8	23	25 01.9	2	78 05.2	56	19 59.9	1	256 04.0	56	19 01.9	1
18	205 36.8	141 57.5	15	22 53.1	15	106 41.6	23	24 59.5	3	79 00.9	56	19 59.2	1	257 00.2	56	19 01.3	1
19	206 35.9	141 42.3	15	23 08.1	14	107 04.4	23	24 56.9	3	79 56.5	55	19 58.3	1	257 56.5	56	19 00.7	1
20	207 35.1	141 26.9	15	23 22.4	14	107 27.2	23	24 54.2	3	80 51.9	55	19 57.4	1	258 52.9	56	19 00.1	1
21	208 34.2	141 11.3	16	N23 36.2	+13	107 49.9	+23	N24 51.4	– 3	81 47.1	+55	N19 56.4	– 1	259 49.3	+57	S18 59.6	+ 1
22	209 33.4	140 55.7	16	23 49.3	13	108 12.5	23	24 48.4	3	82 42.1	55	19 55.4	1	260 45.9	57	18 59.1	1
23	210 32.5	140 39.9	16	24 01.8	12	108 35.1	23	24 45.2	3	83 36.9	55	19 54.4	1	261 42.6	57	18 58.6	+ 1
24	211 31.6	140 24.0	16	24 13.7	11	108 57.7	23	24 41.9	4	84 31.6	54	19 53.3	1	262 39.4	57	18 58.1	0
25	212 30.8	140 08.0	16	24 24.9	11	109 20.2	23	24 38.5	4	85 26.0	54	19 52.1	1	263 36.2	57	18 57.7	0
26	213 29.9	139 52.0	16	N24 35.6	+10	109 42.7	+23	N24 34.9	– 4	86 20.4	+54	N19 51.0	– 1	264 33.2	+57	S18 57.2	0
27	214 29.0	139 35.9	16	24 45.5	9	110 05.2	22	24 31.2	4	87 14.6	54	19 49.8	1	265 30.2	57	18 56.9	0
28	215 28.2	139 19.7	16	24 54.8	9	110 27.6	22	24 27.3	4	88 08.6	54	19 48.5	1	266 27.4	57	18 56.5	0
29	216 27.3	139 03.5	16	25 03.5	8	110 50.0	22	24 23.3	4	89 02.5	54	19 47.2	1	267 24.7	57	18 56.2	0
30	217 26.5	138 47.3	–16	N25 11.4	+ 7	111 12.4	+22	N24 19.1	– 4	89 56.1	+54	N19 45.9	– 1	268 22.0	+57	S18 55.8	0

1991 MARCH, APRIL — SUN AND MOON

0h UT	SUN				MOON 0h–8h				MOON 8h–16h				MOON 16h–24h				HP
	GHA	v	Dec	d	GHA	v	Dec	d	GHA	v	Dec	d	GHA	v	Dec	d	
Mar	(SD 16'.1)						MARCH										
1	176 51.9 + 3		S 7 51.5	+23	355 29	131	N 3 19	−121	111 40	135	N 1 18	−121	227 55	135	S 0 43	−120	58.1
2	176 54.8	3	7 28.8	23	344 10	137	S 2 43	117	100 27	138	S 4 40	116	216 45	138	6 36	112	57.4
3	176 57.8	3	7 05.9	23	333 03	138	8 28	109	89 21	138	10 17	105	205 39	137	12 02	100	56.6
4	177 01.0	3	6 43.0	23	321 56	135	13 42	96	78 11	134	15 18	90	194 25	132	16 48	85	55.9
5	177 04.3	3	6 19.9	23	310 37	131	18 13	78	66 48	128	19 31	73	182 56	127	20 44	65	55.3
6	177 07.6 + 4		S 5 56.7	+23	299 03	124	S 21 49	− 59	55 07	123	S 22 48	− 52	171 10	120	S 23 40	− 44	54.8
7	177 11.1	4	5 33.5	23	287 10	120	24 24	37	43 10	117	25 01	29	159 07	117	25 30	− 21	54.4
8	177 14.6	4	5 10.1	23	275 04	117	25 51	− 13	31 01	116	26 04	− 5	146 57	116	26 09	+ 3	54.3
9	177 18.4	4	4 46.7	23	262 53	117	26 06	+ 11	18 50	117	25 55	+ 19	134 47	119	25 36	26	54.3
10	177 22.1	4	4 23.3	23	250 46	120	25 10	34	6 46	122	24 36	42	122 48	124	23 54	49	54.4
11	177 25.9 + 4		S 3 59.8	+24	238 52	126	S 23 05	+ 56	354 58	129	S 22 09	+ 63	111 07	130	S 21 06	+ 69	54.7
12	177 29.8	4	3 36.2	24	227 17	133	19 57	75	343 30	135	18 42	81	99 45	137	17 21	87	55.2
13	177 33.8	4	3 12.7	24	216 02	139	15 54	92	332 21	141	14 22	96	88 42	141	12 46	101	55.8
14	177 37.9	4	2 49.0	24	205 03	143	11 05	105	321 26	143	9 20	108	77 49	143	7 32	111	56.4
15	177 41.9	4	2 25.3	24	194 12	142	S 5 41	114	310 34	142	S 3 47	116	66 56	141	S 1 51	116	57.0
16	177 46.1 + 4		S 2 01.6	+24	183 17	139	N 0 05	+118	299 36	137	N 2 03	+118	55 53	134	N 4 01	+118	57.6
17	177 50.4	4	1 37.9	24	172 07	130	5 59	116	288 17	127	7 55	114	44 24	123	9 49	112	58.2
18	177 54.7	4	1 14.2	24	160 27	118	11 41	108	276 25	113	13 29	104	32 18	107	15 13	100	58.6
19	177 59.0	4	0 50.5	24	148 05	102	16 53	93	263 47	97	18 26	87	19 24	91	19 53	79	58.9
20	178 03.4	4	0 26.7	24	134 55	85	21 12	71	250 20	80	22 23	62	5 40	75	23 25	53	59.1
21	178 07.8 + 5		S 0 03.0	+24	120 55	72	N 24 18	+ 42	236 07	68	N 25 00	+ 32	351 15	66	N 25 32	+ 20	59.3
22	178 12.3	5	N 0 20.8	24	106 21	65	25 52	+ 9	221 26	64	26 01	− 2	336 30	65	25 59	− 13	59.3
23	178 16.8	5	0 44.4	24	91 35	67	25 46	− 25	206 42	71	25 21	36	321 53	73	24 45	46	59.2
24	178 21.3	5	1 08.1	24	77 06	79	23 59	56	192 25	83	23 03	65	307 48	88	21 58	73	59.1
25	178 25.8	5	1 31.7	24	63 16	94	20 45	82	178 50	100	19 23	89	294 30	105	17 54	95	58.9
26	178 30.4 + 5		N 1 55.3	+24	50 15	110	N 16 19	−100	166 05	115	N 14 39	−106	282 00	120	N 12 53	−109	58.6
27	178 34.9	5	2 18.8	24	38 00	124	11 04	112	154 04	128	9 12	115	270 12	131	7 17	117	58.2
28	178 39.5	5	2 42.3	24	26 23	133	N 5 20	118	142 36	136	N 3 22	118	258 52	137	N 1 24	118	57.8
29	178 44.0	5	3 05.8	23	15 09	139	S 0 34	118	131 28	139	S 2 32	115	247 47	139	S 4 27	114	57.3
30	178 48.6	5	3 29.2	23	4 06	139	6 21	111	120 25	139	8 12	108	236 44	138	10 00	105	56.7
31	178 53.2 + 5		N 3 52.4	+23	353 02	136	S 11 45	−100	109 18	134	S 13 25	− 96	225 32	133	S 15 01	− 90	56.1
Apr	(SD 16'.0)						APRIL										
1	178 57.7 + 5		N 4 15.7	+23	341 45	131	S 16 31	− 85	97 56	129	S 17 56	− 79	214 05	126	S 19 15	− 73	55.6
2	179 02.2	5	4 38.9	23	330 11	124	20 28	66	86 15	123	21 34	59	202 18	120	22 33	52	55.1
3	179 06.7	4	5 01.9	23	318 18	119	23 25	44	74 17	117	24 09	37	190 14	116	24 46	29	54.7
4	179 11.1	4	5 25.0	23	306 10	116	25 15	− 21	62 06	115	25 36	− 13	178 01	115	25 49	− 5	54.4
5	179 15.5	4	5 47.8	23	293 56	116	25 54	+ 3	49 52	117	25 51	+ 11	165 49	118	25 40	+ 18	54.2
6	179 19.8 + 4		N 6 10.7	+23	281 47	120	S 25 22	+ 27	37 47	121	S 24 55	+ 34	153 48	124	S 24 21	+ 41	54.3
7	179 24.1	4	6 33.4	23	269 52	126	23 40	48	25 58	129	22 52	55	142 07	131	21 57	61	54.5
8	179 28.4	4	6 55.9	23	258 18	133	20 56	68	14 31	136	19 48	74	130 47	138	18 34	79	54.8
9	179 32.5	4	7 18.4	22	247 05	140	17 15	85	3 25	141	15 50	89	119 46	143	14 21	95	55.3
10	179 36.7	4	7 40.7	22	236 09	144	12 46	98	352 33	145	11 08	103	108 58	144	9 25	106	56.0
11	179 40.7 + 4		N 8 03.0	+22	225 22	145	S 7 39	+109	341 47	143	S 5 50	+112	98 10	143	S 3 58	+114	56.7
12	179 44.6	4	8 25.1	22	214 33	140	S 2 04	115	330 53	139	S 0 09	117	87 12	135	N 1 48	118	57.5
13	179 48.5	4	8 47.0	22	203 27	132	N 3 46	117	319 39	128	N 5 43	117	75 47	124	7 40	115	58.3
14	179 52.3	4	9 08.8	22	191 51	119	9 35	113	307 50	113	11 28	109	63 43	108	13 17	106	59.0
15	179 56.1	4	9 30.5	22	179 31	101	15 03	101	295 12	95	16 44	94	50 47	89	18 18	88	59.5
16	179 59.7 + 4		N 9 52.0	+21	166 16	82	N 19 46	+ 81	281 38	77	N 21 07	+ 71	36 55	71	N 22 18	+ 63	59.9
17	180 03.3	4	10 13.3	21	152 06	66	23 21	52	267 12	63	24 13	41	22 15	59	24 54	+ 30	60.0
18	180 06.8	3	10 34.5	21	137 14	58	25 24	+ 18	252 12	57	25 42	+ 6	7 09	58	25 48	− 6	59.9
19	180 10.1	3	10 55.4	21	122 07	60	25 42	− 17	237 07	63	25 25	− 28	352 10	67	24 57	40	59.7
20	180 13.4	3	11 16.2	21	107 17	72	24 17	50	222 29	78	23 27	59	337 47	84	22 28	68	59.4
21	180 16.6 + 3		N 11 36.9	+20	93 11	90	N 21 20	− 77	208 41	96	N 20 03	− 83	324 17	103	N 18 40	− 90	58.9
22	180 19.7	3	11 57.3	20	80 00	108	17 10	96	195 48	115	15 34	101	311 43	119	13 53	105	58.5
23	180 22.7	3	12 17.5	20	67 42	125	12 08	108	183 47	129	10 20	111	299 56	132	8 29	112	58.0
24	180 25.6	3	12 37.5	20	56 08	136	6 37	115	172 24	138	N 4 42	115	288 42	140	N 2 47	115	57.5
25	180 28.3	3	12 57.3	20	45 02	142	N 0 52	115	161 24	143	S 1 03	114	277 47	143	S 2 57	112	57.0
26	180 30.9 + 3		N 13 16.9	+19	34 10	143	S 4 49	−111	150 33	143	S 6 40	−108	266 56	141	S 8 28	−105	56.5
27	180 33.4	2	13 36.3	19	23 17	141	10 13	102	139 38	138	11 55	97	255 56	137	13 32	93	56.0
28	180 35.8	2	13 55.5	19	12 13	134	15 05	89	128 27	133	16 34	83	244 40	129	17 57	77	55.5
29	180 38.1	2	14 14.4	19	0 49	127	19 14	72	116 56	125	20 26	64	233 01	122	21 30	58	55.1
30	180 40.3 + 2		N 14 33.0	+19	349 03	121	S 22 28	− 51	105 04	118	S 23 19	− 43	221 02	117	S 24 02	− 36	54.7

5

1991 MAY, JUNE — ARIES AND PLANETS

0h UT	ARIES GHA	VENUS GHA	v	Dec	d	MARS GHA	v	Dec	d	JUPITER GHA	v	Dec	d	SATURN GHA	v	Dec	d
May	° '	° '		° '		° '		° '		° '		° '		° '		°	
									MAY								
1	218 25.6	138 31.1	−16	N25 18.8	+ 7	111 34.7	+22	N24 14.9	− 5	90 49.6	+53	N19 44.5	− 1	269 19.4	+58	S18 55.5	0
2	219 24.7	138 14.9	16	25 25.4	6	111 57.1	22	24 10.4	5	91 43.0	53	19 43.1	1	270 17.0	58	18 55.3	0
3	220 23.9	137 58.8	16	25 31.4	5	112 19.4	22	24 05.8	5	92 36.2	53	19 41.7	2	271 14.6	58	18 55.0	0
4	221 23.0	137 42.7	16	25 36.8	5	112 41.7	22	24 01.1	5	93 29.3	53	19 40.2	2	272 12.4	58	18 54.8	0
5	222 22.1	137 26.6	16	25 41.4	4	113 04.0	22	23 56.2	5	94 22.2	53	19 38.7	2	273 10.2	58	18 54.5	0
6	223 21.3	137 10.6	−16	N25 45.3	+ 3	113 26.2	+22	N23 51.3	− 5	95 15.0	+53	N19 37.1	− 2	274 08.2	+58	S18 54.4	0
7	224 20.5	136 54.8	16	25 48.6	3	113 48.5	22	23 46.1	5	96 07.6	53	19 35.5	2	275 06.2	58	18 54.2	0
8	225 19.6	136 39.0	16	25 51.3	2	114 10.7	22	23 40.7	5	97 00.1	52	19 33.9	2	276 04.3	58	18 54.1	0
9	226 18.7	136 23.3	16	25 53.3	1	114 33.0	22	23 35.3	6	97 52.4	52	19 32.2	2	277 02.6	58	18 54.0	0
10	227 17.8	136 07.8	15	25 54.5	+ 1	114 55.2	22	23 29.7	6	98 44.6	52	19 30.5	2	278 00.9	58	18 53.9	0
11	228 17.0	135 52.5	−15	N25 55.2	0	115 17.5	+22	N23 24.0	− 6	99 36.7	+52	N19 28.7	− 2	278 59.3	+59	S18 53.9	0
12	229 16.1	135 37.4	15	25 55.1	− 1	115 39.7	22	23 18.1	6	100 28.6	52	19 26.9	2	279 57.9	59	18 53.9	0
13	230 15.2	135 22.4	15	25 54.4	1	116 01.9	22	23 12.1	6	101 20.3	52	19 25.1	2	280 56.5	59	18 53.8	0
14	231 14.4	135 07.7	14	25 53.0	2	116 24.1	22	23 06.0	6	102 12.0	52	19 23.2	2	281 55.3	59	18 53.9	0
15	232 13.6	134 53.3	14	25 51.0	3	116 46.3	22	22 59.6	6	103 03.5	51	19 21.3	2	282 54.1	59	18 53.9	0
16	233 12.7	134 39.0	−14	N25 48.3	− 3	117 08.6	+22	N22 53.2	− 7	103 54.8	+51	N19 19.4	− 2	283 53.0	+59	S18 54.0	0
17	234 11.8	134 25.1	14	25 45.0	4	117 30.8	22	22 46.6	7	104 46.1	51	19 17.4	2	284 52.1	59	18 54.1	0
18	235 11.0	134 11.5	13	25 41.0	5	117 53.0	22	22 39.9	7	105 37.3	51	19 15.4	2	285 51.2	59	18 54.2	0
19	236 10.1	133 58.2	13	25 36.5	5	118 15.3	22	22 33.0	7	106 28.3	51	19 13.3	2	286 50.5	59	18 54.4	0
20	237 09.2	133 45.2	13	25 31.2	6	118 37.6	22	22 26.0	7	107 19.1	51	19 11.2	2	287 49.8	60	18 54.5	0
21	238 08.4	133 32.6	−12	N25 25.4	− 7	118 59.9	+22	N22 18.8	− 7	108 09.9	+51	N19 09.1	− 2	288 49.3	+60	S18 54.7	0
22	239 07.5	133 20.4	12	25 18.9	7	119 22.1	22	22 11.6	7	109 00.5	51	19 07.0	2	289 48.8	60	18 55.0	0
23	240 06.7	133 08.5	11	25 11.9	8	119 44.5	22	22 04.2	8	109 51.1	50	19 04.7	2	290 48.4	60	18 55.2	0
24	241 05.8	132 57.1	11	25 04.2	8	120 06.8	22	21 56.6	8	110 41.5	50	19 02.5	2	291 48.2	60	18 55.4	0
25	242 04.9	132 46.1	11	24 56.0	9	120 29.2	22	21 49.0	8	111 31.7	50	19 00.2	2	292 48.0	60	18 55.7	0
26	243 04.1	132 35.6	−10	N24 47.1	− 9	120 51.5	+22	N21 41.1	− 8	112 22.0	+50	N18 58.0	− 2	293 47.9	+60	S18 56.0	0
27	244 03.2	132 25.4	10	24 37.8	10	121 13.9	23	21 33.2	8	113 12.0	50	18 55.6	2	294 47.9	60	18 56.4	0
28	245 02.3	132 15.8	9	24 27.8	11	121 36.4	22	21 25.1	8	114 02.0	50	18 53.2	2	295 48.1	60	18 56.8	0
29	246 01.5	132 06.7	9	24 17.3	11	121 58.8	22	21 16.9	8	114 51.8	50	18 50.8	2	296 48.3	60	18.57.2	0
30	247 00.6	131 58.1	8	24 06.2	12	122 21.3	23	21 08.5	9	115 41.6	50	18 48.4	3	297 48.7	60	18 57.5	0
31	247 59.8	131 50.0	− 8	N23 54.6	−12	122 43.8	+23	N21 00.0	− 9	116 31.3	+50	N18 45.9	− 3	298 49.1	+61	S18 58.0	0
Jun									**JUNE**								
1	248 58.9	131 42.4	− 7	N23 42.6	−13	123 06.4	+23	N20 51.4	− 9	117 20.8	+50	N18 43.4	− 3	299 49.6	+61	S18 58.4	− 1
2	249 58.0	131 35.4	7	23 30.0	13	123 28.9	23	20 42.6	9	118 10.3	49	18 40.9	3	300 50.2	61	18 58.9	1
3	250 57.2	131 28.9	6	23 16.8	14	123 51.5	23	20 33.7	9	118 59.6	49	18 38.3	3	301 50.9	61	18 59.5	1
4	251 56.3	131 23.1	5	23 03.3	14	124 14.1	23	20 24.7	9	119 48.9	49	18 35.7	3	302 51.7	61	19 00.0	1
5	252 55.4	131 17.8	5	22 49.2	15	124 36.8	23	20 15.6	9	120 38.1	49	18 33.1	3	303 52.6	61	19 00.5	1
6	253 54.6	131 13.1	− 4	N22 34.7	−15	124 59.5	+23	N20 06.4	− 9	121 27.2	+49	N18 30.4	− 3	304 53.6	+61	S19 01.1	− 1
7	254 53.8	131 09.0	4	22 19.7	15	125 22.1	23	19 56.9	9	122 16.2	49	18 27.7	3	305 54.6	61	19 01.7	1
8	255 52.9	131 05.5	3	22 04.3	16	125 44.9	23	19 47.5	10	123 05.1	49	18 24.9	3	306 55.8	61	19 02.3	1
9	256 52.0	131 02.7	2	21 48.5	16	126 07.7	23	19 37.8	10	123 53.9	49	18 22.1	3	307 57.1	61	19 02.9	1
10	257 51.2	131 00.6	2	21 32.2	17	126 30.5	23	19 28.0	10	124 42.7	49	18 19.3	3	308 58.4	61	19 03.6	1
11	258 50.3	130 59.1	− 1	N21 15.6	−17	126 53.3	+23	N19 18.2	−10	125 31.3	+49	N18 16.5	− 3	309 59.8	+62	S19 04.3	− 1
12	259 49.4	130 58.2	0	20 58.6	17	127 16.1	23	19 08.2	10	126 19.9	49	18 13.6	3	311 01.3	62	19 04.9	1
13	260 48.5	130 58.0	+ 1	20 41.2	18	127 39.1	23	18 58.0	10	127 08.4	48	18 10.7	3	312 02.9	62	19 05.6	1
14	261 47.7	130 58.5	1	20 23.5	18	128 02.0	23	18 47.8	10	127 56.8	48	18 07.8	3	313 04.6	62	19 06.4	1
15	262 46.9	130 59.8	2	20 05.5	18	128 25.0	23	18 37.4	10	128 45.1	48	18 04.9	3	314 06.4	62	19 07.1	1
16	263 46.0	131 01.8	+ 3	N19 47.1	−19	128 47.9	+23	N18 27.0	−11	129 33.4	+48	N18 01.9	− 3	315 08.2	+62	S19 07.9	− 1
17	264 45.1	131 04.5	3	19 28.3	19	129 11.0	23	18 16.4	11	130 21.6	48	17 58.9	3	316 10.1	62	19 08.7	1
18	265 44.3	131 07.9	4	19 09.4	19	129 34.0	23	18 05.7	11	131 09.7	48	17 55.8	3	317 12.1	62	19 09.5	1
19	266 43.4	131 12.1	5	18 50.1	20	129 57.1	23	17 54.9	11	131 57.8	48	17 52.7	3	318 14.2	62	19 10.4	1
20	267 42.5	131 17.2	6	18 30.6	20	130 20.3	23	17 43.9	11	132 45.8	48	17 49.6	3	319 16.4	62	19 11.2	1
21	268 41.7	131 23.0	+ 7	N18 10.8	−20	130 43.4	+23	N17 32.9	−11	133 33.7	+48	N17 46.5	− 3	320 18.7	+62	S19 12.1	− 1
22	269 40.8	131 29.6	8	17 50.7	20	131 06.7	23	17 21.8	11	134 21.5	48	17 43.3	3	321 20.9	62	19 13.0	1
23	270 40.0	131 37.1	8	17 30.5	21	131 29.9	23	17 10.5	11	135 09.3	48	17 40.1	3	322 23.3	63	19 13.9	1
24	271 39.1	131 45.5	9	17 10.0	21	131 53.2	23	16 59.1	12	135 57.1	48	17 36.9	3	323 25.8	63	19 14.8	1
25	272 38.2	131 54.7	10	16 49.4	21	132 16.6	23	16 47.6	12	136 44.7	48	17 33.7	3	324 28.3	63	19 15.7	1
26	273 37.4	132 04.8	+11	N16 28.6	−21	132 39.9	+23	N16 36.1	−12	137 32.3	+48	N17 30.4	− 3	325 30.9	+63	S19 16.6	− 1
27	274 36.5	132 15.8	12	16 07.6	21	133 03.3	23	16 24.4	12	138 19.9	48	17 27.1	3	326 33.5	63	19 17.6	1
28	275 35.6	132 27.7	13	15 46.5	21	133 26.8	23	16 12.6	12	139 07.4	47	17 23.7	3	327 36.2	63	19 18.5	1
29	276 34.8	132 40.6	14	15 25.3	21	133 50.2	24	16 00.7	12	139 54.8	47	17 20.3	3	328 39.1	63	19 19.5	1
30	277 33.9	132 54.4	+15	N15 04.0	−21	134 13.7	+24	N15 48.7	−12	140 42.2	+47	N17 16.9	− 3	329 41.9	+63	S19 20.5	− 1

1991 MAY, JUNE — SUN AND MOON

0ʰ UT	SUN GHA	v	Dec	d	MOON 0ʰ–8ʰ GHA	v	Dec	d	MOON 8ʰ–16ʰ GHA	v	Dec	d	MOON 16ʰ–24ʰ GHA	v	Dec	d	HP
May	(SD 15'.8)								**MAY**								
	° ′		° ′		° ′		° ′		° ′		° ′		° ′		° ′		′
1	180 42.3	+ 2	N14 51.5	+18	336 59	115	S24 38	− 28	92 54	115	S25 06	− 20	208 49	115	S25 26	− 12	54.4
2	180 44.2	2	15 09.7	18	324 44	115	25 38	− 4	80 39	116	25 42	+ 4	196 35	117	25 38	+ 12	54.2
3	180 45.9	2	15 27.7	18	312 32	118	25 26	+ 20	68 30	120	25 06	27	184 30	123	24 39	34	54.1
4	180 47.5	2	15 45.4	17	300 33	125	24 05	42	56 38	128	23 23	48	172 46	131	22 35	55	54.2
5	180 49.0	1	16 02.8	17	288 57	133	21 40	62	45 10	137	20 38	67	161 27	138	19 31	73	54.4
6	180 50.3	+ 1	N16 19.9	+17	277 45	142	S18 18	+ 78	34 07	143	S17 00	+ 83	150 30	146	S15 37	+ 88	54.8
7	180 51.4	1	16 36.9	17	266 56	147	14 09	92	23 23	148	12 37	96	139 51	149	11 01	100	55.3
8	180 52.4	1	16 53.5	16	256 20	149	9 21	103	12 49	149	7 38	106	129 18	148	5 52	109	56.0
9	180 53.3	1	17 09.9	16	245 46	147	S 4 03	111	2 13	145	S 2 12	113	118 38	142	S 0 19	114 ·	56.8
10	180 54.1	+ 1	17 25.9	16	235 00	140	N 1 35	115	351 20	136	N 3 30	115	107 36	131	N 5 25	114	57.7
11	180 54.7	0	N17 41.7	+15	223 47	127	N 7 19	+114	339 54	121	N 9 13	+112	95 55	115	N11 05	+109	58.6
12	180 55.1	0	17 57.1	15	211 50	109	12 54	106	327 39	101	14 40	101	83 20	95	16 21	96	59.5
13	180 55.4	0	18 12.3	15	198 55	87	17 57	89	314 22	80	19 26	82	69 42	73	20 48	74	60.1
14	180 55.5	0	18 27.2	15	184 55	66	22 02	64	300 01	60	23 06	54	55 01	55	24 00	43	60.6
15	180 55.6	0	18 41.7	14	169 56	51	24 43	+ 31	284 47	49	25 14	+ 19	39 36	47	25 33	+ 6	60.8
16	180 55.4	0	N18 56.0	+14	154 23	48	N25 39	− 6	269 11	50	N25 33	− 19	24 01	53	N25 14	− 30	60.7
17	180 55.1	0	19 09.9	14	138 54	58	24 44	42	253 52	64	24 02	53	8 56	69	23 09	63	60.4
18	180 54.7	− 1	19 23.5	13	124 05	77	22 06	72	239 22	83	20 54	80	354 45	91	19 34	87	59.9
19	180 54.2	1	19 36.7	13	110 16	98	18 07	94	225 54	105	16 33	99	341 39	112	14 54	103	59.2
20	180 53.5	1	19 49.7	13	97 31	117	13 11	107	213 28	123	11 24	110	329 31	128	9 34	113	58.5
21	180 52.7	− 1	N20 02.3	+12	85 39	132	N 7 41	−113	201 51	136	N 5 48	−115	318 07	139	N 3 53	−115	57.8
22	180 51.7	1	20 14.5	12	74 26	141	N 1 58	114	190 47	143	N 0 04	114	307 10	144	S 1 50	112	57.1
23	180 50.6	1	20 26.4	12	63 34	144	S 3 42	110	179 58	145	S 5 32	109	296 23	145	7 21	105	56.4
24	180 49.4	1	20 38.0	11	52 48	143	9 06	102	169 11	143	10 48	99	285 34	140	12 27	95	55.9
25	180 48.1	1	20 49.2	11	41 54	139	14 02	90	158 13	136	15 32	86	274 29	134	16 58	80	55.4
26	180 46.7	− 2	N21 00.0	+11	30 43	132	S18 18	− 74	146 55	128	S19 32	− 69	263 03	127	S20 41	− 62	55.0
27	180 45.1	2	21 10.5	10	19 10	123	21 43	55	135 13	122	22 38	48	251 15	119	23 26	41	54.6
28	180 43.4	2	21 20.6	10	7 14	118	24 07	34	123 12	116	24 41	26	239 08	116	25 07	− 17	54.4
29	180 41.6	2	21 30.4	9	355 04	115	25 24	− 10	110 59	115	25 34	− 2	226 54	116	25 36	+ 6	54.2
30	180 39.7	2	21 39.7	9	342 50	118	25 30	+ 13	98 48	118	25 17	+ 22	214 46	121	24 55	29	54.0
31	180 37.7	− 2	N21 48.7	+ 9	330 47	124	S24 26	+ 36	86 51	126	S23 50	+ 43	202 57	129	S23 07	+ 50	54.0
Jun	(SD 15'.8)								**JUNE**								
1	180 35.5	− 2	N21 57.3	+ 8	319 06	132	S22 17	+ 56	75 18	135	S21 21	+ 63	191 33	138	S20 18	+ 68	54.1
2	180 33.3	2	22 05.6	8	307 51	141	19 10	73	64 12	143	17 57	78	180 35	146	16 39	84	54.4
3	180 31.0	2	22 13.4	8	297 01	149	15 15	87	53 30	150	13 48	92	170 00	152	12 16	95	54.7
4	180 28.6	3	22 20.9	7	286 32	153	10 41	98	43 05	153	9 03	101	159 38	154	7 22	104	55.3
5	180 26.0	3	22 28.0	7	276 12	153	5 38	107	32 45	153	S 3 51	108	149 18	150	S 2 03	110	55.9
6	180 23.4	− 3	N22 34.6	+ 6	265 48	149	S 0 13	+111	22 17	146	N 1 38	+111	138 43	142	N 3 29	+112	56.7
7	180 20.7	3	22 40.9	6	255 05	138	N 5 21	111	11 23	134	7 12	111	127 37	128	9 03	108	57.6
8	180 17.9	3	22 46.8	6	243 45	122	10 51	107	359 47	116	12 38	104	115 43	109	14 22	99	58.6
9	180 15.0	3	22 52.3	5	231 32	101	16 01	95	347 13	93	17 36	90	102 46	86	19 06	82	59.5
10	180 12.1	3	22 57.4	5	218 12	77	20 28	75	333 29	70	21 43	66	88 39	62	22 49	57	60.3
11	180 09.1	− 3	N23 02.1	+ 4	203 41	56	N23 46	+ 45	318 37	51	N24 31	+ 34	73 28	46	N25 05	+ 22	60.9
12	180 06.1	3	23 06.3	4	188 14	44	25 27	+ 10	302 58	43	25 37	− 4	57 41	43	25 33	− 16	61.2
13	180 02.9	3	23 10.2	3	172 24	49	25 17	− 29	287 09	49	24 48	41	41 58	53	24 07	53	61.2
14	179 59.8	3	23 13.6	3	156 51	60	23 14	63	271 51	66	22 11	74	26 57	74	20 57	82	60.9
15	179 56.6	3	23 16.7	3	142 11	81	19 35	90	257 32	88	18 05	97	13 00	96	16 28	103	60.4
16	179 53.4	− 3	N23 19.3	+ 2	128 36	103	N14 45	−107	244 19	110	N12 58	−111	0 09	115	N11 07	−114	59.6
17	179 50.2	3	23 21.6	2	116 04	121	9 13	116	232 05	126	7 17	117	348 11	131	N 5 20	117	58.7
18	179 46.9	3	23 23.4	1	104 22	134	N 3 23	117	220 36	136	N 1 26	117	336 52	139	S 0 31	115	57.9
19	179 43.6	3	23 24.7	1	93 11	141	S 2 26	113	209 32	142	S 4 19	111	325 54	143	6 10	109	57.0
20	179 40.3	3	23 25.8	+ 1	82 17	142	7 59	105	198 39	142	9 44	101	315 01	141	11 25	98	56.2
21	179 37.1	− 3	N23 26.4	0	71 22	140	S13 03	− 93	187 42	138	S14 36	− 88	304 00	136	S16 04	− 84	55.6
22	179 33.8	3	23 26.5	0	60 16	134	17 28	77	176 30	131	18 45	73	292 41	129	19 58	65	55.1
23	179 30.6	3	23 26.2	− 1	48 50	127	21 03	60	164 57	124	22 03	53	281 01	123	22 56	45	54.6
24	179 27.4	3	23 25.6	1	37 04	120	23 41	38	153 04	118	24 19	31	269 02	118	24 50	− 24	54.3
25	179 24.2	3	23 24.5	2	25 00	116	25 14	− 15	140 56	116	25 29	− 7	256 52	117	25 36	0	54.1
26	179 21.0	− 3	N23 23.0	− 2	12 49	117	S25 36	+ 8	128 46	118	S25 28	+ 16	244 44	119	S25 12	+ 24	54.0
27	179 17.8	3	23 21.1	2	0 43	122	24 48	31	116 45	123	24 17	38	232 48	127	23 39	45	54.0
28	179 14.8	3	23 18.8	3	348 55	129	22 54	52	105 04	133	22 02	58	221 17	135	21 04	65	54.0
29	179 11.6	3	23 16.0	3	337 32	139	19 59	69	93 51	141	18 50	75	210 12	145	17 35	80	54.2
30	179 08.6	− 3	N23 12.9	− 4	326 37	147	S16 15	+ 84	83 04	149	S14 51	+ 89	199 33	152	S13 22	+ 92	54.5

1991 JULY, AUGUST — ARIES AND PLANETS

0h UT	ARIES	VENUS				MARS				JUPITER				SATURN			
	GHA	GHA	v	Dec	d	GHA	v	Dec	d	GHA	v	Dec	d	GHA	v	Dec	d
Jul																	
	° ′	° ′		° ′		° ′		° ′		° ′		° ′		° ′		° ′	
1	278 33.1	133 09.1 +16		N14 42.6 −22		134 37.3 +24		N15 36.6 −12		141 29.5 +47		N17 13.5 − 3		330 44.8 +63		S19 21.5 − 1	
2	279 32.2	133 24.9	17	14 21.1	22	135 00.9	24	15 24.4	12	142 16.9	47	17 10.1	4	331 47.8	63	19 22.6	1
3	280 31.3	133 41.7	18	13 59.6	22	135 24.5	24	15 12.2	12	143 04.1	47	17 06.6	4	332 50.8	63	19 23.6	1
4	281 30.5	133 59.6	19	13 38.0	22	135 48.1	24	14 59.8	13	143 51.3	47	17 03.1	4	333 53.8	63	19 24.6	1
5	282 29.6	134 18.5	20	13 16.4	22	136 11.8	24	14 47.3	13	144 38.4	47	16 59.6	4	334 56.9	63	19 25.7	1
6	283 28.7	134 38.4 +21		N12 54.8 −22		136 35.5 +24		N14 34.7 −13		145 25.5 +47		N16 56.0 − 4		336 00.1 +63		S19 26.7 − 1	
7	284 27.9	134 59.6	22	12 33.2	22	136 59.3	24	14 22.0	13	146 12.6	47	16 52.4	4	337 03.4	63	19 27.8	1
8	285 27.1	135 21.8	24	12 11.7	22	137 23.0	24	14 09.3	13	146 59.6	47	16 48.8	4	338 06.6	63	19 28.9	1
9	286 26.2	135 45.3	25	11 50.2	22	137 46.9	24	13 56.4	13	147 46.6	47	16 45.2	4	339 10.0	63	19 29.9	1
10	287 25.3	136 09.9	26	11 28.7	21	138 10.7	24	13 43.5	13	148 33.5	47	16 41.6	4	340 13.3	63	19 31.0	1
11	288 24.5	136 35.8 +27		N11 07.4 −21		138 34.6 +24		N13 30.4 −13		149 20.4 +47		N16 37.9 − 4		341 16.7 +63		S19 32.1 − 1	
12	289 23.6	137 03.0	28	10 46.3	21	138 58.4	24	13 17.3	13	150 07.3	47	16 34.2	4	342 20.1	64	19 33.2	1
13	290 22.7	137 31.4	30	10 25.2	21	139 22.3	24	13 04.1	13	150 54.1	47	16 30.5	4	343 23.6	64	19 34.3	1
14	291 21.9	138 01.2	31	10 04.3	21	139 46.3	24	12 50.8	13	151 40.9	47	16 26.8	4	344 27.1	64	19 35.5	1
15	292 21.0	138 32.5	33	9 43.6	21	140 10.2	24	12 37.4	13	152 27.6	47	16 23.0	4	345 30.6	64	19 36.5	1
16	293 20.2	139 05.1 +34		N 9 23.1 −20		140 34.2 +24		N12 24.0 −14		153 14.3 +47		N16 19.2 − 4		346 34.1 +64		S19 37.7 − 1	
17	294 19.3	139 39.3	36	9 02.9	20	140 58.2	24	12 10.5	14	154 01.0	47	16 15.4	4	347 37.7	64	19 38.8	1
18	295 18.4	140 15.0	37	8 42.9	20	141 22.3	24	11 56.9	14	154 47.7	47	16 11.6	4	348 41.3	64	19 40.0	1
19	296 17.6	140 52.3	39	8 23.3	19	141 46.3	24	11 43.1	14	155 34.3	47	16 07.7	4	349 45.0	64	19 41.1	1
20	297 16.7	141 31.2	41	8 03.9	19	142 10.4	24	11 29.4	14	156 20.9	47	16 03.8	4	350 48.7	64	19 42.2	1
21	298 15.8	142 11.7 +42		N 7 44.9 −19		142 34.6 +24		N11 15.5 −14		157 07.6 +47		N15 59.9 − 4		351 52.3 +64		S19 43.3 − 1	
22	299 15.0	142 54.0	44	7 26.3	18	142 58.7	24	11 01.6	14	157 54.1	47	15 56.0	4	352 56.0	64	19 44.5	1
23	300 14.1	143 38.0	46	7 08.1	18	143 22.9	24	10 47.6	14	158 40.6	47	15 52.1	4	353 59.7	64	19 45.6	1
24	301 13.3	144 23.9	48	6 50.4	17	143 47.0	24	10 33.6	14	159 27.2	47	15 48.2	4	355 03.4	64	19 46.7	1
25	302 12.4	145 11.6	50	6 33.1	17	144 11.2	24	10 19.4	14	160 13.7	46	15 44.2	4	356 07.1	64	19 47.9	1
26	303 11.5	146 01.3 +52		N 6 16.3 −16		144 35.5 +24		N10 05.2 −14		161 00.1 +46		N15 40.2 − 4		357 10.9 +64		S19 49.0 − 1	
27	304 10.7	146 52.9	54	6 00.1	16	144 59.7	24	9 51.0	14	161 46.6	46	15 36.2	4	358 14.6	64	19 50.2	1
28	305 09.8	147 46.5	56	5 44.5	15	145 23.9	24	9 36.7	14	162 33.1	46	15 32.2	4	359 18.3	64	19 51.3	1
29	306 08.9	148 42.2	58	5 29.5	14	145 48.2	24	9 22.3	15	163 19.5	46	15 28.1	4	0 22.0	64	19 52.4	1
30	307 08.1	149 39.9	60	5 15.2	14	146 12.5	24	9 07.8	15	164 05.9	46	15 24.1	4	1 25.7	64	19 53.5	1
31	308 07.3	150 39.7 +62		N 5 01.6 −13		146 36.8 +24		N 8 53.2 −15		164 52.3 +46		N15 20.0 − 4		2 29.5 +64		S19 54.7 − 1	
Aug								**AUGUST**									
1	309 06.4	151 41.7 +64		N 4 48.6 −12		147 01.1 +24		N 8 38.6 −15		165 38.7 +46		N15 15.9 − 4		3 33.2 +64		S19 55.7 − 1	
2	310 05.5	152 45.8	66	4 36.4	11	147 25.4	24	8 24.0	15	166 25.1	46	15 11.8	4	4 36.9	64	19 56.8	1
3	311 04.6	153 52.1	69	4 25.1	11	147 49.7	24	8 09.3	15	167 11.4	46	15 07.6	4	5 40.6	64	19 58.0	1
4	312 03.8	155 00.6	71	4 14.5	10	148 14.0	24	7 54.5	15	167 57.8	46	15 03.5	4	6 44.3	64	19 59.0	1
5	313 02.9	156 11.3	73	4 04.8	9	148 38.3	24	7 39.7	15	168 44.2	46	14 59.3	4	7 47.9	64	20 00.1	1
6	314 02.0	157 24.1 +75		N 3 56.0 − 8		149 02.7 +24		N 7 24.8 −15		169 30.5 +46		N14 55.1 − 4		8 51.5 +64		S20 01.2 − 1	
7	315 01.2	158 39.1	77	3 48.2	7	149 27.0	24	7 09.9	15	170 16.8	46	14 50.9	4	9 55.2	64	20 02.3	1
8	316 00.4	159 56.2	79	3 41.3	6	149 51.4	24	6 54.9	15	171 03.2	46	14 46.7	4	10 58.8	64	20 03.3	1
9	316 59.5	161 15.4	81	3 35.4	5	150 15.7	24	6 39.9	15	171 49.5	46	14 42.5	4	12 02.3	64	20 04.4	1
10	317 58.6	162 36.6	83	3 30.5	4	150 40.0	24	6 24.8	15	172 35.8	46	14 38.3	4	13 05.9	64	20 05.4	1
11	318 57.8	163 59.8 +85		N 3 26.7 − 3		151 04.3 +24		N 6 09.7 −15		173 22.1 +46		N14 34.1 − 1		14 09.4 +63		S20 06.4 − 1	
12	319 56.9	165 24.8	87	3 23.9	2	151 28.7	24	5 54.5	15	174 08.5	46	14 29.8	4	15 12.8	63	20 07.4	1
13	320 56.0	166 51.6	89	3 22.3 − 1		151 53.0	24	5 39.2	15	174 54.8	46	14 25.6	4	16 16.3	63	20 08.5	1
14	321 55.2	168 20.1	90	3 21.7 + 1		152 17.3	24	5 24.0	15	175 41.1	46	14 21.3	4	17 19.7	63	20 09.5	1
15	322 54.3	169 50.0	91	3 22.2	2	152 41.6	24	5 08.7	15	176 27.5	46	14 17.0	4	18 23.0	63	20 10.4	1
16	323 53.5	171 21.4 +93		N 3 23.8 + 3		153 05.9 +24		N 4 53.3 −15		177 13.8 +46		N14 12.7 − 4		19 26.3 +63		S20 11.4 − 1	
17	324 52.6	172 53.9	94	3 26.4	4	153 30.2	24	4 37.9	15	178 00.1	46	14 08.4	4	20 29.6	63	20 12.4	1
18	325 51.7	174 27.4	94	3 30.1	5	153 54.5	24	4 22.5	16	178 46.5	46	14 04.1	4	21 32.9	63	20 13.3	1
19	326 50.9	176 01.8	95	3 34.7	6	154 18.8	24	4 07.0	16	179 32.9	46	13 59.7	4	22 36.1	63	20 14.3	1
20	327 50.0	177 36.8	95	3 40.4	7	154 43.0	24	3 51.5	16	180 19.2	46	13 55.4	4	23 39.2	63	20 15.2	1
21	328 49.1	179 12.2 +96		N 3 46.9 + 8		155 07.3 +24		N 3 36.0 −16		181 05.6 +46		N13 51.1 − 1		24 42.2 +63		S20 16.1 − 1	
22	329 48.3	180 47.7	96	3 54.4	8	155 31.5	24	3 20.5	16	181 52.0	46	13 46.7	4	25 45.2	63	20 17.0	1
23	330 47.4	182 23.2	95	4 02.6	9	155 55.7	24	3 04.9	16	182 38.4	46	13 42.4	4	26 48.2	63	20 17.9	1
24	331 46.6	183 58.4	95	4 11.6	10	156 19.9	24	2 49.2	16	183 24.8	46	13 38.0	4	27 51.1	63	20 18.7	1
25	332 45.7	185 33.1	94	4 21.3	10	156 44.0	24	2 33.5	16	184 11.2	46	13 33.6	4	28 53.9	63	20 19.6	1
26	333 44.8	187 07.1 +93		N 4 31.5 +11		157 08.2 +24		N 2 17.9 −16		184 57.7 +46		N13 29.2 − 4		29 56.8 +63		S20 20.4 − 1	
27	334 44.0	188 40.2	92	4 42.3	11	157 32.3	24	2 02.2	16	185 44.2	46	13 24.8	4	30 59.5	63	20 21.2	1
28	335 43.1	190 12.2	91	4 53.6	12	157 56.4	24	1 46.4	16	186 30.6	47	13 20.5	4	32 02.1	63	20 22.0	1
29	336 42.2	191 42.8	89	5 05.2	12	158 20.5	24	1 30.7	16	187 17.1	47	13 16.1	4	33 04.7	63	20 22.9	1
30	337 41.4	193 11.8	87	5 17.1	12	158 44.5	24	1 14.9	16	188 03.6	47	13 11.6	4	34 07.2	63	20 23.6	1
31	338 40.6	194 39.2 +86		N 5 29.3 +12		159 08.5 +24		N 0 59.1 −16		188 50.2 +47		N13 07.3 − 4		35 09.7 +62		S20 24.4 − 1	

1991 JULY, AUGUST — SUN AND MOON

0h UT	SUN GHA	v	Dec	d	MOON 0h–8h GHA	v	Dec	d	MOON 8h–16h GHA	v	Dec	d	MOON 16h–24h GHA	v	Dec	d	HP
Jul	(SD 15'.8)						JULY										
1	179 05.7 – 3		N23 09.4	– 4	316 05	153	S11 50	+ 96	72 38	155	S10 14	+ 98	189 13	156	S 8 36	+101	54.8
2	179 02.8	3	23 05.5	4	305 49	156	6 55	104	62 25	156	S 5 11	105	179 01	155	S 3 26	107	55.3
3	179 00.0	3	23 01.1	5	295 36	154	S 1 39	108	52 10	153	N 0 09	109	168 43	150	N 1 58	109	55.9
4	178 57.2	3	22 56.4	5	285 13	148	N 3 47	109	41 41	144	5 36	109	158 05	140	7 25	107	56.6
5	178 54.4	3	22 51.3	6	274 25	135	9 12	106	30 40	130	10 58	103	146 50	123	12 41	100	57.4
6	178 51.8 – 3		N22 45.7	– 6	262 53	118	N14 21	+ 97	18 51	110	N15 58	+ 93	134 41	103	N17 31	+ 87	58.3
7	178 49.3	3	22 39.7	6	250 24	95	18 58	81	5 59	87	20 19	73	121 26	80	21 32	66	59.2
8	178 46.8	2	22 33.4	7	236 46	72	22 38	57	351 58	65	23 35	47	107 03	58	24 22	37	60.1
9	178 44.5	2	22 26.7	7	222 01	54	24 59	+ 25	336 55	49	25 24	+ 12	91 44	46	25 36	+ 1	60.7
10	178 42.2	2	22 19.6	8	206 30	46	25 37	– 12	321 16	45	25 25	– 25	76 01	48	25 00	– 37	61.2
11	178 40.0 – 2		N22 12.1	– 8	190 49	51	N24 23	– 50	305 40	55	N23 33	– 60	60 35	60	N22 33	– 72	61.3
12	178 37.9	2	22 04.2	8	175 35	67	21 21	81	290 42	73	20 00	89	45 55	81	18 31	98	61.1
13	178 35.9	2	21 55.9	9	161 16	87	16 53	104	276 43	94	15 09	109	32 17	101	13 20	113	60.6
14	178 34.1	2	21 47.3	9	147 58	106	11 27	117	263 44	113	9 30	119	19 37	117	7 31	121	59.9
15	178 32.4	2	21 38.3	9	135 34	122	N 5 30	121	251 36	126	N 3 29	121	7 42	129	N 1 28	121	59.0
16	178 30.8 – 2		N21 28.9	–10	123 51	132	S 0 33	–118	240 03	134	S 2 31	–117	356 17	135	S 4 28	–114	58.1
17	178 29.3	1	21 19.2	10	112 32	136	6 22	110	228 48	137	8 12	107	345 05	137	9 59	104	57.1
18	178 28.0	1	21 09.1	11	101 22	136	11 43	98	217 38	135	13 21	94	333 53	134	14 55	89	56.3
19	178 26.9	1	20 58.6	11	90 07	133	16 24	83	206 20	131	17 47	77	322 31	129	19 04	71	55.6
20	178 25.8	1	20 47.8	11	78 40	127	20 15	65	194 47	125	21 20	58	310 52	123	22 18	51	55.0
21	178 24.9 – 1		N20 36.6	–12	66 55	121	S23 09	– 44	182 56	120	S23 53	– 36	298 56	118	S24 29	– 29	54.5
22	178 24.2	1	20 24.8	12	54 54	117	24 58	– 21	170 51	117	25 19	– 13	286 48	117	25 32	– 6	54.2
23	178 23.6 – 1		20 13.3	12	42 45	117	25 38	+ 3	158 42	117	25 35	+ 10	274 39	119	25 25	+ 18	54.1
24	178 23.1	0	20 01.1	13	30 38	120	25 07	25	146 38	122	24 42	33	262 40	125	24 09	40	54.0
25	178 22.8	0	19 48.6	13	18 45	127	23 29	47	134 52	129	22 42	53	251 01	133	21 49	60	54.1
26	178 22.6	0	N19 35.7	–13	7 14	135	S20 49	+ 66	123 29	139	S19 43	+ 71	239 48	141	S18 32	+ 76	54.2
27	178 22.6	0	19 22.5	14	356 09	144	17 16	82	112 33	146	15 54	86	228 59	149	14 28	89	54.4
28	178 22.7	0	19 09.0	14	345 28	151	12 59	94	101 59	152	11 25	97	218 31	154	9 48	100	54.7
29	170 23.0 + 1		18 55.2	14	336 06	166	8 08	102	91 40	156	6 26	104	208 16	155	5 42	106	55.1
30	178 23.5	1	18 41.1	14	324 51	155	S 2 56	107	81 26	155	S 1 09	108	198 01	153	N 0 39	109	55.6
31	178 24.1 + 1		N18 26.7	–15	314 34	151	N 2 28	+108	71 05	148	N 4 16	+108	187 33	146	N 6 04	+107	56.1
Aug	(SD 15'.8)						AUGUST										
1	178 24.8 + 1		N18 12.0	–15	303 59	141	N 7 51	+105	60 20	138	N 9 36	+104	176 38	133	N11 20	+101	56.7
2	178 25.6	1	17 56.9	15	292 51	128	13 01	97	48 59	122	14 38	94	165 01	116	16 12	89	57.4
3	178 26.6	1	17 41.5	16	280 57	109	17 41	84	36 46	103	19 05	78	152 29	96	20 23	71	58.1
4	178 27.8	1	17 25.9	16	268 05	88	21 34	63	23 33	82	22 37	55	138 55	76	23 32	46	58.9
5	178 29.1	2	17 10.0	16	254 11	69	24 18	36	9 20	65	24 54	+ 25	124 25	60	25 19	+ 14	59.6
6	178 30.6 + 2		N16 53.8	–16	239 25	57	N25 33	+ 3	354 22	55	N25 36	– 10	109 17	55	N25 26	– 21	60.2
7	178 32.2	2	16 37.4	17	224 12	55	25 05	– 33	339 07	57	24 32	45	94 04	60	23 47	57	60.7
8	178 34.0	2	16 20.7	17	209 04	64	22 50	67	324 08	68	21 43	77	79 16	74	20 26	86	60.9
9	178 35.8	2	16 03.7	17	194 30	79	19 00	94	309 49	86	17 26	101	65 15	91	15 45	108	60.8
10	178 37.9	2	15 46.5	18	180 46	96	13 57	112	296 22	102	12 05	117	52 04	107	10 08	120	60.5
11	178 40.1 + 2		N15 29.0	–18	167 51	112	N 8 08	–122	283 43	116	N 6 06	–123	39 39	119	N 4 03	–123	59.8
12	178 42.4	3	15 11.2	18	155 38	123	N 2 00	123	271 41	125	S 0 03	122	27 46	127	S 2 05	120	59.1
13	178 44.9	3	14 53.2	18	143 53	128	S 4 05	117	260 01	130	6 02	114	16 11	130	7 56	110	58.2
14	178 47.5	3	14 35.0	18	132 21	130	9 46	106	248 31	129	11 32	101	4 40	130	13 13	96	57.3
15	178 50.3	3	14 16.6	19	120 50	128	14 49	91	236 58	127	16 20	85	353 05	125	17 45	78	56.4
16	178 53.2 + 3		N13 57.9	–19	109 10	124	S19 03	– 72	225 14	123	S20 15	– 65	341 17	121	S21 20	– 58	55.6
17	178 56.2	3	13 39.0	19	97 18	120	22 18	51	213 18	118	23 09	44	329 16	117	23 53	35	55.0
18	178 59.3	3	13 19.9	19	85 13	117	24 28	28	201 10	116	24 56	– 20	317 06	115	25 16	– 13	54.6
19	179 02.6	4	13 00.6	20	73 01	116	25 29	– 4	188 57	117	25 33	+ 3	304 54	118	25 30	+ 12	54.3
20	179 06.1	4	12 41.0	20	60 52	119	25 18	+ 18	176 51	120	25 00	27	292 51	123	24 33	34	54.1
21	179 09.6 + 4		N12 21.3	–20	48 54	125	S23 59	+ 40	164 59	127	S23 19	+ 48	281 06	131	S22 31	+ 54	54.1
22	179 13.3	4	12 01.3	20	37 17	132	21 37	61	153 29	136	20 36	66	269 45	138	19 30	72	54.3
23	179 17.1	4	11 41.2	20	26 03	141	18 18	77	142 24	143	17 01	82	258 47	145	15 39	87	54.5
24	179 21.0	4	11 21.0	21	15 12	148	14 12	91	131 40	149	12 41	94	248 09	151	11 07	98	54.8
25	179 25.0	4	11 00.5	21	4 40	152	9 29	101	121 12	153	7 48	103	237 45	153	6 05	105	55.2
26	179 29.1 + 4		N10 39.8	–21	354 18	152	S 4 20	+107	110 50	153	S 2 33	+108	227 23	151	S 0 45	+109	55.7
27	179 33.3	4	10 19.0	21	343 54	150	N 1 04	109	100 24	148	N 2 53	109	216 52	145	N 4 42	108	56.1
28	179 37.6	4	9 58.0	21	333 17	143	6 30	107	89 40	139	8 17	105	205 59	135	10 02	103	56.6
29	179 42.0	5	9 36.8	21	322 14	131	11 45	100	78 25	126	13 25	96	194 31	121	15 01	92	57.1
30	179 46.5	5	9 15.5	21	310 32	115	16 33	86	66 27	110	17 59	82	182 17	103	19 21	75	57.7
31	179 51.1 + 5		N 8 54.1	–22	298 00	98	N20 36	+ 67	53 38	92	N21 43	+ 60	169 10	86	N22 43	+ 52	58.2

1991 SEPTEMBER, OCTOBER — ARIES AND PLANETS

0h UT	ARIES GHA	VENUS GHA	v	Dec	d	MARS GHA	v	Dec	d	JUPITER GHA	v	Dec	d	SATURN GHA	v	Dec	d
Sep								**SEPTEMBER**									
	° ′	° ′		° ′		° ′		° ′		° ′		° ′		° ′		° ′	
1	339 39.7	196 04.7	+84	N 5 41.6	+12	159 32.5	+24	N 0 43.3	−16	189 36.7	+47	N13 02.9	− 4	36 12.0	+62	S20 25.1	− 1
2	340 38.8	197 28.4	82	5 54.0	12	159 56.5	24	0 27.5	16	190 23.3	47	12 58.4	4	37 14.3	62	20 25.8	1
3	341 38.0	198 49.9	79	6 06.4	12	160 20.3	24	N 0 11.6	16	191 09.9	47	12 54.1	4	38 16.6	62	20 26.5	1
4	342 37.1	200 09.2	77	6 18.7	12	160 44.2	24	S 0 04.3	16	191 56.5	47	12 49.6	4	39 18.7	62	20 27.2	1
5	343 36.2	201 26.3	75	6 30.9	12	161 08.0	24	0 20.1	16	192 43.2	47	12 45.2	4	40 20.8	62	20 27.8	1
6	344 35.4	202 41.1	+72	N 6 42.9	+12	161 31.8	+24	S 0 36.0	−16	193 29.9	+47	N12 40.8	− 4	41 22.7	+62	S20 28.5	− 1
7	345 34.5	203 53.5	70	6 54.7	11	161 55.6	24	0 51.9	16	194 16.6	47	12 36.4	4	42 24.6	62	20 29.1	1
8	346 33.7	205 03.6	68	7 06.1	11	162 19.3	24	1 07.8	16	195 03.4	47	12 32.0	4	43 26.5	62	20 29.7	1
9	347 32.8	206 11.3	65	7 17.3	11	162 42.9	24	1 23.7	16	195 50.1	47	12 27.6	4	44 28.2	62	20 30.3	1
10	348 31.9	207 16.6	63	7 28.0	10	163 06.5	24	1 39.6	16	196 36.9	47	12 23.2	4	45 29.8	62	20 30.9	1
11	349 31.1	208 19.5	+61	N 7 38.4	+10	163 30.1	+23	S 1 55.5	−16	197 23.8	+47	N12 18.8	− 4	46 31.4	+61	S20 31.4	− 1
12	350 30.2	209 20.0	58	7 48.3	9	163 53.5	23	2 11.4	16	198 10.6	47	12 14.4	4	47 32.8	61	20 31.9	1
13	351 29.3	210 18.1	56	7 57.7	9	164 17.0	23	2 27.3	16	198 57.5	47	12 10.0	4	48 34.2	61	20 32.5	0
14	352 28.5	211 14.0	54	8 06.6	8	164 40.4	23	2 43.2	16	199 44.5	47	12 05.6	4	49 35.5	61	20 32.9	0
15	353 27.6	212 07.6	51	8 15.0	8	165 03.7	23	2 59.1	16	200 31.4	47	12 01.2	4	50 36.7	61	20 33.4	0
16	354 26.8	212 59.0	+49	N 8 22.9	+ 7	165 27.0	+23	S 3 15.0	−16	201 18.5	+47	N11 56.8	− 4	51 37.8	+61	S20 33.8	− 1
17	355 25.9	213 48.1	47	8 30.2	7	165 50.2	23	3 30.8	16	202 05.5	47	11 52.5	4	52 38.8	61	20 34.3	1
18	356 25.0	214 35.2	45	8 36.9	6	166 13.4	23	3 46.7	16	202 52.6	47	11 48.1	4	53 39.7	61	20 34.7	0
19	357 24.2	215 20.1	43	8 43.0	6	166 36.5	23	4 02.6	16	203 39.8	47	11 43.7	4	54 40.6	61	20 35.1	0
20	358 23.3	216 03.0	41	8 48.5	5	166 59.5	23	4 18.4	16	204 27.0	47	11 39.4	4	55 41.3	61	20 35.5	0
21	359 22.4	216 44.0	+39	N 8 53.4	+ 4	167 22.5	+23	S 4 34.3	−16	205 14.2	+47	N11 35.0	− 4	56 41.9	+61	S20 35.8	− 1
22	0 21.6	217 23.0	37	8 57.7	4	167 45.4	23	4 50.1	16	206 01.5	47	11 30.7	4	57 42.4	60	20 36.1	1
23	1 20.8	218 00.2	35	9 01.3	3	168 08.3	23	5 05.9	16	206 48.8	47	11 26.4	4	58 42.8	60	20 36.4	1
24	2 19.9	218 35.6	34	9 04.3	2	168 31.0	23	5 21.7	16	207 36.2	47	11 22.1	4	59 43.2	60	20 36.7	0
25	3 19.0	219 09.3	32	9 06.6	2	168 53.7	23	5 37.4	16	208 23.6	48	11 17.8	4	60 43.4	60	20 37.0	0
26	4 18.1	219 41.3	+30	N 9 08.4	+ 1	169 16.4	+23	S 5 53.2	−16	209 11.1	+48	N11 13.5	− 4	61 43.6	+60	S20 37.2	0
27	5 17.3	220 11.7	29	9 09.4	0	169 38.9	23	6 08.9	16	209 58.6	48	11 09.2	4	62 43.6	60	20 37.4	0
28	6 16.4	220 40.5	27	9 09.8	0	170 01.4	22	6 24.5	16	210 46.2	48	11 05.0	4	63 43.5	60	20 37.6	0
29	7 15.5	221 07.9	26	9 09.6	− 1	170 23.8	22	6 40.2	16	211 33.8	48	11 00.7	4	64 43.3	60	20 37.7	0
30	8 14.7	221 33.8	+25	N 9 08.7	− 2	170 46.1	+22	S 6 55.8	−16	212 21.5	+48	N10 56.5	− 4	65 43.0	+60	S20 37.9	0
Oct								**OCTOBER**									
1	9 13.9	221 58.4	+23	N 9 07.2	− 2	171 08.3	+22	S 7 11.4	−16	213 09.2	+48	N10 52.3	− 4	66 42.7	+59	S20 38.0	0
2	10 13.0	222 21.7	22	9 05.0	3	171 30.5	22	7 26.9	16	213 57.1	48	10 48.1	4	67 42.1	59	20 38.2	0
3	11 12.1	222 43.7	21	9 02.2	3	171 52.5	22	7 42.5	15	214 44.9	48	10 43.9	4	68 41.5	59	20 38.2	0
4	12 11.3	223 04.4	20	8 58.8	4	172 14.5	22	7 58.0	15	215 32.8	48	10 39.7	4	69 40.9	59	20 38.3	0
5	13 10.4	223 24.1	19	8 54.7	5	172 36.4	22	8 13.4	15	216 20.8	48	10 35.5	4	70 40.1	59	20 38.3	0
6	14 09.5	223 42.7	+18	N 8 50.0	− 5	172 58.1	+22	S 8 28.8	−15	217 08.8	+48	N10 31.4	− 4	71 39.1	+59	S20 38.3	0
7	15 08.7	224 00.2	17	8 44.7	6	173 19.8	22	8 44.2	15	217 56.9	48	10 27.3	4	72 38.2	59	20 38.3	0
8	16 07.8	224 16.8	16	8 38.9	7	173 41.4	22	8 59.5	15	218 45.1	48	10 23.2	4	73 37.0	59	20 38.3	0
9	17 07.0	224 32.4	15	8 32.4	7	174 02.9	21	9 14.7	15	219 33.4	48	10 19.1	4	74 35.8	59	20 38.3	0
10	18 06.1	224 47.0	14	8 25.3	8	174 24.2	21	9 29.9	15	220 21.7	48	10 15.1	4	75 34.5	59	20 38.2	0
11	19 05.2	225 00.8	+13	N 8 17.7	− 8	174 45.5	+21	S 9 45.1	−15	221 10.0	+49	N10 11.0	− 4	76 33.1	+58	S20 38.1	0
12	20 04.4	225 13.8	12	8 09.5	9	175 06.8	21	10 00.1	15	221 58.5	49	10 07.0	4	77 31.5	58	20 38.0	0
13	21 03.5	225 26.0	12	8 00.6	9	175 27.8	21	10 15.2	15	222 47.0	49	10 03.1	4	78 29.9	58	20 37.9	0
14	22 02.6	225 37.5	11	7 51.3	10	175 48.8	21	10 30.2	15	223 35.6	49	9 59.0	4	79 28.1	58	20 37.7	0
15	23 01.8	225 48.2	10	7 41.4	11	176 09.7	21	10 45.1	15	224 24.3	49	9 55.1	4	80 26.3	58	20 37.5	0
16	24 00.9	225 58.2	+ 9	N 7 30.9	−11	176 30.5	+21	S10 59.9	−15	225 13.1	+49	N 9 51.2	− 4	81 24.3	+58	S20 37.3	0
17	25 00.1	226 07.6	9	7 20.0	12	176 51.2	21	11 14.8	15	226 01.9	49	9 47.3	4	82 22.3	58	20 37.1	0
18	25 59.2	226 16.4	8	7 08.5	12	177 11.8	20	11 29.5	15	226 50.8	49	9 43.5	4	83 20.1	58	20 36.8	0
19	26 58.3	226 24.5	8	6 56.4	12	177 32.2	20	11 44.1	15	227 39.8	49	9 39.7	4	84 17.8	58	20 36.6	0
20	27 57.5	226 32.1	7	6 44.0	13	177 52.6	20	11 58.7	15	228 28.9	49	9 35.8	4	85 15.5	58	20 36.3	0
21	28 56.6	226 39.1	+ 7	N 6 30.9	−14	178 12.8	+20	S12 13.2	−14	229 18.0	+49	N 9 32.1	− 4	86 13.0	+57	S20 36.0	0
22	29 55.7	226 45.6	6	6 17.4	14	178 32.9	20	12 27.6	14	230 07.3	49	9 28.3	4	87 10.4	57	20 35.6	0
23	30 54.9	226 51.6	6	6 03.3	15	178 52.9	20	12 41.9	14	230 56.6	49	9 24.7	4	88 07.7	57	20 35.3	0
24	31 54.1	226 57.1	5	5 48.8	15	179 12.8	20	12 56.2	14	231 46.0	50	9 20.9	4	89 04.9	57	20 34.9	0
25	32 53.2	227 02.1	5	5 33.9	16	179 32.5	20	13 10.4	14	232 35.5	50	9 17.3	4	90 02.0	57	20 34.6	0
26	33 52.3	227 06.6	+ 4	N 5 18.4	−16	179 52.1	+20	S13 24.5	−14	233 25.1	+50	N 9 13.7	− 4	90 59.1	+57	S20 34.1	0
27	34 51.5	227 10.8	4	5 02.6	16	180 11.6	19	13 38.5	14	234 14.8	50	9 10.1	4	91 56.0	57	20 33.7	0
28	35 50.6	227 14.5	3	4 46.3	17	180 31.0	19	13 52.4	14	235 04.6	50	9 06.6	4	92 52.8	57	20 33.2	0
29	36 49.7	227 17.8	3	4 29.7	17	180 50.3	19	14 06.2	14	235 54.4	50	9 03.1	4	93 49.6	57	20 32.8	+ 1
30	37 48.9	227 20.8	3	4 12.6	18	181 09.4	19	14 20.0	14	236 44.4	50	8 59.6	3	94 46.1	57	20 32.2	1
31	38 48.0	227 23.4	+ 2	N 3 55.0	−18	181 28.4	+19	S14 33.6	−14	237 34.5	+50	N 8 56.2	− 3	95 42.7	+56	S20 31.7	+ 1

1991 SEPTEMBER, OCTOBER — SUN AND MOON

0h UT	SUN GHA	v	Dec	d	MOON 0h–8h GHA	v	Dec	d	MOON 8h–16h GHA	v	Dec	d	MOON 16h–24h GHA	v	Dec	d	HP
Sep	(SD 15'.9)							**SEPTEMBER**									
1	179 55.7	+5	N 8 32.5	−22	284 36	81	N23 35	+43	39 57	77	N24 18	+33	155 14	72	N24 51	+22	58.7
2	180 00.5	5	8 10.8	22	270 26	69	25 13	+12	25 35	66	25 25	+1	140 41	66	25 26	−10	59.2
3	180 05.3	5	7 48.9	22	255 47	65	25 16	−21	10 52	66	24 55	−32	125 58	67	24 23	43	59.6
4	180 10.1	5	7 26.9	22	241 05	70	23 40	54	356 15	74	22 46	63	111 29	77	21 43	74	60.0
5	180 15.1	5	7 04.9	22	226 46	82	20 29	82	342 08	86	19 07	89	97 34	91	17 38	97	60.1
6	180 20.0	+5	N 6 42.6	−22	213 05	96	N16 01	−104	328 41	100	N14 17	−109	84 21	105	N12 28	−113	60.1
7	180 25.0	5	6 20.3	22	200 06	109	10 35	117	315 55	113	8 38	119	71 48	116	6 39	122	59.8
8	180 30.1	5	5 57.8	23	187 44	119	N 4 37	122	303 43	121	N 2 35	123	59 44	123	N 0 32	121	59.4
9	180 35.2	5	5 35.3	23	175 47	124	S 1 29	121	291 51	126	S 3 30	118	47 57	126	S 5 28	116	58.7
10	180 40.4	5	5 12.7	23	164 03	126	7 24	112	280 09	125	9 16	108	36 14	125	11 04	103	58.0
11	180 45.6	+5	N 4 49.9	−23	152 19	125	S12 47	−99	268 24	123	S14 26	−92	24 27	122	S15 58	−87	57.2
12	180 50.9	5	4 27.1	23	140 29	120	17 25	80	256 29	119	18 45	74	12 28	118	19 59	67	56.4
13	180 56.2	5	4 04.3	23	128 26	117	21 06	59	244 23	115	22 05	52	0 18	114	22 57	44	55.7
14	181 01.4	5	3 41.3	23	116 12	114	23 41	36	232 06	113	24 17	28	347 59	113	24 45	−20	55.1
15	181 06.7	5	3 18.2	23	103 52	113	25 05	−12	219 45	115	25 17	−4	335 40	115	25 21	+4	54.6
16	181 12.1	+5	N 2 55.2	−23	91 35	117	S25 17	+11	207 32	118	S25 06	+20	323 30	121	S24 46	+26	54.3
17	181 17.4	5	2 32.0	23	79 31	123	24 20	34	195 34	125	23 46	41	311 39	129	23 05	48	54.2
18	181 22.7	5	2 08.9	23	67 48	130	22 17	54	183 58	134	21 23	60	300 12	136	20 23	66	54.3
19	181 28.1	5	1 45.7	23	56 28	139	19 17	71	172 47	142	18 06	77	289 09	143	16 49	82	54.5
20	181 33.5	5	1 22.4	23	45 32	146	15 27	86	161 58	147	14 01	90	278 25	149	12 31	94	54.8
21	181 38.8	+5	N 0 59.1	−23	34 54	150	S10 57	+98	151 24	151	S 9 19	+100	267 55	151	S 7 39	+103	55.3
22	181 44.2	5	0 35.8	23	24 26	150	5 56	106	140 56	151	S 4 10	107	257 27	149	S 2 23	108	55.8
23	181 49.4	5	N 0 12.4	23	13 56	148	N 4 54	109	130 24	146	N 1 15	110	246 50	144	N 3 05	109	56.3
24	181 54.7	5	S 0 10.9	23	3 14	141	N 4 54	109	119 35	138	6 43	108	235 53	134	8 31	105	56.9
25	182 00.0	5	0 34.3	23	352 07	129	10 16	103	108 16	125	11 59	100	224 21	121	13 39	96	57.4
26	182 05.2	+5	S 0 57.6	−23	340 22	115	N15 15	+92	96 17	109	N16 47	+86	212 06	104	N18 13	+80	57.9
27	182 10.4	5	1 21.0	23	327 50	99	19 33	73	83 29	93	20 46	65	199 02	88	21 51	58	58.3
28	182 15.5	5	1 44.3	23	314 30	83	22 49	48	69 53	78	23 37	39	185 11	76	24 16	+29	58.6
29	182 20.5	5	2 07.7	23	300 27	72	24 45	+19	55 39	70	25 04	0	170 40	70	25 13	−3	58.9
30	182 25.5	+5	S 2 31.0	−23	285 59	69	N25 10	−13	41 08	70	N24 57	−24	156 18	72	N24 33	−34	59.1
Oct	(SD 16'.1)							**OCTOBER**									
1	182 30.5	+5	S 2 54.4	−23	271 30	75	N23 59	−45	26 45	78	N23 14	−55	142 03	82	N22 19	−63	59.3
2	182 35.3	5	3 17.6	23	257 25	86	21 16	73	12 51	91	20 03	90	128 22	96	18 43	88	59.4
3	182 40.1	5	3 40.9	23	243 57	100	17 15	94	359 37	104	15 41	100	115 21	109	14 01	105	59.3
4	182 44.8	5	4 04.1	23	231 10	112	12 16	110	347 02	116	10 26	112	102 58	119	8 34	116	59.2
5	182 49.4	5	4 27.2	23	218 57	122	6 38	117	334 59	123	N 4 41	119	91 02	126	N 2 42	119	58.9
6	182 53.9	+4	S 4 50.4	−23	207 08	127	N 0 43	−119	323 15	127	S 1 16	−118	79 22	128	S 3 14	−116	58.5
7	182 58.3	4	5 13.4	23	195 30	128	S 5 10	114	311 38	127	7 04	111	67 45	127	8 55	107	58.0
8	183 02.6	4	5 36.4	23	183 52	125	10 42	103	299 57	124	12 25	99	56 01	122	14 04	93	57.4
9	183 06.8	4	5 59.3	23	172 03	120	15 37	87	288 03	119	17 04	81	44 02	116	18 25	75	56.8
10	183 11.0	4	6 22.2	23	159 58	115	19 40	67	275 53	114	20 47	60	31 47	112	21 47	53	56.1
11	183 14.9	+4	S 6 44.9	−23	147 39	111	S22 40	−44	263 30	111	S23 24	−37	19 21	110	S24 01	−28	55.5
12	183 18.8	4	7 07.6	23	135 11	110	24 29	−21	251 01	111	24 50	−12	6 52	112	25 02	−4	55.0
13	183 22.6	4	7 30.1	23	122 44	113	25 06	+4	238 37	116	25 02	+12	354 33	117	24 50	+19	54.6
14	183 26.3	4	7 52.6	22	110 30	120	24 31	27	226 30	123	24 04	34	342 33	125	23 30	41	54.3
15	183 29.8	3	8 14.9	22	98 38	129	22 49	47	214 47	132	22 02	54	330 59	134	21 08	59	54.3
16	183 33.1	+3	S 8 37.1	−22	87 13	138	S20 09	+65	203 31	141	S19 04	+71	319 52	143	S17 53	+76	54.3
17	183 36.4	3	8 59.3	22	76 15	145	16 37	80	192 40	147	15 17	85	309 07	150	13 52	88	54.6
18	183 39.5	3	9 21.2	22	65 37	150	12 24	93	182 07	152	10 51	96	298 39	152	9 15	99	55.0
19	183 42.4	3	9 43.1	22	55 11	152	7 36	101	171 43	151	5 55	104	288 14	151	S 4 11	106	55.6
20	183 45.2	3	10 04.8	22	44 45	150	S 2 25	108	161 15	148	S 0 37	108	277 43	145	N 1 11	109	56.2
21	183 47.9	+3	S10 26.4	−21	34 08	142	N 3 00	+109	150 30	140	N 4 49	+109	266 50	135	N 6 38	+108	56.9
22	183 50.4	2	10 47.8	21	23 05	131	8 26	106	139 16	126	10 12	103	255 22	120	11 55	101	57.6
23	183 52.8	2	11 08.9	21	11 22	116	13 36	96	127 18	109	15 12	92	243 07	103	16 44	87	58.3
24	183 54.9	2	11 30.1	21	358 50	97	18 11	80	114 27	91	19 31	74	229 58	85	20 45	65	58.8
25	183 56.9	2	11 51.0	21	345 23	80	21 50	57	100 43	75	22 47	47	215 58	71	23 34	37	59.2
26	183 58.7	+2	S12 11.7	−21	331 09	67	N24 11	+27	86 16	65	N24 38	+17	201 21	64	N24 55	+5	59.4
27	184 00.3	2	12 32.2	20	316 25	64	25 00	−6	71 29	65	24 54	−17	186 34	67	24 37	−28	59.5
28	184 01.8	1	12 52.5	20	301 41	70	24 09	39	56 51	74	23 30	48	172 05	78	22 42	58	59.5
29	184 03.0	1	13 12.7	20	287 23	83	21 44	67	42 46	88	20 37	75	158 14	94	19 22	82	59.3
30	184 04.0	1	13 32.6	20	273 48	99	18 00	89	29 27	105	16 31	95	145 12	109	14 56	100	59.1
31	184 04.9	+1	S13 52.3	−20	261 01	114	N13 16	−104	16 55	118	N11 32	−108	132 53	122	N 9 44	−110	58.8

5

1991 NOVEMBER, DECEMBER — ARIES AND PLANETS

0ʰ UT	ARIES GHA	VENUS GHA	v	Dec	d	MARS GHA	v	Dec	d	JUPITER GHA	v	Dec	d	SATURN GHA	v	Dec	d
Nov	° ′	° ′		° ′		° ′		° ′		° ′		° ′		° ′		° ′	
								NOVEMBER									
1	39 47.2	227 25.6	+2	N 3 37.2	−18	181 47.3	+19	S14 47.2	−13	238 24.7	+50	N 8 52.8	−3	96 39.1	+56	S20 31.2	+1
2	40 46.3	227 27.5	2	3 18.9	19	182 06.0	19	15 00.6	13	239 14.9	50	8 49.4	3	97 35.4	56	20 30.6	1
3	41 45.4	227 29.1	1	3 00.3	19	182 24.6	19	15 13.9	13	240 05.3	51	8 46.1	3	98 31.6	56	20 30.0	1
4	42 44.6	227 30.3	1	2 41.4	19	182 43.1	18	15 27.1	13	240 55.8	51	8 42.8	3	99 27.8	56	20 29.4	1
5	43 43.7	227 31.2	+1	2 22.1	20	183 01.4	18	15 40.3	13	241 46.4	51	8 39.6	3	100 23.8	56	20 28.8	1
6	44 42.8	227 31.9	0	N 2 02.5	−20	183 19.6	+18	S15 53.3	−13	242 37.1	+51	N 8 36.4	−3	101 19.7	+56	S20 28.1	+1
7	45 42.0	227 32.3	0	1 42.6	20	183 37.7	18	16 06.1	13	243 27.8	51	8 33.2	3	102 15.6	56	20 27.5	1
8	46 41.1	227 32.4	0	1 22.4	21	183 55.6	18	16 18.9	13	244 18.8	51	8 30.1	3	103 11.4	56	20 26.8	1
9	47 40.3	227 32.2	0	1 01.9	21	184 13.4	18	16 31.6	13	245 09.8	51	8 27.1	3	104 07.0	56	20 26.1	1
10	48 39.4	227 31.8	−1	0 41.1	21	184 31.1	18	16 44.1	12	246 01.0	51	8 24.1	3	105 02.6	56	20 25.3	1
11	49 38.5	227 31.1	−1	N 0 20.1	−21	184 48.6	+17	S16 56.5	−12	246 52.2	+51	N 8 21.1	−3	105 58.1	+55	S20 24.6	+1
12	50 37.7	227 30.1	1	S 0 01.2	22	185 06.0	17	17 08.8	12	247 43.6	52	8 18.2	3	106 53.5	55	20 23.8	1
13	51 36.8	227 29.0	1	0 22.7	22	185 23.2	17	17 20.9	12	248 35.1	52	8 15.3	3	107 48.8	55	20 23.0	1
14	52 35.9	227 27.6	2	0 44.4	22	185 40.3	17	17 32.9	12	249 26.7	52	8 12.5	3	108 44.0	55	20 22.2	1
15	53 35.1	227 25.9	2	1 06.3	22	185 57.3	17	17 44.8	12	250 18.5	52	8 09.7	3	109 39.2	55	20 21.4	1
16	54 34.3	227 24.0	−2	S 1 28.5	−22	186 14.1	+17	S17 56.6	−12	251 10.3	+52	N 8 07.0	−3	110 34.2	+55	S20 20.5	+1
17	55 33.4	227 21.8	2	1 50.8	23	186 30.8	17	18 08.2	12	252 02.3	52	8 04.3	3	111 29.2	55	20 19.7	1
18	56 32.5	227 19.4	3	2 13.3	23	186 47.3	16	18 19.7	11	252 54.4	52	8 01.6	3	112 24.1	55	20 18.8	1
19	57 31.7	227 16.8	3	2 36.0	23	187 03.7	16	18 31.0	11	253 46.7	52	7 59.0	3	113 18.8	55	20 17.9	1
20	58 30.8	227 13.9	3	2 58.8	23	187 20.0	16	18 42.1	11	254 39.1	53	7 56.5	2	114 13.6	55	20 16.9	1
21	59 29.9	227 10.8	−4	S 3 21.7	−23	187 36.1	+16	S18 53.2	−11	255 31.6	+53	N 7 54.1	−2	115 08.2	+55	S20 16.0	+1
22	60 29.0	227 07.3	4	3 44.8	23	187 52.1	16	19 04.0	11	256 24.2	53	7 51.7	2	116 02.8	54	20 15.1	1
23	61 28.2	227 03.7	4	4 08.0	23	188 07.9	16	19 14.8	11	257 17.0	53	7 49.3	2	116 57.2	54	20 14.0	1
24	62 27.4	226 59.9	4	4 31.2	23	188 23.7	16	19 25.3	10	258 09.9	53	7 47.0	2	117 51.6	54	20 13.0	1
25	63 26.5	226 55.8	4	4 54.5	23	188 39.2	15	19 35.7	10	259 02.9	53	7 44.8	2	118 45.9	54	20 12.0	1
26	64 25.6	226 51.4	−5	S 5 17.9	−24	188 54.5	+15	S19 46.0	−10	259 56.2	+53	N 7 42.6	−2	119 40.2	+54	S20 11.0	+1
27	65 24.8	226 46.8	5	5 41.5	23	189 09.9	15	19 56.0	10	260 49.5	54	7 40.4	2	120 34.3	54	20 09.9	1
28	66 23.9	226 42.0	5	6 04.9	24	189 25.0	15	20 05.9	10	261 43.0	54	7 38.4	2	121 28.4	54	20 08.8	1
29	67 23.0	226 36.9	5	6 28.4	24	189 39.9	15	20 15.6	10	262 36.6	54	7 36.4	2	122 22.4	54	20 07.7	1
30	68 22.2	226 31.5	−6	S 6 52.0	−24	189 54.7	+15	S20 25.2	−9	263 30.4	54	N 7 34.4	−2	123 16.4	+54	S20 06.7	+1
Dec								**DECEMBER**									
1	69 21.3	226 25.9	−6	S 7 15.5	−24	190 09.4	+15	S20 34.6	−9	264 24.3	+54	N 7 32.6	−2	124 10.3	+54	S20 05.5	+1
2	70 20.5	226 20.0	6	7 39.1	24	190 23.9	15	20 43.8	9	265 18.4	54	7 30.7	2	125 04.1	54	20 04.4	1
3	71 19.6	226 13.9	6	8 02.6	23	190 38.4	14	20 52.8	9	266 12.6	54	7 29.0	2	125 57.8	54	20 03.2	1
4	72 18.7	226 07.5	7	8 26.0	23	190 52.6	14	21 01.6	9	267 07.0	55	7 27.3	2	126 51.5	54	20 02.0	1
5	73 17.9	226 00.8	7	8 49.4	23	191 06.8	14	21 10.3	8	268 01.5	55	7 25.7	2	127 45.1	54	20 00.8	1
6	74 17.0	225 53.8	−7	S 9 12.8	−23	191 20.8	+14	S21 18.7	−8	268 56.1	+55	N 7 24.1	−2	128 38.6	+54	S19 59.6	+1
7	75 16.1	225 46.6	8	9 36.1	23	191 34.6	14	21 27.0	8	269 51.0	55	7 22.6	1	129 32.2	53	19 58.3	1
8	76 15.3	225 39.1	8	9 59.2	23	191 48.4	14	21 35.1	8	270 46.0	55	7 21.2	1	130 25.6	53	19 57.1	1
9	77 14.5	225 31.4	8	10 22.3	23	192 01.9	14	21 43.0	8	271 41.1	55	7 19.8	1	131 18.9	53	19 55.8	1
10	78 13.6	225 23.4	8	10 45.2	23	192 15.4	13	21 50.7	8	272 36.5	56	7 18.5	1	132 12.2	53	19 54.5	1
11	79 12.7	225 15.0	−9	S11 07.9	−23	192 28.7	+13	S21 58.2	−7	273 32.0	+56	N 7 17.3	−1	133 05.5	+53	S19 53.2	+1
12	80 11.9	225 06.4	9	11 30.6	23	192 41.9	13	22 05.4	7	274 27.6	56	7 16.1	1	133 58.6	53	19 51.9	1
13	81 11.0	224 57.5	9	11 53.1	22	192 55.0	13	22 12.5	7	275 23.5	56	7 15.1	1	134 51.7	53	19 50.6	1
14	82 10.1	224 48.3	10	12 15.3	22	193 07.9	13	22 19.4	7	276 19.4	56	7 14.0	1	135 44.8	53	19 49.2	1
15	83 09.2	224 38.8	10	12 37.4	22	193 20.8	13	22 26.1	6	277 15.6	56	7 13.1	1	136 37.8	53	19 47.9	1
16	84 08.4	224 29.1	−10	S12 59.3	−22	193 33.5	+13	S22 32.5	−6	278 11.9	+57	N 7 12.2	−1	137 30.8	+53	S19 46.5	+1
17	85 07.6	224 19.0	10	13 21.0	21	193 46.1	13	22 38.8	6	279 08.4	57	7 11.4	1	138 23.7	53	19 45.1	1
18	86 06.7	224 08.6	11	13 42.4	21	193 58.6	12	22 44.8	6	280 05.0	57	7 10.7	1	139 16.5	53	19 43.7	1
19	87 05.8	223 57.9	11	14 03.6	21	194 10.9	12	22 50.6	6	281 01.8	57	7 10.0	1	140 09.4	53	19 42.2	1
20	88 05.0	223 46.9	11	14 24.4	21	194 23.1	12	22 56.2	5	281 58.8	57	7 09.4	−1	141 02.1	53	19 40.8	1
21	89 04.1	223 35.6	−12	S14 45.1	−20	194 35.3	+12	S23 01.5	−5	282 56.0	+57	N 7 08.9	0	141 54.8	+53	S19 39.4	+2
22	90 03.2	223 24.0	12	15 05.4	20	194 47.3	12	23 06.7	5	283 53.4	58	7 08.5	0	142 47.5	53	19 37.9	2
23	91 02.4	223 12.1	12	15 25.5	20	194 59.2	12	23 11.6	5	284 50.9	58	7 08.1	0	143 40.1	53	19 36.4	2
24	92 01.5	222 59.8	13	15 45.2	19	195 11.0	12	23 16.3	5	285 48.6	58	7 07.8	0	144 32.6	53	19 34.9	2
25	93 00.7	222 47.2	13	16 04.6	19	195 22.7	12	23 20.8	4	286 46.5	58	7 07.6	0	145 25.2	53	19 33.4	2
26	93 59.8	222 34.3	−13	S16 23.6	−19	195 34.3	+12	S23 25.0	−4	287 44.6	+58	N 7 07.4	0	146 17.7	+52	S19 31.9	+2
27	94 58.9	222 21.1	14	16 42.3	18	195 45.8	11	23 29.0	4	288 42.8	59	7 07.3	0	147 10.1	52	19 30.3	2
28	95 58.1	222 07.5	14	17 00.6	18	195 57.2	11	23 32.7	4	289 41.3	59	7 07.3	0	148 02.5	52	19 28.7	2
29	96 57.2	221 53.7	14	17 18.6	18	196 08.5	11	23 36.3	3	290 39.8	59	7 07.4	0	148 54.9	52	19 27.2	2
30	97 56.3	221 39.5	15	17 36.1	18	196 19.7	11	23 39.6	3	291 38.6	59	7 07.6	0	149 47.3	52	19 25.6	2
31	98 55.5	221 25.0	−15	S17 53.2	−17	196 30.8	+11	S23 42.6	−3	292 37.6	+59	N 7 07.8	0	150 39.5	+52	S19 24.1	+2

1991 NOVEMBER, DECEMBER — SUN AND MOON

0ʰ UT	SUN GHA	v	Dec	d	MOON 0ʰ–8ʰ GHA	v	Dec	d	MOON 8ʰ–16ʰ GHA	v	Dec	d	MOON 16ʰ–24ʰ GHA	v	Dec	d	HP
Nov	(SD 16'.2)						**NOVEMBER**										
1	184 05.5 + 1		S14 11.8	−19	248 55	124	N 7 54	−113	4 59	128	N 6 01	−115	121 07	130	N 4 06	−115	58.5
2	184 06.0	0	14 31.1	19	237 17	131	N 2 11	115	353 28	133	N 0 16	116	109 41	133	S 1 40	114	58.1
3	184 06.2	0	14 50.2	19	225 54	133	S 3 34	112	342 07	132	S 5 26	110	98 19	132	7 16	108	57.6
4	184 06.3	0	15 09.0	19	214 31	131	9 04	104	330 42	129	10 48	100	86 51	127	12 28	96	57.2
5	184 06.1	0	15 27.5	18	202 58	125	14 04	91	319 03	123	15 35	86	75 06	120	17 01	79	56.7
6	184 05.7 − 1		S15 45.8	−18	191 06	119	S18 20	− 74	307 05	116	S19 34	− 66	63 01	114	S20 40	− 59	56.1
7	184 05.1	1	16 03.9	18	178 55	112	21 39	52	294 47	111	22 31	44	50 38	110	23 15	36	55.6
8	184 04.3	1	16 21.6	18	166 28	109	23 51	28	282 17	109	24 19	− 20	38 06	110	24 39	− 12	55.1
9	184 03.3	1	16 39.1	17	153 56	111	24 51	− 4	269 47	112	24 55	+ 5	25 39	114	24 50	+ 12	54.7
10	184 02.1	1	16 56.3	17	141 33	116	24 38	+ 20	257 29	119	24 18	27	13 28	123	23 51	34	54.4
11	184 00.7 − 2		S17 13.2	−17	129 31	125	S23 17	+ 42	245 36	129	S22 35	+ 47	1 45	132	S21 48	+ 54	54.2
12	183 59.1	2	17 29.9	16	117 57	135	20 54	60	234 12	139	19 54	65	350 31	142	18 49	70	54.2
13	183 57.3	2	17 46.2	16	106 53	145	17 39	75	223 18	148	16 24	80	339 46	150	15 04	83	54.3
14	183 55.2	2	18 02.2	16	96 16	152	13 41	87	212 48	153	12 14	91	329 21	155	10 43	94	54.6
15	183 52.9	2	18 18.0	15	85 56	156	9 09	97	202 32	155	7 32	99	319 07	156	5 53	102	55.0
16	183 50.5 − 3		S18 33.3	−15	75 43	155	S 4 11	+103	192 18	153	S 2 28	+105	308 51	152	S 0 43	+106	55.6
17	183 47.8	3	18 48.4	15	65 23	149	N 1 03	107	181 52	146	N 2 50	107	298 18	142	N 4 37	106	56.4
18	183 45.0	3	19 03.1	14	54 40	139	6 23	107	170 59	133	8 10	104	287 12	128	9 54	103	57.2
19	183 41.9	3	19 17.5	14	43 20	123	11 37	100	159 23	116	13 17	97	275 19	110	14 54	92	58.1
20	183 38.6	4	19 31.5	14	31 09	103	16 26	88	146 52	95	17 54	81	262 27	89	19 15	75	58.9
21	183 35.1 − 4		S19 45.2	−13	17 56	81	N20 30	+ 67	133 17	75	N21 37	+ 58	248 32	69	N22 35	+ 49	59.6
22	183 31.4	4	19 58.5	13	3 41	64	23 24	39	118 45	60	24 03	+ 28	233 45	56	24 31	+ 17	60.1
23	183 27.6	4	20 11.5	13	348 41	55	24 48	+ 5	103 36	54	24 53	− 7	218 30	55	24 46	− 18	60.4
24	183 23.4	4	20 24.1	12	333 25	57	24 28	− 30	88 22	60	23 58	42	203 22	65	23 16	51	60.4
25	183 19.2	5	20 36.3	12	318 27	70	22 25	62	73 37	75	21 23	70	188 52	82	20 13	79	60.2
26	183 14.6 − 5		S20 48.1	−11	304 14	88	N18 54	− 86	59 42	94	N17 28	− 93	175 16	101	N15 55	− 98	59.8
27	183 10.0	5	20 59.5	11	290 57	106	14 17	103	46 43	112	12 34	107	162 35	116	10 47	109	59.3
28	183 05.2	5	21 10.6	11	278 31	121	8 58	112	34 32	125	7 06	114	150 37	128	N 5 12	115	58.7
29	183 00.1	5	21 21.3	10	266 45	131	N 3 17	114	22 56	133	N 1 23	115	139 09	135	S 0 32	114	58.1
30	182 54.9 − 5		S21 31.5	−10	255 24	135	S 2 26	−112	11 39	135	S 4 18	−110	127 54	136	S 6 08	−107	57.5
Dec	(SD 16'.3)						**DECEMBER**										
1	182 49.5 − 6		S21 41.4	− 9	244 10	135	S 7 55	−105	0 25	134	S 9 40	−101	116 39	132	S11 21	− 97	56.9
2	182 43.9	6	21 50.8	9	232 51	131	12 58	92	349 02	128	14 30	88	105 10	127	15 58	82	56.4
3	182 38.2	6	21 59.8	9	221 17	124	17 20	77	337 21	121	18 37	70	93 22	119	19 47	64	55.9
4	182 32.3	6	22 08.4	8	209 21	117	20 51	57	325 18	115	21 48	49	81 13	114	22 37	42	55.5
5	182 26.3	6	22 16.5	8	197 07	112	23 19	35	312 59	111	23 54	26	68 50	111	24 20	− 19	55.1
6	182 20.1 − 6		S22 24.2	− 7	184 41	110	S24 39	− 10	300 31	112	S24 49	− 2	56 23	113	S24 51	+ 5	54.7
7	182 13.8	6	22 31.5	7	172 16	114	24 46	+ 14	288 10	117	24 32	+ 21	44 07	119	24 11	28	54.4
8	182 07.4	7	22 38.4	6	160 06	122	23 43	36	276 08	125	23 07	42	32 13	129	22 25	49	54.2
9	182 00.8	7	22 44.8	6	148 22	132	21 36	54	264 34	136	20 42	61	20 50	140	19 41	66	54.1
10	181 54.1	7	22 50.7	6	137 10	143	18 35	70	253 33	146	17 25	76	9 59	149	16 09	79	54.0
11	181 47.3 − 7		S22 56.2	− 5	126 28	151	S14 50	+ 84	242 59	154	S13 26	+ 87	359 33	156	S11 59	+ 90	54.2
12	181 40.4	7	23 01.3	5	116 09	158	10 29	93	232 47	159	8 56	95	349 26	159	7 21	98	54.5
13	181 33.5	7	23 05.9	4	106 05	159	5 43	100	222 44	160	S 4 03	101	339 24	158	S 2 22	102	54.9
14	181 26.4	7	23 10.0	4	96 02	157	S 0 40	104	212 39	154	N 1 04	104	329 13	153	N 2 48	104	55.5
15	181 19.3	7	23 13.7	3	85 46	149	N 4 32	104	202 15	145	6 16	103	318 40	140	7 59	102	56.3
16	181 12.1 − 7		S23 17.0	− 3	75 00	136	N 9 41	+100	191 16	130	N11 21	+ 98	307 26	124	N12 59	+ 95	57.1
17	181 04.8	7	23 19.7	2	63 30	117	14 34	91	179 27	110	16 05	87	295 17	103	17 32	82	58.1
18	180 57.5	7	23 22.0	2	51 00	95	18 54	75	166 35	87	20 09	69	282 02	80	21 18	60	59.1
19	180 50.1	7	23 23.8	1	37 22	73	22 18	52	152 35	66	23 10	42	267 41	60	23 52	+ 31	59.9
20	180 42.7	7	23 25.2	− 1	22 41	55	24 23	+ 21	137 36	51	24 44	+ 8	252 27	50	24 52	− 3	60.6
21	180 35.3 − 7		S23 26.0	0	7 17	48	N24 49	− 15	122 05	50	N24 34	− 28	236 55	51	N24 06	− 40	61.1
22	180 27.9	7	23 26.4	0	351 46	55	24 26	50	106 40	59	22 36	62	221 39	65	21 34	72	61.2
23	180 20.5	7	23 26.4	+ 1	336 44	70	20 22	80	91 54	77	19 02	89	207 11	83	17 33	96	61.0
24	180 13.0	7	23 25.8	1	322 34	89	15 57	102	78 03	96	14 15	107	193 39	102	12 28	111	60.5
25	180 05.6	7	23 24.9	2	309 21	108	10 37	114	65 09	112	8 43	116	181 01	117	6 47	118	59.9
26	179 58.1 − 7		S23 23.4	+ 2	296 58	121	N 4 49	−118	52 59	125	N 2 51	−118	169 04	127	N 0 53	−117	59.1
27	179 50.7	7	23 21.5	2	285 11	130	S 1 04	115	41 21	131	S 2 59	114	157 32	132	S 4 53	111	58.2
28	179 43.3	7	23 19.1	3	273 44	132	6 44	108	29 56	132	8 32	104	146 08	132	10 16	100	57.4
29	179 36.0	7	23 16.2	3	262 20	131	11 56	96	18 31	130	13 32	91	134 41	129	15 03	85	56.7
30	179 28.7	7	23 12.8	4	250 50	126	16 28	80	6 56	125	17 48	74	123 01	123	19 02	68	56.0
31	179 21.4 − 7		S23 09.0	+ 4	239 04	120	S20 10	− 61	355 04	119	S21 11	− 54	111 03	117	S22 05	− 47	55.4

5

5.3.9 — INTERPOLATION TABLES — ARIES, SUN, PLANETS 0ʰ–12ʰ

Correction to GHA Aries

UT s	0ᵐ	1ᵐ	2ᵐ	3ᵐ
00	0 00.0	0 15.0	0 30.1	0 45.1
04	01.0	16.0	31.1	46.1
08	02.0	17.0	32.1	47.1
12	03.0	18.0	33.1	48.1
16	04.0	19.1	34.1	49.1
20	0 05.0	0 20.1	0 35.1	0 50.1
24	06.0	21.1	36.1	51.1
28	07.0	22.1	37.1	52.1
32	08.0	23.1	38.1	53.1
36	09.0	24.1	39.1	54.1
40	0 10.0	0 25.1	0 40.1	0 55.2
44	11.0	26.1	41.1	56.2
48	12.0	27.1	42.1	57.2
52	13.0	28.1	43.1	58.2
56	14.0	29.1	44.1	0 59.2
60	0 15.0	0 30.1	0 45.1	1 00.2

Correction to GHA Aries

UT s	4ᵐ	5ᵐ	6ᵐ	7ᵐ
00	1 00.2	1 15.2	1 30.2	1 45.3
04	01.2	16.2	31.2	46.3
08	02.2	17.2	32.3	47.3
12	03.2	18.2	33.3	48.3
16	04.2	19.2	34.3	49.3
20	1 05.2	1 20.2	1 35.3	1 50.3
24	06.2	21.2	36.3	51.3
28	07.2	22.2	37.3	52.3
32	08.2	23.2	38.3	53.3
36	09.2	24.2	39.3	54.3
40	1 10.2	1 25.2	1 40.3	1 55.3
44	11.2	26.2	41.3	56.3
48	12.2	27.2	42.3	57.3
52	13.2	28.2	43.3	58.3
56	14.2	29.2	44.3	1 59.3
60	1 15.2	1 30.2	1 45.3	2 00.3

Correction to GHA Aries

UT s	8ᵐ	9ᵐ	10ᵐ	11ᵐ
00	2 00.3	2 15.4	2 30.4	2 45.5
04	01.3	16.4	31.4	46.5
08	02.3	17.4	32.4	47.5
12	03.3	18.4	33.4	48.5
16	04.3	19.4	34.4	49.5
20	2 05.3	2 20.4	2 35.4	2 50.5
24	06.3	21.4	36.4	51.5
28	07.3	22.4	37.4	52.5
32	08.4	23.4	38.4	53.5
36	09.4	24.4	39.4	54.5
40	2 10.4	2 25.4	2 40.4	2 55.5
44	11.4	26.4	41.4	56.5
48	12.4	27.4	42.4	57.5
52	13.4	28.4	43.4	58.5
56	14.4	29.4	44.4	2 59.5
60	2 15.4	2 30.4	2 45.5	3 00.5

Corr. to GHA / Correction to GHA or Declination for v or d

UT h m	Aries	Sun Planet	1	2	3	4	5	6	7	8	9	10	11	12	13	14	15	16
	° ′	°	Units of 0′.1															
0 00	0 00.0	0	0	0	0	0	0	0	0	0	0	0	0	0	0	0	0	0
12	3 00.5	3	0	0	0	0	0	1	1	1	1	1	1	1	1	1	1	1
24	6 01.0	6	0	0	1	1	1	1	1	1	2	2	2	2	2	2	3	3
36	9 01.5	9	0	1	1	1	1	2	2	2	2	3	3	3	3	4	4	4
0 48	12 02.0	12	0	1	1	1	2	2	2	3	3	3	4	4	4	5	5	5
1 00	15 02.5	15	0	1	1	2	2	3	3	3	4	4	5	5	5	6	6	7
12	18 03.0	18	1	1	2	2	3	3	4	4	5	5	6	6	7	7	8	8
24	21 03.4	21	1	1	2	2	3	4	4	5	5	6	6	7	8	8	9	9
36	24 03.9	24	1	1	2	3	3	4	5	5	6	7	7	8	9	9	10	11
1 48	27 04.4	27	1	2	2	3	4	5	5	6	7	8	8	9	10	11	11	12
2 00	30 04.9	30	1	2	3	3	4	5	6	7	8	8	9	10	11	12	13	13
12	33 05.4	33	1	2	3	4	5	6	6	7	8	9	10	11	12	13	14	15
24	36 05.9	36	1	2	3	4	5	6	7	8	9	10	11	12	13	14	15	16
36	39 06.4	39	1	2	3	4	5	7	8	9	10	11	12	13	14	15	16	17
2 48	42 06.9	42	1	2	4	5	6	7	8	9	11	12	13	14	15	16	18	19
3 00	45 07.4	45	1	3	4	5	6	8	9	10	11	13	14	15	16	18	19	20
12	48 07.9	48	1	3	4	5	7	8	9	11	12	13	15	16	17	19	20	21
24	51 08.4	51	1	3	4	6	7	9	10	11	13	14	16	17	18	20	21	23
36	54 08.9	54	2	3	5	6	8	9	11	12	14	15	17	18	20	21	23	24
3 48	57 09.4	57	2	3	5	6	8	10	11	13	14	16	17	19	21	22	24	25
4 00	60 09.9	60	2	3	5	7	8	10	12	13	15	17	18	20	22	23	25	27
12	63 10.3	63	2	4	5	7	9	11	12	14	16	18	19	21	23	25	26	28
24	66 10.8	66	2	4	6	7	9	11	13	15	17	18	20	22	24	26	28	29
36	69 11.3	69	2	4	6	8	10	12	13	15	17	19	21	23	25	27	29	31
4 48	72 11.8	72	2	4	6	8	10	12	14	16	18	20	22	24	26	28	30	32
5 00	75 12.3	75	2	4	6	8	10	13	15	17	19	21	23	25	27	29	31	33
12	78 12.8	78	2	4	7	9	11	13	15	17	20	22	24	26	28	30	33	35
24	81 13.3	81	2	5	7	9	11	14	16	18	20	23	25	27	29	32	34	36
36	84 13.8	84	2	5	7	9	12	14	16	19	21	23	26	28	30	33	35	37
5 48	87 14.3	87	2	5	7	10	12	15	17	19	22	24	27	29	31	34	36	39
6 00	90 14.8	90	3	5	8	10	13	15	18	20	23	25	28	30	33	35	38	40
12	93 15.3	93	3	5	8	10	13	16	18	21	23	26	28	31	34	36	39	41
24	96 15.8	96	3	5	8	11	13	16	19	21	24	27	29	32	35	37	40	43
36	99 16.3	99	3	6	8	11	14	17	19	22	25	28	30	33	36	39	41	44
6 48	102 16.8	102	3	6	9	11	14	17	20	23	26	28	31	34	37	40	43	45
7 00	105 17.2	105	3	6	9	12	15	18	20	23	26	29	32	35	38	41	44	47
12	108 17.7	108	3	6	9	12	15	18	21	24	27	30	33	36	39	42	45	48
24	111 18.2	111	3	6	9	12	15	19	22	25	28	31	34	37	40	43	46	49
36	114 18.7	114	3	6	10	13	16	19	22	25	29	32	35	38	41	44	48	51
7 48	117 19.2	117	3	7	10	13	16	20	23	26	29	33	36	39	42	46	49	52
8 00	120 19.7	120	3	7	10	13	17	20	23	27	30	33	37	40	43	47	50	53
12	123 20.2	123	3	7	10	14	17	21	24	27	31	34	38	41	44	48	51	55
24	126 20.7	126	4	7	11	14	18	21	25	28	32	35	39	42	46	49	53	56
36	129 21.2	129	4	7	11	14	18	22	25	29	32	36	39	43	47	50	54	57
8 48	132 21.7	132	4	7	11	15	18	22	26	29	33	37	40	44	48	51	55	59
9 00	135 22.2	135	4	8	11	15	19	23	26	30	34	38	41	45	49	53	56	60
12	138 22.7	138	4	8	12	15	19	23	27	31	35	38	42	46	50	54	58	61
24	141 23.2	141	4	8	12	16	20	24	27	31	35	39	43	47	51	55	59	63
36	144 23.7	144	4	8	12	16	20	24	28	32	36	40	44	48	52	56	60	64
9 48	147 24.1	147	4	8	12	16	20	25	29	33	37	41	45	49	53	57	61	65
10 00	150 24.6	150	4	8	13	17	21	25	29	33	38	42	46	50	54	58	63	67
12	153 25.1	153	4	9	13	17	21	26	30	34	38	43	47	51	55	60	64	68
24	156 25.6	156	4	9	13	17	22	26	30	35	39	43	48	52	56	61	65	69
36	159 26.1	159	4	9	13	18	22	27	31	35	40	44	49	53	57	62	66	71
10 48	162 26.6	162	5	9	14	18	23	27	32	36	41	45	50	54	59	63	68	72
11 00	165 27.1	165	5	9	14	18	23	28	32	37	41	46	50	55	60	64	69	73
12	168 27.6	168	5	9	14	19	23	28	33	37	42	47	51	56	61	65	70	75
24	171 28.1	171	5	10	14	19	24	29	33	38	43	48	52	57	62	67	71	76
36	174 28.6	174	5	10	15	19	24	29	34	39	44	48	53	58	63	68	73	77
48	177 29.1	177	5	10	15	20	25	30	34	39	44	49	54	59	64	69	74	79
12 00	180 29.6	180	5	10	15	20	25	30	35	40	45	50	55	60	65	70	75	80

INTERPOLATION TABLES — ARIES, SUN, PLANETS 12ʰ–24ʰ

UT	Corr. to GHA Aries	Sun Planet	1	2	3	4	5	6	7	8	9	10	11	12	13	14	15	16
h m	° ′	′									Units of 0′.1							
12 00	180 29.6	180	5	10	15	20	25	30	35	40	45	50	55	60	65	70	75	80
12	183 30.1	183	5	10	15	20	25	31	36	41	46	51	56	61	66	71	76	81
24	186 30.6	186	5	10	16	21	26	31	36	41	47	52	57	62	67	72	78	83
36	189 31.0	189	5	11	16	21	26	32	37	42	47	53	58	63	68	74	79	84
12 48	192 31.5	192	5	11	16	21	27	32	37	43	48	53	59	64	69	75	80	85
13 00	195 32.0	195	5	11	16	22	27	33	38	43	49	54	60	65	70	76	81	87
12	198 32.5	198	6	11	17	22	28	33	39	44	50	55	61	66	72	77	83	88
24	201 33.0	201	6	11	17	22	28	34	39	45	50	56	61	67	73	78	84	89
36	204 33.5	204	6	11	17	23	28	34	40	45	51	57	62	68	74	79	85	91
13 48	207 34.0	207	6	12	17	23	29	35	40	46	52	58	63	69	75	81	86	92
14 00	210 34.5	210	6	12	18	23	29	35	41	47	53	58	64	70	76	82	88	93
12	213 35.0	213	6	12	18	24	30	36	41	47	53	59	65	71	77	83	89	95
24	216 35.5	216	6	12	18	24	30	36	42	48	54	60	66	72	78	84	90	96
36	219 36.0	219	6	12	18	24	30	37	43	49	55	61	67	73	79	85	91	97
14 48	222 36.5	222	6	12	19	25	31	37	43	49	56	62	68	74	80	86	93	99
15 00	225 37.0	225	6	13	19	25	31	38	44	50	56	63	69	75	81	88	94	100
12	228 37.5	228	6	13	19	25	32	38	44	51	57	63	70	76	82	89	95	101
24	231 37.9	231	6	13	19	26	32	39	45	51	58	64	71	77	83	90	96	103
36	234 38.4	234	7	13	20	26	33	39	46	52	59	65	72	78	85	91	98	104
15 48	237 38.9	237	7	13	20	26	33	40	46	53	59	66	72	79	86	92	99	105
16 00	240 39.4	240	7	13	20	27	33	40	47	53	60	67	73	80	87	93	100	107
12	243 39.9	243	7	14	20	27	34	41	47	54	61	68	74	81	88	95	101	108
24	246 40.4	246	7	14	21	27	34	41	48	55	62	68	75	82	89	96	103	109
36	249 40.9	249	7	14	21	28	35	42	48	55	62	69	76	83	90	97	104	111
16 48	252 41.4	252	7	14	21	28	35	42	49	56	63	70	77	84	91	98	105	112
17 00	255 41.9	255	7	14	21	28	35	43	50	57	64	71	78	85	92	99	106	113
12	258 42.4	258	7	14	22	29	36	43	50	57	65	72	79	86	93	100	108	115
24	261 42.9	261	7	15	22	29	36	44	51	58	65	73	80	87	94	102	109	116
36	264 43.4	264	7	15	22	29	37	44	51	59	66	73	81	88	95	103	110	117
17 48	267 43.9	267	7	15	22	30	37	45	52	59	67	74	82	89	96	104	111	119
18 00	270 44.4	270	8	15	23	30	38	45	53	60	68	75	83	90	98	105	113	120
12	273 44.8	273	8	15	23	30	38	46	53	61	68	76	83	91	99	106	114	121
24	276 45.3	276	8	15	23	31	38	46	54	61	69	77	84	92	100	107	115	123
36	279 45.8	279	8	16	23	31	39	47	54	62	70	78	85	93	101	109	116	124
18 48	282 46.3	282	8	16	24	31	39	47	55	63	71	78	86	94	102	110	118	125
19 00	285 46.8	285	8	16	24	32	40	48	55	63	71	79	87	95	103	111	119	127
12	288 47.3	288	8	16	24	32	40	48	56	64	72	80	88	96	104	112	120	128
24	291 47.8	291	8	16	24	32	40	49	57	65	73	81	89	97	105	113	121	129
36	294 48.3	294	8	16	25	33	41	49	57	65	74	82	90	98	106	114	123	131
19 48	297 48.8	297	8	17	25	33	41	50	58	66	74	83	91	99	107	116	124	132
20 00	300 49.3	300	8	17	25	33	42	50	58	67	75	83	92	100	108	117	125	133
12	303 49.8	303	8	17	25	34	42	51	59	67	76	84	93	101	109	118	126	135
24	306 50.3	306	9	17	26	34	43	51	60	68	77	85	94	102	111	119	128	136
36	309 50.8	309	9	17	26	34	43	52	60	69	77	86	94	103	112	120	129	137
20 48	312 51.3	312	9	17	26	35	43	52	61	69	78	87	95	104	113	121	130	139
21 00	315 51.7	315	9	18	26	35	44	53	61	70	79	88	96	105	114	123	131	140
12	318 52.2	318	9	18	27	35	44	53	62	71	80	88	97	106	115	124	133	141
24	321 52.7	321	9	18	27	36	45	54	62	71	80	89	98	107	116	125	134	143
36	324 53.2	324	9	18	27	36	45	54	63	72	81	90	99	108	117	126	135	144
21 48	327 53.7	327	9	18	27	36	45	55	64	73	82	91	100	109	118	127	136	145
22 00	330 54.2	330	9	18	28	37	46	55	64	73	83	92	101	110	119	128	138	147
12	333 54.7	333	9	19	28	37	46	56	65	74	83	93	102	111	120	130	139	148
24	336 55.2	336	9	19	28	37	47	56	65	75	84	93	103	112	121	131	140	149
36	339 55.7	339	9	19	28	38	47	57	66	75	85	94	104	113	122	132	141	151
22 48	342 56.2	342	10	19	29	38	48	57	67	76	86	95	105	114	124	133	143	152
23 00	345 56.7	345	10	19	29	38	48	58	67	77	86	96	105	115	125	134	144	153
12	348 57.2	348	10	19	29	39	48	58	68	77	87	97	106	116	126	135	145	155
24	351 57.7	351	10	20	29	39	49	59	68	78	88	98	107	117	127	137	146	156
36	354 58.2	354	10	20	30	39	49	59	69	79	89	98	108	118	128	138	148	157
23 48	357 58.6	357	10	20	30	40	50	60	69	79	89	99	109	119	129	139	149	159
24 00	360 59.1	360	10	20	30	40	50	60	70	80	90	100	110	120	130	140	150	160

Correction to GHA or Declination for v or d

Correction to GHA Sun and Planets

UT	0ᵐ	1ᵐ	2ᵐ	3ᵐ
s	° ′	° ′	° ′	° ′
00	0 00	0 15	0 30	0 45
04	01	16	31	46
08	02	17	32	47
12	03	18	33	48
16	04	19	34	49
20	0 05	0 20	0 35	0 50
24	06	21	36	51
28	07	22	37	52
32	08	23	38	53
36	09	24	39	54
40	0 10	0 25	0 40	0 55
44	11	26	41	56
48	12	27	42	57
52	13	28	43	58
56	14	29	44	0 59
60	0 15	0 30	0 45	1 00

Correction to GHA Sun and Planets

UT	4ᵐ	5ᵐ	6ᵐ	7ᵐ
s	° ′	° ′	° ′	° ′
00	1 00	1 15	1 30	1 45
04	01	16	31	46
08	02	17	32	47
12	03	18	33	48
16	04	19	34	49
20	1 05	1 20	1 35	1 50
24	06	21	36	51
28	07	22	37	52
32	08	23	38	53
36	09	24	39	54
40	1 10	1 25	1 40	1 55
44	11	26	41	56
48	12	27	42	57
52	13	28	43	58
56	14	29	44	1 59
60	1 15	1 30	1 45	2 00

Correction to GHA Sun and Planets

UT	8ᵐ	9ᵐ	10ᵐ	11ᵐ
s	° ′	° ′	° ′	° ′
00	2 00	2 15	2 30	2 45
04	01	16	31	46
08	02	17	32	47
12	03	18	33	48
16	04	19	34	49
20	2 05	2 20	2 35	2 50
24	06	21	36	51
28	07	22	37	52
32	08	23	38	53
36	09	24	39	54
40	2 10	2 25	2 40	2 55
44	11	26	41	56
48	12	27	42	57
52	13	28	43	58
56	14	29	44	2 59
60	2 15	2 30	2 45	3 00

5

INTERPOLATION TABLES — SUN, PLANETS 0ʰ–12ʰ

Correction to GHA or Declination for v or d — Units of 0′.1

UT	Corr. to GHA Sun Planet	10	12	14	16	18	20	22	24	26	28	30	32	34	36	38	40	42	44	46	48	50	52	54	56	58	60
h m	°																										
0 00	0	0	0	0	0	0	0	0	0	0	0	0	0	0	0	0	0	0	0	0	0	0	0	0	0	0	0
12	3	1	1	1	1	2	2	2	2	2	2	3	3	3	3	3	3	4	4	4	4	4	4	5	5	5	5
24	6	2	2	2	3	3	3	4	4	4	5	5	5	6	6	6	7	7	7	8	8	8	9	9	9	10	10
36	9	3	3	4	4	5	5	6	6	7	7	8	8	9	9	10	10	11	11	12	12	13	13	14	14	15	15
0 48	12	3	4	5	5	6	7	7	8	9	9	10	11	11	12	13	13	14	15	15	16	17	17	18	19	19	20
1 00	15	4	5	6	7	8	8	9	10	11	12	13	13	14	15	16	17	18	18	19	20	21	22	23	23	24	25
12	18	5	6	7	8	9	10	11	11	12	14	15	16	17	18	19	20	21	22	23	24	25	26	27	28	29	30
24	21	6	7	8	9	11	12	13	14	15	16	18	19	20	21	22	23	25	26	27	28	29	30	32	33	34	35
36	24	7	8	9	11	12	13	15	16	17	19	20	21	23	24	25	27	28	29	31	32	33	35	36	37	39	40
1 48	27	8	9	11	12	14	15	17	18	20	21	23	24	26	27	29	30	32	33	35	36	38	39	41	42	44	45
2 00	30	8	10	12	13	15	17	18	20	22	23	25	27	28	30	32	33	35	37	38	40	42	43	45	47	48	50
12	33	9	11	13	15	17	18	20	22	24	26	28	29	31	33	35	37	39	40	42	44	46	48	50	51	53	55
24	36	10	12	14	16	18	20	22	24	26	28	30	32	34	36	38	40	42	44	46	48	50	52	54	56	58	60
36	39	11	13	15	17	20	22	24	26	28	30	33	35	37	39	41	43	46	48	50	52	54	56	59	61	63	65
2 48	42	12	14	16	19	21	23	26	28	30	33	35	37	40	42	44	47	49	51	54	56	58	61	63	65	68	70
3 00	45	13	15	18	20	23	25	28	30	33	35	38	40	43	45	48	50	53	55	58	60	63	65	68	70	73	75
12	48	13	16	19	21	24	27	29	32	35	37	40	43	45	48	51	53	56	59	61	64	67	69	72	75	77	80
24	51	14	17	20	23	26	28	31	34	37	40	43	45	48	51	54	57	60	62	65	68	71	74	77	79	82	85
36	54	15	18	21	24	27	30	33	36	39	42	45	48	51	54	57	60	63	66	69	72	75	78	81	84	87	90
3 48	57	16	19	22	25	29	32	35	38	41	44	48	51	54	57	60	63	67	70	73	76	79	82	86	89	92	95
4 00	60	17	20	23	27	30	33	37	40	43	47	50	53	57	60	63	67	70	73	77	80	83	87	90	93	97	100
12	63	18	21	25	28	32	35	39	42	46	49	53	56	60	63	67	70	74	77	81	84	88	91	95	98	102	105
24	66	18	22	26	29	33	37	40	44	48	51	55	59	62	66	70	73	77	81	84	88	92	95	99	103	106	110
36	69	19	23	27	31	35	38	42	46	50	54	58	61	65	69	73	77	81	84	88	92	96	100	104	107	111	115
4 48	72	20	24	28	32	36	40	44	48	52	56	60	64	68	72	76	80	84	88	92	96	100	104	108	112	116	120
5 00	75	21	25	29	33	38	42	46	50	54	58	63	67	71	75	79	83	88	92	96	100	104	108	113	117	121	125
12	78	22	26	30	35	39	43	48	52	56	61	65	69	74	78	82	87	91	95	100	104	108	113	117	121	126	130
24	81	23	27	32	36	41	45	50	54	59	63	68	72	77	81	86	90	95	99	104	108	113	117	122	126	131	135
36	84	23	28	33	37	42	47	51	56	61	65	70	75	79	84	89	93	98	103	107	112	117	121	126	131	135	140
5 48	87	24	29	34	39	44	48	53	58	63	68	73	77	82	87	92	97	102	106	111	116	121	126	131	135	140	145
6 00	90	25	30	35	40	45	50	55	60	65	70	75	80	85	90	95	100	105	110	115	120	125	130	135	140	145	150
12	93	26	31	36	41	47	52	57	62	67	72	78	83	88	93	98	103	109	114	119	124	129	134	140	145	150	155
24	96	27	32	37	43	48	53	59	64	69	75	80	85	91	96	101	107	112	117	123	128	133	139	144	149	155	160
36	99	28	33	39	44	50	55	61	66	72	77	83	88	94	99	105	110	116	121	127	132	138	143	149	154	160	165
6 48	102	28	34	40	45	51	57	62	68	74	79	85	91	96	102	108	113	119	125	130	136	142	147	153	159	164	170
7 00	105	29	35	41	47	53	58	64	70	76	82	88	93	99	105	111	117	123	128	134	140	146	152	158	163	169	175
12	108	30	36	42	48	54	60	66	72	78	84	90	96	102	108	114	120	126	132	138	144	150	156	162	168	174	180
24	111	31	37	43	49	56	62	68	74	80	86	93	99	105	111	117	123	130	136	142	148	154	160	167	173	179	185
36	114	32	38	44	51	57	63	70	76	82	89	95	101	108	114	120	127	133	139	146	152	158	165	171	177	184	190
7 48	117	33	39	46	52	59	65	72	78	85	91	98	104	111	117	124	130	137	143	150	156	163	169	176	182	189	195
8 00	120	33	40	47	53	60	67	73	80	87	93	100	107	113	120	127	133	140	147	153	160	167	173	180	187	193	200
12	123	34	41	48	55	62	68	75	82	89	96	103	109	116	123	130	137	144	150	157	164	171	178	185	191	198	205
24	126	35	42	49	56	63	70	77	84	91	98	105	112	119	126	133	140	147	154	161	168	175	182	189	196	203	210
36	129	36	43	50	57	65	72	79	86	93	100	108	115	122	129	136	143	151	158	165	172	179	186	194	201	208	215
8 48	132	37	44	51	59	66	73	81	88	95	103	110	117	125	132	139	147	154	161	169	176	183	191	198	205	213	220
9 00	135	38	45	53	60	68	75	83	90	98	105	113	120	128	135	143	150	158	165	173	180	188	195	203	210	218	225
12	138	38	46	54	61	69	77	84	92	100	107	115	123	130	138	146	153	161	169	176	184	192	199	207	215	222	230
24	141	39	47	55	63	71	78	86	94	102	110	118	125	133	141	149	157	165	172	180	188	196	204	212	219	227	235
36	144	40	48	56	64	72	80	88	96	104	112	120	128	136	144	152	160	168	176	184	192	200	208	216	224	232	240
9 48	147	41	49	57	65	74	82	90	98	106	114	123	131	139	147	155	163	172	180	188	196	204	212	221	229	237	245
10 00	150	42	50	58	67	75	83	92	100	108	117	125	133	142	150	158	167	175	183	192	200	208	217	225	233	242	250
12	153	43	51	60	68	77	85	94	102	111	119	128	136	145	153	162	170	179	187	196	204	213	221	230	238	247	255
24	156	43	52	61	69	78	87	95	104	113	121	130	139	147	156	165	173	182	191	199	208	217	225	234	243	251	260
36	159	44	53	62	71	80	88	97	106	115	124	133	141	150	159	168	177	186	194	203	212	221	230	239	247	256	265
10 48	162	45	54	63	72	81	90	99	108	117	126	135	144	153	162	171	180	189	198	207	216	225	234	243	252	261	270
11 00	165	46	55	64	73	83	92	101	110	119	128	138	147	156	165	174	183	193	202	211	220	229	238	248	257	266	275
12	168	47	56	65	75	84	93	103	112	121	131	140	149	159	168	177	187	196	205	215	224	233	243	252	261	271	280
24	171	48	57	67	76	86	95	105	114	124	133	143	152	162	171	181	190	200	209	219	228	238	247	257	266	276	285
36	174	48	58	68	77	87	97	106	116	126	135	145	155	164	174	184	193	203	213	222	232	242	251	261	271	280	290
11 48	177	49	59	69	79	89	98	108	118	128	138	148	157	167	177	187	197	207	216	226	236	246	256	266	275	285	295
12 00	180	50	60	70	80	90	100	110	120	130	140	150	160	170	180	190	200	210	220	230	240	250	260	270	280	290	300

INTERPOLATION TABLES — SUN, PLANETS 0ʰ–12ʰ

Correction to GHA or Declination for v or d

Units of 0'.1

UT (h m)	Corr. to GHA Sun Planet (°)	60	62	64	66	68	70	72	74	76	78	80	82	84	86	88	90
0 00	0	0	0	0	0	0	0	0	0	0	0	0	0	0	0	0	0
12	3	5	5	5	6	6	6	6	6	6	7	7	7	7	7	7	8
24	6	10	10	11	11	11	12	12	12	13	13	13	14	14	14	15	15
36	9	15	16	16	17	17	18	18	19	19	20	20	21	21	22	22	23
0 48	12	20	21	21	22	23	23	24	25	25	26	27	27	28	29	29	30
1 00	15	25	26	27	28	28	29	30	31	32	33	33	34	35	36	37	38
12	18	30	31	32	33	34	35	36	37	38	39	40	41	42	43	44	45
24	21	35	36	37	39	40	41	42	43	44	46	47	48	49	50	51	53
36	24	40	41	43	44	45	47	48	49	51	52	53	55	56	57	59	60
1 48	27	45	47	48	50	51	53	54	56	57	59	60	62	63	65	66	68
2 00	30	50	52	53	55	57	58	60	62	63	65	67	68	70	72	73	75
12	33	55	57	59	61	62	64	66	68	70	72	73	75	77	79	81	83
24	36	60	62	64	66	68	70	72	74	76	78	80	82	84	86	88	90
36	39	65	67	69	72	74	76	78	80	82	85	87	89	91	93	95	98
2 48	42	70	72	75	77	79	82	84	86	89	91	93	96	98	100	103	105
3 00	45	75	78	80	83	85	88	90	93	95	98	100	103	105	108	110	113
12	48	80	83	85	88	91	93	96	99	101	104	107	109	112	115	117	120
24	51	85	88	91	94	96	99	102	105	108	111	113	116	119	122	125	128
36	54	90	93	96	99	102	105	108	111	114	117	120	123	126	129	132	135
3 48	57	95	98	101	105	108	111	114	117	120	124	127	130	133	136	139	143
4 00	60	100	103	107	110	113	117	120	123	127	130	133	137	140	143	147	150
12	63	105	109	112	116	119	123	126	130	133	137	140	144	147	151	154	158
24	66	110	114	117	121	125	128	132	136	139	143	147	150	154	158	161	165
36	69	115	119	123	127	130	134	138	142	146	150	153	157	161	165	169	173
4 48	72	120	124	128	132	136	140	144	148	152	156	160	164	168	172	176	180
5 00	75	125	129	133	138	142	146	150	154	158	163	167	171	175	179	183	188
12	78	130	134	139	143	147	152	156	160	165	169	173	178	182	186	191	195
24	81	135	140	144	149	153	158	162	167	171	176	180	185	189	194	198	203
36	84	140	145	149	154	159	163	168	173	177	182	187	191	196	201	205	210
5 48	87	145	150	155	160	164	169	174	179	184	189	193	198	203	208	213	218
6 00	90	150	155	160	165	170	175	180	185	190	195	200	205	210	215	220	225
12	93	155	160	165	171	176	181	186	191	196	202	207	212	217	222	227	233
24	96	160	165	171	176	181	187	192	197	203	208	213	219	224	229	235	240
36	99	165	171	176	182	187	193	198	204	209	215	220	226	231	237	242	248
6 48	102	170	176	181	187	193	198	204	210	215	221	227	233	239	244	249	255
7 00	105	175	181	187	193	198	204	210	216	222	228	233	239	245	251	257	263
12	108	180	186	192	198	204	210	216	222	228	234	240	246	252	258	264	270
24	111	185	191	197	204	210	216	222	228	234	241	247	253	259	265	271	278
36	114	190	196	203	209	215	222	228	234	241	247	253	260	266	272	279	285
7 48	117	195	202	208	215	221	228	234	241	247	254	260	267	273	280	286	293
8 00	120	200	207	213	220	227	233	240	247	253	260	267	273	280	287	293	300
12	123	205	212	219	226	232	239	246	253	260	267	273	280	287	294	301	308
24	126	210	217	224	231	238	245	252	259	266	273	280	287	294	301	308	315
36	129	215	222	229	237	244	251	258	265	272	280	287	294	301	308	315	323
8 48	132	220	227	235	242	249	257	264	271	279	286	293	301	308	315	323	330
9 00	135	225	233	240	248	255	263	270	278	285	293	300	308	315	323	330	338
12	138	230	238	245	253	261	268	276	284	291	299	307	314	322	330	337	345
24	141	235	243	251	259	266	274	282	290	298	306	313	321	329	337	345	353
36	144	240	248	256	264	272	280	288	296	304	312	320	328	336	344	352	360
9 48	147	245	253	261	270	278	286	294	302	310	319	327	335	343	351	359	368
10 00	150	250	258	267	275	283	292	300	308	317	325	333	342	350	358	367	375
12	153	255	264	272	281	289	298	306	315	323	332	340	349	357	366	374	383
24	156	260	269	277	286	295	303	312	321	329	338	347	355	364	373	381	390
36	159	265	274	283	292	300	309	318	327	336	345	353	362	371	380	389	398
10 48	162	270	279	288	297	306	315	324	333	342	351	360	369	378	387	396	405
11 00	165	275	284	293	303	312	321	330	339	348	358	367	376	385	394	403	413
12	168	280	289	299	308	317	327	336	345	355	364	373	383	392	401	411	420
24	171	285	295	304	314	323	333	342	352	361	371	380	390	399	409	418	428
36	174	290	300	309	319	329	338	348	358	367	377	387	396	406	416	425	435
11 48	177	295	305	315	325	334	344	354	364	374	384	393	403	413	423	433	443
12 00	180	300	310	320	330	340	350	360	370	380	390	400	410	420	430	440	450

Correction to GHA Sun and Planets

UT (s)	0ᵐ (° ')	1ᵐ (° ')	2ᵐ (° ')	3ᵐ (° ')
00	0 00	0 15	0 30	0 45
04	01	16	31	46
08	02	17	32	47
12	03	18	33	48
16	04	19	34	49
20	0 05	0 20	0 35	0 50
24	06	21	36	51
28	07	22	37	52
32	08	23	38	53
36	09	24	39	54
40	0 10	0 25	0 40	0 55
44	11	26	41	56
48	12	27	42	57
52	13	28	43	58
56	14	29	44	0 59
60	0 15	0 30	0 45	1 00

Correction to GHA Sun and Planets

UT (s)	4ᵐ (° ')	5ᵐ (° ')	6ᵐ (° ')	7ᵐ (° ')
00	1 00	1 15	1 30	1 45
04	01	16	31	46
08	02	17	32	47
12	03	18	33	48
16	04	19	34	49
20	1 05	1 20	1 35	1 50
24	06	21	36	51
28	07	22	37	52
32	08	23	38	53
36	09	24	39	54
40	1 10	1 25	1 40	1 55
44	11	26	41	56
48	12	27	42	57
52	13	28	43	58
56	14	29	44	1 59
60	1 15	1 30	1 45	2 00

Correction to GHA Sun and Planets

UT (s)	8ᵐ (° ')	9ᵐ (° ')	10ᵐ (° ')	11ᵐ (° ')
00	2 00	2 15	2 30	2 45
04	01	16	31	46
08	02	17	32	47
12	03	18	33	48
16	04	19	34	49
20	2 05	2 20	2 35	2 50
24	06	21	36	51
28	07	22	37	52
32	08	23	38	53
36	09	24	39	54
40	2 10	2 25	2 40	2 55
44	11	26	41	56
48	12	27	42	57
52	13	28	43	58
56	14	29	44	2 59
60	2 15	2 30	2 45	3 00

5

INTERPOLATION TABLES — SUN, PLANETS 12ʰ–24ʰ

Correction to GHA or Declination for v or d — Units of 0'.1

UT (h m)	Corr. to GHA Sun Planet (°)	10	12	14	16	18	20	22	24	26	28	30	32	34	36	38	40	42	44	46	48	50	52	54	56	58	60
12 00	180	50	60	70	80	90	100	110	120	130	140	150	160	170	180	190	200	210	220	230	240	250	260	270	280	290	300
12	183	51	61	71	81	92	102	112	122	132	142	153	163	173	183	193	203	214	224	234	244	254	264	275	285	295	305
24	186	52	62	72	83	93	103	114	124	134	145	155	165	176	186	196	207	217	227	238	248	258	269	279	289	300	310
36	189	53	63	74	84	95	105	116	126	137	147	158	168	179	189	200	210	221	231	242	252	263	273	284	294	305	315
12 48	192	53	64	75	85	96	107	117	128	139	149	160	171	181	192	203	213	224	235	245	256	267	277	288	299	309	320
13 00	195	54	65	76	87	98	108	119	130	141	152	163	173	184	195	206	217	228	238	249	260	271	282	293	303	314	325
12	198	55	66	77	88	99	110	121	132	143	154	163	176	187	198	209	220	231	242	253	264	275	286	297	308	319	330
24	201	56	67	78	89	101	112	123	134	145	156	168	179	190	201	212	223	235	246	257	268	279	290	302	313	324	335
36	204	57	68	79	91	102	113	125	136	147	159	170	181	193	204	215	227	238	249	261	272	283	295	306	317	329	340
13 48	207	58	69	81	92	104	115	127	138	150	161	173	184	196	207	219	230	242	253	265	276	288	299	311	322	334	345
14 00	210	58	70	82	93	105	117	128	140	152	163	175	187	198	210	222	233	245	257	268	280	292	303	315	327	338	350
12	213	59	71	83	95	107	118	130	142	154	166	178	189	201	213	225	237	249	260	272	284	296	308	320	331	343	355
24	216	60	72	84	96	108	120	132	144	156	168	180	192	204	216	228	240	252	264	276	288	300	312	324	336	348	360
36	219	61	73	85	97	110	122	134	146	158	170	183	195	207	219	231	243	256	268	280	292	304	316	329	341	353	365
14 48	222	62	74	86	99	111	123	136	148	160	173	185	197	210	222	234	247	259	271	284	296	308	321	333	345	358	370
15 00	225	63	75	88	100	113	125	138	150	163	175	188	200	213	225	238	250	263	275	288	300	313	325	338	350	363	375
12	228	63	76	89	101	114	127	139	152	165	177	190	203	215	228	241	253	266	279	291	304	317	329	342	355	367	380
24	231	64	77	90	103	116	128	141	154	167	180	193	205	218	231	244	257	270	282	295	308	321	334	347	359	372	385
36	234	65	78	91	104	117	130	143	156	169	182	195	208	221	234	247	260	273	286	299	312	325	338	351	364	377	390
15 48	237	66	79	92	105	119	132	145	158	171	184	198	211	224	237	250	263	277	290	303	316	329	342	356	369	382	395
16 00	240	67	80	93	107	120	133	147	160	173	187	200	213	227	240	253	267	280	293	307	320	333	347	360	373	387	400
12	243	68	81	95	108	122	135	149	162	176	189	203	216	230	243	257	270	284	297	311	324	338	351	365	378	392	405
24	246	68	82	96	109	123	137	150	164	178	191	205	219	232	246	260	273	287	301	314	328	342	355	369	383	396	410
36	249	69	83	97	111	125	138	152	166	180	194	208	221	235	249	263	277	291	304	318	332	346	360	374	387	401	415
16 48	252	70	84	98	112	126	140	154	168	182	196	210	224	238	252	266	280	294	308	322	336	350	364	378	392	406	420
17 00	255	71	85	99	113	128	142	156	170	184	198	213	227	241	255	269	283	298	312	326	340	354	368	383	397	411	425
12	258	72	86	100	115	129	143	158	172	186	201	215	229	244	258	272	287	301	315	330	344	358	373	387	401	416	430
24	261	73	87	102	116	131	145	160	174	189	203	218	232	247	261	276	290	305	319	334	348	363	377	392	406	421	435
36	264	73	88	103	117	132	147	161	176	191	205	220	235	249	264	279	293	308	323	337	352	367	381	396	411	425	440
17 48	267	74	89	104	119	134	148	163	178	193	208	223	237	252	267	282	297	312	326	341	356	371	386	401	415	430	445
18 00	270	75	90	105	120	135	150	165	180	195	210	225	240	255	270	285	300	315	330	345	360	375	390	405	420	435	450
12	273	76	91	106	121	137	152	167	182	197	212	228	243	258	273	288	303	319	334	349	364	379	394	410	425	440	455
24	276	77	92	107	123	138	153	169	184	199	215	230	245	261	276	291	307	322	337	353	368	383	399	414	429	445	460
36	279	78	93	109	124	140	155	171	186	202	217	233	248	264	279	295	310	326	341	357	372	388	403	419	434	450	465
18 48	282	78	94	110	125	141	157	172	188	204	219	235	251	266	282	298	313	329	345	360	376	392	407	423	439	454	470
19 00	285	79	95	111	127	143	158	174	190	206	222	238	253	269	285	301	317	333	348	364	380	396	412	428	443	459	475
12	288	80	96	112	128	144	160	176	192	208	224	240	256	272	288	304	320	336	352	368	384	400	416	432	448	464	480
24	291	81	97	113	129	146	162	178	194	210	226	243	259	275	291	307	323	340	356	372	388	404	420	437	453	469	485
36	294	82	98	114	131	147	163	180	196	212	229	245	261	278	294	310	327	343	359	376	392	408	425	441	457	474	490
19 48	297	83	99	116	132	149	165	182	198	215	231	248	264	281	297	314	330	347	363	380	396	413	429	446	462	479	495
20 00	300	83	100	117	133	150	167	183	200	217	233	250	267	283	300	317	333	350	367	383	400	417	433	450	467	483	500
12	303	84	101	118	135	152	168	185	202	219	236	253	269	286	303	320	337	354	370	387	404	421	438	455	471	488	505
24	306	85	102	119	136	153	170	187	204	221	238	255	272	289	306	323	340	357	374	391	408	425	442	459	476	493	510
36	309	86	103	120	137	155	172	189	206	223	240	258	275	292	309	326	343	361	378	395	412	429	446	464	481	498	515
20 48	312	87	104	121	139	156	173	191	208	225	243	260	277	295	312	329	347	364	381	399	416	433	451	468	485	503	520
21 00	315	88	105	123	140	158	175	193	210	228	245	263	280	298	315	333	350	368	385	403	420	438	455	473	490	508	525
12	318	88	106	124	141	159	177	194	212	230	247	265	283	300	318	336	353	371	389	406	424	442	459	477	495	512	530
24	321	89	107	125	143	161	178	196	214	232	250	268	285	303	321	339	357	375	392	410	428	446	464	482	499	517	535
36	324	90	108	126	144	162	180	198	216	234	252	270	288	306	324	342	360	378	396	414	432	450	468	486	504	522	540
21 48	327	91	109	127	145	164	182	200	218	236	254	273	291	309	327	345	363	382	400	418	436	454	472	491	509	527	545
22 00	330	92	110	128	147	165	183	202	220	238	257	275	293	312	330	348	367	385	403	422	440	458	477	495	513	532	550
12	333	93	111	130	148	167	185	204	222	241	259	278	296	315	333	352	370	389	407	426	444	463	481	500	518	537	555
24	336	93	112	131	149	168	187	205	224	243	261	280	299	317	336	355	373	392	411	429	448	467	485	504	523	541	560
36	339	94	113	132	151	170	188	207	226	245	264	283	301	320	339	358	377	396	414	433	452	471	490	509	527	546	565
22 48	342	95	114	133	152	171	190	209	228	247	266	285	304	323	342	361	380	399	418	437	456	475	494	513	532	551	570
23 00	345	96	115	134	153	173	192	211	230	249	268	288	307	326	345	364	383	403	422	441	460	479	498	518	537	556	575
12	348	97	116	135	155	174	193	213	232	251	271	290	309	329	348	367	387	406	425	445	464	483	503	522	541	561	580
24	351	98	117	137	156	176	195	215	234	254	273	293	312	332	351	371	390	410	429	449	468	488	507	527	546	566	585
36	354	98	118	138	157	177	197	216	236	256	275	295	315	334	354	374	393	413	433	452	472	492	511	531	551	570	590
23 48	357	99	119	139	159	179	198	218	238	258	278	298	317	337	357	377	397	417	436	456	476	496	516	536	555	575	595
24 00	360	100	120	140	160	180	200	220	240	260	280	300	320	340	360	380	400	420	440	460	480	500	520	540	560	580	600

INTERPOLATION TABLES — SUN, PLANETS 12ʰ–24ʰ

UT	Corr. to GHA Sun Planet	Correction to GHA or Declination for v or d															
h m	°	60	62	64	66	68	70	72	74	76	78	80	82	84	86	88	90
							Units of 0′.1										
12 00	180	300	310	320	330	340	350	360	370	380	390	400	410	420	430	440	450
12	183	305	315	325	336	346	356	366	376	386	397	407	417	427	437	447	458
24	186	310	320	331	341	351	362	372	382	393	403	413	424	434	444	455	465
36	189	315	326	336	347	357	368	378	389	399	410	420	431	441	452	462	473
12 48	192	320	331	341	352	363	373	384	395	405	416	427	437	448	459	469	480
13 00	195	325	336	347	358	368	379	390	401	412	423	433	444	455	466	477	488
12	198	330	341	352	363	374	385	396	407	418	429	440	451	462	473	484	495
24	201	335	346	357	369	380	391	402	413	424	436	447	458	469	480	491	503
36	204	340	351	363	374	385	397	408	419	431	442	453	465	476	487	499	510
13 48	207	345	357	368	380	391	403	414	426	437	449	460	472	483	495	506	518
14 00	210	350	362	373	385	397	408	420	432	443	455	467	478	490	502	513	525
12	213	355	367	379	391	402	414	426	438	450	462	473	485	497	509	521	533
24	216	360	372	384	396	408	420	432	444	456	468	480	492	504	516	528	540
36	219	365	377	389	402	414	426	438	450	462	475	487	499	511	523	535	548
14 48	222	370	382	395	407	419	432	444	456	469	481	493	506	518	530	543	555
15 00	225	375	388	400	413	425	438	450	463	475	488	500	513	525	538	550	563
12	228	380	393	405	418	431	443	456	469	481	494	507	519	532	545	557	570
24	231	385	398	411	424	436	449	462	475	488	501	513	526	539	552	565	578
36	234	390	403	416	429	442	455	468	481	494	507	520	533	546	559	572	585
15 48	237	395	408	421	435	448	461	474	487	500	514	527	540	553	566	579	593
16 00	240	400	413	427	440	453	467	480	493	507	520	533	547	560	573	587	600
12	243	405	419	432	446	459	473	486	500	513	527	540	554	567	581	594	608
24	246	410	424	437	451	465	478	492	506	519	533	547	560	574	588	601	615
36	249	415	429	443	457	470	484	498	512	526	540	553	567	581	595	609	623
16 48	252	420	434	448	462	476	490	504	518	532	546	560	574	588	602	616	630
17 00	255	425	439	453	468	482	496	510	524	538	553	567	581	595	609	623	638
12	258	430	444	459	473	487	502	516	530	545	559	573	588	602	616	631	645
24	261	435	450	464	479	493	508	522	537	551	566	580	595	609	624	638	653
36	264	440	455	469	484	499	513	528	543	557	572	587	601	616	631	645	660
17 48	267	445	460	475	490	504	519	534	549	564	579	593	608	623	638	653	668
18 00	270	450	465	480	495	510	525	540	555	570	585	600	615	630	645	660	675
12	273	455	470	485	501	516	531	546	561	576	592	607	622	637	652	667	683
24	276	460	475	491	506	521	537	552	567	583	598	613	629	644	659	675	690
36	279	465	481	496	512	527	543	558	574	589	605	620	636	651	667	682	698
18 48	282	470	486	501	517	533	548	564	580	595	611	627	642	658	674	689	705
19 00	285	475	491	507	523	538	554	570	586	602	618	633	649	665	681	697	713
12	288	480	496	512	528	544	560	576	592	608	624	640	656	672	688	704	720
24	291	485	501	517	534	550	566	582	598	614	631	647	663	679	695	711	728
36	294	490	506	523	539	555	572	588	604	621	637	653	670	686	702	719	735
19 48	297	495	512	528	545	561	578	594	611	627	644	660	677	693	710	726	743
20 00	300	500	517	533	550	567	583	600	617	633	650	667	683	700	717	733	750
12	303	505	522	539	556	572	589	606	623	640	657	673	690	707	724	741	758
24	306	510	527	544	561	578	595	612	629	646	663	680	697	714	731	748	765
36	309	515	532	549	567	584	601	618	635	652	670	687	704	721	738	755	773
20 48	312	520	537	555	572	589	607	624	641	659	676	693	711	728	745	763	780
21 00	315	525	543	560	578	595	613	630	648	665	683	700	718	735	753	770	788
12	318	530	548	565	583	601	618	636	654	671	689	707	724	742	760	777	795
24	321	535	553	571	589	606	624	642	660	678	696	713	731	749	767	785	803
36	324	540	558	576	594	612	630	648	666	684	702	720	738	756	774	792	810
21 48	327	545	563	581	600	618	636	654	672	690	709	727	745	763	781	799	818
22 00	330	550	568	587	605	623	642	660	678	697	715	733	752	770	788	807	825
12	333	555	574	592	611	629	648	666	685	703	722	740	759	777	796	814	833
24	336	560	579	597	616	635	653	672	691	709	728	747	765	784	803	821	840
36	339	565	584	603	622	640	659	678	697	716	735	753	772	791	810	829	848
22 48	342	570	589	608	627	646	665	684	703	722	741	760	779	798	817	836	855
23 00	345	575	594	613	633	652	671	690	709	728	748	767	786	805	824	843	863
12	348	580	599	619	638	657	677	696	715	735	754	773	793	812	831	851	870
24	351	585	605	624	644	663	683	702	722	741	761	780	800	819	839	858	878
36	354	590	610	629	649	669	688	708	728	747	767	787	806	826	846	865	885
23 48	357	595	615	635	655	674	694	714	734	754	774	793	813	833	853	873	893
24 00	360	600	620	640	660	680	700	720	740	760	780	800	820	840	860	880	900

Correction to GHA Sun and Planets

UT	0ᵐ	1ᵐ	2ᵐ	3ᵐ
s	° ′	° ′	° ′	° ′
00	0 00	0 15	0 30	0 45
04	01	16	31	46
08	02	17	32	47
12	03	18	33	48
16	04	19	34	49
20	0 05	0 20	0 35	0 50
24	06	21	36	51
28	07	22	37	52
32	08	23	38	53
36	09	24	39	54
40	0 10	0 25	0 40	0 55
44	11	26	41	56
48	12	27	42	57
52	13	28	43	58
56	14	29	44	0 59
60	0 15	0 30	0 45	1 00

Correction to GHA Sun and Planets

UT	4ᵐ	5ᵐ	6ᵐ	7ᵐ
s	° ′	° ′	° ′	° ′
00	1 00	1 15	1 30	1 45
04	01	16	31	46
08	02	17	32	47
12	03	18	33	48
16	04	19	34	49
20	1 05	1 20	1 35	1 50
24	06	21	36	51
28	07	22	37	52
32	08	23	38	53
36	09	24	39	54
40	1 10	1 25	1 40	1 55
44	11	26	41	56
48	12	27	42	57
52	13	28	43	58
56	14	29	44	1 59
60	1 15	1 30	1 45	2 00

Correction to GHA Sun and Planets

UT	8ᵐ	9ᵐ	10ᵐ	11ᵐ
s	° ′	° ′	° ′	° ′
00	2 00	2 15	2 30	2 45
04	01	16	31	46
08	02	17	32	47
12	03	18	33	48
16	04	19	34	49
20	2 05	2 20	2 35	2 50
24	06	21	36	51
28	07	22	37	52
32	08	23	38	53
36	09	24	39	54
40	2 10	2 25	2 40	2 55
44	11	26	41	56
48	12	27	42	57
52	13	28	43	58
56	14	29	44	2 59
60	2 15	2 30	2 45	3 00

5

INTERPOLATION TABLES — MOON 0ʰ–4ʰ, 8ʰ–12ʰ, 16ʰ–20ʰ

UT (h m)	Corr. to GHA (° ′)	5	10	15	20	25	30	35	40	45	50	55	60	65	70	75	80	85	90	95	100	UT (m s)	Corr. to GHA (′)
0 00	0 00	0	0	0	0	0	0	0	0	0	0	0	0	0	0	0	0	0	0	0	0	0 00	00
(8 or 16) 04	0 57	0	0	0	0	0	0	0	0	0	0	0	1	1	1	1	1	1	1	1	1	04	01
08	1 54	0	0	0	0	0	1	1	1	1	1	1	1	1	1	1	1	2	2	2	2	08	02
12	2 51	0	0	0	1	1	1	1	1	1	1	1	2	2	2	2	2	2	2	2	3	12	03
16	3 48	0	0	1	1	1	1	1	1	2	2	2	2	2	2	3	3	3	3	3	3	16	04
0 20	4 45	0	0	1	1	1	1	1	2	2	2	2	3	3	3	3	3	4	4	4	4	0 20	05
24	5 42	0	1	1	1	1	2	2	2	2	3	3	3	3	4	4	4	4	5	5	5	24	06
28	6 39	0	1	1	1	1	2	2	2	3	3	3	4	4	4	4	5	5	5	6	6	28	07
32	7 36	0	1	1	1	2	2	2	3	3	3	4	4	4	5	5	5	6	6	6	7	32	08
36	8 33	0	1	1	2	2	2	3	3	3	4	4	5	5	5	6	6	6	7	7	8	36	09
0 40	9 30	0	1	1	2	2	3	3	3	4	4	5	5	5	6	6	7	7	8	8	8	0 40	10
44	10 27	0	1	1	2	2	3	3	4	4	5	5	6	6	6	7	7	8	8	9	9	44	10
48	11 24	1	1	2	2	3	3	4	4	5	5	6	6	7	7	8	8	9	9	10	10	48	11
52	12 21	1	1	2	2	3	3	4	4	5	5	6	7	7	8	8	9	9	10	10	11	52	12
0 56	13 18	1	1	2	2	3	4	4	5	5	6	6	7	8	8	9	9	10	11	11	12	0 56	13
1 00	14 15	1	1	2	3	3	4	4	5	6	6	7	8	8	9	9	10	11	11	12	13	1 00	14
(9 or 17) 04	15 12	1	1	2	3	3	4	5	5	6	7	7	8	9	9	10	11	11	12	13	13	04	15
08	16 09	1	1	2	3	4	4	5	6	6	7	8	9	9	10	11	11	12	13	13	14	08	16
12	17 06	1	2	2	3	4	5	5	6	7	8	8	9	10	11	11	12	13	14	14	15	12	17
16	18 03	1	2	2	3	4	5	6	6	7	8	9	10	10	11	12	13	13	14	15	16	16	18
1 20	19 00	1	2	3	3	4	5	6	7	8	8	9	10	11	12	13	13	14	15	16	17	1 20	19
24	19 57	1	2	3	4	4	5	6	7	8	9	10	11	11	12	13	14	15	16	17	18	24	20
28	20 54	1	2	3	4	5	6	6	7	8	9	10	11	12	13	14	15	16	17	17	18	28	21
32	21 51	1	2	3	4	5	6	7	8	9	10	11	12	12	13	14	15	16	17	18	19	32	22
36	22 48	1	2	3	4	5	6	7	8	9	10	11	12	13	14	15	16	17	18	19	20	36	23
1 40	23 45	1	2	3	4	5	6	7	8	9	10	11	13	14	15	16	17	18	19	20	21	1 40	24
44	24 42	1	2	3	4	5	7	8	9	10	11	12	13	14	15	16	17	18	20	21	22	44	25
48	25 39	1	2	3	5	6	7	8	9	10	11	12	14	15	16	17	18	19	20	21	23	48	26
52	26 36	1	2	4	5	6	7	8	9	11	12	13	14	15	16	18	19	20	21	22	23	52	27
1 56	27 33	1	2	4	5	6	7	8	10	11	12	13	15	16	17	18	19	21	22	23	24	1 56	28
2 00	28 30	1	3	4	5	6	8	9	10	11	13	14	15	16	18	19	20	21	23	24	25	2 00	29
(10 or 18) 04	29 27	1	3	4	5	6	8	9	10	12	13	14	16	17	18	19	21	22	23	25	26	04	29
08	30 24	1	3	4	5	7	8	9	11	12	13	15	16	17	19	20	21	23	24	25	27	08	30
12	31 21	1	3	4	6	7	8	10	11	12	14	15	17	18	19	21	22	23	25	26	28	12	31
16	32 18	1	3	4	6	7	9	10	11	13	14	16	17	18	20	21	23	24	26	27	28	16	32
2 20	33 15	1	3	4	6	7	9	10	12	13	15	16	18	19	20	22	23	25	26	28	29	2 20	33
24	34 12	2	3	5	6	8	9	11	12	14	15	17	18	20	21	23	24	26	27	29	30	24	34
28	35 09	2	3	5	6	8	9	11	12	14	15	17	19	20	22	23	25	26	28	29	31	28	35
32	36 06	2	3	5	7	8	10	11	13	14	16	17	19	21	22	24	25	27	29	30	32	32	36
36	37 03	2	3	5	7	8	10	11	13	15	16	18	20	21	23	24	26	28	29	31	33	36	37
2 40	38 00	2	3	5	7	8	10	12	13	15	17	18	20	22	23	25	27	28	30	32	33	2 40	38
44	38 57	2	3	5	7	9	10	12	14	15	17	19	21	22	24	26	27	29	31	32	34	44	39
48	39 54	2	4	5	7	9	11	12	14	16	18	19	21	23	25	26	28	30	32	33	35	48	40
52	40 51	2	4	5	7	9	11	13	14	16	18	20	22	23	25	27	29	30	32	34	36	52	41
2 56	41 48	2	4	6	7	9	11	13	15	17	18	20	22	24	26	28	29	31	33	35	37	2 56	42
3 00	42 45	2	4	6	8	9	11	13	15	17	19	21	23	24	26	28	30	32	34	36	38	3 00	43
(11 or 19) 04	43 42	2	4	6	8	10	12	13	15	17	19	21	23	25	27	29	31	33	35	36	38	04	44
08	44 39	2	4	6	8	10	12	14	16	18	20	22	24	25	27	29	31	33	35	37	39	08	45
12	45 36	2	4	6	8	10	12	14	16	18	20	22	24	26	28	30	32	34	36	38	40	12	46
16	46 33	2	4	6	8	10	12	14	16	18	20	22	25	27	29	31	33	35	37	39	41	16	47
3 20	47 30	2	4	6	8	10	13	15	17	19	21	23	25	27	29	31	33	35	38	40	42	3 20	48
24	48 27	2	4	6	9	11	13	15	17	19	21	23	26	28	30	32	34	36	38	40	43	24	48
28	49 24	2	4	7	9	11	13	15	17	20	22	24	26	28	30	33	35	37	39	41	43	28	49
32	50 21	2	4	7	9	11	13	15	18	20	22	24	27	29	31	33	35	38	40	42	44	32	50
36	51 18	2	5	7	9	11	14	16	18	20	23	25	27	29	32	34	36	38	41	43	45	36	51
3 40	52 15	2	5	7	9	11	14	16	18	21	23	25	28	30	32	34	37	39	41	44	46	3 40	52
44	53 12	2	5	7	9	12	14	16	19	21	23	26	28	30	33	35	37	40	42	44	47	44	53
48	54 09	2	5	7	10	12	14	17	19	21	24	26	29	31	33	36	38	40	43	45	48	48	54
52	55 06	2	5	7	10	12	15	17	19	22	24	27	29	31	34	36	39	41	44	46	48	52	55
3 56	56 03	2	5	7	10	12	15	17	20	22	25	27	30	32	34	37	39	42	44	47	49	3 56	56
4 00	57 00	3	5	8	10	13	15	18	20	23	25	28	30	33	35	38	40	43	45	48	50	4 00	57

INTERPOLATION TABLES — MOON 0ʰ–4ʰ, 8ʰ–12ʰ, 16ʰ–20ʰ

UT	Corr. to GHA	100	105	110	115	120	125	130	135	140	145	150	155	160	165	170	175	UT	Corr. to GHA
h m	° ′								Units of 1′									m s	′
0 00	0 00	0	0	0	0	0	0	0	0	0	0	0	0	0	0	0	0	0 00	00
04	0 57	1	1	1	1	1	1	1	1	1	1	1	1	1	1	1	1	04	01
(8 or 16) 08	1 54	2	2	2	2	2	2	2	2	2	2	3	3	3	3	3	3	08	02
12	2 51	3	3	3	3	3	3	3	3	4	4	4	4	4	4	4	4	12	03
16	3 48	3	4	4	4	4	4	5	5	5	5	5	5	5	6	6	6	16	04
0 20	4 45	4	4	5	5	5	5	5	6	6	6	6	6	7	7	7	7	0 20	05
24	5 42	5	5	6	6	6	6	7	7	7	7	8	8	8	8	9	9	24	06
28	6 39	6	6	6	7	7	7	8	8	8	8	9	9	9	10	10	10	28	07
32	7 36	7	7	7	8	8	8	9	9	9	10	10	10	11	11	11	12	32	08
36	8 33	8	8	8	9	9	9	10	10	11	11	11	12	12	12	13	13	36	09
0 40	9 30	8	9	9	10	10	10	11	11	12	12	12	13	13	14	14	15	0 40	10
44	10 27	9	10	10	11	11	11	12	12	13	13	14	14	15	15	16	16	44	10
48	11 24	10	11	11	12	12	13	13	14	14	15	15	16	16	17	17	18	48	11
52	12 21	11	11	12	12	13	14	14	15	15	16	16	17	17	18	18	19	52	12
0 56	13 18	12	12	13	13	14	15	15	16	16	17	18	18	19	19	20	20	0 56	13
1 00	14 15	13	13	14	14	15	16	16	17	18	18	19	19	20	21	21	22	1 00	14
04	15 12	13	14	15	15	16	17	17	18	19	19	20	21	21	22	23	23	04	15
(9 or 17) 08	16 09	14	15	16	16	17	18	18	19	20	21	21	22	23	23	24	25	08	16
12	17 06	15	16	17	17	18	19	20	20	21	22	23	23	24	25	26	26	12	17
16	18 03	16	17	17	18	19	20	21	21	22	23	24	25	25	26	27	28	16	18
1 20	19 00	17	18	18	19	20	21	22	23	23	24	25	26	27	28	28	29	1 20	19
24	19 57	18	18	19	20	21	22	23	24	25	25	26	27	28	29	30	31	24	20
28	20 54	18	19	20	21	22	23	24	25	26	27	28	28	29	30	31	32	28	21
32	21 51	19	20	21	22	23	24	25	26	27	28	29	30	31	32	33	34	32	22
36	22 48	20	21	22	23	24	25	26	27	28	29	30	31	32	33	34	35	36	23
1 40	23 45	21	22	23	24	25	26	27	28	29	30	31	32	33	34	35	36	1 40	24
44	24 42	22	23	24	25	26	27	28	29	30	31	33	34	35	36	37	38	44	25
48	25 39	23	24	25	26	27	28	29	30	32	33	34	35	36	37	38	39	48	26
52	26 36	23	25	26	27	28	29	30	32	33	34	35	36	37	39	40	41	52	27
1 56	27 33	24	25	27	28	29	30	31	33	34	35	36	37	39	40	41	42	1 56	28
2 00	28 30	25	26	28	29	30	31	33	34	35	36	38	39	40	41	43	44	2 00	29
04	29 27	26	27	28	30	31	32	34	35	36	37	39	40	41	43	44	45	04	29
(10 or 18) 08	30 24	27	28	29	31	32	33	35	36	37	39	40	41	43	44	45	47	08	30
12	31 21	28	29	30	32	33	34	36	37	39	40	41	43	44	45	47	48	12	31
16	32 18	28	30	31	33	34	35	37	38	40	41	43	44	45	47	48	50	16	32
2 20	33 15	29	31	32	34	35	36	38	39	41	42	44	45	47	48	50	51	2 20	33
24	34 12	30	32	33	35	36	38	39	41	42	44	45	47	48	50	51	53	24	34
28	35 09	31	32	34	35	37	39	40	42	43	45	46	48	49	51	52	54	28	35
32	36 06	32	33	35	36	38	40	41	43	44	46	48	49	51	52	54	55	32	36
36	37 03	33	34	36	37	39	41	42	44	46	47	49	50	52	54	55	57	36	37
2 40	38 00	33	35	37	38	40	42	43	45	47	48	50	52	53	55	57	58	2 40	38
44	38 57	34	36	38	39	41	43	44	46	48	50	51	53	55	56	58	60	44	39
48	39 54	35	37	39	40	42	44	46	47	49	51	53	54	56	58	60	61	48	40
52	40 51	36	38	39	41	43	45	47	48	50	52	54	56	57	59	61	63	52	41
2 56	41 48	37	39	40	42	44	46	48	50	51	53	55	57	59	61	62	64	2 56	42
3 00	42 45	38	39	41	43	45	47	49	51	53	54	56	58	60	62	64	66	3 00	43
04	43 42	38	40	42	44	46	48	50	52	54	56	58	59	61	63	65	67	04	44
(11 or 19) 08	44 39	39	41	43	45	47	49	51	53	55	57	59	61	63	65	67	69	08	45
12	45 36	40	42	44	46	48	50	52	54	56	58	60	62	64	66	68	70	12	46
16	46 33	41	43	45	47	49	51	53	55	57	59	61	63	65	67	69	71	16	47
3 20	47 30	42	44	46	48	50	52	54	56	58	60	63	65	67	69	71	73	3 20	48
24	48 27	43	45	47	49	51	53	55	57	60	62	64	66	68	70	72	74	24	48
28	49 24	43	46	48	50	52	54	56	59	61	63	65	67	69	72	74	76	28	49
32	50 21	44	46	48	51	53	55	57	60	62	64	66	68	71	73	75	77	32	50
36	51 18	45	47	50	52	54	56	59	61	63	65	68	70	72	74	77	79	36	51
3 40	52 15	46	48	50	53	55	57	60	62	64	66	69	71	73	76	78	80	3 40	52
44	53 12	47	49	51	54	56	58	61	63	65	68	70	72	75	77	79	82	44	53
48	54 09	48	50	52	55	57	59	62	64	67	69	71	74	76	78	81	83	48	54
52	55 06	48	51	53	56	58	60	63	65	68	70	73	75	77	80	82	85	52	55
3 56	56 03	49	52	54	57	59	61	64	66	69	71	74	76	79	81	84	86	3 56	56
4 00	57 00	50	53	55	58	60	63	65	68	70	73	75	78	80	83	85	88	4 00	57

5

INTERPOLATION TABLES — MOON 4ʰ–8ʰ, 12ʰ–16ʰ, 20ʰ–24ʰ

UT	Corr. to GHA	5	10	15	20	25	30	35	40	45	50	55	60	65	70	75	80	85	90	95	100	UT	Corr. to GHA
h m	° ′								Units of 1′													m s	′
4 00	57 00	3	5	8	10	13	15	18	20	23	25	28	30	33	35	38	40	43	45	48	50	0 00	00
(12 or 20) 04	57 57	3	5	8	10	13	15	18	20	23	25	28	31	33	36	38	41	43	46	48	51	04	01
08	58 54	3	5	8	10	13	16	18	21	23	26	28	31	34	36	39	41	44	47	49	52	08	02
12	59 51	3	5	8	11	13	16	18	21	24	26	29	32	34	37	39	42	45	47	50	53	12	03
16	60 48	3	5	8	11	13	16	19	21	24	27	29	32	35	37	40	43	45	48	51	53	16	04
4 20	61 45	3	5	8	11	14	16	19	22	24	27	30	33	35	38	41	43	46	49	51	54	0 20	05
24	62 42	3	6	8	11	14	17	19	22	25	28	30	33	36	39	41	44	47	50	52	55	24	06
28	63 39	3	6	8	11	14	17	20	22	25	28	31	34	36	39	42	45	47	50	53	56	28	07
32	64 36	3	6	9	11	14	17	20	23	26	28	31	34	37	40	43	45	48	51	54	57	32	08
36	65 33	3	6	9	12	14	17	20	23	26	29	32	35	37	40	43	46	49	52	55	58	36	09
4 40	66 30	3	6	9	12	15	18	20	23	26	29	32	35	38	41	44	47	50	53	55	58	0 40	10
44	67 27	3	6	9	12	15	18	21	24	27	30	33	36	38	41	44	47	50	53	56	59	44	10
48	68 24	3	6	9	12	15	18	21	24	27	30	33	36	39	42	45	48	51	54	57	60	48	11
52	69 21	3	6	9	12	15	18	21	24	27	30	33	37	40	43	46	49	52	55	58	61	52	12
4 56	70 18	3	6	9	12	15	19	22	25	28	31	34	37	40	43	46	49	52	56	59	62	0 56	13
5 00	71 15	3	6	9	13	16	19	22	25	28	31	34	38	41	44	47	50	53	56	59	63	1 00	14
(13 or 21) 04	72 12	3	6	10	13	16	19	22	25	29	32	35	38	41	44	48	51	54	57	60	63	04	15
08	73 09	3	6	10	13	16	19	22	26	29	32	35	39	42	45	48	51	55	58	61	64	08	16
12	74 06	3	7	10	13	16	20	23	26	29	33	36	39	42	46	49	52	55	59	62	65	12	17
16	75 03	3	7	10	13	16	20	23	26	30	33	36	40	43	46	49	53	56	59	63	66	16	18
5 20	76 00	3	7	10	13	17	20	23	27	30	33	37	40	43	47	50	53	57	60	63	67	1 20	19
24	76 57	3	7	10	14	17	20	24	27	30	34	37	41	44	47	51	54	57	61	64	68	24	20
28	77 54	3	7	10	14	17	21	24	27	31	34	38	41	44	48	51	55	58	62	65	68	28	21
32	78 51	3	7	10	14	17	21	24	28	31	35	38	42	45	48	52	55	59	62	66	69	32	22
36	79 48	4	7	11	14	18	21	25	28	32	35	39	42	46	49	53	56	60	63	67	70	36	23
5 40	80 45	4	7	11	14	18	21	25	28	32	35	39	43	46	50	53	57	60	64	67	71	1 40	24
44	81 42	4	7	11	14	18	22	25	29	32	36	39	43	47	50	54	57	61	65	68	72	44	25
48	82 39	4	7	11	15	18	22	25	29	33	36	40	44	47	51	54	58	62	65	69	73	48	26
52	83 36	4	7	11	15	18	22	26	29	33	37	40	44	48	51	55	59	62	66	70	73	52	27
5 56	84 33	4	7	11	15	19	22	26	30	33	37	41	45	48	52	56	59	63	67	70	74	1 56	28
6 00	85 30	4	8	11	15	19	23	26	30	34	38	41	45	49	53	56	60	64	68	71	75	2 00	29
(14 or 22) 04	86 27	4	8	11	15	19	23	27	30	34	38	42	46	49	53	57	61	64	68	72	76	04	29
08	87 24	4	8	12	15	19	23	27	31	35	38	42	46	50	54	58	61	65	69	73	77	08	30
12	88 21	4	8	12	15	19	23	27	31	35	39	43	47	50	54	58	62	66	70	74	78	12	31
16	89 18	4	8	12	16	20	24	27	31	35	39	43	47	51	55	59	63	67	71	74	78	16	32
6 20	90 15	4	8	12	16	20	24	28	32	36	40	44	48	51	55	59	63	67	71	75	79	2 20	33
24	91 12	4	8	12	16	20	24	28	32	36	40	44	48	52	56	60	64	68	72	76	80	24	34
28	92 09	4	8	12	16	20	24	28	32	36	40	44	49	53	57	61	65	69	73	77	81	28	35
32	93 06	4	8	12	16	20	25	29	33	37	41	45	49	53	57	61	65	69	74	78	82	32	36
36	94 03	4	8	12	17	21	25	29	33	37	41	45	50	54	58	62	66	70	74	78	83	36	37
6 40	95 00	4	8	13	17	21	25	29	33	38	42	46	50	54	58	63	67	71	75	79	83	2 40	38
44	95 57	4	8	13	17	21	25	29	34	38	42	46	51	55	59	63	67	72	76	80	84	44	39
48	96 54	4	9	13	17	21	26	30	34	38	43	47	51	55	60	64	68	72	77	81	85	48	40
52	97 51	4	9	13	17	21	26	30	34	39	43	47	52	56	60	64	69	73	77	82	86	52	41
6 56	98 48	4	9	13	17	22	26	30	35	39	43	48	52	56	61	65	69	74	78	82	87	2 56	42
7 00	99 45	4	9	13	18	22	26	31	35	39	44	48	53	57	61	66	70	74	79	83	88	3 00	43
(15 or 23) 04	100 42	4	9	13	18	22	27	31	35	40	44	49	53	57	62	66	71	75	80	84	88	04	44
08	101 39	4	9	13	18	22	27	31	36	40	45	49	54	58	62	67	71	76	80	85	89	08	45
12	102 36	5	9	14	18	23	27	32	36	41	45	50	54	59	63	68	72	77	81	86	90	12	46
16	103 33	5	9	14	18	23	27	32	36	41	45	50	55	59	64	68	73	77	82	86	91	16	47
7 20	104 30	5	9	14	18	23	28	32	37	41	46	50	55	60	64	69	73	78	83	87	92	3 20	48
24	105 27	5	9	14	19	23	28	32	37	42	46	51	56	60	65	69	74	79	83	88	93	24	48
28	106 24	5	9	14	19	23	28	33	37	42	47	51	56	61	65	70	75	79	84	89	93	28	49
32	107 21	5	9	14	19	24	28	33	38	42	47	52	57	61	66	71	75	80	85	89	94	32	50
36	108 18	5	10	14	19	24	29	33	38	43	48	52	57	62	67	71	76	81	86	90	95	36	51
7 40	109 15	5	10	14	19	24	29	34	38	43	48	53	58	62	67	72	77	81	86	91	96	3 40	52
44	110 12	5	10	15	19	24	29	34	39	44	48	53	58	63	68	73	77	82	87	92	97	44	53
48	111 09	5	10	15	20	24	29	34	39	44	49	54	59	63	68	73	78	83	88	93	98	48	54
52	112 06	5	10	15	20	25	30	34	39	44	49	54	59	64	69	74	79	84	89	93	98	52	55
7 56	113 03	5	10	15	20	25	30	35	40	45	50	55	60	64	69	74	79	84	89	94	99	3 56	56
8 00	114 00	5	10	15	20	25	30	35	40	45	50	55	60	65	70	75	80	85	90	95	100	4 00	57

INTERPOLATION TABLES — MOON 4ʰ–8ʰ, 12ʰ–16ʰ, 20ʰ–24ʰ

UT	Corr. to GHA	100	105	110	115	120	125	130	135	140	145	150	155	160	165	170	175	UT	Corr. to GHA
h m	° ′								Units of 1′									m s	′
4 00	57 00	50	53	55	58	60	63	65	68	70	73	75	78	80	83	85	88	0 00	00
(12 or 20) 04	57 57	51	53	56	58	61	64	66	69	71	74	76	79	81	84	86	89	04	01
08	58 54	52	54	57	59	62	65	67	70	72	75	78	80	83	85	88	90	08	02
12	59 51	53	55	58	60	63	66	68	71	74	76	79	81	84	87	89	92	12	03
16	60 48	53	56	59	61	64	67	69	72	75	77	80	83	85	88	91	93	16	04
4 20	61 45	54	57	60	62	65	68	70	73	76	79	81	84	87	89	92	95	0 20	05
24	62 42	55	58	61	63	66	69	72	74	77	80	83	85	88	91	94	96	24	06
28	63 39	56	59	61	64	67	70	73	75	78	81	84	87	89	92	95	98	28	07
32	64 36	57	60	62	65	68	71	74	77	79	82	85	88	91	94	96	99	32	08
36	65 33	58	60	63	66	69	72	75	78	81	83	86	89	92	95	98	101	36	09
4 40	66 30	58	61	64	67	70	73	76	79	82	85	88	90	93	96	99	102	0 40	10
44	67 27	59	62	65	68	71	74	77	80	83	86	89	92	95	98	101	104	44	10
48	68 24	60	63	66	69	72	75	78	81	84	87	90	93	96	99	102	105	48	11
52	69 21	61	64	67	70	73	76	79	82	85	88	91	94	97	100	103	106	52	12
4 56	70 18	62	65	68	71	74	77	80	83	86	89	93	96	99	102	105	108	0 56	13
5 00	71 15	63	66	69	72	75	78	81	84	88	91	94	97	100	103	106	109	1 00	14
(13 or 21) 04	72 12	63	67	70	73	76	79	82	86	89	92	95	98	101	105	108	111	04	15
08	73 09	64	67	71	74	77	80	83	87	90	93	96	99	103	106	109	112	08	16
12	74 06	65	68	72	75	78	81	85	88	91	94	98	101	104	107	111	114	12	17
16	75 03	66	69	72	76	79	82	86	89	92	95	99	102	105	109	112	115	16	18
5 20	76 00	67	70	73	77	80	83	87	90	93	97	100	103	107	110	113	117	1 20	19
24	76 57	68	71	74	78	81	84	88	91	95	98	101	105	108	111	115	118	24	20
28	77 54	68	72	75	79	82	85	89	92	96	99	103	106	109	113	116	120	28	21
32	78 51	69	73	76	80	83	86	90	93	97	100	104	107	111	114	118	121	32	22
36	79 48	70	74	77	81	84	88	91	95	98	102	105	109	112	116	119	123	36	23
5 40	80 45	71	74	78	81	85	89	92	96	99	103	106	110	113	117	120	124	1 40	24
44	81 42	72	75	79	82	86	90	93	97	100	104	108	111	115	118	122	125	44	25
48	82 39	73	76	80	83	87	91	94	98	102	105	109	112	116	120	123	127	48	26
52	83 36	73	77	81	04	88	92	95	99	103	106	110	114	117	121	125	128	52	27
5 56	84 33	74	78	82	85	89	93	96	100	104	108	111	115	119	122	126	130	1 56	28
6 00	85 30	75	79	83	86	90	94	98	101	105	109	113	116	120	124	128	131	2 00	29
(14 or 22) 04	86 27	76	80	83	87	91	95	99	102	106	110	114	118	121	125	129	133	04	29
08	87 24	77	81	84	88	92	96	100	104	107	111	115	119	123	127	130	134	08	30
12	88 21	78	81	85	89	93	97	101	105	109	112	116	120	124	128	132	136	12	31
16	89 18	78	82	86	90	94	98	102	106	110	114	118	121	125	129	133	137	16	32
6 20	90 15	79	83	87	91	95	99	103	107	111	115	119	123	127	131	135	139	2 20	33
24	91 12	80	84	88	92	96	100	104	108	112	116	120	124	128	132	136	140	24	34
28	92 09	81	85	89	93	97	101	105	109	113	117	121	125	129	133	137	141	28	35
32	93 06	82	86	90	94	98	102	106	110	114	118	123	127	131	135	139	143	32	36
36	94 03	83	87	91	95	99	103	107	111	116	120	124	128	132	136	140	144	36	37
6 40	95 00	83	88	92	96	100	104	108	113	117	121	125	129	133	138	142	146	2 40	38
44	95 57	84	88	93	97	101	105	109	114	118	122	126	130	135	139	143	147	44	39
48	96 54	85	89	94	98	102	106	111	115	119	123	128	132	136	140	145	149	48	40
52	97 51	86	90	94	99	103	107	112	116	120	124	129	133	137	142	146	150	52	41
6 56	98 48	87	91	95	100	104	108	113	117	121	126	130	134	139	143	147	152	2 56	42
7 00	99 45	88	92	96	101	105	109	114	118	123	127	131	136	140	144	149	153	3 00	43
(15 or 23) 04	100 42	88	93	97	102	106	110	115	119	124	128	133	137	141	146	150	155	04	44
08	101 39	89	94	98	103	107	111	116	120	125	129	134	138	143	147	152	156	08	45
12	102 36	90	95	99	104	108	113	117	122	126	131	135	140	144	149	153	158	12	46
16	103 33	91	95	100	104	109	114	118	123	127	132	136	141	145	150	154	159	16	47
7 20	104 30	92	96	101	105	110	115	119	124	128	133	138	142	147	151	156	160	3 20	48
24	105 27	93	97	102	106	111	116	120	125	130	134	139	143	148	153	157	162	24	48
28	106 24	93	98	103	107	112	117	121	126	131	135	140	145	149	154	159	163	28	49
32	107 21	94	99	104	108	113	118	122	127	132	137	141	146	151	155	160	165	32	50
36	108 18	95	100	105	109	114	119	124	128	133	138	143	147	152	157	162	166	36	51
7 40	109 15	96	101	105	110	115	120	125	129	134	139	144	149	153	158	163	168	3 40	52
44	110 12	97	102	106	111	116	121	126	131	135	140	145	150	155	160	164	169	44	53
48	111 09	98	102	107	112	117	122	127	132	137	141	146	151	156	161	166	171	48	54
52	112 06	98	103	108	113	118	123	128	133	138	143	148	152	157	162	167	172	52	55
7 56	113 03	99	104	109	114	119	124	129	134	139	144	149	154	159	164	169	174	3 56	56
8 00	114 00	100	105	110	115	120	125	130	135	140	145	150	155	160	165	170	175	4 00	57

5.3.10   **STAR DIAGRAM (LHA ARIES 0°-120°)**

The diagrams are explained in 5.2.6 on page 70. Note that when a star is near the zenith its azimuth is liable to a considerable change for a small change in latitude. The magnitude corresponding to the star symbols is shown alongside.

·	Mag	2.1–3.1
○	Mag	1.1–2.0
●	Mag	0.0–1.0
⊙	Mag	–1.6

STAR DIAGRAM (LHA ARIES 120°-240°)

1	Alpheratz	8	Menkar	14	Elnath	20	Procyon	28	Denebola	37	Arcturus	45	Shaula	51	Altair
2	Ankaa	9	Mirfak	15	Alnilam	21	Pollux	29	Gienah	39	Zuben'ubi	46	Rasalhague	53	Deneb
3	Schedar	10	Aldebaran	16	Betelgeuse	23	Suhail	32	Alioth	40	Kochab	47	Eltanin	54	Enif
4	Diphda	11	Rigel	17	Canopus	25	Alphard	33	Spica	41	Alphecca	48	Kaus Aust	55	Al Na'ir
6	Hamal	12	Capella	18	Sirius	26	Regulus	34	Alkaid	42	Antares	49	Vega	56	Fomalhaut
7	Acamar	13	Bellatrix	19	Adhara	27	Dubhe	36	Menkent	44	Sabik	50	Nunki	57	Markab

STAR DIAGRAM (LHA ARIES 240°-360°)

The diagrams are explained in 5.2.6 on page 72. Note that when a star is near the zenith its azimuth is liable to a considerable change for a small change in latitude. The magnitude corresponding to the star symbols is shown alongside.

· Mag 2.1–3.1
○ Mag 1.1–2.0
● Mag 0.0–1.0
⊙ Mag −1.6

5.3.11   **AZIMUTH DIAGRAM A**

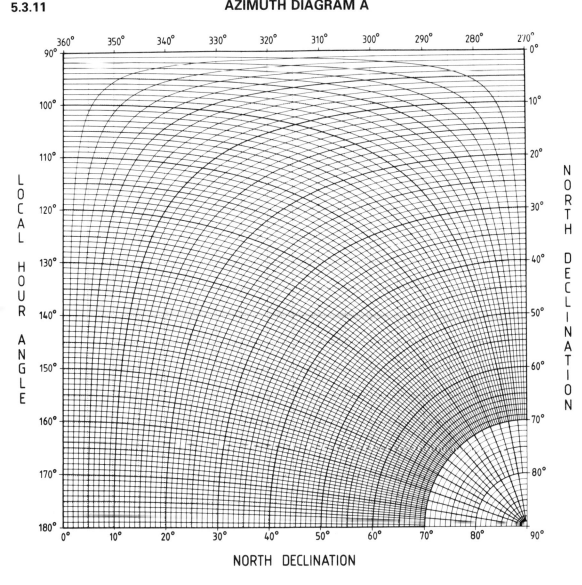

NORTH DECLINATION

Instructions — To determine the Azimuth of an observed body given the latitude of the observer (Lat) and the LHA and Dec of the body.

(1) Plot on the diagrams a position corresponding to the LHA and Dec; if the LHA is greater than 180° use 360° — LHA when plotting.

(2) Read the position of the plotted point on the rectangular graticule, using the scale at the top for the horizontal reading, and the declination scale for the vertical reading.

(3) To the horizontal reading in (2) add the co-latitude (i.e. add 90° and subtract Lat). The vertical co-ordinate is unchanged.

(4) At the point corresponding to the co-ordinates in (3) read the corresponding LHA (= Z).

(5) Z is converted to Azimuth as follows:

LHA (body)	Azimuth
0° to 180°	180° + Z
180° to 360°	180° — Z

Note that in step (4) a reading of the Dec at the same point gives an approximate value of the altitude, and so gives a check on the plotting.

The diagrams A, B and C are portions of a continuous diagram (see p. 111), so that if the movement for co-latitude goes off the diagram on which step (2) is plotted, then the overlap can be found on the previous diagram.

AZIMUTH DIAGRAM B

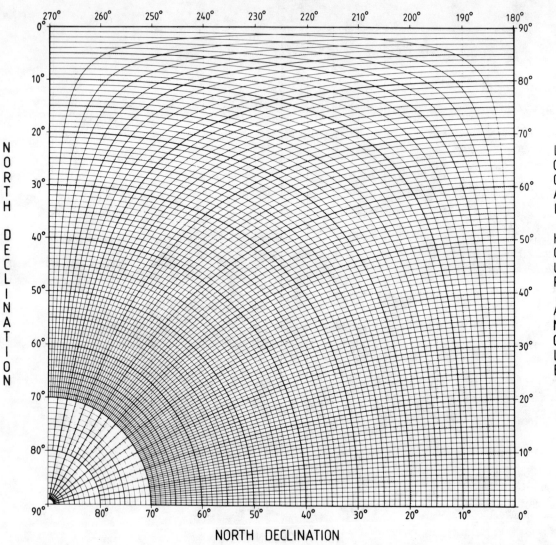

Illustration — On 1991 January 5 at GMT 14^h 40^m 18^s, the Sun is observed from a position N.44°36′ W.2°40′ and it is required to determine the azimuth.

Page 85,	Jan 5,	00^h		GHA	178	44·8′	$v = -6·7′$	Dec S22 41·5′ $d = +$
Interpolation	UT	14^h 36^m			219			
Tables	UT		4^m 18^s		1	04.5		
Page 97	v, d correction					−04.1		+ 4.1
	UT	14^h 40^m 18^s		GHA	398	45.2		
	Longitude W.2°40′				− 2	40.0		
				LHA	396	05.2		
					−360			
				LHA	36	05.2		Dec S22 37.4

Plot on diagram C, LHA = 36°, Dec = S.22°.6; the corresponding graticule co-ordinates are found to be 153° and 57° (down); to the horizontal co-ordinate add 90° and subtract 44°.6; the new co-ordinates being 198°.4 and 57° the corresponding value of LHA (= Z) is 34°. The Dec is 15°. The Azimuth is therefore 180° + 34° = 214°, and the approximate altitude is 15° which can be compared with the observed altitude as a check on the plotting.

AZIMUTH DIAGRAM C

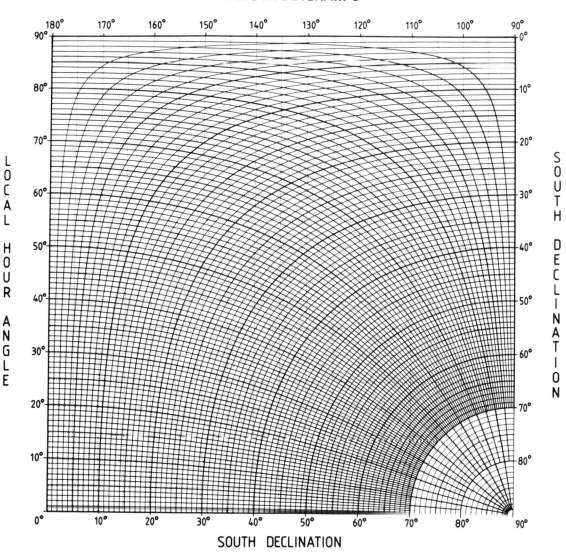

The illustration below shows how A, B and C are portions of a continuous diagram. The points P and Q show the plotting of the example opposite.

5.3.12   CONVERSION TABLES

Arc to Time

°	h m	°	h m	°	h m	′	m s
0	0 00	60	4 00	120	8 00	0	0 00
1	0 04	61	4 04	121	8 04	1	0 04
2	0 08	62	4 08	122	8 08	2	0 08
3	0 12	63	4 12	123	8 12	3	0 12
4	0 16	64	4 16	124	8 16	4	0 16
5	0 20	65	4 20	125	8 20	5	0 20
6	0 24	66	4 24	126	8 24	6	0 24
7	0 28	67	4 28	127	8 28	7	0 28
8	0 32	68	4 32	128	8 32	8	0 32
9	0 36	69	4 36	129	8 36	9	0 36
10	0 40	70	4 40	130	8 40	10	0 40
11	0 44	71	4 44	131	8 44	11	0 44
12	0 48	72	4 48	132	8 48	12	0 48
13	0 52	73	4 52	133	8 52	13	0 52
14	0 56	74	4 56	134	8 56	14	0 56
15	1 00	75	5 00	135	9 00	15	1 00
16	1 04	76	5 04	136	9 04	16	1 04
17	1 08	77	5 08	137	9 08	17	1 08
18	1 12	78	5 12	138	9 12	18	1 12
19	1 16	79	5 16	139	9 16	19	1 16
20	1 20	80	5 20	140	9 20	20	1 20
21	1 24	81	5 24	141	9 24	21	1 24
22	1 28	82	5 28	142	9 28	22	1 28
23	1 32	83	5 32	143	9 32	23	1 32
24	1 36	84	5 36	144	9 36	24	1 36
25	1 40	85	5 40	145	9 40	25	1 40
26	1 44	86	5 44	146	9 44	26	1 44
27	1 48	87	5 48	147	9 48	27	1 48
28	1 52	88	5 52	148	9 52	28	1 52
29	1 56	89	5 56	149	9 56	29	1 56
30	2 00	90	6 00	150	10 00	30	2 00
31	2 04	91	6 04	151	10 04	31	2 04
32	2 08	92	6 08	152	10 08	32	2 08
33	2 12	93	6 12	153	10 12	33	2 12
34	2 16	94	6 16	154	10 16	34	2 16
35	2 20	95	6 20	155	10 20	35	2 20
36	2 24	96	6 24	156	10 24	36	2 24
37	2 28	97	6 28	157	10 28	37	2 28
38	2 32	98	6 32	158	10 32	38	2 32
39	2 36	99	6 36	159	10 36	39	2 36
40	2 40	100	6 40	160	10 40	40	2 40
41	2 44	101	6 44	161	10 44	41	2 44
42	2 48	102	6 48	162	10 48	42	2 48
43	2 52	103	6 52	163	10 52	43	2 52
44	2 56	104	6 56	164	10 56	44	2 56
45	3 00	105	7 00	165	11 00	45	3 00
46	3 04	106	7 04	166	11 04	46	3 04
47	3 08	107	7 08	167	11 08	47	3 08
48	3 12	108	7 12	168	11 12	48	3 12
49	3 16	109	7 16	169	11 16	49	3 16
50	3 20	110	7 20	170	11 20	50	3 20
51	3 24	111	7 24	171	11 24	51	3 24
52	3 28	112	7 28	172	11 28	52	3 28
53	3 32	113	7 32	173	11 32	53	3 32
54	3 36	114	7 36	174	11 36	54	3 36
55	3 40	115	7 40	175	11 40	55	3 40
56	3 44	116	7 44	176	11 44	56	3 44
57	3 48	117	7 48	177	11 48	57	3 48
58	3 52	118	7 52	178	11 52	58	3 52
59	3 56	119	7 56	179	11 56	59	3 56

180° = 12h 00m

Hours, Minutes and Seconds to Decimals of a Day

h m	d	h m	d	m s	d
0 00	0.00000	6 00	0.25000	0 00	0.00000
06	.00417	06	.25417	06	.00007
12	.00833	12	.25833	12	.00014
18	.01250	18	.26250	18	.00021
24	.01667	24	.26667	24	.00028
0 30	0.02083	6 30	0.27083	0 30	0.00035
36	.02500	36	.27500	36	.00042
42	.02917	42	.27917	42	.00049
48	.03333	48	.28333	48	.00056
0 54	.03750	6 54	.28750	0 54	.00062
1 00	0.04167	7 00	0.29167	1 00	0.00069
06	.04583	06	.29583	06	.00076
12	.05000	12	.30000	12	.00083
18	.05417	18	.30417	18	.00090
24	.05833	24	.30833	24	.00097
1 30	0.06250	7 30	0.31250	1 30	0.00104
36	.06667	36	.31667	36	.00111
42	.07083	42	.32083	42	.00118
48	.07500	48	.32500	48	.00125
1 54	.07917	7 54	.32917	1 54	.00132
2 00	0.08333	8 00	0.33333	2 00	0.00139
06	.08750	06	.33750	06	.00146
12	.09167	12	.34167	12	.00153
18	.09583	18	.34583	18	.00160
24	.10000	24	.35000	24	.00167
2 30	0.10417	8 30	0.35417	2 30	0.00174
36	.10833	36	.35833	36	.00181
42	.11250	42	.36250	42	.00188
48	.11667	48	.36667	48	.00194
2 54	.12083	8 54	.37083	2 54	.00201
3 00	0.12500	9 00	0.37500	3 00	0.00208
06	.12917	06	.37917	06	.00215
12	.13333	12	.38333	12	.00222
18	.13750	18	.38750	18	.00229
24	.14167	24	.39167	24	.00236
3 30	0.14583	9 30	0.39583	3 30	0.00243
36	.15000	36	.40000	36	.00250
42	.15417	42	.40417	42	.00257
48	.15833	48	.40833	48	.00264
3 54	.16250	9 54	.41250	3 54	.00271
4 00	0.16667	10 00	0.41667	4 00	0.00278
06	.17083	06	.42083	06	.00285
12	.17500	12	.42500	12	.00292
18	.17917	18	.42917	18	.00299
24	.18333	24	.43333	24	.00306
4 30	0.18750	10 30	0.43750	4 30	0.00312
36	.19167	36	.44167	36	.00319
42	.19583	42	.44583	42	.00326
48	.20000	48	.45000	48	.00333
4 54	.20417	10 54	.45417	4 54	.00340
5 00	0.20833	11 00	0.45833	5 00	0.00347
06	.21250	06	.46250	06	.00354
12	.21667	12	.46667	12	.00361
18	.22083	18	.47083	18	.00368
24	.22500	24	.47500	24	.00375
5 30	0.22917	11 30	0.47917	5 30	0.00382
36	.23333	36	.48333	36	.00389
42	.23750	42	.48750	42	.00396
48	.24167	48	.49167	48	.00403
5 54	.24583	11 54	.49583	5 54	.00410
6 00	0.25000	12 00	0.50000	6 00	0.00417

Decimals of a Degree to Minutes of Arc

°	′	°	′
0.00	0	0.50	30
.01	1	.51	31
.02	1	.52	31
.03	2	.53	32
.04	2	.54	32
0.05	3	0.55	33
.06	4	.56	34
.07	4	.57	34
.08	5	.58	35
.09	5	.59	35
0.10	6	0.60	36
.11	7	.61	37
.12	7	.62	37
.13	8	.63	38
.14	8	.64	38
0.15	9	0.65	39
.16	10	.66	40
.17	10	.67	40
.18	11	.68	41
.19	11	.69	41
0.20	12	0.70	42
.21	13	.71	43
.22	13	.72	43
.23	14	.73	44
.24	14	.74	44
0.25	15	0.75	45
.26	16	.76	46
.27	16	.77	46
.28	17	.78	47
.29	17	.79	47
0.30	18	0.80	48
.31	19	.81	49
.32	19	.82	49
.33	20	.83	50
.34	20	.84	50
0.35	21	0.85	51
.36	22	.86	52
.37	22	.87	52
.38	23	.88	53
.39	23	.89	53
0.40	24	0.90	54
.41	25	.91	55
.42	25	.92	55
.43	26	.93	56
.44	26	.94	56
0.45	27	0.95	57
.46	28	.96	58
.47	28	.97	58
.48	29	.98	59
.49	29	.99	59
0.50	30	1.00	60

This table can also be used for the conversion of decimals of a minute to seconds of arc and vice versa.

PLATE 1 – NAVIGATION LIGHTS (SEE ALSO PLATE 4)

Port sidelight (red) shows from ahead to 22½° abaft the beam

112½°

Abeam

For yachts 12–50m overall, visibility – 2 miles. For yachts under 12m – 1 mile

(May be combined with starboard sidelight in one centreline lantern in boats under 20m overall)

White masthead light shows over arc of 225° – from ahead to 22½° abaft the beam each side. Shown by vessels under power only

Ahead

225°

For yachts 20–50m overall, visibility – 5 miles. For yachts 12–20m – 3 miles. For yachts under 12m – 2 miles

Starboard sidelight (green) shows from ahead to 22½° abaft the beam

112½°

Abeam

For yachts 12–50m overall, visibility – 2 miles. For yachts under 12m – 1 mile

(May be combined with port side light in one centreline lantern in boats under 20m overall)

(Masthead light and stern-light may be combined in one all-round white light in boats under 12m overall)

White sternlight shows over arc of 135°, 67½° on each side of vessel

Astern

For yachts under 50m overall, visibility – 2 miles

135°

Lights for power-driven vessels underway (plan views)

Note: Also apply to sailing yachts or other sailing craft when under power

Motor boat under 7m, less than 7 knots

Motor boat under 12m (combined masthead & sternlight)

Motor yacht under 20m (combined lantern for sidelights)

Motor yacht over 20m

Larger vessel, over 50m, with two masthead lights – the aft one higher

Lights for sailing vessels underway (plan views)

Note: These lights apply to sailing craft when under sail ONLY. If motor-sailing the appropriate lights for a power-driven vessel must be shown, as above

  Masthead tricolour lantern

or

Sailing boat under 7m shows white light to prevent collision. If practicable she should show sidelights and sternlight

Combined sidelights plus stern-light

Tricolour lantern at masthead

Separate sidelights and sternlight for sailing vessel over 20m

Sailing yacht under 20m

Bow view

If not using tri-colour masthead lantern, a sailing yacht may show (in addition to other lights) two all-round lights near masthead, the upper red and the lower green

PLATE 2 – ADMIRALTY METRIC CHART SYMBOLS

A selection of the more common symbols from Admiralty Publication 5011

Reproduced by kind permission of H.M. Stationery Office and the Hydrographer of the Navy.

THE COASTLINE	ARTIFICIAL FEATURES	RADIO AND RADAR
Coast imperfectly known or shoreline unsurveyed.	Sea wall	RC *Non-directional Radiobeacon*
Steep coast	Breakwater	RD RD 269°30′ *Directional Radiobeacon*
Cliffy coast	Submerged jetty (LW) (HW)	RW *Rotating Pattern Radiobeacon*
Sandy shore	Patent slip	RG *Radio Direction Finding Station*
Low Water Line	Lock	**Radio Mast** *Radio mast or tower* **Radio Tr** *Radio tower or scanner* **Radar Tr** **Radar Sc** *Landmarks for visual fixing only*
Foreshore, Mud	Hulk	**TV Mast** **TV Tr** *Television mast or tower*
Foreshore, Sand	Steps	R *Coast Radio Station providing QTG service*
Foreshore, Boulders, Stones, Gravel and Shingle	Telegraph or telephone line, with vertical clearance (above HW) H20m	Ra *Coast Radar Station*
Foreshore, Rock	Sewer, Outfall pipe	**Racon** *Radar Responder Beacon*
Foreshore, Sand and Mud	Bridge (9m)	*Radar Reflector*
Limiting danger line	Fixed bridge with vertical clearance (above HW) H17m	**Ra** (conspic) *Radar conspicuous object.*
Breakers along a shore	Ferry	**Aero RC** *Aeronautical radiobeacon.*
Half-tide channel (on intertidal ground)	Training wall Training Wall (covers)	**Consol Bn** *Consol beacon.*

PLATE 3 – ADMIRALTY METRIC CHART SYMBOLS

A selection of the more common symbols from Admiralty Publication 5011

Reproduced by kind permission of H.M. Stationery Office and the Hydrographer of the Navy.

DANGERS	DANGERS	LIMITS

DANGERS (column 1):

Rock which does not cover (with elevation above MHWS or MHHW, or where there is no tide, above MSL).

Rock which covers and uncovers (with elevation above chart datum).

Rock awash at the level of chart datum.

Submerged rock with 2 metres or less water over it at chart datum, or rock ledge on which depths are known to be 2 metres or less, or a rock or rock ledge over which the exact depth is unknown but which is considered to be dangerous to surface navigation.

Shoal sounding on isolated rock.

Submerged rock not dangerous to surface navigation.

Submerged danger with depth cleared by wire drag.

Wreck showing any portion of hull or superstructure at the level of chart datum. Large scale charts

Wreck of which the masts only are visible. Large scale charts

(Masts) (Funnel) (Mast 3 m) (Mast dries 2.1 m)

Wreck over which the exact depth of water is unknown but is thought to be 28 metres or less, and which is considered dangerous to surface navigation.

DANGERS (column 2):

Wreck over which the depth has been obtained by sounding, but not by wire sweep.

Wreck over which the exact depth is unknown but thought to be more than 28 metres, or a wreck over which the depth is thought to be 28 metres or less, but which is not considered dangerous to surface vessels capable of navigating in the vicinity.

Foul   Foul   Foul

The remains of a wreck, or other foul area no longer dangerous to surface navigation, but to be avoided by vessels anchoring, trawling, etc.

Overfalls and tide-rips

Eddies

Kelp

Breakers

Limiting danger line

LIMITS (column 3):

Leading Bns 089°53′   Bn   Bn
Leading Line

Limit of sector

Traffic separation scheme: one-way traffic lanes (separated by zone).

Submarine cable (telegraph & telephone).

Power Submarine cable (power).

Limits of national fishing zones.

✱ ✱ Small Craft Anchorage.
Anchorage Area.

Type of anchorage is usually indicated by legend, e.g. Small Craft Anchorage, Naval Anchorage, Quarantine Anchorage, etc.

Recommended track for deep draught vessels (track not defined by fixed mark(s)).

Where the minimum safe depth along the recommended track (or section thereof) is guaranteed by the competent harbour regional or national authority, the depth is indicated thus:

>–DW–27m–> – –>–DW–25m–>

DW 27m   DW 25m

PLATE 4 – PRINCIPAL NAVIGATION LIGHTS AND SHAPES

(*Note*: All vessels seen from starboard beam)

Vessel at anchor

All-round white light: if over 50m, a second light aft and lower

Black ball forward

Not under command

Two all-round red lights, plus sidelights and stern-light when making way

Two black balls vertically

Motor sailing

Cone point down, forward

Divers down

Letter 'A' International Code

Vessel aground

Anchor light(s), plus two all-round red lights in a vertical line

Three black balls in a vertical line

Vessels being towed and towing

Vessel towed shows side-lights (forward) and sternlight

Tug shows two masthead lights, sidelights, stern-light, yellow towing light

Towing by day – Length of tow more than 200m

Towing vessel and tow display diamond shapes. By night, the towing vessel shows three masthead lights instead of two as for shorter tows

Vessel fishing

All-round red light over all-round white, plus side-lights and sternlight when underway

Fishing/trawling

Two cones point to point, or a basket if fishing vessel is less than 20m

Vessel trawling

All-round green light over all-round white, plus side-lights and sternlight when underway

Pilot boat

All-round white light over all-round red; plus side-lights and sternlight when underway, or anchor light

Vessel restricted in her ability to manoeuvre

All-round red, white, red lights vertically; plus normal steaming lights when under way

Three shapes in a vertical line – ball, diamond, ball

Dredger

As left, plus two all-round red lights (or two balls) on foul side, and two all-round green (or two diamonds) on clear side

Constrained by draught

Three all-round red lights in a vertical line, plus normal steaming lights. By day – a cylinder

PLATE 5 – IALA BUOYAGE

Lateral marks

Used generally to mark the sides of well defined navigable channels.

Port Hand marks

Light:
Colour – red
Rhythm – any

Navigable channel

Direction of buoyage

Starboard Hand marks

Light:
Colour – green
Rhythm – any

Cardinal marks

Used to indicate the direction from the mark in which the best navigable water lies, or to draw attention to a bend, junction or fork in a channel, or to mark the end of a shoal.

Lights: Always white

NW

NE

Light: VQ or Q

hazard

Light:
VQ (9)
every 10 secs.
or Q (9)
every 15 secs.

Light:
VQ (3)
every 5 secs.
or Q (3)
every 10 secs.

SW

SE

Light: VQ (6) + LFl every 10 secs. or Q (6) + LFl every 15 secs.

Other marks

Isolated danger marks

Use: To mark a small isolated danger with navigable water all round.
Light: Colour – white
Rhythm – group flashing (2)

Safe water marks

Use: Mid-channel or landfall.
Light: Colour – white
Rhythm – Isophase, occulting or 1 long flash every 10 seconds.

Special marks

Any shape not conflicting with lateral or safe water marks.
Light: Colour – yellow
Rhythm – different from other white lights used on buoys.

PLATES 6-7 – INTERNATIONAL CODE OF SIGNALS
CODE FLAGS, PHONETIC ALPHABET, MORSE SYMBOLS AND SINGLE-LETTER SIGNALS

Notes:
1. Single letter signals may be made by any method of signalling. Those marked * when made by sound must comply with the *International Regulations for Preventing Collisions at Sea*, Rules 34 and 35.
2. Signals 'K' and 'S' have special meanings as landing signals for small boats with persons in distress.
3. In the phonetic alphabet, the syllables to be emphasised are in italics.

Code and Answering Pendant

A   Alfa   (*AL* FAH)

I have a diver down; keep well clear at slow speed

*B   Bravo   (*BRAH* VOH)

I am taking in, or discharging, or carrying dangerous goods

*C   Charlie   (*CHAR* LEE)

Yes (affirmative or 'The significance of the previous group should be read in the affirmative)

*D   Delta   (*DELL* TAH)

Keep clear of me; I am manoeuvring with difficulty

*E   Echo   (*ECK* OH)

I am altering my course to starboard

F   Foxtrot   (*FOKS* TROT)

I am disabled; communicate with me

*G   Golf   (*GOLF*)

I require a pilot. When made by fishing vessels operating in close proximity on the fishing grounds it means: I am hauling nets

*H   Hotel   (HOH *TELL*)

I have a pilot on board

*I   India   (*IN* DEE AH)

I am altering my course to port

J   Juliett   (*JEW* LEE *ETT*)

I am on fire and have dangerous cargo on board: keep well clear of me

K   Kilo   (*KEY* LOH)

I wish to communicate with you

L   Lima   (*LEE* MAH)

You should stop your vessel instantly

*M   Mike   (MIKE)

My vessel is stopped and making no way through the water

N   November   (NO *VEM* BER)

No (negative or 'The significance of the previous group should be read in the negative'). This signal may be given only visually or by sound

O   Oscar   (*OSS* CAH)

Man overboard

P   Papa   (PAH *PAH*)

In harbour: all persons should report on board as the vessel is about to proceed to sea. **At sea**: it may be used by fishing vessels to mean 'My nets have come fast upon an obstruction'

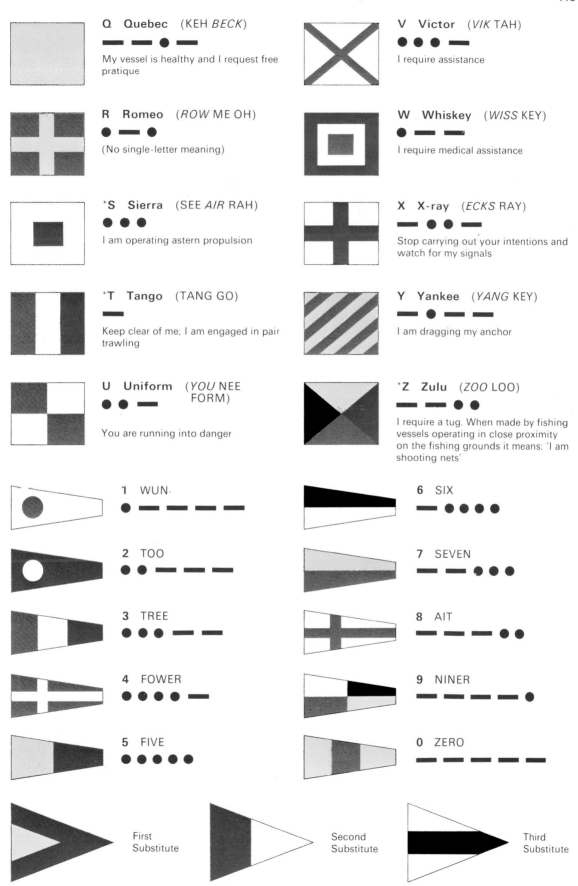

Q Quebec (KEH *BECK*)

━ ━ ● ━

My vessel is healthy and I request free pratique

V Victor (*VIK* TAH)

● ● ● ━

I require assistance

R Romeo (*ROW* ME OH)

● ━ ●

(No single-letter meaning)

W Whiskey (*WISS* KEY)

● ━ ━

I require medical assistance

*S Sierra (SEE *AIR* RAH)

● ● ●

I am operating astern propulsion

X X-ray (*ECKS* RAY)

━ ● ● ━

Stop carrying out your intentions and watch for my signals

*T Tango (TANG GO)

━

Keep clear of me; I am engaged in pair trawling

Y Yankee (*YANG* KEY)

━ ● ━ ━

I am dragging my anchor

U Uniform (*YOU* NEE FORM)

● ● ━

You are running into danger

*Z Zulu (*ZOO* LOO)

━ ━ ● ●

I require a tug. When made by fishing vessels operating in close proximity on the fishing grounds it means: 'I am shooting nets'

1 WUN ● ━ ━ ━ ━

2 TOO ● ● ━ ━ ━

3 TREE ● ● ● ━ ━

4 FOWER ● ● ● ● ━

5 FIVE ● ● ● ● ●

6 SIX ━ ● ● ● ●

7 SEVEN ━ ━ ● ● ●

8 AIT ━ ━ ━ ● ●

9 NINER ━ ━ ━ ━ ●

0 ZERO ━ ━ ━ ━ ━

First Substitute

Second Substitute

Third Substitute

PLATE 8 – INTERNATIONAL PORT TRAFFIC SIGNALS

No	Lights		Main message
1	● ● ●	Flashing	Serious emergency – all vessels to stop or divert according to instructions
2	● ● ●	Fixed or Slow Occulting	Vessels shall not proceed (*Note*: Some ports may use an exemption signal, as in 2a below)
3	● ● ●		Vessels may proceed. One way traffic
4	● ● ○		Vessels may proceed. Two way traffic
5	● ○ ●		A vessel may proceed only when she has received specific orders to do so (*Note*: Some ports may use an exemption signal, as in 5a below)
			Exemption signals and messages
2a	○ ● ● ●	Fixed or Slow Occulting	Vessels shall not proceed, except that vessels which navigate outside the main channel need not comply with the main message
5a	○ ● ○ ●		A vessel may proceed only when she has received specific orders to do so, except that vessels which navigate outside the main channel need not comply with the main message
			Auxiliary signals and messages
	White and/or yellow lights, displayed to the right of the main lights		Local meanings, as promulgated in local port orders

This new system is gradually being introduced, but its general adoption is likely to take many years.

Notes on use:

(1)   The main movement message given by a port traffic signal shall always comprise three lights, disposed vertically. No additional light shall be added to the column carrying the main message. (The fact that the main message always consists of three vertical lights allows the mariner to recognise it as a traffic signal, and not lights of navigational significance). The signals may also be used to control traffic at locks and bridges.

(2)   Red lights indicate 'Do not proceed'.

(3)   Green lights indicate 'Proceed, subject to the conditions stipulated'.
    (For examples, see opposite).
  Note that, to avoid confusion, red and green lights are never displayed together.

(4)   A single yellow light, displayed to the left of the column carrying main messages Nos 2 or 5, at the level of the upper light, may be used to indicate that 'Vessels which can safely navigate outside the main channel need not comply with the main message'. This signal is of obvious significance to yachtsmen.

(5)   Signals which are auxiliary to the main message may be devised by local authorities. Such auxiliary signals should employ only white and/or yellow lights, and should be displayed to the right of the column carrying the main message. Ports with complex entrances and much traffic may need many auxiliary signals, which will have to be documented; but smaller harbours with less traffic may only need one or two of the basic signals, such as 'Vessels shall not proceed' and 'Vessels may proceed, two way traffic'.

  Some signals may be omni-directional – exhibited to all vessels simultaneously: others must be directional, and be shown either to vessels entering or to vessels leaving harbour.

  Signal No 5 is based on the assumption that some other means of communication such as VHF radio, signal lamp, loud hailer, or auxiliary signal will be used to inform a vessel that she may specifically proceed.

  The 'Serious Emergency' signal must be flashing, at least 60 flashes per minute. All other signals must be either fixed or slow occulting (the latter useful when background glare is a problem). A mixture of fixed and occulting lights must not be used.

Chapter 6

Communications

Contents

6

Communications — introduction

It is useful — and sometimes essential — for yachts to be able to communicate with other vessels and with shore stations. A full description of the various methods and procedures is given in Chapter 6 of *The Macmillan & Silk Cut Yachtsman's Handbook*, including:

The International Code; Morse code; phonetic tables; procedure signals; complements; single-letter signals; flag signalling; Morse code by light; sound signals; radio time signals; pratique messages; port signals; tide signals; radiotelephony; flag etiquette. There are also included colour plates showing national maritime flags, flag etiquette, and burgees of selected yacht clubs.

Here in this Almanac explanations are kept to a minimum, and only sufficient information is given to allow limited use of the International Code in cases of emergency, and to permit yachtsmen to pass simple messages. Particular emphasis is placed on the use of VHF radiotelephones. For further information on all aspects of signalling, including the subjects listed above, reference should be made to Chapter 6 of *The Macmillan & Silk Cut Yachtsman's Handbook*.

6.1   INTERNATIONAL CODE

6.1.1   International Code of Signals

Most communication afloat is based on the *International Code of Signals* (HMSO), which provides particularly where there are language problems.

The Code can be used by flags, flashing light, sound signalling, voice (e.g. loud hailer), radio-telegraphy, radiotelephony, or by hand flags.

Signals consist of: single-letter signals which are very urgent or very common; two-letter signals in the General Section; and three-letter signals starting with 'M' in the Medical Section.

Complements

In principle each signal has a complete meaning, but complements (which are numerals from 0 to 9, added to the letters of a signal) are used to supplement the available groups — expressing variations in the meaning of a basic signal, asking or answering questions on the same subject, or giving more detailed information. For example:

YD	What is the wind expected to do?
YD1	The wind is expected to back.
YD2	The wind is expected to veer.
YD3	The wind is expected to increase.
etc.	

Complements should only be used as and when specified in the Code.

6.1.2   Using the International Code

To make full and proper use of the International Code, whereby seamen of nine nations can communicate with each other on matters concerning navigation and safety without knowing any foreign language, it is necessary to hold a copy of the *International Code of Signals*, published by HMSO. It is however possible for yachtsmen to make limited use of the Code so as to pass and receive simple messages, using the information contained in this chapter.

In Plates 6 and 7 on pages 113–120 are shown the International Code flags for the alphabet and for numerals, the phonetic alphabet, the phonetic figure-spelling table, the Morse symbols for letters and numerals, and the single-letter signals of the letters of the alphabet.

6.1.3   General instructions

(1) *Numbers* are signalled: by flags — by numeral pendants; by light — by Morse numerals, but spelt if important; by voice — by phonetic code words, see Plate 7.

(2) *Decimal point* is indicated: by flags — by Answering Pendant; by Light — by $\overline{AAA}$; by voice — by the word 'Decimal'.

(3) *Depths* are signalled in figures followed by 'F' for feet, or 'M' for metres.

(4) *Bearings* are signalled in three figures, denoting degrees (True) from 000 to 359.

(5) *Courses* are signalled as for bearings, with figures prefixed by the letter 'C'.

(6) *Dates* are signalled by two, four or six figures preceded by 'D'. The first two figures show day of month, the next two the month of the year, and the final two (when six are signalled) the year.

(7) *Latitude* is signalled by four figures preceded by 'L', and followed where necessary by 'N' or 'S'. The first two figures indicate degrees, and the second two indicate minutes.

(8) *Longitude* is signalled by four (or five) figures preceded by 'G', and followed by 'E' or 'W'. The last two figures show minutes, and the first two (or three) show degrees.

(9) *Distance* is signalled by figures (in nautical miles) preceded by 'R'.

(10) *Speed* is signalled by figures preceded by 'S' (for knots) or by 'V' (kilometres per hour).

(11) *Time* is signalled by 24 hour clock, preceded by 'T' for local time or by 'Z' for GMT (or UT).

6.1.4   Procedure signals

Note: A bar over the letters of a signal means that the letters are joined together and made as one symbol.

(1) Signals for voice transmissions (R/T or loud hailer)

Signal	Pronunciation	Meaning
INTERCO	IN-TER-CO	International Code group(s) follow(s).
CORRECTION	KOR-REK-SHUN	Cancel my last word or group. The correct word or group follows.
DECIMAL	DAY-SEE-MAL	Decimal point
STOP	STOP	Full stop

(2) Signals for Morse transmissions by light

$\overline{AA}\ \overline{AA}\ \overline{AA}$ etc	Call for unknown station or general call
$\overline{EEEEEE}$ etc	Erase signal.
$\overline{AAA}$	Full stop or decimal point.
TTTT etc	Answering signal.
T	Word or group received.

(3) Signals for flags, radiotelephony and radiotelegraphy transmissions

CQ   Call for unknown station(s) or general call to all stations.

Note: When this signal is used in voice transmission, it should bc pronounced in accordance with the letter-spelling table (i.e. Charlie Quebec).

(4) Signals for use where appropriate in all forms of transmission

AA   'all after . . .' (used after the 'Repeat' signal (RPT) — see below — means 'Repeat all after . . .').

AB   'All before . . .' (used after the 'Repeat' signal (RPT) — see below — means 'Repeat all before . . .').

$\overline{\text{AR}}$ Ending signal, or End of transmission or signal.

$\overline{\text{AS}}$ Waiting signal or period.

BN   'All between . . . and . . .' (used after the 'Repeat' signal (RPT) — means 'Repeat all between . . . and . . .').

C   Affirmative — YES or 'The significance of the previous group should be read in the affirmative'.

CS   'What is the name or identity signal of your vessel (or station)?'

DE   'From . . .' (used to precede the name or identity signal of the calling station).

K   'I wish to communicate with you' or 'Invitation to transmit'.

NO   Negative — NO or 'The significance of the previous group should be read in the negative'. When used in voice transmission the pronunciation should be 'NO'.

OK   Acknowledging a correct repetition or 'It is correct'.

RQ   Interrogative or 'The significance of the previous group should be read as a question'.

R   'Received' or 'I have received your last signal'.

RPT   Repeat signal 'I repeat' or 'Repeat what you have sent' or 'Repeat what you have received'.

WA   'Word or group after . . .' (used after the 'Repeat' signal (RPT) means 'Repeat word or group after . . .').

WB   'Word or group before . . .' (used after the 'Repeat' signal (RPT) means 'Repeat word or group before . . .').

Notes:

1.   The procedure signals 'C', 'NO' and 'RQ' cannot be used in conjunction with single-letter signals.

2.   When these signals are used by voice transmission the letters should be pronounced in accordance with the letter-spelling table, except that 'NO' is pronounced 'NO'.

6.1.5   Selected groups from the International Code

AC   I am abandoning my vessel

AE   I must abandon my vessel

AF   I do not intend to abandon my vessel

AN   I need a doctor

CB   I require immediate assistance

CB4 I require immediate assistance; I am aground

CB5 I require immediate assistance; I am drifting

CB6 I require immediate assistance; I am on fire

CB7 I require immediate assistance; I have sprung a leak

CJ   Do you require assistance?

CK   Assistance is not (or is no longer) required by me (or vessel indicated).

CV   I am unable to give assistance.

DX   I am sinking.

ED   Your distress signals are understood.

EF   SOS/MAYDAY has been cancelled.

FA   Will you give me my position?

IL   I can only proceed at slow speed.

IM   I request to be escorted until further notice.

IT   I am on fire.

IW   Fire is under control.

IX   Fire is gaining.

IZ   Fire has been extinguished.

JG   I am aground. I am in a dangerous situation.

JH   I am aground. I am not in danger.

JI   Are you aground?

JL   You are running the risk of going aground.

JO   I am afloat.

JW   I have sprung a leak.

JX   Leak is gaining rapidly.

KM   I can take you in tow.

KN   I cannot take you in tow.

LO   I am not in my correct position (to be used by a lightvessel).

MG   You should steer course . . .

NC   I am in distress and require immediate assistance.

NG   You are in a dangerous position.

NH   You are clear of all dangers.

PD   Your navigation light(s) is (are) not visible.

PH   You should steer as indicated.

PI   You should maintain your present course.

PP   Keep well clear of me.

QO   You should not come alongside.

QP   I will come alongside.

QR   I cannot come alongside.

QT   You should not anchor. You are going to foul my anchor.

RA   My anchor is foul.

RB   I am dragging my anchor.

RN   My engines are out of action.

RY   You should proceed at slow speed when passing me (or vessels making signal).

SC   I am under way.

SD   I am not ready to get under way.

SQ   You should stop or heave to.

6

UM   The harbour or port is closed to traffic.

UN   You may enter harbour immediately.

UO   You must not enter harbour.

UW   I wish you a pleasant voyage.

YU   I am going to communicate with your station by International Code.

YV   The groups which follow are from the International Code of Signals.

ZD2 Please report me to Lloyd's London.

ZL   Your signal has been received but not understood.

ZM   You should send (or speak) more slowly.

6.1.6   Morse code

When making Morse, it is most important to get the right rhythm and spacing. If a dot is taken as the unit of time, the correct spacing is as follows:

Dot	1 unit
Dash	3 units
Space between each dot/dash in a letter	1 unit
Space between each letter or symbol	3 units
Space between each word or group	7 units

The most likely method whereby a yachtsman will use the Morse code is by light. It helps to have a good light, with a proper flashing key, or trigger.

6.1.7   Flag signalling

The International Code flags (see Plates 6 and 7) consist of 26 alphabetical flags, 11 pendants (numerals 0–9 plus the Answering Pendant or Code Flag), and three triangular flags — the First, Second and Third Substitutes.

Some definitions are important. *Group* — one or more continuous letters and/or numerals comprising a signal. *Hoist* — one or more groups on one halyard. *At the dip* — a signal half-hoisted. *Close up* — a signal fully hoisted. *Tackline* — a line separating two groups. *Superior* — a flag or group above another. *Inferior* — a flag or group below another. *Class* — whether a flag is alphabetical or numeral.

The Answering Pendant is used to answer or acknowledge signals from another vessel. It may also be used as a decimal point.

Substitutes allow for the repetition of one or more letters (or numerals) within a group. The First Sub. repeats the first flag of the group in the class immediately superior to it. The Second Sub. repeats the second flag of that class, and the Third Sub. repeats the third.

A substitute can only repeat a flag of the same class as that immediately preceding it. The Answering Pendant used as a decimal point is disregarded in deciding which substitute to use.

Procedure

The sending ship hoists the identity signal of the ship she is calling: or she hoists the group 'VF' ('You should hoist your identity signal') or 'CS' ('What is the name or identity signal of your vessel/station') — at the same time hoisting her own identity signal.

The sending ship then hoists her message, and when sighted the receiving ship hoists her Answering Pendant at the dip — and close up when the signal has been understood. The procedure is repeated for subsequent hoists.

6.1.8   Radiotelephony (RT)

Plain language is normally used for RT (see 6.3.3), but in the event of language difficulties use the International Code and the following procedure. Letters and figures are spelt in accordance with the spelling tables, see Plates 6 and 7.

(1) *Method of calling.* Call sign or name of station called, not more than three times; the group 'DELTA ECHO'; and the call sign or name of the calling station, not more than three times. After contact is made, the call sign or name need not be sent more than once.

(2) *Reply to call.* Call sign or name of calling station; the group 'DELTA ECHO'; and the call sign or name of the station called.

(3) *Code groups.* The word 'INTERCO' indicates that International Code groups follow. Plain language may be used for names. 'YANKEE ZULU' means 'The words which follow are in plain language'.

(4) For other procedure signals see 6.1.4 (1), (3) and (4).

6.1.9   Morse Code by hand flags, or arms

Exceptionally, it may be useful to signal Morse by hand flags or arms. A dot is made by extending both flags (arms) above the head, and a dash by extending them horizontally at shoulder level. Between dots and dashes the flags (arms) are brought in front of the chest. To separate letters, groups or words the flags (arms) are extended downwards 45° away from the body. Circular motion of the flags (arms) indicates the erase signal if made by the transmitting station, or a request for repetition if made by the receiving station.

A station wishing to communicate by this method sends 'K2' or makes the general Morse call 'AA AA AA'. The station called should make the answering signal (TTTTTT etc) or, if unable to communicate by this method the signal 'YS2' by any means. Other procedure signals as in 6.1.4(4).

6.1.10   Sound signals

The International Code may be sent by sound signal (e.g. whistle, siren, foghorn) but the method is slow, and if misused can cause confusion. In poor visibility it should be reduced to a minimum. Signals other than the single-letter ones should only be used in emergency, and never where there is other traffic around. The signals should be made slowly and distinctly. They may be repeated, if necessary, but at sufficiently long intervals to ensure that no confusion can arise. The single-letter signals of the Code marked by an asterisk, when made by sound, must conform with the *International Regulations for Preventing Collisions at Sea* (Rules 34 and 35), for which see 2.1.7.

6.2   MISCELLANEOUS SIGNALS

6.2.1   Radio time signals

The BBC broadcast time signals at the local times and on the frequencies indicated in the table below. The start of the final, longer pulse marks the minute.

BBC Radio 1 1053 1089 kHz, 97·6–99·8 MHz
BBC Radio 2 88–90·2 MHz
BBC Radio 3 1215 kHz, 90·2–94·4 MHz
BBC Radio 4 198 603 (Tyneside) 720 (N Ireland & London) 1449 (Aberdeen) 1485 (Carlisle) 756 (Redruth) 774 (Plymouth) kHz, 92·5–94·6 MHz
BBC Radio 5 693 909 kHz

Local time	Mon–Fri Radio	Sat Radio	Sun Radio
0000	1,2	1,2	1,2
0530	1		
0600	1,4	1,4	1,4
0700	1,2,3,4	2,3,4	4
0800	1,2,4	2,4	2,4
0900	4	4	2,4
1000	4	4	
1100	4	4	
1200	4		
1300	2,4	1,2,4	4
1400	4	4	
1500	4	4	
1600	4 (not Mon)		4
1700	2,4		1,2,4
1800		2	
1900	2,3,4		4
1930		1,2	
2100			4
2200	1,2		

6.2.2   Pratique messages

All yachts, whether carrying dutiable stores or not, arriving in the United Kingdom from abroad (including the Channel Islands) are subject to Customs, Health and Immigration requirements — see Customs Notice No 8, summarised in Chapter 2 (2.4). The following Health Clearance Messages (International Code) apply:

Q or ZS My vessel is 'healthy' and I request free pratique. (Note: Flag 'Q' to be flown on entering UK waters, illuminated at night).

QQ (Flag 'Q' over First Substitute, or by night a red light over a white light). I require health clearance.

ZT My Maritime Declaration of Health has negative answers to the six health questions.

ZU My Maritime Declaration of Health has a positive answer to question(s) ... indicated.

ZW I require Port Medical Officer.

ZY You have health clearance.

ZZ You should proceed to anchorage for health clearance.

AM Have you a doctor?

6.2.3   Distress signals

A complete list of distress signals, as in Annex IV of the *International Regulations for Preventing Collisions at Sea*, is given in Chapter 2 (2.1.6). Those which are more appropriate for yachts to use are described in 8.1.4. Full details of RT distress messages and procedures, control of distress traffic on RT, the Urgency Signal and the Safety Signal are given in 6.3.10.

Distress signals must only be used when the boat is in serious and immediate danger, and help is urgently required. For lesser emergencies use 'V' (Victor) International Code — 'I require assistance', or one of the groups shown in 6.1.5.

6.2.4   Signals between shore and ships in distress

The following are used if a vessel is in distress or stranded off the coast of the United Kingdom:

(1) Acknowledgment of distress signal
By day: Orange smoke signal, or combined light and sound signal consisting of three single signals fired at about one minute intervals.
By night: White star rocket consisting of three single signals at about one minute intervals.

(2) Landing signals for small boats
'This is the best place to land' — Vertical motion of a white flag or arms (or white light or flare by night), or signalling 'K' (— · —) by light or sound. An indication of direction may be given by placing a steady white light or flare at a lower level.

'Landing here is highly dangerous' — Horizontal motion of a white flag or arms extended horizontally (or white light or flare by night), or signalling 'S' (· · ·). In addition, a better landing place may be signalled by carrying a white flag (or flare, or light), or by firing a white star signal in the direction indicated; or by signalling 'R' (· — ·) if the better landing is to the right in the direction of approach, or 'L' (· — · ·) if it is to the left.

(3) Signals for shore life-saving apparatus
'Affirmative' or specifically 'Rocket line is held', 'Tail block is made fast', 'Hawser is made fast', 'Man is in breeches buoy' or 'Haul away' — Vertical motion of a white flag or the arms (or of a white light or flare).

'Negative' or specifically 'Slack away' or 'Avast hauling' — Horizontal motion of a white flag or the arms (or of a white light or flare).

(4) Warning signal
'You are running into danger' — International Code signal 'U' (· · —) or 'NF'.

Note: Attention may be called to the above signals by a white flare, a white star rocket, or an explosive signal.

6.2.5   Signals used by SAR aircraft
A searching aircraft normally flies at about 3000–5000ft (900–1500m), or below cloud, firing a green Very light every five or ten minutes and at each turning point. On seeing a green flare, a yacht in distress should take the following action:
(1) Wait for the green flare to die out.
(2) Fire one red flare.
(3) Fire another red flare after about 20 seconds (this enables the aircraft to line up on the bearing).
(4) Fire a third red flare when the aircraft is overhead, or appears to be going badly off course.

6.2.6   Directing signals by aircraft
(1) To direct a yacht towards a ship or aircraft in distress — The aircraft circles the yacht at least once; it then crosses low ahead of the yacht, opening and closing the throttle or changing the propeller pitch. Finally it heads in the direction of the casualty.
(2) To indicate that assistance of the yacht is no longer required — The aircraft passes low, astern of the yacht, opening and closing the throttle or changing the propeller pitch.

6.2.7   Port signals
For signals for individual harbours, see Chapter 10. On the Continent traffic signals are to some extent standardised — see 10.14.7 for France, 10.19.7 for the Netherlands, and 10.20.7 for the Federal Republic of Germany.

A new system of International Port Traffic Signals was introduced in 1983, and is illustrated in Plate 8 on page 120. Although this new system has been adopted in a few ports, it is likely to be some time before it is used widely.

VHF channels for port operations are shown for harbours in Chapter 10. Call on the indicated working channel. The following International Code groups refer to port operations.

UH   Can you lead me into port?
UL   All vessels should proceed to sea as soon as possible owing to danger in port.
UM   The harbour (or port indicated) is closed to traffic.
UN   You may enter harbour immediately (or at time indicated).
UO   You must not enter harbour.
UP   Permission to enter harbour is urgently requested. I have an emergency case.
UQ   You should wait outside the harbour (or river mouth). UQ 1 You should wait outside the harbour until daylight.
UR   My estimated time of arrival (at place indicated) is (time indicated). UR 1 What is your estimated time of arrival (at place indicated)?
RZ 1 You should not proceed out of harbour/ anchorage.
RV 2 You should proceed into port.

The following notes apply to individual countries:

British Isles
In an emergency, an Examination Service might be instituted for certain ports, when the following signals would apply:

By day	By night	Meaning
Three red balls shown vertically	Three flashing red lights vertically	Entry to port prohibited
—	Three green lights shown vertically	Entry to port permitted
A blue flag	Red, green, red lights shown vertically	Movement of shipping within port or anchorage prohibited

Vessels of the Examination Service wear a special flag, with a blue border and a square in the centre — the top half white and the bottom half red.

France
See 10.14.7 for simplified and full codes of traffic signals. The simplified code is used in some ports where there is less traffic.

Netherlands
In the event of government control of entry to Dutch harbours, the following signals indicate that

entry is prohibited, and that a yacht should proceed towards the vessel flying the same signal.

By day	By night
Three red balls, disposed vertically, or	Three red lights, disposed vertically, or
Two cones points together over a ball	Three lights, disposed vertically, green over red over white

For other signals see 10.19.7.

Federal Republic of Germany
See 10.20.7.

6.2.8   Visual storm signals
Official storm signals, as previously displayed by Coastguard stations etc, are now discontinued in the British Isles, but signals may be shown in a few places by private arrangement. These should be treated with caution, in case they are not up to date. Signals are shown when a gale is expected within 12 hours, or is already blowing, in the adjacent sea area. The signal is lowered when the wind is below gale force, if a renewal is not expected within six hours. The signals consist of black cones. The North cone, point upwards, indicates gales from a point north of the east–west line. The South cone, point downwards, indicates gales from a point south of the east–west line. A few stations display night signals consisting of a triangle of lights.

International System
An International System of visual storm signals is used in France, the Netherlands, and the Federal Republic of Germany. This is illustrated in 10.14.7.

6.2.9   Tidal signals
Tidal signals are shown for individual harbours in Chapter 10. There is no standard system for British ports, nor for the Netherlands and West Germany. France uses a system for indicating whether the tide is rising or falling, and to show the height of the tide above chart datum by a combination of cones, cylinders and balls by day, and by green, red and white lights at night. See 10.14.7.

6.3   RADIO COMMUNICATIONS

6.3.1   Radiotelephones — general
Many yachts are fitted with radiotelephones, mostly Very High Frequency (VHF) sets with ranges of about 20 miles. Medium Frequency (MF) sets give much greater ranges, but must be Single Sideband (SSB). Double Sideband (DSB) transmissions are prohibited except for emergency transmissions on 2182 kHz, the international MF distress frequency. Full details of the various licences and operating procedures are given in Chapter 6 of *The Macmillan & Silk Cut Yachtsman's Handbook.* The brief notes which follow cover only the most important points.

For a yacht which requires to maintain radio contact with shore on ocean passages it is necessary to use High Frequency (HF) radio, which is more powerful and gives a much bigger range than MF, as is described briefly below.

A Ship Licence for the set is required from the DTI, Marine Licensing Section, Room 613(c), Waterloo Bridge House, Waterloo Road, London, SE1 8UA — who will also give approval for the use of VHF Ch M and Ch M2 for communication between yachts, yacht harbours and yacht clubs, and for race control (see 6.3.2).

A Certificate of Competence and an Authority to Operate are required by the person in charge of a set. For yachtsmen this is likely to be the Certificate of Competence, Restricted VHF Only. The Royal Yachting Association (RYA) is responsible for the conduct of this examination. Details of the syllabus and examination are in RYA booklet G26, available (with application form for the examination) from the RYA.

6.3.2   Radiotelephones — general provisions
For details see the *Handbook for Radio Operators* (Lloyds of London Press). Briefly: operators must not divulge the contents of messages heard; stations must identify themselves when transmitting; except in cases of distress, coast radio stations control communications in their areas; at sea a yacht may call other vessels or shore stations, but messages must not be sent to an address ashore except through a coast radio station; in harbour a yacht may not use inter-ship channels except for safety, and may only communicate with the local Port Operations Service, British Telecom coast stations, or with stations on Ch M or M2; do not interfere with the working of other stations — before transmitting, listen to see that the channel is free; it is forbidden to transmit unnecessary or superfluous signals; priority must be given to distress calls; the transmission of bad language is forbidden; a log must be kept, recording all transmissions, etc.

VHF radio
Very High Frequency (VHF) radio has a range slightly better than the line of sight between the aerials. It pays to fit a good aerial, as high as possible. Maximum power output is 25 watts, and a lower power (usually one watt) is used for short ranges. Most UK coast stations and many harbours now have VHF. So do the principal Coastguard stations and other rescue services.

Marine VHF frequencies are in the band 156·00–174·00 MHz. Ch 16 (156·80 MHz) is for distress and safety purposes, and for calling and answering. Once contact has been made the stations concerned must switch to a working channel, except for safety matters. Yachts at sea are encouraged to listen on Ch 16.

Basic VHF sets are 'simplex', transmitting and receiving on the same frequency, so that it is not possible to speak and listen simultaneously. 'Semi-duplex' sets transmit and receive on different frequencies, while fully 'duplex' sets can do this simultaneously so that conversation is normal.

There are three main groups of frequencies, but certain channels can be used for more than one purpose. They are shown in order of preference.
(1) *Public correspondence* (through coast radio stations). All can be used for duplex. Ch 26, 27, 25, 24 23, 28, 04, 01, 03, 02, 07, 05, 84, 87, 86, 83, 85, 88, 61, 64, 65, 62, 66, 63, 60, 82.
(2) *Inter-ship.* These are all simplex. Ch 06, 08, 10, 13, 09, 72, 73, 69, 67, 77, 15, 17.
(3) *Port operations.* Simplex: Ch 12, 14, 11, 13, 09, 68, 71, 74, 10, 67, 69, 73, 17, 15. Duplex: Ch 20, 22, 18, 19, 21, 05, 07, 02, 03, 01, 04, 78, 82, 79, 81, 80, 60, 63, 66, 62, 65, 64, 61, 84.

Ch 80 (Tx 161·625 MHz Rx 157·025 MHz) is the primary working channel for yachts with yacht harbours, plus Ch M (157·85 MHz) as a stand-by. Yacht clubs may use Ch M2 (161·425 MHz) for race control with Ch M as stand-by (see 6.3.1). Ch 67 (156·375 MHz) is operated in the UK by principal Coastguard stations as the Small Craft Safety Channel, accessed via Ch 16 (see 8.2.2).

Ch 70 is reserved exclusively for digital selective calling for distress and safety purposes.

MF radio

MF radiotelephones operate in the 1605–4200 kHz wavebands. Unlike VHF and HF, MF transmissions tend to follow the curve of the Earth, which makes them suitable for direction finding equipment. For this reason, and because of their good range, the marine distress radiotelephone frequency is in the MF band (2182 kHz). Silence periods are observed on this frequency for three minutes commencing every hour and half hour.

During these silence periods only Distress and Urgency messages may be transmitted (see 6.3.10 below). MF radio equipment must be single side-band (SSB). Double sideband (DSB) transmissions are prohibited except for emergency-only sets operating on 2182 kHz. As for VHF, both the operator and the set must be licenced. MF sets are more complex and more expensive than VHF, and are subject to more regulations.

HF radio

HF radiotelephones use wave bands that are cho-

sen, according to prevailing propagation conditions, from 4, 8, 12, 16 and 22 MHz bands (short wave). HF is more expensive than MF and absorbs more power, but it can provide worldwide coverage—although good installation and correct operation are essential for satisfactory results.

Whereas MF transmissions follow the curve of the earth, HF waves travel upwards and bounce off the ionosphere back to earth. Reception is better at night when the ionosphere is more dense. The directional properties of HF transmissions are poor, and there is no radiotelephone HF distress frequency.

The long-range service in the United Kingdom is provided by Portishead Radio, operated by British Telecom International. Watch is kept on the higher bands during daylight, and on the lower bands at night. A 24-hour watch is kept on the 8 MHz band.

6.3.3   RT procedures

Except for distress, urgency or safety messages, communications between a ship and a coast station are controlled by the latter. Between two ship stations, the station called controls the working. A calling station must use a frequency on which the station called is keeping watch. After making contact, comunication can continue on an agreed working channel. For VHF the name of the station called need normally only be given once, and that of the calling station twice. Once contact is made, each name need only be transmitted once. If a station does not reply, check the settings on the transmitter and repeat the call at three-minute intervals (if the channel is clear).

Prowords

It is important to understand the following:

ACKNOWLEDGE	'Have you received and understood?'
CONFIRM	'My version is . . . is that correct?'
CORRECTION	'An error has been made; the correct version is . . .'
I SAY AGAIN	'I repeat . . . (e.g. important words)'
I SPELL	'What follows is spelt phonetically'
OUT	End of work
OVER	'I have completed this part of my message, and am inviting you to reply'
RECEIVED	'Receipt acknowledged'
SAY AGAIN	'Repeat your message (or part indicated)'
STATION CALLING	Used when a station is uncertain of the identity of a station which is calling

Attention is also called to other procedure signals which can be used for RT, as shown in 6.1.4.

Before making a call, decide exactly what needs to be said. It may help to write the message down. Speak clearly and distinctly. Names or important words can be repeated or spelt phonetically.

For a position, give latitude and longitude, or the yacht's bearing and distance from a charted object. For bearings use 360° True notation. For times use 24 hour notation, and specify GMT, BST etc.

6.3.4   Coast Radio Stations

In the United Kingdom these are operated by British Telecom International, and details are shown in 6.3.15. Coast Stations control communications, and link ship stations with the telephone network ashore. Through them you can call any telephone subscriber in the United Kingdom and in about 200 foreign countries, as described in 6.3.5. At fixed times Coast Stations transmit traffic lists, navigation warnings and weather bulletins. They play an important role in Distress, Urgency and Safety Messages—see 6.3.10.

The major UK Coast Stations operate on both MF and VHF, and they have remotely controlled VHF stations to extend their VHF coverage. The MF stations (and the VHF stations controlled by each) are divided for operational procedures into two regions. The Southern Region comprises Land's End, Niton, North Foreland and Humber Radios. The Northern Region comprises Cullercoats, Stonehaven, Wick/Shetland and Portpatrick Radios.

An incoming call through any station in each region is answered from the first free operating position—not necessarily the nearest manned station. Watch is kept on 2182 kHz by Stonehaven Radio (Northern Region) and Land's End Radio (Southern Region). These stations can engage and speak over all frequencies and channels. Watch may be kept on VHF Ch 16, but distress cover for this primarily rests with HM Coastguard.

Broadcasts are on dedicated MF frequencies and on selected VHF channels (also used for link calls). The Officer in each region making the broadcast can engage and speak over the frequencies and channels of all other stations.

VHF calls to UK Coast Stations

When within range (about 40 miles) you are likely to be able to call a Coast Station. This allows you to make ordinary telephone calls, reverse charge calls, YTD calls (see 6.3.5), or send telegrams. There is also free access to navigational warnings, weather bulletins and gale warnings.

Except in emergency vessels should call a UK Coast Station on one of the working frequencies

shown in 6.3.15. For a Distress or Urgency Call (only) use Ch 16. Avoid using the station's designated broadcast channel at about the time of a scheduled broadcast. Proceed as follows:

(1) Listen for a 'clear' channel, with no transmission at all. A busy channel will have either carrier noise, speech or the engaged signal (a series of pips).

(2) Having located a free channel, the initial call must last at least six seconds in order to activate the Coast Station's ship-call latch equipment. For example: "Land's End Radio, Land's End Radio, this is Yacht Seabird, Seabird—Golf Oscar Romeo India—Channel 85, Over".

(3) When the call is accepted by the Coast Station you will hear engaged pips, indicating that you have activated and engaged the channel. Wait for the operator to speak. If you do not hear the pips and have not activated the station's transmitter you may be out of range. Try another station or call again when you get closer.

(4) When you are answered by the Radio Officer be ready to give the following: Vessel's name, callsign, type of call and billing details (see 6.3.5), the telephone number required (and the name of the person in the case of a personal call).

Telephone calls are normally timed automatically. The timing clock stops when the shore subscriber replaces the handset. Both telephone calls and telegrams can be made or sent to another vessel via a Coast Station.

For receiving calls, you are called on Ch 16 when a message or phone call is ready for you, but it is recommended to listen to the regular traffic lists broadcast from the nearest Coast Station. If your vessel is equipped with a selective call device, you can be alerted by a Coast Station transmitting your Selcal number on Ch 16.

VHF calls to foreign coast stations

French, German and Irish stations are called on a working channel, similarly Belgian and Dutch stations but depending on the position of the yacht. VHF calls to Scheveningen Radio should last several seconds and state the calling channel. A four-tone signal indicates temporary delay but you will be answered when an operator is free.

MF calls to UK Coast Stations

(1) Call the Coast Station concerned on the chosen paired frequency channel, as shown for each station in 6.3.15, in the same way as for VHF calls. Stations have speech detection equipment which recognises and responds to voice patterns, but not to other sounds such as whistling or telex tones.

(2) The speech detector will operate, causing channel engaged pips to be transmitted so that you know that your call has been received.

(3) Wait until the Radio Officer answers—your call will have been queued within the system and will be presented to the first available free position. If you are not answered at once do not change channel, or you may lose your original turn.

(4) If the channel engaged pips are not heard within a few seconds, try again making the call last a little longer—up to 10 seconds.

(5) If the pips are still not heard, or if you think the system has not reacted correctly, call on 2182 kHz. The Coast Station will then answer on 2182 kHz, allocate you a channel, and queue you into the system.

(6) The Radio Officer will request the following information: Vessel's name, callsign, Accounting Code (AAIC—see 6.3.6), and category of traffic (e.g. telegram, telephone call).

Note: Distress and Urgency calls should always be made on 2182 kHz, and will be answered on the same channel. This includes urgent medical calls, which should be preceded by the Urgency Signal "PAN PAN MEDICO"—see 6.3.7. Non-urgent medical calls should be made on working channels.

6.3.5   Link calls
A yacht can be connected, via a coast radio station, into the telephone network. It is possible to make personal calls to certain countries and collect (transferred charge) calls to the UK. World-wide accounting for calls is arranged by quoting the 'Accounting Authority Indicator Code' (AAIC). For British yachts this is 'GB 14', followed by the yacht's callsign. Your AAIC is printed with your callsign on your VHF radio licence. Yacht owners making VHF link calls to the UK through a British coast station can transfer the charge to their home telephone bill by quoting the AAIC 'YTD', followed by their UK telephone number. Or payment may be by British Telecom credit card or transferred charge.

The operator makes the connection. When channels are congested calls may be limited to six minutes. Timing is automatic.

Data may be exchanged on VHF over the telephone network by yachts suitably equipped with V22bis specification modem units. Procedures and charges are as for an ordinary VHF call except that data modems are switched into circuit.

Link call to a yacht
Telephone calls to vessels via BTI Coast Stations are handled by Portishead Radio. By dialling 0800 378389 you will be connected free of charge to the ships radiotelephone service. This number should be used to book calls on VHF, Short Range; the MF, Medium Range; or the HF, Long Range

services. You will be asked for the name of the vessel, station through which vessel normally communicates, voyage details, caller's telephone number (or number to be charged if different), person to whom you wish to speak, and caller's name. Portishead Radio will route the call to the appropriate Coast Station.

6.3.6   Weather information by RT
Sources of weather information are given in Chapter 7 (7.2) and it is possible, for example, to make a link call to a Weather Centre through the nearest coast radio station. Reports on actual weather can be obtained by link calls to Coastguard Stations and lighthouses, as listed in 7.2.16.

MRCCs and MRSCs broadcast strong wind warnings on receipt and local forecasts about every four hours—on Ch 67 after announcement on Ch 16, see 7.2.15. They will also give weather or other safety information on request.

6.3.7   Medical help by RT
Medical advice can be obtained through any UK coast radio station. If medical assistance is required (a doctor, or a casualty to be off-lifted) the request will be passed to the Coastguard. In either case the messages are passed free of charge. Where appropriate, the Urgency Signal PAN PAN MEDICO (see 6.3.10) may be used. For France call: PAN PAN Radiomédical (name of station) in French. For Belgium call: Radiomédical Oostende, in French, Dutch, English or German. For Netherlands call: Radiomédical Scheveningen, in Dutch, English, French or German. For Germany call: Funkarzt (name of station) in German or English.

6.3.8   Flotilla reporting schemes
Where numbers of yachts are required to report on a regular basis to a control centre, BTI offer two schemes. (a) Where vessels are given a window during which to report, and (b) Where vessels report at fixed times. Details from BTI Maritime Radio, 43 Bartholomew Close, London, EC1A 7HP.

6.3.9   Port operations
Many harbours now have VHF RT facilities, while a few also operate on MF (mostly for pilotage). The nominated channels must only be used for messages concerning port operations or (in emergency) the safety of persons, and not for public correspondence. For details of harbour RT information in Chapter 10, see 10.0.1. In a busy port a yacht can learn a great deal by merely listening on the right channel.

6.3.10 Distress messages and procedures

Anybody in the crew should be able to pass a distress message, should this be necessary. But this must only be done if the yacht or a person is in serious danger and requires immediate assistance. The procedure is:

Check main battery switch ON
Switch set ON, and turn power selector to HIGH
Tune to VHF Ch 16 (or 2182 kHz for MF)
If alarm signal generator fitted, operate for at least 30 seconds
Press 'transmit' button, and say slowly and distinctly:

MAYDAY MAYDAY MAYDAY
THIS IS (name of boat, spoken three times)
MAYDAY (name of boat, spoken once)
MY POSITION IS (latitude and longitude, or true bearing and distance from a known point)
Nature of distress (whether sinking, on fire etc)
Aid required
Number of persons on board
Any other important, helpful information (e.g. if the yacht is drifting, whether distress rockets are being fired)
OVER

The yacht's position is of vital importance, and should be repeated if time allows. On completion of the distress message, release the 'transmit' button and listen. In coastal waters an immediate acknowledgment should be expected, in the following form:

MAYDAY (name of station sending the distress message, spoken three times)
THIS IS ... (name of the station acknowledging, spoken three times)
RECEIVED MAYDAY

If an acknowledgment is not received, check the set and repeat the distress call. For 2182 kHz the call should be repeated during the three-minute silence periods which commence every hour and half-hour.

A yacht which hears a distress message from a vessel in her immediate vicinity and which is able to give assistance should acknowledge accordingly, but only after giving an opportunity for the nearest shore station or some larger vessel to do so.

If a yacht hears a distress message from a vessel further away, and it is not acknowledged, she must try to pass on the message in this form:

MAYDAY RELAY, MAYDAY RELAY, MAYDAY RELAY.
This is (name of vessel re-transmitting the distress message, spoken three times)
Followed by the intercepted message.

Control of distress traffic

A distress (MAYDAY) call imposes general radio silence, until the vessel concerned or some other authority (e.g. the nearest MRCC, MRSC or coast station) cancels the distress.

If necessary the station controlling distress traffic may impose radio silence in this form:

SEELONCE MAYDAY, followed by its name or other identification, on the distress frequency.

If some other station nearby believes it necessary to do likewise, it may transmit:

SEELONCE DISTRESS, followed by its name or other identification.

When appropriate the station controlling distress traffic may relax radio silence as follows:

MAYDAY
HELLO ALL STATIONS (spoken three times)
THIS IS (name or identification)
The time
The name of the station in distress
PRU-DONCE

When all distress traffic has ceased, normal working is authorised as follows:

MAYDAY
HELLO ALL STATIONS (spoken three times)
THIS IS (name or identification)
The time
The name of station which was in distress
SEELONCE FEENEE

Urgency Signal

This consists of the words PAN PAN, spoken three times, and indicates that the station has a very urgent message concerning the safety of a ship or person. Messages prefixed by PAN PAN take priority over all traffic except distress, and are sent on VHF Ch 16 or on 2182 kHz. The Urgency Signal is appropriate when urgent medical advice or attention is needed, or when someone is lost overboard. It should be cancelled when the urgency is over.

Safety Signal

This consists of the word SÉCURITÉ (pronounced SAY-CURE-E-TAY) spoken three times, and indicates that the station is about to transmit an important navigational or meteorological warning. Such messages usually originate from a coast station, and are transmitted on a working frequency after an announcement on the distress frequency.

6

6.3.11   INMARSAT

World-wide satellite communication (Satcom) is provided by the International Maritime Satellite Organisation (INMARSAT), through satellites in geostationary orbits above the equator over the Atlantic, Pacific and Indian Oceans. These satellites are the links between the Coast Earth Stations (CESs), operated by organisations such as British Telecom, and the on-board terminals called Ship Earth Stations (SESs). Satcom is more reliable and gives better reception than HF SSB radio.

A CES connects the satellite system with the landbased communication network. A message to a ship originating on land is transmitted by the CES to one of the satellites, and thence to the ship. A call from a ship is received via the satellite by the CES, which then transmits it to its destination over landbased networks.

Standard 'A' terminals have a large antenna about 4ft (1.2m) in diameter inside a radome, and are only suitable for larger vessels. They provide direct dialling facilities, Telex, data and facsimile transmission, and speedy connection to HM Coastguard's MRCC at Falmouth.

New, Standard 'C' terminals are very much smaller and provide Satcom facilities for transmitting and receiving data or text (but not voice) in even a small yacht.

6.3.12   Navigational Warnings — general

The world-wide Navigational Warning Service covers 16 sea areas (NAVAREAS) numbered I–XVI, each with a country nominated as Area Coordinator responsible for issuing long range warnings. These are numbered consecutively through the year and are transmitted in English and in one or more other languages at scheduled times by WT. Other forms of transmission (RT, radiotelex and facsimile) may also be used. Warnings cover items such as failures or changes to navigational aids, wrecks and navigational dangers of all kinds, SAR operations, cable or pipe laying, naval exercises etc.

Within each NAVAREA, Coastal Warnings and Local Warnings may also be issued. Coastal Warnings, up to 100 or 200 n miles offshore, are broadcast in English and in the national language by coast radio stations. Local Warnings are issued by harbour authorities in the national language.

6.3.13   Navigational Warnings — Europe
United Kingdom

The United Kingdom (together with Northern Europe and Scandinavia) come within NAVAREA I, with Britain as the Area Co-ordinator for long range navigational warnings which are broadcast by Portishead Radio (GKA). Messages are numbered in sequence, and the text is published in the weekly *Notices to Mariners* together with a list of warnings still in force.

NAVTEX warnings (see 6.3.14) are broadcast by Niton, Cullercoats and Portpatrick Radio for the areas shown in Fig.6(1).

Coastal Warnings are broadcast by RT at scheduled times from coast radio stations, for the Sea Regions lettered A–N, in Fig.6(2). Important warnings are broadcast at any time on the distress frequencies of 500kHz, 2182kH and VHF Ch 16.

Local warnings from harbour authorities are broadcast by nearby coast radio stations. HM Coastguard broadcasts local warnings for inshore waters outside of harbour limits, on VHF Ch 67 after an announcement on Ch 16.

Vessels which encounter dangers to navigation should notify other craft and the nearest coast radio station, prefacing the message by the safety signal (see 6.3.10).

France

Long range warnings are broadcast in English and French for NAVAREA II, which includes the west coast of France, by St Lys Radio. The north coast comes within NAVAREA I.

AVURNAVS (AVis URgents aux NAVigateurs) are coastal and local warnings issued by regional authorities:

(1) Avurnavs Brest for the west coast of France and the western Channel (Spanish frontier to Mont St Michel).

(2) Avurnavs Cherbourg for the eastern Channel and the North Sea (Mont St Michel to the Belgian frontier).

Avurnavs are broadcast by the appropriate coast radio station, urgent ones on receipt and at the end of the next silence period as well as at scheduled times. RT warnings are prefixed by 'Sécurité Avurnav', followed by the name of the station.

Belgium

Navigational warnings are broadcast by Oostende Radio at scheduled times (see 6.3.16) on 2761kHz MF, 518kHz (NAVTEX) and on Ch 27.

Netherlands

Navigational warnings are broadcast by Scheveningen Radio at scheduled times (see 6.3.16) on 1862kHz (Nes), 1890kHz and 2824kHz MF, and on 518kHz (NAVTEX).

Federal Republic of Germany

Navigational warnings are broadcast by Norddeich Radio on 2614kHz on receipt, after the next silence period, and at scheduled times. Broadcasts commence with the safety signal, the words *Nautische Warnnachricht*, and the serial number; they are in English and German. Decca Warnings for the German and Frisian Islands chains (*Decca Warnnachricht*) are included. Dangers to navigation should be reported to Seewarn Cuxhaven.

6.3.14 NAVTEX

NAVTEX provides navigational and meteorological warnings and other safety information by automatic print-outs from a dedicated receiver, and is a component of the International Maritime Organization (IMO) Global Maritime Distress and Safety System (GMDSS) due for world-wide implementation by August 1991.

At present broadcasts are all in English on a single frequency of 518kHz, with excellent coverage of coastal waters in areas such as NW Europe where the scheme originated. Interference between stations is avoided by time sharing and by limiting the range of transmitters to about 300 n miles, so that three stations cover the United Kingdom. IMO is expected to make a second NAVTEX channel available for broadcasts in the local national language.

The use of a single frequency allows a simple receiver with a printer using cash-roll paper, although some yacht receivers have a video screen. The user programmes the receiver for the vessel's area and for the types of messages required. For example, if Decca is not carried Decca Warnings can be rejected. The receiver automatically rejects messages which are corrupt or ones that have already been printed.

Each message is pre-fixed by a four character group. The first character is the code letter of the transmitting station (in the United Kingdom S for Niton, G for Cullercoats and O for Portpatrick). The second character indicates the category of the message as in the code opposite. The third and fourth are message serial numbers, from 01 to 99. The serial number 00 denotes urgent traffic such as gale warnings and SAR alerts, and messages with this prefix are always printed.

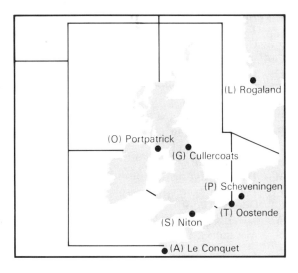

Fig.6(1)   NAVTEX areas around British Isles.

Message categories

A Coastal navigation and hazard warnings
B Gale warnings
C Ice reports (unlikely to apply in UK)
D Search and Rescue information
E Weather forecasts
F Pilot Service messages
G Decca messages
H Loran-C messages
I Omega messages
J Satnav messages
L Oil and gas rig information (UK trial)
Z No messages on hand at scheduled time

Information in a NAVTEX broadcast applies only to the area for which the broadcast station is responsible, as shown in Fig.6(1). A user may accept messages from one or more stations.

NAVTEX stations

The table opposite shows the NAVTEX stations in NAVAREAS I, II and III with their station identity codes and transmission times (GMT). The times of weather bulletins for the British stations are shown in bold.

(P) indicates that the station is provisional or projected.

The diagram above shows the stations and their areas around the British Isles.

NAVAREA I

R – **Reykjavik,** Iceland	0318	0718	1118	1518	1918	2318
B – **Bodø,** Norway	0018	0418	0818	1218	1618	2100
J – **Stockholm,** Sweden	0330	0730	1130	1530	1930	2330
H – **Härnösand,** Sweden	0000	0400	0800	1200	1600	2000
U – **Tallin,** USSR	0030	0430	0830	1230	1630	2030
P – **Netherlands Coast Guard**	0348	0748	1148	1548	1948	2348
T – **Oostende,** Belgium	0248	0648	1048	1448	1848	2248
G – **Cullercoats,** UK	0048	0448	**0848**	1248	1648	**2048**
S – **Niton,** UK	0018	0418	**0818**	1218	1618	**2018**
O – **Portpatrick,** UK	0130	0530	**0930**	1330	1730	**2130**
V – **Vardø,** Norway	0300	0700	1100	1500	1900	2300
L – **Rogaland,** Norway	0148	0548	0948	1348	1748	2148

NAVAREA II

A – **Le Conquet,** France (P)	0000	0400	0800	1200	1600	2000
F – **Brest,** France*	0118	0518	0918	1318	1718	2118
R – **Lisboa,** Portugal	0250	0650	1050	1450	1850	2250
F – **Horta,** Azores	0050	0450	0850	1250	1650	2050
D – **Finisterre,** Spain (P)	0030	0430	0830	1230	1630	2030
I – **Islas Canarias,** Spain (P)	0100	0500	0900	1300	1700	2100

NAVAREA III

G – **Tarifa,** Spain (P)	0100	0500	0900	1300	1700	2100
Z – **Cabo La Nao,** Spain (P)	to be notified (planned)					
Q – **Split,** Yugoslavia	0250	0650	1050	1450	1850	2250
H – **Iraklion,** Greece	0110	0510	0910	1310	1710	2110
L – **Limnos,** Greece	0150	0550	0950	1350	1750	2150
K – **Kerkyra,** Greece	0140	0540	0940	1340	1740	2140
I – **Izmir,** Turkey	0120	0520	0920	1320	1720	2120
E – **Samsun,** Turkey	0040	0440	0840	1240	1640	2040
D – **Istanbul,** Turkey (P)	0030	0430	0830	1230	1630	2030
F – **Antalya,** Turkey	0050	0450	0850	1250	1650	2050
M – **Troodos,** Cyprus	0200	0600	1000	1400	1800	2200
J – **Varna,** Bulgaria	0130	0530	0930	1330	1730	2130
C – **Odessa,** USSR	0230	0630	1030	1430	1830	2230
A – **Novorossiysk,** USSR	0300	0700	1100	1500	1900	2300
N – **Alexandria,** Egypt (P)	0210	0610	1010	1410	1810	2210

* Transmitter on Trial

– **Toulon,** France (P)	to be notified (planned 1992)
– **Ancona,** Italy (P)	to be notified (planned 1990)
– **Cagliari,** Italy (P)	to be notified (planned 1990)
– **Rome,** Italy (P)	to be notified (planned 1990)
– **Haifa,** Israel (P)	to be notified (planned 1990)

6.3.15   UK Coast Radio Stations

Note: Normal primary working frequencies are printed in bold type.

Coast Station: Name Position	MF (Medium Range) RT				VHF Ch	Traffic List Times (GMT)	Navigation Warning Times (GMT)	Weather Bulletin Times (GMT)	Gale Warning Times (GMT) *	Decca Warning Times (GMT) for Chains
	Distress, Urgency, Safety (kHz)	Calling and Working Paired Frequencies (kHz)								
		Channel	Coast Station							
			Transmit	Receive						
Land's End Radio 50°07'N 05°40'W	2182	W X	2782 3610	2002 2120	16	Broadcasts on 2670 kHz and Ch 27 and Ch 64 at:				
					27 88 85 64	Follow Navigation Warnings, Weather Bulletins and Gale Warnings at times shown opposite	0233 0633 1033 1433 1833 2233	0733 1933	0303 0903 1503 2103	As for Navigation Warnings 1B 7D
Tel: 0736 87 1364	Note: VHF Ch 64 directed to Scillies. Selcal (3204): 2170.5 kHz Ch 16									
Pendennis Radio 50°09'N 05°03'W	VHF station remotely controlled from Land's End Radio Selcal (3238): Ch 16				16 62 66	Traffic Lists, Weather Bulletins and Warnings broadcast on Ch 62 at same times as for Land's End Radio above				
Start Point Radio 50°21'N 03°43'W	VHF station remotely controlled from Land's End Radio Selcal (3224): Ch 16				16 26 65 60	Traffic Lists, Weather Bulletins and Warnings broadcast on Ch 26 at same times as for Land's End Radio above				

* Gale warnings — see note at foot of page 135

6.3.15   UK Coast Radio Stations *continued*

Coast Station: Name Position	MF (Medium Range) RT				VHF Ch	Traffic List Times (GMT)	Navigation Warning Times (GMT)	Weather Bulletin Times (GMT)	Gale Warning Times (GMT) *	Decca Warning Times (GMT) for chains
	Distress, Urgency, Safety (kHz)	Calling and Working Paired Frequencies (kHz)								
		Channel	Coast Station							
			Transmit	Receive						
Niton Radio 50°35'N 01°18'W (For Navtex see 6.3.14 p. 133) *Tel: 0983 730496*	2182	U	2628	2009 Note: VHF Ch 04 directed to Brighton. Selcal (3203): 2170.5 kHz Ch 16	16 04 28 81 85 64 87	Broadcasts on 1834 kHz and Ch 28 at: Follow Navigation Warnings, Weather Bulletins and Gale Warnings at times shown opposite	0233 0633 1033 1433 1833 2233	0733 1933	0303 0903 1503 2103	As for Navigation Warnings 1B 5B
Weymouth Bay Radio 50°33'N 02°26'W	VHF station remotely controlled from Niton Radio Selcal (3242): Ch 16				16 05	Traffic Lists, Weather Bulletins and Warnings broadcast on Ch 05 at same times as for Niton Radio above				
St Peter Port Radio 49°27'N 02°32'W Note: Commercial calls only. Link calls available on VHF Ch 62 only. *Tel: 0481 20085*	Ship calls on 2182. Station replies on 1810	1662.5[1] 2182 **1810** (1) Trinity House and SAR only. (2) H24. (3) When 2182 is distress working.	1662.5[1] 2182[2] 2381[3]		16 62[4] 78 67[5] (for notes see right)	Broadcasts on 1810 kHz and Ch 78 at: After navigational warnings. (Ships also called individually on 2182 kHz and Ch 16)	Every 4h from 0133 for local waters	Notes for VHF services: Direct calling on Ch 78. (4) Link calls available Ch 62. (5) Ch 67 available for yacht safety messages.		
Jersey Radio 49°11'N 02°32'W *Tel: 0534 41121*	Ship calls on 2182. Station replies on 1726	**1726** 2182 (1) Foreign vessels (2) UK reg. vessels	2182 2049[1] 2104[2] 2534[2]		16 82 25 67	Broadcasts on 1726 kHz and Ch 25 and 82 at: After weather messages. (Ships also called individually on 2182 kHz and Ch 16)	0433 0645 0745 0833 1245 1633 1845 2033 2245	0645 0745 1245 1845 2245	On receipt and at 0307 0907 1507 2107	(1) on receipt (2) at three minutes past the next two hours 1B
North Foreland Radio 51°22'N 01°25'E *Tel: 0843 291984*	2182	T	2698	2016 Selcal (3201): 2170.5 kHz Ch 16	16 05 26 66 65	Broadcasts on 1848 kHz and Ch 26 at: Follow Navigation Warnings, Weather Bulletins and Gale Warnings at times shown opposite	0133 0533 0933 1333 1733 2133	0733 1933	0303 0903 1503 2103	As for Navigation Warnings 1B 5B 2E
Hastings Radio 50°53'N 00°37'E	VHF station remotely controlled from North Foreland Radio Selcal (3225): Ch 16				16 07 63	Traffic Lists, Weather Bulletins and Warnings broadcast on Ch 07 at same times as for Northforeland Radio above				
Thames Radio 51°20'N 00°20'E	VHF station remotely controlled from North Foreland Radio Selcal (3202): Ch 16				16 02 83	Traffic Lists, Weather Bulletins and Warnings broadcast on Ch 02 at same times as for Northforeland Radio above				
Orfordness Radio 52°00'N 01°25'E	VHF station remotely controlled from North Foreland Radio Selcal (3235): Ch 16				16 62 82	Traffic Lists, Weather Bulletins and Warnings broadcast on Ch 62 at same times as for Northforeland Radio above				
Humber Radio 53°20'N 00°17'E *Tel: 0507 473 448*	2182	Q R S	1925 2684 2810	2569 2111 2562 Note: VHF Ch 85 directed to The Wash. Selcal (3212): 2170.5 kHz Ch 16	16 24 26 85	Broadcasts on 1869 kHz and Ch 26 at: Follow Navigation Warnings, Weather Bulletins and Gale Warnings at times shown opposite	0133 0533 0933 1333 1733 2133	0733 1933	0303 0903 1503 2103	As for Navigation Warnings 5B 2A 2E 9B
Bacton Radio 52°51'N 01°28'E	VHF station remotely controlled from Humber Radio Selcal (3214): Ch 16				16 07 63 64 03	Traffic Lists, Weather Bulletins and Warnings broadcast on Ch 07 same times as for Humber Radio above				
Grimsby Radio 53°34'N 00°05'W	VHF station remotely controlled from Humber Radio Selcal (3239): Ch 16				16 04 27	Traffic Lists, Weather Bulletins and Warnings broadcast on Ch 27 at sames times as for Humber Radio above				

*GALE WARNINGS** are broadcast after the first silence period after receipt and at the next of the times shown or if first broadcast at a scheduled time the warning is repeated at the end of the next silence period.

continued

Fig.6(2) *Coast Radio Stations*

KEY TO MF AND VHF COAST RADIO STATIONS

● = VHF Station, with Channels shown other than Ch 16. Broadcast channels are the first shown.

○ = MF Station

---- = Remote control link

For UK VHF stations call on a working channel, as described in 6.3.4. In emergency use Ch 16.

For French and German VHF stations, call on working frequency. For Dutch and Belgian VHF stations, call on working frequency, as indicated in the panels for Scheveningen Radio and Oostende Radio, below.

The lettered areas (*Alfa, Bravo, Charlie* etc) show the UK Sea Regions for Navigational Warnings — see also 6.3.13.

Scheveningen Radio

Goes	Ch **23** 25
Rotterdam	Ch **24 28** 87
Scheveningen	Ch 26 **83**
Haarlem	Ch **23** 25
Wieringerwerf	Ch **27**
Location L7	Ch **28** 84
Terschelling	Ch **25** 78
Nes	Ch **23**
Appingedam	Ch **27**
Lelystad	Ch **83**

Hours of watch: H24. Call *Scheveningen Radio* in each case on a working channel.

Oostende Radio

Vessels near	*Call on*
Zeebrugge	Ch 27 87
Oostende	Ch 27 85 88
La Panne	Ch 23 78

(Hours of watch: H24 on Ch 16 27)

Antwerpen 24 07 26 27 28 81 (Hours of watch: H24 on Ch 16 24)

Oostende (see below)

Scheveningen (see above)

Norddeich 28 61 86

Collafirth 24
Shetland 27
Norwick

Orkney 26

Alfa

November

Hebrides 26
Lewis 05

Skye 24

Bravo

Cromarty 28 84

Buchan 25 87

Wick

Stonehaven 26

Mike

Charlie

Islay 25 60

Clyde 26

Forth 24 62

NORTHERN REGION

Portpatrick 27

Cullercoats 26

Lima

Whitby 25 28

Morecambe Bay 04 82

Anglesey 26 28 61

28

Grimsby 27 04

Kilo

Humber 26 24 85

Bacton 07 63 64 03

Echo

Cardigan Bay 03

85

SOUTHERN REGION

Orfordness 62 82

Juliett

Celtic 24

07

Ilfracombe 05 07

04

Niton 28 04 81 85 64 87

Thames 02 83

North Foreland 26 66 05 65

Hastings 07 63

Calais 87 01

Dunkerque 61 24

Foxtrot

Weymouth Bay 05

Hotel

India

Boulogne 23 25

Land's End 27 64 85 88 64

Start Pt 26 60 65

Pendennis 62 66

Scillies

St Peter Pt 78 62

Cherbourg 27

Dieppe 02 24

Golf

Jersey 25 82

Cartret 64

Le Havre 82 23 26 28

Port en Bessin 03

Rouen 25 27

Delta

Paimpol 84

Quessant 82 24

Plougasnou 83

St Malo 02 01

Brest-le Conquet 26 28

6.3.15 UK Coast Radio Stations *continued*

Coast Station: Name Position	MF (Medium Range) RT				VHF Ch	Traffic List Times (GMT)	Navigation Warning Times (GMT)	Weather Bulletin Times (GMT)	Gale Warning Times (GMT) *	Decca Warning Times (GMT) for Chains
	Distress, Urgency, Safety (kHz)	Calling and Working Paired Frequencies (kHz)								
		Channel	Coast Station							
			Transmit	Receive						
Cullercoats Radio 55°04′N 01°28′W (For Navtex see 6.3.14 p. 133) *Tel: 091 297 0301*	2182	N O P	1838 2828 3750	2527 1953 2559	16 26	Broadcasts on 2719 kHz and Ch 26 at Follow Navigation Warnings, Weather Bulletins and Gale Warnings at times shown opposite	0233 0633 1033 1433 1833 2233	0703 1903	0303 0903 1503 2103	As for Navigation Warnings 5B 2A 6C 2E 9B 0E
	Selcal (3211): 2170.5 kHz Ch 16									
Whitby Radio 54°29′N 00°36′W	VHF station remotely controlled from Cullercoats Radio Selcal (3231): Ch 16				16 25 28	Traffic Lists, Weather Bulletins and Warnings broadcast on Ch 25 at same times as for Cullercoats Radio above				
Stonehaven Radio 56°57′N 02°13′W *Tel: 0569 62918*	2182	I J K L M	1856 1715 1946 2779 3617	2555 2552 2566 2146 3249	16 26	Broadcast on 2691 kHz and Ch 26 at: Follow Navigation Warnings, Weather Bulletins and Gale Warnings at times shown opposite	0233 0633 1033 1433 1833 2233	0703 1903	0303 0903 1503 2103	As for Navigation Warnings 2A 6C 0E
	Selcal (3222): 2170.5 kHz Ch 16									
Forth Radio 55°56′N 02°27′W	VHF station remotely controlled from Stonehaven Radio Selcal (3228): Ch 16				16 24 62	Traffic Lists, Weather Bulletins and Warnings broadcast on Ch 24 at same times as for Stonehaven Radio above				
Buchan Radio 57°36′N 02°02′W	VHF station remotely controlled from Stonehaven Radio Selcal (3237): Ch 16				16 25 87	Traffic Lists, Weather Bulletins and Warnings broadcast on Ch 25 at same times as for Stonehaven Radio above				
Hebrides Radio 58°14′N 07°02′W Controlled from (Stonehaven Radio) *Tel: 0569 62918*	2182	Z	1866	2534	16 26	Broadcasts on 1866 kHz and Ch 26 at: Follow Navigation Warnings, Weather Bulletins and Gale Warnings at times shown opposite	0203 0603 1003 1403 1803 2203	0703 1903	0303 0903 1503 2103	As for Navigation Warnings 6C 8E
	Selcal (3234): 2170.5 kHz Ch 16									
Lewis Radio 58°28′N 06°14′W	VHF station remotely controlled from Stonehaven Radio Selcal (3216): Ch 16				16 05	Traffic Lists, Weather Bulletins and Warnings broadcast on Ch 05 at same times as for Hebrides Radio above				
Skye Radio 57°28′N 06°41′W	VHF station remotely controlled from Stonehaven Radio Selcal (3232): Ch 16				16 24	Traffic Lists, Weather Bulletins and Warnings broadcast on Ch 24 at same times as for Hebrides Radio above				
Wick Radio 58°26′N 03°06′W **Shetland Radio** (controlled by Wick Radio) *Tel: 0955 2272*	2182 2182	E F G H A B C D	2705 1827 2604 2625 2751 2840.6 3538 —	2524 2548 2013 2381 2006 2277 3335 3328		Broadcasts on 1792 kHz (Wick) and 1824 kHz (Shetland) at: Follow Navigation Warnings, Weather Bulletins and Gale Warnings at times shown opposite	0233 0633 1033 1433 1833 2233	0703 1903	0303 0903 1503 2103	As for Navigation Warnings 6C 8E 0E
	Selcal (3221): 2170.5 kHz									
Cromarty Radio 57°36′N 02°58′W	VHF station remotely controlled from Wick Radio Selcal (3227): Ch 16				16 28 84	Traffic Lists, Weather Bulletins and Warnings broadcast on Ch 28 at same times as for Wick Radio above				
Orkney Radio 58°47′N 02°57′W	VHF station remotely controlled from Wick Radio Selcal (3226): Ch 16				16 26	Traffic Lists, Weather Bulletins and Warnings broadcast on Ch 26 at same times as for Wick Radio above				
Shetland Radio 60°09′N 01°12′W	VHF station remotely controlled from Wick Radio Selcal (3215): Ch 16				16 27	Traffic Lists, Weather Bulletins and Warnings broadcast on Ch 27 at same times as for Wick Radio above				
Collafirth Radio 60°32′N 01°23′W	VHF station remotely controlled from Wick Radio Selcal (3230): Ch 16				16 24	Traffic Lists, Weather Bulletins and Warnings broadcast on Ch 24 at same times as for Wick Radio above				

6

6.3.15   UK Coast Radio Stations *continued*

Coast Station: Name Position	MF (Medium Range) RT				VHF Ch	Traffic List Times (GMT)	Navigation Warning Times (GMT)	Weather Bulletin Times (GMT)	Gale Warning Times (GMT) *	Decca Warning Times (GMT) for chains
	Distress, Urgency, Safety (kHz)	Calling and Working Paired Frequencies (kHz)								
		Channel	Coast Station							
			Transmit	Receive						
Portpatrick Radio 54°51'N 05°07'W (For Navtex see 6.3.14 p. 133) *Tel: 077 681 312*	2182	Y	1883	2104	16	Broadcasts on 1883 kHz and Ch 27 at				
					27	Follow Navigation Warnings, Weather Bulletins and Gale Warnings at times shown opposite	0203 0603 1003 1403 1803 2203	0703 1903	0303 0903 1503 2103	As for Navigation Warnings 8E 3B 7D
	Selcal (3207): 2170.5 kHz Ch 16									
Clyde Radio 55°55'N 04°48'W	VHF station remotely controlled from Portpatrick Radio Selcal (3213): Ch 16				16 26	Traffic Lists, Weather Bulletins and Warnings broadcast on Ch 26 at same times as for Portpatrick Radio above				
Islay Radio 55°46'N 06°27'W	VHF station remotely controlled from Portpatrick Radio Selcal (3233): Ch 16				16 25 60	Traffic Lists, Weather Bulletins and Warnings broadcast on Ch 25 at same times as for Portpatrick Radio above				
Anglesey Radio 53°20'N 04°18'W	VHF station remotely controlled from Portpatrick Radio Note: VHF Ch 28 directed to R Mersey. Selcal (3206): Ch 16				16 26 28 61	Traffic Lists, Weather Bulletins and Warning broadcast on Ch 26 at same times as for Portpatrick Radio above.				
Morecambe Bay Radio 54°10'N 03°12'W	VHF station remotely controlled from Portpatrick Radio Selcal (3240): Ch 16				16 04 82	Traffic Lists, Weather Bulletins and Warnings broadcast on Ch 04 at same times as for Portpatrick Radio above				
Cardigan Bay Radio 52°50'N 04°37'W	VHF station remotely controlled from Portpatrick Radio Selcal (3241): Ch 16				16 03	Traffic Lists, Weather Bulletins and Warnings broadcast on Ch 03 at same times as for Portpatrick Radio above				
Ilfracombe Radio 51°11'N 04°07'W	VHF station remotely controlled from Niton Radio Note: Ch 07 directed to Severn Bridge Selcal (3205): Ch 16				16	Broadcasts on Ch 05 at:				
					05 07	Bulletins and Gale Warnings at times shown opposite Follow Navigation Warnings, Weather	0233 0633 1033 1433 1833 2233	0733 1933	0303 0903 1503 2103	As for Navigation Warnings 1B 7D
Celtic Radio 51°41'N 05°11'W	VHF station remotely controlled from Niton Radio Selcal (3218): Ch 16				16 24	Traffic Lists, Weather Bulletins and Warnings broadcast on Ch 24 at same times as for Ilfracombe Radio				

* Gale warnings — see note at foot of page 135

6.3.16   Irish and Continental Coast Radio Stations

Note: Normal primary working frequencies are printed in bold type.

Coast Station Name Position	Medium Frequency RT Service (kHz)		VHF Ch Tx Rx	Traffic List Times (GMT)	Navigation Warnings Times (GMT)	Weather Bulletin Times (LT)	Gale Warning Times (LT)	Decca Warning Times (GMT)
	Transmits	Receives						
Malin Head Radio 55°22'N See 7°21'W Note 2 *Tel: (077) 70103*	**1841**[1] 2182 2593 (1) When 2182 distress working	2049[1] 2182	16 16 23 23 67[3] 67[3] 85 85	1841 kHz and Ch 23 every odd H+03 (not 0303 0703)	1841 kHz and Ch 23 every 4h from 0033	Ch 23 every 3h from 0103	Ch 23 O/R and next of 0033 0633 1233 1833	1841 kHz and Ch 23 O/R & H+03 for next 2h 6C 3B 7D 8E
Glen Head Radio 54°44'N/8°43'W	VHF station remotely controlled from Malin Head Radio		16 16 24 24 67[3] 67[3]	Ch 24	Ch 24	Ch 24	Ch 24	Ch 24
				Broadcast times as for Malin Head Radio VHF above				
Belmullet Radio 54°16'N/10°03'W	VHF station remotely controlled from Malin Head Radio		16 16 67[3] 67[3] 83 83	Ch 83	Ch 83	Ch 83	Ch 83	Ch 83
				Broadcast times as for Malin Head Radio VHF above				
Dublin Radio 53°23'N/6°04'W	VHF station remotely controlled from Malin Head Radio		16 16 83 83	Ch 83	Ch 83	Ch 83	Ch 83	Ch 83
				Broadcast times as for Malin Head Radio VHF above				

6.3.16 Irish and Continental Coast Radio Stations

Coast Station Name Position	Medium Frequency RT Service (kHz)		VHF Ch		Traffic List Times (GMT)	Navigation Warnings Times (GMT)	Weather Bulletin Times (LT)	Gale Warning Times (LT)	Decca Warning Times (GMT)
	Transmits	Receives	Tx	Rx					
Valentia Radio 51°56'N See 10°21'W Note 4 *Tel: (0667) 6109*	**1827**[1] 2182 2590 2614 (1) When 2182 distress working. Gale Warnings on 1827 kHz S/P1 and at next of 0303 0903 1503 2103 (GMT)	2049[1] 2182	16 24 28 67[3]	16 24 28 67[3]	1827 kHz and Ch 24 every odd H+33 (not 0133 0533)	1827 kHz and Ch 24 every 4h from 0233	1827 kHz 0833 2033 (GMT). Ch 24 every 3h from 0103	1827 kHz see Col 2. Ch 24 O/R and next of 0033 0633 1233 1833	1827 kHz and Ch 24 O/R & H+03 for next 2h 1B 7D
Clifden Radio 53°29'N/10°06'W	VHF station remotely controlled from Valentia Radio				Projected station. Details to be notified later				
Shannon Radio 52°31'N/9°36'W	VHF station remotely controlled from Valentia Radio		16 24 28 67[3]	16 24 28 67[3]	Ch 28	Ch 28	Ch 28	Ch 28	Ch 28
					Broadcast times as for Valentia Radio VHF above				
Bantry Radio 51°38'N/10°00'W	VHF station remotely controlled from Valentia Radio		16 23 67[3] 85	16 23 67[3] 85	Ch 23	Ch 23	Ch 23	Ch 23	Ch 23
					Broadcast times as for Valentia Radio VHF above				
Cork Radio 51°51'N/8°29'W	VHF station remotely controlled from Valentia Radio		16 26 67[3]	16 26 67[3]	Ch 26	Ch 26	Ch 26	Ch 26	Ch 26
					Broadcast times as for Valentia Radio VHF above				
Mine Head Radio 52°00'N/7°35'W	VHF station remotely controlled from Valentia Radio		16 67[3] 83	16 67[3] 83	Ch 83	Ch 83	Ch 83	Ch 83	Ch 83
					Broadcast times as for Valentia Radio VHF above				
Rosslare Radio 52°15'N/6°20'W	VHF station remotely controlled from Valentia Radio		16 23 67[3]	16 23 67[3]	Ch 23	Ch 23	Ch 23	Ch 23	Ch 23
					Broadcast times as for Valentia Radio VHF above				

NOTES (FOR IRISH AND FRENCH COAST STATIONS):
1. When 2182 kHz is distress working.
2. VHF service at Crockalough (55°21'N/7°16'W).
3. Safety information for small craft.
4. VHF service at Kilkeaveragh (51°52'N/10°20'W).
5. H+ ... means commencing at ... minutes past hour.
6. LT means Local Time.
7. O/R means on receipt.

8. S/P1 means after first silence period after receipt.
9. S/P2 means after first and second silence periods after receipt.
10. Make VHF calls to French Coast Stations on a working channel (not Ch 16). For MF call on 2182, or (if busy) on 2321 kHz.
11. VHF broadcasts of weather bulletins and gale warnings refer to coastal waters. (Fr) means 'in French'.
12. For French Forecast areas see Fig. 7(2) on page 161

FRANCE

Bayonne Radio 43°16'N 1°24'W	VHF station remotely controlled from Bordeaux-Arcachon (0700–2200 local time)		16 **24**	24			Ch24 0733 1233 LT (Fr)	Ch 24 O/R & S/P2 (Fr)	
Bordeaux-Arcachon Radio 44°39'N 1°10'W (MF remotely controlled from Brest-Le Conquet 2200–0700 local time. VHF operates 0700–2200 local time) *Tel: 56.83.40.50*	1820 **1862** 2182 2775 3722	At Royan and Cap Ferret: 2182 2049 2056 2069 2153 2167 2506 2541 At Royan: 2449 3161 At Cap Ferret: 2037 2321 2421 2527 3168	16 **28** **82**	28 82	1862 kHz every even H + 07	1820 and 2775 kHz 0703 1703 (in French and English)	1820 kHz 0703 1703 (in French for Areas 23, 24) Ch 82 0733 1233 LT (Fr) (Ile de Ré to Spanish border)	1820 kHz O/R and S/P2 and every even H + 07 (in French for Areas 23, 24) Ch 82 O/R & S/P2 (Fr)	1820 kHz 0703 1703 (in French and English) 1B 8B
Bordeaux Radio 44°53'N 0°30'W	VHF station remotely controlled from Bordeaux-Arcachon (0700–2200 local time)		16 **27**	27					
Royan Radio 45°34'N 0°58'W	VHF station remotely controlled from Bordeaux-Arcachon (0700–2200 local time)		16 **23** **25**	23 25			Ch 23 0733 1233 LT (Fr)	Ch 23 O/R & S/P2 (Fr)	

continued

6.3.16 Continental Coast Radio Stations *continued* (for notes see previous page)

Coast Station Name Position	Medium Frequency RT Service (kHz)		VHF Ch		Traffic List Times (GMT)	Navigation Warning Times (GMT)	Weather Bulletin Times (GMT)	Gale Warning Times (GMT)	Decca Warning Times (GMT)
	Transmits	Receives	Tx	Rx					
La Rochelle Radio 46°20'N 1°05'W	VHF station remotely controlled from Bordeaux-Arcachon (0700–2200 local time)		16 21 26	21 26			Ch 21 0733 1233 LT (Fr)	Ch 21 O/R & S/P2 (Fr)	
St Gilles-Croix-de-Vie Radio 46°44'N 1°59'W	VHF station remotely controlled from Saint Nazaire (0700–2200 local time)		16 **27**	27			Ch 27 0733 1233 LT (Fr)	Ch 27 O/R & S/P2 (Fr)	
Nantes St Herblain Radio 47°13'N 1°37'W	VHF station remotely controlled from Saint Nazaire (0700–2200 local time)		16 **28**	28			Ch 28 0733 1233 LT (Fr)	Ch 28 O/R & S/P2 (Fr)	
Saint Nazaire Radio 47°21'N 2°06'W 47°17'N 2°14'W } VHF (MF service remotely controlled from Brest-Le Conquet 2200–0700 local time) *Tel: 40.22.39.04*	**1687** 2182 2740 3795 1722	2182[1] Also at Batz-sur Mer: 1995 2049 2056 2153 2167 2321 2491 2506 3168 Note: (1) 2182 kHz: H24.	16 **23** **24** (0700–2200 local time)	23 24	1687kHz every odd H + 07	1687 kHz O/R 1722 kHz 0803 1803 (in French)	1722 and 2740 kHz 0803 1803 (Fri) (Areas 14–24) Ch 23 0733 1233 LT (Fr) (Seine to Vendée coast)	1687 kHz O/R & S/P2 & every odd H+07 (Fr) (Areas 14–16) Ch 23 O/R & S/P2 (Fr) (Seine to Vendée coast)	1722kHz O/R 0803 1803 (in French) Chains 1B 8B
Belle Ile Radio 47°21'N 3°09'W	VHF station remotely controlled from Saint Nazaire (0700–2200 local time)		16 **25** **05**	25 05			Ch 25 0733 1233 LT (Fr)	Ch 25 O/R & S/P2 (Fr)	
Pont-l'Abbé Radio 47°53'N 4°13'W	VHF station remotely controlled from Brest-Le Conquet		16 **27**	27			Ch 27 0733 1233 LT (Fr)	Ch 27 O/R & S/P2 (Fr)	
Brest-Le Conquet Radio 48°20'N 4°44'W Located at St Malo 48°38'N 2°02'W Located at Quimperlé 47°53'N 3°30'W (For Navtex see 6.3.14) *Tel: 98.80.40.26*	1673 **1806** 2182 2726 3722 1673 2182 **2691** 1673 1806 **1876** 2182 Notes: 1) Also receives on 2049 2056 2097 2153 2160 2167 2463 2506 3168 kHz 2) Located at Treffiagat 47°49'N 4°16'W	2182 (H24) 2182[1] (H24) 2182[1 2] (H24)	16 **26** **28**	26 28	1806 kHz (Le Conquet) 2691 kHz (St Malo) every even H + 03	1673 kHz (Le Conquet) 2691 kHz (St Malo) 0333 0733 1133 1533 1933 2333 1876 kHz (Quimperlé) 0733 1633 (in English and French)	1673 kHz (Le Conquet) 2691 kHz (St Malo) 1876 kHz (Quimperlé) 0733 1633 2153 and on request (in French for Areas 14–22) Ch 26 0733 1233 LT (Fr)	1673 kHz 1876 kHz 2691 kHz O/R & S/P2 1806 kHz 2691 kHz every even H + 03 (in French for Areas 14–22) Ch 26 O/R & S/P2 (Fr)	
Ouessant Radio 48°27'N 5°05'W	VHF station remotely controlled from Brest-Le Conquet		16 **24** **82**	24 82			Ch 82 0733 1233 LT (Fr)	Ch 82 O/R & S/P2 (Fr)	
Plougasnou Radio 48°42'N 3°48'W	VHF station remotely controlled from Brest-Le Conquet		16 **83**	83			Ch 83 0733 1233 LT (Fr)	Ch 83 O/R & S/P2 (Fr)	
Paimpol Radio 48°45'N 2°59'W	VHF station remotely controlled from Brest-Le Conquet		16 **84**	84			Ch 84 0733 1233 LT (Fr)	Ch 84 O/R & S/P2 (Fr)	
St Malo Radio 48°38'N 2°02'W	VHF station remotely controlled from Saint Nazaire		01 02	01 02			Ch 02 0733 1233 LT (Fr)	Ch 02 O/R & S/P2 (Fr)	

continued

6.3.16 Continental Coast Radio Stations *continued*

Coast Station Name Position	Medium Frequency RT Service (kHz) Transmits	Receives	VHF Ch Tx	Rx	Traffic List Times (GMT)	Navigation Warning Times (GMT)	Weather Bulletin Times (GMT)	Gale Warning Times (GMT)	Decca Warning Times (GMT)
Carteret Radio 49°22′N 1°48′W	VHF station — day service only		16 **64**	64					
Cherbourg Radio 49°38′N 1°36′W	VHF station remotely controlled from Boulogne		16 **27**	27			Ch 27 0733 1233 LT (Fr)	Ch 27 O/R & S/P2 (Fr)	
Port en Bessin Radio 49°20′N 0°42′W	VHF station remotely controlled from Boulogne		**03** 16	03			Ch 03 0733 1233 LT (Fr)	Ch 03 O/R & S/P2 (Fr)	
Rouen Radio 49°27′N 1°02′E	VHF station remotely controlled from Boulogne		16 **25** 27	25 27					
Le Havre Radio 49°31′N 0°05′E Tel: 35.70.90.04	VHF station remotely controlled from Boulogne		16 **23** **26** **28**	23 26 28			Ch 26 0733 1233 LT (Fr)	Ch 26 O/R & S/P2 (Fr)	
Dieppe Radio 49°55′N 1°04′E	VHF station remotely controlled from Boulogne		16 **02** **24**	02 24			Ch 02 0733 1233 LT (Fr)	Ch 02 O/R & S/P2 (Fr)	
Boulogne Radio 50°43′N 1°37′E Escalles: 50°55′N 1°43′E Tel: 21.31.44.00	1694 **1771** 2182 2747 3795	2182[1][2] Also receives on following frequencies at Escalles: 2049 2056 2097 2153 2167 2321 2506 2576 3161 3168 Notes: (1) At Boulogne and Escalles. (2) 2182 kHz: H24.	16 **23** **25**	23 25	1771 kHz every odd H + 03	1694 kHz 0133 0533 0933 1333 1733 2133 (in French and English)	1694 kHz 0703 1733 (in French for Areas 1–14) Ch 23 0733 1233 LT (Fr)	1694 kHz O/R & S/P2 1694 and 1771 kHz every odd H + 03 (Fr) (Areas 1–14) Ch 23 O/R & S/P2 (Fr)	1694 kHz (as Navigation Warning times, in French and English) Chain 5B
Calais Radio 50°55′N 1°43′E	VHF station remotely controlled from Boulogne		**01** 16 **87**	01 87			Ch 87 0733 1233 LT (Fr)	Ch 87 O/R & S/P2 (Fr)	
Dunkerque Radio 51°02′N 2°24′E	VHF station remotely controlled from Boulogne		16 **24** **61**	24 61			Ch 61 0733 1233 LT (Fr)	Ch 61 O/R & S/P2 (Fr)	

BELGIUM (for Oostende Radio see next page)

Antwerpen Radio VHF facilities at following positions. The call in each case is Antwerpen Radio									
Antwerpen	Ch 07 16 **24** 26 27 **28** 83	51°17′N 4°20′E			Ch 24 every H+05	Ch 24 O/R and every H+03 H+48 (in English and Dutch for the Schelde)	Ch 24 Fog warnings O/R and every H+03 H+48 (in English and Dutch)	Ch 24 O/R and every H+03 H+48 (strong breeze warnings in English)	
Kortrijk	Ch 16 **24** 83	50°50′N 3°17′E							
Gent	Ch 16 **24** 26 81	51°02′N 3°44′E							
Vilvoorde	Ch 16 **24** 28	50°56′N 4°25′E							
Ronquières	Ch 16 **24** 27	50°37′N 4°13′E							
Mol	Ch 16 **24** 87	51°11′N 5°07′E							
Liège	Ch 16 **24** 27	50°34′N 5°33′E							

continued

NOTES:

1. H + ... means commencing at ... minutes past the hour.
2. O/R means on receipt.
3. Ch 16 is reserved for calls from French Coast Radio Stations. Vessels should call on a working frequency. For MF, call on 2182 or (if 2182 is busy) on 2321 kHz.
4. LT means Local Time.
5. (Fr) means 'in French'.

6. S/P1 means after first silence period after receipt.
7. S/P2 means after first and second silence periods after receipt.
8. French VHF Bcsts of weather bulletins and gale warnings refer to coastal waters.
9. For French Fcst Areas (MF Bcsts) see Fig. 7(2), page 161.

6.3.16   Continental Coast Radio Stations *continued*

Coast Station Name Position	Medium Frequency RT Service (kHz)		VHF Ch		Traffic List Times (GMT)	Navigation Warning Times (GMT)	Weather Bulletin Times (GMT)	Gale Warning Times (GMT)	Decca Warning Times (GMT)
	Transmits	Receives	Tx	Rx					
Oostende Radio 51°11′N 2°48′E (See note below VHF column concerning which channels to be used in different areas) (For Navtex see 6.3.14)	**1817** **1820**[1] 1905 1908 2087 2090 2170.5 2182 2253 2256 2373 2376 2481 2484 2758 **2761**[1] 2814 **2817**[2] 3629 **3632**[2] 3681 **3684**[1]	2182[3] 2484[4] 3178[4] 2191[5]	16 (H24) **23**[1] **27**[2 3] (H24) 78[1] 85[3] 87[2] 88[3] Used for calls in vicinity of: 1) La Panne 2) Zeebrugge 3) Oostende Hours of watch Ch 16 27: H24		2761 kHz every even H + 20, Ch 27 every H + 20	2761 kHz and Ch 27 O/R S/P2 0233 0633 1033 1433 1833 2233 (in Dutch and English)	2761 kHz and Ch 27 0820 1720 (in Dutch and English for Dover and Thames) Ice Reports on Ch 27 every 4h from 0103 Fog Warnings on 2761 kHz O/R and S/P2 in English and Dutch for the Schelde	2761 kHz and Ch 27 O/R and S/P2 (in Dutch and English for Dover and Thames)	2761 kHz and Ch 27 S/P2 (in English) Chains 5B 2A 6C 8E 2E 9B
Notes 1) Working frequencies for Belgian vessels. 2) Working frequencies for foreign vessels	3) 2182 kHz: H24. 4) 2484 3178 kHz: H24 for Belgian vessels. 5) 2191 kHz: when 2182 kHz is distress working								

NETHERLANDS

Scheveningen Radio 52°06′N 4°16′E Note: Netherlands Coast Guard keeps watch (H24) on 2182 kHz and VHF Ch 16 for safety and distress traffic only.	**1764** **1862**[1] **1890** **1939** **2600** 2824 **3673**	2030 2160[1] 2049[2] 2056 2513 1995 2520[3] (H24) 3191	VHF stations remotely controlled (all H24) Call Scheveningen Radio on working channel of nearest station shown below:		1862 kHz 1890 kHz every odd H + 05 VHF on primary channels every H + 05 2824 kHz 0105 0305 0505 2305	1862 kHz 1890 kHz O/R S/P1 and every 4h from 0333 2824 kHz 0333 2333 (all in Dutch and English)	1862 kHz 1890 kHz every 6h from 0340 (in Dutch and English) VHF on bracketed channels every 6h from 0005 (LT) (in Dutch)	1862 kHz 1890 kHz O/R S/P1 (in Dutch and English) VHF on bracketed channels O/R and every H + 05 (in Dutch)	As for Navigation Warnings (in Dutch and English) Decca Chains 2E 9B
	1) Located at Nes 53°24′N 6°04′E. 2) Keeps watch on 2049 when distress working on 2182 kHz. 3) Calling frequency. Station replies on 2824. Hours of service: 1764 2824 kHz: H24 1862 1939 kHz: Mon–Sat: 0700–2200[4] Sun: 0800–2200[4] 1890 kHz: 0700–2300[4] 2600 kHz: Mon–Sat: 0700–2200[4] 3673 kHz: Occas 4) All 1h earlier when DST is in force.								

Goes	Ch (**23**) 25	51°31′N	3°54′E
Rotterdam	Ch **24 28** (87)	51°56′N	4°28′E
Scheveningen	Ch 26 (**83**)	52°06′N	4°16′E
Haarlem	Ch **23** (25)	52°23′N	4°38′E
Wieringermeer	Ch (**27**)	52°55′N	5°04′E
Location L7	Ch (**28**) 84	53°32′N	4°13′E
Terschelling	Ch (**25**) 78	53°22′N	5°13′E
Nes	Ch (**23**)	53°24′N	6°04′E
Appingedam	Ch (**27**)	53°18′N	6°52′E
Lelystad	Ch (**83**)	52°32′N	5°26′E

Tel: 550 19104

Note: Bracketed channels are those on which Weather Bulletins and Gale Warnings are broadcast.

NOTES:
1. H + … means commencing at … minutes past the hour.
2. LT means Local Time.
3. O/R means on receipt.

4. S/P1 means after first silence period after receipt.
5. S/P2 means after first and second silence periods after receipt.

continued

6.3.16 Continental Coast Radio Stations *continued*

Coast Station Name Position	Medium Frequency RT Service (kHz)		VHF Ch	Traffic List Times (GMT)	Navigation Warning Times (GMT)	Weather Bulletin Times (GMT)	Gale Warning Times (GMT)	Decca Warning Times (GMT)
	Transmits	Receives						

FEDERAL REPUBLIC OF GERMANY

Coast Station Name Position	Transmits	Receives	VHF Ch	Traffic List Times (GMT)	Navigation Warning Times (GMT)	Weather Bulletin Times (GMT)	Gale Warning Times (GMT)	Decca Warning Times (GMT)
Norddeich Radio 53°38'N 7°12'E	1799 1911 2182 **2614**[2] 2799 2848 Notes: 1) 2182 kHz: H24. 2) During Bcsts station replies on 2848 kHz. 3) 2023 kHz 0700–2300 LT 4) 2045 kHz when 2182 is distress working. Only available 2300–0700 LT to German vessels	2491 2541 2182[1] 2023[3] 2045[4] 2128 3161	16 **28** 61 86	2614 kHz and Ch 28 every H + 45 Also on 2614 kHz at 0810 2010 after weather report	2614 kHz O/R S/P1 0133 0533 0933 1333 1733 2133 and on request (In English and German)	2614 kHz 2110 (local times) (in German for North Sea areas and Skagerrak)	2614 kHz 0910 and every 4h from 0133 (in German for North Sea areas and Skagerrak. In English for German Bight)	2614 kHz O/R S/P1 0133 0533 0933 1333 1733 2133 and on request (in English and German) 9B
Bremen Radio 53°05'N 8°48'E	VHF station remotely controlled from Elbe-Weser		16 25 **28**	Ch 28 every H + 40				
Helgoland Radio 54°11'N 7°53'E	VHF station remotely controlled from Elbe-Weser		03 16 **27** 88	Ch 27 every H + 20				
Elbe-Weser Radio 53°50'N 8°39'E	**Note:** Ch 23 28 and 62 are for communication with vessels on the Nord-Ostsee Canal		01 16 **23** 24 **26** 28 62	Ch 23 every H + 20 Ch 26 every H + 50				
Hamburg Radio 53°33'N 9°58'E	VHF station remotely controlled from Elbe-Weser		16 25 **27** 82 83	Ch 27 every H + 40				
Eiderstedt Radio 54°20'N 8°47'E	VHF station remotely controlled from Elbe-Weser		16 **25** 64	Ch 25 every H + 40				
Nordfriesland Radio 54°55'N 8°18'E	VHF station remotely controlled from Elbe-Weser		05 16 **26**	Ch 26 every H + 50				

NOTES:
1. H + ... means commencing at ... minutes past the hour.
2. LT means Local Time.
3. O/R means on receipt.

4. S/P1 means after first silence period after receipt.
5. S/P2 means after first and second silence periods after receipt.

6.4   SHORT NOTES ON FLAG ETIQUETTE

6.4.1   Ensign

A yacht's ensign is the national maritime flag corresponding to the nationality of her owner. Thus a British yacht should wear the Red Ensign, unless she qualifies for a special ensign (see 6.4.2). At sea the ensign must be worn when meeting other vessels, when entering or leaving foreign ports, or when approaching forts, signal and coastguard stations etc. In British harbours the ensign should be hoisted at 0800 (0900 between 1 November and 14 February) and lowered at sunset (or 2100 local time if earlier). The ensign should normally be worn at the stern, but if this is not possible the nearest position should be used, e.g. at the peak in a gaff-rigged boat, at the mizzen masthead in a ketch or yawl, or about two-thirds up the leech of the mainsail.

6.4.2   Special ensigns

Members of certain clubs may apply for permission to wear a special ensign (e.g. Blue Ensign, defaced Blue Ensign, or defaced Red Ensign). For this purpose the yacht must either be a registered ship under Part I of the Merchant Shipping Act 1894 and of at least 2 tons gross tonnage, or be registered under the Merchant Shipping Act 1983 (Small Ships Register) and of at least 7 metres overall length. The owner or owners must be British subjects, and the yacht must not be used for any professional, business or commercial purpose. Full details can be obtained from Secretaries of Clubs concerned.

A special ensign must only be worn when the owner is on board or ashore in the vicinity, and only when the yacht is flying the burgee (or a Flag Officer's flag) of the club concerned. The permit must be carried on board. When the yacht is sold, or the owner ceases to be a member of the Club, the permit must be returned to the Secretary of the Club.

6.4.3   Burgee

A burgee shows that a yacht is in the charge of a member of the club indicated, and does not necessarily indicate ownership. It should be flown at the masthead. If the yacht is on loan, or is chartered, it is correct to use the burgee of the skipper or charterer — not that of the absent owner. Normal practice has been to lower the burgee at night, at the same time as the ensign, but nowadays many owners leave the burgee flying if they are on board or ashore in the vicinity.

6.4.4   Flag officer's flag

Clubs authorise their flag officers to fly special swallow-tailed flags, with the same design as the club burgee and in place of it. The flags of a vice-commodore and a rear-commodore carry one and two balls respectively. A flag officer's flag is flown day and night while he is on board, or ashore nearby. A flag officer should fly his flag with the Red Ensign (or special ensign, where authorised) in preference to the burgee of some other club.

6.4.5   Choice of burgee

An owner who is not a flag officer, and who belongs to more than one club, should normally fly the burgee (and if authorised the special ensign) of the senior club in the harbour where the yacht is lying. An exception may be if another club is staging a regatta or similar function.

6.4.6   Courtesy ensign

It is customary when abroad to fly a small maritime ensign of the country concerned at the starboard crosstrees. The correct courtesy flag for a foreign yacht in British waters is the Red Ensign (not the Union Flag). British yachts do not fly a courtesy flag in the Channel Islands since these are part of the British Isles.

6.4.7   House flag

An owner may fly his personal flag when he is on board in harbour, provided it does not conflict with the design of some existing flag. A house flag is normally rectangular, and is flown at the crosstrees in a sloop or cutter, at the mizzen masthead in a ketch or yawl, or at the foremast head in a schooner.

6.4.8   Salutes

Yachts should salute all Royal Yachts, and all warships of whatever nationality. A salute is made by dipping the ensign (only). The vessel saluted responds by dipping her ensign, and then re-hoisting it, whereupon the vessel saluting re-hoists hers.

Chapter 7

Weather

Contents

7

Weather — introduction

The following subjects are described in detail in Chapter 7 of *The Macmillan & Silk Cut Yachtsman's Handbook*:

Transfer of heat; world weather; air masses; atmospheric pressure; wind; humidity; clouds; depressions and fronts; the passage of a depression; anticyclones; fog; sea and land breezes; thunderstorms; tropical storms; glossary of meteorological terms; forecasting your own weather; bibliography.

Here in the Almanac, emphasis is given to obtaining and interpreting forecasts. For more general information on the weather, including the subjects listed above, reference should be made to Chapter 7 of *The Macmillan & Silk Cut Yachtsman's Handbook*.

7.1 GENERAL WEATHER INFORMATION

7.1.1   Beaufort scale

Force	Wind speed (knots)	Description	State of sea	Probable wave height (m)	Probable max. wave height (m)
0	0–1	Calm	Like a mirror	0	0
1	1–3	Light air	Ripples like scales are formed	0	0
2	4–6	Light breeze	Small wavelets, still short but more pronounced, not breaking	0.1	0.3
3	7–10	Gentle breeze	Large wavelets, crests begin to break; a few white horses	0.4	1
4	11–16	Moderate breeze	Small waves growing longer; fairly frequent white horses	1	1.5
5	17–21	Fresh breeze	Moderate waves, taking more pronounced form; many white horses, perhaps some spray	2	2.5
6	22–27	Strong breeze	Large waves forming; white foam crests more extensive; probably some spray	3	4
7	28–33	Near gale	Sea heaps up; white foam from breaking waves begins to blow in streaks	4	5.5
8	34–40	Gale	Moderately high waves of greater length; edges of crests break into spindrift; foam blown in well marked streaks	5.5	7.5
9	41–47	Severe gale	High waves with tumbling crests; dense streaks of foam; spray may affect visibility	7	10
10	48–55	Storm	Very high waves with long overhanging crests; dense streams of foam make surface of sea white. Heavy tumbling sea; visibility affected	9	12.5
11	56–63	Violent storm	Exceptionally high waves; sea completely covered with long white patches of foam; edges of wave crests blown into froth. Visibility affected	11	16
12	64 plus	Hurricane	Air filled with foam and spray; sea completely white with driving spray; visibility very seriously affected	14	—

Notes: (1) The state of sea and probable wave heights are a guide to what may be expected in the open sea, away from land. In enclosed waters, or near land with an off-shore wind, wave heights will be less but possibly steeper — particularly with wind against tide.

(2) It should be remembered that the height of sea for a given wind strength depends upon the fetch and the duration for which the wind has been blowing. For further information on sea state, see Chapter 9 of *The Macmillan & Silk Cut Yachtsman's Handbook*.

7.1.2   Barometer and thermometer conversion scales

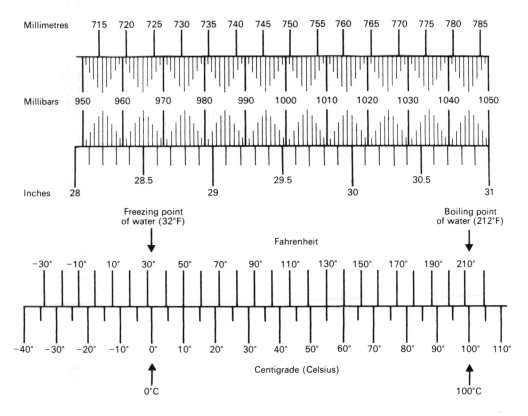

7.1.3   Meaning of terms used in weather bulletins

Visibility

Good	More than 5 miles
Moderate	5–2 miles
Poor	2 miles – 1100 yards (1000 metres)
Fog	Less than 1100 yards (1000 metres)

Timing (of gale warnings)

Imminent	Within 6 hours of time of issue
Soon	6–12 hours
Later	12–24 hours

Speeds (of weather systems)

Slowly	0–15 knots
Steadily	15–25 knots
Rather quickly	25–35 knots
Rapidly	35–45 knots
Very rapidly	Over 45 knots

Barometric pressure changes (tendency)

Now falling) pressure
Rising more slowly (or now steady)) higher than
Rising) 3 hours ago
Steady
Now rising (pressure lower or same as 3 hours ago)
Falling more slowly) Pressure lower than
Falling) 3 hours ago

'Rising' and 'Falling' may be qualified by:

Slowly	Change less than 1.6mb in 3 hours
Quickly	3.5–6mb in 3 hours
Very rapidly	More than 6mb in 3 hours

Gale warnings

Indicate that winds of at least force 8 or gusts reaching 43 knots are expected somewhere in the area. 'Severe gale' implies winds of at least force 9 or gusts of 52 knots. 'Storm' implies winds of force 10 or above, or gusts of 61 knots. Gale warnings remain in force until amended or cancelled ('gales now ceased'). If a gale persists for more than 24 hours the warning is re-issued.

Land area forecasts — wind strength

In land area forecasts winds are given in the following terms, which relate to Beaufort forces as indicated:

Calm	0	Fresh	5
Light	1–3	Strong	6–7
Moderate	4	Gale	8

Land area forecasts — visibility

The following definitions are used in land area forecasts:

Mist	200–1100 yards (183–1000m)
Fog	Less than 200 yards (183m)
Dense fog	Less than 50 yards (46m)

7.2   SOURCES OF WEATHER INFORMATION

7.2.1   BBC Radio Shipping Forecasts

Shipping forecasts cover large sea areas, and in a five minute bulletin it is impossible to include much detail — particularly variations that can and do occur near land — or to convey the right degree of confidence in the weather situation. Hence forecasts for 'Inshore Waters' (see 7.2.2) are often more helpful to yachtsmen cruising near the coast.

Shipping forecasts are broadcast on BBC Radio 4 on 198kHz (1515m) and on local MF frequencies daily at 0033–0038, 0555–0600, 1355–1400 and 1750–1755 (clock times). The 0033–0038 broadcast includes area Trafalgar.

The 0033–0038 and 1355–1400 broadcasts Monday–Friday include a 24-hour forecast for the Minches (between Butt of Lewis and Cape Wrath in the north, and between Barra Head and Ardnamurchan Point in the south), after area Hebrides. For further details see Table 7(2).

The 0033–0038 shipping forecast is also broadcast by Radio Scotland (810kHz), and is followed by a forecast, valid until 1800, for coastal waters of Great Britain up to 12 n miles offshore, and reports from selected stations — see 7.2.2.

The bulletins include a summary of gale warnings in force; a general synopsis of the weather for the next 24 hours and expected changes within that period; forecasts for each sea area for the next 24 hours, giving wind direction and speed, weather and visibility; and the latest reports from selected stations from those shown at the foot of page 155. For each station are given wind direction and Beaufort force, present weather, visibility, and (if available) sea-level pressure and tendency. These stations are marked by their initial letters on the chart for forecast areas on page 154.

Apart from being included in shipping forecasts, gale warnings are broadcast at the earliest juncture in the BBC Radio 4 programme after receipt, and also after the next news bulletin.

Instructions on recording and interpreting the shipping forecasts are given in 7.6.4 of *The Macmillan & Silk Cut Yachtsman's Handbook*.

7.2.2   BBC Inshore Waters Forecasts

Forecasts are given for inshore waters (up to 12 miles offshore) of Great Britain until 1800 next day at the end of English, Welsh and Scottish Radio 4 programmes, and on Radio Scotland, at about 0038 local (or clock) time. The forecast of wind, weather and visibility is followed by the 2200 reports from the following stations: Boulmer, Bridlington, Walton-on-the-Naze, St Catherine's Point, Land's End, Mumbles, Valley, Blackpool, Ronaldsway, Killough, Orlock Head, Larne, Corsewall Point, Prestwick, Benbecula, Stornoway, Lerwick, Wick, Aberdeen and Leuchars.

Radio Ulster (1341kHz) gives forecasts for coastal waters of Northern Ireland at 0010 local time daily.

A forecast, valid until 1800, is broadcast for inshore waters of Great Britain and Northern Ireland on BBC Radio 3, at 0655 local time daily, on 1215kHz.

The schedule of coastal waters forecasts for Great Britain and Ireland is included in Table 7(2) on page 156. For details of local radio station forecasts see 7.2.17 and Table 7(4) on pages 158–159.

7.2.3   BBC General Forecasts

Land area forecasts may include the outlook period (up to 48 hours beyond the shipping forecast) and some reference to weather along the coasts. The more detailed land area forecasts are broadcast on Radio 4 on 198kHz (1515m).

7.2.4   Special forecasts for ships at sea

Forecasts for areas within the region 67°N to 40°N, and 35°W and the coast of Europe (including the Mediterranean) may be obtained by yachtsmen by contacting the Central Meteorological Office Forecast Office. This may be done by telephone (0344) 854913, which may be by link call. No charge is made by the Met Office.

Alternatively, the request may be addressed to the nearest UK Coast Radio Station. Such a call might be in the form: 'North Foreland Radio. Request weather forecast next 24 hours for sea areas Dover and Wight on passage Ramsgate to Cherbourg.'

When telephoning the forecast office it must be realised that during busy periods, such as occasions of bad weather, the staff may be fully occupied and there is likely to be a delay.

If a forecast is required for some future occasion or period, or if the forecast is to be kept under review and up-dated, the request should be addressed to The Meteorological Office, Met.02a, London Road, Bracknell, Berks RG12 2SZ, or sent by telex 849801 WEABKA G, giving full details of the service required and the address to which the account is to be forwarded. Cheques should be crossed and made payable to 'Met Office HQ. Public a/c'.

Weather Centres
Weather Centres provide a range of services at a charge. To arrange a forecast service ring:

Plymouth	(0752) 493377
Southampton	(0703) 220646
London	071-430 5627

Norwich	(0603) 630164
Nottingham	(0602) 384094
Leeds	(0532) 457703
Newcastle	091-232 3808
Aberdeen Airport	(0224) 210572
Kirkwall Airport	(0856) 3802
Glasgow	041-248 7272
Manchester	061-477 1017
Cardiff	(0222) 390420
Bristol	(0272) 279272
Belfast Airport, Crumlin	(08494) 22804
Jersey	(0534) 23660

Irish Republic

Central Forecast Office, Dublin (H24)	(01) 424655
Cork Airport Met. (0900–2000)	(021) 965974
Shannon Airport Met. (H24)	(061) 61333

The numbers of overseas forecast offices and recorded weather messages are shown under 'Telephone' for individual harbours in Areas 14–20 of Chapter 10.

7.2.5   Automatic Telephone Weather Service – Marinecall

Recorded Met Office forecasts are updated twice daily (three times in summer) and cover up to 12 miles offshore including Channel and Irish Sea crossings, Isles of Scilly, Channel Islands, Orkney and the Isle of Man. There are 15 areas, as below. In each case dial 0898 500, and then the three figure number of the area required. The charge is 38p per minute (peak and standard rates) and 25p per minute (evenings and weekends), including VAT. Calls can be made through British Telecom coast stations when the VHF per minute tariff is 95p.

458 South West (Hartland Point to Lyme Regis)
457 Mid-Channel (Lyme Regis to Selsey Bill)
456 Channel East (Selsey Bill to North Foreland)
455 Anglia (North Foreland to The Wash)
454 East (The Wash to Whitby)
453 North East (Whitby to Berwick)
452 Scotland East (Berwick to Rattray Head)
451 Scotland North (Rattray Head to Cape Wrath)
464 Minch (Cape Wrath to Ardnamurchan Point)
463 Caledonia (Ardnamurchan Point to Mull of Kintyre)
462 Clyde (Mull of Kintyre to Mull of Galloway)
461 North West (Mull of Galloway to Colwyn Bay)
460 Wales (Colwyn Bay to St David's Head)
459 Bristol Channel (St David's Head to Hartland Point)
465 Ulster (Carlingford Lough to Lough Foyle)

7.2.6   Facsimile broadcasts

Facsimile recorders that receive pictorial images such as weather maps are now available of a type that makes them suitable for use in yachts and at port locations such as marinas.

The information available is of a general meteorological nature and not all of it is relevant to the average yachtsman, but there are many items that are of direct use such as:

> Isobaric charts (actual and forecast)
> Sea and swell charts
> Representation of cloud satellite images
> Sea temperature charts
> Wind field charts.

Internationally exchanged data is processed at various centres. The main centres in northwest Europe that do this work and make facsimile broadcasts are:

Bracknell (England)	3289·5 8040 9203 11086·5 kHz
Offenbach (Germany)	134·2 kHz

The quality of reception depends on the frequency used and the terrain between transmitter and receiver.

Additional frequencies to those above are also available for limited periods during the 24 hours. Transmission frequencies and schedules are published in the *Admiralty List of Radio Signals, Vol 3*. See also 7.6.12 of *The Macmillan and Silk Cut Yachtsman's Handbook*.

7.2.7   NAVTEX

Gale warnings are broadcast on receipt and are repeated at scheduled times. Weather messages are broadcast at scheduled times. Details of NAVTEX stations, identity codes, message categories and transmission times for NAVAREAS I, II and III are given in Chapter 6 (6.3.14).

7.2.8   Volmet

Volmet broadcasts of weather reports for aircraft in flight can be useful with respect to airfields close to the UK and European coasts. The most useful is the HF SSB (H3E) broadcast by Shannon which operates H24 as follows:

3413 kHz   Sunset to sunrise
5505 kHz   H24
8957 kHz   H24
13264 kHz   Sunrise to sunset

The schedule starts at H+00 at five minute intervals until all airfields are covered. UK and Eire airfield broadcasts are at H+05 and H+35.

7

Royal Air Force SSB VOLMET continuously broadcasts actual weather (H24) for a number of military and civil airfields, mostly in the UK, on 4722 kHz and 11200 kHz.

7.2.9   W/T transmissions

W/T transmissions of weather information in considerable detail are intended for ocean going vessels. The average yachtsman has neither the equipment nor the ability to receive the coded signals at the speed at which they are transmitted by W/T. However, equipment is available which will decode (or encode) Morse signals, and print out the message in English.

Portishead Radio broadcasts Morse transmissions for the Atlantic Weather Bulletin Areas, see *Admiralty List of Radio Signals Vol 3*.

7.2.10   Press forecasts

The delay between the time of issue and the time at which they are available next day make press forecasts of limited value to yachtsmen. However, the better papers publish forecasts which include a synoptic chart which, in the absence of any other chart, can be helpful when interpreting the shipping forecast on first putting to sea.

7.2.11   Television forecasts and Prestel

Some TV forecasts show a synoptic chart which, with the satellite pictures, can be a useful guide to the weather situation at the start of a passage.

Weather information is given on teletext by Ceefax (BBC) and Oracle (ITV). BBC 1 Ceefax gives up to date weather maps on page 581 and standard land area weather forecasts on page 582. Weather statistics for UK and Europe are given on page 584. ITN Oracle shows a marine forecast, updated three times daily, on page 162. Antiope is the French system.

Prestel (operated over a telephone link by British Telecom) has a great deal of weather data supplied by the Met. Office, including shipping forecasts and synopsis for all British sea areas. Main index page, key 209: shipping and sailing 2093: actual weather in UK 20940: actual weather world-wide 2094: aviation Fcsts 20971: European Fcsts 20915: UK weather index 20904: What's New 209091.

Shipping Fcst, 4 times/day 20930 (20p). Gale warnings since last Shipping Fcst 20931 (4p).

Sea crossings. 3 times/day (4p). Southern North Sea 209330. Dover Strait 209331. English Channel (East) 209332. St Georges Channel 209333. Irish Sea 209334.

UK land Fcsts. Caption chart. 3 times/day 20911 (5p). Text, 4 times/day 20910 (5p). 3 day outlook, once a day 20913 (as shown). 7 day outlook, issued Sun 20914 (as shown).

7.2.12   Visual storm signals

Visual storm signals used on the Continent are summarised in 10.14.7, 10.19.7 and 10.20.7.

7.2.13   Radiobeacon wind information

Wind information at La Corbière Lt (49°10′·85N 02°14′·90W is transmitted in Sequence 6 by the Radiobeacon on frequency 305·7 kHz modulated as follows: Callsign CB 4 times at 500 Hz; 1 to 8 dots at 1000 Hz indicates Wind Direction by eight cardinal points (one dot = NE, two dots = E, clockwise to 8 dots = N). Up to 8 dots at 500 Hz indicates average speed on the Beaufort Scale (one dot = Force 1, two dots = Force 2, up to 8 dots = Force 8 or more. One or more dots at 1000 Hz indicates maximum gust above average Beaufort scale.

Similarly, wind information at Chichester Bar (50°45′·88N 00°56′·35W) is transmitted in Sequences 1 and 4 by the Radiobeacon on frequency 303·4 kHz modulated as follows: Callsign CH 4 times; 4s dash; up to eight dashes indicate Wind Direction by eight cardinal points (one dash = NE, two dashes = E, clockwise to eight dashes = N). Up to eight dots indicate average speed on the Beaufort scale (one dot = Force 1, two dots = Force 2, up to eight dots = Force 8 or above).

7.2.14   British and Irish Coast Radio Stations — Weather Bulletins by R/T

Forecasts originating from the Meteorological Office are broadcast by British Telecom Coast Radio Stations, as indicated in Table 7(1) below, by radiotelephone on Medium Frequency, and simultaneously on VHF (where available) after an initial announcement on VHF Ch 16. These stations also give weather information on request — see 7.2.4. Weather messages comprise gale warnings, synopsis and 24-hour forecast for the areas stated.

TABLE 7(1)

Station (*VHF only)	Frequency MF — kHz	VHF Ch	Forecast areas
At 0733 and 1933 (UT)			
Land's End	2670	27	Shannon, Fastnet, Lundy.
Pendennis*		62	Sole, Plymouth,
Start Point*		26	Portland, Wight, Biscay, Finisterre.
Celtic*		24	Lundy, Fastnet.
Ilfracombe*		05	
Niton	1834	28	Portland, Wight,
Weymouth Bay*		05	Dover.

North Foreland	1848	26	Humber, Thames,
Hastings*		07	Dover, Wight.
Thames*		02	
Orfordness*		62	

Humber	1869	26	Humber, German
Bacton*		07	Bight, Thames,
Grimsby*		27	Tyne, Dogger.

At 0703 and 1903 (UT)

Cullercoats	2719	26	Forth, Tyne,
Whitby*		25	Dogger, Fisher,
			German Bight,
			Humber, Thames.

Stonehaven	2691	26	South Utsire,
Forth*		24	Forties, Cromarty,
Buchan*		25	Forth, Fisher.

Wick	1792	1824		Viking, North
Cromarty*			28	Utsire, South
Orkney*			26	Utsire, Forties,
Shetland*			27	Cromarty, Fair Isle,
Collafirth*			24	Faeroes,
				SE Iceland.

Hebrides	1866	26	Malin, Hebrides,
Lewis*		05	Bailey, Rockall.
Skye*		24	

Portpatrick	1883	27	Faeroes, SE
Islay*		25	Iceland, Bailey,
Clyde*		26	Hebrides, Rockall,
			Malin, Irish Sea,
			Lundy, Fastnet,
			Shannon.

Anglesey*		26	Irish Sea.
Morecambe Bay*		04	
Cardigan Bay*		03	

At 0833 and 2033 (UT)

Valentia   1827

Shannon, Fasnet.

At 0103 0403 0703 1003 1303 1603 1903 2203 (UT)

Malin Head*	23
Glen Head*	24
Belmullet*	83
Dublin*	83
Valentia*	24
Shannon*	28
Clifden*	TBN
Bantry*	23
Cork*	26
Mine Head*	83
Rosslare*	23

At 0645 0745 1245 1845 2245 (UT)

Jersey	1726	25	Channel Islands
		82	waters, South of
			50°N and East of
			3°W.

Note: Strong wind warnings for Channel Islands waters are broadcast on receipt, and repeated at next silence period and at 0307, 0907, 1507, and 2107.

Gale Warnings

British Telecom Coast Radio Stations transmit gale warnings on receipt. The R/T MF silence periods are from 00 to 03 and from 30 to 33 minutes past each hour. Gale warnings are repeated at the next of the following times: 0303, 0903, 1503, 2103 UT. Gale warnings are preceded by the R/T Safety Signal SÉCURITÉ (pronounced 'SAY-CURE-E-TAY').

Gale warnings remain in force unless amended or cancelled. If the gale persists for more than 24 hours from the time of origin, the gale warning is re-issued from the local (clock) times shown below. They will also respond to telephone enquiries (for the number see each harbour in Chap 10).

7.2.15   Reports of present weather

Reports of actual local weather conditions prevailing at places around the coast of the British Isles can be obtained by telephone from the following Meteorological Office observation stations, Coastguard stations or from specified lighthouses. The locations are shown in 7(2)):

From Meteorological Offices

Station Name	Telephone No
Blackpool	0253 43061 (night 43063)
Ronaldsway	0624 3311 (night 3313)
(Isle of Man)	
Carlisle	0228 23422, ext 440
Prestwick	0292 79800, ext 2617
(Firth of Clyde)	
Tiree	0879 2456
Benbecula	0870 351
(Hebrides)	
Stornoway	0851 2256 (night) 2282
Wick	0955 2216
Kirkwall	0856 3802
(Orkneys)	
Sella Ness	0806 242069
(Shetlands)	
Kinloss	0309 72161, ext 754
(Moray Firth)	
Shoeburyness	0370 82271, ext 476
(0700–1700 Mon–Fri, except Public Holidays)	

7

From Coastguard stations

The following Coastguard Maritime Rescue Co-ordination Centres (MRCC's) and Sub-Centres (MRSC's), may provide information on actual weather conditions in their immediate locality.

Station Name	Telephone No
MRSC Shetland	0595 2976
MRSC Pentland	0856 3268
MRCC Aberdeen	0224 592334
MRSC Forth	0333 50666
MRSC Tyne/Tees	0912 572691
MRSC Humber	0262 672317
MRCC Yarmouth	0493 851338
MRSC Thames	0255 675518
MRCC Dover	0304 210008
MRSC Solent	0705 552100
MRSC Portland	0305 760439
MRSC Brixham	0803 882704
MRCC Falmouth	0326 317575
MRCC Swansea	0792 366534
MRSC Milford Haven	0646 5218
MRSC Holyhead	0407 2051
MRSC Liverpool	0519 313343
MRSC Belfast	0247 883184
MRCC Clyde	0475 29988
MRSC Oban	0631 63720
MRSC Stornoway	0851 2013

Small craft which require information urgently and are unable to make contact with a Coast Radio Station, may call Coastguard stations listed above on VHF Ch 16 to request the current local forecast.

From Lighthouses

The following lighthouses (LH) and other stations may be able to give information on actual weather locally. Those shown in *italics* are not manned continuously.

Station Name	Telephone No
Lizard	0326 290444
Lizard LH	0326 290431
Portland Bill	0305 820400
Portland Bill LH	0305 820495
St Catherine's LH	0983 730284
Eastbourne	0323 20634
Fairlight (Hastings)	0424 813171
Cromer	0263 512507
Whitby	0947 602107
Strathy Point LH	0641 4210
Cape Wrath LH	0971 81230
Butt of Lewis LH	0851 81201
Hyskeir LH	0688 2423
Rhinns of Islay LH	0496 86223
Pladda LH	0655 31657
Corsewall Point LH	0776 853220
Pointe of Ayre LH	0624 880238
Calf of Man LH	0624 822820
Rhyl	0745 39749
Porth Dinllaën (Caernarfon Bay)	0758 720204
Aberdovey	0654 2327
Lundy South LH	0237 3455
Ballycastle	0265 763519
Portrush	0265 823356

7.2.16   HM Coastguard VHF Ch 67

Each MRCC and MRSC keeps watch on VHF Ch 16 and operates Ch 67 — see 8.2.2. They broadcast strong wind warnings for their local area (only) on receipt on Ch 67 after an announcement on Ch 16; also forecasts for their local area on Ch 67 after an announcement on Ch 16 normally every four hours (every two hours if strong wind or gale warning in force) commencing from the local (clock) times shown below. They will also respond to telephone enquiries (for the number see each harbour in Chap 10).

Forecasts every four (or two) hours from: Swansea 0005, Clyde 0020, Yarmouth 0040, Solent 0040, Brixham 0050, Shetland 0105, Dover 0105, Stornoway 0110, Pentland 0135, Falmouth 0140, Tyne/Tees 0150, Forth 0205, Liverpool 0210, Portland 0220, Holyhead 0235, Oban 0240, Thames 0010, Belfast 0305, Aberdeen 0320, Milford Haven 0335, Humber 0340.

Fig. 7(1) — Reports of present weather

Reports from Meteorological Offices
Reports from Coastguard Stations
Reports from Lighthouses and other Stations

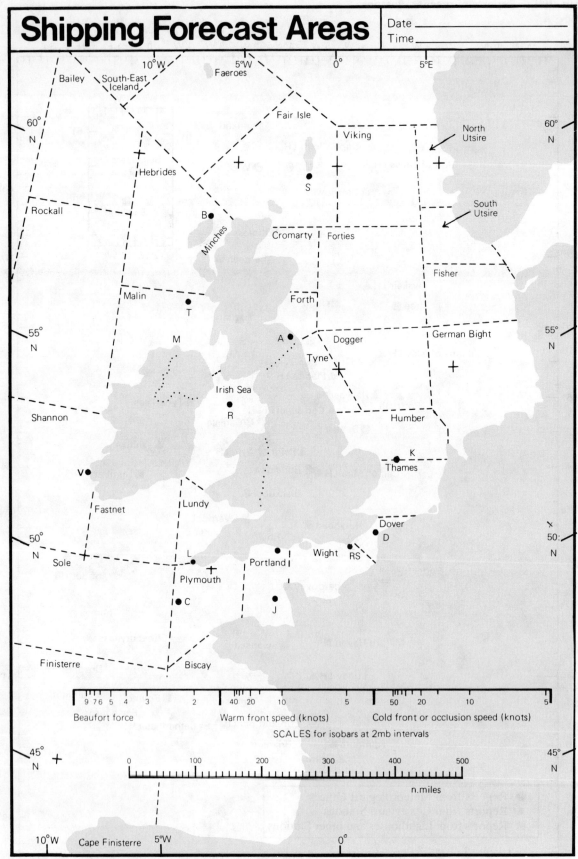

Shipping Forecast Areas

Date _____
Time _____

Bailey
South-East Iceland
Faeroes
Fair Isle
60° N
Viking
North Utsire
Hebrides
S
60° N
Rockall
B
Minches
Cromarty
Forties
South Utsire
Malin
Forth
Fisher
T
55° N
M
A
Dogger
German Bight
55° N
Tyne
Shannon
Irish Sea
R
Humber
V
K
Thames
Fastnet
Lundy
Sole
L
Portland
Wight
Dover
D
50° N
Plymouth
C
J
RS
50° N
Finisterre
Biscay

9 7 6 5 4 3	2	40 20 10 5	50 20 10 5
Beaufort force		Warm front speed (knots)	Cold front or occlusion speed (knots)

SCALES for isobars at 2mb intervals

45° N

0	100	200	300	400	500

n.miles

45° N

10°W
Cape Finisterre
5°W
0°

Note: Capital letters refer to coastal reports; see opposite.

Shipping Forecast Record

GENERAL SYNOPSIS   at _____ UT/BST

System	Present position	Movement	Forecast position	at

Gales	SEA AREA FORECAST	Wind (At first)	Wind (Later)	Weather	Visibility
	VIKING				
	NORTH UTSIRE				
	SOUTH UTSIRE				
	FORTIES				
	CROMARTY				
	FORTH				
	TYNE				
	DOGGER				
	FISHER				
	GERMAN BIGHT				
	HUMBER				
	THAMES				
	DOVER				
	WIGHT				
	PORTLAND				
	PLYMOUTH				
	BISCAY				
	FINISTERRE				
	SOLE				
	LUNDY				
	FASTNET				
	IRISH SEA				
	SHANNON				
	ROCKALL				
	MALIN				
	HEBRIDES				
	BAILEY				
	FAIR ISLE				
	FAEROES				
	SE ICELAND				

COASTAL REPORTS at ____ BST/UT	Wind Direction	Force	Weather	Visibility	Pressure	Change
Tiree (T)						
Butt of Lewis (B)						
Sumburgh (S)						
St Abb's Head (A)						
Smith's Knoll (K)						
Dover (D)						

COASTAL REPORTS	Wind Direction	Force	Weather	Visibility	Pressure	Change
Royal Sovereign (RS)						
Channel Lt V (C)						
Land's End (L)						
Ronaldsway (R)						
Malin Head (M)						
Jersey (J)						

7

TABLE 7(2) British Isles — Daily Shipping Forecasts and Forecasts for Coastal Waters
as broadcast by British Broadcasting Corporation (BBC) and Radio Telefis Eireann (RTE)

Note: All times are local or 'clock' times, unless otherwise stated

Time	Forecast	Contents	Stations and Frequencies
0010	Coastal Waters (Northern Ireland)	Fcst, valid until 1800 for coastal waters of N Ireland up to 12 nm offshore.	*BBC Radio Ulster:* 1341kHz.
0033	Shipping Forecast — Home Waters Fcst Areas	Gale warnings in force, synopsis, 24h Fcst for Home Waters Fcst Areas (including Trafalgar, and Mon-Fri a 24h Fcst for area Minch); reports from selected stations.	*BBC Radio 4:* 198kHz Tyneside 603kHz, London 720kHz, N Ireland 720kHz, Aberdeen 1449kHz, Carlisle 1485kHz, Plymouth 774kHz, Redruth 756kHz. *BBC Radio Scotland:* 810kHz.
0038	Coastal Waters (Great Britain)	Fcst, valid until 1800, for coastal waters of Great Britain up to 12 nm offshore; reports from selected stations.	*BBC Radio 4 and Radio Scotland:* as for 0033 Shipping Forecast.
0555	Shipping Forecast — Home Waters Fcst Areas	Gale warnings in force, synopsis, 24h Fcst for Home Waters Fcst Areas; reports from selected stations.	*BBC Radio 4:* as for 0033 Shipping Forecast. Not London on 720kHz
0633	Coastal Waters (Great Britain)	Fcst, valid until 1800, for coastal waters of Great Britain up to 12 nm offshore.	*BBC Radio 3:* 1215kHz.
0655	Coastal Waters (Ireland)	Gale warnings in force; 24h Fcst for Irish coastal waters up to 30 nm offshore and the Irish Sea.	*RTE – Radio 1:* Tullamore 567kHz, Cork 729kHz.
1253	Coastal Waters (Ireland)	Gale warnings in force; 24h Fcst for Irish coastal waters up to 30 nm offshore and the Irish Sea.	*RTE – Radio 1:* Tullamore 567kHz, Cork 729kHz.
1355	Shipping Forecast — Home Waters Fcst Areas	Gale warnings in force, synopsis, 24h Fcst for Home Waters Fcst Areas; 24h Fcst for area Minch (Mon–Fri); reports from selected stations.	*BBC Radio 4:* as for 0033 Shipping Forecast. (Not London 720 kHz.)
1750	Shipping Forecast — Home Waters Fcst Areas	Gale warnings in force, synopsis, 24h Fcst for Home Waters Fcst Areas; reports from selected stations.	*BBC Radio 4:* as for 0033 Shipping Forecast. (Not London 720 kHz.)
1825 (1823)*	Coastal Waters (Ireland)	Gale warnings in force; 24h Fcst for Irish coastal waters up to 30 nm offshore and the Irish Sea.	*RTE – Radio 1:* Tullamore 567kHz, Cork 729kHz.
2355	Coastal Waters (Ireland)	Gale warnings in force; 24h Fcst for Irish coastal waters up to 30 nm offshore and the Irish Sea.	*RTE – Radio 1:* Tullamore 567kHz, Cork 729kHz.

* 1823 Sat-Sun (Subject to change).

TABLE 7(3) Gale Warnings

Stations	Areas covered	Times
BBC Radio 4: 198kHz, Tyneside 603 kHz, London 720kHz, N Ireland 720kHz, Aberdeen 1449kHz, Carlisle 1485kHz, Plymouth 774kHz, Redruth 756kHz.	Broadcast gale warnings for all Home Waters Fcst Areas, including Trafalgar	At the first available programme junction after receipt and after the first news bulletin after receipt
RTE – Radio 1: Tullamore 567kHz, Cork 729kHz.	Broadcast gale warnings for Irish coastal waters up to 30 nm offshore and the Irish Sea	At first programme junction after receipt and with news bulletins (0630–2352)
RTE – Radio (2 FM): Athlone 612 kHz, Dublin and Cork 1278kHz.		At first programme junction after receipt and with news bulletins (0630–0150).

British Coast Radio Stations broadcast gale warnings for adjacent areas at the end of the first silence period after receipt (i.e. at H + 03 or H + 33) and subsequently at the next of the following times: 0303, 0903, 1503, 2103 GMT. For further details see 7.2.14. For Irish coast stations see 6.3.16 on pages 138–139.

Fig. 7(2) Irish Meteorological Service. Sea area forecasts within 25 n miles of the coast, plus the Irish Sea. Also shown are the stations (starred) from which reports are included in the first and last broadcasts each day and the headlands used to divide up the coastline into smaller areas, depending on the expected weather situation. RTE broadcast stations are also indicated.

Table 7(4) Local Radio Stations — Coastal Weather Forecasts

Station	VHF Transmitter(s)	VHF (MHz)	MF (kHz)	(m)	Coastal Waters Forecasts (local times) (*summer months only)	Small Craft Warnings
BBC Radio Cornwall						
Redruth	Redruth	103·9	630	476	Mon-Fri: 0715 0745 0815 0845 1245 1715 1740	Yes
Bodmin	Caradon Hill	95·2	657	457	Sat: 0715 0745 0815 0845	
Scilly	Scilly	96·0			Sun: 0745 0815 0845 0915	
Plymouth Sound	Plympton	97·0			Daily: Approx 0603 0615	Yes
DevonAir Radio	St Thomas	97·0	660	450	Daily: Every H+00 after the news	Yes
(Exeter/Torquay)	Beacon Hill	96·4	954	314	Brixham Coastguard 0830	
BBC Radio Devon						
Exeter	Exeter	95·8	990	303	Mon-Fri: 0633 0733 0833 1310 1735	Yes*
Plymouth	N Hessary Tor	103·4	855	351	Sat: 0633 0833 1310	
North Devon	Huntshaw Cross	94·8	801	375	Sun: 0833 1310	
Torbay	N Hessary Tor	103·4	1458	206		
Okehampton	Okehampton	96·0				
South West 103	Stockland Hill	103·0			Daily: Every H+00 after news	Yes
					Portland Coastguard 0806	
2CR Bournemouth	Poole	102·3	828	362	Daily: 0710 0810 0906 1310 1710	Yes
BBC Radio Solent	Rowridge IOW	96·1	999	300	Mon-Fri: 0604 0633 0709 0733 0745 0809 0833	Yes
			1359	221	0904 1004 1104 1204 1309 1404 1504	
					1604 1709 1733 1804 2204 2300	
					Sat-Sun: 0633 1709 0733 0745 0809 0833 0904	
					1000 1104 1204 1304 1404 1533 1757	
					1804 1925	
Ocean Sound	Fort Widley	97·5			Daily: 0630 0730 0830	Yes
The Light FM	Crabwood Farm	96·7			Mon-Fri: 1730	
The Gold AM	Farlington Marshes		1170	257		
	Veals Farm		1557	193		
BBC Radio Sussex	Whitehawk Hill	95·3	1485	202	Mon-Fri: 0600 0655 0755 0844 1308 1755	Yes
	Heathfield	104·5	1161	258		
	N Sussex	104·0	1368	219	Sat: 0755 1802 Sun: 0755	
Southern Sound	Brighton	103·5			Daily: Every H+00	Yes
	Newhaven	96·9			Sat-Sun: Every H+00 0730 0830	
	Heathfield	102·4				
	Shoreham		1323	227		
BBC Radio Kent	Wrotham	96·7	1035	290	Mon-Fri: 0645 0745 0845 1305 1708 1808	Yes
	Swingate	104·2	774	388	Sat: 0645 0745 0845 0945 1305	
			1602	187	Sun: 0745 0845 1305	
LBC Crown FM	Croydon	97·3			Daily: After the news, every H+00	
London Talkback	Croydon		1152	261		
Essex Radio	Benfleet	96·3				
	Bakers Wood	102·6	1359	220	Sat-Sun: 0600 0700 0800 0900	Yes
	Rayleigh		1431	210		
Radio Orwell	Foxhall Heath	97·1	1170	257	Daily: Coast Reports 0600 0800 1200 1600 2400	Yes*
BBC Radio Norfolk	Tacolneston	95·1	855	351	Daily: 0850	Yes
	Great Massingham	104·4	873	344		
BBC Radio Lincolnshire	Belmont	94·9	1368	219	Mon-Fri: 0645 0715 0745 0815 0845	0715 0815
BBC Radio Humberside	High Hunsley	95·9	1485	202	Mon-Fri: 0604 0632 0732 0832 1259 1432 1632 1732	Yes
					Sat-Sun: 0730 0830 0930	
BBC Radio Cleveland	Bilsdale	95·0	1548	194	Mon-Fri: 0645 0745 0845 1309 1645	Yes
	Whitby	95.8			Sat: 0745 0845	
					Sun: 0745 0845 0945	
TFM Radio	Bilsdale	96·6	1170	257	Mon-Fri: 0525 0625 0722 0822	Yes
					Sat: 0525 0725 0822 Sun: 0625 0725 0922	

Table 7(4) Local Radio Stations — Coastal Weather Forecasts Continued

Station	VHF Transmitter(s)	Frequencies			Coastal Waters Forecasts (local times) (*summer months only)		Small Craft Warnings
		VHF (MHz)	MF (kHz)	(m)			
BBC Radio Newcastle	Pontop Pike Chatton Fenham	95·4 96·0 104·4	1458 in North	206	*Mon-Fri:* *Sat-Sun:*	0655 0755 0855 1155 1655 1755 0755 0855 0955	Yes
Radio Forth	Craigkelly	97·3	1548	194	*Mon-Sat:* *Sat-Sun*:*	0600–1800 (every hour) 0600 0800 0900 1200 1500 1900	Yes
Radio Tay	Dundee Perth	102·8 96·4	1161 1584	258 189	*Sat-Sun:*	0600 0700 0900 1200 1500 1800 2100 (April-October)	Yes
Radio Clyde	Black Hill	102·5	1152	261	*Daily:*	At regular intervals (0600–1800)	Yes
West Sound, Ayr	Symington Girvan	96·7 97·5	1035	290	*Daily*	Every H+00 and H+30 after news	Yes
BBC Radio Cumbria	Sandale Morecambe Bay Whitehaven	95·6 96·1 104·2	756 837 837	397 358 358	*Mon-Fri:* *Sat:* *Sun:*	0640 0740 0833 1309 1710 0740 0855* 1030 0855* 1030 * = (March to September only)	Yes
BBC Radio Furness	Marton	96·1	837	358	*Mon-Fri:*	0735 0845	Yes
Manx Radio	Snaefell Richmond Hill Jurby	89·0 97.2 103·7	1368	219	*Mon-Fri:* *Sat:* *Sun:*	0700 0800 0900 1310 1740 0700 0800 0900 1200 1700 0800 0859 1300	
BBC Radio Merseyside	Allerton	95·8	1485	202	*Mon-Fri:* *Sat:* *Sun:*	0633 0733 1145 1309 1804 0725 1304 1804 0904 1404 1804	
Radio City	Allerton	96·7	1548	194	*Mon-Fri:*	1315 *Sat-Sun:* 0715	
Swansea Sound	Kilvey Hill	96·4	1170	257	*Mon-Fri:* *Sat-Sun:*	0725 0825 0925 1725 0825 1003	Yes
Red Dragon Radio	Wenallt Christchurch	103·2 97·4	1359 1305	221 230	*Daily:*	0630 0730 0830 1630 1730 H+00 (0600-2400)	Yes
BBC Radio Bristol	Bristol Bath	94.9 104.6	1548	194	*Mon-Fri:* *Sat:* *Sun:*	0605 0632 0659 0733 0759 0833 0859 0805 0905 1105 1302 0905 1105 1305	Yes
GWR FM	Dundry Hill	96.3			*Daily:*	0645	Yes
Brunel Radio	Tor Marton		1260	238	*Daily:*	0645	Yes
Downtown Radio	Limavady Knockbrecken Sheriff's Mountain Brougher Mountain	96·4 102·4 96·6	1026		*Mon-Fri:* *Sat:* *Sun:*	0705 0805 0905 1005 1312 1403 1503 1710 2315 0705 0805 1215 1105 2303 (0003 Mon)	
BBC Radio Guernsey		93·2	1116	269	*Mon-Fri:* *Sat:*	0732* 0832* 1232* 1715 0810 0910 1005 *Sun:* 1005 1205	Yes
BBC Radio Jersey		88·8	1026	292	*Mon-Fri:* *Sat:* *Sun:*	0700 0735 0815 0829 0900 1310 1740 2205 0800 0815 0830 0903 1305 1805 0805 0815 0912 1259	

7.2.17 Local Radio Stations — coastal forecasts

The details and usefulness of forecasts broadcast by local radio stations vary considerably. Some give no more than an indication of the present weather conditions, while others provide more responsible forecasts in conjunction with the local Weather Centre. The timings of weather information from local radio stations most likely to be of interest to yachtsmen in local coastal waters are shown in Table 7(4). Note that many stations are due to change their VHF frequencies shortly.

Many local radio stations in coastal areas participate in a scheme for broadcasting 'Small Craft Warnings' when winds of Force 6 or more are expected within the next 12 hours on the coast or up to five miles offshore. These warnings are handled in much the same way as gale warnings on Radio 4, being broadcast at the first programme junction or at the end of the first news bulletin after receipt. The stations which participate in this scheme are indicated in Table 7(4). In most cases the services operate from Good Friday until 31 October.

Table 7(5) Western Europe — Shipping Forecasts, Coastal Waters Forecasts, Gale Warnings

Notes:
1. All times local or 'clock' times unless otherwise stated.
2. Unless otherwise described, forecasts include gale or near gale warnings, synopsis, 12h Fcst and outlook for further 12h.
3. Forecasts read in English are printed in **bold type** in columns 2 and 3.
4. On receipt and at end of next two silence periods.

Time	Forecast areas	Contents	Stations and Frequencies	Gale Warnings
FRANCE 0655 2005	French Fcst areas 1-24	See note 2; in French	**France Inter Allouis** 164kHz; **Bayonne, Brest & Lille** 1071kHz	
0733 1233	Spanish border to Sables d'Olonne	See note 2; in French	**Bayonne** Ch 24, **Bordeaux-Arcachon** Ch 82, **Royan** Ch 23, **La Rochelle** Ch 21	See note 4 (0700-2200); in French for coastal waters, Spanish border to Sables d'Olonne
0800 1200 1500 2000	Spanish border to Sables d'Olonne	See note 2; in French	**Soulac**, CROSS: Ch 13	See note 4.
0703 GMT 1703 GMT	French Fcst areas 23-24	See note 2; in French	**Bordeaux-Arcachon** 1820kHz (and on request 0700-2200)	See note 4 (0700-2200); in French for areas 23-24. Also 1862kHz every even H+07 (0607-1807) GMT.
0803 GMT 1803 GMT	French Fcst areas 14-24	See note 2; in French	**St Nazaire** 1722kHz	See note 4; in French for areas 14-16. Also 1687 kHz every odd H+07 GMT
0400 1410 0830 1910	Sables d'Olonne to Penmarc'h	See note 2; in French	**Etel**, CROSS: Ch 13	
0733 1233	Sables d'Olonne to Cap de la Hague	See note 2; in French	**St Gilles Croix de Vie** Ch 27, **Nantes St Herblain** Ch 28, **St Nazaire** Ch 23, **Belle Ile** Ch 87, **Pont-l'Abbé** Ch 27, **Brest-Le Conquet** Ch 26, **Ouessant** Ch 82, **Plougasnou** Ch 83, **Paimpol** Ch 84, **St Malo** Ch 02	See note 4; in French for coastal waters, Sables d'Olonne to Cap de la Hague
0733 GMT 1633 GMT 2153 GMT	French Fcst areas 14-22	See note 2; in French	**Brest-Le Conquet**: 1673kHz, **Quimperlé**: 1876kHz, **St Malo**: 2691kHz	See note 4; in French for areas 14-22. 1806 & 2691kHz every even H+03 GMT
Every 3 hours from 0150 GMT	French Fcst areas 14–16	See note 2; **in English** (or French)	**Ouessant Traffic** (Ushant Control Centre, at Corsen): Ch 11 after announcement on Ch 16. General bulletin Ch 11, H+10, H+40	
0900 1900 1600	Penmarc'h to Granville	See note 2; in French	**CROSS**, Ile de Sein Ch 13	
0930 1930 1630	Penmarc'h to Granville	See note 2; in French	**CROSS**, Ile de Batz Ch 13	
0733 1233	Cap de la Hague to Belgian border	See note 2; in French	**Cherbourg** Ch 27, **Port en Bessin** Ch 03, **Le Havre** Ch 26, **Dieppe** Ch 02, **Boulogne** Ch 23, **Calais** Ch 87, **Dunkerque** Ch 61	See note 4; in French for coastal waters Cap de la Hague to Belgian border
0703 GMT 1733 GMT	French Fcst areas 1–14	See note 2; in French	**Boulogne** 1694kHz	See note 4; in French for areas 1-14. 1771kHz every odd H+03 GMT

continued on page 162

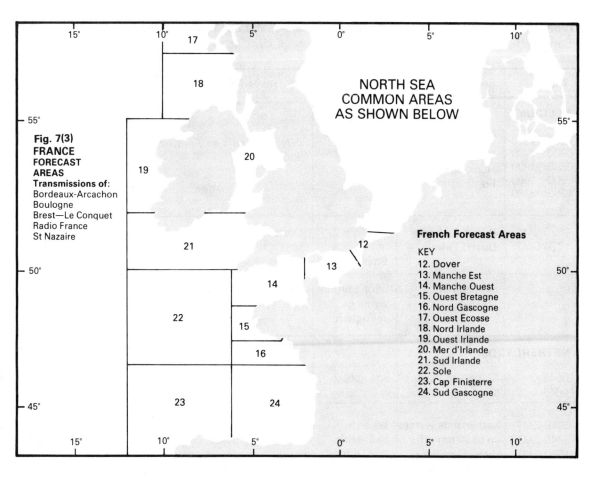

Fig. 7(3)
**FRANCE
FORECAST
AREAS**
Transmissions of:
Bordeaux-Arcachon
Boulogne
Brest—Le Conquet
Radio France
St Nazaire

NORTH SEA
COMMON AREAS
AS SHOWN BELOW

French Forecast Areas
KEY
12. Dover
13. Manche Est
14. Manche Ouest
15. Ouest Bretagne
16. Nord Gascogne
17. Ouest Ecosse
18. Nord Irlande
19. Ouest Irlande
20. Mer d'Irlande
21. Sud Irlande
22. Sole
23. Cap Finisterre
24. Sud Gascogne

Fig. 7(4)

**NORTH SEA COMMON SHIPPING
FORECAST AREAS**
As used for forecasts from:
  Belgium
  Netherlands
  West Germany
  Denmark
  Norway
  United Kingdom

Notes:
(1) Numbers are as for
French Forecast Areas.
(2) Numbers in brackets
with prefix N are as
for German Forecast Areas.

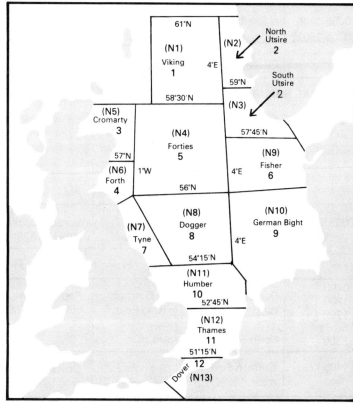

7

Table 7(5) Western Europe — Shipping Forecasts, Coastal Waters Forecasts, Gale Warnings
(Continued. For notes see page 160. All times local or 'clock' times unless otherwise stated.)

Time	Forecast areas	Contents	Stations and Frequencies	Gale Warnings
BELGIUM				
0600 1300 0700 1700 0800 1800 0900 1900 1200 2300	British Fcst areas Dover, Thames, Humber, Wight, Portland	Weather reports; in Dutch	*Belgische Radio en Televisie* 926kHz	
0820 GMT 1720 GMT	**British Fcst areas Dover, Thames**	See note 2; in Dutch and **English**	*Oostende* 2761kHz and VHF Ch 27	See note 4; in Dutch and **English**
(See col. 5)	**Schelde in English**	Strong breeze warnings in **English**	*Antwerpen* Ch 24	Warnings on receipt and every H+03, H+48; in **English**
NETHERLANDS				
0545 0645	Netherlands coastal waters	See note 2; in Dutch	*Hilversum 2* 747 kHz	Every H+00 on 1008 kHz
0340 GMT 0940 GMT 1540 GMT 2140 GMT	**Netherlands waters up to 30 nm off-shore, IJsselmeer and North Sea**	see note 2; **in English** and Dutch	*Scheveningen* 1862 kHz (from Nes) and 1890 kHz. 2824kHz at 0340 GMT only	1862 1890 1939 2600 kHz and VHF on receipt. 1862 1890 kHz after next silence period; in Dutch and **English**
0005 1305 0705 1905	Netherlands waters up to 30 nm off-shore and IJsselmeer	Strong breeze warnings, synopsis, Fcst (in Dutch)	*Scheveningen* VHF Ch 23 25 27 28 83 87 depending on area (see 6.3.16)	Strong breeze warnings on receipt and every H+05 on VHF; in Dutch
FEDERAL REPUBLIC OF GERMANY				
0910 GMT 2110 GMT	German Fcst areas N1-N3, N8-N12	See note 2; in German	*Norddeich* 2614kHz	In English for N10. In German for N1-N4, N8-N12. On receipt, after next silence period, and every 4h from 0133 GMT
0005 (972kHz only) 0930	Southern North Sea and West Baltic	See note 2; in German	*Norddeutscher Rundfunk:* 702kHz, 828kHz, 972kHz	
	Note: Wind Fcst for Areas N9 and N10 (in German) in weather reports after news			
0700 ⎫ 1300 ⎬ 1900 ⎭	Deutsche Bucht, West Baltic	In German, wind Fcst	*Radio Bremen* 936kHz and VHF 89.3, 93.8MHz	
2300	North Sea, Baltic	see note 2;		
0105 1230 0640	German Fcst areas N9–N12	See note 2; in German	*Deutschlandfunk* 1269kHz (and 1539kHz at 0105 only)	Every H+00 (except 2100) in German

Chapter 8

Safety

Contents

Safety — introduction

The following subjects are described in detail in Chapter 8 of *The Macmillan & Silk Cut Yachtsman's Handbook*:

> *Safety equipment — legal requirements and recommended outfits; radar reflectors; bilge pumps; guardrails; fire prevention and fire fighting; lifejackets; safety harnesses; man overboard gear and drill; liferafts; distress signals; SAR organisation; response to distress calls; abandoning ship; liferafts; helicopter rescues; first aid afloat.*

Here in the Almanac is given basic information about safety equipment, distress signals and SAR operations. For further information on these subjects, together with those listed above, reference should be made to Chapter 8 of *The Macmillan & Silk Cut Yachtsman's Handbook*.

8

8.1   SAFETY EQUIPMENT

8.1.1   Safety equipment — general
The skipper is responsible for the safety of the boat and all on board. He must ensure that:
(1) The boat is suitable in design and in construction for her intended purpose.
(2) The boat is maintained in good condition.
(3) The crew is competent and sufficiently strong.
(4) The necessary safety and emergency equipment is carried, is in good condition, and the crew know how to use it.

Individual crew members are responsible for their personal gear. Non-slip shoes or boots are essential. So is foul-weather clothing with close fastenings at neck, wrists and ankles. At least two changes of sailing clothing should be carried, including warm sweaters and towelling strips as neck scarves. Other personal items include a sailor's knife and spike on a lanyard, a waterproof torch, and a supply of anti-seasick pills. Lifejackets and safety harnesses are usually supplied on board, but if individuals bring their own the skipper should make certain they are up to standard.

8.1.2   Safety equipment — legal requirements
Yachts more than 45ft (13.7m) in length are required to carry safety equipment as in the *Merchant Shipping (Life Saving Appliances)* and *Merchant Shipping (Fire Appliances) Rules* (HMSO).

All yachts must carry navigation lights and sound signals which comply with the *International Regulations for Preventing Collisions at Sea*.

Racing yachts are required to carry the safety equipment specified for the class/event concerned.

8.1.3   Safety equipment — recommendations for sea-going yachts 18–45ft (5.5–13.7m) overall length
Full details of recommended safety equipment are given in *The Macmillan & Silk Cut Yachtsman's Handbook*. Below are brief reminders of the minimum equipment which should be carried for (a) coastal and (b) offshore cruising.

But prevention is better than cure, and simple precautions can eliminate accidents. Be particularly careful with bottled gas and petrol. Fit a gas detector. Turn off the gas at the bottle after use. If gas or petrol is smelt — no naked lights, and do not run electrical equipment. Test systems regularly. Insist that crew wear lifejackets and harnesses when necessary, and that they do clip on. Make sure a good look-out is maintained at all times. Listen to every forecast. Double-check all navigational calculations. Take nothing for granted.

Fig. 8(1)   *Putting on a lifejacket — first read the instructions. Hold the jacket up in front of you, put your head through the hole, and secure the waistband at the side or front as appropriate.*

Safety equipment list

	(a) Coastal	(b) Offshore
Safety		
Lifejackets, BS3595, per person	1	1
Harnesses, BS4224, per person	1	1
Navigation		
Charts, almanac, pilot	Yes	Yes
Compass with deviation card	1	1
Hand bearing compass	1	1
Chart table instruments	Yes	Yes
Watch/clock	1	2
Echo sounder	1	1
Leadline	1	1
Radio direction finding set	1	1
Radio receiver (forecasts)	1	1
Barometer	1	1
Navigation lights	Yes	Yes
Radar reflector	1	1
Foghorn	1	1
Powerful waterproof torch	1	1
Anchor with warp or chain	2	2
Towline	1	1
Man overboard		
Lifebuoy, with drogue and light	2	2
Buoyant heaving line	1	1
Dan buoy	–	1
Rope (or boarding) ladder	1	1

Fig. 8(2) *Lifebuoy with dan buoy and flag, automatic light, whistle, dye marker, and drogue.*

	(a) Coastal	(b) Offshore
Fire		
Fire extinguishers	2	3
Fire blanket	1	1
Sinking		
Bilge pumps	2	2
Buckets with lanyards	2	2
Leak stopping gear	Yes	Yes
Distress signals		
Hand flares, red	2	4
Hand flares, white (warning)	4	4
Red parachute rockets	2	4
Hand smoke signals	2	–
Buoyant orange smoke signals	–	2
Emergency radio transmitter	–	1
Abandon ship		
Liferaft for whole crew	1	1
	or	
Dinghy with buoyancy, or inflated inflatable	1	–
Panic bag, extra water etc	–	1

	(a) Coastal	(b) Offshore
Miscellaneous		
First aid kit	1	1
Engine tool kit	1	1
Name/number prominently displayed	Yes	Yes
Storm canvas	Yes	Yes
Emergency steering arrangements	Yes	Yes

8.1.4   Distress signals

A distress signal must only be made if the yacht or a person is in serious and immediate danger, and help is urgently required.

For a lesser emergency, an urgency signal (PAN PAN) as described in 6.3.10 may be appropriate. If help is needed, but the boat is not in immediate danger, the proper signal is 'V' (Victor) International Code, meaning 'I require assistance'. This can be sent as a flag signal (a white flag with a red St Andrew's cross), or by light or sound in Morse code ($\cdots-$). Other signals of an emergency nature in the International Code are given in 6.1.5.

If medical help is required, the proper signal is 'W' (Whiskey) International Code, meaning 'I require medical assistance'.

A full list of the recognised distress signals is given in Annex IV of the *International Regulations for Preventing Collisions at Sea*, and is reproduced in Chapter 2 (2.1.6). The following are those most appropriate for yachts and small craft, together with notes on their use.

(1) **Continuous sounding with any fog signalling apparatus.** In order to avoid confusion, this is best done by a succession of letters SOS in Morse ($\cdots---\cdots$).

(2) **A signal made by radiotelegraphy or by any other signalling method consisting of the group** $\cdots---\cdots$ (SOS) in the Morse Code. For a yacht the most likely methods are by sound signal as in (1) above, or by flashing light.

(3) **A signal sent by radiotelephony consisting of the spoken word MAYDAY.** This procedure is fully described in 6.3.10, but for ease of reference the basic rules are repeated briefly below.

Check the battery switch is ON. Switch the set ON, and select HIGH power. Tune to VHF Ch 16 (or 2182 kHz for MF). If an alarm signal generator is fitted, operate it for at least 30 seconds. Press the 'transmit' button, and say slowly and distinctly:

'MAYDAY MAYDAY MAYDAY — THIS IS (name of boat spoken three times) — MAYDAY — (name of boat spoken once) — MY POSITION IS (latitude and longitude, or true bearing and distance from a known object) — (nature of distress) — (aid required) — (number of persons on board) — (any other important information) — OVER'

8

Release the transmit button, and listen. If no acknowledgment is heard, repeat the message. If transmitting on 2182 kHz, repeat the call during the silence periods commencing each hour and half-hour.

The Urgency Signal (PAN PAN, spoken three times) indicates a lesser emergency than a distress signal, and should be used when there is a very urgent message concerning the safety of a ship or person. For further detail see 6.3.10.

Portable emergency radiotelephones, on 2182 kHz or Ch 16, can be used from the yacht or the liferaft. Also available are Personal Locator Beacons (PLBs) and Emergency Position Indicating Radio Beacons (EPIRBs) operating on 121.5 and 243 MHz. These are primarily for aeronautical purposes and since maritime SAR authorities do not keep watch on these frequencies they are of limited use in coastal waters. More useful is an EPIRB transmitting on 406 MHz, the dedicated COSPAS/SARSAT satellite frequency with full global coverage. Like other radio transmitters, all such equipment must be licensed.

(4) **The International Code signal of distress 'NC'.** This can be made by flag hoist, N being a blue and white chequered flag and C one which is horizontally striped blue, white, red, white, blue.

(5) **A signal consisting of a square flag having above or below it a ball or anything resembling a ball.** This is not too difficult to contrive from any square flag, and a round fender or anchor ball.

(6) **A rocket parachute flare or a hand flare showing a red light.** A red flare is the most effective distress signal at night. Flares serve two purposes — first to raise the alarm, and then to pinpoint the boat's position. Within about three miles from land a hand flare will do both. At greater distances a red parachute rocket (which projects a suspended flare to a height of more than 1000ft, or 300m, and which burns for more than 40 seconds) is needed to raise the alarm, but hand flares are useful to indicate the boat's position. See further comments under (7) below.

(7) **A smoke signal giving off orange-coloured smoke.** By day orange smoke signals (hand held for short distances, or the larger buoyant type for greater ranges) are more effective than flares, although the smoke disperses quickly in a strong wind.

White flares are not distress signals, but are used to indicate the presence of a boat — to another vessel on a collision course for example. An outfit of four is suggested for boats which make night passages. Shield your eyes when using them, to protect night vision.

Pyrotechnics must be stowed where they are accessible, but protected from damp. In good storage conditions they should have a life of three years. Examine them regularly, and replace them by the expiry date. All the crew should know where the flares are stowed, and how to use them. Hold hand flares firmly downwind. Rockets turn into the wind: fire them vertically in normal conditions, or aimed about 15° downwind in strong winds. Do not aim them into the wind, or they will not gain altitude. If there is low cloud, fire rockets at 45° downwind, so that the flare burns under the cloud.

(8) **Slowly and repeatedly raising and lowering arms outstretched to each side.** The arms should be raised and lowered together, above and below the horizontal.

Any of the above distress signals must only be made with the authority of the skipper, and only if the boat or a person is in serious and immediate danger, and help is urgently required: or on behalf of another vessel in distress, which for some reason is unable to make a distress signal. If subsequently the danger is overcome, the distress call must be cancelled by whatever means are available.

8.2   SEARCH AND RESCUE (SAR)

8.2.1   SAR — general

Various authorities are involved in SAR operations. Around the United Kingdom these are: Coast Radio Stations (as shown in 6.3.15, monitoring distress frequencies and controlling communications); HM Coastguard (responsible for initiating and co-ordinating all civil maritime SAR — see below); the RNLI (which supplies and mans the lifeboats — see below); the Royal Navy (which assists with ships and aircraft, including helicopters); the Royal Air Force (operating through Rescue Co-ordination Centres at Edinburgh and Plymouth); and Air Traffic Control Centres. Similar organisations to the above exist in other countries in Western Europe — see 10.12.7 (Republic of Ireland), 10.14.7 (France), 10.19.7 (Belgium, Netherlands), 10.20.7 (West Germany).

8.2.2   HM Coastguard

HM Coastguard initiates and co-ordinates SAR around the United Kingdom and over a large part of the eastern Atlantic. The area is divided into six Maritime Search and Rescue Regions (SRRs), supervised by Maritime Rescue Co-ordination Centres (MRCCs) at Falmouth, Dover, Great Yarmouth, Aberdeen, the Clyde and Swansea. It also includes 'Shannon' area which is the responsibility of the Republic of Ireland. Each SRR is divided into Districts, each with a Maritime Rescue Sub-Centre (MRSC). Their boundaries are shown in the maps at the start of Areas 1–11 in Chapter 10. The telephone number of the nearest MRCC or MRSC (or the equivalent in other countries) is shown for each harbour.

Within each of the 21 districts thus formed there is an organisation of Auxiliary Coastguard watch and rescue stations, grouped within Sectors under the management of Regular Coastguard Officers.

All MRCCs and MRSCs keep watch on VHF Ch 16, and are connected to telex and telephone. A visual look-out is maintained when necessary. The Channel Navigation Information Service (CNIS) keeps a constant radar watch on the Dover Strait, with broadcast of navigational and traffic information on Ch 10 at 10 and 40 minutes past each hour. There are about 560 Regular Coastguard Officers, backed up by more than 4500 Auxiliaries on call for emergencies. HM Coastguard also have a cliff and beach rescue role.

A VHF emergency direction finding service, controlled by HM Coastguard, is operated from various stations round Britain. See 4.3.2.

The radio telephony callsign of an MRCC or MRSC is the geographical name, followed by 'Coastguard' — for example 'SOLENT COAST-GUARD'.

HM Coastguard operates a Local Warning Service relating to hazards which may affect craft in inshore waters, but outside Port and Harbour Authority limits. These local warnings are broad-cast on Ch 67, after an announcement on Ch 16. There is no numerical sequence, and no specific broadcast schedule; any repetition of the broadcast is at the discretion of the originating Coastguard station. Strong wind warnings are broadcast on re-ceipt, and forecasts for local sea areas about every four hours or on request. See also Chapter 7 para 7.2.16.

Yacht and Boat Safety Scheme
This free scheme provides useful information for the Coastguard to mount a successful SAR opera-tion. Owners can obtain a Form CG66 from their local Coastguard station, harbour master or marina. This should be completed with details of the boat and her equipment, and then posted to the local Coastguard Rescue Centre. There is a tear-off section which can be given to a friend or relative so that they know the Coastguard station to contact if they are concerned for the boat's safety.

It is not the function of HM Coastguard to main-tain watch for boats on passage, but they will record information by phone before departure or from intermediate ports, or while on passage by visual signals or VHF Ch 67 (the Small Craft Safety Channel). When using Ch 67 for safety messages it is requested that yachts give the name of the Coastguard Rescue Centre holding the boat's Safety Scheme card. In these circumstances the Coastguard must be told of any change to the planned movements of the boat, and it is important that they are informed of the boat's safe arrival at her ultimate destination.

Raising the alarm
If an accident afloat is seen from shore, dial 999 and ask for the Coastguard. You will be asked to report on the incident, and possibly to stay near the telephone for further communications.

If at sea you receive a distress signal and you are in a position to give assistance, you are obliged to do so with all speed, unless or until you are spe-cifically released.

When alerted, the Coastguard summons the most appropriate help. They might direct a Coast-guard Shore Boat or an Auxiliary (Afloat), if in the vicinity; they might request the launch of a RNLI lifeboat or inflatable lifeboat; the Royal Navy or the Royal Air Force might be asked for a SAR helicopter; other Coastguard stations might be contacted; or shipping might be alerted through nearby Coast Radio Stations.

8.2.3   Royal National Lifeboat Institution (RNLI)
The RNLI, which is supported entirely by volun-tary contributions, has about 200 stations around the United Kingdom, the Republic of Ireland, the Isle of Man, and the Channel Islands. From them are deployed about 130 lifeboats over 10m in length and a similar number of smaller lifeboats. Some of the latter only operate in summer.

When launched on service lifeboats over 10m keep watch on 2182 kHz and Ch 16. They can also use other frequencies (including VHF Ch 0, which is reserved exclusively for SAR) to contact HM Coastguard or Coast Radio Stations. Smaller lifeboats are fitted with VHF. All lifeboats show a quick-flashing blue light.

Similar organisations to the RNLI exist in other countries in Western Europe. The positions of lifeboat stations are indicated on the maps at the start of each Area in Chapter 10.

Yachtsmen can help support the RNLI by joining Shoreline. Details from RNLI, West Quay Road, Poole, Dorset BH15 1HZ.

8.2.4   SAR — communications
For details of signals between shore and ships in distress, signals used by SAR aircraft, and directing signals used by aircraft — see 6.2.4, 6.2.5 and 6.2.6 respectively.

8.2.5   Helicopter rescue
SAR helicopters in the UK are based at Chivenor, Culdrose, Lee-on-Solent, Manston, Woodbridge, Coltishall, Leconfield, Boulmer, Leuchars,

8

Lossiemouth, Sumburgh, Stornoway, Prestwick, Valley and Brawdy.

Wessex helicopters can carry up to ten survivors, but do not usually operate at night, or when the wind exceeds 45 knots. Sea King helicopters can operate to a distance of 300 miles, and at night, and can rescue up to 18 survivors. All can communicate with lifeboats etc on VHF, and some on MF.

When the helicopter is sighted by a boat in distress, a flare, smoke signal, dye marker or a well trained Aldis lamp will assist recognition (very important if there are other vessels in the vicinity). Dodgers with the boat's name or sail number are useful aids to identification.

While hovering the pilot has limited vision beneath him, and relies on instructions from the winch operator. Survivors from a yacht with a mast must be picked up from a dinghy or liferaft streamed at least 100ft (30m) away. It is helpful if the drift of the yacht can be reduced by a sea anchor. In a small yacht with no dinghy, survivors (wearing lifejackets) may have to be picked up from the water, at the end of a long warp. Sails should be lowered.

If a crewman descends from the helicopter, he will take charge. Obey his instructions quickly. Never secure the winch wire to the yacht, and beware that it may carry a lethal static charge if it is not dipped (earthed) in the sea before handling.

Survivors may be lifted by double lift in a strop, accompanied by the crewman in a canvas seat. Or it may be necessary, with no crewman, for a survivor to position himself in the strop. Put your head and shoulders through the strop so that the padded part is in the small of the back and the toggle is in front of the face. Pull the toggle down, as close to the chest as possible. When ready, give a thumbs up sign with an extended arm, and place both arms close down by the side of the body (resist the temptation to hang onto the strop). On reaching the helicopter, do exactly as instructed by the crew.

In some circumstances a 'Hi-line' may be used. This is a rope tail, attached to the winch wire by a weak link, and weighted at its lower end. When it is lowered to the yacht do not make it fast, but coil it

down carefully. The helicopter pays out the winch wire and descends, while the yacht takes in the slack (keeping it outboard and clear of all obstructions) until the winch hook and strop are on board. When ready to lift, the helicopter ascends and takes in the wire. Pay out the tail, and cast it off well clear of the yacht. But if a further lift is to be made the tail should be retained on board (not made fast) to facilitate recovery of the strop for the next lift.

Injured persons can be lifted, strapped into a special stretcher carried in the helicopter.

When alighting from a helicopter, beware of the tail rotor.

8.2.6   Abandon ship

Although preparations must be made, do not abandon a yacht until she is doomed. She is a better target for rescue craft than a liferaft, and while she is still afloat it is possible to use her resources (such as RT, for distress calls) and to select what extra equipment is put in the liferaft or lashed into the dinghy (which should be taken too, if possible).

Before entering the raft, and cutting it adrift:
(1) Send a distress message (Mayday call), saying that yacht is being abandoned, and position.
(2) Dress warmly with sweaters etc under oilskins, and lifejackets on top. Take extra clothes.
(3) Fill any available containers with tops about $\frac{3}{4}$ full with fresh water, so that they will float.
(4) Collect additional food — tins and tin opener.
(5) Collect navigational gear, torch, extra flares, bucket, length of line, first aid kit, knife etc.

Once in the liferaft, plan for the worst. If there has not been time to collect items listed above, collect whatever flotsam is available.
(1) Keep the inside of the raft as dry as possible. Huddle together for warmth. Close the opening as necessary, but keep a good lookout for shipping.
(2) Stream the drogue if necessary for stability, or if it is required to stay near the position.
(3) Ration fresh water to $\frac{3}{4}$ pint ($\frac{1}{2}$ litre) per person per day. Do not drink sea water or urine. Collect rain water.
(4) Use flares sparingly, on the skipper's orders.
(5) Issue and commence anti-seasick pills.

Chapter 9

Tides

Contents

9

Tides — introduction

The following subjects are described in detail in Chapter 9 of *The Macmillan & Silk Cut Yachtsman's Handbook*:

The theory of tides; definitions of terms; calculations of times and heights of HW and LW; calculations of depths of water at specific times; calculations of times at which tide reaches certain heights; Twelfths Rule; tidal calculations by pocket calculator; French tidal coefficients; co-tidal and co-range charts; harmonic constituents; establishment of a port; tidal stream diamonds; tidal stream information on charts and in Sailing Directions ... plus general information on the sea — how waves are formed; freak waves; wind against tide; bars; overfalls and tide races; refraction of waves; reflected waves; ocean currents etc.

Here in the Almanac is given sufficient information for the use of the tidal data provided in Chapter 10, but for fuller details of matters concerning tides and the sea reference should be made to Chapter 9 of *The Macmillan & Silk Cut Yachtsman's Handbook*.

9.1   GENERAL

9.1.1   Explanation

This chapter explains how to use the tidal information contained in Chapter 10, where are given the daily times and heights of High Water (HW) and Low Water (LW) for Standard Ports, together with time and height differences for many other places. Tidal predictions are for average meteorological conditions. In abnormal weather the times and heights of HW and LW may vary considerably.

9.1.2   Times

The times tabulated for the Standard Ports in Chapter 10 — whether inside or outside the tinted areas — are in the Zone Time shown at the top left hand corner of each page. Thus all the times printed for Standard Ports in the UK, Channel Islands and Ireland are in Universal Time (UT) — which for practical purposes corresponds to GMT. All the times printed for Standard Ports in France, Netherlands and the Federal Republic of Germany are in Zone −0100 time. To convert these Zone −0100 times to UT (GMT), you must subtract one hour.

The tinted areas indicate when clock (or local) time is the same as Zone Time. Outside the tinted areas it is necessary to add one hour to the printed times to obtain local Summer Time — often referred to as Daylight Saving Time (DST) on the Continent.

Under each Secondary Port listed in Chapter 10 are its Time Zone, its Standard Port and the data required to calculate time differences — which when applied to the printed times of HW and LW at the Standard Port give the times of HW and LW at the Secondary Port in the Zone Time of that Port. If Summer Time is required, then one hour is added after the Secondary Port time difference has been applied but not before.

9.1.3   Predicted heights

Predicted heights are given in metres and tenths of metres above Chart Datum (see 9.2.1). Care must be taken when using charts which show depths in fathoms/feet. See Conversion Paragraph 9(8).

9.2   DEFINITIONS

Certain definitions are given below and in Fig. 9(1). For further details see Chapter 9 of *The Macmillan & Silk Cut Yachtsman's Handbook*.

9.2.1   Chart datum

Chart datum (CD) is the reference level above which heights of tide are predicted, and below which charted depths are measured. Hence the actual depth of water is the charted depth (at that place) plus the height of tide (at that time).

Tidal predictions for British ports use as their datum Lowest Astronomical Tide (LAT), which is the lowest sea level predicted under average meteorological conditions. All Admiralty charts of the British Isles use LAT as chart datum, but others, particularly fathom charts — do not. Where tidal predications and charted depths are not referenced to the same datum (e.g. LAT), errors resulting in an over estimation of depth by as much as 0·5m can occur.

9.2.2   Charted depth

Charted depth is the distance of the sea bed below chart datum, and is shown in metres and tenths of metres on metric charts, or in fathoms and/or feet on older charts. Make sure which units are used.

9.2.3   Drying height

Drying height is the height above chart datum of the top of any feature occasionally covered by water. The figures are underlined on the chart — in metres and tenths of metres on metric charts, and in feet on older charts. The depth is the height of tide (at the time) minus the drying height. If the result is negative, then that place is above sea level.

9.2.4   Duration

Duration is the time between LW and the next HW, normally slightly more than six hours, and can be used to calculate the time of LW when only the time of HW is known.

9.2.5   Height of tide

The height of the tide is the vertical distance of sea level above (or very occasionally below) chart datum, as defined in 9.2.1.

9.2.6   Interval

The interval is the period of time between a given time and HW, expressed in hours and minutes before (−) or after (+) High Water.

9.2.7   Mean Level

Mean Level (ML) is the average of the heights of Mean High Water Springs (MHWS), Mean High Water Neaps (MHWN), Mean Low Water Springs (MLWS) and Mean Low Water Neaps (MLWN).

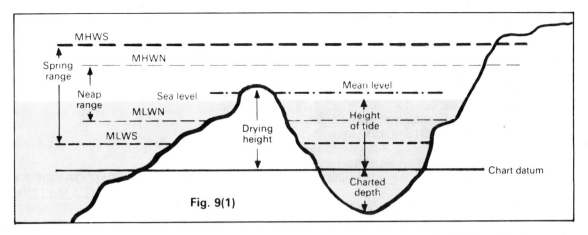

Fig. 9(1)

9.2.8   Range

The range of a tide is the difference between the heights of successive High and Low Waters. Spring range is MHWS–MLWS. Neap range is MHWN–MLWN.

9.3   CALCULATIONS OF TIMES AND HEIGHTS OF HIGH AND LOW WATER

9.3.1   Standard Ports

The times and heights of HW and LW are tabulated for each Standard Port in Chapter 10. The conversion of Zone −0100 time to UT (GMT) and of either Zone UT (GMT) or Zone 0100 time to Local Summer or Daylight Saving Time (DST) is dealt with in 9.1.2. See also 9.7 for the effect of wind and barometric pressure.

9.3.2   Secondary Ports — times of HW and LW

Each Secondary Port listed in Chapter 10 has a data block for the calculation of times of HW and LW as explained in 9.1.2. The following example is for St Peter Port:

TIDES

−0450 Dover; ML 5·0; Duration 0500; Zone 0 (GMT)

Standard Port ST HELIER

Times				Height (metres)			
HW		LW		MHWS	MHWN	MLWN	MLWS
0300	0900	0200	0900	11·1	8·1	4·1	1·3
1500	2100	1400	2100				
Differences ST PETER PORT							
0000	+0012	−0008	+0002	−2·1	−1·4	−0·6	−0·3

Thus −0450 Dover indicates that, on average, HW St Peter Port occurs 4 hours and 50 minutes before HW Dover (the times of HW Dover, in GMT, can be found on the bookmark). Duration 0500 indicates that LW St Peter Port occurs 5 hours before its HW. This is a very rough and ready method.

A more accurate and reliable method uses the Standard Port and Time Differences. Thus when HW at St Helier occurs at 0900 and 2100, the difference is +0012, and HW at St Peter Port occurs at 0912 and 2112. When HW at St Helier occurs at 0300 and 1500, the difference is 0000, and HW St Peter Port occurs also at 0300 and 1500. If, as is likely, HW St Helier occurs at some other time, then the Difference for St Peter Port must be found by interpolation – by eye, by calculator or, when calculating a number of tides, by the graphical method in 9.3.4. Thus when HW St Helier occurs at 1030, the Difference is +0009, and HW St Peter Port occurs at 1039. The same method is used for calculating the times of LW.

The times thus obtained are in the Zone Time indicated in the Secondary Port data block. Care must be taken when the Zone Time at the Secondary Port differs from that at the Standard Port. See 9.1.2 for this and for converting time from one Zone to another and for changing to Summer Time.

These calculations are best done by completing boxes 1, 2, 5, 6, 9 and 10 of the tidal prediction form shown in Fig. 9 (5).

9.3.3   Secondary Ports — heights of HW and LW

The Secondary Port data block also contains height Differences which are applied to the heights of HW and LW at the Standard Port. Thus when the height of HW at St Helier is 11·1m (MHWS), the Difference is −2·1m, and the height of HW at St Peter Port is 9·0m (MHWS). When the height of HW at St Helier is 8·1m (MHWN), the Difference is −1·4m, and the height of HW at St Peter Port is 6·7m (MHWN). If, as is likely, the height of tide at the Standard Port does not exactly equal the Mean Spring or Neap level, then the height Difference is found by interpolation as in 9.3.2. Thus if the height of HW at St Helier is 9·2m, the Difference is −1·7m, and the height of HW at St Peter Port is 7·5m. These calculations are best done by completing boxes 3, 4, 7, 8, 11 and 12 of Fig 9(5).

9

9.3.4 Graphical method for interpolating time and height differences

Any suitable squared paper can be used, see Fig. 9(2), the scales being chosen as required. Using the data for St Peter Port in 9.3.2 above, find the time and height differences for HW St Peter Port if HW St Helier is at 1126, height 8·9m.

Select a scale for the time at St Helier on right-hand side covering 0900 and 1500 when the relevant time differences for St Peter Port are known. At the top, the scale for time differences must cover 0000 and +0012, the two which are shown for times 0900 and 1500.

Plot point A, the time difference (+0012) for HW St Helier at 0900; and point B, the time difference (0000) for HW St Helier at 1500. Join AB. Enter the graph on the right at time 1126 (HW St Helier) and mark C where that time meets AB. From C proceed vertically to the time difference scale at the top, +0007. So that morning HW St Peter Port is 7 minutes after HW St Helier, i.e. 1133.

In the bottom of the diagram, select scales which cover the height of HW at St Helier vertically (i.e. 8·1 to 11·1m and the relevant height differences (−1·4 to −2·1m) horizontally. Plot point D, the height difference (−1·4m) at neaps when the height of HW St Helier is 8·1m; and E, the height

difference −2·1m) at springs when the height of HW St Helier is 11·1m. Join DE. Enter the graph at 8·9m (the height of HW St Helier that morning) and mark F where that height meets DE. From F follow the vertical line to the scale of height differences, −1·6m. So that morning the height of HW St Peter Port is 7·3m.

9.4 CALCULATING HEIGHT OF TIDE AT TIMES BETWEEN HIGH AND LOW WATER

9.4.1 Standard Ports

Intermediate times and heights are best predicted from the Mean Spring and Neap Curves for Standard Ports in Chapter 10. Examples below are for Leith, on a day when the predictions are:

	UT (GMT)	Ht(m)
22	0202	5·3
	0752	1·0
	1417	5·4
TU	2025	0·5

Example: Find the height at Leith at 1200.
(1) On the Leith tidal diagram plot the heights of HW and LW each side of the required time, and join them by a sloping line, Fig. 9(3).
(2) Enter the HW time and other times as necessary in the boxes below the curves.
(3) From the required time, proceed vertically to the curves. The Spring curve is a solid line, and the Neap curve (where it differs) is pecked. Interpolate between the curves by comparing the actual range −4·4m in this example − with the Mean Ranges printed beside the curves. Never extrapolate. Here the Spring curve applies.
(4) Proceed horizontally to the sloping line plotted in (1), and thence vertically to the height scale, to give 4·2m.

Example: To find the time at which the afternoon height of tide falls to 3·7m.
(1) On the Leith tidal diagram, plot the heights of HW and LW each side of the required event, and join them by a sloping line, Fig. 9(4).
(2) Enter the HW time and others to cover the required event, in the boxes below.
(3) From the required height, proceed vertically to the sloping line and thence horizontally to the curves. Interpolate between them as in the previous example and do not extrapolate. Here the actual range is 4·9m, and the Spring curve applies.
(4) Proceed vertically to the time scale, and read off the time required, 1637.

Fig. 9(2)

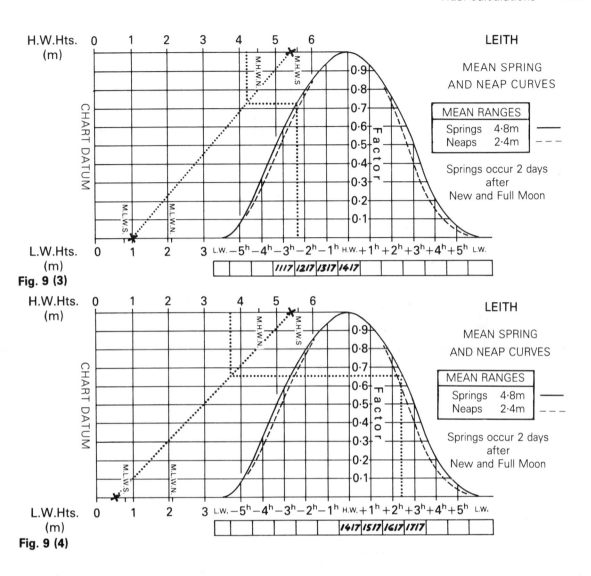

Fig. 9 (3)

Fig. 9 (4)

9.4.2   Secondary Ports

On coasts where there is little change of shape between tidal curves for adjacent Standard Ports, and where the duration of rise or fall at the Secondary Port is like that of the appropriate Standard Port (where the time differences for HW and LW are nearly the same), intermediate times and heights may be predicted from the tidal curves for the Standard Port in a similar manner to 9.4.1 above. The curves are entered with the times and heights of HW and LW at the Secondary Port, calculated as in 9.3.2 and 9.3.3.

Interpolation between the curves can be made by eye, using the range at the Standard Port as argument. Do not extrapolate — use the spring curve for spring ranges or greater, and the neap curve for neap ranges or less. With a large change in duration between springs and neaps the results may have a slight error, greater near LW.

Special curves for places between Swanage and Selsey (where the tide is very complex) are given in 10.2.8.

9.4.3   The use of factors

Tidal curves show the factor of the range attained at times before and after HW. By definition a factor of $1 = HW$, and $0 = LW$. So the factor represents the proportion of the range (for the day in question) by which the height of tide is above the height of LW (that day) at the interval (time) concerned.

Range × factor = Rise above LW

and   Factor = Rise above LW ÷ range

In determining or using the factor it may be necessary to interpolate between the spring and neap curves as described in 9.4.2.

The procedure is shown on the following page, using the tidal prediction form as in Fig. 9(5). Table 9(1) may be used for factor and range calculations.

Fig. 9(5) *Tidal prediction form*   Time or height required ....

	TIME		HEIGHT	
	HW	LW	HW	LW
Standard Port	1	2	3	4
Differences	5	6	7	8
Secondary Port	9	10	11	12

Duration (or time from HW to LW)	13	9–10 or 10–9	Range Stand. Port	14	3 – 4
			Range Secdy. Port	15	11 – 12

* Springs/Neaps/Interpolate

Start: height at given time ↓

9

17 – 16

Time reqd.	16	17 + 18
Time of HW	17	9
Interval	18	

Date ....

Factor	19

Time zone ....

19 x 15

12

20 + 21

Rise above LW	20	22 – 21
Height of LW	21	12
Height reqd.	22	

Start: time for given height ↑

* Delete as necessary

Procedure for diagram in Fig. 9(5). First complete the headings on the left. Then enter in boxes indicated:

- 1 to 4   Predictions for Standard Port
- 5 to 8   Differences for Secondary Port (interpolated if necessary). Not required for Standard Port.
- 9   Sum of 1 and 5 (for Standard Port enter 1)
- 10   Sum of 2 and 6 (for Standard Port enter 2)
- 11   Sum of 3 and 7 (for Standard Port enter 3)
- 12   Sum of 4 and 8 (for Standard Port enter 4)
- 13   Duration (difference of 9 and 10)
- 14   Range at Standard Port (difference of 3 and 4)
- 15   Range at Secondary Port (difference of 11 and 12)

TO FIND HEIGHT AT GIVEN TIME
- 16   Required time
- 17   HW time from 9
- 18   Interval (difference of 16 and 17)
- 19   Factor, from appropriate tidal curve, entered with Interval (18)
- 20   Rise above LW = Factor (19) × Range (15), or for Standard Port use Range (14)
- 21   Height of LW from 12
- 22   Sum of Rise above LW (20) and Height of LW (21)

TO FIND TIME FOR A GIVEN HEIGHT
(start at bottom of diagram)
- 22   Required height
- 21   LW Height from 12
- 20   Rise = Height (22) − LW Height (21)
- 19   Factor = Rise (20) ÷ Range (15). (For Standard Port use 14)
- 18   Interval, from interpolation of appropriate tidal curve, entered with Factor (19)
- 17   HW time from 9
- 16   Interval (18) applied to HW time (17)

TABLE 9(1)

MULTIPLICATION TABLE for use with Fig. 9(5)

RANGE (columns) × FACTOR (rows). Each cell is the product factor × range.

FACTOR	1.00	12.4	12.0	11.6	11.2	10.8	10.4	10.0	9.6	9.2	8.8	8.4	8.0	7.6	7.2	6.8	6.4	6.0	5.6	5.2	4.8	4.4	4.0	3.6	3.2	2.8	2.4	2.0	1.6	1.2	1.00	FACTOR
.98	.98	12.2	11.8	11.4	11.0	10.6	10.2	9.8	9.4	9.0	8.6	8.2	7.8	7.4	7.1	6.7	6.3	5.9	5.5	5.1	4.7	4.3	3.9	3.5	3.1	2.7	2.4	2.0	1.6	1.2	.98	.98
.96	.96	11.9	11.5	11.1	10.8	10.4	10.0	9.6	9.2	8.8	8.4	8.1	7.7	7.3	6.9	6.5	6.1	5.8	5.4	5.0	4.6	4.2	3.8	3.5	3.1	2.7	2.3	1.9	1.5	1.2	.96	.96
.94	.94	11.7	11.3	10.9	10.5	10.2	9.8	9.4	9.0	8.6	8.3	7.9	7.5	7.1	6.8	6.4	6.0	5.6	5.3	4.9	4.5	4.1	3.8	3.4	3.0	2.6	2.3	1.9	1.5	1.1	.94	.94
.92	.92	11.4	11.0	10.7	10.3	9.9	9.6	9.2	8.8	8.5	8.1	7.7	7.4	7.0	6.6	6.3	5.9	5.5	5.2	4.8	4.4	4.0	3.7	3.3	2.9	2.6	2.2	1.8	1.5	1.1	.92	.92
.90	.90	11.2	10.8	10.4	10.1	9.7	9.4	9.0	8.6	8.3	7.9	7.6	7.2	6.8	6.5	6.1	5.8	5.4	5.0	4.7	4.3	4.0	3.6	3.2	2.9	2.5	2.2	1.8	1.4	1.1	.90	.90
.88	.88	10.9	10.6	10.2	9.9	9.5	9.2	8.8	8.4	8.1	7.7	7.4	7.0	6.7	6.3	6.0	5.6	5.3	4.9	4.6	4.2	3.9	3.5	3.2	2.8	2.5	2.1	1.8	1.4	1.1	.88	.88
.86	.86	10.7	10.3	10.0	9.6	9.3	8.9	8.6	8.3	7.9	7.6	7.2	6.9	6.5	6.2	5.8	5.5	5.2	4.8	4.5	4.1	3.8	3.4	3.1	2.8	2.4	2.1	1.7	1.4	1.0	.86	.86
.84	.84	10.4	10.1	9.7	9.4	9.1	8.7	8.4	8.1	7.7	7.4	7.1	6.7	6.4	6.0	5.7	5.4	5.0	4.7	4.4	4.0	3.7	3.4	3.0	2.7	2.4	2.0	1.7	1.3	1.0	.84	.84
.82	.82	10.2	9.8	9.5	9.2	8.9	8.5	8.2	7.9	7.5	7.2	6.9	6.6	6.2	5.9	5.6	5.2	4.9	4.6	4.3	3.9	3.6	3.3	3.0	2.6	2.3	2.0	1.6	1.3	1.0	.82	.82
.80	.80	9.9	9.6	9.3	9.0	8.6	8.3	8.0	7.7	7.4	7.0	6.7	6.4	6.1	5.8	5.4	5.1	4.8	4.5	4.2	3.8	3.5	3.2	2.9	2.6	2.2	1.9	1.6	1.3	1.0	.80	.80
.78	.78	9.7	9.4	9.0	8.7	8.4	8.1	7.8	7.5	7.2	6.9	6.6	6.2	5.9	5.6	5.3	5.0	4.7	4.4	4.1	3.7	3.4	3.1	2.8	2.5	2.2	1.9	1.6	1.2	0.9	.78	.78
.76	.76	9.4	9.1	8.8	8.5	8.2	7.9	7.6	7.3	7.0	6.7	6.4	6.1	5.8	5.5	5.2	4.9	4.6	4.3	4.0	3.6	3.3	3.0	2.7	2.4	2.1	1.8	1.5	1.2	0.9	.76	.76
.74	.74	9.2	8.9	8.6	8.3	8.0	7.7	7.4	7.1	6.8	6.5	6.2	5.9	5.6	5.3	5.0	4.7	4.4	4.1	3.8	3.6	3.3	3.0	2.7	2.4	2.1	1.8	1.5	1.2	0.9	.74	.74
.72	.72	8.9	8.6	8.4	8.1	7.8	7.5	7.2	6.9	6.6	6.3	6.0	5.8	5.5	5.2	4.9	4.6	4.3	4.0	3.7	3.5	3.2	2.9	2.6	2.3	2.0	1.7	1.4	1.2	0.9	.72	.72
.70	.70	8.7	8.4	8.1	7.8	7.6	7.3	7.0	6.7	6.4	6.2	5.9	5.6	5.3	5.0	4.8	4.5	4.2	3.9	3.6	3.4	3.1	2.8	2.5	2.2	2.0	1.7	1.4	1.1	0.8	.70	.70
.68	.68	8.4	8.2	7.9	7.6	7.3	7.1	6.8	6.5	6.3	6.0	5.7	5.4	5.2	4.9	4.6	4.4	4.1	3.8	3.5	3.3	3.0	2.7	2.4	2.2	1.9	1.6	1.4	1.1	0.8	.68	.68
.66	.66	8.2	7.9	7.7	7.4	7.1	6.9	6.6	6.3	6.1	5.8	5.5	5.3	5.0	4.8	4.5	4.2	4.0	3.7	3.4	3.2	2.9	2.6	2.4	2.1	1.8	1.6	1.3	1.1	0.8	.66	.66
.64	.64	7.9	7.7	7.4	7.2	6.9	6.7	6.4	6.1	5.9	5.6	5.4	5.1	4.9	4.6	4.4	4.1	3.8	3.6	3.3	3.1	2.8	2.6	2.3	2.0	1.8	1.5	1.3	1.0	0.8	.64	.64
.62	.62	7.7	7.4	7.2	6.9	6.7	6.4	6.2	6.0	5.7	5.5	5.2	5.0	4.7	4.5	4.2	4.0	3.7	3.5	3.2	3.0	2.7	2.5	2.2	2.0	1.7	1.5	1.2	1.0	0.7	.62	.62
.60	.60	7.4	7.2	7.0	6.7	6.5	6.2	6.0	5.8	5.5	5.3	5.0	4.8	4.6	4.3	4.1	3.8	3.6	3.4	3.1	2.9	2.6	2.4	2.2	1.9	1.7	1.4	1.2	1.0	0.7	.60	.60
.58	.58	7.2	7.0	6.7	6.5	6.3	6.0	5.8	5.6	5.3	5.1	4.9	4.6	4.4	4.2	3.9	3.7	3.5	3.2	3.0	2.8	2.6	2.3	2.1	1.9	1.6	1.4	1.2	0.9	0.7	.58	.58
.56	.56	6.9	6.7	6.5	6.3	6.0	5.8	5.6	5.4	5.2	4.9	4.7	4.5	4.3	4.0	3.8	3.6	3.4	3.1	2.9	2.7	2.5	2.2	2.0	1.8	1.6	1.3	1.1	0.9	0.7	.56	.56
.54	.54	6.7	6.5	6.3	6.0	5.8	5.6	5.4	5.2	5.0	4.8	4.5	4.3	4.1	3.9	3.7	3.5	3.2	3.0	2.8	2.6	2.4	2.2	1.9	1.7	1.5	1.3	1.1	0.9	0.6	.54	.54
.52	.52	6.4	6.2	6.0	5.8	5.6	5.4	5.2	5.0	4.8	4.6	4.4	4.2	4.0	3.7	3.5	3.3	3.1	2.9	2.7	2.5	2.3	2.1	1.9	1.7	1.5	1.2	1.0	0.8	0.6	.52	.52
.50	.50	6.2	6.0	5.8	5.6	5.4	5.2	5.0	4.8	4.6	4.4	4.2	4.0	3.8	3.6	3.4	3.2	3.0	2.8	2.6	2.4	2.2	2.0	1.8	1.6	1.4	1.2	1.0	0.8	0.6	.50	.50
.48	.48	6.0	5.8	5.6	5.4	5.2	5.0	4.8	4.6	4.4	4.2	4.0	3.8	3.6	3.5	3.3	3.1	2.9	2.7	2.5	2.3	2.1	1.9	1.7	1.5	1.3	1.2	1.0	0.8	0.6	.48	.48
.46	.46	5.7	5.5	5.3	5.2	5.0	4.8	4.6	4.4	4.2	4.0	3.9	3.7	3.5	3.3	3.1	2.9	2.8	2.6	2.4	2.2	2.0	1.8	1.7	1.5	1.3	1.1	0.9	0.7	0.6	.46	.46
.44	.44	5.5	5.3	5.1	4.9	4.8	4.6	4.4	4.2	4.0	3.9	3.7	3.5	3.3	3.2	3.0	2.8	2.6	2.5	2.3	2.1	1.9	1.8	1.6	1.4	1.2	1.1	0.9	0.7	0.5	.44	.44
.42	.42	5.2	5.0	4.9	4.7	4.5	4.4	4.2	4.0	3.9	3.7	3.5	3.4	3.2	3.0	2.9	2.7	2.5	2.4	2.2	2.0	1.8	1.7	1.5	1.3	1.2	1.0	0.8	0.7	0.5	.42	.42
.40	.40	5.0	4.8	4.6	4.5	4.3	4.2	4.0	3.8	3.7	3.5	3.4	3.2	3.0	2.9	2.7	2.6	2.4	2.2	2.1	1.9	1.8	1.6	1.4	1.3	1.1	1.0	0.8	0.6	0.5	.40	.40
.38	.38	4.7	4.6	4.4	4.3	4.1	4.0	3.8	3.6	3.5	3.3	3.2	3.0	2.9	2.7	2.6	2.4	2.3	2.1	2.0	1.8	1.7	1.5	1.4	1.2	1.1	0.9	0.8	0.6	0.5	.38	.38
.36	.36	4.5	4.3	4.2	4.0	3.9	3.7	3.6	3.5	3.3	3.2	3.0	2.9	2.7	2.6	2.4	2.3	2.2	2.0	1.9	1.7	1.6	1.4	1.3	1.2	1.0	0.9	0.7	0.6	0.4	.36	.36
.34	.34	4.2	4.1	3.9	3.8	3.7	3.5	3.4	3.3	3.1	3.0	2.9	2.7	2.6	2.4	2.3	2.2	2.0	1.9	1.8	1.6	1.5	1.4	1.2	1.1	1.0	0.8	0.7	0.5	0.4	.34	.34
.32	.32	4.0	3.8	3.7	3.6	3.5	3.3	3.2	3.1	2.9	2.8	2.7	2.6	2.4	2.3	2.2	2.0	1.9	1.8	1.7	1.5	1.4	1.3	1.2	1.0	0.9	0.8	0.6	0.5	0.4	.32	.32
.30	.30	3.7	3.6	3.5	3.4	3.2	3.1	3.0	2.9	2.8	2.6	2.5	2.4	2.3	2.2	2.0	1.9	1.8	1.7	1.6	1.4	1.3	1.2	1.1	1.0	0.8	0.7	0.6	0.5	0.4	.30	.30
.28	.28	3.5	3.4	3.2	3.1	3.0	2.9	2.8	2.7	2.6	2.5	2.4	2.2	2.1	2.0	1.9	1.8	1.7	1.6	1.5	1.3	1.2	1.1	1.0	0.9	0.8	0.7	0.6	0.4	0.3	.28	.28
.26	.26	3.2	3.1	3.0	2.9	2.8	2.7	2.6	2.5	2.4	2.3	2.2	2.1	2.0	1.9	1.8	1.7	1.6	1.5	1.4	1.2	1.1	1.0	0.9	0.8	0.7	0.6	0.5	0.4	0.3	.26	.26
.24	.24	3.0	2.9	2.8	2.7	2.6	2.5	2.4	2.3	2.2	2.1	2.0	1.9	1.8	1.7	1.6	1.5	1.4	1.3	1.2	1.2	1.1	1.0	0.9	0.8	0.7	0.6	0.5	0.4	0.3	.24	.24
.22	.22	2.7	2.6	2.6	2.5	2.4	2.3	2.2	2.1	2.0	1.9	1.8	1.8	1.7	1.6	1.5	1.4	1.3	1.2	1.1	1.1	1.0	0.9	0.8	0.7	0.6	0.5	0.4	0.4	0.3	.22	.22
.20	.20	2.5	2.4	2.3	2.2	2.2	2.1	2.0	1.9	1.8	1.8	1.7	1.6	1.5	1.4	1.4	1.3	1.2	1.1	1.0	1.0	0.9	0.8	0.7	0.6	0.6	0.5	0.4	0.3	0.2	.20	.20
.18	.18	2.2	2.2	2.1	2.0	1.9	1.9	1.8	1.7	1.7	1.6	1.5	1.4	1.4	1.3	1.2	1.2	1.1	1.0	0.9	0.9	0.8	0.7	0.6	0.6	0.5	0.4	0.4	0.3	0.2	.18	.18
.16	.16	2.0	1.9	1.9	1.8	1.7	1.7	1.6	1.5	1.5	1.4	1.3	1.3	1.2	1.2	1.1	1.0	1.0	0.9	0.8	0.8	0.7	0.6	0.6	0.5	0.4	0.4	0.3	0.3	0.2	.16	.16
.14	.14	1.7	1.7	1.6	1.6	1.5	1.5	1.4	1.3	1.3	1.2	1.2	1.1	1.1	1.0	1.0	0.9	0.8	0.8	0.7	0.7	0.6	0.6	0.5	0.4	0.4	0.3	0.3	0.2	0.2	.14	.14
.12	.12	1.5	1.4	1.4	1.3	1.3	1.2	1.2	1.2	1.1	1.1	1.0	1.0	0.9	0.9	0.8	0.8	0.7	0.7	0.6	0.6	0.5	0.5	0.4	0.4	0.3	0.3	0.2	0.2	0.1	.12	.12
.10	.10	1.2	1.2	1.2	1.1	1.1	1.0	1.0	1.0	0.9	0.9	0.8	0.8	0.8	0.7	0.7	0.6	0.6	0.6	0.5	0.5	0.4	0.4	0.4	0.3	0.3	0.2	0.2	0.2	0.1	.10	.10
.08	.08	1.0	1.0	0.9	0.9	0.9	0.8	0.8	0.8	0.7	0.7	0.7	0.6	0.6	0.6	0.5	0.5	0.5	0.4	0.4	0.4	0.4	0.3	0.3	0.3	0.2	0.2	0.2	0.1	0.1	.08	.08
.06	.06	0.7	0.7	0.7	0.7	0.6	0.6	0.6	0.6	0.6	0.5	0.5	0.5	0.5	0.4	0.4	0.4	0.4	0.3	0.3	0.3	0.3	0.2	0.2	0.2	0.2	0.1	0.1	0.1	0.1	.06	.06
.04	.04	0.5	0.5	0.5	0.4	0.4	0.4	0.4	0.4	0.4	0.4	0.3	0.3	0.3	0.3	0.3	0.3	0.2	0.2	0.2	0.2	0.2	0.2	0.1	0.1	0.1	0.1	0.1	0.1	0.0	.04	.04
.02	.02	0.2	0.2	0.2	0.2	0.2	0.2	0.2	0.2	0.2	0.2	0.2	0.2	0.2	0.1	0.1	0.1	0.1	0.1	0.1	0.1	0.1	0.1	0.1	0.1	0.1	0.0	0.0	0.0	0.0	.02	.02

9

9.5   CALCULATIONS OF CLEARANCES UNDER BRIDGES ETC

It is sometimes necessary to calculate whether a boat can pass underneath such objects as bridges or power cables. The heights of such objects are shown on the chart above MHWS, so the clearance will nearly always be greater than the figure shown. The height is shown in metres on metric charts, but in feet on older charts. It is sometimes useful to draw a diagram, as shown in Fig. 9(6), which shows how the measurements are related to chart datum.

Clearance = (Elevation of object + height of MHWS) minus (height of tide at the time + height of mast above above water)

Fig. 9(6)

9.6   TIDAL STREAMS

9.6.1   General

Tidal streams are the horizontal movement of water caused by the vertical rise and fall of the tide. They normally change direction about every six hours and are quite different from ocean currents, such as the Gulf Stream which run for long periods in the same direction.

Tidal streams are important to yachtsmen around the British Isles because they often run at about two knots, and much more strongly in a few areas, and at spring tides. There are a few places where they can attain rates of six to eight knots.

The strength and direction of the tidal stream in the more important areas is shown in *Admiralty Tidal Stream Atlases*, as follows:

NP 209 Edition 4 Orkney and Shetland Islands, 1986
218 Edition 4 North Coast of Ireland, West Coast of Scotland, 1983
219 Edition 1 Portsmouth Harbour and Approaches, 1979
220 Edition 1 Rosyth Harbour and Approaches, 1979

221 Edition 1 Plymouth Harbour and Approaches, 1984
233 Edition 2 Dover Strait, 1975
249 Edition 2 Thames Estuary, 1985
250 Edition 3 English and Bristol Channels, 1973
251 Edition 3 North Sea, Southern Portion, 1976
252 Edition 3 North Sea, Northern Portion, 1975
253 Edition 1 North Sea, Eastern Portion, 1978
256 Edition 3 Irish Sea and Bristol Channel, 1974
257 Edition 3 Approaches to Portland, 1973
264 Edition 4 Channel Islands & Adjacent Coasts of France, 1984
265 Edition 1 France, West Coast, 1978
337 Edition 3 Solent and Adjacent Waters, 1974

Extracts from the above (by permission of the Hydrographer and HMSO) are given in Chapter 10.

The directions of the streams are shown by arrows which are graded in weight and, where possible, in length to indicate the strength of the tidal stream. Thus ⟶ indicates a weak stream and ➤ indicates a strong stream. The figures against the arrows give the mean neap and spring rates in tenths of a knot, thus 19,34 indicates a mean neap rate of 1·9 knots and a mean spring rate of 3·4 knots. The comma indicates the approximate position at which the observations were taken.

9.6.2   Computation of tidal stream rates

Using Table 9(2) it is possible to predict the rate of a tidal stream at intermediate times, assuming that it varies with the range of tide at Dover.

Example

It is required to predict the rate of the tidal stream off the northerly point of the Isle of Skye at 0420 UT (GMT) on a day when the heights of tide at Dover are:

UT (GMT)	Ht(m)
LW 0328	1·4
HW 0819	6·3
LW 1602	1·1
HW 2054	6·4

The range of tide is therefore 6·3 − 1·4 = 4·9m. The appropriate chart is the Tidal Stream Atlas NP 218 or in Chapter 10 Area 8 is that for '4 hours before HW Dover' and this gives a mean neap and a mean spring rate of 09 and 17 respectively (0·9 and 1·7 knots). On Table 9(2), Computation of Rates, on the horizontal line marked Neaps, mark the dot above 09 on the horizontal scale; likewise on the line marked Springs, mark the dot below the

Table 9(2)

	COMPUTATION OF RATES	
Mean Range Dover	TIDAL STREAM RATE (in tenths of a knot): assumed to vary with range of the tide at Dover.	Mean Range Dover

figure 17 on the horizontal scale. Join these two dots with a straight line. On the vertical scale 'Mean Range Dover', find the range 4·9. From this point follow across horizontally until the pencil line just drawn is cut; from this intersection follow the vertical line to the scale of Tidal Stream Rates, either top or bottom, and read off the predicted rate — in this example it is 14 or 1·4 knots.

A perspex sheet or a sheet of tracing paper can be used on top of Table 9(2), so as to preserve it for future use.

It should be remembered that tidal atlases cannot show the details of inshore eddies and the tide often sets towards the coast in bays. Along open coasts the turn of the tidal stream does not necessarily occur at High and Low water. It often occurs at about half tide. The tidal stream usually turns earlier inshore than offshore. On modern charts lettered diamonds give information on the tidal streams by reference to a table showing Set, Spring Rate and Neap Rate at hourly intervals before and after high water at a Standard Port. Where appropriate, normal river currents are included; but currents in the open sea are not included. Information on tidal streams and current streams is also included in *Admiralty Sailing Directions*.

9.7   METEOROLOGICAL CONDITIONS

Meteorological conditions can have a significant effect on tides and tidal streams. Sea level tends to rise in the direction towards which a wind is blowing and be lowered in the other direction. The stronger the wind and the longer it blows, the greater the effect. Also the sudden onset of a gale can set up a wave or 'storm surge' which travels along the coast. Under exceptional conditions this can raise the height of the tide by two or three metres, or a 'negative surge' can lower the height of low water by one or two metres which may be more serious for the yachtsman.

Tidal heights are predicted for average barometric pressure. When the barometer is high, tidal heights are likely to be lower, and vice versa. A change of 34 millibars (one inch of mercury) can cause a change of 0·3 metres in the height of sea level, although it may not be felt immediately. Severe conditions giving rise to a storm surge as described above are likely to be caused by a big depression, and the low barometric pressure tends to raise the sea level still more.

Intense minor depressions can have local effects on the height of water, setting up what is known as a 'seiche' which can raise or lower the sea level a metre or more in the space of a few minutes.

9.8   CONVERSION — FEET TO METRES, AND METRES TO FEET

In the table below the figures in italics are metres.

Feet		6	12	18	24	30	36	42
Fathoms		1	2	3	4	5	6	7
Feet		*1·8*	*3·6*	*5·5*	*7·3*	*9·1*	*10·9*	*12·8*
1	*0·3*	*2·1*	*3·9*	*5·8*	*7·6*	*9·4*	*11·3*	*13·1*
2	*0·6*	*2·4*	*4·2*	*6·1*	*7·9*	*9·7*	*11·6*	*13·4*
3	*0·9*	*2·7*	*4·5*	*6·4*	*8·2*	*10·0*	*11·9*	*13·7*
4	*1·2*	*3·0*	*4·9*	*6·7*	*8·5*	*10·3*	*12·2*	*14·0*
5	*1·5*	*3·3*	*5·2*	*7·0*	*8·8*	*10·6*	*12·5*	*14·3*

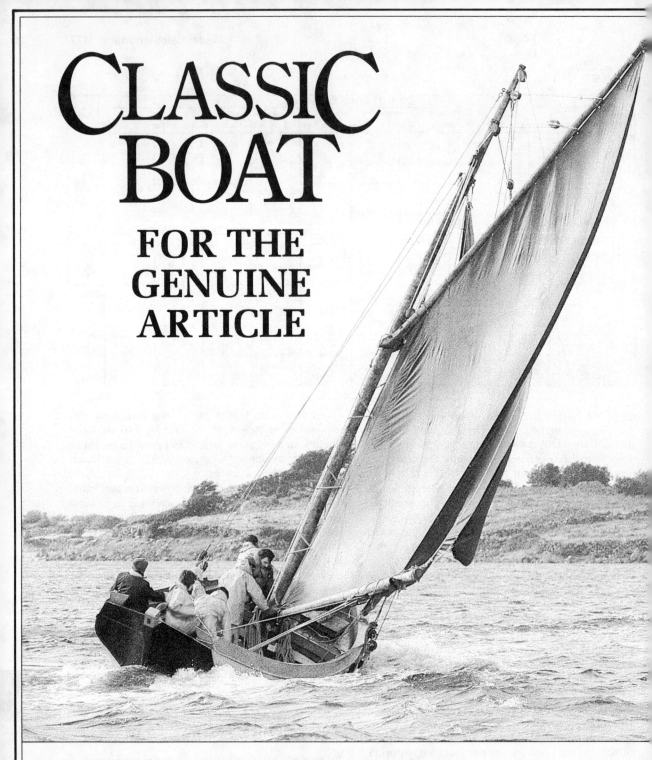

Chapter 10

Harbour, Coastal and Tidal Information

Contents

10

10.0.1.　General information

Harbour, coastal and tidal information is given for the area indicated by the map in 10.0.5, with details of 318 harbours and notes on a further 257 minor harbours and anchorages. The information provided enables a skipper to assess whether he can get into a harbour (tidal height, depth, wind direction etc.), and whether he wants to enter the harbour (shelter, facilities available, early closing days etc.). Each area is arranged as follows:

Index, of the harbours covered in that area.

A sketch of the area showing diagrammatically the positions and characteristics of the harbours covered, principal radiobeacons, coast radio stations, weather information offices, RNLI stations etc.

Tidal stream charts for the area, based on Admiralty tidal stream atlases (by kind permission of the Hydrographer of the Navy and the Controller, HM Stationery Office), showing the strengths and directions of tidal streams for each hour referred to HW Dover and to HW at the nearest Standard Port. For details of the use of tidal stream diagrams see 9.6.2.

A list of principal coastal lights, fog signals and useful waypoints in the area. More powerful lights (ranges 15 miles or more) are in **bold** type; light-vessels and Lanbys are in *CAPITAL ITALICS;* fog signals are in *italics.* Latitude and longitude are shown for more isolated lights and for selected waypoints (underlined). Unless otherwise stated, lights are white. Elevations are in metres (m), and nominal ranges in nautical miles (M). Where appropriate, a brief description is given of the lighthouse or tower. Arcs of visibility, sector limits, and alignment of leading lights etc are true bearings as seen from seward measured in a clockwise direction. Where the latitude and longitude of a light are given (e.g. Bull Point 51 12.ON/4 12.OW) W stands for West. Elsewhere W means white, and except with longitude the word west is written in full to avoid any possible ambiguity. Abbreviations used in the list of lights, fog signals and waypoints are given in 10.0.3.

Passage information, briefly calling attention in note form to some of the principal features of the coast, offlying dangers, tide races, better anhcorages etc.

Table of distances in nautical miles by the most direct route, avoiding dangers, between selected places in that area and in adjacent areas.

In certain areas (Solent, Ireland, France, Belgium, Netherlands and Germany) there follows a section (in the case of the Solent, two sections) giving **special peculiarities** regarding the area − chart references, double tides etc.

Harbour information includes the following:

a. Chartlets. These are based upon Admiralty charts (with the kind permission of Hydrographer of the Navy and the Controller, HM Stationery Office), upon information from Service Hydrographique et Oceanographique de la Marine, France, Deutsches Hydrographisches Institut, Germany, or the Directie Waterhuishouding en Waterbeweging, Netherlands. All depths on the chartlets are in metres. It must be emphasised that these chartlets are not designed or intended for pilotage or navigation, although every effort has been made to ensure that they give an accurate portrayal of the harbour concerned. The publishers and editors disclaim any responsibility for resultant accidents or damage if they are so used. Chartlets do not always cover the whole area referred to in the text (e.g. in E. Anglian rivers). The light tint on the chartlets shows drying area, the dark tint indicates land.

b. After the harbour name, the county (or equivalent abroad) is given, followed by the Admiralty, Stanford (where applicable, Imray Laurie Norie and Wilson (referred to as Imray) chart numbers for the area, and the Ordnance Survey Map numbers in the new 1:50,000 series.

c. The tidal information in these sections is also kindly provided with the permission of the Hydrographer of the Navy, and the Proudman Oceanographic Laboratory (see 1.1.4). Each Standard Port (see 9.3.1) has the times and heights of High and Low Water for every day of the year. In UK and Eire times are given in GMT; this is also known as UT (Universal Time). The Secondary Ports (see 9.3.2) have the differences quoted on the most suitable (not necessarily the nearest) Standard Port. Time and height differences from the nominated Standard Port are given for each Secondary Port. Explanations of tidal calculations are given in Chapter 9.

At the top of each port's tidal information, the average time difference on Dover is given, whereby the GMT for High Water can be quickly obtained to an accuracy of 15 minutes or so. The times of High Water Dover are under Dover (10.3.15) and also on the bookmark for quick reference, both being shown in GMT. By subtracting the Duration, quoted for most ports, the time of the previous Low Water can be approximately obtained.

Mean Level is also quoted. Zone times are given for each port, but no account is taken of BST or other daylight saving times (DST).

d. Tidal curves are given for all Standard Ports and for Portland and Dunkerque. For calculations with tidal data (finding the height of tide at a given time, for example, or the time for a given height), use the tidal curves provided for the appropriate Standard Port.

e. Shelter. Times of lock openings etc are local times (LT), unless stated.

f. Navigation, starting with the lat/long of a waypoint for the approach or entrance.

g. Principal lights, marks and leading lines.

h. Radio telephone. Details of Port Operations and Traffic Management radio services are shown as appropriate for each harbour covered. Other Port Radio stations which may be useful are shown under the nearest harbour covered.

Where significant, the call name of a station is shown in *italics*. Frequencies are indicated by their International Maritime Services Channel (Ch) designator. UK Marina Channel is **80.** MF frequencies are shown in kHz.

Frequencies used for calling and working may be separated by a semi-colon. For example: Ch16; 12 14 indicated that Ch 16 is used for calling, and that Ch 12 and Ch 14 are working frequencies. Where known, primary frequencies are shown in bold type, thus **14.**

Where there is a choice of calling frequency, always indicate the channel that you are using when calling another station. This avoids confusion when the station being called is listening on more than one channel. As example,

'Dover Port Control. This is NONSUCH, NONSUCH on Channel 74'.

Where local times are stated, the letters 'LT' are added. H24 means continuous watch. Time of scheduled broadcasts are shown (for example) as H +20, meaning 20 mins past the hour. HW -3 means 3 hours before local HW; HW +2 means 2 hours after local HW.

i. Telephone numbers are either on the exchange whose dialling code is given after 'Telephone', or on the exchange quoted. E.g. Portsmouth and Gosport numbers are on 0705, so no exchange is shown. But Fareham numbers are on another exchange, as quoted.

Although the numbers of the local Coastguard and the appropriate MRCC or MRSC (see 8.2.2) are given, in emergency dial 999 and ask for the Coastguard. Equivalent numbers are given in 10.14.7, 10.19.7 and 10.20.7.

j. At the end of facilities is indicated whether there is a Post Office (✉) Bank (Ⓑ), Railway Station (⅔) or Commercial Airport (✈) in or near the port. Where there is not, the nearest one is indicated in brackets. For continental ports, the nearest UK ferry link is shown.

Minor harbours and anchorages. Notes on selected places are given at the end of each area.

10.0.2 Abbreviations – harbour facilities with foreign translations

In the harbour facilities, the following abbreviations are used which are also repeated on the book-mark for convenience:

⊕	AB	Alongside berth
	AC	220v AC electrical supplies
	ACA	Admiralty chart agent
	✈	Airport
	Ⓑ	Bank
	Bar	Licensed Bar
	BH	Boat hoist (tons)
	BY	Boatyard
	C	Crane (tons)
	CG	Coastguard
	CH	Chandlery
	⌗	Customs
	D	Diesel fuel
	Dr	Doctor
	EC	Early closing day
	El	Electrical repairs
	Ⓔ	Electronic repairs
	FW	Fresh water supply
	Gas	Calor Gas
	Gaz	Camping Gaz
	Ⓗ	Hospital
	Hr Mr	Harbourmaster
	Kos	Kosangas
⊕	L	Landing place
	▢	Launderette

	LB	Life-boat
⊕	M	Moorings available
	ME	Marine engineering repairs
	MRCC	Maritime Rescue Co-ordination Centre
	MRSC	Maritime Rescue Sub-Centre
	P	Petrol
	✉	Post Office
	R	Restaurant
	⅔	Railway station
	SC	Sailing club
	Sh	Shipwright, hull repairs etc
	Slip	Slipway for launching, scrubbing etc
	SM	Sailmaker
	V	Victuals, food stores etc
		Visitors' berth, or where to report
	WPT	Waypoint
	YC	Yacht Club
		Facilities at Yacht Clubs are normally available to crews who arrive by sea (as opposed to trailing a dinghy by car) and are members of a recognised yacht club.

⊕ Omitted for marinas

Since yachtsmen may be using local information, these and other harbour terms are given
in the following table in French, Dutch and German.

Abbreviations	English	French	German	Dutch
AB	Alongside berth	Accostage	Stegplatz	Aanlegplaats
✈	Airport	Aéroport	Flughafen	Vliegveld
—	Anchorage	Mouillage	Ankerplatz	Ankerplaats
⑧	Bank	Banque	Bank	Bank
BH	Boat hoist	Evateur	Bootslift	Botenlift
BY	Boatyard	Chantier naval	Yachtwerft	Jachwerf
CH	Chandlery	Accastillage	Beschlag-und schiffsbedarfshändler	Beslag en scheepsleverancier
CG	Coast Guard	Garde-Côtière	Küstenwache	Kustwacht
C	Crane	Grue	Kran	Hijskraan
⌗	Customs	Douane	Zoll	Douane
D	Diesel	Gas-oil	Dieselkraftstoff	Dieselolie
Dr	Doctor	Médecin, docteur	Arzt	Huisarts, dokter
EC	Early closing	Demi-congé des magasins	Früher Ladenschluss	Tijden winkelsluiting
El	Electrical repairs	Electrician	Bootselektrik	Elekrische
ⓔ	Electronics	Electroniques	Elektroniks	
FS	Flagstaff	Mât	Flaggenmast	Vlaggestok
FW	Fresh water	Eau potable	Trinkwasser	Drinkwater
Hr Mr	Harbour Master	Chef ou Capitaine du Port	Hafenkapitän Hafenmeister	Havenmeester
Ⓗ	Hospital	Hôpital	Krankenhaus	Ziekenhuis
L	Landing	Escalier du quai	Kaitreppe	Haventrappen
Bar	Licensed bar	Bar	Bar	Bar
◎	Launderette	Laverie	Waschsalon	Waserette
LB	Lifeboat	Canot de Sauvetage	Rettungsboot	Reddingboot
—	Lock	Écluse	Schleuse	Sluis
ME	Marine Engineering	Ingénieur ou Mécanicien	Ingenieur, Bootswerkstatt	Monteur
M	Moorings	Accostage	Festmachebojen	Meerboei
—	Paraffin	Petrole	Petroleum	Petroleum
—	Passport	Passeport	Reisepass	Paspoort
P	Petrol	Essence	Benzin	Benzine
—	Pilot Station	Station de pilotage	Lotsenstation	Loodsstation
⊠	Post Office	Bureau de poste	Postamt	Postkantoor
⅔	Railway Station	Gare	Bahnhof	Station
R	Restaurant	Restaurant	Restaurant	Restaurant
SM	Sailmaker	Voilier	Segelmacher	Zeilmaker
Sh	Shipwright/hull repairs	Constructeur	Schiffswerft	Bouwmeester
Slip	Slipway	Cale	Slip, Schlipp	Sleephelling
—	Traffic Signals	Signaux de Mouvements de navire	Verkehrssignal	Verkeersseinen
V	Victuals/food supplies	Marché	Lebensmittel	Winkelcentrum
YC	Yacht Club	Yacht Club	Yachtclub, Segelclub	Jacht Club
SC	Sailing Club	Club Nautique		
—	Yacht Harbour	Port de plaisance	Yachthafen	Jachthaven

10.0.3   Abbreviations – lights, fog signals and waypoints

Al	Alternating	Dir	Direction light
Bu	Blue	Explos	Explosive signal
Bn	Beacon	F	Fixed
Brg	Bearing (light)	F.Fl	Fixed and flashing
Dia	Diaphone	F.Fl(x)	Fixed and group flashing (no. of flashes)

Fl(x)	Group flashing (no. of flashes)	Q	Quick flashing
G	Green	R	Red
harb	harbour	Racon	Radar responder beacon
(hor)	horizonal	Ra refl	Radar reflector
incr	increasing	RC	Circular radiobeacon
intens	Intensified sector	RD	Directional radiobeacon
IQ	Interrupted quick flashing	RG	Radio direction finding station
Irreg	Irregular	s	seconds
Iso	Isophase	SV	Sodium vapour discharge lamp (orange)
Lanby	Large Automatic Navigational Buoy	(T)	Temporary
Ldg Lts	Leading Lights	TD	Temporarily Discontinued
Lt	Light	TE	Temporarily Extinguished
Lt F	Light-float	Tr	Tower
Lt Ho	Lighthouse	ufn	until further notice
Lt V	Light-vessel	unintens	unintensified
M	Sea miles	(vert)	vertical
m	metres	Vi	Violet
Mo	Morse code light or fog signal	Vis	Visible
min	minutes	VQ	Very quick flashing
obsc	obscured	W	White (see 10.0.1)
Occas	Occasional	Whis	Whistle
Oc	Occulting	WPT	Waypoint
Oc(x)	Group Occulting (no. of eclipses)	Y	Yellow, Orange or Amber
(P)	Provisional		

10.0.4   Glossary of terms used for charts and sailing directions, with foreign translations

1.   Lights – characteristics (examples)

International abbreviations	Older forms	English	French	German	Dutch
F	F	Fixed	Fixe	F.	V
Oc	Occ	Occulting	Occ	Ubr.	O
Oc(2)	Gp Occ(2)	Group Occulting (2)	. . .Occ	Ubr.Grp.(2)	GO
Iso	Isophase	Isophase	Iso	Glt.	Iso
Fl	Fl	Flashing	É,é	Blz.	S
LFl	LFl	Long flashing	Él,él	Blk.	
Fl(3)	GpFl(3)	Group flashing (3)			
Q	QkFl	Quick flashing	Scint,sc	Fkl.	Fl
Q(3)	QkFl(3)	Group quick flashing (3)	. . .É	Blz(. . .)	GS
IQ	IntQkFl	Interrupted quick flashing	Scint.dis.	Fkl.unt.	Int Fl
VQ	VQkFl	Very quick flashing	Scint,rapide		
VQ(3)	VQkFl(3)	Group very quick flashing (3)			
UQ	UQ	Ultra quick flashing			
IUQ	IUQ	Interrupted ultra quick flashing			
Mo(K)	Mo(K)	Morse Code(K)	Mo(K)	Mo(K)	
FFl	FFl	Fixed and flashing	Fix É	Fl. & Blz.Mi.	V & S
Al	Alt.	Alternating	Alt	Wchs	Alt
W	W	White	B,b	w.	w
R	R	Red	R,r	r.(rot)	r
G	G	Green	V,v	gn.(grün)	gn
Y	Y	Yellow	Jaune, J	g.(gelb)	Geel
Y	Or	Orange	org	or.(orange)	gl
Bu	Bl	Blue	bl	bl.(blau)	b
Vi	Vo	Violet	Vio.	viol.	vi
B	B	Black	Noir	s.(schwarz)	Zwart
Gy	gy	Grey	Gris	grau	Grijs

2.   Fog signals

English	French	German	Dutch
Diaphone	Diaphone	Nebelhorn	Diafoon
Horn	Corne de brume	Nautofon	Nautofoon
	Nautophone	Nautophon	Tyfoon
	Typhon	Tyfon	
	Klaxon	Typhon	
Siren	Sirène	Sirene	Mistsirene
			Sirene
Reed	Trompette	Zungenhorn	Mistfluit
Explosive	Explosion	Nebelknallsignal	Knalmistein
	Canon	Kanone	Mistkanon
Bell	Cloche	Glocke	Mistklok
			Mistbel
Gong	Gong	Gong	Mistgong
Whistle	Sifflet	Heulboje	Mist fluit

3.   Other navigational aids and structures

English	French	German	Dutch
Radiobeacon	Radiophone	Funkfeuer	Radiobaken
Light	Feu	Leuchtfeuer	Licht
Lighthouse	Phare	Leuchtturm	Lichttoren
Light-vessel	Feu flottant	Feuerschiff	Lichtschip
	Bateau-feu		
Light-float	Feu flottant	Leuchtfloss	Lichvlot
Beacon	Balise	Bake	Baken
Column	Colonne	Laternenträger	Lantaarnpaal
Dolphin	Duc d'Albe	Dalben	Ducdalf
			Meerpaal
Framework tower	Charpente.Pyl.	Gittermast	Traliemast Geraamte
House	Bâtiment	Haus	Huis
	Maison		
Post	Poteau	Pfahl	Lantaarnpaal
Tower	Tour	Turm	Toren
	Tourelle		
Concrete	Béton	Betonierter	Beton
Metal	de fer	Eiserner	Ijzeren
Stone	Maconnerie	Steinerner	Stenen
Wooden	en bois	Hölzerner	Houten
Band	Bande	Waagerecht gestreift	Horizontaal gestreept
Stripe	Raie	Senkrecht gestreift	Vertikaal gestreept
Chequered	à damier	gewürfelt	Geblokt
Topmark	voy.	Toppzeichen	Topteken
Round	cyl.	rundum	Rond
Cone	Cône	Kegel	Kegel
Conical	Conique	kegelförmig	Kegelvormig
Diamond	los.	Raute,rautenförmig	Ruitvormig
Square	Carré	Viereck, Quadrat	Vierkant
Triangular	Triang	dreieckig	Driehoekig
Destroyed	Détruit	zerstört	Vernield
Occasional	Occasionnel	zeitweise	Facultatief
Temporary	Temporaire	vorübergehend	Tijdelijk
Extinguished	Éteint	gelöscht	Gedoofd

10.0.5   Map of areas

VOLVO PENTA SERVICE

Sales and service centres in area 1

CORNWALL **Marine Engineering Co (Looe) Ltd** The Quay, EAST LOOE PL13 1AQ Tel (05036) 2887. **Penryn Marine** Mylor Yacht Harbour Nr FALMOUTH TR11 5UF Tel (0326) 76202/1/0. DEVON **Marine Engineering Co Ltd** Queen Anne's Marina, Queen Anne's Battery, Coxside, PLYMOUTH PL4 0LP Tel (0752) 226143. **Starey Marine Services** Island Square, Island Street, SALCOMBE TQ8 8DP Tel (054884) 3655. **Philip & Son Ltd** Noss Works, DARTMOUTH TQ6 0EA Tel (08043) 3351. **Pilkington Marine Engineering** 9 Pottery Units, Forde Road, Brunel Trading Estate, NEWTON ABBOT Tel (0626) 52663. **Retreat Boatyard (Topsham) Ltd** Retreat Boatyard, Topsham, EXETER EX3 0LS Tel (039287) 4720.

VOLVO PENTA

Area 1

South-West England
Isles of Scilly to River Exe

188

Isles of Scilly
(see 10.1.8)

For details of traffic
lanes see Fig.2 (8)

6°W

Longships

50°
N

SEPARATION

ZONE

SEPARATION ZONE

SEPARATION ZONE

Round Island
| RC | RR ·—· ·—· |
| 5 | 308 200 |

Seven
Stones

Wolf Rock

CG LB
RG

St. Mary's
ⓘ	10.1.9
P R	VHF 16; 14
RC Aero	STM ··· ——
	321 15

Bishop Rock

Bude**
| P R | VHF 16; 12 |

SEPARATION

5°W

Swansea CG
Falmouth CG

ZONE

Padstow
ⓘ	10.11.23
P R	VHF 16
LB	

Port Isaa

Trevose
Head
RG

50°
30'N

Charlest
| P R | VHF 1 |

NOTE: The coast NE from
St. Ives is covered in Area 11

Newquay**
IL

St. Mawgan
| RC Aero | SM ··· —— |
| | 356·5 50 |

St. Agnes
IL

Mevagissey
| ⓘ | 10.1.14 |
| P R | Ch 16 14 |

Penzance
ⓘ	10.1.11
RC Aero	PH ·—— ····
	333 15
P R	VHF 16; 09 12

Godrevy I.

St. Ives**
LB IL

CG Hayle**

Pendeen
RG

Longships

CG

Sennen
Cove
LB

Mousehole*
LB

Tater-du

Falmouth
ⓘ	10.1.13
C S	Pendennis Radio VHF 16 62
☁	0733 1933
P R	VHF 16; 11 12 13 14 Marinas Ch **80**
LB	IL
Falmouth	CG
RG

Truro*
| ☁ | M–0898 |
| | 500 458 |

Gr
H
Portmell

CG

Goran Hav
Dodman Pt

Porthscatho*

St. Anthony Head

Brixham C
Falmouth CG

St. Michael's Mount*

Newlyn
| ⓘ | 10.1.10 |
| P R | VHF 16; 12 |

Helford
| ⓘ | 10.1.12 |

CG
Porthleven*

IL Coverack*

50°
N

Lands End
Coast Station
| C S | MF 2670 VHF 16 **27 64** 85 88 |
| ☁ | 0733 1933 |

☆ Wolf
Rock

Culdrose CG
Port Mullion*

Cadgwith

Black Head

Lizard
RC	LZ ·—·· ——··
6	298.8 70
LB	

see inset for Isles of Scilly

5°W

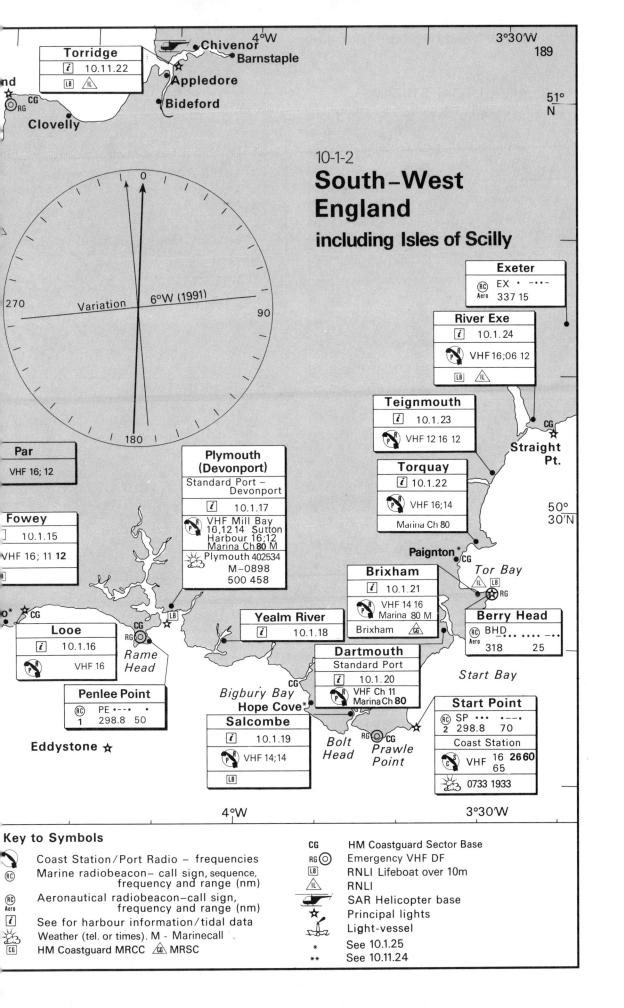

Torridge

| i | 10.11.22 |

Chivenor

Barnstaple

Appledore

Bideford

Clovelly

10-1-2
South–West
England
including Isles of Scilly

Exeter

RC Aero | EX • –•–
337   15

River Exe

| i | 10.1.24 |

VHF 16;06 12

Teignmouth

| i | 10.1.23 |

VHF 12 16 12

Straight
Pt.

CG

Par

VHF 16; 12

**Plymouth
(Devonport)**

Standard Port –
Devonport

| i | 10.1.17 |

VHF Mill Bay
10,12 14   Sutton
Harbour 16;12
Marina Ch **80** M

Plymouth 402534
M–0898
500 458

Torquay

| i | 10.1.22 |

VHF 16;14

Marina Ch 80

50°
30'N

Paignton*
CG

Tor Bay

Fowey

| 10.1.15 |

VHF 16; 11 **12**

Brixham

| i | 10.1.21 |

VHF 14 16
Marina 80 M

Brixham

RG

Berry Head

RC Aero | BHD –••• •••• –••
318   25

Looe

| i | 10.1.16 |

VHF 16

CG
RG

*Rame
Head*

Yealm River

| i | 10.1.18 |

Dartmouth

Standard Port

| i | 10.1.20 |

VHF Ch 11
Marina Ch **80**

Start Bay

Start Point

RC | SP ••• •––•
2   298.8   70

Coast Station

VHF 16 **26 60**
65

0733 1933

Penlee Point

RC | PE •––• •
1   298.8   50

Eddystone ☆

Bigbury Bay
Hope Cove*

CG

Salcombe

| i | 10.1.19 |

VHF 14;14

*Bolt
Head*

RG CG

*Prawle
Point*

Key to Symbols

Coast Station/Port Radio – frequencies
RC   Marine radiobeacon– call sign, sequence,
         frequency and range (nm)
RC Aero   Aeronautical radiobeacon–call sign,
         frequency and range (nm)
i See for harbour information/tidal data
  Weather (tel. or times). M - Marinecall
CG   HM Coastguard MRCC   CG MRSC

CG   HM Coastguard Sector Base
RG ◎   Emergency VHF DF
LB   RNLI Lifeboat over 10m
⚠   RNLI
  SAR Helicopter base
☆   Principal lights
  Light-vessel
*   See 10.1.25
**   See 10.11.24

10.1.3   AREA 1 TIDAL STREAMS

5 Hours before HW Dover (0040 after HW Devonport)

4 Hours before HW Dover (0140 after HW Devonport)

3 Hours before HW Dover (0240 after HW Devonport)

2 Hours before HW Dover (0340 after HW Devonport)

1 Hour before HW Dover (0440 after HW Devonport)

HW Dover (0540 after HW Devonport)

Portland 10.2.13   Isle of Wight 10.2.8   Channel Islands 10.17.3.   Northward 10.11.3   Eastward 10.2.3.   Southward 10.16.3

1 Hour after HW Dover (0545 before HW Devonport) *5 hrs before HW*

2 Hours after HW Dover (0445 before HW Devonport) *4 hrs before HW*

3 Hours after HW Dover (0345 before HW Devonport) *3 hrs before HW*

4 Hours after HW Dover (0245 before HW Devonport) *2 hrs before HW*

5 Hours after HW Dover (0145 before HW Devonport)

6 Hours after HW Dover (0045 before HW Devonport)

1 HR BEFORE HW   *HW FALMOUTH.*

10.1.4 LIGHTS, FOG SIGNALS AND WAYPOINTS

Abbreviations used below are given in 10.0.3. Principal lights are in **bold** print, places in CAPITALS, and light-vessels, light floats and Lanbys in *CAPITAL ITALICS*. Unless otherwise stated lights are white. m—elevation in metres; M—nominal range in n. miles. Fog signals are in *italics*. Useful waypoints are underlined - use those on land with care. See 4.2.2.

ISLES OF SCILLY

Bishop Rock 49°52'·33N 06°26'·68W Fl(2) 15s 44m **29M**; grey round Tr with helicopter platform; part obsc 204°-211°, obsc 211°-233°, 236°-259°; Racon; *Horn Mo(N) 90s*.
Gunner Buoy 49°53'·60N 06°25'·02W; S cardinal.
Round Rock Buoy 49°53'·06N 06°25'·13W; N cardinal.

ST MARY'S.
Bartholomew Ledge Buoy 49°54'·38N 06°19'·80W; port-hand mark.
Spanish Ledge Buoy 49°53'·90N 06°18'·80W; E cardinal; *Bell*.
Peninnis Head 49°54'·24N 06°18'·15W Fl 20s 36m 20M; W round metal Tr on W frame, B cupola; vis 231°-117° but part obsc 048°-083° within 5M. FR Lts on masts to N and NE.
Hats Buoy 49°56'·17N 06°17'·08W; S cardinal.
Round Island 49°58'·70N 06°19'·33W Fl 10s 55m **24M**; W round Tr; vis 021°-288°; H24; RC; *Horn (4) 60s*.

SEVEN STONES Lt V 50°03'·58N 06°04'·28W Fl(3) 30s 12m 25M; R hull, Lt Tr amidships; Racon; *Horn (3) 60s*.

ENGLAND—SOUTH COAST

Longships 50°03'·97N 05°44'·85W Iso WR 10s 35m **W19M, R18/15M**; grey round Tr with helicopter platform; vis R189°-208°, R(unintens) 208°-307°, R307°-327°, W327°-189°; *Horn 10s*. FR on radio mast 4·9M NE.

Wolf Rock 49°56'·70N 05°48'·50W Fl 15s 34m **23M** (H24); *Horn 30s*; Racon.

Runnel Stone Lt Buoy 50°01'·15N 05°40'·30W Q(6) + LFl 15s; S cardinal; *Bell, Whis*.

Tater-du 50°03'·10N 05°34'·60W Fl(3) 15s 34m **23M**; W round Tr; vis 241°-074°. FR 31m 13M (same Tr); vis 060°-074° over Runnel stone and in places 074°-077°.

MOUSEHOLE.
N pier head 50°04'·94N 05°32'·21W 2 FG (vert) 8m 4M; R metal column; replaced by FR when harb closed.
Low Lee Lt Buoy 50°05'·52N 05°31'·32W Q(3) 10s; E cardinal.

NEWLYN.
S Pier head 50°06'·15N 05°32'·50W Fl 5s 10m 9M; W round Tr, R base & cupola; vis 253°-336°; *Siren 60s*.
N Pier head F WG 4m 2M; vis G238°-248°, W over harbour.
Old Quay head FR 3m.
Mary Williams Pier head 2 FR (vert) 8m 2M.

PENZANCE.
S Pier head 50°07'·02N 05°31'·62W Iso WR 2s 11m W9M, R8M; W round Tr, B base; vis R(unintens) 159°-224°, R224°-268°, W268°-345°, R345°-shore.

Albert Pier head 2 FG (vert) 11m 2M.
Mountamopus Buoy 50°04'·60N 05°26'·20W; S cardinal.

PORTHLEVEN.
S pier 50°04'·87N 05°19'·03W FG 10m 4M; G metal column, shown when inner harb is open.
Inside harbour FG 10m 4M; vis 033°-067°.

Lizard 49°57'·58N 05°12'·07W Fl 3s 70m **29M**; W 8-sided Tr; vis 250°-120°, part vis 235°-250°; reflection may be seen inshore of these bearings; RC; *Siren Mo (N) 60s*.

Culdrose Lt Buoy 50°00'·08N 04°59'·60W Fl Y 10s; special mark.
Manacles Lt Buoy 50°02'·77N 05°01'·85W Q(3) 10s; E cardinal mark; *Bell*.
Helston Lt Buoy 50°04'·92N 05°00'·77W Fl Y 2·5s; special mark.
August Rock Buoy 50°06'·07N 05°04'·88W (PA); stbd-hand mark (seasonal).

St Anthony Head 50°08'·43N 05°00'·90W Oc WR 15s 22m **W22/20M, R20M**; W 8-sided Tr; vis W295°-004°, R004°-022° over Manacles, W (unintens) 022°-100°, W100°-172°; (H24); Fog Det Lt LFl 5 min vis 148°-151°; *Horn 30s*.

FALMOUTH.
Black Rock Bn 50°08'·68N 05°01'·95W (unlit); isolated danger mark.
Castle Lt Buoy 50°08'·96N 05°01'·57W Fl G 10s; stbd-hand mark.
St Mawes 50°09'·07N 05°01'·35W; S cardinal mark.
West Narrows Lt Buoy 50°09'·36N 05°02'·00W Fl (2) R 10s; port-hand mark.
The Vilt Lt Buoy 50°09'·95N 05°02'·22W Fl (4) G 15s; stbd-hand mark.
Northbank Lt Buoy 50°10'·32N 05°02'·06W Fl R 4s; port-hand mark
Outer harb E breakwater 50°09'·31N 05°02'·90W Fl R 2s 20m 3M.
North Arm, East head Q 19m 3M.
Inner harbour, Custom House quay head 2 FR (vert) 4m 1M.
Prince of Wales Pier head 2 FR (vert) 6m.
Greenbank Quay Fl R 2s 6m.
St Mawes Quay head 2 FR (vert).

Gwineas Lt Buoy 50°14'·47N 04°45'·30W Q(3) 10s; E cardinal mark; *Bell*.

MEVAGISSEY.
S pier head 50°16'·11N 04°46'·85W Fl(2) 10s 9m 12M; *Dia 30s*.
Cannis Rock Lt Buoy 50°18'·35N 04°39'·88W Q(6) L Fl 15s; S cardinal mark; *Bell*.

FOWEY.
50°19'·59N 04°38'·77W L Fl WR 5s 28m W11M, R9M; W 8-sided Tr, R lantern; vis R284°-295°, W295°-028°, R028°-054°.
Whitehouse Point Iso WRG 3s 11m W11M, R8M, G8M; vis G017°-022°, W022°-032°, R032°-037°.
N pier head 2 FR (vert) 4m 8M; R post.
Udder Rock Buoy 50°18'·90N 04°33'·78W; *Bell*; S cardinal mark.

POLPERRO.
Tidal basin, West pier FW or R 4m 4M; R when harbour closed in bad weather.

LOOE.
Mid main beacon Q(3) W 10s 2M; E cardinal mark.
Banjo Pier head 50°21'·02N 04°27'·00W Oc WR 3s 8m **W15M** R12M; vis W013°-207°, R207°-267°, W267°-313°, R313°-332°.
Nailzee Pt *Siren (2) 30s (occas)*.

Eddystone 50°10'·81N 04°15'·87W Fl(2) 10s 41m **15M**; grey Tr, R lantern. FR 28m 13M (same Tr) vis 112°-129° over Hand deeps; helicopter platform, Racon; *Horn (3) 60s*.

PLYMOUTH SOUND.
Rame Head, S end 50°18'·63N 04°13'·31W (unlit).
Draystone Lt Buoy 50°18'·82N 04°11'·01W Fl(2) R 5s; port-hand mark.
Knap Lt Buoy 50°19'·52N 04°09'·94W FlG 5s; stbd-hand mark.
West Tinker Lt Buoy 50°19'·14N 04°08'·62W Q(9) 15s; W cardinal mark.
Shag Stone 50°19'·03N 02°07'·52W Fl(2) 15s.
Detached Breakwater- West end 50°20'·04N 04°09'·45W Fl WR 10s 19m **W15M**, R12M; grey Tr; vis W262°-208°, R208°-262°. Iso W 4s (same Tr) 12m 12M; vis 031°-039°; *Bell (1) 15s*.
Whidbey 50°19'·5N 04°07'·2W Oc(2) G 10s 29m 3M; Or and W column; vis 000°-160°.
Bovisand Pier Oc(2) G 15s 17m 3M.

E Rutts DZ Lt Buoy 50°12'·60N 03°59'·10W Fl Y 2·5s; special mark. Withdrawn (T).

SALCOMBE.
Sandhill Point Dir Lt 000°Dir Fl WRG 2s 27m W10M, R7M, G7M; R&W diamond on W mast; vis R002·5°-182·5°, G182·5°-357·5°, W357·5°-002·5°.
Blackstone Rock 50°13'·57N 03°46'·43W OWR 4m 2M; G and W Bn; vis R218°-048°, W048°-218°.
Ldg Lts 042°30. Front Q 5m 8M. Rear 180m from front, Oc 4·5s 45m 8M.

Start Point 50°13'·32N 03°38'·47W Fl(3) 10s 62m 25M; W round Tr; vis 184°-068°; RC. FR 55m 12M (same Tr) vis 210°-255° over Skerries bank; *Horn 60s*. FR Lts on radio mast 0·9M WNW.
Skerries Bank Buoy 50°16'·28N 03°33'·70W; port-hand; *Bell*.

DARTMOUTH.
Homestone Buoy 50°19'·56N 03°33'·48W; port-hand mark.
Castle Ledge Lt Buoy 50°19'·96N 03°33'·05W FlG 5s; stbd-hand mark.
Checkstone Lt Buoy 50°20'·42N 03°33'·73W Fl(2) R 5s; port-hand mark.
Kingswear 50°20'·78N 03°34'·02W Iso WRG 3s 9m 8M; vis G318°-325°, W325°-331°, R331°-340°.
Dartmouth (Bayards Cove) 50°20'·81N 03°34'·56W Fl WRG 2s 5m 6M; vis G280°-289°, W289°-297°, R297°-shore.
RDYC 1 50°18'·80N 03°35'·25W; special mark (Apr-Oct).
RDYC 2 50°18'·68N 03°33'·29W; special mark (Apr-Oct).
RDYC 3 50°20'·07N 03°31'·42W; special mark (Apr-Oct).

Berry Head 50°23'·95N 03°28'·94W Fl(2) 15s 58m 18M; W Tr; vis 100°-023°. R Lts on radio mast 5·7M NW.

BRIXHAM.
Victoria Breakwater head 50°24'·29N 03°30'·70W Oc R 15s 9m 6M.

PAIGNTON.
East quay Fl R 7m 3M.

TORQUAY.
Princess Pier head QR 9m 6M.
Haldon Pier head 50°27'·40N 03°31'·67W QG 9m 6M.
Marina South pontoon East end 2 FR (vert) 2m.
South pier head 2 FG (vert) 6m 5M.

TEIGNMOUTH.
The Ness 50°32'·17N 03°29'·80W QWRG 44m W8M, R7M, G7M; vis G229°-243°, W243°-348°, R348°-shore.
The Den, Lts in line 334°. Front FR 10m 6M; grey round Tr; vis 225°-135°. Rear (Powderham Terrace), 62m from front, FR 11m 3M.
Den Pt, SW end 50°32'·38N 03°29'·98W Oc G 5s FG (vert).

EXMOUTH.
Exe Fairway Lt Buoy 50°36'·00N 03°21'·86W Fl 10s; safe water mark; *Bell*.
Straight Point Fl R 10s 34m 7M; vis 246°-071°.
Ldg Lts 305°. Front FY 6m 7M. Rear 57m from front, FY 12m 7M.

Note. For English Channel Waypoints see 10.1.7

10.1.5   PASSAGE INFORMATION

NORTH CORNWALL (charts 1149, 1156)

The coast of North Cornwall is covered in Area 11, to which reference should be made. For Padstow see 10.11.23. For Bude, Newquay, Hayle and St Ives see 10.11.24. For ease of reference, certain general information is repeated below.

Approach to Bristol Chan along N coast of Cornwall is very exposed, with little shelter in bad weather. Padstow is a refuge, but in strong NW winds the sea breaks on bar and prevents entry. Shelter is available under lee of Lundy Island; but there are bad races to NE (White Horses), the NW (Hen and Chickens), and to SE; also overfalls over NW Bank. St Ives (dries) is sheltered from E and S, but exposed to N. So in this area yachts need to be sturdy and well equipped, since if bad weather develops no shelter may be at hand. Streams are moderate W of Lundy, but strong round the island. They get much stronger towards Bristol Chan proper.

ISLES OF SCILLY (10.1.8 and charts 34, 883)

The Scillies comprise 48 islands, extending 21-31M WSW of Land's End. There are many rocky outcrops and offlying dangers, and although they are all well charted care is needed particularly in poor visibility. For pilotage details see *Channel Pilot* or *South England Pilot, Vol 5* (Brandon). There is a useful local publication – *A Yachtsman's Guide to Scilly*.

Several transits are shown on chart 34, and these should be followed, because the tidal streams in and between the islands are difficult to predict with any accuracy. They run harder off points and over rocks, where overfalls may occur.

Conspic landmarks are Bishop Rock Lt Ho, Round Island Lt Ho, the disused Lt Ho on St Agnes, the daymark at the E end of St Martin's, Penninis Lt Ho at the S end of St Mary's, and the TV mast and CG signal station (at the old telegraph tower) both in the NW corner of St Mary's. Yachts must expect to lie to their anchors. There is no one anchorage giving shelter in all wind directions, so it may be necessary to move at short notice. All anchorages may be penetrated by swell. The most popular and useful ones are shown in 10.1.8.

From St Ives to Land's End coast is rugged and exposed. There are overfalls SW of Pendeen Pt (Lt, fog sig). Vyneck Rks lie awash about 3 ca NW of C Cornwall. The Brisons are two rocky islets ½M SW of C Cornwall, and rocky ledges extend inshore and to the S and SW. The Longships (Lt, fog sig) are a group of rks about 1M W of Land's End, with ledges 2 ca further seaward. The inshore passage is not recommended.

LAND'S END/SCILLIES

Between Land's End and the Scillies (chart 1148) streams are rotatory, clockwise. They run ENE from HW Devonport −0100 (1 kn at sp), SSE from HW Devonport +0200 (2 kn at sp), WNW from HW Devonport +0600 (1 kn at sp), and N from HW Devonport −0400 (1¾ kn at sp). The Seven Stones (rks) lie 14M W of the Longships and 7M NE of the Scillies; many of them dry, with ledges in between. They are marked by Lt V (Lt, fog sig) on E side. Wolf Rk (Lt, fog sig) is 8M SW of Land's End, and is steep-to. For traffic schemes see Fig. 2(8).

LAND'S END TO LIZARD HEAD (chart 777)

From Land's End to Gwennap Hd, 2½M SE, rks extend up to 1½ ca offshore, and depths are irregular to seaward causing a bad sea in strong W winds with W-going tide. The Runnel Stone (dries) lies 7 ca S of Gwennap Hd, with rks between it and shore. These dangers are in R sectors of Longships and Tater-du Lts. Do not anch off Porth Curno, due to cables.

Entering Mount's B, the Bucks (dry) are 2 ca SE and E of Tater-du Lt Ho. Gull Rk (24m) is 9 ca NE of Tater-du, close off the E point of Lamorna Cove. Little Heaver (dries) is ½ ca SW of Gull Rk, and Kemyel Rk (dries) is 1¾ ca ENE. Mousehole is a small drying harb, sheltered from W and N, but exposed to winds in E or S, when entrance may be closed: approach from S side of St Clement's I. In W winds there is good anch off the harb. See 10.1.25.

Low Lee, a dangerous steep-to rk, is 4 ca NE of Penlee Pt, marked by buoy. Carn Base Rk lies 3 ca NNW of Low Lee. Newlyn (10.1.10) is only harb in Mount's B safe to approach in strong onshore winds, but only near HW. From here to Penzance (10.1.11) beware Dog Rk and Gear Rk.

From Penzance to St Michael's Mount the head of the b is flat, and dries for 4 ca in places. Dangers include Cressar Rks, Long Rk, Hogus Rks, and Outer Penzeath Rk. Venton chy on with pierheads of St Michael's Mount harb at 084° leads S of these dangers. This tiny harb dries, but is well sheltered, with anch about 1 ca W of entrance, see 10.1.25.

Two dangerous rks, Guthen Rk and Maltman Rk, lie within 2 ca of St Michael's Mount. 1M SE is The Greeb (7m), with rks between it and shore. The Bears (dry) lie 1¾ ca E of The Greeb. The Stone (dries) is ½M S of Cudden Pt, while offshore is Mountamopus shoal marked by buoy which should be passed to seaward. Welloe Rk (dries) lies ½M SW of Trewavas Hd.

Porthleven is small tidal harb, entered between pier on S side and Deazle Rks (dry) on N. Dry out alongside in inner harb, closed in bad weather when approach is dangerous. In fair weather there is good anch off Porth Mellin, about 1½ ca NE of Mullion Island; the harb is not recommended. See 10.1.25.

2½M W of Lizard Hd is The Boa, a rky shoal on which sea breaks in SW gales. The Lizard (Lt, fog sig, RC) is a significant headland (chart 2345) with tidal streams up to 3 kn at sp. The outer rks, all of which dry, from W to E are Mulvin, (2½ ca SW of Lizard Pt), Taylor's Rk (2ca SSW of Lizard Pt), Clidgas Rks (5ca SW of Lt Ho), Men Hyr Rk and the Dales or Stags (5ca SSW of Lt Ho), and Enoch Rk (3ca S of Lt Ho). S of the rks the stream turns E at HW Devonport −0500, and W at HW Devonport +0155. Offshore it turns an hour earlier. A dangerous race extends 2-3M S when stream is strong in either direction, worst in W winds against W-going tide. Then keep at least 3M to seaward. There may be a race SE of the hd.

LIZARD HEAD TO STRAIGHT POINT (chart 442)

Vrogue, a dangerous sunken rk, is 4 ca ESE of Bass Pt, NE of Lizard Hd. Craggan Rks are ½M offshore, and 1M N of Vrogue Rk. From Black Hd to beyond Chynnalls Pt, rks extend at least 1 ca offshore. Coverack gives good anch in W winds, see 10.1.25. From Dolor Pt to E of Lowland Pt are drying rks ¼M offshore.

The Manacles (dry), ¾M E and SE of Manacle Pt, are marked by buoy to seaward and are in R sector of St Anthony Hd Lt. Off the Manacles the stream runs NE from HW Devonport −0345, and SW from HW Devonport +0200, sp rates 1¼ kn. From E of the Manacles there are no offshore dangers on courses NNW to Helford entrance (10.1.12) or N to Falmouth (10.1.13).

Sailing NE from St Anthony Hd, Gull Rk lies 6 ca E of Nare Hd, at W side of Veryan B. The Whelps (dry) are ½M SW of Gull Rk. There is a passage between Gull Rk and the shore. In Veryan B beware Lath Rk 1M SE of Portloe.

On E side of Veryan B, Dodman Pt is a 110m cliff, with a stone cross near SW end. Depths are irregular for 1M S, with heavy overfalls in strong winds, when it is best to pass 2M off. Gorran Haven, a sandy cove with L-shaped pier which dries at sp, is a good anch in offshore winds. See 10.1.25.

2.1M NE of Dodman Pt cross, and 1M ENE of Gorran Haven, is Gwineas Rk (8m). 1 ca E of Gwineas Rk is Yaw Rk (dries 0.9m), marked by buoy on E side. Passage inside Gwineas Rk is possible, but not recommended in strong onshore winds or poor vis. Portmellon and Mevagissey B (see 10.1.25 and 10.1.14) are good anchs in offshore winds. For Charlestown and Par see 10.1.25.

Gribbin Hd has a conspic daymark — a square Tr 25m high with R & W stripes. In bad weather the sea breaks on rks round hd. Cannis Rk (dries) is ¼M SE, and marked by buoy to seaward. 3M E of Fowey (10.1.15) is Udder Rk (dries), ½M offshore in E part of Lantivet B. Larrick Rk (dries) is 1½ ca off Nealand Pt.

Polperro harb dries, but the inlet gives good anch in offshore winds. See 10.1.25. Beware E Polca Rk roughly in mid-chan. There are shoals extending ¼M seaward from Downend Pt, E of Polperro. The chan between Hannafore Pt and St George's (or Looe) Island nearly dries. The Rennies (dry) are rks extending ¼M E and SE of the island. (See 10.1.16). There are overfalls S of Looe Island in bad weather.

Eddystone Rks (chart 1613) lie 8M S of Rame Hd. Shoals extend 3 ca E. Close NW of the Lt Ho (Lt, fog sig) is the stump of old one. The sea can break on Hand Deeps — sunken rks 3½M NW of Eddystone.

Rame Hd is on W side of entrance to Plymouth Sound (10.1.17). It is conspic cone shaped, with small chapel on top. Rks extend about 1 ca off. On the E side of Plymouth Sound, the Mewstone (59m) is a conspic rocky islet 4 ca off Wembury Pt. Drying rks extend 1½ ca SW of Little Mewstone, and the Slimers, which dry, (see 10.1.18) lie 2 ca E of Mewstone. E and W Ebb Rks (awash) lie 2½ ca off Gara Pt (chart 30).

Between Gara Pt and Stoke Pt, 2½M to E, offlying dangers extend about 4 ca offshore in places. In Bigbury B beware Wells Rk and other dangers ½M S of Erme Hd. From Bolt Tail to Bolt Hd keep ½M offshore to clear Greystone Ledge, sunken rks near Ham Stone (11m), and Gregory Rks ½M SE of Ham Stone. The Great and Little Mewstones lie just off Bolt Hd, where coast turns N to Salcombe entrance (10.1.19).

Start Pt (Lt, fog sig, RC) is 3M NE of Prawle Pt, and is a long headland with white Lt Ho near end and conspic radio masts in rear. Rks extend 2½ ca offshore, and the stream runs 4 kn at sp, causing a race extending 1M to seaward. 3M S of Start the stream turns ENE at HW Devonport −0150, and WSW at HW Devonport +0420. Inshore it turns ½ hr earlier. In reasonable weather the overfalls can be avoided by passing close to rks, but in bad weather keep at least 2M off.

Start Pt is W end of Lyme B (chart 3315), stretching 50M NE to Portland Bill, and with no secure harb in its E part. NE of Start Pt is Skerries Bank, on which sea breaks in bad weather (chart 1634). Good anch off Hallsands in offshore winds.

Between Dartmouth (10.1.20) and Brixham (10.1.21) rks extend ½M offshore. Berry Hd (Lt) is steep, flat-topped headland (55m). Here the stream turns N at HW Devonport −0105, and S at HW Devonport +0440, sp rates 1½ kn. In Torbay (chart 26) the more obvious dangers are steep-to, but beware the Sunker ½ ca SW of Ore Stone, and Morris Rogue ½M W of Thatcher Rk.

There are good anchs in Babbacombe B and in Anstey's cove in W winds: beware the Three Brothers (drying rks), S side of Anstey's cove. From Long Quarry Pt for 4M N to Teignmouth (10.1.23) there are no offlying dangers. Off Teignmouth the NNE-going stream begins at HW Devonport −0135, and the SSW-going at HW Devonport +0510. In the entrance the flood begins at HW Devonport −0535, and the ebb at HW Devonport +0040. The stream runs hard off Ferry Pt.

Between Teignmouth and Dawlish rks extend 1 ca offshore. Beware Dawlish Rk (depth 2.1m) about ½M off N end of town. Warren Sands and Pole Sands lie W of entrance to Exmouth (10.1.24), and are liable to shift. Along the NE (Exmouth) side of the chan, towards Orcomb Pt and Straight Pt (Lt), drying rks and shoals extend up to ¼M from shore.

10.1.6 DISTANCE TABLE

Approximate distances in nautical miles are by the most direct route while avoiding dangers and allowing for traffic separation schemes etc. Places in *italics* are in adjoining areas.

	1	2	3	4	5	6	7	8	9	10	11	12	13	14	15	16	17	18	19	20
1 *Fastnet Rock*	1																			
2 *Tuskar Rock*	138	2																		
3 *South Bishop*	162	36	3																	
4 *Lundy Island*	187	85	50	4																
5 *Appledore*	207	103	70	20	5															
6 *Padstow*	186	112	82	40	48	6														
7 Longships	167	130	109	82	89	49	7													
8 Bishop Rock	152	141	132	110	120	76	30	8												
9 Wolf Rock	169	135	117	90	97	57	8	26	9											
10 Lizard Point	190	153	132	105	112	72	23	50	24	10										
11 Falmouth	206	169	148	121	128	88	39	66	40	16	11									
12 Fowey	224	187	166	139	146	106	57	84	58	34	22	12								
13 Plymouth	239	202	181	154	161	121	72	99	73	49	39	22	13							
14 Eddystone	229	192	171	144	151	111	62	89	63	39	31	17	12	14						
15 Start Point	253	216	195	168	175	135	86	113	87	63	55	40	24	24	15					
16 Berry Head	266	229	208	181	188	148	99	126	100	76	68	53	37	37	13	16				
17 Straight Point	280	243	222	195	202	162	113	140	114	90	82	67	51	51	27	14	17			
18 *Portland Bill*	302	265	244	217	224	184	135	162	136	112	104	89	73	73	49	41	36	18		
19 *Le Four*	250	229	208	181	188	148	99	103	95	87	99	109	115	103	113	125	139	153	19	
20 *Casquets*	300	263	142	215	222	182	133	160	134	110	107	96	80	79	57	61	66	48	120	20

ENGLISH CHANNEL
WAYPOINTS   10-1-7

Selected waypoints for use in Channel crossings, listed
from West to East in each Area nominated below.
Waypoints marked with an asterisk (*) are special (yellow)
racing marks, which may be removed in winter. Further
waypoints in coastal waters are given in section 4 of each
relevant area (i.e. to 10.2.4 and 10.3.4 on the English
Coast, and 10.17.4 and 10.18.4 for the French coast and
the Channel Islands).

ENGLISH COAST

Area 1

Bishop Rock Lt	49°52'·33N	06°26'·68W
Seven Stones Lt V	50°03'·58N	06°04'·28W
Wolfe Rock Lt	49°56'·70N	05°48'·50W
Runnel Stone Lt Buoy	50°01'·15N	05°40'·30W
Tater Du Lt	50°03'·10N	05°34'·60W
Low Lee Lt Buoy	50°05'·52N	05°31'·32W
Lizard Point Lt	49°57'·58N	05°12'·07W
Culdrose Lt Buoy	50°00'·08N	05°59'·60W
Manacles Lt Buoy	50°02'·77N	05°01'·85W
Helston Lt Buoy	50°04'·92N	05°00'·77W
August Rk Buoy	50°06'·09N	05°04'·88W
Black Rk Bn	50°08'·68N	05°01'·95W
Castle Lt Buoy	50°08'·96N	05°01'·57W
St Anthony Head Lt	50°08'·43N	05°00'·90W
Gwineas Lt Buoy	50°14'·47N	04°45'·30W
Cannis Rk Lt Buoy	50°18'·35N	04°39'·88W
Udder Rk Buoy	50°18'·90N	04°33'·78W
Eddystone Lt	50°10'·80N	04°15'·87W
Start Point Lt	50°13'·32N	03°38'·47W
Castle Ledge Lt Buoy	50°19'·96N	03°33'·05W
*RDYC No. 1 Buoy	50°18'·80N	03°35'·25W
*RDYC No. 2 Buoy	50°18'·68N	03°33'·29W
*RDYC No. 3 Buoy	50°20'·07N	03°31'·42W
Berry Head Lt	50°23'·95N	03°28'·94W

Area 2

Straight Point Lt	50°36'·46N	03°21'·68W
Portland Bill Lt	50°30'·82N	02°27'·32W
W Shambles Lt Buoy	50°29'·75N	02°24'·33W
E Shambles Lt Buoy	50°30'·75N	02°20'·00W
Anvil Point Lt	50°35'·48N	01°57'·52W
Poole Fairway Lt Buoy	50°38'·95N	01°54'·78W
Needles Fairway Lt Buoy	50°38'·20N	01°38'·90W
Bembridge Ledge Lt Buoy	50°41'·12N	01°02'·74W
Needles Lt	50°39'·70N	01°35'·43W
St Catherine's Point Lt	50°34'·52N	01°17'·80W
Nab Tower Lt	50°40'·05N	00°57'·07W

Area 3

Owers Lanby	50°37'·30N	00°40'·60W
Brighton Marina Lt	50°48'·46N	00°06'·29W
Royal Sovereign Lt	50°43'·38N	00°26'·13E
Dungeness Lt	50°54'·77N	00°58'·67E
S Goodwin Lt Float	51°07'·95N	01°28'·60E

OFFSHORE AIDS

Areas 3 and 17

Channel Lt V	49°54'·42N	02°53'·67W
E Channel Lt Float	49°58'·67N	02°28'·87W

EC1 Lt Buoy	50°05'·90N	01°48'·35W
EC2 Lt Buoy	50°12'·10N	01°12'·40W
EC3 Lt Buoy	50°18'·30N	00°36'·10W
CS1 Lt Buoy	50°33'·67N	00°03'·83W
Greenwich Lanby	50°24'·50N	00°00'·00
CS2 Lt Buoy	50°39'·08N	00°32'·70E
CS3 Lt Buoy	50°52'·00N	01°02'·30E
CS4 Lt Buoy	51°08'·58N	01°34'·03E
Bullock Bank Lt Buoy	50°46'·90N	01°07'·70E
S Varne Lt Buoy	50°55'·60N	01°17'·40E
Varne Lanby	51°01'·25N	01°24'·00E
MPC Lt Buoy	51°06'·17N	01°38'·33E
Sandettie Lt V/Buoy	51°09'·40N	01°47'·20E

FRENCH COAST

Area 16

Quessant SW Lanby	48°31'·68N	05°49'·10W
Créach Lt	48°27'·62N	05°07'·72W
Ouessant NE Lt Buoy	48°45'·90N	05°11'·60W
Basse Paotr Bihan Buoy	48°35'·38N	04°46'·16W
Basse de Portsall Lt Buoy	48°36'·78N	04°46'·05W
Le Relec Lt Buoy	48°36'·05N	04°40'·77W
Ruzven Lt Buoy	48°36'·15N	04°39'·30W
Libenter Lt Buoy	48°37'·57N	04°38'·21W
Trépied Buoy	48°37'·37N	04°37'·45W
Ile Vierge Lt	48°38'·38N	04°34'·00W
Ile de Batz Lt	48°44'·78N	04°01'·55W
Astan Lt Buoy	48°44'·95N	03°57'·55W
Méloine Buoy	48°45'·62N	03°50'·54W
Les Triagoz Lt	48°52'·35N	03°38'·73W
Les Sept Iles Lt	48°52'·78N	03°29'·33W
Basse Crubient Lt Buoy	48°54'·35N	03°11'·09W
La Jument des Héaux Buoy	48°55'·41N	03°07'·96W
Les Heaux Lt	48°54'·53N	03°05'·20W
Rosédo (Bréhat) Lt	48°51'·50N	03°00'·32W
Les Echaudés Buoy	48°53'·44N	02°57'·27W
Roche Gautier Lt Buoy	49°00'·05N	02°52'·92W
Barnouic Lt	49°01'·70N	02°48'·40W
Roches Douvres Lt	49°06'·47N	02°48'·82W

Area 17

Le Légué Lt Buoy	48°34'·39N	02°41'·09W
SW Minquiers Lt Buoy	48°54'·40N	02°19'·30W
NW Minquiers Lt Buoy	48°59'·70N	02°20'·50W
Cap Fréhel Lt	48°41'·10N	02°19'·07W
Banchenou Lt Buoy	48°40'·51N	02°11'·41W
S Minquiers Lt Buoy	48°53'·13N	02°10'·13W
N Minquiers Lt Buoy	49°01'·70N	02°00'·50W
SE Minquiers Lt Buoy	48°53'·50N	02°00'·00W
Basse de Vieux Banc Buoy	48°42'·50N	02°09'·36W

Le Guildo Lt Buoy	48°41'·42N	02°07'·22W
St Malo Fairway Lt Buoy	48°41'·42N	02°07'·21W
Cap de la Hague Lt	49°43'·37N	01°57'·19W
NE Minquiers Lt Buoy	49°00'·91N	01°55'·20W
Basse Bréfort Lt Buoy	49°43'·70N	01°51'·05W
Chausey, Grand Ile Lt	48°52'·23N	01°49'·26W
Cap de Carteret Lt	49°22'·46N	01°48'·35W
Basse Jourdan Lt Buoy	49°06'·90N	01°44'·05W
CH1 Lt Buoy	49°43'·30N	01°42'·10W
Le Videcoq Lt Buoy	48°49'·70N	01°42'·00W
Anvers Lt Buoy	48°53'·91N	01°40'·88W
Cherbourg Fort Ouest Lt	49°40'·50N	01°38'·87W
Le Pierre Noire Lt Buoy	49°43'·57N	01°28'·98W
Cap Lévi Lt	49°41'·80N	01°28'·30W
Basse du Rénier Lt Buoy	49°44'·90N	01°22'·00W
Les Equets Lt Buoy	49°43'·68N	01°18'·28W

CHANNEL ISLANDS
Area 17

Les Hanois Lt	49°26'·20N	02°42'·10W
St Martin's Point Lt	49°25'·37N	02°31'·61W
Reffée Lt Buoy	49°27'·80N	02°31'·18W
Platte Fougère Lt	49°30'·88N	02°29'·05W
Casquets Lt	49°43'·38N	02°22'·55W
Corbière Lt	49°10'·85N	02°14'·90W
Desormes Lt Buoy	49°19'·00N	02°17'·90W
Alderney Main Lt	49°43'·81N	02°09'·77W
Canger Rk Lt Buoy	49°07'·41N	02°00'·30W
Frouquier Aubert Lt Buoy	49°06'·15N	01°58'·70W
Écrevière Lt Buoy	49°15'·33N	01°52'·08W

FRENCH COAST
Area 18

Pointe de Barfleur Lt	49°41'·87N	01°15'·87W
Iles St Marcouf Lt	49°29'·90N	01°08'·90W
Ver-sur-Mer Lt	49°20'·47N	00°31'·15W
LHA Lanby	49°31'·67N	00°09'·80W
Cap de la Hève Lt	49°30'·80N	00°04'·24E
Cap d'Antifer Lt	49°41'·07N	00°10'·00E
Pointe d'Ailly Lt	49°55'·13N	00°57'·56E
Bassurelle Lt Buoy	50°32'·70N	00°57'·80E
Ecovouge Lt Buoy	50°33'·62N	00°59'·00E
Vergoyer SW Lt Buoy	50°26'·90N	01°00'·00E
Vergoyer N Lt Buoy	50°39'·70N	01°22'·30E
ZC1 Lt Buoy	50°44'·85N	01°27'·10E
Ault Lt	50°06'·35N	01°27'·24E
ZC2 Lt Buoy	50°53'·50N	01°31'·00E
Pointe de Haut Blanc Lt	50°23'·90N	01°33'·75E
Cap d'Alprech Lt	50°41'·95N	01°33'·83E
Cap Gris Nez Lt	50°52'·17N	01°35'·07E
CA4 Lt Buoy	50°58'·94N	01°45'·18E
Sangatte Lt	50°57'·23N	01°46'·57E
Dunkerque Lanby	51°03'·00N	01°51'·83E
Walde Lt	50°59'·57N	01°55'·00E

ISLES OF SCILLY   10-1-8

The Isles of Scilly are made up of 48 islands and numerous rocky outcrops, extending approx 10M by 5M and lying 21-31M WSW of Land's End. Only six islands are inhabited, St Mary's, Gugh, St Agnes, St Martin's, Tresco and Bryher. The islands belong to the Duchy of Cornwall and details of arrangements for visiting uninhabited islands are given in the booklet *Duchy of Cornwall − Information for visiting craft* obtainable from the Harbour Master, Hugh Town Harbour, St Mary's. There is a lifeboat and a HM Coastguard Sector Base at St Mary's.

CHARTS
Admiralty 883, 34; passage from Lands End 1148; Stamford 2; Imray C7.

TIDES
Standard Port is Devonport. Tidal differences for St Mary's are given in 10.1.9 below. The tidal heights, times, speeds and directions round islands are irregular.

SHELTER
There are numerous anchorages, the following being but a selection:

HUGH TOWN HARBOUR (St Mary's). See 10.1.9 below.
PORTH CRESSA (St Mary's S of Hugh Town). Beware of dangers on each side of entrance and the submarine cable. Exposed to swell from SE to SW. Anchor in approx 2m. Facilities: all facilities in Hugh Town to N.
NEW GRIMSBY (between Tresco and Bryher). Approach through New Grimsby Sound, or with sufficient rise of tide across Tresco Flats. Good shelter except in NW winds. Anchor between Hangman Is and the quay in 1.5 to 4.5m. Facilities: Bar, R, FW, V, ✉, Ferry to St Mary's.
WATERMILL COVE (NE corner of St Mary's). Excellent shelter in winds NW to S. Anchor in approx 5m.
THE COVE (St Agnes/Gugh). Well sheltered from W and N winds, except when the sand bar between the islands covers near HW sp with a strong NW wind.
PORTH CONGER (St Agnes/Gugh). On the N side of the sand bar, sheltered in winds from E through S to W. May be uncomfortable when the bar is covered. Facilities; L (two quays), ferry to St Mary's; in Middle Town (¼M), St Agnes, V, ✉, R, Bar
OLD GRIMSBY (between Tresco and St Helen's). Green Porth and Raven's Porth, divided by a quay, form the W side of Old Grimsby and both dry. Anchor 2 ca NE of quay in 2.5m. Access more difficult than New Grimsby. Well sheltered in SW winds but open to swell if wind veers N of W. Facilities: L(quay), hotel, slip (hotel).

TEAN SOUND (St Martin's, W side). Requires careful pilotage, but attractive anchorage in better weather. (See St. Martins Hotel below). More suitable for shoal draught boats which can anchor out of main tidal stream in channel. There are several other anchorages which can be used in settled weather, or by shoal draught boats which can take the ground.

NAVIGATION
See chart 34 (essential), 10.1.5 and *A Yachtsman's Guide to Scilly*. For traffic separation schemes, see Chapter 2 Fig. 2(8).

The many offlying dangers need care if the leading lines (lettered on chartlet) cannot be identified, when it is best to lie off. Tidal streams are irregular and run hard off points and over shoals, where overfalls may occur. Many of the channels between the islands have dangerous shallows, often rocky ledges. Beware lobster pots and the ferry entering or leaving. Also beware the grave possibility of normal yacht anchors dragging through the fine sand, even with plenty of scope.

St Mary's Sound (line B) is the normal access to St Mary's Road. From the NE beware the Gilstone (dries) 3ca E of Peninnis Head. An E cardinal bell buoy marks Spanish Ledges which extend from the Gugh shore, and a port-hand buoy marks Bartholomew Ledges (least depth 0.6m). The Woolpack Bn (S cardinal) marks SW end of St Mary's. In the approach to Hugh Town, transit E1 clears Woodcock Ledge, which breaks in bad weather.

Crow Sound (line A) is not difficult with sufficient rise of tide, but is rough in strong winds from E or S. From the NE a yacht can pass close to Menawethan and Biggal Rock. Avoid Trinity Rock and the Ridge, which break in bad weather. Hats buoy (S cardinal) marks a drying shoal with an old boiler on it. The bar (dries) lies off Bar Point, but there is slightly deeper water nearer Bar Point. Leave Crow Rock Bn either side before altering course to SW.

North Channel (line D) is about ¾M wide and provides easy access if the leading marks can be seen. Beware cross tide and Steeple Rock (awash) ¾M SW of Mincarlo. In bad weather the sea breaks on Jeffrey Rock and Spencer's Ledge either side of channel.

Broad Sound (line C) is about ¼M wide at narrowest point, and is entered between Bishop Rock and Fleming's Ledge about ¾M to the N. Leading marks are not conspic, but the channel is shown by Round Rock, Gunner and Old Wreck buoys which mark the main dangers other than Jeffrey Rock.

ISLES OF SCILLY *continued*

LIGHTS AND MARKS
See 10.1.4 for lights. It is wise to study the various marks on the chart before arrival.

RADIO TELEPHONE
For port operations see 10.1.9. Scillies area is served by directional aerial from Land's End Radio on Ch 64. St Mary's Coastguard Ch 16; 67 (manned in bad weather only). Pilot Ch 16.

TELEPHONE (0720)
Hr Mr Hugh Town Harbour 22768; CG 22651; Pilot 22066 ✵ 22571; Info Office 22537; MRSC Falmouth 317575; Airport Reservations 22646; Marinecall 0898 500 458; Ⓗ 22508.

FACILITIES
St Martins Hotel ☎ (0702) 22092 M (6), V, R, Bar, D, FW.

ST MARY'S   10-1-9
Isles of Scilly

CHARTS
Admiralty 34, 883; Stanford 2; Imray C7; OS 203

NOTE: The old Admiralty fathom chart 34 shows more inshore dangers.

TIDES
+0551 Dover; ML 3.1; Duration 0600; Zone 0 (GMT)

Standard Port DEVONPORT (→)

Times				Height (metres)			
HW		LW		MHWS	MHWN	MLWN	MLWS
0000	0600	0000	0600	5.5	4.4	2.2	0.8
1200	1800	1200	1800				

Differences ST MARY'S ROADS

−0030	−0110	−0100	−0020	+0.2	−0.1	−0.2	−0.1

SHELTER
St Mary's Pool gives good shelter in most winds but is exposed to W and NW, when Porth Cressa (see 10.1.8) is

better. Anchoring is not permitted S of a line from the pierhead to the lifeboat slip, off the pierhead where the ferry turns, or in the harbour approaches. Speed limit 3kn.

NAVIGATION
Waypoint St Mary's Sound. Spanish Ledge E cardinal buoy, Bell, 49°53'.90N 06°18'.80W, 128°/308° from/to Great Minalto, 2.4M. See also 10.1.4 and 10.1.8. Other channels into St Mary's Road include Smith Sound between St Agnes and Annet, and with sufficient rise of tide through New Grimsby across Tresco Flats. In the approaches to St Mary's Pool beware Woodcock Ledge (see 10.1.8). Bacon Ledge (depth 0.3m) lies 2½ca W of Newford Island, while further N are The Cow and The Calf (both dry). The 097° transit on the chartlet leads S of Bacon Ledge. If coming from the N, the 151° transit shown leads W of The Cow and E of Bacon Ledge.

LIGHTS AND MARKS
There are two leading marks, rather distant W beacons, bearing 097° for entry into the harbour. Nearest mark is a triangle, the distant mark an X. There are no navigational lights in the harbour except Lt on pier showing FG 4m 3M; vis 072°-192°.

RADIO TELEPHONE
Call: *St Mary's Harbour* VHF Ch 16; 14. (0800-1700 LT).

TELEPHONE (0720)
Hr Mr 22768; CG 22651; MRCC Falmouth 317575; ✵ 22571; Marinecall 0898 500 458; Police 22444; Ⓗ 22392; Dr 22628.

FACILITIES
EC Wednesday (or Thursday according to boat sailings); Harbour Office will hold mail for visiting yachts if addressed c/o the Harbour Master. **Harbour** Slip, M, Gas, Gaz, P (cans), D, L, FW*, C (6 ton); **T. H. Chudleigh** ☎ 22505, Sh, CH; **Chris Jenkins** ☎ 22321, ME; **H.J. Thomas** ☎ 22710, L, ME, CH; **Scillonian Marine** ☎ 22124, CH, El, ACA; **Isles of Scilly YC** ☎ 22352, Bar, Ⓞ, R; **Island Supply Stores** ☎ 22388, Gas; **Hugh Town** has limited shopping facilities. ✉; Ⓑ; ⛴ (ferry to Penzance); ✈ (Helicopter service to Penzance and fixed wing to London and mainland). There are ✉, R, V, Bar etc. at Tresco, Bryher, St Martins and St Agnes.
*0830-1130 except Sat. − see Hr Mr.

NEWLYN   10-1-10
Cornwall

CHARTS
Admiralty 2345, 777; Stanford 13; Imray C7; OS 203

TIDES
+0550 Dover; ML 3.1; Duration 0555; Zone 0 (GMT)

Standard Port DEVONPORT (→)

Times				Height (metres)			
HW		LW		MHWS	MHWN	MLWN	MLWS
0000	0600	0000	0600	5.5	4.4	2.2	0.8
1200	1800	1200	1800				

Differences NEWLYN

−0040	−0105	−0045	−0020	+0.1	0.0	−0.2	0.0

SHELTER
Good except in SE winds when heavy swell occurs in the harbour. In off-shore winds there are good anchorages outside the harbour in Gwavas Lake. Anchoring inside breakwaters is prohibited. No visitors' moorings, overnight stay only.

NAVIGATION
Waypoint Low Lee E cardinal buoy, Q(3) 10s, 50°05'.52N 05°31'.32W, 130°/310° from/to Newlyn pierhead, 1.0M. Approaching from E beware Mountamopus, from S beware Low Lee and Carn Base. Also beware Dog Rk, 3½ ca NE of harbour entrance. Harbour is available at all states of the tide but entrance is narrow, i.e. 45m between pierheads. Leave Lt Ho to port and keep close to New Pier. Newlyn is a commercial fishing port and fishing boats must take priority.

NEWLYN *continued*

LIGHTS AND MARKS
S Pier, head Fl 5s 10m 9M; W Tr, R base and cupola;
Siren 60s. N Pier, head F WG 4m 2M; vis G238°-248°, W
over harbour. Old Quay, head FR 3m 1M.
RADIO TELEPHONE
Call: *Newlyn Harbour*·VHF Ch 16; 12 (Mon-Fri 0800-1700,
Sat 0800-1200 LT).
TELEPHONE (0736)
Hr Mr 62523; CG 871351; MRCC Falmouth 317575;
⌗ (0752) 222929; Marinecall 0898 500 458; Police 62395;
Ⓗ 62382; Dr 63866.
FACILITIES
EC Wednesday; **North Pier** Slip, D, L, FW, ME, El, C
(6 ton); **South Pier** L; **C. K. Jones** ☎ 63095, ME, Sh; **J.
H. Bennetts** ☎ 69988, Gas; **Kernow Marine** ☎ 68606,
El, Ⓔ; **Sea-Com Electronic** ☎ 69695, Ⓔ; **Cosalt**
☎ 63094, CH.
There is a BY with all repair facilities but it is usually
booked up with work on fishing boats.
Town CH, Ⓞ, V, R, Bar; ✉ Ⓑ (AM only); ⇌ (bus to
Penzance); ✈ (Penzance).

PENZANCE   10-1-11
Cornwall

CHARTS
Admiralty 2345, 777; Stanford 13; Imray C7; OS 203
TIDES
−0635 Dover; ML 3.1; Duration 0550; Zone 0 (GMT)

Standard Port DEVONPORT (⟶)

Times				Height (metres)			
HW		LW		MHWS	MHWN	MLWN	MLWS
0000	0600	0000	0600	5.5	4.4	2.2	0.8
1200	1800	1200	1800				

Differences PENZANCE
−0040 −0105 −0045 −0020 +0.1   0.0   −0.2   0.0
PORTHLEVEN
−0045 −0105 −0035 −0025   0.0   −0.1   −0.2   0.0
LIZARD POINT
−0045 −0055 −0040 −0030 −0.2   −0.2   −0.3   −0.2

SHELTER
Perfectly protected within the wet dock. Dock is open
HW−2 to HW+1. Mounts Bay is unsafe anchorage in S
or SE winds. Strong S or SE winds make the harbour
entrance dangerous.
NAVIGATION
Waypoint 50°06'.70N 05°31'.10W, 135°/315° from/to
Penzance S pierhead, 0.48M. Beware Gear Rk coming
from S. Coming from the Lizard in wind or swell approach
on NNW heading to avoid the Boa and Iron Gates.
Cressar (5 ca NE of entrance) and Long Rks are marked
by beacons. There is a harbour speed limit of 5 kn.

▲ Report to Hr Mr

LIGHTS AND MARKS
There are no Ldg Lts or marks. South pierhead Lt
Iso WR 2s 11m 9/8M; vis R159°-268°, W268°-345°,
R345°-shore.
Dock entry signals, shown from FS at N side of Dock
gate (may not be given for yachts).
2B balls (hor) (2FR (vert) by night) — Dock gates open.
2B balls (vert) (FR over FG by night) — Dock gates shut.
RADIO TELEPHONE
VHF Ch 16; 09 **12** (HW−2 to HW+1, and office hours).
TELEPHONE (0736)
Hr Mr 07415; Hr Office 66113; CG 871351; MRCC
Falmouth 317575; ⌗ (0752) 222929; Marinecall
0898 500 458; Police 62395; Dr 63866, Ⓗ 62382
FACILITIES
EC Wednesday (except in summer); **Wet Dock**
(50 visitors) ☎ 66113, Access HW−1½ to HW+1, Slip,
M, D (cans), L, FW, AC, C (3 ton); **Holman Marine**
☎ 63838, Slip (dry dock), ME, El, C, CH, AB; **Matthews
Sail Loft** ☎ 64004, CH, SM; **Cosalt Newlyn** ☎ 63094,
CH; **R. Curnow** ☎ 762025, CH, Sh; **South Pier**
☎ 66113, D, FW, V, R, Bar; **Penzance YC** ☎ 64989, Bar,
L, FW, R; **J. H. Bennetts** ☎ 69988, Gas, Gaz; **Town** Ⓞ,
CH, V, R, Bar. ✉; Ⓑ; ⇌; ✈.

HELFORD RIVER   10-1-12
Cornwall

CHARTS
Admiralty 147, 154; Stanford 13; Imray C6, Y57; OS 204
TIDES
−0613 Dover; ML 3.0; Duration 0550; Zone 0 (GMT).

Standard Port DEVONPORT (⟶)

Times				Height (metres)			
HW		LW		MHWS	MHWN	MLWN	MLWS
0000	0600	0000	0600	5.5	4.4	2.2	0.8
1200	1800	1200	1800				

Differences HELFORD RIVER (Ent)
−0030 −0035 −0015 −0010 −0.2   −0.2   −0.3   −0.2
COVERACK
−0030 −0040 −0020 −0010 −0.2   −0.2   −0.3   −0.2

SHELTER
Excellent shelter except against E winds.
Anchorages:- Durgan Bay, good except in E winds.
     Off Helford but tides strong.
     Navas Creek — good shelter — little room.
Gillan Creek is good but beware rock in middle of
entrance, Car Croc E cardinal spar buoy. (Moorings
administered by Hr Mr). Visitors buoys marked 'Visitors'
on green pick up buoys.
NAVIGATION
Waypoint 50°05'.70N 05°04'.50W, 093°/273° from/to The
Voose N cardinal Bn, 1.5M. If coming from N beware
August Rock (or the Gedges). August Rock buoy G
conical (seasonal). If from SE keep well clear of Nare
Point and Dennis Head. Keep Helford Pt open of Bosahan
Pt to clear rocky reef E end of Bosahan Point (The Voose)
marked by N Cardinal buoy (seasonal). Avoid mud bank
marked by G conical buoy (Bar buoy) on N side of river
opposite Helford Creek. Port and Stbd markers mark
channel from Mawgan Creek to Gweek. Speed limit 6 kn.
LIGHTS AND MARKS
There is a Lt on August Rk Buoy FlG 5s. A useful natural
transit exists as a line from Bosahan Point to Mawnan
Shear (259°) keeps one clear of the dangerous rocks, The
Gedges. Note: There is a local bye-law stating that there
are oyster beds in the river and creeks W of buoy, mid
channel SW of Navas Creek, and yachts must not anchor
or take the ground in that area.

HELFORD RIVER *continued*

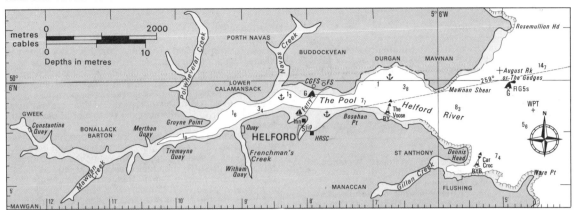

RADIO TELEPHONE
 Helford River SC and Gweek Quay VHF Ch **80**.
TELEPHONE (0326)
 Moorings Officer 280422; MRCC 317575;
 ⌗ (0752) 222929; Marinecall 0898 500 458; Police 72231;
 Ⓗ Helston 572151.
FACILITIES
 EC Wednesday; **Cove Boats** ☎ 250116, M; **Port Navas YC** ☎ 40419, C (1½ ton), Gax, V, L, Bar, R, FW, P, D; **Gweek Quay** ☎ Mawgan 657, C (30 ton), M, CH, R, El, Sh, ME, FW, Ⓔ; **Star Hire Boats** ☎ 260675, M; **Helford Passage** Slip, L, FW; **Helford River SC** ☎ Manaccan 460, Slip, M, L, FW, Bar; **Ferry Boat Inn** ☎ 250278, M, Gas, Gaz, ▣, FW, R, Bar; **J. Badger** (Durgan), Slip, L, FW; **Sailaway** ☎ Manaccan 357, M, FW, Sh, CH, L. ✉ (Helford, Gweek, Mawnan-Smith, Mawgan); Ⓑ Mawnan-Smith (Jan-Sept Mon, Wed, Fri AM only. Oct-May Tues, Fri AM only); ⇌ (bus to Falmouth); ✈ (Penzance or Newquay).
 Note: Ferry will collect yachtsmen from boats, requested during normal ferry operating hours.

RIVER FAL   10-1-13
Cornwall

CHARTS
 Admiralty 32, 18, 154; Stanford 13; Imray C6, Y58; OS 204
TIDES
 −0602 Dover; ML 3.0; Duration 0550; Zone 0 (GMT).

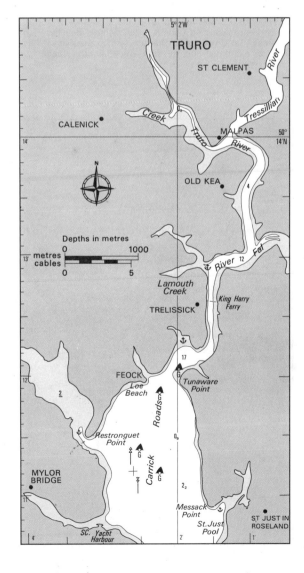

RIVER FAL *continued*

Standard Port DEVONPORT (→)

Times				Height (metres)			
HW		LW		MHWS	MHWN	MLWN	MLWS
0000	0600	0000	0600	5.5	4.4	2.2	0.8
1200	1800	1200	1800				

Differences FALMOUTH

−0030	−0030	−0010	−0010	−0.2	−0.2	−0.3	−0.2

TRURO

−0020	−0025	Dries out		−2.0	−2.0	Dries out	

SHELTER

Excellent. Entrance is a mile wide and deep. It can be approached in any weather or tide although on-shore winds against an ebb tide make it a bit rough. The Visitors Yacht Haven operates in summer months, the pontoons being connected to North Quay. Also there are visitors moorings on the port side of the main channel, clearly marked, operated by the Harbour Commissioner or the Royal Cornwall YC. Port Pendennis is a marina (at present for residents only) to the SW of the commercial port and Falmouth Marina, about ½M beyond Greenbank up the Penryn River, available at all tides. On E side is St Mawes Harbour, with excellent shelter except in SW winds. In these circumstances proceed beyond Amsterdam Pt to anchor. Further up-stream on the W bank is Mylor Yacht Harbour, sheltered from prevailing winds but uncomfortable in strong easterlies. Further up on the W bank is Restronguet Creek, a good anchorage but most of the creek dries. On the E side there is a good anchorage at St Just but uncomfortable in strong W or SW winds. Further up river there are a number of good anchorages including Church Creek, Mopus Reach, Malpas (Bar Creek Yacht Station ¼M up Tresillian R has visitors moorings) and Tolverne. Speed limit in upper reaches is 5kn.

NAVIGATION

Waypoint 50°08'.00N 05°02'.00W, 183°/003° from/to Black Rock Bn, 0.68M. The only hazard is Black Rk which divides the entrance into two. Entrance can be made either side but at night the E channel is advised leaving the buoy Q (3) 10s to port. Beware oyster beds, especially in Penryn River. Falmouth is a deep water port, taking ships up to 90,000 tons; appropriate facilities are available. Take care not to impede shipping or anchor in prohibited areas.
In St Mawes Harbour entrance beware Lugo Rk, which is always covered; leave St Mawes S cardinal buoy to port. Mylor Creek is shallow, approx 1m everywhere except in Mylor Pool itself. Restronguet Creek has as little as 0.6m at MLWS and beware Carrick Carlys Rock just N of entrance, marked with BY posts with N and S cardinal topmarks. At the N end of Carrick Roads Turnaway Pt marks the start of the river; beware strong tides and rips. 'On final approach to Falmouth Yacht Marina leave E cardinal mark to starboard and pass within 20m of outside pontoons to ensure narrow channel is adhered to'.

LIGHTS AND MARKS

St Anthony Head light, R sector covers the Manacles Rocks.

RADIO TELEPHONE

Call: *Falmouth Harbour Radio*, VHF Ch 16; 12 (Mon-Fri 0900-1700, Sat and Sun 0900-1700 in summer. LT). Coastguard − Ch 16 10 67 73. Customs launch Ch 16 12 09 06 10 14. Port Health Ch 16 12 06. Mylor Yacht Harbour, Falmouth Yacht Marina and Royal Cornwall YC Ch **80**. Visitors Yacht Haven Ch 16, 12;

TELEPHONE (0326)

Hr Mrs Falmouth 312285; Truro/Penryn Truro 72130; St Mawes 270553; MRCC 317575; ✆ (0752) 222929; Weather Plymouth 42534; Marinecall 0898 500 458; Police 72231; Dr 312033; Ⓗ Truro 74242.

RIVER FAL *continued*

FACILITIES
FALMOUTH EC Wednesday (winter only). **Falmouth Yacht Marina** (280 + 80 visitors), ☎ 316620, AC, FW, CH, V, P (cans), D, Bar, R, ME, El, Sh, ⊡, BH (30 ton), C (2 ton), Gas, Gaz, SM, Access H24; **Falmouth Harbour Commissioners Visitors Yacht Haven** (40) ☎ 312285, P, D, FW, Access H24; **Port Pendennis Marina** (Residents only at present) Visitors harbour planned to N of Marina, plus YC (R, Bar, ⊡, Ch etc). **Port Falmouth BY** ☎ 313248, ME, El, Sh, M, Slip; **Western Electronic Services** ☎ 317728, Ⓔ; **Penrose** ☎ 312402, SM; **West Country Chandlers** ☎ 312611, CH, Gas, Gaz; **Bosuns Locker** ☎ 312414, CH, ACA; **Nautibits Used Boat Gear** ☎ 317474, CH; **Mainbrace Chandlers** ☎ 318314, CH; **Falmouth Ship Repairers** ☎ 311400, Slip, P, D, FW, ME, El, Sh, C, CH; **Town** V, R, Bar; ⊠; Ⓑ; ⇌; ✈ (Plymouth or Newquay).
PENRYN/FLUSHING **Falmouth Boat Construction** ☎ 74309, M, Slip, El, FW, ME, C (12 ton), Sh; **Williams BY** ☎ 73819, Sh, ME, C; **Penryn Bridge BY** ☎ 73322, BY, ME, El, Sh; **South West Sails** ☎ 752291, SM; **The Boathouse** ☎ 74177, CH, SM, ACA; **Falmouth Chandlers** ☎ 73988, CH, Gas, Gaz; **Falmouth Bass Boat Co.** ☎ 74685, BY, ME, El, Sh; **SKB** ☎ 72107, SM.
MYLOR/RESTRONGUET **Mylor Yacht Harbour** (250 + 20 visitors) ☎ 72121, BH (25 ton), CH, Gas, Gaz, AC, FW, Slip, C (4 ton), Sh, ME, El, Ⓔ, CH, V, D, Bar, ⊡, Access HW∓1; **Mylor Marine Electronics** ☎ 74001, Ⓔ; **Mylor Chandlery** ☎ 75482, CH, Gas, Gaz; **Restronguet Yacht Basin** ☎ 73613, Slip, M, Sh; **Pandora Inn** ☎ 72678, V, R, Bar.
ST MAWES **Freshwater BY** ☎ 270443, M, ME, Sh, El; **Percuil BY** ☎ Portscatho 564, BY, CH; **St Mawes Inner Harbour** FW, Slip; **Pascoes BY** ☎ 270269, ME, El, Sh, M, SM, Gas.
TRURO/MALPAS **Bar Creek Yacht Station** ☎ Truro 73919, BY, M, Slip, ME, Sh, El; **Malpas Marine** ☎ Truro 71260, M, CH, ME, El, Sh; **Reg Langdon** ☎ Truro 72668, CH; **Quay Chandlers** ☎ Truro 72116, CH, Gas;
YACHT CLUBS etc.
Port of Falmouth Sailing Association ☎ 77061.
Royal Cornwall Yacht Club ☎ 311105, M, Slip, FW, R, Bar.
Mylor Yacht Club ☎ 74391, Bar.
St Mawes S.C. ☎ 270686.
Flushing S.C. ☎ 74043.
Restronguet S.C. ☎ 74536.
Note 1 Fuel Barge June to early Sept

NAVIGATION
Waypoint 50°16'.11N 04°46'.54W, 090°/270° from/to pierhead Lt, 0.20M. Beware rock ledges off the N Quay. Harbour entrance between breakwaters is 46m wide. Speed limit in the harbour is 3 kn. Harbour is crowded and is used by large number of fishing boats.
LIGHTS AND MARKS
S Quay Fl (2) 10s 9m 12M; Dia (1) 30s (occas).
RADIO TELEPHONE
Hr Mr VHF Ch 16; 14 (Summer 0900–2100 LT. Winter 0900–1700 LT).
TELEPHONE (0726)
Hr Mr 842496; CG 842353; MRSC Brixham 882704; ⌗ (0752) 222929; Marinecall 0898 500 458; Police 842262; Dr 843701.
FACILITIES
EC Thursday; **N Quay** L, FW; **S Quay** L, FW, AB; **W Quay** P, D, L, FW; **J. Moores BY** ☎ 842962, Slip, Sh (wood), CH; **Jetty Head** L, FW; **Inner Harbour** Slip, M, L; **Village** V, R, ⊡, Gas, Bar. ⊠; Ⓑ (June-Sept 1000-1430, Oct-June 1000-1300); ⇌ (bus to St. Austell); ✈ (Newquay).

MEVAGISSEY 10-1-14
Cornwall

CHARTS
Admiralty 147, 148, 1267; Stanford 13; Imray C6; OS 204
TIDES
−0600 Dover; ML 3.1; Duration 0600; Zone 0 (GMT).

Standard Port DEVONPORT (⟶)

Times				Height (metres)			
HW		LW		MHWS	MHWN	MLWN	MLWS
0000	0600	0000	0600	5.5	4.4	2.2	0.8
1200	1800	1200	1800				

Differences MEVAGISSEY
−0010	−0015	−0005	+0005	−0.1	−0.1	−0.2	−0.1

SHELTER
Harbour is available at all states of the tide but entrance faces NE and is exposed to E winds. Dangerous to approach when there are strong SE winds. Anchorage off is unsuitable when wind is E of S. Inner harbour is reserved for fishing boats except when taking on fuel or water. Visitors berth S Pier.

FOWEY 10-1-15
Cornwall

CHARTS
Admiralty 148, 31, 1267; Stanford 13; Imray C6, Y52; OS 204
TIDES
−0555 Dover; ML 3.1; Duration 0605; Zone 0 (GMT).

Standard Port DEVONPORT (⟶)

Times				Height (metres)			
HW		LW		MHWS	MHWN	MLWN	MLWS
0000	0600	0000	0600	5.5	4.4	2.2	0.8
1200	1800	1200	1800				

Differences FOWEY
−0010	−0015	−0010	−0005	−0.1	−0.1	−0.2	−0.2

PAR
−0005	−0015	0000	−0010	−0.4	−0.4	−0.4	−0.2

SHELTER
Good sheltered harbour but partly exposed to winds from S to SW. Gales from these directions can cause heavy swells in the lower harbour and confused seas, especially on the ebb. Entry at any tide in any conditions. Visitors buoys are white and marked 'FHC − visitors'. Visitors moorings situated in Pont Pill, in the main stream opposite Albert Quay and at Mixtow Pill (1M upstream). Pont Pill offers double berth fore and aft moorings and 60' of moorings on a floating pontoon. In the stream there is a line of single swinging moorings and another 60' of mooring pontoon. Mixtow offers 60' of pontoon morring in quieter conditions. Pontoons are in situ May to October. Albert Quay − there is a 'T' shaped pontoon offering a deep water mooring for a short stay (2 hours), FW available.

FOWEY continued

NAVIGATION
Waypoint 50°19'.30N 04°38'.70W, 205°/025° from/to Whitehouse Pt Lt, Iso WRG, 11/8M. From E beware Udder Rk (3 M E of entrance); from SW beware Cannis Rk (4 ca SE of Gribbin Head). Entering, keep well clear of Punch Cross Ledge. Fowey is a busy commercial port, so take necessary precautions. Speed limit 6 kn. Navigable up to Lostwithiel at HW for boats with shallow draught. Channel is unmarked.

LIGHTS AND MARKS
A daymark on Gribbin Head, RW Tower on headland, 76m, can be seen from all sea directions. Fowey Lt Ho, L Fl WR 5s 28m 11/9M R 284°-295°, W 295°-028°, R 028°-054°.

RADIO TELEPHONE
Call Fowey Harbour Radio VHF Ch 16; 12 (office hours). Boat Marshall Patrol (0900-2000 LT) Ch 16 12. Other stations: Charlestown Ch 16; 14 (HW − 1 to HW + 1 and when vessel expected). Par (call: Par Port Radio) Ch 16; 12 (Office hours and HW − 2 to HW + 1). Water taxi VHF Ch 06.

TELEPHONE (0726) 616
Hr Mr 832471; CG Polruan 228; MRSC Brixham 882704; ⌗ (0752) 222929; Marinecall 0898 500 458; Police 833438; Ⓗ 832241; Dr 832451.

FACILITIES
EC Wednesday and Saturday; **Royal Fowey YC** ☎ 832245, FW, R, Bar; **Upper Deck Marine** ☎ 832287, M, Gas, Gaz, CH; **Troy Chandlery** ☎ 833265, CH, Gas, Gaz, ACA, Ⓔ; **Albert Quay Pontoon** L, FW; **Polruan Quay** Slip, P, D, L, FW, C (3 ton); **C. Toms BY** ☎ Polruan 232, Slip (up to 21m by arrangement), FW, ME, El, Sh, C (7 ton), CH; **Fowey Gallants SC** ☎ 832335, Bar; **Winklepicker** ☎ Polruan 296, CH; **Fowey Refueller** Ch 16 (0900−1800 LT daily − winter Mon−Fri) or ☎ (0836) 519341 P, D; Emergencies ☎ Polruan 697 **Town** ⊡, ✉; Ⓑ; ⇌ (bus to Par); ✈ (Newquay).
A port guide is available from harbour office.

LOOE 10-1-16
Cornwall

CHARTS
Admiralty 147, 148, 1267; Stanford 13; Imray C6; OS 201

TIDES
−0545 Dover; ML 3.0; Duration 0610; Zone 0 (GMT).

Standard Port DEVONPORT (→)

Times				Height (metres)			
HW		LW		MHWS	MHWN	MLWN	MLWS
0000	0600	0000	0600	5.5	4.4	2.2	0.8
1200	1800	1200	1800				
Differences LOOE							
−0010	−0010	−0005	−0005	−0.1	−0.2	−0.2	−0.2
WHITSAND BAY							
0000	0000	0000	0000	0.0	+0.1	−0.1	+0.2

SHELTER
Good except in strong SE winds when the harbour becomes uncomfortable. The whole harbour dries. Visitors berth on W side of Hr marked in Y.

NAVIGATION
Waypoint 50°19'.73N 04°24'.60W, 130°/310° from/to pierhead Lt, 2.0M. Entrance dangerous in strong SE winds, when seas break over the bar heavily. Coming from W, beware Ranneys Rks extending SE and E from Looe Is. From E, beware Longstone Rks extending 1½ ca from shore NE of harbour entrance. At springs, tide runs up to 5 kn. Do not secure to W bank anywhere to S of shops due to rocky outcrops.

LIGHTS AND MARKS
Mid Main Beacon (off Hannafore Pt, halfway between pierhead and Looe Island) Q(3) 10s 2M; E cardinal mark. From West at night keep in W sector (267°-313°) of pierhead Lt Oc WR 3s 8m 15/12M; vis W013°-207°, R207°-267°, W267°-313°, R313°-332°. Nailzee Pt Siren (2) 30s.
R flag is displayed from FS on quay when it is too rough for small craft to put to sea.

RADIO TELEPHONE
VHF Ch 16 (no constant watch).

TELEPHONE (050 36)
Hr Mr 2839; CG 2138; MRSC Brixham 882704; ⌗ (0752) 222929; Marinecall 0898 500 458; Police 2233; Dr 3195.

FACILITIES
EC Thursday (winter only); **East Looe Quay** Access HW ∓3, Slip, P and D (cans), L, FW, ME, El, C (2½ ton), CH; **Looe SC** ☎ 2559, L, R, Bar; **West Looe Quay** Slip, M, P and D (cans), L, FW, ME, El, CH, AB; **Curtis Frank & Pope** ☎ 2332, Slip, M, Sh (Wood); **Marine Engineering Looe** ☎ 2887, ME, El, Ⓔ; **Pearn Norman & Co** ☎ 2244, Slip, M, ME, El, Sh, CH; **Jack Bray & Son** ☎ 2504, CH; **Millendreath Marine** ☎ 3003, CH; **Looe Harbour Chandlers** ☎ 4760, CH, El, Ⓔ, Gas; **Town** P, FW, V, R, Bar, ⊡, ✉; Ⓑ; ⇌; ✈ (Plymouth).

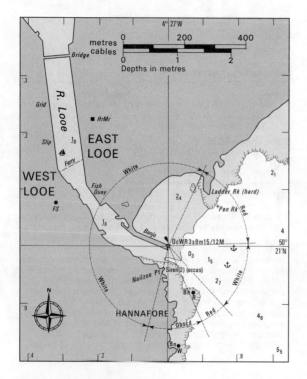

PLYMOUTH   10-1-17
(DEVONPORT)
Devon

CHARTS
Admiralty 30, 1901, 1967, 1902, 871; Stanford 13;
Imray C14, OS 201
TIDES
−0540 Dover; ML 3.3; Duration 0610; Zone 0 (GMT).

Standard Port DEVONPORT (→)

Times				Height (metres)			
HW		LW		MHWS	MHWN	MLWN	MLWS
0000	0600	0000	0600	5.5	4.4	2.2	0.8
1200	1800	1200	1800				

Differences JUPITER POINT
+0010	+0005	0000	−0005	0.0	0.0	+0.1	0.0

SALTASH
0000	+0010	0000	−0005	+0.1	+0.1	+0.1	+0.1

CARGREEN
0000	+0010	+0020	+0020	0.0	0.0	−0.1	0.0

COTEHELE QUAY
0000	+0020	+0045	+0045	−0.9	−0.9	−0.8	−0.4

ST GERMANS
0000	0000	+0020	+0020	−0.3	−0.1	0.0	+0.2

BOVISAND PIER
0000	−0020	0000	−0010	−0.2	−0.1	0.0	+0.1

NOTE: Devonport is a Standard Port and times and
heights of tides are given below.

SHELTER
Excellent shelter. The entrance to the Sound can be made
through either the west or east channel in both of which
there is deep water. The Sound itself has no shallow
patches with less than 3.7m at MLWS. Winds from SE to
W increase the flood and retard the ebb, while winds from
the NW to E have the opposite effect. The R Tamar
which is joined by the R Tavy about 1¼ M above Saltash
offers good shelter, as does the R Lynher. R Tamar is
navigable to Cotehele, and beyond by shallow draught
boats.
BYE LAWS
Plymouth is a Naval Base. The whole harbour comes
under the jurisdiction of the Queen's Harbour Master
although specific parts are allowed local control;
Cattewater Harbour Commissioners; Sutton Harbour
Improvements Co; Associated British Ports run Mill Bay
Docks. There is frequent movement of naval vessels.
These vessels have right of way in the channels. Signals
are hoisted on HM Ships and at the Long Room and Flag
Staff Steps and apply to the waters off the dockyard port
and 125m either side of the deep water channel out to the
western entrance of the breakwater. The Cattewater, Mill
Bay Docks and Sutton Harbour are excluded. Plymouth is
also a busy commercial port principally using Mill Bay
Docks, and a busy fishing port based mainly on the
Barbican area.
NAVIGATION
Waypoint 50°19′.70N 04°09′.80W, 213°/033° from/to
West breakwater Lt, 0.40M. There are no real hazards
entering the harbour as it is very well lit and buoyed. It is
not advised to go between Drake's Island and Mount
Edgcumbe although this is a short cut to the Hamoaze
(known as the Bridge) and has about 1.7m at LWS and is
buoyed. As will be seen from the chart, yachts need not
keep to the deep water channels.
    HMS Cambridge at Wembury has a firing range out to
sea. Firing usually occurs between 0830 and 1700 (LT)
Tuesday to Friday inclusive and when in progress 3 large
red flags are flown at Wembury Point and from Penlee.
HMS Cambridge can be called up on VHF Ch 16 (working
10, 11) if you are worried about being near the closed
area. To enter the Sound during firings, keep to the W of
Eddystone. HMS Cambridge Range Officer ☎ 553740, ext
412 (office hours) or Quartermaster on ext 406 (other
times).

LIGHTS AND MARKS
Wembury Pt Oc Y 10s (occas). W end of breakwater Fl
WR 10s 19m 15/12M (vis W 262°-208°, R 208°-262°) and
Iso 4s 12m 12M (vis 031°-039°). Mallard Shoal Ldg Lts
349°. Front Q.WRG 10/3M (vis G 233°-043°, R 043°-067°,
G 067°-087°, W 087°-099°, R 099°-108°). Rear 396m from
front (on Hoe) Oc G 1.3s (vis 310°-040°).
Dir Lts, with W sectors showing the leading lines, are
established at Withyhedge (070°), Royal Western YC
(315°), Mill Bay (324° and 048°30′), Western Kings
(271°), Raveness (225°), Mount Wise (343°). In each
case above a G sector indicates that the yacht is to stbd
of the leading line, and a R sector that she is to port of it.
In fog the following Dir Lts show white lights as indicated:
Mallard (front) Fl 5s (vis 232°-110°); Royal Western YC F
(vis 313°-317°); Raveness Fl (2) 15s (vis 160°-305°);
Mount Wise F (vis 341°-345°).
Note: Principal lights in Plymouth Sound may show QY in
the event of a mains power failure.
TRAFFIC SIGNALS
See below.
RADIO TELEPHONE
Call: *Long Room Port Control* VHF Ch 16; 08 12 14 (H24).
Call: *Mill Bay Docks* Ch 16; 14 (During ferry operations
only).
Call: *Sutton Harbour Radio* Ch 16; 80 37 (1 Apr- 15 Oct:
0830-2000. 16 Oct-31 Mar: 0900-1800 LT). Mayflower
Marina, Queen Anne's Battery Marina, Sutton Harbour
Marina, Ballast Pound Yacht Harbour and Royal Western
YC Ch 80 Call: *Cattewater Harbour Office* Ch 16; 12
(Mon-Fri, 0900-1700 LT).
TELEPHONE (0752)
Hr Mr QHM 663225; Cattewater Hr Mr 665934; Associated
British Docks at Mill Bay 662191; CG 822239; MRSC
Brixham 882704; Control Centre 53777 Ex 12 or 62;
⌗ (0752) 222929; Marinecall 0898 500 458; Weather Centre
402534; Police 701188; Dr 53533; Ⓗ 668080.
FACILITIES
EC Wednesday
Mayflower International Marina (220 + 60 visitors)
☎ 556633, Slip, P, D, FW, ME, El, Sh, AC, C (2 ton), BH
(25 ton), CH, V, Gas, Gaz, Divers, SM, Bar, BY, YC, ▣;
Sutton Harbour Marina (310) ☎ 664186, P, D, FW, AC,
C (3 ton), Slip, ME, El, Sh, SM; **Queen Anne's Battery
Marina** (240 + 60 visitors) ☎ 671142, Slip, ME, El, Sh, FW,
BH (20 ton), C (50 ton), P, D, CH, Gas, ▣, SM, V, R, AC,
Bar; **Mill Bay Docks** ☎ 662191; facilities here are limited
and yachtsmen should contact the Royal Western YC on
arrival. **Mill Bay Village Marina** No visitors; **Ballast
Pound Yacht Harbour** (50 + 10 visitors) ☎ 813658, FW,
ME, El, Sh, AC, Diver, SM, Access HW∓2; **Boathaven**
(10) ☎ Tavistock 832502, ME, El, SH, C (10 ton); **Royal
Dockyard** has unlimited facilities but is expensive; **A S
Blagdon** ☎ 28155, ME, El, Sh, C (7 ton), P, D; **Eddystone
Marine Repairs** ☎ 509974, El, ME, Sh; **Mashford Bros**
☎ 822232, ME, El, Sh, D, C (10 ton), Slip, Gas; **Sutton
Marine Services** ☎ 662129, C (7 ton), CH, P, D; **Ocean
Marine Services** ☎ 223922, El, CH; **Saltash Marine**
☎ Saltash 3885, CH, ACA; **A E Monsen** ☎ 664384, CH,
ACA; **Fox Haggart** ☎ 662587, ME, Sh; **The Quarterdeck**
☎ 24567, ME, C (12 ton); **Royal Western YC of England**
☎ 660077; Bar, R, M, C (20 ton), D, P, CH, FW, L, ▣, Slip;
Royal Plymouth Corinthian ☎ 664327, M, R, Bar; **RNSA**
c/o QHM ☎ 663225; **Weir Quay YC** ☎ Tavistock 840474;
Retreat BY ☎ 228855, M, BY; **Greenham Marine**
☎ 228114, Ⓔ; **Tolley Marine Electronics** ☎ 222530, Ⓔ;
City P, D, V, R, CH, ✉; Ⓑ; ⇌; ✈.

PLYMOUTH *continued*

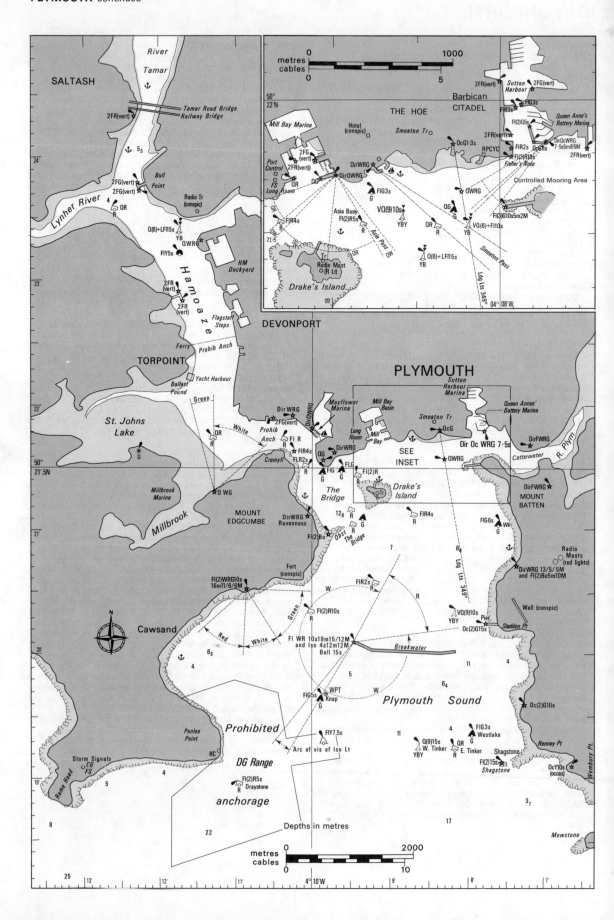

PLYMOUTH *continued*
Traffic signals
Shown from Long Room and Morice Yard controlling the Main Ship Channel between the Breakwater and No1 Jetty

Day	Night		Meaning	Day	Meaning
▨	◌	Red	No movement in Main Channel Small craft keep clear	⬍●	Ship traffic between Sound and Hamoaze stopped
	◌	Green			
	◌	Green			
▨	◌	White	Exit only in Main Channel Small craft keep clear	⬍	Caution necessary between Sound and Hamoaze
●	◌	Green			
●	◌	Green	Entry only in Main Channel Small craft keep clear	⬆	Caution necessary in Sound
▨	◌	White			
▧▷	—Code		Vessels may enter and leave but must give a wide berth to ships displaying Answering Pendant over Numeral Zero	⬇	Caution necessary in Hamoaze
◺	—Pt9				

Flown from HM ships and tugs   ▧▷ Code ◺ Zero   Give wide berth to these vessels

Dock signals-Mill Bay
Shown from the head of Mill Bay Pier

Day	Night		Meaning	Day	Night		Meaning
●	◌	Green	Entry permitted to Outer Mill Bay	●	◌	Red	Exit permitted from Outer Mill Bay
	◌	Green		●	◌	Red	

Shown from the head of Mill Bay Pier and W side of Lock

Day	Night		Meaning	Day	Night		Meaning
●	◌	Green	Entry permitted to the Inner Basin	●	◌	Red	Exit permitted from the Inner Basin
●	◌	Green		●	◌	Red	
●	◌	Green		●	◌	Red	

Note   Coloured flags and lights are waved on occasions but these are only berthing instructions to large vessels and do not concern yachts.

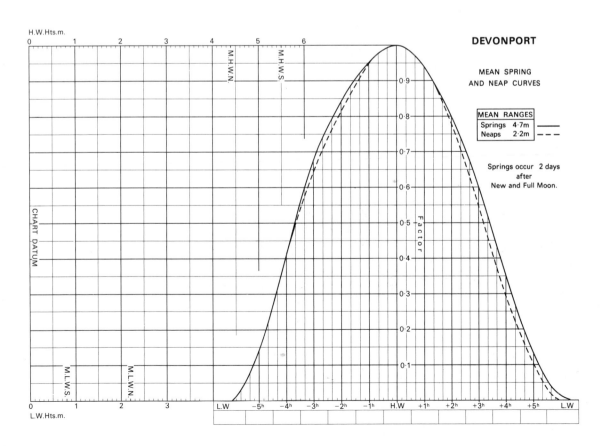

DEVONPORT

MEAN SPRING
AND NEAP CURVES

MEAN RANGES	
Springs 4·7m	——
Neaps 2·2m	- - -

Springs occur 2 days
after
New and Full Moon.

ENGLAND, SOUTH COAST - PLYMOUTH (DEVONPORT)

LAT 50°22'N   LONG 4°11'W

TIMES AND HEIGHTS OF HIGH AND LOW WATERS

YEAR 1991

TIME ZONE **UT (GMT)**
For Summer Time add ONE hour in non-shaded areas

JANUARY

Day	Time	m	Time	m	Time	m	Time	m
1 TU	0555	5.6	1206	0.8	1826	5.4		
2 W	0026	0.8	0643	5.7	1254	0.7	1912	5.4
3 TH	0112	0.8	0727	5.7	1339	0.7	1955	5.4
4 F	0155	0.8	0808	5.6	1422	0.8	2036	5.2
5 SA	0238	1.0	0847	5.5	1504	1.0	2114	5.1
6 SU	0319	1.3	0924	5.3	1545	1.3	2151	4.9
7 M ☾	0400	1.5	1001	5.0	1627	1.6	2230	4.7
8 TU	0443	1.8	1043	4.8	1712	1.9	2317	4.6
9 W	0532	2.1	1134	4.6	1804	2.2		
10 TH	0014	4.5	0630	2.3	1236	4.5	1908	2.3
11 F	0121	4.4	0745	2.4	1347	4.4	2023	2.3
12 SA	0231	4.6	0901	2.2	1500	4.5	2131	2.1
13 SU	0337	4.8	1003	2.0	1606	4.7	2225	1.8
14 M	0434	5.0	1053	1.7	1700	4.9	2311	1.5
15 TU ●	0523	5.2	1135	1.5	1747	5.1	2352	1.3
16 W	0606	5.4	1214	1.2	1829	5.2		
17 TH	0030	1.2	0644	5.4	1251	1.0	1906	5.2
18 F	0106	1.1	0719	5.4	1327	1.0	1940	5.2
19 SA	0141	1.1	0751	5.4	1401	1.0	2011	5.1
20 SU	0216	1.1	0820	5.3	1436	1.1	2038	5.0
21 M	0251	1.3	0845	5.1	1513	1.2	2105	4.9
22 TU	0328	1.4	0913	5.0	1552	1.4	2138	4.7
23 W ☽	0409	1.6	0953	4.8	1636	1.6	2226	4.6
24 TH	0459	1.9	1050	4.6	1731	1.9	2334	4.5
25 F	0603	2.1	1209	4.4	1844	2.1		
26 SA	0059	4.4	0730	2.2	1343	4.4	2015	2.1
27 SU	0231	4.6	0903	1.9	1517	4.6	2136	1.8
28 M	0352	4.9	1013	1.5	1631	4.8	2237	1.3
29 TU	0455	5.2	1108	1.0	1729	5.1	2329	1.0
30 W ○	0547	5.5	1157	0.7	1817	5.4		
31 TH	0014	0.7	0633	5.7	1241	0.5	1900	5.5

FEBRUARY

Day	Time	m	Time	m	Time	m	Time	m
1 F	0057	0.6	0714	5.8	1322	0.4	1938	5.5
2 SA	0137	0.6	0750	5.7	1401	0.6	2013	5.4
3 SU	0215	0.8	0823	5.6	1438	0.8	2043	5.2
4 M	0251	1.0	0851	5.3	1512	1.2	2111	5.0
5 TU	0325	1.3	0919	5.1	1546	1.5	2141	4.8
6 W ☾	0359	1.7	0952	4.8	1620	1.8	2220	4.6
7 TH	0437	2.0	1036	4.5	1659	2.1	2314	4.4
8 F	0525	2.3	1137	4.3	1754	2.4		
9 SA	0023	4.3	0637	2.5	1254	4.2	1924	2.5
10 SU	0144	4.4	0827	2.4	1423	4.2	2106	2.3
11 M	0306	4.5	0945	2.1	1544	4.5	2208	1.9
12 TU	0413	4.8	1036	1.7	1645	4.8	2254	1.5
13 W	0506	5.1	1118	1.3	1733	5.1	2335	1.1
14 TH ●	0550	5.4	1156	0.9	1814	5.3		
15 F	0012	0.9	0629	5.5	1233	0.7	1851	5.4
16 SA	0048	0.7	0704	5.6	1307	0.6	1925	5.4
17 SU	0122	0.7	0737	5.5	1342	0.6	1956	5.3
18 M	0157	0.8	0805	5.4	1416	0.8	2022	5.1
19 TU	0231	0.9	0830	5.2	1451	1.0	2045	5.0
20 W	0307	1.2	0854	5.0	1528	1.3	2113	4.8
21 TH ☽	0346	1.4	0929	4.8	1610	1.6	2158	4.6
22 F	0433	1.8	1027	4.5	1702	1.9	2309	4.4
23 SA	0536	2.1	1153	4.2	1816	2.2		
24 SU	0040	4.3	0712	2.2	1337	4.2	2003	2.2
25 M	0221	4.4	0857	1.9	1516	4.4	2128	1.8
26 TU	0344	4.8	1004	1.4	1625	4.8	2226	1.3
27 W	0445	5.2	1055	1.0	1718	5.1	2314	0.9
28 TH ○	0534	5.5	1140	0.6	1802	5.4	2357	0.6

MARCH

Day	Time	m	Time	m	Time	m	Time	m
1 F	0616	5.7	1221	0.4	1841	5.5		
2 SA	0036	0.5	0653	5.8	1300	0.4	1915	5.5
3 SU	0114	0.5	0726	5.7	1335	0.6	1945	5.4
4 M	0149	0.7	0755	5.5	1408	0.8	2010	5.3
5 TU	0221	1.0	0818	5.3	1438	1.2	2033	5.1
6 W	0251	1.3	0841	5.0	1506	1.5	2100	4.9
7 TH	0320	1.6	0910	4.7	1535	1.8	2136	4.7
8 F ☾	0353	1.9	0952	4.5	1610	2.1	2228	4.4
9 SA	0436	2.2	1053	4.2	1659	2.4	2338	4.3
10 SU	0542	2.5	1213	4.0	1825	2.6		
11 M	0101	4.3	0744	2.5	1347	4.1	2034	2.4
12 TU	0230	4.4	0918	2.1	1516	4.4	2141	1.9
13 W	0343	4.7	1009	1.6	1619	4.7	2228	1.5
14 TH	0439	5.1	1051	1.2	1708	5.1	2308	1.0
15 F	0524	5.4	1129	0.8	1750	5.3	2346	0.7
16 SA ●	0605	5.6	1206	0.5	1828	5.5		
17 SU	0023	0.6	0642	5.6	1243	0.5	1903	5.5
18 M	0059	0.5	0716	5.6	1318	0.5	1935	5.4
19 TU	0135	0.8	0748	5.4	1354	0.7	2004	5.2
20 W	0211	0.8	0817	5.2	1430	0.9	2032	5.1
21 TH	0249	1.1	0848	4.9	1509	1.2	2104	4.9
22 F	0330	1.4	0928	4.7	1552	1.6	2153	4.6
23 SA ☽	0420	1.7	1031	4.4	1647	2.0	2305	4.4
24 SU	0526	2.1	1156	4.2	1806	2.4		
25 M	0032	4.3	0706	2.2	1335	4.2	1952	2.2
26 TU	0208	4.5	0842	1.8	1503	4.5	2110	1.8
27 W	0326	4.8	0944	1.4	1606	4.8	2204	1.3
28 TH	0424	5.2	1033	1.0	1655	5.1	2251	0.9
29 F	0511	5.5	1116	0.7	1737	5.4	2332	0.7
30 SA ○	0551	5.6	1155	0.5	1813	5.5		
31 SU	0011	0.6	0627	5.6	1232	0.6	1846	5.5

APRIL

Day	Time	m	Time	m	Time	m	Time	m
1 M	0047	0.6	0658	5.5	1306	0.7	1914	5.4
2 TU	0120	0.8	0730	5.4	1337	1.0	1938	5.3
3 W	0151	1.1	0748	5.1	1405	1.3	2002	5.1
4 TH	0220	1.4	0811	4.9	1432	1.6	2029	4.9
5 F	0249	1.6	0841	4.7	1501	1.8	2105	4.7
6 SA	0322	1.9	0923	4.4	1536	2.1	2155	4.5
7 SU ☾	0405	2.2	1022	4.2	1626	2.3	2301	4.3
8 M	0507	2.4	1138	4.1	1743	2.5		
9 TU	0018	4.3	0648	2.4	1305	4.1	1940	2.4
10 W	0142	4.4	0829	2.1	1432	4.4	2058	2.0
11 TH	0258	4.7	0928	1.6	1539	4.7	2150	1.5
12 F	0359	5.0	1014	1.2	1632	5.0	2234	1.1
13 SA	0449	5.3	1056	0.8	1717	5.3	2315	0.8
14 SU ●	0533	5.5	1136	0.6	1757	5.5	2355	0.6
15 M	0614	5.6	1215	0.5	1836	5.5		
16 TU	0034	0.5	0652	5.5	1254	0.5	1912	5.5
17 W	0114	0.6	0730	5.4	1333	0.7	1947	5.3
18 TH	0153	0.8	0807	5.2	1413	1.0	2023	5.1
19 F	0235	1.0	0848	4.9	1455	1.3	2104	4.9
20 SA	0321	1.3	0936	4.6	1543	1.6	2156	4.7
21 SU ☽	0414	1.7	1038	4.4	1640	1.9	2301	4.6
22 M	0522	1.9	1152	4.3	1756	2.1		
23 TU	0018	4.5	0649	2.0	1315	4.3	1924	2.1
24 W	0140	4.6	0811	1.8	1432	4.5	2037	1.8
25 TH	0252	4.8	0912	1.4	1532	4.8	2133	1.4
26 F	0350	5.1	1002	1.1	1621	5.1	2221	1.1
27 SA	0438	5.3	1045	1.0	1703	5.4	2304	0.9
28 SU ○	0520	5.4	1125	0.9	1741	5.4	2343	0.9
29 M	0557	5.4	1202	0.9	1814	5.4		
30 TU	0019	0.9	0628	5.3	1237	1.0	1844	5.3

Chart Datum: 3.22 metres below Ordnance Datum (Newlyn)

ENGLAND, SOUTH COAST - PLYMOUTH (DEVONPORT)

TIME ZONE UT(GMT)
For Summer Time add ONE hour in non-shaded areas

LAT 50°22'N   LONG 4°11'W

TIMES AND HEIGHTS OF HIGH AND LOW WATERS

YEAR **1991**

MAY

Day	DoW	Time	m	Time	m	Time	m	Time	m
1	W	0054	1.1	0657	5.2	1309	1.2	1912	5.2
16	TH	0056	0.7	0715	5.3	1316	0.8	1933	5.4
2	TH	0125	1.3	0724	5.0	1338	1.4	1939	5.1
17	F	0140	0.8	0759	5.2	1400	1.0	2015	5.3
3	F	0156	1.5	0751	4.8	1408	1.6	2009	4.9
18	SA	0226	1.0	0845	5.0	1446	1.2	2101	5.1
4	SA	0227	1.6	0824	4.7	1440	1.8	2045	4.8
19	SU	0315	1.2	0935	4.8	1535	1.5	2151	5.0
5	SU	0303	1.8	0906	4.5	1518	2.0	2131	4.6
20	M	0408	1.5	1030	4.6	1630	1.7	2247	4.8
6	M	0347	2.0	1000	4.3	1606	2.2	2229	4.5
21	TU	0508	1.7	1131	4.5	1733	1.9	2350	4.7
7	TU	0444	2.1	1105	4.2	1712	2.3	2335	4.5
22	W	0616	1.8	1238	4.5	1844	1.9		
8	W	0559	2.2	1218	4.3	1837	2.3		
23	TH	0057	4.7	0726	1.8	1346	4.6	1954	1.9
9	TH	0047	4.5	0725	2.0	1335	4.4	1959	2.1
24	F	0205	4.8	0830	1.7	1446	4.7	2054	1.7
10	F	0200	4.7	0835	1.7	1446	4.7	2103	1.7
25	SA	0305	4.9	0924	1.5	1539	4.9	2147	1.5
11	SA	0307	4.9	0931	1.4	1546	4.9	2155	1.3
26	SU	0358	5.0	1012	1.4	1625	5.1	2234	1.4
12	SU	0406	5.1	1020	1.1	1637	5.2	2243	1.0
27	M	0444	5.1	1055	1.3	1707	5.2	2316	1.3
13	M	0458	5.3	1105	0.8	1724	5.4	2328	0.8
28	TU	0525	5.1	1135	1.3	1745	5.3	2355	1.3
14	TU	0545	5.4	1149	0.7	1808	5.5		
29	W	0603	5.1	1212	1.3	1820	5.3		
15	W	0012	0.7	0630	5.4	1233	0.7	1851	5.5
30	TH	0032	1.3	0632	5.0	1247	1.4	1853	5.2
31	F	0107	1.4	0709	4.9	1320	1.5	1925	5.1

JUNE

Day	DoW	Time	m	Time	m	Time	m	Time	m
1	SA	0140	1.5	0742	4.8	1353	1.6	1957	5.0
16	SU	0217	0.8	0836	5.1	1435	1.0	2050	5.4
2	SU	0214	1.5	0816	4.7	1428	1.7	2032	4.9
17	M	0303	1.0	0922	5.0	1521	1.2	2135	5.2
3	M	0251	1.6	0854	4.6	1506	1.8	2111	4.8
18	TU	0351	1.2	1009	4.8	1609	1.4	2222	5.0
4	TU	0333	1.7	0938	4.5	1550	1.9	2157	4.7
19	W	0441	1.4	1058	4.7	1701	1.7	2313	4.9
5	W	0421	1.8	1030	4.5	1642	2.0	2251	4.7
20	TH	0535	1.5	1151	4.6	1758	1.9		
6	TH	0518	1.9	1130	4.5	1745	2.1	2353	4.6
21	F	0008	4.7	0634	1.8	1250	4.6	1901	2.0
7	F	0625	1.9	1237	4.5	1858	2.0		
22	SA	0110	4.6	0739	1.9	1351	4.6	2009	2.0
8	SA	0101	4.6	0737	1.8	1347	4.6	2011	1.9
23	SU	0213	4.6	0842	1.9	1451	4.7	2112	1.9
9	SU	0213	4.7	0830	1.6	1456	4.8	2116	1.6
24	M	0315	4.7	0939	1.8	1547	4.9	2206	1.7
10	M	0322	4.9	0945	1.4	1558	5.0	2213	1.3
25	TU	0411	4.8	1029	1.6	1637	5.0	2254	1.6
11	TU	0425	5.1	1038	1.1	1655	5.2	2306	1.0
26	W	0500	4.9	1114	1.5	1722	5.1	2337	1.4
12	W	0522	5.2	1128	0.9	1746	5.4	2355	0.8
27	TH	0544	4.9	1154	1.4	1803	5.2		
13	TH	0614	5.3	1216	0.8	1835	5.5		
28	F	0016	1.3	0624	5.0	1232	1.3	1841	5.2
14	F	0043	0.7	0703	5.3	1303	0.8	1920	5.5
29	SA	0053	1.3	0701	5.0	1307	1.3	1916	5.2
15	SA	0130	0.7	0750	5.3	1349	0.9	2005	5.5
30	SU	0128	1.3	0735	4.9	1342	1.4	1949	5.2

JULY

Day	DoW	Time	m	Time	m	Time	m	Time	m
1	M	0203	1.3	0808	4.9	1416	1.4	2020	5.1
16	TU	0244	0.7	0859	5.2	1500	0.9	2111	5.4
2	TU	0238	1.3	0840	4.8	1452	1.5	2052	5.0
17	W	0326	1.0	0938	5.0	1542	1.2	2149	5.1
3	W	0315	1.4	0915	4.7	1531	1.6	2127	4.9
18	TH	0408	1.3	1017	4.8	1625	1.5	2230	4.9
4	TH	0356	1.5	0954	4.6	1614	1.7	2210	4.8
19	F	0452	1.6	1101	4.6	1711	1.9	2317	4.7
5	F	0442	1.6	1044	4.5	1704	1.9	2304	4.7
20	SA	0541	1.9	1154	4.5	1806	2.1		
6	SA	0537	1.8	1145	4.5	1806	2.0		
21	SU	0014	4.5	0640	2.2	1256	4.5	1916	2.3
7	SU	0011	4.6	0644	1.9	1257	4.5	1922	2.0
22	M	0122	4.4	0756	2.2	1405	4.5	2038	2.2
8	M	0128	4.6	0802	1.9	1414	4.6	2042	1.8
23	TU	0235	4.4	0911	2.1	1514	4.6	2146	2.0
9	TU	0249	4.6	0917	1.7	1529	4.8	2153	1.5
24	W	0344	4.5	1010	1.9	1614	4.8	2239	1.7
10	W	0405	4.8	1020	1.4	1635	5.1	2252	1.2
25	TH	0442	4.7	1057	1.6	1705	5.1	2322	1.4
11	TH	0508	5.0	1115	1.0	1732	5.4	2344	0.8
26	F	0530	4.8	1139	1.3	1749	5.2		
12	F	0603	5.2	1204	0.8	1822	5.6		
27	SA	0001	1.2	0612	5.1	1217	1.2	1828	5.3
13	SA	0032	0.6	0652	5.3	1251	0.6	1908	5.7
28	SU	0037	1.0	0649	5.1	1252	1.1	1904	5.4
14	SU	0118	0.5	0737	5.4	1335	0.6	1951	5.7
29	M	0112	1.0	0724	5.1	1326	1.0	1936	5.3
15	M	0202	0.5	0819	5.3	1418	0.7	2032	5.6
30	TU	0145	1.0	0756	5.1	1359	1.1	2006	5.2
31	W	0219	1.0	0824	5.0	1433	1.2	2032	5.1

AUGUST

Day	DoW	Time	m	Time	m	Time	m	Time	m
1	TH	0253	1.1	0851	4.9	1508	1.3	2059	5.0
16	F	0332	1.3	0933	4.9	1547	1.5	2145	4.8
2	F	0330	1.3	0920	4.7	1547	1.5	2132	4.8
17	SA	0408	1.7	1011	4.7	1626	1.9	2227	4.5
3	SA	0411	1.5	1001	4.6	1632	1.7	2223	4.6
18	SU	0448	2.1	1102	4.5	1712	2.2	2324	4.3
4	SU	0500	1.8	1103	4.5	1728	2.0	2335	4.4
19	M	0540	2.3	1206	4.3	1820	2.5		
5	M	0604	2.0	1221	4.4	1846	2.1		
20	TU	0036	4.2	0704	2.5	1323	4.3	2007	2.5
6	TU	0102	4.3	0731	2.1	1349	4.5	2023	2.0
21	W	0202	4.2	0848	2.3	1443	4.5	2128	2.1
7	W	0236	4.4	0902	1.9	1514	4.7	2143	1.6
22	TH	0322	4.4	0951	2.0	1551	4.8	2220	1.7
8	TH	0357	4.7	1009	1.5	1623	5.1	2242	1.1
23	F	0423	4.7	1030	1.6	1644	5.1	2301	1.3
9	F	0500	5.0	1103	1.0	1720	5.4	2332	0.7
24	SA	0511	5.0	1117	1.2	1729	5.3	2339	1.0
10	SA	0552	5.3	1150	0.7	1808	5.7		
25	SU	0553	5.2	1154	1.0	1809	5.5		
11	SU	0017	0.4	0636	5.5	1235	0.5	1851	5.8
26	M	0014	0.8	0630	5.3	1230	0.8	1845	5.5
12	M	0100	0.3	0718	5.5	1316	0.4	1931	5.8
27	TU	0049	0.7	0705	5.4	1304	0.8	1918	5.5
13	TU	0140	0.4	0755	5.5	1356	0.5	2007	5.6
28	W	0122	0.7	0737	5.3	1337	0.8	1948	5.4
14	W	0219	0.6	0830	5.3	1434	0.8	2040	5.4
29	TH	0156	0.8	0805	5.2	1411	1.0	2014	5.2
15	TH	0256	0.9	0901	5.1	1510	1.1	2111	5.1
30	F	0230	1.0	0829	5.0	1446	1.2	2037	5.0
31	SA	0306	1.3	0853	4.8	1524	1.4	2106	4.8

Chart Datum: 3.22 metres below Ordnance Datum (Newlyn)

ENGLAND, SOUTH COAST - PLYMOUTH (DEVONPORT)

TIME ZONE UT (GMT)
For Summer Time add ONE hour in non-shaded areas

LAT 50°22′N   LONG 4°11′W

TIMES AND HEIGHTS OF HIGH AND LOW WATERS

YEAR **1991**

SEPTEMBER

Day	TIME	m	TIME	m	TIME	m	TIME	m
1 SU ☾	0346	1.6	0931	4.6	1608	1.7	2158	4.5
16 M	0401	2.1	1015	4.5	1627	2.3	2240	4.2
2 M	0434	1.9	1037	4.4	1705	2.0	2320	4.3
17 TU	0448	2.4	1122	4.3	1729	2.5	2356	4.1
3 TU	0539	2.2	1204	4.3	1828	2.2		
18 W	0609	2.6	1241	4.3	1925	2.6		
4 W	0057	4.2	0717	2.3	1338	4.4	2016	2.0
19 TH	0125	4.1	0814	2.5	1406	4.4	2058	2.2
5 TH	0235	4.4	0852	1.9	1505	4.7	2132	1.6
20 F	0251	4.4	0933	2.0	1518	4.7	2149	1.7
6 F	0350	4.7	0956	1.4	1611	5.1	2227	1.1
21 SA	0354	4.7	1008	1.6	1614	5.1	2231	1.3
7 SA	0447	5.1	1046	1.0	1704	5.5	2313	0.6
22 SU	0443	5.1	1048	1.2	1700	5.4	2309	0.9
8 SU ●	0533	5.4	1131	0.6	1749	5.7	2356	0.4
23 M	0526	5.3	1126	0.9	1742	5.6	○ 2345	0.7
9 M	0615	5.6	1213	0.4	1830	5.8		
24 TU	0605	5.5	1202	0.7	1820	5.6		
10 TU	0036	0.3	0652	5.6	1252	0.4	1906	5.8
25 W	0021	0.6	0640	5.5	1238	0.7	1855	5.6
11 W	0115	0.4	0726	5.6	1330	0.6	1939	5.6
26 TH	0057	0.6	0713	5.5	1314	0.7	1928	5.4
12 TH	0150	0.7	0756	5.4	1405	0.9	2007	5.4
27 F	0132	0.8	0744	5.3	1350	0.9	1958	5.2
13 F	0224	1.1	0823	5.2	1438	1.2	2033	5.1
28 SA	0208	1.0	0812	5.1	1427	1.1	2027	5.0
14 SA	0255	1.5	0850	4.9	1511	1.6	2102	4.8
29 SU	0246	1.3	0840	4.9	1507	1.4	2103	4.7
15 SU ☽	0326	1.8	0923	4.6	1545	2.0	2142	4.5
30 M	0328	1.6	0923	4.7	1554	1.7	2201	4.4

OCTOBER

Day	TIME	m	TIME	m	TIME	m	TIME	m
1 TU ☾	0419	2.0	1031	4.5	1654	2.0	2321	4.2
16 W	0412	2.4	1041	4.4	1651	2.5	2317	4.2
2 W	0528	2.3	1154	4.4	1821	2.2		
17 TH	0523	2.6	1155	4.4	1822	2.5		
3 TH	0054	4.2	0705	2.3	1325	4.5	2001	2.0
18 F	0040	4.2	0710	2.5	1315	4.5	2002	2.3
4 F	0223	4.5	0833	1.9	1447	4.8	2111	1.5
19 SA	0203	4.4	0833	2.2	1430	4.7	2104	1.8
5 SA	0331	4.8	0933	1.5	1549	5.2	2203	1.1
20 SU	0312	4.7	0927	1.8	1532	5.0	2152	1.4
6 SU	0423	5.2	1023	1.0	1640	5.5	2249	0.8
21 M	0405	5.1	1012	1.3	1623	5.3	2234	1.1
7 M	0508	5.4	1107	0.7	1724	5.7	● 2330	0.6
22 TU	0452	5.4	1054	1.0	1709	5.5	2314	0.8
8 TU	0548	5.6	1148	0.6	1804	5.7		
23 W	0534	5.5	1133	0.8	1751	5.6	○ 2353	0.7
9 W	0010	0.6	0624	5.7	1227	0.6	1838	5.7
24 TH	0613	5.6	1213	0.7	1831	5.6		
10 TH	0047	0.7	0656	5.6	1303	0.8	1909	5.5
25 F	0032	0.7	0650	5.6	1252	0.7	1908	5.4
11 F	0121	1.0	0724	5.4	1337	1.1	1936	5.2
26 SA	0111	0.8	0725	5.4	1332	0.9	1946	5.3
12 SA	0153	1.3	0800	5.2	1409	1.4	2000	5.0
27 SU	0151	1.0	0800	5.3	1413	1.1	2024	5.0
13 SU	0222	1.6	0816	5.0	1439	1.7	2028	4.7
28 M	0232	1.3	0838	5.1	1457	1.4	2109	4.8
14 M	0252	1.9	0851	4.8	1512	2.0	2108	4.5
29 TU	0317	1.6	0925	4.9	1547	1.6	2205	4.5
15 TU ☽	0326	2.2	0938	4.6	1553	2.3	2204	4.3
30 W	0411	1.9	1026	4.7	1648	1.9	☾ 2316	4.4
31 TH	0518	2.1	1139	4.6	1805	2.0		

NOVEMBER

Day	TIME	m	TIME	m	TIME	m	TIME	m
1 F	0035	4.4	0640	2.2	1259	4.7	1929	1.9
16 SA	0603	2.4	1217	4.6	1850	2.2		
2 SA	0153	4.6	0759	1.9	1414	4.9	2038	1.6
17 SU	0103	4.5	0726	2.3	1331	4.7	2005	2.0
3 SU	0258	4.9	0902	1.6	1517	5.1	2132	1.3
18 M	0216	4.7	0835	2.0	1440	4.9	2105	1.6
4 M	0352	5.1	0954	1.3	1610	5.3	2220	1.1
19 TU	0320	5.0	0931	1.6	1541	5.1	2156	1.3
5 TU	0438	5.4	1040	1.1	1656	5.5	2303	0.9
20 W	0414	5.2	1021	1.3	1635	5.3	2243	1.1
6 W	0519	5.5	1122	0.9	1736	5.5	● 2343	0.9
21 TH	0502	5.4	1107	1.0	1724	5.4	○ 2328	0.9
7 TH	0556	5.6	1202	1.0	1812	5.5		
22 F	0547	5.6	1151	0.9	1810	5.5		
8 F	0020	1.0	0629	5.5	1239	1.1	1843	5.3
23 SA	0011	0.8	0630	5.6	1235	0.8	1853	5.4
9 SA	0056	1.2	0658	5.4	1314	1.3	1912	5.1
24 SU	0055	0.9	0711	5.6	1319	0.8	1937	5.3
10 SU	0127	1.5	0726	5.3	1346	1.5	1939	5.0
25 M	0138	1.0	0752	5.5	1403	1.0	2020	5.1
11 M	0158	1.7	0755	5.1	1417	1.7	2009	4.8
26 TU	0222	1.2	0814	5.3	1450	1.1	2106	5.0
12 TU	0229	1.9	0828	4.9	1451	1.9	2047	4.6
27 W	0309	1.4	0920	5.2	1539	1.4	2157	4.8
13 W	0304	2.1	0910	4.8	1531	2.1	2136	4.5
28 TH	0400	1.7	1012	5.0	1634	1.6	☾ 2255	4.7
14 TH	0348	2.2	1003	4.7	1622	2.2	☽ 2237	4.4
29 F	0458	1.9	1112	4.9	1737	1.8	2359	4.6
15 F	0446	2.4	1107	4.6	1729	2.3	2348	4.4
30 SA	0604	2.0	1219	4.8	1846	1.9		

DECEMBER

Day	TIME	m	TIME	m	TIME	m	TIME	m
1 SU	0108	4.6	0715	2.0	1330	4.8	1955	1.8
16 M	0003	4.5	0619	2.2	1229	4.6	1900	2.0
2 M	0215	4.8	0823	1.9	1436	4.9	2056	1.7
17 TU	0116	4.6	0736	2.1	1343	4.7	2014	1.9
3 TU	0314	5.0	0922	1.7	1535	5.0	2150	1.5
18 W	0229	4.7	0849	1.9	1457	4.8	2120	1.6
4 W	0406	5.2	1014	1.5	1627	5.1	2237	1.4
19 TH	0336	5.0	0951	1.6	1604	5.0	2217	1.4
5 TH	0451	5.3	1100	1.4	1711	5.2	2320	1.3
20 F	0435	5.2	1045	1.2	1703	5.2	2308	1.1
6 F	0532	5.4	1142	1.3	1751	5.2	●	
21 SA	0527	5.4	1135	1.0	1755	5.3	○ 2356	0.9
7 SA	0000	1.3	0608	5.4	1221	1.3	1826	5.2
22 SU	0615	5.6	1223	0.8	1843	5.4		
8 SU	0037	1.4	0641	5.4	1257	1.4	1858	5.1
23 M	0042	0.8	0700	5.7	1309	0.7	1928	5.4
9 M	0111	1.5	0712	5.3	1331	1.5	1928	5.0
24 TU	0127	0.8	0743	5.7	1354	0.7	2012	5.3
10 TU	0143	1.6	0743	5.2	1403	1.6	1959	4.9
25 W	0211	0.9	0825	5.6	1439	0.8	2055	5.2
11 W	0215	1.7	0814	5.1	1437	1.7	2033	4.8
26 TH	0256	1.0	0907	5.4	1524	1.0	2138	5.0
12 TH	0250	1.8	0849	5.0	1514	1.7	2112	4.7
27 F	0342	1.3	0951	5.2	1611	1.3	2225	4.9
13 F	0329	1.9	0931	4.9	1556	1.8	2159	4.6
28 SA	0430	1.5	1039	5.0	1702	1.6	☾ 2317	4.7
14 SA	0415	2.0	1020	4.9	1647	2.0	☽ 2256	4.5
29 SU	0524	1.8	1134	4.8	1759	1.8		
15 SU	0512	2.2	1120	4.7	1748	2.0		
30 M	0016	4.6	0625	2.0	1238	4.7	1904	2.0
31 TU	0123	4.6	0737	2.1	1348	4.6	2016	2.0

Chart Datum: 3.22 metres below Ordnance Datum (Newlyn)

YEALM RIVER 10-1-18
Devon

CHARTS
Admiralty 28, 1613; Stanford 13; Imray C6, C14; OS 201
TIDES
−0540 Dover; ML 3.2; Duration 0615; Zone 0 (GMT).

Standard Port DEVONPORT (←)

Times				Height (metres)			
HW		LW		MHWS	MHWN	MLWN	MLWS
0000	0600	0000	0600	5.5	4.4	2.2	0.8
1200	1800	1200	1800				

Differences YEALM RIVER ENTRANCE
+0006 +0006 +0002 +0002 −0.1 −0.1 −0.1 −0.1

SHELTER
Very good shelter and easy entrance except in strong onshore winds. Anchorage in Cellar Bay open to NW winds.
NAVIGATION
Waypoint 50°18'.00N 04°06'.00W, 240°/060° from/to Season Pt, 1.4M. The W and E Ebb rocks and the Inner and Outer Slimers are dangerous, lying awash on either side of Wembury Bay. Beware sand bar running S from Season Pt, marked by port hand buoy Fl R 5s (April-Oct), leaving narrow channel on S side. Also sand spit running S from Warren Pt. You cannot beat in on an ebb tide. Strong SW winds hold up the ebb and increase levels, as does the river when in spate. Speed limit 6 kn.
For information about Wembury firing range, see 10.1.17.
LIGHTS AND MARKS
R can buoy, Fl R 5s, marks end of sand bar (Apl-Oct). Ldg Bns at 089°. When abeam of Bn (G triangle on W back) on S shore turn NE towards Bn on N shore. Leave 'spit' R can buoy off Warren Pt to port. From Sand Bar to Misery Pt is only 1.2m at LWS.
RADIO TELEPHONE
None.
TELEPHONE (0752)
Hr Mr 872533; MRSC Brixham 882704; ⌗ (0752) 222929; Marinecall 0898 500 458; Police 701188; Dr 880392.
FACILITIES
EC Thursday; **Yealm Pool** M, L, FW; **Newton Ferrers Village** L, Slip, FW, V, Gas, Gaz, R, Bar; **Yealm Boat Co** ☎ 872564, ME, El, Ⓔ, Sh, Gas, Gaz, CH; **Yealm YC**
☎ 872291, FW, R, Bar; **Bridgend** L, Slip (HW∓2½), FW; **Bridgend Boat Co** ☎ 872162, MF, El, Sh; **Noss Mayo** L, Slip, FW, V, R, Bar; **J. Hockaday** ☎ 872369, El, ME; **A. Hooper** ☎ 872861, SM.
✉ (Newton Ferrers, Noss Mayo); Ⓑ (Newton Ferrers, Tues and Thurs mornings only); ⇌ (Plymouth); ✈ (Plymouth).

SALCOMBE 10-1-19
Devon

CHARTS
Admiralty 28, 1634, 1613; Stanford 13; Imray C6, Y48; OS 202
TIDES
−0535 Dover; ML 3.1; Duration 0615; Zone 0 (GMT).

Standard Port DEVONPORT (←)

Times				Height (metres)			
HW		LW		MHWS	MHWN	MLWN	MLWS
0100	0600	0100	0600	5.5	4.4	2.2	0.8
1300	1800	1300	1800				

Differences SALCOMBE
0000 +0010 +0005 −0005 −0.2 −0.3 −0.1 −0.1
START POINT
+0005 +0030 −0005 +0005 −0.2 −0.4 −0.1 −0.1

SHELTER
Perfectly protected harbour but entrance is affected by S winds. The estuary is 4 M long and has 8 creeks off it, called lakes, which dry. Limited anchorage between ferry and prohibited area. Plenty of visitors deep water moorings. (Hr Mr's launch will contact − on duty 0700-2000 (LT) in season (0600-2200 (LT) in peak season) all have VHF Ch 14). There can be an uncomfortable swell with S winds in the anchorage off the town. Visitors' pontoon and moorings in the Bag are sheltered. New visitors pontoon for short stay by Hr Mr office, Whitestrand.

SALCOMBE *continued*

NAVIGATION
Waypoint 50°12'.40N 03°46'.60W, 180°/000° from/to Sandhill Pt Lt, 1.3M. The bar can be dangerous at spring tides when there are strong on-shore winds on the ebb tide. Speed limit 8 kn. Channel up to Kingsbridge is navigable for vessels with draughts up to 2m. Channel marked by R and W port hand beacons.

LIGHTS AND MARKS
White House in line with Poundstone beacon at 327°. Sandhill Pt beacon in line with Poundstone beacon at 000°. Sandhill Pt Dir Lt 000° Fl WRG 2s 27m 10/7M. R and W diamond on W mast — R002°-182°, G182°-357°, W357°-002°.
Harbour Ldg Lts 042° as shown.
Blackstone Rock QWR 4m 2M vis W048°-218°, R218°-048°.

RADIO TELEPHONE
VHF call *Salcombe Harbour* Ch 14; 14 (11 May–14 Sept 0830–2030 LT; 15 Sept–30 Apl Mon–Fri 0830–1630 LT — Not Sat or Sun). Call Harbour Launch: *Salcombe Harbour Launch*, , Ch 14.
Call: *ICC Base* (clubhouse) and *Egremont* (ICC floating HQ) Ch **80**. Fuel barge Ch 06. Harbour Water taxi service Ch 14.

TELEPHONE (054 884)
Hr Mr 3791; CG Chivelstone 259; MRSC Brixham 882704; ⌗ (0752) 222929; Marinecall 0898 500 458; Police 2107; Dr 2284.

FACILITIES
EC Thursday; **Harbour** (300+50 visitors) ☎ 3791, Slip, Ⓔ, P, D, FW, ME, El, M, L, C (15 ton), Sh, CH, SM; **Salcombe YC** ☎ 2872, L, R, Bar; **Island Cruising Club** ☎ 3481, Bar, ◻; **Winters BY** ☎ 3838, Slip, M, P, D, FW, ME; **Devon Rigging** ☎ 3195 Rigging, ME, CH; **Salcombe Houseboats** ☎ 3479, Gas; **J. Stone** ☎ (0548) 51242, M, FW, ME, El, Sh, CH; **Salcombe Chandlers** ☎ 2620, CH, ACA; **Tideway Boat Construction** ☎ 2987, Slip, CH; **J. Alsop** ☎ 3702, SM; **J. McKillop**

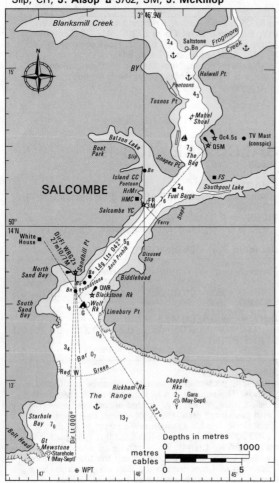

Ⓣ Kingsbridge 2343, SM; **Burwin Marine Electronics** ☎ 3321, Ⓔ; **Sailing** ☎ 2094, ME; **Hudson Thomas Fuel Barge** ☎ (0836) 715644, D, P; **Salcombe Boat Store** ☎ 3708, CH, Ice;
Salcombe is very well equipped with all facilities. FW is available from a boat — if needed, fly a bucket from a halyard. Water boat has Gas, Gaz. Alternatively, FW available from new visitors pontoon by Hr Mr. Public slipways at Batson Creek and at Kingsbridge.
Town ◻; ✉; Ⓑ; ⇌ (bus to Plymouth or Totnes); ✈ (Plymouth).
Note: There is a water taxi service run by the Hr Mr. For timetable contact Hr Mr.

DARTMOUTH 10-1-20
Devon

CHARTS
Admiralty 2253, 1634, 1613; Stanford 12; Imray C5, Y47, Y43; OS 202
TIDES
−0510 Dover; ML 2.8; Duration 0630; Zone 0 (GMT).

NOTE: Dartmouth is a Standard Port and tidal predictions for each day of the year are given below.

SHELTER
Excellent protection inside the harbour but the entrance can be difficult with strong winds from the SE to SW. Anchorages E of fairway opposite Nos 3a to 5 buoys. There are three marinas, as shown on the chartlet, and four sets of pontoons for visiting yachts as follows: — by The Dartmouth YC; near the Hr Mr's office and on N embankment; for short stays only, by the ferry pontoon on the East side.

NAVIGATION
Waypoint 50°19'.50N 03°32'.80W, 148°/328° from/to Kingswear Lt, Iso WRG, 1.5M. To the E of entrance erected on Inner Froward Pt (153m high) is a stone pyramid (24.5m high) which is very conspic. There is no bar and the harbour is always available. The river is navigable on the tide to Totnes. Information from Hr Mr. Speed limit 6 kn.

LIGHTS AND MARKS
Kingswear Main Lt Iso WRG 3s 9m 8M W sector 325°-331°. Dartmouth Lt Fl WRG 2s W sector 289°-297°. Entry buoys as on chartlet.

RADIO TELEPHONE
Hr Mr VHF Ch 11 (Mon–Fri 0900–1700; Sat 0900–1200 LT). Darthaven Marina (Kingswear), Dart Marina, Dart Sailing Centre VHF Ch **80**; Kingswear Marina Noss Works, Call *Dart Marina Four* Ch **80**; Fuel barge Ch 16. Water taxi, Ch 16 or **80**.

TELEPHONE (0803)
Hr Mr 832337; CG & MRSC Brixham 882704; ⌗ Brixham 882130; Marinecall 0898 500 458; Police 832288; Dr 832212; Ⓗ 832255.

FACILITIES
EC Wednesday/Saturday; **Darthaven Marina** (230+12 visitors) ☎ Kingswear 22545, FW, ME, El, Gas, Gaz, ◻, Sh, CH, Bar, R, BH (30 ton), AC; **Kingswear Marina** (110) ☎ 833351, Slip, FW, ME, El, Sh, C (14 ton), CH, BH (16 ton), Gas, Gaz, AC; **Dart Marina** (80+40 visitors) ☎ 833351, Slip, D, FW, AC, ME, El, Sh, C (4 ton), BH (4 ton), Bar, R, ◻, Gas, Gaz, CH; **Dartside Quay Yard** (Galmpton) (40) ☎ 845445 Slip, AC, BH (53, 16), CH, El, Ⓔ, FW, ME, Sh; **Dart Harbour and Navigation Authority** (450+90 visitors), ☎ 832337, Slip, D, FW, ME, El, Sh, CH, V, R; **Royal Dart YC** ☎ Kingswear 272, M, L, FW, Bar; **The Dartmouth YC** ☎ 832305, L, FW, Bar, R; **Creekside BY**(Mill Creek) ☎ 832649, Slip, dry dock, M, ME, Sh, El, C (1 ton), CH, AB; **Philip and Son** ☎ 833351, M, ME, El, Sh, BH, CH; **Bosuns Locker** ☎ 832595, CH, ACA; **Dart Sails** ☎ 832185, SM; **Peter Lucas** ☎ 833094, SM, rigging, masts; **J. W. Upham** ☎ Kingswear 545, El, ME, CH, Sh, Ⓔ; **Burwin Electronics** ☎ 835417, El, Ⓔ; **Torbay Boat Construction** (Dolphin Haven at Galmpton) ☎ Churston 842424, CH, D, FW, L, M, C (27 ton), ME, Sh, Slip, SM, V; **River Taxi** ☎ 833727 (or VHF Ch 16); **Dart Sailing Centre** ☎ 834716, AB, AC, Bar, R; **Misc** Fuel Barge P, D, Slip at Higher Ferry; **Town** V, P (cans), ◻, R, Bar, ✉; Ⓑ; ⇌ (steam train, in season, or bus to Paignton); ✈ (Plymouth or Exeter).

DARTMOUTH *continued*

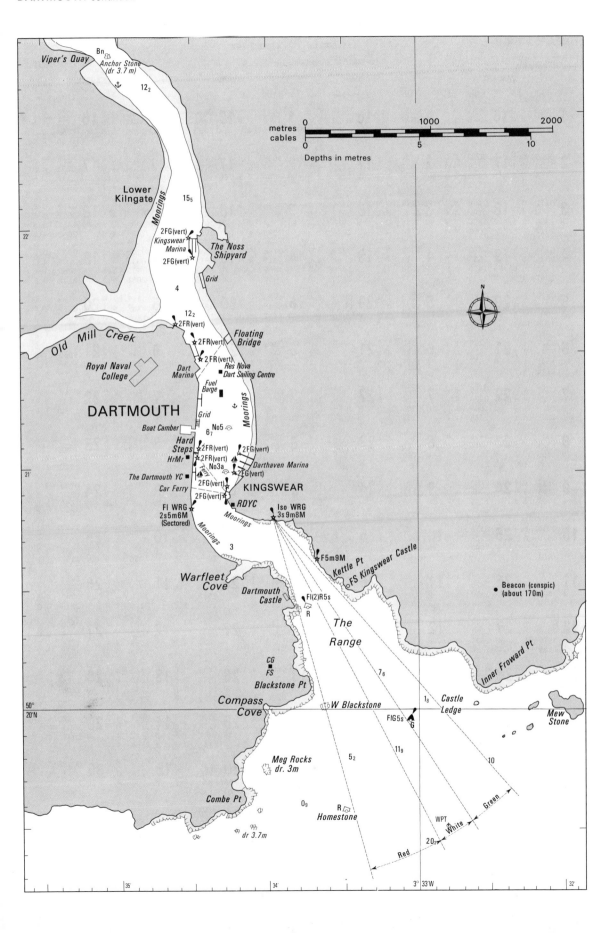

ENGLAND, SOUTH COAST - DARTMOUTH

LAT 50°21′N   LONG 3°34′W

TIMES AND HEIGHTS OF HIGH AND LOW WATERS

YEAR **1991**

TIME ZONE **UT (GMT)**
For Summer Time add ONE hour in non-shaded areas

JANUARY

	TIME	m		TIME	m
1 TU	0620 1205 1851	5.0 0.6 4.8	**16** W	0631 1213 1854	4.8 1.0 4.6
2 W	0025 0707 1254 1936	0.6 5.1 0.5 4.8	**17** TH	0030 0708 1251 1930	1.0 4.8 0.8 4.6
3 TH	0112 0750 1338 2017	0.6 5.1 0.5 4.8	**18** F	0106 0742 1327 2003	0.9 4.8 0.8 4.6
4 F	0154 0830 1421 2057	0.6 5.0 0.6 4.6	**19** SA	0140 0813 1400 2033	0.9 4.8 0.8 4.5
5 SA	0236 0908 1502 2135	0.8 4.9 0.8 4.5	**20** SU	0215 0842 1434 2059	0.9 4.7 0.9 4.4
6 SU	0317 0944 1542 2210	1.1 4.7 1.1 4.3	**21** M	0249 0906 1511 2126	1.1 4.5 1.0 4.3
7 M	0357 1020 1624 2249	1.3 4.4 1.4 4.1	**22** TU	0326 0934 1549 2158	1.2 4.4 1.2 4.1
8 TU	0439 1101 1708 2334	1.6 4.2 1.7 4.0	**23** W	0406 1012 1632 2245	1.4 4.2 1.4 4.0
9 W	0527 1151 1759	1.9 4.0 2.0	**24** TH	0455 1108 1726 2351	1.7 4.0 1.7 3.9
10 TH	0030 0626 1251 1904	3.9 2.1 3.9 2.1	**25** F	0558 1225 1840	1.9 3.8 1.9
11 F	0137 0741 1404 2019	3.9 2.2 3.8 2.1	**26** SA	0114 0726 1359 2011	3.8 2.0 3.8 1.9
12 SA	0249 0858 1519 2129	4.0 2.0 3.9 1.9	**27** SU	0249 0900 1537 2134	4.0 1.7 4.0 1.6
13 SU	0357 1001 1627 2223	4.2 1.8 4.1 1.6	**28** M	0413 1011 1653 2236	4.3 1.3 4.2 1.1
14 M	0456 1052 1723 2310	4.4 1.5 4.3 1.3	**29** TU	0518 1107 1753 2328	4.6 0.8 4.5 0.8
15 TU	0547 1134 1812 ● 2351	4.6 1.2 4.5 1.1	**30** W	0612 1156 1842 ○	4.9 0.5 4.8
			31 TH	0013 0657 1241 1924	0.5 5.1 0.3 4.9

FEBRUARY

	TIME	m		TIME	m
1 F	0057 0738 1322 2001	0.4 5.2 0.2 4.9	**16** SA	0048 0728 1307 1948	0.5 5.0 0.4 4.8
2 SA	0136 0812 1400 2035	0.4 5.1 0.4 4.8	**17** SU	0122 0800 1341 2018	0.5 4.9 0.4 4.7
3 SU	0214 0845 1436 2104	0.6 5.0 0.6 4.6	**18** M	0156 0827 1415 2044	0.6 4.8 0.6 4.5
4 M	0249 0912 1510 2132	0.8 4.7 1.0 4.4	**19** TU	0229 0852 1449 2106	0.7 4.6 0.8 4.4
5 TU	0323 0939 1543 2201	1.1 4.5 1.3 4.2	**20** W	0305 0915 1526 2134	1.0 4.4 1.1 4.2
6 W	0356 1011 1617 ☾ 2239	1.5 4.2 1.6 4.0	**21** TH	0343 0949 1607 2217	1.2 4.2 1.4 4.0
7 TH	0433 1054 1655 2332	1.8 3.9 1.9 3.8	**22** F	0429 1046 1658 2327	1.6 3.9 1.7 3.8
8 F	0521 1154 1749	2.1 3.7 2.2	**23** SA	0531 1209 1811	1.9 3.6 2.0
9 SA	0039 0633 1309 1920	3.7 2.3 3.6 2.3	**24** SU	0055 0708 1353 1959	3.7 2.0 3.6 2.0
10 SU	0200 0823 1441 2103	3.8 2.2 3.6 2.1	**25** M	0239 0854 1536 2125	3.8 1.7 3.8 1.6
11 M	0325 0943 1604 2206	3.9 1.9 3.9 1.7	**26** TU	0404 1002 1647 2224	4.2 1.2 4.2 1.1
12 TU	0434 1035 1708 2253	4.2 1.5 4.2 1.3	**27** W	0508 1054 1742 2313	4.6 0.8 4.5 0.7
13 W	0529 1117 1757 2334	4.5 1.1 4.5 0.9	**28** TH	0558 1139 1827 ○ 2356	4.9 0.4 4.8 0.4
14 TH	0615 1155 1839 ●	4.8 0.7 4.7			
15 F	0011 0654 1233 1915	0.7 4.9 0.5 4.8			

MARCH

	TIME	m		TIME	m
1 F	0641 1220 1905	5.1 0.2 4.9	**16** SA	0630 1205 1853 ●	5.0 0.3 4.9
2 SA	0036 0717 1300 1939	0.3 5.2 0.2 4.9	**17** SU	0022 0706 1243 1927	0.4 5.0 0.3 4.9
3 SU	0114 0749 1334 2008	0.3 5.1 0.4 4.8	**18** M	0059 0739 1318 1958	0.3 5.0 0.3 4.8
4 M	0148 0817 1407 2032	0.5 4.9 0.6 4.7	**19** TU	0134 0810 1353 2026	0.4 4.8 0.5 4.6
5 TU	0220 0840 1436 2054	0.8 4.7 1.0 4.5	**20** W	0210 0839 1429 2053	0.6 4.6 0.7 4.5
6 W	0249 0902 1504 2121	1.1 4.4 1.3 4.3	**21** TH	0247 0909 1507 2125	0.9 4.3 1.0 4.2
7 TH	0318 0931 1532 2156	1.4 4.1 1.6 4.1	**22** F	0328 0948 1549 2212	1.2 4.1 1.4 4.0
8 F	0350 1011 1607 ☾ 2247	1.7 3.9 1.9 3.8	**23** SA	0417 1049 1643 ☽ 2323	1.5 3.8 1.8 3.8
9 SA	0432 1111 1655 2355	2.0 3.6 2.2 3.7	**24** SU	0522 1212 1801	1.9 3.6 2.0
10 SU	0537 1229 1820	2.3 3.4 2.4	**25** M	0047 0702 1351 1948	3.7 2.0 3.6 2.0
11 M	0116 0740 1404 2031	3.6 2.3 3.5 2.2	**26** TU	0225 0839 1522 2107	3.9 1.6 3.9 1.6
12 TU	0248 0915 1536 2139	3.8 1.9 3.8 1.7	**27** W	0346 0942 1627 2202	4.2 1.2 4.2 1.1
13 W	0403 1007 1641 2226	4.1 1.4 4.1 1.3	**28** TH	0446 1032 1718 2250	4.6 0.8 4.5 0.7
14 TH	0501 1050 1731 2307	4.5 1.0 4.5 0.8	**29** F	0534 1115 1801 2331	4.9 0.5 4.8 0.5
15 F	0548 1128 1815 2345	4.8 0.6 4.7 0.5	**30** SA	0616 1154 1838 ○	5.0 0.3 4.9
			31 SU	0010 0652 1232 1910	0.4 5.0 0.4 4.9

APRIL

	TIME	m		TIME	m
1 M	0047 0722 1306 1938	0.4 4.9 0.5 4.8	**16** TU	0034 0716 1254 1936	0.3 4.9 0.3 4.9
2 TU	0120 0748 1336 2001	0.6 4.8 0.8 4.7	**17** W	0114 0753 1332 2009	0.4 4.8 0.5 4.7
3 W	0150 0810 1404 2024	0.9 4.5 1.1 4.5	**18** TH	0152 0829 1412 2045	0.6 4.6 0.8 4.6
4 TH	0219 0833 1430 2051	1.2 4.3 1.4 4.3	**19** F	0233 0909 1453 2125	0.8 4.3 1.1 4.3
5 F	0247 0902 1459 2126	1.4 4.1 1.6 4.1	**20** SA	0319 0956 1540 2215	1.1 4.0 1.4 4.1
6 SA	0320 0943 1533 2214	1.7 3.8 1.9 3.9	**21** SU	0411 1056 1636 ☽ 2319	1.5 3.8 1.7 4.0
7 SU	0402 1041 1623 ☾ 2319	2.0 3.6 2.1 3.7	**22** M	0518 1208 1751	1.8 3.7 1.9
8 M	0503 1155 1738	2.2 3.5 2.3	**23** TU	0034 0645 1331 1920	3.9 1.8 3.7 1.9
9 TU	0034 0644 1320 1936	3.7 2.2 3.5 2.2	**24** W	0156 0807 1450 2034	4.0 1.6 3.9 1.6
10 W	0158 0825 1450 2055	3.8 1.9 3.8 1.8	**25** TH	0311 0909 1552 2131	4.2 1.2 4.2 1.2
11 TH	0317 0925 1559 2148	4.1 1.6 4.1 1.3	**26** F	0411 1000 1643 2219	4.5 1.0 4.5 0.9
12 F	0420 1012 1654 2233	4.4 1.0 4.4 0.9	**27** SA	0500 1044 1726 2303	4.7 0.8 4.7 0.7
13 SA	0512 1055 1741 2314	4.7 0.6 4.7 0.6	**28** SU	0544 1124 1805 ○ 2342	4.8 0.7 4.8 0.7
14 SU	0557 1135 1822 ● 2354	4.9 0.4 4.9 0.4	**29** M	0622 1201 1839	4.8 0.7 4.8
15 M	0639 1214 1900	5.0 0.3 4.9	**30** TU	0018 0653 1237 1908	0.7 4.7 0.0 4.7

Chart Datum: 2.62 metres below Ordnance Datum (Newlyn)

ENGLAND, SOUTH COAST - DARTMOUTH

LAT 50°21'N   LONG 3°34'W

TIMES AND HEIGHTS OF HIGH AND LOW WATERS   YEAR 1991

TIME ZONE UT(GMT)
For Summer Time add ONE hour in non-shaded areas

MAY

Day	TIME	m		Day	TIME	m
1 W	0054 / 0721 / 1309 / 1936	0.9 / 4.6 / 1.0 / 4.6		**16** TH	0056 / 0739 / 1316 / 1956	0.5 / 4.7 / 0.6 / 4.8
2 TH	0125 / 0747 / 1337 / 2002	1.1 / 4.4 / 1.2 / 4.5		**17** F	0139 / 0821 / 1359 / 2037	0.6 / 4.6 / 0.8 / 4.7
3 F	0155 / 0813 / 1407 / 2031	1.3 / 4.2 / 1.4 / 4.3		**18** SA	0225 / 0906 / 1444 / 2122	0.8 / 4.4 / 1.0 / 4.5
4 SA	0226 / 0846 / 1438 / 2106	1.4 / 4.1 / 1.6 / 4.2		**19** SU	0313 / 0955 / 1532 / 2210	1.0 / 4.2 / 1.3 / 4.4
5 SU	0301 / 0927 / 1516 / 2151	1.6 / 3.9 / 1.8 / 4.0		**20** M	0405 / 1049 / 1627 / 2305 ☽	1.3 / 4.0 / 1.5 / 4.2
6 M	0344 / 1019 / 1603 / 2248	1.8 / 3.7 / 2.0 / 3.9		**21** TU	0504 / 1148 / 1728	1.5 / 3.9 / 1.7
7 TU ☽	0440 / 1123 / 1708 / 2352	1.9 / 3.6 / 2.1 / 3.9		**22** W	0006 / 0611 / 1253 / 1840	4.1 / 1.6 / 3.9 / 1.7
8 W	0554 / 1234 / 1833	2.0 / 3.7 / 2.1		**23** TH	0112 / 0722 / 1402 / 1950	4.1 / 1.6 / 4.0 / 1.7
9 TH	0102 / 0721 / 1351 / 1955	3.9 / 1.8 / 3.8 / 1.9		**24** F	0222 / 0827 / 1505 / 2051	4.2 / 1.5 / 4.1 / 1.5
10 F	0217 / 0832 / 1505 / 2100	4.1 / 1.5 / 4.1 / 1.5		**25** SA	0324 / 0921 / 1559 / 2145	4.3 / 1.3 / 4.3 / 1.3
11 SA	0326 / 0929 / 1607 / 2153	4.3 / 1.2 / 4.3 / 1.1		**26** SU	0419 / 1010 / 1647 / 2233	4.4 / 1.2 / 4.5 / 1.2
12 SU	0427 / 1018 / 1659 / 2242	4.5 / 0.9 / 4.6 / 0.8		**27** M	0506 / 1054 / 1730 / 2315	4.5 / 1.1 / 4.6 / 1.1
13 M	0521 / 1104 / 1748 / 2327	4.7 / 0.6 / 4.8 / 0.6		**28** TU ○	0549 / 1134 / 1810 / 2354	4.5 / 1.1 / 4.7 / 1.1
14 TU ●	0610 / 1148 / 1833	4.8 / 0.5 / 4.9		**29** W	0628 / 1211 / 1845	4.5 / 1.1 / 4.7
15 W	0011 / 0655 / 1233 / 1915	0.5 / 4.8 / 0.5 / 4.9		**30** TH	0032 / 0701 / 1247 / 1917	1.1 / 4.4 / 1.2 / 4.6
				31 F	0107 / 0733 / 1320 / 1948	1.2 / 4.3 / 1.3 / 4.5

JUNE

Day	TIME	m		Day	TIME	m
1 SA	0139 / 0805 / 1352 / 2019	1.3 / 4.2 / 1.4 / 4.4		**16** SU	0216 / 0857 / 1433 / 2111	0.6 / 4.5 / 0.8 / 4.8
2 SU	0213 / 0838 / 1427 / 2053	1.3 / 4.1 / 1.5 / 4.3		**17** M	0301 / 0942 / 1519 / 2155	0.8 / 4.4 / 1.0 / 4.6
3 M	0249 / 0915 / 1504 / 2132	1.4 / 4.0 / 1.6 / 4.2		**18** TU	0348 / 1028 / 1606 / 2241	1.0 / 4.2 / 1.2 / 4.4
4 TU	0330 / 0958 / 1547 / 2216	1.5 / 3.9 / 1.7 / 4.1		**19** W	0437 / 1116 / 1657 / 2331 ☽	1.2 / 4.1 / 1.5 / 4.3
5 W	0418 / 1049 / 1638 / 2309 ☽	1.6 / 3.9 / 1.8 / 4.1		**20** TH	0530 / 1207 / 1753	1.5 / 4.0 / 1.7
6 TH	0514 / 1147 / 1740	1.7 / 3.8 / 1.9		**21** F	0024 / 0630 / 1305 / 1857	4.1 / 1.6 / 4.0 / 1.8
7 F	0009 / 0620 / 1252 / 1854	4.0 / 1.7 / 3.9 / 1.8		**22** SA	0125 / 0735 / 1408 / 2005	4.0 / 1.7 / 4.0 / 1.8
8 SA	0116 / 0733 / 1404 / 2007	4.0 / 1.6 / 4.0 / 1.7		**23** SU	0230 / 0839 / 1510 / 2109	4.0 / 1.7 / 4.1 / 1.7
9 SU	0230 / 0842 / 1515 / 2113	4.1 / 1.4 / 4.2 / 1.4		**24** M	0335 / 0937 / 1608 / 2204	4.1 / 1.6 / 4.3 / 1.5
10 M	0342 / 0943 / 1619 / 2211	4.3 / 1.2 / 4.4 / 1.1		**25** TU	0432 / 1027 / 1659 / 2253	4.2 / 1.4 / 4.4 / 1.4
11 TU	0447 / 1037 / 1718 / 2305	4.5 / 0.9 / 4.6 / 0.8		**26** W	0523 / 1113 / 1746 / 2336	4.3 / 1.3 / 4.5 / 1.2
12 W	0546 / 1127 / 1811 / 2354 ○	4.6 / 0.7 / 4.8 / 0.6		**27** TH	0608 / 1153 / 1828	4.3 / 1.2 / 4.6
13 TH	0639 / 1215 / 1859	4.7 / 0.6 / 4.9		**28** F	0015 / 0649 / 1232 / 1905	1.1 / 4.4 / 1.1 / 4.6
14 F	0043 / 0727 / 1303 / 1943	0.5 / 4.7 / 0.6 / 4.9		**29** SA	0053 / 0725 / 1307 / 1939	1.1 / 4.4 / 1.1 / 4.6
15 SA	0130 / 0812 / 1348 / 2027	0.5 / 4.6 / 0.7 / 4.9		**30** SU	0128 / 0758 / 1341 / 2011	1.1 / 4.3 / 1.2 / 4.6

JULY

Day	TIME	m		Day	TIME	m
1 M	0202 / 0830 / 1415 / 2042	1.1 / 4.3 / 1.2 / 4.5		**16** TU	0242 / 0920 / 1458 / 2132	0.5 / 4.6 / 0.7 / 4.8
2 TU	0236 / 0901 / 1450 / 2113	1.1 / 4.2 / 1.3 / 4.4		**17** W	0324 / 0958 / 1539 / 2208	0.8 / 4.4 / 1.0 / 4.5
3 W	0313 / 0936 / 1528 / 2147	1.2 / 4.1 / 1.4 / 4.3		**18** TH	0405 / 1036 / 1622 / 2249 ☽	1.1 / 4.2 / 1.3 / 4.3
4 TH	0353 / 1013 / 1611 / 2229	1.3 / 4.0 / 1.5 / 4.2		**19** F	0448 / 1119 / 1707 / 2334	1.4 / 4.0 / 1.7 / 4.1
5 F	0438 / 1102 / 1700 / 2322 ☽	1.4 / 4.0 / 1.7 / 4.1		**20** SA	0536 / 1210 / 1801	1.7 / 3.9 / 1.9
6 SA	0532 / 1202 / 1801	1.6 / 3.9 / 1.8		**21** SU	0030 / 0636 / 1311 / 1912	3.9 / 2.0 / 3.9 / 2.1
7 SU	0027 / 0640 / 1312 / 1918	4.0 / 1.7 / 3.9 / 1.8		**22** M	0138 / 0752 / 1422 / 2035	3.8 / 2.0 / 3.9 / 2.0
8 M	0144 / 0758 / 1431 / 2039	3.9 / 1.7 / 4.0 / 1.6		**23** TU	0253 / 0908 / 1533 / 2144	3.8 / 1.9 / 4.0 / 1.8
9 TU	0308 / 0914 / 1549 / 2151	4.0 / 1.5 / 4.2 / 1.3		**24** W	0404 / 1008 / 1635 / 2238	3.9 / 1.7 / 4.2 / 1.5
10 W	0426 / 1018 / 1657 / 2251	4.2 / 1.2 / 4.5 / 1.0		**25** TH	0504 / 1056 / 1728 / 2321 ●	4.1 / 1.4 / 4.5 / 1.2
11 TH	0531 / 1114 / 1756 / 2343 ○	4.4 / 0.8 / 4.8 / 0.6		**26** F	0538 / 1138 / 1814	4.4 / 1.1 / 4.6
12 F	0628 / 1203 / 1847	4.6 / 0.6 / 5.0		**27** SA	0000 / 0609 / 1216 / 1853	1.0 / 4.6 / 1.0 / 4.7
13 SA	0032 / 0716 / 1251 / 1932	0.4 / 4.7 / 0.4 / 5.1		**28** SU	0037 / 0713 / 1252 / 1928	0.8 / 4.5 / 0.9 / 4.8
14 SU	0118 / 0800 / 1334 / 2013	0.3 / 4.8 / 0.4 / 5.1		**29** M	0112 / 0747 / 1326 / 1959	0.8 / 4.5 / 0.8 / 4.7
15 M	0201 / 0841 / 1417 / 2053	0.3 / 4.7 / 0.5 / 5.0		**30** TU	0144 / 0818 / 1358 / 2028	0.8 / 4.5 / 0.9 / 4.6
				31 W	0218 / 0846 / 1431 / 2053	0.8 / 4.4 / 1.0 / 4.5

AUGUST

Day	TIME	m		Day	TIME	m
1 TH	0251 / 0912 / 1506 / 2120	0.9 / 4.3 / 1.1 / 4.4		**16** F	0329 / 0953 / 1544 / 2205	1.1 / 4.3 / 1.3 / 4.2
2 F	0328 / 0940 / 1544 / 2152	1.1 / 4.1 / 1.3 / 4.2		**17** SA	0405 / 1030 / 1623 / 2246 ☽	1.5 / 4.1 / 1.7 / 3.9
3 SA	0408 / 1020 / 1628 / 2242	1.3 / 4.0 / 1.5 / 4.0		**18** SU	0444 / 1120 / 1708 / 2341 ☽	1.9 / 3.9 / 2.0 / 3.7
4 SU	0456 / 1121 / 1724 / 2352	1.6 / 3.9 / 1.8 / 3.8		**19** M	0535 / 1222 / 1815	2.1 / 3.7 / 2.3
5 M	0559 / 1237 / 1842	1.8 / 3.8 / 1.9		**20** TU	0051 / 0700 / 1339 / 2003	3.6 / 2.3 / 3.7 / 2.3
6 TU	0117 / 0727 / 1406 / 2019	3.7 / 1.9 / 3.9 / 1.8		**21** W	0219 / 0845 / 1501 / 2125	3.6 / 2.1 / 3.9 / 1.9
7 W	0254 / 0859 / 1533 / 2141	3.8 / 1.7 / 4.1 / 1.4		**22** TH	0342 / 0949 / 1612 / 2218	3.8 / 1.8 / 4.2 / 1.5
8 TH	0418 / 1007 / 1645 / 2241	4.1 / 1.3 / 4.5 / 0.9		**23** F	0445 / 1037 / 1706 / 2300	4.1 / 1.4 / 4.5 / 1.1
9 F	0523 / 1102 / 1744 / 2331	4.4 / 0.8 / 4.8 / 0.5		**24** SA	0534 / 1116 / 1753 / 2338	4.4 / 1.0 / 4.7 / 0.8
10 SA	0617 / 1149 / 1833 ●	4.7 / 0.5 / 5.1		**25** SU	0618 / 1153 / 1834 ○	4.6 / 0.8 / 4.9
11 SU	0016 / 0700 / 1235 / 1915	0.2 / 4.9 / 0.3 / 5.2		**26** M	0013 / 0655 / 1230 / 1909	0.6 / 4.7 / 0.6 / 4.9
12 M	0100 / 0741 / 1316 / 1954	0.1 / 4.9 / 0.2 / 5.2		**27** TU	0049 / 0729 / 1304 / 1941	0.5 / 4.8 / 0.6 / 4.9
13 TU	0139 / 0817 / 1355 / 2029	0.2 / 4.9 / 0.3 / 5.0		**28** W	0122 / 0800 / 1336 / 2010	0.5 / 4.7 / 0.6 / 4.8
14 W	0218 / 0852 / 1432 / 2101	0.4 / 4.7 / 0.6 / 4.8		**29** TH	0155 / 0827 / 1410 / 2036	0.6 / 4.6 / 0.8 / 4.6
15 TH	0254 / 0922 / 1508 / 2132	0.7 / 4.5 / 0.9 / 4.5		**30** F	0229 / 0851 / 1444 / 2058	0.8 / 4.4 / 1.0 / 4.4
				31 SA	0304 / 0914 / 1522 / 2127	1.1 / 4.2 / 1.2 / 4.2

Chart Datum: 2.62 metres below Ordnance Datum (Newlyn)

ENGLAND, SOUTH COAST - DARTMOUTH

LAT 50°21'N   LONG 3°34'W

TIMES AND HEIGHTS OF HIGH AND LOW WATERS

YEAR **1991**

TIME ZONE **UT (GMT)**
For Summer Time add ONE hour in non-shaded areas

SEPTEMBER

Day	Time	m	Time	m	Time	m	Time	m
1 SU ☾	0343	1.4	0951	4.0	1605	1.5	2217	3.9
2 M	0430	1.7	1055	3.8	1701	1.8	2337	3.7
3 TU	0534	2.0	1220	3.7	1823	2.0		
4 W	0112	3.6	0713	2.1	1354	3.8	2012	1.8
5 TH	0253	3.8	0849	1.7	1524	4.1	2130	1.4
6 F	0411	4.1	0954	1.2	1632	4.5	2225	0.9
7 SA	0510	4.5	1045	0.8	1727	4.9	2312	0.4
8 SU ●	0557	4.8	1130	0.4	1814	5.1	2355	0.2
9 M	0640	5.0	1212	0.2	1855	5.2		
10 TU	0036	0.1	0716	5.0	1252	0.2	1930	5.2
11 W	0115	0.2	0749	5.0	1330	0.4	2002	5.0
12 TH	0149	0.5	0818	4.8	1404	0.7	2029	4.8
13 F	0223	0.9	0845	4.6	1436	1.0	2054	4.5
14 SA	0253	1.3	0911	4.3	1509	1.4	2123	4.2
15 SU ☽	0324	1.6	0945	4.1	1542	1.8	2202	3.9
16 M	0358	1.9	1034	3.9	1624	2.1	2258	3.6
17 TU	0444	2.2	1139	3.7	1725	2.3		
18 W	0012	3.5	0604	2.4	1256	3.7	1921	2.4
19 TH	0141	3.5	0810	2.3	1423	3.8	2055	2.0
20 F	0310	3.8	0918	1.8	1538	4.1	2147	1.5
21 SA	0415	4.1	1006	1.4	1635	4.5	2230	1.1
22 SU	0505	4.5	1047	1.0	1723	4.8	2308	0.7
23 M ○	0550	4.7	1125	0.7	1806	5.0	2344	0.5
24 TU	0630	4.9	1201	0.5	1845	5.0		
25 W	0020	0.4	0704	4.9	1238	0.5	1919	5.0
26 TH	0057	0.4	0737	4.9	1314	0.5	1951	4.8
27 F	0131	0.6	0807	4.7	1349	0.7	2020	4.6
28 SA	0207	0.8	0834	4.5	1426	0.9	2049	4.4
29 SU	0244	1.1	0901	4.3	1505	1.2	2124	4.1
30 M	0326	1.4	0943	4.1	1551	1.5	2220	3.8

OCTOBER

Day	Time	m	Time	m	Time	m	Time	m
1 TU ☾	0416	1.8	1049	3.9	1650	1.8	2338	3.6
2 W	0524	2.1	1210	3.8	1816	2.0		
3 TH	0109	3.6	0701	2.1	1341	3.9	1957	1.7
4 F	0241	3.9	0830	1.7	1506	4.2	2108	1.3
5 SA	0351	4.2	0931	1.3	1610	4.6	2201	0.9
6 SU	0445	4.6	1021	0.8	1702	4.9	2248	0.6
7 M	0531	4.8	1106	0.5	1748	5.1	2329	0.4 ●
8 TU	0613	5.0	1147	0.7	1829	5.1		
9 W	0009	0.4	0649	5.1	1226	0.4	1902	5.1
10 TH	0047	0.5	0720	5.0	1303	0.6	1933	4.9
11 F	0121	0.8	0747	4.8	1336	0.9	1959	4.6
12 SA	0152	1.1	0812	4.6	1408	1.1	2022	4.4
13 SU	0221	1.4	0838	4.4	1437	1.5	2050	4.1
14 M	0250	1.7	0912	4.2	1510	1.8	2129	3.9
15 TU	0324	2.0	0943	4.0	1550	2.0	2223	3.7 ☽
16 W	0409	2.2	1059	3.8	1647	2.3	2334	3.6
17 TH	0519	2.4	1211	3.8	1817	2.3		
18 F	0055	3.6	0706	2.3	1331	3.9	1958	2.1
19 SA	0220	3.8	0830	2.0	1448	4.1	2101	1.6
20 SU	0331	4.1	0924	1.6	1552	4.4	2150	1.2
21 M	0426	4.5	1010	1.1	1645	4.7	2233	0.9
22 TU	0515	4.8	1053	0.8	1732	4.9	2313	0.6
23 W ○	0558	4.9	1132	0.6	1816	5.0	2352	0.5
24 TH	0638	5.0	1212	0.5	1855	5.0		
25 F	0032	0.5	0714	5.0	1252	0.5	1932	4.8
26 SA	0111	0.6	0748	4.8	1331	0.7	2008	4.7
27 SU	0150	0.8	0850	4.7	1412	0.9	2046	4.4
28 M	0230	1.1	0859	4.5	1455	1.2	2130	4.2
29 TU	0315	1.7	0945	4.3	1544	1.4	2224	3.9 ☾
30 W	0408	1.7	1045	4.1	1644	1.7	2333	3.8 ☾
31 TH	0514	1.9	1156	4.0	1800	1.8		

NOVEMBER

Day	Time	m	Time	m	Time	m	Time	m
1 F	0050	3.8	0636	2.0	1314	4.1	1925	1.7
2 SA	0210	4.0	0755	1.7	1431	4.3	2035	1.4
3 SU	0317	4.3	0859	1.4	1537	4.5	2130	1.1
4 M	0413	4.5	0952	1.1	1631	4.7	2218	0.9
5 TU	0500	4.8	1039	0.9	1719	4.9	2302	0.7
6 W ●	0543	4.9	1121	0.7	1801	4.9	2342	0.7
7 TH	0621	5.0	1201	0.8	1837	4.9		
8 F	0019	0.8	0654	4.9	1239	0.9	1907	4.7
9 SA	0056	1.0	0722	4.8	1314	1.1	1936	4.5
10 SU	0127	1.3	0749	4.7	1345	1.3	2002	4.4
11 M	0157	1.5	0817	4.5	1416	1.5	2031	4.2
12 TU	0228	1.7	0850	4.3	1449	1.7	2108	4.0
13 W	0302	1.9	0931	4.2	1528	1.9	2156	3.9
14 TH	0345	2.0	1022	4.1	1619	2.0	2255	3.8 ☽
15 F	0442	2.2	1125	4.0	1725	2.1	2333	3.8 ☾
16 SA	0004	3.8	0558	2.2	1233	4.0	1846	2.0
17 SU	0118	3.9	0722	2.1	1347	4.1	2001	1.8
18 M	0234	4.1	0832	1.8	1458	4.3	2102	1.4
19 TU	0340	4.4	0929	1.4	1601	4.5	2154	1.1
20 W	0435	4.6	1019	1.1	1657	4.7	2242	0.9
21 TH	0525	4.8	1106	0.8	1746	4.9	2327	0.7 ○
22 F	0612	5.0	1150	0.7	1835	4.9		
23 SA	0010	0.6	0655	5.0	1235	0.6	1917	4.8
24 SU	0055	0.7	0735	5.0	1319	0.6	2000	4.7
25 M	0137	0.8	0814	4.9	1402	0.8	2042	4.5
26 TU	0221	1.0	0855	4.7	1448	0.9	2127	4.4
27 W	0307	1.2	0940	4.6	1536	1.2	2216	4.2
28 TH	0357	1.5	1031	4.4	1630	1.4	2313	4.1 ☾
29 F	0454	1.7	1130	4.3	1732	1.6	2314	3.9 ☽
30 SA	0015	4.0	0559	1.8	1235	4.2	1842	1.7

DECEMBER

Day	Time	m	Time	m	Time	m	Time	m
1 SU	0123	4.0	0711	1.8	1346	4.2	1951	1.6
2 M	0233	4.2	0819	1.7	1454	4.3	2053	1.5
3 TU	0333	4.4	0919	1.5	1555	4.4	2148	1.3
4 W	0427	4.6	1012	1.3	1649	4.5	2236	1.2
5 TH	0514	4.7	1059	1.2	1734	4.6	2319	1.1
6 F ●	0556	4.8	1141	1.1	1816	4.6	2359	1.1
7 SA	0633	4.8	1220	1.1	1851	4.6		
8 SU	0037	1.2	0705	4.8	1257	1.2	1922	4.5
9 M	0111	1.3	0736	4.7	1330	1.3	1951	4.4
10 TU	0142	1.4	0806	4.6	1402	1.4	2021	4.3
11 W	0214	1.5	0836	4.5	1435	1.5	2054	4.2
12 TH	0248	1.6	0910	4.4	1512	1.5	2133	4.1
13 F	0327	1.7	0951	4.3	1553	1.6	2218	4.0
14 SA	0412	1.8	1039	4.2	1643	1.8	2314	3.9 ☽
15 SU	0508	2.0	1137	4.1	1743	1.8		
16 M	0019	3.9	0614	2.0	1245	4.0	1856	1.8
17 TU	0132	4.0	0732	1.9	1359	4.1	2010	1.7
18 W	0247	4.1	0846	1.7	1516	4.2	2117	1.4
19 TH	0356	4.4	0949	1.4	1625	4.4	2215	1.2
20 F	0457	4.6	1044	1.0	1726	4.6	2307	0.9
21 SA ○	0551	4.8	1134	0.8	1820	4.7	2355	0.7
22 SU	0640	5.0	1222	0.6	1907	4.8		
23 M	0042	0.6	0724	5.1	1309	0.5	1951	4.8
24 TU	0127	0.6	0806	5.1	1353	0.5	2034	4.7
25 W	0210	0.7	0847	5.0	1437	0.6	2116	4.6
26 TH	0254	0.8	0928	4.8	1522	0.8	2158	4.4
27 F	0339	1.1	1010	4.6	1608	1.1	2244	4.3
28 SA	0427	1.3	1057	4.4	1658	1.4	2334	4.1 ☾
29 SU	0520	1.6	1151	4.2	1754	1.6		
30 M	0032	4.0	0620	1.8	1253	4.1	1900	1.8
31 TU	0139	4.0	0733	1.9	1405	4.0	2012	1.8

Chart Datum: 2.62 metres below Ordnance Datum (Newlyn)

DARTMOUTH *continued*

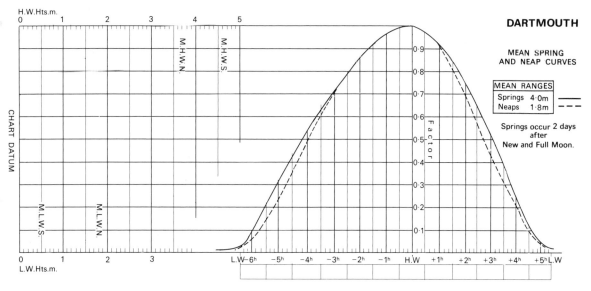

DARTMOUTH

MEAN SPRING
AND NEAP CURVES

MEAN RANGES	
Springs	4·0m ———
Neaps	1·8m - - -

Springs occur 2 days
after
New and Full Moon.

BRIXHAM   10-1-21
Devon

CHARTS
Admiralty 26, 1613; Stanford 12; Imray C5, Y43; OS 202
TIDES
−0505 Dover; ML 2.9; Duration 0635; Zone 0 (GMT).

Standard Port DEVONPORT (←)

Times				Height (metres)			
HW		LW		MHWS	MHWN	MLWN	MLWS
0100	0600	0100	0600	5.5	4.4	2.2	0.8
1300	1800	1300	1800				

Differences BRIXHAM
+0025	+0045	+0010	0000	−0.6	−0.7	−0.2	−0.1

SHELTER
Good, but outer harbour is dangerous in NW winds.
Visitors buoys (white) to E of main channel.
NAVIGATION
Waypoint 50°24'.70N 03°30'.00W, 050°/230° from/to
Victoria breakwater Lt, 0.60M. No dangers — Little run in
tide. Easy access — Inner harbour dries.

LIGHTS AND MARKS
There are no leading marks or leading lights coming into
Brixham. Breakwater head — Oc R 15s. Three R balls or
three R Lts (vert) at entrance indicate 'harbour closed'.
RADIO TELEPHONE
VHF Ch 14 16 (May-Sep: 0900-1300, 1400-1700,
1800-2000. Oct-Apr: Mon-Fri 0900-1300, 1400-1700 LT).
Brixham Coastguard: Ch 16 10 67 73; Yacht Club Ch 80.
TELEPHONE (0803) Prince William Marina Ch 80
Hr Mr 883321; CG & MRSC 882704; Pilot 882214;
Berthing Master 883211; ⌗ 882130; Marinecall
0898 500 458; Police 882231; Dr 882731; Ⓗ 882153.
FACILITIES
EC Wednesday; **Prince William Marina** (535+30 visitors)
☎ 882711, AC, FW, Ⓞ, Access H24; **Harbour Office**
(New Fish Quay) Slip, M, L, FW, C (4 ton), AB; **Brixham
YC** ☎ 883332, M, L, Slip, FW, R, Bar; **Fish Quay** P, D;
Brixham Yacht Supplies ☎ 882290, CH, ACA; **Brixham
Boating Centre** ☎ 51888, CH; **Brixham Net Co**
☎ 886115, CH, ME; **B J R Electrical** ☎ 58158, El, Ⓔ;
R.A. Brewer ☎ 883465, M; **Inner
Harbour** C; **Quay Electrics** Tel. 883030, El, Ⓔ; **Town** Ⓞ,
✉; Ⓑ; ⇌ (bus to Paignton); ✈ (Exeter).

TORQUAY   10-1-22
Devon

CHARTS
Admiralty 26, 1613; Stanford 12; Imray C5, Y43; OS 202
TIDES
−0500 Dover; ML 2.9; Duration 0640; Zone 0 (GMT).

Standard Port DEVONPORT (←)

Times				Height (metres)			
HW		LW		MHWS	MHWN	MLWN	MLWS
0100	0600	0100	0600	5.5	4.4	2.2	0.8
1300	1800	1300	1800				

Differences TORQUAY
+0025	+0045	+0010	0000	−0.6	−0.7	−0.2	−0.1

TORQUAY *continued*

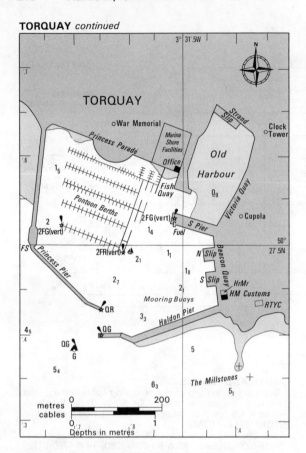

SHELTER
Good shelter but some swell in harbour with strong south easterly winds.

NAVIGATION
Waypoint 50°27'.00N 03°31'.50W, 165°/345° from/to Haldon Pier Lt, 0.40M. Inner harbour (known as Old Harbour) dries completely. Three R balls or three R Lts show harbour closed due to navigational hazard.

LIGHTS AND MARKS
No leading marks. Princess Pier QR 9m 6M. Haldon Pier QG 9m 6M. South Pier 2FG (vert) 5M.

RADIO TELEPHONE
VHF Ch 14 16 (Oct-Mar 0900-1700 Mon-Fri) (Apl-Sept 0900-2000 LT). Marina Ch **80** (H24).

TELEPHONE (0803)
Hr Mr 292429; CG & MRSC Brixham 882704; ⌗ (0752) 222929; Marinecall 0898 500 458; Police 214491; Dr 212489; Ⓗ 614567.

FACILITIES
Torquay Marina (440+60 visitors) ☎ 214624, FW, ME, Gas, Gaz, P, D, Ⓒ, AC, SM, El, Ⓔ, Sh, V, R, Bar; **Haldon Pier** L, FW, AB; **Princess Pier** L; **South Pier** P, D, L, FW, C (6 ton); **Queen Anne Marine** ☎ 294509, P, D; **Royal Torbay YC** ☎ 292006, R, Bar; **Town** All normal facilities, V, R, Ⓒ, Bar, ✉; Ⓑ; ⇌; ✈ (Exeter or Plymouth).

TEIGNMOUTH   10-1-23
Devon

TEIGNMOUTH *continued*

CHARTS
Admiralty 26, 3315; Stanford 12; Imray C5, Y43; OS 192
TIDES
−0450 Dover; ML 2.7; Duration 0625; Zone 0 (GMT).

Standard Port DEVONPORT (←—)

Times				Height (metres)			
HW		LW		MHWS	MHWN	MLWN	MLWS
0100	0600	0100	0600	5.5	4.4	2.2	0.8
1300	1800	1300	1800				

Differences TEIGNMOUTH (Approaches)
+0025 +0040 0000 0000 −0.7 −0.8 −0.3 −0.2

SHELTER
Do not attempt to come in over bar without local knowledge. Harbour completely sheltered but difficult to enter especially with strong winds between NE & S when surf forms on the bar. Access HW∓3.
NAVIGATION
Waypoint 50°32'.40N 03°29'.20W, 076°/256° from/to Training Wall Lt, 0.43M. Bar shifts very frequently.
Beware — rocks off the Ness
— variable extent of Salty flats.
LIGHTS AND MARKS
QWRG 44m 8/7M on The Ness, vis G229°-243°, W243°-348°, R348°-shore. Oc G, FG (vert) on The Point. Two sets of leading lights:- Approaching from SE, lights at 334°. This line keeps clear of the Ness Rocks but does not normally lead through channel through the bar. Once round The Point, lights on the quays at 022°.
RADIO TELEPHONE
VHF Ch 12 16; 12 (Mon-Fri: 0800-1700 LT; Sat 0900-1200 LT).
TELEPHONE (0626)
Hr Mr 772311; CG and MRSC Brixham 882704; ⌗ (0752) 222929; Marinecall 0898 500 458; Police 772433; Dr 774355; Ⓗ 772161.
FACILITIES
EC Thursday; **C Quay Polly Steps** Slip (up to 10m); **DCS Electrics** ☎ 775960, ME, El; **Teignmouth YC** ☎ 772734, M, FW; **Harbour Master** ☎ 772303, M; **Brigantine** ☎ 772400, CH; **Mariners Weigh** ☎ 773698, ME, CH; **Jack Matthews** ☎ 773438, BY; **Chris Humphrey** ☎ 772324, Slip, BY, ME, Sh, D, C (8 ton); **Bobbets Garage** ☎ 774220, P and D (cans); **Sleeman and Hawken** ☎ 872750, ME; **Brigantine** ☎ 772400, Gas, Gaz, FW, CH; **Bartletts** ☎ 773812, Gas; **J & C Engineering** ☎ 778633, ME, Sh; **PFB Electronics** ☎ 776845, Ⓔ. **Town** P, D, L, FW, V, R, Ⓞ, Bar; ✉; Ⓑ; ⇌; ✈ (Exeter).

AGENTS WANTED
Berwick-on-Tweed
Mallaig
Loch Sunart
Loch Aline
Fishguard
Kenmare River

Large number of French Ports

Rotterdam
Norderney
Dornumersiel
Langeoog
Wangerooge
Hooksiel
Bremerhaven

If you are interested in becoming our agent please write to the Editors and get your free copy annually. You do not have to be a resident in a port to be the agent but at least a fairly regular visitor.

RIVER EXE   10-1-24
Devon

CHARTS
Admiralty 2290, 3315; Stanford 12; Imray C5, Y43; OS 192
TIDES
−0445 Dover; ML 2.1; Duration 0625; Zone 0 (GMT).

Standard Port DEVONPORT (←—)

Times				Height (metres)			
HW		LW		MHWS	MHWN	MLWN	MLWS
0100	0600	0100	0600	5.5	4.4	2.2	0.8
1300	1800	1300	1800				

Differences EXMOUTH (Approaches)
+0030 +0050 +0015 +0005 −0.9 −1.0 −0.5 −0.3
STARCROSS
+0040 +0110 No data −1.4 −1.5 No data
TOPSHAM
+0045 +0105 No data −1.5 −1.6 No data

SHELTER
Entrance difficult when wind between S and E. Shelter good in Exe River. Access to Exeter is through the Exeter Canal and passage through locks, S of Topsham, by arrangement with Exeter City Council ☎ Exeter 74306.
NAVIGATION
Waypoint Exe Fairway (safe water) buoy, Fl 10s, Bell, 50°36'.01N 03°21'.97W, 102°/282° from/to channel entrance, 0.60M. Long shallow bar extends SE with rocks to the N of channel. Channel is difficult but well marked. Pole sands are liable to change.
LIGHTS AND MARKS
Ldg Lts FY 6m 7M by The Point in line at 305°; not safe seaward of No 3 Buoy.
RADIO TELEPHONE
Exeter VHF Ch 16; 06 12 (Mon-Fri: 0730-1630 LT, and when vessel expected).
TELEPHONE (0395)
Dockmaster 272009; ⌗ (0752) 222929; CG 263232; MRSC Brixham 882704; Pilot 264036; Marinecall 0898 500 458; Police 264651, Dr 273001; Ⓗ 279684.
FACILITIES
EXMOUTH EC Wednesday; **Dixon & Son** ☎ 263063, ME, Sh, CH; **Exe Sailing Club** ☎ 264607, M, L, AB; **Lavis & Son** ☎ 263095, El, Sh, CH; **Tidal Docks** ☎ 272009, L, FW, ME, C; **Victoria Marine Services** ☎ 265044, ME, Gaz, CH; **Peter Dixon** ☎ 273248, CH, ACA; **M. McNamara** ☎ 264907, SM; **Exmouth Dock Co.** ☎ 272009, C; **Rowsell and Morrison** ☎ 263911, CH, El, SM, Ⓔ, Sh; **Pierhead** V, R, Bar, CH; **Town** P, V, R, Ⓞ, Bar; ✉; Ⓑ; ⇌; ✈ (Exeter).
STARCROSS (0626) **Starcross Fishing and Cruising Club** ☎ 890582; **Wills Starcross Garage** ☎ 890225, P and D (cans), ME, M, Gas; **Starcross YC** ☎ 890470; **Village** P, V, Bar; ✉; Ⓑ; ⇌; ✈ (Exeter).
TOPSHAM (0392) **Topsham SC** Slip, L, FW, Bar; **Retreat BY** ☎ 874720, Access HW ∓2, M, D, ME, El, C, Gas, CH; **Scanes** ☎ 877527, SM; **Foc'sle** ☎ 874105, ACA, CH; **Grimshaw Engineering** ☎ 873539, ME, El; **Trouts BY** ☎ 3044, CH, BY; **Village** P, R, V, Ⓞ, Bar, ✉; Ⓑ; ⇌; ✈ (Exeter).
EXETER (0392) For moorings and anchorages apply Hr Mr Exeter City, ☎ Exeter 74306. No moorings in Exmouth, but some in estuary. **Leisure Warehouse** ☎ 50970, (Exeter Canal Basin) CH, ME.

RIVER EXE *continued*

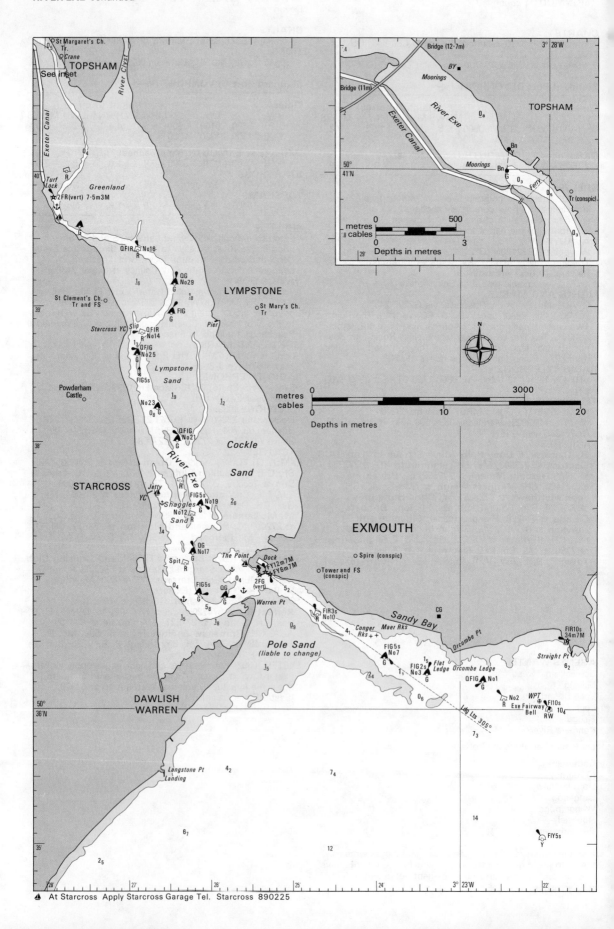

At Starcross Apply Starcross Garage Tel. Starcross 890225

MINOR HARBOURS AND ANCHORAGES 10.1.25

MOUSEHOLE, Cornwall, 50°05′ N, 5°32′ W, Zone 0 (GMT), Admty chart 2345. HW +0550 on Dover, −0024 on Devonport; HW height 0.0 on Devonport; ML 3.2m; Duration 0600. Shelter good except from NE and SE winds; protected by St Clements I. from E winds. Entrance 11m wide; harbour dries at LW. It has depths of 3.8m at MHWS and 2.6m at MHWN. It is closed with timber baulks from Nov−Apl. Lights N Pier 2 FG (vert) 5/6m 4M. R Lt shown when harbour closed. Hr Mr ☎ Penzance 731511. Facilities limited: FW, Slip. Buses to Penzance.

ST MICHAEL'S MOUNT, Cornwall, 50°07′ N, 5°29′ W, Zone 0 (GMT), Admty chart 2345. HW +0550 on Dover, −0024 on Devonport; HW height +0.1m on Devonport; ML 3.2m; Duration 0550. Shelter good from N through E to SE. Harbour dries, it has approx 3.3m at MHWS and 1.4m at MHWN. Beware Hogus Rocks to NW of harbour and Outer Penzeath Rock about 3 ca WSW of Hogus Rocks. Also beware Maltman Rock 1 ca SSW of the Mount. There are no lights. Entrance between piers is 30m wide. No facilities on the island except FW. Marazion, ½ M across the causeway to N has some. EC Wed.

PORTHLEVEN, Cornwall, 50°05′ N, 5°19′ W, Zone 0 (GMT), Admty charts 2345, 777. HW +0551 on Dover, −0055 on Devonport; HW height 0.0 on Devonport; ML 3.1m; Duration 0545. See 10.1.11. Harbour dries above the old LB house but has approx 2.3m in centre of entrance. It is open to W and SW. Beware rocks round pierhead and Deazle Rocks to W. Light on S pier FG 10m 4M shown when inner harbour open. Inside harbour FG vis 033°-067° when required for vessels entering. Visitors go alongside the Quay on E side. Facilities: EC Wed; Hr Mr ☎ Helston 563042; **J. T. Cowis** ME, P and D (in cans); **Handyman** ☎ Helston 562245, CH, Gas, Gaz; **Inner Harbour** C, FW, L, V, Bar; **Village** ✉, ◎, R, Ⓑ.

CADGWITH, Cornwall, 49°59′.2N, 5°10′.7W, Zone 0 (GMT), Admty charts 2345, 154 and 777; HW +0555 on Dover; −0030 on Devonport; −0.2m on Devonport; ML 3.0m. Harbour dries; it is divided into two by a rocky outcrop called The Todden. Beware the extension of this, rocks called The Mare; also beware the rocks to ENE called The Boa which cover at quarter tide. Anchor off The Mare in about 2-3m. Not recommended in on-shore winds. There are no lights. Many local fishing boats operate from here and are hauled up the shingle beach. Facilities: ✉, Bar, R.

PORT MULLION, Cornwall, 50°02′ N, 5°15′ W, Zone 0 (GMT), Admty charts 2345, 777. Lizard HW +0552 on Dover, −0050 on Devonport; HW height −0.2m on Devonport; ML 3.0m; Duration 0545. Harbour dries but has 5.3m at MHWS and 4.2m at MHWN. It is open to all W winds. Anchorage in Mullion Cove is safer especially in lee of Mullion Island where there is approx 3.5m. National Trust owns the island and the harbour. Fin keel boats not allowed in harbour. Visitors not allowed overnight. There are no lights. There is a slip on E side of harbour. Only facilities at Mullion village (1M) EC Wed; Bar, V.

COVERACK, Cornwall, 50°01′ N, 5°05′ W, Zone 0 (GMT), Admty chart 154, 777. HW +0605 on Dover, −0035 on Devonport; HW height −0.2m on Devonport; ML 3.0m; Duration 0550. See 10.1.12. Harbour dries but has 3.3m at MHWS and 2.2m at MHWN. Given good weather and off-shore winds it is better to anchor outside. Harbour is very small and full of fishing boats so berths are unlikely to be available. Beware the Guthens, off Chynhalls Pt, coming from the S, the Dava and other rocks off Lowland Pt coming from the N, and Manacle Rocks to the NE (BYB E cardinal, Q(3) 10s bell). There are no lights. Facilities: Hr Mr ☎ St Keverne 280593; EC Tues; FW (hotel) D, P from garage (in cans), shop, ✉.

PORTSCATHO, Cornwall, 50°11′ N, 4°58′ W, Zone 0 (GMT), Admty chart 154. HW −0600 on Dover, −0025 on Devonport; HW height −0.2m on Devonport; ML 3.0m; Duration 0550. Shelter − small drying harbour but in good weather and off-shore winds there is a good anchorage outside. There are no lights and very few facilities. Hr Mr ☎ 616.

GORRAN HAVEN, Cornwall, 50°14′ N, 4°47′ W, Zone 0 (GMT), Admty charts 148, 1267. HW −0600 on Dover, −0010 on Devonport; HW height −0.1m on Devonport. Shelter good with good flat sand beach for drying out in off-shore wind; good anchorage 100 to 500m E of Hr. Beware Gwineas Rk and Yaw Rk marked by E cardinal buoy. Beware pot markers on approach. Not suitable anchorage when wind is in E. Fin keels without legs should not anchor closer than 300m from Hr wall where depth is 1.8m at MLWS. Facilities: ✉, V, Bar, P (cans), R, L.

PORTMELLON, Cornwall, 50°15′ N, 4°47′ W, Zone 0 (GMT), Admty charts 148, 1267. HW −0600 on Dover, −0010 on Devonport; HW height −0.1m on Devonport; ML 3.1m; Duration 0600. Shelter good but only suitable as a temporary anchorage in settled weather and off-shore winds. There are no lights and few facilities. **G.P. Mitchell** ☎ 842407, BY.

CHARLESTOWN, Cornwall, 50°20′ N, 4°45′ W, Zone 0 (GMT), Admty chart 31, 1267. HW −0555 on Dover, −0010 on Devonport; HW height −0.1m on Devonport; ML 3.1m; Duration 0605. It is a china clay port but has some yacht berths in the inner harbour. Entrance is safe but should only be attempted by day and in off-shore winds with calm weather. N breakwater FG 5m, S breakwater FR 5m. Entry signals − G Lt (night) or R ensign (day) = harbour open. R Lt (night) or B shape (day) = harbour shut. VHF Ch 16; 14 (HW−1 to HW+1 when vessel expected). Yachts should make arrangements before entering on VHF or by telephone, St Austell 3331. Facilities: EC Thurs; Bar, FW, P and D (cans or pre-arranged tanker), R, V.

PAR, Cornwall, 50°21′ N, 4°42′ W, Zone 0 (GMT), Admty chart 31, 1267. HW −0555 on Dover, −0010 on Devonport; HW height −0.1m on Devonport; ML 3.1m; Duration 0605. See 10.1.15. A china clay port which is only suitable as a temporary stop for yachts. Harbour dries. Beware Killyvarder Rocks to SE of entrance marked by a R Bn. Entrance should not be tried except by day, in calm weather with off-shore winds. Entry signals R shape (day) or R Lt (night) = port closed or vessel leaving. VHF Ch 16; 12 (by day and HW−2 to HW+1). Yachts should make arrangements before entering on VHF or by ☎ Par 2282. Facilities: EC Thurs; Bar, D, FW, P, R, V.

POLPERRO, Cornwall, 50°20′ N, 4°31′ W, Zone 0 (GMT), Admty charts 148, 1267. HW −0554 on Dover, −0007 on Devonport; HW height −0.2m on Devonport; ML 3.1m; Duration 0610. Shelter good but harbour dries. There is 3.3m at MHWS and 2.5m at MHWN. The entrance is only 9.8m wide. Entrance closed by hydraulically operated gate in bad weather. Beware The Ranneys to W of entrance, and the rocks to E. Lights: Dir FW (occas) shown from measured distance beacons 1 and 2.2M to ENE. Tidal Basin, W pierhead FW 4m 4M on post, replaced by FR when harbour closed. Facilities: EC Sat; Hr Mr on Fish Quay, FW on quays.

HOPE COVE, Devon, 50°15′ N, 3°49′ W, Zone 0 (GMT), Admty chart 1613. HW −0525 on Dover, River Avon +0015 on Devonport; HW height −0.6m on Devonport; ML 2.6m; Duration 0615. Popular day anchorage but poor holding ground and only safe in off shore winds. Beware rock, which dries 2.7m, ½ ca off shore, 3 ca E off Bolt Tail. There are no lights. Facilities: EC Thurs; very limited facilities at Hope Cove but good at Kingsbridge, (9M bus) or Salcombe, (4M bus).

PAIGNTON, Devon, 50°26′ N, 3°33′ W, Zone 0 (GMT), Admty charts 26, 1613; HW −0500 on Dover, +0035 on Devonport; HW height −0.6m on Devonport; ML 2.9m; Duration 0640. Harbour dries and is only suitable for small boats. E winds cause heavy swell in harbour. Rocks extend 180m E from E wall. Fl R Lt on E arm of entrance. Facilities: Hr Mr (summer only) ☎ 557812. Other telephone numbers and facilities as for Torquay (see 10.1.22). EC Wed. **Paignton SC** ☎ 525817; **Torbay Boating Centre** ☎ 558760, M, ME, Sh, Gas, CH.

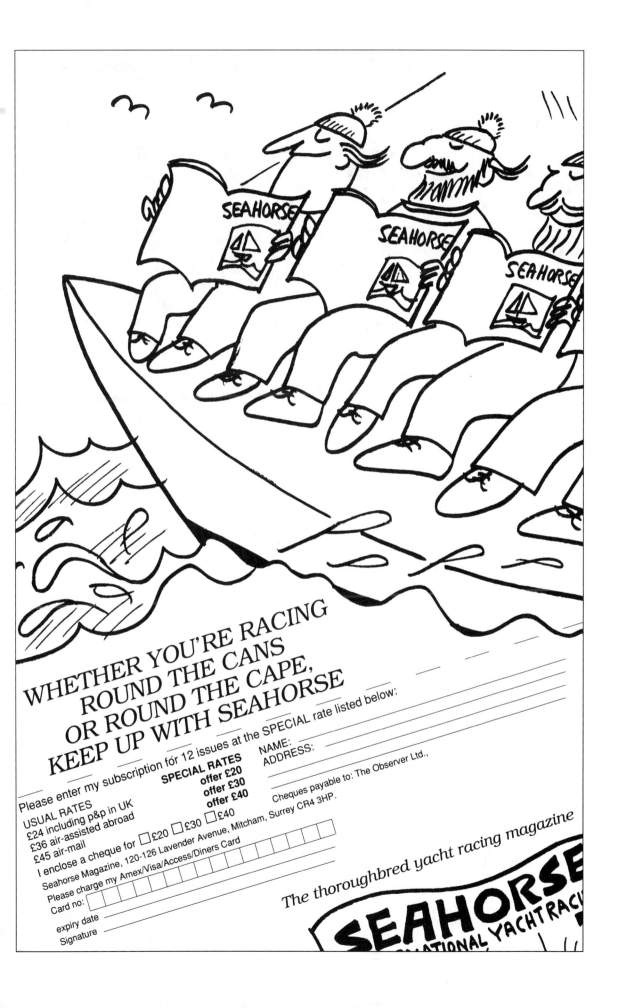

WHETHER YOU'RE RACING
ROUND THE CANS
OR ROUND THE CAPE,
KEEP UP WITH SEAHORSE

Please enter my subscription for 12 issues at the SPECIAL rate listed below:

USUAL RATES
£24 including p&p in UK
£36 air-assisted abroad
£45 air-mail

SPECIAL RATES
offer £20
offer £30
offer £40

NAME:
ADDRESS:

Cheques payable to: The Observer Ltd.,

I enclose a cheque for ☐£20 ☐£30 ☐£40
Seahorse Magazine, 120-126 Lavender Avenue, Mitcham, Surrey CR4 3HP.
Please charge my Amex/Visa/Access/Diners Card
Card no:

expiry date
Signature

The thoroughbred yacht racing magazine

SEAHORSE
INTERNATIONAL YACHT RACING

VOLVO PENTA SERVICE

Area 2

Central Southern England
Lyme Regis to Chichester

51°
N

10-2-2
Central Southern England

Lyme Regis

ℹ️	10.2.11
🅿️	VHF 16;14
⚠️	

Bridport

ℹ️	10.2.12
🅿️	VHF 16;11

Poole Harbour

☁️	M−0898 500 457
RC PO •--• --- 3,6	303.4 10

Weymouth

ℹ️	10.2.14
🅿️	VHF 16;12
LB	

Beer* • CG

R Axe* •

Lyme Bay

War

☆ Straight Point

Lulworth Cove*

CG

Portland CG
Brixham CG

Portland Bill

RC PB •--• ••• 1	291.9 50

Portland
Race

RG

Portland

ℹ️	10.2.13
🅿️	VHF 13 14

50°
30'N

0

270 Variation 5°W (1991) 90

180

Grove Point

Portland ⚠️CG

Weymouth Bay

📞	VHF 05 16
☁️	0733 1933

For details of traffic
lanes see Fig.2(1)

East Channel
Light Buoy

50°
N

Channel LV

RC CR •--• •••	287.3 10

SEPARATION ZONE

3°W

Poole
10.2.16

VHF 14 16;14

Marinas VHF 80

LB   IL

Southampton
ℹ   10.2.24

P R   VHF 16 12
14;18 20 22

☁☀   228844
M–0898
500 457

Hamble River
ℹ   10.2.25

Marinas VHF
Ch **80**

Portsmouth
Standard Port

ℹ   10.2.28

☁☀   M 0898
500 457

P R   VHF 11 16
C&N
Marina Ch **80**

51°N

Chichester
ℹ   10.2.30

RC   CH – · – · · · ·
1,4   303.4   10

P R   VHF 14 16; 14
(0900–1730)

IL

Hythe (Fawley)
RC Aero   FAW · – · · · · –
· – –
370   20

Lee - on - Solent
RC Aero   LS · – · · · · ·
325 10

Solent   CG

Beaulieu River
ℹ   10.2.22

Lymington
ℹ   10.2.19

Marina VHF
Ch **80**   IL

Titchfield Haven

Calshot
CG

Lee-on-Solent

☆ ☆ **Forts**

Hurn
RC Aero   HRN · · · · · – –
· –
394   35

CG   RG

Christchurch
ℹ   10.2.17

IL

CG

Newport*
P R   Ch 16;06

CG

dland
Bay*
an's

*Alban's
edge*

Keyhaven
ℹ   10.2.18

Yarmouth
ℹ   10.2.20

LB

RG

Needles
Radio   HD Ch 88
Lt Ho 337°–097° 30

Newtown
ℹ   10.2.21

Wootton Creek
ℹ   10.2.26

50°
30'N

Swanage
ℹ   10.2.15

LB   CG

St. Catherines Point
RC   CP – · – · · – – ·
2   291.9   50

Bembridge
ℹ   10.2.27

RC Aero   IW · · · – –
276.5 15

Marina VHF
Ch **80**

LB   IL

nvil Point
AL Ch 88
247°–007° 14

Solent CG
Portland CG

Niton
S G   MF 1834
VHF 04 16
28 81 85 87 64

☁☀   0733 1933

Langstone
ℹ   10.2.29

P R   VHF 12 16;12
(0830–1700)

IL

Nab Tower
RC   NB – · · – · · ·
1,3,5 312.6   10

Cowes
ℹ   10.2.23

P R   VHF 16;11 12 14
M **69**
(0830–1700)
Hr Launches 16 69

Marinas VHF
Ch 80

2°W   1°W

Key to Symbols

🎧	Coast Station / Port Radio – frequencies
RC	Marine radiobeacon– call sign, sequence, frequency and range (nm)
RC Aero	Aeronautical radiobeacon–call sign, frequency and range (nm)
ℹ	See for harbour information/tidal data
☁☀	Weather (tel. or times). M - Marinecall
CG	HM Coastguard MRCC CG MRSC

CG	HM Coastguard Sector Base
RG ◎	Emergency VHF DF
LB	RNLI Lifeboat over 10m
IL	RNLI Lifeboat under 10m
🚁	SAR Helicopter base
☆	Principal lights
⚓	Light-vessel
	Lanby
*	See 10.2.31

10.2.3 AREA 2 TIDAL STREAMS

5 Hours before HW Dover (0530 before HW Portsmouth)

4 Hours before HW Dover (0430 before HW Portsmouth)

3 Hours before HW Dover (0330 before HW Portsmouth)

2 Hours before HW Dover (0230 before HW Portsmouth)

1 Hour before HW Dover (0130 before HW Portsmouth)

HW Dover (0030 before HW Portsmouth)

Portland 10.2.13   Isle of Wight 10.2.8   Eastward 10.3.3   Southward 10.17.3   Westward 10.1.3

1 Hour after HW Dover (0030 after HW Portsmouth)

2 Hours after HW Dover (0130 after HW Portsmouth)

3 Hours after HW Dover (0230 after HW Portsmouth)

4 Hours after HW Dover (0330 after HW Portsmouth)

5 Hours after HW Dover (0430 after HW Portsmouth)

6 Hours after HW Dover (0530 after HW Portsmouth)

10.2.4   LIGHTS, FOG SIGNALS AND WAYPOINTS

Abbreviations used below are given in 10.0.3. Principal lights are in **bold** print, places in CAPITALS, and light-vessels, light floats and Lanbys in *CAPITAL ITALICS*. Unless otherwise stated lights are white. m—elevation in metres; M—nominal range in n. miles. Fog signals are in *italics*. Useful waypoints are underlined use those on land with care. See 4.2.2

ENGLAND—SOUTH COAST

AXMOUTH.
Pier head 50°42'·10N 03°'·03.21W Fl 5s 7m 2M.

LYME REGIS.
Ldg Lts 296°. Front at inner pier head 50°43'·14N 02°56'·09W Oc WR 8s 6m 9M; vis R2116°-296°, W296°.-116°. Rear, FG 8m 9M.

BRIDPORT.
East pier head FG 3m 2M.
West pier head 50°42'·52N 02°45'·77W FR 3m 2M.
West pier, root Iso R2s 9m 5M.
DZ Lt Buoy 50°36'·50N 02°42'·00W FlY 3s; special mark.
Portland Bill 50°30'·82N 02°27'·32W Fl(4) 20s 43m **29M**; W round Tr, R band. Changes from 1 flash to 4 flashes 221°-244°, 4 flashes 244°-117°, changes from 4 flashes to 1 flash 117°-141°; RC. FR 19m 13M (same Tr) vis 271°-291° over The Shambles; *Dia 30s maximum power 005°-085°.*

PORTLAND.
Outer breakwater (S end) Oc R 30s 9m 5M.FR on radar Tr 0·68M WSW and on radio mast 2·8M NW.
Outer breakwater (N end) QR 14m 5M; vis 013°-268°.
NE breakwater (SE end) 50°35'·11N 02°24'·99W Fl 10s 22m **20M**; W Tr; *Horn 10s.*
NE breakwater (NW end) 50°35'·62N 02°25'·80W Oc R 15s 11m 5M.
North arm (SE end) Oc G 10s 5M.

WEYMOUTH.
South pier head 50°36'·54N 02°26'·41W Q 10m 9M; traffic sigs 190m SW; *Reed 15s* (when vessels docking). Ldg Lts 237°30 both FR.
North pier head 2 FG (vert) 9m 6M. *Bell* (when vessels expected).
West Shambles Lt Buoy 50°29'·75N 02°24'·33W Q(9) 15s; W cardinal; *Bell.*
East Shambles Lt Buoy 50°30'·75N 02°20'·00W Q(3) 10s; E cardinal; *Whis, Horn (2) 30s.*

Lulworth Cove entrance, East Point 50°36'·97N 02°14'·69W (unlit).
Bindon Hill 50°37'·3N 02°13'·6W and St Alban's Head 50°34'·8N 02°03'·4W Iso R 2s when firing taking place.
Anvil Point 50°35'·48N 01°57'·52W Fl 10s 45m **24M**; W Tr; vis 237°-076°; (H24); RW on trial.

SWANAGE.
Pier head 50°36'·52N 01°56'·88W 2 FR (vert) 6m 3M.
Peveril Ledge Buoy 50°36'·38N 01°56'·02W (unlit); port hand mark.

POOLE.
Poole Fairway Lt Buoy 50°38'·95N 01°54'·78W LFl 10s; safe water mark.

Poole Bar (No. 1) Lt Buoy 50°39.31N 01°55'·10W QG; stbd-hand mark; *Bell* .
(Historic wreck 50°39'·67N 01°54'·79W Fl Y 5s; special mark.
No. 2 Lt Buoy 50°39'·18N 01°55'·17W FlR 2s; port-hand mark.
No. 9 Lt Buoy 50°40'·19N 01°55'·74W Fl G 5s; stbd-hand mark..
No. 10 Lt Buoy 50°40'·11N 01°55'·84W Fl R 4s; port-hand mark.
No. 11 (Hook Sands) Lt Buoy 50°40'·46N 01°56'·05W Fl G 3s; stdb-hand mark.
Training bank, outer end 50°39'·75N 01°55'·76W QR 7m 2M; R framework Tr.
Swash Channel marked by port and stbd-hand buoys, unlit except for
No. 12 (Channel) Lt Buoy 50°40'·41N 01°56'·19W FlR R 2s; port-hand mark.
No. 13 Lt Buoy 50°40'·85N 01°56'·62W FlG 5s; stbd-hand mark, and
No. 14 Lt Buoy 50°40'·76N 01°56'·73W Fl R 4s; port-hand mark.

Sandbanks 50°40'·95N 01°56'·79W FY 10m 4M (RC 80m E).
RMYC pier heads 50°41'·31N 01°56'·73W 2FG (vert) 2M.
East Looe No. 16A Lt Buoy 50°41'·02N 01°56'·03W QR; port- hand mark.
East Looe Dir Lt 50°41'·16N 01°56'·38W Oc WRG 6s 9m W10M, R6M, G6M; vis R234°-294°, W294°-304°, G304°-024°.
Ferry landing, East side 2 FG (vert) either side of ramp.
South Haven Point, ferry landing QR 3m 3M either side of ramp.
North Haven Point Beacon 50°41'·12N 01°57'·10W Q(9) 15s; W cardinal mark.
North channel to Poole Harbour YC marina and Poole Quay marked by port and stbd-hand buoys, mostly lit.
Bullpit Beacon 50°41'·69N 01°56'·62W Q(9) 15s 7m 4M; W cardinal mark.
Salterns Beacon 50°42'·18N 01°57'·12W Q(6)LFl 15s 5m 5M; S cardinal mark.
Parkstone YC platform 50°42'·33N 01°58'·00W Q 8m 1M; hut on dolphin.
Stakes No. 55 Lt Buoy 50°42'·41N 01°58'·92W Q(6)LFl 15s; S cardinal mark.
Little Channel, East side, Oyster Bank 50°42'·59N 01°59'·02W Fl(3)G 5s; stbd-hand mark.
Ro-Ro ferry terminal, two 2FG (vert).
Lts in line 270°30'. Front and Rear QY; vis 180°-000°. Marks centre line of dredged basin.
BP Dock. 2 FG (vert) on E and West sides.
PYC Haven entrance, E side 50°42'·41N 01°59'·70W FlG 5s. West side Fl(3) 10s.
Wareham Channel marked by port and stbd-hand buoys initially, and then by stakes.
South Deep. Marked by Lt beacons and unlit beacons from entrance South of Brownsea Castle to Furzey Island.
Furzey Island, SE corner, slipway 50°40'·88N 01°58'·86W Ldg Lts 305° FlY 2s. Mooring dolphins FlG 5s.

BOURNEMOUTH
Pier head 2 FR (vert) 9/7m 1M; W column. *Reed (2) 120s* when vessel expected.
Boscombe Pier head 2 FR (vert) 7m 1M; R column.
Hengistbury Head, groyne, Bn 50°42'·63N 01°44'·85W (unlit).

Needles Fairway Lt Buoy 50°38'·20N 01°38'·90W LFl 10s; safe water mark; *Whis*.

NOTE: For waypoints of navigational buoys and racing marks in Solent area, see 10.2.9.

Wave Research Structure 50°42'·87N 01°38'·24W Mo(U) 15s and Mo(U)R 15s 10m 5M; *Horn Mo(U) 30s* (temp inop).
Needles Lt 50°39'·70N 01°35'·43W Oc(2) WRG 20s 24m **W17M**, R17°15M, G14M; round Tr, R band and lantern; vis R291°-300°, W300°-083°, R(unintens) 083°-212°, W212°-217°, G217°-224°; *Horn (2) 30s*.

NEEDLES CHANNEL.
SW Shingles Lt Buoy 50°39'·53N 01°37'·24W Fl R 2·5s; port-hand mark.
Bridge Lt Buoy 50°39'·59N 01°36'·80W VQ(9) 10s; W cardinal mark.
Shingles Elbow Lt Buoy 50°40'·31N 01°35'·92W Fl(2)R 5s; port-hand mark.
Mid Shingles Lt Buoy 50°41'·19N 01°34'·59W; Fl(3)R 10s; port-hand mark.
Totland Bay Pier, head 2 FR (vert) 6m 2M.
Warden Lt Buoy 50°41'·46N 01°33'·48W FlG 2.5s; stbd-hand mark; *Bell*.

NORTH CHANNEL.
North Head Lt Buoy 50°42'·65N 01°35'·42W Fl(3)G 10s; stbd-hand mark.
NE Shingles Lt Buoy 50°41'·93N 01°33'·32W Q(3) 10s; E cardinal mark.

Hurst Point Ldg Lts 042°. Front 50°42'·36N 01°33'·05W Iso 4s 15m 14M; R square Tr; vis 029°-053°. Rear 215m from front Iso WR 6s 23m W14/13M, R11M; W round Tr; vis W(unintens) 080°-104°, W234°-244°, R244°-250°, W250°-053°.

LYMINGTON.
Jack in the Basket 50°44'·25N 01°30'·50W Fl R 2s 9m; Ra refl.
Ldg Lts 319°30'. Front 50°45'·2N 01°31'·6W FR 12m 8M; vis 309·5°-329·5°. Rear 363m from front FR 17m 8M; vis as front.
Cross Boom No. 2 Fl R 2s 4m 3M; X and R can on pile.
No. 1 Fl G 2s 2m 3M; G cone on pile. Piles similar to Nos. 1 and 2 mark the channel to Harper's Post 50°45'·05N 01°31'·40W Q(3) 10s 5m 1M.
Lymington Yacht Haven Ldg Lts 244°, both FY.
Ferry pier head 2FG(vert).

Durn's Point obstruction, S end, 50°45'·37N 01°26'·95W QR; Dolphin.
Beaulieu Spit, E end 50°46'·83N 01°21'·67W Fl R 5s 3M; R dolphin; vis 277°-037°. Entrance Channel Beacons No. 5, 9, 19 Fl G 4s; Beacons 12, 20 Fl R 4s.

Stansore Point. 50°46'·7N 01°20'·8W, 50°46'·8N 01°20'·5W, 50°46'·9N 01°20'·4W. In each of these positions is a QR Lt 4m 1M; R triangle, W band, on R pile, marking cables.
Fort Victoria pier head 2 FG (vert) 4M.

YARMOUTH.
Pier head, centre, 2 FR (vert) 2M; G column. High intensity FW (occas).
Jetty head 2 FR (vert) 4m 2M; W mast; second FR shows harbour full. In fog FY 5m from same structure, vis 167°-192°.
Ldg Lts 188°. Front 50°42'·3N 01°30'·0W FG 5m 2M; W diamond on B post. Rear, 63m from front FG 9m 2M; W diamond on B mast.

West Bramble Lt Buoy 50°47'·15N 01°18'·55W VQ(9) 10s; W cardinal mark; *Bell*; Racon.
Outfall 50°48'·25N 01°18'·73W Iso R 10s 6m 5M; column on square structure; Ra refl; FR Lt on each corner; *Horn 20s*.

CALSHOT SPIT Lt F 50°48'·32N 01°17'·55W Fl 5s 12m 11M; R hull, Lt Tr amidships; *Horn (2) 60s*.
Obstn Lts, FR 34m on radar Tr 120m W, and QR on chy 0·9M W.
Fawley Channel No. 2 50°49'·45N 01°18'·75W Fl R 3s.
Ldg Lts 219°. Front QR (occas). Rear Q (occas).
Hamble Point Lt Buoy 50°50'·12N 01°18'·58W Q(6)LFl 15s; S cardinal mark.

RIVER HAMBLE.
Ldg Lts 345°30'. Front No. 6 pile 50°50'·58N 01°18'·74W Oc(2) R 12s 4m 2M. Rear 820m from front QR 12m; W mast; vis 341·5°-349·5°.
No. 1 pile 50°50'·31N 01°18'·57W Fl G 3s 3M; stbd-hand mark.
No. 2 pile 50°50'·36N 01°18'·68W Q(3) 10s 3M; E cardinal mark.
No. 3 pile Fl(2)G 5s.
No. 5 pile Fl(3)G 10s.
No. 7 pile Fl G 3s.
No. 8 pile Fl R 3s.
No. 9 pile Fl(2)G 5s.
No. 10 pile Fl(2)R 5s.
Ldg Lts 026°, Warsash shore. Front 50°51'·0N 01°18'·3W QG; B & W chequered pile Bn. Rear, Sailing Club, Iso G 6s; vis 022°-030°.
Up river Lts 2 FG (vert) or QG are on the E side, and 2 FR (vert) on the West side.

SOUTHAMPTON WATER.
Esso Marine terminal, SE end 50°50'·05N 01°19'·33W 2 FR (vert) 9m 10M; *Whis (2) 20s*.
BP Hamble Jetty 50°50'·8N 01°19'·4W 2 FG (vert) 5/3m 2M (on each side of the 4 dolphins).
Hythe Pier head 50°52'·45N 01°23'·52W 2 FR (vert) 12/5m 5M.
Hythe Marina Village 50°52'·6N 01°23'·8W Q (3) 10s; E cardinal mark.
Lock entrance 2 FG (vert) and 2 FR (vert).
Queen Elizabeth II terminal, South end 50°52'·97N 01°23'·64W 4 FG (vert) 16/14/12/11m 3M.

RIVER ITCHEN.
East side. No. 1 dolphin 50°53'·12N 01°23'·32W QG; stbd-hand mark.
No. 2 dolphin 50°53'·27N 01°23'·28W Fl G 5s 2M; stbd-hand mark.
No.3 dolphin 50°53'·45N 01°23'·18W Fl G 7s; stbd-hand mark.
No.4 pile 50°53'·58N 01°23'·07W QG 4m 2M; stbd-hand mark. Itchen Bridge. FW on bridge span each side marks main channel. 2 FG (vert) 2M each side on E pier. 2 FR (vert) 2M each side on West pier.
Crosshouse Beacon 50°54'·01N 01°23'·10W OcR 5s 5m 2M; port-hand mark, power cable.
Chapel Beacon 50°54'12N 01°23'·13W Fl G 3s 5m 3M; stbd-hand mark.
Shamrock Quay pontoon, SW end 50°54'·45N 01°22'·83W and NE ends 2 FR (vert) 4m. Millstone Point No. 5 Bn Fl G 3s.
No. 6 Bn 50°54'·57N 01°22'·55W Fl R 3s.
No. 7 Bn Fl(2)G 5s.
No. 9 Bn 50°54'·72N 01°22'·38W Fl(4)G 10s.
Kemps Marina 50°54'·80N 01°22'·57W 2 FG (vert),

RIVER TEST.

Lower Foul Ground Lt Bn 50°53'·23N 01°24'·47W Fl (2) R 10s; port-hand Bn.

Upper Foul Ground Lt Bn 50°53'·50N 01°24'·80W Fl (2) R 10s; port hand Bn.

Town Quay Ldg Lts 329°, both FY (occas).

Middle Swinging Ground, Lts in line 336°, both OcG 6s 26m.

COWES.

No. 4 Lt Buoy 50°46'·04N 01°17'·78W QR.

Ldg Lts 164°. Front 50°45'·9N 01°17'·8W Iso 2s 3m 6M. Rear 290m from front Iso R 2s 5m 3M; vis 120°-240°.

East breakwater head Fl R 3s 3M.

Fountain Pontoon 2 FG (vert) each end.

Yacht Haven 2 FG (vert) each end.

East Cowes ferry pontoon 2 FR (vert); *Horn*.

Trinity Wharf 2 FR (vert). Above this point Lts 2 FG (vert) are shown on the W side, and 2 FR (vert) on the E side.

WOOTTON.

Beacon 50°44'·46N 01°12'·08W Q 1M; N cardinal mark.

West side of channel marked by pile beacons: No. 1 Fl G 3s, No. 2 Fl(2) G 5s, No. 3 QG.

RYDE.

Pier, NW corner, N corner and E corner each marked by 2 FR (vert). In fog FY from North corner, vis 045°-165°, 200°-320°.

Fort Gilkicker 50°46'·40N 01°08'·38W Oc G 10s 7M.

Spit Sand Fort, N side 50°46'·20N 01°05'·85W Fl R 5s 18m 7M; large round stone structure.

Horse Sand Fort 50°44'·97N 01°04'·25W Fl 10s 21m **15M**; large round stone structure.

No Man's Land Fort 50°44'·37N 01°05'·61W Fl 5s 21m **15M**; large round stone structure.

St Helen's Fort (IOW) 50°42'·27N 01°04'·95W Fl(3) 10s 16m 8M; large round stone structure.

Brading Harbour entrance, West side, tide gauge 50°42'·55N 01°05'·24W Fl Y 2s 1M.

Sandown Pier head 2 FR (vert) 7/5m 2M.

Shanklin Pier head 2 FR (vert) 6m 4M; TE; *Bell*.

Ventnor Pier 2 FR (vert) 10m 3M.

St Catherine's Point (IOW) 50°34'·52N 01°17'·80W Fl 5s 41m **30M**; W 8-sided tower; vis 257°-117°; RC. FR 35m **17M** (same Tr) vis 099°-116°.

Nab Tower. 50°40'·05N 00°57'·07W Fl(2) 10s 27m **19M**; *Horn(2)30s*; RC; Racon. Fog Det Lt, vis 300°-120°.

PORTSMOUTH.

Outer Spit Lt Buoy 50°45'·55N 01°05'·41W Q(6)LFl 15s; S cardinal mark.

Southsea Castle, N corner 50°46'·66N 01°05'·25W Iso 2s 16m 11M, W stone Tr, B band; vis 339°-066°.

Dir Lt 001°30' (same structure) Dir WRG 11m W13M, R5M, G5M; FG 351·5°-357·5°, AlWG 357·5°-000° (W phase incr with brg), FW 000°-003°, Al WR 003°-005·5° (R phase incr with brg), FR 005·5°-011·5°.

Fort Blockhouse 50°47'·34N 01°06'·65W Dir Lt 320°; Dir WRG 6m W13M, R5M, G5M; OcG 310°-316°, AlWG 316°-318·5° (W phase incr with brg), Oc 318·5°-321·5°, AlWR 321·5°-324° (R phase incr with brg), OcR 324°-330°. 2 FR (vert) 20m E. Dolphin, close E of C&N marina, 50°47'·8N 01°06'·9W, Dir WRG 2m 1M; vis IsoG 2s 322°-330°, AlWG 330°-332°, Iso 2s 332°-335° (main channel), AlWR 335°-337°, IsoR 2s 337°-345° (Small Boat Channel).

Victoria Pile 50°47'·31N 01°06'·40W OcG 15s 1M; stbd-hand mark.

Round Tower 2 FG (vert).

The Point 50°47'·54N 01°06'·48W QG 2M; pile, stbd-hand mark.

In Portsmouth Harbour jetties on the E (Portsmouth) shore are marked by 2 FG (vert) and those on the West (Gosport) shore by 2 FR (vert).

Pile 98 (N of North Corner Jetty) 50°48'·58N 01°06'·69W Q(6)LFl 15s; S cardinal mark.

LANGSTONE.

Roway Wreck beacon 50°46'·08N 01°02'·20W Fl(2) 5s; isolated danger mark.

Langstone Fairway Lt Buoy 50°46'·28N 01°01'·27W LFl 10s; safe water mark.

Eastney Point, drain Bn 50°47'·20N 01°01'·58W QR 2m 2M. FR Lts combined with Y Lts shown when firing taking place. Water intake 50°47'·7N 01°01'·7W Fl R 10s; pile.

Hayling Island ferry landing 2 FG (vert). Langstone Channel, South Lake 50°49'·45N 00°59'·80W FlG 3s 3m 2M; pile, stbd-hand mark.

Binness 50°49'·60N 00°59'·85W FlR 3s 3m 2M; pile, port-hand mark.

CHICHESTER.

Bar beacon 50°45'·88N 00°56'·37W Fl WR 5s 14m W7M, R5M; vis W322°-080°, R080°-322°; Fl(2)R 10s 7m 2M; same structure; vis 020°-080°; RC.

Eastoke Beacon 50°46'·62N 00°56'·08W QR 2m.

West Winner Beacon 50°46'·83N 00°55'·89W QG.

EMSWORTH CHANNEL

Verner 50°48'·33N 00°56'·62W Fl R 10s; pile, port-hand mark.

Marker Point 50°48'·87N 00°56'·62W Fl(2)G 10s 8m; pile, stbd-hand mark.

NE Hayling 50°49'·60N 00°56'·75W Fl(2)R 10s 8m; pile, port-hand mark.

Emsworth 50°49'·63N 00°56'·67W Q(6)LFl 15s; pile, S cardinal mark, tide gauge.

CHICHESTER CHANNEL.

East Head 50°47'·32N 00°54'·70W Fl(4)G 10s; pile, stbd-hand mark, tide gauge.

Camber Beacon 50°47'·84N 00°53'·98W Q(6)LFl 15s; S cardinal mark.

Chalkdock Beacon 50°48'·46N 00°53'·20W Fl(2)G 10s; pile, stbd- hand mark.

Itchenor, jetty 50°48'·44N 00°51'·89W 2 FG (vert); tide gauge.

Birdham 50°48'·30N 00°50'·17W Fl(4)G 10s; pile, stbd-hand mark, depth gauge.

Note. For English Channel Waypoints see 10.1.7

(For Channel Lt V, E Channel Lt F, Channel Islands and adjacent coast of France see 10.17.4).

10.2.5 PASSAGE INFORMATION

LYME BAY (chart 3315)

Between Torbay and Portland there is no harb accessible in onshore winds, and yachtsmen must take care not to be caught on a lee shore. Tides are weak, seldom reaching more than ¾ kn. There are no dangers offshore. In offshore winds there is a good anch off Beer, NE of Beer Hd, the most W chalk cliff in England, see 10.2.31. 3½M E of Lyme Regis (10.2.11) is Golden Cap (186m and conspic). High Ground and Pollock are rks 7 ca offshore, 2M and 3M ESE of Golden Cape.

E of Bridport (10.2.12) is the start of the Chesil Beach, which runs almost straight to N end of Portland peninsula, with its conspic wedge-shaped appearance. In E winds there is anch in Chesil Cove on NW side of Portland, but beware any shift of wind to the W.

PORTLAND

Portland (chart 2255) is mostly steep-to, but rks extend ¼ ca beyond the extremity of the Bill, where there is a stone Bn (18m). Depths S of Bill are irregular. On E side there is rk awash at HW ½ ca off Grove Pt, the E extremity of Portland. From a distance Portland looks like an island, with the highest land (144m) in N, sloping to the Bill where the Lt Ho is conspic.

Tidal streams run very strongly, with eddies either side of Portland. Stream runs S down each side for about 10 hrs out of 12, causing great turbulence where they meet off the Bill. The direction and strength of stream is shown hour by hour, relative to HW Devonport, in 10.2.13. Note that the sp rate reaches 7 kn, but even stronger streams can occur in vicinity of the race. The diagrams show that the race varies in position and extent — usually SE of the Bill on E-going stream, and SW of the Bill on W-going stream.

There is usually a stretch of relatively smooth water ¼ ½M offshore, between the Bill and the race, but yachts using this must take care not to be swept S into the race by the strong stream usually running down either side of Portland. Also beware lobster pots — this is no place for a fouled propeller.

On passage E, unless bound for Weymouth (10.2.14) it is safest to pass 5M S of the Bill, to seaward of the race and of the Shambles bank. If bound for Weymouth, and conditions are suitable for the inshore passage, aim for a point well N of the Bill itself, to allow for tide. It is ideal to round the Bill about HW Devonport − 0130 (HW Portland − 0230) when there will be a favourable tide up the E side of Portland, taking the boat away from the race.

On passage W it is best to round the Bill with the first of the ebb, leaving Weymouth about HW Devonport + 0400 (HW Portland + 0300), so that a yacht will carry the tide well W of Portland.

PORTLAND TO ISLE OF WIGHT (chart 2615)

The Shambles bank is about 3M E of Portland Bill, and should be avoided at all times. In bad weather the sea breaks heavily on it. It is marked by buoys on its E side and at SW end. E of Weymouth are rky ledges extending 3 ca offshore as far as Lulworth Cove, which provides a reasonable anch in fine, settled weather and offshore winds. Rky ledges extend each side of entrance, more so on the W. See 10.2.31.

A firing range extends 5M offshore between Lulworth and St Alban's Hd. Yachts must pass through this area as quickly as possible, when the range is in use. See 10.2.31. Beware Kimmeridge Ledges, which run over ½M seaward. Warbarrow B and Chapman's Pool provide anchs in calm weather and offshore winds. See 10.2.31.

St Alban's Hd (107m and conspic) is steep-to and has a dangerous race off it which may extend 3M seaward. The race lies to the E on the flood and to the W on the ebb; the latter is the more dangerous. An inshore passage about ½M wide avoids the worst of the overfalls. There is an eddy on W side of St Alban's, where the stream runs almost continuously SE. 1M S of St Alban's the ESE stream begins at HW Portsmouth + 0520, and the WNW stream at HW Portsmouth − 0030, with sp rates of 4¾ kn.

There is deep water quite close inshore between St Alban's Hd and Anvil Pt (Lt). 1M NE of Durlston Hd is Peveril Ledge running ¼M seaward, and causing quite a bad race which extends nearly 1M eastwards, particularly on W-going stream against a SW wind. Proceeding towards Poole (10.2.16), overfalls may be met off Ballard Pt and Old Harry on the W-going stream. Studland B (chart 2172) is a good anch except in winds between NE and SE. Anch about 4 ca WNW of Handfast Pt. Avoid foul areas on chart. See 10.2.31.

Poole B offers good sailing in waters sheltered from W and N winds, and with no dangers to worry the average yacht. Tidal streams are weak N of a line between Handfast Pt and Hengistbury Hd. The latter is a dark headland, S of Christchurch harb (10.2.17), with a groyne extending 1 ca S and Beerpan Rks a further ½ ca offshore. Christchurch Ledge extends 2¾M SE from Hengistbury Hd. There are often lobster pots in this area. The tide runs hard over the ledge at sp, and there may be overfalls. Within Christchurch B the streams are weak.

APPROACHES TO SOLENT (charts 2219, 2050)

The Needles with their Lt Ho are conspic landmark for W end of Isle of Wight. There are rks ¼ ca (dries) and ½ ca WNW of Lt Ho, with remains of wreck close SW of inner one. In bad weather broken water and overfalls extend along The Bridge — a reef which runs 8 ca of W of the Lt Ho with extremity marked by buoy.

The NW side of Needles Chan is defined by the Shingles bank, parts of which dry and on which the sea breaks very heavily. The SE side of the bank is fairly steep, the NW side much more gradual in slope. On the ebb the stream sets very strongly in a WSW direction across the Shingles. Gale force winds between S and W against the ebb tide cause a very dangerous sea in Needles Chan. In such conditions the eastern approach to the Solent, via the Forts and Spithead, should be used. In strong winds the North Channel, N of the Shingles, is to be preferred to the Needles Chan. The two join S of Hurst Pt, where overfalls may be met. Beware The Trap, a bank close S of Hurst Fort.

The E approach to the Solent, via Spithead, presents few problems. The main chan is well buoyed and easy to follow, but there is plenty of water for the normal yacht to the S of it when approaching No Man's Land Fort and Horse Sand Fort, which must be passed between. Ryde Sand dries extensively and is a trap for the unwary; so too is Hamilton Bank on the W side of the chan to Portsmouth (10.2.28).

THE SOLENT (charts 2040, 394)

Within the Solent there are few dangers in mid-chan. The most significant is Bramble bank (dries) between Cowes and Calshot. The main chan (buoyed) passes S and W of the Brambles, but yachts can use the North Chan running N of the Brambles at any state of tide.

Tidal stream are strong at sp, but principally follow the direction of the main chans. For details see 10.2.9.

For waypoints of navigational buoys and racing marks see 10.2.10.

There are several spits, banks, rks and ledges which a yachtsmen should know. From the W they include: Pennington and Lymington Spits on the N shore; Black Rk 4 ca W of entrance to Yarmouth (10.2.20); Hamstead Ledge 8 ca W of entrance to Newtown River (10.2.21) and Saltmead Ledge 1½ M to E; Gurnard Ledge 1½ M W of Cowes; Lepe Middle and Beaulieu Spit, S and W of the entrance to Beaulieu River (10.2.22); the shoals off Stone Pt, where three Bns mark cable area; Shrape Mud, which extends N from the breakwater of Cowes harb (10.2.23) and along to Old Castle Pt; the shoals and occasional rks which fringe the Island shore from Old Castle Pt to Ryde, including either side of the entrance to Wootton Creek (10.2.26); and Calshot Spit which extends almost to the Lt F which marks the turn of chan into Southampton Water.

Depending on the direction of wind, there are many good anchs in Solent for yachts which are on passage up or down the coast. For example, in E winds Alum B, close NE of the Needles, is an attractive daytime anch with its coloured cliffs — but beware Long Rk (dries) in middle of b, and Five Fingers Rk 1½ ca SW of Hatherwood Pt on N side. Totland B is good anch in settled weather, but avoid Warden Ledge.

In W winds there is anch on E side of Hurst, as close inshore as depth permits, NE of High Lt. In S winds, or in good weather, anch W of Yarmouth harb entrance, as near shore as possible; reasonably close to town (see 10.2.20).

In winds between W and N there is good anch in Stanswood B, about 1M NE of Stansore Pt. Just N of Calshot Spit there is shelter from SW and W. Osborne B, 2M E of Cowes, is sheltered from winds between S and W. In E winds Gurnard B, the other side of Cowes is preferable. In N winds anch in Stokes B. At E end of IOW there is good anch off Bembridge in winds from S, SW or W; but clear out if wind goes into E.

Within the Solent there are many places which a shoal-draught boat can explore at the top of the tide — such as Ashlett Creek between Fawley and Calshot, Eling up the River Test, and the upper reaches of the Medina.

ISLE OF WIGHT — SOUTH COAST (chart 2045)

From the Needles into Freshwater B the cliffs can be approached to within 1 ca, but beyond the E end of chalk cliffs there are ledges off Brook and again off Atherfield which demand keeping at least ½ M offshore. The E-going stream sets towards these dangers. 4M SSW of the Needles the stream turns E x N at HW Portsmouth + 0530, and W at HW Portsmouth − 0030, sp rate 2 kn. The E-going stream starts running NE, but soon changes to E x N, towards Atherfield ledges. In Freshwater B, 3M E of Needles, the stream turns ESE at HW Portsmouth + 0445, and WNW at HW Portsmouth − 0130, sp rate 1 kn.

St Catherine's Lt Ho (Lt, RC) is conspic. It is safe to pass 2 ca off, but a race occurs off the Pt and can be very dangerous at or near sp with a strong opposing wind, particularly SE of the Pt on a W-going stream in a W gale — when St Catherine's should be given a berth of at least 2M. 1¼ M SE of the Pt the stream turns E x N at HW Portsmouth + 0520, and W x S at HW Portsmouth − 0055, sp rate 3¾ kn.

From St Catherine's Pt to Dunnose, rks extend about 2½ ca in places. A race occurs at Dunnose. In Sandown B, between Dunnose and Culver Cliff, the streams are weak inshore. Off the centre of the B they turn NE x E at HW Portsmouth + 0500, and SW x W at HW Portsmouth − 0100, sp rates 2 kn. Whitecliff B provides an anch in winds between W and N. From here to Foreland (Bembridge Pt) the coast is fronted by a ledge of rks (dry) extending up to 3 ca offshore, and it is advisable to keep to seaward (E) of Bembridge Ledge buoy.

4½ M E of Foreland is Nab Tr (Lt, fog sig, RC), a conspic steel and concrete structure (28m), marking Nab Shoal for larger vessels and of no direct significance to yachtsmen. It is however a most useful landmark when approaching the E end of Isle of Wight, or when making for the harbs of Langstone (10.2.29) or Chichester (10.2.30).

For notes on cross-Channel passages see 10.3.5.

10.2.6   DISTANCE TABLE

Approximate distances in nautical miles are by the most direct route while avoiding dangers and allowing for traffic separation schemes etc. Places in *italics* are in adjoining areas.

	1	2	3	4	5	6	7	8	9	10	11	12	13	14	15	16	17	18	19	20
1 *Le Four*	1																			
2 *Start Point*	113	2																		
3 *Berry Head*	126	13	3																	
4 *Casquets*	120	57	61	4																
5 *Cherbourg*	151	85	86	31	5															
6 Portland Bill	153	49	41	48	62	6														
7 Anvil Point	172	69	61	56	58	20	7													
8 Poole Bar	177	74	66	61	63	25	5	8												
9 Needles	180	84	76	64	61	35	15	12	9											
10 St Catherines	188	95	86	67	58	45	25	25	12	10										
11 Nab Tower	206	110	101	81	66	60	40	30	27	15	11									
12 Lymington	187	91	83	71	68	42	22	19	7	19	25	12								
13 Cowes	194	98	90	78	75	49	29	26	14	25	15	10	13							
14 Hamble	198	102	94	82	79	53	33	30	18	29	19	14	6	14						
15 Portsmouth	203	107	99	87	84	58	38	35	23	20	10	19	10	13	15					
16 Chichester Bar	207	112	104	92	89	63	43	40	28	19	6	23	15	18	8	16				
17 *Owers Lanby*	208	119	110	87	70	69	49	49	36	24	11	34	25	29	20	14	17			
18 *Le Havre*	223	156	151	101	70	118	104	107	98	86	85	105	112	116	95	91	77	18		
19 *Royal Sovereign*	248	163	153	124	102	114	92	92	82	67	54	77	68	72	63	57	43	82	19	
20 *North Foreland*	310	225	215	186	162	176	154	154	144	129	116	139	130	134	125	119	105	137	62	20

SPECIAL TIDAL PROBLEMS BETWEEN SWANAGE AND SELSEY   10-2-8

Owing to the distorted tidal regime in this area, special curves, as shown on the two following pages, are given for certain ports. Since their low water (LW) points are better defined than high water (HW), the times on these curves are referred to LW, but otherwise they are used as described in 9.4. Box 17 of the tidal prediction form shown in Fig.9(5) should be amended to read 'Time of LW'.

Height differences for places between Swanage and Yarmouth always refer to the higher HW (that which reaches a factor of 1.0 on the curves). The time differences, which are not needed for this calculation, also refer to the higher HW.

Since the tides at these places cannot be adequately defined by two curves, a third is shown for the range at Portsmouth (indicated on the right of the graph) at which the two high waters are equal at the port concerned. Interpolation should be between this critical curve and either the spring or neap curve, as appropriate. The higher HW should be used to obtain the range at the Secondary Port.

While the critical curve extends throughout the tidal cycle, the spring and neap curves stop at higher HW. Thus for a range at Portsmouth of 3.5m, the factor for 7 hrs after LW Poole (Town Quay) should be referred to the following LW, whereas had the range at Portsmouth been 2.5m it should be referred to the preceding LW.

For special remarks on Newport, Calshot, Wareham and Tuckton see notes 1, 2 and 3 on the following page.

The procedure to be followed is shown in the example below, referring to the special tidal curve for Swanage, Poole (Entrance) and Bournemouth which is shown at the foot of the page.

Example: Using the tidal data for Swanage below, find the height of tide at Swanage at 0200 on a day when the tidal predictions for Portsmouth are:

19 0100 4.6
M 0613 1.1
   1314 4.5
   1833 0.8

PORTSMOUTH

HW		LW		MHWS	MHWN	MLWN	MLWS
0000	0600	0500	1100	4.7	3.8	1.8	0.6
1200	1800	1700	2300				

Differences **SWANAGE**
−0250 +0105 −0105 −0105 −2.7 −2.2 −0.7 −0.3

(1) Complete the top part of the tidal prediction form, as in Fig.9(5), omitting the HW time column (boxes 1, 5 and 9).
(2) On the left of the Swanage diagram, plot the Secondary Port HW and LW heights (1.9 and 0.6m from (1) above), and join the points by a sloping line.
(3) The time required (0200) is 3h 8m before the time of LW at the Secondary Port, so from this point draw a vertical line to the curve. It is necessary to interpolate from the range at Portsmouth (3.5m), which is midway between the spring range (4.1m) and the critical curve (2.9m). This should give a point level with a factor of 0.84.

Fig. 9(5) *Tidal prediction form*   Time or height required 0200

	TIME		HEIGHT	
	HW	LW	HW	LW
Standard Port *Portsmouth*	1	2 0613	3 4·6	4 1·1
Differences	5	6 −0105	7 −2·7	8 −0·5
Secondary Port *Swanage*	9	10 0508	11 1·9	12 0·6
Duration (or time from HW to LW)	13	9−10 or 10−9	Range Stand. Port 14 3·5	3−4
			Range Secdy. Port 15 1·3	11−12

*Springs/Neaps/Interpolate

Start height at given time 9	Time reqd.	16 0200	17+18
17−16	Time of HW LW	17 0508	9
	Interval	18 −0308	Date. *19th Nov*
	Factor	19 0·84	Time zone. O.(GMT)
19×15	Rise above LW	20 1·1	22−21
12	Height of LW	21 0·6	12 Start: time for given height
20+21	Height reqd.	22 1·7	

*Delete as necessary

(4) From this point draw a horizontal line to meet the sloping line constructed in (2) above.
(5) From the point where the horizontal line meets the sloping line, proceed vertically to the height scale at the top, and read off the height required, 1.7m.

The completed lower part of the tidal prediction form above shows how the calculation is done using the factor method instead of the graphical method just described. The procedure follows that given in 9.4.3. Note that box 9 is amended to read 'Time of LW'.

A less accurate but quick method of finding intermediate heights for certain places is by use of Fig 10A shown later in this section. It is useful to note that the area enclosed by the dotted lines represents the period during which the tide stands and in which a second high tide may occur.

To use this table, note that the first of the three figures given is for mean spring tides, the second for average and the third for mean neap tides. Work out whether the time required is nearer the HW or LW at Portsmouth and find the interval (between time required and the nearest HW or LW at Portsmouth). Extract the height of the corresponding predicted HW (left hand column) or LW (right hand column). By interpolation between the heights of HW or LW, read off the height of tide under the appropriate column (hrs before or after HW or hrs before or after LW).

H.W.Hts.m. SECONDARY PORT
Swanage
Poole (Entrance)
Bournemouth
L.W.Hts.m.
Mean level
Range at Portsmouth
Sp —— 4·1m
------- 2·9m
Np — — — 2·0m

TIDAL CURVES — SWANAGE TO SELSEY

Tidal curves for places between Swanage and Selsey are given below, and their use is explained above. In this area the times of Low Water are defined more sharply than the times of High Water, and the curves are therefore drawn with their times relative to Low Water instead of High Water.

Apart from referring the times to Low Water, the procedure for obtaining intermediate heights with these curves is the same as that used for normal Secondary Ports (see 9.4.2). For most places a third curve is shown, for the range at Portsmouth at which the two High Waters are equal at the port concerned: for interpolation between the curves see the previous page.

Note 1. Owing to constrictions in the River Medina, Newport requires special treatment. The calculation should be made using the time and Low Water height differences for Cowes, and the High Water height differences for Newport. Any height which falls below 1.9m can be disregarded since the tide never falls below this level.

Note 2. Calshot is referred to Southampton as Standard Port. The curves shown below for Calshot should be taken as referring to the Spring and Neap ranges at Southampton (4.0 and 1.9m respectively).

Note 3. Wareham and Tuckton LWs do not fall below 0.7m except under very low river flow conditions.

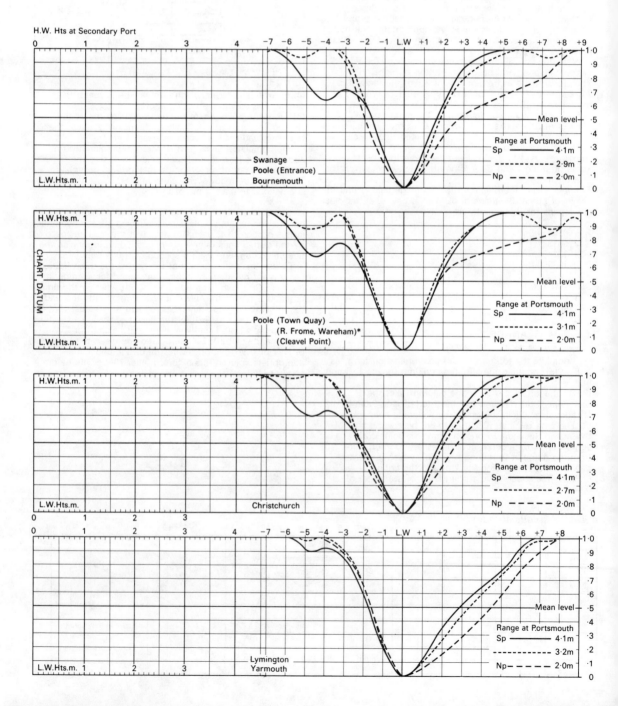

TIDAL CURVES continued

H.W. Hts at Secondary Port

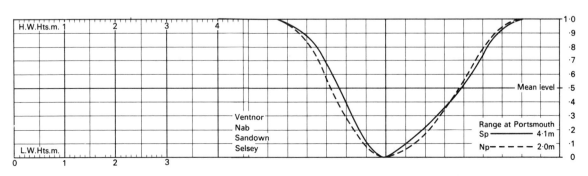

ISLE OF WIGHT TIDAL STREAMS

5 Hours before HW Portsmouth (0445 before HW Dover)

4 Hours before HW Portsmouth (0345 before HW Dover)

3 Hours before HW Portsmouth (0245 before HW Dover)

2 Hours before HW Portsmouth (0145 before HW Dover)

1 Hour before HW Portsmouth (0045 before HW Dover)

HW Portsmouth (0015 after HW Dover)

General Area 2 10.2.3

1 Hour after HW Portsmouth (0115 after HW Dover)

2 Hours after HW Portsmouth (0215 after HW Dover)

3 Hours after HW Portsmouth (0315 after HW Dover)

4 Hours after HW Portsmouth (0415 after HW Dover)

5 Hours after HW Portsmouth (0515 after HW Dover)

6 Hours after HW Portsmouth (0615 after HW Dover)

SWANAGE TO NAB TOWER

FIG 10A   (To be used for finding intermediate heights in metres for places named)

Place	Height of H.W. at Portsmouth	HOURLY HEIGHTS ABOVE CHART DATUM AT THE PLACE													Height of L.W. at Portsmouth
		Hours before or after HIGH WATER AT PORTSMOUTH							Hours before or after LOW WATER AT PORTSMOUTH						
		3b.	2b.	1b.	H.W.	1a.	2a.	3a.	2b.	1b.	L.W.	1a.	2a.	3a.	
	m.	m.	m.	m.	m.	m.	m.	m.	m.	m.	m.	m.	m.	m.	m.
SWANAGE	4.7	1.9	1.8	1.5	1.3	1.4	1.2	0.8	0.6	0.3	0.8	1.3	1.7	1.8	0.6
	4.3	1.6	1.6	1.5	1.5	1.2	1.4	1.1	0.9	0.8	1.0	1.3	1.5	1.6	1.2
	3.8	1.5	1.5	1.5	1.5	1.6	1.5	1.3	1.2	1.1	1.2	1.3	1.4	1.4	1.8
POOLE ENTRANCE	4.7	2.0	1.9	1.6	1.4	1.5	1.4	0.9	0.7	0.3	0.8	1.3	1.6	1.9	0.6
	4.3	1.6	1.6	1.5	1.5	1.5	1.5	1.1	1.0	0.8	0.9	1.2	1.5	1.6	1.2
	3.8	1.4	1.5	1.5	1.5	1.6	1.5	1.3	1.2	1.1	1.1	1.2	1.3	1.4	1.8
POOLE BRIDGE	4.7	2.2	2.2	1.9	1.6	1.6	1.7	1.3	1.1	0.6	0.5	1.0	1.6	1.9	0.6
	4.3	1.8	1.7	1.6	1.7	1.8	1.8	1.5	1.4	1.0	0.8	1.1	1.5	1.7	1.2
	3.8	1.5	1.5	1.6	1.7	1.8	1.8	1.5	1.5	1.3	1.2	1.3	1.5	1.5	1.8
BOURNEMOUTH	4.7	2.1	2.0	1.7	1.5	1.5	1.5	0.9	0.7	0.3	0.6	1.2	1.7	1.9	0.6
	4.3	1.6	1.7	1.6	1.6	1.6	1.5	1.2	1.0	0.8	0.8	1.2	1.4	1.5	1.2
	3.8	1.5	1.5	1.5	1.5	1.6	1.5	1.4	1.3	1.1	1.1	1.2	1.3	1.4	1.8
CHRISTCHURCH HARBOUR †	4.7	1.8	1.8	1.5	1.3	1.5	1.1	0.7	0.7	0.5	0.4	0.9	1.3	1.6	0.6
	4.3	1.5	1.5	1.4	1.5	1.5	1.2	0.9	0.8	0.6	0.6	1.0	1.2	1.4	1.2
	3.8	1.2	1.2	1.3	1.4	1.4	1.1	0.9	0.8	0.6	0.7	0.9	1.0	1.1	1.8
FRESHWATER BAY	4.7	2.4	2.5	2.4	2.2	2.2	1.9	1.1	0.9	0.5	0.8	1.5	2.0	2.2	0.6
	4.3	2.2	2.3	2.2	2.2	2.2	1.9	1.4	1.2	0.9	1.1	1.5	1.8	2.0	1.2
	3.8	1.9	2.0	2.2	2.2	2.2	2.0	1.6	1.6	1.3	1.3	1.6	1.7	1.8	1.8
TOTLAND BAY	4.7	2.3	2.5	2.4	2.3	2.3	2.1	1.4	1.1	0.5	0.8	1.4	1.8	2.1	0.6
	4.3	2.1	2.3	2.3	2.3	2.2	2.1	1.6	1.4	0.9	1.1	1.4	1.7	1.9	1.2
	3.8	2.0	2.1	2.3	2.3	2.2	2.1	1.8	1.7	1.4	1.4	1.6	1.8	1.8	1.8
HURST POINT	4.7	2.3	2.6	2.7	2.5	2.5	2.3	1.6	1.2	0.5	0.7	1.3	1.7	2.0	0.6
	4.3	2.0	2.3	2.5	2.5	2.4	2.3	1.7	1.5	1.1	1.0	1.4	1.7	1.9	1.2
	3.8	1.9	2.1	2.3	2.3	2.3	2.2	1.8	1.7	1.4	1.3	1.5	1.7	1.9	1.8
YARMOUTH I.O.W.	4.7	2.4	2.8	3.0	2.8	2.8	2.7	1.8	1.5	0.7	0.8	1.4	1.8	1.8	0.6
	4.3	2.2	2.5	2.7	2.7	2.7	2.6	1.9	1.6	1.1	1.2	1.6	1.8	2.0	1.2
	3.8	2.0	2.3	2.5	2.5	2.5	2.3	1.9	1.7	1.5	1.5	1.6	1.7	1.8	1.8
LYMINGTON	4.7	2.2	2.6	3.0	2.8	2.9	2.8	2.1	1.7	0.7	0.5	1.1	1.6	1.9	0.6
	4.3	2.0	2.3	2.7	2.7	2.7	2.6	2.1	1.8	1.1	1.0	1.3	1.6	1.7	1.2
	3.8	1.9	2.2	2.4	2.5	2.5	2.4	2.0	1.8	1.5	1.4	1.5	1.6	1.7	1.8
SOLENT BANKS	4.7	2.4	2.9	3.4	3.3	3.2	3.0	2.2	1.8	0.7	0.6	1.2	1.8	2.0	0.6
	4.3	2.2	2.6	3.0	3.1	3.0	2.9	2.2	1.9	1.2	1.1	1.4	1.6	1.9	1.2
	3.8	2.1	2.3	2.6	2.7	2.7	2.6	2.2	2.0	1.6	1.5	1.7	1.9	2.0	1.8
COWES ROAD	4.7	2.5	3.4	4.1	4.2	4.1	3.8	3.0	2.5	1.1	0.6	1.2	1.8	2.1	0.6
	4.3	2.4	3.1	3.7	3.8	3.7	3.5	2.8	2.6	1.5	1.2	1.5	1.8	2.1	1.2
	3.8	2.5	3.0	3.3	3.4	3.4	3.2	2.7	2.5	2.0	1.7	1.9	2.0	2.2	1.8
CALSHOT CASTLE	4.7	2.6	3.6	4.3	4.4	4.3	4.1	3.2	2.6	1.2	0.7	1.3	1.9	2.2	0.6
	4.3	2.6	3.3	3.8	4.0	4.0	3.7	3.0	2.6	1.6	1.2	1.6	2.0	2.2	1.2
	3.8	2.7	3.2	3.5	3.6	3.6	3.4	2.8	2.6	2.0	1.9	2.0	2.2	2.3	1.8
LEE-ON-SOLENT	4.7	2.7	3.6	4.4	4.5	4.4	4.2	3.1	2.5	1.1	0.6	1.2	1.8	2.1	0.6
	4.3	2.7	3.4	3.9	4.1	4.0	3.7	2.9	2.5	1.4	1.2	1.6	2.0	2.2	1.2
	3.8	2.7	3.2	3.6	3.7	3.6	3.3	2.8	2.6	2.1	1.9	2.0	2.2	2.4	1.8
RYDE	4.7	2.7	3.7	4.3	4.5	4.3	4.0	2.9	2.4	1.1	0.7	1.2	1.8	2.1	0.6
	4.3	2.7	3.4	4.0	4.1	4.0	3.7	2.9	2.6	1.6	1.3	1.6	1.9	2.2	1.2
	3.8	2.7	3.2	3.6	3.7	3.6	3.4	2.9	2.7	2.1	1.9	2.0	2.2	2.4	1.8
NAB TOWER	4.7	2.9	3.8	4.4	4.5	4.3	3.6	2.4	2.0	0.9	0.6	1.0	1.5	2.1	0.6
	4.3	2.9	3.6	4.1	4.2	4.0	3.4	2.5	2.2	1.4	1.2	1.4	1.8	2.2	1.2
	3.8	2.9	3.3	3.7	3.7	3.6	3.1	2.6	2.3	1.9	1.7	1.8	2.1	2.4	1.8
SANDOWN	4.7	2.6	3.3	3.8	4.0	3.8	3.3	2.1	1.7	0.8	0.6	1.0	1.5	1.9	0.6
	4.3	2.6	3.0	3.5	3.6	3.5	3.1	2.2	1.9	1.3	1.1	1.4	1.7	2.0	1.2
	3.8	2.6	2.9	3.2	3.3	3.1	2.8	2.3	2.1	1.8	1.6	1.7	1.9	2.2	1.8
VENTNOR	4.7	2.8	3.3	3.7	3.8	3.5	2.9	2.0	1.7	1.0	0.9	1.3	1.7	2.1	0.6
	4.3	2.6	3.1	3.4	3.4	3.2	2.8	2.1	1.9	1.4	1.3	1.6	1.9	2.2	1.2
	3.8	2.5	2.8	3.1	3.1	3.0	2.8	2.3	2.2	1.8	1.7	1.9	2.1	2.3	1.8

Note.—Area enclosed by pecked lines represents the period during which the tide stands, or during which a second high water may occur.
† Heights at Christchurch are for inside the bar; outside the bar, L.W. falls about 0.6 metres lower at Springs.

SOLENT AREA   10-2-9

There are a number of problems and pieces of general information common to all the ports in the Solent area which are collected together in the following paragraphs to avoid repetition.

Yachts and Commercial Shipping. In the interests of the safety of all concerned it is important that good co-operation between yachts and commercial shipping be maintained.

The most crucial point in the central Solent is in the vicinity of the NE Gurnard and W Bramble buoys where the turn to and from the Thorn Channel has to be made. It should be noted that large ships inward bound from the east usually turn first to the southward on passing the Prince Consort buoy before starting the turn into the Thorn Channel somewhere between the Royal Yacht Squadron and Egypt Point, depending on tide and wind. When very large vessels are entering or leaving the Thorn Channel, they are usually preceded by an Associated British Ports Harbour Master's launch (see also 'Local Signals' below).

Other areas in the Solent requiring special co-operation are:—

(a) at the Needles between the Bridge and the SW Shingles buoys; there is plenty of sea-room for yachts to the south of the main channel.

(b) at the turn round Calshot Lt Float. The area bounded by Bourne Gap buoy, Calshot Lt Float, Castle Point buoy, Reach buoy, Calshot buoy and North Thorn buoy is prohibited to yachts and small craft when vessels over 100m (329ft) are navigating the channel between West Bramble buoy and Hook buoy. Southampton Port Radio (SPR)

broadcasts traffic information on Ch 12 every two hours on the hour from 0600-2200, Fri-Sun inclusive and Bank Holiday Mondays, from Easter to end September.

(c) Portsmouth Harbour entrance.

VHF Radio Telephone. The proliferation of VHF radio telephones in yachts is causing problems in port communication networks. Yachtsmen are reminded that CHANNEL 16 is a DISTRESS, SAFETY AND CALLING Channel. Other than for distress, it must only be used to establish contact before going onto a recognised working channel. If another calling channel is available, it should be used in preference to Channel 16. Port Operation channels must not be used for ship to ship communication. The recognised ship to ship channels are 06, 08, 72 and 77. Port Operations channels are as follows:—

12 and 14	— Southampton Port Radio general calling and working channels
11 and 13	— Queen's Harbour Master Portsmouth general working channels
11	— Commercial Harbourmaster Portsmouth general working channel
09	— Pilot working channel
18, 20, 22	— Southampton Port Radio, selected working channels
71 and 74	— Ship/Tug/Pilot/Berthing Master working channels (keep off)

Reports of oil pollution should be made to HM Coastguard (call *Solent Coastguard* VHF Ch 16 67).

SOLENT AREA *continued*

Sailing Information from BBC Radio Solent
999 kHz (300m) and 96.1 MHz VHF.
1359 kHz (221m) in Bournemouth area.
A. Local weather forecasts.
B. Shipping forecasts for Channel sea areas, with general synopsis and Coastal Station reports.
C. Coastguard Station reports.
D. Tidal details.
E. Shipping movements.
F. Gunnery range firing times.

MONDAY TO FRIDAY	SATURDAY
0604 — A	0633 — A B C D E F
0633 — A B C D E F	0709 — A
0709 — A	0733 — A*
0733 — A*	0745 — B C D E F
0745 — B C D E F	0809 — A
0809 — A	0833 — A*
0833 — A*	0904 — A
0904 — A	1000 — A
1004 — A	1104 — A
1104 — A	1204 — A
1204 — A	1304 — A
1309 — A	1404 — A
1404 — A	1533 — A
1504 — A	1804 — A
1604 — A	1925 — A*
1709 — A	
1733 — A* D F	SUNDAY
1804 — A	
2204 — A	0633 — A*
2300 — A*	0709 — A
	0733 — A*
	0745 — B C D E F
	0809 — A
*Live forecast from	0904 — A*
Southampton Weather	1000 — A
Centre.	1104 — A
	1204 — A
	1304 — A
	1504 — A*

The above forecasts can be heard on the telephone by dialling Southampton 8030 or Portsmouth 8030 at the appropriate times.

Local Signals

Outward bound vessels normally hoist the following flag signals during daylight hours.

Signal	Meaning
International 'E' Flag)	
over)	I am bound East (Nab Tower)
Answering Pendant)	
Answering Pendant)	
over)	I am bound West (The
International 'W' Flag)	Needles)

Southampton Patrol launch by day has Harbour Master painted on after cabin in Black lettering on Yellow background. By night it has a blue all round light above the white masthead light.

HM Coastguard — Solent District. The Maritime Rescue Sub Centre (MRSC) at Lee-on-Solent (☎ Lee-on-Solent 552100) controls all Search and Rescue (SAR) activities in HM Coastguard Solent District.

Anyone wishing to obtain the services of any rescue authority should contact the Coastguard and not the rescue authority itself. The Coastguard is able to call on lifeboats and also on the fast inshore boats stationed at Hamble, Lepe, Gosport, Ryde, Cowes, Freshwater Bay and Shanklin; he can also call on the police launch *Ashburton*, helicopters, ships at sea, naval vessels and RAF long range aircraft.

There is an auxiliary Coastguard yacht section made up of yachtsmen willing to assist the Coastguards by making their vessels available for lifesaving purposes; they supplement the lifeboat service. Many of these boats have the Coastguard VHF frequency fitted and so are in touch with all the rescue services. They are all registered and are attached to the MRSC. MRCCs and MRSCs broadcast strong wind warnings and local forecasts.

The area of responsibility for MRSC Solent is bounded on the West by a line from Hengistbury Head South to the Anglo/French median line, and on the East by a line from Beachy Head to the Greenwich buoy.

Radio sets under the control of MRSC Solent (call: *Solent Coastguard*) are:

VHF (Ch 0 06 10 16 67 73)	VHF DF	MF (2182 3023
Needles	Boniface	5680 kHz)
Boniface	Selsey	Lee-on-Solent
Lee-on-Solent	Newhaven	
Selsey	NB. Call	
Newhaven	Portland	
	Coastguard for	
	fix from	
	Highdown, IOW	

To contact Solent Coastguard call on Ch 16; yachtsmen will be transferred to Ch 67 or 73 for traffic.

Sector Stations manned by regular Coastguards and Auxiliaries are sited at Totland (☎ Isle of Wight 753451), Bembridge (☎ Isle of Wight 873943), Calshot (☎ Fawley 893574), Hayling (☎ Portsmouth 464095), Shoreham (☎ Shoreham 2226), Newhaven (☎ Newhaven 514008) and Littlehampton (☎ Littlehampton 715512).

Auxiliary Stations are sited at Needles, Atherfield, Ventnor, Eastney and Selsey.

All Sector and Auxiliary Lookouts are manned for Casualty Risk or heavy traffic periods.

Note: Much useful information is given in the *Solent Year Book* published by the Solent Cruising and Racing Association (SCRA). Also a free booklet *"The Yachtsman's Guide to Southampton Water"*.

SOLENT AREA
WAYPOINTS   10-2-10

Waypoints marked with an asterisk (*) are special (yellow)
racing marks, which may be removed in winter. Racing
buoys marked with a bullet (•) against the longitude are only
laid during Cowes week. Other waypoints are navigational
buoys, unless otherwise stated.

*Alpha	50°46'·40N	01°07'·80W•	East Knoll	50°47'·93N	01°16'·75W
*AFN London	50°46'·55N	01°21'·31W	East Lepe	50°46'·09N	01°20'·81W
After Barn	50°51'·50N	01°20'·73W	East Winner	50°45'·07N	01°00'·01W
*Ashlett	50°49'·95N	01°19'·67W	*Echo	50°46'·50N	01°05'·66W
ASWE No.6	50°45'·32N	01°01'·56W	Eling	50°54'·45N	01°27'·75W
Bald Head	50°49'·88N	01°18'·15W	*Frigate	50°46'·10N	01°22'·10W
Bank Lt Bn	50°53'·58N	01°23'·24W	Fairway	50°38'·20N	01°38'·90W
Bay	50°46'·16N	00°57'·53W	Fawley	50°49'·97N	01°19'·38W
Beaulieu Spit Bn	50°46'·83N	01°21'·67W			
Bembridge Ledge	50°41'·12N	01°02'·74W	*Gamma	50°46'·43N	01°05'·29W
			Greenland	50°51'·08N	01°20'·33W
Bembridge Tide Gauge	50°42'·55N	01°05'·24W	Gurnard	50°46'·18N	01°18'·76W
*Berthon	50°44'·18N	01°29'·13W			
*Beta	50°46'·80N	01°07'·25W•	Gurnard Ledge	50°45'·48N	01°20'·50W
Black Jack	50°49'·10N	01°17'·98W	Gymp	50°53'·15N	01°24'·22W
Black Rock	50°42'·55N	01°30'·55W	Gymp Elbow	50°53'·48N	01°24'·53W
Boulder (Looe Channel)	50°41'·53N	00°49'·00W	Hamble Point	50°50'·12N	01°18'·57W
Bourne Gap	50°47'·80N	01°18'·25W	Hamstead Ledge	50°43'·83N	01°26'·10W
*Bowring Rose	50°47'·28N	01°12'·00W	Hard	50°45'·01N	00°57'·47W
Boyne	50°46'·12N	01°05'·19W	*Hendersons	50°47'·39N	01°15'·82W
Bramble Bn	50°47'·38N	01°17'·05W	Hill Head	50°48'·12N	01°15'·91W
Browndown	50°46'·54N	01°10'·87W			
Bridge	50°39'·59N	01°36'·80W	Hook	50°49'·48N	01°18'·22W
Bury	50°54'·10N	01°27'·03W	Horse Elbow	50°44'·23N	01°03'·80W
			Horse Sand	50°45'·49N	01°05'·18W
Cadland	50°50'·98N	01°20'·45W	Horse Sand Fort Lt	50°44'·97N	01°04'·25W
Calshot	50°48'·40N	01°16'·95W	Hound	50°51'·05N	01°21'·43W
Calshot Splt Lt Float	50°48'·32N	01°17'·55W	Hythe Knock	50°52'·80N	01°23'·73W
Castle Point	50°48'·67N	01°17'·60W			
Castle (NB)	50°46'·43N	01°05'·29W	Jack in Basket	50°44'·24N	01°30'·48W
			*Jib	50°52'·93N	01°22'·97W
*Cathead	50°50'·58N	01°19'·15W			
*Champagne Mumm	50°45'·60N	01°23'·03W	*Keel	50°45'·75N	01°19'·65W
Chichester Bar Bn	50°45'·88N	00°56'·37W	*Kemps	50°45'·15N	01°09'·55W
*Chilling	50°49'·23N	01°17'·42W			
Chi Spit	50°45'·68N	00°56'·48W	Lains Lake	50°51'·55N	01°21'·57W
			*Lambeth	50°41'·50N	01°41'·60W
*Clipper	50°48'·43N	01°15'·63W	Langstone Fairway	50°46'·28N	01°01'·27W
Coronation	50°49'·52N	01°17'·53W	Lee Pt Bn	50°47'·40N	01°11'·85W
Cowes Breakwater Lt	50°45'·84N	01°17'·43W	*Lucas	50°46'·23N	01°08'·67W
Cowes No.3	50°46'·04N	01°17'·95W			
Cowes No.4	50°46'·04N	01°17'·78W	Main Passage	50°45'·98N	01°04'·02W
			Marchwood	50°53'·95N	01°25'·50W
Cracknore	50°53'·92N	01°25'·12W	*Mark	50°49'·53N	01°18'·87W
Crosshouse Lt Bn	50°54'·01N	01°23'·11W	*MDL	50°46'·12N	01°16'·55W
*Cutter	50°49'·47N	01°16'·82W	*Meon	50°49'·15N	01°15'·62W
*Daks-Simpson	50°45'·50N	01°14'·30W	Mid Shingles	50°41'·18N	01°34'·58W
Dean Elbow	50°43'·55N	01°01'·83W	Milbrook	50°54'·08N	01°26'·73W
Deans Elbow	50°52'·13N	01°22'·68W	Mixon Bn	50°42'·35N	00°46'·21W
Deans Lake	50°51'·35N	01°21'·52W	Moorhead	50°52'·52N	01°22'·82W
Dean Tail	50°43'·02N	00°59'·03W	Mother Bank	50°45'·45N	01°11'·13W
*Deck	50°48'·60N	01°16'·57W	Nab 1	50°41'·23N	00°56'·43W
*Delta	50°45'·08N	01°27'·25W	Nab 2	50°41'·70N	00°56'·71W
Dibden Bay	50°53'·67N	01°24'·82W	Nab 3	50°42'·17N	00°57'·05W
Durns Pt obstn (S end)	50°45'·37N	01°26'·95W	Nab East	50°42'·83N	01°07'·20W
			Nab End	50°42'·60N	00°59'·49W
East Bramble	50°47'·20N	01°13'·55W			

Nab Tower	50°40'·05N	00°57'·07W
Needles Fairway	50°38'·20N	01°38'·90W
Netley	50°52'·03N	01°21'·72W
New Grounds	50°41'·97N	00°58'·53W
Newtown G Buoy	50°43'·57N	01°24'·70W
No Mans Land Fort Lt	50°44'·37N	01°05'·61W
Norris	50°45'·94N	01°15'·42W
North East Gurnard	50°47'·03N	01°19'·34W
North East Mining Ground	50°44'·71N	01°06'·30W
North East Ryde Middle	50°46'·18N	01°11'·80W
North East Shingles	50°41'·93N	01°33'·32W
North Head	50°42'·65N	01°35'·42W
North Ryde Middle	50°46'·58N	01°14'·30W
North Sturbridge	50°45'·31N	01°08'·15W
North Thorn	50°47'·88N	01°17'·75W
North West Netley	50°52'·28N	01°22'·65W
No. 2 Yarmouth (mooring)	50°42'·73N	01°29'·54W
*Ossory	50°47'·30N	01°16'·75W
Outer Nab	50°41'·00N	00°56'·56W
Outer Spit	50°45'·55N	01°05'·41W
Peel Bank	50°45'·47N	01°13'·25W
Peel Wreck	50°44'·88N	01°13'·34W
Pier Head	50°53'·63N	01°24'·57W
Poole Fairway	50°38'·95N	01°54'·78W
*Porsche	50°44'·60N	01°21'·80W
Portsmouth No. 4	50°46'·98N	01°06'·27W
Prince Consort	50°46'·38N	01°17'·47W
*Quinnell	50°47'·03N	01°19'·80W
*Ratsey	50°47'·63N	01°13'·56W
Reach	50°49'·02N	01°17'·57W
Ridge	50°46'·42N	01°05'·56W
Roway Wk	50°46'·08N	01°02'·18W
*Royal Thames	50°47'·78N	01°19'·17W
Ryde Pier, head	50°44'·35N	01°09'·51W
RYS flagstaff	50°45'·97N	01°17'·97W
Saddle	50°45'·18N	01°04'·79W
Salt Mead	50°44'·48N	01°22'·95W
Sconce	50°42'·50N	01°31'·35W
Shingles Elbow	50°40'·31N	01°35'·92W
*Short	50°49'·73N	01°19'·32W
South Bramble	50°46'·95N	01°17'·65W
South East Ryde Middle	50°45'·90N	01°12'·00W
South Ryde Middle	50°46'·10N	01°14'·08W
South West Mining Ground	50°44'·63N	01°07'·95W
South West Shingles	50°39'·53N	01°37'·24W
*Spanker	50°47'·08N	01°17'·99W
*Sposa	50°49'·70N	01°17'·50W
Spit Refuge	50°46'·22N	01°05'·37W
Spit Sand Fort Lt	50°46'·20N	01°05'·85W
No. 1 Swinging Ground	50°53'·97N	01°23'·35W
No. 2 Swinging Ground	50°53'·78N	01°25'·03W
*Start	50°47'·05N	01°06'·66W
Stokes Ba	50°46'·64N	01°10'·52W
Street	50°41'·65N	00°48'·80W
Thorn Knoll	50°47'·47N	01°18'·35W
*Trap	50°46'·17N	01°17'·51W
Trinity House (Cowes)	50°46'·10N	01°17'·15W
Warden	50°41'·45N	01°33'·47W
Warner	50°43'·83N	01°03'·92W

West Bramble	50°47'·15N	01°18'·55W
West Knoll	50°47'·52N	01°17'·68W
West Lepe	50°45'·20N	01°24'·00W
West Princessa	50°40'·12N	01°03'·58W
West Ryde Middle	50°46'·45N	01°15'·70W
Weston Shelf	50°52'·68N	01°23'·17W
Wootton Bn	50°44'·46N	01°12'·08W

LYME REGIS   10-2-11
Dorset

CHARTS
Admiralty 3315; Stanford 12; Imray C5; OS 193
TIDES
−0455 Dover; ML 2.4; Duration 0700; Zone 0 (GMT).

Standard Port DEVONPORT (←—)

Times				Height (metres)			
HW		LW		MHWS	MHWN	MLWN	MLWS
0100	0600	0100	0600	5.5	4.4	2.2	0.8
1300	1800	1300	1800				

Differences LYME REGIS
+0040 +0100 +0005 −0005 −1.2 −1.3 −0.5 −0.2

NOTE: Rise is relatively fast for the first hour after LW, then a slackening for the next 1½ hours after which the rapid rate is resumed — there is usually a stand of up to 1½ hours at HW.

SHELTER
The harbour, known as The Cobb, offers excellent shelter except in strong winds from E or SE. Harbour dries at LW. Max length allowed in harbour 9m. Keel boats can dry out alongside Victoria Pier or anchor as shown. Five spherical R visitors buoys available. Access about HW∓2½.
NAVIGATION
Waypoint 50°43'.00N 02°55'.60W, 116°/296° from/to front Ldg Lt. Rock breakwater south of entrance marked by R can beacon. Beware numerous fishing floats in all directions. Red flag on flagpole on Victoria Pier indicates 'Gale warning in force'.
LIGHTS AND MARKS
Ldg Lts 296°.
RADIO TELEPHONE
Call: Lyme Regis Harbour Radio Ch 16; 14. (May-Sept: 0900-1200, 1600-1800 LT).
TELEPHONE (029 74)
Hr Mr 2137; MRSC Weymouth 760439; ∰ (0305) 774747; Marinecall 0898 500 457; Police 2603; Dr 5777; Ⓗ 2254.
FACILITIES
EC Thursday; **Harbour (The Cobb)** ☎ 2137, Slip, M, P and D (cans), L, FW, ME, El, Ⓔ, Sh, AB, V, R, Bar; **Lyme Regis Sailing Club** ☎ 3573, FW, R, Bar; **Lyme Regis Power Boat Club** ☎ 3788, R, Bar; **Axminster Chandlery** ☎ Axminster 33980, CH, ACA; **Town** V, R, Bar; Gas, Gaz, ✉; Ⓑ; ⇌ (bus to Axminster); ✈ (Exeter).

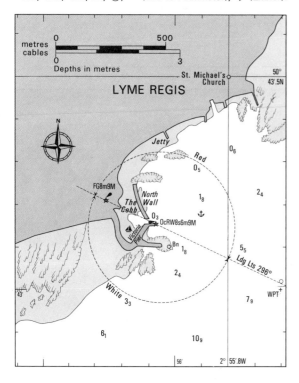

BRIDPORT   10-2-12
Dorset

CHARTS
Admiralty 3315; Stanford 12; Imray C5; OS 193
TIDES
−0500 Dover; ML 2.4; Duration 0650; Zone 0 (GMT).
Standard Port DEVONPORT (←—)

Times				Height (metres)			
HW		LW		MHWS	MHWN	MLWN	MLWS
0100	0600	0100	0600	5.5	4.4	2.2	0.8
1300	1800	1300	1800				

Differences BRIDPORT (West Bay)
+0025 +0040 0000 0000 −1.4 −1.4 −0.6 −0.2

NOTE: Rise is relatively fast for first hour after LW thence a slackening for the next 1½ hours after which the rapid rise is resumed. There is usually a stand of up to 1½ hours at HW.

SHELTER
Good once inside the 12m wide, 180m long entrance, but entrance becomes dangerous in even moderate on-shore winds.
NOTE: Bridport town is 1½ M inland of the harbour.
NAVIGATION
Waypoint 50°42'.20N 02°46'.07W, 210°/030° from/to entrance, 0.37M. Concrete block and unlit BY buoy about ¾M S of entrance indicates end of sewer line. Pier lights are only switched on for commercial vessels. It is safe to enter HW∓3, in favourable weather.
LIGHTS AND MARKS
Harbour can be identified at night by Iso R Lt 2s on roof of Hr Mr office at the shore end of W pier.
Entry signals: Night — No lights on pier — unfit to enter. Day — B ball if port closed.
RADIO TELEPHONE
Call: Bridport Radio VHF Ch 16; 11.
TELEPHONE (0308)
Hr Mr 23222; CG & MRSC Weymouth 760695; ∰ (0305) 774747; Marinecall 0898 500 457; Police 22266; Dr 23771.
FACILITIES
Quay ☎ 23222, Access HW∓3, Slip, P, Ⓞ, Sh, M, FW, ME, CH, AB, V; **D. Ackerman** ☎ 56815, ME. **Town** P, D, V, R, Bar; ✉; Ⓑ; ⇌ (bus to Axminster); ✈ (Exeter).

PORTLAND 10-2-13 TIDAL STREAMS
Dorset

5 Hours before HW Devonport (0145 after HW Dover)

4 Hours before HW Devonport (0245 after HW Dover)

3 Hours before HW Devonport (0345 after HW Dover)

2 Hours before HW Devonport (0445 after HW Dover)

1 Hour before HW Devonport (0545 after HW Dover)

HW Devonport (0545 before HW Dover)

General Area 2   10.2.3

1 Hour after HW Devonport (0445 before HW Dover)

2 Hours after HW Devonport (0345 before HW Dover)

3 Hours after HW Devonport (0245 before HW Dover)

4 Hours after HW Devonport (0145 before HW Dover)

5 Hours after HW Devonport (0045 before HW Dover)

6 Hours after HW Devonport (0045 after HW Dover)

CHARTS
Admiralty 2268, 2255; Stanford 12; Imray C4, C5; OS 194
TIDES
−0430 Dover; ML 1.0; Zone 0 (GMT).

Standard Port PORTSMOUTH (→)

Times				Height (metres)			
HW		LW		MHWS	MHWN	MLWN	MLWS
0000	0600	0500	1100	4.7	3.8	1.8	0.6
1200	1800	1700	2300				

Differences PORTLAND
−0421 −0525 −0520 −0515 −2.6 −2.4 −1.1 −0.4

NOTE: Double LWs occur and predictions are for the first LW.

SHELTER
Shelter is poor in Portland due to lack of wind breaks. Yachts can anchor off Castletown (best in S or SW winds) or off Castle Cove. East Fleet is only suitable for small craft which can lower their masts.
NAVIGATION
Waypoint 50°35'.07N 02°24'.00W, 090°/270° from/to East Ship Channel, Fort Head, 0.50M. Portland race (see diagram of Portland Tidal Streams) is extremely dangerous. The South Ship Channel is permanently closed.
Due to many naval movements in vicinity, yachts should keep watch on VHF Ch 13 when within 3M of 'A' Head. Speed limit in the harbour is 12 kn. Beware reef of rocks extending 1 ca from foot of Sandsfoot Castle, and new shoal areas forming E of Small Mouth.
At night beware unlit mooring buoys, lighters and rafts. Torpedoes are fired to the east from midway along the Northeastern Breakwater. A red flag is flown from the firing point before firing.
Beware Hovercraft/Hydrofoil services from Weymouth.
LIGHTS AND MARKS
Bill of Portland (S end) Fl (4) 20s 43m 29M; W Tr, R band; gradually changes from 1 flash to 4 flashes 221°-244°, 4 flashes 244°-117°, gradually changes from 4 flashes to 1 flash 117°-141°. FR 19m 13M; same Tr; vis 271°-291° over The Shambles; Dia 30s. NE Breakwater, SE end Fl 10s 22m 20M; Horn 10s. Ldg Lts into East Fleet, 288°, Front QG 3m 2M, Rear Iso G 4s 5m 2M.

RADIO TELEPHONE
Portland Naval Base VHF Ch 13 14. Permission to enter, Ch 13 to QHM in working hours, otherwise to Ops Room. Casquets separation scheme, Portland Coastguard: Ch 16 69; 69. 67.
TELEPHONE (0305)
QHM 820311; CG & MRSC 760695; ∰ (0305) 774747; Marinecall 0898 500 457; Police 63011; Dr 820311 (Emergency only).
FACILITIES
EC Wednesday; **Portland** is a Naval Base and provides facilities only for service personnel. Non-service yachtsmen should use Weymouth, except in an emergency.
Royal Dorset YC ☎ Weymouth 771155; **Castle Cove SC** ☎ Weymouth 783708, M, L, FW; **Ferrybridge Marine Services** ☎ Weymouth 786463, Slip, M, L, FW, ME, El, Sh, C; **Marine Engine Centre** ☎ 821175, ME, El, CH. **Town** ✉; Ⓑ; ⇌ (bus to Weymouth); ✈ (Bournemouth).
Note: Low flying helicopters often operate for long periods, day and night, over S part of harbour.

WEYMOUTH 10-2-14
Dorset

CHARTS
Admiralty 2172, 2255, 2268, 2610; Stanford 12;
Imray C4, C5; OS 194
TIDES
−0438 Dover; ML 1.1; Zone 0 (GMT).

Standard Port PORTSMOUTH (→)

Times				Height (metres)			
HW		LW		MHWS	MHWN	MLWN	MLWS
0000	0600	0500	1100	4.7	3.8	1.8	0.6
1200	1800	1700	2300				

Differences WEYMOUTH
−0421 −0525 −0520 −0515 −2.6 −2.4 −1.1 −0.4

NOTE: Double LWs occur. Predictions are for first LW.

SHELTER
Swell runs up the harbour if strong wind from E,
otherwise shelter is good. Visitors' berth in Cove area or
as directed.
NAVIGATION
Waypoint 50°36'.74N 02°26'.00W, 059°/239° from/to
front Ldg Lt, 0.60M. Town Bridge will open on request (2
hours notice) 0900-1300, 1400-1700, 1800-2000 (LT).
Clearance under is 2.7m to 3.8m at HW, 4.6 to 5.2m at
LW.
NOTE: Due to the eddy effect, tide in Weymouth Roads is
westerly at all times except HW −0510 to HW −0310.
Speed limit in the harbour is 'Dead Slow'.
LIGHTS AND MARKS
Ldg Lts 237°. Traffic signals are shown from position near
root of S pier.

3 Fl R	Port closed (emergency)
2 R over 1 G	Entry & departure forbidden
G W G (vert)	Vessels may only proceed with specific orders
3 G	Departure forbidden
3 R	Entry forbidden
No signals	All clear to enter or leave

RADIO TELEPHONE
VHF Ch 16; 12 (when vessel expected). (See Portland).
TELEPHONE (0305)
Hr Mr 206421; CG and MRSC 760695; ∰ (0752) 669811;
Marinecall 0898 500 457; Police 251212; Ⓗ 772211.
FACILITIES
EC Wednesday; **Weymouth Marina** (580) ☎ 773538;
Outer Harbour M; **Weymouth SC** ☎ 785481, M, Bar;
Custom House Quay D, FW, AB; **Barrets Marine
Services** ☎ 779550, Slip, ME, El, D, Gas, Sh; **W. L.
Bussells** ☎ 785633, CH, Sh, ACA, Gaz, Rigging;
Ladyline ☎ 771603, CH; **Royal Dorset YC** ☎ 786258, M,
Bar; **Small Boat** ☎ 782109, ME, CH, Ⓔ, Sh; **R. J. Davis**
☎ 834415, ME, El, CH; **Moto-sails** ☎ 786710, CH;
Weymouth Chandlers ☎ 771603, CH. **Town** P, D, FW,
V, R, Bar. ✉; Ⓑ; ⇌; ✈ (Bournemouth).

NOTE: If proceeding eastwards, check Lulworth firing
programme − see 10.2.31.

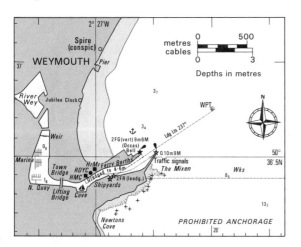

SWANAGE 10-2-15
Dorset

CHARTS
Admiralty 2172, 2610; Stanford 12; Imray C4; OS 195
TIDES
HW Spring −0235, Neap −0515 Dover; ML 1.5
     +0125   +0120   Zone 0 (GMT)
Standard Port PORTSMOUTH (→)

Times				Height (metres)			
HW		LW		MHWS	MHWN	MLWN	MLWS
0000	0600	0500	1100	4.7	3.8	1.8	0.6
1200	1800	1700	2300				

Differences SWANAGE
−0250 +0105 −0105 −0105 −2.7 −2.2 −0.7 −0.3

NOTE: Double HWs occur except at neaps and
predictions are for the higher HW. Near neaps there is a
stand, and the predictions shown are for the middle of the
stand. See 10.2.8

SHELTER
Shelter is good in winds between SW and N. It is bad in
E or SE when winds over Force 4 cause swell. Over Force
6 holding becomes very difficult. Nearest haven Poole.
Pier is for commercial traffic, S side available for yachts
on payment to piermaster.

NAVIGATION
Waypoint 50°36'.70N 01°56'.50W, 054°/234° from/to
Swanage Pier head, 0.30M. Beware Peveril Ledge coming
from S and Tanville Ledges coming from N. On the S side
of the pier there are the ruins of an old pier. It is difficult
to pick up pierhead Lts at night due to confusing street
lights behind.
LIGHTS AND MARKS
The only lights are 2 FR (vert) on the end of the pier.
Peveril Ledge buoy, R can unlit (pass to E).
RADIO TELEPHONE
None
TELEPHONE (0929)
CG 422596; MRSC Weymouth 760695; ∰ (0703) 229251;
Marinecall 0898 500 457; Police 422004; Dr 422676; Ⓗ
422282.
FACILITIES
EC Monday; **Boat Park** (Peveril Point), Slip, FW, L;
Town Jetty, L, AB (HW only); **Swanage SC** ☎ 422987,
Slip, L, FW, Bar; **Diving facilities on Pier** ☎ 423565.
Maritime Services ☎ 424786 Diving, Salvage, Towing;
Town P and D (cans), FW, V, R, Bar. ✉; Ⓑ;
⇌ (bus to Wareham); ✈ (Bournemouth).

POOLE 10-2-16
Dorset

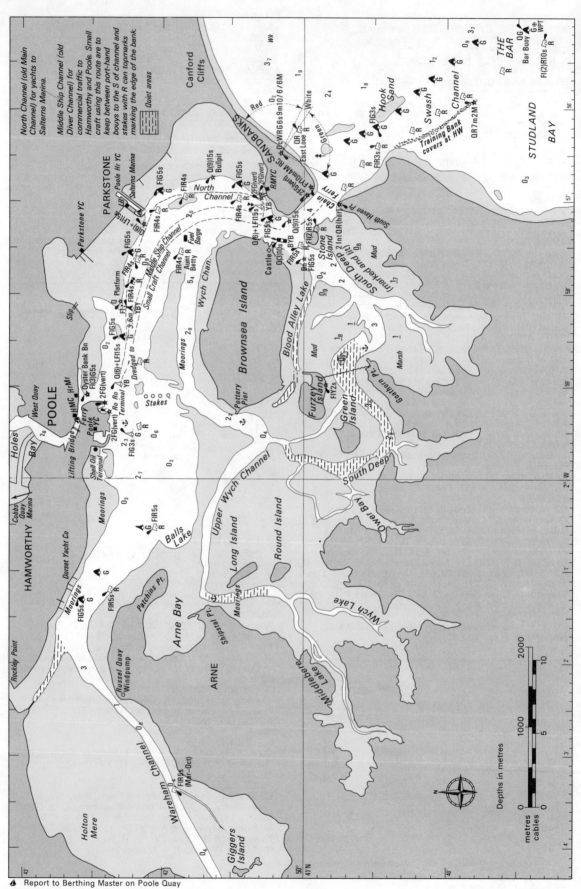

▲ Report to Berthing Master on Poole Quay

ENGLAND, SOUTH COAST - POOLE (TOWN QUAY)

LAT 50°43′N   LONG 1°59′W

TIMES AND HEIGHTS OF HIGH AND LOW WATERS

YEAR **1991**

TIME ZONE UT(GMT)
For Summer Time add ONE hour in non-shaded areas

Chart Datum: 1.40 metres below Ordnance Datum (Newlyn)

(Values given per day as: low-water time / height (m), high-water height (m); ☾ = last quarter, ☽ = first quarter, ○ = full moon, ● = new moon)

JANUARY

Day	Tides (TIME m)
1 TU	0410 0.6 · 2.2 · 1633 0.5
2 W	0457 2.2 · 2.2 · 1721 0.4
3 TH	0546 0.6 · 2.2 · 1808 0.5
4 F	0634 0.6 · 2.1 · 1855 0.5
5 SA	0722 0.7 · 2.0 · 1944 0.6
6 SU	0812 0.8 · 1.9 · 2033 0.8
7 M ☾	0905 0.9 · 1.8 · 2128 0.9
8 TU	1005 1.0 · 1.7 · 2231 1.0
9 W ☽	1122 1.8 · 1.1 · 2351 1.2 · 1.6
10 TH	1240 1.1 · 1.6
11 F	0104 1.2 · 1.7 · 1338 1.0 · 1.6
12 SA	0158 1.1 · 1.7 · 1426 1.0 · 1.7
13 SU	0244 1.0 · 1.8 · 1509 0.9 · 1.7
14 M	0326 1.0 · 1.8 · 1547 0.8 · 1.9
15 TU ●	0403 0.9 · 1.9 · 1621 0.8 · 1.9
16 W	0436 0.9 · 1.9 · 1651 0.7
17 TH	0509 2.0 · 2.0 · 1723 0.6
18 F	0542 2.0 · 2.0 · 1757 0.5
19 SA	0616 2.0 · 2.0 · 1833 0.5
20 SU	0654 2.0 · 1.9 · 1912 0.5
21 M	0736 2.0 · 1.9 · 1953 0.5
22 TU	0819 1.9 · 1.8 · 2040 0.6
23 W ☽	0907 1.9 · 1.7 · 2130 0.8
24 TH	1004 1.8 · 1.7 · 2233 0.9
25 F	1120 1.7 · 1.6
26 SA	0001 1.0 · 1.7 · 1251 1.0 · 1.7
27 SU	0125 1.0 · 1.8 · 1358 0.9 · 1.8
28 M	0224 0.9 · 1.8 · 1450 0.7 · 1.9
29 TU	0314 0.8 · 1.9 · 1537 0.6 · 2.0
30 W ○	0401 0.6 · 2.0 · 1622 0.4 · 2.0
31 TH	0443 0.5 · 2.1 · 1705 0.3 · 2.1

FEBRUARY

Day	Tides (TIME m)
1 F	0528 0.5 · 2.2 · 1749 0.3 · 2.1
2 SA	0612 0.5 · 2.2 · 1833 0.4 · 2.1
3 SU	0655 0.5 · 2.1 · 1916 0.5 · 2.0
4 M	0740 0.6 · 2.0 · 1959 0.6 · 1.9
5 TU	0824 0.8 · 1.8 · 2044 0.8
6 W ☾	0911 1.8 · 1.7 · 2133 1.0
7 TH	1011 1.7 · 1.5 · 2250 1.2
8 F	1213 1.2 · 1.5
9 SA	0046 1.2 · 1.5 · 1320 1.1 · 1.5
10 SU	0142 1.2 · 1.5 · 1408 1.0 · 1.5
11 M	0228 1.1 · 1.6 · 1449 0.9 · 1.7
12 TU	0307 1.0 · 1.7 · 1525 0.8 · 1.8
13 W ○	0341 0.9 · 1.8 · 1557 0.7 · 1.9
14 TH ●	0412 0.8 · 1.9 · 1626 0.6
15 F	0441 · 1.9 · 0.6 · 1655 0.5
16 SA	0514 0.5 · 2.0 · 1730 0.4
17 SU	0550 0.5 · 2.0 · 1806 0.3
18 M	0628 0.4 · 2.0 · 1845 0.3
19 TU	0708 0.4 · 1.9 · 1926 0.3
20 W	0750 0.5 · 1.9 · 2011 0.5
21 TH ☽	0837 0.7 · 1.7 · 2059 0.7
22 F	0929 0.8 · 1.6 · 2159 1.0
23 SA	1045 1.0 · 1.6 · 2351 1.2
24 SU	1246 1.1 · 1.6
25 M	0122 1.0 · 1.7 · 1350 0.9 · 1.7
26 TU	0215 0.9 · 1.8 · 1437 0.7 · 1.9
27 W	0301 0.8 · 1.9 · 1521 0.6 · 2.0
28 TH ○	0344 0.6 · 2.0 · 1603 0.5

MARCH

Day	Tides (TIME m)
1 F	0424 0.5 · 2.1 · 1643 0.3 · 2.0
2 SA	0505 0.4 · 2.2 · 1724 0.3 · 2.1
3 SU	0546 0.4 · 2.2 · 1805 0.4 · 2.0
4 M	0627 0.5 · 2.1 · 1845 0.5 · 2.0
5 TU	0706 0.6 · 2.0 · 1925 0.6 · 1.9
6 W	0746 0.7 · 1.9 · 2004 0.8 · 1.8
7 TH	0825 0.9 · 1.8 · 2045 1.0 · 1.7
8 F ☾	0908 1.0 · 1.6 · 2134 1.2
9 SA	1135 1.2 · 1.5
10 SU	0022 1.3 · 1.4 · 1250 1.2 · 1.4
11 M	0116 1.2 · 1.4 · 1337 1.1 · 1.5
12 TU	0200 1.1 · 1.5 · 1417 1.0 · 1.6
13 W	0235 1.0 · 1.6 · 1451 0.8 · 1.7
14 TH	0309 0.8 · 1.7 · 1522 0.7 · 1.8
15 F ○	0339 0.7 · 1.8 · 1554 0.6 · 1.9
16 SA ●	0411 0.5 · 1.9 · 1626 0.4 · 2.0
17 SU	0444 0.4 · 2.0 · 1702 0.3 · 2.0
18 M	0521 0.3 · 2.0 · 1740 0.3 · 2.0
19 TU	0601 0.3 · 2.0 · 1821 0.3 · 2.0
20 W	0642 0.3 · 2.0 · 1902 0.3 · 2.0
21 TH	0725 0.4 · 1.9 · 1948 0.6 · 1.9
22 F	0813 0.6 · 1.8 · 2039 0.8 · 1.8
23 SA ☽	0907 0.9 · 1.7 · 2145 1.0
24 SU	1034 1.0 · 1.6
25 M	0003 1.2 · 1.5 · 1237 1.0 · 1.7
26 TU	0111 1.0 · 1.6 · 1333 0.9 · 1.8
27 W	0158 0.9 · 1.7 · 1417 0.8 · 1.9
28 TH ○	0240 0.8 · 1.9 · 1500 0.6 · 2.0
29 F	0321 0.6 · 2.0 · 1540 0.5 · 2.1
30 SA ○	0401 0.5 · 2.0 · 1620 0.5 · 2.0
31 SU	0439 0.5 · 2.1 · 1657 0.5 · 2.1

APRIL

Day	Tides (TIME m)
1 M	0519 0.5 · 2.1 · 1738 0.5 · 2.0
2 TU	0558 0.5 · 2.0 · 1816 0.6 · 2.0
3 W	0635 0.6 · 2.0 · 1853 0.7 · 1.9
4 TH	0712 0.7 · 1.9 · 1931 0.9 · 1.8
5 F	0749 0.9 · 1.8 · 2010 1.0 · 1.7
6 SA ☽	0827 1.0 · 1.7 · 2054 1.2
7 SU ☾	0917 1.2 · 1.5 · 2341 1.3
8 M	1204 1.2 · 1.4
9 TU	0037 1.2 · 1.4 · 1255 1.1 · 1.5
10 W	0120 1.1 · 1.5 · 1334 1.0 · 1.6
11 TH	0156 1.0 · 1.5 · 1409 0.9 · 1.7
12 F	0230 0.8 · 1.7 · 1444 0.7 · 1.8
13 SA	0304 0.6 · 1.8 · 1519 0.6 · 1.9
14 SU ●	0340 0.5 · 1.9 · 1557 0.4 · 2.0
15 M	0417 0.3 · 2.0 · 1634 0.3 · 2.1
16 TU	0455 0.3 · 2.0 · 1716 0.3
17 W	0538 0.3 · 2.1 · 1759 0.3
18 TH	0622 0.3 · 2.0 · 1845 0.5
19 F	0708 0.5 · 2.0 · 1933 0.6
20 SA	0758 0.8 · 1.8 · 2030 0.9
21 SU ☽	0900 0.9 · 1.7 · 2148 1.1
22 M	1036 1.0 · 1.7 · 2345 1.1
23 TU	1211 1.0 · 1.6
24 W	0046 1.0 · 1.7 · 1307 0.9 · 1.8
25 TH	0134 0.9 · 1.8 · 1352 0.8 · 1.9
26 F	0216 0.8 · 1.9 · 1434 0.7 · 2.0
27 SA	0257 0.7 · 1.9 · 1516 0.6 · 2.0
28 SU ○	0337 0.6 · 2.0 · 1555 0.6 · 2.0
29 M	0416 0.6 · 2.0 · 1633 0.6 · 2.0
30 TU	0453 0.6 · 2.0 · 1713 0.6

SEA LEVEL IS ABOVE MEAN TIDE LEVEL FROM 2.0 HOURS AFTER L.W. TO 2.0 HOURS BEFORE THE NEXT L.W. AND H.W. WILL OCCUR BETWEEN 5.0 HOURS AFTER L.W. AND 3.0 HOURS BEFORE THE NEXT L.W.

Chart Datum: 1.40 metres below Ordnance Datum (Newlyn)

ENGLAND, SOUTH COAST - POOLE (TOWN QUAY)

LAT 50°43′N   LONG 1°59′W

TIMES AND HEIGHTS OF HIGH AND LOW WATERS

YEAR **1991**

TIME ZONE UT (GMT)
For Summer Time add ONE hour in non-shaded areas

MAY

Day	DOW	Time	m	m	Time	m	m
1	W	0533	2.0	0.6	1752	2.0	0.7
2	TH	0610	2.0	0.6	1830	1.9	0.8
3	F	0647	1.9	0.8	1908	1.9	0.9
4	SA	0724	1.8	0.8	1948	1.8	1.0
5	SU	0804	1.7	0.9	2035	1.7	1.1
6	M	0855	1.6	1.0	2157	1.7	1.2
7 ☾	TU	1026	1.5	1.1	2337	1.6	1.2
8	W	1151	1.5	1.0		(1.6)	
9	TH	0027	1.1	1.5	1242	1.0	1.7
10	F	0110	0.9	1.6	1325	0.9	1.8
11	SA	0151	0.8	1.7	1406	0.8	1.9
12	SU	0231	0.6	1.8	1448	0.6	1.9
13	M	0312	0.5	1.9	1530	0.5	2.0
14 ●	TU	0353	0.4	2.0	1613	0.4	2.1
15	W	0435	0.3	2.0	1657	0.4	
16	TH	0520	2.1	0.3	1744	2.1	0.5
17	F	0607	2.0	0.4	1834	2.0	0.6
18	SA	0657	2.0	0.5	1926	2.0	0.7
19	SU	0752	1.9	0.6	2026	1.9	0.9
20	M	0854	1.8	0.8	☽2139	1.9	1.0
21	TU	1012	1.7	0.9	2307	1.7	1.0
22	W	1133	1.7	0.9		(1.9)	
23	TH	0014	1.0	1.8	1234	0.9	1.9
24	F	0106	0.9	1.8	1324	0.9	1.9
25	SA	0151	0.9	1.8	1409	0.8	1.9
26	SU	0234	0.8	1.9	1453	0.8	2.0
27	M	0317	0.7	1.9	1534	0.8	2.0
28 ○	TU	0357	0.7	1.9	1615	0.8	2.0
29	W	0435	0.6	1.9	1654	0.8	2.1
30	TH	0514	2.0	0.6	1734	1.9	0.8
31	F	0552	1.9	0.7	1812	1.9	0.8

JUNE

Day	DOW	Time	m	m	Time	m	m
1	SA	0629	1.9	0.7	1850	1.9	0.9
2	SU	0707	1.8	0.8	1930	1.8	0.9
3	M	0746	1.8	0.8	2015	1.8	1.0
4	TU	0831	1.7	0.9	2106	1.8	1.0
5	W	0925	1.7	0.9	☾2210	1.7	1.0
6	TH	1030	1.6	0.9	2318	1.7	1.0
7	F	1139	1.6	0.9		(1.7)	
8	SA	0020	0.9	1.6	1239	0.9	1.8
9	SU	0113	0.9	1.7	1333	0.8	1.9
10	M	0202	0.7	1.8	1422	0.7	1.9
11	TU	0249	0.6	1.9	1511	0.6	2.0
12 ●	W	0335	0.5	2.0	1558	0.5	2.1
13	TH	0422	0.4	2.0	1644	0.5	2.1
14	F	0509	0.3	2.1	1735	0.5	
15	SA	0558	2.1	0.4	1824	2.1	0.6
16	SU	0648	2.0	0.5	1916	2.0	0.6
17	M	0740	2.0	0.6	2011	2.0	0.8
18	TU	0835	1.9	0.7	2110	2.0	0.9
19	W	0936	1.8	0.8	☽2218	1.9	1.0
20	TH	1046	1.8	0.9	2332	1.9	1.0
21	F	1157	1.7	1.0		(1.8)	
22	SA	0037	1.0	1.7	1259	1.0	1.8
23	SU	0132	0.9	1.7	1350	1.0	1.8
24	M	0219	0.9	1.8	1436	0.9	1.9
25	TU	0303	0.8	1.8	1520	0.9	1.9
26	W	0344	0.8	1.9	1602	0.9	2.0
27 ○	TH	0423	0.7	1.9	1640	0.8	2.0
28	F	0501	0.7	1.9	1719	0.8	2.1
29	SA	0536	1.9	0.6	1754	1.9	0.8
30	SU	0609	1.9	0.6	1829	1.9	0.8

JULY

Day	DOW	Time	m	m	Time	m	m
1	M	0644	1.9	0.6	1906	1.9	0.8
2	TU	0721	1.9	0.6	1945	1.9	0.8
3	W	0801	1.8	0.6	2028	1.9	0.8
4	TH	0847	1.8	0.7	2117	1.8	0.9
5	F	0938	1.7	0.8	☾2215	1.8	0.9
6	SA	1041	1.7	0.9	2324	1.7	0.9
7	SU	1153	1.6	0.9		(1.8)	
8	M	0038	0.9	1.7	1307	0.9	1.8
9	TU	0141	0.8	1.7	1405	0.8	1.9
10	W	0234	0.7	1.8	1458	0.7	2.0
11 ●	TH	0324	0.5	1.9	1548	0.6	2.0
12	F	0411	0.4	2.0	1634	0.5	2.1
13	SA	0457	0.3	2.2	1722	0.5	
14	SU	0545	2.1	0.3	1808	2.2	0.6
15	M	0631	2.1	0.3	1856	2.2	0.6
16	TU	0718	2.0	0.5	1945	2.1	0.6
17	W	0807	1.9	0.6	2035	2.0	0.8
18	TH	0858	1.8	0.8	☽2131	1.9	0.9
19	F	0956	1.7	0.9	2241	1.8	0.9
20	SA	1114	1.7	1.1		(1.7)	
21	SU	0013	1.1	1.6	1241	1.1	1.7
22	M	0119	1.0	1.6	1339	1.1	1.7
23	TU	0208	1.0	1.7	1427	1.0	1.8
24	W	0251	0.9	1.7	1510	1.0	1.9
25	TH	0331	0.8	1.8	1548	0.9	1.9
26 ○	F	0407	0.8	1.9	1624	0.8	2.0
27	SA	0439	0.6	1.9	1656	0.8	2.1
28	SU	0511	1.9	0.6	1728	2.0	0.7
29	M	0543	1.9	0.6	1801	2.0	0.6
30	TU	0615	1.9	0.5	1836	2.0	0.6
31	W	0651	1.9	0.5	1913	1.9	0.6

AUGUST

Day	DOW	Time	m	m	Time	m	m
1	TH	0730	1.9	0.5	1954	1.9	0.6
2	F	0813	1.8	0.6	2039	1.9	0.7
3	SA	0900	1.8	0.7	2130	1.8	0.8
4	SU	0955	1.7	0.9	2235	1.7	1.0
5	M	1114	1.6	1.0		(1.7)	
6	TU	0013	1.0	1.6	1255	1.0	1.7
7	W	0132	0.9	1.7	1359	0.9	1.8
8	TH	0226	0.8	1.8	1449	0.8	1.9
9	F	0313	0.6	2.0	1536	0.6	2.0
10 ●	SA	0358	0.4	2.1	1620	0.5	2.1
11	SU	0440	0.3	2.2	1703	0.5	
12	M	0524	2.2	0.3	1747	2.2	0.4
13	TU	0607	2.2	0.3	1830	2.2	0.5
14	W	0651	2.1	0.4	1914	2.1	0.6
15	TH	0735	2.0	0.6	1959	2.0	0.8
16	F	0820	1.8	0.8	2047	1.8	0.9
17	SA	0909	1.7	1.0	☽2143	1.7	1.1
18	SU	1020	1.6	1.2	☾2354	1.6	1.2
19	M	1231	1.5	1.3		(1.6)	
20	TU	0104	1.2	1.5	1326	1.2	1.6
21	W	0151	1.0	1.6	1410	1.1	1.7
22	TH	0232	0.9	1.7	1450	1.0	1.7
23	F	0309	0.9	1.8	1525	0.9	1.8
24	SA	0342	0.8	1.9	1558	0.9	1.9
25 ○	SU	0411	0.6	2.0	1627	0.7	1.9
26	M	0440	0.6	2.0	1657	0.6	
27	TU	0512	2.0	0.5	1729	2.0	0.5
28	W	0546	2.0	0.4	1805	2.0	0.5
29	TH	0623	2.0	0.4	1843	2.0	0.5
30	F	0701	2.0	0.5	1924	1.9	0.5
31	SA	0744	1.9	0.6	2008	1.9	0.6

SEA LEVEL IS ABOVE MEAN TIDE LEVEL FROM 2.0 HOURS AFTER L.W. TO 2.0 HOURS BEFORE THE NEXT L.W. AND H.W. WILL OCCUR BETWEEN 5.0 HOURS AFTER L.W. AND 3.0 HOURS BEFORE THE NEXT L.W.

Chart Datum: 1.40 metres below Ordnance Datum (Newlyn)

2

ENGLAND, SOUTH COAST - POOLE (TOWN QUAY)

LAT 50°43'N   LONG 1°59'W

TIMES AND HEIGHTS OF HIGH AND LOW WATERS

YEAR **1991**

TIME ZONE **UT (GMT)**
For Summer Time add ONE hour in non-shaded areas

SEPTEMBER

Day	Time / m	Day	Time / m
1 SU ☾	0830 1.8 0.8 / 2057 1.8 0.8	**16** M	0926 1.6 1.6 / 2317 1.3
2 M	0925 1.7 1.0 / 2200 1.0	**17** TU	1207 1.5 1.3 1.5
3 TU	1053 1.6 1.2 1.7	**18** W	0034 1.2 1.5 / 1302 1.3 1.5
4 W	0008 1.1 1.7 / 1256 1.2 1.7	**19** TH	0122 1.2 1.6 / 1344 1.2 1.6
5 TH	0124 1.0 1.8 / 1350 1.0 1.8	**20** F	0202 1.0 1.7 / 1422 1.0 1.7
6 F	0212 0.8 1.9 / 1435 0.8 2.0	**21** SA	0236 0.9 1.8 / 1455 0.9 1.8
7 SA	0256 0.6 2.0 / 1518 0.6 2.0	**22** SU	0308 0.8 1.9 / 1525 0.8 1.9
8 SU ●	0338 0.5 2.2 / 1600 0.5 2.2	**23** M ○	0338 0.7 2.0 / 1555 0.6 2.0
9 M	0419 0.3 2.2 / 1640 0.4	**24** TU	0408 0.6 2.1 / 1626 0.6 2.0
10 TU	0459 2.2 0.3 2.2 / 1721 0.4	**25** W	0441 0.5 2.1 / 1701 0.5
11 W	0541 2.2 2.2 / 1802 0.5	**26** TH	0517 2.1 0.4 2.1 / 1738 0.4
12 TH	0623 2.1 0.5 2.1 / 1843 0.6	**27** F	0556 2.1 0.4 2.1 / 1816 0.4
13 F	0704 2.0 0.6 2.0 / 1925 0.8	**28** SA	0637 2.0 0.5 2.0 / 1858 0.5
14 SA	0745 1.9 1.8 / 2008 0.9	**29** SU	0721 1.9 1.9 / 1945 0.7
15 SU ☽	0829 1.7 1.1 1.7 / 2054 1.2	**30** M	0810 1.8 0.9 1.8 / 2037 0.9

OCTOBER

Day	Time / m	Day	Time / m
1 TU ☾	0909 1.7 1.1 1.7 / 2146 1.1	**16** W	1124 1.6 1.4 / 2348 1.3
2 W	1104 1.7 1.3 1.7	**17** TH	1223 1.6 1.3 1.5
3 TH	0000 1.2 1.8 / 1244 1.2 1.7	**18** F	0040 1.2 1.7 / 1307 1.2 1.6
4 F	0106 1.0 1.9 / 1333 1.0 1.8	**19** SA	0122 1.1 1.8 / 1345 1.1 1.7
5 SA	0152 0.8 2.0 / 1416 0.8 2.0	**20** SU	0157 1.0 1.9 / 1418 0.9 1.8
6 SU	0234 0.7 2.2 / 1457 0.6 2.1	**21** M	0230 0.9 2.0 / 1450 0.8 1.9
7 M ●	0316 0.6 2.2 / 1537 0.6 2.2	**22** TU	0303 0.7 2.0 / 1523 0.6 2.0
8 TU	0356 0.5 2.3 / 1617 0.5 2.2	**23** W ○	0338 0.6 2.2 / 1558 0.5 2.1
9 W	0435 0.5 2.3 / 1656 0.5 2.0	**24** TH	0414 0.5 2.2 / 1634 0.5 2.2
10 TH	0515 2.2 0.5 / 1737 0.5	**25** F	0453 0.5 2.2 / 1715 0.4
11 F	0555 2.1 0.6 2.1 / 1815 0.6	**26** SA	0535 2.2 0.5 2.2 / 1757 0.5
12 SA	0636 2.0 0.8 2.0 / 1855 0.8	**27** SU	0620 2.1 0.6 2.1 / 1842 0.8
13 SU	0716 1.9 0.9 / 1936 0.9	**28** M	0707 2.0 0.8 2.0 / 1930 0.7
14 M	0758 1.8 1.2 / 2019 1.1	**29** TU	0800 1.9 0.9 1.8 / 2027 0.9
15 TU	0851 1.7 1.3 / 2123 1.3	**30** W ☾	0906 1.9 1.2 / 2142 1.0
		31 TH	1051 1.9 1.2 / 2329 1.1

NOVEMBER

Day	Time / m	Day	Time / m
1 F	1217 1.9 1.2 1.8	**16** SA	1216 1.7 1.6 1.8
2 SA	0036 1.0 2.0 / 1308 1.0 1.9	**17** SU	0026 1.2 1.8 / 1259 1.1 1.7
3 SU	0127 0.9 2.1 / 1353 0.9 2.0	**18** M	0110 1.0 1.8 / 1337 1.0 1.8
4 M	0210 0.8 2.2 / 1434 0.8 2.1	**19** TU	0151 0.9 2.1 / 1415 0.9 1.9
5 TU	0253 0.7 2.2 / 1516 0.6 2.2	**20** W	0231 0.8 2.0 / 1454 0.7 2.0
6 W ●	0334 0.7 2.2 / 1556 0.6 2.0	**21** TH ○	0312 0.7 2.1 / 1534 0.6 2.0
7 TH	0414 0.7 2.2 / 1634 0.6 2.2	**22** F	0353 0.6 2.2 / 1615 0.5 2.2
8 F	0453 0.7 2.2 / 1715 0.6 2.2	**23** SA	0435 0.6 2.2 / 1657 0.5
9 SA	0535 0.8 2.1 / 1755 0.7	**24** SU	0520 0.6 2.2 / 1744 0.5
10 SU	0614 0.9 2.0 / 1834 0.8	**25** M	0608 2.1 0.6 / 1832 0.5
11 M	0655 1.0 1.9 / 1914 0.9	**26** TU	0658 2.1 0.8 2.0 / 1923 0.6
12 TU	0739 1.1 1.8 / 1956 1.0	**27** W	0754 0.9 1.9 / 2020 0.9
13 W	0828 1.2 1.7 / 2047 1.2	**28** TH	0857 1.0 1.9 / 2126 0.9
14 TH ☽	0943 1.3 1.7 / 2206 1.2	**29** F	1014 1.1 1.8 / 2245 1.0
15 F	1121 1.3 1.6 / 2334 1.2	**30** SA	1136 1.1 1.8 / 2308 1.1

DECEMBER

Day	Time / m	Day	Time / m
1 SU	0000 1.0 2.0 / 1239 1.0 1.9	**16** M	1154 1.8 1.1 1.6
2 M	0059 1.0 2.0 / 1330 0.9 1.9	**17** TU	0014 1.0 1.8 / 1253 1.0 1.7
3 TU	0148 0.9 2.0 / 1415 0.9 2.0	**18** W	0112 1.0 1.9 / 1343 0.9 1.8
4 W	0234 0.9 2.1 / 1458 0.8 2.0	**19** TH	0204 0.9 1.9 / 1431 0.8 1.9
5 TH	0317 0.9 2.1 / 1540 0.8 2.0	**20** F	0251 0.8 2.0 / 1517 0.6 2.0
6 F ●	0359 0.8 2.1 / 1621 0.7 2.0	**21** SA ○	0338 0.7 2.1 / 1602 0.5 2.1
7 SA	0439 0.8 2.1 / 1701 0.7 2.2	**22** SU	0424 0.6 2.2 / 1646 0.4
8 SU	0520 2.0 0.9 / 1740 0.7	**23** M	0511 2.2 0.5 / 1734 0.4
9 M	0600 2.0 0.9 / 1819 0.8	**24** TU	0559 2.2 0.5 / 1822 0.4
10 TU	0640 2.0 0.9 / 1855 0.8	**25** W	0648 2.2 0.6 / 1912 0.5
11 W	0719 1.9 1.0 / 1933 0.9	**26** TH	0740 2.2 0.7 / 2003 0.6
12 TH	0800 1.8 1.0 / 2015 0.9	**27** F	0834 2.1 0.8 / 2058 0.8
13 F	0847 1.7 1.1 / 2102 1.0	**28** SA ☾	0934 2.0 0.9 / 2200 0.9
14 SA	0941 1.2 1.8 / 2158 1.0	**29** SU	1046 1.0 1.9 / 2315 1.0
15 SU	1048 1.2 1.8 / 2308 1.1	**30** M	1205 1.0 1.8 1.8
		31 TU	0031 1.1 1.9 / 1310 1.0 1.8

SEA LEVEL IS ABOVE MEAN TIDE LEVEL FROM 2.0 HOURS AFTER L.W. TO 2.0 HOURS BEFORE THE NEXT L.W. AND H.W. WILL OCCUR BETWEEN 5.0 HOURS AFTER L.W. AND 3.0 HOURS BEFORE THE NEXT L.W.

Chart Datum: 1.40 metres below Ordnance Datum (Newlyn)

POOLE continued

CHARTS
Admiralty 2611, 2175, 2615; Stanford 15, 12, 7; Imray C4, Y23; OS 195

TIDES
−0221, +0114 Dover; ML 1.5; Zone 0 (GMT).

Standard Port PORTSMOUTH (→)

Times				Height (metres)			
HW		LW		MHWS	MHWN	MLWN	MLWS
0000	0600	0500	1100	4.7	3.8	1.8	0.6
1200	1800	1700	2300				

Differences POOLE ENTRANCE
−0240 +0105 −0100 −0030 −2.7 −2.2 −0.7 −0.3
TOWN QUAY
−0210 +0140 −0015 −0005 −2.6 −2.2 −0.7 −0.2
WAREHAM (River Frome)
−0140 +0205 +0110 +0035 −2.5 −2.1 −0.7 +0.1

NOTE: Times and heights of LW for each day of the year are given above. Double HWs occur except at neaps and predictions are for the higher HW. Near neaps there is a stand and the predictions shown are for the middle of the stand. See 10.2.8.

SHELTER
An excellent harbour with narrow entrance from sea, accessible in all conditions except very strong E and SE winds. Anchorages may be found in most parts of the harbour, anywhere sheltered from the wind and free from moorings. Speed limit throughout harbour 8 kn; in quiet areas 6 kn.

NAVIGATION
Waypoint Poole Bar (stbd-hand) buoy, QG, 50°39′.42N 01°55′.15W, 147°/327° from/to Haven Hotel, 1.8M. The Bar is dangerous in strong SE-S winds especially on the ebb. Beware number of lobster pots round Studland Bay and close to training bank. A recreational boat channel has been established in the Swash Way on the western side of the channel, from Poole Bar to Shell Bay. Suitable for craft up to 3m draught. There are two channels up to Poole; the Middle Ship Channel (formerly the Diver Channel) and the North Channel (formerly the Main Channel). The former is dredged to 5m for traffic to the ferry terminal at Hamworthy, and is mostly only 60m wide. Recreational traffic must keep out of the Middle Ship Channel but may use the small vessel channel running to the S of the dredged channel between port hand buoys to the S and stakes having R can topmarks marking the edge of the bank. Depth in this channel is 2.0m above CD except close to the stakes where it drops to 1.5m. Alternatively yachts can use the North Channel (formerly the main channel). Both channels are clearly marked by lateral buoys, mostly lit, with divisions marked by cardinal buoys. The Harbour is changing to adapt to the needs of the Oil Industry and cross channel traffic. Changes to buoyage and channels are now frequent. Yachts departing westwards should note regulations regarding Lulworth gunnery range (see 10.2.31). Information is shown in Hr Mr's mooring office on Poole Quay and broadcast on Radio Solent at times given in 10.2.9.

LIGHTS AND MARKS
Radio beacon 303.4 kHz PO 10 M located on Haven Hotel at harbour entrance.
Chain Ferry Sandbanks
Moving: Day—B Ball For'd; Night—WGR Lts For'd;
Fog—1 long, 2 short blasts every 2 mins.
Stationary: Night—W Lt.; Fog—5 sec bell every min.
Poole Bridge (Lights shown from tower)
FR —   Do not approach bridge;
Fl Or — Bridge opening, proceed with caution;
FG —   Proceed;
Bridge opened on request (large vessels) and at routine times for small — Mon-Fri 0930, 1130, 1430, 1630, 1830, 2130, 2330. Sat, Sun & Bank holidays 0730, 0930, 1130, 1330, 1530, 1730, 1930, 2130, 2330. (LT)
Salterns Marina
Lts 2FG (vert) to stbd, 2FR (vert) to port.
Poole YC Haven
Entrance E side FlG 5s. W side Fl (3) 10s.

RADIO TELEPHONE
Call: *Poole Harbour Control* VHF Ch 14 16; 14. (H24). Salterns Marina (call: *Gulliver Base*) and Cobbs Quay Marina, Ch **80**.

TELEPHONE (0202)
Hr Mr 685261; CG (Poole Sector) 670776; MRSC Weymouth 760695; Pilots 673320; Bridge 674115; Harbour Control 666464; Hamworthy Bridge 674115;
✳ (0202) 674567; Weather Southampton 228844; Marinecall 0898 500 457; Police 22099; Ⓗ 675100.

FACILITIES
EC Wednesday. The facilities in Poole Harbour are very extensive and the following is not an exhaustive list.
Salterns Marina (340, some visitors) ☎ 709971, ME, El, Ⓔ, Sh, C (5 ton), BH (40 ton), AC, FW, CH, Bar, Gas, Gaz, P, D, R, ▢; **Cobbs Quay Marina** (600, some visitors) ☎ 674299, Slip, P, D, Gas, ▢, SM, FW, AC, ME, El, Ⓔ, Sh, C (10 ton), CH, R, Bar; **Sunseekers International Marina** (50) ☎ 685335, Slip, BH (2 ton), C (40 ton), AC, Sh, D, FW, ME, El, CH, V, R, Bar; **Dorset Yacht Co** (120+12 visitors) ☎ 674531, Slip, P, D, Gas, Gaz, FW, ME, El, Sh, C (5 ton), Bar, AC;
Harbour Office ☎ 685261 is opposite the quay. There is an office on the quay for Berthing Officer open 0900-2300.
Landing Places: Public landing places on Poole Quay, at Holes Bay and by ferry hards at Sandbanks.
Fresh water is available at Town Quay, at all marinas and boatyards.
Fuel (P and D) and FW is available from Esso barge when on station near Aunt Betty buoy (No 50) and all major yards.
Yacht Clubs
Poole YC ☎ 672687; **Poole Quay YC** ☎ 680746; **Poole Harbour YC** ☎ 707321; **Parkstone YC** ☎ 743610; **Royal Motor YC** ☎ 707227, Bar, R, M; **Cobb's Quay YC** ☎ 673690.
Note: **Poole Quay** (AB, C (24 ton) FW) is close to town centre and many facilities listed below.
Arthur Bray ☎ 676469, M, L, FW, C (2 ton), AB;
J. Harvey ☎ 666226, M; **Marine Engine Centre** ☎ 672082, FW, ME, El, Sh, CH, AB, C (4 ton); **Rockley Boating Centre** ☎ 665001, Slip, M, C (5 ton), FW, CH, AB; **Quay Sails** ☎ 681128, SM; **Tab Sails** ☎ 684638, SM; **Crusader Sails** ☎ 670580, SM; **Sandbanks Yacht Co.** ☎ 707500, Slip, M, D, P, L, FW, ME, El, CH, V, Sh; **Mitchell BY** ☎ 747857, Slip, M, FW, ME, El, L, C (18 ton), Sh, CH; **Lilliput Yacht Station** ☎ 707176, Slip, L, M, FW, Sh; **Latham and Sons** ☎ 748029, Slip, L, FW, C (4 ton), CH, ME, El, Sh; **H. Pipler** ☎ 673056, L, CH, ACA; **Marine Power** ☎ 676469, Spares; **Greenham Marine** ☎ 676363, El, Ⓔ; **Melmarine** ☎ 680462, CH; **Danlea** ☎ 590468, Ⓔ; **Poole Inflatables** ☎ 677777, Safety Equipment and Inflatables; **Town** ✉; Ⓑ; ⇌; ✈ (Bournemouth).

CHRISTCHURCH   10-2-17
Dorset

CHARTS
Admiralty 2172, 2175, 2615; Stanford 7, 12; Imray C4; OS 195

TIDES
HW Spring −0210 Neap −0140 Dover; ML 1.2
         +0120   +0105   Zone 0 (GMT)

Standard Port PORTSMOUTH (→)

Times				Height (metres)			
HW		LW		MHWS	MHWN	MLWN	MLWS
0000	0600	0500	1100	4.7	3.8	1.8	0.6
1200	1800	1700	2300				

Differences CHRISTCHURCH (Ent)
−0230 +0030 −0035 −0035 −2.9 −2.4 −1.2 −0.2
CHRISTCHURCH (Tuckton)
−0205 +0110 +0110 +0105 −3.0 −2.5 −1.0 +0.1
BOURNEMOUTH
−0240 +0055 −0050 −0030 −2.7 −2.2 −0.8 −0.3

NOTE: Double HWs occur except near neaps and predictions are for the higher HW. Near neaps there is a stand and the predictions shown are for the middle of the stand. Tidal levels are for inside the bar. Outside the bar the tide falls about 0.6m lower at springs. Floods (or drought) in the 2 rivers cause considerable variations from predicted heights. See 10.2.8

CHRISTCHURCH *continued*

SHELTER
Good shelter in lee of Hengistbury Head but otherwise very exposed to prevailing SW winds. The Stour is navigable at HW up to Tuckton Bridge and the Avon up to the first bridge across to the island, and both give good shelter from all winds. Recommend entry or departure on the stand. All anchorage areas in the harbour dry. Anchoring forbidden in main channel. It is also forbidden to secure alongside ferry terminal on Mudeford sandbank. Christchurch SC offers limited moorings to monohulls up to 7.9m.

NAVIGATION
Waypoint 50°43'.50N 01°43'.50W, 090°/270° from/to channel entrance, 0.30M. The position of the bar is liable to change after storms. The entrance is difficult on the ebb tide due to very strong streams, 4 to 5 kn in 'The Run'. Beware groynes S of Hengistbury Head and also Beerpan Rks and Yarranton (or Clarendon) Rks.
There is a speed limit in the harbour of 5 kn.

LIGHTS AND MARKS
Buoyage in harbour and entrance is carried out privately by the Christchurch Harbour Association and buoys are often withdrawn in winter. Information can be obtained from Christchurch Marine ☎ 483250. Outer Portland buoy Fl (2) R 10s (May—Sept incl). E end of Mudeford Quay 2 FG (vert).

RADIO TELEPHONE
None.

TELEPHONE (0202)
Quay & Moorings Supt. Highcliffe 274933; CG 425204; MRSC Weymouth 760695; ⌗ (0703) 229251; Marinecall 0898 500 457; Police 486333; Ⓗ 486361.

FACILITIES
Mudeford Quay (Apl-Sept), Slip, M, P (cans, ½M), L, FW, C (mobile), AB, V; **Christchurch Marine** ☎ 483250, Slip, M, FW, ME, El, Sh, CH, ACA; **John Lack** ☎ 483191, FW, ME, El; **RIBS Marine** ☎ 477327, M, FW, ME, El, Sh; **Leak Hayes** ☎ 483141, C (8 ton); **Bob Hoare** ☎ 485708, Sh, CH; **Slaters Marine** ☎ 482751, CH; **R. A. Stride** ☎ 485949, CH.
Town ✉; Ⓑ; ⇌; ✈ (Bournemouth).

KEYHAVEN   10-2-18
Hampshire

CHARTS
Admiralty 2021, 2219, 2040; Stanford 11, 7; Imray C4, C3, Y20; OS 196

TIDES
−0020, +0105 Dover; ML 2.0; Zone 0 (GMT).

Standard Port PORTSMOUTH (→)

Times				Height (metres)			
HW		LW		MHWS	MHWN	MLWN	MLWS
0000	0600	0500	1100	4.7	3.8	1.8	0.6
1200	1800	1700	2300				

Differences HURST POINT
−0115 −0005 −0030 −0025 −2.0 −1.5 −0.5 −0.1

NOTE: Double tides occur at or near springs and on other occasions there is a stand which lasts about 2 hours. Predictions refer to the first HW when there are two. At other times they refer to the middle of the stand. See 10.2.8.
River is administered by New Forest District Council aided by the Keyhaven Consultative Committee.

SHELTER
Good, but the river gets extremely congested. All moorings and anchorages are exposed to winds across the marshland. Access HW ∓4½.

NAVIGATION
Waypoint 50°42'.70N 01°32'.50W, 115°/295° from/to channel entrance, 0.40M. Bar is constantly changing. Entrance should not be attempted in strong E winds. Approaching from W, beware Shingles over which seas break and which very occasionally dry. Give 'The Trap' a wide berth. Leave channel marker buoys well to Stbd. Beware lobster pots.

LIGHTS AND MARKS
When E of the High Lt, two leading beacons in line ('X' topmarks) at 283° lead to entrance of buoyed channel.
NOTE: Ldg Lts 042° do *not* lead into the harbour but keep clear of the Shingles.

RADIO TELEPHONE
None.

TELEPHONE (0590)
River Warden (042 128) 45695; CG Bournemouth 425204; MRSC Lee-on-Solent 552100; New Forest District Council Lyndhurst 3121; ⌗ (0703) 229251; Marinecall 0898 500 457; Police 75411; Dr 72179; Ⓗ (Lymington) 77011.

FACILITIES
EC (Milford-on-Sea) Wednesday; **Keyhaven YC** ☎ 42165, Bar, C, M, L (on beach), FW; **West Solent Boat Builders** ☎ 42080, Slip, ME, El, Sh, C (9 ton), CH; **New Forest District Council** ☎ Lyndhurst 3121, Slip, M; **Milford-on-Sea** P, D, FW, CH, V, R, Bar; **Hurst Castle SC** M, L, FW; **Quay** Slip, L.
Village R, Bar, CH, V, ✉ (Milford-on-Sea); Ⓑ(Milford-on-Sea); ⇌ (bus to New Milton); ✈ (Bournemouth).

LYMINGTON   10-2-19
Hampshire

CHARTS
Admiralty 2021, 2040, 2045; Stanford 7, 11;
Imray C3, Y20, Y30; OS 196

TIDES
Spring −0040, Neap +0020 Dover; ML 2.0; Zone 0 (GMT)
+0100

Standard Port PORTSMOUTH (→)

Times				Height (metres)			
HW		LW		MHWS	MHWN	MLWN	MLWS
0000	0600	0500	1100	4.7	3.8	1.8	0.6
1200	1800	1700	2300				

Differences LYMINGTON
−0110 +0005 −0020 −0020 −1.7 −1.2 −0.5 −0.1
NOTE: Double high waters occur at or near springs and
on other occasions there is a stand which lasts about
2 hrs. Predictions refer to the first HW when there are
two. At other times they refer to the middle of the stand.
See 10.2.8

SHELTER
There are two large marinas and river is accessible at all
states of the tide. Anchoring in the river is prohibited, but
in off-shore winds yachts can anchor off the mud flats
outside. Yachts may use Town Quay or Customs House
Quay (see Hr Mr) and there are up to 100 visitors
moorings in the river opposite Town Quay (W moorings).

NAVIGATION
Waypoint 50°44'.04N 01°30'.00W, 139°/000° from/to
front Ldg Lt, 1.5M. Min. depth in mid-channel from
entrance to Railway Pier/Lymington Marina 1.8m; from
there to Town Quay min depth 1.1m. There are extensive
mud banks round the entrance but they are well marked.
Two sewer outlets to the W are dangerous. Entering,
leave Jack-in-the-Basket about 45m to port to clear Cross
Boom.

LIGHTS AND MARKS
Ldg Lts 319°, both FR 12/17m 8M. Entrance marked by
Jack-in-the-Basket, Fl R 2s. Channel marked by R piles
with can topmarks, with radar reflectors, to port, G piles
with G triangular topmarks to starboard. Port side has
four lights Fl R 2s and Harper Post Q (3) 10s and to
starboard seven lights Fl G 2s. Ldg Lts into Lymington
Yacht Haven 244° both FY. There are two sets of Ldg
marks on the central section; two RW posts on flats to
SSE of Seymore's Post in line at 187°30' for outgoing
craft; two BW posts on flats to SE of Cage Boom in line
at 007°30' for incoming craft.

RADIO TELEPHONE
Marinas VHF Ch 80 (office hours).

TELEPHONE (0590)
Hr Mr 672014; MRSC Lee-on-Solent 552100;
⌗ (0703) 229251; Marinecall 0898 500 457; Police 675411;
Dr 677011.

FACILITIES
EC Wednesday; **Lymington Marina** (300 + 100 visitors)
☎ 675444, Slip, P, AC, D, FW, ME, El, Sh, CH, BH
(40 ton), C, Gas, Gaz; **Lymington Yacht Haven**
(450 + 100 visitors) ☎ 677071, P, D, FW, ME, AC, El, Sh,
C (10 ton), BH (45 ton), CH, Gas, Gaz, ◻; **Berthon Boat
Co.** ☎ 673312, M, P, FW, ME, El, Sh, C, CH, AB; **Royal
Lymington YC** ☎ 672677, R, Bar; **Lymington Town SC**
☎ 674514, AB, R, Bar; **Town Quay** Slip, M, FW, AB
(see Hr Mr); **Aquaboats** ☎ 674266, ME, Sh, CH; **J.G.
Claridge** ☎ 674821, CH; **Shipmates** ☎ 672765, CH;
Greenham Marine ☎ 671144, Ⓔ; **Brookes and
Gatehouse** ☎ 675200, Ⓔ; **Hood** ☎ 673797, SM;
Lymington Sail and Tent ☎ 673139, SM, CH; **Haven
BY** ☎ 673489, ACA; **Sanders** ☎ 673981, SM; **Yachtmail**
☎ 672784, CH; **Mariner Electronics** ☎ 676511, El, Ⓔ;
S.A.L. Marine ☎ 679588, ME, El; **Quayside
Marine** ☎ 679582, Sh (Wood and GRP); **Datayacht**
☎ 671252, Ⓔ; **Bath Road** public pontoon, FW; **Town
Quay** FW, AB (see Hr Mr); **Regis Marine Electronics**
☎ 679251, Ⓔ; **Town** has every facility including ⊠; Ⓑ;
⇌; ✈ (Bournemouth or Southampton).

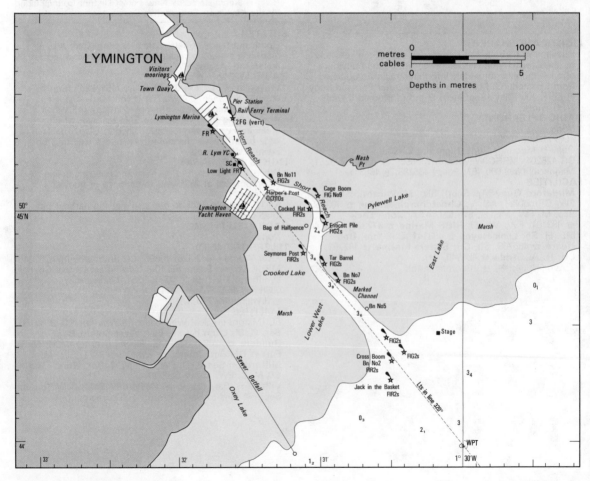

YARMOUTH 10-2-20
Isle of Wight

CHARTS
Admiralty 2021, 2040 2045; Stanford 11; Imray C3, Y20; OS 196

TIDES
Spring −0050, Neap +0020 Dover; ML 2.0; Zone 0 (GMT) +0150

Standard Port PORTSMOUTH (→)

Times				Height (metres)			
HW		LW		MHWS	MHWN	MLWN	MLWS
0000	0600	0500	1100	4.7	3.8	1.8	0.6
1200	1800	1700	2300				

Differences YARMOUTH
−0105	+0005	−0025	−0030	−1.6	−1.3	−0.4	0.0

FRESHWATER
−0210	+0025	−0040	−0020	−2.1	−1.5	−0.4	0.0

TOTLAND BAY
−0130	−0045	−0040	−0040	−2.0	−1.5	−0.5	−0.1

NOTE: Double HWs occur at or near springs; at other times there is a stand which lasts about 2hrs. Predictions refer to the first HW when there are two. At other times they refer to the middle of the stand. See 10.2.8

SHELTER
Harbour affords complete shelter from all directions of wind and sea. Harbour gets very full, and on occasions, closed. Boats over 15m length, 4m beam or 2.4m draft should give notice of arrival by telephone or VHF.

NAVIGATION
Waypoint 50°42'.60N 01°29'.93W, 008°/188° from/to front Ldg Lt, 0.28M. Dangers on approach are Black Rock and shallow water to the N of the breakwater. There are four large Admiralty buoys (two unlit), three E of pier, one W of pier. The most E and the most W are lit. Beware ferries entering and leaving. The road bridge across the R Yar opens on request (Oct−Apr) for boats proceeding up the river to their moorings or the boatyard above the bridge. Bridge opening times (May−Sept) 0805, 0900, 1000, 1200, 1400, 1600, 1730, 1830, 2000 (LT). Speed limit in harbour 4 kn and outside the harbour as far as the pierhead, 6kn.

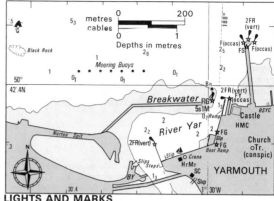

LIGHTS AND MARKS
Leading beacons (two W diamonds) or Ldg Lts (FG), on quay, 188°. When harbour is closed (eg when full in summer at week-ends) a R flag is hoisted at seaward end of Ferry jetty by day and an illuminated board displayed saying 'Harbour Full', by night.

RADIO TELEPHONE
Hr Mr Ch 16 (0800−1700 LT). Call on Ch 80 for berthing instructions.

TELEPHONE (0983)
Hr Mr 760321; Berthing Master 760300 MRSC Lee-on-Solent 552100; ⌗ 760406; Marinecall 0898 500 457; Police 528000; Dr 760434.

FACILITIES
EC Wednesday, **South Quay** ☎ 760300, Slip, P, D, L, M, FW, C; **Harold Hayles Yacht Yard** ☎ 760373, Slip, M, ME, El, Sh, CH, Gas, Gaz; **Richardson Yacht Repairs** ☎ 761091 Sh; **Royal Solent YC** ☎ 760270, Bar, R, L, M, Slip; **Yarmouth Outboards** ☎ 760436, ME, Sh, CH; **Brookes & Gatehouse Services** ☎ 760309, El, Ⓔ; **Buzzard International** ☎ 760707, M, ME, El, Sh, CH; **Salterns Sail Loft** ☎ 760521 SM; **Harwoods Chardley** ☎ 760258 CH, Gas, Gaz; **Hylton Mortimer** ☎ 760120, SM; **Yarmouth Marine Services** ☎ 760309, ME, El, Sh, Divers; **Town** V, R, Bar, ✉; Ⓑ (Sept-May AM only, May-Sept 1000-1445); ⇌ (Ferry to Lymington); ✈ (Bournemouth, IoW airport or Southampton).

NEWTOWN 10-2-21
Isle of Wight

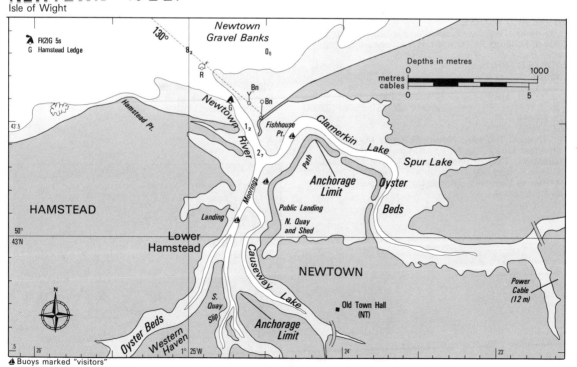

⚐ Buoys marked "visitors"

CHARTS
Admiralty 2021, 2040, 1905; Stanford 11; Imray C3, Y20; OS 196

TIDES
Spring −0108 Dover; ML 2.3; Zone 0 (GMT)
Neap +0058

Standard Port PORTSMOUTH (→)

Times				Height (metres)			
HW		LW		MHWS	MHWN	MLWN	MLWS
0000	0600	0500	1100	4.7	3.8	1.8	0.6
1200	1800	1700	2300				

Differences SOLENT BANK
−0100	0000	−0015	−0020	−1.3	−1.0	−0.3	−0.1

NOTE: Double HWs occur at or near springs; at other times there is a stand which lasts about 2 hrs. Predictions refer to the first HW when there are two. At other times they refer to the middle of the stand. See 10.2.8

SHELTER
3½M E of Yarmouth, Newtown gives good shelter although exposed to winds from the N. Best entrance is on the flood before the mud flats cover. Ent between two shingle spits and can be rough in N winds especially near HW. There are four visitors buoys (conspic W) in Clamerkin Lake and thirteen (conspic W) in the main arm leading to Shalfleet − check with Hr Mr. Do not anchor above boards showing "Anchorage Limit" on account of oyster beds. Fin keel boats can stay afloat from entrance to Hamstead landing or to Clamerkin Limit Boards. Public landing on E side of river N of quay. The whole peninsular ending in Fishouse Pt is a nature reserve. Yachtsmen are asked not to land there between April and June inclusive.

NAVIGATION
Waypoint 50°44'.00N 01°25'.00W, 335°/155° from/to Fishouse Pt 0.67M. From W, make Hamstead Ledge G Conical Buoy; from E beware Newtown gravel banks; leave bar buoy to port. There is only about 0.9m over the bar. After entry there are so many perches that confusion may result. Perches mark the mud banks. Near junction to Causeway Lake depth is down to 0.9m and beyond this water quickly shoals. Clamerkin Lake is deep (1.2m); channel is marked by occasional perches and one small G buoy. Keep to E to avoid gravel spit off W shore, marked by three perches. Beware numerous oyster beds. Speed limit in harbour 5 kn.
Note: There is a rifle range at top of Clamerkin Lake and in Spur Lake. R flags flown during firing.
High Voltage power line across Clamerkin at 50°42'.79N 1°22'.52W clearance of 12m − no shore markings.

LIGHTS AND MARKS
Ldg marks. Two Bns on posts on mud to E of Ent on NE side of Fishouse Pt. Outer Bn RW stripes with Y topmark; inner Bn W with W disc with B circle.

RADIO TELEPHONE
None.

TELEPHONE (0983 for 6 figs; 098 378 for 3 figs)
Hr Mr 424; MRSC Lee-on-Solent 552100;
☎ (0703) 827350; Marinecall 0898 500 457; Police 528000; Dr 760434.

FACILITIES
EC Newport Thursday; **Newtown Quay** M, L, FW; **Shalfleet Quay** Slip, M, L, AB; **Lower Hamstead Landing** L, FW; **R. Seabroke** ☎ 213, Sh; **Shalfleet Village** V, Bar; ✉ (Newport); Ⓑ (Yarmouth or Newport); ⇌ (bus to Yarmouth, ferry to Lymington); ✈ (Southampton).

BEAULIEU RIVER   10-2-22
Hampshire

CHARTS
Admiralty 2021, 2040, 1905; Stanford 11; Imray C3, Y20; OS 196

TIDES
−0100 and +0140 Dover; ML 2.4; Zone 0 (GMT)

Standard Port PORTSMOUTH (→)

Times				Height (metres)			
HW		LW		MHWS	MHWN	MLWN	MLWS
0000	0600	0500	1100	4.7	3.8	1.8	0.6
1200	1800	1700	2300				

BUCKLERS HARD
−0040	−0010	+0010	−0010	−1.0	−0.8	−0.2	−0.3

STANSORE POINT
−0050	−0010	−0005	−0010	−0.9	−0.6	−0.2	0.0

NOTE: Double HWs occur at or near springs; on other occasions there is stand which lasts about 2 hours. The predictions refer to the first HW when there are two, or to the middle of the stand.

SHELTER
Very good shelter from all winds. Anchorage possible in reach between Lepe and Needs Oar Point but preferable to proceed up to Bucklers Hard.

NAVIGATION
Waypoint 50°46'.50N 01°21'.47W, 159°/339° from/to Beaulieu Spit Bn, Fl R 5s, 0.3M. The swatchway at W end of Beaulieu Spit is closed.
There are shoal depths of 0.5m to 0.8m below CD from 100 to 300m out from Beaulieu spit dolphin on line of Ldg marks from pile No 2 and shore. Entrance dangerous LW∓2. Leave Ldg marks open to E for best water. A speed limit of 5 knots applies to the whole river.

LIGHTS AND MARKS
Entrance beacons in line at 339°, N beacon is triangle over a square fluorescent topmark, S beacon is R and carries a W fluorescent topmark. Beaulieu Spit, E end, R dolphin with Fl R 5s 3M vis 277°-037°; ra refl. Lt. River is clearly marked by R and G beacons and perches. Stbd 5, 9 and 19, Fl G 4s; Port 12 and 20, Fl R 4s.

RADIO TELEPHONE
None.

TELEPHONE (0590)
Hr Mr 616200; CG Portsmouth 840200;
MRSC Lee-on-Solent 552100; ⌗ (0703) 229251; Marinecall 0898 500 457; Police Lymington 75411; Dr 612451 or Hythe 845955; Ⓗ Lymington 77011.

FACILITIES
EC Village Shop opens 7 days a week; **Bucklers Hard Yacht Harbour** (110+20 visitors) ☎ 616314, Slip, M, P, D, AC, FW, ME, El, Sh, C (2 ton), BH (26 ton), SM, Gas, Gaz, CH, V, R, Bar; **Palace Quay BY** ☎ 612338, M, ME, El, Sh, CH; **Agamemnon BY** ☎ 616214/5, ME, El, Sh; **Village** V, R, Bar. ✉ (Beaulieu); Ⓑ (Mon, Wed, Fri AM or Hythe); ⇌ (bus to Brockenhurst); ✈ (Bournemouth or Southampton).

COWES 10-2-23
Isle of Wight

CHARTS
Admiralty 2793, 2040, 394, 2045; Stanford 7, 11; Imray C3, Y20; OS 196

TIDES
+0023 Dover; ML 2.7; Zone 0 (GMT)

Standard Port PORTSMOUTH (→)

Times				Height (metres)			
HW		LW		MHWS	MHWN	MLWN	MLWS
0000	0600	0500	1100	4.7	3.8	1.8	0.6
1200	1800	1700	2300				

Differences COWES
−0015	+0015	0000	−0020	−0.5	−0.3	−0.1	0.0

FOLLY INN
−0015	+0015	0000	−0020	−0.6	−0.4	−0.1	+0.2

NEWPORT
−0020	+0020	0000	−0015	−0.6	−0.4	+0.1	+1.3

NOTE: Double high tides occur at or near springs; on other occasions a stand occurs which lasts up to 2 hrs. Times given represent the middle of the stand. See 10.2.8

SHELTER
Good, but outer harbour is exposed to N and NE winds. R Medina is navigable to Newport but the upper reaches dry. Visitors may pick up any mooring so labelled: buoys off the Parade; piles S of Ancasta Marina, opposite Lallows; Thetis Pontoon Landing, between Shepards Wharf and Spencer Thetis Wharf (for short stay and overnight only, dredged to 2m); piles S of the chain ferry, Whitegates area; and considerable berthing alongside pontoon opposite the Folly Inn. Marina berths at Ancasta Marina (W Cowes), Cowes Marina (E Cowes, above chain ferry), and Island Harbour on E shore beyond Folly Inn, see 10.2.31.

NAVIGATION
Waypoint 50°46'.20N 01°17'.90W, 344°/164° from/to front Ldg Lt, 0.35M. On the E side of the entrance, the Shrape (mud flats) extend to Old Castle Point. Yachts are required to use the main channel near W shore. It is forbidden to sail through or anchor in the mooring area. Beware of the floating bridge, ferries and commercial shipping. Speed limit 6 kn in harbour. Board sailing forbidden within fairway and approaches. Floating bridge (chain ferry) normally operates Mon-Sat: 0530-2315, then 2400. Sunday 0700-2315, then 2400 (all LT).

LIGHTS AND MARKS
Entrance is marked by No 3 buoy Fl (G) and No 4 buoy (QR). Ldg Lts 164°. Front Iso 2s 3m 6M; post by Customs House. Rear, 290m from front, Iso R 2s 5m 3M; dolphin by Jubilee Pontoon; vis 120°-240°; No 8 buoy Fl (2) R5s. E breakwater head Fl R 3s 3M. The ends of jetties and certain dolphins are marked by 2FR (vert) on E side of harbour, and by 2FG (vert) on W side.

RADIO TELEPHONE
VHF Ch 16; 11 12 14 69. (0830-1730, LT) Island Harbour and Cowes Marina Ch 80; Ancasta Marina Ch 80 (office hours). Harbourmaster's launches Ch 16 69. Chain Ferry Ch 69 (when ferry operating). Vessels are required to advise ferry of their intention to pass, ferry will acknowledge. Water Bus Service, call: *Yachting World Ferry* Ch 08. HM Coastguard liaison Ch 67.

TELEPHONE (0983)
Hr Mr 293952; MRSC Lee-on-Solent 552100; ✝ (0703) 229251; Waterguard 293132; Folly Reach Harbour Office 295722; Weather Centre Southampton 228844; Marinecall 0898 500 457; Police 528000; Ⓗ 524081; Ⓗ (Frank James) 296504; Dr 295251.

FACILITIES
EC Wednesday; **Cowes Marina** (E. Cowes) (120 + 130 visitors) ☎ 293983, FW, BH (10 ton), D, ME, El, Sh, AC, Gas, V; **Ancasta Marina** (80 + 120 visitors) ☎ 294861, D, FW, ME, El, Sh, AC, Gas, Gaz, Kos, R, SM, V, Ⓒ, CH, C (6 ton), BH (30 ton); **Pascall Atkey** ☎ 292381, ME, CH, ACA, Gas, Gaz; **Clare Lallow** ☎ 292112, Gas, Slip, P, D, L, FW, CH, ME, El, Sh; **Souters Shipyard** ☎ 294711, Slip, P, D, FW, AB, ME, El, Sh, C (50 ton); **FBM Marine** ☎ 292561, ME, El, Sh; **Spencer Rigging** ☎ 292022, CH, M, Rigging; **Marine Bazaar** ☎ 298869, CH; **The Book Cabin** ☎ 295409, Books and charts;

McWilliam ☎ 298855, SM; **Ratsey and Lapthorn** ☎ 294051, SM; **RHP Marine** ☎ 290421, ME, El; **Eddie Richards** ☎ 298949, Sh; **Adrian Stone** ☎ 297898, Sh; **Island Boat Repairs** ☎ 298015, Sh; **Martin Marine** ☎ 292892, ME; **Regis Marine Electronics** ☎ 293996, El, Ⓔ; **Martec** ☎ 296913, El, Ⓔ; **Mustang Marine** ☎ 290565, ME, El, Sh; **Powerplus Marine** ☎ 200036, ME; (H24 − ☎ (0860) 435476) **Britannia Wharf** ☎ 292724, Slip, Sh, ME; **D. Floyd** ☎ 295408, Divers; **Aquatogs** ☎ 295071, CH; **UK Sailing Centre** ☎ 294941, AB, Slip, Bar, FW; **Euro Marine Services** ☎ 290284, ME, CH.

Yacht Clubs: **Royal Yacht Squadron** ☎ 292743; **Royal London YC** ☎ 299727 **Royal Corinthian YC** ☎ **Cowes Corinthian YC** ☎ 296333; **Cowes Combined Clubs** ☎ 295744; **Island SC** ☎ 293061. **Castle Rock YC** ☎ 293581;

Casualties − (Ch 67) land at W. Cowes Fountain Pier for ambulance or as directed.

FW is available at Town Quay, Whitegates Public Pontoon, Watch House slipway (by Customs), in marinas and Folly Pier. **Do-It-Yourself** at Shepard's Wharf ☎ 297821, CH, C (6 ton), AB, BH (20 ton), Gas, AC, Tools etc; Thetis Public Pontoon Landing.
Town P, D, Bar, R, V, Slip, ✉, Ⓑ; ⚓ (Ferry to Southampton); ✈ (Southampton).
Ferry Services: Red Funnel ferries ☎ 292101; Hydrofoil ☎ 292101.
WHIPPINGHAM: **Folly Inn** ☎ 297171, L, Bar, R, M, Slip, Ⓒ.

SOUTHAMPTON   10-2-24
Hampshire

SOUTHAMPTON
MEAN SPRING AND NEAP CURVES
Springs occur 2 days after New and Full Moon

MEAN RANGES
Springs 4·0m
Neaps 1·9m

CHARTS
Admiralty 2041, 1905, 394, 2045; Stanford 11; Imray C3; OS 196

TIDES
HW (1st) −0001 Dover; ML 2.9; Zone 0 (GMT)

Southampton is a Standard Port and tidal predictions for each day of the year are given below. See Sections 10.2.8 and 10.2.9. A NE gale combined with high barometer may lower sea level by 0.6m. At springs there are two separate HWs about 2 hours apart; at neaps there is a long stand. Predictions are for the first HW where there are two or for the middle of the stand.

SHELTER
Good from most wind directions although a heavy chop develops in SE winds above force 4. It is better to shelter in marinas.
There are no specific yacht anchorages but temporary anchoring is permitted (subject to Hr Mr) off club moorings at Netley, Hythe, Weston & Marchwood in about 2m. Keep clear of main or secondary channels and Hythe Pier. Public moorings for large yachts opposite Royal Pier near Gymp Shoal in 4m by arrangement with the Hr Mr. The nearest landing is a slipway at Town Quay Marina. Visitors berths available in Hythe Marina (with lock entrance), at Shamrock Quay Marina (R Itchen), at Kemp's Quay Marina (R Itchen) and at Ocean Village Marina.

NAVIGATION
Waypoint Weston Shelf (stbd-hand) buoy, Fl(3)G 15s, 50°52′.68N 01°23′.16W, 138°/318° from/to Port Sig Stn, 0.40M. There are no hidden dangers or navigational hazards. Main channels are well marked. There are several unlit large mooring buoys at Hythe both to E and W of the main channel. Other isolated buoys exist and yachtsmen entering the port during darkness should keep just outside the lighted buoyed fairway. Very large tankers operate from Fawley and very large passenger and container ships from Southampton. It is essential to keep clear of ocean-going shipping; see 10.2.9.
R Test   Eling Creek dries. There is foul ground at Marchwood and Royal Pier.
R Itchen   Care is necessary, particularly at night, above Itchen Bridge; the channel bends sharply to port and favours the W side. There are unlit moorings in the centre of the river. Navigation above Northam Bridge (14′6″, 4.4m) is not advisable.
There is a speed limit of 6 kn. in both rivers above the line Hythe Pier to Weston Shelf.

LIGHTS AND MARKS
These are too numerous to elaborate and reference should be made to the charts.
The following should be noted:
(1)   Southampton Water bifurcates at Dock Head which is clearly marked by a high lattice mast showing traffic signals which are mandatory for commercial vessels but may be disregarded by yachts navigating outside the main channels. The signals are shown on the side of Test or Itchen as appropriate thus:

(a)	A green shape or light	A vessel may enter or leave the docks
(b)	A red shape or light	Entry or departure forbidden
(c)	A red shape or light over a green shape or light	Departure forbidden to facilitate entry of large vessel.
(d)	A green shape or light over a red shape or light	Entry forbidden to facilitate entry of large vessel.

(2)   Hythe Marina Village, close NW of Hythe Pier, marked by Q (3) 10s; E cardinal Bn. Lock entrance, N side 2 FG (vert); S side 2 FR (vert).
(3)   Dock Head, West side (Queen Elizabeth II Terminal, S end) 4 FG (vert) 3M; framework Tr; mark entrance to R Test.
(4)   Entrance to R Itchen marked by Lt Buoy Oc G 4s, beyond which piles with G Lts mark E side of channel leading under road bridge.
(5)   Above Itchen Bridge, which is marked by 2 FR (vert) and 2 FG (vert), the principal marks are Crosshouse Bn Oc R 5s, Chapel Bn Fl G 3s, Shamrock Quay pontoons 2 FR (vert) at SW and NE ends, No 5 Bn Fl G 3s, No 7 Bn Fl (2) G 5s, Millstone Pt jetty 2 FR (vert), No 9 Bn Fl (4) G 10s and Kemps Quay Marina 2 FG (vert).

RADIO TELEPHONE
Vessel Traffic Services (VTS) Centre Southampton. Call: *Southampton VTS* VHF Ch 12 14 16 (H24). Traffic information for small craft on Ch every even H+00 0600-2200 Fri-Sun and Bank Holiday Mondays from Easter − 30 Sept.
Southampton Harbour Patrol Call: *Southampton Patrol* VHF Ch 12 16; 01-28, 60-88 (H24) both have Ch 10, 12, 14, 16, 18, 22, 71 & 74.
Marinas VHF Ch **80**.

ENGLAND, SOUTH COAST – SOUTHAMPTON

Lat 50°54′ N   Long 1°24′ W

TIMES AND HEIGHTS OF HIGH AND LOW WATERS

YEAR **1991**

TIME ZONE **UT (GMT)**
For Summer Time add ONE
hour in non-shaded areas

Chart Datum: 2.74 metres below Ordnance Datum (Newlyn)

JANUARY

Day	Time	m	Time	m	Time	m	Time	m
1 Tu	0428	0.7	1050	4.5	1654	0.4	2326	4.6
16 W	0437	1.0	1107	4.3	1654	0.8	2340	4.3
2 W	0520	0.6	1138	4.6	1744	0.3		
17 Th	0511	1.1	1141	4.4	1728	0.7		
3 Th	0015	4.7	0609	0.5	1226	4.6	1829	0.3
18 F	0013	4.4	0547	0.8	1213	4.4	1802	0.6
4 F	0103	4.7	0653	0.6	1314	4.5	1913	0.4
19 Sa	0043	4.4	0621	0.8	1245	4.4	1835	0.6
5 Sa	0151	4.6	0736	0.7	1403	4.4	1953	0.6
20 Su	0117	4.4	0656	0.8	1320	4.3	1907	0.7
6 Su	0240	4.4	0816	0.9	1452	4.2	2034	0.9
21 M	0150	4.4	0730	0.9	1358	4.3	1940	0.9
7 M ☾	0330	1.2	0859	1.2	1546	3.9	2118	1.2
22 Tu	0230	4.3	0806	1.1	1442	4.1	2018	1.1
8 Tu	0425	4.0	0947	1.5	1645	3.7	2212	1.6
23 W ☽	0317	4.2	0849	1.3	1534	4.0	2107	1.4
9 W	0524	3.8	1046	1.7	1753	3.6	2317	1.8
24 Th	0414	4.0	0947	1.6	1641	3.6	2214	1.6
10 Th	0628	3.7	1154	1.9	1907	3.6		
25 F	0524	3.9	1103	1.7	1804	3.8	2339	1.7
11 F	0029	1.9	0733	3.7	1306	1.8	2016	3.6
26 Sa	0642	3.9	1230	1.6	1931	3.9		
12 Sa	0137	1.9	0829	3.8	1407	1.7	2110	3.8
27 Su	0108	1.6	0757	4.0	1349	1.3	2042	4.1
13 Su	0233	1.7	0916	3.9	1458	1.4	2154	4.0
28 M	0224	1.3	0900	4.2	1456	0.9	2140	4.3
14 M	0319	1.5	0956	4.1	1541	1.1	2233	4.1
29 Tu	0325	1.0	0953	4.4	1553	0.6	2229	4.5
15 Tu ●	0400	1.2	1033	4.2	1619	0.9	2308	4.2
30 W ○	0419	0.7	1042	4.5	1643	0.3	2316	4.7
31 Th	0507	0.5	1127	4.6	1728	0.2	2359	4.8

FEBRUARY

Day	Time	m	Time	m	Time	m	Time	m
1 F	0552	0.4	1210	4.6	1811	0.2		
16 Sa	0529	0.6	1152	4.5	1743	0.4		
2 Sa	0042	4.7	0632	0.4	1252	4.6	1850	0.3
17 Su	0020	4.6	0604	0.5	1224	4.5	1816	0.4
3 Su	0123	4.6	0708	0.5	1334	4.4	1925	0.5
18 M	0049	4.6	0637	0.5	1256	4.5	1848	0.5
4 M	0204	4.5	0742	0.7	1416	4.2	1956	0.8
19 Tu	0123	4.5	0708	0.6	1334	4.4	1919	0.6
5 Tu	0245	4.2	0813	1.0	1417	4.0	2029	1.1
20 W	0200	4.4	0741	0.8	1417	4.3	1954	0.9
6 W ☾	0328	4.0	0849	1.4	1548	3.8	2109	1.6
21 Th	0246	4.3	0821	1.1	1510	4.1	2040	1.3
7 Th	0417	3.8	0935	1.7	1647	3.5	2205	2.0
22 F	0342	4.1	0916	1.5	1617	3.9	2149	1.7
8 F	0518	3.6	1042	2.0	1805	3.4	2325	2.2
23 Sa ☽	0455	3.9	1034	1.8	1749	3.8	2324	1.9
9 Sa	0632	3.5	1209	2.1	1935	3.5		
24 Su	0626	3.8	1216	1.7	1926	3.9		
10 Su	0053	2.1	0749	3.6	1333	1.9	2046	3.6
25 M	0102	1.7	0751	3.9	1343	1.3	2039	4.1
11 M	0205	1.9	0851	3.8	1436	1.6	2135	3.9
26 Tu	0218	1.3	0855	4.1	1448	0.9	2132	4.4
12 Tu	0259	1.6	0936	4.0	1523	1.2	2215	4.1
27 W	0317	0.9	0946	4.3	1541	0.5	2217	4.6
13 W	0341	1.2	1015	4.1	1600	0.9	2248	4.3
28 Th ○	0405	0.6	1029	4.5	1626	0.4	2258	4.7
14 Th ●	0417	0.9	1049	4.3	1635	0.7	2320	4.4
15 F	0454	0.7	1122	4.4	1709	0.5	2350	4.5

MARCH

Day	Time	m	Time	m	Time	m	Time	m
1 F	0449	0.4	1110	4.6	1708	0.2	2338	4.7
16 Sa ●	0426	0.6	1054	4.4	1643	0.4	2320	4.6
2 Sa	0528	0.3	1149	4.6	1747	0.2		
17 Su	0503	0.3	1128	4.5	1719	0.3	2351	4.6
3 Su	0014	4.7	0605	0.3	1227	4.5	1821	0.3
18 M	0541	0.3	1200	4.6	1756	0.3		
4 M	0050	4.6	0636	0.4	1304	4.4	1853	0.5
19 Tu	0022	4.6	0616	0.3	1235	4.5	1830	0.4
5 Tu	0126	4.4	0705	0.6	1340	4.2	1919	0.8
20 W	0057	4.6	0649	0.4	1316	4.4	1904	0.6
6 W	0201	4.2	0732	0.9	1419	4.0	1946	1.2
21 Th	0137	4.5	0725	0.7	1402	4.3	1941	0.9
7 Th	0238	4.0	0800	1.3	1502	3.8	2020	1.6
22 F	0226	4.3	0806	1.0	1459	4.1	2031	1.3
8 F ☾	0323	3.8	0841	1.7	1556	3.6	2109	2.0
23 Sa ☽	0326	4.0	0904	1.4	1615	3.9	2143	1.7
9 Sa	0418	3.6	0941	2.0	1710	3.4	2227	2.2
24 Su	0445	3.8	1028	1.6	1749	3.8	2321	1.8
10 Su	0533	3.5	1112	2.1	1848	3.4		
25 M	0619	3.8	1207	1.6	1921	4.0		
11 M	0006	2.2	0703	3.5	1251	2.0	2011	3.6
26 Tu	0055	1.6	0744	3.9	1329	1.3	2028	4.2
12 Tu	0130	2.0	0817	3.9	1403	1.6	2105	3.8
27 W	0205	1.3	0841	4.1	1432	0.9	2117	4.4
13 W	0230	1.6	0907	3.9	1452	1.2	2144	4.1
28 Th	0259	0.9	0931	4.3	1520	0.6	2158	4.6
14 Th	0313	1.2	0947	4.1	1531	0.9	2218	4.3
29 F	0343	0.6	1012	4.4	1603	0.4	2236	4.6
15 F	0350	0.8	1021	4.3	1607	0.6	2250	4.4
30 Sa ○	0423	0.4	1042	4.5	1642	0.3	2312	4.6
31 Su	0500	0.4	1125	4.5	1718	0.3	2345	4.6

APRIL

Day	Time	m	Time	m	Time	m	Time	m
1 M	0534	0.4	1201	4.4	1750	0.5		
16 Tu	0516	0.3	1139	4.5	1733	0.4	2359	4.6
2 Tu	0018	4.5	0604	0.5	1236	4.3	1819	0.6
17 W	0556	0.3	1219	4.5	1815	0.4		
3 W	0049	4.3	0631	0.6	1310	4.2	1846	0.9
18 Th	0038	4.5	0636	0.4	1305	4.4	1855	0.6
4 Th	0123	4.2	0656	0.9	1347	4.0	1913	1.2
19 F	0124	4.4	0717	0.6	1358	4.3	1939	0.9
5 F	0159	4.0	0726	1.2	1430	3.8	1947	1.6
20 Sa	0217	4.2	0802	0.9	1500	4.1	2034	1.3
6 Sa	0242	3.8	0805	1.6	1522	3.6	2036	1.9
21 Su ☽	0321	4.0	0904	1.2	1616	4.0	2146	1.6
7 Su ☾	0337	3.6	0902	1.8	1632	3.5	2149	2.1
22 M	0441	3.9	1021	1.4	1743	4.0	2312	1.6
8 M	0449	3.5	1024	2.0	1801	3.5	2320	2.1
23 Tu	0608	3.8	1149	1.4	1903	4.1		
9 Tu	0614	3.5	1159	1.9	1921	3.6		
24 W	0033	1.5	0724	3.9	1303	1.2	2005	4.2
10 W	0045	1.9	0730	3.6	1315	1.6	2019	3.8
25 Th	0139	1.2	0823	4.1	1404	1.0	2052	4.4
11 Th	0147	1.5	0826	3.8	1408	1.3	2101	4.0
26 F	0231	0.9	0910	4.2	1452	0.7	2133	4.4
12 F	0233	1.1	0905	4.1	1452	0.9	2137	4.2
27 Sa	0315	0.7	0950	4.3	1534	0.6	2209	4.5
13 Sa	0313	0.8	0948	4.2	1531	0.6	2212	4.4
28 Su ○	0354	0.6	1028	4.3	1611	0.6	2244	4.4
14 Su ●	0353	0.6	1024	4.4	1611	0.5	2246	4.5
29 M	0429	0.6	1102	4.3	1647	0.6	2316	4.4
15 M	0434	0.4	1101	4.5	1652	0.4	2321	4.6
30 Tu	0502	0.6	1138	4.3	1721	0.7	2347	4.3

ENGLAND, SOUTH COAST – SOUTHAMPTON

Lat 50°54′ N Long 1°24′ W

TIMES AND HEIGHTS OF HIGH AND LOW WATERS

YEAR **1991**

TIME ZONE UT (GMT)
For Summer Time add ONE hour in non-shaded areas

Chart Datum: 2.74 metres below Ordnance Datum (Newlyn)

MAY

Day	Time	m		Day	Time	m
1 W	0533 / 1213 / 1750	0·6 / 4·2 / 0·9		16 Th	0540 / 1209 / 1803	0·3 / 4·5 / 0·5
2 Th	0020 / 0602 / 1247 / 1819	4·2 / 0·7 / 4·1 / 1·0		17 F	0024 / 0626 / 1300 / 1850	4·5 / 0·4 / 4·4 / 0·7
3 F	0054 / 0631 / 1325 / 1850	4·1 / 0·9 / 4·0 / 1·2		18 Sa	0116 / 0712 / 1357 / 1940	4·4 / 0·5 / 4·4 / 0·9
4 Sa	0131 / 0703 / 1407 / 1927	4·0 / 1·2 / 4·0 / 1·5		19 Su	0212 / 0801 / 1459 / 2034	4·2 / 0·7 / 4·3 / 1·1
5 Su	0215 / 0743 / 1458 / 2015	3·8 / 1·4 / 3·7 / 1·7		20 M	0316 / 0858 / 1607 / 2136	4·1 / 1·0 / 4·2 / 1·3
6 M	0307 / 0836 / 1600 / 2119	3·7 / 1·6 / 3·6 / 1·9		21 Tu	0427 / 1004 / 1721 / 2246	3·9 / 1·2 / 4·1 / 1·4
7 Tu	0411 / 0944 / 1713 / 2235	3·6 / 1·8 / 3·6 / 1·9		22 W	0542 / 1117 / 1831 / 2357	3·9 / 1·3 / 4·1 / 1·4
8 W	0525 / 1103 / 1825 / 2350	3·6 / 1·8 / 3·7 / 1·8		23 Th	0655 / 1227 / 1932	3·9 / 1·3 / 4·2
9 Th	0637 / 1216 / 1924	3·6 / 1·6 / 3·8		24 F	0102 / 0755 / 1327 / 2024	1·3 / 4·0 / 1·2 / 4·2
10 F	0055 / 0737 / 1315 / 2012	1·5 / 3·8 / 1·3 / 4·0		25 Sa	0156 / 0846 / 1418 / 2106	1·1 / 4·1 / 1·1 / 4·2
11 Sa	0147 / 0827 / 1405 / 2054	1·2 / 4·0 / 1·0 / 4·2		26 Su	0243 / 0928 / 1503 / 2143	1·0 / 4·1 / 1·0 / 4·3
12 Su	0233 / 0910 / 1451 / 2135	0·9 / 4·1 / 0·8 / 4·4		27 M	0324 / 1007 / 1544 / 2219	0·8 / 4·2 / 0·9 / 4·3
13 M	0318 / 0953 / 1538 / 2215	0·6 / 4·3 / 0·6 / 4·5		28 Tu	0402 / 1044 / 1621 / 2252	0·8 / 4·2 / 1·0 / 4·2
14 Tu	0405 / 1037 / 1626 / 2255	0·4 / 4·4 / 0·5 / 4·5		29 W	0437 / 1121 / 1655 / 2325	0·8 / 4·2 / 1·0 / 4·2
15 W	0452 / 1122 / 1715 / 2339	0·3 / 4·5 / 0·5 / 4·5		30 Th	0509 / 1156 / 1728 / 2358	0·8 / 4·2 / 1·0 / 4·2
				31 F	0541 / 1233 / 1801	0·8 / 4·1 / 1·1

JUNE

Day	Time	m		Day	Time	m
1 Sa	0033 / 0613 / 1310 / 1836	4·1 / 0·9 / 4·1 / 1·2		16 Su	0107 / 0706 / 1348 / 1932	4·4 / 0·4 / 4·5 / 0·7
2 Su	0111 / 0649 / 1350 / 1913	4·0 / 1·0 / 4·0 / 1·3		17 M	0201 / 0753 / 1443 / 2021	4·3 / 0·5 / 4·4 / 0·9
3 M	0153 / 0726 / 1436 / 1956	3·9 / 1·2 / 3·9 / 1·5		18 Tu	0258 / 0842 / 1543 / 2112	4·2 / 0·8 / 4·3 / 1·1
4 Tu	0241 / 0812 / 1526 / 2049	3·9 / 1·4 / 3·8 / 1·6		19 W	0400 / 0934 / 1644 / 2210	4·0 / 1·0 / 4·2 / 1·3
5 W	0335 / 0905 / 1623 / 2148	3·8 / 1·5 / 3·8 / 1·7		20 Th	0506 / 1035 / 1749 / 2312	3·9 / 1·3 / 4·1 / 1·4
6 Th	0435 / 1008 / 1725 / 2254	3·7 / 1·6 / 3·8 / 1·7		21 F	0615 / 1141 / 1851	3·8 / 1·4 / 4·0
7 F	0542 / 1115 / 1827 / 2359	3·7 / 1·6 / 3·9 / 1·5		22 Sa	0018 / 0721 / 1245 / 1948	1·5 / 3·8 / 1·5 / 4·0
8 Sa	0647 / 1220 / 1924	3·8 / 1·4 / 4·0		23 Su	0118 / 0820 / 1345 / 2037	1·4 / 3·9 / 1·5 / 4·0
9 Su	0100 / 0746 / 1320 / 2014	1·3 / 3·9 / 1·2 / 4·2		24 M	0212 / 0910 / 1436 / 2120	1·3 / 3·9 / 1·4 / 4·1
10 M	0155 / 0839 / 1417 / 2102	1·0 / 4·1 / 1·0 / 4·3		25 Tu	0259 / 0952 / 1521 / 2158	1·2 / 4·0 / 1·3 / 4·1
11 Tu	0249 / 0930 / 1512 / 2148	0·8 / 4·2 / 0·8 / 4·4		26 W	0340 / 1032 / 1559 / 2233	1·0 / 4·1 / 1·2 / 4·1
12 W	0343 / 1020 / 1608 / 2236	0·6 / 4·4 / 0·7 / 4·5		27 Th	0418 / 1108 / 1637 / 2308	0·9 / 4·1 / 1·1 / 4·2
13 Th	0436 / 1110 / 1702 / 2324	0·4 / 4·5 / 0·6 / 4·5		28 F	0452 / 1144 / 1712 / 2342	0·8 / 4·2 / 1·0 / 4·2
14 F	0528 / 1202 / 1754	0·3 / 4·5 / 0·6		29 Sa	0526 / 1218 / 1746	0·8 / 4·2 / 1·0
15 Sa	0016 / 0617 / 1254 / 1844	4·5 / 0·3 / 4·5 / 0·6		30 Su	0017 / 0601 / 1253 / 1821	4·2 / 0·8 / 4·2 / 1·1

JULY

Day	Time	m		Day	Time	m
1 M	0052 / 0634 / 1329 / 1857	4·2 / 0·9 / 4·2 / 1·1		16 Tu	0140 / 0734 / 1417 / 1958	4·4 / 0·4 / 4·5 / 0·7
2 Tu	0129 / 0709 / 1406 / 1934	4·1 / 0·9 / 4·1 / 1·2		17 W	0230 / 0815 / 1506 / 2039	4·3 / 0·6 / 4·4 / 0·9
3 W	0210 / 0746 / 1448 / 2015	4·0 / 1·1 / 4·1 / 1·3		18 Th	0323 / 0858 / 1601 / 2125	4·1 / 0·9 / 4·1 / 1·2
4 Th	0257 / 0829 / 1536 / 2104	3·9 / 1·3 / 4·0 / 1·5		19 F	0422 / 0948 / 1659 / 2220	3·9 / 1·3 / 3·9 / 1·5
5 F	0350 / 0919 / 1632 / 2201	3·8 / 1·4 / 3·9 / 1·6		20 Sa	0528 / 1049 / 1803 / 2327	3·7 / 1·7 / 3·8 / 1·7
6 Sa	0451 / 1021 / 1734 / 2308	3·8 / 1·6 / 3·9 / 1·6		21 Su	0643 / 1201 / 1909	3·6 / 1·9 / 3·7
7 Su	0602 / 1134 / 1841	3·8 / 1·6 / 4·0		22 M	0039 / 0755 / 1312 / 2009	1·8 / 3·7 / 1·9 / 3·8
8 M	0019 / 0714 / 1247 / 1943	1·5 / 3·8 / 1·5 / 4·1		23 Tu	0146 / 0853 / 1412 / 2059	1·7 / 3·8 / 1·7 / 3·9
9 Tu	0128 / 0819 / 1355 / 2040	1·3 / 4·0 / 1·3 / 4·2		24 W	0241 / 0940 / 1503 / 2141	1·4 / 3·9 / 1·5 / 4·0
10 W	0232 / 0916 / 1459 / 2133	1·0 / 4·2 / 1·0 / 4·3		25 Th	0326 / 1020 / 1545 / 2218	1·2 / 4·1 / 1·3 / 4·1
11 Th	0329 / 1011 / 1557 / 2223	0·7 / 4·4 / 0·8 / 4·4		26 F	0404 / 1054 / 1620 / 2253	1·0 / 4·2 / 1·1 / 4·2
12 F	0425 / 1102 / 1652 / 2313	0·4 / 4·5 / 0·6 / 4·5		27 Sa	0437 / 1127 / 1656 / 2325	0·8 / 4·3 / 1·0 / 4·3
13 Sa	0517 / 1151 / 1744	0·3 / 4·6 / 0·5		28 Su	0512 / 1159 / 1729 / 2358	0·7 / 4·3 / 0·9 / 4·3
14 Su	0002 / 0606 / 1240 / 1832	4·5 / 0·2 / 4·7 / 0·5		29 M	0544 / 1230 / 1804	0·7 / 4·4 / 0·8
15 M	0052 / 0652 / 1328 / 1916	4·5 / 0·2 / 4·6 / 0·5		30 Tu	0030 / 0617 / 1300 / 1838	4·3 / 0·7 / 4·4 / 0·8
				31 W	0103 / 0649 / 1333 / 1911	4·3 / 0·7 / 4·3 / 0·9

AUGUST

Day	Time	m		Day	Time	m
1 Th	0140 / 0721 / 1410 / 1946	4·2 / 0·9 / 4·2 / 1·1		16 F	0244 / 0819 / 1512 / 2039	4·1 / 1·0 / 4·1 / 1·3
2 F	0221 / 0756 / 1454 / 2026	4·1 / 1·1 / 4·2 / 1·3		17 Sa	0336 / 0859 / 1605 / 2126	3·8 / 1·5 / 3·8 / 1·6
3 Sa	0311 / 0840 / 1547 / 2118	4·0 / 1·4 / 4·0 / 1·5		18 Su	0438 / 0956 / 1708 / 2232	3·6 / 1·9 / 3·6 / 2·0
4 Su	0412 / 0940 / 1651 / 2228	3·8 / 1·6 / 3·9 / 1·7		19 M	0558 / 1113 / 1822 / 2358	3·5 / 2·2 / 3·5 / 2·1
5 M	0530 / 1101 / 1808 / 2352	3·7 / 1·8 / 3·9 / 1·7		20 Tu	0727 / 1240 / 1939	3·5 / 2·2 / 3·6
6 Tu	0657 / 1230 / 1925	3·8 / 1·7 / 4·0		21 W	0121 / 0836 / 1351 / 2038	1·9 / 3·7 / 2·0 / 3·8
7 W	0114 / 0812 / 1349 / 2029	1·4 / 4·0 / 1·4 / 4·2		22 Th	0223 / 0925 / 1446 / 2124	1·6 / 3·9 / 1·7 / 4·0
8 Th	0225 / 0911 / 1454 / 2124	1·1 / 4·3 / 1·1 / 4·3		23 F	0309 / 1002 / 1527 / 2201	1·3 / 4·1 / 1·3 / 4·1
9 F	0322 / 1002 / 1549 / 2213	0·7 / 4·5 / 0·8 / 4·5		24 Sa	0345 / 1034 / 1602 / 2234	1·0 / 4·2 / 1·0 / 4·3
10 Sa	0414 / 1048 / 1639 / 2300	0·4 / 4·6 / 0·5 / 4·6		25 Su	0417 / 1104 / 1635 / 2305	0·8 / 4·4 / 0·8 / 4·4
11 Su	0502 / 1133 / 1727 / 2345	0·2 / 4·8 / 0·4 / 4·6		26 M	0451 / 1133 / 1709 / 2335	0·6 / 4·4 / 0·7 / 4·4
12 M	0548 / 1218 / 1810	0·1 / 4·8 / 0·3		27 Tu	0524 / 1201 / 1742	0·5 / 4·5 / 0·6
13 Tu	0029 / 0629 / 1259 / 1851	4·6 / 0·2 / 4·7 / 0·4		28 W	0006 / 0556 / 1231 / 1816	4·5 / 0·5 / 4·5 / 0·6
14 W	0113 / 0709 / 1342 / 1927	4·4 / 0·4 / 4·6 / 0·6		29 Th	0037 / 0628 / 1302 / 1848	4·4 / 0·6 / 4·5 / 0·7
15 Th	0157 / 0744 / 1426 / 2002	4·3 / 0·7 / 4·3 / 0·9		30 F	0112 / 0658 / 1338 / 1921	4·3 / 0·7 / 4·4 / 0·9
				31 Sa	0153 / 0732 / 1420 / 1958	4·2 / 1·0 / 4·2 / 1·2

2

ENGLAND, SOUTH COAST – SOUTHAMPTON

Lat 50°54′ N   Long 1°24′ W

TIMES AND HEIGHTS OF HIGH AND LOW WATERS   YEAR **1991**

TIME ZONE **UT(GMT)**
For Summer Time add ONE
hour in non-shaded areas

	SEPTEMBER		OCTOBER		NOVEMBER		DECEMBER
Time m	Time m	Time m	Time m	Time m	Time m	Time m	Time m

SEPTEMBER

1 Su (0243 4.0 / 0815 1.4 / 1513 4.1 / 2050 1.5
16 M   0350 3.6 / 0906 2.0 / 1609 3.6 / 2136 1.8

2 M   0348 3.9 / 0918 1.7 / 1622 3.9 / 2204 1.8
17 Tu   0508 3.4 / 1023 2.3 / 1728 3.5 / 2308 2.2

3 Tu   0515 3.8 / 1048 1.9 / 1751 3.8 / 2340 1.8
18 W   0647 3.4 / 1201 2.3 / 1858 3.5

4 W   0653 3.8 / 1226 1.8 / 1917 3.9
19 Th   0045 2.1 / 0804 3.6 / 1321 2.1 / 2008 3.7

5 Th   0109 1.5 / 0809 4.1 / 1345 1.5 / 2024 4.2
20 F   0153 1.8 / 0855 3.9 / 1418 1.7 / 2057 3.9

6 F   0218 1.1 / 0904 4.4 / 1446 1.1 / 2116 4.4
21 Sa   0241 1.4 / 0931 4.1 / 1500 1.3 / 2133 4.1

7 Sa   0312 0.6 / 0949 4.6 / 1536 0.7 / 2201 4.5
22 Su   0317 1.0 / 1003 4.3 / 1534 1.0 / 2206 4.3

8 Su ●   0359 0.3 / 1030 4.7 / 1621 0.4 / 2243 4.6
23 M ○   0351 0.7 / 1033 4.4 / 1609 0.7 / 2238 4.4

9 M   0443 0.2 / 1110 4.8 / 1704 0.3 / 2324 4.7
24 Tu   0424 0.6 / 1102 4.6 / 1643 0.6 / 2310 4.5

10 Tu   0524 0.2 / 1150 4.8 / 1745 0.3
25 W   0459 0.5 / 1131 4.6 / 1719 0.5 / 2341 4.5

11 W   0004 4.6 / 0603 0.3 / 1229 4.7 / 1821 0.4
26 Th   0534 0.5 / 1202 4.6 / 1755 0.5

12 Th   0043 4.5 / 0638 0.5 / 1307 4.5 / 1854 0.6
27 F   0015 4.5 / 0608 0.5 / 1235 4.6 / 1828 0.6

13 F   0124 4.3 / 0709 0.8 / 1344 4.3 / 1923 0.9
28 Sa   0051 4.4 / 0643 0.7 / 1313 4.5 / 1904 0.8

14 Sa   0205 4.1 / 0740 1.1 / 1425 4.0 / 1955 1.3
29 Su   0136 4.3 / 0719 1.0 / 1359 4.3 / 1942 1.1

15 Su)   0253 3.8 / 0815 1.6 / 1512 3.8 / 2035 1.7
30 M   0229 4.1 / 0805 1.4 / 1454 4.1 / 2036 1.4

OCTOBER

1 Tu (0340 3.9 / 0911 1.7 / 1607 3.9 / 2154 1.7
16 W   0421 3.5 / 0937 2.2 / 1634 3.5 / 2213 2.1

2 W   0511 3.8 / 1043 1.9 / 1741 3.8 / 2330 1.7
17 Th   0550 3.5 / 1108 2.3 / 1801 3.5 / 2348 2.1

3 Th   0646 4.0 / 1219 1.8 / 1908 3.9
18 F   0712 3.6 / 1231 2.1 / 1920 3.6

4 F   0056 1.4 / 0757 4.2 / 1334 1.4 / 2013 4.2
19 Sa   0104 1.8 / 0808 3.8 / 1335 1.7 / 2015 3.8

5 Sa   0202 1.1 / 0848 4.5 / 1431 1.0 / 2102 4.4
20 Su   0158 1.5 / 0851 4.0 / 1421 1.3 / 2057 4.0

6 Su   0254 0.7 / 0931 4.6 / 1518 0.7 / 2144 4.5
21 M   0240 1.1 / 0926 4.3 / 1500 1.0 / 2135 4.2

7 M ●   0337 0.4 / 1009 4.7 / 1600 0.5 / 2223 4.6
22 Tu   0316 0.8 / 0958 4.4 / 1538 0.7 / 2210 4.4

8 Tu   0419 0.3 / 1046 4.7 / 1639 0.4 / 2303 4.6
23 W ○   0353 0.7 / 1033 4.6 / 1616 0.6 / 2243 4.5

9 W   0459 0.3 / 1123 4.7 / 1717 0.4 / 2340 4.6
24 Th   0432 0.6 / 1104 4.6 / 1655 0.5 / 2320 4.6

10 Th   0535 0.5 / 1158 4.6 / 1751 0.5
25 F   0512 0.5 / 1138 4.7 / 1735 0.4 / 2359 4.5

11 F   0017 4.5 / 0609 0.7 / 1233 4.4 / 1822 0.7
26 Sa   0552 0.6 / 1216 4.6 / 1815 0.5

12 Sa   0055 4.3 / 0638 0.9 / 1308 4.2 / 1849 0.9
27 Su   0041 4.5 / 0634 0.7 / 1258 4.5 / 1853 0.7

13 Su   0134 4.1 / 0707 1.3 / 1347 4.0 / 1919 1.3
28 M   0129 4.4 / 0716 1.0 / 1351 4.3 / 1938 0.9

14 M   0218 3.9 / 0740 1.6 / 1429 3.8 / 1956 1.6
29 Tu   0226 4.2 / 0805 1.3 / 1445 4.1 / 2033 1.3

15 Tu)   0312 3.6 / 0827 2.0 / 1523 3.6 / 2051 2.0
30 W   0337 4.1 / 0910 1.6 / 1559 4.0 / 2145 1.5

31 Th   0500 4.0 / 1032 1.7 / 1725 3.9 / 2311 1.5

NOVEMBER

1 F   0624 4.1 / 1156 1.7 / 1847 4.0
16 Sa   0601 3.6 / 1128 2.0 / 1816 3.6 / 2357 1.8

2 Sa   0030 1.4 / 0732 4.2 / 1308 1.4 / 1953 4.1
17 Su   0707 3.8 / 1236 1.8 / 1922 3.7

3 Su   0136 1.1 / 0825 4.4 / 1405 1.1 / 2044 4.3
18 M   0100 1.6 / 0800 4.0 / 1333 1.5 / 2013 3.9

4 M   0228 0.9 / 0909 4.5 / 1452 0.8 / 2127 4.4
19 Tu   0152 1.3 / 0842 4.2 / 1420 1.1 / 2059 4.1

5 Tu   0313 0.7 / 0948 4.6 / 1534 0.6 / 2207 4.5
20 W   0239 1.0 / 0922 4.4 / 1504 0.9 / 2140 4.3

6 W ●   0354 0.6 / 1024 4.6 / 1614 0.6 / 2245 4.5
21 Th ○   0323 0.6 / 1000 4.5 / 1549 0.7 / 2221 4.4

7 Th   0433 0.6 / 1059 4.5 / 1650 0.6 / 2322 4.5
22 F   0409 0.7 / 1039 4.6 / 1634 0.5 / 2304 4.5

8 F   0509 0.7 / 1134 4.5 / 1725 0.6 / 2359 4.4
23 Sa   0456 0.6 / 1119 4.6 / 1720 0.4 / 2347 4.6

9 Sa   0541 0.9 / 1206 4.3 / 1755 0.8
24 Su   0542 0.6 / 1202 4.6 / 1805 0.4

10 Su   0035 4.3 / 0613 1.1 / 1241 4.2 / 1824 1.0
25 M   0035 4.5 / 0628 0.7 / 1249 4.5 / 1850 0.5

11 M   0112 4.1 / 0643 1.3 / 1317 4.1 / 1854 1.2
26 Tu   0126 4.5 / 0714 0.8 / 1340 4.4 / 1936 0.7

12 Tu   0154 3.9 / 0717 1.5 / 1359 3.9 / 1930 1.5
27 W   0222 4.4 / 0804 1.1 / 1437 4.2 / 2028 0.9

13 W   0242 3.8 / 0800 1.8 / 1448 3.8 / 2019 1.7
28 Th   0325 4.3 / 0901 1.3 / 1543 4.1 / 2128 1.2

14 Th)   0339 3.7 / 0857 2.0 / 1547 3.6 / 2121 1.9
29 F   0434 4.2 / 1006 1.5 / 1656 4.0 / 2237 1.3

15 F (0449 3.6 / 0959 2.1 / 1700 3.6 / 2239 1.9
30 Sa   0549 4.1 / 1120 1.5 / 1813 3.9 / 2351 1.4

DECEMBER

1 Su   0657 4.2 / 1230 1.4 / 1923 4.0
16 M   0557 3.8 / 1130 1.8 / 1819 3.7 / 2355 1.7

2 M   0059 1.3 / 0756 4.2 / 1331 1.3 / 2022 4.1
17 Tu   0700 3.9 / 1237 1.6 / 1926 3.8

3 Tu   0158 1.2 / 0845 4.3 / 1425 1.1 / 2111 4.2
18 W   0102 1.5 / 0757 4.0 / 1338 1.4 / 2025 4.0

4 W   0249 1.1 / 0928 4.3 / 1512 0.9 / 2154 4.3
19 Th   0202 1.3 / 0848 4.2 / 1435 1.1 / 2116 4.1

5 Th   0333 1.0 / 1006 4.4 / 1553 0.8 / 2233 4.3
20 F   0257 1.1 / 0934 4.4 / 1527 0.8 / 2204 4.4

6 F ●   0413 1.0 / 1042 4.4 / 1631 0.8 / 2310 4.3
21 Sa ○   0351 0.8 / 1020 4.5 / 1618 0.5 / 2252 4.5

7 Sa   0449 1.0 / 1115 4.3 / 1705 0.8 / 2347 4.3
22 Su   0443 0.7 / 1106 4.6 / 1708 0.4 / 2340 4.6

8 Su   0523 1.0 / 1149 4.3 / 1736 0.8
23 M   0533 0.6 / 1152 4.6 / 1757 0.3

9 M   0021 4.3 / 0555 1.1 / 1223 4.2 / 1808 0.9
24 Tu   0028 4.7 / 0622 0.5 / 1239 4.6 / 1843 0.3

10 Tu   0057 4.2 / 0626 1.2 / 1257 4.2 / 1838 1.0
25 W   0116 4.7 / 0709 0.6 / 1329 4.5 / 1928 0.4

11 W   0134 4.1 / 0700 1.3 / 1335 4.1 / 1912 1.2
26 Th   0207 4.6 / 0754 0.7 / 1421 4.4 / 2012 0.6

12 Th   0213 4.0 / 0737 1.5 / 1418 4.0 / 1952 1.4
27 F   0301 4.5 / 0841 1.0 / 1518 4.2 / 2101 0.9

13 F   0300 3.9 / 0822 1.6 / 1506 3.8 / 2039 1.5
28 Sa   0401 4.3 / 0932 1.2 / 1621 4.0 / 2158 1.2

14 Sa   0352 3.8 / 0916 1.8 / 1603 3.7 / 2135 1.7
29 Su)   0504 4.1 / 1032 1.4 / 1731 3.9 / 2303 1.5

15 Su   0451 3.8 / 1020 1.8 / 1708 3.7 / 2242 1.8
30 M   0613 4.0 / 1142 1.6 / 1848 3.8

31 Tu (0015 1.6 / 0720 4.0 / 1254 1.6 / 1958 3.9

Chart Datum: 2.74 metres below Ordnance Datum (Newlyn)

SOUTHAMPTON *continued*

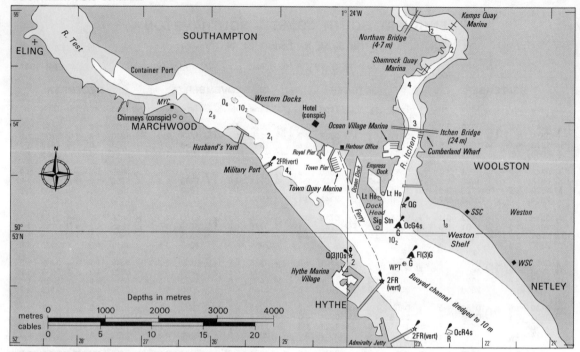

TELEPHONE (0703)
Dock and Harbour Master 339733; MRSC Lee-on-Solent
552100; ✳ (0703) 229251; Southampton Weather Centre
228844; Marinecall 0898 500 457; Police 26222; Dr 226631
(Port Health); Ⓗ 777222.

FACILITIES
Ocean Village Marina (450 + 50 visitors) ☎ 229385, FW,
V, R, Bar, CH, Slip, Gas, Gaz, Kos, ME, Sh, ▣, P, D,
(Access H24); **Shamrock Quay Marina** (220 + 40 visitors)
☎ 229461, BH (50 ton), C (12 ton), ME, El, Sh, SM, ▣,
R, Bar, AC, CH, FW, Gas, Gaz, Kos, V; **Hythe Marina**
(180 + 50 visitors) ☎ 849263, BH (30 ton), C (12 ton), AC,
P, D, El, ME, Sh, CH, FW, SM, (Access H24); **Kemp's
Quay Marina** (180 + 5 visitors) ☎ 632323, AC, C (5 ton),
D, FW, Gas, ME, (Access HW∓3½); **Town Quay Marina**
(400) ☎ 211080, R, Bar; **Itchen Marina** ☎ 631500, D, BY,
C (12 ton); **Royal Southampton YC** ☎ 223352, Bar, R, M,
FW, L, ▣; **Hythe SC** ☎ 846563; **Marchwood YC**
☎ 864641, Bar, M, C (10 ton), FW, L; **Netley SC**
☎ 454272; **Southampton SC** ☎ 446575; **Weston SC**
☎ 452527; **Hythe Marina Yacht Services** ☎ 840460, ME,
El, Sh; **Kelvin Hughes** ☎ 631286, CH, ACA; **Stephen
Ratsey** ☎ 221683, SM; **Pumpkin Marine** ☎ 229713, CH;
Southampton Yacht Services ☎ 335266, Sh; **Solent
Rigging** ☎ 639976, Rigging; **Southern Spar Services**
☎ 331714, Spars; **Alpha Sails** ☎ 553623, SM;
G Sailmakers ☎ 221453, SM; **Ullman Sails** ☎ 335596,
SM; **B. D. Marine** ☎ 220178, ME, El; **Waters Yacht
Engineers** ☎ 220144, ME, El; **Hythe Marine Services**
☎ 848782 ME, El, Sh; **Boat Shop** ☎ 449338, CH; **Belsize
BY** ☎ 671555, CH; **Larry Marks** ☎ 447037, CH;
Shamrock Chandlery ☎ 632725, CH (and at the Hythe
marina); **Captain Pumpkin** ☎ 229713, CH; **Bowdeck**
☎ 331841, Ⓔ; **Hards** at Hythe, Crackmore, Eling,
Mayflower Park (Test), Northam (Itchen). Public landings at
Cross House hand, Cross House slip, Block House hard
(Itchen), Carnation public hard & Cowporters public hard.
City V, R, Bar, Ⓑ; ✉; ⇌; ✈; Ferries/Hydrofoil to
IoW ☎ 333042.

NOTE
Associated British Ports publish a Yachtsman's Guide to
the area. Apply to *Vessel Traffic Services Centre*, Berth 37,
Eastern Docks.

HAMBLE   10-2-25
Hampshire

CHARTS
Admiralty 2022, 1905; Stanford 11; Imray C3; OS 196
TIDES
+0130, −0010 Dover; ML 2.9; Zone 0 (GMT)

Standard Port SOUTHAMPTON (←)

Times				Height (metres)			
HW		LW		MHWS	MHWN	MLWN	MLWS
0400	1100	0000	0600	4.5	3.7	1.8	0.5
1600	2300	1200	1800				

Differences WARSASH

| +0020 | +0010 | +0010 | 0000 | 0.0 | +0.1 | +0.1 | +0.3 |

BURSLEDON

| +0020 | +0020 | +0010 | +0010 | +0.1 | +0.1 | +0.2 | +0.2 |

CALSHOT CASTLE

| +0015 | +0030 | +0015 | +0005 | 0.0 | 0.0 | +0.2 | +0.3 |

NOTE: Double high waters occur at or near springs — on
other occasions there is a stand which lasts about 2
hours. Predictions are for the first HW where there are
two or for the middle of the stand. See 10.2.8.

SHELTER
Excellent with many marinas and boat yards. Anchoring
prohibited.
NAVIGATION
Waypoint Hamble Point S cardinal buoy, Q(6) + LFl 15s,
50°50'.12N 01°18'.57W, 168°/348° from/to front Ldg Lt,
0.48M. Unlit piles and buoys are a danger at night. NE
gales can lower depths up to 0.6m. River is extremely
crowded.
LIGHTS AND MARKS
Ldg Lts 345°. Front Oc(2) R 12s 4m 2M; No 6 pile Bn.
Rear, 820m from front, QR 12m; W mast on shore; vis
341°-349°. No 1 pile FlG 3s 3M; stbd-hand mark. No 2
pile Q(3) 10s 3M; E cardinal mark. No 3 pile Fl(2) G 5s;
stbd-hand mark. No 5 pile Fl(3) G 10s; stbd-hand mark.
Ldg Lts 026° on Warsash shore. Front QG; B&W
chequered pile Bn; Rear Iso G 6s. No 7 pile FlG 3s;
stbd-hand mark. No 8 pile FlR 3s; port-hand mark. No 9
pile Fl(2) G 5s; stbd-hand mark. No 10 pile Fl(2) R 5s;
port-hand mark. Above Warsash, jetties and pontoons etc
on the E side are marked by G Lts, and those on the W
side by R Lts.

HAMBLE *continued*

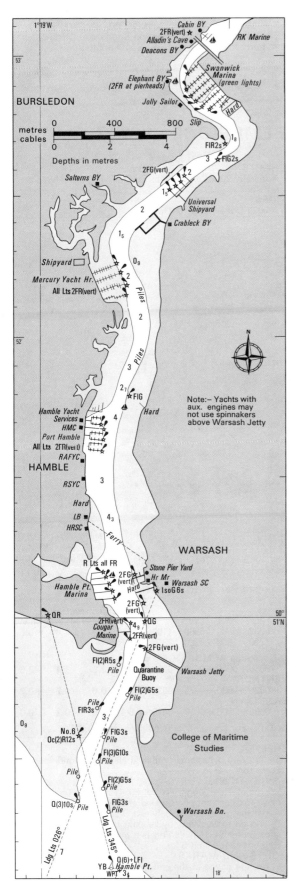

RADIO TELEPHONE
Call: *Hamble Harbour Radio* Ch 16 68 (Mon–Fri 0830-1700; Sat & Sun April–Oct 0900-1830 Nov–Mar 0900-1300). Marinas Ch **80**. See also Southampton 10.2.24.

TELEPHONE (0703)
Hr Mr Locks Heath 576387; CG & MRSC Lee-on-Solent 552100; ⌗ (0703) 229251; Southampton Weather Centre 228844; Marinecall 0898 500 457; Police 581111; Dr Locks Heath 573110.

FACILITIES
EC Wednesday; **Hamble Point Marina** (220 + 10 visitors) ☎ 452741, AC, Bar, BH (40 ton), C (8 ton), CH, D, Ⓔ, FW, Gas, Gaz, ME, Sh, V, YC, (Access H24); **Mercury Yacht Harbour** (364) ☎ 452741, AC, Bar, BH (12 ton), CH, D, Ⓔ, FW, Gas, Gaz, ME, P, Sh, SM, V, (Access H24); **Port Hamble Marina** (369) ☎ 452741, AC, Bar, BH (60 ton), C (7 ton), CH, D, Ⓔ, FW, Gas, Gaz, ME, P, Sh, SM, Slip, V, (Access H24); **Swanwick Marina** (350 + 50 visitors) ☎ Locks Heath 885000 (After 1700, Locks Heath 885262), AC, ACA, BH (60 ton), C (12 ton), CH, D, Ⓔ, FW, Gas, Gaz, ⌗, Ⓞ, ME, P, ✉, Sh, SM, V, (Access H24); **Aladdin's Cave** ☎ Bursledon 2182, CH; **BK Electro-Marine** ☎ Locks Heath 572170, Ⓔ; **Bursledon Riggers** ☎ Bursledon 4263 **Cabin BY** ☎ Bursledon 2516, AB, C (3 ton), Ⓔ, FW, Gas, M, ME, R, Sh, Slip; **Compass Point Chandlery** ☎ 452388, CH; **Cougar Quay** ☎ 453513, BH (18 ton), BY, C (16 ton); D, Ⓔ, FW, ⌗, ME, P, Sh, Slip, (Access HW∓4); **Crableck BY** ☎ Locks Heath 572570, Sh; **Deacons Boatyard** ☎ Bursledon 2253, C (10 ton), Ⓔ, ME, Sh, Slip (16 ton), SM; **Ditty Box** ☎ 453436, CH; **Eastlands Boatyard** ☎ Bursledon 3556, BY; **Elephant BY** ☎ Bursledon 3268, Ⓔ, ME, Sh, Slip; **Foulkes & Son** ☎ Bursledon 6349, C (10 ton), CH; **Greenham Marine** ☎ 455044, Ⓔ, El; **Hamble River BY** ☎ Locks Heath 572318, ME, Sh, Slip; **Hamble River SC** ☎ 452070; **Hamble Yacht Services** ☎ 454111, BY, BH (60 ton), C (5 ton), Ⓔ, ME, Sh, Slip (150 ton), SM; **Hudson Marine Electronics** ☎ 455129, Ⓔ; **Marine Power** ☎ Bursledon 3918, ME; **Marine Technology** ☎ 455743, El; **Piper Marine Services** ☎ 454563, (or call *Piper Fuel* Ch 37), D, P; **RAF YC** ☎ 452208, Bar, R, L; **R K Marine** ☎ Locks Heath 583572, ME; **Royal Southern YC** ☎ 453271; **Salterns Boatyard** ☎ Bursledon 3911, BY; **Sea Fever** ☎ Locks Heath 582804, CH, Gaz; **Seasure** ☎ Locks Heath 885330 CH; **The Solent Trading Co.** ☎ 454849, CH; **Stone Pier Yard** ☎ Locks Heath 885400, BY, C, D, FW, Sh, Slip; **Universal Shipyards** (110) ☎ Locks Heath 574272, ACA, BH (50 ton), BY, C, CH, Ⓔ, FW, M, ME, Sh; **Victoria Rampart** ☎ Locks Heath 885400, BH (25 ton), BY, C (12 ton), CH, D, Ⓔ, FW, ME, P, SM; **Warsash SC** ☎ Locks Heath 583575; **Warsash Nautical Bookshop** ☎ Locks Heath 572384, ACA; **Yachtmail** ☎ 455058, CH.

Divers
Andark ☎ Locks Heath 581755 (emergency/after hours ☎ Botley 786006); **Warsash Divers** ☎ 0860-627800.

Sailmakers
Alpha Sails ☎ 553623; **Bruce Banks** ☎ Locks Heath 582444; **Hamble Sailing Services** ☎ 455868; **Lucas** ☎ 452247; **Relling** ☎ Titchfield 46816; **Richardson Sails** ☎ Bursledon 3914; **Shore Sails** ☎ Locks Heath 589450; **Sobstad** ☎ 456205; **Ullman Sails** ☎ 454254; **W L Sails** ☎ 453109.

Hards at Warsash, Hamble and Swanwick. **Slips** at Warsash, Hamble, Bursledon and Lower Swanwick. ✉ (Hamble, Bursledon, Warsash and Lower Swanwick); Ⓑ (Hamble, Bursledon, Sarisbury Green, Swanwick, Warsash); ⇌ (Hamble and Bursledon); ✈ (Southampton). *'Hamble River Guide'* available from Hr Mr.

WOOTTON CREEK   10-2-26
Isle of Wight

CHARTS
Admiralty 2022, 394; Stanford 11; Imray C3, Y20; OS 196

TIDES
+0023 Dover; ML 2.8; Zone 0 (GMT)

Standard Port PORTSMOUTH (→)

Times				Height (metres)			
HW		LW		MHWS	MHWN	MLWN	MLWS
0000	0600	0500	1100	4.7	3.8	1.8	0.6
1200	1800	1700	2300				

Differences RYDE
−0010	+0010	−0005	−0010	−0.2	−0.1	0.0	+0.1

NOTE: Wootton Creek comes under the authority of the Queen's Harbour Master, Portsmouth but it is exercised through a private association, Wootton Creek Fairways Association. Sec. R. Perraton Tel. 882763. For special tidal information see 10.2.8

SHELTER
Good except when stormy winds in N or E. The creek dries at MLWS above ferry terminal. Anchoring in the fairway prohibited.

NAVIGATION
Waypoint Wootton N cardinal Bn, Q, 50°44'.47N 01°12'.08W, 043°/223° from/to ferry slip, 0.59M. Beware large Sealink ferries; ferries leave astern and turn at Wootton Bn. It is difficult to beat in on the ebb. Speed limit 5 kn.

LIGHTS AND MARKS
Entrance to creek due S of SE Ryde Middle buoy and 1¾ M W of Ryde Pier. Once in channel follow four beacons on stbd side. Keep in W sector of Lt at root of ferry pier Oc WRG 10s G221°-224°, W224°-225½°, R225½°-230½°. By ferry terminal, turn on leading marks on W shore (two marks, an upright and an inverted triangle, which together form a diamond when in line).

RADIO TELEPHONE
None.

TELEPHONE (0983)
Royal Victoria YC 882325; CG 872886; MRSC Lee-on-Solent 552100; Fairways Association 882763; ☷ (0703) 229251; Marinecall 0898 500 457; Police 528000; Dr 882424.

FACILITIES
EC Wootton Bridge — Wednesday, Wootton Village — Thursday; **Royal Victoria YC** ☎ 882325, Slip, M, FW, R, Bar; **Marine Installations** ☎ 883960, Slip, ME, El, Ⓔ, Sh; **Village** ✉ (Ryde, Wootton Bridge); Ⓑ (Ryde); ⛴ (ferry to Portsmouth); ✈ (Southampton).

BEMBRIDGE   10-2-27
Isle of Wight

CHARTS
Admiralty 2022, 2050, 2045; Stanford 11; Imray C3, C9; OS 196

TIDES
+0020 Dover; Zone 0 (GMT)

Standard Port PORTSMOUTH (→)

Times				Height (metres)			
HW		LW		MHWS	MHWN	MLWN	MLWS
0000	0600	0500	1100	4.7	3.8	1.8	0.6
1200	1800	1700	2300				

Differences BEMBRIDGE
−0010	+0005	+0020	0000	−1.6	−1.5	−1.4	−0.6

VENTNOR
−0025	−0030	−0025	−0030	−0.8	−0.6	−0.2	+0.2

SANDOWN
0000	+0005	+0010	+0025	−0.6	−0.5	−0.2	0.0

NOTE: For special tidal conditions, see 10.2.8

SHELTER
Good. Very occasional trouble in NNE gale conditions. Entry HW −3 to HW +2.

NAVIGATION
Waypoint Tide gauge, Fl.Y 2s, 50°42'.54N 01°05'.23W, close N of entrance to buoyed channel. The bar dries. Avoid the gravel banks between St. Helen's Fort, Nodes Pt and on to Seaview, by keeping to entry times above. Area round St. Helen's Fort is a prohibited anchorage. Harbour speed limit 6 kn.

LIGHTS AND MARKS
Lt on tide gauge at the entrance, Fl Y 2s 1M.

BEMBRIDGE continued

RADIO TELEPHONE
Bembridge Marina VHF Ch 16; **80.**
TELEPHONE (0983)
Hr Mr 872828; CG 872886; Berthing Master 874436; MRSC Lee-on-Solent 552100; ✆ (0703) 229251; Marinecall 0898 500 457; Police 528000; Dr 872614
FACILITIES
EC Thursday; **Bembridge Marina** (40 + 100 visitors) ☎ 874436, FW, ME, El, D, AC, ▣, V, R, Bar; Access HW − 3 to HW + 2; **F. Attrill & Sons** ☎ 872319, Slip, M, ME, El, Sh, CH; **Spinnaker Yacht Chandlery** ☎ 874324, CH, Gas; **Alan Coombes** ☎ 872296, Slip, M, FW, ME, D, El, Sh, CH; **St. Helen's Quay** P, D, FW, CH; **Harbour Engineering** ☎ 872306, D, FW, ME; **Bembridge Outboards** ☎ 872817, ME, Sh; **Bembridge BY** ☎ 872423, Slip, M, ME, Sh; **Stratton BY** ☎ 873185, D; **Bembridge SC** ☎ 872683; **Brading Haven YC** ☎ 872289, Bar, R, FW; Various other boatyards with limited facilities. **Town** P, D, CH, V, R, Bar. ✉ (Bembridge, St. Helens); Ⓑ (Bembridge); ⇌ (Brading); ✈ (Southampton).

PORTSMOUTH 10-2-28
Hampshire

CHARTS
Admiralty 2628, 2629, 2625, 2631, 394, 2050, 2045; Stanford 11; Imray C3, C9; OS 197
TIDES
+0023 Dover; ML 2.8; Zone 0 (GMT)
Standard Port PORTSMOUTH (→)

Times				Height (metres)			
HW		LW		MHWS	MHWN	MLWN	MLWS
0500	1000	0000	0600	4.7	3.8	1.8	0.6
1700	2200	1200	1800				
Differences LEE-ON-SOLENT							
−0005	+0005	−0015	−0010	−0.2	−0.1	+0.1	+0.2

Portsmouth is a Standard Port and tidal predictions for each day of the year are given below. See sections 10.2.8 and 10.2.9.

SHELTER
Excellent. This very large harbour affords shelter in some area for any wind. Navigational and shipping information available from Duty Harbour Controller (VHF Ch 11 13). Call *QHM*.
Good shelter in Camber, but this is a busy little commercial dock and often full. Also beware the Isle of Wight car ferry docking near the entrance.

Anchor in Portchester Lake near the Castle, clear of moorings. Otherwise pick up a vacant mooring in the area desired, land and consult local SC.
Old Hard and steps near NE corner of castle are public but piers are private Portchester SC landings.
Yachts fitted with engines must use them between Southsea War Memorial and the Ballast Buoy (2 ca N of Fort Blockhouse). Fishing or anchoring in fairways is forbidden. Yachts must keep 100m clear of submarines berthed in Haslar Creek. If over 20m in length, ask QHM's permission (VHF R/T Ch 11) or telephone for permission to enter, leave or move in harbour, especially in fog.
NAVIGATION
Waypoint Outer Spit S cardinal buoy, Q(6) + LFl 15s, 50°45'.55N 01°05'.41W, 185°/005° from/to Southsea Castle, 1.1M. Portsmouth is a major naval port and all comes under the authority of the Queen's Harbour Master. On approaching from E inshore, yachts may go through the gap in the submerged barrier. The gap is 1 M S of Lumps Fort and is marked by a pile on the N side and a dolphin (QR) on the S side.
Beware: very strong tides in Harbour mouth; Commercial shipping and ferries; Gosport ferry; HM Ships and submarines entering and leaving. (HM Ships hoist a Code pendant, ship's pendants and a pendant Zero).
A Small Boat Channel for craft under 20m in length exists at the entrance to Portsmouth Harbour. It lies to the West of (and parallel to) the main dredged channel, and runs from No 4 Bar Buoy (QR, off Clarence Pier) to the north end of Fort Blockhouse, extending about 50m off the latter. Yachts entering harbour by the Small Boat Channel must keep to the West of the line to the Ballast Buoy until North of same. Yachts entering on the Portsmouth side of the main dredged channel must keep well to starboard, clear of the main channel. All yachts leaving harbour must use the Small Boat Channel, as described above.
Yachts crossing the entrance may only do so to the N of Ballast Buoy or to the S of No 4 Bar Buoy. Dir Lt on dolphin S of Cold Harbour jetty, Dir WRG 2m 1M, Iso G 2s 322.5°-330°, Al WG 330°-332.5°, Iso W 2s 332.5°-335° (covering the main channel), Al WR 335°-337.5°, Iso R 2s 337.5°-345° (covering the small boat channel).
Haslar Creek; a reserved area, prohibited to yachts, exists in Haslar Creek near all submarines berthed at HMS Dolphin. Speed limit within the harbour 10 kn.
FIRING AREAS
Fraser Gunnery Range, Eastney, in use Monday to Friday, 0900-1600.
Details from Portsmouth 822351 ext 6420 or from Radio Solent (see 10.2.9).
Areas and sectors of circles centred on 50°47' N, 01°02' W
Area 1 200 yds 120°-200°
Area 2 6,000 yds 120°-155°
Area 3 18,000 yds 120°-155°
From 30 mins before firing, R Flag with International Numeral (1 for area 1, 2 for area 2, etc) displayed from:
Range Building
Hayling Island YC

PORTSMOUTH

MEAN SPRING AND NEAP CURVES

MEAN RANGES	
Springs	4·1m
Neaps	2·0m

Springs occur 2 days after New and Full Moon

PORTSMOUTH continued

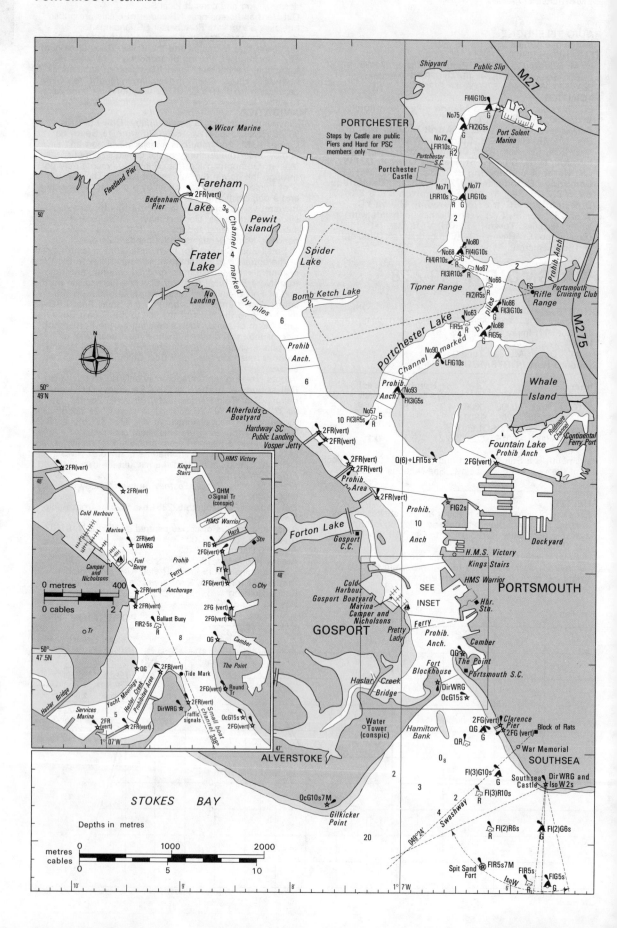

PORTSMOUTH *continued*

Admiralty Trial Station, W of Langstone Harbour
FS by Hr Mr's Office, Langstone
FS by Hr Mr's Office, Itchenor
FS on South Parade Pier
Tipner Firing Range as shown on chartlet; danger area extends 2,500 metres from firing range.
When firing in progress R flags by day or R Lt by night shown on Tipner Range FS. When firing is in progress, yachts should keep clear of the range or pass through the area as quickly as possible.

LIGHTS AND MARKS

St Jude's church spire and Southsea Castle Lt Ho in line at 003° lead between Outer Spit buoy and Horse Sand buoy. At night keep in the W sector (000°-003°) between the Al WG and Al WR sectors of the Dir Lt on Southsea Castle, which also shows an Iso W 2s Lt, vis 339°-066°. Swashway Channel at the NW of Elbow Spit and No 2 buoy, keep War Memorial and RH edge of block of flats in line at 049°24'.

At night the Oc W sector of the Dir Lt on Fort Blockhouse (west side of harbour entrance) shows 318.5°-321.5° between the Al WG and Al WR sectors. The following signals displayed at Central Signal Station, Fort Blockhouse, Gilkicker Point and sometimes in the HM Ship concerned, must be obeyed.

		SIGNAL	MEANING AND APPLICATION	HOISTED/ DISPLAYED BY
1.	DAY	Red Flag with white diagonal bar.	Large vessel underway in Main Channel or Harbour. Other vessels may be required by QHM to wait alongside or hold in a waiting position.	Central Signal Station, Blockhouse Signal Station, Gilkicker Signal Station.
	NIGHT	R G G		
2.	DAY	Red Flag with white diagonal bar over one black ball.	Large vessel leaving Harbour. Vessels entering Harbour will be kept clear by QHM. Vessels leaving harbour will be allowed to proceed clear of the large vessel.	Central Signal Station, Blockhouse Signal Station, Gilkicker Signal Station.
	NIGHT	W W G G		
3.	DAY	One Black Ball over Red Flag and white diagonal bar.	Large vessel entering habour. Vessels leaving harbour will be kept clear of QHM. Vessels entering harbour will be allowed to proceed clear of the large vessel.	Central Signal Station Blockhouse Signal Station
	NIGHT	G G W W		
4.	DAY	Large Black Pennant.	No merchant or private vessel to anchor in Man-of-War Anchorage at Spithead.	Gilkicker Signal Station.
	NIGHT	W G G		
5.	DAY	International Code Pennant. Superior to Pennant Zero.	Warship or RFA underway in Main Channel or Harbour warning signal to other ships. Specific instructions will be given by QHM.	Warship or RFA.
6.	DAY	International Code Pennant Superior to Pennant NINE.	Warship or RFA underway in Main Channel or Harbour warning signal to other ships. Specific instruction will be given by QHM.	Central Signal Station, Blockhouse Signal Station, Gilkicker Signal Station.

	NIGHT	G G G		
7.	DAY	Flag E	Submarine entering or leaving Haslar Creek. Warning signal to other ships. Specific instructions will be given by QHM but all vessels are less than 20m in length are to keep clear	Blockhouse Signal Station, Blockhouse Pierhead (NOTE: The Amber Light at Blockhouse Pierhead will flash when submarines are actually underway).
	NIGHT	R Y		
8.	DAY	International Code Pennant Superior to Flag A.	Have divers down.	Ships or boats employing Divers.
	NIGHT	RR		

Fog Routine. When fog routine comes into force it is broadcast on Ch 11 13 73. Flags will be hoisted as in 1. above. Yacht traffic may continue at the skipper's discretion but must proceed with great caution.

RADIO TELEPHONE

Queens Harbour Master (call: *QHM*) VHF Ch 11 (commercial vessels & yachts), Ch 13 (RN vessels) (H24). Fort Gilkicker (call *Gilkicker*) Ch 16 (H24). Call: *Portsmouth Harbour Radio* (Commercial Port Manager) Ch **11** (H24). Camper and Nicholson Marina Call: *Camper Base* Ch **80** (office hours), Fareham Yacht Harbour Ch **80** (summer 0900-1800, winter Sun 0900-1300 LT).

TELEPHONE (0705)

QHM 822351 Ex 23694; Commercial Port Manager 820436; **Camber Berthing Offices** ☎ 834764 ✚ (0703) 229251; MRSC Lee-on-Solent 552100; Marinecall 0898 500 457; Weather Centre (0703) 228844; Police 321111; Dr Gosport 80922; Fareham Health Centre Fareham 282911; Ⓗ 822331

FACILITIES

PORTSMOUTH EC Wednesday (Southsea Saturday)
Port Solent (900) ☎ 210765, P, D, FW, ME, El, Ⓔ, Sh, BH (30 ton), CH, V, AC, R, Bar, Gas, Gaz, ◎Access H24 via lock (43m × 12.5m); **Vosper Thornycroft** ☎ 379481, FW, ME, El, Ⓔ, Sh; **W G Lucas** ☎ 826629, SM; **Tudor S C** ☎ 662002, Slip, M, FW, Bar; **Royal Albert YC** ☎ 825924, M, Bar; **Ron Hale** ☎ 732985, ME, CH; **Nautech** ☎ 693611, El, Ⓔ; **Chris Hornsey** ☎ 734728, CH; **Gieves & Hawkes** ☎ 821351, ACA; Harbour Moorings ☎ 832484 **Town** ✉, Ⓑ, ⇌, ✈ (Southampton). Ferries to Continent and IoW.
GOSPORT EC Wednesday **Camper & Nicholson Marina** (350, some visitors) ☎ 524811, P, D, FW, ME, El, Sh, BH (150, 40 ton), CH, V, R, AC, Bar, Gas, Gaz, SM, ◎; **W G Lucas** ☎ 504434, CH; **Hardway SC** ☎ 581875, Slip, M, L, FW, C (mast stepping only), AB; **Hardway Marine** ☎ 580420, P, D, ACA, CH; **Solent Marine Services** ☎ 584622, El, Ⓔ, CH; **B & H Sails** ☎ 510204, CH; **Crewsaver** ☎ 528621, CH; **Blake** ☎ 523411, CH; **Camper & Nicholson Yard** ☎ 580221, BY, ME, El, Sh, Ⓔ; **Clarence Marina** ☎ 511555 ME, El, Ⓔ, Sh (also at Port Solent); **R. Arthur** ☎ 526522 CH; **Upper Deck Chandlery** ☎ 504434 CH; **Allday Aluminium** ☎ 587741, Sh; **Barter & Hugget** ☎ 589431, Ⓔ, CH, SM; **Gosport BY** ☎ 586216, Slip, ME, El, Sh, C; **Town** ✉; Ⓑ; ⇌ (Portsmouth); ✈ (Southampton)
Note:— Approval has been given to build a marina at the entrance to Haslar Creek.
FAREHAM EC Wednesday **Fareham Yacht Harbour** ☎ Fareham 232854, Slip, D, FW, ME, El, Ⓔ, Sh, V, Bar, CH; (Access HW∓3); **Ladyline** ☎ Fareham 234297, M, Sh, CH; **Hamper Marine** ☎ Fareham 280203, Sh; **M B Marine Sales** ☎ Fareham 234277, ME, CH; **Wicor Marine** (200) ☎ Fareham 237112, Slip, M, D, ME, Sh, CH, AC, BH (10 ton), C (7 ton), FW, El, Ⓔ, Gas, Gaz; **Portsmouth Marine Engineering** ☎ Fareham 232854, Slip, ME, El, Ⓔ, Sh, D, FW, Gas, AC, C (10 ton), CH; **North Sails (UK)** ☎ Fareham 231525, SM; **Sobstad Sailmakers (UK)** ☎ Fareham 233242, SM; **Portchester SC** ☎ 376375 **Town** ✉; Ⓑ; ⇌; ✈ (Southampton).

ENGLAND, SOUTH COAST - PORTSMOUTH

LAT 50°48'N   LONG 1°07'W

TIMES AND HEIGHTS OF HIGH AND LOW WATERS

YEAR **1991**

TIME ZONE UT(GMT)
For Summer Time add ONE hour in non-shaded areas

JANUARY

Day	TIME	m	TIME	m	TIME	m	TIME	m		Day	TIME	m	TIME	m	TIME	m	TIME	m
1 TU	0424	1.0	1120	4.8	1648	0.7				**16** W	0451	1.4	1143	4.4	1706	1.1		
2 W	0007	4.8	0512	0.9	1210	4.8	1735	0.6		**17** TH	0019	4.5	0523	1.2	1217	4.5	1737	0.9
3 TH	0101	4.9	0559	0.9	1258	4.8	1821	0.7		**18** F	0051	4.5	0555	1.1	1247	4.5	1810	0.8
4 F	0152	4.8	0646	1.0	1347	4.7	1907	0.8		**19** SA	0118	4.5	0629	1.0	1317	4.5	1845	0.7
5 SA	0241	4.7	0733	1.1	1436	4.5	1954	1.0		**20** SU	0147	4.5	0706	0.9	1351	4.4	1923	0.7
6 SU	0332	4.6	0821	1.3	1530	4.3	2042	1.2		**21** M	0221	4.5	0746	0.9	1430	4.3	2003	0.8
7 M ☾	0424	4.4	0913	1.5	1631	4.1	2135	1.5		**22** TU	0300	4.4	0828	1.0	1514	4.2	2048	0.9
8 TU	0517	4.2	1012	1.7	1736	3.9	2237	1.7		**23** W ☽	0347	4.3	0915	1.2	1606	4.0	2137	1.2
9 W	0612	4.1	1128	1.8	1838	3.8	2358	1.9		**24** TH	0445	4.1	1011	1.4	1716	3.9	2239	1.1
10 TH	0705	4.0	1248	1.8	1937	3.8				**25** F	0601	4.0	1126	1.6	1843	3.8		
11 F	0112	1.9	0758	4.0	1348	1.7	2033	3.8		**26** SA	0008	1.7	0715	4.0	1259	1.6	1957	3.9
12 SA	0208	1.8	0849	4.1	1437	1.6	2127	4.0		**27** SU	0134	1.6	0821	4.1	1408	1.4	2104	4.1
13 SU	0256	1.7	0938	4.1	1521	1.5	2217	4.1		**28** M	0235	1.4	0922	4.2	1502	1.1	2211	4.3
14 M	0339	1.6	1024	4.2	1600	1.3	2303	4.3		**29** TU	0326	1.2	1021	4.4	1550	0.9	2322	4.5
15 TU ●	0417	1.5	1115	4.3	1635	1.2	2344	4.4		**30** W ○	0414	1.0	1115	4.6	1636	0.6		
										31 TH	0025	4.7	0458	0.8	1205	4.7	1719	0.5

FEBRUARY

Day	TIME	m	TIME	m	TIME	m	TIME	m		Day	TIME	m	TIME	m	TIME	m	TIME	m
1 F	0110	4.8	0542	0.7	1248	4.7	1802	0.5		**16** SA	0030	4.5	0528	0.8	1224	4.5	1744	0.6
2 SA	0141	4.8	0625	0.7	1328	4.7	1845	0.6		**17** SU	0052	4.6	0603	0.7	1254	4.5	1819	0.5
3 SU	0211	4.7	0707	0.8	1408	4.5	1927	0.8		**18** M	0119	4.6	0640	0.6	1328	4.5	1857	0.4
4 M	0246	4.6	0750	1.0	1451	4.3	2009	1.0		**19** TU	0153	4.5	0719	0.6	1406	4.4	1937	0.5
5 TU	0326	4.3	0833	1.3	1537	4.1	2052	1.3		**20** W	0232	4.4	0800	0.7	1449	4.3	2020	0.8
6 W ☽	0413	4.1	0919	1.5	1634	3.9	2140	1.7		**21** TH ☾	0317	4.2	0845	1.0	1541	4.0	2107	1.1
7 TH	0510	3.9	1017	1.8	1743	3.7	2255	2.0		**22** F	0415	4.0	0936	1.3	1658	3.8	2206	1.6
8 F	0611	3.7	1220	1.9	1849	3.6				**23** SA	0541	3.8	1050	1.7	1833	3.7	2358	1.9
9 SA	0054	2.0	0711	3.7	1329	1.8	1951	3.6		**24** SU	0702	3.8	1254	1.7	1947	3.8		
10 SU	0152	1.9	0810	3.7	1419	1.7	2052	3.7		**25** M	0131	1.7	0809	3.9	1400	1.4	2057	4.0
11 M	0239	1.8	0906	3.8	1501	1.5	2151	3.9		**26** TU	0226	1.5	0914	4.1	1449	1.1	2223	4.3
12 TU	0319	1.6	0959	4.0	1538	1.3	2245	4.1		**27** W	0313	1.2	1021	4.3	1534	0.9	2338	4.5
13 W	0354	1.4	1047	4.1	1610	1.1	2329	4.3		**28** TH ○	0357	0.9	1135	4.5	1617	0.7		
14 TH ●	0426	1.2	1125	4.3	1640	0.9												
15 F	0004	4.4	0456	1.0	1157	4.4	1710	0.7										

MARCH

Day	TIME	m	TIME	m	TIME	m	TIME	m		Day	TIME	m	TIME	m	TIME	m	TIME	m
1 F	0023	4.7	0438	0.7	1213	4.6	1658	0.5		**16** SA ●	0425	0.8	1127	4.4	1640	0.6	2355	4.5
2 SA	0056	4.8	0519	0.6	1236	4.7	1738	0.5		**17** SU	0459	0.6	1156	4.5	1716	0.4		
3 SU	0112	4.8	0559	0.6	1306	4.6	1818	0.6		**18** M	0020	4.6	0535	0.4	1230	4.6	1753	0.4
4 M	0134	4.7	0639	0.7	1340	4.5	1857	0.7		**19** TU	0052	4.6	0614	0.4	1306	4.6	1833	0.4
5 TU	0204	4.5	0717	0.9	1417	4.4	1936	1.0		**20** W	0129	4.6	0654	0.4	1347	4.5	1914	0.5
6 W	0239	4.3	0756	1.1	1456	4.1	2014	1.3		**21** TH	0210	4.4	0736	0.6	1434	4.3	1958	0.9
7 TH	0318	4.1	0834	1.4	1542	3.9	2053	1.6		**22** F	0258	4.2	0822	0.9	1532	4.1	2047	1.3
8 F	0405	3.8	0916	1.7	1644	3.6	2141	2.0		**23** SA ☾	0403	3.9	0915	1.4	1703	3.9	2152	1.7
9 SA	0510	3.6	1141	2.0	1759	3.5				**24** SU	0534	3.8	1040	1.7	1826	3.8		
10 SU	0029	2.1	0621	3.5	1258	1.9	1906	3.5		**25** M	0010	1.9	0649	3.7	1245	1.7	1936	3.9
11 M	0125	2.0	0725	3.5	1347	1.8	2010	3.6		**26** TU	0120	1.7	0757	3.8	1342	1.4	2049	4.1
12 TU	0210	1.8	0826	3.6	1428	1.6	2112	3.8		**27** W	0208	1.4	0908	4.0	1428	1.2	2220	4.3
13 W	0247	1.6	0924	3.8	1503	1.3	2212	4.0		**28** TH	0252	1.1	1039	4.3	1512	1.0	2316	4.6
14 TH	0321	1.3	1015	4.0	1535	1.1	2259	4.2		**29** F	0334	1.0	1130	4.5	1553	0.8	2355	4.7
15 F ○	0352	1.1	1056	4.2	1607	0.9	2333	4.4		**30** SA	0414	0.8	1200	4.6	1634	0.7		
										31 SU	0018	4.7	0454	0.7	1216	4.6	1712	0.7

APRIL

Day	TIME	m	TIME	m	TIME	m	TIME	m		Day	TIME	m	TIME	m	TIME	m	TIME	m
1 M	0034	4.7	0533	0.7	1242	4.6	1751	0.7		**16** TU	0510	0.4	1208	4.6	1730	0.4		
2 TU	0100	4.6	0611	0.8	1314	4.5	1829	0.9		**17** W	0028	4.7	0551	0.4	1251	4.6	1812	0.5
3 W	0131	4.5	0647	0.9	1349	4.4	1905	1.1		**18** TH	0110	4.6	0634	0.5	1337	4.5	1857	0.7
4 TH	0204	4.3	0723	1.1	1426	4.2	1942	1.4		**19** F	0157	4.5	0719	0.7	1431	4.4	1944	1.0
5 F	0240	4.1	0759	1.4	1508	4.0	2019	1.6		**20** SA	0251	4.2	0808	1.0	1542	4.2	2039	1.4
6 SA	0320	3.9	0836	1.6	1600	3.8	2102	1.9		**21** SU ☽	0403	4.0	0908	1.4	1704	4.1	2155	1.8
7 SU ☾	0414	3.7	0925	1.9	1709	3.6	2348	2.1		**22** M	0524	3.9	1042	1.7	1815	4.0	2352	1.8
8 M	0526	3.5	1211	1.9	1818	3.6				**23** TU	0635	3.8	1218	1.6	1921	4.1		
9 TU	0045	2.0	0635	3.5	1303	1.8	1920	3.6		**24** W	0054	1.6	0742	3.9	1315	1.4	2030	4.2
10 W	0129	1.8	0737	3.6	1343	1.6	2020	3.8		**25** TH	0143	1.4	0854	4.1	1402	1.3	2140	4.4
11 TH	0206	1.6	0835	3.7	1420	1.4	2115	4.0		**26** F	0227	1.2	1005	4.3	1445	1.1	2233	4.5
12 F	0241	1.3	0927	4.0	1456	1.1	2202	4.2		**27** SA	0309	1.1	1053	4.4	1528	1.0	2308	4.6
13 SA	0316	1.0	1012	4.2	1532	0.9	2240	4.4		**28** SU ○	0350	0.9	1124	4.5	1608	0.9	2333	4.6
14 SU ●	0353	0.8	1051	4.4	1610	0.6	2314	4.6		**29** M	0430	0.9	1150	4.5	1648	0.9		
15 M	0431	0.5	1129	4.5	1649	0.5	2350	4.7		**30** TU	0000	4.6	0508	0.9	1220	4.5	1727	1.0

Chart Datum: 3.22 metres below Ordnance Datum (Newlyn)

2

ENGLAND, SOUTH COAST - PORTSMOUTH

LAT 50°48'N   LONG 1°07'W

TIMES AND HEIGHTS OF HIGH AND LOW WATERS   YEAR **1991**

TIME ZONE UT(GMT)
For Summer Time add ONE hour in non-shaded areas

MAY

Day	Time	m	Time	m	Time	m	Time	m
1 W	0031	4.6	0546	0.9	1253	4.5	1805	1.1
2 TH	0104	4.5	0623	1.0	1329	4.4	1842	1.3
3 F	0138	4.3	0659	1.2	1406	4.3	1919	1.4
4 SA	0213	4.2	0735	1.3	1445	4.1	1958	1.6
5 SU	0252	4.0	0814	1.5	1531	4.0	2044	1.8
6 M	0338	3.8	0903	1.7	1626	3.9	2204	2.0
7 TU	0436	3.7	1032	1.8	1728	3.8	(2343	1.9
8 W	0543	3.6	1158	1.7	1829	3.8		
9 TH	0035	1.8	0646	3.7	1250	1.6	1926	3.9
10 F	0119	1.5	0745	3.8	1334	1.4	2020	4.1
11 SA	0201	1.3	0839	4.0	1417	1.2	2110	4.3
12 SU	0242	1.0	0931	4.2	1500	0.9	2156	4.4
13 M	0324	0.8	1019	4.4	1543	0.8	2241	4.6
14 TU	0406	0.6	1106	4.5	1627	0.6	● 2325	4.7
15 W	0450	0.5	1153	4.6	1712	0.6		
16 TH	0010	4.7	0534	0.5	1243	4.7	1757	0.7
17 F	0058	4.6	0620	0.6	1336	4.6	1846	0.9
18 SA	0149	4.5	0709	0.8	1437	4.5	1937	1.1
19 SU	0247	4.3	0802	1.0	1547	4.4	2035	1.4
20 M	0356	4.2	0902	1.3	1655	4.3	) 2146	1.6
21 TU	0509	4.0	1018	1.5	1758	4.3	2312	1.7
22 W	0617	4.0	1139	1.5	1900	4.3		
23 TH	0021	1.6	0721	4.0	1242	1.5	1959	4.3
24 F	0114	1.5	0823	4.1	1333	1.4	2054	4.4
25 SA	0201	1.4	0921	4.2	1420	1.3	2143	4.4
26 SU	0246	1.2	1010	4.3	1505	1.3	2223	4.5
27 M	0329	1.1	1050	4.3	1547	1.2	2258	4.5
28 TU	0410	1.1	1125	4.4	1629	1.2	O 2332	4.5
29 W	0450	1.0	1201	4.4	1709	1.2		
30 TH	0007	4.5	0528	1.0	1237	4.4	1747	1.3
31 F	0042	4.4	0605	1.1	1312	4.4	1825	1.3

JUNE

Day	Time	m	Time	m	Time	m	Time	m
1 SA	0117	4.3	0641	1.1	1349	4.3	1902	1.4
2 SU	0152	4.2	0718	1.2	1426	4.2	1941	1.5
3 M	0228	4.1	0756	1.3	1505	4.2	2024	1.6
4 TU	0309	4.0	0840	1.4	1550	4.1	2114	1.7
5 W	0356	3.9	0932	1.5	1641	4.0	(2216	1.7
6 TH	0453	3.8	1036	1.5	1739	4.0	2324	1.7
7 F	0557	3.8	1145	1.5	1839	4.0		
8 SA	0027	1.5	0701	3.8	1247	1.4	1936	4.1
9 SU	0122	1.4	0802	3.9	1342	1.3	2032	4.3
10 M	0212	1.1	0900	4.1	1433	1.1	2125	4.4
11 TU	0301	0.9	0957	4.3	1523	1.0	2217	4.5
12 W	0348	0.7	1051	4.5	1611	0.8	● 2307	4.7
13 TH	0436	0.6	1145	4.6	1659	0.8	2357	4.7
14 F	0523	0.5	1240	4.7	1748	0.8		
15 SA	0048	4.7	0611	0.6	1337	4.7	1836	0.9
16 SU	0140	4.6	0700	0.7	1437	4.7	1927	1.0
17 M	0236	4.5	0750	0.9	1538	4.6	2020	1.2
18 TU	0338	4.3	0844	1.1	1638	4.5	2118	1.4
19 W	0447	4.2	0943	1.3	1734	4.4	) 2224	1.6
20 TH	0551	4.1	1051	1.5	1829	4.3	2338	1.6
21 F	0652	4.0	1204	1.6	1923	4.2		
22 SA	0045	1.6	0749	4.0	1307	1.6	2014	4.2
23 SU	0141	1.6	0844	4.0	1400	1.6	2102	4.2
24 M	0230	1.4	0935	4.1	1448	1.5	2148	4.3
25 TU	0315	1.3	1022	4.2	1533	1.4	2230	4.3
26 W	0357	1.2	1104	4.3	1616	1.4	2309	4.4
27 TH	0437	1.1	1144	4.3	1655	1.3	O 2347	4.4
28 F	0515	1.1	1221	4.4	1733	1.3		
29 SA	0022	4.4	0549	1.0	1257	4.4	1807	1.3
30 SU	0057	4.4	0622	1.0	1330	4.4	1841	1.3

JULY

Day	Time	m	Time	m	Time	m	Time	m
1 M	0129	4.3	0656	1.0	1402	4.4	1917	1.3
2 TU	0203	4.3	0732	1.0	1436	4.3	1955	1.3
3 W	0240	4.2	0811	1.0	1513	4.3	2037	1.3
4 TH	0321	4.1	0855	1.1	1558	4.2	2125	1.4
5 F	0411	4.0	0945	1.3	1652	4.1	(2221	1.5
6 SA	0512	3.9	1046	1.4	1756	4.0	2330	1.5
7 SU	0625	3.8	1200	1.5	1903	4.1		
8 M	0046	1.4	0736	3.9	1315	1.5	2005	4.1
9 TU	0151	1.3	0841	4.0	1416	1.3	2104	4.3
10 W	0246	1.1	0943	4.2	1510	1.1	2200	4.5
11 TH	0337	0.8	1042	4.4	1601	1.0	● 2253	4.6
12 F	0425	0.6	1140	4.6	1649	0.8	2345	4.7
13 SA	0512	0.5	1237	4.8	1736	0.7		
14 SU	0035	4.7	0558	0.5	1333	4.8	1821	0.8
15 M	0125	4.7	0643	0.6	1424	4.8	1908	0.9
16 TU	0215	4.6	0729	0.7	1515	4.7	1955	1.0
17 W	0309	4.4	0816	0.9	1606	4.5	2044	1.3
18 TH	0410	4.2	0906	1.2	1658	4.3	) 2138	1.5
19 F	0515	4.0	1003	1.5	1750	4.2	2246	1.7
20 SA	0615	3.9	1120	1.7	1843	4.0		
21 SU	0020	1.8	0713	3.8	1249	1.8	1935	4.0
22 M	0128	1.7	0809	3.8	1349	1.8	2027	4.0
23 TU	0219	1.6	0906	3.9	1438	1.7	2117	4.1
24 W	0303	1.4	0957	4.0	1522	1.6	2205	4.2
25 TH	0344	1.3	1045	4.2	1601	1.4	2248	4.3
26 F	0421	1.2	1127	4.3	1638	1.3	O 2327	4.3
27 SA	0454	1.0	1205	4.4	1711	1.2		
28 SU	0002	4.4	0525	0.9	1238	4.5	1742	1.1
29 M	0034	4.4	0556	0.9	1306	4.5	1814	1.0
30 TU	0104	4.4	0628	0.8	1333	4.5	1848	1.0
31 W	0135	4.4	0703	0.7	1403	4.4	1924	0.9

AUGUST

Day	Time	m	Time	m	Time	m	Time	m
1 TH	0210	4.3	0741	0.8	1438	4.4	2004	1.0
2 F	0250	4.2	0822	0.9	1520	4.3	2047	1.1
3 SA	0336	4.1	0908	1.1	1611	4.1	(2137	1.3
4 SU	0437	3.9	1002	1.4	1720	4.0	2241	1.6
5 M	0603	3.8	1120	1.7	1841	3.9		
6 TU	0020	1.7	0723	3.8	1303	1.7	1949	4.0
7 W	0141	1.5	0830	4.0	1409	1.5	2050	4.2
8 TH	0237	1.2	0933	4.2	1501	1.2	2147	4.4
9 F	0325	0.9	1035	4.5	1549	1.0	2241	4.6
10 SA	0411	0.6	1139	4.7	1634	0.8	● 2332	4.7
11 SU	0455	0.5	1236	4.9	1717	0.7		
12 M	0019	4.8	0538	0.4	1316	4.9	1800	0.6
13 TU	0103	4.8	0620	0.5	1350	4.8	1842	0.7
14 W	0146	4.7	0703	0.6	1427	4.7	1925	0.9
15 TH	0231	4.5	0745	0.8	1510	4.5	2009	1.2
16 F	0321	4.2	0829	1.3	1600	4.2	2055	1.5
17 SA	0423	4.0	0917	1.6	1658	4.0	) 2150	1.8
18 SU	0531	3.8	1026	2.0	1757	3.8	(2137	1.3
19 M	0001	2.0	0634	3.7	1239	2.1	1855	3.8
20 TU	0112	1.9	0734	3.7	1335	1.9	1952	3.8
21 W	0201	1.7	0833	3.8	1421	1.8	2047	3.9
22 TH	0243	1.5	0930	3.9	1502	1.6	2139	4.0
23 F	0321	1.4	1023	4.1	1538	1.4	2226	4.2
24 SA	0355	1.2	1107	4.3	1611	1.3	2306	4.3
25 SU	0425	1.0	1143	4.5	1641	1.1	O 2339	4.4
26 M	0455	0.9	1211	4.5	1712	1.0		
27 TU	0006	4.5	0526	0.7	1234	4.6	1743	0.9
28 W	0035	4.5	0559	0.6	1259	4.6	1818	0.7
29 TH	0106	4.5	0635	0.6	1330	4.6	1855	0.7
30 F	0142	4.5	0713	0.7	1406	4.5	1935	0.8
31 SA	0223	4.3	0754	0.9	1449	4.3	2017	1.0

Chart Datum: 3.22 metres below Ordnance Datum (Newlyn)

ENGLAND, SOUTH COAST - PORTSMOUTH

LAT 50°48′N   LONG 1°07′W

TIMES AND HEIGHTS OF HIGH AND LOW WATERS

YEAR 1991

TIME ZONE UT(GMT)
For Summer Time add ONE hour in non-shaded areas

SEPTEMBER

Day	TIME	m	TIME	m	Day	TIME	m	TIME	m
1 SU ☾	0311 / 0839 / 1541 / 2105	4.1 / 1.2 / 4.1 / 1.3			16 M	0439 / 0933 / 1702 / 2323	3.8 / 2.1 / 3.8 / 2.1		
2 M	0416 / 0932 / 1658 / 2207	3.9 / 1.6 / 3.9 / 1.7			17 TU	0550 / 1109 / 1810	3.7 / 2.2 / 3.7		
3 TU	0558 / 1058 / 1828	3.8 / 2.0 / 3.9			18 W	0042 / 0654 / 1310 / 1912	2.0 / 3.7 / 2.1 / 3.7		
4 W	0015 / 0714 / 1304 / 1936	1.8 / 3.9 / 1.9 / 4.0			19 TH	0131 / 0755 / 1354 / 2010	1.9 / 3.8 / 1.9 / 3.8		
5 TH	0133 / 0821 / 1400 / 2038	1.6 / 4.1 / 1.6 / 4.2			20 F	0212 / 0854 / 1433 / 2106	1.7 / 4.0 / 1.7 / 4.0		
6 F	0223 / 0926 / 1447 / 2137	1.2 / 4.4 / 1.3 / 4.4			21 SA	0248 / 0949 / 1507 / 2155	1.5 / 4.2 / 1.5 / 4.2		
7 SA	0308 / 1036 / 1531 / 2232	0.9 / 4.6 / 1.0 / 4.6			22 SU	0320 / 1034 / 1538 / 2236	1.3 / 4.4 / 1.3 / 4.4		
8 SU ●	0351 / 1138 / 1613 / 2321	0.7 / 4.8 / 0.8 / 4.8			23 M ○	0351 / 1108 / 1608 / 2308	1.1 / 4.6 / 1.0 / 4.5		
9 M	0433 / 1214 / 1655	0.5 / 4.9 / 0.6			24 TU	0422 / 1133 / 1640 / 2336	0.9 / 4.7 / 0.9 / 4.6		
10 TU	0001 / 0514 / 1238 / 1735	4.9 / 0.5 / 4.9 / 0.6			25 W	0456 / 1158 / 1715	0.7 / 4.7 / 0.7		
11 W	0039 / 0554 / 1308 / 1815	4.8 / 0.6 / 4.9 / 0.7			26 TH	0007 / 0531 / 1227 / 1751	4.7 / 0.6 / 4.7 / 0.6		
12 TH	0117 / 0635 / 1342 / 1855	4.7 / 0.8 / 4.7 / 0.9			27 F	0042 / 0609 / 1302 / 1829	4.7 / 0.6 / 4.7 / 0.6		
13 F	0157 / 0715 / 1420 / 1936	4.5 / 1.0 / 4.5 / 1.2			28 SA	0121 / 0649 / 1342 / 1910	4.6 / 0.8 / 4.6 / 0.8		
14 SA	0240 / 0755 / 1502 / 2017	4.3 / 1.4 / 4.2 / 1.5			29 SU	0205 / 0732 / 1427 / 1955	4.4 / 1.0 / 4.4 / 1.1		
15 SU ☽	0331 / 0838 / 1605 / 2102	4.0 / 1.8 / 4.0 / 1.9			30 M	0258 / 0819 / 1524 / 2045	4.2 / 1.4 / 4.1 / 1.4		

OCTOBER

Day	TIME	m	Day	TIME	m
1 TU ☾	0420 / 0917 / 1652 / 2153	4.0 / 1.8 / 3.9 / 1.8	16 W	0501 / 1130 / 1717 / 2355	3.8 / 2.3 / 3.7 / 2.1
2 W	0555 / 1109 / 1817	4.0 / 2.1 / 3.9	17 TH	0608 / 1230 / 1824	3.8 / 2.2 / 3.7
3 TH	0007 / 0704 / 1252 / 1924	1.9 / 4.1 / 1.9 / 4.0	18 F	0048 / 0709 / 1316 / 1925	2.0 / 3.9 / 2.0 / 3.8
4 F	0114 / 0810 / 1342 / 2028	1.6 / 4.3 / 1.6 / 4.2	19 SA	0131 / 0807 / 1355 / 2022	1.8 / 4.1 / 1.8 / 3.9
5 SA	0202 / 0917 / 1427 / 2130	1.3 / 4.5 / 1.3 / 4.5	20 SU	0207 / 0900 / 1429 / 2113	1.6 / 4.3 / 1.5 / 4.2
6 SU	0246 / 1022 / 1509 / 2228	1.1 / 4.8 / 1.0 / 4.7	21 M	0241 / 0945 / 1502 / 2156	1.4 / 4.5 / 1.3 / 4.4
7 M ●	0328 / 1108 / 1550 / 2309	0.9 / 4.9 / 0.9 / 4.8	22 TU	0315 / 1021 / 1536 / 2233	1.1 / 4.6 / 1.0 / 4.5
8 TU	0409 / 1135 / 1631 / 2342	0.8 / 5.0 / 0.8 / 4.9	23 W ○	0351 / 1053 / 1611 / 2308	0.9 / 4.8 / 0.8 / 4.7
9 W	0450 / 1202 / 1711	0.7 / 5.0 / 0.7	24 TH	0428 / 1126 / 1649 / 2344	0.8 / 4.8 / 0.7 / 4.8
10 TH	0016 / 0529 / 1234 / 1750	4.9 / 0.8 / 4.9 / 0.8	25 F	0508 / 1202 / 1729	0.7 / 4.9 / 0.6
11 F	0052 / 0608 / 1308 / 1828	4.7 / 1.0 / 4.7 / 1.0	26 SA	0024 / 0548 / 1242 / 1810	4.8 / 0.8 / 4.8 / 0.7
12 SA	0129 / 0648 / 1344 / 1907	4.6 / 1.3 / 4.5 / 1.3	27 SU	0108 / 0632 / 1326 / 1854	4.7 / 0.9 / 4.7 / 0.8
13 SU	0210 / 0727 / 1423 / 1946	4.4 / 1.5 / 4.3 / 1.5	28 M	0158 / 0718 / 1416 / 1941	4.6 / 1.2 / 4.5 / 1.1
14 M	0255 / 0808 / 1507 / 2028	4.2 / 1.9 / 4.0 / 1.8	29 TU ☽	0300 / 0810 / 1519 / 2036	4.4 / 1.5 / 4.2 / 1.4
15 TU ☽	0352 / 0859 / 1605 / 2130	4.0 / 2.2 / 3.8 / 2.1	30 W ☾	0427 / 0914 / 1644 / 2149	4.3 / 1.9 / 4.1 / 1.7
			31 TH	0544 / 1056 / 1803 / 2335	4.3 / 2.0 / 4.1 / 1.8

NOVEMBER

Day	TIME	m	Day	TIME	m
1 F	0651 / 1224 / 1911	4.3 / 1.9 / 4.2	16 SA	0616 / 1223 / 1833	4.0 / 2.0 / 3.8
2 SA	0044 / 0754 / 1317 / 2016	1.6 / 4.5 / 1.6 / 4.3	17 SU	0034 / 0713 / 1307 / 1932	1.9 / 4.1 / 1.8 / 3.9
3 SU	0136 / 0856 / 1403 / 2119	1.4 / 4.7 / 1.4 / 4.5	18 M	0119 / 0806 / 1347 / 2027	1.7 / 4.2 / 1.6 / 4.1
4 M	0221 / 0950 / 1446 / 2212	1.3 / 4.8 / 1.2 / 4.7	19 TU	0201 / 0855 / 1426 / 2116	1.5 / 4.4 / 1.4 / 4.3
5 TU	0305 / 1031 / 1528 / 2251	1.1 / 4.9 / 1.0 / 4.8	20 W	0242 / 0939 / 1506 / 2202	1.3 / 4.6 / 1.1 / 4.5
6 W ●	0347 / 1103 / 1609 / 2324	1.1 / 4.9 / 1.0 / 4.8	21 TH ○	0324 / 1020 / 1547 / 2246	1.1 / 4.7 / 0.9 / 4.6
7 TH	0428 / 1134 / 1649 / 2357	1.1 / 4.9 / 0.9 / 4.8	22 F	0406 / 1102 / 1629 / 2330	0.9 / 4.8 / 0.7 / 4.8
8 F	0508 / 1207 / 1729	1.1 / 4.8 / 1.0	23 SA	0450 / 1144 / 1712	0.9 / 4.9 / 0.6
9 SA	0032 / 0548 / 1242 / 1808	4.7 / 1.2 / 4.7 / 1.1	24 SU	0016 / 0534 / 1229 / 1757	4.8 / 0.9 / 4.8 / 0.7
10 SU	0110 / 0627 / 1318 / 1846	4.6 / 1.4 / 4.6 / 1.3	25 M	0105 / 0621 / 1317 / 1844	4.8 / 1.0 / 4.7 / 0.8
11 M	0149 / 0707 / 1356 / 1925	4.5 / 1.6 / 4.4 / 1.5	26 TU	0158 / 0710 / 1410 / 1934	4.7 / 1.2 / 4.6 / 1.0
12 TU	0230 / 0749 / 1436 / 2006	4.3 / 1.8 / 4.2 / 1.7	27 W	0303 / 0804 / 1512 / 2029	4.6 / 1.4 / 4.4 / 1.3
13 W	0317 / 0837 / 1523 / 2055	4.2 / 2.0 / 4.0 / 1.9	28 TH ☾	0418 / 0905 / 1628 / 2133	4.5 / 1.7 / 4.3 / 1.5
14 TH ☾	0413 / 0950 / 1621 / 2213	4.1 / 2.2 / 3.9 / 2.0	29 F	0527 / 1020 / 1744 / 2250	4.5 / 1.8 / 4.2 / 1.7
15 F	0515 / 1127 / 1728 / 2340	4.0 / 2.2 / 3.8 / 2.0	30 SA	0630 / 1142 / 1852	4.5 / 1.8 / 4.2

DECEMBER

Day	TIME	m	Day	TIME	m
1 SU	0007 / 0729 / 1247 / 1955	1.7 / 4.5 / 1.7 / 4.3	16 M	0616 / 1201 / 1840	4.1 / 1.8 / 3.8
2 M	0107 / 0825 / 1339 / 2054	1.6 / 4.6 / 1.5 / 4.4	17 TU	0021 / 0716 / 1301 / 1944	1.7 / 4.1 / 1.7 / 3.9
3 TU	0158 / 0915 / 1426 / 2146	1.5 / 4.6 / 1.4 / 4.5	18 W	0121 / 0812 / 1353 / 2043	1.6 / 4.3 / 1.4 / 4.1
4 W	0245 / 0959 / 1510 / 2230	1.4 / 4.7 / 1.3 / 4.6	19 TH	0214 / 0905 / 1442 / 2139	1.4 / 4.4 / 1.2 / 4.3
5 TH	0329 / 1037 / 1553 / 2307	1.4 / 4.7 / 1.2 / 4.6	20 F	0303 / 0956 / 1529 / 2231	1.2 / 4.6 / 1.0 / 4.5
6 F	0412 / 1112 / 1635 / 2343	1.3 / 4.7 / 1.1 / 4.6	21 SA ○	0351 / 1044 / 1615 / 2322	1.1 / 4.7 / 0.8 / 4.7
7 SA	0454 / 1148 / 1715	1.3 / 4.7 / 1.1	22 SU	0438 / 1132 / 1701	0.9 / 4.8 / 0.6
8 SU	0018 / 0534 / 1224 / 1753	4.6 / 1.4 / 4.6 / 1.1	23 M	0012 / 0525 / 1220 / 1747	4.8 / 0.8 / 4.8 / 0.6
9 M	0055 / 0613 / 1259 / 1831	4.6 / 1.4 / 4.6 / 1.2	24 TU	0103 / 0612 / 1309 / 1834	4.9 / 0.8 / 4.8 / 0.6
10 TU	0132 / 0652 / 1335 / 1907	4.5 / 1.5 / 4.4 / 1.3	25 W	0156 / 0700 / 1400 / 1923	4.9 / 0.9 / 4.7 / 0.7
11 W	0209 / 0730 / 1412 / 1944	4.4 / 1.6 / 4.3 / 1.4	26 TH	0254 / 0750 / 1457 / 2013	4.8 / 1.1 / 4.5 / 0.9
12 TH	0248 / 0810 / 1451 / 2024	4.3 / 1.7 / 4.2 / 1.5	27 F	0359 / 0843 / 1604 / 2106	4.7 / 1.3 / 4.4 / 1.2
13 F	0330 / 0855 / 1535 / 2110	4.2 / 1.8 / 4.0 / 1.6	28 SA ☾	0501 / 0941 / 1718 / 2207	4.5 / 1.5 / 4.2 / 1.5
14 SA ☽	0419 / 0948 / 1628 / 2205	4.2 / 1.9 / 3.9 / 1.7	29 SU	0600 / 1051 / 1824 / 2321	4.4 / 1.7 / 4.1 / 1.7
15 SU	0515 / 1053 / 1732 / 2313	4.1 / 1.9 / 3.8 / 1.8	30 M	0656 / 1212 / 1925	4.3 / 1.7 / 4.1
			31 TU	0039 / 0750 / 1319 / 2023	1.8 / 4.3 / 1.7 / 4.1

Chart Datum: 3.22 metres below Ordnance Datum (Newlyn)

LANGSTONE 10-2-29
Hampshire

CHARTS
Admiralty 3418; Stanford 10, 11; Imray C3, Y33;
OS 196, 197
TIDES
+0022 Dover; Zone 0 (GMT)

Standard Port PORTSMOUTH (←)

Times				Height (metres)			
HW		LW		MHWS	MHWN	MLWN	MLWS
0500	1000	0000	0600	4.7	3.8	1.8	0.6
1700	2200	1200	1800				

Differences LANGSTONE

0000	0000	+0010	+0010	+0.1	+0.1	0.0	0.0

NAB TOWER

+0015	0000	+0015	+0015	−0.2	0.0	+0.2	0.0

SHELTER
Very good shelter but it must be entered with caution
when a heavy sea is running. Shelter in marina to W
inside entrance. Anchorage in Russell's Lake. For
overnight stay apply Hr Mr at the ferry on Hayling Island.
(☎ 3419). Also anchorage in Langstone Channel out of
fairway.
NAVIGATION
Waypoint Langstone Fairway (safe water) buoy, LFl 10s,
50°46'.28N 01°01'.27W, 167°/347° from/to QR Lt at
entrance, 0.94M. Entrance between E Winner bank and W
Winner bank but apart from these the entrance is
straightforward. Tides are strong in the entrance. Harbour
speed limit 10 kn.

LIGHTS AND MARKS
Leading marks (concrete dolphins) 344°. Red flag, with
numeral pendant below, flown at the Fort, Battery and
Hr Mr's flag staff indicates firing from range to W of
harbour entrance (frequently across harbour approach).
See 10.2.28.
RADIO TELEPHONE
VHF Ch 12 16; 12 (Summer 0830-1700. Winter: Mon-Fri
0830-1700; Sat-Sun 0830-1300 LT). Marina Ch **80** (H24).
TELEPHONE (0705)
Hr Mr 463419; MRSC Lee-on-Solent 552100;
⌗ (0703) 229251; Marinecall 0898 500 457; Police 321111;
Dr 465721.
FACILITIES
EC Havant - Wednesday; **Langstone Marina** (300)
☎ 822719 CH, BH (20 ton), D, Gaz, C, AC, FW, Access
HW∓3; **Hayling Pontoons** (Entrance to Sinah Lake),
Slip, D, FW, L, P, AB; **Langstone SC** ☎ Havant 484577,
Slip, M, L, FW, Bar; **Eastney Cruising Ass.** ☎ 734103;
Solartron SC; Locks SC ☎ 829833; **Tudor SC** (Eastney)
☎ 662002.
✉ (Eastney, Hayling); Ⓑ (Havant, Hayling, Emsworth);
⇌ (bus to Havant); ✈ (Southampton).

CHICHESTER 10-2-30
W. Sussex

CHARTS
Admiralty 3418; Stanford 10, 11; Imray C3, C9, Y33;
OS 197
TIDES
+0020 Dover; ML 2.8; Zone 0 (GMT)

Standard Port PORTSMOUTH (←)

Times				Height (metres)			
HW		LW		MHWS	MHWN	MLWN	MLWS
0500	1000	0000	0600	4.7	3.8	1.8	0.6
1700	2200	1200	1800				

Differences HARBOUR ENTRANCE

−0010	+0005	+0015	+0020	+0.2	+0.2	0.0	+0.1

BOSHAM

0000	+0010	No data		+0.2	+0.1	No data	

ITCHENOR

−0005	+0005	+0005	+0025	+0.1	0.0	−0.2	−0.2

DELL QUAY

+0005	+0015	No data		+0.2	+0.1	No data	

SELSEY BILL

−0005	−0005	+0035	+0035	+0.6	+0.6	0.0	0.0

SHELTER
Chichester harbour has excellent shelter in all four main
arms of the harbour, Emsworth, Thorney, Bosham and
Chichester. Beware shallow patches W and S of Bar Bn.
There are a large number of yacht harbours, marinas etc.
Good anchorages at East Head; in Thorney Channel off
Pilsey Is; W of Fairway buoy on S side of channel. No
anchoring E of Cobnor Pt. Advisable to make prior
arrangement for mooring.
NAVIGATION
Waypoint 50°45'.50N 00°56'.50W, 193°/013° from/to Bar
Bn, 0.47M. The entrance is about ½ M wide at HW but
this dries exposing a sandbank known as the Winner from
the East Head side leaving a deep channel close to
Hayling Island. There is a bar 1 M S of the entrance with
a channel giving depths of 0.4m close E of the Bar Bn.
There is a patch drying 0.3m about 2 ca ESE of the Bn. A
port-hand buoy lies 194° 2.2 ca from Bar Bn (Apl-Nov). In
winds above force 5 from S quarter and particularly during
spring ebbs, seas over the bar are confused. It is advised
to cross the bar from HW−3 to HW+1. There is a speed
limit throughout the harbour of 8 kn.
LIGHTS AND MARKS
Bar Bn Fl(2) R 10s; vis 020°-080°; and Fl WR 5s; vis
W322°-080°, R080°-322°; both on W pylon with tide
gauge; RC. All channels well marked.
RADIO TELEPHONE
Harbour Office, Itchenor VHF Ch **14** 16 (Call *Chichester*
on Ch 14). (Apl-Sept 0900-1730. Oct-Mar: Mon-Sat
0900-1300, Mon-Fri 1400-1730 LT). Emsworth and
Northney Marinas Ch **80**.

CHICHESTER continued

TELEPHONE (0243)

Harbour Office Itchenor 512301; CG Hayling 464095, Selsey 602274; ⊞ (0703) 229251; MRSC Lee-on-Solent 552100; Weather information Portsmouth 8091; Marinecall 0898 500 457; Police 784433; Ⓗ 787970.

FACILITIES

EMSWORTH CHANNEL: channel is straight, broad and deep. Good anchorages especially N of Sandy Pt near entrance to channel. Visitors moorings on 5 outer piles. EC Wednesday; **Slips** at South St, Kings St, and Slipper Mill. Contact the Warden ☎ 376422; **Emsworth Yacht Harbour** (200+4 visitors) ☎ 375211, Slip, Gas, ME, El, AC, Sh, P, D, FW, C (20 ton); (Access HW∓2); **David Still Marine** ☎ 374242, ME, Sh, CH; **Ostar Marine** ☎ 376414; **Greenham Marine Ltd** ☎ 378314, El.

HAYLING ISLAND: EC Wednesday; **Northney Marina** (260+17 visitors) ☎ Hayling 466321, D, C (25 ton), Bar, FW, AC, El, Sh, R, CH, ME; **Chichester Harbour Yacht Services** ☎ Hayling 465051 ME, El, Sh, Slip, C, CH; **Hayling Yacht Co.** ☎ Hayling 463592, ME, El, Slip, BH (8 ton), P, D, FW, AB, Sh, CH; **Hayling Is Marine Services** ☎ Hayling 464869; **Sparkes Yacht Harbour** (140) ☎ Hayling 463572, Slip, ME, El, FW, P, D, Gas, Gaz, ▢, Sh, C (20 ton), CH.

THORNEY CHANNEL: Strangers are advised to go up at half flood. Channel is marked by perches. After Thorney village, channel splits, Prinsted Chan to port (full of moorings) and Nutbourne Chan to stbd. There is plenty of room to anchor in Thorney Chan and it is well protected from E and SE winds. **Thornton Marina** (77+6 visitors) ☎ 375335, Slip, P and D (cans), FW, Sh, ME, C (10 ton), BH (12 ton). Prinsted — **Paynes BY** ☎ 572224, Slip, L, FW, ME;

BOSHAM CHANNEL: There are some Harbour Authority moorings in this channel and there is a hard at Bosham Quay. Most of the channel dries. Anchoring in channel is prohibited. EC Wednesday; **Bosham Quay** L, FW, AB; **Capt. Charles Currey** ☎ 573174, CH; **Rockall Sails** ☎ 572149, SM; **Bosham SC** ☎ 572341; **Arun Sails** ☎ 573185 SM;

CHICHESTER CHANNEL: this runs up to Itchenor. From Sandhead buoy proceed 034° to Fl (2) G 10s Chaldock Bn; alter course to 039° to Fairway buoy, Fl (3). Anchoring prohibited in Itchenor Reach.

EC Itchenor Thursday. Hard available at all stages of the tide. There are six visitor's buoys off Itchenor jetty. For single moorings apply Hr Mr. **G. Haines** ☎ 512228, Slip, P, D, CH, Sh; **E. M. Coombes** ☎ 573194, FW, CH, Slip, P and D (cans); **Northshore Yacht Yards** ☎ 512611, Slip, M; **Regis Marine** ☎ 511070, El, Ⓔ; **H. C. Darley** ☎ 512243, P and D (cans), CH; **E. Bailey** ☎ 512374, ME, P, D, Sh; **Francis Marine** ☎ 787987, CH; **Penguin Engineering** ☎ 465607, CH, ME.

CHICHESTER LAKE AND FISHBOURNE CHANNEL: Birdham Pool Yacht Basin, Access HW∓3 when lock gates open. At Chichester Yacht Basin, the approach dries at CD but is dredged to about 1m at normal LWS. Secure to pontoons whilst waiting: lock control boards show 'Red' indicating 'wait' or 'Green' for 'enter'. They are floodlit at night. When the gates are open with a free flow in and out, there is a QY Lt on top of the Control Tr. **Birdham** — **Chichester Yacht Basin** (900+50 visitors) ☎ 512731, Slip, P, D, FW, ME, El, Sh, AC, Gas, Gaz, CH, V, R, BH (20 ton), Access HW∓4½; **Vernons Shipyard** ☎ 512606; **Greenham Marine** ☎ 512995, El, Ⓔ; **Yacht and Sports Gear** ☎ 784572, CH, ACA; **B. A. Peters** ☎ 512923, CH; **Copp Sails** ☎ 533622, SM. Birdham Pool — **Birdham Pool Marina** (230+10 visitors) ☎ 512310, Slip, P, D, FW, El, Ⓔ, AC, Sh, CH, Gas, Gaz, ME, SM, C (3 ton), Access HW∓3; **Birdham Shipyard** ☎ 512310; Slip, M, P, Sh, CH; **Sterndrives** ☎ 512831, ME; **Seahorse Sails** ☎ 512195, SM; **Dell Quay** — Launching is possible on the hard, depending on the tide, on payment of harbour dues. **Ted Bailey (Dell Quay)** ☎ 781110 Sh; **Wyche Marine** ☎ 782768, M, L, Sh.

Clubs: Bosham SC ☎ 572341; **Chichester YC** ☎ 512918, R, Bar, ▢; **Chichester Cruiser and Racing Club; Dell Quay SC** ☎ 785080; **Emsworth SC** ☎ 43065; **Emsworth Slipper SC** ☎ 42523; **Hayling Island SC** ☎ Hayling 463768; **Itchenor SC** ☎ 512400; **Langstone SC** ☎ Havant 484577; **Mengham Rythe SC** ☎ Hayling 463337; **Thorney Island SC; West Wittering SC.**

MINOR HARBOURS AND ANCHORAGES 10.2.31

BEER, Devon, 50°41′N, 3°06′W, Zone 0 (GMT), Admty chart 3315. HW −0440 on Dover, +0045 on Devonport; HW height −1.1m on Devonport; ML 2.3m; Duration 0640. Beer roads afford a sheltered anchorage in winds from W to N. It is open to prevailing winds. Go ashore by boat over open beach. From E beware rocks at the bottom of headland on E side of cove. Facilities: EC Thurs in Beer and Seaton; **Jimmy Green Marine** ☎ 20744, CH; SC, ✉, Bar, BY, R, V.

RIVER AXE, Devon 50°41′N, 3°06′W, Zone 0 (GMT), Admty chart 3315. HW −0440 on Dover, +0045 on Devonport; HW height +1.1m on Devonport; ML 2.3m; Duration 0640. Good shelter for smallish boats; boats up to 1m draught can enter at HW. Cross bar, which dries, then turn sharply to W. Entrance is 7m wide. The channel through the bar is unmarked and shifts constantly. Local knowledge is needed. A road bridge (2m clearance) crosses the river 2 ca within the entrance. Facilities: EC Thurs (Seaton), BY; **Axe YC** ☎ Seaton 20779, Slip, Bar; **Seaton** ✉, R, V, Gas, Gaz, P and D (cans).

LULWORTH COVE, Dorset, 50°37′N, 2°15′W, Zone 0 (GMT), Admty chart 2172. HW −0449 on Dover, −0410 on Portsmouth; HW height −2.4m on Portsmouth; ML 1.2m. Good shelter in offshore winds but S and SW winds cause heavy swell in the cove. The centre of the cove has a depth of about 4m below CD. There is a can buoy in the centre of the cove. Anchor in NE part in 2.5m. Holding ground is poor. Village is on W bank. Facilities: EC Wed and Sat; FW at tap in car park, D and P at garage (cans), Bar, ✉, Slip, R.
Note. There are two danger areas to E, one extending 6M seawards, the other 13M. Firing takes place most weekdays from 0930-1700 (1200 on Fridays), often on Tues and Thurs nights and up to 6 weekends per year. There is NO firing during August. When firing is in progress R flags (Red lights at night) are flown from St Albans Head and Bindon Hill. However, further ashore, mariners may notice some red flags which fly whether or not firing is taking place; these mark the range boundary. No visual signals ashore warn of naval firings, but warships using the range will patrol S of Lulworth Banks and fly red flags. Times of firing are published locally, sent to Hr Mrs and YCs and can be obtained from the Range Officer ☎ Bindon Abbey (0929) 462721 ext. 4819 during normal working hours and from guardroom ext. 4824 at other times. Firing details are broadcast by Radio Solent (999 kHz − 300 AM or 96.1 MHz VHF) daily (see 10.2.9) and Two Counties Radio and can be obtained from Portland CG (Ch 67), Portland Naval Base (Ch 13 & 14), or Range Safety Boats (Ch 08).
All the Land Area and the Inner Sea Danger Area (DO26(INNER)) are subject to the regulations laid down in "The Lulworth Ranges Byelaws 1978 operative from 10th November 1978 − Statutory Instruments 1978 No 1663". A copy may be obtained from HMSO if required. A key passage in the rules is as follows: "The Byelaws shall not apply to any vessel in the ordinary course of navigation not being used for fishing in the Sea Area and remaining in the Sea Area no longer than is reasonably necessary to pass through the Sea Area."

CHAPMAN'S POOL, Dorset, 50°35′N, 2°04′W, Zone 0 (GMT), Admty chart 2172. Tidal data is approx that for Swanage see 10.2.15. Chapman's Pool, like Worbarrow Bay, Brandy Bay and Kimmeridge Bay is picturesque and is convenient anchorage in depths of about 3m when the wind is off-shore. Anchor centre of bay to avoid tidal swirl. Beware large B buoy unlit in centre. There are no lights and no facilities.

STUDLAND BAY, Dorset, 50°39′N, 1°56′W, Zone 0 (GMT), Admty chart 2172. Tidal data is approx that for Swanage. See 10.2.15. Shelter is good except from winds from N and E. Beware Redend Rocks off S shore. Best anchorage in depths of about 3m below CD, 3 ca NW of The Yards (3 strange projections on the chalk cliffs near Handfast Pt). Facilities: EC Thurs; shops, hotel etc in Studland village. No marine facilities. P and D (cans).

WAREHAM, Dorset, 50°41′N, 2°05′W, Zone 0 (GMT), Admty chart 2611. HW −0030 (Np), +0320 (Sp) on Dover, −0140 (Np), +0205 (Sp) on Portsmouth (See 10.2.16). Shelter very good, approach narrow and winding up R Frome but well marked by buoys and posts at entrance. Beware prohibited anchorages (salmon holes) marked on the chart and moored boats. Passage is unlit; keep outside at all bends. Facilities: **Ridge Wharf Yacht Centre** (180 + 6 visitors) (½M upstream of Ent) ☎ 2650, Access HW∓2 approx AB, M, FW, P, D, ME, El, Gas, Gaz, AC, BH (20 ton), Slip, Sh, CH; **Redclyffe YC** ☎ 51227 (½M below bridge); **Wareham Quay** AB, FW, R; **Town** EC Wed, P and D in cans, V, Gas, R, Dr ☎ 3444, Bar, ✉, ⑧, ⟲.

NEWPORT, Isle of Wight, 50°42′N, 1°17′W, Zone 0 (GMT), Admty chart 2793. For tidal predictions see 10.2.8 and 10.2.23. For approaches up R Medina see 10.2.23. Southwards from Folly Inn on E shore the Medina Borough Council is the harbour authority. ½M south of Folly Inn is **Island Harbour Marina** (170) ☎ 526733, AC, Bar, BH (16 ton), CH, D, P, El, FW, Gas, ⊡, ME, R, Sh, Slip, V. Marina has excellent shelter and is approached through dredged channel (access HW∓3½) and lock. Waiting pontoon outside lock.
Channel S from Island Harbour to Newport dries but there is 2m or more from HW Portsmouth −1½ to HW Portsmouth +2. Speed limit 6 kn up to Seaclose (just past Newport Rowing Club) and 4 kn from there to Newport. In Newport depth at pontoons 1.4m HW∓2. Bilge keel boats lie alongside pontoons, and single keel boats at quay wall − these areas are dredged and kept level. Hr Mr will supply rubbing boards. **Newport Yacht Harbour** (40 visitors) Hr Mr ☎ 525994, VHF Ch 16; 06 (office hours or by arrangement), AC, D, FW. **Town** EC Thursday; ⑧, Bar, BY, C (5 ton mobile, 12 ton fixed), CH, D, Dr, El, Gas, Ⓗ; ⊡, ME, P, ✉, R, Sh, Slip, SM, V.

TITCHFIELD HAVEN, Hampshire 50°49′N, 01°14′W, Zone 0 (GMT), Admty charts 1905, 2022. HW +0030 on Dover (GMT); 0000 on Portsmouth; HW height −0.2m on Portsmouth. Short term anchorage for small craft at mouth of R. Meon. Bar dries ¼M offshore. Ent. dries 1.2m at LWS. Entrance marked by Hillhead SC house (white conspic), beacons mark channel, spherical topmarks to port, triangular ones to stbd. Small harbour to W inside ent where yachts can lie in soft mud alongside bank. Facilities: **Hillhead village** EC Thurs, ✉, CH, V, P and D (cans).

AGENTS WANTED
Berwick-on-Tweed
Mallaig
Loch Sunart
Loch Aline
Fishguard
Kenmare River

Large number of French Ports

Rotterdam
Norderney
Dornumersiel
Langeoog
Wangerooge
Hooksiel
Bremerhaven

If you are interested in becoming our agent please write to the Editors and get your free copy annually. You do not have to be a resident in a port to be the agent but at least a fairly regular visitor.

VOLVO PENTA SERVICE

3

Area 3

South-East England
Littlehampton to Havengore Creek

VOLVO PENTA

10-3-2
South-East England

Key to Symbols

Coast Station / Port Radio – frequencies

Marine radiobeacon– call sign, sequence, frequency and range (nm)

Aeronautical radiobeacon–call sign, frequency and range (nm)

i See for harbour information/tidal data

Weather (tel. or times). M - Marinecall

CG HM Coastguard MRCC MRSC

CG HM Coastguard Sector Base

LB RNLI Lifeboat over 10m

IL RNLI Lifeboat under 10m

SAR Helicopter base

★ Principal lights

Light-vessel

Lanby

RG Emergency VHF DF

* See 10.3.24

Weather Centre
071-836 4311
M-0898
500 455

London Bridge
Standard Port
i 10.3.21

St Katharine's*

Graveser
Gravesend Ra
VHF **12** 1
09 18 2
(Thames Navig
Service)

Woolwich
Thames Barrier
Control Zone
Woolwich
Radio
VHF **14** 16 22
(Thames Navigation
Service)

Thames
VHF 16 02 8
0733 1933

270   Variation   5°W (1991)   180   0

Littlehampton
i 10.3.9
Marina VHF
Ch **80**
IL   CG

Brighton Marina
i 10.3.11
BM —••• ——
2,5 303.4 10
VHF Ch **80**
16; 11 68
IL

Brighton
Radio Sussex
1485 kHz
M-0898
500 456

Shoreham
Standard Port
i 10.3.10
VHF 16;14
SHM
••• •••• ——
332 10
LB IL CG

Newhaven
i 10.3.12
NH —• ••••
3,6 303.4 10
VHF 16;12
Marinas
VHF Ch **80**
LB   CG

RG

Eastbourne
CG

Beac
Hea
★

Selsey
LB   IL

RG

Owers

Dover CG
Solent CG

51°
N

0°

0°

Southend-on-Sea

(RC) (Aero) SND
··· ·· ·–··
362.5 20

M–0898
500 455

n-on-Sea

10.3.22

Hole Haven*

1°E

Havengore Creek

i 10.3.23

North Foreland

(S)(C) MF 1848
VHF 16
05 **65** 66

0733 1933

(RC) NF –· ··–·
301.1 50

Kingsferry Bridge

(P)(R) VHF 10

The Swale

i 10.3.18

Thames CG
Dover CG

Margate* LB ⚠️IL RG

CG

Manston

Chatham

Radio Kent
1035 kHz
M–0898
500 455

Ramsgate

i 10.3.16

LB ⚠️IL

Sandwich*

South Goodwin Lt. F.

Sheerness

Standard Port

i 10.3.20

(P)(R) VHF Medway Radio
16 09 11 22 **74**

LB ⚠️IL

Whitstable

i 10.3.17.

(P)(R) VHF 16;09
12

⚠️IL CG

Langdon Bay

Channel Navigation Information Centre

(P)(R) VHF **10** 16

Dover CG

Walmer

LB ⚠️IL

Dover

Standard Port

i 10.3.15

(P)(R) VHF 16 **74**;
12 **74** (H24)

LB

RG

Rye

i 10.3.13

(P)(R) VHF 16;14

⚠️IL

CG

Folkestone

i 10.3.14

M–0898
500 456

Varne Lanby

51°N

astings*

VHF 16
07 63

0733 1933

IB ⚠️IL

Littlestone-on-Sea ⚠️IL

RG (o) CG

Fairlight

Dungeness

(RC) DU –· ··–·
⁶ 310.3 30

LB CG

Lydd

(RC)(Aero) LYX ··· ·–··
397 15 –··–

For details of traffic lanes see Fig.2 (2)

Royal Sovereign

(RC) RY ·–· ·–··
² 310.3 50

☆

SEPARATION ZONE

1°E

10.3.3   AREA 3 TIDAL STREAMS

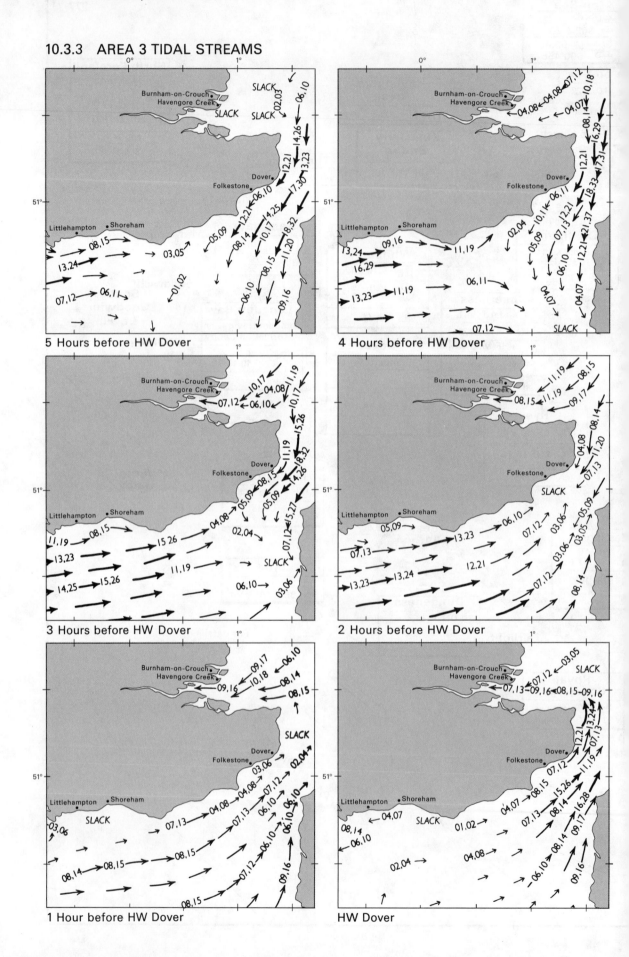

5 Hours before HW Dover

4 Hours before HW Dover

3 Hours before HW Dover

2 Hours before HW Dover

1 Hour before HW Dover

HW Dover

Thames Estuary 10.3.19   Westward 10.2.3   Southward 10.18.3   Northward 10.4.3

3

1 Hour after HW Dover

2 Hours after HW Dover

3 Hours after HW Dover

4 Hours after HW Dover

5 Hours after HW Dover

6 Hours after HW Dover

10.3.4   LIGHTS, FOG SIGNALS AND WAYPOINTS

Abbreviations used below are given in 10.0.3. Principal lights are in **bold** print, places in CAPITALS, and light-vessels, light floats and Lanbys in *CAPITAL ITALICS*. Unless otherwise stated lights are white. m—elevation in metres; M—nominal range in n. miles. Fog signals are in *italics*. Useful waypoints are <u>underlined</u> use those on land with care. See 4.2.2.

ENGLAND—SOUTH COAST

<u>Mixon Beacon</u> 50°42'·35N 00°46'·21W (unlit); port-hand mark.
<u>East Borough Head Lt Buoy</u> 50°41'·50N 00°39'·00W Q3 10s; N cardinal mark.

OWERS LANBY 50°37'·27N 00°40'·60W Fl(3) 20s 12m **22M**; tubular structure on circular buoy; ; *Horn (3) 60s.*

<u>Bognor Regis. Pier head</u> 50°46'·70N 00°40'·42W 2 FR (vert).
<u>Outfall Lt Buoy</u> 50°46'·20N 00°30'·45W Fl Y 5s; special mark.

LITTLEHAMPTON.
<u>West Pier head</u> 50°47'·85N 00°32'·37W 2 FR(vert)7m 6M. Ldg Lts 346°. Front East pierhead FG 6m 7M; B column. Rear 64m from front Oc WY 7·5s 9m 10M; W tower; vis W290°-356°, Y 356°-042°.

WORTHING.
Pier head 2 FR (vert) 6m 1M.
<u>Outfall Lt Buoy</u> 50°48'·45N 00°19'·40W Fl(2)R 10s; port-hand mark.

SHOREHAM.
<u>Lt Buoy</u> 50°47'·00N 00°15'·33W Fl Y 5s; special mark.
<u>West Breakwater head</u> 50°49'·45N 00°14'·79W Fl R 5s 7m 7M.
East Breakwater head Fl G 5s 7m 8M; *Siren 120s.*
Ldg Lts 355° Middle Pier. Front F WR or G 8m W10M, R9M, G9M; W watchhouse, R base; tidal Lts, traffic signals; *Horn 20s.* **Rear** 192m from front Fl 10s 13m **15M**; vis 283°-103°.
West Pier, head F WR 6m; R to seaward.
East pier, head F WG 7m; G to seaward.

BRIGHTON.
<u>Lt Buoy</u> 50°46'·00N 00°08'·30W Fl Y 3s; special mark.
West pier head 2 FR (vert) 13m 4M; *Bell (1) 13s* (when vessel expected).
Palace pier 2 FR (vert) 10m 2M.
BRIGHTON marina.
East breakwater Fl(4) WR 20s 16m W10M, R8M; W pillar, G bands; vis R260°-295°, W295°-100°.
East breakwater head QG 8m 7M.
<u>West Breakwater head</u> 50°48'·46N 00°06'·29W QR 10m 7M; W round structure, R bands; *Horn (2) 30s.*

NEWHAVEN.
Breakwater Head 50°46'·52N 00°03'·60E Oc(2) 10s 17m 12M; *Horn 30s.*
West Pier head 2 FR (vert); RC.
East Pier, head Iso G 5s 12m 6M; W framework Tr.

<u>CS 1 Lt Buoy</u> 50°33'·67N 00°03'·83W Fl Y 2·5s; special mark; *Whis.*

Note. For English Channel Waypoints see 10.1.7

<u>CS 2 Lt Buoy</u> 50°39'·08N 00°32'·70E Fl Y 5s; special mark.
<u>CS 3 Lt Buoy</u> 50°52'·00N 01°02'·30E Fl Y 10s; special mark; *Bell.*
<u>CS 4 Lt Buoy</u> 51°08'·57N 01°34'·02E Fl(4)Y 15s; special mark; *Whis.*

GREENWICH LANBY 50°24'·50N 00°00'·00 Fl 5s 12m **21M**; tubular structure on circular buoy; Racon; Ra refl; *Horn 30s*

Beachy Head 50°44'·00N 00°14'·60E Fl(2) 20s 31m **25M**; W round Tr, R band and lantern; vis 248°-101°; (H24); *Horn 30s.* Fog Det Lt vis 085°-265°.

Royal Sovereign 50°43'·38N 00°26'·13E Fl 20s 28m **15M**; W Tr with R band on W cabin on concrete column; Helicopter platform; *Dia(2) 30s.*
<u>Royal Sovereign Buoy</u> 50°44'·20N 00°25'·95E (unlit); port-hand mark.

EASTBOURNE.
<u>Pier head</u> 50°45'·88N 00°17'·85E 2 FR (vert) 8m 2M.
<u>St Leonard's sewer outfall Lt Buoy</u> 50°49'·27N 00°32'·00E Fl Y 5s; special mark.

HASTINGS.
Pier head 2 FR (vert).
<u>West breakwater head</u> 50°51'·13N 00°35'·70E Fl R 2·5s 5m 4M. Ldg Lts 356°. Front FR 14M 4M. Rear 357m from front FR 55m 4M.

RYE.
<u>Rye Fairway Lt Buoy</u> 50°54'·00N 00°48'·13E LFl 10s; safe water mark.
<u>West groyne head</u> 50°55'·55N 00°46'·65E Fl R 5s 7m 6M; Ra refl.
East Arm, head Q(9) 15s 7m 6M; G cone on structure; *Horn 7s.*

Dungeness 50°54'·77N 00°58'·67E Fl 10s 40m **27M**; B round Tr, W bands and lantern, floodlit; Part obsc 078°-shore; RC; (H24). F RG 37m 11M (same Tr); vis R057°-073°, G073°-078°, R196°-216°; FR Lts shown 2·4 and 5·2M WNW when firing taking place.
QR and FR on radio mast 1·2M NW; *Horn (3) 60s.*

VARNE LANBY 51°01'·25N 01°24'·00E Fl R 20s 12m **19M**; *Horn 30s*; Racon.

FOLKESTONE.
Breakwater head 51°04'·53N 01°11'·79E Fl(2) 10s 14m **22M**; *Dia(4) 60s.* In fog Fl 2s; vis 246°-306°, intens 271·5°-280·5°.
Inner harbour, East Pier head QG.

DOVER.
Admiralty Pier Extension head 51°06'·65N 01°19'·77E Fl 7·5s 21m **20M**; W Tr; vis 096°-090°, obsc in The Downs by South Foreland inshore of 226°; *Horn 10s.*
Prince of Wales Pier head VQ G 14m 4M; W Tr; Fl Y 1·5s (intens, occas).
Southern Breakwater, West head Oc R 30s 21m **18M**; W Tr.

Knuckle Oc WR 10s 15m **W15M**, R13M; W Tr; vis R059°-239°, W239°-059°.
North head 51°07'·17N 01°20'·72E FY 17m 4M.
Eastern Arm head, Port Control Sig Stn; *Horn (2) 30s.*

SOUTH GOODWIN Lt F 51°07'·95N 01°28'·60E Fl(2) 30s 12m**21M**; R hull with Lt Tr amidships; *Horn(2) 60s.*
SW Goodwin Lt Buoy 51°08'·57N 01°28'·80E Q(6)LFl 15s; S cardinal mark.
S Goodwin Lt Buoy 51°10'·57N 01°32'·37E Fl(4)R 15s; port-hand mark.
SE Goodwin Lt Buoy 51°12'·95N 01°34'·55E Fl(3)R 10s; port-hand mark.

EAST GOODWIN Lt F 51°13'·05N 01°36'·31E Fl 15s 12m **21M**; R hull with Lt Tr amidships; Racon; *Horn 30s.*
East Goodwin Lt Buoy 51°16'·00N 01°35'·60E Q(3) 10s; E cardinal mark.

DEAL.
Pier head 51°13'·40N 01°24'·65E 2 FR (vert) 7m 5M.

THE DOWNS.
Deal Bank Lt Buoy 51°12'·90N 01°25'·68; QR; port-hand mark.
Goodwin Fork Lt Buoy 51°13'·25N 01°27'·13E Q(6)LFl 15s; S cardinal mark; *Bell.*
Downs Lt Buoy 51°14'·31N 01°26'·90E Fl(2)R 5s; port-hand mark.

GULL STREAM.
W Goodwin Lt Buoy 51°15'·28N 01°27'·32E FlG 5s; stbd-hand mark.
S Brake Lt Buoy 51°15'·40N 01°27'·00E Fl(3)R 10s; port-hand mark.
NW Goodwin Lt Buoy 51°16'·55N 01°28'·55E Q(9) 15s; W cardinal mark; *Bell.*
Brake Lt Buoy 51°16'·90N 01°28'·40E Fl(4)R 15s; port-hand mark; *Bell.*
N Goodwin Lt Buoy 51°17'·60N 01°30'·03E FlG 2·5s; stbd-hand mark.
Gull Stream Lt Buoy 51°18'·10N 01°30'·02E QR; port-hand mark.
Gull Lt Buoy 51°19'·55N 01°31'·40E VQ(3) 5s; E cardinal mark.
Goodwin Knoll Lt Buoy 51°19'·55N 01°32'·30E Fl(2)G 5s; stbd-hand mark.
NE Goodwin Lt Buoy 51°20'·28N 01°34'·27E Q(3) 10s; E cardinal mark; Racon.

RAMSGATE CHANNEL
B1 Buoy 51°15'·75N 01°25'·70E (unlit); stbd-hand mark.
B2 Buoy 51°18'·05N 01°24'·20E (unlit); stbd-hand mark.

RIVER STOUR.
Channel marked by port and stbd-hand buoys and beacons. Pegwell Bay, Sandwich approach 51°18'·72N 01°23'·05E FlR 10s 3m 4M; framework Tr; moved to meet changes in channel.

RAMSGATE.
East Brake Lt Buoy 51°19'·45N 01°29'·10E Q(3) 10s; E cardinal mark. Dredged approach channel marked by Lt Buoys, Fl(4)Y 10s on South side and Q Fl on North side.
Channel Lt Buoy, South side 51°19'·44N 01°26'·00E Q; N cardinal mark.
North side 51°15'·51N 01°26'·00E Q(6)LFl 15s; S cardinal mark.
South breakwater head VQR 10m 5M; RW Bn.
North breakwater head QG; GW Bn.

West ferry terminal Dir Lt 270°, Dir Oc WRG 10s 10m 5M; vis G259°-269°, W269°-271°, R271°-281°.
Royal Harbour entrance, East side Oc 10s 8m 4M.
West side FR or FG 12m 7M; vis 256°-251°; G when less than 3m of water, R when 3m or more.

BROADSTAIRS.
Broadstairs Knoll Lt Buoy 51°20'·85N 01°29'·57E FlR 2·5s; port-hand mark.
Pier, SE end 51°21'·46N 01 26'·83E 2 FR (vert) 7m 4M.

North Foreland 51°22'·47N 01°26'·80E Fl(5) WR 20s 57m **W21M, R18M, R16M**; W 8-sided Tr; vis W shore-150°, R150°-200°, W200°-011°; RC.

ENGLAND—EAST COAST

FALLS Lt F 51°18'·10N 01°48'·45E Fl(2) 10s 12m **24M**; R hull with Lt Tr amidships; RC; Racon; *Horn Mo(N) 60s.*
F3 LANBY 51°23'·82N 02°00'·62E Fl 10s 12m **22M**; Racon; *Horn 10s.*

Elbow Lt Buoy 51°23'·20N 01°31'·68E Q; N cardinal mark.
Foreness Point, sewer outfall Lt Buoy 51°24'·60N 01°26'·10E FlY 5s; special mark.
Longnose Buoy 51°24'·12N 01°26'·20E (unlit); port-hand mark.
Longnose Spit Buoy 51°23'·90N 01°25'·85E (unlit); N cardinal mark.

MARGATE.
Promenade Pier, N head 51°23'·65N 01°22'·93E Fl (3)R 10s.
Stone Pier head FR 18m 4M.

GORE CHANNEL.
SE Margate Lt Buoy 51°24'·10N 01° 20'·50E Q(3) 10s; E cardinal mark.
S Margate Lt Buoy 51°23'·90N 01°16'·75E FlG 2·5s; stbd-hand mark.
Margate Hook Bn 51°24'·03N 01°12'·68E (unlit); stbd-hand mark.
Hook Spit Buoy 51°24'·03N 01°12'·68E (unlit); stbd-hand mark.
E Last Lt Buoy 51°24'·00N 01°12'·27E QR; port-hand mark.

HERNE BAY.
Pier head (isolated from shore) 51°22'·88N 01°07'·00E Q 8m 4M. (2 FR (vert) near root.

WHITSTABLE.
Whitstable Street Lt Buoy 51°23'·83N 01°01'·70E VQ; N cardinal mark.
Whitstable Oyster Lt Buoy 51°22'·03N 01°01'·16E Fl(2)R 10s; port-hand mark.
On E side of harbour F 15m 8M; W mast; FR 10m 5M (same structure) shown when entry/departure prohibited.
West Quay, dolphin 51°21'·82N 01°01'·55E Fl WRG 2m 5s W5M, R3M, G3M; vis W118°-156°, G156°-178°, R178°-201°.
West quay, NW end 51°21'·806N 01°01'·590E 2 FG (vert).
East Quay, N end 2 FR (vert) 4m 1M.
Ldg Lts 122°30'. Front 51°21'·7N 01°01'·8E FR 7m on mast. Rear, 30m from front FR 13m on mast.

THE SWALE.
Columbine Buoy 51°24'·23N 01°01'·45E (unlit); stbd-hand mark.
Columbine Spit Buoy 51°23'·83N 01°00'·12E (unlit); stbd-hand mark.
Pollard Spit Lt Buoy 51°22'·95N 00° 58'·66E QR; port-hand mark.
Ham Gat Buoy 51°23'·05N 00°58'·41E (unlit); stbd-hand mark.
Sand End Lt Buoy 51°21'·40N 00°56'·00E FlG 5s; stbd-hand mark.
Faversham Spit Buoy 51°20'·72N 00°54'·28E (unlit); N cardinal mark.

QUEENS CHANNEL/FOUR FATHOMS CHANNEL.
East Margate Lt Buoy 51°27'·00N 01°26'·50E FlR 2·5s; port-hand mark.
NE Spit Lt Buoy 51°27'·92N 01°30'·00E VQ(3) 5s; E cardinal mark.
Spaniard Lt Buoy 51°26'·20N 01°04'·10E Q(3) 10s; E cardinal mark.
Spile Lt Buoy 51°26'·40N 00°55'·85E FlG 2·5s; stbd-hand mark.

PRINCES CHANNEL/EDINBURGH CHANNELS.
Outer Tongue Lt Buoy 51°30'·70N 01°26'·50E LFl 10s; safe water mark; Whis; Racon.
Tongue Sand Tower 51°29'·55N 01°22'·10E (unlit N and S cardinal Lt Buoys close N and S).
PRINCES CHANNEL.
E Tongue Lt Buoy 51°28'·73N 01°18'·70E Fl(2)R 5s; port-hand mark.
S Shingles Lt Buoy 51°29'·20N 01°16'·15E Q(6)LFl 15s; S cardinal mark; Bell.
N Tongue Lt Buoy 51°28'·80N 01°13'·20E Fl(3)R 10s; port-hand mark.
SE Girdler Lt Buoy 51°29'·47N 01°10'·00E Fl(3)G 10s; stbd-hand mark.
W Girdler Lt Buoy 51°29'·60N 01°06'·90E Q(9) 15s; W cardinal mark; Bell.
Girdler Lt Buoy 51°29'·15N 01°06'·50E Fl(4)R 15s; port-hand mark.
Shivering Sand Tr 51°29'·90N 01°04'·90E (unlit N and S cardinal Lt Buoys close N and S).
E Redsand Lt Buoy 51°29'·38N 01°04'·12E Fl(2)R 5s; port-hand mark.

OAZE DEEP.
Red Sand Tr 51°28'·60N 00°59'·50E (unlit port and stbd-hand Lt Buoys close NW and E).
S Oaze Lt Buoy 51°30'·00N 01°00'·80E Fl(2)G 5s; stbd-hand mark.
SW Oaze Lt Buoy 51°29'·03N 00°57'·05E Q(6)LFl 15s; S cardinal mark.
W Oaze Lt Buoy 51°29'·03N 00°55'·52E VQ(9) 10s; W cardinal mark.
Cant Bn 51°27'·73N 00°55'·45E (unlit).
E Cant Lt Buoy 51°28'·50N 00°55'·70E QR; port-hand mark.
W Cant Lt Buoy 51°27'·06N 00°45'·24E QR; port-hand mark.

Medway Lt Buoy 51°28'·80N 00°52'·92E Iso 2s; safe water mark.

SHEERNESS.
Garrison Pt Ro Ro Berth No. 10. 51°26'·80N 00°44'·73E 2 FR; on dolphin; Horn(3) 30s .
Isle of Grain 51°26'·6N 00°43'·5E Q WRG 20m W13M,

R7M, G8M; R&W diamond on R Tr; vis R220°-234°, G234°-241°, W241°-013°; Ra refl.

SEA REACH.
No. 1 Lt Buoy 51°29'·42N 00°52'·67E FlY 2·5s; special mark; Racon.
No. 2 Lt Buoy 51°29'·37N 00°49'·85E Iso 5s; safe water mark.
No. 3 Lt Buoy 51°29'·30N 00°46'·65E LFl 10s; safe water mark.
No. 4 Lt Buoy 51°29'·58N 00°44'·28E FlY 2·5s; special mark.
No. 5 Lt Buoy 51°29'·92N 00°41'·54E Iso 5s; safe water mark.
No. 6 Lt Buoy 51°30'·00N 00°39'·94E Iso 2s; safe water mark.
No. 7 Lt Buoy 51°30'·83N 00°37'·15E FlY 2·5s; special mark; Racon.
Mid Blyth Lt Buoy 51°30'·05N 00°32'·50E Q; N cardinal mark.

CANVEY ISLAND.
Jetty head, East end 2 FG (vert); Bell (1) 10s.
West end 2 FG (vert). Lts 2 FR (vert) to port, and 2 FG (vert) to starboard, are shown from wharves etc above this point.
Shornmead 51°27'·0N 00°26'·6E Fl(2) WRG 10s 12m **W17M**, R13M, G13M; vis G shore-080°, R080°-085°, W085°-088°, G088°-141°, W141°-205°, R205°-213°.
Northfleet Lower 51°26'·9N 00°20'·4E Oc WR 5s 15m **W17M**, R14M; vis W164°-271°, R271°-S shore.
Northfleet Upper 51°26'·9N 00°20'·2E Oc WRG 10s 30m **W16M**, R12M, G12M; vis R126°-149°, W149°-159°, G159°-269°, W269°-279°.
Broadness. 51°28'·0N 00°18'·7E Oc R 5s 12m 12M; R metal Tr.

SOUTHEND.
Pier, East end 51°30'·84N 00°43'·51E 2 FG (vert) 7/5m. Horn Mo(N) 30s (temp inop, 1986).
West head 2 FG (vert) 13m 8M.

Shoebury Bn 51°30'·27N 00°49'·40E Fl(3) G 10s.
Inner Bn 51°30'·96N 00°49'·28E Fl Y 2·5s.
Blacktail (West) Bn 51°31'·43N 00°55'·30E Iso G 10s 10m 5M.
Blacktail (East) Bn 51°31'·75N 00°56'·60E Iso G 5s 10m 5M.

IMPORTANT NOTE. Buoyage in the Thames Estuary is subject to continual change.

10.3.5   PASSAGE INFORMATION

This area embraces the greatest concentration of commercial shipping in the world, and it must be recognised that in such waters the greatest danger to a small yacht is being run down by a larger vessel, especially in poor visibility. In addition to the many ships plying up and down the traffic lanes, there are fast ferries, hovercraft and hydrofoils passing to and fro between English and Continental harbs; warships and submarines on exercises; fishing vessels operating both inshore and offshore; many other yachts; and static dangers such as lobster pots and fishing nets which are concentrated in certain places.

Even for coastal cruising it is essential to have knowledge of the traffic separation schemes in force, see Fig. 2(2), observing that the SW-bound lane from the Dover Strait passes only 4M off Dungeness, for example. Radar surveillance of the Dover Strait is maintained continously by the Channel Navigation Information Service (CNIS).

It should be remembered that in the English Chan wind can have a big effect on tidal streams, and on the range of tides. Also N winds, which give smooth water and pleasant sailing off the shores of England, can cause rough seas on the French coast. The rates of tidal streams vary with the locality, and are greatest in the narrowest parts of the Chan and off large headlands: in the Dover Strait sp rates can reach 4 kn, but elsewhere in open water they seldom exceed 2 kn. In strong winds the Dover Strait can become very rough. With strong S winds the English coast between Isle of Wight and Dover is very exposed, and shelter is hard to find.

CROSS-CHANNEL PASSAGES

Various factors need to be considered when planning a passage between, say, England and France in whichever direction. It is an advantage for the average yacht to minimise the length of time out of sight of land, thus reducing not only fatigue (which can soon become apparent in a family crew) but also the risk of navigational error due in part to tidal streams. Thus, when proceeding from Brighton to St Malo for example, it pays to cruise coastwise to Poole or Weymouth before setting off for Cherbourg, Alderney or the Casquets. Such tactics also combine the legal requirement to cross traffic separation schemes at right angles (see 2.1.2). Naturally the coastwise sections of any cruise should be timed to take maximum advantage from favourable tidal streams.

Prevailing winds also need to be considered. If it is accepted (as statistics show) that in the English Channel between Portland and the Channel Islands the wind more commonly blows from a direction between S and W, the likelihood of getting a good slant is improved by sailing from Portland rather than Brighton: departure from Brighton might give a long beat to windward. Such decisions may depend of course on forecast wind directions in the immediate future.

It is also helpful to plan that points of departure and arrival have powerful lights and conspic landmarks, and radio-beacons which can be used in the event of visibility closing down. Do not forget the importance of taking back bearings in the early stages of a Channel crossing, in order to assess the correct course and proper allowance for leeway and tidal stream.

On some passages soundings can be a useful aid to navigation: thus in the example quoted above from Portland to the Casquets, the Hurd Deep is a useful guide to progress made.

THE OWERS (chart 1652)

Selsey Bill is a low headland, and off it lie the Owers — groups of rks and shoals extending 3M to the S, and 5M to the SE. Just W and SW of the Bill, The Streets (awash) extend 1¼M seaward. 1¼M SSW of the Bill are The Grounds (or Malt Owers) and The Dries (dry). 1M E of The Dries, and about 1¼M S of the lifeboat house on E side of Selsey Bill is a group of rks called The Mixon, marked by Bn at E end.

Immediately S of dangers above is the Looe chan, which runs E/W about ¾M S of Mixon Bn, and is marked by buoys at W end, where it is narrowest between Brake (or Cross) Ledge on N side and Boulder Bank to the S. In daylight and in good vis and moderate weather, the Looe chan is an easy and useful short cut. The E-going stream begins at HW Portsmouth +0430, and the W-going at HW Portsmouth −0135, sp rates 2½ kn. Beware lobster pots in this area.

In poor vis or in bad weather (and always in darkness) keep S of the Owers Lanby, moored 7M SE of Selsey Bill, marking SE end of Owers. Over much of Owers there is less than 3m, and large parts virtually dry: so a combination of tidal stream and strong wind produces heavy breaking seas and overfalls over a large area.

SELSEY BILL TO DUNGENESS (charts 1652, 536)

The coast from Selsey Bill to Brighton is low, faced by a shingle beach, and with few offlying dangers. Bognor Rks (dry in places) extend 1¾M E from a point 1M W of the pier, and Bognor Spit extends E and S from the end of them. Middleton ledge are rks running 8 ca offshore, about 1½M E of Bognor pier, with depths of less than 1m. Shelley rks lie ½M S of Middleton ledge, with depths of less than 1m.

Winter Knoll, about 2½M SSW of Littlehampton (10.3.9) has depths of 2.1m. Kingston rks, with depth of 2.0m lie about 3¼M ESE of Littlehampton. Grass Banks, an extensive shoal with depths of 3.0m at W end, lie about 1M S of Worthing: Elbow, with depth of 3.1m, lies 1¾M SE of Worthing pier.

Off Shoreham (10.3.10) Church Rks, with depth of 0.3m, lie 1½M W of entrance and ¼M offshore. Jenny Rks, with depth 0.9m, are 1¼M E of the entrance, 3 ca offshore.

At Brighton (10.3.11) the S Downs join the coastline, and high chalk cliffs are conspic from here to Beachy Hd. There are no dangers more than 3 ca from shore, until Birling Gap, where a rky ledge begins, on which is built Beachy Hd Lt Ho (Lt, fog sig). Below the watch house on cliff top, Head Ledge (dries) extends about 4 ca S. 2M S of Beachy Hd the W-going stream begins at HW Dover +0030, and the E-going at HW Dover −0520, sp rates 2¼ kn. In bad weather there are overfalls off the hd, which should then be given a berth of 2M.

Royal Sovereign Lt Tr (Lt, fog sig) lies about 7M E of Beachy Hd. The extensive Royal Sovereign shoals lie from between 1½M N of the Tr to 3M NW of it, and have a least depth of 3.5m. There are strong eddies over the shoals at sp, and the sea breaks on them in bad weather.

On the direct course from Royal Sovereign Lt Tr to clear Dungeness there are no dangers. Along the coast in Pevensey B and Rye B there are drying rky ledges or shoals extending ½M offshore in places. These include Boulder Bank near Wish Tr, S of Eastbourne; Oyster Reef off Cooden; Bexhill Reef off Bexhill-on-Sea; Bopeep Rks off St Leonards; and the shoals at the mouth of R Rother, at entrance to Rye (10.3.13). There are also shoals 2-3M offshore, on which the sea builds in bad weather.

Dungeness (Lt, fog sig, RC) is at SE extremity of Romney Marsh. The nuclear power station is conspic. The pt is steep-to on SE side. Trinity House has an experimental station at Dungeness: disregard any uncharted light, fog signal or radar beacon therefrom. Good anch close NE of Dungeness.

DUNGENESS TO NORTH FORELAND (charts 1892, 1828)

From Dungeness to Folkestone (10.3.14) the coast forms a b. Beware Roar bank, depth 2.7m, E of New Romney: otherwise there are no offlying dangers. Good anch off Sandgate in offshore winds. Off Folkestone harb the E-going stream begins HW Dover −0155, sp rate 2 kn; the W-going begins HW Dover +0320, sp rate 1½ kn.

Past Dover (10.3.15) and S Foreland keep ½M offshore: do not pass too close to Dover harb because ferries etc leave at speed, and also there can be considerable backwash off harb walls. 8M S of Dover is the Varne, a shoal 5M in extent with least depth 3.7m and a heavy sea in bad weather, marked by Lanby. Between S and N Foreland the N-going stream begins at about HW Dover −0150, and the S-going at about HW Dover +0415.

Goodwin Sands are extensive, shifting shoals, running about 10M from N to S, and 5M from E to W at their widest part. Along the E and N sides large areas dry up to 3m. The sands are well marked by Lt Fs and by buoys. Kellett Gut is a chan about ½M wide, running from SW to NE through the middle of the sands, but it is not regularly surveyed and liable to change. The Gull Stream (buoyed) leads inside Goodwin Sands and outside Brake Sands off Ramsgate (10.3.16). The Ramsgate Channel leads inside the Brake Sands and Cross Ledge.

THAMES ESTUARY (chart 1607)

N Foreland (Lt, RC) marks the S entrance to Thames Estuary, an area encumbered by banks many of which dry. N Foreland (chart 1828) is well marked by Lt Ho and buoys offshore. From HW Dover −0120 to HW Dover +0045 the stream runs N and W from the Downs into Thames Estuary. From HW Dover +0045 to HW Dover +0440 the N-going stream from The Downs meets the E-going stream from Thames Estuary, which in strong winds causes a bad sea. From HW Dover −0450 to HW Dover −0120 the streams turn W into Thames Estuary and S towards The Downs.

The sandbanks shift constantly, and it is important to have corrected charts showing recent buoyage changes. With wind against tide a short, steep sea is raised, particularly in E or NE winds. The stream runs 3 kn at sp in places, mostly in the directions of the chans but sometimes across the shoals in between. The main chans carry much commercial shipping and are well buoyed and lit, but this does not apply to lesser chans and swatchways which are convenient for yachtsmen, particularly when crossing the estuary from N to S, or S to N.

The main chans on the S side of the estuary are as follows. S Chan, which leads W about 1M off the N Kent coast and into Gore Chan, Horse Chan and Four Fathoms Chan across the Kentish Flats (most of this route is sparsely buoyed, and very sparsely lit); Queens Chan; Princes Chan, a main E/W route, passing S of Tongue Sand Tr, where the W-going stream begins at HW Sheerness −0610, and the E-going at HW Sheerness +0030, sp rates 2 kn; the Edinburgh Chans, which run into Knob Chan; and Oaze Deep, a continuation of Knock John Chan and Barrow Deep, which join it from a NE direction.

When crossing the estuary it is essential to study the tides carefully, both to ensure sufficient depth in places and also to make the best use of tidal streams. Good vis is needed to pick out the buoys and marks, and to avoid commercial shipping. Proceeding N from N Foreland to Orford Ness or beyond (or coming in opposite direction) it may be preferable to keep to seaward of the main banks, passing Kentish Knock buoy and thence to Shipwash Lt F 24M further N.

Bound from N Foreland to the Crouch or Blackwater proceed through S Edinburgh Chan, through the swatchway about ½M NE of Knock John Tr into Barrow Deep, and thence round the end of W Barrow Sand. With sufficient rise of tide it is possible to cut across between Maplin Spit and Barrow Sand, but usually it is better to proceed SW to Maplin Bank buoy, and thence into E Swin to the Whitaker buoy. This is just one of many routes which could be followed, depending on wind direction and tidal conditions.

10.3.6   DISTANCE TABLE

Approximate distances in nautical miles are by the most direct route while avoiding dangers and allowing for traffic separation schemes etc. Places in *italics* are in adjoining areas.

	1	2	3	4	5	6	7	8	9	10	11	12	13	14	15	16	17	18	19	20
1 *Casquets*	**1**																			
2 *Cherbourg*	31	**2**																		
3 *Nab Tower*	81	66	**3**																	
4 Owers Lanby	87	70	11	**4**																
5 Shoreham	106	88	32	21	**5**															
6 Brighton Marina	109	90	35	24	5	**6**														
7 Newhaven	114	94	40	29	12	7	**7**													
8 Royal Sovereign	124	102	54	43	27	22	15	**8**												
9 Folkestone	162	140	92	81	65	60	53	38	**9**											
10 Dover	167	145	97	86	70	65	58	43	5	**10**										
11 Ramsgate	182	160	112	101	85	80	73	58	20	15	**11**									
12 North Foreland	186	164	116	105	89	84	77	62	24	19	4	**12**								
13 Whitstable	203	179	133	122	106	101	94	79	41	36	22	17	**13**							
14 Sheerness	216	194	146	135	119	114	107	92	54	49	34	30	14	**14**						
15 London Bridge	258	236	188	177	161	156	149	134	96	91	76	72	55	45	**15**					
16 Shoeburyness	215	193	145	134	118	113	106	91	53	48	33	29	14	4	43	**16**				
17 *Orford Ness*	231	209	161	150	134	129	122	107	69	64	49	45	50	53	92	49	**17**			
18 *Dieppe*	139	108	92	81	75	70	65	55	71	75	90	94	111	124	166	123	135	**18**		
19 *Cap Gris Nez*	175	147	101	90	74	69	62	47	19	19	28	32	49	62	104	61	74	61	**19**	
20 *Goeree Tower*	278	250	204	193	177	172	165	150	106	101	94	91	104	114	154	111	78	164	103	**20**

S.E. ENGLAND
WAYPOINTS   10-3-7

Selected waypoints for use in Area 3 are listed in alphabetical order below. Further waypoints for use in coastal waters are given in section 4 of each relevant area. Selected waypoints for use in Channel crossings are given in 10.1.7.

Brake Lt Buoy	51°16'·90N	01°28'·40E
Broadstairs Knoll Lt Buoy	51°20'·85N	01°29'·58E
Brighton Marina Hd	50°48'·46N	00°06'·29W
Bullock Bank Lt Buoy	50°46'·90N	01°07'·70E
Colbalt N Lt Buoy	50°57'·44N	01°23'·40E
Colbalt SW Lt Buoy	50°48'·82N	01°16'·40E
Columbine Lt Buoy	51°24'·23N	01°01'·45E
Columbine Spit Buoy	51°23'·83N	01°00'·12E
CS 1 Lt Buoy	50°33'·67N	00°03'·83W
CS 2 Lt Buoy	50°39'·10N	00°32'·70E
CS 3 Lt Buoy	50°52'·00N	01°02'·30E
CS 4 Lt Buoy	51°08'·58N	01°34'·03E
Deal Bank Lt Buoy	51°12'·90N	01°25'·68E
Downs Lt Buoy	51°14'·32N	01°26'·92E
Drill Stone Lt Buoy	51°25'·80N	01°43'·00E
Dungeness Lt	50°54'·77N	00°58'·67E
Dungeness Lt Buoy	50°54'·43N	00°58'·33E
East Brake Lt Buoy	51°19'·45N	01°29'·10E
East Borough Hd Lt Buoy	50°41'·50N	00°39'·00W
East Goodwin Lt F	51°13'·05N	01°36'·31E
East Goodwin Lt Buoy	51°16'·00N	01°35'·60E
East Last Lt Buoy	51°24'·00N	01°12'·27E
East Margate Lt Buoy	51°27'·00N	01°26'·50E
East Redsand Lt Buoy	51°29'·38N	01°04'·15E
East Tongue Lt Buoy	51°28'·73N	01°18'·70E
East Varne Lt Buoy	50°58'·20N	01°21'·00E
Elbow Lt Buoy	51°23'·20N	01°31'·70E
F1 Lt Buoy	51°11'·33N	01°45'·10E
F2 Lt Buoy	51°20'·38N	01°56'·30E
Falls Lt F	51°18'·10N	01°48'·50E
Falls Head Lt Buoy	51°28'·20N	01°50'·00E
Falls Mid Lt Buoy	51°20'·50N	01°48'·00E
Goodwin Fork Lt Buoy	51°13'·25N	01°27'·13E
Goodwin Knoll Lt Buoy	51°19'·55N	01°32'·30E
Greenwich Lanby	50°24'·50N	00°00'·0
Gull Lt Buoy	51°19'·55N	01°31'·40E
Gull Stream Lt Buoy	51°18'·10N	01°30'·02E
Hook Spit Lt Buoy	51°24'·03N	01°12'·68E
Margate Hook Bn	51°24'·03N	01°12'·68E
Mid Falls Lt Buoy	51°20'·50N	01°48'·00E
Mid Varne Lt Buoy	50°58'·90N	01°20'·00E
MPC Lt Buoy	51°06'·17N	01°38'·33E
Newhaven Breakwater Hd	50°46'·52N	00°03'·60E
North Goodwin Lt Buoy	51°17'·60N	01°30'·03E
North Goodwin Lt V	51°20'·28N	01°34'·27E
North Redsand Towers		
Lt Buoy	51°28'·70N	00°59'·42E
North East Goodwin Lt Buoy	51°20'·28N	01°34'·27E
North East Spit Lt Buoy	51°27'·92N	01°30'·00E

North East Tongue Sand		
Tr Lt Buoy	51°29'·65N	01°22'·13E
North West Goodwin Lt Buoy	51°16'·55N	01°28'·55E
Outer Owers Buoy	50°38'·75N	00°41'·30W
Outer Tongue Lt Buoy	51°30'·70N	01°26'·50E
Owers Lanby	50°37'·30N	00°40'·60W
Pollard Spit Lt Buoy	51°22'·95N	00°58'·66E
Pullar Buoy	50°40'·45N	00°50'·00W
Quern Lt Buoy	51°19'·39N	01°26'·20E
Ramsgate Channel B.1 Buoy	51°15'·75N	01°25'·70E
Ramsgate Channel B.2 Buoy	51°18'·05N	01°24'·20E
Royal Sovereign Lt	50°43'·38N	00°26'·13E
Rye Fairway Lt Buoy	50°54'·00N	00°48'·13E
Shoreham Lt Buoy	50°47'·00N	00°15'·33W
South Brake Lt Buoy	51°15'·40N	01°27'·00E
South East Goodwin Lt Buoy	51°12'·95N	01°34'·55E
South East Margate Lt Buoy	51°24'·10N	01°20'·50E
South Falls Lt Buoy	51°14'·00N	00°44'·00E
South Goodwin Lt Buoy	51°10'·57N	01°32'·37E
South Goodwin Lt F	51°07'·95N	01°28'·60E
South Inner Gabbard Lt Buoy	51°51'·20N	01°52'·40
South Margate Lt Buoy	51°23'·90N	01°16'·75E
South Redsand Towers		
Lt Buoy	51°28'·57N	00°59'·77E
South East Margate Lt Buoy	51°24'·10N	01°20'·50E
South Varne Lt Buoy	50°55'·60N	01°17'·40E
South West Goodwin Lt Buoy	51°08'·57N	01°28'·80E
South West Sandettie		
Lt Buoy	51°09'·80N	01°45'·70E
South West Tongue Tr		
Lt Buoy	51°29'·40N	01°22'·13E
Spaniard Lt Buoy	51°26'·20N	01°04'·10E
Spile Lt Buoy	51°26'·40N	00°55'·85E
Varne Lanby	51°01'·25N	01°24'·00E
West Girdler Lt Buoy	51°29'·58N	01°06'·82E
West Goodwin Lt Buoy	51°15'·28N	01°27'·32E
Whitstable St Lt Buoy	51°23'·83N	01°01'·70E
WSW Sandettie Lt Buoy	51°12'·40N	01°51'·20E

LITTLEHAMPTON   10-3-9
W. Sussex

CHARTS
Admiralty 1991, 1652; Stanford 9; Imray C9; OS 197
TIDES
+0015 Dover; ML 2.8; Zone 0 (GMT).

Standard Port SHOREHAM (→)

Times				Height (metres)			
HW		LW		MHWS	MHWN	MLWN	MLWS
0500	1000	0000	0600	6.2	5.0	1.9	0.7
1700	2200	1200	1800				

Differences LITTLEHAMPTON (ENT)
+0010 0000 −0005 −0010 −0.4 −0.4 −0.2 −0.2
LITTLEHAMPTON (NORFOLK WHARF)
+0015 +0005 0000 +0045 −0.7 −0.7 −0.3 +0.2
PAGHAM
+0015 0000 −0015 −0025 −0.7 −0.5 −0.1 −0.1
BOGNOR REGIS
+0010 −0005 −0005 −0020 −0.6 −0.5 −0.2 −0.1

NOTE: Tidal heights inside harbour are affected by flow down River Arun. Tide seldom falls lower than 0.7m above datum.

SHELTER
Good. SE winds cause a certain swell up the harbour; SW winds cause roughness on the bar. Entrance dangerous with strong SE winds.
NAVIGATION
Waypoint 50°47'.50N 00°32'.20W, 166°/346° from/to front Ldg Lt 346°, 0.60M. Bar ½ M offshore. Harbour available from HW−4 to HW+3 for boats with about 2m draught. The ebb stream runs so fast at springs that yachts may have difficulty entering. When Pilot boat with P at the bow displays a RW flag by day or W over R lights at night, all boats keep clear of entrance. Speed limit 6½ kn. Depth over the bar is 0.6m less than depth shown on tide gauges. On departure check tide gauge at East Pier to calculate depth on bar.

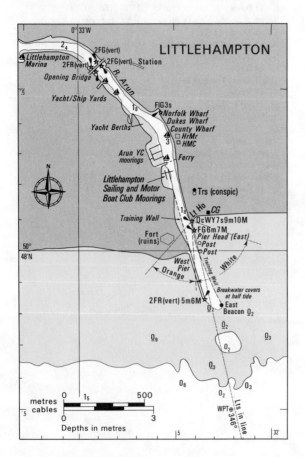

LIGHTS AND MARKS
Leading marks for entrance are lighthouse at inshore end of E breakwater and the black steel column for the light at the outer end of E breakwater; Ldg Lts 346°.
Swing bridge Fl G Lt — Open
Fl R Lt — Closed   from high mast to port.
The central retractable section of the bridge has 2 FR (vert) to port at each end and 2 FG (vert) to stbd at each end. Opening section is 22m wide. Bridge retracted on request provided notice given before 1630 previous day.
RADIO TELEPHONE
Marinas Ch 80 (office hours).
TELEPHONE (0903)
Hr Mr 721215/6; CG 715512; MRSC Lee-on-Solent 552100; ▦ (0703) 229251; Marinecall 0898 500 456; Police 716161; Dr 714113.
FACILITIES
EC Wednesday **Littlehampton Marina** (120+30 visitors) ☎ 713553, Slip, BH (16 ton), CH, P, D, V, R, Bar, FW, AC, Sh, ME, SM; **Ship and Anchor Marina** (182, some visitors) ☎ Yapton 551262, Slip, FW, C (6 ton), ME, Sh, CH, V, R, Bar (Access HW∓4); **Arun YC** (90+10 visitors) ☎ 714533, Slip, AC, FW, L, M, Bar (Access HW∓3); **E side of Harbour** M, C, FW; **Littlehampton Sailing and Motor Club** ☎ 715859, M, FW, Bar; **Wm Osbornes** ☎ 713996, BY; **Delta Yachts** ☎ 717369, BY; **Arrow Marine** ☎ 721686, FW, ME, El, Sh, P, D; **County Wharf** FW, C (5 ton); **Hillyards** ☎ 713327, M, FW, ME, Sh (Wood), C; **Sussex YC** ☎ 464868 Bar, R, M, D, FW, L, Slip.
Town P, D, V, R, Bar. ✉; Ⓑ; ⇌; ✈ (Shoreham).

SHOREHAM   10-3-10
W. Sussex

CHARTS
Admiralty 2044, 1652; Stanford 9; Imray C9; OS 197/8
TIDES
+0005 Dover; ML 3.4; Duration 0605; Zone 0 (GMT)

Standard Port SHOREHAM (→)

Times				Height (metres)			
HW		LW		MHWS	MHWN	MLWN	MLWS
0500	1000	0000	0600	6.2	5.0	1.9	0.7
1700	2200	1200	1800				

Differences WORTHING
+0010 0000 −0005 −0010 −0.1 −0.2 0.0 0.0

NOTE: Shoreham is a Standard Port and tidal predictions for the year are given below.

SHELTER
Excellent. There is complete shelter once through the locks into Southwick Canal. Locks are manned HW∓4. The shallow water at the entrance can be very rough in strong on-shore winds. Berthing space for yachts is very limited and arrangements should be made in advance. Harbour dues are high.
NAVIGATION
Waypoint 50°49'.20N 00°14'.72W, 175°/355° from/to front Ldg Lt 355°, 0.52M. From E, beware Jenny Rks; from W beware Church Rks. Yachtsmen are advised not to use the W arm if possible. Harbour is mainly commercial, so before entering yachtsmen should familiarise themselves with bye-laws, control signals, lock signals, tidal signals etc. Prince George lock usually used for light craft and yachts.
Prince George Lock opens
Outward HW−3¾, −1¾, +½, +2¾
Inward HW−3¼, −1¼, +1, +3¼
Apl to Oct on Sat, Sun and Bank Holidays
Outward HW−3¾, −2½, −1, +¼, +1½, +3
Inward HW−3¼, −2, −½, +½, +1¾, +3¼

SHOREHAM *continued*

LIGHTS AND MARKS

International Port Traffic Signals (see 6.2.7) are displayed from Middle Pier Control Station. In line with High Lighthouse they form leading line for entrance.
Additional signals are displayed as follows. From Lifeboat House: focussed over Eastern Arm, and controlling movement therein. From Lifeboat House: focussed over Western Arm, and controlling movement therein. From Prince George Lock: controlling entrance thereto. From Prince Philip Lock: controlling entrance thereto.

RADIO TELEPHONE

VHF Ch 14 16; 14 (H24). Lady Bee Marina Ch **80**

TELEPHONE (0273)

Hr Mr 592613; MRSC Lee-on-Solent 552100; ⌗ (0703) 229251; Marinecall 0898 500 456; Police 454521; Ⓗ 455622; Dr 461101 (Health Centre).

FACILITIES

EC Wednesday; **Lady Bee Marina** (110 + 10 visitors) ☎ 593801, Slip, P, D, FW, ME, El, Sh, SM, AC, R, V, CH; Access HW∓3½; **Surry BY** ☎ 461491, Slip, M, FW, AR, Access HW ∓2½; **Sussex Motor YC** ☎ 463078, M, L, Bar; **Shoreham Ship Services** ☎ 461274, CH; **Riverside Marine** ☎ 464831, ME, FW, El, Sh, SM, Slip, M; **A. O. Muggeridge** ☎ 592211, CH, Rigging, ACA; **G. P. Barnes** ☎ 591705, Gas.
Town ▢, ✉; Ⓑ; ⇌; ✈.

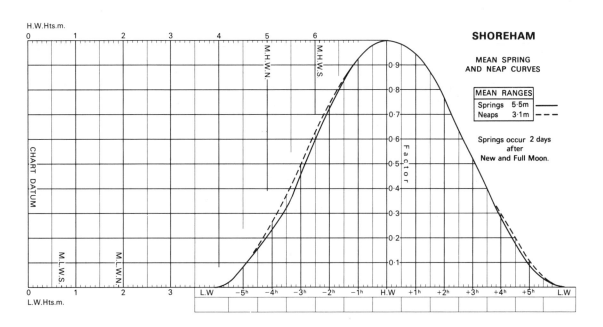

SHOREHAM

MEAN SPRING
AND NEAP CURVES

MEAN RANGES	
Springs	5·5m ———
Neaps	3·1m - - -

Springs occur **2 days** after **New and Full Moon.**

ENGLAND, SOUTH COAST – SHOREHAM

Lat 50°50′ N   Long 0°15′ W

TIMES AND HEIGHTS OF HIGH AND LOW WATERS

YEAR **1991**

TIME ZONE UT(GMT)
For Summer Time add ONE hour in non-shaded areas

Chart Datum: 3.27 metres below Ordnance Datum (Newlyn)

JANUARY

Day	Time	m	Time	m	Time	m	Time	m
1 Tu	0512	0.9	1110	6.3	1742	0.7	2347	6.4
2 W	0601	0.9	1200	6.4	1829	0.8		
3 Th	0036	6.4	0649	1.0	1249	6.3	1915	0.8
4 F	0122	6.4	0735	1.0	1335	6.2	1959	0.8
5 Sa	0205	6.3	0820	1.1	1419	6.0	2042	0.9
6 Su	0247	6.1	0905	1.2	1504	5.7	2126	1.1
7 M (	0328	5.8	0952	1.3	1552	5.4	2212	1.3
8 Tu	0414	5.5	1043	1.6	1644	5.0	2307	1.6
9 W	0510	5.2	1145	1.8	1750	4.7		
10 Th	0013	1.9	0617	4.9	1256	1.9	1905	4.7
11 F	0127	2.0	0729	4.9	1404	1.9	2015	4.8
12 Sa	0234	1.9	0832	5.0	1504	1.7	2114	5.0
13 Su	0328	1.7	0927	5.2	1552	1.4	2203	5.3
14 M	0413	1.5	1012	5.5	1633	1.2	2244	5.6
15 Tu ●	0453	1.3	1051	5.7	1710	1.1	2319	5.8
16 W	0527	1.2	1124	5.8	1743	1.0	2353	5.9
17 Th	0558	1.2	1156	5.9	1815	1.0		
18 F	0024	5.9	0632	1.1	1230	5.9	1850	0.9
19 Sa	0055	6.0	0707	1.1	1304	5.9	1924	0.9
20 Su	0129	6.0	0742	1.0	1341	5.9	2001	0.8
21 M	0202	6.0	0819	1.0	1419	5.8	2037	0.9
22 Tu	0237	5.8	0859	1.0	1458	5.6	2117	1.0
23 W)	0318	5.6	0944	1.2	1544	5.4	2205	1.2
24 Th	0410	5.3	1042	1.4	1643	5.1	2310	1.5
25 F	0521	5.1	1159	1.5	1806	5.0		
26 Sa	0035	1.6	0646	5.1	1326	1.5	1936	5.2
27 Su	0201	1.4	0807	5.4	1445	1.3	2053	5.5
28 M	0314	1.2	0918	5.7	1550	1.0	2154	5.9
29 Tu	0414	1.0	1013	6.0	1644	0.8	2250	6.2
30 W ○	0505	0.8	1103	6.3	1732	0.7	2337	6.4
31 Th	0551	0.8	1149	6.4	1816	0.6		

FEBRUARY

Day	Time	m	Time	m	Time	m	Time	m
1 F	0021	6.5	0635	0.8	1232	6.4	1858	0.6
2 Sa	0102	6.5	0715	0.8	1314	6.3	1937	0.6
3 Su	0139	6.4	0754	0.8	1353	6.1	2013	0.7
4 M	0213	6.2	0832	0.9	1431	5.9	2049	0.9
5 Tu	0246	5.9	0908	1.1	1506	5.5	2127	1.2
6 W (	0321	5.5	0949	1.4	1548	5.1	2211	1.6
7 Th	0407	5.1	1042	1.8	1645	4.7	2313	2.0
8 F	0512	4.7	1154	2.1	1807	4.4		
9 Sa	0035	2.2	0637	4.5	1320	2.1	1938	4.5
10 Su	0159	2.2	0800	4.6	1434	2.0	2049	4.8
11 M	0304	1.9	0906	5.0	1530	1.6	2143	5.2
12 Tu	0353	1.6	0954	5.3	1612	1.3	2224	5.6
13 W	0431	1.3	1032	5.7	1648	1.1	2300	5.8
14 Th ●	0505	1.1	1104	5.9	1722	0.9	2331	6.0
15 F	0536	0.9	1136	6.0	1755	0.8		
16 Sa	0002	6.1	0609	0.8	1210	6.1	1829	0.7
17 Su	0034	6.2	0644	0.7	1245	6.2	1904	0.6
18 M	0107	6.2	0720	0.6	1323	6.2	1939	0.6
19 Tu	0140	6.2	0757	0.6	1359	6.1	2016	0.7
20 W	0212	6.0	0835	0.8	1435	5.8	2054	0.9
21 Th)	0250	5.7	0918	1.0	1517	5.5	2140	1.2
22 F	0341	5.3	1014	1.4	1618	5.1	2246	1.6
23 Sa	0454	5.0	1134	1.6	1750	4.9		
24 Su	0021	1.7	0631	4.9	1316	1.6	1932	5.0
25 M	0157	1.6	0804	5.1	1440	1.4	2051	5.5
26 Tu	0310	1.3	0913	5.6	1542	1.0	2149	5.9
27 W	0407	1.0	1007	6.0	1633	0.7	2239	6.3
28 Th ○	0453	0.7	1051	6.2	1717	0.6	2321	6.4

MARCH

Day	Time	m	Time	m	Time	m	Time	m
1 F	0534	0.6	1132	6.4	1756	0.5	2358	6.5
2 Sa	0613	0.6	1210	6.4	1833	0.5		
3 Su	0033	6.5	0649	0.6	1247	6.3	1908	0.5
4 M	0106	6.4	0723	0.6	1322	6.1	1941	0.6
5 Tu	0136	6.2	0755	0.8	1355	5.9	2013	0.8
6 W	0204	5.9	0828	1.0	1426	5.5	2046	1.2
7 Th	0235	5.5	0903	1.3	1502	5.1	2124	1.6
8 F (	0315	5.0	0945	1.8	1553	4.7	2220	2.1
9 Sa	0414	4.6	1053	2.2	1711	4.4	2341	2.4
10 Su	0544	4.3	1225	2.3	1852	4.4		
11 M	0117	2.4	0723	4.4	1352	2.2	2014	4.7
12 Tu	0229	2.1	0835	4.8	1454	1.8	2112	5.1
13 W	0320	1.7	0927	5.2	1538	1.4	2153	5.6
14 Th	0358	1.3	1003	5.6	1617	1.0	2227	5.9
15 F	0434	1.0	1035	5.9	1651	0.8	2259	6.1
16 Sa ●	0508	0.7	1108	6.1	1726	0.6	2332	6.2
17 Su	0543	0.6	1145	6.2	1804	0.6		
18 M	0008	6.3	0621	0.5	1222	6.3	1841	0.5
19 Tu	0043	6.3	0658	0.5	1302	6.3	1918	0.5
20 W	0119	6.3	0737	0.5	1341	6.2	1957	0.7
21 Th	0154	6.1	0817	0.7	1420	5.9	2038	0.9
22 F	0235	5.8	0901	1.1	1507	5.5	2128	1.3
23 Sa)	0328	5.3	1000	1.4	1612	5.1	2240	1.7
24 Su	0444	4.9	1125	1.7	1748	4.9		
25 M	0018	1.8	0627	4.8	1305	1.7	1926	5.1
26 Tu	0151	1.6	0758	5.1	1426	1.4	2039	5.5
27 W	0258	1.3	0903	5.5	1525	1.0	2134	5.9
28 Th	0349	0.9	0953	5.9	1611	0.8	2218	6.2
29 F	0433	0.7	1033	6.1	1653	0.6	2256	6.4
30 Sa ○	0512	0.6	1109	6.2	1731	0.5	2331	6.4
31 Su	0547	0.6	1145	6.2	1805	0.5		

APRIL

Day	Time	m	Time	m	Time	m	Time	m
1 M	0002	6.3	0620	0.6	1219	6.1	1837	0.6
2 Tu	0033	6.2	0652	0.6	1254	6.0	1908	0.7
3 W	0101	6.3	0722	0.8	1324	5.8	1941	1.0
4 Th	0129	5.8	0753	1.0	1355	5.5	2013	1.3
5 F	0159	5.4	0827	1.3	1430	5.2	2051	1.7
6 Sa	0238	5.0	0909	1.7	1516	4.8	2142	2.1
7 Su (	0333	4.6	1006	2.1	1626	4.5	2255	2.4
8 M	0454	4.3	1126	2.3	1758	4.5		
9 Tu	0022	2.4	0629	4.4	1254	2.2	1923	4.7
10 W	0138	2.1	0748	4.7	1403	1.9	2024	5.1
11 Th	0233	1.7	0843	5.1	1454	1.5	2110	5.5
12 F	0317	1.3	0923	5.4	1536	1.1	2148	5.9
13 Sa	0356	0.9	0959	5.8	1615	0.8	2223	6.1
14 Su ●	0435	0.7	1036	6.1	1656	0.6	2300	6.3
15 M	0516	0.5	1117	6.3	1736	0.6	2340	6.3
16 Tu	0557	0.5	1201	6.3	1818	0.6		
17 W	0021	6.4	0640	0.5	1247	6.3	1900	0.7
18 Th	0101	6.3	0723	0.6	1330	6.2	1944	0.8
19 F	0143	6.1	0807	0.9	1417	5.9	2031	1.1
20 Sa	0230	5.7	0856	1.1	1508	5.6	2127	1.4
21 Su)	0325	5.3	0957	1.4	1616	5.3	2240	1.7
22 M	0442	5.0	1116	1.6	1741	5.1		
23 Tu	0007	1.7	0614	4.9	1245	1.6	1906	5.3
24 W	0128	1.6	0736	5.0	1359	1.4	2013	5.5
25 Th	0233	1.3	0840	5.4	1456	1.1	2106	5.8
26 F	0323	1.0	0929	5.7	1544	0.9	2150	6.0
27 Sa	0407	0.8	1009	5.9	1625	0.8	2227	6.1
28 Su ○	0445	0.7	1044	6.0	1703	0.7	2301	6.1
29 M	0521	0.7	1120	6.0	1738	0.7	2334	6.1
30 Tu	0553	0.7	1155	5.9	1811	0.8		

ENGLAND, SOUTH COAST – SHOREHAM

Lat 50°50' N Long 0°15' W

TIMES AND HEIGHTS OF HIGH AND LOW WATERS

YEAR **1991**

3

TIME ZONE UT(GMT)
For Summer Time add ONE hour in non-shaded areas

MAY

Day	Time	m	Day	Time	m
1 W	0005 / 0625 / 1230 / 1843	6.0 / 0.8 / 5.8 / 1.0	16 Th	0003 / 0625 / 1235 / 1848	6.3 / 0.7 / 6.3 / 0.9
2 Th	0035 / 0655 / 1302 / 1915	5.9 / 0.9 / 5.7 / 1.2	17 F	0049 / 0712 / 1325 / 1936	6.2 / 0.8 / 6.2 / 1.0
3 F	0104 / 0727 / 1336 / 1950	5.7 / 1.1 / 5.5 / 1.4	18 Sa	0138 / 0802 / 1417 / 2028	6.1 / 1.0 / 6.1 / 1.2
4 Sa	0137 / 0802 / 1411 / 2029	5.4 / 1.4 / 5.3 / 1.7	19 Su	0228 / 0854 / 1509 / 2124	5.8 / 1.1 / 5.8 / 1.4
5 Su	0217 / 0844 / 1455 / 2116	5.1 / 1.7 / 5.0 / 2.0	20 M	0324 / 0951 / 1610 / 2229 ☽	5.5 / 1.3 / 5.6 / 1.5
6 M	0307 / 0934 / 1552 / 2215	4.7 / 1.9 / 4.8 / 2.2	21 Tu	0431 / 1057 / 1718 / 2340	5.2 / 1.5 / 5.4 / 1.6
7 Tu	0412 / 1036 / 1704 / 2326 ☾	4.5 / 2.1 / 4.7 / 2.2	22 W	0547 / 1211 / 1830	5.0 / 1.6 / 5.4
8 W	0531 / 1150 / 1819	4.5 / 2.1 / 4.8	23 Th	0053 / 0702 / 1321 / 1935	1.6 / 5.0 / 1.5 / 5.4
9 Th	0038 / 0646 / 1301 / 1925	2.0 / 4.7 / 1.8 / 5.1	24 F	0158 / 0806 / 1420 / 2030	1.4 / 5.1 / 1.4 / 5.6
10 F	0140 / 0748 / 1401 / 2018	1.7 / 5.1 / 1.5 / 5.5	25 Sa	0251 / 0857 / 1513 / 2118	1.3 / 5.3 / 1.2 / 5.7
11 Sa	0231 / 0837 / 1451 / 2103	1.7 / 5.5 / 1.1 / 5.8	26 Su	0338 / 0942 / 1558 / 2159	1.1 / 5.5 / 1.1 / 5.8
12 Su	0319 / 0922 / 1539 / 2146	0.9 / 5.8 / 0.9 / 6.0	27 M	0420 / 1022 / 1639 / 2236	1.0 / 5.6 / 1.0 / 5.8
13 M	0405 / 1006 / 1626 / 2231	0.7 / 6.0 / 0.7 / 6.2	28 Tu	0457 / 1102 / 1716 / 2311 ○	0.9 / 5.7 / 1.0 / 5.8
14 Tu	0451 / 1054 / 1713 / 2317 ●	0.6 / 6.2 / 0.7 / 6.3	29 W	0532 / 1139 / 1751 / 2344	0.9 / 5.7 / 1.1 / 5.8
15 W	0538 / 1144 / 1800	0.6 / 6.2 / 0.8	30 Th	0605 / 1214 / 1824	1.0 / 5.7 / 1.2
			31 F	0016 / 0637 / 1248 / 1858	5.7 / 1.1 / 5.7 / 1.3

JUNE

Day	Time	m	Day	Time	m
1 Sa	0049 / 0710 / 1323 / 1932	5.6 / 1.2 / 5.6 / 1.5	16 Su	0131 / 0757 / 1411 / 2021	6.2 / 0.9 / 6.2 / 1.1
2 Su	0122 / 0747 / 1357 / 2012	5.5 / 1.3 / 5.4 / 1.6	17 M	0221 / 0845 / 1500 / 2111	6.0 / 1.0 / 6.1 / 1.2
3 M	0202 / 0824 / 1436 / 2053	5.2 / 1.5 / 5.3 / 1.7	18 Tu	0312 / 0935 / 1550 / 2205	5.7 / 1.1 / 5.9 / 1.3
4 Tu	0246 / 0908 / 1523 / 2140	5.0 / 1.6 / 5.1 / 1.8	19 W	0406 / 1028 / 1643 / 2305 ☽	5.4 / 1.3 / 5.6 / 1.5
5 W	0337 / 0957 / 1616 / 2236	4.9 / 1.7 / 5.0 / 1.9	20 Th	0506 / 1129 / 1743	5.1 / 1.5 / 5.4
6 Th	0436 / 1055 / 1717 / 2339	4.8 / 1.8 / 5.0 / 1.8	21 F	0009 / 0613 / 1235 / 1846	1.6 / 4.9 / 1.6 / 5.2
7 F	0544 / 1200 / 1823	4.8 / 1.7 / 5.1	22 Sa	0115 / 0721 / 1341 / 1948	1.7 / 4.9 / 1.7 / 5.2
8 Sa	0044 / 0649 / 1308 / 1926	1.6 / 5.0 / 1.5 / 5.3	23 Su	0217 / 0822 / 1440 / 2045	1.6 / 5.0 / 1.6 / 5.3
9 Su	0147 / 0751 / 1411 / 2023	1.4 / 5.3 / 1.3 / 5.6	24 M	0311 / 0916 / 1533 / 2134	1.5 / 5.1 / 1.5 / 5.4
10 M	0246 / 0847 / 1508 / 2117	1.1 / 5.6 / 1.1 / 5.9	25 Tu	0358 / 1004 / 1619 / 2217	1.3 / 5.3 / 1.4 / 5.5
11 Tu	0340 / 0943 / 1604 / 2208	0.9 / 5.9 / 0.9 / 6.1	26 W	0440 / 1047 / 1659 / 2256 ○	1.2 / 5.5 / 1.3 / 5.7
12 W	0434 / 1038 / 1656 / 2300 ●	0.8 / 6.1 / 0.9 / 6.2	27 Th	0516 / 1125 / 1735 / 2331	1.1 / 5.6 / 1.3 / 5.7
13 Th	0526 / 1134 / 1749 / 2351	0.8 / 6.2 / 0.9 / 6.3	28 F	0550 / 1202 / 1810	1.1 / 5.7 / 1.3
14 F	0618 / 1229 / 1840	0.8 / 6.3 / 1.0	29 Sa	0003 / 0623 / 1236 / 1842	5.7 / 1.1 / 5.7 / 1.3
15 Sa	0041 / 0706 / 1321 / 1929	6.3 / 0.9 / 6.3 / 1.0	30 Su	0035 / 0656 / 1308 / 1916	5.7 / 1.2 / 5.7 / 1.4

JULY

Day	Time	m	Day	Time	m
1 M	0110 / 0731 / 1341 / 1953	5.6 / 1.2 / 5.7 / 1.4	16 Tu	0204 / 0826 / 1437 / 2049	6.1 / 0.9 / 6.3 / 1.0
2 Tu	0145 / 0807 / 1416 / 2029	5.5 / 1.2 / 5.6 / 1.4	17 W	0248 / 0909 / 1517 / 2134	5.9 / 1.0 / 6.0 / 1.2
3 W	0223 / 0844 / 1452 / 2109	5.4 / 1.3 / 5.5 / 1.4	18 Th	0332 / 0953 / 1559 / 2222 ☽	5.6 / 1.2 / 5.7 / 1.4
4 Th	0304 / 0923 / 1535 / 2153	5.2 / 1.4 / 5.4 / 1.5	19 F	0419 / 1043 / 1649 / 2318	5.2 / 1.5 / 5.3 / 1.7
5 F	0350 / 1012 / 1626 / 2250	5.1 / 1.5 / 5.2 / 1.6	20 Sa	0518 / 1144 / 1751	4.8 / 1.8 / 5.0
6 Sa	0448 / 1112 / 1729 / 2356	4.9 / 1.6 / 5.1 / 1.6	21 Su	0025 / 0632 / 1257 / 1903	1.9 / 4.6 / 2.0 / 4.8
7 Su	0558 / 1224 / 1840	4.9 / 1.6 / 5.2	22 M	0138 / 0747 / 1409 / 2014	2.0 / 4.6 / 2.0 / 4.9
8 M	0109 / 0714 / 1340 / 1951	1.5 / 5.1 / 1.5 / 5.4	23 Tu	0244 / 0853 / 1511 / 2113	1.8 / 4.8 / 1.9 / 5.1
9 Tu	0221 / 0825 / 1449 / 2056	1.3 / 5.4 / 1.3 / 5.7	24 W	0338 / 0947 / 1601 / 2203	1.6 / 5.1 / 1.7 / 5.3
10 W	0326 / 0930 / 1551 / 2155	1.1 / 5.7 / 1.1 / 6.0	25 Th	0423 / 1033 / 1642 / 2243 ○	1.4 / 5.4 / 1.5 / 5.6
11 Th	0424 / 1029 / 1648 / 2249 ●	0.9 / 6.0 / 1.0 / 6.2	26 F	0500 / 1111 / 1718 / 2316	1.2 / 5.6 / 1.3 / 5.7
12 F	0518 / 1125 / 1740 / 2341	0.8 / 6.2 / 1.0 / 6.3	27 Sa	0533 / 1145 / 1751 / 2347	1.1 / 5.8 / 1.3 / 5.8
13 Sa	0609 / 1218 / 1830	0.8 / 6.4 / 1.0	28 Su	0606 / 1217 / 1822	1.1 / 5.8 / 1.2
14 Su	0031 / 0656 / 1307 / 1917	6.3 / 0.8 / 6.4 / 1.0	29 M	0018 / 0639 / 1248 / 1856	5.8 / 1.1 / 5.9 / 1.2
15 M	0118 / 0742 / 1353 / 2004	6.3 / 0.7 / 6.4 / 1.0	30 Tu	0051 / 0711 / 1319 / 1929	5.8 / 1.0 / 5.9 / 1.1
			31 W	0124 / 0745 / 1350 / 2004	5.8 / 1.0 / 5.9 / 1.1

AUGUST

Day	Time	m	Day	Time	m
1 Th	0159 / 0818 / 1422 / 2039	5.7 / 1.0 / 5.8 / 1.1	16 F	0253 / 0913 / 1512 / 2136	5.7 / 1.2 / 5.7 / 1.4
2 F	0235 / 0855 / 1458 / 2119	5.6 / 1.1 / 5.6 / 1.3	17 Sa	0331 / 0956 / 1555 / 2225 ☽	5.2 / 1.6 / 5.2 / 1.8
3 Sa	0314 / 0937 / 1544 / 2210	5.3 / 1.4 / 5.3 / 1.5	18 Su	0424 / 1053 / 1656 / 2333	4.8 / 2.0 / 4.8 / 2.1
4 Su	0406 / 1035 / 1646 / 2319	5.0 / 1.6 / 5.1 / 1.7	19 M	0540 / 1212 / 1816	4.5 / 2.3 / 4.5
5 M	0521 / 1152 / 1807	4.9 / 1.8 / 5.0	20 Tu	0056 / 0710 / 1337 / 1942	2.3 / 4.4 / 2.4 / 4.6
6 Tu	0044 / 0651 / 1320 / 1934	1.7 / 4.9 / 1.7 / 5.2	21 W	0215 / 0827 / 1447 / 2053	2.1 / 4.7 / 2.2 / 4.9
7 W	0208 / 0816 / 1440 / 2048	1.5 / 5.3 / 1.5 / 5.5	22 Th	0313 / 0925 / 1538 / 2144	1.9 / 5.1 / 1.8 / 5.2
8 Th	0319 / 0925 / 1544 / 2148	1.2 / 5.7 / 1.2 / 5.9	23 F	0400 / 1011 / 1619 / 2223	1.6 / 5.4 / 1.5 / 5.6
9 F	0416 / 1022 / 1640 / 2240	1.0 / 6.1 / 1.0 / 6.2	24 Sa	0436 / 1046 / 1653 / 2255	1.3 / 5.7 / 1.3 / 5.8
10 Sa	0507 / 1114 / 1728 / 2327 ●	0.8 / 6.4 / 0.9 / 6.4	25 Su	0509 / 1117 / 1724 / 2323 ○	1.1 / 5.9 / 1.1 / 5.9
11 Su	0554 / 1200 / 1814	0.7 / 6.5 / 0.8	26 M	0540 / 1200 / 1756 / 2353	1.0 / 6.0 / 1.0 / 6.0
12 M	0012 / 0637 / 1244 / 1858	6.4 / 0.7 / 6.5 / 0.8	27 Tu	0613 / 1219 / 1829	0.9 / 6.1 / 0.9
13 Tu	0056 / 0720 / 1325 / 1939	6.4 / 0.7 / 6.5 / 0.8	28 W	0027 / 0646 / 1250 / 1903	6.0 / 0.9 / 6.1 / 0.9
14 W	0137 / 0758 / 1403 / 2019	6.2 / 0.8 / 6.3 / 0.9	29 Th	0101 / 0719 / 1322 / 1938	6.0 / 0.8 / 6.1 / 0.8
15 Th	0215 / 0836 / 1436 / 2056	6.0 / 0.9 / 6.1 / 1.1	30 F	0134 / 0754 / 1355 / 2014	6.0 / 0.9 / 6.0 / 0.9
			31 Sa	0209 / 0830 / 1431 / 2053	5.8 / 1.1 / 5.7 / 1.2

Chart Datum: 3.27 metres below Ordnance Datum (Newlyn)

ENGLAND, SOUTH COAST – SHOREHAM

Lat 50°50′ N   Long 0°15′ W

TIMES AND HEIGHTS OF HIGH AND LOW WATERS

YEAR 1991

TIME ZONE UT(GMT)
For Summer Time add ONE hour in non-shaded areas

SEPTEMBER

Day	Time	m	Day	Time	m
1 Su (	0248	5.5	16 M	0337	4.8
	0914	1.4		1008	2.2
	1517	5.4		1605	4.7
	2144	1.5		2241	2.2
2 M	0342	5.1	17 Tu	0452	4.5
	1012	1.7		1126	2.5
	1621	5.0		1729	4.4
	2255	1.8			
3 Tu	0502	4.9	18 W	0008	2.4
	1138	1.9		0629	4.4
	1751	4.9		1258	2.6
				1905	4.4
4 W	0030	1.8	19 Th	0135	2.3
	0645	5.0		0751	4.7
	1315	1.8		1411	2.3
	1927	5.1		2021	4.7
5 Th	0201	1.6	20 F	0238	2.0
	0810	5.3		0852	5.1
	1435	1.5		1504	1.9
	2043	5.5		2115	5.2
6 F	0309	1.3	21 Sa	0324	1.6
	0916	5.8		0936	5.5
	1535	1.2		1545	1.5
	2139	5.9		2152	5.6
7 Sa	0403	0.9	22 Su	0401	1.3
	1008	6.2		1012	5.8
	1626	0.9		1619	1.2
	2226	6.2		2223	5.9
8 Su ●	0449	0.7	23 M ○	0435	1.1
	1054	6.4		1042	6.0
	1711	0.7		1653	1.0
	2308	6.4		2253	6.0
9 M	0533	0.6	24 Tu	0508	0.9
	1135	6.5		1114	6.1
	1752	0.7		1726	0.8
	2348	6.4		2323	6.1
10 Tu	0612	0.6	25 W	0543	0.8
	1214	6.5		1147	6.2
	1831	0.7		1801	0.8
11 W	0027	6.4	26 Th	0000	6.2
	0651	0.7		0618	0.8
	1251	6.4		1221	6.2
	1909	0.7		1838	0.7
12 Th	0105	6.2	27 F	0036	6.2
	0726	0.8		0655	0.8
	1325	6.3		1257	6.2
	1943	0.8		1915	0.8
13 F	0140	6.0	28 Sa	0114	6.1
	0800	1.0		0732	0.9
	1355	6.0		1332	6.1
	2018	1.0		1954	0.9
14 Sa	0214	5.7	29 Su	0152	5.9
	0836	1.3		0812	1.1
	1427	5.7		1412	5.8
	2054	1.4		2036	1.2
15 Su)	0250	5.3	30 M	0237	5.6
	0915	1.7		0900	1.5
	1507	5.2		1502	5.4
	2138	1.8		2131	1.5

OCTOBER

Day	Time	m	Day	Time	m
1 Tu (	0335	5.3	16 W	0408	4.6
	1005	1.8		1041	2.5
	1612	5.1		1640	4.5
	2246	1.8		2312	2.4
2 W	0501	5.0	17 Th	0534	4.5
	1133	1.9		1205	2.6
	1745	4.9		1811	4.4
3 Th	0021	1.8	18 F	0038	2.4
	0638	5.1		0658	4.7
	1308	1.8		1321	2.3
	1919	5.1		1932	4.7
4 F	0147	1.6	19 Sa	0146	2.1
	0757	5.5		0802	5.1
	1420	1.5		1417	2.0
	2031	5.5		2028	5.1
5 Sa	0250	1.2	20 Su	0237	1.7
	0857	5.9		0849	5.4
	1518	1.1		1502	1.5
	2123	5.9		2110	5.5
6 Su	0343	0.9	21 M	0319	1.3
	0946	6.2		0927	5.8
	1606	0.8		1540	1.2
	2207	6.2		2144	5.8
7 M	0426	0.7	22 Tu	0358	1.1
	1027	6.4		1002	6.0
	1648	0.7		1618	0.9
●	2245	6.3		2218	6.0
8 Tu	0507	0.6	23 W ○	0435	0.9
	1106	6.5		1037	6.2
	1726	0.7		1655	0.7
	2322	6.3		2255	6.2
9 W	0544	0.7	24 Th	0513	0.8
	1142	6.4		1116	6.3
	1803	0.7		1735	0.7
				2335	6.3
10 Th	0621	0.7	25 F	0554	0.8
	1216	6.3		1156	6.3
	1838	0.8		1816	0.7
11 F	0034	6.1	26 Sa	0018	6.3
	0655	0.9		0634	0.9
	1248	6.2		1236	6.3
	1910	0.9		1858	0.8
12 Sa	0109	5.9	27 Su	0101	6.2
	0728	1.1		0717	1.0
	1319	5.9		1318	6.1
	1943	1.1		1942	1.0
13 Su	0142	5.7	28 M	0146	6.0
	0801	1.4		0804	1.2
	1351	5.6		1405	5.9
	2018	1.4		2030	1.2
14 M	0217	5.3	29 Tu	0236	5.2
	0841	1.8		0858	1.5
	1430	5.2		1459	5.5
	2059	1.8		2127	1.4
15 Tu)	0303	5.0	30 W (	0337	5.5
	0932	2.2		1003	1.7
	1524	4.8		1607	5.2
	2156	2.2		2238	1.6
			31 Th	0454	5.3
				1123	1.8
				1733	5.0

NOVEMBER

Day	Time	m	Day	Time	m
1 F	0002	1.7	16 Sa	0550	4.8
	0619	5.3		1216	2.2
	1246	1.7		1825	4.7
	1858	5.1			
2 Sa	0120	1.5	17 Su	0041	2.0
	0731	5.6		0658	5.0
	1356	1.4		1320	1.9
	2007	5.4		1929	5.0
3 Su	0224	1.3	18 M	0141	1.8
	0829	5.8		0753	5.3
	1453	1.2		1413	1.6
	2059	5.7		2020	5.3
4 M	0316	1.0	19 Tu	0232	1.4
	0917	6.1		0840	5.6
	1542	0.9		1459	1.2
	2143	5.9		2102	5.7
5 Tu	0401	0.9	20 W	0318	1.1
	0959	6.2		0923	5.9
	1624	0.8		1545	0.9
	2221	6.1		2145	5.9
6 W ●	0442	0.8	21 Th ○	0403	0.8
	1037	6.2		1005	6.1
	1702	0.7		1630	0.8
	2258	6.1		2230	6.1
7 Th	0520	0.8	22 F	0448	0.9
	1113	6.2		1050	6.3
	1737	0.8		1715	0.7
	2336	6.1		2316	6.3
8 F	0555	0.9	23 Sa	0534	0.9
	1148	6.1		1136	6.3
	1811	0.9		1800	0.8
9 Sa	0013	6.0	24 Su	0007	6.3
	0628	1.1		0621	1.0
	1220	6.0		1223	6.3
	1844	1.0		1848	0.8
10 Su	0046	5.9	25 M	0055	6.1
	0701	1.3		0709	1.1
	1252	5.9		1311	6.2
	1916	1.2		1937	0.9
11 M	0120	5.7	26 Tu	0145	6.2
	0737	1.5		0800	1.2
	1326	5.6		1402	6.0
	1953	1.4		2027	1.1
12 Tu	0155	5.5	27 W	0236	6.1
	0817	1.8		0852	1.3
	1406	5.3		1455	5.8
	2033	1.6		2121	1.2
13 W	0238	5.2	28 Th (	0332	5.8
	0903	2.0		0952	1.4
	1454	5.0		1556	5.5
	2120	1.9		2222	1.4
14 Th	0331	4.9	29 F	0435	5.6
	0959	2.2		1100	1.6
	1556	4.7		1707	5.2
	2219	2.1		2331	1.5
15 F	0436	4.8	30 Sa	0543	5.5
	1106	2.3		1213	1.6
	1709	4.6		1822	5.1
	2329	2.2			

DECEMBER

Day	Time	m	Day	Time	m
1 Su	0043	1.5	16 M	0547	5.0
	0653	5.5		1215	1.8
	1323	1.5		1822	4.9
	1932	5.2			
2 M	0150	1.4	17 Tu	0040	1.8
	0754	5.6		0653	5.2
	1423	1.3		1320	1.6
	2030	5.4		1927	5.1
3 Tu	0247	1.3	18 W	0146	1.5
	0846	5.7		0754	5.4
	1516	1.1		1421	1.3
	2118	5.6		2026	5.4
4 W	0337	1.1	19 Th	0245	1.3
	0933	5.8		0849	5.7
	1601	1.0		1518	1.1
	2202	5.7		2120	5.8
5 Th	0420	1.1	20 F	0340	1.1
	1015	5.9		0942	6.0
	1643	0.9		1610	0.9
	2242	5.8		2213	6.1
6 F ●	0500	1.0	21 Sa ○	0432	0.9
	1053	6.0		1034	6.2
	1719	0.9		1702	0.8
	2322	5.9		2307	6.3
7 Sa	0537	1.1	22 Su	0522	0.9
	1129	6.0		1124	6.4
	1753	0.9		1752	0.8
	2358	5.9		2359	6.4
8 Su	0611	1.2	23 M	0612	0.9
	1203	5.9		1215	6.4
	1826	1.0		1842	0.8
9 M	0032	5.8	24 Tu	0049	6.5
	0644	1.3		0702	0.9
	1236	5.8		1304	6.4
	1859	1.1		1930	0.8
10 Tu	0106	5.7	25 W	0138	6.4
	0719	1.4		0751	1.0
	1310	5.7		1355	6.3
	1934	1.3		2018	0.8
11 W	0139	5.6	26 Th	0226	6.3
	0756	1.6		0841	1.1
	1348	5.5		1444	6.0
	2011	1.4		2106	0.9
12 Th	0215	5.5	27 F	0313	6.1
	0836	1.7		0932	1.1
	1429	5.2		1535	5.7
	2050	1.5		2156	1.1
13 F	0256	5.3	28 Sa (	0403	5.9
	0919	1.8		1028	1.3
	1516	5.0		1632	5.4
	2135	1.7		2253	1.3
14 Sa	0343	5.1	29 Su	0459	5.8
	1009	1.9		1131	1.5
	1609	4.9		1736	5.1
	2228	1.8		2358	1.5
15 Su	0442	5.0	30 M	0604	5.3
	1108	1.9		1240	1.6
	1713	4.8		1849	5.0
	2332	1.9			
			31 Tu	0110	1.6
				0712	5.2
				1349	1.6
				1957	5.0

Chart Datum: 3.27 metres below Ordnance Datum (Newlyn)

BRIGHTON 10-3-11
E. Sussex

CHARTS
Admiralty 1991, 1652; Stanford 9; Imray C9; OS 198
TIDES
+0001 Dover; ML 3.5; Duration 0605; Zone 0 (GMT)

Standard Port SHOREHAM (←)

Times				Height (metres)			
HW		LW		MHWS	MHWN	MLWN	MLWS
0500	1000	0000	0600	6.2	5.0	1.9	0.7
1700	2200	1200	1800				

Differences BRIGHTON
−0010	−0005	−0005	−0005	+0.3	+0.1	0.0	−0.1

BRIGHTON MARINA
SHELTER
The marina gives good shelter under all conditions, but the approach in strong S winds could be very rough.
NAVIGATION
Waypoint 50°48′.20N 00°06′.29W, 180°/000° from/to West breakwater Lt, 0.26M. 180° safe sector of approach except shallow water to E of entrance in main Lt R sector. Shoaling may occur at entrance after gales.
LIGHTS AND MARKS
E breakwater Fl(4) WR 20s 16m 10/8M; vis R260°-295°, W295°-100°. E breakwater head QG 8m 6M. W breakwater head QR 10m 7M; Horn (2) 30s.
Inner Harbour Lock controlled by normal R and G traffic control.
Times: 0800-2000 LT.
RADIO TELEPHONE
Call: *Brighton Control* VHF Ch 16; 68 11. Marina Ch **80**.
TELEPHONE (0273)
Hr Mr 693636; CG & MRSC Lee-on-Solent 552100;
▒ (0273) 697936; Marinecall 0898 500 456; Police 606744;
Ⓗ 608431; Dr 686863.

FACILITIES
Brighton Marina (1600+200 visitors) ☎ 693636, ▒, FW, P, D, AC, Gas, Gaz, ▣, R, Bar; **Brighton Marina Boatyard** ☎ 609235, BH (60 ton), C (35 ton); **Brighton Marina Yacht Club** ☎ 697049, Bar, R; **Felton Marine Engineering** ☎ 601779, El, ME; **Leonard Marine** ☎ 515987, Me; **Scott Marine** ☎ 671665, ME; **Terry Pachol & Son** ☎ 682724, Sh; **F.A.M. Enterprises** ☎ 684385, Ⓔ; **Nautical Electronics Services** ☎ 693258, Ⓔ; **Wilkinson** ☎ 677758, Sm; **Welch Marine Services** ☎ 675972, SM; **Russeel Simpson** ☎ 697161, CH; **Moores Marine Maintenance** ☎ (0860) 525966 Diving; **Superstore** V; **Town** V, R, Bar, ▒, Ⓑ, ⇌, ✈ Shoreham, Harbour Guides available from Harbour Manager

NEWHAVEN   10-3-12
E. Sussex

CHARTS
Admiralty 2154, 1652; Stanford 9; Imray C9; OS 198
TIDES
0000 Dover; ML 3.6; Duration 0550; Zone 0 (GMT).

Standard Port SHOREHAM (←)

Times				Height (metres)			
HW		LW		MHWS	MHWN	MLWN	MLWS
0500	1000	0000	0600	6.2	5.0	1.9	0.7
1700	2200	1200	1800				

Differences NEWHAVEN

−0015	−0010	0000	0000	+0.4	+0.2	0.0	−0.2

EASTBOURNE

−0010	−0005	+0015	+0020	+1.1	+0.6	+0.2	+0.1

SHELTER
Good, but with strong on-shore winds there is often a difficult sea at the entrance. Accessible in all weathers but with strong on-shore winds pass close to breakwater; there are heavy breaking seas on E side of dredged channel.

NAVIGATION
Waypoint 50°46′.20N 00°03′.70E, 168°/348° from/to West breakwater Lt, 0.32M. Harbour silts up and dredging is in continuous operation. Cargo vessels and ferries often warp off by means of hawsers run across the harbour.

RADIO TELEPHONE
VHF Ch 16; 12 (H24). Newhaven Marina Ch **80**
TELEPHONE (0273)
Hr Mr 514131; CG 514350; MRSC Lee-on-Solent 552100; Harbour Signal Station 514131 ext. 247; ⌗ (0703) 229251; Marinecall 0898 500 456; Police 515801; Dr 515076; Ⓗ 609411 (Accidents (0273) 696955).
FACILITIES
EC Wednesday; **Newhaven Marina** (300 + 50 visitors) ☎ 513881, Slip, FW, ME, El, Sh, AC, BH (18 ton), C (10 ton), CH, V, R, Bar, Gas, Gaz, ▣, (Access HW∓5), fuel pontoon 200 yds N of ent; **Newhaven Marina YC** ☎ 513976; **Sealink Quays** ☎ 514131, Slip, P, D, L, FW, ME, El, Sh, C (3 ton), CH, AB, V, R, Bar; **Ship and Industrial Repairs** ☎ 516298, ME, El, Sh, C; **Cantell & Son** ☎ 514118, ME, Sh, CH, SM, Slip, C, ACA; **Golden Arrow Marine** ☎ 513987, ME; **Newhaven and Seaford SC** ☎ 513770, Slip, M, P, D, ME, El, Sh, CH, AB; **Meeching Boats** (80) ☎ 514907, ME, El, Sh; **Russell Simpson Marine** ☎ 513458 CH, El; **Leonard Marine** ☎ 515987 BY, El, ME, Sh, Slip, SM; **C & E Sports** ☎ 515450, Gas; **L D Electronics** ☎ 56179, Ⓔ; **Nautical Electronic Services** ☎ 693258, Ⓔ.
Town P, V, R, Bar. ✉; Ⓑ; ⇌; ✈ (Shoreham).

LIGHTS AND MARKS
Traffic signals, displayed from Tr on W side of river.

Triangle over ball, or G Lt	— only entry permitted.
Ball over triangle, or R Lt	— only departure permitted.
Ball, triangle, ball (vert) or RGR Lts (vert)	— No entry or departure
Ball or G R Lts (vert)	— Entry and departure permitted with care for vessels under 15m

Swing bridge signals
FIG — Bridge opening or closing
FR — Vessels may pass N to S
FG — Vessels may pass S to N

RYE   10-3-13

E. Sussex

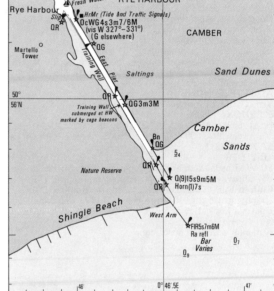

CHARTS
Admiralty 1991, 536; Stanford 9; Imray C8; OS 189

TIDES
0000 Dover; ML 2.0; Zone 0 (GMT).

Standard Port DOVER (→)

Times			Height (metres)			
HW		LW	MHWS	MHWN	MLWN	MLWS
0000	0600	0100	0700	6.7	5.3	2.0	0.8
1200	1800	1300	1900			

Differences RYE HARBOUR

| +0005 | −0010 | No data | −1.4 | −1.7 | Dries | |

HASTINGS

| 0000 | −0010 | −0030 | −0030 | +0.8 | +0.5 | +0.1 | −0.1 |

SHELTER
Very good in river. Entrance requires care when wind strong (force 7 or over) from SE to SW. Enter HW 2 to HW +3. Rye harbour is ¾ M inside entrance and is a small village used by commercial shipping. The town of Rye is another 2M up river; it is a Cinque Port.

NAVIGATION
Waypoint Rye Fairway (safe water) buoy, LFl 10s, 50°54'.00N 00°48'.13E, 150°/330° from/to West Arm head Lt, 1.81M. Beware:
(1) Narrow entrance. Limited width of channel (42m).
(2) Bar at entrance.
(3) Strong flood stream in river — up to 4.5 kn (max HW−3 to HW−1).
(4) Shallow water E & W of entrance with ground swell or surf.
Harbour speed limit 6 kn.

LIGHTS AND MARKS
East Arm, head Q(9) 15s 9m 5M; Horn 7s.
Tide Signals on Hr Mr office: −
Night — FG 2.1-3.0m on bar
　　　　　F Purple Over 3.0m on bar
Day — None, but horizontal timbers on tripod beacon marking W arm indicate depths 5', 10' and 15'.
Traffic signals on Hr Mr office to indicate big ship movements
1 B Ball — Vessel entering
2 B Balls (hor) — Vessel leaving
3 B Balls (triangle) — Vessels entering and leaving.
In addition a Q orange Lt is exhibited at Harbour office.

RADIO TELEPHONE
VHF Ch 16; 14 (0900−1700 LT).

TELEPHONE (0797)
Hr Mr 225225; CG 813171; MRCC Dover 210008;
⌗ (0703) 229251; Marinecall 0898 500 456; Police 222112;
Dr 222031; Ⓗ 222109.

FACILITIES
EC Tuesday; **Admiralty Jetty** Slip, M*, L, FW, AB*;
Strand Quay Slip, M*, P and D (50m, cans), L, FW, AB*; **Rye Yacht Centre** ☎ 223336, M, L, FW, ME, El, C (15 ton), AB; **Phillips BY** ☎ 223234, Slip, M, L, FW, ME, El, C (3 ton); **Sandrock Marine** ☎ 222679, Slip, M, D, L, FW, ME, El, CH, AB; **Sea Cruisers** ☎ 222070, ME, Sh, CH, ACA. **Town** ✉; Ⓑ; ⇌; ✈ (Lydd).
* See Hr Mr.
Note:- Marina under construction (1990)
　　　　½ M from harbour mouth (100+20 visitors).

FOLKESTONE 10-3-14
Kent

CHARTS
Admiralty 1991, 1892; Stanford 9; Imray C8; OS 179
TIDES
−0010 Dover; ML 3.7; Duration 0500; Zone 0 (GMT).

Standard Port DOVER (→)

Times				Height (metres)			
HW		LW		MHWS	MHWN	MLWN	MLWS
0000	0600	0100	0700	6.7	5.3	2.0	0.8
1200	1800	1300	1900				

Differences FOLKESTONE
−0020	−0005	−0010	−0010	+0.4	+0.4	0.0	−0.1

DUNGENESS
−0010	−0015	−0020	−0010	+1.0	+0.6	+0.4	+0.1

SHELTER
Good shelter except in strong E winds.
NAVIGATION
Waypoint 51°04'.30N 01°12'.00E, 150°/330° from/to breakwater head Lt, 0.26M. Beware Copt Rocks and Mole Head Rocks. Also ferries and pulling off wires from the jetty.
LIGHTS AND MARKS
Ldg Lts 295° at ferry terminal, FR and FG (occas). 305° on QG Lt at E pierhead leads to inner harbour. Bu flag or 3FR(vert) at FS on S arm, ¼ hr before ferry sails, indicates port closed.
RADIO TELEPHONE
VHF Ch 16; 22 (occas).
TELEPHONE (0303)
Hr Mr 54947; MRCC Dover 210008; ✉ (0304) 202441; Marinecall 0898 500 456; Police 850055; Port Health Office 57574; Ⓗ 57311.
FACILITIES
EC Wednesday (larger shops open all day); **South Quay BR Slipway** Slip (free), FW; **Folkestone Y and MB Club** ☎ 51574, Bar, D, FW, L, Slip, M; **Sealink** C (by arrangement 5 ton); **Garage** P. and D (100 yds, cans); **Bosun's Locker** ☎ 55752, CH. **Town** P, V, R, Bar. ✉; Ⓑ; ⇌; ✈ (Lydd).
A marina is under construction

metres / cables
500
FOLKESTONE
Slipway
Copt Rocks
Wreckage (DR)
YC The Stade
Inner Harbour
Stage
Bridge
New Mole
Harbour Masters Office FR (occas)
Pilot Station
Ferry Terminal
Outer Harbour Dredged to 6m
Breakwater
Mole Head Rocks
Power cables
Limit of dredged area
295° 305°
Berthing Sig FS Fl(2)10s14m22M Dia(4)
Depths in metres
▲ Contact Hr Mr

DOVER 10-3-15
Kent

CHARTS
Admiralty 1698, 1892; Stanford 9; Imray C8; OS 179
TIDES
0000 Dover; ML 3.7; Duration 0505; Zone 0 (GMT)

Standard Port DOVER (→)

Times				Height (metres)			
HW		LW		MHWS	MHWN	MLWN	MLWS
0000	0600	0100	0700	6.7	5.3	2.0	0.8
1200	1800	1300	1900				

Differences DEAL
+0010	+0020	+0010	+0005	−0.6	−0.3	0.0	0.0

RICHBOROUGH
+0015	+0015	+0030	+0030	−3.4	−2.6	−1.7	−0.7

NOTE: Dover is a Standard Port and tidal predictions for each day of the year are given below.

SHELTER
The small craft anchorage is exposed to winds from NE through S to SW and in gales a heavy sea builds up. Visiting yachts are welcome for up to 14 days. For longer periods, apply in advance. Berthing instructions for Wellington Dock given from Dockmaster's Office at entrance to Granville Dock. Dock gates open HW−1½ to HW+1. Waiting pontoon available. Yachtsmen intending to leave the dock should inform the Dockmaster's Office (manned from HW−2). Small craft may not be left unattended in Outer Harbour.
NAVIGATION
Waypoint from SW 51°06'.15N 01°19'.77E, 180°/000° from/to Admiralty Pier Lt Ho, 0.5M. Waypoint from NE 51°07'.27N 01°21'.51E, 090°/270° from/to S end Eastern Arm, 0.5M. Frequent ferry and hovercraft movements through both entrances. Strong tides across entrances and high walls make entry under sail slow and difficult − use of engine very strongly recommended. Observe traffic signals and follow instructions of harbour patrol launch. Do not pass between buoy marking wreck inside W entrance, Q, and southern breakwater.
LIGHTS AND MARKS
Admiralty Pier head Fl 7.5s 21m 20M; W Tr; vis 096°-090°.
International Port Traffic Signals are in operation, (see 6.2.7) shown for the Eastern entrance, day and night, on panels near Port Control; for Western entrance, day and night, on panels near Admiralty Pier Signal Station.
N.B. Specific permission to enter or leave Eastern or Western entrance *must* first be obtained from Port Control on VHF Ch 74, Ch 12 or, if not fitted with VHF/RT, with Aldis Lamp signals:
SV − I wish to enter port
SW − I wish to leave port.
Port Control will reply 'OK' or 'Wait'.
A Q Fl lamp from the Control Tower means keep clear of entrance you are approaching.
Docking signals
International Port Traffic Signals together with small Fl Y light to be shown 5 min before bridge is swung.
RADIO TELEPHONE
Call: *Dover Port Control* VHF Ch 12 74; 12 **74** (H24). Channel Navigation Information Service (CNIS) − call: *Dover Coastguard* Ch 16 **69**; 11 67 **69** (Ch 80 for yachts). Information broadcasts on Ch 11 at H+40, and also at H+55 when visibility is less than 2M.
TELEPHONE (0304)
Hr Mr 240400; CG 852515; MRCC 210008; ✉ (0304) 202441; Marinecall 0898 500 456; Police 240055; Ⓗ 201624.
FACILITIES
EC Wednesday; **Wellington Dock** ☎ 240400, Slip, L, FW, C, AB; **Royal Cinque Ports YC** ☎ 206262, L, Bar, M, C, FW, R; **Dover Yacht Co** ☎ 201073, D, FW, ME, El, Sh, C; **Dover Marine Supplies** ☎ 201677, D, FW, ME, El, Sh, Slip, C, SM, ACA, CH; **Smye-Rumsby** ☎ 201187, El, Ⓔ.
Town P and D (cans), V, R, Bar. ✉; Ⓑ; ⇌; ✈ (Lydd).
Note: *A Yachtsman's Guide* is available from Harbour House or Dockmaster.

DOVER *continued*

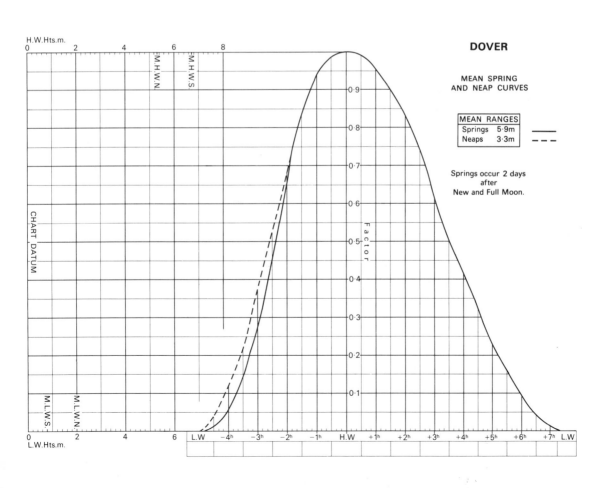

DOVER

**MEAN SPRING
AND NEAP CURVES**

MEAN RANGES	
Springs	5·9m
Neaps	3·3m

Springs occur 2 days
after
New and Full Moon.

ENGLAND, SOUTH COAST – DOVER

Lat 51°07′ N   Long 1°19′ E

TIMES AND HEIGHTS OF HIGH AND LOW WATERS

YEAR **1991**

TIME ZONE **UT(GMT)**
For Summer Time add ONE hour in non-shaded areas

Chart Datum: 3.67 metres below Ordnance Datum (Newlyn)

JANUARY

Day	Time	m	Day	Time	m
1 Tu	0611 / 1057 / 1843 / 2330	0.9 / 6.6 / 0.9 / 6.7	**16** W	0627 / 1123 / 1841 / 2340	1.2 / 6.1 / 1.2 / 6.3
2 W	0703 / 1150 / 1935	0.7 / 6.7 / 0.8	**17** Th	0702 / 1156 / 1913	1.1 / 6.2 / 1.1
3 Th	0019 / 0752 / 1239 / 2022	6.8 / 0.6 / 6.6 / 0.8	**18** F	0012 / 0735 / 1227 / 1945	6.4 / 1.0 / 6.2 / 1.1
4 F	0104 / 0839 / 1326 / 2104	6.7 / 0.9 / 6.5 / 1.0	**19** Sa	0045 / 0808 / 1259 / 2018	6.5 / 1.0 / 6.2 / 1.1
5 Sa	0148 / 0922 / 1411 / 2143	6.6 / 0.8 / 6.3 / 1.2	**20** Su	0117 / 0842 / 1331 / 2050	6.5 / 1.0 / 6.2 / 1.1
6 Su	0232 / 1004 / 1457 / 2221	6.5 / 1.0 / 6.0 / 1.4	**21** M	0149 / 0915 / 1405 / 2124	6.4 / 1.1 / 6.1 / 1.3
7 M ☾	0317 / 1047 / 1545 / 2301	6.3 / 1.3 / 5.8 / 1.7	**22** Tu	0225 / 0950 / 1446 / 2200	6.3 / 1.3 / 6.0 / 1.5
8 Tu	0407 / 1132 / 1641 / 2347	6.0 / 1.7 / 5.5 / 2.0	**23** W ☽	0308 / 1028 / 1536 / 2244	6.2 / 1.5 / 5.8 / 1.7
9 W	0508 / 1227 / 1749	5.6 / 2.0 / 5.2	**24** Th	0403 / 1119 / 1638 / 2344	6.1 / 1.7 / 5.6 / 1.9
10 Th	0049 / 0618 / 1333 / 1904	2.3 / 5.4 / 2.1 / 5.1	**25** F	0511 / 1232 / 1754	5.8 / 1.9 / 5.4
11 F	0206 / 0733 / 1447 / 2015	2.3 / 5.3 / 2.1 / 5.3	**26** Sa	0110 / 0629 / 1404 / 1919	2.0 / 5.7 / 1.8 / 5.5
12 Sa	0322 / 0839 / 1552 / 2112	2.2 / 5.4 / 1.9 / 5.5	**27** Su	0242 / 0749 / 1528 / 2040	1.8 / 5.7 / 1.6 / 5.7
13 Su	0420 / 0932 / 1642 / 2156	1.9 / 5.6 / 1.7 / 5.8	**28** M	0400 / 0903 / 1640 / 2145	1.5 / 6.0 / 1.3 / 6.1
14 M	0508 / 1014 / 1726 / 2234	1.6 / 5.8 / 1.5 / 6.0	**29** Tu	0506 / 1004 / 1743 / 2237	1.1 / 6.3 / 1.0 / 6.4
15 Tu ●	0549 / 1051 / 1804 / 2308	1.4 / 5.9 / 1.3 / 6.2	**30** W ○	0604 / 1057 / 1841 / 2323	0.8 / 6.5 / 0.8 / 6.7
			31 Th	0657 / 1144 / 1930	0.6 / 6.6 / 0.7

FEBRUARY

Day	Time	m	Day	Time	m
1 F	0005 / 0744 / 1225 / 2009	6.8 / 0.5 / 6.6 / 0.7	**16** Sa	0720 / 1203 / 1928	0.8 / 6.4 / 0.9
2 Sa	0045 / 0823 / 1304 / 2043	6.8 / 0.5 / 6.5 / 0.8	**17** Su	0021 / 0751 / 1234 / 1958	6.6 / 0.7 / 6.4 / 0.8
3 Su	0123 / 0900 / 1342 / 2112	6.8 / 0.6 / 6.4 / 1.0	**18** M	0052 / 0822 / 1306 / 2029	6.7 / 0.7 / 6.4 / 0.9
4 M	0201 / 0934 / 1420 / 2141	6.6 / 0.9 / 6.2 / 1.2	**19** Tu	0123 / 0853 / 1340 / 2103	6.6 / 0.8 / 6.3 / 1.0
5 Tu	0240 / 1006 / 1501 / 2210	6.4 / 1.2 / 5.9 / 1.6	**20** W	0158 / 0927 / 1419 / 2138	6.6 / 1.0 / 6.2 / 1.2
6 W ☾	0322 / 1040 / 1546 / 2245	6.0 / 1.6 / 5.5 / 1.9	**21** Th ☽	0240 / 1003 / 1508 / 2220	6.4 / 1.3 / 6.0 / 1.5
7 Th	0412 / 1120 / 1642 / 2336	5.6 / 2.0 / 5.2 / 2.3	**22** F	0335 / 1052 / 1610 / 2319	6.1 / 1.6 / 5.6 / 1.9
8 F	0518 / 1221 / 1805	5.1 / 2.3 / 4.9	**23** Sa	0444 / 1207 / 1733	5.6 / 1.9 / 5.3
9 Sa	0055 / 0652 / 1349 / 1942	2.5 / 4.9 / 2.4 / 4.9	**24** Su	0049 / 0615 / 1348 / 1919	2.0 / 5.4 / 2.0 / 5.3
10 Su	0242 / 0818 / 1519 / 2051	2.4 / 5.1 / 2.2 / 5.2	**25** M	0232 / 0757 / 1522 / 2046	1.8 / 5.5 / 1.6 / 5.6
11 M	0355 / 0917 / 1619 / 2136	2.0 / 5.3 / 1.8 / 5.6	**26** Tu	0353 / 0911 / 1634 / 2142	1.4 / 5.8 / 1.3 / 6.1
12 Tu	0445 / 0957 / 1705 / 2213	1.6 / 5.6 / 1.5 / 5.9	**27** W	0458 / 1004 / 1736 / 2227	1.0 / 6.2 / 1.0 / 6.4
13 W	0529 / 1031 / 1747 / 2244	1.3 / 5.9 / 1.3 / 6.1	**28** Th ○	0556 / 1048 / 1829 / 2308	0.7 / 6.4 / 0.8 / 6.7
14 Th ●	0608 / 1101 / 1824 / 2316	1.0 / 6.1 / 1.1 / 6.4			
15 F	0646 / 1132 / 1857 / 2349	0.9 / 6.3 / 0.9 / 6.5			

MARCH

Day	Time	m	Day	Time	m
1 F	0645 / 1127 / 1912 / 2346	0.5 / 6.6 / 0.6 / 6.6	**16** Sa ●	0622 / 1101 / 1835 / 2318	0.7 / 6.4 / 0.8 / 6.6
2 Sa	0724 / 1204 / 1944	0.4 / 6.6 / 0.6	**17** Su	0657 / 1133 / 1907 / 2350	0.6 / 6.5 / 0.7 / 6.8
3 Su	0021 / 0758 / 1238 / 2012	6.9 / 0.5 / 6.5 / 0.7	**18** M	0730 / 1207 / 1937	0.6 / 6.6 / 0.7
4 M	0056 / 0830 / 1312 / 2039	6.8 / 0.5 / 6.4 / 0.9	**19** Tu	0024 / 0801 / 1241 / 2009	6.8 / 0.6 / 6.6 / 0.7
5 Tu	0130 / 0900 / 1345 / 2105	6.6 / 0.9 / 6.2 / 1.1	**20** W	0057 / 0833 / 1319 / 2046	6.7 / 0.7 / 6.5 / 0.9
6 W	0204 / 0928 / 1419 / 2134	6.3 / 1.2 / 6.0 / 1.4	**21** Th	0137 / 0910 / 1402 / 2125	6.6 / 0.9 / 6.3 / 1.1
7 Th	0239 / 0957 / 1457 / 2204	6.0 / 1.6 / 5.6 / 1.8	**22** F	0223 / 0950 / 1454 / 2210	6.3 / 1.3 / 5.9 / 1.4
8 F ☾	0319 / 1033 / 1545 / 2249	5.5 / 2.0 / 5.2 / 2.2	**23** Sa ☽	0321 / 1042 / 1602 / 2313	5.9 / 1.7 / 5.5 / 1.8
9 Sa	0419 / 1126 / 1701 / 2357	5.0 / 2.4 / 4.8 / 2.5	**24** Su	0438 / 1201 / 1732	5.4 / 2.0 / 5.2
10 Su	0603 / 1245 / 1857	4.7 / 2.6 / 4.7	**25** M	0043 / 0625 / 1345 / 1920	1.9 / 5.3 / 1.9 / 5.3
11 M	0138 / 0748 / 1430 / 2016	2.5 / 4.8 / 2.4 / 5.1	**26** Tu	0225 / 0802 / 1512 / 2033	1.7 / 5.5 / 1.6 / 5.7
12 Tu	0317 / 0849 / 1543 / 2104	2.1 / 5.2 / 1.9 / 5.4	**27** W	0342 / 0905 / 1620 / 2124	1.2 / 5.9 / 1.2 / 6.1
13 W	0413 / 0928 / 1634 / 2139	1.6 / 5.5 / 1.5 / 5.8	**28** Th	0442 / 0950 / 1718 / 2204	0.9 / 6.1 / 1.0 / 6.4
14 Th	0459 / 0959 / 1718 / 2213	1.2 / 5.9 / 1.2 / 6.1	**29** F	0536 / 1028 / 1805 / 2244	0.7 / 6.3 / 0.8 / 6.6
15 F	0542 / 1028 / 1758 / 2245	0.9 / 6.1 / 1.0 / 6.4	**30** Sa ○	0621 / 1104 / 1842 / 2320	0.6 / 6.4 / 0.8 / 6.7
			31 Su	0656 / 1139 / 1910 / 2356	0.6 / 6.5 / 0.7 / 6.7

APRIL

Day	Time	m	Day	Time	m
1 M	0727 / 1212 / 1938	0.6 / 6.5 / 0.8	**16** Tu	0709 / 1140 / 1919 / 2358	0.6 / 6.7 / 0.7 / 6.8
2 Tu	0029 / 0758 / 1243 / 2008	6.6 / 0.7 / 6.4 / 0.9	**17** W	0742 / 1221 / 1955	0.6 / 6.6 / 0.7
3 W	0059 / 0829 / 1314 / 2037	6.5 / 0.7 / 6.2 / 1.1	**18** Th	0039 / 0819 / 1306 / 2036	6.7 / 0.7 / 6.5 / 0.8
4 Th	0130 / 0857 / 1345 / 2107	6.2 / 1.2 / 6.0 / 1.4	**19** F	0124 / 0900 / 1357 / 2119	6.5 / 0.9 / 6.3 / 1.0
5 F	0201 / 0927 / 1422 / 2141	5.9 / 1.5 / 5.7 / 1.7	**20** Sa	0219 / 0946 / 1456 / 2210	6.2 / 1.3 / 6.0 / 1.3
6 Sa	0239 / 1000 / 1507 / 2221	5.5 / 1.9 / 5.4 / 2.0	**21** Su ☾	0325 / 1044 / 1603 / 2315	5.8 / 1.6 / 5.6 / 1.6
7 Su ☽	0335 / 1049 / 1614 / 2320	5.1 / 2.2 / 5.0 / 2.3	**22** M	0445 / 1201 / 1726	5.5 / 1.9 / 5.4
8 M	0511 / 1158 / 1753	4.7 / 2.5 / 4.8	**23** Tu	0041 / 0624 / 1333 / 1857	1.7 / 5.4 / 1.8 / 5.5
9 Tu	0041 / 0656 / 1324 / 1920	2.4 / 4.8 / 2.4 / 5.0	**24** W	0206 / 0744 / 1449 / 2004	1.5 / 5.6 / 1.5 / 5.8
10 W	0213 / 0759 / 1447 / 2015	2.1 / 5.1 / 2.0 / 5.4	**25** Th	0317 / 0840 / 1550 / 2054	1.2 / 5.8 / 1.3 / 6.1
11 Th	0324 / 0842 / 1548 / 2056	1.6 / 5.5 / 1.6 / 5.8	**26** F	0416 / 0924 / 1645 / 2136	1.0 / 6.0 / 1.2 / 6.3
12 F	0417 / 0917 / 1638 / 2134	1.3 / 5.9 / 1.3 / 6.1	**27** Sa	0505 / 1002 / 1730 / 2216	0.9 / 6.2 / 1.1 / 6.4
13 Sa	0506 / 0952 / 1725 / 2209	1.0 / 6.2 / 1.0 / 6.4	**28** Su ○	0547 / 1038 / 1805 / 2255	0.9 / 6.3 / 1.0 / 6.5
14 Su ●	0550 / 1027 / 1807 / 2244	0.8 / 6.4 / 0.8 / 6.7	**29** M	0624 / 1115 / 1838 / 2332	0.9 / 6.3 / 1.0 / 6.5
15 M	0631 / 1102 / 1843 / 2320	0.6 / 6.6 / 0.7 / 6.8	**30** Tu	0656 / 1149 / 1910	0.9 / 6.4 / 0.9

ENGLAND, SOUTH COAST – DOVER

Lat 51°07′ N   Long 1°19′ E

TIMES AND HEIGHTS OF HIGH AND LOW WATERS

YEAR 1991

3

TIME ZONE UT(GMT)
For Summer Time add ONE
hour in non-shaded areas

MAY

Day		Day	
1 W	0005 6·4 / 0730 0·9 / 1221 6·3 / 1942 1·0	16 Th	0730 0·7 / 1210 6·6 / 1947 0·7
2 Th	0036 6·2 / 0801 1·1 / 1252 6·2 / 2015 1·2	17 F	0029 6·6 / 0813 0·8 / 1303 6·5 / 2032 0·7
3 F	0106 6·0 / 0832 1·3 / 1324 6·0 / 2049 1·3	18 Sa	0124 6·4 / 0858 0·9 / 1359 6·3 / 2119 0·9
4 Sa	0138 5·8 / 0904 1·5 / 1401 5·8 / 2124 1·6	19 Su	0225 6·2 / 0948 1·1 / 1456 6·1 / 2212 1·1
5 Su	0218 5·5 / 0939 1·8 / 1446 5·6 / 2203 1·8	20 M ☽	0327 5·9 / 1044 1·4 / 1555 5·9 / 2313 1·3
6 M	0311 5·2 / 1024 2·0 / 1543 5·3 / 2254 2·0	21 Tu	0435 5·7 / 1151 1·6 / 1702 5·8
7 Tu ☾	0427 5·0 / 1120 2·2 / 1657 5·1 / 2357 2·1	22 W	0024 1·4 / 0553 5·5 / 1303 1·7 / 1817 5·7
8 W	0550 5·0 / 1232 2·2 / 1814 5·2	23 Th	0135 1·4 / 0703 5·8 / 1411 1·6 / 1923 5·8
9 Th	0113 1·9 / 0657 5·2 / 1347 2·0 / 1917 5·5	24 F	0240 1·3 / 0801 5·7 / 1516 1·5 / 2018 5·9
10 F	0226 1·7 / 0748 5·5 / 1454 1·7 / 2006 5·8	25 Sa	0339 1·3 / 0850 5·8 / 1606 1·5 / 2105 6·0
11 Sa	0329 1·4 / 0832 5·8 / 1553 1·4 / 2050 6·1	26 Su	0431 1·3 / 0934 5·9 / 1654 1·4 / 2150 6·1
12 Su	0424 1·1 / 0912 6·1 / 1647 1·2 / 2131 6·4	27 M	0515 1·2 / 1014 6·1 / 1734 1·3 / 2233 6·2
13 M	0516 0·9 / 0953 6·4 / 1736 0·8 / 2213 6·6	28 Tu ○	0554 1·2 / 1054 6·2 / 1812 1·3 / 2312 6·2
14 Tu ●	0604 0·8 / 1037 6·6 / 1821 0·8 / 2255 6·8	29 W	0631 1·1 / 1132 6·2 / 1848 1·1 / 2350 6·2
15 W	0648 0·7 / 1122 6·6 / 1903 0·7 / 2340 6·8	30 Th	0706 1·1 / 1207 6·2 / 1923 1·1
		31 F	0022 6·1 / 0738 1·2 / 1239 6·2 / 1958 1·2

JUNE

Day		Day	
1 Sa	0055 6·0 / 0812 1·3 / 1313 6·1 / 2032 1·3	16 Su	0123 6·5 / 0858 0·8 / 1351 6·5 / 2118 0·7
2 Su	0127 5·8 / 0846 1·4 / 1349 6·0 / 2108 1·4	17 M	0218 6·3 / 0946 1·0 / 1440 6·4 / 2207 0·8
3 M	0205 5·7 / 0921 1·5 / 1429 5·8 / 2146 1·5	18 Tu	0310 6·1 / 1034 1·2 / 1531 6·2 / 2258 1·1
4 Tu	0250 5·5 / 1000 1·7 / 1514 5·7 / 2228 1·7	19 W ☽	0404 5·9 / 1125 1·5 / 1626 6·0 / 2354 1·3
5 W	0343 5·3 / 1047 1·9 / 1609 5·5 / 2319 1·8 ☾	20 Th	0505 5·6 / 1221 1·7 / 1729 5·8
6 Th	0447 5·3 / 1144 2·0 / 1712 5·5	21 F	0053 1·5 / 0611 5·5 / 1321 1·8 / 1835 5·7
7 F	0021 1·8 / 0551 5·3 / 1250 2·0 / 1815 5·6	22 Sa	0157 1·6 / 0717 5·5 / 1426 1·9 / 1940 5·7
8 Sa	0131 1·7 / 0652 5·5 / 1402 1·8 / 1914 5·8	23 Su	0300 1·7 / 0818 5·6 / 1529 1·8 / 2039 5·7
9 Su	0240 1·5 / 0747 5·8 / 1508 1·6 / 2008 6·0	24 M	0357 1·6 / 0911 5·7 / 1624 1·7 / 2129 5·8
10 M	0345 1·3 / 0837 6·0 / 1612 1·3 / 2058 6·2	25 Tu	0448 1·5 / 0957 5·9 / 1712 1·5 / 2216 5·9
11 Tu	0444 1·1 / 0928 6·3 / 1709 1·1 / 2149 6·5	26 W	0532 1·4 / 1038 6·0 / 1753 1·3 / 2258 6·0
12 W ●	0540 0·9 / 1016 6·4 / 1803 0·9 / 2240 6·6	27 Th ○	0611 1·3 / 1116 6·1 / 1831 1·2 / 2334 6·1
13 Th	0634 0·8 / 1112 6·6 / 1853 0·7 / 2332 6·6	28 F	0646 1·3 / 1151 6·2 / 1907 1·1
14 F	0723 0·7 / 1207 6·6 / 1942 0·6	29 Sa	0010 6·1 / 0720 1·2 / 1225 6·2 / 1941 1·1
15 Sa	0027 6·6 / 0811 0·7 / 1300 6·6 / 2030 0·6	30 Su	0041 6·1 / 0754 1·2 / 1257 6·2 / 2015 1·1

JULY

Day		Day	
1 M	0113 6·0 / 0826 1·2 / 1331 6·2 / 2050 1·2	16 Tu	0155 6·4 / 0931 0·9 / 1413 6·6 / 2150 0·7
2 Tu	0145 5·9 / 0901 1·3 / 1405 6·1 / 2125 1·3	17 W	0239 6·2 / 1009 1·1 / 1458 6·4 / 2231 1·0
3 W	0220 5·8 / 0936 1·4 / 1440 6·0 / 2202 1·4	18 Th ☽	0325 6·0 / 1047 1·4 / 1546 6·2 / 2313 1·3
4 Th	0301 5·7 / 1014 1·6 / 1522 6·0 / 2242 1·5	19 F	0417 5·7 / 1129 1·8 / 1641 5·8
5 F	0350 5·6 / 1059 1·8 / 1614 5·9 / 2333 1·7 ☾	20 Sa	0003 1·7 / 0518 5·4 / 1747 5·5
6 Sa	0451 5·5 / 1157 1·9 / 1718 5·8	21 Su	0104 2·0 / 0632 5·2 / 1335 2·2 / 1904 5·3
7 Su	0038 1·8 / 0557 5·5 / 1310 1·9 / 1827 5·8	22 M	0218 2·1 / 0749 5·2 / 1456 2·1 / 2016 5·4
8 M	0155 1·7 / 0707 5·6 / 1430 1·7 / 1934 5·9	23 Tu	0329 2·0 / 0853 5·5 / 1602 1·9 / 2115 5·6
9 Tu	0311 1·5 / 0813 5·8 / 1545 1·5 / 2037 6·1	24 W	0427 1·8 / 0942 5·7 / 1652 1·6 / 2203 5·8
10 W	0421 1·3 / 0915 6·1 / 1651 1·2 / 2136 6·3	25 Th	0513 1·6 / 1023 6·0 / 1736 1·4 / 2242 5·9
11 Th ●	0525 1·1 / 1014 6·4 / 1750 0·9 / 2234 6·5	26 F ○	0554 1·4 / 1058 6·1 / 1815 1·2 / 2316 6·0
12 F	0624 0·9 / 1109 6·6 / 1845 0·7 / 2329 6·6	27 Sa	0631 1·3 / 1130 6·2 / 1850 1·1 / 2347 6·1
13 Sa	0719 0·7 / 1200 6·7 / 1937 0·5	28 Su	0703 1·2 / 1203 6·4 / 1924 1·0
14 Su	0021 6·6 / 0808 0·7 / 1246 6·8 / 2025 0·5	29 M	0018 6·2 / 0734 1·1 / 1234 6·5 / 1958 0·9
15 M	0109 6·6 / 0851 0·7 / 1330 6·7 / 2108 0·5	30 Tu	0048 6·2 / 0806 1·1 / 1304 6·4 / 2030 1·0
		31 W	0117 6·2 / 0837 1·2 / 1334 6·4 / 2103 1·1

AUGUST

Day		Day	
1 Th	0148 6·1 / 0911 1·2 / 1405 6·4 / 2135 1·2	16 F	0244 6·1 / 1004 1·4 / 1505 6·3 / 2231 1·5
2 F	0223 6·0 / 0945 1·4 / 1443 6·2 / 2210 1·4	17 Sa ☽	0329 5·7 / 1040 1·8 / 1555 5·8 / 2312 1·9
3 Sa	0307 5·9 / 1023 1·6 / 1531 6·1 / 2254 1·6	18 Su	0426 5·3 / 1127 2·2 / 1658 5·3
4 Su	0404 5·7 / 1115 1·9 / 1634 5·8 / 2356 1·9	19 M	0008 2·3 / 0544 5·0 / 1241 2·5 / 1831 5·0
5 M	0516 5·5 / 1231 2·0 / 1750 5·6	20 Tu	0130 2·4 / 0721 5·0 / 1419 2·4 / 2001 5·1
6 Tu	0121 1·9 / 0642 5·4 / 1404 1·9 / 1916 5·6	21 W	0300 2·3 / 0833 5·3 / 1538 2·0 / 2103 5·4
7 W	0251 1·7 / 0808 5·6 / 1528 1·6 / 2033 5·9	22 Th	0403 1·9 / 0922 5·7 / 1631 1·6 / 2148 5·7
8 Th	0407 1·4 / 0917 6·0 / 1638 1·2 / 2136 6·2	23 F	0451 1·6 / 1000 6·0 / 1715 1·3 / 2221 5·9
9 F	0513 1·1 / 1012 6·4 / 1739 0·9 / 2231 6·5	24 Sa	0532 1·4 / 1031 6·2 / 1754 1·1 / 2249 6·1
10 Sa ●	0614 0·9 / 1059 6·7 / 1835 0·6 / 2319 6·6	25 Su ○	0608 1·2 / 1102 6·4 / 1831 1·0 / 2318 6·3
11 Su	0709 0·7 / 1143 6·8 / 1926 0·4	26 M	0642 1·1 / 1133 6·6 / 1904 0·9 / 2347 6·4
12 M	0004 6·7 / 0754 0·6 / 1224 6·9 / 2009 0·4	27 Tu	0713 1·0 / 1203 6·6 / 1935 0·8
13 Tu	0045 6·7 / 0830 0·7 / 1303 6·9 / 2047 0·5	28 W	0017 6·5 / 0742 1·0 / 1232 6·7 / 2006 0·9
14 W	0124 6·5 / 0903 0·9 / 1342 6·7 / 2122 0·7	29 Th	0046 6·4 / 0813 1·0 / 1302 6·6 / 2037 1·0
15 Th	0204 6·3 / 0934 1·1 / 1422 6·5 / 2156 1·1	30 F	0117 6·4 / 0846 1·1 / 1334 6·5 / 2110 1·2
		31 Sa	0154 6·2 / 0921 1·3 / 1412 6·4 / 2145 1·4

Chart Datum: 3.67 metres below Ordnance Datum (Newlyn)

ENGLAND, SOUTH COAST – DOVER

Lat 51°07′ N   Long 1°19′ E

TIMES AND HEIGHTS OF HIGH AND LOW WATERS

YEAR 1991

TIME ZONE UT (GMT)
For Summer Time add ONE hour in non-shaded areas

Chart Datum: 3.67 metres below Ordnance Datum (Newlyn)

SEPTEMBER

Day	Time	m	Time	m	Time	m	Time	m
1 Su (	0237	6.0	1000	1.6	1500	6.1	2228	1.7
16 M	0336	5.4	1045	2.2	1609	5.2	2318	2.4
2 M	0335	5.7	1054	1.9	1606	5.7	2333	2.0
17 Tu	0451	5.0	1149	2.5	1753	4.8		
3 Tu	0452	5.4	1211	2.1	1734	5.4		
18 W	0034	2.6	0642	4.9	1326	2.5	1937	5.0
4 W	0106	2.1	0638	5.3	1352	2.0	1921	5.5
19 Th	0213	2.5	0802	5.2	1501	2.2	2037	5.3
5 Th	0243	1.8	0813	5.6	1518	1.6	2042	5.9
20 F	0327	2.1	0851	5.6	1557	1.7	2118	5.7
6 F	0357	1.4	0914	6.1	1626	1.1	2136	6.2
21 Sa	0417	1.7	0928	5.9	1642	1.4	2148	6.0
7 Sa	0501	1.1	1000	6.5	1725	0.8	2221	6.5
22 Su	0459	1.4	0957	6.2	1723	1.1	2216	6.2
8 Su ●	0558	0.9	1041	6.7	1818	0.6	2302	6.7
23 M ○	0539	1.2	1028	6.5	1801	0.9	2244	6.4
9 M	0648	0.8	1120	6.9	1903	0.5	2340	6.7
24 Tu	0614	1.1	1059	6.7	1838	0.8	2315	6.6
10 Tu	0726	0.7	1158	7.0	1942	0.5		
25 W	0648	1.0	1130	6.8	1912	0.8	2346	6.6
11 W	0017	6.7	0758	0.8	1235	6.9	2016	0.7
26 Th	0719	1.0	1201	6.8	1942	0.9		
12 Th	0052	6.6	0827	0.9	1310	6.7	2049	0.9
27 F	0018	6.6	0751	1.0	1234	6.8	2015	1.0
13 F	0128	6.4	0857	1.2	1347	6.5	2121	1.2
28 Sa	0053	6.5	0826	1.1	1309	6.6	2049	1.2
14 Sa	0205	6.1	0928	1.5	1425	6.1	2152	1.6
29 Su	0133	6.4	0904	1.3	1351	6.4	2128	1.4
15 Su)	0246	5.8	1002	1.9	1508	5.7	2228	2.0
30 M	0222	6.1	0949	1.6	1444	6.0	2217	1.8

OCTOBER

Day	Time	m	Time	m	Time	m	Time	m
1 Tu (	0324	5.7	1045	1.9	1557	5.6	2325	2.1
16 W	0402	5.2	1109	2.4	1657	4.9	2342	2.6
2 W	0449	5.4	1207	2.0	1740	5.3		
17 Th	0534	5.0	1225	2.5	1845	4.9		
3 Th	0102	2.1	0638	5.4	1344	1.9	1928	5.5
18 F	0104	2.6	0704	5.2	1355	2.3	1949	5.2
4 F	0233	1.8	0801	5.8	1505	1.4	2036	5.9
19 Sa	0226	2.2	0801	5.5	1504	1.9	2032	5.6
5 Sa	0342	1.4	0856	6.1	1607	1.1	2124	6.2
20 Su	0327	1.9	0842	5.9	1557	1.5	2104	5.9
6 Su	0441	1.2	0939	6.5	1704	0.9	2202	6.4
21 M	0416	1.5	0917	6.2	1644	1.2	2136	6.2
7 M	0533	1.0	1017	6.7	1751	0.8	2238	6.6
22 Tu ●	0501	1.3	0950	6.5	1727	1.0	2209	6.4
8 Tu	0615	0.9	1055	6.9	1832	0.7	2315	6.7
23 W ○	0543	1.1	1024	6.7	1808	0.9	2242	6.6
9 W	0649	0.9	1133	6.9	1909	0.7	2350	6.6
24 Th	0622	1.0	1059	6.8	1846	0.9	2318	6.7
10 Th	0721	0.9	1208	6.8	1942	0.9		
25 F	0657	1.0	1134	6.9	1921	0.9	2357	6.7
11 F	0025	6.5	0754	1.1	1242	6.6	2015	1.1
26 Sa	0734	1.0	1212	6.8	1957	1.0		
12 Sa	0059	6.4	0826	1.3	1316	6.4	2047	1.4
27 Su	0038	6.6	0812	1.1	1255	6.6	2036	1.1
13 Su	0134	6.2	0900	1.5	1349	6.0	2118	1.7
28 M	0126	6.4	0856	1.2	1345	6.3	2119	1.4
14 M	0212	5.9	0934	1.8	1430	5.6	2153	2.0
29 Tu	0220	6.1	0945	1.4	1446	6.0	2213	1.7
15 Tu)	0258	5.5	1014	2.2	1527	5.2	2238	2.4
30 W	0327	5.8	1044	1.7	1603	5.6	2322	2.0 (
31 Th	0444	5.6	1201	1.8	1737	5.5		

NOVEMBER

Day	Time	m	Time	m	Time	m	Time	m
1 F	0050	2.0	0615	5.6	1328	1.7	1907	5.6
16 Sa	0005	2.4	0547	5.2	1248	2.2	1835	5.2
2 Sa	0211	1.8	0730	5.8	1442	1.4	2011	5.9
17 Su	0119	2.3	0653	5.4	1401	2.0	1930	5.4
3 Su	0315	1.5	0826	6.1	1542	1.2	2057	6.1
18 M	0227	2.0	0747	5.7	1505	1.7	2015	5.7
4 M	0412	1.3	0911	6.4	1635	1.1	2138	6.3
19 Tu	0329	1.7	0830	6.0	1602	1.4	2054	6.0
5 Tu	0459	1.2	0952	6.5	1722	1.0	2216	6.4
20 W	0423	1.5	0911	6.3	1652	1.2	2135	6.3
6 W ●	0540	1.2	1031	6.6	1801	1.0	2254	6.5
21 Th ○	0513	1.2	0952	6.6	1740	1.0	2216	6.6
7 Th	0617	1.1	1111	6.7	1838	1.0	2330	6.5
22 F	0600	1.1	1033	6.8	1824	0.9	2258	6.7
8 F	0652	1.1	1147	6.6	1913	1.1		
23 Sa	0642	1.0	1116	6.8	1906	0.9	2344	6.7
9 Sa	0005	6.5	0728	1.2	1222	6.4	1947	1.2
24 Su	0723	0.9	1201	6.7	1945	1.0		
10 Su	0039	6.4	0802	1.3	1255	6.2	2019	1.4
25 M	0034	6.7	0806	0.9	1252	6.6	2029	1.1
11 M	0114	6.2	0837	1.5	1328	6.0	2051	1.7
26 Tu	0127	6.5	0853	1.0	1348	6.4	2117	1.3
12 Tu	0151	6.0	0912	1.7	1408	5.7	2127	1.9
27 W	0222	6.4	0942	1.2	1449	6.1	2210	1.5
13 W	0233	5.8	0950	1.9	1456	5.4	2207	2.2
28 Th	0319	6.1	1040	1.4	1553	5.8	2313	1.7 (
14 Th)	0325	5.5	1037	2.1	1602	5.1	2259	2.4
29 F	0421	5.9	1147	1.5	1705	5.6		
15 F	0431	5.3	1136	2.3	1722	5.0		
30 Sa	0025	1.8	0532	5.8	1259	1.6	1822	5.6

DECEMBER

Day	Time	m	Time	m	Time	m	Time	m
1 Su	0134	1.8	0645	5.8	1408	1.5	1928	5.7
16 M	0015	2.2	0542	5.5	1259	2.0	1821	5.3
2 M	0239	1.7	0747	5.9	1510	1.4	2025	5.8
17 Tu	0128	2.2	0645	5.6	1411	1.9	1921	5.5
3 Tu	0338	1.6	0840	6.1	1606	1.4	2112	6.0
18 W	0242	1.9	0742	5.9	1519	1.6	2015	5.8
4 W	0430	1.5	0929	6.2	1654	1.3	2156	6.1
19 Th	0348	1.7	0836	6.1	1621	1.4	2107	6.1
5 Th	0515	1.4	1013	6.3	1736	1.3	2238	6.3
20 F	0447	1.4	0927	6.4	1718	1.1	2157	6.4
6 F ●	0554	1.3	1055	6.4	1814	1.2	2316	6.4
21 Sa ○	0540	1.1	1016	6.6	1808	1.0	2248	6.6
7 Sa	0632	1.2	1134	6.4	1850	1.2	2353	6.4
22 Su	0629	0.9	1106	6.7	1856	0.9	2339	6.7
8 Su	0709	1.2	1210	6.3	1924	1.3		
23 M	0717	0.8	1157	6.7	1942	0.8		
9 M	0028	6.4	0744	1.2	1243	6.1	1958	1.4
24 Tu	0031	6.8	0802	0.7	1250	6.7	2027	0.9
10 Tu	0100	6.3	0818	1.3	1316	6.0	2029	1.5
25 W	0120	6.7	0849	0.7	1342	6.5	2114	1.0
11 W	0135	6.2	0853	1.5	1349	5.8	2103	1.6
26 Th	0209	6.6	0938	0.8	1433	6.3	2200	1.2
12 Th	0211	6.0	0928	1.6	1429	5.7	2139	1.8
27 F	0257	6.5	1027	1.1	1527	6.1	2249	1.4
13 F	0251	5.9	1007	1.8	1515	5.5	2220	2.0
28 Sa	0349	6.2	1120	1.3	1623	5.8	2343	1.7 (
14 Sa	0339	5.7	1052	1.9	1610	5.3	2312	2.1
29 Su	0447	6.0	1218	1.6	1727	5.5		
15 Su	0435	5.5	1150	2.0	1716	5.3		
30 M	0045	1.9	0554	5.7	1324	1.7	1839	5.4
31 Tu	0154	2.0	0706	5.6	1432	1.8	1949	5.4

RAMSGATE 10-3-16
Kent

CHARTS
Admiralty 1827, 1828; Stanford 5, 19; Imray C1, C8; OS 179
TIDES
+0020 Dover; ML 2.6; Duration 0530; Zone 0 (GMT).

Standard Port DOVER (←)

Times				Height (metres)			
HW		LW		MHWS	MHWN	MLWN	MLWS
0000	0600	0100	0700	6.7	5.3	2.0	0.8
1200	1800	1300	1900				

Differences RAMSGATE
+0020 +0020 −0007 −0007 −1.8 −1.5 −0.8 −0.4
HW Broadstairs = HW Dover +0027 approx.

SHELTER
Good in inner harbour (marina). Access HW−2 to HW+2 approx.
NAVIGATION
Waypoint 51°19'.50N 01°26'.00E, 090°/270° from/to new breakwater entrance, 0.25M. Beware Dyke Bank to the N, and Brake and Cross Ledge to the S; all these dry. Access is by main channel from the E. Contact Port Control VHF Ch 14. Reception pontoon in West Gully of Royal Harbour.
LIGHTS AND MARKS
Entrance channel has lateral and cardinal buoys and marks. Breakwater entrance N side QG, S side VQR. Ldg Lts 270°. Front Dir Oc WRG 10s; G259°-269°, W269°-271°, R271°-281°. Rear Oc 5s. International Port Traffic Signals control main channel and entry to Royal Harbour and marina. West Pier Lt refers to depth between piers: — FR over 3m, FG less than 3m.
RADIO TELEPHONE
VHF Ch 14 (H24). Marina Ch 14.
TELEPHONE (0843)
Hr Mr 586251; CG Dover 210008; MRSC Frinton-on-Sea 5518; ⌗ (0304) 202441; Marinecall 0898 500 456; Police 581724; Dr 595061.
FACILITIES
EC Thursday; **Ramsgate Yacht Marina** (400+100 visitors) ☎ 592277, Slip, AC, FW, C (20 ton), ⊡, (Access HW−2 to HW+1; **Royal Temple YC** ☎ 591766, Bar; **Ramsgate Marine** ☎ 593140, Slip, Ⓔ, ME, El, Sh, BH; **Marine Centre** ☎ 596772, Slip, ME, El, Sh, Ⓔ; **Seagear** ☎ 591733, ACA, Gaz, CH; **Foy Boat Marine** ☎ 592662, P, D, L, AB; **Bosun's Locker** ☎ 597158, CH, ACA; **Walkers Marine** ☎ 592176, ME; **Davis Marine** ☎ 586172, ME; **A J C White** ☎ Dover 617800, SM. **Town** P, Gas, Gaz, V, R, Bar. ✉; Ⓑ; ⇌; ✈ (Manston).

WHITSTABLE 10-3-17
Kent

CHARTS
Admiralty 2571; Stanford 5; Imray Y14; OS 179
TIDES
+0135 Dover; ML 3.0; Duration 0605; Zone 0 (GMT).

Standard Port SHEERNESS (→)

Times				Height (metres)			
HW		LW		MHWS	MHWN	MLWN	MLWS
0200	0800	0200	0700	5.7	4.8	1.5	0.6
1400	2000	1400	1900				

Differences WHITSTABLE
−0008 −0011 +0005 0000 −0.3 −0.3 0.0 −0.1
MARGATE
−0050 −0040 −0020 −0050 −0.9 −0.9 −0.1 0.0
HERNE BAY
−0025 −0015 0000 −0025 −0.5 −0.5 −0.1 −0.1

SHELTER
Good shelter except in strong winds from NNW to NE. Berthing is restricted to genuine refuge seekers since priority is given to commercial shipping. Moorings to NW of harbour controlled by YC, Access HW∓1.
NAVIGATION
Waypoint 51°22'.62N 01°01'.20E, 165°/345° from/to West Quay dolphin, 0.83M. Beware shoals near approaches, which are very shallow. Harbour dries. Oyster beds are numerous. Approach should not be attempted before half tide.
LIGHTS AND MARKS
Ldg Lts 122°, both FR, West Quay, off head Fl WRG 5s; dolphin; vis W118°-156°, G156°-178°, R178°-201°. NE arm FW 15m 8M; indicates harbour open; FR below this Lt indicates harbour closed.
RADIO TELEPHONE
VHF Ch 16; 09 12 (Mon-Fri: 0800-1700 LT. Other times: HW−3 to HW+1). Tidal information on request.
TELEPHONE (0227)
Hr Mr 274086; MRSC Frinton-on-Sea 5518; ⌗ (0304) 202441; Marinecall 0898 500 455; Police 770055; Dr 263811.
FACILITIES
EC Wednesday; **Harbour** ☎ 274086, L, FW, D, C (15 ton), AB; **Whitstable YC** ☎ 272942, M, R, Slip, L, FW, Bar; **The Dinghy Store** ☎ 274168, ME, Sh, CH, ACA; **Whitstable Marine** ☎ 262525, ME, El, Sh, CH, C, V; **H. Goldfinch** ☎ 272295, SM; **Waldens** ☎ 272098, Gas; **Barton Marine** ☎ 273917, CH; **W. Grantham** ☎ 273505, ME, El; **ICOM UK** ☎ 363859, Ⓔ. **Town** ⊡, P, V, R, Bar. ✉; Ⓑ; ⇌ (bus to Herne Bay or Canterbury); ✈ (Lydd or Manston).

10.3.19 THAMES ESTUARY TIDAL STREAMS

CAUTION:– Due to very strong rates of
tidal streams in some areas, eddies may
occur. Where possible, some indication of
these is shown but in many areas there is
insufficient information or eddies are
unstable

5 Hours before HW Sheerness(0335 before HW Dover)

4 Hours before HW Sheerness(0235 before HW Dover)

3 Hours before HW Sheerness(0135 before HW Dover)

2 Hours before HW Sheerness (0035 before HW Dover)

1 Hour before HW Sheerness (0025 after HW Dover)

HW Sheerness (0125 after HW Dover)

General Areas 10.3.3 10.4.3

1 Hour after HW Sheerness (0225 after HW Dover)

2 Hours after HW Sheerness (0325 after HW Dover)

3 Hours after HW Sheerness (0425 after HW Dover)

4 Hours after HW Sheerness (0525 after HW Dover)

5 Hours after HW Sheerness (0600 before HW Dover)

6 Hours after HW Sheerness (0500 before HW Dover)

THE SWALE   10-3-19
Kent

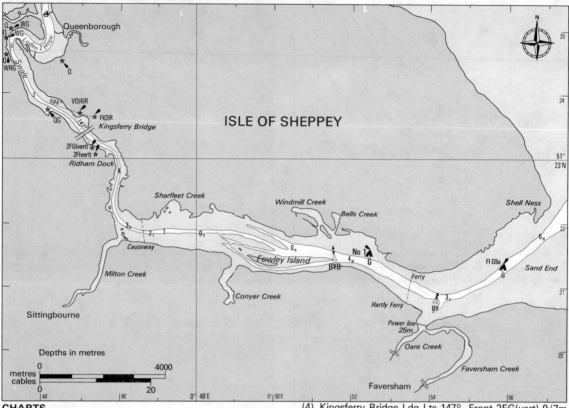

CHARTS
Admiralty 2571, 2572, 1834; Stanford 5;
Imray Y18, Y14; OS 178.

TIDES
Queenborough +0130 Dover; Harty Ferry +0120 Dover;
ML (Harty Ferry) 3.0; Duration 0610; Zone 0 (GMT).

Standard Port SHEERNESS (→)

Times				Height (metres)			
HW		LW		MHWS	MHWN	MLWN	MLWS
0200	0800	0200	0700	5.7	4.8	1.5	0.6
1400	2000	1400	1900				

Differences R. SWALE (Grovehurst Jetty)

−0007	0000	0000	+0016	0.0	0.0	0.0	−0.1

SHELTER
Excellent shelter in the Swale, the passage between the
Isle of Sheppey and the N Kent coast, along its 14M from
Queenborough in the W to Shell Ness in the E. Yachts
can enter Milton Creek, Conyer Creek (dries), Faversham
Creek or Oare Creek. There are two W visitors buoys off
Queenborough, and a concrete lighter to go alongside.

NAVIGATION
Waypoint (E entrance) Columbine Spit stbd-hand buoy,
51°23'.84N, 01°00'.13E, 050°/230° from/to entrance to
buoyed channel 1.3M. E entrance between Pollard Spit
and Ham Gat is well marked, the buoys being moved to
suit the shifting channel. The W entrance is marked by
Queenborough Spit buoy 1M from Garrison Pt on S side.
Direction of buoyage changes at Milton Creek. There are
numerous oyster beds in the area. Beware wreck in
Faversham Creek; lock gates by swing bridge impound
water at top of the harbour.

LIGHTS AND MARKS
No fixed lights at E entrance. In W Swale:
(1) Entrance Dir Lt Q 16m 5M; vis 163°-168°.
(2) Round Loden Hope bend: two QWG and one QWRG
    on Bns; keep in G sectors.
(3) Horse Reach Ldg Lts 113°. Front QG 7m 5M. Rear
    FIG 3s 10m 6M. Ldg Lts 098°. Front VQ(4)R 5s 6m
    5M. Rear Fl(2)R 5s 10m 9M.

(4) Kingsferry Bridge Ldg Lts 147°. Front 2FG(vert) 9/7m.
    Rear 2FW(vert) 11/9m. Lights on bridge 2×2 FG
    (vert) on SW; 2×2 FR (vert) on NE.
Bridge traffic signals: −
No Lts   = Bridge down
Q Or and QG = Centre span lifting
FG   = Bridge open
QR   = Centre span lowering. Keep clear.
Bridge opens for yachts; either call on VHF Ch 10 or hoist
a bucket in the rigging and give one long and four short
blasts.

RADIO TELEPHONE
Call: *Medway Radio* VHF Ch 09 11 **74** 16 22 (H24);
Kingsferry Bridge Ch 10 (H24); Conyer Marine Ch **80**.

TELEPHONE (0795)
Hr Mr (Medway Ports Authority) 580003;
⌗ (0304) 202441; Marinecall 0898 500 455; Police 536639;
Dr or Ⓗ contact Medway Navigation Service 663025.

FACILITIES
QUEENBOROUGH: EC Wednesday. **Town Quay** L, FW,
Slip, M; **Queenborough YC** ☎ Sheerness 663955, M,
Bar; **Calfcastle BY** ☎ 661141, Slip, C, ME, El, Sh; **Jim
Brett Marine** ☎ 667121, ME, Sh, El, AB, C (10 ton);
André Hardy ☎ 873767, Sh, ME; **Bosun's Store**
☎ 662674, CH, Gas; **Town** V, R, Bar. ✉; Ⓑ; ⇌;
✈ (Lydd or Gatwick).
MILTON CREEK (Sittingbourne): EC Wednesday **Crown
Quay** M, FW; **Town** V, R, Bar. ✉; Ⓑ; ⇌;
✈ (Lydd or Gatwick); also the Dolphin Yard Sailing Barge
Museum.
OARE CREEK: **Youngboats** ☎ 536176, M, C (8 ton), ME,
El, Sh, CH; **Hollow Shore Cruising Club** Bar; **Fuller
Marine** ☎ 532294, CH, Gas.
CONYER CREEK: **Swale Marina** ☎ 521562, ME, Sh, M,
BH (15 ton), C (3 ton), Slip, CH; **Conyer Marine**
☎ 521276, ME, Sh, El, Ⓔ, Slip, D, SM; **Conyer
Chandlery** ☎ 522200, CH, V, El; **Conyer Cruising Club**;
Wilkinson ☎ 521503, SM.
FAVERSHAM: EC Thursday; **Brents BY** ☎ 537809, M, AB,
Ⓔ, C (40 ton), AC, FW, ME, El, Sh, SM; **Iron Wharf BY**
☎ 536296, M, AC, C (25 ton), D; **Quay Lane Wharf**
☎ 531660, AC, FW, Sh, ME, CH, SM; **Hollowshore BY**
☎ 532317, Sh, El, C (5 ton), Ⓔ; **Town** V, R, Bar, Gas.
✉; Ⓑ; ⇌; ✈ (Lydd or Gatwick).

RIVER MEDWAY
(SHEERNESS)
Kent

10-3-20

CHARTS
Admiralty 3683, 2482, 1835, 1834, 1183; Stanford 5;
Imray Y18; OS 178

TIDES
+0130 Dover; ML 3.1; Duration 0610; Zone 0 (GMT).

Standard Port SHEERNESS (→)

Times				Height (metres)			
HW		LW		MHWS	MHWN	MLWN	MLWS
0200	0800	0200	0700	5.7	4.8	1.5	0.6
1400	2000	1400	1900				

Differences UPNOR
+0015 +0015 +0015 +0025 +0.2 +0.2 −0.1 −0.1

ROCHESTER (STROOD PIER)
+0018 +0018 +0018 +0028 +0.2 +0.2 −0.2 −0.3

ALLINGTON LOCK
+0050 +0035   No data −2.1 −2.2 −1.3 −0.4

NOTE: Sheerness is a Standard Port and tidal predictions
for each day of the year are given below.

SHELTER
The Medway and Swale give shelter from all directions if
the correct anchorage is chosen. Lower reaches are bad in
strong NE winds; Stangate Creek is good in all weathers.
River is tidal up to Allington Lock (21.6M).

NAVIGATION
Waypoint Medway (safe water) buoy, Iso 2s, 51°28′.80N,
00°52′.92E, 069°/249° from/to Garrison Pt Lt, 5.5M. The
wreck of the ammunition ship 'Richard Montgomery' lies
2 M from the harbour mouth, her masts showing above
the water. Yachtsmen intending to proceed up the
Medway or Swale should obtain a copy of *Medway Ports
River Byelaws 1979* from Medway Ports Authority
Sheerness Docks, Sheerness, Kent. ME 12 IRX.

Bridge Clearances (MHWS):
Rochester   — 5.9m
New Hythe (M20)   — 11.3m
Aylesford (Stone)   — 2.87m
Aylesford (Bailey)   — 3.26m
Maidstone Bypass   — 9.45m
Kingsferry (Shut)   — 3.35m

Speed Limits: –
6 kn — W of Folly Pt Longitude
8 kn — S of Kingsferry Bridge
8 kn — in Queenborough harbour in area between line
         Swale Ness — Queenborough Pt and line 270°
         from Long Pt
For ease of reference the area is split up as follows:-
(1) Lower Medway
(2) Upper Medway

LIGHTS AND MARKS
Garrison Pt Sig Stn, Traffic sigs, Horn (3) 30s.
Isle of Grain Lt Q WRG 20m 13/7M.
Traffic Signals: Powerful Lt, Fl 7s shown from Garrison Pt
Signal Station indicates movement of large vessels; shown
up river, inward bound; shown to seaward, outward
bound.

RADIO TELEPHONE
Call: *Medway Radio* (at Garrison Point, Sheerness) VHF
Ch 09 11 16 22 73 **74** (H24). Yachts should keep watch on
Ch 74 underway and Ch 16 at anchor. Kingsferry Bridge,
West Swale, Ch 10 (H24). Gillingham Marina, Hoo Marina,
Medway Bridge Marina, Ch **80** (0900-1700 LT).

TELEPHONE (0634)
Hr Mr Sheerness 580003; MRSC Frinton-on-Sea 675518;
⌗ (0304) 202441; Marinecall 0898 500 455; Police
Chatham 811281 Sheerness (0795) 661451; Dr Contact
Medway Navigation Service Sheerness 663025.

FACILITIES
EC Wednesday; The Medway estuary and the Swale
provide a huge area to explore, although much of it dries
out to mud. The Medway is well buoyed and perched up
to Rochester. *Medway Ports River Byelaws* obtainable
from Medway Ports Authority.
LOWER MEDWAY Sheerness is a Standard Port and is the
headquarters of Medway Ports Authority. It is a
commercial harbour with Ro-Ro ferry berths and no
accommodation for yachts. Shelter is good except in the
entrance reaches in strong NE winds. In Stangate Creek it
is good in all conditions. There are also good anchorages
in Sharfleet Creek; from about 4 hrs flood it is possible to
go right through into Half Acre Creek. Some minor creeks
are buoyed.
Sheppey YC ☎ Sheerness 663052; **W. Hurst**
☎ Sheerness 662356, ACA.
UPPER MEDWAY Admiralty Chart 1835 Folly Point to
Maidstone. Harbour Master (Medway Ports Authority)
☎ Sheerness 580003. Speed limit above Folly Point is
6 kn. There are landing facilities (only) at Gillingham Pier,
Gillingham Dock steps, Sun Pier (Chatham), Ship Pier,
Town Quay steps (Rochester) and Strood Pier. Medway
Port Authority have two visitors moorings in Tower Reach
just upstream of Rochester Bridge. All other moorings are
administered by YCs or marinas. There are slips at
Commodore Hard, Gillingham and Upnor Causeway
opposite Pier public house. Slips also available at Auto
Marine Boatyard, Cuxton, Rochester (HW ∓3).

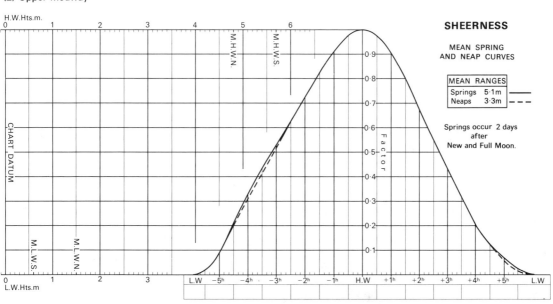

SHEERNESS
MEAN SPRING
AND NEAP CURVES

MEAN RANGES	
Springs	5·1m ———
Neaps	3·3m - - - -

Springs occur 2 days
after
New and Full Moon.

RIVER MEDWAY *continued*

ENGLAND, EAST COAST – SHEERNESS

Lat 51°27' N   Long 0°45' E

TIMES AND HEIGHTS OF HIGH AND LOW WATERS

YEAR 1991

3

TIME ZONE **UT(GMT)**
For Summer Time add ONE hour in non-shaded areas

JANUARY

#	Day	Time	m	Time	m	Time	m	Time	m		#	Day	Time	m	Time	m	Time	m	Time	m
1	Tu	0018	5.7	0642	0.6	1242	5.9	1902	0.7		16	W	0041	5.3	0655	1.0	1303	5.3	1855	1.1
2	W	0107	5.7	0735	0.4	1333	6.0	1947	0.8		17	Th	0114	5.4	0728	0.9	1337	5.4	1928	1.0
3	Th	0152	5.8	0825	0.3	1420	6.0	2029	0.8		18	F	0147	5.5	0805	0.8	1409	5.5	2004	0.9
4	F	0237	5.8	0910	0.3	1505	5.9	2108	0.9		19	Sa	0219	5.5	0842	0.7	1444	5.6	2040	0.9
5	Sa	0321	5.7	0952	0.4	1552	5.7	2146	1.0		20	Su	0251	5.6	0918	0.7	1519	5.6	2115	0.9
6	Su	0403	5.6	1030	0.6	1637	5.5	2223	1.1		21	M	0327	5.6	0952	0.7	1557	5.5	2148	1.0
7	M	0447	5.5	1108	0.8	1722	5.3	2302	1.3 ☾		22	Tu	0403	5.5	1023	0.8	1638	5.4	2223	1.1
8	Tu	0533	5.3	1149	1.0	1811	5.0	2349	1.4		23	W	0444	5.4	1057	0.9	1725	5.2	2306	1.2 ☽
9	W	0627	5.0	1239	1.2	1910	4.8				24	Th	0533	5.3	1143	1.1	1822	5.0		
10	Th	0050	1.6	0733	4.8	1347	1.4	2018	4.6		25	F	0007	1.4	0639	5.1	1252	1.2	1935	4.9
11	F	0213	1.7	0850	4.7	1501	1.5	2129	4.7		26	Sa	0130	1.5	0801	5.0	1426	1.3	2053	4.9
12	Sa	0334	1.6	1003	4.7	1606	1.4	2231	4.9		27	Su	0301	1.4	0922	5.1	1550	1.2	2207	5.1
13	Su	0440	1.4	1102	4.9	1658	1.1	2322	5.0		28	M	0424	1.1	1038	5.3	1701	1.0	2313	5.3
14	M	0533	1.2	1149	5.1	1743	1.3				29	Tu	0537	0.8	1142	5.6	1801	0.9		
15	Tu	0004	5.2	0617	1.1	1228	5.2	1819 ●	1.2		30	W	0008	5.5	0638	0.5	1235	5.8	1850 ○	0.8
											31	Th	0056	5.7	0728	0.3	1321	5.9	1934	0.7

FEBRUARY

#	Day	Time	m	Time	m	Time	m	Time	m		#	Day	Time	m	Time	m	Time	m	Time	m
1	F	0138	5.8	0812	0.2	1405	6.0	2012	0.7		16	Sa	0126	5.6	0749	0.5	1348	5.7	1949	0.7
2	Sa	0219	5.9	0853	0.2	1446	5.9	2049	0.7		17	Su	0158	5.7	0826	0.4	1423	5.8	2026	0.7
3	Su	0258	5.9	0928	0.3	1525	5.8	2122	0.8		18	M	0232	5.8	0901	0.5	1457	5.8	2100	0.7
4	M	0336	5.8	1000	0.5	1603	5.6	2153	0.9		19	Tu	0305	5.8	0934	0.6	1534	5.6	2131	0.8
5	Tu	0413	5.6	1028	0.7	1641	5.3	2224	1.1		20	W	0341	5.7	1000	0.7	1613	5.5	2202	1.0
6	W	0452	5.3	1059	1.0	1722	5.0	2301	1.3 ☾		21	Th	0421	5.6	1030	0.9	1657	5.2	2244	1.1 ☽
7	Th	0537	5.0	1139	1.3	1808	4.7	2351	1.6		22	F	0511	5.3	1113	1.1	1753	4.9	2342	1.3
8	F	0636	4.6	1239	1.6	1912	4.4				23	Sa	0617	5.0	1224	1.4	1906	4.7		
9	Sa	0109	1.9	0758	4.3	1412	1.8	2036	4.3		24	Su	0109	1.5	0744	4.8	1406	1.4	2033	4.7
10	Su	0258	1.8	0934	4.4	1536	1.7	2200	4.5		25	M	0253	1.4	0917	4.9	1538	1.4	2156	4.9
11	M	0417	1.5	1041	4.7	1637	1.5	2258	4.8		26	Tu	0421	1.2	1034	5.3	1651	1.2	2302	5.2
12	Tu	0515	1.3	1129	5.0	1723	1.3	2343	5.1		27	W	0533	0.7	1133	5.6	1749	0.9	2354	5.5
13	W	0600	1.1	1207	5.2	1803	1.1				28	Th	0627	0.4	1222	5.8	1834 ○	0.8		
14	Th	0019	5.3	0636	0.9	1242	5.4	1838 ●	1.0											

MARCH

#	Day	Time	m	Time	m	Time	m	Time	m		#	Day	Time	m	Time	m	Time	m	Time	m
1	F	0038	5.7	0712	0.3	1304	5.9	1914	0.7		16	Sa	0024	5.6	0646	0.6	1248	5.7	1850 ●	0.7
2	Sa	0119	5.9	0751	0.2	1344	5.9	1951	0.6		17	Su	0059	5.7	0724	0.4	1323	5.9	1928	0.6
3	Su	0155	6.0	0826	0.2	1420	5.9	2025	0.6		18	M	0133	5.9	0802	0.4	1358	5.9	2006	0.5
4	M	0232	5.9	0858	0.3	1456	5.7	2057	0.7		19	Tu	0208	6.0	0839	0.4	1433	5.9	2043	0.6
5	Tu	0307	5.8	0927	0.6	1529	5.5	2125	0.8		20	W	0244	5.9	0911	0.5	1511	5.7	2117	0.7
6	W	0341	5.6	0952	0.8	1602	5.3	2152	1.0		21	Th	0322	5.8	0942	0.7	1550	5.5	2152	0.9
7	Th	0416	5.3	1017	1.1	1635	5.0	2221	1.3		22	F	0407	5.6	1014	1.0	1637	5.2	2235	1.0
8	F	0457	4.9	1052	1.4	1716	4.7	2304	1.6 ☾		23	Sa	0501	5.3	1102	1.3	1733	4.9	2336	1.2 ☽
9	Sa	0549	4.5	1143	1.7	1812	4.3				24	Su	0611	5.0	1212	1.6	1848	4.6		
10	Su	0007	1.8	0704	4.2	1307	2.0	1933	4.1		25	M	0106	1.4	0740	4.8	1352	1.7	2018	4.7
11	M	0208	1.9	0847	4.2	1458	1.9	2112	4.4		26	Tu	0247	1.2	0910	5.0	1522	1.5	2141	4.9
12	Tu	0342	1.6	1006	4.6	1603	1.6	2221	4.7		27	W	0412	0.9	1021	5.3	1633	1.2	2244	5.2
13	W	0440	1.2	1055	5.0	1652	1.3	2309	5.0		28	Th	0516	0.6	1116	5.6	1726	1.0	2333	5.5
14	Th	0526	1.0	1136	5.3	1733	1.1	2349	5.3		29	F	0605	0.4	1203	5.7	1810	0.8		
15	F	0607	0.8	1212	5.5	1811	0.9				30	Sa	0015	5.7	0646	0.4	1242	5.8	1848 ○	0.7
											31	Su	0053	5.8	0721	0.3	1317	5.8	1924	0.6

APRIL

#	Day	Time	m	Time	m	Time	m	Time	m		#	Day	Time	m	Time	m	Time	m	Time	m
1	M	0130	5.9	0754	0.4	1352	5.8	1959	0.6		16	Tu	0106	6.0	0737	0.4	1333	5.9	1948	0.5
2	Tu	0205	5.8	0825	0.5	1425	5.7	2032	0.7		17	W	0145	6.0	0815	0.5	1412	5.9	2029	0.5
3	W	0239	5.7	0853	0.7	1456	5.5	2100	0.9		18	Th	0226	6.0	0851	0.6	1453	5.7	2108	0.6
4	Th	0312	5.5	0918	1.0	1527	5.3	2125	1.1		19	F	0311	5.8	0928	0.8	1536	5.5	2150	0.7
5	F	0346	5.2	0943	1.2	1557	5.0	2152	1.3		20	Sa	0402	5.6	1007	1.1	1626	5.2	2238	0.9
6	Sa	0424	4.9	1016	1.5	1635	4.8	2230	1.5		21	Su	0459	5.3	1058	1.3	1723	5.0	2342	1.0 ☽
7	Su	0512	4.6	1104	1.7	1725	4.5	2327	1.7 ☾		22	M	0608	5.1	1205	1.5	1835	4.8		
8	M	0618	4.3	1212	2.0	1836	4.2				23	Tu	0103	1.1	0728	5.0	1331	1.6	1955	4.8
9	Tu	0059	1.8	0745	4.3	1355	1.9	2008	4.3		24	W	0230	1.0	0850	5.1	1451	1.4	2112	5.0
10	W	0244	1.5	0910	4.6	1514	1.6	2127	4.6		25	Th	0345	0.8	0957	5.3	1600	1.2	2216	5.2
11	Th	0348	1.2	1009	5.0	1607	1.3	2221	5.0		26	F	0447	0.6	1051	5.5	1655	1.0	2306	5.4
12	F	0440	0.9	1055	5.3	1654	1.0	2308	5.3		27	Sa	0534	0.6	1136	5.6	1740	0.9	2349	5.5
13	Sa	0527	0.7	1136	5.6	1739	0.8	2349	5.6		28	Su	0614	0.6	1215	5.6	1821	0.8		
14	Su	0612	0.5	1217	5.8	1822 ●	0.7				29	M	0028	5.6	0648	0.6	1252	5.6	1859	0.7
15	M	0028	5.8	0656	0.4	1255	5.9	1906	0.6		30	Tu	0106	5.7	0721	0.6	1326	5.6	1935	0.7

Chart Datum: 2.90 metres below Ordnance Datum (Newlyn)

ENGLAND, EAST COAST – SHEERNESS

Lat 51°27′ N   Long 0°45′ E

TIMES AND HEIGHTS OF HIGH AND LOW WATERS

YEAR **1991**

TIME ZONE UT (GMT)
For Summer Time add ONE hour in non-shaded areas

MAY

Day	Time	m	Time	m		Day	Time	m	Time	m
1 W	0141 / 0752 / 1357 / 2009	5.6 / 0.7 / 5.6 / 0.8				16 Th	0130 / 0755 / 1355 / 2019	6.0 / 0.6 / 5.8 / 0.5		
2 Th	0216 / 0822 / 1427 / 2040	5.5 / 0.9 / 5.4 / 0.9				17 F	0216 / 0837 / 1440 / 2105	6.0 / 0.7 / 5.7 / 0.5		
3 F	0250 / 0850 / 1458 / 2105	5.3 / 1.1 / 5.3 / 1.1				18 Sa	0305 / 0918 / 1527 / 2152	5.9 / 0.9 / 5.5 / 0.6		
4 Sa	0325 / 0918 / 1531 / 2135	5.2 / 1.3 / 5.1 / 1.2				19 Su	0359 / 1002 / 1619 / 2242	5.7 / 1.1 / 5.4 / 0.7		
5 Su	0403 / 0953 / 1609 / 2213	5.0 / 1.4 / 4.9 / 1.3				20 M ☽	0455 / 1051 / 1713 / 2340	5.5 / 1.2 / 5.1 / 0.8		
6 M	0448 / 1037 / 1655 / 2305	4.8 / 1.6 / 4.7 / 1.4				21 Tu	0557 / 1149 / 1815	5.3 / 1.4 / 5.1		
7 Tu ☾	0543 / 1136 / 1754	4.6 / 1.8 / 4.6				22 W	0046 / 0704 / 1257 / 1924	0.8 / 5.2 / 1.5 / 5.0		
8 W	0017 / 0652 / 1252 / 1907	1.5 / 4.5 / 1.8 / 4.5				23 Th	0157 / 0816 / 1409 / 2036	0.9 / 5.2 / 1.4 / 5.1		
9 Th	0140 / 0808 / 1411 / 2025	1.3 / 4.7 / 1.6 / 4.7				24 F	0305 / 0922 / 1518 / 2142	0.8 / 5.2 / 1.3 / 5.2		
10 F	0250 / 0914 / 1514 / 2128	1.1 / 5.0 / 1.3 / 5.0				25 Sa	0406 / 1020 / 1619 / 2237	0.8 / 5.3 / 1.2 / 5.3		
11 Sa	0350 / 1009 / 1609 / 2223	0.9 / 5.3 / 1.1 / 5.3				26 Su	0457 / 1108 / 1711 / 2325	0.8 / 5.4 / 1.0 / 5.3		
12 Su	0445 / 1058 / 1702 / 2312	0.7 / 5.6 / 0.9 / 5.6				27 M	0539 / 1151 / 1756	0.9 / 5.4 / 0.9		
13 M	0537 / 1144 / 1754 / 2358	0.6 / 5.8 / 0.7 / 5.8				28 Tu ○	0008 / 0617 / 1229 / 1838	5.4 / 0.9 / 5.5 / 0.8		
14 Tu ●	0627 / 1229 / 1845	0.5 / 5.9 / 0.6				29 W	0048 / 0652 / 1304 / 1917	5.4 / 0.9 / 5.5 / 0.8		
15 W	0043 / 0713 / 1312 / 1933	5.9 / 0.5 / 5.9 / 0.5				30 Th	0124 / 0726 / 1337 / 1952	5.4 / 0.9 / 5.4 / 0.8		
						31 F	0159 / 0758 / 1409 / 2025	5.4 / 1.0 / 5.4 / 0.9		

JUNE

Day	Time / m		Day	Time / m
1 Sa	0234 / 0829 / 1440 / 2056 — 5.3 / 1.1 / 5.3 / 1.0		16 Su	0300 / 0910 / 1518 / 2150 — 6.0 / 0.8 / 5.7 / 0.4
2 Su	0310 / 0901 / 1515 / 2129 — 5.2 / 1.2 / 5.2 / 1.0		17 M	0349 / 0953 / 1606 / 2237 — 5.7 / 1.0 / 5.6 / 0.4
3 M	0348 / 0938 / 1552 / 2207 — 5.1 / 1.3 / 5.1 / 1.1		18 Tu	0441 / 1037 / 1655 / 2323 — 5.7 / 1.1 / 5.5 / 0.6
4 Tu	0428 / 1019 / 1634 / 2252 — 5.1 / 1.4 / 5.0 / 1.1		19 W ☽	0534 / 1123 / 1749 — 5.5 / 1.2 / 5.4
5 W ☾	0515 / 1106 / 1722 / 2344 — 5.0 / 1.5 / 4.9 / 1.1		20 Th	0014 / 0631 / 1217 / 1848 — 0.7 / 5.3 / 1.3 / 5.2
6 Th	0610 / 1204 / 1821 — 4.9 / 1.5 / 4.9		21 F	0112 / 0734 / 1321 / 1954 — 0.9 / 5.1 / 1.4 / 5.0
7 F	0048 / 0714 / 1312 / 1928 — 1.1 / 4.9 / 1.5 / 4.9		22 Sa	0216 / 0840 / 1433 / 2104 — 1.0 / 5.1 / 1.4 / 5.0
8 Sa	0155 / 0822 / 1422 / 2039 — 1.1 / 5.1 / 1.4 / 5.1		23 Su	0321 / 0945 / 1543 / 2209 — 1.1 / 5.1 / 1.3 / 5.0
9 Su	0303 / 0925 / 1528 / 2142 — 0.9 / 5.3 / 1.2 / 5.3		24 M	0419 / 1041 / 1645 / 2305 — 1.1 / 5.1 / 1.2 / 5.1
10 M	0406 / 1024 / 1630 / 2241 — 0.8 / 5.5 / 1.0 / 5.5		25 Tu	0509 / 1129 / 1739 / 2353 — 1.1 / 5.2 / 1.1 / 5.2
11 Tu	0506 / 1118 / 1730 / 2336 — 0.7 / 5.6 / 0.8 / 5.7		26 W	0553 / 1211 / 1824 — 1.1 / 5.3 / 1.0
12 W ●	0603 / 1208 / 1828 — 0.7 / 5.7 / 0.6		27 Th ○	0035 / 0631 / 1249 / 1904 — 5.3 / 1.1 / 5.4 / 0.9
13 Th	0029 / 0655 / 1257 / 1923 — 5.9 / 0.7 / 5.7 / 0.5		28 F	0113 / 0706 / 1323 / 1940 — 5.3 / 1.1 / 5.4 / 0.9
14 F	0120 / 0741 / 1344 / 2013 — 6.0 / 0.7 / 5.8 / 0.4		29 Sa	0147 / 0740 / 1355 / 2013 — 5.4 / 1.0 / 5.4 / 0.8
15 Sa	0209 / 0826 / 1432 / 2103 — 6.0 / 0.7 / 5.7 / 0.3		30 Su	0220 / 0813 / 1427 / 2049 — 5.4 / 1.0 / 5.4 / 0.8

JULY

Day	Time / m		Day	Time / m
1 M	0254 / 0849 / 1501 / 2124 — 5.4 / 1.0 / 5.4 / 0.8		16 Tu	0332 / 0936 / 1546 / 2217 — 5.9 / 0.8 / 5.8 / 0.3
2 Tu	0329 / 0925 / 1536 / 2159 — 5.4 / 1.1 / 5.4 / 0.8		17 W	0417 / 1013 / 1630 / 2255 — 5.8 / 0.9 / 5.7 / 0.5
3 W	0407 / 1002 / 1613 / 2235 — 5.4 / 1.1 / 5.3 / 0.9		18 Th ☽	0502 / 1052 / 1715 / 2334 — 5.5 / 1.1 / 5.5 / 0.8
4 Th	0447 / 1040 / 1652 / 2313 — 5.3 / 1.2 / 5.3 / 1.0		19 F	0551 / 1134 / 1807 — 5.2 / 1.3 / 5.2
5 F ☾	0533 / 1123 / 1742 — 5.2 / 1.3 / 5.2		20 Sa	0019 / 0646 / 1231 / 1909 — 1.1 / 5.0 / 1.5 / 4.9
6 Sa	0001 / 0629 / 1221 / 1842 — 1.0 / 5.0 / 1.4 / 5.1		21 Su	0121 / 0751 / 1347 / 2026 — 1.3 / 4.8 / 1.6 / 4.7
7 Su	0103 / 0737 / 1333 / 1955 — 1.1 / 5.0 / 1.4 / 5.1		22 M	0237 / 0905 / 1514 / 2145 — 1.5 / 4.7 / 1.6 / 4.8
8 M	0220 / 0847 / 1451 / 2110 — 1.1 / 5.1 / 1.3 / 5.2		23 Tu	0348 / 1014 / 1627 / 2249 — 1.4 / 4.9 / 1.4 / 5.0
9 Tu	0336 / 0955 / 1604 / 2219 — 1.0 / 5.3 / 1.1 / 5.4		24 W	0447 / 1109 / 1726 / 2339 — 1.4 / 5.1 / 1.2 / 5.2
10 W	0444 / 1057 / 1713 / 2322 — 0.9 / 5.4 / 0.9 / 5.6		25 Th	0533 / 1154 / 1811 — 1.3 / 5.2 / 1.0
11 Th ●	0546 / 1154 / 1819 — 0.7 / 5.6 / 0.7		26 F ○	0019 / 0614 / 1232 / 1850 — 5.3 / 1.2 / 5.3 / 0.9
12 F	0019 / 0641 / 1246 / 1916 — 5.8 / 0.7 / 5.7 / 0.4		27 Sa	0056 / 0649 / 1306 / 1924 — 5.4 / 1.1 / 5.4 / 0.8
13 Sa	0112 / 0730 / 1334 / 2006 — 6.0 / 0.7 / 5.8 / 0.3		28 Su	0128 / 0723 / 1338 / 1958 — 5.5 / 1.0 / 5.5 / 0.7
14 Su	0201 / 0815 / 1419 / 2054 — 6.0 / 0.7 / 5.9 / 0.2		29 M	0201 / 0757 / 1409 / 2033 — 5.6 / 0.9 / 5.6 / 0.6
15 M	0247 / 0857 / 1503 / 2136 — 6.0 / 0.7 / 5.9 / 0.2		30 Tu	0233 / 0832 / 1442 / 2108 — 5.7 / 0.8 / 5.6 / 0.6
			31 W	0307 / 0908 / 1514 / 2142 — 5.6 / 0.9 / 5.6 / 0.7

AUGUST

Day	Time / m		Day	Time / m
1 Th	0342 / 0941 / 1548 / 2212 — 5.6 / 1.0 / 5.6 / 0.8		16 F	0427 / 1019 / 1640 / 2251 — 5.5 / 1.1 / 5.5 / 1.0
2 F	0419 / 1012 / 1624 / 2241 — 5.5 / 1.1 / 5.5 / 0.9		17 Sa ☽	0508 / 1054 / 1725 / 2327 — 5.2 / 1.3 / 5.1 / 1.3
3 Sa	0501 / 1048 / 1709 / 2319 — 5.3 / 1.2 / 5.3 / 1.1		18 Su	0554 / 1142 / 1822 — 4.8 / 1.5 / 4.7
4 Su	0551 / 1139 / 1807 — 5.1 / 1.4 / 5.1		19 M	0022 / 0655 / 1253 / 1942 — 1.6 / 4.6 / 1.8 / 4.5
5 M	0017 / 0657 / 1252 / 1923 — 1.3 / 4.9 / 1.5 / 5.0		20 Tu	0149 / 0818 / 1444 / 2118 — 1.8 / 4.4 / 1.8 / 4.5
6 Tu	0144 / 0815 / 1425 / 2047 — 1.4 / 4.9 / 1.4 / 5.0		21 W	0318 / 0945 / 1606 / 2227 — 1.8 / 4.6 / 1.5 / 4.9
7 W	0314 / 0932 / 1549 / 2207 — 1.3 / 5.0 / 1.2 / 5.3		22 Th	0421 / 1044 / 1704 / 2316 — 1.5 / 4.9 / 1.2 / 5.1
8 Th	0428 / 1042 / 1706 / 2315 — 1.2 / 5.3 / 0.9 / 5.6		23 F	0511 / 1129 / 1749 / 2356 — 1.3 / 5.2 / 1.0 / 5.4
9 F	0533 / 1142 / 1812 — 1.0 / 5.5 / 0.6		24 Sa	0551 / 1207 / 1825 — 1.2 / 5.4 / 0.8
10 Sa ●	0011 / 0628 / 1232 / 1906 — 5.8 / 0.9 / 5.7 / 0.4		25 Su ○	0031 / 0627 / 1241 / 1900 — 5.5 / 1.0 / 5.6 / 0.7
11 Su	0100 / 0714 / 1317 / 1954 — 6.0 / 0.7 / 5.9 / 0.2		26 M	0103 / 0700 / 1313 / 1934 — 5.6 / 0.9 / 5.7 / 0.6
12 M	0144 / 0757 / 1359 / 2034 — 6.1 / 0.7 / 6.0 / 0.1		27 Tu	0134 / 0735 / 1344 / 2009 — 5.8 / 0.8 / 5.8 / 0.5
13 Tu	0226 / 0836 / 1439 / 2114 — 6.0 / 0.7 / 6.0 / 0.2		28 W	0206 / 0811 / 1415 / 2044 — 5.8 / 0.7 / 5.8 / 0.5
14 W	0307 / 0912 / 1519 / 2149 — 5.9 / 0.7 / 5.9 / 0.4		29 Th	0240 / 0846 / 1447 / 2117 — 5.8 / 0.8 / 5.8 / 0.7
15 Th	0348 / 0946 / 1559 / 2220 — 5.7 / 0.8 / 5.8 / 0.7		30 F	0314 / 0917 / 1522 / 2145 — 5.7 / 0.9 / 5.7 / 0.8
			31 Sa	0350 / 0946 / 1600 / 2210 — 5.6 / 1.1 / 5.6 / 1.0

Chart Datum: 2.90 metres below Ordnance Datum (Newlyn)

ENGLAND, EAST COAST – SHEERNESS

Lat 51°27′ N   Long 0°45′ E

TIMES AND HEIGHTS OF HIGH AND LOW WATERS

YEAR 1991

TIME ZONE UT(GMT)
For Summer Time add ONE hour in non-shaded areas

SEPTEMBER

Day	Time	m	Day	Time	m
1 Su ☾	0431	5·3	16 M	0505	4·8
	1021	1·2		1055	1·6
	1645	5·4		1740	4·6
	2247	1·2		2330	1·8
2 M	0520	5·1	17 Tu	0600	4·5
	1112	1·4		1158	1·9
	1744	5·1		1855	4·3
	2346	1·5			
3 Tu	0627	4·8	18 W	0048	2·1
	1229	1·5		0719	4·3
	1904	4·9		1359	1·9
				2033	4·4
4 W	0120	1·7	19 Th	0239	2·0
	0749	4·7		0856	4·4
	1412	1·5		1529	1·6
	2036	4·9		2150	4·7
5 Th	0258	1·6	20 F	0346	1·7
	0917	4·9		1006	4·8
	1543	1·2		1626	1·2
	2200	5·2		2241	5·1
6 F	0416	1·3	21 Sa	0435	1·4
	1028	5·2		1052	5·2
	1659	0·8		1711	1·0
	2305	5·6		2322	5·4
7 Sa	0518	1·1	22 Su	0518	1·1
	1126	5·5		1132	5·4
	1800	0·5		1750	0·8
	2357	5·8		2357	5·6
8 Su ●	0610	0·9	23 M ○	0554	1·0
	1212	5·8		1207	5·6
	1848	0·3		1827	0·7
9 M	0042	6·0	24 Tu	0031	5·8
	0653	0·8		0631	0·8
	1305	5·9		1241	5·8
	1930	0·2		1903	0·5
10 Tu	0123	6·0	25 W	0104	5·9
	0733	0·7		0709	0·7
	1334	6·0		1314	5·9
	2008	0·3		1940	0·5
11 W	0201	6·0	26 Th	0138	5·9
	0811	0·7		0745	0·7
	1412	6·0		1348	6·0
	2043	0·4		2015	0·6
12 Th	0239	5·9	27 F	0212	5·9
	0846	0·8		0822	0·8
	1450	5·9		1423	5·9
	2114	0·6		2049	0·7
13 F	0314	5·6	28 Sa	0249	5·8
	0917	1·0		0857	0·9
	1528	5·7		1500	5·8
	2142	0·9		2118	0·9
14 Sa	0349	5·4	29 Su	0327	5·6
	0946	1·2		0929	1·0
	1606	5·4		1542	5·6
	2209	1·2		2148	1·1
15 Su ☽	0426	5·1	30 M	0409	5·3
	1016	1·4		1009	1·2
	1647	5·0		1631	5·4
	2241	1·5		2230	1·4

OCTOBER

Day	Time	m	Day	Time	m
1 Tu ☾	0459	5·1	16 W	0513	4·6
	1105	1·3		1115	1·8
	1734	5·1		1807	4·4
	2333	1·6		2353	2·1
2 W	0608	4·8	17 Th	0621	4·4
	1225	1·5		1243	1·8
	1856	4·9		1928	4·4
3 Th	0104	1·8	18 F	0128	2·1
	0733	4·7		0747	4·4
	1405	1·4		1430	1·6
	2027	5·0		2050	4·6
4 F	0239	1·6	19 Sa	0253	1·8
	0858	4·9		0905	4·7
	1532	1·0		1532	1·3
	2146	5·3		2150	5·0
5 Sa	0355	1·4	20 Su	0349	1·5
	1009	5·3		1003	5·1
	1642	0·7		1623	1·0
	2247	5·6		2237	5·3
6 Su	0455	1·1	21 M	0434	1·2
	1104	5·6		1048	5·4
	1737	0·5		1706	0·8
	2336	5·8		2318	5·6
7 M ●	0544	1·0	22 Tu	0516	1·0
	1149	5·7		1129	5·6
	1822	0·5		1749	0·7
				2356	5·8
8 Tu	0018	5·9	23 W ○	0558	0·8
	0627	0·8		1207	5·8
	1229	5·9		1829	0·6
	1902	0·4			
9 W	0057	5·9	24 Th	0034	5·9
	0706	0·7		0641	0·7
	1309	6·0		1245	5·9
	1935	0·5		1909	0·6
10 Th	0134	5·9	25 F	0110	6·0
	0742	0·7		0721	0·7
	1345	5·9		1323	6·0
	2009	0·6		1947	0·6
11 F	0208	5·8	26 Sa	0148	5·9
	0819	0·8		0802	0·7
	1423	5·8		1402	6·0
	2039	0·8		2023	0·8
12 Sa	0242	5·6	27 Su	0227	5·8
	0850	1·0		0843	0·8
	1500	5·6		1446	5·8
	2105	1·1		2058	1·0
13 Su	0314	5·3	28 M	0308	5·6
	0918	1·2		0924	0·9
	1536	5·3		1532	5·7
	2132	1·3		2136	1·2
14 M	0348	5·1	29 Tu	0355	5·4
	0943	1·4		1010	1·0
	1616	5·0		1627	5·4
	2203	1·6		2224	1·4
15 Tu ☽	0424	4·8	30 W	0449	5·1
	1020	1·6		1151	1·2
	1704	4·7		1732	5·2
	2248	1·8		2326	1·6
			31 Th	0556	4·9
				1222	1·2
				1846	5·0

NOVEMBER

Day	Time	m	Day	Time	m
1 F	0045	1·7	16 Sa	0019	1·9
	0712	4·9		0642	4·6
	1348	1·2		1310	1·5
	2008	5·1		1940	4·7
2 Sa	0209	1·6	17 Su	0138	1·8
	0832	5·0		0757	4·7
	1507	1·0		1426	1·3
	2121	5·3		2047	4·9
3 Su	0322	1·4	18 M	0249	1·5
	0939	5·3		0903	5·0
	1614	0·8		1527	1·1
	2220	5·5		2145	5·2
4 M	0423	1·2	19 Tu	0345	1·3
	1035	5·5		0959	5·3
	1708	0·7		1620	0·9
	2311	5·6		2235	5·5
5 Tu	0515	1·1	20 W	0437	1·1
	1123	5·6		1049	5·5
	1751	0·7		1709	0·8
	2353	5·7		2322	5·7
6 W ●	0600	0·9	21 Th ○	0526	0·9
	1207	5·7		1136	5·7
	1829	0·7		1757	0·7
7 Th	0032	5·7	22 F	0005	5·8
	0641	0·8		0615	0·8
	1246	5·7		1221	5·9
	1903	0·7		1842	0·7
8 F	0109	5·7	23 Sa	0048	5·9
	0720	0·8		0703	0·7
	1324	5·7		1304	6·0
	1935	0·8		1926	0·7
9 Sa	0142	5·6	24 Su	0130	5·8
	0757	0·9		0749	0·6
	1402	5·6		1351	6·0
	2006	1·0		2006	0·8
10 Su	0216	5·5	25 M	0213	5·8
	0829	1·0		0836	0·6
	1439	5·4		1437	5·9
	2036	1·2		2047	0·9
11 M	0247	5·3	26 Tu	0258	5·6
	0856	1·2		0924	0·7
	1514	5·2		1528	5·8
	2104	1·3		2131	1·1
12 Tu	0319	5·1	27 W	0348	5·5
	0922	1·3		1013	0·8
	1552	5·0		1623	5·6
	2136	1·5		2219	1·3
13 W	0356	5·0	28 Th	0440	5·3
	0957	1·4		1106	0·9
	1635	4·9		1720	5·4
	2217	1·6		2312	1·4
14 Th ☽	0440	4·8	29 F	0539	5·2
	1047	1·5		1208	0·9
	1726	4·7		1825	5·2
	2312	1·6			
15 F	0534	4·7	30 Sa	0015	1·5
	1151	1·6		0643	5·1
	1829	4·6		1316	1·0
				1935	5·1

DECEMBER

Day	Time	m	Day	Time	m
1 Su	0127	1·6	16 M	0032	1·6
	0757	5·1		0653	4·9
	1427	1·0		1317	1·3
	2046	5·2		1948	4·9
2 M	0240	1·5	17 Tu	0144	1·6
	0907	5·2		0805	4·9
	1535	1·0		1430	1·2
	2149	5·3		2054	5·1
3 Tu	0349	1·3	18 W	0256	1·4
	1009	5·3		0912	5·1
	1634	0·9		1536	1·0
	2244	5·4		2156	5·3
4 W	0448	1·2	19 Th	0359	1·2
	1102	5·4		1014	5·4
	1720	0·9		1635	0·9
	2330	5·4		2251	5·5
5 Th	0539	1·0	20 F	0459	1·0
	1150	5·5		1111	5·6
	1801	1·0		1732	0·8
				2343	5·6
6 F ●	0012	5·5	21 Sa ○	0557	0·8
	0624	0·9		1204	5·8
	1232	5·5		1822	0·8
	1836	1·0			
7 Sa	0050	5·5	22 Su	0032	5·7
	0703	0·9		0652	0·6
	1312	5·5		1255	5·9
	1910	1·0		1912	0·8
8 Su	0126	5·5	23 M	0119	5·8
	0741	0·9		0744	0·5
	1348	5·5		1342	6·0
	1942	1·0		1957	0·8
9 M	0158	5·4	24 Tu	0204	5·8
	0813	1·0		0834	0·4
	1423	5·4		1432	6·0
	2013	1·1		2040	0·8
10 Tu	0230	5·4	25 W	0250	5·8
	0843	1·0		0922	0·4
	1457	5·3		1521	5·9
	2044	1·2		2124	0·9
11 W	0303	5·3	26 Th	0336	5·7
	0914	1·1		1009	0·4
	1534	5·2		1610	5·8
	2118	1·3		2206	1·0
12 Th	0336	5·2	27 F	0424	5·6
	0948	1·1		1054	0·6
	1612	5·1		1701	5·6
	2156	1·4		2251	1·2
13 F	0414	5·1	28 Sa ☾	0515	5·5
	1027	1·2		1142	0·7
	1654	5·0		1756	5·3
	2238	1·5		2342	1·3
14 Sa ☽	0458	5·0	29 Su	0611	5·3
	1115	1·2		1235	0·9
	1742	4·9		1857	5·1
	2330	1·6			
15 Su	0550	4·9	30 M	0041	1·5
	1211	1·3		0717	5·1
	1841	4·8		1340	1·1
				2005	5·0
			31 Tu	0155	1·5
				0830	5·0
				1451	1·2
				2115	5·0

Chart Datum: 2.90 metres below Ordnance Datum (Newlyn)

MEDWAY RIVER *continued*

MARINAS (from seaward)
  Mariners Farm Boatpark ☎ 33179; **Gillingham Marina**
  (250 + 12 visitors) ☎ 280022, Slip, P, D, FW, ME, El, Ⓔ,
  Sh, CH, V, AC, Bar, BH (20 ton), C (1 ton), Gas, Gaz;
  Access W basin HW∓2, E basin (via lock), HW∓4½;
  Medway Pier Marina ☎ 51113, D, FW, BY, Ⓔ,
  C (6 ton), Slip; **Hoo Marina** (245) ☎ 250311, FW, Sh, C
  (20 ton), ME, SM, AC, CH, El, Ⓔ, Gas, Gaz; Access W
  basin HW∓1½, E basin (via lock) HW∓2; **Medway
  Bridge Marina** (160 + 15 visitors) ☎ 43576, Slip, D, P,
  FW, ME, El, Ⓔ, Sh, C (3 ton), BH (10 ton), Gas, Gaz, R,
  SM, AC, CH, V, Bar; **Cuxton Marina** (150 + some
  visitors) ☎ 721941, Slip, FW, ME, El, Ⓔ, Sh, BH (12 ton),
  AC, CH; **Elmhaven Marina** (60) ☎ 240489, Slip, FW,
  ME, El, Sh, C, AC; **Allington Lock Marina** (120)
  ☎ Maidstone 52864, CH, ME, El, Sh, P, D, Slip, C
  (10 ton), FW, Gas, Gaz; (non-tidal). Note: Old HM
  Dockyard basins are being converted to Chatham Maritime
  Marina, ☎ 815081.
Yacht Clubs
  Chatham YC ☎ 723051; **Hoo Ness YC** ☎ 250052, Bar,
  R, M, L, FW; **Medway Cruising Club** ☎ 54752, Bar, M,
  L, FW; **Medway Motor Cruising Club** ☎ 827194;
  Medway Motor YC ☎ 389856; **Medway YC** ☎ 718399;
  Rochester CC ☎ 841350, Bar, R, M, FW, L, ▣; **Strood
  YC** ☎ 718261, Bar, M, C (1.5 ton), FW, L, Slip.
Other Facilities
  Gransden Marine ☎ 826770, CH, ACA; **Letley
  Moorings** (Sufference Wharf), ☎ 814429, ME, El, Sh, dry
  dock, AB; **A + B Textiles** ☎ 579686, SM; **Invicta
  Services** ☎ 574191, Sh; **Cabin Yacht Stores** ☎ 718020,
  CH; **Dave Elliot** ☎ 408160, SM; **Baker Marine** ☎ 843227
  CH **OC Diesel Refuelling Barge** (Ship pier, Rochester)
  ☎ 813773, D, CH;
  Towns − all facilities R, V, ▣, ✉; ⇌; ✈ (Lydd or
  Gatwick).

Hoo Marina

Gillingham Marina

RIVER THAMES 10-3-21
London

CHARTS
Admiralty 3319, 2484, 3337, 2151, 1186, 1185; Stanford 5; Imray C2, C1; OS 176, 177, 178. More details obtainable from *'Nicholsons Guide to the Thames'*, from PLA publications and *'London Waterways Guide'* (Imray).

TIDES
+0245 Dover; ML 3.7; Duration 0555; Zone 0 (GMT).

Standard Port LONDON BRIDGE (→)

Times				Height (metres)			
HW		LW		MHWS	MHWN	MLWN	MLWS
0300	0900	0400	1100	7.1	5.8	1.6	0.5
1500	2100	1600	2300				

Differences WOOLWICH (GALLIONS POINT)
−0020 −0020 −0025 −0040 −0.1 −0.1 +0.1 0.0

CHELSEA BRIDGE
+0020 +0015 +0055 +0100 −0.8 −0.7 −0.6 −0.3

RICHMOND LOCK
+0100 +0055 +0325 +0305 −2.1 −2.2 −1.4 −0.3

NOTE: London Bridge is a Standard Port and tidal predictions for each day of the year are given below. The river is tidal up to Teddington Lock with half-tide lock at Richmond. When the Thames Barrier is closed, water levels will vary considerably from predictions.

TIDES — TIME DIFFERENCES ON LONDON BRIDGE

Place	MHWS	MHWN	MLWN	MLWS
Teddington Lock	+0106	+0056	—	—
Richmond Lock	+0100	+0055	+0325	+0305
Chiswick Bridge	+0049	+0044	+0235	+0224
Hammersmith Bridge	+0038	+0037	+0200	+0156
Putney Bridge	+0032	+0030	+0138	+0137
Battersea Bridge	+0023	+0020	+0109	+0110
Chelsea Bridge	+0020	+0015	+0055	+0100
Westminster Bridge	+0012	+0011	+0031	+0035
London Bridge	0000	0000	0000	0000
Surrey Comm Dock				
Greenland Dock	−0010	−0008	−0013	−0015
Millwall Dock Entrance	−0010	−0008	−0014	−0016
Deptford Creek	−0012	−0011	−0018	−0021
Greenwich Pier	−0014	−0012	−0020	−0023
India and Millwall Dock Entrance	−0018	−0015	−0026	−0029
Royal Victoria Dock Entrance	−0021	−0018	−0031	−0025
Woolwich Ferry	−0028	−0024	−0042	−0047
Royal Albert Dock Entrance	−0029	−0024	−0043	−0050
Southern Outfall (below Crossness)	−0030	−0025	−0048	−0056
Coldharbour Point	−0037	−0030	−0053	−0103
Stoneness Lighthouse	−0048	−0037	−0059	−0114
Broadness Lighthouse	−0052	−0040	−0101	−0119
Tilburyness	−0056	−0042	−0103	−0123
Gravesend Town Pier	−0059	−0044	−0106	−0125

SHELTER
Very good shelter in many places above the Thames Barrier. In Bow Creek (Bugsby's Reach), in Deptford Creek (HW∓2), South Dock Marina, St Katharine's Yacht Haven (see 10.3.24), Lambeth Pier (PLA), Chelsea Harbour Marina, Chelsea Yacht & Boat Co (Cheyne Walk), Cadogan Pier (PLA), Hurlingham YC, Chas Newens (BY, Putney), Alan See (Hammersmith), Hammersmith Pier, Chiswick Quay Marina, Auto Marine Services (Chiswick), Grand Union Canal ent (Brentford), Howlett's BY (Twickenham) and Tough's BY (Teddington) as well as numerous Draw Docks belonging to the PLA.

PIERS WHERE LANDING CAN BE MADE BY ARRANGEMENT

Hampton Court Pier	
Richmond Landing Stage	(071) 930 2641
Kew Pier	
Hammersmith Pier	(081) 748 2715
Putney Pier	(071) 930 2641
Chelsea Harbour Pier	(071) 351 4433
Cadogan Pier	(071) 352 4604
Lambeth Pier	
Westminster Pier	
Charing Cross Pier	(071) 930 2641
London Bridge City Pier	
Swan Lane Pier	(071) 987 1185/ (071) 730 4812
Tower Pier	(071) 930 2641
Cherry Garden Pier	(071) 237 3498/5134
West India Dock Pier	(071) 987 1185/ (071) 730 4812
Greenwich Pier	(071) 930 2641
London City Airport Pier	(071) 474 5555
Barrier Gardens Pier	(081) 854 5555

NAVIGATION
River users are advised to read the Port of London River Bye Laws and *Pleasure Users Guide to the Thames*, obtainable from Thames House, St Andrews Road, Tilbury, Essex, RM18 7JH (☎ Tilbury 3444 Ext 584). When proceeding up or down river, unless impracticable, keep to the starboard side of mid-channel. Boats approaching a bridge against the tide give way to those approaching with the tide. However, vessels over 40m always have priority. Below Wandsworth there is no speed limit. Above, limit is 8 kn.

A triangle of three red discs, or lights, hanging below an arch apex down indicates that that arch is closed. The Thames Tidal Barrier is in the centre of Woolwich Reach and consists of 9 piers between which rotating gates can form a barrier. The spans between piers are designated 'A' to 'K' from South to North. Spans A and from H to K inclusive are not navigable. The main navigational spans are C, D, E and F. Green lights forming arrows, point towards the span in use and clear for traffic. Red lights forming a St Andrews Cross each side of a span indicate that it is closed. Lights may be exhibited from: Thamesmead, False Point, Blackwall Point and Brunswick Wharf. These will indicate: Y flashing − Proceed with extreme caution, barrier about to close; R flashing − all vessels stop, barrier being closed. The Thames Barrier Navigation Centre, call sign *Woolwich Radio*, is the communications centre for that part of the river to the W of Crayfordness. The Traffic Controller regulates all traffic through the barrier, controlling it from Margaret Ness to Blackwall Point. Radio VHF Chs 14 and 22. General shipping information is not available from this centre but from the Thames Navigation Service (Woolwich Radio or Gravesend Radio or ☎ Gravesend 67684). All vessels with VHF (vessels without VHF see below) intending to go through the barrier must inform Woolwich Radio on Ch 14 of their ETA when passing Crayfordness inward bound or Tower Bridge outward bound. Then, when passing Margaret Ness Point inward or Blackwall Point outward obtain permission from the Controller to proceed. Yachts without VHF should proceed with caution, normally using span G (N side) if bound up river or span B (S side) if bound down river, and keeping clear of larger vessels. Note however that depths in spans B and G may only be about 1.5m at LW springs. If possible ring Barrier Control 855 0315, before arrival. The barrier is completely closed monthly for test. Individual spans are closed weekly. When barrier is closed, water levels will differ considerably from predictions.

The Half tide weir at Richmond is operated to maintain a min depth of 1.7m between Teddington and Richmond bridges. When the weir gates are down, lock is available. Other times (approx. HW∓2) sail straight through.

Headway of centre span and height of MHWS.

Name of Bridge	Distance above London Bridge Sea Miles	Headway of Centre Span above Chart Datum (m)	MHWS (m)
Richmond	13.97	7.9	2.6
Richmond Railway	13.67	7.9	2.6
Twickenham	13.64	8.5	2.6
Richmond Footbridge	13.49	9.7	4.8
Kew	11.33	10.6	5.3
Kew Railway	10.98	10.9	5.3
Chiswick	10.22	12.2	5.3
Barnes Railway	9.55	10.9	5.5

RIVER THAMES *continued*

Hammersmith	7.97	9.4	5.7
Putney	6.45	11.4	5.9
Fulham Railway	6.31	12.8	6.1
Wandsworth	5.46	11.9	6.1
Battersea Railway	4.83	12.2	6.1
Battersea	4.27	11.7	6.2
Albert	4.04	11.1	6.2
Chelsea	3.40	12.9	6.3
Victoria Railway	3.31	12.3	6.3
Vauxhall	2.46	12.1	6.5
Lambeth	2.02	13.1	6.6
Westminster	1.64	12.2	6.8
Charing Cross Rly	1.32	13.8	6.8
Waterloo	1.12	15.3	6.8
Blackfriars	0.63	14.0	6.9
Blackfriars Rly	0.62	13.9	6.9
Southwark	0.24	14.3	6.9
Cannon St. Rly	0.16	14.0	6.9
London Bridge	0	16.0	7.1
Tower	below 0.49	15.7	7.1

Note: The tidal Thames is divided by the PLA into two sections
Upper Section – Teddington to Cross Ness
Lower Section – Cross Ness to the Sea

LIGHTS AND MARKS
Margaret Ness or Tripcock Pt Fl(2) W 5s 11m 8M. Tower Bridge sounds horn 20s or gong 30s when bascules open for shipping. When Richmond half-tide barrier is shut, a triangle of red discs (red lights at night) is hung below the centre span of the footbridge.

RADIO TELEPHONE
Call *Woolwich Radio* VHF Ch **14** 16 22 (H24) (for Thames Barrier control)
St Katharines Yacht Haven VHF Ch **80** (HW−2 to HW+1½; 0600-2030 LT in summer, 0800-1800 LT in winter). Chelsea Harbour Marina VHF Ch 14 16 **80** (HW−2 to HW+1½).
Brentford Dock Marina VHF Ch 14 16
Gravesend Radio VHF Ch **12** 16 18 20 (H24)
Information broadcasts every H and H+30 on Ch 12 by Gravesend, and every H+15 and H+45 on Ch 14 by Woolwich. These are repeated by North Foreland Radio Ch 26, Thames Radio Ch 02, Hastings Radio Ch 07 and Orfordness Radio Ch 62 at the end of first silence period after receipt. PLA Patrol Launches (call: *Thames Patrol*) VHF Ch 12 14 16 06. Police Ch 14.

TELEPHONE
Port of London Authority (0375) 852301; Hr Mr (Upper Section) (071) 481 0720; Hr Mr (Lower Section) (0474) 567684; Duty Officer (Woolwich) (081) 855 0315; Duty Officer (Gravesend) (0474) 560311; Richmond Lock & Hr Office (081) 940 0634; General Enquiries (071) 481 8484; London Port Health Authority (071) 606 3030 Ext 1603; River Police (071) 488 5291; Thames Navigation Service (0474) 560311; London Weather Centre (071) 246 8091; Tower Bridge Master (071) 407 0922; ✠ (071) 283 8633 Ext 570 (or night (071) 626 3524); Marinecall 0898 500 455; Ⓗ (071) 987 7011.

FACILITIES (Letters in brackets refer to chartlets)
TEDDINGTON (081)
Tough Shipyards (A) ☎ 977 4494, BY, CH, AC, ME, Gas, C (6 ton), Sh, El, FW; **Swan Island Harbour (B)** ☎ 892 2861, D, M, ME, El, Sh, FW, Gas, Slip.
RICHMOND (081)
J T Howlett (C) ☎ 892 3183, BY, CH, D, Gas, M, FW; **Richmond Slipways** ☎ 892 5062, BY, Gas, ME, El, Sh. **Petersham Boat Services** ☎ 940 0173 M, FW.
BRENTFORD (081)
Brentford Dock Marina (D) (80+10 visitors) ☎ 568 0287 (VHF Ch 14, 16), AC, Bar, CH, El, FW, ME, R, V; Access HW∓2½; **Thames Locks (No 101)** ☎ 560 8942, M, AB, Entrance to Grand Union Canal; **T Norris** ☎ 560 3453, CH, ME.
KEW (081)
Bason and Arnold (F) ☎ 994 2431, CH, D, P, Gas; **Cranfield** ☎ 788 9255, SM. **Red Eye Marine** ☎ 940 8364 M.
CHISWICK (081)
Chiswick Quay Marina (50) ☎ 994 8743 CH, D, Gas, M, ME, El, Sh; (Access HW∓2); **Alan See** ☎ 748 7738, BY, M, ME, El, Sh.
WANDSWORTH (081)
Hurlingham YC ☎ 788 5547, M; **Chas Newens Marina** ☎ 788 4587 CH, ME, FW, M, El.
CHELSEA (071)
Chelsea Harbour (G) see 10.3.24; **Chelsea Yacht & Boat Co (H)** ☎ 352 1427, M, Gas; **Cadogan Pier (I)** ☎ 352 4604, M, L.
KINGS REACH (071)
Threestokes Marine ☎ 247 4595, CH, Gas.
POOL OF LONDON (071)
St Katharines Yacht Haven (J) ☎ 488 2400 (see 10.3.24); **Crawleys (K)** ☎ 481 1774, (Fuel barge), P, D; **Kelvin Hughes** ☎ 709 9076, CH, ACA; **Pumpkin Marine (J)** ☎ 480 6630, CH, P, D.
LIMEHOUSE REACH (071)
South Dock Marina (372) ☎ 252 2244, AC, ME, Sh, El, FW, CH, V, C (20 ton), Bar, R; **Limehouse Lock** ☎ 895 9930, Access HW∓3½; AB, M. Entry to Regents Canal.
GREENWICH (081)
East Greenwich Garage ☎ 858 4881, ME, P, D; **Charlton Marine** ☎ 858 1446, CH, Gas; **W H Donovan** ☎ 858 1143, BY; **Caldergate (L)** P, D; **Greenwich YC** ☎ 858 7339.

NOTE: From 6th May 1990 Inner London 01 code will become 071, Outer London 01 code will become 081.

RIVER THAMES *continued*

ENGLAND, EAST COAST – LONDON BRIDGE

Lat 51°30' N   Long 0°05' W

TIME ZONE UT(GMT)
For Summer Time add ONE hour in non-shaded areas

TIMES AND HEIGHTS OF HIGH AND LOW WATERS

YEAR 1991

JANUARY

Day	Time	m	Time	m	Time	m	Time	m	Day	Time	m	Time	m	Time	m	Time	m
1 Tu	0141	6·8	0827	0·6	1404	7·1	2050	0·8	16 W	0157	6·7	0827	0·7	1422	6·7	2039	0·8
2 W	0229	6·9	0921	0·3	1454	7·3	2138	0·7	17 Th	0233	6·8	0910	0·6	1458	6·9	2121	0·7
3 Th	0315	7·1	1009	0·1	1542	7·5	2220	0·6	18 F	0308	7·0	0950	0·6	1534	7·0	2202	0·8
4 F	0400	7·2	1052	0·0	1628	7·5	2259	0·7	19 Sa	0342	7·0	1028	0·4	1609	7·0	2235	0·9
5 Sa	0444	7·2	1133	0·2	1713	7·3	2334	0·9	20 Su	0414	7·0	1101	0·7	1642	6·9	2305	1·1
6 Su	0526	7·0	1208	0·5	1758	7·0			21 M	0445	6·8	1126	0·8	1718	6·7	2326	1·2
7 M ☾	0610	6·7	1241	0·8	1843	6·6			22 Tu	0518	6·7	1146	0·9	1754	6·5	2351	1·3
8 Tu	0042	1·4	0655	6·4	1316	1·1	1933	6·2	23 W ☽	0554	6·5	1214	0·9	1838	6·2		
9 W	0123	1·6	0748	6·1	1405	1·3	2029	6·0	24 Th	0031	1·3	0639	6·3	1257	1·0	1933	6·0
10 Th	0222	1·8	0854	5·8	1517	1·4	2134	5·9	25 F	0126	1·4	0745	6·1	1359	1·2	2050	5·9
11 F	0348	1·8	1010	5·8	1627	1·4	2248	5·9	26 Sa	0243	1·5	0914	6·0	1538	1·4	2213	6·0
12 Sa	0459	1·5	1127	5·9	1726	1·2	2351	6·1	27 Su	0427	1·4	1041	6·1	1711	1·2	2330	6·3
13 Su	0600	1·3	1222	6·1	1818	1·1			28 M	0557	1·1	1201	6·4	1836	1·1		
14 M	0039	6·2	0652	1·1	1307	6·3	1906	1·0	29 Tu	0036	6·5	0721	0·7	1304	6·8	1947	0·9
15 Tu ●	0120	6·5	0741	0·9	1345	6·5	1952	0·9	30 W ○	0131	6·8	0822	0·4	1358	7·1	2040	0·7
									31 Th	0219	7·0	0914	0·1	1446	7·3	2127	0·6

FEBRUARY

Day	Time	m	Time	m	Time	m	Time	m	Day	Time	m	Time	m	Time	m	Time	m
1 F	0303	7·2	0959	-0·1	1529	7·5	2207	0·6	16 Sa	0246	7·1	0934	0·4	1511	7·2	2145	0·6
2 Sa	0342	7·3	1038	0·0	1610	7·5	2242	0·6	17 Su	0319	7·2	1012	0·4	1545	7·3	2220	0·7
3 Su	0421	7·3	1111	0·2	1649	7·3	2312	0·8	18 M	0352	7·2	1044	0·5	1619	7·2	2248	0·9
4 M	0459	7·1	1137	0·5	1726	7·0	2337	1·0	19 Tu	0423	7·1	1108	0·7	1652	6·9	2308	1·1
5 Tu	0536	6·9	1201	0·8	1804	6·7			20 W	0457	6·9	1123	0·9	1729	6·6	2329	1·1
6 W ☾	0003	1·2	0614	6·5	1228	1·0	1843	6·3	21 Th ☽	0533	6·7	1147	1·0	1810	6·3		
7 Th	0036	1·3	0702	6·1	1306	1·2	1933	6·0	22 F	0007	1·2	0619	6·4	1229	1·1	1902	6·0
8 F	0120	1·5	0802	5·8	1358	1·5	2033	5·7	23 Sa	0059	1·3	0727	6·0	1328	1·4	2019	5·8
9 Sa	0222	1·8	0914	5·5	1524	1·7	2142	5·5	24 Su	0215	1·5	0858	5·9	1511	1·6	2148	5·9
10 Su	0412	1·8	1048	5·5	1648	1·6	2311	5·6	25 M	0410	1·4	1031	6·1	1652	1·4	2313	6·2
11 M	0529	1·5	1200	5·8	1749	1·4			26 Tu	0551	1·0	1153	6·5	1825	1·2		
12 Tu	0012	6·0	0629	1·2	1246	6·1	1843	1·2	27 W	0022	6·6	0713	0·5	1255	6·9	1933	0·8
13 W	0057	6·3	0721	1·0	1324	6·5	1934	1·0	28 Th ○	0117	6·9	0811	0·1	1345	7·2	2025	0·6
14 Th ●	0135	6·6	0809	0·7	1401	6·8	2022	0·8									
15 F	0212	6·9	0853	0·5	1436	7·0	2105	0·6									

MARCH

Day	Time	m	Time	m	Time	m	Time	m	Day	Time	m	Time	m	Time	m	Time	m
1 F	0204	7·1	0857	-0·1	1430	7·4	2108	0·5	16 Sa ●	0142	6·9	0827	0·5	1406	7·1	2040	0·7
2 Sa	0243	7·3	0938	-0·1	1510	7·5	2146	0·5	17 Su	0218	7·2	0908	0·4	1443	7·3	2121	0·6
3 Su	0321	7·3	1013	0·1	1546	7·4	2217	0·6	18 M	0251	7·3	0946	0·3	1518	7·4	2157	0·6
4 M	0356	7·3	1041	0·4	1620	7·2	2242	0·8	19 Tu	0325	7·4	1020	0·5	1553	7·3	2228	0·8
5 Tu	0430	7·1	1102	0·7	1651	6·9	2304	0·9	20 W	0400	7·3	1047	0·7	1630	7·0	2254	0·9
6 W	0502	6·9	1122	0·8	1723	6·7	2327	1·0	21 Th	0440	7·1	1106	0·9	1708	6·6	2320	1·0
7 Th	0539	6·6	1149	0·9	1758	6·4			22 F	0523	6·7	1136	1·1	1751	6·3	2358	1·1
8 F	0000	1·0	0622	6·2	1225	1·1	1841	6·1	23 Sa ☽	0617	6·3	1219	1·3	1848	5·9		
9 Sa	0041	1·2	0717	5·8	1313	1·5	1935	5·7	24 Su	0052	1·3	0727	6·0	1320	1·6	2005	5·8
10 Su	0131	1·6	0827	5·4	1415	1·9	2046	5·4	25 M	0212	1·4	0851	6·0	1458	1·8	2128	5·9
11 M	0243	1·9	0955	5·3	1603	2·0	2214	5·4	26 Tu	0402	1·2	1020	6·2	1634	1·5	2254	6·2
12 Tu	0452	1·7	1122	5·6	1718	1·6	2337	5·7	27 W	0539	0·8	1137	6·7	1804	1·2		
13 W	0558	1·4	1214	6·0	1815	1·3			28 Th	0003	6·6	0655	0·3	1238	7·1	1912	0·8
14 Th	0025	6·2	0653	1·0	1253	6·5	1907	1·0	29 F	0057	7·0	0748	0·1	1327	7·3	2001	0·6
15 F	0106	6·6	0742	0·8	1331	6·8	1957	0·8	30 Sa ○	0141	7·1	0832	0·0	1408	7·4	2043	0·5
									31 Su	0220	7·2	0910	0·2	1444	7·3	2118	0·6

APRIL

Day	Time	m	Time	m	Time	m	Time	m	Day	Time	m	Time	m	Time	m	Time	m
1 M	0256	7·2	0941	0·4	1518	7·2	2148	0·7	16 Tu	0223	7·3	0919	0·5	1451	7·3	2135	0·6
2 Tu	0329	7·2	1006	0·5	1549	7·1	2212	0·8	17 W	0303	7·5	0956	0·5	1529	7·3	2212	0·6
3 W	0400	7·0	1026	0·8	1617	6·9	2233	0·8	18 Th	0345	7·4	1030	0·7	1612	7·0	2247	0·6
4 Th	0433	6·8	1048	0·8	1647	6·7	2259	0·8	19 F	0430	7·2	1101	0·9	1657	6·7	2323	0·8
5 F	0509	6·6	1118	0·9	1719	6·5	2332	0·9	20 Sa	0522	6·9	1137	1·2	1746	6·3		
6 Sa	0550	6·3	1156	1·1	1758	6·2			21 Su ☾	0007	1·0	0621	6·5	1222	1·4	1845	6·1
7 Su	0011	1·0	0639	5·9	1239	1·4	1846	5·8	22 M	0100	1·1	0727	6·3	1323	1·7	1952	6·0
8 M	0057	1·3	0741	5·6	1333	1·8	1948	5·5	23 Tu ☽	0218	1·2	0840	6·2	1446	1·7	2107	6·0
9 Tu	0158	1·6	0901	5·4	1450	2·0	2117	5·4	24 W	0346	1·0	0959	6·4	1609	1·5	2227	6·2
10 W	0332	1·7	1023	5·6	1627	1·8	2241	5·6	25 Th	0511	0·7	1113	6·7	1729	1·2	2337	6·6
11 Th	0505	1·4	1126	6·0	1732	1·5	2340	6·0	26 F	0624	0·4	1212	7·0	1839	1·0		
12 F	0608	1·1	1214	6·4	1829	1·2			27 Sa	0032	6·9	0717	0·3	1302	7·1	1930	0·7
13 Sa	0027	6·5	0704	0·8	1256	6·8	1923	0·9	28 Su ○	0117	7·0	0759	0·4	1342	7·1	2012	0·7
14 Su ●	0107	6·8	0754	0·6	1335	7·1	2011	0·8	29 M	0157	7·0	0834	0·5	1419	7·1	2047	0·7
15 M	0145	7·1	0830	0·5	1413	7·2	2054	0·6	30 Tu	0232	7·0	0905	0·7	1450	7·0	2118	0·7

Chart Datum: 3.20 metres below Ordnance Datum (Newlyn)

ENGLAND, EAST COAST – LONDON BRIDGE

Lat 51°30' N   Long 0°05' W

TIMES AND HEIGHTS OF HIGH AND LOW WATERS   YEAR 1991

TIME ZONE UT(GMT)
For Summer Time add ONE hour in non-shaded areas

MAY

Day	Time	m	Time	m	Time	m	Time	m
1 W	0304	6.9	0931	0.8	1519	6.9	2143	0.8
2 Th	0336	6.8	0955	0.8	1546	6.8	2209	0.8
3 F	0410	6.7	1023	0.9	1617	6.7	2237	0.8
4 Sa	0447	6.5	1055	1.0	1651	6.5	2311	0.8
5 Su	0527	6.3	1132	1.1	1729	6.3	2349	0.9
6 M	0611	6.1	1212	1.3	1812	6.0		
7 Tu ☾	0034	1.1	0703	5.9	1302	1.6	1903	5.8
8 W	0127	1.3	0806	5.7	1401	1.8	2012	5.6
9 Th	0234	1.4	0921	5.7	1518	1.8	2136	5.7
10 F	0356	1.3	1030	6.0	1634	1.6	2245	6.0
11 Sa	0508	1.1	1127	6.4	1739	1.3	2342	6.3
12 Su	0614	0.9	1218	6.7	1841	1.1		
13 M	0031	6.7	0716	0.8	1304	6.9	1938	0.9
14 Tu ●	0116	6.9	0809	0.7	1347	7.0	2029	0.7
15 W	0201	7.2	0856	0.6	1430	7.1	2117	0.5
16 Th	0246	7.3	0938	0.6	1514	7.1	2202	0.4
17 F	0335	7.4	1019	0.6	1600	7.0	2245	0.4
18 Sa	0427	7.3	1059	0.8	1649	6.9	2329	0.5
19 Su	0520	7.1	1140	1.0	1742	6.6		
20 M ☽	0015	0.6	0617	6.9	1225	1.3	1835	6.4
21 Tu	0106	0.8	0716	6.6	1317	1.5	1933	6.3
22 W	0208	0.9	0818	6.5	1422	1.6	2037	6.2
23 Th	0318	0.9	0928	6.4	1535	1.5	2152	6.2
24 F	0427	0.8	1040	6.5	1647	1.3	2304	6.4
25 Sa	0536	0.7	1142	6.7	1756	1.1		
26 Su	0003	6.6	0635	0.7	1232	6.8	1853	1.0
27 M	0052	6.6	0720	0.7	1316	6.8	1938	0.9
28 Tu ○	0133	6.7	0757	0.8	1352	6.8	2016	0.8
29 W	0211	6.7	0830	0.8	1425	6.8	2051	0.8
30 Th	0246	6.7	0901	0.9	1456	6.7	2124	0.8
31 F	0319	6.7	0934	0.9	1527	6.7	2155	0.8

JUNE

Day	Time	m	Time	m	Time	m	Time	m
1 Sa	0355	6.7	1006	0.9	1559	6.6	2227	0.8
2 Su	0431	6.6	1041	1.0	1634	6.5	2301	0.9
3 M	0509	6.5	1116	1.1	1711	6.4	2337	0.9
4 Tu	0549	6.4	1153	1.2	1749	6.3		
5 W ☽	0015	1.0	0632	6.2	1234	1.3	1832	6.1
6 Th	0059	1.0	0721	6.0	1321	1.5	1923	5.9
7 F	0152	1.1	0823	5.9	1422	1.6	2033	5.8
8 Sa	0258	1.2	0935	6.0	1536	1.6	2150	6.0
9 Su	0416	1.1	1042	6.2	1649	1.4	2258	6.2
10 M	0527	1.0	1143	6.5	1800	1.2	2358	6.5
11 Tu	0638	0.9	1238	6.7	1909	1.0		
12 W ●	0053	6.7	0742	0.6	1328	6.8	2011	0.7
13 Th	0147	7.0	0837	0.7	1416	6.9	2105	0.5
14 F	0239	7.2	0927	0.7	1504	7.0	2155	0.3
15 Sa	0329	7.4	1013	0.6	1552	7.1	2242	0.1
16 Su	0420	7.5	1055	0.7	1640	7.1	2329	0.1
17 M	0511	7.4	1136	0.8	1727	7.0		
18 Tu	0012	0.3	0601	7.1	1217	1.0	1815	6.8
19 W ☽	0055	0.5	0652	6.8	1257	1.2	1906	6.6
20 Th	0140	0.7	0747	6.5	1347	1.4	2002	6.4
21 F	0236	0.9	0847	6.3	1450	1.5	2108	6.2
22 Sa	0339	1.0	0956	6.2	1602	1.5	2223	6.1
23 Su	0444	1.0	1105	6.3	1711	1.3	2332	6.2
24 M	0543	1.0	1203	6.3	1812	1.2		
25 Tu	0028	6.3	0635	1.0	1249	6.4	1906	1.0
26 W	0113	6.4	0720	1.0	1330	6.5	1951	0.9
27 Th ○	0154	6.5	0802	0.9	1405	6.6	2033	0.8
28 F	0230	6.6	0842	0.9	1439	6.7	2112	0.8
29 Sa	0305	6.7	0921	0.9	1512	6.7	2149	0.8
30 Su	0341	6.7	0957	0.9	1548	6.7	2224	0.8

JULY

Day	Time	m	Time	m	Time	m	Time	m
1 M	0416	6.7	1033	1.0	1621	6.7	2257	0.8
2 Tu	0451	6.7	1106	1.0	1654	6.6	2327	0.8
3 W	0526	6.6	1136	1.1	1727	6.5	2357	0.9
4 Th	0603	6.4	1205	1.2	1803	6.4		
5 F ☽	0029	0.9	0643	6.2	1243	1.3	1845	6.2
6 Sa	0110	1.0	0735	6.0	1333	1.4	1942	6.0
7 Su	0206	1.1	0846	5.9	1442	1.5	2101	6.0
8 M	0325	1.2	1000	6.0	1609	1.4	2221	6.1
9 Tu	0452	1.1	1112	6.2	1730	1.2	2334	
10 W	0610	1.0	1217	6.5	1850	0.9		
11 Th ●	0042	6.6	0724	0.9	1314	6.6	2001	0.7
12 F	0140	6.9	0826	0.6	1406	6.8	2058	0.4
13 Sa	0232	7.2	0917	0.7	1454	7.0	2149	0.1
14 Su	0321	7.4	1003	0.5	1539	7.2	2235	-0.1
15 M	0407	7.5	1045	0.5	1624	7.3	2318	-0.1
16 Tu	0454	7.4	1123	0.7	1706	7.2	2354	0.2
17 W	0537	7.2	1156	0.9	1749	7.0		
18 Th ☽	0027	0.5	0621	6.8	1228	1.1	1834	6.7
19 F	0059	0.8	0707	6.5	1303	1.3	1923	6.4
20 Sa	0140	1.0	0801	6.2	1351	1.5	2022	6.1
21 Su	0237	1.3	0901	6.0	1505	1.6	2134	5.9
22 M	0353	1.4	1014	5.8	1628	1.6	2259	5.8
23 Tu	0501	1.3	1130	5.9	1740	1.3		
24 W	0005	6.0	0600	1.2	1225	6.1	1841	1.1
25 Th	0055	6.2	0652	1.1	1309	6.3	1933	1.0
26 F ○	0135	6.4	0741	1.0	1347	6.5	2018	0.8
27 Sa	0212	6.6	0826	0.9	1422	6.7	2058	0.7
28 Su	0246	6.8	0907	0.8	1456	6.9	2136	0.6
29 M	0321	6.9	0946	0.8	1529	6.9	2213	0.6
30 Tu	0355	6.9	1021	0.8	1602	6.9	2245	0.7
31 W	0427	6.9	1051	0.9	1631	6.8	2313	0.8

AUGUST

Day	Time	m	Time	m	Time	m	Time	m
1 Th	0459	6.7	1115	1.1	1702	6.7	2334	0.9
2 F	0533	6.5	1137	1.2	1734	6.6	2357	0.9
3 Sa	0611	6.3	1210	1.2	1815	6.4		
4 Su	0032	1.0	0657	6.0	1255	1.3	1907	6.1
5 M	0123	1.1	0802	5.8	1357	1.4	2027	5.9
6 Tu	0240	1.3	0927	5.8	1535	1.5	2157	6.0
7 W	0427	1.3	1048	6.1	1711	1.2	2323	6.3
8 Th	0550	1.1	1203	6.4	1842	0.8		
9 F	0035	6.7	0712	0.9	1303	6.7	1954	0.4
10 Sa ●	0131	7.1	0815	0.7	1354	7.0	2049	0.1
11 Su	0220	7.3	0904	0.5	1439	7.2	2138	-0.1
12 M	0305	7.5	0949	0.4	1521	7.4	2220	-0.2
13 Tu	0348	7.5	1027	0.5	1602	7.4	2257	0.0
14 W	0428	7.4	1059	0.6	1641	7.3	2326	0.3
15 Th	0508	7.1	1126	0.9	1719	7.0	2350	0.7
16 F	0546	6.7	1151	1.0	1758	6.7		
17 Sa ☽	0015	0.9	0625	6.4	1221	1.1	1842	6.3
18 Su ☾	0049	1.1	0710	6.1	1302	1.3	1940	6.0
19 M	0135	1.4	0808	5.8	1357	1.6	2049	5.7
20 Tu	0250	1.7	0917	5.6	1539	1.8	2221	5.7
21 W	0426	1.6	1051	5.6	1712	1.5	2342	5.9
22 Th	0532	1.4	1200	5.9	1817	1.2		
23 F	0032	6.2	0628	1.1	1245	6.3	1909	0.9
24 Sa	0112	6.5	0719	0.9	1323	6.6	1955	0.8
25 Su ○	0147	6.7	0804	0.8	1357	6.8	2036	0.6
26 M	0220	6.9	0846	0.7	1430	7.0	2115	0.5
27 Tu	0253	7.0	0925	0.7	1503	7.1	2150	0.5
28 W	0327	7.1	1000	0.7	1534	7.1	2224	0.6
29 Th	0359	7.1	1030	0.8	1604	7.1	2251	0.7
30 F	0431	6.9	1052	1.0	1637	6.9	2308	0.9
31 Sa	0505	6.6	1112	1.1	1713	6.7	2329	1.0

Chart Datum: 3.20 metres below Ordnance Datum (Newlyn)

ENGLAND, EAST COAST – LONDON BRIDGE

Lat 51°30′ N   Long 0°05′ W

TIMES AND HEIGHTS OF HIGH AND LOW WATERS

YEAR **1991**

TIME ZONE UT(GMT)
For Summer Time add ONE hour in non-shaded areas

SEPTEMBER

Day	Time	m	Time	m	Time	m	Time	m
1 Su (	0543	6·3	1144	1·1	1754	6·4		
16 M	0010	1·1	0624	6·0	1224	1·2	1900	5·9
2 M	0005	1·1	0629	6·0	1231	1·2	1852	6·1
17 Tu	0055	1·4	0717	5·7	1313	1·5	2008	5·5
3 Tu	0057	1·3	0734	5·7	1333	1·4	2015	5·9
18 W	0154	1·8	0827	5·4	1422	1·8	2134	5·5
4 W	0216	1·6	0904	5·7	1519	1·5	2148	6·0
19 Th	0341	1·9	0959	5·4	1638	1·7	2305	5·7
5 Th	0410	1·5	1031	6·0	1701	1·1	2315	6·4
20 F	0501	1·5	1122	5·8	1744	1·3	2358	6·1
6 F	0536	1·1	1149	6·5	1834	0·6		
21 Sa	0558	1·2	1212	6·2	1836	1·0		
7 Sa	0022	6·9	0657	0·8	1248	6·9	1940	0·2
22 Su	0039	6·5	0649	1·0	1250	6·6	1923	0·8
8 Su ●	0117	7·3	0757	0·6	1337	7·2	2032	−0·1
23 M ○	0116	6·7	0735	0·8	1326	6·9	2005	0·6
9 M	0204	7·4	0844	0·4	1419	7·3	2117	−0·1
24 Tu	0149	7·0	0818	0·7	1359	7·1	2046	0·5
10 Tu	0246	7·5	0927	0·4	1458	7·4	2155	0·0
25 W	0223	7·1	0858	0·6	1432	7·2	2122	0·5
11 W	0325	7·4	1002	0·5	1536	7·4	2226	0·3
26 Th	0257	7·2	0935	0·6	1505	7·3	2157	0·5
12 Th	0402	7·2	1030	0·7	1613	7·3	2251	0·6
27 F	0331	7·2	1007	0·7	1539	7·3	2226	0·7
13 F	0435	7·0	1054	0·8	1648	7·0	2312	0·8
28 Sa	0406	7·0	1034	0·8	1617	7·1	2248	0·8
14 Sa	0508	6·7	1116	1·0	1725	6·7	2336	1·0
29 Su	0442	6·7	1059	1·0	1659	6·8	2315	1·0
15 Su ☽	0543	6·4	1146	1·0	1807	6·3		
30 M	0525	6·3	1134	1·1	1749	6·4	2354	1·3

OCTOBER

Day	Time	m	Time	m	Time	m	Time	m
1 Tu (	0615	5·9	1222	1·3	1852	6·1		
16 W	0022	1·4	0631	5·8	1241	1·4	1927	5·6
2 W	0049	1·6	0724	5·7	1331	1·4	2012	5·9
17 Th	0116	1·7	0737	5·5	1340	1·7	2043	5·5
3 Th	0212	1·7	0849	5·8	1518	1·3	2138	6·2
18 F	0227	2·0	0903	5·4	1512	1·8	2203	5·6
4 F	0355	1·5	1014	6·1	1652	0·9	2259	6·6
19 Sa	0410	1·8	1024	5·6	1654	1·4	2309	6·0
5 Sa	0516	1·1	1129	6·6	1817	0·4		
20 Su	0515	1·4	1125	6·0	1750	1·1	2357	6·4
6 Su	0005	7·0	0635	0·8	1227	7·0	1919	0·1
21 M	0607	1·1	1210	6·4	1841	0·8		
7 M ●	0057	7·3	0733	0·5	1314	7·2	2008	0·0
22 Tu	0038	6·7	0657	0·9	1249	6·8	1928	0·6
8 Tu	0142	7·4	0819	0·5	1357	7·3	2049	0·1
23 W ○	0116	6·9	0744	0·7	1326	7·0	2013	0·5
9 W	0223	7·3	0858	0·5	1436	7·3	2124	0·3
24 Th	0152	7·1	0829	0·6	1404	7·2	2054	0·5
10 Th	0258	7·3	0932	0·5	1511	7·3	2152	0·5
25 F	0229	7·2	0910	0·6	1442	7·4	2132	0·5
11 F	0332	7·1	0959	0·7	1546	7·2	2214	0·7
26 Sa	0307	7·2	0949	0·6	1521	7·4	2207	0·7
12 Sa	0403	6·9	1026	0·8	1620	6·9	2237	0·9
27 Su	0346	7·1	1026	0·6	1606	7·3	2240	0·8
13 Su	0434	6·6	1048	0·9	1657	6·6	2305	1·0
28 M	0430	6·8	1101	0·8	1654	7·0	2313	1·1
14 M	0506	6·4	1118	1·0	1737	6·3	2340	1·2
29 Tu	0518	6·4	1142	1·0	1750	6·6	2357	1·4
15 Tu ☽	0543	6·1	1154	1·1	1825	5·9		
30 W (	0612	6·1	1232	1·2	1853	6·3		
31 Th	0052	1·6	0717	5·9	1341	1·3	2004	6·2

NOVEMBER

Day	Time	m	Time	m	Time	m	Time	m
1 F	0208	1·7	0830	6·0	1510	1·1	2119	6·3
16 Sa	0140	1·8	0755	5·5	1411	1·5	2100	5·6
2 Sa	0332	1·5	0949	6·2	1628	0·8	2235	6·6
17 Su	0250	1·8	0915	5·6	1529	1·5	2206	5·9
3 Su	0447	1·2	1102	6·6	1746	0·5	2340	7·0
18 M	0409	1·6	1024	5·9	1647	1·2	2305	6·2
4 M	0603	0·9	1203	6·9	1848	0·3		
19 Tu	0515	1·3	1120	6·2	1749	0·9	2356	6·5
5 Tu	0034	7·1	0703	0·7	1252	7·1	1937	0·3
20 W	0614	1·0	1210	6·6	1846	0·7		
6 W ●	0120	7·2	0751	0·6	1335	7·1	2016	0·4
21 Th ○	0042	6·8	0710	0·8	1255	6·9	1940	0·6
7 Th	0159	7·1	0829	0·6	1413	7·1	2050	0·6
22 F	0126	7·0	0802	0·7	1340	7·1	2029	0·6
8 F	0234	7·0	0903	0·6	1450	7·1	2118	0·7
23 Sa	0208	7·1	0851	0·5	1425	7·3	2114	0·5
9 Sa	0305	7·0	0932	0·7	1524	7·0	2143	0·8
24 Su	0251	7·1	0938	0·4	1511	7·4	2156	0·6
10 Su	0336	6·8	0959	0·8	1559	6·6	2212	1·0
25 M	0336	7·1	1023	0·4	1600	7·4	2238	0·7
11 M	0406	6·6	1027	0·9	1635	6·6	2242	1·0
26 Tu	0423	7·0	1108	0·5	1652	7·2	2319	1·0
12 Tu	0440	6·4	1058	1·0	1715	6·4	2318	1·2
27 W	0512	6·8	1153	0·6	1746	7·0		
13 W	0516	6·2	1134	1·1	1758	6·1	2358	1·3
28 Th	0001	1·2	0604	6·5	1242	0·8	1843	6·7
14 Th ☽	0558	6·0	1218	1·2	1849	5·9		
29 F	0050	1·4	0702	6·4	1338	0·9	1945	6·5
15 F	0045	1·6	0649	5·7	1309	1·4	1949	5·7
30 Sa	0149	1·5	0805	6·3	1444	0·9	2051	6·4

DECEMBER

Day	Time	m	Time	m	Time	m	Time	m
1 Su	0300	1·5	0915	6·3	1552	0·8	2203	6·5
16 M	0154	1·7	0801	5·7	1426	1·3	2104	5·8
2 M	0410	1·3	1028	6·4	1701	0·7	2311	6·7
17 Tu	0301	1·7	0919	5·8	1542	1·3	2213	6·0
3 Tu	0522	1·1	1134	6·6	1807	0·7		
18 W	0420	1·5	1030	6·0	1659	1·1	2315	6·3
4 W	0008	6·8	0629	0·9	1229	6·7	1900	0·7
19 Th	0532	1·2	1133	6·4	1808	0·9		
5 Th	0056	6·8	0721	0·8	1316	6·8	1942	0·8
20 F	0012	6·6	0639	0·9	1232	6·7	1912	0·7
6 F ●	0137	6·8	0804	0·8	1355	6·8	2018	0·8
21 Sa ○	0106	6·8	0742	0·7	1326	7·0	2011	0·6
7 Sa	0213	6·8	0842	0·7	1433	6·9	2050	0·8
22 Su	0154	7·0	0840	0·5	1416	7·3	2103	0·6
8 Su	0246	6·8	0915	0·7	1508	6·9	2122	0·8
23 M	0242	7·1	0932	0·3	1505	7·5	2150	0·6
9 M	0317	6·8	0946	0·8	1545	6·8	2156	0·9
24 Tu	0328	7·2	1021	0·1	1555	7·6	2235	0·6
10 Tu	0349	6·7	1017	0·9	1620	6·7	2228	1·0
25 W	0414	7·1	1108	0·1	1644	7·5	2318	0·8
11 W	0423	6·6	1049	0·9	1657	6·6	2304	1·1
26 Th	0501	7·1	1151	0·2	1733	7·3	2356	1·0
12 Th	0458	6·4	1123	1·0	1734	6·4	2339	1·2
27 F	0549	6·9	1232	0·5	1824	6·9		
13 F	0534	6·3	1200	1·1	1815	6·2		
28 Sa (	0035	1·2	0636	6·7	1314	0·7	1917	6·6
14 Sa	0017	1·4	0614	6·1	1241	1·1	1900	6·0
29 Su	0119	1·4	0731	6·5	1404	0·9	2015	6·4
15 Su	0100	1·5	0700	5·9	1328	1·3	1955	5·8
30 M	0215	1·5	0834	6·3	1505	1·0	2121	6·3
31 Tu	0327	1·5	0948	6·1	1613	1·1	2233	6·2

Chart Datum: 3.20 metres below Ordnance Datum (Newlyn)

SOUTHEND-ON-SEA/ LEIGH-ON-SEA 10-3-22
Essex

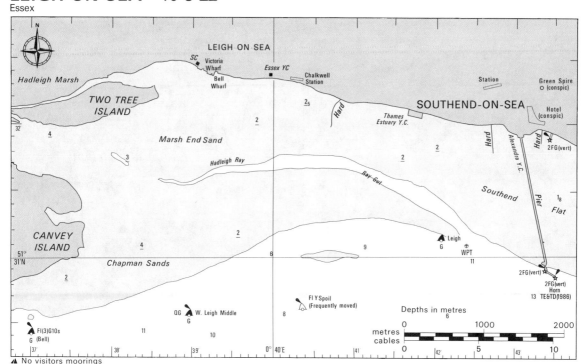

▲ No visitors moorings

CHARTS
Admiralty 1185; Stanford 5; Imray C2, Y6; OS 178
TIDES
+0125 Dover; ML 3.0; Duration 0610; Zone 0 (GMT).

Standard Port SHEERNESS (←—)

Times				Height (metres)			
HW		LW		MHWS	MHWN	MLWN	MLWS
0200	0800	0200	0700	5.7	4.8	1.5	0.6
1400	2000	1400	1900				

Differences SOUTHEND-ON-SEA

−0005	−0005	−0005	−0005	0.0	0.0	−0.1	−0.1

SHELTER
The whole area dries soon after half ebb, except Ray Gut. Some moorings are available at Leigh-on-Sea. Yachts can take the ground alongside Bell Wharf or Victoria Wharf.
NAVIGATION
Waypoint Leigh (stbd-hand) buoy, 51°31′.10N 00°42′.43E, at entrance to Ray Gut. Approaching from Shoeburyness, keep outside the two buoys Mid Shoebury (Con G) and W Shoebury (Con G Fl G 2.5s). Beware some 3000 small boat moorings a mile either side of Southend pier. Speed limit in Canvey Island/Hadleigh Ray areas is 8kn.
NOTE: Southend-on-Sea and Leigh-on-Sea are both part of the lower Port of London Authority Area. Southend BC launches 'Alec White II' and 'Sidney Bates II' patrol area (VHF Ch 16), April-October.
LIGHTS AND MARKS
Pier lights as shown in chartlet.
RADIO TELEPHONE
Police launches, Southend BC launches, Thames Navigation Service all VHF Ch 12.
TELEPHONE (0702)
Hr Mr 611889; Hr Mr Leigh-on-Sea 710561; CG 294998; MRSC Frinton-on-Sea 675518; Essex Police Marine Section Rayleigh 775533; ▦ (0702) 547141 Ext 26; Marinecall 0898 500 455; Police 341212; Dr 49451; Ⓗ 348911.

FACILITIES
SOUTHEND-ON-SEA EC Wednesday. **Alexandra YC** ☎ 340363, Bar, FW; **Thames Estuary YC** ☎ 345967; **Halfway YC** ☎ 582025; **Thorpe Bay YC** ☎ 587563, Bar, L, Slip, R, FW; **Southend Pier** L, FW, Bar; **Cruisermart** ☎ 400055, CH; **IYE (England)** ☎ 511215, Ⓔ; Town V, R, Bar, ✉; Ⓑ; ⇌; ✈.
LEIGH-ON-SEA EC Wednesday. **Essex YC** ☎ 78404, FW, Bar; **Leigh on Sea SC** ☎ 76788, FW, Bar; **Bell Wharf**, AB; **Victoria Wharf** AB, SM, Slip; **Mikes BY** ☎ 713151, Slip, D (cans), L, FW, ME, El, Sh, C, CH; **Sea King** ☎ 73612, Slip, L, D, ME, El, Sh, C, CH; **Johnson and Jago** ☎ 76639, ME, El, Sh, D (cans); **W Sails** ☎ 714550, SM; **Two Tree Island** ☎ 711010, Slip, FW (see Hr Mr).
CANVEY ISLAND. **Halcon Marine** (250) ☎ Canvey Island 685001, Slip, M, D, FW, ME, El, Sh, C, Gas, Access HW∓2. **Island YC** ☎ Canvey Island 683729.
BENFLEET **Benfleet YC** ☎ South Benfleet 792278, Slip, FW, Bar; **Dauntless** ☎ South Benfleet 793782, Slip, D, M, FW, ME, El, Sh, C, Access HW∓2½. **A.J. Long** ☎ South Benfleet 758874 M.

HAVENGORE 10-3-23
Essex

CHARTS
Admiralty 3750, 1185; Stanford 4, 5; Imray C1, Y17; OS 178

TIDES
+0110 Dover; ML 2.7; Duration 0615; Zone 0 (GMT).

Standard Port SHEERNESS (←)

Times				Height (metres)			
HW		LW		MHWS	MHWN	MLWN	MLWS
0200	0700	0100	0700	5.7	4.8	1.5	0.6
1400	1900	1300	1900				

Differences SHIVERING SANDS TOWER
−0025	−0019	−0008	−0026	−0.6	−0.6	−0.1	−0.1

SHELTER
Good shelter and a short cut at spring tides between the Thames and the Crouch for craft drawing less than 1.5m. Recommended to start passage about HW−1 using Yokesfleet, Middleway and Narrow Cuts.

NAVIGATION
Waypoint 51°30'.78N 00°54'.07E, 146°/326° from/to Havengore Creek entrance, 3.0M. Approach crosses Shoeburyness gunnery range which is in use most weekdays. The rules are laid down in *Statutory Rules & Orders No 714 of 1936* obtainable from HMSO. Key paragraph is 'Any vessel wishing to enter Havengore Creek during such time or times as the whole of the target area is not closed in accordance with Bye Law No 3 must enter the target area not later than half an hour

before high water and proceed by the shortest possible course to the Creek'. Red flags are hoisted at many points 1 hour before firing starts. Before setting off to Havengore, ring the Range Operations Officer, ☎ Southend-on-Sea 292271 Ext 3211; permission must be obtained preferably 24 hours in advance. Range is clear on bank holidays and at weekends. No passage allowed in dark hours. Lifting bridge across the creek will normally be opened on request. ☎ Southend-on-Sea 292271 Ext 3436 (Bridge manned HW∓2 sunrise to sunset). There is no charge. When tide gauge at Southend pier shows 5m there is 1.5 over the Broomway. Speed limit in creeks 8 kn.

LIGHTS AND MARKS
There are no lights.

RADIO TELEPHONE
Gravesend Radio VHF Ch 12 gives half hourly navigational information. Range Operations Officer listens on Ch 16 during working hours. Call sign 'Shoe Base'.

TELEPHONE (0702)
CG 4998; ⌗ (071) 626 1515 Ext 5861; MRSC Frinton-on-Sea 675518; Marinecall 0898 500 455; Police 431212; Dr Southend-on-Sea 218678.

FACILITIES
EC Great Wakering Wednesday; **Sutton's BY** ☎ Southend-on-Sea 219422, Slip, P, D, FW, ME, El, Sh, C, CH, AB; **Wakering YC** (0702) 468226, M, L, Bar; **Great Wakering** V, R, Bar. ✉ (Great Wakering & Barling); Ⓑ (Shoeburyness, Thorpe Bay); ⇌ (Shoeburyness); ✈ (Southend).

MINOR HARBOURS AND ANCHORAGES 10.3.24

EASTBOURNE, E Sussex, 50°46′N, 0°17′E, Zone 0 (GMT), Admty chart 536. HW −0005 on Dover, −0007 on Shoreham; HW height +0.9m on Shoreham; ML 3.8m; Duration 0540. See 10.3.12. Anchorage in Eastbourne Bay sheltered from W winds through N to NE and good holding ground. Beware Boulder Bank, rocks dry 0.2m, extend ¼M seaward by Wish Tower. There is a beacon on shore 1 ca E of Tower. Landing steps on pier (NE side). Pierhead Lts 2 FR (vert) 8m 2M. R Lt occas is shown W of lifeboat station as a guide to local fishermen. There are all shore facilities but few marine facilities. A marina is under construction.

HASTINGS, E Sussex, 50°51′N, 0°35′E, Zone 0 (GMT), Admty chart 536. HW −0005 on Dover; HW height +0.7m on Dover; ML 3.8m; Duration 0530. See 10.3.13. Anchorage off Hastings is only recommended in fair weather; beware dangerous wreck 3 ca SW of pier head. Lts: Pierhead 2 FR (vert) 8m 5M from white hut; W breakwater head Fl R 2.5s 5m 4M; No 2 Groyne, E breakwater Fl G 3m 3M; Ldg Lts 356° front FR 14m 4M on W metal column, rear 357m from front, FR 55m 4M on 5-sided W Tr on West Hill. The stone breakwater is in a state of dis-repair and is only for the protection of fishing vessels. Facilities: EC Wed; ⌗ (0304) 202441; all shore facilities at Hastings and St Leonards. Few marine facilities — **Hastings and St Leonards YC** ☎ Hastings 420656. Landing places on pier.

SANDWICH, Kent, 51°18′N, 1°21′E, Zone 0 (GMT), Admty chart 1828. HW +0015 on Dover; HW height −1.0m on Dover; ML 1.4m; Duration 0520. Sandwich is on the S side of the R Stour, Richborough on the N side. Sandwich being 3M above Richborough Wharf. The river is winding but vessels with draught up to 2m can reach Sandwich on spring tides. There are six channel buoys and one fairway buoy marking the entrance, all fitted with rotating reflective beacons. (searchlight needed). There are moorings for visitors at Sandwich Quay (ring Quaymaster ☎ 613283). Facilities: EC Wed, Slip; ⌗ (0304) 202441; **Marina** (120 + some visitors) ☎ (0304) 613783 (max 18m length, 2.1m draught), BH (15 ton), Sh, Slip, FW; Access HW∓2; **A. J. C. White** ☎ (0304) 617800, SM; **Richborough Port** has D by tanker. **Sandwich Sailing and Motorboat Club** ☎ (0304) 611116 and **Sandwich Bay Sailing and Water Ski Clubs** offer some facilities. Both ports are administered by The Sandwich Port and Haven Commissioners.

MARGATE, Kent, 51°23′N, 1°23′E, Zone 0 (GMT), Admty charts 1827, 1607, 1828. HW +0050 on Dover; −0040 on Sheerness; HW height −0.9m on Sheerness; ML 2.6m; Duration 0610. See 10.3.17. There is a small harbour open to NW winds inside Stone Pier — Pierhead Lt FR 18m 4M. Beware remains of old pier, known as Margate Iron Jetty, extending 2½ ca N from root of Stone Pier, Fl(3)R 10s. The harbour dries 2m; alternative anchorages W of Margate or N of pier. Facilities: EC Thurs; Bar, LB, D and P in cans from garage, R, V, all stores. ⌗ (0304) 202441; **Margate YC** ☎ Thanet (0304) 292602, R, Bar. A marina is proposed.

GRAVESEND, Kent, 51°26′N, 0°22′E, Zone 0 (GMT), Admty charts 1186, 2151. HW +0150 on Dover, +0020 on Sheerness; HW height +0.7m on Sheerness; ML 3.3m; Duration 0610. See 10.3.21. Anchorage E of the piers just below entrance to Gravesend Canal Basin. There are two visitors buoys (orange) at the Club. Lock gates open HW −1½ to HW +½ on request to Lockkeeper, Tel. 352392. East end of Gravesend Reach marked by Ovens Buoy Fl 1s Bell. Royal Terrace Pierhead FR. Gravesend Radio (Thames Navigation Service) VHF Ch 12 14 16 18 20 (H24). Broadcasts on Ch 12 every H+00, H+30. Facilities: EC Wed; Bar, C (at canal entrance — ask at Club), CH, FW (standpipe near lock), P (from garage), R, V; ⌗ 626 1515 Ext 5861; **J&R Starbuck** ☎ (0474) 350671 ME, El, Sh; **Gravesend SC**, Bar, C, FW, P&D (cans). ⌗ 363555; **Tame Technology** ☎ 334414 Ⓔ. Note: Boats can be left unattended in canal basin but not at anchorages.

CHELSEA HARBOUR, Greater London, 51°28′N, 0°11′W Zone 0 (GMT), Admty chart 3319. HW times London Bridge + 20mins. See 10.3.21. Good shelter under all conditions. Basin entrance (5.9m width × 2.5m sill depth) with bascule bridge; Access HW−2 to HW+1½, H24. Waiting berths on Chelsea Harbour Pier (keep clear of reserved area for Thames Line fast river service). Radio telephone (call *Chelsea Harbour*) VHF Ch 80. Marina (60+10 visitors) ☎ 071 351 4433, AC, FW, Bar, CH, R, D, Gas, V, YC.

ST KATHARINE YACHT HAVEN, Greater London, 51°30′N, 0°05′W, Admty chart 337, 3319. HW +0245 on Dover. HW times and heights as London Bridge. See 10.3.21. Good shelter under all conditions. Lock (42.7m × 9.1m with 2 lifting bridges), access HW−2 to HW+1½, winter 0800-1800, (lock shut Tues and Wed, Nov to Feb), summer 0600-2030. Moor to St Katharine's Pier 183m downstream whilst waiting (no shore access). Radio telephone (call *St Katharines*) VHF Ch 80. Yacht Haven (100+50 visitors) ☎ (071) 488 2400, AC, Bar, YC, FW, Gas, R, V, ⌗; **Robbins Marine** ☎ (071) 987 5884, ME, El, Sh; **Millwall Marine** ☎ (071) 515 9351, ME, El, Sh; **Captain Pumpkin** ☎ (071) 480 6630, CH.

HOLEHAVEN, Essex, 51°30′N, 0°33′E, Zone 0 (GMT), Admty chart 1185/6. HW +0140 on Dover, +0010 on Sheerness; height as Leigh-on-Sea; (10.3.22) ML 3.0m; Duration 0610. Shelter is good. Moorings S side of pier — very crowded; see Piermaster for mooring. Beware swell from passing traffic; keep to E (Canvey) side on entrance; once over bar, depths increase to 5m; anchor on W side as E side has long stone groynes running out. Lts Coryton Refinery Jetty No 4 2 FG (vert). ½ M up creek a bridge crosses, 9m at MHWS and opening span of 30m. Facilities: EC Thurs; FW (from 'The Lobster Smack' yard), P and D from village (1M); all other facilities at Canvey Island.

AGENTS WANTED
Berwick-on-Tweed
Mallaig
Loch Sunart
Loch Aline
Fishguard
Kenmare River

Large number of French Ports

Rotterdam
Norderney
Dornumersiel
Langeoog
Wangerooge
Hooksiel
Bremerhaven

If you are interested in becoming our agent please write to the Editors and get your free copy annually. You do not have to be a resident in a port to be the agent but at least a fairly regular visitor.

VOLVO PENTA SERVICE

Sales and service centres in area 4

BEDFORDSHIRE **Harry Kitchener Marine Ltd** Barkers Lane, BEDFORD MK41 9RL Tel (0234) 51931. ESSEX **French Marine Motors Ltd** 61/63 Waterside, BRIGHTLINGSEA CO7 0AX Tel (020630) 2133. **Volspec Ltd** Woodrolfe Road, Tollesbury, MALDON CM9 8SE Tel (0621) 869756. NORFOLK **Marinepower Engineering** Grange Walk, WROXHAM NR12 8RX Tel (0603) 782434. NORTHAMPTONSHIRE **C V S Pentapower** St. Andrews Road, NORTHAMPTON NN1 2LF Tel (0604) 38537/38409/36173. SUFFOLK **A D Truman Ltd** Old Maltings Boatyard, Oulton Broad, LOWESTOFT NR32 3PH Tel (0502) 565950. **French Marine Motors Ltd** Suffolk Yacht Harbour, Levington, IPSWICH IP10 0LN Tel (0473) 88882.

VOLVO PENTA

Area 4 4

East England
River Crouch to King's Lynn

10-4-2
East England

320

53°N

2°E

Newarp Lt. F.

Lowestoft
Standard Port
ℹ️	10.4.17
📻P	VHF 14 16;14
LB	CG

Cross Sand

Winterton
CG

Bacton
📻S C	VHF 16 07
	03 63 64
	0733 1933
⚠️	CG

Cromer
📻C	CM --- --
	5 287.3 50
LB	CG ⚠️

Great Yarmouth
ℹ️	10.4.18
📻P	VHF 12 16;
	09 11 12
📻 Aero	ND -- -- --
	397 15
LB	M-0898
	500 455
	☼ ⚠️
Yarmouth	CG

Happisburgh ☆

Norfolk Broads*
See 10.4.22

Trimingham RG ◎

Sheringham

LB

Blakeney
| ℹ️ | 10.4.19 |

Norwich
| ☼ | Norwich |
| | 660 779 |

Coltishall

Variation
4°W (1991)
0
90
180
270

1°E

Burnham
Overy
Staithe*

Hunstanton CG ⚠️

Brancaster Staithe*

**Wells-next-
the-Sea**
ℹ️	10.4.20
📻P	VHF 16;06
	08 12
LB	⚠️ CG

Kings Lynn
ℹ️	10.4.21
📻P	VHF 16; 1114
	M-0898
	500 455/454

53°N

●Wisbech*

River
Welland*

10.4.3 AREA 4 TIDAL STREAMS

5 Hours before HW Dover (0530 before HW Harwich)

4 Hours before HW Dover (0430 before HW Harwich)

3 Hours before HW Dover (0330 before HW Harwich)

2 Hours before HW Dover (0230 before HW Harwich)

1 Hour before HW Dover (0130 before HW Harwich)

HW Dover (0030 before HW Harwich)

Southward 10.3.3   Thames Estuary 10.3.19   Northward 10.5.3   Eastward 10.19.3

1 Hour after HW Dover (0030 after HW Harwich)

2 Hours after HW Dover (0130 after HW Harwich)

3 Hours after HW Dover (0230 after HW Harwich)

4 Hours after HW Dover (0330 after HW Harwich)

5 Hours after HW Dover (0430 after HW Harwich)

6 Hours after HW Dover (0530 after HW Harwich)

10.4.4   LIGHTS, FOG SIGNALS AND WAYPOINTS

Abbreviations used below are given in 10.0.3. Principal lights are in **bold** print, places in CAPITALS, and light-vessels, light floats and Lanbys in *CAPITAL ITALICS*. Unless otherwise stated lights are white. m—elevation in metres; M—nominal range in n. miles. Fog signals are in *italics*. Useful waypoints are <u>underlined</u> use those on land with care. See 4.2.2.

THAMES ESTUARY—NORTHERN PART

OFFSHORE MARKS.
<u>Kentish Knock Lt Buoy</u> 51°38'·50N 01°40'·50E Q(3) 10s; E cardinal mark; *Whis*.
<u>S Knock Lt Buoy</u> 51°34'·73N 01°36'·10E Q(6)LFl 15s; S cardinal mark; *Bell*.
BLACK DEEP
<u>Long Sand Head Lt Buoy</u> 51°47'·87N 01°39'·51E VQ; N cardinal; *Bell*.
<u>Trinity Lt Buoy</u> 51°49'·02N 01°36'·50E Q(6)LFl 15s; S cardinal; *Whis*.
<u>Black Deep No 2 Lt Buoy</u> 51°45'·58N 01°32'·28E VQ(9) 10s; W cardinal.
<u>Sunk Head Tr Lt Buoy</u> 51°46'·59N 01°30'·60E Q; N cardinal.
<u>Black Deep No 1 Lt Buoy</u> 51°44'·00N 01°28'·20E FlG 5s; stbd-hand.
<u>Black Deep No 3 Lt Buoy</u> 51°41'·75N 01°25'·65E Fl(3)G 15s; stbd-hand mark; *Bell*.
<u>Black Deep No 4 Lt Buoy</u> 51°41'·60N 01°28'·60E Fl(2)R 5s; port-hand mark.
<u>Black Deep No 5 Lt Buoy</u> 51°39'·50N 01°23'·10E VQ(3) 5s; E cardinal mark.
<u>Black Deep No 6 Lt Buoy</u> 51°38'·40N 01°24'·40E Q(9) 15s; West cardinal mark.
<u>Black Deep No 7 Lt Buoy</u> 51°37'·05N 01°17'·80E QG; stbd-hand mark.
<u>Black Deep No 8 Lt Buoy</u> 51°35'·60N 01°18'·50E FlR 2·5s; port-hand mark.
<u>Black Deep No 9 Lt Buoy</u> 51°35'·10N 01°15'·20E Q(6)LFl 15s; S cardinal mark.
<u>Black Deep No 10 Lt Buoy</u> 51°34'·70N 01°15'·70E QR; port-hand mark.
<u>Black Deep No 11 Lt Buoy</u> 51°34'·30N 01°13'·50E Fl(3)G 10s; stbd-hand mark.
<u>Black Deep No 12 Lt Buoy</u> 51°33'·80N 01°13'·60E Fl(4)R 15s; port-hand mark.

KNOCK JOHN CHANNEL (selected buoys).
<u>Knock John Lt Buoy</u> 51°33'·46N 01°11'·08E Fl(2)R 5s; port-hand.
<u>Knock John No 5 Lt Buoy</u> 51°32'·75N 01°08'·68E Fl(3)G 10s; stbd-hand.
<u>Knob Lt Buoy</u> 51°30'·66N 01°04'·38E Iso 5s; safe water mark; *Bell*.
(For OAZE DEEP see 10.3.4).

EAST SWIN (KING'S) CHANNEL.
<u>W Sunk Lt Buoy</u> 51°44'·30N 01°25'·90E Q(9) 15s; W cardinal mark.
<u>Gunfleet Spit Lt Buoy</u> 51°45'·30N 01°21'·80E Q(6)LFl 15s; S cardinal mark; *Bell*.
<u>Gunfleet Old Lt Ho</u> 51°46'·08N 01°20'·52E (unlit).
<u>W Sunk Lt Buoy</u> 51°44'·30N 01°25'·90E Q(9) 15s; W cardinal mark.
BARROW DEEP (selected buoys).
<u>Barrow No 2 Lt Buoy</u> 51°41'·95N 01°23'·00E Fl(2)R 5s; port-hand mark.

<u>Barrow No 3 Lt Buoy</u> 51°42'·00N 01°19'·87E Q(3) 10s; E cardinal mark; *Racon*.
<u>Barrow No 4 Lt Buoy</u> 51°39'·75N 01°17'·80E VQ(9) 10s; West cardinal mark.
<u>Barrow No 6 Lt Buoy</u> 51°37'·78N 01°15'·18E Fl(4)R 15s; port-hand mark.
<u>Barrow No 9 Lt Buoy</u> 51°35'·50N 01°10'·40E VQ(3) 5s; E cardinal mark.
<u>Barrow No 11 Lt Buoy</u> 51°33'·73N 01°05'·85E Fl(3)G 10s; stbd-hand mark.
<u>SW Barrow Lt Buoy</u> 51°31'·80N 01°00'·53E Q(6)LFl 15s; S cardinal mark; *Bell*.

EAST SWIN.
<u>N Middle Buoy</u> 51°41'·00N 01°12'·00E (unlit); N cardinal mark.
<u>S Whitaker Lt Buoy</u> 51°40'·20N 01°09'·15E Fl(2)G 10s; stbd-hand mark.
<u>W Hook Middle Buoy</u> 51°39'·13N 01°08'·10E (unlit); port-hand mark.
<u>NE Maplin Lt Buoy</u> 51°37'·43N 01°04'·90E FlG 5s; stbd-hand mark; *Bell*. <u>Maplin Bank Lt Buoy</u> 51°35'·47N 01°04'·80E Fl(3)R 10s; port-hand mark.
<u>Maplin Edge Buoy</u> 51°35'·30N 01°03'·75E (unlit); stbd-hand mark. . <u>Maplin Lt Buoy</u> 51°34'·00N 01°02'·40E Q(3) 10s; E cardinal mark; *Bell*.
<u>W Swin Buoy</u> 51°33'·82N 01°03'·80E (unlit); port-hand mark.
<u>SW Swin Lt Buoy</u> 51°32'·74N 01°01'·18E Fl(2)R 5s; port-hand mark.
WHITAKER CHANNEL.
<u>Whitaker Lt Buoy</u> 51°41'·40N   01°10'·61E Q(3) 10s; E cardinal mark; *Bell*.
<u>Swin Spitway Lt Buoy</u> 51°41'·73N 01°07'·63E Iso 10s; safe water mark; *Bell*.
<u>Whitaker Bn</u> 51°39'·62N 01°06'·30E (unlit); isolated danger mark.
<u>S Buxey Lt Buoy</u> 51°39'·82N 01°02'·60E Fl(2) G 16s; stbd-hand mark.
<u>Sunken Buxey Lt Buoy</u> 51°39'·50N 01°00'·60E Q; N cardinal mark.
<u>Outer Crouch Lt Buoy</u> 51°38'·35N 00°58'·61E Fl G 5s; stbd-hand mark.
<u>Crouch Lt Buoy</u> 51°37'·60N 00°56'·49E Fl R 10s; port-hand mark.
<u>Inner Crouch Lt Buoy</u> 51°37'·19N 00°55'·22E L Fl 10s; safe water mark.
RAY SAND CHANNEL.
<u>Buxey Bn</u> 51°41'·10N 01°01'·38E (unlit); N cardinal mark.
GOLDMER GAT/WALLET.
<u>NE Gunfleet Lt Buoy</u> 51°49'·90N 01°27'·90E Q(3) 10s; E cardinal mark.
<u>Wallet No 4 Lt Buoy</u> 51°46'·50N 01°17'·33E Fl(4)R 10s; port-hand mark.
<u>Wallet Spitway Lt Buoy</u> 51°42'·67N 01°06'·97E LFl 10s; safe water mark; *Bell*.
<u>Knoll Lt Buoy</u> 51°43'·85N 01°05'·17E Q; N cardinal mark.
<u>Eagle Lt Buoy</u> 51°44'·10N 01°03'·92E Q; stbd-hand mark.
<u>NW Knoll Lt Buoy</u> 51°44'·19N 01°02'·50E Fl(2)R 5s; port-hand mark.
<u>Colne Bar Lt Buoy</u> 51°44'·58N 01°02'·65E Fl(2)G 5s; stbd-hand mark.
<u>Bench Head Buoy</u> 51°44'·54N 01°01'·05E; stbd- hand mark.
RIVER BLACKWATER.
<u>The Nass</u> 51°45'·75N 00°54'·88E VQ(3) 5s 6m 2M; E cardinal mark.

4

Bradwell Power Station, barrier, NE end and SW end each 2 FR (vert), 2m apart. Bradwell Creek 51°44'·6N 00°53'·3E QR.

BRIGHTLINGSEA.
Ldg Lts 041°. Front 51°48'·4N 01°01'·3E FR 7m 4M; Y square, W stripe on post; vis 020°-080°. Rear 50m from front FR 10m 4M; Y square, W stripe on post. FR Lts are shown on 7 masts between 1·5M and 3M NW when firing occurs.
Hardway, head 51°48'·2N 01°01'·5E 2 FR (vert) 2m.
RIVER COLNE.
Batemans Tower 51°48'·3N 01°00'·8E FY 12m.
Fingringhoe Wick, Pier head 2 FR (vert) 6/4m (occas).
No 23 51°50'·6N 00°59'·0E Fl G 5s 5m.
Wivenhoe Yacht Club 51°51'·3N 00°57'·6E FY.
Cooks Jetty 51°51'·2N 00°57'·8E 2 FG (vert).
Rowhedge Wharf FY 11m.

CLACTON-ON-SEA.
Berthing arm 51°47'·00N 01°09'·60E 2 FG (vert) 5m 4M; Reed(2) 120s (occas).
WALTON-ON-THE-NAZE.
Pier head 51°50'·60N 01°16'·90E 2 FG (vert) 5m 2M.

OFFSHORE MARKS
S Galloper Lt Buoy 51°43'·95N 01°56'·50E Q(6) LFl 15s; S cardinal mark; Whis; Racon.
OUTER GABBARD Lt V 51°59'·38N 02°04'·63E Fl(4) 20s 12m 23M; R hull with Lt Tr amidships; RC; Horn(4) 60s.
S Inner Gabbard Lt Buoy 51°51'·20N 01°52'·40E Q(6)LFl 15s; S cardinal mark.
N Inner Gabbard Lt Buoy 51°59'·10N 01°56'·10E Q; N cardinal mark.
HARWICH APPROACHES
MEDUSA CHANNEL.
Medusa Lt Buoy 51°51'·20N 01°20'·46E FlG 5s; stbd-hand mark. Naze Tr 51°51'·85N 01°17'·40E (unlit).
Stone Banks Buoy 51°53'·18N 01°19'·32E; port-hand mark, direction of buoyage N to S).
Pye End Buoy 51°55'·00N 01°18'·00E ; safe water mark.
CORK SAND /ROUGH SHOALS.
S Cork Buoy 51°51'·30N 01°24'·20E (unlit); S cardinal mark.
Roughs Tr SE Lt Buoy 51°53'·61N 01°29'·06E Q(3) 10s; E cardinal mark; Bell.
Roughs Tr NW Lt Buoy 51°53'·78N 01°28'·88E Q(9) 15s; W cardinal mark.
Rough Lt Buoy 51°55'·65N 01°31'·30E VQ; N cardinal mark.
Cork Lt Buoy 51° 55'·44N 01°27'·30E QR; port-hand mark.
Cork Sand Bn 51°55'·44N 01°25'·20E (unlit); port-hand mark.
Washington Lt Buoy 51°56'·54N 01°27°·30E QG; stbd-hand mark.
Felixtowe Ledge Lt Buoy 51°56'·30N 01°24'·56E Fl(3) G10s; stdb-hand mark.
SUNK Lt F 51°51'·00N 01°35'·00E Fl(2) 20s 12m 24M; R hull with Lt Tr amidships; RC; Racon; Horn(2) 60s.
SHIPWASH.
Shipwash Lt Buoy 51°52'·65N 01°34'·05E Q(6)LFl 15s; S cardinal mark.
Shiphead Lt Buoy 51°53'·75N 01°34'·05E FlR 5s; port-hand mark.
SW Shipwash Lt Buoy 51°54'·82N 01°34'·10E LFlR 10s; port-hand mark.
E Shipwash Lt Buoy 51°57'·05N 01°38'·00E VQ(3) 5s; E cardinal mark.
N Shipwash Lt Buoy 52°01'·70N 01°38'·38E Q; N cardinal mark; Bell.
SHIPWASH Lt F 52°02'·03N 01°42'05E Fl(3) 20s 12m 24M; R hull with Lt Tr amidships; Horn(3) 60s.

HARWICH CHANNEL.
HA Lt Buoy 51°56'·40N 01°31'·20E Iso 5s; safe water mark; Whis.
Harwich Channel Lt Buoy No. 1 51°56'·11N 01°27·30E FlY 2·5s; special mark; Racon.
Harwich Channel No.3 Lt Buoy 51°55'·96N 01°24'·56E Fl Y 5s; stdb-hand mark.
Harwich Channel No 5 Lt Buoy 51°55'·94N 01°22'·45E Fl Y 10s; stdb-hand mark.
Landguard Lt Buoy 51°55'·35N 01°18'·98E Q; N cardinal.
FELIXSTOWE.
Landguard Point Jetty Elbow 51°56'·2N 01°19'·2E 2 FG (vert) 8/6m;
Jetty Hd 51°56'·3N 01°19'·2E 2 FG (vert) 8/6m; on Dolphin.
Container berth, South end 2 FG (vert).
Crane quay, S end 2 FG (vert). Dock entrance, S pier head FG 3m. North pier head 51°56'·9N 01°19'·1E FR 3m 10M.

HARWICH.
Wharves, jetties and piers show 2 FR (vert).
Shotley Spit 51°57'·26N 01°17'·67E Q(6) L Fl 15s; S cardinal.
Shotley Marina Lock 51°57'·4N 01°16'·7E Dir Lt;on structure.
Shotley Marina Entrance, E side Fl(4)G 15s; G cone on pile.
Shotley Marina, W side VQ(3)W 5s 5s; E cardinal mark.
Erwarton Ness 51°57'·08N 01°13'·35E Q(6) LFl 15s; S cardinal Bn.
Holbrook 51°57'·19N 01°10'·46E VQ(6)LFl 10s; S cardinal Bn.
Shotley Ganges Pier, head 2 FG (vert) 4m 1M; G post.
Mistley, Baltic wharf 51°56'·7N 01°05'·3E 2 FR (vert).
Suffolk Yacht Harbour. Ldg Lts. Front Iso Y Rear Oc Y 4s.
Woolverstone Marina 52°00'·4N 01°11'·8E 2 FR (vert).
Orwell Bridge FY 39m 3M at centre; 2 FR (vert) on pier 9 and 2 FG (vert) on pier 10.
Felixstowe Town Pier, head 51°57'·4N 01°21'·0E 2 FG (vert) 7m.

WOODBRIDGE HAVEN.
Buoy 51°58'·36N 01°24'·17E (unlit); safe water mark.
Ldg Lts FlW or FlY moved as required (on request). Front W triangle on R post. Rear; R line on post.
Ferry landing, E side 2 FG (vert). W side 2 FR (vert).
Groyne, outer end QR; TE.
BAWDSEY BANK.
S Bawdsey Lt Buoy 51°57'·20N 01°30'·32E Q(6)LFl 15s; S cardinal mark; Whis.
Mid Bawdsey Lt Buoy 51°58'·85N 01°33'·70E Fl(3)G 10s; stbd-hand mark.
NE Bawdsey Lt Buoy 52°01'·70N 01°36'·20E FlG 10s; stbd-hand mark.

CUTLER/WHITING BANK.
Cutler Buoy 51°58'·50N 01°27'·60E (unlit); stbd-hand mark.
SW Whiting Buoy 52°01'·22N 01°30'·90E (unlit);S cardinal.
Whiting Hook Buoy 52°02'·95N 01°31'·95E (unlit); port-hand mark.
NE Whiting Buoy 52°03'·75N 01°33'·85E (unlit); E cardinal.
Orford Ness 52°05'·00N 01°34'·55E Fl 5s 28m 30M; W round Tr, R bands. F RG 14m R14M, G15M (same Tr); vis R shore-210°, R038°-047°, G047°-shore.

SIZEWELL. Power station, S pipeline 52°12'·5N 01°37'·7E 2 FR (vert) 12/10m. N pipeline 2 FR (vert) 12/10m.

SOUTHWOLD.
Southwold Lt Ho 52°19'·60N 01°41'·00E Fl(4) WR 20s 37m W22M, R22M, R20M; W round Tr; vis R(intens) 204°-220°, W220°-001°, R001°-032°.

N pier head 52°18'·77N 01°40'·63E FIG 1.5s 4m 4M, and 3 FIR 1·5s (vert); R shown when harb inaccessible.
S pier head QR 4m 2M.
E Barnard Lt Buoy 52°24'·60N 01°46'·20E Q(3) 10s; E cardinal mark.
S Newcome Lt Buoy 52°25'·70N 01°45'·20E FIG 2·5s; stbd-hand mark.
Pakefield Lt Buoy 52°27'·05N 01°45'·30E Fl(2)G 5s; stbd-hand mark.
East Newcome Lt Buoy 52°28'·48N 01°49'·32E Fl(2)R 5s; port-hand mark.
LOWESTOFT ROADS
Claremont Pier 52°27'·9N 01°45'·0E 2 FR (vert) 5/4m 4M; W column. 3 FR mark firing range 1·5M SSW.
LOWESTOFT
Lowestoft 52°29'·2N 01°45'·5E Lt Ho. Fl 15s 37m **28M**; W Tr; part obscd 347°-shore. FR 30m **18M** (same Tr); vis 184°-211°.
Outer harb S pier head Oc R 5s 12m 6M; *Horn (4) 60s.*
N pier head 52°28'·29N 01°45'·50E Oc G 5s 12m 8M.
Corton Lt Buoy 52°31'·10N 01°51'·50E Q(3) 10s; E cardinal.

GREAT YARMOUTH.
Gorleston S pier head Fl R 3s 11m 11M; vis 235°-340°; *Horn (3) 60s.*
Ldg Lts 264°. Front Oc 3s 6m 10M. Rear Oc 6s 7m 10M.
N pier head 52°34'·36N 01°44'·49E QG; vis 176°-078°.
Brush lighthouse FR 20m 6M; R round Tr.
Groyne, head 52°34'·3N 01°44'·4E 2 FG (vert) 4m.
52°34'·3N 01°44'·3E 2 FG (vert). 52°34'·3N 01°44'·2E 2 FG (vert). 5F mark pile structure close West.
Haven Bridge 52°36'·4N 01°43'·5E marked by pairs of 2 FR (vert) and 2 FG (vert) showing up and down stream. 1 FR marks centre of channel.
YARMOUTH ROADS
South Denes, outfall 52°35'·10N 01°44'·50E QR 5m 2M; B and Y triangle.
Wellington Pier head 52°35'·9N 01°44'·4E 2 FR (vert) 8m 3M.
Jetty head 2FR(vert) 7m 2M. Britannia Pier head 52°36'·5N 01°44'·6E 2 FR (vert) 11m 4M; W column.
North Scroby Lt Buoy 52°42'·20N 01°45'·80E VQ; N cardinal; *Bell; Whis.*
Cockle Lt Buoy 52°44'·00N 01°43'·70E VQ(3) 5s; E cardinal.
Cross Sand Lt Buoy 52 37.00N°1 59.25E LFI.10s 6m 5M; W HFP buoy, RWVS; Racon.
E Cross Sand Lt Buoy 52 40.00N° 1 53.80E Fl(4)R 15s; port-hand mark.   NE Cross Sand Lt Buoy 52 43.00N°1 53.80E VQ(3) 5s; E cardinal mark.
SMITH'S KNOLL Lt F 52°43'·50N 02°18'·00E Fl(3) 20s 12m **23M**; R hull with Lt Tr amidships; RC; Racon; *Horn (3) 60s.*
S Winterton Ridge Lt Buoy 52°47'·20N 02°03'·60E Q(6)LFI 15s; S cardinal mark.
N Winterton Ridge Lt Buoy 52°50'·10N 01°59'·87E Q; N cardinal mark.

NEWARP Lt F 52°48'·35N 01°55'·80E Fl 10s 12m **26M** (H24); R hull with Lt Tr amidships; *Horn 20s* (H24), Racon.
S Haisbro Lt Buoy 52°50'·80N 01°48.40E Q(6)LFI 15s; S cardinal mark; *Bell.*   Mid Haisbro Lt Buoy 52 54.20N°1 41.70E Fl(2)G 5s; stbd-hand mark.
N Haisbro Lt Buoy 53°00'·20N 01°32'·40E Q; N cardinal mark; *Bell*; Racon.
Happisburgh 52°49'·20N 01°32'·30E Fl(3) 30s 41m 14M; W Tr, 3 R bands. R Lts on radio mast 1·2M NW.
CROMER
Cromer 52°55'·5N 01°19'·1E Fl 5s 84m **23M**; W 8-sided Tr; RC; vis 102°-307°; Racon.
Lifeboat House 2 FR (vert) 8m 5M.

E Sheringham Lt Buoy 53°02'·20N 01°15'·00E Q(3) 10s; E cardinal mark.
W Sheringham Lt Buoy 53°02'·97N 01°07'·70E Q(9) 15s; W cardinal mark.
Blakeney Overfalls Lt Buoy 53°03'·00N 01°01'·50E Fl(2)R 5s; port-hand mark; *Bell.*

WELLS.
Channel, West side 52°59'·0N 00°50'·2E Fl 5s 2m 3M; metal tripod.   East side Fl R 3s; square on metal tripod.
E Docking Lt Buoy 53°09'·80N 00°50'·50E FIR 2·5s; port-hand mark.
N Docking Lt Buoy 53°14'·80N 00°41'·60E Q; N cardinal mark.
S Race Lt Buoy 53°08'·65N 00°55'·80E Q(6)LFI 15s; S cardinal mark; *Bell .*
N Race Lt Buoy 53°14'·85N 00°44'·20E FIG 5s; stbd-hand mark; *Bell.*
(For marks further N, see 10.5.4).
Burnham Flats Lt Buoy 53°07'·50N 00°35'·00E VQ(9) 10s; W cardinal mark; *Bell.*
North Well Lt Buoy 53°03'·00N 00°28'·00E LFI 10s; safe water mark; *Horn*; Racon.
Lynn Knock Lt Buoy 53°04'·40N 00°27'·31E QG; stbd-hand mark.
Woolpack Lt Buoy 53°02'·65N 00°31'·55E FIR 10s; port-hand mark.
ROARING MIDDLE Lt F 52°58'·50N 00°21'·00E Q 5m 8M; N cardinal mark; *Bell.* Replaced May-June by B&Y pillar and bell buoy, Q.
CORK HOLE.
Sunk Lt Buoy 52°56'·50N 00°23'·85E Q(9) 15s; W cardinal.
No 1 Lt Buoy 52°55'·70N 00°22'·10E VQ; N cardinal; *Bell .*
No 3 Lt Buoy 52°54'·43N 00°24'·50E Q(3) 10s; E cardinal.
No 3A Lt Buoy 52°53'·45N 00°24'·10E FIG 5s; stbd-hand mark. (Buoyage from Cork Hole to Lynn Cut subject to change).

KING'S LYNN.
Beacon B 52°49'·1N 00°21'·2E Fl Y 2s 3m 2M; cone point up on B post.
Beacon E 58°48'·2N 00°21'·5E Fl Y 6s 3m 2M; cone point up on B post.
West Bank 52°47'·4N 00°22'·1E Fl Y 2s 3m 4M; R pile structure.
Marsh Cut Ldg Lts 155°. Front 52°47'·0N 00°22'·6E QR 11m 3M. Rear 233m from front F 16m 4M.
Old Lynn Channel 52°51'·3N 00°15'·7E Fl G 10s 6m 1M; B cone point up on B column.
Trial Bank Beacon 52°50'·5N 00°14'·7E Fl(2) 5s 13m 3M.

WISBECH CHANNEL (Note: beacons are moved as required)
Dale 52°50'·8N 00°12'·8E Fl G 2s 3M.
Double Brush 52°50'·1N 00°13'·1E QG 3M; X on Bn.
Big Tom 52°49'·6N 00°13'·2E Fl(2) R 10s; R Bn.
Walker 52°49'·7N 00°13'·1E Fl G 5s.

RIVER NENE,
Marsh 52°49'·0N 00°13'·0E QR.
West End 52°49'·5N 00°13'·0E Fl G 5s 3M; B mast, Ra refl.
Scottish Sluice, West bank 52°48'·5N 00°12'·7E FG 9m; Mast. QG (vert) 6m.
Stakes on West side of River Nene to Wisbech carry QW Lts, and those on E side QR Lts.

10.4.5 PASSAGE INFORMATION

On the N side of Thames Estuary (chart 1975) the main chans run seaward in a NE direction (e.g. West Swin, Barrow Deep, Black Deep, Knock Deep) lined by banks which dry in places. The main chans are well buoyed. All the sandbanks in Thames Estuary are liable to change, and particular care is needed when crossing the estuary in a NW/SE direction. Bad visibility and much shipping can add to the hazards. Even with a moderate wind against tide, a short and steep sea is easily raised in these shallow waters. For further notes on Thames Estuary, see 10.3.5. For North Sea crossing see 10.19.5. There have been many recent buoyage changes in this area.

FOULNESS TO GREAT YARMOUTH (charts 1975, 2052)

Foulness Sand extends nearly 6M NE from Foulness Pt, the extremity being marked by Whitaker Bn. On N side of Whitaker Chan leading to R Crouch (10.4.8 and chart 3750) lies Buxey Sand, inshore of which is the Ray Sand Chan (dries), a convenient short cut between R Crouch and R Blackwater with sufficient rise of tide. For detailed directions to East Coast harbours (R Swale to Humber) see *East Coast Rivers* (Yachting Monthly). To seaward of Buxey Sand is Wallet Spitway (buoyed), and to NE of this is Gunfleet Sand, marked by buoys and drying in places along much of its 10M length. A conspic disused Lt Tr stands on SE side of Gunfleet Sand, about 6M SSE of Naze Tr, and here the SW- going (flood) streams begins about HW Sheerness +0600, and the NE-going stream at about HW Sheerness −0030, sp rates 2 kn.

Goldmer Gat and the Wallet give access to R Colne (10.4.10) and R Blackwater (10.4.9 and chart 3741). The chan is well marked and always accessible. The final approach 2M S of Colne Pt leads between Knoll (dries) on S side, and Eagle (depth 0.1m) on N side.

11M E of The Naze, the Sunk Lt F (Lt, fog sig, RC) guards the entrance to Harwich (10.4.12), an extensive and well sheltered harb accessible at all times (chart 2693). From the S, approach through Medusa Chan about 1M E of Naze Tr: at N end of this chan, 1M off Dovercourt, is Pye End buoy marking chan to Walton Backwaters (10.4.11). Making Harwich from the E beware Cork Sand (dries), S of which there is a minor chan. The main chan (well buoyed) passes N of Cork Sand and carries much commercial shipping. Approaching from NE beware Wadgate Ledge and the Platters about 1½M ENE of Landguard Pt. S of Landguard Pt the W-going (flood) stream begins at HW Harwich +0600, and the E-going stream at HW Harwich, sp rates about 1½ kn.

From 9M E of Felixstowe to 4M SSE of Orford Ness is the Shipwash shoal, marked by buoys and with a drying patch near its S end. Inshore of this is Bawdsey Bank, marked by buoys, with depths of 1.4m, and on which the sea breaks in E gales. Still further inshore, and slightly S, 2M off the entrance to R Deben (10.4.14) is a rky shoal called Cutler, with least depth of 1.8m, marked by buoy on E side.

Whiting Bank (buoyed) lies close SW of Orford Ness, and has a least depth of 0.9m. Hollesley Chan, about 1M wide, runs inshore W and N of this bank. In the SW part of Hollesley B is the entrance to Orford Haven (10.4.15).

There are overfalls S of Orford Ness on both the ebb and flood streams. 2M S of Orford Ness the SW-going stream begins at HW Harwich +0605, sp rate 2½ kn: the NE-going stream begins at HW Harwich −0010, sp rate 3 kn.

N of Orford Ness the coast is clear of offlying dangers past Aldeburgh and Southwold (10.4.16), as far as Benacre Ness, 5M S of Lowestoft (10.4.17). Sizewell power station is a conspic square building 1½M N of Thorpe Ness.

Lowestoft may be approached from S by buoyed chan to Pakefield Road, Lowestoft South Road (close E of pier heads), W of Lowestoft Bank: beware strong set possibly across harb entrance. From the N, approach through Yarmouth Road and then proceed S through Gorleston, Corton and Lowestoft North Roads (buoyed). From E, approach through Holm Chan. 2M E of harb entrance the S-going stream begins at HW Harwich +0530, and the N-going at HW Harwich −0110, sp rates 3 kn.

In the approaches to Great Yarmouth (10.4.18) from seaward there are frequent changes to the chans. The sea often breaks on North Scroby, Middle Scroby and Caister Shoal (all of which dry), and there are heavy tide rips over parts of Corton and South Scroby Sands, Middle and South Cross Sands, and Winterton Overfalls. 1M E of entrance to Gt Yarmouth Haven the S-going stream begins at HW Harwich +0530, and the N-going at HW Harwich −0050, sp rates 2¼ kn. Breydon Water (tidal) affects streams in the Haven: after heavy rain the out-going stream at Brush Quay may attain over 5 kn. For Norfolk Broads see 10.4.22.

About 12 M NE of Great Yarmouth lie Newarp Banks, on which the sea breaks in bad weather.

NORTH NORFOLK COAST (charts 106, 108)

Haisborough Sand (buoyed) lies 8M off the Norfolk coast, with depths of less than 1.8m in many places, and down to 0.4m. The shoal is steep-to, on its NE side in particular, and there are tidal eddies. Even a moderate sea or swell breaks on the shallower parts. There are dangerous wrecks near the S end. Haisborough Tail and Hammond Knoll (with wreck depth 1.2m) lie to the E of S end of Haisborough Sand.

The streams follow the directions of the coast and of chans between the banks NE of the Norfolk coast. But in the outer chans the stream is somewhat rotary: when changing from SE-going to NW-going it sets SW, and when changing from NW-going to SE-going it sets NE, across the shoals. Close S of Haisborough Sand the SE-going stream begins at HW Harwich +0530, and the NW-going at HW Harwich −0040, sp rates about 2½ kn.

The coast of N Norfolk is unfriendly in bad weather, with no harb accessible when there is any N in the wind. The harbs all dry, and seas soon build up in the entrances or over the bars, some of which are dangerous even in a moderate breeze and an ebb tide. But in settled weather and moderate offshore winds it is a peaceful area to explore, particularly for boats which can take the ground. See 10.4.22.

If proceeding direct from Cromer to the Humber, pass S of Sheringham Shoal (buoyed) where the ESE-going stream begins at HW Immingham −0225, and the WNW-going at +0430. Proceed to NE of Blakeney Overfalls and Docking Shoal, and to SW of Race Bank, so as to fetch Inner Dowsing Lt Tr (Lt, fog sig). Thence pass E of Protector Overfalls, and steer for Rosse Spit buoy at SE side of entrance to Humber (10.5.8).

THE WASH (charts 108, 1190, 1200)

The Wash is a shallow area of shifting sands, formed by the estuaries of the rivers Great Ouse, Nene, Welland and Witham. Important factors are the strong tidal streams, the low shore line, and frequent poor vis. Keep a careful watch on the echo sounder, and remember that buoys may have been moved to accommodate changes in the chan. In general terms the in-going stream begins at HW Immingham −0520, and the out-going at HW Immingham −0045, sp rates about 2 kn. The in-going stream is usually stronger than the out-going, but its duration is less. Prolonged NE winds cause an in-going current, which can increase the rate and duration of the in-going stream and also the height of sea level at the head of the estuary. Do not attempt entry to the rivers too early on the flood, which runs hard in the rivers.

SOUTHERN NORTH SEA
WAYPOINTS   10-4-6

Selected waypoints for use in the Southern North Sea are
nominated below. Further waypoints in coastal waters are
given in 10.4.4 for the English Coast and 10.19.4 for the
Belgium and Dutch coasts.

Aldeburgh Ridge Lt Buoy	51°06'·82N	01°37'·60E
Barrow No.3 Lt Buoy	51°42'·00N	01°19'·87E
Blakeney Overfalls Lt Buoy	53°03'·00N	00°01'·50E
Burnham Flats Lt Buoy	53°07'·50N	00°35'·00E
Buxey No 1 Lt Buoy	51°39'·02N	01°00'·86E
Colne Bar Lt Buoy	51°44'·58N	01°02'·65E
Cockle Lt Buoy	52°44'·00N	01°43'·70E
Corton Lt Buoy	52°31'·10N	01°51'·50E
Cross Sand Lt Buoy	52°37'·00N	01°59'·25E
Crouch Lt Buoy	51°37'·60N	00°56'·49E
Eagle Lt Buoy	51°44'·10N	01°03'·92E
East Barnard Lt Buoy	51°24'·60N	01°46'·20E
East Cross Sand Lt Buoy	52°40'·00N	01°53'·80E
East Newcome Lt Buoy	52°28'·48N	01°49'·32E
East Sheringham Lt Buoy	53°02'·20N	01°15'·00E
East Shipwash Lt Buoy	51°57'·05N	01°38'·00E
Foulness Lt Buoy	51°39'·82N	01°03'·92E
Gunfleet Spit Lt Buoy	51°45'·30N	01°21'·80E
Harwich HA Lt Buoy	51°56'·40N	01°31'·20E
Horse Shoal Lt Buoy	51°37'·07N	00°51'·62E
Inner Crouch Lt Buoy	51°37'·19N	00°55'·22E
Knoll Lt Buoy	51°43'·85N	01°05'·17E
Long Sand Head Lt Buoy	51°47'·87N	01°39'·53E
Medusa Lt Buoy	51°51'·20N	01°20'·46E
Newarp Lt F	52°48'·35N	01°55'·80E
North Caister Lt Buoy	52°41'·00N	01°45'·00E
North Docking Lt Buoy	53°14'·80N	00°41'·60E
North East Gunfleet	51°49'·90N	01°27'·90E
North Galloper Lt Buoy	51°50'·00N	01°59'·50E
North Haisbro Lt Buoy	53°00'·20N	01°32'·40E
North Inner Gabbard Lt Buoy	51°59'·10N	01°56'·10E
North Scroby Lt Buoy	52°42'·20N	01°45'·80E
North Shipwash Lt Buoy	52°01'·70N	01°38'·38E
North Well Lt Buoy	53°03'·00N	00°28'·00E
North West Scroby Lt Buoy	52°40'·00N	01°46'·20E
Orford Haven Buoy	52°01'·78N	01°27'·98E
Outer Crouch Lt Buoy	51°38'·35N	00°58'·61E
Outer Gabbard Lt V	51°59'·38N	02°04'·63E
Ridge Lt Buoy	51°40'·10N	01°04'·99E
Rough Lt Buoy	51°55'·65N	01°31'·30E
Scott Patch Lt Buoy	51°11'·10N	00°36'·50E
Scroby Elbow Lt Buoy	52°37'·70N	01°46'·50E
Shiphead Lt Buoy	51°53'·75N	01°34'·05E
Shipwash Lt F	52°02'·03N	01°42'·05E
Smiths Knoll Lt F	52°43'·50N	02°18'·00E
South Cork Lt Buoy	51°51'·30N	01°24'·20E
South Inner Gabbard Lt Buoy	51°51'·20N	01°52'·40E
South Galloper Lt Buoy	51°43'·95N	01°56'·50E
South Haisbro Lt Buoy	52°50'·80N	01°48'·40E
South Newcome Lt Buoy	51°25'·70N	01°45'·20E
South Race Lt Buoy	53°08'·65N	00°55'·80E
South West Scroby Lt Buoy	52°35'·81N	01°46'·55E
Sunk Lt F	51°51'·00N	01°35'·00E
Sunk Head Tr Lt Buoy	51°46'·60N	01°30'·60E
Sunken Buxey Lt Buoy	51°39'·50N	01°00'·60E

Swin Spitway Lt Buoy	51°41'·73N	01°07'·65E
Trinity Lt Buoy	51°49'·00N	01°36'·50E
Wallet No.2 Lt Buoy	51°48'·85N	01°23'·10E
Wallet No.4 Lt Buoy	51°46'·50N	01°17'·33E
Wells Fairway Lt Buoy	53°00'·15N	00°51'·12E
West Sheringham Lt Buoy	53°02'·97N	01°07'·70E
Whitaker Lt Buoy	51°41'·40N	01°10'·61E
Whitaker No 1 Lt Buoy	51°41'·15N	01°09'·77E
Woodbridge Haven Lt Buoy	51°58'·36N	01°24'·17E
Woolpack Lt Buoy	53°02'·65N	00°31'·55E
Areas 18 and 19		
Abbeville Lt Buoy	50°56'·08N	01°37'·42E
Akkaert NE Lt Buoy	51°27'·31N	02°59'·38E
Akkaert Midden Lt Buoy	51°24'·23N	02°53'·50E
Akkaert SW Lt Buoy	51°22'·30N	02°46'·40E
A-Noord Lt Buoy	51°23'·50N	02°37'·00E
A-Zuid Lt Buoy	51°21'·50N	02°37'·00E
Bergues N Lt Buoy	51°19'·90N	02°24'·62E
Bergues Lt Buoy	51°16'·20N	02°18'·70E
Bergues S Lt Buoy	51°15'·16N	02°19'·50E
Binnenstroombank Lt Buoy	51°14'·50N	02°53'·73E
BT Ratel Lt Buoy	51°11'·58N	02°28'·00E
Buitenstroombank Lt Buoy	51°15'·20N	02°51'·80E
Dunkerque Lanby	51°03'·00N	01°51'·83E
Dyck E Lt Buoy	51°05'·70N	02°05'·80E
Fairy S Lt Buoy	51°21'·22N	02°17'·35E
Fairy W Lt Buoy	51°23'·90N	02°09'·44E
F3 Lanby	51°23'·80N	02°00'·60E
Goote Bank Lt Buoy	51°27'·00N	02°52'·70E
Hinder 1	51°20'·90N	02°11'·06E
Kwintebank Lt Buoy	51°21'·75N	02°43'·00E
LST "420" Lt Buoy	51°15'·50N	02°40'·70E
Middelkirkebank N Lt Buoy	51°20'·87N	02°46'·40E
Middelkirkebank S Lt Buoy	51°14'·78N	02°42'·00E
Middelkirkebank Lt Buoy	51°18'·25N	02°42'·80E
Nautica Ena Lt Buoy	51°18'·12N	02°52'·85E
Nieuwpoortbank Lt Buoy	51°10'·21N	02°36'·16E
Oost Dyck W Lt Buoy	51°17'·18N	02°26'·42E
Oostendebank N Lt Buoy	51°21'·25N	02°53'·00E
Oostendebank Oost Lt Buoy	51°17'·36N	02°52'·00E
Oostendebank W Lt Buoy	51°16'·25N	02°44'·85E
Ruytingen SW Lt Buoy	51°05'·00N	01°46'·85E
Ruytingen SE Lt Buoy	51°09'·18N	01°08'·98E
Sandettié Lt V	51°09'·30N	01°47'·20E
Sandettié N Lt Buoy	51°18'·42N	02°04'·80E
Sandettié SW Lt Buoy	51°09'·70N	01°45'·70E
Sandettié WSW Lt Buoy	51°12'·32N	01°51'·10E
SW Wandelaar Lt Buoy	51°22'·00N	03°01'·00E
SCH 3 Lt Buoy	51°24'·35N	03°02'·90E
SCH 4 Lt Buoy	51°25'·05N	03°03'·10E
Scheur-Zand Lt Buoy	51°23'·70N	03°07'·68E
SW Thornton Lt Buoy	51°31'·01N	02°51'·00E
Trapegeer Lt Buoy	51°08'·45N	02°34'·45E
Wenduinebank E Lt Buoy	51°18'·88N	03°01'·71E
Wenduinebank W Lt Buoy	51°17'·30N	02°52'·87E
West Hinder Lt V	51°22'·98N	02°26'·40E
Westroombank Lt Buoy	51°11'·39N	02°43'·15E
Wielingen Zand Lt Buoy	51°22'·60N	03°10'·80E
Zand Lt Buoy	51°22'·50N	03°10'·12E
Zuidstroombank Lt Buoy	51°12'·33N	02°47'·50E

10.4.7 DISTANCE TABLE

Approximate distances in nautical miles are by the most direct route while avoiding dangers and allowing for traffic separation schemes etc. Places in *italics* are in adjoining areas.

1 *Cap Gris Nez*	**1**																			
2 *North Foreland*	32	**2**																		
3 *Shoeburyness*	61	29	**3**																	
4 Burnham-on-Crouch	68	36	27	**4**																
5 West Mersea	67	35	30	22	**5**															
6 Walton-on-Naze	68	36	31	25	18	**6**														
7 Harwich	74	42	37	31	24	6	**7**													
8 River Deben	75	43	41	35	28	10	8	**8**												
9 Orford Ness	74	44	49	43	36	18	15	8	**9**											
10 Southwold	91	59	64	58	51	33	30	23	15	**10**										
11 Lowestoft	101	69	74	68	61	43	40	33	25	10	**11**									
12 Great Yarmouth	109	77	82	76	69	51	48	41	33	18	7	**12**								
13 Wells	157	125	130	124	117	99	96	89	81	66	56	50	**13**							
14 Kings Lynn	184	152	157	151	144	126	123	116	108	93	83	77	33	**14**						
15 *Grimsby*	201	169	174	168	161	143	140	133	125	110	100	94	54	61	**15**					
16 *Flamborough Head*	224	192	197	191	184	166	163	156	148	133	123	117	77	86	44	**16**				
17 *Oostende*	50	58	80	91	88	74	76	73	72	81	83	93	143	187	194	211	**17**			
18 *Goeree Tower*	103	91	111	108	104	100	99	85	78	79	81	83	125	152	169	186	51	**18**		
19 *IJmuiden*	149	137	155	151	140	125	126	122	110	105	102	102	143	170	182	193	97	46	**19**	
20 *Brunsbüttel*	362	337	348	342	337	320	320	312	306	296	288	287	310	343	332	330	314	263	221	**20**

BURNHAM-ON-CROUCH
Essex   **10-4-8**

CHARTS
Admiralty 3750, 1975, 1183; Stanford 4, 5; Imray C1, Y17; OS 168/178

TIDES
+0110 Dover; ML 3.0; Duration 0610; Zone 0 (GMT).

Standard Port SHEERNESS (←)

Times				Height (metres)			
HW		LW		MHWS	MHWN	MLWN	MLWS
0000	0600	0100	0700	5.7	4.7	1.5	0.6
1200	1800	1300	1900				

Differences BURNHAM-ON-CROUCH

−0020 −0020 −0005 −0005 −0.5 −0.5 −0.5 −0.4

NOTE: Rivers Crouch and Roach, out as far as Foulness Point, are controlled by the Crouch River Authority. The Crouch is navigable up to Battlesbridge, 15 M from Foulness.

SHELTER
Rivers are exposed to all winds. Anchoring prohibited in fairway but is possible just above or below the moorings. Sometimes anchoring is possible to W of moorings by Crouch YC. Cliff Reach is important to yachtsmen as it provides shelter from SW winds. There are many moorings and landing places in the R Roach S of Wallasea Island. See 10.4.22.

NAVIGATION
Waypoint Outer Couch Lt Buoy 51° 38'.35N, 00° 58'61E. There are few landmarks to assist entering the Crouch. By day, the buoys marking Whitaker Channel are easily found. Channel now lit Lt Buoys from Outer Crouch to westward. There is a 'Firing Danger Area' just to S of Foulness Point. Speed limit in river is 8kn.
N.B. Landing on Bridgemarsh Is (up river) is strictly forbidden.

LIGHTS AND MARKS
From Sunken Buxey N cardinal Lt Buoy, St Mary's church spire bearing 233° leads to Outer Crouch stbd-hand buoy and from here 240° leads into river. Channel marked 8QG & 1QR.

RADIO TELEPHONE
Essex Marina VHF Ch **80** (0900-1700 LT). West Wick Marina Ch **80** (1000-1700 LT).

TELEPHONE (0621)
Hr Mr 783602; CG Shoeburyness 4998; MRSC Frinton-on-Sea 675518; ✵ (0473) 219401; Marinecall 0898 500 455; Police 782121; Dr 782054.

FACILITIES
BURNHAM EC Wednesday; **Burnham Yacht Harbour** (350) ☎ 782150, ME, El, Sh, BH (30 ton), CH, ◎, R, Access H24; **Royal Corinthian YC** ☎ 782105, AB, FW, M, L, R, Bar; **Royal Burnham YC** ☎ 782044, FW, L, R, Bar; **Tucker Brown** ☎ 782150, BY, C (5 ton), CH, El, FW, M, Gas, Gaz, L, ME, Sh, AB, D, Slip, AC, BH; **R. J. Prior** ☎ 782160, AB, BY, C (15 ton), D, FW, L, ME, El, Sh, M, Slip; **Kelvin Aqua** ☎ 782659, L, CH, FW, ACA, Gas, Gaz; **W. Yardley** ☎ 782076, BY, D, FW, M, ME, CH, M; **Petticrow** (200) ☎ 782115, BY, C (4 ton), D, El, FW, M, ME, Sh, Slip; **Rice and Cole** ☎ 782063, BY, C (4½ ton), CH, D, M, Sh, L, Gas, Gaz, M, FW; **Crouch YC** ☎ 782252, L, FW, R, Bar; **Sadler Sails** ☎ 782124, SM; **Hood** ☎ 782821, SM; **Cranfield Sails** ☎ 782669, SM; **Crouch Engineering** ☎ 782130, D, El, L, ME, P, AB; **Duerr Engineering** ☎ 782726, El, ME (H24); **Peter Barker** ☎ 782403, Sh; **Tubby Lee Yachting Services** ☎ 783562, Rigging;
Town V, R, Bar, ✉; ⑧; ⇌; ✈ (Southend).
WALLASEA **Essex Marina** (400) ☎ Canewdon 531, AB, BY, Gas, Bar, C (13 ton), BH (40 ton), CH, D, El, FW, L, M, ME, P, R, Sh, Slip, V, YC; **Essex YC.**
FAMBRIDGE **West Wick Marina** (Stow Creek) (180) ☎ 741268, AB, Gas, Gaz, CH, El, Slip, FW, D, C (5 ton), YC, Bar; **North Fambridge Yacht Station** (150) ☎ 740370, CH, Sh, M, ME, BY, C (5 ton), El, FW, L, Slip, Gas, Gaz, Access HW∓5; **Brandy Hole Yacht Station** (120) ☎ Southend-on-Sea 230248, L, M, ME, Sh, Slip, Gas, Gaz, Bar, BY, D, FW, Access HW∓4.

BURNHAM-ON-CROUCH *continued*

BLACKWATER RIVER 10-4-9
Essex

CHARTS
Admiralty 3741, 1183; Stanford 4, 5; Imray C1, Y17; OS 168

TIDES
+0105 Dover; ML 2.8; Duration 0620; Zone 0 (GMT).

Standard Port SHEERNESS (←)

Times				Height (metres)			
HW		LW		MHWS	MHWN	MLWN	MLWS
0000	0600	0100	0700	5.7	4.7	1.5	0.6
1200	1800	1300	1900				

Differences TOLLESBURY (Mill Creek)
−0027 −0027 −0019 −0019 −0.9 −0.8 −0.6 −0.4
OSEA ISLAND
−0005 −0005 −0016 −0016 −0.4 −0.4 −0.2 −0.1
MALDON
+0005 +0005   No data   −2.8 −2.4   No data

SHELTER
By choosing the appropriate area good shelter can always be found. Entrance to the Chelmer and Blackwater canal by Heybridge basin at Maldon. Lock opens HW−1 to HW. For moorings, ring River Bailiff.

NAVIGATION
Waypoint Knoll N cardinal buoy, Q, 51°43'.85N 01°05'.18E, 107°/287° from/to Nass Bn, 6.7M.
WEST MERSEA Beware oyster beds between Cobmarsh Is and Packing Marsh Is and in Salcott Chan.
BRADWELL No dangers but only suitable for small craft and area gets very crowded.
TOLLESBURY FLEET Proceeding up Woodrolfe Creek, a tide mark shows the depth over the yacht harbour entrance sill (approx 3m at MHWS and 2m at MHWN). Speed limits: Woodrolfe Creek 4 kms upper reaches and at Osea Is, Tollesbury Fleet S.Channel 8 kms.

⛵ Contact YCs

LIGHTS AND MARKS
Bradwell Yacht Marina entrance W side has two beacons B triangular topmarks; E side has beacon with R square topmark.
MALDON After rounding S of Osea Is, 'The Doctor', Blackwater SC Lt showing Iso G 5s at 300° leads approximately up the channel. Alternatively No 3 and No 8 buoys in line at 305°.

RADIO TELEPHONE
Bradwell Marina VHF Ch **80** (office hours). Tollesbury Marina Ch **80** (office hours).

TELEPHONE (0621)
Hr Mr 853646; River Bailiff 854477; CG (MRSC) Frinton-on-Sea 675518; Canal Lockmaster 853506; ⌗ (0473) 219481; Marinecall 0898 500 455; Police (0245) 491212 (West Mersea (0206) 762212); Dr 854118, West Mersea 382015.

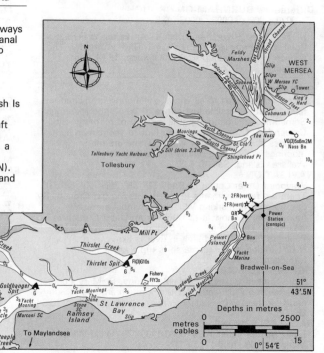

BLACKWATER RIVER *continued*

FACILITIES
EC W Mersea, Tollesbury, Maldon — Wednesday.
TOLLESBURY: **Tollesbury Marina** (240 + 20 visitors)
☎ 868471, Slip, D, AC, BH (10 ton), Gas, Gaz, FW, ME,
El, Sh, C (5 ton), CH, V, R, Bar, Ⓞ, Access HW ∓ 1½;
Tollesbury Cruising Club ☎ 869561, Bar, R, M, C (20
ton), D, CH, FW, L, Slip, AC, ME, El, Sh; **Pier** FW;
Volspec ☎ 869756, ME; **Tollesbury Saltings** ☎ 868421,
Access HW ∓ 2 Slip, FW, ME, El, Sh; **A.P. Marine**
☎ 869589, CH. **Village** P, V, R, Bar. ✉; Ⓑ (Tues, Thurs
1000-1430); ⇌ (bus to Witham); ✈ (Southend or
Cambridge).
WEST MERSEA: (0206) **Clarke & Carter BY** ☎ 382244,
Slip (+ dock), M, L (at high water), FW, ME, El, C (10
ton), CH; **William Wyatt** ☎ 382856, Slip, M, ME, El, CH;
Causeway P and D (A. Clark), L, FW, ME, El, V;
Gowen Sails ☎ 382922, SM; **West Mersea YC**
☎ 382947, M (see boatman), R, Bar; **Mersea Chandlers**
☎ 384433, CH, ACA;
Town P, D, FW, ME, El, CH, V, R, Bar. ✉; Ⓑ;
⇌ (bus to Colchester); ✈ (Southend or Cambridge).
BRADWELL: **Bradwell Marina** (280, some visitors)
☎ 76235, Slip, AC, Gas, Gaz, D, P, FW, ME, El, Sh, BH
(16 ton), CH, R, Bar, Access HW ∓ 4½; **Bradwell Quay**
Slip, L; **Bradwell Quay YC** ☎ 76539, M, FW, Bar, L,
Slip. **Town** ✉; Ⓑ (Maldon); ⇌ (bus to Southminster);
✈ (Southend).
MALDON: **Maldon Quay** Slip, M, P, D, FW, AB; **Dan
Webb & Feesey** ☎ 854280, Slip, D, Sh, CH, M;
Fairways Marine Engineers ☎ 852866, ME, El;
Heybridge Basin ☎ 854022, D, ME, El, Sh, CH, Bar;
Blackwater SC ☎ 853923, L, FW; **Holt and James**
☎ 854022, Slip, D, L, M, FW, CH; **Mantsbrite Marine
Electronics** ☎ 853003, Ⓔ, El; **A Taylor** ☎ 853456, SM;
Anglian Yacht Services ☎ 852290 emergencies.
Town ✉; Ⓑ; ⇌ (bus to Chelmsford); ✈ (Southend,
Cambridge or Stanstead).
MAYLANDSEA: **Marina** Access HW ∓ 2; **Dan Webb and
Feesey** (350) ☎ 740264, Slip, D, Sh, CH.

SHELTER
Suitable shelter can be found for most winds. Anchorages
in Brightlingsea Creek; to the W of Mersea Stone Pt; in
Pyefleet, E of Pewit Is; R Colne navigable up to Wivenhoe
(1.6m draught) or Hythe, Colchester (3m draught). Outer
harbour is exposed to westerly winds.
NAVIGATION
Waypoint Colne Bar (stbd-hand) buoy, 51°44'.58N
01°02'.66E, 158°/338° from/to Mersea Stone, 3.6M. See
also 10.4.9. Extensive mud and sand banks flank the
entrance channel. The entrance to Brightlingsea creek is
very narrow at LW. River traffic in the Colne is
considerable. Large coasters use the Brightlingsea
channels. Speed limits — 8kn; Buoy 13 to Fingringhoe
(except Buoy 12 to 16) 5kn; Fingringhoe to Colchester
4kn.
LIGHTS AND MARKS
Up as far as Wivenhoe, where the river dries out, it is
extremely well buoyed. Brightlingsea has FR Ldg Lts
adjusted according to the channel and channel buoys Fl
(3) G 8s and Fl (2) R 8s. A Y Lt is exhibited from The
Tower by Westmarsh Pt.
RADIO TELEPHONE
Colchester Harbour Radio VHF Ch 16; **14** 11 (Office hrs &
HW − 2 to HW + 1). Tel. Colchester 575858.
TELEPHONE (0621)
Hr Mr 52110; Harbour Office Brightlingsea 2200; CG &
MRSC Frinton-on-Sea 675518; Canal Lockmaster 53506;
▦ (0473) 219481; Marinecall 0898 500 455; Police 52255;
Dr 52535, West Mersea 382015.
FACILITIES
BRIGHTLINGSEA: (020 630) **Town Hard** ☎ 3535, L, FW;
Colne YC ☎ 2594, L, FW, R, Bar; **L.H. Morgan** ☎ 2003,
M, Gas, D, L, FW, ME, El, Ⓔ, Sh, CH, ACA;
Cox Marine ME, El, Sh; **French Marine Motors**
☎ 2133, CH, P, D, ME, El, Ⓔ; **Brightlingsea SC** Slip,
Bar; **James Lawrence** ☎ 2863, SM; **The Boatcentre**
☎ 2003, CH; **St Osyth BY** ☎ St Osyth 820005, M, L,
FW, ME, C, Sh, El, Slip; **Town** P, D, FW, ME, El, Sh, C
(mobile), CH, V, R, Bar; ✉; Ⓑ; ⇌ (bus to Wivenhoe or
Colchester); ✈ (Southend or Cambridge).
WIVENHOE: (020 622) **Colne Marine Yacht** ☎ 2417, L,
ME, El, Sh, C; **Wivenhoe SC**; **Village near quay** P, V,
Bar; ✉; Ⓑ (AM only); ⇌; ✈ (Southend or Cambridge).
Note: A marina is planned at Brightlingsea shipyard.

RIVER COLNE   10-4-10
Essex

CHARTS
Admiralty 3741, 1183; Stanford 5, 4; Imray C1, Y17;
OS 168
TIDES
+ 0055 Dover; ML 2.5; Duration 0615; Zone 0 (GMT).
Standard Port SHEERNESS (←)

Times				Height (metres)			
HW		LW		MHWS	MHWN	MLWN	MLWS
0200	0800	0100	0700	5.7	4.7	1.5	0.6
1400	2000	1300	1900				

Differences BRIGHTLINGSEA
−0035 −0035 −0025 −0025 −0.7 −0.9 −0.3 −0.2
WIVENHOE
−0011 −0011 No data   No data

WALTON-ON-THE-NAZE
Essex

10-4-11

CHARTS
Admiralty 2695, 2052; Stanford 5, 6; Imray C1, Y16; OS 169

TIDES
+0040 Dover; ML 2.3; Duration 0615; Zone 0 (GMT).

Standard Port HARWICH (→)

Times				Height (metres)			
HW		LW		MHWS	MHWN	MLWN	MLWS
0000	0600	0000	0600	4.0	3.4	1.1	0.4
1200	1800	1200	1800				

Differences WALTON-ON-THE-NAZE

−0008 −0011 +0008 +0005 +0.2   0.0   0.0   0.0

SHELTER
The 'Walton Backwaters' give good shelter in any weather. Go alongside in marina in The Twizzle or anchor in Hamford Water, or in Walton Channel. W & F Yacht Trust Basin, Tel. Frinton 675873, entry HW−1 to HW. Keel boats can stay afloat in Walton Channel (N end 7m, S end 5m) or in the Twizzle (E end 5m).

NAVIGATION
Waypoint Pye End (safe water) buoy, 51°55'.00N 01°18'.00E, 054°/234° from/to buoyed channel entrance, 1.0M. Beware lobster pots off the Naze, Pye Sands and oyster beds S and W of Horsey I.

LIGHTS AND MARKS
Whether approaching from N or S it is necessary to find Pye End buoy marking the N extremity of Pye sand. The most conspic landmark is the Naze tower just N of Walton- on-the-Naze. There are no lights so the Backwaters cannot be entered at night.

RADIO TELEPHONE
None.

TELEPHONE (0255)
Hr Mr Harwich 243030; CG & MRSC Frinton-on-Sea 675518; ▓ (0473) 219481; Marinecall 0898 500 455; Police 241312; Ⓗ 502446.

FACILITIES
EC Wednesday; **Titchmarsh Marina** (450+10 visitors), ☎ 672185, Slip, D, FW, Gas, Gaz, AC, ME, C (25 ton), BH (10 ton), CH, YC, Sh, Access HW∓4½; **Walton Channel** M; **Walton & Frinton YC** ☎ 675526, L, FW, AB, Bar; **Twizzle Creek** M, L; **Bedwell & Co** ☎ 675873, Slip, M, D, C (½ ton), Sh, CH; **Frank Halls** ☎ 675596,

Slip, M, FW, D, Sh, CH, ME, El, Sh; **Bateson** ☎ 671348, El; **Town** P, V, R, Bar. ✉; Ⓑ; ⇌; ✈ (Southend or Cambridge).

RIVER STOUR (HARWICH)
Essex/Suffolk

10-4-12

RIVER STOUR (HARWICH) *continued*

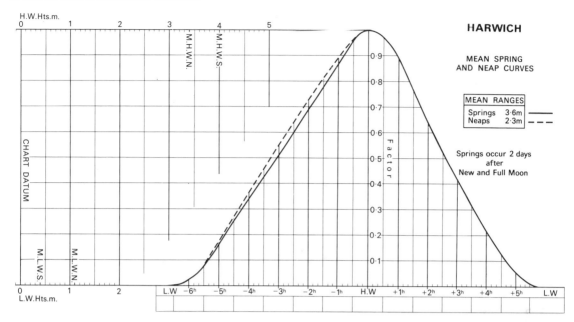

HARWICH

MEAN SPRING
AND NEAP CURVES

MEAN RANGES
Springs   3·6m ———
Neaps   2·3m - - -

Springs occur 2 days
after
New and Full Moon

CHARTS
Admiralty 1491, 1593, 1594, 2693; Stanford 5, 6;
Imray C1, Y16; OS 169

TIDES
+0040 Dover; ML 2.2; Duration 0630; Zone 0 (GMT)

Standard Port HARWICH (→)

Times				Height (metres)			
HW		LW		MHWS	MHWN	MLWN	MLWS
0000	0600	0000	0600	4.0	3.4	1.1	0.4
1200	1800	1200	1800				

Differences MISTLEY

+0025	+0025	0000	+0020	+0.2	0.0	−0.1	−0.1

NOTE: Harwich is a Standard Port and times and heights
of tidal predicitions for each day of the year are given
below.

SHELTER
Good. Anchor off Erwarton Ness, Wrabness or Holbrook
Creek. Alongside berths at Shotley Point Marina, Harwich
Quay (dries) for short periods near HW, and at New
Mistley and Manningtree (dry; off chartlet). No facilities
for yachts at Felixstowe.

NAVIGATION
Waypoint Cork Sand (port-hand) buoy, QR, 01°55'.43N
01°25'.70E, 086°/266° from/to position 0.7M S of
Landguard Pt, 4.0M. Beware commercial shipping. Yachts
must keep clear of deep water channel: recommended
track to S of it from Cork Sand Bn and thence to W of it
past Harwich. Entrance to Shotley Point Marina through
marked channel, with outer limits lit, to lock gate at all
states of tide. The channel up the R Stour is well marked.
Beware 'The Horse' 2 ca NW of Stone Pt and also the
drying bank 1½ ca NW of Wrabness Point. The channel
from Mistley Quay to Manningtree is narrow and tortuous,
local knowledge is invaluable.

Special Local Sound Signals
Commercial vessels may use these additional signals:

Four short and rapid blasts
followed by one short blast } = I am turning short
around to starboard.

Four short and rapid blasts
followed by two short blasts) } = I am turning short
around to port.

One prolonged blast = I am leaving a dock,
quay or anchorage.

LIGHTS AND MARKS
The channel West from Harwich past Parkeston Quay to
Harkstead Pt (off chartlet) is marked by G conical
stbd-hand buoys, Fl G or QG. There is a conspic factory
chimney at Cattawade, straight up the river about 8 M.

If kept dead ahead on course 270° it will lead through the
best water up to Harkstead Pt. Shotley Pt Marina Dir Lt
339° on E side of lock entrance indicates dredged
channel. Entrance to marina assisted by Inogen Visual
Guidance Marker Lights which are square, ambered
displays on which a vertical black line indicates position
on the approach centre line. Off the centre line, arrows
indicate the direction to steer to regain the correct
approach line.

RADIO TELEPHONE
Call: *Harwich Harbour Control* VHF Ch 16 11 14 **71** (H24).
Yachts are requested not to use Ch 71 but it is useful to
monitor the channel to obtain information on shipping.
Local weather, tidal information etc available on request.
The Harwich Harbour Board Patrol launch, *Godwit* keeps
regular patrol and listening watch of VHF Ch 11. Shotley
Point Marina Ch **80** (lock master).
See also River Orwell. (10.4.13).

TELEPHONE (0255)
Hr Mr 243030; CG & MRSC Frinton-on-Sea 675518;
Harwich Haven Authority 243030; Harbour Operations
Room 243111; ☎ (0473) 219481; Marinecall 0898 500 455;
Police 241312; Dr 506451; Ⓗ 502446.

FACILITIES
EC Wednesday
HARWICH: **Town Pier** L, FW, AB (tidal); **Royal Harwich
YC** ☎ Woolverstone 319; **Dolphin Sails** ☎ 243366, SM;
F.M. Services ☎ 506808, Gas; **R & J Marine** ☎ 502849,
El;
Town P, D, ME, El, Sh, V, R, Bar. ✉; Ⓑ; ⇌;
✈ (Cambridge or Norwich).
SHOTLEY: **Shotley Point Marina** (350 – visitors welcome)
☎ Shotley 348908, FW, AC, D, P, ▣, ME, El, Ⓔ, Sh,
Slip, BH (30 ton), C, V, CH, SM, Bar, R; Access H24 via
lock; entrance controlled by INOGEN lights. **Shotley SC**
☎ Shotley 500, Slip, L, FW, Bar; **Harwich and
Dovercourt SC** ☎ Harwich 240672, M, L, FW, C (5 ton),
AB, V, R, Bar. **Shotley BY** ☎ Shotley 714, Slip, M, ME,
El, Sh.
WRABNESS: M, FW, V, Bar.
MISTLEY: AB, M, FW, V, P, D, Bar.
MANNINGTREE: M, AB, FW, V, Bar; **Stour SC**
☎ Colchester 393924, FW, M, Bar; **DN Howells**
☎ 392577, Gas.

RIVER ORWELL   10-4-13
Suffolk

CHARTS
Admiralty 2693, 2052, 1491; Stanford 5, 6; Imray C1, Y16;
OS 169

ENGLAND, EAST COAST – HARWICH

Lat 51°57′ N   Long 1°17′ E

TIMES AND HEIGHTS OF HIGH AND LOW WATERS

YEAR **1991**

TIME ZONE UT(GMT)
For Summer Time add ONE hour in non-shaded areas

JANUARY

Day	Time	m	Time	m	Time	m	Time	m
1 Tu	0520	0.4	1158	4.1	1743	0.5		
2 W	0022	3.9	0611	0.2	1248	4.2	1828	0.5
3 Th	0109	4.0	0657	0.1	1334	4.2	1912	0.6
4 F	0151	4.0	0744	0.1	1419	4.1	1954	0.6
5 Sa	0233	4.0	0829	0.1	1504	4.0	2036	0.7
6 Su	0315	3.9	0914	0.2	1548	3.8	2119	0.8
7 M ☾	0359	3.8	1000	0.4	1634	3.6	2204	1.0
8 Tu	0444	3.6	1049	0.6	1723	3.4	2258	1.1
9 W	0537	3.4	1147	0.8	1821	3.2		
10 Th	0004	1.2	0642	3.3	1256	1.0	1928	3.1
11 F	0126	1.2	0801	3.2	1412	1.0	2042	3.2
12 Sa	0247	1.1	0915	3.2	1515	1.0	2143	3.3
13 Su	0348	1.0	1013	3.4	1606	1.0	2231	3.4
14 M	0434	0.8	1059	3.5	1645	1.0	2313	3.5
15 Tu ●	0513	0.7	1139	3.6	1719	0.9	2351	3.6
16 W	0546	0.6	1215	3.7	1751	0.8		
17 Th	0027	3.7	0618	0.5	1249	3.7	1822	0.7
18 F	0059	3.7	0652	0.3	1324	3.8	1856	0.6
19 Sa	0133	3.8	0727	0.3	1358	3.8	1931	0.6
20 Su	0206	3.8	0802	0.4	1433	3.8	2006	0.7
21 M	0240	3.8	0837	0.4	1511	3.7	2043	0.7
22 Tu	0317	3.8	0915	0.5	1552	3.6	2124	0.8
23 W ☽	0359	3.7	0957	0.5	1638	3.5	2212	0.9
24 Th	0449	3.6	1051	0.7	1736	3.4	2316	1.0
25 F	0553	3.5	1207	0.8	1846	3.3		
26 Sa	0041	1.0	0712	3.4	1330	0.9	2002	3.3
27 Su	0202	0.9	0834	3.5	1446	0.8	2121	3.4
28 M	0317	0.7	0955	3.6	1552	0.7	2227	3.6
29 Tu	0421	0.5	1058	3.8	1647	0.6	2323	3.7
30 W ○	0515	0.3	1150	4.0	1732	0.5		
31 Th	0011	3.9	0601	0.1	1238	4.1	1812	0.5

FEBRUARY

Day	Time	m	Time	m	Time	m	Time	m
1 F	0053	4.0	0643	0.0	1320	4.1	1853	0.4
2 Sa	0134	4.1	0724	0.0	1401	4.0	1931	0.5
3 Su	0212	4.1	0805	0.0	1439	3.9	2011	0.5
4 M	0249	4.0	0843	0.2	1517	3.8	2047	0.7
5 Tu	0327	3.9	0922	0.4	1553	3.6	2125	0.8
6 W ☾	0404	3.7	1002	0.6	1633	3.4	2209	1.0
7 Th	0448	3.6	1048	0.9	1719	3.1	2305	1.2
8 F	0546	3.1	1151	1.1	1821	3.0		
9 Sa	0028	1.3	0712	2.9	1312	1.2	1949	2.9
10 Su	0218	1.2	0850	3.0	1449	1.2	2112	3.0
11 M	0328	1.0	0952	3.2	1545	1.1	2209	3.2
12 Tu	0414	0.8	1038	3.4	1626	0.9	2252	3.4
13 W	0451	0.6	1119	3.6	1706	0.8	2330	3.6
14 Th ●	0525	0.5	1154	3.7	1730	0.7		
15 F	0005	3.7	0557	0.4	1229	3.8	1803	0.6
16 Sa ●	0041	3.8	0631	0.2	1303	3.9	1835	0.5
17 Su	0114	3.9	0704	0.2	1338	3.9	1909	0.4
18 M	0147	3.9	0738	0.2	1413	3.9	1944	0.5
19 Tu	0220	3.9	0812	0.3	1449	3.8	2020	0.5
20 W	0256	3.9	0849	0.4	1527	3.7	2100	0.6
21 Th ☽	0336	3.8	0929	0.5	1612	3.5	2146	0.8
22 F	0426	3.6	1021	0.7	1705	3.3	2249	0.9
23 Sa	0530	3.4	1137	0.9	1817	3.2		
24 Su	0019	1.0	0655	3.3	1312	1.0	1941	3.1
25 M	0151	0.8	0829	3.3	1436	0.9	2108	3.3
26 Tu	0314	0.6	0950	3.6	1543	0.8	2216	3.5
27 W	0416	0.4	1049	3.8	1634	0.7	2309	3.7
28 Th ○	0504	0.2	1137	3.9	1715	0.5	2353	3.9

MARCH

Day	Time	m	Time	m	Time	m	Time	m
1 F	0544	0.0	1219	4.0	1753	0.4		
2 Sa	0034	4.0	0624	0.0	1259	4.0	1829	0.4
3 Su	0110	4.1	0700	0.0	1335	4.0	1907	0.4
4 M	0145	4.1	0737	0.1	1409	3.9	1944	0.4
5 Tu	0220	4.0	0811	0.3	1442	3.7	2018	0.6
6 W	0254	3.8	0844	0.5	1514	3.5	2051	0.7
7 Th	0329	3.6	0918	0.8	1548	3.4	2127	0.9
8 F ☾	0407	3.3	0959	1.0	1624	3.1	2214	1.1
9 Sa	0455	3.1	1055	1.2	1713	2.9	2330	1.2
10 Su	0611	2.8	1224	1.4	1835	2.8		
11 M	0128	1.2	0812	2.9	1408	1.3	2029	2.9
12 Tu	0249	1.0	0921	3.1	1510	1.1	2134	3.1
13 W	0339	0.7	1009	3.4	1552	0.9	2220	3.4
14 Th	0419	0.6	1049	3.6	1628	0.8	2259	3.6
15 F	0452	0.4	1126	3.7	1701	0.6	2337	3.8
16 Sa ●	0527	0.3	1203	3.9	1736	0.5		
17 Su	0014	3.9	0603	0.2	1239	4.0	1810	0.4
18 M	0049	4.0	0638	0.1	1314	4.0	1846	0.3
19 Tu	0126	4.0	0712	0.2	1351	3.9	1923	0.4
20 W	0201	4.0	0748	0.3	1427	3.8	2001	0.4
21 Th	0239	3.9	0826	0.4	1505	3.7	2043	0.5
22 F	0322	3.8	0910	0.6	1550	3.5	2134	0.6
23 Sa ☽	0414	3.6	1006	0.9	1644	3.3	2241	0.8
24 Su	0522	3.4	1125	1.1	1756	3.1		
25 M	0011	0.8	0649	3.3	1256	1.1	1924	3.1
26 Tu	0144	0.7	0825	3.4	1422	1.0	2051	3.2
27 W	0303	0.5	0936	3.4	1527	0.9	2156	3.5
28 Th	0400	0.3	1031	3.8	1613	0.7	2247	3.7
29 F	0444	0.2	1116	3.9	1652	0.6	2330	3.8
30 Sa ○	0522	0.1	1157	3.9	1730	0.5		
31 Su	0008	3.9	0557	0.1	1234	3.9	1807	0.4

APRIL

Day	Time	m	Time	m	Time	m	Time	m
1 M	0045	4.0	0632	0.1	1307	3.9	1843	0.4
2 Tu	0119	4.0	0707	0.3	1338	3.8	1919	0.4
3 W	0152	3.9	0740	0.4	1409	3.7	1951	0.6
4 Th	0225	3.7	0811	0.7	1439	3.6	2022	0.7
5 F	0258	3.5	0842	0.9	1510	3.4	2056	0.8
6 Sa	0336	3.3	0918	1.1	1545	3.2	2138	1.0
7 Su ☾	0420	3.1	1012	1.3	1630	3.0	2247	1.1
8 M	0520	2.9	1133	1.4	1733	2.9		
9 Tu	0027	1.1	0700	2.9	1307	1.3	1913	2.9
10 W	0149	0.9	0830	3.1	1416	1.1	2037	3.1
11 Th	0249	0.7	0925	3.4	1507	0.9	2135	3.3
12 F	0335	0.5	1010	3.6	1549	0.7	2220	3.6
13 Sa	0416	0.3	1052	3.8	1628	0.6	2304	3.8
14 Su ●	0454	0.2	1132	3.9	1706	0.4	2344	3.9
15 M	0533	0.2	1212	4.0	1746	0.3		
16 Tu	0025	4.0	0611	0.2	1252	4.0	1825	0.3
17 W	0104	4.1	0649	0.2	1330	4.0	1904	0.3
18 Th	0145	4.1	0728	0.2	1409	3.8	1948	0.3
19 F	0227	4.0	0812	0.4	1450	3.7	2036	0.4
20 Sa	0315	3.8	0900	0.7	1536	3.5	2132	0.5
21 Su ☽	0410	3.6	0959	0.9	1633	3.3	2240	0.6
22 M	0518	3.5	1112	1.1	1742	3.2		
23 Tu	0001	0.6	0639	3.4	1234	1.1	1903	3.2
24 W	0126	0.5	0802	3.5	1354	1.0	2022	3.3
25 Th	0239	0.4	0911	3.6	1457	0.9	2128	3.5
26 F	0334	0.3	1004	3.7	1546	0.8	2220	3.7
27 Sa	0417	0.3	1051	3.8	1628	0.6	2304	3.8
28 Su ○	0455	0.3	1130	3.8	1706	0.5	2343	3.8
29 M	0530	0.3	1205	3.8	1744	0.4		
30 Tu	0019	3.9	0605	0.4	1239	3.8	1822	0.4

Chart Datum: 2.02 metres below Ordnance Datum (Newlyn)

ENGLAND, EAST COAST – HARWICH

Lat 51°57′ N   Long 1°17′ E

TIMES AND HEIGHTS OF HIGH AND LOW WATERS

YEAR **1991**

TIME ZONE **UT(GMT)**
For Summer Time add ONE hour in non-shaded areas

Chart Datum symbols: ☾ Last Quarter, ● New Moon, ☽ First Quarter, ○ Full Moon

MAY

Day				
1 W	0055 3.8	0639 0.5	1310 3.8	1857 0.5
2 Th	0128 3.7	0712 0.6	1341 3.7	1930 0.6
3 F	0202 3.6	0742 0.8	1411 3.6	2002 0.7
4 Sa	0236 3.5	0815 0.9	1442 3.5	2037 0.8
5 Su	0314 3.4	0853 1.1	1518 3.4	2121 0.8
6 M	0357 3.2	0942 1.2	1603 3.2	2220 0.9
7 Tu ☾	0449 3.1	1049 1.3	1659 3.1	2337 0.9
8 W	0558 3.1	1208 1.3	1812 3.1	
9 Th	0052 0.8	0717 3.2	1319 1.1	1930 3.2
10 F	0154 0.6	0826 3.4	1416 0.9	2037 3.4
11 Sa	0247 0.5	0924 3.6	1507 0.8	2135 3.6
12 Su	0336 0.4	1014 3.8	1555 0.6	2227 3.8
13 M	0421 0.3	1102 3.9	1640 0.5	2316 3.9
14 Tu ●	0506 0.3	1147 4.0	1725 0.4	
15 W	0003 4.1	0549 0.3	1231 4.0	1810 0.3
16 Th	0048 4.1	0632 0.3	1313 4.0	1855 0.2
17 F	0134 4.1	0716 0.5	1357 3.9	1942 0.2
18 Sa	0220 4.0	0802 0.6	1440 3.7	2033 0.3
19 Su	0311 3.9	0853 0.8	1528 3.6	2129 0.3
20 M ☽	0406 3.8	0948 0.9	1623 3.5	2231 0.4
21 Tu	0508 3.6	1049 1.0	1723 3.4	2340 0.6
22 W	0615 3.5	1200 1.1	1832 3.4	
23 Th	0053 0.4	0727 3.5	1314 1.1	1944 3.4
24 F	0204 0.4	0834 3.5	1422 1.0	2051 3.5
25 Sa	0301 0.5	0932 3.6	1518 0.8	2149 3.6
26 Su	0349 0.5	1021 3.7	1606 0.7	2238 3.6
27 M	0430 0.5	1104 3.7	1649 0.6	2322 3.7
28 Tu ○	0508 0.6	1142 3.7	1729 0.6	
29 W	0001 3.7	0544 0.6	1217 3.7	1807 0.5
30 Th	0038 3.7	0618 0.7	1249 3.7	1843 0.6
31 F	0113 3.7	0650 0.8	1321 3.7	1916 0.6

JUNE

Day				
1 Sa	0147 3.6	0723 0.8	1352 3.6	1951 0.6
2 Su	0220 3.6	0758 0.9	1425 3.5	2027 0.6
3 M	0257 3.5	0836 1.0	1501 3.5	2110 0.7
4 Tu	0338 3.4	0919 1.0	1543 3.4	2156 0.7
5 W ☾	0424 3.4	1012 1.1	1655 3.5	2254 0.7
6 Th	0519 3.3	1113 1.1	1730 3.3	2358 0.7
7 F	0622 3.3	1224 1.1	1838 3.3	
8 Sa	0104 0.6	0731 3.4	1330 1.0	1947 3.4
9 Su	0205 0.6	0837 3.6	1429 0.8	2053 3.6
10 M	0301 0.5	0938 3.7	1524 0.7	2156 3.7
11 Tu	0355 0.4	1034 3.8	1617 0.5	2254 3.9
12 W ●	0445 0.4	1200 3.9	1709 0.4	2347 4.0
13 Th	0534 0.4	1214 3.9	1800 0.3	
14 F	0036 4.1	0621 0.5	1300 3.9	1848 0.3
15 Sa	0126 4.1	0706 0.5	1345 3.9	1937 0.1
16 Su	0213 4.1	0752 0.6	1430 3.9	2026 0.1
17 M	0301 4.0	0839 0.7	1517 3.8	2117 0.1
18 Tu	0352 3.9	0928 0.8	1604 3.8	2210 0.2
19 W ☽	0445 3.7	1020 0.9	1658 3.7	2308 0.4
20 Th	0542 3.6	1120 1.0	1756 3.6	
21 F	0012 0.5	0643 3.4	1229 1.1	1902 3.4
22 Sa	0121 0.6	0751 3.4	1344 1.1	2013 3.4
23 Su	0226 0.7	0857 3.4	1453 1.0	2121 3.4
24 M	0324 0.8	0953 3.5	1550 0.8	2217 3.5
25 Tu	0410 0.8	1041 3.6	1638 0.7	2305 3.6
26 W	0452 0.8	1123 3.6	1720 0.7	2346 3.6
27 Th ○	0529 0.8	1200 3.7	1757 0.6	
28 F	0024 3.7	0603 0.8	1235 3.7	1831 0.5
29 Sa	0059 3.7	0635 0.8	1307 3.7	1904 0.5
30 Su	0133 3.7	0707 0.8	1340 3.7	1938 0.5

JULY

Day				
1 M	0205 3.7	0741 0.8	1412 3.7	2013 0.6
2 Tu	0240 3.7	0818 0.8	1446 3.7	2050 0.5
3 W	0317 3.6	0856 0.9	1524 3.7	2129 0.5
4 Th	0357 3.6	0936 0.9	1606 3.6	2213 0.6
5 F ☾	0445 3.5	1026 1.0	1655 3.5	2306 0.7
6 Sa	0540 3.4	1129 1.1	1756 3.5	
7 Su	0014 0.7	0648 3.4	1245 1.1	1906 3.5
8 M	0126 0.7	0758 3.6	1355 0.9	2020 3.5
9 Tu	0233 0.7	0907 3.6	1500 0.7	2134 3.7
10 W	0335 0.6	1012 3.7	1603 0.6	2238 3.8
11 Th ●	0433 0.6	1109 3.8	1701 0.4	2336 4.0
12 F	0523 0.5	1201 3.9	1751 0.2	
13 Sa	0028 4.1	0608 0.5	1249 4.0	1839 0.1
14 Su	0116 4.2	0652 0.5	1333 4.1	1924 0.0
15 M	0201 4.2	0735 0.5	1416 4.1	2009 0.0
16 Tu	0246 4.1	0818 0.6	1458 4.0	2054 0.1
17 W	0329 3.9	0901 0.7	1541 4.0	2141 0.2
18 Th ☽	0414 3.8	0946 0.8	1626 3.8	2228 0.4
19 F	0502 3.6	1037 1.0	1716 3.6	2323 0.6
20 Sa	0556 3.4	1140 1.1	1817 3.4	
21 Su	0031 0.9	0700 3.2	1303 1.2	1935 3.2
22 M	0149 1.0	0818 3.2	1430 1.1	2057 3.3
23 Tu	0300 1.0	0927 3.3	1536 0.9	2200 3.4
24 W	0353 1.0	1020 3.5	1626 0.7	2249 3.5
25 Th	0437 0.9	1104 3.6	1706 0.7	2330 3.6
26 F ○	0513 0.9	1143 3.7	1740 0.6	
27 Sa	0007 3.7	0544 0.8	1218 3.7	1812 0.5
28 Su	0041 3.8	0615 0.7	1254 3.8	1843 0.4
29 M	0114 3.8	0646 0.6	1323 3.9	1917 0.3
30 Tu	0147 3.8	0720 0.6	1354 3.9	1951 0.3
31 W	0219 3.8	0754 0.7	1426 3.9	2023 0.4

AUGUST

Day				
1 Th	0254 3.8	0829 0.7	1500 3.8	2058 0.5
2 F	0331 3.7	0905 0.8	1538 3.8	2135 0.6
3 Sa ☾	0413 3.6	0948 1.0	1623 3.7	2221 0.7
4 Su	0505 3.5	1044 1.1	1720 3.5	2327 0.9
5 M	0610 3.4	1204 1.1	1834 3.4	
6 Tu	0053 0.9	0724 3.3	1328 1.0	1957 3.4
7 W	0212 0.9	0843 3.4	1446 0.8	2121 3.6
8 Th	0322 0.8	0956 3.6	1555 0.6	2230 3.8
9 F	0421 0.7	1057 3.8	1648 0.5	2326 4.0
10 Sa ●	0509 0.6	1147 3.9	1740 0.1	
11 Su	0015 4.1	0553 0.5	1232 4.1	1824 0.0
12 M	0100 4.2	0632 0.5	1314 4.2	1904 0.0
13 Tu	0141 4.2	0713 0.5	1353 4.2	1945 0.0
14 W	0222 4.1	0752 0.5	1433 4.2	2026 0.2
15 Th	0300 3.9	0833 0.7	1511 4.0	2105 0.4
16 F	0339 3.7	0912 0.8	1550 3.8	2148 0.5
17 Sa ☽	0419 3.5	0956 1.0	1635 3.6	2233 0.9
18 Su	0504 3.3	1051 1.2	1730 3.3	2334 1.2
19 M	0603 3.1	1215 1.3	1853 3.1	
20 Tu	0104 1.3	0730 3.0	1406 1.2	2033 3.1
21 W	0233 1.3	0857 3.2	1515 1.0	2139 3.3
22 Th	0331 1.1	0955 3.4	1603 0.8	2227 3.5
23 F	0413 1.0	1040 3.6	1641 0.6	2306 3.7
24 Sa	0448 0.9	1118 3.7	1715 0.5	2343 3.8
25 Su ○	0519 0.8	1153 3.8	1746 0.4	
26 M	0017 3.9	0549 0.7	1225 3.9	1817 0.3
27 Tu	0049 4.0	0621 0.6	1257 4.0	1849 0.3
28 W	0121 4.0	0653 0.5	1330 4.0	1921 0.3
29 Th	0155 4.0	0727 0.6	1404 4.0	1954 0.4
30 F	0229 3.9	0802 0.7	1437 4.0	2027 0.5
31 Sa	0305 3.8	0839 0.8	1514 3.9	2104 0.6

Chart Datum: 2.02 metres below Ordnance Datum (Newlyn)

ENGLAND, EAST COAST – HARWICH

Lat 51°57′ N   Long 1°17′ E

TIMES AND HEIGHTS OF HIGH AND LOW WATERS

YEAR 1991

TIME ZONE UT (GMT)
For Summer Time add ONE hour in non-shaded areas

Chart Datum: 2.02 metres below Ordnance Datum (Newlyn)

SEPTEMBER

Date	Time	m	Time	m	Time	m	Time	m
1 Su (	0345	3·7	0921	0·9	1559	3·7	2150	0·8
16 M	0416	3·3	1007	1·2	1647	3·5	2241	1·3
2 M	0434	3·5	1017	1·0	1657	3·5	2257	1·0
17 Tu	0504	3·1	1123	1·3	1801	3·0		
3 Tu	0537	3·3	1139	1·1	1814	3·4		
18 W	0007	1·5	0622	2·9	1321	1·3	1954	3·0
4 W	0028	1·1	0657	3·2	1313	1·0	1945	3·4
19 Th	0149	1·4	0812	3·0	1436	1·0	2105	3·3
5 Th	0157	1·1	0825	3·3	1437	0·8	2114	3·6
20 F	0254	1·2	0917	3·3	1527	0·8	2155	3·5
6 F	0310	0·9	0942	3·6	1545	0·5	2220	3·8
21 Sa	0338	1·0	1004	3·5	1606	0·6	2234	3·7
7 Sa	0406	0·8	1040	3·8	1638	0·3	2312	4·0
22 Su	0414	0·9	1044	3·7	1640	0·5	2311	3·9
8 Su ●	0451	0·7	1129	4·0	1722	0·1	2357	4·1
23 M ○	0445	0·7	1120	3·8	1712	0·4	2346	4·0
9 M	0530	0·6	1211	4·1	1801	0·1		
24 Tu	0519	0·6	1156	4·0	1744	0·3		
10 Tu	0039	4·2	0610	0·5	1250	4·2	1841	0·1
25 W	0021	4·1	0553	0·5	1231	4·1	1818	0·3
11 W	0117	4·1	0648	0·5	1328	4·2	1917	0·2
26 Th	0055	4·1	0627	0·5	1306	4·1	1852	0·3
12 Th	0152	4·0	0727	0·5	1405	4·2	1955	0·3
27 F	0130	4·1	0702	0·5	1341	4·1	1926	0·4
13 F	0227	3·9	0804	0·7	1440	4·0	2032	0·6
28 Sa	0205	4·0	0740	0·6	1418	4·0	2002	0·6
14 Sa	0301	3·7	0842	0·8	1518	3·8	2107	0·8
29 Su	0242	3·8	0819	0·7	1457	3·9	2043	0·7
15 Su)	0336	3·5	0919	1·0	1557	3·5	2146	1·1
30 M	0324	3·7	0905	0·8	1546	3·7	2132	1·0

OCTOBER

Date	Time	m	Time	m	Time	m	Time	m
1 Tu (	0413	3·5	1006	0·9	1647	3·5	2241	1·2
16 W	0419	3·2	1038	1·2	1709	3·1	2312	1·5
2 W	0516	3·3	1129	1·0	1804	3·4		
17 Th	0519	3·0	1210	1·2	1842	3·0		
3 Th	0010	1·3	0638	3·2	1300	0·9	1937	3·4
18 F	0043	1·5	0653	3·0	1334	1·0	2011	3·2
4 F	0137	1·2	0805	3·4	1425	0·7	2100	3·6
19 Sa	0157	1·3	0818	3·2	1433	0·8	2107	3·5
5 Sa	0250	1·0	0921	3·6	1528	0·4	2202	3·9
20 Su	0249	1·1	0915	3·5	1518	0·7	2153	3·7
6 Su	0343	0·9	1017	3·8	1617	0·2	2251	4·0
21 M	0331	0·9	1002	3·7	1557	0·5	2233	3·9
7 M ●	0427	0·7	1105	4·0	1658	0·2	2334	4·1
22 Tu	0409	0·8	1042	3·9	1635	0·4	2312	4·0
8 Tu	0506	0·6	1147	4·1	1736	0·2		
23 W ○	0447	0·6	1123	4·0	1712	0·4	2350	4·1
9 W	0014	4·1	0546	0·5	1225	4·2	1812	0·3
24 Th	0525	0·5	1203	4·1	1749	0·4		
10 Th	0049	4·0	0624	0·5	1302	4·1	1849	0·4
25 F	0029	4·1	0603	0·5	1242	4·2	1827	0·4
11 F	0123	4·0	0703	0·6	1338	4·1	1924	0·6
26 Sa	0107	4·1	0642	0·5	1323	4·1	1904	0·5
12 Sa	0157	3·8	0740	0·7	1413	3·9	1958	0·8
27 Su	0145	4·0	0829	0·5	1404	4·1	1944	0·7
13 Su	0227	3·7	0813	0·8	1449	3·7	2032	1·0
28 M	0225	3·8	0809	0·6	1449	3·9	2030	0·8
14 M	0300	3·5	0849	1·0	1528	3·5	2108	1·2
29 Tu	0310	3·7	0900	0·7	1541	3·8	2124	1·0
15 Tu)	0335	3·4	0932	1·1	1612	3·3	2157	1·4
30 W	0400	3·5	1003	0·7	1641	3·6	2228	1·2
31 Th	0504	3·4	1118	0·8	1756	3·5	2346	1·3

NOVEMBER

Date	Time	m	Time	m	Time	m	Time	m
1 F	0618	3·4	1241	0·7	1917	3·5		
16 Sa	0544	3·2	1225	1·0	1849	3·2		
2 Sa	0107	1·2	0737	3·4	1359	0·6	2032	3·6
17 Su	0050	1·3	0700	3·3	1330	0·8	2001	3·4
3 Su	0219	1·1	0850	3·6	1503	0·5	2134	3·8
18 M	0151	1·1	0811	3·4	1425	0·7	2100	3·6
4 M	0315	1·0	0949	3·8	1552	0·4	2224	3·9
19 Tu	0244	1·0	0911	3·6	1514	0·6	2150	3·8
5 Tu	0403	0·8	1038	3·9	1634	0·5	2308	3·9
20 W	0331	0·8	1003	3·8	1600	0·5	2237	3·9
6 W ●	0445	0·7	1122	4·0	1711	0·5	2347	3·9
21 Th ○	0417	0·7	1052	4·0	1642	0·5	2323	4·0
7 Th	0526	0·6	1203	4·0	1747	0·5		
22 F	0501	0·6	1139	4·1	1726	0·5		
8 F	0024	3·9	0605	0·6	1241	4·0	1824	0·6
23 Sa	0007	4·1	0544	0·5	1225	4·2	1807	0·5
9 Sa	0057	3·9	0643	0·6	1316	3·9	1859	0·7
24 Su	0049	4·0	0629	0·4	1310	4·2	1849	0·6
10 Su	0130	3·8	0720	0·7	1352	3·8	1931	0·9
25 M	0131	4·0	0716	0·4	1355	4·1	1934	0·7
11 M	0201	3·7	0754	0·8	1427	3·6	2004	1·0
26 Tu	0215	3·9	0804	0·4	1443	4·0	2022	0·8
12 Tu	0233	3·6	0829	0·9	1504	3·5	2040	1·2
27 W	0301	3·8	0856	0·4	1535	3·9	2112	0·9
13 W	0307	3·5	0910	0·9	1545	3·4	2125	1·3
28 Th (	0352	3·7	0953	0·5	1633	3·7	2210	1·1
14 Th	0349	3·4	1003	1·0	1633	3·3	2224	1·4
29 F	0448	3·6	1058	0·5	1736	3·6	2315	1·2
15 F	0440	3·3	1112	1·0	1734	3·2	2337	1·4
30 Sa	0553	3·5	1210	0·6	1845	3·5		

DECEMBER

Date	Time	m	Time	m	Time	m	Time	m
1 Su	0028	1·2	0702	3·5	1324	0·6	1955	3·5
16 M	0603	3·4	1231	0·8	1856	3·4		
2 M	0142	1·1	0813	3·6	1430	0·6	2101	3·6
17 Tu	0056	1·2	0714	3·4	1335	0·8	2005	3·5
3 Tu	0247	1·0	0921	3·6	1525	0·6	2157	3·7
18 W	0159	1·0	0823	3·5	1434	0·7	2108	3·6
4 W	0342	0·9	1016	3·7	1612	0·7	2244	3·7
19 Th	0257	0·9	0928	3·7	1529	0·6	2206	3·8
5 Th	0430	0·8	1104	3·8	1652	0·7	2326	3·8
20 F	0352	0·7	1027	3·9	1620	0·6	2259	3·9
6 F ●	0513	0·7	1146	3·8	1729	0·7		
21 Sa ○	0444	0·5	1122	4·0	1709	0·6	2349	3·9
7 Sa	0004	3·8	0554	0·6	1225	3·8	1805	0·8
22 Su	0533	0·4	1212	4·1	1754	0·5		
8 Su	0039	3·8	0631	0·6	1302	3·8	1839	0·8
23 M	0036	4·0	0622	0·3	1300	4·2	1839	0·5
9 M	0112	3·7	0706	0·6	1335	3·7	1912	0·9
24 Tu	0121	4·0	0709	0·2	1348	4·2	1924	0·6
10 Tu	0142	3·7	0740	0·7	1409	3·7	1944	0·9
25 W	0206	4·0	0757	0·1	1436	4·1	2009	0·6
11 W	0215	3·6	0813	0·7	1444	3·6	2019	1·0
26 Th	0250	3·9	0846	0·2	1524	4·0	2056	0·7
12 Th	0249	3·6	0851	0·7	1521	3·5	2100	1·0
27 F	0336	3·9	0935	0·2	1613	3·8	2145	0·9
13 F	0327	3·6	0935	0·8	1603	3·5	2145	1·1
28 Sa (	0426	3·8	1030	0·4	1708	3·5	2241	1·0
14 Sa	0410	3·5	1024	0·8	1651	3·4	2240	1·2
29 Su	0520	3·7	1132	0·6	1807	3·5	2346	1·1
15 Su	0501	3·4	1123	0·8	1749	3·3	2346	1·2
30 M	0624	3·5	1242	0·7	1913	3·4		
31 Tu	0103	1·1	0737	3·4	1355	0·8	2025	3·4

RIVER ORWELL *continued*

TIDES
Pin Mill +0100 Dover; Ipswich +0115 Dover; ML 2.4;
Duration 0555; Zone 0 (GMT)

Standard Port HARWICH (←)

Times				Height (metres)			
HW		LW		MHWS	MHWN	MLWN	MLWS
0000	0600	0000	0600	4.0	3.4	1.1	0.4
1200	1800	1200	1800				
Differences IPSWICH							
+0015	+0025	0000	+0010	+0.2	0.0	−0.1	−0.1

SHELTER
Good. Entrance and river well marked. Anchorages above
Shotley Pt on W side, or in Buttermans Bay. No facilities
for yachts at Felixstowe. Berths available by arrangement
in Suffolk Yacht Harbour, Woolverstone Marina and Fox
Marina (Ipswich). For berths in Ipswich Dock it is essential
to contact Ipswich Port Radio before arrival (Tel. 53999) or
call *Wherry Quay* Ch 14. Then call Ipswich Port Radio
(Ch 14) for lock to open. Keep clear of commercial
shipping at all times.

NAVIGATION
Waypoint Shotley Spit S cardinal Bn, Q(6) + LFl 15s,
51°57'.22N 01°17'.70E, at river entrance. Main danger is
the large amount of merchant shipping, ferries etc
entering and leaving Harwich, Felixstowe and passing up
river to Ipswich. Ipswich dock opens from HW−1 to HW
but mainly for commercial vessels.
There is a speed limit of 6 knots in the R Orwell.

LIGHTS AND MARKS
Entrance between Shotley Spit Lt Bn Q(6) + L Fl 15s to
port and Walton buoy, Fl (3) G 10s to stbd. For detail see
R Stour Chartlet. (←) 10.4.12.
Suffolk Yacht Harbour approach marked by four Bns. Ldg
Lts Front Iso Y, Rear Oc Y 4s. Woolverstone Marina Lts 2
FR (vert). R and G Lts control entry to Ipswich Dock
(H24).

New Cut, W of Ipswich Dock, 3 FR (vert) indicates cut
closed.
Bridge Lts − Centre FY

| | No 9 Pier 2 FR (vert) | shown up and |
| | No 10 Pier 2 FG (vert) | down stream. |

RADIO TELEPHONE
Call: *Ipswich Port Radio* VHF Ch **14** 16; 12 **14** (H24). Once
above the bridge keep constant listening watch on Ch 14.
Fox Marina, Woolverstone Marina, Suffolk Yacht Harbour
Ch **80**.(0800 − 1730 LT).

TELEPHONE (0473)
Hr Mr Orwell Navigation Service 231010; CG & MRSC
Frinton-on-Sea 675518; ⌗ (0473) 219481; Marinecall
0898 500 455; Police 233000; Ⓗ 712238.

FACILITIES
EC Chelmondiston - Thursday; Ipswich - Wednesday;
PIN MILL/WOOLVERSTONE: **Woolverstone Marina**
(300 + 22 visitors) ☎ 84206, Slip, P (cans), D, FW, ME, El,
Sh, AC, Gas, Gaz, ▣, C (25 ton mobile), CH, V; **Royal
Harwich YC** ☎ 84319, R, Bar; **Pin Mill SC** ☎ 84271;
J. Ward ☎ 84276, Slip, M, (10 visitors), D, L, FW, ME,
El, Sh, CH, AB, V, R, Bar; **F. A. Webb BY** ☎ 84291,
ME, El, Sh, Slip.
Town ✉; Ⓑ (Ipswich); ⇌ (Ipswich); ✈ (Cambridge).
LEVINGTON: **Suffolk Yacht Harbour** (390 + 10 visitors)
☎ Nacton 240, Slip, P, D, FW, ME, El, Ⓔ, Sh, C (9 ton),
BH (10 ton), CH, V, Gas, Gaz, AC, SM, Bar Access H24;
J. Parker ☎ 88878, SM; **Bob Spalding** ☎ 88674, ME.
Town ✉; Ⓑ (Felixstowe); ⇌ (bus to Ipswich);
✈ (Cambridge or Norwich).
IPSWICH: **Fox's Marina** (100 + some visitors) ☎ 689111
FW, AC, D, Gas, Gaz, BH (26 and 44 ton), C (7 ton),
ME, El, Ⓔ, Sh, Bar, CH, ACA; **Neptune Marina**
(18 visitors) ☎ 34578, Sh, ME, FW; **Wherry Quay Yacht
(Oysterworld)** (30) ☎ 53999, AB, M, FW, AC, R, Access
via lock (HW−2 to HW+½; **Orwell YC** ☎ 55288, Slip,
L, FW, Bar; **Orwell Auto Electrics** ☎ 49624, El, Ⓔ;
Austin Farrar ☎ 622666, SM.
Town ✉; Ⓑ; ⇌; ✈ (Cambridge or Norwich).

RIVER DEBEN   10-4-14

Suffolk

CHARTS
Admiralty 2693, 2052; Stanford 3, 6; Imray C28, Y15; OS 169

TIDES
Woodbridge Haven +0025 Dover; Woodbridge +0125 Dover; ML 2.0; Duration 0635; Zone 0 (GMT)

Standard Port HARWICH (←)

Times				Height (metres)			
HW		LW		MHWS	MHWN	MLWN	MLWS
0000	0600	0000	0600	4.0	3.4	1.1	0.4
1200	1800	1200	1800				

Differences WOODBRIDGE HAVEN

+0010	0000	+0010	+0010	−0.3	−0.5	−0.1	+0.1

WOODBRIDGE

+0055	+0030	+0055	+0015	0.0	−0.3	−0.2	0.0

SHELTER
Good at all times in yacht harbour at Woodbridge. Also good at anchorages up the river, above Horse Sand, at Ramsholt, at Waldringfield and at Woodbridge. Entrance gets dangerously choppy with strong on-shore winds and is only 1 ca wide.

NAVIGATION
Waypoint Woodbridge Haven (safe water) buoy, 51°58'.36N 01°24'.17E, 150°/330° approx from/to buoyed channel entrance (shifts), 0.40M. There is a shifting shingle bar at the entrance but the channel is well buoyed and marked. Beware the Horse Sand just up river of Felixstowe ferry. It is entirely free of commercial traffic. From Wilford Bridge to the entrance of Creek at lower end of Ramsholt Reach, speed limit is 8 kn.

LIGHTS AND MARKS
If a pilot is required, dip the burgee when passing Martello Tower T. The Woodbridge Haven Buoy is unlit. Leading marks, Front W triangle on R background, Rear R rectangle, are moved according to the channel. There are 2 FR (vert) on Felixstowe side, 2 FG (vert) on Bardsey side.

RADIO TELEPHONE
Tide Mill Yacht Harbour VHF Ch **80** Pilot Ch 08.

TELEPHONE (0394 — for 4 fig nos 03943)
Hr Mr 5118; CG Aldeburgh 2779; MRSC Frinton-on-Sea 675518; Pilot Felixstowe 283469; ⌗ (0473) 219481; Marinecall 0898 500 455; Police 3377; Dr 2046.

FACILITIES
EC Wednesday.
WOODBRIDGE: **Tide Mill Yacht Harbour** (150+50 visitors) ☎ 385745, Slip, D, L, FW, ME, El, Sh, C (10 ton), AC, V, Access HW−3½ to HW+2½; **Granary Yacht Harbour** ☎ 36327, CH, ME, Slip, C, Sh; **Whisstocks BY** ☎ 4222, Slip, MD, FW, ME, El, Sh, C (20 ton), CH, V; **Eversons BY** ☎ 4358, Access HW∓4, Slip, M, D, ME, El, Sh, C (6 ton), CH; **Frank Knights BY** ☎ 2318, M, D, FW, ME, Sh; **Robertsons** ☎ 2305, Slip, M, D, L, Sh, CH; **Small Craft Deliveries** ☎ 2600, ACA; **Webb Bros** ☎ 2183, Gas; **Town** P, D, L (opp Everson BY), FW, CH, V, R, Bar, ⊠; Ⓑ; ⇌; ✈ (Cambridge or Norwich).
RAMSHOLT **George Collins** ☎ Shottisham 229, M, FW, ME, Bar;
WALDRINGFIELD **Waldringfield BY** ☎ Waldringfield 260, C, Slip, BH (40 ton), D, L, FW, V, Bar;
FELIXSTOWE FERRY QUAY Slip, M, L, FW, ME, El, Sh, CH, V, R, Bar; **Felixstowe Ferry SC** ☎ 283785; **Felixstowe Ferry BY** (200) ☎ 282173, ME, El, Sh, CH, Gas.

RIVER ORE/ALDE   10-4-15

Suffolk

CHARTS
Admiralty 2695, 1543, 2052, 2693; Stanford 6, 3; Imray Y15, C28; OS 169

TIDES
Ent. +0010 Dover Slaughden Quay +0155 Dover; ML 1.5; Duration 0620; Zone 0 (GMT).

Standard Port LOWESTOFT (→)

Times				Height (metres)			
HW		LW		MHWS	MHWN	MLWN	MLWS
0300	0900	0200	0800	2.4	2.1	1.0	0.5
1500	2100	1400	2000				

Differences ALDEBURGH

+0120	+0120	+0120	+0110	+0.4	+0.6	0.0	0.0

ORFORDNESS

+0135	+0135	+0135	+0125	+0.4	+0.6	−0.1	0.0

Standard Port HARWICH (←)

Times				Height (metres)			
HW		LW		MHWS	MHWN	MLWN	MLWS
0000	0600	0000	0600	4.0	3.4	1.1	0.4
1200	1800	1200	1800				

Differences ORFORD HAVEN BAR

−0025	−0025	−0040	−0015	−0.8	−0.8	−0.2	−0.1

ORFORD QUAY

+0021	+0021	+0053	+0053	−1.4	−1.3	+0.2	0.0

RIVER ORE/ALDE *continued*

Differences at Slaughden Quay are +0115 on Harwich:
Snape Bridge +0315 on Harwich

SHELTER

R Ore changes name to R Alde between Orford and
Aldeburgh, and is navigable up to Snape. Good
anchorages where shown, also between Slaughden Quay
and Martello Tower and at Iken. Upper reaches of river
are shallow and winding, and although marked by withies
these may be damaged. Landing prohibited on MoD land
and on Havergate Island bird sanctuary.

NAVIGATION

Waypoint Orford Haven (safe water) buoy, 52°01'.78N
01°27'.98E, although this is moved from time to time
dependent on changes to the bar. The bar shifts after
onshore gales and is dangerous in rough or confused
seas. Ebb runs up to 6 kn. Up to date plan of entrance
available from Orford Chandlery or Secretary, Aldeburgh
YC. In absence of local information do not enter before
half flood. Beware shoals off the orange tipped Bn on W
shore just inside entrance (keep well to E side), and S to
SW of Dove Pt (the most SW point of Havergate Island).

LIGHTS AND MARKS

Shingle Street, about 0.2M S of entrance, is located by a
Martello Tower and CG Stn. Buoy and Bn are moved
according to channel.

RADIO TELEPHONE

VHF Ch 16; 67 (H24).

TELEPHONE (Aldeburgh, 0728; Orford and Shottisham, 0394)

Hr Mr Aldeburgh 452896 and Orford c/o 450210; MRSC
Frinton-on-Sea 675518; CG Aldeburgh 452061 and Shingle
Street (week ends, bad weather), Shottisham 411558;
⌗ (0473) 219481; Marinecall 0898 500 455; Police 452716;
Dr Orford 450315, 450369, Shottisham 411214, and
Aldeburgh 452027.

FACILITIES

ORFORD. EC Wed; **Orford Quay** Slip, AB (short-stay), M,
L, FW, C (5 ton), SC, ⌗, Bar; **Orford Chandlery**
☎ 450210, CH, D (cans), Gas, Gaz, R, Sh (small craft);
Orford SC Slip, L, FW. **Village** (¼M). P and D (cans),
✉, V, R, Bar, ⇌ (occ. bus to Woodbridge).
ALDEBURGH. EC Wed; **Slaughden Quay** L, FW, ⌗;
R. F. Upson ☎ 452896, Slip, M, D (cans), ME, Sh;
D. G. Cable ☎ Leiston 0119, M, Sh; **Aldeburgh BY**
☎ 452019, Slip, Gas, Gaz, P, D, ME, Sh, CH; **Aldeburgh
YC** ☎ 452562, Slip, L, FW, Bar, R, D, P, CH. **Town**
(¾ M), V, R, Bar, ✉; Ⓑ; ⇌ (bus to Wickham Market);
✈ (Norwich).

SOUTHWOLD   10-4-16
Suffolk

CHARTS

Admiralty 2695, 1543; Stanford 3; Imray C28; OS 156

TIDES

−0105 Dover; ML 1.3; Duration 0620; Zone 0 (GMT).

Standard Port LOWESTOFT (→)

Times				Height (metres)			
HW		LW		MHWS	MHWN	MLWN	MLWS
0300	0900	0200	0800	2.4	2.1	1.0	0.5
1500	2100	1400	2000				

Differences SOUTHWOLD
+0035 +0035 +0040 +0030 +0.1   +0.1 −0.1 −0.1

SHELTER

Good shelter and a stage, 100m beyond the LB on N bank
opposite the Harbour Inn, is reserved for visiting
yachtsmen. In strong winds from S through E to N
entrance is dangerous.

NAVIGATION

Waypoint 52°18'.06N 01°41'.80E, 135°/315° from/to
North Pier Lt, 1.0M. Entry should be made on the flood
since the ebb runs up to 5 kn. Some shoals are
unpredictable. A sand and shingle bar lies off the harbour
entrance, whose extent varies. Obtain details of approach
channels from Hr Mr before entering or ask for a pilot
(Ch 12 or 09 or Tel. 724712). Shoal forms inside N pier.
Unlit low bridge ¾ M upstream of entrance.

SOUTHWOLD HARBOUR

Depths in metres

⚓ Visitors berths at pontoon ¼M up river on Stbd. side past LB
house and Hr Mr office

LIGHTS AND MARKS

N Pier Lt & Lt Ho in line - 010°
N Pier Lt & Water Tr (conspic) - 342°
N Pier Lt & Walberswick Church - 268°
Harbour mouth opens on - 300°
Two red flags or 3Fl R 1.5s (vert) at N pier means entry
inadvisable or shipping movements in harbour.
NOTE: Lt Ho is in Southwold town, about 1 M N from
harbour entrance, Fl (4) WR 20s 37m 22/20M; vis R
(intens) 204°-220°, W220°-001°, R001°-032°.

RADIO TELEPHONE

Call: *Southwold Port Radio* VHF Ch 12; 16 (0800-1800
LT). Pilots Ch 12 09.

TELEPHONE (0502)

Hr Mr 724712; CG 722360; MRCC Great Yarmouth 851338;
⌗ (0473) 219481; Marinecall 0898 500 455; Weather
Norwich 660779; Police 722666; Dr 722326;
Ⓗ 723333.

FACILITIES

EC Wednesday (both Southwold and Walberswick);
Hr Mr Slip, L, FW, Sh, C (10 ton), AB; **Harbour Marine
Services** ☎ 724721 D, CH, ME, Sh, Slip; **Harbour Inn**
(on quay), Bar; **Southwold SC; Jeckells** ☎ 565007, SM;
Town (¾ M) V, R, Gas, Gaz, Kos, ✉; Ⓑ;
⇌ (bus to Brampton or Darsham); ✈ (Norwich).

LOWESTOFT   10-4-17
Suffolk

CHARTS

Admiralty 1536, 1543; Stanford 3; Imray C28; OS 156/134

TIDES

−0145 Dover; ML 1.6; Duration 0620; Zone 0 (GMT).
Lowestoft is a standard port and tidal predictions for each
day of the year are given below.

SHELTER

Harbour is always available. Yacht basin in the SW
corner. Yachts lie in 3 tiers on the North side (bad in E
winds). Yacht basin is controlled by Royal Norfolk &
Suffolk YC. Mooring on inner side of S Pier is dangerous
due to bad state of the pier. Bridge to inner harbour (and
Lake Lothing) opens (LT)

October to April
Mon – Sat	0700	0930	1900	2100	
Sunday	0800	0930	1400	1900	2100
May to September					
Mon – Sat	0700	0930	1900	2100	
Sunday	0730	0930	1400	1900	2100

and also when ships pass through. Bridge clearance 2.2m
at MHWS. Small craft may pass under the bridge at any
time but VHF Ch 14 contact advisable (see 10.4.22).

ENGLAND, EAST COAST – LOWESTOFT

Lat 52°28′ N   Long 1°45′ E

TIMES AND HEIGHTS OF HIGH AND LOW WATERS

YEAR 1991

TIME ZONE UT (GMT)
For Summer Time add ONE hour in non-shaded areas

JANUARY

Day	Time	m		Day	Time	m
1 Tu	0328 / 0928 / 1541 / 2137	0.5 / 2.5 / 0.7 / 2.6		**16** W	0350 / 1007 / 1524 / 2143	0.7 / 2.2 / 0.9 / 2.4
2 W	0420 / 1022 / 1630 / 2224	0.3 / 2.5 / 0.7 / 2.6		**17** Th	0426 / 1039 / 1601 / 2216	0.6 / 2.2 / 0.8 / 2.5
3 Th	0507 / 1115 / 1715 / 2309	0.1 / 2.4 / 0.7 / 2.7		**18** F	0500 / 1109 / 1639 / 2254	0.5 / 2.2 / 0.7 / 2.5
4 F	0552 / 1203 / 1758 / 2354	0.1 / 2.4 / 0.8 / 2.6		**19** Sa	0535 / 1143 / 1715 / 2330	0.4 / 2.2 / 0.7 / 2.5
5 Sa	0637 / 1252 / 1837	0.2 / 2.3 / 0.9		**20** Su	0611 / 1216 / 1752	0.4 / 2.1 / 0.8
6 Su	0039 / 0722 / 1343 / 1916	2.6 / 0.3 / 2.1 / 0.9		**21** M	0007 / 0646 / 1254 / 1830	2.5 / 0.5 / 2.1 / 0.8
7 M ☾	0128 / 0807 / 1435 / 2000	2.5 / 0.5 / 2.1 / 1.0		**22** Tu	0045 / 0724 / 1339 / 1913	2.4 / 0.5 / 2.0 / 0.9
8 Tu ☽	0220 / 0856 / 1533 / 2050	2.4 / 0.7 / 2.0 / 1.1		**23** W ☽	0126 / 0807 / 1433 / 2001	2.4 / 0.6 / 2.0 / 1.0
9 W	0318 / 0956 / 1639 / 2158	2.3 / 0.8 / 2.0 / 1.2		**24** Th	0218 / 0901 / 1541 / 2105	2.3 / 0.7 / 2.0 / 1.1
10 Th	0428 / 1105 / 1745 / 2335	2.2 / 0.9 / 2.1 / 1.2		**25** F	0333 / 1013 / 1650 / 2231	2.2 / 0.8 / 2.0 / 1.1
11 F	0546 / 1213 / 1845	2.1 / 1.0 / 2.1		**26** Sa	0500 / 1128 / 1754 / 2358	2.2 / 0.8 / 2.1 / 1.0
12 Sa	0058 / 0707 / 1307 / 1935	1.1 / 2.1 / 1.0 / 2.2		**27** Su	0615 / 1235 / 1850	2.2 / 0.8 / 2.2
13 Su	0156 / 0809 / 1348 / 2015	1.0 / 2.1 / 1.0 / 2.2		**28** M	0116 / 0726 / 1339 / 1945	0.8 / 2.3 / 0.8 / 2.3
14 M	0239 / 0856 / 1420 / 2045	0.9 / 2.1 / 1.0 / 2.3		**29** Tu	0226 / 0831 / 1439 / 2035	0.5 / 2.3 / 0.7 / 2.4
15 Tu ●	0315 / 0933 / 1450 / 2113	0.8 / 2.2 / 0.9 / 2.3		**30** W ○	0320 / 0928 / 1530 / 2122	0.3 / 2.4 / 0.7 / 2.5
				31 Th	0407 / 1015 / 1615 / 2207	0.1 / 2.4 / 0.6 / 2.6

FEBRUARY

Day	Time	m		Day	Time	m
1 F	0450 / 1100 / 1654 / 2252	0.0 / 2.4 / 0.6 / 2.7		**16** Sa	0437 / 1046 / 1624 / 2235	0.3 / 2.2 / 0.6 / 2.5
2 Sa	0531 / 1141 / 1733 / 2333	0.0 / 2.3 / 0.6 / 2.7		**17** Su	0511 / 1116 / 1700 / 2311	0.3 / 2.2 / 0.6 / 2.5
3 Su	0613 / 1222 / 1809	0.1 / 2.2 / 0.7		**18** M	0545 / 1150 / 1733 / 2346	0.3 / 2.2 / 0.6 / 2.5
4 M	0015 / 0650 / 1303 / 1843	2.6 / 0.3 / 2.1 / 0.8		**19** Tu	0618 / 1226 / 1809	0.4 / 2.1 / 0.7
5 Tu	0058 / 0730 / 1346 / 1920	2.5 / 0.5 / 2.0 / 0.9		**20** W	0024 / 0654 / 1305 / 1848	2.5 / 0.5 / 2.1 / 0.7
6 W ☾	0145 / 0809 / 1435 / 2003	2.3 / 0.7 / 2.0 / 1.0		**21** Th ☽	0107 / 0735 / 1354 / 1937	2.4 / 0.6 / 2.0 / 0.8
7 Th	0241 / 0856 / 1533 / 2100	2.2 / 1.0 / 2.0 / 1.1		**22** F	0203 / 0830 / 1456 / 2043	2.2 / 0.8 / 2.0 / 0.9
8 F	0350 / 1001 / 1641 / 2245	2.0 / 1.1 / 2.0 / 1.2		**23** Sa	0324 / 0943 / 1613 / 2215	2.1 / 0.9 / 2.0 / 0.9
9 Sa	0516 / 1137 / 1750	2.0 / 1.2 / 2.0		**24** Su	0454 / 1111 / 1724 / 2352	2.1 / 1.0 / 2.0 / 0.8
10 Su	0043 / 0654 / 1246 / 1858	1.1 / 2.0 / 1.1 / 2.0		**25** M	0616 / 1228 / 1828	2.1 / 1.0 / 2.1
11 M	0139 / 0758 / 1331 / 1945	1.0 / 2.0 / 1.1 / 2.1		**26** Tu	0115 / 0735 / 1333 / 1928	0.6 / 2.2 / 0.9 / 2.1
12 Tu	0218 / 0843 / 1405 / 2018	0.8 / 2.1 / 1.0 / 2.2		**27** W	0215 / 0833 / 1426 / 2020	0.4 / 2.3 / 0.8 / 2.4
13 W	0254 / 0918 / 1435 / 2050	0.7 / 2.1 / 0.9 / 2.3		**28** Th ○	0303 / 0918 / 1511 / 2107	0.2 / 2.3 / 0.6 / 2.5
14 Th ●	0328 / 0948 / 1511 / 2124	0.5 / 2.2 / 0.7 / 2.4				

MARCH

Day	Time	m		Day	Time	m
1 F	0346 / 0958 / 1552 / 2150	0.0 / 2.3 / 0.6 / 2.6		**16** Sa ●	0331 / 0946 / 1524 / 2135	0.3 / 2.2 / 0.6 / 2.5
2 Sa	0428 / 1037 / 1630 / 2231	0.0 / 2.3 / 0.5 / 2.6		**17** Su	0407 / 1016 / 1601 / 2213	0.3 / 2.3 / 0.5 / 2.5
3 Su	0507 / 1113 / 1705 / 2311	0.1 / 2.3 / 0.5 / 2.6		**18** M	0443 / 1050 / 1639 / 2250	0.3 / 2.3 / 0.5 / 2.5
4 M	0543 / 1150 / 1739 / 2350	0.2 / 2.2 / 0.6 / 2.5		**19** Tu	0518 / 1124 / 1715 / 2330	0.3 / 2.3 / 0.5 / 2.5
5 Tu	0616 / 1226 / 1811	0.4 / 2.2 / 0.7		**20** W	0552 / 1200 / 1752	0.4 / 2.2 / 0.6
6 W	0030 / 0648 / 1301 / 1846	2.4 / 0.7 / 2.1 / 0.8		**21** Th	0009 / 0628 / 1239 / 1837	2.4 / 0.6 / 2.2 / 0.6
7 Th	0113 / 0720 / 1341 / 1926	2.2 / 0.9 / 2.0 / 0.9		**22** F	0058 / 0711 / 1326 / 1931	2.3 / 0.7 / 2.1 / 0.7
8 F	0207 / 0758 / 1430 / 2016	2.1 / 1.0 / 2.0 / 1.0		**23** Sa ☽	0201 / 0809 / 1424 / 2041	2.2 / 0.9 / 2.0 / 0.8
9 Sa	0316 / 0850 / 1533 / 2135	1.9 / 1.2 / 1.9 / 1.1		**24** Su	0328 / 0926 / 1539 / 2213	2.1 / 1.1 / 2.0 / 0.8
10 Su	0445 / 1035 / 1641	1.9 / 1.3 / 1.9		**25** M	0501 / 1100 / 1658 / 2345	2.1 / 1.1 / 2.0 / 0.6
11 M	0007 / 0622 / 1215 / 1748	1.0 / 1.9 / 1.2 / 1.9		**26** Tu	0626 / 1216 / 1807	2.1 / 1.0 / 2.1
12 Tu	0101 / 0730 / 1300 / 1850	0.9 / 2.0 / 1.1 / 2.0		**27** W	0058 / 0731 / 1316 / 1909	0.4 / 2.2 / 0.9 / 2.2
13 W	0143 / 0815 / 1333 / 1937	0.7 / 2.1 / 1.0 / 2.1		**28** Th	0154 / 0820 / 1405 / 2001	0.3 / 2.2 / 0.8 / 2.4
14 Th	0218 / 0848 / 1409 / 2018	0.6 / 2.1 / 0.8 / 2.2		**29** F	0241 / 0900 / 1446 / 2048	0.2 / 2.3 / 0.7 / 2.5
15 F	0254 / 0916 / 1446 / 2056	0.4 / 2.2 / 0.7 / 2.4		**30** Sa ○	0322 / 0935 / 1528 / 2130	0.1 / 2.3 / 0.6 / 2.5
				31 Su	0401 / 1011 / 1605 / 2211	0.2 / 2.3 / 0.5 / 2.6

APRIL

Day	Time	m		Day	Time	m
1 M	0437 / 1045 / 1641 / 2248	0.3 / 2.3 / 0.5 / 2.5		**16** Tu	0413 / 1022 / 1620 / 2231	0.3 / 2.4 / 0.5 / 2.5
2 Tu	0511 / 1116 / 1713 / 2326	0.3 / 2.3 / 0.6 / 2.4		**17** W	0450 / 1100 / 1703 / 2315	0.4 / 2.3 / 0.5 / 2.5
3 W	0539 / 1148 / 1746	0.6 / 2.2 / 0.7		**18** Th	0530 / 1137 / 1748	0.5 / 2.3 / 0.5
4 Th	0003 / 0605 / 1216 / 1818	2.3 / 0.8 / 2.2 / 0.7		**19** F	0001 / 0611 / 1218 / 1841	2.4 / 0.7 / 2.3 / 0.5
5 F	0045 / 0631 / 1250 / 1858	2.1 / 1.0 / 2.1 / 0.8		**20** Sa	0056 / 0700 / 1305 / 1939	2.3 / 0.9 / 2.2 / 0.5
6 Sa	0137 / 0707 / 1333 / 1948	2.0 / 1.1 / 2.0 / 0.9		**21** Su ☽	0207 / 0800 / 1403 / 2045	2.2 / 1.0 / 2.1 / 0.6
7 Su ☾	0246 / 0800 / 1431 / 2056	1.9 / 1.2 / 2.0 / 1.0		**22** M	0335 / 0911 / 1515 / 2203	2.1 / 1.2 / 2.1 / 0.6
8 M	0409 / 0916 / 1541 / 2246	1.9 / 1.3 / 1.9 / 1.0		**23** Tu	0500 / 1035 / 1630 / 2322	2.1 / 1.2 / 2.1 / 0.5
9 Tu	0528 / 1109 / 1650	1.9 / 1.3 / 1.9		**24** W	0611 / 1148 / 1741	2.1 / 1.1 / 2.2
10 W	0005 / 0639 / 1211 / 1754	0.8 / 2.0 / 1.1 / 2.0		**25** Th	0030 / 0711 / 1246 / 1846	0.4 / 2.2 / 1.0 / 2.2
11 Th	0052 / 0730 / 1254 / 1850	0.7 / 2.0 / 1.0 / 2.1		**26** F	0126 / 0756 / 1337 / 1941	0.4 / 2.2 / 0.8 / 2.3
12 F	0135 / 0807 / 1335 / 1941	0.5 / 2.1 / 0.8 / 2.2		**27** Sa	0213 / 0835 / 1422 / 2028	0.3 / 2.2 / 0.7 / 2.4
13 Sa	0215 / 0839 / 1415 / 2024	0.4 / 2.2 / 0.7 / 2.4		**28** Su ○	0254 / 0911 / 1503 / 2111	0.4 / 2.3 / 0.6 / 2.4
14 Su ●	0254 / 0913 / 1458 / 2107	0.3 / 2.3 / 0.6 / 2.5		**29** M	0331 / 0943 / 1543 / 2150	0.4 / 2.3 / 0.6 / 2.4
15 M	0333 / 0946 / 1539 / 2148	0.3 / 2.3 / 0.5 / 2.5		**30** Tu	0407 / 1016 / 1620 / 2230	0.6 / 2.3 / 0.6 / 2.4

Chart Datum: 1.50 metres below Ordnance Datum (Newlyn)

ENGLAND, EAST COAST – LOWESTOFT

Lat 52°28′ N   Long 1°45′ E

TIMES AND HEIGHTS OF HIGH AND LOW WATERS   YEAR **1991**

TIME ZONE **UT(GMT)**
For Summer Time add ONE
hour in non-shaded areas

4

MAY

Day	Time	m	Day	Time	m
1 W	0435 / 1046 / 1656 / 2307	0.7 / 2.3 / 0.6 / 2.3	16 Th	0430 / 1037 / 1700 / 2305	0.5 / 2.5 / 0.4 / 2.5
2 Th	0500 / 1113 / 1730 / 2345	0.8 / 2.3 / 0.7 / 2.2	17 F	0516 / 1118 / 1752 / 2358	0.6 / 2.4 / 0.3 / 2.4
3 F	0522 / 1141 / 1803	0.8 / 2.3 / 0.7	18 Sa	0603 / 1203 / 1843	0.8 / 2.4 / 0.3
4 Sa	0026 / 0552 / 1213 / 1845	2.1 / 1.0 / 2.2 / 0.7	19 Su	0058 / 0654 / 1252 / 1937	2.3 / 0.9 / 2.4 / 0.3
5 Su	0116 / 0633 / 1256 / 1931	2.0 / 1.1 / 2.2 / 0.8	20 M	0207 / 0748 / 1348 / 2035 ☽	2.2 / 1.0 / 2.3 / 0.3
6 M	0218 / 0726 / 1348 / 2030	2.0 / 1.2 / 2.1 / 0.8	21 Tu	0322 / 0846 / 1450 / 2139	2.1 / 1.1 / 2.2 / 0.4
7 Tu ☾	0328 / 0831 / 1448 / 2139	1.9 / 1.2 / 2.0 / 0.8	22 W	0433 / 0956 / 1558 / 2250	2.1 / 1.1 / 2.2 / 0.5
8 W	0437 / 0950 / 1556 / 2258	2.0 / 1.2 / 2.0 / 0.8	23 Th	0539 / 1107 / 1709 / 2356	2.1 / 1.1 / 2.2 / 0.5
9 Th	0537 / 1111 / 1703 / 2358	2.0 / 1.2 / 2.1 / 0.6	24 F	0637 / 1213 / 1818	2.1 / 1.0 / 2.2
10 F	0631 / 1209 / 1805	2.1 / 1.0 / 2.1	25 Sa	0052 / 0728 / 1309 / 1918	0.5 / 2.2 / 0.9 / 2.3
11 Sa	0048 / 0718 / 1258 / 1901	0.5 / 2.1 / 0.9 / 2.2	26 Su	0143 / 0809 / 1401 / 2011	0.6 / 2.2 / 0.8 / 2.3
12 Su	0133 / 0758 / 1345 / 1952	0.5 / 2.2 / 0.8 / 2.3	27 M	0226 / 0845 / 1448 / 2056	0.6 / 2.3 / 0.8 / 2.3
13 M	0216 / 0837 / 1431 / 2041	0.4 / 2.3 / 0.6 / 2.4	28 Tu ○	0303 / 0918 / 1530 / 2139	0.7 / 2.3 / 0.7 / 2.3
14 Tu ●	0301 / 0916 / 1520 / 2128	0.4 / 2.4 / 0.6 / 2.5	29 W	0335 / 0950 / 1609 / 2218	0.8 / 2.4 / 0.7 / 2.2
15 W	0345 / 0956 / 1609 / 2216	0.4 / 2.4 / 0.5 / 2.5	30 Th	0401 / 1018 / 1646 / 2258	0.8 / 2.4 / 0.7 / 2.2
			31 F	0426 / 1046 / 1722 / 2335	0.9 / 2.4 / 0.6 / 2.1

JUNE

Day	Time	m	Day	Time	m
1 Sa	0454 / 1116 / 1758	0.9 / 2.4 / 0.6	16 Su	0556 / 1148 / 1835	0.8 / 2.6 / 0.1
2 Su	0015 / 0531 / 1152 / 1835	2.1 / 1.0 / 2.3 / 0.6	17 M	0050 / 0641 / 1237 / 1922	2.3 / 0.8 / 2.5 / 0.1
3 M	0058 / 0613 / 1231 / 1916	2.0 / 1.0 / 2.3 / 0.6	18 Tu	0144 / 0728 / 1330 / 2013	2.2 / 0.9 / 2.5 / 0.3
4 Tu	0146 / 0701 / 1318 / 2003	2.0 / 1.0 / 2.2 / 0.7	19 W	0248 / 0816 / 1424 / 2107 ☽	2.1 / 1.0 / 2.4 / 0.4
5 W	0245 / 0756 / 1409 / 2056 ☾	2.0 / 1.1 / 2.2 / 0.7	20 Th	0354 / 0911 / 1526 / 2211	2.1 / 1.1 / 2.3 / 0.5
6 Th	0345 / 0856 / 1507 / 2158	2.0 / 1.1 / 2.1 / 0.7	21 F	0456 / 1020 / 1635 / 2316	2.1 / 1.1 / 2.2 / 0.7
7 F	0446 / 1007 / 1615 / 2303	2.0 / 1.2 / 2.1 / 0.7	22 Sa	0558 / 1137 / 1748	2.1 / 1.1 / 2.2
8 Sa	0543 / 1120 / 1724	2.1 / 1.1 / 2.2	23 Su	0018 / 0654 / 1250 / 1901	0.7 / 2.1 / 1.0 / 2.2
9 Su	0003 / 0633 / 1220 / 1826	0.6 / 2.1 / 1.0 / 2.2	24 M	0113 / 0743 / 1350 / 2001	0.8 / 2.2 / 0.9 / 2.2
10 M	0054 / 0720 / 1315 / 1924	0.6 / 2.2 / 0.9 / 2.3	25 Tu	0200 / 0822 / 1441 / 2050	0.9 / 2.3 / 0.8 / 2.2
11 Tu	0145 / 0805 / 1411 / 2018	0.5 / 2.3 / 0.7 / 2.4	26 W	0239 / 0858 / 1522 / 2135	0.9 / 2.3 / 0.7 / 2.2
12 W ●	0233 / 0850 / 1509 / 2113	0.5 / 2.4 / 0.5 / 2.4	27 Th ○	0309 / 0928 / 1600 / 2215	0.9 / 2.4 / 0.7 / 2.2
13 Th	0326 / 0933 / 1605 / 2207	0.6 / 2.5 / 0.6 / 2.5	28 F	0337 / 0956 / 1635 / 2250	0.9 / 2.4 / 0.6 / 2.2
14 F	0418 / 1018 / 1658 / 2300	0.6 / 2.5 / 0.2 / 2.5	29 Sa	0407 / 1026 / 1709 / 2326	0.9 / 2.4 / 0.5 / 2.1
15 Sa	0507 / 1103 / 1746 / 2354	0.7 / 2.6 / 0.1 / 2.4	30 Su	0441 / 1100 / 1745	0.9 / 2.4 / 0.5

JULY

Day	Time	m	Day	Time	m
1 M	0000 / 0518 / 1135 / 1818	2.1 / 0.9 / 2.4 / 0.5	16 Tu	0030 / 0618 / 1218 / 1900	2.3 / 0.7 / 2.6 / 0.1
2 Tu	0035 / 0558 / 1213 / 1856	2.0 / 0.9 / 2.4 / 0.5	17 W	0118 / 0700 / 1307 / 1945	2.2 / 0.8 / 2.6 / 0.3
3 W	0113 / 0639 / 1252 / 1933	2.1 / 0.9 / 2.3 / 0.5	18 Th	0209 / 0743 / 1358 / 2031 ☽	2.1 / 0.9 / 2.4 / 0.5
4 Th	0200 / 0724 / 1335 / 2018	2.0 / 1.0 / 2.3 / 0.6	19 F	0303 / 0830 / 1456 / 2126	2.1 / 1.0 / 2.3 / 0.7
5 F	0252 / 0815 / 1426 / 2109 ☾	2.0 / 1.0 / 2.2 / 0.6	20 Sa	0405 / 0931 / 1603 / 2233	2.0 / 1.1 / 2.2 / 0.9
6 Sa	0356 / 0915 / 1530 / 2215	2.0 / 1.1 / 2.2 / 0.7	21 Su	0511 / 1105 / 1724 / 2345	2.1 / 1.1 / 2.1 / 1.0
7 Su	0458 / 1031 / 1648 / 2322	2.1 / 1.1 / 2.2 / 0.7	22 M	0616 / 1239 / 1850	2.1 / 1.1 / 2.1
8 M	0556 / 1148 / 1800	2.1 / 1.0 / 2.2	23 Tu	0050 / 0715 / 1343 / 1958	1.0 / 2.2 / 0.9 / 2.1
9 Tu	0024 / 0648 / 1254 / 1903	0.7 / 2.2 / 0.9 / 2.3	24 W	0141 / 0800 / 1410 / 2046	1.0 / 2.2 / 0.8 / 2.1
10 W	0120 / 0739 / 1400 / 2005	0.7 / 2.3 / 0.7 / 2.3	25 Th	0222 / 0837 / 1507 / 2128	1.0 / 2.3 / 0.7 / 2.1
11 Th ●	0216 / 0828 / 1503 / 2105	0.7 / 2.4 / 0.4 / 2.4	26 F ○	0252 / 0907 / 1543 / 2201	1.0 / 2.3 / 0.6 / 2.2
12 F	0315 / 0915 / 1558 / 2201	0.7 / 2.5 / 0.2 / 2.4	27 Sa	0320 / 0937 / 1616 / 2235	0.9 / 2.4 / 0.5 / 2.2
13 Sa	0407 / 1001 / 1646 / 2252	0.6 / 2.6 / 0.1 / 2.4	28 Su	0354 / 1009 / 1648 / 2305	0.8 / 2.4 / 0.4 / 2.2
14 Su	0454 / 1048 / 1731 / 2341	0.6 / 2.7 / 0.0 / 2.4	29 M	0428 / 1043 / 1722 / 2335	0.7 / 2.5 / 0.4 / 2.2
15 M	0537 / 1133 / 1816	0.7 / 2.7 / 0.0	30 Tu	0503 / 1116 / 1756	0.7 / 2.5 / 0.4
			31 W	0005 / 0539 / 1152 / 1828	2.1 / 0.7 / 2.5 / 0.5

AUGUST

Day	Time	m	Day	Time	m
1 Th	0039 / 0615 / 1230 / 1903	2.1 / 0.8 / 2.4 / 0.5	16 F	0126 / 0709 / 1330 / 1952	2.1 / 0.8 / 2.4 / 0.7
2 F	0118 / 0654 / 1309 / 1941	2.1 / 0.9 / 2.4 / 0.6	17 Sa	0215 / 0754 / 1424 / 2037 ☽	2.1 / 0.9 / 2.3 / 0.9
3 Sa	0205 / 0741 / 1356 / 2030	2.1 / 0.9 / 2.3 / 0.7	18 Su	0311 / 0848 / 1533 / 2139	2.1 / 1.1 / 2.1 / 1.1
4 Su	0305 / 0837 / 1501 / 2131	2.0 / 1.0 / 2.2 / 0.8	19 M	0416 / 1026 / 1701 / 2315	2.0 / 1.2 / 2.0 / 1.2
5 M	0415 / 0954 / 1628 / 2250	2.0 / 1.1 / 2.1 / 0.9	20 Tu	0526 / 1222 / 1835	2.1 / 1.1 / 2.0
6 Tu	0520 / 1124 / 1745	2.1 / 1.0 / 2.2	21 W	0031 / 0635 / 1322 / 1943	1.2 / 2.1 / 0.9 / 2.1
7 W	0001 / 0618 / 1243 / 1854	0.9 / 2.2 / 0.8 / 2.2	22 Th	0122 / 0730 / 1405 / 2030	1.1 / 2.2 / 0.8 / 2.1
8 Th	0105 / 0715 / 1356 / 2003	0.8 / 2.3 / 0.6 / 2.3	23 F	0158 / 0809 / 1441 / 2107	1.1 / 2.2 / 0.7 / 2.2
9 F	0207 / 0807 / 1454 / 2101	0.8 / 2.4 / 0.3 / 2.4	24 Sa	0228 / 0841 / 1515 / 2139	0.9 / 2.3 / 0.5 / 2.2
10 Sa ●	0303 / 0858 / 1543 / 2152	0.7 / 2.5 / 0.1 / 2.4	25 Su ○	0258 / 0911 / 1546 / 2207	0.8 / 2.4 / 0.4 / 2.2
11 Su	0350 / 0945 / 1628 / 2237	0.7 / 2.7 / 0.0 / 2.4	26 M	0331 / 0945 / 1620 / 2235	0.7 / 2.5 / 0.4 / 2.3
12 M	0433 / 1030 / 1711 / 2320	0.6 / 2.7 / -0.1 / 2.4	27 Tu	0407 / 1020 / 1654 / 2303	0.7 / 2.5 / 0.4 / 2.3
13 Tu	0515 / 1113 / 1752	0.6 / 2.7 / 0.0	28 W	0443 / 1056 / 1726 / 2333	0.6 / 2.5 / 0.4 / 2.2
14 W	0001 / 0552 / 1158 / 1831	2.3 / 0.6 / 2.7 / 0.2	29 Th	0516 / 1130 / 1758	0.7 / 2.5 / 0.5
15 Th	0043 / 0630 / 1241 / 1913	2.2 / 0.7 / 2.6 / 0.4	30 F	0007 / 0552 / 1207 / 1831	2.2 / 0.7 / 2.5 / 0.6
			31 Sa	0045 / 0630 / 1246 / 1909	2.2 / 0.8 / 2.4 / 0.7

Chart Datum: 1.50 metres below Ordnance Datum (Newlyn)

ENGLAND, EAST COAST – LOWESTOFT

Lat 52°28′ N   Long 1°45′ E

TIME ZONE UT(GMT)
For Summer Time add ONE hour in non-shaded areas

TIMES AND HEIGHTS OF HIGH AND LOW WATERS

YEAR 1991

SEPTEMBER

Day		Time	m		Time	m
1	Su ☾	0128 / 0716 / 1337 / 1956	2.1 / 0.9 / 2.3 / 0.8	16 M	0216 / 0813 / 1505 / 2039	2.1 / 1.1 / 2.1 / 1.3
2	M	0222 / 0815 / 1450 / 2101	2.1 / 0.9 / 2.2 / 1.0	17 Tu	0316 / 0933 / 1633 / 2211	2.1 / 1.1 / 2.0 / 1.4
3	Tu	0333 / 0937 / 1618 / 2228	2.1 / 1.0 / 2.1 / 1.1	18 W	0422 / 1146 / 1803	2.0 / 1.1 / 2.0
4	W	0448 / 1113 / 1741 / 2348	2.1 / 0.9 / 2.2 / 1.0	19 Th	0000 / 0531 / 1245 / 1911	1.3 / 2.1 / 0.9 / 2.1
5	Th	0552 / 1235 / 1856	2.2 / 0.7 / 2.2	20 F	0046 / 0633 / 1328 / 1958	1.2 / 2.1 / 0.8 / 2.1
6	F	0054 / 0652 / 1341 / 2001	0.9 / 2.3 / 0.4 / 2.3	21 Sa	0120 / 0722 / 1403 / 2035	1.1 / 2.2 / 0.6 / 2.2
7	Sa	0152 / 0748 / 1435 / 2050	0.8 / 2.4 / 0.2 / 2.4	22 Su	0152 / 0801 / 1437 / 2105	1.0 / 2.3 / 0.5 / 2.2
8	Su ●	0243 / 0839 / 1522 / 2133	0.7 / 2.6 / 0.1 / 2.4	23 M ○	0228 / 0905 / 1513 / 2133	0.8 / 2.4 / 0.5 / 2.3
9	M	0328 / 0926 / 1605 / 2213	0.6 / 2.7 / 0.0 / 2.4	24 Tu	0303 / 0916 / 1546 / 2201	0.7 / 2.5 / 0.4 / 2.3
10	Tu	0409 / 1009 / 1646 / 2252	0.6 / 2.8 / 0.1 / 2.4	25 W	0341 / 0954 / 1622 / 2231	0.7 / 2.6 / 0.4 / 2.4
11	W	0448 / 1052 / 1724 / 2330	0.6 / 2.7 / 0.2 / 2.3	26 Th	0418 / 1031 / 1654 / 2303	0.6 / 2.6 / 0.5 / 2.4
12	Th	0526 / 1133 / 1801	0.6 / 2.7 / 0.4	27 F	0456 / 1153 / 1728 / 2339	0.7 / 2.6 / 0.5 / 2.3
13	F	0007 / 0603 / 1216 / 1835	2.3 / 0.7 / 2.5 / 0.7	28 Sa	0533 / 1148 / 1801	0.7 / 2.5 / 0.7
14	Sa	0046 / 0639 / 1301 / 1911	2.2 / 0.8 / 2.3 / 0.9	29 Su	0016 / 0615 / 1233 / 1841	2.3 / 0.7 / 2.4 / 0.8
15	Su ☽	0128 / 0722 / 1356 / 1948	2.2 / 0.9 / 2.2 / 1.1	30 M	0100 / 0707 / 1331 / 1933	2.3 / 0.8 / 2.3 / 1.0

OCTOBER

Day		Time	m		Time	m
1	Tu ☾	0152 / 0813 / 1448 / 2043	2.2 / 0.8 / 2.2 / 1.1	16 W	0218 / 0850 / 1556 / 2054	2.1 / 1.0 / 2.0 / 1.4
2	W	0301 / 0933 / 1620 / 2211	2.1 / 0.8 / 2.1 / 1.2	17 Th	0324 / 1030 / 1711 / 2241	2.1 / 1.0 / 2.0 / 1.4
3	Th	0418 / 1101 / 1741 / 2331	2.2 / 0.7 / 2.2 / 1.1	18 F	0430 / 1148 / 1818 / 2350	2.1 / 0.9 / 2.1 / 1.3
4	F	0528 / 1218 / 1852	2.2 / 0.6 / 2.2	19 Sa	0533 / 1237 / 1913	2.1 / 0.8 / 2.2
5	Sa	0035 / 0631 / 1320 / 1946	1.0 / 2.3 / 0.4 / 2.3	20 Su	0035 / 0630 / 1316 / 1952	1.1 / 2.2 / 0.7 / 2.2
6	Su	0130 / 0728 / 1411 / 2031	0.9 / 2.5 / 0.3 / 2.4	21 M	0115 / 0718 / 1356 / 2024	1.0 / 2.3 / 0.6 / 2.3
7	M ●	0218 / 0818 / 1456 / 2111	0.8 / 2.6 / 0.2 / 2.4	22 Tu	0154 / 0803 / 1433 / 2054	0.9 / 2.4 / 0.5 / 2.4
8	Tu	0301 / 0846 / 1539 / 2148	0.7 / 2.7 / 0.3 / 2.4	23 W ○	0235 / 0846 / 1511 / 2126	0.8 / 2.5 / 0.5 / 2.4
9	W	0345 / 0948 / 1618 / 2224	0.6 / 2.7 / 0.4 / 2.4	24 Th	0316 / 0928 / 1548 / 2201	0.7 / 2.6 / 0.5 / 2.5
10	Th	0424 / 1030 / 1654 / 2300	0.6 / 2.6 / 0.5 / 2.4	25 F	0358 / 1009 / 1624 / 2237	0.7 / 2.6 / 0.6 / 2.5
11	F	0503 / 1111 / 1728 / 2333	0.7 / 2.5 / 0.7 / 2.4	26 Sa	0441 / 1052 / 1701 / 2315	0.6 / 2.6 / 0.7 / 2.5
12	Sa	0539 / 1137 / 1756	0.7 / 2.4 / 0.9	27 Su	0526 / 1137 / 1741 / 2354	0.6 / 2.5 / 0.8 / 2.4
13	Su	0007 / 0616 / 1237 / 1824	2.3 / 0.8 / 2.3 / 1.1	28 M	0616 / 1228 / 1828	0.6 / 2.4 / 0.9
14	M	0041 / 0658 / 1330 / 1858	2.3 / 0.9 / 2.1 / 1.2	29 Tu	0039 / 0713 / 1331 / 1924	2.4 / 0.6 / 2.3 / 1.1
15	Tu ☽	0124 / 0746 / 1437 / 1946	2.2 / 1.0 / 2.0 / 1.3	30 W ☾	0131 / 0815 / 1450 / 2030	2.3 / 0.7 / 2.2 / 1.2
				31 Th	0237 / 0924 / 1616 / 2146	2.3 / 0.7 / 2.2 / 1.2

NOVEMBER

Day		Time	m		Time	m
1	F	0348 / 1041 / 1728 / 2301	2.3 / 0.6 / 2.2 / 1.2	16 Sa	0333 / 1033 / 1716 / 2239	2.2 / 0.9 / 2.1 / 1.3
2	Sa	0501 / 1150 / 1831	2.3 / 0.5 / 2.2	17 Su	0439 / 1137 / 1811 / 2343	2.2 / 0.8 / 2.1 / 1.2
3	Su	0007 / 0607 / 1252 / 1924	1.1 / 2.4 / 0.5 / 2.3	18 M	0543 / 1226 / 1858	2.2 / 0.7 / 2.2
4	M	0101 / 0707 / 1343 / 2007	1.0 / 2.5 / 0.4 / 2.3	19 Tu	0035 / 0637 / 1311 / 1939	1.1 / 2.3 / 0.7 / 2.3
5	Tu	0154 / 0800 / 1430 / 2046	0.9 / 2.5 / 0.5 / 2.4	20 W	0122 / 0730 / 1354 / 2016	1.0 / 2.4 / 0.6 / 2.4
6	W ●	0241 / 0846 / 1511 / 2122	0.8 / 2.6 / 0.5 / 2.4	21 Th ○	0207 / 0816 / 1435 / 2054	0.9 / 2.5 / 0.6 / 2.4
7	Th	0326 / 0930 / 1548 / 2156	0.7 / 2.6 / 0.6 / 2.5	22 F	0256 / 0905 / 1518 / 2133	0.7 / 2.5 / 0.6 / 2.5
8	F	0407 / 1013 / 1622 / 2230	0.7 / 2.5 / 0.8 / 2.5	23 Sa	0345 / 0952 / 1601 / 2215	0.6 / 2.6 / 0.6 / 2.6
9	Sa	0446 / 1054 / 1652 / 2301	0.7 / 2.4 / 0.9 / 2.5	24 Su	0437 / 1039 / 1646 / 2256	0.5 / 2.6 / 0.7 / 2.6
10	Su	0524 / 1135 / 1715 / 2331	0.8 / 2.3 / 1.0 / 2.4	25 M	0528 / 1131 / 1735 / 2339	0.5 / 2.5 / 0.8 / 2.6
11	M	0601 / 1218 / 1741	0.8 / 2.2 / 1.1	26 Tu	0618 / 1226 / 1824	0.4 / 2.4 / 0.9
12	Tu	0003 / 0641 / 1307 / 1818	2.4 / 0.8 / 2.1 / 1.2	27 W	0026 / 0711 / 1328 / 1916	2.5 / 0.4 / 2.3 / 1.0
13	W	0043 / 0724 / 1403 / 1909	2.3 / 0.9 / 2.1 / 1.2	28 Th	0116 / 0805 / 1437 / 2011	2.5 / 0.4 / 2.2 / 1.1
14	Th ☽	0133 / 0816 / 1509 / 2007	2.3 / 0.9 / 2.0 / 1.3	29 F	0215 / 0903 / 1552 / 2111	2.4 / 0.5 / 2.2 / 1.2
15	F	0230 / 0918 / 1615 / 2116	2.2 / 0.9 / 2.0 / 1.3	30 Sa	0320 / 1011 / 1700 / 2222	2.4 / 0.6 / 2.1 / 1.2

DECEMBER

Day		Time	m		Time	m
1	Su	0431 / 1118 / 1801 / 2331	2.4 / 0.6 / 2.2 / 1.1	16 M	0346 / 1035 / 1716 / 2245	2.2 / 0.8 / 2.1 / 1.2
2	M	0541 / 1220 / 1856 / 2343	2.4 / 0.6 / 2.2 / 1.2	17 Tu	0458 / 1137 / 1811 / 2354	2.2 / 0.8 / 2.1 / 1.2
3	Tu	0035 / 0646 / 1315 / 1943	1.1 / 2.4 / 0.7 / 2.3	18 W	0601 / 1231 / 1858	2.3 / 0.7 / 2.2
4	W	0135 / 0745 / 1403 / 2024	1.0 / 2.4 / 0.7 / 2.4	19 Th	0052 / 0700 / 1320 / 1943	1.0 / 2.3 / 0.7 / 2.3
5	Th	0230 / 0835 / 1446 / 2100	0.9 / 2.4 / 0.8 / 2.4	20 F	0146 / 0754 / 1407 / 2028	0.9 / 2.4 / 0.7 / 2.4
6	F ●	0316 / 0920 / 1524 / 2133	0.8 / 2.4 / 0.9 / 2.5	21 Sa ○	0243 / 0848 / 1458 / 2111	0.7 / 2.5 / 0.7 / 2.5
7	Sa	0358 / 1003 / 1556 / 2205	0.8 / 2.3 / 0.9 / 2.5	22 Su	0341 / 0941 / 1550 / 2154	0.5 / 2.5 / 0.7 / 2.6
8	Su	0437 / 1045 / 1620 / 2235	0.7 / 2.3 / 1.0 / 2.5	23 M	0433 / 1033 / 1641 / 2239	0.3 / 2.5 / 0.7 / 2.6
9	M	0513 / 1124 / 1646 / 2305	0.7 / 2.2 / 1.0 / 2.5	24 Tu	0522 / 1126 / 1728 / 2324	0.2 / 2.5 / 0.7 / 2.7
10	Tu	0548 / 1203 / 1718 / 2339	0.7 / 2.2 / 1.0 / 2.4	25 W	0609 / 1218 / 1813	0.2 / 2.4 / 0.8
11	W	0624 / 1243 / 1756	0.7 / 2.1 / 1.0	26 Th	0011 / 0658 / 1313 / 1858	2.6 / 0.2 / 2.3 / 0.9
12	Th	0016 / 0701 / 1328 / 1841	2.4 / 0.7 / 2.1 / 1.1	27 F	0100 / 0745 / 1409 / 1945	2.6 / 0.2 / 2.2 / 1.0
13	F	0100 / 0745 / 1418 / 1930	2.4 / 0.8 / 2.0 / 1.1	28 Sa ☾	0152 / 0837 / 1511 / 2035	2.5 / 0.4 / 2.1 / 1.1
14	Sa	0146 / 0831 / 1516 / 2024	2.3 / 0.8 / 2.0 / 1.2	29 Su	0252 / 0935 / 1618 / 2137	2.4 / 0.6 / 2.1 / 1.1
15	Su	0243 / 0928 / 1618 / 2128	2.3 / 0.8 / 2.0 / 1.2	30 M	0401 / 1041 / 1724 / 2256	2.3 / 0.7 / 2.1 / 1.2
				31 Tu	0516 / 1148 / 1824	2.3 / 0.8 / 2.2

Chart Datum: 1.50 metres below Ordnance Datum (Newlyn)

LOWESTOFT *continued*

Depths in metres

NAVIGATION
Sands are continually shifting. Beware shallows and drying areas, and do not cross banks in bad weather or strong tidal conditions. From S, waypoint East Barnard E cardinal buoy, Q(3) 10s, 52°24'.60N 01°46'.20E; then follow buoyed channel inshore of S Newcome and Pakefield buoys. From N or E, waypoint Corton E cardinal buoy, Q(3) 10s, 52°31'.10N 01°51'.50E; then follow Holm Channel (buoyed) into Corton Road. Speed limit in harbour 4 kn. Passage to Oulton Broad Wednesday p.m., passing two swing bridges and a lock; give Oulton Broad Hr Mr at least 48 hours notice.

LIGHTS AND MARKS
Entry Signals: Fl W Lt (obsc 232°-286°) below the Oc R Lt on South Pier Lt Ho − vessels may proceed to sea (with clearance from harbour control on Ch 14 or tel 572286) but entry prohibited. When signal not shown: No vessel to proceed to sea but entry permitted.
Bridge Signals: when bridge is lifting, vessels may not approach within 137m until G Lt is shown on N wall of entrance channel. When G Lt shown: vessels may enter or leave Inner Harbour.

RADIO TELEPHONE
VHF Ch **14** 16; 14 (H24). Pilot Ch 14.

TELEPHONE (0502)
Hr Mr 572286 Ext 41; Hr Mr Oulton Broad 574946; CG 565365; MRCC Great Yarmouth 851338; Bridge Control 572286 Ext 42; Pilot 560277; ⌗ (0473) 219481; Weather Norwich 660779; Marinecall 0898 500 455; Police 562121; Ⓗ 600611.

FACILITIES
EC Thursday; **Royal Norfolk & Suffolk YC** ☎ 566726, Slip, M, D, L, FW, C (2ton), R, Bar; **Oulton Broad — Jeckells Y. Co.** ☎ 565007, L, ME, El, Sh, CH, SM; **Oulton Broad Calor Centre** Gas, Gaz; **Knights Creek** ☎ 572599, El, CH; **J. E. Fletcher** ☎ 574951, Slip, Sh; **F. Newson** ☎ 574902, Slip, M, L, El, Sh; **A. D. Truman** ☎ 565950, Slip, M, L, ME, El, Sh; **Lowestoft Cruising Club** ☎ 574376, Slip, M, L, FW, AB; **Charity and Taylor** ☎ 581529, ACA. **Town** V, R, Bar. ✉; Ⓑ; ⇌; ✈ (Norwich).

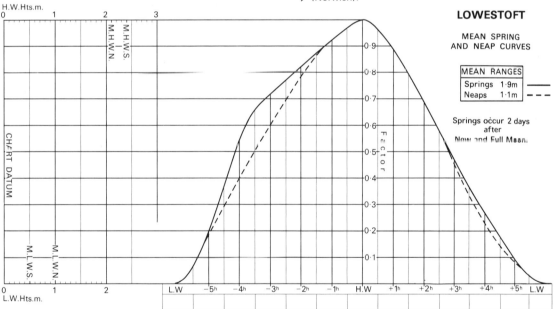

LOWESTOFT

MEAN SPRING AND NEAP CURVES

MEAN RANGES	
Springs	1·9m
Neaps	1·1m

Springs occur 2 days after New and Full Moon.

GREAT YARMOUTH   10-4-18
Norfolk

CHARTS
Admiralty 1536, 1543; Stanford 3; Imray C28; OS 134
TIDES
−0210 Dover; ML 1.5; Duration 0620; Zone 0 (GMT).

Standard Port LOWESTOFT (←)

Times				Height (metres)			
HW		LW		MHWS	MHWN	MLWN	MLWS
0300	0900	0200	0800	2.4	2.1	1.0	0.5
1500	2100	1400	2000				

Differences GORLESTON
−0035 −0035 −0030 −0030 0.0 −0.1 0.0 0.0
CAISTER-ON-SEA
−0130 −0130 −0100 −0100 0.0 −0.1 0.0 0.0

Rise of tide occurs mainly during 3½ hours after LW. Level is usually within 0.3m of predicted HW height, from 3 hours before HW Lowestoft, until HW Lowestoft. Flood tide runs for about 1½ hrs after predicted HW and Ebb for about 2-2½ hrs after predicted LW.

GREAT YARMOUTH *continued*

SHELTER
Anchoring is prohibited within the harbour but shelter is excellent on the East side on Town Hall Quay which is immediately south of the Haven Bridge.

NAVIGATION
Waypoint 52°34'.40N 01°45'.67E, 084°/264° from/to front Ldg Lt 264°, 1.0M. Subject to clearance, the harbour is available at all times but small craft should not attempt entrance when strong SE winds cause dangerous seas especially on the ebb tide. Other than at slack water there are strong tidal streams at the entrance. Temporary shoaling is liable to occur in the harbour entrance during strong easterly winds when depths of 1m less than those charted may be expected. The harbour is a busy commercial port, traffic signals and instructions from the Vessel Traffic Service (VTS) should be complied with at all times. Beware the strong tidal streams that sweep through the Haven Bridge.

Bridge clearances (at MHWS)

Haven Bridge (C/L centre span closed)	2.3m
Vauxhall (old railway bridge)	2.3m
Bure (A47 road bridge)	2.3m
Breydon (C/L centre span closed)	4.0m
Breydon (side spans)	4.5m

LIGHTS AND MARKS
Main Lt (S Pier) Fl R 3s. 11m 11M vis. 235°-340°. Fog sig Horn (3) 60s. N Pier Lt Q G 8m 6M vis. 176°-078° (through 270°). Ldg Lts 264°-Front Oc 3s 6m 10M. Rear Oc 6s 7m 10M. Tidal signal (S Pier) Q Y vis. 235°-340°, when tide flooding between the piers.

TRAFFIC CONTROL SIGNALS
S Pier 3 F R (vert) vis. 235°-295°. Entrance to Port Prohibited. VTS Office — 3 F R (vert) no vessel to proceed down river south of the Life-boat shed.
Haven Bridge — when bridge is lifting and passage prohibited 3 F R (vert) exhibited from the Eastern or Western Buttresses.
Breydon Bridge — when bridge is lifting and passage through the centre span is prohibited 3 F R (vert) exhibited from the S Buttress or Bridge Control Building. Both the Haven and Breydon Bridges when manned operate on VHF Ch 12.

RADIO TELEPHONE
Call: *Great Yarmouth Harbour* VHF Ch 12, 16 (H24). Breydon and Haven Bridges Ch 12.

TELEPHONE (0493)
Hr Mr 855151; CG & MRCC 851338; ▦ 843686; Police 842222; Port Health Authority 856100; Breydon Bridge 651275; Broads Navigation Authority (0603) 610734.

FACILITIES
EC Thursday; **Burgh Castle Marina** (90 + 10 visitors) ☎ 780263, Slip, D, FW, ME, El, Sh, C (6 ton), ▢, Gas, Gaz, CH, V, R, Bar, Access HW∓4; **Goodchild Marine** 852442; BY, D, ME, El, FW, Slip, Diving; **Bure Marine** 656996, Slip, AB, FW, L, M, ME, El, Sh; **Breydon Marine** 780379, AB, P, D, L, FW; **Paul Williment** ☎ 662710 (by LB station) D; **Yarmouth Stores** 842289, SM; **Gorleston Marine** 661883, ACA; **Town** P, D, CH, V, R, Bar, ✉, Ⓑ, ⇌, ✈ (Norwich).

BLAKENEY   10-4-19
Norfolk

Depths in metres

▲ Ring Hr Mr

BLAKENEY *continued*

CHARTS
Admiralty 108; Imray C28; OS 133
TIDES
−0445 Dover; Duration 0530; Zone 0 (GMT).

Standard Port IMMINGHAM (→)

Times				Height (metres)			
HW		LW		MHWS	MHWN	MLWN	MLWS
0100	0700	0100	0700	7.3	5.8	2.6	0.9
1300	1900	1300	1900				
Differences BLAKENEY							
+0115	+0055	No data		−3.9	−3.8	No data	
BLAKENEY BAR							
+0035	+0025	+0030	+0040	−1.6	−1.3	No data	
CROMER							
+0050	+0030	+0050	+0130	−2.1	−1.7	−0.5	−0.1

SHELTER
Very good shelter but harbour inaccessible with fresh on-
shore winds. Conditions in the entrance deteriorate very
quickly with on-shore winds, especially on the ebb. Entry,
springs HW ∓2½, neaps HW ∓1. Moorings in The Pit or
at Stiffkey Sluices.
NAVIGATION
Waypoint 53°00'.15N 00°51'.12E, 020°/200° from/to
channel entrance 0.67M. Large wreck to W of harbour
entrance channel; very dangerous, unlit, marked by buoy.
The bar is shallow and changes frequently. The channel is
marked by B buoys to be left to stbd. Beware mussel lays
in the channel off Blakeney spit. Speed limit 8 kn. For
pilotage contact Stratton Long Marine (below).
LIGHTS AND MARKS
Orange leading beacons established on dunes at Blakeney
Pt, moved according to changes in the channel (not
always reliable). Conspic marks are Blakeney Church and
Langham Church. There is a conspic chimney on the
house on Blakeney Point neck. A Lt buoy, QY, is placed
(April-Oct) marking entrance, 1½ ca N of wreck.
RADIO TELEPHONE
None.
TELEPHONE (0263)
Hr Mr 740362; CG Wells 219; MRCC Great Yarmouth
851338; ⌗ (0473) 219481; Marinecall 0898 500 455;
Dr 740314.
FACILITIES
EC Wednesday; **Blakeney Quay** Slip, M, D, L, FW, El, C
(15 ton), CH, AB; **Stratton Long Marine** ☎ 740362, M,
P, D, FW, ME, El, Sh, CH, Slip, L, C, AB, BY, SM, Gas,
Gaz, AC; **Village** V, R, Bar. ✉; Ⓑ; ≉ (Sherringham);
✈ (Norwich).
Note: The areas of Blakeney Point and Dunes are
National Trust Property and contain a bird sanctuary.
Note 2: There is a plan to build a marina at Cromer.

WELLS-NEXT-THE-SEA 10-4-20
Norfolk

CHARTS
Admiralty 108; Imray C28, Y9; OS 132
TIDES
−0445 Dover; Duration 0540; Zone 0 (GMT).

Standard Port IMMINGHAM (→)

Times				Height (metres)			
HW		LW		MHWS	MHWN	MLWN	MLWS
0100	0700	0100	0700	7.3	5.8	2.6	0.9
1300	1900	1300	1900				
Differences WELLS-NEXT-THE-SEA							
+0035	+0045	+0340	+0310	−3.8	−3.8	No data	
WELLS BAR							
+0020	+0020	+0020	+0020	−1.3	−1.0	No data	
HUNSTANTON							
+0010	+0020	+0105	+0025	+0.1	−0.2	−0.1	0.0
BURNHAM OVERY STAITHE							
+0045	+0055	No data	−5.0	−4.9		No data	

SHELTER
The shelter is good except in strong N winds. Max draft
3m at springs. Entrance possible from HW −1½ to HW
+1 but recommended on the flood. Entrance impossible
to small craft with strong on-shore winds.
NAVIGATION
Waypoint Wells Fairway buoy, 53°00'.15N, 00°51'.12E,
020°/200° from/to channel entrance, 0.67M. The bar and
entrance vary in depth and position. The position of buoys
is altered to suit. Channel is marked with Q buoys to stbd,
QR to port, reaching No. 16 (port). Keep to port side of
channel from No 12 to quay. Advisable to take a pilot or
follow fishing boat.

LIGHTS AND MARKS
Harbour ent has a conspic W Lifeboat Ho with R roof on
the West point.
RADIO TELEPHONE
VHF Ch 16; 06 08 12 (when vessels expected)
TELEPHONE (0328 − Fakenham)
Hr Mr 710655; CG 710587; Pilot 710739; MRCC Gt.
Yarmouth 851338; ⌗ (0473) 219481; Marinecall
0898 500 455; Police 710212; Ⓗ 710218.
FACILITIES
EC Thursday; **East Quay** Slip, M, L; **Main Quay** M (see
Hr Mr), L, FW, ME, El, Sh, C (5 ton mobile), CH, AB, V,
R, Bar; **Wells SC** Slip, Bar; **Standard House Chandlery**
☎ 710593, M, L, ME, El, Sh, CH, AB, V, ACA;
R. Bicknell ☎ 710593, CH; **M. Walsingham** ☎ 710438,
Gas; **Preston** ☎ 2414, Ⓔ; **Town** P and D (bowser on
quay − up to 500 galls), CH, V, R, Bar. ✉; Ⓑ;
≉ (bus to Norwich or King's Lynn); ✈ (Norwich).

KING'S LYNN 10-4-21
Norfolk

CHARTS
Admiralty 1200, 1190; Imray Y9; OS 132

TIDES
−0450 Dover; ML 3.6; Duration 0340 Sp, 0515 Np;
Zone 0 (GMT).

Standard Port IMMINGHAM (⟶)

Times				Height (metres)			
HW		LW		MHWS	MHWN	MLWN	MLWS
0100	0700	0100	0700	7.3	5.8	2.6	0.9
1300	1900	1300	1900				

Differences KING'S LYNN

+0030	+0030	+0305	+0140	−0.5	−0.8	−0.8	+0.1

WISBECH CUT

+0020	+0025	+0200	+0030	−0.3	−0.7	−0.4	No data

SHELTER
Harbour is 1½ M within the river mouth and consequently well sheltered. Entry recommended HW ∓3. The dock is open from about HW−1½ to HW and yachts can be left there with the Dockmaster's permission. Drying moorings at Fisher Fleet, S Quay, S side of Mill Fleet or Friar's Wharf.

metres
cables
0   2000
0   10
Depths in metres

⚓ Report to Hr Mr at Common Staithe Quay

NAVIGATION
Waypoint North Well (RW) buoy LFl 10s Horn Racon 53°03'.N, 00°00'.28E, 022°/202° From/to Cork Hole 7.0M. Extensive shifting sand banks extend several miles into the Wash. The best and safest approach is via the Cork Hole route, marked by Lt buoys. Channels are subject to frequent changes particularly between No 7 Light Buoy and Lynn Cut. S of West Stones Bn the deeper water is on E side of channel.

LIGHTS AND MARKS
Ldg Lts 155°. Front QR 11m 3M, Rear FW 16m 4M, both on masts.
Entry signals for Alexander Dock:
Bu flag or R Lt — Vessels can enter
R flag or G Lt — Vessels leaving dock.

RADIO TELEPHONE
VHF Ch 16; 11 14 (Mon-Fri: 0800-1730 LT. Other times: HW−4 to HW+1).
King's Lynn Docks Ch **14** 16; 11 (HW−2½ to HW+1).
Other station: Wisbech Ch 16; 09 **14** (HW−4 to HW when vessel expected).

TELEPHONE (0553)
Hr Mr 773411, Dock 691555; CG and MRCC Gt. Yarmouth 851338; ⌗ (0473) 219481; Marinecall 0898 500 455; Dr Ring Hr Mr.

FACILITIES
EC Wednesday; There are virtually no facilities for visiting yachts; **Docks** ☎ 691555, M, L, FW, C (32 ton), AB; **N.C. Shipp** ☎ 772831, ME, El; **V. Pratt** ☎ 764058, El, CH; **Downham Components** ☎ (0366) 500737, Ⓔ. **Commercial and Marine Communications** ☎ 672206 El, Ⓔ; **Town** P, D, ME, El, Sh, CH, V, R, Bar. ✉; Ⓑ; ⇌; ✈ (Humberside or Norwich).
Note 24 miles up the Great Ouse river **Ely Marina** ☎ Ely 664622, (Lock at Denver Sluice and low bridges above this point), Slip, M, P, D, FW, ME, El, Sh, C (10 ton), CH.

MINOR HARBOURS AND ANCHORAGES 10.4.22

RIVER ROACH, Essex 51°35' N, 0°43' E, Zone 0 (GMT), Admty chart 3750. At Rochford HW +0115 on Dover, −0010 on Sheerness; HW height −2.4m on Sheerness. Excellent shelter. Very good anchorage and shelter about ¼M up R Roach close to W bank. River runs into R Crouch and is ¼M wide at the mouth, but mud extends from both banks, the Wallasea Ness bank being marked by Branklet Spit Buoy (Y spher). Few boats go above Barling Ness. For moorings and anchorages, see chartlet 10.3.23 and 10.4.8. A riding light is needed when anchored since R Roach is used by freighters both day and night. Facilities: most facilities in **Rochford** EC Wed. **Shuttlewoods** (100) ☎ 226, D, BY, Slip, M; **Paglesham** FW, (from yard), V (at East End), Sh, Bar. **Wakering** El, FW, ME, Sh; Stores at **Great Wakering; Wakering YC**.

NORFOLK BROADS. There are about 130 miles of navigable rivers and tributaries in Norfolk and Suffolk together with meres and lakes, known as Broads. The main rivers are the Bure, the Yare and the Waveney which all flow into Breydon Water and thence into the sea at Great Yarmouth (see 10.4.18). This is the principal entrance. Licences are compulsory and Norfolk Broads temporary licences are obtainable from The Broads Authority Thomas Harvey House 18 Colegate Norwich NR3 1BQ ☎ (0603) 610734. Pass up R Yare, under Haven Bridge (headroom when closed 2.4m at MHWS) which is a lifting bridge (contact the Bridge Officer on Yarmouth 663476 or on VHF Ch 12). Bridge is manned 0800-1700 Mon-Thurs, 0800-1600 Fri. It does not open 0800-0900 or 1700-1800. Lifts are co-ordinated to pass small craft in groups. Thence to Breydon Water or to the R Bure, under two bridges (headroom 2m at MHWS.) Once past the two fixed bridges, some other bridges on the broads open — to open swing bridges, give three long blasts. A number of broads are closed to navigation. Tides: LW at Breydon (mouth of R Yare) is 1 hour before LW at Yarmouth Yacht Station (mouth of R Bure). Tide will start to flood on Breydon Water whilst still ebbing from R Bure. LW R Bure mouth = HW at Yarmouth Bar +0700. Tidal differences are quoted on LW at Yarmouth Yacht Station, which is Gorleston (see 10.4.18) +0100. For LW times at the following, add to time of LW at Yarmouth Yacht Station

Acle Bridge +0230	St Olaves +0115
Horning +0300	Beccles +0320
Reedham +0115	Oulton Broad +0300
Cantley +0200	Potter Heigham +0400
Norwich +0430	Burney Arms +0100

The Broads can also be entered at Lowestoft from the sea, via Oulton Dyke and Mutford Lock (opens Wed) into the R Waveney (see 10.4.17).

BURNHAM OVERY STAITHE, Norfolk, 52°59' N, 0°45' E, Zone 0 (GMT), Admty chart 108. HW −0420 on Dover, +0021 on Immingham; HW height −2.6m on Immingham. See 10.4.20. Small harbour which dries; anchorage off the Staithe only suitable in good weather. No lights. Scolt Hd conspic to W and Gun Hill to E. Channel varies constantly and buoys moved to suit. Local knowledge advisable. Facilities: (0328) **Burnham Overy Staithe SC** ☎ 738348, M, L; **The Boathouse** ☎ 738348, CH, M, ME, Sh, Slip, FW; **Burnham Market** EC Wed; Bar, P and D (cans), R, V.

BRANCASTER STAITHE, Norfolk, 52°58' N, 0°39' E, Zone 0 (GMT), Admty chart 108. HW −0425 on Dover, Hunstanton +0020 on Immingham; HW height −0.6m on Immingham. Small unlit harbour which dries; dangerous to enter except in daylight in fine weather. Speed limit 6 kn. Approach from due N. Conspic Golf Club House with Lt Fl 5s 8m 3M marks the start of channel buoys. Beware wreck shown on chart. Sandbanks vary continuously and buoys changed to suit. Scolt Hd conspic to E. Pilot advised. Facilities: (0485) Hr Mr ☎ 210638, visitors mooring available occasionally; Bar, BY, CH, D, El, FW, P and D (cans), ME, R, Sh, V; **Brancaster Staithe SC** ☎ 210249, R, Bar; **Scolt Head Nat Trust Warden** ☎ 210330 (Access HW∓3); **Brancaster Sailing Centre** ☎ 210236, CH.

WISBECH, Cambridgeshire, 52°40' N, 0°10' E, Zone 0 (GMT), Admty charts 1200. HW −0450 on Dover, Wisbech Cut +0020 on Immingham; HW height −0.5m on Immingham; ML 3.5m; Duration 0520. See 10.4.21. Excellent shelter. Vessels of 4.8m draught at sp can reach Wisbech (3.4m at nps). Entrance to R Nene and inland waterways. Moorings W bank ½M downstream from Sutton Bridge at Sutton Port or at Wisbech Town Quay. Entrance well marked from wreck to Nene Towers with lit stbd Bns. Best entrance HW −3. Wisbech Cut to Sutton Br is 3½M call on VHF Ch 16 09 14 or ☎ Holbeach 350364. Sutton Br to Wisbech 12M with Fl R Lts to port. Take care when ships entering or leaving the berthing area. Facilities: (0945) Hr Mr ☎ 582125; EC Wed; **Bodger Bros** ☎ 582864, Gas; **Town** P and D (cans), Bar, R, V, L at Western Tower.

WELLAND RIVER, Lincolnshire, 52°56' N, 0°05' E, Zone 0 (GMT), Admty charts 1200, 1190. At Welland Bridge HW −0440 on Dover, +0030 on Immingham; HW height −0.1m on Immingham; ML 0.3m; Duration 0520. Enter by Welland Cut, Iso R 2s to SE and Iso G 2s to NW. Entrance HW ∓3. Beware tides of up to 5 kn on flood at sp. Secure at small quay ½M NE of bridge on stbd side. Dries.
Recommended for short stay only (at Fosdyke). Very limited facilities.

4

YACHTING
MONTHLY
Britain's top cruising magazine

Cruising under sail – that's the cover to cover theme of Yachting Monthly. From beginner to expert, creek crawler to blue water yachtsman there's something for everyone in each issue.

The *Practical Seamanship* section discusses and analyses seamanship problems in a down to earth and easily understood fashion. Then there's cruising narrative near and far to whet the appetite and technical features on navigation and pilotage. Each month there are authoritative test reports on new boats from our experienced team and also reviews of the latest equipment for boats of all types and sizes. And rounded off by our Around the Coast regional cruising news section it makes a complete package for the cruising yachtsman.

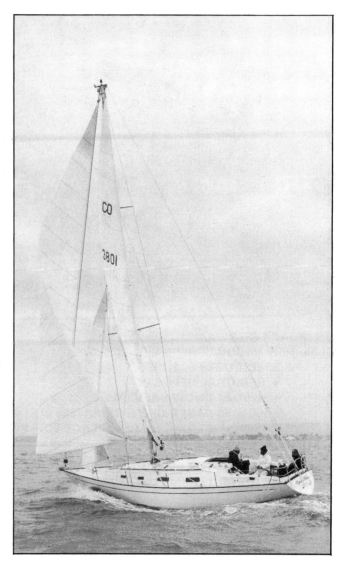

Editor: Andrew Bray
01-261 6040

Advertisement Manager: David Williams
01-261 5582

Fax 01-261 6704

IPC Magazines Ltd, Kings Reach Tower, Stamford Street, London SE1 9LS

BOAT*MART*
INTERNATIONAL

TAKE OUT A SUBSCRIPTION NOW! FOR YOU OR YOUR FRIENDS

FOR ONLY £13.00* YOU CAN HAVE YOUR COPIES POSTED PROMPTLY TO YOUR HOME

* 12 ISSUES / 1 YEAR

★ **BOAT TESTS**
  ★ **NEW PRODUCT REVIEWS**
    ★ **SPECIALIST FEATURES**
      ★ **REGIONAL REPORTS**
        ★ **BOAT SHOW PREVIEWS**
          ★ **40 PAGES OF INFORMATIVE EDITORIAL**
            ★ **MARINE MARKETPLACE FOR SERVICES AND ACCESSORIES**

VOLVO PENTA SERVICE

Sales and service centres in area 5

HUMBERSIDE **Hall Brothers (Bridlington) Ltd** Bessingby Way, Bessingby Industrial Estate, BRIDLINGTON YO16 4SJ Tel (0262) 673346/676604. YORKSHIRE **Auto Unit Repairs (Leeds) Ltd** Henshaw Works, Yeadon, LEEDS LS19 7XY Tel (0532) 501222. **Yacht Services Ltd** Naburn, YORK YO1 4RW Tel (0904) 621021.

Area 5

North-East England
Boston to Berwick-on-Tweed

5

VOLVO PENTA

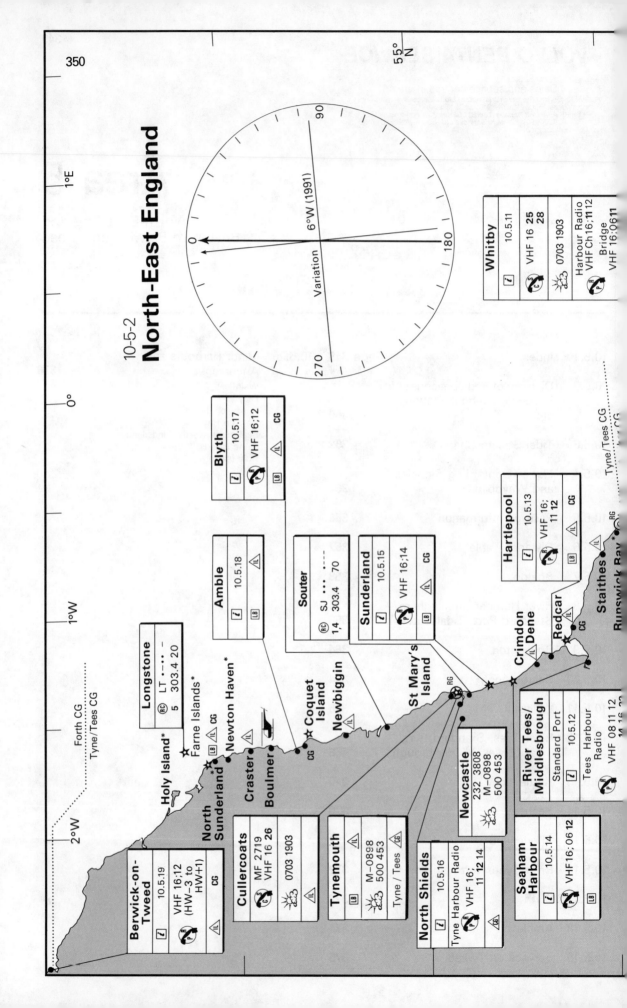

10-5-2
North-East England

6°W (1991)

Variation

Longstone
Ⓡ️Ⓒ LT ·—·· —
5   303.4 20

Berwick-on-Tweed
10.5.19
ℹ️   VHF 16;12
(HW−3 to HW+1)
⚓ CG

Cullercoats
Ⓢ️Ⓒ MF 2719
VHF 16 26
☀️ 0703 1903
⚓

Tynemouth
🛟   ⚓
☀️ M−0898
500 453
Tyne / Tees 📻

North Shields
10.5.16
ℹ️
Tyne Harbour Radio
📻 VHF 16;
11 **12** 14

Seaham Harbour
10.5.14
ℹ️   📻 VHF16; 06 **12**
🛟

Newcastle
232 3808
M−0898
500 453
☀️

Blyth
10.5.17
ℹ️   📻 VHF 16;12
🛟   ⚓ CG

Amble
10.5.18
ℹ️   ⚓
🛟

Souter
Ⓡ️Ⓒ SJ ··· ·———
1,4   303.4 70

Sunderland
10.5.15
ℹ️   📻 VHF 16;14
🛟   ⚓ CG

River Tees/ Middlesbrough
Standard Port
10.5.12
ℹ️
Tees Harbour Radio
📻 VHF 08 11 12
11 16 22

Hartlepool
10.5.13
ℹ️   📻 VHF 16;
11 **12**   ⚓ CG
🛟   ⚓

Whitby
10.5.11
ℹ️
Ⓢ️Ⓒ VHF 16 **25**
28
☀️ 0703 1903
Harbour Radio
VHF Ch16; **11** 12
Bridge
VHF 16; 06 **11**

Holy Island*
Farne Islands*
North Sunderland*
Newton Haven*
Craster
Boulmer
Coquet Island
Newbiggin
St Mary's Island
Crimdon Dene
Redcar
Staithes
Runswick Bay*

Forth CG
Tyne/Tees CG

Tyne/Tees CG
Tyne/Tees CG

55°
N

10.5.3 AREA 5 TIDAL STREAMS

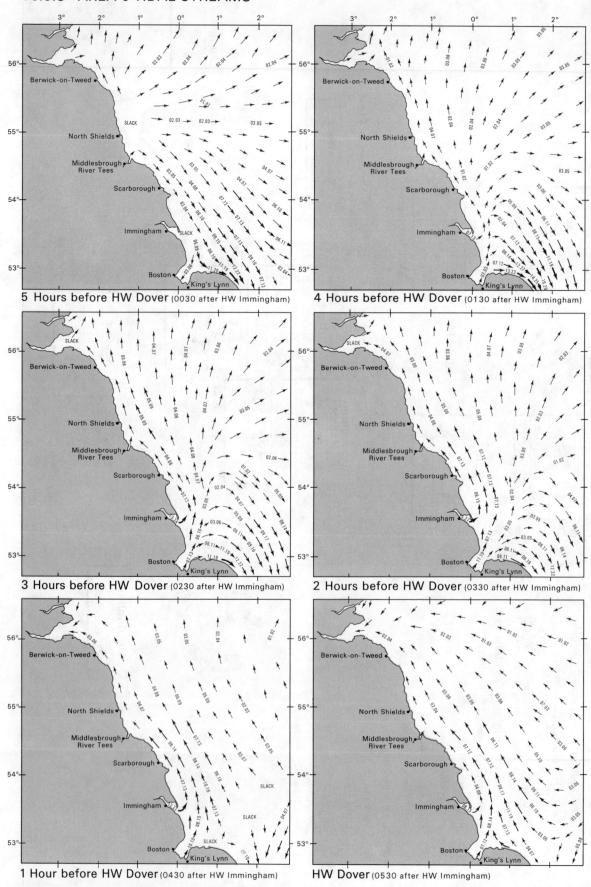

5 Hours before HW Dover (0030 after HW Immingham)

4 Hours before HW Dover (0130 after HW Immingham)

3 Hours before HW Dover (0230 after HW Immingham)

2 Hours before HW Dover (0330 after HW Immingham)

1 Hour before HW Dover (0430 after HW Immingham)

HW Dover (0530 after HW Immingham)

Northward 10.6.3   Southward 10.4.3

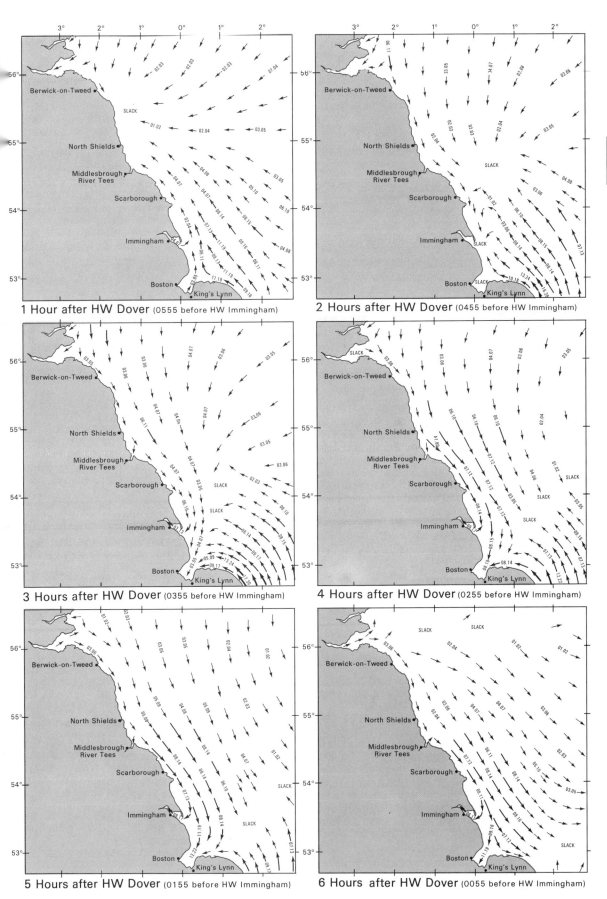

1 Hour after HW Dover (0555 before HW Immingham)

2 Hours after HW Dover (0455 before HW Immingham)

3 Hours after HW Dover (0355 before HW Immingham)

4 Hours after HW Dover (0255 before HW Immingham)

5 Hours after HW Dover (0155 before HW Immingham)

6 Hours after HW Dover (0055 before HW Immingham)

10.5.4   LIGHTS, FOG SIGNALS AND WAYPOINTS

Abbreviations used below are given in 10.0.3. Principal lights are in **bold** print, places in CAPITALS, and light-vessels, light floats and Lanbys in *CAPITAL ITALICS*. Unless otherwise stated lights are white. m—elevation in metres; M—nominal range in n. miles. Fog signals are in *italics*. Useful waypoints are <u>underlined</u> use those on land with care. See 4.2.2.

ENGLAND—NORTH-EAST COAST

BOSTON. <u>Boston Roads Lt Buoy</u> 52°57'·55N 00°16'·23E LFl 10s; safe water mark.

FREEMAN CHANNEL. <u>Boston No. 1 Lt Buoy</u> 52°57'·87N 00°15'·16E FlG 3s; stbd-hand mark.
<u>Alpha Lt Buoy</u> 52°57'·66N 00°15'·06E FlR 3s; port-hand mark. <u>No. 3 Lt Buoy</u> 52°58'·10N 00°14'·15E FlG 6s; stbd-hand mark. <u>Bravo Lt Buoy</u> 52°57'·98N 00°14'·00E FlR 6s; port-hand mark. <u>No. 5 Lt Buoy</u> 52°58'·52N 00°12'·78E FlG 3s; stbd-hand mark. <u>Charlie Lt Buoy</u> 52°58'·43N 00°12'·54E FlR 3s; port-hand mark. <u>Freeman Inner Lt Buoy</u> 52°58'·45N 00°11'·50E Q(9) 15s; W cardinal mark. <u>Delta Lt Buoy</u> 52°58'·34N 00°11'·68E FlR 6s; port-hand mark.

BOSTON DEEP. <u>Lynn Knock Lt Buoy</u> 53°04'·35N 00°27'·30E QG; stbd-hand mark. <u>Pompey Buoy</u> 53°02'·20N 00°19'·37E (unlit); stbd-hand mark. <u>Long Sand Buoy</u> 53°01'·10N 00°18'·30E (unlit); stbd-hand mark. <u>Friskney Buoy</u> 53°00'·48N 00°16'·68E (unlit); stbd-hand mark. <u>Scullridge Buoy</u> 52°59'·68N 00°14'·00E (unlit); stbd-hand mark.

LOWER ROAD. <u>Boston No. 7 Lt Buoy</u> 52°58'·57N 00°10'·05E FlG 3s; stbd-hand mark. <u>Echo Lt Buoy</u> 52°58'·34N 00°10'·15E FlR 3s; port-hand mark. <u>Boston No. 9 Lt Buoy</u> 52° 57'·58N 00°08'·45E FlG 3s; stbd-hand mark. <u>Foxtrot Lt Buoy</u> 52°57'·55N 00°09'·00E FlR 3s; port-hand mark. <u>Boston No. 11 Lt Buoy</u> 52°56'·65N 00°08'·10E FlG 6s; stbd-hand mark. <u>Golf Lt Buoy</u> 52°56'·66N 00°08'·50E FlR 3s; port-hand mark. <u>Hotel Lt Buoy</u> 52°56'·28N 00°07'·54E FlR 3s; port-hand mark. <u>Boston No.13 Lt Buoy</u> 52°56'·18N 00°06'·93E FlG 3s; stbd-hand mark. <u>Juliett Lt Buoy</u> 52°56'·08N 00°06'·72E FlR 3s; port-hand mark. <u>India Lt Buoy</u> 56°12'·05N 00°06'·72E FlR 6s; port-hand mark. <u>Boston No.15 Lt Buoy</u> 52°56'·30N 00°05'·73E FlG 3s; stbd-hand mark.

<u>Welland</u> 52°56'·06N 00°05'·37E QR 5m; R square on Bn. Entrance, N side, <u>Dollypeg</u> 52°56'·10N 00°05'·15E QG 4m 1M; B triangle on Bn; Ra refl. Tabs Head Q WG 4m 1M; R square on W mast; vis W shore-251°, G251°-shore; Ra refl. New Cut 52°56'·0N 00°04'·8E Fl G 3s. New Cut Ldg Lts 240°. Both F 5M.
River to Boston marked by FR and FG Lts, and by FW Ldg Lts.

WELLAND CUT. SE side Iso R 2s; NW side Iso G 2s. Lts QR (to port) and QG (to starboard) mark the channel upstream. Wainfleet Range UQR, with FR on Trs SW & NE.
Wainfleet Swatchway. <u>Swatchway Buoy</u> 53°03'·76N 00°19'·80E (unlit); stbd-hand mark (direction of buoyage S). <u>Inner Knock Buoy</u> 53°04'·85N 00°20'·50E (unlit); port-hand mark. <u>Wainfleet Roads Buoy</u> 53°06'·20N 00°21'·40E (unlit); port-hand mark. <u>Skegness South Buoy</u> 53°06'·70N 00°23'·35E (unlit); stbd-hand mark. <u>Skegness Buoy</u> 53°08'·42N 00°23'·80E (unlit); stbd-hand mark. Skegness Pier 2 FR (vert). <u>Scott Patch Lt Buoy</u> 53°11'·10N 00°36'·50E VQ(3) 5s; E cardinal mark.   <u>S Inner Dowsing Lt Buoy</u> 53°12'·10N 00°33'·80E Q(6)LFl 15s; S cardinal mark; *Bell.*

DUDGEON Lt V 53°16'·60N 01°17'·00E Fl(3) 30s 12m **25M**; R hull with Lt Tr amidships; RC; Racon; *Horn(4) 60s.*
<u>E Dudgeon Lt Buoy</u> 53°19'·70N 00°58'·80E Q(3) 10s; E cardinal mark; *Bell.* <u>W Ridge Lt Buoy</u> 53°19'·05N 00°44'·60E Q(9) 15s; W cardinal mark.

Inner Dowsing 53°19'·70N 00°33'·96E Fl 10s 41m **21M**; R pylon on W house, on platform on B piles; Racon; *Horn 60s;* FlR 2s Lts (synchronized) on each corner of house, when main Lt is not displayed.
<u>Protector Lt Buoy</u> 53°24'·83N 00°25'·25E FlR 2·5s; port-hand mark. <u>DZ No. 4 Lt Buoy</u> 53°27'·12N 00°19'·17E FlY 5s; special mark. <u>DZ No. 3 Lt Buoy</u> 53°28'·40N 00°19'·20E FlY 2·5s; special mark. <u>Rosse Spit Lt Buoy</u> 53°30'·40N 00°17'·05E Fl(2)R 5s; port-hand mark. <u>Haile Sand No. 2 Buoy</u> 53°32'·14N 00°12'·80E Fl(3)R 10s; port-hand mark.
<u>Mid Outer Dowsing Lt Buoy</u> 53°24'·80N 01°07'·90E Fl(3)G 10s; stbd-hand mark; *Bell.* <u>N Outer Dowsing Lt Buoy</u> 53°33'·50N 00°59'·70E Q; N cardinal mark.

DOWSING Lt V 53°34'·00N 00°50'·17E Fl(2) 10s 12m **23M**; R hull with Lt Tr amidships; *Horn(2) 60s;* Racon.
<u>Humber Lt Buoy</u> 53°36'·72N 00°21'·60E L Fl 10s; safe water mark; *Bell;* Racon. <u>N Binks Lt Buoy</u> 53°36'·22N 00°18'·70E FlY 2·5s; special mark.   <u>Outer Haile Lt Buoy</u> 53°35'·25N 00°19'·00E Fl(4)Y 15s; special mark.
<u>S Binks Lt Buoy</u> 53°34'·70N 00°16'·60E FlY 5s; special mark.
SPURN Lt F 53°33'·53N 00°14'·33E Q(3) 10s 10m 8M; E cardinal mark; *Horn 20s;* Racon.

EAST CHEQUER Lt F 53°33'·4N 00°12'·6E L Fl 10s 6m 6M; B hull; Ra refl; *Horn 30s.* FW Riding Lt.
<u>No. 3 Chequer Lt Buoy</u> 53°33'·05N 00°10'·70E Q(6)LFl 15s; S cardinal mark. <u>Tetney Monobuoy</u> 53°32'·34N 00°06'·85E 2 VQY (vert); Y SBM; *Horn Mo(A) 60s;* QY on 290m floating hose. Spurn Point Beacon Fl G 3s 11m 5M; G triangle on frame tripod. Military Pier (head) and Pilot Jetty each show 2 FG (vert) Lts 6m 2M.
BULL Lt F 53°33'·78N 00°05'·64E VQ 8m 6M; N cardinal mark; *Horn (2) 20s.* <u>Bull Sand Fort</u> 53°33'·70N 00°04'·14E Fl(2) 5s 20m 4M; *Horn 20s.*
Killingholme Lts in line 292°. Front Iso R 2s 10m 14M. Rear, 189m from front, Oc R 4s 21m 14M. *Bell.* <u>Haile Sand Fort</u> 53°32'·05N 00°02'·14E 2 FR (vert) 21m 3M.
<u>Wreck Lt Buoy</u> 53°42'·35N 00°07'·30E VQ(3) 5s; E cardinal .
<u>DZ Lt Buoy</u> 53°47'·82N 00°00'·25E QY; special mark.
<u>DZ South Lt Buoy</u> 53°50'·35N 00°01'·50W FlY 2s; special mark. <u>DZ No. 5 Lt Buoy</u> 53°50'·40N 00°04'·00W FlY 5s; special mark. <u>DZ No. 4 Lt Buoy</u> 53°51'·50N 00°00'·00 FlY 10s; special mark. <u>DZ No. 3 Lt Buoy</u> 53°54'·10N 00°02'·00W FlY 10s; special mark.
<u>DZ No. 2 Lt Buoy</u> 53°54'·05N 00°04'·00W FlY 10s; special mark.   <u>DZ North Lt Buoy</u> 53°53'·10N 00°05'·50W FlY 2s; special mark. <u>DZ No. 1 Lt Buoy</u> 53°52'·10N 00°07'·00W FlY 5s; special mark. <u>Hornsea Sewer Outfall Lt Buoy</u> 53°55'·00N 00°01'·70E FlY 20s; special mark. <u>Atwick Sewer Outfall Lt Buoy</u> 53°57'·10N 00°10'·20W FlY 10s; special mark.

BRIDLINGTON. <u>SW Smithic Lt Buoy</u> 54°02'·40N 00°09'·10W Q(9) 15s; W cardinal. <u>N pier head</u> 54°04'·77N 00°11'·08W Fl 2s 7m 9M; *Horn 60s.* S pier FR or G R12m, G8m, R4M, G3M. (Tidal Lts). <u>N Smithic Lt Buoy</u> 54°06'·20N 00°03'·80W Q; N cardinal mark.

Flamborough Head 54°06'·95N 00°04'·87W Fl(4) 15s 65m **29M**; W round Tr; RC; *Horn(2) 90s.*
FILEY. On cliff above CG Stn FR 31m 1M; vis 272°-308°.

Filey Brigg Lt Buoy 54°12'·74N 00°14'·48W Q(3)10s; E cardinal mark; *Bell*.

SCARBOROUGH. E pier head 54°16'·87N 00°23'·27W QG 8m 3M. West pier head 2 FR (vert) 5m 4M when 1·8m on bar. Lighthouse Pier Iso 5s 17m 9M and FY 8m (tide signals); *Dia 60s*.

WHITBY. Whitby Lt Buoy 54°30'·32N 00°36'·48W Q; N cardinal; *Bell*. **High Lt, Ling Hill** 54°28'·67N 00°34'·00W Iso WR 10s 73m **23M**; W 8-sided Tr and dwellings; vis R128°-143°, W143°-319°. E Pier head FR 14m 3M. West Pier head FG 14m; *Horn 30s*. Ldg Lts 169° Church Steps, Rear FR 46m (between E and W Pier Lts, leads into harbour). Ldg Lts 029°. Front FY. Rear 25m from front FY.
Redcar, The High. Outfall Lt Buoy 54°36'·63N 01°00'·30W FIY 10s; special mark. Salt Scar Lt Buoy 54°38'·15N 01°00'·00W Q; N cardinal mark; *Horn(1) 15s*; *Bell*.

REDCAR. Luffway Ldg Lts 197°. Front, on Esplanade, FR 8m 7M; vis 182°-212°. Rear, 115m from front, FR 12m 7M; vis 182°-212°. High Stone Ldg Lts 247°. Both Oc R 2·5s 9/11m 7M; vis 232°-262°.

Tees Fairway Lt Buoy 54°40'·93N 01°06'·37W Iso 4s 9m 8M; safe water mark; *Horn(1) 5s*; Racon. Tees North (Fairway) Lt Buoy 54°40'·28N 01°07'·20W FIG 5s; stbd-hand mark. Tees South (Fairway) Lt Buoy 54°40'·17N 01°06'·95W FIR 5s; port-hand mark.

RIVER TEES. Breakwater head, **South Gare**. 54°38'·83N 01°08'·16W FI WR 12s 16m **W20M**, **R17M**; W round Tr; vis W020°-274°, R274°-357°; *Horn 30s*. Ldg Lts 210°. Both FR 18/20m 13/10M.

HARTLEPOOL. Longscar Lt Buoy 54°40'·85N 01°09'·80W Q(3) 10s; E cardinal mark; *Bell*. The Heugh 54°41'·78N 01°10'·47W FI(2) 10s 19m **19M** (H24); W Trs.
Old Pier head 54°41'·59N 01°10'·99W QG 13m 7M; B Tr. Dir Lt 324°53'. 54°42'·00N 01°11'·60W Dir Iso WRG 3s 42m; vis G323·2°-324·4°, W324·4°-325·4°, R325·4°-326·6°.
Pipe jetty head 54°42'·80N 01°12'·40W 2 FR (vert) 1M; *Bell(1) 15s*.
SEAHAM HARBOUR. North Pier head 54°50'·25N 01°19'·15W FI G 10s 12m 5M; W column, B bands; *Dia 30s*. S Pier head 2 FR (vert) 10m 5M. Hendon Rock Buoy 54°54'·21N 01°19'·44W (unlit); port-hand mark; *Bell*.
Ballast Buoy 54°54'·53N 01°18'·39W (unlit); special mark.

SUNDERLAND. **Roker Pier** head 54°55'·27N 01°21'·05W FI 5s 25m **23M**; W round Tr, R bands and cupola: vis 211°-357°; *Siren 20s*. New South pier head FI 10s 14m 10M; W Tr. South side FI R 5s 9m 2M. Old North pier head QG 12m 8M; Y Tr; *Horn 10s*.
Whitburn Steel Buoy 54°56'·30N 01°20'·80W (unlit); port-hand mark.
WHITBURN FIRING RANGE. 54°57'·2N 01°21'·3W and 54°57'·7N 01°21'·2W both FR when firing is taking place.
Special buoys 54°57'·04N 01°18'·81W and 54°58'·58N 01°19'·80W, both FIY 2·5s.
Lt Buoy 55°00'·17N 01°23'·60W FI(3)R 10s; port-hand mark.
Lizard Point, Souter 54°58'·23N 01°21'·80W FW 43m; W round Tr, Or Band and Lantern; vis 230°-270°.

TYNEMOUTH. **Entrance**, N pier head 55°00'·87N 01°24'·08W FI(3) 10s 26m **26M**; grey round Tr, W lantern; *Horn 10s*. S pier head Oc WRG 10s 15m W13M, R9M, G8M; grey round Tr, R&W lantern; vis W075°-161°, G161°-179° over Bellhues rock, W179°-255°, R255°-075°; *Bell (1) 10s* (TD 1988).
Herd Groyne, head Oc WR 10s 13m W13M, R11M, R1M; R pile structure, R&W lantern; vis R(unintens) 080°-224°, W224°-255°, R255°-277°; *Bell (1) 5s (TD 1988)*.

NORTH SHIELDS. **Fish Quay** Ldg Lts 258°. **Front** F 25m **20M**; W square Tr. **Rear** 220m from front F 39m **20M**; W square Tr.

CULLERCOATS. Ldg Lts 256°. Front 55°02'·1N 01°25'·8W FR 27m 3M. Rear 38m from front FR 35m 3M.

BLYTH. Fairway Lt Buoy 55°06'·58N 01°28'·50W FIG 3s; *Bell*. **E Pier head** FI(4) 10s 10m **21M**; W Tr. FR 13m 13M (same Tr); vis 152°-249°; *Horn (3) 30s*. West Pier head 2FR(vert) 7m 8M; W Tr. Training wall, S end FI R 6s 6m 1M. South Harbour, Inner West Pier, N end 2 FI(2) R 6s (vert) 5m 5M; W metal structure. Ldg Lts 324°. Front 55°07'·4N 01°29'·8W F Bu 11m 10M; Or diamond on framework Tr. Rear, 180m from front, F Bu 17m 10M; Or diamond on framework Tr. Blyth Snook Ldg Lts 338°. Front F Bu 5m 5M; W sided Tr. Rear, 87m from front, F Bu 11m 5M; W triangle on mast.
Hauxley Buoy 55°19'·28N 01°31'·54W (unlit); port-hand mark.

COQUET CHANNEL. **Coquet** 55°20'·01N 01°32'·25W FI(3) WR 30s 25m **W23M**, **R19M**; W square Tr, turreted parapet, lower half grey; vis R330°-140°, W140°-163°, R163°-180°, W180°-330°; *Horn 30s*.
NE Coquet Buoy 55°20'·55N 01°32'·00W (unlit); port-hand mark.
NW Coquet Buoy 55°20'·41N 01°32'·71W (unlit); stbd-hand mark.
Pan Bush Buoy 55°20'·67N 01°33'·22W (unlit); port-hand mark.
Outfall Lt Buoy 55°20'·32N 01°33'·63W FIR 5s; port-hand mark; *Bell*.

WARKWORTH. S breakwater FI R 5s 9m 5M; W Tr, R bands. N breakwater 55°20'·38N 01°34'·15W FI G 6s 12m 6M; W pylon.

ALNMOUTH BAY. Boulmer Stile Buoy 55°23'·75N 01°32'·60W (unlit); port-hand mark. BEADNALL BAY. Newton Rock Buoy 55°32'·08N 01°35'·45W (unlit); port-hand mark.

NORTH SUNDERLAND. NW pier head FG 11m 3M; W Tr; vis 159°-294°; *Siren 90s* (occas). Breakwater head 55°35'·05N 01°38'·79W FI R 2·5s 6m.

Black Rock Point, **Bamburgh** 55°37'·00N 01°43'·35W Oc(2) WRG 15s 12m **W17M**, R13M, G13M; W building; vis G122°-165°, W165°-175°, R175°-191°, W191°-238°, R238°-275°, W275°-289°, G289°-300°.

FARNE ISLANDS, near SW point L FI(2) WR 15s 27m W13M, R9M; W round Tr; vis R119°-277°, W277°-119°. **Longstone**, West side 55°38'·63N 01°36'·55W FI 20s 23m **29M**; R Tr, W band; RC; *Horn (2) 60s*.

Swedman Buoy 55°37'70N 01°41'·50W (unlit); stbd-hand mark.
HOLY ISLAND. Ridge Buoy 55°39'·70N 01°45'87W (unlit); W cardinal mark.
Triton Buoy 55°39'·61N 01°46'49W (unlit); stbd-hand mark.

BERWICK. Breakwater head 55°45'·88N 01°58'·95W FI 5s 15m 10M; W round Tr, R cupola and base; vis 154°-010°. FG (same Tr) 8m 1M; vis 010°-154°; *Reed 60s* (occas).

10.5.5   PASSAGE INFORMATION

For general notes on The Wash see 10.4.5. The W shore of The Wash (chart 108) is fronted by extensive flats which extend 2 – 3M offshore and which dry up to 4m, and provide a bombing range. The Wainfleet Swatchway should only be used in good vis: the chan shifts constantly, and beware the various dangers off Gibraltar Pt, 3M S of Skegness. For Wainfleet see 10.5.20. The better route N from Boston (10.5.7) is through Freeman Chan into Lynn Deep which, if bound E, also gives access to Sledway which runs S of Woolpack and Burnham Flats. Near N end of Lynn Deep there are overfalls over Lynn Knock at sp tides.

Inner Dowsing is a narrow N/S sandbank with a least depth of 1.2m, 10M off Mablethorpe. There are overfalls off the W side of the bank at the N end. Inner Dowsing Lt Ho (Lt, fog sig) stands close NE of the bank.

In the outer approaches to R Humber and The Wash there are many offlying banks, but few of them are of direct danger to yachts. The sea however breaks on some of them in bad weather, when they should be avoided. Fishing vessels may be encountered, and there are oil/gas installations offshore (see below).

TIDAL STREAMS IN RIVERS

Tidal streams in rivers are influenced by local weather conditions as well as by the phases of the Moon. At or near springs, in a river which is obstructed, for example, by sandbanks at the entrance, the time of HW gets later going up river: the time of LW also gets later, but more rapidly. So the duration of rise of tide becomes shorter, and duration of fall of tide becomes longer. At the entrance the flood stream starts at an inverval after LW which increases with the degree of obstruction of the channel: this interval between local LW and the start of the flood increases with the distance up river. The ebb begins soon after local HW along the length of the river. Hence the duration of the flood is less than that of the ebb, and the difference increases with distance up river.

The flood stream is normally stronger than the ebb, and runs harder during the first half of the rise of tide.

At neaps the flood and ebb both start soon after local LW and HW respectively, and their durations and rates are roughly equal.

Both at springs and neaps, the streams can be affected by recent precipitation, whereby the duration and rate of the ebb are increased, and of the flood are reduced.

OIL AND GAS INSTALLATIONS

Any yacht crossing the North Sea is likely to encounter oil or gas installations. These are shown on Admiralty charts where the scale permits, and are listed in the *Annual Summary of Admiralty Notices to Mariners* and in the *Admiralty List of Lights and Fog Signals*. Safety zones of radius 500 metres are established round all permanent platforms, mobile exploration rigs, and tanker loading moorings. Yachts must not enter these zones except in emergency or due to stress of weather.

Platforms show a main, white light, flashing Morse U every 15 seconds with a range of 15M. In addition there are secondary red lights, flashing Morse U every 15 seconds with a range of 3M, synchronised with the main light and situated at each corner of the platform if not marked by a white light. Platforms sound a fog signal, Horn Morse U every 30 seconds.

RIVER HUMBER (charts 109, 1188, 3497)

R Humber is formed by R Ouse and R Trent, which join 15M above Kingston upon Hull, and is important for the access provided to the inland waterways by these rivers. By the time

R Humber reaches the sea between Donna Nook and Spurn Hd it is 6M wide, draining as it does most of Yorkshire and the Midlands.

Approaching from the S, a yacht should make for Rosse Spit buoy and then for Haile Sand buoy, before altering course any more W to meet and follow the main buoyed chan, which leads in from a NE direction through New Sand Hole. Beyond Bull Sand Fort (Lt, fog sig) it is advisable to follow one of the buoyed chans, since shoals are liable to change.

If proceeding to or coming from the N, beware The Binks — a shoal (dries in places) extending 3M E from Spurn Hd, with a rough sea when wind is against tide.

10M E of Spurn Hd the tidal streams are not affected by the river; the S-going stream begins at HW Immingham −0455, and the N-going at HW Immingham +0130. Nearer the entrance the direction of the S-going stream becomes more W, and that of the N-going stream more E. ½M S of Spurn Hd the in-going stream runs NW and begins about HW Immingham −0520, sp rate 3½ kn: the out-going stream runs SE and begins about HW Immingham, sp rate 4 kn. In this area the worst seas are experienced in NW gales on a strong flood tide.

HUMBER TO WHITBY (charts 107, 121, 129)

For the coast, harbs, anchs N from R Humber refer to *Sailing Directions Humber Estuary to Rattray Head* (R Northumberland YC). Bridlington B (chart 1882) is clear of dangers apart from Smithic Shoals (buoyed), about 3M off Bridlington (10.5.9): the seas break on these shoals in strong N or E winds.

Flamborough Hd (Lt, fog sig, RC) is a steep, white cliff with conspic Lt Ho on summit. The Lt may be obsc by cliffs when close inshore. An old Lt Ho, also conspic, is 2½ ca WNW. From here the coast runs NW, with no offshore dangers until Filey Brigg where rky ledges extend ½M ESE, marked by buoy. There is anch in Filey B (10.5.20) in N or offshore winds. NW of Filey Brigg beware Horse Rk and foul ground ½M offshore; maintain this offing past Scarborough (10.5.10) to Whitby High Lt. Off Whitby (10.5.11) beware Whitby Rk and The Scar (dry in places) to E of harb, and Upgang Rks (dry in places) 1M to WNW: the sea breaks on all these rks.

WHITBY TO COQUET ISLAND (charts 134, 152, 156)

From Whitby to Hartlepool (10.5.13) there are no dangers more than 1M offshore. Runswick B (10.5.20 and chart 1612), 5M NW of Whitby, provides anch in winds from S and W but is dangerous in onshore winds. The little harb of Staithes is only suitable for yachts which can take the ground, and only in good weather and offshore winds.

Redcliff, dark red and 205m high is a conspic feature of this coast which, along to Hunt Cliff is prone to landslides and is fringed with rky ledges which dry for about 3 ca. There is a conspic radio mast 4 ca SW of Redcliff. Off Redcar and Coatham beware West Scar and Salt Scar — detached rky ledges (dry) lying 1-8 ca offshore. Other ledges lie close SW and S of Salt Scar which is marked by buoy.

Between R Tees (10.5.12) and Hartlepool (10.5.13) beware Long Scar — detached rky ledge (dries) with extremity marked by buoy. From the Heugh an offing of 1M clears all dangers until approaching Sunderland (10.5.15), where White Stones, rky shoals with depth 3.0m, lie 1¾M SSE of Roker Pier Lt Ho, and Hendon Rk, depth 1.5m, lies 1¼M SE of the Lt Ho. N of Sunderland, Whitburn Steel, a rk with less than 2m over it, lies 1M S of Souter Pt, and an obstruction (dries) lies 1 ca SE of Whitburn Steel. Along this stretch of coast industrial smoke haze may reduce vis and obsc Lts.

The coast N of Tynemouth (10.5.16) is foul, and on passage to Blyth (10.5.17) it should be given an offing of 1M. 3½M N of Tynemouth is St Mary's Island (with disused Lt Ho), connected to land by causeway. The harb of Seaton Sluice, 1M NW of St Mary's Island, is closed.

Proceeding N from Blyth, keep well seaward of The Sow and Pigs buoy, and set course to clear Newbiggin Pt and Beacon Pt by about 1M. Vessels conduct trials on measured distance here. Near Beacon Pt is conspic chy of aluminium smelter. Snab Pt is 2M NNW of Beacon Pt. Cresswell Skeres, rky patches with depth 3.0m, lie 1¼M and 1¾m NNE of Snab Pt. Cresswell Pt is 8 ca NW of Snab Pt, and between the two are rks extending 3 ca seaward. S of Hauxley Hd rks extend 6 ca offshore, with depths of 1.2m, marked by buoy.

COQUET ISLAND AND AMBLE (chart 1627)

Coquet Island (Lt, fog sig) lies about ½M offshore at SE end of Alnmouth B, and nearly 1M NNE of Hauxley Pt — off which drying ledges extend 5½ ca E and 6½ ca NNE towards the island (marked by buoys). On passage, normally pass 1M E of Coquet Island, but Coquet Chan inshore is available in good vis by day. It is very narrow, but no longer buoyed, with least depth of 1.2m near the centre, and the stream runs strongly, S-going from HW Tyne −0515 and N-going from HW Tyne +0045. There are good anchs in Coquet Road, W of the island, in winds from S or W.

Amble (Warkworth) Harb entrance (10.5.18) is about 1M W of Coquet Island, and 1½M SE of Warkworth Castle (conspic). 4 ca NE and ENE of entrance is Pan Bush, rky shoal with least depth of 0.3m on which dangerous seas can build in any swell. The bar off entrance has varying depths, down to less than 1m. Once inside, the harb is safe, but the entrance is dangerous in strong winds from N or E when broken water may extend to Coquet Island.

Between Coquet Island and the Farne Islands, 19M to N, keep at least 1M offshore to avoid various dangers. To seaward, Dicky Shad and Newton Skere lie 1¾M and 4½M E of Baednell Pt, and Craster Skeres lie 5M E of Castle Pt: these are three rky banks on which the sea breaks heavily in bad weather. For Newton Haven and Seahouses (N Sunderland) see 10.5.20.

FARNE ISLANDS AND HOLY ISLAND (chart 111, 1192)

The coast between N Sunderland Pt and Berwick upon Tweed, 16M NW, is a dangerous area. The Farne Islands and offlying shoals extend 4½M offshore, and are worth visiting in good weather. The area is a bird sanctuary, owned and operated by the National Trust, with large colonies of sea birds and also grey seals. For details of this area refer to R Northumberland YC sailing directions. The group of islands, rks and shoals is divided by Farne Sound running NE/SW, and by Staple Sound running NW/SE. Farne Island (Lt) is the innermost I, separated from mainland by Inner Sound, which in good conditions is a better N/S route than keeping outside the whole group: but the stream runs 3 kn at sp, and with strong wind against tide there is rough water. Beware Swedman reef (dries, marked by buoy) 4 ca WSW of Megstone, which is a rk 5m high 1M NW of Farne Lt Ho. N of Inner Sound, off Holy Island, Goldstone Chan passes between Goldstone Rk (dries) on E side and Plough Seat Reef and Plough Rk (both dry) on W side. See 10.5.20.

On NE side of Farne Island there is anch called The Kettle, sheltered except from NW, but anch out of stream close to The Bridges connecting Knock's Reef and W Wideopen.

If course is set outside Farne Islands, pass 1M E of Longstone (Lt, fog sig, RC) to clear Crumstone Rk 1M to S, and Knivestone (dries) and Whirl Rks (depth 0.6m) respectively 5 ca and 6 ca NE of Longstone Lt Ho. The sea breaks on these rks. Also watch for shipping.

Near the Farne Islands and Holy Island the SE-going stream begins at HW Tyne −0430, and the NW-going at HW Tyne +0130. 1M NE of Longstone the sp rate is about 3½ kn, decreasing seaward. There is an eddy S of Longstone on NW-going stream.

Holy Island (Lindisfarne) lies 6M WNW of Longstone, and is linked to mainland by a causeway covered at HW. There is a good anch on S side (chart 1612). From a point about ½M S of Plough Seat Reef, obelisks on Old Law lead 260° S of Triton Shoal (least depth 0.4m, 4 ca SSE of Castle Pt) to the bar, from where Heugh Bn on with belfry of St Mary's Church leads 310° to anch. The stream runs strongly in and out of harb, W-going from HW Tyne +0510, and E-going from HW Tyne −0045. See 10.5.20.

10.5.6 DISTANCE TABLE

Approximate distances in nautical miles are by the most direct route while avoiding dangers and allowing for traffic separation schemes etc. Places in *italics* are in adjoining areas.

1 *North Foreland*	1																			
2 *Goeree Tower*	91	2																		
3 *IJmuiden*	137	46	3																	
4 *Brunsbüttel*	337	263	221	4																
5 Boston	160	161	175	344	5															
6 Grimsby	169	169	182	332	58	6														
7 Bridlington	194	188	196	329	83	44	7													
8 Flamborough Head	192	186	193	325	84	45	5	8												
9 Scarborough	206	200	207	336	98	59	19	14	9											
10 Whitby	222	116	223	345	114	75	35	30	16	10										
11 River Tees	243	237	244	367	135	96	56	50	37	21	11									
12 Hartlepool	245	239	246	370	137	98	58	53	39	24	4	12								
13 Seaham	253	247	254	373	145	106	66	61	47	33	15	11	13							
14 Sunderland	257	251	258	375	149	110	70	65	51	36	20	16	5	14						
15 Tynemouth	262	256	262	378	154	115	75	70	56	41	27	23	12	7	15					
16 Blyth	270	264	267	382	162	123	83	78	64	49	35	31	20	15	8	16				
17 Longstone (Farne)	298	292	295	388	190	151	111	105	92	76	67	63	52	46	40	32	17			
18 Berwick-on-Tweed	313	307	310	402	205	166	126	120	107	91	82	78	67	61	55	47	15	18		
19 *St Abbs Head*	322	316	322	410	214	175	135	129	116	110	91	87	76	70	64	56	24	12	19	
20 Peterhead	404	391	378	439	296	257	217	212	200	186	173	170	161	155	149	143	112	105	97	20

BOSTON 10-5-7
Lincs.

⚓ Visitors berths at River Quay, report to Hr Mr (alongside Lock)

CHARTS
Admiralty 108, 1200; Imray Y9; OS 131
TIDES
−0500 Dover; ML 3.4; Duration Flood 0500, Ebb 0700; Zone 0 (GMT).

Standard Port IMMINGHAM (→)

Times				Height (metres)			
HW		LW		MHWS	MHWN	MLWN	MLWS
0100	0700	0100	0700	7.3	5.8	2.6	0.9
1300	1900	1300	1900				

Differences BOSTON

0000	+0010	+0140	+0050	−0.5	−1.0	−0.9	−0.5

SKEGNESS

+0010	+0015	+0030	+0020	−0.4	−0.5	−0.1	0.0

SHELTER
Very good but mooring in the Dock is not permitted except in emergency. Yachts which can lower masts should pass through the Grand Sluice into fresh water (24 hrs notice required); marina is on the stbd side immediately beyond the sluice. This leads into the R Witham Navigation which goes 31 miles up to Lincoln. The lock is 22.7m x 4.6m and opens approx HW∓1. Moorings may be possible (on S side) below first fixed bridge. British Waterways have 50 moorings, with electricity, above the sluice.
NAVIGATION
Waypoint Boston Roads safe water buoy, LFl 10s, 52°57'.53N 00°16'.23E, 100°/280° from/to Freeman Channel entrance, 0.70M. The channel is liable to change but is well marked. Tabs Head marks the entrance to the river which should be passed not earlier than HW−3 to enable the Grand Sluice to be reached before the start of the ebb. On reaching Boston Dock, masts should be lowered to negotiate swing bridge (cannot always be opened) and three fixed bridges. Channel through town is narrow and un-navigable at LW.

LIGHTS AND MARKS
New Cut and R Witham are marked by Bns with topmarks. FW Lts mark leading lines — six pairs going upstream and six pairs going downstream. St Boltoph's Church tower, known as the Boston Stump is conspicuous landmark. Entry signals for Boston Dock are not given since yachts are not allowed in. Yachts in difficulty secure just above dock entrance and see Hr Mr. The port is administered by Port of Boston Authority.
RADIO TELEPHONE
Call: *Boston Dock* VHF Ch 12 (Mon to Fri 0700-1700 LT and HW−3 to HW+2). Call: *Grand Sluice* Ch 74.
TELEPHONE (0205)
Hr Mr 362328; MRCC Great Yarmouth 851338; Port Signal Stn 362328; ⌗ (0205) 63070; Lock Keeper 364864; Marinecall 0898 500 455; Police 366222; Ⓗ 364801.
FACILITIES
EC Thursday; **Boston Marina** (50 and some visitors) ☎ 364420, D, ACA, FW, CH; C in dock by arrangement with Hr Mr (emergency only) Access HW∓2; **Boston Diesel** ☎ 364568, ME, El, Sh, Gas; **Town** V, R, Bar, ✉, Ⓑ, ≈, ✈ (Norwich or Humberside).

RIVER HUMBER 10-5-8
Humberside

CHARTS
Admiralty 109, 3497, 1188; Associated British Ports; Imray C29; OS 107
TIDES
−0510 Dover; ML 4.1; Duration 0555; Zone 0 (GMT).

RIVER HUMBER *continued*

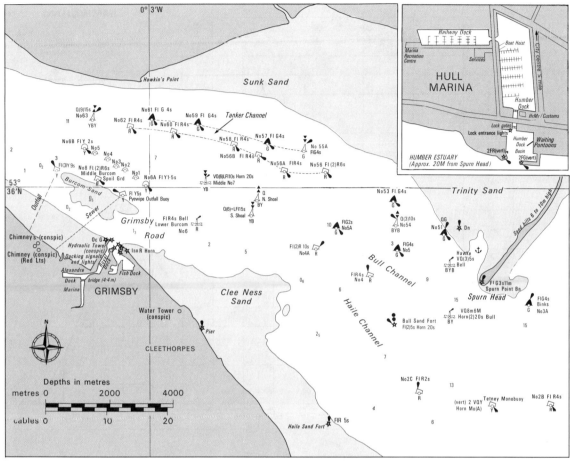

Standard Port IMMINGHAM (→)

Times				Height (metres)			
HW		LW		MHWS	MHWN	MLWN	MLWS
0100	0700	0100	0700	7.3	5.8	2.6	0.9
1300	1900	1300	1900				

Differences HULL

+0005	+0015	+0010	+0020	+0.2	0.0	−0.2	−0.2

GRIMSBY

−0003	−0011	−0015	−0002	−0.3	−0.2	0.0	+0.1

BULL SAND FORT

−0020	−0030	−0035	−0015	−0.4	−0.3	+0.1	+0.2

BURTON STATHER

+0105	+0045	+0335	+0305	−2.1	−2.3	−2.3	Dries

KEADBY

+0135	+0125	+0415	+0355	−2.7	−3.1	Dries	Dries

BLACKTOFT

+0055	+0050	+0310	+0255	−1.5	−1.8	−1.9	−0.8

GOOLE

+0130	+0115	+0355	+0350	−1.6	−2.1	−1.9	−0.6

NOTE: Immingham is a standard Port and details of daily HW and LW times and heights are given below.

SHELTER

R Humber is the estuary of R Ouse and R Trent. Yachts can anchor inside Spurn Head except in strong SW to NW winds. There are marinas at Hull, Grimsby, South Ferriby and Naburn. In Grimsby, visiting yachts now use the Fish Dock where lock charges are high. The approach to South Ferriby Marina should not be attempted without reference to up-to-date Associated British Ports Chart. Immingham should be used only in emergency. South Ferriby available HW∓2½, Grimsby Dock HW∓2½, Hull Marina HW∓3. Yachts are welcome at Brough and Winteringham (30M up river from Spurn Head), but contact club first.

NAVIGATION

Waypoint 53°33'.50N 00°08'.00E, 095°/275° from/to Bull Sand Fort, 2.3M. There is a whirlpool effect at confluence of Rivers Hull and Humber. In flood it runs W into Humber and NE into Hull (reaches 2½ kn at springs). N.B. Associated British Ports is the Navigational and Conservancy Authority for the Humber Estuary and are owners of the ports of Hull, Grimsby, Immingham and Goole. They issue up-to-date information about the buoyed channel up river from Hull which is constantly changing.

LIGHTS AND MARKS

The Humber is well marked for its whole length. International Port Traffic Signals control entry to Grimsby (Royal Dock) shown W of entrance; Immingham; Killingholme; Hull; Goole. Entry to Winteringham Haven and Brough Haven should not be attempted without first contacting Humber Yawl Club for up-to-date approach channel details and mooring availability. Havens available HW∓2 approx.

RADIO TELEPHONE

Humber Vessel Traffic Service − call: *VTS Humber* (Queen Elizabeth Dock, Hull, ☎ Hull 701787) VHF Ch 12, 16; **10 12** 13. Weather reports, tidal information and navigational warnings broadcast every odd H+03 on Ch 12. Grimsby Docks call *Royal Dock* Ch 16; 09 **18** (H24). Immingham Docks Ch 16; 09 22 (H24). River Hull Port Operations Service call: *Drypool Radio* Ch 16; 06 **14** (Mon-Fri: 0800−1800; Sat 0830−1300 LT. HW−2 to HW+½). Goole Docks Ch 16; 14 (H24). Booth Ferry Bridge Ch 16; 12 (H24). Selby Railway Bridge Ch 09; **09** 12. Selby Toll Bridge Ch 09; 09. South Ferriby Yacht Harbour, Humber Yawl Club, Hull Marina, Ch **80** (H24). Grimsby Marina Ch 09 18.

RIVER HUMBER *continued*

H.W. Hts. m.

CHART DATUM

M.H.W.N.

M.H.W.S.

M.L.W.N.

M.L.W.S.

Factor

IMMINGHAM

MEAN SPRING
AND NEAP CURVES

MEAN RANGES	
Springs	6·4m
Neaps	3·2m

Springs occur 2 days
after
New and Full Moon.

L.W. Hts. m.

L.W −5ʰ −4ʰ −3ʰ −2ʰ −1ʰ H.W +1ʰ +2ʰ +3ʰ +4ʰ +5ʰ L.W

TELEPHONE (Hull 0482 Grimsby 0472)
HULL Hr Mr 783538; Lock Tower 215357; MRSC
Bridlington 672317; ✆796161; Marinecall 0898 500 454;
Police 26111; Dr − contact Humber Vessel Traffic Service
701787.
GRIMSBY Port Manager 359181; ✆ 45441; CG Cleethorpes
698300; Marinecall 0898 500 454; Police 59171; Ⓗ 74111.
FACILITIES
HULL **Hull Marina** (310 + 20 visitors) ☎ 25048
(open 0700-2200 LT Fri, Sat, Sun, 0800 − 1800 LT
weekdays), P, D, FW, CH, BH (50 ton), C (2 ton), AC,
Gas, ✆, ME, El, Sh, Slip, Ⓠ, SM, (Access HW∓3);
B. Cooke ☎ 223454, ACA; **Locat Developments**
☎ 25163, Ⓔ.
GRIMSBY EC Thursday; **Grimsby Marina** (150 + 25
visitors). ☎ 360404, D, FW, ME, AC, Gas, Gaz, El, Sh, BH
(30 ton), R, CH, Bar, (Access HW∓3, bridge clearance
4.45m); **Grimsby and Cleethorpes YC** ☎ 356678; Bar, R,
M, FW, Ⓠ; **Grahams** ☎ 46673, ACA; **Fish Dock**
☎ 361343, M; **Royal Dock** ☎ 361344.
SOUTH FERRIBY **South Ferriby Marina** (100 + 20 visitors)
☎ Barton-on-Humber 635620, D, FW, ME, El, Sh, C
(30 ton), CH, Gas, Gaz, (Access HW∓3). **Village** V,
Bar, P.
WINTERINGHAM HAVEN (belongs to Humber Yawl
Club) ☎ Scunthorpe 734452, ✉.
BROUGH HAVEN **Humber Yawl Club** ☎ Hull 667224,
Slip, FW, AB*, Bar. *Limited − contact club.
Note. There is a marina at Naburn, up R Ouse near York
(approx 80M from Spurn Pt). **Naburn Marina** (450 +
50 visitors) ☎ York 21021, VHF Ch **80** 37, CH, P, D, FW,
AC, Sh, ME, BH (16 ton), R.

ENGLAND, EAST COAST – IMMINGHAM

Lat 53°38′ N   Long 0°11′ W

TIMES AND HEIGHTS OF HIGH AND LOW WATERS

YEAR **1991**

TIME ZONE **UT (GMT)**
For Summer Time add ONE hour in non-shaded areas

5

Chart Datum: 3.90 metres below Ordnance Datum (Newlyn)

JANUARY

	Time	m		Time	m
1 Tu	0558 1215 1812	7·2 1·3 7·3	**16** W	0007 0619 1218 1818	1·6 6·6 1·8 6·9
2 W	0046 0652 1303 1859	0·8 7·3 1·3 7·5	**17** Th	0043 0653 1253 1850	1·4 6·7 1·6 7·0
3 Th	0135 0741 1348 1942	0·7 7·3 1·3 7·5	**18** F	0117 0726 1327 1923	1·3 6·7 1·6 7·1
4 F	0222 0827 1430 2026	0·7 7·1 1·5 7·4	**19** Sa	0152 0759 1401 1957	1·2 6·8 1·6 7·1
5 Sa	0304 0912 1510 2110	0·9 6·9 1·7 7·1	**20** Su	0225 0833 1433 2030	1·2 6·7 1·6 7·0
6 Su	0345 0956 1548 2153	1·2 6·5 1·9 6·8	**21** M	0257 0908 1507 2107	1·3 6·6 1·7 6·9
7 M	0426 1040 1628 2240	1·5 6·2 2·2 6·5	**22** Tu	0331 0945 1542 2146	1·4 6·4 1·9 6·7
8 Tu	0509 1127 1718 2334	1·9 5·9 2·5 6·1	**23** W	0410 1027 1627 2235	1·6 6·2 2·1 6·5
9 W	0603 1225 1819	2·3 5·6 2·8	**24** Th	0501 1122 1727 2342	1·9 5·9 2·4 6·2
10 Th	0043 0710 1335 1940	5·8 2·6 5·6 2·9	**25** F	0608 1238 1849	2·2 5·8 2·5
11 F	0205 0822 1446 2057	5·6 2·6 5·7 2·8	**26** Sa	0107 0734 1404 2020	6·0 2·3 5·9 2·3
12 Sa	0318 0925 1543 2157	5·8 2·5 6·0 2·5	**27** Su	0240 0900 1521 2142	6·1 2·2 6·2 1·9
13 Su	0417 1017 1630 2247	6·0 2·3 6·3 2·1	**28** M	0359 1013 1624 2251	6·4 1·9 6·6 1·4
14 M	0504 1102 1709 2329	6·2 2·1 6·5 1·8	**29** Tu	0504 1113 1716 2349	6·8 1·6 7·0 1·0
15 Tu	0543 1142 1746	6·4 2·0 6·7	**30** W	0557 1205 1803	7·1 1·3 7·3
			31 Th	0039 0645 1252 1846	0·6 7·3 1·1 7·5

FEBRUARY

	Time	m		Time	m
1 F	0124 0727 1333 1926	0·5 7·3 1·1 7·6	**16** Sa	0100 0706 1310 1903	1·0 6·9 1·2 7·3
2 Sa	0205 0806 1409 2005	0·5 7·2 1·2 7·5	**17** Su	0134 0738 1344 1937	0·9 7·0 1·2 7·3
3 Su	0240 0844 1443 2042	0·8 6·9 1·4 7·3	**18** M	0206 0811 1416 2012	0·9 6·9 1·2 7·3
4 M	0312 0918 1515 2118	1·1 6·6 1·6 7·0	**19** Tu	0237 0844 1445 2047	1·0 6·8 1·4 7·1
5 Tu	0343 0952 1548 2156	1·5 6·3 1·9 6·5	**20** W	0310 0918 1522 2127	1·2 6·6 1·6 6·9
6 W	0417 1028 1626 2238	1·9 6·0 2·3 6·1	**21** Th	0345 0957 1604 2214	1·5 6·3 1·9 6·5
7 Th	0459 1113 1715 2340	2·4 5·6 2·7 5·6	**22** F	0431 1049 1704 2323	1·9 6·0 2·2 6·0
8 F	0600 1224 1836	2·8 5·4 3·0	**23** Sa	0540 1208 1831	2·4 5·7 2·4
9 Sa	0116 0728 1355 2019	5·3 3·0 5·4 2·9	**24** Su	0102 0717 1348 2015	5·8 2·6 5·8 2·3
10 Su	0251 0853 1512 2134	5·4 2·8 5·7 2·6	**25** M	0244 0851 1512 2141	5·9 2·4 6·1 1·8
11 M	0357 1006 1606 2227	5·7 2·5 6·0 2·1	**26** Tu	0402 1006 1616 2245	6·4 2·0 6·6 1·3
12 Tu	0447 1041 1649 2311	6·1 2·2 6·4 1·8	**27** W	0501 1104 1706 2339	6·8 1·6 7·0 0·8
13 W	0527 1123 1726 2350	6·4 1·9 6·7 1·4	**28** Th	0547 1151 1749	7·0 1·3 7·3
14 Th	0601 1200 1800	6·6 1·6 6·9			
15 F	0027 0645 1235 1831	1·2 6·8 1·4 7·1			

MARCH

	Time	m		Time	m
1 F	0025 0628 1232 1828	0·6 7·2 1·1 7·5	**16** Sa ●	0000 0607 1211 1807	1·0 6·9 1·2 7·2
2 Sa	0104 0704 1310 1904	0·5 7·2 1·0 7·6	**17** Su	0036 0639 1248 1841	0·5 7·1 1·0 7·4
3 Su	0140 0738 1344 1940	0·6 7·1 1·0 7·5	**18** M	0112 0713 1323 1916	0·7 7·1 1·0 7·4
4 M	0211 0811 1415 2013	0·8 7·0 1·2 7·2	**19** Tu	0145 0747 1357 1952	0·8 7·1 1·0 7·4
5 Tu	0239 0842 1443 2047	1·1 6·7 1·4 6·9	**20** W	0218 0822 1432 2032	0·9 6·9 1·1 7·2
6 W	0305 0910 1512 2119	1·5 6·5 1·7 6·5	**21** Th	0251 0858 1510 2115	1·2 6·7 1·4 6·8
7 Th	0335 0941 1545 2157	1·9 6·1 2·1 6·0	**22** F	0329 0939 1555 2210	1·6 6·4 1·7 6·4
8 F	0409 1019 1628 2252	2·3 5·8 2·5 5·5	**23** Sa	0417 1034 1657 2326	2·1 6·0 2·1 5·9
9 Sa	0501 1120 1739	2·8 5·4 2·9	**24** Su	0530 1157 1831	2·5 5·7 2·3
10 Su	0028 0631 1300 1935	5·1 3·2 5·2 3·0	**25** M	0109 0710 1338 2012	5·7 2·7 5·8 2·0
11 M	0215 0815 1432 2100	5·2 3·1 5·5 2·6	**26** Tu	0243 0840 1500 2131	6·0 2·4 6·2 1·6
12 Tu	0327 0924 1534 2156	5·6 2·7 5·9 2·1	**27** W	0353 0950 1600 2230	6·4 2·0 6·6 1·2
13 W	0417 1013 1619 2241	6·0 2·3 6·3 1·7	**28** Th	0445 1044 1648 2319	6·7 1·6 6·9 0·9
14 Th	0458 1055 1658 2322	6·4 1·9 6·6 1·3	**29** F	0527 1129 1729	6·9 1·3 7·2
15 F	0534 1134 1733	6·7 1·5 6·9	**30** Sa ○	0001 0604 1207 1805	0·7 7·0 1·1 7·3
			31 Su	0036 0636 1243 1839	0·7 7·1 1·0 7·3

APRIL

	Time	m		Time	m
1 M	0110 0707 1316 1914	0·8 7·1 1·1 7·2	**16** Tu	0046 0646 1302 1856	0·8 7·2 0·9 7·4
2 Tu	0140 0738 1347 1947	1·0 7·0 1·2 7·0	**17** W	0124 0724 1341 1938	0·8 7·2 0·9 7·3
3 W	0206 0836 1415 2020	1·3 6·8 1·4 6·7	**18** Th	0201 0804 1420 2025	1·0 7·1 1·0 7·1
4 Th	0233 0836 1444 2054	1·6 6·6 1·6 6·4	**19** F	0240 0844 1504 2115	1·3 6·8 1·2 6·7
5 F	0301 0907 1517 2132	1·9 6·3 2·0 6·0	**20** Sa	0322 0931 1555 2216	1·7 6·5 1·5 6·3
6 Sa	0335 0943 1557 2223	2·3 5·9 2·3 5·5	**21** Su	0414 1030 1702 2334	2·2 6·2 1·8 6·0
7 Su	0420 1037 1659 2346	2·8 5·6 2·7 5·2	**22** M	0527 1150 1829	2·5 6·0 1·9
8 M	0536 1204 1842	3·1 5·3 2·8	**23** Tu	0103 0656 1319 1955	5·9 2·6 6·0 1·8
9 Tu	0126 0721 1337 2009	5·2 3·1 5·5 2·5	**24** W	0225 0818 1434 2105	6·1 2·4 6·3 1·5
10 W	0239 0837 1444 2111	5·6 2·8 5·8 2·1	**25** Th	0328 0922 1534 2203	6·3 2·1 6·5 1·3
11 Th	0334 0932 1536 2202	6·0 2·3 6·2 1·7	**26** F	0419 1016 1623 2249	6·5 1·8 6·7 1·1
12 F	0419 1019 1620 2247	6·3 1·9 6·6 1·3	**27** Sa	0459 1104 1704 2330	6·7 1·6 6·9 1·1
13 Sa	0459 1101 1659 2327	6·6 1·5 6·9 0·9	**28** Su ○	0534 1140 1740	6·8 1·4 7·0
14 Su ●	0536 1142 1737	6·9 1·2 7·2	**29** M	0005 0607 1217 1817	1·1 6·9 1·3 7·0
15 M	0008 0611 1222 1815	0·8 7·1 1·0 7·4	**30** Tu	0039 0638 1250 1852	1·2 6·8 1·2 6·9

ENGLAND, EAST COAST – IMMINGHAM

Lat 53°38′ N   Long 0°11′ W

TIMES AND HEIGHTS OF HIGH AND LOW WATERS

YEAR **1991**

TIME ZONE UT(GMT)
For Summer Time add ONE hour in non-shaded areas

MAY

Day	Time	m	Day	Time	m
1 W	0110 / 0709 / 1323 / 1927	1.3 / 6.9 / 1.3 / 6.7	16 Th	0106 / 0706 / 1330 / 1931	1.0 / 7.2 / 0.8 / 7.2
2 Th	0140 / 0740 / 1354 / 2002	1.5 / 6.8 / 1.5 / 6.5	17 F	0149 / 0749 / 1416 / 2023	1.2 / 7.2 / 0.9 / 7.0
3 F	0208 / 0811 / 1425 / 2037	1.7 / 6.6 / 1.6 / 6.3	18 Sa	0234 / 0836 / 1505 / 2118	1.4 / 7.0 / 1.1 / 6.8
4 Sa	0239 / 0843 / 1458 / 2117	2.0 / 6.4 / 1.8 / 6.0	19 Su	0321 / 0927 / 1559 / 2219	1.7 / 6.8 / 1.3 / 6.4
5 Su	0312 / 0919 / 1539 / 2204	2.3 / 6.1 / 2.1 / 5.7	20 M ⟨	0413 / 1024 / 1659 / 2325	2.1 / 6.5 / 1.5 / 6.2
6 M	0355 / 1007 / 1633 / 2309	2.6 / 5.8 / 2.3 / 5.5	21 Tu	0515 / 1130 / 1810	2.3 / 6.3 / 1.6
7 Tu (	0454 / 1113 / 1747	2.9 / 5.6 / 2.4	22 W	0036 / 0625 / 1245 / 1921	6.0 / 2.5 / 6.2 / 1.7
8 W	0027 / 0615 / 1234 / 1909	5.4 / 3.0 / 5.6 / 2.3	23 Th	0148 / 0738 / 1357 / 2027	6.0 / 2.4 / 6.3 / 1.6
9 Th	0140 / 0735 / 1344 / 2015	5.6 / 2.8 / 5.8 / 2.0	24 F	0251 / 0844 / 1458 / 2125	6.1 / 2.3 / 6.4 / 1.6
10 F	0240 / 0639 / 1443 / 2112	5.9 / 2.4 / 6.1 / 1.7	25 Sa	0343 / 0942 / 1552 / 2214	6.2 / 2.1 / 6.4 / 1.6
11 Sa	0332 / 0934 / 1535 / 2204	2.1 / 2.1 / 6.5 / 1.4	26 Su	0427 / 1030 / 1638 / 2258	6.4 / 1.9 / 6.5 / 1.5
12 Su	0419 / 1024 / 1623 / 2252	6.5 / 1.7 / 6.8 / 1.2	27 M	0505 / 1113 / 1719 / 2336	6.5 / 1.7 / 6.6 / 1.5
13 M	0501 / 1112 / 1709 / 2339	6.8 / 1.3 / 7.1 / 1.0	28 Tu ○	0539 / 1153 / 1758	6.7 / 1.5 / 6.6
14 Tu ●	0542 / 1158 / 1754	7.0 / 1.1 / 7.2	29 W	0011 / 0612 / 1229 / 1836	1.5 / 6.8 / 1.5 / 6.6
15 W	0022 / 0624 / 1243 / 1842	0.9 / 7.2 / 0.9 / 7.3	30 Th	0046 / 0646 / 1304 / 1913	1.5 / 6.8 / 1.5 / 6.5
			31 F	0119 / 0719 / 1338 / 1949	1.7 / 6.8 / 1.5 / 6.4

JUNE

Day	Time	m	Day	Time	m
1 Sa	0151 / 0752 / 1412 / 2026	1.8 / 6.7 / 1.6 / 6.3	16 Su	0229 / 0826 / 1503 / 2114	1.3 / 7.2 / 0.8 / 6.9
2 Su	0223 / 0826 / 1446 / 2104	2.0 / 6.6 / 1.7 / 6.1	17 M	0314 / 0915 / 1552 / 2206	1.6 / 7.1 / 1.0 / 6.6
3 M	0257 / 0903 / 1525 / 2146	2.1 / 6.4 / 1.8 / 6.0	18 Tu	0400 / 1006 / 1642 / 2259	1.8 / 6.9 / 1.2 / 6.3
4 Tu	0335 / 0943 / 1609 / 2234	2.3 / 6.2 / 2.0 / 5.8	19 W))	0448 / 1101 / 1736 / 2357	2.1 / 6.6 / 1.5 / 6.1
5 W	0421 / 1033 / 1702 / 2330	2.5 / 6.0 / 2.1 / 5.7	20 Th	0544 / 1201 / 1835	2.3 / 6.3 / 1.8
6 Th	0519 / 1133 / 1805	2.6 / 5.9 / 2.1	21 F (	0059 / 0649 / 1310 / 1940	5.9 / 2.5 / 6.1 / 2.0
7 F	0035 / 0628 / 1241 / 1913	5.7 / 2.6 / 6.0 / 2.0	22 Sa	0204 / 0759 / 1419 / 2043	5.8 / 2.5 / 6.1 / 2.1
8 Sa	0141 / 0738 / 1348 / 2019	5.8 / 2.5 / 6.1 / 1.9	23 Su	0304 / 0905 / 1524 / 2139	5.9 / 2.4 / 6.1 / 2.0
9 Su	0243 / 0847 / 1451 / 2121	6.1 / 2.2 / 6.3 / 1.6	24 M	0356 / 1003 / 1619 / 2228	6.1 / 2.2 / 6.2 / 2.0
10 M	0339 / 0949 / 1550 / 2220	6.4 / 1.9 / 6.6 / 1.4	25 Tu	0440 / 1052 / 1705 / 2311	6.3 / 2.0 / 6.3 / 1.9
11 Tu	0430 / 1045 / 1647 / 2313	6.7 / 1.5 / 6.9 / 1.3	26 W	0518 / 1136 / 1747 / 2350	6.5 / 1.8 / 6.4 / 1.8
12 W ●	0519 / 1140 / 1742	6.9 / 1.2 / 7.1	27 Th ○	0554 / 1214 / 1827	6.7 / 1.6 / 6.5
13 Th	0005 / 0605 / 1232 / 1835	1.1 / 7.1 / 0.9 / 7.2	28 F	0028 / 0629 / 1250 / 1903	1.7 / 6.8 / 1.5 / 6.5
14 F	0055 / 0652 / 1324 / 1928	1.1 / 7.3 / 0.7 / 7.2	29 Sa	0103 / 0702 / 1326 / 1937	1.7 / 6.9 / 1.4 / 6.5
15 Sa	0142 / 0740 / 1413 / 2020	1.2 / 7.3 / 0.7 / 7.1	30 Su	0137 / 0735 / 1359 / 2012	1.7 / 6.8 / 1.4 / 6.5

JULY

Day	Time	m	Day	Time	m
1 M	0209 / 0809 / 1433 / 2046	1.8 / 6.8 / 1.4 / 6.3	16 Tu	0256 / 0856 / 1532 / 2139	1.3 / 7.4 / 0.8 / 6.8
2 Tu	0242 / 0843 / 1508 / 2122	1.9 / 6.7 / 1.5 / 6.3	17 W	0335 / 0939 / 1612 / 2223	1.5 / 7.1 / 1.2 / 6.4
3 W	0315 / 0919 / 1543 / 2200	2.0 / 6.6 / 1.6 / 6.1	18 Th))	0416 / 1024 / 1654 / 2308	1.8 / 6.7 / 1.6 / 6.1
4 Th	0352 / 0959 / 1624 / 2244	2.1 / 6.4 / 1.8 / 5.9	19 F	0459 / 1116 / 1742 / 2358	2.2 / 6.3 / 2.0 / 5.8
5 F	0437 / 1047 / 1713 / 2337	2.3 / 6.3 / 1.9 / 5.8	20 Sa ⟨	0556 / 1221 / 1845	2.5 / 6.0 / 2.4
6 Sa	0533 / 1147 / 1817	2.4 / 6.1 / 2.0	21 Su	0109 / 0710 / 1340 / 1958	5.6 / 2.7 / 5.7 / 2.5
7 Su	0045 / 0648 / 1300 / 1931	5.7 / 2.5 / 6.1 / 2.1	22 M	0222 / 0834 / 1500 / 2108	5.7 / 2.7 / 5.7 / 2.5
8 M	0158 / 0808 / 1419 / 2046	5.9 / 2.3 / 6.2 / 1.9	23 Tu	0327 / 0943 / 1604 / 2204	5.9 / 2.4 / 5.9 / 2.3
9 Tu	0307 / 0921 / 1532 / 2155	6.2 / 2.0 / 6.4 / 1.7	24 W	0419 / 1037 / 1654 / 2251	6.2 / 2.1 / 6.2 / 2.1
10 W	0407 / 1028 / 1638 / 2257	6.5 / 1.6 / 6.7 / 1.5	25 Th	0501 / 1120 / 1736 / 2333	6.4 / 1.8 / 6.4 / 1.9
11 Th ●	0502 / 1130 / 1737 / 2353	6.9 / 1.2 / 7.0 / 1.3	26 F ○	0537 / 1200 / 1812	6.9 / 1.6 / 6.5
12 F	0553 / 1227 / 1832	7.2 / 0.8 / 7.2	27 Sa	0011 / 0611 / 1236 / 1846	1.7 / 6.8 / 1.4 / 6.6
13 Sa	0045 / 0641 / 1317 / 1923	1.1 / 7.4 / 0.6 / 7.3	28 Su	0046 / 0645 / 1310 / 1919	1.6 / 7.0 / 1.3 / 6.7
14 Su	0131 / 0727 / 1405 / 2011	1.1 / 7.5 / 0.5 / 7.3	29 M	0119 / 0716 / 1342 / 1949	1.5 / 7.0 / 1.2 / 6.7
15 M	0216 / 0812 / 1450 / 2056	1.1 / 7.5 / 0.6 / 7.1	30 Tu	0151 / 0748 / 1415 / 2022	1.5 / 7.0 / 1.2 / 6.7
			31 W	0223 / 0820 / 1446 / 2054	1.6 / 6.9 / 1.3 / 6.5

AUGUST

Day	Time	m	Day	Time	m
1 Th	0254 / 0854 / 1517 / 2127	1.7 / 6.9 / 1.4 / 6.4	16 F	0339 / 0948 / 1609 / 2219	1.7 / 6.7 / 1.8 / 6.1
2 F	0327 / 0929 / 1550 / 2204	1.8 / 6.7 / 1.6 / 6.2	17 Sa))	0417 / 1033 / 1649 / 2304	2.1 / 6.3 / 2.2 / 5.8
3 Sa	0404 / 1013 / 1634 / 2251	2.0 / 6.5 / 1.9 / 6.0	18 Su	0505 / 1133 / 1747	2.5 / 5.8 / 2.7
4 Su	0455 / 1111 / 1733 / 2358	2.3 / 6.3 / 2.2 / 5.8	19 M	0010 / 0621 / 1303 / 1913	5.5 / 2.9 / 5.5 / 3.0
5 M	0610 / 1231 / 1855	2.5 / 6.0 / 2.3	20 Tu	0140 / 0804 / 1437 / 2039	5.5 / 2.9 / 5.5 / 2.8
6 Tu	0126 / 0742 / 1405 / 2025	5.8 / 2.4 / 6.0 / 2.3	21 W	0257 / 0921 / 1546 / 2142	5.7 / 2.5 / 5.8 / 2.5
7 W	0247 / 0908 / 1528 / 2142	6.1 / 2.0 / 6.3 / 2.0	22 Th	0355 / 1016 / 1635 / 2230	6.1 / 2.1 / 6.2 / 2.2
8 Th	0356 / 1021 / 1637 / 2247	6.5 / 1.6 / 6.7 / 1.6	23 F	0438 / 1059 / 1715 / 2311	6.4 / 1.6 / 6.4 / 1.9
9 F	0452 / 1123 / 1733 / 2342	6.9 / 1.1 / 7.0 / 1.3	24 Sa	0515 / 1137 / 1750 / 2349	6.7 / 1.5 / 6.7 / 1.7
10 Sa ●	0542 / 1217 / 1822	7.3 / 0.7 / 7.3	25 Su ○	0549 / 1214 / 1822	6.9 / 1.3 / 6.8
11 Su	0031 / 0627 / 1304 / 1907	1.1 / 7.5 / 0.4 / 7.4	26 M	0022 / 0621 / 1248 / 1853	1.1 / 7.1 / 1.1 / 6.9
12 M	0114 / 0709 / 1348 / 1949	0.9 / 7.7 / 0.4 / 7.3	27 Tu	0056 / 0652 / 1320 / 1923	1.3 / 7.2 / 1.1 / 6.9
13 Tu	0154 / 0749 / 1426 / 2029	1.0 / 7.6 / 0.6 / 7.1	28 W	0128 / 0723 / 1351 / 1954	1.3 / 7.2 / 1.1 / 6.9
14 W	0230 / 0829 / 1503 / 2105	1.1 / 7.5 / 0.9 / 6.8	29 Th	0201 / 0757 / 1422 / 2026	1.3 / 7.2 / 1.2 / 6.8
15 Th	0305 / 0908 / 1535 / 2141	1.3 / 7.2 / 1.3 / 6.5	30 F	0232 / 0830 / 1451 / 2058	1.5 / 7.1 / 1.4 / 6.6
			31 Sa	0304 / 0907 / 1524 / 2134	1.6 / 6.8 / 1.6 / 6.4

Chart Datum: 3.90 metres below Ordnance Datum (Newlyn)

ENGLAND, EAST COAST – IMMINGHAM

Lat 53°38′ N   Long 0°11′ W

TIMES AND HEIGHTS OF HIGH AND LOW WATERS   YEAR **1991**

TIME ZONE UT(GMT)
For Summer Time add ONE hour in non-shaded areas

5

SEPTEMBER

Day	Time	m		Day	Time	m
1 Su ☾	0342 / 0950 / 1606 / 2220	1·9 / 6·5 / 2·0 / 6·1		16 M	0423 / 1052 / 1654 / 2313	2·5 / 5·6 / 2·9 / 5·5
2 M	0433 / 1052 / 1705 / 2330	2·2 / 6·1 / 2·4 / 5·8		17 Tu	0533 / 1224 / 1822	2·9 / 5·3 / 3·2
3 Tu	0553 / 1224 / 1836	2·5 / 5·8 / 2·6		18 W	0049 / 0724 / 1404 / 2004	5·4 / 2·9 / 5·4 / 3·1
4 W	0109 / 0735 / 1406 / 2015	5·8 / 2·4 / 6·0 / 2·5		19 Th	0218 / 0847 / 1514 / 2111	5·6 / 2·6 / 5·8 / 2·7
5 Th	0237 / 0904 / 1528 / 2134	6·1 / 1·9 / 6·4 / 2·1		20 F	0319 / 0942 / 1603 / 2159	6·0 / 2·2 / 6·2 / 2·3
6 F	0346 / 1014 / 1631 / 2234	6·5 / 1·4 / 6·8 / 1·7		21 Sa	0406 / 1027 / 1644 / 2241	6·4 / 1·8 / 6·5 / 2·0
7 Sa	0440 / 1111 / 1722 / 2326	7·0 / 1·0 / 7·1 / 1·3		22 Su	0444 / 1106 / 1719 / 2319	6·7 / 1·5 / 6·7 / 1·7
8 Su ●	0526 / 1200 / 1805	7·3 / 0·6 / 7·3		23 M ○	0519 / 1143 / 1751 / 2354	7·0 / 1·2 / 6·9 / 1·4
9 M	0010 / 0607 / 1243 / 1843	1·1 / 7·6 / 0·5 / 7·4		24 Tu	0551 / 1218 / 1822	7·2 / 1·1 / 7·0
10 Tu	0050 / 0646 / 1321 / 1920	0·9 / 7·7 / 0·5 / 7·3		25 W	0029 / 0624 / 1252 / 1853	1·2 / 7·3 / 1·0 / 7·1
11 W	0127 / 0723 / 1357 / 1955	0·9 / 7·6 / 0·8 / 7·2		26 Th	0103 / 0657 / 1326 / 1926	1·2 / 7·4 / 1·1 / 7·1
12 Th	0202 / 0801 / 1429 / 2029	1·1 / 7·4 / 1·1 / 6·9		27 F	0138 / 0733 / 1357 / 1959	1·2 / 7·3 / 1·2 / 7·0
13 F	0233 / 0837 / 1457 / 2100	1·4 / 7·1 / 1·5 / 6·6		28 Sa	0212 / 0811 / 1430 / 2034	1·3 / 7·1 / 1·5 / 6·8
14 Sa	0305 / 0914 / 1528 / 2134	1·7 / 6·6 / 2·0 / 6·3		29 Su	0247 / 0853 / 1505 / 2112	1·5 / 6·9 / 1·8 / 6·5
15 Su ☽	0339 / 0955 / 1603 / 2213	2·1 / 6·1 / 2·4 / 5·9		30 M	0329 / 0943 / 1549 / 2203	1·8 / 6·5 / 2·2 / 6·2

OCTOBER

Day	Time	m		Day	Time	m
1 Tu ☾	0426 / 1052 / 1654 / 2318	2·1 / 6·1 / 2·6 / 5·9		16 W	0451 / 1139 / 1725 / 2349	2·7 / 5·4 / 3·3 / 5·5
2 W	0551 / 1229 / 1828	2·4 / 5·9 / 2·8		17 Th	0627 / 1310 / 1907	2·9 / 5·4 / 3·3
3 Th	0057 / 0731 / 1404 / 2004	5·9 / 2·2 / 6·1 / 2·6		18 F	0121 / 0755 / 1423 / 2022	5·6 / 2·6 / 5·7 / 3·0
4 F	0223 / 0854 / 1518 / 2117	6·2 / 1·8 / 6·5 / 2·2		19 Sa	0229 / 0854 / 1518 / 2115	5·9 / 2·2 / 6·0 / 2·5
5 Sa	0328 / 0957 / 1614 / 2214	6·6 / 1·3 / 6·8 / 1·8		20 Su	0321 / 0943 / 1602 / 2202	6·2 / 1·9 / 6·4 / 2·1
6 Su	0420 / 1049 / 1701 / 2302	7·0 / 1·0 / 7·1 / 1·4		21 M	0404 / 1027 / 1641 / 2242	6·6 / 1·6 / 6·7 / 1·8
7 M	0504 / 1136 / 1740 / 2344	7·3 / 0·8 / 7·2 / 1·2		22 Tu	0442 / 1108 / 1716 / 2322	6·9 / 1·3 / 6·9 / 1·5
8 Tu	0543 / 1215 / 1815	7·4 / 0·8 / 7·3		23 W ○	0519 / 1146 / 1750	7·1 / 1·2 / 7·1
9 W	0024 / 0621 / 1252 / 1849	1·1 / 7·5 / 0·9 / 7·3		24 Th	0001 / 0556 / 1224 / 1824	1·3 / 7·3 / 1·1 / 7·2
10 Th	0100 / 0657 / 1324 / 1921	1·1 / 7·4 / 1·1 / 7·1		25 F	0039 / 0634 / 1300 / 1859	1·1 / 7·4 / 1·1 / 7·2
11 F	0133 / 0734 / 1355 / 1954	1·2 / 7·2 / 1·4 / 7·0		26 Sa	0119 / 0716 / 1337 / 1937	1·1 / 7·3 / 1·3 / 7·2
12 Sa	0205 / 0811 / 1423 / 2025	1·4 / 6·9 / 1·7 / 6·7		27 Su	0158 / 0759 / 1415 / 2018	1·2 / 7·2 / 1·5 / 7·0
13 Su	0236 / 0847 / 1453 / 2057	1·7 / 6·5 / 2·1 / 6·4		28 M	0239 / 0849 / 1456 / 2103	1·4 / 6·9 / 1·9 / 6·7
14 M	0308 / 0927 / 1527 / 2134	2·0 / 6·1 / 2·5 / 6·1		29 Tu	0327 / 0945 / 1545 / 2156	1·6 / 6·5 / 2·2 / 6·4
15 Tu ☽	0349 / 1019 / 1612 / 2226	2·4 / 5·7 / 2·9 / 5·7		30 W	0428 / 1057 / 1649 / 2309	1·9 / 6·2 / 2·6 / 6·1
				31 Th	0549 / 1221 / 1814	2·1 / 6·0 / 2·7

NOVEMBER

Day	Time	m		Day	Time	m
1 F	0035 / 0714 / 1344 / 1938	6·1 / 2·0 / 6·2 / 2·6		16 Sa	0007 / 0643 / 1316 / 1912	5·7 / 2·6 / 5·6 / 3·1
2 Sa	0157 / 0829 / 1454 / 2049	6·3 / 1·7 / 6·4 / 2·3		17 Su	0121 / 0752 / 1419 / 2018	5·8 / 2·4 / 5·9 / 2·8
3 Su	0301 / 0931 / 1549 / 2146	6·6 / 1·5 / 6·7 / 2·0		18 M	0225 / 0850 / 1511 / 2114	6·1 / 2·1 / 6·2 / 2·4
4 M	0355 / 1023 / 1634 / 2235	6·8 / 1·3 / 6·6 / 1·7		19 Tu	0317 / 0942 / 1557 / 2203	6·4 / 1·8 / 6·6 / 2·0
5 Tu	0440 / 1106 / 1712 / 2319	7·0 / 1·2 / 7·0 / 1·5		20 W	0404 / 1030 / 1640 / 2249	6·7 / 1·5 / 6·8 / 1·6
6 W ●	0520 / 1146 / 1747 / 2358	7·1 / 1·2 / 7·1 / 1·3		21 Th ○	0449 / 1115 / 1719 / 2334	7·0 / 1·4 / 7·0 / 1·3
7 Th	0558 / 1222 / 1819	7·2 / 1·3 / 7·1		22 F	0533 / 1158 / 1758	7·2 / 1·2 / 7·2
8 F	0035 / 0636 / 1255 / 1852	1·3 / 7·1 / 1·4 / 7·1		23 Sa	0019 / 0618 / 1241 / 1839	1·1 / 7·3 / 1·2 / 7·3
9 Sa	0109 / 0713 / 1327 / 1924	1·4 / 6·9 / 1·6 / 7·0		24 Su	0104 / 0706 / 1324 / 1921	1·0 / 7·3 / 1·3 / 7·3
10 Su	0142 / 0751 / 1357 / 1957	1·5 / 6·7 / 1·9 / 6·8		25 M	0151 / 0755 / 1408 / 2006	1·0 / 7·2 / 1·5 / 7·2
11 M	0213 / 0827 / 1427 / 2030	1·7 / 6·4 / 2·2 / 6·6		26 Tu	0239 / 0849 / 1453 / 2056	1·1 / 7·0 / 1·8 / 7·0
12 Tu	0247 / 0907 / 1501 / 2107	1·9 / 6·2 / 2·4 / 6·3		27 W	0329 / 0945 / 1542 / 2149	1·3 / 6·7 / 2·1 / 6·8
13 W	0327 / 0952 / 1541 / 2150	2·2 / 5·9 / 2·7 / 6·0		28 Th	0426 / 1048 / 1640 / 2251	1·5 / 6·4 / 2·4 / 6·5
14 Th ☽	0416 / 1051 / 1635 / 2251	2·4 / 5·6 / 3·0 / 5·8		29 F	0530 / 1156 / 1746	1·7 / 6·2 / 2·5
15 F	0523 / 1203 / 1750	2·6 / 5·5 / 3·2		30 Sa	0003 / 0641 / 1309 / 1857	6·4 / 1·8 / 6·1 / 2·6

DECEMBER

Day	Time	m		Day	Time	m
1 Su	0117 / 0751 / 1416 / 2009	6·3 / 1·8 / 6·2 / 2·4		16 M	0005 / 0638 / 1309 / 1907	5·9 / 2·4 / 5·7 / 2·8
2 M	0227 / 0854 / 1517 / 2114	6·4 / 1·8 / 6·3 / 2·2		17 Tu	0117 / 0748 / 1415 / 2020	6·0 / 2·3 / 5·9 / 2·6
3 Tu	0327 / 0950 / 1604 / 2209	6·5 / 1·8 / 6·5 / 2·0		18 W	0227 / 0854 / 1514 / 2124	6·2 / 2·1 / 6·1 / 2·2
4 W	0419 / 1037 / 1645 / 2255	6·6 / 1·7 / 6·7 / 1·8		19 Th	0329 / 0953 / 1607 / 2221	6·4 / 1·8 / 6·4 / 1·8
5 Th	0504 / 1119 / 1722 / 2337	6·7 / 1·7 / 6·8 / 1·6		20 F	0426 / 1048 / 1655 / 2316	6·7 / 1·6 / 6·9 / 1·4
6 F ●	0544 / 1157 / 1757	6·8 / 1·6 / 7·0		21 Sa ○	0519 / 1139 / 1740	7·0 / 1·4 / 7·2
7 Sa	0017 / 0624 / 1232 / 1831	1·5 / 6·8 / 1·7 / 7·0		22 Su	0007 / 0611 / 1228 / 1825	1·1 / 7·3 / 1·3 / 7·4
8 Su	0052 / 0700 / 1306 / 1904	1·5 / 6·7 / 1·8 / 7·0		23 M	0057 / 0702 / 1316 / 1912	0·9 / 7·3 / 1·3 / 7·5
9 M	0126 / 0737 / 1338 / 1937	1·5 / 6·6 / 1·9 / 6·9		24 Tu	0147 / 0752 / 1402 / 1958	0·8 / 7·3 / 1·3 / 7·3
10 Tu	0159 / 0812 / 1409 / 2011	1·6 / 6·5 / 2·0 / 6·8		25 W	0236 / 0843 / 1446 / 2044	0·8 / 7·2 / 1·5 / 7·3
11 W	0232 / 0849 / 1443 / 2044	1·7 / 6·3 / 2·2 / 6·6		26 Th	0322 / 0934 / 1531 / 2132	0·9 / 6·9 / 1·7 / 7·1
12 Th	0307 / 0927 / 1518 / 2122	1·8 / 6·1 / 2·4 / 6·4		27 F	0410 / 1024 / 1617 / 2224	1·2 / 6·6 / 2·0 / 6·8
13 F	0346 / 1009 / 1557 / 2206	2·0 / 5·9 / 2·6 / 6·2		28 Sa ☾	0459 / 1119 / 1708 / 2322	1·5 / 6·3 / 2·3 / 6·3
14 Sa	0433 / 1058 / 1647 / 2259	2·2 / 5·8 / 2·8 / 6·0		29 Su	0556 / 1219 / 1810	1·8 / 6·0 / 2·5
15 Su	0530 / 1200 / 1751	2·3 / 5·7 / 2·9		30 M	0029 / 0702 / 1328 / 1923	6·2 / 2·0 / 5·9 / 2·6
				31 Tu	0147 / 0812 / 1436 / 2039	6·0 / 2·3 / 5·9 / 2·5

Chart Datum: 3.90 metres below Ordnance Datum (Newlyn)

BRIDLINGTON   10-5-9
Humberside

CHARTS
Admiralty 1882, 121, 129, 1190; Imray C29; OS 101
TIDES
+0542 Dover; ML 3.6; Duration 0610; Zone 0 (GMT).

Standard Port RIVER TEES ENT. (→)

Times				Height (metres)			
HW		LW		MHWS	MHWN	MLWN	MLWS
0000	0600	0000	0600	5.5	4.3	2.0	0.9
1200	1800	1200	1800				

Differences BRIDLINGTON
+0100 +0050 +0055 +0050 +0.6   +0.4   +0.3   +0.2
FILEY BAY
+0042 +0042 +0047 +0034 +0.3   +0.6   +0.4   +0.1

SHELTER
Good shelter except in winds from E, SE and S. Harbour available from HW∓3 (for draft of 2.7m).
NAVIGATION
Waypoint SW Smithic W cardinal buoy, Q(9) 15s, 54°02'.41N 00°09'.10W, 153°/333° from/to entrance, 2.6M. Beware bar, 1m at MLWN, could dry out at MLWS. Air gunnery and bombing practice is carried out off Cowden 17M south. Range marked by 5 small conical buoys; 3 seaward ones flashing every 10 secs, the 2 shoreward ones every 5 secs.
LIGHTS AND MARKS
Run in keeping the N Pier head light 002°. Tidal signals displayed from Sig Stn 50m from S Pierhead.
Less than 2.7m in harbour:- FG (No signal by day).
More than 2.7m in harbour:- FR (R flag by day).
When harbour is not clear, a W flag with a B circle in it below a R flag.
RADIO TELEPHONE
VHF Ch 16; **12** 14 (occas).
TELEPHONE (0262)
Hr Mr 670148; CG 672317; MRSC Bridlington 672317; ⌗ Scarborough 366631; Marinecall 0898 500 454; Police 672222; Ⓗ 673451.
FACILITIES
EC Thursday; **S Pier** ☎ 670148, FW, C (7 ton), CH; **Royal Yorkshire YC** ☎ 672041, L, FW, R, Bar; **West end of Harbour** Slip; **C & M Marine** ☎ 672212, Slip, M, Sh, C, CH. See Hr Mr for M, AB.
Town P, D, ME, El, V, R, Bar. ✉; Ⓑ; ⇌; ✈ (Humberside).

⚓ Call to Hr Mr's Watchkeeper

SCARBOROUGH   10-5-10
N. Yorkshire

CHARTS
Admiralty 1612, 129, 1191; Imray C29; OS 101
TIDES
+0527 Dover; ML 3.5; Duration 0615; Zone 0 (GMT).

Standard Port RIVER TEES ENT. (→)

Times				Height (metres)			
HW		LW		MHWS	MHWN	MLWN	MLWS
0000	0600	0000	0600	5.5	4.3	2.0	0.9
1200	1800	1200	1800				

Differences SCARBOROUGH
+0040 +0040 +0030 +0030 +0.2   +0.3   +0.3   0.0

⚓ Contact Watchman on duty at Lt Ho

SHELTER
The old harbour is reserved strictly for fishing fleet. E harbour cannot be entered in strong E-SE winds, otherwise available HW∓3.
NAVIGATION
Waypoint 54°16'.50N 00°22'.00W, 122°/302° from/to East Pier Lt, 0.83M. Beware rocks SW of E pier running out for approx 20 m. Keep well clear of Ramsdale Scar. Keep careful watch for salmon nets to E and SE of entrance.
LIGHTS AND MARKS
No leading lights or marks. B ball at Lt Ho masthead (or Iso 5s Lt) — more than 3.7m on the bar. FY — more than 1.8m, less than 3.7m. R flag — do not enter. These depths refer to Old Harbour; East Harbour entrance is about 1.5m less.
RADIO TELEPHONE
Call *Scarborough Lt Ho.* VHF Ch 16; 12 14 (H24).
TELEPHONE (0723)
Hr Mr Working hrs 373530, non-working hrs 360684; CG 372323; MRSC Bridlington 672317; ⌗ 366631; Marinecall 0898 500 454; Police 363333; Ⓗ 368111.
FACILITIES
EC Wednesday; **North Wharf** Slip, C (20 ton); **Scarborough YC** ☎ 373821, Slip, M*, L, FW, ME, El, C (10 ton), AB; **Old Pier** M*, L, FW, ME, El, AB; **Scarborough Marine** ☎ 375199, L, ME, El, Sh, CH, P and D (cans); **Vincent Pier** C (15 ton); **A. H. Parcell** ☎ 375754, Ⓔ; **G. Kendall** ☎ 367021, Ⓔ; **West Pier** Slip, D, L; **Quay Marine** P, D, ME, El, Sh, CH; **Fisherman's Chandlers** ☎ 365266 CH; *Long waiting list — some berths available for visitors.
Town P, D, V, R, Bar, ✉; Ⓑ; ⇌; ✈ (Humberside).

WHITBY   10-5-11
N. Yorkshire

CHARTS
Admiralty 1612, 134, 129; Imray C29; OS 94
TIDES
+0500 Dover; ML 3.2; Duration 0605; Zone 0 (GMT).

Standard Port RIVER TEES ENT. (→)

Times				Height (metres)			
HW		LW		MHWS	MHWN	MLWN	MLWS
0000	0600	0000	0600	5.5	4.3	2.0	0.9
1200	1800	1200	1800				

Differences WHITBY
+0014	+0014	+0011	+0011	−0.1	0.0	0.0	−0.1

SHELTER
Good shelter except in lower harbour in strong NW to NE winds. Harbour available from HW∓3 for drafts of approx 2m. In strong winds from NW through N to SE the sea breaks a long way out and entry is difficult. Marina is run by Scarborough Borough Council. Bridge opens at ½ hour intervals HW∓2; and from May to Sept inclusive on Sat and Sun at 0900 and 1800.
NAVIGATION
Waypoint 54°30′.30N 00°36′.90W, 349°/169° from/to entrance, 0.65M. Harbour can be approached safely from any direction except SE. From SE beware Whitby Rock; keep Whitby Rock Buoy to port. Beware strong set to E when approaching piers from HW−2 to HW. Swing bridge is manned HW∓2, shows fixed G Lts when open, fixed R Lts when closed.
LIGHTS AND MARKS
Leading lines
(1) Chapel spire in line with Lt Ho — 176°.
(2) FR Lt, seen between East and West Pier Extension, Lts (FR and FG), leads 169° into harbour. Continue on this line until beacons (W triangle and W circle with B stripe) on East Pier (two FY Lts at night) are abeam.
(3) On course 209° leave marks in line astern.
Entry signal G Lt by night shown from top of W Pier Lt Ho indicating 'Enter', only applies to vessels over 30m in length.

RADIO TELEPHONE
VHF Ch 16; 11 12 (0830-1730 LT). Whitby Bridge Ch 16; 06 11 (listens on Ch 16 HW−2 to HW+2).
TELEPHONE (0947)
Hr Mr 602354; CG 602107; MRSC Humber (0262) 672317; ⌗ 602074 (working hours); Marinecall 0898 500 454/453; Police 603443; Dr 820888.
FACILITIES
EC Wednesday; **Whitby Marina** (200 + 10 visitors) ☎ 600165, Slip, P, AC, D, FW, ME, El, Sh, C, CH, Access HW∓2; **Fish Quay** M, D, L, FW, C (1 ton), CH, AB, R, Bar; **Whitby Marine Services** ☎ 600361, ME, El, Sh, CH; **M.R. Coates Marine** ☎ 604486, ME, El, Sh, CH, BH, ACA; **Whitby Port Services** ☎ 602272, Sh (up to 30 ton); **Whitby YC** ☎ 603623, M, L, Bar; **North East Sails** ☎ 604710 SM; **Endeavour Marine** ☎ 603484, ME, Sh, CH; **Collier** ☎ 602068 Gas, Gaz;
Town ✉; Ⓑ; ⇌; ✈ (Teesside).

RIVER TEES
MIDDLESBROUGH   10-5-12
Cleveland

CHARTS
Admiralty 2566, 2567, 134; Imray C29; OS 93
TIDES
+0450 Dover; ML 3.2; Duration 0605; Zone 0 (GMT).

Standard Port RIVER TEES ENT. (→)

Times				Height (metres)			
HW		LW		MHWS	MHWN	MLWN	MLWS
0000	0600	0000	0600	5.5	4.3	2.0	0.9
1200	1800	1200	1800				

Differences MIDDLESBROUGH (Dock Ent)
0000	+0002	0000	−0003	+0.1	+0.2	+0.1	−0.1

NOTE: River Tees Entrance is a Standard Port and detailed tide tables are given below.

SHELTER
Entry is not recommended for small craft during periods of heavy weather especially with NE, E or SE strong winds. Berthing may be arranged at Paddy's Hole (Bran Sands), at Stockton Castlegate Marine Club or elsewhere by arrangement with Hr Mr.
NAVIGATION
Waypoint Tees Fairway safe water buoy, Iso 4s, Horn, Racon, 54°40′.94N 01°06′.39W, 030°/210° from/to S Gare breakwater, 2.4M. Beware Saltscar, Eastscar and Longscar Rocks on approaching. Bridges up river have following clearances:
(1) ½ mile above Middlesbrough Dock — Transporter Bridge—49m at MHWS;
(2) 2 miles from there, Newport Bridge, 6.4m at MHWS.
(3) ½ mile from there, A 19 Road Bridge 18.3m at MHWS;
(4) 2 miles from there, Stockton-Victoria Bridge 5.6m at MHWS.
LIGHTS AND MARKS
QW Lt, or 3FR (vert) at Old CG Stn, means no entry without approval of Hr Mr. Ldg Lts 210°, FR on framework Trs. Channel well marked to beyond Middlesbrough.
RADIO TELEPHONE
Call: Tees Harbour Radio VHF Ch 16; 08 11 12 14 22 (H24). Information service Ch 14 22.
TELEPHONE (0642)
Hr Mr 452541; MRSC North Shields 257 2691; ⌗ 091 257 2691; Marinecall 0898 500 453; Police 326326; Ⓗ (North Tees) 672122, (South Tees) 850850.

RIVER TEES/MIDDLESBROUGH *continued*

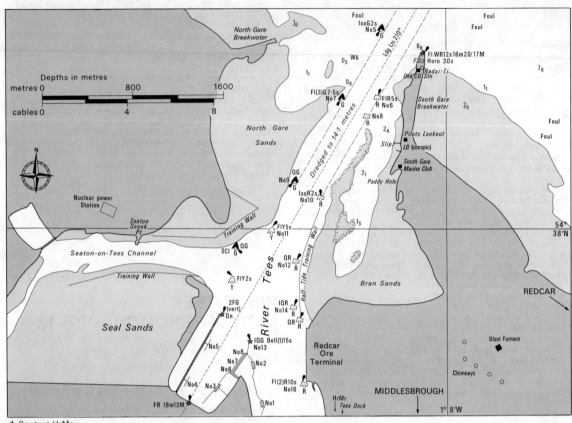

⚓ Contact HrMr

FACILITIES

EC Wednesday; Limited accommodation on River Tees for small pleasure craft. Prior arrangements must be made with Club secretaries or Hr Mr. **South Gare Marine Club** ☎ 482015, Slip, M (check with Warden), L, FW, Bar; **Castlegate Marine Club** ☎ 583299 Slip, M, FW, ME, EI, Sh, CH, L, V; **Tees Motor Boat Club** M (check with secretary); **Tees Docks** ☎ 452541, M (check), L, FW, C (30 ton), AB (check); **CTC Marine** ☎ 211756, Ⓔ, CH, ACA; **D.A.V. Engineering and Marine** ☎ 468272, EI, ME. **Town** ✉; Ⓑ; ⇌; ✈.

RIVER TEES ENTRANCE

MEAN SPRING AND NEAP CURVES

MEAN RANGES	
Springs	4·6m ——
Neaps	2·3m - - -

Springs occur 2 days after New and Full Moon.

ENGLAND, EAST COAST – RIVER TEES ENTRANCE

Lat 54°38′ N Long 1°09′ W

TIMES AND HEIGHTS OF HIGH AND LOW WATERS

YEAR 1991

TIME ZONE UT (GMT)
For Summer Time add ONE hour in non-shaded areas

5

JANUARY

Day	Time	m	Time	m	Time	m	Time	m
1 Tu	0339	5·5	0957	1·0	1557	5·6	2228	0·5
16 W	0402	4·8	1003	1·4	1607	5·1	2231	1·1
2 W	0430	5·6	1044	1·0	1644	5·7	2316	0·4
17 Th	0435	4·9	1037	1·3	1638	5·2	2305	1·0
3 Th	0518	5·6	1129	1·0	1729	5·7		
18 F	0508	4·9	1109	1·2	1709	5·2	2337	0·9
4 F	0003	0·4	0605	5·5	1212	1·2	1814	5·6
19 Sa	0540	4·9	1143	1·2	1742	5·2		
5 Sa	0049	0·6	0653	5·2	1256	1·4	1900	5·4
20 Su	0012	0·9	0615	4·9	1218	1·3	1817	5·2
6 Su	0134	0·9	0740	5·0	1340	1·7	1948	5·1
21 M	0048	1·0	0652	4·8	1253	1·4	1855	5·1
7 M ☾	0222	1·2	0830	4·7	1427	1·9	2040	4·8
22 Tu	0127	1·1	0735	4·7	1334	1·5	1940	4·9
8 Tu	0311	1·5	0924	4·4	1519	2·2	2138	4·6
23 W ☽	0211	1·3	0825	4·5	1422	1·7	2034	4·7
9 W	0407	1·8	1021	4·3	1623	2·3	2244	4·4
24 Th	0304	1·6	0925	4·4	1524	1·9	2142	4·5
10 Th	0509	2·0	1125	4·2	1740	2·3	2353	4·3
25 F	0413	1·8	1037	4·3	1645	2·0	2304	4·4
11 F	0617	2·1	1228	4·3	1856	2·2		
26 Sa	0539	1·9	1154	4·4	1821	1·9		
12 Sa	0100	4·3	0719	2·1	1327	4·4	1957	2·0
27 Su	0028	4·6	0703	1·7	1307	4·6	1941	1·5
13 Su	0158	4·5	0808	1·9	1416	4·6	2043	1·7
28 M	0142	4·8	0809	1·5	1411	5·0	2042	1·1
14 M	0246	4·6	0851	1·8	1458	4·8	2122	1·5
29 Tu	0244	5·1	0904	1·2	1503	5·3	2134	0·6
15 Tu ●	0327	4·7	0928	1·6	1535	5·0	2157	1·3
30 W ○	0335	5·4	0950	1·0	1549	5·6	2220	0·4
31 Th	0421	5·5	1033	0·9	1633	5·7	2304	0·2

FEBRUARY

Day	Time	m	Time	m	Time	m	Time	m
1 F	0504	5·5	1113	0·9	1712	5·8	2344	0·3
16 Sa	0444	5·1	1051	1·0	1645	5·4	2316	0·6
2 Sa	0544	5·5	1151	1·0	1751	5·7		
17 Su	0515	5·1	1123	0·9	1716	5·5	2350	0·6
3 Su	0024	0·5	0622	5·3	1228	1·1	1831	5·5
18 M	0547	5·1	1156	1·0	1751	5·4		
4 M	0102	0·8	0702	5·0	1304	1·4	1910	5·2
19 Tu	0024	0·7	0624	5·0	1231	1·1	1829	5·3
5 Tu	0140	1·1	0742	4·7	1341	1·7	1954	4·9
20 W	0102	0·9	0704	4·9	1312	1·2	1916	5·1
6 W ☾	0219	1·6	0826	4·5	1422	2·0	2046	4·5
21 Th ☽	0144	1·2	0754	4·6	1358	1·5	2011	4·7
7 Th	0304	1·9	0918	4·2	1514	2·2	2149	4·2
22 F	0236	1·6	0847	4·4	1500	1·8	2122	4·4
8 F	0400	2·3	1023	4·1	1630	2·4	2306	4·0
23 Sa	0346	1·9	1007	4·2	1626	1·9	2251	4·3
9 Sa	0519	2·4	1140	4·0	1817	2·4		
24 Su	0520	2·0	1133	4·3	1811	1·8		
10 Su	0031	4·0	0646	2·4	1255	4·2	1937	2·1
25 M	0024	4·4	0656	1·9	1255	4·5	1934	1·4
11 M	0138	4·2	0749	2·1	1352	4·5	2026	1·8
26 Tu	0140	4·7	0801	1·6	1358	4·9	2032	1·0
12 Tu	0229	4·4	0834	1·9	1437	4·7	2104	1·5
27 W	0236	5·0	0851	1·3	1450	5·2	2119	0·6
13 W	0308	4·7	0911	1·6	1514	5·0	2139	1·2
28 Th ○	0322	5·2	0934	1·1	1532	5·5	2202	0·3
14 Th ●	0343	4·8	0945	1·3	1546	5·2	2212	0·9
15 F	0414	5·0	1019	1·1	1616	5·3	2244	0·7

MARCH

Day	Time	m	Time	m	Time	m	Time	m
1 F	0403	5·4	1013	0·9	1612	5·6	2241	0·3
16 Sa ●	0342	5·1	0952	1·1	1545	5·4	2216	0·6
2 Sa	0440	5·4	1049	0·8	1648	5·7	2318	0·4
17 Su	0414	5·2	1026	0·9	1617	5·5	2249	0·5
3 Su	0513	5·4	1123	0·9	1723	5·6	2351	0·6
18 M	0447	5·3	1059	0·8	1652	5·6	2325	0·6
4 M	0547	5·2	1156	1·0	1758	5·4		
19 Tu	0520	5·3	1134	0·8	1730	5·5		
5 Tu	0025	0·9	0621	5·0	1228	1·2	1835	5·2
20 W	0003	0·7	0600	5·2	1214	0·9	1814	5·3
6 W	0057	1·2	0656	4·8	1302	1·5	1914	4·8
21 Th	0042	1·0	0643	5·0	1257	1·1	1903	5·1
7 Th	0131	1·6	0735	4·6	1340	1·8	2002	4·5
22 F	0127	1·3	0733	4·7	1348	1·4	2005	4·7
8 F ☾	0211	2·0	0823	4·3	1426	2·1	2101	4·2
23 Sa ☽	0222	1·7	0834	4·5	1454	1·6	2119	4·4
9 Sa	0301	2·3	0925	4·1	1532	2·3	2219	3·9
24 Su	0334	2·0	0949	4·3	1620	1·7	2248	4·3
10 Su	0416	2·5	1042	4·0	1711	2·4	2347	3·9
25 M	0508	2·2	1115	4·3	1758	1·6		
11 M	0556	2·5	1204	4·1	1850	2·2		
26 Tu	0015	4·4	0639	2·0	1232	4·5	1914	1·3
12 Tu	0102	4·1	0713	2·3	1310	4·3	1947	1·8
27 W	0123	4·7	0740	1·7	1335	4·8	2008	0·9
13 W	0155	4·4	0802	2·0	1358	4·6	2029	1·5
28 Th	0215	4·9	0827	1·4	1425	5·1	2053	0·7
14 Th	0234	4·7	0842	1·6	1437	4·9	2105	1·1
29 F	0257	5·1	0908	1·2	1507	5·3	2134	0·6
15 F	0310	4·9	0917	1·3	1512	5·2	2141	0·8
30 Sa ○	0335	5·2	0945	1·0	1543	5·4	2210	0·6
31 Su	0409	5·2	1020	1·0	1619	5·5	2244	0·7

APRIL

Day	Time	m	Time	m	Time	m	Time	m
1 M	0440	5·2	1052	1·0	1654	5·4	2316	0·9
16 Tu	0419	5·4	1037	0·8	1631	5·6	2302	0·7
2 Tu	0511	5·2	1125	1·1	1727	5·2	2347	1·1
17 W	0458	5·4	1119	0·8	1716	5·5	2343	0·9
3 W	0543	5·0	1157	1·2	1805	5·0		
18 Th	0542	5·3	1203	0·9	1807	5·3		
4 Th	0019	1·4	0618	4·9	1232	1·4	1846	4·8
19 F	0028	1·2	0629	5·1	1252	1·0	1903	5·0
5 F	0055	1·7	0659	4·7	1312	1·7	1934	4·5
20 Sa	0119	1·5	0723	4·9	1348	1·2	2008	4·8
6 Sa	0135	2·0	0748	4·4	1359	1·9	2032	4·2
21 Su ☽	0216	1·8	0826	4·6	1456	1·4	2121	4·6
7 Su ☾	0226	2·3	0847	4·1	1500	2·1	2142	4·0
22 M	0327	2·1	0938	4·5	1613	1·5	2238	4·5
8 M	0334	2·5	0957	4·1	1619	2·2	2258	4·0
23 Tu	0449	2·1	1052	4·5	1734	1·4	2351	4·5
9 Tu	0459	2·5	1109	4·2	1744	2·1		
24 W	0607	2·0	1203	4·6	1842	1·2		
10 W	0008	4·2	0618	2·3	1214	4·4	1850	1·8
25 Th	0052	4·7	0707	1·8	1302	4·8	1935	1·1
11 Th	0104	4·4	0716	2·0	1307	4·6	1941	1·5
26 F	0142	4·8	0755	1·6	1352	5·0	2020	1·0
12 F	0149	4·7	0801	1·7	1352	4·9	2023	1·2
27 Sa	0225	5·0	0837	1·4	1436	5·1	2100	0·9
13 Sa	0229	5·0	0842	1·4	1432	5·2	2104	0·9
28 Su ○	0301	5·0	0915	1·2	1515	5·2	2136	1·0
14 Su ●	0305	5·1	0919	1·1	1511	5·4	2143	0·7
29 M	0335	5·1	0950	1·2	1552	5·2	2210	1·1
15 M	0342	5·3	0959	0·9	1550	5·5	2221	0·7
30 Tu	0407	5·1	1024	1·1	1628	5·1	2241	1·2

Chart Datum: 2.85 metres below Ordnance Datum (Newlyn)

ENGLAND, EAST COAST – RIVER TEES ENTRANCE

Lat 54°38′ N   Long 1°09′ W

TIMES AND HEIGHTS OF HIGH AND LOW WATERS

YEAR 1991

TIME ZONE UT (GMT)
For Summer Time add ONE hour in non-shaded areas

MAY

Day	Time	m	Time	m	Time	m	Time	m
1 W	0440	5·1	1058	1·2	1705	5·0	2315	1·4
2 Th	0515	5·0	1133	1·3	1744	4·9	2350	1·6
3 F	0553	4·9	1212	1·4	1828	4·7		
4 Sa	0028	1·8	0636	4·8	1255	1·6	1916	4·5
5 Su	0112	2·0	0724	4·6	1342	1·8	2011	4·3
6 M	0202	2·2	0819	4·4	1437	1·9	2111	4·2
7 Tu ⦅	0303	2·3	0919	4·3	1541	2·0	2214	4·2
8 W	0412	2·4	1021	4·4	1648	1·9	2316	4·3
9 Th	0520	2·3	1122	4·5	1753	1·7		
10 F	0012	4·5	0624	2·1	1217	4·7	1850	1·5
11 Sa	0102	4·7	0716	1·8	1307	4·9	1941	1·3
12 Su	0148	5·0	0805	1·5	1357	5·1	2029	1·1
13 M	0232	5·2	0850	1·2	1443	5·3	2114	0·9
14 Tu ●	0314	5·4	0935	1·0	1531	5·5	2159	0·9
15 W	0357	5·5	1021	0·8	1620	5·5	2244	0·9
16 Th	0442	5·5	1108	0·8	1711	5·5	2330	1·1
17 F	0530	5·4	1158	0·8	1805	5·3		
18 Sa	0019	1·3	0621	5·3	1250	0·9	1903	5·1
19 Su	0112	1·5	0716	5·1	1348	1·0	2005	4·9
20 M ⦆	0209	1·8	0816	4·9	1450	1·1	2110	4·7
21 Tu	0311	2·0	0919	4·8	1556	1·3	2214	4·6
22 W	0419	2·0	1026	4·7	1702	1·3	2318	4·6
23 Th	0527	2·0	1129	4·7	1804	1·3		
24 F	0015	4·7	0628	1·9	1228	4·8	1859	1·3
25 Sa	0106	4·7	0721	1·7	1320	4·8	1945	1·3
26 Su	0151	4·8	0808	1·6	1408	4·9	2027	1·3
27 M	0232	4·9	0850	1·5	1451	4·9	2105	1·3
28 Tu ○	0310	5·0	0929	1·3	1532	5·0	2142	1·4
29 W	0345	5·0	1006	1·3	1612	4·9	2217	1·4
30 Th	0420	5·0	1042	1·3	1651	4·9	2252	1·5
31 F	0458	5·0	1120	1·3	1730	4·8	2330	1·6

JUNE

Day	Time	m	Time	m	Time	m	Time	m
1 Sa	0536	5·0	1158	1·3	1812	4·7		
2 Su	0010	1·7	0618	4·9	1241	1·4	1857	4·6
3 M	0052	1·8	0703	4·8	1324	1·5	1945	4·5
4 Tu	0138	2·0	0751	4·6	1412	1·6	2036	4·4
5 W ⦅	0229	2·1	0842	4·6	1518	1·7	2131	4·6
6 Th	0325	2·2	0936	4·5	1602	1·7	2228	4·4
7 F	0427	2·2	1034	4·6	1704	1·7	2325	4·5
8 Sa	0532	2·1	1133	4·7	1805	1·6		
9 Su	0021	4·7	0634	1·9	1232	4·8	1904	1·4
10 M	0114	4·9	0733	1·6	1330	5·1	2001	1·2
11 Tu	0205	5·1	0829	1·3	1425	5·3	2053	1·1
12 W ●	0256	5·3	0850	1·0	1519	5·4	2143	1·0
13 Th	0343	5·5	1013	0·8	1613	5·5	2233	1·0
14 F	0433	5·5	1104	0·6	1706	5·5	2322	1·1
15 Sa	0522	5·6	1154	0·6	1800	5·4		
16 Su	0010	1·2	0611	5·5	1245	0·6	1853	5·3
17 M	0059	1·4	0703	5·4	1337	0·7	1948	5·1
18 Tu	0151	1·6	0757	5·2	1432	0·9	2043	4·9
19 W ⦆	0244	1·8	0854	5·0	1527	1·2	2141	4·7
20 Th ⦅	0342	1·9	0953	4·8	1626	1·7	2238	4·6
21 F	0444	2·0	1055	4·7	1725	1·5	2336	4·5
22 Sa	0549	2·0	1156	4·6	1824	1·6		
23 Su	0032	4·5	0652	1·9	1255	4·6	1917	1·7
24 M	0124	4·6	0747	1·8	1349	4·6	2005	1·6
25 Tu	0212	4·7	0834	1·6	1437	4·7	2047	1·6
26 W	0254	4·9	0918	1·5	1522	4·8	2125	1·5
27 Th ○	0334	5·0	0957	1·3	1602	4·8	2203	1·5
28 F	0409	5·0	1034	1·2	1640	4·8	2238	1·4
29 Sa	0445	5·1	1109	1·2	1716	4·8	2315	1·4
30 Su	0520	5·1	1146	1·2	1753	4·8	2353	1·5

JULY

Day	Time	m	Time	m	Time	m	Time	m
1 M	0557	5·0	1222	1·2	1832	4·7		
2 Tu	0031	1·5	0636	5·0	1302	1·3	1913	4·6
3 W	0110	1·6	0716	4·9	1342	1·3	1957	4·5
4 Th	0152	1·8	0801	4·8	1427	1·5	2046	4·4
5 F ⦅	0240	1·9	0851	4·7	1518	1·6	2141	4·4
6 Sa	0336	2·0	0950	4·6	1619	1·7	2241	4·4
7 Su	0444	2·0	1057	4·6	1727	1·7	2346	4·5
8 M	0600	1·9	1207	4·7	1839	1·6		
9 Tu	0049	4·7	0713	1·6	1314	4·9	1945	1·4
10 W	0149	5·0	0818	1·3	1416	5·1	2043	1·2
11 Th ●	0244	5·2	0914	0·9	1514	5·4	2135	1·1
12 F	0335	5·5	1006	0·6	1606	5·6	2223	0·9
13 Sa	0423	5·7	1055	0·4	1657	5·6	2309	0·9
14 Su	0509	5·7	1142	0·3	1744	5·5	2354	1·0
15 M	0554	5·7	1228	0·4	1831	5·4		
16 Tu	0038	1·1	0641	5·6	1314	0·6	1919	5·2
17 W	0123	1·3	0728	5·3	1402	0·9	2006	4·9
18 Th ⦆	0208	1·6	0819	5·1	1450	1·2	2058	4·6
19 F	0258	1·8	0915	4·8	1543	1·6	2153	4·4
20 Sa ⦅	0356	2·1	1017	4·5	1642	1·8	2255	4·3
21 Su	0508	2·2	1126	4·4	1749	2·0		
22 M	0000	4·3	0627	2·1	1234	4·4	1853	2·0
23 Tu	0102	4·4	0734	1·9	1335	4·5	1949	1·9
24 W	0155	4·6	0826	1·7	1427	4·6	2034	1·7
25 Th	0242	4·8	0908	1·5	1511	4·7	2114	1·6
26 F ○	0321	5·0	0946	1·2	1549	4·8	2150	1·4
27 Sa	0355	5·1	1020	1·1	1623	4·9	2224	1·3
28 Su	0427	5·2	1052	1·0	1655	4·9	2257	1·2
29 M	0458	5·2	1126	0·9	1727	4·9	2330	1·2
30 Tu	0530	5·2	1158	0·9	1800	4·9		
31 W	0004	1·2	0604	5·2	1234	1·0	1836	4·8

AUGUST

Day	Time	m	Time	m	Time	m	Time	m
1 Th	0039	1·3	0639	5·1	1310	1·1	1916	4·7
2 F	0117	1·5	0721	4·9	1351	1·3	2002	4·5
3 Sa ⦅	0201	1·7	0811	4·7	1440	1·6	2057	4·4
4 Su	0257	1·9	0914	4·5	1541	1·8	2203	4·3
5 M	0409	2·0	1030	4·4	1659	1·9	2318	4·3
6 Tu	0539	1·9	1151	4·5	1825	1·8		
7 W	0032	4·6	0704	1·6	1309	4·7	1938	1·6
8 Th	0138	4·9	0812	1·2	1412	5·1	2034	1·3
9 F	0233	5·2	0905	0·7	1507	5·3	2124	1·0
10 Sa ●	0322	5·5	0953	0·4	1555	5·5	2207	0·9
11 Su	0406	5·8	1038	0·3	1638	5·6	2249	0·8
12 M	0448	5·8	1120	0·2	1720	5·6	2330	0·8
13 Tu	0529	5·8	1203	0·3	1801	5·4		
14 W	0010	1·0	0610	5·6	1243	0·6	1842	5·2
15 Th	0048	1·2	0653	5·3	1324	1·0	1924	4·9
16 F	0128	1·5	0738	5·0	1405	1·4	2009	4·6
17 Sa ⦆	0212	1·8	0832	4·7	1451	1·8	2103	4·4
18 Su	0305	2·1	0935	4·3	1549	2·2	2206	4·2
19 M	0420	2·3	1052	4·2	1705	2·4	2320	4·2
20 Tu	0600	2·3	1212	4·2	1829	2·3		
21 W	0035	4·3	0719	2·1	1321	4·3	1933	2·1
22 Th	0134	4·5	0809	1·9	1412	4·5	2018	1·9
23 F	0219	4·8	0849	1·4	1453	4·7	2054	1·6
24 Sa	0257	5·0	0922	1·2	1527	4·9	2128	1·4
25 Su ○	0329	5·0	0955	1·0	1557	5·0	2202	1·1
26 M	0400	5·3	1027	0·8	1627	5·1	2233	1·1
27 Tu	0428	5·4	1058	0·7	1657	5·1	2304	1·0
28 W	0458	5·4	1130	0·8	1727	5·1	2336	1·1
29 Th	0530	5·4	1203	0·9	1801	5·0		
30 F	0010	1·2	0607	5·2	1239	1·1	1839	4·8
31 Sa	0048	1·3	0650	5·0	1319	1·3	1926	4·6

Chart Datum: 2.85 metres below Ordnance Datum (Newlyn)

ENGLAND, EAST COAST – RIVER TEES ENTRANCE

Lat 54°38′ N   Long 1°09′ W

TIME ZONE UT(GMT)
For Summer Time add ONE hour in non-shaded areas

TIMES AND HEIGHTS OF HIGH AND LOW WATERS

YEAR **1991**

5

SEPTEMBER

Day	Time	m	Day	Time	m
1 Su ☾	0134 / 0742 / 1409 / 2023	1.5 / 4.7 / 1.6 / 4.4	**16** M	0222 / 0854 / 1454 / 2117	2.1 / 4.2 / 2.4 / 4.2
2 M	0232 / 0851 / 1514 / 2134	1.8 / 4.5 / 1.9 / 4.3	**17** Tu	0332 / 1014 / 1612 / 2234	2.3 / 4.0 / 2.6 / 4.1
3 Tu	0350 / 1016 / 1640 / 2257	1.9 / 4.3 / 2.1 / 4.3	**18** W	0515 / 1142 / 1750 / 2354	2.4 / 4.0 / 2.6 / 4.2
4 W	0530 / 1147 / 1817	1.9 / 4.4 / 2.0	**19** Th	0645 / 1252 / 1900	2.1 / 4.2 / 2.3
5 Th	0018 / 0657 / 1304 / 1927	4.5 / 1.5 / 4.7 / 1.7	**20** F	0056 / 0735 / 1342 / 1947	4.5 / 1.8 / 4.5 / 2.0
6 F	0124 / 0759 / 1404 / 2020	4.9 / 1.0 / 5.0 / 1.4	**21** Sa	0144 / 0813 / 1420 / 2025	4.8 / 1.5 / 4.7 / 1.7
7 Sa	0216 / 0849 / 1451 / 2105	5.3 / 0.6 / 5.3 / 1.1	**22** Su	0222 / 0849 / 1454 / 2058	5.0 / 1.2 / 4.9 / 1.4
8 Su ●	0303 / 0934 / 1535 / 2146	5.6 / 0.3 / 5.5 / 0.9	**23** M ○	0256 / 0922 / 1525 / 2132	5.2 / 0.9 / 5.1 / 1.2
9 M	0343 / 1014 / 1613 / 2224	5.8 / 0.2 / 5.6 / 0.8	**24** Tu	0327 / 0955 / 1555 / 2204	5.4 / 0.8 / 5.2 / 1.1
10 Tu	0423 / 1054 / 1649 / 2302	5.8 / 0.3 / 5.5 / 0.8	**25** W	0356 / 1027 / 1624 / 2237	5.5 / 0.7 / 5.3 / 1.0
11 W	0459 / 1130 / 1726 / 2337	5.8 / 0.5 / 5.4 / 1.0	**26** Th	0428 / 1101 / 1657 / 2311	5.5 / 0.7 / 5.3 / 1.0
12 Th	0537 / 1207 / 1801	5.6 / 0.8 / 5.2	**27** F	0504 / 1134 / 1732 / 2347	5.5 / 0.9 / 5.2 / 1.1
13 F	0012 / 0617 / 1242 / 1839	1.2 / 5.3 / 1.2 / 5.0	**28** Sa	0544 / 1212 / 1812	5.3 / 1.1 / 5.0
14 Sa	0049 / 0700 / 1319 / 1921	1.5 / 4.9 / 1.6 / 4.7	**29** Su	0029 / 0632 / 1256 / 1902	1.2 / 5.0 / 1.4 / 4.8
15 Su ☽	0130 / 0751 / 1401 / 2012	1.8 / 4.6 / 2.0 / 4.4	**30** M	0120 / 0731 / 1348 / 2002	1.5 / 4.7 / 1.8 / 4.5

OCTOBER

Day	Time	m	Day	Time	m
1 Tu ☾	0222 / 0844 / 1457 / 2115	1.7 / 4.4 / 2.1 / 4.4	**16** W ☾	0254 / 0934 / 1521 / 2148	2.3 / 4.0 / 2.6 / 4.2
2 W	0345 / 1012 / 1626 / 2238	1.8 / 4.3 / 2.2 / 4.4	**17** Th	0417 / 1054 / 1649 / 2302	2.3 / 4.0 / 2.7 / 4.3
3 Th	0522 / 1140 / 1800 / 2357	1.7 / 4.4 / 2.1 / 4.6	**18** F	0543 / 1204 / 1808	2.2 / 4.2 / 2.5
4 F	0641 / 1250 / 1907	1.4 / 4.7 / 1.8	**19** Sa	0005 / 0643 / 1256 / 1903	4.5 / 1.9 / 4.5 / 2.2
5 Sa	0102 / 0738 / 1344 / 1958	4.9 / 1.0 / 5.0 / 1.5	**20** Su	0056 / 0728 / 1338 / 1945	4.7 / 1.6 / 4.7 / 1.9
6 Su	0154 / 0825 / 1429 / 2042	5.2 / 0.7 / 5.3 / 1.2	**21** M	0140 / 0808 / 1415 / 2023	5.0 / 1.3 / 5.0 / 1.6
7 M ●	0237 / 0907 / 1508 / 2121	5.5 / 0.5 / 5.4 / 1.0	**22** Tu	0218 / 0846 / 1450 / 2101	5.2 / 1.1 / 5.2 / 1.3
8 Tu	0318 / 0945 / 1545 / 2157	5.6 / 0.5 / 5.5 / 0.9	**23** W ○	0253 / 0922 / 1522 / 2136	5.4 / 0.9 / 5.3 / 1.1
9 W	0355 / 1021 / 1619 / 2233	5.7 / 0.6 / 5.4 / 0.9	**24** Th	0328 / 0957 / 1556 / 2213	5.5 / 0.8 / 5.4 / 1.0
10 Th	0431 / 1057 / 1652 / 2308	5.6 / 0.8 / 5.4 / 1.1	**25** F	0406 / 1035 / 1633 / 2252	5.6 / 0.8 / 5.4 / 0.9
11 F	0508 / 1129 / 1726 / 2342	5.4 / 1.1 / 5.2 / 1.2	**26** Sa	0448 / 1113 / 1712 / 2334	5.5 / 1.0 / 5.4 / 1.0
12 Sa	0547 / 1203 / 1801	5.2 / 1.4 / 5.0	**27** Su	0534 / 1156 / 1757	5.4 / 1.2 / 5.2
13 Su	0018 / 0629 / 1243 / 1843	1.5 / 4.8 / 1.8 / 4.8	**28** M	0021 / 0628 / 1243 / 1849	1.1 / 5.1 / 1.5 / 5.0
14 M	0059 / 0720 / 1319 / 1933	1.8 / 4.5 / 2.1 / 4.5	**29** Tu	0116 / 0730 / 1338 / 1949	1.3 / 4.8 / 1.8 / 4.8
15 Tu ☽	0149 / 0820 / 1412 / 2034	2.0 / 4.2 / 2.4 / 4.3	**30** W	0220 / 0842 / 1446 / 2101	1.5 / 4.6 / 2.1 / 4.6
			31 Th ☾	0338 / 1002 / 1607 / 2217	1.6 / 4.5 / 2.2 / 4.6

NOVEMBER

Day	Time	m	Day	Time	m
1 F	0501 / 1118 / 1730 / 2330	1.5 / 4.5 / 2.1 / 4.7	**16** Sa	0435 / 1104 / 1702 / 2309	2.1 / 4.2 / 2.5 / 4.4
2 Sa	0612 / 1224 / 1838	1.3 / 4.7 / 1.9	**17** Su	0542 / 1201 / 1807	2.0 / 4.4 / 2.3
3 Su	0034 / 0709 / 1317 / 1930	4.9 / 1.1 / 4.9 / 1.6	**18** M	0005 / 0638 / 1252 / 1902	4.6 / 1.7 / 4.6 / 2.0
4 M	0127 / 0757 / 1402 / 2015	5.1 / 0.9 / 5.1 / 1.4	**19** Tu	0056 / 0727 / 1335 / 1948	4.8 / 1.5 / 4.9 / 1.7
5 Tu	0213 / 0839 / 1443 / 2056	5.3 / 0.9 / 5.2 / 1.2	**20** W	0142 / 0811 / 1416 / 2032	5.1 / 1.3 / 5.1 / 1.4
6 W ●	0256 / 0918 / 1518 / 2134	5.4 / 0.9 / 5.3 / 1.1	**21** Th ○	0226 / 0854 / 1457 / 2115	5.3 / 1.1 / 5.3 / 1.2
7 Th	0334 / 0953 / 1552 / 2210	5.4 / 1.0 / 5.3 / 1.1	**22** F	0310 / 0936 / 1536 / 2157	5.5 / 1.0 / 5.5 / 1.0
8 F	0412 / 1027 / 1626 / 2245	5.3 / 1.1 / 5.3 / 1.2	**23** Sa	0355 / 1019 / 1619 / 2242	5.6 / 1.0 / 5.5 / 0.9
9 Sa	0448 / 1059 / 1659 / 2320	5.2 / 1.3 / 5.2 / 1.3	**24** Su	0442 / 1102 / 1702 / 2330	5.5 / 1.0 / 5.5 / 0.8
10 Su	0527 / 1133 / 1737 / 2357	5.0 / 1.6 / 5.1 / 1.5	**25** M	0533 / 1147 / 1750	5.4 / 1.2 / 5.4
11 M	0610 / 1210 / 1818	4.8 / 1.8 / 4.9	**26** Tu	0019 / 0628 / 1236 / 1841	0.9 / 5.2 / 1.4 / 5.3
12 Tu	0039 / 0656 / 1250 / 1904	1.7 / 4.5 / 2.1 / 4.7	**27** W	0114 / 0727 / 1331 / 1938	1.0 / 5.0 / 1.7 / 5.1
13 W	0126 / 0751 / 1340 / 1959	1.9 / 4.3 / 2.3 / 4.5	**28** Th	0213 / 0830 / 1432 / 2042	1.2 / 4.8 / 1.9 / 4.9
14 Th	0220 / 0851 / 1439 / 2101	2.0 / 4.2 / 2.5 / 4.4	**29** F	0319 / 0938 / 1539 / 2150	1.3 / 4.6 / 2.1 / 4.8
15 F	0325 / 0957 / 1549 / 2206	2.1 / 4.1 / 2.6 / 4.3	**30** Sa	0428 / 1045 / 1652 / 2259	1.4 / 4.6 / 2.1 / 4.7

DECEMBER

Day	Time	m	Day	Time	m
1 Su	0537 / 1149 / 1803	1.4 / 4.6 / 2.0	**16** M	0435 / 1102 / 1704 / 2312	2.0 / 4.3 / 2.3 / 4.5
2 M	0004 / 0638 / 1246 / 1903	4.8 / 1.4 / 4.7 / 1.8	**17** Tu	0543 / 1203 / 1812	1.9 / 4.5 / 2.2
3 Tu	0103 / 0730 / 1337 / 1954	4.9 / 1.3 / 4.9 / 1.6	**18** W	0014 / 0646 / 1257 / 1916	4.6 / 1.7 / 4.7 / 1.9
4 W	0154 / 0816 / 1420 / 2039	5.0 / 1.3 / 5.0 / 1.5	**19** Th	0113 / 0742 / 1349 / 2011	4.9 / 1.5 / 5.0 / 1.5
5 Th	0240 / 0856 / 1500 / 2119	5.1 / 1.3 / 5.1 / 1.3	**20** F	0208 / 0834 / 1437 / 2103	5.1 / 1.3 / 5.2 / 1.2
6 F ●	0322 / 0932 / 1536 / 2157	5.1 / 1.3 / 5.2 / 1.2	**21** Sa ○	0300 / 0922 / 1524 / 2150	5.4 / 1.1 / 5.5 / 0.9
7 Sa	0400 / 1007 / 1610 / 2234	5.1 / 1.4 / 5.2 / 1.2	**22** Su	0350 / 1010 / 1609 / 2238	5.5 / 1.0 / 5.6 / 0.6
8 Su	0438 / 1041 / 1645 / 2309	5.0 / 1.4 / 5.2 / 1.2	**23** M	0440 / 1055 / 1655 / 2327	5.6 / 1.0 / 5.7 / 0.5
9 M	0515 / 1115 / 1720 / 2344	4.9 / 1.5 / 5.1 / 1.3	**24** Tu	0530 / 1142 / 1742	5.6 / 1.0 / 5.7
10 Tu	0554 / 1151 / 1758	4.8 / 1.7 / 5.0	**25** W	0015 / 0621 / 1228 / 1829	0.5 / 5.4 / 1.2 / 5.6
11 W	0022 / 0635 / 1229 / 1839	1.4 / 4.7 / 1.8 / 4.9	**26** Th	0104 / 0713 / 1316 / 1921	0.6 / 5.2 / 1.4 / 5.4
12 Th	0103 / 0719 / 1312 / 1924	1.6 / 4.5 / 2.0 / 4.7	**27** F	0157 / 0806 / 1408 / 2016	0.8 / 5.0 / 1.6 / 5.1
13 F	0147 / 0808 / 1358 / 2012	1.7 / 4.4 / 2.2 / 4.6	**28** Sa ☾	0253 / 0904 / 1504 / 2117	1.1 / 4.7 / 1.9 / 4.9
14 Sa	0236 / 0901 / 1450 / 2108	1.9 / 4.3 / 2.3 / 4.5	**29** Su	0352 / 1004 / 1609 / 2223	1.4 / 4.6 / 2.1 / 4.7
15 Su	0332 / 1000 / 1553 / 2209	1.9 / 4.2 / 2.4 / 4.4	**30** M	0457 / 1109 / 1723 / 2333	1.6 / 4.5 / 2.1 / 4.6
			31 Tu	0604 / 1214 / 1836	1.7 / 4.5 / 2.0

Chart Datum: 2.85 metres below Ordnance Datum (Newlyn)

HARTLEPOOL 10-5-13
Cleveland

CHARTS
Admiralty 2566; Imray C29; OS 93
TIDES
+0437 Dover; ML 3.0; Duration 0600; Zone 0 (GMT).

Standard Port RIVER TEES ENT. (←)

Times				Height (metres)			
HW		LW		MHWS	MHWN	MLWN	MLWS
0000	0600	0000	0600	5.5	4.3	2.0	0.9
1200	1800	1200	1800				

Differences HARTLEPOOL
| −0004 | −0004 | −0006 | −0006 | −0.1 | −0.1 | −0.2 | −0.1 |

SHELTER
Strong winds from E cause swell to build up making entrance channel hazardous. Once inside there is good shelter. Best berth at Hartlepool YC pontoons, SE corner of Victoria Dock, depth 5m (apply Dock Office Tel. 66127). West Harbour (dries) available for small craft. Access to enclosed docks HW∓1.
NAVIGATION
Waypoint Longscar E cardinal buoy, Q(3) 10s, Bell, 54°40'.85N 01°09'.79W, 137°/317° from/to entrance, 1.0M. Beware from S — Longscar rocks, 6 ca S of bottom of chartlet (Buoy BYB. Q (3) 10s). From N — 'The Stones' NE of breakwater head, 1 ca.
LIGHTS AND MARKS
Leading line 324°53' into main harbour (Dir Iso WRG 3s 42m). Amber Lt near front Dir Lt means vessels may enter but not leave. When not shown vessels may leave but not enter. Traffic to and from enclosed docks 1G Lt — Vessel may enter N Basin. 2G Lts — Vessel may pass through N Basin. 1R Lt — Vessel may not approach dock.
RADIO TELEPHONE
Call: *Hartlepool Dock Radio* VHF Ch 16; 11 **12** (H24).
TELEPHONE (0429)
Hr Mr 266127; CG & MRSC North Shields 572691; Tees & Hartlepool Port Authority 276771; ⌗ 861390; Marinecall 0898 500 453; Police 221151; Dr 274570.
FACILITIES
EC Wednesday; **Harbour** (400) ☎ 266127, FW, D, Slip, C (10 ton); **Irvings Quay** Slip, M, L, AB; **Fish Quay** P (in cans), D, FW, CH; **A. M. Marine** ☎ 233820 ME, El, Sh, CH, C (Mobile); **Cliff Reynolds** ☎ 272049, ME, El, CH; **Dock** ☎ 266127, M, FW, ME, El, C (3 ton, 10 ton), AB; **Hartlepool YC** ☎ 274931, Bar; **Tees SC** ☎ 267151, ME, El; **Town** P, V, R, ⌷, Bar. Gas, Gaz, ✉; Ⓑ; ⇌; ✈ (Teesside).
Note:— South docks are being converted into a marina complex.

SEAHAM 10-5-14
Durham

CHARTS
Admiralty 1627; Imray C29; OS 88
TIDES
+0435 Dover; ML 3.0; Duration 0600; Zone 0 (GMT).

Standard Port RIVER TEES ENT. (←)

Times				Height (metres)			
HW		LW		MHWS	MHWN	MLWN	MLWS
0000	0600	0000	0600	5.5	4.3	2.0	0.9
1200	1800	1200	1800				

Differences SEAHAM
| −0015 | −0015 | −0015 | −0015 | −0.3 | −0.2 | 0.0 | −0.2 |

SHELTER
Small boats normally berth in N Dock where shelter is excellent but it dries. Larger boats may enter S Dock; gates open from HW−2 to HW+1.
NAVIGATION
Waypoint 54°50'.20N 01°18'.50W, 094°/274° from/to entrance, 0.40M. Shallow water and rocks to S of S breakwater (Liddle Scars). Entrance should not be attempted during strong on-shore winds. Speed limit 5 kn.
LIGHTS AND MARKS
No leading lights or marks but harbour is easily identified by lighthouse on N Pier (W with B bands). FS at NE corner of S dock in line with N Lt Ho leads in clear of Tangle Rks. Anchorage good ¾ M off shore with Clock Tower in transit with St John's church tower.
Traffic signals, S Dock:
R Lt — Vessels enter
G Lt — Vessels leave
RADIO TELEPHONE
VHF Ch 16; 06 **12** (HW−2½ to HW+1½ — office hours 0800 − 1800 LT Mon−Fri).
TELEPHONE (091)
Hr Mr 581 3246; MRSC North Shields 257 2691; Seaham Harbour Operations Office 581 3877; ⌗ Sunderland 565 7113; Marinecall 0898 500 453; Police 581 2255; Dr 581 2332.
FACILITIES
EC Wednesday; **South Dock** ☎ 581 3877, L, FW, C (40 ton), AB; **North Dock** M; **Town** (½ M) P, D, FW, ME, El, CH (5 M), V, R, Bar. ✉; Ⓑ; ⇌; ✈ (Teesside or Newcastle).

SUNDERLAND   10-5-15
Tyne and Wear

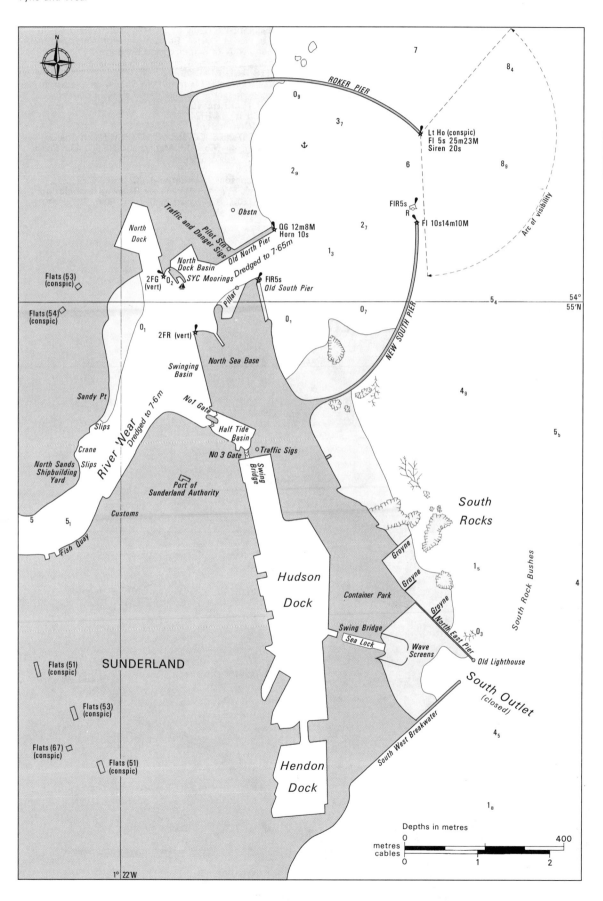

N

ROKER PIER

0_9

7

8_4

3_7

⚓

Lt Ho (conspic)
Fl 5s 25m23M
Siren 20s

2_9

6

8_9

FlR5s
R

Fl 10s14m10M

Arc of visibility

○ Obstn

Traffic and Danger Sigs

Pilot Stn

North
Dock

QG 12m8M
Horn 10s

2_7

Old North Pier   Dredged to 7·65m

North
Dock Basin

1_3

Flats (53)
(conspic)

2FG
(vert) 0_2

SYC Moorings

FlR5s
Old South Pier

Pillar

5_4

54°
55′N

Flats (54)
(conspic)

0_1

NEW SOUTH PIER

0_7

0_1

2FR (vert)

North Sea Base

Swinging
Basin

River Wear   Dredged to 7·6m

No1 Gate

4_9

Sandy Pt

Half Tide
Basin

5_b

Slips

Crane

No 3 Gate

○ Traffic Sigs

North Sands
Shipbuilding
Yard

Swing
Bridge

South
Rocks

5

5_1

Customs

Port of
Sunderland Authority

South Rock Bushes

Fish Quay

1_5

Groyne

Groyne

4

Hudson
Dock

Container Park

Groyne

North East Pier

0_3

Flats (51)
(conspic)

Swing Bridge

Sea Lock

SUNDERLAND

Wave
Screens

Old Lighthouse

Flats (53)
(conspic)

South Outlet
(closed)

Flats (67)
(conspic)

Flats (51)
(conspic)

4_5

Hendon
Dock

South West Breakwater

1_8

Depths in metres

0   400
metres
cables
0   1   2

1° 22′W

5

SUNDERLAND *continued*

CHARTS
Admiralty 1627; Imray C29; OS 88
TIDES
+0430 Dover; ML 2.9; Duration 0600; Zone 0 (GMT).

Standard Port RIVER TEES ENT. (←)

Times				Height (metres)			
HW		LW		MHWS	MHWN	MLWN	MLWS
0000	0600	0000	0600	5.5	4.3	2.0	0.9
1200	1800	1200	1800				

Differences SUNDERLAND

−0017	−0017	−0016	−0016	−0.3	−0.1	0.0	−0.1

SHELTER
Shelter is good but no facilities for private yachts except through Sunderland YC, or Wear Boating Association. Strong winds between NE and SE cause heavy swell in entrance and outer harbour. Yachts normally berthed in North Dock, just up river from North Dock Basin.

NAVIGATION
Waypoint 54°55'.20N 01°20'.00W, 098°/278° from/to Roker Pier Lt, 0.61M. Beware wreck at Whitburn Steel about 1 M N of entrance, and Hendon Rk (0.9m), 1.2M SE of entrance, marked by R can bell buoy on its E side.
LIGHTS AND MARKS
Three flashing R Lts from Pilot Station on Old North Pier indicate danger in harbour − no entry or departure.
RADIO TELEPHONE
VHF Ch 16; 14 (H24)
TELEPHONE (091)
Hr Mr 567 2626; CG 567 4255; MRSC North Shields 557 2691; ⌗ 565 7113; Marinecall 0898 500 453; Police 586 2621; Ⓗ 565 6256.
FACILITIES
EC Wednesday; **Sunderland YC** ☎ 567 5133, Slip (Dinghy), FW, AB, Bar; **Wear Boating Association** ☎ 567 5313, AB; **Town** P, D, V, R, Bar. ✉; Ⓑ; ⇌; ✈ (Newcastle).

RIVER TYNE/NORTH SHIELDS
Tyne and Wear
10-5-16

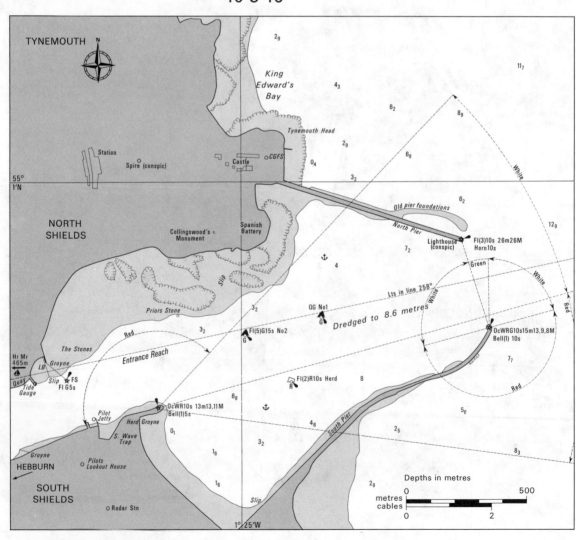

RIVER TYNE / NORTH SHIELDS *continued*

CHARTS
Admiralty 152, 1934; Imray C29; OS 88
TIDES
+0430 Dover; ML 2.9; Duration 0604; Zone 0 (GMT)

Standard Port RIVER TEES ENT. (←)

Times				Height (metres)			
HW		LW		MHWS	MHWN	MLWN	MLWS
0000	0600	0000	0600	5.5	4.3	2.0	0.9
1200	1800	1200	1800				

Differences NORTH SHIELDS
−0016 −0018 −0017 −0022 −0.5 −0.4 −0.2 −0.2
NEWCASTLE-UPON-TYNE
−0013 −0015 −0009 −0014 −0.2 −0.2 −0.1 −0.1

SHELTER
Good shelter in all weathers. The approach is difficult for small craft in E and NE strong winds. Yachts may go into Albert Edward Dock giving excellent shelter and protection from heavy river traffic; obtain permission from Hr Mr by VHF or telephone first. Entrance 1M up river from Fl G 5s Lt on No 1 Groyne, on N bank.
NAVIGATION
Waypoint 55°01'.00N 01°22'.22W, 078°/258° from/to front Ldg Lt 258°, 2.2M. From S — No dangers. From N — Beware Bellhues Rock (approx 1 M N of harbour and ¾ M off shore) — Beware old N Pier; give it a wide berth.
LIGHTS AND MARKS
Ldg Lts 258° — two W Trs with W Lts. Buoys mark the dredged channel in Lower Harbour. Tynemouth Castle forms prominent landmark on cliff 26m high on N side of harbour.
RADIO TELEPHONE
Call: *Tyne Harbour Radio* VHF Ch 12 16; 11 **12** 14 (H24).
TELEPHONE (091)
Hr Mr 257 0407; CG & MRSC 257 2691; ⌗ 257 9441; Weather: 232 6453; Marinecall 0898 500 453; Police 232 3451; Dr Radio through Tyne Harbour 257 2080.
FACILITIES
EC Wednesday
Limited berthing accommodation on the River Tyne for small pleasure craft. Prior arrangements must be made with club Secretaries or Harbour Master.
St Peter's Basin Marina (140 + 20 visitors)
☎ (0665) 712168 Approx 1.5M seaward of Tyne bridge. AC, FW, D, P, Access HW∓4. **Hebburn Marina** (50) ☎ 483 2876, FW, Slip; **Friars Goose Marina** (50) ☎ 469 2545, FW, ME, El, CH, Slip; **Robsons Boatyard** ☎ 455 5187, Slip, L, FW, ME, El, AB; **Tyne Slipway** ☎ 456 6209, Slip, M, L, FW; **Jim Marine** ☎ 257 7610, Slip, FW, ME, El, Sh, C, CH, AB, V, R, Bar; **John Lillie and Gillie** ☎ 257 2217 ACA; **A.N.D. Electronics** ☎ 258 1635, Ⓔ; **Kelvin Hughes** ☎ 257 1318, Ⓔ; **Sperry** ☎ 257 1413, Ⓔ; **Town**, P (cans), D, V, R, Bar. ✉; Ⓑ; ⇌ (Tynemouth or South Shields), ✈ (Newcastle).

BLYTH   10-5-17
Northumberland

CHARTS
Admiralty 1626; Imray C29; OS 81, 88
TIDES
+0415 Dover; ML 2.8; Duration 0558; Zone 0 (GMT).

Standard Port RIVER TEES ENT. (←)

Times				Height (metres)			
HW		LW		MHWS	MHWN	MLWN	MLWS
0000	0600	0000	0600	5.5	4.3	2.0	0.9
1200	1800	1200	1800				

Differences BLYTH
−0011 −0025 −0018 +0013 −0.5 −0.4 −0.3 −0.1

SHELTER
Very good — Yachts normally berth in South Harbour, eastern section. At low tide in strong SE winds, seas break across entrance.
NAVIGATION
Waypoint Fairway stbd-hand buoy, FIG 3s, Bell, 55°06'.58N 01°28'.50W, 140°/320° from/to East Pier Lt, 0.53M. Beware The Pigs, The Sow and Seaton Sea Rocks when approaching from the N. No dangers from the S.
LIGHTS AND MARKS
Ldg Lts 324°, F Bu on framework Trs with Or diamonds 11/17m. Second pair of Ldg Lts 338°, F Bu at 5m and 11m respectively.
RADIO TELEPHONE
Call: *Blyth Harbour Control* VHF Ch 16; 12 (H24).
TELEPHONE (0670)
Hr Mr 352678; CG & MRSC North Shields 257 2691; ⌗ 361521; Marinecall 0898 500 453; Police (0661) 72555; Dr 353226.
FACILITIES
EC Wednesday; **R Northumberland YC** ☎ 353636, Slip, M, L, FW, C (30 ton), D, CH, ME, El, Sh, Bar; **South Harbour** ☎ 352678, M, D, L, FW, C (3 ton 25 ton), CH, Gas, Gaz, AB; **Boat Yard** ☎ 353207, Slip, D, ME, El, Sh; **Town** P, V, R, Bar. ✉; Ⓑ; ⇌ (bus to Newcastle); ✈ (Newcastle).

AMBLE   10-5-18
Northumberland

CHARTS
Admiralty 1627; Imray C29; OS 81

TIDES
+0412 Dover; ML 3.0; Duration 0606; Zone 0 (GMT).

Standard Port RIVER TEES ENT. (←)

Times				Height (metres)			
HW		LW		MHWS	MHWN	MLWN	MLWS
0000	0600	0000	0600	5.5	4.3	2.0	0.9
1200	1800	1200	1800				

Differences AMBLE
−0039	−0033	−0040	−0036	−0.5	−0.2	0.0	−0.1

NORTH SUNDERLAND
−0104	−0102	−0115	−0124	−0.7	−0.6	−0.4	−0.2

HOLY ISLAND
−0059	−0057	−0122	−0132	−0.7	−0.6	−0.5	−0.3

SHELTER
The harbour, known as Warkworth Harbour, is safe in all weathers but entrance is dangerous in strong N to E winds or in swell which causes breakers on the bar (Pan Bush). In NE gales, broken water can extend to Coquet Island. Yachts should go to the Braid Yacht Marina on S bank of Coquet River, approx 1000m from ent; or the river above fish dock (ask at Coquet YC). There is a speed limit throughout the harbour of 4 kn.

NAVIGATION
Waypoint 55°21'.00N 01°33'.00W, 045°/225° from/to harbour entrance, 0.9M. Entrance recommended from NE, passing N and W of Pan Bush shoal. A wreck, min depth 1.7m, lies 1.75 ca ENE of breakwater head. Alternative approach in good conditions and with sufficient rise of tide through Coquet channel (buoyed, min depth 0.3m). The S-going stream sets strongly across entrance.

LIGHTS AND MARKS
Coquet Island Lt Ho, (conspic) W square Tr, turreted parapet, lower half grey; Fl (3) WR 30s 25m 23/19M R330°-140°, W140°-163°, R163°-180°, W180°-330°. Horn 30s.

RADIO TELEPHONE
Call *Amble Harbour* VHF Ch 16 14 (Mon-Fri 0900-1700 LT). Coquet YC Ch 16. Marina, Call *Amble Braid Marina* Ch **80** (H24).

TELEPHONE (0665)
Hr Mr 710306; MRSC North Shields 572691; CG 710575; ⌗ Blyth 361521; Marinecall 0898 500 453; Ⓗ 602661.

FACILITIES
EC Wednesday; **Braid Marina** (250+40 visitors) ☎ 712168 AC, BY, C, Gas, FW, D, P, R, Gaz, Slip, BH (20 ton), ME, El, Sh, Bar; V, CH, Ⓞ; Access HW∓4 via sill; **Harbour** D, AB; **J and J Harrison** ☎ 710267 ME, Slip, CH, El, Sh, D; **Coquet YC** Slip, Bar, M, FW, L; **Amble Marine** ☎ 711069 SM, El, Ⓔ; **Marina Filling Station** P (cans); **Town** V, R, Bar, ✉, ⇌ (Alnmouth), ✈ (Newcastle).

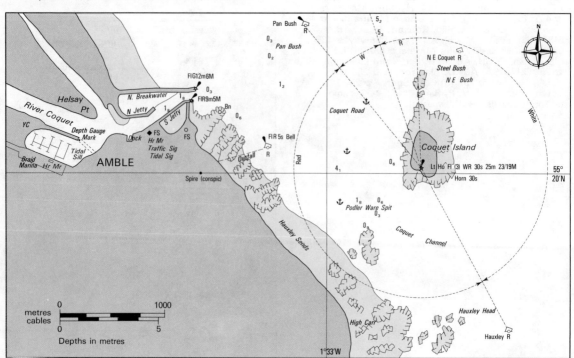

BERWICK-ON-TWEED 10-5-19
Northumberland

CHARTS
Admiralty 1612, 111, 160; OS 75
TIDES
+0330 Dover; ML 2.5; Duration 0620; Zone 0 (GMT).

Standard Port RIVER TEES ENT. (←)

Times				Height (metres)			
HW		LW		MHWS	MHWN	MLWN	MLWS
0000	0600	0000	0600	5.5	4.3	2.0	0.9
1200	1800	1200	1800				

Differences BERWICK

−0109	−0111	−0126	−0131	−0.8	−0.5	−0.7	−0.3

SHELTER
Good shelter or anchorage except in strong winds from
E and SE. Yachts lie at W end of Fish Jetty or in Tweed
Dock (opens HW−2 to HW). There are also good
anchorages at Holy Is. See 10.5.20.
NAVIGATION
Waypoint 55°45'.80N 01°58'.00W, 098°/278° from/to
breakwater Lt Ho, 0.54M. On-shore winds and ebb tides
cause very confused state over the bar. From HW−2 to
HW+1 strong flood tide sets across the entrance — keep
well up to breakwater. The sands at the mouth of the
Tweed shift so frequently that local knowledge is useful
when entering Berwick Harbour.
LIGHTS AND MARKS
Town hall clock tower and lighthouse in line at 294°.
When past Crabwater Rock, pick up transit beacons at
Spittal in line at 207°. Beacons are B and Y with
triangular top marks.
RADIO TELEPHONE
VHF CG: Ch 16 (0900-1700 LT); Pilot and Hr Mr; Ch 16;
12 (HW−3 to HW+1, when shipping expected).
TELEPHONE (0289)
Hr Mr 7404; CG 6005; MRSC North Shields 572691;
⌗ 307547; Marinecall 0898 500 453/452; Police 307111;
Dr 7484
FACILITIES
EC Thursday; **Dock** ☎ 7404, Slip, M (See Hr Mr), P, D,
L, FW, ME, El, Sh, C (Mobile 3 ton), AB; **Town** P, V, R,
Bar. ✉; Ⓑ; ⇌; ✈ (Newcastle or Edinburgh).

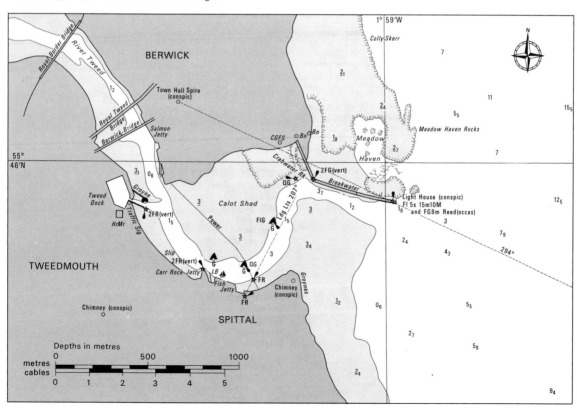

MINOR HARBOURS AND ANCHORAGES   10.5.20

WAINFLEET, Lincolnshire, 53°06' N, 0°20' E, Zone 0 (GMT), Admty chart 1190. Skegness HW +0500 on Dover, −0009 on Immingham; HW height −0.4m on Immingham; ML 4.0m; Duration 0600. Shelter good. Swatchway buoyed but not lit; channel through saltings marked with posts with radar reflectors, R can tops to port, G triangular tops to stbd. Enter HW∓1½. No lights. Facilities: EC Thurs, M, AB (larger boats at fishing jetties, smaller at YC), FW at Field Study Centre on stbd side at entrance. All shore facilities at Skegness (3½ miles).

FILEY, N Yorkshire, 54°13' N, 0°16' W, Zone 0 (GMT), Admty charts 1882, 129. HW +0532 on Dover, +0042 on River Tees Ent; HW height + 0.4m on River Tees Ent.; ML 3.5m; Duration 0605. See 10.5.9. Good anchorage in winds from NNE through W to S. Anchor in 4 to 5m on hard sandy bottom. Light on cliff above CG Station, G metal column, FR 31m 1M vis 272° − 308°. The natural breakwater, Filey Brigg marked by Lt Buoy, Q(3)10s, Bell. Beware the Horse Rock, N of Filey Brigg, foul ground extending ½M from shore. Facilities; EC Wed, V, R, Bar, L, Ⓗ. ☎ 68111, ✉, Ⓑ, ⇌.

RUNSWICK BAY, N. Yorkshire, 54°32' N, 0°45' W; Zone 0 (GMT). Admty chart 1612. HW +0505 on Dover: +0010 on River Tees Ent; HW height −0.1m on River Tees Ent; ML 3.1m; Duration 0605. Good shelter in all winds from NW by W to SSE. Enter bay at 270° keeping clear of many rocks at base of cliffs. Two white posts (2FY by night when required by lifeboat) 18m apart are leading marks to LB house and can be used to lead into anchorage. Good holding in 6m to 9m in middle of bay. Facilities: **Runswick Bay Rescue Boat Station** ☎ Whitby 840965; **Runswick Bay Hotel** ☎ 840210 Bar, R; **Runswick Bay Stores** ☎ 840880 V.

NEWTON HAVEN (St Mary's), Northumberland, 55° 31' N, 1° 36'.5W, Zone 0 (GMT), Admty chart 156. HW +0342 on Dover, −0102 on River Tees Ent; HW height −0.7m on River Tees Ent.; ML 2.6m; Duration 0625. A safe anchorage in winds from NNW to SE via S but susceptible to swell. Entrance to S of Newton Point. Beware Fills Rks. Anchor between Fills Rks and Low Newton by the Sea in 4/5m. A very attractive anchorage with no lights, marks or facilities except a pub.

SEAHOUSES (North Sunderland Harbour), Northumberland, 55°35' N, 1°39' W, Zone 0 (GMT), Admty chart 1612. HW +0340 on Dover, −0102 on River Tees Ent; HW height −0.7m on River Tees Ent.; ML 2.7m; Duration 0618. See 10.5.18. Good shelter except in on-shore winds when swell makes outer harbour berths very uncomfortable and dangerous. Access HW∓3. Inner harbour has excellent berths but usually full of fishing boats. Beware The Tumblers (rocks) to the W of entrance and rocks protruding NE from E breakwater. Lights − Breakwater head Fl R 2.5s 6m; NW pier head FG 11m 3M; vis 159° − 294°, on W Tr; traffic signals; Siren 90s when vessels expected. When it is dangerous to enter a R Lt is shown over the G Lt (or R flag over a Bu flag) on NW pier head. Facilities: EC Wed; **J. Davidson** ☎ 720347, Gas; all facilities available.

FARNE ISLANDS, Northumberland, 55°37' N, 1°39' W, Zone 0 (GMT), Admty chart 111. HW +0345 on Dover, −0102 on River Tees Ent.; HW height −0.7m on River Tees Ent; ML 2.6m; Duration 0630. The islands are a nature reserve belonging to the National Trust. Landing is only allowed on Inner Farne, Staple I and Longstone. In the Inner Islands, yachts can anchor in The Kettle on the E side of Inner Farne, near the Bridges (which connect Knox Reef to West Wideopens) or to the S of West Wideopens. In the Outer Islands yachts can anchor in Pinnacle Haven (between Staple I and Brownsman). Beware turbulence over Knivestone and Whirl Rks and eddy S of Longstone during NW tidal streams. Lights Black Rock Point Oc(2) WRG 15s 12m 17/13M; G122° − 165°, W165° − 175°, R175° − 191°, W191° − 238°, R238° − 275°, W275° − 289°, G289° − 300°. Farne Is Lt Ho at SW Pt LFl(2) WR 15s 27m 13/9M; W round Tr; R119° − 277°, W277° −119°. Longstone Fl 20s 23m 29M, R Tr with W band, RC, Siren (2) 60s. It is a beautiful area with no facilities, and should only be attempted in good weather.

HOLY ISLAND, Northumberland, 55°40' N, 1°47' W, Zone 0 (GMT), Admty chart 1612. HW +0344 on Dover, −0058 on River Tees Ent.; HW height −0.7m on River Tees Ent; ML 2.6m; Duration 0630. See 10.5.18. Shelter is complete in The Ooze (or Ouse) aground on soft mud; anchorage good just to E of St Cuthbert's I to the S of The Heugh except in W winds. Beware Plough Rks and the rocks all round them. Keep to Ldg Line 260° with Old Law Bns in line until church and Bn come in line at 310° which leads in to the anchorage S of The Heugh. There are no lights. Facilities: FW from tap on village green; P and D at Beale (5 miles); limited provisions in village. Hr Mr ☎ Holy Island 207 or 217. Note Lindisfarne is the ancient name for Holy Island; it is linked to the mainland by a causeway which is covered at HW.

AGENTS WANTED
Berwick-on-Tweed
Mallaig
Loch Sunart
Loch Aline
Fishguard
Kenmare River

Large number of French Ports

Rotterdam
Norderney
Dornumersiel
Langeoog
Wangerooge
Hooksiel
Bremerhaven

If you are interested in becoming our agent please write to the Editors and get your free copy annually. You do not have to be a resident in a port to be the agent but at least a fairly regular visitor.

VOLVO PENTA SERVICE

Sales and service centres in area 6
LOTHIAN **Port Edgar Marine Services Ltd** Port Edgar Marina, Shore Road,
South Queensferry, Nr EDINBURGH EH30 9SQ Tel (031-331) 1233.

Area 6

South-East Scotland
Eyemouth to Peterhead

VOLVO PENTA

6

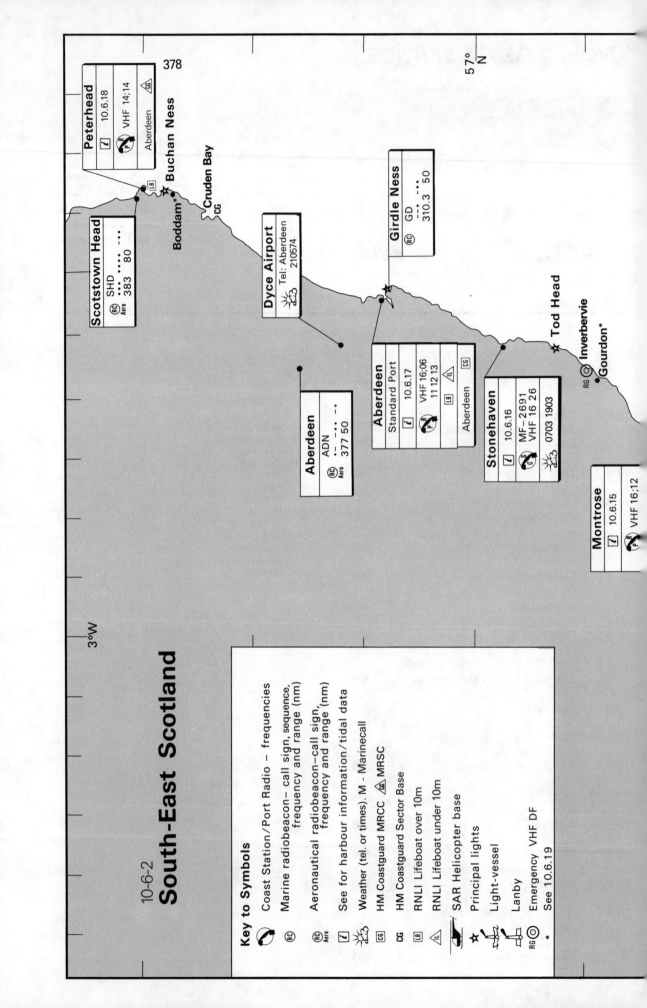

378

10·6·2 South-East Scotland

Peterhead
i	10.6.18
☎	VHF 14;14
	Aberdeen CG

Buchan Ness

Cruden Bay

Boddam* CG

Scotstown Head
| RC Aero | SHD ▪▪▪ ▪▪▪▪ ▪▪ 383 80 |

Dyce Airport
| | Tel: Aberdeen 210574 |

Aberdeen
| RC Aero | ADN ▪— —▪▪ —▪ 377 50 |

Aberdeen
	Standard Port
i	10.6.17
☎	VHF 16:06 11 12 13
	LB ⚠
	Aberdeen CG

Girdle Ness
| RC | GD —▪ —▪▪ ▪▪▪ 310.3 50 |

Stonehaven
i	10.6.16
☎ CG	MF – 2691 VHF 16 26
⛅	0703 1903

Tod Head

Inverbervie

RG ⊙ Gourdon*

Montrose
| i | 10.6.15 |
| ☎ | VHF 16;12 |

3°W

57° N

Key to Symbols

Symbol	Description
🕾	Coast Station/Port Radio – frequencies
RC	Marine radiobeacon– call sign, sequence, frequency and range (nm)
RC Aero	Aeronautical radiobeacon–call sign, frequency and range (nm)
i	See for harbour information/tidal data
⛅	Weather (tel. or times). M - Marinecall
CG	HM Coastguard MRCC CG MRSC
CG	HM Coastguard Sector Base
LB	RNLI Lifeboat over 10m
⚠	RNLI Lifeboat under 10m
🚁	SAR Helicopter base
★	Principal lights
	Light-vessel
	Lanby
RG ⊙	Emergency VHF DF
*	See 10.6.19

379

Forth CG

Forth CG

7°W (1991)

Variation

Bell Rock ☆

Arbroath
| *i* | 10.6.14 | | CG |
| LB | ⚠ | |

River Tay
i	10.6.13
📞	VHF 16;10 11 12 13 14
☼	M-0898 500 452

Broughty Ferry

Tayport ☆

Leuchars
| RC | LU •-•• --• 255.5 100 | ⛵ Aero |

Fife Ness
| RC | FP ••-• •--• 6 303.4 100/70 | ⬛ Forth |

Crail* RG

St Monans* ☆ May Island 🐝

Anstruther
| *i* | 10.6.12 |
| LB | |

Elie* ☆ Elie Ness

Methil
| *i* | 10.6.11 |
| 📞 | VHF 16;14 |

Leven CG

Fidra
| RC | FD ••-• -•• 289.6 10 |

☆ Bass Rock

Dunbar
| *i* | 10.6.8 |
| LB | ⚠ |

Barns Ness ☆

Burntisland
| *i* | 10.6.10 |

Kirkaldy*

Kinghorn ⚠

Inchkeith
| RC | NK -• -•- 296.5 10 |

North Berwick* ☆

Forth Coast Station
| G | VHF 16 24 62 |
| ☼ | 0703 1903 |

Aberdour*

Inchcolm* ☆

Cramond* ⚠

Granton CG

Fisherrow*

Edinburgh
| ☼ | M-0898 500 452 |

Firth of Forth
	Standard Port (Leith)	
i	10.6.9	
📞	VHF 16 71;09 10 11 12 13 14 **20 71**	
	(Forth Navigation Service)	
	Marina VHF 80	

Rosyth/ Firth of Forth
| 📞 | VHF 16 13 71 |
| ☼ | Inverkeithing 412566 |

South Queensferry

St Abbs Head* ☆
RG

Eyemouth
| *i* | 10.6.7 | | CG |
| LB | | |

Burnmouth*

56° N

56° N

3°W

2°W

10.6.3   AREA 6 TIDAL STREAMS

5 Hours before HW Dover (0340 after HW Leith)

4 Hours before HW Dover (0440 after HW Leith)

3 Hours before HW Dover (0540 after HW Leith)

2 Hours before HW Dover (0545 before HW Leith)

1 Hour before HW Dover (0445 before HW Leith)

HW Dover (0345 before HW Leith)

Northward 10.7.3   Southward 10.5.3

1 Hour after HW Dover (0245 before HW Leith)

2 Hours after HW Dover (0145 before HW Leith)

3 Hours after HW Dover (0045 before HW Leith)

4 Hours after HW Dover (0015 after HW Leith)

5 Hours after HW Dover (0115 after HW Leith)

6 Hours after HW Dover (0215 after HW Leith)

10.6.4   LIGHTS, FOG SIGNALS AND WAYPOINTS

Abbreviations used below are given in 10.0.3. Principal lights are in **bold** print, places in CAPITALS, and light-vessels, light floats and Lanbys in *CAPITAL ITALICS*. Unless otherwise stated lights are white.   m—elevation in metres; M—nominal range in n. miles. Fog signals are in *italics*. Useful waypoints are underlined use those on land with care. See 4.2.2.

SCOTLAND—SOUTH-EAST COAST

BURNMOUTH
Ldg Lts. Front 55°50'·6N 02°04'·1W FR 29m 4M. Rear 45m from front FR 35m 4M. Both on W posts.

EYEMOUTH.
Ldg Lts 174°. West breakwater head, front FG 9m 5M. Rear 55m from front FG 10m 4M. Both Or columns.
East breakwater 55°52'·51N 02°05'·18W Iso R 2s 8m 8M.

ST ABB'S.
Ldg Lts. Front, head of inside jetty, FR 4m 1M. Rear, SW corner of old harbour, FR 8m 1M.
St Abb's Head 55°54'·97N 02°08'·20W Fl 10s 68m **29M**; W Tr; Racon.
Torness Power Station, pier head Fl R 5s 10m 5M.
Barns Ness 55°59'·2N 02°26'·6W Iso W 4s 30s 36m 10M; W Tr.

DUNBAR.
Bayswell Hill Ldg Lts 198°. Front Oc G 6s 15m 3M; W triangle on Y column; intens 188°-208°. Rear Oc G 6s 22m 3M; synchronised with front, intens 188°-208°.
Victoria Harbour, middle quay, QR 6m 3M; vis over harbour entrance.
Bass Rock, South side, 56°04'·60N 02°38'·37W Fl(3) 20s 46m 10M; W Tr; vis 241°-107°.

NORTH BERWICK.
North pier head 56°03'·73N 02°42'·92W F WR 7m 3M; vis R seaward, W over harbour. Not lit if entrance closed by weather.
Fidra, near summit 56°04'·40N 02°47'·00W Fl(4) 30s 34m **24M**; W Tr; RC; obsc by Bass Rock, Craig Leith and Lamb island.
Wreck Lt Buoy 56°04'·40N 02°52'·30W Fl(2)R 10s; port-hand mark.
Port Seton, East pier head, Iso WR 4s 10m W9M, R6M; R shore-105°, W105°-225°, R225°-shore; *Bell (occas).*
Cockenzie Power Station, jetty head QR 6m 1M.
Fisherrow, East pier head Oc W 6s 5m 6M; framework Tr.
South Channel Approach Lt Buoy 56°01'·42N 03°02'·14W LFl 10s; safe water mark.
Narrow Deep Lt Buoy 56°01'·48N 03°04'·51W Fl(2)R 10s; port-hand mark.
Herwit Lt Buoy 56°01'·05N 03°06'·43W Fl(3)G 10s; stbd-hand mark; *Bell.*
Craigh Waugh Lt Buoy 56°00'·27N 03°04'·38W Q; N cardinal mark.
Leith Approach Lt Buoy 55°59'·95N 03°11'·42W FlR 3s; port- hand mark.
Inchkeith Fairway Lt Buoy 56°03'·50N 03°00'·00W Iso 2s; safe water mark; Racon.
No. 1 Lt Buoy 56°03'·23N 03°03'·63W FlG 9s; stbd-hand mark.

No. 2 Lt Buoy 56°02'·91N 03°03'·63W FlR 9s; port-hand mark.
No. 3 Lt Buoy 56°03'·23N 03°06'·00W FlG 6s; stbd-hand mark.
No. 4 Lt Buoy 56°02'·91N 03°06'·00W FlR 6s; port-hand mark.
No. 5 Lt Buoy 56°03'·20N 03°07'·80W FlG 3s; stbd-hand mark.
No. 6 Lt Buoy 56°03'·05N 03°08'·35W FlR 3s; port-hand mark.
No. 8 Lt Buoy 56°02'·95N 03°09'·54W FlR 9s; port-hand mark.
Inchkeith, summit 56°02'·01N 03°08'·09W Fl 15s 67m **22M**; RC. Stell Point *Horn 15s.*
Pallas Rock Lt Buoy 56°01'·50N 03°09'·21W VQ(9) 10s; W cardinal mark.
East Gunnet Lt Buoy 56°01'·42N 03°12'·29W Q(3) 10s; E cardinal mark.
West Gunnet Lt Buoy 56°01'·35N 03°10'·98W Q(9) 15s; W cardinal mark.
North Channel (cont).
No. 7 Lt Buoy 56°02'·80N 03°10'·87W QG; *Bell*; Racon.
No. 9 Lt Buoy 56°02'·37N 03°13'·38W FlG 6s; stbd-hand mark.
No. 10 Lt Buoy 56°02'·05N 03°13'·30W FlR 6s; port-hand mark.
No. 11 Lt Buoy 56°02'·08N 03°15'·15W FlG 3s; stbd-hand mark.
No. 12 Lt Buoy 56°01'·77N 03°15'·05W FlR 3s; port-hand mark.
No. 13 Lt Buoy 56°01'·77N 03°16'·94W FlG 9s; stbd-hand mark.
No. 14 Lt Buoy 56°01'·52N 03°16'·82W FlR 9s; port-hand mark.

LEITH.
East breakwater head 55°59'·48N 03°10'·85W Iso R 4s 7m 9M; *Horn (3) 30s.*
West breakwater head FlG 6s.

GRANTON.
East pier head 55°59'·28N 03°13'·17W FlR 2s 5m 6M.
West pier head FlG 2s 5m 7M; W Tr.
Oxcars 56°01'·36N 03°16'·74W Fl(2) WR 7s 16m W13M, R12M; W Tr, R band; vis W072°-087°, R087°-196°, W196°-313°, R313°-072°; Ra refl.
Inchcolm, E ast point, 56°01'·73N 03°17'·75W Fl(3) 15s 20m 10M; part obsc 075°-145°; *Horn (3) 45s.*
No. 15 Lt Buoy 56°01'·43N 03°18'·70W FlG 6s; stbd-hand mark.
No. 16 Lt Buoy 56°00'·75N 03°19'·80W FlR 3s; port-hand mark.
No. 17 Lt Buoy 56°01'·17N 03°20'·12W FlG 3s; stbd-hand mark.
No. 19 Lt Buoy 56°00'·71N 03°22'·38W FlG 9s; stbd-hand mark.

FIRTH OF FORTH, NORTH SHORE (INWARD).
Hawkcraig Point Ldg Lts 292°. Front 56°03'·04N 03°16'·98W Q 12m 14M; W Tr; vis 282°-302°. Rear, 96m from front, Iso 5s 16m 14M; W Tr; vis 282°-302°.
Braefoot Bay Terminal.
Western Jetty. Ldg Lts 247°. **Front** 56°02'·15N 03°18'·63W Fl 3s 6m **15M**; W triangle on E dolphin; vis 237°-257°; four dolphins marked by 2FG(vert). **Rear**, 88m from front, Fl 3s

12m **15M**; W triangle on approach gangway; vis 237°-257°; synchronised with front.
Mortimer's Deep.
No. 1 Lt Buoy 56°02'·82N 03°15'·65W QG; stbd-hand mark.
No. 2 Lt Buoy 56°02'·65N 03°16'·08W QR; port-hand mark.
No. 3 Lt Buoy 56°02'·51N 03°17'·44W Fl(2)G 5s; stbd-hand mark.
No. 4 Lt Buoy 56°02'·38N 03°17'·35W Fl(2)R 5s; port-hand mark.
No. 5 Lt Buoy 56°02'·37N 03°17'·86W FlG 4s; stbd-hand mark.
No. 6 Lt Buoy 56°02'·28N 03°17'·78W FlR 4s; port-hand mark.
No. 7 Lt Buoy 56°01'·94N 03°18'·92W Fl(2)G 5s; stbd-hand mark.
No° 8 Lt Buoy 56°02'·10N 03°18'·17W FlR 2s; port-hand mark.
No. 9 Lt Buoy 56°01'·69N 03°19'·08W QG; stbd-hand mark.
No. 10 Lt Buoy 56°01'·83N 03°18'·48W Fl(2)R 5s; port-hand mark.
No. 14 Lt Buoy 56°01'·56N 03°18'·96W Q(9) 15s; W cardinal mark.
Inchcolm. South Lts in line 066°. Front, 84m from rear, Q 7m 7M; W Tr; vis 062°-082°. Common Rear 56°01'·80N 03°18'·13W Iso 5s 11m 7M; W Tr; vis 062°-082°.
North Lts in line 077°. Front, 80m from rear, Q 7m 7M; W Tr; vis 062°-082°.
Deep Channel
No. 16 Lt Buoy 56°00'·75N 03°19'·81W FlR 3s; port-hand mark.
No. 17 Lt Buoy 56°01'·17N 03°20'·10W FlG 3s; stbd-hand mark.
No. 19 Lt Buoy 56°00'·72N 03°22'·40W FlG 9s; stbd-hand mark.
Hound Point Terminal.
NE dolphin 56°00'·37N 03°21'·52W FR 7m 5M; Dn; *Siren(3) 90s.*
Centre pier 2 Aero FR 47m 5M.
SW dolphin FR 7m 5M, Dn.
Inch Garvie, NW end 56°00'·01N 03°23'·29W LFl 5s 9m 11M; B Bn, W lantern.
North Queensferry. Oc 5s and QR or QG traffic signals.
Forth Rail Bridge. Centres of spans have W Lts and ends of cantilevers R Lts, defining N and S channels.
Forth Road Bridge. N suspension Tr Iso G 4s 7m 6M on East and West sides; 2 Aero FR 155m 11M and 2 FR 109m 7M on same Tr. Main span, N part QG 50m 6M on East and West sides. Main span, centre Iso 4s 52m 8M on East and West sides. Main span, S part QR 50m 6M on East and West sides. S suspension Tr Iso R 4s 7m 6M on East and West sides; 2 Aero FR 155m and 2 Fr 109m 7M on same Tr.

PORT EDGAR.
Dir Lt 244°. West breakwater head 55°59'·85N 03°24'·69W Dir FlR 4s 4m 8M; W blockhouse; 4 QY mark floating breakwater.
3 2 FR (vert) mark North ends of marina pontoons inside harbour.
Beamer Rock 56°02'·28N 03°24'·66W Fl 3s 6m 9M; W Tr, R top; *Horn 20s.*

HM NAVAL BASE, ROSYTH.
Main Channel Dir Lt 323°. Beacon A 56°01'·19N 03°25'·53W Dir Oc WRG 7m 4M; R square on W post with R bands, on B&W diagonal square on W Bn; vis G318°-322°, W322°-325°, R325°-328° (H24).
Dir Lt 115°, Beacon C Dir Oc WRG 6s 7m 4M; vis R110°-114°, W114°-116°, G116°-120°.

Dir Lt 295°, Beacon E Dir Oc 6s 11m 4M: vis 293°-297°.
South Arm Jetty, head 56°01'·08N 03°26'·48W LFl(2)WR 12s 5m W9M; R6M; vis W010°-280°, R280°-010°.
Rosyth Main Channel.
Whale Bank No. 2 Lt Buoy 56°00'·70N 03°25'·10W Q(3) 10s; E cardinal mark.
No. 3 Lt Buoy 56°00'·87N 03°24'·98W FlG 5s; stbd-hand mark.
No. 4 Lt Buoy 56°00'·82N 03°25'·18W FlR 3s; port-hand mark.
No. 5 Lt Buoy 56°01'·08N 03°25'·80W QG; stbd-hand mark.
No. 6 Lt Buoy 56°01'·01N 03°25'·94W QR; port-hand mark.
Charlestown. Lts in line. Front 56°02'·2N 03°30'·6W FG 4m 10M; Y triangle on Y pile; vis 017°-037°; marks line of HP gas main. Rear FG 6m 10M; Y triangle on Y pile; vis 017°-037°.
Crombie Jetty, downstream dolphin 2 FG (vert) 8m 4M.
Crombie Jetty, upstream dolphin 2 FG (Vert) 8m 4M.
Bo'ness.
Carriden outfall 56°01'·3N 03°33'·6W FlY 5s 3M; Y pile Bn.
Torry 56°02'·5N 03°35'·2W FlG 10s 5m 7M; G structure.
Bo'ness Platform 56°01'·9N 03°36'·1W QR 3m 2M; R pile Bn.

GRANGEMOUTH.
No. 1 pile 56°02'·2N 03°37'·9W Fl(3)R 20s 4m 6M.
No. 2 pile 56°02'·4N 03°38'·8W FlG 5s 4m 6M;.
No. 3 pile FlR 5s 4m 6M.
No. 4 pile FlG 2s 4m 5M.
No. 5 pile FlR 2s 4m 5M.
Dock entrance, East jetty *Horn 30s*; docking signals.
Longannet Power Station, intake LFlG 10s 5m 6M.

KINCARDINE.
Swing bridge 56°03'·9N 03°43'·5W FW at centre of each span; FR Lts mark each side of openings.

KIRKCALDY.
East pier head 56°06'·78N 03°08'·81W Fl WG 10s 12m 8M; vis G156°-336°, W336°-156°; South pier head 2 FR (vert) 7m 5M.
West Rockheads Buoy 56°07'·00N 03°06'·90W (unlit); stbd hand mark.
East Rockheads Buoy 56°07'·15N 03°06'·33W (unlit); stbd-hand mark.
Kirkcaldy Wreck Lt Buoy 56°07'·26N 03°05'·20W Fl(3)G 18s; stbd-hand mark.

METHIL.
Outer pier head 56°10'·77N 03°00'·39W Oc G 6s 8m 5M; W Tr; vis 280°-100°.
Elie Ness 56°11'·05N 02°48'·65W Fl 6s 15m **18M**; W Tr.

ST MONANCE.
Breakwater head 56°12'·20N 02°45'·80W Oc WRG 6s 5m W7M, R4M, G4M; vis G282°-355°, W355°-026°, R026°-038°.
East pier, head 2 FG (vert) 6m 4M; Or tripod; *Bell (occas).*
West pier, near head, 2 FR (vert) 6m 4M.

PITTENWEEM.
Ldg Lts 037° Middle pier head. Front FR 4m 5M. Rear FR 8m 5M. Both W columns, R bands.
East pier head extension 56°12'·68N 02°43'·53W Oc G 6s 5m 5M.
Beacon Rock QR 3m 2M.
West pier, Elbow, *Horn 90s (occas).*

ANSTRUTHER.
West pier head 2 FR (vert) 5m 4M; grey post; *Reed (3) 60s (occas) .*

East pier head 56°13'·15N 02°41'·72W Fl G 3s 6m 4M; R column.

Isle of May, Summit. 56°11'·13N 02°33'·30W Fl (2) 15s 73m **22M**; square Tr on stone dwelling.

CRAIL.
Ldg Lts 295°. Front FR 24m 6M (not lit when harbour closed). Rear 30m from front FR 30m 6M.
Fife Ness 56°16'·73N 02°35'·10W Iso WR 10s 12m **W21M, R20M**; vis W143°-197°, R197°-217°, W217°-023°; RC.
North Carr Lt Buoy 56°18'·07N 02°32'·85W Q(3) 10s; E cardinal mark.
Bell Rock 56°26'·05N 02°23'·07W Fl 5s 32m **18M**; W round Tr; Racon.

RIVER TAY.
Tay Fairway Lt Buoy 56°28'·60N 02°37'·15W LFl 10s; safe water mark; *Whis*.
Middle Lt Buoy (North) 56°28'·26N 02°38'·87W Fl(3)G 18s; stbd-hand mark.
Middle Lt Buoy (South) 56°28'·00N 02°38'·57W Fl(2)R 12s; port-hand mark.
Abertay Lt Buoy 56°27'·41N 02°40'·66W Q(3) 10s; E cardinal mark; Racon.
Abertay (Elbow) Lt Buoy 56°27'·15N 02°40'·70W FlR 6s; port-hand mark.
Inner Lt Buoy 56°27'·10N 02°44'·23W Fl(2)R 12s; port-hand mark.
North Lady Lt Buoy 56°27'·36N 02°46'·80W Fl(3)G 18s; stbd-hand mark.
South Lady Lt Buoy 56°27'·20N 02°46'·76W Fl(3)R 18s; port-hand mark.
Pool Lt Buoy 56°27'·15N 02°48'·50W FlR 6s; port-hand mark.
Horse Shoe Lt Buoy 56°27'·28N 02°50'·11W VQ(6)LFl 10s; S cardinal mark.
Scalp Lt Buoy 56°27'·18N 02°51'·50W Fl(2)R 12s; port-hand mark.
Tentsmuir Point 56°26'·6N 02°49'·5W FlY 5s; Y Bn; vis 198°-208°; marks gas pipeline.
Monifieth 56°28'·9N 02°47'·8W FlY 5s; Y Bn; vis 018°-028°; marks gas pipeline.
Broughty Castle 56°27'·76N 02°52'·10W 2 FG (vert) 10/8m 4M; FR is shown at foot of old Lt Ho at Buddon Ness, 4M to E, and at other places on firing range when practice is taking place.

TAYPORT.
High Lighthouse, Dir Lt 269°, 56°27'·17N 02°53'·85W Dir Iso WRG 3s 24m **W22M**, **R17M**, **G16M**; W Tr; vis G267°-268°, W268°-270°, R270°-271°.

ARBROATH.
Outfall Lt Buoy 56°32'·66N 02°34'·96W FlY 3s; special mark.
Ldg Lts 299°. Front FR 7m 5M; W column. Rear, 50m from front, FR 13m 5M; W column.
West breakwater, E end, VQ(2) 6s 6m 4M; W metal post.
East pier, South elbow 56°33'·26N 02°34'·89W FlG 3s 8m 5M; W Tr; shows FR when harbour closed; *Siren(3) 60s (occas)*.
Scurdie Ness 56°42'·12N 02°26'·15W Fl(3) 20s 38m **23M**; Racon.

MONTROSE..
Scurdie Rocks Lt Buoy 56°42'·15N 02°25'·42W QR; port-hand mark.
Annat Lt Buoy 56°42'·38N 02°25'·53W Fl G 3s; stbd-hand mark.

Ldg Lts 272°. Front FR 11m 5M; W twin pillars, R bands. Rear, 272m from front, FR 18m 5M; W Tr, R cupola.
Inner Ldg Lts 265°. Front FG 21m 5M; Or triangle on pylon. Rear, 180m from front, FG 33m 5M; Or triangle on pylon.

JOHNSHAVEN.
Ldg Lts 316°. Front FR 5m; R structure. Rear, 85m from front, FG 20m; shows R when unsafe to enter harbour.

GOURDON HARBOUR.
Ldg Lts 358°. Front 56°49'·6N 02°17'·1W FR 5m 5M; W Tr; shows G when unsafe to enter; *Siren(2) 60s (occas)*. Rear 120m from front FR 30m 5M; W Tr.
West pier head Fl WRG 3s 5m W9M, R7M, G7M; vis G180°-344°, W344°-354°, R354°-180°.
East breakwater head Q 3m 7M.

Tod Head 56°53'·0N 02°12'·8W Fl(4) 30s 41m **29M**; W Tr.

STONEHAVEN.
Outer pier head 56°57'·59N 02°11'·89W Iso WRG 4s 7m W11M, R7M, G8M; vis G214°-246°, W246°-268°, R268°-280°.
Inner harbour Ldg Lts 273°. Front F 6m 5M. Rear FR 8m 5M.

Girdle Ness 57°08'·35N 02°02'·82W Fl(2) 20s 56m **22M**; W Tr; obsc by Greg Ness when bearing more than about 020°; RC; Racon.

ABERDEEN.
Fairway Lt Buoy 57°09'·33N 02°01'·85W LFl 10s; safe water mark; Racon.
South breakwater head Fl(3) R 8s 23m 7M.
North pier head Oc WR 6s 11m 9M; W Tr; vis W145°-055°, R055°-145°. In fog FY (same Tr) vis 136°-336°; *Bell (3) 12s*.
Old South breakwater QR 3m 2M; R column.
Abercromby Jetty head Oc G 4s 5m 4M; G column; vis 230°-080°.
South Jetty head, QR 5m 4M; vis 063°-243°.
Torry. Ldg Lts 236°. Front FR or G 14m 5M; W Tr; R when entrance safe, FG when dangerous to navigation; vis 195°-279°. Rear 205m from front FR 19m 5M; W Tr; vis 195°-279°.

Buchan Ness 57°28'·23N 01°46'·37W Fl 5s 40m **28M**; W Tr, R bands; Racon; *Horn (3) 60s*.

PETERHEAD.
Kirktown Ldg Lts 314°. Front 57°30'·2N 01°47'·1W FR 13m 8M; R mast, W triangle point up. Rear 65m from front FR 17m 8M; R mast, W triangle point down.
South breakwater head Fl(2) R 12s 24m 7M; W Tr with B base.
North breakwater head 57°29'·85N 01°46'·22W Iso RG 6s 19m 7M; tripod; vis R165°-230°, G230°-165°; *Horn 30s*.

Rattray Head. Ron Rock. 57°36'·6N 01°48'·9W Fl(3) 30s 28m **24M**; W Tr; *Horn (2) 45s*.

10.6.5   PASSAGE INFORMATION

From Berwick-upon-Tweed to the Firth of Forth there is no good harbour which can be approached with safety in strong onshore winds. So, if on passage with strong winds from N or E, it is advisable to keep well to seaward. Northward from Firth of Forth to Rattray Hd the coast is mostly rky and steep-to, and there are no out-lying dangers within 2M of the coast except those off R Tay, and Bell Rk. Throughout this area reference should be made to *North Sea (West) Pilot* and *Sailing Directions Humber Estuary to Rattray Head* (R Northumberland YC). For the Firth of Forth, refer to the *Forth Yacht Clubs Association Pilot Handbook*, which covers the coast from Berwick-upon-Tweed to Fraserburgh.

BERWICK-UPON-TWEED TO BASS ROCK (chart 175)

The coast N from Berwick is rky with cliffs rising in height to Burnmouth. Keep ½M offshore to avoid outlying rks. Burnmouth has more alongside berths than Eyemouth, which is a busy fishing harb. N of Burnmouth the cliffs fall gradually to Eyemouth Bay.

Close S of St Abb's Hd is St Abb's Harb: the inner harb dries, but outer harb has depth of 2m in places. Do not approach in strong onshore wind or sea, and beware rky ledges close each side of leading line. Temp anchorage in offshore winds in Coldingham Bay. See 10.6.19.

St Abb's Hd (Lt) is a bold, steep headland, 92m high, with no offlying dangers. The stream runs strongly round the hd, causing turbulence with wind against tide; this can be largely avoided by keeping well inshore. The ESE-going stream begins at HW Leith – 0345, and the WNW-going at HW Leith + 0240. There is a good anch in Pettico Wick, on NW side of hd, in S winds, but dangerous if the wind shifts onshore. There are no off-lying dangers between St Abb's Hd and Fast Castle Hd, 3M WNW. Between Fast Castle Hd and Barns Ness, about 8M NW, is the attractive little harb of Cove, which however dries and should only be approached in very good conditions.

Barns Ness (Lt) lies 2½M ESE of Dunbar (10.6.8) and is fringed with rks: tidal streams as for St Abb's Hd. A conspic chy is ¾M WSW of Barns Ness, and Torness Power Station (conspic) is 1¾M SE of Barns Ness. Between here and Dunbar keep at least ¼M offshore to clear rky patches. Sicar Rk lies about 1¼M ENE of Dunbar, and sea breaks on it in onshore gales.

The direct course from Dunbar to Bass Rk (Lt) is clear of all dangers: inshore of this line beware Wildfire Rks (dry) on NW side of Bellhaven B. In offshore winds there is anch in Scoughall Road. Great Car is ledge of rks, nearly covering at HW, 1M ESE of Gin Hd, with Car Bn (stone Tr surmounted by cross) at its N end. Drying ledges of rks extend 1M SE of Great Car, up to 3 ca offshore. Keep at least ½M off Car Bn in strong onshore winds. Tantallon Castle (ruins) is on cliff edge 1M W of Great Car. Bass Rk lies 1¼M NNE of Gin Hd, and is a steep, conspic rk with no offlying dangers.

BASS ROCK TO INCHKEITH (chart 734)

Westward of Bass Rk Craigleith, Lamb Island and Fidra lie ½M or more offshore, while the coast is generally foul. Craigleith is steep-to, but temporary anchorage can be found on SE and SW sides; if passing inshore of it keep well to N side of chan. N Berwick Harb (dries) lies S of Craigleith, but is unsafe in onshore winds. Lamb Island is 1½M WNW of N Berwick (see 10.6.19) and has a rky ledge extending ¼M SW. Inshore, between Craigleith and Lamb Island, beware drying rks up to 3 ca from land. Fidra Island (Lt, RC) is a bird reserve, nearly connected to the shore by rky ledges, and should be passed to the N. There are anchorages on E, S or W sides, depending on wind, in good weather.

In the B between Fidra and Edinburgh some shelter can be found in SE winds in Aberlady B and Gosford B. The best

anch is SW of Craigielaw Pt. Port Seton is ¾M E of the conspic Chys of Cockenzie Power Station, and the E side of this fishing harb (dries) can be entered HW – 3 to HW + 3, but not advisable in strong on-shore wind or sea. Cockenzie (dries) is close to power station; beware Corsik Rk 400m to E. Access HW – 2½ to HW + 2½, but no attractions except boatyard. For Fisherrow see 10.6.19.

There are no dangers on the direct course from Fidra to Inchkeith (Lt, RC), which stands in the centre of entrance to Leith, Granton (10.6.9), and the higher reaches of Firth of Forth. Rks extend ¾M SE from Inchkeith, and ½M off the SW side. There is a small harb on W side, below the Lt Ho; landing is forbidden without permission. N Craig and Craig Waugh (least depth 0.6m) are shallow patches 2½M SE from Inchkeith Lt Ho, and are buoyed. The deep water chans N and S of Inchkeith are buoyed. In N Chan, close to Inchkeith the W-going (flood) stream begins about HW Leith – 0530, and the E-going at HW Leith + 0030, sp rates about 1 kn. The streams gather strength towards the Forth bridges, where they reach 2¼ kn and there may be turbulence. For Cramond and Inchcolm see 10.6.19.

INCHKEITH TO FIFE NESS (charts 734, 190)

From Burntisland (10.6.10) the N shore of Firth of Forth leads E to Kinghorn Ness. 1M SSW of Kinghorn Ness Blae Rk (buoyed) has least depth of 4.6m, but the sea breaks on it in E gales. Rost Bank lies halfway between Kinghorn Ness and Inchkeith, with tide rips at sp tides or in strong winds.

Between Kinghorn Ness and Kirkcaldy, drying rks lie up to 3 ca offshore. Kirkcaldy Harb is primarily commercial but by arrangement yachts can enter inner dock near HW. The entrance is dangerous in strong E winds, when the sea breaks a long way out. For Kirkcaldy see 10.6.19.

Between Kirkcaldy and Methil (10.6.11) the only dangers more than 2 ca offshore are The Rockheads, extending 4 ca SE of Dysart, and marked by buoys. Largo B provides anch near E side, well sheltered from N and E. Off Chapel Ness beware W Vows (dries) and E Vows (dries, marked by refuge Bn). There is anch close W of Elie Ness, see 10.6.19. Ox Rk (dries) lies ½M ENE of Elie Ness, and ¼M offshore: otherwise there are no dangers more than 2 ca offshore past St Monans (10.6.19), Pittenweem and Anstruther (10.6.12), but in bad weather the sea breaks on Shield Rk 4 ca off Pittenweem. From Ansthruther to Crail and on to Fife Ness keep 3 ca offshore to clear Caiplie Rk and other dangers. For Crail see 10.6.19.

May Island (Lt, RC) lies about 5M S of Fife Ness: its shores are bold except at NW end where rks extend 1 ca off. In good weather it is possible to land. Anch on W side, near N end, in E winds; or on E side, near N end, in W winds. Lt Ho boats use Kirkhaven, close SE of Lt Ho. See 10.6.19.

FIFE NESS TO MONTROSE (chart 190)

Fife Ness is fringed by rky ledges, and a reef extends 1M NE to N Carr Rk (dries, marked by Bn). In strong onshore winds keep to seaward of N Carr Lt buoy. From here keep ½M offshore to clear dangers entering St Andrews B, where there is anch: the little harb dries, and should not be approached in onshore winds.

R Tay (10.6.13) entrance is between Tentsmuir Pt and Buddon Ness (chart 1481), and has many sandbanks which are liable to shift. Abertay Sands extend nearly 4M E of Tentsmuir Pt on S side of chan (buoyed), and Gaa Sands run 1¾M E from Buddon Ness. Passage across Abertay and Gaa Sands is very dangerous. Abertay Lt buoy (Racon) is on N side of chan 1¾M ESE of Buddon Ness. Elbow is an extension of Abertay Sands, to S and SE of Lt buoy. The Bar, NE of Abertay Lt buoy, is dangerous in heavy weather, particularly in strong onshore wind or swell. S of Buddon Ness the W-going (flood) stream begins about HW Aberdeen −0400, and the E-going at about HW Aberdeen +0230, sp rates 2 kn.

Bell Rk (Lt, Racon) lies about 11½M E of Buddon Ness. 2M E of Bell Rk the S-going stream begins HW Aberdeen −0220, and the N-going at HW Aberdeen +0405, sp rates 1 kn. W of Bell Rk the streams begin earlier.

N from Buddon Ness the coast is sandy. 1¼M SW of Arbroath (10.6.14) beware Elliot Houses, rky patches with depth 1.8m, which extend about ½M offshore. Between Whiting Ness and Scurdie Ness, 9½M NNE, the coast is clear of out-lying dangers, but is mostly fringed with drying rks up to 1 ca off. In offshore winds there is anch in Lunan B, off Ethie Haven.

Scurdie Ness (Lt, Racon) stands on S side of entrance to Montrose (10.6.15). Scurdie Rks (dry) extend 2 ca E of the ness. On N side of chan Annat Bank dries up to about ½M E of the shore, opposite Scurdie Ness (chart 1438). The in-going stream begins at HW Aberdeen −0500, and the outgoing at HW Aberdeen +0115; both streams are very strong, up to 7 kn at sp, and there is turbulence off the entrance on the ebb. The entrance is dangerous in strong onshore winds, with breaking seas extending to Scurdie Ness on the ebb. In marginal conditions the last quarter of the flood is best time to enter.

MONTROSE TO RATTRAY HEAD (charts 210, 213)

N from Montrose the coast is sandy for 5M to Milton Ness, where there is anch on S side in N winds. Johnshaven, 2¼M SW of Gourdon, is a small harb (dries), which should not be approached with onshore wind or swell. ½M NE, off Brotherton Castle, drying rks extend 4 ca offshore. Gourdon has a small harb (mostly dries) approached by winding chan marked by Bns: inner harbour has storm gates. Outside Gourdon Harb rks extend ¾M S of entrance, and the sea breaks heavily in strong E winds. See 10.6.19.

N to Inverbervie the coast is fringed with rky ledges up to 2 ca offshore. Just N of Tod Hd (Lt) is Catterline, a small b which forms a natural anch in W winds, but open to E. Downie Pt lies close SE of Stonehaven (10.6.16). The b has a sandy bottom, but is encumbered by rky ledges up to 2 ca from shore. Anch 6 ca E of Bay Hotel. In E gales the b is dangerous, and sea breaks well outside harb entrance.

From Garron Pt to Girdle Ness the coast is mostly steep-to. Fishing nets may be met off headlands during fishing season. Craigmaroinn and Seal Craig (dry) are parts of reef 3 ca offshore SE of Portlethen, a fishing village with landing sheltered by rks. Cove B has a very small fishing harb, off which there is anch in good weather: Cove Rks (dry) lie 1½ ca offshore. From Cove to Girdle Ness keep ½M offshore, avoiding The Hasman, a rk which dries 1 ca off Altens village.

Greg Ness and Girdle Ness (Lt, RC, Racon) are fringed by rks. Girdlestone is a rky patch, depth less than 2m, 2 ca ENE of Lt Ho. A drying patch lies 2 ca SE of Lt Ho. Off Girdle Ness the S-going stream begins at HW Aberdeen −0430, and the N-going at HW Aberdeen +0130, sp rates 2½ kn. A race forms on S-going stream. Girdle Ness lies at SE corner of Aberdeen B (10.6.17).

Northward from Aberdeen there are few offshore dangers to Buchan Ness. R Ythan, 1¾M SSW of Hackley Hd, is navigable by small craft, but chan shifts constantly. 3M N is the very small harb of Collieston (mostly dries), only accessible in fine weather. 4¾M NNE of Hackley Hd lie The Skares, rks (marked by buoy) extending 3½ ca from S point of Cruden B − where there is anch in offshore winds. On N side of Cruden B is Port Erroll (dries).

Buchan Ness (Lt, fog sig, Racon) is a rky peninsula. 2 ca N is the islet Meikle Mackie, close W of which is the small harb of Boddam (dries). 3 ca NE of Meikle Mackie is The Skerry, a rk 6m high on S side of Sandford B; rks on which the sea breaks extend 2 ca NNE. There is a chan between The Skerry and the coast, which can be used when making for Peterhead (10.6.18). See also 10.6.19 for Boddam.

Rattray Hd (Lt, fog sig on Ron Rk, 3 ca E of hd) has rky foreshore, drying for 2 ca. Rattray Briggs is a detached reef, depth 0.6m, 2 ca E of Lt Ho. Rattray Hard is a rky patch, depth 0.2m, 1½M ENE of Lt Ho, which raises a dangerous sea during strong onshore winds. Off Rattray Hd the S-going stream begins at HW Aberdeen −0420, and the N-going at HW Aberdeen +0110, sp rates 3 kn. In normal conditions keep about 1M E of Rattray Hd, but in bad weather pass 5M off, preferably at slack water. Conspic radio masts with R Lts lie 2.5M WNW and 2.2M W of Lt Ho.

For notes on offshore oil and gas installations, see 10.5.5.

10.6.6   DISTANCE TABLE

Approximate distances in nautical miles are by the most direct route while avoiding dangers and allowing for traffic separation schemes etc. Places in *italics* are in adjoining areas.

	1	2	3	4	5	6	7	8	9	10	11	12	13	14	15	16	17	18	19	20
1 *Brunsbüttel*	1																			
2 *Flamborough Head*	325	2																		
3 *Longstone (Farne)*	388	105	3																	
4 Eyemouth	406	126	21	4																
5 St Abbs Head	408	129	24	3	5															
6 Dunbar	422	143	38	17	14	6														
7 Granton	449	170	65	44	41	27	7													
8 Port Edgar	456	177	72	51	48	34	7	8												
9 Burntisland	448	169	64	43	40	26	5	8	9											
10 Methil	441	162	57	36	33	20	14	20	12	10										
11 Anstruther	431	155	50	29	26	14	23	29	22	11	11									
12 Fife Ness	428	155	50	29	26	17	28	34	27	16	5	12								
13 Dundee	446	174	69	49	46	37	48	54	47	36	25	20	13							
14 Arbroath	433	169	64	44	41	34	45	51	44	33	22	17	15	14						
15 Montrose	433	175	69	51	48	43	55	61	54	43	32	27	27	12	15					
16 Stonehaven	434	185	82	66	63	60	72	78	71	60	49	44	45	30	20	16				
17 Aberdeen	436	194	93	78	75	73	84	90	83	72	61	56	57	42	32	13	17			
18 Peterhead	439	212	112	98	95	93	106	112	105	94	83	78	80	64	54	35	25	18		
19 *Duncansby Head*	504	292	192	179	176	174	186	192	185	174	163	158	161	145	135	115	105	82	19	
20 *Lerwick*	514	358	271	256	253	251	264	270	263	252	241	236	238	222	212	193	183	158	110	20

EYEMOUTH   10-6-7

Berwick

CHARTS
Admiralty 1612, 160; OS 67
TIDES
+0330 Dover; ML No data; Duration 0610; Zone 0 (GMT).

Standard Port LEITH (⟶)

Times				Height (metres)			
HW		LW		MHWS	MHWN	MLWN	MLWS
0300	0900	0300	0900	5.6	4.5	2.1	0.8
1500	2100	1500	2100				

Differences EYEMOUTH
−0015 −0025 −0014 −0004 −0.9   −0.8   No data

SHELTER
Good shelter in harbour in all weathers but entry should not be attempted in strong winds from N through NE to E. There are many fishing boats. Yachts normally berth outer end of E pier in 2m approx. Anchor in bay only in off-shore winds.
NAVIGATION
Waypoint 55°53'.00N 02°05'.28W, 354°/174° from/to E breakwater Lt, 0.50M. Approach can be made N or S of Hurcar Rocks but there are no leading marks to the S. To the N, beware Blind Buss. Entrance and basin dredged to 0.9m.
LIGHTS AND MARKS
Ldg Lts 174° (pillars painted orange) both FG 7/10m 4M on West pier. FR or red flag − unsafe to enter.
RADIO TELEPHONE
VHF Ch 16; 12 (No regular watch).
TELEPHONE (08907)
Hr Mr 50223; CG 50348; MRSC Crail 50666; ⌗ Edinburgh 554 2421; Marinecall 0898 500 452; Police 50217; Dr 50599.
FACILITIES
EC Wednesday; **Jetty** Slip, D (By delivery), P (cans), FW, AB; **Fishermans Mutual Assoc.** ☎ 50360 CH, Gas; **Eyemouth BY** ☎ 50231, Slip, BH, ME, El, Sh, C (12 ton mobile); **Collins** ☎ 50308, El; **Eyemouth Marine** ☎ 50594, ME; **Leith & Son** ☎ Berwick 307264 SM; **Marconi Marine** ☎ 51252 Ⓔ; **Coastal Marine** ☎ 50328 ME, Sh; **The Boat Shop** ☎ 51327 CH; **Town** LB, P, D, CH, V, R, Bar. ✉, Ⓞ, Gas, Gaz, Ⓑ, ⇌ (bus to Berwick-on-Tweed); ✈ (Edinburgh).
Note: − limited facilities in town on Sundays.

▲ Report to Hr Mr

DUNBAR   10-6-8

East Lothian

CHARTS
Admiralty 734, 175; Imray 27; OS 67
TIDES
+0330 Dover; ML 3.1; Duration 0600; Zone 0 (GMT).

Standard Port LEITH (⟶)

Times				Height (metres)			
HW		LW		MHWS	MHWN	MLWN	MLWS
0300	0900	0300	0900	5.6	4.5	2.1	0.8
1500	2100	1500	2100				

Differences DUNBAR
−0005 −0010 +0010 +0017 −0.4   −0.3   −0.1   −0.1
FIDRA
−0005 −0005 −0010 −0010 −0.4   −0.1   0.0   −0.2

SHELTER
Outer (Victoria) Harbour is dangerous in strong NW to NE winds but Inner (Old or Cromwell) Harbour (dries) is safe at all times: entry through a bridge which is opened on request to Hr Mr.
NAVIGATION
Waypoint 56°00'.70N 02°30'.80W, 018°/198° from/to front Ldg Lt 198°, 0.50M. Min depth at entrance 0.9m. Entrance is unsafe in heavy on-shore swell. N side of Victoria harbour dries but pool 1.25m at LWS in SW corner. Beware Outer Buss Rk (0.6m). Keep to port on entry to avoid rockfall off castle.
LIGHTS AND MARKS
The entrance is to port of the 198° leading line which is marked by two marks to S of Doo Rks, both Oc G 6s, with W triangles on Or columns intens 188°-208° (synchronised). Entrance on Ldg line 132°, QR seen between the cliffs. Port Authority is the Lothian Regional Council.
RADIO TELEPHONE
None.
TELEPHONE (0368)
Hr Mr 63005; CG 63342; MRSC Crail 50666; ⌗ Edinburgh 554 2421; Marinecall 0898 500 452; Police 62718; H (0620) 824141; Dr 62327.
FACILITIES
EC Wednesday; **Quay** Slip, L, FW, D (delivery), P (cans); **North Wall** M, L, AB; **Inner Harbour** Slip, L, AB; **F & P Blair** ☎ 62371 ME; **Lawrence Turnbull** ☎ 63228 Gas, Gaz; **Town** LB, P, Ⓞ, V, R, Bar. ✉; Ⓑ; ⇌; ✈ (Edinburgh).

FIRTH OF FORTH   10-6-9
Lothian/Fife

CHARTS
Admiralty 734, 735, 736; Imray C27; OS 66

TIDES
+0340 Dover; ML 3.3; Duration 0620; Zone 0 (GMT).

Standard Port LEITH (→)

Times				Height (metres)			
HW		LW		MHWS	MHWN	MLWN	MLWS
0300	0900	0300	0900	5.6	4.5	2.1	0.8
1500	2100	1500	2100				

Differences COCKENZIE
−0007	−0015	−0013	−0005	−0.2	0.0	No data	

GRANTON
0000	0000	0000	0000	0.0	0.0	0.0	0.0

Kincardine:— Time difference Leith +0030.
Alloa:— Time difference Leith +0048.
Leith is a Standard Port and tidal predictions for each day of the year are given below.

SHELTER
Rosyth does not offer any facilities to yachts except in emergency. Leith Docks are an impounded dock and accordingly yachts are not normally accepted. Yachts are advised to shelter in Granton or Port Edgar at S Queensferry or in Forth Yacht Marina at N Queensferry. Granton — Yachts go to E of Middle Pier. Buoys are run by Royal Forth and Forth Corinthian YCs.

NAVIGATION
Waypoint Granton 56°00'.00N 03°13'.22W, 000°/180° from/to entrance, 0.72M. Beware Forth Railway Bridge — Forth Road Bridge — H.M. Ships entering and leaving Rosyth Dockyard — Hound Pt Oil Terminal — Braefoot Gas Terminal.
Note: Control of Forth Estuary, all commercial impounded docks and Granton Harbour is exercised by Forth Ports Authority.

LIGHTS AND MARKS
Granton — R Flag with W diagonal cross (or G Lt by night) on signal mast at middle pierhead — Entry prohibited.
Leith — R Lt on both walls — Port closed.
     — G Lt on both walls — Vessels may proceed.
     — G Lt on one wall — Vessels moor on that side.
Port Edgar — On West Pier Dir Lt Fl R 4s 4m 8M 244°; 4 QY Lts mark floating breakwater; 3 x 2 FR (vert) mark N ends of marina pontoons inside harbour.
A Protected Channel 150m wide extends from Nos 13 & 14 light-buoys NNW of Oxcars, under the bridges (N of Inch Garvie and Beamer Rk), to the entrance of Rosyth Dockyard. When the Protected Channel is in operation an Oc 5s Lt and a QR Lt are shown from N Queensferry Naval Sig Stn, and all other vessels must clear the channel for naval traffic.

RADIO TELEPHONE
North Queensferry Naval Signal Station at Battery Point (call: *Queensferry*) VHF Ch 16; 13 **71** (H24).
Rosyth Naval Base (call: *QHM*) Ch 13 (Mon-Fri: 0730-1700 LT).
Forth Navigation Service (at Leith) Ch 16 **71** (H24); **20** 12 (use 71 within area for calling and for short messages).
Grangemouth Docks Ch 16; 14 (H24).
Port Edgar Marina Ch 80 (Apl – Sept 0900 – 1900; Oct – Mar 0900 – 1700 LT).

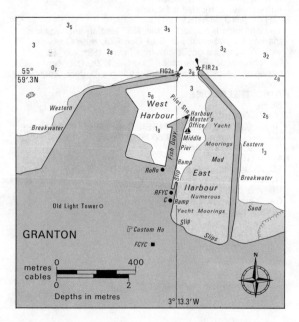

SCOTLAND, EAST COAST – LEITH

Lat 55°59′ N   Long 3°10′ W

TIMES AND HEIGHTS OF HIGH AND LOW WATERS

YEAR 1991

TIME ZONE UT(GMT)
For Summer Time add ONE hour in non-shaded areas

JANUARY

Day	Time	m	Time	m	Time	m	Time	m
1 Tu	0223	5·6	0834	0·9	1448	5·7	2115	0·5
16 W	0255	5·1	0835	1·5	1501	5·3	2103	1·2
2 W	0315	5·7	0925	0·9	1538	5·8	2206	0·5
17 Th	0328	5·2	0906	1·4	1533	5·4	2136	1·1
3 Th	0403	5·8	1010	1·0	1625	5·8	2250	0·5
18 F	0359	5·3	0939	1·3	1605	5·4	2209	1·0
4 F	0450	5·7	1051	1·1	1713	5·7	2329	0·7
19 Sa	0432	5·2	1012	1·3	1640	5·4	2240	1·0
5 Sa	0537	5·4	1129	1·3	1803	5·5		
20 Su	0508	5·2	1048	1·3	1717	5·3	2313	1·1
6 Su	0004	1·0	0626	5·2	1207	1·6	1853	5·2
21 M	0546	5·0	1124	1·4	1758	5·2	2349	1·2
7 M (	0041	1·3	0717	4·9	1249	1·9	1944	5·0
22 Tu	0629	4·9	1205	1·6	1843	5·1		
8 Tu	0127	1·7	0810	4·7	1344	2·1	2038	4·7
23 W)	0031	1·5	0716	4·7	1255	1·8	1932	5·0
9 W	0227	2·0	0908	4·5	1459	2·3	2139	4·6
24 Th	0125	1·8	0811	4·6	1400	2·0	2032	4·8
10 Th	0342	2·2	1012	4·5	1624	2·4	2248	4·5
25 F	0240	2·0	0918	4·5	1528	2·0	2146	4·7
11 F	0454	2·2	1119	4·5	1735	2·2	2354	4·6
26 Sa	0413	2·0	1036	4·6	1705	1·9	2310	4·8
12 Sa	0555	2·2	1218	4·7	1830	2·0		
27 Su	0537	1·8	1152	4·8	1820	1·5		
13 Su	0049	4·7	0644	2·0	1308	4·8	1915	1·8
28 M	0024	5·0	0643	1·5	1258	5·1	1922	1·0
14 M	0136	4·8	0726	1·8	1350	5·0	1954	1·5
29 Tu	0126	5·3	0738	1·2	1351	5·4	2016	0·7
15 Tu ●	0219	5·0	0802	1·6	1428	5·1	2029	1·3
30 W ○	0219	5·5	0827	1·0	1440	5·7	2104	0·4
31 Th	0304	5·7	0912	0·8	1524	5·8	2149	0·3

FEBRUARY

Day	Time	m	Time	m	Time	m	Time	m
1 F	0347	5·7	0954	0·8	1607	5·8	2227	0·4
16 Sa	0334	5·4	0921	1·0	1542	5·6	2148	0·7
2 Sa	0427	5·7	1029	0·8	1650	5·7	2258	0·5
17 Su	0406	5·4	0954	1·0	1615	5·6	2219	0·7
3 Su	0510	5·5	1059	1·0	1734	5·5	2325	0·8
18 M	0441	5·3	1028	1·0	1652	5·5	2250	0·8
4 M	0553	5·2	1129	1·2	1817	5·2	2352	1·2
19 Tu	0519	5·2	1103	1·1	1734	5·4	2324	1·0
5 Tu	0636	4·9	1200	1·5	1903	4·9		
20 W	0600	5·0	1143	1·2	1818	5·2		
6 W	0025	1·6	0721	4·6	1241	1·9	1950	4·7
21 Th)	0002	1·4	0647	4·8	1229	1·5	1908	5·0
7 Th	0113	2·0	0810	4·4	1342	2·2	2044	4·4
22 F	0054	1·8	0743	4·6	1333	1·8	2013	4·7
8 F	0225	2·4	0912	4·3	1521	2·4	2159	4·2
23 Sa	0209	2·1	0855	4·5	1512	2·0	2137	4·5
9 Sa	0404	2·5	1031	4·2	1705	2·3	2321	4·3
24 Su	0401	2·2	1024	4·5	1703	1·8	2308	4·7
10 Su	0528	2·4	1146	4·4	1812	2·1		
25 M	0535	2·0	1146	4·7	1818	1·4		
11 M	0027	4·4	0626	2·1	1245	4·6	1858	1·7
26 Tu	0021	4·9	0639	1·6	1250	5·1	1913	1·0
12 Tu	0116	4·6	0710	1·8	1329	4·8	1937	1·4
27 W	0119	5·2	0728	1·3	1342	5·4	2000	0·6
13 W	0158	4·9	0745	1·5	1407	5·1	2011	1·2
28 Th ○	0207	5·5	0812	0·9	1425	5·7	2043	0·4
14 Th ●	0234	5·1	0817	1·3	1439	5·3	2043	0·9
15 F	0305	5·3	0848	1·1	1510	5·5	2117	0·8

MARCH

Day	Time	m	Time	m	Time	m	Time	m
1 F	0248	5·6	0851	0·7	1506	5·8	2121	0·3
16 Sa ●	0235	5·3	0820	1·0	1441	5·5	2049	0·6
2 Sa	0326	5·7	0927	0·7	1544	5·8	2154	0·3
17 Su	0305	5·5	0854	0·8	1513	5·7	2122	0·5
3 Su	0403	5·6	0958	0·7	1622	5·7	2222	0·5
18 M	0338	5·5	0930	0·7	1550	5·7	2155	0·6
4 M	0440	5·4	1025	1·0	1702	5·5	2244	0·8
19 Tu	0414	5·4	1009	0·7	1630	5·7	2228	0·7
5 Tu	0518	5·1	1050	1·0	1744	5·2	2306	1·2
20 W	0456	5·3	1047	0·8	1715	5·5	2303	1·0
6 W	0557	4·9	1117	1·3	1823	4·9	2334	1·6
21 Th	0540	5·1	1128	1·1	1803	5·2	2344	1·4
7 Th	0636	4·6	1153	1·7	1907	4·5		
22 F)	0628	4·9	1219	1·4	1859	4·9		
8 F	0013	2·0	0718	4·4	1245	2·1	1958	4·3
23 Sa)	0037	1·9	0728	4·6	1327	1·8	2008	4·6
9 Sa	0115	2·4	0816	4·2	1411	2·4	2110	4·1
24 Su	0158	2·3	0844	4·5	1513	1·9	2135	4·5
10 Su	0257	2·6	0933	4·1	1622	2·3	2238	4·1
25 M	0356	2·3	1013	4·6	1656	1·7	2300	4·7
11 M	0447	2·5	1103	4·2	1738	2·1	2352	4·3
26 Tu	0524	2·1	1133	4·8	1802	1·4		
12 Tu	0554	2·2	1208	4·4	1829	1·7		
27 W	0007	5·0	0622	1·7	1235	5·1	1851	1·0
13 W	0045	4·6	0640	1·8	1256	4·7	1907	1·4
28 Th	0101	5·2	0707	1·3	1324	5·4	1933	0·7
14 Th	0127	4·8	0716	1·5	1335	5·0	1940	1·0
29 F	0146	5·4	0746	1·0	1405	5·6	2011	0·5
15 F	0204	5·1	0828	1·2	1409	5·3	2013	0·8
30 Sa ○	0225	5·5	0828	0·8	1442	5·7	2046	0·5
31 Su	0300	5·5	0854	0·7	1519	5·7	2118	0·6

APRIL

Day	Time	m	Time	m	Time	m	Time	m
1 M	0334	5·4	0924	0·7	1556	5·5	2143	0·7
16 Tu	0310	5·5	0910	0·6	1527	5·8	2133	0·6
2 Tu	0409	5·3	0951	0·8	1634	5·3	2206	1·0
17 W	0351	5·5	0954	0·6	1612	5·7	2212	0·8
3 W	0444	5·1	1017	1·0	1711	5·1	2228	1·3
18 Th	0436	5·4	1039	0·8	1702	5·5	2252	1·1
4 Th	0519	4·9	1044	1·3	1750	4·9	2256	1·6
19 F	0526	5·2	1126	1·0	1757	5·2	2337	1·5
5 F	0556	4·6	1119	1·6	1833	4·5	2335	2·0
20 Sa	0620	5·0	1220	1·3	1856	5·0		
6 Sa	0640	4·3	1208	1·9	1924	4·3		
21 Su)	0033	1·9	0723	4·7	1330	1·6	2005	4·7
7 Su (	0032	2·3	0734	4·2	1323	2·2	2029	4·1
22 M	0152	2·2	0836	4·6	1504	1·8	2121	4·7
8 M	0159	2·5	0844	4·1	1515	2·3	2146	4·1
23 Tu	0334	2·3	0954	4·7	1629	1·6	2237	4·8
9 Tu	0346	2·5	1002	4·2	1645	2·0	2300	4·3
24 W	0455	2·1	1108	4·8	1729	1·4	2341	5·0
10 W	0504	2·2	1114	4·4	1741	1·7	2358	4·5
25 Th	0552	1·8	1209	5·1	1818	1·2		
11 Th	0556	1·9	1209	4·7	1824	1·4		
26 F	0033	5·2	0636	1·5	1257	5·3	1900	1·0
12 F	0044	4·8	0635	1·5	1254	5·0	1901	1·1
27 Sa	0119	5·3	0715	1·2	1340	5·4	1938	0·9
13 Sa	0124	5·1	0711	1·2	1332	5·3	1938	0·8
28 Su ○	0156	5·3	0750	1·0	1418	5·5	2012	0·9
14 Su ●	0158	5·3	0747	0·9	1408	5·5	2015	0·6
29 M	0232	5·3	0824	0·9	1455	5·4	2043	0·9
15 M	0234	5·5	0828	0·7	1446	5·7	2054	0·5
30 Tu	0306	5·3	0855	0·9	1532	5·3	2111	1·0

Chart Datum: 2.90 metres below Ordnance Datum (Newlyn)

6

SCOTLAND, EAST COAST – LEITH

Lat 55°59′ N   Long 3°10′ W

TIMES AND HEIGHTS OF HIGH AND LOW WATERS

YEAR **1991**

TIME ZONE **UT(GMT)**
For Summer Time add ONE hour in non-shaded areas

MAY

Day	Time	m	Day	Time	m
1 W	0340 / 0924 / 1609 / 2137	5·2 / 1·0 / 5·2 / 1·2	16 Th	0333 / 0947 / 1601 / 2203	5·5 / 0·6 / 5·7 / 0·9
2 Th	0415 / 0953 / 1647 / 2203	5·1 / 1·2 / 5·0 / 1·4	17 F	0422 / 1038 / 1654 / 2249	5·5 / 0·7 / 5·5 / 1·2
3 F	0450 / 1023 / 1726 / 2233	4·9 / 1·3 / 4·8 / 1·7	18 Sa	0516 / 1129 / 1749 / 2335	5·3 / 0·9 / 5·3 / 1·5
4 Sa	0528 / 1100 / 1808 / 2313	4·7 / 1·6 / 4·6 / 1·9	19 Su	0613 / 1221 / 1847	5·2 / 1·1 / 5·1
5 Su	0612 / 1147 / 1856	4·5 / 1·8 / 4·4	20 M ☽	0028 / 0713 / 1321 / 1948	1·8 / 5·0 / 1·4 / 4·9
6 M	0005 / 0702 / 1247 / 1951	2·2 / 4·4 / 2·0 / 4·3	21 Tu	0135 / 0816 / 1434 / 2054	2·0 / 4·9 / 1·5 / 4·8
7 Tu ☾	0115 / 0802 / 1407 / 2055	2·3 / 4·3 / 2·0 / 4·2	22 W	0255 / 0925 / 1547 / 2204	2·1 / 4·8 / 1·6 / 4·8
8 W	0240 / 0907 / 1533 / 2200	2·4 / 4·3 / 2·0 / 4·3	23 Th	0412 / 1032 / 1649 / 2307	2·1 / 4·9 / 1·5 / 4·9
9 Th	0359 / 1013 / 1641 / 2301	2·2 / 4·5 / 1·8 / 4·5	24 F	0513 / 1135 / 1740	1·9 / 5·0 / 1·5
10 F	0501 / 1114 / 1733 / 2354	1·9 / 4·7 / 1·5 / 4·8	25 Sa	0000 / 0603 / 1227 / 1827	5·0 / 1·7 / 5·1 / 1·4
11 Sa	0549 / 1206 / 1819	1·6 / 5·0 / 1·2	26 Su	0048 / 0645 / 1314 / 1909	5·1 / 1·5 / 5·2 / 1·3
12 Su	0040 / 0633 / 1252 / 1901	5·0 / 1·3 / 5·2 / 0·9	27 M	0130 / 0725 / 1357 / 1946	5·1 / 1·3 / 5·2 / 1·3
13 M	0122 / 0717 / 1338 / 1946	5·2 / 0·9 / 5·5 / 0·7	28 Tu ○	0208 / 0800 / 1437 / 2019	5·1 / 1·2 / 5·2 / 1·3
14 Tu ●	0204 / 0806 / 1424 / 2032	5·4 / 0·7 / 5·6 / 0·7	29 W	0244 / 0834 / 1515 / 2050	5·1 / 1·1 / 5·1 / 1·3
15 W	0247 / 0856 / 1511 / 2117	5·5 / 0·6 / 5·7 / 0·7	30 Th	0318 / 0907 / 1552 / 2119	5·1 / 1·2 / 5·1 / 1·4
			31 F	0352 / 0940 / 1630 / 2148	5·1 / 1·2 / 5·0 / 1·5

JUNE

Day	Time	m	Day	Time	m
1 Sa	0428 / 1012 / 1706 / 2221	5·0 / 1·3 / 4·9 / 1·7	16 Su	0504 / 1124 / 1735 / 2329	5·5 / 0·6 / 5·5 / 1·3
2 Su	0506 / 1048 / 1745 / 2259	4·9 / 1·4 / 4·7 / 1·8	17 M	0556 / 1210 / 1828	5·4 / 0·8 / 5·3
3 M	0549 / 1129 / 1828 / 2344	4·8 / 1·5 / 4·6 / 1·8	18 Tu	0014 / 0652 / 1256 / 1924	1·5 / 5·2 / 1·1 / 5·1
4 Tu	0633 / 1218 / 1915	4·7 / 1·6 / 4·5	19 W ☽	0104 / 0749 / 1351 / 2022	1·7 / 5·0 / 1·4 / 4·9
5 W ☾	0037 / 0723 / 1315 / 2008	2·0 / 4·6 / 1·7 / 4·4	20 Th	0206 / 0849 / 1454 / 2123	1·9 / 4·9 / 1·6 / 4·8
6 Th	0141 / 0819 / 1425 / 2105	2·1 / 4·6 / 1·8 / 4·4	21 F	0319 / 0953 / 1601 / 2226	2·1 / 4·8 / 1·7 / 4·8
7 F	0253 / 0918 / 1536 / 2206	2·1 / 4·6 / 1·8 / 4·6	22 Sa	0431 / 1057 / 1703 / 2325	2·0 / 4·8 / 1·8 / 4·8
8 Sa	0404 / 1019 / 1642 / 2305	2·0 / 4·7 / 1·6 / 4·7	23 Su	0532 / 1158 / 1759	1·9 / 4·8 / 1·8
9 Su	0506 / 1121 / 1740	1·7 / 4·9 / 1·4	24 M	0020 / 0623 / 1252 / 1846	4·8 / 1·7 / 4·9 / 1·7
10 M	0000 / 0603 / 1220 / 1834	4·9 / 1·4 / 5·1 / 1·2	25 Tu	0107 / 0708 / 1341 / 1928	4·9 / 1·5 / 4·9 / 1·6
11 Tu	0052 / 0657 / 1315 / 1926	5·1 / 1·0 / 5·3 / 0·9	26 W	0149 / 0747 / 1424 / 2004	5·0 / 1·4 / 5·0 / 1·5
12 W ●	0141 / 0753 / 1409 / 2018	5·3 / 0·7 / 5·5 / 0·8	27 Th ○	0227 / 0824 / 1504 / 2037	5·0 / 1·2 / 5·0 / 1·4
13 Th	0231 / 0849 / 1501 / 2109	5·5 / 0·5 / 5·6 / 0·8	28 F	0304 / 0858 / 1539 / 2108	5·1 / 1·2 / 5·1 / 1·4
14 F	0321 / 0944 / 1553 / 2158	5·6 / 0·4 / 5·7 / 0·9	29 Sa	0337 / 0931 / 1613 / 2138	5·1 / 1·1 / 5·1 / 1·4
15 Sa	0410 / 1036 / 1644 / 2245	5·6 / 0·5 / 5·6 / 1·1	30 Su	0410 / 1004 / 1645 / 2210	5·1 / 1·1 / 5·0 / 1·5

JULY

Day	Time	m	Day	Time	m
1 M	0445 / 1036 / 1722 / 2243	5·1 / 1·2 / 4·9 / 1·5	16 Tu	0535 / 1145 / 1804 / 2349	5·6 / 0·6 / 5·4 / 1·2
2 Tu	0523 / 1110 / 1800 / 2321	5·0 / 1·2 / 4·8 / 1·6	17 W	0626 / 1221 / 1854	5·4 / 0·9 / 5·1
3 W ☽	0605 / 1148 / 1842 / 1946	4·9 / 1·3 / 4·7 / 4·9	18 Th ☽	0027 / 0718 / 1301 / 1946	1·4 / 5·1 / 1·3 / 4·9
4 Th	0005 / 0648 / 1235 / 1927	1·7 / 4·9 / 1·4 / 4·6	19 F	0115 / 0812 / 1355 / 2041	1·7 / 4·9 / 1·7 / 4·7
5 F ☾	0056 / 0737 / 1331 / 2019	1·8 / 4·8 / 1·6 / 4·6	20 Sa	0219 / 0911 / 1506 / 2143	2·0 / 4·7 / 2·0 / 4·5
6 Sa	0158 / 0832 / 1439 / 2118	1·9 / 4·7 / 1·8 / 4·6	21 Su	0345 / 1020 / 1626 / 2251	2·1 / 4·5 / 2·1 / 4·5
7 Su	0313 / 0936 / 1556 / 2223	1·9 / 4·7 / 1·8 / 4·6	22 M	0505 / 1132 / 1734 / 2355	2·1 / 4·5 / 2·1 / 4·6
8 M	0432 / 1048 / 1713 / 2330	1·8 / 4·8 / 1·6 / 4·8	23 Tu	0607 / 1234 / 1831	1·9 / 4·6 / 1·9
9 Tu	0545 / 1200 / 1818	1·4 / 4·9 / 1·4	24 W	0049 / 0655 / 1326 / 1916	4·7 / 1·6 / 4·7 / 1·8
10 W	0033 / 0648 / 1304 / 1916	5·0 / 1·0 / 5·2 / 1·1	25 Th	0134 / 0736 / 1410 / 1953	4·9 / 1·4 / 4·9 / 1·6
11 Th ●	0129 / 0748 / 1402 / 2011	5·3 / 0·7 / 5·4 / 0·9	26 F ○	0214 / 0811 / 1449 / 2025	5·0 / 1·2 / 5·0 / 1·4
12 F	0221 / 0844 / 1455 / 2102	5·5 / 0·4 / 5·6 / 0·8	27 Sa	0247 / 0844 / 1521 / 2054	5·1 / 1·1 / 5·1 / 1·3
13 Sa	0310 / 0937 / 1542 / 2149	5·7 / 0·3 / 5·8 / 0·8	28 Su	0318 / 0917 / 1552 / 2125	5·3 / 1·0 / 5·2 / 1·2
14 Su	0357 / 1025 / 1629 / 2234	5·8 / 0·2 / 5·7 / 0·8	29 M	0348 / 0947 / 1622 / 2154	5·3 / 0·9 / 5·2 / 1·2
15 M	0445 / 1108 / 1716 / 2312	5·7 / 0·4 / 5·6 / 1·0	30 Tu	0421 / 1017 / 1654 / 2224	5·3 / 0·9 / 5·1 / 1·2
			31 W	0457 / 1048 / 1731 / 2258	5·3 / 0·9 / 5·0 / 1·3

AUGUST

Day	Time	m	Day	Time	m
1 Th	0536 / 1122 / 1811 / 2336	5·2 / 1·0 / 4·9 / 1·4	16 F	0645 / 1212 / 1909	5·1 / 1·3 / 4·8
2 F	0618 / 1201 / 1853	5·1 / 1·3 / 4·8	17 Sa ☽	0027 / 0735 / 1254 / 1958	1·6 / 4·8 / 1·8 / 4·5
3 Sa	0022 / 0705 / 1251 / 1942	1·6 / 4·9 / 1·5 / 4·6	18 Su	0122 / 0830 / 1402 / 2056	2·0 / 4·5 / 2·2 / 4·4
4 Su	0118 / 0800 / 1357 / 2042	1·8 / 4·7 / 1·8 / 4·5	19 M	0253 / 0942 / 1540 / 2210	2·2 / 4·3 / 2·4 / 4·3
5 M	0237 / 0910 / 1525 / 2155	1·9 / 4·6 / 2·0 / 4·5	20 Tu	0438 / 1104 / 1709 / 2327	2·2 / 4·3 / 2·3 / 4·5
6 Tu	0415 / 1033 / 1659 / 2315	1·8 / 4·6 / 1·9 / 4·7	21 W	0547 / 1213 / 1812	2·0 / 4·5 / 2·1
7 W	0541 / 1154 / 1813	1·5 / 4·8 / 1·6	22 Th	0027 / 0637 / 1306 / 1857	4·6 / 1·7 / 4·6 / 1·8
8 Th	0024 / 0646 / 1300 / 1912	4·9 / 1·0 / 5·1 / 1·2	23 F	0114 / 0716 / 1348 / 1934	4·8 / 1·4 / 4·8 / 1·6
9 F	0121 / 0741 / 1355 / 2003	5·3 / 0·6 / 5·4 / 0·9	24 Sa	0151 / 0749 / 1426 / 2004	5·0 / 1·1 / 5·1 / 1·3
10 Sa ●	0211 / 0833 / 1444 / 2050	5·6 / 0·3 / 5·7 / 0·7	25 Su ○	0223 / 0821 / 1456 / 2033	5·2 / 0·9 / 5·2 / 1·2
11 Su	0256 / 0920 / 1527 / 2134	5·8 / 0·1 / 5·8 / 0·6	26 M	0253 / 0852 / 1525 / 2103	5·4 / 0·8 / 5·3 / 1·0
12 M	0340 / 1002 / 1609 / 2211	5·9 / 0·1 / 5·8 / 0·6	27 Tu	0322 / 0923 / 1555 / 2132	5·5 / 0·7 / 5·4 / 1·0
13 Tu	0423 / 1039 / 1651 / 2246	5·8 / 0·2 / 5·6 / 0·7	28 W	0354 / 0954 / 1627 / 2205	5·5 / 0·7 / 5·3 / 1·0
14 W	0509 / 1111 / 1737 / 2316	5·7 / 0·5 / 5·4 / 0·9	29 Th	0430 / 1025 / 1702 / 2238	5·5 / 0·8 / 5·2 / 1·0
15 Th	0557 / 1138 / 1823 / 2348	5·4 / 0·9 / 5·1 / 1·2	30 F	0511 / 1058 / 1742 / 2316	5·4 / 1·0 / 5·0 / 1·2
			31 Sa	0554 / 1135 / 1826 / 2359	5·2 / 1·3 / 4·9 / 1·4

Chart Datum: 2.90 metres below Ordnance Datum (Newlyn)

SCOTLAND, EAST COAST – LEITH

Lat 55°59′ N   Long 3°10′ W

TIMES AND HEIGHTS OF HIGH AND LOW WATERS   YEAR **1991**

TIME ZONE UT(GMT)

For Summer Time add ONE
hour in non-shaded areas

SEPTEMBER

	Time	m		Time	m
1 Su ☾	0643 1223 1917	5·0 1·6 4·7	**16** M	0034 0753 1304 2010	2·0 4·4 2·3 4·3
2 M	0056 0743 1331 2021	1·7 4·7 2·0 4·5	**17** Tu	0158 0904 1439 2123	2·3 4·2 2·5 4·2
3 Tu	0222 0900 1511 2142	1·9 4·6 2·2 4·5	**18** W	0400 1027 1630 2245	2·3 4·2 2·5 4·3
4 W	0414 1029 1656 2307	1·8 4·6 2·1 4·7	**19** Th	0516 1138 1740 2352	2·0 4·4 2·2 4·5
5 Th	0539 1149 1808	1·5 4·9 1·7	**20** F	0605 1231 1827	1·7 4·6 1·9
6 F	0015 0636 1252 1902	5·0 1·0 5·2 1·3	**21** Sa	0040 0644 1314 1903	4·7 1·4 4·9 1·6
7 Sa	0111 0725 1342 1947	5·3 0·6 5·5 1·0	**22** Su	0118 0717 1352 1934	5·0 1·1 5·1 1·3
8 Su ●	0157 0810 1426 2029	5·6 0·7 5·7 0·7	**23** M ○	0152 0749 1423 2003	5·2 0·9 5·3 1·1
9 M	0238 0853 1506 2109	5·8 0·2 5·8 0·6	**24** Tu	0223 0821 1454 2036	5·5 0·7 5·4 0·9
10 Tu	0318 0931 1545 2143	5·9 0·2 5·7 0·6	**25** W	0253 0855 1525 2110	5·6 0·6 5·5 0·8
11 W	0359 1003 1625 2215	5·8 0·3 5·6 0·7	**26** Th	0328 0929 1559 2145	5·7 0·7 5·5 0·8
12 Th	0442 1030 1706 2242	5·6 0·6 5·3 0·9	**27** F	0407 1003 1638 2223	5·6 0·8 5·3 0·9
13 F	0527 1057 1748 2311	5·3 1·0 5·0 1·2	**28** Sa	0449 1040 1720 2305	5·5 1·0 5·2 1·1
14 Sa	0612 1125 1831 2345	5·0 1·4 4·8 1·6	**29** Su	0537 1120 1807 2351	5·2 1·4 5·0 1·4
15 Su ☽	0659 1204 1916	4·7 1·9 4·5	**30** M	0632 1211 1904	5·0 1·8 4·8

OCTOBER

	Time	m		Time	m
1 Tu ☾	0053 0738 1321 2013	1·7 4·7 2·2 4·6	**16** W	0110 0820 1342 2035	2·2 4·2 2·5 4·3
2 W	0225 0858 1506 2134	1·9 4·6 2·3 4·6	**17** Th	0255 0933 1525 2147	2·3 4·2 2·6 4·3
3 Th	0410 1022 1646 2255	1·8 4·7 2·2 4·8	**18** F	0422 1045 1647 2256	2·1 4·3 2·4 4·5
4 F	0523 1134 1752	1·5 5·0 1·8	**19** Sa	0519 1142 1741 2350	1·9 4·6 2·1 4·7
5 Sa	0000 0616 1233 1842	5·1 1·1 5·3 1·4	**20** Su	0601 1230 1823	1·6 4·8 1·8
6 Su	0053 0700 1321 1924	5·4 0·8 5·5 1·1	**21** M	0035 0639 1310 1858	5·0 1·3 5·1 1·4
7 M ●	0136 0741 1403 2003	5·6 0·5 5·6 0·8	**22** Tu	0113 0713 1347 1933	5·2 1·0 5·3 1·1
8 Tu	0217 0820 1442 2040	5·8 0·5 5·7 0·7	**23** W ○	0149 0750 1420 2010	5·5 0·8 5·5 0·9
9 W	0255 0857 1518 2114	5·8 0·5 5·8 0·7	**24** Th	0225 0828 1457 2051	5·6 0·7 5·6 0·8
10 Th	0335 0928 1556 2144	5·7 0·7 5·5 0·8	**25** F	0305 0907 1535 2133	5·7 0·8 5·6 0·8
11 F	0415 0955 1636 2213	5·5 0·9 5·3 1·0	**26** Sa	0349 0949 1618 2219	5·7 0·9 5·5 0·9
12 Sa	0458 1022 1713 2242	5·2 1·2 5·1 1·3	**27** Su	0437 1022 1704 2305	5·5 1·2 5·3 1·1
13 Su	0540 1050 1754 2315	4·9 1·6 4·8 1·6	**28** M	0529 1115 1757 2355	5·3 1·5 5·1 1·4
14 M	0626 1129 1838	4·6 2·0 4·6	**29** Tu	0627 1209 1856	5·1 1·9 4·9
15 Tu ☽	0001 0718 1222 1930	2·0 4·4 2·3 4·4	**30** W ☾	0058 0732 1317 2003	1·6 4·9 2·2 4·8
			31 Th	0219 0844 1448 2117	1·8 4·8 2·3 4·8

NOVEMBER

	Time	m		Time	m
1 F	0347 0959 1618 2231	1·7 4·9 2·2 4·9	**16** Sa	0305 0941 1536 2151	2·2 4·4 2·4 4·5
2 Sa	0454 1108 1725 2334	1·5 5·0 1·9 5·2	**17** Su	0414 1042 1644 2252	2·0 4·5 2·2 4·7
3 Su	0546 1206 1815	1·3 5·3 1·6	**18** M	0510 1138 1737 2346	1·8 4·8 1·9 4·9
4 M	0028 0632 1255 1858	5·4 1·1 5·4 1·4	**19** Tu	0557 1225 1822	1·5 5·0 1·7
5 Tu	0113 0712 1338 1937	5·5 1·0 5·5 1·1	**20** W	0032 0640 1308 1905	5·2 1·2 5·2 1·3
6 W ●	0155 0752 1417 2015	5·6 0·9 5·5 1·0	**21** Th ○	0117 0724 1350 1950	5·4 1·0 5·4 1·0
7 Th	0235 0827 1455 2050	5·6 0·9 5·5 1·0	**22** F	0203 0808 1432 2039	5·6 0·9 5·6 0·8
8 F	0314 0900 1532 2121	5·5 1·0 5·4 1·0	**23** Sa	0249 0855 1516 2129	5·7 0·9 5·6 0·8
9 Sa	0354 0929 1608 2152	5·3 1·2 5·3 1·2	**24** Su	0337 0941 1603 2220	5·7 1·0 5·6 0·8
10 Su	0435 0958 1644 2222	5·1 1·5 5·1 1·4	**25** M	0427 1028 1653 2310	5·6 1·2 5·5 0·9
11 M	0515 1028 1724 2255	4·9 1·7 4·9 1·6	**26** Tu	0519 1115 1748 2359	5·5 1·5 5·4 1·1
12 Tu	0557 1105 1806 2337	4·7 2·0 4·7 1·9	**27** W	0615 1205 1845	5·3 1·7 5·2
13 W	0643 1152 1853	4·5 2·2 4·6	**28** Th ☾	0052 0715 1304 1946	1·4 5·1 2·0 5·1
14 Th ☽	0030 0736 1255 1948	2·1 4·3 2·4 4·5	**29** F	0155 0818 1416 2050	1·6 5·0 2·2 5·0
15 F	0143 0837 1414 2049	2·2 4·3 2·5 4·4	**30** Sa	0308 0926 1536 2158	1·7 4·9 2·2 5·0

DECEMBER

	Time	m		Time	m
1 Su	0416 1033 1648 2303	1·7 5·0 2·1 5·1	**16** M	0303 0941 1541 2153	2·0 4·5 2·2 4·7
2 M	0512 1134 1746	1·6 5·1 1·9	**17** Tu	0414 1042 1650 2257	1·9 4·6 2·0 4·8
3 Tu	0000 0604 1227 1834	5·2 1·5 5·2 1·6	**18** W	0518 1142 1751 2358	1·7 4·8 1·7 5·0
4 W	0051 0649 1314 1917	5·3 1·4 5·3 1·4	**19** Th	0614 1237 1847	1·5 5·0 1·4
5 Th	0137 0731 1356 1958	5·3 1·4 5·3 1·3	**20** F	0055 0705 1327 1940	5·2 1·2 5·3 1·0
6 F ●	0220 0809 1435 2035	5·3 1·3 5·3 1·2	**21** Sa ○	0148 0756 1416 2034	5·4 1·0 5·5 0·8
7 Sa	0300 0842 1513 2109	5·3 1·4 5·3 1·2	**22** Su	0238 0847 1503 2128	5·6 0·9 5·7 0·6
8 Su	0340 0914 1548 2141	5·2 1·4 5·3 1·3	**23** M	0327 0937 1552 2219	5·8 0·9 5·8 0·6
9 M	0417 0943 1623 2211	5·1 1·6 5·2 1·4	**24** Tu	0416 1024 1640 2306	5·8 1·0 5·8 0·6
10 Tu	0452 1014 1658 2242	5·0 1·7 5·1 1·5	**25** W	0505 1109 1732 2350	5·7 1·2 5·6 0·8
11 W	0530 1047 1738 2316	4·8 1·8 4·9 1·6	**26** Th	0556 1153 1824	5·5 1·4 5·5
12 Th	0610 1128 1819 2357	4·7 2·0 4·8 1·8	**27** F	0032 0650 1239 1921	1·1 5·2 1·7 5·3
13 F	0654 1216 1906	4·6 2·1 4·7	**28** Sa ☾	0120 0746 1334 2018	1·4 5·0 1·9 5·1
14 Sa ☽	0048 0744 1315 1957	1·9 4·5 2·2 4·6	**29** Su	0219 0848 1445 2121	1·7 4·9 2·1 4·9
15 Su	0151 0840 1425 2053	2·0 4·5 2·3 4·6	**30** M	0328 0954 1605 2228	1·9 4·8 2·2 4·9
			31 Tu	0438 1102 1718 2334	2·0 4·8 2·1 4·9

Chart Datum: 2.90 metres below Ordnance Datum (Newlyn)

FIRTH OF FORTH *continued*

TELEPHONE (031)
Hr Mr Leith 554-3661; CG & MRSC Crail 50666;
☰ 554-2421; Forth Yacht Clubs Assn 331 1118. Weather,
Glasgow 248-3451 or for Port Edgar Inverkeithing 412475;
Marinecall 0898 500 452; Police (S. Queensferry) 331 1798;
Dr (Hosps) Dunfermline 73777, Leith 332 2525.
FACILITIES
SOUTH QUEENSFERRY EC Wednesday; **Port Edgar
Marina** (300+8 visitors) ☎ 331-3330, Slip, AC, CH, D, El,
Ⓔ, ME, Sh, SM, Gas, FW, R, C (5 ton); Access H24;
Forth Area Marine Electronics ☎ 331 4343, El, Ⓔ, **Port
Edgar Marine Services** ☎ 331 1233, ME; **Bosun's
Locker** ☎ 331-3875, D, Sh, Gas, Gaz, CH; **Town** P, V,
R, Bar. ✉, Ⓑ, ⇌ (Dalmeny), ✈ (Edinburgh).

NORTH QUEENSFERRY **Forth Yacht Marina** (100+some
visitors) ☎ Inverkeithing 416101, Slip, D (cans), ME, El,
Sh, C (20 ton), CH, SM; **Town** D, V, R, Bar, ✉,
Ⓑ, ⇌ (Inverkeithing), ✈ (Edinburgh).
GRANTON Hr Mr ☎ 552-3385, Slip, AB, FW; **Royal Forth
YC** ☎ 552-3006, Slip, M, L, FW, C (5 ton), D, ME, El,
Sh, Bar; **Forth Corinthian YC** ☎ 552-5939, Slip, M, L,
Bar; Access HW∓3½; **Seaspan** ☎ 552-2224, Gas, Gaz,
Sh, CH; **Scott, Walter and Watson** ☎ 552-6695, ME; **J
C Forbes** ☎ 552-8201, Sh; **Granton Marine Engineering**
☎ 552-0164 ME **Town** D, P, V, R, Bar. ✉, Ⓑ, ⇌,
✈ (Edinburgh).
EDINBURGH **Chattan Shipping Services** ☎ 557-0988,
ACA.

LEITH
MEAN SPRING
AND NEAP CURVES

MEAN RANGES	
Springs	4·8m
Neaps	2·4m

Springs occur 2 days
after
New and Full Moon.

BURNTISLAND   10-6-10
Fife

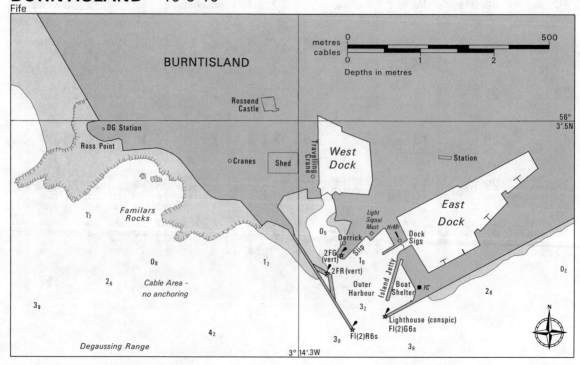

BURNTISLAND *continued*

CHARTS
Admiralty 739; Imray C27; OS 66
TIDES
+0340 Dover; ML 2.9; Duration 0625; Zone 0 (GMT).

Standard Port LEITH (←)

Times				Height (metres)			
HW		LW		MHWS	MHWN	MLWN	MLWS
0300	0900	0300	0900	5.6	4.5	2.1	0.8
1500	2100	1500	2100				

Differences BURNTISLAND
+0002	−0002	−0002	−0004	0.0	0.0	0.0	0.0

SHELTER
Shelter is very good in the docks but only fair in the outer harbour; unsuitable for yachts in strong winds. E dock can be entered from HW−2 to HW.
NAVIGATION
Waypoint 56°03'.00N 03°14'.00W, 163°/343° from/to entrance, 0.23M. To the E of the port, beware Black Rocks (off chartlet) and to the W, Familars Rocks. Keep clear of ships using DG ranges SW of port. Commercial barge operations can cause delays.
LIGHTS AND MARKS
By night and day
FR − Docks closed, bring up in roads
FG − Clear to enter Outer harbour
FR }
FG } − Dangerous to enter
FR }
FW } − Clear to enter E dock
FR }
2FW } Clear to enter W dock
The above signals are shown from HW −3 until both dock gates are closed at HW.
RADIO TELEPHONE
Forth Navigation VHF Ch 16; 71 12 20 (H24).
TELEPHONE (0592)
Hr Mr (Port Superintendent) Leven 26725; CG & MRSC Crail 50666; # 260730; Marinecall 0898 500 452; Police 872708; Dr 872761.
FACILITIES
EC Wednesday; **Dock** ☎ 872236, L, FW, C (10 ton), AB (Limited); **Outer Harbour** ☎ 872236, Slip, L, FW, AB (Limited); **Lammerlaws** ☎ 874270 ME, El, Sh, CH; **Briggs Marine** ☎ 872939 D, ME, El, Sh, C (30 ton); **Burntisland YC** ☎ 873375, M, L, FW, C (5 cwt); **Starlyburn BY** ☎ 872458, Slip, L, FW, ME, El, Sh, C, (25 ton); **Pop's Stores** ☎ 873524, Gas; **Town** P, D, ME, El, C, V, R, Bar. ✉; Ⓑ; ➔; ✈ Edinburgh.

METHIL 10-6-11
Fife

CHARTS
Admiralty 739; Imray C27; OS 59
TIDES
+0330 Dover; ML 3.2; Duration 0615; Zone 0 (GMT)

Standard Port LEITH (←)

Times				Height (metres)			
HW		LW		MHWS	MHWN	MLWN	MLWS
0300	0900	0300	0900	5.6	4.5	2.1	0.8
1500	2100	1500	2100				

Differences METHIL
−0006	−0012	−0007	−0001	−0.1	−0.1	−0.1	−0.1

SHELTER
Principally a commercial port but good shelter in emergency.
NAVIGATION
Waypoint 56°10'.50N 03°00'.00W, 140°/320° from/to pier head Lt, 0.34M. Beware silting. A sand bar forms rapidly to seaward of the lighthouse and the dredged depth cannot always be maintained.

LIGHTS AND MARKS
By day and night
FR over FG Dangerous to enter. Bring up in roads.
FR over FW Clear to enter No 2 dock
FR Remain in roads until another signal is made.
RADIO TELEPHONE
VHF Ch 16; 14 (HW−3 to HW).

TELEPHONE (0592)
Hr Mr (Port Superintendent) Leven 26725; CG & MRSC Crail 50666; # Kirkcaldy 260730; Marinecall 0898 500 452; Police 712881; Dr Leven 26913.
FACILITIES
EC Thursday; **Harbour** 2 Docks; C (7 ton); **Jas Donaldson** ☎ 26118, Gas; **Town** P, D, V, R, Bar, ✉; Ⓑ; ➔ (bus to Markinch or Kirkcaldy); ✈ (Edinburgh).

ANSTRUTHER 10-6-12
Fife

CHARTS
Admiralty 734, 175; Imray C27; OS 59
TIDES
+0315 Dover; ML 3.2; Duration 0620; Zone 0 (GMT).

Standard Port LEITH (←)

Times				Height (metres)			
HW		LW		MHWS	MHWN	MLWN	MLWS
0300	0900	0300	0900	5.6	4.5	2.1	0.8
1500	2100	1500	2100				

Differences ANSTRUTHER
−0010	−0035	−0020	−0020	−0.1	−0.1	−0.1	−0.1

SHELTER
Good shelter but entry should not be attempted when strong winds are blowing from the E and S.

ANSTRUTHER *continued*

NAVIGATION
Waypoint 56°12'.60N 02°42'.10W, 198°/018° from/to entrance, 0.60M. Harbour dries. Beware lobster pots and fishing vessels.

LIGHTS AND MARKS
Conspic Lt Tr on W Pier. Ldg Lts 018°, both FG. Fog horn (Reed) (3) 60s

RADIO TELEPHONE
Forth Navigation Service. See 10.6.9.

TELEPHONE (0333)
Hr Mr 310836; CG & MRSC Crail 50666;
⌗ Dundee 29171; Marinecall 0898 500 452; Police 310333; Dr 310352.

FACILITIES
EC Wednesday; **Fisherman's Mutual Association** ☎ Pittenweem 311263, CH, D; **Harbour** Slip, M, FW, CH, AC, AB; **Christie & Co** Tel. 311339, ME; **Gray + Pringle** ☎ 310508, Gas, Gaz; **R. R. Bett** ☎ 310369, El; **Town** ✉; Ⓑ; ⇌ (bus Cupar or Leuchars); ✈ Edinburgh, or Dundee (Riverside).

RIVER TAY   10-6-13
Fife/Angus

CHARTS
Admiralty 1481, 190; OS 54, 59

TIDES
+0350 Dover; ML 3.0; Duration 0610; Zone 0 (GMT).

Standard Port ABERDEEN (→)

Times				Height (metres)			
HW		LW		MHWS	MHWN	MLWN	MLWS
0000	0600	0100	0700	4.3	3.4	1.6	0.6
1200	1800	1300	1900				

Differences BAR

+0100	+0100	+0050	+0110	+0.9	+0.8	+0.3	+0.1

DUNDEE

+0140	+0120	+0055	+0145	+1.1	+0.9	+0.3	+0.1

NEWBURGH

+0215	+0200	+0250	+0335	−0.2	−0.4	−1.1	−0.5

SHELTER
Good shelter in the Tay estuary but the entrance is dangerous in strong winds from SE to E or in an on-shore swell. Tayport is best place for yachts on passage, access HW∓2½. Dundee docks (commercial) gates open HW−2 to HW. Anchorages as shown on chartlet; the one off the city is exposed and landing difficult. There are anchorages up river at Balmerino, Newburgh, Inchyra and Perth. Note:- Area is administered by the Dundee Port Authority.

NAVIGATION
Waypoint Tay Fairway safe water buoy, LFl 10s, Whis, 56°28'.62N 02°37'.15W, 060°/240° from/to Middle Bar buoys, 1.0M. The river is navigable right up to Perth. Entrance to river across Abertay sands is forbidden due to stakes. Channel is well buoyed but caution should be exercised as depths are liable to change. Tayport harbour dries except W side of NE pier; S side is full of yacht moorings.

LIGHTS AND MARKS
There are no leading lights but channel is well marked. The high focal plane buoy "*Abertay*" (Racon) at E end of Gaa Sands is a clear visual mark.

RADIO TELEPHONE
Dundee Harbour Radio VHF Ch 16; 10 11 **12** 13 14 (H24). Perth Harbour Ch 09.

RIVER TAY *continued*

TELEPHONE (0382)
Hr Mr (Dundee) 24121; Perth Hr Mr Perth 24056; MRSC Crail 50666; ⌗ 22412; Tayport Boatowners' Assn 553679; Marinecall 0898 500 452; Police (Tayport) 552222 (Dundee) 23200; Dr 21953; Ⓗ 23125.

FACILITIES
NORTH BANK: EC Dundee Wednesday; **Camperdown Dock** FW, ME, El, C (8 ton), AB; **Victoria Dock** FW, ME, C (8 ton), AB; **Royal Tay YC** (Broughty Ferry) ☎ 77516, M, L, R, Bar; **Allison-Gray** ☎ 27444, CH, ACA, SM; **Scotcraig Boat Co** ☎ 553230, M, L, ME, El, Sh, C (2 ton), CH; **Broughty Ferry** Slip, M; **Sea and Shore** ☎ 451816; **Dundee Town** P, D, CH, V, R, Bar, ✉, Ⓑ, ⇌, ✈.
SOUTH BANK: **Tayport Harbour** ☎ 553679 Slip, L, FW, AB, AC; **Wormit Boating Club** ☎ 541400 Slip, L, FW, V.

ARBROATH   10-6-14
Angus

CHARTS
Admiralty 1438, 190; OS 54
TIDES
+0335 Dover; ML 2.9; Duration 0620; Zone 0 (GMT).

Standard Port ABERDEEN (→)

Times				Height (metres)			
HW		LW		MHWS	MHWN	MLWN	MLWS
0000	0600	0100	0700	4.3	3.4	1.6	0.6
1200	1800	1300	1900				

Differences ARBROATH
+0056 +0037 +0034 +0055 +0.7 +0.7 +0.2 +0.1

▲ Report to Senior Harbour Assistant

SHELTER
Good, especially in Dock, but entrance can be dangerous in moderate SE swell. Dock gates normally remain open, but will be closed on request. Entry should not be attempted LW ∓ 2½.

NAVIGATION
Waypoint 56°33'.00N 02°34'.10W, 119°/299° from/to entrance, 0.50M. Beware Knuckle rocks to stbd and Cheek Bush rocks to port on entering. Arbroath is a very busy fishing harbour so beware heavy traffic.

LIGHTS AND MARKS
Leading lights (FR) in line at 299°. By day St Thomas' church towers in line with the gap between Lt Ho on N pier and Bn on West breakwater.
Entry signals:- Fl G — Entry safe
　　　　　　　FR — Entry dangerous

RADIO TELEPHONE
Contact AFA on VHF Ch 16.
TELEPHONE (0241)
Hr Mr 72166; CG 72113; MRSC Crail 50666; ⌗ Dundee 22412; Marinecall 0898 500 452; Police 72222; Dr 76836.

FACILITIES
EC Wednesday; **Pier** Slip, D, L, FW, AB; **Mackays BY** ☎ 72879, Slip, L, ME, El, Sh, C (8 ton) Ⓔ; **Arbroath Fisherman's Association** ☎ 72928, M, D, Gas, CH; **Gerrards** ☎ 73177, Slip, Sh; **W. M. Teviotdale** ☎ 73104, ME; **Elbar Shop** ☎ 73141, Gas; **A. Copland** ☎ 73212 ME; **J. Connely** ☎ 70121 ME; **Town** P, D, V, R, Bar. ✉; Ⓑ; ⇌; ✈ (Dundee).

AGENTS WANTED
Berwick-on-Tweed
Mallaig
Loch Sunart
Loch Aline
Fishguard
Kenmare River

Large number of French Ports

Rotterdam
Norderney
Dornumersiel
Langeoog
Wangerooge
Hooksiel
Bremerhaven

If you are interested in becoming our agent please write to the Editors and get your free copy annually. You do not have to be a resident in a port to be the agent but at least a fairly regular visitor.

MONTROSE   10-6-15
Angus

CHARTS
Admiralty 1438, 190; OS 54
TIDES
+0320 Dover; ML 2.8; Duration 0645; Zone 0 (GMT).

Standard Port ABERDEEN (→)

Times				Height (metres)			
HW		LW		MHWS	MHWN	MLWN	MLWS
0000	0600	0100	0700	4.3	3.4	1.6	0.6
1200	1800	1300	1900				

Differences MONTROSE
+0100 +0100 +0030 +0040 +0.5 +0.5 +0.3 +0.1

SHELTER
Good with quayside berths usually available but beware wash from other traffic. Channel depth min 5m; best entry LW to LW+1; tidal streams are strong (up to 6 kn). It is a busy commercial port. Call up Hr Mr or report to Port Control Office.

NAVIGATION
Waypoint 56°42'.20N 02°25'.00W, 091°/271° from/to front Ldg Lt, 1.25M. Beware Annat Bank to N and Scurdie Rks to S on entering. Entrance to harbour is dangerous with strong on-shore winds during ebb tide as heavy overfalls develop.

LIGHTS AND MARKS
Two sets of Ldg Lts. Outer 271°, both FR 5M. Inner 265°, both FG, 5M.
RADIO TELEPHONE
VHF Ch 16; 12 (H24).
TELEPHONE (0674)
Hr Mr 72302, 73153; CG 72101; MRCC Aberdeen 592334; ⌗ 74444; Marinecall 0898 500 452; Police 72222; Dr 73400.

FACILITIES
EC Wednesday; **Riverside Quay** ☎ 72302, D, L, FW, ME, El, C (1½ to 40 ton), CH, AB; **South Esk Boats** ☎ 76580, Slip, Sh; **Elbar Shop** ☎ 73981, Gas; **Town** V, R, P, Bar. ✉; Ⓑ; ⇌; ✈ (Aberdeen).

MONTROSE continued

⚠ Report to Port Control Office

STONEHAVEN   10-6-16
Kincardine

CHARTS
Admiralty 1438, 210; OS 45
TIDES
+0235 Dover; ML 2.7; Duration 0620; Zone 0 (GMT).

Standard Port ABERDEEN (→)

Times				Height (metres)			
HW		LW		MHWS	MHWN	MLWN	MLWS
0000	0600	0100	0700	4.3	3.4	1.6	0.6
1200	1800	1300	1900				

Differences STONEHAVEN
+0013 +0008 +0013 +0009 +0.2   +0.2   +0.1   0.0

SHELTER
Good shelter especially from S through W to N winds.
Inner harbour dries; storm gates closed in severe weather.
Speed limit in harbour 3 kn.

NAVIGATION
Waypoint 56°57'.60N 02°10'.50W, 090°/270° from/to
breakwater Lt, 0.77M. Give Downie Pt a wide berth. Do
not enter in strong on-shore winds.
LIGHTS AND MARKS
When harbour is closed, a G Lt is displayed.
RADIO TELEPHONE
None.
TELEPHONE (0569)
Hr Mr 62741; CG & MRCC Aberdeen 592334;
⌗ Aberdeen 586258; Marinecall 0898 500 452;
Police 62963; Dr 62945.
FACILITIES
EC Wednesday; **Aberdeen and Stonehaven YC** Slip,
Bar; **Harbour** ☎ 65323, M, L, FW, AC, Slip, C (1.5 ton);
AB; **Town** LB, V, R, Bar. ✉; Ⓑ; ⇌; ✈ (Aberdeen).

ABERDEEN   10-6-17
Aberdeen

CHARTS
Admiralty 210, 1446; OS 38
TIDES
+0220 Dover; ML 2.5; Duration 0620; Zone 0 (GMT).

Note: Aberdeen is a Standard Port and tidal predictions
for each day of the year are given below.

SHELTER
Good shelter in harbour. Entry should not be attempted
when winds are strong from NE through E to ESE. Yachts
are not encouraged and it is very expensive. A busy
commercial port and although all facilities are available,
they are geared to commercial traffic. There are no special
berths for yachts, so using commercial berths entails all
the usual obligations and risks. Yachtsmen intending to
call should contact the Hr Mr beforehand. Harbour open
at all states of tide. Anchorage in Aberdeen Bay.
NAVIGATION
Waypoint Fairway safe water buoy, LFl 10s, Racon,
57°09'.34N 02°01'.83W, 058°/238° from/to N pier Lt,
1.1M. Give Girdle Ness a berth of at least ¼M (more in
bad weather) and do not pass close round pier heads.
Strong tidal streams and, with river in spate, possible
overfalls. Channel dredged to 6m on leading line.

ABERDEEN *continued*

LIGHTS AND MARKS
Leading Lts 236° (FR when port open — FG when port closed).
Traffic signals at root of N Pier:

FG   Entry prohibited
FR   Departure prohibited
FR & FG Port closed

RADIO TELEPHONE
VHF Ch 16; 10 11 12 13 (H24).

TELEPHONE (0224)
Hr Mr 592571; CG and MRCC 592334; ⌗ 586258;
Weather: Dyce 722334; Marinecall 0898 500 452;
Police 639111; Dr 55142.

FACILITIES
EC Wednesday/Saturday; **Enterprise Ship Stores**
☎ 590329, CH; **Woodsons of Aberdeen** ☎ 722884, El,
Ⓔ; **Kelvin Hughes** ☎ 580823, CH, ACA; **North Sea
Stores** ☎ 591896, CH; **Furuno (UK)** ☎ 595351, Ⓔ;
Seametrix ☎ 873060, Ⓔ; **Town** P, D, V, R, Bar. ⊡; Ⓑ;
⇌; ✈.

⚠ After berthing, report to harbour control at HrMr

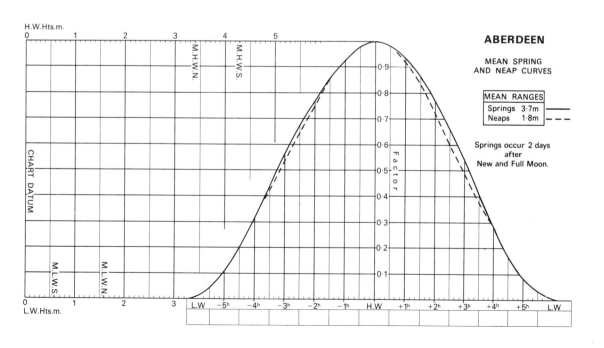

ABERDEEN

MEAN SPRING
AND NEAP CURVES

MEAN RANGES	
Springs	3·7m ———
Neaps	1·8m - - -

Springs occur 2 days
after
New and Full Moon.

SCOTLAND, EAST COAST – ABERDEEN

Lat 57°09′ N   Long 2°04′ W

TIMES AND HEIGHTS OF HIGH AND LOW WATERS

YEAR 1991

TIME ZONE UT (GMT)
For Summer Time add ONE hour in non-shaded areas

JANUARY

Day	Time	m	Day	Time	m
1 Tu	0110 / 0713 / 1324 / 1942	4.4 / 0.9 / 4.5 / 0.5	16 W	0137 / 0726 / 1333 / 1954	3.9 / 1.2 / 4.2 / 0.9
2 W	0202 / 0759 / 1411 / 2032	4.4 / 0.9 / 4.6 / 0.4	17 Th	0211 / 0758 / 1405 / 2026	4.0 / 1.2 / 4.2 / 0.8
3 Th	0253 / 0844 / 1456 / 2118	4.4 / 1.0 / 4.6 / 0.4	18 F	0244 / 0830 / 1437 / 2058	4.0 / 1.2 / 4.3 / 0.8
4 F	0342 / 0928 / 1542 / 2206	4.3 / 1.1 / 4.5 / 0.5	19 Sa	0319 / 0904 / 1511 / 2134	4.0 / 1.1 / 4.3 / 0.8
5 Sa	0428 / 1010 / 1628 / 2252	4.1 / 1.2 / 4.3 / 0.7	20 Su	0353 / 0938 / 1546 / 2210	4.0 / 1.2 / 4.3 / 0.8
6 Su	0515 / 1054 / 1716 / 2342	3.8 / 1.4 / 4.1 / 1.0	21 M	0431 / 1016 / 1626 / 2249	3.9 / 1.2 / 4.2 / 1.0
7 M ☾	0604 / 1142 / 1810	3.6 / 1.5 / 3.8	22 Tu	0512 / 1058 / 1711 / 2334	3.7 / 1.3 / 4.0 / 1.1
8 Tu	0034 / 0657 / 1239 / 1909	1.3 / 3.4 / 1.7 / 3.6	23 W ☽	0601 / 1147 / 1805	3.6 / 1.5 / 3.9
9 W	0135 / 0759 / 1351 / 2018	1.5 / 3.3 / 1.8 / 3.4	24 Th	0029 / 0702 / 1250 / 1913	1.3 / 3.5 / 1.6 / 3.7
10 Th	0243 / 0908 / 1514 / 2132	1.6 / 3.3 / 1.8 / 3.3	25 F	0138 / 0813 / 1409 / 2033	1.4 / 3.5 / 1.7 / 3.6
11 F	0350 / 1013 / 1628 / 2240	1.6 / 3.4 / 1.7 / 3.4	26 Sa	0258 / 0928 / 1536 / 2157	1.5 / 3.5 / 1.5 / 3.7
12 Sa	0449 / 1106 / 1725 / 2334	1.6 / 3.6 / 1.5 / 3.5	27 Su	0417 / 1037 / 1652 / 2311	1.4 / 3.7 / 1.2 / 3.9
13 Su	0536 / 1151 / 1810	1.5 / 3.8 / 1.3	28 M	0522 / 1134 / 1753	1.2 / 4.0 / 0.9
14 M	0021 / 0617 / 1228 / 1846	3.7 / 1.4 / 3.9 / 1.2	29 Tu	0011 / 0617 / 1225 / 1846	4.1 / 1.1 / 4.3 / 0.6
15 Tu ●	0100 / 0652 / 1302 / 1921	3.8 / 1.3 / 4.0 / 1.0	30 W ○	0104 / 0703 / 1312 / 1933	4.3 / 0.9 / 4.5 / 0.3
			31 Th	0151 / 0745 / 1355 / 2016	4.4 / 0.8 / 4.6 / 0.2

FEBRUARY

Day	Time	m	Day	Time	m
1 F	0234 / 0825 / 1437 / 2058	4.4 / 0.8 / 4.6 / 0.3	16 Sa	0219 / 0808 / 1415 / 2034	4.1 / 0.9 / 4.4 / 0.6
2 Sa	0315 / 0903 / 1518 / 2138	4.2 / 0.8 / 4.5 / 0.4	17 Su	0251 / 0840 / 1447 / 2107	4.1 / 0.8 / 4.4 / 0.6
3 Su	0355 / 0939 / 1557 / 2217	4.1 / 0.9 / 4.4 / 0.6	18 M	0324 / 0914 / 1524 / 2142	4.1 / 0.8 / 4.4 / 0.6
4 M	0433 / 1017 / 1638 / 2255	3.9 / 1.1 / 4.1 / 0.9	19 Tu	0400 / 0952 / 1603 / 2221	4.0 / 0.9 / 4.3 / 0.8
5 Tu	0513 / 1057 / 1722 / 2336	3.6 / 1.3 / 3.8 / 1.3	20 W	0440 / 1033 / 1648 / 2305	3.8 / 1.1 / 4.1 / 1.0
6 W ☾	0557 / 1142 / 1814	3.4 / 1.5 / 3.5	21 Th	0527 / 1120 / 1744 / 2357	3.7 / 1.3 / 3.8 / 1.3
7 Th	0024 / 0650 / 1241 / 1919	1.6 / 3.2 / 1.8 / 3.2	22 F	0628 / 1224 / 1857	3.5 / 1.5 / 3.6
8 F ☾	0128 / 0759 / 1412 / 2044	1.8 / 3.1 / 1.9 / 3.1	23 Sa ☽	0109 / 0742 / 1351 / 2027	1.6 / 3.4 / 1.6 / 3.5
9 Sa	0300 / 0921 / 1556 / 2212	1.9 / 3.2 / 1.8 / 3.2	24 Su	0244 / 0907 / 1531 / 2159	1.7 / 3.4 / 1.4 / 3.6
10 Su	0423 / 1031 / 1704 / 2316	1.8 / 3.3 / 1.6 / 3.4	25 M	0414 / 1023 / 1648 / 2311	1.6 / 3.6 / 1.1 / 3.8
11 M	0518 / 1123 / 1749	1.7 / 3.5 / 1.3	26 Tu	0518 / 1123 / 1746	1.3 / 3.9 / 0.8
12 Tu	0003 / 0558 / 1204 / 1827	3.6 / 1.5 / 3.8 / 1.1	27 W	0005 / 0607 / 1212 / 1834	4.0 / 1.1 / 4.2 / 0.5
13 W	0041 / 0634 / 1239 / 1859	3.8 / 1.3 / 4.0 / 0.9	28 Th ○	0052 / 0648 / 1256 / 1916	4.2 / 0.8 / 4.4 / 0.3
14 Th ●	0114 / 0706 / 1312 / 1931	4.0 / 1.1 / 4.1 / 0.7			
15 F	0147 / 0737 / 1342 / 2002	4.1 / 1.0 / 4.3 / 0.6			

MARCH

Day	Time	m	Day	Time	m
1 F	0133 / 0726 / 1337 / 1955	4.3 / 0.7 / 4.5 / 0.2	16 Sa ●	0117 / 0710 / 1316 / 1933	4.1 / 0.8 / 4.2 / 0.5
2 Sa	0211 / 0802 / 1415 / 2032	4.3 / 0.6 / 4.5 / 0.3	17 Su	0149 / 0742 / 1349 / 2006	4.1 / 0.7 / 4.4 / 0.4
3 Su	0246 / 0837 / 1453 / 2107	4.2 / 0.6 / 4.4 / 0.4	18 M	0222 / 0816 / 1425 / 2042	4.2 / 0.6 / 4.4 / 0.5
4 M	0321 / 0911 / 1528 / 2139	4.0 / 0.7 / 4.3 / 0.7	19 Tu	0257 / 0853 / 1504 / 2118	4.1 / 0.6 / 4.4 / 0.6
5 Tu	0353 / 0945 / 1606 / 2213	3.9 / 0.9 / 4.0 / 1.0	20 W	0335 / 0932 / 1548 / 2159	4.1 / 0.7 / 4.2 / 0.8
6 W	0428 / 1021 / 1645 / 2247	3.7 / 1.1 / 3.7 / 1.3	21 Th	0416 / 1017 / 1640 / 2244	3.9 / 0.9 / 4.0 / 1.1
7 Th	0506 / 1102 / 1732 / 2326	3.5 / 1.4 / 3.4 / 1.6	22 F	0506 / 1109 / 1742 / 2340	3.7 / 1.1 / 3.7 / 1.5
8 F ☾	0551 / 1153 / 1834	3.3 / 1.6 / 3.2	23 Sa ☽	0608 / 1218 / 1900	3.5 / 1.3 / 3.5
9 Sa	0019 / 0653 / 1309 / 1957	1.9 / 3.1 / 1.8 / 3.0	24 Su	0057 / 0726 / 1351 / 2032	1.8 / 3.4 / 1.4 / 3.4
10 Su	0152 / 0815 / 1510 / 2135	2.1 / 3.1 / 1.8 / 3.1	25 M	0243 / 0853 / 1527 / 2157	1.8 / 3.4 / 1.2 / 3.5
11 M	0348 / 0942 / 1628 / 2247	2.0 / 3.2 / 1.6 / 3.3	26 Tu	0407 / 1009 / 1637 / 2302	1.6 / 3.6 / 0.9 / 3.7
12 Tu	0449 / 1045 / 1716 / 2334	1.8 / 3.4 / 1.3 / 3.5	27 W	0504 / 1108 / 1729 / 2351	1.3 / 3.8 / 0.7 / 3.9
13 W	0532 / 1132 / 1754	1.5 / 3.6 / 1.0	28 Th	0549 / 1156 / 1814	1.0 / 4.0 / 0.5
14 Th	0012 / 0605 / 1208 / 1829	3.7 / 1.2 / 3.9 / 0.8	29 F	0032 / 0628 / 1238 / 1853	4.0 / 0.8 / 4.2 / 0.4
15 F	0045 / 0638 / 1242 / 1900	3.9 / 1.0 / 4.1 / 0.6	30 Sa ○	0110 / 0703 / 1316 / 1930	4.1 / 0.7 / 4.3 / 0.3
			31 Su	0144 / 0738 / 1352 / 2004	4.1 / 0.6 / 4.3 / 0.4

APRIL

Day	Time	m	Day	Time	m
1 M	0218 / 0812 / 1427 / 2036	4.1 / 0.6 / 4.2 / 0.6	16 Tu	0157 / 0755 / 1406 / 2019	4.2 / 0.6 / 4.4 / 0.5
2 Tu	0250 / 0846 / 1504 / 2107	4.0 / 0.7 / 4.0 / 0.8	17 W	0234 / 0836 / 1451 / 2100	4.2 / 0.6 / 4.3 / 0.7
3 W	0321 / 0919 / 1541 / 2138	3.9 / 0.9 / 3.8 / 1.1	18 Th	0317 / 0921 / 1542 / 2143	4.1 / 0.6 / 4.1 / 0.9
4 Th	0353 / 0956 / 1620 / 2210	3.8 / 1.0 / 3.5 / 1.3	19 F	0403 / 1010 / 1648 / 2234	4.0 / 0.8 / 3.9 / 1.2
5 F	0428 / 1035 / 1706 / 2249	3.6 / 1.3 / 3.4 / 1.6	20 Sa	0457 / 1109 / 1747 / 2334	3.8 / 1.0 / 3.7 / 1.5
6 Sa	0511 / 1123 / 1805 / 2340	3.4 / 1.5 / 3.2 / 1.9	21 Su ☽	0600 / 1221 / 1903	3.6 / 1.1 / 3.5
7 Su ☾	0605 / 1229 / 1920	3.2 / 1.6 / 3.1	22 M	0055 / 0714 / 1348 / 2025	1.8 / 3.5 / 1.2 / 3.5
8 M	0056 / 0719 / 1408 / 2047	2.1 / 3.1 / 1.7 / 3.1	23 Tu	0227 / 0834 / 1508 / 2139	1.7 / 3.5 / 1.1 / 3.5
9 Tu	0249 / 0843 / 1536 / 2200	2.0 / 3.1 / 1.5 / 3.2	24 W	0342 / 0946 / 1614 / 2238	1.5 / 3.6 / 0.9 / 3.7
10 W	0402 / 0955 / 1631 / 2252	1.8 / 3.3 / 1.3 / 3.4	25 Th	0437 / 1045 / 1706 / 2326	1.3 / 3.8 / 0.7 / 3.7
11 Th	0449 / 1048 / 1715 / 2333	1.5 / 3.5 / 1.0 / 3.7	26 F	0523 / 1133 / 1750	1.1 / 3.9 / 0.6
12 F	0529 / 1130 / 1751	1.2 / 3.8 / 0.8	27 Sa	0008 / 0603 / 1217 / 1828	3.8 / 0.9 / 4.0 / 0.6
13 Sa	0010 / 0604 / 1208 / 1828	3.8 / 1.0 / 4.0 / 0.6	28 Su	0045 / 0641 / 1256 / 1903	3.9 / 0.8 / 4.0 / 0.6
14 Su ●	0045 / 0639 / 1246 / 1903	4.0 / 0.8 / 4.2 / 0.5	29 M	0119 / 0717 / 1333 / 1937	4.0 / 0.7 / 4.0 / 0.7
15 M	0120 / 0716 / 1324 / 1940	4.1 / 0.7 / 4.3 / 0.4	30 Tu	0152 / 0752 / 1408 / 2009	4.0 / 0.7 / 3.9 / 0.8

Chart Datum: 2.25 metres below Ordnance Datum (Newlyn)

SCOTLAND, EAST COAST – ABERDEEN

Lat 57°09′ N   Long 2°04′ W

TIMES AND HEIGHTS OF HIGH AND LOW WATERS   YEAR **1991**

MAY

Day	Time	m	Day	Time	m
1 W	0223	4·0	16 Th	0218	4·2
	0827	0·8		0825	0·5
	1444	3·8		1446	4·3
	2040	1·0		2047	0·8
2 Th	0256	3·9	17 F	0303	4·2
	0901	0·9		0915	0·5
	1524	3·7		1541	4·2
	2112	1·2		2136	1·0
3 F	0327	3·8	18 Sa	0353	4·1
	0938	1·0		1009	0·6
	1604	3·6		1640	4·0
	2148	1·4		2228	1·2
4 Sa	0403	3·7	19 Su	0448	4·0
	1019	1·2		1108	0·8
	1651	3·4		1743	3·8
	2227	1·6		2327	1·5
5 Su	0444	3·6	20 M	0549	3·8
	1104	1·3		1215	0·9
	1743	3·3		1849	3·6
	2316 (☽	1·8		(☽	
6 M	0534	3·4	21 Tu	0036	1·6
	1201	1·4		0656	3·7
	1845	3·2		1328	1·0
				1958	3·5
7 Tu	0018	1·9	22 W	0151	1·6
	0636	3·3		0808	3·6
	1313	1·5		1440	1·0
	1952 (☾	3·2		2104	3·4
8 W	0138	1·9	23 Th	0301	1·5
	0747	3·3		0915	3·6
	1432	1·4		1543	1·0
	2101	3·2		2204	3·5
9 Th	0256	1·8	24 F	0402	1·3
	0857	3·3		1016	3·7
	1536	1·3		1637	0·9
	2159	3·4		2255	3·5
10 F	0355	1·6	25 Sa	0454	1·2
	0956	3·5		1109	3·7
	1627	1·1		1722	0·9
	2248	3·5		2340	3·7
11 Sa	0444	1·3	26 Su	0540	1·0
	1047	3·7		1156	3·8
	1711	0·9		1803	0·9
	2330	3·7			
12 Su	0527	1·1	27 M	0019	3·8
	1133	3·9		0622	0·9
	1753	0·7		1236	3·8
				1841	0·9
13 M	0011	3·9	28 Tu	0056	3·9
	0610	0·9		0700	0·9
	1218	4·1		1316	3·8
	1835	0·6		1914 (○	0·9
14 Tu	0052	4·1	29 W	0130	3·9
	0653	0·7		0737	0·9
	1304	4·3		1354	3·8
	1917 (●	0·6		1948	1·0
15 W	0134	4·2	30 Th	0202	3·9
	0738	0·6		0813	0·9
	1354	4·3		1432	3·8
	2001	0·6		2022	1·1
			31 F	0234	3·9
				0849	0·9
				1511	3·7
				2056	1·2

JUNE

Day	Time	m	Day	Time	m
1 Sa	0307	3·9	16 Su	0341	4·3
	0924	0·9		1000	0·4
	1550	3·7		1628	4·1
	2131	1·4		2214	1·1
2 Su	0342	3·8	17 M	0433	4·2
	1002	1·0		1055	0·6
	1633	3·6		1723	3·9
	2210	1·5		2306	1·2
3 M	0421	3·7	18 Tu	0527	4·0
	1044	1·1		1151	0·7
	1718	3·5		1818	3·7
	2254	1·6			
4 Tu	0508	3·6	19 W	0001	1·4
	1132	1·2		0627	3·8
	1807	3·4		1252	1·0
	2344	1·7		1917 (☽	3·5
5 W	0600	3·5	20 Th	0103	1·5
	1227	1·3		0730	3·7
	1902 (☾	3·3		1357	1·1
				2019	3·3
6 Th	0043	1·7	21 F	0212	1·5
	0657	3·5		0836	3·5
	1330	1·3		1501	1·2
	2001	3·3		2121	3·3
7 F	0149	1·7	22 Sa	0322	1·5
	0801	3·5		0942	3·5
	1434	1·3		1602	1·3
	2103	3·3		2220	3·4
8 Sa	0256	1·6	23 Su	0426	1·4
	0904	3·5		1042	3·5
	1535	1·2		1654	1·2
	2200	3·5		2311	3·5
9 Su	0357	1·4	24 M	0520	1·2
	1004	3·7		1136	3·5
	1630	1·0		1740	1·2
	2252	3·7		2356	3·6
10 M	0454	1·2	25 Tu	0607	1·1
	1102	3·9		1222	3·6
	1722	0·9		1821	1·2
	2342	3·9			
11 Tu	0546	1·0	26 W	0034	3·8
	1157	4·0		0648	1·0
	1812	0·8		1303	3·7
				1857	1·2
12 W	0028	4·1	27 Th	0109	3·9
	0636	0·7		0724	0·9
	1252	4·2		1342	3·8
	1900 (●	0·7		1933 (○	1·2
13 Th	0114	4·2	28 F	0142	3·9
	0727	0·5		0759	0·9
	1345	4·3		1419	3·8
	1949	0·7		2006	1·2
14 F	0202	4·3	29 Sa	0213	4·0
	0818	0·4		0833	0·8
	1440	4·3		1454	3·8
	2037	0·8		2040	1·2
15 Sa	0251	4·3	30 Su	0247	4·0
	0908	0·4		0907	0·8
	1535	4·2		1531	3·8
	2125	0·9		2114	1·2

JULY

Day	Time	m	Day	Time	m
1 M	0321	4·0	16 Tu	0409	4·4
	0942	0·9		1028	0·4
	1607	3·8		1652	3·9
	2149	1·3		2235	1·0
2 Tu	0357	3·9	17 W	0457	4·2
	1020	0·9		1116	0·7
	1647	3·7		1739	3·7
	2227	1·3		2322	1·2
3 W	0437	3·9	18 Th	0549	3·9
	1059	1·0		1207	1·0
	1727	3·6		1829 (☾	3·5
	2309 (☽	1·4			
4 Th	0522	3·8	19 F	0014	1·4
	1144	1·1		0645	3·6
	1814	3·4		1303	1·3
	2358	1·5		1926	3·3
5 F	0614	3·7	20 Sa	0119	1·6
	1238	1·2		0751	3·4
	1909 (☾	3·4		1409	1·5
				2032	3·2
6 Sa	0056	1·6	21 Su	0239	1·6
	0714	3·6		0905	3·3
	1338	1·3		1522	1·6
	2011	3·4		2141	3·3
7 Su	0205	1·6	22 M	0400	1·6
	0822	3·5		1019	3·3
	1447	1·3		1627	1·6
	2117	3·5		2241	3·4
8 M	0318	1·5	23 Tu	0504	1·4
	0934	3·6		1119	3·4
	1556	1·2		1720	1·5
	2220	3·6		2330	3·6
9 Tu	0428	1·3	24 W	0553	1·2
	1042	3·8		1207	3·5
	1659	1·1		1803	1·4
	2318	3·9			
10 W	0530	1·0	25 Th	0012	3·7
	1146	4·0		0632	1·1
	1757	1·0		1248	3·7
				1841	1·3
11 Th	0010	4·1	26 F	0048	3·9
	0627	0·7		0707	0·8
	1245	4·2		1324	3·8
	1849 (●	0·9		1914 (○	1·2
12 F	0059	4·3	27 Sa	0120	4·0
	0719	0·4		0740	0·8
	1338	4·3		1359	3·9
	1938	0·8		1947	1·1
13 Sa	0147	4·4	28 Su	0152	4·1
	0808	0·3		0812	0·7
	1429	4·4		1432	4·0
	2023	0·8		2019	1·1
14 Su	0234	4·5	29 M	0223	4·1
	0856	0·2		0844	0·7
	1518	4·3		1504	4·0
	2108	0·8		2050	1·1
15 M	0321	4·5	30 Tu	0256	4·2
	0942	0·3		0917	0·7
	1606	4·2		1538	3·9
	2150	0·9		2124	1·1
			31 W	0329	4·1
				0950	0·8
				1612	3·8
				2157	1·1

AUGUST

Day	Time	m	Day	Time	m
1 Th	0406	4·1	16 F	0508	3·9
	1027	0·9		1119	1·1
	1649	3·7		1740	3·5
	2237	1·2		2327	1·4
2 F	0448	3·9	17 Sa	0600	3·6
	1108	1·0		1205	1·5
	1733	3·6		1832 (☽	3·3
	2322 (☽	1·4			
3 Sa	0537	3·8	18 Su	0027	1·6
	1156	1·2		0703	3·3
	1827	3·5		1306	1·8
				1937	3·2
4 Su	0017	1·5	19 M	0151	1·8
	0639	3·6		0639	3·1
	1256	1·4		1433	1·9
	1931	3·4		2056	3·2
5 M	0130	1·6	20 Tu	0336	1·7
	0755	3·5		0953	3·2
	1412	1·5		1600	1·9
	2044	3·5		2207	3·3
6 Tu	0256	1·5	21 W	0445	1·5
	0918	3·5		1059	3·3
	1536	1·5		1659	1·7
	2157	3·6		2304	3·5
7 W	0417	1·3	22 Th	0533	1·3
	1037	3·7		1147	3·5
	1649	1·3		1743	1·5
	2301	3·9		2346	3·7
8 Th	0522	0·9	23 F	0611	1·1
	1142	4·0		1227	3·7
	1747	1·1		1818	1·3
	2356	4·1			
9 F	0617	0·6	24 Sa	0022	3·9
	1236	4·2		0643	0·9
	1836	0·9		1300	3·9
				1850	1·2
10 Sa	0043	4·4	25 Su	0055	4·1
	0706	0·3		0716	0·7
	1326	4·3		1333	4·0
	1921 (●	0·8		1921 (○	1·0
11 Su	0130	4·6	26 M	0126	4·2
	0751	0·1		0745	0·7
	1411	4·4		1404	4·1
	2002	0·7		1952	1·0
12 M	0213	4·6	27 Tu	0157	4·3
	0834	0·1		0816	0·6
	1453	4·3		1434	4·1
	2043	0·7		2023	0·9
13 Tu	0257	4·6	28 W	0229	4·3
	0917	0·2		0847	0·6
	1535	4·2		1505	4·0
	2121	0·8		2056	0·9
14 W	0339	4·5	29 Th	0303	4·3
	0957	0·5		0921	0·7
	1614	4·0		1539	4·0
	2200	0·9		2131	1·0
15 Th	0423	4·2	30 F	0339	4·2
	1037	0·8		0956	0·9
	1657	3·7		1616	3·9
	2242	1·1		2209	1·1
			31 Sa	0421	4·0
				1037	1·1
				1659	3·7
				2255	1·3

Chart Datum: 2.25 metres below Ordnance Datum (Newlyn)

SCOTLAND, EAST COAST – ABERDEEN

Lat 57°09' N Long 2°04' W

TIMES AND HEIGHTS OF HIGH AND LOW WATERS

YEAR 1991

TIME ZONE UT(GMT)
For Summer Time add ONE hour in non-shaded areas

SEPTEMBER

Day	Time	m	Day	Time	m
1 Su ☾	0515	3·8	16 M	0624	3·2
	1125	1·3		1207	1·9
	1756	3·6		1842	3·3
	2354	1·5			
2 M	0624	3·6	17 Tu	0103	1·8
	1228	1·6		0745	3·1
	1906	3·5		1335	2·1
				2002	3·2
3 Tu	0113	1·6	18 W	0300	1·8
	0748	3·5		0919	3·1
	1355	1·7		1528	2·0
	2026	3·5		2127	3·3
4 W	0250	1·5	19 Th	0414	1·6
	0918	3·6		1030	3·3
	1531	1·7		1630	1·8
	2145	3·7		2228	3·5
5 Th	0413	1·2	20 F	0502	1·4
	1034	3·7		1118	3·6
	1642	1·4		1713	1·6
	2248	3·9		2315	3·7
6 F	0515	0·8	21 Sa	0540	1·1
	1134	4·0		1156	3·8
	1734	1·2		1749	1·3
	2342	4·2		2351	3·9
7 Sa	0604	0·5	22 Su	0614	0·9
	1222	4·2		1229	3·9
	1819	0·9		1821	1·1
8 Su ●	0028	4·4	23 M ○	0025	4·1
	0649	0·3		0645	0·8
	1306	4·3		1300	4·1
	1900	0·7		1852	1·0
9 M	0110	4·6	24 Tu	0057	4·3
	0730	0·2		0716	0·7
	1347	4·3		1331	4·1
	1938	0·6		1923	0·9
10 Tu	0151	4·6	25 W	0130	4·4
	0809	0·2		0747	0·6
	1425	4·3		1404	4·2
	2016	0·6		1957	0·8
11 W	0230	4·6	26 Th	0204	4·4
	0847	0·4		0819	0·6
	1501	4·2		1436	4·2
	2053	0·7		2030	0·9
12 Th	0310	4·4	27 F	0240	4·4
	0922	0·6		0854	0·7
	1538	4·0		1511	4·1
	2129	0·9		2108	0·9
13 F	0350	4·1	28 Sa	0321	4·3
	0957	1·0		0932	0·9
	1614	3·8		1550	3·8
	2207	1·1		2152	1·1
14 Sa	0433	3·8	29 Su	0410	4·1
	1034	1·3		1016	1·2
	1655	3·6		1638	3·9
	2251	1·4		2242	1·3
15 Su ☽	0522	3·5	30 M	0511	3·8
	1113	1·6		1108	1·5
	1742	3·4		1737	3·7
	2343	1·7		2346	1·4

OCTOBER

Day	Time	m	Day	Time	m
1 Tu ☾	0624	3·6	16 W	0021	1·8
	1218	1·8		0706	3·2
	1852	3·6		1242	2·2
				1907	3·3
2 W	0112	1·5	17 Th	0158	1·7
	0751	3·5		0832	3·2
	1354	1·9		1429	2·1
	2015	3·6		2030	3·3
3 Th	0247	1·4	18 F	0324	1·7
	0917	3·6		0943	3·4
	1524	1·7		1545	1·9
	2132	3·7		2141	3·5
4 F	0403	1·1	19 Sa	0419	1·4
	1026	3·8		1037	3·5
	1627	1·5		1633	1·7
	2234	4·0		2233	3·7
5 Sa	0459	0·8	20 Su	0501	1·2
	1119	4·0		1118	3·7
	1716	1·2		1712	1·4
	2325	4·2		2315	3·8
6 Su	0546	0·6	21 M	0536	1·0
	1204	4·1		1154	3·9
	1758	0·9		1747	1·2
				2351	4·1
7 M ●	0010	4·4	22 Tu	0611	0·9
	0628	0·4		1228	4·1
	1243	4·2		1821	1·0
	1838	0·8			
8 Tu	0050	4·5	23 W ○	0028	4·3
	0707	0·4		0645	0·7
	1321	4·3		1300	4·2
	1916	0·7		1856	0·9
9 W	0130	4·5	24 Th	0103	4·4
	0744	0·5		0719	0·7
	1357	4·2		1334	4·3
	1952	0·7		1934	0·8
10 Th	0208	4·4	25 F	0142	4·4
	0818	0·6		0755	0·7
	1432	4·2		1411	4·3
	2029	0·8		2013	0·8
11 F	0246	4·2	26 Sa	0226	4·4
	0851	0·9		0834	0·9
	1505	4·0		1450	4·3
	2105	1·0		2056	0·9
12 Sa	0325	4·0	27 Su	0314	4·3
	0917	1·2		0917	1·1
	1539	3·9		1534	4·2
	2142	1·2		2143	1·0
13 Su	0407	3·8	28 M	0410	4·1
	0959	1·4		1004	1·3
	1616	3·7		1626	4·0
	2224	1·4		2240	1·1
14 M	0455	3·5	29 Tu	0513	3·9
	1037	1·7		1102	1·6
	1659	3·6		1727	3·8
	2313	1·6		2346	1·3
15 Tu ☽	0553	3·3	30 W	0625	3·7
	1127	2·0		1214	1·8
	1756	3·4		1839	3·7
			31 Th ☾	0107	1·3
				0744	3·6
				1341	1·9
				1958	3·7

NOVEMBER

Day	Time	m	Day	Time	m
1 F	0232	1·2	16 Sa	0212	1·6
	0900	3·7		0843	3·4
	1501	1·7		1434	2·0
	2111	4·0		2039	3·5
2 Sa	0341	1·1	17 Su	0318	1·5
	1004	3·8		0943	3·5
	1603	1·5		1538	1·8
	2213	4·0		2139	3·6
3 Su	0437	0·9	18 M	0410	1·3
	1057	3·9		1033	3·7
	1654	1·2		1627	1·6
	2305	4·1		2231	3·8
4 M	0523	0·8	19 Tu	0454	1·2
	1142	4·0		1115	3·8
	1737	1·0		1711	1·4
	2351	4·2		2316	4·0
5 Tu	0605	0·7	20 W	0534	1·0
	1221	4·1		1154	4·0
	1818	0·9		1753	1·2
6 W ●	0034	4·3	21 Th ○	0000	4·2
	0643	0·7		0614	0·9
	1259	4·2		1232	4·2
	1857	0·8		1835	1·0
7 Th	0113	4·3	22 F	0043	4·3
	0719	0·8		0655	0·8
	1333	4·2		1312	4·4
	1935	0·8		1917	0·8
8 F	0151	4·2	23 Sa	0130	4·4
	0757	0·9		0737	0·8
	1406	4·2		1352	4·4
	2012	0·9		2002	0·7
9 Sa	0230	4·1	24 Su	0219	4·4
	0826	1·1		0822	0·9
	1439	4·1		1436	4·4
	2049	1·0		2050	0·7
10 Su	0310	3·9	25 M	0312	4·3
	0858	1·3		0908	1·1
	1512	4·0		1522	4·4
	2125	1·1		2141	0·8
11 M	0350	3·8	26 Tu	0409	4·2
	0934	1·5		0957	1·3
	1548	3·9		1616	4·2
	2204	1·3		2237	0·9
12 Tu	0435	3·6	27 W	0509	4·0
	1013	1·7		1052	1·5
	1628	3·8		1713	4·1
	2249	1·4		2339	1·0
13 W	0526	3·5	28 Th	0612	3·9
	1059	1·9		1156	1·7
	1718	3·6		1818	3·9
	2344	1·6			
14 Th ☽	0627	3·4	29 F	0048	1·1
	1158	2·1		0720	3·7
	1817	3·5		1307	1·7
				1928	3·9
15 F ☾	0055	1·7	30 Sa	0201	1·2
	0734	3·3		0829	3·6
	1316	2·1		1422	1·7
	1927	3·4		2040	3·8

DECEMBER

Day	Time	m	Day	Time	m
1 Su	0310	1·1	16 M	0206	1·5
	0934	3·7		0842	3·4
	1529	1·6		1430	1·9
	2145	3·9		2040	3·6
2 M	0409	1·1	17 Tu	0311	1·5
	1030	3·7		0941	3·5
	1628	1·4		1538	1·7
	2244	3·9		2143	3·7
3 Tu	0459	1·1	18 W	0409	1·3
	1118	3·9		1034	3·7
	1719	1·2		1635	1·5
	2334	4·0		2242	3·8
4 W	0543	1·0	19 Th	0501	1·2
	1200	3·9		1123	4·0
	1804	1·1		1729	1·3
				2337	4·0
5 Th	0019	4·0	20 F	0550	1·0
	0622	1·0		1208	4·2
	1239	4·1		1818	1·0
	1846	1·0			
6 F ●	0100	4·0	21 Sa ○	0029	4·2
	0659	1·1		0638	0·9
	1314	4·2		1252	4·4
	1924	1·0		1906	0·7
7 Sa	0140	4·0	22 Su	0121	4·4
	0734	1·1		0724	0·9
	1347	4·2		1337	4·5
	2001	0·9		1955	0·6
8 Su	0218	4·0	23 M	0213	4·5
	0808	1·2		0811	0·9
	1419	4·2		1423	4·6
	2036	1·0		2043	0·5
9 M	0256	3·9	24 Tu	0305	4·4
	0840	1·3		0858	1·0
	1450	4·1		1511	4·6
	2111	1·0		2132	0·4
10 Tu	0335	3·9	25 W	0357	4·3
	0915	1·5		0945	1·1
	1525	4·1		1600	4·5
	2148	1·1		2224	0·5
11 W	0414	3·8	26 Th	0451	4·2
	0952	1·6		1034	1·2
	1602	4·0		1654	4·3
	2227	1·2		2318	0·7
12 Th	0458	3·7	27 F	0544	3·9
	1033	1·7		1126	1·4
	1644	3·8		1750	4·1
	2311	1·3			
13 F	0544	3·5	28 Sa	0015	1·0
	1119	1·8		0643	3·7
	1733	3·7		1225	1·6
				1852	3·9
14 Sa ☽	0003	1·4	29 Su	0120	1·2
	0638	3·4		0745	3·5
	1214	1·9		1333	1·7
	1829	3·6		2001	3·7
15 Su	0102	1·5	30 M	0229	1·3
	0738	3·4		0851	3·4
	1320	1·9		1450	1·7
	1934	3·5		2112	3·6
			31 Tu ☾	0335	1·4
				0957	3·5
				1603	1·6
				2221	3·6

Chart Datum: 2.25 metres below Ordnance Datum (Newlyn)

PETERHEAD   10-6-18
Aberdeen

CHARTS
Admiralty 1438, 213; OS 30
TIDES
+0140 Dover; ML 2.3; Duration 0620; Zone 0 (GMT).

Standard Port ABERDEEN (←)

Times				Height (metres)			
HW		LW		MHWS	MHWN	MLWN	MLWS
0000	0600	0100	0700	4.3	3.4	1.6	0.6
1200	1800	1300	1900				

Differences PETERHEAD

−0035	−0045	−0035	−0040	−0.5	−0.3	−0.1	−0.1

SHELTER
Excellent shelter. Can be entered in any weather at any tide. The bay is enclosed by breakwaters behind which yachts can anchor. Alongside berths in the inner harbours are sometimes available. Contact Hr Mr on VHF before entering or leaving.
NAVIGATION
Waypoint 57°29'.14N 01°45'.00W, 134°/314° from/to entrance, 1.0M. Peterhead is a major commercial port with all the implications. No navigational dangers. Yachts should give construction area a wide berth. Buoys are frequently moved.

LIGHTS AND MARKS
Leading lights into Peterhead Bay 314°.
Fishing Harbour signals (on Control Tower over Hr office on West pier)
3 Fl R (hor) — Bay closed to inward traffic
3 FR (hor) — Fishing Hr closed to inward traffic
2 Fl R (hor) — No exit from Bay to sea
2 FR (hor) — No exit from Fishing Hr
4 Fl R (hor) — Bay and harbour closed — No traffic movement permitted.
4 FR (hor) — Fishing harbour closed
When no signals showing, vessels may enter or leave with permission from Control Tower, call on Ch 16.
RADIO TELEPHONE
VHF Ch Port, Ch 14; 14. Emergency only, Ch 16.
TELEPHONE (0779)
Hr Mr 74281/3; CG 74278; MRCC Aberdeen 592334; ⌗ 73592; Marinecall 0898 500 452; Police 72571; Dr 74841.
FACILITIES
EC Wednesday; **A.J. Buchan** ☎ 72348, Slip, ME, El, Sh, C; **Northern Engineering** ☎ 72406, ME, El, Sh, C; **R. Irvin** ☎ 72044, ME, El, Sh, C; **Racal Decca** ☎ 73005, Ⓔ; **Woodsons** ☎ 70931, Ⓔ; **A. M. Campbell** ☎ 76433, El; **Murisons** ☎ 72173, Gas; **Town** P, D, V, R, Bar, ✉; Ⓑ; ⇌ (bus to Aberdeen); ✈ (Aberdeen).

▲ Vessels without radio, report to harbour office after berthing

MINOR HARBOURS AND ANCHORAGES   10.6.19

BURNMOUTH, Berwick, 55°50′N, 2°04′W, Zone O (GMT), Admty charts 1407, 1192. HW +0315 on Dover, −0025 on Leith; Duration 0615. Good shelter especially in inner harbour (dries). With on-shore winds a swell makes outer harbour uncomfortable. Min depth at entrance at LWS is 0.6m. From S beware Quarry Shoal Rocks; from N beware East and West Carrs. Leading line at 274° with two Bns or FR at night 29/35m 4M, 45m apart run in towards the harbour mouth until the Lts in the inner basin at root of W pier (2FG (vert)) come in line with outer harbour entrance. Facilities: FW, limited stores, Bar at top of valley.

ST ABBS, Berwick, 55°54′N, 2°08′W, Zone O (GMT), Admty chart 175. HW +0330 on Dover, −0017 on Leith; HW height −0.6m on Leith; Duration 0605; Shelter good. In strong on-shore winds outer harbour suffers from waves breaking over E pier. Inner harbour is best but often full of fishing boats and dries out. Hr Mr will direct visitors. On E side of entrance channel, beware Hog's Nose and on W side the Maw Carr, Ldg Line S face of Maw Carr on village hall (conspic) runs in until the harbour entrance opens to port when the second Ldg Line can be seen, front on head of jetty FR 4m 1M, rear on SW corner of old harbour FR 8m 1M. Access HW∓3. Facilities: FW on quay (tap), V (local grocer), LB, R, more facilities including bar at Coldingham (½ M).

NORTH BERWICK, East Lothian, 56°04′N, 2°43′W Zone O (GMT), Admty chart 734. Fidra HW +0344 on Dover, −0005 on Leith; HW height −0.2m on Leith; ML 3.1m; Duration 0625. Shelter good with winds S to W but harbour is dangerous with on-shore winds. Entrance is closed by boom in bad weather. Entrance is 8m wide. Harbour dries out. Beware The Maidenfoot, marked by Bn 1 ca NW of N pierhead. Ldg line − W face of North Berwick Law (conspic) in line with post on N pierhead (160°). Lights: N pierhead FWR 7m 3M R to seaward, W over harbour. Extinguished when vessels cannot enter harbour due to bad weather. Facilities: EC Thurs; **East Lothian YC** ☎ 2698 Bar, P and D (cans), FW on pier, stores etc obtainable in town; **Lawrence Turnbull** ☎ 2134, Gas; Ⓑ, ✉, ⇌ & Bus services to Edinburgh.

FISHERROW, Midlothian, 55°57′N, 3°04′W, Zone O (GMT), Admty chart 734. HW +0345 on Dover, −0005 on Leith; HW height −0.1m on Leith; ML 3.0m; Duration 0620. Shelter good except in winds from NW. Mainly a pleasure craft harbour. Approach dangerous in on-shore winds. Harbour dries; available HW∓2. Light − E pier head, Oc 6s 5m 6M on metal framework tower. Berth on E pier. Facilities: EC Wed; stores and FW. P and D from garage. Hr Mr ☎ Edinburgh 665-5900; CG 665-5639; **Fisherrow YC** ☎ 665-2576; **Town** V, R, Bar, Ⓑ, ✉, SM.

CRAMOND, Midlothian, 55°59′N, 3°18′W, Zone O (GMT), Admty chart 736. Tidal details as Granton (see 10.6.9). Enter R Almond, W of Cramond Island, marked by buoys and posts. At shore line is a sill. Access HW∓2. **Cramond Boat Club** ☎ 336-1356 FW, M, Bar; **Village** V, R, Pub, Bus.

INCHCOLM, Fife, 56°02′N, 3°18′W, Zone O (GMT), Admty chart 736. Tidal details as Aberdour. Best anchorage N of abbey (conspic). Beware Meadulse Rocks (dry). Ends of island foul. Lt Fl(3) 15s (obsc 075°−145°) at SE point, Horn(3) 45s. Land at jetty E of abbey (fee payable). No facilities.

ABERDOUR, Fife, 56°03′N, 3°18′W, Zone O (GMT), Admty charts 735. HW +0345 on Dover; +0005 on Leith; HW height 0.0m on Leith; ML 3.3m; Duration 0630. Good shelter except in SE winds when a swell occurs. The anchorage between The Little Craigs and the disued pier is good but exposed to winds from E to SW. Temporary berths are available in harbour (dries) alongside the quay wall. Beware Little Craigs (dries 2.1m) and outfall 2ca N marked by Bn. There are no lights or marks. Facilities: EC Wed; Hr Mr ☎ 860140, FW (tap on pier), P, R, V, Bar in village. **Aberdour Boat Club** ☎ 860206.

KIRKCALDY, Fife, 56°07′N, 3°09′W, Zone O (GMT), Admty chart 739. HW +0345 on Dover, −0005 on Leith; HW height −0.1m on Leith; ML 3.2m; Duration 0620.

Shelter good except in strong E winds. Yachts can berth on E pier in outer harbour (known as Pier Harbour) or, by arrangement with Hr Mr, enter the Wet Dock (HW−2 to HW) if space allows. If possible make arrangements before arrival (Methil Hr. Radio Ch 16, 14 will relay messages). A special Lt Buoy FlY 5s, lies ½ M E of harbour. If approaching from E, keep S of the Bn 60m SSE of East Pier Lt. Lights; E pier head, Fl WG 10s 10m 8M; G156°−336°, W336°−156°. S pier head 2 FR (vert) 7m, 5M. W pier, inner head FW 5m. Dock entrance W side FR 6m, E side FG 6m. Entry signals, day and night: FR-Port closed, bring up in roads. FG-Entry permitted. Harbour is administered by Forth Ports Authority. Contact Methil ☎ 26725. Facilities: EC Wed; Bar, D (by road tanker); FW, R, V. Small repairs can be arranged. ✉, Ⓑ.

ELIE, Fife, 56°11′N, 2°46′W, Zone O (GMT), Admty chart 734. HW +0325 on Dover, −0015 on Leith; HW height −0.1m on Leith; ML 3.2m; Duration 0620; Elie Bay provides good shelter from winds in the N sectors to small craft but local knowledge is needed. Anchor to W of pier or take the mud alongside it. Beware ledge off end of pier which dries. Coming from E beware Ox Rock (dries 1m) ½ M ENE of Elie Ness; coming from W beware rocks off Chapel Ness, West Vows, East Vows (surmounted by cage Bn) and Thill Rock, the E extremity of the latter pair marked by R can buoy. Light; Elie Ness Fl 6s 15m 18M, white Tr. Facilities: In villages of Elie and Earlsferry, FW, R, V, Bar, ✉, Ⓑ; **Shell Bay** ☎ 330283, Gas.

ST MONANS, Fife, 56°12′N, 2°49′W, Zone O (GMT), Admty chart 734. HW +0335 on Dover, −0020 on Leith; HW height −0.1m on Leith; ML 3.2m; Duration 0620. Shelter good except in strong SE to SW winds when scend occurs in the harbour. Harbour dries. Lie alongside E pier until contact with Hr Mr. Coming from NE keep at least 2½ ca from coast. Lights Breakwater head Oc WRG 6s 5m 7/4M; E pier head 2 FG (vert) 6m 4M. W pier head 2 FR (vert) 6m 4M. Facilities: EC Wed; Bar, D (by road tanker), El, FW, ME, Sh, Slip (by root of E pier), R, V, ✉, AC, Ⓑ; **Millers BY** ☎ 864; **Bass Rk Oil** ☎ 501, P, D, Gas.

CRAIL, Fife, 56°15′N, 2°38′W, Zone O (GMT), Admty chart 175. HW +0320 on Dover, −0020 on Leith; HW height −0.2m on Leith; ML 3.0m; Duration 0615. Good shelter but only for boats able to take the ground alongside. Harbour is protected by timber booms dropped into grooves at the pier heads in foul weather. Entrance between S pier and Bn on rocks to S following Ldg Line 295° − two W concrete pillars with FR Lts, 24m 6M and 30m 6M. Vessels should contact Forth Coastguard on VHF Ch 16 before entering. Facilities: EC Wed; Bar, C, R, Slip, V, ✉, Ⓑ. Coastguard ☎ 50666.

MAY ISLAND, Fife, 56°11′N, 2°33′W, Zone O (GMT), Admty chart 734. HW +0325 on Dover, −0025 on Leith. Anchorages at W Tarbert or E Tarbert according to the wind. Landing at Altar Stones. There is a harbour at Kirk Haven. Beware rocks N and S of island, Norman Rock to N and Maiden Hair Rock to S. At summit of island, a square Tr on stone house Fl(2) 15s 73m 22M. There are no facilities. The island is a nature reserve.

GOURDON, Kincardine, 56°50′N, 2°17′W, Zone O (GMT), Admty chart 210. HW +0240 on Dover; +0020 on Aberdeen; HW height +0.4m on Aberdeen; ML 2.7m; Duration 0620. Shelter good and inner harbour protected by storm gates. Beware rocks running S from W pier end marked by Bn. Lights − Ldg Lts 358°, both FR. Front Lt shows G when not safe to enter. West pier head Fl WRG 3s 5m 9/7M, vis G180°−344°, W344°−354°, R354°−180°. E breakwater head Q 3m 7M. Facilities: Hr Mr ☎ Inverbervie 61779 − Slip, FW from standpipe, V, R, Bar, D, ME, AC, M.

BODDAM, Aberdeen, 57°28′N, 1°46′W, Zone O (GMT), Admty chart 213. HW +0145 on Dover, −0040 on Aberdeen; HW height −0.4m on Aberdeen; ML 2.3m; Duration 0620. Good shelter, being protected by Meikle Mackie, the island just off Buchan Ness; harbour dries. Beware rocks all round Meikle Mackie and to the SW of it. There are no lights. Yachts lie along N wall. Very limited facilities, but all facilities at Peterhead, 4 miles away.

POWER PLUS

As the most experienced motor boating team in the United Kingdom, we deliver total coverage for cruising under power both in Britain and overseas.

Don't miss an issue this year – or you'll miss out on an exceptional package of features, boat and equipment reports and special supplements:

PLUS   Our quarterly Which Boat? buyer's guide

PLUS   Our annual guide to Mediterranean boating

PLUS   The latest update on our aerial River Guide series

All this AND crew cards, competitions, cruise accounts, backed up by practical advice and expert evaluation – and we carry the largest selection of new and secondhand boats for sale.

We're committed to helping you take full advantage of your boating, offering the most comprehensive read on the market today. So SAVE time and money by subscribing now AND add power to your reading with

MOTOR BOAT
A N D   Y A C H T I N G

Britain's biggest selling motor boating magazine.

RACING OR
CRUISING ?

FOR FULL SCOTTISH COVERAGE, REA[D]

Yachting
⊠*Life.*

THE NATIONAL MAGAZINE NORTH OF THE BORDER
Available at Chandlers, Marinas, Boatyards and Newsagents
or by subscription (£9 p.a.) from 113 West Regent Street, Glasgow.

80p
EVER[Y]
MONT[H]

VOLVO PENTA SERVICE

Sales and service centres in area 7
GRAMPIAN *Henry Fleetwood & Sons Ltd* Baker Street, LOSSIEMOUTH
IV31 6NZ Tel (034381) 3015. HIGHLANDS AND ISLANDS *Caley Marina* Canal
Road, Muirtown, INVERNESS IV3 6NF Tel (0463) 236539.

Area 7

North-East Scotland
Fraserburgh to Scrabster
including Orkney and Shetland Islands

VOLVO PENTA

7

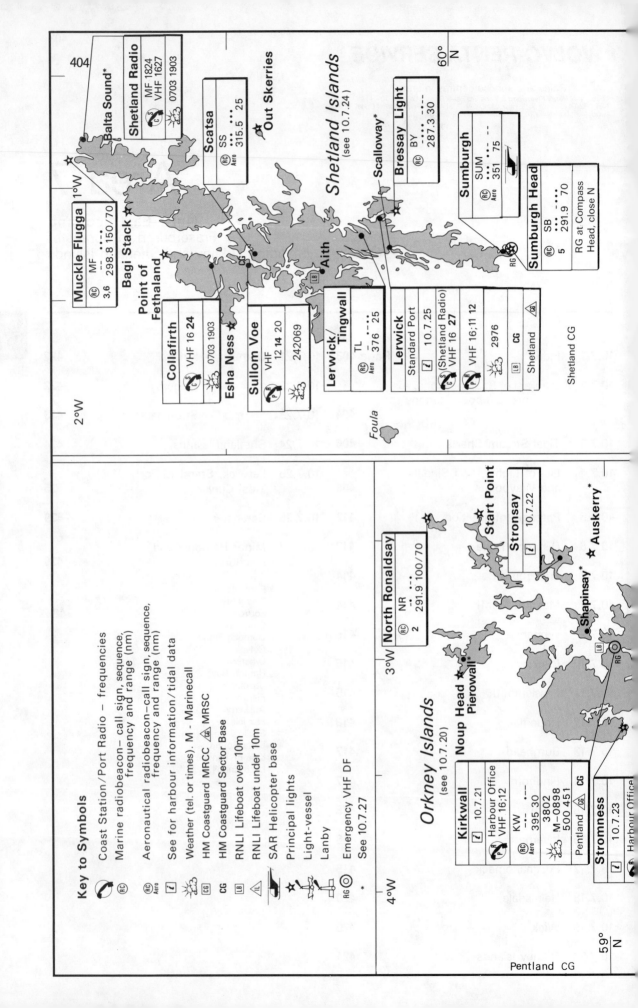

Key to Symbols

📞 Coast Station/Port Radio – frequencies

🔵RC Marine radiobeacon– call sign, sequence, frequency and range (nm)

🔵RC Aero Aeronautical radiobeacon–call sign, sequence, frequency and range (nm)

ℹ️ See for harbour information/tidal data

🌦️ Weather (tel. or times). M - Marinecall

CG HM Coastguard MRCC 🔺CG MRSC

CG HM Coastguard Sector Base

LB RNLI Lifeboat over 10m

LB RNLI Lifeboat under 10m

🚁 SAR Helicopter base

★ Principal lights

⚓ Light-vessel

⚓ Lanby

RG◎ Emergency VHF DF

* See 10.7.27

404

60° N

Shetland Islands
(see 10.7.24)

Balta Sound*

Shetland Radio
🔵RC 📞 MF 1824
VHF 1627
🌦️ 0703 1903

Scatsa
🔵RC Aero SS ••• ••• •••
315.5 25

Out Skerries

1°W

Muckle Flugga
🔵RC MF ••• ••
3,6 298.8 150/70

Bagi Stack ★

Point of Fethaland

Esha Ness ★

Collafirth
📞S CG VHF 16 **24**
🌦️ 0703 1903

Sullom Voe
📞R P VHF
12 **14** 20
🌦️ 242069

Aith LB

Scalloway*

Bressay Light
🔵RC BY –••• –•–•• ––
287.3 30

Sumburgh
🔵RC Aero SUM ••• ••– ––
351 75

Sumburgh Head
🔵RC SB ••• –•••
5 291.9 70
RG at Compass Head, close N

RG

Lerwick/Tingwall
🔵RC Aero TL – •–••
376 25

Lerwick
Standard Port
ℹ️ 10.7.25
📞S CG (Shetland Radio)
VHF 16 **27**
📞R P VHF 16;11 12
🌦️ 2976
LB CG Shetland

Shetland CG

2°W

Foula

Orkney Islands
(see 10.7.20)

Noup Head ★

Pierowall*

North Ronaldsay
🔵RC NR –• •–•
2 291.9 100/70

Start Point ★

Stronsay
ℹ️ 10.7.22

★ **Auskerry***

● **Shapinsay***

Kirkvall
ℹ️ 10.7.21
📞R P Harbour Office
VHF 16;12
🔵RC Aero KW –•– •––
395 30
🌦️ 3802
M–0898
500 451
Pentland 🔺CG CG

Stromness
ℹ️ 10.7.23
📞R Harbour Office

LB

RG◎

3°W

4°W

59° N

Pentland CG

10-7-2
North-East Scotland, Orkney and Shetland

8°W (1991)

90

Variation

180

270

Buchan Radio
| ⓈⒸ | VHF 16 25 87 |
| ☀️3 | 0703 1903 |

1°W

Fraserburgh
| ⓘ | 10.7.7 |
| Ⓟ | VHF 16;12 |
| LB |

Rattray Head

Moray CG

Pentland CG
Aberdeen CG

Kinnaird's Head
| Ⓡⓒ | KD |
| 1,4 | 291.9 100/70 |

2°W

Buckie
ⓘ	10.7.10
ⓈⒸ	Cromarty VHF 16 84 28
Ⓟ	VHF 12 16;14
LB

RG ⊙

Banff/Macduff
ⓘ	10.7.8
Ⓟ	VHF 16;12
⚠️	CG

Whitehills
| ⓘ | 10.7.9 |

Cullen*

Lossiemouth
ⓘ	10.7.11
Ⓟ	VHF 16;12
	CG

Findochty Portknockie

Kinloss
| Ⓡⓒ | KS |
| Aero | 370 50 |

3°W

Orkney Harbour Radio
| ☀️3 | 0703 1903 |
| Ⓟ | Orkney Harbour Radio VHF 16 20;C9 11 |

Duncansby Head

Cantick Head Muckle Skerry

Noss Head

Wick
ⓘ	10.7.19
ⓈⒸ	MF 1792 1824
Ⓟ	VHF 16;14
Ⓡⓒ Aero	WIK 344 40
LB

Lybster*

Burghead
| ⓘ | 10.7.13 |
| Ⓟ | VHF 16;14 |

Hopeman
| ⓘ | 10.7.12 |

Covesea Skerries

Clythness

Thurso
| M–0898 500 451 |

RG ⊙

Dunnet Head
RG ⊙

3.6 291.9 50

Scrabster
| ⓘ | 10.7.26 |
| Ⓟ | VHF 16;12 |

Dounreay/Thurso
| Ⓡⓒ Aero | DO 364.5 15 |

Kyle of Tongue*

CG

LB

Helmsdale
| ⓘ | 10.7.18 |

Golspie*

Dornoch F*

Portmahomack
| ⓘ | 10.7.17 |

Tarbat Ness

Invergordon
| Ⓟ | VHFCh 11 16 13 |
| LB |

Cromarty F*
Fortrose*

Findhorn
| ⓘ | 10.7.14 |

Nairn
| ⓘ | 10.7.15 |

Inverness
ⓘ	10.7.16
Ⓟ	VHF 12 16; 12 14
☀️3	M–0898 500 451

CG

58°
N

10.7.3 AREA 7 TIDAL STREAMS

5 Hours before HW Dover (0500 after HW Aberdeen)

4 Hours before HW Dover (0600 after HW Aberdeen)

3 Hours before HW Dover (0520 before HW Aberdeen)

2 Hours before HW Dover (0420 before HW Aberdeen)

1 Hour before HW Dover (0320 before HW Aberdeen)

HW Dover (0220 before HW Aberdeen)

Southward 10.6.3   Westward 10.8.3

1 Hour after HW Dover (0120 before HW Aberdeen)

2 Hours after HW Dover (0020 before HW Aberdeen)

3 Hours after HW Dover (0040 after HW Aberdeen)

4 Hours after HW Dover (0140 after HW Aberdeen)

5 Hours after HW Dover (0240 after HW Aberdeen)

6 Hours after HW Dover (0340 after HW Aberdeen)

10.7.4   LIGHTS, FOG SIGNALS AND WAYPOINTS

Abbreviations used below are given in 10.0.3. Principal lights are in **bold** print, places in CAPITALS, and light-vessels, light floats and Lanbys in *CAPITAL ITALICS*. Unless otherwise stated lights are white. m—elevation in metres; M—nominal range in n. miles. Fog signals are in *italics*. Useful waypoints are underlined - use those on land with care. See 4.2.2.

SCOTLAND—NORTH-EAST COAST

FRASERBURGH.
Cairnbulg Briggs 57°41'·12N 01°56'·37W Fl 3s 9m 5M; Bn.
Balaclava breakwater head 57°41'·53N 01°59'·63W Fl(2) G 8s 26m 6M; vis 178°-326°; *Siren 20s* (occas).
South breakwater head LFl R 6s 9m 5M.
Ldg Lts 291° Middle Jetty, Elbow. Front QR 12m 5M. Rear 75m from front Oc R 6s 17m 5M. G Lts indicate when basins open, R when shut.

Kinnaird's Head 57°41'·87N 02°00'·15W Fl 15s 37m **25M**; W Tr; RC.
Bombing range Lt Buoy 57°43'·80N 02°00'·75W FlY 5s; special mark.
Target float 57°42'·00N 02°10'·00W FlY 10s; bombing target; Ra refl.

MACDUFF.
Lighthouse pier head 57°40'·26N 02°29'·90W Fl(2) WRG 6s 12m W9M, R7M; W Tr; vis G shore-115°, W115°-174°, R174°-210°; *Horn (2) 20s* .
Ldg Lts 127° Front FR 44m 3M; White cone, black stripes on roof of building. Rear 60m from front FR 55m 3M; W mast, B bands.
West pier head QG 4m 5M.
Whitehills Pier head Fl WR 3s 7m W9M, R6M; W Tr; vis R132°-212°, W212°-245°.

PORTSOY.
Pier Ldg Lts 160°. Front 57°41'N 02°41'W F 12m 5M; Tr. Rear FR 17m 5M; X on mast.

BUCKIE.
West Muck 57°41'·07N 02°57'·93W QR 5m 7M; tripod.
North breakwater head 2 FR (vert) 7m 11M.
Ldg Lts 125°. **Front** Oc R 10s 15m **15M**; W Tr; *Siren (2) 60s*.
Rear 365m from front Iso WG 2s 30m **W16M**, G12M; vis G090°-110°, W110°-225°.
West Pier, NW corner 2 FG (vert) 4m 9M.

LOSSIEMOUTH.
Sewer outfall Lt Buoy 57°43'·78N 03°15'·83W FlY 5s; special mark.
South pier head 57°43'·44N 03°16'·59W Fl R 6s 11m 5M; *Siren 60s* .
Middle jetty Ldg Lts 292°. Front FR 5m; rear 44m from front FR 8m, (occas).

Covesea Skerries 57°43'·5N 03°20'·2W Fl WR 20s 49m **W24M, R20M**; W Tr; vis W076°-267°, R267°-282°.

HOPEMAN.
South pier head 57°42'·71N 03°26'·20W Oc G 4s 8m 4M shown 1/8-30/4.
North quay Ldg Lts 081°. Front FR and rear 10m from front FR 3m shown 1/8-30/4.

BURGHEAD.
North breakwater head 57°42'·10N 03°29'·94W Oc 8s 7m 5M.
Spur head QR 3m 5M; vis from SW only.
South pier head QG 3m 5M; vis from SW only.

NAIRN.
West pier head 57°35'·62N 03°51'·56W QG 5m 1M.
East pier head Oc WRG 4s 6m 5M; 8-sided Tr; vis G shore-100°, W100°-207°, R207°-shore.
Whiteness Head, McDermott Base Iso WRG 4s 6m 10M; vis G138°-141°, W141°-144°, R144°-147°.

INVERNESS FIRTH.
Riff Bank East Lt Buoy 57°38'·40N 03°58'·07W FlY 10s; special mark.
Navity Bank Lt Buoy 57°38'·20N 04°01'·10W Fl(3)G 15s; stbd-hand mark.
Riff Bank North Lt Buoy 57°37'·18N 04°02'·30W Fl(2)R 12s; port-hand mark.
Riff Bank West Lt Buoy 57°35'·80N 04°03'·95W FlY 5s; special mark.
SOUTH CHANNEL
Riff Bank South Lt Buoy 57°36'·75N 04°00'·87W Q(6)LFl 15s; S cardinal mark.
Craigmee Lt Buoy 57°35'·32N 04°04'·95W FlR 6s; port-hand mark.
Chanonry 57°34'·46N 04°05'·48W Oc 6s 12m **15M**; W Tr; vis 148°-073°.
Avoch 57°34'·0N 04°09'·8W 2 FR (vert) 7/5m 5M.
Munlochy Lt Buoy 57°32'·93N 04°07'·55W LFl 10s; safe water mark.
Meikle Mee Lt Buoy 57°30'·27N 04°11'·94W FlG 3s; stbd-hand mark.
Longman Point 57°30'·02N 04°13'·22W Fl WR 2s 7m W5M, R4M; R conical Bn; vis W078°-258°, R258°-078°.
Graigton Point 57°30'·07N 04°14'·01W Fl WRG 4s 6m W11M, R7M, G7M; vis W312°-048°, R048°-064°, W064°-085°, G085°-shore.
Kessock Bridge. N Trs OcG 6s and QG; S Trs OcR 6s and QR. Y Lts mark bridge centre.

INVERNESS.
Outer Beacon 57°29'·84N 04°13'·85W QR 3m 4M.
Inner Beacon 57°29'·7N 04°14'·0W QR 3m 4M.
Embankment head Fl G 2s 8m 4M; G framework Tr.
East side Fl R 3s 7m 6M.
CALEDONIAN CANAL. Clachnaharry, South training wall 57°29'·5N 04°15'·8W Iso 4s 5m; W triangle on W mast; traffic signals.

CROMARTY.
Fairway Lt Buoy 57°39'·98N 03°54'·10W LFl 10s; safe water mark; Racon.
The Ness Oc WR 10s 18m **W15M**, R11M; W Tr; vis R079°-088°, W088°-275°, obsc by North Sutor when brg less than 253°.
Nigg Ferry jetty, SE corner, 2 FG (vert) 6m 2M.
SW corner 2 FG (vert) 6m 2M.
Nigg Oil Terminal Pier, head Oc G 5s 31m 5M; grey Tr, floodlit.
East and West ends marked by 2 FG (vert) 9/7m 4M.
British Aluminium Co jetty head QG 17m 5M.

INVERGORDON.
Dockyard pier head Fl(3) G 10s 15m 4M.

Supply Base, SE corner Iso G 4s 9m 6M; grey mast.
Quay, West end Oc G 8s 9m 6M; grey mast.
Queen's Dock, West Arm, Iso G 2s 9m 6M.
Three Kings Lt Buoy 57°43'·75N 03°54'·17W Q(3) 10s; E cardinal mark.
Tarbat Ledge/Culloden Rock Buoy 57°52'·45N 03°45'·45W (unlit); port-hand mark.
Lt Buoy 57°53'·00N 03°47'·00W FlY 5s; special mark.
Tarbat Ness 57°51'·92N 03°46'·52W Fl(4) 30s 53m **24M**; W Tr, R bands; Racon.
Tain Bar Buoy (moved as requisite) 57°51'·6N 03°52'·9W (unlit); safe water mark.
TAIN firing range 57°49'·5N 03°57'·4W FR, when firing occurs.

HELMSDALE.
Ldg Lts 313°. Front FG (or FR when harbour closed), rear FG. NW pier; *Horn 30s* (occas).
Ben-a-chielt 58°19'·8N 03°22'·8W Aero 5 FR (vert) 448-265m; radio mast.
Lybster, South pier Oc R 6s 10m 3M; W Tr; occas.
Clythness 58°19'N 03°13'W Fl(2) 30s 45m **16M**; W Tr, R band.

WICK.
South pier head 58°26'·36N 03°04'·65W Fl WRG 3s 12m W5M, R3M, G3M; W 8-sided Tr; vis G253°-269°, W269°-286°, R286°-329°; *Bell (2) 10s* (occas).
South pier root Ldg Lts 234°. Front FR 5m on 5m mast. Rear, 20m from front, FR 8m on 8m mast. Dir Lt 290° 58°26'·6N 03°05'·2W Dir F WRG 9m W10M, R7M, G7M; column on N end of bridge; vis G285°-289°, W289°-292°, R292°-295°.
Noss Head 58°28'·8N 03°03'·0W Fl WR 20s 53m **W25M, R 21M**; W stone Tr; vis R shore-191°, W191°-shore.

SCOTLAND—NORTH COAST

Duncansby Head 58°38'·67N 03°01'·43W Fl 12s 67m **24M**; W Tr; Racon.
Pentland Skerries 58°41'·4N 02°55'·4W Fl(3) 30s 52m **25M**; W Tr; *Horn 45s.*
Lother Rock 58°43'·80N 02°58'·58W Q 11m 6M; Racon.
South Ronaldsay, Burwick jetty 2 FG (vert) 6m 2M.
Swona, near SW end Fl 8s 17m 9M; W column; vis 261°-210°.
North head Fl(3) 10s 16m 10M.
Stroma, Swilkie Point 58°41'·78N 03°06'·92W Fl(2) 20s 32m **26M**; W Tr; RC; *Horn (2) 60s* .
Inner sound, John O'Groats, pier head Fl R 3s 4m 2M; W post; Ra refl.
Dunnet Head Fl(4) 30s 105m **23M**; W Tr; RG.

THURSO.
Holburn Head Fl WR 10s 23m **W15M**, R11M; W Tr; vis W198°-358°, R358°-shore.
Breakwater head QG 5m 4M; G post; shown 1/9-30/4.
Ldg Lts 195°. Front FG 5m 4M; W post. Rear FG 6m 4M; W mast.

SCRABSTER.
Outer pier head 58°36'·63N 03°32'·48W QG 6m 4M.
East pier head 2 FG (vert) 6m 4M; shown 1/8-31/5.
West pier head 2 FR (vert) 6m 4M; shown 1/8-31/5.
Strathy Point 58°36'N 04°01'W Fl 20s 45m **27M**; W low Tr on dwelling.
Sule Skerry 59°05'·10N 04°24'·30W Fl(2) 15s 34m **19M**; W Tr; RC; Racon.
North Rona 59°07'·3N 05°48'·8W Fl(3) 20s 114m **24M**; W Tr.

Sula Sgeir 59°05'·65N 06°09'·50W Fl 15s 74m 11M.
Loch Eriboll, White Head 58°31'·1N 04°38'·8W Fl WR 3s 18m W13M, R12M; W Tr and building; vis W030°-172°, R172°-191°, W191°-212°.
Cape Wrath 58°37'·55N 04°59'·87W Fl (4) 30s 122m **24M**; W Tr; RC; *Horn (3) 45s.*

ORKNEY ISLANDS
Tor Ness 58°46'·7N 03°17'·6W Fl 3s 20m 9M; W Tr.
South Walls, SE end, **Cantick Head** 58°47'·2N 03°07'·8W Fl 20s 38m **18M**; W Tr.

SCAPA FLOW AND APPROACHES.
Ruff Reef, off Cantick Head, Fl(2) 10s 10m 6M; B Bn.
Long Hope, South Ness Pier, head, 58°48'·1N 03°12'·2W Fl WRG 3s 6m W7M, R5M, G5M; vis G082°-242°, W242°-252°, R252°-082°.
Hoxa Head 58°49'·3N 03°02'·0W Fl WR 3s 15m W9M, R6M; W Tr; vis W026°-163°, R163°-201°, W201°-215°.
Stanger Head 58°49'·0N 03°04'·6W Fl R 5s 25m 8M.
Roan Head 58°50'·8N 03°03'·8W Fl(2) R 6s 12m 7M.
Nevi Skerry 58°50'·7N 03°02'·6W Fl(2) 6s 7m 6M.
Calf of Flotta 58°51'·3N 03°03'·9W QR 8m 4M.
Flotta Terminal. N end of jetty. East 2 FR (vert) 10/8m 3M. West 2 FR (vert) 10/8m 3M; *Bell 10s.*
Mooring dolphins, East and West, both QR 8m 3M.
Single Point Mooring No.1 58°52'·2N 03°07'·3W FlY 5s 12m 3M; *Horn Mo(A) 60s.* Single Point Mooring No. 2 58°52'·3N 03°05'·8W Fl(4)Y 15s 12m 3M; *Horn Mo(N) 60s.*
Gibraltar Pier 58°50'·3N 03°07'·8W 2 FG (vert) 7/5m 3M.
Golden Wharf, N end 58°50'·2N 03°11'·4W 2 FR (vert) 3M.
Lyness Wharf, S end 58°50'·0N 03°11'·3W 2 FR (vert) 7/5m 3M.
St Margaret's Hope, Needle Point Reef 58°50'·1N 02°57'·3W Fl G 3s 6m 3M; diamond on post.
Pierhead 2 FG (vert) 6/4m 2M.
Ldg Lts 196°, both FR 7/11m.
Rose Ness 58°52'·4N 02°49'·9W Fl 6s 24m 8M; W Tr.
Scapa Pier 58°57'·4N 02°58'·3W Fl G 3s 6m 8M; W mast.
Barrel of Butter 58 53'·4N 03°07'·5W Fl(2) 10s 6m 7M.

Cava 58°53'·2N 03°10'·6W Fl WR 3s 12m W10M, R8M; W round Tr; vis W351°-143°, R143°-196°, W196°-251°, R251°-271°, W271°-298°.
Houton Bay Ldg Lts 316°. Front 58°55'·00N 03°11'·46W Fl G 3s 8m. Rear 200m from front FG 16m both R triangle on W pole, B bands, vis 312°-320°.
Ro-Ro terminal, South end Iso R 4s 5M.

CLESTRAN SOUND.
Peter Skerry Lt Buoy 58°55'·32N 03°13'·43W Fl G 6s; stbd-hand mark.
Riddock Shoal Lt Buoy 58°55'·88N 03°15'·07W Fl(2)R 12s; port-hand mark.

HOY SOUND.
Ebbing Eddy Rocks Lt Buoy 58°56'·62N 03°16'·90W Q; N cardinal mark.
Graemsay Island Ldg Lts 104°. **Front** 58°56'·46N 03°18'·50W Iso 3s 17m **15M**; W Tr; vis 070°-255°. **Rear** 1·2M from front Oc WR 8s 35m **W20M, R16M**; W Tr; vis R097°-112°, W112°-163°, R163°-178°, W178°-332°; obsc on leading line within 0·5M.
Skerry of Ness 58°56'·98N 03°17'·73W Fl WG 4s 7m W7M, G4M; vis W shore-090°, G 090°-shore.

STROMNESS.
Pier, SE corner Iso R 6s 15m 5M.

Ldg Lts 317°. Front 58°57'·6N 03°18'·0W FR 29m 11M; post on W Tr. Rear, 55m from front FR 39m 11M; both vis 307°-327°.
North pier, head FIR 3s 8m 5M.
Copinsay 58°53'·8N 02°40'·2W Fl(5) 30s 79m **21M**; W Tr; *Horn (4) 60s.*
Auskerry 59°01'·6N 02°34'·2W Fl 20s 34m **18M**; W Tr.
Helliar Holm, South end 59°01'·17N 02°53'·95W Fl WRG 10s 18m W14M, R10M; W Tr; vis G256°-276° W276°-292° R292°-098° W098°-116° G116°-154°.
Balfour, pier 59°01'·9N 02°54'·4W Q WRG 5m W3M, R2M, G2M; vis G270°-010°, W010°-020°, R020°-090°.

KIRKWALL.
Scargun Shoal Buoy 59°00'·83N 02°58'·57W (unlit); stbd-hand mark.
Pier, N end 58°59'·26N 02°57'·58W Iso WRG 5s 8m **W15M**, R13M, G13M; W Tr; vis G153°-183°, W183°-192°, R192°-210°.

WIDE FIRTH.
Linga Skerry Lt Buoy 59°02'·42N 02°57'·46W Q(3) 10s; E cardinal mark.
Boray Skerries Lt Buoy 59°03'·68N 02°57'·55W Q(6)LFl 15s; S cardinal mark.
Skertours Lt Buoy 59°04'·15N 02°56'·61W Q; N cardinal mark.
The Galt Lt Buoy 59°05'·25N 02°54'·15W Q; N cardinal mark.
Brough of Birsay 59°08'·25N 03°20'·30W Fl(3) 25s 52m **18M**; white castellated Tr and building.
Papa Stronsay, NE end, The Ness 59°09'·38N 02°34'·80W Iso 4s 8m 9M; W Tr.

STRONSAY, PAPA SOUND.
Quiabow Buoy 59°09'·85N 02°36'·20W (unlit); stbd-hand mark.
No. 1 Lt Buoy (off Jacks Reef) 59°09'·20N 02°36'·40W FlG 5s; stbd-hand mark.
No. 2 Lt Buoy 59°08'·95N 02°36'·50W FlR 5s; port-hand mark.
No. 3 Lt Buoy 59°08'·73N 02°36'·08W Fl(2)G 5s; stbd-hand mark.
No. 4 Lt Buoy 59°08'·80N 02°36'·37W Fl(2)R 5s; port-hand mark.
Whitehall Pier 50°08'·61N 02°35'·79W 2 FG (vert) 8/6m 4M.

SANDAY.
Start Point 59°16'·70N 02°22'·50W Fl(2) 20s 24m **19M**; W Tr, B stripes.
Kettletoft, pier Fl WRG 3s 7m W7M, R5M, G5M; W Tr; vis W351°-011°, R011°-180°, G180°-351°.
North Ronaldsay. NE end, 59°23'·40N 02°22'·80W Fl 10s 43m **19M**; R Tr, W bands; RC; Racon; *Horn 60s.*
Nouster, pier head 59°21'·4N 02°26'·3W QR 5m.

EDAY.
Calf of Eday 59°14'·2N 02°45'·7W Iso WRG 5s 8m W8M, R7M, G6M; W Tr; vis R shore-216°, W216°-223°, G223°-302°, W302°-307°.
Backaland pier Fl R 3s 5m 4M; vis 192°-250°.

WESTRAY.
Noup Head 59°19'·90N 03°04'·10W Fl 30s 79m **22M**; W Tr; vis 335°-242°, 248°-282°; obsc on easterly bearings within 0·8M, part obsc 240°-275°.
Pierowall, E pier head Fl WRG 3s 7m W11M, R7M, G7M; vis G254°-276°, W276°-291°, R291°-308°, G308°-215°.
West pier head 2 FR (vert).

Papa Westray, Moclett Bay pier head Fl WRG 5s 7m W5M, R3M, G3M; vis G306°-341°, W341°-040°, R040°-074°.
Egilsay pier, South end Fl G 3s 4m 4M.

SHETLAND ISLES
FAIR ISLE.
Skadan, S end 59°30'·85N 01°39'·08W Fl(4) 30s 32m **24M**; W Tr; vis 260°-146°, obsc inshore 260°-282°; *Horn(2) 60s.*
Skroo, N end 59°33'·16N 01°36'·49W Fl(2) 30s 80m **22M**; W Tr; vis 087°-358°; *Horn (3) 45s.*

MAINLAND.
Sumburgh Head 59°51'·30N 01°16'·37W Fl(3) 30s 91m **23M**; W Tr; RC.

HOSWICK and SANDWICK.
Mousa, Perie Bard, Fl 3s 20m 10M; W Tr.

BRESSAY.
Kirkabister Ness, 60°07'·25N 01°07'·18W Fl(2) 20s 32m **23M**; W Tr; RC; FR Lts on radio masts 0·95M NE.

LERWICK.
Twageos Point 60°08'·95N 01°07'·83W L Fl 6s 8m 6M.
Maryfield, Ferry Terminal Oc WRG 6s 5m 5M; vis W008°-013°, R013°-106°, W106°-111°, G111°-008°.
Breakwater, North head 2 FR (vert) 5m 4M.
Victoria Pier, North head, FIR 3s 5m 1M.
Victoria Pier, East Elbow, 2 FG (vert) 5m 4M.
North Jetty QR 5m 1M.
North Ness 60°09'·6N 01°08'·7W Iso WG 4s 4m 5M; vis G158°-216°, W216°-158°. Loofa Baa 60°09'·75N 01 08'·67W Q(6) LFl 15s 4m 5M; S cardinal mark.
North entrance Dir Lt 215°. Dir Oc WRG 6s 27m 8M; vis R211°-214°, W214°-216°, G216°-221°.
Gremista Marina, South breakwater head Iso R 4s 3m 2M.
Greenhead Q(4) R 10s 4m 3M.
Rova Head 60°11'·45N 01°08'·45W Fl(3) WRG 18s 10m W8M, R7M, G6M; W Tr; vis R shore-180°, W180°-194°, G194°-213°, R213°-241°, W241°-261°, G261°-009°, W009°-shore.
Dales Voe 60°11'·8N 01°11'·1W Fl(2)WRG 8s 5m W4M, R3M, G3M; vis G220°-227°, W227°-233°, R233°-240°.
Dales Voe Quay 2 FR (vert) 9/7m.
Hoo Stack 60°14'·99N 01°05'·25W Fl(4)WRG 12s 40m W7M, R5M, G5M; W pylon; vis R169°-180°, W180°-184°, G184°-193°, W193°-169°.
Dir Lt 182°. DirFl(4)WRG 12s 33m W9M, R6M, G6M; same structure; vis R177°-180°, W180°-184°, G184°-187°; synchronised with upper Lt.
Moul of Eswick Fl WRG 3s 50m W9M, R6M, G6M; W Tr; vis R shore-200°, W200°-207°, G207°-227°, R227°-241°, W241°-028°, R028°-shore.

WHALSAY.
Symbister Ness 60°20'·46N 01°02'·15W Fl(2) WG 12s 11m W8M, G6M; vis W shore-203°, G203°-shore.
Symbister Bay, South breakwater head 60°20'·6N 01°01'·5W QG 4m 2M. North breakwater head Oc G 7s 3m 3M.
East breakwater head Oc R 7s 3m 3M.
Marina North pontoon 2 FG (vert) 2m 3M.
Skate of Marrister 60°21'·4N 01°01'·3W FlG 6s 4m 4M; G mast with platform.
Suther Ness Fl WRG 3s 8m W10M, R8M, G7M; vis W shore-038°, R038°-173°, W173°-206°, G206°-shore.
Mainland. Laxo Voe ferry terminal 60°21'·1N 01°10'·0W 2 FG (vert) 4m 2M.

Out Skerries 60°25'·50N 00°43'·50W Fl 20s 44m **20M**; W Tr.

Bruray ferry berth 60°25'·4N 00°45'·0W 2 FG (vert) 6m 4M (TE). Muckle Skerry 60°26'·4N 00°51'·7W Fl(2) WRG 10s 13m W7M, R5M, G5M; W Tr; vis W046°-192°, R192°-272°, G272°-348°, W348°-353°, R353°-046°.

YELL SOUND.

S entrance, Lunna Holm 60°27'·38N 01°02'·39W Fl(3)WRG 15s 19m W10M, R7M, G7M; W round Tr; vis R shore-090°, W090°-094°, G094°-209°, W209°-275°, R275°-shore.

Firths Voe, N shore 60°27'·2N 01°10'·6W Oc WRG 8s 9m **W15M**, R10M, G10M; W Tr; vis W189°-194°, G194°-257°, W257°-263°, R263°-339°, W339°-066°.

Linga Is. Dir Lt DirQ(4)WRG 8s 10m W9M, R9M, G9M; concrete column; vis R145°-148°, W148°-152°, G152°-155°. Q(4)WRG 8s 10m W7M, R4M, G4M; same structure; vis R052°-146°, G154°-196°, W196°-312°; synchronized with Dir Lt. Yell, Ulsta ferry terminal, breakwater head Oc RG 4s 7m R5M, G5M; vis G shore-354°, R044°-shore. Oc WRG 4s 5m W8M, R5M, G5M; same structure; vis G shore-008°, W008°-036°, R036°-shore.

Toft ferry terminal 60°28'·0N 01°12'·4W 2 FR (vert) 5/3m 2M.

Ness of Sound, West side, Iso WRG 5s 18m W9M, R6M, G6M; vis G shore-345°, W345°-350°, R350°-160°, W160°-165°, G165°-shore.

Brother Island, Dir Lt 329°, Dir Fl(4) WRG 8s 16m W10M, R7M, G7M; vis G323°-328°, W328°-330°, R330°-333°.

Mio Ness 60°29'·7N 01°13'·5W Q(2)WR 10s 12m W7M, R4M; W round Tr; W282°-238°, R238°-282°.

Tinga Skerry 60°30'·5N 01°14'·7W Q(2)G 10s 9m 5M; W Tr.

YELL SOUND, NORTH ENTRANCE.

Bagi Stack 60°43'·55N 01°07'·40W Fl(4) 20s 45m 10M; W Tr.

Gruney Island 60°39'·20N 01°18'·03W Fl WR 5s 53m W7M, R4M; W Tr; vis R064°-180°, W180°-012°; Racon.

Point of Fethaland Fl(3) WR 15s 65m **W24M, R20M**; W Tr; vis R080°-103°, W103°-160°, R160°-206°, W206°-340°.

Muckle Holm 60°34'·85N 01°15'·90W Fl(2) 10s 32m 10M; W Tr.

Little Holm Iso 4s 12m 6M; W Tr.

Outer Skerry Fl 6s 12m 8M; B column, W bands.

Quey Firth Oc WRG 6s 22m W12M, R8M, G8M; W Tr; vis W shore (through S and W)-290°, G290°-327°, W327°-334°, R334°-shore.

Lamba, S side, Fl WRG 3s 30m W8M, R5M, G5M; W Tr; vis G shore-288°, W288°-293°, R293°-327°, W327°-044°, R044°-140°, W140°-shore.

SULLOM VOE.

Gluss Isle Ldg Lts 195° (H24). **Front** F 39m **19M**. Both Lts 9M by day. **Rear** F 69m **19M**. Little Roe 60°30'·05N 01°16'·35W Fl(3) WR 10s 16m W5M, R4M; Y and W structure; vis R036°-095°, W095°-036°.

Skaw Taing 60°29'·1N 01°16'·7W Fl(2)WRG 5s 21m W8M, R5M, G5M; Or and W structure; vis W049°-078°, G078°-147°, W147°-154°, R154°-169°, W169°-288°.

Ness of Bardister 60°28'·2N 01°19'·5W Oc WRG 8s 20m W9M, R6M, G6M; Or and W structure; vis W180°-240°, R240°-310°, W310°-314°, G314°-030°.

Vats Houllands 60°28'·0N 01°17'·5W Oc WRGY 3s 73m 6M; grey Tr; vis W343°-029°, Y029°-049°, G049°-074°, R074°-098°, G098°-123°, Y123°-148°, W148°-163°.

Fugla Ness. Lts in line 212°. Rear 60°27'·3N 01°19'·7W Iso 4s 45m 14M. Common front 60°27'·5N 01°19'·4W Iso 4s 27m 14M; synchronized with rear Lts. Lts in line 203°. Rear 60°27'·3N 01°19'·6W Iso 4s 45m 14M.

Sella Ness. Upper Lt 60°26'·9N 01°16'·5W Q WRG 14m 7M; vis G084°-099°, W099°-100°, W126°-128°, R128°-174°; by day F WRG 2M (occas).

Sella Ness. Lower Lt. Q WRG 10m 7M; vis G084°-106°, W106°-115°, R115°-174°; by day F WRG 2M (occas).

Tug jetty finger, pier head Iso G 4s 4m 3M. Garth Pier, North arm, head 60°26'·7N 01°16'·2W Fl(2)G 5s 4m 3M.

Scatsa Ness. Upper Lt 60°26'·5N 01°18'·1W Oc WRG 5s 14m 7M; vis G161°-187°, W187°-188°, W207°-208°, R208°-251°; by day F WRG 2M (occas).

Scatsa Ness. Lower Lt Oc WRG 5s 10m 7M; vis G161°-197°, W197°-202°, R202°-251°; by day F WRG 2M (occas).

Ungam Island 60°27'·3N 01°18'·5W VQ(2) 5s 2m 2M; W column; Ra refl.

Whitehill 60°34'·85N 01°00'·01W Fl WR 3s 24m W9M, R6M; vis W shore-163°, R163°-211°, W211°-349°, R349°-shore.

Uyea Sound 60°41'·2N 00°55'·3W Fl(2) 8s 8m 7M; R & W Bn.

Balta Sound 60°44'·5N 00°47'·6W Fl WR 10s 17m 10/7M; vis W249°-010°, R010°-060°, W060°-154°; Q Lt (occas) marks Unst Aero RC 0·7M W.

NORTH UNST.

Muckle Flugga 60°51'·33N 00°53'·00W Fl(2) 20s 66m **25M**; W Tr; RC. **Auxiliary Lt** FR 52m **15M** (same Tr); vis 276°-311°. Yell. Cullivoe breakwater head 60°41'·9N 00°59'·7W Oc R 7s 5m 2M. **Esha Ness** 60°29'·35N 01°37'·55W Fl 12s 61m **25M**; W square Tr.

Hillswick, S end of Ness 60°27'·2N 01°29'·7W Fl(4) WR 15s 34m W9M, R6M; W house: vis W217°-093°, R093°-114°.

Muckle Roe, Swarbacks Minn, 60°21'·05N 01°26'·90W Fl WR 3s 30m W9M, R6M; vis W314°-041°, R041°-075°, W075°-137°. Aith breakwater. RNLI berth 60°17'·2N 01°22'·3W QG 5s 3M. West Burra Firth. Transport Pier, head 60°17'·7N 01°32'·3W Iso G 4s 4m 4M.

Ve Skerries 60°22'·40N 01°48'·67W Fl(2) 20s 17m 11M; Racon.

VAILA SOUND.

Rams Head 60°12'·00N 01°33'·40W Fl WG 8s W9m, G6M, R6M; 16m; W house; vis G265°-355°, W355°-012°, R012°-090°, W090°-136°, obsc by Vaila I when brg more than 030°.

Vaila Pier. 60°13'·5N 01°34'·0W 2 FR (vert) 4m.

Skeld Voe. Skeld Pier, head 60°11'·2N 01°26'·1W 2 FR (vert) 4/2m 3M.

North Havra 60°09'·88N 01°20'·17W Fl WRG 12s 24m 7/5M; W Tr; vis G 001°-053·5°, W053·5°-060·5°, R060·5°-182°, G274°-334°, W334°-337·5°, R337·5°-001°.

Point of the Pund 60°08'·02N 01°18'·20W Fl WRG 5s 20m 7/5M; W Tr; vis R350°-090°, G090°-111°, R111°-135°, W135°-140°, G140°-177°, W267°-350°.

SCALLOWAY.

Whaleback Skerry Lt Buoy 60°07'·98N 01°18'·79W Q; N cardinal mark.

Moores slipway, jetty head 60°08'·2N 01°16'·7W 2 FR (vert) 4/3m 1M.

Blacksness, West Pier, head 2 FG (vert) 6/4m 3M.

East Pier, head Oc R 7s 5m 3M.

Centre Pier: Oc WRG 10s 7m W14, G11, R11; vis G045.7°-056.8°, W056.8°-058.8°, R058.8°-069.9°.

Fugla Ness 60°06'·40N 01°20'·75W Fl(2)WRG 10s 20m W10M, R7M, G7M; W Tr; vis G014°-032°, W032°-082°, R082°-134°, W134°-shore.

FOULA.

60°06'·78N 02°03'·72W Fl(3) 15s 36m **18M**; W Tr.

10.7.5   PASSAGE INFORMATION

RATTRAY HEAD TO DUNCANSBY HEAD (chart 115)

On direct route from Rattray Hd (Lt, fog sig) to Duncansby Hd (Lt, Racon) heavy seas may be met in strong W winds. For oil installations see 10.5.5. Tidal streams are moderate off Rattray Hd and strong in inner part of Moray Firth, but weak elsewhere in the firth. 5M NE of Rattray Hd the NE-going stream begins at HW Aberdeen +0140, and the SE-going stream at HW Aberdeen −0440, sp rates 2 kn.

In strong winds the sea breaks over Steraton Rk in the E approach to Fraserburgh (10.7.7), and over Colonel Rk 1¼M E of Kinnairds Hd (Lt). Banff B is shallow: beware Collie Rks N of Macduff (10.7.8). Banff harb dries, and should not be approached in fresh NE-E winds, when sea breaks well offshore.

From Meavie Pt to Scarnose dangers extend up to 3 ca from shore in places. Beware Caple Rk (depth 0.2m) ¾M W of Logie Hd. Spey B is clear of dangers more than ¾M from shore: anch here, but only in offshore winds. Beware E Muck (dries) ½M SW of Craigan Roan, an above-water rky patch ½M SW of Craig Hd, and Middle Muck and W Muck in approach to Buckie (10.7.10). For Portknockie see 10.7.27.

Halliman Skerries (dry) lie 1½M WNW of Stotfield Hd, and are marked by Bn. Covesea Skerries Lt Ho is 2M W of Stotfield Hd, and Covesea Skerries (dry) lie ½M NW of the Lt Ho.

Inverness Firth is approached between Nairn (10.7.15) and S Sutor. In heavy weather there is a confused sea with overfalls on Guillam Bank, 9M S of Tarbat Ness. The sea also breaks on Riff Bank (S of S Sutor) which dries in places. Chans run both N and S of Riff Bank. Off Fort George, on E side of entrance to Inverness Firth (chart 1078), the SW-going stream begins HW Aberdeen +0605, sp rate 2½ kn; the NE-going stream begins at HW Aberdeen −0105, sp rate 3½ kn. There are eddies and turbulence between Fort George and Chanonry Pt when stream is running hard. Most of Inverness Firth is shallow, but a deeper chan skirts the NW shore to within 1M of Craigton Pt, NE of which is a bank called Meikle Mee with depths of less than 1m. There is a clearance of 29m under the bridge, where tidal stream is very strong (see Inverness 10.7.16). For Fortrose see 10.7.27.

Cromarty Firth (chart 1889) is entered between N Sutor and S Sutor, both fringed by rks, some of which dry. Off the entrance the in-going stream begins at HW Aberdeen +0605, and the out-going at HW Aberdeen −0105, sp rates 1½ kn. Good sheltered anchs within the firth. See 10.7.27.

The coast running NE to Tarbat Ness (Lt) is fringed with rks. Beware Three Kings (dries) about 3M NE of N Sutor. Culloden Rk, a shoal with depth of 1.8m, extends ¼M NE of Tarbat Ness, where stream is weak. Beware salmon nets on coast between Tarbat Ness and Portmahomack (10.7.17). Dornoch Firth (10.7.27) is shallow, with shifting banks, and in strong E winds the sea breaks heavily on the bar E of Dornoch Pt.

At Lothbeg Pt, between Brora Pt and Helmsdale (10.7.18), there is a rk ledge extending ½M offshore. Near Berriedale, 7M NE of Helmsdale, is The Pinnacle, a detached rk 61m high, standing close offshore. The Beatrice oil field lies on Smith Bank, 28M NE of Tarbat Ness, and 11M off Caithness coast. Between Dunbeath and Lybster (10.7.27) there are no dangers more than 2 ca offshore. Clyth Ness is fringed by detached and drying rks. From here to Wick (10.7.19) the only dangers are close offshore. There is anch in Sinclair's B in good weather, but Freswick B further N is better while waiting for tide in Pentland Firth (beware wreck in centre of bay). Baxter Rk (depth 2.7m) lies 4 ca S of Duncansby Hd, and Stacks of Duncansby 6 ca further SSW.

PENTLAND FIRTH (chart 2162)

This dangerous chan should only be attempted in moderate winds and good vis, and not at sp tides. At E end the firth is entered between Duncansby Hd and Old Hd (S Ronaldsay), between which lie Pentland Skerries. At W end the firth is entered between Dunnet Hd and Tor Ness (Hoy). Near the centre of firth are the islands of Swona (N side) and Stroma (S side). Outer Sound is between Swona and Stroma; Inner Sound is between Stroma and the Scottish coast E of St John's Pt. Other than as above there are no dangers more than about 2 ca offshore, but the tide runs extremely strongly, and causes very severe eddies and races and a most confused sea at different times and places depending on conditions. See *North Coast of Scotland Pilot*.

In general the E-going stream begins at HW Aberdeen +0500, and the W-going at HW Aberdeen −0105. On both streams eddies form S of Muckle Skerry and around Stroma. Between Pentland Skerries and Duncansby Hd the sp rate is 8-10 kn. On the SE-going stream Duncansby Race extends first towards Muckle Skerry but then swings anti-clockwise until by HW Aberdeen −0440 it extends in a NW direction from Duncansby Hd. At HW Aberdeen −0140 it starts to subside. By HW Aberdeen +0245 the race forms again for about 2h in a ENE direction towards Muckle Skerry. This race is violent in strong E or SE winds against SE going stream.

The stream runs 8-9 kn at sp through Outer Sound, causing a persistent and dangerous race off Swilkie Pt at N end of Stroma, especially with a W-going stream and a strong W wind.

The most dangerous and extensive race in the firth is Merry Men of Mey, which forms off St John's Pt on W-going stream at HW Aberdeen −0150 and for a while extends right across to Tor Ness with heavy breaking seas even in fine weather. By HW Aberdeen +0315 the SE end of race detaches from Men of Mey Rks off St John's Pt, and by HW Aberdeen +0435 the race begins to subside off Tor Ness. With the start of the E-going stream, at about HW Aberdeen +0515, the race subsides in mid-chan.

Any yacht going through Pentland Firth, even in ideal conditions, must avoid Duncansby Race, Swilkie Race, and Merry Men of Mey. A safe passage depends on correct timing and positioning to avoid the worst races mentioned above, regular fixes to detect any dangerous set, and sufficient power to cope with the very strong tidal stream.

ORKNEY ISLANDS (10.7.20 and charts 2249, 2250)

The islands are mostly indented and rky, but with sandy beaches especially on NE sides. Pilotage is easy in good vis, but in other conditions great care is needed since tides run strongly. For details refer to Clyde Cruising Club sailing directions and *North Coast of Scotland Pilot*, which apply also to Shetland Islands.

When cruising in Orkney it is essential to understand and use the tidal streams to the best advantage, while at the same time considering the various tide races and overfalls, particularly near sp. A good engine is needed since, for example, there are many places where it is dangerous to get becalmed. It must also be remembered that swell from the Atlantic or North Sea can contribute to dangerous sea conditions, or penetrate to some of the anchorages. During summer months winds are not normally unduly strong, and can be expected to be Force 7 or more on about two days a month. But in winter the wind reaches this strength for 10-15 days per month, and gales can be very severe in late winter and early spring. Cruising conditions are best near midsummer, when of course the hours of daylight are much extended.

Stronsay Firth and Westray Firth run from SE to NW through the group. Races and/or tide rips, often dangerous in bad weather with wind against tide, occur off Mull Head, over Dowie Sand, between Muckle Green Holm and War Ness (where violent turbulence may extend right across the firth), between Faraclett Hd and Wart Holm, and off Sacquoy Hd. Off War Ness the SE-going stream begins at HW Aberdeen +0435, and the NW going at HW Aberdeen −0200, sp rates 7 kn.

Tide races and dangerous seas occur at the entrances to most of the firths or sounds when the stream is against strong winds. This applies particularly to Hoy Sound, Eynhallow Sound, Papa Sound (Westray), Lashy Sound, and North Ronaldsay Firth.

There are many good anchs among the islands, including: Deer Sound (W of Deer Ness); B of Firth, B of Isbister, and off Balfour in Elwick B (all leading from Wide Firth); Rysa Sound, B of Houton, Hunda Sound (in Scapa Flow); Rousay Sound; and Pierowall Road (Westray). Plans for some of these are on chart 2622. For Shapinsay, Auskerry, Houton Bay and Pierowall see 10.7.27. There is a major oil terminal and prohibited area at Flotta, on S side of Scapa Flow.

SHETLAND ISLANDS (10.7.24 and charts 3281, 3282, 3283)

These islands mostly have bold cliffs and are relatively high, separated by narrow sounds through which the tide runs strongly, so that in poor vis great care is needed. The Clyde Cruising Club sailing directions are almost indispensable.

As an introduction to these waters, a most violent and dangerous race forms off Sumbrugh Hd (at S end of mainland) on both streams. Other dangerous areas include between Ve Skerries and Papa Stour; the mouth of Yell Sound with strong wind against N-going stream; and off Holm of Skaw (N end of Unst).

Although there are many secluded and attractive anchs, it must be remembered that the weather can change very quickly, with sudden shifts of wind. Also beware salmon fisheries and mussel rafts (unlit) in many Voes, Sounds and harbours. For Scalloway and Balta Sound see 10.7.27.

Fair Isle (North Haven) is a useful port of call when bound to/from Shetland Is. Note that races form off both ends of the island, especially S, during the strength of tidal stream in both directions. See 10.7.27.

SCOTLAND — NORTH COAST (chart 1954)

Dunnet B, S of Dunnet Hd (Lt) gives temp anch in E or S winds, but dangerous seas roll in from NW. On W side of Thurso B is Scrabster (10.7.26).

Between Holborn Hd and Strathy Pt the E-going stream begins at HW Ullapool −0150, and the W going at HW Ullapool +0420, sp rates 2½ kn. Close to Brims Ness off Ushat Hd the sp rate is 3 kn, and there is often turbulence. SW of Ushat Hd the buildings of Dounreay are conspic, near shore. Dangers extend ¼M seaward off this coast.

Along E side of Strathy Pt an eddy gives almost continuous N-going stream, but there is usually turbulence off the pt where this eddy meets the main E or W stream. Several small bs along this coast give temp anch in offshore winds, but must not be used or approached with wind in a N quarter.

Kyle of Tongue (10.7.27) is entered from E through Caol Raineach, S of Eilean nan Ron, or from N between Eilean Iosal and Cnoc Glass. There is no chan into the kyle W of Rabbit Islands, to which a drying spit extends ½M NNE from the mainland shore. Further S there is a bar across entrance to inner part of kyle. There are anchs on SE side of Eilean nan Ron, SE side of Rabbit Islands, off Skullomie, or S of Eilean Creagach off Talmine. Approach to the latter runs close W of Rabbit Islands, but beware rks to N and NW of them.

Loch Eriboll (see chart 2720 and 10.7.27) provides secure anchs, but in strong winds violent squalls blow down from mountains. Eilean Cluimhrig lies on W side of entrance; the other (E) shore is fringed with rks up to 2 ca offshore. At White Hd (Lt) the loch narrows to 6½ ca. There are chans W and E of Eilean Choraidh. Best anchs in Camas an Duin (S of Ard Neackie) or in Rispond B close to entrance (but not in E winds, and beware Rispond Rk which dries). Westward to C Wrath (see 10.8.5) the coast is indented, with dangers extending 3 ca from the shore and from offlying rks and islets. A firing exercise area extends 8M E of C Wrath, and 4M offshore. When in use, R flags or pairs of R Lts (vert) are shown from E and W limits, and yachts should keep clear.

10.7.6   DISTANCE TABLE

Approximate distances in nautical miles are by the most direct route while avoiding dangers and allowing for traffic separation schemes etc. Places in *italics* are in adjoining areas.

	1	2	3	4	5	6	7	8	9	10	11	12	13	14	15	16	17	18	19	20
1 *Flamborough Head*	1																			
2 *Fife Ness*	155	2																		
3 *Peterhead*	212	78	3																	
4 Fraserburgh	227	94	16	4																
5 Banff	244	111	33	18	5															
6 Buckie	257	124	46	31	15	6														
7 Lossiemouth	267	134	56	41	25	11	7													
8 Findhorn	280	147	69	54	38	24	13	8												
9 Inverness	301	168	90	75	59	45	34	23	9											
10 Tarbat Ness	283	150	72	57	41	27	18	14	27	10										
11 Helmsdale	285	152	74	59	44	33	26	28	43	16	11									
12 Wick	283	150	72	57	50	46	44	51	69	42	29	12								
13 Duncansby Head	292	158	82	67	62	58	57	63	81	54	41	13	13							
14 Scrabster	310	176	100	85	80	76	75	81	99	72	59	31	18	14						
15 Kirkwall	325	191	115	100	95	91	90	96	114	87	74	46	34	50	15					
16 Stromness	314	180	104	89	84	80	79	85	103	76	63	35	22	25	32	16				
17 Noup Head	342	208	132	117	112	108	107	113	131	104	91	63	50	47	23	28	17			
18 Lerwick	356	238	160	150	156	160	162	170	190	162	148	120	109	124	95	110	82	18		
19 Sullom Voe	385	268	190	180	186	190	192	200	220	192	178	150	139	154	125	136	108	38	19	
20 *Cape Wrath*	355	221	145	130	125	121	120	126	144	117	104	76	63	47	79	58	73	155	176	20

FRASERBURGH   10-7-7
Aberdeen

CHARTS
Admiralty 1462, 222; OS 30
TIDES
+0120 Dover; ML 2.3; Duration 0615; Zone 0 (GMT).

Standard Port ABERDEEN (←)

Times				Height (metres)			
HW		LW		MHWS	MHWN	MLWN	MLWS
0000	0600	0100	0700	4.3	3.4	1.6	0.6
1200	1800	1300	1900				

Differences FRASERBURGH

−0105	−0115	−0120	−0110	−0.6	−0.5	−0.2	0.0

SHELTER
Good shelter but entrance is dangerous in on-shore gales. Yachts normally use South Harbour.
NAVIGATION
Waypoint 57°41'.32N 01°58'.71W, 111°/291° from/to entrance, 0.57M. This is a very busy fishing port and fishing vessels come and go day and night. There are no particular facilities for yachtsmen but it is a safe refuge. Large boulders have been deposited in SW part of harbour ent, reducing depth over an area which extends NE to the 291° ldg line. Take care on entering or leaving.
LIGHTS AND MARKS
Ldg Lts (Front QR, Rear Oc R 6s) lead in between the piers at 291°.
Entry signals at South Pier
2 B Balls or 2 R Lts (vert): No entry. R flag or one R Lt: Harbour open but special care needed.
Docking signals (from head of Burnett Pier, SE end of West Pier, and NE end of head of North Pier). By day, semaphore arm: 45° above horizontal − clear inwards; horizontal − closed to all traffic; 45° below horizontal − clear outwards. By night G Lt shows relevant basin open, R Lt shows relevant basin closed.
RADIO TELEPHONE
VHF Ch 16; 12 (H24).
TELEPHONE (0346)
Hr Mr 23323; Port Office 25858; CG 24279; MRCC Aberdeen 592334; ▓ 28033; Marinecall 0898 500 451; Police 23121; Dr 22088.
FACILITIES
EC Wednesday; **Port** ☎ 25858, Slip, P, D, L, FW, ME, El, Sh, C (70 ton mobile), CH, AB, V, R, Bar; **Caleys** ☎ 23241, P, D; **Mitchells** ☎ 22021, ME, El; **Buchan, Hall and Mitchell** ☎ 23336, ME, El, Sh; **May & Bruce** ☎ 25222, ME; **C. Will** ☎ 23364, C (30 ton); **G Walker** ☎ 23211 Slip, SM, Sh, C; **J. Noble** ☎ 3179, El, Sh; **Murisons** ☎ 23376, Gas. **Town** ✉, Ⓑ; ⇌ (bus to Aberdeen); ✈ (Aberdeen).

MACDUFF   10-7-8
(BANFF)
Banff

CHARTS
Admiralty 1462, 222; OS 29
TIDES
+0055 Dover; ML 2.0; Duration 0615; Zone 0 (GMT).

Standard Port ABERDEEN (←)

Times				Height (metres)			
HW		LW		MHWS	MHWN	MLWN	MLWS
0200	0900	0400	0900	4.3	3.4	1.6	0.6
1400	2100	1600	2100				

Differences BANFF

−0100	−0150	−0150	−0050	−0.8	−0.6	−0.5	−0.2

SHELTER
Reasonably good shelter but the entrance is open to westerly winds. Entry not recommended in strong NW winds. Harbour is three basins with entrance 17m wide. A busy cargo and fishing port.
NAVIGATION
Waypoint 57°40'.50N 02°30'.50W, 307°/127° from/to Macduff ent, 0.40M. Same waypoint 056°/236° from/to Banff entrance, 0.44M.
Beware rocky coast to the N and S of harbour entrance. There is a slight to moderate surge in the outer harbour with N to NE gales.
LIGHTS AND MARKS
Ldg Lts 127°, both FR. A B ball (FG Lt at night) over pierhead Lt means harbour closed.
RADIO TELEPHONE
VHF Ch 16; 12 (H24).

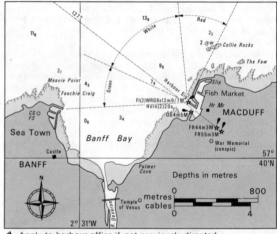

TELEPHONE (Macduff 0261, Banff 02612)
Hr Mr (Macduff) 32236; Hr Mr (Banff) 5093; CG Banff 2415; MRCC Aberdeen 592334; ▓ 32217; Marinecall 0898 500 451; Police (Macduff) 32222, (Banff) 2555; Dr Banff 2021.
FACILITIES
EC Wednesday; **Harbour** ☎ 32236, Slip, P, D, FW, ME, El, Sh, CH, V, R, Bar; **Macduff Boat Building & Engineering Co** ☎ 32234, ME, El, Sh. **Banff SC.**
W. Thompson ☎ 32388, Gas; **Town** ✉ (Macduff, Banff); Ⓑ (Banff); ⇌ (bus to Keith); ✈ (Aberdeen).
Note: Banff harbour, controlled by Grampian Region Council, is a popular yachting port. When entrance to Macduff is very rough with winds from SW to N, Banff can be a safe refuge. When winds are strong between N and ENE, Banff is unapproachable. Harbour dries. FW on quays. Town has P, D, ⇌, V, R, Bar.

WHITEHILLS 10-7-9
Banff

CHARTS
Admiralty 115, 222; OS 29
TIDES
+0050 Dover; ML 2.4; Duration 0610; Zone 0 (GMT).

Standard Port ABERDEEN (←—)

Times				Height (metres)			
HW		LW		MHWS	MHWN	MLWN	MLWS
0200	0900	0400	0900	4.3	3.4	1.6	0.6
1400	2100	1600	2100				

Differences WHITEHILLS
−0122 −0137 −0117 −0127 −0.4   −0.3 +0.1 +0.1

SHELTER
Safe. Swell in the outer basin in strong N to W winds.
NAVIGATION
Waypoint 57°42'.00N 02°34'.80W, 000°/180° from/to breakwater Lt, 1.2M. Reefs on S side of channel marked by two beacons. Beware numerous fishing floats.
LIGHTS AND MARKS
Fl WR 3s on pier head — approach in R sector vis R132°-212°, W212°-245°; Siren 10s (occas).
RADIO TELEPHONE
Whitehills Harbour Radio VHF Ch 16; 09.
TELEPHONE (026 17)
Hr Mr 5229; CG Banff 2415; MRCC Aberdeen 592334; ⌗ Peterhead 74867; Marinecall 0898 500 451; Police (0542) 32222; Dr Banff 2027.
FACILITIES
EC Wednesday; **Pier** ☎ 5229, P, D, FW, ME, El, CH, V, Bar; **End of Harbour** Slip; **Paterson** ☎ 5219, P, D, CH. **Town** V, R, Bar. ✉; Ⓑ (AM only); ⇌ (bus to Keith); ✈ (Aberdeen).

Apply to harbour office if not previously directed

BUCKIE 10-7-10
Banff

CHARTS
Admiralty 1462, 222; OS 28
TIDES
+0040 Dover; ML 2.4; Duration 0550; Zone 0 (GMT).

Standard Port ABERDEEN (←—)

Times				Height (metres)			
HW		LW		MHWS	MHWN	MLWN	MLWS
0200	0900	0400	0900	4.3	3.4	1.6	0.6
1400	2100	1600	2100				

Differences BUCKIE
−0130 −0145 −0125 −0140 −0.2   −0.2   0.0 +0.1

Apply to harbour office if not previously directed

SHELTER
Overnight only. Good shelter and can be entered in all weathers. Hr entrance is 9m wide. Portknockie has good shelter. See 10.7.27.
NAVIGATION
Waypoint 57°41'.32N 02°58'.80W, 306°/126° from/to entrance, 0.80M. Beware West Muck, Middle Muck and East Muck Rocks, 3 ca off shore. There is a dangerous swell over the bar in harbour entrance in strong N to W winds.
LIGHTS AND MARKS
Lights in line at 125° lead SW of West Muck. Entry signals:
W Pier B ball or Fl G Lt — Entrance depth less than 3m
B ball or FG over Fl G Lts — Entrance dangerous
2 B balls or 2 FR Lts — Harbour closed.
RADIO TELEPHONE
VHF Ch 12 16; 12. (Ch 16 H24)
TELEPHONE (0542)
Hr Mr 31700; CG Banff 2415; MRCC Aberdeen 592334; ⌗ 32254; Marinecall 0898 500 451; Police 32222; Dr 31555.
FACILITIES
EC Wednesday; **No 4 Basin (East)** ☎ 31700, Slip, D, (Lorry delivery), AB, FW; **Aberdeen Boat Centre** Sh, CH; **Herd and Mackenzie** ☎ 31245, Slip, ME, El, Sh, C (15 ton); **Jones, Buckie SY** ☎ 32727, ME, El, Sh, CH, ACA, SM, BH; **Moravian Motors** ☎ 33977, Gas. **Town** ✉; Ⓑ; ⇌ (bus to Elgin); ✈ (Aberdeen or Inverness).

LOSSIEMOUTH 10-7-11
Moray

CHARTS
Admiralty 1462; OS 28
TIDES
+0040 Dover; ML 2.3; Duration 0605; Zone 0 (GMT)

Standard Port ABERDEEN (←—)

Times				Height (metres)			
HW		LW		MHWS	MHWN	MLWN	MLWS
0200	0900	0400	0900	4.3	3.4	1.6	0.6
1400	2100	1600	2100				

Differences LOSSIEMOUTH
−0125 −0200 −0130 −0130 −0.2   −0.2   0.0   0.0

SHELTER
Very good from winds from N through W to SSE. From NE to SE it is dangerous and E winds bring swell in outer harbour. Visiting yachts moor in East Basin.
NAVIGATION
Waypoint 57°43'.40N 03°16'.00W, 097°/277° from/to entrance, 0.30M. Rocks to N & S of harbour entrance — approach from East. At night leading lights (FR 292°) are shown when safe to enter. When entering the harbour, beware current from R Lossie setting in northerly direction and causing confused water.

LOSSIEMOUTH *continued*

LIGHTS AND MARKS
By day — B ball at S pier } Dangerous
By night — R Lt over G Lt } to enter
R Flag at South Jetty when merchant vessels entering or
leaving. Leading lights 292°, both FR.

RADIO TELEPHONE
VHF Ch 16; 12 (0800-1700 LT, and 1h before vessel
expected).

TELEPHONE (034 381)
Hr Mr 3066; CG 2009; MRCC Aberdeen 592334; ⌗ Elgin
547518; Marinecall 0898 500 451; Police 2022; Dr 2277.

⚓ Apply to harbour office if not previously directed

FACILITIES
EC Thursday; **Harbour** Slip, D, M (See Hr Mr), FW (on
quay), ME, El, Sh, C, AB, SM, BH (15 ton); **Jones
Buckie Shipyard** ☎ 2029, ME, El, Sh, CH. **Lossiemouth
SC** ☎ 2928; **Mallard** ☎ 3001, Gas.
Town P, V, R, Bar. ✉; Ⓑ; ⇌ (bus to Elgin);
✈ (Inverness).
Note:- East Basin will probably become a marina.

AGENTS WANTED
Berwick-on-Tweed
Mallaig
Loch Sunart
Loch Aline
Fishguard
Kenmare River

Large number of French Ports

Rotterdam
Norderney
Dornumersiel
Langeoog
Wangerooge
Hooksiel
Bremerhaven

If you are interested in becoming our agent please write to
the Editors and get your free copy annually. You do not have
to be a resident in a port to be the agent but at least a fairly
regular visitor.

HOPEMAN   10-7-12
Moray

CHARTS
Admiralty 1462, 223; OS 28
TIDES
+0050 Dover; ML 2.4; Duration 0610; Zone 0 (GMT)

Standard Port ABERDEEN (←)

Times				Height (metres)			
HW		LW		MHWS	MHWN	MLWN	MLWS
0200	0900	0400	0900	4.3	3.4	1.6	0.6
1400	2100	1600	2100				

Differences HOPEMAN
−0120	−0150	−0135	−0120	−0.2	−0.2	0.0	0.0

SHELTER
A popular yachting harbour with alongside berths and
good facilities; controlled by Grampian Regional Council.
Entrance is difficult in winds from NE to SE. Once in SW
basin, shelter good from all winds. Harbour dries. Access
HW∓2 (for 1.5m draught).

NAVIGATION
Waypoint 57°42′.68N, 03°26′.50W, 263°/083° from/to
entrance, 0.17M. Dangerous rocks lie off harbour
entrance. Harbour dries. Do not attempt entry in heavy
weather. Beware salmon stake nets E and W of harbour
Mar to Aug and lobster pot floats.

LIGHTS AND MARKS
Ldg Lts 081°, Front FR 3m, Rear FR 4m (1 August –
30th April). West Quay elbow OcG 4s 8m 4M.

RADIO TELEPHONE
None.

TELEPHONE (0343)
Hr Mr 830650; MRCC Aberdeen 592334; ⌗ Elgin 547518;
Marinecall 0898 500 451; Police 830222; Dr Elgin 543141.

FACILITIES
EC Wednesday. **John More** ☎ 830221 CH, ME, Gas;
North East Sailing ☎ 830889 Sh; **J Sutherland**
☎ 830236 ME, El, D, P (cans); **Harbour** Slip, AB, D, FW;
Town V, R, Bar, ✉; Ⓑ; ⇌ (bus to Elgin); ✈ (Inverness).

⚓ Apply to harbour office if not previously directed

BURGHEAD 10-7-13
Moray

⚓ Apply to harbour office if not previously directed

CHARTS
Admiralty 1462, 223; OS 28
TIDES
+0035 Dover; ML 2.4; Duration 0610; Zone 0 (GMT).

Standard Port ABERDEEN (←—)

Times				Height (metres)			
HW		LW		MHWS	MHWN	MLWN	MLWS
0200	0900	0400	0900	4.3	3.4	1.6	0.6
1400	2100	1600	2100				

Differences BURGHEAD
−0120	−0150	−0135	−0120	−0.2	−0.2	0.0	0.0

SHELTER
One of the few harbours open in Moray Firth with strong E winds. NE wall of basin dries. Go alongside where available and contact Hr Mr's office. Can become very congested with fishing vessels.
NAVIGATION
Waypoint 57°42'.30N 03°30'30W, 317°/137° from/to N Pier Lt, 0.28M. Channel is subject to variations due to sand movement. Details from Hr Mr. Approach from SW. Access HW∓4.
LIGHTS AND MARKS
No leading lights but night entrance is safe after identifying the two outer pier Lts, QR and Oc 8s.
RADIO TELEPHONE
Hr Mr VHF Ch 16; 14 (office hours and when vessel expected).
TELEPHONE (0343)
Hr Mr 835337, CG Lossiemouth 2009; MRCC Aberdeen 592334; ✚ Elgin 547518; Marinecall 0898 500 451; Dr Lossiemouth 2277.
FACILITIES
EC Thursday; **Harbour** D, FW, AB, C (15 ton mobile), L, Slip. **Ernest Colburn** ☎ 835088 BY, Sh; **Town** Bar, ✉; V, P (cans), Ⓑ; ≉ (bus to Elgin); ✈ (Inverness).

FINDHORN 10-7-14
Moray

CHARTS
Admiralty 223; OS 27
TIDES
+0110 Dover; ML 2.5; Duration 0615; Zone 0 (GMT)

Standard Port ABERDEEN (←—)

Times				Height (metres)			
HW		LW		MHWS	MHWN	MLWN	MLWS
0200	0900	0400	0900	4.3	3.4	1.6	0.6
1400	2100	1600	2100				

Differences FINDHORN
−0120	−0150	−0135	−0130	0.0	−0.1	0.0	+0.1

SHELTER
Anchor off north pier and enquire at YC. Do not attempt entry in strong winds from NW to NE or when big swell is running.
THE OLD BAR. The original mouth of Findhorn River 4M SW of Findhorn gives excellent shelter in all weathers. Channel changes − local knowledge needed.
NAVIGATION
Waypoint 57°41'.00N 03°38'.80W 328°/148° from/to Ee Point, 1.4M. From waypoint, proceed to spar buoy, thence SSW to the R buoy which marks the channel entrance. Thence to four poles to be left a boat's length to port. Bar is constantly changing; strangers are advised to enter near HW. Once past The Ee turn to port, leaving two green buoys to stbd. Beware The Sturdy, a drying bank NW of anchorage on chartlet.
LIGHTS AND MARKS
There are no lights. There is a windsock on a flagpole by The Ee.
RADIO TELEPHONE
VHF Ch **80** (when yacht racing in progress).
TELEPHONE (0309)
MRCC Aberdeen 592334; ✚ Elgin 547518; W. Macdonald (Findhorn Pilot) 30236; Marinecall 0898 500 451; Police 72224; Dr 72221.
FACILITIES
Royal Findhorn YC ☎ 30247, M, FW, Bar; **Findhorn BY** ☎ 30099, C (16 ton), CH, D and P (cans), El, FW, L, M, ME, ACA, R, Slip, Gas; **Reids Engineering** (Forres) ☎ 72175, ME, El; **Norman Whyte** ☎ 30504, AC, L, ME, FW, BY, Sh; **Town** V, R, Bar, ✉; Ⓑ (Nairn and Forres); ≉ (Forres), ✈ (Inverness).

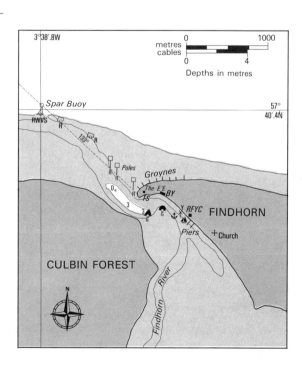

NAIRN 10-7-15
Nairn

CHARTS
Admiralty 1462, 223; OS 27
TIDES
+0110 Dover; ML 2.2; Duration 0615; Zone 0 (GMT).

Standard Port ABERDEEN (←)

Times				Height (metres)			
HW		LW		MHWS	MHWN	MLWN	MLWS
0200	0900	0400	0900	4.3	3.4	1.6	0.6
1400	2100	1600	2100				

Differences NAIRN
−0120	−0150	−0135	−0130	0.0	−0.1	0.0	+0.1

McDERMOTT BASE
−0110	−0140	−0120	−0115	−0.1	−0.1	+0.1	+0.3

SHELTER
Entry channel faces NNE so winds from that direction make entry difficult. Pontoons in harbour with six visitors places.
NAVIGATION
Waypoint 57°35'.90N, 03°51'.80W, 335°/155° from/to entrance, 0.30M. Advisable to enter between HW∓1½. Harbour is no longer used by commercial shipping.
LIGHTS AND MARKS
Lt Ho on E pier head, sectored Oc WRG 4s, G shore-100°, W100°-207°, R207°-shore. Keep in W sector.
RADIO TELEPHONE
None. Ch 37 (weekends only).
TELEPHONE (0667)
Hr Mr 54704; MRCC Aberdeen 592334; ⚓ Inverness 231608; Marinecall 0898 500 451; Police 52222; Dr 53421; Clinic 5092.
FACILITIES
EC Wednesday: **Grants** ☎ 52243 D and P (drums); **Nairn Basin** FW (standpipes), Slip, AC (110 volts), P, D; **Nairn SC** ☎ 53897, Bar; **Town** V, R, Bar, ✉; Ⓑ; ⇌; ✈ (Inverness).
A major marina – village project is under way (1990).

⏏ Nairn, apply to YC

INVERNESS 10-7-16
Inverness

CHARTS
Admiralty 115, 1077, 1078; OS 26/27
TIDES
+0100 Dover; ML 2.7; Duration 0620; Zone 0 (GMT).

Standard Port ABERDEEN (←)

Times				Height (metres)			
HW		LW		MHWS	MHWN	MLWN	MLWS
0300	1000	0000	0700	4.3	3.4	1.6	0.6
1500	2200	1200	1900				

Differences INVERNESS
−0050	−0150	−0200	−0105	+0.5	+0.3	+0.2	+0.1

FORTROSE
−0125	−0125	−0125	−0125	0.0	0.0	No data	

CROMARTY
−0120	−0155	−0155	−0120	0.0	0.1	+0.1	+0.2

INVERGORDON
−0105	−0200	−0200	−0110	+0.1	+0.1	+0.1	+0.1

DINGWALL
−0045	−0145	No data		+0.1	+0.2	No data	

SHELTER
Good shelter in all weathers. Inverness is the NE entrance to the Caledonian Canal, entrance to which can be difficult in strong tides. Caledonian Canal — See 10.8.15. Fortrose offers some safe anchorages at the entrance to the inner part of the Moray Firth. See 10.7.27.
NAVIGATION
Waypoint Meikle Mee stbd-hand buoy, FlG 3s, 57°30'.28N 04°11'.93W, 070°/250° from/to Longman Pt Bn, 0.74M. Tidal streams strong S of Craigton Pt (East going stream at springs exceeds 5 kn). Beware marine farms S of Avoch. (Off chartlet).
LIGHTS AND MARKS
Entrance to river is very narrow but deep. Craigton Pt Lt is Fl WRG 4s 6m 11/7M vis W312°-048°, R048°-064°, W064°-085°, G085°-shore.
RADIO TELEPHONE
Call: *Inverness Harbour Office* VHF Ch 12 16; 12 06 14 (Mon-Fri: 0800-1700 LT). Caley Marina Ch **80**. Inverness Boat Centre Ch **80** (0900-1800 LT). Other station: Cromarty Firth Port Control Ch 16; 06 08 **11** 12 13 14 (H24).
Call: *Clachnaharry Sea Lock* Ch 74. For canal office call: *Caledonian Canal* Ch 74.
TELEPHONE (0463)
Hr Mr 233291 (after hours 231725); CG Cromarty 967211; MRCC Aberdeen 592334; ⚓ 231608; Marinecall 0898 500 451; Police 239191; Dr 234151.
FACILITIES
EC Wednesday; **Caley Marina** (25+25 visitors) ☎ 236539 ACA, AC, C (20 ton), CH, D, ME, El, Sh, FW, (Access H24); **Muirtown Marina** (20+20 visitors) ☎ 239745 AC, D, FW, Gas, Gaz, ME, Ⓞ, C (4 ton), CH, Sh, El; Access HW∓4; **Shore Street Quay** ☎ 233291, Slip, P, D, L, FW, ME, El, C (2 mobiles), CH, AB; **Citadel Quay** ☎ 233291, Slip, P, D, L, FW, ME, El, AB; **Inverness Boatbuilding and Engineering** ☎ 243585, Slip, M, ME, El, Sh, C (100 ton); **P. T. McHardy** ☎ 233632, Gas; **Inverness Boat Centre** ☎ 73383, CH, FW, L, M, ME, P, Slip, SM. **Town** V, R, Bar. ✉; Ⓑ; ⇌; ✈.

INVERNESS *continued*

⚓ Apply to Harbour office if not previously directed

PORTMAHOMACK 10-7-17
Ross and Cromarty

CHARTS
Admiralty 115, 223; OS 21

TIDES
+0035 Dover; ML 2.5; Duration 0600; Zone 0 (GMT).

Standard Port ABERDEEN (←)

Times				Height (metres)			
HW		LW		MHWS	MHWN	MLWN	MLWS
0300	0800	0200	0800	4.3	3.4	1.6	0.6
1500	2000	1400	2000				

Differences PORTMAHOMACK
−0120	−0210	−0140	−0110	−0.2	−0.1	+0.1	+0.1

SHELTER
Uncomfortable in W to SW winds, but otherwise good shelter. Access to harbour at HW only. Harbour dries but good anchorage close SW of pier.

NAVIGATION
Waypoint Special buoy, Fl.Y 5s, 57°53'.03N 03°47'.02W, 346°/166° from/to Tarbat Ness Lt, 1.13M. Beware Curach Rocks which lie from 2ca SW of pier to the shore. Rocks extend to N and W of the pier. Beware lobster pot floats and salmon nets to N of harbour.

PORTMAHOMACK *continued*

LIGHTS AND MARKS
There are no lights or marks.
RADIO TELEPHONE
None.
TELEPHONE (086 287)
CG 564; MRCC Aberdeen 592334; ⌗ Invergordon 852221; Marinecall 0898 500 451; Dr 358 Tain 2759.
FACILITIES
EC Wednesday; **Harbour** C (6 ton), M, P and D (¾ M on Tain road in cans), L, FW, CH, AB; **Port Service Stn** ☎ 231, Gas; **Town** ✉; ⑧ (Mobile from Dingwall 1235-1345); ⇌ (bus to Tain); ✈ (Inverness).

⚓ Anchor off and wait

⚓ Apply to Harbour office if not previously directed

FACILITIES
EC Wednesday; **NW Pier** ☎ 354, Slip, M (See Hr Mr), L, FW, AB; **E Pier** ☎ 354, M (See Hr Mr), L, FW, AB; **A. R. McLeod** ☎ 338, Gas; **A. R. McLeod** ☎ 234, El; **Town** P, D, V, R, Bar. ✉; ⑧ (Brora); ⇌; ✈ (Wick).

HELMSDALE   10-7-18
Sutherland

CHARTS
Admiralty 115, 1462; OS 17
TIDES
+0035 Dover; ML 2.2; Duration 0615; Zone 0 (GMT).

Standard Port ABERDEEN (←)

Times				Height (metres)			
HW		LW		MHWS	MHWN	MLWN	MLWS
0300	0800	0200	0800	4.3	3.4	1.6	0.6
1500	2000	1400	2000				

Differences HELMSDALE

−0140	−0200	−0150	−0135	−0.5	−0.4	−0.1	−0.1

GOLSPIE

−0130	−0215	−0155	−0130	−0.3	−0.3	−0.1	0.0

SHELTER
Good in all weathers except strong SE winds.
NAVIGATION
Waypoint 58°06'.61N 03°38'.30W, 133°/313° from/to entrance, 0.35M. Beware spate coming down river after heavy rains. Shallow both sides of channel and bar builds up in river when in spate.
LIGHTS AND MARKS
Ldg Lts 313°. Front FG (harbour open) or FR (harbour closed). Rear FG; both on W masts.
RADIO TELEPHONE
VHF Ch 16.
TELEPHONE (043 12)
Hr Mr 347; CG Wick 2332; MRCC Aberdeen 592334; ⌗ Wick 3125; Marinecall 0898 500 451; Dr 225 (Home) or 221 (Surgery).

WICK   10-7-19
Caithness

CHARTS
Admiralty 1462, 115; OS 12
TIDES
+0010 Dover; ML 2.0; Duration 0625; Zone 0 (GMT).

Standard Port ABERDEEN (←)

Times				Height (metres)			
HW		LW		MHWS	MHWN	MLWN	MLWS
0300	0800	0200	0800	4.3	3.4	1.6	0.6
1500	2000	1400	2000				

Differences WICK

−0155	−0220	−0210	−0220	−0.9	−0.7	−0.2	−0.1

DUNCANSBY HEAD

−0320	−0320	−0320	−0320	−1.2	−1.0	No data	

SHELTER
Shelter good except in strong E winds. NB. The river harbour is leased and must *not* be entered without prior permission.
NAVIGATION
Waypoint 58°26'.20N 03°03'.30W, 104°/284° from/to South Pier Lt, 0.72M. Harbour entrance dangerous in strong E winds as boats have to make a 90° turn at the end of S Pier. Unlit pole beacon S side of bay marks seaward end of ruined breakwater.
LIGHTS AND MARKS
Harbour inaccessible — a black ball (G light at night) on look-out tower over CG Station on South Head.
South pier Lt — Fl WRG 3s 12m 5/3M G253°-269°, W269°-286°, R286°-329°
Dir Lt on N end of bridge, W sector 289°-292°.
When harbour temporarily obstructed B ball or R Lt at S Pier head. Leading Lts 234°, both FR.

WICK *continued*

RADIO TELEPHONE
VHF Ch 16; 14 (when vessel expected).
TELEPHONE (0955)
Hr Mr 2030; CG 2332; MRSC Kirkwall 3268; ⌗ 3650;
Police 3551; Ⓗ 2434, 2261.
FACILITIES
EC Wednesday; **Inner N Pier** Slip, L, ME, AB (see
Hr Mr), V; **Harbour Quays** L, ME; **Outer S Pier** L;
Jetty ☎ Tel. 2689, D, L, FW, CH; **James McCaughey**
☎ 3701 or 2858, ME, El, Sh, CH, Slip, Gas; **Town** Slip,
P, ME, El, Sh, C, CH, V, R, Bar. ✉; Ⓑ; ≉; ✈.

▲ Contact Hr Mr

ORKNEY ISLANDS   10-7-20
The Orkneys consist of some 70 islands, of which about 24
are inhabited. They extend 5 to 50M NNE from Duncansby
Head, and are mostly low-lying, but Hoy in the SW of the
group reaches 475m (1560ft). Coasts are generally rocky and
much indented, but there are many sandy beaches. A
passage with least width of about 3M runs from NW to SE
through the group. The islands are divided from Scotland
by Pentland Firth, a very dangerous stretch of water (see
10.7.5). The climate is mild but windy, and very few trees
grow. The principal island is Mainland (or Pomona) on
which stands Kirkwall, the capital. There is a small naval
base at Lyness in Scapa Flow.
   Beware the many lobster pots (creels) all round the coast.
Severe gales blow in winter and early spring (see 10.7.5).
There are lifeboats at Longhope, Stromness and Kirkwall.
There is a MRSC at Kirkwall, ☎ (0856) 3268, with Auxiliary
(Watch and Rescue) Stations at Longhope (South Walls),
Brough Ness (South Ronaldsay), Stromness (Mainland),
Deerness (Mainland), Westray, Papa Westray, Sanday,
North Ronaldsay and all inhabited islands except Egilsay and
Wyre.

CHARTS
Charts 2249 and 2250 cover the islands. For larger scale
charts, see under individual harbours.
TIDES
Tidal information is related to Aberdeen (10.6.17) as
Standard Port. Tidal streams are strong, particularly in
Pentland Firth and in the firths and sounds among the
islands (see 10.7.5.).

SHELTER
There are piers at all the main islands, and there are many
anchorages, of which the following are a selection.
MAINLAND
SCAPA BAY: good except in S winds. No yacht berths
alongside pier due to heavy harbour traffic.
STROMNESS: see 10.7.23
KIRKWALL: see 10.7.21
HOUTON BAY: see 10.7.27
ST MARY'S: N side of Kirk Sound; anchor in Bay of Ayre
or go alongside E side of pier.
KIRK SOUND (E entrance): anchor N or E end of Lamb
Holt.
DEER SOUND: anchor in Pool of Mirkady or off pier on
NW side of sound; very good shelter, no facilities.
BURRAY
EAST WEDDEL SOUND: excellent anchorage E side of
Churchill Barrier in centre of Weddel Bay.
HUNDA SOUND: good anchorage in all winds.
SOUTH RONALDSAY
ST MARGARET'S HOPE: anchor in centre of bay; beware
Flotta ferries using the pier.
HOY
LONG HOPE: anchor E of the pier on South Ness, which
is used by steamers/ferries or go alongside pier (safest at
slack water). Facilities: FW, ✉, V.
PEGAL BAY: good anchorage except in strong W winds.
ROUSAY
WYRE SOUND: anchor to E of Rousay pier, or go
alongside pier. Facilities: ✉, shop.
EDAY
FERS NESS BAY: good holding, and shelter from all
S winds.
WESTRAY
PIEROWALL: see 10.7.27
BAY OF MOCLETT: Excellent anchorage but open to
S winds.
SOUTH WICK: Small vessel anchorage on E of Papa
Westray, off the old pier or ESE of pier off Holm of Papa.
SANDAY
OTTERSWICK: good anchorage except in N or E winds.
NORTH BAY: on NW side of island, exposed to NW.
KETTLETOFT BAY: anchor in bay or go alongside pier;
very exposed to SE winds. Facilities: ✉, shop, hotel.
NORTH RONALDSAY
SOUTH BAY: anchor in middle of bay or go alongside
pier; open to S and E, and subject to swell.
LINKLET BAY: not a safe anchorage, open to E.
STRONSAY: see 10.7.22
AUSKERRY: see 10.7.27
NAVIGATION
Apart from the strong tidal streams and associated races,
navigation is easy in clear weather; see 10.7.5.
LIGHTS AND MARKS
The main harbours and sounds are well lit; for details see
10.7.4. Powerful lights are shown from Cantick Head,
Graemsay Island, Copinsay, Auskerry, Kirkwall, Brough of
Birsay, Sanday Island, North Ronaldsay and Noup Head.
RADIO TELEPHONE
Orkney Harbours Navigation Service (call: *Orkney Harbour
Radio*, Ch 16 20; 09 11 (H24)) covers Scapa Flow, Wide
Firth and Shapinsay Sound; see 10.7.21. For other local
stations see individual harbours. The local Coast Radio
Station is Orkney Radio (VHF Ch 16 26 (H24)), remotely
controlled from Wick Radio.
MEDICAL SERVICES
There are doctors available at Kirkwall, Stromness,
Rousay, Shapinsay, Eday, North Ronaldsay, Stronsay,
Sanday and Westray (Pierowall). Papa Westray is looked
after from Westray. The only hospital is at Kirkwall.
Serious cases are flown to Aberdeen (1 hour). The only
dental services are at Kirkwall.

ORKNEY ISLANDS *continued*

SALMON CAGES

Beware salmon cages in the following areas: —

Rysa Sound	Pegal Bay
Lyrawa Bay	Hunda Sound
Ore Bay	Kirk Sound
Widewall Bay	Carness Bay
St Margaret's Hope	Bay of Ham

OYSTERS AND LONGLINES

Beware Oysters and Longlines located as follows: —

Widenall Bay	Bay of Firth
Swandister Bay	Damsay Sound
Water Sound	Gairsay Milldurnday
Hunda Sound	Pierowall
Deer Sound	Bay of Skaill (Westray)
Inganess Bay	Longhope

KIRKWALL   10-7-21
Orkney Islands

CHARTS
Admiralty 2250, 1553, 2584; OS 6
TIDES
− 0045 Dover; ML 1.7; Duration 0620; Zone 0 (GMT).

Standard Port ABERDEEN (←)

Times				Height (metres)			
HW		LW		MHWS	MHWN	MLWN	MLWS
0300	1100	0200	0900	4.3	3.4	1.6	0.6
1500	2300	1400	2100				

Differences KIRKWALL

− 0305	− 0245	− 0305	− 0250	− 1.4	− 1.2	− 0.5	− 0.2

MUCKLE SKERRY

− 0230	− 0230	− 0230	− 0230	− 1.7	− 1.4	− 0.6	− 0.2

BURRAYNESS

− 0200	− 0200	− 0155	− 0155	− 1.0	− 0.9	− 0.3	0.0

SHELTER
Harbour well sheltered except in N winds or W gales
when there is a surge at the entrance. Safe anchorage for
small yachts between W pier head and Crowness Pt.
NAVIGATION
Waypoint 59°01'.40N 02°57'.00W, 008°/188° from/to
pierhead Lt, 2.2M. SW of the bay is a shoal.

LIGHTS AND MARKS
St Magnus Cathedral is very conspic.
RADIO TELEPHONE
VHF Ch 16; 12 (0900-1700 LT). Orkney Harbours
Navigation Service, call: *Orkney Harbour Radio* Ch 16 20;
09 11 (H24). Local Weather on Ch 11 at 0915 and
1715 LT.
TELEPHONE (0856)
Hr Mr 2292; Port Office 3636; CG & MRSC 3268;
⌗ 2108; Weather 3802; Marinecall 0898 500 451;
Police 2241; Dr 2763 or 3201.
FACILITIES
EC Wednesday; **Pier** P, D, FW CH; **N & E Quays** M;
Ellewick (Pier) M, D, FW, V; **Orkney SC** ☎ 2331, M, L,
C, AB; **Hatston Slip**; **John Scott and Millar** ☎ 3146,
Gas; **Town** P, D, ME, El, Sh, CH, V, Gas, R, Bar. ✉; Ⓑ
⇌ (Ferry to Scrabster, bus to Thurso); ✈.

STRONSAY   10-7-22
Orkney Islands

CHARTS
Admiralty 2622; OS 6
TIDES
− 0140 Dover; ML 1.7; Duration 0620; Zone 0 (GMT).

Standard Port ABERDEEN (←)

Times				Height (metres)			
HW		LW		MHWS	MHWN	MLWN	MLWS
0300	1100	0200	0900	4.3	3.4	1.6	0.6
1500	2300	1400	2100				

Differences DEER SOUND

− 0245	− 0245	− 0245	− 0245	− 1.1	− 0.9	− 0.3	0.0

SHELTER
Good from winds in all directions. Good anchorage
between seaward end of piers. Many other good sheltered
anchorages round the bay.

STRONSAY *continued*

NAVIGATION
Waypoint Quiabow stbd-hand buoy, 59°09'.83N 02°36'.20W, 009°/189° from/to No 1 Lt Buoy, 6.5 ca.
800m NE of Huip Ness is Quiabow, a submerged rock marked by G conical buoy.
Jack's Reef extends 400m E from Huip Ness, and is marked by G conical buoy.
A bank extends 350m SW from Papa Stronsay. Crampie Shoal is in mid-channel, marked by a buoy. The buoyed channel to Whitehall pier is dredged to 3.5 m.
Spit to E of Whitehall pier extends 400m N.
The E entrance is narrow and shallow.

LIGHTS AND MARKS
Pierhead Lts, 2FG (vert).

RADIO TELEPHONE
See Kirkwall.

TELEPHONE (085 76)
Hr Mr 257; CG & MRSC Kirkwall 3268; ⌗ Kirkwall 2108; Marinecall 0898 500 451; Police (0856) 2251; Dr 321.

FACILITIES
EC Thursday; **W. Pier** M, L, AB; **Main Pier** M, L, FW, AB; **Village (Whitehall)** P, D, V, Bar. ⊠; Ⓑ; ⇌ (ferry to Scrabster, bus to Thurso); ✈.

STROMNESS 10-7-23
Orkney Islands

CHARTS
Admiralty 2249, 2568; OS 6

TIDES
−0145 Dover; ML 2.0; Duration 0620; Zone 0 (GMT).

Standard Port ABERDEEN (←)

Times				Height (metres)			
HW		LW		MHWS	MHWN	MLWN	MLWS
0300	1100	0200	0900	4.3	3.4	1.6	0.6
1500	2300	1400	2100				

Differences **STROMNESS**
−0430	−0355	−0415	−0420	−0.7	−0.8	−0.1	−0.1

OTTERSWICK
−0355	−0355	−0355	−0355	−0.8	−0.7	−0.1	+0.1

PIEROWALL
−0355	−0355	−0355	−0355	−0.6	−0.6	−0.2	0.0

EYNHALLOW SOUND
−0400	−0400	−0355	−0355	−0.6	−0.6	−0.2	−0.1

SHELTER
Very good shelter with no tidal stream in harbour.
Anchorage in harbour or berth alongside.
The southern pier is the Northern Lights Pier and is for no other use. Berthing piers further N.

⚓ Contact Hr Mr

NAVIGATION
Waypoint 58°57'.00N 03°16'.90W, 137°/317° from/to front Ldg Lt, 0.88M. Tides in Hoy sound are very strong, entry should not be attempted in bad weather or when strong winds are against the tide. Spring tides can exceed 7 kn.

LIGHTS AND MARKS
Ldg Lts 317°, both FR 29/39m 11M (H24); W Trs; vis 307°-327°. Skerry of Ness Lt, Fl WG 4s 7m 7/4M; W shore-090°, G090°-shore.

RADIO TELEPHONE
VHF Ch 16; 12 (0900-1700 LT). (See also Kirkwall).

TELEPHONE (0856)
Hr Mr 850744; CG & MRSC Kirkwall 3268; ⌗ Kirkwall 2108; Marinecall 0898 500 451; Police 850222; Dr 850205.

FACILITIES
EC Thursday; **I. Richardson** ☎ 850321, Sh; **R. J. Merriman** ☎ 850361, El; **Walker Stewart** ☎ 850613, Ⓔ; **Marine Electronics** ☎ 850247, Ⓔ; **Town** FW, D, V, R, Bar, Gas, ⊠; Ⓑ; ⇌ (Ferry to Scrabster, bus to Thurso); ✈ (Kirkwall).
Note: Yachtsmen may contact, for help, **J. Stout** ☎ 850100, **I. Mackenzie** ☎ 850587 or **S. Mowat** ☎ 850624

SHETLAND ISLANDS   10-7-24

The Shetland Islands consist of approx 100 islands, holms and rocks of which fewer than 20 are inhabited. They lie 90 to 150 miles NNE of the Scottish mainland. By far the biggest island is Mainland with Lerwick, the capital, on the E side and Scalloway, the only other town and old capital, on the W side. At the very S there is the airport at Sumbrugh.

Two islands of the Shetland group not shown on the chartlet are Fair Isle, lying 20M SSW of Sumburgh Head (see 10.7.27) and owned by the National Trust for Scotland, and Foula lying 16M W of Mainland.

There are lifeboats at Lerwick and Aith, and there is a MRSC at Lerwick (0595) 2976. There is a Sector Base at Sella Ness (Sullom Voe), and an Auxiliary Station (Watch and Rescue) at Fair Isle.

CHARTS

Admiralty; general 3281, 3282, 3283; also 3291, 3292, 3294, 3295, 3297, 3298.

TIDES

Tidal information is related to Lerwick, Standard Port, see 10.7.25 below. In open waters tidal streams are mostly weak but in some sounds and other places rates of 6 kn or more can be attained and there are some dangerous races and overfalls. Tidal streams run mostly N and S or NW and SE, and cause dangerous disturbances at the N and S extremities of the islands and in the two main sounds (Yell Sound and Bluemull Sound/Colgrave Sound).

SHELTER

Weather conditions are bad in winter, and yachts should restrict visits to April to September. Around mid-summer it is light during all 24 hours. There are numerous anchorages but the following are those which it is safe to enter in all weathers.
LERWICK: see 10.7.25
CAT FIRTH: excellent shelter, anchor in approx 6m. Facilities: ✉ (Skellister), FW, V (both at Lax Firth).
GRUNNA VOE: off S side of Dury Voe, good shelter, anchor in 5-10m, good holding, beware prohibited anchoring areas. Facilities: V, FW, ✉ (Lax Firth).
SCALLOWAY: see 10.7.27.
VAILA SOUND: on SW of Mainland, use Easter Sound entrance (Wester Sound entrance is dangerous), very good shelter, anchor N of Salt Ness in 4 to 5m in mud. Facilities: FW, V, ✉.
GRUTING VOE: tides −0150 on Lerwick, anchor in main voe or in Browland, Seli or Scutta voes. Facilities: Stores and ✉ at Bridge of Walls (at head of Browland Voe).
SWARBACKS MINN: a large complex of voes and islands SE of St Magnus Bay. Best anchorages Uyea Sound or Aith Voe, both well sheltered and good holding. Facilities: former none; Aith FW, ✉, V, Bar, LB.
OLNA FIRTH: NE of Swarbacks Minn, beware rk 1 ca off S shore which dries. Anchor in firth, 4-8m or in Gon Firth or go alongside pier at Voe. Facilities: (Voe) FW, V, D, ✉, Bar.
URA FIRTH: NE of St Magnus Bay, anchor in Hills Wick on W side or in Hamar Voe on E side. The latter has excellent shelter in all weathers and good holding. Facilities: Hamar Voe, none; Hills Wick V, R, FW, V, ✉, D, ME, El, Sh, Bar.
HAMNA VOE: tides − 0200 on Lerwick, very good shelter, ldg line 153° old house on S shore with prominent rk on pt of W shore 3 ca within ent. Facilities: ✉ (½M), Stores, D (1½M), L (at pier).
S OF YELL SOUND: in the complex there are a number of good anchorages; Hamna Voe, Boatsroom Voe, West Lunna Voe, Dales Voe, Colla Firth. Tides − 0025 on Lerwick; all well protected and good holding. Facilities: none except at West Lunna Voe where there is a small hotel.
SULLOM VOE: tides −0130 on Lerwick. 6½M long deep water voe which has partly been taken over by the oil industry. Anchor above the narrows. Facilities at Brae, FW, V, ✉, D, ME, El, Sh, Bar.
MID YELL VOE: tides −0040 on Lerwick, enter through South Sd or Hascosay Sd, good anchorage in wide part of voe 2½-10m. Facilities: ✉, FW at pier on S side, D, Stores, ME, Sh, El.
BASTA VOE: good anchorage above shingle bank in 5-15m; good holding in places. Facilities: FW, Stores,

Motel, ✉.
BALTA SOUND; see 10.7.27.

NAVIGATION

A careful lookout must be kept for salmon farming cages and low lying mussel rafts (approx 100 in no), mostly marked by plastic yellow buoys and combinations of Y lights. The Clyde Cruising Club *Shetland Sailing Directions and Anchorages* is a most valuable publication for visitors. For general passage information see 10.7.5. Local magnetic anomalies may be experienced.

LIGHTS AND MARKS

See 10.7.4.

RADIO TELEPHONE

For Port Radio services see 10.7.25. Local Coast Radio Stations are Shetland Radio (Ch 16 27), and Collafirth Radio (Ch 16 24). Weather messages are broadcast by Shetland Radio (Ch 27) and Collafirth Radio (Ch 24) at 0703 and 1903 GMT. Gale warnings after next silence period and at 0303 0903 1503 2103 GMT.

TELEPHONE (0595)

Hr Mr Lerwick 2828; Sullom Voe 242551; Scalloway 636; Weather 2239.

FACILITIES

See shelter above.

LERWICK 10-7-25
Shetland Islands

CHARTS
Admiralty 3290, 3283, 3291; OS 4
TIDES
−0008 Dover; ML 1.3; Duration 0620; Zone 0 (GMT).

Standard Port LERWICK (→)

Times				Height (metres)			
HW		LW		MHWS	MHWN	MLWN	MLWS
0000	0600	0100	0800	2.2	1.6	0.9	0.5
1200	1800	1300	2000				

Differences FAIR ISLE
−0020 −0025 −0020 −0035 0.0 +0.1 0.0 −0.1
BLUE MULL SOUND
−0135 −0135 −0155 −0155 +0.4 +0.3 +0.1 0.0

Lerwick is a Standard Port and tidal predictions for each day of the year are given below.

SHELTER
Good. Hr Mr allocates berths in Small Dock or Albert Dock. Fishing boats occupy most alongside space. Anchoring prohibited for about 2 ca off the waterfront. Gremista marina is in North Harbour, mainly for local boats, and is a long way from the town.
NAVIGATION
Waypoint 60°06'.00N 01°08'.45W, 185°/005° from/to Twageos Pt Lt, 3.0M. From S, Bressay Sound is clear of dangers. From N, beware Soldian Rock (dries), Nive Baa (0.6m) and Green Holm (10m high) and the Brethren (two rocks 2m and 1.5m high).
LIGHTS AND MARKS
Kirkabister Ness Lt Fl(2) 30s 32m 21M on Bressay. Twageos Pt Lt LFl 6s 8m 6M. Loofa Baa S Cardinal Bn marks shoal between North and South Harbours. Light-buoys mark Middle Ground in North Harbour.
RADIO TELEPHONE
VHF Ch 16; 11 **12** (H24).
Other stations: Sullom Voe Ch 16; 12 **14** 20 (H24). Traffic information is available on request on Ch 14 or 16. Local weather forcasts will be broadcast on request on Ch 14 or 16. Scalloway Ch 16; 12 (Mon-Fri: 0800-1700. Sat: 0800-1200 LT). Balta Sound Ch 16 20 (occas).
TELEPHONE (0595)
Hr Mr 2828; CG Sullom Voe 2561; MRSC 2976; ☰ 4040; Weather 2239; Police 2110; Dr 3201.
FACILITIES
EC Wednesday (all day); **Harbour** Slip, M, P, D, L, FW, ME, Sh, Gas; **Malakoff** ☎ 5544, ME, El, Ⓔ, Sh, Slip, BY, CH, Sh, SM; **Thulecraft** ☎ 3192, CH, ME, Gas; **Hay** ☎ 3057, ACA; **Lerwick Harbour Trust** ☎ 2991, M, FW, D, P, AB; **Rearo Supplies** ☎ 2636, Gas; **Lerwick Boating Club** ☎ 2407, L, C, Bar, Ⓞ; **Town** V, R, Bar, CH, ✉; Ⓑ; ⇌ (ferry to Aberdeen); ✈.

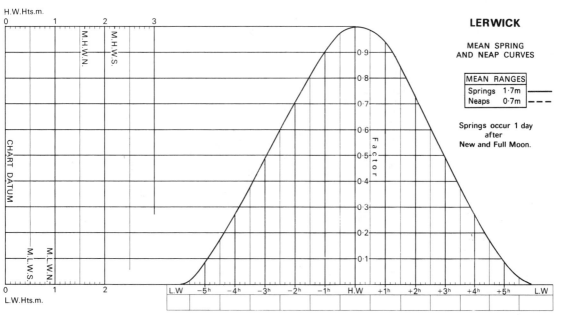

H.W.Hts.m.

LERWICK

MEAN SPRING AND NEAP CURVES

MEAN RANGES	
Springs	1·7m
Neaps	0·7m

Springs occur 1 day after New and Full Moon.

SHETLAND ISLANDS - LERWICK

LAT 60°09'N   LONG 1°08'W

TIMES AND HEIGHTS OF HIGH AND LOW WATERS   YEAR 1991

TIME ZONE UT(GMT)
For Summer Time add ONE hour in non-shaded areas

JANUARY

Day	Time	m	Time	m	Time	m	Time	m
1 TU	0443	0.6	1056	2.3	1714	0.3	2332	2.2
16 W	0453	0.8	1107	2.1	1726	0.6	2340	2.0
2 W	0529	0.6	1141	2.4	1802	0.3		
17 TH	0526	0.7	1140	2.2	1758	0.5		
3 TH	0019	2.2	0613	0.6	1227	2.4	1850	0.3
18 F	0014	2.0	0559	0.7	1215	2.2	1830	0.5
4 F	0105	2.1	0657	0.7	1311	2.3	1937	0.3
19 SA	0049	2.0	0633	0.7	1250	2.2	1904	0.5
5 SA	0150	2.0	0741	0.7	1357	2.2	2026	0.4
20 SU	0125	1.9	0708	0.7	1325	2.1	1939	0.5
6 SU	0236	1.8	0826	0.8	1443	2.1	2116	0.6
21 M	0202	1.9	0745	0.8	1404	2.1	2018	0.6
7 M	0323	1.7	0916	0.9	1533	1.9	2210	0.7
22 TU	0243	1.8	0827	0.8	1446	2.0	2103	0.7
8 TU	0415	1.6	1016	1.0	1630	1.8	2314	0.9
23 W	0328	1.8	0916	0.9	1536	1.9	2157	0.8
9 W	0520	1.6	1141	1.0	1746	1.7		
24 TH	0424	1.7	1020	0.9	1640	1.8	2308	0.9
10 TH	0025	0.9	0637	1.6	1308	1.0	1911	1.6
25 F	0536	1.7	1147	0.9	1808	1.8		
11 F	0130	1.0	0744	1.6	1412	1.0	2018	1.7
26 SA	0037	0.9	0700	1.8	1319	0.9	1940	1.8
12 SA	0222	1.0	0836	1.8	1502	0.9	2109	1.7
27 SU	0156	0.9	0811	1.9	1430	0.7	2050	1.9
13 SU	0306	1.9	0919	1.9	1544	0.8	2152	1.8
28 M	0256	0.8	0908	2.0	1527	0.5	2146	2.0
14 M	0345	0.9	0957	2.0	1620	0.7	2230	1.9
29 TU	0347	0.7	0957	2.2	1617	0.3	2235	2.1
15 TU	0420	0.8	1032	2.1	1654	0.6	2306	1.9
30 W	0432	0.6	1043	2.3	1704	0.2	2319	2.1
31 TH	0515	0.6	1126	2.4	1748	0.2		

FEBRUARY

Day	Time	m	Time	m	Time	m	Time	m
1 F	0001	2.1	0555	0.5	1209	2.4	1830	0.2
16 SA	0537	0.6	1151	2.2	1804	0.4		
2 SA	0042	2.1	0635	0.5	1250	2.3	1911	0.3
17 SU	0022	2.0	0610	0.6	1227	2.2	1837	0.4
3 SU	0121	2.0	0713	0.6	1331	2.2	1951	0.4
18 M	0058	2.0	0645	0.6	1303	2.2	1913	0.4
4 M	0159	1.9	0752	0.7	1412	2.0	2030	0.6
19 TU	0134	2.0	0722	0.6	1342	2.1	1951	0.5
5 TU	0238	1.8	0831	0.8	1454	1.9	2109	0.8
20 W	0214	1.9	0803	0.7	1425	2.0	2034	0.7
6 W	0318	1.7	0916	0.9	1540	1.7	2154	0.9
21 TH	0258	1.8	0852	0.8	1517	1.9	2128	0.8
7 TH	0406	1.6	1020	1.0	1642	1.6	2303	1.0
22 F	0351	1.7	0958	0.9	1624	1.7	2242	1.0
8 F	0517	1.6	1226	1.1	1831	1.5		
23 SA	0504	1.7	1133	0.9	1801	1.7		
9 SA	0049	1.1	0701	1.6	1353	1.0	2000	1.6
24 SU	0026	1.0	0638	1.7	1314	0.8	1940	1.7
10 SU	0200	1.1	0810	1.7	1447	0.9	2055	1.6
25 M	0151	0.9	0756	1.7	1424	0.6	2047	1.8
11 M	0249	1.0	0857	1.8	1527	0.8	2136	1.7
26 TU	0249	0.8	0854	2.0	1519	0.4	2138	1.9
12 TU	0327	0.9	0935	1.9	1601	0.7	2211	1.8
27 W	0335	0.7	0942	2.1	1606	0.3	2221	2.0
13 W	0401	0.8	1010	2.0	1632	0.6	2244	1.9
28 TH	0417	0.6	1026	2.2	1648	0.2	2300	2.0
14 TH	0433	0.7	1044	2.1	1702	0.5	2316	2.0
15 F	0505	0.6	1117	2.2	1733	0.4	2349	2.0

MARCH

Day	Time	m	Time	m	Time	m	Time	m
1 F	0456	0.5	1108	2.3	1728	0.2	2338	2.1
16 SA	0438	0.5	1050	2.2	1702	0.3	2320	2.1
2 SA	0534	0.4	1148	2.3	1805	0.2		
17 SU	0512	0.5	1126	2.2	1736	0.3	2355	2.1
3 SU	0014	2.0	0610	0.4	1227	2.2	1840	0.3
18 M	0548	0.4	1203	2.2	1812	0.3		
4 M	0049	2.0	0645	0.5	1305	2.1	1914	0.5
19 TU	0031	2.1	0624	0.5	1243	2.2	1849	0.4
5 TU	0123	1.9	0720	0.6	1342	2.0	1946	0.6
20 W	0110	2.0	0704	0.5	1326	2.1	1930	0.5
6 W	0158	1.8	0756	0.7	1420	1.8	2018	0.8
21 TH	0151	2.0	0749	0.6	1413	2.0	2016	0.7
7 TH	0234	1.7	0835	0.8	1502	1.7	2054	0.9
22 F	0237	1.8	0843	0.7	1509	1.8	2112	0.9
8 F	0315	1.7	0926	1.0	1555	1.5	2144	1.1
23 SA	0332	1.7	0932	0.7	1622	1.7	2232	1.0
9 SA	0410	1.6	1112	1.0	1736	1.4	2337	1.1
24 SU	0445	1.7	1132	0.7	1803	1.6		
10 SU	0548	1.5	1323	1.0	1937	1.5		
25 M	0020	1.0	0619	1.7	1307	0.6	1935	1.7
11 M	0130	1.1	0738	1.6	1419	0.9	2031	1.6
26 TU	0140	0.9	0738	1.8	1412	0.5	2035	1.7
12 TU	0222	1.0	0824	1.7	1458	0.7	2110	1.7
27 W	0233	0.8	0836	1.9	1503	0.4	2121	1.8
13 W	0300	0.9	0905	1.8	1530	0.6	2143	1.8
28 TH	0318	0.6	0924	2.0	1547	0.3	2200	1.9
14 TH	0333	0.7	0941	2.0	1600	0.5	2215	1.9
29 F	0357	0.5	1007	2.1	1626	0.2	2236	2.0
15 F	0405	0.6	1015	2.1	1630	0.4	2247	2.0
30 SA	0435	0.4	1047	2.2	1702	0.3	2311	2.0
31 SU	0511	0.4	1126	2.2	1736	0.3	2345	2.0

APRIL

Day	Time	m	Time	m	Time	m	Time	m
1 M	0546	0.4	1203	2.1	1809	0.4		
16 TU	0527	0.4	1144	2.2	1749	0.4		
2 TU	0018	2.0	0620	0.5	1240	2.0	1839	0.5
17 W	0008	2.1	0608	0.4	1229	2.2	1831	0.5
3 W	0052	1.9	0655	0.5	1317	1.9	1910	0.7
18 TH	0050	2.1	0653	0.4	1316	2.1	1916	0.6
4 TH	0126	1.9	0730	0.7	1355	1.8	1941	0.8
19 F	0134	2.0	0744	0.5	1408	1.9	2006	0.7
5 F	0202	1.8	0810	0.8	1437	1.6	2017	0.9
20 SA	0223	1.9	0842	0.5	1507	1.8	2106	0.9
6 SA	0242	1.7	0859	0.9	1529	1.5	2105	1.0
21 SU	0319	1.8	0955	0.6	1620	1.6	2224	1.0
7 SU	0333	1.6	1013	0.9	1646	1.4	2222	1.1
22 M	0429	1.7	1125	0.6	1752	1.6		
8 M	0442	1.5	1223	0.9	1845	1.4		
23 TU	0000	1.0	0554	1.7	1248	0.5	1914	1.6
9 TU	0031	1.1	0619	1.6	1330	0.8	1949	1.5
24 W	0115	0.9	0712	1.8	1350	0.4	2011	1.7
10 W	0137	1.0	0733	1.6	1412	0.7	2030	1.6
25 TH	0209	0.7	0812	1.8	1440	0.4	2055	1.7
11 TH	0220	0.9	0822	1.8	1447	0.6	2105	1.8
26 F	0254	0.6	0902	1.9	1522	0.4	2134	1.8
12 F	0257	0.7	0903	1.9	1521	0.5	2140	1.9
27 SA	0335	0.5	0945	2.0	1600	0.4	2210	1.9
13 SA	0333	0.6	0943	2.0	1555	0.4	2215	2.0
28 SU	0413	0.5	1026	2.0	1635	0.4	2244	1.9
14 SU	0409	0.5	1022	2.1	1632	0.3	2251	2.1
29 M	0450	0.4	1105	2.0	1708	0.5	2318	2.0
15 M	0447	0.4	1102	2.2	1710	0.3	2329	2.1
30 TU	0526	0.4	1142	2.0	1740	0.5	2352	2.0

Chart Datum: 1.22 metres below Ordnance Datum (Newlyn)

SHETLAND ISLANDS - LERWICK

LAT 60°09'N   LONG 1°08'W
TIMES AND HEIGHTS OF HIGH AND LOW WATERS

YEAR **1991**

TIME ZONE **UT(GMT)**
For Summer Time add ONE hour in non-shaded areas

Chart Datum: 1.22 metres below Ordnance Datum (Newlyn)

MAY

Day					Day				
1 W	0602	0.5	1219	1.9	16 TH	0558	0.3	1218	2.1
	1811	0.6				1818	0.5		
2 TH	0026	2.0	0637	0.5	17 F	0034	2.1	0647	0.3
	1257	1.8	1843	0.7		1309	2.0	1906	0.6
3 F	0102	1.9	0714	0.6	18 SA	0121	2.1	0740	0.3
	1337	1.7	1917	0.8		1402	1.9	1957	0.7
4 SA	0139	1.8	0754	0.7	19 SU	0211	2.0	0839	0.4
	1419	1.6	1956	0.9		1500	1.8	2055	0.8
5 SU	0219	1.7	0841	0.8	20 M	0306	1.9	0946	0.4
	1508	1.5	2043	1.0		1606	1.6	) 2203	0.9
6 M	0306	1.7	0938	0.8	21 TU	0409	1.8	1102	0.5
	1607	1.5	2143	1.0		1721	1.6	2323	0.9
7 TU	0401	1.6	1051	0.8	22 W	0523	1.7	1217	0.5
(2302	1.0	1723	1.4			1837	1.6		
8 W	0508	1.6	1210	0.8	23 TH	0038	0.8	0638	1.7
	1841	1.5				1319	0.5	1936	1.6
9 TH	0025	1.0	0623	1.6	24 F	0139	0.7	0744	1.7
	1309	0.7	1936	1.6		1410	0.5	2024	1.7
10 F	0126	0.9	0728	1.7	25 SA	0229	0.7	0838	1.8
	1356	0.6	2021	1.7		1454	0.5	2105	1.7
11 SA	0214	0.7	0822	1.8	26 SU	0314	0.6	0924	1.8
	1439	0.5	2102	1.9		1533	0.6	2144	1.8
12 SU	0259	0.6	0910	1.9	27 M	0355	0.6	1007	1.8
	1521	0.4	2143	2.0		1609	0.6	2220	1.9
13 M	0342	0.5	0956	2.0	28 TU	0434	0.5	1047	1.9
	1604	0.4	2224	2.1		1643	0.6	O 2256	2.0
14 TU	0426	0.4	1043	2.1	29 W	0511	0.5	1125	1.8
● 2307	2.1	1647	0.4			1717	0.7	2331	2.0
15 W	0511	0.3	1130	2.1	30 TH	0548	0.5	1203	1.8
	1732	0.4	2350	2.2		1750	0.7		
					31 F	0007	2.0	0624	0.5
						1242	1.8	1824	0.7

JUNE

Day					Day				
1 SA	0043	2.0	0700	0.6	16 SU	0108	2.2	0731	0.2
	1321	1.7	1900	0.8		1350	1.9	1943	0.6
2 SU	0120	1.9	0739	0.6	17 M	0156	2.1	0826	0.3
	1401	1.7	1938	0.8		1442	1.8	2034	0.7
3 M	0159	1.8	0820	0.6	18 TU	0247	2.0	0924	0.4
	1444	1.6	2020	0.9		1537	1.7	2131	0.8
4 TU	0240	1.8	0905	0.7	19 W	0342	1.9	1027	0.5
	1531	1.5	2109	0.9		1637	1.6	) 2238	0.8
5 W	0326	1.7	0956	0.7	20 TH	0446	1.8	1135	0.6
	1624	1.5	(2207	0.9		1745	1.5	2354	0.8
6 TH	0419	1.7	1055	0.7	21 F	0559	1.7	1240	0.7
	1726	1.5	2314	0.9		1852	1.6		
7 F	0521	1.7	1159	0.7	22 SA	0106	0.8	0713	1.6
	1833	1.6				1337	0.7	1950	1.6
8 SA	0026	0.9	0632	1.7	23 SU	0206	0.8	0815	1.7
	1303	0.7	1933	1.7		1426	0.7	2038	1.7
9 SU	0132	0.8	0741	1.8	24 M	0257	0.7	0906	1.7
	1400	0.6	2027	1.8		1509	0.7	2121	1.8
10 M	0228	0.7	0842	1.9	25 TU	0341	0.7	0951	1.7
	1453	0.6	2116	2.0		1548	0.7	2200	1.9
11 TU	0320	0.5	0937	2.0	26 W	0422	0.6	1032	1.8
	1543	0.5	2202	2.1		1624	0.7	2238	2.0
12 W	0410	0.4	1029	2.1	27 TH	0459	0.6	1111	1.8
	1631	0.5	● 2248	2.2		1659	0.7	O 2313	2.0
13 TH	0500	0.3	1119	2.1	28 F	0534	0.5	1148	1.8
	1719	0.5	2334	2.2		1734	0.7	2349	2.0
14 F	0550	0.2	1209	2.1	29 SA	0609	0.5	1224	1.8
	1807	0.5				1807	0.7		
15 SA	0020	2.2	0640	0.2	30 SU	0024	2.0	0642	0.5
	1259	2.0	1854	0.6		1300	1.8	1841	0.7

JULY

Day					Day				
1 M	0059	2.0	0717	0.5	16 TU	0136	2.2	0802	0.3
	1337	1.8	1917	0.8		1413	1.9	2006	0.6
2 TU	0135	2.0	0752	0.5	17 W	0223	2.1	0851	0.4
	1415	1.7	1954	0.8		1500	1.8	2054	0.7
3 W	0213	1.9	0831	0.6	18 TH	0311	1.9	0943	0.6
	1455	1.7	2036	0.8		1549	1.7	) 2150	0.8
4 TH	0254	1.8	0913	0.6	19 F	0406	1.8	1042	0.7
	1540	1.6	2124	0.9		1646	1.6	2303	0.9
5 F	0340	1.8	1003	0.7	20 SA	0514	1.6	1152	0.9
	1632	1.6	(2223	0.9		1758	1.6		
6 SA	0436	1.7	1104	0.7	21 SU	0033	0.9	0640	1.6
	1736	1.6	2336	0.9		1303	0.9	1913	1.6
7 SU	0548	1.7	1217	0.8	22 M	0147	0.9	0756	1.6
	1849	1.7				1401	0.9	2013	1.7
8 M	0056	0.8	0711	1.8	23 TU	0244	0.8	0852	1.6
	1331	0.8	1957	1.8		1450	0.9	2101	1.8
9 TU	0207	0.7	0825	1.8	24 W	0329	0.7	0938	1.7
	1434	0.7	2054	1.9		1531	0.9	2142	1.9
10 W	0306	0.6	0925	2.0	25 TH	0408	0.7	1017	1.8
	1529	0.6	2145	2.1		1608	0.8	2219	2.0
11 TH	0400	0.4	1019	2.1	26 F	0443	0.6	1053	1.9
	1619	0.6	● 2233	2.2		1642	0.7	O 2254	2.1
12 F	0450	0.3	1109	2.1	27 SA	0515	0.5	1127	1.9
	1706	0.5	2319	2.3		1714	0.7	2327	2.1
13 SA	0539	0.2	1156	2.1	28 SU	0546	0.5	1201	1.9
	1752	0.5				1746	0.7		
14 SU	0005	2.3	0627	0.1	29 M	0617	0.5	1234	1.9
	1243	2.1	1836	0.5		1818	0.7		
15 M	0051	2.3	0714	0.2	30 TU	0035	2.1	0648	0.5
	1328	2.0	1921	0.6		1308	1.9	1852	0.7
					31 W	0110	2.1	0722	0.5
						1343	1.9	1927	0.7

AUGUST

Day					Day				
1 TH	0146	2.0	0757	0.6	16 F	0239	2.0	0855	0.7
	1421	1.8	2006	0.8		1502	1.8	2105	0.8
2 F	0225	2.0	0837	0.7	17 SA	0328	1.8	0942	0.9
	1502	1.8	2050	0.8		1550	1.7	) 2208	1.0
3 SA	0311	1.9	0924	0.8	18 SU	0429	1.6	1047	1.0
	1553	1.7	2146	0.9		1654	1.7	2358	1.0
4 SU	0407	1.8	1025	0.9	19 M	0607	1.5	1225	1.1
	1654	1.7	2302	0.9		1831	1.6		
5 M	0522	1.7	1147	0.9	20 TU	0129	1.0	0739	1.6
	1815	1.7				1340	1.1	1947	1.7
6 TU	0036	0.9	0658	1.7	21 W	0228	0.9	0838	1.7
	1316	0.9	1935	1.8		1432	1.0	2038	1.8
7 W	0156	0.8	0817	1.8	22 TH	0311	0.8	0920	1.7
	1424	0.8	2037	2.0		1512	0.9	2119	1.9
8 TH	0257	0.5	0917	2.0	23 F	0346	0.7	0956	1.8
	1518	0.7	2130	2.1		1547	0.8	2155	2.0
9 F	0350	0.4	1008	2.1	24 SA	0418	0.6	1029	1.9
	1607	0.6	2216	2.3		1618	0.6	2228	2.1
10 SA	0438	0.2	1054	2.1	25 SU	0447	0.5	1100	2.0
	1651	0.5	● 2302	2.4		1649	0.7	O 2302	2.2
11 SU	0523	0.2	1138	2.1	26 M	0517	0.5	1132	2.0
	1733	0.5	2346	2.4		1721	0.6	2335	2.2
12 M	0607	0.2	1219	2.1	27 TU	0547	0.5	1204	2.1
	1814	0.5				1753	0.6		
13 TU	0029	2.4	0649	0.2	28 W	0009	2.2	0618	0.5
	1300	2.0	1854	0.5		1238	2.1	1826	0.6
14 W	0112	2.3	0731	0.4	29 TH	0045	2.2	0651	0.5
	1340	2.0	1935	0.6		1313	2.0	1902	0.7
15 TH	0155	2.1	0812	0.5	30 F	0122	2.1	0727	0.6
	1420	1.9	2018	0.7		1351	1.9	1941	0.7
					31 SA	0203	2.0	0808	0.7
						1432	1.9	2027	0.8

7

SHETLAND ISLANDS - LERWICK

LAT 60°09'N   LONG 1°08'W

TIMES AND HEIGHTS OF HIGH AND LOW WATERS

YEAR 1991

TIME ZONE UT(GMT)
For Summer Time add ONE hour in non-shaded areas

SEPTEMBER

Day	Time	m	Time	m	Time	m	Time	m
1 SU ☾	0251	1.9	0856	0.9	1522	1.8	2126	0.9
16 M	0351	1.6	0940	1.1	1600	1.7	2311	1.1
2 M	0352	1.8	1001	1.0	1626	1.8	2249	0.9
17 TU	0526	1.5	1131	1.2	1729	1.7		
3 TU	0516	1.7	1134	1.1	1752	1.8		
18 W	0102	1.0	0716	1.6	1313	1.2	1908	1.7
4 W	0030	0.9	0657	1.8	1310	1.0	1917	1.8
19 TH	0200	0.9	0813	1.7	1406	1.1	2006	1.8
5 TH	0149	0.7	0812	1.9	1415	0.9	2021	2.0
20 F	0241	0.8	0853	1.8	1445	1.0	2048	1.9
6 F	0247	0.5	0907	2.0	1506	0.8	2113	2.2
21 SA	0314	0.7	0927	1.9	1518	0.9	2124	2.0
7 SA	0336	0.4	0953	2.1	1550	0.6	2200	2.3
22 SU	0344	0.6	0958	2.0	1549	0.8	2158	2.1
8 SU ●	0421	0.3	1035	2.1	1631	0.5	2244	2.4
23 M ○	0413	0.6	1029	2.1	1621	0.7	2232	2.2
9 M	0502	0.2	1114	2.2	1711	0.5	2326	2.4
24 TU	0443	0.5	1101	2.2	1653	0.6	2307	2.3
10 TU	0542	0.3	1152	2.2	1750	0.5		
25 W	0515	0.6	1134	2.2	1728	0.6	2344	2.3
11 W	0007	2.4	0620	0.4	1230	2.1	1828	0.5
26 TH	0549	0.5	1209	2.2	1804	0.6		
12 TH	0048	2.3	0657	0.5	1306	2.1	1906	0.6
27 F	0022	2.3	0625	0.6	1247	2.2	1842	0.7
13 F	0128	2.1	0733	0.7	1343	2.0	1946	0.7
28 SA	0104	2.1	0704	0.7	1327	2.1	1925	0.7
14 SA	0209	1.9	0809	0.9	1422	1.9	2029	0.9
29 SU	0149	2.1	0748	0.8	1411	2.0	2016	0.8
15 SU ☽	0254	1.8	0848	1.0	1505	1.8	2125	1.0
30 M	0243	2.0	0841	1.0	1503	1.9	2121	0.9

OCTOBER

Day	Time	m	Time	m	Time	m	Time	m
1 TU ☾	0348	1.8	0951	1.1	1608	1.8	2247	0.9
16 W	0436	1.6	1013	1.2	1628	1.7		
2 W	0516	1.8	1129	1.1	1733	1.8		
17 TH	0008	1.0	0625	1.6	1217	1.2	1759	1.7
3 TH	0023	0.8	0652	1.8	1259	1.1	1857	1.9
18 F	0114	0.9	0732	1.7	1323	1.1	1914	1.8
4 F	0136	0.6	0800	1.9	1400	0.9	2002	2.0
19 SA	0157	0.9	0814	1.8	1406	1.0	2005	1.9
5 SA	0231	0.5	0853	2.0	1448	0.8	2054	2.2
20 SU	0232	0.8	0849	1.9	1442	0.9	2046	2.0
6 SU	0317	0.4	0932	2.1	1531	0.7	2141	2.3
21 M	0304	0.7	0922	2.0	1516	0.8	2125	2.1
7 M	0359	0.4	1011	2.1	1611	0.6	2224	2.3 ●
22 TU	0337	0.6	0956	2.1	1551	0.7	2203	2.2
8 TU	0438	0.4	1048	2.2	1650	0.5	2305	2.3
23 W ○	0411	0.6	1031	2.2	1628	0.6	2242	2.3
9 W	0515	0.5	1125	2.2	1728	0.5	2345	2.2
24 TH	0447	0.5	1107	2.3	1706	0.6	2323	2.3
10 TH	0551	0.6	1200	2.2	1805	0.6		
25 F	0525	0.6	1146	2.3	1747	0.6		
11 F	0024	2.2	0624	0.7	1236	2.1	1842	0.6
26 SA	0006	2.3	0605	0.6	1227	2.3	1830	0.6
12 SA	0104	2.1	0657	0.8	1312	2.1	1921	0.8
27 SU	0052	2.2	0649	0.8	1310	2.2	1918	0.6
13 SU	0144	1.9	0731	0.9	1350	2.0	2003	0.9
28 M	0142	2.1	0737	0.9	1357	2.1	2013	0.7
14 M	0228	1.8	0808	1.0	1431	1.9	2055	1.0
29 TU	0238	2.0	0833	1.0	1450	2.0	2119	0.7
15 TU ☾	0321	1.7	0857	1.2	1521	1.8	2210	1.0
30 W	0344	1.8	0942	1.1	1553	1.9	2239	0.7
31 TH	0505	1.8	1110	1.1	1710	1.9		

NOVEMBER

Day	Time	m	Time	m	Time	m	Time	m
1 F	0005	0.7	0631	1.8	1235	1.0	1831	1.9
16 SA	0620	1.6	1205	1.2	1759	1.8		
2 SA	0115	0.6	0737	1.8	1337	0.9	1939	2.0
17 SU	0052	0.9	0718	1.7	1310	1.1	1908	1.8
3 SU	0209	0.6	0826	1.9	1427	0.8	2034	2.1
18 M	0139	0.8	0804	1.9	1358	1.0	2003	1.9
4 M	0255	0.5	0908	2.0	1511	0.7	2121	2.1
19 TU	0221	0.8	0844	2.0	1442	0.8	2051	2.0
5 TU	0336	0.5	0947	2.1	1552	0.6	2205	2.2
20 W	0302	0.7	0924	2.1	1524	0.7	2137	2.1
6 W ●	0414	0.6	1024	2.1	1632	0.6	2246	2.2
21 TH ○	0343	0.6	1004	2.2	1606	0.6	2222	2.2
7 TH	0450	0.6	1100	2.2	1710	0.6	2326	2.2
22 F	0425	0.6	1045	2.3	1650	0.6	2308	2.3
8 F	0524	0.7	1136	2.2	1748	0.6		
23 SA	0508	0.6	1127	2.3	1735	0.5	2354	2.3
9 SA	0005	2.1	0557	0.8	1212	2.2	1825	0.7
24 SU	0553	0.7	1211	2.3	1822	0.5		
10 SU	0044	2.0	0630	0.9	1248	2.1	1903	0.7
25 M	0043	2.2	0639	0.7	1256	2.3	1912	0.5
11 M	0124	1.9	0705	1.0	1326	2.0	1944	0.8
26 TU	0134	2.1	0728	0.8	1344	2.2	2007	0.5
12 TU	0207	1.8	0743	1.0	1406	2.0	2030	0.9
27 W	0229	2.0	0821	0.9	1436	2.1	2108	0.6
13 W	0254	1.7	0828	1.1	1450	1.9	2124	0.9
28 TH ☾	0329	1.9	0923	1.0	1534	2.0	2218	0.6
14 TH ☽	0350	1.6	0924	1.2	1542	1.8	2232	1.0
29 F	0437	1.8	1036	1.0	1642	1.9	2335	0.7
15 F	0500	1.6	1039	1.2	1645	1.7	2351	0.9
30 SA	0553	1.7	1157	1.0	1759	1.9		

DECEMBER

Day	Time	m	Time	m	Time	m	Time	m
1 SU	0045	0.7	0702	1.8	1308	0.9	1912	1.9
16 M	0604	1.7	1158	1.1	1803	1.8		
2 M	0143	0.7	0758	1.8	1405	0.8	2013	2.0
17 TU	0036	0.9	0710	1.8	1310	1.0	1917	1.8
3 TU	0232	0.7	0844	1.9	1454	0.8	2105	2.0
18 W	0138	0.8	0806	1.9	1410	0.9	2022	1.9
4 W	0314	0.7	0925	2.0	1538	0.7	2150	2.0
19 TH	0232	0.8	0856	2.0	1502	0.7	2117	2.1
5 TH	0353	0.7	0942	2.1	1619	0.7	2232	2.0
20 F	0321	0.7	0942	2.2	1551	0.7	2208	2.2
6 F ●	0429	0.8	1041	2.1	1658	0.6	2311	2.0
21 SA ○	0409	0.7	1027	2.3	1638	0.5	2257	2.2
7 SA	0504	0.8	1117	2.2	1736	0.6	2350	2.0
22 SU	0456	0.6	1112	2.3	1726	0.4	2345	2.2
8 SU	0538	0.8	1153	2.2	1812	0.6		
23 M	0542	0.6	1157	2.4	1814	0.3		
9 M	0027	2.0	0611	0.9	1229	2.1	1848	0.7
24 TU	0033	2.2	0627	0.6	1243	2.4	1903	0.3
10 TU	0106	1.9	0646	0.9	1305	2.1	1925	0.7
25 W	0121	2.1	0714	0.7	1329	2.3	1954	0.3
11 W	0144	1.8	0722	0.9	1342	2.0	2003	0.8
26 TH	0211	2.0	0803	0.8	1418	2.2	2048	0.4
12 TH	0225	1.8	0801	1.0	1422	1.9	2044	0.8
27 F	0302	1.9	0855	0.8	1510	2.1	2147	0.6
13 F	0309	1.7	0846	1.0	1504	1.9	2131	0.9
28 SA ☾	0359	1.9	0956	0.8	1609	1.9	2254	0.7
14 SA	0358	1.7	0938	1.1	1553	1.8	2225	0.9
29 SU	0503	1.7	1111	0.9	1721	1.8		
15 SU	0456	1.7	1042	1.1	1652	1.8	2328	0.9
30 M	0006	0.8	0616	1.7	1235	0.9	1843	1.8
31 TU	0113	0.8	0725	1.7	1345	0.9	1955	1.8

Chart Datum: 1.22 metres below Ordnance Datum (Newlyn)

SCRABSTER 10-7-26
Caithness

CHARTS
Admiralty 1462, 2162, 1954; OS 12
TIDES
−0240 Dover; ML 3.2; Duration 0615; Zone 0 (GMT).

Standard Port ABERDEEN (←)

Times				Height (metres)			
HW		LW		MHWS	MHWN	MLWN	MLWS
0300	1000	0100	0800	4.3	3.4	1.6	0.6
1500	2200	1300	2000				

Differences SCRABSTER
−0455	−0510	−0500	−0445	+0.7	+0.3	+0.5	+0.2

STROMA
−0320	−0320	−0320	−0320	−1.2	−1.1	−0.3	−0.1

SHELTER
Very good except in strong NE winds. Anchoring is not recommended. Secure alongside NE wall and contact Hr Mr. Yachts normally use Inner Basin.
NAVIGATION
Waypoint 58°36′.60N 03°32′.00W, 098°/278° from/to E pier Lt, 0.25M. Can be entered at all tides in all weathers. Do not confuse harbour lights with those of Thurso. Beware fishing vessels, merchant ships and the Orkney ferries.
LIGHTS AND MARKS
There are no leading marks or lights. Entry is straightforward once the Lt on end of pier QG 6m 4M has been located.
RADIO TELEPHONE
VHF Ch 16; 12 (0800-2200 LT).
TELEPHONE (0847)
Hr Mr 62779; CG Wick 62332; MRSC Kirkwall 3268; ✠ 62727; Marinecall 0898 500 451; Police 63222; Dr. 63154.
FACILITIES
EC Thurso — Thursday; **Harbour** Slip, D, L, FW, ME, El, C (30 ton mobile), CH, AB, R, Bar; **Pentland Firth YC** M, R, Bar; **Thurso** V, R, Bar. ✉; Ⓑ; ⇌; ✈ (Wick).

MINOR HARBOURS AND ANCHORAGES 10.7.27

CULLEN, Banff, 57°41′N, 2°49′W, Zone 0 (GMT), Admty Chart 222. HW +0045 on Dover, −0135 on Aberdeen; HW height −0.3m on Aberdeen; ML 2.4m; Duration 0555. Shelter good but entrance hazardous in strong winds from N and W. Harbour, consisting of two basins, dries, access HW∓4 approx. Moor in inner basin if under 1m draught. Beware local boat mooring right across inner basin entrance. There are no lights or marks. Popular recreational harbour. Facilities: Hr Mr ☎ 41116; **Cullen Bay Hotel** ☎ 40432 R, Bar; **Town** V, R, Bar, ✉.

PORTKNOCKIE, Banff, 57°42′N, 2°51′W, Zone 0 (GMT), Admty chart 222. HW +0045 on Dover, −0135 on Aberdeen; HW height −0.3m on Aberdeen; ML 2.3m; Duration 0555. Shelter is good and is one of the safest harbours on S side of Moray Firth but care is needed entering in strong N winds. Scend is often experienced. Most of inner harbour dries but berth on W or N wall — firm sandy bottom. W Tr on S pier head. Yachts use NW jetties. Orange street lights surround the harbour — two conspic white lights are the leading lights of approx 130°, on S pier. Facilities: Hr Mr ☎ Cullen 40705; EC Wed; AB, FW, C (15 ton), CH; **D Reid** Slip, L, Sh. Dr. ☎ Cullen 40272, **Town** Ⓑ, P, ✉, V, Bar.

FINDOCHTY, Banff, 57°42′N, 2°54′W, Zone 0 (GMT), Admty chart 222. HW +0045 on Dover, −0140 on Aberdeen; HW height −0.2m on Aberdeen; ML 2.3m; Duration 0550. Good shelter in inner basin which has pontoon berths for 60 yachts. Access (1.5m draught) HW∓4. Outer basin dries and has numerous rocky outcrops. Entrance faces N and is 20m wide. There are two FW Ldg Lts leading into Outer Basin. Facilities: Hr Mr ☎ Cullen 40715. **Town** V, R, Bar, ✉.

FORTROSE, Ross and Cromarty, 57°35′N, 4°08′W, Zone 0 (GMT), Admty charts 1078, 223. HW +0055 on Dover, −0125 on Aberdeen; HW height 0.0m on Aberdeen; ML 2.5m; Duration 0620. See 10.7.16. Small Hr which dries, well protected by Chanonry Ness on E. Beware Craigan Rock ESE of Hr entrance. Ldg line 296°, Broomhill House (conspic on hill to NW) in line with school house spire. Follow line until just beyond G buoy Iso G, then turn W to avoid Craigan Rock. There are no Hr Lts. Lt Ho on Chanonry Pt Oc 6s 12m 15M, vis 148°−073°. Facilities: EC Thurs; AB, P, ✉, Ⓑ, D, Dr, L, M, R, YC, Slip, V; **Chanonry SC** (near pier); **Fortrose YC**; **Pagwari** ☎ 20356, Gas.

CROMARTY FIRTH, Ross and Cromarty, 57°41′N, 4°02′W, Zone 0 (GMT), Admty charts 1889, 1890. HW +0100 on Dover, −0135 on Aberdeen; HW height 0.0m on Aberdeen; ML 2.5m; Duration 0625. See 10.7.16. Excellent harbour extending 7.5M W and then 9M SW. Good shelter can always be found depending on the direction of the wind. The harbour is run by Cromarty Firth Ports Authority. Visitors should report to the Port Manager (VHF Ch 16). Beware rocks and reefs round N and S Sutor, N and S of entrance. Cromarty harbour is protected by two piers, and dries. Cromarty Lt Ho, on the Ness, Oc WR 10s 18m 14/11M, R079°−088°, W088°−275°, obsc by N Sutor when bearing less than 253°. A Lt is shown 5m from head of S pier 1st Oct to 31st Mar. Anchorage in approx 6m 2 ca W of S pier head. Cromarty Firth Port Control VHF Ch 11 16 13 (H24). Facilities: EC Wed; AB, Bar, C(3 ton) D, FW, ✉, P, R, V, L; **Invergordon Boating Club**; **Tomlinson** ☎ 852233, Gas.

7

MINOR HARBOURS AND ANCHORAGES *Continued*

DORNOCH FIRTH, Ross and Cromarty/Sutherland 57°51' N, 4°08' W, Zone 0 (GMT), Admty charts 223, 115. HW + 0115 on Dover, −0120 on Aberdeen; HW height +0.1m on Aberdeen; ML 2.5m; Duration 0605. Excellent shelter but difficult entrance. Firth extends 15M inland, entered between N edge of Whiteness Sands and S edge of Gizzen Briggs. There are many shifting sandbanks, especially near the entrance. Anchorages in 7m ¾M ESE of Dornoch Pt (sheltered from NE swell by Gizzen Briggs), in 7m 2 ca SSE of Ard na Cailc, in 3.3m 1M below Bonar Bridge. (Admiralty chart coverage ceases ¼M E of Ferry Pt.) Light on Tarbat Ness Fl(4) 30s 53m 24M. R Lt shown on Tain bombing range when firing in progress. Very limited facilities at Ferrytown and Bonar Bridge. Dornoch:- EC Thur; V, P, ✉, Dr, Ⓑ, R, Bar. Note: A bridge is under construction southwards from Ard na Cailc which will have min clearance of 11m at MHWS under the centre arch.

GOLSPIE, Sutherland, 57°58' N, 3°59' W, Zone 0 (GMT), Admty chart 223. HW +0045 on Dover, −0130 sp, −0215 np on Aberdeen; HW height −0.3m on Aberdeen; ML 2.3m; Duration 0610. See 10.7.18. Golspie pier projects 60m across foreshore with arm projecting SW at the head, giving shelter during NE winds. Beware The Bridge, a bank (0.3m to 1.8m) running parallel to the shore ¼M to seaward of pier head. Seas break heavily over The Bridge in NE winds. There are no lights. To enter, keep Duke of Sutherlands Memorial in line with boathouse SW of pier at 316° until Church spire in middle of village in line with head of pier at 006°, then keep on those marks. Harbour gets very congested; good anchorage off pier. Facilities: EC Wed; **Lindsay** ☎ 3212, Gas; **Town** Bar, D, Dr, Ⓗ, L, M, P, ✉, R, ⇌, V, Ⓑ.

LYBSTER, Caithness, 58°18' N, 3°17' W, Zone 0 (GMT), Admty chart 115. HW +0020 on Dover, −0150 sp −0215 np on Aberdeen; HW height −0.6m on Aberdeen; ML 2.1m; Duration 0620. Excellent shelter in Inner Hr. Berth on E side of W pier at N end. Beware rocks on E side of entrance; entrance difficult in strong E winds. Min depth 2.5m in entrance. S pier head Lt Oc R 6s 10m 3M shown during fishing season. Facilities: EC Thurs; FW on S quay, **Town** Bar, D, P, R, V.

HOUTON BAY, Orkney Islands, 58°55' N, 3°11' W, Zone 0 (GMT), Admty chart 2568. HW −0140 on Dover, −0400 on Aberdeen; HW height +0.3m on Kirkwall; ML 1.8m; Duration 0615. Anchorage in the bay in approx 5.5m at centre, sheltered from all winds. The entrance is to the E of the island Holm of Houton; entrance channel dredged 3.5m for 15m each side of Ldg line. Care should be taken not to obstruct merchant vessels & ferries plying to Flotta. Ldg Lts in line at 316°, Front Fl G 3s 8m, Rear FG 16m. Ro Ro terminal in NE corner marked by Iso R 4s. There are no facilities, except a slip close E of piers.

SHAPINSAY, Orkney Islands, 59°03' N, 2°54' W, Zone 0 (GMT), Admty charts 2249, 2250. HW −0015 on Dover, −0330 on Aberdeen; HW height −1.0m on Aberdeen. Good shelter in Ellwick Bay off Balfour on SW end of island in 2½ to 3m. Enter bay passing W of Helliar Holm which has Lt (Fl WRG 10s) on S end. Keep mid-channel. Balfour Pier Lt Q WRG 5m 3/2M; vis G270°-010°, W010°-020°, R020°-090°. Tides in The String reach 5 kn at springs. Facilities: ✉, P (from garage), shop.

PIEROWALL, Orkney Islands, 59°19' N, 2°58' W, Zone 0 (GMT), Admty chart 2622. HW −0135 on Dover, −0355 on Aberdeen; HW height +0.7m on Kirkwall; ML 2.2m; Duration 0620. See 10.7.23. The bay is a good anchorage in 2m to 7m and well protected. Deep water berths at Gill Pt. are available − consult Hr Mr (Tel. Westray 273). Beware Skelwick Skerry rocks approaching from S and the rocks off Vest Ness (extent approx 1 ca off shore) coming from the N. The N entrance through Papa Sound should not be used unless local knowledge is available. There is a dangerous tide race off Mull Head at the N of Papa Westray. Lights: E pier head Fl WRG 3s 7m 11/7M; G254°−276°, W276°−291°, R291°−308°, G308°−215°. W pier head 2 FR (vert) 4/6m 3M. Facilities: Hr Mr VHF Ch 16 FW (at Gill Pier) P and D at garage in Pierowall, Bar, ✉, R, V.

AUSKERRY, Orkney Islands 59°02' N, 2°34' W, Zone 0 (GMT), Admty chart 2250. HW −0010 on Dover, −0315 on Aberdeen; HW height −1.0m on Aberdeen. Small island at entrance to Stronsay Firth has small harbour on W side. Safe entrance and good shelter except in SW winds. Auskerry Sound and Stronsay Firth are dangerous with wind over tide. Ent min 3.5m and alongside pier 1.2m. Yachts can lie secured between ringbolts at entrance and the pier. Auskerry Lt at S end Fl 20s 34m 18M from W Tr. There are no facilities.

FAIR ISLE, Shetland Islands, 59°32' N, 1°37' W, Zone 0 (GMT), Admty chart 2622. HW −0030 on Dover, −0020 on Lerwick; HW height −0.1m on Lerwick; ML 1.4m; Duration 0620. See 10.7.25. Good shelter in North Haven although open to NE winds. Lie alongside pier or anchor in approx 2m. Beware rocks all round the island particularly in the 'so called' South Harbour which is not recommended. There is a light at each end; Skadan in the S Fl (4) 30s 32m 24M; vis 260°−146° but obscured close inshore from 260°−282°; Horn(2) 60s. In the N, Skroo Fl (2) 30s 80m 22M (vis about 087°−358°), Horn (3) 45s. Ldg Marks at 199°, the Stack of North Haven in line with top of Sheep Craig leads into North Haven. Facilities: there is a shop and ✉ at N Shriva, and a bi-weekly ferry to Shetland.

SCALLOWAY, Shetland Islands, 60°08' N, 1°17' W, Zone 0 (GMT), Admty chart 3294. HW −0200 on Dover, −0150 on Lerwick; HW height −0.5m on Lerwick; ML 0.9m; Duration 0620. A good sheltered anchorage available in all weathers but care is needed passing through the islands in strong SW winds. Anchor off Scalloway 6 to 10m, in Hamna Voe (W Burra), almost land-locked, in 6m approx, but bottom foul with old moorings. Lights; Scalloway Hr, Moores Slipway jetty head 2 FR (vert) 4/2m 3M; Blacksness W pier head 2 FG (vert) 6/4m 3M; E pier head Oc R 7s 5m 3M; Fugla Ness Fl (2) WRG 10s 20m 10/7M; W Tr; vis G014°−032°, W032°−082°, R082°−134°, W134°−shore. Lt Oc WRG 10s 7m 14/11M, in posn 60°08'.11N 01°16'.39W, vis G045.7°−056.8°, W056.8°−058.8°, R058.8°−069.9°. VHF Ch 16; 12 (office hours). Facilities: EC Thurs; Bar, C, D, El, FW, ME, ✉, Sh, Slip, R, V, AB, SM, BY, CH, M, P; **Scalloway Boating Club** ☎ 408; **W. Moore** ☎ 215, Slip, ME, El, Sh; **H. Williamson** ☎ 645, El.

BALTA SOUND, Shetland Islands, 60°44' N, 0°48' W, Zone 0 (GMT), Admty chart 3293. HW −0105 on Dover, −0055 on Lerwick; HW height +0.2m on Lerwick; ML 1.3m; Duration 0640. The Sound and Balta Hr form a large landlocked harbour with good shelter from all winds. Beware kelp which causes bad holding. R can buoys mark 4m patches. Anchor near Sandisons Wharf in approx 6m. Light on S end of Balta I Fl WR 10s 17m 10/)M; W249°−010°, R010°−060°, W060°−154°. Safest entry is between Huney I and Balta I. VHF Ch 16; 20 (office hours) Facilities: at BY FW, D, El, ME, Sh; Hotel by pier; **Baltasound village**, Bar, R, V, ✉.

KYLE OF TONGUE, Sutherland, 58°32' N, 4°24' W (Rabbit I.), Zone 0 (GMT), Admty Charts 1954, 2720. HW −0325 on Dover, +0050 on Ullapool; HW height −0.4m on Ullapool. The Kyle runs about 7M inland and contains many sheltered anchorages. Entry (see 10.7.5) should not be attempted in strong N winds. Anchorages at Talmine (W of Rabbit I.) protected from all but NE winds; at Skullomie Hr, protected from E winds; off Mol na Coinne, a small bay on SE side of Eilean nan Ron, protected from W and N winds; off S of Rabbit I., protected from W to N winds. There are no lights or leading marks. Facilities: Limited supplies at Talmine shop (½M from slip) or at Coldbachie (1½M from Skullomie).

LOCH ERIBOLL, Sutherland, 58°29' N, 4°39' W, Zone 0 (GMT), Admty chart 2076. Tidal figures taken at Rispond: HW −0345 on Dover, +0035 on Ullapool; HW height −0.5m on Ullapool; ML 2.7m; Duration 0610. See 10.8.7. Two good anchorages; in Rispond Bay on W side of loch, entrance good in all but E winds, in approx 5m; in bays to N and S of peninsular at Heilam on E side of loch. Yachts can enter Rispond Hr, access approx HW∓3, where they can dry out alongside. There are no lights or marks. Facilities at Rispond are extremely limited.

VOLVO PENTA SERVICE

Sales and service centres in area 8
ARGYLL *Kilmelford Yacht Haven* Kilmelford, OBAN PA34 4XD
Tel (085 22) 248.

Area 8

North-West Scotland
Stornoway to Craobh Haven

VOLVO PENTA

8

North-West Scotland

10-8-2

432

Key to Symbols

☎	Coast Station/Port Radio – frequencies
RC	Marine radiobeacon– call sign, sequence, frequency and range (nm)
RC Aero	Aeronautical radiobeacon–call sign, frequency and range (nm)
ⓘ	See for harbour information/tidal data
☼	Weather (tel. or times). M - Marinecall
CG	HM Coastguard MRCC ⚠ MRSC
CG	HM Coastguard Sector Base
LB	RNLI Lifeboat over 10m
⚠	RNLI Lifeboat under 10m
✈	SAR Helicopter base
☆	Principal lights
⚓	Light-vessel
☸	Lanby
RG	Emergency VHF DF
*	See 10.8.19

Kilda Radio
☎℗	VHF 16;08
RC Aero	KL 338 ···-·· 30

Loch Maddy*
☎℗	VHF 16;12

Skye Radio
☎℗⊙	VHF 16 24
☼	0703 1903

Portree
ⓘ	10.8.9
☎℗	VHF 16;08

Eilean Glas
RC	LG ··-· ---·· 6 294.2 50

Stornoway
ⓘ	10.8.7
☎℗	VHF 16;12
RC Aero	STN ···- - ---· 669.5 60 Stornoway ⚠CG

Ullapool
	Standard Port
ⓘ	10.8.8
☎℗	VHF 16;12
☼	M 0898 500 464

Cape Wrath
RC	CW -·-· ·-- 1 298.8 50

Butt of Lewis
RC	BL -··· ·-·· 2,5 298.8 150

Lewis Radio
☎℗⊙	VHF 16 05
☼	0703 1903

Gallan Head
☎℗⊙	Hebrides Radio MF1866 VHF 16 26
☼	0703 1903

St Kilda*

West Loch Tarbert*

East Loch Tarbert*

Loch Shell*

Loch Seaforth

Harris

North Uist

Benbecula

Lewis

Tiumpan Head

Stoerhead

Loch Laxford*

Lochinver*

Loch Ewe*

Loch Gairloch*

Loch a'Bhraige*

Sound of Raasay

Rona

Uig

Loch Torridon

Rubn'Re (Rubha Reidh)

Summer Isles

Badcall Bay

Loch Inchard

Loch Eriboll

Pentland CG

Cape Wrath

Stornoway CG

Stornoway CG

Oban CG

Oban CG

58°N

58° N

57° 30'N

57° 30'N

5°W

6°W

7°W

8°W

433

Caledonian Canal 10.8.15
ⓘ

Fort William 10.8.14
ⓘ

Oban
Standard Port
ⓘ 10.8.16 📻 VHF 16;12
M–0898
500 463
☀️ Oban

Mallaig 10.8.10
ⓘ 📻 VHF 16;09
📞ᴾ/ᴿ M–0898
☀️ 500 464

Connel/Oban
Ⓡ CNL •––• –•
Aero 404 15

Corpach
CG

Loch Melfort 10.8.17
ⓘ 📞ᴾ/ᴿ VHF 16 **80**

Loch Sunart 10.8.11
ⓘ

Loch Linnhe

Glenelg

Loch Hourn

Loch Nevis*

Arisaig*

Eigg*

Sound of Sleat
LB

Dunstaffnage*
LB

Lismore I.
☆

Scotport

Gulf of Corryvrecken

Oigh Sgeir
Ⓡ OR •–– ––• –••
5 294.2 50

Canna*

Rhum

Muck

Ardnamurchan Point ☆

Rubha nan Gall
CG

Tobermory 10.8.12
ⓘ 📻 VHF 16;12
📞ᴾ/ᴿ

Loch Aline 10.8.13
ⓘ

Mull

Bunessan*

Iona

Craobh Haven 10.8.18
ⓘ 📞ᴾ/ᴿ VHF 16 **80** 74

Jura

Colonsay

Oronsay

Coll*

Arinagour*

Tiree
RG ☆ Tiree

Skerryvore ☆

Dubh Artach ☆

Oban CG
Clyde CG

Loch Boisdale*

Barra Island

Barra

Castle Bay*

Stornoway CG
Oban CG

Barra Head
Ⓡ BD –••• –••
1 308 200/70

LB

Variation
9°W (1991)

0

90

180

270

10.8.3 AREA 8 TIDAL STREAMS

5 Hours before HW Dover (0050 before HW Ullapool)

4 Hours before HW Dover (0010 after HW Ullapool)

3 Hours before HW Dover (0110 after HW Ullapool)

2 Hours before HW Dover (0210 after HW Ullapool)

1 Hour before HW Dover (0310 after HW Ullapool)

HW Dover (0410 after HW Ullapool)

Eastward 10.7.3   Southward 10.9.3

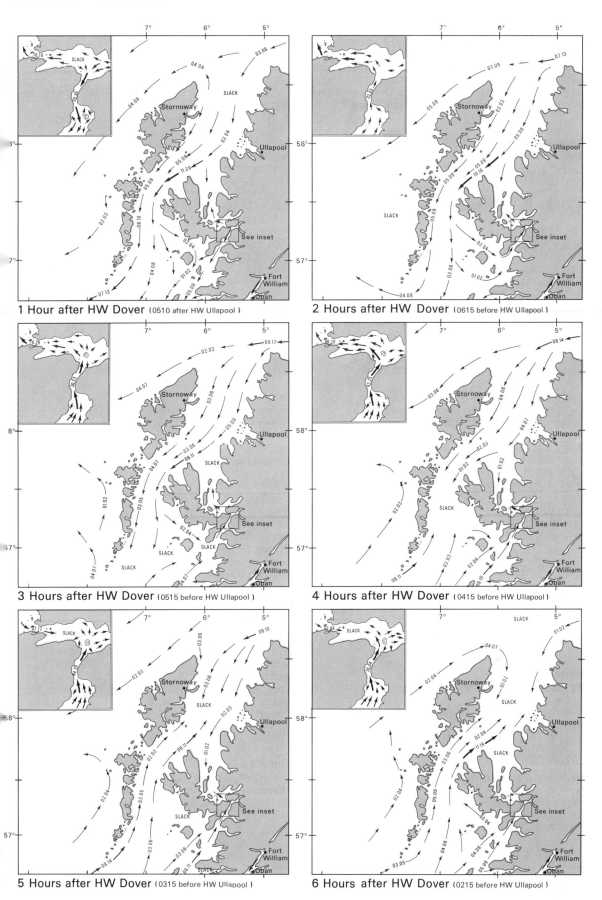

1 Hour after HW Dover (0510 after HW Ullapool)

2 Hours after HW Dover (0615 before HW Ullapool)

3 Hours after HW Dover (0515 before HW Ullapool)

4 Hours after HW Dover (0415 before HW Ullapool)

5 Hours after HW Dover (0315 before HW Ullapool)

6 Hours after HW Dover (0215 before HW Ullapool)

8

10.8.4   LIGHTS, FOG SIGNALS AND WAYPOINTS

Abbreviations used below are given in 10.0.3. Principal lights are in **bold** print, places in CAPITALS, and light-vessels, light floats and Lanbys in *CAPITAL ITALICS*. Unless otherwise stated lights are white. m—elevation in metres; M—nominal range in n. miles. Fog signals are in *italics*. Useful waypoints are underlined use those on land with care. See 4.2.2.

Cape Wrath 58°37'·55N 04°59'·87W Fl (4) 30s 122m **24M**; W Tr; RC; *Horn(3) 45s.*
Rockall 57°35'·8N 13°41'·3W Fl 15s 19m 13M (unreliable).

SCOTLAND—WEST COAST

LOCH INCHARD
Rubha na Lecaig 58°27'·43N 05°04'·51W Fl(2) 10s 30m 8M.
Loch Bervie Ldg Lts 327°. Front 58°27'·5 05°03'·03W Oc G 8s 16m 9M; W square, Or triangle on Gy Tr. Rear, 330m from front, Oc G 8s 26m 8M; W square, Or triangle, on Gy Tr.
Stoer Head 58°14'·4N 05°24'·0W Fl 15s 59m **24M**; W Tr.

LOCH INVER
Glas Leac 58°08'·7N 05°16'·3W Fl WRG 3s 7m; vis W071°-080°, R080°-090°, G090°-103°, W103°-111°, R111°-243°, W243°-251°, G251°-071°.
Off Aird Ghlas QG 3m 1M; B column, W bands.
Culag Harbour, breakwater head 2 FG (vert) 6m.
Soyea Island Fl(2) 10s 34m 6M.
Summer Isles, Old Dornie, new pier head Fl G 3s 5m.
Rubha Cadail 57°55'·53N 05°13'·30W Fl WRG 6s 11m W9M, R6M, G6M; W Tr; vis G311°-320°, W320°-325°, R325°-103°, W103°-111°, G111°-118°, W118°-127°, R127°-157°, W157°-199°.
Ullapool Pt 57°53'·62N 05°09'·85W Iso R 4s 8m 6M; vis 258°-108°.
Ferry Pier 57°37'·7N 05°09'·5W 2 FR (vert) 6m; on post.
Extension, SE corner 57°53'·7N 05°09'·3W Fl R 3s 6m 1M; on pole.
Cailleach Head 57°55'·83N 05°24'·15W Fl(2) 12s 60m 9M; W Tr; vis 015°-236°.
Loch Ewe, NATO jetty, NW corner Fl G 4s 5m 3M.
Dolphins off N and S ends of jetty Fl G 4s.
Rubha Reidh 57°51'·4N 05°48'·6W Fl(4) 15s 37m **24M**.
LOCH GAIRLOCH, Glas Eilean 57°42'·8N 05°42'·3W Fl WRG 6s 9m W6M, R 4M; vis W080°-102°, R102°-296°, W296°-333°, G333°-080°.

RONA
NE point Fl 12s 69m **19M**; W Tr; vis 050°-358°.
LOCH A'BHRAIGE.
Sgeir Shuas 57°35'·04N 05°58'·54W Fl R 2s 6m 3M; vis 070°-199°.
Jetty, SW end, 2FR (vert). 57°34'·6N 05°57'·9W FlR 5s.
Ldg Lts 136°30' Front. No 9 Bn Q WRG 3m W4M, R3M; W and Or Bn; vis W135°-138°, R138°-318°, G318°-135°.
No.10 Iso 6s 28m 5M; W Bn.
No. 1 Bn Fl G 3s 91m 3M, Or Bn.
Rubha Chuiltairbh Fl 3s 6m 5M; W Bn.
No. 11 Bn QY 6m 4M; Or Bn.
No. 3 Bn Fl(2) 10s 9m 4M; W and Or Bn.

No. 12 Bn QR 5m 3M; Or Bn.
Garbh Eilean, SE point, No. 8 Bn Fl 3s 8m 5M; W Bn.

SOUND OF RAASAY.
Portree Pier, head, 57°24'·66N 06°11'·34W 2 FR (vert) 6m 4M; occas.
Ru Na Lachan 57°29'·04N 05°52'·07W Oc WR 8s 21m 10M; framework Tr; vis W 337°-022°, R022°-117°, W117°-162°.
Applecross Pier FlG 3s 3m 3M.
McMillan's Rock Lt Buoy 57°21'·13N 06°06'·24W Fl(2)G 12s; stbd-hand mark.
Suisnish 2 FG (vert) 8/6m 2M.
Raasay, SE point, Eyre Point 57°20'·03N 06°01'·22W Fl WR 3s 5m W9M, R6M; vis W215°-266°, R266°-288°, W288°-063°.
Skye, Loch Sligachan, Sconser ferry terminal QR 8m 3M.
Crowlin, Eilean Beag 57°21'·23N 05°51'·33W Fl 6s 32m 6M; W Bn.

KYLE AKIN
 Eilean Ban 57°16'·68N 05°44'·48W Iso WRG 4s 16m W9M, R6M, G6M; W Tr; vis W278°-282°, R282°-096°, W096°-132°, G132°-182°; Racon.
Allt-an-Avaig, jetty 2 FR (vert) 10m; vis 075°-270°.
S shore, ferry slipway QR (vis in Kyle of Loch Alsh).
Mooring dolphin 57°16'·4N 05°43'·4W Q 5m 3M.

KYLE OF LOCH ALSH.
Ferry pier, West and E sides, 2 FG (vert) 6/5m 5M.
Fishery Pier, E end Fl G 3s 6m 2M.
Butec Jetty 57°16'·7N 05°42'·4W Oc G 6s 5m 3M each end, synchronized.
Sgeir-na-Caillich 57°15'·63N 05°38'·83W Fl(2)R 6s 3m 4M.

SOUND OF SLEAT,
Kyle Rhea 57°14'·20N 05°39'·90W Fl WRG 3s 7m W11M, R9M, G8M; W Bn; vis R shore-219°, W219-228°, G228°-338°, W338°-346°, R346°-shore.
Sandaig Island, NW point Fl 6s 12m 8M; W 8-sided Tr.
Ornsay, SE end Oc 8s 18m **15M**; W Tr; vis 157°-030°.
Eilean Iarmain, off pier head 2 FR (vert) 3/2m 2M.
Armadale Bay, pier Oc R·6s 6m 6M.
Point of Sleat 57°01'N 06 01'W Fl 3s 20m 9M; W Tr.

MALLAIG.
Northern Pier, E end 57°00'·48N 05°49'·45W Iso WRG 4s 6m W9M, R6M, G6M; grey pylon on concrete base; vis G181°-185°, W185°-197°, R197°-201°. FlG 3s 14m 6M; same structure. 3 FR (vert) 12M shown when entry prohibited.
Sgeir Dhearg 57°00'·64N 05°49'·53W Fl(2)WG 8s 6m 5M; grey Bn; vis G190°-055°, W055°-190°.
On reef 2 FG (vert) 5/3m 4M; B pylon.

SCOTLAND—THE HEBRIDES
Butt of Lewis 58°30'·93N 06°15'·72W Fl 5s 52m **25M**; R Tr; vis 056°-320°; RC; *Horn(2) 30s.*
Tiumpan Head 58°15'·6N 06°08'·3W Fl(2) 15s 55m **25M**.
Eitshal 58°10'·7N 06°35'·0W 4FR(vert) on radio mast.

STORNOWAY,
Arnish Point 58°11'·50N 06°22'·17W FlWR 10s 17m **W19M**, **R15M**; W round Tr; vis W088°-198°, R198°-302°, W302°-013°.
Sandwick Bay, NW side Oc WRG 6s 10m 9M; vis G334°-341°, W341°-347°, R347°-354°.
Stoney Field 58°11'·6N 06°21'·3W Fl WRG 3s 8m 11M; vis G shore-073°, R073°-102°, W102°-109°, G109°-shore.

LOCH ERISORT.
Tavag Beag 58 07.22N°6 23.15W Fl 3s 13m 3M.
Eilean Chalabrigh 58°06'·81N 06°26'·62W QG 5m 3M.
Gob na Milaid 58°01'·0N 06°21'·8W Fl 15s 14m 10M; W Tr.
Rubh' Uisenish 57°56'·2N 06°28'·2W Fl 5s 24m 11M; W Tr.

EAST LOCH TARBERT,
Scalpay, **Eilean Glas** 57°51'·43N 06°38'·45W Fl(3) 20s 43m **23M**; W Tr, R bands; RC; Racon.
Sgeir Griadach Lt Buoy 57°50'·38N 06°41'·31W Q(6)LFl 15s; S cardinal mark.
Sgeir Ghlas 57°52'·38N 06°45'·18W Iso WRG 4s 9m W9M, R6M, G6M; vis G282°-319°, W319°-329°, R329°-153°, W153°-164°. G164°-171°.
Scalpay, North Harbour Lt Buoy 57°52'·58N 06°42'·16W Fl G 2s; stbd-hand mark.
Dun Cor Mor Fl R 5s 10m 5M.

SOUND OF HARRIS
Dubh Sgeir 57°45'·5N 07°02'·6W Q(2) 5s 9m 6M; R Tr, B bands.
Jane's Tower 57°45'·8N 07°02'·0W Q(2)G 5s 6m 4M; obsc 273°-318°.
Leverburgh, pier head 57°46'·0N 07°01'·6W Oc WRG 8s 5m 2M; vis G305°-059°, W059°-066°, R066°-125°.
Berneray. Bays Loch, breakwater head Iso R 4s 4M; on Gy column.
Drowning Rock Q(2) G 8s 2m 2M.
Reef Channel No. 1 QG 2m 4M.
Reef Channel No. 2 Iso G 4s 2m 4M.
Eilean Fuam 57°41'·9N 07°10'·6W Q 6m 2M.
North Uist, Newton jetty 57°41'·5N 07°11'·5W 2 FG (vert) 9m 8M.
Griminish Harbour, Sgeir Dubh 57°40'·0N 07°26'·8W Q(2) G 10s 4m 4M.
Pier Hd 57°39'·3N 07°26'·3W 2 FG (vert) 4m G. Metal column (shown Mar-Oct).

LOCH MADDY,
Weaver's Point 57°36'·61N 07°05'·95W Fl 3s 21m 7M; W hut.
Glas Eilean Mor 57°35'·98N 07°06'·64W Fl(2) 6s 8m.
Rudna Nam Pleac 57°35'·8N 07°06'·7W Fl R 4s 7m 5M; W post.
Ruigh Liath, E islet 57°35'·73N 07°08'·36W QG 6m.
Vallaquie Island 57°35'·5N 07°09'·3W Fl(3)WRG 8s 11m W7M, R5M, G5M; W pillar; vis G shore-205°, W205°-210°, R210°-240°, G240°-254°, W254°-257°, R257°-shore.
Lochmaddy Ldg Lts 298°. Front, Ro Ro pier 57°35'·8N 07°09'·3W 2 FG (vert) 8/6m 4M. Rear, 112m from front, OcG 8s 10m 4M; column on dolphin; vis 284°-304°.
Grimsay. Kellin Harbour breakwater, NE corner 57°28'·9N 07°12'·3W 2 FR (vert) 6m 5M.

LOCH CARNAN.
Landfall Lt Buoy 57°22'·30N° 07°11'·45W LFl 10s; safe water mark.

No. 2 Lt Buoy 57°22'·33N 07°14'·87W Fl R 2s; port-hand mark.
No .3 Lt Buoy 57°22'·35N 07°15'·55W Fl R 5s; port-hand mark.
No. 4 Lt Buoy 57°22'·27N 07°16'·13W QR; port-hand mark.
Ldg Lts 222°. Front 57°22'·00N 07°16'·28W Fl R 2s 7m 5M; W diamond on post. Rear 58m from front Iso R 10s 11m 5M; W diamond on post.
Usinish 57°17'·91N 07°11'·50W Fl WR 20s 54m **W19M**, **R15M**; W Tr; vis W193°-356°, R356°-013°.

LOCH BOISDALE,
Calvay, E End 57°08'·5N 07°15'·3W Fl(2) WRG 10s 16m W7M, R4M, G4M; W framework Tr; vis G190°-202°, W202°-286°, R286°-111°, W111°-190°.
N side QG 3m 3M. Gasay Island FlWR 5s 10m W7M, R4M; W framework Tr; vis R284°-120°, W120°-284°.
Jetty, head 57°09'·2N 07°18'·2W Iso RG 4s 12m 2M; framework Tr; vis G shore-283°, R283°-shore; 2 FG (vert) 8m 3M on dolphin 84m W.
Ludaig Dir Lt 297° 57°06'·2N 07°19'·7W Dir Oc WRG 6s 8m W7M, R4M, G4M; vis G287°-296°, W296°-298°, R298°-307°.
Ludaig Pier 2 FG (vert) 5/3m 3M.
Stag Rock 57°05'·9N 07°18'·3W Fl(2) 8s 7m 4M.
Bank Rock 57°05'·6N 07°17'·5W Q(2) 4s 5m 4M.
Haun Dir Lt 236° Dir Oc WRG 3s 9m W7M, R4M, G4M; vis G226°-234°, W234°-237°, R237°-246°.

BARRA.
Curachan Lt Buoy 56°58'·58N 07°20·45W Q(6)LFl 15s; S cardinal mark.

ERISKAY.
Pier 2 FG (vert) 5m.
Acairseid Mhor Ldg Lts 285°. Front 57°03'·9N 07°17'·2W Oc R 6s 9m 4M. Rear 24m from front Oc R 6s 10m 4M. Both grey columns.

VATERSAY SOUND,
Dubh Sgeir 56°56'·4N 07°28'·9W Fl(2)WG 6s 6m W7M, G5M; vis W280°180°, G180°-280°.
Sgeir Leadh 56°56'·7N 07°30'·7W Fl 3s 7m 8M; W building.
Rudha Glas. Ldg Lts 295°. Front 56°56'·8N 07°30'·6W FR 9m 4M; R triangle on W Tr. Rear 550m from front FR 22m 4M; R triangle on W Tr.
South Uist. Falconet Tower 57°21'·5N 07°23'·6W FR 25m 8M (3M by day); shown 1h before firing, changes to Iso R 2s 15min before firing until completion; similar Lts 1·2M NNW and 7·5M SSW.

BERNERAY,
West side, **Barra Head** 56°47'·13N 07°39'·18W Fl 15s 208m **21M**; W Tr; obsc by islands to NE; RC.
Flannan Islands, Eilean Mor 58°17'·32N 07°35'·23W Fl(2) 30s 101m **20M**; W Tr; obsc in places by islands to west.

EAST LOCH ROAG,
Aird Laimishader, Carloway 58°17'·1N 06°49'·5W L Fl 12s 61m 8M; W hut; obsc on some brgs.
Ardvanich Point 58°13'·5N 06°47'·7W Fl G 3s 2m 2M. T Tidal Rock 58°13'·5N 06°47'·6W Fl R 3s 2m 2M (synchronised with previous Lt).
Great Bernera, Kirkibost jetty 2 FG (vert) 6/5m 2M.
Greinam 58°13'·3N 06°46'·2W Fl WR 6s 8m W8M, R7M; W Bn; vis R143°-169°, W169°-143°.
Rudha Arspaig, jetty 2 FR (vert) 10/7m 4M.

8

ST KILDA
Ldg Lts 270°. <u>Front</u> 57°48'·36N 08°34'·27W Oc 5s 26m 3M. Rear, 100m from front, Oc 5s 38m 3M; synchronised.

SCOTLAND—WEST COAST

<u>Eilean Trodday</u> 57°43'·6N 06°17'·8W Fl(2) WRG 10s 49m W12M, R9M, G9M; W Bn; vis W062°-088°, R088°-130°, W130°-322°, G322°-062°.

SKYE
Uig. Pier head Iso WRG 4s 9m W7M, R4M, G4M; vis W180°-008°, G008°-052°, W052°-075°, R075°-180°.
Waternish Point 57°36'·5N 06°38'·0W Fl 20s 21m 8M; W Tr.
Loch Dunvegan, Uiginish point 57°26'·8N 06°36'·5W Fl WG 3s 14m W7M, G5M; W hut; vis G040°-128°, W128°-306°, obsc by Fiadhairt point when brg more than 148°.
Neist Point 57°25'·4N 06°47'·2W Fl 5s 43m **16M**; W Tr.
Loch Harport, Ardtreck Point 57°20'·4N 06°25'·8W Iso 4s 17m 9M; small W Tr.

CANNA
East end, Sanday Island 57°02'·8N 06°27'·9W Fl 6s 32m 9M; W Tr; vis 152°-061°.
Oigh Sgeir, near S end, **Hyskeir** 56°58'·13N 06°40'·80W Fl(3) 30s 41m **24M**; W Tr; RC. N end *Horn 30s.*

EIGG
<u>SE point of Eilean Chathastail</u> 56°52'·25N 06°07'·20W Fl 6s 24m 8M; W Tr; vis 181°-shore.
<u>Bo Faskadale Lt Buoy</u> 56°48'·18N 06°06'·35W Fl(3)G 18s; stbd- hand mark.
Ardnamurchan 56°43'·64N 06°13'·46W Fl(2) 20s 55m **24M**; grey Tr; vis 002°-217°; *Horn (2) 20s.*
Cairns of Coll, <u>Suil Ghorm</u> 56°42'·27N 06°26'·70W Fl 12s 23m 11M; W Tr.

COLL
Loch Eatharna, <u>Bogha Mor Lt Buoy</u> 56°36'·67N 06°30'·90W FlG 6s; stbd-hand mark.
Arinagour pier 2 FR (vert) 10m.

TIREE,
Scarinish, S side of entrance 56°30'·02N 06°48'·20W Fl 3s 11m **16M**; W square Tr; vis 210°-030°.
Ldg Lts 286°30. Front 56°30'·6N 06°47'·9W FR (when vessel expected). Rear 30m from front FR.
Skerryvore 56°19'·40N 07°06'·75W Fl 10s 46m **26M**; grey Tr; Racon; *Horn 60s.*
Dubh Artach 56°08'·0N 06°37'·9W Fl(2) 30s 44m **20M**; grey Tr, R band; *Horn 45s.*
Eileanan na Liathanaich, SE end, Bunessan 56°20'·5N 06°16'·2W Fl WR 6s 12m W8M, R6M; W Bn; vis R088°-108°, W108°-088°.

SOUND OF MULL.
<u>Ardmore Point</u> 56°39'·4N 06°07'·6W Fl(2) 10s 17m 8M; W column.
Rubha nan Gall 56°38'·33N 06°03'·91W Fl 3s 17m **15M**, W Tr.
<u>Eileanan Glasa, Green Island</u> 56°32'·3N 05°54'·7W Fl 6s 7m 8M; W Tr.
<u>Ardtornish Point</u> 56°31'·1N 05°45'·1W Fl(2) WRG 10s 7m W8M, R5M, G5M; W Tr; vis G shore-302°, W302°-310°, R310°-342°, W342°-057°, R057°-095°, W095°-108°, G108°-shore.

<u>Glas Eileanan, Grey Rocks</u> 56°29'·8N 05°42'·7W Fl 3s 10m 6M; W round Tr on W base.

LOCH LINNHE.
Entrance, west side, <u>Corran Point</u> 56°43'·27N 05°14'·47W Iso WRG 4s 12m W10M, R7M; W Tr; vis R shore-195°, W195°-215°, G215°-305°, W305°-030°, R030°-shore.
<u>Corran Narrows, NE</u> 56°43'·62N 05°13'·83W Fl 5s 4m 4M; W framework Tr; vis S shore-214°.
<u>Jetty</u> 56°43'·42N 05°14'·56W FlR 5s 7m 3M.

FORT WILLIAM,
Pier head Fl G 2s 6m 4M. Corpach, Caledonian Canal lock entrance Iso WRG 4s 6m 5M; W Tr; vis G287°-310°, W310°-335°, R335°-030°.
Sgeir Bhuidhe, Appin 56°33'·6N 05°24'·6W Fl(2) WR 7s 7m 9M; W Bn; vis R184°-220°, W220°-184°.

LOCH CRERAN,
off Airds Point Fl WRG 2s 2m W3M, R1M, G1M; vis R196°-246°, W246°-258°, G258°-041°, W041°-058°, R0093°-139°. obscured 139°-196°.
Eriska, NE point, QG 2m 2M; vis 128°-329°.
Lismore, <u>SW end</u> 56°27'·4N 05°36'·4W Fl 10s 31m **19M**; W Tr; vis 237°-208°.
<u>Lady's Rock</u> 56°27'·0N 05°37'·0W Fl 6s 12m 5M; R structure on W Bn.
<u>Duart Point</u> 56°26'·9N 05°38'·7W Fl(3) WR 18s 14m W5M, R3M; grey building; vis W162°-261°, R261°-275°, W275°-353°, R353°-shore.

DUNSTAFFNAGE BAY.
Pier head, NE end 2 FG (vert) 4m 2M.

OBAN,
<u>North spit of Kerrera</u> 56°25'·50N 05°29'·50W FlR 3s 9m 5M; W column. R bands.
Dunollie Fl(2) WRG 6s 7m W5M, G4M, R4M; vis G351°-009°, W009°-047°, R047°-120°, W120°-138°, G138°-143°.
Rubbh a Chruidh QR 3m 2M.
Kerrera Sound, <u>Dubh Sgeir</u> 56°22'·82N 05°32'·20W Fl(2) 12s 7m 5M; W Tr.
Port Lathaich 56°22'·8N 05°31'·3W OcG 6s 6M; vis 037°-072°.
<u>Fladda</u> 56°14'·9N 05°40'·8W Fl(3) WR 18s 13m W14M, R11M; W Tr; vis R169°-186°, W186°-001°.
<u>Dubh Sgeir</u> 56°14'·8N 05°40'·1W Fl 6s 7m 6M; W tank.
The Garvellachs, <u>Eileach an Naoimh, SW end</u> 56°13'·1N 05°48'·9W Fl 6s 21m 9M; W Bn; vis 240°-215°.

COLONSAY,
<u>Scalasaig, Rubha Dubh</u> 56°04'·02N 06°10'·83W Fl(2) WR 10s 6m W8M, R5M; W building; vis R shore-230°, W230°-337°, R337°-354°.
Pier Ldg Lts 262°, FR 10m (occas).
Loch Melfort, <u>Fearnach Bay pier</u> 56°16'·2N 05°30'·1W 2 FR (vert) 6/5m 3M; shown 1/4 to 31/10.

For Sound of Jura and Sound of Islay see 10.9.4.

10.8.5 PASSAGE INFORMATION

SCOTLAND — WEST COAST

This provides splendid, if sometimes boisterous, sailing and unmatched scenery. In summer the long hours of daylight and warmth of Gulf Stream compensate for lower air temp and higher wind speeds experienced when depressions run typically N of Scotland. Inshore the wind is often unpredictable, due to geographical effects of lochs, mountains and islands offshore: calms and squalls can occur in rapid succession. Magnetic anomalies occur.

A yacht must rely on good anchors. Particularly in N of area, facilities are very dispersed. It is essential to carry good large scale charts, and pilotage information as in *West Coast of Scotland Pilot* or as provided by the Clyde Cruising Club. Also useful is *Scottish West Coast Pilot*, by Mark Brackenbury.

It is helpful to know at least some of the more common Gaelic terms, as follows. *Acairseid*: anchorage. *Ailean*: meadow. *Aird, ard*: promontory. *Aisir, aisridh*: passage between rocks. *Beag*: litttle. *Beinn*: mountain. *Bo, boghar, bodha*: rock. *Cala*: harbour. *Camas*: channel, bay. *Caol*: strait. *Cladach*: shore, beach. *Creag*: cliff. *Cumhamn*: narrows. *Dubh, dhubh*: black. *Dun*: castle. *Eilean, eileanan*: island. *Garbh*: rough. *Geal, gheal*: white. *Glas, ghlas*: grey, green. *Inis*: island. *Kyle*: narrow strait. *Linn, Linne*: pool. *Mor, mhor*; large. *Mull*: promontory. *Rinn, roinn*: point. *Ruadh*: red, brown. *Rubha, rhu*: cape. *Sgeir*: rock. *Sruth*: current. *Strath*: river valley. *Tarbert*: isthmus. *Traigh*: beach. *Uig*: bay.

CAPE WRATH TO SKYE (charts 1785, 1794)

C Wrath (Lt, fog sig, RC) is a steep headland (110m). To N of it the E-going stream begins at HW Ullapool −0350, and W-going at HW Ullapool +0235, sp rates 3 kn. Eddies close inshore cause almost continuous W-going stream E of cape, and N-going stream SW of it. Where they meet is turbulence, with dangerous sea in bad weather. Duslic Rk, 7 ca NE of Lt Ho, dries. 6M SW of C Wrath is islet of Am Balg (45m), foul for 2 ca offshore.

There are anchs in Loch Inchard (chart 2503), the most sheltered being in Loch Bervie on N shore. Good anchs among Is along S shore of Loch Laxford, entered between Ardmore Pt and Rubha Ruadh (see 10.8.19). Handa I to WSW is bird sanctuary. Handa Sound is navigable with care, but beware Bogha Morair in mid-chan and associated overfalls. Tide turns 2h earlier in the sound than offshore.

With strong wind against tide there is bad sea off Pt of Stoer. S lies Enard B. The best shelter is Loch Inver (10.8.19 and chart 2504), with good anch off hotel near head of loch.

Summer Isles (chart 2501) lie NW of Ullapool (10.8.8) and provide several good anchs, but approaches are often difficult. The best include the b on E side of Tanera Mor; off NE of Tanera Beg (W of Eilean Fada Mor); and in Caolas Eilean Ristol, between the island and mainland.

Gruinard Island, SW of entrance to Little Loch Broom, is dangerously contaminated and landing is prohibited.

Loch Ewe (chart 3146) provides good shelter and is easy of access. Best anchs are in Poolewe B (beware Boor Rks off W shore) and in SW corner of Loch Thuirnaig (entering, keep close to S shore to avoid rks extending from N side). See 10.8.19.

Off Rubha Reidh (Lt) the NE-going stream begins at HW Ullapool −0335, and the SW-going at HW Ullapool +0305. Sp rates 3 kn, but streams lose strength SW of pt.

Longa Island lies N of entrance to Loch Gairloch (10.8.19 and chart 2528). The chan N of it is navigable but narrow at E end. Outer loch is free of dangers, but exposed to swell. Best anch is Caolas Bad a Chrotha on W side of Eilean Horrisdale, on S side of loch.

Loch Torridon (chart 2210) has few dangers, and streams are weak except in narrows between Loch Shieldaig and Upper Loch Torridon, where they run 2-3 kn. Entering Loch Torridon from S or W beware Murchadh Breac (dries) 3 ca NNW of Rubha na Fearna. Best anchs are SW of Eilean Mor (to W of Ardheslaig); in Loch a 'Chracaich, on S shore 3M from entrance; E of Shieldaig Island in Loch Shieldaig; and near head of Upper Loch Torridon.

OUTER HEBRIDES (charts 1785, 1794, 1795)

The E sides of these islands have many good, sheltered anchs, but W coasts give little shelter. The Outer Hebrides sailing directions of Clyde Cruising Club are recommended. The Sea of the Hebrides and the Little Minch can be very rough, particularly between Skye and Harris, and around Shiant Islands where tide runs locally 4 kn at sp, and heavy overfalls can be met. Beware fish farms in many inlets.

Between Skerryvore and Neist Pt the stream runs generally N and S, starting N-going at HW Ullapool +0550, and S-going at HW Ullapool −0010. Mostly it does not exceed 1 kn; but it is stronger near Skerryvore, around headlands of The Small Isles, and over rks and shoals. Between N point of Skye and S Harris the NE-going stream begins at HW Ullapool −0335, and the SW-going stream at HW Ullapool +0250, sp rates 2½ kn.

From N to S, the better harbs in Outer Hebrides include: *Lewis*. Stornoway (see 10.8.7); Loch Grimshader (beware Sgeir a'Chaolais, dries in entrance); Loch Erisort; Loch Odhairn; Loch Shell (10.8.19). Proceeding S from here, or to E Loch Tarbert beware Sgeir Inoe (dries) 3M ESE of Eilean Glas Lt Ho at SE end of Scalpay.

Harris. E Loch Tarbert (10.8.19); Loch Scadaby; Loch Stockinish; Loch Finsby. W Loch Tarbert (10.8.19).

N Uist. Loch Maddy (10.8.19); Loch Eport.

S Uist. Loch Skiport; Loch Eynort; Loch Boisdale (10.8.19).

Barra. Castlebay (10.8.19).

Berneray. On N side, E of Shelter Rk.

SKYE (charts 1795, 2210, 2209, 2208)

Skye and the islands around it provide many good and attractive anchs, of which the most secure are: Acairseid Mhor on the W side of Rona; Portree (see 10.8.9); Isleornsay; Portnalong, near the entrance to Loch Harport, and Carbost at the head: Dunvegan; and Uig B in Loch Snizort.

Anch behind Fladday Island near the N end of Raasay can be squally and uncomfortable except in settled weather, and Loch Scavaig more so, though the latter is so spectacular as to warrant a visit in fair weather. Soay has a small, safe harb on its N side, but the bar at entrance almost dries at LW sp.

Tides are strong off Rubha Hunish at N end of Skye, and heavy overfalls occur with weather-going tide against fresh or strong winds.

Between Skye and the coast there is the choice of Sound of Raasay and Inner Sound. Using the former, coming S from Portree, beware Sgeir Chnapach (3m) and Ebbing Rk (dries 2.4m) NNW of Oskaig Pt. At the Narrows (chart 2534) the S-going stream begins at HW Ullapool −0605, and the N-going at HW Ullapool −0040. Sp rate 1½ kn in mid-chan, but more near shoals each side. Beware McMillan's Rk in mid-chan, marked by buoy. The direction of buoyage here is now N-wards.

8

The chan between Scalpay and Skye narrows to 2½ ca 2M W of Guillamon Island, where a reef has least depth of 0.3m. There is a Lt Bn on N side of narrows, where N-going stream begins at HW Ullapool +0550, and S-going at HW Ullapool −0010, sp rates about 1 kn.

Inner Sound is a wider, easier chan than Sound of Raasay: the two are connected by Caol Rona and Caol Mor, respectively N and S of Raasay. Dangers extend about 1M N of Rona, and Cow Island lies off the mainland 8M to S; otherwise approach from N is clear to Crowlin Islands, which should be passed to W. There is a platform construction site with prohibited area S of Crowlin Island. There is a good anch between the two S islands, More and Meadhonach. See 10.8.19.

The British Underwater Test and Evaluation Centre (BUTEC) torpedo range exists in the Inner Sound. While passage through the Sound is normally unrestricted, vessels passing through the area may be requested to keep to the eastern side of the Sound while the range is active. This is indicated by RED FLAGS and International Code NE4 flown at the range head building at Applecross, by all range vessels and at the naval pier at Kyle of Lochalsh.

Approaching Kyle Akin from W, beware dangerous rks to N, off Bleat Island (at S side of entrance to Loch Carron); Bogha Beag (dries 0.6m) on S side of chan, 6½ ca W of Kyle Akin Lt Ho; and Black Eye Rk 4 ca W of Lt Ho with least depth 3.8m. For Plockton (Loch Carron) see 10.8.19.

Pass at least ½ ca distant either N or S of Eileanan Dubha off Kyle of Lochalsh. On S side of main chan String Rk (dries) is marked by buoy. For Loch Alsh see 10.8.19.

Kyle Rhea connects Loch Alsh with NE end of Sound of Sleat. The tidal streams are very strong: N-going stream begins HW Ullapool +0600, sp rate 6-7 kn; S-going stream begins at HW Ullapool, sp rate 8 kn. Eddies form both sides of the Kyle and there are heavy overfalls off S end in strong S winds on S-going stream. Temp anch in Sandaig Bay.

THE SMALL ISLES (charts 2207, 2208)

These consist of Rhum, Eigg, Muck and Canna. Dangers extend SSW from Canna: at 1M Jemina Rk (depth 1.5m) and Belle Rk (depth 3.6m); at 2M Humla Rk (5m high), marked by Lt buoy and with offlying shoals close W and ½ ca N of it; at 5M Oigh Sgeir (Lt, fog sig, RC), the largest of a group of small islets; and at 7M Mill Rks (with depths of 1.8m). The tide runs hard in these areas, and in bad weather the sea breaks heavily up to 15M SW of Canna.

On the N side of Muck, 1M offshore, are Godag Rks, some above water but with submerged dangers extending 2 ca further to N. Most other dangers around The Small Isles are closer inshore, but there are banks on which the sea breaks heavily in bad weather. Local magnetic anomalies exist around the islands.

The best harb is Eigg (10.8.19). Others are Loch Scresort (Rhum) and Canna Harbour (between Canna and Sanday), but both are exposed to E. For Canna see 10.8.19.

SOUTH OF ARDNAMURCHAN POINT (chart 2171)

6M NE of Ardnamurchan Pt (Lt, fog sig) is Bo Faskadale, with two heads, the N one awash and the S with depth of 1.2m, marked by buoy. Ardnamurchan Pt has no offlying dangers, but it is exposed, and a heavy sea can build up even in moderate winds. Here the N-going stream begins at HW Oban −0525, and the S-going at HW Oban +0100, sp rates 1½ kn.

Proceeding S (chart 2171) there is the choice of Passage of Tiree (exposed to SW, and with heavy overfalls in bad weather) or the sheltered route via Sound of Mull, Firth of Lorne and Sound of Jura. The latter denies a visit to Coll or Tiree, where best anchs are at Arinagour and Gott B respectively. Beware Cairns of Coll, off the N point.

The Sound of Mull gives access to Tobermory (10.8.12), Dunstaffnage (10.8.19), Oban (10.8.16), and up Loch Linnhe through Corran Narrows (where tide runs strongly) to Fort William (10.8.14) and to Corpach for the Caledonian Canal (10.8.15). But, apart from these places, there are dozens of lovely anchs in the sheltered lochs inside Mull, as for example in Loch Sunart (10.8.11). For Loch Aline see 10.8.13.

The W coast of Mull is rewarding in really calm and settled weather, but careful pilotage is needed. Beware tide rip off Caliach Pt (NW corner) and Torran Rks off SW end of Mull. Buressan, N side of Ross of Mull, is an anch with boatyard etc. (see 10.8.19). Apart from the attractions of Iona and of Staffa (Fingal's Cave), the remote Treshnish Islands are worth visiting. The best anchs in this area are at Ulva, Gometra, and Bull Hole and Tinker's Hole in Iona Sound. Passage through Iona Sound avoids overfalls W of Iona, but care is needed.

On the mainland shore Eilean nam Beathach is a sheltered anch. For passage S through Sound of Jura, and Gulf of Corryvreckan, see 10.9.5. For Loch Melfort see 10.8.17.

10.8.6   DISTANCE TABLE

Approximate distances in nautical miles are by the most direct route while avoiding dangers and allowing for traffic separation schemes etc. Places in *italics* are in adjoining areas.

	1	2	3	4	5	6	7	8	9	10	11	12	13	14	15	16	17	18	19	20
1 *Lerwick*	1																			
2 *Kirkwall*	95	2																		
3 *Duncansby Head*	109	34	3																	
4 *Cape Wrath*	155	79	63	4																
5 Butt of Lewis	183	118	103	40	5															
6 Stornoway	208	132	116	53	30	6														
7 Ullapool	208	132	116	53	52	43	7													
8 Portree	238	162	146	83	69	50	53	8												
9 Neist Point	247	171	155	92	72	49	65	48	9											
10 Mallaig	265	189	173	110	100	83	82	38	41	10										
11 Barra Head	295	219	203	140	120	97	113	96	48	63	11									
12 Oigh Sgeir	274	198	182	119	99	76	92	67	27	29	33	12								
13 Ardnamurchan Pt	284	218	202	139	119	96	104	60	47	22	47	21	13							
14 Tobermory	304	228	212	149	129	106	114	70	57	32	56	31	10	14						
15 Fort William	347	271	255	192	171	149	157	113	100	75	99	74	53	43	15					
16 Oban	328	252	236	173	153	130	138	94	81	56	80	55	34	24	29	16				
17 Crinan	344	268	252	189	169	146	154	110	97	72	92	71	50	42	50	24	17			
18 *Mull of Kintyre*	387	311	295	232	212	189	203	159	140	111	112	103	99	89	98	70	51	18		
19 *Altacarry Head*	379	303	287	224	204	181	197	151	132	103	104	95	91	92	101	73	54	12	19	
20 *Tory Island*	385	309	293	230	210	187	203	170	138	132	95	113	110	115	143	114	110	86	74	20

STORNOWAY 10-8-7
Lewis (Outer Hebrides)

CHARTS
Admiralty 2529, 1794; OS 8
TIDES
−0428 Dover; ML 2.9; Duration 0610; Zone 0 (GMT).
Standard Port ULLAPOOL (—→)

Times				Height (metres)			
HW		LW		MHWS	MHWN	MLWN	MLWS
0100	0700	0300	0900	5.2	3.9	2.1	0.7
1300	1900	1500	2100				

Differences STORNOWAY
−0010	−0010	−0010	−0010	−0.4	−0.2	−0.1	0.0

LOCH ERIBOLL (Portnancon)
+0055	+0105	+0055	+0100	0.0	+0.1	+0.1	+0.2

KYLE OF DURNESS
+0030	+0030	+0050	+0050	−0.6	−0.4	−0.3	−0.1

LOCH SHELL (Hebrides)
−0023	−0010	−0010	−0027	−0.4	−0.3	−0.2	0.0

EAST LOCH TARBERT (Hebrides)
−0035	−0020	−0020	−0030	−0.2	−0.2	0.0	+0.1

LOCH MADDY (Hebrides)
−0054	−0024	−0026	−0040	−0.4	−0.3	−0.2	0.0

LOCH SKIPORT (Hebrides)
−0110	−0035	−0034	−0034	−0.6	−0.6	−0.4	−0.2

LOCH BOISDALE (Hebrides)
−0105	−0040	−0030	−0050	−1.1	−0.9	−0.4	−0.2

CASTLEBAY (Hebrides)
−0125	−0050	−0055	−0110	−0.9	−0.8	−0.4	−0.1

BARRA HEAD (Hebrides)
−0125	−0050	−0055	−0105	−1.2	−0.9	−0.3	+0.1

WEST LOCH TARBERT (Hebrides)
−0103	−0043	−0024	−0044	−1.0	−0.7	−0.8	−0.3

LITTLE BERNERA (Hebrides)
−0031	−0021	−0027	−0037	−0.9	−0.8	−0.5	−0.2

CARLOWAY (Hebrides)
−0050	+0010	−0045	−0025	−1.0	−0.7	−0.5	−0.1

Standard Port ULLAPOOL (—→)

Times				Height (metres)			
HW		LW		MHWS	MHWN	MLWN	MLWS
0000	0600	0300	0900	5.2	3.9	2.1	0.7
1200	1800	1500	2100				

VILLAGE BAY (St Kilda)
−0110	−0040	−0100	−0100	−1.9	−1.4	−0.9	−0.3

FLANNAN ISLES
−0036	−0026	−0026	−0036	−1.3	−0.9	−0.7	−0.2

ROCKALL
−0115	−0115	−0125	−0125	−2.4	−1.8	−1.0	−0.3

SHELTER
Good except S swells make the anchorages uncomfortable. Anchorages: Poll nam Portan opposite commercial quays, clear of LB moorings; Glumaig Harbour in W sector is best anchorage but oil industry works may preclude this; Eilean na Gobhail in bay NW of island; or yachts can go alongside Cromwell Street Quay. It is possible to berth alongside fishing boats in the inner harbour. Visitors land at steps N of FG Ldg Lts and report to Hr Mr or enter Inner Harbour and berth at Cromwell St quay.

NAVIGATION
Waypoint 58°10′.00N 06°20′.80W, 163°/343° from/to Oc WRG Lt, 2.3M. Reef rocks, W side of entrance marked by lighted R can buoy. The rocky patch off Holm Point is marked by an unlit R beacon. Ferries to Ullapool use the harbour. A local magnetic anomaly exists over a small area 1.75 ca N of Seid Rks.

LIGHTS AND MARKS
Arnish Point Fl WR 10s 17m 19/15M; W Tr; vis W088° − 198°, R198° − 302°, W302° − 013°. R can buoy QR marking Reef Rock. Stoney Field Fl WRG 3s 8m 11M; vis G shore − 073°, R073° − 102°, W102° − 109°, G109° − shore. Sandwick Bay, NW side (close E of power station and water Tr) Oc WRG 6s 10m 9M; vis G334° − 341°, W341° − 347°, R347° − 354°; in line with conspic chy bears 343°. Ldg Lts 325° to Ro Ro jetty, both FG.

RADIO TELEPHONE
VHF Ch 16; 12 (H24)

TELEPHONE (0851)
Hr Mr 2688; CG 2013; MRSC 2013; ⌗ 3626; Marinecall 0898 500 464; Police 2222; Dr 3145

FACILITIES
EC Wednesday; **Pier N end of Bay** FW, C(10 ton), CH, AB; **W Pier** Slip, P, FW; **Steamer Pier** FW; **Duncan MacIver** ☎ 2010 CH, ACA; **Electronic Services** ☎ 2909 El, Ⓔ; **Stornoway Boatbuilding Co.** ☎ 3488, ME, El, Sh; **Town** P, D, El, V, R, Bar, Gas, ✉, Ⓑ; ⇌ (ferry to Ullapool, bus to Garve); ✈.

8

ULLAPOOL   10-8-8
Ross and Cromarty

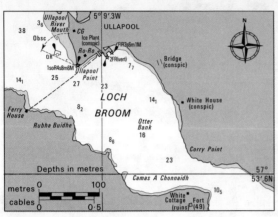

CHARTS
Admiralty 2500; OS 19
TIDES
−0415 Dover; ML 3.0; Duration 0610; Zone 0 (GMT).
Standard Port ULLAPOOL (—→)

Times				Height (metres)			
HW		LW		MHWS	MHWN	MLWN	MLWS
0000	0600	0300	0900	5.2	3.9	2.1	0.7
1200	1800	1500	2100				

Differences LOCH LAXFORD
+0015 +0015 +0005 +0005 −0.3   −0.4   −0.2   0.0
LOCH BERVIE
+0030 +0010 +0010 +0020 −0.3   −0.3   −0.2   0.0
LOCH INVER
−0005 −0005 −0005 −0005 −0.2   0.0   0.0   +0.1
BADCALL BAY
+0005 +0005 +0005 +0005 −0.7   −0.5   −0.5   +0.2
LOCH EWE (Mellon Charles)
−0010 −0010 −0010 −0010 −0.1   −0.1   −0.1   0.0
LOCH GAIRLOCH
−0020 −0020 −0010 −0010 0.0   +0.1   −0.3   −0.1
SUMMER ISLES (Tanera Mor)
−0005 −0005 −0010 −0010 −0.1   +0.1   0.0   +0.1

Ullapool is a Standard Port and detailed tidal predictions for each day of the year are given below.

SHELTER
Good shelter in anchorage behind Ullapool Point. Note that Ullapool is primarily a fishing port from Aug to Mar and the pier is extremely congested. Moorings sometimes available (see Hr Mr).
NAVIGATION
Waypoint Loch Broom entrance 57°55'.80N 05°15'.00W, 309°/129° from/to Ullapool Pt Lt, 3.5M. North of Ullapool point is an extensive flat at the mouth of Ullapool River which dries out: deep water marked by QR buoy. Beware fish pens and unlit buoys S of narrows off W shore.
LIGHTS AND MARKS
Ullapool Point Iso R 4s 8m 6M; grey mast; vis 258°−108°. Pier SE corner, Fl R 3s 6m 1M; SW corner 2FR (vert).
RADIO TELEPHONE
VHF Ch 16; 12 (July-Nov: H24. Dec-June: office hours).
TELEPHONE (0854)
Hr Mr 2091 & 2165; Port Officer 2724; CG 2014; MRSC Stornoway 2013; ⌗ (Aug−Mar) 2253; Marinecall 0898 500 464; Police 2017; Dr 2015.
FACILITIES
EC Tuesday (but open all day in summer); **Pier** ☎ 2091 & 2165, D, L, FW, CH, AB; **Ardmair Boat Centre** ☎ 2054, Sh, CH; **Ullasport** ☎ 2621, CH, ACA; **Summer Isles Charters** ☎ (085 483) 230, ME, El, Sh; **Ullapool YC** Gas; **Highland Coastal Trading Co** ☎ 2488 CH; **Village** P, ⊙, ME, El, Ⓔ, V, R, Bar. ✉; Ⓑ; ⇌ (bus to Garve); ✈ (Inverness).
Note: daily buses to Inverness and ferries to Stornoway.

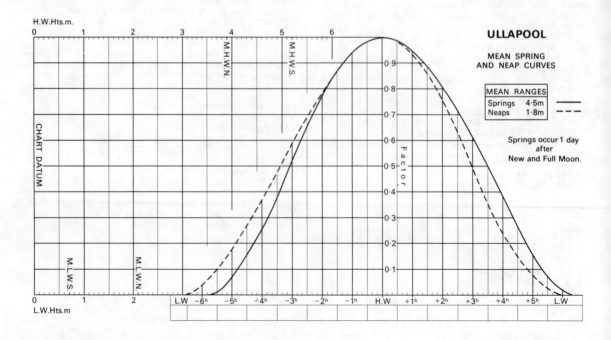

SCOTLAND, WEST COAST - ULLAPOOL

LAT 57°54′N   LONG 5°10′W

TIMES AND HEIGHTS OF HIGH AND LOW WATERS

YEAR **1991**

TIME ZONE UT(GMT)
For Summer Time add ONE hour in non-shaded areas

8

JANUARY

Day	Time	m	Time	m	Time	m	Time	m
1 TU	0058	0.9	0702	5.3	1333	0.6	1930	5.2
2 W	0144	0.7	0747	5.4	1420	0.4	2017	5.1
3 TH	0228	0.7	0833	5.4	1505	0.4	2105	5.0
4 F	0311	0.8	0920	5.2	1550	0.6	2153	4.8
5 SA	0355	1.0	1008	5.0	1635	0.8	2244	4.5
6 SU	0439	1.3	1058	4.7	1721	1.2	2338	4.3
7 M ☾	0526	1.6	1152	4.4	1812	1.6		
8 TU ☽	0039	4.1	0618	2.0	1253	4.1	1909	1.9
9 W	0146	3.9	0721	2.2	1405	4.0	2018	2.1
10 TH	0254	3.9	0837	2.4	1519	3.9	2130	2.1
11 F	0356	4.0	0953	2.3	1623	4.0	2232	2.1
12 SA	0447	4.2	1057	2.1	1714	4.1	2322	1.9
13 SU	0530	4.4	1147	1.9	1755	4.3		
14 M	0004	1.7	0606	4.7	1230	1.7	1829	4.5
15 TU ●	0041	1.6	0639	4.9	1306	1.5	1901	4.6
16 W	0115	1.4	0710	5.0	1341	1.3	1930	4.7
17 TH	0148	1.3	0740	5.1	1413	1.2	2000	4.8
18 F	0220	1.3	0812	5.2	1446	1.1	2031	4.8
19 SA	0253	1.3	0845	5.2	1519	1.1	2104	4.7
20 SU	0328	1.3	0920	5.1	1554	1.2	2141	4.7
21 M	0406	1.4	1000	4.9	1632	1.3	2224	4.5
22 TU	0448	1.6	1046	4.7	1714	1.5	2315	4.3
23 W ☽	0536	1.8	1140	4.5	1805	1.7		
24 TH	0023	4.1	0636	2.0	1252	4.3	1909	1.9
25 F	0152	4.0	0756	2.1	1421	4.1	2034	2.0
26 SA	0318	4.1	0929	2.0	1544	4.2	2200	1.8
27 SU	0427	4.3	1048	1.7	1652	4.5	2309	1.5
28 M	0523	4.7	1149	1.3	1748	4.8		
29 TU	0003	1.2	0610	5.0	1240	0.8	1835	5.0
30 W ○	0050	0.9	0654	5.3	1325	0.5	1919	5.2
31 TH	0132	0.7	0735	5.5	1406	0.3	2000	5.3

FEBRUARY

Day	Time	m	Time	m	Time	m	Time	m
1 F	0212	0.6	0815	5.5	1446	0.3	2040	5.2
2 SA	0251	0.6	0854	5.4	1525	0.5	2119	5.0
3 SU	0329	0.8	0932	5.2	1602	0.8	2158	4.8
4 M	0407	1.1	1010	4.9	1640	1.2	2239	4.4
5 TU	0445	1.5	1050	4.5	1719	1.6	2327	4.1
6 W ☽	0527	1.9	1137	4.1	1804	2.0		
7 TH	0032	3.9	0617	2.3	1252	3.8	1904	2.3
8 F	0158	3.8	0732	2.5	1435	3.7	2039	2.5
9 SA	0317	3.8	0919	2.5	1558	3.8	2208	2.4
10 SU	0420	4.0	1043	2.3	1656	4.0	2306	2.1
11 M	0507	4.3	1135	2.0	1739	4.2	2348	1.9
12 TU	0546	4.6	1214	1.7	1812	4.4		
13 W	0024	1.6	0618	4.8	1249	1.4	1841	4.7
14 TH ●	0056	1.4	0648	5.1	1320	1.2	1909	4.8
15 F	0128	1.2	0718	5.2	1351	1.0	1936	5.0
16 SA	0159	1.1	0748	5.4	1422	0.9	2006	5.1
17 SU	0232	1.0	0820	5.4	1454	0.8	2037	5.1
18 M	0307	1.0	0855	5.3	1528	0.9	2112	5.0
19 TU	0344	1.1	0934	5.1	1605	1.1	2151	4.7
20 W	0424	1.3	1018	4.8	1645	1.3	2238	4.4
21 TH	0509	1.6	1112	4.4	1732	1.7	2344	4.1
22 F	0606	1.9	1232	4.1	1834	2.0		
23 SA	0128	3.9	0731	2.1	1416	3.9	2011	2.2
24 SU	0306	4.0	0926	2.0	1543	4.1	2156	2.0
25 M	0418	4.2	1047	1.6	1649	4.4	2304	1.6
26 TU	0513	4.6	1142	1.1	1740	4.7	2353	1.2
27 W	0559	5.0	1227	0.7	1822	5.0		
28 TH ○	0035	0.9	0638	5.3	1307	0.4	1900	5.2

MARCH

Day	Time	m	Time	m	Time	m	Time	m
1 F	0114	0.6	0715	5.5	1345	0.3	1936	5.3
2 SA	0150	0.5	0750	5.5	1420	0.3	2010	5.3
3 SU	0226	0.6	0824	5.4	1454	0.5	2042	5.1
4 M	0301	0.8	0856	5.2	1528	0.9	2115	4.9
5 TU	0335	1.1	0928	4.8	1601	1.3	2149	4.6
6 W	0410	1.4	1001	4.5	1634	1.7	2227	4.3
7 TH	0448	1.8	1041	4.1	1712	2.0	2321	3.9
8 F ☾	0533	2.1	1146	3.7	1801	2.4		
9 SA	0054	3.7	0637	2.4	1349	3.5	1934	2.6
10 SU	0229	3.7	0838	2.5	1524	3.6	2137	2.5
11 M	0340	3.9	1017	2.3	1627	3.8	2240	2.2
12 TU	0433	4.2	1108	1.9	1711	4.1	2322	1.9
13 W	0514	4.5	1146	1.6	1745	4.4	2357	1.6
14 TH	0548	4.7	1219	1.3	1814	4.7		
15 F	0029	1.3	0619	5.0	1250	0.9	1841	4.9
16 SA ●	0102	1.1	0650	5.3	1322	0.8	1909	5.1
17 SU	0135	0.9	0722	5.5	1354	0.7	1940	5.2
18 M	0209	0.8	0756	5.4	1426	0.7	2012	5.2
19 TU	0245	0.8	0833	5.3	1503	0.8	2048	5.1
20 W	0324	0.9	0914	5.1	1541	1.0	2128	4.8
21 TH	0405	1.1	1002	4.7	1623	1.3	2217	4.4
22 F	0453	1.4	1106	4.3	1711	1.7	2332	4.1
23 SA ☽	0555	1.8	1238	3.9	1817	2.0		
24 SU	0122	3.9	0730	2.0	1417	3.8	2005	2.2
25 M	0253	4.0	0924	1.8	1536	4.0	2148	1.9
26 TU	0402	4.3	1034	1.4	1636	4.3	2248	1.6
27 W	0456	4.6	1124	1.0	1723	4.6	2333	1.2
28 TH	0539	4.9	1205	0.7	1802	4.9		
29 F	0013	0.9	0617	5.1	1243	0.5	1837	5.1
30 SA ○	0050	0.7	0651	5.3	1318	0.5	1909	5.2
31 SU	0125	0.7	0724	5.3	1351	0.5	1940	5.2

APRIL

Day	Time	m	Time	m	Time	m	Time	m
1 M	0200	0.7	0755	5.2	1424	0.7	2010	5.1
2 TU	0233	0.9	0825	4.9	1455	1.0	2041	4.9
3 W	0307	1.1	0856	4.7	1527	1.3	2113	4.6
4 TH	0342	1.4	0930	4.3	1600	1.6	2151	4.3
5 F	0420	1.7	1012	4.1	1636	2.0	2242	4.0
6 SA ☽	0504	2.0	1116	3.7	1722	2.3		
7 SU ☾	0000	3.8	0603	2.2	1301	3.5	1836	2.5
8 M	0132	3.7	0744	2.3	1435	3.5	2040	2.5
9 TU	0246	3.8	0926	2.2	1542	3.7	2155	2.3
10 W	0344	4.0	1023	1.9	1630	4.0	2242	2.0
11 TH	0431	4.3	1105	1.6	1707	4.3	2320	1.7
12 F	0510	4.6	1141	1.3	1740	4.7	2356	1.3
13 SA	0546	4.9	1216	1.0	1811	4.9		
14 SU ●	0032	1.1	0621	5.2	1251	0.8	1843	5.1
15 M	0109	0.8	0657	5.3	1327	0.6	1916	5.2
16 TU	0147	0.7	0736	5.3	1404	0.6	1952	5.2
17 W	0227	0.7	0817	5.2	1443	0.7	2032	5.0
18 TH	0309	0.8	0904	4.9	1524	0.9	2117	4.8
19 F	0355	1.0	1001	4.5	1609	1.3	2216	4.4
20 SA	0448	1.3	1050	4.1	1702	1.6	2339	4.1
21 SU ☽	0556	1.5	1242	3.9	1812	1.9		
22 M	0112	4.0	0729	1.6	1406	3.9	1952	2.0
23 TU	0231	4.1	0901	1.5	1516	4.0	2120	1.8
24 W	0336	4.2	1006	1.3	1613	4.3	2219	1.5
25 TH	0430	4.5	1055	1.0	1659	4.5	2305	1.3
26 F	0515	4.7	1137	0.9	1738	4.7	2346	1.1
27 SA	0554	4.8	1214	0.8	1813	4.9		
28 SU ○	0024	1.0	0628	4.9	1250	0.8	1844	5.0
29 M	0101	0.9	0700	4.9	1324	0.8	1915	5.0
30 TU	0136	0.9	0731	4.8	1356	1.0	1945	4.9

Chart Datum: 2.75 metres below Ordnance Datum (Newlyn)

SCOTLAND, WEST COAST - ULLAPOOL

LAT 57°54′N   LONG 5°10′W

TIMES AND HEIGHTS OF HIGH AND LOW WATERS

YEAR 1991

TIME ZONE UT (GMT)
For Summer Time add ONE hour in non-shaded areas

MAY

Day	TIME	m	TIME	m	Day	TIME	m	TIME	m
1 W	0211 / 0803 / 1429 / 2017	1.0 / 4.7 / 1.2 / 4.8			16 TH	0214 / 0810 / 1428 / 2025	0.6 / 5.0 / 0.7 / 5.0		
2 TH	0247 / 0836 / 1501 / 2052	1.2 / 4.5 / 1.4 / 4.6			17 F	0301 / 0902 / 1513 / 2117	0.6 / 4.8 / 0.9 / 4.8		
3 F	0323 / 0913 / 1535 / 2131	1.3 / 4.2 / 1.6 / 4.4			18 SA	0351 / 1003 / 1602 / 2219	0.8 / 4.5 / 1.2 / 4.5		
4 SA	0402 / 0958 / 1613 / 2220	1.6 / 4.0 / 1.8 / 4.2			19 SU	0446 / 1113 / 1656 / 2333	1.0 / 4.2 / 1.4 / 4.3		
5 SU	0445 / 1055 / 1657 / 2322 ☽	1.8 / 3.7 / 2.1 / 4.0			20 M	0550 / 1227 / 1802	1.2 / 4.0 / 1.7		
6 M	0538 / 1211 / 1757	2.0 / 3.6 / 2.3			21 TU	0048 / 0705 / 1338 / 1920	4.2 / 1.3 / 4.0 / 1.8		
7 TU	0033 / 0649 / 1333 / 1926 ☾	3.9 / 2.1 / 3.6 / 2.4			22 W	0158 / 0822 / 1444 / 2037	4.2 / 1.4 / 4.0 / 1.8		
8 W	0143 / 0815 / 1442 / 2051	3.9 / 2.0 / 3.7 / 2.2			23 TH	0302 / 0927 / 1541 / 2140	4.2 / 1.3 / 4.1 / 1.7		
9 TH	0246 / 0923 / 1538 / 2150	4.0 / 1.8 / 4.0 / 2.0			24 F	0359 / 1020 / 1631 / 2233	4.3 / 1.3 / 4.3 / 1.5		
10 F	0340 / 1015 / 1624 / 2238	4.2 / 1.6 / 4.3 / 1.7			25 SA	0449 / 1106 / 1713 / 2319	4.4 / 1.2 / 4.5 / 1.4		
11 SA	0429 / 1059 / 1704 / 2321	4.5 / 1.3 / 4.6 / 1.4			26 SU	0532 / 1147 / 1750	4.4 / 1.2 / 4.6		
12 SU	0513 / 1141 / 1742	4.8 / 1.0 / 4.8			27 M	0001 / 0609 / 1225 / 1824	1.3 / 4.5 / 1.1 / 4.7		
13 M	0003 / 0555 / 1222 / 1819	1.1 / 5.0 / 0.8 / 5.0			28 TU	0041 / 0644 / 1301 / 1856 ○	1.2 / 4.6 / 1.2 / 4.8		
14 TU	0046 / 0638 / 1303 / 1858 ●	0.9 / 5.1 / 0.7 / 5.1			29 W	0119 / 0717 / 1335 / 1929	1.2 / 4.6 / 1.2 / 4.8		
15 W	0129 / 0722 / 1345 / 1939	0.7 / 5.2 / 0.6 / 5.1			30 TH	0156 / 0750 / 1409 / 2002	1.2 / 4.5 / 1.3 / 4.8		
					31 F	0232 / 0824 / 1443 / 2037	1.2 / 4.4 / 1.4 / 4.7		

JUNE

Day	TIME	m	Day	TIME	m
1 SA	0309 / 0901 / 1518 / 2115	1.3 / 4.2 / 1.5 / 4.5	16 SU	0344 / 0952 / 1552 / 2208	0.5 / 4.7 / 0.9 / 4.8
2 SU	0347 / 0941 / 1555 / 2158	1.4 / 4.1 / 1.7 / 4.4	17 M	0435 / 1052 / 1642 / 2308	0.7 / 4.4 / 1.2 / 4.6
3 M	0427 / 1027 / 1636 / 2246	1.5 / 3.9 / 1.8 / 4.2	18 TU	0528 / 1154 / 1737	0.9 / 4.2 / 1.4
4 TU	0511 / 1122 / 1726 / 2341	1.7 / 3.8 / 2.0 / 4.1	19 W	0012 / 0627 / 1259 / 1837 ☽	4.4 / 1.2 / 4.1 / 1.7
5 W	0603 / 1227 / 1828	1.8 / 3.8 / 2.1	20 TH	0117 / 0732 / 1403 / 1945	4.2 / 1.4 / 4.0 / 1.8
6 TH	0041 / 0706 / 1336 / 1941	4.0 / 1.8 / 3.8 / 2.1	21 F	0223 / 0839 / 1505 / 2055	4.1 / 1.6 / 4.0 / 1.9
7 F	0146 / 0816 / 1442 / 2052	4.1 / 1.8 / 4.0 / 2.0	22 SA	0327 / 0942 / 1601 / 2200	4.0 / 1.7 / 4.1 / 1.9
8 SA	0250 / 0921 / 1541 / 2154	4.2 / 1.6 / 4.2 / 1.8	23 SU	0426 / 1036 / 1650 / 2256	4.0 / 1.6 / 4.2 / 1.8
9 SU	0350 / 1018 / 1632 / 2249	4.3 / 1.4 / 4.4 / 1.5	24 M	0516 / 1124 / 1732 / 2345	4.1 / 1.6 / 4.4 / 1.6
10 M	0446 / 1110 / 1719 / 2340	4.6 / 1.2 / 4.7 / 1.2	25 TU	0557 / 1205 / 1809	4.2 / 1.5 / 4.6
11 TU	0537 / 1159 / 1803	4.8 / 1.0 / 4.9	26 W	0028 / 0633 / 1244 / 1842	1.4 / 4.4 / 1.4 / 4.7
12 W	0030 / 0626 / 1246 / 1847 ●	0.9 / 5.0 / 0.8 / 5.0	27 TH	0107 / 0706 / 1320 / 1915 ○	1.3 / 4.4 / 1.3 / 4.8
13 TH	0119 / 0715 / 1333 / 1932	0.7 / 5.0 / 0.7 / 5.1	28 F	0144 / 0738 / 1354 / 1947	1.2 / 4.5 / 1.3 / 4.8
14 F	0207 / 0805 / 1418 / 2020	0.5 / 5.0 / 0.7 / 5.1	29 SA	0219 / 0810 / 1427 / 2020	1.1 / 4.5 / 1.3 / 4.8
15 SA	0255 / 0857 / 1505 / 2112	0.4 / 4.9 / 0.8 / 5.0	30 SU	0253 / 0842 / 1501 / 2054	1.1 / 4.4 / 1.4 / 4.8

JULY

Day	TIME	m	Day	TIME	m
1 M	0327 / 0916 / 1536 / 2130	1.2 / 4.4 / 1.4 / 4.7	16 TU	0411 / 1017 / 1618 / 2232	0.5 / 4.7 / 0.9 / 4.8
2 TU	0403 / 0954 / 1613 / 2210	1.3 / 4.3 / 1.6 / 4.5	17 W	0456 / 1110 / 1703 / 2325	0.8 / 4.4 / 1.3 / 4.5
3 W	0440 / 1037 / 1655 / 2256	1.4 / 4.2 / 1.7 / 4.4	18 TH	0543 / 1208 / 1753 ☽	1.2 / 4.1 / 1.6
4 TH	0523 / 1129 / 1745 / 2349	1.5 / 4.1 / 1.9 / 4.2	19 F	0025 / 0636 / 1314 / 1851	4.1 / 1.6 / 3.9 / 1.9
5 F	0613 / 1233 / 1845 ☾	1.7 / 4.0 / 2.0	20 SA	0138 / 0742 / 1424 / 2006	3.9 / 1.9 / 3.9 / 2.1
6 SA	0052 / 0715 / 1349 / 1957	4.1 / 1.7 / 4.0 / 2.0	21 SU	0256 / 0900 / 1531 / 2130	3.7 / 2.1 / 3.9 / 2.2
7 SU	0207 / 0829 / 1503 / 2115	4.1 / 1.8 / 4.1 / 1.9	22 M	0406 / 1011 / 1628 / 2242	3.8 / 2.0 / 4.1 / 2.0
8 M	0323 / 0942 / 1608 / 2225	4.2 / 1.6 / 4.3 / 1.7	23 TU	0502 / 1107 / 1714 / 2335	3.9 / 1.9 / 4.3 / 1.8
9 TU	0430 / 1048 / 1703 / 2327	4.4 / 1.4 / 4.5 / 1.3	24 W	0545 / 1151 / 1752	4.1 / 1.7 / 4.5
10 W	0528 / 1144 / 1752	4.6 / 1.2 / 4.8	25 TH	0018 / 0620 / 1229 / 1825	1.5 / 4.3 / 1.5 / 4.7
11 TH	0021 / 0619 / 1235 / 1838 ●	0.9 / 4.8 / 0.9 / 5.1	26 F	0055 / 0651 / 1303 / 1856 ○	1.3 / 4.5 / 1.4 / 4.9
12 F	0111 / 0707 / 1322 / 1923	0.6 / 5.0 / 0.7 / 5.2	27 SA	0128 / 0720 / 1336 / 1926	1.1 / 4.6 / 1.2 / 5.0
13 SA	0158 / 0754 / 1407 / 2009	0.3 / 5.1 / 0.5 / 5.3	28 SU	0200 / 0748 / 1407 / 1956	1.0 / 4.7 / 1.2 / 5.0
14 SU	0243 / 0841 / 1451 / 2055	0.2 / 5.1 / 0.6 / 5.3	29 M	0231 / 0816 / 1439 / 2027	1.0 / 4.7 / 1.2 / 5.0
15 M	0327 / 0928 / 1534 / 2142	0.2 / 4.9 / 0.7 / 5.1	30 TU	0302 / 0846 / 1512 / 2100	1.0 / 4.7 / 1.2 / 5.0
			31 W	0335 / 0919 / 1548 / 2136	1.1 / 4.6 / 1.3 / 4.8

AUGUST

Day	TIME	m	Day	TIME	m
1 TH	0409 / 0957 / 1626 / 2217	1.2 / 4.5 / 1.5 / 4.6	16 F	0459 / 1108 / 1711 / 2324	1.4 / 4.2 / 1.6 / 4.1
2 F	0448 / 1042 / 1710 / 2307	1.3 / 4.3 / 1.7 / 4.4	17 SA	0543 / 1214 / 1802 ☽	1.8 / 3.9 / 2.0
3 SA	0533 / 1141 / 1804 ☾	1.5 / 4.1 / 1.9	18 SU	0044 / 0640 / 1340 / 1914	3.7 / 2.2 / 3.7 / 2.4
4 SU	0011 / 0628 / 1305 / 1915	4.1 / 1.8 / 3.9 / 2.1	19 M	0224 / 0812 / 1458 / 2105	3.6 / 2.4 / 3.8 / 2.3
5 M	0141 / 0746 / 1438 / 2049	3.9 / 1.9 / 3.9 / 2.0	20 TU	0346 / 0950 / 1602 / 2231	3.6 / 2.3 / 4.0 / 2.1
6 TU	0311 / 0920 / 1553 / 2217	4.0 / 1.9 / 4.1 / 1.7	21 W	0445 / 1050 / 1651 / 2322	3.8 / 2.1 / 4.2 / 1.8
7 W	0423 / 1037 / 1653 / 2322	4.2 / 1.6 / 4.5 / 1.3	22 TH	0527 / 1133 / 1729	4.1 / 1.8 / 4.5
8 TH	0521 / 1136 / 1742	4.5 / 1.2 / 4.8	23 F	0000 / 0600 / 1209 / 1802	1.5 / 4.3 / 1.6 / 4.7
9 F	0014 / 0610 / 1225 / 1826	0.8 / 4.9 / 0.9 / 5.2	24 SA	0033 / 0628 / 1241 / 1832	1.3 / 4.5 / 1.4 / 4.9
10 SA	0100 / 0654 / 1308 / 1908 ●	0.5 / 5.1 / 0.6 / 5.4	25 SU	0104 / 0655 / 1312 / 1900 ○	1.1 / 4.7 / 1.2 / 5.1
11 SU	0142 / 0736 / 1350 / 1949	0.1 / 5.3 / 0.4 / 5.5	26 M	0134 / 0720 / 1343 / 1929	0.9 / 4.9 / 1.1 / 5.2
12 M	0223 / 0816 / 1430 / 2029	0.1 / 5.3 / 0.4 / 5.5	27 TU	0203 / 0747 / 1414 / 1959	0.8 / 5.0 / 1.0 / 5.2
13 TU	0302 / 0856 / 1509 / 2109	0.2 / 5.1 / 0.6 / 5.2	28 W	0234 / 0816 / 1447 / 2031	0.8 / 5.0 / 1.0 / 5.2
14 W	0341 / 0937 / 1548 / 2150	0.5 / 4.9 / 0.8 / 4.9	29 TH	0306 / 0847 / 1522 / 2107	0.9 / 4.9 / 1.1 / 5.0
15 TH	0419 / 1019 / 1628 / 2233	0.9 / 4.5 / 1.2 / 4.5	30 F	0340 / 0924 / 1601 / 2147	1.0 / 4.7 / 1.3 / 4.7
			31 SA	0418 / 1006 / 1644 / 2238	1.2 / 4.5 / 1.5 / 4.4

Chart Datum: 2.75 metres below Ordnance Datum (Newlyn)

SCOTLAND, WEST COAST - ULLAPOOL

LAT 57°54'N   LONG 5°10'W

TIMES AND HEIGHTS OF HIGH AND LOW WATERS

YEAR **1991**

TIME ZONE **UT(GMT)**

For Summer Time add ONE
hour in non-shaded areas

8

SEPTEMBER

	TIME	m		TIME	m
1 SU ☾	0502 1104 1737 2351	1.5 4.1 1.8 4.0	**16** M	0548 1247 1830	2.3 3.7 2.3
2 M	0557 1240 1852	1.9 3.9 2.0	**17** TU	0147 0718 1417 2031	3.5 2.5 3.7 2.4
3 TU	0136 0721 1426 2044	3.8 2.1 3.9 2.0	**18** W	0314 0919 1525 2204	3.6 2.4 3.9 2.1
4 W	0308 0913 1543 2214	3.9 2.0 4.1 1.6	**19** TH	0415 1022 1617 2253	3.8 2.2 4.1 1.8
5 TH	0418 1031 1641 2313	4.2 1.6 4.5 1.1	**20** F	0458 1104 1657 2329	4.1 1.9 4.4 1.5
6 F	0511 1124 1728 2359	4.6 1.2 4.9 0.7	**21** SA	0531 1139 1731	4.3 1.6 4.7
7 SA	0556 1208 1810	4.9 0.8 5.2	**22** SU	0002 0559 1212 1801	1.3 4.6 1.4 4.9
8 SU ●	0041 0635 1248 1848	0.3 5.2 0.6 5.5	**23** M O	0033 0625 1243 1831	1.1 4.8 1.2 5.1
9 M	0120 0712 1327 1925	0.1 5.3 0.4 5.5	**24** TU	0103 0651 1315 1901	0.9 5.0 1.0 5.3
10 TU	0157 0748 1404 2001	0.1 5.3 0.4 5.4	**25** W	0134 0719 1348 1933	0.8 5.1 0.9 5.3
11 W	0233 0822 1441 2036	0.3 5.2 0.6 5.2	**26** TH	0206 0749 1423 2007	0.7 5.2 0.9 5.2
12 TH	0308 0857 1518 2111	0.6 4.9 0.9 4.8	**27** F	0240 0822 1501 2046	0.8 5.1 1.0 5.0
13 F	0343 0933 1555 2147	1.0 4.6 1.3 4.4	**28** SA	0316 0900 1541 2130	1.0 4.8 1.2 4.7
14 SA	0419 1015 1635 2231	1.5 4.0 1.7 4.0	**29** SU	0356 0945 1627 2228	1.2 4.5 1.4 4.3
15 SU ☽	0458 1113 1722 2347	1.9 3.9 2.0 3.6	**30** M	0442 1050 1725 2356	1.6 4.1 1.7 3.9

OCTOBER

	TIME	m		TIME	m
1 TU ☾	0542 1237 1848	1.9 3.9 1.9	**16** W	0055 0624 1320 1933	3.5 2.5 3.8 2.3
2 W	0138 0713 1414 2042	3.8 2.1 4.0 1.8	**17** TH	0225 0821 1432 2110	3.5 2.5 3.9 2.1
3 TH	0301 0905 1526 2200	3.9 2.0 4.2 1.4	**18** F	0329 0935 1529 2207	3.7 2.3 4.1 1.9
4 F	0404 1014 1623 2253	4.2 1.6 4.5 1.0	**19** SA	0417 1023 1615 2247	4.2 2.0 4.3 1.6
5 SA	0454 1103 1709 2337	4.6 1.2 4.9 0.7	**20** SU	0453 1104 1654 2323	4.3 1.7 4.6 1.4
6 SU	0536 1145 1750	4.9 0.9 5.1	**21** M	0525 1138 1729 2357	4.6 1.5 4.8 1.1
7 M ●	0017 0613 1225 1826	0.5 5.1 0.7 5.3	**22** TU	0555 1213 1803	4.8 1.2 5.1
8 TU	0054 0647 1303 1901	0.4 5.3 0.6 5.3	**23** W O	0030 0624 1249 1837	0.9 5.1 1.0 5.2
9 W	0130 0720 1339 1935	0.4 5.3 0.6 5.2	**24** TH	0105 0655 1326 1913	0.8 5.2 0.9 5.3
10 TH	0204 0753 1416 2008	0.6 5.1 0.8 5.0	**25** F	0141 0729 1404 1952	0.7 5.2 0.8 5.2
11 F	0238 0825 1452 2042	0.9 4.9 1.0 4.7	**26** SA	0219 0806 1446 2036	0.8 5.1 0.9 5.0
12 SA	0312 0900 1529 2118	1.2 4.7 1.3 4.3	**27** SU	0259 0849 1531 2127	1.0 4.9 1.0 4.6
13 SU	0346 0939 1609 2202	1.6 4.4 1.6 4.0	**28** M	0343 0942 1621 2234	1.2 4.6 1.2 4.3
14 M	0424 1032 1655 2310	1.9 4.1 1.9 3.7	**29** TU	0433 1055 1723	1.6 4.3 1.5
15 TU	0511 1152 1756	2.2 3.8 2.2	**30** W ☾	0000 0536 1229 1844	4.0 1.8 4.1 1.6
			31 TH	0127 0703 1352 2019	3.9 2.0 4.1 1.6

NOVEMBER

	TIME	m		TIME	m
1 F	0240 0837 1501 2131	4.1 1.9 4.3 1.3	**16** SA	0226 0827 1427 2102	3.8 2.4 4.0 2.0
2 SA	0341 0945 1558 2225	4.3 1.6 4.5 1.1	**17** SU	0323 0930 1523 2155	4.0 2.2 4.2 1.8
3 SU	0431 1036 1647 2310	4.5 1.4 4.7 0.9	**18** M	0409 1019 1611 2240	4.2 1.9 4.5 1.5
4 M	0514 1120 1730 2351	4.8 1.2 4.9 0.8	**19** TU	0449 1102 1655 2321	4.5 1.7 4.7 1.3
5 TU	0552 1201 1808	5.0 1.0 5.0	**20** W	0526 1144 1737	4.8 1.4 4.9
6 W ●	0028 0626 1241 1842	0.8 5.1 0.9 5.0	**21** TH O	0001 0601 1226 1818	1.1 5.0 1.1 5.1
7 TH	0105 0659 1319 1916	0.8 5.1 0.9 4.9	**22** F	0042 0638 1309 1900	0.9 5.2 0.9 5.1
8 F	0140 0731 1356 1950	0.9 5.0 1.0 4.8	**23** SA	0123 0751 1352 1945	0.8 5.2 0.8 5.1
9 SA	0214 0804 1433 2024	1.1 4.9 1.1 4.6	**24** SU	0205 0800 1438 2033	0.8 5.2 0.7 5.0
10 SU	0248 0840 1511 2102	1.3 4.7 1.3 4.3	**25** M	0249 0847 1526 2129	0.9 5.0 0.8 4.7
11 M	0323 0919 1551 2145	1.6 4.5 1.5 4.1	**26** TU	0336 0941 1618 2233	1.1 4.8 1.0 4.4
12 TU	0401 1006 1634 2240	1.8 4.3 1.8 3.8	**27** W	0427 1050 1716 2345	1.4 4.6 1.2 4.2
13 W	0445 1104 1725 2353	2.1 4.1 2.0 3.7	**28** TH	0526 1205 1824	1.6 4.4 1.3
14 TH ☽	0541 1213 1831 1939	2.3 4.0 2.1 1.4	**29** F	0058 0636 1319	4.1 1.8 4.3
15 F	0114 0702 1324 1952	3.6 2.4 4.0 2.1	**30** SA	0208 0754 1427 2051	4.1 1.9 4.3 1.7

DECEMBER

	TIME	m		TIME	m
1 SU	0311 0906 1529 2151	4.2 1.8 4.4 1.4	**16** M	0218 0823 1424 2053	4.0 2.3 4.2 1.9
2 M	0405 1005 1625 2242	4.4 1.7 4.4 1.3	**17** TU	0321 0930 1529 2155	4.1 2.1 4.3 1.7
3 TU	0453 1057 1713 2327	4.5 1.5 4.5 1.2	**18** W	0415 1028 1626 2248	4.4 1.9 4.5 1.5
4 W	0534 1143 1754	4.7 1.4 4.6	**19** TH	0502 1121 1718 2338	4.6 1.6 4.7 1.3
5 TH	0007 0610 1226 1831	1.2 4.8 1.3 4.7	**20** F	0546 1210 1806	4.9 1.3 5.0
6 F ●	0046 0645 1306 1905	1.2 4.9 1.2 4.7	**21** SA O	0025 0628 1258 1853	1.0 5.1 0.9 5.1
7 SA	0122 0718 1344 1939	0.9 5.0 1.2 4.7	**22** SU	0111 0711 1345 1940	0.9 5.3 0.7 5.2
8 SU	0157 0751 1421 2013	1.3 5.0 1.2 4.6	**23** M	0156 0755 1432 2028	0.8 5.3 0.5 5.1
9 M	0231 0825 1458 2048	1.4 4.9 1.3 4.4	**24** TU	0241 0843 1519 2120	0.8 5.3 0.5 5.0
10 TU	0306 0901 1534 2125	1.5 4.8 1.4 4.3	**25** W	0326 0934 1607 2215	0.9 5.2 0.6 4.7
11 TH	0342 0941 1612 2207	1.7 4.6 1.6 4.1	**26** TH	0414 1030 1657 2314	1.1 5.0 0.9 4.5
12 TH	0421 1024 1654 2256	1.9 4.4 1.7 4.2	**27** F	0504 1131 1751	1.3 4.7 1.2
13 F	0505 1114 1740 2356	2.1 4.3 1.9 3.9	**28** SA ☽	0018 0600 1237 1852	4.3 1.6 4.4 1.5
14 SA	0600 1212 1837	2.2 4.2 2.0	**29** SU	0126 0705 1347 2001	4.1 1.9 4.2 1.7
15 SU	0106 0708 1317 1945	3.9 2.3 4.1 2.0	**30** M	0234 0819 1458 2112	4.1 2.0 4.1 1.8
			31 TU	0338 0933 1605 2215	4.2 2.0 4.1 1.8

Chart Datum: 2.75 metres below Ordnance Datum (Newlyn)

PORTREE   10-8-9
Skye

CHARTS
Admiralty 2534, 2209; Imray C66; OS 23

TIDES
−0445 Dover; ML 2.9; Duration 0610; Zone 0 (GMT).
Standard Port ULLAPOOL (←)

Times				Height (metres)			
HW		LW		MHWS	MHWN	MLWN	MLWS
0000	0600	0300	0900	5.2	3.9	2.1	0.7
1200	1800	1500	2100				
Differences PORTREE (Skye)							
−0025	−0025	−0025	−0025	+0.1	−0.2	−0.2	0.0
SHEILDAG (Loch Torridon)							
−0020	−0020	−0015	−0015	+0.4	+0.3	+0.1	0.0
PLOCKTON (Loch Carron)							
+0005	−0025	−0005	−0010	+0.5	+0.5	+0.5	+0.2
LOCH SNIZORT-(Uig Bay, Skye)							
−0045	−0020	−0005	−0025	+0.1	−0.4	0.0	0.0
LOCH DUNVEGAN (Skye)							
−0105	−0030	−0020	−0040	0.0	−0.1	0.0	0.0
LOCH HARPORT (Skye)							
−0115	−0035	−0020	−0100	−0.1	−0.1	0.0	+0.1
KYLE OF LOCHALSH							
−0040	−0020	−0005	−0025	+0.1	0.0	+0.1	+0.1
GLENELG BAY (Kyle Rhea)							
−0105	−0034	−0034	−0054	−0.4	−0.4	−0.9	−0.1
LOCH HOURN							
−0125	−0050	−0040	−0110	−0.2	−0.1	−0.1	+0.1

SHELTER
Secure shelter in all but strong SW winds but holding
ground not reliable. There are eight HIDB moorings for
visitors for vessels up to 15 tons, in Portree. There are a
number of anchorages round Skye, so choose one
according to wind direction and forecast. There are four
HIDB moorings off Stein in NW.

NAVIGATION
Waypoint 57°24'.70N 06°07'.50W, 090°/270° from/to
Sgeir Mhor rock, 1.6M. Approaching from S, keep clear
of shore round An Tom Pt (off chartlet) where there are
rocks.

LIGHTS AND MARKS
The only lights in the harbour are 2 FR (vert) (occas) on
the pier.

RADIO TELEPHONE
VHF Ch 16; 08 (occas).

TELEPHONE (0478)
Hr Mr office on pier ☎ 2926; MRSC Oban 63720;
CG 2663; ▒ Inverness 231608; Marinecall 0898 500 464;
Police 2888; Dr 2013; Ⓗ 2704

FACILITIES
EC Wednesday; **Pier** D (cans), L, FW; **West End Garage**
P, Gas; **Town** P, V, Gaz, Ⓞ, R, Bar. ✉; Ⓑ; ≉ (bus to
Kyleakin, ferry to Kyle of Lochalsh); ✈ (Inverness).

MALLAIG   10-8-10
Inverness

CHARTS
Admiralty 2534, 2208; Imray C65, C66; OS 40
TIDES
−0515 Dover; ML 2.9; Duration 0605; Zone 0 (GMT).
Standard Port OBAN (→)

Times				Height (metres)			
HW		LW		MHWS	MHWN	MLWN	MLWS
0000	0600	0100	0700	4.0	2.9	1.8	0.7
1200	1800	1300	1900				
Differences MALLAIG							
+0040	+0020	+0035	+0030	+1.0	+0.9	+0.3	0.0
INVERIE BAY							
+0030	+0020	+0035	+0020	+1.0	+0.9	+0.2	0.0
BAY OF LAIG (Eigg)							
+0015	+0030	+0040	+0005	+0.7	+0.6	−0.2	−0.2
LOCH MOIDART							
+0015	+0015	+0040	+0020	+0.8	+0.6	−0.2	−0.2
LOCH EATHARNA (Coll)							
+0025	+0010	+0015	+0025	+0.4	+0.3	No data	
GOTT BAY (Tiree)							
+0015	0000	0000	+0015	+0.1	+0.1	−0.1	−0.1

SHELTER
Good shelter in SW winds but open to the N. Anchor
near the head or go alongside Fish Pier. Access H24.

⚓ No visitors moorings

NAVIGATION
Waypoint 57°00'.70N 05°49'.80W, 330°/150° from/to
Steamer Pier Lt, 0.28M. Red Rocks lie in entrance to the
harbour (marked by beacon on centre rock) but can be
passed either side, the E side being easier. Harbour is
often congested with fishing boats. Also used by car ferry
service to Skye.

LIGHTS AND MARKS
Sgeir Dhearg Fl(2)WG 8s 6m 5M; vis G190°−055°,
W055°−190° (liable to be obsc by town lights). Steamer
Pier, E end Iso WRG 4s 6m 9/6M; vis G181°−185°,
W185°−197°, R197°−201°. Int Port Traffic Sigs for
ferries (May−Sep).

RADIO TELEPHONE
Call: *Mallaig Harbour Radio* VHF Ch 16; 09 (office hours).

TELEPHONE (0687)
Hr Mr 2154; CG 2336; MRSC Oban 63720; ▒ Fort William
2948; Marinecall 0898 500 464; Police 2177; Dr 2202

FACILITIES
EC Wednesday; **Jetty** Slip, M, P, D, L, FW, ME, El, Sh,
C (10 ton mobile), CH, AB; **Mallaig Boat Bldg Co.**
☎ 2304, ME, El, Sh, CH; **Western Battery Service**
☎ 2044, Ⓔ; **Johnson Bros** ☎ 2215 CH, ACA; **Town** V,
R, Gas, Gaz, Bar. ✉; Ⓑ; ≉; ✈ (Inverness).

LOCH SUNART (Drumbuie and Salen)   10-8-11
Argyll

CHARTS
Admiralty 2392, 2394; Imray C65; OS 45, 47, 49
TIDES
Salen −0500 Dover; ML 2.0; Zone 0 (GMT).
Standard Port OBAN (——►)

Times				Height (metres)			
HW		LW		MHWS	MHWN	MLWN	MLWS
0100	0700	0100	0800	4.0	2.9	1.8	0.7
1300	1900	1300	2000				

Differences SALEN
−0015 +0015 +0010 +0005 +0.6   +0.5   −0.1   −0.1

SHELTER
Anchorages in Loch na Droma Buidhe (S of Oronsay) sheltered in all winds, between Oronsay and Carna, in Loch Teacuis (very difficult entrance), E of Carna, Salen Bay, Garbh Eilean (NW of Rubha an Daimh), and E of sand spit near head of loch by Strontian R.
NAVIGATION
Waypoints − from W 56°39'.70N 06°03'.00W, 263°/083° from/to Creag nan Sgarbh 3.7M: from S 56°38'00N, 06°00'65W 1M to S of Auliston Pt. Beware Ross Rk S of Risga; Broad Rk E of Risga; Dun Ghallain Rk; shoals extending 3 ca NNW from Eilean mo Shlinneag off S shore; rk which dries 1 ca W of S end of Garbh Eilean and strong streams at sp in Laudale Narrows.
LIGHTS AND MARKS
There are no Lts. There are numbers of transits shown on the chart. Coming from S, Eilean Mor Peak at 052°; from W, Risga in line with N point of Oronsay at 083°. Further up the loch, 339° and 294°, as shown in chartlet are useful.
RADIO TELEPHONE
None.
TELEPHONE (096 785)
MRSC and CG Oban 63720; ✆ Oban 2948; Marinecall 0898 500 463; Ⓗ Fort William 2481; Dr 231.
FACILITIES
SALEN EC Monday Jack Walters ☎ 648, M, V, Gas; The Jetty Shop ☎ 648, CH, V, Gas, M, (ME, El, Sh, P, D by arrangement); Conyer Marine ☎ 654, M, ME, Sh, El, CH; Salen Hotel ☎ 661 R, Bar; Village V, FW (at pier), CH, ✉, Ⓑ (mobile Tues and Wed), ⇌ (bus to Loch Ailort), ✈ (Oban).
STRONTIAN V, hotel, ✉, Gas, Bar, FW.

TOBERMORY   10-8-12
Mull

CHARTS
Admiralty 2474, 2171; Imray C65; OS 47
TIDES
−0519 Dover; ML 2.5; Duration 0610; Zone 0 (GMT).
Standard Port OBAN (——►)

Times				Height (metres)			
HW		LW		MHWS	MHWN	MLWN	MLWS
0100	0700	0100	0800	4.0	2.9	1.8	0.7
1300	1900	1300	2000				

Differences TOBERMORY (Mull)
+0025 +0010 +0015 +0025 +0.4   +0.4   0.0   0.0
IONA (Mull)
−0010 −0005 −0020 +0015   0.0   +0.1   −0.3   −0.2
LOCH LATHAICH (Bunessan, Mull)
−0015 −0015 −0010 −0015 +0.3   +0.1   0.0   −0.1
ULVA SOUND (Mull)
−0010 −0015   0000 −0005 +0.4   +0.3   0.0   −0.1

TOBERMORY *Continued*

SHELTER
Good except for some swell when strong winds from NW or N. Anchor off Old Distillery pierhead (where there are some Bu spherical mooring buoys marked 'HIDB visitors only'), off Aros pier in SW corner of bay, close to NW side of Calve Is or in bay at NW end of Calve Is.

NAVIGATION
Waypoint 56°38'.00N 06°02'.00W, 058°/238° from/to MacBraynes Pier, 1.1M. South entrance is only 80m wide at HW, with a dangerous wreck, and dries at LW. North entrance is recommended, the only danger being Sgeit Calve on NE of Calve Island.

LIGHTS AND MARKS
Coming up Doirlinn passage Tobermory Free Church spire in line with West entrance Pt to Doirlinn, about 300° leads through the channel.

RADIO TELEPHONE
VHF Ch 16 (office hours. Listens only).

TELEPHONE (0688)
Hr Mr 2017; CG 2200; MRSC Oban 63720; ✉ 231608; Marinecall 0898 500 463; Police 2016; Dr 2013

FACILITIES
EC Wednesday; **Pier** P, FW, AB, V: **Seafare** (listens on Ch 16 office hours) ☎ 2277, M, P, D, Sh, CH, V, ACA; **Archebald Brown** ☎ 2020, FW, AB; **Western Isles YC** ☎ 2097; **Iain MacDonald** ☎ 2023 Gas. **Town** V, R, Bar, ✉; Ⓑ; Ⓞ, ⇌ (ferry to Oban); ✈ (Mull).

LOCH ALINE   10-8-13
Argyll

CHARTS
Admiralty 2390; Imray C65; OS 49
TIDES
−0523 Dover; Duration 0610; Zone 0 (GMT).
Standard Port OBAN (→)

Times				Height (metres)			
HW		LW		MHWS	MHWN	MLWN	MLWS
0100	0700	0100	0800	4.0	2.9	1.8	0.7
1300	1900	1300	2000				

Differences LOCH ALINE

No data	+0012	+0012	No data	+0.5	+0.3	No data	No data

CRAIGNURE

+0030	+0005	+0010	+0015	0.0	+0.1	−0.1	−0.1

SHELTER
Very good shelter but only good anchorage is in S end of loch to E of entrance. There are numerous hazards in N part of loch. Yachts can use the pier outside the loch, 3 ca W of entrance temporarily, or go alongside the old stone pier in the entrance on W side.

NAVIGATION
Waypoint 56°31'.50N, 05°46'30W 356°/176° from/to front Ldg Bn, 0.9M. The entrance is easy and is buoyed. The Ldg Bns 356° lead 0.5 ca W of Bogha Lurcain, a drying rock off Bolorkle Pt on E side of ent. Beyond Bolorkle Pt the ent is narrow with a bar (min depth 2.1m, 1985). Here stream runs 2½ kn at sp. Beware coasters from the sand mine going to/from the jetty and ferries to and from Mull.

LIGHTS AND MARKS
Ardtornish Pt Lt Ho, 1M SE of ent, Fl (2) WRG 10s 7m 8/5M; vis G shore-302°, W302°-310°, R310°-342°, W342°-057°, R057°-095°, W095°-108°, G108°-shore. Three buoys mark entrance channel QR, QG and Fl R 2s. End of ferry slip 2FR (vert). A War Memorial Cross (conspic 9m high) stands on W side of entrance. The Ldg Lts are FW 2m/4m (H24). Half mile up the loch on E side is a Y iron Bn with spherical topmark marking a reef, and ½M further up is a similar Bn marking a larger reef.

RADIO TELEPHONE
None.

TELEPHONE (096 784)
✉ Oban 62892; Marinecall 0898 500 463; MRSC Oban 63720; Ⓗ Oban 63636; Dr 252.

FACILITIES
K. Masters ☎ 2301, Gas; **J. Hodgson** ☎ 204, M, P, D, FW, Gas, R, Ⓞ; **Lochaline Stores** ☎ 220, V; **Lochaline Hotel** ☎ 657, R, Bar; **Village** Bar, Shop, V, P, ✉, Ⓑ (Oban or Fort William), ⇌ (Oban); ✈ (Oban); Ferry to Fishmish.

FORT WILLIAM/CORPACH
Inverness
                                          10-8-14

CHARTS
Admiralty 2372, 2380; Imray C65; OS 41
TIDES
−0535 Dover; ML 2.5; Duration 0610; Zone 0 (GMT).
Standard Port OBAN (→)

Times				Height (metres)			
HW		LW		MHWS	MHWN	MLWN	MLWS
0100	0700	0100	0800	4.0	2.9	1.8	0.7
1300	1900	1300	2000				

Differences CORPACH

0000	+0020	+0040	0000	0.0	0.0	−0.2	−0.2

CORRAN NARROWS

+0007	+0007	+0004	+0004	+0.4	+0.4	−0.1	0.0

LOCH LEVEN HEAD

+0045	+0045	+0045	+0045	No data		No data	

LOCH LINNHE (Port Appin)

−0005	−0005	−0030	0000	+0.2	+0.2	+0.1	+0.1

BARCALDINE PIER (Loch Creran)

+0010	+0020	+0040	+0015	+0.1	+0.1	0.0	+0.1

FORT WILLIAM/CORPACH *Continued*

SHELTER
Exposed to NE through N to SW winds. Anchorages in Bishop's Bay (Loch Leven), Ardgour Bay (beware ferry moorings and fish farm), Camus na Gal Bay (good shelter), Corpach Basin or SW of Eilean A Bhealaidh.

NAVIGATION
Corpach waypoint 56°50'.30N 05°07'.00W, 135°/315° from/to lock entrance, 0.30M. There are no dangers round Fort William but when coming up Loch Linnhe, the Corran Narrows may present a danger. On the port side is Salachan shoal running from Salachan Pt to the narrows and on the starboard is Culchenna spit. These are well marked and buoyed. Spring tide makes up to 6 kn through the narrows.

LIGHTS AND MARKS
There is a Fl G 2s Lt at Fort William pierhead.
NOTE: Corpach is the entrance to the Caledonian Canal (see 10.8.15). There is an Iso WRG 4s Lt at N jetty of lock entrance.

RADIO TELEPHONE
Call: *Corpach Lock* VHF Ch 74.
TELEPHONE (0397)
Hr Mr 7249; CG 7762; MRSC Oban 63720; ⌗ 2948; Marinecall 0898 500 463; Police 2361; Dr 3136, 2947.
FACILITIES
FORT WILLIAM. EC Wednesday; **Pier** ☎ 3881, L, AB; **Slip** ☎ 3701, L; **Town** P, ME, El, Sh, YC, V, R, Bar; Ⓗ; ✉; Ⓑ; ⇌.
CORPACH. **Corpach Basin** ☎ 249, AB, L, FW; **Lochaber Marine** ☎ 861, ME, El, Sh, D (cans), M, CH, C, (18 ton), Slip, Divers; **Lochaber YC** ☎ 3576, M, FW, L, Slip; **Village** P, V, R, Bar, ✉; Ⓑ; ⇌; ✈ (Oban).

CALEDONIAN CANAL   10.8.15
Inverness

CHARTS
Admiralty 1791. OS 41 34 26
TIDES
Tidal differences: Clachnaharry +0116 on Dover, −0104 on Aberdeen; Corpach −0455 on Dover, +0035 on Oban.
SHELTER
Corpach is the SW end of the Caledonian Canal. It is best to pass through the sea lock and lie between that and the first canal lock. The canal consists of three lochs, Lochs Lochy, Oich and Ness connected by canals with 29 locks totalling in all 60M. There are 14 locks between Loch Linnhe (Corpach), through Lochs Lochy and Oich to the summit (100' above sea level) and 15 locks from the summit through Loch Ness to Inverness. 22 miles are through canals and 38 through lochs. It normally takes two full days to pass through and in the summer It may take longer.

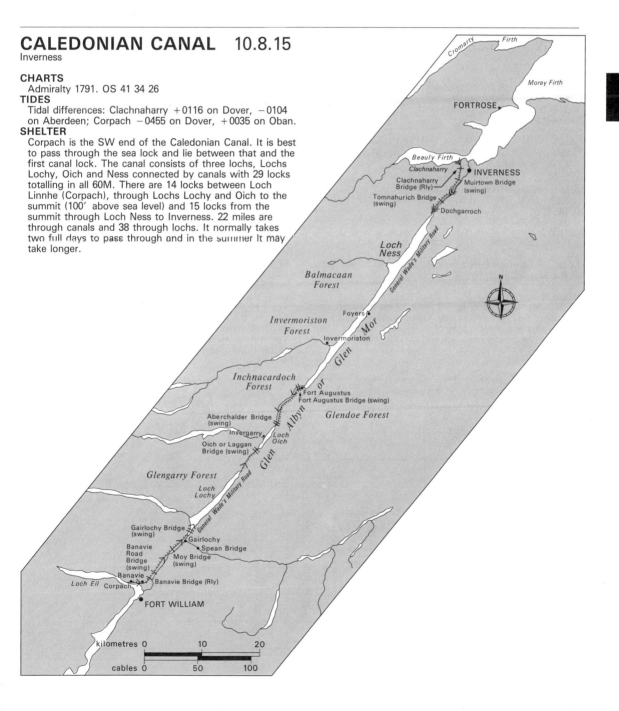

CALEDONIAN CANAL *Continued*

NAVIGATION
There is a speed limit of 5.2 kn in the canal sections.
There are eight swing bridges. All locks are manned and
operate from 0800-1200 and 1300-1645 LT, May-Oct
7 days a week; winter, Mon-Sat. Sea locks will open
outside these hours for extra payment. Dues are payable
at the Corpach end. Canal is available for vessels up to
48m LOA, 11m beam and 4m draught, max mast height
36.5m. Entrance is available HW−4 to HW+4 (springs);
H24 (neaps). Ring Lockkeeper on Corpach 249. For rules
and regulations etc apply to the Engineer and Manager,
Caledonian Canal Office, Clachnaharry,
Tel. Inverness 233140.
Loch Oich is part of an Hydro-Electric Scheme and for
this reason the water level can vary. Do not pass bridges
at either end without keeper's instructions.

LIGHTS & MARKS
Channel is marked by posts, cairns and buoys, R on the
NW side of the channel and G on the SE side — none are
lit. There is an Iso WRG 4s light at canal entrance at
Corpach, and an Iso 4s at the sea lock in Inverness.

OBAN   10-8-16
Argyll

CHARTS
Admiralty 1790, 2171, 2487; Imray C65; OS 49
TIDES
−0530 Dover; ML 2.4; Duration 0610; Zone 0 (GMT).
Standard Port OBAN (→)

Times				Height (metres)			
HW		LW		MHWS	MHWN	MLWN	MLWS
0100	0700	0100	0800	4.0	2.9	1.8	0.7
1300	1900	1300	2000				

Differences DUNSTAFFNAGE BAY
+0005 0000 0000 +0005 +0.1 +0.1 +0.1 +0.1
CONNEL
+0020 +0005 +0010 +0015 −0.3 −0.2 −0.1 +0.1
BONAWE
+0150 +0205 +0240 +0210 −2.0 −1.7 −1.3 −0.5

Oban is a Standard Port and tidal predictions for each day
of the year are given below.

SHELTER
Good except in SW-NW strong winds. Also at Little
Horseshoe Bay, Horseshoe Bay, Gallanachbeg, Ardantrive
and Bandystone. Anchorages off town, but water is deep.
There are no visitors moorings and no alongside berths
available.

RADIO TELEPHONE
Call: *Corpach Lock* VHF Ch 74. Call: *Laggan Lock* Ch 74.
Call: *Fort Augustus Lock* Ch 74. Call: *Dochgarroch Lock*
Ch 74. For Clachnaharry office, call: *Caledonian Canal* Ch
74. Call: *Clachnaharry Sea Lock* Ch 74.
TELEPHONES
Head Office Inverness 233140; Corpach Sea Lock Corpach
249; Clachnaharry Sea Lock Inverness 235439.
FACILITIES
 − Corpach see 10.8.14.
 − Gairlochy AB.
 − NE end of Loch Lochy V, M, AB, R.
 − Oich Bridge D, AB, R.
 − Invergarry V, L, FW, AB.
 − Fort Augustus FW, P, L, ME, El, AB, P, V, ✉, Dr,
   Bar.
 − Dochgarroch FW, P, V.
 − Caley Marina (25+25 visitors) ☎ Inverness
   236539 (Muirtown top lock) FW, C, ACA, CH, D,
   ME, El, Sh, AC.
 − Muirtown Marina (20 visitors) (Muirtown
   basin) ☎ Inverness 239745, D, El, ME, Sh, FW,
   Gas, Gaz, ▣, C (4 ton), CH, AC.

NAVIGATION
Waypoint 56°25'.80N 05°30'.00W, 306°/126° from/to
Dunollie Lt, 0.71M. Beware Sgeir Rathaid in middle of the
bay marked by buoys, also MacBraynes ferries run
services from Railway Quay.
LIGHTS AND MARKS
North Spit of Kerrera Fl R 3s 9m 5M; W column, R
bands. Dunollie Fl(2) WRG 6s 7m 5/4M; vis G351°−009°,
W009°−047°, R047°−120°, W120°−138°, G138°−143°.
North Pier 2FG(vert). South Quay 2FG(vert). Northern
Lights Wharf OcG 6s. FR Lts mark works in progress on
Railway Quay (T).
RADIO TELEPHONE
CG-VHF Ch 16 (H24). Port Office, N pier Ch 16; 12
(0900 − 1700 LT).
TELEPHONE (0631)
CG 63720; Piermaster 62892; MRSC 63720; ⌗ 63079;
Marinecall 0898 500 463; Police 62213; Dr 63175.
FACILITIES
EC Thursday; **N. Pier** ☎ 62892, L, FW, C (15 ton mobile);
Cal Mac Pier ☎ 62285, Slip, D, L, FW, CH; **Curries BY**
☎ 62102, Slip, CH; **Oban Yacht Services BY** ☎ 63666,
Slip, M, D, L, FW, ME, Sh, C, CH, AB; **Nancy Black**
☎ 62550, CH, ACA; **Ardantrive Bay** M, P, D, FW (on
pier); **Railway Pier** D.
West Highland Gas Services ☎ 64050 Gas; **Ardoran**
Marine ☎ 66123 D, Sh, ME, Slip, C, M; **Oban Divers**
☎ 62755 divers; **Vale Engineering** ☎ 64531 ME, El;
Town P, V, R, Bar. ✉; Ⓑ; ⇌; ✈.
Note: Royal Highland YC, Andentallan, by Oban,
☎ 63309.

H.W.Hts.m.

OBAN

MEAN SPRING
AND NEAP CURVES

MEAN RANGES
Springs 3·3m
Neaps   1·1m

Springs occur 2 days
after
New and Full Moon.

L.W.Hts.m.

OBAN *continued*

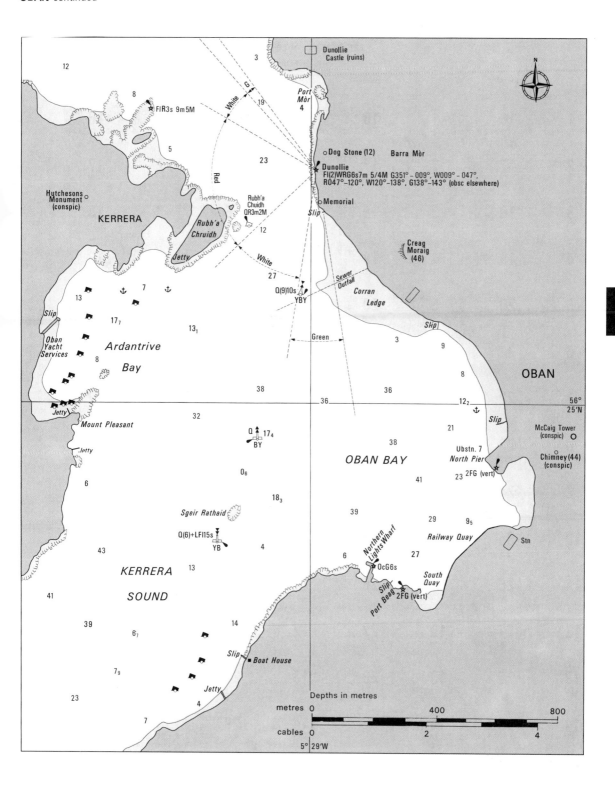

12

3

Dunollie
Castle (ruins)

8

Port
Mòr
4

White

G

19

23

Red

☆ FlR3s 9m5M

5

Dog Stone (12)   Barra Mòr

Dunollie
Fl(2)WRG6s7m 5/4M G351°–009°, W009°–047°,
R047°–120°, W120°–138°, G138°–143° (obsc elsewhere)

Hutchesons
Monument
(conspic)

KERRERA

Rubh'a
Chuidh
QR3m2M

Memorial

Rubh'a'
Chruidh

Slip

Creag
Moraig
(46)

Jetty

12

White

27

Q(9)10s
YBY

Sewer
Outfall

Corran
Ledge

Slip

13   ⚓   7   ⚓

Slip

Oban
Yacht
Services

17₇

13₁

Green

3

9

Ardantrive
Bay

8

8

OBAN

Jetty

38

36

36

56°
25′N

12₂

⚓

Slip

Mount Pleasant

32

21

McCaig Tower
(conspic)   ○

Jetty

Q   17₄
BY

38

Ubstn. 7
North Pier

23 2FG (vert)

Chimney (44)
(conspic)

OBAN BAY

6

0₆

41

Sgeir Rathaid

18₃

39

29

9₅

Railway Quay

Q(6)+LFl15s
YB

43

4

13

KERRERA
SOUND

6

Northern
Lights Wharf

27

South
Quay

Stn

OcG6s

41

39

6₇

14

Slip
Port Bead

2FG (vert)

7₉

Slip   ■ Boat House

Jetty

23

4

Depths in metres

7

metres 0   400   800

cables 0   2   4

5° 29′W

SCOTLAND, WEST COAST - OBAN

LAT 56°25'N   LONG 5°29'W

TIMES AND HEIGHTS OF HIGH AND LOW WATERS

YEAR **1991**

TIME ZONE UT (GMT)
For Summer Time add ONE hour in non-shaded areas

JANUARY

Day	TIME	m		Day	TIME	m
1 TU	0549	4.1		**16** W	0005	1.2
	1214	0.8			0607	3.9
	1831	4.0			1218	1.3
					1824	3.7
2 W	0024	0.5		**17** TH	0036	1.1
	0634	4.2			0638	4.0
	1305	0.7			1252	1.2
	1913	4.0			1853	3.8
3 TH	0109	0.5		**18** F	0106	1.0
	0716	4.2			0708	4.0
	1354	0.8			1324	1.2
	1953	3.9			1920	3.8
4 F	0153	0.5		**19** SA	0136	1.0
	0757	4.1			0738	4.0
	1439	1.0			1358	1.2
	2030	3.7			1947	3.7
5 SA	0236	0.7		**20** SU	0207	1.0
	0836	3.9			0810	3.9
	1523	1.2			1434	1.2
	2107	3.5			2017	3.7
6 SU	0319	0.9		**21** M	0241	1.1
	0917	3.6			0845	3.8
	1608	1.5			1513	1.3
	2147	3.3			2049	3.5
7 M	0405	1.2		**22** TU	0320	1.3
	1002	3.4			0925	3.6
	1654	1.7			1556	1.4
	☾ 2235	3.1			2128	3.4
8 TU	0456	1.5		**23** W	0406	1.4
	1057	3.2			1014	3.4
	1748	1.9			1647	1.6
	2341	3.0			☽ 2217	3.2
9 W	0555	1.8		**24** TH	0504	1.6
	1211	3.0			1123	3.2
	1853	2.0			1749	1.7
					2327	3.0
10 TH	0110	3.0		**25** F	0620	1.7
	0705	1.9			1302	3.1
	1340	3.0			1905	1.7
	2011	2.0				
11 F	0236	3.1		**26** SA	0114	3.0
	0821	1.9			0752	1.7
	1459	3.1			1446	3.2
	2123	1.9			2028	1.6
12 SA	0338	3.2		**27** SU	0307	3.2
	0927	1.9			0923	1.5
	1557	3.2			1602	3.4
	2216	1.7			2143	1.3
13 SU	0424	3.4		**28** M	0417	3.5
	1020	1.7			1032	1.2
	1642	3.4			1659	3.6
	2257	1.5			2241	0.9
14 M	0501	3.6		**29** TU	0508	3.8
	1104	1.6			1127	0.9
	1720	3.5			1745	3.8
	2332	1.3			2329	0.6
15 TU	0535	3.8		**30** W	0550	4.1
	1142	1.4			1214	0.7
	1754	3.6			1824	4.0
	●				○	
				31 TH	0013	0.4
					0628	4.2
					1256	0.6
					1859	4.0

FEBRUARY

Day	TIME	m		Day	TIME	m
1 F	0054	0.3		**16** SA	0043	0.8
	0703	4.2			0646	4.1
	1336	0.7			1302	0.9
	1931	4.0			1859	3.9
2 SA	0133	0.3		**17** SU	0113	0.7
	0736	4.1			0716	4.2
	1413	0.8			1334	0.9
	2001	3.9			1925	3.9
3 SU	0211	0.5		**18** M	0144	0.7
	0807	3.9			0747	4.1
	1448	1.0			1408	0.9
	2031	3.7			1954	3.7
4 M	0249	0.8		**19** TU	0218	0.8
	0839	3.7			0820	3.8
	1524	1.3			1446	1.0
	2103	3.5			2025	3.7
5 TU	0329	1.1		**20** W	0257	1.0
	0912	3.4			0857	3.7
	1602	1.6			1528	1.2
	2139	3.3			2101	3.5
6 W	0412	1.5		**21** TH	0342	1.3
	0950	3.2			0942	3.3
	1647	1.8			1617	1.4
	☾ 2228	3.0			2146	3.4
7 TH	0505	1.8		**22** F	0441	1.5
	1043	2.9			1047	3.0
	1747	2.0			1719	1.6
	2358	2.9			2254	3.0
8 F	0616	2.0		**23** SA	0603	1.7
	1227	2.8			1307	2.8
	1917	2.1			1841	1.7
9 SA	0206	2.9		**24** SU	0129	2.9
	0746	2.1			0801	1.7
	1447	2.8			1502	3.0
	2059	2.0			2019	1.6
10 SU	0322	3.1		**25** M	0327	1.4
	0915	2.0			0940	1.4
	1555	3.0			1605	3.2
	2201	1.7			2138	1.2
11 M	0409	3.3		**26** TU	0421	3.5
	1013	1.8			1037	1.1
	1637	3.2			1652	3.5
	2242	1.5			2231	0.9
12 TU	0445	3.5		**27** W	0502	3.8
	1054	1.5			1121	0.8
	1711	3.4			1731	3.7
	2315	1.3			2315	0.5
13 W	0518	3.7		**28** TH	0538	4.0
	1128	1.3			1159	0.6
	1741	3.6			1805	3.9
	2346	1.1			○ 2354	0.3
14 TH	0549	3.9				
	1200	1.1				
	1808	3.7				
	●					
15 F	0014	0.9				
	0617	4.1				
	1231	1.0				
	1834	3.9				

MARCH

Day	TIME	m		Day	TIME	m
1 F	0609	4.2		**16** SA	0550	4.1
	1235	0.6			1201	0.8
	1835	4.0			1806	3.9
					●	
2 SA	0031	0.3		**17** SU	0014	0.6
	0638	4.2			0619	4.2
	1308	0.6			1233	0.7
	1902	4.0			1832	4.0
3 SU	0108	0.3		**18** M	0046	0.6
	0707	4.1			0651	4.2
	1341	0.7			1308	0.6
	1930	4.0			1900	4.0
4 M	0143	0.5		**19** TU	0120	0.6
	0735	3.9			0724	4.1
	1412	1.0			1344	0.7
	1958	3.8			1931	4.0
5 TU	0218	0.8		**20** W	0158	0.7
	0803	3.7			0759	3.9
	1444	1.2			1423	0.8
	2027	3.6			2004	3.8
6 W	0255	1.1		**21** TH	0240	0.9
	0833	3.4			0839	3.6
	1519	1.4			1507	1.0
	2059	3.4			2043	3.5
7 TH	0334	1.5		**22** F	0330	1.2
	0905	3.2			0926	3.2
	1558	1.7			1558	1.3
	2139	3.1			2130	3.2
8 F	0424	1.8		**23** SA	0435	1.5
	0944	2.9			1041	2.8
	1653	1.9			1702	1.5
	☾ 2253	2.8			☽ 2248	2.9
9 SA	0533	2.0		**24** SU	0610	1.7
	1108	2.7			1328	2.7
	1821	2.1			1828	1.6
10 SU	0131	2.8		**25** M	0207	2.9
	0711	2.1			0819	1.6
	1419	2.7			1452	2.9
	2020	2.0			2007	1.5
11 M	0252	3.0		**26** TU	0318	3.2
	0853	2.0			0935	1.3
	1529	2.9			1548	3.2
	2133	1.8			2120	1.2
12 TU	0339	3.2		**27** W	0405	3.5
	0951	1.7			1022	1.1
	1611	3.1			1630	3.4
	2214	1.5			2210	0.9
13 W	0416	3.5		**28** TH	0442	3.7
	1028	1.5			1100	0.9
	1644	3.3			1706	3.7
	2247	1.3			2251	0.6
14 TH	0449	3.7		**29** F	0513	3.9
	1100	1.2			1134	0.7
	1713	3.6			1737	3.8
	2316	1.0			2329	0.5
15 F	0519	3.9		**30** SA	0541	4.0
	1130	1.0			1206	0.7
	1740	3.8			1805	3.9
	2345	0.8			○	
				31 SU	0005	0.4
					0608	4.0
					1238	0.7
					1832	4.0

APRIL

Day	TIME	m		Day	TIME	m
1 M	0040	0.5		**16** TU	0020	0.5
	0636	3.9			0628	4.2
	1309	0.8			1243	0.5
	1900	3.9			1837	4.1
2 TU	0115	0.7		**17** W	0100	0.5
	0704	3.8			0704	4.0
	1340	1.0			1323	0.6
	1929	3.8			1913	4.0
3 W	0150	0.9		**18** TH	0143	0.7
	0733	3.6			0747	3.8
	1412	1.1			1406	0.7
	1958	3.6			1951	3.8
4 TH	0226	1.2		**19** F	0232	0.9
	0803	3.4			0831	3.5
	1446	1.4			1454	0.9
	2031	3.4			2035	3.5
5 F	0305	1.5		**20** SA	0329	1.2
	0835	3.1			0927	3.1
	1524	1.6			1547	1.2
	2110	3.1			2131	3.2
6 SA	0353	1.8		**21** SU	0442	1.4
	0913	2.9			1101	2.8
	1613	1.8			1652	1.4
	2213	2.9			☽ 2310	3.0
7 SU	0459	2.0		**22** M	0618	1.6
	1018	2.7			1306	2.8
	1728	2.0			1811	1.5
	☾					
8 M	0040	2.8		**23** TU	0145	3.1
	0628	2.0			0757	1.5
	1320	2.6			1421	2.9
	1915	2.0			1937	1.4
9 TU	0205	3.0		**24** W	0250	3.2
	0801	1.9			0905	1.3
	1439	2.8			1515	3.1
	2040	1.8			2047	1.2
10 W	0255	3.2		**25** TH	0335	3.4
	0903	1.7			0952	1.2
	1526	3.0			1558	3.3
	2129	1.6			2139	1.0
11 TH	0335	3.4		**26** F	0411	3.6
	0945	1.5			1029	1.1
	1603	3.2			1634	3.5
	2205	1.3			2222	0.8
12 F	0410	3.6		**27** SA	0442	3.7
	1019	1.2			1103	1.0
	1634	3.5			1706	3.7
	2238	1.1			2301	0.8
13 SA	0443	3.9		**28** SU	0510	3.7
	1053	1.0			1136	0.9
	1703	3.7			1736	3.8
	2310	0.8			○ 2338	0.8
14 SU	0517	4.1		**29** M	0540	3.7
	1128	0.7			1206	0.9
	1733	3.9			1806	3.8
	● 2344	0.6				
15 M	0552	4.2		**30** TU	0014	0.8
	1204	0.6			0609	3.7
	1804	4.0			1242	0.9
					1835	3.8

Chart Datum: 2.10 metres below Ordnance Datum (Newlyn)

SCOTLAND, WEST COAST - OBAN

LAT 56°25'N   LONG 5°29'W

TIMES AND HEIGHTS OF HIGH AND LOW WATERS   YEAR 1991

TIME ZONE UT(GMT)
For Summer Time add ONE hour in non-shaded areas

MAY

Day	TIME	m	TIME	m	Day	TIME	m	TIME	m
1 W	0051	1.0	0641	3.6	16 TH	0048	0.6	0658	3.9
	1314	1.0	1906	3.8		1309	0.5	1903	4.0
2 TH	0126	1.1	0712	3.5	17 F	0138	0.7	0745	3.7
	1347	1.2	1938	3.6		1355	0.6	1947	3.8
3 F	0204	1.3	0744	3.3	18 SA	0233	0.9	0835	3.4
	1422	1.3	2013	3.4		1445	0.8	2037	3.6
4 SA	0244	1.5	0819	3.2	19 SU	0334	1.1	0934	3.1
	1500	1.5	2053	3.2		1538	1.0	2137	3.4
5 SU	0332	1.7	0858	3.0	20 M	0442	1.3	1050	2.9
	1544	1.7	2149	3.0		1637	1.2	☽ 2308	3.2
6 M	0430	1.9	0954	2.8	21 TU	0555	1.5	1218	2.9
	1642	1.8	2332	2.9		1744	1.3		
7 TU	0539	1.9	1144	2.7	22 W	0058	3.1	0710	1.5
☾	1800	1.9				1332	2.9	1856	1.4
8 W	0102	3.0	0652	1.9	23 TH	0206	3.2	0816	1.5
	1325	2.8	1922	1.8		1431	3.0	2005	1.3
9 TH	0200	3.2	0756	1.7	24 F	0256	3.3	0910	1.4
	1424	2.9	2025	1.7		1520	3.2	2103	1.3
10 F	0244	3.3	0847	1.5	25 SA	0335	3.3	0954	1.3
	1508	3.2	2113	1.4		1602	3.3	2152	1.2
11 SA	0325	3.6	0932	1.3	26 SU	0410	3.4	1033	1.2
	1547	3.4	2154	1.2		1639	3.5	2235	1.2
12 SU	0405	3.8	1014	1.0	27 M	0444	3.5	1110	1.2
	1624	3.6	2235	0.9		1713	3.6	2316	1.1
13 M	0447	3.9	1056	0.8	28 TU	0518	3.5	1146	1.1
	1702	3.8	2316	0.7	O	1747	3.7	2354	1.1
14 TU	0529	4.0	1139	0.6	29 W	0553	3.5	1221	1.1
●	1741	4.0				1820	3.7		
15 W	0000	0.6	0613	4.0	30 TH	0032	1.2	0627	3.5
	1224	0.5	1821	4.0		1256	1.1	1852	3.7
					31 F	0111	1.3	0702	3.5
						1330	1.1	1926	3.7

JUNE

Day	TIME	m	TIME	m	Day	TIME	m	TIME	m
1 SA	0149	1.4	0736	3.4	16 SU	0232	0.8	0833	3.6
	1404	1.2	2001	3.6		1434	0.6	2035	3.8
2 SU	0229	1.5	0810	3.2	17 M	0326	1.0	0920	3.3
	1440	1.4	2039	3.4		1523	0.8	2127	3.6
3 M	0312	1.6	0847	3.1	18 TU	0420	1.2	1012	3.1
	1519	1.5	2125	3.3		1614	1.0	2228	3.3
4 TU	0359	1.7	0930	3.0	19 W	0516	1.4	1113	3.0
	1604	1.6	2225	3.1		1710	1.2	☽ 2341	3.1
5 W	0451	1.8	1026	2.9	20 TH	0614	1.6	1223	2.9
	1659	1.7	☾ 2341	3.1		1812	1.4		
6 TH	0548	1.8	1141	2.9	21 F	0058	3.1	0716	1.6
	1805	1.7				1336	2.9	1919	1.5
7 F	0050	3.2	0648	1.7	22 SA	0204	3.0	0821	1.7
	1259	2.9	1913	1.7		1441	3.0	2025	1.6
8 SA	0148	3.3	0748	1.5	23 SU	0259	3.1	0920	1.6
	1404	3.1	2016	1.5		1536	3.2	2125	1.5
9 SU	0240	3.4	0845	1.4	24 M	0348	3.1	1010	1.5
	1459	3.3	2113	1.3		1621	3.3	2216	1.5
10 M	0333	3.6	0940	1.1	25 TU	0431	3.2	1053	1.3
	1551	3.5	2206	1.1		1700	3.5	2301	1.4
11 TU	0426	3.7	1032	0.9	26 W	0512	3.3	1131	1.2
	1641	3.7	2259	0.9		1735	3.6	2342	1.3
12 W	0518	3.8	1122	0.7	27 TH	0549	3.4	1207	1.1
●	1728	3.9	O 2351	0.7		1809	3.7		
13 TH	0610	3.9	1210	0.5	28 F	0021	1.3	0623	3.5
	1815	4.0				1242	1.1	1841	3.8
14 F	0044	0.6	0658	3.8	29 SA	0059	1.3	0656	3.5
	1258	0.5	1901	4.0		1314	1.1	1914	3.8
15 SA	0138	0.7	0746	3.7	30 SU	0135	1.3	0727	3.5
	1346	0.5	1947	4.0		1347	1.1	1947	3.7

JULY

Day	TIME	m	TIME	m	Day	TIME	m	TIME	m
1 M	0211	1.3	0757	3.4	16 TU	0302	0.8	0851	3.6
	1419	1.2	2020	3.6		1459	0.6	2059	3.7
2 TU	0248	1.4	0828	3.3	17 W	0346	1.1	0930	3.4
	1453	1.3	2057	3.5		1544	0.9	2141	3.4
3 W	0327	1.5	0902	3.2	18 TH	0431	1.4	1013	3.2
	1531	1.4	2138	3.4	☽	1633	1.2	2230	3.1
4 TH	0409	1.5	0942	3.1	19 F	0520	1.6	1111	3.0
	1615	1.5	2230	3.3		1729	1.5	2333	2.9
5 F	0458	1.6	1032	3.0	20 SA	0618	1.8	1234	2.9
	1709	1.6	☾ 2335	3.2		1836	1.7		
6 SA	0554	1.6	1139	3.0	21 SU	0100	2.8	0731	1.8
	1816	1.7				1410	2.9	1952	1.8
7 SU	0050	3.2	0658	1.6	22 M	0237	2.9	0851	1.8
	1303	3.0	1931	1.6		1521	3.1	2107	1.8
8 M	0206	3.2	0808	1.5	23 TU	0345	3.0	0954	1.6
	1425	3.1	2046	1.4		1610	3.3	2207	1.7
9 TU	0317	3.3	0916	1.3	24 W	0432	3.1	1040	1.4
	1535	3.4	2154	1.2		1649	3.4	2253	1.5
10 W	0423	3.5	1017	1.0	25 TH	0510	3.3	1118	1.3
	1635	3.6	2255	1.0		1723	3.6	2333	1.4
11 TH	0520	3.7	1111	0.7	26 F	0543	3.4	1152	1.1
	1726	3.9	● 2351	0.7	O	1755	3.8		
12 F	0610	3.8	1200	0.5	27 SA	0008	1.3	0614	3.6
	1813	4.1				1224	1.0	1825	3.9
13 SA	0043	0.6	0654	3.9	28 SU	0042	1.2	0642	3.6
	1247	0.3	1856	4.2		1254	0.9	1855	3.9
14 SU	0132	0.6	0735	3.9	29 M	0114	1.1	0709	3.7
	1332	0.3	1938	4.1		1324	0.9	1925	3.9
15 M	0218	0.7	0813	3.8	30 TU	0146	1.1	0735	3.6
	1415	0.4	2019	3.9		1353	1.0	1955	3.9
					31 W	0219	1.1	0802	3.6
						1425	1.1	2027	3.7

AUGUST

Day	TIME	m	TIME	m	Day	TIME	m	TIME	m
1 TH	0254	1.2	0832	3.5	16 F	0346	1.4	0925	3.3
	1500	1.2	2102	3.6		1556	1.3	2135	3.2
2 F	0333	1.3	0907	3.4	17 SA	0430	1.6	1013	3.1
	1541	1.4	2144	3.4		1649	1.7	☽ 2223	2.9
3 SA	0419	1.4	0950	3.2	18 SU	0527	1.8	1136	2.9
	1632	1.5	2240	3.1		1757	1.9	2356	2.7
4 SU	0515	1.5	1049	3.0	19 M	0646	1.9	1348	2.9
	1740	1.7				1925	2.0		
5 M	0006	3.0	0623	1.8	20 TU	0229	2.7	0826	1.9
	1222	2.9	1906	1.7		1506	3.0	2056	1.9
6 TU	0159	3.0	0744	1.5	21 W	0338	2.9	0937	1.7
	1421	3.1	2042	1.5		1552	3.3	2157	1.7
7 W	0325	3.2	0904	1.3	22 TH	0420	3.1	1022	1.5
	1542	3.3	2159	1.2		1628	3.5	2239	1.5
8 TH	0428	3.4	1009	1.0	23 F	0454	3.3	1057	1.3
	1637	3.7	2258	0.9		1701	3.7	2314	1.3
9 F	0517	3.7	1101	0.6	24 SA	0524	3.5	1129	1.1
	1723	4.0	2347	0.6		1731	3.9	2346	1.2
10 SA	0600	3.9	1147	0.4	25 SU	0552	3.7	1158	1.0
●	1804	4.2			O	1801	4.0		
11 SU	0031	0.5	0637	4.0	26 M	0016	1.0	0618	3.8
	1230	0.2	1841	4.3		1227	0.9	1830	4.1
12 M	0113	0.5	0712	4.0	27 TU	0046	0.9	0643	3.9
	1311	0.2	1916	4.2		1255	0.8	1858	4.1
13 TU	0152	0.6	0744	3.9	28 W	0116	0.9	0708	3.9
	1351	0.3	1950	4.0		1325	0.8	1928	4.0
14 W	0230	0.8	0816	3.7	29 TH	0149	0.9	0735	3.9
	1431	0.6	2023	3.8		1357	0.9	1959	3.9
15 TH	0307	1.1	0849	3.6	30 F	0224	1.0	0805	3.7
	1512	0.9	2057	3.5		1433	1.1	2033	3.7
					31 SA	0304	1.2	0839	3.5
						1515	1.3	2113	3.4

8

Chart Datum: 2.10 metres below Ordnance Datum (Newlyn)

SCOTLAND, WEST COAST - OBAN

LAT 56°25′N   LONG 5°29′W

TIMES AND HEIGHTS OF HIGH AND LOW WATERS   YEAR **1991**

TIME ZONE UT(GMT)
For Summer Time add ONE hour in non-shaded areas

Chart Datum: 2.10 metres below Ordnance Datum (Newlyn)

SEPTEMBER

Days 1–15

Day	Time m	Time m	Time m	Time m
1 SU ☾	0350 1.3	0921 3.3	1609 1.5	2208 3.1
2 M	0447 1.5	1020 3.3	1724 1.7	2353 2.9
3 TU	0601 1.6	1214 2.9	1909 1.7	
4 W	0216 2.9	0732 1.6	1443 3.1	2057 1.5
5 TH	0328 3.1	0856 1.8	1544 3.4	2203 1.2
6 F	0420 3.4	0957 0.9	1629 3.8	2250 0.9
7 SA	0502 3.7	1044 0.6	1708 4.0	2331 0.7
8 SU ●	0539 3.9	1127 0.4	1744 4.2	
9 M	0009 0.5	0611 4.0	1816 4.3	
10 TU	0046 0.5	0642 4.1	1245 0.3	1848 4.2
11 W	0121 0.7	0712 4.0	1323 0.4	1918 4.0
12 TH	0155 0.8	0742 3.9	1401 0.7	1948 3.8
13 F	0229 1.1	0813 3.7	1440 1.1	2019 3.5
14 SA	0306 1.4	0847 3.4	1522 1.5	2052 3.2
15 SU ☽	0348 1.6	0929 3.1	1613 1.8	2132 2.9

Days 16–30

Day	Time m	Time m	Time m	Time m
16 M	0442 1.9	1045 2.9	1722 2.0	2253 2.7
17 TU	0603 2.0	1317 2.9	1856 2.1	
18 W	0157 2.7	0748 2.0	1435 3.1	2033 1.8
19 TH	0307 2.9	0906 1.8	1520 3.3	2132 1.8
20 F	0349 3.1	0952 1.6	1557 3.5	2211 1.6
21 SA	0423 3.3	1027 1.3	1629 3.7	2243 1.3
22 SU	0453 3.5	1058 1.2	1700 3.9	2313 1.1
23 M O	0521 3.7	1126 1.0	1730 4.1	2343 1.0
24 TU	0547 3.9	1155 0.9	1800 4.2	
25 W	0013 0.8	0612 4.0	1225 0.8	1830 4.2
26 TH	0046 0.8	0640 4.0	1257 0.8	1902 4.2
27 F	0121 0.8	0709 4.0	1333 0.9	1935 4.0
28 SA	0159 0.9	0742 3.9	1413 1.0	2013 3.7
29 SU	0241 1.1	0819 3.6	1500 1.3	2056 3.4
30 M	0330 1.3	0905 3.4	1601 1.6	2158 3.0

OCTOBER

Days 1–15

Day	Time m	Time m	Time m	Time m
1 TU ☾	0431 1.5	1011 3.1	1727 1.7	
2 W	0024 2.8	0547 1.6	1306 3.0	1924 1.7
3 TH	0211 2.9	0719 1.5	1438 3.3	2054 1.5
4 F	0312 3.2	0839 1.3	1530 3.6	2148 1.2
5 SA	0358 3.4	0936 1.0	1610 3.8	2230 1.0
6 SU	0437 3.7	1021 0.7	1646 4.0	2307 0.8
7 M ●	0512 3.9	1102 0.5	1718 4.1	2342 0.7
8 TU	0543 4.0	1141 0.5	1749 4.1	
9 W	0016 0.7	0613 4.1	1219 0.6	1818 4.1
10 TH	0050 0.8	0643 4.0	1256 0.7	1849 3.9
11 F	0123 1.0	0712 4.0	1333 1.0	1919 3.7
12 SA	0158 1.2	0745 3.7	1411 1.3	1950 3.5
13 SU	0234 1.4	0820 3.5	1453 1.6	2023 3.3
14 M	0314 1.6	0901 3.3	1543 1.9	2102 3.0
15 TU ☽	0404 1.8	1006 3.0	1649 2.1	2207 2.8

Days 16–31

Day	Time m	Time m	Time m	Time m
16 W	0516 2.0	1222 3.0	1815 2.1	
17 TH	0050 2.7	0651 2.0	1346 3.1	1942 2.1
18 F	0215 2.9	0815 1.9	1437 3.3	2045 1.9
19 SA	0305 3.1	0908 1.7	1517 3.5	2128 1.7
20 SU	0342 3.3	0947 1.5	1552 3.7	2203 1.4
21 M	0414 3.5	1020 1.3	1625 3.9	2235 1.2
22 TU	0444 3.7	1051 1.1	1658 4.1	2308 1.0
23 W O	0513 3.9	1123 0.9	1731 4.2	2343 0.8
24 TH	0543 4.1	1157 0.8	1806 4.2	
25 F	0020 0.7	0615 4.1	1235 0.8	1843 4.2
26 SA	0059 0.7	0650 4.1	1316 0.9	1922 4.0
27 SU	0141 0.8	0728 4.0	1403 1.1	2004 3.7
28 M	0227 1.0	0811 3.7	1457 1.3	2055 3.4
29 TU	0319 1.2	0902 3.5	1605 1.5	2206 3.0
30 W ☾	0419 1.4	1018 3.2	1731 1.7	
31 TH	0010 2.9	0531 1.5	1253 3.2	1907 1.7

NOVEMBER

Days 1–15

Day	Time m	Time m	Time m	Time m
1 F	0140 3.0	0653 1.5	1413 3.4	2026 1.5
2 SA	0241 3.2	0808 1.3	1504 3.6	2120 1.4
3 SU	0329 3.4	0907 1.1	1545 3.7	2203 1.2
4 M	0409 3.6	0955 1.0	1620 3.8	2240 1.1
5 TU	0445 3.8	1038 0.9	1652 3.9	2316 1.0
6 W ●	0518 3.9	1117 0.9	1724 3.9	2350 1.0
7 TH	0550 4.0	1156 0.9	1756 3.9	
8 F	0025 1.0	0621 4.0	1234 1.1	1827 3.8
9 SA	0100 1.1	0653 3.9	1312 1.2	1859 3.7
10 SU	0135 1.2	0726 3.8	1350 1.4	1932 3.5
11 M	0210 1.4	0802 3.6	1431 1.7	2007 3.4
12 TU	0249 1.5	0842 3.4	1518 1.9	2045 3.2
13 W	0333 1.7	0935 3.2	1615 2.0	2136 3.0
14 TH ☽	0428 1.9	1105 3.1	1722 2.1	2305 2.9
15 F	0540 2.0	1240 3.2	1833 2.1	

Days 16–30

Day	Time m	Time m	Time m	Time m
16 SA	0054 2.9	0700 2.0	1342 3.3	1938 2.0
17 SU	0202 3.0	0806 1.9	1429 3.5	2031 1.8
18 M	0250 3.2	0856 1.7	1510 3.6	2115 1.6
19 TU	0330 3.4	0937 1.5	1549 3.8	2156 1.3
20 W	0406 3.7	1015 1.3	1628 4.0	2237 1.1
21 TH O	0443 3.9	1055 1.1	1709 4.1	2318 0.9
22 F	0521 4.0	1137 0.9	1752 4.1	
23 SA	0001 0.7	0600 4.1	1222 0.9	1835 4.1
24 SU	0045 0.7	0641 4.2	1310 0.9	1919 4.0
25 M	0130 0.8	0724 4.1	1402 1.0	2006 3.7
26 TU	0218 0.8	0810 3.9	1500 1.2	2058 3.5
27 W	0309 1.0	0904 3.7	1603 1.4	2200 3.2
28 TH ☾	0405 1.2	1014 3.4	1712 1.6	2320 3.1
29 F	0507 1.3	1158 3.3	1825 1.7	
30 SA	0046 3.0	0616 1.4	1330 3.3	1938 1.7

DECEMBER

Days 1–15

Day	Time m	Time m	Time m	Time m
1 SU	0158 3.1	0728 1.5	1431 3.4	2041 1.6
2 M	0255 3.3	0834 1.4	1520 3.5	2133 1.5
3 TU	0344 3.4	0929 1.3	1600 3.5	2216 1.4
4 W	0425 3.6	1017 1.3	1636 3.6	2256 1.3
5 TH	0502 3.7	1100 1.3	1711 3.7	2333 1.2
6 F ●	0536 3.8	1140 1.3	1745 3.7	
7 SA	0009 1.2	0608 3.9	1220 1.3	1818 3.7
8 SU	0044 1.1	0641 3.9	1258 1.4	1851 3.7
9 M	0119 1.2	0714 3.9	1336 1.5	1924 3.6
10 TU	0153 1.3	0749 3.8	1414 1.6	1957 3.5
11 W	0228 1.4	0825 3.6	1455 1.7	2031 3.4
12 TH	0304 1.6	0907 3.5	1539 1.8	2108 3.2
13 F	0345 1.7	0958 3.3	1628 1.9	2154 3.1
14 SA	0434 1.8	1108 3.2	1722 2.0	2257 3.0
15 SU	0535 1.9	1225 3.2	1822 2.0	

Days 16–31

Day	Time m	Time m	Time m	Time m
16 M	0021 3.0	0645 1.9	1329 3.3	1924 1.9
17 TU	0139 3.1	0753 1.8	1425 3.4	2025 1.7
18 W	0241 3.3	0853 1.7	1517 3.6	2121 1.5
19 TH	0334 3.5	0947 1.4	1609 3.8	2212 1.2
20 F	0423 3.7	1038 1.2	1700 3.9	2301 0.9
21 SA	0509 4.0	1128 1.0	1749 4.0	2349 0.7
22 SU	0555 4.1	1219 0.8	1836 4.1	
23 M	0035 0.6	0639 4.2	1310 0.8	1920 4.0
24 TU	0121 0.5	0723 4.2	1401 0.8	2004 3.9
25 W	0207 0.6	0808 4.1	1453 1.0	2048 3.7
26 TH	0254 0.7	0855 3.9	1544 1.2	2133 3.5
27 F	0344 0.9	0948 3.6	1637 1.4	2226 3.2
28 SA ☾	0437 1.2	1051 3.4	1735 1.6	2332 3.1
29 SU	0537 1.4	1214 3.2	1839 1.8	
30 M	0057 3.0	0645 1.6	1347 3.1	1953 1.8
31 TU	0222 3.1	0759 1.7	1502 3.2	2104 1.8

LOCH MELFORT 10-8-17
Argyll

CHARTS
Admiralty 2326; Imray C65; OS 55
TIDES
Loch Shuna −0615 Dover; ML Seil Sound 1.4; Duration Seil Sound 0615; Zone 0 (GMT).
Standard Port OBAN (←)

Times				Height (metres)			
HW		LW		MHWS	MHWN	MLWN	MLWS
0100	0700	0100	0800	4.0	2.9	1.8	0.7
1300	1900	1300	2000				

Differences SEIL SOUND
−0035 −0015 −0040 −0015 −1.3 −0.9 −0.7 −0.3
SCALASAIG (Colonsay)
−0020 −0005 −0015 +0005 −0.1 −0.2 −0.2 −0.2
GLENGARRISDALE BAY (Jura)
−0020 0000 −0010 0000 −0.4 −0.2 0.0 −0.2

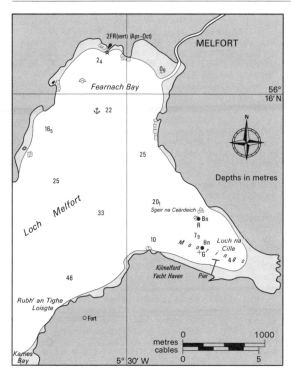

SHELTER
Loch Melfort provides several sheltered anchorages. There is a bay with moorings ½M inside the entrance on S shore, but beware rock which dries 1.5m. 1M further E is Kames Bay with some room to anchor clear of moorings, rocks and fish farm, and sheltered from S and W. Fearnach Bay at NE end of loch is a good anchorage in N winds and moorings are available. Best shelter of all is in Loch na Cille, where Kilmelford Yacht Haven provides swinging and pontoon moorings.
NAVIGATION
Waypoint 56°14'.00N 05°35'.00W, 210°/030° from/to summit Eilean Gamhna, 4ca. Pass either side of Eilean Gamhna. 8ca NE lies Campbell Rock (1.8m). A rock which dries 0.9m lies 1½ca ESE of the FS on Eilean Coltair. The S side of Loch Melfort is mostly steep-to, except in Kames Bay. Approaching Kilmelford Yacht Haven beware drying reef which extends ¾ca from NE shore and is marked by a red and black (port-hand) perch, and also a rock near S shore marked by green (stbd-hand) perch.
LIGHTS AND MARKS
2FR(vert) on the pier in Fearnach Bay.
RADIO TELEPHONE
Camus Marine VHF Ch 16 **80** (working hours).
TELEPHONE (085 22)
Hr Mr 248; CG and MRSC Oban 63720; ⌗ Oban 63079; Marinecall 0898 500 463; Police (0631) 62213; Ⓗ Lochgilphead 2323.

FACILITIES
Kilmelford Yacht Haven ☎ 248, BH (12 ton), Slip, ME, El, Sh, CH, Gas, Gaz, D, FW. **Melfort Marine** (Fearnach Bay) ☎ 257, M, AB, Gas, D, FW, R, Bar, P, D, AC, Sh, V; **Village** (¾M) V, Bar, ⊠.

CRAOBH HAVEN
(Loch Shuna) 10-8-18
Argyll

CHARTS
Admiralty 2326; Imray C65; OS 55
TIDES
HW Loch Shuna −0615 Dover; ML Seil Sound 1.4; Duration Seil Sound 0615; Zone 0 (GMT). For tidal figures see 10.8.17 opposite.

SHELTER
Craobh (pronounced Creuve) Haven is a yacht harbour on E shore of Loch Shuna. It is enclosed by Eilean Buidhe on the NE side, and by Eilean an Duin and Fraoch Eilean to the NW and W. Each island has a causeway to the shore. The entrance on the N side is formed by breakwaters. Very good shelter within. There are anchorages in Asknish Bay 1M to the N, and in the bays S of Craobh Haven — E of Eilean Arsa and in Bagh an Tight-Stoir.
NAVIGATION
Waypoint 56°12'.84N 05°33'.40W, 270°/090° from/to entrance, 0.5M. Tidal streams in Loch Shuna are weak. Beware un-marked reefs Eich Donna NE of the island Eilean Gamhna. A stbd-hand buoy marks a rock (1m) which lies ¾ca NNW of the N breakwater head. Port-hand buoys mark a shoal area close S of the E breakwater. A pink perch on W corner of harbour marks a spit. Elsewhere there is ample depth in the marina.
LIGHTS AND MARKS
There are no lights or marks.
RADIO TELEPHONE
VHF Ch 16 **80** (summer 0800−1900 LT; winter 0900−1700 LT).
TELEPHONE (085 25)
Hr Mr 222; CG and MRSC Oban 63720; ⌗ Oban 63079; Marinecall 0898 500 463; Police (0631) 62213; Ⓗ Lochgilphead 2323.
FACILITIES
Craobh Haven Marina (175+25 visitors) ☎ 222, AC, FW, D, P, SM, V, Bar, Access H24; **Camus Marine** (200) ☎ 622 Slip, BH (15 ton), C (12 ton), Gas, Gaz, CH, ME, El, Sh.
Craobh Haven Bank (Wednesday or at Lochgilphead), ⊠ (Kilmelford); ⇌ (Oban by bus); ✈ (Glasgow).

8

MINOR HARBOURS AND ANCHORAGES   10.8.19

LOCH LAXFORD, Sutherland, 58°25′ N, 5°08′ W, Zone 0 (GMT), Admty chart 2503. HW −0410 on Dover, +0010 on Ullapool. See 10.8.8. Ent between Rubha Ruadh and Ardmore Pt, 1M ENE, clearly identified by three isolated mountains Ben Stack, Ben Arkle and Foinaven inland. There are many anchorages in the loch including: Loch a'Chadh-fi on NE side (John Ridgway's Adventure School has moorings − check with school on Pt on W side of narrows); Bagh nah-Airde Beag, next bay to E, (beware rk ½ ca off SE shore which covers at MHWS); Fanagmore Bay on SW shore (beware head of bay foul with old moorings); Bagh na Fionndalach Mor on SW shore (4-6m); Weaver's Bay on SW shore, 3M from ent (beware drying rock off NW Pt of ent). Beware many fish farming cages. Facilities: none, nearest at Scourie (5M).

LOCH INVER, Sutherland, 58°09′ N, 5°15′ W, Zone 0 (GMT), Admty chart 2504. HW −0433 on Dover, −0005 on Ullapool; HW height −0.1m on Ullapool; ML 3.1m. See 10.8.8. Entrance between Soya I and Kirkaig Pt. Beware rk about 50m off Kirkaig Pt which dries. About 1M up the loch is the islet Glas Leac with a Lt Fl WRG 3s 7m; W071°-080°, R080°-090°, G090°-103°, W103°-111°, R111°-243°, W243°-251°, G251°-071°. Anchor at top of loch in 6m approx in middle of bay off the pier. Perfect shelter from all winds. Facilities: Shop, ✉, Hotel, Gas, FW, P, D.

LOCH SHELL, Harris, 58°00′ N, 6°25′ W, Zone 0 (GMT), Admty chart 1794. HW −0437 on Dover, −0016 on Ullapool; HW height −0.4m on Ullapool; ML 2.7m. See 10.8.7. Pass S of Eilean luvard; beware rks to W of Is. Anchor in Tob Eishken, 2½M up loch on N shore (beware rk awash on E side of entrance), or at head of loch (exposed to E winds, and dries some distance). Facilities: ✉/Stores at Lemrevay.

WEST LOCH TARBERT, Harris, 57°55′ N, 6°55′ W, Zone 0 (GMT), Admty chart 2841. HW −0515 on Dover, −0055 on Ullapool; HW height −0.8m on Ullapool; Duration 0550. See 10.8.7. Good shelter once beyond Taransay. Safest entrance to N of Taransay thence up the S side of loch. Beware rks and islets on N shore. Anchor at head of loch in approx 10m off Tarbert village. There are three small lochs off N shore which provide good alternative anchorages − Lochs Leosavay, Meavaig and Bunavoneadar. Facilities: FW only but Tarbert is only ¼M away.

EAST LOCH TARBERT, Harris, 57°54′ N, 6°48′ W, Zone 0 (GMT), Admty chart 2905. HW −0500 on Dover, −0039 on Ullapool; HW height −0.2m on Ullapool; ML 2.8m; Duration 0605. See 10.8.7. Approach through Sound of Scalpay; beware Elliot Rk (depth 2m) 2½ ca SSW of Rubha Crago. Eilean Glas Lt Ho at E end of Scalpay, Fl (3) 20s 43m 23M; W Tr, R bands. In Sound of Scalpay, stream sets W from HW+3, and E from HW−3. Anchor off Tarbert WSW of steamer pier in about 2.5m. Facilities: EC Thurs; Bar, D, Dr, FW at pier, P, ✉, R, V, ferry to Uig (Skye).

Alternatively Scalpay North Harbour gives good shelter. Beware rk ½ ca off Aird an Aiseig, E side of entrance. Stbd hand buoy marks wreck off Coddem. ½ ca E of the buoy is a rk, depth 1.1m. Fish pier at S end of harbour has 2FG (vert) lights; anchor ¾ ca N, in about 3m. Facilities FW at pier, ✉, V, ferry to Harris.

ST KILDA, 57°50′ N, 8°30′ W, Zone 0 (GMT), Admty chart 2524. Tidal figures taken at Village Bay; HW −0510 on Dover, −0055 on Ullapool; HW height −1.6m on Ullapool; ML 1.9m; Duration 0615. See 10.8.7. A group of four Is and three stacks now taken over by the Army. Anchor in Village Bay, facing SE, in approx 5m about 1.5 ca off the Army pier. If wind is between S and NE big swells come into the bay; poor holding and untenable if winds are strong. Reef lies parallel to and ½ ca off N shore. Ldg Lts 270°, both Oc 5s 26/38m 3M. Yachts with VHF call *Kilda Radio* VHF Ch 16;08 for permission to land. Alternative anchorage is Glen Bay on N side which is only satisfactory in S and E winds. Facilities: FW from wells near landings (by courtesy of the Army); Food, FW, ☎.

LOCH EWE, Ross and Cromarty, 57°51′ N, 5°38′ W, Zone 0 (GMT), Admty charts 3146, 2509. Tidal figures taken at Mellon Charles; HW −0415 on Dover, −0010 on Ullapool; HW height −0.1m on Ullapool; ML 2.9m; Duration 0610.

See 10.8.8. Excellent shelter in all winds except N. Easy entrance with no dangers in loch except Boor Rks on W shore about 0.7M from loch head. Loch approx 7M long with Isle Ewe with two small Islets about 2M from entrance in centre of loch which can be passed on either side. Beware unlit mooring buoys and also dolphins near MoD (Navy) pier E side of entrance. Loch divides beyond Isle Ewe. MoD fuelling pier, dolphins and marker buoys opposite E end of Isle Ewe. Excellent anchorage in Loch Thurnaig to E. Aultbea Pier, partly derelict, to NE. Beware fish farming cages. Facilities: Dr., P, ✉, R, V, Bar. On pier D, L, S of Poolewe Bay (3.5m), **Inverewe Gdns** FW, Bar, D, L, P (at garage), ✉, R, V, Gas.

LOCH GAIRLOCH, Ross and Cromarty, 57°43′ N, 5°45′ W, Zone 0 (GMT), Admty charts 2528, 2210. HW −0440 on Dover, −0020 on Ullapool; HW height +0.1m on Ullapool; ML 2.9m; Duration 0600. See 10.8.8. A wide loch facing W. Entrance clear of dangers. Quite heavy seas roll in bad weather. Yachts can take shelter in Badachro to W of Eilean Horrisdale on S side of loch or in Loch Shieldaig at SE end of the loch. At the head of the loch, Flowerdale Bay, the N branch of the loch, anchor in approx 6m near the head of the pier. Lights: Glas Eilean Fl WRG 6s 9m 6/4M W080°-102°, R102°-296°, W296°-333°, G333°-080°. Pierhead, QR 9m. Facilities: Loch Shirlaig Hotel (½M), P, D, FW; stores ½M.

LOCH MADDY, North Uist, 57°36′ N, 7°07′ W, Zone 0 (GMT), Admty chart 2825 HW −0500 on Dover, −0039 on Ullapool. See 10.8.7. With strong wind against tide there can be bad seas off ent. Approaches clear but from S inside Madadh Mor beware submerged rk ½ ca N of Leac nam Madadh. Lights: Weaver's Pt Fl 3s 21m 7M; Glas Eilean Mor Fl(2) 6s; Rudna Nam Fl R 4s 7m 5M; inside loch Ruigh Liath QG, Lochmaddy pier Ldg Lts 298°. Front 2FG(vert) 4M. Rear OcG 8s 10m 4M; vis 284°−304°. Anchorages: off Steamer Pier; in Charles Harbour; Oronsay − go alongside private pier but anchoring not recommended owing to moorings; Sponish Harbour; Loch Portain; Vallaquie. VHF Ch 16; 12. Port Manager ☎ 63337 (day), 63226 (night). Facilities: Lochmaddy, EC Wed, Shop, Gas, ✉, P, D, FW; Loch Portain ✉, Shop.

LOCH A'BHRAIGE, Rona, 57°34′ N, 5°58′ W, Zone 0 (GMT), Admty chart 2534. HW −0438 on Dover, −0023 on Ullapool; HW height +0.2m on Ullapool; ML 2.9m; Duration 0605. A good safe anchorage in NW of the island except in NNW winds. Beware rocks on the NE side lying up to a ca off shore. Lights Sgeir Shuas, NE of entrance, Fl R 2s 6m 3M; vis 070°−199°. Harbour in NE corner of loch, Lt on SW corner 2 FR (vert). Ldg Lts 137°. Front Q WRG 3m 4/3M, W135°−138°, R138°−318°, G318°−135°. Rear Iso 6s 28m 5M. Facilities very limited. There is a pier, FW and a helipad. Alternative shelter at Acarseid Mhor at SW of Island. (Sketch chart of rocks at entrance is necessary). Loch is used by MoD (Navy) − call on VHF Ch 16 to Rona Naval Establishment before entering.

CROWLIN ISLANDS, Ross and Cromarty, 57°21′ N, 5°51′ W. Zone 0 (GMT), Admty charts 2534, 2209. HW −0435 on Dover, −0020 on Ullapool; HW height +0.3 on Ullapool. Anchor between Eilean Meadhonach and Eilean Mor, approaching from N, keep E of Eilean Beg. Excellent shelter except in strong N winds. There is an inner anchorage with 3½m but entrance channel dries. Eilean Beg Lt Ho FlW 6s 32m 6M. There are no facilities.

LOCH HARPORT, Isle of Skye, 57°20′ N, 6°25′ W, Zone 0 (GMT), Admty chart 1795. HW −0447 (Sp), −0527 (Np) on Dover, −0035 (Sp) −0115 (Np) on Ullapool; HW height −0.1m on Ullapool. See 10.8.9. On E side of Loch Bracadale, entered between Oronsay I and Ardtreck Pt (W Lt Ho, Iso 4s 17m 9M). SW end of Oronsay has conspic rock pillar, called The Castle; keep ¼M off-shore here and off E coast of Oronsay which is joined to Ullinish Pt by drying reef. Anchorages: Oronsay Is, N side of drying reef (4m), or on E side, but beware rk (dries) 0.5ca off N shore of Oronsay. Fiskavaig Bay 1M S of Ardtreck (7m); Loch Beag on N side of loch, exposed to W winds; Port na Long E of Ardtreck, sheltered except from E winds (beware fish farm); Carbost on SW shore. Facilities: (Carbost) EC Wed; V (local shop), Bar, R, P (garage), ✉, FW. (Port na Long) Bar, FW.

MINOR HARBOURS AND ANCHORAGES *Continued*

PLOCKTON, LOCH CARRON, Ross and Cromarty, 57°20' N, 5°39' W, Zone 0 (GMT), Admty charts 2528, 2209. HW −0435 on Dover, −0020 on Ullapool; HW height +0.3m on Ullapool; ML 3.2m; Duration 0600. See 10.8.9. Good anchorage on S side of Outer Loch Carron. Safest entrance between Sgeir Bhuidhe and Sgeir Golach, thence S to pass between Dubgh Sgeir and Hawk Rks off Cat I (with conspic stone tower). Beware Plockton Rks off Yellow Cliff Isle. Lts established 57°21'.93N, 5°37'.32W Dir Fl (3) WRG 10s vis: G060°-063°, W063°-067°, R067°-070°. At 57°20'.33N 5°37'.65 W Dir Fl (3) WRG 10s vis G157°-162°, W162°-166°, R166°-171°. At 57°21'.58N, 5°34'.53W Dir Fl (3) WRG 10s G318°-041°, W041°-044°, R044°-050°. Sgeir Golach marked by G Bn with cone. Anchor in centre of bay in approx 3.5m. Facilities: **Leisure Marine** D, CH; **Village** Bar, FW, ✉, R, ⛟, Gas, V, airstrip.

LOCH ALSH, Ross and Cromarty, 57°17' N, 5°34' W, Zone 0 (GMT), Admty charts 2540, 2541. Tidal figures taken at Dornie Bridge; HW −0450 on Dover, −0025 on Ullapool; HW height 0.0 on Ullapool; ML 3.0m; Duration 0555. See 10.8.9. Almost land-locked between the SE corner of Skye and the mainland. Safe anchorages can be found for most winds; off the hotel at Kyle of Lochalsh in 11m; in Ardintoul Bay on S shore opposite Racoon Rk in 5.5m; in Totaig (or Ob Aonig) opposite Loch Long entrance in 3.5m; in Ratigan Bay in SW corner of the loch in 7m; in Avernish Bay, W of Rubh' an Aisig in 3m (open to SW); inside the pier at Kyleakin. Kyle of Lochalsh is an important ferry port and railhead; yachts can go alongside E end of pier to fuel. Pier head Lts 2 FG (vert) 6/5m 5M on W side, 2 FG (vert) 6/5m 4M on E side. Facilities (at Kyle of Lochalsh): Hr Mr ☎ Kyle 4167, Bar, D, FW, ✉, R, ⛟, V, airstrip, CH, P. Bus to Glasgow or Inverness.

LOCH BOISDALE, South Uist, 57°09' N, 7°18' W, Zone 0 (GMT), Admty chart 2770. HW −0510 on Dover, −0045 on Ullapool; HW height −0.9m on Ullapool; ML 2.4m; Duration 0600. See 10.8.7. Good shelter except in SE gales when swell runs right up the 2M loch. Safest entrance from N passing between Rubha na Crulbe and Calvay I. From S beware Clan Ewan Rk, dries 1m, and McKenzie Rk. Channel up to Boisdale Hr N of Gasay I (beware rks off E end). Anchor off pier in approx 4m, or SW of Gasay I in approx 9m. There are fish cages W of Ru Bhuaitt. Calvay I E end Fl(2) WRG 10s 16m 7/4M; vis G190°−202°, W202°−286°, R286°−111°, W111°−190°. Gasay I Fl WR 5s 10m 7/4M; vis W120°−284°, R284°−120°. Gasay I, N side QG (TE 1985). Ludaig Dir Lt 297°, Dir Oc WRG 6s 8m 7/4M; G287°−296°, W296°−298°, R298°−307°. N pier 2 FG (vert). Ro Ro terminal Iso RG 4s Gshore−283°, R283°−shore. N entrance Ldg line, pier in line with Hollisgeir at 245°. Facilities: EC Tues; Bar, FW (tap on pier); P, ✉, R, V, ferry to mainland.

CANNA, The Small Islands, 57°03' N, 6°29' W, Zone 0 (GMT), Admty chart 1796. HW −0457 (Sp), −0550 (Np) on Dover, −0035 on Ullapool; HW height −0.4m on Ullapool; Duration 0605. Good shelter except in strong E winds. Hr lies between Canna and Sanday I. Most of Hr dries. Anchor in 3m to 4m having entered Hr along Sanday I shore: beware drying patch W of pier on Canna side. Lights: Sanday I Fl 6s 32m 8M, vis 152°−061°. Beware abnormal magnetic variations off NE Canna. Facilities: FW only. **Note:** Canna is a National Trust for Scotland island and yachtsmen are asked to refrain from ditching rubbish.

LOCH NEVIS, Inverness, 57°02' N, 5°44' W, Zone 0 (GMT), Admty chart 2208. HW −0515 on Dover, +0030 on Oban. HW height +1.0m on Oban. Anchorage NE of Eilean na Glaschoille, good except in S winds. Beware rocks Bogha cas Sruth (dries 1.8m), Bogha Don and Sgeirean Glasa both marked by Bns. Upper parts of the loch subject to very violent unpredictable squalls. Yachts can pass into the inner loch with care, and anchor N or SE of Eilean Maol, but this passage should be undertaken with caution.

CASTLEBAY, Barra, 56°57' N, 7°29' W, Zone 0 (GMT), Admty chart 2769. HW −0525 on Dover, −0105 on Ullapool; HW height −0.8m on Ullapool; ML 2.3m; Duration 0600. See 10.8.7. Very good shelter and holding ground. Best anchorage NW of Kiessimul Castle (on an island) in approx 8m; NE of castle are rocks. Alternative anchorage in Vattersay Bay in approx 9m. Beware rks NNW of Dubh Sgeir; Dubh Sgeir Lt Fl(2) WG 6s 6m 7/5M; vis W280°-180°, G180°-280°. Sgeir Liath Lt Fl 3s 7m 8M. Ldg Lts 295°, Front on Rudha Glas, FR 9m 4M, R △ on W framework Tr, rear, 550m from front, FR 22m 4M, R on W framework Tr. Facilities: Bar, D, FW, P, ✉, R, V. Ferry to mainland.

EIGG HARBOUR, Eigg, 56°53' N, 6°08' W, Zone 0 (GMT), Admty chart 2207. HW −0523 on Dover, +0025 on Oban, HW height +0.7m on Oban. See 10.8.10. Most of Hr dries but yachts can anchor NE of Galmisdale Pt which is good anchorage, except in NE winds when yachts should go through the narrows and anchor in South Bay in 6/8m. Tide runs strongly in the narrows. Coming from N beware Garbh Sgeir and Flod Sgeir, both marked by Bns. SE point of Eilean Chathastail Fl 6s 24m 8M, vis 181°−shore. VHF, call *Eigg Harbour*, Ch 16; 08. Facilities: FW, D, repairs can be arranged by Hr Mr; **Village** (2M) Bar, ✉, R, V, Gas.

ARISAIG, (Loch Nan Ceall), Inverness, 56°54' N, 5°55' W, Zone 0 (GMT), Admty chart 2207. HW −0515 on Dover, +0030 on Oban; HW height +0.9m on Oban; ML 2.9m; Duration 0605. Anchorage above Cave Rock, approx 1M within the entrance, is well sheltered. South channel is winding but is marked by perches. Ldg line into loch is S point of Eigg and N point of Muck. There are numerous unmarked rocks. There are no lights. VHF, Call *Arisaig Harbour* Ch 16. Facilities: EC Thurs; FW at hotel; **Sea Leisure Centre** ☎ 224 C (10 ton), CH, D, El, M, ME, P, Sh, V. **Village** Bar, ✉, R, ⛟, V.

ARINAGOUR, Loch Eatharna, Coll, 56°37' N, 6°31' W. Zone 0 (GMT). Admty chart 2474. HW −0530 on Dover, +0015 on Oban; HW height +0.4m on Oban; ML 1.4m; Duration 0600; see 10.8.10. Good shelter except with SE swell or strong S winds. Entrance marked by Arinagour pier, NW of G buoy (Fl G 6s) marking Bogha Mor. Continue N towards old pier, pick up a buoy or anchor to S of it. Beware McQuarry's Rock (dries) 1 ca E of Arinagour pier. Lt on Arinagour pier head 2 FR(vert), 10m on metal column. Facilities: six visitors moorings on W side of harbour, N of pier. Alternative anchorage N of Eilean Eatharna. **Highlands and Islands Development Board Trading Post** M, D, FW, Gas, V, CH, R; **Village** ◎, FW, P, Hotel, ✉.

DUNSTAFFNAGE, Argyll, 56°27' N, 5°26' W, Zone 0 (GMT), Admty chart 2378. HW −0500 on Dover; local tidal figures approx as for Oban. See 10.8.16. Good sheltered anchorage approached between Rubhagarbh and Eilean Mor. No navigational hazards. Anchor near castle in approx 5m or S part of bay or enter yacht harbour. Lts on pier head on NW side of bay 2 FG (vert) 4m 2M. Facilities: Land at pier; **Dunstaffnage Yacht Haven** ☎ Oban 66555 P, D, V, CH, R, BH (20 ton), AB, M, AC, Gas; **Ardtalla Yachts** ☎ Oban 65630 ME, El, Sh, ◎, SM, CH.

LOCH LATHAICH, Mull, 56°19' N, 6°14' W, Zone 0 (GMT), Admty chart 2617. HW −0545 on Dover, −0015 on Oban; HW height +0.2m on Oban. ML 2.4. See 10.8.12. Excellent shelter with easy access. Eileanan na Liathanaich (a group of islets) lie off the ent marked by a W Bn at the E end, Fl WR 6s 12m 8/6M, R088°-108°, W108°-088°. Keep to W side of loch and anchor behind White I at the head of loch (approx 5m). Facilities: (Bunessan) Shop, ✉, Bar, R, P (cans, 3M), FW (90m).

VOLVO PENTA SERVICE

Sales and service centres in area 9
STRATHCLYDE *J N MacDonald & Co* 47-49 Byron Street, GLASGOW G11 6LP.
Tel (041 334) 6171. *Troon Marine Services Ltd* Harbour Road, TROON KA10 6DJ
Tel: (0292) 316180.

Area 9

South-West Scotland
Loch Craignish to Kirkcudbright

VOLVO PENTA

9

460

Helensburgh 10.9.15
Rhu Marina VHF Ch **80**

Greenock/Gourock 10.9.16
Standard Port
Clydeport Estuary Radio
VHF 16;12
041-248 3451
M–0898
500 462
Clyde CG

Clyde Radio VHF 16 26
0703 1903

Ardrossan VHF 16;12 14

Ayr M–0898
500 462

Troon 10.9.19
VHF 16;14

Lamlash 10.9.13

Kip Marina 10.9.17
Marina VHF Ch 80

Largs* 10.9.18
Marina VHF Ch 80

Rothesay 10.9.14
VHF 16;12
Marina VHF 80

Loch Craignish* 10.9.8

Ardrishaig 10.9.12

East Loch Tarbert 10.9.11

Pladda DA
RC

Crinan 10.9.9
M–0898
500 463

Campbeltown 10.9.10
VHF 16;12 14
CG

Islay Radio VHF 16 25
0703 1903

Port Ellen/Islay LAY
Aero RC
395 30

Rhinns of Islay RN
RC
4 294.2 70

Arrochar

Loch Goil
Loch Long
Gareloch

Inverary*

5°W

Toward Point

Largs*
Millport*

Cumbraes
Little Cumbrae

Holy Island

Caladh
Tighnabruaich

Bute

Loch Fyne

Loch Ranza*

Arran

Brodick*

Carradale*

5°30′W

6°W

Scarba

Gulf of Corryvrecken

Sound of Jura

Crinan Canal

Loch Sween*

West Loch Tarbert

Jura

Colonsay
Oransay

Scalasaig*

Loch Tarbert*

Craighouse*

Rubha A'Mhail

*Port Askaig

Gigha*

Islay

Rhinns of Islay

Oban CG
Clyde CG

Prestwick

56°N

55°

56°N

55°30′N

CG

CG

CG

CG

RG

10-9-2

South West Scotland

461

Key to Symbols

📞 ℝℂ	Coast Station/Port Radio – frequencies
	Marine radiobeacon– call sign, sequence, frequency and range (nm)
ℝℂ Aero	Aeronautical radiobeacon–call sign, frequency and range (nm)
i	See for harbour information/tidal data
🌦	Weather (tel. or times). M - Marinecall
ℂ𝔾	HM Coastguard MRCC 🔺 MRSC
C G	HM Coastguard Sector Base
LB	RNLI Lifeboat over 10m
🔺	RNLI Lifeboat under 10m
✈	SAR Helicopter base
☆	Principal lights
⚓	Light-vessel
⚓	Lanby
*	See 10.9.22

NOTE: For summary of navigational aids etc. in Northern Ireland, see 10.13.2

SEPARATION ZONE

For details see Fig.2(7)

Variation 8°W (1991)

Clyde CG
Liverpool CG

Turnberry Point ☆

Ailsa Craig ✦

Sanda I. ☆

Girvan*
| 📞 P | VHF 16;12 |
| LB | |

| ℝℂ Aero | TRN
- · - · - 355 25 ✈ |

Stranraer
| 📞 P | VHF 16;14 |
| 🔺 | |

Loch Ryan*

Corsewall Point ☆

Black Head ☆

Portpatrick
i	10.9.20
📞 C	MF–1883 VHF 16 27
🌦	0703 1903
LB	C G

Crammag Head ☆

Mull of Galloway ☆

55°
N

Wigtown Bay*

Kirkcudbright
i	10.9.21
📞	VHF 16;12
LB	

Isle of Whithorn*

Luce Bay

5°W

5°30′W

6°W

Fair Head

55°
N

10.9.3. AREA 9 TIDAL STREAMS

5 Hours before HW Dover (0050 before HW Ullapool)

4 Hours before HW Dover (0010 after HW Ullapool)

3 Hours before HW Dover (0110 after HW Ullapool)

2 Hours before HW Dover (0210 after HW Ullapool)

1 Hour before HW Dover (0310 after HW Ullapool)

HW Dover (0410 after HW Ullapool)

Northward 10.8.3   Irish Sea 10.10.3   North Ireland 10.13.3

1 Hour after HW Dover (0510 after HW Ullapool)

2 Hours after HW Dover (0615 before HW Ullapool)

3 Hours after HW Dover (0515 before HW Ullapool)

4 Hours after HW Dover (0415 before HW Ullapool)

5 Hours after HW Dover (0315 before HW Ullapool)

6 Hours after HW Dover (0215 before HW Ullapool)

10.9.4 LIGHTS, FOG SIGNALS AND WAYPOINTS

Abbreviations used below are given in 10.0.3. Principal lights are in **bold** print, places in CAPITALS, and light-vessels and Lanbys in *CAPITAL ITALICS*. Unless otherwise stated lights are white. m—elevation in metres; M—nominal range in n. miles. Fog signals are in *italics*. Useful waypoints are underlined use those on land with care. See 4.2.2.

SCOTLAND—WEST COAST

SOUND OF JURA

Reisa an t-Sruith, S end of island 56°07'·8N 05°38'·8W Fl(2) 12s 12m 7M; W column.

CRINAN CANAL

E of lock entrance 56°05'·48N 05°33'·30W Fl WG 3s 8m 4M; W Tr, R band; vis W shore-146°, G146°-shore.
Ruadh Sgeir 56°04'·3N 05°39'·7W Fl 6s 13m 8M; W Tr.
Skervuile 55°52'·47N 05°49'·80W Fl 15s 22m 9M; W Tr.
Eilean nan Gabhar 55°50'·05N 05°56'·15W Fl 5s 7m 8M; framework Tr; vis 225°-010°.
Na Cuiltean 55°48'·65N 05°54'·85W Fl 10s 9m 9M; column on W building.

SOUND OF ISLAY

Rhuda Mhail 55°56'·20N 06°07'·35W Fl(3) WR 15s 45m **W24M**, **R21M**; W Tr; vis R075°-180°, W180°-075°.
Carragh an t-Struith 55°52.'·3N 06°05'·7W Fl WG 3s 8m W9M, G6M, W Tr; vis W354°-078°, G078°-170°, W170°-185°.
Carragh Mhor 55°50'·4N 06°06'·0W Fl(2) WR 6s 7m W8M, R6M; W Tr; vis R shore-175°, W175°-347°, R347°-shore.
McArthur's Head, S end 55°45'85N 06°02'·80W Fl(2) WR 10s 39m W14M, R11M; W Tr; W in Sound of Islay from NE coast—159°, R159°-244°, W244°-E coast of Islay.
Eilean a Chuirn 55°40'·14N 06°01'·15W Fl(3) 18s 26m 8M; W Bn; obsc when bearing more than 040°.
Otter Rock Lt Buoy 55°33'·92N 06°07'·85W Q(6)LFl 15s; S cardinal mark.

PORT ELLEN

Lt Buoy 55°37'·00N 06°12'·22W QG; stbd-hand mark.
Carraig Fhada Fl WRG 3s 19m W8M, R6M, G6M; W square Tr; vis W shore-248°, G248°-311°, W311°-340°, R340°-shore.
Ro Ro terminal 2 FG (vert) 7/6m 3M.

LOCH INDAAL

Bruichladdich pier head 2 FR (vert) 6m 5M.
Rudha an Duin 55°44'·70N 06°22'·35W Fl(2) WR 7s 15m W13M, R12M; W Tr; vis W218°-249°, R249°-350°, W350°-036°.

Orsay Island, **Rinns of Islay** 55°40'·38N 06°30'·70W Fl 5s 46m **24M**; W Tr; vis 256°-184°; *Horn (3) 45s.* RC.

WEST LOCH TARBERT

Dunskeig Bay, N end Q(2) 10s 11m 8M.
Eileen Traighe, off S side, 55°45'·40N 05°35'·70W QR 5m 3M; R post; Ra refl.
Corran Point QG 3m 3M; G post; Ra refl. Sgeir Mhein QR 3m 3M; R post; Ra refl.
Black Rocks QG 3M; G post; Ra refl.
Kennacraig ferry terminal 2 FG (vert) 7/6m 3M; silver post.

Mull of Kintyre 55°18'·6N 05°48'·1W Fl(2) 20s 91m **29M**; Tr on W building; vis 347°-178°; *Horn Mo(N) 90s.*

Sanda Island, S side 55°16'·50N 05°34'·90W L Fl WR 24s

50m **W19M**, **R16M**; W Tr; vis R245°-267°, W267°-shore; Racon. (Fl 10s 55m 15M with no red sector (T) ufn).
Arranman Barrels Lt Buoy 55°19'·40N 05°32'·80W Fl(2)R 12s; port-hand mark.

CAMPBELTOWN LOCH

Davaar N point 55°25'·69N 05°32'·37W Fl(2) 10s 37m **23M**; W Tr; vis 073°-330°; *Horn (2) 20s.*
Methe Bank Lt Buoy 55°25'·30N 05°34'·36W Iso 10s; safe water mark.
Otterard Lt Buoy 55°27'·07N 05°31'·05W Q(3)10s; E cardinal mark.
Kilbrannan Sound. Port Crannaich, breakwater head 55°35'·7N 05°27'·8W Fl R 10s 5m 6M; vis 099°-279°.
Skipness range 55°46'·7N 05°19'·0W Iso R 8s 7m 10M; concrete building; vis 292°-312°. Oc(2)Y 10s **24M** when range in use (occas).

LOCH FYNE

Sgat More, S end 55°50'·85N 05°18'·42W Fl 3s 9m 12M; W Tr.
Portavadie breakwater 2 FG (vert) 6/4m 4M.

EAST LOCH TARBERT

Madadh Maol, entrance S side 55°52'·02N 05°24'·18W Fl R 2·5s 4m.
Eilean aChoic, off SE side QG 3m.

ARDRISHAIG

Breakwater head 56°00'·76N 05°26'·53W L Fl WRG 6s 9m 4M; W Tr; vis G287°-339°, W339°-350°, R350°-035°. 2FG (vert) on pier 120m NW.
Otter Spit 56°00'·63N 05°21'·03W Fl G 3s 7m 8M; G tank on concrete pyramid.
Glas Eilean, S end 56°01'·10N 05°21'·10W Fl R 5s 12m 7M; R column on pedestal.
Sgeir an Eirionnaich 56°06'·5N 05°13'·5W Fl WRG 3s 7m 8M; B framework Tr on B round Tr, W stripes; vis R044°-087°, W087°-192°, R192°-210°, W210°-044°.

KYLES OF BUTE

Ardlamont Point No. 47 Lt Buoy 55°49'·59N 05°11'·70W Fl R 4s; port-hand mark.
Carry Point No. 46 Lt Buoy 55°51'·40N 05°12'·18W Fl R 4s; port-hand mark.
Rubha Ban Lt Buoy 55°54'·95N 05°12'·33W Fl R 4s; port-hand mark.
Burnt Islands No. 42 Lt Buoy (S of Eilean Buidhe) 55°55'·77N 05°10'·32W Fl R 2s; port-hand mark.
Rubha Bodach Lt Buoy 55°55'·39N 05°09'·53W Fl G; stbd-hand mark.
Ardmaleish Point No. 41 Lt Buoy 55°53'·03N 05°04'·63W Q; N cardinal mark.

ARRAN ISLAND

Pladda 55°25'·50N 05°07'·07W Fl(3) 30s 40m **23M**; W Tr; RC. **Holy Island**, Pillar Rock Point 55°31'·05N 05°03'·57W Fl(2) 20s 38m **25M**; W square Tr.
Holy Island, SW end Fl G 3s 14m 10M; W Tr; vis 282°-147°.
Brodick Bay, pier head 2 FR (vert) 9/7m 4M.

FIRTH OF CLYDE

Runnaneun Point 55°43'·79N 05°00'·17W Fl R 6s 8m 12M; W Tr.
Little Cumbrae 55°43'·27N 04°57'·95W Fl 3s 31m **23M**; W

Tr; vis 334°-210°; shown by day if fog signal operating; *Horn (3) 40s* .

Portachur Lt Buoy 55°44'·35N 04°58'·44W FIG 3s; stbd-hand mark.

Mountstuart Lt Buoy 55°48'·00N 04°57'·50W LFl 10s; safe water mark.

GREAT CUMBRA
MILLPORT. Eileans, West end 55°44'·89N 04°55'·52W QG 5m 2M; shown 1/9-30/4.
Ldg Lts 333°. Pier head front FR 7m 5M. Rear 137m from front FR 9m 5M.

FAIRLIE
Hunterston Jetty, S end 55°45'·10N 04°52'·80W 2 FG (vert); N end 2 FG (vert).
NATO Pier, 2 FG (vert) N and S ends.

LARGS
Yacht Haven S breakwater head 55°46'·35N 04°51'·67W OcG 10s 4m 4M.
West breakwater head OcR 10s 4m 4M.
Approach Lt buoy 55°46'·50N 04°51'·78W LFl 10s; safe water mark.
Largs Pier, head 2 FG (vert) 7/5m 5M (H24).
Ascog Patches No. 13 55°49'·71N 05°00'·17W Fl(2) 10s 5m 5M; isolated danger mark.
Toward Point 55°51'·73N 04°58'·73W Fl 10s 21m **22M**; W Tr; shown by day if fog signal operating; *Horn 20s*.
Toward Bank No. 35 Lt Buoy 55°51'·05N 04°59'·93W FIG 3s; stbd-hand mark.

ROTHESAY
N Quay, E end 55°50'·32N 05°03'·03W 2 FG (vert) 7m 5M.
West end 2 FR (vert) 7m 5M.
Albert Quay, near N end 2 FR (vert) 8m 5M.
Skelmorlie Lt Buoy 55°51'·65N 04°56'·28W Iso 5s; safe water mark.
Wemyss Bay, pier 2 FG (vert) 7/5m 5M.
Inverkip oil jetty, S and N ends 2 FG (vert) 11m 2M.
No. 12 55°52'·9N 04°53·7W Oc(2)Y 10s 5m 3M; special mark.
Kip Lt Buoy 55°54'·49N 04°52'·95W QG; stbd-hand mark.
Cowal Lt Buoy 55°56'·00N 04°54'·77W LFl 10s; safe water mark.
Lunderston Bay No. 8 55°55'·5N 04°52'·9W Fl(4)Y 10s 5m 3M.
Gantock Beacon 55°56'·46N 04°55'·00W Fl R 2·5s 12m **18M**; W round Tr.

DUNOON
Pier, S end and N end 2 FR (vert) 5m 6M.
Cloch Point Fl 3s 24m 8M; W round Tr, B band, W dwellings; *Horn (2) 30s* .
McInroy's Point RoRo terminal 2 FG (vert) 5/3m 6M.
No. 5 55°57'·0N 04°51'·6W Oc(2)Y 10s 5m 3M; special mark.
Hunter's Quay RoRo terminal 2 FR (vert) 6/4m 6M.
Holy Loch, pier 55°59'·0N 04°56'·7W 2 FR (vert) 6/4m 3M.

LOCH LONG.
Loch Long Lt Buoy 55°59'·17N 04°52'·33W Oc 6s; safe water mark.
Baron's Point, No. 3 55°59'·2N 04°51'·0W Oc(2)Y 10s 3M.
Ravenrock Point 56°02'·1N 04°54'·3W Fl 4s 12m 10M; W framework Tr on W column.
Dir Lt 204°, Dir WRG 9m (same Tr); vis R201·5°-203°, Al WR203°-203·5° (W phase incr with brg), W203·5°-204·5°, Al WG204·5°-205° (G phase incr with brg), G205°-206·5°.
Portdornaige 56° 03.7N°4 53.6W Fl 6s 8m 11m; W column; vis 026°-206°.

Carraig nan Ron (Dog Rock) 56°06'·0N 04°51'·6W Fl 2s 7m 11M; W column.
Finnart Oil Terminal, Cnap Point 56°07'·4N 04°49'·9W Ldg Lts 031°. Front Q 8m 10M; W column. Rear, 87m from front F 13m; R line on W Tr.
Ashton Lt Buoy 55°58'·11N 04°50'·58W Iso 5s; safe water mark.

GOUROCK
Railway pier head 55°57'·8N 04°49'·0W 2 FG (vert) 10/8m 3M; grey framework Tr.
Kempock Point No. 4 55°57'·7N 04°49'·3W Oc(2)Y 10s 6m 3M.
Whiteforeland Lt Buoy 55°58'·11N 04°47'·20W LFl 10s; safe water mark.
Rosneath Patch, S end 55°58'·52N 04°47'·37W Fl(2) 10s 5m 10M.
Ldg Lts 356° Ardencaple Castle Centre; Front 56°00'·6N 04°45'·3W 2 FG (vert) 26/23m 12M; Tr on NW corner of castle; vis 335°-020°. Rear 822m from front FG 10M.

ROSNEATH
8N Lt Buoy 55°59'·09N 04°44'·13W Fl Y 3s 3m 3M; special mark.
Beacon No. 1 55°59'·12N 04°43'·81W VQ(4)Y 5s 9m and Dir Q WRG 7m W3M, R2M, G2M; vis G078°-079°, W079°-080°, G080°-082°.
Row Lt Buoy 55°59'·85N 04°45'·05W FIG 5s; stbd-hand mark.
7N Lt Buoy 56°00'·06N 04°45'·29W Oc G 6s 3m 3M; stbd-hand mark.
Cairndhu Lt Buoy 56°00'·36N 04°45'·93W FIG 2·5s; stbd-hand mark.
Rosneath. Dir Lt 291°. Dir Oc WRG 3s 7m 14M; vis G288°-290°, W290°-292°, R292°-296°; (H24).
Ldg Lts 291°. Front 56°00'·6N 04°47'·7W FR 4m. Rear 0·66M from front FR.
Castle Point 56°00'·20N 04°46'·43W Fl(2) R 10s 8m 6M; R mast.
Rosneath DG Jetty 2 FR (vert) 5M; W column; vis 150°-030°.
Rhu Narrows 56°00'·9N 04°47'·1W Q(3) WRG 6s 9m W10M, R7M, G7M; vis G270°-000°, W000°-114°, R114°-188°.
Dir Lt 318°, Dir Oc WRG 6s; same Tr; vis G313°-317°, W317°-319°, R319°-320°; (H24).
Rosneath Bay Ldg Lts 163°. Front 56°00'·0N 04°47'·1W FG 11m 12M; framework Tr; vis 149°-177°. Rear 683m from front FG 24m 12M; stone Tr; vis 149°-177°.

GARELOCH
Rhu South Lt Buoy 56°00'·66N 04°47'·35W FIG 3s; stbd-hand mark.
Mambeg Dir Lt 330°, Dir Q(4) WRG 8s 8m 14M; W column; vis G327°-329°, W329°-331°, R331°-332°; (H24).
Faslane Base, wharf, S elbow Fl G 5s 11m 5M. Floating dock, E side Fl R, middle 2 FG (vert) 14m 5M, N side Q WRG 14m W9M, R6M, G6M; vis G333°-084°, W084°-161°, R161°-196°; (H24).
Garelochhead, S fuel jetty 56°04'·23N 04°49'·62W 2 FG (vert) 10m 5M.
North fuel jetty, elbow Iso WRG 4s 10m; vis G351°-356°, W356°-006°, R006°-011°.

GREENOCK
Anchorage Lts in line 196°. Front 55°57'·6N 04°46'·5W FG 7m 12M. Rear 32m from front FG 9m 12M.
Lts in line 194°30'. Front 55°57'·4N 04°45'·8W FG 18m. Rear 360m from front FG 33m.
Clydeport Container Terminal NW corner QG 8m 8M.
Victoria Harbour, entrance West side 2 FG (vert).

9

Garvel Embankment, <u>West end</u> 55°56'·81N 04°43'·48W Oc G 10s 9m 4M.

<u>E end, Maurice Clark Point</u> 55°56'·61N 04°42'·78W QG 7m 2M.

PORT GLASGOW
Beacon off entrance 55°56'·3N 04°41'·2W FG 7m 9M; B&W chequered Tr and cupola.

Steamboat Quay, West end FG 12m 12M; B&W chequered column; vis 210°-290°. From here to Glasgow Lts on S bank are Fl G and Lts on N bank are Fl R.

SCOTLAND—WEST COAST

ARDROSSAN
Approach Dir 055°, 55°38'·7N 04°49'·1W Dir FWRG 15m 9M; vis G048·5°-053·5°, W053·5°-056·5°, R056·5°-061·5°. FR 9m 9M (same Tr); vis 340°-130°.

N breakwater head Fl WR 2s 12m 5M; R gantry; vis R041°-126°, W126°-041°.

<u>Lighthouse pier head</u> 55°38'·47N 04°49'·50W Iso WG 4s 11m 9M; W Tr; vis W035°-317°, G317°-035°.

IRVINE
<u>Entrance, N side</u> 55°36'·21N 04°42'·00W Fl R 3s 6m 5M; R mast. S side Fl G 3s 6m 5M; G column.

Ldg Lts 051°. Front FG 10m 5M. Rear 101m from front FR 15m 5M; both on G masts, vis 019°-120°.

TROON
<u>Troon Lt Buoy</u> 55°30'·07N 04°41'·28W Fl G 4s; stbd- hand mark.

<u>West pier head</u> 55°33'·07N 04°40'·95W Oc WR 6s 11m 5M; W Tr; vis R036°-090°, W090°-036°; *Siren 30s.*

14m SE of West pier head, Fl WG 3s 7m 5M; post on dolphin; vis G146°-318°, W318°-146°.

E pier head Fl R 10s 6m 3M; R column; obsc brg more than 199°.

<u>Lady Isle</u> 55°31'·63N 04°43'·95W Fl(4) 30s 19m 8M; W Bn.

AYR
<u>Bar Lt Buoy</u> 55°28'·12N 04°39'·38W Fl G 2s; stbd-hand mark.
<u>N breakwater head</u> 55°28'·22N 04°38'·71W QR 9m 5M.
S pier head Q 7m 7M; vis 012°-161°. FG 5m 5M; same Tr; vis 012°-066° over St Nicholas rocks.

Ldg Lts 098°. Front 55°28'·2N 04°38'·3W FR 10m 5M. Rear 130m from front OcR 10s 18m 9M.

Turnberry Point, near castle ruins 55°19'·55N 04°50'·60W Fl 15s 29m **24M**; W Tr.

Ailsa Craig 55°15'·12N 05°06'·42W Fl(6) 30s 18m **17M**; W Tr; vis 145°-028°.

GIRVAN
<u>N groyne head</u> 55°14'·75N 04°51'·70W Iso 4s 3m 4M.
S pier head 2 FG (vert) 8m 4M; W Tr.
N breakwater head 55°14'·74N 04°51'·77W Fl(2)R 6s 7m 4M.

LOCH RYAN
<u>Cairn Point</u> 54°58'·5N 05°01'·8W Fl(2) R 10s 14m 12M; W Tr.
Cairnryan 54°57'·8N 05°00'·9W Fl R 5s 5m 5M.

Stranraer approach, No. 1 Bn 54°56'·6N 05°01'·3W Oc G 6s.
No. 3 Bn 54°55'·9N 05°01'·6W QG.
No. 5 54°55'·1N 05°01'·8W Fl G 3s.

STRANRAER
Centre pier, head 2 F Bu (vert).
E pier, head 2FR(vert) 9m.
Ross pier, head 2 FG (vert) 10m 4M; R column.

Corsewall Point 55°00'·43N 05°09'·50W Al Fl WR 74s 34m **18M**; W Tr; vis 027°-257°.

Killantringan, <u>Black Head</u> 54°51'·71N 05°08'·75W Fl(2) 15s 49m **25M**; W Tr.

PORTPATRICK. Ldg Lts 050°. Front 54°50'·5N 05°06'·9W FG (occas). Rear, 68m from front, FG 8m (occas).

Crammag Head 54°39'·90N 04°57'·80W Fl 10s 35m **18M**; W Tr.

Mull of Galloway, <u>SE end</u> 54°38'·05N 04°51'·35W Fl 20s 99m **28M**; W Tr; vis 182°-105°.

Port William. Ldg Lts 105°. Front, <u>pier head</u> 54°45'·65N 04°35'·10W Fl G 3s 7m 3M. Rear, 130m from front, FG 10m 2M.

Isle of Whithorn Harbour 54°41'·8N 04°21'·7W QG 4m 5M. Ldg Lts 335°. Front OcR 8s 7m 7M. Rear, 35m from front, OcR 8s 9m 7M, synchronised.

<u>Little Ross</u> 54°45'·93N 04°05'·02W Fl 5s 50m 12M; W Tr; obsc in Wigton Bay when brg more than 103°.

KIRKCUDBRIGHT BAY
<u>No 1 Lifeboat House</u> 54°'·47.68N 04°03'·66W Fl 3s 7m 3M.
No. 12 54°49'·1N 04°04'·8W Fl R 3s 3m.
<u>Perch No.14</u> 54°49'·25N 04°04'·76W Fl 3s 5m.
Perch No. 22 54°50'·1N 04°03'·9W Fl R 3s 2m.
Outfall 54°50'·2N 04°03'·8W Fl Y 5s 3m 2M; Y framework Tr.

<u>Hestan Island, E end</u> 54°50'·0N 03°48'·4W Fl(2) 10s 38m 7M; W house.
Annan, S end of quay 54°59'N 03°16'W 2FR(vert) 4m 5M.
Barnkirk Point 54°58'·0N 03°15'· 9W Fl 2s 18m 2M.

10.9.5   PASSAGE INFORMATION

SCOTLAND – SOUTH WEST COAST

Although conditions in the South-West of Scotland are in general less rugged than from Mull northwards, some of the remarks at the start of 10.8.5 are equally applicable to this area.

The W coasts of Colonsay and Oronsay (chart 2169) are fringed with dangers up to 2M offshore. The two islands are separated by a narrow chan which dries and has an overhead cable (10m). For Scalasaig see 10.9.22.

Sound of Luing (chart 2326) between Scarba, Lunga, Fiola Meadlonach, Rubha Fiola and Pladda (or Fladda) on the W side, and Luing and Dubh Sgeir on the E side, is the normal chan to or from Sound of Jura – despite dangers at the N end and strong tidal streams. The N-going stream begins at HW Oban + 0430, and the S-going at HW Oban − 0155. Sp rates are 2½-3 kn at S end of sound, increasing to 6 kn or more in ls off N entrance – where there are eddies, races and overfalls. Good shelter in Ardinmar B, SW of Torsa.

CORRYVRECKAN/CRINAN (charts 2326, 2343)

Between Scarba and Jura is the Gulf of Corryvreckan (chart 2343), with a least width of 6 ca and free of dangers, but noted for its very strong tides which, in conjunction with an uneven bottom, cause extreme turbulence. This is particularly dangerous with strong W winds over a W-going (flood) tide which spews out several miles to seaward of the gulf, with overfalls extending 3M from the W of entrance. The gulf is best avoided, and should never be attempted by yachts except at slack water and in calm conditions. Keep to the S side of the gulf to avoid the whirlpool known as The Hag. The W-going stream in the gulf begins at HW Oban + 0410, and the E-going at HW Oban − 0210. Sp rate W-going is 8½ kn, and E-going rather less.

The range of tide at sp can vary nearly 2m between the E end of the gulf (1.5m) and the W end (3.4m), with HW ½ h earlier at the E end. Slack water lasts about 1h at nps, but only ½ h at sps. On the W-going (flood) stream eddies form both sides of the gulf, but the one on the N (Scarba) shore is more important. Where this eddy meets the main stream off Camas nam Bairneach there is violent turbulence, with heavy overfalls extending W at the division of the eddy and the main stream. There are temp anchs with the wind in the right quarter in Bagh Gleann a Mhaoil in the SE corner of Scarba, and in Bagh Gleann nam Muc at N end of Jura but the latter has rocks in approaches E and SW of Eilean Beag.

At N end of Sound of Jura is Loch Craignish (chart 2326). There are very strong tides in Dorus Mor, if approaching from the N. The W-going stream begins at HW Oban + 0330, and the E-going at HW Oban − 0215, sp rates 8 kn. The main chan up Loch Craignish is clear 1½ ca offshore, but beware charted rks off Eilean Dubh and Eilean Mhic Chrion when approaching head of loch and the Ardfern Yacht Centre, which is behind Eilean Inshaig on W shore. See 10.9.22.

S of Loch Craignish is Loch Crinan, which leads to the Crinan Canal (10.9.9). Beware Black Rk, 2m high and 2 ca N of the canal sea lock, and dangers extending ½ ca from the rk.

SOUND OF ISLAY (chart 2481)

An alternative N/S route is through the Sound of Islay (chart 2481). The chan presents no difficulty: hold to the Islay shore, where all dangers are close in. The N-going stream begins at HW Oban + 0440, and the S-going at HW Oban − 0140. The sp rates are 2½ kn at N entrance and 1½ kn at S entrance, but increasing in the narrows and reaching 5 kn off Port Askaig. There are overfalls off McArthur's Head (Islay side of S entrance) during the S-going stream. There are anchs in the sound, but mostly holding ground is poor. The best places are alongside at Port Askaig (10.9.22), or at anch off the distillery in Bunnahabhain B, 2½ M to N.

The W coast of Islay is very exposed. Off Orsay, Frenchman's Rks and W Bank the NW-going stream begins at HW Oban + 0530, and the SE-going at HW Oban − 0040. Sp rates are 8 kn off Orsay and Frenchman's Rks, and 6 kn over W bank, but decrease to 3 kn 5M offshore. There are races and overfalls in these areas. In the N of Islay there is anch E of Nave Island at entrance to Loch Gruinart: beware Balach Rks which dry, just to N. Loch Indaal gives some shelter: beware rks extending from Laggan Hd on E side of entrance. Port Ellen (chart 2474) has several dangers in approach, and is exposed to S. See 10.9.22.

SOUND OF JURA TO MULL OF KINTYRE

From Crinan to Gigha the Sound of Jura is safe if a mid-chan course is held. Skervuile (Lt) is a reef roughly in middle of sound. Loch Sween (chart 2397) can be approached N or SE of MacCormaig Islands, where there is an attractive anch on NE side of Eilean Mor, but exposed to NE. Coming from N beware Keills Rk and Danna Rk. Sgeirean a Mhain is a rk in fairway 1½ M NE of Castle Sween (conspic on SE shore). Anch at Tayvallich, near head of loch on W side. See 10.9.22.

W Loch Tarbert (chart 2477) is long and narrow, with good anchs but unmarked shoals. On entry give a berth of at least 2½ ca to Eilean Traighe off N shore, E of Ardpatrick Pt. Dun Skeig, an isolated hill, is conspic on S shore. Good anch near head of loch, 1M by road from E Loch Tarbert (see 10.9.11).

On other side of sound, near S end of Jura, are The Small Isles (chart 2396) between Rubh' an Leanachais and Rubha na Caillich. Beware Goat Rk (dries) 1½ ca off southernmost I, Eilean nan Gabhar, behind which is good anch. Also possible to go alongside Craighouse Pier (10.9.22). Another anch exists in Lowlandman's B, about 3M to N, but exposed to S winds: Ninefoot Rks with depth of 2.4m lie off entrance.

S of W Loch Tarbert, and about 2M off the Kintyre shore, is Gigha Island (chart 2475), with Cara Island and Gigalum Island off its S end. See 10.9.22. Dangers extend 1M W off S end of Gigha Island. Outer and Inner Red Rks (least depth 2m) lie 2M SW of N end of Gigha Island.

Gigha Sound need very careful pilotage, since there are several dangerous rks. The N-going stream begins at HW Oban + 0430, and S-going at HW Oban − 0155, sp rates 1½ kn. Good anchs in Druimyeon B and Ardminish B, respectively N and S of Ardminish Pt on E side of Gigha.

From Crinan to Mull of Kintyre is about 50M, and this long peninsula has great effect on tidal stream in North Channel. Off Mull of Kintyre (Lt, fog sig) the N-going stream begins at HW Oban + 0400, and the S-going at HW Oban − 0225, sp rates 5 kn. A strong race and overfalls exist S and SW of Mull of Kintyre, dangerous in strong S winds against S-going tide. Careful timing is needed. There is a traffic scheme in N Channel – see Fig. 2(7).

Sanda Sound separates Sanda Island (LT) and its neighbouring rks and islets, from Kintyre. Beware Macosh Rks (dry) forming part of Barley Ridges, 2 ca offshore, E of Rubha McShannuick; Arranman Barrels, drying and submerged, 2½ ca E from Du-na-h-Oighe and marked by buoy; and Blindman rk (depth 2m) 2 ca off Ru Stafnish, where there are 3 radio masts ½ M to W. 3 ca off N of Sanda Island is Sheep Island. Paterson's Rk (dries) is 1M E of Sheep Island. There is anch in Sanda Harb. In Sanda Sound the E-going stream begins at HW Greenock + 0340, and the W-going at HW Greenock − 0230, sp rates 5 kn. Tide races extend N and W from Sheep Island, and in strong S or SW winds the Sound is dangerous. In these conditions pass E of Paterson's Rk, and 2M S of Sanda and Mull of Kintyre.

MULL OF KINTYRE TO MULL OF GALLOWAY (charts 2199, 2198)

Once E of Mull of Kintyre, tidal and pilotage conditions improve greatly. Campbeltown (10.9.10) is entered N of Davaar Island (Lt, fog sig). 1½M N of Lt Ho is Otterard Rk (depth 3m), with Long Rk (dries) 5 ca W of it; both are marked by buoys. E of Davaar Island tide runs 4 kn at sp, and there are overfalls.

Kilbrannan Sound runs 21M from Davaar Island to Skipness Pt, where it joins Inchmarnock Water and Bute Sound. There are few dangers apart from overfalls on Erins Bank, 10M S of Skipness, on S-going stream. Good anch in Carradale B, off Torrisdale Castle. There are overfalls off Carradale Pt on S-going stream. For Carradale see 10.9.22.

Loch Fyne (chart 2381) is relatively clear of dangers to E Loch Tarbert (10.9.11). On E shore beware rks off Ardlamont Pt, and 4M to NW is Skate Island which is best passed to W.

3M from Ardrishaig (10.9.12) beware Big Rk (depth 2.1m). Further N, at entrance to Loch Gilp (much of which dries) note shoals round Gulnare Rk with least depth 1.5m, and Duncuan Island with dangers extending SW to Sgeir Sgalag (depth 0.8m) marked by buoy.

Where Loch Fyne turns NE it is largely obstructed by Otter Spit (dries), extending 8 ca WNW from E shore. Outer end of spit is marked by Bn (lit), but dangers extend somewhat beyond. The stream runs up to 2 kn here. A rk with depth less than 2m lies about ¾M SW of Otter Spit Bn. In Upper Loch Fyne (chart 2382) Minard Narrows are formed by rks and islets in the fairway, but there are charted chans between. For Inveraray see 10.9.22.

Bute Sound leads into Firth of Clyde, and is clear in fairway. Sannox Rk (depth 1.2m) is ¼M off Arran coast 8M N of Lamlash (10.9.13). 1 ca off W side of Inchmarnock is Tra na-h-uil, a rk which dries. In Inchmarnock Sound, Shearwater Rk (depth 0.9m) lies in centre of S entrance.

Arran's mountains tend to cause squalls or calms, but it has good anchs at Lamlash (10.9.13), Brodick (10.9.22) and Loch Ranza (10.9.22).

Kyles of Bute are attractive chan between Inchmarnock Water and Firth of Clyde, and straightforward apart from Burnt Islands. Here it is best to take N chan, narrow but well buoyed, passing S of Eilean Buidhe, and N of Eilean Fraoich and Eilean Mor. Care is needed, since stream may reach 5 kn at sp.

In contrast, the N lochs in Firth of Clyde are less attractive. Loch Goil is worth a visit but Loch Long is squally and has few anchs, while Gareloch has little to attract cruising yachts. For Millport (Great Cumbrae) see 10.9.22. There is anch in Kilchattan Bay (E Bute) sheltered from SSE to WNW.

Navigation in Firth of Clyde presents few problems since chans are well marked, but beware unlit moorings and also the considerable amount of commercial and naval shipping (see 10.9.15). Tidal streams are generally weak, seldom exceeding 1 kn.

S of Largs (10.9.18) the coast is generally uninviting, with mostly commercial harbs until Troon (10.9.19). There are various dangers in Ayr B (10.9.22); beware Troon Rk (depth 5.6m, but sea can break), Lappock Rk (dries, marked by Bn), and Mill Rk (dries, buoyed).

There is a serious race off Bennane Hd (8M SSE of Ailsa Craig) when tide is running strongly. Loch Ryan offers little for yachtsmen but there is anch S of Kirkcolm Pt, inside the drying spit which runs in SE direction 1½M from the point. There is also useful anch in Lady Bay, sheltered except from NE. Between Corsewall Pt and Mull of Galloway the S-going stream begins HW Greenock +0310, and the N-going at HW Greenock −0250. Sp rate off and S of Black Hd is 5 kn; N of Black Hd it decreases, to 2-3 kn off Corsewall Pt. Races occur off Morroch B, Money Hd, Mull of Logan and SE of Crammag Hd.

Mull of Galloway (Lt) is S point of Scotland, a tall headland (83m) and steep-to, but beware dangerous race extending nearly 3M to S. On E-going stream the race extends NNE into Luce B; on W-going stream it extends SW and W.

The Scares are rks in middle of Luce B. Elsewhere b is clear more than ¼M offshore, but there is practice bombing range. Best anch at E Tarbert B, or alongside in Drummore which is sheltered but dries. Off Burrow Hd there is bad race in strong W winds with W-going tide. In Wigtown B (10.9.22) the best anch is in l of Whithorn B, but exposed to S. It is also possible to dry out in Garlieston.

There is a tank firing range extending 14M offshore between Kirkcudbright (10.9.21) and Abbey Head, 4M to E. If unable to avoid the area, cross it at N end close inshore. For information telephone 'Range control' Dundrennan 055 723236 or contact the Range safety boat "Gallovidian" which keeps watch on VHF Ch 16. The range operates from 0900-1600 LT Mon-Fri.

10.9.6   DISTANCE TABLE

Approximate distances in nautical miles are by the most direct route while avoiding dangers and allowing for traffic separation schemes etc. Places in *italics* are in adjoining areas.

1 *Tory Island*	1																			
2 *Barra Head*	95	2																		
3 *Oigh Sgeir*	113	33	3																	
4 *Ardnamurchan Pt*	110	47	21	4																
5 Port Askaig	87	77	75	60	5															
6 Mull of Kintyre	86	112	103	99	33	6														
7 Campbeltown	106	132	123	119	53	20	7													
8 E Loch Tarbert	131	157	148	144	78	45	31	8												
9 Ardrishaig	140	166	157	153	87	54	39	10	9											
10 Toward Point	139	165	156	152	86	53	45	23	31	10										
11 Kip Marina	144	170	161	157	91	58	50	28	36	5	11									
12 Helensburgh	153	179	170	166	100	67	59	37	45	14	9	12								
13 Lamlash	120	146	137	133	67	34	24	25	34	21	25	33	13							
14 Troon	130	156	147	143	77	44	33	33	40	24	29	38	16	14						
15 Portpatrick	119	148	139	135	69	36	39	66	74	65	68	77	44	49	15					
16 Mull of Galloway	134	164	155	151	85	52	56	82	90	81	84	93	60	65	16	16				
17 Kirkcudbright	164	196	187	183	117	84	88	114	122	113	116	125	92	97	48	32	17			
18 *Mew Island*	116	149	140	136	69	37	44	72	80	74	77	86	54	60	16	22	54	18		
19 *Point of Ayre*	160	186	177	173	107	74	78	104	112	103	106	115	82	87	38	22	25	44	19	
20 *St Bees Head*	177	207	198	194	128	95	99	125	133	124	127	136	103	108	59	43	24	65	26	20

CLYDE AREA WAYPOINTS
10-9-7

Selected waypoints for use in the Clyde area are listed in alphabetical order below. Further waypoints for use in coastal waters are given in section 4 of each relevant area.

AE Lt Buoy	55°51'·68N	05°02'·31W
Ailsa Craig Lt	55°15'·12N	05°06'·42W
Ardgowan Pt Buoy	55°54'·93N	04°54'·00W
Ardmaleish No.41 Lt Buoy	55°53'·03N	05°04'·62W
Ardmore No.4 Lt Buoy	55°58'·75N	04°48'·30W
Ardmore No.5 Lt Buoy	55°58'·67N	04°47'·44W
Ardmore No. 8 Lt Buoy	55°58'·95N	04°46'·66W
Ardmore No.10 Lt Buoy	55°59'·03N	04°45'·62W
Ardyne Lt Buoy	55°52'·00N	05°03'·16W
Arranman Barrels Lt Buoy	55°19'·40N	05°32'·80W
Ascog Patches Lt Bn (No. 13)	55°49'·71N	05°00'·17W
Ashton Lt Buoy	55°58'·11N	04°50'·58W
Ayr Bar Lt Buoy	55°28'·12N	04°39'·38W
Cairndhu Lt Buoy	56°00'·36N	04°45'·93W
Cowal Lt Buoy	55°56'·00N	04°54'·77W
Dunoon Bank Lt Buoy	55°56'·63N	04°54'·09W
Eagle Rock Lt Buoy	55°38'·21N	04°49'·62W
Fairlie Patch Lt Buoy	55°45'·48N	00°52'·30W
Fullerton Rk Lt Buoy	55°30'·64N	05°04'·50W
Gantock Bn Lt	55°56'·46N	04°55'·00W
Hun 1 Lt Buoy	55°48'·10N	05°54'·15W
Hun 3 Lt Buoy	55°47'·60N	04°53'·43W
Hun 5 Lt Buoy	55°45'·86N	04°52'·45W
Hun 7 Lt Buoy	55°44'·96N	04°53'·86W
Hun 8 Lt Buoy	55°44'·80N	04°53'·62W
Hun 9 Lt Buoy	55°44'·68N	04°54'·38W
Hun 10 Lt Buoy	55°44'·15N	04°54'·79W
Hun 11 Lt Buoy	55°43'·45N	04°55'·09W
Hun 12 Lt Buoy	55°43'·45N	04°55'·55W
Hun 13 Lt Buoy	55°42'·52N	04°55'·10W
Hun 14 Lt Buoy	55°42'·52N	04°55'·54W
Kip Lt Buoy	55°54'·49N	04°52'·95W
Kilcreggan No.1 Lt Buoy	55°58'·68N	04°50'·19W
Kilcreggan No.2 Lt Buoy	55°59'·20N	04°51'·39W
Lady Isle Lt	55°31'·63N	04°43'·95W
Lamont Shelf Lt Buoy	55°48'·40N	05°13'·48W
Largs Lt Buoy	55°46'·50N	04°51'·78W
Loch Long Lt Buoy	55°59'·17N	04°52'·33W
Methe Bank Lt Buoy	55°25'·30N	05°34'·36W
Millbeg Bank Lt Buoy	55°25'·53N	05°33'·93W
Mountstuart Lt Buoy	55°27'·07N	05°31'·04W
Outer St Nicholas Lt Buoy	55°28'·11N	04°39'·37W

Outfall Lt Buoy	55°43'·56N	04°54'·74W
Pillar Rk Lt Ho	55°31'·05N	05°03'·57W
Pladda Lt Ho	55°25'·50N	05°11'·70W
Perch Rock Buoy	55°59'·45N	04°45'·58W
Portachur Lt Buoy	55°44'·35N	04°58'·44W
Portachur Spit Lt Buoy	55°44'·42N	04°57'·05W
Rhu South Lt Buoy	56°00'·67N	04°47'·34W
Row Lt Buoy	55°59'·85N	04°45'·05W
Skelmorlie Lt Buoy	55°51'·65N	04°56'·28W
Skipness Pt No. 51 Lt Buoy	55°45'·57N	05°19'·60W
Toward Bank Lt Buoy No.35	55°51'·05N	04°59'·93W
Troon Lt Buoy	55°33'·07N	04°41'·27W
Warden Bank Lt Buoy	55°57'·78N	04°54'·48W
West Crinan Lt Buoy	55°38'·46N	04°49'·82W
Whiteforeland Lt Buoy	55°58'·12N	04°47'·20W
7N Lt Buoy	56°00'·06N	04°45'·29W
8N Lt Buoy	55°59'·09N	04°44'·13W

9

LOCH CRAIGNISH   10-9-8
Argyll

CHARTS
Admiralty 2326, 2169; Imray C63, C65; OS 55
TIDES
−0540 Dover; ML (Seil Sound) 1.5;
Duration (Seil Sound) 0615; Zone 0 (GMT).
Standard Port OBAN (←)

Times				Height (metres)			
HW		LW		MHWS	MHWN	MLWN	MLWS
0100	0700	0100	0800	4.0	2.9	1.8	0.7
1300	1900	1300	2000				

Differences SEIL SOUND
−0035 −0015 −0040 −0015 −1.3   −0.9   −0.7   −0.3
GLENGARRISDALE BAY (Jura)
−0020   0000 −0010   0000 −0.4   −0.2   0.0   −0.2
Tidal heights are very much affected by wind and
barometric pressure causing differences of up to 1m above
or below predicted height.

SHELTER
Entrance between Garbh Reisa and Liath-sgier Mhor.
Beware squalls in easterlies, especially on E side of loch.
Yachts can go to Ardfern Yacht Centre or anchor off.
Anchorages include
− Goat Island (Eilean nan Gabhar), approach from
  E channel and anchor between the island and the
  skerry
− Eilean Righ, off the E side in middle of the Is.
− Bagh na Cille, NE of Craignish Pt.
− Eilean Dubh in the "lagoon" between the Is and
  Craignish peninsular.

NAVIGATION
Waypoint 56°07′ N, 05°35′.5W. Beware strong tidal
streams (up to 8kn) in the Dorus Mor. Beware a reef
extending one ca SSW of the SE chain of islands. Also
beware rock 1½ca SSW of Eilean Dubh. The main
fairway is free from hazards, except a rock Sgeir Dubh
due E of the easterly point of Mhic Chrion which has a
reef extending about ½ ca all round it. Beware fish cages
especially on E side of loch. At Ardfern, beware drying
rock at N end of anchorage with a rock awash ¼ca E of
it. These two are ½ca S of the more southerly of little
islets close to the mainland.
LIGHTS AND MARKS
There are no lights.
RADIO TELEPHONE
VHF Ch 16 37 watched by Ardfern Yacht Centre during
working hours and Ch **80** (0830 − 1800 LT).
TELEPHONE (085 25)
Hr Mr (Yacht Centre) 247; MRSC (Oban) 63720; Marinecall
0898 500 463; ⊞ Oban 63079; Dr (0546) 2921;
Ⓗ (0546) 2449
FACILITIES
Ardfern Yacht Centre (87 + 20 visitors); ☎ 247, AC,
BH (16 ton), Slip, ME, El, Sh, ACA, C (6 ton), FW, D,
CH, Gas, Gaz, R; **Galley of Lorne Hotel** ☎ 284, R, V,
P (cans); **Ardfern Village Store** V; **Ardfern Village**
Ⓑ (Wednesday); ✉ (AM only); ⇌ (Oban); ✈ (Glasgow).

CRINAN   10-9-9
Argyll

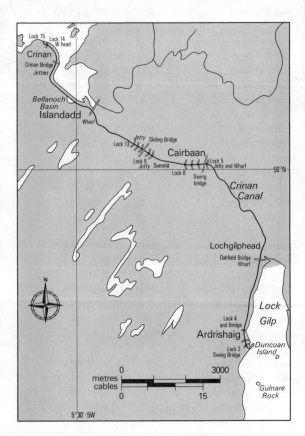

Depths in metres

CHARTS
Admiralty 2320, 2326; Imray C65; OS 55

TIDES
−0608 Dover; ML 2.1; Duration 0605; Zone 0 (GMT)
Standard Port OBAN (←)

Times				Height (metres)			
HW		LW		MHWS	MHWN	MLWN	MLWS
0100	0700	0100	0800	4.0	2.9	1.8	0.7
1300	1900	1300	2000				

SCALASAIG (Colonsay)
−0020 −0005 −0015 +0005 −0.1 −0.2 −0.2 −0.2
RUBHA A'MHAIL (Islay)
−0020 0000 +0005 −0015 −0.3 −0.1 −0.3 −0.1
ORSAY ISLAND (Islay)
−0110 −0110 −0040 −0040 −1.4 −0.6 −0.5 −0.2
BRUICHLADDICH (Islay)
−0100 −0005 −0110 −0040 −1.7 −1.4 −0.4 +0.1
PORT ELLEN (Islay)
−0530 −0050 −0045 −0530 −3.1 −2.1 −1.3 −0.4
PORT ASKAIG (Islay)
−0110 −0030 −0020 −0020 −1.9 −1.4 −0.8 −0.3
CRAIGHOUSE (Sound of Jura)
−0430 −0130 −0050 −0500 −2.8 −2.0 −1.4 −0.4
LOCH BEAG (Sound of Jura)
−0110 −0045 −0035 −0045 −1.6 −1.2 −0.8 −0.4
GIGHA SOUND (Sound of Jura)
−0450 −0210 −0130 −0410 −2.5 −1.6 −1.0 −0.1
MACHRIHANISH
−0520 −0350 −0340 −0540   Mean range 0.5 metres.
High water in Loch Crinan is 0045 before HW Oban.

SHELTER
Complete shelter in canal basin, but often many fishing boats lie there. Good shelter in Crinan Harbour to E of Eilean da Mheim, but full of moorings. Except in strong winds from W or N there is anchorage off the canal entrance, clear of fairway. R Add is available to small shoal-draught boats in good weather at HW. Not advised without local knowledge.

NAVIGATION
Waypoint 56°05′.80N 05°33′.69W, 326°/146° from/to Fl WG 3s Lt, 0.38M. Beware the Black Rocks and other nearby rocks in approach and near Ldg line.
CRINAN CANAL. Canal runs from Crinan, 9 miles to Ardrishaig and has 15 locks. All bridges open and canal can be entered at any tide. Max size, 26.5m length, 6m beam, 2.9m draught, mast height 28.9m. Vessels proceeding West have right of way. Canal dues are payable at Ardrishaig or Crinan sea lock. Passage time is between 5 to 6 hours. Locks operate (LT): −
Sea locks 0600-1200, 1230-2130 Mon-Sat.
Inland bridges and locks 0800-1200, 1230-1615 Mon-Sat.
Sunday opening times are flexible (summer months only).

LIGHTS AND MARKS
W wing of entrance 2 FG (vert)
E wing of entrance 2 FR (vert)
Light to E of entrance Fl WG 3s 8m 4M,
W shore-146°, G146°-shore.

RADIO TELEPHONE
VHF Ch 16; 74.

TELEPHONE (054 683)
MRSC Oban 63720; ⌗ 52261; Marinecall 0898 500 463;
Police Lochgilphead (0546) 2222; Dr Lochgilphead 2921

FACILITIES
Canal Office ☎ Lochgilphead 3210, M, L, FW; **Crinan Boats** ☎ 232, Slip, M, L, FW, ME, El, Sh, Gas, C, (5 ton) ⊡, CH, ACA; **Sea Basin** P (cans), D, AB, V, R, Bar; **Crinan Hotel** ☎ 235, D, R, Bar; **Fyneside Service Station** ☎ Lochgilphead 2229, C. **M. Murray** ☎ 238 M; **Village** ✉; Ⓑ (Ardrishaig); ⇌ (Oban); ✈ (Glasgow or Campbeltown).
Note: There are some Bu spherical buoys marked 'HIDB visitors only'.

9

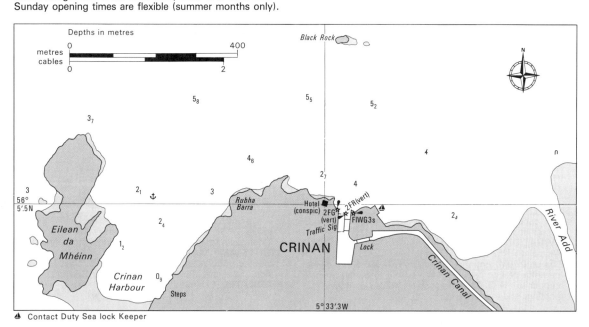

▲ Contact Duty Sea lock Keeper

CAMPBELTOWN   10-9-10
Argyll

CHARTS
Admiralty 1864 2126; Imray C63; OS 68
TIDES
+0045 Dover; ML 1.7; Duration 0630; Zone 0 (GMT).
Standard Port GREENOCK (⟶)

Times				Height (metres)			
HW		LW		MHWS	MHWN	MLWN	MLWS
0000	0600	0000	0600	3.4	2.9	1.0	0.4
1200	1800	1200	1800				

Differences CAMPBELTOWN
+0010 +0005 +0005 +0020 −0.5   −0.3   +0.1   +0.2
SANDA ISLAND
−0040 −0040   No data −1.0   −0.9   No data
SOUTHEND, KINTYRE
−0020 −0040 −0040 +0035 −1.3   −1.2   −0.5   −0.2

SHELTER
Good shelter from all directions. Excellent anchorage.
NAVIGATION
Waypoint 55°26'.30N 05°31'.39W, 060°/240° from/to
front Ldg Bn 240°, 2.6M. Strong winds gust over the hills
to the SW when wind in that direction.
LIGHTS AND MARKS
Davaar Fl(2) 10s 37m 23M. Ldg Lts 240°, Front FY 7m
6M, Rear FY 28m 6M.
RADIO TELEPHONE
VHF Ch 16; 12 14 (0845-1645 LT)
TELEPHONE (0586)
Hr Mr 52552; CG 52770; MRCC Greenock 29988;
⌗ 52261; Marinecall 0898 500 462; Police 52253; Dr 52105
FACILITIES
EC Wednesday; **Piers** ☎ 52552, Slip, P, D, L, FW, ME,
El, Sh, C (4 ton mobile), CH, AB, V, R, Bar; **Town Jetty**
L, FW, ME, CH, AB; **New Quay** Slip; **Campbeltown
Shipyard** ☎ 52881 L, FW, ME, Sh, CH, AB; **New Quay
Chandlers** ☎ 54381 CH; **Campbeltown S.C.** Slip
(dinghies only), M, L, FW, ME, CH, AB; **Duncan
McPhee** ☎ 52115/52772, Slip, M, ME, El, Sh, C, CH;
County Garage ☎ 52235 Gas; **Town** P, D, V, R, Bar.
✉; Ⓑ; ⇌ (Air or bus to Glasgow); ✈.

EAST LOCH TARBERT   10-9-11
Argyll

CHARTS
Admiralty 2381; Imray C63; OS 62
TIDES
+0120 Dover; ML 1.9; Duration 0640; Zone 0 (GMT).
Standard Port GREENOCK (⟶)

Times				Height (metres)			
HW		LW		MHWS	MHWN	MLWN	MLWS
0000	0600	0000	0600	3.4	2.9	1.0	0.4
1200	1800	1200	1800				

Differences EAST LOCH TARBERT
+0005 +0005 −0020 +0015   0.0   0.0   +0.1   −0.1

SHELTER
Very good indeed in all weathers but gets very crowded.
Access at all times.
NAVIGATION
Waypoint 55°52'.02N 05°22'.96W, 090°/270° from/to FIR
2.5s Lt, 0.70M. Entrance is very narrow. Cock Isle divides
the entrance into two. Buteman's Hole to the N, Main
harbour to the S. N anchorages are fouled by heavy
moorings and lost chains.

LIGHTS AND MARKS
Leading marks, Bn, G column (QG Lt) in line with tower
(conspic) at 239°
RADIO TELEPHONE
VHF Ch 16 (0900-1700 LT)
TELEPHONE (08802)
Hr Mr 344; CG 540; MRCC Greenock 29988;
⌗ Greenock 28311; Marinecall 0898 500 462; Police 200;
Ⓗ Lochgilphead 2323.

FACILITIES
EC Wednesday; **Old Quay** D, FW; **Tarbert YC** Slip, L;
W. B. Leitch & Son ☎ 287, SM, ▣, ACA; **M. Elliot**
☎ 560, ME; **A. MacCallum** ☎ 209, Sh. **Tarbert (Argyll)**
Fishermen ☎ 421, D, V, CH; **Yacht Berthing Facility**
AB, FW, L, AC; **A. McKay** ☎ 215 Gas;
Town P and D (cans), Gas, Gaz, L, V, R, Bar. ✉
(Tarbert); Ⓑ (Tarbert); ⇌ (bus to Glasgow); ✈ (Glasgow
or Campbeltown).

ARDRISHAIG   10-9-12
Argyll

CHARTS
Admiralty 2381; Imray C63; OS 55
TIDES
+0110 Dover; ML 1.9; Duration 0640; Zone 0 (GMT).
Standard Port GREENOCK (⟶)

Times				Height (metres)			
HW		LW		MHWS	MHWN	MLWN	MLWS
0000	0600	0000	0600	3.4	2.9	1.0	0.4
1200	1800	1200	1800				

Differences ARDRISHAIG
+0006 +0006 −0015 +0020   0.0   0.0   +0.1   −0.1
INVERARY
+0011 +0011 +0034 +0034 −0.1   +0.1   −0.5   −0.2

SHELTER
Harbour is sheltered except in strong easterly winds. Lock
into the Crinan Canal opens at all states of the tide. (See
10.9.9). Shelter can be obtained by going into the canal
basin. Canal tolls payable at Ardrishaig or Crinan sea lock.
NAVIGATION
Waypoint No 48 port-hand buoy, FIR 4s, 56°00'.18N
05°26'.24W, 165°/345° from/to breakwater Lt, 0.61M.
Tidal rocks to east of approach channel are dangerous.
LIGHTS AND MARKS
Lighted buoy W side of channel Fl R 4s. Unlit B buoy E
side of channel. Both to the S of Sgeir Sgalag.
RADIO TELEPHONE
VHF Ch 16; 74.

ARDRISHAIG *continued*

▲ Contact Duty Sea lock Keeper

TELEPHONE (0546)
Hr Mr 3210; CG Oban 3729; MRCC Greenock 29988;
⌗ 52261; Marinecall 0898 500 462; Police 3233; Dr 2921.

FACILITIES
EC Wednesday; **Ardrishaig Pier/Harbour** ☎ 3210, Slip,
L, FW, AB; **Crinan Canal** M, L, FW, AB, R, Bar; **Crinan
BY** ☎ 83 232, Slip, L, FW, ME, El, Sh, CH, V;
Ardrishaig BY ☎ 3280 ME, El, Sh, CH, C, D (cans);
Cranes up to 20 ton available Lochgilphead (2 M); **Mid-
Argyll Caravans** ☎ 2003 Gas. **Village** P and D (cans),
CH, V, R, Bar. ✉; Ⓑ; ⇌ (bus to Oban); ✈ (Glasgow or
Campbeltown).

LAMLASH   10-9-13
Isle of Arran, Bute

CHARTS
Admiralty 1864; Imray C63; OS 69
TIDES
+0050 Dover; ML no data; Duration 0635; Zone 0 (GMT).
Standard Port GREENOCK (→)

Times				Height (metres)			
HW		LW		MHWS	MHWN	MLWN	MLWS
0000	0600	0000	0600	3.4	2.9	1.0	0.4
1200	1800	1200	1800				

Differences LAMLASH
−0016 −0036 −0024 −0004 −0.2 −0.2 No data
BRODICK BAY
0000   0000 +0005 +0005 −0.2 −0.2 0.0 0.0
LOCH RANZA
−0015 −0005 −0005 −0010 −0.4 −0.3 −0.1 0.0

SHELTER
Very good in all weathers. Anchorages — off Lamlash
except in E. winds; off Kingscross, good except in N or
NW strong winds; off the Farm on NW of Holy Is in E
winds. Alternative Loch Ranza to the N (where new
marina is planned see 10.9.22).

NAVIGATION
Waypoint 55°32'.63N 05°03'.00W, 090°/270° from/to
North Channel buoy (FlR 5s), 1.0M. Beware submarines
which exercise frequently in this area, and also wreck of
landing craft (charted) off farmhouse on Holy Island.
LIGHTS AND MARKS
Lights as shown on chartlet. There are two consecutive
measured miles marked by poles north of Sannox, courses
322° or 142° (about 12 miles N of Lamlash).
RADIO TELEPHONE
None.
TELEPHONE (077 06)
MRCC Greenock 29988; ⌗ Ardrossan 63017;
Marinecall 0898 500 462; Police Brodick 2573; Ⓗ 214.
FACILITIES
EC Wednesday (Brodick and Lamlash); **Lamlash Jetty**
Slip, M, L, V; **Brodick Pier** L, FW, AB. **Johnston's
Marine Stores** ☎ 333, AB, Slip, FW, M, L.
Village Bar, R, ME, P and D (cans), V, CH, ✉; Ⓑ;
⇌ (bus to Brodick, ferry to Ardrossan); ✈ (Glasgow or
Prestwick).

ROTHESAY   10-9-14
Isle of Bute, Bute

CHARTS
Admiralty 1867, 1907; Imray C63; OS 63
TIDES
+0100 Dover; ML 1.9; Duration 0640; Zone 0 (GMT).
Standard Port GREENOCK (→)

Times				Height (metres)			
HW		LW		MHWS	MHWN	MLWN	MLWS
0000	0600	0000	0600	3.4	2.9	1.0	0.4
1200	1800	1200	1800				

Differences ROTHESAY BAY
−0020 −0015 −0010 −0002 +0.2 +0.2 +0.2 +0.2

SHELTER
Good shelter except in strong N to NE winds. Good
anchorage in bay. In N to NE winds, yachts advised to go
to Kyles of Bute or Kames Bay. Major pier reconstruction
in progress.
NAVIGATION
Waypoint 55°51'.00N 05°02'.69W, 014°/194° from/to
Albert Pier Lt, 0.69M. Keep 1 ca off Bogany Pt coming
from E, and Ardbeg Pt coming from W. Admiralty
mooring buoys, unlit, in Rothesay Bay (painted with
Dayglo paint).
LIGHTS AND MARKS
Approaching the harbour, 'A' buoy Fl Y 2s is the most
southerly of the mooring buoys.

ROTHESAY continued

RADIO TELEPHONE
VHF Ch 16; 12 (1 May-30 Sept; 0600-2100, 1 Oct-30 Apl, 0600-1900 LT).
TELEPHONE (0700)
Hr Mr 3842; CG Ardrossan 61014; MRCC Greenock 29988; ⌗ Greenock 26331; Marinecall 0898 500 462; Police 2121; Dr 3985; Ⓗ 3938
FACILITIES
EC Wednesday; **Outer Harbour (E)** ☎ 3842, Slip, D*, L, FW, ME, El, AB; **Outer Harbour (W)** ☎ 3842, D*, L, FW, ME, El, Sh, CH, AB; **Inner Harbour** L, FW, AB; **Main Pier** FW, R; **Albert Pier** D*, L, FW, C (4 ton mobile); **Town** P, D, CH, V, R, Bar; ✉; Ⓑ; ⇌ (ferry to Wemyss Bay); ✈ (Glasgow).
*By arrangement (min 200 galls).
Note: There is a marina planned for Dunoon.

HELENSBURGH/RHU   10-9-15
Dumbarton

CHARTS
Admiralty 2000, 1994; Imray C63; OS 56, 63
TIDES
+0110 Dover; ML 1.9; Duration 0640; Zone 0 (GMT).

SHELTER
Excellent in Gareloch — Entrance not difficult. Helensburgh Pier may be used, but rather exposed.
NAVIGATION
Waypoint 55°59'.30N 04°45'.19W, 176°/356° from/to front Ldg Lt 356°, 1.3M. Beware submarines from Faslane Base and large unlit MoD mooring buoys and barges off W shore of Gareloch. Gareloch entrance narrows to about

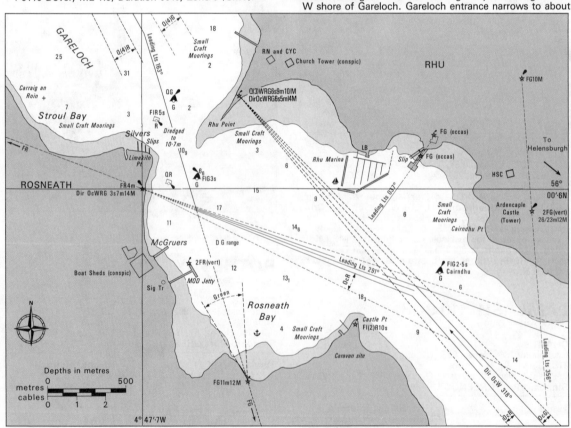

Standard Port GREENOCK (→)

Times				Height (metres)			
HW		LW		MHWS	MHWN	MLWN	MLWS
0000	0600	0000	0600	3.4	2.9	1.0	0.4
1200	1800	1200	1800				
Differences HELENSBURGH							
0000	0000	0000	0000	0.0	0.0	0.0	0.0
COULPORT							
−0005	−0005	−0005	−0005	0.0	0.0	−0.1	−0.1
ARROCHAR							
−0005	−0005	−0005	−0005	0.0	0.0	−0.1	−0.1
GARELOCHHEAD							
0000	0000	0000	0000	0.0	0.0	0.0	−0.1

150m at Rhu Pt. Shingle spit is being removed to widen channel. If using Helensburgh Pier keep outside line of pierhead. Beware occasional steamer.
Beaches between Helensburgh Pier and Cairndhu Pt strewn with large boulders above and below MLWS.
Major construction and marine works are in hand at Faslane Naval Base. Faslane Bay area contains numerous obstructions and underwater cables. Gareloch Fuel Depot area immediately to N. of Base is included.
Craft proceeding to Garelochhead keep to W shore until well clear of Base area.
Construction lights and unlit obstructions make night passages in the Base area most inadvisable. Gareloch Oil Fuel Depot sectored light is clearly visible from S of construction areas.

HELENSBURGH/RHU *continued*

LIGHTS AND MARKS
Leading lights into Gareloch 356°, 318°, 291° and 163°.

RADIO TELEPHONE
VHF Ch 16. Rhu Marina Ch **80** (office hours). See also Greenock/Gourock.

TELEPHONE (0436)
Queen's Hr Mr 74321; MRCC Greenock 29988 & 29014; ☏ Greenock 28311; Marinecall 0898 500 462; Police 72141; Ⓗ Alexandria 54121; Dr 72277.

FACILITIES
EC Wednesday; **Rhu Marina** (150) ☎ 820652, D, FW, CH, AC, BH (4½ ton), Gas, Gaz; **Royal Northern & Clyde YC** ☎ 820322, L, R, Bar; **Helensburgh SC** ☎ 72778 Slip (dinghies) L, FW; **McGruer (Rosneath)** ☎ 831313, Sh, ME, El, M, L, BH (25 ton), Slip; **Timbacraft** ☎ 810391, Sh, ME, El, Slip; **Silvers Marine** ☎ 831222 FW, Sh, ME, El, Ⓔ, L, M, BH (18 ton); **Nicolson Hughes** ☎ 831356, SM; **Gareloch Moorings and Engineers** ☎ 820062 ME, El, M; **R. McAlister** ☎ Dumbarton 62396 Sh, ME, El, M, Slip, BH (10 ton), AB, FW, CH, D; **Harken Barbarossa** ☎ 71415, CH: **Machspeed** ☎ 76351 CH; **Helensburgh** EC Wednesday, Slip, FW, CH, V, R, Bar, P, D, L, ✉; Ⓑ; ⇌; ✈ (Glasgow).

🔲 Restricted Area-Max Speed 7Kn
– – – Southern Limit of Dockyard Port

NOTE: There are many restricted areas which are closed to all vessels during Nuclear Submarine movements (see W Coast of Scotland Pilot APP 2). Vessels are never allowed within 150m of naval installations; MoD police launches patrol area.
The S limit of restricted area marked by two Or posts with St Andrews Cross topmarks on Shandon foreshore. The W limit marked by three-sectored Lt at Gareloch Oil fuel depot N jetty. When restrictions are in force
1. Holy Loch, Coulport, Faslane
    by day : 3 G Lts (vert) supplemented by International
                Code pendant over pendant Nine.
    by night : 3 FG (vert) in conspic position
2. Entrance to Gareloch
    by day : R G G Lts (vert) supplemented by R flag
               with W diagonal bar.
    by night : R G G Lts (vert)

GREENOCK/GOUROCK
Renfrew

10-9-16

CHARTS
Admiralty 1994; Imray C63; OS 63

TIDES
+0115 Dover; ML 2.0; Duration 0640; Zone 0 (GMT)
Standard Port GREENOCK (→)

Times				Height (metres)			
HW		LW		MHWS	MHWN	MLWN	MLWS
0000	0600	0000	0600	3.4	2.9	1.0	0.4
1200	1800	1200	1800				

Differences PORT GLASGOW
+0010 +0005 +0010 +0020 +0.2 +0.1 0.0 0.0

BOWLING
+0020 +0010 +0030 +0055 +0.6 +0.5 +0.3 +0.1

NOTE: Harbours are all controlled by Clyde Port Authority, 16 Robertson St., Glasgow. Tel. Glasgow 221-8733. Greenock is a Standard Port and tidal predictions for each day of the year are given below.

SHELTER
Greenock — Commercial port
Gourock — very good anchorages on W side of bay but exposed to NE to N winds.

NAVIGATION
Gourock waypoint 55°58'.00N 04°49'.00W, 000°/180° from/to Kempock Pt Lt, 0.22M. No navigational dangers except the continuous shipping using the Clyde estuary and steamers using Railway Pier. Beware the bottom being fouled with lost tackle.

LIGHTS AND MARKS
(Gourock). At the end of the pier 2 FG (vert).

RADIO TELEPHONE
Call: *Clydeport Estuary Radio* VHF Ch 16; 14 12 (H24). Other station: Dunoon (call: *Dunoon Pier*) Ch 31; 12 16 **31** (0700-2035 LT Mon-Sat; 0900-2015 LT Sun).

TELEPHONE (0475)
Hr Mr 26221; CG 29988; MRCC 29988; ☏ 28311; Weather Glasgow 246 8091; Marinecall 0898 500 462; Police 24444; Dr 20000.

FACILITIES
EC Wednesday; **Greenock** All facilities available by prior arrangement with Harbour Dept, but small craft not particularly welcome; **Jas. Adam & Son** ☎ 31346 Slip, ME, El, C (5 ton), Ⓔ; **R. McAlister & Son** ☎ Dumbarton 62396, CH, D, Gas, ME, Sh; **Garvel Dry Dock** ☎ 25372, AB, AC, C (45 ton), El, Ⓔ, FW, L, ME, Sh; **Mackenzie** ☎ 36196, SM; **Royal Gourock YC** ☎ 32983 M, L, FW, ME, V, R, Bar; **Ritchie Bros** ☎ 32125, M; **Mackenzie** ☎ 36196, SM; **Ashton Bay** M; **Gourock Bay** M, L; **Maybank** Slip; **Town (Gourock)** P, D, V, R, Bar. ✉; Ⓑ; ⇌; ✈ (Glasgow).
Note: Clyde Yacht Clubs Assn is at Anchor House, Blackhall Lane, Paisley 041-887-8296. The Clyde Cruising Club is aboard S.V. Carrick, Glasgow 041-552-2183.

SCOTLAND, WEST COAST - GREENOCK

LAT 55°57'N   LONG 4°46'W

TIMES AND HEIGHTS OF HIGH AND LOW WATERS

YEAR **1991**

TIME ZONE UT(GMT)
For Summer Time add ONE hour in non-shaded areas

JANUARY

Day	Time	m	Time	m	Time	m	Time	m
1 TU	0019	3.4	0546	0.4	1226	3.7	1806	0.2
2 W	0108	3.5	0633	0.4	1312	3.9	1853	0.1
3 TH	0155	3.5	0718	0.4	1356	4.0	1940	0.1
4 F	0240	3.5	0803	0.5	1440	4.0	2026	0.2
5 SA	0325	3.5	0849	0.7	1524	3.9	2113	0.4
6 SU	0409	3.4	0937	0.8	1608	3.8	2202	0.6
7 M ☾	0455	3.2	1028	1.0	1653	3.6	2254	0.8
8 TU	0544	3.1	1126	1.1	1742	3.4	2355	1.0
9 W	0639	3.0	1236	1.2	1835	3.1		
10 TH	0112	1.2	0747	2.9	1354	1.2	1941	2.9
11 F	0230	1.2	0902	2.9	1501	1.1	2106	2.8
12 SA	0330	1.2	1007	2.9	1555	1.0	2222	2.7
13 SU	0417	1.1	1100	3.1	1641	0.9	2318	2.8
14 M	0457	1.1	1144	3.2	1720	0.8		
15 TU ●	0003	2.9	0531	1.0	1223	3.3	1755	0.7
16 W	0041	3.0	0603	1.0	1258	3.3	1828	0.6
17 TH	0115	3.1	0634	0.9	1330	3.4	1900	0.6
18 F	0148	3.2	0707	0.8	1403	3.5	1935	0.5
19 SA	0222	3.2	0741	0.8	1436	3.5	2011	0.4
20 SU	0258	3.3	0819	0.7	1511	3.5	2051	0.4
21 M	0336	3.3	0859	0.7	1549	3.5	2134	0.4
22 TU	0417	3.2	0944	0.8	1630	3.4	2223	0.5
23 W ☾	0502	3.2	1034	0.8	1714	3.3	2319	0.6
24 TH	0550	3.1	1133	0.9	1804	3.1		
25 F	0028	0.7	0645	3.0	1247	1.0	1907	2.9
26 SA	0148	0.8	0755	2.9	1410	0.9	2044	2.9
27 SU	0258	0.7	0917	3.0	1519	0.7	2216	2.9
28 M	0356	0.6	1027	3.2	1616	0.5	2321	3.1
29 TU	0446	0.5	1124	3.4	1706	0.3		
30 W ○	0014	3.3	0532	0.4	1213	3.7	1752	0.1
31 TH	0100	3.4	0616	0.3	1258	3.8	1837	0.1

FEBRUARY

Day	Time	m	Time	m	Time	m	Time	m
1 F	0142	3.5	0659	0.3	1340	3.9	1919	0.1
2 SA	0222	3.5	0740	0.4	1421	3.9	2001	0.2
3 SU	0300	3.4	0822	0.4	1501	3.8	2042	0.3
4 M	0338	3.3	0903	0.6	1540	3.7	2123	0.6
5 TU	0416	3.2	0947	0.7	1620	3.4	2205	0.8
6 W ☾	0456	3.0	1035	0.9	1701	3.2	2252	1.0
7 TH	0539	2.9	1135	1.1	1745	2.9	2355	1.3
8 F	0631	2.7	1310	1.2	1837	2.6		
9 SA	0202	1.4	0751	2.6	1438	1.2	1958	2.5
10 SU	0311	1.3	0934	2.7	1534	1.0	2204	2.5
11 M	0358	1.2	1038	2.8	1619	0.9	2306	2.6
12 TU	0437	1.1	1125	3.0	1656	0.8	2349	2.8
13 W	0510	0.9	1204	3.2	1730	0.6		
14 TH ●	0024	3.0			1239	3.3	1802	0.5
15 F	0057	3.1	0611	0.7	1311	3.4	1835	0.4
16 SA	0129	3.2	0644	0.6	1344	3.5	1909	0.2
17 SU	0202	3.3	0718	0.5	1417	3.5	1946	0.2
18 M	0237	3.3	0755	0.4	1451	3.5	2025	0.1
19 TU	0313	3.3	0834	0.4	1528	3.4	2106	0.2
20 W	0352	3.3	0917	0.4	1607	3.3	2153	0.4
21 TH	0433	3.2	1005	0.5	1650	3.1	2247	0.6
22 F	0518	3.0	1102	0.7	1738	2.9	2358	0.8
23 SA	0610	2.9	1221	0.9	1838	2.8		
24 SU	0132	0.9	0715	2.9	1358	0.8	2040	2.7
25 M	0246	0.9	0853	2.9	1508	0.6	2215	2.8
26 TU	0341	0.7	1012	3.1	1602	0.4	2315	3.1
27 W	0429	0.5	1109	3.4	1650	0.3		
28 TH ○	0002	3.2	0513	0.4	1158	3.6	1734	0.1

MARCH

Day	Time	m	Time	m	Time	m	Time	m
1 F	0044	3.3	0555	0.3	1240	3.7	1815	0.1
2 SA	0121	3.4	0635	0.2	1320	3.8	1855	0.1
3 SU	0157	3.4	0714	0.2	1358	3.7	1932	0.2
4 M	0231	3.3	0752	0.3	1434	3.6	2009	0.4
5 TU	0304	3.2	0830	0.4	1509	3.4	2044	0.5
6 W	0338	3.1	0909	0.6	1545	3.2	2119	0.8
7 TH	0413	2.9	0950	0.8	1622	2.9	2156	1.0
8 F ☾	0450	2.8	1040	1.0	1702	2.7	2241	1.2
9 SA	0534	2.6	1202	1.2	1747	2.5		
10 SU	0037	1.4	0630	2.5	1401	1.2	1847	2.3
11 M	0236	1.4	0839	2.5	1459	1.0	2130	2.4
12 TU	0324	1.2	1003	2.7	1543	0.9	2236	2.6
13 W	0402	1.0	1054	2.9	1621	0.7	2319	2.8
14 TH	0436	0.9	1134	3.1	1657	0.5	2355	3.0
15 F	0509	0.7	1210	3.2	1731	0.3		
16 SA ●	0028	3.1	0542	0.5	1244	3.4	1806	0.2
17 SU	0102	3.2	0617	0.3	1318	3.4	1842	0.1
18 M	0136	3.3	0653	0.2	1353	3.4	1920	0.0
19 TU	0211	3.3	0731	0.1	1430	3.4	2000	0.2
20 W	0248	3.3	0811	0.1	1508	3.3	2042	0.2
21 TH	0327	3.3	0855	0.2	1548	3.2	2130	0.4
22 F	0409	3.2	0945	0.4	1632	3.0	2225	0.6
23 SA	0453	3.1	1045	0.6	1722	2.8	2342	0.9
24 SU	0544	3.0	1210	0.7	1831	2.6		
25 M	0118	1.0	0650	2.9	1345	0.7	2045	2.6
26 TU	0227	0.8	0832	2.9	1450	0.6	2204	2.8
27 W	0320	0.7	0951	3.1	1542	0.4	2257	3.0
28 TH	0407	0.5	1049	3.3	1629	0.3	2341	3.2
29 F	0451	0.4	1136	3.5	1711	0.2		
30 SA ○	0020	3.3	0532	0.3	1218	3.5	1750	0.2
31 SU	0055	3.3	0611	0.2	1256	3.5	1828	0.2

APRIL

Day	Time	m	Time	m	Time	m	Time	m
1 M	0129	3.2	0649	0.2	1332	3.4	1903	0.3
2 TU	0201	3.2	0725	0.2	1406	3.3	1936	0.4
3 W	0232	3.1	0801	0.3	1440	3.1	2008	0.6
4 TH	0303	3.0	0837	0.5	1513	2.9	2040	0.8
5 F	0336	2.9	0917	0.7	1549	2.8	2115	0.9
6 SA ☾	0413	2.8	1003	0.9	1628	2.6	2159	1.2
7 SU	0454	2.7	1110	1.1	1713	2.5	2310	1.4
8 M	0545	2.6	1257	1.1	1811	2.4		
9 TU	0132	1.4	0704	2.5	1408	1.0	2015	2.4
10 W	0233	1.2	0904	2.6	1457	0.8	2145	2.6
11 TH	0316	1.0	1006	2.8	1540	0.6	2236	2.8
12 F	0356	0.8	1053	3.0	1619	0.4	2316	3.0
13 SA	0433	0.6	1134	3.2	1658	0.2	2354	3.1
14 SU ●	0511	0.4	1213	3.3	1737	0.1		
15 M	0031	3.2	0549	0.2	1251	3.3	1816	0.0
16 TU	0108	3.3	0629	0.2	1330	3.4	1857	0.0
17 W	0146	3.4	0710	-0.1	1410	3.4	1939	0.0
18 TH	0225	3.4	0754	0.0	1451	3.3	2025	0.2
19 F	0306	3.3	0841	0.1	1535	3.1	2115	0.4
20 SA	0349	3.3	0934	0.3	1624	3.0	2215	0.7
21 SU ☾	0436	3.2	1039	0.5	1720	2.8	2331	0.9
22 M	0529	3.1	1201	0.6	1842	2.7		
23 TU	0054	0.9	0636	3.0	1323	0.6	2025	2.8
24 W	0200	0.9	0805	3.0	1426	0.5	2136	2.9
25 TH	0254	0.7	0922	3.1	1518	0.4	2229	3.0
26 F	0342	0.5	1021	3.2	1604	0.4	2313	3.1
27 SA	0427	0.4	1110	3.3	1647	0.3	2352	3.2
28 SU ○	0509	0.3	1154	3.3	1727	0.4		
29 M	0028	3.2	0549	0.3	1233	3.2	1803	0.4
30 TU	0101	3.1	0627	0.3	1309	3.1	1837	0.5

Chart Datum: 1.26 metres below Ordnance Datum (Newlyn)

SCOTLAND, WEST COAST - GREENOCK

LAT 55°57'N   LONG 4°46'W

TIMES AND HEIGHTS OF HIGH AND LOW WATERS

YEAR 1991

TIME ZONE UT(GMT)
For Summer Time add ONE hour in non-shaded areas

Moon symbols: (last quarter, ● new moon,) first quarter, O full moon

MAY

Day		Time	m	Time	m	Time	m	Time	m
1	W	0133	3.1	0703	0.3	1342	3.0	1909	0.6
2	TH	0204	3.1	0739	0.4	1415	2.9	1941	0.7
3	F	0236	3.0	0815	0.5	1449	2.8	2014	0.8
4	SA	0309	3.0	0855	0.6	1525	2.8	2053	1.0
5	SU	0346	2.9	0942	0.8	1606	2.7	2141	1.1
6	M	0428	2.9	1040	0.9	1653	2.6	2245	1.2
7	TU (	0516	2.8	1153	0.9	1751	2.6		
8	W	0012	1.3	0618	2.7	1306	0.9	1911	2.6
9	TH	0129	1.2	0746	2.7	1405	0.7	2041	2.7
10	F	0226	1.0	0906	2.8	1456	0.5	2144	2.8
11	SA	0314	0.8	1006	2.9	1542	0.3	2234	3.0
12	SU	0359	0.5	1056	3.1	1627	0.2	2318	3.1
13	M	0442	0.3	1142	3.2	1711	0.1		
14	TU ●	0001	3.2	0525	0.1	1227	3.2	1754	0.0
15	W	0043	3.3	0609	0.0	1311	3.3	1839	0.0
16	TH	0124	3.4	0655	-0.1	1355	3.3	1925	0.1
17	F	0206	3.5	0742	-0.1	1441	3.2	2013	0.3
18	SA	0250	3.5	0833	0.0	1529	3.2	2105	0.5
19	SU	0336	3.5	0927	0.2	1621	3.1	2203	0.7
20	M)	0424	3.4	1029	0.3	1719	3.0	2309	0.8
21	TU	0517	3.4	1138	0.5	1829	2.9		
22	W	0020	0.9	0618	3.3	1251	0.6	1947	2.9
23	TH	0127	0.9	0731	3.2	1355	0.6	2055	2.9
24	F	0225	0.7	0845	3.1	1451	0.6	2152	3.0
25	SA	0317	0.6	0949	3.1	1540	0.6	2241	3.1
26	SU	0405	0.5	1044	3.1	1626	0.6	2324	3.1
27	M	0450	0.4	1131	3.0	1707	0.6		
28	TU O	0003	3.1	0532	0.4	1214	2.9	1745	0.7
29	W	0039	3.1	0611	0.4	1251	2.9	1820	0.7
30	TH	0113	3.1	0648	0.4	1326	2.8	1853	0.8
31	F	0146	3.1	0724	0.5	1400	2.8	1926	0.8

JUNE

Day		Time	m	Time	m	Time	m	Time	m
1	SA	0219	3.1	0801	0.5	1435	2.8	2001	0.9
2	SU	0253	3.1	0839	0.6	1512	2.8	2041	0.9
3	M	0330	3.1	0923	0.6	1554	2.9	2127	1.0
4	TU	0411	3.1	1012	0.7	1640	2.9	2220	1.1
5	W)	0456	3.0	1108	0.7	1732	2.8	2321	1.1
6	TH	0547	2.9	1210	0.7	1832	2.8		
7	F	0028	1.1	0648	2.9	1314	0.6	1940	2.8
8	SA	0134	0.9	0802	2.8	1414	0.5	2049	2.9
9	SU	0233	0.8	0916	2.9	1509	0.4	2150	3.0
10	M	0327	0.6	1020	3.0	1601	0.3	2244	3.1
11	TU	0418	0.3	1116	3.1	1650	0.2	2334	3.2
12	W ●	0507	0.2	1208	3.2	1738	0.2		
13	TH	0020	3.4	0555	0.0	1258	3.3	1825	0.2
14	F	0106	3.5	0643	-0.1	1346	3.3	1912	0.2
15	SA	0152	3.6	0732	-0.1	1434	3.3	2000	0.3
16	SU	0237	3.7	0822	0.0	1521	3.3	2050	0.5
17	M	0323	3.7	0913	0.1	1610	3.3	2142	0.6
18	TU	0410	3.7	1007	0.3	1702	3.2	2239	0.7
19	W)	0500	3.6	1106	0.5	1757	3.1	2340	0.8
20	TH	0553	3.4	1211	0.7	1859	3.0		
21	F	0047	0.9	0652	3.2	1320	0.8	2005	2.9
22	SA	0154	0.8	0801	3.0	1425	0.8	2110	2.9
23	SU	0254	0.8	0913	2.9	1521	0.8	2208	2.9
24	M	0348	0.7	1019	2.8	1611	0.8	2259	3.0
25	TU	0436	0.6	1115	2.8	1655	0.9	2343	3.0
26	W	0520	0.6	1201	2.8	1734	0.9		
27	TH O	0023	3.1	0559	0.6	1242	2.8	1809	0.9
28	F	0100	3.1	0635	0.6	1318	2.8	1842	0.9
29	SA	0134	3.2	0709	0.6	1351	2.9	1914	0.9
30	SU	0207	3.2	0743	0.5	1425	3.0	1948	0.9

JULY

Day		Time	m	Time	m	Time	m	Time	m
1	M	0241	3.2	0819	0.5	1501	3.0	2025	0.8
2	TU	0316	3.2	0858	0.5	1539	3.1	2106	0.8
3	W	0353	3.2	0941	0.5	1621	3.1	2151	0.9
4	TH	0434	3.2	1030	0.5	1706	3.0	2241	0.9
5	F (	0519	3.1	1124	0.6	1755	3.0	2339	0.9
6	SA	0609	3.0	1228	0.6	1851	2.9		
7	SU	0045	0.9	0708	2.9	1337	0.6	1956	2.9
8	M	0156	0.8	0827	2.8	1443	0.6	2108	2.9
9	TU	0302	0.6	0951	2.9	1542	0.5	2214	3.0
10	W	0400	0.4	1100	3.0	1635	0.4	2312	3.3
11	TH ●	0453	0.2	1157	3.2	1724	0.3		
12	F	0004	3.5	0542	0.1	1249	3.3	1811	0.3
13	SA	0052	3.7	0630	0.0	1336	3.4	1857	0.3
14	SU	0137	3.8	0717	0.0	1421	3.5	1942	0.3
15	M	0222	3.9	0803	0.0	1505	3.5	2028	0.4
16	TU	0306	3.9	0850	0.2	1548	3.4	2114	0.5
17	W	0350	3.8	0937	0.4	1632	3.3	2204	0.6
18	TH)	0435	3.6	1028	0.6	1718	3.1	2258	0.8
19	F	0521	3.4	1124	0.8	1808	3.0		
20	SA	0002	0.9	0630	3.1	1236	1.0	1906	2.9
21	SU	0120	1.0	0710	2.9	1401	1.1	2020	2.8
22	M	0234	0.9	0832	2.7	1508	1.1	2137	2.8
23	TU	0333	0.9	1001	2.7	1600	1.1	2238	2.9
24	W	0422	0.8	1105	2.7	1643	1.0	2328	3.0
25	TH	0505	0.7	1153	2.8	1721	1.0		
26	F O	0010	3.1	0542	0.7	1232	2.9	1754	0.9
27	SA	0047	3.2	0615	0.6	1306	3.0	1824	0.9
28	SU	0120	3.3	0647	0.6	1337	3.1	1855	0.8
29	M	0152	3.3	0719	0.6	1409	3.2	1927	0.8
30	TU	0224	3.4	0753	0.4	1442	3.2	2002	0.7
31	W	0257	3.4	0830	0.4	1518	3.3	2039	0.6

AUGUST

Day		Time	m	Time	m	Time	m	Time	m
1	TH	0332	3.4	0910	0.4	1556	3.2	2120	0.7
2	F	0410	3.3	0955	0.5	1637	3.2	2206	0.7
3	SA	0451	3.2	1046	0.6	1722	3.1	2300	0.8
4	SU	0537	3.1	1148	0.7	1811	3.0		
5	M	0005	0.9	0630	2.9	1307	0.8	1910	2.9
6	TU	0129	0.9	0747	2.8	1426	0.8	2028	2.9
7	W	0246	0.7	0938	2.9	1528	0.7	2151	3.1
8	TH	0347	0.5	1053	3.0	1621	0.6	2255	3.3
9	F	0440	0.3	1149	3.2	1708	0.4	2348	3.6
10	SA ●	0527	0.2	1237	3.4	1753	0.4		
11	SU	0035	3.8	0612	0.1	1320	3.5	1836	0.3
12	M	0120	3.9	0656	0.0	1401	3.6	1918	0.3
13	TU	0202	4.0	0739	0.1	1440	3.5	2001	0.3
14	W	0243	3.9	0821	0.3	1519	3.4	2043	0.4
15	TH	0323	3.8	0903	0.5	1557	3.3	2127	0.6
16	F	0404	3.6	0946	0.7	1637	3.2	2216	0.8
17	SA)	0446	3.3	1033	1.0	1719	3.0	2314	1.0
18	SU (	0530	3.0	1134	1.3	1808	2.8		
19	M	0041	1.1	0619	2.8	1336	1.4	1914	2.7
20	TU	0213	1.1	0734	2.6	1451	1.4	2101	2.7
21	W	0313	1.0	0945	2.6	1541	1.3	2215	2.9
22	TH	0400	0.9	1051	2.7	1621	1.2	2307	3.1
23	F	0440	0.8	1135	2.9	1657	1.1	2348	3.2
24	SA	0515	0.7	1211	3.0	1728	1.0		
25	SU O	0024	3.3	0547	0.6	1243	3.2	1757	0.9
26	M	0057	3.4	0618	0.5	1313	3.3	1828	0.7
27	TU	0128	3.4	0650	0.4	1344	3.3	1900	0.6
28	W	0200	3.5	0725	0.4	1417	3.4	1935	0.5
29	TH	0233	3.5	0801	0.3	1452	3.4	2012	0.5
30	F	0308	3.4	0841	0.4	1529	3.4	2053	0.5
31	SA	0346	3.3	0925	0.5	1609	3.3	2138	0.6

Chart Datum: 1.26 metres below Ordnance Datum (Newlyn)

9

SCOTLAND, WEST COAST - GREENOCK

LAT 55°57′N   LONG 4°46′W

TIMES AND HEIGHTS OF HIGH AND LOW WATERS

YEAR **1991**

TIME ZONE **UT(GMT)**
For Summer Time add ONE hour in non-shaded areas

Chart Datum: 1.26 metres below Ordnance Datum (Newlyn)

SEPTEMBER

Day	Time	m	Time	m	Time	m	Time	m		Day	Time	m	Time	m	Time	m	Time	m
1 SU ☾	0427	3.2	1015	0.7	1652	3.2	2231	0.7		16 M	0450	2.9	1031	1.4	1719	2.9	2352	1.3
2 M	0512	3.1	1118	0.9	1740	3.1	2340	0.9		17 TU	0536	2.7	1227	1.6	1813	2.8		
3 TU	0605	2.9	1247	1.1	1836	3.1				18 W	0140	1.3	0638	2.6	1417	1.6	2002	2.8
4 W	0114	0.9	0733	2.8	1412	1.0	1958	3.0		19 TH	0241	1.2	0912	2.6	1507	1.4	2137	2.9
5 TH	0234	0.8	0938	2.9	1512	0.9	2132	3.2		20 F	0327	1.0	1019	2.8	1547	1.3	2232	3.1
6 F	0333	0.6	1045	3.1	1602	0.7	2237	3.4		21 SA	0406	0.9	1103	3.0	1622	1.1	2315	3.3
7 SA	0422	0.4	1135	3.4	1648	0.5	2329	3.7		22 SU	0441	0.7	1138	3.2	1654	1.0	2352	3.4
8 SU ●	0508	0.2	1218	3.5	1731	0.4				23 M O	0514	0.6	1211	3.3	1726	0.8		
9 M	0015	3.8	0550	0.2	1258	3.6	1812	0.3		24 TU	0026	3.4	0547	0.5	1244	3.6	1758	0.6
10 TU	0058	3.9	0631	0.2	1335	3.6	1853	0.3		25 W	0100	3.5	0621	0.4	1316	3.5	1833	0.5
11 W	0137	3.9	0711	0.3	1411	3.5	1933	0.3		26 TH	0133	3.5	0657	0.3	1351	3.5	1910	0.4
12 TH	0216	3.8	0750	0.4	1447	3.5	2013	0.4		27 F	0209	3.5	0736	0.3	1427	3.5	1949	0.4
13 F	0254	3.6	0827	0.6	1522	3.3	2054	0.6		28 SA	0246	3.4	0817	0.4	1505	3.5	2032	0.4
14 SA	0331	3.4	0905	0.9	1558	3.2	2137	0.8		29 SU	0325	3.3	0901	0.6	1545	3.5	2119	0.5
15 SU ☽	0410	3.2	0944	1.1	1636	3.1	2230	1.1		30 M	0408	3.2	0953	0.8	1628	3.4	2215	0.7

OCTOBER

Day	Time	m	Time	m	Time	m	Time	m		Day	Time	m	Time	m	Time	m	Time	m
1 TU	0457	3.1	1101	1.1	1717	3.3	2329	0.9		16 W	0503	2.8	1056	1.7	1731	3.0		
2 W	0557	2.9	1232	1.2	1815	3.2				17 TH	0042	1.3	0602	2.7	1310	1.7	1843	2.9
3 TH	0104	0.9	0751	2.9	1352	1.2	1939	3.2		18 F	0152	1.2	0759	2.7	1415	1.6	2035	2.9
4 F	0217	0.8	0927	3.0	1450	1.0	2110	3.4		19 SA	0242	1.1	0927	2.8	1501	1.4	2142	3.1
5 SA	0313	0.6	1026	3.3	1540	0.8	2215	3.5		20 SU	0324	0.9	1017	3.1	1540	1.2	2232	3.2
6 SU	0401	0.4	1113	3.4	1625	0.6	2306	3.7		21 M	0402	0.7	1058	3.2	1617	1.0	2314	3.3
7 M	0446	0.3	1154	3.6	1708	0.5	2352	3.8		22 TU	0440	0.6	1135	3.4	1653	0.8	2352 ●	3.4
8 TU	0527	0.3	1232	3.6	1749	0.4				23 W O	0517	0.4	1212	3.5	1731	0.6		
9 W	0033	3.8	0606	0.4	1308	3.6	1829	0.4		24 TH	0030	3.5	0555	0.3	1248	3.6	1809	0.4
10 TH	0112	3.7	0644	0.5	1343	3.5	1908	0.4		25 F	0109	3.5	0634	0.3	1325	3.6	1849	0.3
11 F	0149	3.5	0720	0.6	1416	3.5	1947	0.5		26 SA	0148	3.5	0715	0.3	1404	3.7	1932	0.3
12 SA	0225	3.4	0755	0.8	1449	3.4	2026	0.7		27 SU	0229	3.4	0759	0.4	1444	3.7	2018	0.4
13 SU	0300	3.2	0829	1.0	1523	3.3	2108	0.9		28 M	0312	3.4	0847	0.7	1526	3.7	2109	0.5
14 M	0337	3.0	0905	1.2	1600	3.2	2157	1.1		29 TU	0359	3.2	0942	0.9	1612	3.6	2208	0.7
15 TU	0417	2.9	0948	1.5	1641	3.1	2304	1.3		30 W	0453	3.1	1049	1.1	1702	3.5	2321	0.8
										31 TH	0603	3.0	1209	1.3	1802	3.5		

NOVEMBER

Day	Time	m	Time	m	Time	m	Time	m		Day	Time	m	Time	m	Time	m	Time	m
1 F	0043	0.8	0740	3.0	1324	1.2	1919	3.4		16 SA	0045	1.2	0651	2.8	1302	1.6	1915	3.0
2 SA	0153	0.8	0900	3.2	1423	1.1	2041	3.5		17 SU	0146	1.1	0816	2.9	1404	1.4	2037	3.0
3 SU	0249	0.7	0958	3.3	1515	0.9	2147	3.5		18 M	0238	0.9	0922	3.1	1454	1.2	2141	3.1
4 M	0338	0.6	1046	3.4	1603	0.7	2241	3.6		19 TU	0324	0.7	1014	3.2	1540	1.0	2234	3.2
5 TU	0424	0.5	1128	3.5	1647	0.6	2328	3.6		20 W	0408	0.6	1059	3.4	1624	0.7	2321	3.3
6 W ●	0506	0.5	1207	3.6	1730	0.5				21 TH O	0451	0.4	1141	3.5	1707	0.5		
7 TH	0011	3.5	0545	0.6	1243	3.5	1810	0.5		22 F	0005	3.4	0534	0.3	1223	3.6	1750	0.4
8 F	0050	3.4	0622	0.7	1318	3.5	1849	0.5		23 SA	0050	3.5	0617	0.3	1304	3.7	1834	0.3
9 SA	0127	3.3	0657	0.8	1351	3.5	1928	0.6		24 SU	0133	3.5	0701	0.4	1345	3.8	1920	0.2
10 SU	0202	3.2	0731	0.9	1424	3.4	2006	0.7		25 M	0218	3.5	0748	0.5	1428	3.9	2009	0.3
11 M	0237	3.1	0804	1.1	1457	3.4	2047	0.9		26 TU	0305	3.4	0837	0.7	1513	3.9	2100	0.4
12 TU	0313	3.0	0841	1.2	1534	3.3	2132	1.0		27 W	0355	3.4	0931	0.9	1600	3.8	2157	0.5
13 W	0354	3.0	0925	1.4	1614	3.2	2227	1.1		28 TH ☾	0449	3.3	1030	1.0	1650	3.8	2301	0.7
14 TH ☽	0440	2.9	1022	1.5	1701	3.2	2333	1.2		29 F	0552	3.2	1138	1.1	1747	3.6	2341	1.0
15 F	0537	2.9	1140	1.6	1759	3.1				30 SA	0011	0.8	0706	3.2	1249	1.2	1852	3.5

DECEMBER

Day	Time	m	Time	m	Time	m	Time	m		Day	Time	m	Time	m	Time	m	Time	m
1 SU	0121	0.8	0820	3.2	1353	1.1	2006	3.4		16 M	0046	1.0	0711	3.0	1302	1.3	1928	3.0
2 M	0223	0.8	0923	3.3	1451	0.9	2116	3.4		17 TU	0150	0.9	0821	3.0	1408	1.2	2045	3.0
3 TU	0317	0.8	1017	3.3	1543	0.8	2217	3.3		18 W	0249	0.8	0927	3.1	1506	1.0	2155	3.1
4 W	0406	0.8	1103	3.4	1631	0.7	2309	3.3		19 TH	0342	0.6	1023	3.2	1559	0.7	2255	3.2
5 TH	0450	0.8	1145	3.4	1716	0.6	2355	3.2		20 F	0431	0.5	1059	3.4	1648	0.5	2348	3.3
6 F	0531	0.8	1224	3.5	1757	0.6				21 SA O	0518	0.3	1201	3.6	1736	0.3		
7 SA	0036	3.2	0608	0.9	1300	3.5	1836	0.6		22 SU	0037	3.4	0604	0.4	1246	3.8	1822	0.2
8 SU	0114	3.1	0643	0.9	1334	3.5	1914	0.7		23 M	0124	3.5	0649	0.4	1331	3.9	1909	0.1
9 M	0149	3.1	0717	1.0	1407	3.4	1951	0.7		24 TU	0211	3.5	0735	0.4	1415	4.0	1957	0.1
10 TU	0223	3.1	0750	1.1	1441	3.4	2028	0.8		25 W	0257	3.5	0823	0.5	1500	4.0	2046	0.2
11 W	0259	3.1	0826	1.2	1516	3.4	2108	0.9		26 TH	0344	3.5	0912	0.7	1545	4.0	2137	0.4
12 TH	0338	3.1	0907	1.2	1554	3.4	2152	0.9		27 F	0433	3.4	1004	0.8	1633	3.9	2232	0.5
13 F	0421	3.1	0954	1.3	1636	3.3	2243	1.0		28 SA ☾	0525	3.3	1102	0.9	1724	3.7	2333	0.7
14 SA	0510	3.0	1049	1.4	1724	3.2	2341	1.0		29 SU	0623	3.2	1208	1.0	1820	3.5		
15 SU	0606	3.0	1153	1.4	1820	3.1				30 M	0043	0.9	0730	3.1	1321	1.1	1925	3.3
										31 TU	0157	1.0	0842	3.1	1429	1.0	2042	3.1

GREENOCK/GOUROCK *continued*

Note: There is a scheme to re-open the Forth and Clyde Canal from Dalmuir (on the Clyde) via Kirkintilloch, Castlecary, Bonnybridge to the Carron R flowing into the Forth at Grangemouth.

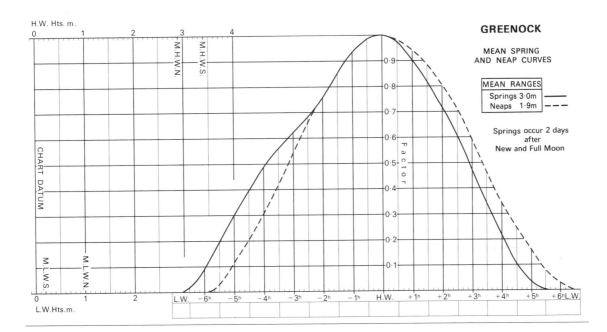

GREENOCK

MEAN SPRING AND NEAP CURVES

MEAN RANGES
Springs 3·0m ———
Neaps 1·9m – – –

Springs occur 2 days after New and Full Moon

INVERKIP (KIP MARINA)
Renfrew

10-9-17

CHARTS
Admiralty 1907; Imray C63; OS 63
TIDES
+0110 Dover; ML 1.8; Duration 0640; Zone 0 (GMT).
Standard Port GREENOCK (←)

Times				Height (metres)			
HW		LW		MHWS	MHWN	MLWN	MLWS
0000	0600	0000	0600	3.4	2.9	1.0	0.4
1200	1800	1200	1800				

Differences WEMYSS BAY
−0005 −0005 −0005 −0005 0.0   0.0 +0.1 +0.1

SHELTER
Excellent and is navigable at all states of the tide (2.4m at MLWS). Inverkip Bay is exposed to winds NW through W to SW.
NAVIGATION
Waypoint Kip stbd-hand buoy, QG, 55°54'.48N 04°52'.95W, at entrance to buoyed channel. Entrance ½M N of conspic chimney (238m). Beware shifting bank to N of entrance to buoyed channel. No areas in marina dry.
LIGHTS AND MARKS
From Kip G buoy, QG, three G buoys to starboard and three R buoys to port, 30m apart form navigable channel 365 metres long.
RADIO TELEPHONE
VHF Ch **80** (H24).
TELEPHONE (0475)
Hr Mr 521485; CG 29014; MRCC 29988; ⌗ 28311; Marinecall 0898 500 462; Police 521222; Dr 520248; Ⓗ 33777.
FACILITIES
EC Wednesday; **Kip Marina** (700+40 visitors) ☎ 521485, D, FW, AC, ME, El, Ⓔ, Sh, BH (40 ton), ACA, SM, CH, V, R, Bar, ▣, Gas, Gaz, YC; **Town** ✉; Ⓑ (Gourock); ⇌; ✈ (Glasgow).

LARGS 10-9-18
Ayr

FACILITIES
EC Wednesday. **Largs Yacht Haven** (500 – some visitors) ☎ 675333, FW, D, P, BH (45 ton), ⊙, CH, AC, SM, BY, C (12 ton), Gas, Gaz, Slip (Access H24); **Clyde Motor Co.** ☎ 687139, ME, diving; **Largs Chandlers** ☎ 686026, CH; **Yacht Electrical and Electronic Services** ☎ 686463, El, Ⓔ; **Regattas** ☎ 686684, Bar, R; **The Ship's Galley** ☎ 675625, V; **Largs SC** ☎ 674782; **Town** LB, V, R, Bar, ✉, Ⓑ; ⇌; ✈ (Glasgow).

CHARTS
Admiralty 1907, 1867; Imray C63; OS 63

TIDES
+0105 Dover; ML 1.9; Duration 0640; Zone 0 (GMT).
Standard Port GREENOCK (←)

Times				Heights (metres)			
HW		LW		MHWS	MHWN	MLWN	MLWS
0000	0600	0000	0600	3.4	2.9	1.0	0.4
1200	1800	1200	1800				

Differences ARDROSSAN

−0020	−0010	−0010	−0010	−0.2	−0.2	+0.1	+0.1

SHELTER
Excellent shelter in Yacht Haven (1M S of Largs pier) accessible at all tides. Largs bay exposed to winds from N to W and from S. Temporary anchorage in 10m about ½ca N of pier opposite Royal Hotel.

NAVIGATION
Waypoint 55°46'.40N 04°51'.77W; RW mid channel buoy off entrance to marina. Approaching from S beware Hunterston and Southannan sands. The area between the S breakwater and the NATO pier is restricted and anchoring is forbidden.

LIGHTS AND MARKS
Yacht Haven (1M S of Largs pier): entrance buoy RW LFl 10s; S breakwaterhead Oc G 10s; N breakwaterhead Oc R 10s. Largs; N end of pier, 2 FG (vert) 7/5m 5M, shown when vessel expected.

RADIO TELEPHONE
Yacht Haven Ch **80** (H24).

TELEPHONE (0475)
Hr Mr (Yacht Haven) 675333; CG 29014; MRCC 29988; ⌗ 28311; Marinecall 0898 500 462; Dr 673380; Ⓗ 33777.

TROON   10-9-19
Ayr

CHARTS
Admiralty 1866 2220; Imray C63; OS 70
TIDES
+0050 Dover; ML 1.9; Duration 0630; Zone 0 (GMT).
Standard Port GREENOCK (←)

Times				Height (metres)			
HW		LW		MHWS	MHWN	MLWN	MLWS
0000	0600	0000	0600	3.4	2.9	1.0	0.4
1200	1800	1200	1800				
Differences TROON							
−0025	−0025	−0020	−0020	−0.2	−0.2	0.0	0.0
IRVINE							
−0020	−0020	−0030	−0010	−0.3	−0.3	−0.1	0.0
AYR							
−0025	−0025	−0030	−0015	−0.4	−0.3	+0.1	+0.1
GIRVAN							
−0025	−0040	−0035	−0010	−0.3	−0.3	−0.1	0.0

SHELTER
Completely sheltered from all winds. Berth in Yacht Marina.
NAVIGATION
Waypoint 55°33'.20N 04°42'.00W, 283°/103° from/to West Pier Lt, 0.61M. Beware the Mill Rock ½ M NE of West Pier (R buoy on S side). Keep clear of water off Ailsa Shipbuilding yard.
LIGHTS AND MARKS
As on chartlet. No leading lights. Sheds of Ailsa shipyard (35m) are conspic. Recommended approach Troon on bearing S to SW. Entry signals: Day—2B balls, Night—2RLts (vert) Entry and Exit prohibited: these refer to commercial traffic only.
RADIO TELEPHONE
Marina VHF Ch **80** (H24). Other stations: Ardrossan Ch 16; 12 14 (H24). Girvan Ch 16; 12 (Mon-Fri: 0900-1700 LT).
TELEPHONE (0292)
Hr Mr 313412; CG Greenock 29014; MRCC Greenock 29988; ☎ 262088; Marinecall 0898 500 462; Police 313100; Ⓗ 68621; Marina officials will give telephone numbers of doctors on call 315553.

TROON

FACILITIES
EC Wednesday; **Marina** (345+40 visitors) ☎ 315553 (Access all tides), Slip, D, FW, ME, El, Sh (on-site repairs ☎ 316180), BH (12 ton), C (2 ton), CH, AC, V, R, Bar; Ⓞ, Gas, Gaz; **Harbour Pier** FW, Sh, AB, V. **Ailsa Shipyard** has all normal 'big ship' repair facilities. **Troon Cruising Club** ☎ 311190; **Marine Mechanical** ☎ 313400, ME; **Boat Electrics and Electronics** ☎ 315355, El, Ⓔ. **Town** ✉; Ⓑ; ≷; ✈ (Glasgow).

PORTPATRICK   10-9-20
Wigtown

CHARTS
Admiralty 2198; Imray C62; OS 82

TIDES
+0032 Dover; ML 2.1; Duration 0615; Zone 0 (GMT).
Standard Port LIVERPOOL (→)

Times				Heights (metres)			
HW		LW		MHWS	MHWN	MLWN	MLWS
0000	0600	0200	0800	9.3	7.4	2.9	0.9
1200	1800	1400	2000				
Differences PORTPATRICK							
+0018	+0026	0000	−0035	−5.5	−4.4	−2.0	−0.6

Stranraer Differences Liverpool +0046 (see 10.10.11)

SHELTER
Good but is a difficult entrance in winds from SW to NW when strong. Inner harbour has good shelter and berthing facilities.
NAVIGATION
Waypoint 54°50'.00N 05°08'.00W, 235°/055° from/to entrance, 0.70M. Entrance to outer harbour by way of short narrow entrance with adjacent hazards including rocky shelf submerged at HW. Barrel marks end of rocks.
LIGHTS AND MARKS
Two FG Ldg Lts 050°, 6 and 8m: Front on sea wall, Rear on building; 2 vert orange lines by day. There is a conspic hotel approx 100m NW of Inner Harbour.
RADIO TELEPHONE
None. Other station: Stranraer VHF Ch 16; 14 (H24). Portpatrick Coast Radio Station VHF Ch 16; 27.
TELEPHONE (077 681)
Hr Mr 355; CG and MRSC Greenock 29988; ☎ Newton Stewart 2718; Marinecall 0898 500 462; Police 222; Ⓗ Stranraer 2323
FACILITIES
EC Thursday. **Harbour** Slip (very small craft), M, FW, L, AB. **Village** P, D, Gas, V, R, Bar. ✉; Ⓑ (Stranraer); ≷ (bus to Stranraer); ✈ (Carlisle).

KIRKCUDBRIGHT   10-9-21
Kirkcudbrightshire

CHARTS
Admiralty 1344, 1346, 2094; Imray C62; OS 84

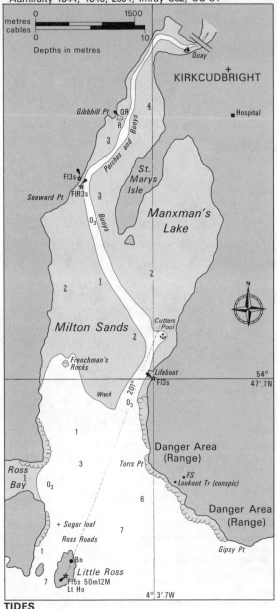

TIDES
+0030 Dover; ML 4.1; Duration 0545; Zone 0 (GMT).
Standard Port LIVERPOOL (→)

Times				Heights (metres)			
HW		LW		MHWS	MHWN	MLWN	MLWS
0000	0600	0200	0800	9.3	7.4	2.9	0.9
1200	1800	1400	2000				

Differences KIRKCUDBRIGHT BAY
+0015 +0015 +0010 0000 −1.8 −1.5 −0.5 −0.1
DRUMMORE
+0030 +0040 +0015 +0020 −3.4 −2.5 −0.9 −0.3
ISLE OF WHITHORN
+0020 +0025 +0025 +0005 −2.4 −2.0 −0.8 −0.2

SHELTER
Very good shelter. Complete shelter at town quays, which dry. Boats can stay afloat in 2m off the wooden jetty. Good shelter behind Ross Is and in Flint Bay 1 ca N of Torrs Pt except in winds between SSW and ESE which cause heavy swell.
NAVIGATION
Waypoint 54°45'.50N 04°04'.00W, 185°/005° from/to Torrs Pt, 1.4M. The Bar is 7 ca N of Torrs Pt. Note that spring tides run up to 3 kn.

LIGHTS AND MARKS
Little Ross Lt Ho West of entrance Fl 5s 50m 12M, (obsc in Wigtown bay when bearing more than 103°).
Note: The harbour authority is the Dumfries & Galloway Regional Council.
RADIO TELEPHONE
VHF Ch 12, 16. (HW∓2).
TELEPHONE (0557)
Hr Mr 31135; CG 31133; ☎ Newton Stewart 2718; Marinecall 0898 500 461; Police 30600; Dr 30755.
FACILITIES
EC Thursday. **Town Quay** P, D, L, FW, AB, El, CH; **Gordon Burns** ☎ 30420, ME; **Wooden Pier** AB; **Kirkcudbright YC** ☎ 30963; **SC** ☎ 30032, Slip, M, FW; **Scallop Gear** ☎ 30399, CH; **Town** V, R, Bar. ⊠; Ⓑ; ⇌ (bus to Dumfries); ✈ (Glasgow).

MINOR HARBOURS AND ANCHORAGES   10.9.22

SCALASAIG, Colonsay, 56°04' N, 6°11' W, Zone 0 (GMT), Admty chart 2474. HW −0600 on Dover, −0012 on Oban; HW height −0.1m on Oban; ML 2.2m. See 10.9.9. There is a swell running most of the time so anchor close to the shore, preferably to the S of pier head in approx 2.5m (works in progress 1987). Inner harbour safe, but dries. Beware group of rocks N of pier head marked by Bn. Lts: Rubha Dubh to S of harbour, Fl (2) WR 10s 6m 8/5M; R shore−230°, W230°−337°, R337°−354°. Ldg Lts 262°, front on pier head FR 8m, rear 60m from front, FR 10m. Facilities: D, P, V (all at ⊠), FW.

LOCH TARBERT, Jura, 55°57' N, 6°00' W, Zone 0 (GMT), Admty charts 2481, 2169. Tides at Rubha A'Mhail HW −0540 on Dover, −0010 on Oban; HW height −0.2m on Oban; ML 2.1m; Duration 0600. Excellent shelter inside the loch; anchor outside in Glenbatrick Bay in approx 6m in S winds, or at Bagh Gleann Righ Mor in approx 2m in N winds. To enter inner loch there are four pairs of ldg marks (white stones) at approx 120°, 150°, 077°, and 188°, the latter astern, to be picked up in sequence. There are no facilities.

LOCH SWEEN, TAYVALLICH, Argyll, 56°01' N, 5°37' W, Zone 0 (GMT), Admty chart 2397. HW +0550 on Dover, −0015 on Oban; HW height −1.1m on Oban; ML 1.5m; Duration 0610. Good shelter; anchor in Port Lunna SSW of Barr Mor, in Loch a Bhealaich (outside Tayvallich in approx 7m) or enter inner harbour and anchor by central reef. Beware Sgeirean a Mhain, a rock in the middle of the loch to S of Taynish I, 3M from entrance. There are no lights. Facilities: **Livingstone** ☎ 226, Gas, Bar, FW (tap by ⊠), ⊠, R, V.

CRAIGHOUSE, Jura, 55°50' N, 5°57' W, Zone 0 (GMT), Admty charts 2168, 2396, 2481. HW +0600 on Dover, −0430 np, −0130 sp on Oban; HW height −2.0m on Oban; ML 0.7m; Duration 0640 np 0530 sp. See 10.9.9. Good shelter but squalls occur in W winds. Enter between Lt Bn on SW end of Eilean nan Gabhar, Fl 5s 7m 8M vis 225°−010°, and the beacon to the SW. Yachts may go alongside the pier or anchor in 5m N end of Loch na Mile. Facilities: very limited. There are eight spherical Bu buoys marked 'HIDB visitors only'. Bar, FW, ⊠, R, V; **Paton** ☎ 242, Gas.

GIGHA ISLAND, Argyll, 55°41' N, 5°44' W, Zone 0 (GMT), Admty chart 2475. HW +0600 on Dover, −0450 np, −0210 sp on Oban; HW height −2.0m on Oban; ML 0.9m; Duration 0530. See 10.9.9. By careful selection, good shelter can be found round the island in any conditions. Main anchorage is Ardminish Bay but Druimyeon Bay and the bay N of West Tarbert Bay are popular alternatives, the latter being good in NE winds. Beware numerous rocks in Gigha Sound, reefs extending off both points of Ardminish Bay and the Kiln Rk off the jetty. There are no lights but there is a W cardinal buoy Fl (9) 15s marking Gigalum Rks, opposite N end of Gigalum I. There are 12 spherical buoys marked 'HIDB for visitors' in Ardminish Bay. Facilities are limited; Bar, FW in hut at end of jetty, ⊠, R, V; **Gigha Engineering Services** ☎ 261, ME. **Bannatyne** ☎ 220, Gas.

PORT ASKAIG, Islay, 55°51' N, 6°07' W, Zone 0 (GMT), Admty chart 2481. HW +0610 on Dover, −0050 on Oban; HW height −1.6m on Oban; ML 1.2m. Harbour on W side of Sound of Islay. Anchor close inshore in 4m or secure to ferry pier. Beware strong tides with eddies. Facilities: Hotel, Gas, FW (hose on pier), P, R, Bar, V, ⊠, ferries to Jura and Kintyre.

MINOR HARBOURS AND ANCHORAGES *Continued*

PORT ELLEN, Islay, 55°38′ N, 6°12′ W, Zone 0 (GMT), Admty chart 2474. HW −0620 sp +0130 np on Dover; −0050 sp −0530 np on Oban; the tide seldom exceeds 0.6m and the level of the sea is greatly affected by the weather; at neaps the tide is often not appreciable. See 10.9.9. Good shelter except in S winds when a swell sets into the bay. In these conditions, anchor N of Carraig Fhada. At other times anchor in 3m in NE corner. Beware rocks all along E side of entrance. Carraig Fhada, Lt Ho (conspic) on W side Fl WRG 3s 19m 8/6M; W shore-248°, G248°−311°, W311°−340°, R340°−shore. Keep in W sector until past the G can buoy, QG; Ro Ro terminal shows 2 FG (vert). Facilities: **Bridgend Sawmills** ☎ 598, Gas; **Village** Bar, FW, ✉, R, V.

CARRADALE BAY, Argyll, 55°32′ N, 5°27′ W, Zone 0 (GMT), Admty chart 2131, HW +0115 on Dover, 0000 on Greenock; HW height −0.2m on Greenock. Good anchorage in 7m off Torrisdale Castle in SW corner of bay. With S winds a swell sets into bay and better anchorage to be found N of Carradale Pt, in Port Cranaig. Off Carradale Pt is R buoy Fl(2)R 12s marks outer end of foul ground. Good shelter inside breakwater. Facilities: V, R, Bar, ✉.

BRODICK, Arran, 55°35′ N, 5°09′ W, Zone 0 (GMT), Admty chart 1864. HW +0115 on Dover, 0000 on Greenock; HW height −0.2m on Greenock; ML 1.8m; Duration 0635. See 10.9.13. Shelter is good except in E winds. Anchor W of pier in approx 3m, just below the Castle in 4.5m or further N off Merkland Pt in 3 to 4m. There are no navigational dangers but the bay is in a submarine exercise area. Only Lts are 2FR (vert) 9/7m 4M on pier head and Fl Y on two Admiralty buoys. Facilities: EC Wed; Ⓑ, Bar, P and D in cans, FW (at pier head), ME, ✉, R, V.

LOCH RANZA, Arran, 55°43′ N, 5°17′ W, Zone 0 (GMT), Admty charts 2221, 2131. HW +0120 on Dover, −0005 on Greenock; HW height −0.3m on Greenock; ML 1.7m; Duration 0635. See 10.9.13. Good shelter but swell comes into the harbour with N winds. The 850m mountain 4M to S causes fierce squalls in the loch with S winds. Beware rocky spit extending seaward from S of Newton Pt. Anchor off castle in 5m. Facilities: Bar, FW (tap near pier), ✉, R, V. Marina is planned.

INVERARY, Argyll, 56°14′ N, 5°04′ W, Zone 0 (GMT), Admty chart 2382. HW +0126 on Dover, +0011 on Greenock; HW height −0.1m (sp), +0.1m (np) on Greenock (see 10.9.12). For Upper Loch Fyne see 10.9.5. Beware An Oitir extending 2 ca offshore, ½M S of pier. Anchor NNE of pier in 4m or pick up a buoy (some reserved for visitors). Facilities: FW (on pier), ✉, V, R, Bar, Gas, bus to Glasgow.

CALADH HARBOUR, Argyll, 55°56′ N, 5°12′ W, Zone 0 (GMT), Admty chart 1906. HW (Tighnabruaich) +0015 on Dover; as Greenock; HW height +0.1m on Greenock; ML 2.1m. Perfectly sheltered natural harbour on W side of mouth of Loch Riddon. This delightful anchorage lies behind Eilean Dush, a tiny uninhabited island at the mouth of Loch Riddon. There are two passages into Caladh Harbour, N and S of Eilean Dush; keep to the middle of the S passage; between R and G beacons when using the N. It is best to fetch up in the middle of the harbour, avoiding a nasty drying rock which lurks off the N shore. Land at a stone slip on the S side. There are no facilities or stores. Tighnabruaich has all stores, a yacht yard and D in cans.

LOCH LONG/LONG GOIL, Argyll/Dumbartonshire, 56°02′ to 12′ N, 4°45′ to 54′ W; Zone 0 (GMT); Admty chart 3746. HW (Arrochar) +0010, (Lochgoilhead) +0022 on Dover; (Arrochar) −0005, (Lochgoilhead) +0007 on Greenock; HW height (Arrochar) 0.0m, (Lochgoilhead) −0.3m on Greenock; ML 1.75m; Duration 0645. See 10.9.15. Loch Long is about 15M long and there are anchorages at Cove, Portincaple, Blairmore (unsuitable in S winds), Ardentinny, Coilessan (about 1M S of Ardgartan Pt), Arrochar (anchor N of the pier or opposite, off the W shore). In Loch Goil by Carrick Castle (Anchor S of the pier, in N winds a swell develops), or at Lochgoilhead; the whole of the head of the loch is crowded with moorings, so find a free one or anchor with tripping line. Avoid anchoring near Douglas Pier. Beware large tankers going up to Finnart and nuclear submarines going up to Coulport. There is a submarine noise range in Loch Goil, marked 'Experimental Area' on the chart. Contact range vessel on Ch 13 if present. Lights: Coulport Jetty, 2FG (vert) each end; Portdornaige Fl W6s 8m 11M,

vis. 026°-206°; Dog Rock (Carraig nan Ron) Fl W2s 11M; Finnart Ocean Oil Terminal has numerous lights for the benefit of tankers. Facilities: Loch Long (Cove) shops, FW (on pier); (Portincaple) shops, hotel, ✉, FW; (Ardentinny) shop, V.R. hotel, M; (Blairmore) shops, ✉, Slip, FW; (Arrochar) shops, hotel, FW, Gas, ✉. Loch Goil (Carrick Castle) has ✉, shop, hotel; (Lochgoilhead) has all stores, ✉, hotel, FW, Gas.

MILLPORT, Great Cumbrae, Bute, 55°45′ N, 4°55′ W, Zone 0 (GMT), Admty chart 1867. HW +0100 on Dover, −0015 on Greenock; HW height 0.0m on Greenock; ML 1.9m; Duration 0640. Good shelter except with S winds. Anchor E of the inner of The Eileans in approx 3m, or off pier in approx 3m. Beware The Spoig and The Clach to W of Ldg Line, and the rocks off The Eileans to E of Ldg Line. Ldg Lts 333°, front FR 7m 5M, rear FR 9m 5M. Facilities: EC Wed; Hr Mr ☎ Largs 530826, Bar, Gas, D, P, FW, ✉, R, Slip, V.

AYR, Ayr, 55°28′ N, 4°38′ W, Zone 0 (GMT), Admty chart 1866. HW +0050 on Dover, −0025 on Greenock; HW height −0.3m on Greenock; ML 1.8m. Duration 0630. See 10.9.19. Good shelter except in W winds when shelter can be found in the dock. Beware St Nicholas Rock to S of entrance and large amounts of debris being washed down the R Ayr after heavy rains. Entrance is not easy for larger yachts. Ldg Lts 098° Front, by Pilot Stn, FR 10m 5M R Tr, also traffic signals; rear (130m from front) Oc R 10s 18m 10M. N breakwater head QR 9m 5M. S pier head QW 7m 7M; vis 012°−161°, and FG 5m 5M; vis 012°−066°, over St Nicholas Rocks. North Quay head, 2 B balls (vert) or 2FR (vert) = harbour closed. 1 B ball (1 R Lt or 1 GLt) = proceed with caution. Hr Mr Tel. 281687. VHF Ch 16 14. Facilities: EC Wed; Ⓑ, Bar, CH, Gas, D, El, FW, ME, ✉, R, ⚓, Sh, V; **Saturn Sails** ☎ 286241 SM; **Ayr Yacht & Cruising Club** (40) ☎ 267963, Bar, R, M. **J. W. Mackay** ☎ 281586, Sh, ME, El; **J. Goodwin** ☎ 263837, CH.

GIRVAN, Ayr, 55°15′ N, 4°52′ W, Zone 0 (GMT), Admty chart 1866 2199. HW +0043 on Dover, −0032 on Greenock; HW height −0.3m on Greenock; ML 1.8m; Duration 0630. See 10.9.19. Good shelter. Harbour used by fishing vessels and coasters but yachts may find berths available on quay. Beware Girvan Patch, 2.4m, 4 ca SW of entrance, and Brest Rocks, 3.5M N of harbour extending 6 ca offshore, marked by W Lt Bn Fl(2) 6s 7m 4M. Entrance between breakwater to N and pier to S. Lts: Breakwater head Iso 4s 3m 4M; S pier head 2FG (vert) 8m 4M South pier head − 2 B discs (hor), at night 2FR (hor) = harbour closed. VHF Ch 16; 12 (office hours). Facilities: EC Wed; Harbour Office ☎ 3048; FW, Slip; **Town** Ⓑ, Bar, ✉, R, ⚓, V.

LOCH RYAN, Wigtown, 54°55′ N, 5°03′ W, Zone 0 (GMT), Admty chart 1403. HW (Stranraer) +0055 on Dover, −0020 on Greenock; HW height −0.4m on Greenock; ML 1.6m; Duration 0640. Very good shelter except in strong NW winds. Entrance between Milleur Pt and Finnarts Pt. Anchorages in Lady Bay, 1.3M SSE of Milleur Pt; in The Wig in 3m; off Stranraer NE of steamer pier in 3m or lie alongside quay at Stranraer. Beware The Beef Barrel, rk 1m high 6 cables SSE of Milleur Pt; the sand spit running 1.5M to SE from W shore opposite Cairn Pt Lt Ho Fl (2) R 10s 14m 12M. Lt at Cairnryan ferry terminal Fl R 5s 5m 5M. Lts at Stranraer − centre pier head 2FBu (vert), E pier head 2FR (vert), W Ross pier head 2 FVi (vert) 10m 4M. Facilities (Stranraer): EC Wed; Ⓑ, Bar, D, FW, P, ✉, R, ⚓, V.

ISLE OF WHITHORN, Wigtown, 54°42′ N, 4°22′ W, Zone 0 (GMT), Admty chart 2094. HW +0035 on Dover, +0020 on Liverpool; HW height −2.2m on Liverpool; ML 3.7m; Duration 0545. See 10.9.21. Shelter good but Hr dries having approx 2.5m at HW∓3. Beware the Skerries, a ledge on W side of entrance marked by a thin iron stake. E pier head has QG 4m 5M; Ldg Lts 335°, front Oc R 8s 7m 7M; orange mast; Rear, 35m from front, Oc R 8s 9m 7M; orange mast; synchronised with front. Berth alongside quay. Facilities: Hr Mr ☎ Whithorn 246, Slip, P, D, FW, ME, Sh, CH, V, Bar, ✉, VHF Ch 80 (occas).

WIGTOWN BAY, Kirkcudbrightshire, 54°47′ N, 4°21′ W, Zone 0 (GMT), Admty chart 2094. HW (Garlieston) +0100 on Dover, +0030 on Liverpool; HW height −2.0m on Liverpool; ML 3.8m; Duration 0545. Garlieston harbour affords complete shelter but dries. Access (2m) HW∓3. Pier head Lt 2FR (vert) 5m 3M. Beware rocky outcrops in W side of bay marked by a perch. Facilities: Hr Mr ☎ Garlieston 259. FW, AC on quay & visitors moorings, stores, ME, P, D and slip in town.

9

VOLVO PENTA SERVICE

Sales and service centres in area 10
CUMBRIA **Waterhead Marine Ltd** AMBLESIDE LA22 0EX Tel (053 94) 32424.
Windermere Aquatic Ltd Glebe Road, BOWNESS-ON-WINDERMERE LA23 3HE
Tel (09662) 2121. MANCHESTER **Pilkington Motor Marine** Watson Street,
MANCHESTER M3 4LP Tel (061 834) 5392.

Area 10

North-West England, Isle of Man and North Wales
Maryport to Pwllheli

VOLVO PENTA

10

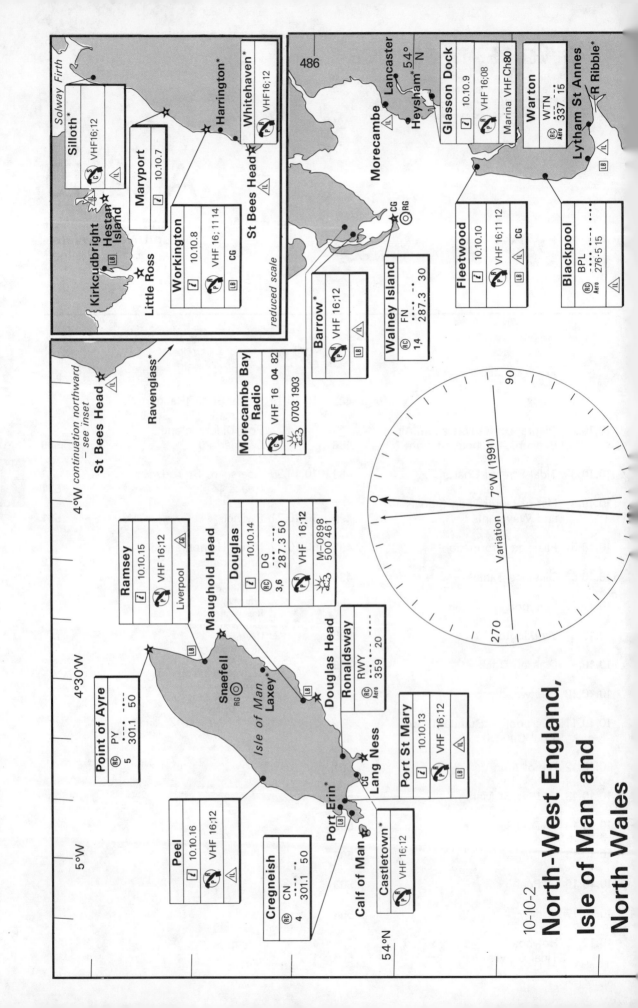

10-10-2

North-West England, Isle of Man and North Wales

10.10.3   AREA 10 TIDAL STREAMS

5 Hours before HW Dover (0515 before HW Liverpool)

4 Hours before HW Dover (0415 before HW Liverpool)

3 Hours before HW Dover (0315 before HW Liverpool)

2 Hours before HW Dover (0215 before HW Liverpool)

1 Hour before HW Dover (0115 before HW Liverpool)

HW Dover (0015 before HW Liverpool)

Northward 10.9.3   Southward 10.11.3   North Ireland 10.13.3   South Ireland 10.12.3

1 Hour after HW Dover (0045 after HW Liverpool)

2 Hours after HW Dover (0145 after HW Liverpool)

3 Hours after HW Dover (0245 after HW Liverpool)

4 Hours after HW Dover (0345 after HW Liverpool)

5 Hours after HW Dover (0445 after HW Liverpool)

6 Hours after HW Dover (0545 after HW Liverpool)

10

10.10.4 LIGHTS, FOG SIGNALS AND WAYPOINTS

Abbreviations used below are given in 10.0.3. Principal lights are in **bold** print, places in CAPITALS, and light-vessels, light floats and Lanbys in *CAPITAL ITALICS*. Unless otherwise stated lights are white. m—elevation in metres; M—nominal range in n. miles. Fog signals are in *italics*. Useful waypoints are underlined use those on land with care. See 4.2.2.

ENGLAND—WEST COAST

SILLOTH.
Corner Lt Buoy 54°49'·40N 03°31'·30W Fl G; stbd-hand mark.
Lees Scar 54°51'·80N 03°24'·75W QG 11m 8M; W structure on piles; vis 005°-317°.
East Cote Dir Lt 052°, Dir FG 15m 12M; W structure on piles; vis 046°-058°, intens 052°.
Groyne head 54°52'·1N 03°24'·0W 2 FG (vert) 4m 4M; Fl Bu traffic signals close by.

MARYPORT.
S pier head 54°43'·05N 03°30'·60W Fl 1·5s 10m 4M.

WORKINGTON.
South pier 54°39'·13N 03°34'·71W Fl 5s 11m 8M; R building; *Siren 20s*.
Ldg Lts 132°. Front 54°38'·9N 03°34'·1W FR 10m 3M. Rear 134m from front FR 12m 3M; both on W pyramidal Tr, Y bands.

WHITEHAVEN.
West pier head 54°33'·16N 03°35'·84W Fl G 5s 16m 13M; W round Tr.
North pier head 2 FR (vert) 8m 9M; W round Tr.

Saint Bees Head 54°30'·80N 03°38'·15W Fl(2) 20s 102m **21M**; W round Tr; obsc shore—340°; (H24).
Selker Lt Buoy 54°16'·13N 03°29'·50W Fl(3)G 10s; stbd-hand mark; *Bell*.

BARROW-IN-FURNESS.
Lightning Knoll Lt Buoy 53°59'·83N 03°14'·20W LFl 10s; safe water mark; *Bell*.
Isle of Walney 54°02'·92N 03°10'·65W Fl 15s 21m **23M**; stone Tr; obsc 122°-127° within 3M of shore; RC.
Walney Channel Ldg Lts 041°. Front 54°03'·3N 03°08'·9W Q 6m 6M; B pile structure, W daymark. Rear 640m from front Iso 2s 12m 6M; R column, W face.
Haws Point, NE of point QR 8m 6M.
Rampside Sands Ldg Lts 006°. Front 54°04'·4N 03°09'·7W Q 6m 6M; B pile structure, W daymark. Rear 0·77M from front Iso 2s 14m 6M; R column, W face.
No. 3A 54°04'·4N 03°09'·7W QG 8m 9M.

MORECAMBE.
Morecambe Lt Buoy 53°52'·00N 03°24'·00W Q(9)15s; W cardinal mark; *Whis*.
Lune Deep Lt Buoy 53°55'·80N 03°11'·00W Q(6)LFl 15s; S cardinal mark; *Whis*; Racon.
Sewer outfall 54°04'·3N 02°53'·7W Fl G 2s 4m 2M; metal framework Tr.
Lts in line about 090°. Front 54°04'·4N 02°52'·5W FR 10m 2M; G mast. Rear 140m from front FR 14m 2M; G mast.
Central Promenade Pier 2 FG (vert) 9m 4M.

HEYSHAM.
S outfall 54°01'·73N 02°55'·73W Fl(2)G 10s 5m 2M; metal post.
North outfall FlG 5s 5m 2M; metal post.
South jetty head 54°01'·90N 02°55'·64W 2 FG (vert) 9/7m 5M; W pylon; Ra refl; *Siren 30s*.
SW Quay Ldg Lts 102°, both F Bu 11/14m 2M; Or&B diamonds on masts.
South pier head Oc G 7·5s 9m 6M; W Tr, R base.
North pier head 2 FR (vert) 11m 2M; obsc from seaward.

RIVER LUNE.
Ldg Lts 084°. Front, Plover Scar 53°58'·87N 02°52'·88W Fl 2s 6m 6M; W Tr, B lantern. Rear, Cockersand Abbey 854m from front F 18m 8M; R framework Tr.
Crook Perch, No. 7, 53°59'·5N 02°52'·3W FlG 5s 3M; G mast.
Bazil Perch, No. 16 54°00'·2N 02°51'·6W Fl(3)R 10s 3M; R mast.
Glasson Quay FG 1M.
Outfall 54°01'·3N 02°49'·7W Fl (TE 1985).

FLEETWOOD.
Fairway No. 1 Lt Buoy 53°57'·65N 03°02'·15W Q; N cardinal mark; *Bell*.
Esplanade Ldg Lts 156°. Front 53°55'·7N 03°00'·4W Fl Y 2s 14m. Rear 320m from front Fl Y 4s 28m. Both buff-coloured square Trs, B bases, R lanterns and vis on leading line only.
Steep Breast Perch 53°55'·8N 03°00'·5W Iso G 2s 3m 2M.
Knott End slipway, head 53°55'·7N 03°00'·0W 2 FR (vert) 3m 2M.

BLACKPOOL.
North Pier head 2 FG (vert) 3M.
Central Pier head 2 FG (vert) 4M.
South Pier head 2 FG (vert) 4M.

RIVER RIBBLE.
Gut Lt Buoy 53°41'·74N 03°08'·91W LFl 10s, safe water mark.
Perches show FlR on N side, and FlG on S side of channel.
S side, 14·25 mile perch 53°42.75N°3 04'·85W FlG 5s 6m 3M; B framework Tr and tripod.
Southport Pier, head, 52°39'·35N 03°01'·25W 2 FG (vert) 6m 5M; W post; vis 033°-213°.

El Oso Wreck Lt Buoy 53°37'·55N 03°23'·45W Q; N cardinal mark.
Jordan's Spit Lt Buoy 53°35'·75N 03°19'·20W Q(9) 15s; W cardinal mark.
FT Lt Buoy 53°34'·55N 03°13'·12W Q; N cardinal mark.
Spoil Ground Lt Buoy 53°34'·25N 03°17'·30W FlY 3s; special mark.

ENGLAND—WEST COAST, RIVER MERSEY

RIVER MERSEY.
BAR LANBY 53°32'·00N 03°20'·90W Fl 5s 12m **21M**; tubular structure on buoy; Racon; *Horn*.
FORMBY Lt F 53°31'·10N 03°13'·45W Iso 4s 11m 6M; R hull, W stripes.
CROSBY Lt F 53°30'·7N 03°06'·2W Oc 5s 11m 8M; R hull, W stripes.

SEACOMBE FERRY, N and S corners 3 FG 5m 5M; near N corner FY 8m 6M; *Bell (3) 20s* .
Cammell Laird slip, SE corner Fl(2) G 6s 5m 5M.
BIRKENHEAD Woodside landing stage, N end 3 FG and S end 2 FG (vert) with *Bell (4) 15s*.
TRANMERE TERMINAL, N dolphin 53°22'·9N 03°00'·0W Fl G 3s 7m 7M.
N stage, S end 2 FG (vert) 10m 5M; *Bell (2) 10s*.

ENGLAND—WEST COAST

RIVER DEE.
HE2 Lt Buoy 53°26'·20N 03°16'·80W QR; port- hand mark.
Hilbre Island, N end 53°22'·97N 03°13'·70W Fl R 3s 14m 5M; W metal framework Tr.
MOSTYN, training wall head Fl R 1·3s 8m 4M; B mast.
Ldg Lts 216°. Front 53°19'·2N 03°16'·1W FR 12m; W diamond on B mast. Rear 135m from front FR 22m; W diamond on B mast.
North training wall, head Fl R 3s 4m 6M; framework Tr.
South training wall, head Fl G 10s 3m 6M; framework Tr.
Summersby Wharf FR.
Connah's Quay, power station 2 FR (vert).
South Hoyle Lt Buoy 53°21'·45N 03°24'·78W Fl(3)R 10s; port- hand mark.

ISLE OF MAN

Point of Ayre 54°24'·95N 04°22'·03W Al L Fl WR 60s 32m **19M**; W Tr, two R bands; RC; Racon.
Low Lt 54°25'·1N 04°21'·8W Fl 3s 10m 8M; R Tr, lower part W, on B Base; part obsc 335°-341°; *Siren (3) 90s*.

JURBY
Cronk y Cliwe 54°22'·3N 04°31'·4W 2 FlR 5s (vert); synchronized, 2m apart.
Orrisdale 54°19'·3N 04°34'·1W 2 FlR 5s (vert); synchronized, 2m apart.
North DZ buoy 54°23'·6N 04°36'·7W Fl Y 10s (unreliable).
South DZ buoy 54°21'·5N 04°38'·8W Fl Y 10s (unreliable); with QY on target floats 1·5M ENE and 2·1M E.

PEEL.
Pier head, East side of entrance Oc R 7s 8m 5M; W Tr with R band; vis 156°-249°.
Groyne, head Iso R 2s.
Castle Jetty, head Oc G 7s 5m 4M; W Tr, G bands.
Breakwater head 54°13'·67N 04°41'·62W Oc 7s 11m 6M; W Tr; *Bell* (occas).

PORT ERIN.
Ldg Lts 099°. Front 54°05'·3N 04°45'·4W FR 10m 5M; W Tr, R band. Rear 39m from front FR 19m 5M; W column, R band.
Raglan Pier, head Oc G 5s 8m 5M; W Tr, G band.
Thousla Rock 54°03'·7N 04°48'·0W Fl R 3s 9m 4M; 8-sided tapered pillar.

Calf of Man, West point Fl 15s 93m **28M**; W 8-sided Tr; vis 274°-190°; FR Lts on conspic radio mast 3·2M NE; *Horn 45s*.
Chicken Rock 54°02'·3N 04°50'·1W Fl 5s 38m 13M; *Horn 60s*.

PORT ST MARY.
The Carrick 54°04'·30N 04°42'·60W Q(2) 5s 6m 3M; isolated danger mark.
Alfred Pier, head Oc R 10s 8m 5M; W Tr, R band; *Bell* (occas).
Inner Pier, head Oc R 3s 8m 5M; W Tr, R band.

CASTLETOWN.
New Pier, head Oc R 15s 8m 5M; W Tr, R band.

North side of entrance Oc G 4s 3m.
Irish Quay Oc R 4s 5m 5M; W Tr, R band; vis 142°-322°.

Langness, Dreswick Point 54°03'·28N 04°37'·45W Fl(2) 30s 23m **21M**; W Tr.
Derby Haven, breakwater, SW end Iso G 2s 5m 5M; W Tr, G band (TE 1985).
Douglas Head 54°08'·58N 04°27'·88W Fl 10s 32m **24M**; W Tr; obsc brg more than 037°. FR Lts on radio masts 1 and 3M West.

DOUGLAS.
Princess Alexandra Pier, head 54°08'·85N 04°27'·80W Fl R 5s 16m 8M; R mast; *Whis (2) 40s*.
Battery Pier, 140m from breakwater head, QR 12m 1M; W Tr, R band; vis 038°-218°.
Ldg Lts 229°, Front Oc 10s 9m 5M; W and R triangle on mast. Rear, 60m from front, Oc 10s 12m 5M; W and R triangle on mast; synchronised with front.
Victoria Pier, head Oc G 8s 10m 3M; W column; vis 225°-327°; RC; International Port Traffic Signals; *Bell (1) 2s*.
Fort Anne Jetty, head Oc R 4s 6m; W Tr, R band; vis 107°-297°.
King Edward VIII Pier, South side, Oc G 4s 6m; W framework Tr, G band; vis 253°-005°.
FR each side of swing bridge, 365m West, when closed.

LAXEY.
Pier, head Oc R 3s 7m 5M; W Tr, R band; obsc when brg less than 318°.
Breakwater, head Oc G 3s 7m; W Tr, G band.

Maughold Head 54°17'·70N 04°18'·50W Fl(3) 30s 65m **22M**; W Tr.
Bahama Lt Buoy 54°20'·00N 04°08'·45W Q(6)LFl 15s; S cardinal mark; *Bell*.

RAMSEY.
South Pier, head 54°19'·42N 04°22'·42W Oc R 5s 8m 4M; W Tr, R band, B base; *Bell* (occas).
North Pier, head Oc G 5s 9m 5M; W Tr, B base.

WALES—NORTH COAST

Chester Flat Lt Buoy 53°21'·65N 03°27'·40W Fl(2)R 5s; port- hand mark.
Middle Patch Spit Lt Buoy 53°21'·80N 03°31'·55W FlR 5s; port- hand mark.
North Rhyl Lt Buoy 53°22'·75N 03°34'·50W Q; N cardinal mark.
W Constable Lt Buoy 53°23'·13N 03°49'·17W Q(9) 15s; W cardinal mark.

Rhyl, River Clwyd, breakwater head 53°19'·50N 03°30'·30W QR 7m 2M; Bn.
Llanddulas, Llysfaen jetty 53°17'·55N 03°39'·45W Fl G 10s.
Raynes Quarry, jetty head 2 FG (vert).

COLWYN BAY
Victoria Pier, head 53°17'·90N 03°43'·25W 2 FG (vert) 5m 3M.
Llandudno Pier, head 53°19'·90N 03°49'·40W 2 FG (vert) 8/6m 4M.
Great Ormes Head Lt Ho 53°20'·55N 03°52'·10W (unlit).

CONWY
Entrance, South side 53°18'·0N 03°50'·9W Fl WR 5s 5m 2M; B column; vis W076°-088°, R088°-171°, W171°-319°, R319°-076°.

MENAI STRAIT.
Trwyn-Du 53°18'·76N 04°02'·38W Fl 5·5s 19m **15M**; W round castellated Tr, B bands; vis 101°-023°; *Bell (1) 30s*, sounded continuously. FR on radio mast 2M SW.
Mountfield 53°16'·15N 04°05'·10W Fl WG 2s 8m 6M; vis G221°-226°, W226°-341°.
Beaumaris, Pier FWG 5m 6M; vis G212°-286°, W286°-041°, G041°-071°.
St George's Pier Fl G 10s.
East side of channel 53°13'·2N 04°09'·5W QR 4m; R mast; vis 064°-222°.
Price Point Fl WR 2s 5m 3M; W Bn; vis R059°-239°, W239°-259°.
Britannia tubular bridge, South channel Ldg Lts 231° E side. Front FW. West side, Rear 45m from front FW.
Centre span of bridge Iso 5s 27m 3M, one either side.
South end of bridge, FR 21m 3M either side.
North end of bridge FG 21m 3M either side.
Port Dinorwic, pier head F WR 5m 2M; vis R225°-357°, W357°-225°.

Point Lynas 53°24'·97N 04°17'·30W Oc 10s 39m **20M**; W castellated Tr; vis 109°-315°; (H24); Fog Det Lt vis 212°-214°; *Horn 45s*; RC.
Pilot station pier 54°24'·9N 04°17'·1W 2 FR (vert).
Amlwch, SBM 53°26'·7N 04°19'·8W Mo(U) 15s 8M; mooring buoy; Ra refl. Fl Y 5s 3M marks floating hose 285m from buoy; *Horn Mo(U) 30s*.

AMLWCH.
Main breakwater 53°25'·0N 04°19'·8W 2 FG (vert) 11/9m 5M; W mast; vis 141°-271°.
Inner breakwater 2 FR (vert) 12/10m 5M; W mast; vis 164°-239°.
Inner harbour FW 9m 8M; W post; vis 233°-257°.
Wylfa power station 2 FG (vert) 13m 6M.

The Skerries 53°25'·25N 04°36'·45W Fl(2) 10s 36m **22M**; W round Tr, R band; RC; Racon. FR 26m **16M**; same Tr; vis 231°-254°; *Horn (2) 20s*.

HOLYHEAD.
Clipera Lt Buoy 53°20'·08N 04°36'·14W Fl(4)R 15s; port-hand mark; *Bell*.
Breakwater, head 53°19'·83N 04°37'·08W Fl(3) 15s 21m 14M; W square Tr, B band; *Siren 20s*.
Old Harbour, Admiralty Pier dolphin 53°18'·85N 04°37'·00W 2 FG (vert) 8m 5M; *Bell (occas)*.

South Stack 53°18'·4N 04°41'·9W Fl 10s 60m **28M**; (H24); W Tr; obsc to north by North Stack and part obsc in Penrhos bay. *Horn 30s*. Fog Det Lt vis 145°-325°.
Ynys Meibion 53°11'·4N 04°30'·2W Fl R 5s 37m 10M (occas) 2 FR (vert) shown from flagstaffs 550m NW and 550m SE when firing taking place.

WALES—WEST COAST

CAERNARFON BAY AND MENAI STRAIT (SOUTHERN PART).
Llanddwyn Island, S end 53°08'·04N 04°24'·70W Fl WR 2·5s 12m W7M, R4M; W Tr; vis R280°-015°, W015°-120°.
Cl Lt Buoy 53°07'·46N 04°24'·90W Fl G 5s; stbd-hand mark.
Abermenai Point 53°07'·60N 04°19'·64W Fl WR 3·5s 6m 3M; W mast; vis R065°-245°, W245°-065°.
Caernarfon Harbour, Tidal Basin, South Pier head 2FG(vert).
Poole Lt Buoy 53°00'·00N 04°34'·00W Fl Y 6s; special mark; (Apr-Oct).
Porth Dinllaen. Careg y Chwislen 52°56'·96N 04°33'·44W isolated danger mark (unlit).

Bardsey Island 52°44'·97N 04°47'·93W Fl(5) 15s 39m **26M**; W square Tr, R bands; obsc by Bardsey Island 198°-250° and in Tremadoc bay when brg less than 260°; Horn *Mo(N) 45s*; RC.

St Tudwal's, West Island 52°47'·90N 04°28'·20W Fl WR 20s 46m **W15**/12M, R13M; W round Tr; vis W349°-169°, R169°-221°, W221°-243°, R243°-259°, W259°-293°, R293°-349°; obsc by East Island 211°-231°.

PWLLHELI.
Sewer outfall 52°53'·18N 04°23'·69W QR. F WRG 12m; vis G155°-175°, R175°-245°, W245°-045°.

10.10.5   PASSAGE INFORMATION

ENGLAND – NORTH WEST COAST

On the boundaries of Areas 9 and 10 lles Solway Firth (chart 1346), most of which is encumbered by shifting sandbanks. There are navigable, buoyed channels as far as Annan on the N shore, but buoys are moved as conditions dictate. Particularly in the upper firth, the stream runs very strongly in the chans when the banks are dry, and less strongly over the banks when these are covered. In Powfoot Chan for example the in-going stream begins at HW Liverpool − 0300, and the outgoing at HW Liverpool + 0100, sp rates up to 6 kn. Off the entrances to Firth of Solway, and in the approaches to Workington (10.10.8) beware shoals over which strong W winds raise a heavy sea. Southwards along the Cumbria coast past St Bees Hd to Walney Island there are no dangers more than 2M offshore, but no shelter either.

For Silloth, Harrington, Whitehaven and Ravenglass see 10.10.22.

BARROW TO RIVER MERSEY (charts 1961, 1981, 1951)

Entrance to Barrow-in-Furness (chart 3164) is about 1M S of Hilpsford Pt at S end of Walney Island. Two chys of Roosecote power station are conspic, 3¼M N of Walney Lt Ho (Lt, RC). Coming from S it is possible to cross the sands between Fleetwood and Barrow with sufficient rise of tide. The stream sets across the chan, which is narrow and shallow but well marked. W winds cause rough sea in the entrance. Moorings and anch off Piel Island, but space is limited and stream runs hard on ebb. See 10.10.22.

Lune Deep, 2M NW of Rossall Pt, is entrance to Morecambe B (chart 2010), gives access to Fleetwood (10.10.10), Glasson Dock (10.10.9), and the commercial port of Heysham (10.10.22). It is well buoyed. Streams runs 3½ kn at sp. Most of b is encumbered with drying sands, intersected by chans which are subject to change. S of Morecambe B, beware shoals extending 4M W of Rossall Pt.

Gut Channel in estuary of R Ribble gives access to the port of Preston. This is now closed to commercial shipping. Many of navigational aids have been withdrawn, dredging of docks has ceased and silting has occurred (10.10.22).

Queen's Chan and Crosby Chan (charts 1951 and 1978) which are well buoyed, dredged and preserved by training banks, give main access to R Mersey, and are entered E of the Bar Lanby. Be careful not to obstruct commercial shipping. From the N the old Formby chan is abandoned, but possible near HW. Towards HW and in moderate winds a yacht can cross the training bank (level of which varies between 2m and 3m above CD) E of Great Burbo Bank, if coming from the W. Rock Chan, parts of which dry and which is unmarked, may also be used but beware wrecks.

In good weather and at nps, the Dee Estuary (charts 1953, 1978) is interesting for boats prepared to take the ground. Most of estuary dries and banks extend 6M seaward. Chans shift, and buoys are moved as required. Stream runs hard in chans when banks are dry. Main entrance is Welsh Chan, but if coming from N Hilbre Swash runs W of Hilbre Island (lit).

Sailing W from the Dee on the ebb, it is feasible to take the inshore passage (buoyed) S of West Hoyle Spit, and this enjoys some protection from onshore winds at half tide or below. Rhyl is a tidal harbour, not accessible in strong onshore winds, but gives shelter for yachts able to take the ground. Abergele Road, Colwyn B and Llandudno B are possible anchs in settled weather and S winds.

Between Pt of Air and Great Ormes Hd the E-going stream begins at HW Liverpool + 0600, and the W-going at HW Liverpool − 0015, sp rates 3 kn.

ISLE OF MAN (charts 2094, 2696)

There are choices when rounding S of IOM. In bad weather or in darkness, keep S of Chicken Rk (Lt, fog sig), noting the traffic scheme offshore − see Fig. 2(7). In good conditions, take chan between Chicken Rk and Calf of Man (Lt, fog sig). Alternatively use Calf Sound (chart 2696) between Calf of Man and coast, passing S of Kitterland Island but N of Thousla Island, which is marked by lit Bn and is close to Calf of Man shore. There is also a minor chan, called Little Sound, N of Kitterland Island.

The stream runs strongly through Calf Sound, starting N-going at HW Liverpool − 0145, and S-going at HW Liverpool + 0345, sp rates 3½ kn. W of Calf of Man the stream runs N and S, but changes direction off Chicken Rk and runs W and E between Calf of Man and Langness Pt 6M to E. Overfalls extend E from Chicken Rk on E-going stream, which begins at HW Liverpool + 0610, and N from the rk on W-going stream, which begins at HW Liverpool.

Off Langness Pt (Lt) the Skerranes (dry) extend 1 ca SW, and tidal stream runs strongly, with eddies and a race. E side of Langness peninsula is foul ground, over which a dangerous sea can build in strong winds. Here the NE-going stream begins at HW Liverpool + 0545, and the SW-going at HW Liverpool − 0415, sp rates 2¼ kn.

There is anch in Derby Haven, N of St Michael's Island, but exposed to E. Between Derby Island and Douglas (10.10.14) and on to Maughold Hd, there are no dangers more than 4 ca offshore. Near the land the SW-going stream runs for 9 hours and the NE-going for 3 hours, since an eddy forms during the second half of the main NE-going stream. Off Maughold Hd the NE-going stream begins at HW Liverpool + 0500, and the SW-going at HW Liverpool − 0415.

SE, E and NW of Pt of Ayre are dangerous shoals, over which the sea breaks in bad weather. They are Bahama Bank (least depth 1.5m), Whitestone Bank (0.6m), Ballacash Bank (2.4m), King William Banks (3.7m), and Strunakill Bank (5.5m).

The W coast of IOM has few pilotage features. A spit with depths less than 1.8m runs 4 ca offshore ½M E of Rue Pt. Jurby Rk (depth 2.7m) lies 4 ca off Jurby Hd, and up to 3M offshore there is a target area marked by buoys and Y Lts: yachts are advised to pass to seaward or to keep well inshore by passing close to Jurby Rk (above). Craig Rk (depth 3.7m) and shoals lie 2½M NNE of St Patricks I.

For general pilotage information, tidal streams and harbour details of IOM, see *Isle of Man Sailing Directions, Tidal Streams and Anchorages*, published by the Manx Sailing and Cruising Club.

MENAI STRAIT

The main features of this narrow chan (chart 1464) are: Puffin Island, seaward of NE end; Beaumaris (10.10.19); Garth Pt at Bangor (10.10.19), where NE end of Strait begins; Menai Suspension Bridge (30.5m); The Swellies (10.10.19), a narrow 1M stretch with strong tide and dangers mid-stream; Britannia Rail Bridge, with cables close W at elevation of 24m; Port Dinorwic (10.10.19); Caernarfon (10.10.19); Abermenai Pt, where narrows mark SW end of Strait; and Caernarfon Bar.

The Swellies should be taken near HW slack, and an understanding of tidal streams is essential. The tide is about 1h later, and sp range about 2.7m more, at NE end of Strait than at SW end. Levels differ most about HW + 0100 at NE end (when level there is more than 1.8m above level at SW end), and about HW − 0445 at NE end (when level there is more than 1.8m below level at SW end). Normally the stream runs as follows (times referred to HW Holyhead). HW − 0040 to HW + 0420: SW between Garth Pt and Abermenai Pt. HW + 0420 to HW + 0545: outwards from about The Swellies, NE towards Garth Pt and SW towards Abermenai Pt. HW + 0545 to HW − 0040: NE between Abermenai Pt and Garth Pt. Sp rates generally about 3 kn, but more in narrows, e.g. 5 kn off

Abermenai Pt, 6 kn between the bridges, and 8 kn at The Swellies. The timings and rates of streams may be affected by strong winds in either direction.

Note that direction of lateral buoyage changes at Caernarfon.

The following brief notes only cover very basic pilotage. From NE, enter chan W of Puffin Island, taking first of ebb to arrive Swellies at slack HW (HW Holyhead −0100). Slack HW only lasts about 20 mins at sps, a little more at nps. Pass under centre of Suspension Bridge span, and steer to leave Swelly buoy close to stbd, and Platters (dry) on mainland shore to port. From Swelly buoy to Britannia Bridge hold mainland shore, leaving Bn on Price Pt to port, and Gored Goch and Gribbin Rk to stbd. Leave Britannia Rk (centre pier of bridge) to stbd. Thence to SW hold to buoyed chan near mainland shore. Port Dinorwic is useful to await right tidal conditions for onward passage in either direction. Caernarfon Bar is impassable even in moderately strong winds against ebb, but narrows at Abermenai Pt demand a fair tide, or slackish water, since tide runs strongly here. Going seaward on first of ebb, when there is water over the banks, it may not be practicable to return to the Strait if conditions on the bar are bad. Then it is best to anch near Mussel Bank buoy and await slack water, before returning to Caernarfon (say). Leaving Abermenai Pt on last of ebb means banks to seaward are exposed and there is little water in chan or over bar.

Going NE it is safe to arrive at Swellies with last of flood, leaving Caernarfon about HW Holyhead −0230. Do not leave too late, or full force of ebb will be met before reaching Bangor. For detailed instructions see *West Coasts of England and Wales Pilot*, or *Cruising Anglesey* (North West Venturers Yacht Club).

ANGLESEY TO BARDSEY ISLAND (charts 1970, 1971)

On N of Anglesey, off Lynas Pt (Lt, fog sig, RC) a race extends ½M on E-going stream. Off Amlwch is a mooring/unloading buoy for supertankers, which must be given a wide berth. Amlwch is a small commercial harb (mostly dries) 1½M W of Lynas Pt. A drying rk lies ½ ca offshore on W side of approach, which should not be tried in strong onshore winds. From here to Carmel Hd beware E Mouse (and shoals to SE), Middle Mouse, Harry Furlong's Rks (dry), Victoria Bank (least depth 1.6m), Coal Rk (awash), and W Mouse (with dangers to W and SW). The outermost of these dangers is 2M offshore. There are overfalls and races at headlands and over many rks and shoals along this coast.

Between Carmel Hd and the Skerries (Lt, fog sig, Racon, RC) the NE-going stream begins at HW Holyhead +0550, and the SW-going at HW Holyhead −0010, sp rates 5 kn. 1M NW of Skerries the stream turns 1½h later, and runs less strongly. Simplest passage, or at night or in bad weather, is to pass 1M off Skerries, remembering traffic scheme off shore − see Fig. 2(7). In good conditions by day the inshore passage may be taken, close round Carmel Hd, but there is a confused sea here with wind against tide, and good timing is then needed.

Races also occur off N Stack and (more severe) off S Stack (Lt, fog sig), up to 1½M offshore on NNE-going stream which begins at HW Holyhead −0605, sp rate 5 kn. Races do not extend so far on SSW-going stream which begins at HW Holyhead +0020, sp rate 5 kn.

Along W coast of Anglesey, S from Holyhead (10.10.18), coast is rugged with rks, some drying, up to 1½M offshore. There are races off Penrhyn Mawr and Rhoscolyn Hd. Pilot's Cove, E of Llanddwyn Island, is good anch while waiting right conditions for Menai Strait. Porth Dinllaen is good anch, but exposed to N and NE. Beware rks off the pt, and Carreg-y-chad ¾M to SW. Give Carreg-y-Chwislen (a drying rk with Bn, and with shoals extending 2½ ca E) a berth of at least 3½ ca in rough weather. See 10.10.22.

Braich y Pwll is a steep and rky point at end of Lleyn Peninsula (chart 1971). About 1M N of it and about 1M offshore lie The Tripods, a bank on which there are overfalls and a bad sea with wind against tide.

Bardsey Sound can be used in daylight and moderate winds. Stream reaches 6 kn at sp, and passage should be made at slack water, ½h before HW or LW Holyhead. Avoid Carreg Ddu on N side and Maen Bugail on S side of Sound, where there are dangerous races. Passing outside Bardsey Island (Lt, fog sig, RC) make a good offing to avoid overfalls which extend 1½M W of I and 2½M S of it. Turbulence occurs over Bastram Shoal, Devil's Tail and Devil's Ridge, which lie S and E of Bardsey Island. In the approaches to St Tudwal's Island (lit) and Abersoch (10.10.20) there may be overfalls off Trwyn Cilan.

10.10.6   DISTANCE TABLE

Approximate distances in nautical miles are by the most direct route while avoiding dangers and allowing for traffic separation schemes etc. Places in *italics* are in adjoining areas.

	1	2	3	4	5	6	7	8	9	10	11	12	13	14	15	16	17	18	19	20
1 *Strangford*	1																			
2 *Mew Island*	29	2																		
3 *Mull of Galloway*	34	23	3																	
4 *St Bees Head*	70	65	43	4																
5 Point of Ayre	44	43	21	26	5															
6 Douglas	63	62	40	37	19	6														
7 Barrow	95	96	74	39	53	52	7													
8 Glasson Dock	109	107	85	53	64	63	22	8												
9 Fleetwood	103	113	79	47	58	57	17	10	9											
10 Liverpool	109	121	101	75	80	70	50	52	46	10										
11 Conwy	90	105	94	77	72	59	59	62	56	46	11									
12 Beaumaris	89	102	91	77	71	58	62	66	60	49	12	12								
13 Holyhead	74	90	79	80	68	50	72	79	73	68	36	32	13							
14 Caernarfon	92	111	105	87	81	68	72	76	70	59	22	10	26	14						
15 Bardsey Island	103	120	115	116	107	88	103	107	101	90	53	41	38	31	15					
16 Abersoch	117	134	129	126	121	102	117	121	115	104	67	55	52	45	14	16				
17 Pwllheli	121	138	133	130	125	106	121	125	119	108	71	59	56	49	18	5	17			
18 *South Bishop*	151	172	169	174	159	143	163	167	161	150	113	101	98	91	60	70	74	18		
19 *Tuskar Rock*	136	155	152	163	152	132	159	170	164	152	115	103	91	93	63	75	79	36	19	
20 *Dun Laoghaire*	71	90	93	113	93	78	119	126	120	118	88	84	56	69	61	75	79	90	70	20

MARYPORT 10-10-7
Cumbria

CHARTS
Admiralty 1346, 2013; Imray C62; OS 89
TIDES
+0038 Dover; ML 4.7; Duration 0550; Zone 0 (GMT).
Standard Port LIVERPOOL (→)

Times				Height (metres)			
HW		LW		MHWS	MHWN	MLWN	MLWS
0000	0600	0200	0800	9.3	7.4	2.9	0.9
1200	1800	1400	2000				

Differences MARYPORT
+0017 +0032 +0020 +0005 −0.7 −0.8 −0.4 0.0
SILLOTH
+0030 +0040 +0045 +0055 −0.1 −0.3 −0.6 −0.1
TORDUFF POINT
+0105 +0140 +0520 +0410 −4.1 −4.9 — —

SHELTER
Complete shelter in Elizabeth Dock. Harbour dries. Entry
HW ∓1½. Nearest anchorage Workington Basin.
NAVIGATION
Waypoint 54°43'.08N 03°32'.39W, 270°/090° from/to
South Pier Lt, 1.0M. 1.8m over bar between piers at
entrance at half tide and in river channel. Mud banks
cover HW−2. Channel not buoyed.
LIGHTS AND MARKS
South Pier. Fl 1.5s.
RADIO TELEPHONE
VHF Ch 16; 12 (occas).
TELEPHONE (0900)
Hr Mr 817440; CG 2238; MRSC Liverpool 931-3341;

⌗ 4611; Marinecall 0898 500 461; Police 812601;
Dr 815544; Ⓗ 812634.
FACILITIES
EC Wednesday. **Maryport Marina** (200) ☎ 813331, AC,
BY, CH, El, FW, ◎, ME, Slip Access over sill 1.75m
HW∓2½ (P and D from Fisherman's Co-op via marina);
Elizabeth Dock Slip (at HW), M, Sh, AB. **Town** P, D,
ME, V, R, Bar; ✉; Ⓑ; ⇌; ✈ (Newcastle)

WORKINGTON 10-10-8
Cumbria

CHARTS
Admiralty 1346, 1826, 2013; Imray C62; OS 89
TIDES
+0025 Dover; ML 4.4; Duration 0545; Zone 0 (GMT).
Standard Port LIVERPOOL (→)

Times				Height (metres)			
HW		LW		MHWS	MHWN	MLWN	MLWS
0000	0600	0200	0800	9.3	7.4	2.9	0.9
1200	1800	1400	2000				

Differences WORKINGTON
+0020 +0020 +0020 +0010 −1.1 −1.0 −0.1 +0.3
WHITEHAVEN
+0005 +0015 +0010 +0005 −1.3 −1.1 −0.5 +0.1
TARN POINT
+0005 +0005 +0010 0000 −1.0 −1.0 −0.4 0.0

SHELTER
Good shelter in Turning Basin. Tidal harbour dries and
bridge clearance is only 1.8m.
NAVIGATION
Waypoint 54°39'.58N 03°35'.30W, 311°/131° from/to
front Ldg Lt, 1.0M. No navigational dangers but in periods
of heavy rain a strong freshet may be encountered. Debris
from collapsed wall marked by sign-boards river-side wall
of dock.
LIGHTS AND MARKS
End of breakwater QG, end of S pier Fl 5s. Leading Lts
on W pyramidal Trs with Y bands both FR at 132°.
RADIO TELEPHONE
VHF Ch 16; 14 (HW−2½ to HW+2).
TELEPHONE (0900)
Hr Mr 602301; CG 2238; ⌗ 604601;
MRSC Liverpool 931-3341; Police 812601; Dr 64866;
Hosp 602244.
FACILITIES
EC Thursday; **Dock** D, FW, ME, El; **Vanguard SC**
☎ 826886, M, FW; **Town** P, V, R, Bar. ✉; Ⓑ; ⇌;
✈ (Carlisle or Newcastle).

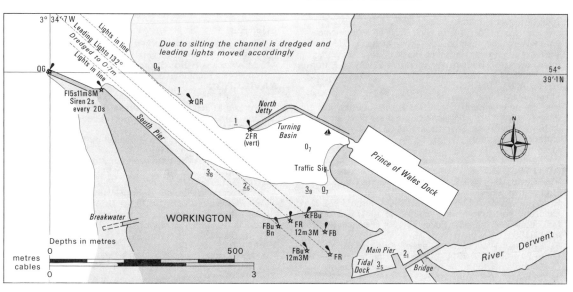

GLASSON DOCK   10-10-9
Lancashire

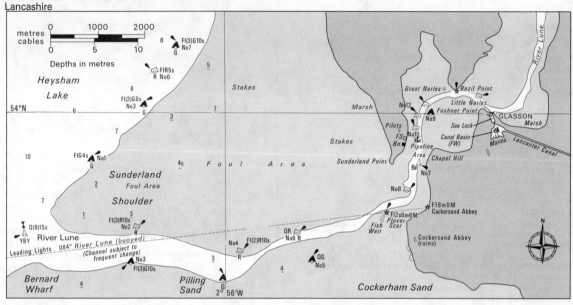

CHARTS
Admiralty 2010, 1552; Imray C62; OS 102, 97
TIDES
+0020 Dover; ML Wyre Lt Ho 11.7, Lancaster 5.2;
Duration 0535; Zone 0 (GMT).
Standard Port LIVERPOOL (——>)

Times				Height (metres)			
HW		LW		MHWS	MHWN	MLWN	MLWS
0000	0600	0200	0700	9.3	7.4	2.9	0.9
1200	1800	1400	1900				

Differences GLASSON DOCK

+0020	+0030	+0220	+0240	−2.7	−3.0	No data	

LANCASTER

+0110	+0030	No data		−5.0	−4.9	Dries out	

BARROW-IN-FURNESS (Ramsden Dock)

+0015	+0015	+0020	+0020	−0.2	−0.3	−0.1	+0.1

MORECAMBE

+0005	+0010	+0030	+0015	+0.2	0.0	0.0	+0.2

HEYSHAM

+0005	+0005	+0015	0000	+0.1	0.0	0.0	+0.2

SHELTER
Very sheltered anchorage. Even more so up towards
Lancaster; navigable for small boats but pilot is advised.
Dock connects with British Waterways basin of Lancaster
canal. Marina is in canal.
NAVIGATION
Waypoint R Lune entrance 53°58'.40N 03°00'.00W,
264°/084° from/to front Ldg Lt 084°, 4.2M. Dock gates
are open from HW−1½ to HW. Wait at R Lune buoy
until HW−2 and then go up. Abbey Lt has a tide gauge
showing depth over the sill at Glasson Dock. Beware
three wrecks on Bernard Wharf within 2½ miles E from
Nos 2 and 8 Fleetwood buoys.
LIGHTS AND MARKS
Plover Scar Lt and Cockersand Abbey Lt in line at 084°
lead up the channel between Nos 2 and 3 buoys. Lts
difficult to pick out at R Lune buoy; steer 085° until
Abbey Lt identified. Channel is buoyed up to dock
entrance. Buoys no 6, 8, 10, 12, 14, 16 (Bn) and 18 are Fl
or QR; no 5, 7 (Bn) and 9 are QG. Harbour authority is
the Lancaster Port Commission.
RADIO TELEPHONE
VHF Ch 16; 08 (HW−2 to HW+1). Marina Ch 80.
TELEPHONE (0524)
Hr Mr 751724 or 751307; CG & MRSC Liverpool 931-3341;
Lancaster Port Commission 751304; ⌗ (051) 933 4292;
Marinecall 0898 500 461; Police 791239; Ⓗ Lancaster 65944.
FACILITIES
EC Lancaster Wednesday; **Glasson Dock Marina**
(240+20 visitors) ☎ 751491, Slip, D, FW, ME, El, Ⓔ, Sh,
C, (50 ton), BH (50 ton), AC, CH; **Glasson Basin**
☎ 751724, M, AB; **Glasson SC** ☎ 751089 Slip, M, C;

Lune Cruising Club Access HW∓2; **Town** P, V, R, Bar,
✉; Ⓑ (Lancaster); ⇌ (bus to Lancaster); ✈ (Blackpool).
Note: There is a proposal to build a 500 berth marina at
Morecambe.

FLEETWOOD   10-10-10
Lancashire

CHARTS
Admiralty 2010, 1552; Imray C62; OS 102
TIDES
+0015 Dover; ML 5.0; Duration 0540; Zone 0 (GMT).
Standard Port LIVERPOOL (——>)

Times				Height (metres)			
HW		LW		MHWS	MHWN	MLWN	MLWS
0000	0600	0200	0700	9.3	7.4	2.9	0.9
1200	1800	1400	1900				

Differences FLEETWOOD

0000	0000	+0005	0000	−0.1	−0.1	+0.1	+0.3

BLACKPOOL

−0015	−0005	−0005	−0015	−0.4	−0.4	−0.1	+0.1

SHELTER
Very good shelter except in strong winds from N to W.
Boats can pass Fleetwood and proceed up to Skipool
(5 M) where is HQ of Blackpool & Fleetwood YC. Passage
up river not recommended on tides less than 8.0m.
NAVIGATION
Waypoint 53°57'.78N 03°01'.90W, 338°/158° from/to
front Ldg Lt 156°, 2.25M. Beware Ro Ro vessels turning
in the harbour and dredgers working continuously.
LIGHTS AND MARKS
Channel well buoyed, five G conical buoys and one Bn to
starboard, eight R can buoys to port. Fleetwood Ldg Lts
156° (only to be used between No 7 buoy and Black Scar
(No 11) perch). Lts are Front Fl Y 2s and Rear Fl Y 4s.
RADIO TELEPHONE
Call: *Fleetwood Harbour Control* VHF Ch 16; 11 **12** (H24).
Call: *Fleetwood Docks* Ch 16; 12 (HW−2 to HW+2).
Information from Harbour Control on request. Other
stations: Ramsden Docks Ch 16; 12 (H24); Heysham
Ch 16; 14 (H24).
TELEPHONE (039 17)
Hr Mr 872323; CG 873780; MRSC (051) 931-3341;
⌗ 79211; Marinecall 0898 500 461; Police 876611;
Dr Cleveleys 826280.

FLEETWOOD *continued*

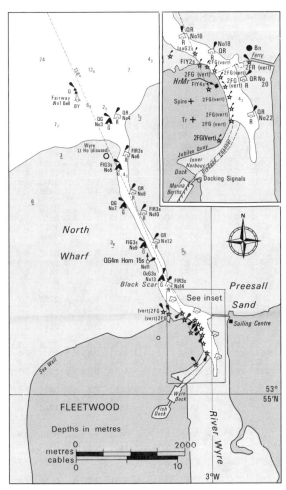

FLEETWOOD

Depths in metres

metres 0 2000
cables 0 10

FACILITIES

EC Wednesday; **Harbour** ☎ 872323, FW, ME, El, CH;
Wyre dock (70) M (No deep water moorings), FW, ME,
El, Sh, C (by arrangement 25 ton); **Blackpool and
Fleetwood YC (Skipool Creek)** ☎ Blackpool 884205,
Slip (at Stanah), L, FW, AB (Skipool), Bar, M;
Fleetwood Trawler Supply Co ☎ 873470, CH, ACA;
Wardleys Marine ☎ Hambleton 700117, AB, CH, D, El,
FW, L, M (drying), ME, Sh, Slip; **David Moss**
☎ Blackpool 893830, D (cans), FW, ME, El, Sh, C (mobile
50 ton), CH; **Marine Electronics** ☎ 779174, Ⓔ
Town P, D, ME, El, Sh, CH, V, R, Bar. ✉; Ⓑ; ⇌ (bus
to Poulton-le-Fylde or Blackpool); ✈ (Blackpool).

Note: – The Wyre Dock area is to be converted to a
Marina Village with berths for 400 yachts.

POULTON-LE-FYLDE. P, D, ME, El, Sh, V, R, Bar;
Lytham Marine ☎ 735531, Slip, D, FW, ME, El, Sh, C
(4 ton), CH, AB; **Fylde Coast Sailmaking Co** ☎ 873476,
SM, CH.

LIVERPOOL   10-10-11
Merseyside

CHARTS
Admiralty 3490, 1978, 1951, 1978; Imray C62; OS 108
TIDES
+0015 Dover; ML 5.2; Duration 0535; Zone 0 (GMT).

Standard Port LIVERPOOL (→)

Times				Height (metres)			
HW		LW		MHWS	MHWN	MLWN	MLWS
0000	0600	0200	0700	9.3	7.4	2.9	0.9
1200	1800	1400	1900				
Differences FORMBY							
−0015	−0010	−0020	−0020	−0.3	−0.1	0.0	+0.1
ROCK CHANNEL							
−0030	−0030	−0030	−0030	−0.4	−0.2	−0.2	0.0
Differences R. MERSEY							
EASTHAM							
+0003	+0006	+0015	+0030	+0.4	+0.3	−0.1	−0.1
WIDNES							
+0040	+0045	+0400	+0345	−4.2	−4.4	−2.5	−0.3
Differences R. DEE							
MOSTYN QUAY							
−0020	−0015	−0020	−0020	−0.8	−0.7	No data	
CHESTER							
+0105	+0105	+0500	+0500	−5.3	−5.4	Dries out	

NOTE: Liverpool is a Standard Port and tidal predictions
for each day of the year are given below.

SHELTER
Yachts should go to marina in Brunswick and Coburg
Docks. Shelter good in Stanley, Canning, Albert or
Salthouse Docks. There are no other facilities for berthing
or anchoring yachts on the NE side. (Anchoring possible
on Birkenhead side but only in fair weather).
NAVIGATION
Liverpool waypoint Bar Lanby 53°32′.00N 03°20′.90W, Fl
5s, Horn, Racon, 280°/100° from/to Queen's Channel,
3.0M. River Dee waypoint Hilbre Swash HE2 port-hand
buoy, QR, 53°26′.20N 03°16′.80W (channel shifts). Wind
against tide causes steep seas in outer reaches of Mersey.
Do not go outside buoys marking fairway. Advisable to
enter by Bar and Queens Channel. The whole area from
River Dee, River Mersey to River Alt and up to
Morecambe Bay is littered with sandbanks. R Mersey is
safe within commercial channel, but everywhere else great
caution and local knowledge is needed. R Alt is only
available HW∓2 and only suitable for shallow draught
(1.2m) boats. See 10.10.22.

10

statute miles
0 15

LIGHTS AND MARKS
The entrance to the Mersey is marked by the Bar Lanby Fl
5s 12m 21M, Horn 20s, Racon.

ENGLAND, WEST COAST – LIVERPOOL

Lat 53°25′ N   Long 3°00′ W

TIMES AND HEIGHTS OF HIGH AND LOW WATERS

YEAR **1991**

TIME ZONE UT(GMT)
For Summer Time add ONE hour in non-shaded areas

Chart Datum: 4.93 metres below Ordnance Datum (Newlyn)

JANUARY

Day	Time	m	Day	Time	m
1 Tu	0539 / 1118 / 1815 / 2346	1.1 / 9.6 / 0.7 / 9.6	16 W	0547 / 1132 / 1812 / 2351	1.8 / 9.0 / 1.6 / 8.7
2 W	0628 / 1207 / 1904	0.9 / 9.8 / 0.5	17 Th	0621 / 1205 / 1848	1.6 / 9.1 / 1.4
3 Th	0034 / 0716 / 1253 / 1952	9.6 / 0.9 / 9.8 / 0.5	18 F	0024 / 0656 / 1239 / 1923	8.8 / 1.5 / 9.2 / 1.3
4 F	0120 / 0759 / 1338 / 2037	9.4 / 1.1 / 9.6 / 0.7	19 Sa	0056 / 0731 / 1313 / 1958	8.8 / 1.5 / 9.2 / 1.3
5 Sa	0205 / 0842 / 1423 / 2121	9.1 / 1.4 / 9.3 / 1.1	20 Su	0130 / 0805 / 1347 / 2032	8.8 / 1.6 / 9.1 / 1.4
6 Su	0249 / 0924 / 1507 / 2204	8.7 / 1.8 / 8.9 / 1.6	21 M	0205 / 0840 / 1422 / 2107	8.7 / 1.8 / 9.0 / 1.6
7 M	0334 / 1009 / 1553 / 2249	8.3 / 2.2 / 8.4 / 2.2	22 Tu	0242 / 0918 / 1503 / 2146	8.5 / 2.0 / 8.8 / 1.9
8 Tu	0423 / 1058 / 1645 / 2343	7.8 / 2.7 / 7.9 / 2.7	23 W	0325 / 1002 / 1550 / 2233	8.2 / 2.3 / 8.5 / 2.3
9 W	0520 / 1158 / 1749	7.4 / 3.1 / 7.4	24 Th	0420 / 1058 / 1651 / 2336	7.9 / 2.7 / 8.1 / 2.6
10 Th	0045 / 0631 / 1310 / 1904	3.0 / 7.3 / 3.3 / 7.2	25 F	0530 / 1215 / 1810	7.7 / 2.8 / 7.8
11 F	0154 / 0744 / 1425 / 2016	3.1 / 7.4 / 3.2 / 7.4	26 Sa	0100 / 0657 / 1348 / 1935	2.7 / 7.7 / 2.7 / 7.9
12 Sa	0257 / 0846 / 1527 / 2115	2.9 / 7.7 / 2.9 / 7.7	27 Su	0226 / 0816 / 1510 / 2051	2.5 / 8.0 / 2.2 / 8.3
13 Su	0350 / 0936 / 1617 / 2202	2.6 / 8.1 / 2.5 / 8.0	28 M	0338 / 0924 / 1619 / 2155	2.0 / 8.6 / 1.6 / 8.8
14 M	0434 / 1019 / 1659 / 2242	2.3 / 8.5 / 2.2 / 8.3	29 Tu	0440 / 1020 / 1716 / 2249	1.5 / 9.1 / 1.0 / 9.2
15 Tu	0512 / 1057 / 1737 / 2318	2.1 / 8.7 / 1.9 / 8.5	30 W	0532 / 1111 / 1808 / 2337	1.1 / 9.6 / 0.5 / 9.5
			31 Th	0618 / 1156 / 1853	0.8 / 9.8 / 0.2

FEBRUARY

Day	Time	m	Day	Time	m
1 F	0021 / 0702 / 1238 / 1935	9.6 / 0.6 / 9.9 / 0.2	16 Sa	0001 / 0639 / 1217 / 1904	9.1 / 1.1 / 9.5 / 0.9
2 Sa	0100 / 0740 / 1317 / 2013	9.5 / 0.7 / 9.8 / 0.5	17 Su	0034 / 0713 / 1250 / 1937	9.2 / 1.0 / 9.5 / 0.9
3 Su	0140 / 0816 / 1355 / 2049	9.3 / 1.0 / 9.5 / 0.9	18 M	0107 / 0747 / 1324 / 2011	9.2 / 1.1 / 9.5 / 1.0
4 M	0216 / 0820 / 1432 / 2122	8.9 / 1.4 / 9.4 / 1.5	19 Tu	0141 / 0820 / 1359 / 2043	9.1 / 1.3 / 9.3 / 1.3
5 Tu	0253 / 0927 / 1510 / 2157	8.5 / 2.0 / 8.5 / 2.2	20 W	0218 / 0856 / 1439 / 2118	8.8 / 1.6 / 9.0 / 1.7
6 W	0332 / 1003 / 1553 / 2237	8.0 / 2.6 / 7.8 / 2.8	21 Th	0258 / 0936 / 1525 / 2202	8.5 / 2.0 / 8.5 / 2.2
7 Th	0420 / 1051 / 1648 / 2333	7.5 / 3.1 / 7.2 / 3.4	22 F	0350 / 1033 / 1627 / 2305	8.0 / 2.5 / 7.9 / 2.7
8 F	0526 / 1204 / 1808	7.0 / 3.6 / 6.8	23 Sa	0505 / 1154 / 1754	7.5 / 2.8 / 7.5
9 Sa	0059 / 0655 / 1341 / 1945	3.6 / 6.9 / 3.5 / 6.8	24 Su	0039 / 0642 / 1338 / 1930	3.0 / 7.4 / 2.7 / 7.6
10 Su	0223 / 0818 / 1500 / 2056	3.4 / 7.2 / 3.2 / 7.3	25 M	0216 / 0809 / 1505 / 2049	2.7 / 7.9 / 2.1 / 8.1
11 M	0327 / 0918 / 1557 / 2145	3.0 / 7.8 / 2.6 / 7.8	26 Tu	0332 / 0917 / 1613 / 2149	2.1 / 8.5 / 1.4 / 8.7
12 Tu	0414 / 0959 / 1641 / 2224	2.5 / 8.3 / 2.1 / 8.2	27 W	0431 / 1010 / 1706 / 2238	1.5 / 9.1 / 0.8 / 9.2
13 W	0454 / 1037 / 1719 / 2258	2.0 / 8.7 / 1.7 / 8.6	28 Th	0520 / 1057 / 1753 / 2320	1.0 / 9.6 / 0.4 / 9.5
14 Th	0529 / 1111 / 1756 / 2330	1.6 / 9.0 / 1.3 / 8.9			
15 F	0604 / 1144 / 1829	1.3 / 9.3 / 1.0			

MARCH

Day	Time	m	Day	Time	m
1 F	0603 / 1137 / 1834 / 2358	0.7 / 9.8 / 0.2 / 9.6	16 Sa	0540 / 1115 / 1804 / 2334	1.1 / 9.4 / 0.8 / 9.3
2 Sa	0641 / 1215 / 1910	0.6 / 9.8 / 0.3	17 Su	0617 / 1150 / 1839	0.8 / 9.6 / 0.7
3 Su	0035 / 0716 / 1252 / 1942	9.5 / 0.6 / 9.7 / 0.6	18 M	0008 / 0652 / 1225 / 1914	9.4 / 0.7 / 9.7 / 0.6
4 M	0109 / 0748 / 1326 / 2013	9.3 / 0.9 / 9.4 / 1.0	19 Tu	0042 / 0727 / 1302 / 1948	9.4 / 0.8 / 9.7 / 0.8
5 Tu	0141 / 0819 / 1358 / 2042	9.0 / 1.3 / 8.9 / 1.6	20 W	0119 / 0804 / 1340 / 2022	9.3 / 1.0 / 9.4 / 1.2
6 W	0215 / 0849 / 1432 / 2110	8.6 / 1.9 / 8.4 / 2.2	21 Th	0158 / 0842 / 1422 / 2100	9.0 / 1.4 / 9.0 / 1.7
7 Th	0250 / 0919 / 1511 / 2141	8.1 / 2.4 / 7.8 / 2.8	22 F	0242 / 0927 / 1514 / 2148	8.6 / 1.9 / 8.4 / 2.3
8 F	0332 / 1000 / 1559 / 2227	7.6 / 3.0 / 7.1 / 3.4	23 Sa	0338 / 1026 / 1621 / 2254	8.0 / 2.4 / 7.8 / 2.8
9 Sa	0431 / 1102 / 1713 / 2351	7.0 / 3.5 / 6.6 / 3.8	24 Su	0457 / 1154 / 1751	7.6 / 2.7 / 7.4
10 Su	0600 / 1246 / 1904	6.7 / 3.6 / 6.6	25 M	0032 / 0632 / 1334 / 1924	3.0 / 7.5 / 2.5 / 7.6
11 M	0141 / 0737 / 1420 / 2026	3.7 / 7.0 / 3.2 / 7.0	26 Tu	0206 / 0757 / 1454 / 2037	2.7 / 7.9 / 1.9 / 8.1
12 Tu	0254 / 0842 / 1522 / 2115	3.2 / 7.5 / 2.6 / 7.6	27 W	0318 / 0901 / 1556 / 2132	2.1 / 8.5 / 1.3 / 8.7
13 W	0345 / 0928 / 1610 / 2153	2.6 / 8.1 / 2.1 / 8.2	28 Th	0414 / 0952 / 1647 / 2217	1.5 / 9.0 / 0.8 / 9.1
14 Th	0426 / 1006 / 1649 / 2228	2.0 / 8.7 / 1.6 / 8.6	29 F	0459 / 1034 / 1729 / 2257	1.1 / 9.4 / 0.6 / 9.3
15 F	0504 / 1041 / 1727 / 2301	1.5 / 9.4 / 1.1 / 9.0	30 Sa	0539 / 1113 / 1805 / 2333	0.9 / 9.5 / 0.6 / 9.4
			31 Su	0614 / 1150 / 1839	0.8 / 9.5 / 0.7

APRIL

Day	Time	m	Day	Time	m
1 M	0007 / 0648 / 1224 / 1910	9.4 / 0.8 / 9.4 / 0.9	16 Tu	0631 / 1201 / 1850	0.7 / 9.7 / 0.7
2 Tu	0039 / 0719 / 1256 / 1938	9.2 / 1.1 / 9.1 / 1.3	17 W	0021 / 0710 / 1243 / 1928	9.6 / 0.7 / 9.7 / 0.8
3 W	0110 / 0749 / 1328 / 2006	9.0 / 1.4 / 8.7 / 1.7	18 Th	0102 / 0751 / 1327 / 2008	9.4 / 0.8 / 9.4 / 1.2
4 Th	0142 / 0818 / 1401 / 2033	8.7 / 1.9 / 8.4 / 2.2	19 F	0145 / 0836 / 1415 / 2051	9.1 / 1.2 / 8.9 / 1.7
5 F	0216 / 0850 / 1439 / 2104	8.3 / 2.3 / 7.8 / 2.8	20 Sa	0236 / 0927 / 1511 / 2143	8.7 / 1.7 / 8.4 / 2.3
6 Sa	0257 / 0929 / 1524 / 2148	7.8 / 2.8 / 7.2 / 3.3	21 Su	0336 / 1031 / 1621 / 2252	8.2 / 2.1 / 7.8 / 2.7
7 Su	0350 / 1026 / 1630 / 2255	7.2 / 3.2 / 6.7 / 3.7	22 M	0451 / 1153 / 1743	7.8 / 2.3 / 7.6
8 M	0508 / 1151 / 1805	6.9 / 3.4 / 6.6	23 Tu	0021 / 0614 / 1316 / 1904	2.8 / 7.8 / 2.1 / 7.7
9 Tu	0041 / 0638 / 1324 / 1933	3.7 / 7.0 / 3.2 / 7.0	24 W	0144 / 0731 / 1427 / 2012	2.6 / 8.1 / 1.8 / 8.1
10 W	0202 / 0751 / 1432 / 2029	3.3 / 7.4 / 2.6 / 7.5	25 Th	0251 / 0833 / 1528 / 2105	2.1 / 8.5 / 1.4 / 8.5
11 Th	0300 / 0843 / 1525 / 2112	2.7 / 8.0 / 2.1 / 8.1	26 F	0346 / 0924 / 1617 / 2150	1.7 / 8.8 / 1.2 / 8.8
12 F	0346 / 0925 / 1612 / 2150	2.1 / 8.6 / 1.6 / 8.6	27 Sa	0431 / 1007 / 1659 / 2230	1.4 / 9.0 / 1.1 / 9.0
13 Sa	0430 / 1004 / 1654 / 2227	1.5 / 9.0 / 1.1 / 9.0	28 Su	0511 / 1047 / 1734 / 2305	1.3 / 9.1 / 1.1 / 9.1
14 Su	0511 / 1042 / 1733 / 2304	1.1 / 9.4 / 0.8 / 9.3	29 M	0547 / 1123 / 1808 / 2340	1.2 / 9.1 / 1.2 / 9.1
15 M	0551 / 1122 / 1812 / 2342	0.8 / 9.6 / 0.7 / 9.5	30 Tu	0621 / 1158 / 1839	1.2 / 9.0 / 1.3

ENGLAND, WEST COAST – LIVERPOOL

Lat 53°25' N   Long 3°00' W

TIMES AND HEIGHTS OF HIGH AND LOW WATERS

YEAR 1991

TIME ZONE UT(GMT)
For Summer Time add ONE hour in non-shaded areas

MAY

Day	Time/m	Time/m	Time/m	Time/m
1 W	0012 9.0	0653 1.4	1231 8.8	1907 1.6
16 Th	0004 9.6	0659 0.7	1231 9.6	1914 0.9
2 Th	0045 8.9	0724 1.6	1304 8.5	1937 1.9
17 F	0050 9.5	0745 0.7	1320 9.3	1959 1.2
3 F	0117 8.7	0755 1.9	1338 8.2	2006 2.2
18 Sa	0140 9.3	0836 1.0	1412 9.0	2047 1.6
4 Sa	0154 8.4	0830 2.2	1415 7.9	2042 2.6
19 Su	0233 8.9	0929 1.3	1508 8.5	2141 2.0
5 Su	0233 8.0	0911 2.5	1458 7.5	2125 3.0
20 M ☽	0331 8.6	1030 1.6	1612 8.1	2244 2.3
6 M	0322 7.6	1002 2.8	1555 7.1	2223 3.3
21 Tu	0435 8.3	1136 1.8	1719 7.9	2356 2.5
7 Tu ☾	0424 7.3	1108 3.0	1706 6.9	2339 3.4
22 W	0544 8.1	1245 1.9	1829 7.8	
8 W	0537 7.3	1224 2.9	1824 7.1	
23 Th	0107 2.5	0655 8.1	1351 1.9	1935 8.0
9 Th	0059 3.2	0648 7.5	1334 2.6	1928 7.5
24 F	0213 2.3	0758 8.2	1451 1.8	2032 8.2
10 F	0205 2.7	0747 8.0	1434 2.1	2022 8.0
25 Sa	0311 2.1	0853 8.3	1542 1.7	2119 8.4
11 Sa	0301 2.2	0839 8.4	1528 1.7	2108 8.5
26 Su	0400 1.9	0941 8.5	1627 1.7	2202 8.6
12 Su	0352 1.7	0925 8.9	1617 1.3	2152 9.0
27 M	0444 1.8	1023 8.6	1705 1.7	2241 8.8
13 M	0440 1.3	1012 9.3	1704 1.0	2235 9.3
28 Tu ○	0523 1.7	1101 8.6	1612 1.7	2318 8.9
14 Tu ●	0526 1.0	1057 9.5	1749 0.8	2319 9.5
29 W	0558 1.6	1137 8.6	1812 1.7	2351 8.9
15 W	0612 0.7	1143 9.6	1832 0.8	
30 Th	0634 1.6	1212 8.5	1843 1.8	
31 F	0027 8.8	0706 1.7	1246 8.4	1916 1.9

JUNE

Day	Time/m	Time/m	Time/m	Time/m
1 Sa	0100 8.7	0740 1.8	1321 8.3	1949 2.1
16 Su	0133 9.5	0832 0.6	1404 9.2	2040 1.2
2 Su	0137 8.5	0816 1.9	1358 8.1	2026 2.3
17 M	0223 9.3	0921 0.8	1454 8.8	2129 1.6
3 M	0215 8.3	0857 2.1	1439 7.8	2107 2.6
18 Tu	0314 9.0	1012 1.2	1548 8.4	2221 2.0
4 Tu	0258 8.1	0941 2.3	1524 7.6	2155 2.8
19 W ☽	0407 8.6	1106 1.6	1644 8.1	2319 2.3
5 W ☾	0348 7.9	1031 2.5	1619 7.4	2251 3.0
20 Th	0506 8.2	1204 2.0	1746 7.8	
6 Th	0444 7.7	1130 2.5	1720 7.4	2358 3.0
21 F	0021 2.6	0611 7.9	1306 2.3	1852 7.7
7 F	0547 7.8	1236 2.5	1828 7.6	
22 Sa	0128 2.7	0719 7.8	1409 2.4	1955 7.8
8 Sa	0109 2.8	0653 8.0	1344 2.3	1931 7.9
23 Su	0234 2.6	0822 7.8	1507 2.4	2051 8.0
9 Su	0216 2.4	0755 8.3	1447 1.9	2029 8.4
24 M	0332 2.4	0917 8.0	1557 2.2	2139 8.3
10 M	0317 2.0	0853 8.7	1545 1.6	2122 8.8
25 Tu	0421 2.2	1004 8.1	1641 2.1	2221 8.5
11 Tu	0413 1.5	0946 9.0	1638 1.3	2213 9.2
26 W	0505 2.0	1045 8.3	1719 2.0	2301 8.7
12 W ●	0508 1.1	1040 9.3	1729 1.0	2304 9.4
27 Th ○	0544 1.9	1123 8.4	1754 1.9	2337 8.8
13 Th	0600 0.8	1130 9.5	1818 0.9	2353 9.6
28 F	0619 1.7	1158 8.5	1827 1.8	
14 F	0652 0.6	1222 9.5	1906 0.9	
29 Sa	0011 8.9	0653 1.6	1232 8.5	1900 1.8
15 Sa	0043 9.6	0741 0.5	1313 9.4	1952 1.0
30 Su	0046 8.9	0727 1.6	1306 8.5	1934 1.8

JULY

Day	Time/m	Time/m	Time/m	Time/m
1 M	0121 8.8	0802 1.6	1340 8.4	2011 1.9
16 Tu	0204 9.6	0901 0.6	1429 9.0	2107 1.3
2 Tu	0157 8.7	0839 1.7	1415 8.3	2049 2.1
17 W	0247 9.2	0943 1.1	1514 8.6	2149 1.7
3 W	0233 8.5	0917 1.9	1453 8.1	2128 2.3
18 Th ☽	0332 8.8	1027 1.7	1600 8.2	2237 2.3
4 Th	0312 8.4	0957 2.1	1536 7.9	2213 2.6
19 F	0421 8.2	1116 2.3	1654 7.7	2332 2.8
5 F ☾	0400 8.2	1045 2.3	1630 7.7	2308 2.7
20 Sa	0520 7.6	1215 2.7	1800 7.4	
6 Sa	0457 8.0	1144 2.5	1734 7.7	
21 Su	0042 3.1	0635 7.3	1326 3.0	1916 7.4
7 Su	0017 2.8	0605 7.9	1256 2.5	1849 7.8
22 M	0159 3.1	0754 7.3	1436 2.9	2025 7.6
8 M	0135 2.6	0720 8.1	1412 2.3	1959 8.1
23 Tu	0310 2.8	0858 7.6	1534 2.7	2121 8.0
9 Tu	0250 2.2	0830 8.4	1519 1.9	2103 8.6
24 W	0406 2.5	0950 7.9	1623 2.4	2206 8.4
10 W	0356 1.7	0932 8.8	1620 1.5	2200 9.0
25 Th	0451 2.1	1031 8.2	1702 2.1	2245 8.7
11 Th ●	0457 1.2	1030 9.2	1716 1.2	2254 9.4
26 F ○	0530 1.8	1108 8.5	1737 1.8	2320 8.9
12 F	0553 0.7	1123 9.6	1807 0.9	2344 9.7
27 Sa	0604 1.6	1142 8.6	1811 1.7	2354 9.1
13 Sa	0643 0.4	1212 9.6	1856 0.7	
28 Su	0638 1.4	1212 8.8	1843 1.5	
14 Su	0032 9.9	0733 0.2	1300 9.6	1941 0.7
29 M	0027 9.2	0710 1.3	1245 8.8	1917 1.5
15 M	0119 9.8	0818 0.3	1345 9.4	2025 0.9
30 Tu	0059 9.2	0744 1.3	1316 8.8	1951 1.5
31 W	0131 9.1	0816 1.4	1348 8.7	2026 1.7

AUGUST

Day	Time/m	Time/m	Time/m	Time/m
1 Th	0205 8.9	0850 1.6	1423 8.5	2101 2.0
16 F	0254 8.7	0945 1.9	1517 8.2	2153 2.3
2 F	0242 8.7	0925 1.9	1501 8.3	2141 2.3
17 Sa ☽	0338 8.1	1024 2.6	1604 7.7	2242 3.0
3 Sa	0324 8.4	1006 2.2	1549 8.0	2230 2.6
18 Su	0431 7.4	1119 3.2	1708 7.2	2351 3.4
4 Su	0419 8.1	1102 2.6	1652 7.7	2339 2.9
19 M	0550 6.9	1239 3.5	1835 7.1	
5 M	0532 7.8	1218 2.8	1817 7.6	
20 Tu	0126 3.5	0727 6.9	1406 3.4	1959 7.3
6 Tu	0109 2.8	0659 7.7	1348 2.6	1941 7.9
21 W	0247 3.1	0842 7.3	1512 3.0	2100 7.9
7 W	0234 2.4	0819 8.1	1505 2.2	2053 8.4
22 Th	0345 2.6	0931 7.8	1602 2.5	2145 8.4
8 Th	0348 1.8	0927 8.6	1609 1.7	2152 9.0
23 F	0430 2.1	1010 8.3	1641 2.1	2223 8.8
9 F	0449 1.1	1023 9.1	1705 1.2	2244 9.5
24 Sa	0506 1.7	1045 8.6	1716 1.8	2257 9.1
10 Sa ●	0543 0.5	1112 9.5	1756 0.8	2332 9.9
25 Su ○	0540 1.4	1116 8.8	1749 1.5	2329 9.3
11 Su	0631 0.2	1157 9.7	1839 0.6	
26 M	0614 1.2	1147 9.0	1822 1.3	
12 M	0015 10.0	0714 0.1	1239 9.7	1921 0.6
27 Tu	0001 9.4	0646 1.1	1218 9.1	1856 1.2
13 Tu	0056 10.0	0754 0.2	1320 9.5	1959 0.8
28 W	0032 9.4	0719 1.0	1249 9.1	1930 1.3
14 W	0137 9.7	0832 0.6	1358 9.2	2037 1.2
29 Th	0104 9.4	0751 1.2	1321 9.0	2002 1.5
15 Th	0215 9.3	0908 1.2	1436 8.7	2114 1.7
30 F	0138 9.2	0823 1.5	1355 8.8	2037 1.8
31 Sa	0215 8.9	0857 1.8	1433 8.5	2115 2.2

10

Chart Datum: 4.93 metres below Ordnance Datum (Newlyn)

ENGLAND, WEST COAST – LIVERPOOL

Lat 53°25′ N   Long 3°00′ W

TIMES AND HEIGHTS OF HIGH AND LOW WATERS

YEAR **1991**

TIME ZONE **UT(GMT)**
For Summer Time add ONE hour in non-shaded areas

SEPTEMBER

Day	Time / m	Time / m	Time / m	Time / m
1 Su ☾	0257 8.5	0938 2.3	1521 8.1	2206 2.6
16 M	0349 7.3	1021 3.5	1620 7.2	2302 3.5
2 M	0355 8.0	1034 2.8	1628 7.7	2319 2.9
17 Tu	0504 6.7	1144 3.9	1747 6.9	
3 Tu	0513 7.5	1157 3.1	1800 7.5	
18 W	0043 3.6	0652 6.7	1328 3.7	1923 7.2
4 W	0059 2.9	0650 7.5	1335 2.9	1931 7.8
19 Th	0211 3.3	0812 7.2	1439 3.2	2027 7.7
5 Th	0227 2.3	0815 8.0	1456 2.3	2044 8.5
20 F	0310 2.7	0901 7.7	1529 2.7	2112 8.3
6 F	0339 1.6	0918 8.7	1559 1.7	2141 9.1
21 Sa	0355 2.2	0939 8.2	1610 2.2	2150 8.8
7 Sa	0437 0.9	1009 9.2	1651 1.2	2228 9.6
22 Su	0434 1.7	1013 8.6	1645 1.7	2224 9.1
8 Su ●	0526 0.5	1054 9.6	1736 0.8	2312 9.9
23 M ○	0509 1.4	1045 9.0	1720 1.4	2258 9.4
9 M	0608 0.2	1134 9.7	1818 0.6	2353 10.0
24 Tu	0544 1.1	1116 9.2	1756 1.2	2330 9.5
10 Tu	0648 0.3	1214 9.7	1856 0.6	
25 W	0618 1.0	1149 9.3	1832 1.1	
11 W	0031 9.9	0724 0.5	1250 9.5	1931 0.9
26 Th	0004 9.6	0652 1.0	1221 9.4	1907 1.2
12 Th	0107 9.6	0758 0.9	1326 9.2	2006 1.3
27 F	0039 9.5	0726 1.1	1256 9.3	1942 1.4
13 F	0142 9.1	0830 1.5	1401 8.8	2040 1.8
28 Sa	0116 9.3	0759 1.4	1333 9.0	2019 1.7
14 Sa	0219 8.6	0901 2.2	1437 8.3	2115 2.5
29 Su	0157 9.0	0836 1.9	1415 8.7	2103 2.1
15 Su ☽	0258 7.9	0935 2.8	1521 7.8	2157 3.1
30 M	0244 8.5	0919 2.4	1507 8.2	2157 2.5

OCTOBER

Day	Time / m	Time / m	Time / m	Time / m
1 Tu ☾	0346 7.9	1020 2.9	1619 7.8	2316 2.8
16 W	0419 6.8	1045 3.8	1655 7.1	2346 3.6
2 W	0511 7.5	1149 3.2	1750 7.6	
17 Th	0551 6.7	1228 3.9	1824 7.1	
3 Th	0053 2.7	0643 7.6	1324 2.9	1917 8.0
18 F	0113 3.3	0719 7.0	1347 3.5	1935 7.5
4 F	0216 2.1	0802 8.1	1440 2.3	2026 8.6
19 Sa	0218 2.8	0816 7.5	1443 2.9	2027 8.1
5 Sa	0322 1.5	0901 8.7	1539 1.7	2121 9.2
20 Su	0308 2.3	0858 8.1	1528 2.4	2110 8.6
6 Su	0416 1.0	0949 9.2	1630 1.3	2206 9.6
21 M	0352 1.8	0935 8.6	1610 1.9	2146 9.0
7 M ●	0502 0.7	1031 9.4	1712 1.0	2248 9.8
22 Tu	0433 1.5	1009 9.0	1649 1.5	2223 9.3
8 Tu	0542 0.6	1111 9.6	1751 0.8	2327 9.8
23 W ○	0511 1.2	1044 9.3	1729 1.3	2259 9.6
9 W	0618 0.7	1147 9.6	1828 0.8	
24 Th	0550 1.0	1119 9.5	1808 1.1	2339 9.7
10 Th	0004 9.6	0652 0.9	1221 9.4	1903 1.2
25 F	0627 1.0	1157 9.5	1848 1.1	
11 F	0039 9.3	0724 1.3	1255 9.2	1937 1.5
26 Sa	0018 9.6	0704 1.1	1236 9.5	1928 1.4
12 Sa	0113 8.9	0758 1.8	1328 8.8	2011 2.0
27 Su	0100 9.4	0742 1.4	1319 9.2	2011 1.5
13 Su	0148 8.5	0825 2.3	1405 8.4	2044 2.5
28 M	0147 9.0	0825 1.8	1406 8.9	2100 1.9
14 M	0226 7.9	0856 2.9	1447 7.9	2124 3.0
29 Tu	0240 8.5	0914 2.3	1504 8.4	2200 2.2
15 Tu ☽	0314 7.3	0938 3.4	1541 7.4	2220 3.4
30 W	0345 8.0	1016 2.8	1613 8.1	2316 2.4
31 Th	0502 7.7	1137 2.9	1733 8.0	

NOVEMBER

Day	Time / m	Time / m	Time / m	Time / m
1 F	0038 2.3	0624 7.8	1302 2.8	1852 8.2
16 Sa	0004 3.2	0601 7.0	1236 3.5	1825 7.5
2 Sa	0151 2.0	0735 8.1	1413 2.4	1959 8.6
17 Su	0114 2.9	0710 7.4	1344 3.1	1927 7.9
3 Su	0254 1.6	0834 8.5	1512 1.9	2054 8.9
18 M	0213 2.5	0804 7.8	1440 2.6	2020 8.3
4 M	0348 1.3	0924 8.9	1603 1.6	2142 9.2
19 Tu	0307 2.1	0850 8.3	1531 2.2	2105 8.8
5 Tu	0434 1.2	1006 9.2	1647 1.4	2224 9.3
20 W	0355 1.7	0932 8.8	1617 1.7	2150 9.1
6 W ●	0513 1.1	1045 9.3	1727 1.3	2304 9.3
21 Th ○	0440 1.4	1014 9.2	1704 1.4	2234 9.4
7 Th	0550 1.2	1122 9.3	1804 1.3	2340 9.2
22 F	0523 1.2	1057 9.5	1749 1.2	2319 9.6
8 F	0624 1.4	1157 9.0	1839 1.5	
23 Sa	0607 1.1	1140 9.6	1835 1.0	
9 Sa	0017 9.0	0655 1.6	1231 9.1	1914 1.7
24 Su	0004 9.6	0649 1.1	1225 9.6	1921 1.0
10 Su	0050 8.7	0726 2.0	1306 8.9	1947 2.0
25 M	0052 9.5	0734 1.3	1313 9.4	2009 1.2
11 M	0126 8.4	0755 2.3	1341 8.5	2020 2.4
26 Tu	0142 9.2	0819 1.6	1404 9.2	2101 1.4
12 Tu	0204 8.0	0829 2.7	1420 8.2	2100 2.7
27 W	0236 8.8	0910 2.0	1458 8.9	2157 1.7
13 W	0246 7.6	0910 3.1	1508 7.8	2148 3.0
28 Th ☾	0335 8.4	1007 2.3	1559 8.6	2301 1.9
14 Th ☽	0338 7.2	1003 3.5	1606 7.5	2249 3.2
29 F ☽	0440 8.1	1115 2.6	1705 8.3	2301 2.8
15 F ☾	0445 7.0	1115 3.6	1715 7.3	2316 2.4
30 Sa	0007 2.0	0550 7.9	1227 2.6	1815 8.2

DECEMBER

Day	Time / m	Time / m	Time / m	Time / m
1 Su	0114 2.1	0700 8.0	1337 2.5	1924 8.3
16 M	0005 2.9	0556 7.4	1238 3.2	1824 7.7
2 M	0219 2.0	0802 8.2	1442 2.3	2026 8.4
17 Tu	0116 2.7	0704 7.6	1349 2.9	1928 8.0
3 Tu	0317 1.9	0857 8.5	1536 2.1	2118 8.6
18 W	0222 2.4	0806 8.1	1453 2.5	2029 8.4
4 W	0406 1.8	0943 8.7	1626 1.9	2204 8.7
19 Th	0321 2.0	0901 8.5	1550 2.0	2124 8.8
5 Th	0448 1.7	1026 8.9	1708 1.8	2247 8.8
20 F	0414 1.6	0952 9.0	1644 1.5	2216 9.2
6 F ●	0526 1.7	1104 9.0	1747 1.7	2325 8.8
21 Sa ○	0505 1.3	1041 9.4	1736 1.1	2306 9.5
7 Sa	0601 1.7	1140 9.1	1824 1.7	
22 Su	0553 1.1	1129 9.7	1827 0.8	2356 9.6
8 Su	0001 8.7	0634 1.8	1215 9.0	1857 1.8
23 M	0641 0.9	1218 9.8	1916 0.6	
9 M	0035 8.6	0704 1.9	1249 8.9	1931 1.9
24 Tu	0046 9.6	0727 0.9	1306 9.8	2005 0.6
10 Tu	0109 8.5	0735 2.1	1324 8.8	2004 2.0
25 W	0134 9.5	0813 1.1	1354 9.6	2053 0.8
11 W	0144 8.3	0811 2.3	1401 8.5	2040 2.2
26 Th	0223 9.2	0900 1.4	1443 9.4	2142 1.1
12 Th	0220 8.0	0849 2.6	1440 8.3	2121 2.4
27 F	0314 8.8	0949 1.8	1535 9.0	2233 1.5
13 F	0303 7.7	0931 2.9	1524 8.0	2207 2.7
28 Sa ☾	0407 8.3	1042 2.2	1630 8.5	2329 2.0
14 Sa ☽	0350 7.5	1021 3.1	1616 7.8	2301 2.8
29 Su	0506 7.9	1143 2.6	1733 8.1	
15 Su	0448 7.3	1125 3.3	1716 7.7	
30 M	0031 2.3	0615 7.7	1253 2.8	1845 7.8
31 Tu	0140 2.5	0726 7.7	1408 2.8	1957 7.8

Chart Datum: 4.93 metres below Ordnance Datum (Newlyn)

LIVERPOOL *continued*

RADIO TELEPHONE
Call: *Mersey Radio* (Port of Liverpool Building) VHF Ch **12** 16; 09 12 18 19 22 (H24). Traffic movements, local navigational warnings and weather reports broadcast on Ch 09 at 3h and 2h before HW. Local navigational and gale warnings broadcast on receipt on Ch 12, and on Ch 09 every 4h commencing 0000 local time. Alfred Dock Ch 05 (H24). Tranmere Stages Ch 19 (H24). Garston Dock Ch 20 (H24). Waterloo Dock Ch 20 (H24). Langton Dock Ch 21 (H24). Gladstone Dock Ch 05 (H24). Eastham Locks (Manchester Ship Canal) Ch 07 14 (H24). Latchford Locks (Manchester Ship Canal) Ch 14 20 (H24). Weaver Navigation. Weston Point Dock, call *Weston Point* Ch 74. Yachts entering or leaving Weaver Navigation should call on Ch 74 when approaching locks. For other BWB stations call: *Marsh Lock, Dutton Lock, Saltisford Lock, Anderton Depot* all on Ch 74.

TELEPHONE (051)
Hr Mr 200 4124; CG & MRSC 931 3341; ⌗ (051) 933 4292; Marinecall 0898 500 461; Police 709 6010; Ⓗ 709 0141.

FACILITIES
EC Wednesday; **Liverpool Marina** (500) ☎ 708 5228. 0600-2130 Mar to Oct. Min depth 3.5m. Slip, BH, AC, FW, C (50 ton), Bar, Ⓞ, R, CH, V; Ent via Brunswick Dock lock; Access HW∓2; **Albert Dock** Access HW−2 to HW (VHF Ch 37 when entrance manned) AB, FW, AC; **West Kirby SC** ☎ 625 5579, Slip, M (in Dee Est), L, FW, C (30 ton), AB (at HW), Bar; **Blundellsands SC** ☎ 929 2101; Slip, L (at HW), FW, Bar; **Hoylake SC** ☎ 632 2616, Slip, M, FW, Bar; **AMP Marine** ☎ 647 4787 Sh; **Royal Mersey YC** ☎ 645 3204, Slip, M, P, D, L, FW, R, Bar; **Perrys Yacht Centre** ☎ 647 5751, CH; **Davey Jones Marine** ☎ 263 4700, ME, El, CH; **Ship Shape** ☎ 928 4471, Sh, CH; **J. Sewill** ☎ 227 1376, ACA, Nautical Instruments; **Dubois − Phillips and McCallum** ☎ 236 2776, CH, ACA; **MGR Services** ☎ 653 3437, Ⓔ; **Robins Marine** ☎ 709 5431, Ⓔ.
Town ✉; Ⓑ; ⇌; ✈.
Note: Access to East Coast via Leeds and Liverpool Canal (British Waterways Board). Liverpool to Goole 161 miles, 103 locks. Maximum draught 3ft, air draught 8ft, beam 13ft 6in, length 60ft.

H.W.Hts.m.

LIVERPOOL

MEAN SPRING AND NEAP CURVES

MEAN RANGES	
Springs	8·4m
Neaps	4·5m

Springs occur 2 days after New and Full Moon.

10

L.W.Hts.m.

ISLE OF MAN   10-10-12

CHARTS
Admiralty 2696, 2094

The Isle of Man is one of the British Islands, set in the Irish Sea almost equidistant from England, Scotland and Ireland but it is not part of the United Kingdom. It has a considerable degree of self-government. The island comes under the same customs umbrella as the rest of the United Kingdom, so no customs formalities are necessary on landing or returning to UK ports.
Manx harbours are administered by the Isle of Man Government and the lights are maintained by the Commissioners of Northern Lighthouses in Scotland. Besides the four main harbours given below, there are good anchorages at Castletown in the SE, Laxey Bay in the E and Port Erin in the SW — see 10.10.22. There are also good anchorages in Derby Haven in the SE; this is a rather

bleak area and the inner harbour dries. Most of the harbours are on the E and S sides but a visit to the W coast with its characteristic cliffs is worth while. For passage through Calf Sound, see 10.10.5.
When contact with local Harbour Masters cannot be established on VHF, vessels should call *Douglas Radio* Ch 16 12 for urgent messages or other information. Since the closure of MRSC Ramsey, calls have to be made to Liverpool but there is no loss of radio coverage on VHF as the existing Snaefell (IoM) aerial has been retained and linked to Liverpool by land line. Weather forecasts can be obtained from local radio programmes or by telephone from the Met Office Ronaldsway (0624) 823313 between 0630 and 2030 (LT). Visitors are recommended to obtain *Sailing directions, tidal streams and anchorages of the Isle of Man* produced by the Manx Sailing and Cruising Club in Ramsey, Tel. (0624) 813494.

PORT ST MARY 10-10-13
Isle of Man

CHARTS
Admiralty 2696, 2094; Imray C62, Y70; OS 95
TIDES
+0020 Dover; ML 3.2; Duration 0605; Zone 0 (GMT).

Depths in metres

Standard Port LIVERPOOL (←)

Times				Height (metres)			
HW		LW		MHWS	MHWN	MLWN	MLWS
0000	0600	0200	0700	9.3	7.4	2.9	0.9
1200	1800	1400	1900				
Differences PORT ST MARY							
+0005	+0015	−0010	−0030	−3.4	−2.7	−1.2	−0.3
CALF SOUND							
+0005	+0005	−0015	−0025	−3.2	−2.6	−0.9	−0.3
PORT ERIN							
−0005	+0015	−0010	−0050	−4.1	−3.2	−1.3	−0.5

SHELTER
Very good shelter except in E or SE winds. Inner harbour dries out. Anchorages off Gansey Pt; poor holding. Visitors moorings.
NAVIGATION
Waypoint 54°03'.60N 04°43'.00W, 150°/330° from/to breakwater Lt, 0.84M. Carrick Rock, 7 ca E of breakwater Q(2) 5s 6m 3M. Rock outcrops to E of breakwater to 2 ca offshore. Beware of lobster and crab pots, especially offshore from Calf Island to Langness Pt.
LIGHTS AND MARKS
Alfred Pier, head Oc R 10s 8m 5M; W Tr, R band. Inner Pier, head Oc R 3s 8m 5M; W Tr, R band. These two Lts in line 295° lead clear S of The Carrick.
RADIO TELEPHONE
Call: *Port St Mary Harbour* VHF Ch 16; 12 (0830-1630 LT when manned or through Douglas Harbour Radio).
TELEPHONE (0624)
Hr Mr 833206; CG and MRSC Liverpool 931 3341; Weather 823313; ⌗ 74321; Marinecall 16622; Police 822222; Dr 832281.
FACILITIES
EC Thursday; **Breakwater** Slip, D (by road tanker), L, FW, C (20 ton mobile), AB; **Inner Harbour** Slip, D, L, FW, C (20 ton mobile), AB; **Bay** M, L; **Ballasalla Marine & Auto Eng** ☎ 822715, ME; **Isle of Man YC** ☎ 832088, FW, Bar. **Town** CH, V, R, Bar. ✉; Ⓑ; ⇌ (bus to Douglas, ferry to Heysham); ✈ (I.o.M.).

DOUGLAS 10-10-14
Isle of Man

CHARTS
Admiralty 2696, 2094; Imray C62, Y70; OS 95
TIDES
+0020 Dover; ML 3.8; Duration 0600; Zone 0 (GMT).
Standard Port LIVERPOOL (←)

Times				Height (metres)			
HW		LW		MHWS	MHWN	MLWN	MLWS
0000	0600	0200	0700	9.3	7.4	2.9	0.9
1200	1800	1400	1900				
Differences DOUGLAS							
−0004	−0004	−0022	−0032	−2.4	−2.0	−0.5	−0.1

SHELTER
Shelter is good except with north-easterly winds. Very heavy seas run in during NE gales. The Harbour Board provides one B can buoy for visitors, between Lifeboat slip and Fort Anne Jetty, and a mooring pontoon at inner end of Battery Pier.
NAVIGATION
Waypoint 54°09'.00N 04°27'.60W, 049°/229° from/to front Ldg Lt, 0.47M. Inner harbour dries; access HW ∓2. It becomes very full in summer. There is no bar. Beware swing bridge and also concrete step at end of dredged area (diamond mark on King Edward pier). SE and SW corners of linkspan, SE of pier, marked with 2 FG (vert). Concrete dolphin at seaward end of Princess Alexandra Pier 2FR (vert). Approach to N of No 1 buoy and await port entry signal. If available call on VHF Ch 12. Keep clear of larger vessels and ferries.
LIGHTS AND MARKS
Ldg Lts 229°, both Oc 10s 9/12m 5M, synchronised. International Port Traffic Signals Nos 2, 3 and 5 shown from mast at head of Victoria Pier. Signals below are shown from near head of Victoria Pier in panels with FIY Lts in top corners.

X (red)   Unspecified vessels may not proceed
→ (white)   Vessels may proceed in direction shown

Depths in metres

RADIO TELEPHONE
VHF Ch 16; 12 (H24). Broadcasts Ch 12 at 0133, 0533, 0733, 0933, 1333, 1733 and 2133 giving navigational warnings for IoM coastal waters.
TELEPHONE (0624)
Hr Mr 23813; CG and MRSC Liverpool 931 3341; ⌗ 74321; Marinecall 0898 500 461; Police 26222; Dr 73661.
FACILITIES
EC Thursday; **Outer Harbour** ☎ 23813, Slip, M, P, D, L, FW, ME, El, Sh, C (10, 5 ton), CH; **Inner Harbour (N & S Quays)** ☎ 23813, Slip, M (N & S Quays), P, D, L, FW, ME, El, Sh, C, CH, AB; **Manx Marine** ☎ 74842, CH, ACA; **Auto Electrical Centre** ☎ 28123, El, Diving; **Douglas Motor Boat & Sailing Club** ☎ 73965, Bar, Slip, L; **Rileys** ☎ 75166, Gas, Gaz, Kos. **Town** V, R, Bar. ✉; Ⓑ; ⇌ (ferry to Heysham; also in summer to Belfast and Liverpool); ✈ (I.o.M.).

RAMSEY 10-10-15
Isle of Man

CHARTS
Admiralty 2696, 2094; Imray C62, Y70; OS 95
TIDES
+0020 Dover; ML 4.0; Duration 0545; Zone 0 (GMT).
Standard Port LIVERPOOL (←)

Times				Height (metres)			
HW		LW		MHWS	MHWN	MLWN	MLWS
0000	0600	0200	0700	9.3	7.4	2.9	0.9
1200	1800	1400	1900				

Differences RAMSEY

+0005	+0015	−0005	−0015	−1.7	−1.5	−0.6	+0.1

SHELTER
Very good except in strong winds between NE and SE, through E. The harbour dries. Access HW−2½ to HW+2. Berth alongside SW quay — instructions given by Hr Mr as vessels enter between piers. The Manx S.C. has visitors moorings N of Queens Pier.
NAVIGATION
Waypoint 54°19'.40N 04°21'.60W, 095°/275° from/to entrance, 0.48M. The foreshore dries out 100m to seaward of the pier heads. Entrance to the harbour is only permitted from HW−2½ to HW+2.
LIGHTS AND MARKS
There are no leading lights or marks. Lights as shown on chartlet. There is FR Lt in centre of swing bridge.
RADIO TELEPHONE
VHF Ch 16; 12 (0830-1630 LT when manned or through Douglas Harbour Radio).
TELEPHONE (0624)
Hr Mr 812245; CG and MRSC Liverpool 931 3341; ⌗ 74321; Marinecall 0898 500 461; Police 812234; Dr 813881; Ⓗ 813254.
FACILITIES
EC Wednesday; **Entrance Channel** L, FW, AB; C*, **North Quay** L, FW, ME, El, Sh, AB; **East Quay** ☎ 812245, L, FW, ME, El, Sh, AB; **West Quay** Slip (Grid), L, FW, ME, El, AB, Ⓠ; **Shipyard Quay** Slip, ME, El, Sh; **Old Harbour** Slip, M, L, ME, ∧B; **Calor Manx Gas** ☎ 813143, Gas; **Booth W. Kelly** ☎ 812322, ME; **Freedom Yachts** ☎ 897717, Sh; **Bevan** ☎ 812583, El, Ⓔ; **Manx Sailing and Cruising Club** ☎ 813494, Bar, D, P, Ⓔ, FW, L, Ⓠ, Slip, V; **Town** P, D, V, R, Gas, Gaz, Kos, Bar, ✉; Ⓑ; ⇌ (bus to Douglas, ferry to Heysham); ✈ (I.o.M.).
Fuels from local suppliers but none situated on harbour estate.
*Various mobile cranes on hire from suppliers through Douglas.

⚠ Report to HrMr

PEEL 10-10-16
Isle of Man

CHARTS
Admiralty 2696, 2094; Imray C62, Y70; OS 95
TIDES
+0005 Dover; ML 2.9; Duration 0540; Zone 0 (GMT).

⚠ Report to HrMr

Standard Port LIVERPOOL (←)

Times				Height (metres)			
HW		LW		MHWS	MHWN	MLWN	MLWS
0000	0600	0200	0700	9.3	7.4	2.9	0.9
1200	1800	1400	1900				

Differences PEEL

−0015	+0010	0000	−0010	−4.0	−3.2	−1.4	−0.4

SHELTER
Good shelter except in strong NW to NE winds. Inner harbour has water HW∓3; bottom is flat sand.
NAVIGATION
Waypoint 54°14'.00N 04°41'.20W, 037°/217° from/to breakwater Lt, 0.42M. Entry should not be attempted in strong NW to NE winds. Beware groyne running ENE from mouth of River Neb submerged at half tide. Harbour dries out and is very crowded from June to October.
LIGHTS AND MARKS
There are no leading marks or lights. Lt on end of groyne, Iso R 2s. Pier head Oc R 7s 8m 5M; vis 156°-249°. Breakwater Oc 7s 11m 6M.
RADIO TELEPHONE
VHF Ch 16; 12 (0830-1630 LT when manned or through Douglas Harbour Radio).
TELEPHONE (0624)
Hr Mr 842338; CG and MRSC Liverpool 931 3341; ⌗ 74321; Weather 16622; Marinecall 0898 500 461; Police 842208; Dr 843636.
FACILITIES
EC Thursday; **Breakwater** Slip, L, FW, ME, El, Sh, C (7½ ton mobile), AB; **Inner Pier** ☎ 842338, L, FW, ME, El, Sh, AB; **East Quay** Slip, L, FW, ME, El, C (7½ ton mobile), AB; **West Quay** L, FW, ME, El, Sh, Slip, C (7½ ton mobile), AB; **J. D. Faulkner** ☎ 842296, ME, D (cans); **Manx Gas Service Centre** ☎ 842281, Gas; **West Marine** ☎ 842604, BY, CH, ME; **Manx Marine** ☎ 74842, CH, ACA; **Peel Sailing and Cruising Club** ☎ 842390, P and D (cans), R, Ⓠ, Bar; **T and J Autos** ☎ 842096, ME; **Town** P and D (cans), CH, V, R, Bar, ✉; Ⓑ; ⇌ (bus to Douglas, ferry to Heysham); ✈ (I.o.M.).

CONWY   10-10-17
Gwynedd

CHARTS
Admiralty 1978, 1977; Imray C61; OS 115
TIDES
−0015 Dover; ML 4.3; Duration 0545; Zone 0 (GMT).
Standard Port HOLYHEAD (⟶)

Times				Height (metres)			
HW		LW		MHWS	MHWN	MLWN	MLWS
0000	0600	0500	1100	5.7	4.5	2.0	0.7
1200	1800	1700	2300				

Differences CONWY
+0020 +0020 No data +0050 +2.1 +1.6 +0.3 No data

Standard Port LIVERPOOL (⟵)

Times				Height (metres)			
HW		LW		MHWS	MHWN	MLWN	MLWS
0000	0600	0200	0700	9.3	7.4	2.9	0.9
1200	1800	1400	1900				

LLANDUDNO
−0035 −0025 −0025 −0035 −1.9 −1.5 −0.5 −0.2

NOTE: HW Conwy is −0040 springs and −0020 neaps
HW Liverpool approx.

SHELTER
Good except for strong winds from NW. Anchorage off
town quay or ask Hr Mr for vacant mooring.
NAVIGATION
Waypoint Fairway (safe water) buoy, 53°17'.90N
03°55'.47W, 290°/110° from/to Penmaen-bach Point,
1.7M. Channel is variable with depths of about 0.5m and
strong stream. Keep at least ¼ ca clear of Perch Lt to
stbd on entry. Many mussel beds in harbour entrance.
Beware unlit moorings. Entry recommended during
daylight only and between HW−2 and HW. Entry via
'Inshore Passage' not recommended. Speed limit from the
Perch Lt to ½ M above bridges is 10 kn.
Vessels must proceed only within the buoyed channel.
Vessels must check with harbour authorities before arrival.
LIGHTS AND MARKS
None of the channel marks has either light or bell except
the most inshore one, Fl WR 5s 5m 2M; W 076°-088°,
R 088°-171°; W 171°-319°, R 319°-076°. The 'Inshore
Passage' to E of Perch Lt can be used for vessels up to
2m draught, Neaps HW ∓1, Springs HW ∓3, passing
inshore of Or liferaft (on station Apl-Oct).
RADIO TELEPHONE
VHF Ch 16; 06 08 **12** 14 72 (Apl-Sept 0900-1700. Oct-Mar
Mon-Fri 0900-1700 LT). N Wales Cruising Club on
Ch **80** Llanddulas Ch 16; 14 (0900 − 1230, 1400-1700 LT).

TELEPHONE (0492)
Hr Mr 596253; CG Llangoed 224; MRSC Holyhead 2051;
⌗ (0407) 2336; Marinecall 0898 500 460; Police 2222;
Dr 593385.
FACILITIES
EC Wednesday; **Conwy Quay Harbour** ☎ 596253,
(dries − limited stay for loading, watering, etc.), M, D, L,
FW, AB (up to 40 ft); **Conwy Harbour Boat Shop**
☎ 592366, D, ME, Gas, Gaz, CH; **Conwy River
Boatyard** ☎ 592489, M, ME, El, Slip, Gas, Gaz, Sh;
Deganwy Dock (dries), L, FW, C (mobile), AB;
Sailtronic Marine ☎ Glanconwy 536, El, Ⓔ; **Deganwy
Entrance** Slip, L; **Beacons** Slip, L; **Conwy YC** ☎ 83690,
Slip, M, L, FW, R, Bar; **N Wales Cruising Club**
☎ 593481, M, L, FW, AB, Bar; **Town** P and D (in cans),
V, R, Bar. ✉; Ⓑ; ⇌; ✈ (Liverpool).

HOLYHEAD   10-10-18
Gwynedd

CHARTS
Admiralty 2011, 1970; Imray C61; OS 114
TIDES
−0045 Dover; ML 3.2; Duration 0615; Zone 0 (GMT).
Standard Port HOLYHEAD (⟶)

Times				Height (metres)			
HW		LW		MHWS	MHWN	MLWN	MLWS
0000	0600	0500	1100	5.7	4.5	2.0	0.7
1200	1800	1700	2300				

Differences AMLWCH
+0020 +0010 +0035 +0025 +1.6 +1.3 +0.5 +0.2

PORTH TRECASTEL
−0045 −0025 −0005 −0015 −0.6 −0.6 0.0 0.0
Holyhead is a Standard Port and tidal predictions for each
day of the year are given below.

SHELTER
Very good. Anchor in New Harbour only. NE winds cause
a slight sea.
NAVIGATION
Waypoint 53°20'.00N 04°36'.47W, 019°/199° from/to
Admiralty Pier Old Lt Ho, 1.2M. Cliperau Rocks (R can
bell buoy) Fl (4) 15s. Beware ferries, especially crossing
the entrance to New Harbour passing down to go to Inner
Harbour. Also beware large unlit mooring buoys in NW
part of harbour.
LIGHTS AND MARKS
Entrance between Cliperau Rks and breakwater lighthouse.
Entry signals:- R Lt or R Flag — Inner harbour closed.
2R Lts or 2R Flags — Old and Inner harbours blocked.
RADIO TELEPHONE
VHF Ch 16 14 (H24). Other station: Anglesey Marine
Terminal (Amlwch) Ch 10 12 16 19. SC Ch 80.
TELEPHONE (0407)
Hr Mr 2304; CG & MRSC 2051; ⌗ (0407) 2714;
Marinecall 0898 500 460; Police Beaumaris 810222;
Dr via CG.
FACILITIES
EC Tuesday; **Harbour** ☎ 2304, Slip, M, D, L, FW, ME,
El, Sh, C (many), CH, AB; **Holyhead SC** ☎ 2526, Slip,
M, L, FW, R (Summer only), Bar; **Holyhead BY**
☎ 50111, ACA, FW, CH, D, ME, El, Sh, C (20 ton);
Trinity Marine ☎ 3855, BH, BY, D, FW, ME, Sh, Slip;
Holyhead Chandlery ☎ 3632, CH, ME, El, Ⓔ, ACA;
Trearddur Bay BY ☎ Trearddur Bay 860501, D, FW, Sh,
CH; **Trearddur Bay** M (Small craft only), L; **Trearddur
Bay Village** P, V, R, Bar. **Town** P, V, R, Bar, ⊡, ✉; Ⓑ;
⇌; ✈ (Liverpool). Ferry to Dun Laoghaire.

HOLYHEAD *continued*

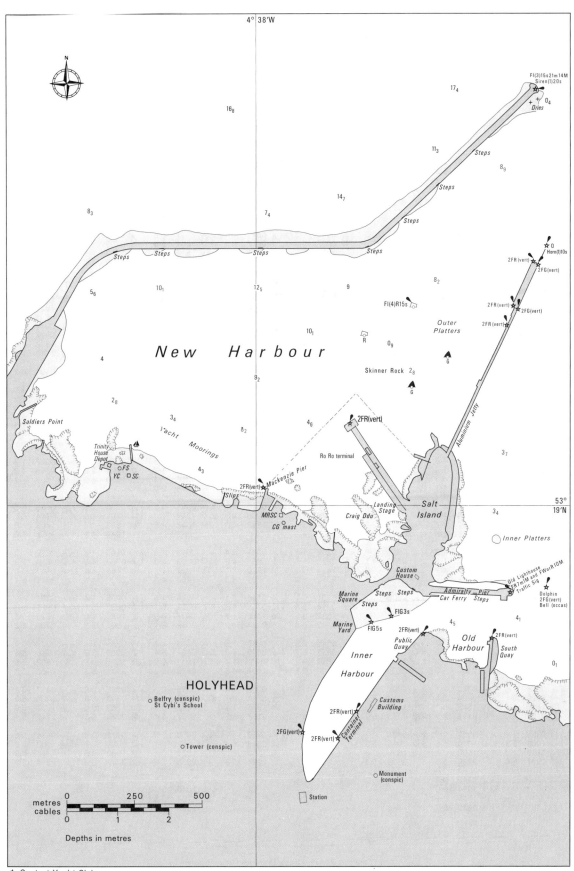

4° 38′W

Fl(3)15s21m14M
Siren(1)20s

Dries   0₄

17₄

16₈

11₃   *Steps*

8₉

14₇   *Steps*

8₃   *Steps*

7₄   *Steps*

O
Horn(1)10s

2FR(vert)
2FG(vert)

Steps   *Steps*   *Steps*   *Steps*

5₆   10₁   12₅   9   8₂   2FR(vert)
2FG(vert)

N e w   H a r b o u r   Fl(4)R15s

Outer Platters   2FR(vert)

4   10₁   R   0₉   G

9₂   Skinner Rock 2₈   G

Yacht   Moorings   2₈

Soldiers Point   3₄   8₂   4₆   2FR(vert)

Trinity House Depot   4₃

FS   YC   SC

Slips   2FR(vert)   *Mackenzie Pier*

Aluminium Jetty

3₇

3₄   53°
19′N

MRSC   *Ro Ro terminal*

CG mast   *Craig Ddu*   *Landing Stage*   *Salt Island*   *Inner Platters*

Custom House

Old Lighthouse
FR7mIM and FWorR10M
Traffic Sig

Marine Square   *Steps*   *Steps*   *Admiralty Pier*   *Car Ferry*   *Steps*

Dolphin
2FG(vert)
Bell (occas)

Steps   4₁

Marine Yard   FIG3s   4₅

FIG5s   2FR(vert)   *Old Harbour*   2FR(vert)

Public Quay   *South Quay*

HOLYHEAD   *Inner*   0₁

o Belfry (conspic)
St Cybi's School   *Harbour*   *Customs Building*

2FR(vert)

2FG(vert)   2FR(vert)   *Container Terminal*

o Tower (conspic)

o Monument
(conspic)

□ Station

metres
cables   0   250   500

0   1   2

Depths in metres

10

▲ Contact Yacht Club

WALES – HOLYHEAD

Lat 53°18′ N   Long 4°38′ W

TIMES AND HEIGHTS OF HIGH AND LOW WATERS

YEAR **1991**

TIME ZONE **UT (GMT)**
For Summer Time add ONE hour in non-shaded areas

JANUARY

Day	Time	m	Day	Time	m
1 Tu	0404 / 1019 / 1638 / 2248	0.8 / 5.8 / 5.7 / 5.7	**16** W	0427 / 1035 / 1651 / 2258	1.3 / 5.4 / 1.1 / 5.1
2 W	0454 / 1105 / 1729 / 2337	0.7 / 5.9 / 0.4 / 5.7	**17** Th	0459 / 1108 / 1725 / 2330	1.2 / 5.5 / 1.0 / 5.5
3 Th	0542 / 1153 / 1817	0.7 / 5.9 / 0.4	**18** F	0533 / 1142 / 1758	1.1 / 5.5 / 0.9
4 F	0025 / 0628 / 1239 / 1904	5.5 / 0.8 / 5.8 / 0.5	**19** Sa	0004 / 0607 / 1215 / 1832	5.2 / 1.1 / 5.5 / 0.9
5 Sa	0112 / 0714 / 1326 / 1952	5.3 / 1.0 / 5.6 / 0.8	**20** Su	0038 / 0642 / 1250 / 1907	5.1 / 1.1 / 5.5 / 1.0
6 Su	0159 / 0801 / 1413 / 2040	5.1 / 1.3 / 5.3 / 1.1	**21** M	0114 / 0719 / 1328 / 1945	5.1 / 1.2 / 5.4 / 1.1
7 M	0249 / 0850 / 1504 / ☾2134	4.8 / 1.6 / 5.0 / 1.5	**22** Tu	0154 / 0759 / 1409 / 2029	5.0 / 1.4 / 5.2 / 1.3
8 Tu	0343 / 0946 / 1603 / 2234	4.5 / 1.9 / 4.7 / 1.8	**23** W	0239 / 0847 / 1458 / ☽2121	4.8 / 1.6 / 5.0 / 1.5
9 W	0447 / 1054 / 1713 / 2342	4.4 / 2.1 / 4.5 / 2.0	**24** Th	0335 / 0949 / 1603 / 2227	4.6 / 1.8 / 4.8 / 1.7
10 Th	0600 / 1210 / 1831	4.3 / 2.2 / 4.4	**25** F	0452 / 1106 / 1727 / 2349	4.5 / 1.9 / 4.7 / 1.8
11 F	0048 / 0709 / 1320 / 1940	2.0 / 4.4 / 2.1 / 4.4	**26** Sa	0618 / 1232 / 1852	4.6 / 1.8 / 4.7
12 Sa	0148 / 0806 / 1419 / 2034	2.0 / 4.6 / 1.9 / 4.6	**27** Su	0107 / 0733 / 1347 / 2005	1.7 / 4.8 / 1.5 / 5.0
13 Su	0237 / 0851 / 1505 / 2117	1.8 / 4.9 / 1.7 / 4.8	**28** M	0213 / 0833 / 1450 / 2104	1.4 / 5.2 / 1.2 / 5.2
14 M	0318 / 0929 / 1543 / 2153	1.6 / 5.1 / 1.4 / 4.9	**29** Tu	0310 / 0924 / 1543 / 2153	1.1 / 5.5 / 0.7 / 5.5
15 Tu	0353 / 1003 / 1619 / ●2227	1.4 / 5.3 / 1.3 / 5.0	**30** W	0357 / 1010 / 1630 / ○2238	0.8 / 5.8 / 0.4 / 5.6
			31 Th	0442 / 1054 / 1715 / 2320	0.6 / 6.0 / 0.2 / 5.7

FEBRUARY

Day	Time	m	Day	Time	m
1 F	0525 / 1136 / 1757	0.5 / 6.0 / 0.3	**16** Sa	0509 / 1118 / 1732 / 2337	0.8 / 5.7 / 0.7 / 5.4
2 Sa	0003 / 0605 / 1217 / 1838	5.6 / 0.6 / 5.9 / 0.4	**17** Su	0542 / 1150 / 1804	0.7 / 5.7 / 0.6
3 Su	0042 / 0646 / 1257 / 1919	5.4 / 0.7 / 5.7 / 0.7	**18** M	0011 / 0617 / 1225 / 1838	5.4 / 0.8 / 5.7 / 0.7
4 M	0121 / 0726 / 1337 / 1958	5.2 / 1.0 / 5.4 / 1.1	**19** Tu	0046 / 0653 / 1303 / 1916	5.3 / 0.9 / 5.6 / 0.9
5 Tu	0202 / 0808 / 1419 / 2042	4.9 / 1.4 / 5.0 / 1.5	**20** W	0124 / 0733 / 1344 / 1958	5.2 / 1.1 / 5.3 / 1.1
6 W	0244 / 0854 / 1507 / ☾2131	4.6 / 1.7 / 4.6 / 1.9	**21** Th	0208 / 0820 / 1433 / 2050	5.0 / 1.4 / 5.0 / 1.5
7 Th	0338 / 0953 / 1609 / 2238	4.4 / 2.1 / 4.3 / 2.2	**22** F	0303 / 0922 / 1539 / 2159	4.7 / 1.7 / 4.7 / 1.8
8 F	0449 / 1115 / 1737	4.2 / 2.3 / 4.1	**23** Sa	0421 / 1048 / 1713 / 2332	4.5 / 1.9 / 4.5 / 2.0
9 Sa	0003 / 0622 / 1246 / 1917	2.4 / 4.2 / 2.3 / 4.1	**24** Su	0601 / 1224 / 1850	4.5 / 1.7 / 4.6
10 Su	0120 / 0740 / 1357 / 2019	2.2 / 4.4 / 2.0 / 4.4	**25** M	0100 / 0726 / 1342 / 2005	1.8 / 4.8 / 1.4 / 4.9
11 M	0218 / 0832 / 1446 / 2103	2.0 / 4.7 / 1.7 / 4.6	**26** Tu	0208 / 0826 / 1444 / 2058	1.5 / 5.1 / 0.9 / 5.2
12 Tu	0300 / 0914 / 1524 / 2136	1.7 / 5.0 / 1.4 / 4.9	**27** W	0301 / 0914 / 1532 / 2142	1.1 / 5.5 / 0.6 / 5.4
13 W	0335 / 0943 / 1557 / 2206	1.4 / 5.2 / 1.1 / 5.1	**28** Th	0345 / 0955 / 1614 / ○2220	0.8 / 5.7 / 0.3 / 5.5
14 Th	0407 / 1014 / 1628 / ●2235	1.2 / 5.4 / 0.9 / 5.2			
15 F	0438 / 1045 / 1659 / 2305	0.9 / 5.6 / 0.8 / 5.3			

MARCH

Day	Time	m	Day	Time	m
1 F	0424 / 1034 / 1654 / 2258	0.5 / 5.9 / 0.2 / 5.6	**16** Sa	0409 / 1016 / 1732 / ●2235	0.8 / 5.6 / 0.7 / 5.4
2 Sa	0502 / 1112 / 1732 / 2334	0.4 / 5.9 / 0.3 / 5.6	**17** Su	0441 / 1048 / 1701 / 2308	0.6 / 5.7 / 0.5 / 5.5
3 Su	0540 / 1150 / 1808	0.5 / 5.8 / 0.5	**18** M	0515 / 1123 / 1734 / 2343	0.5 / 5.8 / 0.5 / 5.6
4 M	0011 / 0617 / 1228 / 1843	5.4 / 0.6 / 5.5 / 0.8	**19** Tu	0551 / 1201 / 1812	0.6 / 5.8 / 0.6
5 Tu	0046 / 0653 / 1304 / 1919	5.3 / 0.9 / 5.3 / 1.1	**20** W	0021 / 0632 / 1242 / 1852	5.5 / 0.7 / 5.6 / 0.8
6 W	0121 / 0731 / 1341 / 1957	5.0 / 1.3 / 4.9 / 1.5	**21** Th	0102 / 0716 / 1327 / 1938	5.3 / 0.9 / 5.3 / 1.2
7 Th	0159 / 0813 / 1423 / 2039	4.8 / 1.6 / 4.6 / 1.9	**22** F	0149 / 0808 / 1422 / 2033	5.1 / 1.2 / 4.9 / 1.6
8 F	0246 / 0904 / 1518 / ☾2136	4.5 / 2.0 / 4.2 / 2.3	**23** Sa	0247 / 0904 / 1535 / ☽2149	4.8 / 1.6 / 4.6 / 1.9
9 Sa	0348 / 1009 / 1642 / 2308	4.2 / 2.3 / 3.9 / 2.5	**24** Su	0410 / 1045 / 1715 / 2325	4.5 / 1.7 / 4.4 / 2.0
10 Su	0520 / 1200 / 1839	4.1 / 2.3 / 4.0	**25** M	0551 / 1217 / 1848	4.5 / 1.6 / 4.5
11 M	0041 / 0657 / 1320 / 1951	2.4 / 4.3 / 2.1 / 4.3	**26** Tu	0049 / 0712 / 1331 / 1954	1.8 / 4.8 / 1.2 / 4.8
12 Tu	0145 / 0758 / 1412 / 2034	2.1 / 4.6 / 1.7 / 4.6	**27** W	0154 / 0809 / 1427 / 2043	1.5 / 5.1 / 0.9 / 5.1
13 W	0230 / 0843 / 1451 / 2107	1.8 / 4.9 / 1.4 / 4.8	**28** Th	0243 / 0858 / 1512 / 2122	1.1 / 5.4 / 0.6 / 5.3
14 Th	0305 / 0912 / 1525 / 2136	1.4 / 5.1 / 1.1 / 5.1	**29** F	0325 / 0935 / 1552 / 2157	0.8 / 5.6 / 0.5 / 5.4
15 F	0338 / 0943 / 1556 / 2204	1.1 / 5.4 / 0.8 / 5.3	**30** Sa	0403 / 1012 / 1628 / ○2233	0.6 / 5.7 / 0.4 / 5.5
			31 Su	0438 / 1048 / 1704 / 2306	0.6 / 5.7 / 0.5 / 5.5

APRIL

Day	Time	m	Day	Time	m
1 M	0515 / 1125 / 1737 / 2342	0.6 / 5.6 / 0.7 / 5.4	**16** Tu	0451 / 1059 / 1709 / 2320	0.5 / 5.8 / 0.5 / 5.7
2 Tu	0550 / 1201 / 1811	0.7 / 5.4 / 0.9	**17** W	0533 / 1143 / 1751	0.5 / 5.7 / 0.6
3 W	0015 / 0627 / 1236 / 1845	5.3 / 1.0 / 5.1 / 1.2	**18** Th	0003 / 0618 / 1229 / 1838	5.6 / 0.6 / 5.5 / 0.9
4 Th	0050 / 0703 / 1313 / 1920	5.1 / 1.2 / 4.8 / 1.6	**19** F	0049 / 0703 / 1321 / 1928	5.4 / 0.8 / 5.2 / 1.2
5 F	0127 / 0744 / 1352 / 2001	4.9 / 1.6 / 4.5 / 1.9	**20** Sa	0142 / 0808 / 1418 / 2030	5.2 / 1.1 / 5.0 / 1.6
6 Sa	0209 / 0832 / 1444 / 2053	4.6 / 1.9 / 4.2 / 2.3	**21** Su	0244 / 0917 / 1539 / ☽2145	4.9 / 1.3 / 4.6 / 1.9
7 Su	0304 / 0935 / 1557 / ☾2209	4.4 / 2.1 / 4.0 / 2.5	**22** M	0404 / 1038 / 1709 / 2309	4.7 / 1.4 / 4.5 / 1.9
8 M	0423 / 1101 / 1739 / 2346	4.2 / 2.2 / 4.0 / 2.4	**23** Tu	0533 / 1158 / 1828	4.7 / 1.3 / 4.6
9 Tu	0554 / 1224 / 1859	4.2 / 2.0 / 4.2	**24** W	0027 / 0646 / 1307 / 1930	1.7 / 4.9 / 1.2 / 4.8
10 W	0056 / 0704 / 1323 / 1949	2.2 / 4.5 / 1.7 / 4.5	**25** Th	0128 / 0744 / 1402 / 2018	1.5 / 5.1 / 1.0 / 5.0
11 Th	0145 / 0754 / 1406 / 2026	1.8 / 4.8 / 1.4 / 4.8	**26** F	0219 / 0830 / 1447 / 2057	1.2 / 5.2 / 0.8 / 5.1
12 F	0225 / 0832 / 1443 / 2058	1.4 / 5.1 / 1.0 / 5.1	**27** Sa	0301 / 0911 / 1525 / 2132	1.0 / 5.3 / 0.7 / 5.2
13 Sa	0301 / 0908 / 1518 / 2131	1.1 / 5.3 / 0.8 / 5.3	**28** Su	0339 / 0949 / 1602 / ○2207	0.9 / 5.4 / 0.7 / 5.3
14 Su	0336 / 0943 / 1553 / ●2204	0.8 / 5.6 / 0.6 / 5.5	**29** M	0417 / 1026 / 1637 / 2242	0.8 / 5.3 / 0.8 / 5.4
15 M	0412 / 1020 / 1630 / 2241	0.6 / 5.7 / 0.5 / 5.6	**30** Tu	0454 / 1102 / 1711 / 2316	0.8 / 5.3 / 0.9 / 5.3

Chart Datum: 3.05 metres below Ordnance Datum (Newlyn)

WALES – HOLYHEAD

Lat 53°18′ N   Long 4°38′ W

TIMES AND HEIGHTS OF HIGH AND LOW WATERS

YEAR 1991

TIME ZONE UT (GMT)
For Summer Time add ONE hour in non-shaded areas

MAY

Day	Time 1	m	Time 2	m	Time 3	m	Time 4	m
1 W	0529	0.9	1139	5.1	1744	1.1	2351	—
2 Th	0605	1.1	1215	5.0	1819	1.3		
3 F	0027	5.1	0642	1.2	1252	4.8	1855	1.6
4 Sa	0103	5.0	0723	1.4	1333	4.6	1935	1.8
5 Su	0145	4.8	0808	1.7	1420	4.4	2025	2.1
6 M	0234	4.6	0903	1.8	1519	4.2	2125	2.3
7 Tu ☾	0336	4.4	1007	1.9	1637	4.1	2240	2.3
8 W	0452	4.4	1119	1.9	1751	4.2	2353	2.1
9 Th	0604	4.5	1222	1.7	1850	4.5		
10 F	0052	1.8	0700	4.7	1316	1.4	1938	4.7
11 Sa	0140	1.5	0748	5.0	1401	1.1	2019	5.0
12 Su	0223	1.2	0832	5.2	1442	0.9	2058	5.3
13 M	0305	0.9	0914	5.5	1524	0.7	2138	5.5
14 Tu ●	0348	0.6	0956	5.6	1606	0.6	2219	5.6
15 W	0433	0.5	1042	5.7	1651	0.6	2304	5.7
16 Th	0520	0.4	1132	5.6	1739	0.7	2351	5.7
17 F	0612	0.5	1224	5.5	1829	0.9		
18 Sa	0042	5.5	0707	0.6	1320	5.2	1924	1.1
19 Su	0137	5.3	0805	0.8	1420	4.9	2023	1.4
20 M ☽	0239	5.1	0910	1.0			2129	1.6
21 Tu	0348	4.9	1019	1.2	1644	4.6	2241	1.7
22 W	0504	4.8	1129	1.3	1754	4.6	2351	1.7
23 Th	0612	4.8	1234	1.2	1856	4.7		
24 F	0055	1.6	0713	4.9	1330	1.1	1948	4.8
25 Sa	0151	1.4	0804	4.9	1419	1.2	2032	4.9
26 Su	0237	1.3	0849	5.0	1501	1.1	2110	5.1
27 M	0321	1.2	0929	5.0	1539	1.1	2146	5.2
28 Tu ○	0400	1.1	1007	5.0	1614	1.2	2223	5.2
29 W	0437	1.1	1045	5.0	1649	1.2	2258	5.3
30 Th	0513	1.1	1122	5.0	1725	1.2	2333	5.2
31 F	0550	1.1	1158	4.9	1800	1.3		

JUNE

Day	Time 1	m	Time 2	m	Time 3	m	Time 4	m
1 Sa	0008	5.2	0627	1.2	1235	4.8	1836	1.5
2 Su	0045	5.1	0704	1.3	1314	4.7	1916	1.6
3 M	0126	5.0	0747	1.4	1357	4.5	1959	1.8
4 Tu	0209	4.8	0832	1.5	1444	4.4	2049	1.9
5 W ☾	0258	4.7	0924	1.6	1542	4.3	2146	2.0
6 Th	0357	4.6	1021	1.6	1648	4.3	2251	2.0
7 F	0505	4.6	1125	1.6	1753	4.5	2356	1.9
8 Sa	0610	4.7	1225	1.4	1852	4.7		
9 Su	0056	1.6	0707	4.9	1321	1.3	1942	4.9
10 M	0149	1.3	0801	5.1	1412	1.1	2032	5.2
11 Tu	0242	1.0	0851	5.3	1501	0.9	2118	5.4
12 W ●	0332	0.8	0933	5.5	1550	0.7	2204	5.6
13 Th	0423	0.5	1033	5.6	1709	0.6	2254	5.7
14 F	0515	0.4	1125	5.6	1730	0.6	2343	5.8
15 Sa	0607	0.5	1217	5.5	1822	0.7		
16 Su	0034	5.7	0659	0.4	1310	5.3	1913	0.9
17 M	0126	5.6	0752	0.6	1405	5.1	2006	1.1
18 Tu	0220	5.4	0847	0.8	1503	4.9	2103	1.4
19 W ☽	0318	5.1	0946	1.1	1604	4.7	2203	1.6
20 Th	0423	4.9	1049	1.3	1711	4.6	2311	1.7
21 F	0532	4.7	1154	1.5	1815	4.5		
22 Sa	0018	1.8	0639	4.6	1256	1.6	1916	4.6
23 Su	0123	1.7	0740	4.6	1351	1.6	2008	4.7
24 M	0219	1.6	0832	4.7	1439	1.5	2051	4.9
25 Tu	0305	1.5	0917	4.8	1521	1.4	2131	5.0
26 W	0348	1.3	0956	4.9	1559	1.3	2207	5.2
27 Th ○	0426	1.2	1033	4.9	1634	1.3	2242	5.3
28 F	0501	1.1	1108	4.9	1709	1.2	2318	5.3
29 Sa	0534	1.1	1142	5.0	1743	1.2	2351	5.3
30 Su	0610	1.1	1217	4.9	1818	1.3		

JULY

Day	Time 1	m	Time 2	m	Time 3	m	Time 4	m
1 M	0027	5.3	0645	1.1	1252	4.9	1853	1.4
2 Tu	0103	5.2	0721	1.2	1330	4.8	1931	1.5
3 W	0141	5.1	0759	1.3	1409	4.7	2013	1.6
4 Th	0223	5.0	0843	1.4	1456	4.6	2101	1.7
5 F ☾	0311	4.9	0932	1.5	1550	4.5	2157	1.8
6 Sa	0410	4.7	1033	1.6	1658	4.5	2306	1.9
7 Su	0522	4.7	1142	1.6	1810	4.6		
8 M	0019	1.7	0634	4.8	1250	1.5	1916	4.8
9 Tu	0127	1.5	0741	4.9	1352	1.3	2013	5.1
10 W	0227	1.2	0840	5.2	1449	1.1	2107	5.4
11 Th ●	0324	0.8	0935	5.4	1541	0.8	2156	5.6
12 F	0416	0.5	1026	5.6	1630	0.6	2244	5.8
13 Sa	0505	0.3	1113	5.6	1719	0.5	2330	5.9
14 Su	0554	0.2	1201	5.6	1805	0.6		
15 M	0018	5.9	0642	0.2	1249	5.4	1852	0.7
16 Tu	0104	5.8	0728	0.5	1337	5.2	1938	0.9
17 W	0152	5.5	0816	0.8	1425	5.0	2027	1.2
18 Th ☽	0242	5.2	0907	1.2	1518	4.7	2121	1.5
19 F	0338	4.8	1004	1.5	1617	4.5	2224	1.8
20 Sa	0444	4.5	1111	1.8	1727	4.4	2339	2.0
21 Su	0601	4.3	1221	1.9	1842	4.4		
22 M	0056	2.0	0719	4.3	1327	1.9	1947	4.6
23 Tu	0202	1.9	0820	4.5	1422	1.8	2037	4.8
24 W	0254	1.6	0905	4.6	1507	1.6	2118	5.0
25 Th	0335	1.4	0943	4.8	1543	1.4	2152	5.2
26 F ○	0410	1.2	1017	4.9	1617	1.3	2226	5.3
27 Sa	0442	1.1	1050	5.0	1649	1.1	2257	5.4
28 Su	0513	1.0	1119	5.1	1722	1.1	2329	5.5
29 M	0546	0.9	1151	5.1	1754	1.1		
30 Tu	0001	5.5	0618	0.9	1224	5.1	1827	1.1
31 W	0035	5.4	0650	1.0	1257	5.0	1902	1.2

AUGUST

Day	Time 1	m	Time 2	m	Time 3	m	Time 4	m
1 Th	0112	5.3	0726	1.1	1334	4.9	1940	1.3
2 F	0149	5.2	0805	1.2	1415	4.8	2023	1.5
3 Sa ☾	0233	5.0	0851	1.4	1505	4.7	2117	1.7
4 Su	0329	4.8	0950	1.7	1612	4.6	2228	1.9
5 M	0447	4.6	1108	1.8	1737	4.5	2356	1.8
6 Tu	0615	4.6	1231	1.7	1859	4.7		
7 W	0114	1.6	0733	4.8	1341	1.5	2005	5.1
8 Th	0220	1.2	0836	5.1	1440	1.2	2057	5.4
9 F	0315	0.7	0927	5.4	1531	0.9	2145	5.7
10 Sa ●	0404	0.4	1013	5.6	1617	0.6	2228	6.0
11 Su	0449	0.2	1057	5.7	1701	0.4	2312	6.1
12 M	0533	0.1	1139	5.7	1743	0.4	2354	6.0
13 Tu	0615	0.3	1221	5.5	1825	0.6		
14 W	0036	5.8	0657	0.5	1303	5.3	1907	0.8
15 Th	0120	5.5	0740	0.8	1345	5.1	1951	1.2
16 F	0204	5.1	0825	1.3	1430	4.8	2039	1.6
17 Sa ☽	0253	4.7	0915	1.7	1524	4.5	2138	2.0
18 Su	0353	4.4	1020	2.1	1633	4.3	2258	2.2
19 M	0520	4.1	1142	2.3	1803	4.3		
20 Tu	0028	2.2	0700	4.2	1300	2.2	1923	4.5
21 W	0142	2.0	0805	4.4	1402	2.0	2016	4.7
22 Th	0233	1.7	0849	4.6	1446	1.7	2056	5.0
23 F	0312	1.4	0924	4.8	1521	1.5	2129	5.2
24 Sa	0345	1.2	0953	5.0	1553	1.2	2200	5.4
25 Su ○	0414	1.0	1021	5.1	1623	1.0	2230	5.5
26 M	0444	0.9	1051	5.3	1654	0.9	2301	5.6
27 Tu	0515	0.8	1120	5.3	1725	0.9	2333	5.7
28 W	0546	0.8	1153	5.3	1757	0.9		
29 Th	0005	5.6	0618	0.8	1227	5.3	1832	1.0
30 F	0042	5.5	0653	1.0	1303	5.2	1910	1.2
31 Sa	0120	5.3	0734	1.2	1344	5.0	1955	1.4

10

Chart Datum: 3.05 metres below Ordnance Datum (Newlyn)

WALES – HOLYHEAD

Lat 53°18′ N   Long 4°38′ W

TIMES AND HEIGHTS OF HIGH AND LOW WATERS

YEAR **1991**

TIME ZONE UT (GMT)
For Summer Time add ONE hour in non-shaded areas

Chart Datum: 3.05 metres below Ordnance Datum (Newlyn)

SEPTEMBER

Day	Time	m		Day	Time	m
1 Su (	0206 / 0820 / 1434 / 2053	5.1 / 1.5 / 4.8 / 1.7		**16** M	0310 / 0928 / 1539 / 2212	4.3 / 2.3 / 4.4 / 2.3
2 M	0305 / 0922 / 1545 / 2210	4.8 / 1.8 / 4.6 / 1.9		**17** Tu	0434 / 1055 / 1711 / 2349	4.0 / 2.5 / 4.2 / 2.3
3 Tu	0431 / 1049 / 1720 / 2346	4.5 / 2.0 / 4.5 / 1.9		**18** W	0627 / 1225 / 1843	4.1 / 2.4 / 4.4
4 W	0611 / 1221 / 1849	4.5 / 1.9 / 4.8		**19** Th	0107 / 0737 / 1328 / 1942	2.1 / 4.3 / 2.2 / 4.7
5 Th	0107 / 0730 / 1333 / 1954	1.5 / 4.8 / 1.6 / 5.1		**20** F	0159 / 0819 / 1413 / 2023	1.8 / 4.6 / 1.8 / 5.0
6 F	0212 / 0827 / 1429 / 2044	1.1 / 5.1 / 1.2 / 5.5		**21** Sa	0237 / 0853 / 1450 / 2057	1.5 / 4.8 / 1.5 / 5.2
7 Sa	0303 / 0914 / 1515 / 2128	0.7 / 5.4 / 0.9 / 5.8		**22** Su	0310 / 0921 / 1521 / 2128	1.2 / 5.1 / 1.3 / 5.4
8 Su ●	0348 / 0955 / 1557 / 2207	0.4 / 5.6 / 0.6 / 6.0		**23** M ○	0341 / 0949 / 1552 / 2157	1.0 / 5.3 / 1.1 / 5.6
9 M	0428 / 1033 / 1637 / 2248	0.2 / 5.7 / 0.5 / 6.0		**24** Tu	0410 / 1017 / 1623 / 2230	0.8 / 5.4 / 0.9 / 5.7
10 Tu	0508 / 1112 / 1718 / 2327	0.3 / 5.7 / 0.5 / 6.0		**25** W	0441 / 1048 / 1655 / 2302	0.7 / 5.5 / 0.8 / 5.8
11 W	0547 / 1150 / 1757	0.4 / 5.6 / 0.6		**26** Th	0513 / 1122 / 1730 / 2339	0.7 / 5.5 / 0.8 / 5.7
12 Th	0008 / 0625 / 1229 / 1836	5.7 / 0.7 / 5.4 / 0.9		**27** F	0549 / 1158 / 1808	0.8 / 5.5 / 0.9
13 F	0048 / 0703 / 1307 / 1917	5.4 / 1.1 / 5.1 / 1.2		**28** Sa	0018 / 0628 / 1238 / 1850	5.6 / 1.0 / 5.4 / 1.1
14 Sa	0128 / 0744 / 1348 / 2002	5.0 / 1.5 / 4.9 / 1.6		**29** Su	0100 / 0712 / 1324 / 1941	5.3 / 1.3 / 5.2 / 1.4
15 Su)	0213 / 0820 / 1436 / 2057	4.7 / 1.9 / 4.6 / 2.0		**30** M	0152 / 0804 / 1419 / 2044	5.0 / 1.6 / 4.9 / 1.7

OCTOBER

Day	Time	m		Day	Time	m
1 Tu (	0300 / 0911 / 1534 / 2206	4.7 / 1.9 / 4.7 / 1.8		**16** W	0348 / 0957 / 1612 / 2252	4.1 / 2.5 / 4.3 / 2.3
2 W	0431 / 1041 / 1711 / 2337	4.5 / 2.1 / 4.7 / 1.7		**17** Th	0526 / 1129 / 1740	4.1 / 2.5 / 4.4
3 Th	0607 / 1208 / 1834	4.6 / 1.9 / 4.9		**18** F	0011 / 0645 / 1239 / 1849	2.1 / 4.3 / 2.3 / 4.6
4 F	0055 / 0719 / 1317 / 1935	1.4 / 4.9 / 1.6 / 5.2		**19** Sa	0109 / 0734 / 1328 / 1938	1.9 / 4.5 / 2.0 / 4.9
5 Sa	0155 / 0811 / 1411 / 2025	1.0 / 5.1 / 1.3 / 5.5		**20** Su	0152 / 0812 / 1409 / 2016	1.6 / 4.8 / 1.7 / 5.2
6 Su	0243 / 0854 / 1456 / 2107	0.7 / 5.4 / 0.9 / 5.7		**21** M	0229 / 0844 / 1444 / 2051	1.3 / 5.1 / 1.3 / 5.4
7 M ●	0325 / 0932 / 1535 / 2146	0.5 / 5.6 / 0.7 / 5.9		**22** Tu	0301 / 0914 / 1518 / 2125	1.0 / 5.3 / 1.1 / 5.6
8 Tu	0403 / 1009 / 1614 / 2224	0.5 / 5.6 / 0.6 / 5.9		**23** W ○	0335 / 0946 / 1552 / 2159	0.8 / 5.5 / 0.9 / 5.7
9 W	0441 / 1045 / 1652 / 2304	0.5 / 5.6 / 0.7 / 5.8		**24** Th	0410 / 1020 / 1630 / 2237	0.7 / 5.6 / 0.7 / 5.8
10 Th	0518 / 1122 / 1732 / 2342	0.7 / 5.6 / 0.8 / 5.5		**25** F	0447 / 1058 / 1709 / 2318	0.7 / 5.7 / 0.8 / 5.7
11 F	0554 / 1200 / 1811	1.0 / 5.4 / 1.0		**26** Sa	0527 / 1139 / 1753	0.8 / 5.7 / 0.8
12 Sa	0021 / 0631 / 1236 / 1850	5.3 / 1.3 / 5.2 / 1.3		**27** Su	0003 / 0611 / 1224 / 1842	5.6 / 1.0 / 5.5 / 1.0
13 Su	0059 / 0709 / 1314 / 1933	4.9 / 1.6 / 4.9 / 1.7		**28** M	0052 / 0700 / 1314 / 1938	5.3 / 1.3 / 5.3 / 1.2
14 M	0142 / 0751 / 1359 / 2023	4.6 / 2.0 / 4.7 / 2.0		**29** Tu	0149 / 0757 / 1412 / 2043	5.0 / 1.6 / 5.1 / 1.5
15 Tu)	0233 / 0843 / 1456 / 2127	4.3 / 2.3 / 4.5 / 2.2		**30** W (	0300 / 0905 / 1525 / 2159	4.7 / 1.9 / 4.9 / 1.6
				31 Th	0426 / 1027 / 1652 / 2320	4.6 / 2.0 / 4.9 / 1.5

NOVEMBER

Day	Time	m		Day	Time	m
1 F	0549 / 1146 / 1810	4.7 / 1.9 / 5.0		**16** Sa	0532 / 1132 / 1743	4.3 / 2.3 / 4.6
2 Sa	0031 / 0655 / 1252 / 1912	1.3 / 4.9 / 1.6 / 5.2		**17** Su	0005 / 0634 / 1232 / 1842	1.9 / 4.5 / 2.1 / 4.8
3 Su	0130 / 0748 / 1347 / 2002	1.1 / 5.1 / 1.4 / 5.4		**18** M	0059 / 0723 / 1323 / 1931	1.7 / 4.7 / 1.8 / 5.0
4 M	0219 / 0832 / 1433 / 2046	0.9 / 5.2 / 1.2 / 5.5		**19** Tu	0144 / 0804 / 1406 / 2015	1.4 / 5.0 / 1.6 / 5.2
5 Tu	0301 / 0910 / 1515 / 2125	0.8 / 5.4 / 1.0 / 5.6		**20** W	0225 / 0842 / 1447 / 2056	1.2 / 5.2 / 1.2 / 5.6
6 W ●	0341 / 0946 / 1556 / 2204	0.8 / 5.5 / 0.9 / 5.6		**21** Th ○	0305 / 0919 / 1528 / 2136	1.0 / 5.5 / 1.0 / 5.6
7 Th	0417 / 1023 / 1634 / 2244	0.9 / 5.5 / 0.9 / 5.5		**22** F	0345 / 0959 / 1612 / 2220	0.8 / 5.7 / 0.8 / 5.7
8 F	0454 / 1059 / 1713 / 2322	1.0 / 5.5 / 1.0 / 5.3		**23** Sa	0427 / 1041 / 1657 / 2306	0.8 / 5.8 / 0.7 / 5.7
9 Sa	0529 / 1136 / 1751	1.2 / 5.4 / 1.2		**24** Su	0513 / 1126 / 1746 / 2356	0.8 / 5.8 / 0.7 / 5.6
10 Su	0000 / 0605 / 1212 / 1831	5.1 / 1.4 / 5.3 / 1.4		**25** M	0601 / 1215 / 1838	1.0 / 5.7 / 0.8
11 M	0038 / 0642 / 1250 / 1910	4.9 / 1.6 / 5.1 / 1.6		**26** Tu	0048 / 0653 / 1307 / 1934	5.4 / 1.1 / 5.6 / 0.9
12 Tu	0119 / 0723 / 1331 / 1955	4.7 / 1.9 / 4.9 / 1.8		**27** W	0145 / 0749 / 1404 / 2034	5.2 / 1.4 / 5.4 / 1.1
13 W	0205 / 0809 / 1419 / 2047	4.5 / 2.1 / 4.7 / 2.0		**28** Th	0249 / 0851 / 1508 / 2139	4.9 / 1.6 / 5.2 / 1.3
14 Th)	0301 / 0907 / 1518 / 2150	4.3 / 2.3 / 4.6 / 2.1		**29** F)	0402 / 0959 / 1621 / 2249	4.7 / 1.8 / 5.0 / 1.4
15 F	0416 / 1017 / 1631 / 2301	4.2 / 2.3 / 4.5 / 2.1		**30** Sa	0515 / 1112 / 1734 / 2358	4.7 / 1.8 / 5.0 / 1.4

DECEMBER

Day	Time	m		Day	Time	m
1 Su	0622 / 1221 / 1841	4.7 / 1.7 / 5.0		**16** M	0526 / 1129 / 1744	4.4 / 2.2 / 4.7
2 M	0100 / 0720 / 1321 / 1938	1.4 / 4.9 / 1.6 / 5.1		**17** Tu	0001 / 0629 / 1234 / 1846	1.8 / 4.6 / 2.0 / 4.8
3 Tu	0154 / 0809 / 1415 / 2027	1.3 / 5.0 / 1.4 / 5.2		**18** W	0100 / 0726 / 1331 / 1942	1.6 / 4.8 / 1.7 / 5.0
4 W	0240 / 0851 / 1501 / 2111	1.2 / 5.2 / 1.3 / 5.2		**19** Th	0154 / 0815 / 1423 / 2033	1.4 / 5.1 / 1.4 / 5.3
5 Th	0322 / 0931 / 1543 / 2152	1.2 / 5.3 / 1.2 / 5.2		**20** F	0242 / 0900 / 1512 / 2121	1.2 / 5.4 / 1.0 / 5.5
6 F ●	0400 / 1007 / 1623 / 2231	1.2 / 5.4 / 1.1 / 5.2		**21** Sa ○	0329 / 0945 / 1600 / 2210	1.0 / 5.6 / 0.8 / 5.6
7 Sa	0437 / 1044 / 1701 / 2308	1.2 / 5.5 / 1.1 / 5.2		**22** Su	0416 / 1030 / 1649 / 2258	0.8 / 5.8 / 0.5 / 5.7
8 Su	0512 / 1120 / 1737 / 2344	1.3 / 5.4 / 1.2 / 5.1		**23** M	0505 / 1118 / 1740 / 2349	0.7 / 5.9 / 0.4 / 5.7
9 M	0547 / 1156 / 1814	1.4 / 5.4 / 1.3		**24** Tu	0553 / 1205 / 1829	0.7 / 5.9 / 0.4
10 Tu	0019 / 0622 / 1231 / 1850	5.0 / 1.5 / 5.3 / 1.4		**25** W	0038 / 0643 / 1255 / 1921	5.6 / 0.8 / 5.8 / 0.8
11 W	0057 / 0700 / 1309 / 1930	4.8 / 1.6 / 5.1 / 1.5		**26** Th	0130 / 0734 / 1347 / 2013	5.3 / 1.0 / 5.6 / 0.8
12 Th	0137 / 0740 / 1349 / 2012	4.7 / 1.8 / 5.0 / 1.6		**27** F	0225 / 0826 / 1442 / 2110	5.1 / 1.3 / 5.3 / 1.1
13 F	0220 / 0825 / 1434 / 2100	4.5 / 2.0 / 4.8 / 1.8		**28** Sa	0324 / 0924 / 1543 / 2212	4.8 / 1.6 / 5.1 / 1.4
14 Sa)	0314 / 0918 / 1529 / 2155	4.4 / 2.1 / 4.7 / 1.9		**29** Su	0430 / 1031 / 1654 / 2319	4.6 / 1.8 / 4.8 / 1.6
15 Su	0417 / 1020 / 1635 / 2257	4.4 / 2.2 / 4.6 / 1.9		**30** M	0540 / 1144 / 1807	4.6 / 1.9 / 4.7
				31 Tu	0028 / 0649 / 1256 / 1917	1.7 / 4.6 / 1.9 / 4.7

HOLYHEAD *continued*

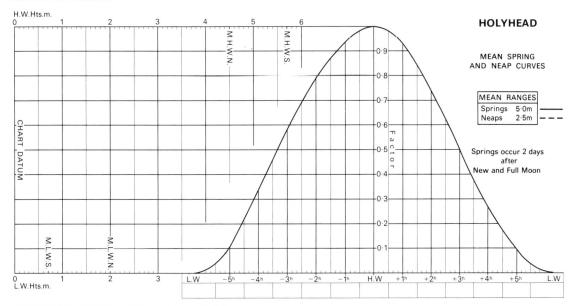

HOLYHEAD

MEAN SPRING AND NEAP CURVES

MEAN RANGES	
Springs	5·0m
Neaps	2·5m

Springs occur 2 days after New and Full Moon

MENAI STRAIT 10-10-19
Gwynedd

CHARTS
Admiralty 1464; Imray C61; OS 114, 115
TIDES
Beaumaris — 0025, Caernarfon — 0130 Dover;
ML Beaumaris 3.9; Caernarfon 2.9; Duration 0540;
Zone 0 (GMT).
Standard Port HOLYHEAD (←)

Times				Height (metres)			
HW		LW		MHWS	MHWN	MLWN	MLWS
0000	0600	0500	1100	5.7	4.5	2.0	0.7
1200	1800	1700	2300				

Differences BEAUMARIS
+0025 +0010 +0055 +0035 +2.0 +1.6 +0.5 +0.1
MENAI BRIDGE
+0030 +0010 +0100 +0035 +1.7 +1.4 +0.3 0.0
PORT DINORWIC
−0015 −0025 +0030 0000 0.0 0.0 0.0 +0.1
CAERNARFON
−0030 −0030 +0015 −0005 −0.4 −0.4 −0.1 −0.1
PORTH DINLLAEN
−0120 −0105 −0035 −0025 −1.0 −1.0 −0.2 −0.2
BARDSEY ISLAND
−0220 −0240 −0145 −0140 −1.2 −1.2 −0.5 −0.1

HW in The Swellies −0045 HW Port Dinorwic;
−0200 HW Liverpool; −0115 HW Holyhead.

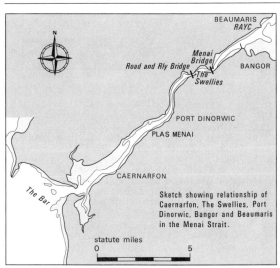

Sketch showing relationship of Caernarfon, The Swellies, Port Dinorwic, Bangor and Beaumaris in the Menai Strait.

statute miles
0   5

SHELTER
Very good shelter and facilities at Beaumaris, Bangor, Port Dinorwic (fresh water marina), Caernarfon (only available near HW).
NAVIGATION
NE entrance waypoint 53°20'.00N 04°00'.00W, 045°/225° from/to NE end Puffin Island, 1.0M. Caernarfon Bar waypoint 53°07'.60N 04°26'.00W, 270°/090° from/to Abermenai Pt Lt, 3.8M. From N end of Strait keep to buoyed channel near Anglesey shore. Night pilotage not recommended — many unlit buoys. The bridges and power cables have minimum clearance of 24m at MHWS. Between the bridges is a stretch of water called the Swellies which should only be attempted at slack HW which normally occurs about one hour before HW Holyhead. For further notes see Menai Strait 10.10.5.
LIGHTS AND MARKS
A light FWG exhibited at the end of Beaumaris pier. Menai Strait is marked by lateral marks, lights and light buoys; direction of buoyage changes off Caernarfon. From N approach in G sector of Mountfield Lt. Between the bridges is Price Pt, Fl WR 2s 5m 3M; R059° – 239°, W239° – 259°. At S end of Strait, Abermenai Pt Lt, Fl WR 3.5s; R065° – 245°, W245° – 065°.

Depths in metres

⚓ Apply to Royal Anglesey YC

MENAI STRAIT *continued*

BEAUMARIS
RADIO TELEPHONE
None.
TELEPHONE (0248)
Hr Mr 750057 Ex. 212; CG & MRSC Holyhead 2051;
⌗ (0248) 2336; Marinecall 0898 500 460; Police 810222;
Dr 810501.
FACILITIES
EC Beaumaris – Wednesday. **Pier** FW, L; **Royal
Anglesey YC** ☎ 810295, Slip, M, L, R, Bar; P.
Brimecombe ☎ 810310, M; **Northwest Venturers YC**
☎ 810023, M, L, FW; **Anglesey Boat Co** ☎ 810359, Slip,
P and D (in cans), FW, ME, BH (20 ton), Sh, C (2 ton),
CH, El, Ⓔ Gas: **Town** ⊠; Ⓑ; ⇌ (bus to Bangor);
✈ (Liverpool).

BANGOR
RADIO TELEPHONE
None.
TELEPHONE (0248)
Hr Mr 722920 Ex. 212; CG & MRSC Holyhead 2051;
⌗ (0407) 2336; Dr 364567.

FACILITIES
Dickies Tel. 352775, Slip, D, FW, ME, El, Sh, C, CH, Ⓔ,
SM, BH (30 ton), Gas, Gaz; **Port Penrhyn**, Slip, D;
Town ⊠; Ⓑ; ⇌; ✈ (Chester).

THE SWELLIES
NAVIGATION
For general pilotage notes on Menai Strait, including the
Swellies, see 10.10.5. The (Swellies) passage between the
bridges is dangerous for yachts and small craft except at
or immediately before slack HW. At other times the
stream can run up to 8 kn. At slack HW there is 3m over
The Platters and over the outcrop off Price Pt, and these
can be ignored. Passage is also possible for shallow-
draught boats at slack LW at neaps, but there are charted
depths of 0.4m close E of Britannia Bridge. Passage at
night not recommended.
LIGHTS AND MARKS
St George's Pier FIG 10s.
E side of channel QR 4m; R mast; vis 064°-222°.
Price Pt FIWR 2s 5m 3M; W Bn: vis R059°-239°,
W239°-259°. Britannia Bridge, E side, Ldg Lts 231°. Both
FW. Centre span of bridge Iso 5s 27m 3M; either side. S
end of bridge FR 21m 3M; either side. N end FG 21m 3M;
either side.

PORT DINORWIC
RADIO TELEPHONE
Port Dinorwic Yacht Harbour, Call *Dinorwic Marine* VHF
Ch **80** (office hours).
TELEPHONE (0248)
Hr Mr 670441; CG & MRSC Holyhead 2051;
⌗ (0407) 2336; Dr 670423.
FACILITIES
Outer harbour dries. **Port Dinorwic Yacht Harbour** (230)
☎ 670559 D, AC, CH, SM; **J. Dawson** ☎ 670103, SM;
P. D. Marine ☎ 670441, ME, El, Sh, Slip, C;
M. J. Stallard ☎ 670010, El, CH; **Town** Ⓔ, ⊠ (Bangor
or Caernarfon); Ⓑ; ⇌ (Bangor); ✈ (Liverpool).
Note: Between Port Dinorwic and Caernarfon is **Plas
Menai** ☎ 670964, the Sport Council for Wales Sailing and
Sports Centre. VHF Ch **80** 37.
Call: *Menai Base.* Day moorings only. All forms of water
sport.

⚓ Apply to HrMr

CAERNARFON
RADIO TELEPHONE
VHF Ch 16; 12 14 (day service only).
TELEPHONE (0286)
Hr Mr 672118; CG & MRSC Holyhead 2051; ⌗ (0407)
2336; Police 673333; Dr 673224; Ⓗ 370007.
FACILITIES
Harbour ☎ 672118, FW, Slip, L, C (2 ton), V;
Caernarfon Marine ☎ 674322, P, D, ME, El, Ⓔ, Sh, CH;
Caernarfon SC ☎ 672861, L, Bar; **Royal Welsh YC**
☎ 672599, P, FW, Bar; **Arfon Oceaneering** ☎ 76055,
Slip, CH, El, Ⓔ, ME; **Town** ⊠; Ⓑ; ⇌ (Bangor);
✈ (Liverpool).

ABERSOCH 10-10-20
Gwynedd

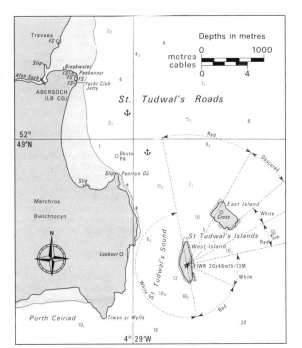

CHARTS
Admiralty 1484, 1512, 1971; Imray C61; OS 123
TIDES
−0315 Dover; ML 2.5; Duration 0520; Zone 0 (GMT).
Standard Port MILFORD HAVEN (→)

Times				Height (metres)			
HW		LW		MHWS	MHWN	MLWN	MLWS
0100	0800	0100	0700	7.0	5.2	2.5	0.7
1300	2000	1300	1900				

Differences ST TUDWAL'S ROADS
+0155 +0145 +0240 +0310 −2.2 −1.9 −0.7 −0.2
ABERDARON
+0210 +0200 +0240 +0310 −2.4 −1.9 −0.6 −0.2

SHELTER
There are few moorings for visitors. Apply to Hr Mr or SC. Anchorage in St Tudwal's Roads clear of area of moored yachts is sheltered from SSE through S to NE.
NAVIGATION
Waypoint 52°48'.50N 04°26'.06W, 113°/293° from/to Yacht Club jetty, 2.4M. There are no navigational dangers but steer well clear of the rocks to the E of St Tudwal's Islands, which dry out. The islands themselves are fairly steep to, except at N ends. St Tudwal's Sound is clear of dangers.
LIGHTS AND MARKS
The only major light is that on St Tudwal's West Island as shown on the chartlet.
RADIO TELEPHONE
South Caernarfon YC Ch **80.**
TELEPHONE (075 881)
Hr Mr 812684; CG & MRSC Holyhead 2051; ∰ (0407) 2336; Marinecall 0898 500 460; Police 2022; Dr Pwllheli 612535.
FACILITIES
EC Wednesday. **S. Caernarvonshire YC** ☎ 2338, Slip, M, L, FW, R, Bar (May-Sept), D; **Abersoch BY** ☎ 2213, Slip, ME, El, Sh, C (5 ton), ACA, CH; **Abersoch Land & Sea Services** ☎ 3434, ME, El, Sh, FW, P, D, C (12 ton), CH; **Hookes Marine** ☎ 2458, ME, El, Sh; **Abersoch Power Boat Club** ☎ 2027; **Town** CH, V, R, Bar. ✉; Ⓑ; ⇌ (Pwllheli); ✈ (Chester).

PWLLHELI 10-10-21
Gwynedd

CHARTS
Admiralty 1971, 1512; Imray C61; OS 123
TIDES
−0300 Dover; ML 2.6; Duration 0510; Zone 0 (GMT).
Standard Port MILFORD HAVEN (→)

Times				Height (metres)			
HW		LW		MHWS	MHWN	MLWN	MLWS
0100	0800	0100	0700	7.0	5.2	2.5	0.7
1300	2000	1300	1900				

Differences PWLLHELI
+0210 +0150 +0245 +0320 −2.0 −1.8 −0.6 −0.2
CRICCIETH
+0210 +0155 +0255 +0320 −2.0 −1.8 −0.7 −0.3

SHELTER
Small secure harbour with good shelter. Strong winds from SW to E cause breakers off shore. Inner harbour has good shelter but dries. Entry HW ∓2. No anchoring in harbour. Mooring enquiries to Hr Mr.
NAVIGATION
Waypoint 52°52'.50N 04°23'.00W, 150°/330° from/to Pwllheli Pt Lt (QR), 0.80M. The bar has often less than 0.3m. It is safe to cross in any wind direction. Boats with 1.5m draught can cross HW ∓2. Tide runs up to 3 kn at sp. Harbour speed limit 5 kn.
LIGHTS AND MARKS
F WRG 12m; vis G155°-175°, R175°-245°, W245°-045°. Buoyed entrance channel in G sector. Outer No 1 Lt Buoy, QG, G conical.
RADIO TELEPHONE
VHF Ch 16 (occas).

⚓ Secure to mooring and see Hr Mr

TELEPHONE (0758)
Hr Mr 613131 ex 281; MRSC Holyhead 2051; CG 720204; ∰ (0407) 2336; Marinecall 0898 500 460; Police Abersoch 2022; Dr 612535
FACILITIES
EC Thursday. **Pier**, P, D, L, FW, AB, V; **Pwllheli SC** ☎ 612219; **Marina Club** ☎ 612611, Slip, L, FW; **Partington BY** ☎ 612808, Slip, L, FW, ME, Gas, Sh, C (10 ton), CH, ACA; **Firmhelm BY** ☎ 612251, Slip, D, L, FW, ME, Sh, C (14 ton), CH; **Harbour Authority** Slip, M, L, FW, AB; **Tony Evans Marine Engineering** ☎ 613219, ME, El; **Rowlands Marine Electronics** ☎ 613193, Ⓔ, El; **J.K.A. Sails** ☎ 613266, SM; **Tudor Sails** ☎ 613141, SM.
Town V, R, Bar; ✉; Ⓑ; ⇌; ✈ (Chester).

10

MINOR HARBOURS AND ANCHORAGES 10.10.22

SILLOTH, Cumbria, 54°52′N, 3°24′W, Zone 0 (GMT), Admty charts 1346, 2013. HW −0050 on Dover, +0035 on Liverpool; HW height −0.3m on Liverpool; ML 4.9m; Duration 0520. See 10.10.7. Two channels marked on stbd side. Approx 8M long, East channel and Middle channel. Anchorage off Lees Scar in about 4m, exposed to SW winds; outer harbour dries; or berth in the new wet dock, but this is principally commercial. Beware constantly changing channels and sandbanks. East Cote Dir Lt 052° FG 15m 12M; vis 046°−058°, intens 052°. Lees Scar, S of entrance, QG 11m 8M; vis 005°−317°. Groyne head 2 FG (vert). Entry signals on mast at New Dock − no entry unless Y signal arm raised by day or Q Bu Lt by night. VHF Ch 16; 12 (HW−2½ to HW+1½). Facilities: EC Tues; Hr Mr ☎ 31358; FW on quays, all stores available, Ⓑ, Bar, ✉, R, V.

HARRINGTON, Cumbria, 54°37′N, 3°34′W, Zone 0 (GMT), Admty chart 1346. HW +0025 on Dover, +0015 on Liverpool; HW height −1.1m on Liverpool; ML 4.6m; Duration 0540. Good shelter in small harbour only used now by local fishermen and yachts. Entrance by stone pier. Inner harbour dries. Contact Cockermouth 823761 Ext. 148 for moorings. Very limited facilities.

WHITEHAVEN, Cumbria, 54°33′N, 3°36′W, Zone 0 (GMT), Admty chart 1346. HW +0015 on Dover, +0010 on Liverpool; HW height −1.2m on Liverpool; ML 4.5m; Duration 0550. See 10.10.8. All harbour dries except Queens Dock, but outer harbour has over 5m at MHWS. Very good shelter and entrance safe in most conditions. Access HW∓2½. W pier head Fl G 5s 16m 13M. N pier head 2 FR (vert) 8m 9M. N Wall Quay 2 FR (vert) 8m 2M. Old Quay head 2 FG (vert) 8m 2M. VHF Ch 16; 12 (HW−2½ to HW+1½). Facilities: EC Wed; berthing see Hr Mr. ☎ 692435, FW, D, Slip, C (7½ ton), P (on Fish Quay), Bar, Ⓑ, CH, ✉, R, V.

RAVENGLASS, Cumbria, 54°21′N, 3°25′W, Zone 0 (GMT), Admty chart 1346. HW +0020 on Dover, +0005 on Liverpool; HW height −1.0m on Liverpool; ML 4.6m; Duration 0545. Large harbour formed by estuaries of R Mite, R Irt and R Esk, which dries; there is approx 2.5m in entrance at HW−2. From N beware Drigg Rock and from S Selker Rks. Also beware gun testing range at Eskmeals (R flag when in use). There is a FG Lt (occas). Facilities: FW (in village), but no other facilities.

BARROW-IN-FURNESS, Cumbria, 54°06′N, 3°12′W, Zone 0 (GMT), Admty chart 3164. HW +0030 on Dover, +0015 on Liverpool; HW height −0.25m on Liverpool; ML 5.2m; Duration 0530. See 10.10.9. Good shelter. Harbour dries except for Walney Channel which must be kept clear. Landing places at Piel I and Roa I. Depths of under 2m may be encountered even on Ldg lines. Lights: Walney I Fl 15s 21m 23M (when within 3M of shore, obsc 122°−127°), RC. Ldg Lts leading in from Lightning Knoll By (RW Lfl 10s) at 041° front Q 6m 6M (B structure with W daymark), rear (640m from front) Iso 2s 12m 6M (R column with W face). VHF *Ramsden Dock* Ch 16; 12 (H24). Facilities: EC Thurs; all facilities available in Barrow; **Rawlinson** ☎ 832806, SM.

HEYSHAM, Lancashire, 54°02′N, 2°55′W, Zone 0 (GMT), Admty charts 1552, 2010. HW +0015 on Dover, +0001 on Liverpool; HW height +0.1m on Liverpool; ML 5.3m; Duration 0545. See 10.10.9. Good shelter but yachts not normally accepted without special reason. Beware ferries and 'rig' supply vessels. Ldg Lts 102°, front FBu 11m 2M, Y+B diamond on mast; rear (137m from front) FBu 14m 2M, Y+B diamond on mast. S pier head Oc G 7.5s 9m 6M. N pier head 2FR (vert) 11m, obsc from seaward. Entry sigs; R flag or R Lt = no entry; no signal = no departure; 2R flags or 2R Lts = no entry or departure. VHF Ch 16; 14 74 (H24). Facilities: EC Wed (Heysham and Morecambe); Bar, FW, R, V. All stores at Morecambe (2M).

RIVER RIBBLE, Lancashire, 53°45′N, 2°47′W, Zone 0 (GMT), Admty chart 1981. HW +0013 on Dover; Preston 0000, St Anne's −0004 on Liverpool; HW height Preston −3.9m, St Anne's −0.1m on Liverpool; ML Preston 2.4m, St Anne's 5.4m; Duration St Anne's 0520. Preston closed as a commercial port in 1981. Many navigational aids in R Ribble have been withdrawn and silting has

occurred. Entrance marked by Gut buoy, RW, lit. Training wall breached and channel now runs through S Gut (unmarked). Local knowledge needed. Contact **Ribble Cruising Club** ☎ Lytham 739983. Yachts berth nearby at Lytham, at Freckleton or near River Douglas entrance. Facilities: AB, C (7 ton), CH, D, FW, Sh, Slip. **Douglas Boatyard**, access HW∓2, ☎ Hesketh Bank 812462, ME, Sh, CH. Other facilities very limited except at Preston. Hr Mr (Preston) ☎ Preston 726711. **Preston Marina** ☎ 741031 (30), FW, Slip, Access HW−2 to HW+1 via lock.

RIVER ALT, Merseyside, 53°30′N, 3°04′W, Zone 0 (GMT), Admty chart 1951. HW −0008 on Dover, −0021 on Liverpool, see 10.10.11. Good shelter but only available to small craft. Access HW∓1½ for draught of 1.2m. Channel shifts frequently. Entrance channel marked by can buoy N side of groyne between Crosby and Hall Road beach marks. Channel from there marked by perches arranged by Blundellsands SC. Anchor between perches marking channel; local knowledge advised. Facilities very limited. **Blundellsands SC** at Hightown ☎ Liverpool 929 2101 (occas).

CASTLETOWN, Isle of Man, 54°04′N, 4°39′W, Zone 0 (GMT), Admty chart 2696. HW +0025 on Dover, +0010 on Liverpool; HW height −2.9m on Liverpool; ML 3.4m; Duration 0555. All 4 harbours dry. Secure in Inner Hr below fixed bridge or in Irish Hr below swing bridge. Anchorage between Lheeah−rio Rks and pier in 3m; at Langness Pt; in Derby Haven (drying). The bay gives good shelter except in SW to SE winds. Beware Lheeah-rio Rocks in W of bay, marked by R can buoy Fl R 3s, Bell. Beware race off Langness Pt, which should be given a good berth. Lt to E of Langness Pt, on Dreswick Pt Fl(2) 30s 23m 21M. N side of entrance Oc G 4s 3m (W metal post on concrete column). S side of entrance, Irish Quay, Oc R 4s 5m 5M vis 142°−322°. 150m NW is swing bridge marked by 2 FR (hor). To SE, New Pier head Oc R 15s 8m 5M. VHF Ch 16; 12 (when vessel expected). Facilities: EC Thurs; Hr Mr ☎ 823549; Dr 823597 **Outer Hr** Slip, L, C (20 ton) AB; **Irish Quay** AB, C, FW; **Inner Hr** AB, C, FW; **Moon's Garage** ☎ 823211 P, D, Gas; **Ballasalla Marine and Auto Eng** ☎ 822715, ME; **J. J. Clague** ☎ 822525, Gas.

LAXEY, Isle of Man, 54°13′N, 4°23′W, Zone 0 (GMT), Admty chart 2094. HW +0025 on Dover, +0010 on Liverpool; HW height −2.0m on Liverpool; ML 4.0m; Duration 0550. The bay gives good shelter in N to SW winds through W. The harbour is only suitable for small yachts; it dries and has approx 2m at MHWN. Access HW∓3. Beware rocks on N side of the narrow entrance. Keep close to pier after entering to avoid training wall to N. Pier head Lt Oc R 3s 7m 5M, obsc when bearing less than 318°. Breakwater head Lt Oc G 3s 7m. Facilities are few other than FW, R, ✉, Ⓑ, Bar.

PORT ERIN, Isle of Man, 54°05′N, 4°46′W, Zone 0 (GMT), Admty charts 2696, 2094. HW −0020 on Dover, +0005 on Liverpool; HW height −3.7m on Liverpool; ML 2.9m; Duration 0555. See 10.10.13. The bay has good anchorage in 3m to 8m, and protection from winds except those from SW to NW. There is a small drying harbour on the S side which has 3.6m at MHWN. Beware the ruined breakwater running N from the SW corner, the end being marked with B con buoy. Ldg Lts 099°, front FR 10m 5M, rear FR 19m 5M, lead into middle of the bay. Raglan Pier (E arm of harbour) Oc G 5s 8m 5M. Facilities: EC Thurs; Bar, D, FW, P, R, Slip, V. Two visitors buoys W of Raglan Pier − Call Hr Mr Port St. Mary (VHF).

PORTH DINLLAEN, Gwynedd, 52°57′N, 4°34′W, Zone 0 (GMT), Admty charts 1512, 1971. HW −0240 on Dover, −0120 on Holyhead; HW height −1.0m on Holyhead; ML 2.5m; Duration 0535. Shelter good in S to W winds but strong NNW to NNE winds cause heavy seas in the bay. Beware Carreg-y-Chad (1.8m) 0.75M SW of the point, and Carreg-y-Chwislen (dries, with Bn unlit) 2 ca ENE of the point. Best anchorage 0.1M S of LB house in approx 2m. Facilities: EC Wed; Hr Mr ☎ Nefyn 720295; CG ☎ Nefyn 720204, Bar, V by landing stage; Other facilities are at Morfa Nefyn (IM), Bar, P. R. V.

VOLVO PENTA SERVICE

Sales and service centres in area 11

AVON **Bristol Marine Engineering** Hanover Place, Albion Dockside Estate, BRISTOL BS1 1UT Tel (0272) 262923. WORCESTERSHIRE **Upton Marina** Upton-on-Severn, WORCESTER WR8 0PB Tel (06846) 4540. DYFED **Burry Port Yacht Services** The Harbour, BURRY PORT SA16 0ER Tel (05546) 2740. **Dale Sailing Co Ltd** DALE SA62 3RB Tel (06465) 349. GLAMORGAN **Swansea Marine Engineering Co** Swansea Yacht Haven, SWANSEA SA1 1WN Tel (0792) 51600. GWYNEDD **Arfon Oceaneering** Victoria Dock Slipway, Balaclava Road, CAERNARFON LL55 1TG Tel (0286) 76055 **Hookes Marine** Sarn Bach Road, ABERSOCH LL53 7ER Tel (075 881) 2458. PEMBROKESHIRE **Dale Sailing Co Ltd** Brunel Quay, Neyland, MILFORD HAVEN SA73 1PY Tel (0646) 601636.

VOLVO PENTA

Area 11

South Wales and Bristol Channel
Porthmadog to St Ives

11

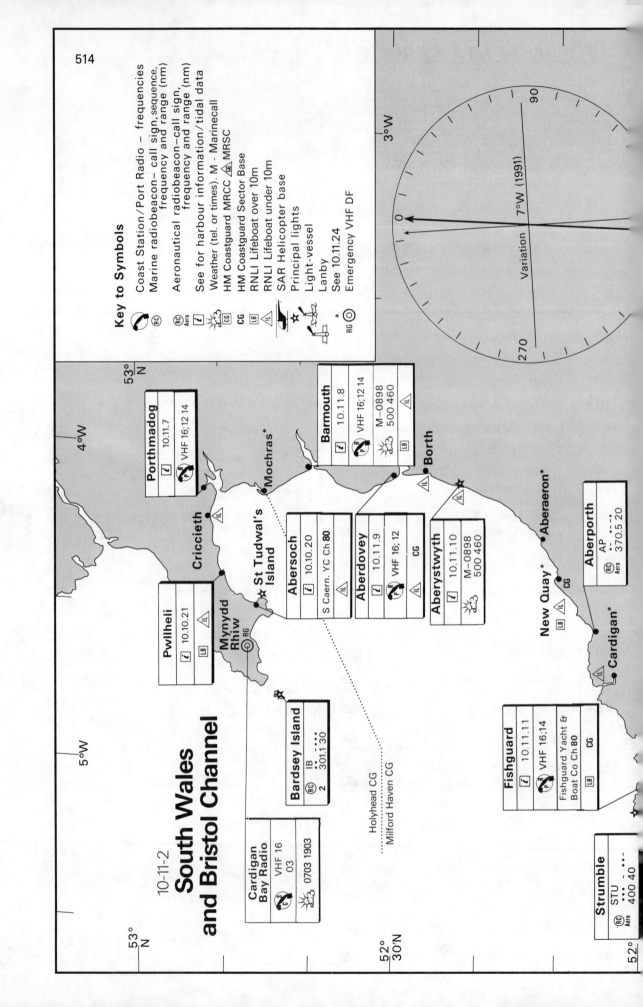

514

10.11.2
South Wales
and Bristol Channel

Key to Symbols

Coast Station/Port Radio – frequencies
Marine radiobeacon– call sign, sequence, frequency and range (nm)
Aeronautical radiobeacon–call sign, frequency and range (nm)
See for harbour information/tidal data
Weather (tel. or times). M - Marinecall
HM Coastguard MRCC / MRSC
HM Coastguard Sector Base
RNLI Lifeboat over 10m
RNLI Lifeboat under 10m
SAR Helicopter base
Principal lights
Light-vessel
Lanby
See 10.11.24
Emergency VHF DF

Variation 7°W (1991)

Cardigan Bay Radio
VHF 16
03
0703 1903

Bardsey Island
IB ·· – ···
2 301.1 30

Holyhead CG
Milford Haven CG

Strumble
STU ··· – ··· –
400 40

Pwllheli
10.10.21

Fishguard
10.11.11
VHF 16;14
Fishguard Yacht & Boat Co Ch 80

Mynydd Rhiw RG

St Tudwal's Island

Criccieth

Abersoch
10.10.20
S Caern. YC Ch 80

Aberdovey
10.11.9
VHF 16; 12
CG

Aberystwyth
10.11.10
M–0898 500 460

New Quay* CG

Aberporth
AP · – · · – –
370.5 20

Aberaeron*

Cardigan*

Porthmadog
10.11.7
VHF 16;12 14

Mochras*

Barmouth
10.11.8
VHF 16;12 14
M–0898 500 460

Borth

10.11.3 AREA 11 TIDAL STREAMS

5 Hours before HW Dover (HW Milford Haven)

4 Hours before HW Dover (0100 after HW Milford Haven)

3 Hours before HW Dover (0200 after HW Milford Haven)

2 Hours before HW Dover (0300 after HW Milford Haven)

1 Hour before HW Dover (0400 after HW Milford Haven)

HW Dover (0500 after HW Milford Haven)

Southward 10.1.3   Northward 10.10.3   South Ireland 10.12.3

1 Hour after HW Dover (0600 after HW Milford Haven)

2 Hours after HW Dover (0525 before HW Milford Haven)

3 Hours after HW Dover (0425 before HW Milford Haven)

4 Hours after HW Dover (0325 before HW Milford Haven)

5 Hours after HW Dover (0225 before HW Milford Haven)

6 Hours after HW Dover (0125 before HW Milford Haven)

10.11.4   LIGHTS, FOG SIGNALS AND WAYPOINTS

Abbreviations used below are given in 10.0.3. Principal lights are in **bold** print, places in CAPITALS, and light-vessels, light floats and Lanbys in *CAPITAL ITALICS*. Unless otherwise stated lights are white.   m—elevation in metres; M—nominal range in   n. miles. Fog signals are in *italics*. Useful waypoints are underlined - use those on land with care. See 4.2.2.

WALES—WEST COAST (see also 10.10.4)

Porthmadog Fairway Lt Buoy 52°53'·58N 04°11'·55W LFl 10s; safe water mark.
Shell Island 52°49'·54N 04°07'·64W Fl WRG 4s; vis G079°-124°, W124°-134°, R134°-179°.

BARMOUTH.
Barmouth Outer Lt Buoy 52°42'·60N 04°04'·76W LFl 10s; safe water mark.
North Bank Y perch 52°42'·81N 04°03'·67W QR 4m 2M.
Ynys y Brawd, SE end 52°42'·97N 04°03'·07W Fl R 5s. Bridge, NW end 2 FR (hor).

Sarn Badrig Causeway Lt Buoy 52°41'·17N 04°25'·30W Q(9) 15s; W cardinal mark; *Bell*.
Sarn-y-Bwch. Bwch Buoy 52°34'·80N 04°13'·50W (unlit); W cardinal mark.

ABERDOVEY.
Aberdovey Outer Buoy 52°31'·75N 04°06'·20W (unlit); safe water mark.
Cynfelyn Patches. Patches Buoy 52°25'·80N 04°16'·30W (unlit); W cardinal mark.

ABERYSTWYTH.
S breakwater head 52°24'·39N 04°05'·46W Fl(2) WG 10s 12m 10M; B column; vis G030°-053°, W053°-210°. 4FR(vert) on radio tower 2·8M S.
Ldg Lts 138°. Front FR 4m 5M. Rear 52m from front FR 7m 6M.

ABERAERON.
S pier 52°14'·60N 04°15'·87W Fl(3) G 10s 6M; vis 125°-200°.
N pier Fl(4) R 15s 6M; vis 104°-178°.

Carreg Ina Buoy 52°13'·09N 04°20'·47W (unlit); N cardinal mark.
New Quay Pier head 52°12'·94N 04°21'·27W Fl WG 3s 12m W8M, G5M; vis W135°-252°, G252°-295°.

CARDIGAN
Bridge, Iso Y 2s on upstream and downstream sides.

FISHGUARD.
Northern breakwater head 52°00'·74N 04°58'·15W Fl G 4·5s 18m 13M; 8-sided Tr; *Bell (1) 8s* .
East breakwater, head Fl R 3s 10m 5M.
Lts in line 282°. Front 52°00'·7N 04°59'·2W FG 77m 5M; W diamond on W mast. Rear 46m from front FG 89m 5M; W diamond on W mast.
Penanglas, 152m S of point *Dia (2) 60s*; W obelisk.

Strumble Head 52°01'·8N 05°04'·3W Fl(4) 15s 45m **29M**; W round Tr; vis 038°-257°; (H24).
South Bishop 51°51'·15N 05°24'·65W Fl 5s 44m **24M**; W round Tr; (H24); RC; *Horn (3) 45s*.
St Brides Bay. Research Area, seaward Lt Buoys.

Lt Buoy A1 51°49'·30N 05°20'·00W Fl(4)Y 20s; special mark.
Lt Buoy B1 51°48'·30N 05°20'·00W Fl(4)Y 20s; special mark.

The Smalls 51°43'·25N 05°40'·15W Fl(3) 15s 36m **25M**; W round Tr, R bands; Racon. FR 33m 13M; same Tr; vis 253°-285° over Hats and Barrels rock; both Lts shown H24; *Horn (2) 60s*.

Skokholm Island, SW end 51°41'·60N 05°17'·17W Fl R 10s 54m **17M**; W 8-sided Tr; part obsc 226°-258°; (H24); *Horn 15s*.

WALES—SOUTH COAST

St Ann's Head 51°40'·85N 05°10'·35W Fl WR 5s 48m **W23M.R22/19M**; W 8-sided Tr; vis W233°-247°, R247°-285°, R (intens) 285°-314°, W314°-332°, W332°-124°, W129°-131°; *Horn (2) 60s*.
St Anne's Head Lt Buoy 51°40'·23N 05°10'·43W Fl R 2·5s; port-hand mark.
Mid Channel Rocks Lt Buoy 51°40'·16N 05°10'·07W Q(9) 15s; S cardinal mark.
Middle Channel Rocks Lt 51°40'·29N 05°09'·77W Fl(3) G 7s 18m 8M; B round Tr, aluminium lantern.
Sheep Lt Buoy 51°40'·03N 05°08'·23W QG; stbd-hand mark.
Millbay Lt Buoy 51°41'·02N 05°09'·38W Fl(2) R 5s; port-hand mark.
West Chapel Lt Buoy 51°40'·97N 05°08'·60W Fl G 10s; stbd-hand mark.
East Chapel Lt Buoy 51°40'·85N 05°08'·08W Fl R 5s; port-hand mark.
Rat Lt Buoy 51°40'·77N 05°07'·80W Fl G 5s; stbd-hand mark.
Angle Lt Buoy 51°41'·60N 05°08'·20W VQ; S cardinal mark.
Thorn Rock Lt Buoy 51°41'·50N 05°07'·70W Q(9) 15s; W cardinal mark.
Dakotian Lt Buoy 51°42'·13N 05°08'·22W Q(3) 10s; E cardinal mark.
Chapel Lt Buoy 51°41'·63N 05°06'·80W Fl G 5s; stbd-hand mark.
Stack Lt Buoy 51°42'·00N 05°06'·46W Fl R 2·5s; port-hand mark.
South Hook Lt Buoy 51°40'·80N 05°06'·03W Q(6) +L Fl 15s; S cardinal mark.
Esso Lt Buoy 51°41'·72N 05°05'·17W Q Fl; N cardinal mark.
East Angle Lt Buoy 51°41'·68N 05°04'·20W Fl(3) G 10s; stbd-hand mark.

MILFORD HAVEN.
West Blockhouse Point F 54m 13M; W stripe on B ground, on W Tr; vis 004·5°-040·5°; Q WR 21m W9M, R7M; vis W220°-250°, R250°-020°, W020°-036°, R036°-049°.
Watwick Point F 80m **15M**; vis 013·5°-031·5°. Dale Fort Fl(2) WR 5s 20m W5M, R3M; vis R222°-276°, W276°-019°.
Great Castle Head F WRG 27m W5M, R3M, G3M; W square Tr, B stripe; vis R243°-281°, G281°-299°, W299°-029°; Oc 4s 27m **15M**; same Tr; vis 031°-048°.
Little Castle Head Oc 8s 53m **15M**; vis 031°-048°.
Pembroke Dock Ldg Lts 153°. Front QG 5m; W diamond, B stripe. Rear, 82m from front, QG 9m; W diamond, B stripe.
Turbot Bank Lt Buoy 51°37'·40N 05°10'·00W VQ(9) 10s; W cardinal mark.

WALES—SOUTH COAST—BRISTOL CHANNEL

SAINT GOWAN LT V 51°30'·50N 04°59'·80W Fl 20s 12m
26M; R hull with Lt Tr amidships; *Horn (3) 60s*; Racon.

Caldey Island 51°37'·86N 04°41'·00W Fl(3) WR 20s 65m
W14M, R12M; W round Tr; vis R173°-212°, W212°-088°,
R088°- 102°.

Eel Point Buoy 51°38'·83N 04°42'·17W (unlit); stbd-hand
mark.

Giltar Spit Buoy 51°39'·00N 04°42'·05W (unlit); port-hand
mark.

Spaniel Buoy 51°38'·03N 04°39'·67W (unlit); E cardinal mark.

Woolhouse Buoy 51°39'·32N 04°39'·62W (unlit); S cardinal
mark.

North Highcliff Buoy 51°39'·35N 04°40'·70W (unlit); N cardinal mark.

TENBY.

Pier, head 51°40'·37N 04°41'·81W FR 7m 7M.

Saundersfoot Pier 51°42'·55N 04°41'·68W Fl R 5s 6m 7M.

CARMARTHEN BAY.

DZ1 Buoy 51°42'·05N 04°35'·90W (unlit); special mark.

DZ2 Lt Buoy 51°39'·95N 04°37'·62W Fl Y 2·5s; special mark.

DZ3 Buoy 51°37'·35N 04°37'·70W (unlit); special mark.

DZ7 Lt Buoy 51°38'·08N 04°30'·05W Fl Y 10s; special mark.

DZ4 Lt Buoy 51°35'·70N 04°29'·95W Fl Y 5s; special mark.

DZ8 Buoy 51°41'·50N 04°24'·30W (unlit); special mark.

DZ6 Buoy 51°38'·00N 04°24'·30W (unlit); special mark.

DZ5 Lt Buoy 51°36'·35N 04°24'·30W Fl Y 2·5s; special mark.

Burry Port 51°40'·5N 04°14'·9W Barrel Post QR (occas).
West breakwater FR.

Whiteford Lt Ho Fl 5s (occas).

West Helwick (W.HWK) Lt Buoy 51°31'·37N 04°23'·58W
Q(9) 15s; W cardinal mark; *Whis*; Racon.

East Helwick Lt Buoy 51°31'·77N 04°12'·60W VQ(3) 5s; E
cardinal mark; *Bell*.

SWANSEA BAY.

Ledge Lt Buoy 51°29'·90N 03°58'·70W VQ(6)LFl 10s; S
cardinal mark.

Mixon Buoy 51°33'·10N 03°58.70W (unlit); port-hand mark;
Bell.

Grounds Lt Buoy 51°32'·'90N 03°53'·40W VQ(3) 5s; E
cardinal mark.

Mumbles 51°34'·00N 03°58'·20W Fl(4) 10s 35m **17M**; W 8-
sided Tr, Fog Det Lt; vis 331°-336°; *Horn(3) 60s*.

Railway Pier, head 2FR(vert).

SW Inner Green Grounds Lt Buoy 51°34'·04N 03°56'·95W
Q(6)LFl 15s; S cardinal mark; *Bell*.

SWANSEA.

Outer Fairway Lt Buoy 51°35'·50N 03°56'·06W QG; stbd-
hand mark; *Bell*.

West pier head Fl(2)R 10s 11m 9M; FR Lts on radio mast
1·3M NNE.

East breakwater head 51°36'·35N 03°55'·55W 2 FG (vert)
10m 6M; W framework Tr; *Horn 30s*.

Lts in line 020°. Front 2 FG (vert) 5m 2M. Rear 250m from
front FG 6M (mark E limit of dredged area, obsc bearing less
than 020°).

RIVER NEATH.

Approach Channel Lt Buoy 51°35'·70N 03°52'·75W Fl G 5s;
stbd-hand mark.

SE training wall, near S end 51°36'·30N 03°51'·89W 2FG(vert)
6m 5M.

Training wall, middle FG 6m 5M.

Training wall, N end 3 FG (vert) 6m 5M.

PORT TALBOT.

Cabenda Lt Buoy 51°33'·43N 03°52'·27W VQ(6)LFl 10s; S
cardinal mark.

Outer channel buoys: 51°33'·67N 03°51'·22W Fl G 5s; stbd-
hand mark.

Port Talbot, N Outer Lt Buoy 51°33'·76N 03°51'·30W Fl R
5s; port-hand mark.

Port Talbot, N Inner Lt Buoy 51°34'·19N 03°50'·17W Fl R 3s;
port-hand mark; *Horn*.

Ldg Lts 060° (occas). Front Oc R 4s 12m 6M. Rear Oc R 6s
32m 6M; both Y and Or diamonds on pylons.

N breakwater head Fl(4)R 10s 11m 3M; metal pylon.

S breakwater head 51°34'·43N 03°48'·95W Fl G 3s 11m 3M.

Sker Point. Kenfig Lt Buoy 51°29'·71N 03°46'·52W Q(3)
10s; E cardinal mark.

BRISTOL CHANNEL—EASTERN PART (NORTH SHORE)

W Scarweather (W.SCAR) Lt Buoy 51°28'·28N 03°55'·50W
Q(9) 15s; W cardinal mark; *Bell*; Racon.

S Scarweather (S.SCAR) Lt Buoy 51°27'·58N 03°51'·50W
Q(6)LFl 15s; S cardinal mark.

Hugo Buoy 51°28'·80N 03°48'·30W (unlit); port-hand mark.

E Scarweather Buoy 51°28'·12N 03°46'·23W (unlit); E cardinal mark.

PORTHCAWL

Fairy Buoy 51°27'·83N 03°42'·00W (unlit); W cardinal mark.

Tusker Lt Buoy 51°26'·97N 03°40'·55W Fl(2)R 5s; port-hand
mark.

Porthcawl breakwater, head 51°28'·33N 03°41'·95W F WRG
10m W6M, R4M, G4M; W 6-sided Tr, B base; vis G302°-036°,
W036°-082°, R082°-122°. In line with Saint Hilary radio mast
(Aero QR) 094° leads through Shord Channel.

West Nash Lt Buoy 51°25'·95N 03°45'·88W VQ(9) 10s; W
cardinal mark.

Middle Nash Buoy 51°25'·00N 03°40'·00W (unlit); S cardinal
mark.

East Nash Lt Buoy 51°24'·03N 03°34'·03W Q(3) 10s; E
cardinal mark.

Nash 51°24'·00N 03°33'·05W Fl(2) WR 10s 56m **W21M**,
R20/17M; W round Tr; vis R280°-290°, W290°-097°, R097°-
100°, R (intens) 100°-104°, R104°-120°, W120°-128°; *Siren
(2) 45s*; RC.

Saint Hilary 51°27'·4N 03°24'·1W Aero QR 346m 11M; radio
mast; 4 FR (vert) on same mast 6M.

Breaksea Point, intake 51°22'·5N 03°24'·5W Fl R 11m. FR Lt
on radio mast 3·4M ENE.

BREAKSEA LANBY 51°19'·85N 03°19'·00W Fl 15s 11m
16M; Racon; F riding Lt; *Horn (2) 36s*.

Wenvoe 51°27'·5N 03°16'·8W Aero Fl W 364m 12M; radio
mast.

Merkur Lt Buoy 51°21'·85N 03°15'·87W Fl R 2·5s; port-hand
mark.

Welsh Water Barry West Lt Buoy 51°22'·23N 03°16'·84W
Fl R 5s; port-hand mark.

BARRY.

West breakwater, head Fl2·5s 12m 10M; W round Tr.

E breakwater, head 51°23'·50N 03°15'·37W QG 7m 8M.

W One Fathom Lt Buoy 51°20'·40N 03°14'·50W Q(9) 15s;
W cardinal mark.

N One Fathom Lt Buoy 51°21'·10N 03°11'·75W Q; N cardinal
mark.

Mackenzie Lt Buoy 51°21'·72N 03°08'·15W QR; port-hand
mark.

Wolves Lt Buoy 51°2310N 03°08'·81W VQ; N cardinal mark.

11

Flat Holm, SE point 51°22'·52N 03°07'·05W Fl(3) WR 10s 50m **W16M**, R13M; W round Tr; vis R106°-140°, W140°-151°, R151°-203°, W203°-106°; (H24); *Horn 30s.*
Weston Lt Buoy 51°22'·80N 03°05'·20W Fl(2)R 5s; port-hand mark.
Monkstone Rock Lt 51°24'·86N 03°05'·93W Fl 5s 13m 13M; R column on round Tr.

CARDIFF/PENARTH ROADS.
Ranie Lt Buoy 51 24.22N° 3 09.30W Fl(2)R 5s; port-hand mark.
S Cardiff Lt Buoy 51°24'·15N 03°08'·48W Q(6)LFl 15s; S cardinal mark; *Bell* .
Mid Cardiff Lt Buoy 51°25'·57N 03°08'·00W Fl(3)G 10s; stbd-hand mark.
Cardiff Spit Buoy 51°25'·53N 03°06'·42W (unlit); port hand mark.
N Cardiff Lt Buoy 51°27'·77N 03°05'·28W QG; stbd-hand mark.

PENARTH.
Promenade Pier, near head 2 FR (vert) 8/6m 3M; *Reed Mo(BA) 60s,* sounded 10 min before a steamer is expected.
Club pontoon 51°26'·8N 03°10'·5W Q.

CARDIFF.
Outer Wrach Lt Buoy 51°26'·17N 03°09'·38W Q(9) 15s; W cardinal mark.
Ldg Lts 349°. **Front** 51°27'·7N 03°09'·9W F 4m **17M**. **Rear** 520m from front F 24m **17M**.
Queen Alexandra Dock entrance, S jetty head 2 FG (vert); *Dia 60s.*

Tail Patch Lt Buoy 51°23'·50N 03°03'·59W QG; stbd-hand mark.
Hope Lt Buoy 51°24'·82N 03°02'·60W Q(3) 10s; E cardinal mark.
NW Elbow Lt Buoy 51°26'·10N 02°59'·95W VQ(9) 10s; W cardinal mark; *Bell.*

ENGLISH AND WELSH GROUNDS Lt F 51°26'·90N 03°00'·10W L Fl 10s 11m 12M; R hull, W name on sides, Lt Tr; Racon; *Horn (2) 20s.*

NEWPORT DEEP. Newport Deep Lt Buoy 51°29'·33N 02°59'·03W Fl(3)G 10s; stbd-hand mark; *Bell.*

RIVER USK.
East Usk 51°32'·38N 02°57'·93W Fl(2) WRG 10s 11m **W15M**, R11M, G11M; W round Tr; vis W284°-290°, R290°-017°, W017°-037°, G037°-115°, W115°-120°. Also Oc WRG 10s 10m W11M, R9M, G9M; vis G018°-022°, W022°-024°, R024°-028°.
Alexandra Dock, South Lock, West pier head 2FR(vert) 9/7m 6M; *Horn 60s.*
E pier head 2 FG (vert) 9/7m 6M.
Julians Pill Ldg Lts 057°. Rear, 61m from front, FG 8m 4M. Front 51°33'·3N 02°57'·9W FG 5m 4M (common front).
Ldg Lts 149°. Rear, 137m from front FG 9m 4M.
Bellport Jetty 51°33'·6N 02°58'·0W 2 FG (vert).
Dallimores Wharf 51°33'·8N 02°58'·4W 2 FG (vert) 6m.
Transporter Bridge, West side 2 FR (vert); 2 FY (vert) shown on transporter car; E side 2 FG (vert).
Centres of George Street and Newport Bridges marked by FY Lts.

BRISTOL DEEP.
N Elbow Lt Buoy 51°27'·12N 02°57'·08W QG; stbd-hand mark; *Bell* .
S Mid Grounds Lt Buoy 51°27'·78N 02°57'·13W Fl(4)R 15s; port-hand mark.

E Mid Grounds Lt Buoy 51°27'·93N 02°54'·58W FlR 5s; port-hand mark.
Clevedon Lt Buoy 51°27'·33N 02°54'·18W VQ; N cardinal mark.
Welsh Hook Lt Buoy 51°28'·40N 02°52'·00W Fl(2)R 5s; port-hand mark; *Bell* .
Avon Lt Buoy 51°27'·77N 02°51'·65W FlG 2·5s; stbd-hand mark.
Clevedon Pier, detached head FlG 10s 7m 3M.
Walton Bay, Old signal station Fl 2·5s 35m 2M.

Black Nore Point 51°29'·05N 02°47'·95W Fl(2) 10s 11m **15M**; W round Tr; obsc by Sand point when brg less than 049°; vis 044°-243°.

Newcome Lt Buoy 51°29'·93N 02°46'·95W Fl(3)R 10s; port-hand mark.
Cockburn Lt Buoy 51°30'·43N 02°44'·00W Fl R 2·5s; port-hand mark.
Portishead Point 51°29'·64N 02°46'·34W Q(3) 10s 9m **16M**; B framework Tr, W base; vis 060°-262°; *Horn 20s.*

PORTISHEAD.
Pier head 51°29'·66N 02°45'·18W Iso G 2s 5m 3M; W column; *Horn 15s,* sounded from HW4 to HW3.
Lock, E side 2FR(vert) 7/5m 1M. Lock, West side 2 FG (vert) 7/5m 1M.
Portbury Wharf. Lts in line 192°. Front 51°29'·5N 02°44'·1W Oc G 5s 7m 10M; vis 171°-211°. Rear 100m from front Oc G 5s 12m 10M; vis 171°-211°.
Seabank. Lts in line 103°. Front 51°30'·0N 02°43'·7W Oc(2) 10s 13m 5M; vis 086°-119°. Rear, 150m from front Oc(2) 10s 16m 5M; vis 086°-119°.
Royal Portbury Dock 51°30'·1N 02°43'·6W Fl G 15s 5m 6M. Pier corner Fl G 2s 7m 7M; *Dia 30s,* sounded HW4 to HW3.
Knuckle 51°29'·92N 02°43'·60W Oc G 5s 6m 6M.

AVONMOUTH.
Royal Edward Dock, N Pier, head Fl 10s 15m 10M; round Tr; vis 060°-228°. Ldg Lts 184°. Front QG 5m 6M; vis 129°-219°. Rear 220m from front.
S pier head 51°30'·34N 02°43'·02W Oc RG 30s 9m 10M; round Tr; vis R294°-036°, G036°-194°; *Bell 10s.*
King Road Ldg Lts 072°. N pier head. Front 51°30'·5N 02°43'·0W Oc R 5s 5m 9M; W obelisk, R bands; vis 062°-082°. Rear, 546m from front, QR 15m 10M; B&W striped circle on framework Tr, Or bands; vis 066°-078°.
Royal Edward Lock, N side 2 FR (vert), S side 2 FG (vert).
Oil Jetty, head, 51°30'·6N 02°42'·8W 2 FG (vert) 2M. Gypsum effluent pipe Fl Y 3s 3m 2M.

RIVER AVON.
Ldg Lts 127°. Front 51°30'·05N 02°42'·47W FR 7m 3M; vis 010°-160°. Rear 142m from front FR 17m 3M; vis 048°-138°.
Monoliths 51°30'·2N 02°42'·7W FlR 5s 5m 3M; vis 317°-137°.
Saint George Ldg Lts 173°, both OcG 5s 1M, on Or columns, synchronised.
Nelson Point 51°29'·82N 02°42'·43W FlR 3s 9m 3M; W mast.
Broad Pill 51°29'·6N 02°41'·8W QY 11m 1M; W framework Tr.
Avonmouth Bridge, NE end LFl R 10s, SW end LFl G 10s, both 5m 3M showing up and downstream. From here to City Docks, Oc G Lts are shown on S bank, and R or Y Lts on N bank.
CUMBERLAND BASIN. Entrance, N side 2 FR (vert) 6m 1M; S side 2 FG (vert) 7m 1M; Plimsoll Bridge, centre Iso 5s 6m each side.

AVON BRIDGE. N side FR 6m 1M on bridge pier. Centre of span Iso 5s 6m 1M. S side FG 6m 1M on bridge pier.

ENGLAND—WEST COAST—RIVER SEVERN

Bedwin Lt Buoy 51°32'·33N 02°43'·15W Q(3) 10s; E cardinal mark.
THE SHOOTS.
Lower Shoots Bn 51°33'·62N 02°42'·05W (unlit); stbd-hand mark.
Upper Shoots Bn 51°34'·20N 02°41'·79W (unlit); W cardinal mark. Charston Rock 51°35'·32N 02°41'·60W Fl 5s 5m 9M; W round Tr, B stripe; vis 203°-049°.
Ldg Lts 013° Front F Bu 16m. Rear 320m from front F Bu 33m 10M. Chapel Rock 51°36'·40N 02°39'·13W Fl WRG 2·6s 6m W8M, G5M; B framework Tr, W lantern; vis W213°-284°, R284°-049°, W049°-051°, G051·5°-160°.
RIVER WYE, Wye Bridge, 2 F Bu (hor); centre of span.

SEVERN BRIDGE.
West Tr 3QR (hor) on upstream and downstream sides; Horn (3) 45s. Centre of span Q Bu, each side. E Tr 3QG (hor) on upstream and downstream sides. Obscured 040°-065°.
Aust 51°36'·1N 02°37'·9W 2 QG (vert) 11/5m 6M; power cable pylon.
Lyde Rock 51°36'·9N 02°38'·6W QR 5m 5M; B framework Tr, W lantern. Sedbury 2 FR (vert) 10m 3M.
Slime Road Ldg Lts 210°. Front F Bu 9m 5M; W hut. Rear, 91 m from front, F Bu 16m 5M; B framework Tr; W lantern.
Inward Rocks Ldg Lts 252°. Front F 6m 6M; B framework Tr. Rear, 183m from front, F 13m 2M; W hut and mast.
Sheperdine Ldg Lts 070°. Front F 7m 5M; B framework Tr, W lantern. Rear, 168m from front, F 13m 5M; B framework Tr, W lantern; Bell (26) 60s.
Narlwood Rocks Ldg Lts 225°. Front Fl 2s 5m 8M; Y Bn, B lantern. Rear, 198m from front Fl 2s 9m 8M; Y Bn, B lantern.
Conigre Ldg Lts 077°. Front F Vi 21m 8M. Rear, 213m from front F Vi 29m 8M.
Fishing House Ldg Lts 218°. Front F 5m 2M: W hut and post. Rear F 11m 2M; W hut and mast.
BERKELEY Power Station 3x2 FG (vert); Siren (2) 30s.
Bull Rock Iso 2s 6m 8M.
Lydney Docks, pier head FW or R (tidal); Gong (tidal).
Berkeley Pill Ldg Lts 188°. Front FG 5m 2M. Rear, 152m from front, FG 11m 2M; both B Trs, W lanterns.
Panthurst Pill F Bu 6m 1M; W post on concrete hut.

SHARPNESS Docks, S pier head 2 FG (vert) 6m 3M; Siren 20s. N Pier 2 FR (vert) 6m 3M.
Old entrance, S side, Siren 5s (tidal).

ENGLAND—BRISTOL CHANNEL (SOUTH SHORE)

WESTON-SUPER-MARE.
Pier head 51°20'·85N 02°59'·17W 2 FG (vert) 6/5m.
East Culver Lt Buoy 51°17'·70N 03°14'·50W Q(3) 10s; E cardinal mark.
West Culver Lt Buoy 51°16'·85N 03°19'·20W VQ(9) 10s; W cardinal mark. Gore Lt Buoy 51°13'·93N 03°09'·70W Iso 5s; safe water mark; Bell.

BURNHAM-ON-SEA. **Entrance**, 51°14'·90N 02°59'·85W Fl 7·5s 28m **17M**; W round Tr, R stripe; vis 074°-164°. **Dir Lt** 078·5°. Dir F WRG 24m **W16M**, R12M, G12M; same Tr; vis G073°-077°, W077°-079°, R079°-083°. Seafront Lts in line 112°, moved for changing channel, Front FR 6m 3M. Rear FR 12m 3M; church Tr. Brue 51°13'·5N 03°00'·2W QR 4m 3M; W mast, R bands. Stert Reach 51°11'·3N 03°01'·9W Fl 3s 4m 7M; vis 187°-217°.
Hinkley Point, water intake 51°12'·9N 03°07'·8W 2FG(vert) 7/5m 3M.

WATCHET. West breakwater head 51°11'·03N 03°19'·67W FG 9m 9M; R 6-sided Tr, W lantern, G cupola. FR Lts on radio masts 1·6M SSW. E pier 2FR(vert) 3M.

MINEHEAD, breakwater head Fl(2)G 5s 4M; vis 127°-262°. Sewer Outfall outer end 51°12'·95N 03°28'·22W QG 6m 7M; stbd-hand Bn.
Lynmouth Foreland 51°14'·70N 03°47'·13W Fl(4) 15s 67m **26M**; W round Tr; vis 083°-275° (H24).
LYNMOUTH. River training arm 2 FR (vert) 6m 5M. Harbour arm 2 FG (vert) 6m 5M.
Sand Ridge Buoy 51°14'·98N 03°49'·70W (unlit); stbd-hand mark. Copperas Rock Buoy 51°13'·77N 04°00'·50W (unlit); stbd- hand mark.

ILFRACOMBE. Lantern Hill 51°12'·64N 04°06'·70W FR 39m 6M; W lantern on chapel. Promenade Pier, N end 3x2 FG (vert) (occas).
Horseshoe Lt Buoy 51°15'·00N 04°12'·85W Q; N cardinal mark.
Bull Point 51°11'·95N 04°12'·05W Fl(3) 10s 54m **25M**; W round Tr. FR 48m 12M; same Tr; vis 058°-096°.
Morte Stone Buoy 51°11'·30N 04°14'·85W (unlit); stbd-hand mark. Baggy Leap Buoy 51°08'·90N 04°16'·90W (un-lit); stbd- hand mark.

BIDEFORD. Bideford Fairway Lt Buoy 51°05'·23N 04°16'·17W LFl 10s; safe water mark; Bell. Bideford Bar Buoy 51°04'·86N 04°14'·63W; stdb-hand mark. **Instow** Ldg Lts 118°. **Front** Oc 6s 22m . **Rear** 427m from front Oc 10s 38m **15M**. Both on W Trs and vis 103°-133°; (H24). Crow Point Fl R 5s 8m 4M; W framework Tr; vis 225°-045°.

LUNDY. **Near N point** 51°12'·07N 04°40'·57W Fl(2) 20s 50m **24M**; W round Tr; vis 009°-285°.
SE point 51°09'·70N 04°39'·30W Fl 5s 53m **24M**; W round Tr; vis 170°-073°; RC; Horn 25s.
Hartland Point 51°01'·3N 04°31'·4W Fl(6) 15s 37m **26M**; (H24); W round Tr; Horn 60s.
PADSTOW. Stepper Point 50°34'·11N 04°56'·63W L Fl 10s 12m 4M.
Trevose Head 50°32'·93N 05°02'·06W Fl R 5s 62m **25M**; W round Tr.

NEWQUAY. N pier head 2 FG (vert) 5m 2M. S pier head 2FR(vert) 4m 2M; round stone Tr.
The Stones Lt Buoy 50°15'·60N 05°25'·40W Q; N cardinal mark; Bell; Whis. Godrevy Island 50°14'·50N 05°23'·95W FlWR 10s 37m W12M, R9M; W 8-sided Tr; vis W022°-101°, R101°-145°, W145°-272°. 4 FR (vert) Lts on radio mast 6·5M SE.

HAYLE
Lts in line 180°. Front 50°11'·5N 05°26'·1W 17m 4M. Rear 110m from front. Both F (occas) on pile structures with R&W lanterns.
ST IVES. E pier head 2 FG (vert) 8m 5M; W pier head 2 FR (vert) 5m 3M.
Pendeen 50°09'·8N 05°40'·2W Fl(4) 15s 59m **27M**; W round Tr; vis 042°-240°; in bay between Gurnard head and Pendeen it shows to coast; Siren 20s.
For Lts further SW see 10.1.4.

11

10.11.5   PASSAGE INFORMATION

CARDIGAN BAY (charts 1971, 1972, 1973)

Harbs are mostly on a lee shore, and most have bars which make them dangerous to approach in bad weather. In N part of b there are three major dangers to coasting yachts, as are described briefly below. St Patrick's Causeway runs 11M SW from Mochras Pt. It is mostly large loose stones, and dries for much of its length. In strong winds the sea breaks heavily at all states of tide. The outer end is marked by a Lt buoy. At the inner end there is a chan about ½M offshore, which can be taken with care at half tide.

Sarn-y-Bwch runs 4M WSW from Pen Bwch Pt. It is composed of rocky boulders, drying in places 6 ca offshore and with depths of 0.3m extending nearly 3M seaward. There is a buoy off W end. Sarn Cynfelyn and Cynfelyn Patches extend a total of 6½M offshore, with depths of 1.5m in places, from a point about 2M N of Aberystwyth (10.11.10). There is a buoy off outer end. Not quite halfway along the bank is Main Chan, 3 ca wide, running roughly N and S, but not marked.

Firing exercises take place in the S part of Cardigan B (chart 1973). Beware targets and mooring buoys, some unlit.

THE BISHOPS AND THE SMALLS (chart 1478)

If bound N or S along St George's Chan (ie not proceeding to Cardigan B or Milford Haven) the easiest route is W of the Bishops and the Smalls, but note the traffic scheme (see Fig. 2(8)). This is the best route by night but, if bound to/from Milford Haven or S Wales harbours, it is possible to pass inside both the Smalls and Grassholm Island. Even shorter is the route inside the Bishops, passing close W of Ramsey Island, and outside Skomer Island and Skokholm Island. The shortest route of all involves the passage of Ramsey Sound and Jack Sound, but this is not recommended except by daylight, in good weather, and with the right tidal conditions − preferably at neaps. The main features (only) of these various chans are described below, but for full directions refer to the *West Coasts of England and Wales Pilot*, or to *Irish Sea Cruising Guide*.

The Bishops and the Clerks (chart 1482) are islets and rks 2½M W and NW of Ramsey Island, a bird sanctuary SSW of St David's Hd. N Bishop is the N islet of the group, but Bell Rk which has depth of 2.2m lies 3 ca ENE of N Bishop and between them is a ridge with heavy overfalls and tide rips. S Bishop (Lt, fog sig, RC) is the SW islet, with rks extending ½ ca NE and NW. Between S Bishop and Ramsey Island are several dangers, including Daufraich (islet 7 ca NE of S Bishop) with Maen Daufraich (dries) close N of it; Cribog (dries) and Moelyn (dries) respectively 2 and 3½ ca ENE of Daufraich; there are heavy overfalls SE of Moelyn. There is however a chan ¼M W of Ramsey Island, if care is taken to avoid dangers S and close W of Ramsey Island. This chan passes E of Llechau-uchaf (rk 1.5m high) and Llechau-isaf (dries) which are near N and S ends respectively of foul ground with heavy overfalls about 6½ ca W of Ramsey Island. Beware also Carreg Rhoson, with rks extending from it to NE and SW, roughly between N Bishop and S Bishop; Maen Rhoson (rk 9m high) 2 ca NW of Careg Rhoson; and Carreg-trai (dry) 1¾M NE of Carreg Rhoson. Note also Gwahan, a rk 1.5m high, about 4 ca N of Ramsey Island. 2M W of The Bishops the S-going stream begins at HW Milford Haven +0400, and the N-going at HW Milford Haven −0225, sp rates 2 kn. Between The Bishops and Ramsey Island the SW-going stream begins at HW Milford Haven +0330, and the NE-going at HW Milford Haven −0255, sp rates 5 kn.

Ramsey Sound (chart 1482) should be taken at slack water (see also above). The S-going stream begins at HW Milford Haven +0300, and the N-going at HW Milford Haven −0325, sp rates 6 kn at The Bitches where chan is narrowest (2 ca) and decreasing N and S. The Bitches are rks extending 2 ca E from middle of E side of Ramsey Island. Other dangers are Gwahan and Carreg-gafeiliog, respectively on W and E sides of N end of chan: Horse Rk (dries) and associated overfalls

about ½M NNE of The Bitches; Shoe Rk (dries) on E side of chan at S end; and rks extending ½M SSE from S end of Ramsey I.

St Brides B provides anch in settled weather or offshore winds, but is a trap in westerlies. Solva is a little harb with shelter for boat capable of taking ground, or anch E of Black Rk off the entrance. See 10.11.24.

If passing outside The Smalls (Lt, fog sig, Racon) beware SW Rk (dries) 3 ca SW of Lt Ho, the only danger W of it. Near The Smalls the S-going stream begins at HW Milford Haven +0515, and the N-going at HW Milford Haven −0045, sp rates 5 kn near the rks but decreasing to 3 kn when 2M S, W or N of them.

As mentioned above, there are various chans inside The Smalls (chart 1478). Hats and Barrels are shallow rky areas respectively about 1¾M and 4M E of The Smalls. They are usually marked by tide rips and overfalls, and by breaking seas in bad weather. The chan between The Smalls and Hats is over 1M wide, but beware E Rk 2½ ca E of Lt Ho. Chan between Hats and Barrels is 2M wide. There are no leading marks for either of these chans.

Grassholm is 7M E of The Smalls, and has no dangers extending more than ½ ca, although there is a race either end and strong tidal eddies so that it is advisable to pass about 1M off. The chan between Barrels and Grassholm is 2½M wide, and here the S-going stream begins at HW Milford Haven +0440, and the N-going at HW Milford Haven −0135, sp rates 5 kn. 5M of clear water lie between Grassholm and Skomer Island/Skokholm Island to the E. But Wildgoose Race, which forms W of Skomer and Skokholm is very dangerous, so it is necessary to keep 2M W of these two islands.

To E of Skomer Island is Midland Island, and between here and Wooltack Pt is Jack Sound (chart 1482) which is only 1 ca wide and should not be attempted without detailed pilotage directions, and only at slack water. Among the dangers which should be identified on the chart are: The Crab Stones, extending E from Midland Island; The Cable, a drying rk on E side of chan; Tusker Rk, steep-to on its W side, off Wooltack Pt; the Black Stones; and The Anvil and other rks off Anvil Pt. In Jack Sound the S-going stream begins at HW Milford Haven +0200, and the N-going at HW Milford Haven −0425, sp rates 6 kn.

BRISTOL CHANNEL (chart 1179, 1076, 1165, 1164)

Sailing E from Milford Haven, along N shore of Bristol Chan, there are few significant dangers to St Gowan's Hd. Crow Rk (dries) is 5½ ca SSE of Linney Hd, and The Toes are dangerous submerged rocks close W and SE of Crow Rk. There is a passage inshore off these dangers. There are overfalls on St Gowan Shoals which extend 4M SW of St Gowan's Hd, and the sea breaks on the shallow patches in bad weather.

Caldy Island (Lt) lies S of Tenby (10.11.13). Off its NW pt is St Margaret's Island connected by a rky reef. Caldy Sound is between St Margaret's Island and Giltar Pt (chart 1482). It is buoyed, but beware Eel Spit near W end of Caldy Island where there can be a nasty sea with wind against tide, and Woolhouse Rks (dry) 1¼ ca NE of Caldy Island.

Carmarthen B (10.11.24) has no offshore dangers for yachts, other than the charted sands at head of b and on its E side off Burry Inlet (10.11.14). There is a harb (dries) at Saundersfoot 2M N of Tenby, with anch off well sheltered from N and W but subject to swell. Streams are weak here. See 10.11.24.

Helwick Sands extend 7M W from Port Eynon Pt. Near their W end are depths of 1.8 m. Stream sets across the sands. There is a narrow chan inshore, close to Port Eynon Pt. Between here and Mumbles Hd the stream runs roughly along coast, sp rates 3 kn off pts, but there are eddies in Port Eynon B and Oxwich B, and overfalls off Oxwich Pt.

Off Mumbles Hd (Lt, fog sig) beware Mixon Shoal (dries), marked by buoy. In good conditions pass N of shoal, 1 ca off Mumbles Hd. Anch N of Mumbles Hd, good holding but exposed to swell. Green Grounds, rky shoals, cover W side of b in approach to Swansea (10.11.15).

Scarweather Sands, much of which dry and where sea breaks heavily, extend 7M W from Porthcawl (10.11.24) and are marked by buoys (chart 1161). There is a chan between the sands and coast to E, but beware Hugo Bank (dries) and rky patches with overfalls up to ¾M offshore between Sker Pt and Porthcawl.

Nash Sands extend 7½M WNW from Nash Pt. Depths vary and are least at inshore end (dries), but there is chan 1 ca wide between sand and rky ledge off Nash Pt. On E-going stream there are heavy overfalls off Nash Pt and at W end of Nash Sands. Between Nash Pt and Breaksea Pt the E-going stream begins at HW Avonmouth +0535, and the W-going at HW Avonmouth −0035, sp rates 3 kn. Off Breaksea Pt there may be overfalls.

From Rhoose Pt to Lavernock Pt the coast if fringed with foul ground. Lavernock Spit extends 1¾M from Lavernock Pt, and E of the spit is main chan to Cardiff (10.11.17), the other side of the chan being Cardiff Grounds − a drying bank which runs parallel with the shore and about 1½M from it. Further offshore is Monkstone Rk (dries), and E of this runs the buoyed chan to Avonmouth and Bristol (10.11.19) S of extensive drying banks along the N shore (chart 1176).

Near the centre of Bristol Chan, and close to main fairway are the Is of Flat Holm (Lt, fog sig) and Steep Holme. 7M SW of Flat Holm lies Culver Sand (dries), 4M in length, marked by buoys. Between Flat Holm and Steep Holme the E-going stream begins at HW Avonmouth −0610, sp rate 3 kn, and the W-going at HW Avonmouth +0015, sp rate 4 kn.

W from Burnham-on-Sea (10.11.20), the S shore of Bristol Chan has fewer obstructions than N shore. There is also less shelter since harbs such as Watchet, Minehead, Porlock Weir or Watermouth dry out. See 10.11.24. In bad weather dangerous overfalls occur NW and NE of Foreland Pt. 5M to W there is a race off Highveer Pt. Between Ilfracombe (10.11.21) and Bull Pt the E-going stream begins at HW Milford Haven +0540, and the W-going at HW Milford Haven −0025, sp rates 3 kn. Overfalls occur up to 1½M N of Bull Point and over Horseshoe Rks, which lie 3M N. There is a dangerous race off Morte Pt, 1½M to W of Bull Pt.

NORTH CORNWALL (charts 1149, 1156)

Approach to Bristol Chan along N coast of Cornwall is very exposed, with little shelter in bad weather. Padstow is a refuge, but in strong NW winds the sea breaks on bar and prevents entry. Shelter is available under lee of Lundy Island; but there are bad races to NE (White Horses), the NW (Hen and Chickens), and to SE; also overfalls over NW Bank. St Ives (dries) is sheltered from E and S, but exposed to N. So in this area yachts need to be sturdy and well equipped, since if bad weather develops no shelter may be at hand. Streams are moderate W of Lundy, but strong round the island. They get much stronger towards Bristol Chan proper.

Proceeding SW from Taw/Torridge (10.11.22), keep 3M off to avoid the race N of Hartland Pt (Lt, fog sig). There is shelter off Clovelly in winds S-SW. Bude Haven dries, and is not approachable in W winds; but it is accessible in calm weather or offshore winds. Near HW a chan leads to canal lock, marked by Ldg marks at 075° and 131°. See 10.11.24.

Boscastle is a tiny harb (dries) 3M NE of Tintagel Hd. Only approach in good weather or offshore winds: anch off or (if room) dry out alongside.

For dangers in Padstow approaches see 10.11.23. Off Trevose Hd (Lt) beware Quies Rks which extend 1M to W. From here S the coast is relatively clear to Godrevy Island, apart from Bawden Rks 1M N of St Agnes Hd. Newquay B (10.11.24) is good anch in offshore winds, and the harb (dries) is sheltered but uncomfortable in N winds. Off Godrevy Island (Lt) are the Stones, extending 1M from island and marked by buoy.

In St Ives B (chart 1168), Hayle (dries) is a commercial port: seas break heavily on bar in strong onshore winds. Stream is strong, so enter just before HW. The bottom is mostly sand. St Ives (dries) gives sheltered anch outside in winds from E to SW, but very exposed to N; there is sometimes room to dry out alongside. See 10.11.24.

From St Ives to Land's End coast is rugged and exposed. There are overfalls SW of Pendeen Pt (Lt, fog sig). Vyneck Rks lie awash about 3 ca NW of C Cornwall. The Brisons are two rocky islets ½M SW of C Cornwall, and rocky ledges extend inshore and to the S and SW. The Longships (Lt, fog sig) are a group of rks about 1M W of Land's End, with ledges 2 ca further seaward. The inshore passage is unwise.

For continuation south, see 10.1.5.

10.11.6 DISTANCE TABLE

Approximate distances in nautical miles are by the most direct route while avoiding dangers and allowing for traffic separation schemes etc. Places in *italics* are in adjoining areas.

		1	2	3	4	5	6	7	8	9	10	11	12	13	14	15	16	17	18	19	20
1	*Bardsey Island*	1																			
2	*Abersoch*	14	2																		
3	Aberdovey	31	26	3																	
4	Aberystwyth	33	30	10	4																
5	Fishguard	45	54	47	40	5															
6	South Bishop	60	70	67	61	25	6														
7	Milford Haven	83	93	90	84	48	23	7													
8	Tenby	106	116	113	107	71	46	28	8												
9	Swansea	129	139	136	130	94	69	55	36	9											
10	Barry	151	161	158	152	116	91	77	57	37	10										
11	Newport	168	178	175	169	133	108	94	75	54	17	11									
12	Sharpness	191	201	198	192	156	131	117	106	75	39	32	12								
13	Avonmouth	174	184	181	175	139	114	100	89	58	22	15	17	13							
14	Burnham-on-Sea	168	178	175	169	133	108	94	70	48	18	28	50	33	14						
15	Minehead	148	158	155	149	113	88	76	55	32	14	29	51	34	20	15					
16	Ilfracombe	127	137	134	128	92	67	53	35	25	35	51	74	57	45	25	16				
17	Lundy Island	110	120	117	111	75	50	38	30	37	54	71	95	78	66	46	22	17			
18	*Longships*	168	178	175	169	133	108	105	110	120	130	146	169	152	140	121	95	82	18		
19	*Tuskar Rock*	63	75	84	80	48	36	59	82	105	127	144	167	150	144	124	103	85	130	19	
20	*Dun Laoghaire*	61	75	92	94	94	90	113	136	159	181	198	221	204	198	178	157	140	199	70	20

PORTHMADOG   10-11-7
Gwynedd

CHARTS
Admiralty 1971, 1512; Imray C61; OS 124
TIDES
−0232 Dover; ML 2.8; Duration 0455; Zone 0 (GMT).
Standard Port MILFORD HAVEN (→)

Times				Height (metres)			
HW		LW		MHWS	MHWN	MLWN	MLWS
0100	0800	0100	0700	7.0	5.2	2.5	0.7
1300	2000	1300	1900				

Differences PORTHMADOG
+0235 +0210   No data   −1.9   −1.8   No data
Differences on Liverpool −0245

SHELTER
Inner Harbour — Good all year round. Outer Harbour — Summer only and exposed to S winds.
NAVIGATION
Waypoint Fairway (safe water) buoy, LFI 10s, 52°53′.58N 04°11′.55W (channel shifts). Depth at Bar MLWS is only 0.8m. When wind is in SW, waves are steep sided and close, especially on the ebb tide. Bar changes frequently. Up to date situation is supplied by Hr Mr upon request. Advise entering HW∓1½.
LIGHTS AND MARKS
Fairway buoy RW L Fl 10s. Remainder of channel markers (16) have reflective top marks, G to stbd, R to port.
RADIO TELEPHONE
Madoc YC: VHF Ch 16 80. Hr Mr Ch 16; 12 (0900-1700 LT).
TELEPHONE (0766)
Hr Mr 512927; CG Nefyn 720204; MRSC Holyhead 2051; Pilot 75684; Harbour Authority Dwyfor District Council, (0758) 613131; ⌗ (0407) 2714; Marinecall 0898 500 460; Police 512226; Dr 512239.
FACILITIES
EC Wednesday; **Harbour** (265) ☎ 512927, D, FW, C, Slip; **Pen-y-Cei** Slip, V, R, Bar; **Madoc YC** ☎ 512976, M, L, FW, AB, Bar; **Glaslyn Marine Supplies** ☎ 513545, CH, ACA; **Robert Owen** ☎ 513435, D, ME; **D. Hardie** ☎ 512776, Sh; **Kyffin BY** El, C (3½ ton), CH, AB; **Madog BY** ☎ 514205, AB; **Porthmadog & Transfynydd SC** ☎ 513546, Slip, AB, M, FW; **Harbour Filling Station** P (45 gall drums). **Town** ⌧; Ⓑ; ≷; ✈ (Chester).

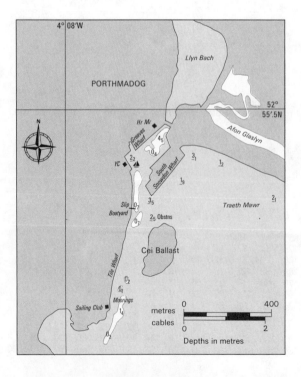

BARMOUTH   10-11-8
Gwynedd

CHARTS
Admiralty 1484, 1971; Imray C61; OS 124
TIDES
−0250 Dover; ML 2.8; Duration 0515; Zone 0 (GMT).
Standard Port MILFORD HAVEN (→)

Times				Height (metres)			
HW		LW		MHWS	MHWN	MLWN	MLWS
0100	0800	0100	0700	7.0	5.2	2.5	0.7
1300	2000	1300	1900				

Differences BARMOUTH
+0215 +0205 +0310 +0320 −2.0 −1.7 −0.7   0.0

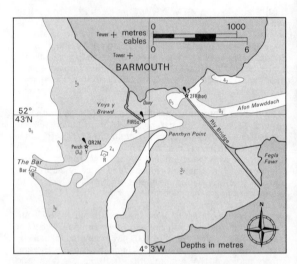

Depths in metres

SHELTER
Good shelter. Entry HW∓2½ safe except in strong on-shore winds; entry impossible with strong SW winds. The river (Afon Mawddach) and estuary are tidal and river is navigable for about 7 miles above railway bridge. It is not buoyed and sandbanks move constantly. Local knowledge is essential. Clearance under railway bridge approx 5.5m. Exposed anchorage W of Barmouth Outer buoy in 6 to 10m. In harbour secure to mooring as directed by Hr Mr on account of submarine cables and strong tidal streams. A quay, which dries at half-tide, fronts the town.
NAVIGATION
Waypoint, Barmouth Outer (safe water) buoy, L Fl 10s, 52°42′.60N 04°04′.75W, 253°/073° from/to Y perch Lt, QR, 0.7M. Approach from SW between St Patrick's Causeway (Sarn Badrig) and Sarn-y-Bwch (see 10.11.5). Barmouth can be identified by Cader Idris, a mountain 890m high, 5M ESE. Fegla Fawr, a rounded hill, lies on S side of harbour. Bar lies 0.75M W of Penrhyn Pt, min depth 0.3m but subject to considerable change. Channel marked by two port-hand buoys, moved as necessary. Tidal stream runs 3 to 5 kn on ebb at springs.
LIGHTS AND MARKS
Y perch, QR 4m 2M marks S end of stony ledge extending 3 ca SW from Ynys y Brawd across North Bank. Ynys y Brawd groyne, SE end, marked by Bn with Lt, Fl R 5s. NW end of Rly bridge 2 FR(hor).
RADIO TELEPHONE
Call *Barmouth Harbour* VHF Ch 12, 16; 12 (Apl-Sept 0900-2200 LT; Oct-Mar 0900-1600 LT).
TELEPHONE (0341)
Hr Mr 280671; CG 280176; ⌗ (0407) 2336; Marinecall 0898 500 460; Police 280222; Dr 280521.
FACILITIES
EC Wednesday; There are some visitors' moorings; **Quay** D, FW, El, AC, Slip; **J. Stockford** ☎ 280742, Slip, M, D, L; **Seafarer Chandlery** ☎ 280978, CH, ACA; **Barmouth YC** ☎ 280000; **Marine Stores** ☎ 280742, Slip, M; **Merioneth YC** ☎ 280000; **Town** P, D, V, R, Bar; ⌧; Ⓑ; ≷; ✈ (Chester); Ferry across to Penrhyn Pt.

ABERDOVEY   10-11-9
Gwynedd

CHARTS
Admiralty 1484, 1972; Imray C61; OS 135
TIDES
−0320 Dover; ML 2.6; Duration 0535; Zone 0 (GMT).
Standard Port MILFORD HAVEN (→)

Times				Height (metres)			
HW		LW		MHWS	MHWN	MLWN	MLWS
0100	0800	0100	0700	7.0	5.2	2.5	0.7
1300	2000	1300	1900				

Differences ABERDOVEY

+0215	+0200	+0230	+0305	−2.0	−1.7	−0.5	0.0

SHELTER
Good except in strong W to SW winds. Berth alongside jetty.
NAVIGATION
Waypoint Aberdovey Outer (safe water) buoy, 52°31'.75N 04°06'.22W, 250°/070° from/to jetty, 2.3M (channel shifts). Bar is hazardous below ½ tide and is constantly changing position. Visitors are advised to contact Hr Mr before entering, or telephone the Pilot. There are no lights. Submarine cables (prohibited anchorages) marked by beacons with R diamond top marks. There is heavy silting E of jetty.
LIGHTS AND MARKS
No lights or marks. Buoys in the channel are all G conical and are left to stbd — Bar, S Spit and Inner, leading to jetty.
RADIO TELEPHONE
Call *Aberdovey Harbour* VHF Ch 12; 16.
TELEPHONE (065 472)
Hr Mr 626; CG 327; MRSC Dale 218; Pilot 247; ⌗ (0407) 2714 Ext 262; Marinecall 0898 500 460; Police 222; Dr Tywyn 710414; Ⓗ Tywyn 710411.
FACILITIES
EC Wednesday (winter only); **Jetty** L, FW, AB; **Wharf** Slip, L, FW, C, AB; **West Wales Marina BY** ☎ 478, ME, El, Sh, CH; **Frongoch BY** ☎ 644, Slip (Patent 10 ton), ME, El, Sh, CH; **Dovey YC** ☎ (0827) 286514, Bar, Slip, L, FW; **Dovey Marine** ☎ 581, CH, ACA; **Bruce Morris** ☎ Tywyn 711541, Ⓔ. **Town** P and D (in cans), ME, El, CH, V, R, Bar. ✉; Ⓑ; ⇌; ✈ (Chester).

ABERYSTWYTH   10-11-10
Dyfed

CHARTS
Admiralty 1484, 1972; Imray C61; OS 135
TIDES
−0330 Dover; ML 2.7; Duration 0540; Zone 0 (GMT)
Standard Port MILFORD HAVEN (→)

Times				Height (metres)			
HW		LW		MHWS	MHWN	MLWN	MLWS
0100	0800	0100	0700	7.0	5.2	2.5	0.7
1300	2000	1300	1900				

Differences ABERYSTWYTH

+0145	+0130	+0210	+0245	−2.0	−1.7	−0.7	0.0

NEW QUAY

+0150	+0125	+0155	+0230	−2.1	−1.8	−0.6	−0.1

ABERPORTH

+0135	+0120	+0150	+0220	−2.1	−1.8	−0.6	−0.1

PORT CARDIGAN

+0140	+0120	+0220	+0130	−2.3	−1.8	−0.5	0.0

SHELTER
Good but harbour dries. Lie alongside quays. Advise entering between HW∓2; dangerous in strong on-shore winds. Visitors berth halfway up Town Quay, marked 'Visiting Yachts only' — Access HW∓2½.
NAVIGATION
Waypoint 52°24'.80N 04°06'.00W, 318°/138° from/to front Ldg Lt 138°, 0.62M. Beware Castle Rocks when approaching from N. Narrow entrance with right-angle turn inside the pier head.
LIGHTS AND MARKS
Harbour located by Pen-y-Dinas, conspic hill 120m high, with Wellington monument, which lies to S of entrance. The head of the N breakwater in line with Wellington monument bearing 140° leads S of Castle Rock. Leading lights 138°, both FR on Ystwyth Bridge; white markers for daytime. N jetty Q WR 4M, R sector covering Castle Rock. S jetty Fl(2) WG 10s 10M.

⚓ Report to HrMr

RADIO TELEPHONE
VHF (portable) Ch 16 14 (for harbour control only).
TELEPHONE (0970)
Hr Mr 611433; CG 612220; MRSC Dale 218; ⌗ (0222) 399123; Marinecall 0898 500 460; Police 612791; Dr 4855.
FACILITIES
Town Quay Slip, CH, C (3 ton), L, FW, Access HW∓2½; **Inner Basin** Slip, L, C (up to 15 ton by arrangement); **F. L. Steelcraft** ☎ Borth 713, CH, D, Ⓔ, ME, Sh, M, Slip; C (25 ton); **Lucas Service** ☎ 617013, El; **AJ Plant** ☎ 828983, C (25 ton mobile); **Aberystwyth YC** ☎ 612907, Slip, M, L, FW, Bar; **Primrose Gdn Centre** ☎ 4631, Gas; **Town** P and D (cans), CH, V, R, Bar. ✉; Ⓑ; ⇌; ✈ (Swansea).
Note: − A marina is planned here.

11

FISHGUARD   10-11-11
Dyfed

CHARTS
Admiralty 1484, 1973; Imray C61/60; OS 157
TIDES
−0400 Dover; ML 2.5; Duration 0550; Zone 0 (GMT).
Standard Port MILFORD HAVEN (→)

Times				Height (metres)			
HW		LW		MHWS	MHWN	MLWN	MLWS
0100	0800	0100	0700	7.0	5.2	2.5	0.7
1300	2000	1300	1900				

Differences FISHGUARD
+0115 +0100 +0110 +0135 −2.2   −1.8   −0.5   +0.1
CARDIGAN TOWN
+0220 +0150   No data −2.2 −1.6   No data
PORTHGAIN
+0055 +0045 +0045 +0100 −2.5   −1.8   −0.6   0.0
RAMSEY SOUND
+0030 +0030 +0030 +0030 −1.9   −1.3   −0.3   0.0
SOLVA
+0015 +0010 +0035 +0015 −1.5   −1.0   −0.2   0.0
LITTLE HAVEN
+0010 +0010 +0025 +0015 −1.1   −0.8   −0.2   0.0
MARTIN'S HAVEN
+0010 +0010 +0015 +0015 −0.8   −0.5   +0.1   +0.1

SHELTER
Good shelter except in strong winds between NE & NW and can be entered at any time.
NAVIGATION
Waypoint 52°01'.00N 04°57'.50W, 057°/237° from/to Northern Breakwater Lt, 0.48M. The harbour can be entered in any weather.
Beware large swell against quay near station especially in strong N winds, 340°-010°.
LIGHTS AND MARKS
N Breakwater FIG 4.5s 18m 13M, Bell 8s. E Breakwater FIR 3s 10m 5M. Lts in line 282°, both FG; W diamonds on masts.
RADIO TELEPHONE
VHF Ch 16; 14 (H24). Fishguard Yacht & Boat Co and Goodwick Marina Ch **80**.
TELEPHONE (0348)
Hr Mr 872247; MRSC Dale 218; ≋ (0222) 399123; Marinecall 0898 500 460; Police 873073; Dr 872802.
FACILITIES
EC Wednesday; **Goodwick Marine** ☎ 874590 D, AC, CH; **No 3 Berth** L, FW, C (6 ton); **No 4 Berth** L, FW, C (6 ton); **Lower Fishguard** Slip; **Fishguard Marine** ☎ 873377, Slip, ME, Sh, CH; **Harbour** ☎ 872881, Slip (small S end), M (see Hr.Mr.); **Fishguard Bay YC** ☎ 872866, FW, Bar; **Fishguard Yacht and Boat Co.** ☎ 873377, BY, ACA; **Fishguard Harbour Garage** ☎ 873814, Gas; **Town** P, D, CH, V, R, Bar. ⊠; Ⓑ; ⇌; ✈ (Swansea).

MILFORD HAVEN   10-11-12
Dyfed

CHARTS
Admiralty 1478, 3274, 3275, 2878; Imray C60; OS 157
TIDES
−0500 Dover; ML 3.8; Duration 0605; Zone 0 (GMT).
Standard Port MILFORD HAVEN (—➤)

Times				Height (metres)			
HW		LW		MHWS	MHWN	MLWN	MLWS
0100	0800	0100	0700	7.0	5.2	2.5	0.7
1300	2000	1300	1900				

Differences SKOMER IS
−0005	−0005	+0005	+0005	−0.4	−0.1	0.0	0.0

DALE ROADS
−0005	−0005	−0008	−0008	0.0	0.0	0.0	−0.1

NEYLAND
+0002	+0010	0000	0000	0.0	0.0	0.0	0.0

HAVERFORDWEST
+0010	+0025	No data		−4.8	−4.9	Dries out	

LLANGWM (Black Tar)
+0010	+0020	+0005	0000	+0.1	+0.1	0.0	−0.1

NOTE: Milford Haven is a Standard Port and all tidal predictions for the year are given below.

SHELTER
Very good shelter in various places round the harbour, especially in Westfield Marina at Neyland. Anchorages – Dale Bay; Off Ellen's Well and Angle Point on S shore; Off Scotch Bay by Milford, above the town; and many others above Pembroke Dock. River Cleddau is navigable, at certain tides, up to Haverfordwest for boats with moderate draughts. Clearance under Cleddau Bridge above Neyland is 37m; under power cable 1M upstream, 25m. Check low headroom under bridges and cables approaching Haverfordwest. Contact Milford Haven Signal Station to ascertain most suitable anchorage or berth. Majority of moorings are 'all-tide afloat'. It is possible to dry out safely, depending on weather conditions at inshore areas of Dale, Sandy Haven and Angle Bay.
NAVIGATION
Waypoint Mid Channel Rocks W cardinal buoy, Q(9) 15s, 51°40'.09N 05°10'.04W, 222°/042° from/to Mid Channel Rocks Lt Ho, 0.27M. There is considerable tidal set across the entrance to the Haven particularly at springs. In bad weather avoid passing over Mid Channel Rocks in entrance, where a confused sea and swell will be found. Give St Ann's Head a wide berth, as there is a confused sea there in bad weather. Beware large tankers entering and leaving the haven.
NOTE:– The Port Authority is the Milford Haven Port Authority with jetty, Signal Station and offices at Hubberston Point. Their launches have green hulls and white upperworks and fly a Pilot flag (white over red horizontal) when on pilotage duties or a blue flag with the word 'Harbourmaster' in white letters while on patrol. Their instructions must be obeyed. No vessel may operate within 100 metres of any terminal or any tanker whether at anchor or under way. Milford Dock opens from HW−2 to HW and berths may be had on application to the Dockmaster (Tel. 692275).

▲ Contact Milford Haven Signal Station

WALES – MILFORD HAVEN

Lat 51°42' N Long 5°01' W

TIMES AND HEIGHTS OF HIGH AND LOW WATERS

YEAR 1991

TIME ZONE UT(GMT)
For Summer Time add ONE hour in non-shaded areas

Moon phase symbols: ● new moon · ○ full moon · (last quarter ·) first quarter

JANUARY

Day	Time	m	Time	m	Time	m	Time	m
1 Tu	0011	0.9	0612	7.1	1242	0.6	1842	7.1
2 W	0102	0.7	0702	7.3	1331	0.5	1930	7.1
3 Th	0148	0.6	0749	7.4	1419	0.5	2016	7.0
4 F	0233	0.7	0834	7.2	1504	0.7	2100	6.8
5 Sa	0317	1.0	0918	7.0	1546	1.0	2142	6.5
6 Su	0357	1.3	1002	6.6	1628	1.4	2226	6.1
7 M (	0440	1.7	1047	6.2	1712	1.9	2312	5.7
8 Tu	0526	2.1	1134	5.7	1801	2.2		
9 W	0005	5.4	0622	2.4	1223	4.8	1903	2.5
10 Th	0114	5.2	0735	2.6	1348	5.2	2023	2.6
11 F	0234	5.2	0900	2.6	1507	5.3	2136	2.4
12 Sa	0341	5.5	1006	2.3	1607	5.5	2231	2.2
13 Su	0433	5.8	1055	2.0	1655	5.8	2315	1.9
14 M	0516	6.1	1137	1.7	1736	6.0	2353	1.6
15 Tu ●	0554	6.4	1214	1.5	1812	6.2		
16 W	0028	1.4	0629	6.6	1248	1.3	1848	6.4
17 Th	0100	1.2	0704	6.7	1321	1.1	1920	6.5
18 F	0133	1.1	0737	6.8	1354	1.0	1954	6.6
19 Sa	0205	1.1	0811	6.8	1427	1.0	2026	6.5
20 Su	0239	1.1	0844	6.7	1501	1.0	2101	6.5
21 M	0312	1.3	0921	6.6	1538	1.3	2138	6.3
22 Tu	0350	1.5	0959	6.4	1617	1.5	2219	6.1
23 W)	0433	1.8	1044	6.1	1704	1.8	2308	5.8
24 Th	0526	2.0	1139	5.8	1804	2.1		
25 F	0011	5.5	0638	2.3	1252	5.6	1924	2.3
26 Sa	0133	5.5	0809	2.3	1422	5.6	2053	2.1
27 Su	0303	5.7	0936	1.9	1545	5.9	2210	1.7
28 M	0414	6.2	1047	1.4	1649	6.4	2312	1.3
29 Tu	0513	6.7	1144	0.9	1743	6.8		
30 W ○	0004	0.8	0604	7.1	1234	0.5	1831	7.1
31 Th	0050	0.6	0650	7.4	1319	0.3	1914	7.2

FEBRUARY

Day	Time	m	Time	m	Time	m	Time	m
1 F	0133	0.4	0733	7.5	1359	0.3	1955	7.2
2 Sa	0212	0.5	0813	7.4	1437	0.5	2033	7.0
3 Su	0249	0.7	0851	7.1	1514	0.8	2110	6.7
4 M	0324	1.0	0928	6.7	1548	1.3	2146	6.3
5 Tu	0359	1.5	1004	6.2	1621	1.7	2224	5.9
6 W (	0434	1.9	1042	5.8	1658	2.2	2306	5.5
7 Th	0518	2.4	1129	5.3	1746	2.6		
8 F	0004	5.1	0622	2.8	1238	4.9	1907	2.9
9 Sa	0134	4.9	0805	2.9	1423	4.8	2058	2.8
10 Su	0310	5.1	0939	2.6	1543	5.1	2207	2.4
11 M	0410	5.6	1034	1.9	1634	5.6	2254	2.0
12 Tu	0454	6.0	1116	1.3	1715	5.9	2332	1.6
13 W	0532	6.3	1153	1.3	1751	6.3		
14 Th ●	0007	1.2	0607	6.6	1227	1.0	1825	6.5
15 F	0039	1.0	0642	6.9	1259	0.8	1859	6.8
16 Sa	0112	0.8	0714	7.0	1331	0.6	1931	6.9
17 Su	0144	0.7	0748	7.1	1404	0.6	2004	6.9
18 M	0218	0.7	0822	7.1	1437	0.7	2037	6.8
19 Tu	0251	0.9	0857	6.9	1512	1.0	2112	6.6
20 W	0327	1.2	0935	6.6	1550	1.4	2152	6.3
21 Th)	0407	1.5	1017	6.2	1634	1.7	2240	5.9
22 F	0458	1.9	1112	5.7	1733	2.1	2343	5.5
23 Sa	0614	2.3	1229	5.3	1900	2.4		
24 Su	0116	5.3	0801	2.3	1415	5.3	2047	2.3
25 M	0258	5.6	0938	1.9	1542	5.7	2206	1.8
26 Tu	0409	6.1	1042	1.3	1641	6.3	2302	1.2
27 W	0502	6.7	1133	0.8	1730	6.7	2350	0.8
28 Th ○	0549	7.1	1218	0.5	1814	7.0		

MARCH

Day	Time	m	Time	m	Time	m	Time	m
1 F	0032	0.5	0631	7.3	1257	0.6	1853	7.2
2 Sa	0110	0.3	0710	7.4	1334	0.3	1930	7.2
3 Su	0147	0.3	0747	7.3	1408	0.5	2004	7.0
4 M	0219	0.6	0820	7.0	1439	0.8	2037	6.8
5 Tu	0250	0.9	0853	6.7	1508	1.2	2110	6.4
6 W	0321	1.3	0925	6.2	1538	1.6	2142	6.0
7 Th	0353	1.7	1000	5.7	1609	2.1	2220	5.6
8 F (	0431	2.3	1040	5.2	1648	2.5	2309	5.1
9 Sa	0527	2.7	1139	4.8	1800	2.9		
10 Su	0032	4.8	0706	2.9	1327	4.6	2005	2.9
11 M	0227	4.9	0900	2.7	1511	4.9	2134	2.5
12 Tu	0336	5.4	1002	2.2	1604	5.4	2223	2.0
13 W	0423	5.9	1045	1.7	1645	5.9	2302	1.5
14 Th	0501	6.3	1122	1.2	1722	6.3	2339	1.1
15 F	0537	6.7	1157	0.9	1757	6.7		
16 Sa ●	0012	0.8	0612	7.0	1231	0.6	1831	6.9
17 Su	0046	0.6	0648	7.2	1304	0.4	1904	7.1
18 M	0120	0.5	0723	7.3	1340	0.4	1940	7.1
19 Tu	0155	0.5	0759	7.2	1415	0.5	2015	7.0
20 W	0230	0.7	0836	7.0	1451	0.8	2053	6.7
21 Th	0310	1.0	0917	6.6	1531	1.2	2135	6.4
22 F	0355	1.4	1003	6.1	1617	1.7	2226	5.9
23 Sa)	0451	1.9	1102	5.6	1720	2.2	2334	5.5
24 Su	0614	2.3	1227	5.2	1856	2.4		
25 M	0113	5.3	0804	2.2	1413	5.3	2042	2.2
26 Tu	0250	5.6	0929	1.8	1531	5.7	2153	1.7
27 W	0353	6.2	1027	1.2	1624	6.2	2245	1.2
28 Th	0444	6.6	1113	0.8	1709	6.6	2329	0.8
29 F	0527	7.0	1154	0.6	1750	6.9		
30 Sa ○	0008	0.6	0607	7.1	1232	0.5	1828	7.0
31 Su	0045	0.5	0645	7.1	1306	0.5	1902	7.0

APRIL

Day	Time	m	Time	m	Time	m	Time	m
1 M	0119	0.6	0719	7.0	1337	0.7	1935	6.9
2 Tu	0149	0.7	0751	6.8	1406	0.9	2006	6.7
3 W	0220	1.0	0823	6.5	1436	1.3	2039	6.4
4 Th	0251	1.4	0854	6.1	1504	1.6	2111	6.0
5 F	0324	1.8	0928	5.7	1535	2.0	2148	5.7
6 Sa	0402	2.2	1007	5.3	1614	2.4	2234	5.2
7 Su (	0454	2.5	1101	4.9	1715	2.8	2344	4.9
8 M	0617	2.8	1229	4.6	1859	2.9		
9 Tu	0126	4.9	0801	2.6	1415	4.8	2040	2.6
10 W	0247	5.3	0914	2.2	1519	5.3	2139	2.1
11 Th	0339	5.7	1003	1.7	1604	5.8	2223	1.6
12 F	0423	6.2	1044	1.3	1644	6.3	2302	1.2
13 Sa	0502	6.6	1122	0.9	1722	6.6	2340	0.8
14 Su ●	0540	7.0	1200	0.6	1800	7.0		
15 M	0018	0.6	0619	7.2	1238	0.4	1838	7.2
16 Tu	0056	0.4	0659	7.3	1316	0.4	1917	7.2
17 W	0135	0.5	0740	7.2	1355	0.5	1957	7.1
18 Th	0218	0.7	0822	6.9	1437	0.8	2040	6.8
19 F	0303	1.0	0903	6.5	1522	1.2	2128	6.4
20 Sa	0353	1.4	1000	6.0	1616	1.8	2224	6.0
21 Su	0457	1.8	1104	5.6	1722	2.1	2334	5.6
22 M)	0617	2.0	1224	5.4	1849	2.2		
23 Tu	0102	5.5	0748	2.0	1354	5.4	2018	2.1
24 W	0225	5.8	0904	1.7	1504	5.8	2127	1.7
25 Th	0327	6.1	1000	1.3	1557	6.1	2219	1.3
26 F	0417	6.4	1047	1.1	1642	6.4	2302	1.1
27 Sa	0501	6.6	1127	0.9	1723	6.6	2342	0.9
28 Su ○	0542	6.7	1204	0.9	1801	6.7		
29 M	0018	0.9	0618	6.7	1238	0.9	1836	6.8
30 Tu	0053	0.9	0653	6.7	1309	1.0	1910	6.7

Chart Datum: 3.71 metres below Ordnance Datum (Newlyn)

WALES – MILFORD HAVEN

Lat 51°42′ N   Long 5°01′ W

TIMES AND HEIGHTS OF HIGH AND LOW WATERS   YEAR **1991**

TIME ZONE UT(GMT)
For Summer Time add ONE hour in non-shaded areas

MAY

Day	Time	m	Time	m		Day	Time	m	Time	m
1 W	0126 / 0726 / 1340 / 1942	1.0 / 6.5 / 1.1 / 6.6				16 Th	0123 / 0726 / 1342 / 1945	0.5 / 7.1 / 0.6 / 7.1		
2 Th	0158 / 0759 / 1411 / 2016	1.2 / 6.3 / 1.4 / 6.4				17 F	0211 / 0813 / 1430 / 2033	0.6 / 6.9 / 0.9 / 6.9		
3 F	0230 / 0833 / 1442 / 2050	1.4 / 6.0 / 1.6 / 6.1				18 Sa	0301 / 0904 / 1521 / 2125	0.9 / 6.5 / 1.2 / 6.6		
4 Sa	0304 / 0908 / 1515 / 2128	1.7 / 5.7 / 1.9 / 5.8				19 Su	0356 / 0957 / 1614 / 2221	1.2 / 6.2 / 1.5 / 6.2		
5 Su	0343 / 0946 / 1555 / 2212	2.0 / 5.4 / 2.2 / 5.5				20 M)	0455 / 1057 / 1719 / 2323	1.5 / 5.8 / 1.8 / 5.9		
6 M	0433 / 1035 / 1649 / 2309	2.3 / 5.1 / 2.5 / 5.2				21 Tu	0601 / 1204 / 1824	1.7 / 5.6 / 2.0		
7 Tu (	0537 / 1142 / 1804	2.5 / 4.9 / 2.6				22 W	0034 / 0713 / 1317 / 1938	5.8 / 1.8 / 5.5 / 2.0		
8 W	0024 / 0656 / 1303 / 1930	5.1 / 2.4 / 5.0 / 2.5				23 Th	0147 / 0823 / 1426 / 2047	5.8 / 1.8 / 5.6 / 1.8		
9 Th	0140 / 0811 / 1416 / 2039	5.3 / 2.2 / 5.3 / 2.2				24 F	0251 / 0924 / 1524 / 2145	5.9 / 1.6 / 5.9 / 1.7		
10 F	0243 / 0910 / 1514 / 2134	5.7 / 1.8 / 5.7 / 1.8				25 Sa	0345 / 1014 / 1613 / 2233	6.0 / 1.5 / 6.1 / 1.5		
11 Sa	0335 / 0959 / 1602 / 2221	6.1 / 1.4 / 6.1 / 1.4				26 Su	0433 / 1058 / 1657 / 2316	6.2 / 1.4 / 6.3 / 1.4		
12 Su	0423 / 1044 / 1647 / 2306	6.5 / 1.1 / 6.5 / 1.0				27 M	0516 / 1137 / 1737 / 2356	6.3 / 1.3 / 6.4 / 1.3		
13 M	0508 / 1129 / 1730 / 2351	6.8 / 0.8 / 6.9 / 0.7				28 Tu ○	0556 / 1214 / 1814	6.3 / 1.3 / 6.5		
14 Tu ●	0553 / 1212 / 1814	7.0 / 0.6 / 7.1				29 W	0032 / 0632 / 1248 / 1850	1.2 / 6.3 / 1.3 / 6.5		
15 W	0036 / 0639 / 1257 / 1859	0.5 / 7.1 / 0.5 / 7.2				30 Th	0106 / 0707 / 1320 / 1924	1.2 / 6.3 / 1.3 / 6.5		
						31 F	0140 / 0742 / 1352 / 1959	1.3 / 6.2 / 1.4 / 6.3		

JUNE

Day	Time	m		Day	Time	m
1 Sa	0215 / 0816 / 1426 / 2034	1.4 / 6.0 / 1.5 / 6.2		16 Su	0257 / 0856 / 1512 / 2115	0.6 / 6.7 / 0.9 / 6.9
2 Su	0250 / 0851 / 1501 / 2111	1.6 / 5.9 / 1.7 / 6.0		17 M	0346 / 0945 / 1602 / 2206	0.9 / 6.4 / 1.2 / 6.6
3 M	0328 / 0929 / 1539 / 2152	1.7 / 5.7 / 1.9 / 5.8		18 Tu	0437 / 1035 / 1652 / 2258	1.2 / 6.1 / 1.5 / 6.2
4 Tu	0412 / 1012 / 1624 / 2238	1.9 / 5.5 / 2.1 / 5.6		19 W)	0530 / 1129 / 1747 / 2354	1.5 / 5.8 / 1.8 / 5.9
5 W	0501 / 1102 / 1719 / 2333	2.1 / 5.3 / 2.3 / 5.5		20 Th	0628 / 1229 / 1849	1.8 / 5.5 / 2.0
6 Th	0600 / 1203 / 1825	2.2 / 5.3 / 2.3		21 F	0057 / 0731 / 1337 / 1958	5.7 / 2.0 / 5.4 / 2.1
7 F	0035 / 0706 / 1309 / 1934	5.5 / 2.1 / 5.3 / 2.2		22 Sa	0205 / 0839 / 1443 / 2105	5.5 / 2.1 / 5.5 / 2.1
8 Sa	0141 / 0811 / 1415 / 2040	5.6 / 1.9 / 5.6 / 2.0		23 Su	0311 / 0930 / 1542 / 2204	5.6 / 2.0 / 5.7 / 1.9
9 Su	0246 / 0912 / 1517 / 2139	5.9 / 1.7 / 5.9 / 1.6		24 M	0407 / 1031 / 1633 / 2255	5.7 / 1.8 / 5.9 / 1.8
10 M	0345 / 1009 / 1613 / 2235	6.2 / 1.3 / 6.3 / 1.3		25 Tu	0455 / 1115 / 1716 / 2337	5.9 / 1.7 / 6.1 / 1.6
11 Tu	0440 / 1102 / 1705 / 2330	6.5 / 1.0 / 6.7 / 0.9		26 W	0537 / 1154 / 1757	6.0 / 1.5 / 6.3
12 W ●	0533 / 1154 / 1757	6.8 / 0.8 / 7.0		27 Th ○	0015 / 0615 / 1231 / 1834	1.4 / 6.1 / 1.4 / 6.4
13 Th	0022 / 0625 / 1245 / 1846	0.7 / 7.0 / 0.7 / 7.1		28 F	0052 / 0652 / 1304 / 1909	1.3 / 6.2 / 1.3 / 6.5
14 F	0114 / 0716 / 1334 / 1937	0.5 / 7.0 / 0.6 / 7.2		29 Sa	0126 / 0726 / 1337 / 1942	1.3 / 6.2 / 1.3 / 6.5
15 Sa	0205 / 0806 / 1423 / 2026	0.5 / 6.9 / 0.7 / 7.1		30 Su	0159 / 0759 / 1409 / 2018	1.3 / 6.2 / 1.3 / 6.4

JULY

Day	Time	m		Day	Time	m
1 M	0233 / 0833 / 1443 / 2051	1.3 / 6.1 / 1.4 / 6.3		16 Tu	0325 / 0921 / 1538 / 2141	0.6 / 6.7 / 0.9 / 6.8
2 Tu	0308 / 0908 / 1519 / 2128	1.4 / 6.0 / 1.5 / 6.2		17 W	0407 / 1004 / 1620 / 2224	1.0 / 6.3 / 1.3 / 6.4
3 W	0345 / 0945 / 1556 / 2206	1.5 / 5.9 / 1.7 / 6.0		18 Th)	0449 / 1049 / 1705 / 2311	1.5 / 5.9 / 1.7 / 5.9
4 Th	0426 / 1026 / 1640 / 2251	1.7 / 5.7 / 1.9 / 5.9		19 F	0536 / 1139 / 1756	1.9 / 5.6 / 2.1
5 F	0512 / 1115 / 1732 / 2343	1.9 / 5.6 / 2.1 / 5.7		20 Sa	0004 / 0631 / 1241 / 1900	5.5 / 2.3 / 5.3 / 2.4
6 Sa	0610 / 1214 / 1838	2.0 / 5.5 / 2.2		21 Su	0113 / 0745 / 1359 / 2026	5.2 / 2.5 / 5.2 / 2.5
7 Su	0048 / 0719 / 1324 / 1952	5.6 / 2.1 / 5.5 / 2.1		22 M	0236 / 0907 / 1515 / 2142	5.1 / 2.4 / 5.4 / 2.3
8 M	0202 / 0832 / 1439 / 2108	5.7 / 1.9 / 5.7 / 1.9		23 Tu	0345 / 1010 / 1613 / 2238	5.3 / 2.2 / 5.7 / 2.0
9 Tu	0317 / 0942 / 1549 / 2217	5.9 / 1.6 / 6.1 / 1.5		24 W	0437 / 1058 / 1659 / 2322	5.6 / 1.9 / 6.0 / 1.7
10 W	0423 / 1045 / 1649 / 2318	6.3 / 1.3 / 6.5 / 1.0		25 Th	0520 / 1137 / 1739	5.9 / 1.6 / 6.3
11 Th ●	0522 / 1143 / 1746	6.6 / 0.9 / 6.9		26 F ○	0000 / 0558 / 1212 / 1815	1.5 / 6.1 / 1.4 / 6.5
12 F	0014 / 0615 / 1235 / 1836	0.7 / 6.9 / 0.7 / 7.2		27 Sa	0034 / 0634 / 1246 / 1849	1.3 / 6.3 / 1.2 / 6.6
13 Sa	0106 / 0706 / 1324 / 1926	0.4 / 7.1 / 0.5 / 7.3		28 Su	0106 / 0706 / 1317 / 1923	1.1 / 6.4 / 1.1 / 6.7
14 Su	0155 / 0752 / 1411 / 2012	0.3 / 7.1 / 0.5 / 7.3		29 M	0138 / 0738 / 1349 / 1955	1.0 / 6.5 / 1.0 / 6.7
15 M	0242 / 0837 / 1454 / 2057	0.3 / 7.0 / 0.6 / 7.1		30 Tu	0211 / 0809 / 1420 / 2027	1.0 / 6.5 / 1.1 / 6.7
				31 W	0243 / 0842 / 1454 / 2100	1.1 / 6.4 / 1.2 / 6.5

AUGUST

Day	Time	m		Day	Time	m
1 Th	0317 / 0915 / 1528 / 2135	1.2 / 6.3 / 1.4 / 6.4		16 F	0407 / 1007 / 1621 / 2227	1.5 / 6.0 / 1.7 / 5.9
2 F	0352 / 0953 / 1606 / 2216	1.5 / 6.1 / 1.7 / 6.1		17 Sa)	0444 / 1051 / 1705 / 2313	2.0 / 5.6 / 2.2 / 5.4
3 Sa	0433 / 1035 / 1651 / 2305	1.7 / 5.8 / 1.9 / 5.8		18 Su	0532 / 1146 / 1805	2.5 / 5.2 / 2.6
4 Su	0526 / 1132 / 1756	2.0 / 5.6 / 2.2		19 M	0018 / 0646 / 1310 / 1942	4.9 / 2.8 / 4.9 / 2.8
5 M	0010 / 0639 / 1248 / 1923	5.5 / 2.2 / 5.4 / 2.3		20 Tu	0159 / 0836 / 1449 / 2121	4.8 / 2.8 / 5.1 / 2.6
6 Tu	0135 / 0808 / 1419 / 2056	5.4 / 2.2 / 5.5 / 2.1		21 W	0325 / 0950 / 1552 / 2219	5.1 / 2.4 / 5.5 / 2.1
7 W	0305 / 0932 / 1539 / 2212	5.7 / 1.9 / 6.0 / 1.6		22 Th	0417 / 1037 / 1637 / 2301	5.5 / 2.0 / 6.0 / 1.7
8 Th	0416 / 1038 / 1641 / 2312	6.1 / 1.4 / 6.5 / 1.0		23 F	0458 / 1116 / 1716 / 2336	5.9 / 1.6 / 6.3 / 1.4
9 F	0513 / 1133 / 1734	6.6 / 0.9 / 7.0		24 Sa	0534 / 1150 / 1751	6.2 / 1.3 / 6.6
10 Sa ●	0004 / 0603 / 1222 / 1824	0.6 / 7.0 / 0.5 / 7.3		25 Su ○	0010 / 0608 / 1222 / 1824	1.1 / 6.5 / 1.1 / 6.8
11 Su	0052 / 0649 / 1307 / 1909	0.3 / 7.2 / 0.3 / 7.5		26 M	0041 / 0641 / 1253 / 1856	0.9 / 6.7 / 0.9 / 6.9
12 M	0135 / 0733 / 1349 / 1951	0.2 / 7.3 / 0.3 / 7.5		27 Tu	0113 / 0712 / 1324 / 1928	0.8 / 6.8 / 0.8 / 7.0
13 Tu	0216 / 0812 / 1429 / 2030	0.3 / 7.1 / 0.5 / 7.3		28 W	0144 / 0744 / 1355 / 2001	0.7 / 6.8 / 0.8 / 6.9
14 W	0254 / 0851 / 1507 / 2110	0.6 / 6.9 / 0.8 / 6.9		29 Th	0215 / 0815 / 1427 / 2033	0.8 / 6.7 / 1.0 / 6.8
15 Th	0331 / 0929 / 1543 / 2148	1.0 / 6.5 / 1.2 / 6.4		30 F	0249 / 0849 / 1503 / 2110	1.0 / 6.5 / 1.2 / 6.5
				31 Sa	0324 / 0927 / 1539 / 2149	1.3 / 6.3 / 1.6 / 6.2

11

Chart Datum: 3.71 metres below Ordnance Datum (Newlyn)

WALES – MILFORD HAVEN

Lat 51°42′ N   Long 5°01′ W

TIMES AND HEIGHTS OF HIGH AND LOW WATERS

YEAR 1991

TIME ZONE UT(GMT)
For Summer Time add ONE hour in non-shaded areas

SEPTEMBER

Day	Time	m	Day	Time	m
1 Su ☾	0404	1.7	16 M	0441	2.6
	1009	5.9		1101	5.2
	1627	1.9		1719	2.7
	2240	5.8		2332	4.8
2 M	0458	2.1	17 Tu	0551	2.9
	1108	5.5		1221	4.9
	1734	2.3		1856	2.9
	2350	5.4			
3 Tu	0618	2.4	18 W	0114	4.6
	1231	5.3		0754	3.0
	1916	2.4		1413	5.0
				2047	2.7
4 W	0128	5.2	19 Th	0256	5.0
	0802	2.4		0919	2.6
	1415	5.5		1522	5.4
	2058	2.1		2148	2.2
5 Th	0305	5.6	20 F	0349	5.4
	0929	1.9		1009	2.1
	1535	6.0		1607	5.9
	2209	1.5		2230	1.7
6 F	0410	6.2	21 Sa	0430	5.9
	1030	1.3		1047	1.6
	1631	6.6		1645	6.3
	2302	0.9		2306	1.4
7 Sa	0501	6.7	22 Su	0505	6.3
	1120	0.8		1120	1.3
	1720	7.1		1720	6.6
	2349	0.5		2340	1.0
8 Su ●	0546	7.1	23 M ○	0539	6.6
	1204	0.5		1154	1.0
	1805	7.4		1754	6.9
9 M	0032	0.3	24 Tu	0012	0.8
	0628	7.3		0611	6.8
	1246	0.3		1227	0.8
	1846	7.5		1828	7.1
10 Tu	0112	0.3	25 W	0045	0.7
	0707	7.3		0645	7.0
	1324	0.3		1259	0.7
	1924	7.4		1902	7.2
11 W	0148	0.4	26 Th	0117	0.6
	0744	7.2		0717	7.0
	1401	0.5		1331	0.7
	2002	7.2		1935	7.1
12 Th	0222	0.7	27 F	0151	0.8
	0819	6.9		0751	6.9
	1436	0.9		1406	0.9
	2037	6.8		2012	6.9
13 F	0256	1.2	28 Sa	0226	1.0
	0854	6.5		0827	6.7
	1510	1.3		1444	1.2
	2112	6.3		2051	6.6
14 Sa	0327	1.6	29 Su	0304	1.3
	0931	6.1		0908	6.4
	1543	1.8		1527	1.5
	2149	5.8		2135	6.2
15 Su ☽	0400	2.1	30 M	0349	1.8
	1010	5.6		0956	6.0
	1623	2.3		1620	2.0
	2231	5.3		2231	5.7

OCTOBER

Day	Time	m	Day	Time	m
1 Tu ☾	0448	2.2	16 W	0509	2.9
	1101	5.6		1137	5.0
	1737	2.3		1808	2.9
	2349	5.3			
2 W	0615	2.5	17 Th	0018	4.7
	1231	5.4		0649	3.0
	1920	2.3		1313	5.0
				1949	2.7
3 Th	0131	5.3	18 F	0202	4.9
	0801	2.3		0827	2.7
	1411	5.6		1434	5.3
	2053	1.9		2101	2.3
4 F	0257	5.7	19 Sa	0307	5.3
	0918	1.8		0925	2.3
	1522	6.2		1527	5.8
	2155	1.4		2149	1.9
5 Sa	0355	6.2	20 Su	0350	5.8
	1014	1.3		1009	1.8
	1614	6.7		1607	6.2
	2244	0.9		2228	1.5
6 Su	0442	6.7	21 M	0430	6.2
	1101	0.9		1047	1.4
	1701	7.0		1645	6.6
	2327	0.7		2305	1.2
7 M ●	0525	7.0	22 Tu	0505	6.6
	1143	0.6		1122	1.1
	1743	7.2		1723	6.9
				2342	0.9
8 Tu	0008	0.5	23 W ○	0542	6.9
	0604	7.2		1158	0.9
	1222	0.5		1800	7.1
	1822	7.3			
9 W	0045	0.5	24 Th	0017	0.7
	0642	7.2		0617	7.1
	1259	0.6		1235	0.7
	1859	7.2		1838	7.2
10 Th	0120	0.7	25 F	0053	0.7
	0717	7.1		0655	7.2
	1334	0.7		1313	0.7
	1935	7.0		1916	7.1
11 F	0152	1.0	26 Sa	0131	0.8
	0752	6.9		0734	7.1
	1408	1.1		1352	0.9
	2009	6.6		1958	6.8
12 Sa	0223	1.3	27 Su	0212	1.0
	0826	6.5		0817	6.9
	1442	1.4		1437	1.1
	2043	6.2		2043	6.6
13 Su	0254	1.7	28 M	0257	1.3
	0901	6.1		0901	6.5
	1515	1.9		1527	1.5
	2119	5.8		2132	6.2
14 M	0328	2.1	29 Tu	0348	1.7
	0941	5.7		0955	6.2
	1555	2.3		1627	1.8
	2200	5.3		2233	5.8
15 Tu ☽	0407	2.5	30 W	0451	2.1
	1027	5.3		1101	5.8
	1647	2.6		1742	2.1
	2255	4.9		2347 ☾	5.5
			31 Th	0611	2.3
				1222	5.7
				1909	2.1

NOVEMBER

Day	Time	m	Day	Time	m
1 F	0114	5.5	16 Sa	0043	5.0
	0740	2.2		0710	2.7
	1348	5.8		1321	5.3
	2029	1.8		1954	2.5
2 Sa	0232	5.8	17 Su	0159	5.2
	0854	1.9		0823	2.5
	1457	6.2		1427	5.6
	2131	1.5		2054	2.1
3 Su	0329	6.2	18 M	0258	5.6
	0950	1.5		0919	2.1
	1550	6.5		1519	5.9
	2221	1.2		2143	1.8
4 M	0419	6.5	19 Tu	0346	6.0
	1038	1.2		1006	1.7
	1638	6.8		1606	6.3
	2305	1.0		2228	1.4
5 Tu	0502	6.8	20 W	0430	6.4
	1120	1.0		1049	1.4
	1720	6.9		1651	6.7
	2344	0.9		2311	1.1
6 W ●	0542	6.9	21 Th ○	0512	6.8
	1201	0.9		1132	1.1
	1801	6.9		1734	6.9
				2353	0.9
7 Th	0021	1.0	22 F	0554	7.0
	0619	6.9		1215	0.8
	1238	0.9		1818	7.1
	1838	6.8			
8 F	0056	1.0	23 Sa	0035	0.8
	0656	6.9		0638	7.2
	1313	1.1		1300	0.7
	1913	6.7		1903	7.1
9 Sa	0128	1.2	24 Su	0120	0.8
	0731	6.8		0723	7.2
	1347	1.3		1347	0.8
	1948	6.5		1949	7.0
10 Su	0201	1.4	25 M	0206	0.9
	0805	6.5		0809	7.0
	1422	1.5		1436	0.9
	2023	6.2		2039	6.7
11 M	0233	1.7	26 Tu	0254	1.2
	0842	6.2		0900	6.8
	1457	1.8		1529	1.2
	2058	5.9		2131	6.4
12 Tu	0307	2.0	27 W	0348	1.4
	0919	5.9		0953	6.5
	1535	2.1		1626	1.4
	2138	5.5		2226	6.1
13 W	0346	2.3	28 Th ☽	0445	1.7
	1003	5.6		1052	6.2
	1621	2.4		1727	1.7
	2226	5.2		2329	5.8
14 Th	0437	2.6	29 F	0550	2.0
	1057	5.3		1157	6.0
	1722	2.6		1838	1.9
	2326 ☽	5.0			
15 F	0547	2.8	30 Sa	0039	5.6
	1205	5.2		0702	2.1
	1838	2.6		1310	5.9
				1949	1.9

DECEMBER

Day	Time	m	Day	Time	m
1 Su	0152	5.7	16 M	0039	5.2
	0816	2.0		0707	2.5
	1420	6.0		1314	5.5
	2057	1.8		1947	2.3
2 M	0257	5.9	17 Tu	0149	5.4
	0919	1.8		0818	2.4
	1522	6.1		1423	5.7
	2153	1.7		2053	2.1
3 Tu	0352	6.1	18 W	0256	5.7
	1014	1.6		0922	2.0
	1614	6.3		1525	6.0
	2241	1.5		2152	1.8
4 W	0440	6.4	19 Th	0355	6.1
	1101	1.5		1019	1.7
	1701	6.4		1621	6.4
	2325	1.4		2244	1.4
5 Th	0523	6.6	20 F	0447	6.5
	1144	1.3		1112	1.3
	1743	6.5		1715	6.7
				2334	1.1
6 F ●	0003	1.3	21 Sa ○	0537	6.9
	0603	6.7		1203	0.9
	1222	1.3		1805	7.0
	1821	6.5			
7 Sa	0039	1.3	22 Su	0024	0.8
	0639	6.7		0627	7.2
	1259	1.3		1253	0.7
	1857	6.5		1855	7.1
8 Su	0113	1.3	23 M	0112	0.7
	0716	6.7		0714	7.3
	1333	1.3		1342	0.5
	1933	6.4		1942	7.1
9 M	0145	1.4	24 Tu	0159	0.7
	0751	6.6		0802	7.3
	1406	1.4		1432	0.6
	2008	6.2		2030	7.0
10 Tu	0218	1.6	25 W	0247	0.8
	0825	6.4		0851	7.2
	1440	1.6		1519	0.7
	2042	6.1		2118	6.8
11 W	0251	1.7	26 Th	0335	1.0
	0901	6.2		0939	6.9
	1517	1.8		1609	1.0
	2118	5.9		2207	6.5
12 Th	0327	1.9	27 F	0424	1.3
	0938	6.0		1030	6.6
	1556	2.0		1659	1.4
	2156	5.6		2258	6.1
13 F	0407	2.2	28 Sa ☽	0516	1.7
	1020	5.8		1123	6.2
	1640	2.2		1754	1.8
	2241	5.4		2356	5.8
14 Sa	0455	2.4	29 Su	0615	2.0
	1109	5.6		1224	5.8
	1734	2.4		1857	2.1
	2334 ☽	5.3			
15 Su	0556	2.5	30 M	0102	5.5
	1207	5.5		0726	2.2
	1838	2.4		1304	5.6
				2012	2.2
			31 Tu	0216	5.5
				0843	2.3
				1449	5.6
				2122	2.2

Chart Datum: 3.71 metres below Ordnance Datum (Newlyn)

MILFORD HAVEN *continued*

LIGHTS AND MARKS
Middle Channel Rocks Fl(3)G 7s 18m 8M; B Tr, steel lantern. Ldg Lts (for West channel) 040°. Front Oc 4s 27m 15M. Rear Oc 8s 53m 15M; both vis 031°-048° (H24). Milford Dock Ldg Lts 348° both FG, with W circular daymarks. Dock entry signals on E side of lock: Blue flag or 2FG(vert) means gates open, vessels may enter. Exit signals are given via VHF Ch 12. VHF is used normally by day for entry instead of Bu flag.

RADIO TELEPHONE
Call: *Milford Haven Radio* (Port Signal Station), VHF Ch 11 12 14 16 (H24); 09 10 11 **12** 14 16 67. Local weather forecasts broadcast on Ch 12 and 14 at approx. 0300, 0900, 1500 and 2100 GMT. Gale Warnings broadcast on receipt Ch 12 and 14. Shipping movements for next 24 hours on Ch 12 between 0800−0830 and 2000−2030 LT.
Milford Haven Patrol/Pilot Launches, VHF Ch 11 16 12 (H24); 06 08 11 12 14 16 67.
Milford Docks Ch 09 12 14 16 (HW−2½ to HW+½).
Westfield Marina and Lawrenny Yacht Stn Ch **80**.

TELEPHONE
Hr Mr Milford Haven Signal Station 692342/3; Dock Master 692275; CG & MRSC 636218; ☎ (0646) 681310; Marinecall 0898 500 459; Police (Milford Haven) 692351; Police (Pembroke) 682121, (Neyland) 600221; Dr via Milford Haven Signal Station 692342/3.

FACILITIES
EC Wednesday (Pembroke Dock and Neyland): Thursday (Milford Haven, Haverfordwest); **Westfield Marina** (at Neyland) (380+40 visitors) ☎ 601601; FW, D, R, CH, V, AC, Ⓔ, P, Gas, Gaz, ▣, C (15 ton); SM, SC, ME, EI, Sh; Access Lower basin H24, Upper basin HW∓3½ **Brunel Chandlery** ☎ 601667, ACA, CH, Gas, Gaz, V; **Dale SC** ☎ Dale 636349/Neyland 601636, C (23 ton), BY, ME, EI, Sh, CH, D, V, FW, L, M, Ⓔ, P, R (Dale), Slip (Dale), Gas, Gaz, ACA; **Milford Haven Port Authority Jetty** ☎ 692342/3 (occasional use by visiting yachtsmen with special permission from Harbourmaster − contact Signal Station) AB, FW, L, M; **Milford Docks** (150) ☎ 692271 (contact Pierhead for permission to enter, VHF Ch 14) AB, C (various), CH, EI, Ⓔ, V, FW, ⌗, D, L, ME, Sh; **Dudley Marine** ☎ 692787, BY, AB, FW, L, ME, CH, Sh, EI; **Pennar Park Marine** ☎ 684608, AB, Bar, FW, L, M, R, Slip, V; **Marine and Port Services** ☎ 682271, AB, BY, C, D, EI, FW, L, M, CH, ME, Sh, Slip; **Rudders BY** ☎ 600288, C, EI, Ⓔ, FW, L, M, ME, Sh, Slip, SM; **Kelpie Boats** ☎ 683661, BY, CH, D, FW, L, ACA, SM,

ME; **Bridge Boats** ☎ 601661, ME, Sh, BY, EI, CH; **Copp Sails** ☎ 601561, SM; **East Llanion Marine** ☎ 686866, BY, D (cans), Slip, Ⓔ, EI, FW, Sh; **Lawrenny Yacht Station** (100) ☎ 651212, AB, Bar, BY, C (30 ton), CH, D, ▣, FW, L, M, ME, P, R, Slip, V (Sub ✉ in village). **Milford Haven Calor Gas Centre** ☎ 692252, Gas.
Yacht Clubs − **Dale YC** ☎ Dale 636362,
Pembrokeshire YC ☎ 692799,
Neyland YC ☎ 600267,
Pembroke Haven YC ☎ 684403, Bar, M, L, FW, Slip;
Towns − Milford Haven, ✉; Ⓑ; ⇌.
Pembroke Dock, ✉; Ⓑ; ⇌; Ⓗ.
Neyland, ✉; Ⓑ.
Haverfordwest, ✉; Ⓗ; Ⓑ; ⇌; ✈ (Swansea).
Note: The Castlemartin Range Danger Area extends 12M S from St Govans Head and from there in an arc to a point 12M WNW of Linney Head. The Danger Area operative on any one day however depends on the ranges used. Call Castlemartin Control Tower on Channel 16 VHF, ☎ 661321 Ext 336, Range Safety Boats on Ch 16 or 12, or Milford Haven Coastguard. When firing is in progress R flags are flown (R flashing lights at night), along the coast from St Govans Head to Linney Head to Freshwater West. Times of firing are published locally and can be obtained from the Range Officer on 661321 Ext 336 or 287, or Ext 364 (the Chief Clerk).

During the firing period (April to December) firing takes place between 0900 and 1630. Night firing takes place from 1830 to 2359 normally on Tuesdays and Thursdays. (These times vary according to the hours of darkness). Firing also takes place for two weeks in January and February.

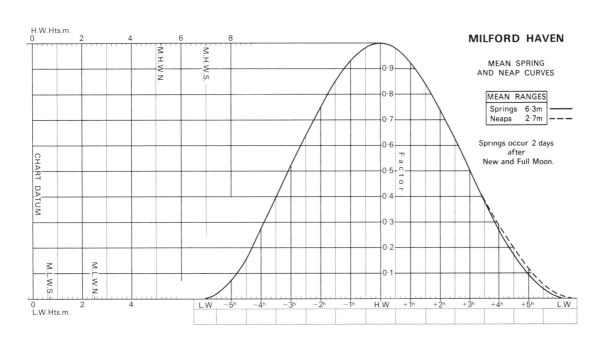

MILFORD HAVEN — MEAN SPRING AND NEAP CURVES. MEAN RANGES: Springs 6·3m, Neaps 2·7m. Springs occur 2 days after New and Full Moon.

TENBY   10-11-13
Dyfed

CHARTS
Admiralty 1482 1076; Stanford 14; Imray C60; OS 158
TIDES
−0510 Dover; ML 4.5; Duration 0610; Zone 0 (GMT)
Standard Port MILFORD HAVEN (←)

Times				Height (metres)			
HW		LW		MHWS	MHWN	MLWN	MLWS
0100	0800	0100	0700	7.0	5.2	2.5	0.7
1300	2000	1300	1900				

Differences TENBY

−0015	−0010	−0015	−0020	+1.4	+1.1	+0.5	+0.2

STACKPOLE QUAY

−0005	+0025	−0010	−0010	+0.9	+0.7	+0.2	+0.3

SHELTER
Harbour dries out but shelter good. (Access HW∓2½).
Sheltered anchorages in Tenby Roads, Caldey Roads,
Jones Bay or Lydstep Haven depending on wind direction.
NAVIGATION
Waypoint 51°40'.00N 04°38'.00W, 099°/279° from/to FS
on Castle Hill, 2.2M. Beware Woolhouse Rocks (buoy
unlit) and Sker Rocks (unbuoyed). It is recommended that
boats enter Tenby harbour HW∓2½. On approaching
Tenby Roads, keep outside the line of buoys.
LIGHTS AND MARKS
FR 7m 7M on pierhead. Inside Hr FW 6m 1M marks
landing steps. Tenby church spire and N side of St
Catherine's Is in line at 276°. R can Bn (unlit) marks rock
outcrop off North Walk on north beach near Hr.
RADIO TELEPHONE
VHF Ch 16 (listening during office hours).
TELEPHONE (0834)
Hr Mr 2717 (end May-end Sept); MRSC Dale 636218;
▦ (0222) 399123; Marinecall 0898 500 459; Police 2303;
Dr. 4161; Hosp 2040.

FACILITIES
EC Wednesday; **Harbour** ☎ 2717, Slip (up to 4.2m), L,
FW; **Pier** L; **Tenby YC** ☎ 2762, M; **Morris Bros** ☎ 2105,
Gas, CH;
Town P, D, CH, V, R, Bar. ✉; Ⓑ; ⇌; ✈ (Swansea).

BURRY PORT   10-11-14
Dyfed

CHARTS
Admiralty 1167; Stanford 14; Imray C59, C60; OS 159

⏶ Report to Burry Port Yacht Services   The above is under development

TIDES
−0500 Dover; ML 4.7; Duration 0555; Zone 0 (GMT).
Standard Port MILFORD HAVEN (←)

Times				Height (metres)			
HW		LW		MHWS	MHWN	MLWN	MLWS
0100	0800	0100	0700	7.0	5.2	2.5	0.7
1300	2000	1300	1900				

Differences BURRY PORT

+0003	+0003	+0007	+0007	+1.6	+1.4	+0.5	+0.4

LLANELLI

−0003	−0003	+0150	+0020	+0.8	+0.6	No data	

FERRYSIDE

0000	−0010	+0220	0000	−0.3	−0.7	−1.7	−0.6

CARMARTHEN

+0010	0000	No data		−4.4	−4.8	dries out	

SHELTER
Shelter in outer harbour is good but it dries out; as it is
entirely filled with moorings, entry without prior inspection
at LW is not practical. Can be approached HW∓2. The
dock is not available to yachtsmen, but gates have been
removed and it could be useful in emergency. Port is
owned by Llanelli Borough Council and rate payers have
first priority.
NAVIGATION
Waypoint 51°37'.10N 04°18'.20W. 320°/140° from/to
Minor Pt 0.34M. Proceed on stern transit 198° with
Worms Head in the Sound between Burry Holms and
Limekiln Pt. When Whiteford Lt Ho bears E, head for
three chimneys of Power Stn, approx NE, leading to
barrel post off harbour. No dangers in Carmarthen Bay
but ground swell develops into rollers on the bar. Bar
should not be attempted by small craft in W winds of
Force 5 or over. Best time to enter is HW−2 to HW+1,
but the channel is not buoyed. Before entry, check which
sections of Carmarthen Bay are closed for range practice.
(See 10.11.12). Channel through the sandbanks is liable to
vary and is unlit.
LIGHTS AND MARKS
A barrel post with a QR light is about 1 ca S of conspic
Tr and FS on West breakwater. Entrance to Burry Inlet
close N of Burry Holms marked by Y buoy Fl Y 2.5s.
Three conspic chimneys east of harbour.
RADIO TELEPHONE
None.

BURRY PORT *continued*

TELEPHONE (055 46)
Superintendent Llanelli 758181; CG and
MRCC Swansea 366534; ⊞ (0222) 399123; Proof and
Experimental Station 09945-243; Marinecall 0898 500 459;
Police (Llanelli) 772222; Dr 2240.

FACILITIES
EC Tuesday; **Outer Harbour West pier** ☎ 3342, Slip,
M (ring Hr Mr); **West Basin** ☎ 3342, Slip (ring Hr Mr), L,
CH; **East Pier** Slip, L; **Burry Port Yacht Services**
☎ 2740, Slip, M, D, L, ME, El, Sh, C, CH; **Burry Port
YC** Bar; **Shoreline Caravan Park** ☎ 2657, Gas.
Town P, D, V, R, Bar. ⊠; Ⓑ; ≽; ✈ (Cardiff).

SWANSEA 10-11-15
West Glamorgan

CHARTS
Admiralty 1161; Stanford 14; Imray C59; OS 159
TIDES
−0515 Dover; ML 5.3; Duration 0620; Zone 0 (GMT)
Standard Port MILFORD HAVEN (←)

Times				Height (metres)			
HW		LW		MHWS	MHWN	MLWN	MLWS
0100	0800	0100	0700	7.0	5.2	2.5	0.7
1300	2000	1300	1900				

Differences SWANSEA							
+0004	+0006	−0006	−0003	+2.6	+2.1	+0.7	+0.3
MUMBLES							
+0005	+0010	−0020	−0015	+2.3	+1.7	+0.6	+0.2
PORTHCAWL							
0000	0000	0000	−0015	+2.9	+2.3	+0.8	+0.3

SHELTER
Very good. Small craft may lie in the river but they dry
out on mud at LW. Good anchorage off Mumbles in W
wind. It is advised to enter the marina in South Dock,
available HW∓3, (Swansea Yacht Haven). There are four
buoys marked SYH for waiting yachts in mid-stream;
moor fore and aft between them.

NAVIGATION
Waypoint stbd-hand buoy, QG, Bell, 51°35'.50N
03°56'.06W, 200°/020° from/to Eastern Breakwater Lt,
0.92M. At springs, yachts should not enter river until
LW+2. Yachts must be under power in the harbour and
approaches, maximum speed 5 kn.

LIGHTS AND MARKS
Ldg Lts 020°. Front 2FG (vert) 5m 2M. Rear FG 6M; mark
E side of dredged channel. When approaching from E,
keep to seaward side of the inner fairway buoy (G conical,
Fl G 2.5s). Marina Master will advise on movements on
VHF Ch **80**. Traffic signals are shown at W side of
entrance to King's Lock. Three FR Lts (vert) mean that
dock and harbour are closed. Three FR Lts (hor) mean
that docks are closed. Other signals consist of three rows
of R or G Lts in three columns. Yachts entering are
controlled by the light in the middle row of the left-hand
column. When red this prohibits movement of yachts in
the port or in the approach channel: when green,
incoming craft may enter between breakwaters and
proceed to river berth or marina, as below:

R R R	
G R R	Yachts may enter river and proceed
R R R	to Yacht Haven

Traffic signals at lock to yacht haven as follows:

2FR	— Lock closed. Do not proceed
R } G }	— Free flow operating; proceed with caution
R	— Proceed only if instructed
G	— Proceed into lock as instructed

RADIO TELEPHONE
Call: *Swansea Docks Radio* VHF Ch 16; 14 (H24). Marina
Ch **80** (working hours).
TELEPHONE (0792)
Hr Mr 650855 Ext 260; CG 366534; MRCC 366534;
⊞ (0222) 399123; Marinecall 0898 500 459; Police 456999;
Ⓗ 205666; Dr 653452.

FACILITIES
Swansea Yacht Haven (350+50 visitors) ☎ 470310, D,
FW, C (1 ton), BH (18 ton), AC, Gas, CH, Gaz, ME, El,
Ⓔ, Sh, ⬚, Bar, R, Access HW∓3¼; **Swansea Yacht &
Sub Aqua Club** ☎ 654863, M, L, FW, C (½ ton static),
AB, Bar; **Near Landing** ME, El, CH; **Westland Engine
Supplies** ☎ 873249 ME; **Cambrian Small Boats and
Chandlery** ☎ 467263, ACA, CH; **Canard Sails** ☎ 367838,
SM; **Swansea Marine Engineering** ☎ 51600 ME; **Barry
Marine** ☎ 458057, ME, El, Ⓔ, CH; **Rainbow Sailing**
☎ 467804, El, Ⓔ, Sh, SM, V; **Arcadia Marine** ☎ 465333,
ME, El, Sh, SM, Ⓔ; **Town** ME, El, Sh, CH, V, R, Bar.
⊠; Ⓑ; ≽; ✈.

During construction of the barrage across the river Tawe
(due for completion in July 1991) visitors to the Yacht
Haven are advised to call the Marina Master on Ch 80 for
instructions.

River Neath Slip, M (entry over bar after ½ flood)
Monkstone Marina (controlled by Monkstone SC)
☎ Briton Ferry 8722. No multihulls.

Mumbles P, D, CH, V, R, Bar; **Bristol Channel YC**
☎ 366000, Slip, M; **Mumbles YC** ☎ 369321, Slip, M, L,
FW, C (by appointment);

BARRY 10-11-16
South Glamorgan

CHARTS
Admiralty 1182; Stanford 14; Imray C59; OS 171
TIDES
−0435 Dover; ML 6.1; Duration 0630; Zone 0 (GMT).
Standard Port BRISTOL (AVONMOUTH) (→)

Times				Height (metres)			
HW		LW		MHWS	MHWN	MLWN	MLWS
0600	1100	0300	0800	13.2	10.0	3.5	0.9
1800	2300	1500	2000				

Differences BARRY							
−0030	−0015	−0125	−0030	−1.8	−1.3	+0.2	0.0

BARRY *Continued*

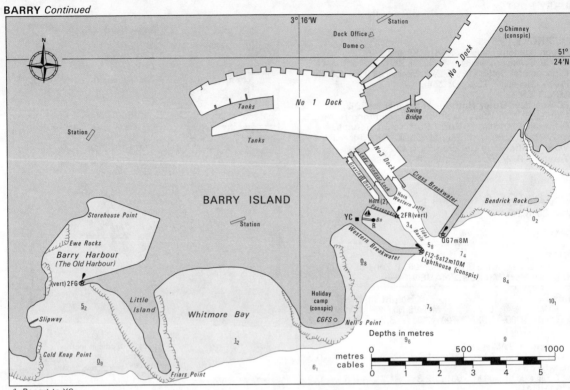

⚠ Report to YC

SHELTER
Good shelter except in strong E to SE winds. In these winds yachts are advised to enter the dock (HW∓3) by prior arrangement. Outer harbour always available (free). Old harbour to W of Barry Island dries out and is no longer any use. A marina is planned for The Old Harbour.

NAVIGATION
Waypoint 51°23'.00N 03°15'.00W, 152°/332° from/to entrance, 0.53M. Beware heavy merchant traffic. Approaching from E keep well out from the shore. Strong tidal stream across entrance.

LIGHTS AND MARKS
W Breakwater Fl 2.5s 10M. E Breakwater QG 8M.

RADIO TELEPHONE
Call: *Barry Radio* VHF Ch 16; 10 (HW−4 to HW+3).

TELEPHONE (0446)
Hr Mr 732311; MRCC Swansea 366534; ▦ (0222) 399123; Marinecall 0898 500 459; Police 734451; Dr 739543.

FACILITIES
EC Wednesday; **Windway Marine** ☎ 737312, L, FW, BY, AB, C; **Ray Harris Marine** ☎ 740924, Slip, P, D, FW, ME, El, Sh, CH, SM; **Barry YC** (130) ☎ 735511, Slip, M, Bar, FW, Access HW∓3½; **ARG Ltd** Gas.
Town P, D, CH, V, R, Bar. ✉; Ⓑ; ⇌; ✈ (Cardiff).

CARDIFF 10-11-17
South Glamorgan

CHARTS
Admiralty 1182; Stanford 14; Imray C59; OS 171

TIDES
−0425 Dover; ML 6.4; Duration 0610; Zone 0 (GMT).
Standard Port BRISTOL (AVONMOUTH) (→)

Times				Height (metres)			
HW		LW		MHWS	MHWN	MLWN	MLWS
0600	1100	0300	0800	13.2	10.0	3.5	0.9
1800	2300	1500	2000				

Differences **CARDIFF**							
−0015	−0015	−0100	−0030	−1.0	−0.6	+0.1	0.0

NEWPORT							
−0020	−0010	0000	−0020	−1.1	−1.0	−0.6	−0.7

⚠ Contact Penarth YC or Cardiff YC

CARDIFF *continued*

SHELTER
Very good within port limits. Small boats anchor in Penarth. In strong winds from NE to SE, safest to N of Penarth Harbour or into Portway Village Marina (access HW∓3¾).

NAVIGATION
Waypoint 51°24'.00N 03°08'.73W, 169°/349° from/to front Ldg Lt 349°, 3.7M. Shipping can be heavy.

LIGHTS AND MARKS
Buoyed channel lighted. Ldg Lts 349°. Ldg Lts into R Ely 304° and 246°. Docking signals:-
Queen Alexandra Dock Lock;

Fl R Lt —	prepare to dock.
FR Lt —	vessels may dock.
FR Lt 9m below docking signal —	outer half of lock only available.
3 R Lts in inverted triangle —	S approach Jetty is occupied.

RADIO TELEPHONE
VHF Ch 16; 11 14 (HW−4 to HW+3). Marina Ch **80**.

TELEPHONE (0222)
Hr Mr 461083; CG Barry 735016; MRCC Swansea 366534; ⌗ (0222) 399123; Weather Centre 397020; Marinecall 0898 500 459; Police 373934; Dr 415258.

FACILITIES
EC Wednesday; **Portway Village Marina** (220 + some visitors) ☎ 705021, ME, El, Sh, C, CH, Access HW∓4; **Docks** ☎ 471311, Slip, P, D, L, FW, ME, El, Sh, C, CH, AB, V, R, Bar; **Cambrian and West Fleet Yacht Chandlers** ☎ 709983 Sh, ME, CH, El, Ⓔ, D, ACA: **Cardiff Boat Bldg** ☎ 488034, D, SM, Sh, C (20 ton); **Blair Nautical Supplies** ☎ 21810, CH, ACA; **Penarth MB & SC** ☎ 26575, Bar, Slip, M, L, FW, C; **Penarth YC** ☎ 708196, Slip, FW, Bar; **Cardiff YC** ☎ 387697, Slip, M, L (Floating Pontoon), FW, Bar; **Barry Marine Centre** ☎ 562000, CH; **E.H. Hewett** ☎ 480624, ME, El; **Cambrian Marine Services** ☎ 43459, ME, El, Sh; **Barda Yachts** ☎ 705106, Sh; **ARG Ltd** ☎ 481076, Gas. **Town** P, D, ME, El, V, R, Bar. ✉; Ⓑ; ⇌; ✈.

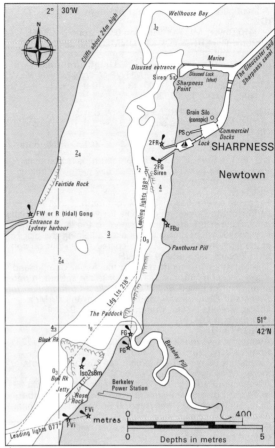

⚓ Report to Docks Hr Mr

SHARPNESS 10-11-18
Gloucestershire

CHARTS
Admiralty 1166; Stanford 14; Imray C59; OS 162

TIDES
−0315 Dover; ML No data; Duration 0415; Zone 0 (GMT).
Standard Port BRISTOL (AVONMOUTH) (→)

Times				Height (metres)			
HW		LW		MHWS	MHWN	MLWN	MLWS
0000	0600	0000	0700	13.2	10.0	3.5	0.9
1200	1800	1200	1900				

Differences SHARPNESS DOCK
+0035 +0050 +0305 +0245 −3.9 −4.2 −3.3 −0.4
SUDBROOK
+0010 +0010 +0025 +0015 +0.2 +0.1 −0.1 +0.1
NARLWOOD ROCKS
+0025 +0025 +0120 +0100 −1.9 −2.0 −2.3 −0.8
BERKELEY
+0030 +0045 +0245 +0220 −3.8 −3.9 −3.4 −0.5

SHELTER
Very good. Yachts pass through Commercial Docks to get to marina and to entrance to Gloucester and Sharpness Canal. Lock normally operates HW−2½ to HW+½.

NAVIGATION
Waypoint 51°42'.80N 02°29'.20W, 208°/028° from/to entrance, 0.20M. The entrance is 15 miles up river from King Road and the river dries out except for a narrow buoyed channel. Yachts should arrive off Sharpness about HW−1; allow for strong flood stream. Watch for entry signals, stemming tide south of the F Bu Lt. Beware strong set across entrance. There are no locks in the canal to Gloucester, but several swing bridges.

LIGHTS AND MARKS
Entry signals are as follows:—

Day	Night	
2 B balls	2 R Lts	Entrance closed
1 B ball	1 R Lt	Entrance not clear (traffic)
1 G flag	1 G Lt	Entrance clear for commercial shipping
1 G flag over 1 B ball	1 G Lt over 1 R Lt	Small vessels are to berth before large ones
No signals	No signals	Yachts may proceed in or out.
2 G flags (one at each yard arm)	2 G Lts	HW or tide ebbing

RADIO TELEPHONE
Call: *Sharpness Control* VHF Ch 16; 14 (H24). Bridges on Gloucester and Sharpness Canal Ch 74.

TELEPHONE (0453)
Hr Mr 811644; ⌗ (0453) 811302; Marinecall 0898 500 459; MRCC Swansea 366534; Police (Berkeley) Dursley 810477; Ⓗ 810777.

FACILITIES
EC Saturday; **Sharpness Marine** ☎ 811476, D, AC, FW, Sh, Gas, CH; **Commercial Docks** ☎ 811644, ME, El, Sh, C, AB. **Town** V, R, Bar. ✉; Ⓑ (Berkeley); ⇌ (Stonehouse); ✈ (Bristol).

BRISTOL (CITY DOCKS)
Avon
10-11-19

CHARTS
Admiralty 1859, 1176; Stanford 14; Imray C59; OS 172
TIDES
−0410 Dover; ML 7.0; Duration 0620; Zone 0 (GMT).
Standard Port BRISTOL (AVONMOUTH) (→)

Times				Height (metres)			
HW		LW		MHWS	MHWN	MLWN	MLWS
0200	0800	0300	0800	13.2	10.0	3.5	0.9
1400	2000	1500	2000				

Differences CUMBERLAND BASIN (Ent)
+0010 +0010   Dries out −2.9 −3.0   Dries out
PORTISHEAD
−0002 0000   No data −0.1 −0.1   No data

NOTE: The Port of Bristol (Avonmouth) is a Standard Port and tidal predictions for each day are given below.

SHELTER
Except in emergency, neither Avonmouth, Royal Portbury or Portishead Docks are available for yachts. Some shelter is available in the approach channel to the locks at Portishead. Yachts must not anchor adjoining the pier or stone jetty and they must be prepared to dry out on soft mud 2 hours each side of MLWS.
The regulations for craft entering the Avon, Cumberland Basin, Floating Harbour or City Docks are set out in detail in a pamphlet called *Bristol City Docks — Information for Owners of Pleasurecraft*, obtainable from the Hr Mr's Office, Underfall Yard, Cumberland Road, Bristol BS1 6XG. ☎ 264797.

NAVIGATION
Avonmouth waypoint 51°30'.40N 02°43'.21W, 307°/127° from/to front Ldg Lt 127°, 0.58M. The channel from Flatholm is buoyed. Tidal stream can run at five knots or more. When approaching Walton Bay, contact Avonmouth Radio on Ch 12 and transfer to either Ch 09 or 14 low power, for instructions to pass Royal Portbury Dock and enter the River Avon. If no radio fitted, signal Avonmouth Signal Station with international flag R or flash morse letter R. The signal station will reply by light or loud hailer.

LIGHTS AND MARKS
R Avon is entered south of S Pier Lt Oc RG 30s; vis R 294°-036°, G036°-194°. Ldg Lts 127° both FR. Saint George Ldg Lts 173°, both Oc G 5s synchronised. Above Pill Creek stbd hand Lts are mostly Oc G 5s, and port hand are FY.
Yachts should arrive Cumberland Basin entrance by HW. Entry signals to Bristol City Docks are shown from two positions on E bank, 1½ and 2½ ca above Clifton Suspension Bridge. FG Lt − come ahead with caution. FR Lt − stop and await orders. Prince's Street and Redcliffe bridges are manned 0600-2230 summer, 0900-1645 winter. Other bridges HW−3 to HW+1. R Lts indicate bridges are closed. Inform Bridgemaster Tel. 299338 in advance, or sound one short blast followed by one long and one short.

RADIO TELEPHONE
Avonmouth Signal Station (South Pier, Royal Edward Dock) Call: *Avonmouth Radio*: VHF Ch **12** (VTS), Port Operations Ch 14 09 11 16 (H24): navigational information provided on request. Royal Portbury Dock Ch 16; 12 **14** (HW−4½ to HW+3½).
Portishead Dock Ch 16; 12 **14** (HW−2½ to HW+1½). City Docks Radio Ch 14; 11 **14** (HW−3 to HW+1). Bristol Floating Harbour Ch 16; 73 (Office hours). Other station: Newport Ch 16; 09 11 (HW∓4). Marina Ch **80**.

TELEPHONE (0272)
Hr Mr 264797; CG Barry 735016; MRCC Swansea 366534; Netham Lock Keeper 776590; Princes St & Redcliffe Bridge Masters 299338; ⊞ (0272) 826451; Dock Master, Cumberland Basin 273633; Bristol Floating Harbour 297608; Weather Centre 279298; Marinecall 0898 500 459; Police 277777; Ⓗ 230000.

FACILITIES
EC Wednesday/Saturday; **Bristol Marina** (80 visitors) ☎ 265730, D, FW, ME, El, Sh, AC, SM, Slip, C, BH (30 ton), Access HW−3 to HW+1; **Baltic Wharf Leisure Centre** ☎ 297608, Slip, L, Bar; **Cabot Cruising Club** ☎ 268318, M, L, FW, AB, Bar; **Mud Dock** FW, C (4 ton); **City Dock** ☎ 264797, AB,C (4 ton), M; gridiron available outside Cumberland Basin − contact Dockmaster ☎ 273633; **Saltford Marine** ☎ Saltford 872226, Slip, C (8 ton), M, L, FW, ME, El, Sh, CH, R; **Marine Electronic Services** ☎ 227409, Ⓔ; **Portavon Marina** ☎ 861626, Slip, M, L, FW, ME, Sh, CH, R; **Enigma Chandlery** ☎ (0454) 416876, CH; **Bristol Boating Centre** ☎ 294160, CH; **Bristol Marine Engineering** ☎ 262923, BY, Gas, Gaz, Kos, ME, El, CH; **SW Petroleum Co** P, D; **W F Price** ☎ 823888, CH, ACA; **City** ✉; Ⓑ; ⇌; ✈.

ENGLAND, WEST COAST – PORT OF BRISTOL (AVONMOUTH)

Lat 51°30′ N   Long 2°43′ W

TIMES AND HEIGHTS OF HIGH AND LOW WATERS

YEAR 1991

TIME ZONE UT (GMT)
For Summer Time add ONE hour in non-shaded areas

JANUARY

	Time	m		Time	m
1 Tu	0147 0714 1416 1945	1·3 13·4 1·1 13·4	**16** W	0148 0730 1411 1947	1·8 12·3 1·7 12·2
2 W	0239 0804 1507 2033	1·0 13·7 0·9 13·6	**17** Th	0229 0804 1450 2020	1·7 12·5 1·6 12·4
3 Th	0325 0850 1550 2118	1·0 13·8 0·9 13·5	**18** F	0305 0836 1527 2053	1·6 12·7 1·5 12·6
4 F	0406 0934 1628 2200	1·1 13·6 1·1 13·1	**19** Sa	0341 0910 1602 2128	1·5 12·8 1·5 12·6
5 Sa	0442 1017 1704 2242	1·4 13·1 1·6 12·5	**20** Su	0413 0945 1633 2202	1·6 12·7 1·6 12·4
6 Su	0515 1058 1734 2322	1·9 12·5 2·0 11·8	**21** M	0442 1020 1701 2237	1·8 12·4 1·8 12·0
7 M (	0546 1139 1805	2·3 11·7 2·6	**22** Tu	0509 1057 1729 2312	2·1 12·0 2·1 11·6
8 Tu	0003 0618 1221 1839	11·1 2·9 11·0 3·1	**23** W)	0539 1134 1801 2353	2·4 11·4 2·5 11·0
9 W	0048 0657 1313 1924	10·4 3·4 10·3 3·7	**24** Th	0617 1225 1846	2·9 10·8 3·0
10 Th	0147 0758 1420 2044	9·9 4·0 9·9 4·0	**25** F	0052 0712 1342 1957	10·5 3·4 10·4 3·5
11 F	0304 0934 1539 2210	9·8 3·9 9·9 3·7	**26** Sa	0222 0850 1512 2148	10·3 3·6 10·6 3·3
12 Sa	0420 1045 1651 2315	10·2 3·4 10·4 3·1	**27** Su	0348 1031 1633 2312	10·9 3·1 11·3 2·7
13 Su	0522 1144 1746	10·9 2·7 11·0	**28** M	0505 1157 1744	11·7 2·4 12·1
14 M	0011 0610 1238 1832	2·5 11·5 2·2 11·5	**29** Tu	0034 0611 1312 1845	1·9 12·5 1·6 12·8
15 Tu ●	0102 0652 1327 1913	2·1 12·0 1·9 11·9	**30** W ○	0138 0706 1409 1935	1·2 13·3 0·9 13·4
			31 Th	0230 0754 1457 2019	0·7 13·8 0·5 13·7

FEBRUARY

	Time	m		Time	m
1 F	0314 0834 1536 2100	0·5 14·0 0·5 13·7	**16** Sa	0250 0816 1511 2033	1·1 13·3 1·0 13·2
2 Sa	0350 0914 1610 2136	0·6 13·9 0·8 13·4	**17** Su	0327 0850 1546 2107	1·0 13·4 0·9 13·2
3 Su	0423 0952 1638 2213	1·0 13·4 1·3 12·9	**18** M	0359 0924 1617 2139	1·1 13·3 1·1 13·0
4 M	0448 1027 1702 2247	1·5 12·8 1·8 12·1	**19** Tu	0427 0959 1642 2213	1·3 12·9 1·4 12·6
5 Tu	0512 1059 1725 2316	2·0 11·9 2·3 11·3	**20** W	0451 1033 1706 2247	1·6 12·4 1·7 12·0
6 W	0534 1130 1749 2347	2·5 11·1 2·8 10·5	**21** Th)	0516 1109 1734 2325	2·0 11·6 2·2 11·3
7 Th	0603 1205 1821	3·2 10·2 3·5	**22** F	0551 1156 1817	2·6 10·8 2·9
8 F	0032 0643 1304 1910	9·6 4·0 9·3 4·3	**23** Sa	0021 0642 1316 1923	10·5 3·3 10·1 3·6
9 Sa	0157 0804 1444 2122	9·1 4·6 9·1 4·5	**24** Su	0157 0827 1454 2129	10·0 3·8 10·2 3·6
10 Su	0339 1013 1617 2245	9·4 4·0 9·7 3·6	**25** M	0334 1019 1624 2301	10·5 3·1 10·9 2·7
11 M	0454 1116 1720 2344	10·4 3·0 10·6 2·7	**26** Tu	0458 1149 1737	11·5 2·2 12·0
12 Tu	0546 1212 1810	11·3 2·3 11·4	**27** W	0022 0601 1259 1834	1·8 12·5 1·3 12·8
13 W	0039 0629 1306 1850	2·1 12·0 1·8 12·0	**28** Th ○	0124 0653 1354 1920	1·0 13·3 0·7 13·4
14 Th ●	0128 0707 1352 1927	1·6 12·5 1·4 12·5			
15 F	0212 0742 1433 1959	1·3 12·9 1·1 12·9			

MARCH

	Time	m		Time	m
1 F	0213 0737 1437 1959	0·5 13·7 0·4 13·7	**16** Sa ●	0148 0714 1411 1934	1·1 13·1 0·9 13·2
2 Sa	0253 0813 1514 2036	0·4 13·9 0·5 13·8	**17** Su	0229 0751 1450 2008	0·8 13·5 0·7 13·5
3 Su	0327 0849 1543 2108	0·5 13·8 0·8 13·5	**18** M	0305 0826 1525 2043	0·7 13·7 0·7 13·5
4 M	0355 0922 1609 2141	0·9 13·4 1·2 13·0	**19** Tu	0339 0901 1556 2118	0·8 13·5 0·8 13·3
5 Tu	0417 0953 1628 2210	1·3 12·7 1·6 12·2	**20** W	0409 0939 1623 2153	1·0 13·1 1·2 12·8
6 W	0438 1021 1648 2235	1·8 11·9 2·1 11·4	**21** Th	0434 1016 1648 2230	1·4 12·4 1·6 12·1
7 Th	0459 1048 1709 2301	2·3 11·0 2·6 10·6	**22** F	0502 1058 1719 2313	1·9 11·6 2·2 11·3
8 F (	0523 1116 1737 2333	2·9 10·1 3·3 9·7	**23** Sa)	0539 1151 1803	2·5 10·7 2·9
9 Sa	0558 1203 1818	3·7 9·2 4·1	**24** Su	0017 0635 1312 1916	10·4 3·3 10·0 3·7
10 Su	0041 0657 1342 1935	8·8 4·5 8·6 4·8	**25** M	0148 0826 1444 2118	10·1 3·6 10·1 3·4
11 M	0254 0936 1538 2213	8·9 4·4 9·2 4·0	**26** Tu	0324 1006 1613 2244	10·6 2·8 11·0 2·5
12 Tu	0417 1045 1645 2312	10·0 3·2 10·3 2·9	**27** W	0444 1130 1720	11·7 2·0 12·0
13 W	0511 1142 1736	11·1 2·3 11·3	**28** Th	0001 0543 1221 1812	1·6 12·5 1·3 12·7
14 Th	0008 0557 1236 1819	2·1 12·0 1·7 12·1	**29** F	0102 0632 1330 1857	1·0 13·1 0·8 13·2
15 F	0102 0638 1327 1857	1·5 12·6 1·2 12·7	**30** Sa ○	0148 0713 1411 1934	0·7 13·4 0·7 13·4
			31 Su	0226 0749 1446 2008	0·7 13·5 0·9 13·5

APRIL

	Time	m		Time	m
1 M	0258 0822 1512 2040	0·9 13·4 1·1 13·3	**16** Tu	0242 0802 1501 2020	0·7 13·6 0·7 13·6
2 Tu	0324 0853 1536 2110	1·1 13·0 1·4 12·8	**17** W	0319 0843 1536 2100	0·7 13·5 0·8 13·4
3 W	0348 0922 1557 2138	1·4 12·5 1·7 12·1	**18** Th	0353 0925 1609 2141	1·0 13·1 1·2 12·9
4 Th	0409 0950 1617 2203	1·8 11·7 2·1 11·4	**19** F	0424 1009 1640 2226	1·3 12·4 1·6 12·2
5 F	0431 1017 1640 2228	2·2 11·0 2·5 10·6	**20** Sa	0458 1057 1715 2316	1·8 11·6 2·2 11·4
6 Sa	0457 1045 1708 2259	2·7 10·2 3·1 9·8	**21** Su)	0540 1154 1803	2·5 10·8 2·9
7 Su (	0530 1127 1746 2357	3·4 9·4 3·8 9·1	**22** M	0019 0642 1306 1920	10·7 3·1 10·3 3·4
8 M	0622 1240 1849	4·1 8·8 4·4	**23** Tu	0138 0816 1427 2057	10·5 3·1 10·4 3·1
9 Tu	0155 0802 1443 2103	8·9 4·3 9·1 4·2	**24** W	0303 0939 1548 2213	10·9 2·6 11·1 2·4
10 W	0327 0957 1556 2224	9·8 3·4 10·1 3·2	**25** Th	0417 1054 1652 2326	11·6 2·0 11·8 1·9
11 Th	0426 1057 1651 2325	10·9 2·5 11·1 2·4	**26** F	0516 1203 1744	12·2 1·7 12·3
12 F	0515 1157 1740	11·8 1·8 12·0	**27** Sa	0028 0604 1256 1829	1·5 12·5 1·5 12·6
13 Sa	0024 0601 1255 1824	1·8 12·5 1·3 12·7	**28** Su	0116 0646 1338 1907	1·4 12·7 1·3 12·8
14 Su ●	0116 0643 1341 1903	1·3 13·1 0·9 13·2	**29** M	0155 0723 1413 1941	1·3 12·7 1·5 12·9
15 M	0202 0723 1423 1942	1·3 13·5 0·7 13·6	**30** Tu	0227 0755 1442 2013	1·4 12·7 1·5 12·8

Chart Datum: 6.50 metres below Ordnance Datum (Newlyn)

ENGLAND, WEST COAST – PORT OF BRISTOL (AVONMOUTH)

Lat 51°30′ N   Long 2°43′ W

TIMES AND HEIGHTS OF HIGH AND LOW WATERS

YEAR **1991**

TIME ZONE UT (GMT)
For Summer Time add ONE hour in non-shaded areas

Time / m

MAY

Day	Time m		Day	Time m	
1 W	0256 1.5 / 0827 12.5 / 1508 1.7 / 2043 12.4		**16** Th	0303 0.9 / 0830 13.4 / 1522 1.0 / 2049 13.4	
2 Th	0322 1.6 / 0857 12.1 / 1532 1.9 / 2112 12.0		**17** F	0343 1.0 / 0917 13.1 / 1602 1.2 / 2135 13.0	
3 F	0346 1.9 / 0927 11.5 / 1556 2.1 / 2141 11.4		**18** Sa	0423 1.3 / 1006 12.6 / 1640 1.6 / 2223 12.5	
4 Sa	0413 2.2 / 0957 11.0 / 1621 2.5 / 2212 10.8		**19** Su	0502 1.7 / 1055 11.9 / 1720 2.1 / 2315 11.9	
5 Su	0441 2.6 / 1031 10.4 / 1651 2.9 / 2248 10.2		**20** M	0547 2.2 / 1150 11.3 / 1808 2.5	
6 M	0516 3.0 / 1113 9.8 / 1729 3.3 / 2340 9.7		**21** Tu	0012 11.4 / 0642 2.6 / 1249 10.9 / 1910 2.8	
7 Tu	0605 3.5 / 1215 9.4 / 1825 3.7		**22** W	0117 11.0 / 0749 2.7 / 1357 10.7 / 2022 2.8	
8 W	0057 9.5 / 0713 3.6 / 1338 9.5 / 1942 3.8		**23** Th	0227 11.0 / 0900 2.6 / 1508 10.9 / 2131 2.6	
9 Th	0225 10.0 / 0842 3.3 / 1458 10.1 / 2115 3.3		**24** F	0338 11.3 / 1006 2.5 / 1614 11.3 / 2238 2.4	
10 F	0332 10.8 / 0957 2.7 / 1600 11.0 / 2227 2.7		**25** Sa	0440 11.5 / 1112 2.4 / 1709 11.6 / 2343 2.3	
11 Sa	0428 11.6 / 1104 2.2 / 1655 11.8 / 2334 2.1		**26** Su	0532 11.7 / 1214 2.3 / 1757 11.9	
12 Su	0522 12.3 / 1208 1.7 / 1746 12.5		**27** M	0038 2.1 / 0618 11.9 / 1300 2.1 / 1839 12.1	
13 M	0038 1.6 / 0611 12.9 / 1306 1.3 / 1834 13.0		**28** Tu	0121 2.0 / 0657 12.0 / 1340 2.0 / 1917 12.2	
14 Tu	0131 1.2 / 0657 13.3 / 1357 1.0 / 1919 13.4		**29** W	0158 1.9 / 0734 12.0 / 1415 1.9 / 1952 12.2	
15 W	0219 0.9 / 0744 13.4 / 1442 0.9 / 2002 13.5		**30** Th	0233 1.8 / 0808 12.0 / 1447 1.9 / 2025 12.1	
			31 F	0304 1.9 / 0840 11.8 / 1517 2.0 / 2056 11.9	

JUNE

Day	Time m		Day	Time m	
1 Sa	0335 2.0 / 0912 11.6 / 1545 2.2 / 2128 11.6		**16** Su	0423 1.1 / 0957 12.9 / 1640 1.4 / 2216 13.0	
2 Su	0404 2.1 / 0946 11.3 / 1613 2.3 / 2203 11.3		**17** M	0504 1.4 / 1044 12.5 / 1719 1.7 / 2302 12.5	
3 M	0435 2.3 / 1021 11.0 / 1644 2.6 / 2241 10.9		**18** Tu	0543 1.8 / 1132 11.9 / 1758 2.1 / 2351 11.9	
4 Tu	0511 2.6 / 1102 10.6 / 1720 2.8 / 2325 10.6		**19** W	0624 2.2 / 1221 11.3 / 1842 2.5	
5 W	0551 2.8 / 1149 10.3 / 1805 3.1		**20** Th	0043 11.3 / 0710 2.6 / 1316 10.8 / 1934 2.9	
6 Th	0018 10.3 / 0641 3.0 / 1246 10.2 / 1900 3.3		**21** F	0142 10.9 / 0806 3.0 / 1418 10.5 / 2040 3.2	
7 F	0124 10.3 / 0741 3.1 / 1357 10.3 / 2009 3.3		**22** Sa	0249 10.6 / 0914 3.2 / 1527 10.6 / 2149 3.2	
8 Sa	0237 10.7 / 0856 2.9 / 1508 10.8 / 2132 3.0		**23** Su	0356 10.7 / 1021 3.1 / 1631 10.8 / 2255 3.0	
9 Su	0343 11.3 / 1013 2.5 / 1613 11.5 / 2247 2.5		**24** M	0458 10.9 / 1126 2.9 / 1727 11.2 / 2357 2.6	
10 M	0444 11.9 / 1123 2.1 / 1712 12.1 / 2357 2.0		**25** Tu	0551 11.2 / 1224 2.5 / 1815 11.6	
11 Tu	0542 12.4 / 1232 1.7 / 1808 12.7		**26** W	0049 2.3 / 0638 11.5 / 1312 2.3 / 1859 11.9	
12 W	0104 1.6 / 0638 12.9 / 1334 1.3 / 1900 13.1		**27** Th	0134 2.1 / 0719 11.7 / 1354 2.1 / 1937 12.0	
13 Th	0202 1.2 / 0731 13.2 / 1426 1.1 / 1951 13.4		**28** F	0215 2.0 / 0755 11.8 / 1432 2.0 / 2011 12.1	
14 F	0253 1.0 / 0822 13.3 / 1515 1.0 / 2040 13.5		**29** Sa	0253 1.9 / 0827 11.9 / 1507 2.0 / 2043 12.1	
15 Sa	0341 1.0 / 0910 13.2 / 1559 1.1 / 2128 13.3		**30** Su	0327 1.9 / 0900 11.9 / 1539 2.0 / 2115 12.1	

JULY

Day	Time m		Day	Time m	
1 M	0359 1.9 / 0932 11.9 / 1610 2.0 / 2150 12.0		**16** Tu	0451 1.1 / 1024 12.9 / 1704 1.4 / 2240 12.9	
2 Tu	0431 1.9 / 1007 11.7 / 1640 2.2 / 2226 11.7		**17** W	0523 1.5 / 1105 12.3 / 1736 1.9 / 2320 12.2	
3 W	0502 2.1 / 1042 11.4 / 1711 2.4 / 2302 11.4		**18** Th	0553 2.1 / 1144 11.5 / 1805 2.4 / 2351 10.9	
4 Th	0533 2.3 / 1110 11.1 / 1744 2.6 / 2343 11.0		**19** F	0003 11.4 / 0624 2.7 / 1227 10.8 / 1841 3.1	
5 F	0610 2.6 / 1203 10.7 / 1824 2.9		**20** Sa	0049 10.6 / 0702 3.3 / 1320 10.1 / 1928 3.7	
6 Sa	0032 10.7 / 0655 2.9 / 1259 10.5 / 1917 3.2		**21** Su	0149 10.0 / 0802 3.9 / 1432 9.8 / 2057 4.0	
7 Su	0141 10.5 / 0757 3.1 / 1416 10.5 / 2037 3.4		**22** M	0308 9.8 / 0939 3.9 / 1553 10.1 / 2221 3.6	
8 M	0301 10.8 / 0931 3.1 / 1535 11.0 / 2212 3.0		**23** Tu	0428 10.2 / 1052 3.3 / 1702 10.7 / 2326 2.9	
9 Tu	0413 11.4 / 1051 2.6 / 1644 11.7 / 2327 2.4		**24** W	0530 10.8 / 1154 2.7 / 1756 11.4	
10 W	0522 12.0 / 1207 2.1 / 1750 12.4		**25** Th	0022 2.4 / 0619 11.3 / 1248 2.3 / 1841 11.9	
11 Th	0046 1.9 / 0625 12.6 / 1319 1.6 / 1849 12.9		**26** F	0113 2.0 / 0702 11.7 / 1335 2.0 / 1920 12.2	
12 F	0152 1.4 / 0721 13.1 / 1418 1.1 / 1942 13.5		**27** Sa	0158 1.8 / 0738 12.0 / 1416 1.8 / 1954 12.4	
13 Sa	0247 0.9 / 0812 13.4 / 1508 0.8 / 2029 13.7		**28** Su	0237 1.6 / 0811 12.2 / 1454 1.7 / 2025 12.6	
14 Su	0334 0.7 / 0858 13.5 / 1552 0.8 / 2114 13.7		**29** M	0314 1.5 / 0840 12.4 / 1528 1.6 / 2056 12.7	
15 M	0416 0.8 / 0942 13.3 / 1630 1.0 / 2157 13.4		**30** Tu	0348 1.5 / 0912 12.5 / 1559 1.7 / 2129 12.6	
			31 W	0419 1.6 / 0945 12.3 / 1628 1.8 / 2203 12.4	

AUGUST

Day	Time m		Day	Time m	
1 Th	0447 1.8 / 1017 12.0 / 1654 2.1 / 2235 11.9		**16** F	0516 2.2 / 1105 11.6 / 1727 2.5 / 2319 11.3	
2 F	0511 2.1 / 1051 11.6 / 1719 2.4 / 2311 11.4		**17** Sa	0540 2.8 / 1137 10.7 / 1754 3.2 / 2354 10.3	
3 Sa	0539 2.4 / 1126 11.1 / 1751 2.8 / 2351 10.9		**18** Su	0610 3.5 / 1219 9.8 / 1831 3.9	
4 Su	0617 2.9 / 1214 10.6 / 1836 3.3		**19** M	0049 9.4 / 0653 4.3 / 1335 9.2 / 1940 4.6	
5 M	0055 10.4 / 0712 3.4 / 1333 10.3 / 1951 3.7		**20** Tu	0225 9.1 / 0849 4.7 / 1521 9.4 / 2156 4.1	
6 Tu	0229 10.3 / 0854 3.5 / 1507 10.6 / 2149 3.4		**21** W	0403 9.6 / 1028 3.8 / 1638 10.4 / 2301 3.1	
7 W	0353 10.9 / 1030 2.9 / 1627 11.4 / 2312 2.6		**22** Th	0506 10.6 / 1129 2.8 / 1732 11.3 / 2357 2.3	
8 Th	0511 11.7 / 1153 2.3 / 1740 12.3 / 2326 2.9		**23** F	0556 11.4 / 1222 2.2 / 1817 12.0	
9 F	0038 1.9 / 0617 12.6 / 1309 1.5 / 1839 13.1		**24** Sa	0049 1.8 / 0638 11.9 / 1312 1.7 / 1855 12.5	
10 Sa	0144 1.2 / 0712 13.2 / 1406 0.9 / 1930 13.7		**25** Su	0135 1.5 / 0714 12.3 / 1355 1.5 / 1928 12.8	
11 Su	0236 0.6 / 0758 13.7 / 1454 0.5 / 2013 14.0		**26** M	0218 1.3 / 0745 12.7 / 1433 1.4 / 1959 13.0	
12 M	0319 0.4 / 0839 13.8 / 1535 0.5 / 2054 14.0		**27** Tu	0254 1.2 / 0816 12.9 / 1508 1.3 / 2032 13.2	
13 Tu	0356 0.6 / 0918 13.6 / 1610 0.8 / 2134 13.7		**28** W	0328 1.2 / 0847 13.0 / 1541 1.4 / 2104 13.1	
14 W	0427 1.0 / 0956 13.1 / 1640 1.3 / 2210 13.0		**29** Th	0359 1.3 / 0919 12.8 / 1610 1.6 / 2138 12.7	
15 Th	0454 1.4 / 1031 12.4 / 1704 1.9 / 2247 12.2		**30** F	0426 1.6 / 0952 12.4 / 1634 1.9 / 2210 12.2	
			31 Sa	0448 2.0 / 1024 11.9 / 1657 2.3 / 2245 11.6	

Chart Datum: 6.50 metres below Ordnance Datum (Newlyn)

ENGLAND, WEST COAST – PORT OF BRISTOL (AVONMOUTH)

Lat 51°30′ N   Long 2°43′ W

TIMES AND HEIGHTS OF HIGH AND LOW WATERS

YEAR **1991**

TIME ZONE UT(GMT)
For Summer Time add ONE hour in non-shaded areas

SEPTEMBER

Day	Time m	Time m	Time m	Time m
1 Su ☾	0513 2.4	1058 11.3	1727 2.7	2326 10.9
16 M	0529 3.6	1127 9.7	1751 4.0	2356 9.2
2 M	0549 2.9	1146 10.6	1812 3.4	
17 Tu	0607 4.3	1236 8.8	1846 4.7	
3 Tu	0032 10.1	0645 3.6	1312 10.0	1930 3.9
18 W	0135 8.6	0719 5.0	1444 9.0	2127 4.6
4 W	0212 10.0	0839 3.8	1453 10.4	2138 3.5
19 Th	0327 9.2	1000 4.2	1606 10.1	2233 3.4
5 Th	0346 10.7	1019 3.0	1620 11.4	2305 2.5
20 F	0433 10.3	1058 3.1	1658 11.2	2325 2.4
6 F	0504 11.8	1144 2.1	1730 12.4	
21 Sa	0522 11.3	1150 2.3	1743 12.0	
7 Sa	0028 1.6	0604 12.7	1255 1.3	1827 13.3
22 Su	0017 1.8	0604 12.0	1241 1.7	1822 12.6
8 Su ●	0128 0.9	0655 13.4	1349 0.7	1913 13.8
23 M ○	0106 1.4	0642 12.5	1327 1.4	1857 13.0
9 M	0216 0.5	0738 13.8	1434 0.5	1952 14.0
24 Tu	0149 1.2	0716 12.9	1408 1.2	1931 13.3
10 Tu	0257 0.5	0815 13.9	1511 0.6	2029 14.0
25 W	0227 1.0	0748 13.2	1444 1.1	2005 13.4
11 W	0329 0.8	0851 13.7	1542 1.0	2105 13.6
26 Th	0304 1.1	0820 13.3	1518 1.2	2040 13.3
12 Th	0357 1.2	0925 13.2	1609 1.5	2139 12.9
27 F	0336 1.2	0854 13.1	1549 1.5	2115 13.0
13 F	0420 1.8	0959 12.4	1631 2.0	2212 12.0
28 Sa	0404 1.6	0929 12.7	1616 1.8	2152 12.4
14 Sa	0441 2.3	1028 11.5	1654 2.6	2241 11.1
29 Su	0428 1.9	1006 12.1	1641 2.2	2231 11.7
15 Su ☽	0502 2.9	1055 10.6	1718 3.2	2311 10.1
30 M	0457 2.4	1047 11.4	1715 2.7	2320 10.8

OCTOBER

Day	Time m	Time m	Time m	Time m
1 Tu ☾	0536 3.0	1143 10.6	1805 3.4	
16 W	0536 4.1	1153 9.1	1812 4.4	
2 W	0032 10.1	0639 3.7	1309 10.1	1935 3.9
17 Th	0039 8.7	0635 4.7	1345 8.9	1942 4.7
3 Th	0205 10.0	0833 3.7	1444 10.5	2127 3.2
18 F	0230 9.0	0849 4.6	1512 9.7	2146 3.8
4 F	0335 10.8	1004 2.8	1609 11.6	2248 2.3
19 Sa	0342 10.0	1013 3.6	1612 10.8	2242 2.8
5 Sa	0448 11.9	1125 2.0	1713 12.5	
20 Su	0435 11.0	1106 2.7	1659 11.7	2334 2.1
6 Su	0005 1.5	0544 12.7	1232 1.3	1805 13.2
21 M	0522 11.8	1200 2.1	1743 12.4	
7 M ●	0103 1.0	0632 13.3	1324 0.9	1850 13.5
22 Tu	0028 1.7	0604 12.5	1252 1.6	1824 12.9
8 Tu	0149 0.8	0713 13.5	1408 0.8	1928 13.7
23 W ○	0116 1.3	0643 13.0	1337 1.3	1902 13.3
9 W	0229 0.9	0749 13.6	1443 1.0	2004 13.6
24 Th	0159 1.1	0720 13.3	1418 1.1	1941 13.5
10 Th	0300 1.2	0823 13.5	1512 1.3	2039 13.3
25 F	0239 1.0	0758 13.5	1456 1.2	2019 13.4
11 F	0327 1.5	0857 13.0	1538 1.7	2111 12.6
26 Sa	0315 1.2	0836 13.3	1532 1.4	2100 13.1
12 Sa	0349 2.0	0925 12.3	1602 2.1	2142 11.8
27 Su	0349 1.5	0921 12.9	1604 1.7	2143 12.5
13 Su	0412 2.4	0957 11.5	1626 2.6	2212 11.0
28 M	0420 1.9	1000 12.4	1638 2.1	2231 11.8
14 M	0434 2.9	1024 10.6	1651 3.2	2240 10.1
29 Tu	0455 2.4	1049 11.7	1718 2.6	2325 11.1
15 Tu	0459 3.5	1057 9.8	1723 3.8	2322 9.3
30 W ☾	0540 3.0	1149 11.0	1814 3.2	
31 Th	0031 10.5	0645 3.4	1302 10.6	1935 3.4

NOVEMBER

Day	Time m	Time m	Time m	Time m
1 F	0149 10.5	0818 3.3	1425 10.9	2103 2.9
16 Sa	0114 9.3	0714 4.2	1404 9.7	2011 3.9
2 Sa	0311 11.0	0936 2.7	1543 11.6	2216 2.3
17 Su	0234 9.8	0847 3.9	1512 10.4	2138 3.3
3 Su	0421 11.8	1049 2.1	1647 12.3	2330 1.9
18 M	0339 10.6	1007 3.2	1609 11.2	2241 2.6
4 M	0518 12.4	1200 1.7	1740 12.7	
19 Tu	0433 11.4	1109 2.5	1659 12.0	2340 2.1
5 Tu	0031 1.6	0605 12.8	1253 1.5	1825 12.9
20 W	0523 12.2	1208 2.0	1749 12.6	
6 W ●	0119 1.5	0648 13.0	1337 1.4	1904 13.0
21 Th ○	0038 1.6	0611 12.8	1303 1.5	1835 13.1
7 Th	0158 1.5	0724 13.1	1413 1.5	1941 12.9
22 F	0128 1.3	0656 13.3	1352 1.2	1921 13.4
8 F	0230 1.6	0759 13.0	1446 1.6	2016 12.7
23 Sa	0216 1.1	0740 13.5	1439 1.2	2006 13.4
9 Sa	0300 1.8	0833 12.7	1514 1.9	2049 12.3
24 Su	0300 1.1	0825 13.5	1522 1.2	2053 13.2
10 Su	0325 2.1	0905 12.2	1541 2.2	2121 11.7
25 M	0342 1.3	0910 13.3	1603 1.5	2141 12.9
11 M	0350 2.4	0935 11.6	1607 2.5	2152 11.1
26 Tu	0421 1.6	0957 12.9	1644 1.8	2228 12.4
12 Tu	0414 2.8	1006 10.9	1634 2.9	2224 10.5
27 W	0501 2.0	1048 12.3	1727 2.2	2320 11.8
13 W	0442 3.2	1041 10.3	1708 3.3	2304 9.9
28 Th ☽	0546 2.5	1142 11.8	1817 2.5	
14 Th	0518 3.6	1127 9.8	1751 3.8	2358 9.4
29 F	0017 11.2	0639 2.8	1243 11.3	1916 2.8
15 F	0607 4.0	1236 9.5	1850 4.0	
30 Sa	0121 10.9	0745 3.0	1352 11.1	2025 2.9

DECEMBER

Day	Time m	Time m	Time m	Time m
1 Su	0233 10.9	0857 2.9	1504 11.2	2134 2.8
16 M	0117 9.9	0730 3.7	1401 10.2	2016 3.5
2 M	0343 11.2	1007 2.7	1612 11.5	2242 2.6
17 Tu	0234 10.2	0854 3.6	1514 10.7	2143 3.2
3 Tu	0445 11.6	1118 2.4	1709 11.8	2350 2.4
18 W	0343 10.9	1019 3.0	1617 11.4	2255 2.5
4 W	0537 12.0	1218 2.2	1800 12.0	
19 Th	0445 11.7	1126 2.4	1718 12.1	
5 Th	0043 2.1	0624 12.3	1306 2.0	1843 12.2
20 F	0000 2.0	0543 12.5	1232 1.8	1814 12.7
6 F ●	0127 2.0	0704 12.5	1347 1.9	1924 12.3
21 Sa ○	0104 1.5	0636 13.1	1334 1.4	1907 13.2
7 Sa	0205 1.9	0742 12.6	1423 1.9	2001 12.3
22 Su	0201 1.2	0728 13.5	1429 1.1	1958 13.5
8 Su	0239 1.9	0818 12.5	1457 1.9	2034 12.1
23 M	0251 1.0	0816 13.7	1518 0.9	2046 13.6
9 M	0310 2.1	0850 12.2	1528 2.1	2105 11.9
24 Tu	0338 1.0	0903 13.7	1603 1.0	2132 13.4
10 Tu	0339 2.3	0921 11.9	1557 2.3	2136 11.6
25 W	0420 1.1	0950 13.5	1644 1.2	2219 13.0
11 W	0406 2.5	0953 11.6	1626 2.5	2210 11.2
26 Th	0459 1.4	1037 13.1	1723 1.5	2305 12.5
12 Th	0434 2.7	1027 11.2	1658 2.7	2245 10.8
27 F	0539 1.8	1123 12.5	1801 2.0	2351 11.8
13 F	0506 2.9	1106 10.7	1733 3.0	2326 10.4
28 Sa ☾	0618 2.3	1212 11.8	1842 2.5	
14 Sa	0544 3.2	1150 10.4	1815 3.2	1916 2.8
29 Su	0043 11.1	0703 2.8	1309 11.1	1933 3.0
15 Su	0014 10.1	0631 3.5	1248 10.1	1907 3.5
30 M	0144 10.6	0804 3.3	1415 10.6	2040 3.4
31 Tu	0254 10.4	0919 3.4	1529 10.6	2156 3.4

Chart Datum: 6.50 metres below Ordnance Datum (Newlyn)

11

BRISTOL *continued*

AVONMOUTH

MEAN SPRING
AND NEAP CURVES

MEAN RANGES	
Springs	12.3m
Neaps	6·5m

Springs occur 2 days
after
New and Full Moon.

BURNHAM-ON-SEA   10-11-20
Somerset

CHARTS
Admiralty 1152; Stanford 14; Imray C59; OS 182
TIDES
−0435 Dover; ML 5.4; Duration 0620; Zone 0 (GMT).
Standard Port BRISTOL (AVONMOUTH) (⟵)

Times				Height (metres)			
HW		LW		MHWS	MHWN	MLWN	MLWS
0200	0800	0300	0800	13.2	10.0	3.5	0.9
1400	2000	1500	2000				

Differences BURNHAM

−0020	−0025	−0030	0000	−2.3	−1.9	−1.4	−1.1

BRIDGWATER

−0015	−0030	+0305	+0455	−8.6	−8.1	dries out	

WESTON-SUPER-MARE

−0020	−0030	−0130	−0030	−1.2	−1.0	−0.8	−0.2

WATCHET

−0035	−0050	−0145	−0040	−1.9	−1.5	+0.1	+0.1

MINEHEAD

−0035	−0045	−0100	−0100	−2.6	−1.9	−0.1	0.0

PORLOCK BAY

−0045	−0055	−0205	−0050	−3.0	−2.2	−0.1	−0.1

BURNHAM-ON-SEA *continued*

SHELTER
Yachts can lie afloat about 40m E of No 2 buoy. Anchor in R Brue or S of town jetty. Local knowledge is necessary to enter.

NAVIGATION
Waypoint 51°13′.56N 03°10′.00W, 258°/078° from/to Upper Lt, 6.5M. Entrance is very choppy in strong winds especially from W to SW or from N to NE. Entry not advised at night. Entry advised from HW−3 to HW. First locate Gore bell buoy and then pick up transit of old light structure with main Lt Ho, keeping the latter open S of former. When past No 2 buoy, steer in transit of white mark in sea wall with Church Tr. Best shelter in R Brue (dries).

LIGHTS AND MARKS
Fl 7.5s 28m 17M; W Tr, R stripe; vis 074°-164°. Dir Lt 078° F WRG 24m 16/12M; same Tr; vis G073°-077°, W077°-079°, R079°-083°. Seafront Lts in line 112° (moved to meet changes in channel). Front FR 6m 3M; W stripe on sea wall. Rear FR 12m 3M; church Tr.

RADIO TELEPHONE
Hr Mr and Pilot VHF Ch 16; 08 (HW−3 to HW+1). Other stations: Watchet VHF Ch 16; 09 12 14 (occas). Minehead Ch 16; 12, 14 (occas). Marina Ch **80**.

TELEPHONE (0278)
Hr Mr and Pilot 782180; CG Watchet 31486; MRCC Swansea 366534; ∰ (0752) 222929; Marinecall 0898 500 459; Police 782288; Ⓗ 782262.

FACILITIES
EC Wednesday; **Burnham-on-Sea YC** Slip, M, L, Bar; **Jetty** Slip; **D. C. Blake** ☎ 783275, FW, ME; **Solway Ltd** ☎ 782908, Gas; **Wessex Marine** ☎ 42255, ME; **Town** ✉; Ⓑ; ⇌ (Highbridge); ✈ (Bristol).

Note: There is a marina at Bridgwater. Yachts should pass Gore Lt Buoy at HW−3.
Bridgwater Marina (50 + 120 visitors) ☎ 422222, AC, ME, El, Sh, C (2 ton), BH (27 ton), CH, Bar, R, V, Gas, Gaz, FW, Access HW∓1½.

⚓ None available

ILFRACOMBE   10-11-21
Devon

CHARTS
Admiralty 1160, 1165; Stanford 14; Imray C59; OS 180

TIDES
−0525 Dover; ML 5.0; Duration 0625; Zone 0 (GMT).
Standard Port MILFORD HAVEN (←)

Times				Height (metres)			
HW		LW		MHWS	MHWN	MLWN	MLWS
0100	0700	0100	0700	7.0	5.2	2.5	0.7
1300	1900	1300	1900				

Differences ILFRACOMBE
−0030	−0015	−0035	−0055	+2.2	+1.7	+0.5	0.0

ILFRACOMBE

Depths in metres

SHELTER
Good except E to NE Winds. On entering obtain directions from pierhead gates on NE side. SW gales cause a very severe surge in the harbour. 12 visitors buoys in outer harbour.

NAVIGATION
Waypoint 51°13′.20N 04°06′.60W, 000°/180° from/to pierhead, 0.55M. Coming from E, beware Copperas Rocks (4M to E), marked by buoy. Do not anchor in line with LB Slip. 1 or 2 balls hoisted on flagpole yard indicates steamer is to berth alongside pier.

LIGHTS AND MARKS
There are no leading marks. Inner Pier Head Lt 2 FG (vert). 3 Lts on Promenade Pier, all 2 FG (vert). Shown 1 Sept-30 Apl. Siren 30s when vessel expected. Lantern Hill Lt FR, 39m 6M.

RADIO TELEPHONE
Call: *Ilfracombe Harbour* VHF Ch 16; 12 (Apl-Oct 0800-2000 when manned. Nov-Mar occas). Ch **80** (occas).

TELEPHONE (0271)
Hr Mr 63969; CG 62117; MRCC Swansea 366534; ∰ (0752) 222929; Marinecall 0898 500 459; Police 63633; Dr 63119.

FACILITIES
EC Thursday; **Harbour** ☎ 62108, Slip, M (See Hr.Mr.), D (cans), L, FW, CH, V, R, Bar; **Ilfracombe YC** ☎ 63969, Bar, R, M, C (35 ton), FW, L, Ⓞ, CH; **Pier** FW; **Watermouth Marine** ☎ 62504, M, FW, Slip, D; **Harbour Chandlery** ☎ 62299, CH, Gas; **Ilfracombe Marine Services** ☎ 66815, ME, El, C (5 ton), Sh; **Town** ✉; Ⓑ; ⇌ (bus to Barnstaple); ✈ (Exeter).

Note: It is planned to turn the harbour into a marina.

11

RIVERS TAW & TORRIDGE
Devon
10-11-22

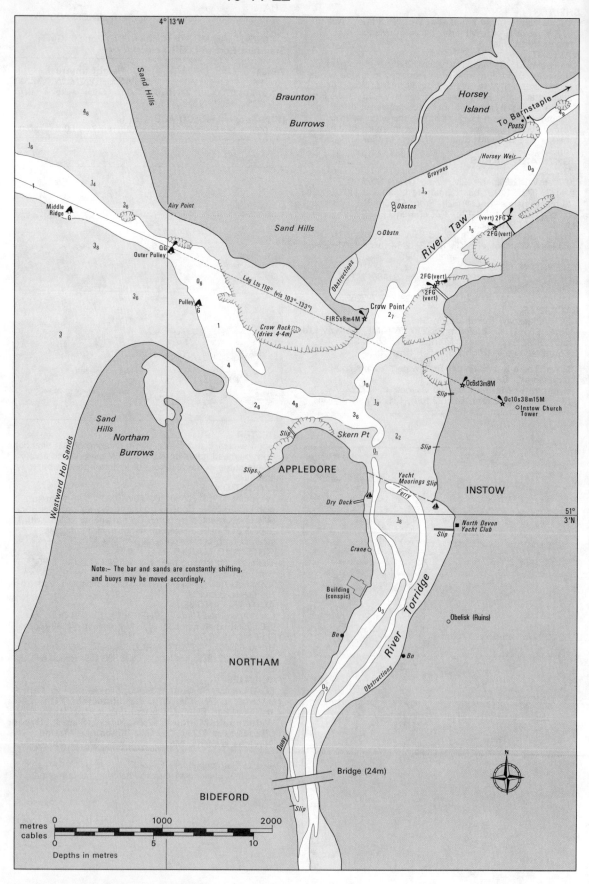

4° 13'W

Sand Hills

Braunton

Burrows

Horsey
Island

To Barnstaple
Posts

4₆

Horsey Weir

0₉

Groynes

1₆

1₄

River Taw

4₈

Middle
Ridge
G

Airy Point

Sand Hills

1₃

Obstns

(vert) 2FG

3₆

QG
Outer Pulley

Obstn

1₅

2FG (vert)

3₈

0₆

Obstructions

2FG (vert)

3₆

Pulley
G

Ldg Lts 118° (vis 103°-133°)

2FG
(vert)

Crow Point

1

Crow Rock
(dries 4·4m)

FIR5s8m4M

2₇

Oc6s13m8M

4

1₈

Slip

Oc10s38m15M
Instow Church
Tower

3

2₆

4₈

3₆

1₈

Sand
Hills
Northam
Burrows

Slip

Skern Pt

2₂

Slip

0₁

APPLEDORE

INSTOW

51°
3'N

Yacht
Moorings Slip

Westward Ho! Sands

Slips

Ferry

Dry Dock

North Devon
Yacht Club

1₈

Slip

Note:– The bar and sands are constantly shifting,
and buoys may be moved accordingly.

Crane

Building
(conspic)

River Torridge

Obelisk (Ruins)

0₃

Bn

NORTHAM

Obstructions

Bn

0₃

N

Quay

Bridge (24m)

BIDEFORD

Slip

metres   0   1000   2000
cables   0   5   10

Depths in metres

RIVERS TAW & TORRIDGE *continued*

CHARTS
Admiralty 1160; Stanford 14; Imray C58; OS 180
TIDES
−0520 Dover; ML 3.6; Duration 0600; Zone 0 (GMT)

Standard Port MILFORD HAVEN (←)

Times				Height (metres)			
HW		LW		MHWS	MHWN	MLWN	MLWS
0100	0700	0100	0700	7.0	5.2	2.5	0.7
1300	1900	1300	1900				

Differences APPLEDORE
−0020 −0025 +0015 −0045 +0.5 0.0 −0.9 −0.5
BARNSTAPLE
0000 −0015 −0155 −0245 −2.9 −3.8 −2.2 −0.4
BIDEFORD
−0020 −0025 0000 0000 −1.1 −1.6 −2.5 −0.7
CLOVELLY
−0030 −0030 −0020 −0040 +1.3 +1.1 +0.2 +0.2
LUNDY ISLAND
−0030 −0030 −0020 −0040 +1.0 +0.7 +0.2 +0.1
BUDE
−0040 −0040 −0035 −0045 +0.7 +0.6 No data

SHELTER
Very well protected, but entry in strong on-shore winds is dangerous. Yachts can anchor or pick up mooring buoy in Appledore Pool. A marina is planned at Northam.
NAVIGATION
Waypoint 51°05'.40N 04°16'.04W, 298°/118° from/to front Ldg Lt 118°, 3.8M (channel shifts). Estuary dries out at low water and entry is only recommended from HW−2 to HW. Once tide is running out, breakers quickly form between Bar Buoy and Middle Ridge. Advice on bar available from Hartland/Swansea Coastguard. Tidal stream off Skern Pt can reach 5kts at springs. Passage up to Bideford is not difficult but boats proceeding to Barnstaple are advised to take a pilot (available at Appledore).
LIGHTS AND MARKS
Apart from jetties etc only the Fairway Buoy, Outer Pulley, Crow Point and the two leading marks are lit. The Torridge has no lights. Entry at night is NOT recommended.
RADIO TELEPHONE
Two Rivers Port/Pilots VHF Ch 16; 12 (Listens from HW−2). Other station: Bude VHF Ch 16; 12 (when vessel expected.)
TELEPHONE (Barnstaple + Instow 0271, Bideford 0237)
Hr Mr Bideford 476711 Ext 317, Barnstaple apply Amenities Officer 72511 Ext 7408; MRCC Swansea 366534; ⌗ (0752) 222929; Marinecall 0898 500 459; Police (Bideford) 476896; Dr Appledore (Bideford 474994), Bideford 476444 or 476363, Barnstaple 75221 or 473443.
FACILITIES
EC Barnstaple & Bideford — Wednesday;
APPLEDORE is a free port so no authority can charge for use of public facilities eg slip at town quay and alongside berths. **RNS Marine** ☎ Bideford 474167, CH; **Marine Electronics (Bideford)** ☎ Torrington 22870, El, Ⓔ; **The Sea Chest** ☎ Bideford 476191, CH;
BIDEFORD: AB (few), V, R, Bar; Berthing arranged through Capt V. Harris ☎ Bideford 474569; **Blanchards** ☎ 472084, Gas;
INSTOW: **F. Johns** ☎ Instow 860578, M, AB, ACA, CH; **N. Devon YC** ☎ Instow 860367, Slip, R, Bar; **Instow Marine Services** ☎ 861081, D, ME, Ⓔ, C (4 ton); **Town** V, R, FW, Bar.
BARNSTAPLE: AB, V, Bar; **Barnstaple Calor Centre** ☎ 75794, Gas.
Towns ✉ (all four); Ⓑ (Barnstaple, Bideford); ⇌ (Barnstaple); ✈ (Exeter).
Note: There are no alongside facilities for FW, D or P. Small quantities supplied in jerrycans. A larger quantity of D or P can be supplied by bowser from Plymouth (see Hr Mr). FW can be collected from the North Devon YC.

PADSTOW 10-11-23
Cornwall

CHARTS
Admiralty 1156, 1168; Stanford 13; Imray C58; OS 200
TIDES
−0550 Dover; ML 4.0; Duration 0600; Zone 0 (GMT)

Standard Port MILFORD HAVEN (←)

Times				Height (metres)			
HW		LW		MHWS	MHWN	MLWN	MLWS
0100	0700	0100	0700	7.0	5.2	2.5	0.7
1300	1900	1300	1900				

Differences PADSTOW
−0055 −0050 −0040 −0050 +0.3 +0.4 +0.1 +0.1
NEWQUAY
−0100 −0110 −0105 −0050 0.0 +0.1 0.0 −0.1
PERRANPORTH
−0100 −0110 −0110 −0050 −0.1 0.0 0.0 +0.1
ST IVES
−0050 −0115 −0105 −0040 −0.4 −0.3 −0.1 +0.1
CAPE CORNWALL
−0130 −0145 −0120 −0120 −1.0 −0.9 −0.5 −0.1

SHELTER
Heavy breaking seas often encountered on Doom Bar and in adjacent channel during strong onshore winds or heavy ground swell. Allow ample rise of tide (least depth in channel at LWS late 1987 was 1.3m). Anchorage just

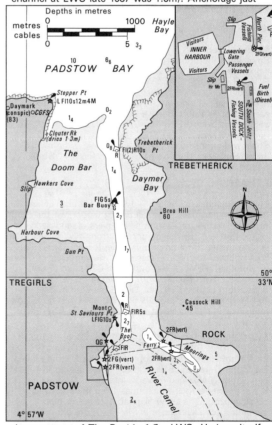

down stream of The Pool in 1.5m LWS. Harbour itself gives alongside berthing in good shelter except in strong SE winds. Harbour dries. Vessels may not be left unattended in harbour. Swinging mooring (drying) sometimes available for small vessels on passage.
NAVIGATION
Waypoint 50°35'.00N 04°58'.50W, 305°/125° from/to Stepper Pt, 1.5M. Coming from S, beware Quies Rks, Gulland Rk, The Hen, Gurley Rk and Chimney Rks and the wreck 5 ca W of Stepper Pt. All are hazardous (off the chartlet). From N, keep well clear of Newland Is and its reefs jutting out. The sandbanks in the estuary change frequently, so local knowledge, care and a rising tide are recommended. Final approach S of St Saviours Pt is close to W shore.

11

PADSTOW *continued*

LIGHTS AND MARKS
Entrance marked by the stone tower (daymark) conspic, W of Stepper Point. Stepper Pt Lt L Fl 10s 12m 4M and harbour entrance marked by 2 FG (vert) to stbd and 2FR (vert) to port.

RADIO TELEPHONE
VHF Ch 16 (HW − 2½ to HW + 1½).

TELEPHONE (0841)
Hr Mr 532239; CG St. Merryn 520407; MRCC Falmouth 317515; ⌗ (0752) 222929; Marinecall 0898 500 458; Police Wadebridge 2216; Dr 532346.

FACILITIES
EC Wednesday; **Harbour** ☎ 532239, Access HW ∓2½, Slip, M, FW, El, C, D, AB, V, R, Bar; **Pier** ☎ 532239, D; **Dock** ☎ 532239, ME, C (6 ton), AB; **Rock SC** ☎ Trebetherick 2431, Slip; **Wadebridge Boat Centre** ☎ Wadebridge 3809, M, ME, El, CH; **Chapman & Hewitt** ☎ Wadebridge 2981, BY; **Westerly Boats** ☎ Trebetherick 3439, Slip, L, Sh; **Cornish Crabbers** ☎ Trebetherick 2666, Slip, ME, Sh, C; **Nettec Marine Chandlers** (on quay), CH, Gas, Gaz.
Town ⊚, P, ✉; Ⓑ; ⇌ (bus to Bodmin Road); ✈ (Newquay or Plymouth).

MINOR HARBOURS AND ANCHORAGES 10.11.24

MOCHRAS, Gwynedd, 52°49′ N, 4°07′ W, Zone 0 (GMT), Admty chart 1512. HW −0245 on Dover, +0205 on Milford Haven. HW height −1.7m on Milford Haven. Small yacht harbour on E end of Shell Island. Mochras lagoon dries. See 10.11.5. Entrance between Shell Is (Lt Fl WRG 4s; G079°-124°, W124°-134°, R134°-179°; shown Apl-Nov) and sea wall. Bar, about 2 ca to seaward. Three R posts mark N side of channel. Tide runs strongly in the narrows on the ebb. Entry advised after HW∓2. Inside, the channel runs NE to Pen-Sarn, marked by posts. To S buoyed channel runs to Shell Island Yacht Harbour. Shallow draught boats can lie afloat below the railway bridge. Facilities (Pen-Sarn) Slip, AB, FW, ⇌. **Shell Island** ☎ Llanbedr 453 M, FW, R, Slip.

ABERAERON, Dyfed, 52°19′ N, 4°09′ W, Zone 0 (GMT), Admty Chart 1484. HW −0325 on Dover, +0140 on Milford Haven; HW height −1.9m on Milford Haven; ML 2.7m; Duration 0540. A small drying harbour at the mouth of the R. Aeron (or Ayron). Short piers extend each side of the river ent. Pierheads dry. In strong NW winds there is little shelter. Foul ground with depths of 1.5m extend 3 ca offshore to SW of Aberaeron. Beware Carreg Gloyn (0.3m) 4 ca WSW of harbour; Sarn Cadwgan (1.8m) extending ½M offshore from Cadwgan Pt to NE of Aberaeron. Lights:− N pier Fl(4)R 15s 6m 6M; vis 104°-178°. S pier Fl(3)G 10s 6m 7M; vis 125°-200°. No radio telephone. Facilities: Hr Mr ☎ 570407; **Aberaeron YC** ☎ 570077.

NEW QUAY, Dyfed, 52°13′ N, 4°21′ W, Zone −0100. Admty charts 1484, 1972. HW −0335 on Dover, +0140 on Milford Haven. HW height −2.0m on Milford Haven; ML 2.6m; Duration 0540. The bay gives shelter in offshore winds, but NW winds make it untenable. On E side of bay is Carreg Ina, a rock which dries 1.6m marked by N cardinal buoy. Bns show alignment of sewer pipe extending 7ca NNW from Ina Point. There are moorings in the bay. The harbour (dries) is protected by a pier with a Lt, FIWG 3s 12m 8/5M; vis W135°-252°, G252°-295°. Rocks, marked by a Bn, extend 50m SSE from pierhead. Facilities: Hr Mr ☎ 560368; CG ☎ 560212; Dr ☎ 560203; YC ☎ 560516; D (from fishermen) ☎ 560375. **Town** D, FW, V, P (3M), ✉, R, Bar.

CARDIGAN, Dyfed, 52°06′ N, 4°41′ W, Zone 0 (GMT), Admty chart 1484. HW −0350 on Dover, +0130 on Milford Haven; HW height −2.1m on Milford Haven; ML 2.7m; Duration 0550. See 10.11.10. Shelter is good but entrance dangerous in strong N to NW winds. Bar dries but has 2.5m at MHWS. Channel between Pen-y-Ergyd and Bryn Du changes continuously. Anchor in pools in R Teifi near St Dogmaels. There are no lights. Facilities: EC Wed; Hr Mr ☎ 612084; **Ynys Marine** ☎ 613179, ME, Sh; **Town** Ⓑ, Bar, CH, D, FW, ME, P, R, ⇌, V.

SOLVA, Dyfed, 51°52′ N, 5°12′ W, Zone 0 (GMT), Admty chart 1478. HW −0450 on Dover, +0012 on Milford Haven, HW height −1.3m on Milford Haven; ML 3.2m; Duration 0555. Good shelter for small boats that can take the ground. Beware Black Rock in centre of entrance (E side entrance recommended) and stone spit at Trwyn Caws on W just inside entrance. Strong S winds make entrance difficult. There are nine visitors buoys painted red and some drying moorings available. Anchor behind the rock in approx 3m. Small craft can go up to the quay. Facilities very limited; stores available in village. FW on quay. Hr Mr St. Davids 721373, M, CH, Access HW∓3; **Solva Boat Owners Assn.** ☎ St Davids 721209.

ST BRIDES BAY, Dyfed, 51°48′ N, 5°10′ W, Zone 0 (GMT), Admty chart 1478. HW (Little Haven) − 0450 on Dover, +0010 on Milford Haven; HW height −1.3m on Milford Haven; ML 3.2m; Duration 0555. Many good anchorages, especially between Little Haven and Borough Head in S or E winds or between Solva and Dinas Fawry in N or E winds, but in W winds boats should shelter in Solva (see above) or Skomer (see below). For approaches from the N or S see 10.11.5. Keep clear of Research Area in the middle of the bay, marked by buoys. Facilities: (Little Haven) CH, V, R, Bar, FW (cans).

SKOMER, Dyfed, 51°44′ N, 5°17′ W, Zone 0 (GMT), Admty charts 2878, 1478. HW −0455 Dover, −0005 on Milford Haven; HW height −0.4m (Sp), −0.1m (Np) on Milford Haven. The island is a nature reserve (fee payable to Warden on landing); anchorage in North Haven or South Haven; in both cases keep close to W shore entering, and land on The Neck (E side). Landing in S Haven is discouraged. Keep at least 100m off coastline 1st Sept-28th Feb to avoid disturbing seals and between 1st Mar-31st July to avoid disturbing nesting sea birds. Do not anchor in N Haven but pick up buoys provided. For Jack Sound see 10.11.5. There are no lights or marks and no facilities.

SAUNDERSFOOT, Dyfed, 51°43′ N, 4°42′ W, Zone 0 (GMT), Admty chart 1482 1076. HW −0510 on Dover, −0013 on Milford Haven. HW height +1.4m on Milford Haven; ML 4.4m; Duration 0605. A half-tide harbour with good shelter with S to SW winds there may be a surge and with E winds it may be rough. On approach, beware buoys marking restricted area (power boats, etc) between Coppett Hall Pt and Perry's Pt. Alongside berths are sometimes available (see Hr Mr) as are moorings in the middle. Light on pierhead Fl R 5s 6m 7M on stone cupola VHF, Hr Mr 16; 11. Facilities: EC Wed; Hr Mr ☎ 812094, CH, FW (on SW wall), Slip; **Jones and Teague** ☎ 813429, ME; **Vox Leisure** ☎ Hr Mr, BH; **Town** V, R, Bar, ✉, Ⓑ, ⇌.

CARMARTHEN, Dyfed, 51°51′ N, 4°18′ W, Zone 0 (GMT), Admty chart 1076. HW −0455 on Dover, +0010 on Milford Haven; HW height −4.6m on Milford Haven. R Towy dries out, except for river water. Beware Carmarthen Bar off mouth of Rivers Towy and Taf. Local knowledge or a pilot are essential. Channel into rivers changes frequently and is not buoyed. Access HW∓2. There are six electric cables crossing between the mouth and the railway bridge in Carmarthen, min clearance 15m. Visitors berths at R Towy YC at Ferryside (9M below Carmarthen), access HW∓3 (liable to dry). Facilities: **Carmarthen** normal facilities of a market town; **Tawe Works** ☎ 236601, Gas; **River Towy YC** (Ferryside) ☎ Ferryside 366, Bar, FW, M; **Town** Normal facilities Ⓑ, Bar, ✉, V, ⇌, ✈ (Swansea).

PORTHCAWL, Mid Glamorgan, 51°24′ N, 3°42′ W; Zone 0 (GMT). Admty chart 1169. HW −0505 on Dover; 0005 on Milford Haven; HW height +2.6m on Milford Haven; ML 5.3m. See 10.11.15. A small tidal harbour protected by breakwater running SE from Porthcawl Pt. Beware rock ledge (dries) to W of breakwater. At end of breakwater Porthcawl Lt Ho, W 6-sided tower with B base; F WRG 10m 6/4M; vis G302°-036°, W036°-082°, R082°-122°. In line 094° with Saint Hilary radio mast leads through Shord channel. Tidal streams can reach 6kn at springs off end of breakwater. Anchor approx 3ca SSE of Lt Ho. Facilities: EC Wed; Hr Mr 2756, 3 visitors moorings (HW∓2); **Porthcawl Marine** ☎ 4785, CH; **Porthcawl Harbour Boating Club** ☎ 2342; **Town** V, R, Bar, P and D (cans), ✉, Ⓑ, ⇌ (Bridgend), ✈ (Cardiff).

MINOR HARBOURS AND ANCHORAGES *Continued*

NEWPORT, Gwent, 51°33′ N, 2°59′ W, Zone 0 (GMT), Admty chart 1176. HW −0425 on Dover, −0015 on Avonmouth, HW height −1.0m on Avonmouth; ML 6.0m; Duration 0620. See 10.11.17. A commercial port controlled by Associated British Ports (☎ 65411) but a safe sheltered port for yachts. Enter R Usk over bar (approx 0.5m) E of West Usk buoy and follow buoyed and lit channel to South Lock entrance; turn NE, yacht moorings on S side between power station pier and YC. W Usk buoy QR Bell, East Usk Lt Ho Fl (2) WRG 10s 11m 15/11M, W284° −290°, R290° −017°, W017° −037°, G037° −115°, W115° −120°. Ldg Lts 057°, both FG. Alexandra Dock, S lock W pier head 2 FR (vert) 9/7m 6M. E pier head 2 FG (vert) 9/7m 6M. VHF Ch 16; 09 11 (HW −4 to HW +4). Facilities: EC Thurs; ⚓ ☎ 273709 **Beechwood Marine** ☎ 277955, CH, El, ME, Sh; **Leeway Leisure** ☎ 276611, CH, El, ME, Sh; **Aquascan** ☎ 841117, Ⓔ; **Town** All facilities.

WESTON-SUPER-MARE, Avon, 51°21′ N, 2°59′ W, Zone 0 (GMT), Admty charts 1152, 1176. HW −0435 on Dover, −0025 on Avonmouth; HW height −1.1m on Avonmouth; ML 6.1m; Duration 0655. See 10.11.20. Good shelter except in S winds in Knightstone Harbour (dries) at N end of bay. Causeway at entrance marked by Bn. Access HW∓2. Grand pierhead 2 FG (vert) 6/5m. Alternative anchorage in good weather in R Axe (dries), entry HW∓2. Facilities: EC Mon, **Passey and Porter** ☎ 628281; CH, El, ME, Sh, Slip; **Uphill Boat Services** ☎ 418617; CH, El, D, FW, Slip, BH (10 ton), ME, Sh; **Weston Bay YC** ☎ 620772; FW, Bar, VHF Ch **80 Town** Bar, Ⓑ; D, FW, P, ✉, R, ⇌, ✈.

WATCHET, Somerset, 51°11′ N, 3°20′ W, Zone 0 (GMT), Admty chart 1160. HW −0455 on Dover, −0043 on Avonmouth; HW height −1.7m on Avonmouth; ML 6.2m; Duration 0655. See 10.11.20. Good shelter but harbour dries; there is approx 6m in entrance at MHWS. Available approx HW∓2. Yachts should berth on W breakwater. Beware tidal streams round W pier head. Rocks and mud dry 0.5M to seaward. W breakwater head FG 9m 9M. E pier head 2 FR (vert) 3M. VHF Ch 16; 14 12 (HW−2 to HW+2). On W breakwater head B ball (Fl G at night) and on E pier 2 FR (vert) − at least 2.4m on flood or 3m on ebb. Facilities: EC Wed; Hr Mr ☎ 3430; ⚓ ☎ 31214, FW, D, P, Slip, CH, V, R, Bar; **Watchet Boat Owners Assn.**

MINEHEAD, Somerset, 51°13′ N, 3°28′ W, Zone 0 (GMT), Admty chart 1160. HW −0450 on Dover, −0040 on Avonmouth; HW height −2.6m (Sp), −1.9m (Np) on Avonmouth; ML 5.7m. There is no bar; access HW∓2. Small harbour formed by pier curving E and then SE, over which seas break in gales at MHWS. Best approach from N or NW; beware The Gables, shingle bank (dries 3.3m) about ¾ M ENE of pier. Berth alongside pier. A sewer outfall runs from a position 2ca S of pierhead to 1¾ ca NNE of it, passing ½ ca E of pierhead. Outer portion is protected by rock covering, rising to 2.8m above sea bed. Outer end marked by stbd-hand Bn QG 6m 7M. Harbour gets very crowded. Pierhead Lt Fl(2)G 5s 4M; vis 127°-262°. Facilities: EC Wed; Hr Mr ☎ 702566; **Tarr and Foy** ☎ 702029, Gas; **Pier** FW, Slip; **Town** normal facilities, Bar, D, El, Gas, ME, P, R, Sh, V, ✉, Ⓑ, ⇌ (Taunton or Barnstaple), ✈ (Exeter).

PORLOCK WEIR, Somerset, 51°13′ N, 3°38′ W, Zone 0 (GMT), Admty chart 1160. HW −0500 on Dover, −0050 on Avonmouth; HW height −2.6m on Avonmouth; ML 5.6m; Duration 0655. See 10.11.20. Shelter very good once in harbour but entrance difficult. Channel between pebble bank to NW and wooden wall to SE approx 15m wide. There is a small pool just inside entrance for shallow draft boats − others dry out inside harbour. There are no lights. Hr Mr ☎ 862106. Facilities: very limited; FW and stores on quay; **Porlock Weir SC** ☎ 862028.

WATERMOUTH, Devon, 51°13′ N, 4°05′ S, Zone 0 (GMT), Admty chart 1165. HW −0525 on Dover, −0020 on Milford Haven; HW height +2.0m on Milford Haven; ML 4.9m; Duration 0625. Good shelter, except from NW winds, but harbour dries. Entrance identified by white CG cottage above Rillage Pt. SW gales cause heavy surge in harbour. Access HW∓3 at sp, outside breakwater only at np. Visitors buoys distinguished by Y handles on R buoys. Facilities: M, D (cans), FW (cans), Slip; **Watermouth Caves** ☎ 62504, Gas; **Watermouth YC** ☎ 65048, Bar.

LUNDY ISLAND, Devon, 51°11′ N, 4°40′ W, Zone 0 (GMT), Admty chart 1164. HW −0530 on Dover, −0030 on Milford Haven; HW height +0.9m on Milford Haven; ML 4.3m; Duration 0605. See 10.11.22. Shelter good if correct side of island is selected according to the wind. In winds from NW to SSW anchor N of SE point of island. In winds from E to N some shelter can be obtained on W side of the island but holding ground is poor. Jenny's Cove on W side is safe so long as there is no W ground swell. The high land (145m) gives considerable shelter. Waters round the island are a Marine Nature Reserve. Near N Pt, Lt Fl (2) 20s 50m 24M; vis 009° −285°. On SE Pt, Lt Fl 5s 53m 24M; vis 170° −073°; RC. Facilities: Landing place by the anchorage in the SW corner; **Lundy Co Landmark Trust** ☎ Woolacombe 870870, CH, Gas, bar and hotel.

BUDE, Cornwall, 50°50′ N, 4°33′ W, Zone 0 (GMT), Admty chart 1156. HW −0540 on Dover, −0040 on Milford Haven; HW height +0.7m on Milford Haven; Duration 0605. See 10.11.22. Limited shelter; Hr dries − available for average yacht HW∓2. Provided prior arrangements have been made, yachts can pass lock and berth in canal (approx 5 m over CD required). Locking fees are high (£50; £75 outside working hours; £100 Sundays), and gates will only open if there is no sea running. Ldg marks, front W spar with Y diamond topmark, rear W flagstaff, in line at 075°. Continue on this line until inner ldg marks in line at 131°, front W pile with Y triangular topmark, rear W spar with Y triangular topmark. There are no lights. VHF Ch 16; 12 (when vessel expected). Facilities: EC Thurs; Hr Mr ☎ 353111; very limited facilities; **N.E. Truscott** ☎ 352423, Gas; **Town** Ⓑ, Bar, ✉, R. V.

NEWQUAY, Cornwall, 50°25′ N, 5°05′ W, Zone 0 (GMT), Admty chart 1168. HW −0604 on Dover, −0100 on Milford Haven; HW height +0.1m on Milford Haven; ML 3.7m; see 10.11.23. Entrance to harbour between two walls, rather narrow. Beware Old Dane Rk and Listrey Rk outside harbour towards Towan Hd. Swells cause a surge in the harbour. Enter HW∓2 but not in strong onshore winds. Hr dries; berth as directed by Hr Mr. Lts − North Pier 2 FG (vert) 2M, South Pier 2 FR (vert) 2M. VHF Ch 16 14 Facilities: EC Wed (winter only); Hr Mr ☎ 872809, FW, Slip, D, V, R, Bar; **H. N. Bennett** ☎ 875900, Gas, Gaz; **J. B. Marine** ☎ 878185, CH. (Shallow draft boats can take the ground in Gannel Creek, close S of Newquay, but only in settled weather. Beware causeway bridge about half way up the creek.).

HAYLE, Cornwall, 50°11′ N, 5°25′ W, Zone 0 (GMT), Admty chart 1168. HW −0605 on Dover, −0100 on Milford Haven; HW height −0.4m on Milford Haven; ML 3.6m; Duration 0555. Shelter is very good but dangerous sea breaks on bar in strong on-shore winds; harbour dries. Approx 5m at entrance at MHWS. The harbour is divided by long arm (approx 300m) stretching almost to Ldg Lts which should be left to W. Beware training bank W of entrance channel marked by perches. Lts in line 180°, front FW 17m 4M, rear FW 23m 4M. E arm of harbour leads to Hayle, the W arm to Lelant Quay. Hayle E pierhead 2 FG (vert), W pierhead 2 FR (vert). (Note: Hayle is closed to commercial traffic. Small craft may cross the bar in good weather within 1h of HW. Charted aids do not necessarily indicate best water). Facilities: EC Thurs; Ⓑ, Bar, FW, ⇌, R, V, P and D (cans).

ST IVES, Cornwall, 50°13′ N, 5°28′ W, Zone 0 (GMT), Admty chart 1168. HW −0605 on Dover, −0100 on Milford Haven; HW height −0.4m on Milford Haven; ML 3.6m; Duration 0555. See 10.11.23. Shelter is good except in on-shore winds when heavy swell builds up. 9 visitors moorings available. Harbour dries but has approx 4.5m at MHWS. Alternative anchorage between the harbour and Porthminster Pt to S in 3m. Beware Hoe Rock off St Ives Hd coming from NW, and The Carracks off Porthminster Pt coming from SE. Keep E of G conical buoy about 1½ ca ENE of Smeaton's pierhead. Lights, E pier head (Smeatons pier) 2 FG (vert) 8m 5M. W pier head 2 FR (vert) 5m 3M. VHF Ch 16. Facilities: EC Thurs; Hr Mr ☎ Penzance 795018; six visitor moorings; **Fisherman's Co-op** ☎ Penzance 796276, Gas, Gaz; **Smeaton's Pier** FW; **Town** Ⓑ, ▢, Bar, FW, P (in cans), ✉, R, ⇌, V.

11

VOLVO PENTA SERVICE

Sales and service centres in area 12
Names and addresses of Volvo Penta dealers in
this area are available from:

IRELAND **Western Marine** Bulloch Harbour, Dalkey, CO. DUBLIN Tel 800321
Telex 800327.

**VOLVO
PENTA**

Area 12

South Ireland
Shannon to Malahide

12

548

Clifden** [LB]

Cashel Bay

10°W

9°W

Slyne Head
(RC) SN
1,3,5 ••• --
289.6 50

Galway Bay
Standard Port
[i] 10.13.19
[P][R] VHF 16; 12

Eeragh Island
Inishmore
Black Head
Kilronan**
[LB]
Aran Islands
Inisheer

53°
N

Liscanor Bay

Ennis
(RC) Aero ENS
352 80 •••

Shannon Airport
061–61333
Shannon [CG]

Kilrush
[i] 10.12.8

Loop Head
(RC) LP
2,4,6 ••• --•--
289.6 50

Limerick
[P][R] VHF 16;12

Shannon Radio
[C][S] VHF 16 24
28 67
0833/2033
On VHF Every
3 Hours From 0103

Kerry Head

River Shannon
[i] 10.12.9

Foynes
(RC) Aero FOY
•--• --- -•--
395 50
[P][R] VHF 16; 12 13

Little Samphire Island

Brandon Bay

Smerwick Harbour

Tralee Bay *

Cork (Cobh)
Standard Port
[i] 10.12.17
[P][R] VHF 16 ;12 14

Ventry* **Dingle***

Inishtearaght

Dingle Bay

Cork Radio
[C][S] VHF 16;26
Every 3 Hours
From 0103

52°
N

Valentia
[C][S] MF–1827
VHF 16 67
0833/2033
On VHF Every
3 Hours From 0103
[LB]

Kenmare River
[i] 10.12.10

Cork Airport
021–965974

Portmagee*

Bantry
[i] 10.12.11
[P][R] VHF 16;11 14

Kinsale
[i] 10.12.16
[P][R] VHF16; 06 14

Oys
Hav

Great Skellig

Kenmare River

Glengariff*•

Castletown*
Bantry Bay

Schull
[i] 10.12.13

Courtmacsherry*•
Glandore*•
[LB]

Bull Rock

Sheep Head

Galley Head

**Old Head
Kinsal**
(RC) OH
2 --- •••
296.5

Bantry Radio
[C][S] VHF 16 23
67 85
Every 3 Hours
From 0103

Mizen Head
(RC) MZ
4 -- --•••
308 200/100

C. Clear

Castle Haven
[i] 10.12.15

Fastnet

Crookhaven
[i] 10.12.12

Baltimore
[i] 10.12.14
[LB]

10°W

9°W

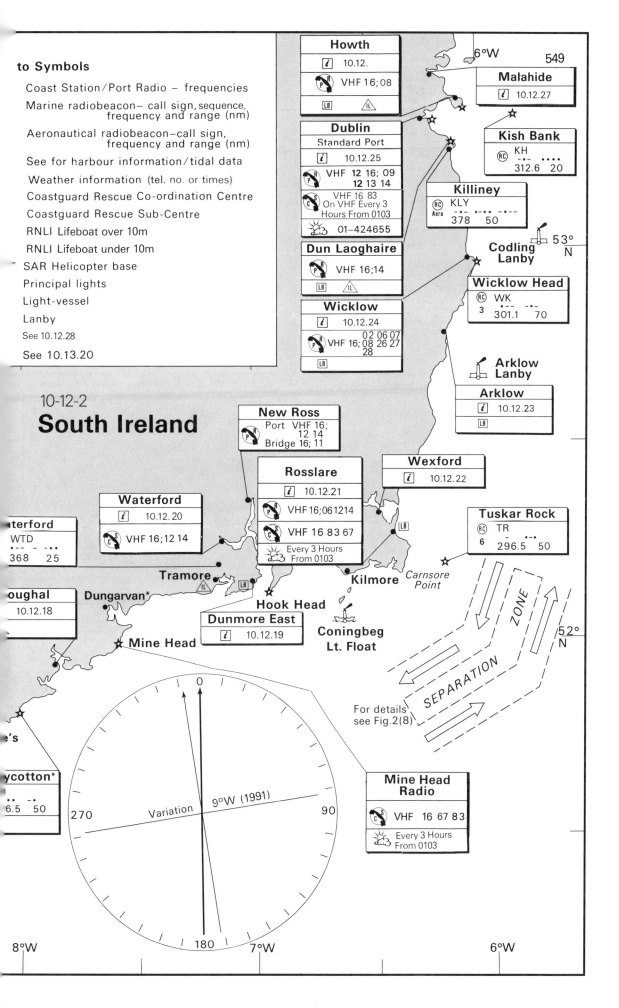

to Symbols

Coast Station/Port Radio – frequencies

Marine radiobeacon– call sign, sequence, frequency and range (nm)

Aeronautical radiobeacon–call sign, frequency and range (nm)

See for harbour information/tidal data

Weather information (tel. no. or times)

Coastguard Rescue Co-ordination Centre

Coastguard Rescue Sub-Centre

RNLI Lifeboat over 10m

RNLI Lifeboat under 10m

SAR Helicopter base

Principal lights

Light-vessel

Lanby

See 10.12.28

See 10.13.20

6°W

Howth
i	10.12.
P R	VHF 16; 08
LB	IL

Malahide
| i | 10.12.27 |

Kish Bank
RC	KH
	─·─ ····
	312.6 20

Dublin
Standard Port
i	10.12.25
P R	VHF **12** 16; 09 **12** 13 14
C S	VHF 16 83 On VHF Every 3 Hours From 0103
☁	01–424655

Killiney
RC Aero	KLY
	─·─ ··· ─·─
	378 50

Dun Laoghaire
| P R | VHF 16;14 |
| LB | IL |

Codling Lanby

53° N

Wicklow Head
RC	WK
3	·─ ─·
	301.1 70

Wicklow
i	10.12.24
P R	VHF 16; 08 26 27 28 / 02 06 07
LB	

Arklow Lanby

Arklow
| i | 10.12.23 |
| LB | |

10-12-2
South Ireland

New Ross
| P R | Port VHF 16; 12 14 |
| | Bridge 16; 11 |

Wexford
| i | 10.12.22 |

Waterford
| i | 10.12.20 |
| C S | VHF 16;12 14 |

Rosslare
i	10.12.21
P R	VHF 16;061214
C S	VHF 16 83 67
☁	Every 3 Hours From 0103

terford
| WTD |
| ·─ ─· |
| 368 25 |

Tuskar Rock
RC	TR
6	─·
	296.5 50

LB

Tramore

IL
LB

oughal
| | 10.12.18 |

Dungarvan*

Kilmore

Carnsore Point

ZONE

SEPARATION

52° N

Hook Head

Dunmore East
| i | 10.12.19 |

Mine Head

Coningbeg Lt. Float

e's

ycotton*
| ·· ─· |
| 6.5 50 |

270

Variation 9°W (1991)

90

180

For details see Fig.2(8)

Mine Head Radio
| C S | VHF 16 67 83 |
| ☁ | Every 3 Hours From 0103 |

8°W

7°W

6°W

10.12.3   AREA 12 TIDAL STREAMS

5 Hours before HW Dover (0530 before HW Dublin)

4 Hours before HW Dover (0430 before HW Dublin)

3 Hours before HW Dover (0330 before HW Dublin)

2 Hours before HW Dover (0230 before HW Dublin)

1 Hour before HW Dover (0130 before HW Dublin)

HW Dover (0030 before HW Dublin)

Northward 10.13.3   South Irish Sea 10.11.3

1 Hour after HW Dover (0030 after HW Dublin)

2 Hours after HW Dover (0130 after HW Dublin)

3 Hours after HW Dover (0230 after HW Dublin)

4 Hours after HW Dover (0330 after HW Dublin)

5 Hours after HW Dover (0430 after HW Dublin)

6 Hours after HW Dover (0530 after HW Dublin)

12

10.12.4   LIGHTS, FOG SIGNALS AND WAYPOINTS

Abbreviations used below are given in 10.0.3. Principal lights are in **bold** print, places in CAPITALS, and light-vessels, light floats and Lanbys in *CAPITAL ITALICS*. Unless otherwise stated lights are white. m—elevation in metres; M—nominal range in n. miles. Fog signals are in *italics*. Useful waypoints are <u>underlined</u> use those on land with care. See 4.2.2.

IRELAND—WEST COAST

RIVER SHANNON.
Ballybunnion Lt Buoy 52°32'·50N 09°46'·92W VQ; N cardinal mark.
<u>Kilcredaun Head</u> 52°34'·78N 09°42'·58W Fl 6s 41m 13M; W Tr; obsc within 1M 224°-247°.
Scattery Island, <u>Rineana Point</u> 52°36'·33N 09°31'·05W Fl(2) 7·5s 15m 10M; W Tr; vis 208°-092° (H24).
Tarbert Island, N point Iso WR 4s 18m W14M, R10M; W round Tr; vis W069°-277°, R277°-287°, W287°-339°.
Jetty 52°35'·4N 09°22'·5W 2 FG (vert) at SW end and at NE end.
Tarbert Ldg Lts 128°. Front Iso 2s 13m 3M; triangle on W framework Tr; vis 123°-133°. Rear, 400m from front, Iso 5s 18m 3M; G stripe on W Bn.
Garraunbaun Point Fl(3) WR 10s 16m W8M, R5M; W square column, vis R shore-072°, W072°-242°, R242°-shore.
Rinealon Point, Rinalan Fl 2·5s 4m 7M; B column, W bands; vis 234°-088°.

FOYNES,
West Channel Ldg Lts 108° (may be moved for changes in channel). Front, Barneen Point 52°36'·9N 09°06'·5W Iso WRG 4s 3m W4M, R3M, G3M; B triangle with W stripe on W column with B bands; vis W273°-038°, R038°-094°, G094°-104°, W104°-108°, R108°-114°. Rear, East Jetty, 540m from front Oc 4s 16m 10M; B triangle with W stripe on W column with B bands.
Colleen Point, No. 3, 52°36'·9N 09°06'·9W QG 2m 2M; W column, B bands.
Weir Point, No. 4, 52°37'·0N 09°07'·0W VQ(4)R 10s 2m 2M; W column, B bands.
Beeves Rock 52°39'·0N 09°01'·3W Fl WR 5s 12m W12M, R9M; vis W064°-091°, R091°-238°, W238°-265°, W(unintens) 265°-064°.
Shannon Airport 52°41'·7N 08°55'·6W Aero AlFl WG 7·5s 40m.
Dernish Island, pier head, 2 FR (vert) 4m 2M each end.
E breakwater head QR 3m 1M.
Conor Rock 52°40'·9N 08°54'·2W Fl R 4s 6m 6M; W framework Tr; vis 228°-093°.
North Channel Ldg Lts 093°. Front, Tradree Rock 52°41'·0N 08°49'·9W Fl R 2s 6m 5M; W framework Tr; vis 246°-110°. Rear 0·65M from front Iso 6s 14m 5M; W Tr, R bands; vis 327°-190°.
Bird Rock 52°40'·9N 08°50'·2W QG 6m 5M; W framework Tr.
Grass Island 52°40'·4N 08°48'·5W Fl G 2s 6m 4M; W column, B bands.
Laheen's Rock 52°40'·3N 08°48'·1W QR 4m 5M.
S side, Spilling Rock 52°40'·0N 08°47'·1W Fl G 5s.
N side, Ldg Lts 061°. Front, Crawford Rock 490m from rear, Fl R 3s 6m 5M. Crawford No. 2, Common rear, 52°40'·8N 08°44'·8W Iso 6s 10m 5M.
Ldg Lts 302°. Flagstaff Rock, 670m from rear, Fl R 2s 7m 5M.
The Whelps 52°40'·6N 08°45'·1W Fl G 3s 5m 5M; W pile structure.

Ldg Lts 106°. Meelick Rock, front 52°40'·2N 08°42'·3W Iso 4s 6m 3M. Meelick No. 2, rear 275m from front Iso 6s 9m 5M; both W pile structures.
Ldg Lts 146°, Braemar Point, front 52°39'·1N 08°41'·9W Iso 4s 5m 5M. Rear Braemar No. 2, 122m from front Iso 6s 6m 4M; both W pile structures.
N side, Clonmacken Point 52°39'·5N 08°40'·6W Fl R 3s 7m 4M. E side, Spillane's Tower 52°39'·3N 08°39'·8W Fl 3s 11m 6M; turret on Tr.

LIMERICK DOCK.
Lts in line 098°. Front 52°39'·5N 08°38'·8W. Rear 100m from front; both F; R diamonds on columns; occas.
North Wharf head, 2 FR (vert) 10m; occas.

TRALEE BAY.
Little Samphire Island 52°16'·23N 09°52'·80W Fl WRG 5s 27m **W16M**, R13M; G13M; Blue round Tr; vis R262°-275°, R280°-090°, G090°-140°, W140°-152°, R152°-172°.
Great Samphire Island 52°16'·1N 09°52'·2W QR 15m 3M; vis 097°-242°.
Fenit Pier, head 52°16'·2N 09°51'·5W 2FR(vert) 12m 3M; vis 148°-058°.
Brandon Pier, head 52°16'·0N 10°09'·6W 2 FG (vert) 5m 4M.

Inishtearaght, West end Blasket Islands 52°04'·60N 10°39'·60W Fl(2) 20s 84m **27M**; W Tr; vis 318°-221° also shown by day in poor visibility.

DINGLE.
NE side of entrance Fl G 3s 20m 6M.
Pier head 52°08'·3N 10°16'·5W 2 FR (vert) 4m 2M.
Ldg Lts 182°. Front 52°07'·4N 10°16'·6W, rear 100m from front, both Oc 3s.

VALENTIA.
Fort (Cromwell) Point 51°56'·00N 10°19'·25W Fl WR 2s 16m **W17M**, **R15M**; W Tr; vis R102°-304°, W304°-351°; obsc from seaward by Doulus head when brg more than 180°.
FR Lts on radio masts on Geokaun hill 1·25M WSW.
Ldg Lts 141°. Front Oc WRG 4s 25m W11M, R8M, G8M; W conical Tr; vis G134°-140°, W140°-142°, R142°-148°. Rear 122m from front Oc 4s 43m 5M; vis 133°-233° synchronised with front.

Skelligs Rock 51°46'·10N 10°32'·43W Fl(3) 10s 53m **27M**; W Tr; vis 262°-115°; part obsc within 6M 110°-115°

DARRYNANE.
Ldg Lts 034°. Front 51°45'·9N 10°09'·2W Oc3s 10m 4M. Rear Oc 3s 16m 4M.
Ballycrovane Harbour 51°42'·6N 09°57'·5W Fl R 3s.

Bull Rock 51°35'·47N 10°18'·05W Fl 15s 83m **31M**; W Tr; vis 220°-186°.

BANTRY BAY
Sheep Head 51°32'·57N 09°51'·00W Fl(3) WR 15s 83m **W18M**, **R15M**; W building; vis R007°-017°, W017°-212°.

BEREHAVEN
West entrance, **Ardnakinna Point** Fl(2) WR 10s 62m **W17M**, R14M; W round Tr; vis R319°-348°, W348°-066°, R066°-shore. FR on radio mast 3·45M 295°.

Castletown Dir Lt 024° 51°38'·80N 09°54'·30W Dir Oc WRG 5s 4m W14M, R11M, G11M; W hut, R stripe; vis G020·5°-024°, W024°-024·5°, R024·5°-027·5°.

CASTLETOWN BERE
Perch Rock QG 4m 1M; W column, B bands. Ldg Lts 010°. Front 51°39'·1N 09°54'·4W Oc 3s 4m 1M; W column, R stripe, B&W chequered sides; vis 005°-015°. Rear 80m from front Oc 3s 7m 1M; W with R stripe; vis 005°-015°.

Roancarrigmore 51°39'·17N 09°44'·80W Fl WR 3s 18m **W18M**, R14M; W round Tr, B band; vis W312°-050°, R050°-122°, R(unintens) 122°-242°, R242°-312°. Reserve Lt W10M, R6M obsc 140°-220°.

WHIDDY ISLAND
West clearing Lt Oc 2s 22m 3M; vis 073°-106°.
SW dolphin QY 10m 2M; *Horn 20s.*
NE dolphin QY 10m 2M.

Mizen Head 51°26'·97N 09°49'·18W Iso 4s 52m **16M**; vis 313°-133°; RC; Racon.

CROOKHAVEN,
Rock Island Point 51°28'·55N 09°42'·23W L Fl WR 8s 20m W13M, R11M; W Tr; vis W over Long Island bay to 281°, R281°-340°; inside harbour R281°-348°, W348° towards N shore.

IRELAND—SOUTH COAST
Fastnet, West end 51°23'·33N 09°36'·13W Fl 5s 49m **28M**; grey Tr; *Horn (4) 60s.*
Copper Point, Long Island, E end 51°30'·22N 09°32'·02W Q(3) 10s 16m 8M; W round Tr.

SCHULL
Ldg Lts 346° Front 51°31'·6N 09°32'·5W Oc 5s 5m 11M, W mast. Rear 91m from front Oc 5s 8m 11M; W mast.

BALTIMORE
Barrack Point 51°28'·33N 09°23'·65W Fl(2) WR 6s 40m W6M, R3M; vis R168°-294°, W294°-038°.

CASTLE HAVEN
Reen Point 51°30'·9N 09°10'·5W Fl WRG 10s 9m W5M, R3M, G3M; W Tr; vis G shore-338°, W338°-001°, R001°-shore.

Galley Head, summit 51°31'·82N 08°57'·13W Fl(5) 20s 53m **28M**; W Tr; vis 256°-065°.

COURTMACSHERRY
Wood Point 51°38'·3N 08°41'·0W Fl(2) WR 5s 15m 5M; vis W315°-332°, R332°-315°.
Old Head of Kinsale, S point 51°36'·23N 08°31'·80W Fl(2) 10s 72m **25M**; B Tr, two W bands; RC; *Horn (3) 45s.*

KINSALE.
Bulman Lt Buoy 51°40'·10N 08°29'·70W Q(6)LFl 15s; S cardinal mark.
Charles's Fort Fl WRG 5s 18m W9M, R6M, G6M; vis G348°-358°, W358°-004°, R004°-168° shown throughout 24 hrs. Marina, each end 2 FG (vert).

CORK.
Roche's Point 51°47'·56N 08°15'·24W Oc WR 20s 30m **W20M, R16M**; vis R shore-292°, W292°-016°, R016°-033°, W(unintens) 033°-159°, R159°-shore; *Dia 30s.*
White Bay Ldg Lts 035°. Front Oc R 5s 11m 5M; W hut. Rear 113m from front Oc R 5s 21m 5M; W hut; synchronised with front.

Fort Davis Ldg Lts 354°. Front Oc 5s 29m 10M. Rear. Dognose Landing Quay, 203m from front Oc 5s 37m 10M; synchronised with front.
Curraghbinney Ldg Lts 252°. Front 51°48'·6N 08°17'·6W F 10m 3M. Rear, 61m from front, F 15m 3M; both white diamonds on columns; vis 229°-274°.
Crosshaven Marina 2 FR (vert) at NE and NW corners. Whitegate Marine Terminal, Jetty, 2 FG (vert) at S and N heads.
East Ferry Marina, East Passage, 2 FR (vert) at N and S ends.
Spit Bank Pile 51°50'·70N 08°16'·41W Iso WR 4s 10m W10M, R7M; W house on R piles; vis R087°-196°, W196°-221°, R221°-358°.

Ballycotton 51°49'·50N 07 59'·00W Fl WR 10s 59m **W22M, R18M**; B Tr, within W walls, B lantern; vis W238°-063°, R063°-238°; RC; *Dia(4) 90s.*

YOUGHAL
West side of entrance 51°56'·55N 07°50'·49W Fl WR 2·5s 24m W12M, R9M; W Tr; vis W183°-273°, R273°-295°, W295°-307°, R307°-351°, W351°-003°.

Mine Head 51°59'·57N 07°35'·60W Fl(4) 20s 87m **28M**; W Tr, B band; vis 228°-shore.
Ballinacourty Point 52°04'·67N 07°33'·10W Fl(2) WRG 10s 16m W12M, R9M, G9M; W Tr; vis G245°-274°, W274°-302°, R302°-325°, W325°-117°.

DUNGARVAN.
Ballinacourty Ldg Lts 083°. Front F 9m 2M; W column, B bands. Rear 46m from front F 12m 2M; W column, B bands.
Esplanade Ldg Lts. Front and Rear FR 8m 2M.

WATERFORD.
Hook Head 52°07'·40N 06°55'·72W Fl 3s 46m **24M**; W Tr, two B bands; Racon; *Horn (2) 45s.*
Dunmore East, E pier head L Fl WR 8s 13m W12M, R9M; grey Tr, W lantern; vis W225°-310°, R310°-004°.
E breakwater extension 52°08'·96N 06°59'·32W Fl R 2s 6m 4M; vis 000°-310°.
West wharf Fl G 2s 6m 4M; vis 165°-246°.
Duncannon Ldg Lts 002°. **Front** Oc 4s 13m **15M**; W Tr, R stripe on fort; vis 340°-030°. Oc WR 4s 13m W9M, R7M; same Tr; vis R119°-149°, W149°-172°. **Rear** 0·54M from front Oc 4s 39m **15M**; W Tr, R stripe; vis 354°-069°.
Middle Bar Lt Buoy 52°11'·83N 06°56'·48W Fl R 5s; port-hand mark.
Duncannon Spit Lt Buoy 52°12'·67N 06°56'·00W Fl(2) G 5s; stbd-hand mark.

Passage Point 52°14'·23N 06°57'·70W Fl WR 5s 7m W6M, R5M; R pile structure; vis W shore-127°, R127°-302°.
Cheek Point 52°16'·1N 06°59'·3W Q WR 6m 5M; W mast; vis W007°-289°, R289°-007°.
Sheagh 52°16'·3N 06°59'·4W Fl R 3s 29m 3M; vis 090°-318°.
Kilmokea 52°16'·4N 06°58'·9W Fl 5s.
Power station jetty, 4 in No 2 FR (vert) 3M.
Railway Bridge 8 FR; traffic signals.
Snowhill Point Ldg Lts 255°. Front Fl WR 2·5s 5m 3M; vis W222°-020°, R020°-057°, W057°-107°. Rear, Flour Mill, 0·4M from front Q 12m 5M.
Queen's Channel Ldg Lts 098°. Front QR 8m 5M; B Tr, W band; vis 030°-210°. Rear 550m from front Q 15m 5M; W mast.
Giles Quay 52°15'·4N 07°04'·2W Fl 3s 9m; vis 255°-086°.
Cove 52°15'·0N 07°05'·1W Fl WRG 6s 6m 2M; W Tr; vis R111°-161°, G161°-234°, W234°-111°.
Smelting House Point 52°15'·1N 07°05'·2W Q 8m 3M; W mast.

Ballycar 52°15'·0N 07°05'·4W Fl RG 3s 5m; vis G127°-212°, R212°-284°.

CONINGBEG Lt F 52°02'·38N 06°39'·45W Fl(3) 30s 12m **24M**; R hull, and Tr, lantern amidships; *Horn (3) 60s*. Racon.
Kilmore, breakwater head Q RG 6m 5M; vis R269°-354°, G354°-003°, R003°-077°.
Carne, pier head Fl R 3s 6m.

IRELAND—EAST COAST

Tuskar 52°12'·15N 06°12'·40W Q(2) 7·5s 33m **28M**; W Tr; RC; Racon; *Horn (4) 45s*.

ROSSLARE.
Pier head 52°15'·41N 06°20'·22W L Fl WRG 5s 15m W13M, R10M, G10M; R Tr; vis G098°-188°, W188°-208°, R208°-246°, G246°-283°, W283°-286°, R286°-320°.
Ldg Lts 124°. Front 52°15'·3N 06°20'·1W. Rear 67m from front. Both FR 2M; vis 079°-169°.
New Ferry Pier, head 52°15'·3N 06°20'·2W Q 10m 3M.
Ldg Lts 146°. Front 52°15'·2N 06°20'·1W, rear 110m from front, both Oc 3s 3M, synchronised.

ARKLOW LANBY 52°39'·50N 05°58'·10W Fl(2) 12s 12m **16M**; tubular structure on buoy; Racon; *Horn Mo(A) 30s* .
Arklow Head, Pier head 52°46'·7N 06°08'·4W Oc R 10s 9m 9M.

ARKLOW.
S pier head 52°47'·59N 06°08'·16W Fl WR 6s 10m 13M; framework Tr; vis R shore-223°, W223°-350°; R350°-shore.
N pier head LFl G 7s 7m 10M; vis shore-287°.

Wicklow Head 52°57'·93N 05°59'·83W Fl(3) 15s 37m **26M**; W Tr; RC.

WICKLOW
E pier head 52°58'·98N 06°02'·01W Fl WR 5s 11m 6M; W Tr, R base and cupola; vis R136°-293°, W293°-136°.
West pier head Fl G 1·5s 5m 6M.

CODLING LANBY 53°03'·02N 05°40'·70W Fl 4s 12m **16M**; tubular structure on buoy; Racon; *Horn 20s*.
Kish Bank 53°18'·68N 05°55'·38W Fl(2) 30s 29m **28M**; W Tr, R band, helicopter platform; RC; Racon; *Horn (2) 30s*.

DUBLIN BAY.
Muglins 53°16'·53N 06°04'·52W Fl 5s 14m 8M; W conical Tr, R band.

DUN LAOGHAIRE
East Breakwater, head 53°18'·13N 06°07'·55W Fl(2) 15s 16m **22M**; stone Tr, W lantern; *Dia 30s or Bell (1) 6s*.
West Breakwater, head Fl(3) G 7·5s 11m 7M; stone Tr, W lantern; vis 188°-062°.
Car Ferry Terminal head 53°17'·31N 06°07'·73W Q WR 6s 3M; vis R030°-131°, W131°-030°; QY traffic signal 80m SW.
Rosbeg East Lt Buoy 53°19'·99N 06°04'·35W Q(3) 10s; E cardinal mark.
Rosbeg South Lt Buoy 53°20'·00N 06°04'·35W Q(6) + LFl 15s; S cardinal buoy.
Bennett Bank Lt Buoy 53°20'·16N 05°55'·07W Q(6)LFl 15s; S cardinal mark; *Horn(3) 30s*.

PORT OF DUBLIN.
Great South Wall, head, **Poolbeg** 53°20'·52N 06°09'·02W Oc(2) R 20s 20m **15M**; R round Tr; *Horn (2) 60s*.
North Bull Wall, **Bull** Fl(3) G 10s 15m **15M**; G round Tr; *Bell (4) 30s*.

North Bank Oc G 8s 10m **16M**; G square Tr on piles; *Bell (3) 20s*.
53°20'·4N 06°11'·3W Aero 2 QR (vert) 205/85m 11M; 3 FR (vert) Lts mark intermediate heights on chimney.

BEN OF HOWTH.
Baily 53°21'·67N 06°03'·10W Fl 20s 41m **27M**; stone Tr; *Dia 60s*.

HOWTH.
Howth Lt Buoy 53°23'·72N 06°03'·53W Fl G 5s; stbd-hand mark.
Rowan Rocks Lt Buoy 53°23'·87N 06°03'·20W Q(3) 10s; E cardinal mark.
E pier head Fl(2) WR 7·5s 13m **W17M**, R 13M; W Tr; vis W256°-295°, R295°-256°.
W pier head Fl G 3s 7m 6M.
Dublin Airport 53°25'·7N 06°14'·7W Aero Al Fl WG 7·5s 95m.

Rockabill 53°35'·80N 06°00'·30W Fl WR 12s 45m **W23M**, **R19M**; W Tr, B band; vis W178°-329°, R329°-178°; *Horn (4) 60s*. Also shown by day when fog signal is operating.

10.12.5   PASSAGE INFORMATION

IRELAND — WEST COAST

This coast gives wonderful cruising, but is exposed to the Atlantic and any swell offshore, but this diminishes mid-summer. In bad weather however the sea breaks dangerously on shoals with quite substantial depths. There is usually a refuge close by, but if caught out in deteriorating weather and poor visibility, a stranger may need to make an offing until conditions improve, so a stout yacht and good crew are required. Tidal streams are weak, except round headlands.

There are few Lts, and inshore navigation is not wise after dark. Coastal navigation is feasible at night in good visibility, and fog is less frequent than in Irish Sea. A good watch must be kept for drift nets off the coast, and for lobster pots in inshore waters.

Stores, fuel and water are not readily available. Even in mid-summer a yacht may meet at least one gale in a two-week cruise. Listen regularly to the Radio Telefis Eireann forecasts, as described in Table 7(2).

For all Irish waters the Sailing Directions published by the Irish Cruising Club are strongly recommended, and particularly on the W coast, where other information is scant.

The stretch of coast from Black Hd to Loop Hd has no safe anchs, and no Lts S of Inisheer. Take care not to be set inshore, although there are few offlying dangers except in Liscanor Bay and near Mutton Island. Loop Hd (Lt, RC) marks the N side of Shannon estuary, and should be passed 3 ca off. Here the stream runs SW from HW Galway +0300, and NE from HW Galway −0300.

RIVER SHANNON (charts 1547, 1548, 1549, 1540)

R Shannon is the longest river in Ireland, running 100M from Lough Allen to Limerick and thence, in the tidal section, 50M from Limerick dock to its mouth between Loop Hd and Kerry Hd.

In the lower reaches, as far as the junction with R Fergus about 15M below Limerick, the tides and streams are those of a deep-water inlet, with roughly equal durations of rise and fall, and equal rates of flood and ebb streams. In the entrance the flood stream begins at HW Galway −0555, and the ebb at HW Galway +0015. Above the junction with R Fergus the tidal characteristics become more like those of most rivers: the flood stream is stronger than the ebb, but it runs for a shorter time. In the Shannon the stream is much affected by the wind: S and W winds increase the rate and duration of the flood stream, and reduce the ebb. Strong N or E winds have the opposite effect. Prolonged or heavy rain increases the rate and duration of the ebb.

Off Kilcredaun Pt the ebb runs at 4 kn at sp, and in strong winds between S and NW it forms a bad race. This can be mostly avoided by keeping near the N shore, which is free from offlying dangers, and thereby avoiding the worst of the tide. When leaving the Shannon in strong W winds, aim to pass Kilcredaun Pt at slack water, and again keep near the N shore.

In the estuary and lower reaches of the Shannon there are several anchs available for yachts on passage up or down the coast. Killala B (chart 1819) is about 3M E of Loop Hd, and is convenient in good weather or in N winds, but exposed to SE and to any swell. Carrigaholt B (chart 1547), entered about 1M N of Kilcredaun Pt, is well sheltered from W winds and has little tidal stream, but is exposed to E. In N winds there is anch SE of Querrin Pt (chart 1547), 4½M further up river on N shore. Off Kilrush (10.12.8) there are anchs E of Scattery Island and N of Hog Island. (Note that there are overfalls ¾M S of Scattery Island with W winds and ebb tide).

For further information on R Shannon see 10.12.9.

LOOP HEAD TO MIZEN HEAD (charts 2254, 2423)

There is no Lt from Loop Hd to Inishtearaght, apart from Little Samphire Island in Tralee Bay, where Fenit Pier provides the only secure refuge along this bit of coast.

There is an anch, but exposed to N winds and to swell, on the W side of Brandon Bay. From here the scenery is spectacular to Smerwick Harb, entered between the Duncapple islets and the E Sister. It is sheltered except from NW or N winds.

Sybil Pt has steep cliffs, and offlying rks extend 3½ca. There is a race in W or NW winds with N-going tide, and often a nasty sea between Sybil Pt and Blasket Sound.

The Blasket Islands are very exposed, with strong tides and overfalls, but worth a visit in settled weather (chart 2970). Gt Blasket and Inishvickillane each have anch and landing on their NE side. Inishtearaght is the most W island (Lt), but further W lie Tearaght rks, and 3M SSW are Little Foze and Gt Foze rks. Extensive rks and shoals form the W side of Blasket Sound; this is the most convenient N-S route, 1M wide, and easy in daylight and reasonable weather with fair wind or tide. The N-going stream starts at HW Galway +0430, and the S-going at HW Galway −0155, with sp rate 3 kn. Wild Bank (or Three Fathom Pinnacle), a shallow patch with overfalls, lies 2½M SSW of Slea Hd. 3M SW of Wild Bank is Barrack Rk, with breakers in strong winds.

Dingle Bay is wide and deep, with few dangers round its shores. The best anchs are at Ventry, Dingle and Valentia — see 10.12.28.

The SW end of Puffin Island is steep-to, but the sound to the E is rocky and not recommended. Rough water is met between Bray Hd and Bolus Hd with fresh onshore winds or swell. Great Skellig (lit) is 6M, and Little Skellig 5M WSW of Puffin Island. Lemon Rk lies between Puffin Island and Little Skellig. Here the stream turns N at HW Cobh +0500, and S at HW Cobh −0110. There is a rk 3 ca SW of Great Skellig. When very calm it is possible to go alongside at Blind Man's Cove on NE side of Great Skellig, where there are interesting ruins.

Ballinskelligs Bay has an anch N of Horse Island, which has two Rks close off E end. Centre of bay is a prohib anch (cables). Darryname is an attractive, sheltered harb N of Lamb Hd. The entrance has Ldg Lts and marks, but is narrow and dangerous in bad weather.

Great Hog (or Scariff) Island has a rk close N, and a reef extending 2 ca W. Little Hog (or Deenish) Island is rocky 1 ca to NE. Moylaun Island lies 1½M E of Deenish, and has a rk 1½ ca SW of it. Two Head Island, off Lamb Hd, is steep-to. Kenmare R (chart 2495) has attractive harbs and anchs, but its shores are rocky, with no Lts. The best places are Sneem (see 10.12.28), Kilmakilloge and Ardgroom.

Dursey Island is steep-to except for rks ¾M NE and 1½ ca SW of Dursey Hd. Bull Rk (Lt, fog sig) and two rks W of it lie 2½M WNW of Dursey Hd. Cow Rk is midway between Bull Rk and Dursey Hd, with clear water each side. Calf and Heifer Rks are ¾M SW of Dursey Hd, where there is often broken water. 2M W of The Bull the stream turns NW at HW Cobh +0150, and SE at HW Cobh −0420. Dursey Sound (chart 2495) is a good short cut, but the stream runs 4 kn at sp. W-going starts at HW Cobh +0135, and E-going at HW Cobh −0450. A rk lies almost awash in mid-chan at the narrows, where there are also cables 24m above MHWS. Hold very close to the island shore. Beware wind changes in the sound, and broken water at N entrance.

Keep 3 ca off Crow Island to clear dangers. Off Blackball Hd at entrance to Bantry B (10.12.11) there can be a nasty race, particularly on W-going stream against the wind. Bantry B (charts 1838, 1840) has excellent harbs — notably Castletown, Adrigole and Glengariff (see 10.12.28). There are few dangers offshore, except around Bere and Whiddy Islands.

12

Sheep Hd (Lt) separates Bantry from Dunmanus B (chart 2552) which has three harbs — Dunmanus, Kitchen Cove and Dunbeacon. Carbery, Cold and Furze Islands lie in middle of bay, and it is best to keep N of them. Three Castle Hd at S end of bay has rks 1 ca W, and sea can break on S Bullig 4 ca off hd.

MIZEN HEAD TO TUSKAR ROCK (charts 2424, 2049)

From Mizen Head to Cork are many natural harbours. Only the best are mentioned here. Offshore the stream seldom exceeds 1½ kn, but it is stronger off headlands causing races and overfalls with wind against tide. Prolonged W winds increase the rate/duration of the E-going stream, and strong E winds have a similar effect on the W-going stream.

Off Mizen Hd the W-going stream starts at HW Cobh +0120, and the E-going at HW Cobh −0500. The sp rate is 4 kn, which with wind against tide forms a dangerous race, sometimes extending to Three Castle Hd or Brow Hd, with broken water right to the shore.

Crookhaven (10.12.12) is a well sheltered harb, accessible at all states of tide, entered between Rock Island Lt Ho and Alderman Rks, ENE of Streek Hd. Anchor off the village. The passage from here to Schull (10.12.13) can be made inside Long Island.

Fastnet Rk (Lt, fog sig) is nearly 4M WSW of C Clear. There is one rk ¼M NE of Fastnet. Long Island Bay can be reached from here or through Gascanane Sound, between C Clear Island and Sherkin Island. Carrigmore Rks lie in the middle of this chan, with Gascanane Rk 1 ca W of them. The chan between Carrigmore Rks and Badger Island is best. If bound for Crookhaven, beware Bullig Reef, N of C Clear Island.

10M E of Baltimore (10.12.14) is Castle Haven (10.12.15), a sheltered and attractive harb, entered between Reen Pt (Lt) and Battery Pt. On passage Toe Hd has foul ground ½ ca S, and ¾M S is a group of rks called the Stags.

Sailing E to Glandore, pass outside or inside High Island and Low Island, but if inside beware Belly Rk (awash) about 3 ca S of Rabbit Island. Good anch off Glandore (10.12.28), or off Union Hall.

Keep at least ½M off Galley Hd to clear Dhulic Rk, and further off in fresh winds. Clonakilty B has little to offer. Offshore the W-going stream makes at HW Cobh +0200, and the E-going at HW Cobh −0420, sp rates 1½ kn.

Rks extend ¼ ca from Seven Heads, and beware Cotton Rk and Shoonta Rk close to the E. In middle of Courtmacsherry B are several dangers — from W to E Horse Rk, Black Tom, Barrel Rk and Blueboy, with a patch called Inner Barrels further inshore. These must be avoided going to or from Courtmacsherry, a rather shallow harb with a bar which breaks in strong S or SE winds. See 10.12.28.

Old Head of Kinsale (Lt, fog sig, RC) is quite steep-to, but a race extends 1M to SW on W-going stream, and to SE on E-going stream. There is an inshore passage in light weather, but in strong winds keep 2M off.

½M S of Hangman Pt at entrance to Kinsale (10.12.16) is Bulman Rk. The Sovereigns are large rks off Oyster Haven — a good harb, clear but for Harbour Rk in mid-chan off Ferry Pt which must be passed on its W side. See 10.12.28.

Daunt Rk is 7 ca SE of Robert's Hd. Little Sovereign on with Reanies Hd 241° leads inshore of it. Ringabella B offers temp anch in good weather, near entrance to Cork (10.12.17).

From Cork to Ballycotton keep 3 ca off as far as Power Hd, and then at least ½M off for dangers including Smiths Rks 1½M WSW of Ballycotton Island (Lt, fog sig, RC). Sound Rk lies between Ballycotton Island and Small Island. Ballycotton Harb (10.12.28) is small and crowded, but usually there is sheltered anch outside. N side of Ballycotton B is foul ½M offshore.

Pass 1 ca S of Capel Island. The sound is not recommended. For Youghal see 10.12.18. To the E, there is a submerged rk ½ ca SE of Ram Hd. Here the W-going stream starts at HW Cobh +0230, and the E-going at HW Cobh −0215, sp rates 1½ kn. Mine Hd (Lt) has two dangerous rks, The Rogue over ¼M E and The Longship 1M SW.

Helvick is a small sheltered harb on S side of Dungarvan B (10.12.28) and is approached along S shore, S of Helvick Rks, N of which other dangers exist towards Ballinacourty Pt. From here to Tramore there are few offlying rks, until Falskirt — a dangerous rk off Swines Pt in W approach to Dunmore East (10.12.19). Beware salmon nets.

From a point 1M S of Hook Hd (avoiding the overfalls known as Tower Race, which extend about 1M S of the hd at times), there are no obstructions on a direct course for Saltee Sound (chart 2740). Jackeen Rk is 1M NW of the S end of North Saltee, and Sebber Bridge extends ¾M N from the NE point of South Saltee, so care is needed through the sound, where the stream runs 3½ kn at sp. There are several rks round the Saltees, including the Bohurs to the E of the sound. From N of Long Bohur steer to pass N of Black Rk, before altering course eastward to pass 2 ca off Carnsore Pt, and thence to Greenore Pt. Watch for lobster pots in this area. In settled weather the little harb of Kilmore Quay (mostly dries) is available, but there are rocks and shoals in the approaches.

There can be a dangerous race off Carnsore Pt. In bad weather or in poor vis, pass S of Coningbeg Lt F, the Barrels and Tuskar Rk (Lt). Dangerous rks lie up to 6½ ca SSW and 2 ca NW of Tuskar Rk.

TUSKAR ROCK TO LAMBAY ISLAND (charts 1787, 1468)

From Carnsore Pt to Dublin (10.12.25) the shallow offshore banks cause dangerous overfalls and dictate the route. This is not a good cruising area, but for passage making it is sheltered from the W winds. Tidal streams run mainly N and S, but the N-going flood sets across the banks on the inside, and the S-going ebb sets across them on the outside.

From Tuskar or Greenore Pt there is the choice of going inside Lucifer and Blackwater Banks, or seawards to fetch the Arklow Lanby. Again, from here either the inshore or seaward passage can be taken. Approaching Dublin B, yachts normally use Dalkey Sound, but with a foul tide or light wind it is better to use Muglins Sound. Muglins (Lt) is steep-to except for a rk about 1 ca WSW of the Lt. Beware Leac Buidhe (dries) 1 ca E of Clare Rk.

Kish Bank and Burford Bank lie offshore in the approaches to Dublin B, and Rosbeg Bank lies on the N side of it. The N-going stream begins at HW Dublin −0600, and the S-going at HW Dublin, sp rates 3 kn. The sea breaks on Burford Bank in E gales.

Ben of Howth, on N side of Dublin B, is steep-to, with no dangers more than 1 ca offshore. Ireland's Eye, a rky island which rises steeply to a height of 99m, lies about ¾M N of Howth (10.12.26) with reefs running SE and SW from Thulla rk at its SE end.

For notes on crossing the Irish Sea, see 10.13.5.

10.12.6 DISTANCE TABLE

Approximate distances in nautical miles are by the most direct route while avoiding dangers and allowing for traffic separation schemes etc. Places in *italics* are in adjoining areas.

	1	2	3	4	5	6	7	8	9	10	11	12	13	14	15	16	17	18	19	20
1 *Galway*	1																			
2 *Slyne Hd*	49	2																		
3 Loop Hd	55	52	3																	
4 Valentia	103	92	48	4																
5 Bantry	155	144	100	58	5															
6 Fastnet Rk	150	139	95	53	34	6														
7 Kinsale	199	188	144	102	83	49	7													
8 Cork	210	199	155	113	94	60	17	8												
9 Youghal	228	217	173	131	112	78	35	25	9											
10 Dunmore East	262	251	207	165	146	112	69	59	34	10										
11 Tuskar Rk	287	276	232	190	171	137	98	85	63	32	11									
12 Arklow	324	313	269	227	208	174	135	122	100	69	37	12								
13 Wicklow	339	328	284	242	223	189	150	137	115	84	52	15	13							
14 Dun Laoghaire	357	346	302	260	241	207	168	155	133	102	70	36	21	14						
15 *Mew Island*	309	260	312	345	326	292	253	240	218	187	155	118	107	90	15					
16 *Douglas*	394	345	364	322	303	269	230	217	195	164	132	102	92	80	62	16				
17 *South Bishop*	310	299	255	214	194	160	123	110	90	61	36	62	72	90	172	143	17			
18 *Lundy Island*	336	325	281	239	220	186	147	140	126	105	85	112	122	140	222	193	50	18		
19 *Bishop Rock*	298	287	243	201	182	148	135	136	134	140	141	175	185	215	290	260	125	110	19	
20 *Ouessant*	396	385	341	299	280	246	235	236	234	234	228	265	275	298	390	361	218	180	100	20

10.12.7 SPECIAL DIFFERENCES IN IRELAND

The Ordnance Survey map numbers refer to the Irish Ordnance Survey maps, scale 1:12670 or ½in to 1 mile, which cover the whole island, including Ulster, in 25 sheets.

Irish Customs: Yachts should preferably make their first port of call at one of the following places where there are customs posts Dublin port, Dun Laoghaire, Dunmore East, Waterford, New Ross, Dungarvan, Cobh, Cork, Crosshaven, Kinsale, Baltimore (summer only), Crookhaven, Bantry, Castletownbere, Cahirciveen, Fenit, Kilrush, Foynes, Limerick, Galway, Westport, Sligo and Killybegs. Yachts, in fact, are permitted to make their first call anywhere and if, after the proper procedures have been gone through, no Customs Officer arrives, report to the Civil Guard station. Passports are not required by UK citizens. Fly flag Q on arrival.

Irish Coast Life Saving Service: This is staffed by volunteers who are trained in first aid and equipped with breeches buoys, cliff ladders etc and their telephone numbers are those of the Leader's residence. Where appropriate these telephone numbers are given for each port.

Irish Marine Rescue Co-ordination Centre: The centre for the whole of the Irish Republic is situated at Shannon Airport. Its telephone numbers are (061) 61219 and (061) 61969. Should these be engaged call Air Traffic Control, Shannon (061) 61233 or Cork (021) 965326 or Dublin (01) 379900. In extreme emergency dial 999. The centre can call on the RNLI, Coast Life Saving Service, Irish Army Air Corps helicopters, search aircraft, Irish naval vessels, civil aircraft, Irish lighthouse service and the Garda Siochana. The Centre liaises with UK and France and acts as a clearing house for all messages received during the rescue operation within 100 miles of the Irish coast.

For Northern Ireland: The HM Coastguard Maritime Rescue Sub-Centre is in Bangor, Co Down, Tel. Donaghadee (0247) 883184. HM Customs have seven main places where yachtsmen should report in the event of a local Customs Officer not being available;

Larne Customs: ☎ (0232) 752511
Londonderry Customs: ☎ (0504) 262273
Kilkeel Customs: ☎ (06937) 62158
Coleraine Customs: ☎ (0265) 4803
Belfast Customs: ☎ (0232) 752511
Warrenpoint Customs: ☎ (069372) 3288
Bangor: No telephone.

Liquefied petroleum gas: In the Republic of Ireland LPG is provided by Kosan, a sister company of Calor Gas Ltd. But the bottles have different connections, and the smallest bottle is taller than the normal Calor one fitted in most yachts. Yachts visiting the Irish Republic are advised to take an ample stock of Calor. Availability of Kosan gas is indicated by symbol Kos.

Telephones: To dial the Irish Republic from the UK, dial 010 (International Exchange) followed by 353 (Irish Republic) followed by the area code (given in UK telephone books, or shown below omitting the initial 0) followed by the number. Dublin is an exception: for Dublin dial 0001 followed by the number. To dial UK from the Irish Republic: prefix the UK code with 03 and retain the 0 at the beginning of the UK area code, eg to call Southampton 123456 dial 03 0703 123456. London is the exception: to call London 246 3456, dial 03 1 246 3456.

Weather: Weather messages (comprising gale warnings, 24 hr forecast for Irish coastal waters up to 30M offshore and Irish Sea) are broadcast by RTE Radio 1. For details see Table 7(2).

Radio weather bulletins on RTE Radio 1 are at:

0633	Coastal waters
1253	Coastal waters
	(1255 on Sun)
1825	Coastal waters
2355	Coastal waters

Note 1. There are two books of sailing directions, published by the Irish Cruising Club, one for the South and West coasts of Ireland, the other for the North and East coasts. These are highly recommended.

Note 2. For further information regarding the Republic of Ireland, write to Irish Yachting Association, 3 Park Rd, Dun Laoghaire, Co Dublin ☎ 800239 or to Irish Tourist Board, 150 New Bond Street, London W1Y 0AQ (☎ 071 493 3201).

Note 3. Currency in Republic of Ireland is the Punt (£IR) divided into 100p.

KILRUSH 10-12-8
Clare

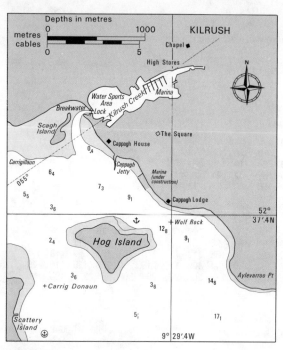

CHARTS
Admiralty 1819, 1547; Irish OS 17
TIDES
−0555 Dover; ML 2.7; Duration 0610; Zone 0 (GMT).

Standard Port GALWAY (→)

Times				Height (metres)			
HW		LW		MHWS	MHWN	MLWN	MLWS
1000	0500	0000	0600	5.1	3.9	2.0	0.6
2200	1700	1200	1800				

Differences KILRUSH
−0006 +0027 +0057 −0016 −0.1   −0.2   −0.3   −0.1

SHELTER
Kilrush harbour dries. The deep water harbour is Cappagh, well sheltered except in SE winds. Pier is in constant use by Shannon pilot boats and tugs.
NAVIGATION
Waypoint 52°37'.00N 09°32'.10W, 235°/055° from/to Watch House Point, 1.5M. See also 10.12.9. Coming between Hog Is and mainland, beware Wolf Rock. Approaching between Scattery Is and mainland, beware Baurnahard Spit and Carrigillaun.
LIGHTS AND MARKS
High store house (Glynn's Mill) in line with conspic white house on Watch House Pt in line at 055° leads into Kilrush Channel until S of Carrigillaun when alter to stbd towards Cappagh Jetty.
RADIO TELEPHONE
VHF Ch 16; 12. Other stations: Foynes Ch 16; 12 13 (occas). Limerick Ch 16; 12 13 (office hours).
TELEPHONE (065)
Hr Mr 51027; MRCC Limerick 61219; Coast Life Saving Service 51004; ⌗ Limerick 44426; Weather Shannon 61333; Police 17; Dr. 51275
FACILITIES
EC Thursday; **Kilrush Creek Marina** (250 + 50 visitors) ☎ 52072, Slip, BH, D, ME, Sh, El, P, ⏚, Bar, R, Access H24; **Cappagh** ☎ 51027, Slip, M, L, FW, CH, AB;
George Brew ☎ 51028, Kos; **Town** P, D, El, CH, AB, V, R, Bar. ✉; Ⓑ; ⇌ (bus to Limerick); ✈ (Shannon). **Note 1:** Car ferry across Shannon from Tarbert to Killimer (4M upstream of Kilrush).
Note 2: A marina for 250 boats is planned for Kilrush Creek.

RIVER SHANNON 10-12-9
CHARTS
Admiralty 1819, 1547, 1548, 1549, 1540. Upper reaches 5080, 5078.
TIDES

HW at	HW Galway	HW Dover
Kilbaha	−0015	+0605
Carrigaholt	−0015	+0605
Tarbert	+0035	−0530
Foynes	+0050	−0515
Limerick	+0130	−0435

SHELTER
The Shannon Estuary is 50M long, from Loop Head to Limerick. Between Kilconly and Kilcredaun Pts in the W and the entrance to R Fergus there are many sheltered anchorages protected from all but E winds. The most convenient for boats on passage N or S is Carrigaholt Bay which gives good shelter from W winds. Kilbaha Bay, 3M inside Loop Head, is sheltered in winds from W to NE but holding is poor and it is exposed to swell. The best anchorage in the estuary is at Foynes on the S bank opposite R Fergus. Above this point the river narrows and becomes shallower although there is a minimum of 2m at LWS. Yachts may proceed up to Limerick Dock but this has all the drawbacks of a commercial port — frequent shifting of berth, dirt and someone constantly on watch.

NAVIGATION
Waypoint 52°33'.50N 09°43'.00W, 236°/056° from/to Tail of Beal Bar buoy, 1.7M. For notes on entrance and tidal streams see 10.12.5. The ebb can reach 4 kn. Yachtsmen intending to visit the Shannon are advised to obtain the Irish Coast Pilot and also the Irish Cruising Club's *Sailing Directions for the South and West Coasts of Ireland*. It is the longest navigable river in the UK or Ireland and is controlled by the Limerick Harbour Commissioners. Pilots can be taken from Cappagh Pier to Limerick and from Limerick Dock to Killaloe. The channel is marked by buoys, beacons and perches. There are six large locks on the upper reaches (above Portumna) and all

are manned (toll). Above Lough Ree the ideal draught is less than a metre (1½m with careful navigation). The river is slow with many lakes; Lough Derg is 24M long and Lough Ree is 16M long. Between them at Shannon Harbour, a canal runs across to Dublin, the Grand Canal with 46 locks; max length 18.6m, beam 3.9m, height 2.74m, draught 1m. The Shannon bridges have a clearance of 4.6m except the swing bridge at Portumna which has 2.4m when closed. Lifting spans at Termonbarry and Rooskey are manned during daylight hours and are controlled by traffic lights. There is little commercial traffic.
LIGHTS AND MARKS
Principal lights are shown in 10.12.4
FACILITIES
Fuel, water and stores are obtainable at many villages.
KILBAHA V, FW, D (cans) at Hehir's Pub, P, ✉; Bus to Limerick (Sat).
CARRIGAHOLT V, P, ✉, R (summer).
KILRUSH and CAPPAGH — see 10.12.8. Pilot Stn ☎ 51027.
TARBERT V, P, ✉; Bus to Limerick.
FOYNES V, D, FW, ✉, R; Bus to Limerick. **Foynes YC** ☎ Foynes 90, Slip, Bar.
Ballina (Logh Derg) Marina with all facilities.
LIMERICK **J & G Boyd** ☎ 44366, Kos; **Shannon Yacht Fitters** ☎ Portumna 41105, Sh, ME, El; **Peter Lawless** ☎ Limerick 51567, CH, arrangement for pilot, ME, El, Sh; **Limerick Harbour Commission** ☎ (661) 315377.

KENMARE RIVER   10-12-10
Kerry

CHARTS
Admiralty 2495; Imray C56; Irish OS 21/24

TIDES
+0515 Dover; ML Dunkerron 2.2;
West Cove 2.0
Duration Dunkerron 0620;   Zone 0 (GMT).
West Cove 0610

Standard Port COBH (RINGASKIDDY) (→)

Times				Height (metres)			
HW		LW		MHWS	MHWN	MLWN	MLWS
0500	1100	0500	1100	4.2	3.3	1.4	0.5
1700	2300	1700	2300				

Differences WEST COVE
−0113 −0033 −0049 −0129 −0.6 −0.5 −0.1   0.0
DUNKERRON HARBOUR
−0117 −0027 −0050 −0140 −0.2 −0.3 +0.1   0.0
BALLYCROVANE HARBOUR (Coulagh Bay)
−0116 −0036 −0053 −0133 −0.6 −0.5 −0.1   0.0

SHELTER
SNEEM HARBOUR entered between Sherky Is and
Rossdohan Is; anchor NE of Gainish Is. Considerable swell
passes each side of Sherky Is making the anchorage
uncomfortable at times.
KENMARE Good shelter. Berth on quay on N side of river,
just below town.
ORMOND HARBOUR gives good shelter but beware rock
2½ca ENE of Hog Is.
KILMAKILLOGE HARBOUR is a safe anchorage for small
boats against all winds. Entering keep W of Spanish Is.
Space is restricted by a number of shoals. Anchor 1ca
SW of Carrigwee; S of Eseadawer Pt or in Collorus Hr.
ARDGROOM HARBOUR affords excellent shelter but has a
hazardous entrance over a rocky bar. Power is needed.
Anchor in Reenvade ½ca E of pier.
CLANDERRY HARBOUR Entrance NE of Illaunbweeheen
(Yellow Is) is only 7m wide. SW of the Is, entrance is
rocky. Anchor ENE of inner harbour.
BALLYCROVANE HARBOUR in Coulagh Bay is a good
anchorage but exposed to W winds. N and E shores are
foul. Anchor ½ca NE of Bird Is.

GARNISH BAY is only good in settled weather and wind in
W. Anchor either W of the Carrigduff concrete beacon or
1ca S of Bn.
There are many other anchorages including West Cove,
Coongar Hr, Blackwater R, Dunkerron Hr, Kenmare, Lehid
Hr, Cleanderry Hr.

NAVIGATION
Waypoint 51°41'.2N 10°04'.8W, 335°/155° from/to
Reenmore Point 0.7M. Three deepwater channels from N;
between Scariff Is and Deenish Is which is clear; between
Deenish Is and Moylaun Is which has shallow rocky
patches; between Moylaun Is and Twohead Is which is
clear and 4½ca wide. From SW approach from NW of
The Bull thence NW of Dursey Is. Above Maiden Rock
keep NW of Lackeen Rks. Beware salmon nets between
June and September.

LIGHTS AND MARKS
Bull Rk Lt — Fl 15s 83m 31M.
Ballycrovane Hr Lt — Fl R 3s.
Kilmakilloge Hr — Ldg Lts 041°, both Iso Y 8s.
Kenmare (on Fadda Is) — 2 white piles mark in line astern
max depth to the quay.
Old Watch Tower on Dursey Is (conspic) 250m.
Eagle Hill (Cod's Head) — 216m.
Conspic hotel NE side of Sneem Hr Ent.
Ardgroom Hr — two W beacons (front on Black Rk, rear
ashore) leads 099° through bar.

RADIO TELEPHONE
None.

TELEPHONE (064)
MRCC (061) 61219; Coast Life-Saving Service
(Waterville) 4320; ⌗ Bantry 50061; Ⓗ 41088.

FACILITIES
SNEEM L (Hotel Parknasilla, Oysterbed House pier or near
town). **Town** (2M from Hr), Bar, ✉, Slip, V, Kos.
KENMARE Kenmare Bay Hotel ☎ 41300, V, R, Bar.
Town ✉, Ⓗ, Ⓑ, ⇌ (Killarney), ✈ (Cork).
KILMAKILLOGE HARBOUR **Bunaw Pier**, L, AB, V, Bar.
ARDGROOM HARBOUR Supplies available at Ardgroom
(2M SSE of quay).

BANTRY   10-12-11
Cork

CHARTS
Admiralty 1838, 1840; Imray C56; Irish OS 24
TIDES
+0600 Dover; ML 1.8; Duration 0610; Zone 0 (GMT).

Standard Port COBH (RINGASKIDDY) (→)

Times				Height (metres)			
HW		LW		MHWS	MHWN	MLWN	MLWS
0500	1100	0500	1100	4.2	3.3	1.4	0.5
1700	2300	1700	2300				

Differences BANTRY

−0045	−0025	−0040	−0105	−0.7	−0.7	−0.1	0.0

FENIT PIER (Tralee Bay)

−0057	−0017	−0029	−0109	+0.5	+0.2	+0.3	+0.1

DINGLE HARBOUR

−0111	−0041	−0049	−0119	−0.3	−0.4	0.0	0.0

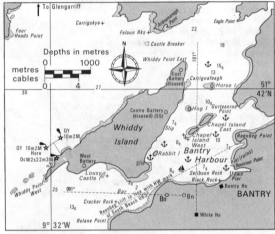

SHELTER
Apart from Bantry there are several good harbours in Bantry Bay — Dunboy Bay on W side of Piper Sound (exposed to E), Castletown (major fishing port, see 10.12.28), Lawrence Cove and Lonehort on Bear Island, Adrigole (attractive anchorage half way along N shore), and Glengariff (see 10.12.28).
NAVIGATION
Waypoint 51°40′.00N 09°36′.00W, 253°/073° from/to Whiddy Point West, 2.5M. Yachts can approach the shore fairly close everywhere except off Bear and Whiddy Islands. Beware Ducalia Rks, awash at LW, 1 M E of Roancarrigmore Lt, and Gerranes Rks 1 M W of Whiddy Is. In Bantry Harbour keep well clear (1½ to 2 ca) of all the islands. Also beware of Carrignafeagh off Whiddy Island. In Bantry harbour beware unlit mussel rafts all round the Chapel Islands.
LIGHTS AND MARKS
The main entrance, marked by buoys, is the N channel (10m depth) to anchorage S of Chapel Is. The S channel is unlit (min depth on bar 1.7m over Cracker Rk). Whiddy Is Lt is sectored Oc W 2s 22m 3M 073°-106°. Ldg marks, White House and S. Chapel Island ruin in line at 181°. Ldg line 091°, Front RW post FW Lt, Rear W post FR Lt.
RADIO TELEPHONE
VHF Ch 16; 14 11 (H24).
TELEPHONE (027)
Lifeboat Valentia 6214; MRCC Limerick 61219; Coast Life-Saving Service — Mizen Head (028) 35115; ☎ 50061; Police 50045; Dr 50404; ℍ 50133.
FACILITIES
EC Wednesday; **Bantry Pier** L, FW; **Glengarriff** FW, V, Bar; **Carroll Shipping** ME; **Donal and Noreen Casey** ☎ 50342, Kos; **Bantry Bay SC** Slip, L; **Town** P and D (cans), L, FW, CH, V, R, Bar. ✉; Ⓑ; ⇌ (bus to Cork); ✈ (Cork or Shannon); Car Ferry (Cork).

CROOKHAVEN   10-12-12
Cork

CHARTS
Admiralty 2184; Imray C56; Irish OS 24
TIDES
+0550 Dover; ML 1.8; Duration 0610; Zone 0 (GMT).
Standard Port COBH (RINGASKIDDY) (→)

Times				Height (metres)			
HW		LW		MHWS	MHWN	MLWN	MLWS
0500	1100	0500	1100	4.2	3.3	1.4	0.5
1700	2300	1700	2300				

Differences CROOKHAVEN

−0057	−0033	−0048	−0112	−0.8	−0.6	−0.4	−0.1

SHELTER
Excellent shelter. Anchorages opposite village in middle of bay in 3m; N of W point of Rock Is; to the E of Granny Is. The last two are a long way from the village.
NAVIGATION
Waypoint 51°28′.50N 09°40′.50W, 094°/274° from/to Lt Ho on Sheemon Pt, 1M. Entrance between Sheemon Pt and Black Horse Rocks (3.5 ca ESE) on which is an N cardinal beacon. From S, keep 1 ca E of Alderman Rocks and 0.5 ca off Black Horse Rks Bn. Passage between Streek Hd and Alderman Rks is not advised. Inside the bay the shores are steep to.
LIGHTS AND MARKS
Lt Ho on Rock Is (conspic W tower) L Fl WR 8s 20m 13/11M. Outside Hr, W over Long Is Bay − 281°, R281°-340°; Inside Hr R281°-348°, W348°-N shore.
RADIO TELEPHONE
None.
TELEPHONE (028)
MRCC (061) 6 12 19; Coast Life Saving Service Goleen 3 51 17; ☎ Bantry 5 00 61; Dr 3 51 48.
FACILITIES
Ron Holland Guest House ☎ 35168, Sh, ME; **Village** V, Kos, Ⓑ (Bantry); ✉; ⇌ (Cork); ✈ (Cork).

SCHULL   10-12-13
Cork

CHARTS
Admiralty 2184; Imray C56; Irish OS 24
TIDES
+0610 Dover; ML 1.8; Duration 0610; Zone 0 (GMT).
Standard Port COBH (RINGASKIDDY) (→)

Times				Height (metres)			
HW		LW		MHWS	MHWN	MLWN	MLWS
0500	1100	0500	1100	4.2	3.3	1.4	0.5
1700	2300	1700	2300				

Differences SCHULL

−0040	−0015	−0015	−0110	−0.9	−0.6	−0.2	−0.1

DUNMANUS HARBOUR

−0107	−0031	−0044	−0120	−0.7	−0.6	−0.2	0.0

SCHULL *Continued*

⚓ Report to Hr Mr

SHELTER
Good shelter except in strong S winds — in these winds, best shelter is behind Long Island. Schull Harbour is available at all times. Anchor SE of pier, clear of fairway.

NAVIGATION
Waypoint 51°29'.60N 09°31'.60W, 166°/346° from/to front Ldg Lt 346°, 2.1M. Entering between Schull Pt on the W and Coosheen Pt on E, beware Bull Rock in middle of channel, marked by a R iron perch.

LIGHTS AND MARKS
Leading lights NE of village in line at 346°, both Oc 5s. The pier is normally lit by street lights all night.

RADIO TELEPHONE
None.

TELEPHONE (028)
Hr Mr 2 81 36; MRCC Limerick 6 12 19; Coast Life Saving Service 3 51 17; ⊞ Bantry 5 00 61; Police 2 81 11; Dr 2 83 11; Ⓗ Bantry 5 01 33.

FACILITIES
EC Tuesday; **Schull Pier** Slip, M, D, L, FW, AC, AB; **Sailing Club** ☎ 2 82 86; **J. O'Reilly** ☎ 2 81 36, Kos; **Rossbrin BY** ☎ 3 73 52, M, Sh, Slip; **Simon Nelson** ☎ 2 85 54, CH.
Village P, ME, El, Sh, CH, V, R, Bar. ✉; Ⓑ; ⇌ (bus to Cork); ✈ (Cork); Car Ferry (Cork)

BALTIMORE   10-12-14
Cork

CHARTS
Admiralty 3725, 2129; Imray C56; Irish OS 24
TIDES
−0605 Dover; ML 2.1; Duration 0610; Zone 0 (GMT)

Standard Port COBH (RINGASKIDDY) (→)

Times				Height (metres)			
HW		LW		MHWS	MHWN	MLWN	MLWS
0500	1100	0500	1100	4.2	3.3	1.4	0.5
1700	2300	1700	2300				

Differences BALTIMORE
−0025	−0005	−0010	−0050	−0.5	−0.3	+0.1	+0.1

CLONAKILTY BAY
−0033	−0011	−0019	−0041	−0.3	−0.2		No data

SHELTER
Excellent shelter and harbour is always available. Anchor N or W of New Pier, or in Church Strand Bay past lifeboat slip in 2-3m. In strong W winds off ruined abbey on Sherkin I. (off chartlet), clear of ferry.

NAVIGATION
Waypoint 51°27'.80N 09°23'.42W, 180°/000° from/to Loo Rock buoy, 0.62M. On entering beware Loo Rock to starboard, marked by a buoy with Lt and Radar reflector. Beware Lousy Rocks and Wallis Rocks in the middle of the harbour. Harbour can be entered from the N but this is tricky and not recommended.

LIGHTS AND MARKS
Entrance easily identified by conspic W Tr called Lot's Wife on Beacon Pt and W Lt Ho on Barrack Pt. Barrack Pt Lt is unreliable.

RADIO TELEPHONE
Call: *Baltimore Harbour Radio* VHF Ch 16 09.

TELEPHONE (028)
Hr Mr 20184; MRCC Limerick 61219; Coast Life Saving Service 20125; ⊞ Bantry 50061; Police 41358; Dr 21488; Ⓗ 21677.

FACILITIES
EC None; **New Pier** Slip, AB; **K. Cotter** ☎ 20106, D, CH, V, Gas, Gaz, Kos, FW; **M. Casey** Bar, P; **H. Skinner** ☎ 20114, Slip, Sh; **Old Pier** FW; **R. Bushe** ☎ 20125, ACA; **T. O'Driscoll** ☎ 20344, ME.
Village P, Bar. ✉; ⇌ (bus to Cork); ✈ (Cork).

CASTLE HAVEN   10-12-15
Cork

CHARTS
Admiralty 2129, 2092; Imray C56; Irish OS 24
TIDES
+0605 Dover; ML 2.2; Duration 0605; Zone 0 (GMT)

Standard Port COBH (RINGASKIDDY) (→)

Times				Height (metres)			
HW		LW		MHWS	MHWN	MLWN	MLWS
0500	1100	0500	1100	4.2	3.3	1.4	0.5
1700	2300	1700	2300				

Differences CASTLETOWNSHEND
−0020	−0030	−0020	−0050	−0.4	−0.3	0.0	+0.2

12

CASTLE HAVEN Continued

SHELTER

Excellent anchorage protected from all weathers and available at all tides, day and night, although the outer part of harbour is subject to swell in S winds. Anchor in midstream SE of the slip at Castletownshend, N of Cat Island, or further upstream as shown on chartlet.

NAVIGATION

Waypoint 51°29'.00N 09°10'.00W, 171°/351° from/to Reen Point Lt, 2M. Enter between Horse I. and Skiddy I. both of which have foul ground all round. Black Rk lies off the SE side of Horse I. and is steep-to along its S side. On the other side of Horse I. is Flea Sound, a narrow boat passage, obstructed by rocks. Colonel Rk (0.5m) lies close to the E shore, 2ca N of Reen Pt. A submarine cable runs E/W across the harbour from the slip close N of Reen Pier to the slip at Castletownshend.

LIGHTS AND MARKS

Reen Point Lt, Fl WRG 10s 9m 5/3M; W Tr; vis G shore-338°, W338°-001°, R001°-shore. A ruined Tr stands on E end of Horse I.

RADIO TELEPHONE

None.

TELEPHONE (028)

MRCC (061) 61219; Coast Life Saving Service 36247; ⌗ Bantry 50061; Dr 21488; Ⓗ 21677.

FACILITIES

Reen Pier L, FW; **SC** ☎ 36100; **Castletownshend Village** Slip, Bar, R, V, FW, ✉, Ⓑ (Skibbereen), ⇌ (Cork), ✈ (Cork).

CASTLETOWNSHEND

KINSALE   10-12-16

Cork

CHARTS

Admiralty 2053, 1765; Imray C56; Irish OS 25

TIDES

−0600 Dover; ML 2.2; Duration 0600; Zone 0 (GMT)

Standard Port COBH (RINGASKIDDY) (→)

Times				Height (metres)			
HW		LW		MHWS	MHWN	MLWN	MLWS
0500	1100	0500	1100	4.2	3.3	1.4	0.5
1700	2300	1700	2300				

Differences KINSALE

−0019	−0005	−0009	−0023	−0.1	−0.1	+0.1	0.0

SHELTER

Excellent sheltered harbour except in very strong SE winds. Accessible in all weathers, at all tides, day and night. Anchorage SW of James Fort between moorings and bridge. Moorings at Kinsale YC.

NAVIGATION

Waypoint 51°40'.00N 08°30'.00W, 181°/001° from/to Charles's Fort Lt, 1.7M. Bulman Rock off Hangman Pt marked by S cardinal buoy. Also beware Farmer Rock ¾ ca off shore on W bank and Carrignarone on E bank opposite Money Pt.

LIGHTS AND MARKS

Charles's Fort Fl WRG 5s; 18m 9/6M vis G348°-358°, W358°-004°, R004°-168°. Port-hand Lt buoys mark chan.

RADIO TELEPHONE

VHF Ch 16; 14. Kinsale YC Ch **16** M.

TELEPHONE (021)

Hr Mr 772503; MRCC Limerick 61219; Coast Life Saving Service 772133; ⌗ 772271; Police 772302; Dr 772253, 772133; Ⓗ Cork 546400.

FACILITIES

EC Thursday; **Kinsale Marina** ☎ 772196, FW, AC, D, P, AB; **Pier** ☎ 772503, Slip, M, P (cans), D, L, FW, ME, El, Sh, AB, V, R, Bar; **Kinsale YC** ☎ 772196, Slip, M, P, D, L, FW, C, R, Bar; **Kinsale Marine Services** ☎ 772611, D, M, CH, Gas, Gaz; **Kilmacsimon BY** ☎ 775134, Slip, ME, Sh, C, D, El; **McWilliam Sails** ☎ 831505, SM; (Several excellent restaurants — the gourmet centre of Ireland).

Town P, D, V, R, Bar. ✉; Ⓑ; ⇌ (bus to Cork); ✈ (Cork).

CORK (COBH) 10-12-17

Cork

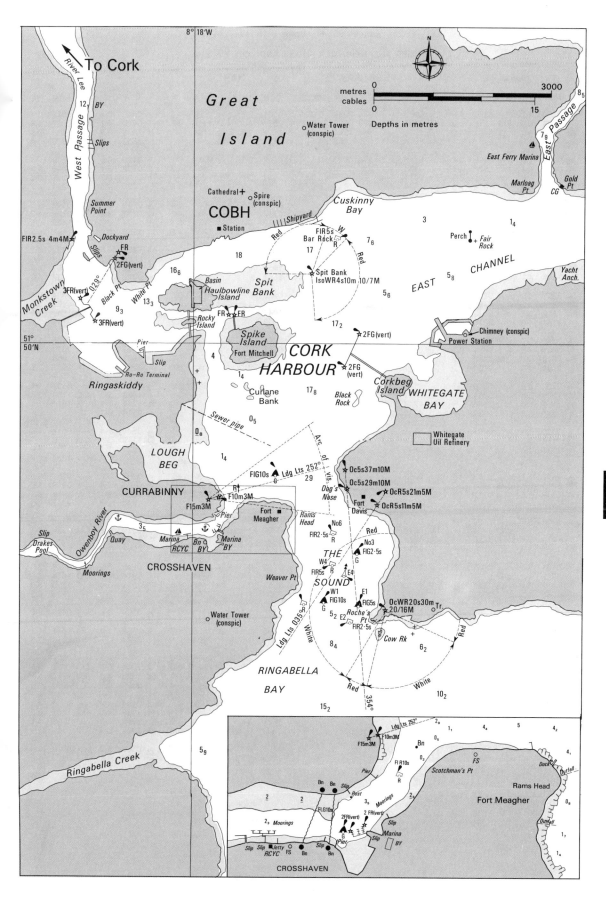

8° 18'W

To Cork

River Lee

12 BY

Slips

West Passage

Great

Island

Water Tower
(conspic)

metres
cables

0   3000

0   15

Depths in metres

N

8·5

East Passage

7·9
Gold
Pt
CG

East Ferry Marina

Marloag
Pt

Summer
Point

Cathedral✝ Spire
(conspic)

COBH

■ Station

Cuskinny
Bay

Water Tower
(conspic)

3

1·4

Perch ✦ Fair
Rock

FlR2.5s 4m4M☆

Dockyard

FR

2FG(vert)

Red   Shipyard

FlR5s W
Bar Rock
R

7·6

Yacht
Anch.

Red

CHANNEL

3FR(vert) 029°

16·6

18

17

☆ Spit Bank
IsoWR4s10m 10/7M

5·8

5·6

EAST

Black Pt

White Pt
13·3

9·3

Basin
Haulbowline
Island

*Spit
Bank*

FR☆☆FR

Monkstown Creek

Slips

Rocky
Island

Spike
Island
Fort Mitchell

17·2

2FG(vert)

Chimney (conspic)

Power Station

51°
50'N

Pier

**CORK
HARBOUR**

2FG
(vert)

*Corkbeg
Island* WHITEGATE
BAY

Slip

Ro-Ro Terminal

Ringaskiddy

4

1·4

+

+

Curlane
Bank

17·8

Black Rock

Whitegate
Oil Refinery

Sewer pipe

0·5

0·8

*LOUGH
BEG*

1·4

Arc of vis.

Oc5s37m10M

Oc5s29m10M

FlG10s ▲ Ldg Lts 252°

29

Dog's
Nose

OcR5s21m5M

OcR5s11m5M

CURRABINNY

R
☆ F10m3M
F15m3M

Fort
Davis

No6
R

Red

Pier

Fort
Meagher

Rams
Head

FlR2·5s
R

No3
FlG2·5s
G

Slip
Drakes
Pool

⚓ Owenboy River

3·5

Quay

Marina
RCYC BY

Bn
BY

Marina
BY

W4
FlR5s
R

E4

THE
SOUND

Moorings

Weaver Pt

W1
FlG10s
G

E1

FlG5s
G

OcWR20s30m
20/16M Tr

CROSSHAVEN

5·2 E2

Roche's
Pt

FlR2·5s

Cow Rk

+

Red

Water Tower
(conspic)

Ldg Lts 035°

White

8·4

6·2

White

RINGABELLA

Red

354°

10·2

BAY

15·2

Ringabella Creek

5·9

Ldg Lts 252°

2·9

1·1

4·4

5

4·2

F15m3M F10m3M

Bn

0·5

FS

Dock
Outfall

Pier
Post

Fl R10s
R

0·2

Scotchman's Pt

4·1

Bn Bn Slip

2

2

FlG10s

Moorings

3·5

2·3

Rams Head

Fort Meagher

0·8

Outfall

2·9 Moorings

2FR(vert)

2 FR(vert)

Slip

Marina
BY

1·7

Slip Slip Jetty
RCYC FS

Pier

Slip
Bn

Slip
Bn

CROSSHAVEN

1·4

12

IRELAND, SOUTH COAST – RINGASKIDDY

Lat 51°50' N   Long 8°19' W

TIMES AND HEIGHTS OF HIGH AND LOW WATERS

YEAR 1991

TIME ZONE UT(GMT)
For Summer Time add ONE hour in non-shaded areas

JANUARY

Day	Time	m		Day	Time	m
1 Tu	0530 / 1205 / 1754	4.3 / 0.6 / 4.3		**16** W	0550 / 1212 / 1804	4.0 / 0.9 / 4.0
2 W	0028 / 0622 / 1257 / 1845	0.5 / 4.4 / 0.5 / 4.3		**17** Th	0028 / 0624 / 1246 / 1836	0.8 / 4.1 / 0.8 / 4.0
3 Th	0117 / 0710 / 1347 / 1931	0.5 / 4.4 / 0.5 / 4.3		**18** F	0102 / 0656 / 1319 / 1907	0.7 / 4.1 / 0.8 / 4.0
4 F	0205 / 0758 / 1434 / 2018	0.5 / 4.4 / 0.6 / 4.2		**19** Sa	0134 / 0727 / 1351 / 1938	0.7 / 4.1 / 0.8 / 4.0
5 Sa	0253 / 0844 / 1522 / 2104	0.5 / 4.2 / 0.7 / 4.0		**20** Su	0206 / 0759 / 1423 / 2012	0.7 / 4.1 / 0.8 / 4.0
6 Su	0341 / 0931 / 1610 / 2150	0.7 / 4.0 / 0.8 / 3.8		**21** M	0240 / 0834 / 1458 / 2050	0.8 / 4.1 / 0.8 / 3.9
7 M	0430 / 1020 / 1659 / (2241	0.8 / 3.8 / 1.0 / 3.6		**22** Tu	0318 / 0914 / 1538 / 2132	0.8 / 4.0 / 0.9 / 3.8
8 Tu	0522 / 1112 / 1753 / 2337	1.0 / 3.6 / 1.2 / 3.5		**23** W	0403 / 1002 / 1627 /) 2224	0.9 / 3.8 / 1.1 / 3.7
9 W	0617 / 1210 / 1849	1.2 / 3.5 / 1.3		**24** Th	0458 / 1058 / 1726 / 2327	1.1 / 3.7 / 1.2 / 3.6
10 Th	0038 / 0719 / 1310 / 1951	3.4 / 1.3 / 3.4 / 1.3		**25** F	0604 / 1204 / 1838	1.2 / 3.6 / 1.3
11 F	0141 / 0822 / 1412 / 2051	3.4 / 1.3 / 3.4 / 1.3		**26** Sa	0041 / 0721 / 1323 / 1958	3.5 / 1.2 / 3.5 / 1.3
12 Sa	0243 / 0922 / 1510 / 2148	3.5 / 1.3 / 3.5 / 1.2		**27** Su	0204 / 0844 / 1444 / 2119	3.6 / 1.2 / 3.6 / 1.1
13 Su	0339 / 1014 / 1602 / 2235	3.7 / 1.2 / 3.7 / 1.1		**28** M	0324 / 1002 / 1557 / 2230	3.8 / 1.0 / 3.8 / 0.8
14 M	0428 / 1058 / 1648 / 2316	3.8 / 1.1 / 3.8 / 1.0		**29** Tu	0430 / 1104 / 1657 / 2327	4.0 / 0.7 / 4.1 / 0.6
15 Tu	0512 / 1137 / 1727 / ● 2354	3.9 / 1.0 / 3.9 / 0.9		**30** W	0525 / 1157 / 1749 / ○	4.3 / 0.5 / 4.2
				31 Th	0017 / 0614 / 1245 / 1834	0.4 / 4.4 / 0.4 / 4.3

FEBRUARY

Day	Time	m		Day	Time	m
1 F	0103 / 0657 / 1328 / 1914	0.3 / 4.4 / 0.4 / 4.3		**16** Sa	0039 / 0631 / 1255 / 1843	0.6 / 4.2 / 0.6 / 4.1
2 Sa	0145 / 0738 / 1411 / 1954	0.3 / 4.4 / 0.4 / 4.2		**17** Su	0110 / 0700 / 1326 / 1913	0.5 / 4.2 / 0.6 / 4.2
3 Su	0226 / 0818 / 1450 / 2032	0.4 / 4.2 / 0.6 / 4.1		**18** M	0141 / 0731 / 1357 / 1944	0.5 / 4.2 / 0.6 / 4.1
4 M	0307 / 0854 / 1529 / 2111	0.6 / 4.0 / 0.8 / 3.9		**19** Tu	0215 / 0805 / 1430 / 2020	0.6 / 4.2 / 0.7 / 4.1
5 Tu	0346 / 0934 / 1609 / 2152	0.8 / 3.8 / 1.0 / 3.7		**20** W	0251 / 0844 / 1511 / 2103	0.7 / 4.1 / 0.8 / 4.0
6 W	0427 / 1017 / 1652 / (2241	1.0 / 3.5 / 1.2 / 3.5		**21** Th	0336 / 0929 / 1600 /) 2155	0.9 / 3.9 / 1.0 / 3.8
7 Th	0516 / 1111 / 1744 / 2342	1.3 / 3.3 / 1.3 / 3.3		**22** F	0434 / 1027 / 1704 / 2301	1.1 / 3.6 / 1.2 / 3.5
8 F	0615 / 1214 / 1848	1.4 / 3.2 / 1.4		**23** Sa	0543 / 1140 / 1818	1.2 / 3.4 / 1.3
9 Sa	0052 / 0726 / 1327 / 2001	3.2 / 1.5 / 3.2 / 1.4		**24** Su	0022 / 0706 / 1309 / 1945	3.4 / 1.3 / 3.3 / 1.3
10 Su	0206 / 0840 / 1439 / 2112	3.3 / 1.4 / 3.3 / 1.3		**25** M	0157 / 0839 / 1440 / 2114	3.5 / 1.2 / 3.5 / 1.1
11 M	0312 / 0945 / 1539 / 2209	3.5 / 1.3 / 3.5 / 1.1		**26** Tu	0321 / 0957 / 1553 / 2223	3.7 / 0.9 / 3.7 / 0.7
12 Tu	0406 / 1034 / 1627 / 2254	3.7 / 1.1 / 3.7 / 0.9		**27** W	0424 / 1055 / 1648 / 2315	4.0 / 0.6 / 4.0 / 0.5
13 W	0449 / 1115 / 1708 / 2333	3.9 / 0.9 / 3.9 / 0.8		**28** Th	0513 / 1143 / 1733 / ○	4.2 / 0.4 / 4.2
14 Th	0527 / 1150 / 1743 / ●	4.0 / 0.7 / 4.0				

MARCH

Day	Time	m		Day	Time	m
1 F	0001 / 0557 / 1227 / 1814	0.3 / 4.4 / 0.3 / 4.3		**16** Sa	0529 / 1154 / 1744 / ●	4.2 / 0.5 / 4.1
2 Sa	0042 / 0635 / 1304 / 1850	0.2 / 4.4 / 0.3 / 4.3		**17** Su	0011 / 0601 / 1227 / 1815	0.5 / 4.3 / 0.5 / 4.3
3 Su	0119 / 0710 / 1340 / 1924	0.3 / 4.3 / 0.4 / 4.2		**18** M	0043 / 0632 / 1259 / 1846	0.4 / 4.3 / 0.5 / 4.3
4 M	0154 / 0742 / 1413 / 1957	0.4 / 4.1 / 0.6 / 4.1		**19** Tu	0117 / 0704 / 1334 / 1920	0.4 / 4.3 / 0.5 / 4.3
5 Tu	0226 / 0815 / 1444 / 2029	0.6 / 3.9 / 0.8 / 3.9		**20** W	0154 / 0740 / 1411 / 1958	0.5 / 4.2 / 0.7 / 4.2
6 W	0258 / 0847 / 1517 / 2104	0.8 / 3.7 / 1.0 / 3.7		**21** Th	0236 / 0822 / 1456 / 2043	0.7 / 4.1 / 0.8 / 4.0
7 Th	0335 / 0924 / 1556 / 2149	1.1 / 3.5 / 1.2 / 3.5		**22** F	0325 / 0911 / 1549 / 2139	0.9 / 3.8 / 1.0 / 3.7
8 F	0420 / 1013 / 1647 / (2247	1.3 / 3.3 / 1.3 / 3.3		**23** Sa	0426 / 1013 / 1657 /) 2251	1.1 / 3.5 / 1.2 / 3.5
9 Sa	0519 / 1118 / 1753	1.4 / 3.1 / 1.5		**24** Su	0537 / 1132 / 1812	1.2 / 3.3 / 1.3
10 Su	0001 / 0631 / 1238 / 1909	3.1 / 1.5 / 3.0 / 1.5		**25** M	0018 / 0703 / 1304 / 1942	3.4 / 1.3 / 3.3 / 1.2
11 M	0123 / 0751 / 1359 / 2029	3.2 / 1.5 / 3.1 / 1.3		**26** Tu	0152 / 0834 / 1433 / 2107	3.5 / 1.1 / 3.5 / 0.8
12 Tu	0236 / 0904 / 1505 / 2134	3.3 / 1.3 / 3.4 / 1.1		**27** W	0310 / 0946 / 1538 / 2209	3.7 / 0.8 / 3.7 / 0.6
13 W	0334 / 0959 / 1556 / 2221	3.6 / 1.0 / 3.6 / 0.9		**28** Th	0406 / 1038 / 1627 / 2257	4.0 / 0.6 / 4.0 / 0.4
14 Th	0417 / 1042 / 1637 / 2302	3.8 / 0.8 / 3.8 / 0.7		**29** F	0452 / 1123 / 1709 / 2339	4.2 / 0.4 / 4.2 / 0.3
15 F	0455 / 1119 / 1712 / 2337	4.0 / 0.7 / 4.0 / 0.5		**30** Sa	0532 / 1201 / 1747 / ○	4.3 / 0.3 / 4.2
				31 Su	0015 / 0607 / 1235 / 1821	0.3 / 4.3 / 0.4 / 4.2

APRIL

Day	Time	m		Day	Time	m
1 M	0049 / 0639 / 1306 / 1852	0.4 / 4.2 / 0.5 / 4.2		**16** Tu	0019 / 0607 / 1238 / 1825	0.4 / 4.4 / 0.5 / 4.4
2 Tu	0120 / 0709 / 1335 / 1923	0.5 / 4.1 / 0.7 / 4.0		**17** W	0059 / 0645 / 1317 / 1903	0.4 / 4.3 / 0.5 / 4.3
3 W	0149 / 0737 / 1404 / 1952	0.5 / 3.9 / 0.8 / 3.9		**18** Th	0142 / 0726 / 1402 / 1947	0.5 / 4.2 / 0.6 / 4.2
4 Th	0220 / 0808 / 1436 / 2027	0.9 / 3.7 / 1.0 / 3.7		**19** F	0229 / 0812 / 1451 / 2037	0.7 / 4.0 / 0.8 / 4.0
5 F	0256 / 0844 / 1515 / 2110	1.1 / 3.6 / 1.1 / 3.5		**20** Sa	0324 / 0907 / 1549 / 2138	0.8 / 3.8 / 1.0 / 3.7
6 Sa	0342 / 0931 / 1607 / 2206	1.2 / 3.4 / 1.3 / 3.3		**21** Su	0426 / 1013 / 1655 /) 2251	1.0 / 3.5 / 1.1 / 3.5
7 Su	0440 / 1033 / 1712 / (2316	1.4 / 3.2 / 1.4 / 3.2		**22** M	0537 / 1130 / 1811	1.1 / 3.4 / 1.1
8 M	0549 / 1149 / 1825	1.4 / 3.1 / 1.4		**23** Tu	0014 / 0659 / 1255 / 1934	3.4 / 1.1 / 3.4 / 1.0
9 Tu	0034 / 0702 / 1307 / 1940	3.2 / 1.4 / 3.1 / 1.3		**24** W	0137 / 0819 / 1411 / 2047	3.5 / 1.0 / 3.5 / 0.8
10 W	0147 / 0813 / 1416 / 2047	3.3 / 1.2 / 3.3 / 1.1		**25** Th	0244 / 0924 / 1510 / 2145	3.7 / 0.8 / 3.7 / 0.6
11 Th	0246 / 0914 / 1511 / 2139	3.5 / 1.0 / 3.6 / 0.9		**26** F	0338 / 1014 / 1559 / 2233	3.9 / 0.6 / 3.9 / 0.5
12 F	0334 / 1002 / 1556 / 2224	3.8 / 0.8 / 3.8 / 0.7		**27** Sa	0423 / 1057 / 1641 / 2313	4.0 / 0.5 / 4.1 / 0.5
13 Sa	0416 / 1044 / 1635 / 2304	4.0 / 0.7 / 4.0 / 0.5		**28** Su	0502 / 1134 / 1719 / ○ 2350	4.1 / 0.5 / 4.1 / 0.5
14 Su	0454 / 1122 / 1712 / ● 2342	4.2 / 0.5 / 4.2 / 0.4		**29** M	0539 / 1207 / 1753	4.1 / 0.6 / 4.1
15 M	0530 / 1200 / 1740 / ○	4.3 / 0.5 / 4.3		**30** Tu	0022 / 0611 / 1236 / 1827	0.6 / 4.0 / 0.7 / 4.1

Chart Datum: 0.13 metres above Ordnance Datum (Dublin)

IRELAND, SOUTH COAST – RINGASKIDDY

Lat 51°50′ N   Long 8°19′ W

TIMES AND HEIGHTS OF HIGH AND LOW WATERS

YEAR **1991**

TIME ZONE **UT (GMT)**
For Summer Time add ONE
hour in non-shaded areas

	MAY			JUNE			JULY			AUGUST		
	Time	m		Time	m		Time	m		Time	m

	MAY Time	m		Time	m		JUNE Time	m		Time	m		JULY Time	m		Time	m		AUGUST Time	m		Time	m

MAY

1 W — 0052 0·7 / 0641 4·0 / 1304 4·0 / 1857 4·0
16 Th — 0049 0·4 / 0634 4·3 / 1310 0·5 / 1857 4·3

2 Th — 0121 0·8 / 0710 3·9 / 1335 0·8 / 1930 3·9
17 F — 0137 0·5 / 0720 4·2 / 1359 0·6 / 1945 4·2

3 F — 0154 0·9 / 0742 3·7 / 1409 0·9 / 2005 3·8
18 Sa — 0229 0·6 / 0811 4·0 / 1453 0·7 / 2040 4·0

4 Sa — 0232 1·0 / 0819 3·6 / 1451 1·0 / 2047 3·6
19 Su — 0325 0·7 / 0908 3·8 / 1549 0·8 / 2139 3·8

5 Su — 0317 1·1 / 0905 3·4 / 1541 1·1 / 2138 3·4
20 — 0426 0·8 / 1010 3·6 / ☽ 1652 0·9 / 2245 3·7

6 M — 0410 1·2 / 1000 3·3 / 1638 1·2 / 2238 3·3
21 Tu — 0532 0·9 / 1119 3·5 / 1800 0·9 / 2357 3·6

7 Tu — 0511 1·3 / 1106 3·2 / 1743 1·3 / ☾ 2346 3·3
22 W — 0642 1·0 / 1229 3·5 / 1912 0·9

8 W — 0615 1·3 / 1215 3·2 / 1850 1·2
23 Th — 0107 3·6 / 0751 0·9 / 1337 3·5 / 2019 0·8

9 Th — 0052 3·4 / 0721 1·2 / 1321 3·3 / 1955 1·1
24 F — 0211 3·6 / 0853 0·8 / 1436 3·7 / 2117 0·7

10 F — 0152 3·5 / 0823 1·0 / 1420 3·5 / 2053 0·9
25 Sa — 0305 3·7 / 0945 0·7 / 1527 3·8 / 2207 0·7

11 Sa — 0247 3·7 / 0918 0·9 / 1512 3·8 / 2145 0·7
26 Su — 0352 3·8 / 1030 0·7 / 1613 3·9 / 2249 0·7

12 Su — 0336 3·9 / 1007 0·7 / 1600 4·0 / 2231 0·6
27 M — 0435 3·9 / 1109 0·7 / 1654 4·0 / 2327 0·7

13 M — 0421 4·1 / 1052 0·6 / 1644 4·2 / 2318 0·5
28 Tu — 0513 3·9 / 1143 0·7 / 1732 4·0 / ○

14 Tu — 0505 4·3 / 1137 0·5 / ● 1727 4·3
29 W — 0001 0·7 / 0549 3·9 / 1215 0·8 / 1808 4·0

15 W — 0003 0·4 / 0549 4·3 / 1222 0·5 / 1811 4·4
30 Th — 0032 0·8 / 0622 3·9 / 1246 0·8 / 1842 4·0

31 F — 0104 0·8 / 0655 3·8 / 1319 0·8 / 1916 3·9

JUNE

1 Sa — 0138 0·9 / 0728 3·8 / 1355 0·9 / 1952 3·8
16 Su — 0226 0·4 / 0811 4·1 / 1447 0·4 / 2037 4·2

2 Su — 0216 0·9 / 0805 3·7 / 1434 0·9 / 2030 3·7
17 M — 0318 0·5 / 0903 4·0 / 1541 0·5 / 2131 4·0

3 M — 0257 1·0 / 0846 3·6 / 1518 1·0 / 2114 3·6
18 Tu — 0413 0·6 / 0957 3·8 / 1637 0·7 / 2228 3·8

4 Tu — 0342 1·0 / 0934 3·5 / 1606 1·0 / 2203 3·5
19 W — 0511 0·8 / 1055 3·6 / 1736 0·8 / ☽ 2327 3·6

5 W — 0431 1·1 / 1026 3·4 / 1659 1·1 / ☾ 2259 3·5
20 Th — 0611 0·9 / 1156 3·5 / 1838 0·9

6 Th — 0527 1·1 / 1125 3·4 / 1758 1·1 / 2358 3·5
21 F — 0029 3·5 / 0713 1·0 / 1259 3·5 / 1942 0·9

7 F — 0627 1·1 / 1227 3·4 / 1902 1·1
22 Sa — 0133 3·5 / 0815 1·0 / 1359 3·5 / 2044 0·9

8 Sa — 0100 3·5 / 0730 1·1 / 1331 3·5 / 2006 1·0
23 Su — 0230 3·5 / 0912 1·0 / 1457 3·6 / 2139 0·9

9 Su — 0201 3·7 / 0833 1·0 / 1432 3·7 / 2107 0·9
24 M — 0324 3·6 / 1003 0·9 / 1548 3·7 / 2228 0·9

10 M — 0300 3·8 / 0934 0·8 / 1529 3·9 / 2204 0·8
25 Tu — 0412 3·7 / 1048 0·9 / 1635 3·8 / 2311 0·9

11 Tu — 0356 4·0 / 1030 0·7 / 1623 4·1 / 2259 0·6
26 W — 0455 3·8 / 1126 0·8 / 1718 3·9 / 2347 0·8

12 W — 0448 4·1 / 1123 0·6 / ● 1715 4·3 / 2351 0·5
27 Th — 0534 3·8 / 1208 0·8 / 1756 4·0 / ○

13 Th — 0540 4·2 / 1214 0·5 / 1805 4·4
28 F — 0021 0·8 / 0611 3·9 / 1235 0·8 / 1831 4·0

14 F — 0043 0·4 / 0629 4·3 / 1304 0·4 / 1856 4·4
29 Sa — 0053 0·8 / 0645 3·9 / 1309 0·7 / 1904 4·0

15 Sa — 0134 0·4 / 0720 4·2 / 1357 0·4 / 1945 4·3
30 Su — 0127 0·8 / 0717 3·8 / 1342 0·7 / 1938 3·9

JULY

1 M — 0159 0·8 / 0751 3·8 / 1416 0·8 / 2012 3·9
16 Tu — 0301 0·4 / 0846 4·1 / 1521 0·4 / 2111 4·1

2 Tu — 0234 0·8 / 0825 3·8 / 1454 0·8 / 2049 3·8
17 W — 0349 0·6 / 0931 3·9 / 1610 0·6 / 2159 3·9

3 W — 0312 0·9 / 0904 3·7 / 1534 0·9 / 2129 3·7
18 Th — 0438 0·8 / 1020 3·7 / 1701 0·8 / ☽ 2249 3·6

4 Th — 0353 0·9 / 0948 3·6 / 1619 1·0 / 2216 3·6
19 F — 0530 1·0 / 1115 3·5 / 1756 1·0 / 2346 3·4

5 F — 0441 1·0 / 1038 3·5 / 1712 1·0 / ☾ 2311 3·6
20 Sa — 0627 1·1 / 1215 3·4 / 1857 1·2

6 Sa — 0537 1·1 / 1139 3·5 / 1814 1·1
21 Su — 0049 3·3 / 0730 1·2 / 1321 3·3 / 2005 1·2

7 Su — 0012 3·5 / 0643 1·1 / 1245 3·5 / 1923 1·1
22 M — 0155 3·3 / 0836 1·2 / 1427 3·4 / 2111 1·2

8 M — 0121 3·5 / 0755 1·1 / 1358 3·6 / 2037 1·0
23 Tu — 0258 3·4 / 0936 1·1 / 1528 3·6 / 2207 1·1

9 Tu — 0233 3·6 / 0908 1·0 / 1508 3·8 / 2146 0·9
24 W — 0353 3·5 / 1028 1·0 / 1619 3·7 / 2254 1·0

10 W — 0341 3·8 / 1014 0·8 / 1613 4·0 / 2249 0·7
25 Th — 0440 3·7 / 1112 0·9 / 1704 3·9 / 2333 0·9

11 Th — 0441 4·0 / 1113 0·6 / 1711 4·2 / ● 2344 0·5
26 F — 0522 3·8 / 1149 0·8 / 1743 4·0 / ○

12 F — 0536 4·2 / 1208 0·4 / 1803 4·4
27 Sa — 0007 0·8 / 0558 3·9 / 1222 0·7 / 1817 4·1

13 Sa — 0036 0·3 / 0627 4·3 / 1257 0·3 / 1852 4·4
28 Su — 0039 0·7 / 0631 4·0 / 1253 0·7 / 1848 4·1

14 Su — 0126 0·3 / 0714 4·3 / 1347 0·2 / 1938 4·4
29 M — 0110 0·7 / 0700 4·0 / 1324 0·6 / 1917 4·1

15 M — 0215 0·3 / 0759 4·2 / 1433 0·3 / 2025 4·3
30 Tu — 0140 0·7 / 0730 4·0 / 1355 0·7 / 1947 4·0

31 W — 0211 0·7 / 0759 3·9 / 1427 0·7 / 2019 4·0

AUGUST

1 Th — 0243 0·8 / 0833 3·9 / 1503 0·8 / 2054 3·9
16 F — 0357 0·9 / 0939 3·8 / 1617 1·0 / 2203 3·6

2 F — 0319 0·9 / 0912 3·8 / 1543 0·9 / 2138 3·8
17 Sa — 0441 1·1 / 1027 3·5 / 1706 1·2 / ☽ 2255 3·3

3 Sa — 0404 1·0 / 0959 3·7 / 1635 1·1 / 2230 3·6
18 Su — 0533 1·3 / 1126 3·3 / 1805 1·4

4 Su — 0501 1·2 / 1058 3·5 / 1739 1·2 / 2334 3·5
19 M — 0000 3·2 / 0636 1·4 / 1238 3·2 / 1917 1·5

5 M — 0610 1·3 / 1211 3·4 / 1853 1·3
20 Tu — 0116 3·1 / 0751 1·4 / 1355 3·3 / 2034 1·4

6 Tu — 0052 3·4 / 0728 1·3 / 1334 3·5 / 2018 1·2
21 W — 0230 3·3 / 0905 1·3 / 1504 3·5 / 2141 1·3

7 W — 0218 3·5 / 0853 1·1 / 1458 3·7 / 2138 1·0
22 Th — 0332 3·5 / 1003 1·1 / 1559 3·7 / 2230 1·0

8 Th — 0335 3·7 / 1006 0·9 / 1609 4·0 / 2242 0·7
23 F — 0420 3·7 / 1049 0·9 / 1642 3·9 / 2311 0·9

9 F — 0438 4·0 / 1106 0·6 / 1706 4·2 / 2337 0·4
24 Sa — 0501 3·9 / 1126 0·8 / 1719 4·1 / 2344 0·7

10 Sa — 0530 4·2 / 1157 0·3 / 1754 4·4 / ●
25 Su — 0536 4·0 / 1200 0·7 / 1753 4·2 / ○

11 Su — 0025 0·2 / 0615 4·4 / 1245 0·2 / 1839 4·5
26 M — 0015 0·7 / 0607 4·1 / 1231 0·6 / 1822 4·2

12 M — 0110 0·2 / 0659 4·4 / 1328 0·2 / 1921 4·5
27 Tu — 0045 0·6 / 0635 4·1 / 1300 0·6 / 1850 4·2

13 Tu — 0154 0·3 / 0738 4·3 / 1411 0·3 / 2001 4·3
28 W — 0114 0·6 / 0703 4·1 / 1330 0·6 / 1919 4·2

14 W — 0234 0·4 / 0818 4·2 / 1451 0·4 / 2040 4·1
29 Th — 0144 0·7 / 0731 4·1 / 1402 0·7 / 1949 4·2

15 Th — 0315 0·6 / 0857 4·0 / 1534 0·7 / 2119 3·9
30 F — 0216 0·8 / 0804 4·1 / 1437 0·8 / 2025 4·1

31 Sa — 0254 0·9 / 0843 4·0 / 1519 1·0 / 2107 3·9

12

Chart Datum: 0.13 metres above Ordnance Datum (Dublin)

IRELAND, SOUTH COAST – RINGASKIDDY

Lat 51°50′ N   Long 8°19′ W

TIMES AND HEIGHTS OF HIGH AND LOW WATERS

YEAR 1991

TIME ZONE UT (GMT)
For Summer Time add ONE hour in non-shaded areas

Chart Datum: 0.13 metres above Ordnance Datum (Dublin)

SEPTEMBER

Day	Time	m	Day	Time	m
1 Su ☾	0341	1.1	16 M	0442	1.4
	0929	3.8		1038	3.4
	1613	1.2		1715	1.5
	2200	3.7		2308	3.2
2 M	0440	1.3	17 Tu	0546	1.5
	1031	3.6		1151	3.2
	1719	1.3		1825	1.6
	2309	3.4			
3 Tu	0551	1.4	18 W	0028	3.1
	1151	3.4		0702	1.6
	1838	1.4		1313	3.3
				1947	1.6
4 W	0035	3.3	19 Th	0149	3.2
	0714	1.4		0822	1.4
	1323	3.5		1427	3.4
	2008	1.3		2100	1.4
5 Th	0211	3.4	20 F	0257	3.4
	0844	1.2		0927	1.2
	1454	3.7		1524	3.7
	2131	1.0		2153	1.1
6 F	0329	3.7	21 Sa	0346	3.7
	0957	0.9		1014	1.0
	1600	4.0		1607	3.9
	2233	0.7		2235	0.9
7 Sa	0427	4.0	22 Su	0428	3.9
	1054	0.6		1054	0.8
	1652	4.3		1645	4.1
	2322	0.5		2312	0.8
8 Su ●	0513	4.3	23 M ○	0504	4.1
	1140	0.3		1129	0.7
	1737	4.5		1719	4.2
				2344	0.7
9 M	0007	0.3	24 Tu	0536	4.2
	0556	4.4		1201	0.7
	1224	0.3		1751	4.3
	1818	4.5			
10 Tu	0048	0.3	25 W	0017	0.7
	0635	4.4		0605	4.3
	1303	0.3		1234	0.6
	1855	4.5		1821	4.3
11 W	0126	0.4	26 Th	0048	0.7
	0710	4.4		0635	4.3
	1341	0.4		1306	0.7
	1930	4.3		1850	4.3
12 Th	0202	0.6	27 F	0121	0.7
	0745	4.2		0707	4.3
	1418	0.6		1341	0.8
	2004	4.1		1924	4.3
13 F	0237	0.8	28 Sa	0157	0.8
	0819	4.0		0741	4.2
	1454	0.9		1420	0.9
	2037	3.9		2002	4.1
14 Sa	0312	1.0	29 Su	0239	1.0
	0857	3.8		0823	4.1
	1532	1.1		1507	1.0
	2115	3.6		2047	3.9
15 Su ☽	0353	1.2	30 M	0329	1.1
	0941	3.6		0915	3.9
	1617	1.4		1603	1.2
	2204	3.4		2145	3.7

OCTOBER

Day	Time	m	Day	Time	m
1 Tu ☾	0431	1.3	16 W	0504	1.5
	1021	3.6		1106	3.4
	1711	1.4		1740	1.6
	2259	3.5		2339	3.2
2 W	0543	1.4	17 Th	0614	1.5
	1143	3.5		1221	3.3
	1831	1.4		1853	1.6
3 Th	0027	3.4	18 F	0056	3.3
	0706	1.4		0728	1.5
	1314	3.5		1333	3.4
	1959	1.3		2005	1.4
4 F	0158	3.5	19 Sa	0204	3.4
	0832	1.1		0836	1.3
	1437	3.8		1433	3.6
	2115	1.0		2104	1.2
5 Sa	0310	3.8	20 Su	0300	3.6
	0941	0.9		0929	1.1
	1530	4.0		1521	3.8
	2213	0.8		2152	1.1
6 Su	0403	4.1	21 M	0345	3.9
	1033	0.6		1013	1.0
	1628	4.3		1603	4.0
	2301	0.6		2233	0.9
7 M	0448	4.3	22 Tu	0424	4.1
	1118	0.5		1052	0.8
	1711	4.4		1642	4.2
	2343 ●	0.5		2311	0.8
8 Tu	0529	4.4	23 W	0501	4.2
	1158	0.4		1130	0.8
	1750	4.4		1718	4.3
				2347 ○	0.8
9 W	0019	0.5	24 Th	0536	4.3
	0607	4.4		1207	0.7
	1236	0.5		1753	4.4
	1825	4.4			
10 Th	0055	0.6	25 F	0024	0.8
	0641	4.4		0611	4.4
	1310	0.7		1245	0.7
	1857	4.2		1829	4.4
11 F	0128	0.8	26 Sa	0103	0.8
	0714	4.2		0649	4.3
	1344	0.8		1326	0.8
	1930	4.1		1907	4.3
12 Sa	0159	0.9	27 Su	0144	0.9
	0745	4.1		0730	4.2
	1418	1.0		1411	0.9
	2001	3.9		1951	4.2
13 Su	0234	1.1	28 M	0232	1.0
	0823	3.9		0816	4.2
	1454	1.2		1454	1.0
	2037	3.7		2042	4.0
14 M	0314	1.3	29 Tu	0325	1.1
	0905	3.7		0912	4.0
	1539	1.4		1600	1.2
	2124	3.5		2142	3.8
15 Tu ☽	0403	1.4	30 W	0427	1.4
	0959	3.5		1019	3.8
	1635	1.5		1706	1.3
	2224	3.3		2254 ☾	3.6
			31 Th	0536	1.3
				1134	3.7
				1821	1.3

NOVEMBER

Day	Time	m	Day	Time	m
1 F	0012	3.5	16 Sa	0632	1.4
	0653	1.2		1232	3.5
	1255	3.7		1903	1.4
	1941	1.2			
2 Sa	0131	3.6	17 Su	0102	3.4
	0811	1.1		0737	1.4
	1408	3.8		1333	3.6
	2050	1.0		2005	1.3
3 Su	0237	3.8	18 M	0202	3.6
	0914	0.9		0836	1.2
	1508	4.0		1429	3.8
	2148	0.9		2101	1.2
4 M	0332	4.0	19 Tu	0256	3.8
	1002	0.7		0928	1.1
	1559	4.1		1518	3.9
	2234	0.7		2150	1.1
5 Tu	0419	4.2	20 W	0343	4.0
	1054	0.7		1016	1.0
	1642	4.2		1604	4.0
	2316	0.7		2237	0.9
6 W ●	0501	4.3	21 Th ○	0428	4.2
	1133	0.7		1101	0.9
	1722	4.3		1648	4.3
	2353	0.7		2320	0.8
7 Th	0539	4.3	22 F	0511	4.3
	1210	0.8		1144	0.8
	1757	4.2		1730	4.4
8 F	0027	0.8	23 Sa	0005	0.8
	0615	4.3		0555	4.4
	1243	0.9		1229	0.7
	1831	4.2		1814	4.4
9 Sa	0059	0.9	24 Su	0050	0.7
	0649	4.2		0638	4.4
	1317	1.0		1317	0.7
	1903	4.1		1859	4.3
10 Su	0131	1.0	25 M	0137	0.8
	0724	4.1		0724	4.4
	1351	1.1		1406	0.8
	1937	3.9		1947	4.2
11 M	0206	1.1	26 Tu	0227	0.8
	0801	4.0		0815	4.3
	1427	1.2		1458	0.9
	2013	3.8		2039	4.1
12 Tu	0246	1.2	27 W	0321	0.9
	0842	3.8		0910	4.1
	1511	1.3		1555	1.0
	2057	3.6		2136	3.9
13 W	0332	1.3	28 Th	0420	1.0
	0929	3.7		1010	3.9
	1600	1.4		1655	1.4
	2149	3.5		2240 ☾	3.7
14 Th	0427	1.4	29 F	0522	1.0
	1026	3.5		1116	3.8
	1657	1.5		1801	1.1
	2251 ☽	3.4		2347	3.7
15 F	0527	1.4	30 Sa	0629	1.1
	1127	3.5		1225	3.7
	1758	1.5		1912	1.1
	2357	3.4			

DECEMBER

Day	Time	m	Day	Time	m
1 Su	0056	3.7	16 M	0632	1.3
	0740	1.0		1231	3.6
	1333	3.8		1900	1.3
	2018	1.1			
2 M	0201	3.9	17 Tu	0102	3.5
	0843	1.0		0735	1.3
	1433	3.8		1333	3.6
	2115	1.0		2005	1.3
3 Tu	0258	3.9	18 W	0205	3.6
	0941	0.9		0840	1.2
	1527	3.9		1433	3.8
	2207	0.9		2107	1.2
4 W	0350	4.0	19 Th	0304	3.8
	1028	0.9		0941	1.1
	1614	4.0		1531	3.9
	2251	0.9		2206	1.0
5 Th	0435	4.1	20 F	0400	4.0
	1112	0.9		1035	0.9
	1657	4.1		1626	4.1
	2330	0.9		2259	0.9
6 F ●	0518	4.1	21 Sa ○	0452	4.2
	1150	0.9		1129	0.8
	1736	4.1		1716	4.3
				2351	0.7
7 Sa	0007	0.9	22 Su	0543	4.4
	0557	4.2		1219	0.7
	1225	1.0		1805	4.3
	1812	4.0			
8 Su	0039	0.9	23 M	0041	0.6
	0634	4.1		0631	4.5
	1259	1.0		1309	0.7
	1848	4.0		1853	4.4
9 M	0113	0.9	24 Tu	0130	0.5
	0709	4.1		0720	4.5
	1333	1.0		1359	0.6
	1921	3.9		1942	4.2
10 Tu	0147	1.0	25 W	0219	0.5
	0744	4.0		0808	4.4
	1408	1.1		1449	0.6
	1957	3.9		2030	4.2
11 W	0225	1.0	26 Th	0310	0.6
	0820	3.9		0858	4.2
	1446	1.1		1541	0.7
	2034	3.8		2122	4.0
12 Th	0304	1.1	27 F	0402	0.7
	0901	3.8		0952	4.1
	1527	1.2		1634	0.9
	2117	3.7		2216	3.9
13 F	0348	1.2	28 Sa	0458	0.8
	0946	3.7		1048	3.9
	1612	1.2		1732	1.0
	2204	3.6		2315 ☾	3.7
14 Sa	0437	1.2	29 Su	0557	1.0
	1035	3.6		1149	3.7
	1702	1.3		1832	1.1
	2258	3.5			
15 Su	0532	1.3	30 M	0018	3.6
	1132	3.6		0702	1.1
	1758	1.3		1253	3.6
	2358	3.5		1938	1.2
			31 Tu	0123	3.6
				0808	1.1
				1358	3.6
				2042	1.2

Chart Datum: 0.13 metres above Ordnance Datum (Dublin)

CORK *continued*

CHARTS
Admiralty 1777, 1773, 1765; Imray C56, C57; Irish OS 25
TIDES
−0535 Dover; ML 2.3; Duration 0555; Zone 0 (GMT)

Standard Port COBH (RINGASKIDDY) (→)

Times				Height (metres)			
HW		LW		MHWS	MHWN	MLWN	MLWS
0500	1100	0500	1100	4.2	3.3	1.4	0.5
1700	2300	1700	2300				

Differences CORK
+0020 +0020 +0020 +0020 +0.3 +0.1 0.0 0.0

NOTE: Cobh is a Standard Port — Times and heights of tides for the year are given below.

SHELTER
Very good shelter under all conditions. Cork itself is largely a commercial port, but berths are available; before proceeding up river contact Port Operations. The main yachting centre is at Crosshaven in Owenboy River, where there are two marinas (Crosshaven Boatyard and Royal Cork YC) and anchorages further upstream, in particular in Drake's Pool. There is also a marina at East Ferry on the E side of Great Island.
NAVIGATION
Waypoint 51°46'.00N 08°15'.30W, 174°/354° from/to front Ldg Lt 354°, 2.8M. There are no navigational dangers for yachtsmen. It is one of the safest harbours to enter in the world. Harbour is deep and well marked. Tidal streams run about 1½ kn in entrance at springs, but more between the forts. Entrance to Owenboy River carries a minimum of 2m at LWS, and the channel is buoyed.

TELEPHONE (021)
Hr Mr 273125; MRCC Limerick (061) 61219; Port Operation & Information Stn. 811380; Coast Life Saving Service (Crosshaven) 831448; ✠ 271322; Weather 964600; Police (Crosshaven) 831222; Dr 831716 (Crosshaven) or 811546 (Cobh); Ⓗ 546400.
FACILITIES
EC Wednesday; **Royal Cork YC Marina** ☎ 831023, AC, M, D, P, L, Ⓞ, Slip, V, FW, Bar, R; **Crosshaven BY Marina** (100+20 visitors) ☎ 831161, AC, BH (25 ton), C (1.5 ton), CH, D, El, FW, Gas, Gaz, ME, P, Sh, Slip; **East Ferry Marina** (60+12 visitors) ☎ 811342, D, AC, FW; **Salve Engineering** ☎ 831145, BY, FW, L, M, ME, Slip; **McWilliam Sailmakers** ☎ 831504, SM; **Union Chandlery** ☎ 271643, ACA, CH; **Glen Marine** ☎ 841163, BY, CH; **Rider Services** ☎ 841176, Ⓔ; **Irish Marine Electronics** ☎ 894155, Ⓔ; **Crosshaven Village** Bar, Dr, L, ✉, R, V, YC; **Cork City** ACA, Bar, CH, Ⓞ, V, Ⓑ; ✉; Ferry Port; ⇌; ✈.

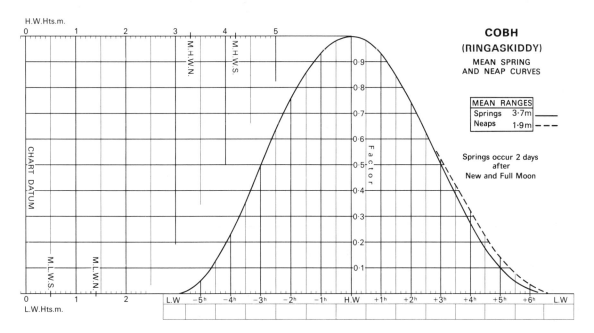

H.W.Hts.m.

COBH
(RINGASKIDDY)
MEAN SPRING AND NEAP CURVES

MEAN RANGES	
Springs	3·7m
Neaps	1·9m

Springs occur 2 days after New and Full Moon

12

L.W.Hts.m.

LIGHTS AND MARKS
The hammer-head water tower S of Crosshaven is a very conspic mark, 24.5m high.
Ldg Lts, two sets, both below Fort Davis on E shore;
(1) Lts Oc 5s, front 29m 10M, rear 37m 10M lead E of Harbour Rocks.
(2) Lts Oc R 5s, front 11m 5M, rear 21m 5M lead W of Harbour Rocks.
FW leading lights with W diamond day marks in line 252° lead to Crosshaven, but not easy to see.
RADIO TELEPHONE
Call: *Cork Harbour Radio* VHF Ch 16; 12 14 (H24); Crosshaven Marina Ch M (Mon-Fri: 0830-1700 LT). Royal Cork YC Marina Ch M (0900-2300 LT). East Ferry Marina Ch M.

YOUGHAL 10-12-18
Cork

CHARTS
Admiralty 2071; Imray C57; Irish OS 22
TIDES
−0545 Dover; ML 2.3; Duration 0555; Zone 0 (GMT).

YOUGHAL *continued*
Standard Port COBH (RINGASKIDDY) (←)

Times				Height (metres)			
HW		LW		MHWS	MHWN	MLWN	MLWS
0500	1100	0500	1100	4.2	3.3	1.4	0.5
1700	2300	1700	2300				

Differences YOUGHAL

−0002	+0014	+0016	0000	0.0	0.0	−0.1	0.0

BALLYCOTTON

−0011	+0001	+0003	−0009	0.0	0.0	−0.1	0.0

DUNGARVAN HARBOUR

+0004	+0012	+0007	−0001	0.0	+0.1	−0.2	0.0

SHELTER
Good, but strong SE to S by W winds cause a swell inside the harbour. Good anchorages off Mall Dock, opposite the most northerly warehouse or N of Ferry Point.

NAVIGATION
East Bar waypoint 51°55'.60N 07°48'.00W, 122°/302° from/to Fl WR 2.5s Lt, 1.8M. Beware Blackball Ledge and Bar Rocks outside harbour entrance in R sector of lighthouse Lt. Do not attempt entry in rough seas. Beware salmon nets in entrance and bay during season; also mussel banks off town quays.

LIGHTS AND MARKS
A 15m white tower on W side of entrance shows Lt Fl WR 2.5s, 24m 12/9M, W 183°-273°, R 273°-295°, W 295°- 307°, R 307°-351°, W 351°-003°, the W sectors leading over the bars. Convent Tr in line with edge of Town Hall at 178° keeps clear of Red Bank to N.

RADIO TELEPHONE
VHF Ch 16.

TELEPHONE (024)
Hr Mr 92365; MRCC Limerick 61219; Coast Life Saving Service 93252; ⌗ Cork 21322; Police 2200; Dr 72253.

FACILITIES
EC Wednesday; **Ferry Point Boat Co** ☎ 94232, ME, El, Sh, CH; **Alan Prim** ☎ 932781, Kos; **Whitegates Gas Depot** ☎ (021) 661269, Gas (refills); **Town** Slip, P, D, L, FW (well), V, R, Bar; ✉; Ⓑ; ⇌ (bus to Cork); ✈ (Cork).

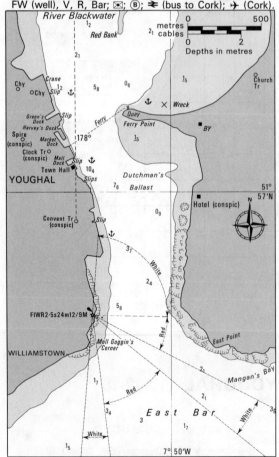

▲ No special visitors berths

DUNMORE EAST   10-12-19
Waterford

CHARTS
Admiralty 2046; Imray C61, C57; Irish OS 23

TIDES
−0535 Dover; ML 2.3; Duration 0605; Zone 0 (GMT).

Standard Port COBH (RINGASKIDDY) (←)

Times				Height (metres)			
HW		LW		MHWS	MHWN	MLWN	MLWS
0500	1100	0500	1100	4.2	3.3	1.4	0.5
1700	2300	1700	2300				

Differences DUNMORE EAST

+0013	+0013	+0001	+0001	0.0	0.0	−0.2	0.0

SHELTER
Very good. Yachts may berth alongside W wharf only. There are no moorings for visiting craft. Yachts may anchor N of the harbour.
Craft stay afloat at all times but can dry out in grid opposite synchrolift. Very good shelter except when wind is from NE, E to SE. Alongside berths occasionally available but it gets very crowded with fishing boats especially in the autumn. Hr depth 2 to 3.4m. On arrival, berth at East Pier and report to Hr Mr.

NAVIGATION
Waypoint (see 10.12.20 for waypoint off Hook Head) 52°08'.0N 06°58'.0W, 137°/317° from/to breakwater Lt, 1.2M. There are no navigational dangers. Enter harbour under power, if available. Approaching by night from E, give Hook Head a wide berth (½M); when clear of Hook Head alter course for Dunmore East in R sector of breakwater Lt. From W, steer for Hook Head until in R sector and then alter course to N.

LIGHTS AND MARKS
East Pier Lt Ho L Fl WR8s 13m 12/9M, W225°-310°, R310°-004°. E Breakwater head Fl R2s 6m 4M, vis 000°-310°. W wharf Fl G 2s 6m 4M, vis 165°-246°.

RADIO TELEPHONE
VHF Ch 16; 14 (Pilot Station).

TELEPHONE (051)
Hr Mr 83166; CG Cork 26552; Pilot 83119; MRCC Limerick (061) 61219; ⌗ 75391; Coast Life Saving Service 83115; Dr 83194.

DUNMORE EAST *Continued*

FACILITIES
Harbour ☎ 83166, BH (230 ton), D, FW (on East Pier); **Waterford Harbour SC** ☎ 83389, R, Bar; **Dunmore East Garage** ☎ 83200, Kos; **Dunmore East Fishermans Co-operative Society** ☎ 83307, CH; **Dunmore Marine Supply Co** ☎ 83165, CH; **Village** Bar, D, P (cans), Slip, R, V, Ⓑ; ✉; ➔ (Waterford); ✈ (Dublin).

WATERFORD   10-12-20
Waterford

CHARTS
Admiralty 2046; Imray C57; Irish OS 23
TIDES
−0520 Dover; ML 2.4; Duration 0605; Zone 0 (GMT).

Standard Port COBH (RINGASKIDDY) (←)

Times				Height (metres)			
HW		LW		MHWS	MHWN	MLWN	MLWS
0500	1100	0500	1100	4.2	3.3	1.4	0.5
1700	2300	1700	2300				

Differences WATERFORD
+0057 +0057 +0046 +0046 +0.4 +0.3 −0.1 −0.1
CARNSORE POINT
+0029 +0019 −0002 +0008 −1.1 −1.0 No data

▲ Dunmore East: Berth W Wharf, report Hr Mr.

SHELTER
Very good and there are many excellent anchorages; off the quays just W of Cheek Pt; W of Little Is on S side of main river about 1½M E of Waterford; in Barrow R on E side just S of New Ross; in Barrow R on the N side of the E/W stretch about 2M S of New Ross.
NAVIGATION
Waypoint 52°06'.50N 07°56'.60W, 182°/002° from/to front Ldg Lt 002°, 6.7M. Beware of Falskirt Rock (2 ca off Swine Head) and Brecaun reef (20 ca NE of Hook Head). Give Tower Race, extending 1M to S of Hook Head, a wide berth.
LIGHTS AND MARKS
Hook Head Fl 3s 46m 24M; W Tr, two B bands. Dunmore East Fl WR 8s 13m 12/9M; vis W225°-310°, R310°-004°. Duncannon Ldg Lts 002°, both Oc 4s. Do not confuse Waterford entrance with Tramore Bay.
RADIO TELEPHONE
New Ross VHF Ch 16; 12 14 (H24).
TELEPHONE (051)
Hr Mr 74499; CG Cork 26552; MRCC Limerick 61219; ▦ 75391; Police 74888; Dr 83194; Ⓗ 75429.
FACILITIES
EC Thursday; **Carrolls BY (Ballyhack)** ME, El, Sh, C; **Town** AB, M, FW, P, D, Gaz, V, R, Bar, ➔; ✈
Note: a marina is planned for Arthurstown.

ROSSLARE HARBOUR
Dublin   **10-12-21**

CHARTS
Admiralty 1772; Imray C61; Irish OS 23
TIDES
−0525 Dover; ML 1.1; Duration 0640; Zone 0 (GMT)

12

ROSSLARE *continued*

Standard Port DUBLIN (NORTH WALL) (→)

Times				Height (metres)			
HW		LW		MHWS	MHWN	MLWN	MLWS
0000	0700	0000	0500	4.1	3.4	1.5	0.5
1200	1900	1200	1700				

Differences ROSSLARE HARBOUR

−0440	−0710	−0710	−0440	−2.2	−2.0	−0.7	−0.3

SHELTER
An artificial harbour and busy ferry port which is a useful stopping place. Yachts can anchor in the shelter of the breakwater or go alongside No 1 berth West Pier. Often uncomfortable in winds WNW to NE and dangerous with even moderate winds WNW to NNE.

NAVIGATION
Waypoint 52°14'.60N 06°15'.00W, 105°/285° from/to breakwater Lt, 3.3M. Main approach channel is South Shear. From S, beware Splaugh Rock off Greenore Point, and overfalls here and further S over The Baillies. South Shear runs S of Holdens Bed, a shallow bank with changeable depths, and the tide sets across the channel. Approach from N through North Shear. If wind shifts to dangerous sector leave immediately, through South Shear.

WEXFORD   10-12-22
Wexford

CHARTS
Admiralty 1772; Imray C61; Irish OS 23

TIDES
Neap −0630 Spring −0330 Dover; ML 1.3; Duration 0630; Zone 0 (GMT)

Standard Port DUBLIN (NORTH WALL) (→)

Times				Height (metres)			
HW		LW		MHWS	MHWN	MLWN	MLWS
0000	0700	0000	0500	4.1	3.4	1.5	0.5
1200	1900	1200	1700				

Differences WEXFORD

−0350	−0720	−0725	−0325	−2.4	−2.0	−1.0	−0.3

TUSKAR ROCK

−0457	−0627	−0601	−0517	−1.5	−1.4		No data

LIGHTS AND MARKS
Two sets of Ldg Lts, 146° both Oc 3s 10/11m, 3M and 124° both FR 10/12m 2M. Lt on the end of breakwater L Fl WRG 5s 15m 13/10M, showing R320°-286° over foul ground from Greenore Pt; W283°-286° over South Shear; G246°-283° over section of Holden's Bed with min depth 5.8m; R208°-246° over N section of Holden's Bed; W188°-208° over North Shear; G098°-188° over South Bay.

RADIO TELEPHONE
Call: *Rosslare Harbour Radio* VHF Ch 16; 06 12 14 (H24).

TELEPHONE (053)
Hr Mr 33114; MRCC Limerick 61219; Coast Life Saving Service 32102; ⌗ 33116; Police 22333; Dr 31154; Ⓗ Wexford 22233.

FACILITIES
EC Thursday; **Pier** ☎ 33114, M, P, D, L, FW, ME, C; **Rosslare Ship Repairers** ☎ 33194, ME, Sh, El, Slip, C; **J. Devereaux** ☎ 33104, Kos; **Town** V, R, Bar, ✉, Ⓑ; ⇌; ✈ (Dublin).

SHELTER
Safe sheltered anchorage off town quays but difficult entrance which should not be attempted in strong winds from E to S when seas break on the bar.

NAVIGATION
Waypoint 52°20'.00N 06°18'.00W, 107°/287° from/to FS on The Raven Point, 2.7M (channel shifts). Bar partly dries and it's position changes. Harbour Board has ceased to function so buoys are not maintained. During summer head in between G local buoys. After 3rd R buoy, N of ruins (awash at HW) head 325°. About ¼M off, keep along shore for approx 1M. Having passed two W posts, head SW towards conspic factory tower, SE end of town. Turn in when 1ca off training wall. There are no pilots but local knowledge is very advisable — try Rosslare harbour for knowledgeable local. (J. Sherwood 22875 or night 22731).

LIGHTS AND MARKS
No lights. Leading marks (local). Dayglo buoys mark the channel in summer.

WEXFORD *continued*

RADIO TELEPHONE
None.

TELEPHONE (053)
Hr Mr 33114; MRCC Limerick 61219; ⌗ 33116;
Police 22333; Dr 31154; Ⓗ 42233.

FACILITIES
EC Thursday; **Wexford Quays** Slip, P, D, L, FW, ME, El,
CH, AB, V; **Wexford Harbour Boat Club** ☎ 22039, Slip,
C (5 ton), Bar; **Barrow Valley Marine** ☎ 21902, CH;
Town ✉; Ⓑ; ⇌; ✈ (Waterford).

ARKLOW   10-12-23
Wicklow

CHARTS
Admiralty 633, 1468; Imray C61; Irish OS 19

TIDES
−0200 Dover; ML 1.3; Duration 0640; Zone 0 (GMT).

Standard Port DUBLIN (NORTH WALL) (→)

Times				Height (metres)			
HW		LW		MHWS	MHWN	MLWN	MLWS
0000	0700	0000	0500	4.1	3.4	1.5	0.5
1200	1900	1200	1700				

Differences ARKLOW
| −0215 | −0255 | −0245 | −0225 | −2.4 | −2.0 | −0.3 | +0.3 |

SHELTER
Good shelter except in strong SE winds, when seas break
across the entrance. Entrance is difficult without power.
Once in dock, shelter is perfect (3m). Temporary
anchorage 1M S of piers in 4m during SE winds off
Roadstone Jetty (Oc R 10s 9m 9M). 2 ca S of jetty a
breakwater extends ENE for 3 ca (QY). Best anchorage
between jetty and breakwater.

NAVIGATION
Waypoint 52°47′.60N 06°07′.50W, 090°/270° from/to
entrance, 0.40M. No navigational dangers. The entrance
to the dock is only 13.5m wide. Due to obstructions it is
dangerous to proceed up river of dock entrance without
local knowledge.

LIGHTS AND MARKS
There are no leading lights or marks. The only two lights
are on the piers. North pier LFI G 7s 7m 10M. South pier

⚓ Stop in Dock Entrance and ask
Fl WR 6s 10m 13M; R shore-223°, W223°-350°,
R350°-shore.

RADIO TELEPHONE
VHF Ch 16 (office hours).

TELEPHONE (0402)
Hr Mr 32426; MRCC Limerick 61219; RNLI 32001; Coast
Life Saving Service 32430; ⌗ 32497; Police 2101;
Dr 32421.

FACILITIES
EC Wednesday; **Tyrrell's Yard** ☎ 32001, Slip, L, FW,
ME, El Sh, C (5 ton mobile), AB; **Dock** ☎ 32426, Slip, M,
D, L, FW, ME, El, C (1 ton) CH, AB; **Jack Fitzgerald**
☎ 32152, El; **J. Annelsey** Kos; **Town** CH, V, R, P and D
(cans), Bar, ✉; Ⓑ; ⇌; ✈ (Dublin).

WICKLOW   10-12-24
Wicklow

52°
59′.2N

Leitrim River

Goods
Station

FIG 1·5s
5m 6M

FIWR5s11m6M

Planet Rk
Pogeen Rk

Slip
BH
Yacht
Yard

FIWG10s
5m 6M

Bar

Slip
LB
Black
Castle
(ruins)

BY

HrMr
Fuel
Station

Packet
Quay

YC

Church

WICKLOW

Corrigen
Head

6° 2′.2W

metres
cables   0   400

0   2
Depths in metres

CHARTS
Admiralty 633, 1468; Imray C61; Irish OS 16

TIDES
−0010 Dover; ML 1.5; Duration 0640; Zone 0 (GMT)

Standard Port DUBLIN (NORTH WALL) (→)

Times				Height (metres)			
HW		LW		MHWS	MHWN	MLWN	MLWS
0000	0700	0000	0500	4.1	3.4	1.5	0.5
1200	1900	1200	1700				

Differences WICKLOW
| −0035 | −0047 | −0044 | −0038 | −1.4 | −1.1 | −0.6 | 0.0 |

SHELTER
Very safe, and always accessible. Outer harbour is open
to NE winds which cause a swell. Inner harbour (river)
gives excellent shelter. Berthing on W pier is not
recommended.

NAVIGATION
Waypoint 52°59′.20N 06°01′.80W, 040°/220° from/to
entrance, 0.27M. Entry presents no difficulty so long as
one keeps in the R sector of the Lt on E Pier. This avoids
Planet Rock and Pogeen Rock. Depth over bar 0.5m.
There is a rock 5m NNW of Packet Quay off the point;
keep at least 10m off at LWS.

LIGHTS AND MARKS
There are no leading marks or lights. The only lights are
those shown on the chartlet on East Pier, West Pier and
Packet Quay.

RADIO TELEPHONE
VHF Ch 16; 02 06 07 08 26 27 28 (when vessel expected).

TELEPHONE (0404)
Hr Mr 67455; MRCC Limerick (061) 61219; Coast Life
Saving Service 67310; ⌗ 67222; Police 67107; Dr 67381.

FACILITIES
EC Thursday; **East Pier** L, AB; **South Quay** Slip, P, D,
L, FW, AB; **Wicklow Marine Services** ☎ 68408, M, ME,
El, Sh, C, AB; **Neil Watson** ☎ 67492, Slip, BH (16 ton),
M, FW, ME, El, Sh, C, CH, AB; **Wicklow SC** ☎ 67526,
M, L, FW, Bar; **J. P. Hopkins** ☎ 67413, Kos, Gaz;
Town CH, V, R, Bar. ✉; Ⓑ; ⇌; ✈ (Dublin).

AGENTS WANTED
Berwick-on-Tweed
Mallaig
Loch Sunart
Loch Aline
Fishguard
Kenmare River

Large number of French Ports

Rotterdam
Norderney
Dornumersiel
Langeoog
Wangerooge
Hooksiel
Bremerhaven

If you are interested in becoming our agent please write to
the Editors and get your free copy annually. You do not have
to be a resident in a port to be the agent but at least a fairly
regular visitor.

12

DUBLIN/DUN LAOGHAIRE
Dublin
10-12-25

CHARTS
Admiralty 1447, 1468, 1415; Imray C61, C62; Irish OS 16
TIDES
Dublin Bar +0015   Dun Laoghaire +0010 Dover; ML 2.4;
Duration 0640; Zone 0 (GMT).

Standard Port DUBLIN (NORTH WALL) (→)

Times				Height (metres)			
HW		LW		MHWS	MHWN	MLWN	MLWS
0000	0700	0000	0500	4.1	3.4	1.5	0.5
1200	1900	1200	1700				

Differences DUBLIN BAR

−0006	−0001	−0002	−0003	0.0	0.0	0.0	+0.1

DUN LAOGHAIRE

−0006	−0001	−0002	−0003	0.0	0.0	0.0	+0.1

NOTE: Dublin is a Standard Port and times and heights of tides for the year are given below.
Since Dun Laoghaire is the principal yachting centre for Dublin, the following all refer to Dun Laoghaire.

SHELTER
The harbour is always available but is open to NE swell and anchor holding ground is poor. In these conditions yachts should proceed to Dublin or Howth unless YCs can provide sheltered moorings.
NAVIGATION
Waypoint 53°18'.40N 06°07'.00W, 060°/240° from/to entrance, 0.47M. Keep clear of the many coasters and ferries. Warning — do not anchor in areas marked 'moorings' or in fairways. Beware — the drying rocks approx 10m from the East Pierhead right in the entrance.
LIGHTS AND MARKS
There are no leading lights or marks. There are lights on both pierheads as shown, on Mail Boat Pierhead and on Trader's Wharf. Light on Car Ferry Pier has R sector to cover moorings, so anchor in W sector outside fairways.

RADIO TELEPHONE
VHF Call *Harbour Office Dun Laoghaire* Ch 16; 14. YCs Ch M. Dublin (Call *Dublin Port Radio*) Ch **12** 16; 09 **12** 13 14 (H24). Dublin lifting bridge (call *Eastlink*) Ch 12 13; Dublin Radio Ch 16 67 65 83 (H24).
TELEPHONE (01)
Hr Mr 801130, Dublin 748772; MRCC Limerick 61219; Coast Life Saving Service 809641 or 376497; ≋ 801321; Weather 424655; Local weather (Dublin Bay) 1199; Police (Dublin) 778141, (Dun Laoghaire) 801285; Dr 859244; Ⓗ 806901.
FACILITIES
National YC ☎ 805725, Slip, M, L, C (4 ton), FW, D, R, Bar; **Royal St. George YC** ☎ 801811, Slip, M, D, L, FW, C (5 ton), R, Bar; **Royal Irish YC** ☎ 809452, Slip, M, D, L, FW, C (5 ton), R, Bar, CH; **Dun Laoghaire Motor YC** ☎ 801371, Slip, FW, AB, Bar; **Cross Berth (Traders Wharf)** FW, C (5 ton), AB; **Downer International Sails (Dun Laoghaire)** ☎ 804286, SM; **B. J. Marine** ☎ 719605, CH; **All Weather Marine** ☎ 713305 CH; **Western Marine** ☎ 800321, CH; **Windmill Leisure & Marine** ☎ 772008, CH, ACA; **Dinghy Supplies** ☎ 322312, CH; **Watson and Jameson** ☎ 326466, SM; **H. Pilsworth** ☎ 822023 ME; **E. Brunker** ☎ 342590, Ⓔ; **Apex Electrical** ☎ 541066, El; **Viking Marine** ☎ 806654, CH, Gas; **Town** P, D, ME, El, Sh, CH, V, R, Bar, ✉; Ⓑ; ⇌; ✈ (Dublin).

IRELAND, EAST COAST – DUBLIN (NORTH WALL)

Lat 53°21' N Long 6°13' W

TIMES AND HEIGHTS OF HIGH AND LOW WATERS

YEAR 1991

TIME ZONE UT(GMT)
For Summer Time add ONE hour in non-shaded areas

Each cell below lists the day's successive readings as Time/height(m).

JANUARY

No.	Day	Times & Heights (m)	No.	Day	Times & Heights (m)
1	Tu	0448/0.7 1129/4.3 1719/0.4	16	W	0516/1.0 1146/4.0 1742/0.8
2	W	0000/4.0 0533/0.6 1218/4.3 1807/0.3	17	Th	0014/3.7 0546/0.9 1219/4.0 1814/0.7
3	Th	0049/4.0 0619/0.6 1307/4.4 1856/0.3	18	F	0048/3.7 0618/0.6 1253/4.1 1846/0.6
4	F	0140/4.0 0707/0.7 1358/4.3 1947/0.4	19	Sa	0121/3.7 0653/0.8 1330/4.1 1923/0.6
5	Sa	0230/3.8 0757/0.8 1449/4.2 2039/0.5	20	Su	0158/3.7 0731/0.8 1406/4.1 2002/0.6
6	Su	0322/3.7 0849/1.0 1543/4.1 2132/0.8	21	M	0237/3.7 0813/0.8 1447/4.0 2044/0.7
7	M ☾	0419/3.5 0945/1.2 1641/3.8 2231/1.1	22	Tu	0322/3.6 0858/0.9 1534/3.9 2132/0.8
8	Tu	0522/3.4 1045/1.4 1747/3.6 2337/1.3	23	W ☽	0413/3.5 0950/1.1 1628/3.8 2226/1.1
9	W	0631/3.3 1158/1.6 1857/3.5	24	Th	0516/3.4 1051/1.2 1734/3.6 2332/1.3
10	Th	0053/1.5 0737/3.3 1321/1.7 2005/3.4	25	F	0629/3.4 1205/1.4 1853/3.5
11	F	0204/1.5 0834/3.4 1433/1.6 2104/3.4	26	Sa	0052/1.4 0742/3.5 1328/1.3 2011/3.6
12	Sa	0258/1.4 0922/3.5 1525/1.4 2153/3.5	27	Su	0208/1.3 0847/3.6 1440/1.1 2118/3.7
13	Su	0341/1.3 1003/3.7 1606/1.1 2233/3.5	28	M	0308/1.1 0943/3.9 1538/0.8 2216/3.8
14	M	0414/1.2 1040/3.8 1641/1.1 2309/3.6	29	Tu	0356/0.9 1035/4.1 1626/0.5 2306/3.9
15	Tu ●	0445/1.1 1113/3.9 1712/0.9 2342/3.6	30	W ○	0440/0.9 1122/4.2 1711/0.3 2353/4.0
			31	Th	0522/0.5 1208/4.3 1754/0.2

FEBRUARY

No.	Day	Times & Heights (m)	No.	Day	Times & Heights (m)
1	F	0036/4.0 0604/0.5 1253/4.4 1838/0.2	16	Sa	0021/3.8 0553/0.5 1229/4.2 1818/0.4
2	Sa	0119/4.0 0648/0.5 1338/4.4 1923/0.3	17	Su	0055/3.9 0627/0.5 1304/4.2 1852/0.3
3	Su	0202/3.9 0731/0.6 1423/4.2 2008/0.5	18	M	0130/3.9 0703/0.5 1341/4.2 1930/0.4
4	M	0247/3.7 0818/0.8 1510/4.0 2056/0.8	19	Tu	0208/3.8 0745/0.5 1423/4.1 2012/0.6
5	Tu	0335/3.6 0907/1.0 1600/3.8 2146/1.1	20	W	0251/3.7 0830/0.7 1510/3.9 2058/0.8
6	W	0427/3.4 1000/1.3 1658/3.5 2244/1.4	21	Th	0341/3.6 0922/0.9 1604/3.7 2152/1.1
7	Th	0530/3.2 1106/1.6 1810/3.2	22	F	0442/3.4 1024/1.1 1713/3.5 2301/1.4
8	F	0000/1.7 0643/3.1 1239/1.7 1928/3.2	23	Sa	0600/3.3 1144/1.3 1841/3.4
9	Sa	0131/1.7 0754/3.2 1411/1.6 2037/3.2	24	Su	0034/1.5 0723/3.4 1320/1.3 2008/3.4
10	Su	0236/1.6 0851/3.3 1507/1.4 2129/3.3	25	M	0201/1.4 0836/3.6 1434/1.0 2117/3.6
11	M	0319/1.4 0938/3.5 1548/1.2 2212/3.4	26	Tu	0300/1.2 0936/3.8 1531/0.7 2213/3.7
12	Tu	0355/1.2 1016/3.7 1619/1.0 2247/3.6	27	W	0346/0.9 1027/4.0 1616/0.5 2258/3.9
13	W	0424/1.0 1049/3.9 1648/0.8 2318/3.7	28	Th ○	0427/0.7 1112/4.2 1657/0.3 2339/3.9
14	Th ●	0452/0.8 1123/4.0 1716/0.6 2350/3.8			
15	F	0522/0.7 1156/4.1 1746/0.4			

MARCH

No.	Day	Times & Heights (m)	No.	Day	Times & Heights (m)
1	F	0506/0.5 1154/4.3 1736/0.2	16	Sa ●	0452/0.5 1126/4.1 2351/4.0
2	Sa	0017/4.0 0544/0.4 1235/4.3 1815/0.2	17	Su	0525/0.4 1201/4.2 1747/0.3
3	Su	0053/4.0 0624/0.4 1316/4.3 1855/0.4	18	M	0025/4.0 0600/0.3 1238/4.2 1824/0.3
4	M	0131/3.9 0704/0.5 1357/4.1 1935/0.6	19	Tu	0102/4.0 0639/0.3 1319/4.2 1902/0.4
5	Tu	0211/3.8 0748/0.7 1437/3.9 2018/0.9	20	W	0142/3.9 0721/0.4 1402/4.1 1945/0.6
6	W	0251/3.6 0833/1.0 1522/3.6 2103/1.2	21	Th	0227/3.8 0809/0.6 1453/3.9 2033/0.9
7	Th	0338/3.4 0922/1.3 1612/3.3 2155/1.5	22	F	0319/3.7 0904/0.8 1552/3.6 2131/1.2
8	F	0431/3.2 1023/1.6 1716/3.1 2304/1.7	23	Sa ☽	0423/3.5 1012/1.1 1705/3.4 2244/1.5
9	Sa	0540/3.1 1150/1.7 1842/3.0	24	Su	0542/3.4 1137/1.2 1836/3.0
10	Su	0042/1.8 0700/3.1 1330/1.6 2001/3.0	25	M	0021/1.6 0709/3.4 1312/1.1 2002/3.4
11	M	0158/1.7 0808/3.2 1432/1.4 2057/3.2	26	Tu	0147/1.5 0823/3.6 1423/0.9 2108/3.6
12	Tu	0246/1.4 0900/3.4 1512/1.1 2139/3.4	27	W	0246/1.2 0924/3.8 1515/0.7 2200/3.7
13	W	0322/1.2 0942/3.6 1546/0.9 2214/3.6	28	Th ○	0331/0.9 1013/4.0 1557/0.5 2242/3.9
14	Th	0353/0.9 1019/3.8 1616/0.7 2247/3.8	29	F	0410/0.7 1057/4.1 1637/0.4 2319/3.9
15	F	0423/0.7 1052/4.0 1644/0.5 2319/3.9	30	Sa ○	0447/0.6 1136/4.2 1713/0.4 2353/4.0
			31	Su	0523/0.5 1214/4.2 1750/0.4

APRIL

No.	Day	Times & Heights (m)	No.	Day	Times & Heights (m)
1	M	0027/3.9 0601/0.5 1252/4.1 1827/0.6	16	Tu	0537/0.3 1215/4.2 1757/0.3
2	Tu	0102/3.9 0641/0.6 1330/3.9 1904/0.8	17	W	0038/4.1 0618/0.3 1300/4.1 1839/0.5
3	W	0137/3.8 0721/0.8 1409/3.7 1944/1.0	18	Th	0121/4.0 0704/0.4 1349/4.0 1924/0.7
4	Th	0216/3.6 0805/1.0 1450/3.5 2026/1.3	19	F	0211/3.9 0757/0.5 1444/3.8 2016/0.9
5	F	0258/3.5 0854/1.2 1536/3.3 2115/1.5	20	Sa	0307/3.8 0856/0.7 1546/3.6 2118/1.2
6	Sa	0348/3.3 0950/1.4 1633/3.1 2216/1.7	21	Su ☽	0412/3.6 1006/0.9 1701/3.4 2233/1.4
7	Su ☾	0445/3.2 1104/1.5 1746/3.0 2339/1.8	22	M	0527/3.5 1127/1.0 1827/3.3
8	M	0558/3.1 1229/1.5 1907/3.0	23	Tu	0001/1.5 0649/3.5 1252/1.0 1945/3.4
9	Tu	0100/1.7 0710/3.2 1337/1.3 2009/3.2	24	W	0121/1.4 0802/3.7 1359/0.9 2047/3.6
10	W	0155/1.5 0811/3.4 1425/1.1 2056/3.4	25	Th	0222/1.2 0901/3.8 1453/0.7 2138/3.7
11	Th	0239/1.2 0857/3.6 1503/0.9 2135/3.6	26	F	0310/1.0 0952/3.9 1536/0.6 2219/3.8
12	F	0315/1.0 0939/3.8 1536/0.6 2212/3.8	27	Sa	0350/0.9 1037/4.0 1614/0.6 2255/3.9
13	Sa	0349/0.7 1017/4.0 1610/0.5 2247/4.0	28	Su ○	0427/0.7 1116/4.0 1651/0.7 2327/3.9
14	Su ●	0423/0.5 1055/4.1 1644/0.3 2322/4.0	29	M	0505/0.7 1153/3.9 1725/0.7
15	M	0458/0.4 1134/4.2 1719/0.3 2358/4.1	30	Tu	0000/3.9 0542/0.7 1229/3.8 1801/0.8

12

Chart Datum: 0.20 metres below Ordnance Datum (Dublin)

IRELAND, EAST COAST – DUBLIN (NORTH WALL)

Lat 53°21′ N   Long 6°13′ W

TIMES AND HEIGHTS OF HIGH AND LOW WATERS

YEAR **1991**

TIME ZONE UT (GMT)
For Summer Time add ONE hour in non-shaded areas

MAY

Day	Time	m	Time	m	Time	m	Time	m
1 W	0034	3.8	0621	0.8	1306	3.7	1838	0.9
2 Th	0110	3.8	0700	0.9	1344	3.5	1916	1.1
3 F	0148	3.7	0744	1.0	1423	3.4	1958	1.3
4 Sa	0229	3.6	0832	1.1	1507	3.2	2044	1.4
5 Su	0314	3.5	0922	1.2	1557	3.1	2138	1.5
6 M	0404	3.4	1020	1.3	1657	3.1	2241	1.6
7 Tu ☾	0504	3.3	1125	1.3	1805	3.1	2349	1.6
8 W	0608	3.3	1229	1.2	1913	3.2		
9 Th	0052	1.4	0713	3.4	1327	1.1	2006	3.4
10 F	0147	1.3	0809	3.6	1415	0.9	2053	3.6
11 Sa	0233	1.0	0858	3.8	1458	0.7	2135	3.8
12 Su	0314	0.8	0943	3.9	1538	0.6	2214	4.0
13 M	0355	0.6	1027	4.0	1616	0.5	2254	4.1
14 Tu ●	0435	0.4	1111	4.1	1655	0.4	2334	4.1
15 W	0519	0.3	1157	4.1	1737	0.5		
16 Th	0018	4.1	0604	0.3	1248	4.0	1822	0.5
17 F	0107	4.1	0655	0.3	1340	3.9	1910	0.7
18 Sa	0159	4.0	0749	0.4	1437	3.8	2005	0.9
19 Su	0257	4.0	0849	0.5	1538	3.6	2107	1.1
20 M ☽	0359	3.8	0955	0.7	1648	3.5	2214	1.3
21 Tu	0509	3.7	1106	0.8	1804	3.4	2330	1.4
22 W	0624	3.7	1221	0.9	1916	3.5		
23 Th	0046	1.4	0734	3.7	1330	0.9	2018	3.5
24 F	0152	1.3	0834	3.7	1426	0.9	2110	3.6
25 Sa	0246	1.2	0928	3.8	1514	0.9	2153	3.7
26 Su	0332	1.0	1014	3.8	1555	0.7	2231	3.8
27 M	0413	1.0	1057	3.8	1631	0.9	2305	3.8
28 Tu	0451	0.9	1134	3.7	1705	0.9	2339	3.8
29 W	0527	0.9	1210	3.6	1740	1.0		
30 Th	0012	3.8	0605	0.9	1246	3.5	1815	1.0
31 F	0048	3.8	0645	0.9	1323	3.5	1853	1.1

JUNE

Day	Time	m	Time	m	Time	m	Time	m
1 Sa	0126	3.7	0726	0.9	1401	3.4	1933	1.2
2 Su	0205	3.7	0808	1.0	1442	3.3	2015	1.2
3 M	0246	3.6	0853	1.0	1525	3.3	2103	1.3
4 Tu	0331	3.6	0939	1.0	1614	3.2	2153	1.4
5 W ☽	0420	3.5	1031	1.1	1712	3.2	2249	1.4
6 Th	0516	3.5	1127	1.1	1815	3.3	2350	1.4
7 F	0618	3.5	1228	1.1	1916	3.4		
8 Sa	0053	1.3	0721	3.6	1327	1.0	2011	3.6
9 Su	0151	1.1	0820	3.7	1422	0.9	2100	3.7
10 M	0244	0.9	0914	3.8	1510	0.8	2146	3.9
11 Tu	0332	0.7	1004	3.9	1555	0.7	2230	4.0
12 W ●	0420	0.5	1054	4.0	1638	0.6	2316	4.1
13 Th ○	0506	0.4	1144	4.0	1722	0.6		
14 F	0004	4.2	0554	0.3	1238	4.0	1808	0.6
15 Sa	0056	4.2	0645	0.2	1331	3.9	1859	0.6
16 Su	0148	4.2	0738	0.3	1426	3.8	1951	0.7
17 M	0244	4.1	0834	0.4	1522	3.7	2049	0.9
18 Tu	0341	4.0	0934	0.6	1624	3.6	2149	1.1
19 W ☽	0444	3.9	1035	0.8	1730	3.5	2254	1.2
20 Th	0551	3.7	1143	1.0	1839	3.4		
21 F	0005	1.4	0700	3.6	1253	1.1	1942	3.5
22 Sa	0120	1.4	0806	3.6	1359	1.2	2039	3.5
23 Su	0225	1.3	0905	3.6	1454	1.2	2127	3.6
24 M	0318	1.2	0956	3.6	1538	1.2	2209	3.7
25 Tu	0403	1.1	1040	3.6	1616	1.1	2247	3.7
26 W	0441	1.0	1118	3.6	1651	1.1	2320	3.8
27 Th ○	0518	0.9	1154	3.5	1723	1.0	2354	3.8
28 F	0553	0.9	1228	3.5	1757	1.0		
29 Sa	0029	3.8	0627	0.8	1302	3.5	1831	1.0
30 Su	0104	3.9	0702	0.8	1337	3.5	1906	1.0

JULY

Day	Time	m	Time	m	Time	m	Time	m
1 M	0140	3.9	0738	0.8	1413	3.5	1945	1.0
2 Tu	0218	3.8	0818	0.8	1453	3.5	2026	1.1
3 W	0258	3.8	0900	0.8	1536	3.4	2112	1.1
4 Th	0342	3.7	0945	0.9	1626	3.4	2203	1.2
5 F	0434	3.7	1037	1.0	1725	3.4	2259	1.3
6 Sa	0534	3.6	1136	1.1	1829	3.4		
7 Su	0005	1.3	0643	3.6	1243	1.2	1934	3.5
8 M	0116	1.2	0752	3.6	1351	1.1	2032	3.7
9 Tu	0222	1.1	0854	3.7	1450	1.0	2125	3.8
10 W	0318	0.8	0952	3.8	1539	0.9	2216	4.0
11 Th ●	0409	0.6	1045	3.9	1626	0.7	2304	4.1
12 F ○	0457	0.4	1136	3.9	1711	0.6	2353	4.3
13 Sa	0544	0.2	1227	4.0	1756	0.5		
14 Su	0043	4.3	0632	0.1	1316	4.0	1842	0.5
15 M	0134	4.4	0721	0.2	1406	3.9	1931	0.6
16 Tu	0225	4.3	0812	0.3	1457	3.8	2023	0.7
17 W	0317	4.2	0904	0.5	1550	3.7	2117	1.0
18 Th ☽	0413	4.0	0959	0.8	1649	3.5	2216	1.2
19 F	0515	3.7	1101	1.1	1756	3.4	2323	1.4
20 Sa ☾	0625	3.5	1214	1.2	1903	3.4		
21 Su	0048	1.5	0737	3.4	1333	1.5	2006	3.4
22 M	0208	1.5	0843	3.4	1436	1.5	2101	3.5
23 Tu	0308	1.4	0938	3.4	1524	1.4	2148	3.6
24 W	0353	1.2	1023	3.5	1602	1.3	2227	3.7
25 Th	0430	1.1	1059	3.5	1634	1.1	2301	3.8
26 F ○	0501	0.9	1133	3.6	1705	1.0	2333	3.9
27 Sa	0532	0.8	1204	3.6	1734	0.9		
28 Su	0005	4.0	0601	0.7	1235	3.7	1805	0.9
29 M	0039	4.0	0632	0.6	1307	3.7	1838	0.8
30 Tu	0113	4.0	0706	0.6	1342	3.7	1914	0.8
31 W	0149	4.0	0741	0.6	1419	3.7	1952	0.8

AUGUST

Day	Time	m	Time	m	Time	m	Time	m
1 Th	0227	4.0	0822	0.7	1500	3.6	2036	0.9
2 F	0311	3.9	0905	0.9	1548	3.6	2125	1.1
3 Sa	0400	3.8	0955	1.0	1644	3.5	2221	1.2
4 Su	0501	3.6	1055	1.3	1751	3.4	2330	1.4
5 M	0615	3.5	1210	1.4	1904	3.5		
6 Tu	0052	1.4	0735	3.5	1331	1.4	2012	3.6
7 W	0211	1.2	0846	3.6	1439	1.2	2112	3.8
8 Th	0311	0.9	0946	3.8	1529	1.0	2206	4.0
9 F	0400	0.6	1038	3.9	1614	0.8	2255	4.2
10 Sa ●	0445	0.3	1126	4.0	1657	0.6	2342	4.4
11 Su	0529	0.2	1211	4.1	1739	0.5		
12 M	0028	4.5	0612	0.1	1255	4.1	1822	0.5
13 Tu	0113	4.5	0657	0.2	1340	4.0	1907	0.5
14 W	0201	4.4	0742	0.4	1426	3.9	1955	0.7
15 Th	0249	4.2	0830	0.7	1514	3.8	2044	0.9
16 F	0341	3.9	0921	1.0	1606	3.6	2139	1.2
17 Sa ☽	0438	3.7	1019	1.4	1708	3.4	2245	1.5
18 Su	0549	3.4	1132	1.6	1819	3.3		
19 M	0015	1.7	0707	3.3	1302	1.7	1931	3.4
20 Tu	0148	1.6	0819	3.3	1413	1.7	2033	3.5
21 W	0250	1.5	0917	3.4	1503	1.5	2121	3.6
22 Th	0332	1.3	0959	3.5	1539	1.3	2200	3.8
23 F	0406	1.1	1034	3.6	1610	1.1	2235	3.9
24 Sa	0435	0.9	1105	3.7	1638	1.0	2306	4.0
25 Su ○	0502	0.7	1134	3.8	1708	0.8	2339	4.1
26 M	0530	0.6	1205	3.8	1736	0.7		
27 Tu	0010	4.2	0600	0.6	1236	3.9	1808	0.7
28 W	0043	4.2	0632	0.5	1310	3.9	1843	0.7
29 Th	0120	4.2	0707	0.6	1347	3.9	1923	0.7
30 F	0159	4.1	0747	0.7	1427	3.8	2006	0.8
31 Sa	0244	4.0	0832	0.9	1515	3.7	2056	1.0

Chart Datum: 0.20 metres below Ordnance Datum (Dublin)

IRELAND, EAST COAST – DUBLIN (NORTH WALL)

Lat 53°21′ N   Long 6°13′ W

TIMES AND HEIGHTS OF HIGH AND LOW WATERS

YEAR **1991**

TIME ZONE UT (GMT)

For Summer Time add ONE
hour in non-shaded areas

SEPTEMBER

	Time	m		Time	m
1 Su ☾	0336 0922 1613 2155	3.8 1.2 3.6 1.2	**16** M	0506 1047 1727 2339	3.3 1.8 3.4 1.7
2 M	0441 1024 1723 2309	3.6 1.4 3.5 1.4	**17** Tu	0629 1221 1846	3.2 1.9 3.3
3 Tu	0603 1149 1843	3.5 1.6 3.5	**18** W	0114 0748 1338 1954	1.7 3.2 1.8 3.4
4 W	0041 0730 1320 1959	1.4 3.5 1.6 3.7	**19** Th	0216 0844 1429 2044	1.5 3.4 1.6 3.6
5 Th	0202 0843 1427 2103	1.2 3.6 1.4 3.9	**20** F	0300 0927 1507 2127	1.3 3.6 1.4 3.8
6 F	0301 0941 1518 2155	0.9 3.8 1.1 4.1	**21** Sa	0332 1000 1538 2202	1.1 3.7 1.2 4.0
7 Sa	0348 1028 1600 2242	0.6 4.0 0.8 4.3	**22** Su	0402 1031 1607 2234	0.9 3.9 1.0 4.1
8 Su ●	0430 1111 1640 2326	0.4 4.1 0.6 4.5	**23** M ○	0430 1102 1637 2306	0.7 4.0 0.8 4.2
9 M	0509 1150 1720	0.3 4.2 0.5	**24** Tu	0458 1133 1708 2340	0.6 4.1 0.7 4.3
10 Tu	0008 0550 1229 1800	4.5 0.3 4.2 0.5	**25** W	0527 1205 1740	0.5 4.1 0.6
11 W	0050 0631 1310 1842	4.5 0.4 4.1 0.6	**26** Th	0015 0601 1241 1817	4.3 0.5 4.1 0.6
12 Th	0134 0713 1351 1927	4.3 0.8 4.0 0.8	**27** F	0055 0638 1319 1857	4.3 0.6 4.1 0.7
13 F	0219 0757 1436 2015	4.1 0.9 3.9 1.0	**28** Sa	0137 0719 1402 1944	4.2 0.8 4.0 0.8
14 Sa	0307 0844 1524 2108	3.8 1.2 3.7 1.3	**29** Su	0226 0805 1453 2037	4.0 1.0 3.9 1.0
15 Su ☽	0400 0938 1620 2212	3.6 1.6 3.5 1.6	**30** M	0322 0900 1552 2141	3.8 1.3 3.7 1.2

OCTOBER

	Time	m		Time	m
1 Tu ☾	0431 1006 1705 2259	3.6 1.6 3.6 1.3	**16** W	0537 1120 1746	3.2 1.9 3.4
2 W	0556 1133 1828	3.5 1.7 3.6	**17** Th	0017 0657 1239 1856	1.7 3.2 1.9 3.5
3 Th	0031 0723 1304 1945	1.3 3.5 1.6 3.8	**18** F	0123 0758 1338 1955	1.5 3.4 1.7 3.6
4 F	0148 0833 1411 2049	1.1 3.7 1.4 4.0	**19** Sa	0212 0843 1423 2042	1.3 3.6 1.5 3.8
5 Sa	0244 0928 1501 2141	0.9 3.9 1.2 4.2	**20** Su	0250 0921 1500 2122	1.1 3.8 1.3 4.0
6 Su	0331 1013 1543 2226	0.7 4.1 0.9 4.4	**21** M	0322 0956 1534 2159	0.9 4.0 1.0 4.1
7 M ●	0410 1052 1621 2308	0.5 4.2 0.8 4.4	**22** Tu	0355 1028 1606 2235	0.8 4.1 0.9 4.2
8 Tu	0448 1127 1701 2349	0.5 4.2 0.7 4.4	**23** W ○	0426 1102 1640 2312	0.6 4.2 0.7 4.3
9 W	0526 1204 1739	0.5 4.2 0.6	**24** Th	0459 1137 1716 2351	0.6 4.2 0.6 4.3
10 Th	0028 0604 1241 1819	4.3 0.7 4.2 0.7	**25** F	0536 1215 1757	0.6 4.3 0.6
11 F	0109 0643 1320 1903	4.2 0.9 4.1 0.9	**26** Sa	0035 0615 1257 1841	4.2 0.7 4.2 0.6
12 Sa	0151 0726 1402 1949	4.0 1.1 3.9 1.1	**27** Su	0121 0659 1344 1931	4.1 0.8 4.1 0.7
13 Su	0236 0811 1447 2042	3.7 1.4 3.8 1.3	**28** M	0215 0748 1437 2027	4.0 1.0 4.0 0.9
14 M	0325 0901 1536 2142	3.5 1.6 3.6 1.5	**29** Tu	0314 0844 1539 2132	3.8 1.3 3.9 1.0
15 Tu ☽	0424 1003 1635 2254	3.3 1.8 3.5 1.7	**30** W ☾	0423 0953 1649 2248	3.6 1.5 3.8 1.2
			31 Th	0544 1113 1808	3.5 1.6 3.8

NOVEMBER

	Time	m		Time	m
1 F	0010 0706 1236 1924	1.2 3.6 1.6 3.9	**16** Sa	0011 0655 1229 1853	1.5 3.3 1.7 3.6
2 Sa	0123 0812 1345 2027	1.1 3.7 1.4 4.0	**17** Su	0109 0751 1327 1951	1.4 3.5 1.6 3.7
3 Su	0222 0907 1439 2121	0.9 3.9 1.2 4.2	**18** M	0159 0837 1415 2040	1.2 3.7 1.4 3.9
4 M	0310 0952 1524 2209	0.8 4.0 1.1 4.2	**19** Tu	0242 0918 1458 2125	1.0 3.9 1.1 4.0
5 Tu	0352 1031 1604 2251	0.8 4.1 0.9 4.2	**20** W	0321 0957 1538 2207	0.9 4.0 0.9 4.1
6 W ●	0430 1108 1644 2330	0.8 4.2 0.9 4.2	**21** Th ○	0359 1035 1619 2249	0.7 4.2 0.7 4.2
7 Th	0506 1142 1723	0.7 4.2 0.8	**22** F	0437 1115 1659 2334	0.7 4.3 0.6 4.2
8 F	0010 0543 1217 1804	4.1 0.9 4.1 1.0	**23** Sa	0516 1157 1743	0.6 4.3 0.5
9 Sa	0048 0621 1255 1846	4.0 1.0 4.1 1.0	**24** Su	0021 0558 1242 1829	4.2 0.7 4.3 0.5
10 Su	0128 0700 1334 1931	3.8 1.2 4.0 1.1	**25** M	0112 0645 1333 1921	4.1 0.8 4.3 0.5
11 M	0209 0742 1416 2019	3.6 1.4 3.8 1.3	**26** Tu	0205 0735 1426 2018	4.0 0.9 4.2 0.6
12 Tu	0254 0829 1501 2111	3.4 1.5 3.7 1.4	**27** W	0304 0832 1525 2119	3.8 1.1 4.1 0.8
13 W	0343 0921 1550 2206	3.3 1.7 3.6 1.5	**28** Th ☾	0409 0935 1630 2226	3.7 1.3 4.0 0.9
14 Th ☽	0440 1020 1645 2308	3.2 1.8 3.5 1.5	**29** F	0520 1045 1743 2339	3.6 1.4 3.9 1.0
15 F	0547 1125 1749	3.2 1.8 3.5	**30** Sa ☾	0636 1200 1856	3.6 1.5 3.9

DECEMBER

	Time	m		Time	m
1 Su	0052 0744 1314 2002	1.1 3.7 1.5 3.9	**16** M	0001 0652 1225 1857	1.3 3.4 1.5 3.6
2 M	0157 0842 1418 2101	1.1 3.8 1.4 4.0	**17** Tu	0104 0751 1328 1959	1.3 3.6 1.4 3.7
3 Tu	0250 0929 1508 2152	1.2 3.9 1.2 4.0	**18** W	0202 0843 1425 2056	1.2 3.7 1.2 3.8
4 W	0335 1013 1553 2237	1.0 4.0 1.1 4.0	**19** Th	0253 0929 1515 2146	1.0 3.9 1.0 3.9
5 Th	0414 1049 1634 2318	1.0 4.0 1.0 3.9	**20** F	0338 1014 1602 2234	0.9 4.1 0.8 4.0
6 F ●	0451 1126 1713 2356	1.0 4.0 1.0 3.9	**21** Sa ○	0420 1058 1647 2322	0.7 4.2 0.6 4.1
7 Sa	0526 1200 1753	1.0 4.0 0.9	**22** Su	0502 1143 1733	0.6 4.3 0.4
8 Su	0032 0603 1236 1832	3.8 1.1 4.0 1.0	**23** M	0011 0547 1231 1821	4.1 0.6 4.4 0.3
9 M	0109 0639 1313 1913	3.7 1.1 4.0 1.0	**24** Tu	0102 0632 1321 1910	4.1 0.6 4.4 0.3
10 Tu	0145 0719 1351 1954	3.6 1.2 3.9 1.1	**25** W	0154 0723 1413 2004	4.0 0.7 4.4 0.4
11 W	0223 0759 1430 2036	3.5 1.3 3.8 1.1	**26** Th	0247 0815 1508 2058	3.9 0.8 4.3 0.5
12 Th	0305 0843 1511 2119	3.4 1.4 3.8 1.2	**27** F	0345 0911 1606 2157	3.8 1.0 4.1 0.8
13 F	0350 0929 1557 2207	3.3 1.5 3.7 1.3	**28** Sa ☾	0448 1012 1712 2302	3.6 1.2 3.9 1.0
14 Sa ☽	0444 1021 1651 2301	3.3 1.5 3.6 1.3	**29** Su	0558 1120 1824	3.5 1.4 3.8
15 Su ☽	0547 1120 1751	3.3 1.6 3.6	**30** M	0014 0709 1239 1935	1.2 3.5 1.5 3.7
			31 Tu	0130 0812 1357 2042	1.3 3.6 1.5 3.7

Chart Datum: 0.20 metres below Ordnance Datum (Dublin)

DUBLIN *continued*

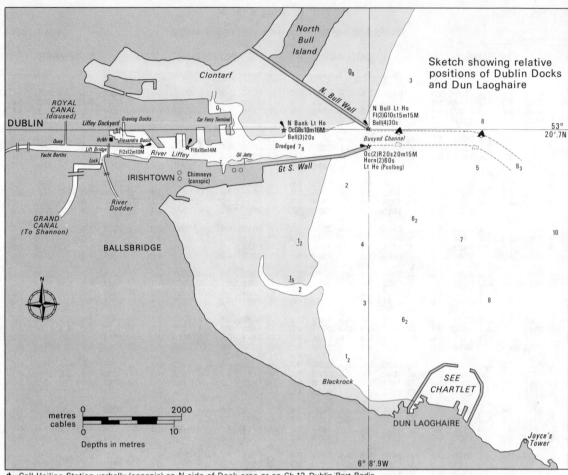

Sketch showing relative
positions of Dublin Docks
and Dun Laoghaire

▲ Call Hailing Station verbally (conspic) on N side of Dock area or on Ch 12, Dublin Port Radio

DUBLIN

MEAN SPRING
AND NEAP CURVES·

MEAN RANGES	
Springs	3·6m
Neaps	1·9m

Springs occur 1 day
after
New and Full Moon.

HOWTH 10-12-26
Dublin

⚓ Call Marina on Ch M

CHARTS
Admiralty 1415; Imray C61, C62; Irish OS 16
TIDES
+0025 Dover; ML 2.4; Duration 0625; Zone 0 (GMT)

Standard Port DUBLIN (NORTH WALL) (←)

Times				Height (metres)			
HW		LW		MHWS	MHWN	MLWN	MLWS
0000	0700	0000	0500	4.1	3.4	1.5	0.5
1200	1900	1200	1700				

Differences HOWTH
−0005	−0015	−0005	+0005	0.0	0.0	−0.3	0.0

SHELTER
Good shelter, and available at all tides and in almost any conditions. No entry to trawler dock for pleasure craft. Marina dredged to 3m.
NAVIGATION
Waypoint Howth stbd-hand buoy, FIG 5s, 53°23'.72N 06°03'.53W, 071°/251° from/to breakwater Lt, 0.30M. Beware Casana Rk on the E side of the Ben of Howth. Also beware Puck Rk on the NE corner, and a rock about 50m off Puck Rk which dries. A mile N is Ireland's Eye with rocks running out SE and SW from Thulla, their ends marked by Rowan Rocks and South Rowan buoys. The best approach is S of Ireland's Eye. Between the Nose and the harbour, watch out for lobster pots. Beware rocks off both pierheads. Keep strictly to marked channel up to marina.
LIGHTS AND MARKS
E Pierhead Lt — Fl(2) WR 7.5s 13m 17/13M; W 256°-295°, R elsewhere. W sector leads safely to NE corner of harbour.
RADIO TELEPHONE
Hr Mr VHF Ch 16; 08. Marina Ch M 16.
TELEPHONE (01)
Hr Mr 322252; MRCC Limerick (061) 61219; ⌗746571; Coast Life Saving Service 773481; Police 322806; Dr 323191; Ⓗ 377755
FACILITIES
EC Saturday. **Howth Marina** (220) ☎ 322141, Slip, FW, AC, D; **Howth YC** ☎ 322141, R (392100), Bar, M, D, FW, Slip, L, C (7 ton); **W Pier** D, FW; **Waton and Jameson** ☎ 326466, SM; **E. Brunker** ☎ 342590, Ⓔ; **M. Hunt** ☎ 390268, Kos; **Summit Stores** ☎ 322136, Kos; **Fish Dock** ☎ 322252 D; **Town** P and D (cans), ✉; Ⓑ; ✈ (Dublin); ✈ (Dublin).

MALAHIDE 10-12-27
Dublin

CHARTS
Admiralty 1468, 633; Imray C61, C62; Irish OS 13, 16
TIDES
+0030 Dover; ML 2.4; Duration 0615; Zone 0 (GMT)

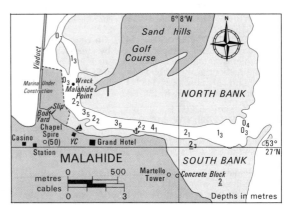

Standard Port DUBLIN (NORTH WALL) (←)

Times				Height (metres)			
HW		LW		MHWS	MHWN	MLWN	MLWS
0000	0700	0000	0500	4.1	3.4	1.5	0.5
1200	1900	1200	1700				

Differences MALAHIDE
−0019	−0013	+0014	+0006	+0.1	+0.1	0.0	0.0

RIVER BOYNE BAR
−0025	−0015	+0110	0000	+0.4	+0.3	No data	

DUNANY POINT
−0028	−0018	−0008	−0006	+0.7	+0.9	No data	

DUNDALK – SOLDIERS POINT
−0010	−0010	0000	+0045	+1.0	+0.8	+0.1	−0.1

SHELTER
A safe anchorage for yachts of up to 2m draught. Entry possible after half flood.
NAVIGATION
Waypoint 53°27'.20N 06°06'.00W, 085°/265° from/to Grand Hotel, 1.6M. The bar off the entrance is 0.3m in depth and there are sandbanks on either side. Do not attempt entry in thick weather or after dark, or in strong onshore winds. The flood stream reaches 3 kn sp, and the ebb 3½ kn. Beware wreck of trawler off the shipyard.
LIGHTS AND MARKS
During the summer only, the S bank is marked with a R buoy, the N bank with a G buoy by the bar. (Laid and altered as necessary by the Malahide YC). There are no navigational Lts. The entry bearing was 267° (1986). A RW mid-channel buoy 0.6M up stream from bar buoys.
RADIO TELEPHONE
Malahide YC. Call *Yacht Base* Ch M (occas).
TELEPHONE (01)
MRCC Limerick 61219; Coast Lifesaving Service Howth 773481; ⌗ Dublin 740459; Police 450216; Dr 451953; Ⓗ 301122
FACILITIES
Malahide YC ☎ 453372, Slip, C; **Malahide Hardware** ☎ 450944, Kos; **Malahide Marine** ☎ 451059, BY; **Town** ▢, ✉; Ⓑ; ✈; ✈ (Dublin).

12

MINOR HARBOURS AND ANCHORAGES 10.12.28

TRALEE BAY, Kerry, 52°16′ N, 09°52′ W, Zone 0 (GMT), Admty chart 2739. HW −0612 on Dover; −0037 on Cork (Ringaskiddy); HW height +0.4m on Cork (Ringaskiddy); ML 2.6m; Duration 0605. See 10.12.11. Entering the bay from W, pass 3M N of Magharee Is. Lt on Little Samphire Is Fl WRG 5s 17m 16/13M, W140°-152° (leading clear into bay) R152°-172°, obsc 172°-262°, R262°-275°, obsc 275°-280°, R280°-090°, G090°-140°. On Samphire Is Lt QR 15m 3M. Fenit Harbour, formed by causeway joining Samphire Is to mainland, is exposed to E and NE winds. A safe harbour in most conditions. Fenit Pier head 2FR (vert) 12m 3M, obsc 058°-148°. Facilities: (Fenit 066) Hr. Mr. 36103; V, Bar, R, ✉, Slip, C, ⚓ ☎ 36115.

VENTRY, Kerry, 52°06′ N, 10°19′ W, Zone 0 (GMT), Admty charts 2790, 2789. HW +0540 on Dover; −0056 on Cork; HW height −0.3m on Cork; ML 2.1m; Duration 0605. Note: there are magnetic anomalies near the Blaskets. Hr exposed to SE winds and mountains cause fierce squalls from W. Beware Reenvare Rks which extend 1 ca SE from Parkmore Pt; also NE shore 0.5M NW of Paddock Pt a ridge 3m on which seas break, extends 2.5 ca offshore. Anchor off beach in approx 4m (church bearing W, the village NE) or in 3m S side of bay. There are no lights. Facilities: L, P, Slip, V, Kos.

DINGLE, Kerry, 52°07′ N, 10°15′ W, Zone 0 (GMT), Admty charts 2790, 2789. HW +0540 on Dover; −0056 on Cork; HW height −0.3m on Cork; ML 2.1m; Duration 0605. See 10.12.11. Landlocked harbour giving excellent shelter. A busy fishing port. Beware Crow Rk (dries 3.7m) 0.8M SW of Reenbeg Pt, running 3 ca off shore; also the rocky ledge extending half way across entrance at Black Pt. Anchor 1M S of pier, W of dredged channel; or, for small craft, 1 ca SSW of pier in 1.5m. Lights: Tr on E side of ent Fl G 3s 20m 6M; Pier head FR 4m 2M; Ldg Lts 182° front and rear Oc W 3s, 100m apart, leading down dredged channel. E side of S end of channel, G cone buoy. Facilities: Coast Life Saving Service (066) 51278; **Pier** D, FW; **Town** Bar, P, ✉, R, V, Kos.

PORTMAGEE, Kerry, 51°53′ N, 10°21′ W, Zone 0 (GMT), Admty chart 2125. HW +0550 on Dover; −0120 sp −0040 np on Cork; HW height −0.4m on Cork; ML 2.3m; Duration 0610. A good safe anchorage but entrance dangerous in heavy seas. There are no hidden dangers but navigation from Reencaragh Pt up to the pier and bridge needs to be very accurate. Anchor off the pier in approx 6m and beware of strong tides; going alongside pier is not recommended. Bridge opens on request − ring Hr Mr ☎ 6101. Facilities: limited to stores in the village, Kos.

CASTLETOWN, (Bearhaven), Cork, 51°39′ N, 9°54′ W, Zone 0 (GMT), Admty chart 1840. HW +0605 on Dover, −0035 on Cork; HW height −0.6m on Cork; ML 1.9m; Duration 0610. Good shelter; entrance chan only 50m wide abreast Came Pt. Anchor to E of Ldg line NW of Dinish I in 3/5m. Perch Rk in ent. chan. marked by Bn with QG Lt. Ldg Lts 010°, both Oc W 3s, 80m apart, 4/7m 1M, vis 005°−015°. There is also a Dir Oc WRG 5s 4m 14/11M with W sector 024°−024.5°. Beware Walter Scott Rk (2.7m) 2 ca S of Dinish I, marked by S Card Lt Buoy Q(6) + LFl 15s; also Carrigaglos (0.6m high) 1.5 ca from SW point of Dinish I. VHF Ch 16; 08. Facilities: FW (on pier and on quay); Synchrolift on Dinish I; Hr Mr on quay, ☎ 70220; **Town** El, ME, Sh, D and P at garage, Bar, Ⓑ, ✉, V, R, Kos.

GLENGARIFF, Cork, 51°44′ N, 9°33′ W, Zone 0 (GMT), Admty chart 1838. HW +0600 on Dover, −0030 on Cork; HW height −0.4m on Cork; ML 2.0m; Duration 0610. Excellent anchorage; ent. between Big Pt and Gun Pt. Keep well to E of Illnacullen and small I to E of it. Chan to W of I is strewn with rks and has power line overhead. Beware Tinker Rks by Big Pt; Yellow Rks S of Illnacullen; Ship I with rks all round in W of ent., E of Illnacullen. Anchor; S of Bark I in 7m; in centre of Hr. in 8/10m. Facilities: **Eccles Hotel** ☎ 63003, Bar, FW, R; **Town** Bar, D, P, ✉, R, V, Kos.

GLANDORE, Cork, 51°33′ N, 9°07′ W, Zone 0 (GMT), Admty chart 2092. HW +0605 on Dover, −0025 on Cork; HW height −0.3m on Cork; ML 2.0m; Duration 0605. Excellent shelter. Safest entrance between Adam I and Goat's Head thence keeping E of Eve I and W of the chain of Rks, Outer Danger, Middle Danger, Inner Danger and Sunk Rk. Anchor between Glandore pier and Coosaneigh Pt in approx 3m. There are no lights, but The Dangers are marked by perches and Sunk Rk by BY N Cardinal buoy. Facilities: Coast Life Saving Service (028) 33115; FW at both piers; **Unionhall** Bar, D, P, ✉, R, V. **Glandore** Bar, CH, ✉, R, V, Kos.

COURTMACSHERRY, Cork, 51°38′ N, 8°41′ W; Zone 0 (GMT), Admty chart 2081. HW −0610 on Dover, −0012 on Cork; HW height −0.4m on Cork; ML 2.0m; Duration 0545. Harbour in NW corner of Courtmacsherry Bay which has a number of hazards; Barrel Rk (dries 2.6m) in centre of bay, marked by unlit S cardinal perch; sunken rocks 2 ca NE of the perch; Blue Boy Rk (0.2m) 4 ca E of the perch; Black Tom (2.3m) 6 ca W of the perch; Inner Barrels (0.5m) 5 ca NW of the perch; Horse Rk (dries 3.6m) 4½ ca off Barry Pt on the W shore. Lights: Wood Point Fl(2) WR 5s 15m 5M, W315°-332°, R332°-315°. Old Head of Kinsale, S point, Fl(2) 10s 72m 25M; RC. Enter over bar (2.3m) between Wood Pt and Coolmain Pt into estuary of Argideen River. Depths may vary. Beware seas break on bar in strong S or SE winds. Anchor NE of Ferry Pt in approx 2.5m or N of the pier. Weed may foul anchor; best to moor with anchors up and down stream. Facilities: Coast Life Saving Service (053) 29637. **Courtmacsherry Hotel** ☎ 46198, Bar, R, P, V; **Quay** FW, D; **Village** V, ✉.

OYSTER HAVEN, Cork, 51°41′ N, 8°27′ W, Zone 0 (GMT), Admty charts 2053, 1765. HW −0600 on Dover, −0018 on Cork; ML 2.2m; Duration 0600. Good shelter but subject to swell in S winds. Enter 0.5M N of Big Sovereign, a steep islet divided into two. Keep to S of Little Sovereign on E side of entrance. There is foul ground off Ballymacus Pt on W side, and off Kinure Pt on E side. Pass W of Harbour Rock (0.9m) off Ferry Pt, the only danger within harbour. Anchor NNW of Ferry Pt or up N arm of harbour off the W shore. Weed in higher reaches may foul anchor. No lights, marks or radio telephone. Coast Life Saving Service (021) 770711. Facilities at Kinsale. See 10.12.16.

BALLYCOTTON, Cork, 51°50′ N, 8°01′ W, Zone 0 (GMT), Admty chart 2424. HW −0555 on Dover, +0006 on Cork; HW height 0.0m on Cork; ML 2.3m; Duration 0550. See 10.12.18. Small Hr. at W end of bay; suffers from scend in strong SE winds. Numerous fishing boats alongside piers, but yachts should go alongside and not anchor in harbour. Good anchorage in offshore winds in 6m NE of breakwater, protected by Ballycotton I. Ballycotton Lt Fl WR 10s 59m 22/18M, B Tr in W walls, on Ballycotton I; W238°−063°, R063°−238°; RC: Dia(4) 90s. Facilities: FW on pier. **Village** Bar, ✉, R, V, LB, Kos.

DUNGARVAN, Waterford, 52°05′ N, 7°34′ W, Zone 0 (GMT), Admty chart 2017. HW −0540 on Dover, +0008 on Cork; HW height +0.1m on Cork; ML 2.3m; Duration 0600. See 10.12.18. A large bay, the W side of which dries. Across the entrance there are Carrickapane Rk, Helvick Rk and The Gainers, all marked. Yachts can anchor off Helvick Hr. in approx 4m, or pass up to Dungarvan Town Hr. Beware salmon nets. Channel from Ballynacourty Pt marked by buoys. Ballynacourty Pt Lt Fl(2) WRG 10s 16m 12/9M, G245°-274°, W274°-302°, R302°-325°, W325°-117°. Ballynacourty Ldg Lts 083°, both FW 9/12m 2M on W columns with B bands, 46m apart; Esplanade Ldg Lts 298°, both FR 8/9m 2M. Facilities: EC Thurs; AB, Bar, Ⓑ, D (from garage), P (on quay), ✉, R, V, Kos.

VOLVO PENTA SERVICE

Sales and service centres in area 13
NORTHERN IRELAND **Robert Craig & Sons Ltd** 15-21 Great Georges Street,
BELFAST BT15 1BW Tel (0232) 232971.

Area 13

North Ireland
Carlingford Lough to Galway

VOLVO PENTA

13

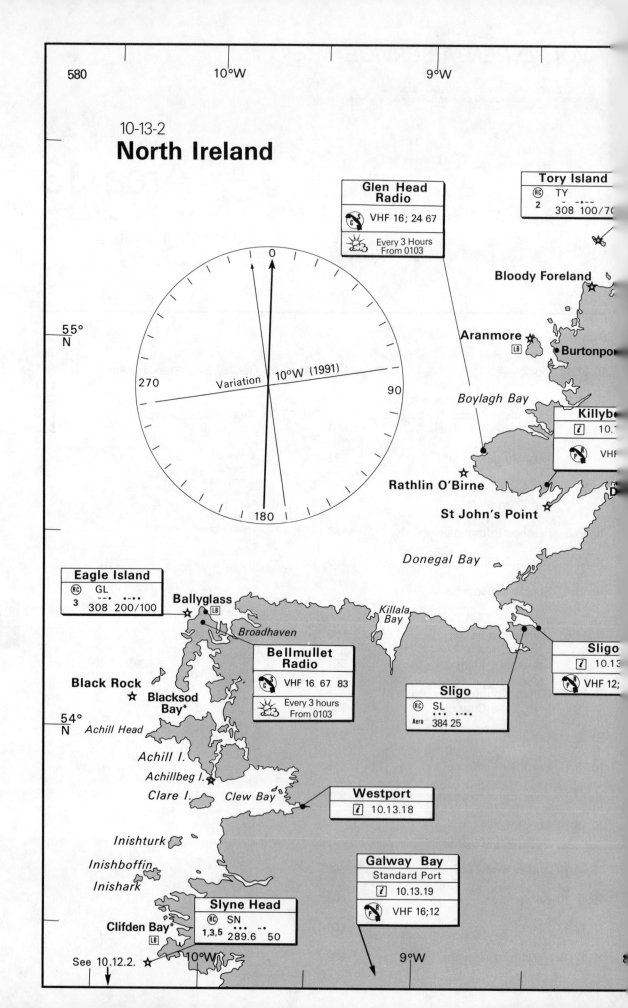

North Ireland

580

10°W

9°W

Glen Head Radio

🌀	VHF 16; 24 67
☀️	Every 3 Hours From 0103

Tory Island

℞₂	TY — -·-·
	308 100/70

Bloody Foreland ☆

55° N

Aranmore ☆ 🄻🄱

Burtonport

Variation 10°W (1991)

270

90

180

Boylagh Bay

Killyb

🛈	10.
🄿ℝ	VHF

Rathlin O'Birne ☆

St John's Point ☆

D

Donegal Bay

Eagle Island

℞₃	GL —· -··
	308 200/100

Ballyglass ☆ 🄻🄱

Broadhaven

Black Rock ☆

Blacksod Bay*

Bellmullet Radio

🌀	VHF 16 67 83
☀️	Every 3 hours From 0103

54° N

Achill Head

Killala Bay

Sligo

🛈	10.13
🄿ℝ	VHF 12;

Sligo

℞ Aero	SL ··· -·-·
	384 25

Achill I.

Achillbeg I. ☆

Clare I.

Clew Bay

Westport

🛈	10.13.18

Inishturk

Inishboffin

Inishark

Galway Bay

Standard Port	
🛈	10.13.19
🄿ℝ	VHF 16;12

Slyne Head

℞ 1,3,5	SN ··· --
	289.6 50

Clifden Bay* 🄻🄱

See 10.12.2. ☆

10°W

9°W

7°W 6°W

☆ Inishtrahull

...n Head ...dio
F 1841
HF 16 23
67 85
VHF Every 3
rs From 0103

...Head
☆

Altacarry Head
RC AH
3   −· ··· ····
    294.2 50

SEPARATION ZONE

For details
see Fig.2(7)

...lroy Bay*

...Haven* Buncrana

Inishowen

CG
Ballycastle RG

Portrush
i 10.13.12
P R VHF 16:14
M−0898
500 465
CG   LB

Red*
Bay IL

Carnlough*
Maidens ☆

Larne
i 10.13.11
P R VHF 16;14

55° N

Swilley
10.13.15

River Bann/ Coleraine
i 10.13.13
P R VHF 16; 12
Marina Ch **80**

Bangor
P R VHF 16; 11 80
Belfast CG CG

Black Head

Mew Island
RC MW
2   −− ·−−
    294.2 50

...ough Foyle
i 10.13.14
M−0898
500 465
VHF 16; 12 14

Belfast Airport/ Aldergrove
Crumlin 52339
M−0898
500 465

Lough
Neagh

RG
☆ ☆ Donaghadee*
LB

South Rock Lt.F.
RC SU
6   ··· ·−−
    301.1 50

Belfast
Standard Port
i 10.13.10
P R VHF 12;08 10
11 12 14 16

Portavogie*
Cloughy
IL

Strangford
i 10.13.9
P R VHF 16;12 14
Marina VHF **80**

Greenore
P R VHF 16;13

7°W

Ardglass* CG
St John's
Point ☆
Newcastle

Warrenpoint
P R VHF 16;12

Carlingford Lough
i 10.13.8

54° N

Kilkeel*
CG IL

Haulbowline
☆

Dundalk
P R VHF 16 ;06 12

☆ **Clogher Head**
LB

☆ **Rockabill**

IL

Dublin/Rush
RC RSH
Aero −· −· ··· ····
      326 30

6°W

...y to Symbols

Coast Station/Port Radio – frequencies

Marine radiobeacon– call sign, sequence, frequency and range (nm)

Aeronautical radiobeacon–call sign, frequency and range (nm)

See for harbour information/tidal data

Weather (tel. or times). M - Marinecall

HM Coastguard MRCC CG MRSC

HM Coastguard Sector Base

RNLI Lifeboat over 10m

RNLI Lifeboat under 10m

SAR Helicopter base

Principal lights

Light-vessel

Lanby

See 10.13.20

Emergency VHF DF

10.13.3 AREA 13 TIDAL STREAMS

5 Hours before HW Dover (0450 before HW Belfast)

4 Hours before HW Dover (0350 before HW Belfast)

3 Hours before HW Dover (0250 before HW Belfast)

2 Hours before HW Dover (0150 before HW Belfast)

1 Hour before HW Dover (0050 before HW Belfast)

HW Dover (0010 after HW Belfast)

Southward 10.12.3   North Irish Sea 10.10.3   SW Scotland 10.9.3

1 Hour after HW Dover (0110 after HW Belfast)

2 Hours after HW Dover (0210 after HW Belfast)

3 Hours after HW Dover (0310 after HW Belfast)

4 Hours after HW Dover (0410 after HW Belfast)

5 Hours after HW Dover (0510 after HW Belfast)

6 Hours after HW Dover (0610 after HW Belfast)

10.13.4   LIGHTS, FOG SIGNALS AND WAYPOINTS

Abbreviations used below are given in 10.0.3. Principal lights are in **bold** print, places in CAPITALS, and light-vessels, light floats and Lanbys in *CAPITAL ITALICS*. Unless otherwise stated lights are white. m—elevation in metres; M—nominal range in n. miles. Fog signals are in *italics*. Useful waypoints are underlined use those on land with care. See 4.2.2.

IRELAND—EAST COAST

Rockabill 53°35'·80N 06°00'·30W Fl WR 12s 45m **W23M, R19M**; W Tr, B band; vis W178°-329°, R329°-178°; *Horn (4) 60s*. Also shown by day when fog signal is operating.
Skerries Bay, pier head Oc R 6s 7m 7M; W column; vis 103°-154°.
Balbriggan 53°36'·7N 06°10'·7W Fl(3) WRG 20s 12m W13M, R10M, G10M; W Tr; vis G159°-193°, W193°-288°, R288°-305°.

DROGHEDA.
Lts in line about 248°. **Front** 53°43'·13N 06°14'·82W Oc 12s 8m **15M**; framework Tr, W lantern; vis 203°-293°. **Rear** 85m from front Oc 12s 12m **17M**; framework Tr; vis 246°-252°.
North light 53°43'·4N 06°15'·2W Fl R 4s 7m **15M**; framework Tr, W lantern; vis 282°-288°.
Drogheda Bar 53°43'·3N 06°13'·7W Fl(3) R 5s 6m 3M; R column; Ra refl.
Aleria Beacon 53°43'·3N 06°14'·2W QG 11m 3M.
Lyons 53°43'·2N 06°41'·2W Fl R 2s. Above this point Lts on starboard hand when entering are green, and on port hand red.

DUNDALK.
N training wall, head, **Pile light** 53°58'·50N 06°17'·68W Fl WR 15s 10m **W21M, R18M**; W house on R piles; vis W124°-151°, R151°-284°, W284°-313°, R313°-124°. Oc G 5s 8m; same Tr; vis 331°-334°; Fog Det Lt, VQ 7m, vis 358°; *Horn (3) 60s*.
No. 2 Bn 53°58'·3N 06°17'·8W Fl(2)R 5s 4m 3M; pile.
No. 8 Bn 53°59'·4N 06°19'·0W Fl R 3s; R pile. Above this point Lts on starboard hand when entering are QG, and on port hand QR.
Giles Quay, pier head 53°59'·1N 06°14'·3W Fl G 3s; occas.

CARLINGFORD LOUGH.
Hellyhunter Lt Buoy 54°00'·34N 06°01'·99W Q(6)LFl 15s; S cardinal mark; *Horn(2) 20s*.
Haulbowline 54°01'·19N 06°04'·68W Fl(3) 10s 32m **20M**; grey Tr; reserve Lt 15M; Fog Det Lt, VQ, vis 330 . Turning Lt FR 21m 9M; same Tr; vis 196°-208°; *Horn 30s*.
Ldg Lts 310° Vidal Bank, Front 54°01'·8N 06°05'·4W Oc 3s 7m 11M; G house on piles; vis 295°-325°. R   , Green Island 457m from front Oc 3s 12m 11M; G house on piles; vis 295°-325°.
Greenore Pier Fl R 7·5s 10m 5M.
Carlingford Quay, head Fl 3s 5m 2M.

NEWRY RIVER.
Ldg Lts 310°. Front 54°06'·4N 06°16'·5W. F   ar 274m from front. Both Iso 4s 2M; stone columns.
Warren Point breakwater, head 54°05'·78N 06°15'·20W Fl G 3s 6m 3M.
Deep water quay Fl G 5s 5m 3M; R post.

KILKEEL.
Pier head 54°03'·45N 05°59'·27W Fl WR 2s 8m 8M; vis

R296°-313°, W313°-017°.
Meeney's Pier Fl G 3s 6m 2M.

ANNALONG.
E breakwater head Oc WRG 5s 8m 9M; framework Tr; vis G204°-249°, W249°-309°, R309°-024°.

DUNDRUM BAY
St John's Point 54°13'·58N 05°39'·23W Q(2) 7·5s 37m **23M**; B round Tr, Y bands. **Auxiliary Lt** Fl WR 3s 14m W15M, R11M; same Tr, vis W064°-078°, R078°-shore; H24 when fog sig operating; *Horn (2) 60s*.
FR on west side of channel outside harbour and 3FR on west side of channel inside harbour when local vessels expected. FR on flagstaffs S and E of entrance when firing takes place.

ARDGLASS.
Inner pier head Iso WRG 4s 10m W8M, R7M, G5M; Tr; vis G shore-310°, W310°-318°, R318°-shore.
Outer pier head 54 15.6N°5 36.0W Fl R 3s 10m 5M.

STRANGFORD LOUGH.
Strangford Lt Buoy 54°18'·61N 05° 28'·63W LFl 10s; safe water mark; *Whis*.
Bar Pladdy Lt Buoy 54°19'·33N 05°30'·45W Q(6)LFl 15s; S cardinal mark.
Angus Rock 54°19'·83N 05°31'·45W Fl R 5s 15m 6M shown throughout 24 hrs.
Ldg Lts 341°. Front, Dogtail Point, Oc(4) 10s 2m 5M. Rear, Gowland Rock 0·8M from front, Oc(2) 10s 6m 5M.
Salt Rock Fl R 3s 8m 3M.
Swan Island Fl(2) WR 6s 5m; W column; vis W115°-334°, R334°-115°.
S Pladdy Fl(3) 10s.
N Pladdy Q.
Church Point Fl(4) R 10s.
Portaferry Pier, head Oc WR 10s 9m W9M, R6M; vis W335°-005°, R005°-017°, W017°-128°.
North Ldg Lts 181°. Rear, 70m from front, Oc R 10s 12m 6M; Y mast; vis 178°-185°.
Pier head, N front Oc WRG 10s 8m W9M, R6M, G6M; Y mast; vis G173°-180°, W180°-183°, R183°-190° (common front); E Front, same mast, Oc WRG 5s 6m; vis R190°-244°, G244°-252°, W252°-260°, R260°-294°.
E Ldg Lts 256°, Rear 46m from front Oc R 5s 10m 6M; Y mast; vis 250°-264°.

SOUTH ROCK Lt F 54°24'·47N 05°21'·92W Fl(3) R 30s 12m **20M**; R hull and Lt Tr, W Mast; RC; Racon; *Horn (3) 45s*.

PORTAVOGIE
Plough Rock Lt Buoy 54°27'·37N 05°25'·07W QR; port-hand mark; *Bell*.
South pier head 54°27'·44N 05°26'·08W, Iso WRG 5s 9m 9M; vis G shore-258°, W258°-275°, R275°-348°.
Skulmartin Lt Buoy 54°31'·83N 05°24'·85W LFl 10s; safe water mark; *Whis*.
Ballywalter, breakwater head 54°32'·67N 05°28'·75W Fl WRG 1·5s 5m 9M; vis G240°-267°, W267°-277°, R277°-314°. Unreliable.
DONAGHADEE
S pier 54°38'·70N 05°31'·81W Iso WR 4s 17m **W18M**, R14M; W Tr; vis W shore-326°, R326°-shore.
Governor Rocks Lt Buoy 54°39'·36N 05°31'·94W Fl R 3s; port- hand mark.

Deputy Reefs Lt Buoy 54°39'·50N 05°31'·90W Fl G 2s; stbd-hand mark.
Foreland Spit Lt Buoy 54°39'·63N 05°32'·25W Fl R 6s; port-hand mark.

BELFAST LOUGH.
Mew Island, NE end 54°41'·92N 05°30'·75W Fl(4) 30s 37m **30M**; B Tr, W band; RC. *Dia (4) 30s*. Briggs Lt Buoy 54°41'·18N 05°35'·67W Fl(2)R 10s; port-hand mark.

BANGOR.
N pier 54°40'·02N 05°40'·30W Iso R 12s 9m 9M.
Belfast No. 1 Channel Lt Buoy 54°41'·67N 05°46'·30W IQG; stbd- hand mark; *Bell*.
Cloghan Jetty Lt Buoy 54°44'·12N 05°41'·52W Fl G 3s; stbd hand mark.
Cloghan Jetty, N end Fl G 3s 2M; *Horn 15s*. S end Fl G 3s.
Kilroot power station, intake 54°43'·2N 05°45'·9W OcG 4s; 2 QR on chimney 500m N.
Kilroot Point. Jetty head Oc G 10s 6m 9M; G framework Tr.

CARRICKFERGUS
E pier head Fl G 7·5s 5m 4M; vis 050°-255°.
West pier head Fl R 7·5s 5m 4M; vis 068°-256°.
Marina E breakwater 54°42'·71N 05°48'·63W QG 8m 3M.
West breakwater QR 7m 3M; vis 125°-065°.

Black Head 54°46'·00N 05°41'·27W Fl 3s 45m **27M**; W 8-sided Tr.
North Hunter Rock Lt Buoy 54°53'·04N 05°45'·06W Q; N cardinal mark.
South Hunter Rock Lt Buoy 54°52'·68N 05°45'·22W Q(6)LFl 15s; S cardinal mark; *Horn(3) 30s*.

LARNE.
Barr Point 54°51'·5N 05°46'·7W; R framework Tr; *Dia 30s*. Reserve fog signal *Horn*.
Chaine Tower 54°51'·27N 05°47'·82W Iso WR 5s 23m 11M; grey Tr; vis W230°-240°, R240°-shore.
Ferris Point 54°51'·08N 05°47'·34W Iso WRG 10s 18m **W17M**, R13M, G13M; lantern on square W Tr; vis W345°-119°, G119°-154°, W154°-201°, R201°-223°.
Entrance Ldg Lts 184°. Front 54°49'·6N 05°47'·7W Oc 4s 6m 12M; W diamond with R stripe on R pile structure; vis 179°-189°. Rear 610m from front Oc 4s 14m 12M; W diamond with R stripe on aluminium round Tr; synchronised with front, vis 179°-189°.

Maidens 54°55'·73N 05°43'·60W Fl(3) 20s 29m **23M**; W Tr, B band. Auxiliary Lt Fl R 5s 15m 8M; same Tr; vis 142°-182° over Russel and Highland Rocks.

CARNLOUGH HARBOUR
N pier 54°59'·6N 05°59'·2W Fl G 3s 4m 5M; W column, B bands.
South pier Fl R 3s 6m 5M; W column, B bands.

RED BAY
Pier 55°03'·9N 06°03'·1W Fl 3s 10m 5M.

RATHLIN ISLAND.
Rue Point 55°15'·53N 06°11'·40W Fl(2) 5s 16m 14M; W 8-sided Tr, B bands.
Altacarry Head, **Rathlin East** 55°18'·07N 06°10'·20W Fl(4) 20s 74m **26M**; W Tr, B band; vis 110°-006° and 036°-058°; RC.
Rathlin West, 0·5M NE of Bull point 55°18'·05N 06°16'·75W Fl R 5s 62m **22M**; W Tr, lantern at base; vis 015°-225°; H24 when fog sig operating; *Horn (4) 60s*.
Manor House Pier 55°17'·5N 06°11'·6W Fl(2) R 6s 5m 4M.

IRELAND—NORTH COAST

Ballycastle pier, head 55°12'·5N 06°14'·3W L Fl WR 9s 6m 5M; vis R110°-212°, W212°-000°.

PORTRUSH.
N pier head Fl R 3s 6m 3M; vis 220°-160°.
S pier head Fl G 3s 6m 3M; vis 220°-100°.
Portstewart Point 55°11'·3N 06°43'·2W Oc R 10s 21m 5M; R square hut; vis 040°-220°.

COLERAINE
River Bann, Ldg Lts 165°. Front 55°09'·9N 06°46'·2W Oc 5s 6m 2M; W Tr. Rear 245m from front Oc 5s 14m 2M; W Tr. River marked by Fl G on starboard hand, and Fl R on port.
West pier, near head Fl G 5s 2M; grey mast.
East pier head Fl R 5s 6m 2M; W Tr.
Ballyaghran 55°09'·9N 06°45'·9W Fl(2) R 5s; square on R Bn.
Lough Foyle Lt Buoy 55°15'·30N 06°52'·50W LFl 10s; safe water mark; *Whis*.
Tuns Lt Buoy 55°14'·01N 06°53'·38W Fl R 3s; port-hand mark.
Inishowen 55°13'·56N 06°55'·70W Fl(2) WRG 10s 28m **W18M**, R14M, G14M; W Tr, 2 B bands; vis G197°-211°, W211°-249°, R249°-000°; *Horn (2) 30s*.

LOUGH FOYLE.
Warren Point 55°12'·58N 06°57'·06W Fl 1·5s 9m 10M; W round Tr, G abutment. G; vis 232°-061°.
Magilligan Point 55°11'·74N 06°57'·97W QR 7m 4M; R pile structure.
McKinney's Bank 55°10'·92N 07°00'·50W Fl R 5s 6m 4M; R pile structure.
Moville 55°11'·00N 07° 02'·06W Fl WR 2.5s 11m 4M; vis W240°-064°, R064°-240°.
Above this point the channel to River Foyle is marked by Lts Fl G, when entering, on starboard hand, and Fl R on port hand. G Lts are shown from W structures on G or B piles; R Lts from W structures on R piles.
Kilderry 55°04'·09N 07°13'·95W Fl G 2s 6m 6M; W structure on B piles.
Muff 55°03'·63N 07°14'·21W Fl G 2s 5m 3M; G structure.
Coneyburrow 55°03'·32N 07°14'·42W Fl G 2.5s 5m 3M; G mast on G piles.
Faughan 55°03'·12N 07°14'·42W Fl R 4s 8m 3M; W lantern on R piles.
Culmore Point 55°02'·78N 07°15'·20W Q 6m 5M; G Tr on B base.
Culmore Bay 55°02'·72N 07°15'·65W Fl G 5s 4m 2M; W lantern on G piles.
Lisahally 55°02'·52N 07°05'·72W QR 2M; port-hand Lt Bn; R refl.
Ballynagard 55°02'·28N 07°16'·37W Fl 3s 6m 3M; W lantern on G structure.
Otter Bank 55°01'·95N 07°16'·65W Fl R 4s 4m 3M; W structure on R Tr.
Brook Hall 55°01'·70N 07°17'·07W QG 4m 3M; W structure on G base.
Mountjoy 55°01'·25N 07°17'·49W QR 5m 3M; W lantern on R piles. Demolished, FW(T).

Inishtrahull 55°25'·85N 07°14'·60W Fl(3) 15s 59m **25M**; W Tr; Racon.

LOUGH SWILLY.
Fanad Head 55°16'·58N 07°37'·85W Fl(5) WR 20s 39m **W18M**, R14M; W Tr; vis R100°-110°, W110°-313°, R313°-345°, W345°-100°. FR on radio mast 3·08M 200°.
Swilly More Lt Buoy 55°15'·15N 07°35'·73W Fl G 3s; stbd-hand mark

Dunree 55°11'·85N 07°33'·20W Fl(2) WR 5s 46m W12M, R9M; vis R320°-328°, W328°-183°, R183°-196°.
Buncrana pier, near head Iso WR 4s 8m W14M, R11M; vis R shore-052° over Inch spit, W052°-139°, R139°-shore over White Strand rock.
Rathmullan, pier head Fl G 3s 5M; vis 206°-345°.

MULROY LOUGH.
Limeburner Buoy 55°18'·54N 07°48'·36W Q Fl; N cardinal mark; *Whis*.
Ravedy island 55°15'·1N 07°46'·7W Fl 3s 9m 3M; concrete Tr; vis 177°-357°.
Dundooan Rocks 55°13'N 07°48'W QG 4m 1M; G concrete Tr.
Crannoge Point 55°12'N 07°48'W FlG 5s 5m 2M; G concrete Tr.

IRELAND—WEST COAST

SHEEPHAVEN.
Downies Bay, Pier head FlR 3s 5m 2M; vis 283° through N till obsc by Downies Point.
Ldg Lts 125°. Front 55°10'·8N 07°55'·6W Oc 6s 7m 2M; B column, W bands. Rear, 81m from front, Oc 6s 12m 2M; B column, W bands.
Tory Island, NW point 55°16'·35N 08°14'·92W Fl(4) 30s 40m **30M**; B Tr, W band; vis 302°-277°; RC; *Horn 60s*.

Inishbofin Pier Fl 8s 3m 3M; part obsc.
Ballyness Harbour. Ldg Lts 119°. Front 55°09'·0N 08°06'·9W Iso 4s 25m 1M. Rear, 61m from front, Iso 4s 26m 1M.
Bloody Foreland 55°09'·5N 08°17'·0W Fl WG 7·5s 14m W6M, G4M; vis W062°-232°, G232°-062°.
Glassagh. Ldg Lts. Front 55°06'·8N 08°18'·9W Oc 8s 12m 3M. Rear 46m from front Oc 8s 17m 3M, synchronised with front.
Inishsirrer, NW end 55°07'·4N 08°20'·9W Fl 3·7s 20m 4M; vis 083°-263°.

BUNBEG.
Gola Island Ldg Lts 171°. Front 55°05'·1N 08°21'·0W Oc 3s 9m 2M; W Bn, B band. Rear, 86m from front, Oc 3s 13m 2M; B Bn, W band; synchronised with front.
Bo Island, E point 55°04'·8N 08°20'·1W FlG 3s 3m; Bn. Inishinny No. 1 55°04'·5N 08°19'·8W QG 3m 1M; square column with steps.
Carrickbullog No. 2 QR. Inishcoole No 4 QR 4m 1M; square column on base, with steps; Neon.
Yellow Rocks No. 6 QR 3m 1M; square column with steps; Neon. Magheralosk No. 5 QG 4m 1M; G square column with steps.
Cruit Island. Owey Sound Ldg Lts 068°. Front Oc 10s. Rear, 107m from front, Oc 10s (TE 1983).
Rinnalea Point 55°02'·5N 08°23'·7W Fl 7·5s 19m 9M; square Tr; vis 132°-167°.
Mullaghdoo Ldg Lts 184°, Front 55°02'·4N 08°21'·6W Iso 8s 19m 2M; W mast. Rear, 358m from front Iso 8s 29m 2M; W mast (TE 1983).

Aranmore, Rinrawros Point 55°00'·9N 08°33'·6W Fl(2) 20s 71m **29M**; W Tr; obsc by land about 234°-007° and about 013°. Auxiliary Lt Fl R 3s 61m 13M, same Tr; vis 203°-234°.

NORTH SOUND OF ARAN.
Ldg Lts 186°. Front 54°58'·9N 08°29'·2W Oc 8s 8m 3M; B Bn, W band. Rear 395m from front Oc 8s 17m 3M; B Bn.
Ballagh Rocks 54°59'·97N 08°28'·80W Fl 2·5s 13m 5M; W structure, B band.
Black Rocks 54°59'·4N 08°29'·6W FlR 3s 3m 1M; R column.

RUTLAND NORTH CHANNEL.
Inishcoo Ldg Lts 119°. Front 54°59'·1N 08°27'·7W Iso 6s 6m 1M; W Bn, B band. Rear 248m from front Iso 6s 11m 1M; B Bn, Y band.
Carrickatine No. 2 54°59'·2N 08°28'·0W QR 6m 1M; R beacon with steps.
Rutland Island Ldg Lts 138°. Front 54°58'·9'.1 08°27'·6W Oc 6s 8m 1M; W Bn, B band. Rear 330m from front Oc 6s 14m 1M; B Bn, Y band.
Inishcoo No. 4 QR 3m 1M.
Nancy's Rock No. 1 QG 3m 1M.
No. 6 QR 3m 1M.

BURTONPORT
Ldg Lts 068°. Front 54°58'·9N 08°26'·4W FG 17m 1M; grey Bn, W band. Rear 355m from front FG 23m 1M; grey Bn, Y band.

SOUTH SOUND OF ARAN.
Illancrone Island 54°56'·28N 08°28'·53W Fl 5s 7m 6M; square Tr.
Wyon Point 54°56'·50N 08°27'·50W Fl(2) WRG 10s 8m W6M, R3M; W square Tr; vis G shore-021°, W021°-042°, R042°-121°, W121°-150°, R 150°-shore.
Turk Rocks 54°57'·30N 08°28'·15W Fl G 5s 6m 2M; G square Tr. Aileen Reef 54°58'·2N 08°28'·8W QR 6m 1M.
Carrickbealatroha, Upper 54°58'·64N 08°28'·58W Fl 5s 3m 2M; square brickwork Tr.

RUTLAND SOUTH CHANNEL.
Corren's Rock 54°58'·12N 08°26'·68W Fl R 3s 4m 2M; R square Tr.
Teige's Rock 54°58'·61N 08°26'·75W Fl 3s 4m 2M; W round Tr, square base.
Dawros Head 54°49'·6N 08°33'·6W L Fl 10s 39m 4M; W square column.
Rathlin O'Birne. West side 54°39'·77N 08°49'·90W Fl WR 20s 35m **W22M, R18M**; W Tr; vis R195°-307°, W307°-195°.
Teelin Point 54°37'·32N 08°37'·72W Fl R 10s; R structure.
Donegal Bay, St John's Point 54°34'·15N 08°27'·60W Fl 6s 30m 14M; W Tr.

KILLYBEGS.
Rotten Island 54°36'·87N 08°26'·39W Fl WR 4s 20m **W15M**, R11M; W Tr; vis W255°-008°, R008°-039°, W039°-208°.
Ldg Lts 338°. Pier, Front Oc R 8s 5m 2M. Rear 65m from front Oc R 8s 7m 2M. Both Y diamonds, on buildings.
W pier head 2 FR (vert).

SLIGO.
Wheat Rock Lt Buoy 54°18'·82N 08°39'·03W Q(6)LFl 15s; S cardinal mark.
Blackrock 54°18'·47N 08°37'·00W Fl 5s 24m 13M; W Tr, B band. Auxiliary Lt Fl R 3s 12m 5M; same Tr; vis 107°-130° over Wheat and Seal rocks.
Lower Rosses, N of point (Cullaun Bwee) 54°19'·72N 08°34'·37W Fl(2) WRG 10s 8m W10M, R8M, G8M; W hut on piles; vis G over Bungar bank-066°, W066°-070°, R070° over Drumcliff bar shown throughout 24 hrs.
Ldg Lts 125°. Front Metal Man 54°18'·22N 08°34'·50W Fl 4s 3m 7M. Rear Oyster Island, 365m from front Oc 4s 13m 10M. Both shown throughout 24 hrs.

KILLALA.
Inishcrone Pier Fl WRG 1·5s 8m 2M; vis W098°-116°, G116°-136°, R136°-187°.
Ldg Lts 230°. Rinnaun Point, Front 54°13'·5N 09°12'·2W Oc 10s 7m 5M. Rear 150m from front Oc 10s 12m 5M.
Dir Lt 215°, Inch Island, 54°13'·3N 09°12'·3W Fl WRG 2s 6m 3M; square Tr; vis G205°-213°, W213°-217°, R217°-225°.

Ldg Lts 196°. Kilroe, Front 54°12'·6N 09°12'·2W Oc 4s 5m 2M; square Tr. Rear 120m from front Oc 4s 10m 2M; square Tr.

Ldg Lts 236°. Pier, Front Iso 2s 5m 2M; W diamond on Tr. Rear, 200m from front, Iso 2s 7m 2M; W diamond on pole. Killala Bay. Bone Rock, NE end 54°15'·8N 09°11'·2W Q 7m; N cardinal mark.

Broadhaven, Gubacashel Point 54°16'·05N 09°53'·28W Iso WR 4s 27m W12M, R9M; W Tr; vis W shore (S side of bay)-355°, R355°-shore.
Ballyglass 54°15'·3N 09°53'·4W Fl G 3s.
Eagle Island, West end 54°16'·98N 10°05'·52W Fl(3) 10s 67m **26M**; W Tr; RC. Shown throughout 24 hrs.

Blackrock 54°04'·0N 10°19'·2W Fl WR 12s 86m **W22M, R16M**; W Tr; vis W276°-212°, R212°-276°.

Blacksod pier root 54°05'·90N 10°03'·63W Fl(2) WR 7·5s 13m W12M, R9M; W Tr on dwelling; vis R189°-210°, W210°-018°.
Pier Head 54°05'·9N 10°03'·6W 2 FR (vert) 6m 3M.
Achill Island, Ridge Pt. 54°01'·8N 09°58'·5W Fl 5s 21m 5M.

ACHILL SOUND.
Innish Biggle QR.
Carrigeenfushta Fl G 3s.
Achill Sound 53°56'·0N 09°55'·4W QG.
Ldg Lts 330° Whitestone, Front and rear both Oc 4s.
Saulia Pier 53°57'·1N 09°55'·5W Fl G 3s 12m. 53°52'·1N 09°56'·5W Fl R 2s 5m; R square Tr.
Carrigin-a-tShrutha 53°52'·3N 09°56'·7W Q (2) R 5s .

CLEW BAY.
Achillbeg Island, S point 53°51'·48N 09°56'·80W Fl WR 5s 56m **W18M, R18M, R15M**; W round Tr on square building; vis R262°-281°, W281°-342°, R342°-060°, W060°-092°, R(intens) 092°-099°, W099°-118°.
Clare Island, E pier Fl R 3s 5m 3M.
Cloghcormick Buoy 53°50'·54N 09°43'·27W (unlit); W cardinal mark.

WESTPORT BAY.
Dorinish Lt Buoy 53°49'·46N 09°40'·61W Fl G 3s; stbd-hand mark.
Inishgort, S point 53°49'·58N 09°40'·17W L Fl 10s 11m 10M; W Tr. Shown throughout 24 hrs.
Westport approach 53°47'·97N 09°34'·30W Fl 3s; G box on conical Bn. Roonagh Quay Ldg Lts 144°, both Iso 10s.

INISHBOFIN.
Inishlyon, Lyon Head 53°36'·7N 10°09'·6W Fl WR 7·5s 13m W7M, R4M; W post; vis W036°-058°, R058°-184°, W184°-325°, R325°-036°.
Gun Rock Fl(2) 6s 8m 4M; W column; vis 296°-253°.

Cleggan Point 52°34'·5N 10°07'·7W Fl(3) WRG 15s 20m W6M, R3M, G3M; W column on W hut; vis W shore-091°, R091°-124°, G124°-221°.

Slyne Head, N Tr, Illaunamid 53°23'·97N 10°14'·00W Fl(2) 15s 35m **28M**; B Tr; RC.
Inishnee 53°22'·7N 09°54'·4W Fl(2) WRG 10s 9m W5M, R3M, G3M; W column on W square base; vis G314°-017°, W017°-030°, R030°-080°, W080°-194°.
Croaghnakeela Island 53°19'·4N 09°58'·3W Fl 3·7s 7m 5M; W column; vis 034°-045°, 218°-286°, 311°-325°.

GALWAY BAY.
Eeragh, E side 53°08'·90N 09°51'·78W Fl 15s 35m **23M**; W Tr, two B bands; vis 297°-262°.

Straw Island 53°07'·05N 09°37'·80W Fl(2) 5s 11m **17M**; W Tr.
Ldg Lts 192°. Front 53°06'·3N 09°39'·7W Oc 5s 6m 3M; W column on W square base; vis 142°-197°. Rear 43m from front Oc 5s 8m 2M; W column on W square base; vis 142°-197°.
Kilronan Pier, head Fl WG 1·5s 5m 3M; W column; vis G240°-326°, W326°-000°.
Kiggaul Bay Fl WR 3s 5m W5M, R3M; vis W329°-359°, R359°-059°, part obsc by West shore of bay.

CASHLA BAY
Entrance, West side Fl(3) WR 10s 8m W6M, R3M; W column on concrete structure; vis W216°-000°, R000°-069°.
Rossaveel Pier Ldg Lts 116° Front Oc 3s 4m; W mast. Rear 90m from front Oc 3s 8m; W mast.
Spiddle Pier, head Fl WRG 7·5s 11m W6M, R4M, G4M; Y column; vis G102°-282°, W282°-024°, R024°-066°.
Lion Pt Dir Lt 53°15'·83N 09°33'·97W Dir Iso WRG 4s 6m W8M, R6M, G6M; W square Tr on column; vis G357°-008°, W008°-011°, R011°-017°.

GALWAY
Mutton Island Lt Buoy 53°15'·05N 09°02'·88W Fl(2)R 6s; port-hand mark.
Leverets 53°15'·32N 09°01'·87W Q WRG 9m 10M; B round Tr, W bands; vis G015°-058°, W058°-065°, R065°-103°, G103°-143.5°, W143·5°-146·5°, R146·5°-015°.
Rinmore Iso WRG 4s 7m 5M; W square Tr; vis G359°-008°, W008°-018°, R018°-027°.
Approach Channel Ldg Lts 325°. Front 53°16'·1N 09°02'·8W Fl R 1·5s 12m 7M; R diamond, Y diagonal stripes on mast; vis 315°-345°. Rear 310m from front Oc R 10s 19m 7M; R diamond, Y diagonal stripes on framework Tr; vis 315°-345°.
Nimmo's Pier 53°15'·99N 09°02'·77W Iso Y 6s 7m 6M.

Black Head 53°09·25N 09°15'·78W Fl WR 5s 20m W11M, R8M; W square Tr; vis W045°-268°, R268°-276°.

Inisheer 53°02'·77N 09°31'·60W Iso WR 20s 34m **W20M, R16M**; W Tr, B band; vis W (part vis beyond 7M) 225°-231°, W231°-245°, R245°-269°, W269°-115°.

Loop Head 52°33'·65N 09°55'·90W Fl(4) 20s 84m **28M**; W Tr; vis 280°-218°; RC.

For Lts further S see 10.12.4.

13

10.13.5 PASSAGE INFORMATION

LAMBAY ISLAND TO FAIR HEAD (charts 44, 2093, 2198)

In general this coast is fairly steep-to except in larger bs, particularly Dundalk. Streams offshore run up to 2½ kn as far as Rockabill, but are weaker further N until approaching Belfast Lough.

Lambay Island is private, and steep-to except on W side, where there can be overfalls. Skerries Islands (Colt, Shenicks and St Patrick's) are 1M E and SE of Red Island, to E of Skerries Harbour. Colt Island and Shenicks Island are connected to shore at LW. Pass between them and St Patrick's Island, but the latter has off-liers 3 ca to S. Rockabill, two steep-to rks with Lt Ho, is 2½M E of St Patrick's Island. Going NE from Carlingford (10.13.8), after rounding Hellyhunter buoy there are no real offshore dangers until Strangford Lough (10.13.9). For Kilkeel and Ardglass see 10.13.20.

N from Strangford keep ½M off Ballyquintin Pt. 3M to NE are Butter Pladdy rks; keep to E of these. 2M further N is South Rock, with disused Lt Ho, part of cluster of rks to be avoided in poor visibility or bad weather by closing South Rock Lt F. In good weather pass inshore of South Rk, and between it and North Rk (chart 2156).

There are three routes for Belfast Lough (10.13.10). E of Mew Island is Ram Race (to the N on the ebb, and the S on the flood). Copeland Sound, between Mew Island and Copeland Island, is passable but not recommended. Donaghadee Sound is buoyed and a good short cut for yachts: the stream runs SSE from HW Belfast +0530 and NW from HW Belfast −0030, and can attain 4½ kn. An eddy extends S to Ballyferris Pt, and about 1M offshore. For Donaghadee see 10.13.20.

N from Belfast Lough, Black Hd is straightforward. Pass E of Muck Island, which is steep-to. Hunter Rk, 2½M off Larne, is marked by buoys. Further offshore are the Maidens, two dangerous groups of rks extending 2M N and S; E Maiden in the S group is lit.

The very small harb of Carnlough (10.13.20) provides shelter for small yachts, but should not be approached in strong onshore winds. There is anch here in offshore winds, and also in Red B 5M further N. Either can provide a useful anch on passage to or from the Western Isles. There is temp anch in good weather in Cushendun B, 5M NW of Garron Pt.

Fair Hd is a bold headland, steep-to all round, and marks the NE corner of Ireland.

CROSSING THE IRISH SEA

Passages across the Irish Sea can range from the fairly long haul from Land's End to Cork (140M), to the relatively short hop from Mull of Kintyre to Torr Pt (11M). But such distances are deceptive, because the average cruising yacht needs to depart from and arrive at a reasonably secure harbour; also in the North Chan strong tidal streams can cause heavy overfalls: so each passage needs to be treated on its merits.

Many yachts use the Land's End/Cork route on their way to (and from) the delightful cruising ground along the S coast of Ireland (see 10.12.5). Penzance B, or one of the Scilly Is anchs, make a convenient place from which to leave, with good Lts and Round Island radiobeacon to take departure. Although the Celtic Sea is exposed to the Atlantic, there are no dangers on passage and the tidal streams are weak. A landfall between Ballycotton and Old Hd of Kinsale (both have good Lts and radiobeacons) presents no offlying dangers, and in poor vis decreasing soundings indicate approach to land. There is likelihood, outward bound under sail, that the boat will be on the wind − a possible benefit on the return passage. If however the wind serves, and if it is intended to cruise along the southern coast, a landfall at the Fastnet with arrival at (say) Baltimore will place the yacht more to windward, with little extra distance.

From Land's End the other likely destination is Dun Laoghaire. A stop at (say) Milford Haven enables the skipper to select the best time for passing the Bishops and Smalls (see 10.11.5), and roughly divides the total passage into two equal parts. From S Bishop onwards there are the options of making the short crossing to Tuskar Rk and going N inside the banks (theoretically a good idea in strong W winds), or of keeping to seaward. But in bad weather the area off Tuskar is best avoided; apart from the traffic scheme, the tide is strong at sp and the sea can be very rough.

The ferry route Holyhead/Dun Laoghaire is another typical crossing, and is relatively straightforward with easy landfalls either end. The tide runs hard round Anglesey at sp, so departure just before slack water minimises the set N or S. Beware also the traffic scheme off The Skerries.

The IOM (see 10.10.5) is a good centre for cruising in the Irish Sea, and its harbs provide convenient staging points whether bound N/S or E/W.

Between Scotland and Northern Ireland there are several possible routes, but much depends on weather and tide. Time of departure must take full advantage of the stream, and avoid tide races and overfalls (see 10.9.5). Conditions can change quickly, so a flexible plan is needed.

FAIR HEAD TO BLOODY FORELAND (chart 2723)

This is a good cruising area, under the lee of land in SW wind, but very exposed to NW or N. Beware fishing boats and nets in many places. Tidal streams are complex, up to 6 kn at sp in Rathlin Sound but weaker further W. The flood runs W from HW Galway −0500, but at HW Galway −0300 an E eddy starts inshore between Bloody Foreland and Malin Hd. The ebb runs E from HW Galway +0130, but at HW Galway +0330 a W eddy starts inshore from Malin Hd to Bloody Foreland. These eddies initially run only 1M or so offshore but gradually extend seawards, and if timed correctly can be used when sailing in either direction.

A fair tide is essential through Rathlin Sound where the stream runs 6 kn at sp, and causes dangerous overfalls. The main stream runs NW from HW Galway −0600 for five hrs, and SE from HW Galway +0100 for four hrs. A W-going eddy runs from Fair Hd close inshore towards Carrickmannanon Rk from HW Galway +0100, and an E-going eddy runs from HW Galway −0500 to −0100. The worst overfalls in the chan are from HW Galway −0500 to −0300, and it is best to enter W-bound at the end of this period, on the last of favourable tide. Keep seaward of Carrickmannanon Rk and Sheep Island. A harb has been built in Church Bay, on the W side of Rathlin Island.

Proceeding to Portrush (10.13.12), use Skerries Sound in good weather. For Lough Foyle use either the main chan W of The Tuns, or S chan passing 2 ca N of Magilligan Pt and allowing for set towards The Tuns on the ebb (up to 3½ kn).

Torr Rks, Inishtrahull and Garvan Islands lie N and E of Malin Hd. Inishtrahull is lit and is about 1M long, with rks extending N about 3 ca into Torr Sound. Inishtrahull Sound, between Inishtrahull and Garvan Islands, is exposed, and tidal stream up to 4 kn at sp can cause a dangerous sea with no warning. Stream also sets hard through Garvan Islands, S of which Garvan Sound can be passed safely in daylight avoiding two sunken rks — one 1½ ca NE of Rossnabartan, and the other 5 ca NW. The main stream runs W for only 3 hrs, from HW Galway −0500 to −0200; otherwise it runs E. W of Malin Hd a W-going eddy starts at HW Galway +0400, and an E-going one at HW Galway −0300. In bad weather it is best to pass at least 3M N of Torr Rks.

From Malin Hd to Dunaff Hd, at entrance to Lough Swilly (10.13.15), keep ½M offshore. Trawbreaga Lough gives shelter, but is shallow, and sea can break on bar: only approach when no swell, and at half flood. Entrance to Lough Swilly is clear except for Swilly Rks off the W shore, SSE of Fanad Head.

W from Lough Swilly the coast is very foul. Beware Limeburner Rk 3M N of Melmore Hd. Mulroy B has good anchs but needs accurate pilotage, as in Irish Cruising Club Sailing Directions. See 10.13.20.

Between Mulroy B and Sheephaven there is inshore passage S of Frenchman Rk, and between Guill Rks and Carnabollion, safe in good weather. Otherwise keep 1M offshore. Sheephaven B has good anchs except in strong NW or N winds, and is easy to enter between Rinnaflagla Pt and Horn Hd. Beware Wherryman Rks, which dry, 1 ca off E shore.

Between Horn Hd and Bloody Foreland are three low islands — Inishbofin, Inishdooey and Inishbeg. The first is almost part of the mainland, but there is a temp anch on S side. 6M offshore is Tory Island (Lt, fog sig, RC) with rks for 5 ca on SW side. Temp anch in good weather in Camusmore B. In Tory Sound the stream runs W from HW Galway + 0230, and E from HW Galway − 0530, sp rates 2 kn.

BLOODY FORELAND TO ARAN IS. (charts 2725, 2420)

Off Bloody Foreland there is often heavy swell. The coast and islands S to Aranmore give good cruising. Offlying dangers are Buniver and Brinlack shoals, which can break; Bullogconnell 1M NW of Gola Island; and Stag Rks 2M NNW of Owey Island. Anchs include Bunbeg and Gweedore Harb (chart 1883), and Cruit B which is easier access. Behind Aranmore are several good anchs. Use N entrance, since S one is shallow (chart 2792). Rutland N Channel is main approach to Burtonport — general facilities, see 10.13.20.

Boylagh B has shoals and rks N of Roaninish Island. Connell Rk is 1M N of Church Pool — a good anch, best approached from Dawros Hd 4½M to W. There is temp anch (but not in W or NW winds) just E of Rinmeasa Pt, on S side of Glen B. Rathlin O'Birne has steps E side. Anch SE of them ¾ ca offshore. The sound is ½M wide; keep island side to avoid rks off Malin Beg Head.

In Donegal B beware uncharted rks W of Teelin, a good natural harb but exposed to S and W. Killybegs (10.13.16) has better shelter and is always accessible. Good shelter with fair access in Donegal Harb (chart 2792). Moderate anch at Mullaghmore in good weather with winds from SE through S to NW. Inishmurray is worth a visit in good weather: anch off S side. There are shoals close E and NE of the island, and rks 1½M to N. Keep well clear of coast S to Sligo (10.13.17) in onshore winds, and watch for lobster pots.

Killala B has temp anch 1M S of Kilcummin Pt, on W side. Proceeding to Killala beware St Patrick's Rks. Entrance has Ldg Lts and marks, but bar is dangerous in strong NE winds. The coast W to Broadhaven is inhospitable. Only Belderg and Portacloy give a little shelter. Stag Rks are steep-to. Broadhaven (chart 2703) is good anch and refuge, but in N/NW gales sea can break in entrance. In approaches beware Slugga Rk on E side with off-lier, and Monastery Rk on S side.

The coast from Eagle Island to Slyne Hd has many inlets, some sheltered. Streams are weak offshore. There are few Lts. Keep ½M off Erris Hd, and further in bad weather. Unless calm, keep seaward of Eagle Island (Lt, RC) where there is race to N. Frenchport (chart 2703) is good temp anch except in strong W winds. Inishkea Is (chart 2704) can be visited in good weather: anch N or S of Rusheen Island. The sound off Mullett Peninsula is clear, but for Pluddany Rks 6 ca E of Inishkea N.

Blacksod B (chart 2704) has easy entrance, but in W gales beware breakers 1M SE of Duvillaunmore. From N, in good weather, there is chan between Duvillaunbeg and Gaghty Island. Black Rk (Lt) has rks up to 1¼M SW, but entry at night is possible. See 10.13.20.

Rough water is likely off Achil Hd. Achill Sound (chart 2667) is obstructed by cables 11m high at swing bridge. Anchs each end of Sound, but the stream runs strongly.

Clare Island has Two Fathom Rk 1½M off NW coast, and Deace's Rk ½M to the N. In Clew B both Newport and Westport (see chart 2057 and 10.13.18) need detailed pilotage instructions. S of Clare Island beware Meemore Shoal 1½M W of Roonagh Hd. 2M further W is the isolated rk Mweelaun. The offshore islands Coher, Bullybeg, Inishturk (with anch on E side) and Inishdalla have few hidden dangers, but the coast to the E must be given a berth of 1½M even in calm weather, while in strong winds breakers extend much further seaward.

Killary B (chart 2706) and Little Killary both have good anchs in magnificent scenery. Consult sailing directions, and only approach in reasonable weather and good visibility.

Ballynakill (chart 2706), easily entered either side of Freaghillaun South, has excellent shelter. Beware Mullaghadrina and Ship Rk in N chan. Anch in Fahy, Derryinver or Barnaderg B. Rks and breakers exist E of Inishbofin and S of Inishshark: see chart 2707 for clearing lines. Carrickmahoga is dangerous rk between Inishbofin and Cleggan. Lecky Rks lie 1M SSE of Davillaun. There is anch on S side of Inishbofin (Lt), but difficult in strong SW wind or swell.

Cleggan B is moderate anch, exposed to NW but easy access. High Island sound can be used, but not Friar I Sound or Aughrus Passage. Clifden B (chart 2708) has offlying dangers with breakers: enter 3 ca S of Seal Rks Bn and anch between Drinagh Pt and Larner's Rk. See 10.13.20.

Slyne Hd (Lt and RC) marks SW end of rks and islets stretching 2M WSW from coast. Here the stream turns N at HW Galway − 0320, and S at HW Galway + 0300. It runs 3 kn at sp, and in bad weather causes a dangerous race. The sea may break on Barret Shoal, 3M NW of Slyne Hd.

The Connemara coast (charts 2709, 2096) and Aran Islands (chart 3339) gives excellent cruising in good vis. But there are many rks, and few navigational marks. Between Slyne Hd and Roundstone B are many offlying dangers. Further E the better harbs are Roundstone B, Cashel B, Killeany Bay, Greatman B and Cashla B. Kilronan (10.13.20) on Inishmore is only reasonable harb in Aran Islands, but is exposed in E winds. Cruising coastwise keep well offshore of Skird Rks.

Normal approach to Galway B is through N Sound or S Sound. N Sound is 3M wide between Eagle Rk and other dangers off Lettermullan shore, and banks on S side which break in strong winds. S Sound is wider, with no dangers except Finnis Rk ½M SE of Inisheer. The other chans are Gregory Sound, 1M wide between Inishmore and Inishmaan, and Foul Sound between Inishmaan and Inisheer. The latter has one danger — Pipe Rk and the reef inshore of it, extending 3 ca NW of Inisheer.

The N side of Galway B is exposed, with no shelter. Galway (10.13.19) is a commercial port, and New Harb (chart 1984) is a more pleasant anch.

For all Irish waters the Sailing Directions published by the Irish Cruising Club are strongly recommended, and particularly on the W coast, where other information is scant.

13

10.13.6 DISTANCE TABLE

Approximate distances in nautical miles are by the most direct route while avoiding dangers and allowing for traffic separation schemes etc. Places in *italics* are in adjoining areas.

1	*Dun Laoghaire*	**1**																		
2	*Pt of Ayre*	93	**2**																	
3	*Mull of Galloway*	93	21	**3**																
4	*Barra Hd*	238	184	163	**4**															
5	Rockabill	20	75	73	218	**5**														
6	Carlingford	50	70	60	203	30	**6**													
7	Strangford	71	44	34	175	51	36	**7**												
8	Mew Island	92	43	23	146	72	57	29	**8**											
9	Bangor	96	48	29	149	76	61	34	6	**9**										
10	Larne	108	59	37	135	88	73	45	16	16	**10**									
11	Altacarry Hd	135	85	64	104	117	102	74	45	45	31	**11**								
12	Portrush	150	98	79	103	130	115	87	58	58	48	19	**12**							
13	Londonderry	177	127	106	120	157	142	114	85	85	75	45	30	**13**						
14	Rathmullan	200	149	128	105	181	166	138	109	109	96	65	51	65	**14**					
15	Tory Island	209	156	135	95	189	174	146	117	117	105	74	61	74	35	**15**				
16	Killybegs	267	214	193	153	247	232	204	175	175	163	132	119	132	93	58	**16**			
17	Sligo	281	228	207	167	261	246	218	189	189	177	146	133	146	107	72	30	**17**		
18	Eagle Island	297	244	223	183	277	262	234	205	205	193	162	149	162	123	88	62	59	**18**	
19	Slyne Hd	352	299	278	238	332	317	289	260	260	248	217	204	217	178	143	117	114	55	**19**
20	Galway	348	348	327	287	381	366	338	309	309	297	266	253	266	227	192	166	163	104	49	**20**

CARLINGFORD LOUGH

Louth/Down   10-13-8

CHARTS
Admiralty 44, 2800; Imray C62; Irish OS 9

TIDES
Cranfield Point +0025 and Warrenpoint +0035 Dover; ML 2.9; Duration Cranfield Point 0615, Warrenpoint 0540; Zone 0 (GMT).

Standard Port DUBLIN (NORTH WALL) (←)

Times				Height (metres)			
HW		LW		MHWS	MHWN	MLWN	MLWS
0000	0700	0000	0500	4.1	3.4	1.5	0.5
1200	1900	1200	1700				

Differences CRANFIELD POINT
−0027 −0011 +0017 −0007 +0.7   +0.9   +0.3   +0.2
WARRENPOINT
−0020 −0010 +0040 +0040 +1.0   +0.9   +0.1   +0.2
Note: NE coast is Ulster, SW coast the Republic of Ireland.

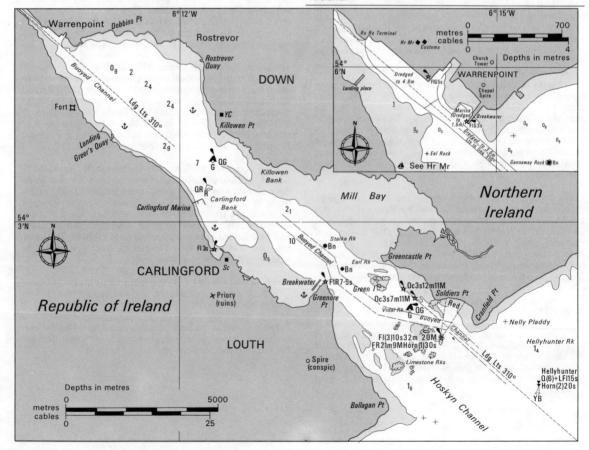

CARLINGFORD LOUGH *continued*

SHELTER
Good shelter. Anchorages at Greenore between quay and breakwater; off Greer's Quay; between Killowen Pt and Rostrevor; N of Carlingford Hr. Alongside berth at pier in Hr (dries).

NAVIGATION
Waypoint 54°00'.23N 06°02'.20W, 130°/310° from/to front Ldg Lt 310°, 2.4M. The lough becomes choppy in S winds and with on-shore winds the bar becomes impassable. Beware sudden squalls. Tides run up to 5 kn off Greenore. Drying rocks and shoals extend nearly across the entrance. The main channel is Carlingford Cut, about 3 ca SW of Cranfield Point, and passing 2 ca N of Haulbowline Lt Ho.

LIGHTS AND MARKS
Haulbowline Fl(3) 10s 32m 20M; granite Tr. Turning Lt FR 21m 9M; same Tr; vis 196°-208°; Horn 30s. Ldg Lts 310° both Oc 3s 7/12m 11M; G houses on piles, vis 295°-325°. Greenore Pier FIR 7.5s 10m 5M. Newry River Ldg Lts 310° both Iso 4s 5/15m 2M, stone columns.

RADIO TELEPHONE
Warrenpoint VHF Ch 16; 12 (H24). Greenore (call: *Ferry Greenore*) Ch 16; 13 (H24). Other stations: Dundalk Ch 16; 06 12. Kilkeel Ch 16; **12** 14 (Mon-Fri: 0900-2000 LT).

TELEPHONE
(Carlingford 042; Newry 0693) Hr Mr Warrenpoint 73381; CG Kilkeel 62232; MRCC Limerick 61219 or Donaghadee 883184; Coast Life Saving Service Clogerhead 22263; ⌗ (0232) 752511; Irish ⌗ Dundalk 34114; Marinecall 0898 500 465; Police (Carlingford) 73102 (Warrenpoint) 722222; Dr Dundalk 31470; Ⓗ Newry 2543, Dundalk 34701

FACILITIES
EC, Warrenpoint Wednesday. **Carlingford Marina** (50), AC, D, FW, P, Slip; **Harbour** Slip; **Carlingford YC** ☎ 73238 Bar, M, V, FW, Slip; **Dundalk SC** FW, Slip; **Greenore Pt** FW; **Warrenpoint** FW, P, D, AB; **D.A. Stukins** ☎ 72322, ME, El, Sh; **T. McArdle** ☎ 73100 Kos; **P. A. McGill** ☎ 73278, Gas.
✉ (Warrenpoint, Rostrevor, Carlingford); Ⓑ (Dundalk, Warrenpoint); ⇌ (Dundalk, Newry); ✈ (Dublin).

STRANGFORD LOUGH   10-13-9
Co. Down

CHARTS
Admiralty 2156, 2159; Imray C62; Irish OS 5, 9

TIDES
Killard Pt. 0000, Strangford Quay +0200 Dover; ML 2.0; Duration 0610; Zone 0 (GMT).

Standard Port BELFAST (→)

Times				Height (metres)			
HW		LW		MHWS	MHWN	MLWN	MLWS
0100	0700	0000	0600	3.5	3.0	1.1	0.4
1300	1900	1200	1800				

Differences STRANGFORD
+0147 +0157 +0148 +0208 +0.1 +0.1 −0.2 0.0
KILLYLEAGH
+0157 +0207 +0211 +0231 +0.3 +0.3 No data
KILKEEL
+0010 +0010 0000 0000 +1.8 +1.4 +0.8 +0.3

SHELTER
Excellent — largest inlet on E coast. Good anchorages in the Narrows at Cross Roads, Strangford Creek, Audley Roads and in Ballyhenry Bay. Berthing at piers in Strangford or Portaferry dependent on state of tide. Good anchorages up the lough in Quoile, Ringhaddy Sound and Whiterock. Some visitors moorings available.

NAVIGATION
Waypoint Strangford Fairway buoy, LFl 10s, Whis, 54°18'.62N 05°28'.62W, 126°/306° from/to Angus Rock Lt, 2.05M. Beware overfalls in the SE approaches and at the bar, which can be dangerous when ebb from narrows is running against strong SSW to E winds. Tidal flow in narrows, and hence the overfalls, relates to HW Strangford Quay (+0200 Dover) not to HW Killard Pt. During flood the bar presents no special problem but for preference enter when tide in the narrows is slack or on the young flood. Visitors should use the East Channel. Strong tidal streams flow through the Narrows, up to 7 kn at springs. Beware St Patricks Rk, Bar Pladdy and Pladdy Lug and whirlpool at Routen Wheel. Beware car ferry between Strangford and Portaferry. Up the lough, beware drying patches, known as pladdies and often un-marked. Swan Is, seen as grassy mound at HW, is edged with rocks and a reef extends 32m E ending at W Bn (Fl (2) WR 6s).

LIGHTS AND MARKS
Entrance identified by Strangford Fairway (safe water) buoy, W Tr on Angus Rk, Pladdy Lug Bn (W) and St Patrick's Rk perch. Leading marks to clear St Quintin Rks are perch on St Patrick's Rks and obelisk in line at 224°. Leading marks to Cross Roads anchorage are stone Bns in line at 260°, difficult to see due to trees.

Bar Pladdy Buoy	Q (6) + one long ev 15s
Angus Rk	Fl R 5s (on Tower)
Dogtail Pt	Oc (4) 10s Ldg Lts 341°
Salt Rk Bn	Fl R 3s
Gowland Rk Bn	Oc (2) 10s Ldg Lts 341°
Swan Is Bn	Fl (2) WR 6s
SW outlier (S Pladdy)	Fl (3) 10s
N outlier (N Pladdy)	Q
Church Pt Bn	Fl (4) R 10s
Portaferry Quay	Oc WR 10s
Ballyhenry Is Bn	Q G
Limestone Rk	Q R

RADIO TELEPHONE
Killyleagh Port VHF Ch 16; 12 (occas). *Strangford Harbour Port* Ch 16; 12 14 (Mon-Fri 0900-1700 LT) . In Strangford Lough most YCs and Seaquip Ch **80**

TELEPHONE
Strangford (039 686) Strangford Port 637; MRSC (Donaghadee) 883184; ⌗ (0232) 752511; Marinecall 0898 500 465; Police 222; Medical Clinic (Downpatrick) 612971; Casualty (Downpatrick) 613311.

FACILITIES
STRANGFORD M, L, FW, CH, AB, V, R, Bar, ✉; **Seaquip** ☎ 303, D (cans), El, Ⓔ, Sh, CH; **Milligan** ☎ 233, Gas.
PORTAFERRY M, P and D (cans), V, R, Bar, ✉, Ⓑ, L, LB, Gas.
KILLYLEAGH M, P and D (cans), L, C (mobile), CH, V, R, Bar, ✉, YC; **Seaboard Sailing Centre** ☎ (Killyleagh) 828511; **East Down YC** ☎ (Killyleagh) 828375; **Maguire** ☎ Killyleagh (828439), Gas.
SKETRICK ISLAND R, Bar, L; **Irwin Yachts** ☎ Killinchy 541592, CH, SM.
KIRCUBBIN **Maxwell Bros** ☎ (Kircubbin) 211, Gas.
Note: A marina is planned near Killyleagh.

13

STRANGFORD LOUGH

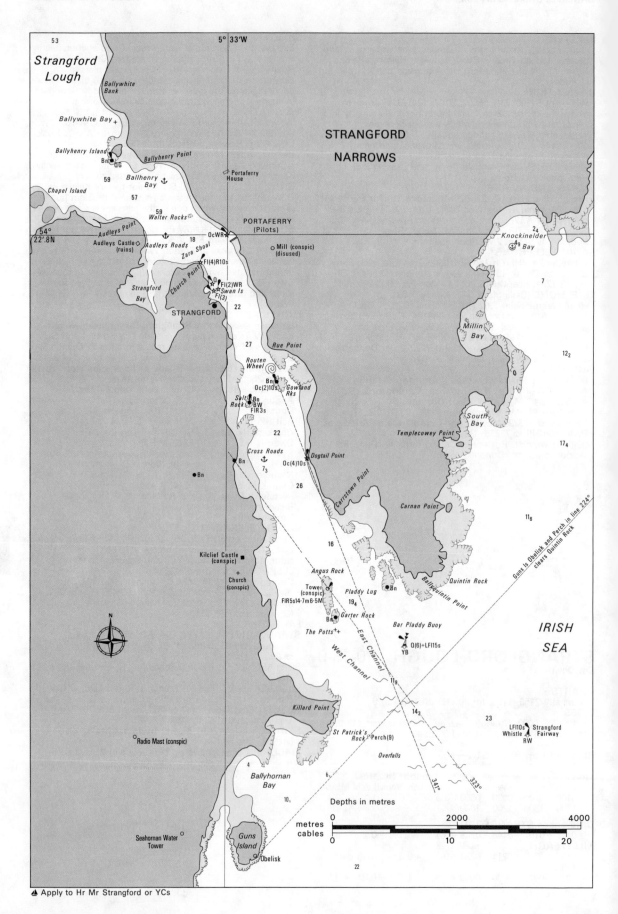

53

Strangford Lough

5° 33'W

Ballywhite Bank

Ballywhite Bay +

Ballyhenry Island
Bn QG

Chapel Island

Ballyhenry Point

59   Ballhenry Bay ⚓

57

59   Walter Rocks

54°
22'.8N   *Audleys Point*

Audleys Castle (ruins) ◇   Audleys Roads ⚓   18   OcWR

Zara Shoal

Fl(4)R10s

Q Fl(2)WR
Swan Is
Fl(3)

STRANGFORD

22

STRANGFORD
NARROWS

Portaferry
House

PORTAFERRY
(Pilots)

Mill (conspic)
(disused)

Knockinelder
Bay   24

7

27   Rue Point

Routen Wheel

Bn
Oc(2)10s   Gowland
Rks

Salt Rock Bn
BW
Fl R3s

22

Cross Roads

Bn   7₃   Oc(4)10s Dogtail Point

Bn

26

16

Kilclief Castle
(conspic) ■

+ Church
(conspic)

Angus Rock
Tower
(conspic)
Fl R5s14·7m6·5M

Bn

The Potts ++

Killard Point

Radio Mast (conspic)

Seahornan Water
Tower

Guns
Island
Obelisk

West Channel

Pladdy Lug

19₄   Garter Rock

East Channel

St Patrick's
Rock Perch(9)

Overfalls

Ballyhornan
Bay   4

6₁

10₁

Millin
Bay

12₂

South
Bay

Templecowey Point   17₄

Carstown Point

Carnan Point   11₆

Quintin Rock

Ballyquintin Point

Bar Pladdy Buoy
Q(6)+LFl15s
YB

Bn

11₉

14₃

23

IRISH
SEA

Guns Is Obelisk and Perch in line 224°
clears Quintin Rock

LFl10s Strangford
Whistle ♦ Fairway
RW

341°   323°

Depths in metres

metres   0   2000   4000
cables   0   10   20

N

BELFAST LOUGH   10-13-10
County Down and County Antrim

CHARTS
Admiralty 1753; Imray C62, C64; Irish OS 5

TIDES
+0001 Dover; ML 2.0; Duration 0620; Zone 0 (GMT).

Standard Port BELFAST (→)

Times				Height (metres)			
HW		LW		MHWS	MHWN	MLWN	MLWS
0100	0700	0000	0600	3.5	3.0	1.1	0.4
1300	1900	1200	1800				

Differences DONAGHADEE
+0020 +0020 +0023 +0023 +0.5 +0.4 0.0 +0.1
PORTAVOGIE
+0010 +0020 +0010 +0020 +1.2 +0.9 +0.3 +0.2
CARRICKFERGUS
+0005 +0005 +0005 +0005 −0.3 −0.3 −0.2 −0.1
SOUTH ROCK
+0023 +0023 +0025 +0025 +1.0 +0.8 +0.1 +0.1

NOTE: Belfast is a Standard Port and tidal predictions for every day of the year are given below. Belfast is a commercial port and main sailing centres in Belfast Lough are Bangor, Cultra and Carrickfergus.

SHELTER
Belfast — excellent.
Cultra — good.
Ballyholme Bay — good in offshore winds.
SSE of Carrickfergus Pier — good except in E winds.
Carrickfergus — very good in marina.
Bangor — exposed to N winds; good for small boats.

NAVIGATION
Waypoint Bangor 54°41'.00N 05°40'.00W, 010°/190° from/to breakwater Lt, 1.0M. Rounding Orlock Pt beware Briggs Rks extending ¾ M offshore. The Lough is well marked. Beware Carrickfergus Bank extends 15 ca SSW from the harbour, and from Carrickfergus E to Kilroot Pt there is a sand bank drying up to 4 ca from shore.

LIGHTS AND MARKS
Channel up to Belfast is well marked by buoys and beacons. Once the pile beacons are reached it is dangerous to leave the channel. Tie up where directed by the Berthing Master at the Hailing House.
Carrickfergus entry signal — when sufficient water to enter — Square flag hoisted by day or extra R light on West Pierhead by night.

RADIO TELEPHONE
Call: *Belfast Harbour Radio* (at Clarendon Dock) VHF Ch 12; 08 11 **12** 14 16 (H24).
Bangor Ch 16; 11 (when vessel expected).
Carrickfergus Ch 16; 12 14 (HW−3 to HW+1, when vessel expected). Copelands Marina, Royal Northern Ireland YC and Carrickfergus Marina, Ch 16; 11 80 (Ch 11 H24).

TELEPHONE (0232)
Hr Mr Belfast 234422, Bangor (0247) 472596; MRSC & CG Donaghadee 883184; ☗ 234466; Weather: Crumlin 22339, Marinecall 0898 500 465; Police Belfast 58411, Carrickfergus 62021, Bangor 464444; Dr 464444.

FACILITIES
EC Belfast Wednesday; Bangor Thursday.
BELFAST (0232)**Harbour** ☎ 38506, Slip, P, D, L, FW, ME, El, Sh, C (up to 20 ton), CH, AB; **James Tedford** ☎ 226763, SM, Gas, ACA, CH; **J. McCready** CH; **Town** P, CH, V, R, Bar; ✉; Ⓑ; ⇌; ✈.
HOLYWOOD (023 17)**McCready** (Sailboat) ☎ Holywood 2888, ME, El, Sh, CH; **R N Ireland YC, Cultra** ☎ Holywood 2041, Slip, M, P (½ M), D, L, FW, AB, R, Bar; **Town** P, CH, V, R, Bar; ✉; Ⓑ; ⇌; ✈ (Belfast).
BANGOR (0247) **Bangor Marina** (350 + 40 visitors) ☎ 453297; FW, AC, Ⓞ CH, BH (40 ton), ME, El, Sh, Gas, Gaz, Slip, C, SM, V, P, D, Ⓔ; Access **R Ulster YC** ☎ 270568, R, Bar; **Doun Diving & Marina** ☎ 450831, Diving; **Hamilton** ☎ 461013, Gas; **Bangor Shipyard** ☎ 270939, ME, El, Sh, Slip, CH; **Munster Simms Engineering** ☎ 270531, ME, El, Sh; **Ballyholme YC** ☎ 462467, M, L; **Bangor Marine Services** ☎ 469916, ME; **Town** M, L, ME, El, Sh, CH, V, R, Bar; ✉; Ⓑ; ⇌; ✈ (Belfast).
DONAGHADEE (0247) Hr Mr 882377 **Copelands Marina** ☎ 882184, D, FW, C (20 ton); **County Hardware** ☎ 883300, Gas. **Town** V, R, Bar; ✉; Ⓑ; ⇌ (Bangor); ✈ (Belfast).

13

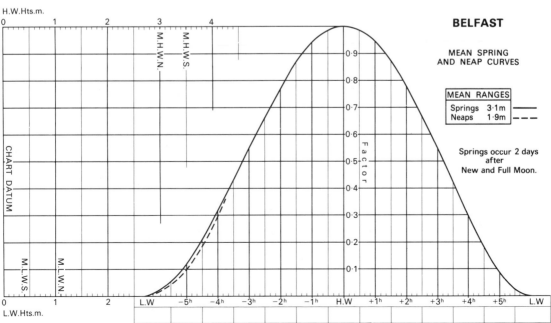

IRELAND, EAST COAST – BELFAST

Lat 54°36′ N Long 5°55′ W

TIMES AND HEIGHTS OF HIGH AND LOW WATERS

YEAR **1991**

TIME ZONE UT(GMT)
For Summer Time add ONE hour in non-shaded areas

JANUARY

Day	Time	m	Day	Time	m
1 Tu	0458	0.6	**16** W	0502	0.8
	1106	3.7		1118	3.4
	1723	0.4		1737	0.6
	2342	3.5		2339	3.1
2 W	0547	0.6	**17** Th	0534	0.7
	1156	3.8		1150	3.4
	1814	0.3		1810	0.5
3 Th	0034	3.4	**18** F	0011	3.2
	0636	0.6		0607	0.6
	1243	3.8		1221	3.5
	1902	0.3		1841	0.5
4 F	0124	3.3	**19** Sa	0043	3.2
	0723	0.7		0642	0.6
	1331	3.8		1252	3.5
	1949	0.3		1914	0.4
5 Sa	0212	3.2	**20** Su	0119	3.2
	0811	0.7		0719	0.6
	1419	3.7		1328	3.5
	2039	0.4		1952	0.4
6 Su	0303	3.1	**21** M	0155	3.2
	0858	0.8		0759	0.6
	1510	3.5		1408	3.5
	2128	0.5		2034	0.5
7 M	0353	2.9	**22** Tu	0239	3.2
	0950	0.9		0843	0.7
	1603	3.4		1453	3.5
☾	2221	0.7		2121	0.6
8 Tu	0448	2.8	**23** W	0327	3.1
	1048	1.0		0934	0.9
	1659	3.2		1545	3.4
	2320	0.9	☽	2214	0.8
9 W	0547	2.8	**24** Th	0423	3.1
	1153	1.1		1033	1.0
	1801	3.1		1647	3.2
				2319	0.9
10 Th	0022	1.0	**25** F	0532	3.0
	0646	2.8		1146	1.1
	1259	1.1		1803	3.1
	1903	3.0			
11 F	0124	1.0	**26** Sa	0036	1.0
	0742	2.9		0649	3.0
	1401	1.0		1310	1.1
	2002	3.0		1926	3.1
12 Sa	0219	1.0	**27** Su	0154	1.0
	0834	3.0		0804	3.2
	1457	0.9		1426	0.9
	2056	3.0		2043	3.2
13 Su	0308	1.0	**28** M	0301	0.9
	0922	3.1		0908	3.4
	1545	0.8		1529	0.7
	2143	3.0		2149	3.3
14 M	0352	0.9	**29** Tu	0359	0.8
	1004	3.3		1004	3.5
	1627	0.7		1624	0.5
	2226	3.1		2245	3.4
15 Tu	0428	0.8	**30** W	0449	0.7
	1044	3.3		1055	3.7
	1705	0.6		1713	0.3
●	2304	3.1	○	2336	3.4
			31 Th	0536	0.6
				1142	3.8
				1758	0.2

FEBRUARY

Day	Time	m	Day	Time	m
1 F	0021	3.4	**16** Sa	0546	0.5
	0618	0.5		1156	3.4
	1227	3.8		1815	0.3
	1841	0.2			
2 Sa	0102	3.3	**17** Su	0018	3.2
	0659	0.5		0619	0.5
	1309	3.8		1228	3.5
	1923	0.3		1849	0.3
3 Su	0141	3.2	**18** M	0052	3.3
	0740	0.6		0655	0.4
	1351	3.7		1303	3.5
	2004	0.4		1926	0.4
4 M	0220	3.1	**19** Tu	0128	3.3
	0820	0.7		0734	0.5
	1434	3.5		1344	3.5
	2046	0.6		2006	0.4
5 Tu	0301	3.0	**20** W	0211	3.3
	0904	0.8		0818	0.6
	1521	3.4		1430	3.4
	2129	0.8		2051	0.6
6 W	0348	2.9	**21** Th	0258	3.2
	0953	1.0		0908	0.8
	1614	3.2		1524	3.3
☽	2220	1.0		2146	0.8
7 Th	0442	2.9	**22** F	0357	3.1
	1055	1.1		1009	0.9
	1715	3.0		1631	3.1
	2322	1.1		2255	1.0
8 F	0547	2.8	**23** Sa	0509	3.0
	1210	1.2		1130	1.1
	1821	2.9		1757	2.9
9 Sa	0035	1.2	**24** Su	0025	1.2
	0655	2.8		0634	3.0
	1327	1.1		1306	1.0
	1928	2.8		1928	2.9
10 Su	0145	1.2	**25** M	0149	1.1
	0759	2.9		0752	3.1
	1430	1.0		1422	0.9
	2029	2.8		2046	3.0
11 M	0243	1.1	**26** Tu	0256	1.0
	0854	3.0		0857	3.3
	1522	0.9		1522	0.6
	2121	2.9		2146	3.2
12 Tu	0329	1.0	**27** W	0349	0.8
	0941	3.1		0952	3.5
	1606	0.7		1612	0.4
	2204	3.0		2237	3.3
13 W	0407	0.8	**28** Th	0435	0.6
	1021	3.2		1040	3.6
	1642	0.6		1657	0.3
	2242	3.1	○	2320	3.4
14 Th	0442	0.7			
	1057	3.3			
	1715	0.5			
●	2316	3.1			
15 F	0513	0.6			
	1126	3.4			
	1744	0.4			
	2347	3.2			

MARCH

Day	Time	m	Day	Time	m
1 F	0516	0.5	**16** Sa	0447	0.6
	1123	3.7		1057	3.3
	1737	0.2		1715	0.3
	2358	3.4	●	2319	3.2
2 Sa	0556	0.5	**17** Su	0520	0.5
	1203	3.8		1129	3.4
	1815	0.3		1747	0.3
				2351	3.3
3 Su	0032	3.3	**18** M	0556	0.4
	0632	0.5		1204	3.5
	1242	3.7		1822	0.3
	1850	0.3			
4 M	0106	3.3	**19** Tu	0027	3.3
	0707	0.5		0634	0.4
	1320	3.6		1242	3.5
	1927	0.5		1902	0.3
5 Tu	0140	3.2	**20** W	0106	3.3
	0744	0.6		0714	0.4
	1359	3.5		1326	3.4
	2004	0.7		1944	0.5
6 W	0216	3.2	**21** Th	0149	3.3
	0823	0.7		0801	0.5
	1443	3.3		1416	3.3
	2043	0.9		2032	0.7
7 Th	0258	3.1	**22** F	0242	3.2
	0908	0.9		0854	0.7
	1531	3.1		1515	3.1
	2128	1.1		2131	0.9
8 F	0349	3.0	**23** Sa	0343	3.1
	1003	1.1		1000	0.9
	1630	2.9		1630	2.9
☽	2223	1.2	☽	2249	1.1
9 Sa	0452	2.9	**24** Su	0459	3.0
	1119	1.2		1130	0.9
	1739	2.8		1804	2.8
	2339	1.3			
10 Su	0605	2.8	**25** M	0025	1.2
	1245	1.2		0624	3.0
	1850	2.7		1302	0.9
				1931	2.9
11 M	0100	1.3	**26** Tu	0142	1.1
	0716	2.8		0738	3.1
	1355	1.0		1411	0.7
	1955	2.7		2040	3.0
12 Tu	0205	1.2	**27** W	0242	0.9
	0816	2.9		0840	3.3
	1449	0.9		1505	0.5
	2050	2.8		2134	3.1
13 W	0256	1.0	**28** Th	0331	0.7
	0907	3.0		0932	3.4
	1532	0.7		1552	0.4
	2135	2.9		2219	3.2
14 Th	0336	0.9	**29** F	0414	0.6
	0948	3.1		1019	3.6
	1609	0.6		1633	0.3
	2213	3.0		2257	3.3
15 F	0413	0.7	**30** Sa	0454	0.5
	1024	3.2		1059	3.6
	1642	0.4		1711	0.3
	2247	3.1	○	2330	3.3
			31 Su	0530	0.5
				1137	3.6
				1746	0.4

APRIL

Day	Time	m	Day	Time	m
1 M	0001	3.3	**16** Tu	0534	0.4
	0604	0.5		1143	3.4
	1214	3.6		1801	0.3
	1819	0.5			
2 Tu	0032	3.4	**17** W	0007	3.4
	0639	0.5		0617	0.3
	1250	3.5		1228	3.4
	1853	0.6		1843	0.4
3 W	0104	3.3	**18** Th	0050	3.4
	0714	0.6		0703	0.4
	1328	3.4		1317	3.3
	1927	0.8		1930	0.6
4 Th	0141	3.3	**19** F	0138	3.3
	0752	0.7		0754	0.5
	1409	3.2		1413	3.1
	2005	0.9		2023	0.7
5 F	0222	3.2	**20** Sa	0234	3.2
	0836	0.9		0853	0.6
	1457	3.0		1518	3.0
	2047	1.1		2129	0.9
6 Sa	0310	3.1	**21** Su	0339	3.1
	0928	1.0		1004	0.7
	1552	2.9		1638	2.8
	2139	1.2	☽	2251	1.1
7 Su	0407	3.0	**22** M	0452	3.1
	1034	1.1		1129	0.7
	1657	2.7		1804	2.8
☾	2247	1.3			
8 M	0513	2.9	**23** Tu	0012	1.1
	1153	1.1		0607	3.1
	1807	2.7		1245	0.6
				1919	2.9
9 Tu	0005	1.3	**24** W	0121	1.0
	0622	2.8		0716	3.2
	1303	1.0		1348	0.5
	1912	2.7		2019	3.0
10 W	0114	1.2	**25** Th	0218	0.8
	0724	2.9		0815	3.3
	1359	0.9		1440	0.4
	2006	2.8		2110	3.1
11 Th	0209	1.1	**26** F	0307	0.7
	0818	2.9		0907	3.4
	1446	0.7		1527	0.4
	2054	2.9		2152	3.2
12 F	0256	0.9	**27** Sa	0349	0.6
	0904	3.1		0953	3.4
	1527	0.6		1607	0.4
	2135	3.0		2228	3.2
13 Sa	0336	0.7	**28** Su	0428	0.5
	0943	3.2		1034	3.4
	1604	0.4		1644	0.5
	2213	3.1	○	2301	3.3
14 Su	0416	0.6	**29** M	0506	0.5
	1023	3.3		1113	3.4
	1642	0.3		1719	0.5
●	2249	3.3		2333	3.4
15 M	0455	0.5	**30** Tu	0542	0.5
	1102	3.4		1150	3.4
	1720	0.3		1751	0.6
	2326	3.3			

Chart Datum: 2.01 metres below Ordnance Datum (Belfast)

IRELAND, EAST COAST – BELFAST

Lat 54°36′ N   Long 5°55′ W

TIMES AND HEIGHTS OF HIGH AND LOW WATERS

YEAR 1991

TIME ZONE UT(GMT)

For Summer Time add ONE
hour in non-shaded areas

	MAY				JUNE				JULY				AUGUST		
	Time m		Time m		Time m		Time m		Time m		Time m		Time m		Time m

MAY

1 W 0004 3·4 / 0615 0·6 / 1227 3·3 / 1824 0·7
16 Th 0608 0·3 / 1221 3·3 / 1834 0·5

2 Th 0038 3·4 / 0652 0·6 / 1303 3·2 / 1857 0·8
17 F 0042 3·5 / 0659 0·3 / 1316 3·2 / 1926 0·6

3 F 0114 3·4 / 0730 0·7 / 1344 3·1 / 1935 0·9
18 Sa 0134 3·4 / 0754 0·3 / 1416 3·1 / 2022 0·7

4 Sa 0155 3·3 / 0812 0·8 / 1429 3·0 / 2018 1·0
19 Su 0230 3·4 / 0853 0·4 / 1522 3·0 / 2127 0·8

5 Su 0239 3·2 / 0901 0·9 / 1518 2·9 / 2107 1·1
20 M 0331 3·3 / 1000 0·5 / 1634 2·9 / ☽ 2235 0·9

6 M 0328 3·1 / 0956 0·9 / 1614 2·8 / 2203 1·2
21 Tu 0437 3·2 / 1109 0·5 / 1746 2·8 / 2346 0·9

7 Tu 0423 3·0 / 1059 1·0 / 1715 2·8 / ☾ 2309 1·2
22 W 0543 3·2 / 1217 0·5 / 1850 2·9

8 W 0523 2·9 / 1203 0·9 / 1817 2·8
23 Th 0050 0·9 / 0646 3·2 / 1317 0·5 / 1948 2·9

9 Th 0015 1·2 / 0624 2·9 / 1302 0·8 / 1913 2·8
24 F 0147 0·8 / 0745 3·2 / 1411 0·5 / 2036 3·0

10 F 0117 1·1 / 0721 3·0 / 1354 0·7 / 2006 2·9
25 Sa 0237 0·7 / 0839 3·2 / 1457 0·5 / 2119 3·1

11 Sa 0211 1·0 / 0813 3·1 / 1443 0·6 / 2053 3·1
26 Su 0324 0·6 / 0927 3·3 / 1541 0·6 / 2157 3·2

12 Su 0300 0·8 / 0904 3·2 / 1528 0·5 / 2138 3·2
27 M 0407 0·6 / 1010 3·3 / 1619 0·6 / 2234 3·3

13 M 0348 0·6 / 0953 3·3 / 1743 0·4 / 2221 3·3
28 Tu 0447 0·6 / 1051 3·2 / 1655 0·7 / ○ 2309 3·3

14 Tu 0434 0·5 / 1041 3·4 / 1659 0·4 / ● 2306 3·4
29 W 0523 0·6 / 1129 3·2 / 1729 0·7 / 2343 3·4

15 W 0520 0·4 / 1130 3·4 / 1744 0·4 / 2353 3·5
30 Th 0600 0·6 / 1207 3·2 / 1801 0·8

31 F 0018 3·4 / 0635 0·6 / 1243 3·1 / 1835 0·8

JUNE

1 Sa 0053 3·4 / 0713 0·7 / 1321 3·1 / 1913 0·9
16 Su 0126 3·6 / 0747 0·2 / 1411 3·1 / 2011 0·6

2 Su 0131 3·4 / 0751 0·7 / 1402 3·0 / 1952 0·9
17 M 0219 3·6 / 0840 0·2 / 1508 3·0 / 2107 0·7

3 M 0211 3·3 / 0834 0·7 / 1446 3·0 / 2037 1·0
18 Tu 0314 3·5 / 0938 0·3 / 1609 2·9 / 2206 0·8

4 Tu 0253 3·2 / 0921 0·8 / 1534 2·9 / 2127 1·0
19 W 0412 3·4 / 1037 0·4 / 1711 2·9 / ☽ 2308 0·8

5 W 0339 3·2 / 1012 0·8 / 1624 2·9 / ☾ 2223 1·1
20 Th 0512 3·3 / 1139 0·5 / 1810 2·9

6 Th 0431 3·1 / 1108 0·8 / 1720 2·9 / 2323 1·1
21 F 0011 0·9 / 0614 3·2 / 1239 0·6 / 1906 2·9

7 F 0529 3·1 / 1207 0·8 / 1819 2·9
22 Sa 0112 0·8 / 0713 3·1 / 1335 0·7 / 1958 3·0

8 Sa 0025 1·1 / 0629 3·1 / 1306 0·8 / 1917 3·0
23 Su 0208 0·8 / 0806 3·1 / 1427 0·7 / 2046 3·0

9 Su 0128 1·0 / 0731 3·1 / 1404 0·7 / 2015 3·1
24 M 0300 0·7 / 0901 3·1 / 1515 0·8 / 2129 3·1

10 M 0227 0·9 / 0832 3·2 / 1458 0·6 / 2110 3·1
25 Tu 0348 0·7 / 0949 3·1 / 1557 0·8 / 2210 3·2

11 Tu 0324 0·7 / 0931 3·3 / 1552 0·6 / 2202 3·4
26 W 0430 0·6 / 1031 3·1 / 1635 0·8 / 2248 3·3

12 W 0417 0·6 / 1028 3·3 / 1644 0·5 / ● 2252 3·5
27 Th 0509 0·6 / 1111 3·1 / 1709 0·8 / ○ 2325 3·4

13 Th 0509 0·4 / 1123 3·3 / 1734 0·5 / 2343 3·6
28 F 0546 0·6 / 1147 3·1 / 1743 0·8 / 2358 3·4

14 F 0601 0·3 / 1218 3·3 / 1827 0·5
29 Sa 0619 0·6 / 1222 3·1 / 1815 0·8

15 Sa 0034 3·6 / 0653 0·2 / 1314 3·2 / 1917 0·6
30 Su 0032 3·4 / 0652 0·6 / 1257 3·1 / 1850 0·7

JULY

1 M 0106 3·4 / 0727 0·6 / 1333 3·1 / 1927 0·7
16 Tu 0157 3·7 / 0815 0·2 / 1439 3·1 / 2036 0·6

2 Tu 0141 3·4 / 0805 0·6 / 1412 3·1 / 2008 0·8
17 W 0247 3·6 / 0904 0·3 / 1529 3·0 / 2128 0·7

3 W 0219 3·4 / 0846 0·6 / 1454 3·1 / 2053 0·8
18 Th 0339 3·4 / 0956 0·5 / 1623 2·9 / ☽ 2223 0·8

4 Th 0303 3·3 / 0931 0·6 / 1541 3·0 / 2142 0·9
19 F 0435 3·3 / 1052 0·7 / 1719 2·9 / 2326 0·9

5 F 0350 3·3 / 1023 0·7 / 1633 3·0 / ☾ 2238 1·0
20 Sa 0536 3·1 / 1154 0·8 / 1818 2·9

6 Sa 0445 3·2 / 1120 0·8 / 1732 3·0 / 2343 1·1
21 Su 0032 1·0 / 0638 3·0 / 1257 0·9 / 1916 2·9

7 Su 0550 3·1 / 1225 0·8 / 1838 3·1
22 M 0138 0·9 / 0740 3·0 / 1358 1·0 / 2011 3·0

8 M 0053 1·1 / 0700 3·1 / 1333 0·9 / 1945 3·1
23 Tu 0237 0·9 / 0830 2·9 / 1450 1·0 / 2101 3·1

9 Tu 0204 1·0 / 0813 3·2 / 1437 0·8 / 2049 3·3
24 W 0328 0·8 / 0927 3·0 / 1536 1·0 / 2148 3·2

10 W 0308 0·8 / 0919 3·2 / 1538 0·7 / 2146 3·4
25 Th 0413 0·7 / 1012 3·0 / 1616 0·9 / 2228 3·3

11 Th 0406 0·6 / 1021 3·3 / 1633 0·6 / ● 2240 3·6
26 F 0451 0·6 / 1051 3·0 / 1651 0·8 / ○ 2305 3·3

12 F 0459 0·4 / 1118 3·3 / 1725 0·6 / 2332 3·7
27 Sa 0526 0·6 / 1126 3·1 / 1722 0·7 / 2337 3·4

13 Sa 0550 0·2 / 1211 3·3 / 1812 0·5
28 Su 0557 0·5 / 1158 3·1 / 1753 0·7

14 Su 0021 3·7 / 0639 0·1 / 1302 3·3 / 1900 0·5
29 M 0007 3·4 / 0627 0·5 / 1229 3·1 / 1825 0·6

15 M 0109 3·7 / 0727 0·1 / 1351 3·2 / 1948 0·6
30 Tu 0038 3·4 / 0659 0·4 / 1302 3·2 / 1900 0·6

31 W 0110 3·5 / 0733 0·4 / 1337 3·2 / 1938 0·6

AUGUST

1 Th 0147 3·5 / 0812 0·5 / 1418 3·2 / 2020 0·7
16 F 0301 3·4 / 0910 0·7 / 1529 3·0 / 2135 0·9

2 F 0229 3·4 / 0854 0·6 / 1503 3·2 / 2107 0·8
17 Sa 0355 3·2 / 1000 0·9 / 1623 2·9 / ☽ 2235 1·0

3 Sa 0318 3·3 / 0943 0·7 / 1555 3·1 / ☾ 2202 1·0
18 Su 0455 3·0 / 1101 1·1 / 1726 2·9 / 2350 1·1

4 Su 0414 3·2 / 1042 0·9 / 1657 3·1 / 2309 1·1
19 M 0601 2·9 / 1214 1·2 / 1832 2·9

5 M 0525 3·1 / 1154 1·0 / 1808 3·1
20 Tu 0106 1·1 / 0709 2·8 / 1324 1·2 / 1935 3·0

6 Tu 0029 1·1 / 0645 3·0 / 1314 1·0 / 1924 3·1
21 W 0212 1·0 / 0809 2·8 / 1422 1·1 / 2032 3·1

7 W 0149 1·0 / 0805 3·1 / 1426 1·0 / 2033 3·3
22 Th 0304 0·9 / 0901 2·9 / 1510 1·0 / 2119 3·1

8 Th 0257 0·8 / 0915 3·2 / 1527 0·8 / 2132 3·5
23 F 0348 0·7 / 0946 2·9 / 1550 0·9 / 2202 3·2

9 F 0355 0·5 / 1014 3·3 / 1620 0·7 / 2226 3·6
24 Sa 0426 0·6 / 1026 3·0 / 1624 0·8 / 2237 3·3

10 Sa 0445 0·3 / 1106 3·4 / 1708 0·6 / ● 2315 3·8
25 Su 0458 0·5 / 1059 3·1 / 1657 0·7 / ○ 2309 3·3

11 Su 0532 0·2 / 1154 3·4 / 1753 0·5
26 M 0527 0·5 / 1129 3·1 / 1726 0·6 / 2337 3·4

12 M 0000 3·8 / 0617 0·2 / 1238 3·4 / 1836 0·5
27 Tu 0556 0·4 / 1158 3·2 / 1758 0·6

13 Tu 0045 3·8 / 0659 0·2 / 1319 3·3 / 1919 0·5
28 W 0007 3·4 / 0628 0·4 / 1231 3·3 / 1834 0·5

14 W 0128 3·7 / 0741 0·3 / 1359 3·2 / 2001 0·6
29 Th 0041 3·5 / 0702 0·4 / 1306 3·3 / 1910 0·6

15 Th 0213 3·6 / 0825 0·5 / 1442 3·1 / 2046 0·7
30 F 0119 3·5 / 0740 0·5 / 1345 3·3 / 1952 0·6

31 Sa 0202 3·4 / 0823 0·6 / 1432 3·3 / 2040 0·8

13

Chart Datum: 2.01 metres below Ordnance Datum (Belfast)

IRELAND, EAST COAST – BELFAST

Lat 54°36′ N   Long 5°55′ W

TIMES AND HEIGHTS OF HIGH AND LOW WATERS

YEAR **1991**

TIME ZONE **UT (GMT)**
For Summer Time add ONE hour in non-shaded areas

Chart Datum: 2.01 metres below Ordnance Datum (Belfast)

SEPTEMBER

Day	Time	m	Time	m	Time	m	Time	m
1 Su ☾	0253	3.3	0914	0.8	1525	3.2	2136	0.9
16 M	0414	3.0	1007	1.3	1634	3.0	2304	1.2
2 M	0355	3.1	1016	1.0	1631	3.1	2248	1.1
17 Tu	0522	2.8	1120	1.4	1744	2.9		
3 Tu	0512	3.0	1137	1.2	1750	3.1		
18 W	0028	1.2	0632	2.8	1241	1.4	1853	2.9
4 W	0019	1.1	0642	2.9	1306	1.2	1910	3.1
19 Th	0135	1.1	0735	2.8	1345	1.2	1954	3.0
5 Th	0141	0.9	0804	3.0	1416	1.0	2018	3.3
20 F	0229	0.9	0830	2.9	1434	1.1	2044	3.1
6 F	0246	0.7	0908	3.2	1514	0.9	2115	3.5
21 Sa	0312	0.8	0915	3.0	1515	0.9	2127	3.2
7 Sa	0339	0.5	1002	3.3	1603	0.7	2207	3.7
22 Su	0349	0.6	0953	3.1	1552	0.8	2203	3.2
8 Su ●	0426	0.3	1048	3.4	1647	0.6	2252	3.8
23 M ○	0421	0.5	1027	3.1	1626	0.7	2234	3.3
9 M	0508	0.2	1129	3.4	1729	0.5	2336	3.8
24 Tu	0454	0.5	1058	3.2	1658	0.6	2305	3.4
10 Tu	0549	0.3	1207	3.4	1808	0.5		
25 W	0525	0.4	1129	3.3	1733	0.5	2339	3.5
11 W	0017	3.8	0628	0.3	1242	3.4	1846	0.5
26 Th	0558	0.5	1203	3.4	1808	0.5		
12 Th	0057	3.7	0706	0.5	1319	3.3	1926	0.6
27 F	0015	3.5	0635	0.6	1239	3.4	1849	0.5
13 F	0140	3.6	0745	0.7	1358	3.3	2006	0.8
28 Sa	0057	3.5	0716	0.5	1323	3.4	1933	0.6
14 Sa	0225	3.4	0825	0.9	1442	3.2	2053	0.9
29 Su	0145	3.3	0801	0.7	1412	3.3	2023	0.7
15 Su ☽	0314	3.2	0911	1.1	1532	3.1	2149	1.1
30 M	0240	3.2	0854	0.9	1508	3.2	2125	0.9

OCTOBER

Day	Time	m	Time	m	Time	m	Time	m
1 Tu ☾	0348	3.0	1003	1.1	1619	3.1	2244	1.0
16 W	0438	2.8	1026	1.4	1654	3.0	2334	1.2
2 W	0513	2.9	1133	1.2	1737	3.1		
17 Th	0547	2.8	1142	1.4	1801	3.0		
3 Th	0014	0.9	0643	2.9	1257	1.2	1855	3.2
18 F	0043	1.1	0650	2.8	1252	1.3	1903	3.0
4 F	0130	0.8	0757	3.0	1402	1.0	1959	3.4
19 Sa	0140	1.0	0747	2.9	1347	1.2	1957	3.0
5 Sa	0229	0.6	0856	3.2	1456	0.8	2056	3.5
20 Su	0226	0.8	0833	3.0	1433	1.0	2042	3.1
6 Su	0318	0.5	0943	3.3	1542	0.7	2145	3.7
21 M	0307	0.7	0914	3.1	1515	0.9	2122	3.2
7 M ●	0402	0.4	1026	3.4	1624	0.6	2230	3.7
22 Tu	0343	0.6	0950	3.2	1553	0.7	2159	3.3
8 Tu	0442	0.4	1102	3.4	1704	0.6	2311	3.8
23 W ○	0420	0.5	1026	3.3	1631	0.6	2237	3.4
9 W	0520	0.4	1136	3.5	1742	0.5	2350	3.7
24 Th	0457	0.5	1102	3.4	1711	0.5	2316	3.5
10 Th	0557	0.5	1210	3.5	1818	0.6		
25 F	0534	0.5	1140	3.5	1751	0.5	2358	3.5
11 F	0029	3.6	0634	0.7	1245	3.5	1856	0.7
26 Sa	0615	0.5	1222	3.5	1835	0.5		
12 Sa	0109	3.5	0700	0.6	1323	3.4	1935	0.8
27 Su	0045	3.4	0700	0.6	1309	3.5	1924	0.5
13 Su	0151	3.3	0747	1.0	1405	3.3	2020	0.9
28 M	0137	3.3	0749	0.8	1401	3.4	2019	0.6
14 M	0239	3.1	0830	1.1	1453	3.2	2112	1.1
29 Tu	0237	3.1	0849	1.0	1501	3.3	2124	0.7
15 Tu ☽	0334	2.9	0921	1.3	1549	3.1	2219	1.2
30 W ☾	0349	3.0	1000	1.1	1609	3.2	2241	0.8
31 Th	0512	2.9	1123	1.2	1723	3.2		

NOVEMBER

Day	Time	m	Time	m	Time	m	Time	m
1 F	0000	0.8	0634	2.9	1238	1.1	1835	3.3
16 Sa	0553	2.8	1149	1.3	1801	3.0		
2 Sa	0109	0.8	0740	3.0	1340	1.0	1938	3.4
17 Su	0039	1.0	0650	2.9	1250	1.2	1859	3.1
3 Su	0205	0.6	0834	3.1	1433	0.8	2033	3.5
18 M	0133	0.9	0744	3.0	1347	1.1	1952	3.1
4 M	0254	0.5	0919	3.3	1519	0.7	2122	3.6
19 Tu	0222	0.8	0832	3.1	1437	1.0	2042	3.2
5 Tu	0339	0.5	1000	3.4	1603	0.6	2207	3.6
20 W	0307	0.7	0917	3.3	1524	0.8	2129	3.3
6 W ●	0420	0.5	1037	3.4	1642	0.6	2249	3.6
21 Th ○	0350	0.6	0959	3.4	1610	0.7	2216	3.4
7 Th	0457	0.6	1111	3.5	1720	0.6	2329	3.5
22 F	0434	0.5	1042	3.5	1655	0.6	2304	3.4
8 F	0533	0.7	1146	3.5	1758	0.7		
23 Sa	0519	0.5	1126	3.6	1742	0.5	2351	3.4
9 Sa	0007	3.5	0607	0.8	1221	3.6	1835	0.7
24 Su	0605	0.6	1212	3.6	1831	0.4		
10 Su	0045	3.4	0642	0.9	1257	3.5	1914	0.8
25 M	0042	3.4	0653	0.6	1302	3.6	1921	0.4
11 M	0126	3.2	0719	1.0	1337	3.5	1957	0.9
26 Tu	0137	3.2	0747	0.7	1355	3.6	2018	0.4
12 Tu	0209	3.1	0844	1.1	1420	3.4	2043	1.0
27 W	0237	3.1	0844	0.9	1453	3.5	2118	0.5
13 W	0258	3.0	0846	1.2	1510	3.2	2136	1.0
28 Th ☾	0343	3.0	0949	1.0	1556	3.4	2226	0.6
14 Th	0352	2.9	0941	1.3	1603	3.1	2237	1.1
29 F	0457	2.9	1059	1.0	1702	3.3	2334	0.6
15 F ☾	0451	2.8	1042	1.3	1701	3.1	2340	1.1
30 Sa	0608	2.9	1210	1.0	1810	3.3		

DECEMBER

Day	Time	m	Time	m	Time	m	Time	m
1 Su	0039	0.6	0712	3.0	1312	0.9	1912	3.3
16 M	0551	2.9	1156	1.2	1803	3.1		
2 M	0138	0.6	0806	3.1	1408	0.8	2009	3.4
17 Tu	0039	1.0	0653	3.0	1300	1.2	1907	3.1
3 Tu	0230	0.6	0854	3.2	1458	0.8	2101	3.4
18 W	0140	0.9	0752	3.1	1404	1.1	2009	3.2
4 W	0318	0.7	0936	3.3	1545	0.7	2149	3.4
19 Th	0236	0.8	0847	3.3	1501	0.9	2108	3.3
5 Th	0400	0.7	1016	3.4	1628	0.7	2233	3.4
20 F	0329	0.7	0939	3.4	1555	0.7	2204	3.4
6 F ●	0438	0.8	1052	3.5	1708	0.7	2312	3.4
21 Sa ○	0420	0.6	1030	3.5	1647	0.5	2257	3.4
7 Sa	0515	0.8	1127	3.5	1744	0.7	2350	3.3
22 Su	0511	0.6	1118	3.7	1736	0.4	2349	3.4
8 Su	0549	0.8	1203	3.6	1821	0.7		
23 M	0558	0.5	1207	3.7	1825	0.3		
9 M	0027	3.3	0621	0.9	1238	3.6	1857	0.7
24 Tu	0041	3.4	0648	0.6	1255	3.7	1916	0.2
10 Tu	0103	3.2	0656	0.9	1314	3.5	1934	0.8
25 W	0133	3.3	0738	0.6	1345	3.7	2006	0.2
11 W	0142	3.1	0734	0.9	1352	3.5	2015	0.8
26 Th	0226	3.2	0830	0.7	1439	3.6	2100	0.3
12 Th	0223	3.1	0816	1.0	1433	3.4	2058	0.8
27 F	0324	3.1	0925	0.8	1535	3.5	2157	0.5
13 F	0308	3.0	0903	1.1	1517	3.3	2148	0.9
28 Sa ☾	0426	3.0	1027	0.9	1635	3.4	2259	0.6
14 Sa	0357	3.0	0953	1.1	1607	3.2	2241	0.9
29 Su	0529	2.9	1133	0.9	1739	3.3		
15 Su	0452	2.9	1052	1.2	1702	3.1	2339	1.0
30 M	0004	0.7	0634	2.9	1239	0.9	1843	3.2
31 Tu	0109	0.8	0733	3.0	1342	0.9	1945	3.2

BELFAST LOUGH *continued*

GROOMSPORT (0247) Hr Mr ☎ Bangor 464733, M, Slip, FW; **Cockle Island Boat Club**, Slip, M, FW, L, R. **Murphy's** ☎ 337, Gas. **Town** ✉ (Bangor); Ⓑ (Bangor); ⇌ (Bangor); ✈ (Belfast).

CARRICKFERGUS. (096 03) Easily recognised by conspic castle to E of commercial port. Marina depths 1.9m to 2.4m. **Carrickfergus Marina** (270 + 30 visitors) ☎ 453297, AC, BH (10½ ton), CH, D, El, FW, Sh; **Carrickfergus S.C.** ☎ 51402, M, L, FW, C, AB; **Caters Carrick** ☎ 51919 CH, Gas, Rigging; **W.W. Marine** ☎ 69895 ME, El, Sh; **Belfast Lough Marine Electronics** ☎ 65565, El, Ⓔ; **Town** V, R, Ⓑ; ✉; ⇌; ✈ (Belfast).

LARNE 10-13-11
Antrim

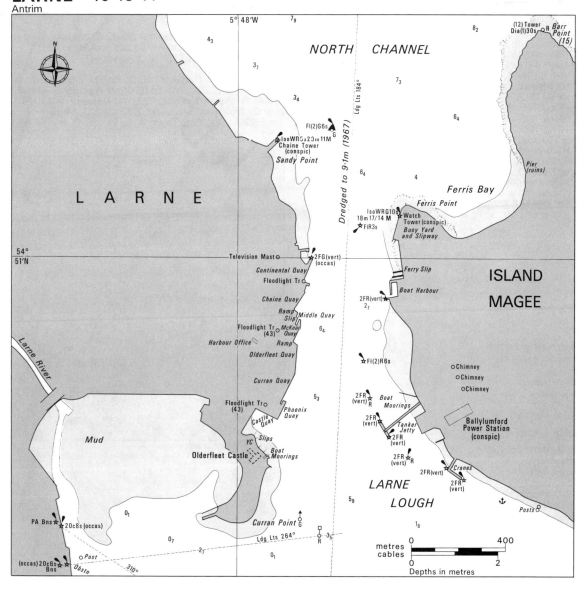

LARNE *continued*

CHARTS
Admiralty 1237; Imray C62, C64; Irish OS 5
TIDES
0000 Dover; ML 1.6; Duration 0620; Zone 0 (GMT).

Standard Port BELFAST (←)

Times				Height (metres)			
HW		LW		MHWS	MHWN	MLWN	MLWS
0100	0700	0000	0600	3.5	3.0	1.1	0.4
1300	1900	1200	1800				

Differences LARNE
+0005 0000 +0010 −0005 −0.7 −0.5 −0.3 0.0
RED BAY
+0022 −0010 +0007 −0017 −1.9 −1.5 −0.8 −0.2

SHELTER
Secure shelter in Larne Lough. Anchorage S of Ballylumford Power Stn. Harbour can be entered day or night in any conditions. W side is commercial until Curran Pt where there are two YCs with moorings.
NAVIGATION
Waypoint 54°51'.70N 05°47'.47W, 004°/184° from/to front Ldg Lt 004°, 2.1M. Beware Hunter Rock 2M NE of harbour entrance. N.B. Abnormal magnetic variation exists near Hunter Rock and between it and the mainland. Larne is a busy commercial port. Tide in the entrance runs at up to 3½ kn. Beyond the narrow entrance, the only recommended channel is close along the E shore.
LIGHTS AND MARKS
Entrance Ldg Lts 184°, Oc 4s, synchronised and vis 179°-189°; W diamonds with R stripes.
RADIO TELEPHONE
VHF Ch 16 14.
TELEPHONE (0574)
Hr Mr 79221; CG 74447; MRSC Donaghadee 883184; Pilot 73785; ⌗ (0232) 249606; Marinecall 0898 500 465; Police 72266; Dr 75331; Ⓗ (Casualty) 75431.
FACILITIES
EC Tuesday; **Pier** ☎ 79221, M, L, FW, C (32 ton); **Larne Harbour** M, L, FW; **E.A. BC** ☎ 77204, Slip, M, L, FW, V, Bar; **A.C. Hutcheson** ☎ 73207, El, Ⓔ; **Alan Lyttle** ☎ 72850, D; **Curran Saw Mills** ☎ 72241, CH; **T. R. Fulton** ☎ 72288, Gas; **Howdens** ☎ 60222, D; **East Antrim YC** ☎ 77204, Slip, M, L, V, FW, Bar; **Rea Bros** Sh; **Old Mill Electrics** ☎ 83201, El; **Town** P and D (delivered), CH, V, R, Bar, ✉; Ⓑ; ⇌; ✈ (Belfast).

AGENTS WANTED
Berwick-on-Tweed
Mallaig
Loch Sunart
Loch Aline
Fishguard
Kenmare River

Large number of French Ports

Rotterdam
Norderney
Dornumersiel
Langeoog
Wangerooge
Hooksiel
Bremerhaven

If you are interested in becoming our agent please write to the Editors and get your free copy annually. You do not have to be a resident in a port to be the agent but at least a fairly regular visitor.

PORTRUSH   10-13-12
Antrim

CHARTS
Admiralty 49, 2499, 2798; Imray C64; Irish OS 2
TIDES
−0410 Dover; ML 1.1; Duration 0610; Zone 0 (GMT).

Tidal figures based on Londonderry (→)

Times		Height (metres)			
HW	LW	MHWS	MHWN	MLWN	MLWS
−0105	−0105	−0.8	−0.6	−0.2	0.0

SHELTER
Anchorage on E side of Ramore Head in Skerries Roads gives good shelter in most conditions, but exposed to sea/swell from N. Harbour is sheltered except in strong NW-N winds.
NAVIGATION
Waypoint 55°13'.00N 06°41'.00W, 308°/128° from/to N Pier Lt, 1.1M. Entrance with on-shore winds over force 4 is difficult. Beware submerged breakwater projecting 20m SW from N pier.
LIGHTS AND MARKS
Ldg Lts 028° (occas, for lifeboat use) both FR 6/8 1M; R triangles on metal Bn and metal mast. N pier Fl R 3s 6m 3M; vis 220°-160°. S pier Fl G 3s 6m 3M; vis 220°-100°. Fixed Bu Lt on CG look-out, Ramore Hd.
RADIO TELEPHONE
VHF Ch 16; 14 (0900-1730 LT, Mon−Fri. Extended evening hours Sat−Sun, June−Sept.)
TELEPHONE (0265)
Hr Mr 822307; CG 823356; MRSC (0247) 883184; ⌗ Coleraine 44803; Marinecall 0898 500 465; Police 822721; Dr 823767; Ⓗ Coleraine 44177.
FACILITIES
EC Wednesday; **Harbour** AB, D, FW, M, Slip; **Portrush YC** ☎ 823932, Bar, FW; **Todd Chart Agency** ☎ 824176, ACA; **S. Stewart** ☎ 822951, El; **A. Doherty** ☎ 824735, Ⓔ; **C. Trolan** ☎ Portstewart 2221, Gas; **J. Mullan** ☎ 822209, Gas, Gaz; **Town** V, R, Bar, ▣, P, ✉; Ⓑ; ⇌; ✈ (Belfast).

⚓ Berth N Quay and ask Hr Mr

RIVER BANN 10-13-13
Londonderry/Antrim

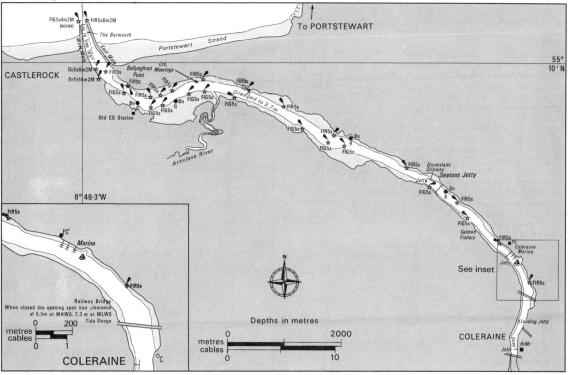

CHARTS
Admiralty 2499, 2723, 2798; Imray C64; Irish OS 2
TIDES
−0345 Dover (Coleraine); ML 1.1; Duration 0540; Zone 0 (GMT).

Tidal figures based on Londonderry (—→)

Times		Height (metres)			
HW	LW	MHWS	MHWN	MLWN	MLWS
−0117	−0050	−0.6	−0.4	−0.3	−0.1

SHELTER
The Mouth, known as The Barmouth, is between two moles, running 2 ca N from the beaches. Once inside shelter is good. Do not attempt entry in strong on-shore winds or when waves breaking across the entrance. If in doubt call Coleraine Harbour Radio (Ch 16, 12) or ring Coleraine 42012. Anchor upstream of old CG Station, or go up to Drumslade Slipway or Coleraine Marina, 3½M & 4½M from entrance on NE bank.
NAVIGATION
Waypoint 55°11′.00N, 06°47′.07W, 022°/202° from/to Barmouth entrance breakwaters, 1M. Approach from E of N to bring Ldg Lts into line at Mole ends. The sand bar is constantly moving but has a dredged depth of approx 3.5m. Beware salmon nets across the width of the river during the salmon fishing season at 2M or 4M from entrance. Also beware commercial traffic.
LIGHTS AND MARKS
Ldg Lts 165°, front Oc 5s 6m 2M on W metal tower; rear Oc 5s 14m 2M.
RADIO TELEPHONE
VHF Ch 12 (Mon-Fri: 0900-1700 LT). Coleraine Marina Ch 80 .
TELEPHONE (0265)
Hr Mr 42012; ⌗ (0232) 752511; CG Portrush 823356; MRSC Donaghadee 883184; Rly Bridge 42403; Marinecall 0898 500 465; Police (Portrush) 44122; Ⓗ 44177; Dr 44831.
FACILITIES
COLERAINE EC Thursday. **Coleraine (Borough Council) Marina** (45 + 15 visitors), ☎ 44768, Slip, D, FW, R, BH (15 ton), AC; **Coleraine Yacht Supplies** ☎ 52525, CH; **Coleraine YC** ☎ 44503, Bar M; **Seaton Sail & Power (Drumslade Slipway)** ☎ 832086, Slip, CH; **Calor Kosangas Gas Centre** ☎ 57057, Gas, Kos; **Alan Doherty** ☎ 824735, Ⓔ. **Coleraine Harbour** ☎ 42012 BH (35 ton) **Town** P, D, V, R, ✉; Ⓑ; ➹; ✈ (Belfast).

LOUGH FOYLE 10-13-14
Londonderry/Donegal

CHARTS
Admiralty 2486, 2499; Imray C64; Irish OS 2
TIDES
Culmore Point −0025 Londonderry
Moville (−0055 Londonderry
(−0300 Dover
(−0400 Belfast
Warren Point −0400 Dover
Londonderry −0300 Dover
ML 1.5; Duration 0615; Zone 0 (GMT)

Standard Port GALWAY (—→)

Times				Height (metres)			
HW		LW		MHWS	MHWN	MLWN	MLWS
0200	0900	0200	0800	5.1	3.9	2.0	0.6
1400	2100	1400	2000				

Differences LONDONDERRY

+0254	+0319	+0322	+0321	−2.4	−1.8	−0.8	−0.1

SHELTER
The SE side of the Lough is low lying and shallow. The NW rises steeply and has a number of village harbours between the entrance and Londonderry (often referred to as Derry).
GREENCASTLE — a busy fishing harbour, safe in NNW to WSW winds. Anchor off or go alongside fishing boats.
MOVILLE — the pier is close to the village and has 1.5m at the end (shops closed all day Wed).

LOUGH FOYLE *continued*

CARRICKARORY — has a good pier/quay, the end 25m of which has a depth of 2m. Good shelter with winds NNW to SW.

CULMORE BAY — Complete shelter (anchor 1½ ca W of Culmore Pt). 4M from Londonderry.

LONDONDERRY — Good shelter — anchor close below Craigavon Bridge Berth on non-commercial quay (down from Guildhall). There is a bridge at Rosses Pt about 2M downstream, clearance 32m.

NAVIGATION

Waypoint Tuns (port-hand) buoy, FIR 3s, 55°04'.01N 06°53'.38W, 055°/235° from/to Warren Point Lt, 2.5M. Outside entrance beware The Tuns which run 3M NE from E side of entrance. The main channel ¾ M wide is the North Channel NW of The Tuns but there is a channel, min depth 4m, 3 ca off shore along NE side of Magilligan Pt. Beware commercial traffic; in June and July the channel is at times obstructed by salmon nets at night. N channel tides reach 3½ kn, and up in the river the ebb runs up to 6 kn.

LIGHTS AND MARKS

Inishowen Fl(2) WRG 10s 28m 18/14M; W Tr, two B bands; vis G197°-211°, W211°-249°, R249°-000°; Horn(2) 30s. Warren Point Fl 1.5s 9m 10M; W Tr, G abutment; vis 232°-061°. Magilligan Point FIR 2s 7m 4M; R structure. The main channel up to Londonderry is very well lit. Foyle Bridge centre FW each side; VQG on W pier; VQR on E pier.

RADIO TELEPHONE

VHF Ch 16; 12 14 (H24). Safety and Distress Ch 16; Information on Shipping movements and navigation Ch 14.

TELEPHONE (0504)

Hr Mr (Berthing Master) 263680; CG Portrush 823356; MRSC Donaghadee 883184; ✆ 261937; Marinecall 0898 500 465; Police 261893; Dr 264868; Ⓗ 45171.

FACILITIES (Londonderry)

EC Thursday; **Harbour Office** ☎ 263680, M, FW, C (10 ton mobile), AB; **8 & 9 Sheds** M, FW, C (2 x 1½ ton elec), AB; **7 Shed** M, FW, AB; **14/15 Berth** M, FW, AB; **Dolphins** M, FW, El, AB; **NR Quay** P, D, ME, El; **Prehen Boat Club** ☎ 43405; **Town** P, D, ME, El, CH, V, R, Bar. ✉; Ⓑ; ⇌; ✈.

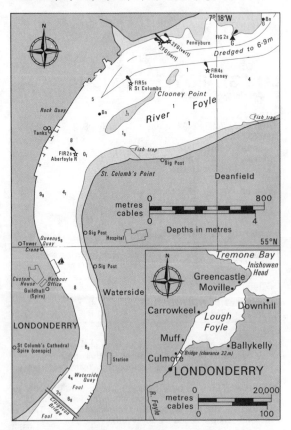

LOUGH SWILLY   10-13-15

Donegal

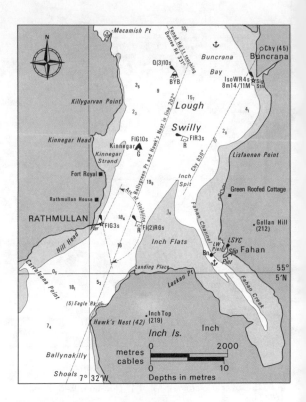

CHARTS

Admiralty 2697; Irish OS 1

TIDES

−0500 Dover; ML 2.5; Duration 0605; Zone 0 (GMT)

Standard Port GALWAY (→)

Times				Height (metres)			
HW		LW		MHWS	MHWN	MLWN	MLWS
0200	0900	0200	0800	5.1	3.9	2.0	0.6
1400	2100	1400	2000				

Differences RATHMULLAN
+0125 +0050 +0126 +0118 −0.8 −0.7 −0.1 −0.1
FANAD HEAD
+0115 +0040 +0125 +0120 −1.1 −0.9 −0.5 −0.1
MULROY BAY BAR
+0108 +0052 +0102 +0118 −1.2 −1.0 No data
SHEEPHAVEN (DOWNIES BAY)
+0057 +0043 +0053 +0107 −1.1 −0.9 No data

SHELTER

Entrance easy in all weathers but swell can render anchorages below Inch Island uncomfortable. Anchorages — Port Salon Bay when wind not in E, but liable to swell (off chartlet to NW); Fahan Creek E of Inch Is entered at HW; W of Macamish Pt sheltered from SE to N through W; Rathmullan Road S of pier off town.

NAVIGATION

Lough Swilly waypoint 55°17'.50N 07°34'.50W, 352°/172° from/to Dunree Head Lt, 5.7M. Six lit lateral buoys and one lit cardinal buoy mark main channel. Beware Swilly More Rks, Kinnegar Spit, Colpagh rks off E shore, Kinnegar Strand, Inch Flats and fish farms.

LIGHTS AND MARKS

Leading lines into Lough Swilly
(1) Fanad Hd Lt touching Dunree Head at 331°.
(2) Ballygreen Pt and Hawk's Nest in line at 202°.

RADIO TELEPHONE

None.

TELEPHONE (074)

Hr Mr 58177; MRSC Limerick 61219; ✆ 21935; Police 58113; Dr 58135.

LOUGH SWILLY *continued*

FACILITIES
RATHMULLAN EC Wednesday; **Pier** AB, AC, C (5 ton),
FW, L, M, Slip; **E. Toomey** ☎ 58125, CH; **Rathmullan
House Hotel** ☎ 58117, M, L, R, Bar; **Fort Royal Hotel**
☎ 58100, M, L, R, Bar; **Town** D and P (cans), Kos, Bar,
R, V, ✉; Ⓑ; ⇌ (bus to Londonderry); ✈ (Londonderry).
RAMELTON **Quay** AB, L; **Town** Bar, P and D (cans), FW,
Kos, R, V, ✉.
FAHAN Slip, FW, L, M (ask YC), R; **Lough Swilly YC**
☎ Fahan 6 01 89, Bar; **Bradley's Garage** (1M SE), Kos,
V, P and D (cans).

KILLYBEGS   10-13-16
Donegal

CHARTS
Admiralty 2702, 2792; Irish OS 3
TIDES
−0520 Dover; ML 2.2; Duration 0620; Zone 0 (GMT).

Standard Port GALWAY (→)

Times				Height (metres)			
HW		LW		MHWS	MHWN	MLWN	MLWS
0600	1100	0000	0700	5.1	3.9	2.0	0.6
1800	2300	1200	1900				

Differences KILLYBEGS
+0040 +0050 +0055 +0035 −1.0   −0.9   −0.5   0.0
BURTONPORT
+0042 +0055 +0115 +0055 −1.2   −1.0   −0.6   −0.1
DONEGAL HARBOUR (SALTHILL QUAY)
+0038 +0050 +0052 +0104 −1.2   −0.9   No data
MULLAGHMORE
+0036 +0048 +0047 +0059 −1.4   −1.0   −0.4   −0.2

⚓ See Hr Mr on Fish Quay

SHELTER
A secure harbour although SSW winds cause a little
swell. Accessible in all weathers day and night.
NAVIGATION
Waypoint 54°36'.00N 08°27'.00W, 202°/022° from/to
Rotten Island Lt, 0.94M. Beware of Fintragh. Note that
Manister Rock is covered at HW and dries at LW.
LIGHTS AND MARKS
Keep mid channel until off Rough Pt then follow the
leading lights into harbour by Fish Quay. Ldg Lts 338°,
both Oc R 8s.
RADIO TELEPHONE
VHF Ch 16.
TELEPHONE (073)
Hr Mr 31032; MRCC Limerick 61219; ♯ 31070;
Police 31002; Dr 31181 (Home) 31148 (Surgery).
FACILITIES
EC Wednesday; **Landing Pier** ☎ 31032, Slip, M, D, P,
FW, L, ME, El, CH, AB, V, R, Bar; **Berthing Quay** Slip,
M, D, AB; **Mooney Boats** ☎ 31152, Sh, C (12 ton), ME,
El, Sh; **Gallaher Bros** ☎ 31004, Kos; **Barry Electronics**
☎ 31215, Ⓔ.
Town ✉; Ⓑ; ⇌ (bus to Sligo); ✈ (Strandhill).

SLIGO   10-13-17
Sligo

CHARTS
Admiralty 2852, 2767; Irish OS 7
TIDES
−0511 Dover; ML 2.3; Duration 0620; Zone 0 (GMT).

Standard Port GALWAY (→)

Times				Height (metres)			
HW		LW		MHWS	MHWN	MLWN	MLWS
0600	1100	0000	0700	5.1	3.9	2.0	0.6
1800	2300	1200	1900				

Differences SLIGO HARBOUR (Oyster Is)
+0043 +0055 +0042 +0054 −1.0   −0.9   −0.5   −0.1
KILLALA BAY (INISHCRONE)
+0035 +0055 +0030 +0050 −1.3   −1.2   −0.7   −0.2
BROADHAVEN
+0040 +0050 +0040 +0050 −1.4   −1.1   −0.4   −0.1
BLACKSOD QUAY
+0025 +0035 +0040 +0040 −1.2   −1.0   −0.6   −0.2
BLACKSOD BAY (BULL'S MOUTH)
+0101 +0057 +0109 +0105 −1.5   −1.0   −0.6   −0.1

SHELTER
The lower harbour is fairly exposed but Sligo town is 5M
from open sea and gives good shelter.
NAVIGATION
Waypoint 54°18'.62N 08°39'.00W, 248°/068° from/to
Cullaun Bwee Lt, 3.0M. The passage between Oyster
Island and Coney Island is marked 'Dangerous'. Pass N of
Oyster Is leaving Blennick Rks to Port. Passage up to
Sligo town between training walls. Some perches are in
bad repair. Pilots at Raghley Head and Rosses Pt. Channel
up to quays dredged to 2.4m.
LIGHTS AND MARKS
Ldg Lts into harbour 125°, lead to Metal Man Rocks.
Channel lights up the harbour are under repair.
RADIO TELEPHONE
Pilots VHF Ch 16; 14.
TELEPHONE (071)
Harbour Office 61197; MRCC Limerick 61219; ♯ 61064;
Police 42031; Dr 42886.
FACILITIES
EC Monday, all day; **Deepwater Pier** P and D (in cans),
L, FW, ME, El, Sh, C (15 ton), CH, AB; **Ballast Quay**
☎ 61197, M, L, FW, ME, El, C, CH, AB; **Rodney Lomax**
☎ 66124, Slip, ME, El, Sh; **Sligo YC** ☎ 77168, M, FW,
Bar, Slip; **Sligo Bedding Centre** ☎ 2303, Kos.
Town V, R, Bar. ✉; Ⓑ; ⇌; ✈ (Strandhill).

13

SLIGO HARBOUR *continued*

WESTPORT (CLEW BAY)
Mayo

10-13-18

CHARTS
Admiralty 2057; Irish OS 10 and 11
TIDES
−0545 Dover; ML 2.5; Duration 0610; Zone 0 (GMT)

Standard Port GALWAY (→)

Times				Height (metres)			
HW		LW		MHWS	MHWN	MLWN	MLWS
0600	1100	0000	0700	5.1	3.9	2.0	0.6
1800	2300	1200	1900				

Differences INISHRAHER							
+0030	+0012	+0058	+0026	−0.6	−0.5	−0.3	−0.1
CLARE ISLAND							
+0019	+0013	+0029	+0023	−1.0	−0.7	−0.4	−0.1
KILLARY HARBOUR							
+0021	+0015	+0035	+0029	−1.0	−0.8	−0.4	−0.1
CLIFDEN BAY							
+0005	+0005	+0016	+0016	−0.7	−0.5		No data

SHELTER
Westport Bay affords secure anchorage amongst the islands and is available at all states of tide.

NAVIGATION
Waypoint 53°49′.20N 09°42′.10W, 251°/071° from/to Inishgort Lt Ho, 1.2M. Pilot for Westport lives on Inishlyre. Beware of the Spit and Mondelly (or Monkelly) Rks which are unmarked.
LIGHTS AND MARKS
Westport Bay entrance — Inishgort Lt L Fl 10s 11m 10M. North of hotel ruins in line with South of Lt Bn (Fl 3s) at 080°. Passage from Westport Bay to Westport, 5 miles, is marked by Bns.
RADIO TELEPHONE
None.
TELEPHONE (098)
MRCC (061) 61219; ⌗ 25230; Police 25555; Ⓗ (094) 21733
FACILITIES
EC Wednesday; **Quays** M, L, AB, V, R, Bar; **M O'Grady** ☎ 25072, Kos. **T.P. Lynn** ☎ 25230 El, Ⓔ; **Mayo SC** ☎ 26260 L, C (3 ton), Bar; **Town** ✉, Ⓑ; ⇌; ✈ (Enniskillen or Knock).
Note: — Between Westport and Galway, repair facilities at **Aster Boats**, Drimagh Harbour, Errislannan ☎ Clifden (095) 21323. See 10.13.20.

GALWAY BAY   10-13-19
Galway

CHARTS
Admiralty 2173, 3339, 1984, 1903; Irish OS 14
TIDES
−0605 Dover; ML 2.9; Duration 0620; Zone 0 (GMT).

Standard Port GALWAY (—→)

Times				Height (metres)			
HW		LW		MHWS	MHWN	MLWN	MLWS
0600	1100	0000	0700	5.1	3.9	2.0	0.6
1800	2300	1200	1900				

Differences KILKIERAN COVE

0005	+0005	+0016	+0016	−0.3	−0.2	−0.1	0.0

INISHBOFIN HARBOUR

+0013	+0009	+0021	+0017	−1.0	−0.8	−0.4	−0.1

KILLEANY BAY (Aran Islands)

−0008	−0008	+0003	+0003	−0.4	−0.3	−0.2	−0.1

LISCANNOR

−0003	−0007	+0006	+0002	−0.4	−0.3	No data	

NOTE: Galway is a Standard Port and tidal information for each day of the year are given below.

SHELTER
Galway Bay is sheltered from large swells by Aran Islands, but seas get up in the 20M from Aran Is to Galway. There are numerous anchorages in Galway Bay, but the principal ones are:
KIGGAUL BAY. Easy entrance, day or night, anchor close to Lt (Fl 3s WR 5/3M) to W or NW. Depth 3 to 4m; exposed to S and SE winds.
GREATMAN BAY. Beware English Rk (dries 1.2m), Keeraun Shoal (breaks in heavy weather), Arkeena Rk, Trabaan Rk, Rin Rks and Chapel Rks. Anchor off Natawny Quay or go alongside at Maumeen Quay.
CASHLA BAY. Easiest harbour on this coast; enter in any weather. Anchor off Clashnacally pier.
There is no safe harbour from Cashla to Galway (20M).
GALWAY HARBOUR gives very good protection, being sheltered from SW by Mutton Is. Dock gates open HW−2 to HW. Enter inner dock and secure in SW corner of basin. New Harbour (home of Galway Bay SC) is nearest safe anchorage to Galway.
CREEKS E of Black Head have rocks and shallows but give excellent shelter. Ballyvaghan Bay, Aughinish Bay, South Bay, and Kinvarra Bay are the main ones.
MUTTON ISLAND. (52°48'.6N, 09° 31'.5W) Anchorage about 1 to 1½ ca off SE end of Is, called Tobacco Cove, in approx 3m, sheltered except from S.
ARAN ISLANDS. The only reasonable shelter is in Killeany Bay in Inishmore. Anchor S of Kilronan pier. Alternatively, anchor off Trawmore Strand or in good weather at Portmurvy.

NAVIGATION
Galway Waypoint 53°14'.80N 09°03'.40W, 241°/061° from/to Leverets Lt, 1.1M.
Approaches:
North Sound between Inishmore and mainland, 4½M wide, is easiest but beware Brocklinmore Bank in heavy weather.
Gregory Sound between Inishmore and Inishmaan, is free of dangers but give Straw Is a berth of 2 to 3 ca.
Foul Sound between Inishmaan and Inisheer; only danger is Pipe Rk (dries) at end of reef extending 3 ca from NW end of Inisheer.
South Sound between Inisheer and mainland. Only danger Finnis Rk (dries 0.4m) 4½ ca SE of E point of Inisheer (marked by E cardinal Lt buoy Q(3) 10s). Approaching from S, beware Kilstiffin Rks off Liscannor Bay.
In Galway it is dangerous to lie in the 'Layby' (a dredged cut E of pier extending from dock gates) when wind is S or SE. When wind is strong from these points, seas sweep round the pierhead.
LIGHTS AND MARKS
Kiggaul Bay Lt Fl.WR 3s 5/3M.
Cashla Bay Killeen Pt Fl(3) WR 10s 6/3M; Lion Pt Dir (010°) Iso WRG 4s 8/6M.
Galway Leverets Q WRG 9m 10M; B Tr W bands; vis G015°-058°, W058°-065°, R065°-103°, G103°-143°, W143°-146°, R146°-015°. Ldg Lts 325° Front Fl R 1.5s, Rear Oc R 10s; both R diamonds with Y diagonal stripes on masts vis 315°-345°.
Black Head Lt Fl WR 5s 20m 11/8M, R sector covering Illanloo Rk (268°-293°).
Aran Islands Inishmore Rock Is Fl 15s 35m 23M
Straw Is Fl(2) 5s 11m 17M
Inisheer Iso WR 20s 34m 20/16M (R sector covers Finnis Rk) R269°-245°, W245°-231°, obsc 231°-115°, W115°-269°.

RADIO TELEPHONE
Call *Harbour Master Galway* VHF Ch 16; 12 (HW−2½ to HW+1).
TELEPHONE (091)
Hr Mr 61874; Coast Life-Saving Service (099) 61107; MRCC Limerick (061) 61219; Harbour Office 61874; ⌗ 62539; Police 63161; Dr 62453.

13

GALWAY BAY *continued*

FACILITIES
GALWAY EC Monday; **Dock** L, FW, El, ME, C (35 ton), CH, AB (see Hr Mr), V, R, Bar; **Galway YC** Slip, M, L, FW, C, CH, Bar; **Galway Maritime Services** ☎ 66568, CH, ACA; **Galway Bay SC** ☎ 94527, M, CH, Bar; **Town** Slip, P, D, L, FW, ME, El, C, V, R, Bar, ⊠; Ⓑ; ⇌; ✈.
KIGGAUL BAY Bar (no phone), shop at Lettermullen (1M).
GREATMAN BAY Maumeen V, P (1M), Bar.
CASHLA BAY No facilities. **Carraroe** (1M) Shop, Hotel, phone; **Costelloe** (1½M), Hotel, ⊠, Garage.
KILRONAN V, D, FW, Good shelter but very crowded with fishing boats ⊠, Ferry to Galway; ✈ to Galway from airstrip on beach.

GALWAY

MEAN SPRING
AND NEAP CURVES

MEAN RANGES	
Springs	4·5m
Neaps	1·9m

Springs occur 1 day
after
New and Full Moon.

IRELAND, WEST COAST – GALWAY

Lat 53°16′ N   Long 9°03′ W

TIMES AND HEIGHTS OF HIGH AND LOW WATERS

YEAR **1991**

TIME ZONE UT(GMT)
For Summer Time add ONE hour in non-shaded areas

JANUARY

Day	Time	m	Time	m	Time	m	Time	m
1 Tu	0457	5.4	1111	0.5	1727	5.3	2323	0.8
16 W	0522	4.8	1132	1.0	1750	4.6	2342	1.2
2 W	0544	5.5	1157	0.4	1817	5.3		
17 Th	0556	4.9	1204	0.9	1822	4.7		
3 Th	0010	0.8	0632	5.5	1243	0.5	1904	5.2
18 F	0014	1.1	0629	4.9	1235	0.8	1855	4.7
4 F	0055	0.9	0720	5.4	1330	0.6	1951	5.0
19 Sa	0046	1.1	0704	4.9	1307	0.8	1928	4.7
5 Sa	0140	1.1	0806	5.1	1415	0.9	2037	4.8
20 Su	0120	1.1	0740	4.9	1342	0.9	2004	4.6
6 Su	0226	1.3	0853	4.8	1503	1.2	2125	4.5
21 M	0157	1.2	0818	4.8	1419	1.0	2042	4.5
7 M ☾	0315	1.6	0943	4.5	1553	1.6	2217	4.2
22 Tu	0237	1.4	0858	4.6	1501	1.2	2125	4.4
8 Tu	0410	1.9	1038	4.2	1652	1.8	2318	4.0
23 W ☽	0324	1.6	0948	4.4	1552	1.5	2217	4.2
9 W	0518	2.1	1147	3.9	1801	2.1		
24 Th ☽	0423	1.8	1048	4.2	1655	1.7	2325	4.1
10 Th	0028	4.0	0638	2.2	1306	3.8	1914	2.1
25 F	0542	1.9	1205	4.1	1815	1.8		
11 F	0138	4.0	0752	2.1	1416	3.9	2018	2.1
26 Sa	0046	4.1	0710	1.8	1330	4.1	1938	1.7
12 Sa	0236	4.1	0851	1.9	1512	4.0	2110	1.9
27 Su	0204	4.3	0826	1.5	1442	4.4	2047	1.5
13 Su	0325	4.3	0939	1.7	1559	4.2	2155	1.7
28 M	0307	4.6	0927	1.1	1542	4.7	2142	1.1
14 M	0407	4.5	1021	1.4	1638	4.4	2233	1.5
29 Tu	0402	5.0	1017	0.7	1633	5.0	2230	0.8
15 Tu ●	0445	4.7	1058	1.2	1715	4.5	2308	1.3
30 W ○	0449	5.3	1102	0.4	1719	5.2	2313	0.6
31 Th	0534	5.4	1144	0.2	1803	5.2	2354	0.5

FEBRUARY

Day	Time	m	Time	m	Time	m	Time	m
1 F	0618	5.5	1225	0.2	1845	5.2		
16 Sa	0607	5.0	1210	0.5	1829	4.9		
2 Sa	0035	0.5	0659	5.4	1304	0.4	1926	5.0
17 Su	0021	0.6	0641	5.1	1241	0.5	1902	4.9
3 Su	0114	0.7	0741	5.1	1344	0.7	2006	4.8
18 M	0055	0.6	0714	5.0	1313	0.5	1935	4.8
4 M	0155	1.0	0822	4.8	1425	1.0	2047	4.5
19 Tu	0130	0.7	0752	4.9	1349	0.7	2012	4.7
5 Tu	0237	1.3	0905	4.4	1507	1.4	2131	4.2
20 W	0209	1.0	0834	4.7	1430	1.1	2054	4.5
6 W ☾	0324	1.7	0952	4.1	1556	1.8	2221	3.9
21 Th ☽	0254	1.3	0922	4.4	1519	1.4	2145	4.2
7 Th	0421	2.0	1051	3.7	1701	2.2	2327	3.7
22 F	0353	1.6	1023	4.1	1624	1.8	2254	3.9
8 F	0543	2.2	1217	3.5	1834	2.3		
23 Sa	0518	1.8	1147	3.9	1757	2.0		
9 Sa	0053	3.7	0726	2.2	1355	3.6	2001	2.2
24 Su	0027	3.9	0704	1.7	1324	3.9	1937	1.8
10 Su	0213	3.8	0839	2.0	1503	3.8	2101	2.0
25 M	0158	4.1	0826	1.4	1442	4.2	2046	1.5
11 M	0311	4.0	0929	1.7	1549	4.0	2143	1.7
26 Tu	0303	4.5	0921	0.9	1536	4.6	2135	1.1
12 Tu	0353	4.3	1007	1.3	1626	4.2	2220	1.4
27 W	0352	4.8	1006	0.5	1621	4.9	2217	0.7
13 W	0430	4.5	1040	1.0	1658	4.5	2251	1.1
28 Th ○	0435	5.1	1045	0.3	1702	5.1	2255	0.4
14 Th ●	0504	4.7	1111	0.8	1729	4.6	2320	0.9
15 F	0534	4.9	1139	0.6	1758	4.8	2350	0.7

MARCH

Day	Time	m	Time	m	Time	m	Time	m
1 F	0516	5.3	1123	0.1	1742	5.2	2333	0.3
16 Sa ●	0506	4.9	1108	0.4	1727	4.9	2322	0.4
2 Sa	0556	5.3	1200	0.1	1819	5.1		
17 Su	0539	5.1	1139	0.3	1758	5.0	2354	0.3
3 Su	0011	0.3	0635	5.2	1236	0.3	1857	5.0
18 M	0614	5.1	1211	0.3	1832	5.0		
4 M	0048	0.5	0713	5.0	1313	0.6	1934	4.8
19 Tu	0029	0.3	0650	5.1	1246	0.4	1909	5.0
5 Tu	0126	0.8	0752	4.7	1349	1.0	2012	4.5
20 W	0106	0.5	0731	5.0	1324	0.7	1948	4.8
6 W	0204	1.1	0832	4.3	1426	1.4	2051	4.2
21 Th	0148	0.8	0815	4.7	1408	1.1	2033	4.5
7 Th	0246	1.5	0912	4.0	1510	1.8	2135	3.9
22 F	0237	1.1	0907	4.3	1500	1.5	2127	4.2
8 F ☾	0335	1.9	1003	3.6	1606	2.2	2231	3.6
23 Sa ☽	0341	1.5	1012	4.0	1610	1.9	2240	3.9
9 Sa	0449	2.2	1120	3.4	1744	2.4	2357	3.5
24 Su	0512	1.7	1142	3.8	1753	2.0		
10 Su	0645	2.2	1323	3.4	1934	2.3		
25 M	0017	3.8	0700	1.6	1321	3.9	1931	1.8
11 M	0140	3.6	0811	2.0	1439	3.6	2036	2.0
26 Tu	0148	4.1	0812	1.3	1430	4.2	2032	1.4
12 Tu	0243	3.8	0901	1.6	1524	3.9	2118	1.6
27 W	0247	4.4	0903	0.9	1519	4.5	2117	1.1
13 W	0327	4.1	0938	1.3	1559	4.2	2152	1.3
28 Th	0334	4.7	0943	0.6	1600	4.8	2156	0.7
14 Th	0402	4.4	1009	0.9	1630	4.4	2223	0.9
29 F	0414	4.9	1021	0.4	1638	5.0	2233	0.5
15 F	0434	4.7	1038	0.6	1658	4.7	2252	0.7
30 Sa ○	0454	5.1	1057	0.3	1716	5.0	2309	0.4
31 Su	0532	5.1	1132	0.3	1753	5.1	2346	0.4

APRIL

Day	Time	m	Time	m	Time	m	Time	m
1 M	0610	5.0	1207	0.5	1828	5.0		
16 Tu	0549	5.2	1144	0.4	1807	5.1		
2 Tu	0022	0.6	0646	4.8	1242	0.8	1904	4.8
17 W	0007	0.3	0629	5.1	1224	0.5	1846	5.1
3 W	0059	0.8	0724	4.6	1317	1.1	1941	4.6
18 Th	0049	0.5	0714	5.0	1306	0.8	1931	4.9
4 Th	0135	1.1	0802	4.3	1354	1.5	2018	4.3
19 F	0135	0.7	0804	4.7	1354	1.2	2020	4.6
5 F	0216	1.5	0843	4.0	1433	1.8	2058	4.0
20 Sa	0230	1.1	0900	4.4	1451	1.6	2118	4.3
6 Sa	0304	1.8	0929	3.7	1525	2.1	2150	3.7
21 Su ☽	0339	1.4	1007	4.1	1604	1.9	2231	4.0
7 Su ☾	0410	2.0	1034	3.4	1651	2.3	2302	3.5
22 M	0506	1.6	1130	3.9	1739	1.9		
8 M	0547	2.1	1219	3.4	1841	2.3		
23 Tu	0000	4.0	0630	1.5	1259	4.0	1904	1.8
9 Tu	0039	3.5	0716	1.9	1349	3.6	1949	2.0
24 W	0123	4.1	0742	1.3	1405	4.2	2004	1.5
10 W	0154	3.7	0812	1.6	1442	3.8	2036	1.7
25 Th	0222	4.3	0833	1.1	1453	4.5	2050	1.2
11 Th	0242	4.0	0853	1.3	1518	4.1	2112	1.3
26 F	0308	4.5	0914	0.9	1534	4.7	2131	1.0
12 F	0321	4.3	0928	1.0	1550	4.4	2146	1.0
27 Sa	0349	4.7	0952	0.8	1612	4.8	2209	0.8
13 Sa	0356	4.6	1000	0.7	1621	4.7	2219	0.7
28 Su ○	0428	4.8	1028	0.7	1649	4.9	2245	0.7
14 Su ●	0433	4.9	1034	0.5	1654	4.9	2252	0.4
29 M	0508	4.8	1105	0.7	1726	4.9	2323	0.7
15 M	0509	5.1	1108	0.3	1729	5.1	2329	0.3
30 Tu	0546	4.7	1140	0.9	1801	4.9		

Chart Datum: 0.20 metres above Ordnance Datum (Dublin)

13

IRELAND, WEST COAST – GALWAY

Lat 53°16′ N   Long 9°03′ W

TIMES AND HEIGHTS OF HIGH AND LOW WATERS

YEAR **1991**

TIME ZONE **UT(GMT)**
For Summer Time add ONE hour in non-shaded areas

MAY

Day	Time	m	Day	Time	m
1 W	0000	0.8	16 Th	0615	5.1
	0624	4.6		1208	0.7
	1215	1.1		1831	5.2
	1838	4.8			
2 Th	0038	1.0	17 F	0039	0.5
	0702	4.4		0704	5.0
	1252	1.3		1255	0.9
	1914	4.6		1920	5.0
3 F	0116	1.2	18 Sa	0130	0.7
	0740	4.2		0757	4.8
	1328	1.6		1347	1.2
	1952	4.4		2013	4.8
4 Sa	0157	1.4	19 Su	0227	1.0
	0820	4.0		0853	4.5
	1411	1.8		1444	1.5
	2033	4.1		2111	4.5
5 Su	0243	1.7	20 M	0331	1.2
	0905	3.8		0955	4.3
	1501	2.0		1550	1.7
	2121	3.9		2216	4.3
6 M	0339	1.8	21 Tu	0441	1.4
	1002	3.6		1105	4.1
	1607	2.2		1706	1.8
	2219	3.8		2329	4.1
7 Tu	0448	1.9	22 W	0556	1.5
	1112	3.6		1219	4.1
	1727	2.2		1824	1.8
	2329	3.7			
8 W	0603	1.8	23 Th	0045	4.1
	1235	3.6		0702	1.4
	1843	2.1		1327	4.2
				1928	1.6
9 Th	0043	3.8	24 F	0148	4.2
	0706	1.6		0757	1.4
	1338	3.8		1419	4.3
	1940	1.8		2020	1.5
10 F	0144	4.0	25 Sa	0240	4.3
	0758	1.4		0843	1.3
	1426	4.1		1504	4.5
	2026	1.5		2105	1.3
11 Sa	0233	4.3	26 Su	0325	4.4
	0840	1.1		0925	1.2
	1505	4.4		1545	4.6
	2107	1.1		2146	1.1
12 Su	0317	4.6	27 M	0407	4.5
	0921	0.9		1004	1.2
	1543	4.7		1624	4.7
	2146	0.8		2227	1.0
13 M	0400	4.8	28 Tu	0448	4.5
	1000	0.7		1042	1.2
	1623	5.0		1702	4.8
	2226	0.6		2306	1.0
14 Tu	0444	5.0	29 W	0527	4.5
	1041	0.6		1120	1.2
	1702	5.1		1740	4.8
	2308	0.4		2344	1.0
15 W	0527	5.1	30 Th	0607	4.5
	1123	0.6		1157	1.3
	1746	5.2		1817	4.7
	2353	0.4			
			31 F	0022	1.0
				0645	4.4
				1235	1.4
				1855	4.6

JUNE

Day	Time	m	Day	Time	m
1 Sa	0102	1.2	16 Su	0123	0.5
	0724	4.3		0747	4.9
	1313	1.5		1337	1.0
	1933	4.5		2002	5.0
2 Su	0141	1.3	17 M	0215	0.7
	0804	4.2		0839	4.7
	1354	1.6		1429	1.2
	2013	4.3		2054	4.8
3 M	0223	1.4	18 Tu	0308	1.0
	0844	4.0		0932	4.5
	1437	1.8		1524	1.4
	2056	4.2		2150	4.5
4 Tu	0308	1.5	19 W	0406	1.2
	0931	3.9		1030	4.3
	1528	1.9		1626	1.7
	2142	4.0		2251	4.2
5 W	0359	1.6	20 Th	0509	1.5
	1021	3.8		1134	4.1
	1626	2.0		1736	1.8
	2237	3.9			
6 Th	0457	1.6	21 F	0001	4.0
	1122	3.8		0615	1.6
	1732	2.0		1242	4.1
	2339	3.9		1848	1.8
7 F	0558	1.6	22 Sa	0112	4.0
	1228	3.9		0719	1.7
	1838	1.8		1344	4.1
				1951	1.7
8 Sa	0046	4.0	23 Su	0213	4.0
	0700	1.5		0815	1.7
	1330	4.1		1436	4.2
	1937	1.6		2044	1.6
9 Su	0148	4.2	24 M	0305	4.1
	0755	1.3		0903	1.6
	1422	4.3		1522	4.4
	2030	1.3		2132	1.4
10 M	0243	4.4	25 Tu	0352	4.2
	0847	1.1		0948	1.5
	1510	4.6		1604	4.5
	2119	1.0		2214	1.2
11 Tu	0335	4.7	26 W	0435	4.3
	0935	0.9		1028	1.4
	1556	4.9		1645	4.6
	2207	0.7		2255	1.1
12 W	0424	4.9	27 Th	0515	4.3
	1023	0.8		1108	1.3
	1644	5.1		1723	4.7
	2255	0.5		2333	1.0
13 Th	0515	5.0	28 F	0554	4.4
	1111	0.7		1144	1.3
	1732	5.2		1801	4.7
	2344	0.4			
14 F	0604	5.1	29 Sa	0010	1.0
	1158	0.7		0631	4.4
	1821	5.3		1221	1.2
				1838	4.7
15 Sa	0034	0.4	30 Su	0046	1.0
	0656	5.0		0707	4.4
	1246	0.8		1256	1.3
	1912	5.2		1914	4.6

JULY

Day	Time	m	Day	Time	m
1 M	0121	1.0	16 Tu	0151	0.5
	0742	4.3		0815	4.8
	1333	1.3		1404	0.9
	1951	4.5		2030	4.5
2 Tu	0157	1.1	17 W	0237	0.8
	0819	4.3		0901	4.6
	1411	1.4		1451	1.2
	2027	4.4		2119	4.5
3 W	0234	1.2	18 Th	0327	1.2
	0857	4.2		0952	4.3
	1451	1.6		1545	1.5
	2108	4.3		2213	4.2
4 Th	0317	1.3	19 F	0421	1.5
	0941	4.1		1048	4.1
	1538	1.7		1648	1.8
	2155	4.1		2316	3.9
5 F	0404	1.4	20 Sa	0527	1.8
	1030	4.0		1156	3.9
	1634	1.8		1807	1.9
	2251	4.0			
6 Sa	0502	1.5	21 Su	0035	3.7
	1130	4.0		0643	2.0
	1743	1.8		1309	3.9
				1928	1.9
7 Su	0000	4.0	22 M	0152	3.7
	0610	1.6		0754	1.9
	1241	4.0		1412	4.0
	1857	1.7		2033	1.7
8 M	0113	4.1	23 Tu	0254	3.8
	0720	1.5		0851	1.8
	1348	4.2		1505	4.1
	2005	1.4		2124	1.5
9 Tu	0219	4.3	24 W	0343	4.0
	0823	1.3		0938	1.6
	1447	4.5		1550	4.3
	2104	1.1		2206	1.3
10 W	0319	4.5	25 Th	0424	4.2
	0921	1.1		1019	1.4
	1541	4.8		1631	4.5
	2157	0.7		2244	1.1
11 Th	0414	4.8	26 F	0502	4.3
	1013	0.8		1054	1.2
	1633	5.1		1708	4.6
	2248	0.4		2318	0.9
12 F	0505	5.0	27 Sa	0537	4.4
	1101	0.6		1129	1.1
	1722	5.3		1743	4.7
	2336	0.2		2351	0.8
13 Sa	0554	5.1	28 Su	0611	4.5
	1147	0.5		1200	1.0
	1810	5.4		1817	4.8
14 Su	0021	0.1	29 M	0022	0.7
	0642	5.1		0643	4.5
	1232	0.5		1232	0.9
	1856	5.3		1850	4.8
15 M	0106	0.2	30 Tu	0053	0.7
	0728	5.0		0714	4.5
	1317	0.7		1304	1.0
	1944	5.2		1924	4.7
			31 W	0126	0.8
				0748	4.5
				1338	1.1
				1959	4.6

AUGUST

Day	Time	m	Day	Time	m
1 Th	0159	0.9	16 F	0247	1.2
	0823	4.4		0914	4.3
	1416	1.2		1505	1.5
	2037	4.5		2135	4.1
2 F	0237	1.1	17 Sa	0336	1.7
	0903	4.3		1004	4.0
	1458	1.4		1604	1.9
	2121	4.3		2234	3.7
3 Sa	0322	1.3	18 Su	0441	2.0
	0949	4.1		1109	3.8
	1552	1.6		1727	2.1
	2216	4.1		2357	3.5
4 Su	0420	1.6	19 M	0612	2.2
	1049	4.0		1232	3.7
	1704	1.8		1909	2.1
	2326	3.9			
5 M	0534	1.7	20 Tu	0135	3.5
	1205	3.9		0740	2.1
	1832	1.8		1352	3.8
				2020	1.9
6 Tu	0052	3.9	21 W	0243	3.7
	0700	1.7		0839	1.9
	1327	4.1		1450	4.0
	1955	1.5		2110	1.6
7 W	0209	4.1	22 Th	0329	4.0
	0815	1.5		0922	1.6
	1436	4.4		1534	4.3
	2058	1.1		2149	1.3
8 Th	0312	4.5	23 F	0407	4.2
	0914	1.1		1000	1.4
	1532	4.8		1612	4.5
	2152	0.6		2223	1.0
9 F	0406	4.8	24 Sa	0441	4.4
	1003	0.8		1033	1.1
	1621	5.1		1645	4.7
	2237	0.3		2254	0.8
10 Sa	0454	5.0	25 Su	0512	4.5
	1048	0.5		1104	0.9
	1708	5.4		1718	4.8
	2320	0.0		2322	0.6
11 Su	0537	5.2	26 M	0543	4.7
	1130	0.3		1133	0.8
	1751	5.5		1749	4.9
				2351	0.5
12 M	0001	0.0	27 Tu	0612	4.7
	0621	5.2		1204	0.7
	1211	0.3		1821	4.9
	1835	5.4			
13 Tu	0042	0.1	28 W	0021	0.5
	0703	5.1		0643	4.8
	1252	0.5		1235	0.7
	1919	5.2		1855	4.9
14 W	0121	0.4	29 Th	0052	0.7
	0745	4.9		0716	4.7
	1334	0.7		1309	0.8
	2001	4.9		1930	4.8
15 Th	0204	0.8	30 F	0127	0.8
	0827	4.6		0751	4.6
	1418	1.1		1345	1.0
	2046	4.5		2009	4.6
			31 Sa	0205	1.1
				0832	4.4
				1429	1.3
				2056	4.3

Chart Datum: 0.20 metres above Ordnance Datum (Dublin)

IRELAND, WEST COAST – GALWAY

Lat 53°16′ N   Long 9°03′ W

TIMES AND HEIGHTS OF HIGH AND LOW WATERS

YEAR 1991

TIME ZONE UT(GMT)
For Summer Time add ONE hour in non-shaded areas

SEPTEMBER

Day	Time	m	Day	Time	m
1 Su ((	0250 / 0919 / 1524 / 2153	1.4 / 4.2 / 1.6 / 4.1	16 M	0356 / 1026 / 1648 / 2316	2.2 / 3.8 / 2.2 / 3.5
2 M	0350 / 1021 / 1641 / 2309	1.7 / 4.0 / 1.8 / 3.9	17 Tu	0534 / 1150 / 1838	2.4 / 3.7 / 2.2
3 Tu	0515 / 1147 / 1827	2.0 / 3.9 / 1.8	18 W	0109 / 0713 / 1321 / 1952	3.5 / 2.3 / 3.8 / 2.0
4 W	0045 / 0656 / 1319 / 1952	3.9 / 1.9 / 4.1 / 1.4	19 Th	0219 / 0813 / 1422 / 2040	3.7 / 2.0 / 4.0 / 1.7
5 Th	0206 / 0811 / 1427 / 2051	4.2 / 1.5 / 4.5 / 1.0	20 F	0304 / 0856 / 1505 / 2118	4.0 / 1.7 / 4.3 / 1.3
6 F	0305 / 0904 / 1521 / 2138	4.5 / 1.1 / 4.9 / 0.6	21 Sa	0339 / 0931 / 1541 / 2150	4.3 / 1.4 / 4.5 / 1.0
7 Sa	0352 / 0948 / 1606 / 2219	4.9 / 0.8 / 5.2 / 0.2	22 Su	0410 / 1003 / 1614 / 2220	4.5 / 1.1 / 4.7 / 0.8
8 Su ●	0435 / 1028 / 1648 / 2257	5.1 / 0.5 / 5.4 / 0.1	23 M ○	0440 / 1033 / 1645 / 2248	4.7 / 0.9 / 4.9 / 0.6
9 M	0515 / 1108 / 1729 / 2334	5.2 / 0.3 / 5.4 / 0.1	24 Tu	0509 / 1102 / 1718 / 2318	4.9 / 0.7 / 5.0 / 0.5
10 Tu	0556 / 1147 / 1810	5.3 / 0.3 / 5.4	25 W	0539 / 1133 / 1751 / 2349	5.0 / 0.6 / 5.1 / 0.5
11 W	0012 / 0635 / 1225 / 1850	0.2 / 5.2 / 0.5 / 5.1	26 Th	0611 / 1207 / 1827	5.0 / 0.6 / 5.1
12 Th	0050 / 0714 / 1304 / 1931	0.5 / 5.0 / 0.8 / 4.8	27 F	0022 / 0645 / 1243 / 1906	0.6 / 5.0 / 0.8 / 4.9
13 F	0130 / 0755 / 1347 / 2015	1.0 / 4.7 / 1.2 / 4.4	28 Sa	0059 / 0724 / 1323 / 1949	0.9 / 4.8 / 1.0 / 4.7
14 Sa	0209 / 0837 / 1432 / 2100	1.4 / 4.4 / 1.6 / 4.1	29 Su	0141 / 0808 / 1411 / 2039	1.2 / 4.6 / 1.3 / 4.4
15 Su)	0256 / 0925 / 1527 / 2156	1.8 / 4.0 / 1.9 / 3.7	30 M	0230 / 0900 / 1511 / 2141	1.6 / 4.4 / 1.6 / 4.1

OCTOBER

Day	Time	m	Day	Time	m
1 Tu ((	0335 / 1007 / 1635 / 2302	1.9 / 4.1 / 1.8 / 3.9	16 W	0444 / 1058 / 1742	2.5 / 3.8 / 2.2
2 W	0509 / 1136 / 1821	2.1 / 4.0 / 1.8	17 Th	0012 / 0622 / 1225 / 1900	3.6 / 2.4 / 3.8 / 2.1
3 Th	0041 / 0649 / 1307 / 1938	4.0 / 1.9 / 4.2 / 1.4	18 F	0134 / 0730 / 1335 / 1954	3.8 / 2.2 / 4.0 / 1.8
4 F	0155 / 0757 / 1412 / 2032	4.3 / 1.6 / 4.6 / 1.0	19 Sa	0223 / 0816 / 1423 / 2034	4.0 / 1.9 / 4.2 / 1.5
5 Sa	0249 / 0846 / 1501 / 2114	4.7 / 1.2 / 4.9 / 0.7	20 Su	0301 / 0854 / 1501 / 2110	4.3 / 1.6 / 4.5 / 1.2
6 Su	0332 / 0927 / 1545 / 2153	4.9 / 0.9 / 5.1 / 0.5	21 M	0332 / 0928 / 1536 / 2141	4.6 / 1.3 / 4.7 / 1.0
7 M ●	0412 / 1006 / 1626 / 2231	5.1 / 0.7 / 5.3 / 0.4	22 Tu	0403 / 1000 / 1612 / 2213	4.8 / 1.0 / 5.0 / 0.8
8 Tu	0451 / 1045 / 1705 / 2308	5.3 / 0.5 / 5.3 / 0.4	23 W ○	0434 / 1033 / 1647 / 2245	5.0 / 0.8 / 5.1 / 0.7
9 W	0529 / 1123 / 1744 / 2344	5.3 / 0.5 / 5.2 / 0.6	24 Th	0506 / 1106 / 1725 / 2320	5.2 / 0.7 / 5.2 / 0.7
10 Th	0607 / 1201 / 1825	5.2 / 0.7 / 5.0	25 F	0543 / 1144 / 1804 / 2358	5.2 / 0.7 / 5.2 / 0.8
11 F	0021 / 0645 / 1239 / 1904	0.9 / 5.0 / 1.0 / 4.8	26 Sa	0621 / 1225 / 1848	5.2 / 0.8 / 5.1
12 Sa	0059 / 0724 / 1320 / 1947	1.2 / 4.8 / 1.3 / 4.4	27 Su	0039 / 0705 / 1310 / 1935	1.0 / 5.1 / 1.0 / 4.9
13 Su	0137 / 0805 / 1405 / 2032	1.6 / 4.5 / 1.6 / 4.1	28 M	0126 / 0752 / 1402 / 2030	1.3 / 4.9 / 1.3 / 4.6
14 M	0222 / 0850 / 1457 / 2124	2.0 / 4.2 / 2.0 / 3.8	29 Tu	0220 / 0849 / 1507 / 2134	1.7 / 4.6 / 1.6 / 4.3
15 Tu)	0318 / 0945 / 1609 / 2233	2.3 / 4.0 / 2.2 / 3.6	30 W ((	0328 / 0957 / 1627 / 2251	2.0 / 4.4 / 1.7 / 4.2
			31 Th	0454 / 1119 / 1757	2.1 / 4.3 / 1.7

NOVEMBER

Day	Time	m	Day	Time	m
1 F	0018 / 0624 / 1242 / 1909	4.2 / 2.0 / 4.4 / 1.5	16 Sa	0018 / 0624 / 1225 / 1849	3.8 / 2.3 / 4.0 / 1.9
2 Sa	0130 / 0730 / 1347 / 2002	4.4 / 1.7 / 4.6 / 1.2	17 Su	0123 / 0723 / 1326 / 1940	4.0 / 2.1 / 4.2 / 1.7
3 Su	0223 / 0820 / 1437 / 2047	4.7 / 1.5 / 4.8 / 1.0	18 M	0211 / 0809 / 1415 / 2022	4.3 / 1.8 / 4.4 / 1.5
4 M	0307 / 0904 / 1522 / 2127	4.9 / 1.2 / 5.0 / 0.9	19 Tu	0249 / 0850 / 1458 / 2101	4.5 / 1.5 / 4.6 / 1.2
5 Tu	0348 / 0945 / 1603 / 2206	5.1 / 1.0 / 5.1 / 0.9	20 W	0325 / 0928 / 1539 / 2141	4.8 / 1.2 / 4.9 / 1.0
6 W ●	0426 / 1024 / 1644 / 2242	5.2 / 0.9 / 5.1 / 0.9	21 Th ○	0402 / 1006 / 1621 / 2220	5.1 / 1.0 / 5.1 / 0.9
7 Th	0504 / 1102 / 1725 / 2320	5.2 / 0.9 / 5.0 / 1.0	22 F	0441 / 1047 / 1705 / 2301	5.3 / 0.8 / 5.2 / 0.9
8 F	0542 / 1142 / 1804 / 2357	5.2 / 1.0 / 4.9 / 1.2	23 Sa	0522 / 1130 / 1750 / 2343	5.4 / 0.7 / 5.3 / 0.9
9 Sa	0619 / 1221 / 1845	5.1 / 1.1 / 4.7	24 Su	0605 / 1215 / 1838	5.4 / 0.7 / 5.2
10 Su	0035 / 0659 / 1302 / 1926	1.5 / 4.9 / 1.4 / 4.5	25 M	0029 / 0653 / 1304 / 1928	1.0 / 5.3 / 0.9 / 5.0
11 M	0114 / 0740 / 1345 / 2009	1.7 / 4.7 / 1.6 / 4.2	26 Tu	0119 / 0745 / 1358 / 2023	1.3 / 5.1 / 1.1 / 4.8
12 Tu	0158 / 0822 / 1433 / 2056	2.0 / 4.4 / 1.8 / 4.0	27 W	0213 / 0840 / 1457 / 2121	1.5 / 4.9 / 1.3 / 4.6
13 W	0247 / 0911 / 1529 / 2152	2.2 / 4.2 / 2.0 / 3.9	28 Th ((	0314 / 0941 / 1603 / 2227	1.8 / 4.7 / 1.5 / 4.4
14 Th))	0350 / 1007 / 1635 / 2259	2.4 / 4.0 / 2.1 / 3.8	29 F	0424 / 1049 / 1715 / 2340	1.9 / 4.5 / 1.6 / 4.4
15 F	0508 / 1115 / 1746	2.4 / 4.0 / 2.1	30 Sa	0542 / 1204 / 1827	2.0 / 4.4 / 1.6

DECEMBER

Day	Time	m	Day	Time	m
1 Su	0052 / 0655 / 1316 / 1928	4.4 / 1.9 / 4.4 / 1.6	16 M	0003 / 0612 / 1221 / 1835	4.0 / 2.2 / 4.1 / 1.9
2 M	0151 / 0754 / 1413 / 2019	4.6 / 1.7 / 4.5 / 1.5	17 Tu	0107 / 0717 / 1326 / 1934	4.1 / 2.0 / 4.2 / 1.7
3 Tu	0240 / 0843 / 1503 / 2104	4.7 / 1.5 / 4.6 / 1.4	18 W	0202 / 0812 / 1423 / 2027	4.4 / 1.7 / 4.4 / 1.5
4 W	0324 / 0928 / 1548 / 2146	4.9 / 1.4 / 4.7 / 1.3	19 Th	0251 / 0901 / 1514 / 2115	4.6 / 1.4 / 4.7 / 1.3
5 Th	0404 / 1010 / 1630 / 2226	5.0 / 1.2 / 4.8 / 1.3	20 F	0338 / 0949 / 1603 / 2203	4.9 / 1.1 / 5.0 / 1.1
6 F ●	0445 / 1049 / 1711 / 2305	5.1 / 1.1 / 4.8 / 1.3	21 Sa ○	0423 / 1035 / 1652 / 2249	5.2 / 0.8 / 5.2 / 0.9
7 Sa	0523 / 1130 / 1751 / 2343	5.1 / 1.1 / 4.7 / 1.4	22 Su	0509 / 1122 / 1740 / 2336	5.4 / 0.6 / 5.3 / 0.8
8 Su	0603 / 1210 / 1831	5.0 / 1.2 / 4.7	23 M	0557 / 1210 / 1829	5.5 / 0.5 / 5.3
9 M	0021 / 0641 / 1249 / 1910	1.5 / 4.9 / 1.3 / 4.6	24 Tu	0022 / 0645 / 1257 / 1919	0.8 / 5.5 / 0.5 / 5.2
10 Tu	0059 / 0720 / 1328 / 1949	1.6 / 4.8 / 1.4 / 4.4	25 W	0110 / 0734 / 1345 / 2008	0.9 / 5.4 / 0.7 / 4.9
11 W	0138 / 0759 / 1408 / 2030	1.7 / 4.6 / 1.5 / 4.3	26 Th	0159 / 0825 / 1436 / 2100	1.1 / 5.1 / 0.9 / 4.8
12 Th	0220 / 0840 / 1451 / 2112	1.9 / 4.5 / 1.7 / 4.2	27 F	0250 / 0918 / 1529 / 2153	1.4 / 4.9 / 1.3 / 4.6
13 F	0307 / 0924 / 1538 / 2202	2.1 / 4.3 / 1.8 / 4.0	28 Sa ((	0348 / 1016 / 1630 / 2255	1.7 / 4.5 / 1.6 / 4.4
14 Sa ●	0400 / 1014 / 1631 / 2258	2.2 / 4.2 / 1.9 / 4.0	29 Su	0454 / 1122 / 1739	1.9 / 4.3 / 1.8
15 Su	0504 / 1113 / 1732	2.3 / 4.1 / 1.9	30 M	0005 / 0611 / 1239 / 1852	4.2 / 2.0 / 4.1 / 1.9
			31 Tu	0116 / 0727 / 1349 / 1955	4.3 / 1.9 / 4.1 / 1.9

13

Chart Datum: 0.20 metres above Ordnance Datum (Dublin)

MINOR HARBOURS AND ANCHORAGES 10.13.20

KILKEEL, Down, 54°04′N, 5°59′W, Zone 0 (GMT), Admty chart 2800. HW +0015 on Dover, +0025 on Belfast; HW height +1.6m on Belfast; ML 2.9m; Duration 0620. See 10.13.9. Shelter is complete in inner basin, but it becomes very crowded. Depth off quays approx 1m. There are drying banks both sides of entrance channel and SE gales cause sand bank right across entrance. This is removed by dredging or is slowly washed away in E winds. CG stn is conspic mark for entering, red brick with W flagstaff to W of entrance. Secure in inner basin and see Hr Mr. Breakwater Lt is Fl WR 2s 8m 8M, R296° – 313°, W313° – 017°, storm signals. Meeney's pier Fl G 3s. VHF Ch 16 **12** 14 (Mon-Fri: 0900 – 2000). Facilities: EC Thurs; Hr Mr ☎ 62287 FW on quay; **Shipyard** (between fish market and dock) El, ME, Sh, Slip; **Town** (¾M) Bar, ✉, R, V, Gas.

ARDGLASS, Down, 54°16′N, 5°36′W, Zone 0 (GMT), Admty chart 633. HW +0025 on Dover, +0030 on Belfast; HW height +1.1m on Belfast; ML 2.6m; Duration 0620. A rocky bay partly sheltered by breakwater with quays on inside. Further up hr on SW side is old tidal dock giving excellent shelter. Safe harbour except in strong winds from E to S. Yachts should consult Hr Mr who will allocate berth or anchorage clear of fishing vessels. Yachts can go alongside E wall of inner hr. VHF Ch 16 14 12. Lts on inner pier head E of Tidal Dock, Iso WRG 4s 10m 8/5M G shore – 310°, W310° – 318°, R318° – shore. Breakwater Fl R 3s 10m 5M. Facilities: Hr Mr ☎ (0396) 841291; FW (on quay); **Town** P and D nearby; Bar, ✉, R, V, Gas.

PORTAVOGIE, Down, 54°27′N, 5°26′W, Zone 0 (GMT), Admty chart 2156. HW +0016 on Dover, +0015 on Belfast; HW height +1.1m on Belfast; ML 2.6m; Duration 0620. See 10.13.10. Good shelter; harbour very full of fishing boats. Beware Plough Rks to S, and McCammon Rks to N of ent. Keep in W sector of Lt on Outer Breakwater Iso WRG 5s 12m 9M G shore-258°, W258°-275°, R275°-348°. Inner Breakwater 2 FG (vert) 6m 4M. About 3 ca NE of Plough Rk is a R can buoy, Bell, Fl(2) R 10s. VHF Ch 16; 14 12 (Mon-Fri: 0900 – 2000 LT). Facilities: EC Thurs; Hr Mr ☎ 71470; Slip, FW (on central quay) Sh, ME, El; **Town** CH, D, P, ✉, R, Gas, V. No licenced premises.

DONAGHADEE, Down, 54°38′N, 5°32′W, Zone 0 (GMT), Admty chart 3709. HW +0025 on Dover, +0020 on Belfast; HW height +0.5m on Belfast; ML 2.2m; Duration 0615. See 10.13.10. Hr is small and very full; scend often sets in. Best berth alongside SE quay. Depth in harbour approx 3m. Beware ledge with less than 2m extends 1.5 ca ENE from S pier head. Alternatively go to the Marina 3 ca S of hr., excellent shelter and facilities but tricky entrance (pilots available). South Pier Lt, Iso WR 4s 17m 18/14M W shore – 326°, R326° – shore. No lights on marina. Facilities: Hr Mr ☎ 882377; **Copeland's Marina** ☎ 882184 Access HW∓4; all facilities. **Town** Bar, D, Gas, FW, P, ✉, R, V.

CARNLOUGH HARBOUR, Antrim, 54°59′N, 05°58°W, Zone 0 (GMT), Admty chart 2198. HW +0006 on Dover, +0005 on Belfast; HW height – 1.6m on Belfast; ML 0.9m; Duration 0625. Small Hr accommodating yachts & small fishing boats, visitors welcome. Good shelter except in SE gales. Entrance dredged annually in May to 1.6m, harbour 2.0m. Entrance difficult in strong onshore winds. Beware rocks which cover at HW on either side of entrance. N pier Lt, Fl G 3s; S Pier Fl R 3s. VHF Ch 16 (occas.). Facilities: EC Wed, Hr Mr ☎ (0574) 84486; **Quay** AB, AC (see Hr Mr), FW, L, Slip; **Town** Bar, P and D (cans), Gas, Gaz, ✉, R, V.

RED BAY, Antrim, 55°04′N, 6°03′W, Zone 0 (GMT), Admty chart 2199. HW +0006 on Dover, +0022 sp – 0010 np on Belfast; HW height – 1.7m on Belfast; ML 0.9m; Duration 0625. See 10.13.11. Good anchorage but open to N and E winds. Beware rks and two ruined piers W of Garron Pt. In S and E winds anchor 2 ca off W stone arch near head of bay in approx 3.5m; in N or W winds anchor S of small pier in 2/5m 0.5M NE of Waterfoot village. Facilities: **Cushendall** (1M N of pier) Bar, D, P, ✉, R, V, Gas.

MULROY BAY, Donegal, 55°15′N, 7°47′W, Zone 0 (GMT), Admty chart 2699; HW (bar) – 0455 on Dover, +0100 on Galway; HW height – 1.1m on Galway. Beware Limeburner Rk, (marked by buoy) 2½M N of ent and the bar which is dangerous in swell or onshore winds. Channel runs between Black Rks and Sessiagh Rks thence through First, Second and Third Narrows (with strong tides) to Broad Water. HW at the head of the lough is 2¼ hrs later than at the bar. Anchorages: Close SW of Ravedy Is (Fl 3s); Fanny's Bay (2m), excellent; Rosnakill Bay (3.5m) in SE side; Cranford Bay; Milford Port (3 to 4m). Beware electric cable 6m, over Moross channel, barring North Water to high masted boats. Facilities: **Milford Port** AB, FW, V; **Fanny's Bay** ✉, Shop at Downings village (1M), hotel at Rosepenna (¾M).

SHEEP HAVEN, Donegal, 55°11′N, 7°51′W, Zone 0 (GMT), Admty chart 2699. HW – 0515 on Dover, +0050 on Galway; HW height – 1.0m on Galway. See 10.13.15. Bay is 4M wide with numerous anchorages, easily accessible in daylight, but exposed to N winds. Beware rocks for 3ca off Rinnafaghla Pt; also Wherryman Rocks, which dry, 1ca off E shore 2¼M S of Rinnafaghla Pt. Anchor in Downies (or Downings) Bay to SW of pier; in Pollcormick Inlet close W in 3m; in Ards Bay for excellent shelter, but beware the bar in strong winds. Lights: Portnablahy Ldg Lts 125°, both Oc 6s 7/12m 2M; Downies pier head Fl R 3s 5m 2M. Facilities: (Downies) EC Wed, V, FW, P(cans, 300m), R, Bar; (Portnablahy Bay) V, P (cans), R, Bar.

BURTONPORT, Donegal, 54°59′N, 8°26′W, Zone 0 (GMT), Admty charts 2792, 1879. HW – 0525 on Dover, +0050 on Galway; HW height – 0.9m on Galway; ML 2.2m; Duration 0605. See 10.13.16. Normal ent. via North Channel. Hr very full. Berth on local boat on pier or go to Rutland Hr or Aran I. Ent. safe in all weathers except NW gales. N Channel Ldg Lts 119° on Inishcoo, Front Iso 6s 6m 1M. Rear, 248m from front, Iso 6s 11m 1M. Rutland I Ldg Lts 138° Front Oc 6s 8m 1M. Rear, 330m from front, Oc 6s 14m 1M. Burtonport Ldg Lts 068°, Front FG, 17m 1M, rear, 355m from front, FG 23m 1M. Facilities: D (just inside pier), FW (root of pier), P (0.5M inland), **Village** Bar, ✉, R, V, Kos.

BLACKSOD BAY, Mayo, 54°06′N, 10°04′W, Zone 0 (GMT), Admty chart 2704. HW – 0525 on Dover, +0030 on Galway; HW height – 1.1m on Galway; ML 2.2m; Duration 0610. See 10.13.17. Safe anchorage with no hidden dangers, accessible by day or night. Beware Rk which dries 3.5 ca SSE of Ardmore Pt. Good anchorages at Elly Bay (1.8m); NW of Blacksod Quay (3m); Saleen Bay; Elly Hr; N of Claggan Pt. Blacksod Pier root Lt, Fl(2) WR 7.5s 13m 12/9M, R189° – 210°, W210° – 018°. Blacksod pier head Lt 2 FR (vert) 6m 3M. There are no facilities but normal supplies can be obtained at Belmullet 2.5M N of Claggan Pt.

INISHBOFIN, Mayo, 53°37′N, 10°13′W, Zone 0 (GMT) Admty chart 2707. HW – 0555 on Dover, – 0010 on Galway. HW height – 0.9m on Galway; ML 1.9m. See 10.13.19. Very secure harbour once through narrow entrance. Ldg line, 2 conspic W Trs at 032°. Lt on Gun Rock Fl (2) 6s 8 m 4M; vis 296°–253°. Facilities: FW, R, Bar, V, Hotel, ☎ (095) 45803

CLIFDEN BAY, Galway, 53°29′N, 10°01′W, Zone 0 (GMT), Admty chart 2708. HW – 0600 on Dover, +0005 on Galway; HW height – 0.6m on Galway; ML 2.3m; Duration 0610. See 10.13.18. It is essential to identify the high W beacon on Carrickarana Rks, 2.8M SW of Fishing Pt before entering. Ldg Marks 080° W Bn on Fishing Pt in line with Clifden Castle. Beware bar at ent by Fishing Pt and another SE of creek going up to Clifden; also Doolick Rks, Coghan Rks and Rks off Errislannon Pt. Anchor between Larner Rks and Drinagh Pt, dry out alongside Clifden Quay or anchor beyond Yellow Slate Rks in 3.4m in Ardbear Bay. Keep clear of fish farming cages. Facilities: EC Thurs; **A. O'Connell** ☎ 21332, El, FW, M, ME, Sh, Slip; **Aster Boats** ☎ 21332 Slip, L, FW, D, AB, C, CH, M, ME, El, Sh; **Town** Bar, Ⓑ, CH, D, P, ✉, R, V, Kos, FW, V, R, Dr, Ⓗ.

SELLING?
BUYING?

USE

Yachts

and Yachting

- **26 issues a year.**

- **Up to date list of boats for sale.**

- **Minimum delay in advertising your boat.**

- **The largest number of private sailing boats for sale of any UK Yachting Magazine.**

Yachts
and Yachting

196 Eastern Esplanade, Southend-on-Sea, Essex
Tel: 0702 582245
Fax: 0702 588434

VOLVO PENTA SERVICE

Sales and service centres in area 14
Names and addresses of Volvo Penta dealers in
this area are available from:

FRANCE **Volvo Penta France SA,** Chemin de la Nouvelle, F78130 Les Mureaux
Tel (01) 3 474 72 01, Telex 695221 F.
SPAIN **Volvo Concesionarios SA,** Paeso De La Castellana 130, 28046 Madrid 16,
Tel 1-262 2207, Telex 47508 VOLCO E.

**VOLVO
PENTA**

Area 14

South Biscay
Spanish Border to Pornic

Hendaye
St Jean-de-Luz
Anglet
Bayonne
Capbreton
La Vigne
Pauillac
Bordeaux
Blaye
Douhet
Ile d'Aix
La Flotte, Ile de Ré
Ars-en-Ré
L'Aiguillon-la Faute-sur-Mer
Jard-sur-Mer
Fromentine

14

10·14·2
South Biscay

47° N
0°
46° N

La Rochelle
ⓘ 10.14.16
(RC) RE ••• – •
291.9   5
🅢🅒 VHF 16 21
26
🅟🅡 Les Minimes
VHF 09
Ch 21 0733
1233 LT
46.41.29.14

Rochefort
ⓘ 10.14.15
🅟🅡 VHF 16;12

Cognac/Chateaubernard
(RC) CGC
Aero ––• –•• –•• 75
354

Royan
ⓘ 10.14.12
🅢🅒 VHF 16 23 25
🅟🅡 VHF   09

46° N

La Pallice
🅟🅡 VHF 12 16
LB

La Seudre
ⓘ 10.14.13

Pornic
ⓘ 10.14.23
VHF   09
🅟🅡
LB   ⚓

Les Sables d'Olonne
ⓘ 10.14.19
(RC) SO ••• – –
291.9   5
🅟🅡 Yacht harbour
VHF 09
LB   ⚓

St-Gilles-Croix-de-Vie
ⓘ 10.14.20
🅢🅒 VHF 16 27
🅟🅡 VHF   09
Ch 27 0733
1233 LT
LB   ⚓

Ile d'Aix*
Le Chateau
Marennes
L'Aiguillon*
La Flotte*
La Flotte*
Jard*
Ars*
Douhet*
Boyardville
LaCotinière
La Tremblade
Cordouan
Montalivet

Les Baleines
(RC) BN –••• –•
6   303.4   50

St Martin de Ré
ⓘ 10.14.17
🅟🅡 VHF   09

Ile d'Oleron
ⓘ 10.14.14
🅟🅡 Boyardville and
Douhet VHF 09

Pte de la Coubre
(RC) LK •– • –•–
4   303.4   100

Port Bloc/La Gironde
ⓘ 10.14.10
🅟🅡 Le Verdon

CROSS / Soulac
VHF 16; 06 09 10

Bourgenay
ⓘ 10.14.18
🅟🅡 VHF 09 16

Rochebonne Plateau

L'Herbaudière
Fromentine*

See 10.15.2

Ile du Pilier
(RC) PR •– • –••
298.8   10

Ile Noirmoutier
ⓘ 10.14.22
🅟🅡 L'Herbaudière
VHF 09

Ile d'Yeu
ⓘ 10.14.21
(RC) YE – •– • ••
3   312.6   70
🅟🅡 Port Joinville
VHF 09
LB   ⚓

Pte de St Gildas
(RC) NZ –• ––••
289.6   10

Variation
4°W (1991)
0
90
270

4°W
3°W
2°W
1°W
47° N
46° N

611

Key to symbols

📻	Coast Station/Port Radio-frequencies
RC	Marine radiobeacon-call sign, sequence, frequency and range (nm)
RC Aero	Aeronautical radio beacon-call sign, frequency and range (nm)
ℹ	See for harbour information/tidal data
☁	Weather information (tel. no. or times)
CG	Coastguard Rescue Co-ordination Centre
⚠	Coastguard Rescue Sub-Centre or VHF relay
LB	Life-boat
IL	Inshore Life-boat
🚁	SAR Helicopter base
☆	Principal lights
⚓	Light-vessel
⚓	Lanby
*	See 10.14.24

45°N

44°N

FRANCE

SPAIN

Bordeaux/Merignac
RC Aero	BD – ··· – ··· – 393 30
☁	56.34.20.11

Cap Ferret
RC	FT ··· – · – 296.5 100
1,2	
LB	⚠

Arcachon
ℹ	10.14.9
📻S/C	VHF 16 28 82 MF 1862 2182 kHz
📻P/R	VHF 09
☁	Ch 82 0733 1233 LT 0703 1703 on 1820 kHz. 56.83.84.85
	⚠

Bordeaux*
📻S/C	VHF 16 28 82
📻P/R	VHF 12 16
☁	56.90.91.21

Cazaux
RC Aero	CAA – · – · – – · · 382 80

Bayonne*
📻S/C	VHF 16 24
📻P/R	VHF 12 09
☁	Ch 24 0733 1233 LT
LB	

Biarritz
RC Aero	BZ – · · · · – – – · · 341 35
☁	59.23.84.15

Capbreton*
📻P/R	VHF 09

San Sebastian
RC Aero	HIG · · · · · · – – – · · 328 50

Choritoquieta
📻S/C	VHF 16; 20 25 26 27

C Machichaco
RC	MA – – · – 296.5 100
3,4	
📻S/C	VHF **04** 16 23 26 27 MF 1704 kHz

Bilbao
RC Aero	BLO – · · · – · · · – – – · · 370 70
📻S/C	VHF 16; **20** 25 **26** 27
📻P/R	VHF 12 16; 12 13 14

Praves
📻S/C	VHF 16; 24 26 27 **28**

Cabo Mayor
RC	MY – – · – – – 296.5 50
5,6	

📻P/R VHF 09 12   Yacht harbour 09   LB

Ares

La Vigne*

Contis

Vieux-Boucau -les-Bains

Anglet

St Jean de Luz* Hendaye* La Rhune

San Sebastian

San Sebastian

Santander

Danger Area

0°

1°W

2°W

3°W

0°

10.14.3   AREA 14 TIDAL STREAMS

5 Hours before HW Brest
(0010 after HW Dover)

4 Hours before HW Brest
(0110 after HW Dover)

3 Hours before HW Brest
(0210 after HW Dover)

2 Hours before HW Brest
(0310 after HW Dover)

1 Hour before HW Brest
(0410 after HW Dover)

HW Brest
(0510 after HW Dover)

CAUTION:- Due to the very strong rates of the
tidal streams in some of the areas, many eddies
may occur. Where possible some indication of
these eddies has been included. In many areas
there is either insufficient information or the
eddies are unstable.
Generally tidal streams are weak offshore and
strong winds have a very great effect on the rate
and direction of the tidal streams.

Northward 10.15.3

1 Hour after HW Brest
(0610 after HW Dover)

2 Hours after HW Brest
(0515 before HW Dover)

3 Hours after HW Brest
(0415 before HW Dover)

4 Hours after HW Brest
(0315 before HW Dover)

5 Hours after HW Brest
(0215 before HW Dover)

6 Hours after HW Brest
(0115 before HW Dover)

10.14.4   LIGHTS, FOG SIGNALS AND WAYPOINTS

Abbreviations used below are given in 10.0.3. Principal lights are in **bold** print, places in CAPITALS, and light-vessels and Lanbys in *CAPITAL ITALICS*. Unless otherwise stated lights are white. m—elevation in metres; M—nominal range in n. miles. Fog signals are in *italics*. Useful waypoints are underlined use those on land with care. See 4.2.2.

FRANCE—WEST COAST
ST JEAN DE LUZ, Socoa Ldg Lts 138°. Front 43°23'8N 01°41'·1W Q WR 36m W12M, R8M; W square Tr, B stripe; vis W shore-264°, R264°-282°, W282°-shore. Rear **Bord-again**, 0·77M from front, Q 67m **20M**; synchronised with front; intens 135°-141°.
Digue des Criquas, head 43°23'·92N 01°40'·59W Iso G 4s 11m 7M; G square Tr; *Horn 15s.*
Ldg Lts 151°, **Front** QG 18m **17M**; W square Tr, R stripe; intens 150°-152°. **Rear**, 410m from front, QG 27m **17M**; W square Tr, G stripe; intens 150°-152°.
Ste Barbe Ldg Lts 101°. **Front** Dir Oc(31)R 12s 30m **18M**; W triangle point up; intens 095°-107°. **Rear**, 340m from front, Dir Oc(31)R 12s 47m **18M**; B triangle point down on W Tr; synchronised with front; intens 095°-107°.

Guethary Ldg Lts 133°. Front 43°25'·6N 01°36'·5W QR 11m; W mast, R top. Rear, 66m from front, QR 33m; W tower.

BIARRITZ
Ldg Lts 174°. Both Fl R 2s. Aero Mo(L)7·5s 80m; part obsc (occas).
Pte Saint-Martin 43°29'·69N 01°33'·17W Fl(2) 10s 73m **29M**; W Tr, B top.

L'ADOUR.
BA buoy 43°32'·66N 01°32'·68W LFl 10s 8m 8M; safe water mark.
Digue exterieure, Sud Q(9) 15s; W cardinal mark.
Jetée Sud, head Iso G 4s 9m 7M; W square Tr, G top.
Jetée Nord, head Oc(2)R 6s 12m 8M; R&W mast.
Digue du large, head QR 11m 7M; W Tr, R top.
Boucau Ldg Lts 090°. Front Dir Q 9m 14M. Rear Dir Q 15m 14M; both W framework Trs, R tops, intens 087°-093°.
Entrance Ldg Lts 111° (moved as necessary and lit when channel practicable).
Front Dir FG 6m 14M. Rear Dir FG 10m 14M; W Tr, G bands; intens 109°-114°.
Digue Nord, head Fl(2)R 6s 9m 6M; W Tr, R top; vis 296°-091°.
Training wall root (marina entrance) Fl G 2s; W framework Tr, G top.
From Port d'Anglet to Bayonne Ldg Lts 322°, Front QR, Rear Iso R 4s.
Ldg Lts 205°, both Dir FG.
Ldg Lts 345°, both FG.
Pont de l'Aveugle QG 8m 8M; W column, G top.

CAPBRETON.
Estacade Sud Iso G 4s 7m 9M; grey Tr.
Digue Nord, head Fl(2)R 6s 13m 10M; W Tr, R top; *Horn 30s.*
Contis 44°05'·7N 01°19'·2W Fl(4) 25s 50m **23M**; W round Tr, B diagonal stripes.
ZDS buoy 44°28'·00N 01°19'·30W Fl(3)Y 12s 8m 7M; Y buoy.
Emissaire buoy 44°30'·5N 01°17'·6W Fl(2) 6s 8m 5M; isolated danger mark; Ra refl.
La Salie, wharf head 44°30'·9N 01°15'·6W Q(9)15s 19m 10M; W cardinal mark.

ARCACHON.
Cap Ferret 44°38'·83N 01°15'·02W FlR 5s 53m **27M**; W Tr, R top; RC. Oc(3) 12s 46m 14M; same Tr; vis 045°-135°.
Arcachon, West breakwater head QG 6M.
E breakwater head QR 6M. Port de la Vigne Iso R 4s 7m 4M.
Hourtin 45°08'·5N 01°09'·7W Fl 5s 55m **24M**; R square Tr.

LA GIRONDE, PASSE SUD.
Cordouan 45°35'·25N 01°10'·34W Oc(21) WRG 12s 60m **22/18M**; W conical Tr, dark grey band and top; vis W014°-126°, G126°-178°, W178°-250°, W(unintens)250°-267°, R(unintens)267°-294°, R294°-014°; obsc in estuary when brg more than 285°.
Ldg Lts 063°. **St Nicolas Front** 45°33'·80N 01°04'·93W Dir QG 22m **17M**; W square Tr; intens 060°-066°. **Rear Pte de Grave**, 0·84M from front, Oc WRG 4s 26m **W19M**, R15M, G15M; W square Tr, B corners and top; vis W(unintens)033°-054°, W054°-234°, R234°-303°, W303°-312°, G312°-330°, W330°- 341°, W(unintens) 341°-025°.
Ldg Lts 041°, **Le Chay Front**, 45°37'·35N 01°02'·40W Dir QR 33m **18M**; W Tr, R top; intens 039°-042°. **Rear St Pierre**, 0·97M from front, Dir QR 61m **18M**; R water Tr; intens 039°-043°.
Pointe de Grave Jetée Nord, head QW 6m 2M; intens 039°-043°.

LA GIRONDE, GRANDE PASSE DE L'OUEST.
BXA Lt Buoy 45°37'·60N 01°28'·60W Iso 4s 8m 8M; R&W buoy; Ra refl; Racon; *Whis.*
Pte de la Coubre 45°41'·87N 01°13'·93W Fl(2) 10s 64m **28M**; W Tr, R top; RC; Sig Stn. F RG 42m 12M; same Tr; vis R030°-043°, G043°-060°, R060°-110°.
Ldg Lts 081°. **Front, La Palmyre**, 1·1M from rear, Dir Oc 4s 21m **22M**; W mast on dolphin; intens 080°-082°; Q(2) 5s 10m 3M; same structure. **Common rear** 45°39'·8N 01°07'·2W Q 53m **27M**; W radar Tr; intens 080°-082°. Dir FR 57m **17M**; same Tr; intens 326°-328°. Ldg Lts 327°.
Terre-Nègre, Front, 1·1M from rear, Oc(3) WRG 12s 39m **W16M**, R13M, G13M; W Tr, R top on west side; vis R304°-319°, W319°-327°, G327°-000°, W000°-004°, G004°-097°, W097°-104°, R104°-116°.

LA SEUDRE.
Pont de la Seudre QW 20m 10M each side, vis 054°-234° and 234°-054°.
Pte de Mus de Loup Oc G 4s 8m 6M; G&W house, W to seaward; vis 118°-147°.

ILE D'OLERON.
St Trojan-les-Bains FlG 4s 8m; Viaduct d'Oleron marked by F 1·1M ENE.
Le Chateau Ldg Lts 319°. Front QR 11m 7M; R line on W Tr; vis 191°-087°. Rear, 240m from front, QR 24m 7M; W Tr, R top; synchronised with front.
Tourelle Juliar Q(3)WG 10s 12m W11M; G8M; E cardinal mark; vis W147°-336°, G336°-147°.
La Pérrotine Oc(2) R 6s 8m 7M; W framework Tr, R top; obsc by Pte des Saumonards when brg less than 150°.
Rocher d'Antioche 46°04'·00N 01°23'·70W Q 20m 11M; N cardinal mark.
ATT Maumusson 45°47'·00N 01°17'·80W L Fl 10s; safe water mark.
S Denis d' Oléron, Jetée head 46°02'·1N 01°21'·9W Fl(2) G 6s 4m 5M; on G pole.

Pte de Chassiron 46°02'·80N 01°24'·60W Fl 10s 50m **28M**; W round Tr, B bands, part obsc 297°-351°; Sig Stn.

LA COTINIERE.
Dir Lt 048°. Dir Oc WRG 4s 13m W9M, R7M, G7M; W stripe with B border on W column; vis G033°-046°, W046°-050°, R050°-063°.
Entrance Ldg Lts 339°. Front Dir Oc(2) 6s 6m 13M; W Tr, R top; vis 329°-349°; *Horn(2) 20s (HW-3 to HW+3)*. Rear, 425m from front, Dir Oc(2) 6s 14m 12M; W framework Tr, R bands; synchronised with front; intens 329°-349°.
Grande Jetée, elbow Oc R 4s 11m 8M; W Tr, R top.
Digue Sud, head Iso G 4s 9m 7M; W Tr, G top.

LA CHARENTE.
Ile d'Aix 46°00'·67N 01°10'·60W Fl WR 5s 24m **W24M, R20M**; two W round Trs, one for Lt, one to screen R sector; vis R103°-118°, W118°-103°.
Ldg Lts 115°. **Front, Fort de la Pointe** 45°58'·0N 01°04'·3W Dir QR 8m **19M**; W square Tr, R top; intens 113°-117°. **Rear**, 600m from front, Dir QR 21m **20M**; W square Tr, R top; intens 113°-117°. QR 21m 8M; same Tr; vis 322°-067° over Port-des-Barques anchorage.
Port Nord de Fouras, pier head 45°59'·88N 01°05'·75W Oc(3+1) WG 12s 9m W11M, G8M; W&G framework Tr; vis G084°-127°, W127°-084°.
Port Sud de Fouras, Passe aux Filles, Lts in line 042°30'. Front 45°59'·0N 01°05'·7W Oc(2) R 6s 8m 5M; W structure, R top; vis 315°-135°. Rear, 75m from front, Oc(2) R 6s 19m 5M; synchronised with front; vis 315°-135°.

ÎLE DE RÉ.
Buoy PA 46°05'·7N 01°42'·4W Iso 4s 8m 7M; safe water mark; *Whis*; Ra refl.
Chanchardon 46°09'·72N 01°28'·45W Fl WR 4s 15m W11M, R9M; B 8-sided Tr, W base; vis R118°-290°, W290° 118°.
Chauveau 46°08'·09N 01°16'·33W Oc(2+1) WR 12s 23m **W15M**, R11M; W Tr, R top; vis W057°-094°, R094°-104°, W104°-342°, R342°-057°.
Pte de Sablanceaux 46°09'·82N 01°15'·08W Q Vi 7m 1M; W mast and hut, G top.
Rivedoux-Plage Ldg Lts 200°. Front QG 6m 6M; W Tr, G top. Rear, 100m from front, QG 9m 7M; W and G chequered column.
La Flotte 46°11'·3N 01°19'·3W Fl WG 4s 10m W12M, G9M; W Tr, G top; vis G130°-205°, W205°-220°, G220°-257°; *Horn(3) 30s (by day HW-2 to HW+2)*.

St MARTIN DE RÉ,
Breakwater West Head 46°12'·57N 01°21'·82W Fl R 2·5s 7m 4M; W post, R top.
46°12'·5N 01°21'·9W on ramparts E of entrance Oc(2) WR 6s 18m W10M, R7M; W Tr, R top; vis W shore-245°, R245°-281°, W281°-shore.
Mole head, 90m 328°, Iso G 4s 10m 6M; W tripod, G top; obsc by Pte de Loix when brg less than 124°.
Le Fier d'Ars Ldg Lts 265°. Front 46°14'·0N 01°28'·8W Iso 4s 8m 10M; W stripe on grey framework Tr; vis 141°-025°. Rear, 237m from front, Dir Iso G 4s 12m 13M; G square Tr on dwelling; synchronised with front, intens 263°-267°.
ARS-EN-RÉ Ldg Lts 232°. Front 46°12'·8N 01°30'·5W Q 5m 9M; W hut, R lantern. Rear, 370m from front, Q 13m 11M; B stripe on W framework Tr, G top; vis 142°-322°.
Les Baleines 46°14'·70N 01°33'·60W Fl(4) 15s 53m **27M**; grey 8-sided Tr, R lantern; RC.
Les Baleineaux 46°15'·85N 01°35.20W Oc(2) 6s 23m 11M; pink Tr, R top.

LA ROCHELLE.
Chauveau Lt Buoy 46°06'·62N 01°15'·98W VQ(6)LFl 10s; S cardinal mark; *Whis*.

Roche du Sud Lt Buoy 46°06'·43N 01°15'·15W Q(9) 15s; W cardinal mark.
Le Lavardin 46°08'·15N 01°14'·45W Fl(2) WG 6s 14m W11M, G8M; B Tr, R band; vis G160°-169°, W169°-160°.
Tour Richelieu 46°08'·95N 01°10'·27W Fl(4)R 12s 10m 9M; R Tr; RC; *Siren(4) 60s (HW-1 to HW+1)*.
Ldg Lts 059°. Front 46°09'·4N 01°09'·1W Dir Q 15m 14M; R Tr, W bands; intens 056°-062°; by day Fl 4s. Rear, 235m from front, Q 25m 14M; W 8-sided Tr, G top; synchronised with front, vis 350°-125°, obsc 061°-065° by St Nicolas Tr; by day Fl 4s.

LA PALLICE.
Mole d'Escale, head, 46°09'·42N 01°14'·43W Dir Lt 016°. DirQ WRG 33m W14M, R13M, G13M; grey Tr; vis G009°-015°, W015°-017°, R017°-031°.
Mole, SE corner Oc(2)R 6s 7m 6M; W framework Tr, R top.
Mole, NW corner Fl G 4s 5m 6M; G structure.
Oil jetty, head, Q(6)LFl 15s 6m 9M; S cardinal mark.
Bassin Chef-de-Baie, head Fl(3)G 12s 13m 9M; W Tr, G top.
Jetée Sud *Reed(3) 30s*. Ldg Lts 126°, both QG.
Avant Port, Jetée Nord, head Oc(2)R 6s 10m 7M; vis 234°-144°, unintens 164°-184°; Gy Round Tr.
Basin Ldg Lts 085°, both QR 7M; synchronised.

PERTUIS BRETON, NORTH SHORE.
Port du Plomb, West mole 46°12'·4N 01°12'·1W Fl R 4s 9m 7M; W column R top.
Sèvre Niortaise, entrance, Port du Pavé 46°18'·1N 01°08'·0W Fl G 4s 9m 7M; W column, G top.
La Tranche-sur-Mer, pier head 46°20'·7N 01°25'·5W Fl(2) R 6s 6m 7M; R column.
Pte du Grouin-du-Cou 46°20'·68N 01°27'·80W Fl WRG 5s 29m **W20M, R16M, G16M**; W 8-sided Tr, B top; vis R034°-061°, W061°-117°, G117°-138°, W138°-034°.

PLATEAU DE ROCHEBONNE.
Rochebonne NW buoy 46°12'·9N 02°31'·9W Q(9) 15s 8m 7M; W cardinal mark; *Whis*; Ra refl.
Rochebonne SW buoy 46°10'·1N 02°27'·0W Fl(2)R 6s 9m 3M; R buoy; Ra refl.
Rochebonne SE buoy 46°09'·2N 02°21'·2W Q(3) 10s 8m 8M; E cardinal mark; *Bell*; Ra refl.
Rochebonne NE buoy 46°12'·7N 02°25'·0W Iso G 4s 8m 5M; G buoy; Ra refl.

BOURGENAY
Ldg Lts 040°. Front 46°26'·4N 01°40'·5W QG 9M. Rear QG 9M.
Digue West, head Fl R 4s 9M.
Roches du Joanne Lt Buoy 46°25'·35N 01°41'·90W L Fl 10s; safe water mark.

LES SABLES D'OLONNE.
Nouch Sud Lt Buoy 46°28'·63N 01°47'·43W Q(6)LFl 15s; S cardinal mark.

PASSE DU SW
Ldg Lts 033°. **Front** 46°29'·5N 01°46'·3W Iso R 4s 14m **16M**; mast; H24. **Rear**, 330m from front, Iso R 4s 33m **16M**; W square Tr; H24.
Ldg Lts 320°, Jetée des Sables, Front 46°29'·45N 01°47'·52W QG 11m 8M; W Tr, G top. Rear, Tour de la Chaume Oc(21) 12s 33m 13M; large grey Tr, W turret; RC.
Ldg Lts 327°, Front FR 6m 11M; R line on W hut. Rear, 65m from front, FR 9m 11M; R line on W Tr; intens 324°-330°.
Jetée St Nicolas, head UQ(2)R 1s 16m 10M; W Tr, R top; vis 094°-043°.
L'Armandèche Fl(2+1) 15s 42m **23M**; W 6-sided Tr, R top; vis 295°-130°.

14

LA PETITE BARGE LANBY 46°28'·9N 01°50'·6W Q(6) LFl 15s 8m 7M; S cardinal mark; *Whis*; Ra refl.
Les Barges 46°29'·7N 01°50'·4W Fl(2) R 10s 25m **17M**; grey Tr, helicopter platform; vis 265°-205°.

St GILLES-SUR-VIE.
Pill'Hours Lt Buoy 46°41'·1N 01°58'·2W Q(6)LFl 15s; S cardinal mark; *Bell*. Ldg Lts 043°. Front Oc(31)R 12s 7m **13M**; W square Tr, R top; intens 033°-053°. **Rear**, 260m from front, Oc(31)R 12s 28m **13M**; W square Tr, R top; synchronised with front; intens 033°-053°.
Jetée de la Garenne, head Iso WG 4s 7m W8M, G5M; G Tr; vis G220°-335°, W335°-220°.
Jetée de Boisvinet Fl(2) WR 6s 8m W10M, R7M; R column; vis R045°-225°, W225°-045°; *Reed(2) 20s*.
Pte de Grosse Terre Fl(4) WR 12s 25m **W17M**, R13M; W truncated conical Tr; vis W290°-125°, R125°-145°.
St Jean de Monts, jetty head 46°47'·1N 02°05'·1W Q(2) R 5s 10m 3M; W mast, R top.

ILE D'YEU.
Pte des Corbeaux 46°41'·4N 02°17'·1W Fl(21)R 15s 25m **20M**; W square Tr, R top; obsc 083°-143°.

PORT JOINVILLE
Jetty NW head Oc(3) WG 12s 6m W11M, G9M; W 8-sided Tr, G top; vis G shore-150°, W150°-232°, G232°-279°, W279°-285°, G285°-shore; *Horn(3) 30s*.
Quai de Canada. Ldg Lts 219° both QR; vis 169°-269°.
Quai de Canada, head Iso G 4s 7m 6M.
Les Chiens Perrins 46°43'·6N 02°24'·6W Q(9)WG 15s 16m W8M, G4M; W cardinal mark; vis G330°-350°, W350°-200°.
Pte du Butte *Horn 60s*.
Petite Foule 46°43'·1N 02°22'·9W Fl 5s 56m **24M**; W square Tr, G lantern; RC.
La Meule 46°41'·7N 02°20'·6W Oc WRG 4s 9m W9M, R6M, G5M; grey square column, R top; vis G007°-018°, W018°-027°, R027°-041°.

FROMENTINE.
Pte de Notre Dame-de-Monts 46°53'·3N 02°08'·5W Oc(2) WRG 6s 21m W13M, R10M, G10M; W Tr, B top; vis G000°-043°, W043°-063°, R063°-073°, W073°-094°, G094°-113°, W113°-116°, R116°-175°, G175°-196°, R196°-230°.
Bridge, each side on centre span Iso 4s 32m **18M**; H24.
Tourelle Milieu 46°53'·6N 02°09'·6W Fl(4)R 12s 6m 5M; R Tr.

ILE DE NOIRMOUTIER.
Passage du Gois, E shore FlR 4s 6m 6M; R hut; vis 038°-218°.
E turning point Fl 2s 5m 6M; grey pyramid structure.
W turning point Fl 2s 5m 3M; grey pyramid structure.
Bassotière FlG 2s 7m 2M; W tripod, G lantern; vis 180°-000°.
Noirmoutier, jetty Oc(2) R 6s 6m 7M.
Pte des Dames 47°00'·7N 02°13'·3W Oc(3) WRG 12s 34m **W19M, R15M, G15M**; W square Tr; vis G016°-057°, R057°-124°, G124°-165°, W165°-191°, R191°-267°, W267°-357°, R357°-016°.
Pierre Moine 47°03'·43N 02°12'·30W Fl(2) 6s 14m 9M; isolated danger mark.
Basse du Martroger 47°02'·65N 02°17'·05W Q WRG 10m W9M, R6M, G6M; N cardinal mark; vis G033°-055°, W055°-060°, R060°-095°, G095°-124°, W124°-153°, R153°-201°, W201°-240°, R240°-033°.
Port de l'Herbaudière Jetée Ouest, head Oc(21) WG 12s 9m W10M, G7M; W column and hut, G top; vis W187°-190°, G190°-187°.
Jetée Est, head Fl(2) R 6s 8m 5M; R tripod.
Ile du Pilier 47°02'·62N 02°21'·53W Fl(3) 20s 33m **29M**; grey square Tr. Auxiliary Lt QR 10m 11M, same Tr; vis 321°-034; *Reed(3) 60s*; RC.

Pte de Devin 46°59'·1N 02°17'·6W Oc(4) WRG 12s 10m W11M, R8M, G8M; W column and hut, G top; vis G314°-028°, W028°-035°, R035°-134°.

BAIE DE BOURGNEUF.
Bec de l'Époids 46°56'·4N 02°04'·5W Dir Iso WRG 4s 6m W12M, R9M, G8M; W square Tr, R top; vis G106°-113°, R113°-122°, G122°-157°, W157°-158°, R158°-171°, W171°-176°.
Étier des Brochets 46°59'·9N 02°01'·9W Oc(21) WRG 12s 8m W10M, R7M, G7M; G Tr, W band; vis G071°-091°, W091°-102°, R102°-116°, W116°-119°, R119°-164°.
Le Collet 47°01'·8N 01°59'·0W Oc(2) WR 6s 7m W9M, R6M; vis W shore-093°, R093°-shore.
Ldg Lts 118° both QG 6M; W pylons, G tops.
La Bernerie-en-Retz 47°04'·6N 02°02'·4W Fl R 2s 3m 2M; W structure, R top.

PORNIC
Jetée SW, elbow Fl(2+1) 7s 4m 3M.
Head 46°06'·53N 02°06'·61W Fl(2) R 6s 4m 4M; B&R column.
Jetée Est, head Fl G 2·5s 4m 2M; B&G column.
Pte de Noveillard Oc(31) WRG 12s 22m W13M, R9M, G9M; W square Tr, G top, W dwelling; vis G shore-051°, W051°-079°, R079°-shore.
Pte de Gourmalon, breakwater head Fl(2) G 6s 4m 8M; W mast, G top.

Pointe de St-Gildas 47°08'·10N 02°14'·67W Q WRG 23m **W15M**, R12M, G10M; framework Tr on W house; vis R264°-308°, G308°-078°, W078°-088°, R088°-174°, W174°-180°, G180°-264°; RC.

10.14.5   PASSAGE INFORMATION

For general notes on French waters see 10.14.7. Further passage information appears in 10.15.5. A glossary of French terms used on charts or in sailing directions is given in 10.16.5.

BAY OF BISCAY (chart 1104)

Despite its reputation, weather in B of Biscay is no worse than in English Chan, and the S part generally enjoys a warmer and more settled climate. Bigger seas and longer swells from the Atlantic may be met. Although W winds mostly prevail, NE winds are often experienced with anticyclones over the continent. In summer the wind is seldom from SE or S. Often the wind varies in speed and direction from day to day. Gales may be expected once a month in summer. S of La Gironde, sea and land breezes are well developed in summer months. Coastal rainfall is moderate, increasing in the SE corner, where thunder is more frequent. Sea fog may be met from May to October, but is less common in winter.

The general direction of the surface current in summer is SE, towards the SE corner of B of Biscay, where it swings W along N coast of Spain. Rate and direction much depend on wind. With W gales in winter, the current runs E along N coast of Spain, sometimes at 3kn or more. When crossing B of Biscay, allow for a likely set to the E, particularly after strong W winds. Tidal streams are weak offshore, but can be strong in estuaries and channels, and around headlands. It is wise to study the prevailing current and stream from fish floats etc.

Larger scale French charts are often more suitable for inshore waters. The *Bay of Biscay Pilot* is recommended, as are *South Biscay Pilot* and *North Biscay Pilot* (Adlard Coles Ltd) and *French Pilot Volume Four* (Nautical Books).

BAIE DE FONTARABIE (chart 1343)

Known to the Spanish as Rada de Higuer, this lies on the border of Spain and France, and is entered between Cabo Higuer (a bare, rugged cape with Lt Ho, connected by drying reefs to Isla Amuitz, 24m high) and Pte Ste Anne 1¾ M ESE. Les Briquets (dry) lie 1M N of Pte Ste Anne. In strong W winds pass to W of Banc Chicharvel in entrance to b.

In the middle of the roadstead is a neutral area, marked by Bns and shown on chart. Outside this area the boundary line (approximately 1°46′.2W) runs N from a white pyramid on the S shore, about 1M SW of Pte Ste Anne. Ria Fuenterrabia is entered between breakwaters in SW corner of the b, giving access to Hendaye-Plage (see 10.14.24). Entry should not be attempted with strong onshore winds or heavy swell.

POINTE SAINT ANNE TO L'ADOUR (chart 2665)

In bad weather the sea breaks on Plateau de St Jean de Luz, a chain of rky shoals lying 1-4M offshore along this coast, which as far as Pte St Martin has mostly a sandy beach and rky cliffs, with mountains inland.

St Jean de Luz (chart 1343 and 10.14.24) may be approached through four passes. Passe d'Illarguita (between Illarguita and Belhara Perdun) is recommended in bad weather: follow the 138° transit (Le Socoa in line with Bordagain) until the Ste Barbe Ldg Lts (101°) are in line, and thence by Passe de l'Ouest on the 151° transit of the St Jean de Luz Ldg Lts.

N of Pte St Martin the coast changes to sand dunes. The sea breaks over Loutrou shoal in strong W winds. At L'Adour entrance the flood runs E and SE, sp rate 2-4 kn; the ebb runs W, sp rate 3-5 kn.

L'ADOUR TO LA GIRONDE (charts 2665, 2664)

Apart from the entrance to Arcachon (10.14.9), this is a featureless coast bordered by sand dunes and fir trees, with no shelter from W winds. 5M offshore a current usually sets N at about ½ kn, particularly with a S wind: In winter this may be stronger after W winds. Within 1M of the coast there may be a counter-current setting S.

A submerged canyon, the Fosse (or Gouf) de Capbreton, runs at right angles to and within 2M of the coast. In strong W winds a dangerous sea develops along the N and S sides of this. A firing area lies offshore, bounded to the S by a line 295° from Capbreton Bn, and to the N by a line 245° from Pte de la Négade Bn, and extending to 2°25′ W. The inshore limit is 3M off, but connected to the shore at three places, two between Biscarosse and Pte d'Arcachon, and one at Hourtin. The area is divided into 31S and 31N, which are S and N of a clear chan 8M wide running 270° from Arcachon. 31S and 31N are further divided into areas indicated by distance from coast. Thus, 31S 27.45 means the S section, 27-45M offshore. Areas in use are bcst by Bordeaux-Arcachon Radio at 0803 and 1803 (zone −0100). Sectors 31S 12.27 and 31N 12.27 are used on working days from 0800-1800 (zone −0100).

LA GIRONDE − APPROACHES (chart 2910)

La Gironde estuary is formed by the Garonne and the Dordogne, which join at Bec d'Ambes, 38M above Pte de Grave. BXA Lt buoy is moored about 11M WSW of Pte de la Coubre, off which lies Banc de la Mauvaise, the S end of which dries. Cordouan Lt Ho is on a large rky bank in the middle of the estuary. Grande Passe de l'Ouest starts about 4M E of BXA buoy and is dredged through Grand Banc − the outer bar of La Gironde. Enter to seaward of Buoys Nos 1 and 2, and keep in buoyed channel with Ldg Lts. Off Terre-Nègre Lt the SE-going stream begins at HW −0500 (sp rate 1½ kn), and the NW-going at HW +0130 (sp rate 2½ kn).

Passe Sud, a lesser chan, is entered 5½ M W of Pte de la Négade, and runs NE past Pte de Grave. There are two sets of Ldg Lts; the second lead over Platin de Grave, but it is better to pass NW of this shoal. Both entrance chans are dangerous in strong on-shore winds, due to breakers and also the mascaret (bore) on the outgoing stream. Westerly swell breaks on La Mauvaise and around Cordouan, and sandbanks shift constantly. In places tidal stream runs 4 kn or more, and with wind against tide a dangerous sea can build up.

ILE D'OLERON (chart 2648, 2746)

From Pte de l'Epinette 13M N to Pte de Chassiron, the W coast is bounded by drying rks and shoals. In bad weather the sea breaks 4 or 5M offshore, where tidal streams are weak, sp rate 1 kn, starting NW at +0300 HW Pte de Grave and SE at −0505 HW Pte de Grave, but often overcome by current due to prevailing wind. The rate however increases towards Pte de Gatseau, where Pertuis de Maumusson separates the island from mainland. Its entrance is marked by buoy (safe water mark) about 2¾ M W of Pte d'Arvert. Banc des Mattes and Banc de Gatseau, both of which dry in places, lie S and N of the chan, and are joined by a sand bar which usually has a depth of about 1.5m. Depth and position vary, and buoys are moved accordingly. Any swell forms breakers, and the chan is very dangerous then or in even moderately strong W winds, especially on the ebb (sp rate 3½ kn). In good weather and with no swell, enter about HW−1.

14

Coureau d'Oleron, joined by La Seudre (10.14.13) near its S end, leads between ledges and oyster beds, and constantly changes, with buoys moved to conform. It is crossed by a bridge, clearance 15m, about 2M SE of Le Chateau (10.14.14): chan (prohibited anch) is marked by boards at road level, triangular W&G to be left to stbd, rectangular R&W to be left to port, illuminated at night. S-going stream starts − 0230 HW Pte de Grave, N-going at + 0500 HW Pte de Grave, sp rates 2 kn. Just N of bridge is Fort du Chapus, connected to mainland by causeway.

The N end of Coureau d'Oleron leads into Grande Rade, where good anch is found except in fresh NW winds. At N end of Grande Rade is entrance to La Charente (10.14.15). From the N, Grande Rade is entered from Pertuis d'Antioche through Passage de l'Est close to Ile d'Aix (10.14.24) or Passage de l'Ouest, which run each side of La Longe du Boyard − an extensive sandbank on which stands a fort.

PERTUIS D'ANTIOCHE (chart 2746)

A buoy (safe water mark) is moored in W approach to Pertuis d'Antioche which runs between Ile d'Oleron and Ile de Ré, giving access to Rochefort (10.14.15) and La Rochelle (10.14.16). Its shores are low. Off Pte de Chassiron (Lt Ho, Sig Stn) reefs extend ½M W, 1½M N to Rocher d'Antioche (lit), and 1½M E, and there is often a nasty sea. Ile de Ré forms the N shore, and its coast is fringed by rky ledges extending 2½M SE from Pte de Chanchardon (Lt) and nearly 1M from Pte de Chauveau (marked by Bn and Lt Tr).

Plateau de Rochebonne, with depths of less than 4m, is a large rky flat 35-40M W of Ile de Ré, marked by buoys. It is steep-to on all sides, and the sea breaks dangerously on it.

PERTUIS BRETON (chart 2641)

Pertuis Breton is entered between Pte des Baleines (Ile de Ré) and Pte du Grouin du Cou (both lit). It gives access to the harbs on N shore of Ile de Ré, to L'Aiguillon (10.14.24) and Marans on the mainland shore, and provides (except in NW winds) a sheltered route to La Pallice and La Rochelle, through Coureau de la Pallice. Beware rocky ledges (dry) extending 2½M NW from Les Baleines. There are shallows and drying areas all along the N coast of Ile de Ré. Near St Martin and La Flotte there are extensive fisheries, with seaward limits marked by buoys (special marks).

On N shore, Pte du Grouin du Crou has steep cliffs: with fresh NW winds against NW-going stream a bad sea builds on the bank which extends 8M W. 1M S of the point is Roche de l'Aunis (depth 0.3m). From the point sand dunes run 8M ESE to the entrance to Rivière Le Lay, which is fronted by a bar (dries 1m), dangerous in bad weather. The chan to L'Aiguillon (10.14.24) is marked by Bns and buoys. 4M further E is entrance to Anse de l'Aiguillon, in which are extensive mussel beds. In NE corner is entrance to Sèvre Niortaise which, after 3½M, gives access to the canal leading to the port of Marans. The lock operates at HW.

BAIE DE BOURGNEUF (charts 2646, 2647)

B de Bourgneuf is entered between Pte de l'Herbaudière, the NW extremity of Ile de Noirmoutier, and Pte de St Gildas about 7M NNE. The S entrance through Goulet de Fromentine is obstructed by a causeway, Route du Gois, which dries 3m. The b is sheltered except in W winds, which can raise a heavy sea with the ebb stream. There are good anchs but the S and E sides of the b are encumbered with shoals, rocks and oyster or mussel fisheries.

From the S, beware Chaussée des Boeufs, marked by buoys, extending 3½M W and 7½M SW of Ile de Noirmoutier. Some of these dry, and the tide sets on to them. Chenal de la Grise (chart 3216) between Ile du Pilier and Pte de l'Herbaudière has 2.7m in the W sector of Basse du Martroger Lt, and gives access to L'Herbaudière marina (10.14.22). If proceeding E to Pornic (10.14.23), pass N of Basse du Martroger, and beware Roches des Pères about 1M ENE.

From the N (chart 3216) the approach is simple, but beware La Couronnée, dries 1.8m and marked by buoys, on a rky bank about 2M WSW of Pte de St Gildas. 2M S of Pte de St Gildas, Banc de Kerouars extends 3M in an E/W direction with depths of 1m, where the sea breaks.

From westward, approach Pornic in the W sector of Pte de Noveillard Lt − S of Banc de Kerouars and N of Notre Dame Bn Tr, which lies 2M SW of Pornic and marks end of a line of rks extending WNW from La Bernerie. Pierre du Chenal is an isolated rk about 1M SSE of Notre Dame. Within the b are Noirmoutier (10.14.22) and minor drying harbs − Bec de l'Epoids, Port des Brochets, Le Collet and La Bernerie-en-Retz − with a good anch at Pte des Dames.

10.14.6   DISTANCE TABLE

Approximate distances in nautical miles are by the most direct route while avoiding dangers and allowing for traffic separation schemes etc. Places in *italics* are in adjoining areas.

1 *Pointe du Raz*	1																			
2 *Le Palais (Belle Ile)*	81	2																		
3 Pornic	125	45	1 3																	
4 Port Joinville (Ile d'Yeu)	126	50	30	4																
5 St-Gilles-Croix-de-Vie	141	64	40	18	5															
6 Les Sables d'Olonne	156	79	55	31	20	6														
7 St Martin (Ile de Ré)	177	105	75	55	44	27	7													
8 La Rochelle	186	110	92	66	51	36	12	8												
9 Pointe de Chassiron	185	107	84	58	46	32	17	13	9											
10 Royan	224	146	115	97	85	71	56	52	39	10										
11 Bordeaux	278	200	169	151	139	125	110	106	93	54	11									
12 Castets (canal lock)	308	230	199	181	169	155	140	136	123	84	30	12								
13 Cap Ferret (Arcachon)	253	185	160	138	130	113	102	98	85	68	118	152	13							
14 Capbreton	298	235	215	192	186	171	162	158	145	124	174	208	58	14						
15 Bayonne	307	242	223	200	195	178	149	166	153	132	182	216	70	12	15					
16 St Jean de Luz	310	250	230	206	200	186	153	174	161	136	186	220	76	19	16	16				
17 *San Sebastian*	307	249	233	210	204	191	159	178	165	142	192	226	85	31	29	17	17			
18 *Santander*	280	239	241	212	210	201	190	198	185	173	223	257	130	104	102	95	83	18		
19 *La Coruna*	321	334	357	335	340	342	365	354	341	348	398	432	327	315	317	314	298	223	19	
20 *Cabo Finisterre*	369	385	408	386	391	393	416	405	392	399	449	483	378	366	368	365	349	274	59	20

SPECIAL NOTES FOR FRENCH AREAS (Areas 14, 15, 16, 17 and 18) 10-14-7

There are certain differences in the harbour information where French ports are concerned. Instead of 'County' the 'Department' is given. The word Customs is used instead of HMC. It should also be remembered that the Time Zone for France is − 0100 (i.e. 1300 Standard Time in France is 1200 GMT), daylight saving schemes not having been taken into account (see 9.1.2.)

For special information about passports, visas, triptyques, carnets, Permis de Circulation, etc. see the relevant sections in earlier chapters or, for greater detail apply to the French Government Tourist Office, 178 Piccadilly, London, W1V 0AL. Tel. 01-499-6911.

AFFAIRES MARITIMES

In every French port there is a representative of the central government, L'Administration Maritime, known as Affaires Maritimes. This organisation watches over all maritime activities and helps them develop harmoniously − commercial, fishing, pleasure, etc. All information about navigation and any other maritime problems can be supplied by the local representative. If in doubt whom to consult, the Affaires Maritimes is the best place to start. Their headquarters is at

Bureau de la Plaisance − 3 Place Fonteroy, 75007 Paris. Tel: (1) 45.67.55.05

and the telephone number of their local representative is given under each port in the Almanac.

CHARTS

Two French chart numbers are given; SHOM are those issued by the 'Service Hydrographique et Oceanographique de la Marine', the Hydrographic Service of the French Navy; also ECM 'Éditions Cartographiques Maritimes', which are charts for sea and river navigation (Carte-Guide de navigation maritime et fluviale).

The letters SHOM after entries in the 'Facilities' indicates an agent for SHOM charts.

SIGNALS

There are standard sets of signals for Traffic, Storm Warnings, Distress and Tidal, and these apply in all French ports unless otherwise stated.

Traffic Signals

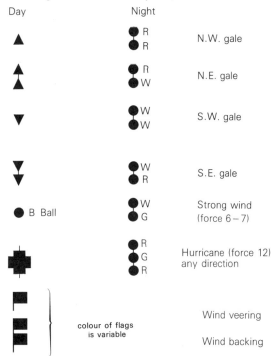

Day		Night		
Full Code	Simplified Code	Full Code	Simplified Code	
● ▲ ●	or **R** Flag	●R ●W ●R	or ●R	ENTRY PROHIBITED
▼ ▲ ●	**R** Flag over **G** Flag	●G ●W ●R	or ●R ●G	ENTRY AND DEPARTURE PROHIBITED
▼ ▲ ▼	or **G** Flag	●G ●W ●G	or ●G	DEPARTURE PROHIBITED
● ● ●	R R Balls R	●R ●R ●R		EMERGENCY — ENTRY PROHIBITED
INTERNATIONAL CODE SIGNAL		●G ●G ●G		PORT OPEN

A Black Flag displayed indicates a shipping casualty in the area.

Flag 'P' is sometimes displayed to indicate that lock or dock gates are open.

Distress Signals (from Lighthouse) or Danger Signals

Most isolated French lighthouses have radiotelephones, but the following signals may be displayed:

A ball above or below a square flag — Require immediate assistance

A black flag at the masthead — Shipwreck in vicinity of lighthouse

Storm Signals (International System)

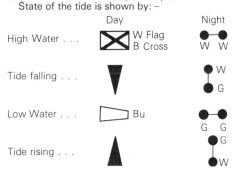

Day	Night	
▲	●R ●R	N.W. gale
▲ ▲	●R ●W	N.E. gale
▼	●W ●W	S.W. gale
▼ ▼	●W ●R	S.E. gale
● B Ball	●W ●G	Strong wind (force 6 − 7)
✚	●R ●G ●R	Hurricane (force 12) any direction
▬ ▬	colour of flags is variable	Wind veering / Wind backing

In France, flashing white lights, by day only, indicate wind over Force 6, as follows: − Quick flashing − within three hours; Interrupted quick flashing − within six hours.

Tidal Signals

There are two sets of signals, one showing the state of the tide and the other showing the depth of water.

State of the tide is shown by: −

	Day	Night	
High Water . . .	⊠ W Flag / B Cross	●—● W W	
Tide falling . . .	▼	● ●W ●G	
Low Water . . .	▭ Bu	●—● G G	
Tide rising . . .	▲	●G ●W	

The depth of water signals show the depth above Chart Datum and to ascertain the figure the various shapes have to be added together;

by day: a cone point down = 0.2 m, a cylinder = 1.0 m, a ball = 5.0 m.

by night: G light = 0.2 m, R light = 1.0 m, W light = 5.0 m.

The three different shapes are shown horizontally, with cones to the left of cylinders and balls to the right, viewed from seaward. Lights are disposed similarly.

The following examples will help to explain.

BY DAY

0.2 m 1.0 m 5.0 m	0.2 m 1.0 m 5.0 m	0.2 m 1.0 m 5.0 m
0.2 m 2.0 m	0.8 m 4.0 m	0.6 m 3.0 m 5.0 m
2.2 m	4.8 m	8.6 m

14

SPECIAL NOTES FOR FRENCH AREAS *continued*

BY NIGHT

2.2 m	4.8 m	8.6 m
0.2 m 2.0 m	0.8 m 4.0 m	0.6 m 3.0 m 5.0 m

The following French equivalents may be useful for understanding tidal data published on notice boards etc in French harbours:

High water (HW)	Pleine mer (PM)
Low water (LW)	Basse mer (BM)
Springs (Sp)	Vive eau (VE)
Neaps (Np)	Morte eau (ME)
Mean high water springs (MHWS)	Pleine mer moyenne de VE
Mean high water neaps (MHWN)	Pleine mer moyenne de ME
Mean low water neaps (MLWN)	Basse mer moyenne de ME
Mean low water springs (MLWS)	Basse mer moyenne de VE
Mean level	Niveau moyen (ou niveau de mi-marée)
Chart datum (CD)	Zero des cartes
Lowest astronomical tide (LAT)	Plus basse mer connue (PBM)
Flood (tide)	Flot (ou flux)
Ebb (tide)	Reflux (ou jusant)
Range	Marnage (ou amplitude)
Stand (at high water)	Etale
Greenwich Mean Time (GMT)	Temps universel (TU)

TIDAL COEFFICIENTS

The French use tidal coefficients which vary from 45 at mean neaps (Morte Eau) to 95 at mean springs (Vive Eau), but which with exceptional tides can be as little as 20 or as much as 120. For an average tide the coefficient is 70. The coefficients, which are published in France for every tide of the year, therefore indicate the size of each tide. The ratio of the coefficients of different tides equals the ratio of their ranges. For example, from the figures given above it can be seen that the range of the largest spring tide (coefficient 120) is six times the range of the smallest neap tide (coefficient 20).

SAFETY AT SEA

Control of Search and Rescue is exercised by the CROSS organisation (Centres Régionaux Operationnels de Surveillance et de Sauvetage) available 24 hrs a day.
The organisation is divided as follows:-
Spanish border to Pointe du Raz: CROSS Etel, Tel. 97.55.35.35, (2182 kHz and VHF Ch 16).
Pointe du Raz to Mont St Michel: CROSS Corsen, Tel. 98.89.31.31, (2182 kHz and VHF Ch 11 16).
Mont St Michel to Antifer: CROSS Jobourg, Tel. 33.52.72.13, (2182 kHz and VHF Ch 11 16).
Antifer to Belgian border: CROSS Gris Nez; Tel. 21.87.21.87, (2182kHz and VHF Ch 16 69).
Note: CROSS Soulac, near Pointe du Grave, is a subsidiary station of CROSS Etel, Tel. 56.59.82.00, (2182 kHz and VHF Ch 16, 0600-2100).
Besides the Search and Rescue function CROSS will provide urgent up-to-date navigational information such as buoys adrift, lights not working etc.
The following CROSS VHF relay stations keep watch on Ch 16; La Rhune (near Spanish border), Cap Ferret, Chassiron (Ile de Oléron), Ile d'Yeu, Belle Ile and Penmarc'h. CROSS can be contacted by radiotelephone, by telephone, through coast radio stations, via the semaphore system (French Navy on Ch 16) as shown below, or via the National Gendarmerie or Affaires Maritimes.
Naval 'Semaphore' stations keep watch on Ch 16 (working channel Ch 10) or by telephone as follows:

SEMAPHORE	TELEPHONE
● SOCOA	59.47.18.54
CAP FERRET	56.60.60.03
POINTE-DE-GRAVE	56.09.60.03
LA COUBRE	46.22.41.73
ILE D'AIX	46.88.66.07
CHASSIRON (Oléron)	46.47.85.43
LES BALEINES (Ré)	46.29.42.06
ST-SAUVEUR (Yeu)	51.58.31.01
● CHEMOULIN	40.91.99.00
PIRIAC-SUR-MER	40.23.59.87
ST-JULIEN	97.50.09.35
TALUT (Belle-Ile)	97.31.85.07
TAILLEFER (Belle-Ile)	97.31.83.18
BEG MELEN (Groix) (PEN MEN)	97.05.80.13
ETEL	97.55.35.59
● PORT-LOUIS	97.85.52.10
BEG MEIL	98.94.98.92
● PENMARCH	98.58.61.00
● POINTE-DU-RAZ	98.70.66.57
CAP-DE-LA-CHEVRE	98.27.09.55
TOULINGUET	98.27.90.02
● MINOU (Vigie)	98.22.10.43
● ST-MATHIEU	98.89.01.59
OUESSANT CREACH	98.48.80.49.
● OUESSANT STIFF	98.48.81.50
● BRIGNOGAN	98.83.50.84
● ST QUAY-PORTRIEUX	96.70.42.18
BATZ	98.61.76.06
● PLOUMANACH	96.23.21.50
BREHAT	96.20.00.12
ST-CAST	96.41.85.30
LE GROUIN	99.89.60.12
LE ROC	33.50.05.85
CARTERET	33.53.85.08
LA HAGUE	33.52.71.87
● LE HOMET	33.92.60.08
LEVY	33.54.31.17
● BARFLEUR	33.54.04.37
ST-VAAST	33.54.44.50
● PORT-EN-BESSIN	31.21.81.51
VILLERVILLE	31.88.11.13
● LA HEVE	35.46.07.81
FECAMP	35.28.00.91
DIEPPE	35.84.23.82
AULT	22.60.47.33
BOULOGNE	21.31.32.10
● DUNKERQUE	20.66.86.18

● H24. Remainder sunrise to sunset.

Whereas in UK, lifeboats should be contacted only through HM Coastguard, in France, although the lifeboat service comes under the CROSS organisation, it is encouraged to contact the lifeboat stations (Societe Nationale de Sauvetage en Mer, SNSM) direct. Where appropriate, therefore, the telephone numbers of local SNSMs are given.

MEDICAL

Telephone numbers of doctors and/or hospitals are given for each port. There is also the Services d'Aide Médicale Urgente (SAMU), which liaises closely with CROSS, which can be contacted as follows: —

PYRÉNÉES-ATLANTIQUE (Bayonne)	59.63.33.33
LANDES (Mont-de-Marsan)	58.75.44.44
GIRONDE (Bordeaux)	56.96.70.70
CHARENTE-MARITIME (La Rochelle)	46.27.15.15
VENDEE (La Roche-sur-Yon)	51.62.62.15
LOIRE-ATLANTIQUE (Nantes)	40.48.35.35
MORBIHAN (Vannes)	97.54.22.11
FINISTERE (Brest)	98.46.11.33
CÔTES-DU-NORD (Saint Brieuc)	96.94.40.15
CALVADOS (Caen)	31.44.88.88
SEINE-MARITIME (Le Havre)	35.21.11.00
SOMME (Amiens)	22.44.33.33
PAS-DE-CALAIS (Arras)	21.71.51.51
NORD (Lille)	20.54.22.22

SPECIAL NOTES FOR FRENCH AREAS *continued*

PUBLIC HOLIDAYS
New Year's Day, Easter Sunday and Monday, Labour Day (1 May), Ascension Day, Armistice Day 1945 (8 May), Whit Sunday and Monday, National (Bastille) Day (14 July), Feast of the Assumption (15 August), All Saints' Day (1 November), Remembrance Day (11 November), Christmas Day.

METEO (Weather)
The BQR (Bulletin Quotidien des Renseignements) is a daily information bulletin displayed in Harbour Masters' Offices and in yacht clubs, and is very informative.

Telephone numbers of the principal coastal Bureaux Meteorologiques (Met. Offices) are given in 7.2.4. This also shows numbers for Repondeurs Automatiques (recorded messages) which are sufficiently detailed for short coastal passages.

For details of weather information from French radio stations see — Table 7 (5).

TELEPHONES
To telephone France from UK, dial 010 33 followed by the number. For all exchanges outside Paris, area codes have been added on to individual numbers. All numbers therefore have eight digits. From inside France, dial the eight figures shown in the Almanac. From UK dial 010 33 followed by the eight digit number shown. There are two sorts of ringing tone: one consists of three second bursts of tone separated by three seconds silence; the other consists of one and a half second bursts of tone followed by three and a half seconds silence. Engaged is similar to that in UK. Number unobtainable is indicated by a recorded announcement. A rapid series of pips indicates your call is being connected. For Police dial 17. For Fire or Hospital dial 18.
To telephone UK from France dial 19; wait for the second dialling tone then dial 44 followed by the area dialling code (omitting the first 0) and then the number.
Phonecards for public telephones may be bought at the PTT or at some cafés and tabacs. Cheap rates are from 2130 to 0800 Mon-Sat; and all day Sun.
Note 1.
See 2.5.3 regarding French Customs regulations.
Note 2.
Speed under power is limited in France to 5 kn. when within 300 m of the shore.
Note 3.
There are strict penalties for infringing the International Regulations for Prevention of Collision at Sea and for French yachts not carrying the correct documentation or safety equipment.
Note 4.
The following abbreviations are used in telephone numbers:

Capitaine du Port	Hr Mr
Affaires Maritimes	Aff Mar
Centre régional opérationnel de surveillance et sauvetage	CROSS
Societe Nationale de Sauvetage en Mer (Lifeboats)	SNSM
Meteorologie/Weather	Meteo
Meteo Repondeur Automatique	Auto

Note 5.
Foreign vessels over 25m must get permission to navigate or anchor in French internal waters and keep watch on Ch 16 or other nominated frequency.

FRENCH TERMS
When cruising in French waters it is essential to know some directions: *Anse:* bay. *Arrière port:* inner harbour. *Avant port:* outer harbour. *Baie:* shoal. *Bassin:* basin. *Canal:* canal, channel. *Cap:* cape. *Chaussée:* bank. *Chenal:* channel. *Clocher:* steeple. *Digue:* breakwater, mole. *Ecluse:* lock. *Est:* east. *Étang:* lagoon, lake. *Falaise:* cliff. *Fleuve:* river. *Golfe:* gulf. *Goulet:* narrows. *Grand:* great. *Île:* island. *Jetée:* jetty. *Miason:* house. *Menhir:* large stone. *Môle:* mole. *Mont:* mountain. *Mouillage:* anchorage. *Moulin:* mill. *Nord:* north. *Ouest:* west. *Passe:* channel. *Pertuis:* strait. *Petit:* small. *Pierre:* stone. *Pointe:* point. *Pont:* bridge. *Port:* harbour, port. *Presqu'île:* peninsula. *Quai:* quay. *Rade:* roadstead. *Récif:* reef. *Rivière:* river. *Roche(r):* rock. *Sable:* sand. *Sud:* south. *Tour:* tower. *Ville:* town.

TIDAL INFORMATION FOR NORTH COAST OF SPAIN   10-14-8
Standard Port POINTE DE GRAVE (——►)

Times				Height (metres)			
HW		LW		MHWS	MHWN	MLWN	MLWS
0000	0600	0500	1200	5.3	4.3	2.1	1.0
1200	1800	1700	2400				
Differences CORUNA							
−0110	−0050	−0030	−0100	−1.7	−1.5	−0.8	−0.5
ORTIGUEIRA							
−0020	+0010	+0020	0000	−1.7	−1.5	−0.8	−0.5
LUARCA							
−0030	−0020	+0005	−0025	−1.4	−1.3	−0.6	−0.5
GIJON							
−0050	−0040	−0015	−0045	−1.3	−1.2	−0.6	−0.5
SANTANDER							
−0020	−0100	0000	−0050	−0.9	−0.8	−0.2	−0.1
BILBAO							
−0045	−0030	−0010	−0030	−1.3	−1.2	−0.7	−0.5
LEQUEITO							
−0100	−0050	−0025	−0045	−1.2	−1.2	−0.6	−0.5
SAN SEBASTIAN							
−0055	−0040	−0020	−0035	−1.2	−1.2	−0.6	−0.5

ARCACHON   10-14-9
Gironde

CHARTS
Admiralty 2664; SHOM 6766, 6787; ECM 255
TIDES
+0620 Dover; ML 2.2; Zone −0100
Standard Port POINTE DE GRAVE (——►)

Times				Height (metres)			
HW		LW		MHWS	MHWN	MLWN	MLWS
0000	0600	0500	1200	5.3	4.3	2.1	1.0
1200	1800	1700	2400				
Differences ARCACHON							
+0005	+0030	+0015	+0040	−1.1	−1.1	−1.0	−0.8
ST JEAN DE LUZ (SOCOA)							
−0050	−0045	−0025	−0040	−1.0	−1.0	−0.5	−0.5
L'ADOUR (BOUCAU)							
−0035	−0030	−0010	−0030	−1.0	−0.9	−0.3	−0.2
CAP FERRET							
−0015	0000	+0005	+0015	−1.2	−1.0	−0.7	−0.6

SHELTER
Good shelter in marina in Bassin d'Arcachon. Entry impossible at night or in strong winds from SW to N. Max length 15m. Besides the Port d'Arcachon there are numerous other small drying harbours round the basin. On the West, La Vigne, Le Canon, Piquey and Claouey; on the South La Teste and Gujan; on the NE Port de Lège, Ares, Andernos, Port de Fontaine Vielle, Lanton (Cassy) and Audenge.
NAVIGATION
Waypoint ATT ARC (safe water) buoy, LFl 10s, Whis, 44°31'.76N 01°18'.27W, approx 260°/080° from/to Nos 1 and 2 channel buoys, 1.0M. Beware shifting sand banks in entrance channel, the sea breaks on these banks in any wind but the entrance channel can be seen through the breakers. With a strong on-shore wind the bar is impassable from HW+1 until LW, and it is best to wait until LW+3. Buoys are adjusted each spring but channel can change later. Latest information from Service de la Marine Gironde at Arcachon 56.82.32.97 or at Bordeaux 56.83.03.00. Average depth over bar is 4.5m. Beware firing ranges to seaward and S of Arcachon. See 10.14.5.
LIGHTS AND MARKS
Cap Ferret Fl R 5s 53m 27M and Oc (3) 12s vis 045°-135°. Arcachon harbour W breakwater QG, E breakwater QR. Port de la Vigne Iso R 4s 7m 4M.
La Salie Q (9) 15s 19m 10M.
RADIO TELEPHONE
VHF Ch 09.
TELEPHONE (56)
Hr Mr 56.83.22.44; Aff Mar 56.83.03.00; ⌗ 56.83.05.89; SNSM 56.83.22.44; CROSS 56.09.82.00; Auto 56.34.88.34; Police 56.83.04.63; Dr 56.83.04.72; ⊞ 56.83.39.50; Brit Consul 56.52.28.35.

14

ARCACHON *continued*

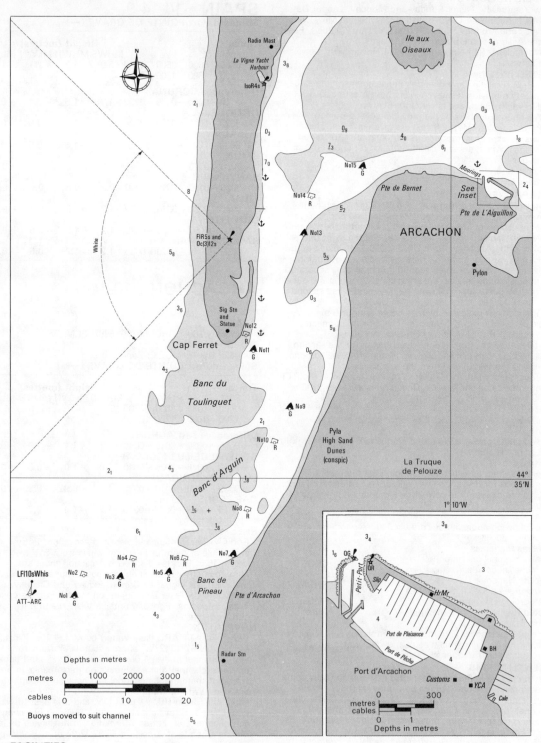

Radio Mast

Ile aux Oiseaux

La Vigne Yacht Harbour

IsoR4s

3_6

3_6

0_9

O_3

0_9 4_0 1_8

2_1 7_3

6_1

7_0 No15
G

5_2 Moorings

No14
R   *Pte de Bernet*   See Inset

2_4

Pte de L'Aiguillon

8 ARCACHON

FIR5s and Oc(3)12s

No13 5_5

5_8

O_3 Pylon

3_6 Sig Stn and Statue 5_8

Cap Ferret   No12
R O_6

No11
G

4_3

Banc du Toulinguet

No9
G

2_1 *Pyla High Sand Dunes (conspic)*

No10
R

La Truque de Pelouze   44° 35'N

4_3 1_8

Banc d'Arguin   1° 10'W

2_1

1_5 +   No8
R 1_8 3_8

6_1 3_4

No4
R   No6
R   No7 1_6 QG
QR   *Petit Port* 3

LFl10sWhis   No2   No3
G   No5
G   Slip   HrMr 3

4

Banc de Pineau   *Port de Plaisance*   BH

No1
G 4_3 *Pte d'Arcachon*   *Port de Pêche* 4

ATT-ARC

1_5 Radar Stn   Customs   YCA
Cale

Depths in metres   *Port d'Arcachon*

metres   0   1000   2000   3000

cables   0   10   20   metres   0   300

Buoys moved to suit channel   cables   0   1

5_5 Depths in metres

FACILITIES

Marina (2243+57 visitors), FW, AC, Slip, C (20 ton), BH (45 ton), D, Access HW∓3; **Station Elf** ☎ 56.83.29.72, P, D; **Y C d'Arcachon** ☎ 56.83.22.11, P, D, FW, Slip, Bar, R; **Arcachon Plaisance** ☎ 56.83.31.31, P, D, L, FW, ME, Ⓔ, El, Sh, CH; **Arcachon Shipchandler** ☎ 56.83.23.69 CH, ME, El, Sh, Ⓔ; **Nautic Service** ☎ 56.83.84.10, ME, El, Sh, CH; **Service Nautique** ☎ 56.83.27.45, SHOM; **Voiles Assistance** ☎ 56.83.58.55, SM; **N Jetty** ☎ 56.83.22.44, Slip, L, FW, C (10 ton), AB; **Town** AB, V, R, Gaz, ✉, Ⓑ, ⇌, ✈ (Bordeaux).
Ferry UK — Roscoff—Plymouth; St Malo—Portsmouth.

PORT BLOC/
LA GIRONDE 10-14-10
Gironde

CHARTS
Admiralty 2910, 2664; SHOM 7028, 6335, 6336; ECM 554
TIDES
(Pauillac) +0720 Dover; ML 3.0; Duration: Springs 0615;
Neaps 0655; Zone −0100
Standard Port POINTE DE GRAVE (→)

Times				Height (metres)			
HW		LW		MHWS	MHWN	MLWN	MLWS
0000	0600	0500	1200	5.3	4.3	2.1	1.0
1200	1800	1700	2400				
Differences ROYAN							
0000	−0020	−0010	−0005	−0.2	−0.2	−0.2	−0.1
LAMENA							
+0035	+0045	+0100	+0130	+0.2	+0.1	−0.4	−0.3
PAUILLAC							
+0045	+0110	+0140	+0220	+0.2	0.0	−0.8	−0.5
LA REUILLE							
+0120	+0155	+0230	+0320	−0.2	−0.4	−1.4	−0.9
LE MARQUIS							
+0130	+0205	+0250	+0340	−0.2	−0.4	−1.6	−1.0
BORDEAUX							
+0155	+0235	+0330	+0425	−0.1	−0.3	−1.7	−1.0

SHELTER
Good shelter. Port Bloc is 4 ca (740m) S of Pointe de
Grave at the entrance to the Gironde. It is dredged to 3m.
Yachts use the W side of the harbour on pontoons or
moor between buoys.
NAVIGATION
Waypoint BXA (safe water) buoy, Iso 4s, Whis, Racon,
45°37'.60N 01°28'.60W, 261°/081° from/to Grande Passe
de l'Ouest Nos 1 and 2 buoys, 4.8M. The approaches to
the Gironde can be dangerous see 10.14.5. There are very
strong tidal streams and currents encountered between
the entrance and Pointe de Grave. Also beware shipping
entering and leaving.

LIGHTS AND MARKS
Ldg Lts 041°. Front QR 33m 18M, intens 039°-043°. Rear,
0.97M from front, QR 61m 18M, intens 039°-043°. Ldg
line E of Pointe de Grave 327° astern with Tèrre Negre Lt
in line with rear of La Palmyre. FR. Lts on NW jetty Fl G
4s 8m 6M, SE jetty Iso R 4s 8m 6M.
RADIO TELEPHONE
Le Verdon VHF Ch 16; 11 12 14 (H24). Pauillac Ch 09 12
(H24). Ambès Ch 12 16 (H24). Bordeaux Ch 11 12 16
(H24). Water level reports on Ch 71. Reports on sea state
from Semaphore (La Coubre) Ch 16; 06 12.
TELEPHONE (56)
Hr Mr 56.09.63.91; Aff Mar 56.09.60.23; CROSS
56.09.82.00; ✠ 56.09.65.14; Police 56.09.60.13; Dr
56.09.60.37; Meteo 56.34.20.11; Brit Consul 56.52.28.35.
FACILITIES
Quai FW, C (10 ton); **Nautic Pointe de Grave**
☎ 56.59.63.27; ME, El, Sh, CH; **Médoc Loisirs** (Verdon)
☎ 56.59.64.91, ME, El, Sh, CH; **La Boutique du Marin**
(Verdon) ☎ 56.59.63.75, ME, El, CH; **Moto Yachting**
Club de la Pointe de Grave ☎ 56.09.61.58; **Town** P, D,
AB, Gaz, V, R, ✉ (Verdon); Ⓑ (Verdon); ≈;
✈ (Bordeaux);
Ferry UK — Roscoff—Plymouth; St Malo—Portsmouth.

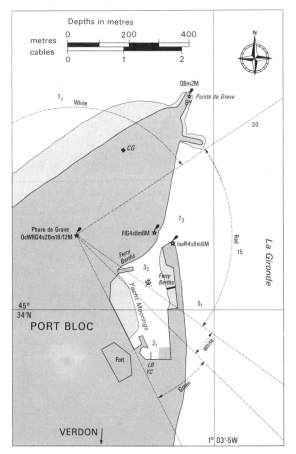

La Gironde is the estuary of the rivers Dordogne and
Garonne. There are a number of havens in the 50 M from
the mouth to Bordeaux including Pauillac (see 10.14.24),
Lamarque and Blaye. In Bordeaux there is a marina
opposite Lormont, just after passing under the first bridge
(see 10.14.24). About 27 M up the Garonne from Bordeaux,
at Castets, there is the first lock into the Canal Lateral à la
Garonne which leads into the Canal du Midi. In the
Garonne at springs, the flood stream starts with a small
bore and then runs at about 3 kn, while the ebb runs at
5 kn. In the other rivers the spring rate does not exceed
3 kn on the flood and 4 kn, on the ebb.
NOTE: A major marina is due to be built at Verdon.

14

FRANCE, WEST COAST - POINTE DE GRAVE

LAT 45°34'N   LONG 1°04'W

TIMES AND HEIGHTS OF HIGH AND LOW WATERS

YEAR **1991**

TIME ZONE –0100
(French Standard Time)
Subtract 1 hour for GMT
For French Summer Time add
ONE hour in non-shaded areas

JANUARY

Day	Time	m	Time	m	Time	m	Time	m
1 TU	0509	5.4	1114	0.8	1740	5.3	2331	0.9
2 W	0557	5.5	1204	0.7	1826	5.3		
3 TH	0019	0.9	0645	5.5	1251	0.8	1911	5.2
4 F	0104	1.0	0731	5.4	1336	0.9	1955	5.1
5 SA	0149	1.1	0816	5.2	1420	1.2	2038	4.8
6 SU	0235	1.3	0901	5.0	1505	1.4	2124	4.6
7 M	0322	1.5	0948	4.7	1553	1.7	(2216	4.4
8 TU	0413	1.8	1044	4.4	1648	2.0	2324	4.2
9 W	0513	2.1	1159	4.2	1755	2.2		
10 TH	0043	4.1	0623	2.2	1321	4.1	1909	2.2
11 F	0152	4.2	0735	2.2	1428	4.2	2013	2.1
12 SA	0245	4.4	0836	2.0	1517	4.3	2104	1.9
13 SU	0327	4.6	0925	1.8	1556	4.5	2146	1.7
14 M	0404	4.8	1006	1.6	1630	4.7	2224	1.6
15 TU	0440	4.9	1044	1.4	1703 ●	4.8	2259	1.4
16 W	0514	5.0	1120	1.3	1734	4.9	2334	1.3
17 TH	0546	5.1	1155	1.3	1803	4.9		
18 F	0007	1.3	0618	5.1	1229	1.2	1832	4.9
19 SA	0042	1.3	0651	5.1	1303	1.2	1904	4.9
20 SU	0117	1.3	0726	5.1	1339	1.2	1939	4.9
21 M	0154	1.3	0805	5.0	1417	1.3	2020	4.8
22 TU	0234	1.4	0850	4.9	1459	1.4	2108	4.6
23 W	0321	1.6	0944	4.7	1548	1.6	) 2212	4.4
24 TH	0417	1.8	1054	4.5	1650	1.9	2335	4.3
25 F	0529	1.9	1219	4.4	1807	2.0		
26 SA	0101	4.4	0652	1.9	1343	4.5	1930	1.9
27 SU	0216	4.6	0811	1.6	1455	4.7	2041	1.6
28 M	0319	4.9	0918	1.3	1554	5.0	2140	1.3
29 TU	0413	5.2	1014	1.0	1644	5.2	2232	1.0
30 W	0501	5.5	1104	0.8	1728 O	5.3	2319	0.8
31 TH	0546	5.6	1150	0.7	1809	5.4		

FEBRUARY

Day	Time	m	Time	m	Time	m	Time	m
1 F	0004	0.8	0628	5.6	1233	0.7	1849	5.3
2 SA	0046	0.8	0708	5.5	1313	0.8	1926	5.2
3 SU	0126	0.9	0745	5.3	1352	1.1	2001	5.0
4 M	0205	1.1	0820	5.0	1429	1.3	2035	4.7
5 TU	0244	1.4	0855	4.7	1508	1.6	2114	4.5
6 W	0327	1.7	0936	4.4	1554	2.0	(2206	4.2
7 TH	0420	2.1	1035	4.0	1655	2.3	2327	4.0
8 F	0531	2.3	1215	3.9	1819	2.4		
9 SA	0105	4.0	0656	2.3	1356	3.9	1940	2.3
10 SU	0216	4.2	0809	2.2	1457	4.2	2040	2.1
11 M	0306	4.5	0903	1.9	1539	4.4	2125	1.8
12 TU	0347	4.7	0946	1.6	1613	4.6	2204	1.6
13 W	0422	4.9	1024	1.4	1645	4.8	2240	1.3
14 TH	0456	5.1	1100	1.2	1715	5.0	● 2315	1.2
15 F	0529	5.2	1135	1.1	1744	5.1	2349	1.1
16 SA	0600	5.3	1209	1.0	1814	5.1		
17 SU	0023	1.0	0633	5.4	1243	1.0	1846	5.1
18 M	0058	1.0	0708	5.3	1318	1.0	1920	5.1
19 TU	0133	1.0	0745	5.2	1354	1.1	1957	5.0
20 W	0212	1.2	0827	5.0	1433	1.3	2042	4.7
21 TH	0255	1.4	0918	4.7	1520	1.6	) 2142	4.5
22 F	0350	1.7	1030	4.4	1620	1.9	2308	4.3
23 SA	0506	1.9	1203	4.2	1745	2.1		
24 SU	0046	4.3	0642	1.9	1337	4.3	1919	2.0
25 M	0209	4.6	0806	1.7	1450	4.6	2032	1.7
26 TU	0313	4.9	0909	1.3	1545	4.9	2128	1.3
27 W	0404	5.2	1001	1.0	1630	5.2	2217	1.0
28 TH	0448	5.3	1047	0.8	1710	5.3	O 2302	0.8

MARCH

Day	Time	m	Time	m	Time	m	Time	m
1 F	0528	5.6	1130	0.7	1747	5.4	2344	0.7
2 SA	0605	5.6	1209	0.7	1821	5.3		
3 SU	0023	0.7	0640	5.4	1246	0.8	1854	5.2
4 M	0100	0.9	0711	5.2	1321	1.0	1925	5.1
5 TU	0134	1.1	0742	5.0	1354	1.3	1956	4.8
6 W	0209	1.3	0813	4.7	1428	1.6	2032	4.6
7 TH	0246	1.7	0851	4.4	1507	1.9	2118	4.3
8 F	0332	2.0	0944	4.0	1600	2.3	(2226	4.0
9 SA	0439	2.3	1110	3.8	1727	2.5		
10 SU	0004	3.9	0613	2.4	1309	3.8	1859	2.4
11 M	0135	4.1	0734	2.2	1422	4.1	2005	2.2
12 TU	0234	4.4	0831	1.9	1508	4.3	2054	1.8
13 W	0318	4.6	0916	1.6	1544	4.6	2135	1.5
14 TH	0356	4.9	0955	1.4	1616	4.8	2213	1.3
15 F	0430	5.1	1033	1.1	1648	5.0	2250	1.1
16 SA	0504	5.3	1109	1.0	1720	5.2	● 2326	0.9
17 SU	0538	5.4	1145	0.8	1753	5.3		
18 M	0002	0.8	0613	5.5	1220	0.8	1827	5.3
19 TU	0038	0.8	0650	5.4	1256	0.8	1903	5.2
20 W	0115	0.9	0729	5.2	1334	1.0	1943	5.0
21 TH	0155	1.0	0814	5.0	1414	1.3	2030	4.8
22 F	0240	1.3	0909	4.6	1503	1.6	2133	4.5
23 SA	0339	1.7	1024	4.3	1607	1.9	) 2258	4.3
24 SU	0501	1.9	1159	4.2	1738	2.1		
25 M	0036	4.4	0637	1.9	1329	4.3	1907	1.9
26 TU	0159	4.6	0836	1.6	1436	4.6	2015	1.6
27 W	0259	4.9	0852	1.3	1526	4.9	2109	1.3
28 TH	0347	5.2	0940	1.0	1608	5.1	2156	1.0
29 F	0429	5.3	1024	0.9	1646	5.2	2240	0.8
30 SA	0506	5.4	1105	0.8	1720	5.3	O 2320	0.8
31 SU	0540	5.3	1143	0.8	1753	5.3	2358	0.8

APRIL

Day	Time	m	Time	m	Time	m	Time	m
1 M	0611	5.2	1218	1.0	1824	5.2		
2 TU	0033	0.9	0641	5.1	1250	1.1	1855	5.0
3 W	0106	1.1	0710	4.9	1321	1.3	1927	4.8
4 TH	0139	1.3	0743	4.6	1354	1.6	2003	4.6
5 F	0214	1.6	0821	4.3	1431	1.9	2047	4.4
6 SA	0257	1.9	0911	4.0	1519	2.2	2147	4.1
7 SU	0356	2.2	1027	3.8	1635	2.4	(2309	4.0
8 M	0523	2.3	1209	3.8	1807	2.4		
9 TU	0038	4.1	0645	2.2	1329	4.0	1917	2.2
10 W	0146	4.3	0747	1.9	1422	4.3	2011	1.9
11 TH	0237	4.6	0836	1.6	1503	4.6	2056	1.6
12 F	0320	4.8	0919	1.3	1541	4.8	2138	1.3
13 SA	0359	5.1	0959	1.1	1617	5.0	2219	1.0
14 SU	0437	5.3	1039	0.9	1653	5.2	● 2300	0.8
15 M	0515	5.4	1118	0.8	1731	5.3	2340	0.7
16 TU	0555	5.4	1158	0.8	1810	5.3		
17 W	0020	0.7	0636	5.4	1237	0.8	1851	5.3
18 TH	0101	0.8	0720	5.2	1318	1.0	1936	5.1
19 F	0145	1.0	0810	4.9	1403	1.3	2029	4.8
20 SA	0235	1.3	0909	4.6	1456	1.6	2133	4.6
21 SU	0338	1.6	1023	4.3	1605	1.9	) 2253	4.5
22 M	0457	1.7	1149	4.3	1726	1.9		
23 TU	0021	4.5	0619	1.7	1308	4.4	1843	1.8
24 W	0137	4.6	0729	1.6	1410	4.6	1948	1.6
25 TH	0236	4.8	0826	1.4	1500	4.8	2043	1.3
26 F	0325	5.0	0915	1.2	1542	4.9	2132	1.2
27 SA	0406	5.1	0959	1.1	1620	5.0	2216	1.0
28 SU	0442	5.1	1039	1.0	1654	5.1	O 2256	1.0
29 M	0515	5.1	1116	1.1	1727	5.1	2333	1.0
30 TU	0546	5.0	1150	1.1	1758	5.1		

Chart Datum: 2.93 metres below Lallemand System (Mean Sea level, Marseilles)

FRANCE, WEST COAST - POINTE DE GRAVE

LAT 45°34′N   LONG 1°04′W

TIMES AND HEIGHTS OF HIGH AND LOW WATERS   YEAR **1991**

TIME ZONE –0100
(French Standard Time)
Subtract 1 hour for GMT
For French Summer Time add
ONE hour in non-shaded areas

MAY

Day	TIME	m	Day	TIME	m
1 W	0008 / 0616 / 1223 / 1831	1.1 / 4.9 / 1.2 / 5.0	**16** TH	0005 / 0627 / 1222 / 1843	0.7 / 5.3 / 0.9 / 5.3
2 TH	0041 / 0647 / 1254 / 1904	1.2 / 4.7 / 1.4 / 4.8	**17** F	0051 / 0716 / 1308 / 1934	0.7 / 5.1 / 1.0 / 5.2
3 F	0115 / 0720 / 1328 / 1940	1.3 / 4.6 / 1.6 / 4.7	**18** SA	0140 / 0808 / 1357 / 2029	0.9 / 4.9 / 1.2 / 5.0
4 SA	0151 / 0758 / 1405 / 2023	1.5 / 4.4 / 1.8 / 4.5	**19** SU	0233 / 0906 / 1452 / 2130	1.1 / 4.7 / 1.4 / 4.8
5 SU	0232 / 0845 / 1451 / 2115	1.7 / 4.2 / 2.0 / 4.3	**20** M	0332 / 1011 / 1554 / 2238 ☽	1.4 / 4.5 / 1.6 / 4.7
6 M	0323 / 0948 / 1552 / 2222	2.0 / 4.0 / 2.2 / 4.2	**21** TU	0437 / 1123 / 1702 / 2352	1.5 / 4.4 / 1.7 / 4.6
7 TU	0431 / 1109 / 1708 / 2338 ☾	2.1 / 3.9 / 2.2 / 4.2	**22** W	0547 / 1234 / 1810	1.6 / 4.4 / 1.7
8 W	0545 / 1226 / 1817	2.1 / 4.1 / 2.1	**23** TH	0104 / 0654 / 1337 / 1915	4.6 / 1.6 / 4.5 / 1.6
9 TH	0049 / 0650 / 1327 / 1917	4.3 / 1.9 / 4.3 / 1.9	**24** F	0206 / 0754 / 1430 / 2014	4.6 / 1.6 / 4.6 / 1.5
10 F	0148 / 0746 / 1417 / 2010	4.5 / 1.7 / 4.5 / 1.6	**25** SA	0258 / 0847 / 1515 / 2106	4.7 / 1.5 / 4.7 / 1.4
11 SA	0239 / 0836 / 1502 / 2100	4.8 / 1.4 / 4.8 / 1.3	**26** SU	0342 / 0933 / 1555 / 2152	4.7 / 1.4 / 4.8 / 1.3
12 SU	0325 / 0923 / 1545 / 2147	5.0 / 1.1 / 5.0 / 1.1	**27** M	0419 / 1013 / 1630 / 2233	4.8 / 1.3 / 4.9 / 1.2
13 M	0410 / 1009 / 1628 / 2233	5.2 / 1.0 / 5.2 / 0.9	**28** TU	0453 / 1051 / 1704 / 2311 ○	4.8 / 1.3 / 5.0 / 1.2
14 TU	0454 / 1053 / 1711 / 2319 ●	5.3 / 0.8 / 5.3 / 0.7	**29** W	0526 / 1126 / 1738 / 2347	4.8 / 1.3 / 5.0 / 1.2
15 W	0540 / 1137 / 1756	5.3 / 0.8 / 5.3	**30** TH	0558 / 1200 / 1811	4.7 / 1.3 / 4.9
			31 F	0021 / 0630 / 1233 / 1845	1.3 / 4.7 / 1.4 / 4.9

JUNE

Day	TIME	m	Day	TIME	m
1 SA	0056 / 0703 / 1308 / 1921	1.3 / 4.6 / 1.5 / 4.7	**16** SU	0132 / 0758 / 1347 / 2020	0.8 / 5.0 / 1.0 / 5.2
2 SU	0132 / 0738 / 1345 / 2000	1.4 / 4.5 / 1.7 / 4.6	**17** M	0221 / 0850 / 1438 / 2113	1.0 / 4.8 / 1.2 / 5.0
3 M	0211 / 0819 / 1428 / 2046	1.6 / 4.3 / 1.8 / 4.5	**18** TU	0313 / 0944 / 1531 / 2210	1.2 / 4.6 / 1.4 / 4.8
4 TU	0255 / 0910 / 1517 / 2140	1.7 / 4.2 / 1.9 / 4.4	**19** W	0407 / 1044 / 1629 / 2313 ☽	1.4 / 4.5 / 1.5 / 4.6
5 W	0347 / 1012 / 1615 / 2242 ☾	1.8 / 4.2 / 2.0 / 4.4	**20** TH	0507 / 1152 / 1731	1.6 / 4.3 / 1.7
6 TH	0447 / 1122 / 1718 / 2350	1.8 / 4.2 / 2.0 / 4.4	**21** F	0023 / 0612 / 1259 / 1837	4.4 / 1.8 / 4.3 / 1.8
7 F	0551 / 1231 / 1821	1.8 / 4.3 / 1.8	**22** SA	0131 / 0718 / 1400 / 1942	4.3 / 1.8 / 4.4 / 1.8
8 SA	0056 / 0654 / 1332 / 1923	4.5 / 1.7 / 4.5 / 1.7	**23** SU	0231 / 0818 / 1450 / 2040	4.4 / 1.8 / 4.5 / 1.7
9 SU	0157 / 0754 / 1426 / 2021	4.6 / 1.5 / 4.7 / 1.4	**24** M	0320 / 0908 / 1532 / 2130	4.4 / 1.6 / 4.6 / 1.6
10 M	0254 / 0849 / 1517 / 2117	4.8 / 1.3 / 4.9 / 1.2	**25** TU	0400 / 0951 / 1610 / 2213	4.5 / 1.5 / 4.8 / 1.5
11 TU	0347 / 0942 / 1606 / 2211	5.0 / 1.1 / 5.1 / 0.9	**26** W	0436 / 1030 / 1645 / 2252	4.6 / 1.4 / 4.9 / 1.4
12 W	0438 / 1032 / 1655 / 2302 ●	5.2 / 1.0 / 5.3 / 0.8	**27** TH	0509 / 1106 / 1720 / 2328 ○	4.7 / 1.4 / 4.9 / 1.3
13 TH	0528 / 1121 / 1745 / 2353	5.2 / 0.9 / 5.4 / 0.7	**28** F	0542 / 1141 / 1754	4.7 / 1.3 / 4.9
14 F	0618 / 1210 / 1836	5.2 / 0.9 / 5.4	**29** SA	0003 / 0614 / 1215 / 1827	1.3 / 4.7 / 1.4 / 4.9
15 SA	0042 / 0708 / 1258 / 1927	0.7 / 5.2 / 0.9 / 5.3	**30** SU	0038 / 0644 / 1250 / 1901	1.3 / 4.7 / 1.4 / 4.9

JULY

Day	TIME	m	Day	TIME	m
1 M	0113 / 0716 / 1325 / 1936	1.3 / 4.6 / 1.5 / 4.8	**16** TU	0200 / 0821 / 1415 / 2044	0.9 / 5.0 / 1.0 / 5.1
2 TU	0149 / 0752 / 1403 / 2016	1.4 / 4.6 / 1.5 / 4.8	**17** W	0245 / 0907 / 1501 / 2131	1.1 / 4.7 / 1.2 / 4.8
3 W	0227 / 0833 / 1444 / 2101	1.4 / 4.5 / 1.6 / 4.7	**18** TH	0331 / 0956 / 1551 / 2223 ☽	1.4 / 4.5 / 1.5 / 4.5
4 TH	0310 / 0923 / 1532 / 2154	1.5 / 4.4 / 1.7 / 4.5	**19** F	0423 / 1057 / 1648 / 2329	1.7 / 4.3 / 1.8 / 4.2
5 F	0359 / 1024 / 1627 / 2258 ☾	1.6 / 4.3 / 1.8 / 4.5	**20** SA	0525 / 1213 / 1756	2.0 / 4.1 / 2.0
6 SA	0458 / 1137 / 1732	1.7 / 4.3 / 1.8	**21** SU	0051 / 0638 / 1328 / 1910	4.1 / 2.1 / 4.2 / 2.0
7 SU	0010 / 0605 / 1251 / 1842	4.4 / 1.8 / 4.4 / 1.7	**22** M	0205 / 0749 / 1427 / 2016	4.1 / 2.0 / 4.3 / 1.9
8 M	0122 / 0715 / 1357 / 1951	4.5 / 1.7 / 4.6 / 1.6	**23** TU	0302 / 0845 / 1513 / 2109	4.2 / 1.9 / 4.5 / 1.8
9 TU	0230 / 0821 / 1456 / 2055	4.7 / 1.5 / 4.8 / 1.3	**24** W	0344 / 0931 / 1551 / 2152	4.4 / 1.7 / 4.7 / 1.6
10 W	0331 / 0921 / 1551 / 2155	4.9 / 1.3 / 5.1 / 1.0	**25** TH	0418 / 1010 / 1626 / 2231	4.5 / 1.5 / 4.8 / 1.4
11 TH	0426 / 1016 / 1643 / 2250 ●	5.1 / 1.1 / 5.3 / 0.8	**26** F	0451 / 1046 / 1700 / 2308 ○	4.7 / 1.4 / 5.0 / 1.3
12 F	0517 / 1108 / 1734 / 2341	5.2 / 0.9 / 5.5 / 0.7	**27** SA	0522 / 1121 / 1734 / 2343	4.8 / 1.3 / 5.0 / 1.2
13 SA	0605 / 1156 / 1823	5.3 / 0.8 / 5.5	**28** SU	0552 / 1155 / 1805	4.8 / 1.3 / 5.1
14 SU	0029 / 0652 / 1244 / 1911	0.6 / 5.3 / 0.8 / 5.5	**29** M	0016 / 0621 / 1229 / 1837	1.2 / 4.8 / 1.2 / 5.1
15 M	0116 / 0737 / 1329 / 1958	0.7 / 5.2 / 0.8 / 5.4	**30** TU	0050 / 0650 / 1302 / 1910	1.2 / 4.8 / 1.3 / 5.0
			31 W	0123 / 0723 / 1337 / 1946	1.2 / 4.8 / 1.3 / 5.0

AUGUST

Day	TIME	m	Day	TIME	m
1 TH	0158 / 0800 / 1414 / 2026	1.2 / 4.7 / 1.4 / 4.8	**16** F	0253 / 0904 / 1511 / 2127	1.5 / 4.5 / 1.6 / 4.4
2 F	0237 / 0843 / 1456 / 2115 ☽	1.4 / 4.6 / 1.5 / 4.7	**17** SA	0338 / 0955 / 1603 / 2225	1.8 / 4.2 / 1.9 / 4.1
3 SA	0321 / 0938 / 1547 / 2218 ☾	1.5 / 4.4 / 1.7 / 4.5	**18** SU	0436 / 1111 / 1713 / 2359	2.2 / 4.0 / 2.2 / 3.9
4 SU	0415 / 1054 / 1651 / 2337	1.7 / 4.3 / 1.8 / 4.3	**19** M	0556 / 1249 / 1837	2.3 / 4.0 / 2.3
5 M	0526 / 1219 / 1811	1.9 / 4.3 / 1.9	**20** TU	0140 / 0718 / 1401 / 1950	3.9 / 2.3 / 4.2 / 2.1
6 TU	0100 / 0647 / 1337 / 1932	4.4 / 1.9 / 4.5 / 1.7	**21** W	0241 / 0819 / 1451 / 2044	4.1 / 2.1 / 4.4 / 1.9
7 W	0216 / 0804 / 1443 / 2043	4.5 / 1.7 / 4.8 / 1.4	**22** TH	0323 / 0906 / 1530 / 2128	4.3 / 1.8 / 4.6 / 1.6
8 TH	0320 / 0907 / 1540 / 2143	4.6 / 1.4 / 5.1 / 1.1	**23** F	0356 / 0946 / 1604 / 2206	4.5 / 1.6 / 4.9 / 1.4
9 F	0413 / 1002 / 1631 / 2235	5.1 / 1.1 / 5.4 / 0.8	**24** SA	0426 / 1022 / 1637 / 2242	4.7 / 1.4 / 5.0 / 1.3
10 SA	0501 / 1052 / 1718 / 2324 ●	5.2 / 0.8 / 5.6 / 0.6	**25** SU	0456 / 1057 / 1709 / 2317 ○	4.8 / 1.2 / 5.1 / 1.2
11 SU	0545 / 1139 / 1803	5.3 / 0.7 / 5.6	**26** M	0525 / 1131 / 1740 / 2350	4.9 / 1.1 / 5.2 / 1.1
12 M	0009 / 0627 / 1223 / 1846	0.6 / 5.3 / 0.7 / 5.6	**27** TU	0554 / 1204 / 1811	5.0 / 1.1 / 5.2
13 TU	0052 / 0707 / 1306 / 1928	0.7 / 5.2 / 0.8 / 5.4	**28** W	0023 / 0624 / 1238 / 1843	1.0 / 5.0 / 1.1 / 5.2
14 W	0133 / 0746 / 1347 / 2006	0.9 / 5.1 / 1.0 / 5.1	**29** TH	0057 / 0656 / 1311 / 1918	1.1 / 5.0 / 1.1 / 5.1
15 TH	0212 / 0824 / 1428 / 2045	1.2 / 4.8 / 1.2 / 4.8	**30** F	0131 / 0731 / 1348 / 1958	1.1 / 4.9 / 1.1 / 4.9
			31 SA	0208 / 0813 / 1428 / 2046	1.3 / 4.7 / 1.4 / 4.7

14

Chart Datum: 2.93 metres below Lallemand System (Mean Sea level, Marseilles)

FRANCE, WEST COAST - POINTE DE GRAVE

LAT 45°34′N   LONG 1°04′W

TIMES AND HEIGHTS OF HIGH AND LOW WATERS

YEAR 1991

TIME ZONE –0100
(French Standard Time) Subtract 1 hour for GMT
For French Summer Time add ONE hour in non-shaded areas

SEPTEMBER

Day	TIME	m	Day	TIME	m
1 SU ☽	0251 / 0907 / 1518 / 2153	1.5 / 4.5 / 1.7 / 4.4	16 M	0348 / 1014 / 1627 / 2300	2.3 / 4.0 / 2.3 / 3.8
2 M	0345 / 1027 / 1626 / 2320	1.8 / 4.3 / 1.9 / 4.2	17 TU	0511 / 1153 / 1758	2.5 / 3.9 / 2.4
3 TU	0500 / 1201 / 1757	2.1 / 4.3 / 2.0	18 W	0100 / 0639 / 1322 / 1916	3.8 / 2.4 / 4.1 / 2.0
4 W	0052 / 0633 / 1326 / 1925	4.3 / 2.0 / 4.5 / 1.7	19 TH	0207 / 0745 / 1418 / 2013	4.0 / 2.2 / 4.3 / 2.0
5 TH	0209 / 0752 / 1434 / 2033	4.5 / 1.7 / 4.8 / 1.4	20 F	0250 / 0834 / 1500 / 2056	4.3 / 1.9 / 4.6 / 1.7
6 F	0308 / 0853 / 1529 / 2128	4.8 / 1.4 / 5.2 / 1.1	21 SA	0323 / 0914 / 1535 / 2135	4.5 / 1.6 / 4.9 / 1.5
7 SA	0357 / 0945 / 1616 / 2217	5.1 / 1.1 / 5.4 / 0.8	22 SU	0354 / 0951 / 1608 / 2211	4.8 / 1.4 / 5.1 / 1.3
8 SU ●	0440 / 1033 / 1659 / 2302	5.3 / 0.8 / 5.6 / 0.7	23 M ○	0424 / 1028 / 1640 / 2246	4.9 / 1.2 / 5.2 / 1.1
9 M	0520 / 1117 / 1739 / 2345	5.3 / 0.7 / 5.6 / 0.7	24 TU	0455 / 1103 / 1712 / 2321	5.1 / 1.1 / 5.3 / 1.0
10 TU	0558 / 1200 / 1817	5.3 / 0.7 / 5.5	25 W	0526 / 1138 / 1745 / 2356	5.1 / 1.0 / 5.3 / 1.0
11 W	0025 / 0634 / 1239 / 1853	0.8 / 5.2 / 0.8 / 5.3	26 TH	0558 / 1214 / 1820	5.2 / 1.0 / 5.3
12 TH	0102 / 0709 / 1317 / 1927	1.0 / 5.1 / 1.0 / 5.0	27 F	0031 / 0633 / 1249 / 1857	1.0 / 5.1 / 1.2 / 5.1
13 F	0138 / 0743 / 1354 / 2000	1.3 / 4.8 / 1.3 / 4.7	28 SA	0107 / 0711 / 1328 / 1939	1.1 / 5.0 / 1.2 / 4.9
14 SA	0214 / 0820 / 1433 / 2039	1.6 / 4.6 / 1.7 / 4.3	29 SU	0146 / 0756 / 1411 / 2032	1.3 / 4.8 / 1.4 / 4.6
15 SU ☽	0254 / 0907 / 1520 / 2133	1.9 / 4.3 / 2.0 / 4.0	30 M	0232 / 0855 / 1504 / 2144	1.6 / 4.5 / 1.7 / 4.3

OCTOBER

Day	TIME	m	Day	TIME	m
1 TU ☽	0330 / 1017 / 1617 / 2315	1.9 / 4.3 / 1.9 / 4.2	16 W	0419 / 1052 / 1706 / 2354	2.5 / 4.0 / 2.4 / 3.8
2 W	0451 / 1151 / 1752	2.1 / 4.4 / 2.0	17 TH	0547 / 1223 / 1826	2.5 / 4.1 / 2.3
3 TH	0045 / 0623 / 1316 / 1914	4.3 / 2.0 / 4.6 / 1.7	18 F	0113 / 0656 / 1329 / 1927	4.0 / 2.3 / 4.3 / 2.1
4 F	0156 / 0735 / 1422 / 2016	4.6 / 1.7 / 4.9 / 1.4	19 SA	0203 / 0750 / 1418 / 2015	4.3 / 2.0 / 4.6 / 1.8
5 SA	0251 / 0834 / 1514 / 2108	4.8 / 1.4 / 5.2 / 1.2	20 SU	0243 / 0835 / 1459 / 2057	4.5 / 1.7 / 4.8 / 1.5
6 SU	0337 / 0924 / 1558 / 2154	5.1 / 1.1 / 5.3 / 1.0	21 M	0318 / 0916 / 1536 / 2136	4.8 / 1.5 / 5.0 / 1.3
7 M	0417 / 1011 / 1638 / 2238	5.2 / 0.9 / 5.4 / 0.9	22 TU	0352 / 0955 / 1612 / 2214	5.0 / 1.3 / 5.2 / 1.1
8 TU	0454 / 1054 / 1715 / 2318	5.3 / 0.8 / 5.4 / 0.9	23 W ○	0426 / 1035 / 1647 / 2253	5.1 / 1.1 / 5.3 / 0.9
9 W	0530 / 1135 / 1749 / 2356	5.3 / 0.9 / 5.3 / 1.0	24 TH	0501 / 1114 / 1724 / 2331	5.2 / 1.0 / 5.3 / 1.0
10 TH	0604 / 1213 / 1821	5.2 / 1.0 / 5.1	25 F	0538 / 1153 / 1803	5.3 / 0.9 / 5.3
11 F	0032 / 0636 / 1249 / 1852	1.2 / 5.0 / 1.2 / 4.9	26 SA	0009 / 0617 / 1233 / 1845	1.0 / 5.2 / 1.0 / 5.1
12 SA	0106 / 0710 / 1324 / 1925	1.4 / 4.9 / 1.4 / 4.6	27 SU	0050 / 0701 / 1315 / 1933	1.2 / 5.1 / 1.1 / 4.9
13 SU	0140 / 0747 / 1401 / 2004	1.7 / 4.6 / 1.7 / 4.3	28 M	0133 / 0751 / 1403 / 2030	1.4 / 4.9 / 1.4 / 4.6
14 M	0218 / 0831 / 1444 / 2054	2.0 / 4.4 / 2.0 / 4.1	29 TU	0223 / 0854 / 1501 / 2142	1.6 / 4.7 / 1.6 / 4.4
15 TU ☽	0307 / 0930 / 1542 / 2209	2.3 / 4.1 / 2.3 / 3.8	30 W ☽	0325 / 1011 / 1614 / 2306	1.9 / 4.5 / 1.8 / 4.3
			31 TH	0443 / 1138 / 1736	2.0 / 4.5 / 1.9

NOVEMBER

Day	TIME	m	Day	TIME	m
1 F	0027 / 0601 / 1257 / 1851	4.4 / 1.9 / 4.7 / 1.7	16 SA	0003 / 0553 / 1227 / 1827	4.0 / 2.3 / 4.3 / 2.1
2 SA	0134 / 0711 / 1402 / 1953	4.6 / 1.7 / 4.8 / 1.5	17 SU	0107 / 0654 / 1328 / 1924	4.2 / 2.1 / 4.5 / 1.9
3 SU	0229 / 0810 / 1455 / 2045	4.8 / 1.5 / 5.0 / 1.3	18 M	0157 / 0747 / 1418 / 2014	4.4 / 1.9 / 4.7 / 1.7
4 M	0315 / 0902 / 1539 / 2132	5.0 / 1.3 / 5.1 / 1.2	19 TU	0241 / 0836 / 1503 / 2100	4.7 / 1.6 / 4.9 / 1.4
5 TU	0355 / 0949 / 1618 / 2214	5.1 / 1.2 / 5.1 / 1.2	20 W	0322 / 0923 / 1545 / 2144	4.9 / 1.4 / 5.1 / 1.2
6 W ●	0432 / 1033 / 1654 / 2254	5.1 / 1.1 / 5.1 / 1.2	21 TH ○	0402 / 1008 / 1627 / 2227	5.1 / 1.1 / 5.2 / 1.1
7 TH	0506 / 1113 / 1726 / 2331	5.1 / 1.1 / 5.1 / 1.2	22 F	0442 / 1052 / 1710 / 2310	5.2 / 1.0 / 5.3 / 1.0
8 F	0539 / 1150 / 1757	5.1 / 1.2 / 4.9	23 SA	0524 / 1137 / 1754 / 2354	5.3 / 0.9 / 5.3 / 1.0
9 SA	0006 / 0612 / 1225 / 1828	1.3 / 5.0 / 1.3 / 4.8	24 SU	0610 / 1222 / 1841	5.3 / 0.9 / 5.2
10 SU	0039 / 0646 / 1300 / 1901	1.5 / 4.9 / 1.5 / 4.6	25 M	0039 / 0659 / 1310 / 1932	1.1 / 5.2 / 1.0 / 5.0
11 M	0113 / 0722 / 1336 / 1938	1.7 / 4.7 / 1.7 / 4.4	26 TU	0127 / 0752 / 1400 / 2028	1.3 / 5.1 / 1.2 / 4.8
12 TU	0150 / 0803 / 1416 / 2022	1.9 / 4.5 / 1.9 / 4.2	27 W	0219 / 0852 / 1456 / 2130	1.5 / 4.9 / 1.4 / 4.6
13 W	0235 / 0853 / 1505 / 2120	2.1 / 4.4 / 2.1 / 4.0	28 TH ☾	0317 / 0958 / 1558 / 2240	1.6 / 4.8 / 1.6 / 4.5
14 TH ☽	0332 / 0957 / 1609 / 2239	2.1 / 4.2 / 2.2 / 4.0	29 F	0421 / 1111 / 1706 / 2354	1.8 / 4.7 / 1.8 / 4.4
15 F	0443 / 1113 / 1721	2.4 / 4.2 / 2.2	30 SA	0530 / 1227 / 1816	1.8 / 4.6 / 1.8

DECEMBER

Day	TIME	m	Day	TIME	m
1 SU	0104 / 0639 / 1335 / 1923	4.5 / 1.8 / 4.7 / 1.7	16 M	0552 / 1228 / 1826	2.1 / 4.4 / 2.0
2 M	0203 / 0743 / 1434 / 2021	4.6 / 1.7 / 4.7 / 1.6	17 TU	0107 / 0657 / 1334 / 1928	4.3 / 2.0 / 4.5 / 1.8
3 TU	0254 / 0841 / 1522 / 2111	4.8 / 1.6 / 4.8 / 1.5	18 W	0204 / 0757 / 1431 / 2025	4.6 / 1.7 / 4.7 / 1.6
4 W	0337 / 0931 / 1603 / 2155	4.9 / 1.4 / 4.8 / 1.4	19 TH	0255 / 0853 / 1524 / 2118	4.8 / 1.5 / 4.9 / 1.4
5 TH	0415 / 1015 / 1639 / 2234	5.0 / 1.4 / 4.9 / 1.4	20 F	0343 / 0946 / 1613 / 2208	5.0 / 1.2 / 5.1 / 1.2
6 F ●	0449 / 1055 / 1711 / 2311	5.0 / 1.3 / 4.9 / 1.4	21 SA ○	0430 / 1037 / 1701 / 2256	5.3 / 1.0 / 5.3 / 1.0
7 SA	0523 / 1132 / 1742 / 2346	5.1 / 1.3 / 4.8 / 1.4	22 SU	0517 / 1126 / 1749 / 2343	5.4 / 0.8 / 5.3 / 1.0
8 SU	0555 / 1207 / 1813	5.0 / 1.4 / 4.8	23 M	0606 / 1215 / 1837	5.5 / 0.8 / 5.3
9 M	0019 / 0628 / 1241 / 1844	1.5 / 5.0 / 1.4 / 4.7	24 TU	0031 / 0656 / 1303 / 1926	1.0 / 5.5 / 0.8 / 5.2
10 TU	0053 / 0702 / 1316 / 1917	1.6 / 4.9 / 1.5 / 4.6	25 W	0118 / 0747 / 1351 / 2015	1.0 / 5.4 / 1.0 / 5.0
11 W	0129 / 0739 / 1353 / 1953	1.7 / 4.8 / 1.7 / 4.5	26 TH	0207 / 0838 / 1440 / 2106	1.1 / 5.2 / 1.2 / 4.8
12 TH	0209 / 0820 / 1434 / 2037	1.8 / 4.6 / 1.8 / 4.3	27 F	0258 / 0933 / 1532 / 2203	1.3 / 5.0 / 1.4 / 4.6
13 F	0254 / 0909 / 1522 / 2132	2.0 / 4.5 / 1.9 / 4.2	28 SA ☾	0353 / 1033 / 1629 / 2310	1.5 / 4.7 / 1.7 / 4.4
14 SA ☾	0346 / 1008 / 1617 / 2242	2.1 / 4.4 / 2.0 / 4.1	29 SU	0453 / 1145 / 1735	1.7 / 4.5 / 1.9
15 SU	0447 / 1117 / 1721 / 2359	2.1 / 4.3 / 2.1 / 4.2	30 M	0025 / 0602 / 1303 / 1847	4.3 / 1.9 / 4.4 / 2.0
			31 TU	0136 / 0714 / 1414 / 1956	4.4 / 1.9 / 4.4 / 1.9

Chart Datum: 2.93 metres below Lallemand System (Mean Sea level, Marseilles)

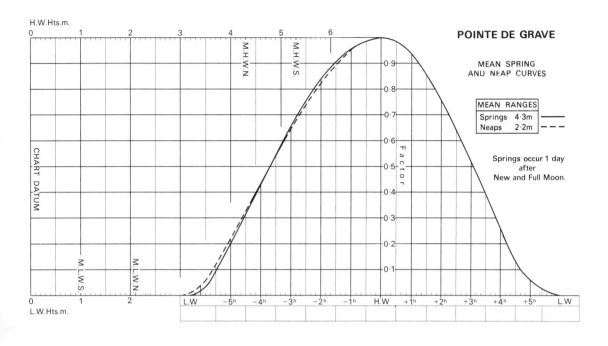

POINTE DE GRAVE

MEAN SPRING
AND NEAP CURVES

MEAN RANGES	
Springs	4·3m
Neaps	2·2m

Springs occur 1 day
after
New and Full Moon.

CANAL
CONNECTIONS 10-14-11

The Canal Latéral à la Garonne and the Canal du Midi provide a popular route to the Mediterranean, despite the large number of locks to be negotiated. If necessary the transit can be done in about a week, but this is not recommended.

Masts can be unstepped at Royan, Pauillac or Bordeaux. Leave Bordeaux at LW Pointe de Grave for the passage up river to the first lock at Castets-en-Dorthe. If necessary a tow can usually be arranged.

Plenty of stout fenders (for example car tyres in strong canvas bags) are needed. Commercial traffic and boats bound west have right of way. On the Canal Latéral à la Garonne most of the locks are automatic. On the Canal du Midi there are many hire cruisers in the summer months. Fuel is available alongside at Agen, Castelnaudary and Port de la Robine, and at other places by can. Food and water are readily obtained along the route. Further information from Service de la Navigation de Toulouse, 2 Port St Etienne, Toulouse. Tel. 61.80.79.91.

Canal	From	To	Km/ Locks	Min Depth (m)	Min Height (m)
Lateral à la Garonne	Castets	Toulouse	193/ 53	2.2	3.5
Du Midi	Toulouse	Sete	240/ 65	1.8	3.0
De la Nouvelle	Salleles	Port la Nouvelle	37/ 14	1.8	3.1

Notes: Max length 30m. Max beam 5.5m.
Headroom of 3.0m is to top of arch. Over a width of 4m, clearance is about 2.50m. Speed limit 8 km/hour (about 4½ kn), but 3 km/hour over aquaducts and under bridges.

ROYAN   10-14-12
Charente Maritime

CHARTS
Admiralty 2910, 2916, 2664; SHOM 7028; ECM 553
TIDES
+0530 Dover; ML 3.0; Duration 0615 Springs, 0655
Neaps; Zone −0100
Standard Port POINTE DE GRAVE (←)

Times				Height (metres)			
HW		LW		MHWS	MHWN	MLWN	MLWS
0000	0600	0500	1200	5.3	4.3	2.1	1.0
1200	1800	1700	2400				

Differences ROYAN

0000	−0020	−0010	−0005	−0.2	−0.2	−0.2	−0.1

SHELTER
Good shelter and easy access day and night except with strong winds from the W or NW. The entrance channel is dredged to 1.0m. Yachts use N basin. A good port of call for Canal du Midi with crane for masts.
NAVIGATION
Waypoint No 12 (port-hand) buoy, OcR 4s, 45°36'.45N 01°03'.00W, 237°/057° from/to Jetée Sud Lt, 1.1M. The approaches to La Gironde can be dangerous − see 10.14.5 and 10.14.10. The sandbanks off Royan shift and buoys are consequently altered. Give the Mauvaise bank and shoals round Cordouan a wide berth. Off harbour entrance, there is an eddy, running S at about 1 kn on the flood and 3 kn on the ebb. Beware ferries.
LIGHTS AND MARKS
La Coubre light − Fl (2) W 10s 64m 31M RC, also FRG 42m 12M R030°-043°, G043°-060°, R060°-110°. Channel buoyed past Courdouan Lt Oc(2+1) WRG 12s 60m 21/17M, W014°-126°, G126°-178.5°, W178.5°-250°, W (unintens) 250°-267°, R (unintens) 267°-294.5°, R294.5°-014°. Obscured in estuary when bearing over 285°.
RADIO TELEPHONE
VHF Ch 09(in season 0800−2000; out of season 0900−1800 LT). Le Verdon Ch 12 16.
TELEPHONE (46)
Hr Mr 46.38.72.22; Aff Mar 46.38.32.75; CROSS 56.09.82.00; SNSM 46.38.75.79; ≋ 46.38.51.27; Meteo 56.34.20.11; Police 46.38.34.22; Dr 46.05.68.69; Ⓗ 46.38.01.77; Brit Consul 56.52.28.35.

FACILITIES
Marina (570 + 60 visitors) Slip, P, D, FW, ME, AC, El, Sh, C (6 ton), BH (26 ton); **Les Regates de Royan** ☎ 46.38.59.64; **Quai Nord** P, D; **Quai Sud** P, D, C (4.5 ton); **Loca Marine** ☎ 46.38.45.99 ME, El, Sh, CH, Ⓔ; **Winckel** (la Voilerie) ☎ 46.38.36.95, SM, CH, Ⓔ; **Royan Marine Service** ☎ 46.38.54.00, CH, SHOM; **Evasion Maritime 17** ☎ 46.05.06.44, Sh, ME, El, Ⓔ, CH; **Meneau Marine** ☎ 46.39.81.27, ME. **Town** Slip, P, D, FW, V, R, Bar, Gaz, ✉; Ⓑ; ≥; ✈ (Bordeaux).
Ferry UK − Roscoff−Plymouth, St Malo−Portsmouth.

PORT DE ROYAN

SEUDRE RIVER   10-14-13
Charente Maritime

CHARTS
Admiralty 2648; SHOM 6335, 6912, 6037; ECM 552
TIDES
+0545 Dover; ML 3.5; Duration Springs 0545, Neaps 0700; Zone −0100
Standard Port POINTE DE GRAVE (←)

Times				Height (metres)			
HW		LW		MHWS	MHWN	MLWN	MLWS
0000	0600	0500	1200	5.3	4.3	2.1	1.0
1200	1800	1700	2400				

Differences LA CAYENNE

−0015	−0035	−0020	0000	+0.5	+0.3	+0.3	+0.1

SHELTER
La Seudre is navigable to lock at Riberou. There are secure anchorages at La Cayenne, La Grève (½M upstream), and off entrance to Chenal de la Tremblade; or yachts can lock into the basin near Marennes, 2M from the river.

SEUDRE RIVER *continued*

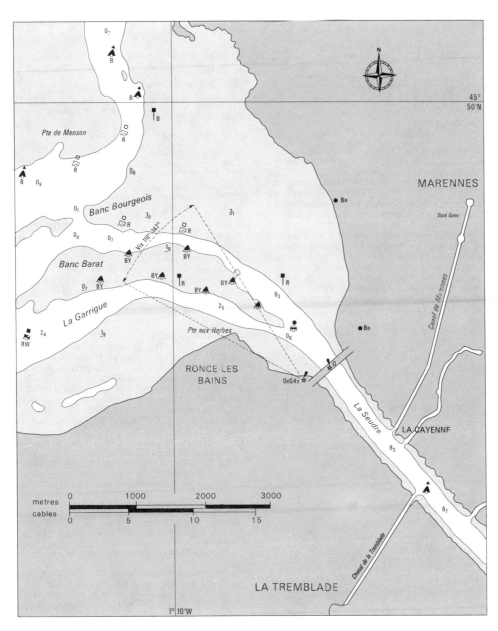

NAVIGATION
Waypoint Pertuis de Maumusson (safe water) buoy, Whis, 45°47'.70N 01°17'.85W, 260°/080° from/to Pte de Gatseau, 2.7M. Pertuis de Maumusson can be used only in good weather, at about HW − 1, see 10.14.5. In even moderate weather it is extremely dangerous, particularly with out-going stream or any swell. It is advisable to approach La Seudre from N, through Coreau d'Oleron, and thence through Chenal de la Soumaille (dries about 0.7m). Chenal de la Garrigue carries slightly more water. Both are marked by Bns and buoys. Beware oyster beds. Pont de Seudre has clearance of 18m. An overhead cable (16m) spans Canal de Marennes.

LIGHTS AND MARKS
There are no leading lights or marks. Lights: Pte de Mus de Loup Oc G 4s 8m 6M vis 118°-147°. On bridge between piers 6 and 7; downstream Q 20m 10M vis 054°-234°; upstream Q 20m 10M vis 234°-054°. Channel is marked by W boards.

RADIO TELEPHONE
VHF Ch 09.

TELEPHONE (46)
Hr Mr (Marennes) 46.85.02.68; Aff Mar, Marennes 46.85.14.33, La Tremblade 46.36.00.22; ⌗ 46.36.03.03; Police 46.85.00.19; Dr Marennes 46.85.23.06, La Tremblade 46.36.16.35; Brit Consul 56.36.16.35.

FACILITIES
MARENNES **Quay (Claude)** ☎ 46.85.15.11, ME, CH; **Paraveau** ☎ 46.85.10.77, Sh; **Ocean 17** ☎ 46.85.36.27, ME, CH; **Quay** ☎ 46.85.15.11, ME, CH; **Town** Slip, M, P, D, L, FW, V, R, Bar.
LA TREMBLADE **Quay** Slip, P, D, FW, C (5 ton); **Bernard Frères** ☎ 46.36.09.00, ME, Sh; **Jamain** ☎ 46.36.01.50 SM, CH; **Boulanger** ☎ 46.36.01.34, ME, Sh; **Atlantic Garage** ☎ 46.36.00.67, ME; **Town** Slip, P, D, L, FW, Gaz, V, R, Bar, ✉; ⒷⒷ; ⇌; ✈ (La Rochelle).
Ferry UK — Roscoff—Plymouth; St Malo—Portsmouth.

14

ILE D'OLÉRON   10-14-14
Charente Maritime

CHARTS
Admiralty 2648, 2746; SHOM 3711, 6334, 6335, 6913, 6914; ECM 552

TIDES
+0545 Dover; ML 3.8; Duration 0540; Zone −0100
Standard Port POINTE DE GRAVE (←)

Times				Height (metres)			
HW		LW		MHWS	MHWN	MLWN	MLWS
0000	0600	0500	1200	5.3	4.3	2.1	1.0
1200	1800	1700	2400				

Differences ROCHEFORT
+0015 −0020 +0045 +0120 +1.1 +0.9 +0.1 +0.4

There are two harbours, Le Chateau d'Oléron and Boyardville. A third on W coast, La Cotiniere, suffers almost constantly from Atlantic swells.

SHELTER
LE CHATEAU: Good shelter, but very full of oyster boats which use inner harbour. Yachts lie on quay SW side (dries 3m) − check with Hr Mr. Access ∓3.
BOYARDVILLE: Good anchorage, sheltered from S and W, in 3m (sand) ½M N of La Perrotine Lt. Landing jetty inshore. Good shelter alongside quays (dry) on N side of harbour. Access HW∓2. Boyardville yacht harbour, non-tidal, entered through automatic gates which open when height of tide is 2.4m. (Approx HW∓2½).
DOUHET: At end of Plage des Saumonards − Well protected from W winds. Berth in marina.

NAVIGATION
Waypoint Pertuis d'Antioche PA (safe water) buoy, Iso 4s,

Whis, 46°05'.55N 01°42'.60W, 283°/103° from/to Pte de Chassiron Lt, 13M.
LE CHATEAU: Bridge to mainland lies 2M S, 15m clearance under spans 20-24, channel marked by boards − W&G to stbd, W&R to port, illuminated at night. Beware Grande Mortanne, a drying ledge, marked by Bns. From N, beware Rocher du Doux (dries) and Rocher Juliar (dries). Mortanne Sud Bn marks entrance to channel (depth 0.8m) indicated by Ldg Lts.
BOYARDVILLE: Bar dries 2m and extends 3 ca (560m) E of breakwater head. Inside bar the channel mostly dries. Beware ferries.
DOUHET: Access by channel d'Est en Ouest

LIGHTS AND MARKS
LE CHATEAU: Ldg Lts 319°, Both QR 11/24m 7M; W Tr with R top; synchronised. Tourelle Juliar Q(3) WG 10s 12m 11/8M; E cardinal mark; vis W147°-336°, G336°-147°.
BOYARDVILLE: Breakwater head Oc(2) R 6s 8m 6M; W Tr with R top; obsc by Pte des Saumonards when brg less than 150°.
DOUHET: No lights

RADIO TELEPHONE
Boyardville VHF Ch 09.

TELEPHONE (46)
Hr Mr (Le Chateau) 46.47.00.01; Hr Mr (Boyardville) 46.47.23.71; Hr Mr Douhet 46.76.71.13 ⌗ 46.47.62.53; Aff Mar 46.47.60.01; CROSS 56.09.82.00; Meteo 46.41.29.14; Auto 46.41.11.11; Police 46.47.61.77; Dr 46.47.60.68; Brit Consul 56.52.28.35.

FACILITIES
LE CHATEAU **Jetty**, Slip, L, FW, C (2.5 ton); **Blondel** ☎ 46.47.61.89, ME, El; **Sorlut Marine** ☎ 46.47.54.08, ME, El, Ⓔ, Sh, CH; **Oléron-Motors-Cycles** ☎ 46.47.62.78, ME, El, CH; **Dubois** ☎ 46.47.62.57, ME, Sh, El, CH; **Magasin 2000** ☎ 46.47.61.43, CH;
BOYARDVILLE **Marina** (150+50 visitors) ☎ 46.47.01.36, AC, FW, C (7 ton), Slip; **Môle chenal de la Perrotine** P, D; **Sodinautic** ☎ 46.47.25.65, ME, Sh, CH; **Marine Oléron** ☎ 46.47.01.36, ME, El, Sh, CH; **Barbaud** ☎ 46.47.01.10, ME.
DOUHET **Marina** (350) FW, AC, Slip Access HW∓2½ **Géron** ☎ 46.76.53.96 ME, El, Sh, Ⓔ, CH. **Town** (Le Chateau) V, Gaz, R, Bar, ✉; Ⓑ; ⇌ (Marennes); ✈ (La Rochelle).
Ferry UK − Roscoff−Plymouth, St Malo−Portsmouth

ROCHEFORT   10-14-15
Charente Maritime

CHARTS
Admiralty 2748, 2746; SHOM 4333; ECM 552

TIDES
+0610 Dover; Zone −0100
Standard Port POINTE DE GRAVE (←)

Times				Height (metres)			
HW		LW		MHWS	MHWN	MLWN	MLWS
0000	0600	0500	1200	5.3	4.3	2.1	1.0
1200	1800	1700	2400				

Differences ROCHEFORT
+0015 −0020 +0045 +0120 +1.1 +0.9 +0.1 +0.4

ILE D'AIX
−0005 −0035 −0025 −0015 +0.9 +0.7 +0.4 0.0

SHELTER
Rochefort is on N bank of Charente, about 10M from the mouth. Entry advised on late flood, as bar breaks on ebb. Anchor out of channel at Martrou or Soubise, or enter Port de Plaisance in Basin No1 (access HW∓1), first basin on W bank: pontoon on N side of entrance for waiting. No 3 Basin, 2½ ca (400m) N, is for commercial craft only. The river is navigable to Tonnay-Charente.

NAVIGATION
Waypoint Les Palles N cardinal buoy, Q, 45°59'.58N 01°09'.53W, 293°/113° from/to front Ldg Lt 115°, 4.0M. Stream in river runs about 2 kn (4 kn in narrows), and at springs there is a bore. Beware wreck just S of first Ldg Line (115°). When WSW of Fouras pick up second (Port-des-Barques) Ldg Line (135°). The bar at Fouras carries about 0.5m. From Port-des-Barques follow the alignment of lettered pairs of Bns. There is a lifting bridge at Martrou, with moorings above and below it.

ROCHEFORT *continued*

LIGHTS AND MARKS
Ile d'Aix Fl WR 5s 24m 24/20M; twin W Trs with R tops; vis R103°-118°, W118°-103°. Ldg Lts 115°, both QR; W square Trs with R tops; intens 113°-117°. Port Sud de Fouras, pierhead, Fl WR 4s 6m, 9/6M; vis R117°-177°, W177°-117°. Port-des-Barques Ldg Lts 135°, both Iso G 4s; W square Trs; synchronised and intens 125°-145°.

RADIO TELEPHONE
VHF Ch 09 16. Yacht harbour CH 09 (HW∓1).

TELEPHONE (46)
Hr Mr 46.84.30.30; Aff Mar 46.84.22.67; CROSS 56.09.82.00; ⌗ 46.99.03.90; Meteo 46.41.29.14; Police 46.87.38.10; Dr 46.99.61.11; Brit Consul 56.52.28.35.

FACILITIES
Marina (180 + 20 visitors) ☎ 46.84.30.30, FW, ME, El, Sh, AC, C (30 ton); **Port Neuf** Slip, FW; **Club Nautique Rochefortais** ☎ 46.87.34.61 Slip; **Rochefort Marine** ☎ 46.87.52.08, ME, El, Ⓔ, Sh, CH; **Town** P, D, V, Gaz, R, Bar, ✉; Ⓑ; ⇌; ✈ (La Rochelle).
Ferry UK — Roscoff—Plymouth; St Malo—Portsmouth.

LA ROCHELLE   10-14-16
Charente Maritime

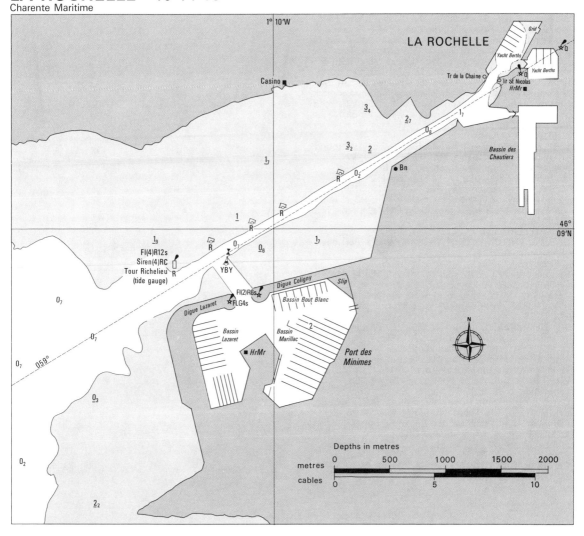

LA ROCHELLE *continued*

CHARTS
Admiralty 2743, 2746, 2648, 2641; SHOM 6334, 6468; ECM 551, 1022

TIDES
+0515 Dover; ML 3.6; Zone −0100
Standard Port POINTE DE GRAVE (←)

Times				Height (metres)			
HW		LW		MHWS	MHWN	MLWN	MLWS
0000	0600	0500	1200	5.3	4.3	2.1	1.0
1200	1800	1700	2400				

Differences LA ROCHELLE
+0005 −0035 −0020 −0015 +0.8 +0.6 +0.4 0.0
LA PALLICE
+0005 −0035 −0020 −0015 +0.8 +0.6 +0.4 0.0

NOTE: La Pallice is the commercial port of La Rochelle and yachts are not welcome there, nor are any facilities provided. La Rochelle has two ports for yachts, La Rochelle-Ville and the Port des Minimes (a large marina).

SHELTER
La Rochelle-Ville harbour, in the old town, is entered between the two towers of St Nicolas and La Chaine. It has an outer basin (tidal), and an inner basin (non-tidal with depth of 3m) on the E side which is entered by a gate (open HW−2 to HW+ ½). In outer basin (100 berths), the first pontoon is reserved for fishing boats. Port des Minimes is a marina with a depth of 2m (max length 14m). All the above give excellent shelter. There is a water bus from Minimes to the town.

NAVIGATION
Waypoint Chauveau S cardinal buoy, VQ(6)+LFl 10s, Whis, 46°06′.63N 01°15′.98W, 240°/060° from/to Tour Richelieu, 4.6M. Approach from about 1M S of Le Lavardin Lt Tr on Ldg Line 059°. Drying rocks off Pte des Minimes (SW of marina) extend ¼M offshore. Tour Richelieu marks S extremity of rocks extending from N shore. Least depth in channel 0.2m. Just past Tour Richelieu (tide gauge for channel), entrance to Port des Minimes is marked by W cardinal buoy, and buoys mark NE side of channel to marina. For La Rochelle-Ville keep on 059° Ldg Line in channel marked by buoys on N side, least depth 0.2m.

LIGHTS AND MARKS
Ldg Lts 059°. Front Q 15m 14M (Fl 4s by day); R round Tr, W bands. Rear Q 25m 14M (Fl 4s by day); W octagonal Tr, G top; synchronised with front, obsc 061°-065° by St Nicolas Tr. Le Lavardin Fl(2) WG 6s 14m 11/8M; B Tr, R band; vis G160°-169°, W169°-160°. Tourelle Richelieu Fl(4)R 12s 10m 9M; R Tr; RC; Siren(4) 60s. Port des Minimes W Mole head FlG 4s, E Mole head Fl(2)R 6s.

RADIO TELEPHONE
La Pallice VHF Ch 12 16 (HW−2 to HW+1). Port des Minimes Ch 09 (H24).

TELEPHONE (46)
Port des Minimes Hr Mr 46.44.41.20, Aff Mar 46.41.43.91, CROSS 56.09.82.00; ⌗ 46.42.64.64; Meteo 46.41.29.14; Auto 46.41.11.11; Police 46.34.67.55; Dr 46.42.19.22; Ⓗ 46.27.33.33; Brit Consul 56.52.28.35.

FACILITIES
PORT DES MINIMES **Marina** (2,800+250 visitors pontoons 14 and 15), ☎ 46.44.69.,86, Gaz, AC, Slip, C (10 ton), P, D, FW, BH (15 ton), R: (also control berths in wet dock in town); **Société des Regates Rochellaises** ☎ 46.44.62.44; **Atlantic Loisirs** ☎ 46.44.21.35, ME, Sh, CH, Ⓔ; **Atlanticoque** ☎ 46.41.39.26, ME, El, Sh, **Label Bleu** ☎ 46.45.10.54, ME, El, Sh, Ⓔ, CH; **Comptoir Maritime Rochelais** ☎ 46.44.34.97, ME, Sh, SHOM, El, Ⓔ, CH; **Fabre Marine** ☎ 46.41.33.25, El; **Proust** ☎ 46.44.13.66, ME, El, Sh, CH; **Pochon** ☎ 46.41.30.53, Ⓔ; **Accastillage Diffusion** ☎ 46.45.49.49, ME, El, Ⓔ, Sh, CH, SHOM; **Chantier Pinta** ☎ 46.44.40.70, ME, El, Sh; **La Rochelle Boat Centre** ☎ 46.45.42.72. ME, El, Sh, CH, Ⓔ; **Voile Système** ☎ 46.41.83.52, SM;

LA ROCHELLE-VILLE **Quay** Slip, FW, C (10 ton), SM, ME, Sh, CH; **Outer Basin** (100)
Town P, D, V, Gaz, R, Bar, ✉; Ⓑ, ⇌; ✈.
Ferry to the Ile de Ré; internal air services from Laleu airport (2½km N of port).
Ferry UK — Roscoff—Plymouth; St Malo—Portsmouth.
Note: Bridge under construction between Pte de La Repentie (on mainland) and Pte de Sablanceaux (on Ile de Ré). Passage to/from Rade de La Pallice must be made N-bound between piles Nos 13 and 14, and S-bound between piles Nos 11 and 12. The passages are buoyed.

ST MARTIN, Ile de Ré   10-14-17
Charente Maritime

CHARTS
Admiralty 2641; SHOM 6521, 6668; ECM 551
TIDES
+0535 Dover; ML 3.4; Zone −0100
Standard Port POINTE DE GRAVE (←)

Times				Height (metres)			
HW		LW		MHWS	MHWN	MLWN	MLWS
0000	0600	0500	1200	5.3	4.3	2.1	1.0
1200	1800	1700	2400				

Differences ST. MARTIN, Ile de Ré
−0025 −0045 −0005 −0005 +0.8   +0.4   +0.1   −0.3

SHELTER
Approach channel dries 1.2m; access HW−3 to HW+1. Avant port protected by mole on W side, and break water to NE. This leads to drying basin where fishing boats lie. Wet dock (with marina) entered by gates which open about HW−1 to HW+1, with sill 0.8m above CD. Complete shelter in wet dock (depth 3m), but often very crowded. Berthing instructions from Hr Mr. 15 m wide area inside NW mole dredged to 2.5m and pontoon provided. Four W mooring buoys for yachts awaiting this tide provided off entrance.

NAVIGATION
Waypoint Rocha N cardinal buoy, Q, 46°14'.75N 01°20'.80W, 020°/200° from/to St Martin mole head, 2.4M. Time arrival for dock gates opening. From the NW, pass N and E of Le Rocha, a rocky bank running 2½M ENE from Pte du Grouin. Approach with church Tr in transit with mole head Lt (202°). From SE, pass well N of Le Couronneau N cardinal Bn, about ¾M NE of entrance, marking a drying ledge in R sector of St Martin Lt (245°-281°).

LIGHTS AND MARKS
Ldg Line, church and Lt Ho in line 210°. NW of entrance Iso G 4s 10m 7M obscured by Pte de Loix when bearing less than 124°. SE of entrance, Oc(2)WR 6s 18m 10/7M W shore-245°, R245°-281°, W281°-shore.

RADIO TELEPHONE
VHF Ch 09 (0800-1900 LT in summer season).

TELEPHONE (46)
Hr Mr 46.09.26.69; Aff Mar 46.09.68.89; ▦ 46.09.21.78; Meteo 46.41.29.14; Auto 46.41.11.11; CROSS 56.09.82.00; Police 46.09.21.17; Dr 46.09.20.08; Ⓗ 46.09.20.01; Brit Consul 56.52.28.35.

FACILITIES
Marina (135+50 visitors), P, D, FW, ME, El, Sh; **Garage du Port** ☎ 46.09.20.41, ME; **YC St Martin** ☎ 46.09.22.07; **Chantiers Naval** ☎ 46.09.21.06, ME, El, Ⓔ, Sh, CH, SHOM; **Quay** FW, C (4 ton); **Ré-Multiservices** ☎ 46.09.40.74, ME, El, Sh, CH. **Town** P, D, V, Gaz, R, Bar, ✉; Ⓑ; ≈ (La Rochelle); ✈ (La Rochelle).
Ferry UK − Roscoff-Plymouth; St Malo-Portsmouth.

14

BOURGENAY   10-14-18
Vendee

CHARTS
Admiralty 2648; SHOM 6522, 6337; ECM 1022
TIDES
+0600 Dover; ML 3.1; Duration 0640; Zone −0100
Standard Port BREST (→)

Times				Height (metres)			
HW		LW		MHWS	MHWN	MLWN	MLWS
0500	1100	0500	1100	7.5	5.9	3.0	1.4
1700	2300	1700	2300				

Differences BOURGENAY
−0030	+0015	−0035	−0030	−2.2	−1.7	−0.9	−0.6

SHELTER
Good shelter in the marina. In bad weather, especially with SW winds, a big swell can break at the entrance. Yachts can anchor off in good weather with off-shore winds.
NAVIGATION
Waypoint 46°25'.40N, 1°41'.60W, 220°/040° from/to pierhead, 1.3M. Entrance channel leads 040° from safe water Lt Buoy to seaward of Roches de Joanne (which are dangerous in bad weather). Beware shallow patch to W of entrance, marked by stbd-hand Bn.
LIGHTS AND MARKS
Ldg Lts 040°, both QG 9M; G panels. Digue Ouest head Fl R 4s 9M; R structure. Mole E head Iso G 4s 5M; not vis to seaward. Breakwater elbow Fl (2) R 6s 5M, not vis to seaward.
RADIO TELEPHONE
VHF Ch 09 16 (office hours; in summer 0800-2100 LT).
TELEPHONE (51)
Hr Mr 51.22.20.36; Port Office 51.22.20.36; SNSM 51.22.20.36; CROSS 97.55.35.35; Auto 51.62.45.99; ⌗ 51.32.02.33; Aff Mar 51.21.01.80; Police 51.33.20.07; Dr 51.90.62.68; Ⓗ 51.21.86.33; Brit Consul 56.52.28.35.
FACILITIES
Marina (410+100 visitors) ☎ 51.22.20.36, Slip, FW, AC, C (15 ton), **Fuel Point** ☎ 51.22.22.41 P, D; **Atlantica** ☎ 51.22.29.54 Ch; **Nauticea** ☎ 51.22.28.46 CH; **Quai 85** ☎ 51.22.24.36 ME, Slip, El, Gaz, Sh; **Super 2000** Gaz; **Rousseau-Bateaux** 51.22.24.75, ME, El, Sh, divers, CH, Gaz; **Association Nautique de Bourgenay** ☎ 51.22.29.41; **Town** R, ▢, C (15 ton), V, Bar, ⊠; Ⓑ; ⇌ (Les Sables d'Olonne); ✈ (La Lande, Chateau d'Olonne). Ferry UK — Roscoff—Plymouth; St. Malo—Portsmouth.

LES SABLES D'OLONNE   10-14-
Vendee

CHARTS
Admiralty 2648; SHOM 6523, 6552, 6551; ECM 1022
TIDES
+0530 Dover; ML 3.1; Duration 0640; Zone −0100
Standard Port BREST (→)

Times				Height (metres)			
HW		LW		MHWS	MHWN	MLWN	MLWS
0500	1100	0500	1100	7.5	5.9	3.0	1.4
1700	2300	1700	2300				

Differences LES SABLES D'OLONNE
−0030	+0015	−0035	−0030	−2.2	−1.7	−0.9	−0.6

SHELTER
Available at all states of tide, and entry is good except in winds from SE to SW when approaches get rough. There are two main channels − the navigation controlled (SW) channel with La Potence Lt bearing 033°, which leads into E channel on Ldg Line 320°. In bad weather use the E channel. Sailing is forbidden in the access channel to harbour. Visitors marina pontoons A, C, E and F. Access to basin forbidden to yachts. Access to Port Olona Marina H24. There are also 110 berths in harbour for yachts on passage.
NAVIGATION
Waypoint Nouch Sud S cardinal buoy, Q(6)+LFl 15s, 46°28'.63N 01°47'.43W, 220°/040° from/to front Ldg Lt 033°, 1.2M. To the W, beware Les Barges d'Olonne, extending 3M W from Pte de Aiguille. Le Noura and Le Nouch are two isolated rocks on shallow patches SSE of Jetée St Nicolas. Further SE, Barre Marine breaks, even in moderate weather. A buoyed wreck (dries) lies off harbour entrance, to E of 320° Ldg Line. From port to marina, dredged channel (2m) is on W side.
LIGHTS AND MARKS
SW passage Ldg Lts 033°. Front Iso R 4s 14m 14M. Rear, 330m from front, Iso R 4s 33m 14M; (both H24).
E passage Ldg Lts 320°. Front QG 11m 8M. Rear, 465m from front, Oc (2+1) 12s 33m 13M; RC. Port signals St Nicolas jetty head UQ(2)R 1s 16m 10M vis 094°-043°; Horn(2) 30s.
RADIO TELEPHONE
Port VHF Ch 16 12; 12 (HW−2 to HW+2). Marina Ch 09 16 (0600-2400 LT in season; 0800-2000 LT out of season and occasionally outside these times).
TELEPHONE (51)
Hr Mr Port de Plaisance 51.32.51.16; Aff Mar 51.21.01.80; CROSS 97.55.35.35; Meteo 51.36.10.78; Auto 51.62.45.99; ⌗ 51.32.02.33; SNSM 51.21.20.55; Police 51.32.69.91; Dr 51.95.14.47; Ⓗ 51.21.06.33; Brit Consul 56.52.28.35.
FACILITIES
Port Olona Marina (800+50 visitors), ☎ 51.32.51.16, Slip, P, D, FW, ME, El, AC, Sh, BH (27 ton), Access H24; **Plaisance 85** ☎ 51.95.07.38, ME, El, Sh, CH, BH (27 ton), Ⓔ; **Heriaud** ☎ 51.21.06.88, ME, El, Sh, CH; **Parisot Marine** ☎ 51.32.59.97, ME, CH; **Sablais Nautique** ☎ 51.32.62.16, ME, CH, El, Ⓔ, Sh, SHOM; **Voilerie Olane** ☎ 51.21.12.92 SM; **A. Masson** ☎ 51.32.01.07 Ⓔ; **Voilerie Tarot** ☎ 51.21.22.87 SM; **La Jeune Marine** ☎ 51.32.30.24 ME, El, CH, Divers, Ⓔ; **Espace Mer** ☎ 51.21.14.64 ME, El; **Compagnie Radio Marine** ☎ 51.32.07.73, Ⓔ, El; **Town** P, D, V, Gaz, R, Bar, ⊠; Ⓑ; ⇌; ✈.
Ferry UK − Roscoff−Plymouth; St Malo−Portsmouth.

LA SABLES D'OLONNE *continued*

ST GILLES-CROIX-DE-VIE   10-14-20
Vendee

CHARTS
Admiralty 2647; SHOM 6613, 6853; ECM 1022, 549

TIDES
+0500 Dover; ML 3.1; Duration 0600; Zone −0100
Standard Port BREST (→)

Times				Height (metres)			
HW		LW		MHWS	MHWN	MLWN	MLWS
0500	1100	0500	1100	7.5	5.9	3.0	1.4
1700	2300	1700	2300				

Differences ST GILLES-SUR-VIE
−0030	−0015	−0030	−0035	−2.2	−1.7	−0.9	−0.6

SHELTER
Good shelter, and easy access except in strong SW winds or swell when breakers form off entrance. Channel is dredged, but very shallow near breakwater heads. Access HW−2 to HW. In harbour, channel 1.5m deep. On N bank lie: − small yacht basin inside Grand Môle; two tidal fishing boat basins; beyond them the marina nominally dredged to 1.5m. Up river on E bank at St-Gilles-sur-Vie yachts can lie alongside quay (dries). In good weather anchor off entrance, close SE of leading line. Anchoring prohibited in channel.

NAVIGATION
Waypoint Pill'Hours S cardinal buoy, Q(6) + LFl 15s, Bell, 46°41'.10N 01°58'.33W, 233°/053° from/to Jetée de la Garenne Lt, 0.90M. Landmarks are Pte de Grosse-Terre (rocky headland) with Lt Ho, the rear Ldg Lt structure, two spires, and water towers round town. Beware Rocher Pill'Hours and drying reefs extending 1 ca (180m) SE. Tide runs strongly in entrance, particularly on ebb.

LIGHTS AND MARKS
Ldg Lts at 043°. Both Oc(3+1)R 12s 7/28m 13M; intens 033.5°-053.5° synchronized. Pointe de Grosse Terre Fl(4)WR 12s 25m 17/13M; vis W290°-125°, R125°-145°. SE Mole head Iso WG 4s 7m 8/5M, G220°-335°, W335°-220°. NW Mole head Fl(2)WR 6s 8m 9/6M; R045°-225°, W225°-045°, Reed(2) 20s.

RADIO TELEPHONE
VHF Ch 09 (season 0600-2200; out of season 0800-1200, 1400-1800 LT).

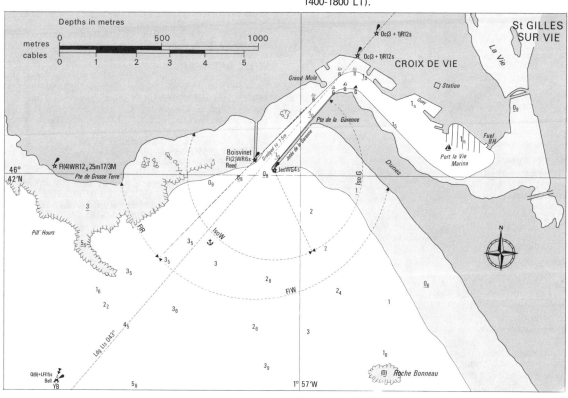

ST GILLES-CROIX-DE-VIE *continued*

TELEPHONE (51)
Hr Mr Port de Plaisance 51.55.30.83; Aff Mar 51.55.10.58;
▦ 51.55.10.58; CROSS 97.55.35.35; SNSM 51.55.01.19;
Meteo 51.36.10.78; Auto 51.62.45.99; Police 51.55.01.19;
Dr 51.55.11.93; Brit Consul 40.63.16.02.

FACILITIES
Port la Vie Marina (750 + 60 visitors) ☎ 51.55.30.83, Bar,
CH, Gaz, R, SM, V, BH (26 ton), P, D, FW, ME, El, AC,
Slip (Access H24); **Quay** Slip, FW, C (6 ton); **Force 5**
☎ 51.55.83.57 ME, El, Sh, CH; **Ship Shop** ☎ 51.54.24.14
ME, El, Ⓔ, Sh, CH; **Massif Marine** ☎ 51.55.45.17, ME,
El, Ⓔ, Sh, CH, C (15 ton); **Cooperative Maritime des
Marins-Pecheurs** ☎ 51.55.31.39, CH, SHOM; **Meca
Marine** ☎ 51.55.42.93, ME, El, Sh, CH; **CN de Havre de
Vie** ☎ 51.55.87.91; **BM Sails** ☎ 51.55.50.48, SM;
Transnav ☎ 51.55.31.60, Ⓔ;
Town V, Gaz, R, Bar, ✉; Ⓑ; ⇌. There is a ferry to Ile
d'Yeu.
Ferry UK — Roscoff—Plymouth; St Malo—Portsmouth.

ILE D'YEU   10-14-21
Vendee

CHARTS
Admiralty 2647; SHOM 6853, 6513, 6890; ECM 549
TIDES
+0550 Dover; ML 3.1; Duration 0600; Zone −0100
Standard Port BREST (→)

Times				Height (metres)			
HW		LW		MHWS	MHWN	MLWN	MLWS
0500	1100	0500	1100	7.5	5.9	3.0	1.4
1700	2300	1700	2300				

Differences PORT JOINVILLE (Ile d'Yeu)
−0035	−0010	−0035	−0035	−2.2	−1.8	−0.9	−0.6

Although Port de la Meule is a fine weather small port
(dries) on the S coast all information following refers to
Port Joinville unless otherwise stated.
SHELTER
Swell runs in the entrance in winds from N to NE but
shelter is good once in the marina in the NE part of the
harbour. Marina gets very crowded mid-season. Yachts
can anchor fore and aft (rafted together) between Gare
Maritime and the ice factory, leaving room for commercial
traffic to west.
NAVIGATION
Waypoint Basse Mayence N cardinal buoy, 46°44'.65N
02°19'.10W, 055°/235° from/to breakwater Lt, 1.4M.
Harbour gets very full in summer. Approach with care at
LW. Beware Basse du Bouet 3ca (500m) NW, La Sablaire
shoal to the E and rocks along the coast both sides of
harbour entrance. Anchoring in outer harbour is
prohibited. In the main harbour a forbidden zone is
marked by R&W paint. At night keep in W sector of Dir
Q WRG Lt.
LIGHTS AND MARKS
There is a conspic water tower behind the town; NW jetty
head Oc(3)WG 12s 9m 11/9M; G shore-150°, W150°-232°,
G232°-279°, W279°-285°, G285°-shore. Horn (3) 30s; tidal
signals. Quai de Canada Ldg Lts 219°, Front QR 11m 6M;
pylon; Rear (85m from front) QR 16m 6M; mast, both vis
169°-269°. Quai de Canada head Iso G 4s 7m 6M unintens
337°-067°. Galiote jetty root Fl(2)R 5s 1M.
RADIO TELEPHONE
VHF Ch 09 (office hours).
TELEPHONE (51)
Hr Mr 51.58.38.11; Harbour Office 51.58.51.10; Aff Mar
51.58.32.45; ▦ 51.58.37.88, CROSS 97.55.35.35; Meteo
51.36.10.78; Auto 51.62.45.99; SNSM 51.58.35.39;
Police 51.58.30.05; Dr 51.58.31.70; Ⓗ 51.68.30.23;
Brit Consul 40.63.16.02.
FACILITIES
Marina (100 + 40 visitors), FW, AB, P, D, ME, El, Sh;
2nd Tidal Basin ☎ 51.58.38.11, Slip, L, FW, C (5 ton);
Berlivet ☎ 51.58.33.11, CH; **CN Ile d'Yeu** ☎ 51.58.31.50;
Comptoln Nautique ☎ 51.58.73.40 ME, El, Sh, CH; **Oya
Nautique** ☎ 51.58.35.54, ME, El, CH; **Poiraud**
☎ 51.58.50.69, ME; **Radio Maritime** ☎ 51.58.32.83, Ⓔ;
M. Naud Gilbert ☎ 51.58.32.44, Gaz; **Town** V, Gaz, R,
Bar, ✉; Ⓑ; ⇌ (St-Gilles-Croix-de-Vie); ✈ (Nantes).
Flights to Nantes and (summers only) to Les Sables
d'Olonne. (Airfield 2M westward).
Ferry UK — Roscoff—Plymouth; St Malo—Portsmouth.
Note: There are no cash telephones —
Phone-cards available from PTT or at some tabacs
and cafés.

ILE D'YEU *continued*

ILE DE NOIRMOUTIER   10-14-22
Vendee

CHARTS
Admiralty 2647, 3216; SHOM 5039; ECM 549
TIDES
+0500 Dover; ML 2.8; Zone −0100
Standard Port BREST (⟶)

Times				Height (metres)			
HW		LW		MHWS	MHWN	MLWN	MLWS
0500	1100	0500	1100	7.5	5.9	3.0	1.4
1700	2300	1700	2300				

Differences BOIS DE LA CHAISE

−0030	−0020	0000	−0005	−2.1	−1.9	−1.4	−1.0

FROMENTINE

−0025	−0020	−0005	+0015	−2.2	−1.9	−1.3	−0.9

SHELTER
Anchor in Bois de la Chaise, exposed to N and E winds. Good shelter alongside in Noirmoutier-en-l'Ile but harbour dries 1.8m-2.4m, access HW∓1. L'Herbaudière comprises fishing harbour (W side) and marina (E side), dredged 2m-3m with good shelter. Visitors report to Pontoon F.
NAVIGATION
Waypoint Baie de Bourgneuf SN3 (safe water) buoy, LFl 10s, 47°06'.00N 02°21'.50W, 318°/138° from/to Basse du Martroger Lt Bn, 4.5M. Chaussée des Boeufs extends 3½M W and 6M SW of island, which is fringed by rocks and banks on N and E sides. W sector (187.5°-190°) of L'Herbaudière West breakwater Lt leads into entrance channel, dredged to 1.3m and passing close W of two 0.8m patches. W breakwater obscures vessels leaving. For Noirmoutier-en-l'Ile, a long channel marked by beacons leads through rocks. La Vendette is one of the highest parts of rocky ledges, E of entrance to Noirmoutier-en-l'Ile.
For Fosse de Fromentine see 10.14.24.

LIGHTS AND MARKS
Noirmoutier jetty Oc(2)R 6s 6m 6M; L'Herbaudière E jetty Fl(2)R 6s 8m 5M; W jetty Oc(2+1)WG 12s 9m 10/7M; W187.5°-190°, G elsewhere.
RADIO TELEPHONE
L'Herbaudière VHF Ch 09. (Hr Mr in working hours).
TELEPHONE (51)
Hr Mr (L'Herbaudière) 51.39.05.05; Aff Mar 51.39.01.64; SNSM 51.39.33.90; CROSS 97.55.35.35; Meteo 40.75.80.07; Auto 40.04.15.15; ⌗ 51.39.06.80; Police 51.39.04.36; Dr 51.39.05.64; Brit Consul 40.63.16.02.
FACILITIES
L'HERBAUDIÈRE. **Marina** (442+50 visitors), ☎ 51.39.05.05, P, D, AC, C (25 ton), Slip, FW, ME, V, SM, Ⓘ, R, Gas, Gaz, Bar (July, Aug), Sh, SC; **Quay** P, D, Bar, R, Gaz, ME, Sh, SM, V; **Gendron Plaisance** ☎ 51.39.18.69, ME, C, El, Ⓔ, Sh, CH; **Gendron Yvon** ☎ 51.39.12.06, ME; **Massif Marine** ☎ 51.39.05.86, ME, C, El, Ⓔ, Sh, CH, Gaz; **Voilerie Burgaud** ☎ 51.39.23.89, SM; **Voilerie Simonin** ☎ 51.39.41.87, SM.
NOIRMOUTIER. **Quay** FW, C (4 ton); **Nautique 85** ☎ 51.39.05.78, ME, El, Ⓔ, Sh, CH; **Quincaillerie de la Mer** ☎ 51.39.47.67, CH; **Voilerie Burgaud** ☎ 51.39.12.66, SM.
Town P, D, V, Gaz, R, Bar, Ⓘ, ⊠; Ⓑ; ⇌ (ferry to Pornic, bus to Nantes); ✈ (Nantes).
Ferry UK — Roscoff—Plymouth; St Malo—Portsmouth.

ILE DE NOIRMOUTIER *continued*

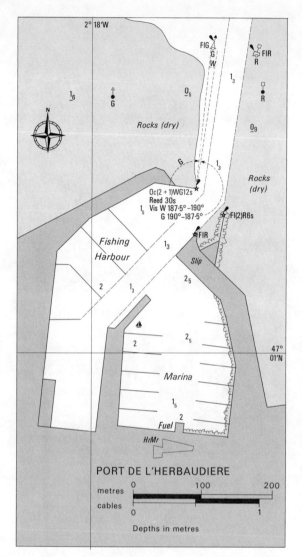

PORT DE L'HERBAUDIERE

metres 0 — 100 — 200

cables 0 — — 1

Depths in metres

PORNIC   10-14-23
Loire Atlantique

CHARTS
Admiralty 2646, 2985, 3216; SHOM 5039, 6854; ECM 549
TIDES
+0515 Dover; ML 2.9; Duration 0540; Zone −0100
Standard Port BREST (⟶)

Times				Height (metres)			
HW		LW		MHWS	MHWN	MLWN	MLWS
0500	1100	0500	1100	7.5	5.9	3.0	1.4
1700	2300	1700	2300				

Differences PORNIC

−0035	−0015	+0005	+0005	−2.1	−1.9	−1.4	−1.1

SHELTER
Very good shelter in the large Pornic-Noëveilland marina, P1, P2 and P3 pontoons reserved for visitors. Old harbour dries (1.8m); access HW∓2½. Entry dangerous in strong winds from SE to W. Marina Access HW∓5.
NAVIGATION
Waypoint Notre Dame Bn, isolated danger mark, 47°05'.49N 02°08'.20W, 227°/047° from/to jetty head, 1.5M. Beware Banc de Kerouars in N of bay; all other hazards are well marked. There is an exit to the S (possible HW∓1 near springs) but a drying causeway joins Ile de Noirmoutier to the mainland. The S end of bay is devoted to oyster beds, and there are many obstructions.

LIGHTS AND MARKS
Marina SW elbow Fl(2+1) 7s 4m 3M; SW jetty head Fl(2)R 6s 4m 4M; E jetty head FlG 2.5s 4m 2M; Pointe de Noëveilland Oc(3+1)WRG 12s 22m 13/9M; G shore-051°, W051°-079°, R079°-shore. Entry signals (simplified).
RADIO TELEPHONE
VHF Ch 09 (H24).
TELEPHONE (40)
Hr Mr 40.82.05,40; Aff Mar 40.82.01.69; ⌗ 40.82.03.17; SNSM 40.82.01.54; Meteo 40.04.15.15; CROSS 97.55.35.35; Police 40.82.00.29; Dr 40.82.01.80; Brit Consul 40.63.16.02.
FACILITIES
Port-la-Noëveillard Marina (750 + 165 visitors)
☎ 40.82.05.40, P, D (on pontoon), FW, ME, AC, El, Sh, BH (20 ton), C (6 ton) CH; **CN de Pornic** ☎ 40.82.42.26; **Pornic Nautic** ☎ 40.82.04.64, ME, El, Ⓔ, Sh, CH; **MEP** ☎ 40.82.52.60 ME, El, Sh, Ⓔ; **Technic Marine** ☎ 40.82.24.44 ME, El, Ⓔ, Sh, CH; **Ouest Voile** ☎ 40.82.26.57, SM; **Town** V, Gaz, R, Bar, ✉; Ⓑ; ⇌; ✈ (Nantes).
Ferry UK — Roscoff—Plymouth; St Malo—Portsmouth.

MINOR HARBOURS AND
ANCHORAGES   10.14.24

HENDAYE, Pyrénées Atlantique, 43°22′ N, 1°47′ W, Zone
−0100; Admty charts 1343, 2665, SHOM 6556, 6558. HW
+0450 on Dover (GMT), −0030 on Pointe de Grave (zone
−0100). HW height −1.1m on Pointe de Grave, ML
2.3m. Hendaye lies on the French bank of the Rio
Bidasoa, the other bank being Fuenterrabia in Spain.
Access to river HW∓3. Beware Les Briquets lying to the
E of the bay. Lt Ho on W end of bay, Cabo Higuer, Fl(2)
60s 63m 23M. River ent breakwater heads, East L Fl R 10s
7m 9M, West FG 9m 4M. River dredged to 2m. Yacht
anchorage 1 ca (185m) SW of landing place at Hendaye
Plage in 3.5m, or in about 3m off Roca Punta at root of
W breakwater, or S of Hendaye quay. Much of bay dries.
Facilities: Hr Mr ☎ 59.20.16.97; ⚓ ☎ 59.20.01.98; Aff
Mar 59.55.06.68; **Quay** C (20 ton), D, FW; **Club
Maritime Hendaye** ☎ 59.20.03.02, VHF Ch 09, P, C
(20 ton); **Jabin** ☎ 59.20.08.96, ME, CH; **Comption
Marina Basque** ☎ 59.20.22.14 CH, Ⓔ; **Town** V, R, Bar,
✉; Ⓑ; ⇌; ✈.

ST JEAN-DE-LUZ, Pyrénées Atlantique, 43°23′ N, 1°40′ W,
Zone −0100; Admty chart 1343, SHOM 6526, 6558. HW
+0435 on Dover (GMT), −0045 on Pointe de Grave (zone
−0100); HW height −1.0m on Pointe de Grave; ML
2.5m. There are two harbours, St Jean-de-Luz on SE of
bay and Socoa to the W of the bay. Approaching from N,
keep W of Les Esquilletac, a rock ½M off Pointe St
Barbe. The bay can be entered at all times except in
strong NW winds, and good anchorage found in approx
4m. There is a small yacht harbour in SW corner of St
Jean-de-Luz. Socoa harbour dries. Enter bay via W
passage between Digue des Criquas and Digue d'Artha.
Sailing is forbidden in the port. Beware a submerged
obstruction in SE corner of the bay. Ldg Lts at 101° both
Oc(3+1)R 12s 30/47m 18M lead in from W, S of Belhara
Perdun. Ldg Lts 138° Front QWR 12/8M, Rear Q 20M
lead between Illarguita and Belhara Perdun. Inner Ldg Lts
151° both Oc(2)G 6s. Le Socoa Lt Ho QWR 36m 12/8M,
W shore-264°, R264°-282°, W282°-264°. Socoa
breakwater head QG 11m 9M. Facilities:
ST JEAN-DE-LUZ Hr Mr ☎ 59.26.26.81; Aff Mar
☎ 59.47.14.55; **Quay** FW, P, C; **CRM** ☎ 59.47.05.85 Ⓔ;
Stream Service Marine ☎ 59.47.05.85 ME, El, Sh, CH,
Ⓔ, Meteo 59.23.84.15.
SOCOA Hr Mr ☎ 59.47.18.44; Aff Mar ☎ 59.47.14.55;
⚓ ☎ 59.47.18.61; **Jetty** C (1 ton), FW, P, D, AC;
Yacht Club Basque ☎ 59.47.26.81; **Arrantzalat**
☎ 59.47.02.02, ME, CH; **Larmanou-Marine**
☎ 59.47.99.97, ME, El, Sh, CH: **Town** V, R, Bar, ✉;
Ⓑ; ⇌.

ANGLET, Pyrénées Atlantique, 43°32′ N, 1°31′ W, Zone
−0100; Admty charts 1343, 2665, SHOM 6571. HW at
Boucau (1½M up river) +0450 on Dover (GMT), −0035
on Pointe de Grave (zone −0100); HW height −1.0m on
Pointe de Grave; ML 2.6m. Access good except in strong
winds from SW to NW when entry may be impracticable.
Tidal stream is strong, up to 5 kn on ebb at springs. The
marina is on the S side ¾M from ent to R Adour. There
are yacht moorings W of marina ent. Pointe St Martin
Fl(2) 10s 73m 29M is approx 2½M SSW of ent. BA buoy
(safe water mark) L Fl 10s is moored 9 ca (1650m) NW of
breakwater head which has QR Lt. Ldg Lts 090°, both Q
intens 087°-093°, W Trs with R tops. N jetty head Oc(2)R
6s 12m 8M. S jetty head Iso G 4s 9m 7M. Inner Ldg Lts
approx 111°, both FG moved as necessary. Traffic signals
(full code, see 10.14.7) shown from Tr S of entrance.
Facilities: Hr Mr ☎ 59.63.05.45; Aff Mar and ⚓ at
Bayonne; Meteo 59.23.84.15; **Marina** (390+10 visitors),
☎ 59.63.05.45; P, D, FW, ME, El, AC, C (1.3 ton), BH
(13 ton), Slip, Sh; **YC Adour Atlantique** ☎ 59.63.16.22,
Nivadour Nautique ☎ 59.63.16.85, ME, El, Sh, CH, Ⓔ.

BAYONNE, Pyrénées Atlantique, 43°30′ N, 1°29′ W, Zone
−0100; Admty chart 1343, SHOM 6536, 6557/8. Details
of tides, entry lights etc are as shown under Anglet
above. Bayonne is 3M upstream from Anglet, the channel
being well marked with Ldg Lts, buoys and beacons.
There are numerous commercial wharves. Yachts berth on
S bank below the bridge near town hall where R Nive
joins the R Adour. VHF Ch 09 12 (H24). Facilities: Hr Mr
☎ 59.63.11.57; Aff Mar ☎ 59.55.06.68; ⚓ ☎ 59.59.08.29;
Port C (30 ton), Slip, FW, P, D; **Club Nautique de
Bayonne; Sorin** ☎ 59.59.16.87, CH, SHOM.

CAPBRETON, Landes, 43°39′ N, 1°26′ W, Zone −0100;
Admty chart 2665, SHOM 6557, 6586. HW +0450 on
Dover (GMT), −0030 on Pointe de Grave (zone −0100);
HW height −1.1m on Pointe de Grave, ML 2.3m. Good
shelter, narrow entrance dangerous in strong winds from N
and W. Do not enter if waves break in mid-channel. Access
at all times except LW; recommended HW∓4. Visitors
Pontoon B. Marina is entered through gap in training wall
on SE side of Boucaret Channel. Harbour dredged to 1.5 to
2.5m. S jetty head Iso G 4s 7m 9M.
N jetty head Fl(2)R 6s 13m 11M, Horn 30s. VHF Ch 09
(0600-2200 in season). Facilities: Hr Mr ☎ 58.72.21.23;
Meteo 89.24.58.80; Aff Mar ☎ 58.72.10.43;
⚓ ☎ 58.72.07.47; **Quay** P, D, Slip, FW; **Marina**
(700+70 visitors), Slip, BH (28 ton), AC, P, D, FW, ME, El,
C (1.5 ton), Sh; **YC Landais; Club Nautique
Capbreton-Hossegor-Seignone** ☎ 58.72.05.25; **Erick
Yachting** ☎ 58.72.14.32, ME, El, Sh, CH, Ⓔ.

LA VIGNE, Gironde, 44°40′ N, 01°14′ W; Zone −0100.
Admty chart 2664, SHOM 6766, ECM 255. HW +0620 on
Dover (GMT); +0030 on Pointe de Grave (zone −0100);
HW height (Cap Ferret) −1.1m on Pointe de Grave; ML
2.3m. Access HW∓2. There are two perches marking the
entrance and a Lt on the SW point, Iso R 4s. Good shelter
but beware strong currents across harbour mouth. There is
a small breakwater (unlit) protruding into the entrance from
the NE side. Facilities: Aff Mar ☎ 56.60.52.76, **Marina**
(268) ☎ 56.60.85.80, FW, AC, Slip, CH, C, P, D.

PAUILLAC, Gironde, 45°12′ N, 0°45′ W, Zone −0100;
Admty charts 2916, 2910; SHOM 6139; HW +0620 on
Dover (GMT), +0045 on Pointe de Grave (zone −0100);
HW height +0.2m on Pointe de Grave; ML 3.0m. Excellent
shelter in marina about half way to Bordeaux from the sea
on W bank, 25M from Le Verdon. Access at all tides (depth
3m). Visitors berth on left of entrance. Beware current in
the river when entering or leaving. Facilities: Hr Mr (Port de
Plaisance) ☎ 56.59.12.16, VHF Ch 09 Aff Mar 56.59.01.58;
Cross 56.09.82.00; ⚓ 56.59.04.01; Meteo 56.34.20.11;
SNSM 56.09.82.00. There are facilities for stepping and
un-stepping masts; **Quay** FW, D, P, C (15 ton); **Marina**
(185+15 visitors), ☎ 56.59.04.53, P, D, FW, AC, Slip, ME,
El, Sh; fuel (on quay); **CN de Pauillac** ☎ 56.59.12.58;
Guiet ☎ 56.59.02.66, CH, ME, El, Sh.

BORDEAUX, Gironde, 44°50′ N, 0°34′ W, Zone −0100;
Admty chart 2916, SHOM 6140, 4610. HW +0715 on
Dover (GMT), +0155 on Pointe de Grave (zone −0100);
HW height −0.1m on Pointe de Grave; ML 2.4m. Bordeaux
is about 55M up the Gironde estuary and River Garonne.
Beware large merchant vessels, strong currents (up to 5 kn
when river in spate) and large bits of flotsam. Point du Jour
marina is 2M from Bordeaux, on W bank just S of
suspension bridge (Pont d'Aquitaine, clearance 51m), with
visitors berths and crane for masts. Moorings may be
available just upstream. No 1 Basin, 1½M above bridge,
access HW−2 to HW+½, may be dirty; crane available.
Or go alongside wharves between No 1 Basin and Pont de
Pierre, but stream is strong. The channel up to Bordeaux is
well marked and lit. VHF Ch 12. Facilities: Hr Mr
☎ 56.90.58.00; Aff Mar ☎ 56.52.26.23; ⚓ ☎ 56.44.47.10;
Meteo 56.90.91.21; **Sport Nautique de la Gironde**
☎ 56.50.84.14; **Cercle de la Voile de Bordeaux**; **Agence
Nautique du Sud Ouest** ☎ 56.91.23.83, ME, El, Sh, CH;
Le Compas ☎ 56.50.60.02, ME, El, Sh, CH, Ⓔ; **Poitevin-
Duault** ☎ 56.52.55.50, CH, Ⓔ, SHOM; **Quay** Slip, C
(5 ton).

BLAYE, Charente Maritime, 45°07′ N, 0°40′ W, Zone −0100,
Admty chart 2916, SHOM 6140. HW +0175 on Dover
(GMT), +0145 on Pointe de Grave (zone −0100); HW
height −0.3m on Pointe de Grave; ML 2.4m. Good shelter;
access good except in winds S to SW. Entrance to NE of
Ile du Paté, marked by Lt Fl G on S bank. Max stay 24
hours. VHF Ch 12 (H24). Facilities: Hr Mr ☎ 57.42.13.49;
⚓ ☎ 57.42.01.11. **Quay** FW, AC, P, D, C (25 ton), Slip,
Access HW∓2½; **Auxemerry** ☎ 57.42.13.43, ME;
A. Moulinier ☎ 57.42.11.94, ME.

14

MINOR HARBOURS *continued*

DOUHET, Ile d'Oleron, Charente Maritime, 46°00' N, 1°20' W, Zone −0100; Admty charts 2648, 2746, SHOM 6334. HW +0545 on Dover (GMT) −0020 on Pointe de Grave (zone −0100); HW height +0.8m on Pointe de Grave; ML 3.7m. In the NE part of the island, access approx HW∓4. There are no lights. Beware rocks E and W of ent channel. Yacht harbour in wet dock, 1.5m. Max length 7m. Facilities: Hr Mr 46.76.71.13, Auto 46.41.11.11; Aff Mar and ⊞ − Le Chateau; **Geron** ☎ 46.76.53.96 ME, El, Ⓔ, Sh, CH; **Quay** FW, AB, Slip. Correspondence with Hr Mr Boyardville.

ILE D'AIX, Charente Maritime, 46°01' N, 1°10' W, Zone −0100; Admty charts 2746, 2748, SHOM 6334, 6468. HW +0545 on Dover (GMT), −0020 on Pointe de Grave (zone −0100); HW height +0.8m on Pointe de Grave; ML 3.7m. Only a fine weather anchorage; anchor or pick up a buoy off the landing jetty at St Catherine's Point, the most southerly tip of the island. Lt on the point is FlWR 5s 24m 23/19M. Mooring available E of St Catherine's Pt (shallow), four W buoys to West of St Catherine's Pt (deeper) and another four SE of the point. Facilities: C (1.5 ton), Slip, AB (SE jetty), shop and restaurant.

PORT D'ANTIOCHE (Port St Denis), Ile d'Oleron, 46°02' N, 1°22' W zone −0100. Admty chart 2648, 2746. SHOM 6333. HW +0545 on Dover (GMT); as for Rochefort (zone −0100). HW height +1.0m on Pointe de Grave. ML 3.8m. Easy entrance. Conspic mark − tower of St Denis; keep at 260°. Light 2FR (west) on jetty. VHF Ch 09. Depth in basin 1.5m. Capacity 600 plus 50 for visitors. Hr Mr 46.47.97.97. (0800–2000) in season. Port de Plaisance ☎ 46.47.24.68, Slip, FW, AC. Yacht Club de l'Ocean ☎ 46.47.93.64, open all year. **Barbancon** ☎ 46.47.86.80 ME;

LA FLOTTE, Ile de Ré, Charente Maritime, 46°11' N, 1°19' W, Zone −0100; Admty charts 2648, 2641, 2746, SHOM 6521, 6668. HW +0535 on Dover (GMT), −0025 on Pointe de Grave (zone −0100); HW height +0.6m on Pointe de Grave; ML 3.4m. La Flotte lies 2M SE of St Martin (see 10.14.17). From NW keep clear of Le Couronneau; from E, keep N of Bn off Pointe des Barres. Approach with La Flotte Lt Ho (W Tr with G top) bearing 215° in W sector. La Flotte Lt Fl WG 4s 10m 12/7M; vis G180°-205°, W205°-220°, G220°-257°, Horn (3)30s by day HW−2 to HW+2. Avant port is sheltered by mole and dries (2.4m); inner harbour dries (2.7m). Access HW∓3. There is an anchorage off La Flotte in 3m, sheltered from S and W. Facilities: Visitors use North Jetty; Hr Mr on Quai Senac Ouest; Aff Mar and ⊞ at St Martin; **Quay** Slip, FW; **Cercle Nautique de la Flotte-en-Ré** (CNLF) (open July-15 Sept); **Chauffour** ☎ 46.09.60.25, ME.

ARS-EN-RÉ, Ile de Ré, Charente Maritime, 46°12' N, 1°31' W, Zone −0100; Admty chart 2648, SHOM 6333, 6334 HW +0540 on Dover (GMT), −0045 on Pointe de Grave (zone −0100); HW height +0.6m; ML 3.4m. Port d'Ars is at the head of a creek in the SW corner of the bay Mer du Fier, the entrance obstructed by rocks which dry. Channel through Mer du Fier marked by buoys and bns; Access HW∓3. There are two quays (dry) and a wet dock with sill gate, 2.9m above CD. Ldg Lts to Fiers d'Ars 265°, Front Iso 4s 5m 11M W square on hut; vis 141°-025°. Rear 370m from front, Dir Iso G 4s 13m 15m, G square Tr on dwelling (synchronised with front and intens 264°-266°). Port d'Ars Ldg Lts 232°, front Q 5m 9M, W rectangle with R lantern, rear 370m from front, Q 13m 11M, B rectangle on W framework Tr, G top; vis 142°-322°. There is an anchorage close S of Pte du Fier with min depth of 2.4m; most of the bay dries. VHF Ch 09. Facilities: Hr Mr ☎ 46.29.40.19, Aff Mar and ⊞ at St Martin (see 10.14.17); SNSM ☎ 46.29.41.49; **Cercle Nautique d'Ars-en-Ré** ☎ 46.29.41.13 (open Apl to Nov); **Blanchard** ☎ 46.29.40.43, ME, El, Sh; **Blondeau Marine** ☎ 46.29.40.39, ME; **Jetties** Slip, FW, C (6 ton).

L'AIGUILLON-LA-FAUTE-SUR-MER, Vendée, 46°20' N, 1°18' W, Zone −0100; Admty charts 2641, 2648, SHOM 6521. HW +0535 on Dover (GMT), −0030 on Pointe de Grave (zone −0100); HW height +0.6m on Pointe de Grave; ML 3.4m. Shelter good except in strong winds from W or S; entry only safe in fine weather with off-shore winds. Access HW∓2½. Beware mussel bed timber piers which cover at HW. Also beware oyster beds. The area is very flat and, being shallow, waves build up quickly in any wind. The bar to seaward dries and is dangerous in bad weather. Entrance can be identified by a hill, La Dive, opposite side of entrance to Pointe d'Arcay, with a conspic transformer on it. Enter with transformer bearing 033°. Anchor in R Lay or go alongside on YC pontoons, (40). Facilities: Hr Mr ☎ 51.56.45.02 Aff Mar ☎ 51.56.45.35; CROSS 56.09.82.00; Dr ☎ 51.56.46.17; **Club Nautique Aiguillonais et Fautais** (CNAF) open July-Sept; ☎ 51.56.44.42; **Groisard-Hériaud** ☎ 51.97.08.73 ME; **Co-operative Maritimes** ☎ 51.56.44.89, CH.

JARD-SUR-MER, Vendee, 46°24' N, 1°35' W, Zone −0100; Admty chart 2648, SHOM 6522. HW +0600 on Dover (GMT), −0010 on Brest (zone −0100); HW height −2.0m on Brest; ML 3.1m; Duration 0640. White daymarks 4 ca (740m) E of harbour lead 038° between Roches de l'Islatte (dry) and Roches de la Brunette (dry), marked by buoys. Then pick up 293° transit of RW marks on W side of harbour, leading to entrance. There are no lights. Facilities: Hr Mr ☎ 51.33.40.17; ⊞ ☎ 51.95.11.33; **Jetty** FW, C (5 ton); **Jard Marine** ☎ 51.33.46.84, CH; **Morineau** ☎ 51.33.42.05 Divers.

FROMENTINE, Vendée, 46°54' N, 2°08' W, Zone −0100; Admty chart 2647, SHOM 5039. HW +0550 on Dover (GMT), −0025 on Brest (zone −0100); HW height −2.1m on Brest; ML 2.9m; Duration 0540. Do not approach from Baie de Bourgneuf as there is a road causeway which dries 3m, connecting Ile de Noirmoutier with the mainland. Enter through Goulet de Fromentine, under the bridge (clearance 27m). The channel is marked by buoys, moved as necessary but it is very shallow, so dangerous in bad weather. The ebb stream runs at more than 5 kn at springs. Do not attempt night entry. Anchor W of pier. Coming from N, beware Les Boeufs. Tourelle Milieu lies on the N side of Le Goulet de Fromentine, Fl(4)R 12s 6m 5M, R Tr. Pointe de Notre Dames-de-Monts Lt Oc(2)WRG 6s 21m 13/10M, G000°-043°, W043°-063°, R063°-073°, W073°-094°, G094°-113°, W113°-116°, R116°-175°, G175°-196°, R196°-230°. Fromentine light-buoy (safe water mark) 46°53'.1N, 2°11'.5W Fl 10s Bell is about 1.5M WSW of Pointe du Notre Dames-de-Monts. Bridge W end Iso W 4s 32m 18M; E end Iso W 4s 32m 18M. Facilities: Aff Mar at Noirmoutier; ⊞ at Beauvois-sur-Mer; **Quay** Slip, C (3 ton), FW; **Cercle Nautique de Fromentine-Barfatre** (CNFB); **Marine Motoculture** ☎ 51.68.53.77, ME, El, Sh, CH;

VOLVO PENTA SERVICE

Sales and service centres in area 15
Names and addresses of Volvo Penta dealers in
this area are available from:

FRANCE *Volvo Penta France SA,* Chemin de la Nouvelle, F78130 Les Mureaux
Tel (01) 3 474 72 01, Telex 695221 F

Area 15

South Brittany
River Loire to Camaret

VOLVO PENTA

15

48°
30'N

See 10.16.2

Pte St Mathieu
(RC) SM
3 ••• ‒‒
289.6 20

Lanvéoc/Poulmic
(RC) Aero BST
‒••• ••• ••• ‒
316 80

Brest ●

Le Conquet ●☆

Camaret
ℹ 10.15.26
LB

Morgat
ℹ 10.15.25

Lorient
ℹ 10.15.19
📞 R P VHF 16; 11
☀☁ 97.64.34.86
LB ⚠IL

Audierne
ℹ 10.15.23
LB ⚠IL

Douarnenez
ℹ 10.15.24
LB ⚠IL

Quimperlé
(Brest-le
Conquet)
S C MF‒1876

Raz de Sein ☆
Cross Corsen
Cross Étel

Pte du Raz Sig. Stn.
VHF 16

Quimper/Pluguffan
(RC) Aero Q R
‒••‒ •‒•
380 •••

Quimper ●

La Forêt
ℹ 10.15.21
⚠IL VHF Ch 09

Concarneau
ℹ 10.15.20
📞 R P VHF 16; 12
⚠IL

48°
N

Ile de Sein
(RC) SN
3 ••• ‒•
303.4 100
LB ⚠IL

Pont l'Abbé
S C VHF 16 27

St Guenolé ●
Pte de Penmarc'h ☆

Guilvinec ●*

LB LB ⚠IL

Beg
Meil Pont-Aven*
Trévignon ● Port Manech
LB ⚠IL
LB ⚠IL
Döelan* LB

Eckmühl Lt
(RC) ÜH
1 •••‒ ••••
289.6 50

CG LB

*Loctudy

☆ Ile aux Moutons

Iles des Glénans

☆ Penfret

Lorient/Lann-Bihoué
(RC) Aero LOR
•‒•• ‒‒‒ •‒•
294.2 80

⚠IL Port Loui
LB Port T
☆ ☆ Ile
Gro

Pte de Combrit
(RC) CT
4 ‒•‒• ‒
289.6 20

Bénodet
ℹ 10.15.22
☀☁ 98.94.00.57
LB ⚠IL

Ile de Groix/Pen Men Lt
(RC) GX
‒‒• ‒‒••
301·1 10

47°
30'N

Port Haliguen-Quiberon
ℹ 10.15.17
Marina VHF 09
LB

*Sa

10-15-2

South Brittany

Belle Ile
S C VHF 05 16 2
CG

47°
N

Key to Symbols

Coast Station/Port Radio – frequencies
Marine radiobeacon– call sign, sequence, frequency and range (nm)
Aeronautical radiobeacon–call sign, frequency and range (nm)
See for harbour information/tidal data
Weather information (tel. no. or times)
Coastguard Rescue Co-ordination Centre

Coastguard Rescue Sub-Centre or VHF relay
Life-boat
Inshore Life-boat
SAR Helicopter base
Principal lights
Light-vessel
Lanby
* See 10.15.27

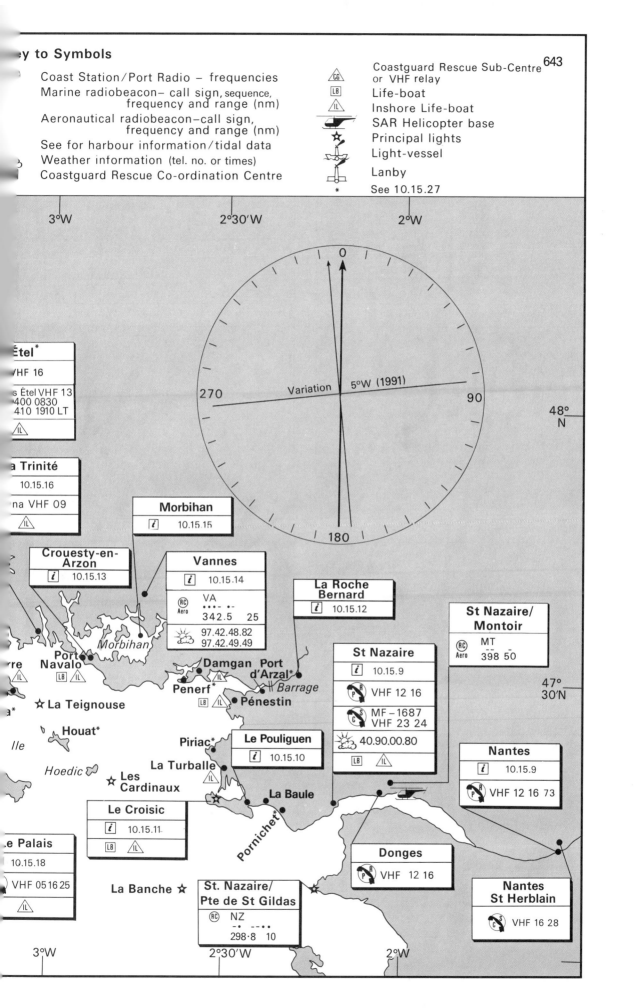

3°W 2°30'W 2°W

Variation 5°W (1991)

0
270 90
180

48° N

Étel*
VHF 16

s Étel VHF 13
400 0830
410 1910 LT

a Trinité
10.15.16

na VHF 09

Morbihan
i 10.15.15

Crouesty-en-Arzon
i 10.15.13

Vannes
i 10.15.14

RC Aero VA
• • • – • –
342.5 25

97.42.48.82
97.42.49.49

La Roche Bernard
i 10.15.12

St Nazaire/Montoir
RC Aero MT
– – – –
398 50

47° 30'N

Morbihan

Port Navalo LB

re

* La Teignouse

\ Houat*

Ile

Hoedic Les Cardinaux

a*

Damgan Port d'Arzal*
Penerf* || Barrage
LB • **Pénestin**

St Nazaire
i 10.15.9

P R VHF 12 16

C S MF – 1687 VHF 23 24

40.90.00.80

LB

Piriac*
La Turballe

Le Pouliguen
i 10.15.10

Nantes
i 10.15.9

P R VHF 12 16 73

Le Croisic
i 10.15.11
LB

La Baule

Pornichet*

Donges
P R VHF 12 16

e Palais
10.15.18

VHF 05 16 25

La Banche ☆

St. Nazaire/Pte de St Gildas
RC NZ
– • – – • •
298·8 10

Nantes St Herblain
C S VHF 16 28

3°W 2°30'W 2°W

10.15.3   AREA 15 TIDAL STREAMS

5 Hours before HW Brest (0010 after HW Dover)

4 Hours before HW Brest (0110 after HW Dover)

3 Hours before HW Brest (0210 after HW Dover)

2 Hours before HW Brest (0310 after HW Dover)

1 Hour before HW Brest (0410 after HW Dover)

HW Brest (0510 after HW Dover)

Northward 10.16.3   Southward 10.14.3

1 Hour after HW Brest (0610 after HW Dover)

2 Hours after HW Brest (0515 before HW Dover)

3 Hours after HW Brest (0415 before HW Dover)

4 Hours after HW Brest (0315 before HW Dover)

5 Hours after HW Brest (0215 before HW Dover)

6 Hours after HW Brest (0115 before HW Dover)

15

10.15.4   LIGHTS, FOG SIGNALS AND WAYPOINTS

Abbreviations used below are given in 10.0.3. Principal lights are in **bold** print, places in CAPITALS, and light-vessels, light floats and Lanbys in *CAPITAL ITALICS*. Unless otherwise stated lights are white. m—elevation in metres; M—nominal range in n. miles. Fog signals are in *italics*. Useful waypoints are underlined use those on land with care. See 4.2.2.

FRANCE—WEST COAST

LOIRE APPROACH LANBY SN1 47°00'05N 02°39'·95W Iso 4s 8m 9M; safe water mark; *Whis*; Racon.
LOIRE APPROACH LANBY SN2 47°03'·00N 02°30'·70W Oc 4s 8m 8M; safe water mark; Ra refl.
NW BANCHE LANBY 47°12'·90N 02°30'·95W Q 8m 8M; N cardinal; *Bell*; Ra refl.
LA COURONNEE LANBY 47°07'·65N 02°20'·00W QG 8m 6M; stbd hand mark; Ra refl.

Pointe de Saint Gildas 47°08'·10N 02°14'·67W Q WRG 23m **W15M**, R12M, G10M; framework Tr on W house; vis R264°-308°, G308°-078°, W078°-088°, R088°-174°, W174°-180°, G180°-264°. RC.
Port de La Gravette, jetty head 47°09'·80N 02°12'·60W Fl(3) WG 12s 7m W8M, G5M; W structure, G top; vis G224°-124°, W124°-224°.
Port de Comberge, S jetty 47°10'·60N 02°09'·95W Oc WG 4s 7m W9M, G5M; W Tr, G top; vis W123°-140°, G140°-123°.
Le Pointeau 47°14'·05N 02°10'·90W Fl WG 4s 4m W10M, G6M; W round Tr, G top; vis G050°-074°, W074°-149°, G149°-345°, W345°-050°.
Les Morées 47°15'·05N 02°12'·95W Oc(2) WR 6s 12m W9M, R6M; G Tr; vis W058°-224°, R300°-058°.
Point de Minden, West mole and E mole, both FIG 2s.

DONGES
West dolphin 47°18'·1N 02°05'·0W Iso G 4s 12m 7M.
E dolphin (close ENE) Iso G 4s; G structure.
Paimboeuf, mole head 47°17'·4N 02°02'·0W Oc(3) WG 12s 9m **W16M**, G11M; W round Tr, G top; vis G shore-123°, W123°-shore.
Île du Petit Carnet 47°17'·3N 02°00'·3W Iso G 4s 9m 6M; W framework Tr, G top.
From Paimboeuf to Nantes lights on S side are G, and on N side R.
Portcé Ldg Lts 025°. **Front** 47°14'·6N 02°15'·4W Q 6m **23M**; W mast; intens 024°-026°. **Rear**, 0.75M from front, 47°15'·3N 02°14'·9W Q 36m **27M**; W Tr; intens 024°-026° (H24).
Pointe d'Aiguillon 47° 14'·60N 02°15'·70W Oc(4) WR 12s 27m 14M; W Tr; vis W233°-293°, W297°-300°, R300°-327°, W327°-023°, W027°-089°.
Villèz-Martin, jetty head, 47°15'·3N 02°13'·7W Fl(2) 6s 10m 12M; W Tr, R top.

SAINT-NAZAIRE
West jetty Oc(4) R 12s 11m 10M; W Tr, R top. E jetty Oc(4) G 12s 11m 11M; W Tr, G top.
Old Mole head Oc (21) 12s 18m 12M; W Tr, R top; weather signals.
Bridge, Iso 4s each side mark channel. *Horn (2) 20s.*
Gron 47°17'·7N 02°09'·6W Iso R 4s 5m 7M; R pedestal.
Le Village No.1 47°18'·1N 02°08'·8W QR 7m 8M; vis 225°-135°.
Oiling jetty Oc R 4s 10m 9M; W Tr, R top.
Le Grand Charpentier 47°12'·90N 02°19'·05W Q WRG 22m W14M, R10M, G 10M; grey Tr, G lantern; vis G020°-049°, W049°-111°, R111°-310°, W310°-020°; helicopter platform;

FIG 2s 2m 3M.
N breakwater head FIR 2s 2m 3M.

LE POULIGUEN
South jetty QR 13m 9M. Les Petits Impairs Fl(2) G 6s 6m 4M.
La Banche 47°10'·70N 02°28'·00W Fl(21) WR 15s 22m **W17M**, R12M; B Tr, W bands; vis R266°-280°, W280°-266°.

LE CROISIC.
Jetée de Tréhic, head 47°18'·5N 02°31'·4W Iso WG 4s 12m W13M, G10M; grey Tr, G top; vis G042°-093°, W093°-137°, G137°-345°. *Horn 15s.*
Ldg Lts 156°. **Front** 47°18'·0N 02°31'·0W Oc(21) 12s 10m **18M**; Or topmark on W pylon; intens 154°-158°. **Rear**, 116m from front, Oc(21) 12s 14m **18M**; Or topmark on W pylon, G top; synchronised with front, intens 154°-158°.
Ldg Lts 174° both QG 5/8m 11M; vis 171°-178° on G and W structures, vis on leading line.
Ldg Lts 134° both Dir QR 6/10m 11M; intens 126°-144°; RW pylons.
Le Grand Mabon 47°18'·1N 02°31'·0W Fl R 2·5s 6m 5M, R pylon and pedestal on base.
Le Four 47°17'·9N 02°38'·0W Fl 5s 23m **19M**; W Tr, B stripes.

ILE DE HOEDIC.
Port de l'Argol 47°20'·7N 02°52'·5W Fl WG 4s 10m W10M, G7M; W Tr, G top; vis W143°-163°, G163°-183°, W183°-203°, G203°-143°.
Les Grands Cardinaux 47°19'·3N 02°50'·1W Fl(4) 15s 28m 13M; R and W Tr.

ILE DE HOUAT.
Port de Saint-Gildas, Môle Nord 47°23'·5N 02°57'·4W Oc(2) WG 6s 8m W8M, G5M; W Tr, G top; vis W168°-198°, G198°-210°, W210°-240°, G240°-168°.

LA TURBALLE.
Ldg Lts 006° both Dir F Vi 3M, intens 004°-009°.
Jetée Garlahy Fl(4) WR 12s 13m W10M, R7M; W pylon, R top; vis R060°-315°, W315°-060°.
Digue Tourlandroux Fl G 4s 7m 6M; W pedestal, G top; *Siren 10 min.*

PIRIAC-SUR-MER.
Pipeline 47°22'·1N 02°32'·8W Oc(21) WRG 12s 14m W12M, R9M, G9M; W square, R stripe on R framework Tr; vis G300°-036°, W036°-068°, R068°-120°.
Inner mole, head 47°22'·9N 02°32'·7W Oc(2) WRG 6s 8m W10M, R7M, G6M; W column; vis R066°-185°, W185°-201°, G201°-224°; *Siren 120s.*
Breakwater heads FIG 4s and FIR 4s 5m 5M.

Mesquer, jetty head 47°25'·3N 02°28'·1W Oc(31) WRG 12s 7m W12M, R8M, G7M; W column and building; vis W067°-072°, R072°-102°, W102°-118°, R118°-293°, W293°-325°, G325°-067°.

Île Dumet 47°24'·7N 02°37'·2W Fl(21) WRG 15s 14m W8M, R6M, G6M; W column, G top on fort; vis G090°-272°, W272°-285°, R285°-325°, W325°-090°.
Basse de Kervoyal Dir QWR W8M, R6M; vis W269°-271°, R271°-269°; S cardinal mark on black Tr.

LA VILAINE.
Basse Bertrand 47°31'·1N 02°30'·7W Iso WG 4s 6m W9M, G6M; G Tr; vis W040°-054°, G054°-227°, W227°-234°, G234°-040°.

Penlan 47°31'·0N 02°30'·2W Oc(2) WRG 6s 26m **W16M**, R12M, G11M; W Tr, R bands; vis R292°-025°, G025°-052°, W052°-060°, R060°-138°, G138°-180°.
Pointe du Scal, 47°29'·7N 02°26'·8W Oc(3)G 12s 8m 6M; W square Tr, G top.

PENERF.
Le Pignon 47°30'·1N 02°38'·9W Fl(3) WR 12s 6m W9M, R6M; R Tr; vis R028°-167°, W167°-175°, R175°-349°, W349°-028°.
Saint-Jacques-en-Sarzeau 47°29'·2N 02°47'·4W Oc(2) R 6s 5m 6M; W 8-sided Tr, R top.

CROUESTY EN ARZON.
Ldg Lts 058°. **Front** 47°32'·6N 02°53'·9W Q 10m **19M**; framework Tr; intens 057°-059°. **Rear**, 315m from front, Q 27m **19M**; intens 057°-059°.
N jetty head Oc(2) R 6s 9m 7M; R and W Tr.
S jetty head Fl G 4s 9m 7M; G and W Tr.
Port-Navalo 47°32'·90N 02°55'·12W Oc(3) WRG 12s 32m **W16M**, R12M, G11M; W Tr and dwelling; vis W155°-220°, G317°-359°, W359°-015°, R015°-105°.
Le Grande Mouton 47°33'·8N 02°54'·8W QG 4m 3M; G tripod.
Rivière D'Auray. Le Gregan Q(6) LFl 15s 3m 8M.

RIVIÉRE DE CRAC'H.
Ldg Lts 347°. Front 47°34'·1N 03°00'·4W Q WRG 10m W10M, R7M, G7M; W Tr, G top; vis G321°-345°, W345°-013°, R013°-080°. **Rear**, 560m from front, Q 21m **15M**; W Tr, G top; synchronised with front, intens 337°-357°.
Dir Lt 347° 47°35'·0N 03°01'·0W Dir Oc WRG 4s 9m W14M, R11M, G11M; W Tr; vis G345°-346°, W346°-348°, R348°-349°.
La Trinité-sur-Mer S pier head Oc(2) WR 6s 6m W10M, R7M; W Tr, R top; vis R090°-293°, W293°-300°, R300°-329°. Jetty head Iso R 4s 8m 5M; W Tr, R top.

BELLE ILE
Goulphar 47°18'·67N 03°13'·67W Fl(2) 10s 87m **24M**; grey Tr; 0·7M SW.
Pointe de Kerdonis 47°18'·6N 03°03'·6W Fl(3) R 15s 35m **15M**; W square Tr and dwelling; obsc by Pointes d'Arzic and de Taillefer 025°-129°.

LE PALAIS
Jetée Sud Oc(2) R 6s 11m 11M; W Tr; obsc 298°-170°.
Jetée Nord Fl(21) G 12s 11m 7M; W Tr, G top; obsc 298°-168°. Sauzon QG 9m 6M; W Tr, G top; vis 194°-045°.
Pointe des Poulains 47°23'·3N 03°15'·1W Fl 5s 34m **24M**; W square Tr and dwelling; vis 023°-291°.

PASSAGE DE LA TEIGNOUSE.
La Teignouse 47°27'·5N 03°02'·8W Fl WR 4s 19m 15/11M; vis W033°-039°, R039°-033°; W Tr, R top.
BASSE DU MILIEU LANBY 47°25'·9N 03°04'·2W Fl(2) G 6s 9m 5M; stbd-hand mark.

PORT HALIGUEN.
Marina, old breakwater head Fl R 4s 10m 5M; W Tr, R top.
New breakwater head 47 29.4N°3 06.0W Oc(2) WR 6s 10m W12M, R9M; W Tr, R top; vis W233°-240°, R240°-299°, W299°-306°, R306°-233°.

PORT MARIA.
Ldg Lts 006°. Front 47°28'·6N 03°07'·2W QG 5m 13M; W Tr, B band; intens 005°-008°. Rear, 230m from front, QG 13m 13M; W Tr, B band; intens 005°-008°.
Main light 47°28'·8N 03°07'·5W Q WRG 28m **W15M**, R11M, G11M; W Tr; vis W246°-252°, W291°-297°, G297°-340°,

W340°-017°, R017°-051°, W051° 081°, G081°-098°, W098°-143°.
Brise-lames Sud, head Oc(2) R 6s 9m 7M; W Tr, R top. Môle Est, head Iso G 4s 9m 7M; W Tr, G top.
Plateau des Birvideaux 47°29'·20N 03°17'·45W Fl(2) 6s 24m 9M; B 8-sided Tr, R bands.

Rivière d'Étel, West side, entrance 47°38'·7N 03°12'·8W Oc(2) WRG 6s 13m W9M, R6M, G6M; R framework Tr; vis W022°-064°, R064°-123°, W123°-330°, G330°-022°; 2 FR on radio mast 2·3M NW; FR and F on radio mast 2·4M NW.

LORIENT.
Ldg Lts Passe Sud 008°. **Front, Fish market** 47°43'·8N 03°21'·7W QR 16m **15M**; W square on grey framework Tr; intens 006°-011°. Rear, **Kergroise-La Perrière** 515m from front QR 28m **16M**; R square, W stripe on grey framework Tr; synchronised with front, intens 006°-011°.
Ldg Lts Passe Ouest 057°. Front, Les Soeurs 47°42'·22N 03°21'·43W Dir QW 13m W3M, G2M; R Tr;R Tr, W bands. Rear, **Port Louis** 740m from front Dir QW **18M**; W daymark, red bands on building; Lt intens 042·5°-058·5°, (4M) 058·5°-048·5°.
Ile aux Soris Dir Q WG 6m W3M, G2M; G framework Tr; vis W041·5°-043·5°, G043·5°-041·5°.
Les Trois Pierres 47°41'·58N 03°22'·40W Q RG 11m R6M, G6M; W Tr, R bands; vis G060°-196°, R196°-002°.
"L" Banc des Truics Lt Buoy 47°40'·82N 03°24'·40W Q(9) 15s; W cardinal mark.
A2 Locqueltas Lt Buoy 47°41'·00N 03°24'·90W FlR 2.5s; port-hand mark.
Bastresse Sud Lt Buoy 47°40'·83N 03°22'·01W QG; stdb-hand mark; Bell.
Les Errants Lt Buoy 47°41'·16N 03°22'·29W Fl(2)R 6s; port-hand mark.

Passe de la Citadelle Ldg Lts 016°. **Front** Oc(3) G 12s 8m **16M**; W Tr, G top. Rear, 306m from front, Oc(3) G 12s 14m 14M; W Tr, G top; synchronised with front.
West side, La Jument Oc R 4s 5m 6M; R Tr; vis 182°-024°.
E side, Tourelle de la Citadelle Oc G 4s 6m 6M; G Tr; vis 009°-193°.
Port-Louis jetty Iso G 4s 7m 6M; W Tr, G top; vis 043°-301°.
West side, Le Cochon Fl R 4s 5m 6M; R Tr.
Kéroman, submarine base Ldg Lts 350°. **Front** Dir Oc(2) R 6s 25m **17M**. **Rear**, 91m from front, Dir Oc(2) R 6s 31m **17M**; grey pylon, R & W bands; Lts synchronised and intens 348°-353°.
Fishing harbour, SE side of entrance Fl RG 4s 7m 6M; W Tr, G top; vis G000°-235°, R235°-360°.
Kernevel Ldg Lts 217°. Front Dir Oc(4) R 12s 10m 14M; R square on R and W framework Tr; intens 215°-219°. Rear, 290m from front Dir Oc(4) R 12s 18m 14M; W square Tr, R top; synchronised with front, intens 215°-219°.
Pengarne Fl G 2·5s 3m 4M; G Tr.
Pointe de l'Espérance Dir Lt 037°. Dir Q WRG 8m W10M, R8M, G8M; W column; vis G034°-037°, W037°, R037°-047°.
Landing stage Fl(4) WR 12s 7m W10M, R7M; W dolphin, R top; vis W110°-347°, R347°-355°, W355°-035°.

ILE DE GROIX
Pointe des Chats 47°37'·30N 03°25'·25W Fl R 5s 16m **19M**; W square Tr and dwelling.
Pointe de la Croix Oc WR 4s 16m W12M, R9M; W pedestal, R lantern; vis W169°-336°, R336°-345°, W345°-353°.
Port Tudy, Môle Est, head Fl(2) R 6s 11m 6M; W Tr, R top; vis 112°-226°.
Port Tudy, Môle Nord, head Iso G 4s 12m 6M; W Tr, G top.
Pen Men 47°38'·87N 03°30'·48W Fl(4) 25s 59m **29M**; W square Tr, B top; vis 309°-275°; RC.

15

Kerroc'h 47°42'·0N 03°27'·7W Oc(2) WRG 6s 22m W11M, R8M, G8M; W Tr, R top; vis R096°-112°, G112°-132°, R132°-302°, W302°-096°.

DOËLAN

Ldg Lts 014°. Front 47°46'·3N 03°36'·5W Oc(3)WG 20m 12s W13M, G10M; W Tr, G band and lantern; vis W shore-305°, G305°-314°, W314°-shore. Rear 326m from front, QR 27m 9M; W Tr, R band and lantern.

MERRIEN

47°47'·1N 03°39'·0W QR 26m 7M; W square Tr, R top; vis 004°-009°.

BRIGNEAU

Mole head 47°46'·9N 03°40'·2W Oc(2) WRG 6s 7m W12M, R9M, G9M; W column, R top: vis G280°-329°, W329°-339°, R339°-034°.

PORT MANECH

Pointe de Beg-ar-Vechen 47°48'·0N 03°44'·4W Oc(4) WRG 12s 38m W10M, R7M, G7M; W & R Tr; vis W(unintens) 050°-140°, W140°-296°, G296°-303°, W303°-311°, R311°-328° over Les Verres, W328°-050°; obsc by Pointe de Beg-Morg when brg less than 299°.

TRÉVIGNON.

Breakwater 47°47'·6N 03°51'·3W Oc(31) WRG 12s 11m W14M, R11M, G11M; W square Tr, G top; vis W004°-051°, G051°-085°, W085°-092°, R092°-127°, R322°-351°.
Mole head Fl G 4s 5m 8M; W column, G top.
Baie de Pouldohan 47°51'·0N 03°53'·7W Fl G 4s 7m 8M; G square Tr, W band; vis 053°-065°.

CONCARNEAU.

Ldg Lts 028.5°. Front La Croix 47°52'·22N 03°55'·00W Oc(3) 12s 14m 13M; R and W Tr; vis 006°-093°. **Rear Beuzec**, 1·34M from front, Dir Q 87m **23M**; Belfry; intens 026°-030°.
Lanriec QG 13m 8M; G stripe on W gable; vis 063°-078°.
La Medée Fl R 2·5s 6m 4M; R Tr.
Passage de Lanriec 47°52'·3N 03°54'·8W Oc(2) WR 6s 4m W8M, R6M; R Tr; vis R209°-354°, W354°-007°, R007°-018°; Fl R 4s and Fl(2) R 6s shown on West side, Fl G 4s and Fl(2) G 6s on E side of passage.
Le Cochon 47°51'·53N 03°55'·47W Fl(3) WRG 12s 5m W9M, R6M, G6M; G Tr; vis G048°-205°, R205°-352°, W352°-048°.
Basse du Chenal QR 6m 5M; R Tr; vis 180°- 163°.

LA FORÊT.

Cap Coz, mole head 47°53'·55N 03°58'·20W Fl(2) R 6s 5m 6M.
Kerleven, mole head Fl G 4s 8m 6M. Inner mole head Iso G 4s 5m 5M.

ÎLES DE GLÉNAN.

Penfret 47°43'·32N 03°57'·10W Fl R 5s 36m **21M**; W square Tr, R top; auxiliary Lt Dir Q 34m 12M; same Tr; vis 295°-315°.
Fort Cigogne Q(2) RG 5s 2M; vis G106°-108°, R108°-262°, G262°-268°, obsc 268°-106°; shown in summer.
Île-aux-Moutons 47°46'·5N 04°01'·7W Oc(2) WRG 6s 18m **W15M**, R11M, G11M; W square Tr and dwelling; vis W035°-050°, G050°-063°, W063°-081°, R081°-141°, W141°-292°, R292°-035°; **auxiliary Lt** DirOc(2) 6s 17m **24M**; same Tr; synchronised with main Lt, intens 278°-283°.
Jaune de Glenan Lt Buoy 47°42'·6N 03°49'·8W Q(3) 10s; E cardinal mark; Whis.
Jument de Glenan Lt Buoy 47°38'·8N 04°01'·3W Q(6) LFl 15s 10m 8M; S cardinal; Whis; Ra refl.
Basse Perrenes Lt Buoy 47°41'·1N 04°06'·3W Q(9) 15s 8m 8M; W cardinal; Whis; Ra refl.

Rouge de Glenan Lt Buoy 47°45'·5N 04°03'·9W VQ(9) 10s 8m 8M; W cardinal; Whis; Ra refl.
Beg-Meil, quay head 47°51'·72N 03°58'·85W Fl R 2s 6m 2M; R and W column.

BENODET.

Ldg Lts 345.5°. Front **Pointe du Coq**, 336m from rear, Oc(2+1) G 12s 11m **17M**; W Tr, G stripe; intens 345°-347°.
Common rear Pyramide Oc(21) 12s 48m 11M; W Tr, G top; vis 338°-016°, synchronised with previous Lt.
Ldg Lts 000°.
Pointe de Combrit, 47°51'·92N 04°06'·70W, front 0·63M from rear, Oc(31) WR 12s 19m W12M, R9M; W Tr, grey corners; vis W325°-017°, R017°-325°; RC.
Pointe du Toulgoet Fl R 2s 2m 2M.
Pont de Cornouaille, NE side 2 FG 3M, West 2 FR 3M.

LOCTUDY.

Pointe de Langoz S side 47°49'·94N 04°09'·48W Fl(4) WRG 12s 12m **W15M**, R11M, G11M; W Tr, R top; vis W115°-257°, G257°-284°, W284°-295°, R295°-318°, W318°-328°, R328°-025°.
Les Perdrix 47°50'·3N 04°10'·0W Fl WRG 4s 15m W11M, R8M, G8M; vis G090°-285°, W285°-295°, R295°-090°.
Karek-Saoz 47°50'·08N 04°09'·30W QR 3m 1M; R truncated Tr.
Le Blas 47°50'·3N 04°10'·1W Fl(3)G 12s 26m 8M; G triangle on truncated column.

LESCONIL.

Men-ar-Groas 47°47'·8N 04°12'·6W Fl(3) WRG 12s 14m W13M, R9M, G9M; W Tr, G top; vis G268°-313°, W313°-333°, R333°-050°.
 E breakwater head 47°47'·77N 04°12'·56W QG 5m 9M; G Tr.
West breakwater Oc R 4s 5m 8M.

GUILVINEC.

Ldg Lts 053°. Mole de Léchiagat, spur, front 47°47'·5N 04°17'·0W Q 7m 8M; W pylon; vis 233°-066°.
Rocher Le Faoute's, middle, 210m from front Q WG 17m W14M, G11M; R circle on W pylon; vis W006°-293°, G293°-006°; synchronised with front. Rear, 0·58M from front, Dir Q 26m 8M; R circle on W pylon; vis 051·5°-054·5°; synchronised with front.
Lost Moan 47°47'·07N 04°16'·69W Fl(3) WRG 12s 8m W9M, R6M, G6M; W Tr, R top; vis R327°-014°, G014°-065°, R065°-140°, W140°-160°, R160°-268°, W268°-273°, G273°-317°, W317°-327°.
Môle de Lechiagat Fl G 4s 5m 7M; W hut, G top.
Môle Ouest Fl R 4s 11m 9M; W Tr, R top.
Pier Head Fl(2) R 6s 4m 5M; R structure.
Kérity. Men Hir 47°47'·3N 04°20'·6W Fl(2)G 6s 5m 1M.
Detached breakwater Fl(2)G 6s 5m 1M.
Locarec 47°47'·3N 04°20'·3W Iso WRG 4s 11m W9M, R6M, G6M; W pedestal on rock; vis G063°-068°, R068°-271°, W271°-285°, R285°-298°, G298°-340°, R340°-063°.

POINTE DE PENMARC'H.

Eckmühl 47°47'·95N 04°22'·35W Fl 5s 60m **24M**; grey 8-sided Tr; RC; Siren 60s.
Le Menhir 47°47'·8N 04°23'·9W Fl(2) WG 6s 19m W8M, G5M; W Tr, B band; vis G135°-315°, W315°-135°.
Scoedec 47°48'·5N 04°23'·1W Fl G 2·5s 6m 3M; G Tr.

SAINT GUÉNOLÉ.

Ldg Lts 026°. Front 47°49'·1N 04°22'·6W QR 8m 4M; R mast. Rear, 51m from front, QR 12m 4M; mast, R and W bands; synchronised with front.
Roches de Groumilli Ldg Lts 123°. Front FG 9m 9M; W Tr, B

bands. Rear, 300m from front, FG 13m 9M; W Tr, B bands. Ldg Lts 055°. Front 47°48'·7N 04°22'·7W VQ 5m 2M; G and W column. Rear, 320m from front F Vi 12m 1M; G and white column; vis 040°-070°.

Pors Poulhan, West side of entrance 47°59'·1N 04°28'·0W QR 14m 9M; W square Tr, R lantern.

AUDIERNE.
Gamelle Ouest Lt Buoy 47°59'·53N 04°32'·76W VQ(9) 10s; W cardinal mark; Whis.

Passe de l'Est Ldg Lts 331°. Front Jetée de Raoulic 48°00'·60N 04°32'·37W Oc(2+1) WG 12s 11m W14M, G9M; W Tr; vis W shore-034°, G034°-shore, but may show W037°-055°. Rear, 0·5M from front, FR 9M; W 8-sided Tr, R top; intens 321°-341°.

Kergadec Dir Lt 006° 48°01'·0N 04°32'·8W Dir Q WRG 43m W12M, R9M, G9M; same Tr as previous Lt; vis G000°-005°, W005°-007°, R007°-017°.

Jetée de Sainte-Evette Oc(2) R 6s 2m 7M; R lantern.

Pointe de Lervily 48°00'·1N 04°34'·0W Fl(2+1) WR 12s 20m W14M, R11M; W Tr, R top; vis W211°-269°, R269°-294°, W294°-087°, R087°-121°.

RAZ DE SEIN.
Le Chat 48°01'·44N 04°48'·80W Fl(2) WRG 6s 27m W9M, R6M, G6M; South cardinal mark; vis G096°-215°, W215°-230°, R230°-271°, G271°-286°, R286°-096°; Ra refl.

La Plate 48°02'·36N 04°45'·50W VQ(9) 10s 19m 8M; West cardinal mark.

La Vieille 48°02'·5N 04°45'·4W Oc(2+1) WRG 12s 33m **W17M**, R14M, G13M; grey square Tr; vis W290°-298°, R298°-325°, W325°-355°, G355°-017°, W017°-035°, G035°-105°, W105°-123°, R123°-158°, W158°-205°; R Lt on radio mast 3·4M ENE; Siren (2+1) 60s.

Tévennec 48°04'·3N 04°47'·6W Q WR 28m W9M, R6M; W square Tr and dwelling; vis W090°-345°, R345°-090°; Dir Lt Iso 4s 24m 12M; same Tr; intens 324°-332°.

CHAUSSEE DE SEIN.
Île de Sein 48°02'·70N 04°51'·95W Fl(4) 25s 49m **29M**; W Tr, B top; RC.

Ar Guéveur 48°02'·0N 04°51'·4W Dia 60s; W Tr. Men-Brial, 0·8M 115° from main Lt, Oc(2) WRG 6s 16m W12M, R9M, G7M; W Tr, G top; vis G149°-186°, W186°-192°, R192°-221°, W221°-227°, G227°-254°.

Ar-Men 48°03'·0N° 04°59'·9W Fl(3) 20s 29m **23M**; W Tr, B top. Siren (3) 60s.

CHAUSSÉE DE SEIN LANBY 48°03'·80N 05°07'·70W VQ(9) 10s 9m 8M; W cardinal mark; Whis; Racon; Ra refl.

Pointe du Millier 48°05'·9N 04°27'·9W Oc(2) WRG 6s 34m **W16M**, R12M, G11M; W house; vis G080°-087°, W087°-113°, R113°-120°, W120°-129°, G129°-148°, W148°-251°, R251°-258°; part obsc 255°-082°.

TRÉBOUL.
Épi de Biron, head 48°06'·1N 04°20'·4W QG 7m 6M; W column, G top.

Île Tristan 48°06'·2N 04°20'·3W Oc(3) WR 12s 35m W13M, R10M; grey Tr, W band, B top; vis W shore-138°, R138°-153°, W153°-shore; obsc by Pointe de Leidé when brg less than 111°.

DOUARNENEZ.
Bassin Nord, N mole head 48°06'·0N 04°19'·3W Iso G 4s 9m 4M; W & G framework Tr.

S mole head Oc(2) R 6s 6m 6M; W & R framework Tr.

Elbow, Môle de Rosmeur, head Oc G 4s 6m 6M; W framework Tr, G top; vis 170°-097°.

BASSE VIEILLE LANBY 48°08'·40N 04°35'·58W Fl(2) 6s 8m 8M; isolated danger mark; Whis; Ra refl.

Basse le Bouc Lt Buoy 48°11'·50N 04°37'·34W Q(9) 15s; W cardinal mark; Whis.

Pointe de Morgat 48°13'·2N 04°29'·9W Oc(4) WRG 12s 77m **W15M**, R11M, G10M; W square Tr, R top, W dwelling; vis W shore-281°, G281°-301°, W301°-021°, R021°-043°; obsc by Pointe du Rostudel when brg more than 027°. Morgat mole head 48°13'·5N 04°30'·0W Oc(2) WR 6s 8m W9M, R6M; W & R framework Tr; vis W015°-265°, R265°-015°.

BASSE DU LIS LANBY 48°13'·05N 04°44'·46W Q(6) LFl 15s 9m 8M; S cardinal mark; Whis.

La Parquette 48°15'·91N 04°44'·25W Fl RG 4s 17m R6M, G5M; W 8-sided Tr, B diagonal stripes; vis R244°-285°, G285°-244°.

Vandrée Lt Buoy 48°15'·06N 04°48'·23W VQ(9) 10s; Whis; W cardinal mark.

Roc du Charles Martel Lt Buoy 48°18'·82N 04°42'·20W QR; Whis port-hand mark.

Swansea Vale Lt Buoy 48°18'·58N 04°39'·52W Fl(2) 6s; Whis; isolated danger mark.

Pointe du Toulinguet 48°16'·87N 04°37'·64W Oc(3) WR 12s 49m **W15M**, R11M; W square Tr on building; vis W shore-028°, R028°-090°, W090°-shore.

CAMARET.
Môle Nord, head 48°16'·92N 04°35'·20W Iso WG 4s 7m W12M, G8M; W framework Tr, G top; vis W135°-182°, G182°-027°; obsc by Pointe des Capucins when brg more than 187°.

Môle Sud, head Fl(2) R 6s 9m 5M; R framework Tr; obsc by Pointe du Grande Gouin when brg less than 143°, and by Pointe des Capucins when brg more than 185°.

15

10.15.5   PASSAGE INFORMATION

BAY OF BISCAY — NORTH PART (chart 20)

In crossing the B of Biscay, allowance should be made for possible set to E. Onshore winds carry cloud which may cause mist or fog rising over land, sometimes obscuring high Lts. Swell usually comes from W or NW. In summer the sea is usually calm or slight. Wind may be changeable in speed and direction, predominantly from SW to NW in summer. Offshore the tidal stream is weak, but gets stronger in N part of B of Biscay towards English Channel, and may run strongly near the coast, off headlands. French charts are often on larger scale than Admiralty charts, and hence are more suitable for inshore waters. Yachts are recommended to carry the *Bay of Biscay Pilot* and *North Biscay Pilot* (Adlard Coles Ltd). Malcolm Robson's *French Pilot Volume Four* (Nautical Books) covers the Biscay coast from the Gironde to the Morbihan, while his *French Pilot Volume Three* continues from Belle Ile to the Raz de Sein. For French terms see 10.16.5.

Many of the more attractive French harbours dry completely, so it is best to have a boat which can take the ground. For this purpose bilge keels are ideal — or otherwise a boat with a long, straight keel, and fitted with legs.

La Loire (chart 2985) carries much commercial traffic. The estuary is divided by two shoals, Plateau de la Banche and Plateau de La Lambarde, which lie about 10M and 6M WNW of Pte de St Gildas. Chenal du Nord runs between these two shoals on S side and the coast on N side. Chenal du Sud, the main chan, leads between Plateau de La Lambarde and Pte de St Gildas. In the approaches to St Nazaire (10.15.9) beware Le Vert, Les Jardinets and La Truie (all dry) which lie SW of Le Pointeau. In Grande Rade the in-going stream begins at HW Brest −0500, and the out-going at HW Brest +0050, sp rates about 2¾ kn.

From Chenal du Nord, B de Pouliguen (10.15.10) is entered between Pte de Penchâteau and Pte du Bec, 3M to E. In SE corner of b is the yacht harb of Pornichet (10.15.27). The B is part sheltered from S by rks and shoals extending SE from Pte de Penchâteau, but a heavy sea develops in strong S-SW winds. The chan through these rks runs between Basse Martineau and Les Guérandaises.

Between Pte de Penchâteau and Pte du Croisic, Basse Lovre is a rky shoal with depths of 0.9m, ½M offshore. Off Pte du Croisic dangers extend 1M to W and to N. Plateau du Four, a dangerous drying bank of rks, lies about 4M W and WSW of Pte du Croisic, marked by buoys and Lt Ho near N end. Off Pte du Castelli, Les Bayonelles (dry) extend ½M W, and Plateau de Piriac extends about 1¾M NW with depths of 3m and drying rks closer inshore. There is chan between Plateau de Piriac and Île Dumet (Lt), which is fringed by drying rks and shoals particularly on N and E sides.

In the approaches to La Vilaine (10.15.12) beware Basse du Bile, a rky shoal depth 0.6m, 1M W of Île du Bile; Basse de Loscolo, depth 0.6m, about 1M to N; and La Grande Accroche, an extensive shoal with depths of less than 1.8m, astride the entrance. The main chan is lit and runs NW of La Grande Accroche, to the bar on N side thereof. Here the flood stream begins at HW Brest −0515, and the ebb at HW Brest +0035, sp rates 2½ kn. In SW winds against the stream the sea breaks heavily in this area, and then the chan ½M off Pte du Halguen is better, but beware La Varlingue (dries).

S of Penerf (10.15.27), which provides good anch, Plateau des Mats is an extensive rky bank, drying in places, up to 1¾M offshore. Dangers extend 1M seaward of Pte de St Jacques, and 3M offshore lies Plateau de la Recherche with depths of 1.8m.

BAIE DE QUIBERON (chart 2353)

The S side of B is enclosed by a long chain of islands, islets, rks and shoals from Presqu'île de Quiberon to Les Grands Cardinaux 13M SE. This chain includes the attractive islands of Houat (10.15.27) and Höedik, well worth visiting, preferably mid-week, and through it the main chan is Passage de la Teignouse which is well marked. In this chan the NE-going (flood) stream begins at HW Brest −0610, and the SW-going at HW Brest −0005, sp rates 3¾ kn: in strong winds it is best to pass at slack water. A good alternative chan is Passage du Béniguet, NW of Houat.

B de Quiberon is an important and attractive yachting area, with major centres at Crouesty (10.15.13), the Morbihan (10.15.15), La Trinite (10.15.16), Port Haliguen (10.15.17) and Port Maria (10.15.27).

BELLE ILE (chart 2353)

Apart from rks which extend ¾M W of Pte des Poulains, and La Truie (dries) marked by Bn Tr ½M off the S coast, there are no dangers more than ¼M offshore. The S coast is much indented and exposed to swell from W: in good settled weather (only) and in absence of swell there is an attractive anch in Port du Vieux Chateau, 1M S of Pte des Poulains — see *North Biscay Pilot*. On the NE coast lie Le Palais (10.15.18) and Sauzon (10.15.27), which dries but has good anch off and is sheltered from S and W. Off Le Palais the ESE-going (flood) stream begins at HW Brest −0610, and the WNW- going at HW Brest +0125, sp rates 1½ kn. 6M NNW of Pte des Poulains lies Plateau des Birvideaux (Lt), a rky bank (depth 2m) on which the sea breaks in bad weather. Between here and Lorient, Etel River (chart 2352) is an attractive harb, but must only be approached in good weather and on the last of the flood. The chan over the bar is shallow and shifts; local semaphore signals indicate the best water, or when entry is impossible. See 10.15.27.

ILE DE GROIX (chart 2352)

Île de Groix lies in SW approach to Lorient (10.15.19). The main offlying dangers are shoals off Pte de la Croix, Les Chats which extend 1M SE from Pte des Chats, and shoals extending ¾M seaward off Port Loc Maria.

Port Tudy, on N coast, is the main harb, and is easy of access and well sheltered except from NE see 10.15.27. The inner harb has a sill and pontoon berths — entry HW∓2. Port Loc Maria is ¾M W of Pte des Chats. The unspoiled little harb is open to the S, but provides an attractive anch in offshore winds, and particularly near nps.

LORIENT TO BENODET (chart 2352)

Between Pte du Talat and Pte de Trévignon sandy beaches give way to rky cliffs. Grand Cochon and Petit Cochon lie about 1M offshore 2M NW of Pte de Keroch. There are many shoals in approaches to Rivière de Bélon and L'Aven. To the W, Ile Verte lies 6 ca S of Ile de Raguénès, with foul ground another 2 ca to S; Men an Tréas, a rk which dries, is 1M WSW of Ile Verte and marked by buoy; Corn Vas, depth 1.8m, is 1¾M SE of Pte de Trévignon, marked by a buoy; Men Du, a rk 0.3m high, lies about 1¼M SE of the same pt, and is marked by a Bn. From Pte de Trévignon to Pte de Cabellou (1M S of Concarneau, 10.15.20) rks extend nearly 1½M offshore in places. Chaussée de Beg Meil extends 8½ ca SE, where Linuen rk (dries) is marked by Bn. The coast W from Beg Meil is fringed by rks, many of which dry, extending 1M offshore, and 1¾M S of Pte de Mousterlin.

Along this coast are several nice harbs and anchs, but most are dangerous to approach in strong onshore winds. They include Le Pouldu (Rivière de Quimperlé); Doëlan (but most of harb dries); Merrien (also mostly dries); Brigneau; and Rivières de Bélon and L'Aven. All are described in *North Biscay Pilot*. For Doëlan and Pont-Aven see 10.15.27.

ILES DE GLÉNAN (chart 3640, French chart 6648)

Îles de Glénan lie off entrance to Benodet (10.15.22). The main island is Penfret (Lt), well known for its Centre Nautique, at NE corner of the group which, with its offlying dangers, stretches 5M from E to W and 4M from N to S. There are buoys on SE, S and SW sides. The islands are interesting to explore, but anchs are rather exposed. Easiest approach is from N, to W side of Penfret; anch there or proceed W to La Chambre, S of Île de St Nicolas. 3½M E of Penfret lies Basse Jaune, a shallow bank part of which dries, marked by buoy. Between Îles de Glénan and Benodet lie Les Pourceaux, reefs which dry, and Île aux Moutons which has dangers extending SW and NW.

BENODET TO RAZ DE SEIN (chart 2351)

Between Benodet and Raz de Sein lies Pte de Penmarc'h (Lt, fog sig, RC) off which dangers extend 3M to SE, and 1M to S, W and NW, and breaking seas occur in strong winds. The harbs of Loctudy, Lesconil and Le Guilvinec all provide sheltered anchs. See 10.15.27.

Chausée de Sein (chart 2351) is a chain of islands, rks and shoals extending 12M W from a position 3M WSW of Pte du Raz. The outer end is marked by a Lt buoy, and near inner end is Île de Sein (Lt, RC). 5M W of Île de Sein is Ar-Men Tr (Lt, fog sig), ½M E of which is a narrow N/S chan. Île de Sein is interesting to visit in fair weather and good vis, preferably near nps. Best approach is through Chenal d'Ezaudi, with Men-Brial Lt Ho, Oc(2) WRG 6s, on with third house (W with B stripe) from left, close S of Lt Ho, at 187°. Drying rocks lie each side, and tide sets across the chan. Anchor off or inside mole, but exposed to N and E. Harb partly dries. For directions on Île de Sein and Raz de Sein see *North Biscay Pilot* (Adlard Coles Ltd).

RAZ DE SEIN (chart 798)

Raz de Sein is the chan between Le Chat Bn Tr at E end of Chaussée de Sein and the dangers extending 8 ca off Pte du Raz, the extremity of which is marked by La Plate Lt Tr. 2M N of Raz de Sein is the Plateau de Tévennec, consisting of islets, rks and shoals which extend ½M in all directions from the Lt Ho thereon. Other dangers on the N side of the Raz are rks and shoals extending nearly 1M W and 8 ca WSW from Pointe du Van, and Basse Jaune (dries) 1M to N. On the S side the main dangers are: Cornoc Bras, a rk with depth of 3m, 1½M SW of La Vieille Lt Tr; Masclougreiz, rky shoals on which sea can break heavily, 1½M S of La Vieille; and Roche Moullec 1½M SE of La Vieille.

In the middle of Raz de Sein the NE-going (flood) stream begins at HW Brest +0550, sp rate 6½ kn; the SW-going (ebb) stream begins at HW Brest −0030, sp rate 5½ kn. There are eddies near La Vieille on both streams. In good weather, near neaps, and with wind and tide together, the Raz presents no difficulty, but in moderately strong winds it should be taken at slack water, which lasts for about ½ hour at end of flood stream. In strong winds the chan must not be used with wind against tide, when there are overfalls with a steep breaking sea.

L'IROISE

Entering B de Douarnenez (chart 798) from Raz de Sein beware Basse Jaune, an isolated rk (dries) about 1M N of Pte du Van. 4½M to E lies Duello Rk (4m high) ½M offshore, with other rks extending 1M to E. Otherwise the S shore of the b is clear of dangers more than 2 ca offshore. Approaching Douarnenez (10.15.24) beware Basse Veur and Basse Neuve. On N side of b beware group of drying rks including La Pierre-Profonde and Le Taureau close SSW of Les Verrès (rk 9m high) which lies nearly 2½M ESE of Morgat (10.15.25).

Off C de la Chèvre various dangers, on which the sea can break, extend SW for 2¼M to Basse Vieille (dries) which is marked by Lanby. 2½M NW of C de la Chèvre is Le Chevreau (dries), with La Chèvre ½M to NE of it (1¼M WSW of Pte de Dinan). 7M W of Pte de Dinan lies Basse du Lis, rky shoals with depth of 1.8m, marked by Lanby.

On the NE side of L'Iroise (chart 2643) a chain of rks extends 7M W from Pte du Toulinguet. There are several chans through these rks, of which the most convenient for Camaret (10.15.26) and for Brest (10.16.9) is the inshore one − Chenal du Toulinguet, which runs between La Louve Bn Tr (1 ca W of Pte du Toulinguet) on E side and a rk called Le Pohen on the W side. Keep in the middle of the chan, which is about 3 ca wide. Here the N-going stream begins at HW Brest −0550, and the S-going at HW Brest +0015, sp rates 2¾ kn.

10.15.6   DISTANCE TABLE

Approximate distances in nautical miles are by the most direct route while avoiding dangers and allowing for traffic separation schemes etc. Places in *italics* are in adjoining areas.

	1	2	3	4	5	6	7	8	9	10	11	12	13	14	15	16	17	18	19	20
1 *Le Four*	1																			
2 *Brest*	25	2																		
3 Camaret	21	8	3																	
4 Morgat	32	23	16	4																
5 Douarnenez	42	27	21	11	5															
6 Pointe du Raz	30	24	18	17	20	6														
7 Audierne	40	34	28	27	30	10	7													
8 Pte de Penmarc'h	52	46	40	39	42	22	15	8												
9 Benodet	70	64	58	57	60	40	33	18	9											
10 Concarneau	74	68	62	61	64	44	37	22	11	10										
11 Lorient	98	92	86	85	88	68	61	46	36	32	11									
12 Port Haliguen	117	111	105	104	107	87	80	65	57	53	32	12								
13 Le Palais	111	105	99	98	101	81	74	59	52	47	26	11	13							
14 La Trinité	122	116	110	109	112	92	85	70	62	58	37	8	16	14						
15 Crouesty	122	116	110	109	112	92	85	70	62	58	37	9	16	8	15					
16 Roche Bernard	146	140	134	133	136	116	109	94	86	82	61	35	40	35	30	16				
17 Le Croisic	136	130	124	123	126	106	99	84	76	72	51	27	27	28	23	25	17			
18 St Nazaire	150	144	138	137	140	120	113	98	91	87	66	42	41	45	40	43	20	18		
19 *Ile d'Yeu*	156	150	144	143	146	126	119	104	98	95	76	56	50	60	56	61	38	34	19	
20 La Rochelle	216	210	204	203	206	186	179	164	158	155	136	116	110	120	116	121	98	94	60	20

15

CANAL CONNECTIONS IN BRITTANY 10.15.8

Canals across Brittany enable boats of limited size to go from the Channel to the Bay of Biscay avoiding the passage around Finistere.

SUMMARY

Channel — Biscay (Ille et Rance Canal and Vilaine)

Section	No of locks	Length nm	km	Speed limit kn
St. Malo—Dinan	2	20.5	38	7.5
Dinan—Tinteniac	14	17.3	32	4.3
Tinteniac—Rennes	33	25.4	47	4.3
Rennes—Redon	12	48	89	4.3
Redon— La Roche-Bernard	0	21.1	39	—

Nantes — Lorient Link (Nantes — Brest Canal and Blavet)

Nantes—Redon	16	51.3	95	4.5
Redon—Josselin	17	34	63	4.3
Josselin—Pontivy	72	25.9	48	4.3
Pontivy—Lorient	28	39.2	72	4.3

L'Aulne

Chateaulin— Port de Carhaix	34	41	76	4.3

Max length	25 m
Max draught	1.1 m (Ille et Rance Canal)
	0.8 m (Josselin—Pontivy)
Max beam	4.6m
Max height	2.4m

Contact: Channel—Biscay   — Rennes 99.59.20.60
                            Redon 99.71.10.66

Nantes—Lorient (Brest) —   Nantes 40.71.70.70
                            Hennebont 97.65.20.82
                            Lorient 97.21.21.54

Locks — shut in winter each Wednesday (approx first week in November to last week in March) for repairs. July and August, in order to conserve water, open on the hour only (and at half hour if traffic demands).

Channel—Biscay Assembly   —Northbound—
                            Lengager Lock.
                            Southbound—
                            Madeleine Lock.

For information and guide books write (with addressed envelope) to
Comité des Canaux Bretons,
Service de Documentation du Comité,
12 rue de Jemmapes,
44000 Nantes (Tel. 40.47.42.94)

RIVER LOIRE/ST NAZAIRE
Loire Atlantique

10-15-9

CHARTS
Admiralty 2985, 3216, 2989; SHOM 6854, 6493, 6797, 6260, 6261, 5992; ECM 248, 547
TIDES
St Nazaire-Dover: Springs +0445, Neaps −0540; ML 3.0; Duration: Springs 0640; Neaps 0445; Zone −0100

RIVER LOIRE/ST. NAZAIRE *continued*

Between Paimboeuf and Nantes, channel marked by Ldg Lts, and by R lights on N side of river, and G on S side

Standard Port BREST (→)

Times				Height (metres)			
HW		LW		MHWS	MHWN	MLWN	MLWS
0000	0600	0000	0600	7.5	5.9	3.0	1.4
1200	1800	1200	1800				

Differences ST NAZAIRE

+0030 −0025 −0005 −0010 −2.0 −1.7 −1.1 −0.8

NANTES (Chantenay)

+0155 +0140 +0330 +0245 −1.7 −1.3 −1.1 +0.2

SHELTER

In strong winds from West the bar is only safe HW−3 to HW. St Nazaire is principally commercial although yachts can stop temporarily. Yachts enter the Dassin de St Nazaire through E lock and berth at S end of Bassin Penhoët. Port Control and Hr Mr NW side of Avant Port. Anchorages in Bonne Anse and Villez Martin.

NAVIGATION

Waypoint Chenal du Sud 47°07'.95N 02°20'.00W, 205°/025° from/to front Ldg Lt 025°, 7.3M. Entrance to Loire divided by La Danche bank with well marked channels N and S. River is shallow beyond Nantes but is navigable in optimum conditions for small craft West of Angers. At Nantes the Brittany canal system can be entered through canal Saint-Felix by Malakoff Lock (see 10.15.8); also there are places reserved for visiting yachts at Trentemoult near the Bureau du Port, accessible at all times.

LIGHTS AND MARKS

Ldg Lts over bar, 025°; both Q 27M, intens 022°-028°.

RADIO TELEPHONE

St Nazaire Port VHF Ch 12 16 (H24). Other stations: Donges VHF Ch 12 16 (H24). Pte de Chémoulin Sig Stn Ch 16.
Nantes VHF Ch 12 16 (H24); water level reports bcst on Ch 73 every 15 min commencing H+00.

TELEPHONE

ST NAZAIRE Hr Mr 40.22.08.46; Aff Mar 40.22.46.32; CROSS 97.55.35.35; SNSM 40.61.03.20; ✠ 40.66.82.65; Meteo 40.90.00.80; Auto 40.90.19.19; Police 40.70.55.00; Dr 40.22.15.32; Ⓗ 40.90.60.60.
NANTES Hr Mr 40.44.20.54; Aff Mar 40.73.18.70; ✠ 40.73.39.55; Meteo 40.84.80.19; Auto 40.04.15.15; Dr 40.47.03.19; Ⓗ 40.48.33.33; Brit Consul 40.63.16.02.

FACILITIES

ST NAZAIRE **La Société Nautique de St Nazaire** ☎ 40.70.10.47, M; **Genet-Loisirs** ☎ 40.22.44.52, M, ME, El, Sh, CH; **Quai** P, D, L, FW, C; **Perraud** ☎ 40.22.51.39, ME, El; **Burodess** ☎ 40.22.11.12; SHOM; **CRM** ☎ 40.66.25.99, Ⓔ; **Emtec** ☎ 40.66.42.10, Ⓔ. **Town** V, Gaz, R, Bar. ✉; Ⓑ; ⇌; Air.
NANTES **Quai** FW, C; **Librairie Beaumont** ☎ 40.48.24.21, CH, SHOM; **Ancre Marine** ☎ 40.73.86.22, ME, CH, SHOM, El, Ⓔ. **Town** all facilities; ✉; Ⓑ; ⇌; ✈.
Ferry UK — St Malo—Portsmouth; Roscoff—Plymouth.

LE POULIGUEN   10-15-10
(PORT OF LA BAULE)
Loire Atlantique

CHARTS

Admiralty 3216; SHOM 6825, 4902; ECM 547

TIDES

Dover: Springs +0435 Neaps +0530; ML 2.9; Duration: Springs 0530 Neaps 0645; Zone −0100

Standard Port BREST (→)

Times				Height (metres)			
HW		LW		MHWS	MHWN	MLWN	MLWS
0000	0600	0000	0600	7.5	5.9	3.0	1.4
1200	1800	1200	1800				

Differences LE POULIGUEN

+0015 −0040 0000 −0020 −2.1 −1.8 −1.2 −0.8

SHELTER

Very good shelter, protected from all winds except SE. Approach from West between Pte de Penchateau and the Grand Charpentier. Best approach HW−1. Visitors berths (30) on Quai Rageot de la Touche.

NAVIGATION

Waypoint 47°15'.00N 02°25'.00W, 232°/052° from/to Basse Martineau buoy, 0.58M. Beware rocks extending 4 M to the Grand Charpentier Lt Ho and breakers in shallow water when wind in S. It is not advisable to enter at night. Beware strong ebb tide.

LIGHTS AND MARKS

From Basse Martineau leave La Vieille and Les Impairs as on chartlet to stbd, and two Bns off Penchateau to port. S Jetty QR 13m 9M; vis 171°-081°.

RADIO TELEPHONE

Pouliguen VHF Ch 09. Pornichet Ch 09.

TELEPHONE (40)

Hr Mr 40.60.37.40; Aff Mar 40.42.32.55; CROSS 97.55.35.35; SNSM 40.61.03.20; ✠ 40.61.32.04; Meteo 40.90.00.80; Auto 40.90.19.19; Police 40.24.48.17; Dr Le Pouliguen 40.60.51.73; Dr La Baule 40.60.17.20; Brit Consul 40.63.16.02.

FACILITIES

Quai (Pontoons 620) ☎ 40.60.03.50, Slip, P, D, AC, L, FW, C (18 ton); **Callaghan Naval** ☎ 40.60.78.43, M, ME, Sh, CH; **Petit Breton Nautique** ☎ 40.42.10.14, M, ME, Ⓔ, El, Sh, CH; **Prat** ☎ 40.60.31.30, Sh, Divers; **SOS Atlantique** ☎ 40.42.33.29, ME, El, CH; **Voilerie X Voiles** ☎ 40.60.47.52, SM; **Le Baule YC** ☎ 40.60.20.90 (allocates berths for visitors); **Town** V, Gaz, R, Bar. ✉ (Le Pouliguen and La Baule); Ⓑ (Le Pouliguen and La Baule); ⇌ (La Baule); ✈ (St Nazaire, La Baule). Ferry UK — St Malo—Portsmouth; Roscoff—Plymouth.

15

LE POULIGUEN *continued*

LE CROISIC 10-15-11
Loire Atlantique

CHARTS
Admiralty 2353; SHOM 6826, 5482; ECM 546, 547
TIDES
+0450 Dover; ML 3.0; Duration 0605; Zone −0100
Standard Port BREST (→)

Times				Height (metres)			
HW		LW		MHWS	MHWN	MLWN	MLWS
0000	0600	0000	0600	7.5	5.9	3.0	1.4
1200	1800	1200	1800				

Differences LE CROISIC
+0030 −0030 −0015 −0010 −2.3 −1.8 −1.1 −0.8
ILE DE HÖEDIC
−0005 −0025 −0030 −0020 −2.3 −1.9 −1.1 −0.8

SHELTER
Safest anchorage is up Pen Bron creek. Alongside berths, called *Chambres* formed by islands called *Jonchères*, dry out. Access HW ∓ 1. Yachts use the fifth *Chambre*. A mooring may be available in Le Poul.
NAVIGATION
Waypoint 47°19′.00N 02°31′.80W, 336°/156° from/to front Ldg Lt 156°, 1.2M. At springs, tides run up to 4 kn. Safest entry then is HW−1. Beware the rocks at Hergo tower. Beware that the Tréhic Lt, which leads clear of distant dangers, will lead onto close dangers.
LIGHTS AND MARKS
Ldg Lts 156°. Front Dir Oc(2+1) 12s 10m 11M; Y topmark on W pylon. Rear Dir Oc(2+1) 12s 14m 18M; Y topmark on W pylon, G top; both intens 154°-158°, synchronized. Ldg Lts 174° both QG 5/8m 11M; G & W structures; vis 170°-177°. Ldg Lts 134° both QR. The sanatorium and hospital are conspic.
RADIO TELEPHONE
VHF Ch 16.
TELEPHONE (40)
Hr Mr 40.23.05.38; Port de Plaisance 40.23.10.95; Aff Mar 40.23.06.56; CROSS 97.55.35.35; SNSM 40.23.01.17; ⌗ 40.23.05.38; Meteo 40.90.08.80; Police 40.23.00.19; Dr 40.23.01.70; Ⓗ 40.23.01.12; Brit Consul 40.63.16.02.

FACILITIES
Marina (220 + 15 visitors), P, D, F.W, C, ME, El, Sh; **Quai** Slip, M, FW, ME, El, Sh, C (10 ton), CH, V, R, Bar; **Bollore** ☎ 40.23.00.85, ME; **Le Croisic Marine** ☎ 40.23.26.39, ME, El, Sh, Ⓔ, CH; **Lemerie** ☎ 40.42.92.12, M, ME, El, Ⓔ, Sh, CH; **Meca Navale** ☎ 40.23.04.10, ME, El, Sh. **Town** V, Gaz, R, Bar. ✉; Ⓑ; ⇌; ✈ (St Nazaire, La Baule). Ferry UK — St Malo—Portsmouth; Roscoff—Plymouth.

LA ROCHE BERNARD 10-15-12
Morbihan

CHARTS
Admiralty 2353; SHOM 5418, 2381; ECM 546
TIDES
+0500 Dover; ML (Pénerf) 3.1; Duration 0610; Zone −0100
Standard Port BREST (→)

Times				Height (metres)			
HW		LW		MHWS	MHWN	MLWN	MLWS
0000	0600	0000	0600	7.5	5.9	3.0	1.4
1200	1800	1200	1800				

Differences PÉNERF
−0010 −0020 −0025 −0020 −2.0 −1.7 −1.0 −0.7

SHELTER
Good shelter, on S bank of La Vilaine, about 7M E of Tréhiguier. There are two marinas — Nouveau Port close to bridge (clearance 30m) and Vieux Port (or Quai de Sainte-Antoine) ¼ M downstream. Anchor at Tréhiguier or at Vieille Roche while waiting for lock at Arzal (see 10.15.27).

LA ROCHE BERNARD *continued*

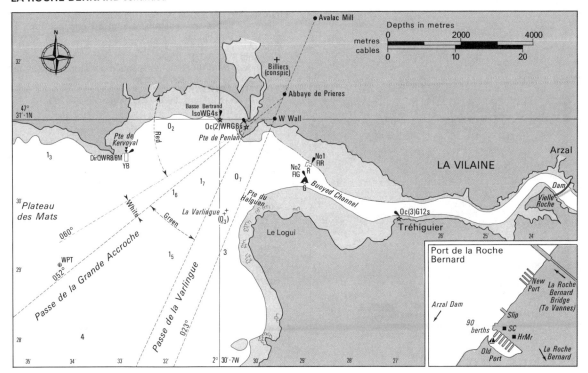

NAVIGATION

La Vilaine waypoint Passe de la Grande Accroche
47°29'.00N 02°34'.28W, 234°/054° from/to Penlan Lt,
3.5M. Approach to La Vilaine has a bar (min 0.5m except
for La Varlingue rocks which dry 0.3m off Pte du Halguen
— beware this when sailing channel 1 below). Sea breaks
on the bar in strong on-shore winds especially with low or
ebb tides. Follow the line of cockle beds for deep water.
The dam, Le Barrage d'Arzal, down river, has a lock
which opens on the hour 0700 to 2200 (LT) in July and
August; in other months 0730, 0900, 1030, 1200, 1400,
1600, 1730, 1900, 2000 LT. Yachts should keep strictly to
the channel above and below the dam. Yachts with masts
can reach Redon where there is a marina and access to
Brittany canal system (see 10.15.8). There is a swing
bridge at Pont Cran, before reaching Redon.

LIGHTS AND MARKS

There are two approaches to river entrance:
(1) Passe de la Varlingue (W wall, Abbey de Prieres and
Avalac Mill in line at 023°), unlit.
(2) Passe de la Grande Accroche (Lt Ho and Abbey de
Prieres in line at 052°).
Two principal lights
(1) Basse Bertrand G Tr, Iso WG 4s 6m 9/6M
W040°-054°, G054°-227°, W227°-234°, G234°-040°.
(2) Penlan W Tr with R bands Oc (2) WRG 6s 26m
16/11M, R292°-025°, G025°-052°, W052°-060°,
R060°-138°, G138°-180°.
Channel from Pte du Halguen to Tréhiguier marked by R
and G numbered buoys.

RADIO TELEPHONE

None.

TELEPHONE (99)

Hr Mr 99.90.62.17; Aff Mar 97.41.12.43; CROSS
97.55.35.35; ☰ (Vannes) 97.63.18.71; Meteo 40.75.80.07;
Police 99.90.61.06; Dr 99.90.61.25; Ⓗ 99.90.61.20;
Brit Consul 40.63.16.02.

FACILITIES

Marina (New Port) (70), ☎ 99.90.65.91, FW, AC, C, CH;
Marina (Old Port) (200), ☎ 99.90.66.77, P, D, ▣
FW, Slip; **Chantier Naval de la Couronne**
☎ 99.90.66.77, M, ME, El, Ⓔ, Sh, CH. **Arvor Marine**
☎ 99.90.64.98, ME, El, Ⓔ, Sh, CH; **Town** V, Gaz, R,
Bar. ✉; Ⓑ; ⇌ (Pontchateau); ✈ (Nantes or Rennes).
Ferry UK — St Malo—Portsmouth; Roscoff—Plymouth.

CROUESTY-EN-ARZON
Morbihan   **10-15-13**

CHARTS

Admiralty 2359, 2358; SHOM 5420, 3165, 5554; ECM 546

TIDES

+0505 Dover; ML 3.0; Duration 0555; Zone −0100
Standard Port BREST (→)

Times				Height (metres)			
HW		LW		MHWS	MHWN	MLWN	MLWS
0000	0600	0000	0600	7.5	5.9	3.0	1.4
1200	1800	1200	1800				

Differences PORT NAVALO
| +0025 | −0005 | −0010 | −0005 | −2.5 | −2.0 | −1.1 | −0.7 |

SHELTER

Good shelter, protected from all winds by Quiberon
peninsular. A very large marina gives added protection.

NAVIGATION

Waypoint 47°32'.12N 02°55'.00W, 238°/058° from/to
front Ldg Lt, 0.85M. There are no navigational dangers,
the entrance being well marked.

LIGHTS AND MARKS

Ldg Lts 058°, Front Q 10m 19M on metal tower, Rear Q
27m 19M on W column: both intens 056°-060°. Marina
breakwater heads: N Oc (2) R 6s, S Fl G 4s.

RADIO TELEPHONE

VHF Ch 09.

TELEPHONE (97)

Hr Mr 97.53.73.33; Aff Mar 97.41.84.10; CROSS
97.55.35.35; Meteo 97.64.34.86; Auto 97.84.82.83; SNSM
97.41.27.40; ☰ 97.53.25.66; Police 97.53.71.65;
Dr 97.51.60.05; Dr (Arzon) 97.26.23.23; Brit Consul
40.63.16.02.

FACILITIES

Marina (1000+120 visitors) ☎ 97.53.73.33, BH (45 ton),
P, D, L, FW, ME, El, Sh, Slip, CH, AB, Bar, C (3 ton);
Amor Nautic ☎ 97.53.78.42, M, ME, El, Sh, CH;
Ateliers Maritimes du Crouesty ☎ 97.53.71.30, M, ME,
El, Ⓔ, Sh, CH; **Chantier Naval du Redo** ☎ 97.53.78.70,
ME, El, Ⓔ, Sh, CH; **Technique Voile** ☎ 97.53.78.58,
SM; **Town** V, Gaz, R, Bar. ✉ (Arzon); Ⓑ (Arzon);
⇌ (Vannes); ✈ (Lorient—Nantes)
Ferry UK — St Malo—Portsmouth; Roscoff—Plymouth.

15

CROUESTY-EN-ARZON continued

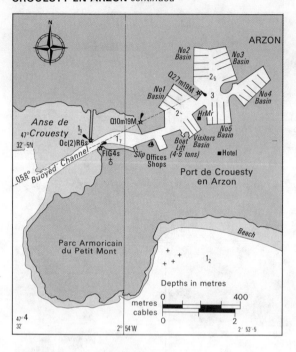

LIGHTS AND MARKS
There are buoys and perches marking the channel from Pointe de Bararac up to Vannes.
G Lt over R Lt = Port closed
No lights   = Port open
Lts shown from the lock, but boats must stop and wait at the S end of the approach canal.

RADIO TELEPHONE
VHF Ch 09. (Summer 0800-2100; winter 0900-1200, 1330-1800 LT)

TELEPHONE (97)
Hr Mr 97.54.16.08; Aff Mar 97.63.40.95; CROSS 97.55.35.35; SNSM 97.26.00.56; ⚑ 97.63.18.71; Meteo 97.42.48.82; Auto 97.42.49.49; Police 97.54.22.56; Dr 97.47.47.25; Ⓗ 97.42.66.42; Brit Consul 40.63.16.02.

FACILITIES
Marina (190 + 80 visitors), ☎ 97.54.16.08, Slip, Ⓞ, FW, AC, ME, Sh, C (12 ton), V, R, P and D (1400−1700); **La Corderie** ☎ 97.47.15.52, CH; **Vannes Nautique** ☎ 97.63.20.17, ME, Sh, El, Ⓔ, CH; **Voilerie Daniel** ☎ 97.47.14.41, Gas, CH, SM, SHOM; **Voilerie Le Pors** ☎ 97.42.54.01, CH, SM, Gaz, Ⓔ; **Marin Tronics** ☎ 97.42.58.75, Ⓔ; **Quai visiteurs** Slip, FW; **Le Pennec** ☎ 97.47.32.09, P, D, ME, El, Sh (on E side of approach canal).
Town all facilities. ✉; Ⓑ; ⇌; ✈ (Lorient).
Ferry UK — St Malo—Portsmouth; Roscoff—Plymouth.

VANNES   10-15-14
Morbihan

CHARTS
Admiralty 2358; SHOM 5420, 3165; ECM 546

TIDES
−0515 Dover; ML 2.7; Duration −; Zone −0100
Standard Port BREST (⟶)

Times				Height (metres)			
HW		LW		MHWS	MHWN	MLWN	MLWS
0000	0600	0000	0600	7.5	5.9	3.0	1.4
1200	1800	1200	1800				

Differences VANNES
+0145 +0155 +0200 +0105 −4.1 −3.2 −2.0 −1.0

SHELTER
Very good shelter, protected from all winds. Access to the port by day only. Marina boat will meet and indicate pontoon. Lock into wet basin opens HW∓2½ (0800-2000 (LT) in season; 0830-1900 (LT) other periods). Lock sill 1.3m above CD.

NAVIGATION
Waypoint − see 10.15.15. Beware very strong streams off the Réchauds, after passing between the Ile aux Moines and the mainland — Réchauds rocks marked by two beacons to stbd. Thereafter passage to Conleau is straightforward and well marked. Passage on to Vannes only advisable near HW.

MORBIHAN   10-15-15
Morbihan

CHARTS
Admiralty 2358; SHOM 3165, 5554, 5420; ECM 546.

TIDES
−0515 Dover; ML 3.1; Zone −0100
Standard Port BREST (⟶)

Times				Height (metres)			
HW		LW		MHWS	MHWN	MLWN	MLWS
0000	0600	0000	0600	7.5	5.9	3.0	1.4
1200	1800	1200	1800				

Differences AURAY
+0025 −0005 +0025 −0005 −2.6 −2.0 −1.1 −0.6
PORT NAVALO
+0025 −0005 −0010 −0005 −2.5 −2.0 −1.1 −0.7

SHELTER
Golfe du Morbihan is an inland sea with deep approaches and entrance. It is about 50 sq miles and thick with islands, most of which are privately owned. There are numerous anchorages, some of which are shown on the chartlet below and some are as follows (see chart 2358):
PORT NAVALO — anchor in bay but exposed to W to NW winds. All facilities.
LE ROCHER — in Auray river. Good shelter.
AURAY — anchor in middle of river (3.5m) or go alongside at St Goustan.
LARMOR BADEN — perfect anchorage to N (2 to 4m).
ILE AUX MOINES — one of the public islands. Anchor off N end, landing at Pt. de Drech or Pt. de Réchauds, or secure to yacht moorings (see Hr Mr).
ILE PIREN — good anchorage but in tidal stream.
ILE D'ARS — one of the public islands. Anchor NE of Pt de Beluré where there is a landing.
VANNES — see 10.15.14.
PORT BLANC MARINA 1¼ M WSW of Pt d'Aradon.
NOYALLO RIVER — anchor in Anse de Truscatte or between Le Passage and Ile de Pechit.
KERNES — off the Anse de Kernes in 3 to 6m.
AR GAZEK — in Ile de Jument in perfect shelter.

NAVIGATION
Waypoint 47°32'.00N 02°55'.13W, 180°/000° from/to Port-Navalo Lt, 0.90M. Beware very strong tides, max 8 kn, which run in the entrance and between some of the islands. Channels and dangers are well marked.

MORBIHAN *continued*

TOWNS

PORT NAVALO. all facilities. ⊞ ☎ 97.41.21.53;
  Police 97.24.17.17.
AURAY. All facilities. Aff Mar ☎ 97.24.01.43;
  Accastillage Diffusion ☎ 97.24.18.89, ME, El, Sh,
  CH, SHOM; **Miran** ☎ 97.24.07.19, ME, Sh, CH;
  Chatenay et Cie 'La Chateyne' ☎ 97.24.91.52, CH.
LE BONO — Anchorage. **Boursicot** ☎ 97.57.82.57, ME.
LARMOR BADEN. Aff Mar ☎ 97.57.05.66.
ILE AUX MOINES. Bureau du Port ☎ 97.26.30.57, M,
  FW. Yachts can secure to moorings − see Hr Mr.
LOCMARIAQUER. Protected anchorage. **Madec**
  ☎ 97.24.92.56, ME.

ARRADON — good anchorage. Slip; Hr Mr 97.26.01.23;
  Mechanique Marine (Pramer) ☎ 97.26.01.16, ME.
CONLEAU — Anchorage in bight just S of village.
  Le Mée (Michelet), ME, El, Sh.
VANNES (see 10.15.14).
SÉNÉ — **Le Gal** ☎ 97.66.96.90, ME.
ILE D'ARS — Rudevent. Visitors anchorage, slip; exposed
  to winds from S and E. **Toussaint Guy**
  ☎ 97.26.30.01, ME, El, Sh.
PORT BLANC — Hr Mr 97.57.01.00. Limited facilities.

LA TRINITÉ-SUR-MER
Morbihan   10-15-16

CHARTS
  Admiralty 2358; SHOM 5352, 5420; ECM 546, 545
TIDES
  +0455 Dover; ML 3.1; Duration 0610; Zone −0100
Standard Port BREST (→)

Times				Height (metres)			
HW		LW		MHWS	MHWN	MLWN	MLWS
0000	0600	0000	0600	7.5	5.9	3.0	1.4
1200	1800	1200	1800				

Differences LA TRINITÉ
  +0010 −0020 −0025 −0015 −2.1 −1.7 −0.9 −0.7

SHELTER
  Very good shelter except in strong SE to S winds when
  the sandbank La Vanererse is covered. Anchorage in the
  river is forbidden. Marina boat will meet and indicate
  pontoon. Access day and night at all tides.
NAVIGATION
  Waypoint 47°31′.90N 02°59′.63W, 167°/347° from/to
  front Ldg Lt 347°, 2.3M. Beware many oyster beds,
  marked with perches. There are no navigational dangers
  and the river is well marked by buoys and perches.
  Deepest water close to E shore. Anchoring and fishing
  prohibited. Speed limit 5 kn.

LIGHTS AND MARKS
  Ldg Lts 347°. Front Q WRG (W345°-013°). Rear QW 21m
  17M; synchronised; intens 337°-357°. Dir Lt 347° Oc
  WRG 4s (W346°-348°).
RADIO TELEPHONE
  Marina VHF Ch 09.
TELEPHONE (97)
  Hr Mr Port de Plaisance 97.55.71.49; Aff Mar 97.55.73.46;
  CROSS 97.55.35.35; SNSM 97.24.00.14; ⊞ 97.55.73.46;
  Meteo 97.64.34.86; Auto 97.84.82.83; Police 97.55.71.62;
  Dr 97.55.74.03; Brit Consul 40.63.16.02.
FACILITIES
  Marina (900 + 100 visitors) ☎ 97.55.71.27, AC, P, D, FW,
  BH (36 ton), Gridiron; **Kervilor** ☎ 97.55.71.69, M, ME, El,
  CH; **Madame Lecuillier** ☎ 97.55.72.59, CH, SHOM;
  Rioux ☎ 97.55.72.43, ME, CH; **S.E.E.M.A.**
  ☎ 97.55.78.06, Ⓔ; **Technique Voile** ☎ 97.55.78.08, CH,
  SM; **Club Nautique** ☎ 97.55.73.48; **Voilerie Le Port**
  ☎ 97.55.72.07, CH, SHOM, Ⓔ. **Town** V, Gaz, R, Bar. ✉;
  Ⓑ; ⇌ (Auray); ✈ (Lorient).
  Ferry UK — Roscoff—Plymouth; St Malo—Portsmouth.

LA TRINITE-SUR-MER *continued*

▲ Marina boat will indicate

PORT HALIGUEN-QUIBERON
Morbihan
10-15-17

CHARTS
Admiralty 2353; Imray C38; SHOM 5420, 5352, 135, 5439;
ECM 545

TIDES
+0500 Dover; ML 3.0; Duration 0615; Zone −0100
Standard Port BREST (——➤)

Times				Height (metres)			
HW		LW		MHWS	MHWN	MLWN	MLWS
0000	0600	0000	0600	7.5	5.9	3.0	1.4
1200	1800	1200	1800				

Differences PORT HALIGUEN-QUIBERON

0000	−0020	−0025	−0015	−2.3	−1.9	−1.0	−0.8

SHELTER
Good shelter but strong winds from NW to NE make it
uncomfortable. Yachts usually moor stern to pontoons.
Secure to visitors' pontoon and ask the Hr Mr. Access at
all tides, day and night.

NAVIGATION
Waypoint 47°29'.80N 03°05'.00W, 060°/240° from/to
breakwater Lt, 0.75M. Approach from E or SE. Beware
shoal (1.8m) ENE of breakwater Lt in R sector 240°-299°.

LIGHTS AND MARKS
W sector 246°-252° of Port Maria Lt (Q WRG) leads N of
Banc de Quiberon; W sector 299°-306° of Haliguen Lt
(Oc(2)WR 6s) leads S of it.

RADIO TELEPHONE
VHF Ch 09.

TELEPHONE (97)
Hr Mr 97.50.20.56; Aff Mar 97.50.08.71; CROSS
97.55.35.35; SNSM 97.50.14.39; ⌗ 97.40.14.81; Meteo
97.64.34.86; Auto 97.84.82.83; Police 97.50.07.39;
Dr 97.50.13.94 (Quiberon); Brit Consul 40.63.16.02.

FACILITIES
Marina (640 + 80 visitors) ☎ 97.50.20.56, Slip, P, D, C
(2 ton), BH (13 ton), ME, El, Sh, Bar, R, AC, CH, FW, ▢,
SM, V; **Société Nautique de Quiberon** ☎ 97.50.17.45;
Loc'Haliguen Marine ☎ 97.50.25.03, CH, ME, El, Sh;
Chantier Nautique Rouzenn ☎ 97.30.40.81 ME, El, Sh,
CH; **Chantier Naval Kergroix** ☎ 97.50.07.16 ME, El, Sh,
CH; **Town** (Quiberon) V, Gaz, R, Bar. ✉; Ⓑ; ⇌; ✈.
Ferry UK — Roscoff—Plymouth.

LE PALAIS (BELLE ÎLE)
Morbihan
10-15-18

CHARTS
Admiralty 2353; Imray C38; SHOM 5911, 135; ECM 545

TIDES
+0450 Dover; ML 3.0; Duration 0615; Zone −0100
Standard Port BREST (——➤)

Times				Height (metres)			
HW		LW		MHWS	MHWN	MLWN	MLWS
0000	0600	0000	0600	7.5	5.9	3.0	1.4
1200	1800	1200	1800				

Differences LE PALAIS

−0015	−0030	−0030	−0025	−2.3	−1.9	−1.0	−0.6

SHELTER
Good shelter except during strong E winds when a
marked swell builds up. Yachts can lock into the Bassin à
Flot HW−1½ to HW+1 (0600-2200 LT) and thence
through lifting bridge into marina. Inner harbour partly
dredged. Usual berth for deep keel yachts on three lines
of mooring buoys inside Mole Bourdelle. Gets very
crowded in summer. As an alternative, Sauzon has space
in outer harbour with approx 2m over CD (see 10.15.27).

NAVIGATION
Waypoint 47°21'.20N 03°08'.00W, 065°/245° from/to
Jetée Nord Lt, 0.80M. There are no navigational dangers
but beware ferries which leave and enter at high speed.
Anchorage between Sauzon and Le Palais is prohibited.

LIGHTS AND MARKS
Mole Bourdelle (N) Fl (2+1) G 12s 11m 7M
Mole Bonnelle (S) Oc (2) R 6s 11m 8M.

RADIO TELEPHONE
VHF Ch 09.

LE PALAIS *continued*

TELEPHONE (97)
Harbour Office 97.31.42.90; Aff Mar 97.31.83.17; CROSS 97.55.35.35; SNSM 97.47.48.49; ⊞ 97.31.85.95; Police 97.31.80.22; Dr 97.31.40.90; Ⓗ 97.31.81.82; Brit Consul 40.63.16.02.

FACILITIES
Marina ☎ 97.52.83.17, P, D, AC, FW, ME, El, Sh, Access HW + 1; **Quai** Slip, FW, C (10 + 5 ton), AB; **Belle-Ile Plaisances** ☎ 97.31.80.23, ME, El, Sh, CH; **YC de Belle Ile** ☎ 97.31.80.46, M; **Guidal** ☎ 97.31.83.75, ME, El; **Kan Ar Mor** ☎ 97.31.82.05, M, CH, ME, El, **Marec** ☎ 97.31.83.60, M, ME, El; **Station Total** ☎ 97.31.80.68, P, D (cans), CH.
Town V, Gaz, R, Bar. ⊠; Ⓑ; ⇌ (ferry to Quiberon); ✈.
Ferry UK — Roscoff—Plymouth.

⚓ proceed up to Marina

LORIENT   10-15-19
Morblhan

CHARTS
Admiralty 304, 2352; Imray C38; SHOM 5912, 6470; ECM 544

TIDES
+0455 Dover; ML 3.0; Duration 0620; Zone −0100
Standard Port BREST (→)

Times				Height (metres)			
HW		LW		MHWS	MHWN	MLWN	MLWS
0000	0600	0000	0600	7.5	5.9	3.0	1.4
1200	1800	1200	1800				

Differences LORIENT
+0005 −0025 −0025 −0015 −2.4 −1.9 −1.0 −0.5
PORT LOUIS
−0010 −0025 −0020 −0020 −2.4 −1.9 −0.9 −0.5
PORT TUDY (Ile de Groix)
−0005 −0035 −0030 −0025 −2.4 −1.9 −0.9 −0.5
PENFRET (Iles de Glenan)
−0010 −0025 −0030 −0020 −2.6 −2.0 −1.2 −0.6

SHELTER
The Ile de Groix shelters the entrance from SW winds. Good shelter in all weathers. Anchorage N of Kernével. Lock into Marina HW∓1. Waiting berths are provided outside lock. Anchorage very full of mooring buoys. An alternative is to pick up vacant mooring N of Port Louis for the night. In both cases passing traffic makes it uncomfortable. Access day and night at all tides.

NAVIGATION
Waypoint Passe du Sud 47°40'.50N 03°22'.40W, 189°/009° from/to front Ldg Lt 008°, 3.4M.
Waypoint Passe de l'Ouest 47°40'.80N 03°24'.80W, 240°/060° from/to front Ldg Lt 060°, 3.0M. There are few navigational dangers entering Lorient so long as leading lines are kept to, but yachts must keep clear of shipping in the main channel. There is a secondary channel for yachts to the W of the main channel (see inset). Depths in this channel are 1m less than shown on panel.

LIGHTS AND MARKS
There are the following leading or directional lights:
(1) Passe de l'Ouest: Ldg Lts 057°. Front, Les Soeurs,

Dir Q 13M; R Tr, W bands. Rear, Port Louis, 740m from front, Dir Q 18M; W daymark, R bands, on building.

(2) Ile aux Soris: Dir QWG 6m 3/2M; G Tr, W041.5°-043.5°, G043.5°-041.3°.
(3) Passe Sud: Ldg Lts 008.5°; Front, Fish Market, Dir QR 16m 15M; R square, G bands on Gy Tr; intens 006°-011°. Rear, Kergroise-La Perriere, 515m from front, Dir QR 28m **16M**; R square, W stripe on Gy Tr; intens 006°-011°.
(4) Ile Saint-Michel: Ldg Lts 016.5°. Front Dir Oc (3) G 12s 8m **16M**; W Tr, G top; intens 015°-018°. Rear, 306m from front, Dir Oc(3) G 12m 12s **16M**; W Tr, G Top; intens 015°-018°.
(5) Les Trois Pierres: QRG 11m 6/6M; B Tr, W bands G 060°-196°, R196°-002°.
(6) Kernével: Ldg Lts 217°; Front, Dir Oc(4)R 12s 10m 14M. Rear, 290m from front, Dir Oc(4)R 12s 18m 14M; W square Tr, R top; intens 215°-219°.
(7) Pointe de l'Esperance: Dir Lt 037°: Dir Q WRG 8m 10/8M; G034.2°-036.7°, W036.7°-037.2°, R037.2°-047.2°.
(8) Pont Gueydon: Dir Lt 352°: Dir Iso WRG 4s 11/9M; G168°-169.5°, W169.5°-170.5°, R170.5°-173.5°.
(9) Pointe de Keroman: Ldg Lts 350°. Front, Dir Oc (2) R 6s 25m **17M**; R house, W bands; intens 348°-353°. Rear, 91m from front, Dir Oc (2) R 6s 31m **17M**; RW Topmark on Gy pylon, R top. intens 348°-353°.

RADIO TELEPHONE
Call: *Vigie Port Louis* VHF Ch 16; 11 (H24). Marinas Ch 09 (office hours).

TELEPHONE (97)
Hr Mr Port de Plaisance 97.21.10.14; Aff Mar 97.37.16.22; CROSS 97.55.35.35; SNSM 97.64.32.42; ⊞ 97.37.29.57; Meteo 97.64.34.86; Auto 97.84.83.44; Police 97.64.27.17; Ⓗ 97.37.51.33; Brit Consul 40.63.16.02.

FACILITIES
Marina Kerneval (410 + 60 visitors) ☎ 97.33.63.56, P, D, FW, AC, ▣, Slip, BH (25 ton), C (100 ton), YC (☎ 97.21.14.01), Access H24; **Marina Lorient** (320 + 50 visitors) ☎ 97.21.10.14, P, D, FW, AC, ▣, Slip, BH (25 ton), C (100 ton); **Co-opérative Maritimes Lorient** ☎ 97.37.07.91, ME, El, Ⓔ, Sh, CH, SHOM; **Guillet** ☎ 97.37.26.76, Sh; **Intership** ☎ 97.37.00.97, ME, CH, Ⓔ, SHOM; **Lorient Marine** ☎ 97.37.34.78, M, ME, El, Ⓔ, CH, Sh; **V. V. Tonnerre** ☎ 97.37.23.55, CH, SM; **Club Nautique de Lorient** ☎ 97.84.81.30. Bar, C (1½ ton), FW, Slip; **Town** All facilities, ⊠; Ⓑ; ⇌; ✈.
Ferry UK — Roscoff—Plymouth.

15

CONCARNEAU 10-15-20
Finistere

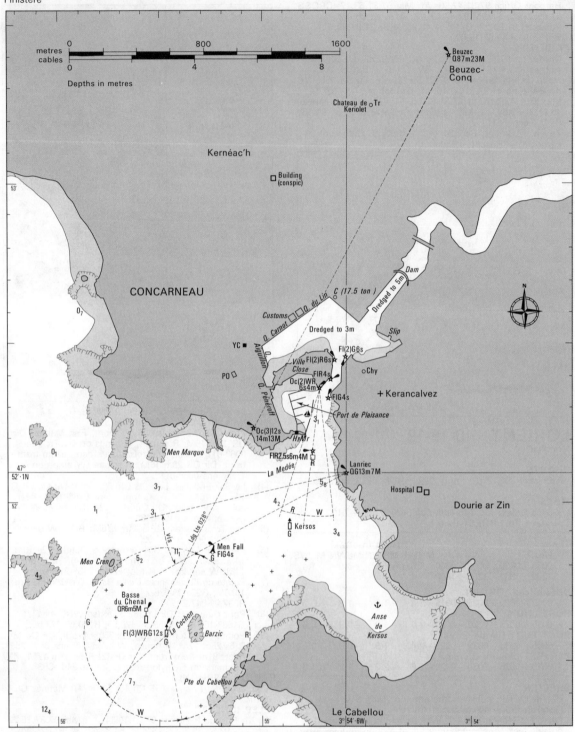

CHARTS
Admiralty 2352, 3641; Imray C38; SHOM 6650, 5368; ECM 544

TIDES
+0455 Dover; ML 2.9; Duration 0615; Zone -0100
Standard Port BREST (→)

Times				Height (metres)			
HW		LW		MHWS	MHWN	MLWN	MLWS
0000	0600	0000	0600	7.5	5.9	3.0	1.4
1200	1800	1200	1800				

Differences CONCARNEAU
-0005 -0035 -0030 -0020 -2.5 -2.0 -1.0 -0.6

SHELTER
Very good shelter in the marina which has the added protection of an anti-wash barrier but exposed to strong S winds. The inner quays are reserved for fishing boats.

NAVIGATION
Waypoint 47°50'.00N 03°56'.80W, 208°/028° from/to front Ldg Lt 028°, 2.52M. Following the leading lights, beware rocks round Men Cren and Le Cochon.

LIGHTS AND MARKS
Ldg Lts 028°, front Oc (3) 12s 14m 13M rear, 1.35M from front, Q. 87m 23M. Lanriec Lt, QG 13m 7M vis 063°-078°.

RADIO TELEPHONE
VHF Ch 16; 12 (H 24). Marina Ch 09.

CONCARNEAU *continued*

TELEPHONE (98)
Hr Mr 98.97.33.80; Marina Office 98.97.57.96; Aff Mar 98.97.53.45; CROSS 97.55.35.35; 97.64.32.42; Meteo 98.94.00.57; Auto 98.94.00.69; ☎ 98.97.09.41; Police 98.97.00.71; Ⓗ 98.50.30.30; Brit Consul 40.63.16.02.
FACILITIES
Marina (267 + 40 visitors), P, D, FW, ME, AC, El, C (17 ton), Slip, Sh; **Quay Pénéroff** P, D, FW, AB; **Barzic** ☎ 98.97.01.57, CH, SHOM; **Chantiers Nautique du Minaouet Grignallou** ☎ 98.97.46.79, M, ME, El, Sh, CH; **Concarneau Marine** ☎ 98.97.19.63, ME, El, Sh; **Voilerie Le Bras** ☎ 98.97.04.28 SM; **Techni Plaisance** ☎ 98.97.22.02 ME, El, Ⓔ, Sh, CH; **Concarneau Plaisance** ☎ 98.97.00.50, M, ME, El, Sh, CH; **Gloaguen** ☎ 98.97.04.08, ME, El, Sh; **Nautisme-Motor Club Dolliou** ☎ 98.97.12.05, ME, El, Sh, CH.
Town V, Gaz, R, Bar. ✉; Ⓑ; ⇌ (bus to Quimper); ✈ (Quimper). Ferry UK — Roscoff—Plymouth.

LA FORÊT 10-15-21
Finistere

CHARTS
Admiralty 2352, 3641; Imray C37, C38; SHOM 6650, 5368; ECM 543, 544
TIDES
+0450 Dover; ML 2.9; Duration 0615; Zone −0100
Standard Port BREST (→)

Times				Height (metres)			
HW		LW		MHWS	MHWN	MLWN	MLWS
0000	0600	0000	0600	7.5	5.9	3.0	1.4
1200	1800	1200	1800				

Differences CONCARNEAU
−0005 −0035 −0030 −0020 −2.5 −2.0 −1.0 −0.6

SHELTER
Good shelter in the Port de Plaisance in all weathers. There is an anchorage inside Cap Coz.
NAVIGATION
Waypoint 47°52'.70N 03°57'.80W, 162°/342° from/to Cap-Coz Lt, 0.9M. Beware Basse Rouge 6.5ca (1200m) S of Cape Coz and Le Scoré to the SE of Cape Coz.
LIGHTS AND MARKS
Channel is marked by buoys and beacons. Cape Coz Lt is Fl (2) R 6s 5m 6M and that on the breakwater to the NNW, Fl G 4s 8m 6M. Breakwater Lts in line at 334°.
RADIO TELEPHONE
VHF Ch 09.
TELEPHONE (98)
Hr Mr 98.56.98.45; Aff Mar 98.56.01.98; CROSS 97.55.35.35; Auto 98.94.00.57; SNSM 98.56.98.45; ☎ (Concarneau) 98.97.01.73; Police 98.56.00.11; Ⓗ (Concarneau) 98.97.10.60; Brit Consul 40.63.16.02.
FACILITIES
Marina (690 + 70 visitors) ☎ 98.56.98.45, ME, El, Sh, CH, AC, D, P, FW, Gaz, R, ▢, SM, V, Bar, BH (16 ton), C (2 ton), Slip (multi hull); **Pontoons** SM, P, AC, D, FW, C (2.5 ton), V, Bar; **Horizons** ☎ 98.56.99.72, ME, El, Sh, CH; **Kerleven (Chantier Naval)** ☎ 98.56.96.85, M, ME, El, Sh, Ⓔ; **PLF Marine** ☎ 98.56.96.04, ME, El, Sh.
Town Gaz, ✉, Ⓑ; ⇌ (Quimper); ✈ (Quimper). Ferry UK — Roscoff—Plymouth.

BÉNODET 10-15-22
Finistere

CHARTS
Admiralty 3640, 2352; Imray C37; SHOM 6649, 6679, 5368; ECM 543
TIDES
+0450 Dover; ML 2.7; Duration 0610; Zone −0100
Standard Port BREST (→)

Times				Height (metres)			
HW		LW		MHWS	MHWN	MLWN	MLWS
0000	0600	0000	0600	7.5	5.9	3.0	1.4
1200	1800	1200	1800				

Differences BÉNODET
−0010 −0025 −0040 −0015 −2.6 −2.2 −1.2 −0.8
CORNIGUEL
+0015 +0010 −0015 −0010 −2.6 −2.1 −1.4 −1.1
LOCTUDY
−0010 −0030 −0030 −0025 −2.6 −2.1 −1.2 −0.9

SHELTER
Anchor in Anse du Trez in offshore winds; or go to one of two marinas; Anse de Penfoul (apply to berthing master on quay); or go to Sainte Marine marina on the W bank. Access day and night at any tide. River Odet easily navigable up to Quimper, but bridge at Poulguinan (just before city) necessitates lowering the mast, or mooring there.
NAVIGATION
Waypoint 47°51'.00N 04°06'.10W, 166°/346° from/to front Ldg Lt 346°, 1.43M. Beware Roches de Mousterlin at the E end of the bay and various rocks round Loctudy at the West end of this bay. In the centre it is clear for small craft. There is a tanker channel past the Ile aux Moutons off the West horn of the bay. Speed limit 3 kn in harbour.
LIGHTS AND MARKS
Ile-aux-Moutons Oc (2) WRG 6s 18m 15/11M and Dir Oc (2) 6s 17m 24M; intens 278°-283°. Ldg Lts 346°. Front Pte du Coq Oc (2+1) G 12s 11m 17M. Rear Oc (2+1) 12s 48m 11M; both W Trs, G tops, synchronized.
RADIO TELEPHONE
VHF Ch 09 (0800-2000 LT in season); both marinas.
TELEPHONE (98)
Hr Mr 98.57.05.78; Aff Mar 98.57.03.82; CROSS 97.55.35.35; SNSM 97.57.02.00; ☎ 98.55.04.19; Police 98.56.00.11; Dr 98.57.22.21; Brit Consul 40.63.16.02.

15

BENODET *continued*

FACILITIES
BENODET **Anse de Penfoul Marina** (250 + 40 visitors on pontoons; also 175 moorings + 15 for visitors)
☎ 98.57.05.78, AC, FW, Ⓞ, R, CH, ME, V, P, D;
Accasting 29 ☎ 98.57.20.83, M, ME, El, Ⓔ, Sh, CH;
Le Gai Matelot ☎ 98.57.19.73, C, M, ME, El, Divers;
Town Quay C (10 ton); **Le Bihan Voiles** ☎ 98.57.18.03,
SM; **Cornouaille Nautique** ☎ 98.57.00.87, ME, El, Ⓔ,
Sh, CH; **Town** All facilities, Gaz, ✉, Ⓑ; ⇌
(bus to Quimper); ✈ (Quimper).
SAINTE MARINE **Ste Marine Marina** (250 + 40 visitors)
has few facilities. **Village** V, R, Bar, Ⓞ, Ⓔ.

AUDIERNE 10-15-23
Finistere

CHARTS
Admiralty 3640; SHOM 6594, 6609, 7147; Imray C36, C37;
ECM 541
TIDES
+0440 Dover; ML 3.1; Duration 0605; Zone −0100
Standard Port BREST (⟶)

Times				Height (metres)			
HW		LW		MHWS	MHWN	MLWN	MLWS
0000	0600	0000	0600	7.5	5.9	3.0	1.4
1200	1800	1200	1800				

Differences AUDIERNE
−0020	−0040	−0040	−0020	−2.3	−1.8	−0.9	−0.5

GUILVINEC
−0010	−0035	−0035	−0020	−2.4	−1.9	−1.0	−0.5

ILE DE SEIN
−0010	−0010	−0010	−0015	−1.1	−0.9	−0.5	−0.3

SHELTER
River is accessible above half tides in all but strong S-SW
winds. Breakwater by Ste Evette gives shelter in all but
SE winds although there may be a swell there when wind
is S or SW. Keep clear of slip area as vedettes enter with
much verve. Visitors buoys are white and marked
'Payant-Visiteurs'.
NAVIGATION
Waypoint 47°59'.00N 04°31'.03W, 151°/331° from/to
front Ldg Lt, 1.85M. Access is difficult in strong S-SW
winds. There are two rock outcrops, Le Sillon de Galets
to the W and La Gamelle in the middle of the bay. A
good drying anchorage opposite quays (E side of river).
Fishermen resent yachts on quays except in NW corner,
which is foul.
LIGHTS AND MARKS
Ldg Lts at 331°, Front Oc (2 + 1) WG 12s 11m 14/9M,
Rear FR 44m 9M. Dir Q WRG 43m 12/9M
G 000°-005°, W 005°-007°, R 007°-017°. This latter Lt in
line with Old Lt Ho gives Ldg line at 006°.
RADIO TELEPHONE
None. Other station Pointe du Raz Ch 16.
TELEPHONE (98)
Hr Mr 98.70.07.91; Aff Mar 98.70.03.33; CROSS
97.55.35.35; SNSM 98.70.03.31; ⌗ 98.70.70.97; Meteo
98.94.03.43; Auto 98.94.00.57; Police 98.70.04.38;
Ⓗ 98.70.00.18; Brit Consul 40.63.16.02.
FACILITIES
Port de Plaisance (70) ☎ 98.70.08.47 Bar, R, CH, ME,
El, Sh, FW, Ⓞ, V; **Poulgoazec** C (15 ton), Slip, P and D
(cans); **Marine Service** ☎ 98.70.22.85, ME, El, Sh;
Bosser ☎ 98.70.10.52, El, Ⓔ; **Club Nautique de la Baie
d'Audierne** ☎ 98.70.21.69.

Town V, Gaz, R, Bar. ✉; Ⓑ; ⇌ (bus to Quimper);
✈ (Quimper).
Ferry UK — Roscoff—Plymouth.

DOUARNENEZ 10-15-24

Finistere

CHARTS
Admiralty 798; SHOM 5316, 6677, 6099; Imray C36; ECM 542.

TIDES
+0500 Dover; ML 4.2; Duration 0615; Zone −0100
Standard Port BREST (→)

Times				Height (metres)			
HW		LW		MHWS	MHWN	MLWN	MLWS
0000	0600	0000	0600	7.5	5.9	3.0	1.4
1200	1800	1200	1800				

Differences DOUARNENEZ

−0015	−0010	−0015	−0020	−0.5	−0.5	−0.2	0.0

SHELTER
Very good shelter and open in all weathers and tides. Yachts are not allowed in the Fishing Harbour but can use the marina (Port de Plaisance) in Treboul, Port Rhu, further up river or Port de Rosmeur. Visitors berths are scarce in the marina at Quai de l'Yser. Access day and night at all tides.

NAVIGATION
Waypoint 48°07'.00N 04°20'.30W, 000°/180° from/to Ile Tristan Lt, 0.83M. There are three rocks to the NW of Ile Tristan, Basse Veur, Petite Basse Neuve and Basse Neuve from 3 to 9 ca (555 to 1665m). All are in the R sector of Ile Tristan Lt.

LIGHTS AND MARKS
Approx 5 M to W is Pte du Millier Lt, Oc (2) WRG 6s 34m 16/11M G 080°-087°, W 087°-113°, R 113°-120°, W 120°-129°, G 129°-148°, W 148°-251°, R 251°-258°. There are no leading lights or marks but the entrance through the Grande Passe is 158°.

RADIO TELEPHONE
VHF Ch 09 (0800−1200 and 1330−2000 LT in season).

TELEPHONE (98)
Hr Mr (Plaisance) 98.74.02.56; Aff Mar 98.92.00.91; CROSS 98.89.31.31; SNSM 98.89.63.16; ⌗ 98.92.01.45; Meteo 98.84.60.64; Auto 98.84.82.83; Police 98.92.01.22; Ⓗ 98.92.25.00; Brit Consul 40.63.16.02.

FACILITIES
Marina (380+30 visitors) ☎ 98.92.09.99, Slip, FW, AC, P, D, C (6 ton), ME, El, Sh; **Port Rhu** AB, R, Bar; **Quai de l'Yser** P, D, L, FW, C, AB, V, R, Bar; **Bateau Baloin** ☎ 98.92.10.40, M, Sh, ME, El, CH; **Riou Louis** ☎ 98.92.15.76, ME, El, Sh; **Ste des Regates de Douarnenez** ☎ 98.92.27.28; **Henri Fiacre** ☎ 98.92.06.28, ME, El, Sh, BH (12 ton), CH, SM; **Bideau** ☎ 98.92.05.71, Ⓔ; **Town** Slip, P, D, FW, CH, AB, Gaz, V, R, Bar. ✉; Ⓑ; ⇌; ✈ (Quimper).
Ferry UK — Roscoff—Plymouth.

MORGAT   10-15-25
Finistere

CHARTS
Admiralty 798, 2690; SHOM 6676, 6678, 6099; Stanford 17; Imray C36; ECM 541, 542.

TIDES
+0500 Dover; ML 4.2; Duration No data; Zone −0100
Standard Port BREST (→)

Times				Height (metres)			
HW		LW		MHWS	MHWN	MLWN	MLWS
0000	0600	0000	0600	7.5	5.9	3.0	1.4
1200	1800	1200	1800				

Differences MORGAT
−0010	−0010	−0015	−0015	−0.5	−0.5	−0.2	0.0

SHELTER
The port is exposed to winds from the W and N but the marina is protected by concrete pontoons.

NAVIGATION
Waypoint 48°12'.00N 04°28'.00W, 147°/327° from/to E breakwater head, 1.9M. Few dangers in approaches. There are rocks under the cliffs S of Pte de Morgat, and Les Verres 2M ESE of entrance.

LIGHTS AND MARKS
Morgat Lt Oc (4) WRG 12s 77m 15/10M G sector covers Les Verres.

RADIO TELEPHONE
VHF Ch 25 87 Marina 09 16.

TELEPHONE (98)
Hr Mr 98.27.01.97; Aff Mar 98.27.09.95; CROSS 98.89.31.31; Meteo 98.84.82.83; SNSM 98.27.00 41; ⌗ 98.27.93.02; Police 98.27.00.22; Ⓗ 98.27.05.33; Brit Consul 40.63.16.02.

FACILITIES
Marina (525+60 visitors), AC, FW, C (8 ton), Slip, CH, D, P, ME, Access H24; **Alemany** ☎ 98.27.01.97, Slip, M, L, FW, ME, C (6 ton), AB, V, R, Bar; **Quay by Hr Mr** P, D; **Service-Plaisance** ☎ 98.27.95.90, M, ME, El, Sh, CH, Ⓔ; **YC du Crozon-Morgat** ☎ 88.27.01.98.
Town (Crozon), V, Gaz, R, Bar. ✉, Ⓑ; ⇌; ✈ (Brest or Quimper). Ferry UK — Roscoff—Plymouth.

CAMARET   10-15-26
Finistere

CHARTS
Admiralty 2690, 3427; SHOM 6678, 6099; Imray C36; Stanford 17; ECM 542.

TIDES
+0500 Dover; ML 4.1; Duration 0610; Zone −0100
Standard Port BREST (→)

Times				Height (metres)			
HW		LW		MHWS	MHWN	MLWN	MLWS
0000	0600	0000	0600	7.5	5.9	3.0	1.4
1200	1800	1200	1800				

Differences CAMARET
−0015	−0015	−0015	−0020	−0.5	−0.5	−0.2	−0.1

SHELTER
Harbour gives good shelter except from strong E winds, but much of it dries and there is a restricted area: see chartlet. Shelter in both marinas, Plaisance La Pointe or Plaisance Styvel, is always good.

NAVIGATION
Waypoint 48°18'.00N 04°36'.00W, 335°/155° from/to North Mole Lt, 1.2M. Beware rocks W of Pointe du Grand Gouin. Anchoring in harbour forbidden.

LIGHTS AND MARKS
Lt Ho at end of N Mole Iso WG 4s W135°-182°, G182°-027°; Ldg line at 148° with front — top of the old fort, back — Keraudren water tower on hill behind.

RADIO TELEPHONE
None. For Ouessant Traffic see Chapter 2 Fig.2(1).

TELEPHONE (98)
Hr Mr 98.27.95.99; Bureau de Port 98.27.93.30; Aff Mar 98.27.93.28; CROSS 98.89.31.31; SNSM 98.27.94.76, ⌗ 98.27.93.02; Meteo 98.84.82.83; Police 98.27.00.22; Dr 98.27.91.35; Brit Consul 40.63.16.02.

FACILITIES
Plaisance 'La Pointe (30+120 visitors), ☎ 98.27.95.99, FW, AC, C (8 ton), D, Access H24; **Plaisance 'Styvel'** (180+30 visitors), FW, AC, Access HW∓3; **Service Plaisance** ☎ 98.27.95.90, M, L, FW, ME, El, Ⓔ, Sh, CH, AB; **Boennec Frères** ☎ 98.27.90.61; ME; **Le Roy** ☎ 98.27.94.32, ME; **Quai Tephany** P, D, L, C (5 ton); **Voileire Lastennet** ☎ 98.27.92.32, SM; **Hugot** ☎ 98.27.90.88, SHOM;
Town V, Gaz, R, Bar. ✉, Ⓑ; ⇌ (Brest); ✈ (Brest or Quimper).
Ferry UK — Roscoff—Plymouth.

MINOR HARBOURS AND ANCHORAGES   10.15.27

PORNICHET, Loire-Atlantique, 47°15'N, 2°20'W, Zone −0100, Admty chart 2989, SHOM 6797. HW +0500 on Dover (GMT), −0040 sp, +0015 np on Brest (zone −0100); HW height −1.9m on Brest; ML 2.9m; Duration 0530 sp 0645 np. Excellent shelter in artificial harbour. No navigational dangers; available at all tides (up to 3.5m draught). Lt on S breakwater head WG 4s 11m 12/9M, G084°−081°, W081°−084°. S breakwater FIG 2s. N breakwater FIR 2s. VHF Ch 09. Facilities are extensive; Hr Mr ☎ 40.47.23.71. ⌗ ☎ 40.61.32.04. Meteo ☎ 40.90.08.80; Aff Mar ☎ 40.60.56.13; CROSS ☎ 97.55.35.35. **Marina** (1100+150 visitors), ☎ 40.61.03.20, AC, Slip, FW, P, D, BH (24 ton), V, R, Bar; **L'Ancre Marine** ☎ 40.61.09.37 ME, El, Ⓔ, Sh, CH SHOM; **Town** Bar, Dr, ✉, R, ⇌, V.

PIRIAC, Loire-Atlantique, 47°23'N, 2°32'W, Zone −0100, Admty chart 2353, SHOM 5482. HW +0505 on Dover (GMT), −0015 on Brest (zone −0100); HW height −1.9m on Brest; ML 3.1m; Duration 0605. A small resort and fishing village with good small harbour. Available HW∓3, 30 berths for visitors, ask at Cercle Nautique ☎ 40.23.52.32 (July-Aug only). Lt Oc(2) WRG 6s 8m 10/6M, vis R066°−185°, W185°−201°, G201°−224°. Facilities: D, P on quay. **Piriac Marine Service** ☎ 40.23.50.86, CH, Ⓔ, El, ME, Sh; **Town** Bar, Dr, R, V.

PORT D'ARZAL, Morbihan, 47°30′ N, 2°24′ W, Zone −0100, Admty chart 2353, SHOM 2381, 5482. Tidal figures below dam as for St Nazaire. Access HW∓3. See 10.15.12 and 10.15.9. Keep to outside of bends going up river. Lock on N side of dam opens as boats approach (no charges); 0700−2000 May to Oct, 0800−1900 in winter. Facilities: Hr Mr 97.90.05.06; **Arzal Nautique** ☎ 97.45.03.52, ME, El, Ⓔ, Sh; **N shore above dam**. C (15 ton) D, El, FW, ME, Sh. **Port de Plaisance, Camoel** (on S shore above dam) (660+50 visitors), ☎ 99.90.05.86 AC, C (15 ton), CH, P, D, El, FW, Gas, Gaz, ME, R, Sh, V.

PENERF, Morbihan, 47°31′ N, 2°37′ W, Zone −0100, Admty chart 2353, SHOM 5418, 5420. HW +0515 on Dover (GMT), −0010 on Brest (zone −0100); HW height −1.9m on Brest; ML 3.0m; Duration 0610. See 10.15.12. Shelter very good in all weathers. Entrances are all difficult. Passe de l'Est has 4m but is narrow and rocky; it leads E of La Traverse, a reef which dries, marked by Bn 1¼M ENE of Pte de Penvins, and thence between Le Pignon and Petite Bayonelle to join Passe du Centre. Passe du Centre is the widest and easiest, leading close W of La Traverse, N of which the depth is 0.1m, and then close E of Le Pignon. Passe de l'Ouest, which leads W of Plateau des Passes, is shallow and not well marked. Beware oyster beds in the river. Anchor in 3.5m near quay. Light, Le Pignon, in the river entrance Fl (3) WR 12s 6m 9/6M on R Tr: R028°−167°, W167°−175°, R175°−349°, W349°−028°. Facilities: P and D (on quay), Slip. **Penerf Marine** ☎ 97.41.13.86, CH, El, ME, Sh; **Town** Bar, Dr, R, V.

ÎLE DE HOUAT, 47°24′ N, 2°57′ W, Zone −0100, Admty chart 2353, SHOM 135. HW +0505 on Dover (GMT), −0017 on Brest (zone −0100); HW height −1.9m on Brest; ML 2.9m; Duration 0605. See 10.15.11 (Île de Höedic). Good shelter at Port St Gildas, towards E end of the N coast, protected by wave-break. Beware rock in the middle (1m) and rocks protruding 6m from breakwater. Anchor inside breakwater in approx 2m. S part of harbour dries. Lt on N mole Oc (2) WG 6s 8m 8/5M from W Tr with G top. W168°−198°, G198°−210°, W210°−240°, G240°−168°. Facilities very limited. Ferries to Quiberon (Port Maria) and Île de Höedic.

PORT MARIA, Morbihan, 47°28′ N, 3°08′ W, Zone −0100, Admty chart 2353, SHOM 5420, 5352, 135. HW +0505 on Dover (GMT), −0010 on Brest (zone −0100); HW height −2.1m on Brest; ML 2.9m; Duration 0615. Shelter good in all winds. Access dangerous in strong winds from SE to SW. Half harbour dries. E mole reserved for ferries. Anchor in S of harbour in approx 2m. Beware rocks at base of S mole. Ldg Lts 006°, both QG intens 005°−008°. E mole head Iso G 4s 9m 6M. S end of wave-break Oc (2) R 6s 9m 8M. Main Lt Ho Q WRG 28m 15/10M, W246°−252°, W291°−297°, G297°−340°, W340°−017°, R017°−051°, W051°−081°, G081°−098°, W098°−143°. Facilities: Hr Mr and Aff Mar ☎ 97.50.08.71. ⌗ ☎ 97.50.14.81. C (6 ton), FW at E quay. **Monvoisin** ☎ 97.50.09.67 SHOM; **Ateliers Normand** ☎ 97.50.26.17 El, ME, Sh; **Town** (and at Quiberon 0.5M) Bar, V, R.

SAUZON, Belle Ile, 47°22′ N, 3°13′ W, Zone −0100, Admty Chart 2353, SHOM 135, ECM 545; HW +0450 on Dover (GMT), −0020 on Brest (zone −0100); HW height −2.0m on Brest; ML 3.0m; Duration 0615. Small attractive harbour which dries, 4M N of Le Palais. See 10.15.18. Good shelter except in E winds. Moorings available (17 deep water buoys) just inside E and W moles, or go into inner harbour and dry out. Main Lt QG 9m 5M. NW Jetée FlG 4s. SE Jetée FlR 4s. Facilities: FW on quay; **Société Nautique de Sauzon** ☎ 97.31.84.56. V, R, Bar in village.

RIVER ÉTEL, Morbihan, 47°39′ N, 3°12′ W, Zone −0100, Admty chart 2352, SHOM 5560. HW +0505 on Dover (GMT), −0020 on Brest (zone −0100); ML 2.8m; Duration 0617. Shelter excellent but approach should only be made on flood tide, by day in good weather at about HW−1½. Bar dries. There is a small marina inside the town quay. Ldg line at 042° is marked by two water towers. Hoist ensign to mast-head or call Mat Fenoux Ch 16; 12. Semaphore arms will be rotated, one turn to acknowledge and then as follows: Arrow vertical = remain on course. Arrow inclined = alter course in direction indicated. Arrow horizontal with ball over = no

entry. R flag = insufficient depth at bar. Light W side of ent Oc (2) WRG 6s 13m 9/6M W022°−064°, R064°−123°, W123°−330°, G330°−022°. Anchoring prohibited within ½M of this Lt. VHF Ch 16; 13. In Etel town, anchor S of LB house SW of quay, above town (beware strong currents) or go alongside quay (end of quay reserved for ferries) or alongside in yacht harbour beyond quay. Facilities: Hr Mr ☎ 97.55.46.62; Aff Mar ☎ 97.55.90.32; Semaphore tower ☎ 97.55.35.59; Sig.Stn. ☎ 97.52.35.29; Auto ☎ 97.64.54.43; **Kenkiz Marine** ☎ 97.55.34.58. CH, El, ME, Sh; **Town** Bar, Dr, FW, R, V.

PORT TUDY, Ile de Groix, 47°39′ N, 3°27′ W, Zone −0100, Admty chart 2352, SHOM 5479, 5912. HW +0505 on Dover (GMT), −0035 on Brest (zone −0100); HW height −2.2m on Brest; ML 3.1m; Duration 0610. See 10.15.19. Very good shelter in marina in inner harbour, but some swell in NE winds. Access HW∓2 (0600-2200). Beware large unlit mooring buoys NE of entrance and rocks both sides of approach. Ldg line at 220°, spire of St Tudy church in line with W end of N jetty. Lights: E mole head Fl (2) R 6s 11m 6M vis 112°−226°. N mole head Iso G 4s 12m 6M. Facilities limited. Hr Mr ☎ 98.05.80.90; ⌗ ☎ 97.05.80.93; **Marina** (150), FW, P, D, ME, El, Sh; **An C' Hanot** ☎ 97.05.81.86 ME, El, Sh, CH; **Coopérative Maritime** ☎ 97.05.80.03, CH; **Town** V, R, Bar, ferry to Lorient.

DOËLAN, Finistere, 47°46′ N, 3°36′ W, Zone −0100, Admty chart 2352, SHOM 5479. HW +0450 on Dover (GMT), −0035 on Brest (zone −0100); HW height −2.2m on Brest; ML 3.1m; Duration 0607. Shelter is good except in bad onshore weather. Harbour dries. Anchorage in outer part of creek or just inside breakwater. Ldg Lts 014°, front Oc (3) WG 12s 20m 13/10M, W shore−305°, G305°−314°, W314°−shore. Rear QR 27m 9M. Facilities: Aff Mar ☎ 98.96.62.38. **Doëlan-Nautic** ☎ 98.71.50.76 CH, El, Ⓔ, ME, Sh; **Town** Bar, D, Dr, FW, P, ✉, R, V.

PONT-AVEN, Finistere, 47°49′ N, 3°44′ W, Zone −0100, Admty chart 2352, SHOM 5479. HW +0450 on Dover (GMT), −0030 on Brest (zone −0100). HW height −1.9m on Brest; ML 2.8m; Duration 0610. Very good shelter at Pont-Aven. Moorings in 2.5m; alongside the quay dries 2.5m. Pont-Aven is 3.6M from Port Manech where there are visitors buoys and a good anchorage in 2.5m outside the bar which dries 0.9m. Beware Les Cochons de Rousbicout to W of entrance (dry 0.3m) and Les Verres to E. The only Lt is at Port Manech on Pte Beg ar Vechen Oc (4) WRG 12s 38m 10/6M. Facilities: **YC de l'Aven** at Port Manech. Aff Mar ☎ 98.06.00.73; **Derrien** ☎ 98.06.01.35, ME; **Town** Bar, C, D, FW, P, R, Slip, V.

LOCTUDY, Finistere, 47°50′ N, 4°10′ W, Zone −0100, Admty chart 3641, SHOM 6649. HW +0505 on Dover (GMT), −0020 on Brest (zone −0100). HW height −2.4m on Brest; ML 2.8m; Duration 0615. (All tidal figures taken at Pont l'Abbé, 3M from entrance). See 10.15.22. Shelter good. Buoys for yachts W of Ile Tudy or anchor NW of the quay. Beware mussel beds. Lights: Langoz Fl (4) WRG 12s 12m 15/10M, W115°−257°, G257°−284°, W284°−295°, R295°−318°, W318°−328°, R328°−025°. Basse Bilien buoy (2M off entrance) VQ (3) 5s. Les Perdrix Lt on N of entrance Fl WRG 4s 15m 11/8M. Facilities: Aff Mar ☎ 98.87.41.79; **wet basin** C (10 ton), D, FW, P; **Club Nautique Loctudy** ☎ 98.87.42.84; **SO.ME.CO.** ☎ 98.87.50.00, El, ME, Sh.

GUILVINEC, Finistere, 47°48′ N, 4°17′ W, Zone −0100, Admty chart 3640, SHOM 6646, 5368. HW +0447 on Dover (GMT), −0023 on Brest (zone −0100); HW height −2.1m on Brest; ML 3.0m. See 10.15.23. Good shelter; harbour always available (unless over 2.5m draught). Good anchorage off entrance protected by reef but keep clear of fairway. Beware Lost Moan Rks SE of entrance marked by RW Bn Tr, Fl (3) WRG 12s 8m 9/6M. Ldg Lts 053°. Front, Mole de Lechiagat Q 7m 8m; W pylon; vis 233°-066°. Middle, Rocher Le Faoute's, 210m from front QWG 12m W14M, G11M; R sphere on W pylon; vis W006°-293°, G293°-006°; synchronised with front. Rear, 0.58M from front, DirQW 26m 8M; R sphere on W pylon; vis 051.5°-054.5°; synchronised with front. VHF Ch 12. Secure to buoy marked 'Port de Plaisance' at N end of harbour. Facilities: Hr Mr ☎ 98.58.05.67; Aff Mar ☎ 98.58.13.13; ⌗; C, D, FW, P; **Glehen** ☎ 98.58.12.00. El, ME, Sh; **Biguais** ☎ 98.58.27.43. CH. **CRM** ☎ 98.58.09.58 Ⓔ, El;

15

VOLVO PENTA SERVICE

Sales and service centres in area 16
Names and addresses of Volvo Penta dealers in
this area are available from:

FRANCE **Volvo Penta France SA,** Chemin de la Nouvelle, F78130 Les Mureaux
Tel (01) 3474 72 01, Telex 695221 F

Area 16

North Brittany
Brest to Paimpol

**VOLVO
PENTA**

16

668

5°W

4°30'W

Variation 6°W (1991)

49°
N

48°
30'N

48°
N

SEPARATION
ZONE

SEPARATION
ZONE

For details see Fig.2(1)

Île Vierge

(RC) VG
5   ─ • • • ─ ─ ─
     298.8   70

Pont
(Brign

L'Aberwrac'h

ℹ️   10.16.14

LB   ⚠️IL

Brest

Standard Port

ℹ️   10.16.9

(P)(R) VHF 08 16

☀️ 98.84.60.6
    98.84.82.8

CG

Pte. de Créac'h

(RC) CA
6   ─ ─ • • ─ • ─
     308   100

*Portsall

⚠️IL
LB

**Brest-
Le Conquet**

(S)(C) MF–1806
      VHF 16 26 28

Cross Corsen

Ouessant Traffic
VHF 11 16; 11 79

CG

Argenton*

L' Aberbenoit

ℹ️   10.16.13

Rade de Bres

ℹ️   10.16.1

RG

Le Conquet

ℹ️   10.16.11

LB

L'Aberildut*

Lampaul

ℹ️   10.16.12

Ouessant
Coast Station

(S)(C) VHF 16 24
          82

LB

Île Molène

LB ⚠️IL

Les Pierres
Noires

L'Iroise

Pte. St Mathieu

(RC) SM
3   • • • ─ ─
     289.6   20

Traffic
management VHF 16

Camaret

LB

Rade
de Brest

Pte.du Toulinguet

Ile de Sein

(RC) SN
3   • • • ─ •
     303.4   70

LB

Pte du Raz

Traffic management
VHF 16

Ar-Men ✫

5°W

See 10.15.2

10-16-2
North Brittany

Roches Douvres

| (RC) 4 | RD •–• –•• 298·8 70 |

⊛ RG

Barnouic ★

49° N

Perros Guirec

| [i] | 10.16.18 |
| ⚠IL | |

Ile de Bréhat

[i]	10.16.21
(RC) 1,5	DO –•• ––– 294. 2 10
☼	96.20.01.92

Tréguier

| [i] | 10.16.19 |
| ⚠IL | |

Les Sept Iles*

ff/Bloscon

| | 10.16 .15. |
| BC | –••• ––•– 287·3 10 |
| VHF 16;12 |
| ⚠IL |

Plateau de Triagoz ☆

Ploumanach
Tregastel*
Ile Grande

LB

Port Blanc*

Pontrieux*

LB

Plougasnou

| (C) S | VHF 16 83 |

Kerprigent

Trébeurden
Bec-Léger

Lézardrieux

| [i] | 10.16.20 |

Primel*

LB ⚠IL

Locquémeau*

St Pol
e Leon

LB

z*

⚠IL

⚠LB

Carantec*

Locquirec

LB ⚠IL

Lannion

| (RC) Aero | LN •–•• –• 345·5 50 |

Paimpol

[i]	10.16.22
(C) S	VHF 16 84
⚠IL	

Lannion

| [i] | 10.16.17 |
| ⚠IL | |

Morlaix

| [i] | 10.16.16 |
| ☼ | 98.88.34.04 |

See 10.17.2

48° 30'N

St. Brieuc

| (RC) Aero | SB ••• –••• 353 25 |
| ☼ | 96.94.94.09 96.78.51.51 |

Key to Symbols

(C)	Coast Station/Port Radio – frequencies	🛈CG	Coastguard Rescue Sub-Centre
(RC)	Marine radiobeacon– call sign, sequence, frequency and range (nm)	LB	Life-boat
(RC) Aero	Aeronautical radiobeacon–call sign, frequency and range (nm)	⚠IL	Inshore Life-boat
[i]	See for harbour information/tidal data	✈	SAR Helicopter base
☼	Weather information (tel. no. or times)	☆	Principal lights
CG	Coastguard Rescue Co-ordination Centre	⚓	Light-vessel
		‡	Lanby
		*	See 10.16.23

10.16.3 AREA 16 TIDAL STREAMS

5 Hours before HW Dover (0215 after HW Brest)

4 Hours before HW Dover (0315 after HW Brest)

3 Hours before HW Dover (0415 after HW Brest)

2 Hours before HW Dover (0515 after HW Brest)

1 Hour before HW Dover (0615 after HW Brest)

HW Dover (0510 before HW Brest)

Southward 10.15.3   Eastward 10.17.3   Northward 10.1.3

1 Hour after HW Dover (0410 before HW Brest)

2 Hours after HW Dover (0310 before HW Brest)

3 Hours after HW Dover (0210 before HW Brest)

4 Hours after HW Dover (0110 before HW Brest)

5 Hours after HW Dover (0010 before HW Brest)

6 Hours after HW Dover (0050 after HW Brest)

16

10.16.4   LIGHTS, FOG SIGNALS AND WAYPOINTS

Note. For English Channel Waypoints see 10.1.7

Abbreviations used below are given in 10.0.3. Principal lights are in **bold** print, places in CAPITALS, and light-vessels, light floats and Lanbys in *CAPITAL ITALICS*. Unless otherwise stated lights are white. m—elevation in metres; M—nominal range in n. miles. Fog signals are in *italics*. Useful waypoints are underlined   use those on land with care. See 4.2.2.

FRANCE—WEST COAST

GOULET DE BREST.
Charles Martel Lt Buoy 48°18'·90N 04°42'·10W QR; port-hand mark; *Whis*.

Pointe du Petit-Minou 48°20'·26N 04°36'·80W Dir Q 30m **23M**; intens 065·5°-070·5°; *Horn 60s* and Fl(2) WR 6s 32m **W19M R15M**; Gy Tr, R top; vis R shore-252°, W252°-260°, R260°-307°, W (unintens) 307°-015°; W015°-065·5°, W 070·5°-shore. FR 1·5M and 2·7M NE.
Ldg Lts 068°. Front from Pointe du Petit-Minou Tr, rear from Pointe du Portzic Tr, both QW **23M**, intensified on leading line.
Roche Mengam 48°20'·40N 04°34'·48W Fl(3) WR 12s 11m W11M, R8M; R Tr, B bands; vis R034°-054°, W054°-034°.

Pointe du Portzic 48°21'·56N 04°31'·97W Oc(2) WR 12s 56m **W19M, R15M**; grey 8-sided Tr; vis R219°-259°, W259°-338°, R338°-000°, W000°-065°, W070°-219°. Dir Q(6)LFl 15s 54m **23M**; same Tr; intens 045°-050°.

BREST.
Port Militaire, Jetée Sud, head QR 10m 5M; W Tr, R top; vis 094°-048°.
Jetée Est, head QG 10m 5M; W Tr, G top; vis 299°-163°.
Terre-pleine du Château Dir Oc(2) WRG 6s 19m W11M, R8M, G8M; on roof of building; vis G335°-344°, W344°-350°, R350°-014°.
La Penfeld, E side of entrance, Iso G 3s 11m 7M; vis 316°-180°.
Quai de l'Artillerie Iso R 3s 8m 7M; vis 144°-350°.
Ldg Lts 314° Front Iso R 5s 9m 10M. Rear, 17m from front, Iso R 5s 16m 12M; both intens 309°-319°.
Port de Commerce. E entrance, S side Oc(2) R 6s 8m 5M; W framework Tr, R top; vis 018°-301°.
Mole de l'Est Oc(2) G 6s 8m 7M.
Jetée Ouest Iso R 4s 10m 7M.
Jetée Sud Fl G 4s 10m 6M; vis 022°-257°.
Moulin Blanc Lt Buoy 48°22'·80N 04°26'·07W Oc(2)R 6s; port-hand mark.

CHENAL DU FOUR (S PART)

Pte de St Mathieu 48°19'·85N 04°46'·17W. Ldg Lts 158° with Kermorvan (below) Fl 15s 56m **29M**; W Tr, R top. Dir F 54m **28M**; same Tr; intens 158°; RC. 54m 291° from St Mathieu Q WRG 26m W14M, R11M, G11M; W Tr; vis G086°-107°, W107°-116°, R116°-134°.
Les Pierres Noires 48°18'·73N 04°54'·80W Fl R 5s 27m **19M**; W Tr, R top; *Siren (2) 60s*.
Les Vieux-Moines 48°19'·40N 04°46'·55W FlR 4s 16m 5M; R 8-sided Tr; vis 280°-133°.

Lochrist 48°20'·6N 04°45'·9W Oc (21) 12s 49m **22M**; W 8-sided Tr, R top; intens 136°-140°; Rear Ldg Lt 138° for Chenal de la Helle with Kermorvan.

Kermorvan 48°21'·80N 04°47'·30W Fl 5s 20m **22M**; W square Tr; obsc by Pte de St Mathieu when brg less than 341°; front Ldg Lt for Chenal de la Helle with Lochrist. Common front Ldg Lt 158° with Pte de St Mathieu (above), and 007° with Trézien (below); *Reed 60s*.
Trézien Ldg Lt 007°; Rear 48°25'·4N 04°46'·8W Oc (2) 6s 84m **21M**; grey tower, W on S side; intens 003°-011°.
Corsen 48°24'·9N 04°47'·7W Dir Q WRG 33m W12M, R8M, G8M; vis R008°-012°, W012°-015°, G015°-021°.

CONQUET
Mole 48°21'·6N 04°47'·1W Oc G 4s 3m 6M; G mast.
La Grande Vinotière, 48°22'·00N 04°48'·30W Oc R 6s 15m 5M; R 8-sided Tr.
Rouget Lt Buoy 48°22'·00N 04°48'·80W Iso G 4s; stbd-hand mar; *Whis*.

ÎLE DE MOLÈNE.
Molène mole head Dir Lt 191°, Dir Fl(3) WRG 12s 6m W9M, R7M, G7M; vis G183°-190°, W190°-192°, R192°-203°.
Chenal des Las, Dir Lt 261°, Dir Fl(2) WRG 6s 9m W9M, R7M, G7M; same structure; vis G252°-259°, W259°-262°, R262°-269°.

CHENAL DE LA HELLE.
Les Trois-Pierres 48°24'·75N 04°56'·75W Iso WRG 4s 15m W9M, R6M, G6M; W column; vis G070°-147°, W147°-185°, R185°-191°, G191°-197°, W197°-213°, R213°-070°.
Le Faix 48°25'·80N 04°53'·82W VQ; 16m 8M; N cardinal mark; in line with Le Stiff (below) bears 293°.

CHENAL DU FOUR (N PART)

Les Plâtresses 48°26'·35N 04°50'·85W Fl RG 4s 17m 6M; W Tr; vis R343°-153°, G153°-333°.
La Valbelle Lt Buoy 48°26'·55N 04°49'·90W Oc R 6s; port-hand mark; *Whis*.
L'Aberildut 48°28'·3N 04°45'·6W Dir Oc (2) WR 6s 12m **W25M, R20M**; W buildings; vis W081°-085°, R085°-087°.
Le Four 48°31'·45N 04°48'·23W Fl(5) 15s 28m **21M**; grey Tr; *Siren (3+2) 75s*.

OUESSANT
OUESSANT SW LANBY 48°31'·68N 05°49'·10W Fl 4s 12m **20M**; RC; Racon.
NE Lt Buoy 48°45'·90N 05°11'·60W L Fl 10s 9m 8M; *Whis*; Racon.

La Jument 48°25'·40N 05°07'·95W Fl(3) R 15s 36m **18M**; grey 8-sided Tr, R Top; obsc by Ouessant 199°-241°; *Reed (3) 60s*.
Pierre-Vertes Lt Buoy 48°22'·2N 05°04'·7W VQ(9) 10s 9m 8M; W cardinal mark; *Whis*.

Kéréon (Men-Tensel) 48°26'·30N 05°01'·45W Oc (21) WR 24s 38m **W19M, R15M**; grey Tr; vis W019°-248°, R248°-019°. *Siren (21) 120s*.
Men-Korn 48°27'·95N 05°01'·22W VQ(3) WR 5s 29m W8M, R8M; E Cardinal mark; vis W145°-040°, R040°-145°.
Le Stiff 48°28'·60N 05°03'·10W Fl(2) R 20s 85m **24M**; two adjoining W Trs.
Créac'h 48°27'·62N 05°07'·72W Fl(2) 10s 70m **34M**; W Tr, B bands; obsc 247°-255°; Racon, RC, RG; *Horn(2) 120s*.
Nividic 48°26'·80N 05°08'·95W VQ(9) 10s 28m 9M; W 8-sided Tr, R bands; obsc by Ouessant 225°-290°. Helicopter platform.
Port du Stiff. Mole Est, head 48°28'·18N 05°03'·16W Dir QWRG 11m W10M, R7M, G7M; W Tr, G top; vis G251°-254°, W254°-264°, R264°-267°.

FRANCE—NORTH COAST

Basse de Portsall Lt Buoy 48°36'·78N 04°46'·05W VQ(9)10s
9m 8M; W cardinal mark; *Whis*; Ra refl.
Portsall 48°33'·9N 04°42'·3W Oc (31) WRG 12s 9m **W16M**,
R13M, G13M; W column, R top; vis G058°-084°, W084°-
088°, R088°-058°.
Corn-Carhai 48°35'·2N 04°43'·9W Fl(3) 12s 19m 9M; W 8-
sided Tr, B top.
Libenter Lt Buoy 48°37'·5N 04°38'·4W Q(9) 15s 8m 8M; W
cardinal mark; Ra refl; *Whis*.

L'ABERWRAC'H.
Ldg Lts 100° Front Ile Vrac'h 48°36'·9N 04°34'·6W QR 20m
7M; W square Tr, R top, W dwelling. Rear, Lanvaon 1·63M
from front Q 55m 12M; grey square Tr, W on west side;
intens 090°-110°.
Breac'h Ver 48°36'·70N 04°35'·40W FlG 2·5s 6m 3M; Bn Tr,
stbd-hand mark.
Dir Lt 128°, La Palue 48°35'·9N 04°33'·9W Dir Oc(2). WRG 6s
5m W13M, R11M, G11M; vis G126°-127°, W127°-129°,
R129°-130°.

Île-Vierge 48°38'·38N 04°34'·00W Fl 5s 77m **27M**; grey Tr;
vis 337°-325°; RC; *Siren 60s*.
Pontusval, Pte de Beg-Pol 48°40'·7N 04°20'·8W Oc(3) WR
12s 16m W10M, R7M; W square Tr, B top, W dwelling; vis
W shore-056°, R056°-096°, W096°-shore. QY and FR Lts on
towers 2·4M S.
Lizen Ven Ouest Lt Buoy 48°40'·57N 04°33'·68W VQ(9)10s
8m 8M ; W cardinal mark; *Whis* .
Aman-ar-Ross Lt Buoy 48°41'·9N 04°27'·0W Q 9m 7M; N
cardinal mark; *Whis*.

PORT DE MOGUÉRIEC.
Ldg Lts 162°. Front, jetty head Iso WG 4s 9m W11M, G6M;
vis W158°-166°, G166°-158°. Rear, 440m from front FG 22m
7M; W column, G top; vis 142°-182°.

Île de Batz 48°44'·78N 04°01'·55W Fl(4) 25s 69m **23M**;
auxiliary Lt FR 67m 7M; same Tr; vis 024°-059°.

ROSCOFF.
Astan Lt Buoy 48°44'·95N 03°57'·55W VQ(3) 5s 12m 8M; E
cardinal mark; *Whis*; Ra refl.
Ar-Chaden 48°43'·99N 03°58'·15 W Q(6)LFl WR 15s 14m
W9M, R6M; S cardinal mark; vis R262°-288°, W288°-294°,
R294°-326°, W326°-110°.
Men-Guen-Bras 48°43'·81N 03°57'·95W Q WRG 14m W9M,
R6M, G6M; N cardinal mark; vis W068°-073°, R073°-197°,
W197°-257°, G257°-068°.
Basse de Bloscon Lt Buoy 48°43'·77N 03°57'·48W VQ; N
cardinal mark.
Le Menk Lt Tr 48°43'·35N 03°56'·60W Q(9) WR 15s 6m 5/
3M; W cardinal Bn Tr; vis W160°-188°.
Ldg Lts 209°. Front, NW mole Oc(21) G 12s 7m 7M; W
column, G top; vis 078°-318°. **Rear** 430m from front Oc(2+1)
12s 24m **15M**; grey square Tr, W on NE side; vis 062°-242°.
Jetty head 48°44'·0N 03°59'·0W F Vi 5m 1M.
Slip 48°44'·3N 04°00'·5W VQ(6) + LFl 10s 13m 7M; S cardinal
mark.

BLOSCON.
Jetty head 48°43'·30N 03°57'·65W Fl WG 4s 9m W10M,
G7M; W Tr, G top, vis W210°-220°, G220°-210°; RC.
BAIE DE MORLAIX.
Ldg Lts 190°. Front, Île Noire 48°40'·39N 03°52'·58W Oc(2)
WRG 6s 15m W11M, R8M, G8M; W square Tr, R top; vis
G051°-135°, R135°-211°, W211°-051°; obsc in places. Rear
(common with Île Louet 176°) **La Lande** 48°38'·2N 03°53'·1W

Fl 5s 85m **23M**; W square Tr, B top; obsc by Pointe Annelou-
esten when brg more than 204°.
Ldg Lts 176°. Front **Île Louet** 48°40'·5N 03°53'·4W Oc(3) WG
12s 17m **W15M**; G10M; W square Tr, B top; vis W305°-244°,
G244°-305°, vis 139°-223° from offshore, except when obsc
by islands. Rear, La Lande above.

ANSE DE PRIMEL.
Ldg Lts 152°. Front FR 35m 6M; W square, R stripe, on
framework Tr; vis 134°-168°. Rear, 202m from front FR 56m
6M; W square, red stripe.
Jetty head 48°42'·82N 03°49'·53W Fl G 4s 6m 7M; W
column, G top.

LOCQUEMEAU.
Ldg Lts 121°. Front FR 21m 6M; W framework Tr, R top; vis
068°-228°. Rear, 484m from front Oc(21) R 12s 39m 7M; W
gabled house; vis 016°-232°.

Beg-Léguer 48°44'·40N 03°32'·83W Oc(4) WRG 12s 60m
W13M, R10M, G10M; west face of W house, R lantern; vis
G007°-084°, W084°-098°, R098°-129°.
Les Triagoz 48°52'·35N 03°38'·73W Oc(2) WR 6s 31m
W15M, R11M; grey square Tr, R lantern; vis W010°-339°,
R339°-010°; obsc in places 258°-268° by Les Sept-Îles.

Les Sept-Îles, **Île-aux-Moines** 48°52'·78N 03°29'·33W Fl(3)
15s 59m **24M**; grey Tr and dwelling; obsc by Ilot Rouzic and
E end of Île Bono 237°-241°, and in Baie de Lannion when brg
less than 039°.

Ploumanac'h Méan-Ruz 48°50'·32N 03°28'·90W Oc WR 4s
26m W13M, R10M; pink square Tr; vis W226°-242°, R242°-
226°; obsc by Pte de Trégastel when brg less than 080°, and
part obsc by Sept-Îles 156°-207°, and by Île Tomé 264°-278°.

PERROS-GUIREC.
Passe de l'Ouest. **Kerjean** Dir Lt 144°. Dir Oc(21) WRG 12s
78m **W15M**, R13M, G13M; W Tr, B top; vis G134°-143°,
W143°-144°, R144°-154°.
Passe de l'Est Ldg Lts 225°. Front **Le Colombier** Oc(4) 12s
28m **18M**; W house; intens 219°-229°. Rear, **Kerprigent**
1·5M from front Q 79m **20M**; W Tr; intens 221°-228°.
Jetée Est (Linkin) 48°48'·26N 03°26'·23W Fl(2) G 6s 4m 7M;
W pile, G top.
Mole Ouest Fl(2) R 6s 4m 8M; W pile, R top.

Port Blanc, Le Voleur Fl WRG 4s 17m W14M, R11M, G11M;
W Tr; vis G140°-148°, W148°-152°, R152°-160°.

TRÉGUIER.
La Corne 48°51'·40N 03°10'·53W Fl(3) WRG 12s 14m W11M,
R8M, G8M; W Tr, R base; vis W052°-059°, R059°-173°,
G173°-213°, W213°-220°, R220°-052°.
Grande Passe Ldg Lts 137°. Front, Port de la Chaîne Oc 4s
12m 12M; W house. Rear **St Antoine** 0·75M from front OcR
4s 34m **15M**; W house, R roof; synchronised with front,
intens 134°-140°.

Les Heaux 48°54'·53N 03°05'·20W Oc(3) WRG 12s 48m
W17M, R12M, G12M; grey Tr; vis R227°-247°, W247°-270°,
G270°-302°, W302°-227°.

LE TRIEUX.
Moisie Rk Bn Tr 48°53'·85N 03°02'·22W (unlit); E cardinal
mark.
Noguejou Bihan Bn 48°53'·43N 03°01'·93W (unlit); E cardinal mark.
Les Sirlots Buoy 48°52'·97N 02°59'·60W (unlit); stbd-hand
mark; *Whis*.
Vieille du Tréou Bn Tr 48°52'·02N 03°01'·12W (unlit); stbd-
hand mark.

16

Rocher Men-Grenn 48°51'·3N 03°03'·9W Q(9) 15s 7m 8M; W cardinal mark.

Ldg Lts 225°. Front **La Croix** 48°50'·25N 03°03'·25W Oc 4s 15m **19M**; two Trs joined, W on NE side, R tops; intens 215°-235°. Rear **Bodic**, 2·1M from front Q 55m **22M**; W house with G gable; intens 221°-229°.

Coatmer Ldg Lts 219°. Front 48°48'·30N 03°05'·78W F RG 16m R9M, G8M; W gable; vis R200°-250°, G250°-053°. Rear, 660m from front, FR 50m 9M; W gable; vis 197°-242°.

Les Perdrix 48°47'·77N 03°05'·83W Fl(2) WG 6s 5m W9M, G6M; G Tr; vis G165°-197°, W197°-202°, G202°-040°.

3 FBu Lts mark marina pontoons, 0·4M SSW.

ILE DE BRÉHAT.

Rosédo 48°51'·5N 03°00'·3W Fl 5s 29m **20M**; W Tr; RC.

Le Paon 48°51'·95N 02°59'·17W F WRG 22m W12M, R9M, G8M; Y square concrete tower; vis W033°-078°, G078°-181°, W181°-196°, R196°-307°, W307°-316°, R316°-348°.

Men-Joliguet 48°50'·14N 03°00'·23W Iso WRG 4s 6m W13M, R10M, G8M; Y Tr, B band; vis R255°-279°, W279°-283°, G283°-175°.

Chenal de Ferlas, Roche Quinonec, Dir Lt 257°, Dir Q WRG 12m W10M, R8M, G8M; vis G254°-257°, W257°-258°, R258°-261°.

Embouchure du Trieux, Dir Lt 271°, Dir Fl WRG 2s 16m W10M, R8M, G8M; W column; vis G267°-270°, W270°-272°, R272°-274°.

La Horaine 48°53'·55N 02°55'·30W Fl(3) 12s 13m 11M; grey 8-sided Tr on B hut.

PAIMPOL.

Pte de Porz-Don Oc(2) WR 6s 13m **W15M**, R11M; W house; vis W269°-272°, R272°-279°.

Ldg Lts 264°. Jetée de Kernoa, front FR 5m 7M; W hut, R top. Rear 360m from front FR 12m 14M; W pylon, R top; intens 261°-267°.

L'Ost Pic 48°46'·75N 02°56'·45W Oc WR 4s 20m W11M, R8M; 2 W Trs, R tops; vis W105°-116°, R116°-221°, W221°-253°, R253°-291°, W291°-329°; obsc by islets near Bréhat when brg less than 162°.

Barnouic 49°01'·70N 02°48'·40W VQ(3) 5s 15m 9M; East cardinal mark, B Tr, Y band, W base.

Roches Douvres 49°06'·47N 02°48'·82W Fl 5s 60m **28M**; pink Tr on dwelling with G roof; RC; RG; *Siren 60s*.

Grand Lejon 48°44'·95N 02°39'·90W Fl(5) WR 20s 17m **W18M**, R14M; R Tr, W bands; vis R015°-058°, W058°-283°, R283°-350°, W350°-015°.

10.16.5 PASSAGE INFORMATION

FRENCH TERMS

When cruising in French waters it is essential to know some French words commonly used on charts or in sailing directions: *Anse*: bay. *Arrière port*: inner harbour. *Avant port*: outer harbour. *Baie*: bay. *Balise*: beacon. *Banc*: bank. *Barre*: bar. *Basse*: shoal. *Bassin*: basin. *Canal*: canal, channel. *Cap*: cape. *Chaussée*: bank. *Chenal*: channel. *Clocher*: steeple. *Digue*: breakwater, mole. *Écluse*: lock. *Est*: east. *Étang*: lagoon, lake. *Falaise*: cliff. *Fleuve*: river. *Golfe*: gulf. *Goulet*: narrows. *Grand*: great. *Île*: island. *Jetée*: jetty. *Maison*: house. *Menhir*: large stone. *Môle*: mole. *Mont*: mountain. *Mouillage*: anchorage. *Moulin*: mill. *Nord*: north. *Ouest*: west. *Passe*: channel. *Pertuis*: strait. *Petit*: small. *Pierre*: stone. *Pointe*: point. *Pont*: bridge. *Port*: harbour, port. *Presqu'île*: peninsula. *Quai*: quay. *Rade*: roadstead. *Récif*: reef. *Rivière*: river. *Roche(r)*: rock. *Sable*: sand. *Sud*: south. *Tour*: tower. *Ville*: town.

OUESSANT (USHANT) (chart 2694)

Ouessant is 10M off the W end of coast of France (chart 2694). It is rky island, with dangers extending ½ M to NE, ¾ M to SE, 1½ M to SW and 1M to NW (where Chaussée de Keleren is a dangerous chain of drying and submerged rks running 1M W of Île de Keleren).

Tidal streams are strong close to the island, and in chans between it and mainland. Off Créach Pt (Lt, fog sig, RC) the stream turns NNE at HW Brest −0550, and SSW at HW Brest +0045, sp rate 5½ kn.

Apart from Lampaul (10.16.12) the only other anch is Baie du Stiff which gives some shelter in moderate winds between S and NW: beware the rk awash about 3½ ca SSW of the rk with isolated danger Bn in middle of b.

Ouessant is something of a barrier between W and N coasts of France, but in fair weather and with reasonable vis the pilotage in the chans between it and the mainland is not very demanding. They are well buoyed and marked, but the tide runs hard in places, causing overfalls when against wind of over force 5. The route outside Ouessant has little to commend it: unless bound to or from Spain or Portugal it adds much to the distance, it is exposed to sea and swell, and the traffic scheme — see Fig.2(1) — restricts the free passage of yachts. In thick weather this is an unhealthy area, and it is prudent to stay in harbour until the vis improves.

There are three main chans between the island and mainland. The inshore one, Chenal du Four, is most direct and most popular. Chenal de la Helle, partly used for access to Ile Molène, is not so direct but better in bad weather. Passage du Fromveur, immediately SE of Ouessant, is easiest but can become extremely rough.

The tide runs strongest at S end of Chenal du Four, entered 1M W of Pte St Mathieu, with Kermorvan and Trézien Ldg Lts on at 007°. Here the N-going stream begins at HW Brest −0550 and reaches 5½ kn at sp. The S-going stream starts at HW Brest +0015, reaching 4¾ kn. Further N, off Pte de Corsen, the stream is weaker, less than 3 kn at sp. Bound homeward, or along the N coast of France, enter the S end of Chenal du Four at LW Brest: then the strongest tide off Kermorvan will be avoided, since it runs at about HW Brest −0300, while full use can be made of the NE stream past Ile Vierge.

Compared to larger vessels, there are several routes for a yacht through Chenal du Four. The following can be used day or night, if necessary from buoy to buoy if marks are obscured. The 007° transit above is followed until the Q WRG St Mathieu Lt is abeam (in G sector). Then alter course to make good 325° (Le Faix Tr on with Grande Courleau Bn) for about 1M until La Grande Vinotière and Pte de Corsen Lts are in transit at 009°. At this point steer to make good 005° to pass between La Grande Vinotière and Roche du Rouget buoy which are 1¼ M away. Aim to pass 1 ca W of La Grande Vinotiére, and continue on this course until the transit of Kermorvan and Pte St Mathieu is picked up at 158°. Then alter to port to follow this stern transit. There are buoys marking chan if difficult to follow the marks (or powerful Lts) astern. Do not confuse St Mathieu with Lochrist; the latter is rear Ldg Lt for outer part of Chenal de la Helle. Follow the 158° transit until Le Four is abeam, although in fact open water is reached once past L'Aberildut.

Coming S, the reverse procedure is followed. It may be difficult to identify the Kermorvan/St Mathieu 158° transit, but assuming moderate vis locate Le Four Tr E of the approach, and then Les Plâtresses slightly W of the transit, and only 5M from Kermorvan.

For Chenal de la Helle from S, follow the above route until Trézien is in transit with Corsen, bearing 050°. At this point pick up transit of Le Faix Tr with Stiff (NE corner of Ouessant) at 293°. Follow this transit for 2M until Kermorvan comes on with Lochrist astern at 138°. Take this stern transit out into open water, passing 6 ca NE of Le Faix. From the N, if difficult to see the 138° Ldg marks, the positions of Les Plâtresses to E of Ldg Line, and of Le Faix Tr and La Helle rk (12m elevation, and 7 ca W of Le Faix) to the W of it, will help locate them. At N end of Chenal de la Helle the ENE stream starts at HW Brest −0520 (sp rate 2¾ kn), and the SW stream at HW Brest −0045 (sp rate 3¾ kn).

Passage du Fromveur is 1M wide, between Ouessant and the dangers round Kéréon Lt Tr. But the stream runs 7 kn at sp, and with wind against tide the chan can be very dangerous. In good conditions it is safe and convenient with a fair tide.

In fair weather access to Molène is easy from Chenal de la Helle. The key transit is Les Trois Pierres on with North Mill at 215°, picked up ½ M W of La Helle Rk. North Mill may be obsc by Tr of Les Trois Pierres: as the latter is approached alter to stbd to skirt it at 1 ca. When 1 ca W of Les Trois Pierres, alter to 190° to pass close E of Bazou Real Bn Tr, which brings South Mill over the bow and in line with white patch on mole. Do not borrow to port, where there are rks, and anch about 1 ca N of mole.

LE FOUR TO ROCHES DOUVRES (charts 2644, 2668)

Proceeding NE from Le Four, and E towards Roscoff (10.16.15) there are many off-lying dangers, in places 3M offshore. Swell may break on shoals even further to seaward. The tide runs strongly, and in poor vis or bad weather it is a coast to avoid. 1M W of Le Four the E-going stream begins at HW Brest −0545, sp rate 3½ kn; the W-going stream begins at HW Brest +0100, sp rate 4 kn. Off Le Libenter, at N side of L'Aberwrac'h entrance the E-going stream starts at HW Brest −0500, sp rate 3¾ kn, and the W-going stream at HW Brest +0110. But in good conditions this is an admirable cruising ground with delightful harbours such as Argenton and Portsall (10.16.23), L'Aberbenoit (10.16.13), L'Aberwrac'h (10.16.14), Correjou, Pontusval and L'Aberildut (10.16.23), and Mogueriec.

16

E of Le Four is an inshore passage leading to Portsall, and thence to L'Aberwrac'h entrance. This is convenient and sheltered, but must only be used by day and in good conditions. French chart 5772 and full pilotage directions, as in *North Brittany Pilot*, are needed. N of L'Aberwrac'h is Ile Vierge Lt Ho, the tallest in the world, and a conspic landmark.

In daylight and above half tide there is a useful short cut to Roscoff through the Canal de l'Ile de Batz, between the island and the mainland at half tide or above. See chart 2745 or French chart 5828. Coming from the W, steer just N of Basse Plate Bn Tr, with Le Loup (a rk with white patch at N end) in transit with St Barbe (a white pyramid beyond Roscoff harb) brg 106°. This transit leads to L'Oignon N cardinal mark, where course is altered to 083° for Pen ar Cleguer at S end of Ile de Batz. Short of this point, when Per Roch N cardinal Bn bears 45° on starboard bow, alter course to leave it ½ ca to starboard. When Per Roch is passed, alter course slightly to starboard to leave An Oan S cardinal Bn to port, and steer for the violet Bn at end of the conspic Roscoff ferry pier. Pass 30m N of this Bn, and at this point alter to 095° which leads to Ar Chaden. For Ile de Batz see 10.16.23.

Approaching from NE, pass E of Basse Astan (marked by buoy) and steer with Men Guen Bras (lit) in transit with Chapelle St Barbe 213° until Ar Chaden is nearly abeam, when course is altered to pass S of Ar Chaden and N of Roc'h Zu N cardinal Bn. Beware rather isolated rk (dries) about 0.8 ca S by W from Ar Chaden. Then pass S of Duslen S cardinal Bn, and N of the ferry pier, and follow the route previously described from W. There are several fair-weather anchs in Canal de l'Ile de Batz, but anch is prohib in the narrows immediately W of the Roscoff ferry pier.

N of Ile de Batz the E-going stream begins at HW Brest − 0435, and the W-going stream at HW Brest + 0105, sp rates both 3¾ kn.

There are many offlying dangers fringing approaches to Rade de Morlaix (10.16.16 and chart 2745). The more important ones by Grand Chenal are Plateau des Duons (with Tour de Duon about 1½ M N of Ile de Callot), La Vieille (with Bn Tr 1M NE of N end of Ile de Callot), Stolvezen (dries) ½ M E of La Vieille, and La Fourche and Pierre a l'Évêque (both dry) ½ M S of La Vieille. S of this point the 176° Ldg Line passes close E of Bn Trs 1 ca NE and I ca SE of Ile Ricard. When Calhic Bn Tr is abeam, alter slightly to port to pass ½ ca E of Le Corbeau Bn Tr, and ½ ca W of Taureau Bn Tr. Pass 1 ca E of Ile Louet, and enter the buoyed chan ¼ M beyond.

Sailing E from Roscoff, Bloscon or Morlaix pass inside or outside Plateau de la Méloine; the former is obvious choice if bound for Lannion (10.16.17). The radome NE of Trébeurden is conspic. For Trébeurden see 10.16.23.

Plateau des Triagoz has offlying dangers WSW and NE of the Lt, where the sea breaks heavily. Here the stream turns ENE at HW Brest − 0325, and WSW at HW Brest + 0245, sp rates both 3¾ kn.

Les Sept Îles consist of four main islands and several islets, through which the tide runs strongly. Île aux Moines is lit, and there is an open anch between it and Île de Bono, which is a bird sanctuary.

Between Ploumanac'h and Perros-Guirec (10.16.18) there is a nice anch in Anse Trestraou, sheltered from S and W winds.

A useful inshore passage, avoiding detour round Les Heaux, is Passage de la Gaine between Tréguier River (10.16.19) and Lézardrieux (10.16.20). It should only be used by day, and in good vis. Front Ldg mark is Men Noblance Bn Tr (white, with B stripe). The rear mark (in transit at 242°) is less conspic, and is a white mark with vertical B stripe on a wall just below the skyline, to right of Plougrescant church (conspic). This mark is easier to see from W end of transit, than from Les Heaux. However, there are three Bns which mark the SE side of Basses des Heaux, and should be passed close on required side. If the passage is made at above half tide it presents no problem in fair weather.

Le Ferlas chan (chart 2557) runs S of Île de Brehat, and is useful if entering or leaving Pontrieux R from or to the E. It is well marked and not difficult, but there are unmarked rks in chan almost awash at or near LW, so is best tackled at half tide.

La Horaine (lit) marks NE part of rks extending seawards from Île de Brehat, but there are rky patches ½ M N and E, and also up to 2M SE, of the Lt Ho.

NNE of Île de Brehat are Plateau de Barnouic (lit) and Plateau des Roches Douvres (Lt, fog sig, RC), both with drying and submerged rks, to be avoided particularly in poor vis.

10.16.6　DISTANCE TABLE

Approximate distances in nautical miles are by the most direct route while avoiding dangers and allowing for traffic separation schemes etc. Places in *italics* are in adjoining areas.

	1	2	3	4	5	6	7	8	9	10	11	12	13	14	15	16	17	18	19	20
1 *Le Palais*	1																			
2 *Pointe du Raz*	81	2																		
3 Brest	105	24	3																	
4 Pointe St Mathieu	99	18	13	4																
5 Le Four	111	30	25	12	5															
6 L'Aberwrac'h	127	46	41	28	15	6														
7 Ile Vierge	124	43	38	25	13	6	7													
8 Roscoff	152	71	66	53	41	34	28	8												
9 Morlaix	163	82	77	64	52	45	39	12	9											
10 Les Sept Iles	171	90	85	72	60	53	47	21	26	10										
11 Perros Guirec	175	94	89	76	64	57	51	25	30	5	11									
12 Tréguier	191	110	105	92	80	73	61	41	46	20	20	12								
13 Lézardrieux	199	118	113	100	88	81	75	49	54	28	28	22	13							
14 *Roches Douvres*	200	119	114	101	89	82	76	50	55	29	31	26	22	14						
15 St Malo	233	152	147	134	122	115	109	83	88	62	62	54	49	42	15					
16 *Les Hanois*	216	135	130	117	105	98	92	66	71	45	·48	45	42	20	56	16				
17 *Casquets*	231	150	145	132	120	113	107	89	94	68	71	68	65	43	70	23	17			
18 *Bishop Rock*	212	131	127	114	102	109	105	119	131	129	134	150	155	148	187	147	160	18		
19 *Eddystone*	214	133	128	115	103	99	93	88	98	84	89	96	109	86	128	74	79	89	19	
20 *Portland Bill*	264	183	178	165	153	146	140	125	129	108	115	1130	113	87	118	67	48	162	73	20

BREST 10-16-9
Finistere

CHARTS
Admiralty 3427, 3428; SHOM 6542; ECM 542; Stanford 17; Imray C36

TIDES
Dover +0510; ML 4.4; Duration 0605; Zone −0100

NOTE: Brest is a Standard Port and the tidal predictions for each day of the year are given below.

SHELTER
Excellent shelter in Brest, and in many anchorages round the Rade du Brest (50 sq miles). Yachts should not use the Port du Commerce but the Port de Plaisance in the Anse du Moulin Blanc. Access at any tide day or night.

NAVIGATION
Waypoint 48°18'.30N 04°44'.00W, 248°/068° from/to front Ldg Lt 068° (Pte du Petit Minou), 5.3M. Moulin Blanc port-hand buoy, Oc(2)R 6s, 48°22'.82N 04°26'.06W, 207°/027° from/to MB1 and MB2 channel buoys, 0.55M. There are two forbidden areas — the Port Militaire in Brest and the zone round the Ile Longue. Fast tidal streams run in the Goulet de Brest. Brest is a busy commercial, naval and fishing port.

LIGHTS AND MARKS
Approaches marked by Lts at Pte St Mathieu, Pte du Petit Minou and Pte du Portzic. Marina 2 M E of the Port de Commerce, marked by buoys.

RADIO TELEPHONE
Call: *Brest Port* (at Pointe du Petit Minou) VHF Ch 08 16 (controls approaches to Brest). Moulin Blanc Marina Ch 09 16 (H24).
Saint Mathieu Ch 16 is part of Ouessant traffic management system, for vessels proceeding in Chenal de la Helle or Chenal du Four. PC Rade (Tour César) Ch 08 16. All vessels entering keep watch on Ch 16.

TELEPHONE (98)
Hr Mr Brest 98.44.13.44; Moulin Blanc 98.02.20.02; Aff Mar 98.80.62.25; CROSS 98.89.31.31; ▦ 98.44.35.20; Meteo 98.84.60.64; Auto 98.84.82.83; Dr 98.44.38.70; Police 98.22.83.90; Ⓗ 98.22.33.33; Brit Consul 99.46.26.64.

FACILITIES
Moulin Blanc Marina (1100+ 100 visitors), ☎ 98.02.20.02, Slip, P (in cans), D, FW, ME, El, Sh, BH (14 ton), AC, Bar, Gaz, R, Ⓞ, SM, V, C (3 ton), CH, Access H24; **Société des Régates de Brest** (at Moulin Blanc) ☎ 98.02.53.36 R, all facilities; **Occase Mer** ☎ 98.42.03.01, Sh, CH, ME; **Comptoirs Maritime** ☎ 98.02.30.04, CH, ME, El, Ⓔ, Sh;

Service Plaisance ☎ 98.02.60.07, ME, El, Sh, CH, Ⓔ; **Loisir Expo** ☎ 98.42.34.37, CH, Sh, ME; **Voiles Cudennec** ☎ 98.40.50.44, SM; **Voiles Océan** ☎ 98.80.28.32, CH, SM; **Accastillage Diffusion** ☎ 98.42.03.57 ME, El, Ⓔ, Sh, CH; **Jouanneau** ☎ 98.44.36.14, SHOM; **Cooperative des Marins Pecheurs** ☎ 98.44.62.77, CH, Ⓔ, SHOM, Gaz; **Town** all facilities, Gaz; ✉; Ⓑ; ⇌; ✈ (Brest-Guipavas). Ferry UK — Roscoff—Plymouth.

RADE DE BREST 10-16-10
Finistere

CHARTS
Admiralty 3427, 3428; SHOM 6542, 6426 6427, 5316; Stanford 17; Imray C36

The Rade de Brest provides a sheltered cruising ground, useful in bad weather, with many attractive anchorages. Beyond Pont Albert-Louppe (28m) it is possible to explore L'Elorn (or R de Landerneau) for about 6M. There is a good anchorage at Le Passage, ½M above the bridge. The port of Landerneau dries.

L'Aulne (or R de Chateaulin) is a lovely river with steep and wooded banks. Near the mouth of the estuary, on the N shore, is a good anchorage in Anse de l'Auberlach. Other anchorages near Landévennec, below Térénez bridge (27m), and also 1½M above the bridge. At Port Launay, 14M above Landévennec, there is a lock, open HW −2 to shortly after HW, leading into a basin where yachts can lie afloat.

Three small rivers run into the Aulne from the N — R Daoulas, R de l'Hôpital and R du Faou. They mostly dry, but provide sheltered berths for boats which can take the ground.

Along the S side of Rade de Brest are various naval installations, with prohibited anchorage around Ile Longue. There are however anchorages at Le Fret, on SE side of Ile Longue, and also at Roscanvel on E side of the Quelern peninsula.

In most of the bays in Rade de Brest the tidal streams are weak, but in the main rivers they can attain 2 kn or more at springs.

RADE DE BREST *continued*

FRANCE, WEST COAST - BREST

LAT 48°23'N   LONG 4°29'W

TIMES AND HEIGHTS OF HIGH AND LOW WATERS

YEAR **1991**

TIME ZONE **-0100**
(French Standard Time)
Subtract 1 hour for GMT
For French Summer Time add
ONE hour in non-shaded areas

JANUARY

Day	TIME	m	Day	TIME	m
1 TU	0500 / 1121 / 1725 / 2346	7.6 / 1.3 / 7.4 / 1.4	**16** W	0520 / 1137 / 1737 / 2354	6.9 / 1.9 / 6.7 / 2.0
2 W	0550 / 1211 / 1815	7.7 / 1.2 / 7.4	**17** TH	0554 / 1210 / 1810	7.1 / 1.8 / 6.9
3 TH	0035 / 0639 / 1259 / 1902	1.3 / 7.7 / 1.2 / 7.3	**18** F	0027 / 0627 / 1243 / 1844	1.8 / 7.1 / 1.7 / 6.9
4 F	0122 / 0725 / 1345 / 1946	1.4 / 7.5 / 1.4 / 7.1	**19** SA	0100 / 0700 / 1317 / 1916	1.8 / 7.2 / 1.7 / 6.9
5 SA	0208 / 0808 / 1430 / 2030	1.7 / 7.3 / 1.7 / 6.8	**20** SU	0134 / 0733 / 1352 / 1951	1.8 / 7.1 / 1.7 / 6.8
6 SU	0252 / 0852 / 1515 / 2114	2.0 / 6.9 / 2.1 / 6.4	**21** M	0210 / 0808 / 1429 / 2028	1.9 / 6.9 / 1.9 / 6.7
7 M	0338 / 0937 / 1603 / ☾ 2202	2.4 / 6.5 / 2.5 / 6.1	**22** TU	0249 / 0847 / 1510 / 2108	2.1 / 6.7 / 2.1 / 6.4
8 TU	0428 / 1029 / 1656 / 2300	2.7 / 6.1 / 2.9 / 5.8	**23** W	0333 / 0932 / 1550 / ☽ 2158	2.3 / 6.4 / 2.4 / 6.2
9 W	0526 / 1132 / 1759	3.0 / 5.8 / 3.1	**24** TH	0426 / 1028 / 1658 / 2304	2.6 / 6.1 / 2.7 / 6.0
10 TH	0008 / 0635 / 1244 / 1911	5.7 / 3.2 / 5.7 / 3.2	**25** F	0534 / 1142 / 1813	2.8 / 6.0 / 2.9
11 F	0122 / 0747 / 1357 / 2021	5.7 / 3.1 / 5.7 / 3.1	**26** SA	0025 / 0655 / 1309 / 1937	6.0 / 2.8 / 6.0 / 2.8
12 SA	0229 / 0851 / 1457 / 2118	5.9 / 2.9 / 5.9 / 2.9	**27** SU	0150 / 0817 / 1429 / 2054	6.2 / 2.5 / 6.3 / 2.4
13 SU	0323 / 0943 / 1546 / 2205	6.1 / 2.7 / 6.1 / 2.6	**28** M	0303 / 0927 / 1535 / 2157	6.6 / 2.1 / 6.7 / 2.0
14 M	0407 / 1025 / 1627 / 2244	6.4 / 2.4 / 6.4 / 2.4	**29** TU	0403 / 1025 / 1630 / 2250	7.1 / 1.6 / 7.1 / 1.5
15 TU	0445 / 1102 / 1703 / ● 2320	6.7 / 2.1 / 6.6 / 2.2	**30** W	0455 / 1114 / 1718 / ○ 2337	7.5 / 1.2 / 7.4 / 1.2
31 TH	0541 / 1159 / 1802	7.8 / 1.0 / 7.5			

FEBRUARY

Day	TIME	m	Day	TIME	m
1 F	0021 / 0623 / 1241 / 1843	1.1 / 7.8 / 0.9 / 7.5	**16** SA	0005 / 0605 / 1221 / 1821	1.5 / 7.4 / 1.3 / 7.2
2 SA	0101 / 0703 / 1320 / 1921	1.1 / 7.7 / 1.1 / 7.3	**17** SU	0037 / 0637 / 1253 / 1853	1.3 / 7.5 / 1.2 / 7.3
3 SU	0139 / 0739 / 1358 / 1957	1.4 / 7.4 / 1.4 / 7.0	**18** M	0110 / 0709 / 1326 / 1926	1.3 / 7.4 / 1.3 / 7.2
4 M	0216 / 0815 / 1435 / 2032	1.7 / 7.0 / 1.8 / 6.6	**19** TU	0144 / 0743 / 1402 / 2000	1.5 / 7.2 / 1.5 / 6.9
5 TU	0254 / 0852 / 1514 / 2111	2.1 / 6.6 / 2.3 / 6.2	**20** W	0221 / 0820 / 1441 / 2040	1.8 / 6.9 / 1.9 / 6.6
6 W	0334 / 0932 / 1557 / ☾ 2156	2.6 / 6.1 / 2.8 / 5.8	**21** TH	0303 / 0902 / 1528 / ☽ 2128	2.1 / 6.5 / 2.4 / 6.2
7 TH	0423 / 1024 / 1653 / 2258	3.0 / 5.6 / 3.3 / 5.5	**22** F	0356 / 0958 / 1629 / 2235	2.6 / 6.0 / 2.8 / 5.9
8 F	0529 / 1139 / 1812	3.3 / 5.3 / 3.5	**23** SA	0508 / 1118 / 1754	2.9 / 5.7 / 3.0
9 SA	0025 / 0658 / 1313 / 1943	5.4 / 3.4 / 5.3 / 3.4	**24** SU	0009 / 0643 / 1300 / 1932	5.8 / 2.9 / 5.7 / 2.9
10 SU	0156 / 0823 / 1433 / 2056	5.5 / 3.2 / 5.5 / 3.1	**25** M	0147 / 0815 / 1428 / 2053	6.0 / 2.6 / 6.1 / 2.4
11 M	0303 / 0923 / 1528 / 2147	5.9 / 2.8 / 5.9 / 2.7	**26** TU	0302 / 0924 / 1531 / 2152	6.5 / 2.1 / 6.6 / 1.9
12 TU	0350 / 1008 / 1610 / 2227	6.2 / 2.4 / 6.2 / 2.3	**27** W	0357 / 1017 / 1620 / 2239	7.0 / 1.5 / 7.0 / 1.4
13 W	0428 / 1045 / 1645 / 2301	6.6 / 2.0 / 6.6 / 2.0	**28** TH	0442 / 1101 / 1703 / ○ 2321	7.5 / 1.1 / 7.4 / 1.1
14 TH	0502 / 1118 / 1718 / ● 2334	7.0 / 1.7 / 6.9 / 1.7			
15 F	0534 / 1150 / 1749	7.2 / 1.4 / 7.1			

MARCH

Day	TIME	m	Day	TIME	m
1 F	0523 / 1140 / 1742 / 2359	7.7 / 0.9 / 7.5 / 1.0	**16** SA	0505 / 1121 / 1721 / ● 2337	7.3 / 1.2 / 7.3 / 1.2
2 SA	0600 / 1217 / 1817	7.8 / 0.9 / 7.5	**17** SU	0537 / 1153 / 1753	7.6 / 1.0 / 7.5
3 SU	0034 / 0635 / 1251 / 1852	1.0 / 7.7 / 1.1 / 7.4	**18** M	0009 / 0610 / 1226 / 1827	1.1 / 7.6 / 1.0 / 7.5
4 M	0108 / 0707 / 1325 / 1924	1.3 / 7.4 / 1.4 / 7.1	**19** TU	0043 / 0644 / 1301 / 1902	1.1 / 7.5 / 1.1 / 7.4
5 TU	0141 / 0740 / 1358 / 1956	1.6 / 7.0 / 1.8 / 6.7	**20** W	0120 / 0720 / 1339 / 1939	1.3 / 7.3 / 1.5 / 7.1
6 W	0215 / 0812 / 1432 / 2030	2.1 / 6.5 / 2.3 / 6.3	**21** TH	0200 / 0801 / 1422 / 2022	1.7 / 6.9 / 1.9 / 6.7
7 TH	0251 / 0849 / 1511 / 2109	2.5 / 6.0 / 2.8 / 5.8	**22** F	0246 / 0846 / 1513 / 2114	2.1 / 6.4 / 2.4 / 6.2
8 F	0334 / 0933 / 1601 / ☾ 2203	3.0 / 5.5 / 3.2 / 5.4	**23** SA	0344 / 0948 / 1621 / ☽ 2227	2.6 / 5.9 / 2.9 / 5.8
9 SA	0434 / 1040 / 1716 / 2328	3.4 / 5.2 / 3.5 / 5.2	**24** SU	0504 / 1116 / 1753	2.9 / 5.6 / 3.0
10 SU	0605 / 1223 / 1858	3.5 / 5.1 / 3.5	**25** M	0009 / 0643 / 1258 / 1929	5.8 / 2.8 / 5.7 / 2.8
11 M	0115 / 0744 / 1358 / 2022	5.4 / 3.3 / 5.4 / 3.2	**26** TU	0143 / 0809 / 1419 / 2042	6.1 / 2.4 / 6.1 / 2.3
12 TU	0231 / 0852 / 1458 / 2117	5.7 / 2.9 / 5.8 / 2.7	**27** W	0249 / 0910 / 1516 / 2135	6.6 / 2.0 / 6.6 / 1.8
13 W	0320 / 0938 / 1540 / 2158	6.2 / 2.4 / 6.2 / 2.3	**28** TH	0339 / 0958 / 1601 / 2219	7.0 / 1.5 / 7.0 / 1.5
14 TH	0359 / 1015 / 1616 / 2232	6.6 / 1.9 / 6.6 / 1.8	**29** F	0421 / 1038 / 1640 / 2257	7.3 / 1.2 / 7.3 / 1.2
15 F	0432 / 1048 / 1649 / 2305	7.0 / 1.5 / 7.0 / 1.5	**30** SA	0458 / 1123 / 1716 / ○ 2332	7.5 / 1.1 / 7.4 / 1.2
31 SU	0533 / 1149 / 1749	7.5 / 1.1 / 7.4			

APRIL

Day	TIME	m	Day	TIME	m
1 M	0006 / 0606 / 1222 / 1822	1.2 / 7.4 / 1.3 / 7.3	**16** TU	0543 / 1200 / 1802	7.6 / 1.1 / 7.6
2 TU	0038 / 0638 / 1254 / 1855	1.4 / 7.2 / 1.6 / 7.0	**17** W	0020 / 0622 / 1240 / 1843	1.1 / 7.5 / 1.2 / 7.4
3 W	0111 / 0710 / 1327 / 1926	1.7 / 6.8 / 1.9 / 6.7	**18** TH	0102 / 0704 / 1324 / 1926	1.3 / 7.2 / 1.6 / 7.1
4 TH	0144 / 0743 / 1401 / 2000	2.1 / 6.4 / 2.4 / 6.3	**19** F	0148 / 0750 / 1413 / 2015	1.7 / 6.8 / 2.0 / 6.7
5 F	0220 / 0818 / 1440 / 2038	2.5 / 6.0 / 2.8 / 5.9	**20** SA	0240 / 0843 / 1511 / 2114	2.1 / 6.3 / 2.4 / 6.3
6 SA	0302 / 0901 / 1528 / 2129	2.9 / 5.6 / 3.2 / 5.6	**21** SU	0345 / 0950 / 1623 / ☽ 2231	2.5 / 5.9 / 2.9 / 6.0
7 SU	0358 / 1002 / 1635 / ☾ 2244	3.2 / 5.3 / 3.4 / 5.3	**22** M	0505 / 1115 / 1748	2.7 / 5.7 / 2.8
8 M	0519 / 1133 / 1807	3.4 / 5.2 / 3.4	**23** TU	0001 / 0631 / 1243 / 1910	6.0 / 2.6 / 5.9 / 2.6
9 TU	0022 / 0652 / 1306 / 1931	5.4 / 3.2 / 5.4 / 3.1	**24** W	0121 / 0745 / 1354 / 2016	6.2 / 2.4 / 6.2 / 2.3
10 W	0141 / 0804 / 1411 / 2031	5.7 / 2.9 / 5.8 / 2.7	**25** TH	0222 / 0843 / 1448 / 2108	6.5 / 2.0 / 6.5 / 2.0
11 TH	0236 / 0855 / 1458 / 2116	6.1 / 2.4 / 6.2 / 2.2	**26** F	0311 / 0930 / 1533 / 2151	6.8 / 1.8 / 6.8 / 1.7
12 F	0318 / 0935 / 1536 / 2153	6.6 / 1.9 / 6.7 / 1.8	**27** SA	0353 / 1011 / 1612 / 2230	7.0 / 1.6 / 7.0 / 1.6
13 SA	0355 / 1011 / 1612 / 2229	7.0 / 1.5 / 7.1 / 1.4	**28** SU	0431 / 1048 / 1649 / ○ 2306	7.1 / 1.5 / 7.1 / 1.5
14 SU	0430 / 1047 / 1648 / ● 2305	7.3 / 1.2 / 7.4 / 1.1	**29** M	0506 / 1123 / 1723 / 2340	7.2 / 1.6 / 7.1 / 1.6
15 M	0506 / 1123 / 1724 / 2341	7.5 / 1.1 / 7.6 / 1.0	**30** TU	0540 / 1157 / 1757	7.0 / 1.7 / 7.0

16

Chart Datum: 4.45 metres below Lallemand System (Mean Sea Level, Marseilles)

FRANCE, WEST COAST - BREST

LAT 48°23′N   LONG 4°29′W

TIMES AND HEIGHTS OF HIGH AND LOW WATERS

YEAR **1991**

TIME ZONE −0100
(French Standard Time)
Subtract 1 hour for GMT
For French Summer Time add
ONE hour in non-shaded areas

MAY

Day	Time	m	Time	m	Time	m	Time	m
1 W	0014	1.7	0614	6.9	1230	1.9	1831	6.9
16 TH	0004	1.2	0607	7.4	1227	1.4	1831	7.4
2 TH	0047	1.9	0648	6.6	1304	2.1	1904	6.6
17 F	0052	1.4	0656	7.1	1317	1.6	1921	7.2
3 F	0122	2.2	0722	6.3	1340	2.4	1939	6.4
18 SA	0143	1.6	0747	6.8	1411	1.9	2014	6.9
4 SA	0159	2.4	0759	6.0	1420	2.7	2019	6.1
19 SU	0239	1.9	0842	6.4	1510	2.2	2112	6.5
5 SU	0242	2.7	0841	5.7	1506	3.0	2106	5.8
20 M	0342	2.2	0945	6.1	1615	2.5	2219	6.3
6 M	0334	3.0	0936	5.5	1605	3.2	2209	5.6
21 TU	0450	2.4	1056	6.0	1726	2.6	2333	6.2
7 TU	0440	3.1	1046	5.4	1717	3.2	2325	5.6
22 W	0601	2.5	1209	6.0	1835	2.6		
8 W	0555	3.0	1204	5.5	1831	3.0		
23 TH	0043	6.2	0708	2.4	1316	6.1	1938	2.4
9 TH	0039	5.8	0704	2.8	1311	5.8	1934	2.7
24 F	0145	6.3	0802	2.3	1412	6.3	2033	2.3
10 F	0140	6.1	0801	2.5	1405	6.2	2025	2.3
25 SA	0238	6.5	0858	2.2	1502	6.5	2121	2.1
11 SA	0229	6.5	0848	2.1	1451	6.6	2110	1.9
26 SU	0324	6.6	0943	2.1	1545	6.7	2204	2.0
12 SU	0313	6.9	0932	1.7	1534	7.0	2153	1.6
27 M	0406	6.7	1024	2.0	1625	6.8	2243	1.9
13 M	0355	7.2	1014	1.4	1616	7.3	2235	1.3
28 TU	0444	6.7	1102	2.0	1703	6.8	2320	1.9
14 TU	0437	7.5	1056	1.3	1659	7.5	2318	1.2
29 W	0521	6.7	1138	2.0	1739	6.8	2355	1.9
15 W	0521	7.4	1141	1.3	1744	7.5		
30 TH	0556	6.6	1213	2.1	1814	6.8		
31 F	0030	2.0	0631	6.5	1248	2.2	1849	6.7

JUNE

Day	Time	m	Time	m	Time	m	Time	m
1 SA	0106	2.1	0706	6.4	1324	2.3	1925	6.5
16 SU	0137	1.4	0740	7.0	1404	1.7	2006	7.2
2 SU	0143	2.3	0743	6.2	1403	2.5	2002	6.3
17 M	0230	1.6	0831	6.7	1457	1.9	2057	6.9
3 M	0224	2.5	0824	6.0	1446	2.7	2045	6.2
18 TU	0324	1.9	0924	6.5	1551	2.2	2152	6.6
4 TU	0309	2.6	0909	5.9	1535	2.8	2135	6.0
19 W	0419	2.2	1021	6.2	1648	2.5	2251	6.3
5 W	0402	2.7	1002	5.8	1630	2.9	2233	5.9
20 TH	0519	2.5	1123	6.0	1750	2.6	2355	6.1
6 TH	0500	2.8	1105	5.8	1732	2.8	2337	6.0
21 F	0621	2.7	1228	6.0	1853	2.7		
7 F	0603	2.7	1210	5.9	1834	2.7		
22 SA	0100	2.7	0725	2.7	1333	6.0	1956	2.7
8 SA	0040	6.0	0704	2.5	1311	6.1	1934	2.4
23 SU	0203	6.0	0825	2.7	1431	6.1	2052	2.6
9 SU	0140	6.3	0802	2.3	1408	6.4	2029	2.2
24 M	0258	6.1	0918	2.6	1523	6.3	2142	2.4
10 M	0235	6.6	0856	2.0	1501	6.8	2122	1.8
25 TU	0346	6.3	1004	2.4	1607	6.5	2225	2.3
11 TU	0327	6.9	0947	1.8	1552	7.1	2213	1.6
26 W	0428	6.4	1045	2.3	1647	6.6	2305	2.1
12 W	0418	7.1	1038	1.5	1643	7.4	2304	1.3
27 TH	0506	6.5	1123	2.2	1724	6.8	2341	2.0
13 TH	0508	7.3	1129	1.4	1734	7.5	2355	1.2
28 F	0542	6.6	1158	2.1	1759	6.8		
14 F	0559	7.3	1220	1.4	1825	7.5		
29 SA	0016	2.0	0616	6.6	1233	2.1	1834	6.8
15 SA	0046	1.2	0651	7.2	1312	1.5	1915	7.4
30 SU	0050	2.0	0651	6.6	1308	2.1	1907	6.8

JULY

Day	Time	m	Time	m	Time	m	Time	m
1 M	0125	2.0	0725	6.5	1343	2.2	1942	6.7
16 TU	0208	1.3	0808	7.0	1431	1.6	2030	7.1
2 TU	0202	2.1	0800	6.4	1421	2.3	2020	6.5
17 W	0253	1.7	0852	6.7	1516	2.0	2115	6.7
3 W	0241	2.2	0839	6.3	1502	2.4	2059	6.4
18 TH	0340	2.1	0939	6.3	1604	2.4	2204	6.3
4 TH	0324	2.4	0922	6.1	1547	2.5	2147	6.2
19 F	0430	2.6	1032	6.0	1659	2.8	2303	5.9
5 F	0413	2.5	1013	6.0	1640	2.6	2242	6.1
20 SA	0530	2.9	1137	5.7	1805	3.0		
6 SA	0509	2.6	1113	6.0	1741	2.7	2347	6.0
21 SU	0013	5.7	0641	3.1	1251	5.7	1918	3.1
7 SU	0614	2.7	1222	6.0	1848	2.6		
22 M	0129	5.6	0755	3.1	1404	5.8	2028	2.9
8 M	0057	6.1	0723	2.6	1333	6.2	1957	2.4
23 TU	0236	5.8	0858	2.9	1504	6.0	2125	2.7
9 TU	0206	6.3	0831	2.3	1439	6.6	2102	2.1
24 W	0329	6.0	0949	2.7	1552	6.3	2211	2.4
10 W	0310	6.6	0933	2.0	1539	6.9	2201	1.7
25 TH	0413	6.2	1031	2.4	1632	6.6	2249	2.2
11 TH	0408	6.9	1029	1.7	1635	7.3	2256	1.3
26 F	0451	6.5	1107	2.2	1708	6.8	2324	1.9
12 F	0501	7.2	1122	1.4	1727	7.6	2347	1.1
27 SA	0525	6.6	1141	2.0	1741	6.9	2357	1.8
13 SA	0552	7.4	1212	1.2	1816	7.7		
28 SU	0558	6.8	1214	1.8	1814	7.0		
14 SU	0036	1.0	0640	7.4	1259	1.2	1903	7.7
29 M	0030	1.7	0630	6.8	1246	1.8	1846	7.1
15 M	0123	1.1	0725	7.3	1346	1.3	1947	7.5
30 TU	0102	1.7	0702	6.8	1318	1.8	1917	7.0
31 W	0135	1.7	0733	6.8	1352	1.9	1951	6.9

AUGUST

Day	Time	m	Time	m	Time	m	Time	m
1 TH	0210	1.9	0808	6.6	1428	2.0	2027	6.7
16 F	0258	2.2	0856	6.3	1519	2.5	2117	6.2
2 F	0248	2.1	0846	6.4	1509	2.3	2107	6.4
17 SA	0343	2.7	0942	5.9	1609	2.9	2210	5.7
3 SA	0332	2.4	0931	6.2	1558	2.5	2159	6.1
18 SU	0439	3.2	1044	5.6	1715	3.3	2323	5.4
4 SU	0427	2.7	1029	6.0	1700	2.8	2306	5.9
19 M	0556	3.4	1209	5.4	1841	3.3		
5 M	0537	2.9	1146	5.9	1818	2.8		
20 TU	0055	5.4	0725	3.4	1338	5.6	2005	3.1
6 TU	0030	5.9	0700	2.8	1313	6.1	1941	2.6
21 W	0215	5.6	0838	3.1	1445	5.9	2106	2.8
7 W	0154	6.1	0820	2.5	1430	6.4	2055	2.2
22 TH	0311	5.9	0930	2.7	1533	6.2	2151	2.4
8 TH	0304	6.5	0927	1.8	1534	6.9	2156	1.7
23 F	0353	6.2	1011	2.4	1612	6.6	2228	2.1
9 F	0401	6.9	1022	1.6	1627	7.4	2248	1.2
24 SA	0429	6.5	1045	2.0	1645	6.9	2301	1.8
10 SA	0452	7.3	1111	1.2	1715	7.7	2334	0.9
25 SU	0501	6.8	1117	1.8	1717	7.1	2332	1.5
11 SU	0537	7.6	1156	1.0	1759	7.9		
26 M	0532	7.0	1148	1.6	1747	7.3		
12 M	0018	0.8	0620	7.6	1238	1.0	1841	7.8
27 TU	0003	1.4	0603	7.2	1218	1.5	1818	7.4
13 TU	0059	0.9	0701	7.5	1319	1.2	1919	7.6
28 W	0034	1.4	0634	7.2	1250	1.5	1849	7.3
14 W	0138	1.3	0738	7.2	1358	1.5	1957	7.2
29 TH	0106	1.5	0705	7.1	1322	1.6	1922	7.1
15 TH	0217	1.7	0816	6.8	1437	2.0	2035	6.7
30 F	0140	1.7	0739	6.9	1358	1.8	1957	6.9
31 SA	0218	2.0	0817	6.6	1439	2.2	2038	6.5

Chart Datum: 4.45 metres below Lallemand System (Mean Sea Level, Marseilles)

FRANCE, WEST COAST - BREST

LAT 48°23'N   LONG 4°29'W

TIMES AND HEIGHTS OF HIGH AND LOW WATERS

YEAR **1991**

TIME ZONE –0100
(French Standard Time)
Subtract 1 hour for GMT
For French Summer Time add
ONE hour in non-shaded areas

SEPTEMBER

Date	Day	Time	m	Time	m	Time	m	Time	m
1	SU (	0302	2.4	0901	6.3	1529	2.6	2130	6.1
2	M	0359	2.8	1003	5.9	1636	2.9	2244	5.8
3	TU	0518	3.0	1130	5.8	1806	3.0		
4	W	0021	5.7	0654	2.9	1309	6.0	1938	2.6
5	TH	0151	6.1	0817	2.5	1427	6.5	2051	2.1
6	F	0258	6.6	0920	2.0	1526	7.0	2146	1.6
7	SA	0350	7.1	1010	1.5	1614	7.5	2233	1.1
8	SU ●	0435	7.5	1054	1.1	1658	7.8	2314	0.9
9	M	0516	7.7	1134	0.9	1736	7.9	2353	0.8
10	TU	0554	7.7	1212	1.0	1813	7.8		
11	W	0030	1.0	0631	7.5	1248	1.2	1849	7.5
12	TH	0106	1.3	0706	7.2	1324	1.6	1924	7.1
13	F	0142	1.8	0741	6.8	1400	2.0	2000	6.6
14	SA	0219	2.3	0818	6.4	1439	2.5	2038	6.1
15	SU)	0301	2.8	0900	5.9	1526	3.0	2126	5.6
16	M	0354	3.3	0957	5.5	1629	3.4	2237	5.3
17	TU	0512	3.5	1124	5.4	1800	3.5		
18	W	0016	5.3	0649	3.5	1305	5.5	1932	3.3
19	TH	0144	5.5	0808	3.2	1416	5.8	2037	2.9
20	F	0242	5.9	0901	2.8	1504	6.2	2122	2.5
21	SA	0323	6.3	0940	2.3	1541	6.6	2158	2.1
22	SU	0358	6.7	1014	2.0	1615	7.0	2230	1.7
23	M O	0430	7.0	1046	1.6	1646	7.3	2302	1.4
24	TU	0501	7.3	1117	1.4	1717	7.5	2333	1.3
25	W	0533	7.4	1149	1.3	1749	7.6		
26	TH	0005	1.3	0605	7.5	1221	1.3	1822	7.5
27	F	0039	1.4	0639	7.4	1256	1.5	1858	7.3
28	SA	0115	1.6	0716	7.1	1335	1.8	1935	6.9
29	SU	0156	2.0	0757	6.7	1419	2.2	2021	6.5
30	M	0245	2.5	0847	6.3	1515	2.6	2118	6.0

OCTOBER

Date	Day	Time	m	Time	m	Time	m	Time	m
1	TU (	0349	2.9	0955	6.0	1630	2.9	2239	5.7
2	W	0516	3.1	1129	5.9	1804	2.9		
3	TH	0019	5.8	0650	2.9	1305	6.2	1932	2.5
4	F	0143	6.2	0807	2.4	1415	6.6	2037	2.1
5	SA	0243	6.7	0904	1.9	1508	7.1	2128	1.6
6	SU	0331	7.1	0950	1.5	1553	7.5	2211	1.3
7	M ●	0413	7.4	1031	1.2	1632	7.7	2250	1.1
8	TU	0451	7.6	1108	1.2	1710	7.7	2327	1.1
9	W	0528	7.6	1145	1.2	1745	7.6		
10	TH	0002	1.3	0603	7.5	1220	1.4	1820	7.3
11	F	0037	1.6	0638	7.2	1255	1.8	1855	7.0
12	SA	0112	2.0	0712	6.8	1330	2.2	1930	6.5
13	SU	0149	2.4	0748	6.4	1408	2.6	2007	6.1
14	M	0229	2.9	0829	6.0	1453	3.0	2053	5.7
15	TU)	0320	3.3	0921	5.7	1552	3.3	2156	5.4
16	W	0429	3.5	1038	5.5	1713	3.4	2324	5.3
17	TH	0558	3.5	1212	5.5	1841	3.3		
18	F	0052	5.5	0718	3.2	1327	5.8	1949	3.0
19	SA	0156	5.9	0816	2.8	1420	6.2	2039	2.6
20	SU	0241	6.3	0859	2.4	1501	6.6	2118	2.1
21	M	0319	6.7	0936	2.0	1537	7.0	2154	1.8
22	TU	0354	7.1	1011	1.7	1612	7.3	2228	1.5
23	W O	0429	7.4	1045	1.4	1646	7.5	2303	1.3
24	TH	0504	7.5	1121	1.3	1722	7.6	2339	1.3
25	F	0540	7.6	1158	1.3	1800	7.5		
26	SA	0018	1.4	0620	7.5	1238	1.5	1841	7.3
27	SU	0059	1.7	0702	7.2	1322	1.9	1925	6.9
28	M	0146	2.1	0749	6.9	1412	2.2	2015	6.5
29	TU	0241	2.5	0844	6.5	1513	2.5	2117	6.1
30	W (	0349	2.8	0954	6.2	1628	3.0	2237	5.9
31	TH	0510	2.9	1121	6.2	1753	2.7		

NOVEMBER

Date	Day	Time	m	Time	m	Time	m	Time	m
1	F	0004	6.0	0633	2.7	1243	6.3	1910	2.5
2	SA	0119	6.3	0742	2.6	1350	6.6	2012	2.2
3	SU	0217	6.6	0838	2.1	1443	6.9	2102	1.9
4	M	0306	7.0	0925	1.8	1528	7.2	2146	1.7
5	TU	0348	7.2	1006	1.6	1608	7.3	2226	1.6
6	W ●	0428	7.3	1045	1.6	1703	7.3	2304	1.6
7	TH	0505	7.3	1122	1.6	1723	7.2	2340	1.7
8	F	0541	7.3	1158	1.7	1759	7.1		
9	SA	0015	1.9	0616	7.1	1233	1.9	1834	6.8
10	SU	0051	2.2	0652	6.9	1309	2.2	1909	6.5
11	M	0128	2.5	0728	6.6	1347	2.5	1947	6.2
12	TU	0207	2.8	0807	6.3	1429	2.8	2030	5.9
13	W	0253	3.0	0854	6.0	1520	3.1	2121	5.7
14	TH)	0350	3.3	0952	5.8	1623	3.2	2227	5.5
15	F	0458	3.3	1106	5.7	1735	3.2	2344	5.6
16	SA	0611	3.2	1220	5.8	1845	3.0		
17	SU	0052	5.8	0715	2.9	1322	6.1	1943	2.7
18	M	0148	6.2	0808	2.6	1408	6.4	2031	2.4
19	TU	0234	6.6	0853	2.2	1456	6.8	2114	2.0
20	W	0317	6.9	0935	1.9	1538	7.1	2156	1.8
21	TH O	0358	7.3	1016	1.6	1619	7.3	2237	1.6
22	F	0440	7.5	1058	1.4	1701	7.5	2320	1.5
23	SA	0523	7.6	1142	1.3	1745	7.6		
24	SU	0005	1.5	0608	7.6	1228	1.4	1832	7.3
25	M	0052	1.6	0656	7.4	1317	1.6	1921	7.0
26	TU	0143	1.9	0746	7.1	1410	1.9	2013	6.7
27	W	0239	2.2	0841	6.8	1509	2.2	2111	6.4
28	TH (	0340	2.5	0944	6.6	1613	2.4	2217	6.2
29	F	0448	2.6	1053	6.4	1723	2.5	2330	6.2
30	SA	0558	2.7	1207	6.4	1833	2.6		

DECEMBER

Date	Day	Time	m	Time	m	Time	m	Time	m
1	SU	0041	6.2	0706	2.6	1314	6.4	1937	2.5
2	M	0144	6.4	0806	2.4	1412	6.5	2033	2.4
3	TU	0238	6.6	0859	2.3	1503	6.7	2123	2.2
4	W	0326	6.8	0945	2.1	1548	6.8	2207	2.1
5	TH	0410	6.9	1028	2.0	1630	6.9	2247	2.1
6	F ●	0449	7.0	1106	1.9	1708	6.9	2325	2.0
7	SA	0526	7.1	1143	1.9	1744	6.8		
8	SU	0001	2.1	0602	7.0	1219	2.0	1820	6.7
9	M	0036	2.2	0637	6.9	1254	2.1	1855	6.6
10	TU	0112	2.3	0712	6.8	1330	2.3	1930	6.4
11	W	0149	2.5	0748	6.5	1408	2.4	2007	6.2
12	TH	0228	2.7	0828	6.3	1450	2.6	2049	6.0
13	F	0312	2.8	0911	6.1	1537	2.8	2137	5.9
14	SA	0403	3.0	1004	6.0	1632	2.9	2234	5.8
15	SU	0502	3.0	1106	5.9	1733	3.0	2339	5.8
16	M	0605	3.0	1213	6.0	1838	2.9		
17	TU	0045	6.0	0709	2.8	1317	6.2	1939	2.7
18	W	0146	6.3	0808	2.5	1415	6.4	2036	2.4
19	TH	0242	6.6	0903	2.2	1508	6.7	2129	2.1
20	F	0334	7.0	0954	1.8	1559	7.0	2219	1.8
21	SA O	0423	7.3	1044	1.5	1648	7.3	2308	1.5
22	SU	0512	7.6	1133	1.3	1737	7.4	2357	1.4
23	M	0601	7.7	1219	1.2	1826	7.4		
24	TU	0046	1.4	0651	7.7	1311	1.2	1915	7.3
25	W	0136	1.5	0739	7.5	1401	1.4	2003	7.1
26	TH	0226	1.7	0828	7.2	1452	1.7	2053	6.8
27	F	0318	2.0	0918	6.9	1545	2.1	2146	6.5
28	SA (	0413	2.4	1014	6.5	1642	2.4	2245	6.2
29	SU	0513	2.7	1118	6.3	1746	2.7	2352	6.0
30	M	0620	2.8	1228	6.0	1855	2.9		
31	TU	0105	6.0	0730	2.9	1339	6.0	2003	2.8

Chart Datum: 4.45 metres below Lallemand System (Mean Sea Level, Marseilles)

16

LE CONQUET   10-16-11
Finistere

CHARTS
Admiralty 2694, 3345; SHOM 5159, 5287; ECM 540; Stanford 17; Imray C36

TIDES
Dover +0535; ML 4.3; Duration 0600; Zone −0100

Standard Port BREST (←)

Times				Height (metres)			
HW		LW		MHWS	MHWN	MLWN	MLWS
0000	0600	0000	0600	7.5	5.9	3.0	1.4
1200	1800	1200	1800				

Differences LE CONQUET

0000	0000	+0010	0000	−0.3	−0.3	−0.1	0.0

SHELTER
Good shelter except in strong winds from the W. Anchor inside the mole, Pierre Glissant. Yachts can go further up harbour but it dries. Six visitors buoys on N side of harbour.

NAVIGATION
Waypoint 48°21'.50N 04°48'.50W, 263°/083° from/to Mole Pierre Glissante Lt, 1.0M. Coming from the NW, beware the Grande Vinotière rocks. Also note strong cross streams in the Chenal du Four.

LIGHTS AND MARKS
Leading line — Lt on end of mole, Pierre Glissant, Oc G 4s in line with spire of Le Conquet church at 095°. Tr beacon and end of Mole St Christophe in line at 079°.

RADIO TELEPHONE
St Mathieu Sig Stn (call: *St Mathieu*) VHF Ch 16 for Chenal du Four and Chenal de la Helle (see 10.16.12).

TELEPHONE (98)
Hr Mr 98.89.00.05; Aff Mar 98.89.00.05; Meteo 98.84.60.64; CROSS 98.89.31.31; SNSM 98.89.02.07; Police 98.89.00.13; Dr 98.89.01.86; Brit Consul 99.46.26.64.

FACILITIES
Bay Slip, M, L; **Garage Tanniou** ☎ 98.89.00.29, ME, El; **Coopérative Maritime** ☎ 98.89.01.85, CH; **Plasti-Bois** ☎ 98.89.11.73 ME; **Town** P, D, FW, ME, El, V, Gaz, R, Bar. ✉; Ⓑ; ⇌ (bus to Brest); ✈ (Brest).
Ferry UK — Roscoff—Plymouth.

LAMPAUL (ILE D'OUESSANT/ USHANT)
Finistere   10-16-12

CHARTS
Admiralty 2694; SHOM 5567, 5287; ECM 540; Stanford 17; Imray C36

TIDES
Dover +0505; ML 4.4; Duration 0555; Zone −0100

Standard Port BREST (←)

Times				Height (metres)			
HW		LW		MHWS	MHWN	MLWN	MLWS
0000	0600	0000	0600	7.5	5.9	3.0	1.4
1200	1800	1200	1800				

Differences BAIE DE LAMPAUL

0000	+0005	−0005	−0005	0.0	−0.1	0.0	+0.1

ILE MOLENE

+0010	+0010	+0015	+0015	0.0	+0.1	−0.1	−0.2

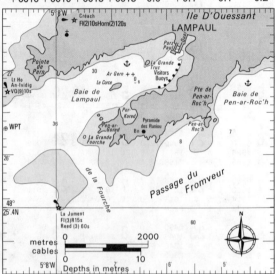

SHELTER
Lampaul Bay is open to strong SW winds and is not recommended except in settled weather. There is normally no room for visitors in the small harbour to E of piers; entrance 15 m wide.

NAVIGATION
Waypoint 48°26'.30N 05°09'.00W, 250°/070° from/to Le Corce Rk, 1.4M. Bring Le Stiff Lt Ho 055° open N of Le Corce, which may be passed on either side; Bn Trs mark Me-ar-Blanh and Kargroe Rks further inshore. Beware ferries whch use the T shaped new quay. Ferries also use the Chenal de la Fourche but this should be attempted with great caution.

LIGHTS AND MARKS
La Jument Fl (3) R 15s 36m 18M; grey 8-sided Tr, R top; obsc 199°-241°; Reed (3) 60s. An-Ividig (Nividic) VQ(9) 10s 28m 9M; W 8-sided Tr, R bands; obsc 225°-290°; helicopter platform. Creac'h Fl (2) 10s 70m 34M; W Tr, B bands; obsc 247°-255°; Horn (2) 120s; RC; Racon.

RADIO TELEPHONE
None.

TELEPHONE (98)
Hr Mr 98.89 20 05; Aff Mar 94.48.80.27; CROSS 98.89.31.31; Meteo 98.84.60.64; SNSM 98.89.70.04; Police 98.68.10.39; Dr 98.89.92.70; Brit Consul 99.46.26.64.

FACILITIES
There are few facilities in Lampaul; L, AB, FW, P and D (in cans), Slip.
Town Gaz, ✉; Ⓑ; ⇌ (ferry to Brest); ✈.
Ferry UK — Roscoff—Plymouth.

L'ABERBENOIT   10-16-13
Finistere

CHARTS
Admiralty 1432; SHOM 7094, 7150; ECM 539; Stanford 17; Imray C35

TIDES
Dover +0535; ML 4.7; Duration 0555; Zone −0100

Standard Port BREST (←)

Times				Height (metres)			
HW		LW		MHWS	MHWN	MLWN	MLWS
0000	0600	0000	0600	7.5	5.9	3.0	1.4
1200	1800	1200	1800				

Differences L'ABERBENOIT
+0020	+0020	+0035	+0035	+0.6	+0.5	+0.1	−0.2

SHELTER
Good shelter, but do not enter at night or in strong WNW winds; best near LW when dangers can be seen. River navigable to bridge at Treglonou. Anchor as shown on chartlet, where there are also six vistors buoys.

NAVIGATION
Waypoint 48°37'.10N 04°39'.00W, 332°/152° from/to La Jument de Guénioc, 1.15M. Beware Plateau de Rusven (buoyed) about 1.7M NW of Ile Garo, and other dangers to NE and SW. From 2ca (370m) W of Ile Guénioc steer to pass close W of Poul Orvil port-hand buoy, and thence to La Jument off Ile Garo.

LIGHTS AND MARKS
There are no Lts. As alternative to route above, La Jument de Garo on with Le Chien 143° avoids most dangers, but leads close to Men Renéat (rk 1m high).

RADIO TELEPHONE
None.

TELEPHONE (98)
Hr Mr none; CROSS 98.89.31.31; ⌗ 98.04.90.27; Meteo 98.84.60.64; Police (Landéda) 98.04.00.18; Dr 98.04.91.96; Brit Consul 99.46.26.64.

FACILITIES
Le Passage Slip, M, L, FW; **Treglonou** Slip; **Chantier Naval des Abers** ☎ 98.89.86.55, Sh, ME, El, M; **Town** Gaz, ✉ (Ploudalmezeau); Ⓑ (Ploudalmezeau); ⇌ (bus to Brest); ✈ (Brest). Ferry UK — Roscoff—Plymouth.

L'ABERWRAC'H   10-16-14
Finistere

CHARTS
Admiralty 1432; SHOM 964, 5772; ECM 539, 540; Stanford 17; Imray C35

TIDES
Dover +0540; ML 4.5; Duration 0600; Zone −0100

Standard Port BREST (←)

Times				Height (metres)			
HW		LW		MHWS	MHWN	MLWN	MLWS
0000	0600	0000	0600	7.5	5.9	3.0	1.4
1200	1800	1200	1800				

Differences ABERWRAC'H, FORT CÉZON
+0020	+0030	+0035	+0020	+0.5	+0.2	−0.1	−0.3

SHELTER
Good except in strong NW winds when it is better to proceed up river to Paluden where there are fore and aft moorings for visitors. At La Palue (approx 3km up river from St Antoine), pick up a buoy or secure bows to pontoon, stern lines to buoys. Max length 10 m. Vessels at these moorings may collide at slack water or when wind and tide conflict. If anchoring, beware oyster beds. Free water tax in summer.

NAVIGATION
Waypoint Grand Chenal 48°37'.40N 04°38'.40W, 280°/100° from/to front Ldg Lt 100°, 2.6M. W cardinal Lt buoy (Whis), 2.6M WxN from Ile Vrac'h, marks Le Libenter shoal. Also beware Basse Trousquennou to S. There are two channels to inner Ldg line 128° (1) From W and best for strangers. Grand Chenal running S of Libenter, Grand Pot de Beurre and Petit Pot de Beurre. (2) From N, Chenal de la Malouine, only by day and in good weather. Transit Petit Pot de Beurre on Pain Sucre (Ile de Croix). Great precision is required.

LIGHTS AND MARKS
For the Grand Chenal the first pair of Ldg Lts at 100° are Ile Vrac'h (QR) and Lanvaon (QW, 1.63M to the rear). Then Dir Lt 128° takes one to the jetty at La Palue. There are no lights further up river but there is a jetty at Paluden (to the E, off chartlet).

RADIO TELEPHONE
VHF Ch 09 16 (0700-2100 LT).

TELEPHONE (98)
Hr Mr 98.04.91.62; Aff Mar 98.04.90.13; CROSS 98.89.31.31; SNSM 98.04.91.54; ⌗ 98.04.90.27; Meteo 98.84.60.64; Police 98.04.00.18; Ⓗ 98.46.11.33; Dr 98.04.91.87; Brit Consul 99.46.26.64.

FACILITIES
Pontoons (80, some visitors) ☎ 98.04.91.62, M, AC, D, BH (12 ton), C (13 ton), FW, ME, El, CH, AB; **Y.C. des Abers** ☎ 98.04.92.60, Bar; **Tech' Marine** ☎ 98.04.99.36 ME, El, Sh, CH; **Slipway** Slip, M, D, L, FW, ME, El, Sh, C (3 ton mobile), CH, AB, V, R, Bar; **Town** P, V, Gaz, R, Ⓞ, P, Bar. ✉; Ⓑ (Lannilis); ⇌ (bus to Brest); ✈ (Brest). Ferry UK — Roscoff—Plymouth.

ROSCOFF   10-16-15
Finistere

CHARTS
Admiralty 2745; SHOM 5828, 5827; ECM 538; Stanford 17; Imray C35

TIDES
Dover −0605; ML 5.2; Duration 0600; Zone −0100

Standard Port BREST (←)

Times				Height (metres)			
HW		LW		MHWS	MHWN	MLWN	MLWS
0000	0600	0000	0600	7.5	5.9	3.0	1.4
1200	1800	1200	1800				

Differences ROSCOFF
+0055	+0105	+0115	+0050	+1.4	+1.1	+0.5	−0.1

ILE DE BATZ
+0045	+0100	+0105	+0050	+1.4	+1.1	+0.5	0.0

16

ROSCOFF *continued*

SHELTER
Good shelter in Roscoff (dries) except with strong winds from N and E. Berth on inner side of jetty in Yacht Harbour or secure to visitors buoy in SW corner. Access HW∓2. A sill is under construction (1988) to maintain deep water in the harbour. Entry to ferry harbour at Bloscon is forbidden without Capitaine du Port's permission. Yachts moor or anchor to the S and well clear of ferry jetty.

NAVIGATION
Waypoint 48°46′.00N 03°55′.80W, 033°/213° from/to Men Guen Bras Lt, 2.6M. The entrance to Roscoff is difficult due to the numerous large rocks in the area. Yachsmen are advised to enter near high tide. The channels are well marked and must be kept to. Bloscon is easier to approach.

LIGHTS AND MARKS
Ile de Batz Lt Ho (conspic) Fl(4) 25s 69m 23M. Off Roscoff are Ar Chaden Q(6) + LFIWR 15s, S cardinal mark, and Men-Guen-Bras Q WRG, N cardinal mark. Ldg Lts 210°. Front on NW mole Oc(2 + 1)G 12s. Rear Oc(2 + 1) 12s. Bloscon jetty head FlWG 4s; W sector 206°-216° shows correct approach.

RADIO TELEPHONE
VHF Ch 09 16 (0700-1100, 1300-2200 l T).

TELEPHONE (98)
Hr Mr (Roscoff) 98.69.76.37; Hr Mr (Bloscon) 98.61.27.84; Harbour Office (Port de Plaisance) 98.69.76.37; Aff Mar 98.69.70.15; CROSS 98.89.31.31; SNSM 98.69.74.08; ⌗ (Roscoff) 98.69.19.67; ⌗ (Bloscon) 98.61.27.86; Meteo 98.84.60.64; Auto 98.88.34.04; Police 98.69.00.48; Ⓗ 98.88.40.22; Dr 98.69.71.18; Brit Consul 99.46.26.64.

FACILITIES
Vieux Port (220 + 30 visitors) ☎ 98.69.76.37, FW, AC, ME, BY; **Quai Neuf** Reserved for fishing vessels, C (5 ton); **Harbour** M; **Centre Nautique de Roscoff** ☎ 98.69.72.79; **Club Nautique de Roscoff** ☎ 98.69.72.79, Bar; **Chantier Naval Le Coz** ☎ 98.69.13.83 ME, El, Sh, CH; **Le Got** ☎ 98.69.71.86, BY. **Town** P, D, ME, El, Sh, CH, Gaz, V, R, Bar. ✉; Ⓑ; ⇌; ✈ (Morlaix).
Ferry UK — Plymouth.

MORLAIX   10-16-16
Finistere

CHARTS
Admiralty 2745; SHOM 5827, 966, 970, 5950; ECM 538; Stanford 17; Imray C34, C35

TIDES
Dover −0610; ML 5.2; Duration 0610; Zone −0100

Standard Port BREST (←)

Times				Height (metres)			
HW		LW		MHWS	MHWN	MLWN	MLWS
0000	0600	0000	0600	7.5	5.9	3.0	1.4
1200	1800	1200	1800				

Differences MORLAIX (CHÂTEAU DU TAUREAU)
+0100 +0115 +0115 +0050 +1.5   +1.1   +0.5   −0.1

MORLAIX *continued*

SHELTER
Good shelter in the bay and in Dourduff although the latter dries. Yachts can proceed up to Morlaix town and enter the lock into the Bassin à Flot where there is a marina and shelter is complete. Lock opens HW−1½ to HW+1 during daytime. Waiting moorings at 'Pen a Lann'.

NAVIGATION
Waypoint Grand Chenal 48°43'.00N 03°53'.50W, 356°/176° from/to Ile Louet Lt, 2.5M. Morlaix Bay is divided by the Ile de Callot on E side of which lies Morlaix River. There are three entrances and all have rocky dangers
(1) Grand Chenal E of Ricard Is (shallower but lit 176°).
(2) Chenal Ouest, W of Ricard Is. Big ship channel, not lit.
(3) Chenal de Treguier (190° and best at night).

LIGHTS AND MARKS
Grand Chenal Lts in line 176° (Ile Louet and La Lande). Treguier Chenal Lts in line 190° (Ile Noire and La Lande). River up to Morlaix town is well buoyed, a distance of 3¾ M.

⏶ Inside lock gates at Morlaix

RADIO TELEPHONE
VHF Ch 09 16.

TELEPHONE (98)
Hr Mr 98.62.13.14; Lock 98.88.54.92; Aff Mar 98.62.10.47; CROSS 98.89.31.31; SNSM 98.88.00.76; ⌗ 98.88.06.31; Auto 98.88.34.04; Police 98.88.58.13; Ⓗ 98.88.40.22; Brit Consul 99.46.26.64.

FACILITIES
Marina (100+60 visitors) ☎ 98.62.13.14, AC, FW, C (8 ton), (Access HW−1½ to HW+1); **Rio L** ☎ 98.88.13.54, Sh, ME, El; **Trégor Marine** ☎ 98.88.24.68, El, CH; **YC de Morlaix** ☎ 98.62.08.51, Slip, M, P, D, L, FW, ME, El, Sh, CH, AB; **Loisirs Nautique** ☎ 98.88.27.30, ME, CH, El; **Cap Mer** ☎ 98.88.25.85, CH, Ⓔ; **Jegou Ritz** ☎ 98.88.04.15, SHOM; **Société Morlaisienne de la Mer** ☎ 98.62.19.21, CH, ME; **Town** P, D, V, Gaz, R, Bar. ✉; Ⓑ; ⇌; ✈.
Ferry UK — Roscoff—Plymouth.

LANNION RIVER   10-16-17
Côtes du Nord

CHARTS
Admiralty 3669, 2668; SHOM 5950, 6056, 967; ECM 538; Stanford 17; Imray C34

TIDES
Dover −0605; ML 5.3; Duration −; Zone −0100

Standard Port BREST (←)

Times				Height (metres)			
HW		LW		MHWS	MHWN	MLWN	MLWS
0000	0600	0000	0600	7.5	5.9	3.0	1.4
1200	1800	1200	1800				

Differences TRÉBEURDEN
+0105	+0110	+0120	+0100	+1.6	+1.3	+0.5	−0.1

SHELTER
Good shelter except in strong winds from NW to W. Anchor in estuary or in river by Guiodel. There are drying berths at Lannion.

NAVIGATION
Waypoint 48°46'.65N 03°42'.20W, 302°/122° from/to front Locquemeau Ldg Lt 122°, 6M. There are non-drying pools off Le Yaudet and Le Beguen. Beware sandbank N and NE of Pt de Dourvin, running about 2 ca (370m), which dries. Pass up the channel near to the Trs; this is impossible at very low water especially with strong NW winds which cause sea to break on the bar.

LIGHTS AND MARKS
The large radome 3.5 M NNE of entrance is conspic landmark. Lt on Pt Beg-Léguer Oc (4) WRG 60m 13/10M; vis W084°-098°, R098°-129°, G007°-084°. Channel to Lannion is narrow and marked by towers and beacons.

RADIO TELEPHONE
None.

TELEPHONE (96)
Hr Mr 96.37.06.52; Aff Mar 96.37.06.52; CROSS 98.89.31.31; SNSM 96.23.52.07; ⌗ 96.37.45.32; Police 96.37.03.78; Dr 96.37.42.52; Brit Consul 99.46.26.64.

FACILITIES
Quai de Loguivy Slip, L, FW, C (1 ton mobile), AB; **Coopérative Maritime** ☎ 96.37.03.18, CH; **Lesbleiz** ☎ 96.48.35.01, M, ME, El, Sh, SHOM, Ⓔ, CH; **Town** M, CH, V, Gaz, R, Bar. ✉; Ⓑ; ⇌; ✈ (Morlaix, Lannion). Ferry UK — Roscoff—Plymouth.

16

PERROS-GUIREC 10-16-18
(PLOUMANAC'H)
Côtes du Nord

CHARTS
Admiralty 3672, 3670, 2668; SHOM 974, 967; ECM 537, 538; Stanford 17; Imray C34

TIDES
Dover −0550; ML 5.1; Duration 0605; Zone −0100

Standard Port ST MALO (⟶)

Times				Height (metres)			
HW		LW		MHWS	MHWN	MLWN	MLWS
0100	0800	0200	0700	12.2	9.2	4.4	1.5
1300	2000	1400	1900				

Differences PERROS-GUIREC
−0034 −0044 −0130 −0050 −2.8   −1.9   −0.9   −0.2
PLOUMANAC'H
−0034 −0039 −0130 −0050 −3.2   −2.1   −1.0   −0.4

SHELTER
Anchorage with good shelter but exposed to NE winds. Shelter in the marina is very good. Access HW∓1. Shelter is good in Ploumanac'h and sill is 4.75M lower than in Perros-Guirec; channel is well marked. Entrance and exit difficult in strong NW winds.

NAVIGATION
Waypoint 48°52'.40N 03°20'.00W, 045°/225° from/to front Ldg Lt 225° (Le Colombier), 6.4M. Beware Ile Tomé in the entrance to Anse de Perros. Rocks extend 7 ca (1300m) off the W side and 6 ca (1110m) E of the N side. Gate into marina opens at HW, day and night, for 1 to 4 hours according to the height of tide. May be closed for 3 days at nps. The sill is 7m above CD. Sill is marked at high water by R and W poles. No anchoring allowed in non-tidal harbour.

LIGHTS AND MARKS
From E of Ile Tomé, Ldg Lts 225° — Front Le Colombier Oc (4) 12s 28m 18M, intens 220°-230°. Rear Kerprigent (1.5M from front) Q 79m 20M, intens 221°-228°. Passe de l'Ouest. Kerjean Dir Lt 144° Oc (2+1) WRG 12s 78m 15/13M vis G134°-143°, W143°-144°, R144°-154°.

RADIO TELEPHONE
VHF Ch 09 16.

TELEPHONE (96)
Hr Mr 96.23.37.82; Gate 96.23.19.03; Aff Mar 96.23.13.78; CROSS 98.89.31.31; SNSM 96.23.20.16; ⌗ 96.23.18.12; Auto 96.20.01.92; Police 96.23.20.17; Dr 96.23.20.01; Brit Consul 99.46.26.64.

FACILITIES
Marina (550+50 visitors) ☎ 96.23.19.03, P, D, FW, ME, AC, El, Sh, C (7 ton), CH, V, R, SM, Gas, Gaz, Kos, Ⓞ, Bar; **Le Locat Marine** ☎ 96.23.05.08, ME, El, Ⓔ, Sh, CH; **Ponant Loisirs** ☎ 96.23.18.38, ME, El, Ⓔ, Sh, CH, SHOM; **Ship Marine** ☎ 96.91.11.88, D, P, CH, ME, El, Ⓔ Sh; **PMP Marine** ☎ 96.91.16.07 ME, El, Ⓔ, Sh, CH;

Town P, FW, CH, V, Gaz, R, Bar. ✉; Ⓑ; ⇌ (Lannion); ✈ (Morlaix/Lannion).
Booking for pontoons and moorings — at Town Hall ☎ 96.23.22.64;
PLOUMANAC'H (230+20 visitors) Sill 2.25m above CD — min depth 1.5m. **Quai Bellevue** FW, AC, Slip. **Société des Régates de Perros Guirec.**
Ferry UK — Roscoff—Plymouth.

TRÉGUIER 10-16-19
Côtes du Nord

CHARTS
Admiralty 3672, 3670, 2668; SHOM 973, 972, 967; ECM 537, 538; Stanford 17; Imray C34

TIDES
Dover −0540; ML 5.5; Duration 0600; Zone −0100

Standard Port ST MALO (⟶)

Times				Height (metres)			
HW		LW		MHWS	MHWN	MLWN	MLWS
0100	0800	0200	0700	12.2	9.2	4.4	1.5
1300	2000	1400	1900				

Differences TRÉGUIER
−0038 −0032 −0130 −0035 −2.4   −1.7   −1.1   −0.4

SHELTER
Good shelter can be found from most winds; SW of La Corne Lt Tr, exposed to NE to NW; off Roche Jaune village; up in Tréguier by the quay; by Palamos.

NAVIGATION
Waypoint 48°55'.00N 03°12'.80W, 317°/137° from/to front Ldg Lt 137°, 5M.
There are three entrance channels:
(1) Grande Passe. Well marked, but strong tidal streams across the channel.
(2) Passe de la Gaine. Navigable with care by day in good visibility.
(3) Passe du Nord-Est. Dangerous with winds from W and NW as sea breaks across the channel.
Speed limit 6kns above La Roche Jaune.

TRÉGUIER *continued*

LIGHTS AND MARKS

Important marks are Men Noblance Bn Tr (BW) on SE corner of Ile d'Er, Skeiviec Bn Tr (W), and La Corne Lt Tr (WR) Fl(3) WRG 12s. Leading marks:
(1) For Grande Passe. Port de la Chaine and St Antoine Lts at 137°.
(2) For Passe de la Gaine. Men Noblance and Plougrescant wall Bn at 242°.
(3) For approach to La Corne. Tréguier cathedral spire and Skeiviec (from SW of La Jument) at 207°.

RADIO TELEPHONE
Tréguier Marina Ch 09.

TELEPHONE (96)
Hr Mr 96.92.42.37; Aff Mar 96.92.30.38; CROSS 96.54.11.11; ✠ 96.92.31.44; Auto 96.20.01.92; Police 96.92.30.33; Dr 96.92.32.14; Ⓗ 96.92.30.72; Brit Consul 99.46.26.64.

FACILITIES
EC Sunday; **Marina** (200 + 130 visitors), ☎ 96.92.42.37, Slip, FW, ME, C (8 ton), CH, AC, Bar, Gaz; **Station Service** ☎ 96.92.30.52, P and D (cans); **Jetties** M, L, FW, ME, El, Sh, CH, AB; **Marina Sports** ☎ 96.92.47.60, M, ME, Sh, CH; **Co-Per Marine** ☎ 96.92.35.72, M. CH; **Club Nautique du Tregor** ☎ 96.92.42.37, excellent facilities, open all year.
Town P, FW, CH, V, Gaz, R, Bar. ✉; Ⓑ; ⇌ (bus to Paimpol); ✈ (St Brieuc).
Ferry UK — Roscoff—Plymouth.

LÉZARDRIEUX   10-16-20
Côtes du Nord

CHARTS
Admiralty 3673, 3670, 2668; SHOM 2845, 832; ECM 537; Stanford 17, 16; Imray C34

TIDES
Dover −0510; ML 5.6; Duration 0610; Zone −0100

Standard Port ST MALO (→)

Times				Height (metres)			
HW		LW		MHWS	MHWN	MLWN	MLWS
0100	0800	0200	0700	12.2	9.2	4.4	1.5
1300	2000	1400	1900				

Differences LÉZARDRIEUX

−0008	−0006	−0050	−0015	−2.0	−1.6	−0.9	−0.5

SHELTER
Very good in all weathers. Harbour and marina can be entered at all tides day or night. Multi-hulls and boats over 12.5 m are not welcome at pontoons, so should moor on visitors buoys in front of marina. Yachts can proceed up river to Pontrieux, about 12 km beyond Lézardrieux, and go into the basin.

NAVIGATION
Waypoint 48°55'.00N 02°56'.20W, 045°/225° from/to front Ldg Lt 225° (La Croix), 6.7M. Outlying dangers are Barnouic Rks and Roches Douvres. There are four entrance channels, Moisie channel, Men du Castric channel (very dangerous at LW), Grand Chenal which is recommended for strangers and the Ferlas Channel from the E. Bridge clearance 18m (above MHWS).

LIGHTS AND MARKS
(1) Moisie channel — Amer du Rosédo W pyramid in line with St Michael's chapel at 160°.
(2) Men du Castric channel — Vieille du Tréou Tr (difficult to see) in line with Arcouest Tr at 174°.
(3) Grand Chenal Lts in line at 225°.
    Front — La Croix Oc 4s 15m 19M; two Trs joined, W on NE side with R tops. Intens 215°-235°.
    Rear — Bodic (2.1 M from front) Q 55m 21M (intens 221°-229°).
(4) Ferlas channel.
    W sector of Joliguet Lt Ho
    W sector of Loguivy
    W sector of Ile à Bois lead to Coatmer line
(5) Coatmer Ldg Lts 219°. Front F RG 16m 9/8M; vis R200°-250°, G250°-053°. Rear, 660m from front, FR 50m 9M.

RADIO TELEPHONE
VHF Ch 09 (0800-2000 July Aug: 0800-1200 and 1400-1800 rest of year LT).

TELEPHONE (96)
Hr Mr 96.20.14.22; Aff Mar at Paimpol 96.20.84.30; CROSS 98.89.31.31; ✠ at Paimpol 96.20.81.87; Auto 96.20.01.92; Police 96.20.10.17; Dr 96.20.10.30; Brit Consul 99.46.26.64.

FACILITIES
EC Sunday; **Marina** (404 + 120 visitors), ☎ 96.20.14.22, Slip, P, D, FW, ME, El, C (6 ton), CH, AC, Bar, Gaz, R, SM, Sh; **Ruffloc'h** ☎ 96.22.13.16, ME, El, CH, Ⓔ; **Trieux Marine** ☎ 96.20.14.71, ME, CH, Sh, Divers; **YC de Trieux** ☎ 96.20.10.39.
Town P, D, V, Gaz, R, Bar. ✉; Ⓑ; ⇌ (bus to Paimpol); ✈ (Lannion/St Brieuc).
Ferry UK — Roscoff—Plymouth.

ILE DE BRÉHAT   10-16-21
Côtes du Nord

CHARTS
Admiralty 2668, 3673; SHOM 832, 2845; ECM 537; Stanford 16; Imray C34

TIDES
Dover −0525; ML 5.8; Duration 0605; Zone −0100

Standard Port ST MALO (→)

Times				Height (metres)			
HW		LW		MHWS	MHWN	MLWN	MLWS
0100	0800	0200	0700	12.2	9.2	4.4	1.5
1300	2000	1400	1900				

Differences ILE DE BRÉHAT

−0014	−0004	−0055	−0035	−1.7	−1.2	−0.7	−0.3

ILE DE BRÉHAT *continued*

SHELTER
Good shelter in Port Clos although harbour dries. Also good shelter in Port de la Corderie at neaps when it is possible to anchor out of the strong tides, and in the Chambre de Bréhat in the SE, each depending on the direction of the wind. There are no alongside berths.

NAVIGATION
Waypoint Ferlas channel 48°49'.45N 02°55'.00W, 098°/278° from/to La Croix Lt, 5.5M. See also 10.16.20. On approach, beware the Barnouic and Roches Douvres (12 and 17 M NNE) and La Horaine, Men March and Ringue Bras closer in. La Chambre and Port Clos best approached from seaward in Ferlas channel (see 10.16.20). There is a prohibited anchorage SW of Port Clos, between Brehat and the mainland.

LIGHTS AND MARKS
There are three principal lights on Ile de Bréhat:
(1) In the N, Phare du Paon F WRG 22m 12/8M; Y Tr; vis W033°-078°, G078°-181°, W181°-196°, R196°-307°, W307°-316°, R316°-348°.
(2) In NW part, Rosédo Fl 5s 29m 20M; W Tr and G gallery; RC.
(3) In the S, on E side of Port Clos entrance, Men-Joliguet Iso WRG 4s 6m 13/8M; Y Tr with B band; vis R255°-279°, W279°-283°, G283°-175°.

RADIO TELEPHONE
None.

TELEPHONE (96)
Hr Mr none; CROSS 98.89.31.31; SNSM 96.20.00.14; Auto 96.20.01.92; ⌗ 96.20.81.87; Police 96.20.80.17; Dr 96.20.00.99; Brit Consul 99.46.26.64.

FACILITIES
Club Nautique de Bréhat ☎ 96.20.00.69, M, FW, Bar; **Mervel** ☎ 96.20.01.39, ME; **Harbours** Slip, M, FW; **Village** V, Gaz, Bar. ⊠; Ⓑ (Paimpol); ⇌ (ferry to Pointe de l'Arcouest, bus to Paimpol); ✈ (St Brieuc). Ferry UK — Roscoff—Plymouth.

PAIMPOL   10-16-22
Côtes du Nord

CHARTS
Admiralty 2668, 3673; SHOM 3670, 832; ECM 537; Stanford 16; Imray C34

TIDES
Dover −0525; ML 5.5; Duration 0600; Zone −0100

Standard Port ST MALO (→)

Times				Height (metres)			
HW		LW		MHWS	MHWN	MLWN	MLWS
0100	0800	0200	0700	12.2	9.2	4.4	1.5
1300	2000	1400	1900				

Differences PAIMPOL
−0009	−0006	−0040	−0010	−1.7	−1.4	−1.2	−0.9

SHELTER
There is good shelter in Paimpol from all winds but the whole Anse de Paimpol dries. Lock opens HW−1½ to HW springs, HW−1 to HW neaps, (when sufficient rise of tide, 8m). Visitors' berths at Pontoon A, as available.

NAVIGATION
Waypoint 48°47'.40N 02°51'.50W, 090°/270° from/to Pte de Porz-Don Lt, 6.6M. There are rocks which dry very close to the leading lines. The Anse de Paimpol is divided by rocks (El Paimpol and El Bras) down the centre. If intending to anchor in Port de Texier, keep to the N of rocks on entering.

LIGHTS AND MARKS
Leading marks — Paimpol church tower and the top of Pt Brividic 260°. Second leading line, lights on Jetée de Kernoa and Paimpol front (both FR) 264°. Pointe de Porz-Don Lt Oc (2) WR 6s 13m 15/11M; vis W269°-272°, R272°-279°

RADIO TELEPHONE
VHF Ch 09 (0800-1200 LT and lock opening hours HW∓2).

TELEPHONE (96)
Hr Mr 96.20.47.67; Port de Plaisance 96.20.47.65; Aff Mar 96.20.84.30; CROSS 98.89.31.31; ⌗ 96.20.81.87; Meteo 96.20.01.92; Police 96.20.80.17; Ⓗ 96.20.86.02; Dr 96.20.80.04; Brit Consul 99.46.26.64.

FACILITIES
Bassin No 2 (marina 260+10 visitors), FW, AB, D, P, ME, El, C (6 ton, 3 ton); **Quai de Kernoa** P, ME; **Quai neuf** Slip, M, FW, AB; **Dauphin** ☎ 96.20.81.38, Sh, CH, SHOM; **Despretz** ☎ 96.20.82.00, M, ME, Sh, CH; **Le Lionnaise Marine** ☎ 96.20.85.18, ME, El, Sh, CH; **MEE** ☎ 96.20.74.47, Ⓔ; **Town** P, D, CH, V, Gaz, R, Bar. ⊠; Ⓑ; ⇌; ✈ (St Brieuc). Ferry UK — Roscoff—Plymouth.

MINOR HARBOURS AND ANCHORAGES 10.16.23

L'ABERILDUT, Finistere, 48°28' N, 4°45' W, Zone −0100, Admty charts 3345, 2694; SHOM 5721. HW +0520 on Dover (GMT), +0007 on Brest (zone −0100). From N beware Les Liniou Rks 2M S of Le Four Lt (Fl(5)15s). Good shelter but exposed to W winds and harbour partly dries. Beware strong cross tides in approach. For Chenal du Four see 10.16.5. Aberildut Lt Dir Oc(2) WR 6s, vis W081°-085°, R085°-087°. Ldg marks Brélès spire and Lanildut spire at 079° lead into fairway between rks which dry, marked by Bn Trs. Facilities: several slips, village shop; **Cariou** ☎ 98.04.30.44, ME. **Hélies Marine** ☎ 98.04.39.16 Sh, ME, El, CH, M.

ARGENTON, Finistere, 48°31' N, 4°46' W, Zone −0100, Admty chart 2694, SHOM 5772, 5287. HW +0535 on Dover (GMT), +0020 on Brest (zone −0100); HW height +0.5m on Brest; ML 4.6m; Duration 0600. Small drying Hr giving good shelter except in W winds when a swell comes up the bay into the Hr. Access HW∓3. Approach is well marked. Beware strong E−W tides. Anchorage in deep water off Hr ent. 10 visitors moorings. There are no lights. Facilities: FW, P on quay; **SC** ☎ 98.89.54.04; **Town** Bar, R, V.

PORTSALL, Finistere, 48°33' N, 4°42' W, Zone −0100, Admty charts 1432, 20, SHOM 5772, 5287. HW +0535 on Dover (GMT), +0020 on Brest (zone −0100); HW height +0.5m on Brest; ML 4.6m; Duration 0600. Small drying harbour at head of bay. Access HW∓3. Good shelter except in strong N winds. Entrance to bay marked by two Bn Trs. Beware numerous rocks lying off-shore for about 2M. Anchor to W of ent. or go alongside quay in Hr. Facilities: **Aff.Mar.** ☎ 98.80.62.25; **SNSM** ☎ 98.48.65.92; **Dr** ☎ 98.48.10.46. **Quay** C (0.5 ton), D, FW, P, Slip; **Club Nautique** (CNPK) ☎ 98.48.63.10. **Coopérative de Pêcheurs** ☎ 98.48.63.26, CH; **Town** Bar, ✉, R, V.

PONTUSVAL, Finistere, 48°40' N, 4°19' W, Zone −0100, Admty chart 2643, SHOM 966. HW +0605 on Dover (GMT), +0055 on Brest (zone −0100); HW height +0.7m on Brest; ML 4.7m Duration 0600. Entrance between An Neudenn Bn Tr to E and three white topped rks to W. Hr, port of Brignogan-Plage, is open to N winds and is often full of fishing boats. Ldg line into Hr, Bn on shore in line with church steeple at 178°. Entry at night forbidden. Facilities: Bar, FW, R, V.

ILE DE BATZ, Finistere, 48°44' N, 4°00' W, Zone −0100, Admty chart 2745; SHOM 5828. HW +0610 Dover (GMT), +0055 on Brest (zone −0100); HW height +1.3m on Brest. For Canal de l'Ile de Batz see 10.16.15. Porz-Kernoc'h gives good shelter but dries. E slip is reserved for ferries. Anchor in E or W parts of the channel depending on wind, but holding ground poor. Anchorage prohibited in area W of Roscoff landing slip. Ile de Batz Lt Fl(4) 25s. Facilities: there are a few shops.

CARANTEC, Finistere, 48°40' N, 3°55' W, Zone −0100, Admty chart 2745, SHOM 5827. HW +0610 on Dover (GMT), +0105 on Brest (zone −0100); HW height +1.2m on Brest; ML 5.0m; Duration 0605. Approach as for Morlaix, (10.16.16) but pass W of Ile Callot. La Penzé Rivière is narrow and tortuous. Yachts can dry out in shelter off Penpoul on the W shore. The anchorage off Carentec is exposed, especially to NW; landing stage dries about 4.6m. Further S the river is not marked but shelter is better SW of Pte de Lingos, or off the old ferry slipways which provide landing places. Beyond the bridge (15m) the river is navigable on the tide for 3M to Penzé. No lights. Facilities: **Aff.Mar.** ☎ 98.67.03.80; **Centre Nautique Carantec-Henvic** ☎ 98.67.01.12; **Elies** ☎ 98.67.03.61. El, ME, Sh, M; **Marine Service** ☎ 98.67.00.04; Ⓔ, CH; **Comptoirs Maritime** ☎ 98.67.01.85, CH, P, D; **Lebras** ☎ 98.67.04.50, ME, El, Sh; **Town** Ⓑ, Bar, ✉, R, V.

PRIMEL, Finistere, 48°42' N, 3°50' W, Zone −0100, Admty chart 3670, 3699, SHOM 5827, 5950. HW −0610 on Dover (GMT), +0100 on Brest (zone −0100); HW height +0.9m on Brest; ML 4.8m; Duration 0600. Good deep anchorage well protected; seas break across ent in strong winds. Beware rks off Pte de Primel to E of ent. and Le Zamegues to W. Ldg Lts 152°, front FR 35m 6M; vis 134°−168°, rear, 202m from front, FR 56m 6M; both

have framework Tr with W square with R vert stripe. Jetty head Lt Fl G 4s 6m 7M. Anchor in channel in 2 to 9m or go alongside quay (1m). VHF Ch 09 16 (summer). Facilities: Bar, C (12 ton), FW, R. Slip, V; **Rolland Marine** ☎ 98.72.32.76. CH, El, ME, Sh, Ⓔ.

LOCQUEMEAU, Côtes du Nord, 48°43' N, 3°34' W, Zone −0100, Admty charts 2644, 2668, SHOM 5950. HW −0600 on Dover (GMT), +0110 on Brest (zone −0100); HW height +1.5m on Brest; ML 5.3m. A small drying Hr by ent. to Lannion River. (10.16.17). There are two quays, the outer being accessible at LW, but this quay is open to W winds. Yachts can dry out at inner quay, on S side. Ldg Lts 122°, leading to outer quay, Front FR 21m 6M; vis 068°−228°. Rear 484m from front, Oc (2+1) R 12s 39m 7M. Facilities: **Ateliers Mecaniques de Lannion** ☎ 96.48.72.32 ME, El, Sh; **Town** Bar.

TREBEURDEN, Côtes du Nord, 48°46' N, 03°35' W; Zone −0100; Admty charts 2668, 2644; SHOM 5950, 6056. HW −0605 on Dover (GMT), +0105 on Brest (zone −0100); ML 5.3m; Duration 0605. A good safe deep water anchorage in settled weather. Very exposed to winds from W to NW. Visitors buoys available. Approach from a position 1.5M S of Basse Blanche W cardinal buoy, marking the W end of Le Crapaud (a reef which dries 3.9m). From here make good a course of 065° towards the N end of Ile Milliau, to pass S of Ar Goureudeg S cardinal Lt Buoy VQ(6) + LFl 10s. When past Ar Goureudeg buoy, alter to E and SE, so as to anchor NE of Ile Milliau. There are no lights in the port. Facilities: Harbour Office ☎ 96.23.66.93; SNSM 96.23.53.82, ⌗ ☎ 96.92.31.44; **Harbour** (340+10 visitors), FW, AC, M; **YC de Trébeurden** ☎ 96.37.00.40 (open July-Aug); **Chantier Naval du Trégor** ☎ 96.23.52.09, BY, ME, El, Sh, CH.

TRÉGASTEL, Côtes du Nord, 48°50' N, 3°31' W, Zone −0100, Admty charts 2644, 2668, SHOM 5950, 967. HW −0550 on Dover (GMT), +0005 on Brest (zone −0100); HW height −1.8m on Brest; ML 5.1m; Duration 0605. See 10.16.18. (Ploumanac'h). Good anchorage in 2m but very exposed to winds from W to N. Entrance channel marked by port and stbd Bns. Ldg line at 149°, Pavillon in line with Chapelle St Anne leads between Ile Dhu and Le Taureau. Thence keep between Bns round to S of Ile Ronde to the anchorage. Facilities: Slip; **Club Nautique de Tregastel** ☎ 96.23.45.05; **Neptune Tregastel Marine** ☎ 96.23.46.13 CH. **Town** Bar, Bank, ✉, R, V.

LES SEPT ILES, Côtes du Nord, 48° 52'.8N, 3°29' .5W. Zone −0100. Admty charts 3669, 3670; SHOM 967. HW −0550 on Dover (GMT), +0005 on Brest (zone−0100). HW height −1.8m on Brest. ML 5.2m. All seven islands are a bird sanctuary. Main anchorage between Île aux Moines and Ile Bono. Landing on latter is prohibited. Anchor due E of jetty; below the Old Fort or close to S side of Ile Bono. Lighthouse on Île aux Moines, Grey Tr, FL (3) W 15s 59m 24M, obsc 237°−241° and in Baie de Lannion when bearing less than 039°. There are no facilities.

PORT BLANC, Côtes du Nord, 48°50' N, 3°19' W, Zone −0100, Admty charts 3672, 2668, SHOM 974, 967. HW −0545 on Dover (GMT), +0007 on St Helier (zone −0100); HW height −1.3m on St Helier; ML 5.3m; Duration 0600. Good natural Hr but exposed to winds between NW and NNE. Ldg marks in line at 150°, Moulin de la Comtesse and Le Voleur Lt; Le Voleur Dir Lt 150°, Fl WRG 4s 17m 14/11M, G140°−148°, W148°−152°, R152°−168°. Yachts can anchor off or dry out alongside quays (known as Port Bago). Facilities: AB, FW on quay, Slip; **Gelgon Nautisme** ☎ 96.92.67.00. CH, El, ME, Sh; **Town** Bar, R, V.

PONTRIEUX, Côtes du Nord, 48°41' N, 3°08' W, Zone −0100, Admty chart 3673, SHOM 2845. Pontrieux is above the lock; for tides below the lock see 10.16.20 Lezardrieux. Complete shelter above lock. Pass under Lezardrieux suspension bridge (18m clearance) and proceed the 7M up river, not well marked. Access up river from mid-tide; lock opens HW−2 to HW+1. VHF Call *L'ecluse de Pontrieux* Ch 12 16. Yachts can go alongside quay in approx 4m. Facilities: Hr Mr ☎ 96.95.64.66, VHF Ch 12 16. **Quay** FW, C (6 ton), AC; **Club Nautique** Bar, R; **Town** Bar, FW, R, Slip, V, Gaz, P, D, Ⓑ, ✉.

16

VOLVO PENTA SERVICE

Sales and service centres in area 17

CHANNEL ISLANDS **Chicks Marine Ltd,** Collings Road, St. Peter Port,
GUERNSEY Tel (0481) 23716/24536. **DK Collins Ltd,** South Pier, St. Helier,
JERSEY, C.I. Tel (0534) 32415.
FRANCE For details of local service dealers in France contact **Volvo Penta France SA,** Chemin de la Nouvelle, F78130 Les Mureaux Tel (01) 3 474 72 01,
Telex 695221 F.

VOLVO PENTA

Area 17

Channel Islands and adjacent coast of France
Portrieux to Cherbourg

17

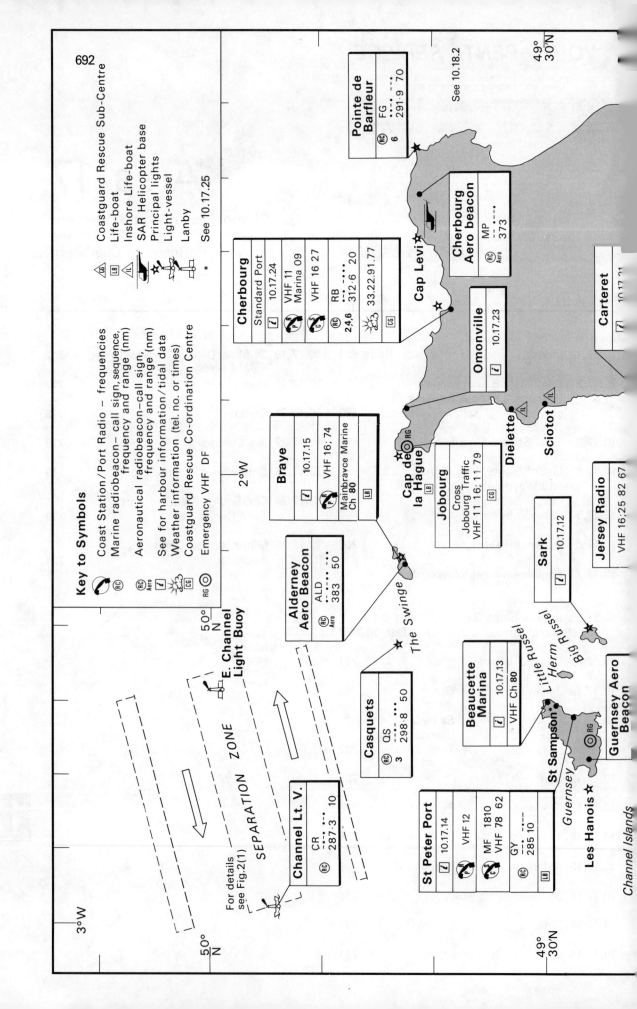

Key to Symbols

Coast Station/Port Radio – frequencies
Marine radiobeacon– call sign, sequence, frequency and range (nm)
Aeronautical radiobeacon–call sign, frequency and range (nm)
See for harbour information/tidal data
Weather information (tel. no. or times)
Coastguard Rescue Co-ordination Centre
Emergency VHF DF

Coastguard Rescue Sub-Centre
Life-boat
Inshore Life-boat
SAR Helicopter base
Principal lights
Light-vessel
Lanby

*   See 10.17.25

3°W

50°N

E. Channel Light Buoy

SEPARATION ZONE

For details see Fig.2(1)

Channel Lt. V.
RC	CR
	287·3 10
LB	

Casquets
RC	QS
	3 298·8 50

The Swinge

Alderney Aero Beacon
RC Aero	ALD
	383 50

Braye
i	10.17.15
P R	VHF 16; 74
	Mainbravce Marine Ch 80
LB	

2°W

Cherbourg
	Standard Port
i	10.17.24
P R	VHF 11 Marina 09
S C	VHF 16 27
RC	RB 24,6 312·6 20
	33.22.91.77
CG	

Pointe de Barfleur
RC	FG
6	291·9 70

See 10.18.2

49°30N

Cap Levi

Cherbourg Aero beacon
RC Aero	MP
	373

Omonville
| i | 10.17.23 |

Carteret
| i | 10.17.21 |

Cap de la Hague

Jobourg
	Cross Jobourg Traffic
	VHF 11 16; 11 79
CG	

Dielette

Sciotot

Sark
| i | 10.17.12 |

Jersey Radio
VHF 16; 25 82 67

St Sampson*

Guernsey

Les Hanois ☆

Beaucette Marina
i	10.17.13
	VHF Ch 80

Little Russel
Herm
Big Russel

Guernsey Aero Beacon

St Peter Port
i	10.17.14
P R	VHF 12
S C	MF 1810 VHF 78 62
RC	GY 285 10
LB	

Channel Islands

49°30N

50°N

693

10·17·2

Channel Islands and adjacent coast of France

10.17.3 AREA 17 TIDAL STREAMS

Notes:
1. Due to very strong tidal stream rates, eddies may occur. Where possible some indication of these has been shown, but in many areas there is either insufficient information or the eddies are unstable.
2. For details of tidal streams round Alderney , see NP 264 part 2.

5 Hours before HW Dover (HW St. Helier)

4 Hours before HW Dover (0100 after HW St. Helier)

3 Hours before HW Dover (0200 after HW St. Helier)

2 Hours before HW Dover (0300 after HW St. Helier)

1 Hour before HW Dover (0400 after HW St. Helier)

HW Dover (0500 after HW St. Helier)

Westward 10.16.3   Eastward 10.18.3   Northward 10.2.3   Isle of Wight 10.2.8   Portland 10.2.13

1 Hour after HW Dover (0600 after HW St. Helier)

2 Hours after HW Dover (0530 before HW St. Helier)

3 Hours after HW Dover (0430 before HW St. Helier)

4 Hours after HW Dover (0330 before HW St. Helier)

5 Hours after HW Dover (0230 before HW St. Helier)

6 Hours after HW Dover (0130 before HW St. Helier)

10.17.4   LIGHTS, FOG SIGNALS AND WAYPOINTS

Abbreviations used below are given in 10.0.3. Principal lights are in **bold** print, places in CAPITALS, and light-vessels , light floats and Lanbys in *CAPITAL ITALICS*. Unless otherwise stated lights are white. m—elevation in metres;
M—nominal range in n. miles. Fog signals are in *italics*. Useful waypoints are underlined use those on land with care. See 4.2.2.

FRANCE—NORTH COAST

PORTRIEUX.
Île Harbour, Roches de Saint-Quay 48°40'.05N 02°48'º42W Oc(2) WRG 6s 16m W11M, R8M, G8M; W square Tr and dwelling, R top; vis R011°-080°, W080°-133°, G133°-270°, R270°-306°, G306°-358°, W358°-011°.
Portrieux jetty 48°38'.7N 02°49'.4W Iso WG 4s 11m W12M, G7M; W 8-sided Tr, G top; vis G(unintens) 020°-110°, G110°-305°, W305°-309°, G309°-020°.
New mole, head Fl R 4s 9m 7M; W mast, R top.

BINIC
Mole head Oc(3) 12s 12m 12M; W Tr, G gallery; unintens 020°-110°.

Pointe à l'Aigle 48°32'.2N 02°43'.1W QG 13m 8M; W Tr, G top; vis 160°-070°.
Le Rohein 48°38'.9N 02°37'.8W VQ(9) WRG 10s 13m W10M, R8M, G8M; West cardinal mark; vis R072°-105°, W105°-180°, G180°-193°, W193°-237°, G237°-282°, W282°-301°, G301°-330°, W330°-072°.

PORT DE DAHOUET.
La Petite-Muette 48°34'.9N 02°34'.3W Fl WRG 4s 10m W9M, R6M, G6M; G and W Tr; vis G055°-114°, W114°-146°, R146°-196°.

ERQUY.
Mole, S end, head 48°38'.13N 02°28'.60W Oc(21) WRG 12s 11m W11M, R9M, G9M; W Tr, R top; vis R055°-081°, W081°-094°, G094°-111°, W111°-120°, R120°-134°.
Inner jetty, head Fl R 2·5s 10m 3M; R and W Tr.

Cap Fréhel 48°41'.10N 02°19'.07W Fl(2) 10s 85m **28M**; grey square Tr; *Horn (2) 60s*; RC.

St Cast, mole head 48°38'.47N 02°14'.50W Iso WG 4s 11m W11M, G8M; G and W structure; vis W204°-217°, G217°-233°, W233°-245°, G245°-204°.

ST MALO.
Fairway Lt Buoy 48°41'.42N 02°07'.21W LFl 10s; safe water mark; *Whis*.
Les Courtis 48°40'.5N 02°05'.8W Fl(3) G 12s 14m 9M; G Tr.
Brunel Lt Buoy 48°40'.88N 02°05'.26W Q(9) 15s; W cardinal mark; *Bell*.
Chenal de la Grand Porte, No. 2 Lt Buoy 48°47'.27N 02°07'.48W Fl(3) R 12s; port-hand pillar buoy; *Whis*.
No. 1 Lt Buoy 48°40'.24N 02°05'.97W Fl G4s; stbd-hand pillar buoy; *Whis*.
Ldg Lts 089°. Front **Le Grand Jardin** 48°40'.27N 02°04'.90W Fl(2) R 10s 24m **15M**; grey Tr; in line with La Ballue, below, leads through channel of Petite Port; obsc by Cap Fréhel when brg less than 097°, by Île de Cézembre 220°-233°, by Grande Conchée 241°-243°, and by Grande Chevruen and

Note. For English Channel Waypoints see 10.1.7

Pte du Meinga when brg more than 251°; RC. Rear **Rochebonne** 4·2M from front 48°40'.3N 01°58'.7W FR 40m **24M**; square Tr, R top; intens 088°-090°.

Ldg Lts 129°. Front **Les Bas-Sablons** 48°38'.2N 02°01'.2W FG 20m **16M**; W square Tr, B top; intens 127°-130°. Rear **La Ballue**, 0·9M from front FG 69m **25M**; grey square Tr; intens 128°-130°.
Le Buron 48°39'.38N 02°03'.60W Fl(2)G 6s 15m 9M; G Tr.
Môle des Noires, head 48°38'.58N 02°01'.85W Fl R 5s 11m 13M; W Tr, R top; obsc 155°-159°, 171°-178°, and when brg more than 192°; *Horn(2) 20s*.
Ecluse du Naye Ldg Lts 071°. Front 48°38'.6N 02°01'.5W FR 6m 3M; on arm over lock gate. Rear 580m from front FR 23m 8M; vis 030°-120°. F Vi Lts in line 071° marks S limits of dredged channel.
Bas-Sablons marina, mole head Fl G 4s 7m 5M; grey mast.
Dinard mole 48°38'.2N 02°02'.8W Oc G 4s 6m 6M; W column, G top; vis 195°-015°.

Embouchure du Fremur. Dir Lt 125° 48°37'.1N 02°08'.2W Dir Iso WRG 4s 20m W14M, R11M, G11M; vis G121°-124°, W124°-126°, R126°-129°.
La Rance, La Jument Fl (5) G 20s.
Tidal barrage NW wall Fl G 4s 5M.
NE dolphin Fl(2) R 6s 5M, SE.
La Plate 48°40'.83N 02°01'.83W VQ WRG 11m W9M, R6M, G6M; N cardinal mark; vis W140°-203°, R203°-210°, W210°-225°, G225°-140°.

La Houle-sous-Cancale, jetty 48°40'.1N 01°51'.1W Oc(3) G 12s 12m 8M; W framework Tr, G top; obsc when brg less than 223°.
La Pierre-de-Herpin 48°43'.83N 01°48'.83W Oc(2) 6s 20m **17M**; W Tr, B top and base; *Siren Mo (N) 60s*.

GRANVILLE.
Hérel, marina 48°49'.9N 01°35'.9W Fl R 4s 12m 7M; W Tr, R top; *Horn (2) 40s*.
Le Loup 48°49'.63N 01°36'.17W Fl(2) 6s 8m 11M; isolated danger mark.
Jetée Est, head Iso G 4s 11m 6M; W framework Tr, G top.
Jetée Ouest, head Iso R 4s 12m 6M; R framework Tr.
Tourelle Fourchie *Horn (4) 60s*.
Pointe du Roc 48°50'.11N 01°36'.70W Fl(4) 15s 49m **23M**; grey Tr, R top.

ILES CHAUSEY.
Le Pignon 48°53'.5N 01°43'.4 W Oc(2) WR 6s 10m W11M, R8M; B Tr, Y band; vis R005°-150°, W150°-005°.
La Crabière Est 48°52'.5N 01°49'.4W Oc WRG 4s 5m W10M, R7M, G7M; B Tr, Y top; vis W079°-291°, G291°-329°, W329°-335°, R335°-079°.
Grande Ile 48 52'.2N 01°49'.3W Fl 5s 39m **23M**; grey square Tr; *Horn 30s*.

PLATEAU DES MINQUIERS.
SE Minquiers Lt Buoy 48°53'.50N 02°00'.00W Q(3) 10s; E cardinal mark; *Bell*
S Minquiers Lt Buoy 48°53'.13N 02°10'.13W Q(6)LFl 15s; S cardinal mark.
SW Minquiers Lt Buoy 48°54'.40N 02°19'.30W Q(9) 15s; W cardinal mark; *Whis*.
NW Minquiers Lt Buoy 48°59'.70N 02°20'.50W Q; N cardinal mark; *Bell*.

N Minquiers Lt Buoy 49°01'·70N 02°00'·50W Q; N cardinal mark.
NE Minquiers Lt Buoy 49°00'·91N 01°55'·20W VQ(3) 5s; E cardinal mark; *Bell.*

REGNÉVILLE,
Pte d'Agon 49°00'·2N 01°34'·6W Oc(2) WR 6s 12m W10M, R7M; W Tr, R top, W dwelling; vis R063°-110°, W110°-063°. Dir Lt 49°00'·7N 01°33'·3W Dir Oc WRG 4s 9m W9M, R7M, G7M; W structure; vis G026°-029°, W029°-031°, R031°-035°.

Le Sénéquet 49°05'·5N 01°39'·7W Fl(3) WR 12s 18m W13M, R10M; W Tr; vis R083°-116°, W116°-083°.

PORTBAIL.
Ldg Lts 042°. Front La Caillourie Q 14m 11M; W pylon, R top. Rear 870m from front Q 20m 9M; belfry.
Training wall, head Q(2)R 5s 5m 2M; W mast, R top.

CARTERET.
Jetée Ouest, head 49°22'·2N 01°47'·4W Oc R 4s 6m 8M; W column, R top. Training wall head Fl(2) G 5s; W mast, G top.
Trois-Grunes Lt Buoy 49°21'·85N 01°54'·76W Q(9) 15s; W cardinal mark.

Cap de Carteret 49°22'·46N 01°48'·35W Fl(21) 15s 81m **26M**; grey Tr, G top; *Horn (3) 60s.*

DIÉLETTE.
Ldg Lts 125°. Front, Jetée Ouest Oc WRG 4s 12m W8M, R6M, G6M; W Tr, G top; vis G shore-072°, W072°-138°, R138°-206°, G206°-shore. Rear 460m from front FR 23m 11M; intens 121°-130°.

CHANNEL ISLANDS

JERSEY.
Ldg Lts 082°. Front La Gréve d'Azette 49°10'·21N 02°05'·00W Oc 5s 23m 14M; vis 034°-129°. Rear, Mont Ubé 1M from front Al WR 6s 46m W14M, R12M; vis 250°-095°; Racon.
Demie de Pas 49°09'·07N 02°06'·05W Mo(D) WR 12s 11m W14M, R10M; B Tr, Y top; vis R130°-303°, W303°-130°; Racon; *Horn (3) 60s.*

ST HELIER.
Small Roads Ldg Lts 023°. Front, Albert Pier Oc G 5s 8m 11M; W bracket and lantern on sea wall. Rear, esplanade 576m from front Oc R 5s 20m 12M; W framework Tr; synchronised with front.
Platte Rock 49°10'·22N 02°07'·27W Fl R 1·5s 6m 5M; R framework Tr. Ldg Lts 078°. Front FG. Rear, 90m from front, FG; both W columns.
Victoria Pier head *Bell*; in reply to vessels' fog signals; traffic signals.

Canger Rock Lt Buoy 49°07'·41N 02°00'·30W Q(9) 15s; W cardinal mark.
Violet Lt Buoy 49°07'·87N 01°57'·05W LFl 10s; safe water mark.

GOREY.
Ldg Lts 298°. Front, pier head 49°11'·9N 02°01'·3W Oc RG 5s 8m 12M; W framework Tr; vis R304°-352°, G352°-304°. Rear 490m from front Oc R 5s 24m 8M.
Verclut breakwater 49°13'·39N 02°00'·57W Fl 1·5s 18m 13M; framework Tr.

Bonne Nuit Bay Ldg Lts 223°. Front, Pierhead FG 7m 6M. Rear, 170m from front FG 34m 6M.
Rozel Bay Dir Lt 245° Dir FWRG 11m 5M; vis G240°-244°, W244°-246°, R246°-250°.
Sorel Point 49°15'·64N 02°09'·45W L Fl WR 7·5s 50m **15M**; B and W chequered Tr; vis W095°-112°, R112°-173°, W173°-230°, R230°-269°, W269°-273°.
Grosnez Point 49°15'·55N 02°14'·75W Fl(2) WR 15s 50m **W19M, R17M**; W concrete hut; vis W081°-188°, R188°-241°.
La Corbière 49°10'·85N 02°14'·90W Iso WR 10s 36m **W18M, R16M**; Round stone Tr; vis W shore-294°, R294°-328°, W328°-148°, R148°-shore; RC; *Horn Mo (C) 60s.*
Noirmont Point Fl(4) 12s 18m 13M; B Tr, W band.
Saint Aubin Harbour, N pierhead Iso R 4s 12m 10M; and Dir Lt 252° F WRG, vis G246°-251°, W251°-253°, R253°-258°. Fort, pierhead Fl(2) Y 5s 8m 1M.

SARK.
Point Robert 49°26'·25N 02°20'·67W Fl 15s 65m **18M**; W 8-sided Tr; vis 138°-353°; *Horn (2) 60s.*
Blanchard Lt Buoy 49°25'·42N 02°17'·35W Q(3) 10s; E cardinal mark; *Bell.*

Courbée du Nez 49°27'·15N 02°22'·08W Fl(4)WR 15s 14m 8M; vis W057°-230°, R230°-057°.
Big Russel, Noire Pute 49°28'·27N 02°24'·93W Fl(2) WR 15s 8m 6M; vis W220°-040°, R040°-220°. Destroyed (T).

HERM.
Fourquies Lt Buoy 49°27'·34N 02°26'·47W Q; N cardinal mark.
Lower Heads Lt Buoy 49°25'·91N 02°28'·48W Q(6)LFl 15s; S cardinal mark; *Bell* .
Alligando 49°27'·9N 02°28'·8W Fl(3) G 5s; Orange A on black mast; shown 1/4-1/11; Ra refl.
Épec Beacon 49°28'·0N 02°27'·9W Fl G 3s; Black E on G mast; shown 1/4-1/11.
Vermerette Beacon 49°28'·3N 02°27'·8W Fl(2) Y 5s; Orange V on Bn; shown 1/4-1/11.
Percée Pass, Gate Rock 49°27'·9N 02°27'·4W Q(9)15s; West cardinal Bn.

GUERNSEY.
St Peter Port Ldg Lts 220°. **Front**, Castle breakwater Al WR 10s 14m **16M**; dark round Tr, W on NE side; vis 187°-007°; RC; *Horn 15s.* Rear Belvedere Oc 10s 61m 14M; W square with Y stripe on W Tr; vis 179°-269°.
White Rock Pier, head 49°27'·43N 02°31'·60W Oc G 5s 11m 14M; round stone Tr; intens 174°-354°.
South pier head Oc R 5s 10m 14M; W framework Tr, R lantern.
North Beach Marina. Dir Lt Oc WRG 10s 5m 6M; vis G264°-268°, W268°-272°, R272°-276°.

St Sampson.
Crocq Pier FR 11m 5M; R column; vis 250°-340°.
N pier head FG 3m 5M; vis 230°-340°.
Ldg Lts 286°. Front S pier head 49°28'·9N 02°30'·8W FR 3m 5M; vis 230°-340°. Rear, 390m from front FG 13m; clock Tr. 2 FR (vert) on chimneys 300m N.
Brehon 49°28'·3N 02°29'·2W Iso 4s 19m 9M; Bn.
Platte 49°29'·1N 02°29'·5W Fl WR 3s 6m W7M, R5M; G Tr; vis R024°-219°, W219°-024°.
Roustel, S end, 49°29'·28N 02°28'·71W Q 8m 7M; B and W chequered Tr, G lantern.
Tautenay 49°30'·2N 02°26'·7W Q(3) WR 6s 7m W7M, R6M; B and W Bn; vis W050°-215°, R215°-050°.

17

Beaucette Marina.
Ldg Lts 276°. Front FR; W board with R stripe. Rear 185m from front FR; R board with W stripe.
Petite Canupe Lt Qk Fl (6) + LFl 15s; S cardinal mark.

Platte Fougère 49°30'·88N 02°29'·05W LFl WR 10s 15m **16M**; W 8-sided Tr, B band; vis W155°-085°, R085°-155°; Racon; *Horn 45s.*

Les Hanois 49°26'·2N 02°42'·1W Q(2) 5s 33m **23M**; grey round Tr, B lantern, helicopter platform; vis 294°-237°; 4 FR on masts 1·27M ESE; *Horn (2) 60s.*

St Martin's Point 49°25'·37N 02°31'·61W Fl(3) WR 10s 15m 14M; flat-roofed, W building; vis R185°-191°, W191°-011°, R011°-081°. *Horn (3) 30s.*

ALDERNEY.
Alderney (Quenard Pt.)) 49°43'·81N 02°09'·77W Fl(4) 15s 37m **18M**; W round Tr, B band; vis 085°-027°; *Siren (4) 60s.* Braye Harbour Ldg Lts 215°. **Front**, elbow of old pier Q 8m **17M**; vis 210°-220°. **Rear** 335m from front Iso 10s 17m **18M**; vis 210°-220°. Both metal posts on W columns.
Chateau a l'Etoc Point 49°44'·00N 02°10'·55W Iso WR 4s 20m W10M, R7M; W column; vis R071°-111°, W111°-151°; in line 111° with main Lt.

Casquets 49°43'·38N 02°22'·55W Fl(5) 30s 37m **28M**; W Tr, the highest and NW of three; RC; Racon; *Dia (2) 60s.*

CHANNEL LT V 49°54'·42N 02°53'·67W Fl 15s 12m **25M**; R hull with Lt Tr amidships; RC; Racon; *Horn(1) 20s.*
E. CHANNEL LT BUOY 49°58'·67N 02°28'·87W Fl Y 5s; X on Y HFP Buoy; Racon; *Horn (2) 30s.*
Lt Buoy EC 1 50°05'·90N 01°48'·35W FlY 2·5s; X on Y HFP buoy; Racon; *Whis.*
Lt Buoy EC 2 50°12'·10N 01°12'·40W Fl(4)Y 15s; X on Y HFP buoy; Racon; *Whis.*
Lt Buoy EC 3 50°18'·30N 00°36'·10W FlY 5s; X on Y HFP buoy; Racon; *Whis.*

FRANCE—NORTH COAST

Cap de la Hague (Gros du Raz) 49°43'·37N 01 57'·19W Fl 5s 48m **23M**; grey Tr, W top; FR Lts on chimney and radio mast 3·8M and 4·5M SE; *Horn 30s.*
La Foraine 49°42'·70N 01°58'·78W; W cardinal pillar buoy; Whis; (occasionally submerged).
La Plate 49°44'·03N 01°55'·64W Fl(21) WR 12s 11m W9M, R6M; 8-sided Tr, Y with B top; vis W115°-272°, R272°-115°.
Basse Bréfort Lt Buoy 49°43'·70N 01°51'·05W VQ 8m 8M; N cardinal mark; *Whis.*
Omonville, La Rogue 49°42'·3N 01°50'·2W Iso WRG 4s 13m W11M, R8M, G8M; W framework Tr, R top; vis G180°-252°, W252°-262°, R262°-287°.

CHERBOURG.
CH1 Lt Buoy 49°43'·30N 01°42'·10W L Fl 10s; safe water mark; *Whis.*
Digue de Querqueville, head Oc(3) WG 12s 8m W11M, G8M; W column, G top; vis W120°-290°, G290°-120°.
Passe de l'Ouest Ldg Lts 140° and 142°. Front, Jetée du Homet 2 Q(hor) 5m **15M**; W triangles on parapet at root of jetty; 63m apart; intens 138°-144°. Rear, **Gare Maritime** 0·98M from front DirQ 23m **21M**; grey framework with triangle point down on building; intens 140°-142·5°.
Fort de l'Ouest 49°40'·50N 01°38'·87W Fl(3) WR 15s 19m

W24M, **R20M**; grey Tr, R top, on fort; vis W122°-355°, R355°-122°; RC; *Reed (3) 60s.*
Fort Central VQ (6) LFl 10s 5m 8M; column; vis 322°-032°.
Fort de l'Est 49°40'·33N 01°35'·93W Iso WG 4s 19m W13M, G10M; W framework Tr, G top; vis W008°-229°, G229°-008°.
Passe Est, Forte d'Île Pelée Oc (2) WR 6s 19m W11M, R8M; W and R pedestal on fort; vis W055°-120°, R120°-055°.
Passe Cabart-Danneville, South side Fl(2) R 6s 5m 6M.
Fort des Flamands 49°39'·1N 01°35'·6W Dir Q WRG 13m W12M, R11M, G11M; vis G173°-176°, W176°-183°, R183°-193°.

LE BECQUET.
Ldg Lts 186°30'. **Front** Oc(21) 12s 8m **16M**; W 8-sided Tr; intens 183°-190°. Rear 50m from front Oc (2+1) R 12s 13m 11M; W 8-sided Tr, R top; synchronised with front, intens 183°-190°.

Port de Lévi 49°41'·3N 01°28'·3W F WRG 7m W11M, R8M, G8M; vis G050°-109°, R109°-140°, W140°-184°.
Cap Lévi 49°41'·80N 01°28'·30W Fl R 5s 36m **22M**; grey square Tr, W top.
La Pierre Noire Lt Buoy 49°43'·57N 01°28'·98W Q(9) 15s 8m 9M; W cardinal mark.
Basse du Renier Lt Buoy 49°44'·90N 01°22'·00W VQ 8m 8M; N cardinal mark; *Whis.*

10.17.5 PASSAGE INFORMATION

Sailing directions for this popular cruising area are listed in Chapter 15 (15.5) of the *The Macmillan & Silk Cut Yachtsman's Handbook*. Particular features are a rugged shoreline, but with sandy bays, numerous offlying rks, strong tidal streams, and a big range of tide. It is important to have large scale charts, and to use recognised leading marks (of which there are plenty) when entering or leaving many of the harbs and anchs. Neap tides are best, particularly for a first visit, and tidal streams need to be worked carefully. Boats which can take the ground have an advantage for exploring the quieter harbs. Be careful to avoid lobster pots, and oyster beds in some rivers. For French terms see 10.16.5.

ST BRIEUC TO ST MALO (chart 2669)

To seaward of B de St Brieuc is Grand Léjon (Lt), a rky shoal 10½M E of Pte de Minard. Rks extend 2½ ca W and 8 ca NNE of the Lt Ho. Petit Léjon (dries) lies 3½M SSE of Lt Ho. B de St Brieuc is encumbered by two rky shoals: on the W side, Roches de St Quay and offlying patches extend 4M E from Portrieux (10.17.16), and on the E side the Plateau du Rohein, at W end of long ridge, is 6M W of C d'Erquy. Between these two shoals is a chan 3M wide leading to the harbs of Binic (10.17.17), Le Légué (10.17.18), Port de Dahouet and Erquy (10.17.25). On the E side of the b, Chenal d'Erquy runs in a WSW/ENE direction about 3 ca off C d'Erquy and inshore of the various rky patches close to seaward. There are several rky shoals within the b itself, some extending nearly 2M from shore. Erquy is a pleasant, drying harb, but often crowded with fishing boats.

From C d'Erquy to C Fréhel and St Malo (10.17.19) there are no worthwhile harbs, but there are anchs in B de la Fresnaie and in B de l'Arguenon. Beware Le Vieux-Banc (dries) 6M ENE of C Fréhel. Here the E-going stream begins at HW St Helier −0555, and the W-going at HW St Helier −0015, sp rates 2½ kn. There are W-going eddies very close inshore on the E-going stream.

In the approaches to St Malo (chart 2700) are many islets, rks and shoals, between which are several chans that can be used in good vis. Tidal streams reach 4 kn at sp, and can set across chans. Chenal de la Grande Porte and Chenal de la Petite Porte are the easiest routes and are well marked. With sufficient rise of tide, and good vis, Chenal du Décollé, Chenal de la Petite Conchée, Chenal de la Grande Conchée, Chenal des Petis Pointus or Chenal de la Bigne can be used, but they all pass over or near to drying patches.

By passing through the lock at W end of the Rance barrage it is possible to cruise up river to Dinan, via the lock at Châtelier (French chart 4233). Beware very rapid changes in level caused by the hydro-electric scheme, explained in pamphlet available at lock, or from harb office St Malo. At Dinan is entrance to Canal d'Ille et Rance (see 10.15.8).

ST MALO TO ALDERNEY RACE

4M E of St Malo is the large drying harb of Rothéneuf (10.17.25 and chart 2700), with anch off in good weather. Proceeding E, beware many dangers off Pte du Grouin, 3M S of which is the drying harb of Cancale, with many oyster beds. There is anch SE of Île des Rimains in good weather. To E of Cancale is the drying expanse of B du Mont St Michel. See 10.17.25.

The W coast of the Cherbourg peninsula is exposed to the W, and is mostly rky and inhospitable. Granville (10.17.20) is the only harb where a yacht can lie afloat. The two main chans to/from the Alderney Race are Passage de la Déroute and Déroute de Terre. The former passes W of Îles Chausey, SE and E of Les Minquiers and Les Ardentes, between Chaussée de Boeufs and Plateau de l'Arconie, between Basses de Taillepied and Les Écrehou, and W of Plateau des Trois Grunes. Parts of this chan are not well marked, and it is advisable not to use it at night.

Déroute de Terre leads between Pte du Roc (off Granville) and Îles Chausey, between Le Sénéquet Lt Tr and Les Boeufs, between Basses de Portbail and Bancs Félés, and E of Plateau des Trois Grunes. For detailed directions see *Channel Pilot*. The S end of this chan, E of Îles Chausey, is very shallow, and along much of this coast as far N as Carteret there is little depth of water, so that a nasty sea can build up. There are drying harbs at Portbail, Carteret (10.17.21) and at Dielette, 11M S of C de la Hague. In approaches to Alderney Race (see below) beware Les Huquets de Jobourg, an extensive bank of drying and submerged rks 5M S of C de la Hague, and Les Huquets de Vauville (dry) close SE of them.

CHANNEL ISLANDS − GENERAL (10.17.9 and chart 2669)

For detailed instructions, refer to sailing directions. In the following paragraphs brief mention is made only of some of the most important navigational features.

Approaching the islands from N, note the traffic scheme off the Casquets − see Fig. 2(1); soundings of Hurd Deep can help navigation. Coming from the W, Guernsey slopes down from S to N, and Jersey from N to S. Individually and collectively the islands are fringed by many rky dangers: there is considerable range of tide (most in Jersey, and least in Alderney), and the streams run very hard through the chans and around headlands; strong W winds cause a heavy sea, usually worst from local HW −0300 to local HW +0300. In bad vis it is prudent to stay in harb.

Tidal streams are rotatory anti-clockwise, particularly in open water and in wider chans. The E-going (flood) stream is of less duration than the W-going, but is stronger. The islands lie across the main direction of the streams, so eddies are common along the shores.

Apart from the main harbs described in 10.17.10 − 10.17.15, there are many delightful anchs in offshore winds. For St Aubin and St Sampson see 10.17.25.

ALDERNEY AND THE CASQUETS (chart 60)

Casquets Lt Ho (Lt, fog sig, RC) is on the largest islet of this group of rocks 5½M W of Alderney (10.17.15). Off-lying dangers extend 4 ca W and WSW (The Ledge and Noire Roque) and 4 ca E (Pte Colotte). The tide runs very hard round and between these various obstructions. A shallow bank, on which are situated Fourquie and l'Equet rks (dry), lies from ½M to 1M E of Casquets, and should not be approached.

3½M E of Casquets is Ortac rk (24m). Ortac Chan runs N/S ½M W of Ortac: here the stream begins to run NE at HW St Helier −0230, and SW at HW St Helier +0355, with sp rates 7 kn. Ortac Chan should not be used in bad weather, when there are very heavy overfalls in this area.

In the approaches to Casquets, overfalls may also be met over Eight-fathom Ledge (8½ ca W of Casquets), Casquets SW bank, Casquets SSW bank, and Casquets SSE bank.

The Swinge (chart 60) lies between Burhou and its bordering rks, and the NW coast of Alderney. It can be a dangerous chan, and should only be used in reasonable vis and in fair weather. The tide runs very hard, and in strong or gale force winds from S or W there are very heavy overfalls on the SW-going stream between Ortac and Les Etacs (off W end of Alderney). In strong E winds, on the NE-going stream, overfalls occur between Burhou and Braye breakwater. These overfalls can mostly be avoided by choosing the best time and route (see below), but due to the uneven bottom and strong tides broken water may be met even in calm conditions.

The NE-going stream begins at HW St Helier −0245, and the SW stream at HW St Helier +0340, sp rates 7 or 8 kn. On the NE-going stream, beware the very strong northerly component of the set in vicinity of Ortac.

17

On N side of the Swinge the main dangers are Boues des Kaines, almost awash at LW about ¾ M ESE of Ortac, and North Rk ¼ M SE of Burhou. On S side of the Swinge beware Pierre au Vraic (dries) almost in the fairway 1¾ M S of Ortac, Barsier Rk (dries) 3½ ca NNW of Clonque Rk, and Corbet Rk with outliers ½ M N of Clonque Rk.

Heading NE, avoid the worst overfalls in W-going tide by keeping near SE side of chan. Great Nannel on with E end of Burhou clears Pierre au Vraic to the E, but passes close W of Les Etacs. When on this transit Roque Tourgis fort is abeam, alter slightly to stbd to pass 1 ca W of Corbet Rk.

The best time to pass SW through the Swinge is when the NE-going stream slackens at about HW St Helier +0400, when the reverse route to that described above should be followed. But after HW St Helier +0500 keep close to Burhou and Ortac, avoiding North Rk and Boues des Kaines, to clear the worst of the overfalls.

Alderney Race (chart 3653) lies between Alderney and C de la Hague (Lt, fog sig), and is so called due to very strong tidal streams. In mid-chan the NNE-going stream starts at HW St Helier −0210, and the SSW stream at HW St Helier +0405, sp rates both 5½ kn. The times at which stream turns do not vary much for various places, but the rates do. For example, 1M W of C de la Hague the sp rates are 7 or 8 kn. In strong winds against the tide the sea breaks almost everywhere, and there are heavy overfalls over submerged rks and banks as shown on chart. Going S through the race, the best time is HW St Helier +0500, before the overfalls get established.

APPROACHES TO GUERNSEY (chart 3654)

The Little Russel between Guernsey and Herm (chart 808) gives the most convenient access to/from N for St Peter Port (10.17.14), and also leads to Beaucette Marina (10.17.13). But it needs care, due to rks which fringe the chan and approaches, and the strong tide which also sets across the entrance. The Big Russel is wider and easier. Doyle Passage, which runs on a line 146°/326° off Doyle Point, can be used with local knowledge by day.

In mid chan, S of Platte and NW of Brehon, the NE-going stream begins at HW St Helier −0250, and the SW stream at HW St Helier +0325, sp rates both 5¼ kn which can cause a very steep sea with wind against tide.

With Lts on Platte Fougère, Tautenay, Roustel, Platte and Bréhon, plus the Ldg Lts (220°) for St Peter Port, the Little Russel can be navigated day or night in reasonable vis, even at LW.

In bad weather or in poor vis it is better to approach St Peter Port from the S, round St Martin's Pt, and this is the natural route when coming from S or W. In onshore winds keep well clear of the W coast of Guernsey, where the sea breaks on dangers up to 4M from land in bad weather.

JERSEY (charts 3655, 1136, 1137, 1138)

To N and NE of Jersey, Les Pierres de Lecq, Les Dirouilles and Les Ecrehou are groups of drying rks, 2-4M offshore. Coming from N, a convenient landfall is Desormes W cardinal Lt Buoy, 4M NNW of Grosnez Pt. Keep ¾ M clear of La Corbière Lt, SE of which begins the Western Passage (buoyed) leading E past Noirmont Pt towards St Helier.

Around the SE point of Jersey runs the Violet Channel (chart 1138). Although marked it is not easy, and should be avoided in bad weather or poor vis. There are dangers to seaward of this chan.

CAP DE LA HAGUE TO POINTE DE BARFLEUR

The N coast of the Cotentin peninsula (chart 1106) runs for 26M, mostly bordered by rks which reach 1M offshore between C de la Hague and Pte de Jardeheu, and 2½M offshore from C Lévi to Pte de Barfleur. Tidal streams run 5 kn at sp, and raise a steep sea with wind against tide. Between C de la Hague and Cherbourg (10.17.24) an eddy runs W close inshore during the last of the E-going stream.

There is anch in Anse de St Martin, about 2M E of C de la Hague, exposed to N, but useful while waiting tide for Alderney Race, as alternative to Omonville (10.17.23).

E of Cherbourg Port de Becquet and Port Lévi are two small drying harbs. Off C Lévi a race develops with wind against tide, and extends nearly 2M to N. Pte de Barfleur has dangers up to 2M offshore, and a race in which the sea breaks heavily, extending 3-4M NE and E from Lt Ho: in bad weather, particularly with winds from NW or SE against the tide, it is necessary to keep at least 6M to seaward to avoid the worst effects.

10.17.6 DISTANCE TABLE

Approximate distances in nautical miles are by the most direct route while avoiding dangers and allowing for traffic separation schemes etc. Places in *italics* are in adjoining areas.

	1	2	3	4	5	6	7	8	9	10	11	12	13	14	15	16	17	18	19	20
1 *Le Four*	1																			
2 *Isle de Batz*	37	2																		
3 Roches Douvres	89	52	3																	
4 Portrieux	100	63	28	4																
5 St Malo	122	83	42	35	5															
6 Granville	134	97	51	54	23	6														
7 Carteret	132	95	44	64	50	38	7													
8 St Helier	119	82	30	44	39	30	26	8												
9 St Peter Port	114	74	25	51	54	55	31	29	9											
10 Les Hanois	105	67	20	48	56	58	37	32	10	10										
11 Casquets	120	90	43	71	70	63	32	43	18	23	11									
12 Braye, Alderney	133	96	46	73	73	66	28	46	23	29	8	12								
13 Cap de la Hague	139	102	50	74	73	61	23	45	28	35	17	9	13							
14 Cherbourg	153	116	64	88	87	75	37	59	42	49	31	23	14	14						
15 *Le Havre*	223	186	134	158	157	145	107	129	112	119	101	93	84	70	15					
16 *Cap Gris Nez*	297	260	208	232	231	219	181	203	186	193	175	167	158	147	108	16				
17 *Start Point*	113	90	76	103	117	120	89	93	70	61	57	67	77	91	156	210	17			
18 *Portland Bill*	153	123	87	115	118	111	75	91	66	67	48	49	52	62	118	161	49	18		
19 *Needles*	178	149	108	132	131	119	81	103	82	86	64	62	59	61	98	126	84	35	19	
20 *Royal Sovereign*	248	212	154	184	183	171	133	155	138	145	124	119	110	102	82	47	163	114	82	20

THE CHANNEL ISLANDS
10-17-9

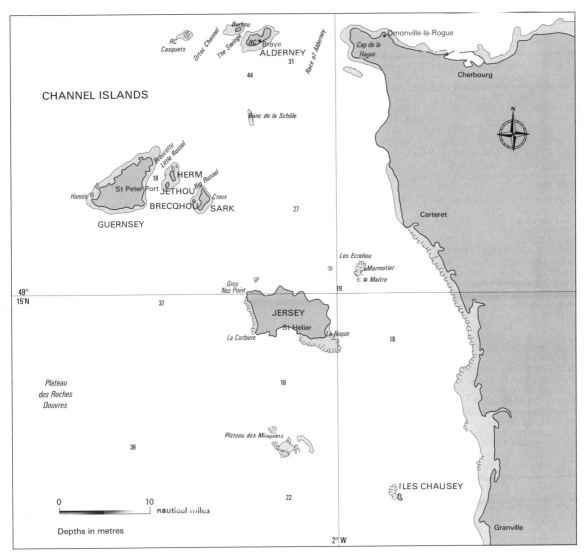

CHANNEL ISLANDS

Depths in metres

The Channel Islands (Jersey, Guernsey, Alderney, Sark and other small islands) lie, not in the Channel, but in the Bay of St. Malo. Alderney is part of the Bailiwick of Guernsey and the States of Alderney have seats in the States of Guernsey. Brecqhou belongs to Sark which in turn with Herm and Jethou are part of Guernsey. Although the eastern ends of Jersey (15 miles) and Alderney (8½ miles) are close to France, the Channel Islands have never been French. They were part of Normandy and became British with William of Normandy, William the Conqueror in 1066. The French call them the Iles Anglo-Normandes (Jersey, Guernsey, Aurigny and Sercq).

The Islands are British but are not part of the United Kingdom. They are self governing and have their own customs regulations and laws. No special documentation is needed for British yachts entering Channel Island ports but they will be subject to customs formalities on return to U.K. Yachts going to France need the normal documentation (passports etc.) and British yachts returning to the Channel Islands from France, must, like all French yachts, wear the Q flag. (It is advisable to do so when arriving from U.K., but not mandatory, except in Alderney). All Channel Islands have a reciprocal medical arrangement with U.K.

Customs and Immigration clearance formalities are carried out at St. Helier and Gorey (Jersey), St Peter Port, St Sampson and Beaucette (Guernsey) and Braye (Alderney). Unlike U.K., there are no coastguards but lifeboats are stationed at St Helier, St Catherines (Jersey), St Peter Port (Guernsey) and Braye (Alderney).

The main problems around the Channel Islands are steep seas which get up very quickly, overfalls, fog and thick weather and the very large tidal range.

17

GOREY 10-17-10
Jersey (Channel Islands)

CHARTS
Admiralty 3655, 1138; SHOM 6939; ECM 1014; Stanford
16; Imray C33A
TIDES
−0454 Dover; ML 6.1; Duration 0545; Zone 0 (GMT)

Standard Port ST HELIER (→)

Times				Height (metres)			
HW		LW		MHWS	MHWN	MLWN	MLWS
0300	0900	0200	0900	11.1	8.1	4.1	1.3
1500	2100	1400	2100				

Differences ST. CATHERINE'S BAY

0000	+0010	+0010	+0010	0.0	−0.1	0.0	+0.1

SHELTER
Good shelter in the harbour which dries out completely.
Access HW∓3. Good anchorage in Gorey Roads and in
St Catherine's Bay to the N of Gorey, except in S to SE
winds; deep water.
NAVIGATION
Waypoint 49°10'.50N 01°57'.33W, 118°/298° from/to
front Ldg Lt 298°, 2.9M. Beware the very large tidal
range. On approaching harbour, keep well outside all local
beacons until the leading marks are picked up. Beware
Banc du Chateau 1M offshore to N of Ldg Line and
Azicot Rk (dries 2.2m) just S of Ldg Line 2 ca from ent.
LIGHTS AND MARKS
(1) Ldg Lts 298°. Front Gorey pier Oc RG 5s 8m 12M; W
framework Tr; vis R304°-352°, G352°-304°. Rear, 490m
from front, OcR 5s 24m 8M; W square with R border.
(2) Gorey pier Lt on with church spire 304° leads over
Road Rk (3.3m), and Azicot Rk.
(3) Gorey pier Lt on with Fort William 250° leads close to
Pacquet Rk (0.6m).
RADIO TELEPHONE
Gorey Harbour Ch 74 (HW−3 to HW+3 summer only).
TELEPHONE (0534)
Hr Mr 53616; ∰ 32302; Marinecall 0898 500 457;
Dr Contact Hr Mr.
FACILITIES
EC Thursday; **Jetty** FW; **Gorey Yacht Services**
☎ 53958, M, P, D, ME, El, Sh, Gas, CH; **Pier** ☎ 53616,
M, P, D, L, FW, C (7 ton), AB.
Town P, CH, V, R, Bar. ✉, ⑧; ⇌ (ferry to Poole,
St Malo or Granville); ✈ (Jersey Airport).
Ferry UK — St Helier — Poole..

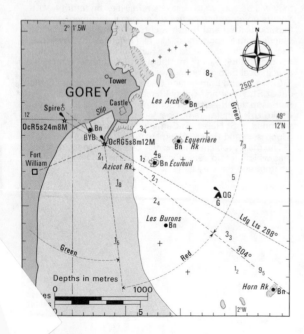

ST HELIER 10-17-11
Jersey (Channel Islands)

CHARTS
Admiralty 3278, 3655, 1137, 1136, 1138; SHOM 6938,
6937; ECM 1014; Stanford 16; Imray C33B
TIDES
−0455 Dover; ML 6.5; Duration 0545; Zone 0 (GMT)

Standard Port ST HELIER (→)

Times				Height (metres)			
HW		LW		MHWS	MHWN	MLWN	MLWS
0300	0900	0200	0900	11.1	8.1	4.1	1.3
1500	2100	1400	2100				

Differences LES MINQUIERS

+0007	0000	−0008	+0013	+0.5	+0.8	−0.1	+0.1

LES ECREHOU

+0004	+0012	+0010	+0020	−0.2	+0.3	−0.3	0.0

NOTE: St Helier is a Standard Port and the tidal
predictions for each day of the year are shown below.

Depths in metres

SHELTER
Excellent shelter in marina and good in La Collette. For St
Aubin's Bay see 10.17.25. Anchoring prohibited in St
Helier Roads due to shipping.
NAVIGATION
Waypoint 49°10'.01N 02°07'.30W, 203°/023° from/to
front Ldg Lt 023°, 0.87M. Note the very large tidal range,
and many offlying rks. Four main channels are Western
Passage, Danger Rk Passage, Red and Green Passage,
and South Passage. In Western Passage beware race off
Noirmont Pt. Entering harbour note Oyster Rks (RW Bn)
to West of Red and Green Passage, and Dog's Nest Rks
(W Bn with globe topmark) to E. Speed limit 10 kn N of
Platte Rk, and 5 kn N of La Collette. Ldg Lts difficult to
see against town lights.
LIGHTS AND MARKS
Western Passage Ldg Lts and Dog's Nest Bn 082° lead N
of Les Fours and Ruaudière Lt Buoys, to position close to
East Rk Lt Buoy, where course is altered to 023° on the
Red and Green Passage Ldg Line (Front Oc G 5s. Rear Oc
R 5s, synchronised). Port-hand buoy beyond Platte Rk (Fl
R 1.5s) marks channel. Main harbour Ldg Lts 078°, both
FG on W columns. Bell at Victoria Pierhead is rung in

ST. HELIER *continued*

answer to vessel's fog signals.

Entry Signals (Port Control Stn and Marina)

FG or Fl G Lt at Port Control Stn. — Vessels may enter
but not leave

FR or Fl R Lt at Port Control Stn. — Vessels may leave
but not enter

R and G Lts together at Port Control Stn. — No vessel
may enter
or leave

QY Lts on NW and NE of Port Control Stn indicate power
driven craft of under 25m length may enter or leave
against the signals displayed (keeping to stbd at entrance).
Marina sill fixed (CD + 5m) and hinged flap which lifts
1.4m over sill to maintain 5.0m.

RADIO TELEPHONE

Call: *St Helier Port Control* VHF Ch 14 (H24). Messages
can be routed through Jersey Radio, the Coast Radio
Station, VHF Ch 16; 25 82 (H24). Weather forecasts on
Ch 25, 82 at 0645, 1245, 1845 and 2245 GMT.

TELEPHONE (0534)

Hr Mr 34451; Marina Office 79549; ⌗ 30232 and 73561;
Duty Forecaster 0077007; Recorded weather forecast
0077002; Marinecall 0898 500 457; Police 75511; Dr 35742
and 53178; Ⓗ 71000.

FACILITIES

EC Thursday; **St Helier Marina** (180 + 200 visitors),
☎ 79549, Grid, CH, ME, El, Sh, FW, V, AC, Gas, Gaz,
Kos, (Visitors area — fingers E, F and G. Vessels over
12m use N side of A finger); Access HW + 3; **Marina
Shop** ☎ 36955, V, Gas, Gaz; **La Collette Yacht Basin**
☎ 74434 (holding area when marina is inaccessible and a
few visitors berths for up to 24 hours), FW, AC, V, R;
St Helier Yacht Club ☎ 32229, P, D, R, Bar; **Boat Yard**
☎ 31907, M, P, D, FW, ME, El, Sh, C (15 ton), CH, AB;
South Pier Slip, M, P, D, L, FW, C (1 ton & 2 ton), AB;
Channel Islands Yacht Services ☎ 42071, ME, SM, Ⓔ,
CH, Gas; **Battrick BY** ☎ 43412, CH; **Bernard Amy**
☎ 42071, CH; **Silva Yates** ☎ 36980, CH; **D.K. Collins**
☎ 32415, ME; **South Pier Shipyard** ☎ 31907, ME, El,
Sh, CH, ACA, Gas; **Raffray** ☎ 23151, ME; **IPCO Marine**
☎ 44651, ME, El, Sh. ☎ 77044, CH, ACA; **Fox Marine
Services** ☎ 21312, ME; **Jersey Marine Electronics**
☎ 21603, El, Ⓔ.

Town P, D, CH, V, R, Bar. ✉; Ⓑ; ⇌ (ferry to Poole,
St Malo, Granville), ✈ (Jersey Airport).

Ferry UK (Poole daily; Torbay twice weekly in summer,
weekly in winter).

Hydrofoil to Weymouth, Guernsey and St Malo.

ST HELIER

MEAN SPRING
AND NEAP CURVES

MEAN RANGES		
Springs	9·8m	———
Neaps	4·0m	– – –

Springs occur 2 days
after
New and Full Moon.

17

CHANNEL ISLANDS – ST. HELIER

Lat 49°11′ N   Long 2°07′ W

TIMES AND HEIGHTS OF HIGH AND LOW WATERS

YEAR **1991**

TIME ZONE UT (GMT)
For Summer Time add ONE hour in non-shaded areas

JANUARY

Day	Time	m	Time	m	Time	m	Time	m
1 Tu	0048	1.7	0629	11.1	1320	1.3	1902	11.0
2 W	0138	1.4	0717	11.4	1408	1.0	1948	11.1
3 Th	0226	1.3	0804	11.4	1454	1.1	2034	11.0
4 F	0310	1.5	0847	11.1	1538	1.4	2118	10.7
5 Sa	0353	1.9	0931	10.7	1619	1.9	2202	10.2
6 Su	0434	2.4	1013	10.1	1659	2.5	2245	9.6
7 M ☾	0515	3.0	1057	9.5	1740	3.1	2330	9.1
8 Tu	0557	3.5	1144	8.9	1824	3.7		
9 W	0021	8.6	0648	4.0	1239	8.4	1917	4.1
10 Th	0120	8.3	0747	4.3	1347	8.0	2020	4.3
11 F	0229	8.3	0857	4.3	1500	8.2	2129	4.2
12 Sa	0335	8.5	1007	4.0	1606	8.5	2234	3.8
13 Su	0433	9.0	1108	3.5	1659	9.0	2327	3.4
14 M	0520	9.5	1157	2.9	1744	9.5		
15 Tu ●	0014	2.8	0601	9.9	1239	2.4	1825	9.9
16 W ●	0055	2.4	0641	10.3	1319	2.0	1902	10.2
17 Th	0131	2.1	0716	10.5	1354	1.8	1937	10.3
18 F	0205	2.0	0751	10.6	1426	1.7	2011	10.3
19 Sa	0237	2.0	0823	10.6	1456	1.8	2042	10.2
20 Su	0307	2.2	0854	10.4	1525	2.0	2112	10.1
21 M	0336	2.4	0927	10.2	1556	2.2	2146	9.8
22 Tu	0409	2.6	1002	9.9	1631	2.6	2224	9.5
23 W ☽	0449	3.0	1044	9.5	1718	3.0	2311	9.1
24 Th	0543	3.5	1137	8.9	1818	3.5		
25 F	0012	8.7	0656	3.8	1255	8.4	1937	3.8
26 Sa	0141	8.4	0827	3.9	1437	8.3	2111	3.7
27 Su	0319	8.7	1006	3.5	1609	8.9	2240	3.2
28 M	0437	9.4	1123	2.6	1715	9.7	2347	2.4
29 Tu	0534	10.3	1224	1.7	1808	10.4		
30 W ○	0042	1.6	0624	11.0	1313	1.0	1855	11.0
31 Th	0130	1.0	0709	11.5	1358	0.6	1937	11.3

FEBRUARY

Day	Time	m	Time	m	Time	m	Time	m
1 F	0213	0.8	0751	11.6	1439	0.6	2018	11.3
2 Sa	0253	0.9	0830	11.5	1517	0.9	2056	11.0
3 Su	0329	1.3	0908	11.0	1550	1.5	2132	10.5
4 M	0402	1.9	0943	10.3	1621	2.2	2206	9.9
5 Tu	0433	2.6	1019	9.7	1651	2.9	2241	9.3
6 W ☾	0505	3.3	1054	9.0	1723	3.6	2318	8.6
7 Th	0544	3.9	1133	8.3	1807	4.2		
8 F	0004	8.1	0639	4.4	1234	7.8	1909	4.6
9 Sa	0121	7.7	0754	4.7	1411	7.6	2033	4.7
10 Su	0301	7.9	0927	4.5	1542	7.9	2202	4.3
11 M	0413	8.4	1045	3.8	1644	8.5	2309	3.6
12 Tu	0505	9.1	1140	3.1	1729	9.2		
13 W	0000	2.9	0546	9.8	1224	2.3	1807	9.9
14 Th ●	0041	2.2	0624	10.4	1302	1.7	1843	10.4
15 F	0117	1.8	0659	10.9	1337	1.4	1917	10.7
16 Sa	0149	1.5	0731	11.1	1408	1.2	1949	10.9
17 Su	0220	1.4	0804	11.1	1437	1.3	2020	10.8
18 M	0249	1.6	0834	11.0	1505	1.5	2051	10.7
19 Tu	0318	1.8	0907	10.7	1536	1.9	2122	10.4
20 W	0350	2.2	0941	10.3	1612	2.3	2159	9.9
21 Th	0430	2.7	1020	9.6	1655	3.0	2241	9.3
22 F	0523	3.3	1111	8.8	1756	3.6	2342	8.6
23 Sa	0636	3.9	1231	8.1	1919	4.1		
24 Su	0121	8.1	0815	4.0	1437	8.0	2101	4.0
25 M	0318	8.4	1003	3.5	1610	8.7	2235	3.2
26 Tu	0433	9.3	1119	2.5	1709	9.6	2342	2.2
27 W	0526	10.2	1214	1.5	1756	10.5		
28 Th ○	0032	1.3	0611	11.0	1259	0.8	1838	11.1

MARCH

Day	Time	m	Time	m	Time	m	Time	m
1 F	0116	0.8	0652	11.5	1340	0.7	1917	11.4
2 Sa	0154	0.5	0731	11.7	1416	0.5	1954	11.4
3 Su	0229	0.7	0808	11.5	1449	0.8	2027	11.1
4 M	0301	1.1	0842	11.0	1517	1.4	2100	10.6
5 Tu	0329	1.7	0912	10.4	1543	1.9	2129	10.0
6 W	0355	2.4	0942	9.7	1607	2.8	2156	9.3
7 Th	0423	3.1	1009	9.0	1635	3.5	2224	8.7
8 F ☾	0458	3.7	1040	8.3	1715	4.1	2259	8.1
9 Sa	0547	4.3	1126	7.7	1812	4.6		
10 Su	0004	7.6	0702	4.7	1310	7.2	1940	4.9
11 M	0219	7.4	0840	4.6	1514	7.5	2125	4.6
12 Tu	0346	8.0	1013	4.0	1617	8.3	2244	3.8
13 W	0438	8.9	1113	3.1	1702	9.1	2334	2.9
14 Th	0519	9.7	1158	2.3	1740	9.9		
15 F	0017	2.1	0557	10.5	1236	1.6	1815	10.6
16 Sa ●	0053	1.6	0632	11.0	1310	1.2	1850	11.4
17 Su	0127	1.2	0706	11.4	1344	1.0	1923	11.2
18 M	0159	1.1	0740	11.4	1415	1.0	1957	11.2
19 Tu	0232	1.3	0813	11.3	1447	1.3	2029	11.0
20 W	0304	1.6	0849	10.9	1522	1.8	2103	10.6
21 Th	0341	2.0	0925	10.3	1600	2.4	2141	10.1
22 F	0424	2.6	1007	9.5	1648	3.0	2227	9.3
23 Sa ☽	0520	3.3	1104	8.7	1751	3.7	2333	8.5
24 Su	0635	3.8	1236	8.0	1914	4.1		
25 M	0121	8.1	0812	3.9	1439	8.1	2056	3.9
26 Tu	0308	8.5	0953	3.3	1556	8.8	2224	3.1
27 W	0416	9.3	1104	2.3	1649	9.7	2325	2.1
28 Th	0505	10.2	1154	1.5	1733	10.4		
29 F	0011	1.4	0549	10.8	1236	0.9	1812	11.0
30 Sa ○	0052	0.9	0628	11.2	1314	0.7	1850	11.2
31 Su	0128	0.7	0704	11.3	1348	0.8	1924	11.2

APRIL

Day	Time	m	Time	m	Time	m	Time	m
1 M	0201	0.9	0740	11.2	1418	1.1	1958	11.0
2 Tu	0230	1.3	0813	10.7	1444	1.7	2027	10.5
3 W	0258	1.8	0843	10.2	1510	2.3	2056	9.9
4 Th	0325	2.4	0909	9.5	1535	2.9	2119	9.4
5 F	0353	3.0	0935	8.9	1604	3.0	2146	8.8
6 Sa	0428	3.6	1004	8.3	1642	4.0	2221	8.2
7 Su ☾	0515	4.1	1049	7.8	1736	4.4	2318	7.7
8 M	0621	4.4	1214	7.3	1853	4.7		
9 Tu	0114	7.4	0748	4.5	1420	7.4	2029	4.5
10 W	0256	7.9	0919	4.0	1532	8.1	2156	3.9
11 Th	0355	8.6	1028	3.2	1621	9.0	2255	3.1
12 F	0441	9.5	1119	2.4	1702	9.8	2342	2.3
13 Sa	0522	10.3	1201	1.8	1742	10.5		
14 Su ●	0022	1.7	0601	10.9	1239	1.3	1819	11.0
15 M	0100	1.4	0639	11.3	1317	1.1	1856	11.3
16 Tu	0138	1.1	0716	11.4	1355	1.1	1933	11.1
17 W	0216	1.2	0755	11.3	1433	1.3	2011	11.2
18 Th	0256	1.5	0834	10.9	1514	1.8	2050	10.7
19 F	0338	1.9	0917	10.2	1559	2.0	2134	10.1
20 Sa	0427	2.5	1007	9.5	1651	3.0	2227	9.4
21 Su ☽	0525	3.0	1111	8.7	1753	3.5	2337	8.7
22 M	0635	3.4	1242	8.3	1910	3.8		
23 Tu	0112	8.4	0759	3.5	1416	8.4	2037	3.6
24 W	0240	8.7	0925	3.1	1525	9.4	2155	3.1
25 Th	0345	9.3	1031	2.5	1619	9.6	2254	2.4
26 F	0435	9.9	1123	1.9	1702	10.1	2342	1.8
27 Sa	0519	10.4	1205	1.5	1742	10.5		
28 Su ○	0022	1.4	0600	10.7	1242	1.4	1819	10.8
29 M	0059	1.3	0636	10.7	1316	1.4	1855	10.8
30 Tu	0133	1.5	0713	10.6	1347	1.7	1928	10.6

Chart Datum: 5.88 metres below Ordnance Datum (Local)

CHANNEL ISLANDS – ST. HELIER

Lat 49°11′ N   Long 2°07′ W

TIMES AND HEIGHTS OF HIGH AND LOW WATERS   YEAR **1991**

TIME ZONE **UT(GMT)**
For Summer Time add ONE hour in non-shaded areas

MAY

Day	Time	m	Time	m	Time	m	Time	m
1 W	0204	1·6	0745	10·3	1415	2·0	1959	10·2
2 Th	0233	2·0	0816	9·8	1443	2·4	2029	9·8
3 F	0303	2·4	0846	9·4	1512	2·9	2056	9·4
4 Sa	0334	2·9	0915	8·9	1545	3·3	2125	8·9
5 Su	0410	3·3	0948	8·5	1621	3·7	2203	8·5
6 M	0452	3·7	1033	8·0	1709	4·0	2254	8·1
7 Tu ☽	0547	3·9	1137	7·7	1811	4·2		
8 W	0011	7·8	0655	4·0	1306	7·7	1926	4·2
9 Th	0144	8·0	0812	3·8	1427	8·1	2049	3·9
10 F	0256	8·5	0925	3·4	1528	8·8	2200	3·3
11 Sa	0353	9·2	1028	2·7	1619	9·5	2258	2·6
12 Su	0442	9·9	1120	2·1	1705	10·2	2349	2·0
13 M ○	0529	10·5	1208	1·7	1749	10·8		
14 Tu ●	0035	1·5	0612	11·0	1253	1·4	1832	11·2
15 W	0120	1·3	0657	11·2	1338	1·3	1914	11·3
16 Th	0205	1·2	0742	11·1	1423	1·4	1958	11·2
17 F	0250	1·3	0827	10·8	1510	1·7	2044	10·8
18 Sa	0338	1·7	0917	10·3	1557	2·1	2134	10·3
19 Su	0427	2·1	1010	9·7	1649	2·6	2227	9·7
20	0522	2·6	1112	9·2	1747	3·1	2332	9·2
21 Tu	0624	2·9	1222	8·8	1852	3·4		
22 W	0043	8·9	0731	3·1	1335	8·7	2002	3·4
23 Th	0158	8·8	0843	3·1	1442	8·9	2112	3·2
24 F	0303	9·0	0948	2·9	1538	9·2	2213	2·9
25 Sa	0357	9·1	1042	2·6	1626	9·6	2305	2·5
26 Su	0445	9·7	1129	2·4	1709	9·9	2350	2·2
27 M	0529	9·9	1208	2·2	1749	10·1		
28 Tu	0029	2·0	0610	10·1	1245	2·1	1827	10·2
29 W	0106	1·9	0648	10·1	1320	2·1	1903	10·2
30 Th	0141	2·0	0724	9·9	1354	2·3	1938	10·1
31 F	0215	2·1	0758	9·7	1426	2·5	2011	9·8

JUNE

Day	Time	m	Time	m	Time	m	Time	m
1 Sa	0247	2·3	0832	9·4	1458	2·7	2043	9·5
2 Su	0319	2·6	0904	9·1	1531	3·0	2115	9·2
3 M	0355	2·8	0938	8·8	1604	3·2	2150	8·9
4 Tu ☽	0431	3·1	1017	8·6	1645	3·5	2234	8·7
5 W	0515	3·3	1105	8·4	1733	3·7	2327	8·5
6 Th	0607	3·5	1205	8·3	1832	3·8		
7 F	0035	8·4	0709	3·5	1316	8·3	1942	3·8
8 Sa	0149	8·5	0820	3·4	1427	8·7	2100	3·5
9 Su	0301	8·9	0934	3·1	1534	9·2	2213	3·0
10 M	0404	9·4	1041	2·6	1631	9·8	2318	2·4
11 Tu	0502	10·0	1142	2·1	1725	10·4		
12 W ●	0014	1·8	0556	10·5	1235	1·7	1815	10·9
13 Th	0106	1·4	0646	10·9	1327	1·4	1904	11·2
14 F	0157	1·1	0735	11·0	1416	1·3	1952	11·3
15 Sa	0244	1·0	0825	10·9	1504	1·4	2040	11·1
16 Su	0332	1·2	0912	10·6	1552	1·7	2128	10·7
17 M	0420	1·6	1003	10·2	1640	2·1	2217	10·2
18 Tu	0508	2·0	1054	9·7	1729	2·6	2309	9·7
19 W ☽	0558	2·6	1149	9·2	1819	3·0		
20 Th	0005	9·2	0652	3·0	1248	8·9	1917	3·4
21 F	0109	8·8	0751	3·4	1349	8·7	2019	3·6
22 Sa	0213	8·6	0854	3·5	1451	8·7	2124	3·6
23 Su	0317	8·7	0955	3·5	1548	8·9	2224	3·3
24 M	0413	8·9	1049	3·2	1638	9·2	2318	3·0
25 Tu	0504	9·2	1137	3·0	1723	9·6		
26 W	0004	2·6	0549	9·5	1221	2·7	1807	9·9
27 Th ○	0046	2·3	0629	9·7	1300	2·4	1846	10·0
28 F	0124	2·1	0709	9·8	1337	2·3	1923	10·1
29 Sa	0159	2·0	0744	9·8	1412	2·3	1958	10·1
30 Su	0233	2·0	0819	9·7	1444	2·3	2030	9·9

JULY

Day	Time	m	Time	m	Time	m	Time	m
1 M	0305	2·1	0850	9·6	1515	2·5	2103	9·7
2 Tu	0335	2·3	0922	9·4	1546	2·7	2134	9·5
3 W	0407	2·5	0955	9·2	1619	2·9	2209	9·3
4 Th	0442	2·7	1033	9·0	1658	3·1	2251	9·1
5 F	0526	3·0	1119	8·8	1749	3·4	2343	8·8
6 Sa	0621	3·3	1218	8·6	1852	3·6		
7 Su	0052	8·5	0730	3·5	1333	8·6	2012	3·7
8 M	0216	8·5	0851	3·4	1456	8·8	2139	3·4
9 Tu	0339	8·9	1013	3·1	1610	9·4	2258	2·7
10 W	0448	9·5	1125	2·5	1713	10·1		
11 Th ●	0003	2·0	0547	10·2	1225	1·8	1808	10·8
12 F	0057	1·3	0641	10·8	1319	1·2	1857	11·3
13 Sa	0148	0·8	0728	11·2	1406	0·9	1945	11·5
14 Su	0234	0·6	0815	11·2	1453	0·9	2030	11·5
15 M	0319	0·7	0900	11·1	1536	1·2	2114	11·1
16 Tu	0402	1·2	0943	10·6	1619	1·7	2156	10·6
17 W	0442	1·8	1026	10·1	1659	2·3	2240	10·0
18 Th ☽	0523	2·5	1109	9·5	1742	2·9	2325	9·3
19 F	0605	3·1	1157	8·9	1827	3·5		
20 Sa	0015	8·7	0653	3·7	1252	8·4	1921	4·0
21 Su	0119	8·2	0752	4·1	1401	8·2	2029	4·2
22 M	0234	8·1	0903	4·2	1512	8·3	2143	4·0
23 Tu	0348	8·3	1014	3·9	1616	8·7	2251	3·6
24 W	0445	8·7	1113	3·5	1706	9·2	2344	3·0
25 Th	0532	9·2	1203	2·9	1750	9·7		
26 F ○	0029	2·4	0614	9·7	1245	2·4	1829	10·1
27 Sa	0107	2·0	0650	10·0	1321	2·1	1906	10·4
28 Su	0142	1·7	0727	10·2	1355	1·9	1940	10·5
29 M	0215	1·6	0759	10·3	1426	1·9	2012	10·5
30 Tu	0244	1·7	0830	10·2	1456	2·0	2042	10·3
31 W	0312	1·9	0858	10·0	1524	2·2	2111	10·1

AUGUST

Day	Time	m	Time	m	Time	m	Time	m
1 Th	0341	2·1	0928	9·8	1553	2·5	2143	9·9
2 F	0413	2·4	1002	9·6	1628	2·8	2220	9·5
3 Sa	0452	2·9	1041	9·2	1715	3·2	2305	9·0
4 Su	0546	3·3	1134	8·8	1819	3·7		
5 M	0011	8·4	0657	3·7	1253	8·4	1944	3·9
6 Tu	0149	8·1	0826	3·8	1437	8·4	2122	3·6
7 W	0334	8·5	1000	3·4	1604	9·1	2249	2·8
8 Th	0447	9·4	1116	2·6	1708	10·0	2356	1·9
9 F	0542	10·2	1217	1·7	1800	10·9		
10 Sa ●	0048	1·0	0631	11·0	1307	1·0	1846	11·5
11 Su	0135	0·5	0714	11·4	1352	0·6	1930	11·8
12 M	0218	0·3	0757	11·6	1434	0·6	2011	11·7
13 Tu	0258	0·6	0836	11·3	1512	0·9	2050	11·4
14 W	0335	1·1	0914	10·9	1549	1·5	2128	10·8
15 Th	0409	1·8	0950	10·2	1624	2·2	2204	10·0
16 F	0442	2·6	1027	9·5	1658	3·0	2241	9·2
17 Sa ☽	0516	3·4	1105	8·8	1737	3·7	2322	8·5
18 Su	0558	4·0	1151	8·2	1828	4·3		
19 M	0021	7·8	0656	4·5	1304	7·8	1938	4·6
20 Tu	0155	7·6	0815	4·7	1444	7·8	2107	4·5
21 W	0328	7·8	0943	4·4	1557	8·4	2227	3·9
22 Th	0428	8·5	1054	3·7	1648	9·0	2325	3·1
23 F	0513	9·2	1143	3·0	1730	9·7		
24 Sa	0008	2·4	0551	9·8	1225	2·3	1808	10·3
25 Su ○	0046	1·8	0628	10·3	1300	1·8	1842	10·8
26 M	0120	1·5	0702	10·7	1334	1·6	1916	11·0
27 Tu	0151	1·3	0733	10·8	1404	1·6	1947	11·0
28 W	0220	1·4	0804	10·7	1433	1·7	2018	10·9
29 Th	0249	1·6	0832	10·6	1501	1·9	2047	10·6
30 F	0317	2·0	0901	10·3	1531	2·3	2118	10·2
31 Sa	0349	2·4	0934	9·9	1607	2·8	2155	9·7

17

Chart Datum: 5.88 metres below Ordnance Datum (Local)

CHANNEL ISLANDS – ST. HELIER

Lat 49°11′ N   Long 2°07′ W

TIMES AND HEIGHTS OF HIGH AND LOW WATERS

YEAR **1991**

TIME ZONE **UT (GMT)**
For Summer Time add ONE hour in non-shaded areas

SEPTEMBER

Day	Time	m	Time	m	Time	m	Time	m
1 Su ☾	0431	3.0	1013	9.4	1657	3.3	2240	9.0
16 M	0509	4.2	1054	8.2	1742	4.4	2323	7.7
2 M	0526	3.6	1108	8.8	1804	3.8	2350	8.2
17 Tu	0607	4.7	1203	7.6	1855	4.8		
3 Tu	0643	4.0	1234	8.2	1935	4.0		
18 W	0110	7.3	0731	4.9	1411	7.6	2027	4.7
4 W	0151	7.9	0819	4.0	1437	8.3	2118	3.7
19 Th	0301	7.7	0910	4.6	1531	8.2	2156	4.1
5 Th	0335	8.5	0956	3.4	1600	9.2	2242	2.7
20 F	0402	8.4	1051	2.4	1621	8.9	2254	3.3
6 F	0440	9.5	1108	2.5	1657	10.1	2343	1.7
21 Sa	0444	9.2	1116	3.1	1701	9.7	2337	2.5
7 Sa	0529	10.4	1203	1.5	1744	11.0		
22 Su	0522	9.9	1157	2.4	1739	10.4		
8 Su ●	0032	0.9	0612	11.1	1249	0.8	1828	11.6
23 M ○	0015	1.9	0557	10.5	1234	1.8	1812	10.9
9 M	0114	0.5	0652	11.6	1331	0.5	1907	11.8
24 Tu	0050	1.5	0631	10.9	1307	1.5	1846	11.2
10 Tu	0154	0.4	0731	11.6	1409	0.6	1947	11.7
25 W	0123	1.3	0703	11.2	1338	1.4	1920	11.3
11 W	0230	0.7	0808	11.4	1444	1.0	2022	11.3
26 Th	0154	1.4	0734	11.2	1411	1.6	1952	11.2
12 Th	0303	1.3	0842	10.9	1515	1.6	2057	10.6
27 F	0225	1.6	0806	11.0	1442	1.9	2025	10.8
13 F	0332	2.1	0914	10.2	1546	2.4	2128	9.9
28 Sa	0258	2.0	0839	10.6	1517	2.3	2100	10.3
14 Sa	0359	2.9	0945	9.5	1616	3.1	2159	9.1
29 Su	0335	2.6	0914	10.1	1559	2.8	2139	9.7
15 Su ☽	0430	3.6	1014	8.8	1652	3.8	2233	8.4
30 M	0421	3.2	0957	9.5	1652	3.4	2231	8.9

OCTOBER

Day	Time	m	Time	m	Time	m	Time	m
1 Tu ☾	0522	3.8	1058	8.7	1803	3.8	2353	8.2
16 W	0527	4.7	1112	7.8	1812	4.6		
2 W	0641	4.1	1235	8.2	1933	3.9		
17 Th	0011	7.4	0643	4.9	1306	7.6	1937	4.6
3 Th	0157	8.1	0815	4.0	1429	8.5	2111	3.5
18 F	0208	7.6	0816	4.7	1442	8.0	2103	4.2
4 F	0322	8.8	0945	3.3	1543	9.3	2227	2.6
19 Sa	0315	8.2	0936	4.1	1538	8.7	2207	3.5
5 Sa	0420	9.7	1051	2.4	1637	10.2	2322	1.8
20 Su	0403	9.0	1034	3.4	1623	9.5	2257	2.8
6 Su	0505	10.5	1142	1.6	1722	10.9		
21 M	0444	9.8	1119	2.7	1702	10.2	2339	2.2
7 M ●	0008	1.2	0547	11.1	1225	1.1	1803	11.4
22 Tu	0520	10.5	1200	2.1	1740	10.8		
8 Tu	0048	0.9	0625	11.4	1304	0.9	1842	11.5
23 W ○	0017	1.7	0557	11.0	1238	1.7	1817	11.2
9 W	0124	0.9	0702	11.4	1341	1.0	1919	11.4
24 Th	0053	1.5	0632	11.3	1314	1.5	1853	11.3
10 Th	0158	1.2	0737	11.2	1413	1.4	1954	11.0
25 F	0130	1.5	0709	11.3	1351	1.4	1930	11.3
11 F	0227	1.8	0809	10.7	1443	1.9	2026	10.4
26 Sa	0208	1.7	0745	11.2	1430	1.8	2009	10.9
12 Sa	0256	2.4	0840	10.1	1512	2.5	2056	9.7
27 Su	0247	2.1	0823	10.9	1511	2.2	2050	10.4
13 Su	0324	3.1	0911	9.5	1542	3.2	2125	9.0
28 M	0331	2.6	0905	10.3	1559	2.7	2136	9.7
14 M	0355	3.7	0938	8.9	1619	3.8	2157	8.4
29 Tu	0421	3.1	0955	9.7	1654	3.2	2235	9.0
15 Tu ☽	0433	4.2	1013	8.3	1706	4.3	2244	7.8
30 W	0522	3.6	1059	9.0	1801	3.5	2357	8.5
31 Th	0635	3.9	1228	8.6	1921	3.6		

NOVEMBER

Day	Time	m	Time	m	Time	m	Time	m
1 F	0134	8.5	0758	3.8	1401	8.8	2046	3.3
16 Sa	0045	7.8	0707	4.6	1320	8.0	1951	4.2
2 Sa	0251	9.0	0918	3.3	1512	9.0	2156	2.8
17 Su	0205	8.1	0827	4.3	1434	8.4	2103	3.8
3 Su	0349	9.6	1021	2.7	1607	9.9	2252	2.2
18 M	0307	8.7	0938	3.8	1532	9.1	2203	3.3
4 M	0435	10.2	1113	2.1	1654	10.5	2337	1.8
19 Tu	0357	9.4	1035	3.2	1621	9.7	2257	2.7
5 Tu	0518	10.7	1157	1.7	1736	10.8		
20 W	0442	10.1	1125	2.6	1706	10.0	2343	2.2
6 W ●	0018	1.6	0557	10.9	1236	1.5	1815	10.9
21 Th ○	0525	10.7	1210	2.1	1750	10.8		
7 Th	0055	1.6	0634	11.0	1313	1.5	1852	10.8
22 F	0028	1.9	0607	11.1	1255	1.7	1832	11.1
8 F	0128	1.8	0709	10.8	1345	1.8	1927	10.5
23 Sa	0112	1.7	0649	11.3	1338	1.6	1916	11.2
9 Sa	0159	2.2	0742	10.5	1418	2.1	2001	10.1
24 Su	0157	1.7	0733	11.3	1423	1.6	2001	11.0
10 Su	0229	2.6	0813	10.1	1449	2.6	2033	9.6
25 M	0242	1.9	0816	11.1	1508	1.8	2047	10.6
11 M	0258	3.1	0844	9.6	1521	3.0	2105	9.1
26 Tu	0329	2.3	0904	10.7	1557	2.2	2138	10.1
12 Tu	0331	3.5	0915	9.1	1556	3.5	2139	8.6
27 W	0420	2.7	0955	10.1	1651	2.6	2235	9.5
13 W	0407	3.9	0952	8.6	1638	3.9	2221	8.2
28 Th ☾	0515	3.1	1054	9.6	1749	3.0	2340	9.1
14 Th ☽	0454	4.3	1040	8.2	1730	4.2	2322	7.9
29 F	0617	3.5	1203	9.1	1855	3.3		
15 F	0554	4.5	1151	7.9	1836	4.3		
30 Sa	0055	8.9	0724	3.6	1317	9.0	2005	3.4

DECEMBER

Day	Time	m	Time	m	Time	m	Time	m
1 Su	0206	9.0	0836	3.5	1429	9.1	2114	3.2
16 M	0039	8.3	0710	4.2	1313	8.3	1949	3.9
2 M	0308	9.2	0943	3.2	1531	9.4	2214	3.0
17 Tu	0155	8.5	0829	4.1	1430	8.6	2104	3.7
3 Tu	0402	9.6	1040	2.8	1623	9.7	2305	2.7
18 W	0305	9.6	0945	3.6	1539	9.1	2214	3.2
4 W	0448	10.0	1127	2.5	1709	10.0	2349	2.5
19 Th	0406	9.5	1052	3.0	1638	9.7	2315	2.7
5 Th	0530	10.3	1211	2.2	1751	10.2		
20 F	0501	10.2	1150	2.4	1732	10.4		
6 F	0028	2.3	0610	10.5	1249	2.1	1832	10.3
21 Sa ○	0010	2.1	0551	10.8	1242	1.8	1822	10.9
7 Sa	0104	2.3	0648	10.5	1326	2.1	1909	10.2
22 Su	0100	1.7	0639	11.3	1330	1.3	1910	11.1
8 Su	0138	2.4	0724	10.4	1401	2.2	1945	10.0
23 M	0149	1.4	0727	11.5	1418	1.2	1957	11.2
9 M	0212	2.5	0758	10.1	1433	2.4	2019	9.7
24 Tu	0236	1.4	0813	11.5	1504	1.2	2044	11.0
10 Tu	0243	2.8	0832	9.8	1505	2.7	2053	9.4
25 W	0322	1.6	0900	11.2	1550	1.5	2132	10.7
11 W	0315	3.1	0904	9.5	1538	3.0	2125	9.0
26 Th	0409	2.0	0946	10.7	1637	1.9	2220	10.2
12 Th	0348	3.2	0936	9.2	1613	3.2	2200	8.8
27 F	0457	2.5	1035	10.2	1725	2.5	2312	9.6
13 F	0424	3.7	1014	8.8	1652	3.5	2241	8.5
28 Sa ☾	0547	3.0	1129	9.6	1818	3.0		
14 Sa ☽	0508	3.9	1059	8.6	1740	3.9	2333	8.3
29 Su	0008	9.1	0642	3.5	1229	9.0	1916	3.5
15 Su	0603	4.1	1200	8.4	1839	3.9		
30 M	0113	8.8	0745	3.8	1338	8.7	2020	3.8
31 Tu	0220	8.7	0854	3.8	1450	8.6	2129	3.8

Chart Datum: 5.88 metres below Ordnance Datum (Local)

SARK 10-17-12
Sark (Channel Islands)

CHARTS
Admiralty 808, 3654; SHOM 6904; ECM 1014; Stanford
16; Imray C33A

TIDES
−0450 Dover; ML 4.9; Duration 0550; Zone 0 (GMT).

Standard Port ST HELIER (←)

Times				Height (metres)			
HW		LW		MHWS	MHWN	MLWN	MLWS
0300	0900	0200	0900	11.1	8.1	4.1	1.3
1500	2100	1400	2100				

Differences SARK (MASELINE PIER)
+0005 +0015 +0005 +0010 −2.1 −1.5 −0.6 −0.3

SHELTER
Many sheltered anchorages, shown on chartlet, depending
on wind direction. Main harbours are Creux (dries) and
Maseline. Goulet passage for N-bound traffic only.

Berthing at jetties prohibited when steamers due, and
always when boat is unattended. Remaining in Creux
harbour for longer than it takes to disembark passengers,
is forbidden without prior permission of the Hr Mr (or call
the Tourist office, call sign Tango Oscar, on Ch 74).

NAVIGATION
Creux waypoint 49°25'.30N 02°20'.30W, 164°/344°
from/to entrance, 0.57M. Beware large tidal range and
strong tidal streams. There are numerous rocks all round
Sark but the centres of the bays are clear of dangers for
the most part. Sark is not a comfortable place to lie
except in settled weather. Beware numerous lobster pots.

LIGHTS AND MARKS
From S, Pinnacle Rock on with E side of Grand Moie at
001°; or W patch on Creux Hr pierhead in line with Pt
Robert Lt Ho at 350°. Point Robert Fl 15s 65m 28M; W
8-sided Tr; vis 138°-353°; Horn(2) 30s.

RADIO TELEPHONE
None.

SARK *continued*

TELEPHONE (0481 83)
Lighthouse Keeper 2021; # 2021; Marinecall
0898 500 457; Police (Guernsey) 25111; Dr 2045.
FACILITIES
EC Thursday and Saturday — Winter only; **Harbour
(east)** ☎ 2025, Slip, M, L, FW, C (1 ton), AB; **Maseline
Jetty** ☎ 2070, M, C (3 ton); **Landing (west)** M, L;
Gallery Stores ☎ 2078, Gas, Gaz, Kos; **Village** P and D
(cans), V, R, Bar. ✉; Ⓑ; ⇌ (ferry to Guernsey-
Weymouth, Poole, St Malo or Granville); ✈ (Guernsey).
Ferry UK — Guernsey (St. Peter Port)—Weymouth/
Poole
Hydrofoil — Guernsey, Alderney, Jersey, St Malo,
Weymouth.

BEAUCETTE 10-17-13
Guernsey (Channel Islands)

CHARTS
Admiralty 808, 807, 3654; SHOM 6903, 6904; ECM 1014;
Stanford 16; Imray C33A
TIDES
−0450 Dover; ML 5.0; Duration 0500; Zone 0 (GMT)

Standard Port ST HELIER (←)

Times				Height (metres)			
HW		LW		MHWS	MHWN	MLWN	MLWS
0300	0900	0200	0900	11.1	8.1	4.1	1.3
1500	2100	1400	2100				

Differences ST PETER PORT
0000 +0012 −0008 +0002 −2.1 −1.4 −0.6 −0.3

NOTE: To ascertain the depth of water over the sill at the
Channel Island Yacht Marina at Beaucette
1. Calculate the predicted *Height* of HW at St Peter Port
for the day.
2. Calculate the *Time* of LW for the day.
3. On following table, select the line corresponding to the
predicted Height of HW. The seven columns at the right
of the table show the depth of water over the sill at
hourly intervals either side of LW.

Predicted height of HW at St Peter Port HW metres	Depth of Water over the Sill in metres (sill dries 2.1m)						
	L.W.	∓1hr	∓2hr	∓3hr	∓4hr	∓5hr	∓6hr
9.75	—	—	0.30	2.74	5.18	6.79	7.62
9.44	—	—	0.15	2.74	5.03	6.55	7.31
9.14	—	—	0.60	2.74	4.87	6.31	7.01
8.83	—	—	0.76	2.74	4.72	6.03	6.70
8.53	—	—	0.91	2.74	4.57	5.79	6.40
8.22	—	—	1.06	2.74	4.42	5.54	6.09
7.92	—	0.18	1.21	2.74	4.26	5.27	5.79
7.61	—	0.42	1.37	2.74	4.11	5.03	5.48
7.31	0.30	0.70	1.52	2.74	3.96	4.78	5.18
7.00	0.60	0.94	1.67	2.74	3.81	4.51	4.87
6.70	0.91	1.21	1.82	2.74	3.65	4.27	4.57
6.39	1.21	1.46	1.98	2.74	3.50	4.02	4.27
6.09	1.52	1.70	2.13	2.74	3.35	3.75	3.96

SHELTER
Excellent shelter but entry restricted as above, and not
advised in strong onshore winds or heavy swell. Secure to
mooring buoy (see chartlet) while waiting. Space inside is
very limited.
NAVIGATION
Waypoint 49°30'.15N 02°28'.50W, 096°/276° from/to
entrance, 1.1M. Approach either from N or S along Little
Russel until between Platte Fougère Lt Ho (W with B
     25m) and Roustel Lt Tr (BW checked). Half way
  n, pick up the leading marks, but beware the Petit
   Rks (buoyed) to the N. Running in, there are
       rying areas to the S. Entrance channel buoyed
        buoys. The entrance is very narrow indeed.
    ARKS
    t FR; R stripe on W background at N
    Rear FR; W stripe on R background, on
    , with windsock.

RADIO TELEPHONE
VHF Ch 16; **80** 37. Other station: St Sampson Ch 16; 12
(H24).

Note: Entrance channel marked by 4 port and 4 starboard hand buoys in summer months

TELEPHONE (0481)
Hr Mr 45000; # 45000; Marinecall 0898 500 457;
Police 25111; Dr 25211 (St Johns Ambulance St Peter
Port).
FACILITIES
EC Thursday; **Channel Island Yacht Marina** (200+50
visitors), ☎ 45000, D, FW, C, AC, Gas, Gaz, V, R, ▣,
BH (30 ton), Slip, Bar; ✉; Ⓑ (St Sampson),
✈ (Guernsey).
Ferry UK — St Peter Port—Weymouth/Poole.

ST PETER PORT 10-17-14
Guernsey (Channel Islands)

CHARTS
Admiralty 3140, 808, 3654, 807; SHOM 6903, 6904; ECM
1014; Stanford 16; Imray C33A
TIDES
−0450 Dover; ML 5.0; Duration 0500; Zone 0 (GMT)

Standard Port ST HELIER (←)

Times				Height (metres)			
HW		LW		MHWS	MHWN	MLWN	MLWS
0300	0900	0200	0900	11.1	8.1	4.1	1.3
1500	2100	1400	2100				

Differences ST PETER PORT
0000 +0012 −0008 +0002 −2.1 −1.4 −0.6 −0.3

SHELTER
Good shelter especially in the Victoria Marina which has a
sill 4.4 m above CD. Access approx HW∓3. Approach via
buoyed channel along S side of harbour. Marina waiting
pontoon and some visitors' moorings to E of marina
entrance. Local boat moorings occupy centre of harbour,
but there is also a fairway to N of them. Albert Dock
Marina and Queen Elizabeth II Marina are for local boats
only. Alternative anchorages in Guernsey are Havelet Bay,
Icart Pt, Fermain Bay, St Sampsons (see 10.17.25) and
Bordeaux. Customs/immigration at St Peter Port, St
Sampson and Beaucette (10.17.13).
NAVIGATION
Waypoint 49°27'.88N 02°30'.70W, 040°/220° from/to
front Ldg Lt 220°, 0.68M. Offlying dangers, big tidal range
and strong tidal streams demand careful navigation.
Easiest approach from N via Big Russel between Herm
and Sark passing S of Lower Heads Lt buoy: slightly more
direct, the Little Russel which needs care — see 10.17.5.

ST. PETER PORT *continued*

Coming round W and S of Guernsey, give Les Hanois a wide berth. Beware ferries and shipping.

LIGHTS AND MARKS

Ldg Lts: Front Castle Breakwater head Al WR 10s 14m 16M (vis 187°-007°) Horn 15s: Rear Belvedere Oc 10s 61m 14M in line at 220°.

On White Rock Pierhead

FR (vis from seaward) — No entry

FR (vis from landward) — No exit

On SW corner of New Pier

FR (vis from landward) — No exit

These signals do not apply to small boats, less than 15m LOA, under power and keeping clear of the fairways.

RADIO TELEPHONE

Call: *Port Control* VHF Ch **12** 78 (H24). Messages may be sent through St Peter Port Radio — See 6.3.15.

TELEPHONE (0481)

Hr Mr 20229; Signal Station (CG) 20085; ⌗ 26911; Marina Office 25987; Marinecall 0898 500 457; Police 25111; Dr 25211 (St John's Ambulance).

FACILITIES

EC Thursday; **Victoria Marina** (280, all visitors) ☎ 25987, Slip, FW, AC, ▣, R, Max stay 14 days (Access HW∓3 sill maintains level CD+4.2m); **North Pier** ☎ 20085, C (32 ton 20 ton 7 ton), AB; **Jetty Harbour Office** ☎ 20229, AB; **Castle Pier** P, D; **Marquand Bros.** ☎ 20962, CH, Gas, Gaz; **Guernsey Marine Services** ☎ 47158, ME, El, BY; **Navigation and Marine Suppliers** ☎ 25838, CH, ACA; **G. Scott** ☎ 28989, SM; **Herm Seaway Marine** ☎ 26829, ME, El, Gas, Gaz; **Seaward Marine** ☎ 45353, ME, El, BY, CH; **John Webster (Marine Management)** ☎ 27030; **Royal Channel Islands YC** ☎ 25500; Bar, **Guernsey YC** ☎ 22838; **Auto Electrical & Diesel Service** ☎ 26811, El; **Boatwork+** ☎ 26071, Ⓔ, CH, ME, El, ACA; **Norman Piette** ☎ 45801, Gas, Gaz; **Greenway Marine** ☎ 45805 ME, El; **Town** P, D, V, CH, R, ▣, Bar. ✉; Ⓑ; ⇌ (ferry to Weymouth, Poole, Cherbourg, St. Malo); Hydrofoil to Sark, Weymouth, Jersey, St Malo; ✈ (Guernsey Airport).

Ferry UK—Weymouth/Poole.

HERM. Herm belongs to the States of Guernsey and landing is permitted on payment of a landing fee. The best anchorages are: off Rosière steps in the SW (almost landlocked but poor holding); Herm Harbour just N — dries; Belvoir Bay on the E side.

Herm harbour office ☎ 22377.

BRAYE 10-17-15

Alderney (Channel Islands)

CHARTS

Admiralty 2845, 3653, 2669, 60; SHOM 6934; ECM 1014; Stanford 16; Imray C33A

TIDES

−0410 Dover; ML 3.6; Duration 0545; Zone 0 (GMT).

Standard Port ST HELIER (←)

Times				Height (metres)			
HW		LW		MHWS	MHWN	MLWN	MLWS
0300	0900	0200	0900	11.1	8.1	4.1	1.3
1500	2100	1400	2100				

Differences BRAYE

+0050 +0040 +0025 +0105 −4.8 −3.4 −1.5 −0.5

SHELTER

Good shelter in Braye (Alderney) Harbour except in strong N and NE winds. There are 80 visitors' yellow mooring buoys in the western part of the harbour and the area near Fort Albert. Anchorage in harbour is good, but keep clear of the jetty because of steamer traffic. Landing on Admiralty Pier is forbidden. The old derelict length of pier extending in NE direction has been removed. There is a FY Lt on end of remaining quay, as shown. Harbour speed limit 4 kn.

NAVIGATION

Waypoint 49°44'.32N 02°10'.90W, 035°/215° from/to front Ldg Lt 215°, 1.05M. The principal dangers are the strong tidal streams, but the N coast of Alderney is covered with detached rocks. The safest approach is from the NE and even if coming from the S, it may be worth going the long way round, giving the Casquets a wide berth and coming down from the N. Beware the Swinge and Alderney Race (see 10.17.5). In harbour entrance, beware the breakwater submerged extension.

LIGHTS AND MARKS

Clearing line for the Nannels:

N side of Fort Albert and end of Admiralty Pier 115°.

Ldg Lts 215° lead into harbour. Front Q 8m 17M vis 210°-220° Rear Iso 10s 17m 18M vis 210°-220°

Daymarks — St Anne's church spire in line with W beacon on Douglas Quay at 210°

There is a sector Lt at Chateau à l'Etoc Pt E of the harbour, Iso WR 4s; vis R071°-111°, W111°-151°. This is in line 111° with the Quenard Pt Lt Ho Fl (4) 15s.

Lt buoys QR and QG mark fairway.

RADIO TELEPHONE

Call: *Alderney Radio* VHF Ch 16; 74 (Nov-Mar 0800-1700, Apl, May and mid Sept to end Oct 0800-1800; June to mid Sept 0800-2200: all LT). Outside these hours call St Peter Port. Mainbrayce Marine Ch **80** 37 (Apl-mid Sept: 0800-2000 LT). For Casquets traffic scheme see Cherbourg (10.17.24).

TELEPHONE (048 182)

Hr Mr 2620; ⌗ 2620; Marinecall 0898 500 457; Police 2731; Dr 2077; Ⓗ 2822.

FACILITIES

EC Wednesday; **Marine Engine Services** ☎ 3586, ME, El, Sh; **Mainbrayce** ☎ 2772, Slip, D, FW, ME, El, Ⓔ, Gas, SM, ACA, Sh, CH, P, D (inner harbour HW∓2); (For Water Taxi service, call Mainbrayce on Ch 16 **80** 37); **Harbour** M, FW, C, ▣; **Jetty** FW; **Sapper Slip** FW; **Alderney SC** ☎ 2758, Bar; **Riduna Garage** ☎ 2919, P, D (cans), Gaz, Gas, Kos. **Blanchard's Building Supplies** ☎ 2722 P and D (cans), Gas; **Town** V, R, ▣, Bar. ✉; Ⓑ;

✈ — to Guernsey, Jersey, Hurn, Southampton or Cherbourg

Ferry UK — via Guernsey—Weymouth/Poole (Direct to Torquay, Tuesdays mid-June — early Sept)

BRAYE (ALDERNEY) *continued*

SAINT QUAY-PORTRIEUX
Côtes du Nord

10-17-16

CHARTS
Admiralty 3672, 2668, 2669; SHOM 5725, 833, 878;
ECM 536; Stanford 16; Imray C33B, C34

TIDES
−0520 Dover; ML 6.4; Duration 0550; Zone −0100

Standard Port ST-MALO (→)

Times				Height (metres)			
HW		LW		MHWS	MHWN	MLWN	MLWS
0805	0120	0749	0256	12.2	9.2	4.4	1.5
2005	1320	1949	1456				

Differences ST QUAY-PORTRIEUX

−0005	−0006	−0021	−0032	−0.8	−0.6	−0.3	−0.1

SHELTER
There is reasonable shelter in the harbour but in winds
from SE to N, a surge occurs. Anchorage in the Rade de
Portrieux is good but affected by winds from N to SE.
Harbour dries. Max stay three days in season.

NAVIGATION
Waypoint 48°41′.00N 02°49′.70W, 347°/167° from/to
Moulières de Portrieux E cardinal Bn, 1.7M. Portrieux lies
inside the Roches de St Quay the channel between being
about ½ M wide. N end of the Roches de St Quay is the
Île Harbour Lt Ho. Beware the Moulières de Portrieux.

~HTS AND MARKS
~arbour (off chartlet) Oc (2) WRG 6s 16m 11/8M; W
~ Tr and dwelling, R top. Jetty head Iso WG 4s 11m
~ W 8-sided Tr, G top; vis G (unintens) 020°-110°,
~ W305°-309°, G309°-020°; in line with
~pic) leads 260°. Mole head FlR 4s 9m 7M;

~~E
~30; 1330-1830 LT. H24 in season).

~31; Aff Mar 96.70.42.27; CROSS

98.89.31.31; SNSM 96.70.52.04; ⌗ 96.33.33.03;
Meteo 99.46.10.46; Police 96.70.61.24; Dr 96.70.41.31;
Brit Consul 99.46.26.64.

FACILITIES
Harbour (500+8 visitors) − Max 3 days in July/Aug.
Slip, M, P, D, L, FW, Sh, C (1.5 ton), ME, El, Sh, CH,
AB, R, Bar; **Cercle de la Voile de Portrieux**
☎ 96.70.41.76, M, FW, C (1 ton), Bar; **Mathurin Cras**
☎ 96.70.57.83, ME, El, C (5 ton), Sh, Ⓔ, CH;
Town V, Gaz, R, Bar. ✉; Ⓑ; ⇌ (bus to St Brieuc);
✈ (St Brieuc—Armor).
Ferry UK − St Malo—Portsmouth.

BINIC 10-17-17
Côtes du Nord

CHARTS
Admiralty 3674, 2668, 2669; SHOM 833, 5725; ECM 536;
Stanford 16; Imray C33B

TIDES
−0525 Dover; ML 5.6; Duration 0550; Zone −0100

Standard Port ST-MALO (→)

Times				Height (metres)			
HW		LW		MHWS	MHWN	MLWN	MLWS
0805	0120	0749	0256	12.2	9.2	4.4	1.5
2005	1320	1949	1456				

Differences BINIC
−0002	−0004	−0018	−0029	−0.8	−0.5	−0.3	−0.1

SHELTER
Good shelter especially in Bassin à Flot (yacht harbour).
Gate opens in working hours when tide reaches 9.5m (not
near neaps). Access to Port de Penthièvre about HW∓3.

NAVIGATION
Waypoint 48°37'.00N 02°42'.00W, 078°/258° from/to
entrance, 4.7M. Best approach from E, from Baie de St
Brieuc (see 10.17.5) keeping E of Caffa W cardinal buoy,
from which entrance is 246°; or from N through Rade de
Portrieux. Entrance between moles, dries 4.2m.

LIGHTS AND MARKS
N mole head Oc(3) 12s 12m 12M; W Tr, G gallery. Gate
and sliding bridge signals on mast N of gate:
By day — St Andrew's Cross, B on W flag — Gate open
By night — W and R Lts (hor)   No entry
           — W and G Lts (hor)   No exit
           — R and G Lts (hor)   No
                                        movements

RADIO TELEPHONE
VHF Ch 09.

TELEPHONE (96)
Hr Mr 96.73.61.86; Aff Mar 96.73.61.86; CROSS
98.89.31.31; ⌗ 96.42.61.84; Auto 96.20.01.92;
Police 96.70.61.24; Dr 96.42.61.05; Brit Consul
99.46.26.64.

FACILITIES
Basin Slip, FW, AB; Jean Bart Marine ☎ 96.73.75.28,
CH, SHOM; Marinarmor ☎ 96.73.60.55, CH, ME, El, Ⓔ,
Sh, SM; Club Nautique de Binic ☎ 96.61.93.55; Town
P, V, Gaz, R, Bar. ✉; Ⓑ; ⇌ (bus to St Brieuc);
✈ (St Brieuc). Ferry UK — St Malo—Portsmouth.

LE LÉGUÉ (ST BRIEUC)
Côtes du Nord   10-17-18

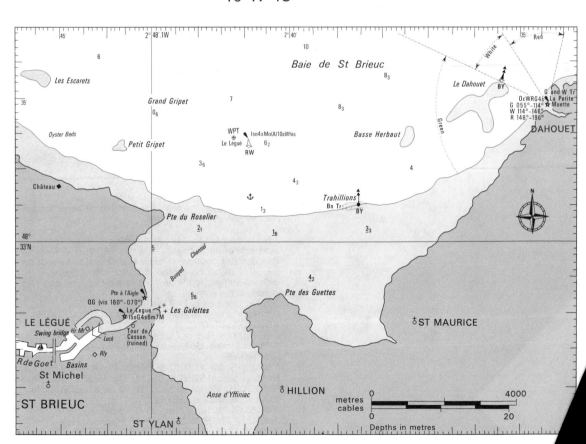

CHARTS
Admiralty 3674; SHOM 833, 5725; ECM 536; Stanford 16; Imray C34, C33B

TIDES
−0520 Dover; ML 5.6; Duration 0550; Zone −0100

Standard Port ST-MALO (→)

Times				Height (metres)			
HW		LW		MHWS	MHWN	MLWN	MLWS
0805	0120	0749	0256	12.2	9.2	4.4	1.5
2005	1320	1949	1456				

Differences LE LÉGUÉ
−0002	−0004	−0018	−0029	−0.8	−0.5	−0.3	−0.1

DAHOUET
−0007	−0005	−0009	−0035	−0.9	−0.5	−0.5	−0.2

SHELTER
Le Légué is the port for St Brieuc and offers very good shelter especially in the wet basin. Le Quai Gilette is a commercial quay but yachts can lie there whilst waiting for lock to open (HW −2 to HW +1 springs; HW ∓1 neaps). Yachts use Bassin No 2 (min 3m) near viaduct.

NAVIGATION
Waypoint Le Légué (safe water) buoy, Iso 4s Mo (A) 10s Whis, 48°34′.40N 02°41′.20W, 032°/212° from/to Pte à l'Aigle Lt, 2.6M. The area dries beyond Pte du Roselier. See 10.17.5. Keep close to Pte à l'Aigle to avoid the Galettes Rks. Channel buoyed (with some gaps). The lock sill is 5.0m above CD.

LIGHTS AND MARKS
There are no leading lines, but there are two Lts on the N side of the river de Gouet ent.
Pte à l'Aigle QG vis 160°-070° 13m 7M. Jetée de la Douane (W column with G top) Iso G 4s 6m 7M.

RADIO TELEPHONE
Call: *Légué Port* VHF Ch 12 16 (occas).

TELEPHONE (96)
Hr Mr 96.33.35.41; Aff Mar 96.61.22.61; CROSS 98.89.31.31; Meteo 96.94.94.09; Auto 96.78.51.51; SNSM 96.88.35.47; ⌗ 96.33.33.03; Police 96.94.52.25; Dr St Brieuc 96.61.49.07; Brit Consul 99.46.26.64.

FACILITIES
Quai AB, C (30 ton); **22 Voiles** ☎ 96.33.14.04, SM; **Inter-Nautic** ☎ 96.33.28.71, ME, Sh, Ⓔ, El, CH; **Lecoq** ☎ 96.33.16.68, Sh, ME, El, CH; **Travadon** ☎ 96.33.38.54, ME. **Town (St Brieuc)** P, D, FW, ME, El, CH, Gaz, V, R, Bar, ✉; Ⓑ; ≠; ✈.
Ferry UK — St Malo—Portsmouth.

ST MALO/DINARD　10-17-19
Ille et Vilaine

CHARTS
Admiralty 2700, 3659; SHOM 5645, 844; ECM 535; Stanford 16; Imray C33B

TIDES
−0515 Dover; ML 6.8; Duration 0535; Zone −0100

Standard Port ST-MALO (→)

Times				Height (metres)			
HW		LW		MHWS	MHWN	MLWN	MLWS
0805	0120	0749	0256	12.2	9.2	4.4	1.5
2005	1320	1949	1456				

Differences ERQUY
−0005	−0004	−0013	−0028	−0.8	−0.5	−0.3	−0.1

SAINT CAST
−0002	0000	−0006	−0018	−0.1	−0.1	0.0	0.0

CANCALE
+0005	+0002	+0012	+0012	+1.3	+1.1	+0.8	+0.6

Saint-Malo is a Standard Port and the tidal predictions for each day of the year are given below.

SHELTER
Excellent shelter in Bassin Vauban or Bassin Duguay-Trouin, min depth 6m. Lock opens HW −2½ to HW +1½. Also good shelter in Port des Bas Sablons Marina entered over sill 2m above CD. There is a yacht anchorage at Dinard.

NAVIGATION
Waypoint Fairway (safe water) buoy, LFl, Whis, 48°41′.42N 02°07′.20W, 307°/127° from/to Grand Jardin Lt, 1.9M. There are numerous dangerous rocks round the entrance channel and there are strong tidal streams. There are three principal entrance channels, Grande Porte channel, Petite Porte channel and the Grande Conchée channel. Care needs to be exercised on all three. Lights at night are very good for the first two. Speed limit in basins is 3 kn. Anchoring in basins is forbidden.

LIGHTS AND MARKS
Chenal de la Grande Porte; Outer Ldg Lts at 089° are:
Front — Le Grand Jardin Fl (2) R 10s 24m 15M grey Tr.
Rear — Rochebonne (off chartlet) 4.2M from Front, FR 40m 25M leads into Chenal de la Petite Porte.
Leading Lts (Les Bas Sablons FG 20m 16M in front and La Ballue FG 69m 25M at rear) at 129° lead in from the Grand Jardin Lt Ho.
La Plate Lt VQ WRG, 11m 9/6M W140°-203°, R203°-210°, W210°-225°, G225°-140°.
St Malo Lock signals

G
W } No entry to lock without instructions
G

G
G } Boats may enter lock
G

R
R } No entry. Keep 200m from gates
R

A Y Lt alongside the top Lt shows that all gates are open but instructions are the same.

2 R Lts over G Lt — all movements prohibited except departure of large ships
Port des Bas Sablons — there is a sill and the depth over the sill is shown on a neon indicator; white figures indicate metres, red figures indicate decimetres and zero indicates 'No entry'.
Ldg Lts into basin, 2 FR, at 071°.
Les Bas Sablons Marina Lt Fl G 4s.

RADIO TELEPHONE
Call: *St Malo Port* or *Grand Jardin* VHF Ch 12 (H24). Bas Sablons Marina, St Servan Ch 09. Port Vauban Ch 09.

TELEPHONE
ST MALO Hr Mr 99.81.62.86; Hr Mr (Sablons) 99.81.71.34; Hr Mr (Vauban) 99.56.51.91; Aff Mar 99.56.87.00; CROSS 98.89.31.31; SNSM 98.89.31.31; ⌗ 99.81.65.90; Meteo 99.46.10.46; Police 99.81.52.30; Ⓗ 99.56.56.19; Brit Consul 99.46.26.64
DINARD Hr Mr 99.46.65.55; ⌗ 99.46.12.42; Meteo 99.46.10.46; Auto 99.46.18.77; Ⓗ 99.46.18.68.

ST MALO *continued*

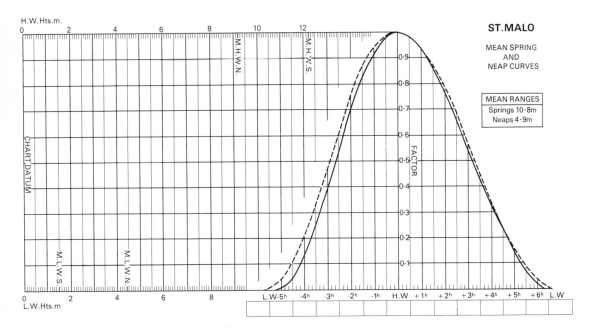

H.W.Hts.m.

ST.MALO

MEAN SPRING
AND
NEAP CURVES

MEAN RANGES
Springs 10·8m
Neaps 4·9m

CHART DATUM

M.H.W.N.

M.H.W.S.

FACTOR

M.L.W.S.

M.L.W.N.

L.W.Hts.m.

L.W -5ʰ -4ʰ -3ʰ -2ʰ -1ʰ H.W +1ʰ +2ʰ +3ʰ +4ʰ +5ʰ +6ʰ L.W

Depths in metres

metres
cables

DINARD

FRANCE NORTH COAST – SAINT MALO

Lat 48°38'N   Long 2°02'W

TIMES AND HEIGHTS OF HIGH AND LOW WATERS

YEAR **1991**

Time Zone -0100
(French Standard Time)
Subtract one hour for GMT For French Summer Time add ONE hour in non-shaded areas

JANUARY

Day	Time	m	Time	m	Time	m	Time	m
1 Tu	0145	1.8	0714	12.4	1414	1.3	1939	12.1
2 W	0241	1.5	0803	12.6	1508	1.1	2027	12.2
3 Th	0332	1.4	0850	12.6	1554	1.2	2111	12.0
4 F	0413	1.6	0932	12.4	1630	1.5	2150	11.6
5 Sa	0447	2.0	1009	11.9	1704	2.0	2227	11.1
6 Su	0521	2.5	1047	11.3	1739	2.7	2306	10.5
7 M	0557	3.2	1126	10.5	1817	3.4	2348	9.7
8 Tu	0638	3.9	1213	9.7	1903	4.1		
9 W	0043	9.2	0733	4.4	1318	9.1	2009	4.6
10 Th	0158	8.8	0849	4.7	1439	8.8	2129	4.8
11 F	0320	8.9	1010	4.6	1559	8.9	2249	4.6
12 Sa	0434	9.3	1123	4.3	1705	9.3	2355	4.2
13 Su	0532	9.8	1223	3.8	1757	9.8		
14 M	0048	3.7	0619	10.4	1311	3.2	1840	10.3
15 Tu	0132	3.2	0659	10.9	1353	2.8	1917	10.7
16 W	0213	2.8	0734	11.3	1431	2.4	1950	11.0
17 Th	0250	2.5	0807	11.6	1507	2.1	2022	11.2
18 F	0324	2.2	0839	11.7	1539	1.9	2054	11.3
19 Sa	0355	2.1	0909	11.8	1609	1.9	2124	11.4
20 Su	0422	2.2	0939	11.6	1635	2.0	2154	11.1
21 M	0449	2.3	1009	11.4	1703	2.3	2226	10.9
22 Tu	0519	2.7	1042	11.0	1735	2.8	2301	10.4
23 W	0553	3.1	1121	10.4	1813	3.3	2344	9.9
24 Th	0636	3.6	1212	9.8	1905	3.9		
25 F	0048	9.5	0742	4.0	1329	9.4	2024	4.1
26 Sa	0217	9.5	0911	4.0	1506	9.5	2158	3.9
27 Su	0351	9.9	1045	3.5	1634	10.0	2327	3.3
28 M	0511	10.8	1205	2.7	1745	10.9		
29 Tu	0039	2.5	0615	11.6	1311	1.8	1844	11.6
30 W	0139	1.7	0709	12.3	1407	1.2	1932	12.1
31 Th	0231	1.2	0754	12.7	1455	0.7	2015	12.3

FEBRUARY

Day	Time	m	Time	m	Time	m	Time	m
1 F	0318	1.0	0835	12.8	1538	0.7	2053	12.3
2 Sa	0356	1.1	0912	12.6	1612	1.0	2128	12.0
3 Su	0426	1.4	0944	12.2	1640	1.5	2159	11.5
4 M	0453	2.0	1015	11.5	1708	2.2	2230	10.8
5 TU	0523	2.8	1047	10.7	1738	3.1	2303	9.9
6 W	0554	3.7	1121	9.7	1821	4.1	2343	9.1
7 Th	0633	4.4	1208	8.7	1901	4.9		
8 F	0042	8.4	0737	5.1	1326	8.1	2023	5.3
9 Sa	0217	8.2	0914	5.2	1510	8.1	2205	5.2
10 Su	0358	8.5	1052	4.7	1639	8.5	2329	4.6
11 M	0511	9.2	1201	4.1	1738	9.3		
12 Tu	0028	3.9	0601	10.0	1252	3.3	1823	10.0
13 W	0113	3.1	0641	10.8	1334	2.6	1859	10.7
14 Th	0152	2.5	0716	11.4	1411	2.0	1932	11.2
15 F	0228	1.9	0748	11.9	1445	1.6	2002	11.7
16 Sa	0301	1.6	0817	12.2	1518	1.3	2033	11.9
17 Su	0334	1.4	0848	12.3	1549	1.2	2103	12.0
18 M	0403	1.4	0918	12.2	1616	1.4	2133	11.8
19 Tu	0429	1.6	0948	11.9	1643	1.7	2202	11.4
20 W	0457	2.1	1019	11.3	1713	2.4	2237	10.8
21 Th	0529	2.8	1056	10.5	1749	3.2	2318	10.0
22 F	0611	3.6	1144	9.5	1839	4.0		
23 Sa	0018	9.2	0715	4.2	1303	8.9	2004	4.5
24 Su	0159	9.0	0857	4.2	1457	8.9	2153	4.2
25 M	0348	9.6	1042	3.6	1633	9.7	2326	3.3
26 Tu	0510	10.6	1202	2.6	1741	10.7		
27 W	0034	2.3	0609	11.5	1302	1.7	1833	11.5
28 Th	0127	1.6	0656	12.2	1352	1.0	1917	12.1

MARCH

Day	Time	m	Time	m	Time	m	Time	m
1 F	0214	1.0	0737	12.6	1435	0.6	1955	12.4
2 Sa	0255	0.8	0813	12.7	1514	0.6	2029	12.4
3 Su	0331	0.9	0846	12.6	1547	0.9	2102	12.1
4 M	0402	1.3	0916	12.2	1615	1.5	2131	11.6
5 Tu	0427	1.9	0945	11.5	1640	2.2	2158	10.9
6 W	0453	2.6	1012	10.6	1706	3.0	2227	10.1
7 Th	0520	3.5	1044	9.6	1736	4.0	2302	9.2
8 F	0554	4.3	1122	8.6	1815	4.9	2349	8.4
9 Sa	0643	5.1	1223	7.8	1923	5.5		
10 Su	0115	7.9	0816	5.3	1415	7.6	2114	5.4
11 M	0313	8.2	1006	4.9	1600	8.2	2251	4.7
12 Tu	0436	8.9	1125	4.1	1706	9.0	2354	3.9
13 W	0529	9.8	1218	3.2	1750	9.9		
14 Th	0040	3.0	0611	10.7	1300	2.4	1829	10.8
15 F	0119	2.2	0646	11.5	1337	1.7	1903	11.5
16 Sa	0156	1.6	0719	12.1	1414	1.2	1935	12.0
17 Su	0231	1.0	0750	12.4	1448	0.9	2006	12.3
18 M	0306	0.0	0822	12.5	1523	0.8	2039	12.3
19 Tu	0339	1.0	0854	12.4	1556	1.1	2111	12.1
20 W	0412	1.3	0928	12.0	1626	1.6	2144	11.6
21 Th	0441	1.9	1002	11.2	1658	2.4	2221	10.9
22 F	0516	2.7	1042	10.3	1737	3.3	2306	9.9
23 Sa	0602	3.6	1135	9.2	1832	4.1		
24 Su	0011	9.2	0711	4.2	1301	8.7	2002	4.4
25 M	0159	9.1	0857	4.1	1455	8.9	2149	4.0
26 Tu	0344	9.7	1036	3.3	1623	9.8	2313	3.1
27 W	0456	10.7	1146	2.5	1725	10.7		
28 Th	0014	2.2	0549	11.5	1240	1.7	1813	11.4
29 F	0104	1.6	0634	12.0	1326	1.3	1854	11.9
30 Sa	0147	1.2	0712	12.3	1408	1.0	1930	12.2
31 Su	0226	1.1	0747	12.4	1444	1.1	2002	12.2

APRIL

Day	Time	m	Time	m	Time	m	Time	m
1 M	0302	1.2	0818	12.2	1519	1.4	2034	11.9
2 Tu	0335	1.2	0849	11.8	1549	1.8	2104	11.5
3 W	0404	2.0	0919	11.1	1617	2.4	2133	10.9
4 Th	0429	2.7	0948	10.4	1642	3.2	2202	10.2
5 F	0457	3.4	1017	9.5	1712	4.0	2235	9.3
6 Sa	0529	4.2	1055	8.6	1749	4.7	2319	8.6
7 Su	0613	4.8	1148	8.0	1844	5.2		
8 M	0027	8.1	0726	5.1	1319	7.8	2018	5.2
9 Tu	0214	8.3	0908	4.8	1502	8.2	2152	4.7
10 W	0341	8.9	1030	4.1	1614	9.0	2301	3.9
11 Th	0442	9.8	1128	3.2	1706	9.9	2353	3.0
12 F	0527	10.7	1214	2.4	1746	10.9		
13 Sa	0035	2.1	0607	11.4	1255	1.7	1825	11.6
14 Su	0115	1.5	0644	12.0	1336	1.2	1902	12.1
15 M	0156	1.1	0720	12.4	1416	0.9	1938	12.4
16 Tu	0236	0.9	0756	12.5	1456	0.9	2015	12.4
17 W	0317	1.0	0834	12.3	1537	1.2	2053	12.2
18 Th	0357	1.4	0913	11.8	1615	1.8	2133	11.7
19 F	0432	1.9	0953	11.0	1651	2.5	2215	10.9
20 Sa	0512	2.7	1039	10.1	1736	3.3	2306	10.1
21 Su	0603	3.4	1137	9.3	1833	4.0		
22 M	0014	9.5	0712	3.9	1300	9.0	1957	4.1
23 Tu	0150	9.5	0844	3.7	1437	9.3	2128	3.7
24 W	0319	10.0	1008	3.2	1556	9.9	2244	3.0
25 Th	0426	10.6	1114	2.6	1655	10.6	2343	2.5
26 F	0520	11.1	1209	2.1	1743	11.1		
27 Sa	0032	2.0	0604	11.5	1255	1.8	1825	11.5
28 Su	0117	1.8	0645	11.7	1337	1.7	1903	11.7
29 M	0158	1.7	0720	11.7	1416	1.8	1937	11.7
30 Tu	0235	1.8	0753	11.5	1453	2.0	2010	11.6

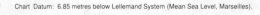

Chart Datum: 6.85 metres below Lellemand System (Mean Sea Level, Marseilles).

FRANCE NORTH COAST – SAINT MALO

Lat 48°38'N   Long 2°02'W

TIMES AND HEIGHTS OF HIGH AND LOW WATERS

YEAR **1991**

Time Zone -0100
(French Standard Time) Subtract one hour for GMT For French Summer Time add ONE hour in non-shaded areas

MAY

Day	Time	m	Time	m	Time	m	Time	m
1 W	0311	2.0	0826	11.2	1527	2.3	2042	11.2
2 Th	0343	2.3	0858	10.8	1558	2.7	2113	10.8
3 F	0413	2.8	0929	10.2	1626	3.2	2144	10.3
4 Sa	0440	3.3	1001	9.6	1657	3.8	2218	9.7
5 Su	0513	3.9	1037	9.0	1732	4.3	2259	9.1
6 M	0554	4.3	1125	8.5	1818	4.7	2354	8.7
7 Tu	0649	4.6	1229	8.3	1924	4.7		
8 W	0111	8.7	0805	4.5	1353	8.5	2044	4.4
9 Th	0233	9.1	0921	4.0	1508	9.1	2155	3.8
10 F	0340	9.8	1026	3.3	1608	9.9	2254	3.1
11 Sa	0434	10.5	1120	2.7	1658	10.7	2346	2.4
12 Su	0522	11.2	1211	2.0	1744	11.4		
13 M	0035	1.8	0607	11.8	1258	1.6	1829	12.0
14 Tu	0122	1.4	0651	12.1	1346	1.3	1913	12.3
15 W	0211	1.2	0735	12.2	1436	1.3	1957	12.4
16 Th	0300	1.2	0819	12.1	1524	1.5	2042	12.2
17 F	0348	1.4	0905	11.7	1609	1.8	2128	11.8
18 Sa	0428	1.9	0951	11.1	1650	2.4	2214	11.2
19 Su	0511	2.4	1038	10.4	1735	3.0	2304	10.7
20 M	0600	2.9	1133	9.8	1827	3.4		
21 Tu	0004	10.2	0658	3.3	1240	9.5	1933	3.6
22 W	0119	10.0	0811	3.4	1359	9.5	2049	3.6
23 Th	0237	10.0	0926	3.3	1514	9.8	2200	3.3
24 F	0346	10.2	1033	3.1	1615	10.2	2303	3.0
25 Sa	0444	10.5	1132	2.9	1710	10.6	2358	2.8
26 Su	0533	10.7	1223	2.7	1756	10.9		
27 M	0047	2.6	0618	10.9	1310	2.6	1838	11.1
28 Tu	0131	2.4	0658	10.9	1353	2.5	1917	11.2
29 W	0213	2.4	0735	10.9	1432	2.6	1952	11.2
30 Th	0251	2.4	0809	10.8	1510	2.7	2026	11.1
31 F	0327	2.5	0842	10.6	1544	2.9	2059	10.9

JUNE

Day	Time	m	Time	m	Time	m	Time	m
1 Sa	0400	2.8	0915	10.3	1615	3.1	2132	10.6
2 Su	0428	3.0	0948	9.9	1643	3.4	2204	10.2
3 M	0500	3.4	1022	9.6	1716	3.7	2241	9.8
4 Tu	0534	3.7	1102	9.3	1755	4.0	2324	9.5
5 W	0616	3.9	1148	9.0	1839	4.1		
6 Th	0016	9.4	0707	4.0	1249	9.1	1940	4.1
7 F	0124	9.5	0813	3.9	1400	9.3	2048	3.8
8 Sa	0234	9.7	0921	3.5	1508	9.8	2155	3.3
9 Su	0340	10.2	1027	3.1	1611	10.5	2258	2.8
10 M	0441	10.8	1129	2.6	1709	11.1		
11 Tu	0000	2.2	0537	11.3	1228	2.1	1803	11.7
12 W	0057	1.8	0631	11.7	1326	1.7	1857	12.1
13 Th	0155	1.4	0722	11.9	1423	1.5	1948	12.3
14 F	0251	1.2	0812	12.0	1517	1.5	2037	12.3
15 Sa	0342	1.3	0901	11.8	1605	1.6	2123	12.2
16 Su	0424	1.5	0945	11.5	1644	1.9	2207	11.8
17 M	0504	1.8	1029	11.0	1725	2.4	2252	11.3
18 Tu	0546	2.4	1114	10.5	1807	2.9	2339	10.7
19 W	0630	2.9	1205	9.9	1856	3.3		
20 Th	0034	10.2	0726	3.4	1309	9.6	1959	3.7
21 F	0144	9.8	0833	3.8	1420	9.4	2109	3.9
22 Sa	0257	9.6	0945	3.9	1533	9.5	2220	3.8
23 Su	0405	9.8	1054	3.8	1636	9.8	2325	3.6
24 M	0500	9.8	1155	3.6	1732	10.2		
25 Tu	0022	3.3	0557	10.1	1247	3.3	1819	10.5
26 W	0111	3.0	0641	10.4	1334	3.0	1901	10.8
27 Th	0156	2.7	0730	10.6	1416	2.9	1938	11.0
28 F	0236	2.5	0755	10.7	1454	2.7	2012	11.1
29 Sa	0313	2.5	0828	10.7	1530	2.7	2045	11.1
30 Su	0346	2.4	0901	10.7	1602	2.7	2116	11.0

JULY

Day	Time	m	Time	m	Time	m	Time	m
1 M	0415	2.5	0932	10.6	1628	2.8	2147	10.9
2 Tu	0443	2.7	1002	10.4	1657	3.0	2219	10.7
3 W	0513	2.9	1036	10.1	1729	3.2	2253	10.3
4 Th	0546	3.2	1113	9.8	1804	3.5	2335	10.0
5 F	0625	3.5	1158	9.6	1849	3.7		
6 Sa	0025	9.7	0716	3.7	1258	9.6	1949	3.8
7 Su	0135	9.6	0826	3.8	1414	9.6	2103	3.7
8 M	0253	9.8	0943	3.6	1533	10.0	2222	3.3
9 Tu	0409	10.2	1101	3.1	1645	10.7	2336	2.7
10 W	0519	10.8	1212	2.5	1749	11.4		
11 Th	0044	2.0	0620	11.4	1315	1.9	1849	12.0
12 F	0146	1.4	0715	11.9	1415	1.4	1941	12.4
13 Sa	0242	1.0	0805	12.1	1509	1.2	2028	12.6
14 Su	0333	0.8	0851	12.2	1554	1.2	2112	12.5
15 M	0414	1.0	0932	12.0	1631	1.4	2151	12.3
16 Tu	0447	1.4	1009	11.5	1705	1.9	2228	11.7
17 W	0522	2.0	1047	10.9	1739	2.6	2307	10.9
18 Th	0559	2.8	1127	10.2	1818	3.3	2350	10.1
19 F	0639	3.6	1215	9.5	1906	4.0		
20 Sa	0046	9.3	0738	4.2	1324	8.9	2016	4.4
21 Su	0203	8.8	0855	4.6	1447	8.9	2137	4.5
22 M	0328	8.8	1019	4.5	1607	9.1	2257	4.2
23 Tu	0442	9.0	1132	4.2	1712	9.6		
24 W	0003	3.8	0539	9.5	1230	3.7	1803	10.2
25 Th	0055	3.2	0626	10.0	1318	3.2	1846	10.7
26 F	0138	2.8	0705	10.5	1359	2.8	1922	11.1
27 Sa	0217	2.4	0739	10.8	1436	2.5	1954	11.4
28 Su	0253	2.1	0811	11.1	1511	2.2	2026	11.6
29 M	0327	1.9	0841	11.2	1542	2.1	2056	11.6
30 Tu	0357	1.9	0911	11.2	1610	2.1	2125	11.5
31 W	0423	2.0	0939	11.1	1635	2.3	2154	11.3

AUGUST

Day	Time	m	Time	m	Time	m	Time	m
1 Th	0449	2.3	1009	10.8	1703	2.6	2225	10.9
2 F	0518	2.7	1042	10.5	1734	3.0	2300	10.4
3 Sa	0552	3.2	1120	9.9	1813	3.5	2345	9.8
4 Su	0637	3.8	1213	9.5	1907	4.0		
5 M	0050	9.3	0745	4.1	1334	9.3	2030	4.1
6 Tu	0223	9.3	0917	4.1	1510	9.6	2203	3.7
7 W	0356	9.7	1048	3.5	1635	10.5	2328	2.9
8 Th	0512	10.6	1205	2.6	1744	11.4		
9 F	0038	1.9	0613	11.4	1308	1.8	1840	12.2
10 Sa	0137	1.2	0706	12.0	1403	1.2	1929	12.7
11 Su	0228	0.7	0750	12.4	1452	0.8	2012	12.9
12 M	0315	0.5	0832	12.5	1535	0.8	2052	12.8
13 Tu	0354	0.7	0910	12.3	1611	1.1	2127	12.5
14 W	0425	1.2	0943	11.8	1640	1.7	2159	11.8
15 Th	0454	1.9	1016	11.1	1710	2.5	2232	10.9
16 F	0526	2.9	1050	10.2	1742	3.4	2308	9.9
17 Sa	0601	3.9	1130	9.3	1822	4.2	2355	8.9
18 Su	0648	4.7	1227	8.6	1922	4.9		
19 M	0109	8.3	0806	5.2	1359	8.4	2055	5.0
20 Tu	0251	8.2	0945	5.1	1538	8.6	2231	4.7
21 W	0419	8.6	1109	4.5	1652	9.3	2341	4.0
22 Th	0520	9.3	1209	3.9	1743	10.0		
23 F	0032	3.3	0604	10.0	1255	3.2	1825	10.7
24 Sa	0114	2.7	0642	10.7	1334	2.6	1859	11.3
25 Su	0152	2.1	0715	11.2	1410	2.1	1931	11.7
26 M	0226	1.7	0746	11.5	1443	1.8	2000	12.0
27 Tu	0259	1.5	0816	11.8	1515	1.6	2030	12.1
28 W	0331	1.5	0845	11.8	1546	1.6	2059	12.0
29 Th	0400	1.6	0914	11.7	1613	1.8	2129	11.7
30 F	0426	1.9	0944	11.3	1640	2.2	2159	11.2
31 Sa	0455	2.5	1017	10.8	1711	2.8	2235	10.5

Chart Datum: 6.85 metres below Lellemand System (Mean Sea Level, Marseilles).

FRANCE NORTH COAST – SAINT MALO

Lat 48°38'N   Long 2°02'W

TIMES AND HEIGHTS OF HIGH AND LOW WATERS

YEAR **1991**

Time Zone -0100
(French Standard Time)
Subtract one hour for GMT For French Summer Time add ONE hour in non-shaded areas

SEPTEMBER

Day	TIME	m	Day	TIME	m
1 Su	0529 / 1055 / 1750 / 2320	3.2 / 10.1 / 3.6 / 9.7	16 M	0610 / 1143 / 1839	4.9 / 8.6 / 5.1
2 M	0614 / 1149 / 1845	4.0 / 9.4 / 4.2	17 Tu	0020 / 0719 / 1310 / 2010	8.0 / 5.5 / 8.2 / 5.3
3 Tu	0027 / 0725 / 1317 / 2017	9.0 / 4.5 / 9.1 / 4.3	18 W	0207 / 0904 / 1501 / 2153	7.9 / 5.3 / 8.5 / 4.9
4 W	0213 / 0910 / 1506 / 2200	9.0 / 4.3 / 9.6 / 3.7	19 Th	0345 / 1034 / 1620 / 2308	8.5 / 4.7 / 9.2 / 4.2
5 Th	0352 / 1045 / 1632 / 2324	9.7 / 3.5 / 10.6 / 2.7	20 F	0448 / 1135 / 1712	9.2 / 3.9 / 10.0
6 F	0506 / 1157 / 1736	10.7 / 2.5 / 11.6	21 Sa	0000 / 0532 / 1220 / 1752	3.4 / 10.1 / 3.1 / 10.8
7 Sa	0027 / 0601 / 1254 / 1827	1.8 / 11.6 / 1.6 / 12.3	22 Su	0040 / 0610 / 1258 / 1828	2.6 / 10.9 / 2.4 / 11.5
8 Su	0120 / 0649 / 1344 / 1910	1.0 / 12.2 / 1.0 / 12.8	23 M	0117 / 0644 / 1335 / 1900	2.0 / 11.5 / 1.9 / 12.0
9 M	0207 / 0730 / 1428 / 1949	0.6 / 12.6 / 0.7 / 12.9	24 Tu	0153 / 0715 / 1410 / 1931	1.6 / 11.9 / 1.5 / 12.3
10 Tu	0248 / 0807 / 1509 / 2025	0.5 / 12.6 / 0.8 / 12.8	25 W	0227 / 0747 / 1444 / 2002	1.3 / 12.2 / 1.3 / 12.4
11 W	0327 / 0842 / 1544 / 2059	0.8 / 12.4 / 1.2 / 12.4	26 TH	0301 / 0817 / 1518 / 2034	1.3 / 12.2 / 1.4 / 12.3
12 Th	0400 / 0915 / 1615 / 2131	1.4 / 11.9 / 1.8 / 11.7	27 F	0336 / 0850 / 1551 / 2107	1.5 / 12.1 / 1.6 / 11.9
13 F	0428 / 0946 / 1641 / 2202	2.2 / 11.2 / 2.6 / 10.8	28 Sa	0408 / 0924 / 1623 / 2141	1.9 / 11.7 / 2.1 / 11.3
14 Sa	0456 / 1017 / 1711 / 2235	3.1 / 10.3 / 3.5 / 9.7	29 Su	0438 / 0959 / 1656 / 2220	2.6 / 11.0 / 2.9 / 10.5
15 Su	0528 / 1054 / 1747 / 2316	4.1 / 9.4 / 4.4 / 8.7	30 M	0516 / 1042 / 1739 / 2309	3.4 / 10.2 / 3.7 / 9.6

OCTOBER

Day	TIME	m	Day	TIME	m
1 Tu	0606 / 1142 / 1839	4.2 / 9.5 / 4.2	16 W	0639 / 1221 / 1920	5.4 / 8.4 / 5.3
2 We	0022 / 0723 / 1316 / 2015	9.0 / 4.5 / 9.3 / 4.2	17 Th	0110 / 0808 / 1402 / 2055	8.1 / 5.3 / 8.6 / 5.0
3 Th	0210 / 0905 / 1501 / 2153	9.1 / 4.1 / 9.9 / 3.5	18 F	0248 / 0937 / 1526 / 2212	8.5 / 4.8 / 9.2 / 4.3
4 F	0344 / 1033 / 1619 / 2308	9.9 / 3.3 / 10.8 / 2.6	19 Sa	0358 / 1044 / 1624 / 2310	9.2 / 4.1 / 10.0 / 3.5
5 Sa	0450 / 1139 / 1716	10.9 / 2.4 / 11.7	20 Su	0447 / 1133 / 1709 / 2355	10.1 / 3.2 / 10.8 / 2.8
6 Su	0006 / 0541 / 1231 / 1804	1.8 / 11.7 / 1.7 / 12.3	21 M	0528 / 1215 / 1747	10.9 / 2.5 / 11.4
7 M	0055 / 0626 / 1318 / 1846	1.3 / 12.2 / 1.3 / 12.6	22 Tu	0036 / 0605 / 1255 / 1825	2.1 / 11.6 / 1.9 / 12.0
8 Tu	0139 / 0705 / 1400 / 1924	1.0 / 12.4 / 1.1 / 12.6	23 W	0114 / 0642 / 1334 / 1900	1.7 / 12.1 / 1.5 / 12.3
9 W	0221 / 0742 / 1440 / 1958	1.1 / 12.4 / 1.2 / 12.4	24 Th	0154 / 0718 / 1414 / 1936	1.4 / 12.4 / 1.3 / 12.4
10 Th	0258 / 0816 / 1517 / 2032	1.4 / 12.2 / 1.6 / 12.0	25 F	0234 / 0753 / 1454 / 2013	1.4 / 12.4 / 1.4 / 12.3
11 F	0334 / 0849 / 1550 / 2104	1.9 / 11.8 / 2.1 / 11.4	26 Sa	0315 / 0832 / 1535 / 2052	1.6 / 12.3 / 1.6 / 11.9
12 Sa	0405 / 0921 / 1619 / 2136	2.5 / 11.2 / 2.8 / 10.6	27 Su	0354 / 0911 / 1613 / 2132	2.0 / 11.9 / 2.1 / 11.3
13 Su	0433 / 0952 / 1647 / 2208	3.3 / 10.5 / 3.6 / 9.7	28 M	0431 / 0952 / 1650 / 2215	2.6 / 11.2 / 2.8 / 10.6
14 M	0503 / 1027 / 1722 / 2247	4.1 / 9.6 / 4.3 / 8.8	29 Tu	0513 / 1040 / 1737 / 2308	3.4 / 10.5 / 3.5 / 9.8
15 Tu	0543 / 1112 / 1808 / 2343	4.9 / 8.8 / 5.0 / 8.2	30 W	0606 / 1141 / 1838	4.0 / 9.9 / 3.9
			31 Th	0020 / 0717 / 1307 / 2002	9.4 / 4.2 / 9.8 / 3.9

NOVEMBER

Day	TIME	m	Day	TIME	m
1 F	0153 / 0846 / 1437 / 2128	9.6 / 3.9 / 10.2 / 3.4	16 Sa	0132 / 0822 / 1411 / 2100	8.7 / 4.8 / 9.2 / 4.4
2 Sa	0317 / 1004 / 1551 / 2239	10.1 / 3.3 / 10.8 / 2.8	17 Su	0248 / 0934 / 1520 / 2205	9.2 / 4.2 / 9.8 / 3.9
3 Su	0421 / 1109 / 1650 / 2336	10.8 / 2.7 / 11.4 / 2.3	18 M	0349 / 1034 / 1615 / 2301	9.9 / 3.6 / 10.5 / 3.2
4 M	0514 / 1203 / 1738	11.4 / 2.2 / 11.8	19 Tu	0440 / 1126 / 1704 / 2350	10.7 / 2.9 / 11.1 / 2.6
5 Tu	0027 / 0559 / 1249 / 1820	2.0 / 11.8 / 1.9 / 12.0	20 W	0526 / 1214 / 1748	11.4 / 2.3 / 11.6
6 W	0112 / 0641 / 1334 / 1900	1.8 / 12.0 / 1.8 / 12.0	21 Th	0038 / 0610 / 1301 / 1832	2.1 / 11.9 / 1.8 / 12.0
7 Th	0155 / 0719 / 1415 / 1937	1.8 / 12.1 / 1.8 / 11.9	22 F	0125 / 0654 / 1348 / 1915	1.8 / 12.3 / 1.5 / 12.2
8 F	0235 / 0754 / 1454 / 2012	2.0 / 11.9 / 2.0 / 11.6	23 Sa	0213 / 0737 / 1437 / 1958	1.6 / 12.5 / 1.4 / 12.2
9 Sa	0312 / 0828 / 1530 / 2045	2.4 / 11.6 / 2.4 / 11.1	24 Su	0301 / 0820 / 1525 / 2043	1.6 / 12.4 / 1.5 / 12.0
10 Su	0347 / 0902 / 1603 / 2118	2.8 / 11.2 / 2.9 / 10.6	25 M	0348 / 0905 / 1609 / 2128	1.9 / 12.2 / 1.8 / 11.5
11 M	0417 / 0934 / 1631 / 2151	3.4 / 10.7 / 3.4 / 9.9	26 Tu	0428 / 0950 / 1649 / 2213	2.3 / 11.7 / 2.3 / 11.0
12 Tu	0447 / 1008 / 1703 / 2227	3.9 / 10.0 / 4.0 / 9.3	27 W	0511 / 1037 / 1734 / 2303	2.9 / 11.2 / 2.8 / 10.4
13 W	0522 / 1048 / 1743 / 2312	4.5 / 9.5 / 4.5 / 8.8	28 Th	0559 / 1132 / 1825	3.3 / 10.7 / 3.3
14 Th	0607 / 1139 / 1833	4.9 / 9.0 / 4.8	29 F	0002 / 0656 / 1237 / 1930	10.0 / 3.7 / 10.4 / 3.5
15 F	0011 / 0705 / 1250 / 1943	8.6 / 5.0 / 8.9 / 4.8	30 Sa	0117 / 0808 / 1357 / 2046	9.8 / 4.3 / 10.3 / 3.5

DECEMBER

Day	TIME	m	Day	TIME	m
1 Su	0235 / 0923 / 1511 / 2158	10.0 / 3.6 / 10.4 / 3.4	16 M	0126 / 0816 / 1403 / 2052	9.2 / 4.3 / 9.5 / 4.1
2 M	0345 / 1032 / 1615 / 2303	10.3 / 3.3 / 10.7 / 3.2	17 Tu	0240 / 0927 / 1515 / 2201	9.6 / 4.0 / 9.9 / 3.8
3 Tu	0444 / 1133 / 1711	10.7 / 3.0 / 10.9	18 W	0347 / 1034 / 1619 / 2306	10.1 / 3.5 / 10.4 / 3.2
4 W	0001 / 0536 / 1226 / 1759	2.9 / 11.1 / 2.7 / 11.1	19 Th	0448 / 1137 / 1716	10.8 / 2.8 / 11.0
5 Th	0051 / 0623 / 1314 / 1844	2.7 / 11.4 / 2.5 / 11.2	20 F	0008 / 0544 / 1236 / 1811	2.7 / 11.5 / 2.2 / 11.6
6 F	0136 / 0703 / 1358 / 1922	2.6 / 11.5 / 2.4 / 11.2	21 Sa	0104 / 0636 / 1332 / 1902	2.1 / 12.1 / 1.7 / 12.0
7 Sa	0219 / 0740 / 1438 / 1957	2.6 / 11.6 / 2.4 / 11.2	22 Su	0200 / 0726 / 1427 / 1950	1.7 / 12.4 / 1.3 / 12.2
8 Su	0257 / 0815 / 1516 / 2032	2.7 / 11.5 / 2.5 / 11.0	23 M	0253 / 0814 / 1519 / 2038	1.5 / 12.6 / 1.1 / 12.2
9 M	0333 / 0848 / 1549 / 2104	2.8 / 11.3 / 2.7 / 10.7	24 Tu	0342 / 0901 / 1604 / 2123	1.4 / 12.4 / 1.2 / 12.0
10 Tu	0405 / 0921 / 1619 / 2136	3.1 / 11.0 / 3.0 / 10.4	25 W	0423 / 0944 / 1642 / 2205	1.6 / 12.3 / 1.3 / 11.6
11 W	0433 / 0952 / 1647 / 2208	3.4 / 10.7 / 3.3 / 10.0	26 Th	0501 / 1026 / 1721 / 2247	2.0 / 11.9 / 2.0 / 11.1
12 Th	0503 / 1026 / 1720 / 2244	3.8 / 10.2 / 3.7 / 9.6	27 F	0541 / 1109 / 1803 / 2334	2.6 / 11.3 / 2.7 / 10.5
13 F	0536 / 1103 / 1756 / 2326	4.1 / 9.8 / 4.0 / 9.3	28 Sa	0625 / 1159 / 1850	3.2 / 10.6 / 3.3
14 Sa	0617 / 1150 / 1841	4.3 / 9.5 / 4.3	29 Su	0028 / 0720 / 1303 / 1955	9.9 / 3.8 / 10.0 / 3.9
15 Su	0017 / 0709 / 1250 / 1941	9.1 / 4.4 / 9.4 / 4.3	30 M	0141 / 0832 / 1420 / 2111	9.6 / 4.1 / 9.6 / 4.1
			31 Tu	0301 / 0951 / 1539 / 2228	9.5 / 9.6 / 9.6 / 4.1

Chart Datum: 6.85 metres below Lellemand System (Mean Sea Level, Marseilles).

FACILITIES

ST MALO: **Marina des Bas-Sablons** (1216 + 60 visitors, visitors Pontoon A) ☎ 99.81.71.34, (sill 2m above CD), Slip, P and D (in cans), AC, BH (10 ton), FW, CH, Gaz, R, YC, Bar; **Port Vauban** ☎ 99.56.51.91, FW, C (1 ton), AC; **Chantier Naval de la Ville Audrain** ☎ 99.56.48.06, El, Ⓔ, ME, CH, Sh; **Chantier Labbé** ☎ 99.56.31.72, ME, El, C, Sh, CH; **Chantier Naval de la Plaisance** ☎ 99.82.62.97, M, ME, El, Sh, CH; **Chatelais et le Gall** ☎ 99.56.14.67, ME,El, Sh, CH; **Richard** ☎ 99.81.63.81, SM, CH; **Armor Voile** ☎ 99.81.49.30, SM; **Société Nautique de la Baie de Saint-Malo** ☎ 99.40.84.42, Bar (visitors welcome); **F. Lessard** ☎ 99.56.13.61, P, D; **Libraire Marine** ☎ 99.40.91.73, Nautical Books, SHOM; **Town** Slip, P, Gaz, D, ME, El, Sh, C, V, R, Bar, ✉; Ⓑ; ⇌; ✈ (Dinard); Ferry UK—Portsmouth; or Jersey.

DINARD: **Port de Dinard** ☎ 99.46.65.55, Slip, M, P, D, L, FW, AB; **Kerbrat Daniel** ☎ 99.46.49.82 ME, El, Ⓔ, Sh, M; **YC de Dinard** ☎ 99.46.14,32, Bar; **G. L. Voile** ☎ 99.46.48,99, SM; **Town** P, D, ME, El, CH, V, Gaz, R, Bar; ✉; Ⓑ; ⇌; ✈.

GRANVILLE   10-17-20
Manche

CHARTS
Admiralty 3672, 2669; SHOM 5897, 824; ECM 535; Stanford 16; Imray C33B

TIDES
−0510 Dover; ML 7.2; Duration 0525; Zone −0100

Standard Port ST—MALO (←)

Times				Height (metres)			
HW		LW		MHWS	MHWN	MLWN	MLWS
0805	0120	0749	0256	12.2	9.2	4.4	1.5
2005	1320	1949	1456				

Differences GRANVILLE
+0003 +0006 +0007 +0022 +0.7   +0.5   +0.2   −0.1

SHELTER
Shelter is good in the marina, Port de Hérel. Approach is rough in strong W winds. The old harbour is only for commercial and fishing vessels: yachts use the marina. Enter and leave under power. Access HW − 2½ to HW + 3½. Speed limit 4 kn; 2 kn between pontoons.

NAVIGATION
Waypoint 48°49'.40N 01°37'.00W, 235°/055° from/to Digue Principale Lt (Fl R 4s), 0.95M. From W, Le Videcoq rks (dry 0.8m) lie 3¼ M W of Pte du Roc, marked by W cardinal whis buoy. Beware rks off Pte du Roc and La Fourchie Bn, and Banc de Tombelaine 1M SSW of Le Loup Lt Tr.

LIGHTS AND MARKS
Port de Hérel marina is a half-tide harbour and depths at the entrance are shown by illuminated figures. W numbers are metres, Or numbers decimetres. Zero means no entry. Ldg Lts as on chartlet.

RADIO TELEPHONE
VHF Ch 12 16 (HW − 1½ to HW + 1). Marina Ch 09.

TELEPHONE (33)
Hr Mr 33.50.00.59; Hr Mr (Hérel) 33.50.20.06; Aff Mar 33.50.00.59; CROSS 33.52.72.13; SNSM 33.61.26.51; ▦ 33.50.19.90; Meteo 33.50.10.00; Auto 33.50.10.00; Police 33.50.01.00; Dr 33.50.00.07; Hosp 33.90.74.75; Brit Consul 33.44.20.13.

FACILITIES
Hérel Marina (850 + 150 visitors) ☎ 33.50.20.06, Slip, P, D, FW, ME, AC, BH (12 ton), C (10 ton), CH, Gaz, R, ◻, V, Bar, SM, El, Sh; **YC de Granville** ☎ 33.50.04.25, L, M, BH, D, P, CH, ◻, Slip FW, AB, Bar; **Comptoir Maritime** ☎ 33.50.18.71, CH; **Granville Plaisance** ☎ 33.50.23.82, ME, El, Ⓔ, M, Sh, CH; **Lecoulant Marine** ☎ 33.50.20.34, M, ME, El, Ⓔ, Sh, CH; **La Marine** ☎ 33.50.71.31, SHOM; **Voiles Mora** ☎ 33.50.38.69, SM; **Town** P, D, ME, V, Gaz, R, Bar. Ⓑ; ⇌; ✈ (Dinard).
Ferry UK via Jersey or Cherbourg—Weymouth/Poole

CARTERET   10-17-21
Manche

CHARTS
Admiralty 3655, 2669; SHOM 827; ECM 535; Stanford 16; Imray C33A

TIDES
−0440 Dover; ML 6.3; Duration 0545; Zone −0100

Standard Port ST—MALO (←)

Times				Height (metres)			
HW		LW		MHWS	MHWN	MLWN	MLWS
0805	0120	0749	0256	12.2	9.2	4.4	1.5
2005	1320	1949	1456				

Differences CARTERET
+0027 +0025 +0025 +0018 −1.0 −0.7 −0.3   0.0

SHELTER
Shelter good but harbour dries completely — entry only possible at HW∓2. Exposed to winds from W and SW which make entrance rough. There are no safe anchorages off shore. It dries ½ M to seaward. Bar at right angles to pier-head rises up to 3m and 15m long. The Petit Port provides the best shelter but is only suitable for shallow draught yachts able to take the bottom. Bar forms after NW winds but is removed by local sand company.

NAVIGATION
Waypoint 49°21'.00N 01°52'.25W, 250°/070° from/to Jetée Ouest Lt, 3.5M. From N keep well off shore on approach to avoid rocks 1 M N of Cap de Carteret extending about 1M from coast. From W, about 4 M off shore, beware Trois Grune Rks (dry 1.6m) marked by W cardinal Lt Buoy.

LIGHTS AND MARKS
Cap de Carteret Fl (2+1) 15s 81m 26M; grey Tr, G top; Horn (3) 60s. Training wall, head Fl (2) G 5s; in line with lifeboat house leads 007°. Jetée Ouest, head Oc R 4s 6m 8M; W column, R top.

RADIO TELEPHONE
Ch 16 64 (remotely controlled from Boulogne).

TELEPHONE (33)
44.00.13; CROSS 33.52.72.13; ▦ 33.04.90.08; 2.91.17; Auto 33.43.20.40; Police 33.53.80.17; 33.40.14.39; Brit Consul 33.44.20.13.

W, AB, R, Bar; **Cercle Nautique de** 33.53.88.29, Slip, M, Bar; **Port de** M, AB; **Garage Tollemer** D (cans). **Town** V, Gaz, R, (Valognes); ✈ (Cherbourg). —Portsmouth; Weymouth (summer

---

Note: 5M to S, Portbail is a safe harbour although choppy in E winds. See 10.17.25.
Note: A marina is planned.

ILES CHAUSEY   10-17-22
Manche

CHARTS
Admiralty 3656, 3659; SHOM 829, 824, 830, 4599; ECM 534; Stanford 16; Imray C33B

TIDES
−0500 Dover; ML 7.5; Duration 0530, Zone −0100

Standard Port ST—MALO (←)

Times				Height (metres)			
HW		LW		MHWS	MHWN	MLWN	MLWS
0805	0120	0749	0256	12.2	9.2	4.4	1.5
2005	1320	1949	1456				

Differences ILES CHAUSEY (Grande Ile)
+0008 +0010 +0011 +0014 +0.8 +0.7 +0.5 +0.5

SHELTER
Shelter good except in strong NW or SE winds. When anchoring remember the big tidal range. Visitors buoys are provided for mooring fore and aft.

NAVIGATION
Waypoint 48°51'.50N 01°48'.48W, 152°/332° from/to La Crabière Est Lt, 1.2M. Although very large range of tide (see above), tidal streams are not excessive. The most direct route into Sound of Chausey is from the S, but beware rocks extending from Pte de la Tour. Alternative route from N with sufficient height of tide but refer to detailed sailing directions for transits to be followed. Local knowledge is needed. Dangerous wreck reported N of La Petite Entrée (off chartlet).
Note:— Yachts may not visit the Iles Chausey without having first made official entry elsewhere, such as Granville.
Harbour gets very crowded in summer weekends.

ILES CHAUSEY *continued*

LIGHTS AND MARKS
Grande Ile, Pte de la Tour Fl 5s 39m 23M; Horn 30s. La
Crabière Est Oc WRG 4s 5m 10/7M; B pylon, Y top; vis
W079°-291°, G291°-329°, W329°-335°, R335°-079°.
From N, L'Enseigne Bn Tr (19m) in line with Pte de la
Tour Lt Ho leads 156°. From S, La Crabière in line with
L'Enseigne leads 333°.
Note:— The island is private property.
RADIO TELEPHONE
None.
TELEPHONE (33)
Police 33.52.72.02.
FACILITIES
R. Tourelle L; Town FW, Gaz, V, R, Bar.
⊠ (Granville); Ⓑ (Granville); ⇌ (Granville); ✈ (Dinard).
Ferry UK via Granville and Jersey—Weymouth/Poole.

OMONVILLE-la-ROGUE
Manche   **10-17-23**

CHARTS
Admiralty 1106, 2669; SHOM 5636, 5631, 828; ECM 528,
1014; Stanford 16, 7; Imray C33A
TIDES
−0330 Dover; ML 3.8; Duration 0545; Zone −0100

Standard Port CHERBOURG (→)

Times				Height (metres)			
HW		LW		MHWS	MHWN	MLWN	MLWS
0300	1000	0400	1000	6.3	5.0	2.5	1.1
1500	2200	1600	2200				

Differences OMONVILLE

−0015	−0010	−0020	−0025	−0.1	0.0	+0.1	0.0

GOURY

−0100	−0045	−0110	−0120	+1.6	+1.5	+1.0	+0.1

SHELTER
Good shelter except in strong winds from N to SE
through E. Pick up a vacant mooring or anchor S of
breakwater but beware rocks at outer end.
NAVIGATION
Waypoint 49°42'.50N 01°48'.60W, 075°/255° from/to
Omonville Lt, 1.0M. Narrow entrance, ½ ca (93m) wide,
between rocks. On S side rocks run N from Omonville
Fort, and to N rocks running ESE from breakwater are
marked by G Bn Tr, Le Tunard. From W or N, keep clear
of Basse Bréfort (depth 1m, marked by N cardinal Lt
buoy) 6ca (1100m) N of Pte de Jardeheu. Approach on
195° transit (below), but pass ½ca (93m) E of Le Tunard
and into W sector of Lt before altering 95° to stbd for
mooring area, heading 290° for old Custom House. From
E, approach on 255° transit (below), in W sector of Lt,
until to S of Le Tunard.
To ENE of port is a military firing area.

LIGHTS AND MARKS
Omonville Lt Iso WRG 4s 13m 11/8M on W framework Tr
with R top; vis G180°-252°, W252°-262°, R262°-287°. Lt
in transit with church steeple, 650m beyond, leads 255° S
of Le Tunard. Le Tunard Bn Tr in line with centre of
Omonville Fort leads 195°, but pass ½ca (93m) E of Le
Tunard.
RADIO TELEPHONE
None. For Casquets traffic scheme see Cherbourg
(10.17.24).
TELEPHONE (33)
Hr Mr Cherbourg 33.53.05.60; Aff Mar Cherbourg
33.53.21.76; ⌗ Cherbourg 33.53.05.60; CROSS
33.52.72.13; 33.52.71.33; Meteo 33.22.91.17;
Police 33.52.72.02; Dr 33.53.08.69; Brit Consul
33.44.20.13.
FACILITIES
Jetty M, L, FW, AB, V, R, Bar; Village V, Gaz, R, Bar.
⊠ (Beaumont Hague); Ⓑ (Beaumont Hague); ⇌ (bus to
Cherbourg); ✈ (Cherbourg).
Ferry UK — Cherbourg—Portsmouth; Weymouth (summer
only).

CHERBOURG   **10-17-24**
Manche

CHARTS
Admiralty 2602, 1106; SHOM 6737D, 5628, 5627, 6966;
ECM 528; Stanford 16, 7; Imray C32, C33A
TIDES
−0320 Dover; ML 3.8; Duration 0535; Zone −0100

Cherbourg is a Standard Port and tidal predictions for
every day of the year are given below.

SHELTER
Shelter is excellent and harbour can be entered in all
states of tide and weather. Good shelter in marina in Port
de Chantereyne. Lock into Bassin à Flot (HW−1 to
HW+1) is normally for commercial vessels only. It is
forbidden to anchor in the port.
NAVIGATION
Waypoints Passe de l'Ouest 49°41'.10N 01°39'.80W,
321°/141° from/to front Ldg Lt 141°, 1.9M. Passe de l'Est
49°41'.00N 01°35'.70W, 000°/180° from/to Fort des
Flamands Lt, 1.85M. For coast between Cap de la Hague
and Pte de Barfleur see 10.17.5. CH1 Lt buoy lies about
3M N × W from Fort de l'Ouest.
There are three entrances:
(1) Passe de l'Ouest is the easiest. Rocks extend about
80m from breakwaters each side. From West, the W
sector of Fort de l'Ouest Lt (bearing more than 122° by
day) keeps clear of all dangers E of Cap de la Hague.
(2) Passe de l'Est carries 6m. Keep to W side of channel
(but at least 80m off Fort de l'Est) to avoid dangers off Ile
Pelée marked by Lt buoy on W side, and by two Bn Trs
on N side which must be given a wide berth.
(3) Passe Cabart Danneville is a shallow channel ½ca
(93m) wide through Digue de l'Est, near the shore. Not
recommended except in good conditions and near HW.
LIGHTS AND MARKS
There are three powerful Lts near Cherbourg. To the W
Cap de la Hague, Fl 5s 48m 23M; to the E Cap Levi, Fl R
5s 36m 22M, and Pte de Barfleur, Fl(2) 10s 72m 29M. For
details see 10.17.4 and 10.18.4.
Fort de l'Ouest Lt, at W end of Digue Centrale, Fl(3)WR
15s 19m 24/20M; vis W122°-355°, R355°-122°; RC;
Reed(3) 60s.
Passe de l'Ouest Ldg Lts 140°30'. Gare Maritime Lt (Q
35m 21M) in line with centre of 2Q(hor) 5m 15M at base
of Digue du Homet.
Grande Rade Ldg Lts 124°. Front FG 10m 10M; W pylon
G top, on blockhouse; Reed(2+1) 60s. Rear, 0.75M fro
front, Iso G 4s 16m 11M; W column, B bands, W top;
intens 114°-134°.
Passe de l'Est is indicated by W sector (176°-183°) o
Q WRG Lt at Fort des Flamands.

CHERBOURG *continued*

RADIO TELEPHONE
Marina Ch 09. (0800-2000 LT).
Call: *COM Cherbourg* VHF Ch 16 (H24). Casquets traffic
scheme, Ship Movement Report System (MAREP), call
Jobourg Traffic (near Cap de la Hague) Ch **11**; 16 11 79
(H24). Information broadcasts in English and French on
Ch 11 at H+20 and H+50, also at H+05 and H+35
when visibility is less than 2M.

TELEPHONE (33)
Hr Mr 33.44.00.13; Hr Mr (Port de Plaisance) 33.53.75.16;
Aff Mar 33.44.00.13; CROSS 33.52.72.13; ⌗ 33.44.16.00;
Marina 33.53.79.65; Meteo 33.22.91.77; Auto 33.43.20.40;
Police 33.44.21.24; Ⓗ 33.52.61.45; Dr 33.53.05.68;
Brit Consul 33.44.20.13.

FACILITIES
Marina (670+130 visitors), Slip, P, D, FW, ME, El, Sh,
BH (27 ton), CH; *Access* H24; **YC de Cherbourg**
☎ 33.53.02.83, FW, Bar; **Aries Cherbourg** ☎ 33.94.15.50
ME, El, Ⓔ, Sh, CH, M: **Legrand** ☎ 33.53.27.34 ME, El,
Ⓔ, Sh, M, SM, CH; **Cotentin Marine** ☎ 33.53.07.30,
ME, El, Sh, CH; **Cherbourg Général Yachting**
☎ 33.53.63.73, ME, El, Ⓔ, SM, CH; **Nordie**
☎ 33.53.02.67, V; **Daily Tanker** D; **Nicollet**
☎ 33.53.11.74, SHOM; **Serelle** ☎ 33.43.70.11, ME, El, Ⓔ,
Sh. **Town** P, D, Gaz, V, R, Bar. ✉; Ⓑ; ⇌; ✈.
Ferry UK—Portsmouth; Weymouth (summer only).

CHERBOURG

MEAN SPRING
AND NEAP CURVES

MEAN RANGES	
Springs	5·2m
Neaps	2·5m

Springs occur 2 days
after
New and Full Moon

FRANCE, NORTH COAST - CHERBOURG

LAT 49°39'N   LONG 1°38'W

TIMES AND HEIGHTS OF HIGH AND LOW WATERS   YEAR **1991**

TIME ZONE −0100
(French Standard Time)
Subtract 1 hour for GMT
For French Summer Time add ONE hour in non-shaded areas

JANUARY

Day	Time	m	Time	m	Time	m	Time	m
1 TU	0318	1.2	0858	6.4	1544	1.0	2123	6.3
16 W	0343	1.8	0918	5.9	1601	1.5	2136	5.7
2 W	0410	1.1	0949	6.6	1635	0.9	2213	6.3
17 TH	0418	1.6	0953	6.0	1634	1.4	2208	5.9
3 TH	0458	1.1	1037	6.6	1722	1.0	2259	6.2
18 F	0451	1.5	1025	6.1	1706	1.3	2242	5.9
4 F	0544	1.2	1121	6.4	1806	1.1	2342	6.1
19 SA	0523	1.4	1057	6.1	1739	1.3	2313	5.9
5 SA	0628	1.3	1203	6.2	1849	1.3		
20 SU	0556	1.4	1130	6.1	1813	1.4	2347	5.8
6 SU	0024	5.8	0710	1.6	1246	5.9	1931	1.7
21 M	0630	1.5	1203	5.9	1848	1.5		
7 M ☽	0108	5.5	0753	2.0	1330	5.5	2018	2.0
22 TU	0022	5.7	0707	1.7	1241	5.7	1927	1.7
8 TU	0154	5.2	0844	2.3	1421	5.2	2113	2.4
23 W ☽	0102	5.5	0748	1.9	1325	5.5	2013	2.0
9 W	0250	5.0	0945	2.6	1524	5.0	2221	2.7
24 TH	0150	5.3	0842	2.2	1420	5.3	2115	2.3
10 TH	0401	4.8	1059	2.7	1640	4.8	2336	2.8
25 F	0254	5.1	0954	2.4	1535	5.1	2236	2.4
11 F	0518	4.9	1212	2.7	1754	4.9		
26 SA	0420	5.1	1119	2.4	1705	5.1		
12 SA	0045	2.7	0626	5.0	1314	2.5	1855	5.0
27 SU	0002	2.3	0547	5.3	1241	2.1	1826	5.3
13 SU	0141	2.5	0721	5.3	1405	2.2	1944	5.2
28 M	0117	2.0	0701	5.6	1350	1.7	1933	5.7
14 M	0227	2.2	0805	5.5	1447	2.0	2025	5.4
29 TU	0219	1.6	0801	6.1	1447	1.3	2028	6.0
15 TU ●	0307	2.0	0843	5.7	1525	1.7	2101	5.6
30 W ○	0313	1.2	0853	6.4	1537	1.0	2116	6.3
31 TH	0401	1.0	0940	6.6	1623	0.8	2201	6.4

FEBRUARY

Day	Time	m	Time	m	Time	m	Time	m
1 F	0445	0.9	1021	6.7	1704	0.7	2241	6.4
16 SA	0429	1.2	1003	6.3	1645	1.0	2219	6.2
2 SA	0524	0.9	1100	6.6	1742	0.9	2318	6.3
17 SU	0500	1.1	1035	6.4	1716	1.0	2251	6.2
3 SU	0600	1.1	1135	6.4	1818	1.1	2352	6.0
18 M	0532	1.1	1107	6.3	1748	1.0	2322	6.1
4 M	0635	1.4	1210	6.0	1853	1.5		
19 TU	0605	1.2	1139	6.2	1822	1.2	2356	5.9
5 TU	0027	5.7	0712	1.7	1246	5.6	1930	1.9
20 W	0640	1.4	1215	5.9	1859	1.5		
6 W ☽	0105	5.3	0749	2.2	1325	5.2	2012	2.4
21 TH	0034	5.6	0720	1.7	1256	5.5	1943	1.9
7 TH	0149	4.9	0839	2.6	1416	4.8	2110	2.8
22 F	0121	5.3	0811	2.1	1350	5.2	2045	2.4
8 F	0249	4.7	0948	2.9	1531	4.6	2235	3.0
23 SA	0226	5.0	0926	2.5	1509	4.9	2215	2.6
9 SA	0420	4.6	1122	2.9	1709	4.5		
24 SU	0403	4.9	1107	2.5	1656	4.9	2357	2.4
10 SU	0008	3.0	0553	4.7	1247	2.7	1830	4.7
25 M	0544	5.2	1239	2.1	1825	5.2		
11 M	0119	2.7	0701	5.0	1346	2.4	1926	5.0
26 TU	0116	2.0	0700	5.6	1347	1.6	1929	5.6
12 TU	0209	2.3	0748	5.3	1430	2.0	2008	5.3
27 W	0214	1.5	0755	6.0	1439	1.2	2018	6.0
13 W	0249	1.9	0826	5.6	1508	1.6	2043	5.6
28 TH ○	0302	1.1	0840	6.4	1524	0.9	2101	6.3
14 TH ●	0324	1.6	0900	6.0	1541	1.4	2116	5.9
15 F	0358	1.3	0933	6.2	1614	1.1	2148	6.1

MARCH

Day	Time	m	Time	m	Time	m	Time	m
1 F	0344	0.9	0921	6.6	1604	0.7	2141	6.4
16 SA ●	0328	1.2	0903	6.3	1544	1.0	2119	6.2
2 SA	0423	0.8	0959	6.6	1641	0.7	2215	6.4
17 SU	0401	0.9	0936	6.4	1617	0.8	2152	6.4
3 SU	0458	0.8	1033	6.5	1714	0.8	2250	6.3
18 M	0433	0.8	1008	6.5	1650	0.8	2225	6.4
4 M	0530	1.0	1105	6.3	1747	1.1	2321	6.1
19 TU	0506	0.9	1042	6.4	1724	0.9	2259	6.3
5 TU	0602	1.3	1136	6.0	1818	1.4	2351	5.7
20 W	0542	1.0	1117	6.2	1800	1.2	2335	6.1
6 W	0634	1.7	1207	5.6	1851	1.9		
21 TH	0620	1.3	1155	5.9	1841	1.5		
7 TH	0024	5.4	0709	2.1	1243	5.2	1927	2.3
22 F	0016	5.7	0704	1.7	1240	5.4	1929	2.0
8 F ☽	0103	5.0	0749	2.5	1326	4.7	2016	2.8
23 SA ☽	0108	5.3	0759	2.1	1341	5.0	2037	2.4
9 SA	0155	4.7	0851	2.9	1431	4.5	2134	3.1
24 SU	0219	5.0	0921	2.5	1507	4.8	2214	2.6
10 SU	0320	4.5	1027	3.0	1617	4.4	2322	3.1
25 M	0403	4.9	1107	2.4	1654	4.9	2354	2.3
11 M	0511	4.6	1209	2.8	1755	4.6		
26 TU	0540	5.2	1233	2.0	1816	5.2		
12 TU	0046	2.7	0628	4.9	1315	2.4	1856	4.9
27 W	0105	1.9	0647	5.6	1333	1.6	1914	5.6
13 W	0140	2.3	0718	5.3	1400	2.0	1938	5.3
28 TH	0157	1.5	0737	6.0	1420	1.2	1959	6.0
14 TH	0220	1.9	0757	5.6	1437	1.6	2014	5.7
29 F	0241	1.2	0819	6.3	1501	1.0	2038	6.2
15 F	0254	1.5	0830	6.0	1511	1.2	2047	6.0
30 SA ○	0320	1.0	0856	6.4	1538	0.9	2114	6.3
31 SU	0355	0.9	0932	6.4	1613	0.9	2148	6.3

APRIL

Day	Time	m	Time	m	Time	m	Time	m
1 M	0430	1.0	1004	6.3	1646	1.0	2220	6.2
16 TU ●	0405	0.8	0942	6.5	1624	0.8	2201	6.5
2 TU	0501	1.1	1036	6.1	1717	1.3	2253	6.0
17 W	0444	0.9	1020	6.4	1703	1.0	2241	6.3
3 W	0533	1.4	1108	5.8	1749	1.6	2322	5.7
18 TH	0525	1.0	1102	6.2	1746	1.2	2322	6.1
4 TH	0605	1.7	1139	5.5	1821	1.9	2355	5.4
19 F	0609	1.3	1146	5.8	1832	1.6		
5 F	0639	2.0	1213	5.1	1858	2.3		
20 SA	0010	5.7	0658	1.7	1237	5.4	1927	2.0
6 SA	0032	5.1	0719	2.4	1255	4.8	1943	2.7
21 SU ☽	0108	5.4	0800	2.1	1343	5.0	2039	2.3
7 SU ☽	0122	4.7	0813	2.8	1354	4.5	2052	3.0
22 M	0222	5.2	0922	2.3	1506	4.9	2209	2.4
8 M	0235	4.6	0937	2.9	1525	4.4	2229	3.0
23 TU	0354	5.2	1054	2.2	1639	5.0	2335	2.2
9 TU	0416	4.6	1116	2.8	1702	4.6	2356	2.7
24 W	0517	5.3	1210	1.9	1751	5.3		
10 W	0538	4.9	1229	2.4	1808	4.9		
25 TH	0040	1.9	0619	5.6	1306	1.6	1846	5.6
11 TH	0055	2.3	0634	5.2	1318	2.0	1856	5.3
26 F	0131	1.4	0709	5.8	1353	1.4	1931	5.8
12 F	0139	1.8	0716	5.6	1357	1.6	1934	5.7
27 SA	0213	1.4	0751	6.0	1433	1.3	2010	6.0
13 SA	0215	1.4	0753	6.0	1433	1.2	2010	6.1
28 SU	0252	1.3	0829	6.1	1511	1.2	2047	6.1
14 SU ●	0251	1.1	0828	6.3	1510	1.0	2046	6.3
29 M	0329	1.2	0904	6.1	1546	1.3	2121	6.1
15 M	0328	0.9	0904	6.4	1546	0.8	2122	6.4
30 TU	0404	1.3	0939	6.0	1621	1.3	2156	6.0

Chart Datum: 3.70 metres below Lallemand System (Mean Sea Level, Marseilles)

TIME ZONE −0100
(French Standard Time)
Subtract 1 hour for GMT
For French Summer Time add ONE hour in non-shaded areas

FRANCE, NORTH COAST - CHERBOURG

LAT 49°39′N   LONG 1°38′W

TIMES AND HEIGHTS OF HIGH AND LOW WATERS

YEAR **1991**

MAY

Day	Time	m	Time	m	Time	m	Time	m
1 W	0438	1.4	1012	5.9	1654	1.5	2229	5.9
2 TH	0510	1.5	1046	5.6	1726	1.7	2302	5.7
3 F	0544	1.8	1119	5.4	1801	2.0	2335	5.4
4 SA	0619	2.0	1154	5.2	1839	2.3		
5 SU	0014	5.2	0700	2.3	1235	4.9	1923	2.5
6 M	0100	5.0	0749	2.5	1329	4.7	2020	2.7
7 TU	0201	4.8	0857	2.7	1437	4.6	2135	2.7
8 W	0317	4.8	1017	2.6	1557	4.7	2254	2.6
9 TH	0435	5.0	1129	2.3	1707	5.0	2359	2.2
10 F	0537	5.2	1226	2.0	1802	5.3		
11 SA	0049	1.9	0626	5.5	1311	1.7	1849	5.6
12 SU	0133	1.5	0711	5.9	1355	1.4	1932	6.0
13 M	0215	1.3	0753	6.1	1436	1.2	2014	6.2
14 TU	0258	[illegible]	0835	6.3	1519	1.0	2057	6.4
15 [W]	[0...]	0.9	[....]	6.3	[....]	1.0	[....]	[..]
16 TH	0428	1.0	1005	6.3	1651	1.1	2229	6.3
17 F	0515	1.1	1054	6.1	1739	1.3	2318	6.1
18 SA	0604	1.3	1143	5.8	1830	1.5		
19 SU	0009	5.9	0657	1.6	1236	5.5	1927	1.8
20 M	0106	5.6	0757	1.8	1338	5.3	2031	2.0
21 TU	0211	5.4	0907	2.0	1447	5.1	2145	2.1
22 W	0325	5.3	1023	2.0	1603	5.2	2259	2.1
23 TH	0439	5.3	1133	2.0	1712	5.2		
24 F	0003	2.0	0542	5.4	1231	1.9	1809	5.4
25 SA	0056	1.9	0636	5.5	1321	1.8	1900	5.5
26 SU	0144	1.7	0722	5.6	1405	1.7	1943	5.7
27 M	0226	1.6	0804	5.7	1446	1.6	2023	5.8
28 TU	0306	1.6	0842	5.7	1525	1.6	2101	5.8
29 W	0343	1.5	0919	5.7	1602	1.6	2138	5.8
30 TH	0419	1.5	0955	5.7	1637	1.7	2212	5.8
31 [F]	0454	1.6	[.]029	5.6	[....]	1.8	[....]	5.7

JUNE

Day	Time	m	Time	m	Time	m	Time	m
1 SA	0528	1.7	1104	5.4	1746	1.9	2321	5.6
2 SU	0604	1.9	1139	5.3	1823	2.0	2358	5.4
3 M	0643	2.0	1218	5.2	1904	2.2		
4 TU	0039	5.3	0726	2.2	1303	5.0	1950	2.3
5 W	0128	5.2	0817	2.3	1354	4.9	2046	2.4
6 TH	0224	5.1	0917	2.3	1455	4.9	2151	2.4
7 F	0329	5.1	1025	2.3	1604	5.1	2258	2.2
8 SA	0436	5.2	1129	2.1	1707	5.3	2359	2.0
9 SU	0537	5.4	1227	1.9	1805	5.5		
10 M	0053	1.8	0633	5.6	1319	1.6	1859	5.8
11 TU	0145	1.5	0725	5.9	1409	1.4	1950	6.1
12 W	0235	1.2	0816	6.1	1501	1.2	2041	6.3
13 TH	0327	1.1	0906	6.2	1552	1.1	2133	6.4
14 F	0419	1.0	0958	6.2	1644	1.1	2223	6.4
15 SA	0509	1.0	1049	6.2	1734	1.2	2312	6.3
16 SU	0558	1.1	1136	6.0	1824	1.3		
17 M	0002	6.1	0649	1.3	1226	5.7	1914	1.5
18 TU	0051	5.9	0740	1.5	1318	5.5	2006	1.8
19 W	0145	5.6	0835	1.8	1413	5.3	2105	2.0
20 TH	0242	5.4	0937	2.0	1515	5.2	2211	2.2
21 F	0349	5.2	1044	2.2	1623	5.1	2317	2.3
22 SA	0456	5.2	1150	2.3	1730	5.1		
23 SU	0021	2.2	0600	5.2	1249	2.2	1828	5.2
24 M	0115	2.1	0656	5.3	1341	2.1	1921	5.4
25 TU	0204	2.0	0744	5.4	1426	2.0	2005	5.5
26 W	0247	1.8	0826	5.5	1508	1.9	2045	5.7
27 TH	0328	1.7	0904	5.5	1546	1.8	2122	5.8
28 F	0405	1.6	0941	5.6	1622	1.7	2158	5.8
29 SA	0440	1.6	1014	5.6	1657	1.7	2232	5.8
30 SU	0513	1.6	1049	5.6	1730	1.7	2305	5.8

JULY

Day	Time	m	Time	m	Time	m	Time	m
1 M	0547	1.6	1121	5.5	1804	1.8	2338	5.7
2 TU	0622	1.7	1156	5.5	1840	1.8		
3 W	0015	5.6	0659	1.8	1233	5.4	1919	2.0
4 TH	0053	5.4	0740	1.9	1316	5.3	2002	2.1
5 F	0140	5.3	0829	2.1	1405	5.2	2057	2.2
6 SA	0233	5.2	0927	2.2	1504	5.1	2201	2.2
7 SU	0340	5.2	1037	2.2	1616	5.2	2312	2.2
8 M	0453	5.2	1148	2.1	1730	5.3		
9 TU	0022	2.0	0603	5.4	1255	1.9	1837	5.6
10 W	0125	1.7	0708	5.6	1355	1.6	1937	5.9
11 TH	0223	1.4	0806	5.9	1451	1.3	2033	6.2
12 F	0319	1.1	0859	6.2	1545	1.1	2125	6.5
13 SA	0411	0.9	0951	6.3	1636	1.0	2214	6.6
14 SU	0459	0.8	1038	6.3	1722	0.9	2300	6.5
15 M	0545	0.9	1121	6.2	1807	1.1	2343	6.4
16 TU	0628	1.1	1203	6.0	1850	1.3		
17 W	0025	6.1	0711	1.4	1246	5.7	1932	1.6
18 TH	0109	5.7	0755	1.7	1332	5.4	2019	2.0
19 F	0156	5.4	0846	2.1	1423	5.1	2116	2.1
20 SA	0253	5.1	0949	2.5	1529	4.9	2227	2.6
21 SU	0407	4.8	1105	2.7	1647	4.8	2343	2.6
22 M	0525	4.8	1220	2.6	1801	4.9		
23 TU	0052	2.5	0634	4.9	1321	2.5	1902	5.2
24 W	0148	2.2	0727	5.1	1411	2.2	1950	5.4
25 TH	0233	2.0	0811	5.3	1453	2.0	2030	5.6
26 F	0312	1.8	0849	5.5	1530	1.8	2106	5.8
27 SA	0347	1.5	0923	5.7	1605	1.6	2140	5.9
28 SU	0421	1.4	0957	5.8	1638	1.5	2212	6.0
29 M	0454	1.3	1028	5.8	1709	1.4	2244	6.1
30 TU	0525	1.3	1059	5.8	1740	1.4	2314	6.0
31 W	0556	1.4	1130	5.8	1813	1.5	2347	5.9

AUGUST

Day	Time	m	Time	m	Time	m	Time	m
1 TH	0630	1.5	1203	5.7	1847	1.6		
2 F	0021	5.7	0706	1.7	1240	5.5	1926	1.9
3 SA	0101	5.5	0747	1.9	1324	5.3	2013	2.1
4 SU	0151	5.3	0843	2.2	1421	5.1	2117	2.3
5 M	0257	5.1	0957	2.4	1539	5.0	2241	2.4
6 TU	0425	5.0	1124	2.4	1709	5.2		
7 W	0006	2.2	0551	5.2	1244	2.1	1827	5.5
8 TH	0118	1.8	0702	5.5	1350	1.7	1932	5.9
9 F	0218	1.3	0759	5.9	1444	1.3	2025	6.3
10 SA	0311	1.0	0850	6.3	1534	1.0	2113	6.6
11 SU	0358	0.7	0936	6.4	1620	0.8	2158	6.7
12 M	0442	0.7	1018	6.5	1701	0.8	2239	6.7
13 TU	0522	0.7	1058	6.4	1741	0.9	2316	6.5
14 W	0559	1.0	1135	6.2	1818	1.2	2352	6.2
15 TH	0636	1.3	1211	5.8	1855	1.6		
16 F	0030	5.7	0715	1.8	1250	5.4	1935	2.0
17 SA	0111	5.3	0706	2.3	1335	5.1	2025	2.5
18 SU	0202	4.9	0856	2.7	1435	4.8	2133	2.8
19 M	0315	4.6	1018	2.9	1603	4.7	2305	2.9
20 TU	0451	4.6	1150	2.9	1735	4.8		
21 W	0029	2.7	0612	4.7	1301	2.6	1843	5.0
22 TH	0129	2.4	0709	5.0	1353	2.3	1931	5.3
23 F	0213	2.0	0751	5.3	1433	1.9	2010	5.6
24 SA	0250	1.7	0827	5.6	1508	1.6	2043	5.9
25 SU	0324	1.4	0859	5.8	1540	1.4	2115	6.1
26 M	0355	1.2	0931	6.0	1612	1.2	2146	6.2
27 TU	0427	1.1	1002	6.1	1642	1.2	2216	6.3
28 W	0458	1.1	1032	6.2	1713	1.2	2247	6.2
29 TH	0528	1.2	1103	6.1	1744	1.3	2319	6.1
30 F	0601	1.3	1135	5.9	1818	1.5	2352	5.9
31 SA	0637	1.6	1212	5.7	1857	1.8		

Chart Datum: 3.70 metres below Lallemand System (Mean Sea Level, Marseilles)

FRANCE, NORTH COAST - CHERBOURG

LAT 49°39'N   LONG 1°38'W

TIMES AND HEIGHTS OF HIGH AND LOW WATERS

YEAR **1991**

TIME ZONE −0100
(French Standard Time)
Subtract 1 hour for GMT
For French Summer Time add
ONE hour in non-shaded areas

SEPTEMBER

	TIME	m		TIME	m
1 SU ☾	0032 0719 1255 1944	5.5 2.0 5.4 2.1	**16** M	0120 0809 1349 2045	4.8 2.8 4.7 2.9
2 M	0123 0814 1355 2053	5.2 2.3 5.1 2.4	**17** TU	0228 0930 1516 2222	4.8 3.1 4.6 3.0
3 TU	0235 0936 1522 2228	4.9 2.6 5.0 2.5	**18** W	0410 1113 1701 2357	4.5 3.0 4.7 2.8
4 W	0415 1118 1705	4.9 2.5 5.2	**19** TH	0541 1232 1813	4.7 2.7 5.0
5 TH	0003 0548 1241 1824	2.2 5.2 2.1 5.5	**20** F	0100 0640 1324 1902	2.4 5.0 2.3 5.3
6 F	0114 0656 1343 1924	1.7 5.6 1.6 6.0	**21** SA	0145 0721 1402 1939	2.0 5.4 1.9 5.7
7 SA	0208 0748 1432 2012	1.3 6.1 1.2 6.4	**22** SU	0220 0756 1436 2013	1.7 5.7 1.6 5.9
8 SU ●	0255 0833 1517 2054	0.9 6.4 0.9 6.7	**23** M ○	0252 0828 1509 2044	1.4 6.0 1.3 6.2
9 M	0337 0914 1558 2135	0.7 6.5 0.8 6.7	**24** TU	0325 0859 1540 2115	1.1 6.2 1.1 6.4
10 TU	0417 0953 1636 2211	0.7 6.6 0.8 6.7	**25** W	0356 0932 1613 2148	1.0 6.3 1.0 6.4
11 W	0454 1029 1711 2247	0.8 6.4 1.0 6.4	**26** TH	0429 1003 1645 2220	1.0 6.4 1.0 6.4
12 TH	0528 1104 1746 2321	1.1 6.2 1.3 6.1	**27** F	0502 1037 1719 2255	1.1 6.3 1.2 6.2
13 F	0603 1137 1820 2355	1.4 5.8 1.6 5.6	**28** SA	0537 1113 1756 2332	1.3 6.1 1.4 5.9
14 SA	0638 1213 1857	1.9 5.4 2.1	**29** SU	0616 1152 1838	1.6 5.7 1.8
15 SU ☽	0032 0718 1254 1942	5.2 2.4 5.1 2.6	**30** M	0016 0703 1241 1931	5.5 2.0 5.4 2.2

OCTOBER

	TIME	m		TIME	m
1 TU ☾	0112 0804 1348 2046	5.2 2.4 5.1 2.5	**16** W	0149 0845 1429 2131	4.6 3.1 4.7 3.0
2 W	0230 0934 1521 2226	4.9 2.6 5.1 2.5	**17** TH	0316 1020 1606 2305	4.5 3.0 4.7 2.8
3 TH	0413 1114 1701 2357	5.0 2.4 5.3 2.1	**18** F	0448 1143 1723	4.7 2.8 5.0
4 F	0540 1231 1812	5.3 2.0 5.7	**19** SA	0014 0553 1240 1817	2.5 5.0 2.4 5.3
5 SA	0100 0641 1327 1906	1.7 5.7 1.5 6.1	**20** SU	0102 0639 1322 1859	2.1 5.4 2.0 5.6
6 SU	0151 0729 1412 1951	1.3 6.1 1.2 6.4	**21** M	0141 0717 1358 1935	1.7 5.7 1.6 6.0
7 M	0233 0811 1453 2030	1.0 6.3 1.0 6.5	**22** TU	0216 0752 1433 2010	1.4 6.1 1.3 6.2
8 TU	0313 0849 1531 2108	0.9 6.5 0.9 6.6	**23** W ○	0250 0827 1508 2044	1.2 6.3 1.1 6.4
9 W	0350 0926 1609 2144	0.9 6.5 1.0 6.5	**24** TH	0326 0902 1544 2120	1.1 6.4 1.0 6.5
10 TH	0426 1002 1644 2218	1.1 6.4 1.2 6.3	**25** F	0403 0939 1622 2159	1.0 6.5 1.0 6.4
11 F	0500 1036 1718 2253	1.3 6.1 1.4 6.0	**26** SA	0442 1018 1701 2239	1.1 6.4 1.2 6.2
12 SA	0534 1109 1752 2326	1.6 5.8 1.8 5.6	**27** SU	0522 1059 1744 2321	1.4 6.2 1.4 5.9
13 SU	0610 1144 1828	2.0 5.5 2.1	**28** M	0607 1145 1831	1.7 5.9 1.8
14 M	0003 0648 1224 1911	5.2 2.4 5.2 2.5	**29** TU ☽	0010 0659 1238 1929	5.5 2.0 5.5 2.1
15 TU ☽	0047 0736 1315 2007	4.8 2.8 4.8 2.9	**30** W ☾	0111 0804 1347 2044	5.2 2.3 5.3 2.3
31 TH				0228 0928 1513 2214	5.1 2.4 5.3 2.3

NOVEMBER

	TIME	m		TIME	m
1 F	0357 1057 1639 2335	5.2 2.3 5.4 2.0	**16** SA	0337 1034 1614 2309	4.8 2.7 5.0 2.6
2 SA	0515 1207 1747	5.4 2.0 5.7	**17** SU	0448 1140 1718	5.0 2.5 5.2
3 SU	0036 0614 1301 1841	1.8 5.7 1.7 5.9	**18** M	0008 0545 1232 1809	2.3 5.3 2.1 5.5
4 M	0125 0704 1348 1926	1.5 6.0 1.4 6.1	**19** TU	0055 0632 1316 1854	1.9 5.6 1.8 5.8
5 TU	0208 0746 1428 2006	1.3 6.2 1.3 6.2	**20** W	0137 0715 1357 1936	1.6 5.9 1.5 6.1
6 W ●	0248 0826 1508 2044	1.3 6.2 1.2 6.3	**21** TH ○	0218 0756 1438 2017	1.4 6.2 1.3 6.3
7 TH	0327 0903 1545 2121	1.3 6.3 1.3 6.2	**22** F	0300 0838 1521 2059	1.2 6.4 1.1 6.4
8 F	0404 0940 1622 2158	1.4 6.2 1.4 6.0	**23** SA	0343 0921 1606 2144	1.2 6.5 1.1 6.4
9 SA	0439 1014 1657 2232	1.5 6.1 1.5 5.8	**24** SU	0429 1006 1652 2230	1.2 6.3 1.1 6.2
10 SU	0514 1050 1731 2307	1.8 5.9 1.8 5.6	**25** M	0515 1054 1739 2318	1.3 6.3 1.3 6.0
11 M	0550 1124 1808 2343	2.0 5.6 2.0 5.3	**26** TU	0604 1142 1830	1.5 6.1 1.5
12 TU	0627 1203 1848	2.3 5.3 2.4	**27** W	0008 0657 1235 1926	5.7 1.7 5.8 1.8
13 W	0024 0711 1248 1936	5.0 2.6 5.1 2.6	**28** TH ☽	0105 0755 1337 2029	5.5 2.0 5.6 2.0
14 TH ☽	0115 0805 1345 2039	4.8 2.8 4.9 2.8	**29** F	0209 0905 1444 2141	5.3 2.2 5.5 2.1
15 F	0219 0915 1457 2155	4.7 2.9 4.9 2.7	**30** SA	0322 1020 1600 2257	5.3 2.3 5.4 2.1

DECEMBER

	TIME	m		TIME	m
1 SU	0437 1131 1710	5.3 2.1 5.5	**16** M	0331 1027 1607 2302	5.0 2.5 5.1 2.4
2 M	0002 0541 1230 1809	2.0 5.5 2.0 5.6	**17** TU	0441 1134 1713	5.2 2.3 5.3
3 TU	0056 0636 1322 1901	1.9 5.6 1.9 5.7	**18** W	0004 0543 1232 1812	2.2 5.4 2.1 5.5
4 W	0146 0724 1407 1946	1.8 5.8 1.7 5.8	**19** TH	0059 0640 1326 1906	2.0 5.7 1.8 5.7
5 TH	0229 0808 1450 2028	1.7 5.9 1.6 5.9	**20** F	0152 0732 1416 1957	1.7 6.0 1.5 6.0
6 F ●	0310 0847 1529 2106	1.7 6.0 1.5 5.9	**21** SA ○	0241 0821 1507 2046	1.4 6.3 1.2 6.2
7 SA	0348 0924 1607 2143	1.6 6.1 1.5 5.8	**22** SU	0331 0910 1557 2136	1.2 6.5 1.0 6.3
8 SU	0425 1001 1643 2218	1.7 6.0 1.6 5.7	**23** M	0421 1000 1646 2224	1.1 6.6 0.9 6.4
9 M	0459 1035 1717 2253	1.8 5.9 1.7 5.6	**24** TU	0509 1049 1733 2312	1.1 6.6 1.0 6.3
10 TU	0534 1109 1752 2326	1.9 5.8 1.9 5.5	**25** W	0557 1135 1821 2359	1.2 6.4 1.1 6.1
11 W	0610 1144 1828	2.0 5.6 2.0	**26** TH	0645 1222 1910	1.4 6.2 1.4
12 TH	0003 0647 1222 1908	5.3 2.2 5.4 2.2	**27** F	0047 0734 1312 2000	5.8 1.6 5.9 1.7
13 F	0043 0728 1305 1952	5.2 2.4 5.3 2.4	**28** SA ☾	0139 0829 1406 2059	5.5 1.9 5.6 2.0
14 SA	0130 0818 1356 2048	5.0 2.5 5.1 2.5	**29** SU	0236 0931 1509 2207	5.3 2.2 5.3 2.3
15 SU	0225 0919 1457 2152	5.0 2.6 5.1 2.5	**30** M	0345 1043 1623 2319	5.2 2.4 5.2 2.4
31 TU				0501 1155 1736	5.1 2.4 5.2

Chart Datum: 3.70 metres below Lallemand System (Mean Sea Level, Marseilles)

MINOR HARBOURS AND ANCHORAGES   10.17.25

ST AUBIN, Jersey, 49°11' N, 2°10' W, Zone 0 (GMT), Admty chart 1137. HW −0455 on Dover; local times and heights, as St Helier; ML 6.1m; Duration 0545. See 10.17.11. Good quiet anchorage in bay with off-shore winds, or yachts can go alongside N quay and dry. Alternative Belcroute Bay on E of Noirmont Pt − steep to, deep water, excellent shelter from W to SW winds; landing by dinghy. Ent to N of St Aubin Fort (on I) in W sector of Lt. N pier head Iso R 4s 12m 10M and Dir Lt 252°, Dir F WRG 5m, G246°−251°, W251°−253°, R253°−258°. St Aubin Fort I pier head Fl (2) Y 5s 8m 1M. Facilities: FW on N quay, Slip; **Royal Channel Islands YC** ☎ 41023 Bar, R, M, Slip; **Battricks** ☎ 43412, BY, Gas; **Jacksons Yacht Services** ☎ 43819. CH, El, ME, Sh; **St Aubin BY** ☎ 45499 ME, El, Sh, CH; **J. Fox** ☎ 44877 ME; **M. Paddock** ME, Sh; **Ken Reece** ☎ 44651, ME, El; **Town** Bar, D, FW, ⬚, P, R, V, buses to St Helier.

ST SAMPSON, Guernsey, 49°29' N, 2°31' W, Zone 0 (GMT), Admty chart 808. HW −0450 on Dover. See 10.17.14. Harbour dries. Guernsey's second harbour and very commercial. Official port of entry. Good shelter but the disadvantages of a commercial port. Lt on Crocq pier head FR 11m 5M; vis 250°−340°, and traffic signals. N pier head FG 3m 5M; vis 230°−340°. Ldg Lts 286°, Front on S pier head FR 3m 5M; vis 230°−340°; Rear, 390m from front, on clocktower, FG 13m. VHF Ch 12 (H24). Facilities: See Hr Mr for AB, C, FW. All facilities at BY for commercial shipping. There are no facilities for yachts. **Marine and General** ☎ 45808, Slip, ME, El, Sh, C. Buses to St Peter Port.

DAHOUET, Côtes du Nord, 48°35' N, 2°34' W, Zone −0100, Admty charts 2668, 2669, SHOM 833. HW −0520 on Dover (GMT), −0006 on Saint-Malo (zone −0100); HW height −0.7m on Saint-Malo; ML 6.1m; Duration 0550. See 10.17.18. Good shelter except in strong NW winds. Outer basin dries, access HW∓2. Approach channel is marked and there is a Lt Tr, La Petite-Muette, Fl WRG 4s 10m 9/6M, G055°−114°, W114°−146°, R146°−196°. Fishing boats use outer Hr, yachts inner wet Hr on Vieux Quai. Facilities: **Quay** Hr Mr, ⌗, C (5 ton), P, D; **YC du Val-André** ☎ 96.72.21.68; **Bouguet** ☎ 96.72.97.00. CH, El, ME, Sh; **Town** Bar, R, V. A marina is under construction

VAL-ANDRÉ, Côtes du Nord, 48°36' N, 2°33' W, Zone −0100, Admty charts 2668, 2669, SHOM 833. HW −0520 on Dover (GMT), −0006 on Saint-Malo (zone −0100); HW height −0.7m on Saint-Malo; ML 6.1m; Duration 0550. A small drying harbour exposed to S and SW winds. Beware Verdelet coming from E and Platier des Trois Têtes from W. Yachts can go alongside the quay, ask YC for mooring off Le Piegu or anchor off. Hr accessible HW∓3. Facilities: Hr Mr ☎ 96.72.83.20, FW, Slip; **YC du Val-André** ☎ 96.72.21.68. Bar, R; **Troalen** ☎ 96.72.20.20. CH, El, ME, Sh; **Town** Bar, R, V.

ERQUY, Côtes du Nord, 48°38' N, 2°28' W, Zone −0100, Admty charts 3672, 2668, 2669, SHOM 833, 5724. HW −0515 on Dover (GMT), −0005 on Saint-Malo (zone −0100); HW height −0.7m on Saint-Malo; ML 6.1m; Duration 0550. See 10.17.19. Sheltered from E, but exposed to SW or W winds. Hr dries and is usually full of fishing boats. Beware Plateau des Portes d'Erquy (dry) about 2M to West. Coming from S, beware of rks off Pte de la Houssaye. Lt on mole-head Oc(2+1) WRG 12s 11m ⅛M R055°−081°, W081°−094°, G094°−111°, ⌐⌐°−120°, R120°−134°. Inner jetty, head Fl R 2.5s ⌐M. Facilities: Hr Mr and ⌗ ☎ 96.72.19.32; **Quay** ⌐, D, FW, P; **Cercle de la Voile d'Erquy** ⌐0; **Régina Plaisance** ☎ 96.72.13.70. CH, El, Bar, R, V.

SAINT-CAST, Côtes du Nord, 48°38' N, 2°15' W, Zone −0100, Admty charts 3659, 2669, SHOM 5646. HW −0515 on Dover (GMT), −0001 on Saint-Malo (zone −0100); HW height −0.1m on Saint-Malo; ML 6.3m; Duration 0550. See 10.17.19. Good shelter from S through W to NW, and moorings are available in 1.8m. Beware Les Bourdinots (dry 2m) with E cardinal buoy ¾M NE of Pte de Saint-Cast, and La Feuillâtre (marked by Bn) and Bec Rond off harbour. Mole-head Lt Iso WG 4s 11m 11/8M, W204°−217°, G217°−233°, W233°−245°, G245°−204°. Facilities: Hr Mr ☎ 96.41.88.34. SNSM ☎ 96.41.88.34. Signal Tr 99.41.85.30; **YC de Saint-Cast** ☎ 96.41.91.77. **La Maison Blanche** ☎ 96.41.81.40. CH, El, ME, Sh; **L.M.B. Marine** ☎ 96.41.80.23. CH, El, ME, Sh; **Town** ⒷＢ; Bar, D, P, ✉, R, V.

LA RICHARDAIS, Ille-et-Vilaine, 48°34' N, 2°02' W, Zone −0100, Admty chart 2669, SHOM 4233. HW (at lock) −0515 on Dover (GMT). Pass through the lock in the dam above St Servan, on W side, opens every hour on the hour when tide is over CD+4m. Port of La Richardais approx 1M beyond lock to W. Complete shelter except from NE winds. R Rance navigable up to Dinan with ease. For water levels in Rance basin and times of operation of power station ☎ 99.46.14.46. Facilities: Hr Mr ☎ 99.46.24.20. **Naviga Voile** ☎ 99.46.99.25. CH, El, ME, Sh; **Town** Bar, D, P, ✉, R, V, Ⓑ.

ROTHENEUF, Ille-et-Vilaine, 48°42' N, 1°56' W, Zone −0100, Admty charts 2700, 3659, SHOM 5644. HW −0510 on Dover (GMT), HW times and heights as for Saint-Malo (zone −0100); ML 7.0m; Duration 0540. Complete shelter in Hr which dries completely. Anchor outside in 4m just N of spar Bn marking ent. Rocks on both sides of ent which is less than 170m wide. Safest to enter when rks uncovered. There are no lights; ldg line at 163° W side of Pte Benard and old converted windmill. Facilities: FW, Slip; **Village** Bar, D, P, R, V.

CANCALE, Ille-et-Vilaine, 48°40' N, 1°51' W, Zone −0100, Admty chart 3659, SHOM 5644, 824. HW −0510 on Dover (GMT), +0004 on Saint-Malo (zone −0100); HW height +1.2m on Saint-Malo; ML 7.5m; Duration 0535. See 10.17.20. A drying Hr just inside Bay of Mont St Michel, 1M SW of Point de la Chaine. Area dries to about 1M off-shore; anchor off end of Pte de la Chaine in deep water. Drying berths usually available in La Houle, the Hr in Cancale. Exposed to winds SW to SE. Jetty-head Lt Oc(3)G 12s 12m 8M, obsc when bearing less than 223°. Facilities: **Quay** C (1.5 ton) D, FW, P; **Club Nautique de Cancale** ☎ 99.89.90.22; **Froc** ☎ 99.89.61.74. El, M, ME, Sh; **Town** (famous for oysters), Ⓑ, Bar, D, P, ✉, R, V.

PORTBAIL, Manche, 49°19' N, 1°43' W, Zone −0100, Admty chart 2669, SHOM 827. HW −0440 on Dover (GMT), +0026 on Saint-Malo (zone −0100); HW height −0.9m on Saint-Malo; ML 6.3m; Duration 0545. See 10.17.21. Good shelter. Hr dries but access HW∓½ at np, HW∓2½ at sp for a draught of 1m. Beware very strong tide over bar. Passage through sand banks buoyed to Training Wall (covers at HW) which is marked by R spar Bns. Drying harbour E of jetty − 1st line of buoys parallel to jetty for visitors; slip to W of jetty. Training Wall head Q(2)R 5s 5m 2M. Ldg Lts 042°, Front (La Caillourie) QW 14m 11M. Rear, 870m from front, QW 20m 9M. VHF Ch 09. Facilities: Hr Mr ☎ 33.04.33.48; **Quay** C (5 ton) D, FW, P; **Cercle Nautique de Portbail-Denneville** ☎ 33.04.86.15. Bar, R; **YC de Portbail** ☎ 33.04.83.48. AB, C, Slip; **Gérard** ☎ 33.04.80.07. El, ME, Sh; **Le Cornec** Sh (wood); **Fleury** Sh, ME, El; **Flambard** Sh, ME, El; **Town** Bar, Ⓑ, ✉, R, ⇌ (Valognes), V.

VOLVO PENTA SERVICE

Sales and service centres in area 18
Names and addresses of Volvo Penta dealers in
this area are available from:

FRANCE **Volvo Penta France SA,** Chemin de la Nouvelle, F78130 Les Mureaux
Tel (01) 3 474 72 01, Telex 695221 F.
BELGIUM **Volvo Penta Belgium,** Wolvwelaan 9 B-1800 Vilvorde Tel (02) 254-14-79,
Telex 65249, Volvo BMB

Area 18

North-East France
Barfleur to Dunkerque

VOLVO PENTA

Key to Symbols

Symbol	Description
Coast Station/Port Radio – frequencies
(RC)	Marine radiobeacon– call sign, sequence, frequency and range (nm)
(RC) Aero	Aeronautical radiobeacon–call sign, frequency and range (nm)
[i]	See for harbour information/tidal data
	Weather information (tel. no. or times)
CG	Coastguard Rescue Co-ordination Centre
CG	Coastguard Rescue Sub-Centre
LB	Life-boat
IL	Inshore Life-boat
	SAR Helicopter base
☆	Principal lights
	Light-vessel
	Lanby
*	See 10.18.29

51°
N

1°W

10-18-2
North-East France

50°
N

See 10.17.2

Cross Gris Nez
Cross Jobourg

Le Havre

Standard Port	
[i]	10.18.19
S C	VHF 23 26 16 28 82
R P	VHF 12 20 67 69
	35.42.21.06
LB	

Fécamp

[i]	10.18.20
R P	VHF 12
Yacht harbou
LB   IL

LHA Lanby

(RC)	LH •−•• ••••
4	291·9 30

Pte. de Barfleur

(RC)	FG •−•• −−−
6	291·9 70

Barfleur

[i]	10.18.9
LB IL	

Ouistreham

[i]	10.18.15
R P	VHF 12 16 68
LB IL	

Etretat
IL
☆

☆ **Cap de**

St Vaast la Hougue

[i]	10.18.10
Marina VHF 09	
IL	

Iles St Marcouf
☆

Vér-sur-Mer

(RC)	ÉR •• −•• •−•
5	291·9 20
IL	

Grandcamp

[i]	10.18.12
LB IL	

IL **Isigny***

Carentan

[i]	10.18.11
R	VHF 09

Port-en-Bessin

[i]	10.18.13
(RC)	BS −••• ••• 313·5 5
S C	VHF 03 16
R P	VHF 18 Lock Ch18
LB IL	

Cabourg-Dives*

Courseulles-sur-Mer

[i]	10.18.14
LB IL	

Deau Trou

[i]	10.18
Marina V	
	31.8
LB	

Caen*

	31.74.48.11

0°

1°W

18

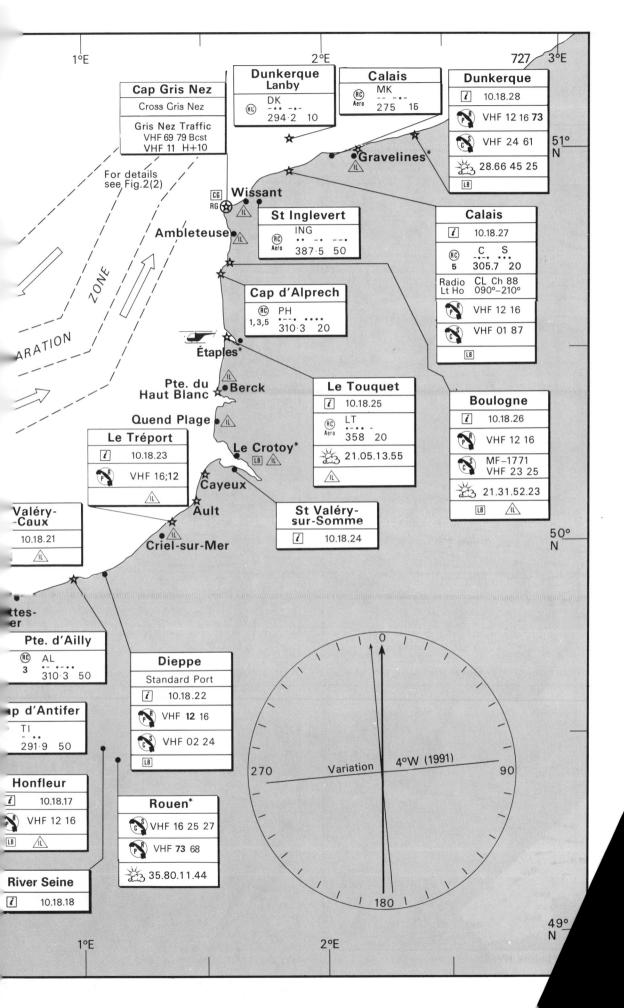

1°E   2°E   3°E

Cap Gris Nez

Cross Gris Nez

Gris Nez Traffic
VHF 69 79 Bcst
VHF 11 H+10

Dunkerque Lanby

(HC) DK
– • • – • –
294·2   10

Calais

(RC Aero) MK
– – – • –
275   15

Dunkerque

ℹ 10.18.28

VHF 12 16 **73**

VHF 24 61

28.66 45 25

LB

For details
see Fig.2(2)

ZONE

ARATION

CG
RG   **Wissant**

Ambleteuse

St Inglevert

(RC Aero) ING
• • – • – – •
387·5   50

Calais

ℹ 10.18.27

(RC 5) C   S
– • – • • •
305.7   20

Radio   CL Ch 88
Lt Ho   090°–210°

VHF 12 16

VHF 01 87

LB

Cap d'Alprech

(RC 1,3,5) PH
• – – • • • • •
310·3   20

Étaples*

Pte. du
Haut Blanc   **Berck**

Quend Plage

Le Tréport

ℹ 10.18.23

VHF 16;12

IL

Le Crotoy*

LB   IL

Le Touquet

ℹ 10.18.25

(RC Aero) LT
• – • – • •
358   20

21.05.13.55

IL

Boulogne

ℹ 10.18.26

VHF 12 16

MF–1771
VHF 23 25

21.31.52.23

LB   IL

Cayeux

Ault

Criel-sur-Mer

St Valéry-sur-Somme

ℹ 10.18.24

Valéry-
-Caux

10.18.21

IL

50°
N

51°
N

...ttes-
...er

Pte. d'Ailly

(RC 3) AL
• – • – • •
310·3   50

...p d'Antifer

TI
– • •
291·9   50

Dieppe

Standard Port

ℹ 10.18.22

VHF **12** 16

VHF 02 24

LB

Honfleur

ℹ 10.18.17

VHF 12 16

LB   IL

Rouen*

VHF 16 25 27

VHF **73** 68

35.80.11.44

River Seine

ℹ 10.18.18

270   Variation   4°W (1991)   90

0

180

49°
N

1°E   2°E

10.18.3   AREA 18 TIDAL STREAMS

5 Hours before HW Dover (0345 before HW Le Havre)

4 Hours before HW Dover (0245 before HW Le Havre)

3 Hours before HW Dover (0145 before HW Le Havre)

2 Hours before HW Dover (0045 before HW Le Havre)

...W Dover (0015 after HW Le Havre)

HW Dover (0115 after HW Le Havre)

Westward 10.17.3   North-eastward 10.19.3   Northward 10.3.3   Isle of Wight 10.2.8

1 Hour after HW Dover (0215 after HW Le Havre)

2 Hours after HW Dover (0315 after HW Le Havre)

3 Hours after HW Dover (0415 after HW Le Havre)

4 Hours after HW Dover (0515 after HW Le Havre)

5 Hours after HW Dover (0615 after HW Le Havre)

6 Hours after HW Dover (0510 before HW Le Havre)

18

10.18.4   LIGHTS, FOG SIGNALS AND WAYPOINTS

Abbreviations used below are given in 10.0.3. Principal lights are in **bold** print, places in CAPITALS, and light-vessels, light floats and Lanbys in *CAPITAL ITALICS*. Unless otherwise stated lights are white. m—elevation in metres; M—nominal range in n. miles. Fog signals are in *italics*. Useful waypoints are underlined use those on land with care. See 4.2.2.

FRANCE—NORTH COAST

Cap Lévi 49°41'·80N 01°28'·30W Fl R 5s 30m **22M**; grey square Tr, W top.
Anse de Vicq Ldg Lts 158°. Front FR 8m 6M; W pylon, R top. Rear 428m from front FR 14m 6M; W pylon, R top.
Les Équets Lt Buoy 49°43'·68N 01°18'·28W Q 8m 4M; N cardinal mark.
Pointe de Barfleur-Gatteville 49°41'·87N 01°15'·87W Fl(2) 10s 72m **29M**; grey Tr, B top; obsc when brg less than 088°; RC; *Réed (2) 60s.*

BARFLEUR.
Ldg Lts 2ˈ19°30'. Front Oc(3) 12s 7m 10M; W square Tr. Rear 283m from front Oc (3) 12s 13m 10M; grey and W square Tr, G top; synchronised with front.
Jetée Est, head 49°40'·4N 01°15'·4W Oc R 4s 5m 6M; W hut, R top.
Jetée Ouest, near root Fl G 4s 8m 6M; W framework Tr, G top.
Pte de Saire 49°36'·44N 01°13'·75W Oc(2ı) 12s 11m 13M; W Tr, G top.

ST VAAST-LA-HOUGUE.
Jetty head 49°35'·22N 01°15'·33W Oc(2) WR 6s 12m W11M, R8M; W Tr, R top; vis R219°-247°, W247°-219°. Obsc by Pte de Saire when brg less than 223° and by Île de Tatihou 230°-249°. *Siren Mo(N) 30s.*
NE side, breakwater head Iso G 4s 6m 5M; W pedestal, G top.
SW side, groyne head Oc(4) R 12s 6m 7M; W hut, R top.

MORSALINES.
Ldg Lts 267°. Front 49°34'·28N 01°16'·45W Oc 4s 9m 10M; W framework Tr, G top; obsc by Île de Tatihou when brg less than 228°. Rear 1·8M from front 49°34'·2N 01°19'·1W Oc(3ı) WRG 12s 90m W12M, R9M, G8M; W 8-sided Tr, G top; vis W 171°-316°, G316°-321°, R321°-342°, W342°-355°.

Îles Saint-Marcouf, Île du Large 49°29'·90N 01°08'·90W VQ(3) 5s 18m 9M; grey Tr, G top.

CARENTAN.
CI Lt Buoy 49°25'·50N 01°07'·08W Iso 4s; safe water mark.
Ldg Lts 209°30'. **Front** Oc(3) R 12s 6m **17M**; W post, R top; intens 209°-211°. Rear 723m from front Oc(3) 12s 14m 11M; W gantry, G top; vis 120°-005°; synchronised with front.

ISIGNY-SUR-MER.
Ldg Lts 173°. **Front** Oc(2ı) 12s 7m **18M**; intens 171°-175°.
Rear 600m from front Oc(2ı) 12s 19m **18M**; W framework Tr, B top; synchronised with front, intens 171°-175°.

GRANDCAMP-LES-BAINS.
Maresquerie 49°23'·2N 01°02'·7W Oc 4s 28m 12M; vis 090°-270°.
Jetée Ouest, head Fl G 4s 9m 6M.
Jetée Est, head 49°23'·50N 01°03'·00W Oc(2) R 6s 10m 9M; *Siren Mo(N) 30s.*
Perré 49°23'·4N 01°02'·5W Oc 4s 8m 13M; G framework Tr

Note. For English Channel Waypoints see 10.1.7

on W hut; vis 083°-263°.
Ldg Lts 146°, both Q 4m 7M; vis 136°-156°.

PORT-EN-BESSIN.
Ldg Lts 204°. Front 49°21'·0N 00°45'·5W Oc(3) 12s 25m 10M; W framework Tr; *Siren 20s* — sounded over a sector of 90° each side of leading line, continuous in the western sector, interrupted in the eastern. Rear, 93m from front Oc(3) 12s 42m 11M; W house; synchronised with front; RC.
Jetée Est, head Oo R 4ₒ 14m 7M; R framework Tr.
Jetée Ouest, head 49°21'·21N 00°45'·42W Fl WG 4s 14m W10M, G7M; G framework Tr; vis W114°-065°, G065°-114°. Oc(2) R 6s and Fl(2) G 6s mark the pier hds.

Ver 49°20'·47N 00°31'·15W Fl(3) 15s 42m **26M**; W Tr, grey top; obsc by cliffs of St Aubin when brg more than 275°; RC.

COURSEULLES-SUR-MER.
Jetée Ouest 49°20'·47N 00°27'·28W Iso WG 4s 7m W9M, G5M; brown framework Tr on dolphin, G top; vis W135°-235°, G235°-135°; *Horn 30s* sounded from 2 hours before to 2 hours after HW.
Jetée Est Oc(2) R 6s 9m 7M; brown framework Tr, R top.

Lion-sur-Mer 49°18'·2 00°18'·8W Iso 4s 16m 7M; building with W and R front. TE 1985.

OUISTREHAM.
OC Lt Buoy 49°19'·89N 00°14'·53W Iso 4s 8m 4M; safe water mark; *Whis.*
Ouistreham Oc WR 4s 37m **W17M**, R 13M; W Tr, R top; vis W151°-115°, R115°-151°.
Jetée Ouest, head Iso G 4s 12m 9M; W framework Tr, G top, on dolphin; *Horn 10s,* sounded from 2 hours before to 3 hours after HW. Ldg Lts 185°.
Front, Jetée Est Oc(3+1) R 12s10m13M; W pylon, R top.
Rear 610m from front Dir Oc(3+1) R 12s 13m **22M**; W pylon, R top; synchronised with front; intens 183°-187°.
Enrochements Est, head 49°18'·08N 00°14'·56W Oc(2) R 6s 7m 8M; R Tr; Ra refl.

Canal de Caen marked by QR and OcR 4s Lts on E side, and by QG and IsoG 4s Lts on West side.
Viaduc de Calix Iso 4s on upstream and downstream sides; FG on N side, FR on S side.

Dives-sur-Mer Oc(2+1) WRG 12s 6m W12M, R9M, G9M; vis G124°-154°, W154°-157°, R157°-193°.

TROUVILLE.
Trouville SW Lt Buoy 49°22'·68N 00°02'·64E VQ(9) 10s; W cardinal mark.
West jetty 49°22'·44N 00°04'·17E Fl WG 4s 10m W12M, G9M; B framework mast on dolphin; vis W005°-176°, G176°-005°.
East jetty Fl(4) WR 12s 8m W10M, R7M; W framework Tr, R top; vis W131°-175°, R175°-131°.
Ldg Lts 148°. Front Oc R 4s 11m 12M; W Tr, R top; vis 330°-150°; *Reed (2) 30s.* Rear 217m from front Oc R 4s 17m 10M; W framework Tr, R top; synchronised with front vis 120°-170°.
West jetty QG 11m 9M; W and G Tr.
Breakwater Iso G 4s 9m 5M; G mast.

HONFLEUR.
Digue du Ratier 49°25'·97N 00°06'·66E VQ 8m 8M; Tank on

B column; Ra refl.
Spillway 49°25'·8N 00°12'·8E VQ(9) 10s 15m 6M; W cardinal mark.
Falaise des Fonds 49°25'·5N 00°12'·9E Fl(3) WRG 12s 15m **W17M**, R13M, G13M; W square Tr, G top; vis G040°-080°, R080°-084°, G084°-100°, W100°-109°, R109°-162°, G162°-260°.

Digue Ouest, head QG 10m 6M; G pylon.
Digue Est, head Q 10m 9M; N cardinal mark; *Reed (5) 40s.*
Mole, head Oc(2) R 6s.
Jetée Transit F Vi 10m 6M; B & W pylon.
Quay, West, 2 FG (vert) 6m 5M.
Quay, East 2 FG (vert) 6m 5M.

LA SEINE MARITIME.
La Risle, Digue Sud, 49°26'·3N 00°22'·0E Iso G 4s 11m 7M; W framework Tr and hut, G top; Ra refl.
Digue Nord, Tourelle Ygou, VQR 7m 5M; R pedestal on grey tank.
Digue Sud, Épi de la Roque, QG 8m 6M; W column, G top.
Marais-Vernier Fl G 4s 8m 5M; W column, G top.
Digue Nord, Tancarville, QR 9m 6M; W column, R top. Aero Fl R 3s on each of 2 bridge pillars.

Cap de la Hève 49°30'·80N 00°04'·24E Fl 5s 123m **24M**; W 8-sided Tr, R top; 2 FR (hor) on Octeville belfry 3·2M NE; Aero obstruction Lt 1·6M ENE.

LE HAVRE LANBY 49°31'·67N 00°09'·80W Q(2) R 10s 10m **20M**; W buoy, R stripes; RC; Racon.

LE HAVRE.
Digue Sud, head 49°29'·10N 00°05'·45E VQ(3) G 2s 15m 11M; W Tr, G top.
Digue Nord, head Fl R 5s 15m **21M**; W Tr, R top; *Reed 15s.* Ldg Lts 107°. Front **Quai Roger Meunier** F 36m **25M**; grey Tr, G top; intens 106°-108°; (H24). Rear **Quai Joannes Couvert** 0·73M from front F 78m **25M**; grey Tr, G top; intens 106°-108°; (H24).
Ldg Lts 090°. **Front** 49°29'·5N 00°05'·8E FR 21m **18M**; W Tr, R top; intens 089°-091°. **Rear**, 620m from front, FR 43m **18M**; square column on house; intens 089°-091° (both occas).
Yacht harbour, Digue Augustin Normand, Q(2) G 5s 5m 2M.
Quai des Abeilles QR 9m 7M; W and R mast; *Bell (1) 2·5s.*

PORT D'ANTIFER.
Bassin de Caux, Mole Ouest, head Fl R 4s 13m 5M; W mast, R top.
Mole Est Fl G 4s 13m 5M; W mast, G top.
Antifer 49°39'·5N 00°09'·2E Oc WRG 4s 24m W14M, R13M, G13M; W Tr; vis G068°-078°, W078°-088°, R088°-098°.
Jetty head 49°39'·8N 00°07'·1E QR 20m 9M; W Tr, R top.
Port D'Antifer Ldg Lts 127°. **Front** 49°38'·3N 00°09'·2E Oc 4s 105m **22M**; W mast, G top vis 127°-128°. **Rear**, 430m from front, Oc 4s 124m **22M**; W mast, G top. By day both show FW Lts **33M** vis 126·5°-128·5°, occasl.

Cap d'Antifer 49°41'·07N 00°10'·00E Fl 20s 128m **29M**; grey 8-sided Tr, G top; vis 021°-222°; RC.

YPORT
Ldg Lts 165°. Front Oc 4s 11m. Rear 30m from front Oc 4s 14m.

FECAMP.
Jetée Nord 49°46'·00N 00°21'·87E Fl(2) 10s 15m **16M**; grey Tr, R top; *Reed (2) 30s.* Lts in line 085°.

Front Jetée Sud, head, QG 14m 9M; grey Tr, G top; vis 072°-217°.
Rear, Jetée Nord, root, QR 10m; R circle on W mast.

SAINT VALERY-EN-CAUX
Jetée Ouest 49°52'·45N 00°42'·50E Oc(2+1) G 12s 13m 14M; G Tr.
Jetée Est Fl(2) R 6s 8m 4M; W mast, R top.

Pointe d'Ailly 49°55'·13N 00°57'·56E Fl(3) 20s 95m **31M**; W square Tr, G top; RC; *Horn (3) 60s* (TD).
D1 Lt Buoy 49°57'·10N 01°01'·26E VQ(3) 5s; E cardinal mark.

DIEPPE.
Jetée Est, head 49°56'·22N 01°05'·17E Oc(4) R 12s 19m 8M; W Tr, R top.
Jetée Ouest, head 49°56'·20N 01°05'·02E Iso WG 4s 10m W12M, G8M; W Tr, G top on building; vis W095°-164°, G164°-095°; *Reed 30s.* Ldg Lts 138°. Front QR 19m 9M; W framework Tr, R top. Rear 200m from front QR 35m 9M; W hut, R top; vis 106°-170°.
Daffodils Lt Buoy 50°02'·50N 01°04'·15E VQ(9) 10s; W cardinal mark.

LE TRÉPORT.
Jetée Ouest 50°03'·94N 01°22'·22E Fl(2) G 10s 15m **20M**; W Tr, G top; *Reed Mo(N) 30s.* Jetée Est Oc R 4s 8m 6M; W column, R top.

Ault 50°06'·35N 01°27'·24E Oc(3) WR 12s 95m **W18M**, R14M, W Tr, R top; vis W040°-175°, R175°-220°.

Cayeux-sur-Mer 50°11'·75N 01°30'·70E Fl R 5s 32m **22M**; W Tr, R top.
Pte du Hourdel 50°12'·95N 01°34'·00E Oc(3) WG 12s 19m W12M, G9M; W Tr, G top; vis W053°-248°, G248°-323°; *Reed (3) 30s.*

PORT DU CROTOY.
Le Crotoy 50°12'·9N 01°37'·4E Oc(2) R 6s 19m 9M; W pylon; vis 285°-135°.
Yacht harbour, West side jetty Fl R 2s 4m 2M.
Yacht harbour, E side Fl G 2s 4m 2M.

SAINT VALERY-SUR-SOMME
50°11'·5N 01°37'·6E Iso G 4s 9m 9M; W pylon, G top; vis 347°-222°.
Embankment head 50°12'·3N 01°35'·9E Q(3) G 6s 2m 2M; G pylon; Ra refl.
Mole head 50°11'·2N 01°38'·6E Fl R 4s 9m 9M; W column, R top; vis 000°-250°.

Pointe du Haut-Blanc 50°23'·90N 01°33'·75E Fl 5s 44m **23M**; W Tr, R bands, G top.

Pointe du Touquet 50°31'·4N 01°35'·6E Fl(2) 10s 54m **25M**; Y Tr, brown band; W and G top.

Camiers, Riviere Canche entrance, N side Oc(2) WRG 6s 17m W9M, R7M, G6M; R framework Tr; vis G015°-090°, W090°-105°, R105°-141°.

Bassurelle Lt Buoy 50°32'·70N 00°57'·80E Fl(4) R 15s 6M; Racon; *Whis.*

Cap d'Alprech 50°41'·95N 01°33'·83E Fl(3) 15s 62m **23M**; W Tr, B top; RC; FR Lts on radio mast 600m NE.

Hoverport Ldg Lts 119° both FR 14M; W columns, grey tops; occas.

18

BOULOGNE.
Approaches Lt Buoy 50°45'·25N 01°31'·15E VQ(6)LFl 10s; S cardinal mark; *Whis.*
Digue Sud (Carnot) 50°44'·48N 01°34'·13E Fl(21) 15s 25m **19M**; W Tr, G top; *Horn(2+1) 60s.*
Digue Nord QR 10m 6M; R Tr.
Ro Ro berth Ldg Lts 197°. Front 50°43'·7N 01°34'·1E FG 16m; dolphin; vis 107°-287°. Rear, 480m from front FR 23m; R mast, W band; vis 187°-207°.
Darse Sarraz-Bournet, entrance E side Oc(2) R 6s 8m 6M; W framework Tr, R top. West side Iso G 4s 0m 5M; W framework Tr, G top.
Jetée NE, head FR 11m 9M; R Tr.
Jetée SW, FG 17m 5M; W column, G top; *Horn 30s.*

ZC1 Lt Buoy 50°44'·85N 01°27'·10E Fl(4)Y 15s; special mark.
ZC2 Lt Buoy 50°53'·50N 01°31'·00E Fl(21)Y 15s; special mark.

Cap Gris-Nez 50°52'·17N 01°35'·07E Fl 5s 72m **29M**; W Tr, B top; obsc 232°-005°; RG; *Siren 60s.*

Sangatte 50°57'·23N 01°46'·57E Oc WG 4s 12m W9M, G6M; W column, B top; vis G065°-089°, W089°-152°, G152°-245°; Racon.

CALAIS.
CA4 Lt Buoy 50°58'·90N 01°45'·15E VQ(9) 10s; W cardinal mark; *Whis.*
Jetée Ouest, head 50°58'·30N 01°50'·48E Iso G 3s 12m 9M; (in fog Iso 3s); W Tr, G top; *Bell (1) 5s.*
Jetée Est, head Fl(2)R 6s 12m **17M**; (in fog Fl(2) 6s on request); grey Tr, R top; *Reed(2) 40s*; Ra refl.
Calais 50°57'·7N 01°51'·2E Fl(4) 15s 59m **23M**; W 8-sided Tr, B top; obsc by Cap Blanc-Nez when brg less than 073°; RC.

SANDETTIE LT F 51°09'·40N 01°47'·20E Fl 5s 12m **24M**; R hull, Lt Tr amidships; *Horn 3s*; Racon.
MPC Lt buoy 51°06'·17N 01°38'·33E Fl Y 2·5s 10m 6M; special mark.
DUNKERQUE LANBY 51°03'·00N 01°51'·83E Fl 3s 10m **25M**; R tubular structure on circular buoy; Racon.

Walde 50°59'·7N 01°54'·9E Fl(3) 12s 13m 4M; B pylon.
DKA Lt Buoy 51°02'·59N 01°57'·06E LFl 10s; safe water mark.

GRAVELINES.
Jetée Ouest 51°00'·93N 02°05'·68E Fl(2)WG 6s 14m W9M, G6M; vis W317°-327°, G078°-085°, W085°-244°. Jetée Est Fl(3)R 12s 5m 4M.

DUNKERQUE PORT OUEST.
Ldg Lts 120°. **Front** Dir FG 16m **19M**; W column, G top; intens 119°-121°. **Rear**, 600m from front, Dir FG 30m **22M**; W column, G top; intens 119°-121°. By day both show FW **28M**.
Jetée du Dyck, head 51°02'·3N 02°09'·9E Fl G 4s 24m 10M; W column, G top.
Jetée Clipon, head Fl(4) 12s 24m 13M; W column, R top; vis 278°-243°; *Siren (4) 60s.* Dir Lt 167° Dir Iso WRG 4s 12m 11M; vis G162°-166°, W166°-168°, 168°172°.
DUNKERQUE.
Dunkerque 51°03'·0N 02°21'·9E Fl(2) 10s 59m **29M**; W Tr, B top. Ldg Lts 185°. Front F Vi 10m 3M; W column, R top; intens 183°-187°. Common rear F Vi 24m 4M; grey framework Tr; intens 184°-186°, 178°-180°.
Front Ldg Lt 179° F Vi 10m 3M; W column, G top; intens 177°-181°.

Jetée Est, head Oc(3) R 12s 11m 10M; W framework Tr, R top. *Horn (3) 30s.*
Jetée Ouest, head 51°03'·68N 02°21'·05E Oc(21) WG 12s 35m **W17M**, G13M; W Tr, brown top; vis G252°-310°, W310°-252°; *Dia(2+1) 60s.*

10.18.5 PASSAGE INFORMATION

The coasts of Normandy and Picardy are convenient to harbours along the South Coast of England — the distance from (say) Brighton to Fécamp being hardly more than an overnight passage. It should be noted however that many of the harbs dry, so that a boat which can take the ground is an advantage. For details of traffic schemes in Dover Strait see Fig. 2(2). Notes on the English Channel and on cross Channel passages appear in 10.3.5. For detailed sailing directions, refer to *Normandy Harbours and Pilotage* (Adlard Coles Ltd), which conveniently covers this area. *The Shell Pilot to the English Channel* (Faber and Faber) covers the French coast from Dunkerque to Brest, and the Channel Islands. For French terms see 10.16.5.

POINTE DE BARFLEUR TO DEAUVILLE (chart 2613)

Raz de Barfleur (10.17.5) must be avoided in bad weather. Pte de Barfleur marks the W end of B de Seine, which stretches 53M E to C de la Heve, close NW of Le Havre. There are no obstructions on a direct course across the b, but a transhipment area for large tankers is centred about 10M ESE of Pte de Barfleur. A feature of B de Seine is the stand of tide at HW.

S from Barfleur (10.18.9) the coast runs SSE 4M to Pte de Saire, with rks and shoals up to 1 ¼ M offshore. 2M S of Pte de Saire is St Vaast-la-Hougue (10.18.10): approach S of Île de Tatihou, but beware La Tourelle (rk which dries) 4 ½ ca E of island, and Le Gavendest (dries) and La Dent (dries) which lie 6 ca SE and 5 ca SSE of island and are marked by buoys. There is a chan inshore of Île de Tatihou which can be used near HW. Anch in Grande Rade in offshore winds, exposed to E and S.

Îles St Marcouf (chart 2073) lie 7M SE of St Vaast-la-Hougue, about 4M offshore, and consist of Île du Large (Lt) and Île de Terre about ¼ M apart. (See 10.18.29). Banc de St Marcouf with depths of 2.4m extends 2 ½ M NW from the islands, and the sea breaks on this in strong N or NE winds. There is anch, rather exposed, SW of Lt Ho. Landing is possible by dinghy in the small harb on W side of Île du Large from about local HW −0200 to HW +0200. There is a bird sanctuary on Île de Terre.

At the head of B du Grand Vey, about 10M S of Îles St Marcouf, are the (very) tidal harbs of Carentan (10.18.11) and Isigny (10.18.29). Entry is only possible near HW. The Carentan chan is well buoyed and adequately lit. It trends SSW across sandbanks for about 4M, beyond which it runs between two breakwaters leading to a lock gate, and thence into canal to town of Carentan. The Isigny chan is deeper, but the harb dries. Neither chan should be attempted in strong onshore winds.

On E side of B du Grand Vey, Roches de Grandcamp (dry) extend more than 1M offshore, N and W of Grandcamp (10.18.12), but they are flat and can be crossed from the N in normal conditions from about HW −0130 to HW +0130. Heavy kelp can give false echo soundings.

Between Pt de la Percée and Port-en-Bessin (10.18.13) a bank lies offshore, with drying ledges extending 3 ca. A race forms over this bank with wind against tide. Off Port-en- Bessin the E-going stream begins about HW Le Havre −0500, and the W-going at about HW Le Havre +0050, sp rates 1 ¼ kn.

From Port-en-Bessin the coast runs E 4M to C Manvieux, E of which lies the wartime harb of Arromanches, where there is anch. Between C Manvieux and Langrune, 10M E, Plateau du Calvados lies offshore. Rocher du Calvados (dries) lies on the W part of this bank, and there are several wrecks in this area.

Roches de Ver (dry) lie near centre of Plateau du Calvados, extending 8 ca offshore about 1M W of Courseulles-sur-Mer (10.18.14). The approach to this harb is dangerous in strong onshore winds. Les Essarts de Langrune (dry) lie E of Courseulles-sur-Mer, and extend up to 2 ¼ M seaward off Langrune: at their E end lie Roches de Lion (dry), which reach up to 1 ½ M offshore in places and extend to a point 2 ½ M W of the harb of Ouistreham (10.18.15).

6M E of Ouistreham is R Dives, where a yacht can dry out (if there is room) alongside the jetty at Cabourg. The banks dry for 1M to seaward, and entry is only possible near HW and in reasonable conditions. See 10.18.29.

Deauville, 8M ENE of Dives, is an important yachting harb (see 10.18.16). Beware Banc de Trouville (dries) which extends ENE from a point 2M N of entrance. The sands dry more than ½ M offshore, and in strong winds from W or N the entrance is dangerous. In marginal conditions it is best attempted within 15 mins of HW, when the stream is slack. At other times, or in worse weather, the sea breaks between the jetties.

ESTUAIRE DE LA SEINE/LE HAVRE (chart 2990)

The Seine estuary is entered between Dives and Le Havre, and is encumbered by shallow and shifting banks which extend seawards to Banc de Seine, 15M W of Le Havre. With wind against tide there is a heavy sea on this bank. Here the SW-going stream begins at HW Le Havre +0400, and the NE-going at HW Le Havre −0300, sp rates 1 ½ kn. Between Deauville and Le Havre the sea can be rough in W winds.

Chenal du Rouen is the main chan into R Seine, and carries a great deal of commercial traffic. The S side of the chan is contained by Digue du Ratier, a training wall which extends E to Honfleur (10.18.17). Note that for tidal reasons Honfleur is not a useful staging port when bound up-river. For notes on R Seine see 10.18.18, and for Rouen see 10.18.29.

Le Havre (10.18.19) is a large commercial port, as well as a yachting centre. Approaching from the NW, the most useful mark is the Lanby moored about 9M W of C de la Hève (Lt). The approach chan, which runs 6M WNW from the harb entrance, is well buoyed and lit. Strong W winds cause rough water over shoal patches either side of the chan. Coming from the N or NE, there is deep water close off C de la Hève, but from here steer S to join the main entrance chan. Beware Banc de l'Éclat (depth 0.1m), which lies on N side of main chan and about 1 ½ M from harb entrance.

CAP D'ANTIFER TO Pte DU HAUT BLANC (chart 2612)

Immediately S of C d'Antifer (Lt, RC) is the large oil tanker harb of Port d'Antifer. A breakwater extends about 1 ½ M seaward, and should be given a berth of about 1M, or more in heavy weather when there may be a race with wind against tide. Off C d'Antifer the NE-going stream begins about HW Le Havre −0430, and the SW-going at about HW Le Havre +0140. There are eddies close inshore E of C d'Antifer on both streams.

From C d'Antifer to Fécamp (10.18.20) drying rks extend up to ¼ M offshore. At Fécamp pierheads the E-going stream begins about HW Le Havre −0500, and the W-going at about HW Le Havre +0025, sp rates 2 ¾ kn. Off Pte Fagnet, close NE of Fécamp, lie Les Charpentiers (rks which dry, about 1 ½ ca offshore).

From Fécamp to St Valéry-en-Caux (10.18.21), which lies 15M ENE, the coast consists of chalk cliffs broken by valleys. There are rky ledges, extending 4 ca offshore in places. The nuclear power station at Paluel 3M W of St Valéry-en-Caux is conspic. Immediately E of St Valéry-en-Caux shallow sandbanks, Les Ridins de St Valéry, with a least depth of 0.6m, extend about 6 ½ ca offshore. At St Valéry-en-Caux entrance the E-going stream begins about HW Dieppe −0550, and the W-going stream begins about HW Dieppe −0015, sp rates 2 ¾ kn. E of the entrance a small eddy runs W on the E-going stream.

18

Between St Valéry-en-Caux and Pte d'Ailly (Lt, fog sig, RC) there are drying rks 4 ca offshore in places. About 1½M E of Pte de Sotteville a rky bank (depth 4.2m) extends about 1M NNW; a strong eddy causes a race over this bank.

From Pte d'Ailly to Dieppe (10.18.22) the coast is fringed by a bank, drying in places, up to 4 ca offshore. Off Pte d'Ailly are Roches d'Ailly, which dry and extend ½M: on this reef is La Galère, a rk which dries, about 3 ca N of Lt Ho. About 6M N of Pte d'Ailly, Les Ecamias are banks with depths of 11m, dangerous in a heavy sea. E of Pte d'Ailly an eddy runs W close inshore on first half of E-going stream. Off Dieppe the ENE-going stream begins about HW Dieppe −0505, and the WSW-going at about HW Dieppe +0030, sp rates 2 kn.

Between Dieppe and Le Tréport, 14M NE, rky banks, drying in places, extend ½M offshore. A prohibited area extends ¾M offshore of Penly nuclear power station and is marked by Lt Buoys. There are no dangers further to seaward, nor in outer approaches to Le Tréport except Ridins du Tréport (depth 4.9m) about 3M NW of entrance, which should be avoided in bad weather.

Between Le Tréport and B de Somme, Banc Franc-Marqué (depth 3.1m) lies 2M offshore, and about 3M N of Le Tréport. B de Somme, entered between Cayeux-sur-Mer and Pte de St Quentin 6M NNE, is a shallow and drying area of shifting sands. Offshore there are two shoals, Bassurelle de la Somme and Quémer, on parts of which the sea breaks in bad weather.

4½M NW of Cayeux-sur-Mer the stream is rotatory anticlockwise. The E-going stream begins about HW Dieppe −0200, and reaches 2½ kn at sp in a direction 070°: the W-going stream begins about HW Dieppe +0600, and reaches 1½ kn at sp in a direction 240°. The chan, which runs close to Pte du Hourdel, is buoyed, but the whole estuary dries out 3M to seaward, and should not be approached in strong W or NW winds. For St Valéry-sur-Somme see 10.18.24, and for Le Crotoy see 10.18.29.

From Pte de St Quentin the coast runs 7M N to Pte du Haut Blanc, with a shallow coastal bank which dries for about ½M offshore.

LE TOUQUET TO DUNKERQUE (charts 2451, 323)

Le Touquet (10.18.25) lies in the Embouchure de la Canche, entered between Pte du Touquet and Pte de Lornel, and with a drying bank which extends 1M seaward of a line joining these two points. Le Touquet-Paris-Plage Lt is shown from a conspic Tr, 1M S of Pte du Touquet. Off the entrance the N-going stream begins about HW Dieppe −0335, sp rate 1¾ kn; and the S-going stream begins about HW Dieppe +0240, sp rate 1¾ kn.

In the approaches to Pas de Calais a number of shoals lie offshore − La Bassurelle, Le Vergoyer, Bassure de Baas, Le Battur, Les Ridens, and The Ridge (or Le Colbart). In bad weather, and particularly with wind against tide in most cases, the sea breaks heavily on all these shoals.

From Pte de Lornel to Boulogne (10.18.26) the coast dries up to ½M offshore. Beware hovercraft traffic S of the harb (chart 438). Off Digue Carnot the N-going stream begins HW Dieppe −0130, and the S-going at HW Dieppe +0350, sp rates 1¾ kn.

Between Boulogne and C Gris Nez (Lt, fog sig) the coastal bank dries about 4 ca offshore. The NE-bound traffic lane lies only 3M off C Gris Nez. 1M NW of C Gris Nez the NE-going stream begins at HW Dieppe −0150, and the SW-going at HW Dieppe +0355, sp rates 4 kn.

In bad weather the sea breaks heavily on Ridens de Calais, 3M N of Calais (10.18.27), and also on Ridens de la Rade about 1½M NE of the harb. Midway between Calais and Dunkerque (10.18.28) is the drying harb of Gravelines which should not be used in strong onshore winds.

Offshore lie Sandettié bank (about 14M to N), Outer Ruytingen midway between Sandettié and the coast, and the Dyck banks which extend in a NE direction for 30M from a point 5M NE of Calais. There are chans between these banks, and they are well buoyed, but great care is needed in poor vis. In general the banks are steep-to on the inshore side, and slope seaward. In bad weather the sea breaks on the shallower parts.

10.18.6   DISTANCE TABLE

Approximate distances in nautical miles are by the most direct route while avoiding dangers and allowing for traffic separation schemes etc. Places in *italics* are in adjoining areas.

	1	2	3	4	5	6	7	8	9	10	11	12	13	14	15	16	17	18	19	20
1 *Casquets*	1																			
2 *Cherbourg*	31	2																		
3 *Portland Bill*	48	62	3																	
4 *Needles*	64	60	35	4																
5 *Nab Tower*	81	66	60	27	5															
6 *Royal Sovereign*	124	102	114	82	54	6														
7 *Dover*	167	145	157	125	97	43	7													
8 Barfleur	48	20	70	60	62	91	138	8												
9 Port en Bessin	76	48	98	88	80	98	143	28	9											
10 Ouistreham	94	66	112	99	88	95	134	46	22	10										
11 Deauville	104	76	126	102	89	90	127	56	36	14	11									
12 Honfleur	110	82	132	107	91	91	126	62	40	24	10	12								
13 Rouen	179	151	201	176	160	160	195	131	109	93	79	69	13							
14 Le Havre	101	70	118	98	85	85	120	56	36	19	8	9	75	14						
15 Fécamp	111	80	120	93	75	60	95	64	52	39	32	34	100	25	15					
16 Dieppe	139	108	143	115	92	55	75	94	81	68	61	63	129	54	29	16				
17 Boulogne	167	142	160	128	100	46	25	128	125	115	108	110	176	101	76	54	17			
18 Cap Gris Nez	175	147	157	126	101	47	19	135	132	122	115	117	183	108	83	61	7	18		
19 Calais	188	160	174	142	114	60	22	148	145	135	128	130	196	121	96	74	20	13	19	
20 Dunkerque	210	182	196	164	136	82	43	170	167	157	150	152	218	143	118	96	42	35	22	20

BARFLEUR 10-18-9
Manche

CHARTS
Admiralty 1349, 2073, 1106; SHOM 5618, 5609, 847; ECM 528; Stanford 7; Imray C32

TIDES
Dover −0250; ML 3.9; Duration 0550; Zone −0100

Standard Port CHERBOURG (←)

Times				Height (metres)			
HW		LW		MHWS	MHWN	MLWN	MLWS
0300	1000	0400	1000	6.3	5.0	2.5	1.1
1500	2200	1600	2200				

Differences BARFLEUR
+0100 +0100 +0050 +0040 +0.2 +0.3 0.0 +0.1

SHELTER
Excellent shelter although entrance difficult in E to NE winds. Harbour dries. Normally yachts lie along NW wall. Beware rocks in SE of harbour. Anchorage outside harbour is safe in off-shore winds. Access HW∓3. Moorings controlled by Capitaine du Port.

NAVIGATION
Waypoint 49°41'.30N 01°14'.21W, 039°/219° from/to front Ldg Lt, 1.35M. Beware Barfleur Race, about 3½ M E and NE of Barfleur Pt, in rough weather. There are numerous rocks between Barfleur Pt and the harbour, and also cross currents. Keep ¼ M E of La Grotte Rks (buoyed). Beware Le Hintar Rks (buoyed) and La Raie (Bn) to E of Ldg Line.

LIGHTS AND MARKS
Pte de Barfleur Fl (2) 10s 72m 29M; grey Tr, B top (conspic); Reed (2) 60s. Ldg Lts 219°30'. Front Oc (3) 12s 7m 10M; W square Tr. Rear Oc (3) 12s 13m 10M; grey and W square Tr, G top; synchronized, not easy to see by day. Jetée Est Oc R 4s 5m 6M. Jetée Ouest Fl G 4s 8m 6M.

RADIO TELEPHONE
None.

TELEPHONE (33)
Hr Mr 33.54.43.61; Aff Mar 33.44.00.13; CROSS 33.52.72.13; SNSM 33.54.04.62; ⌗ 33.54.48.81; Meteo 33.22.91.17; Auto 33.53.11.55; Police 33.54.12.11; Dr 33.54.00.02; Brit Consul 33.44.20.13.

FACILITIES
NW Quay Slip, P, L, FW, AB; Harbour (100+45 visitors) M; Bouly ☎ 33.54.02.66 P, ME, El; Chantier Bellot ☎ 33.54.04.29, Sh; Garage Marine ☎ 33.54.00.23, D. Town P, D, Sh, CH, V, Gaz, R, Bar. ✉; Ⓑ; ≈ (bus to Cherbourg); ✈ (Cherbourg).
Ferry UK — Cherbourg—Portsmouth/Weymouth (latter in summer only).

Depths in metres

ST VAAST-LA-HOUGUE
Manche

10-18-10

CHARTS
Admiralty 1349, 2073, 2613; SHOM 5522, 847; ECM 527; Stanford 2; Imray C32

TIDES
Dover −0240; ML 3.8; Duration 0530; Zone −0100

Standard Port CHERBOURG (←)

Times				Height (metres)			
HW		LW		MHWS	MHWN	MLWN	MLWS
0300	1000	0400	1000	6.3	5.0	2.5	1.1
1500	2200	1600	2200				

Differences ST VAAST-LA-HOUGUE
+0105 +0055 +0120 +0100 +0.3 +0.3 −0.2 −0.2

SHELTER
The harbour is protected from all sides. If harbour full, anchorage in the approach channel is satisfactory except in strong winds from E to S. Marina lock gates open HW−3 to HW+3. Visitors pontoons A, B and C.

NAVIGATION
Waypoint 49°34'.40N 01°13'.50W, 087°/267° from/to La Hougue Lt (Oc 4s), 1.8M. Do not confuse with Lt on jetty. From waypoint head 267° until Reville Point de Saire Lt is just concealed by the Fort de l'Ilet, turn on to 346°. Head for St Vaast la Hougue jetty Lt leaving the Bout du Roc & Balise de Creux buoys to port. Watch out for cross currents.
"Le Run" approach is not recommended and should not be attempted with a boat of over 1.2m draft. The entrance is wide and well marked. Harbour gets very full in summer. Beware oyster beds.

LIGHTS AND MARKS
There are two prominent towers to indicate position—one on Ile de Tatihou and an identical one on La Hougue Pt. Prominent light structure on the end of the outer jetty, Oc (2) WR 6s, R219°-247°, W elsewhere. Siren Mo (N) 30s. Control of traffic in and out of marina by R & G lights.

RADIO TELEPHONE
VHF Ch 09.

TELEPHONE (33)
Hr Mr 33.44.00.13; Aff Mar 33.54.43.61; CROSS 33.52.72.13; SNSM 33.54.42.52; ⌗ 33.44.16.00; Meteo 33.43.20.40; Auto 33.43.20.40; Police 33.54.12.11; Dr 33.54.43.42; Brit Consul 33.44.20.13.

FACILITIES
Marina (500+150 visitors) ☎ 33.54.48.81, FW, C (15 ton), ME, El, Sh, Gaz, D, P, CH, Bar, R, ▣, V, AC, Slip; Access HW−2½ to HW+3; Bernard ☎ 33.54.43.47, ME,

18

ST VAAST-LA-HOUGUE *continued*

El, Sh, CH; **CCE Saint-Vaast** ☎ 33.54.55.08 Ⓔ;
E. Massieu ☎ 33.54.41.00, ME, El; **Cercle Nautique de
la Hougue** ☎ 33.54.55.73, Bar, R, C (3 ton), P, D, CH,
FW, V; **Town** P, D, V, Gaz, R, Bar, ▢, ✉; Ⓑ; ⇌ (bus to
Valognes); ✈ (Cherbourg).
Ferry UK — Cherbourg—Portsmouth/Weymouth (summer
only).

CARENTAN   10-18-11
Manche

CHARTS
Admiralty 2073; SHOM 7056; ECM 527; Stanford 1; Imray
C32

TIDES
Dover −0025; ML (Port-en-Bessin) 4.2; Duration
(Port-en-Bessin) 0520; Zone −0100

Standard Port LE HAVRE (⟶)

Times				Height (metres)			
HW		LW		MHWS	MHWN	MLWN	MLWS
0000	0500	0000	0700	7.9	6.6	3.0	1.2
1200	1700	1200	1900				

Differences PORT-EN-BESSIN
−0045 −0040 −0040 −0045 −0.7   −0.6   −0.3   −0.1
HW Carentan is HW Cherbourg +0100

SHELTER
Safe anchorage N of buoyed channel in winds up to force
5. Complete shelter in the canal/river and in the marina.
Entrance protected from prevailing winds W to S. Entry
not advisable in on-shore winds above force 5. In
emergency the Iles St. Marcouf close by provide shelter
from NNE, N and W see 10.18.29. Depth in locked marina
basin max/min 3.5/2.9m.

NAVIGATION
Waypoint CI safe water buoy, Iso 4s, 49°25′.50N
01°07′.00W, 034°/214° from/to entrance to buoyed
channel, 1.6M. Iles St Marcouf are a good landmark,
4.5M to N. Channel shifts and buoys (six of which are lit,
Fl R or G(3) 12s) are moved as required. All buoys have R
or G reflective panels. Start from CI buoy between
HW −2 and HW −1½. After about 4M the channel enters
between two breakwaters, marked by Bns. 3.5M further
on the channel divides into three, forming a small pool.
Enter the lock ahead (opens HW −2 to HW +3, traffic
sigs) and proceed up the canal to marina. There are
waiting pontoons on E side above and below the lock.

LIGHTS AND MARKS
Breakwaters are marked by Bns, the second of which
inwards are lit port and stbd, Fl R(3) 12s and Fl G(3) 12s
respectively. Ldg Lts 209°30′, Front Oc(3)R 12s and Rear
Oc(3) 12s, lead through the part of the channel 1.6M
inwards from the ends of the breakwaters and immediately
outside (not for the buoyed channel). Lock signals: FG =
lock open, FR = lock closed.

RADIO TELEPHONE
VHF Ch 09 (0800 −1800 LT and during lock opening
hours.)

TELEPHONE (33)
Hr Mr 33.44.00.13; Aff Mar 33.44.00.13; ⌗ 33.44.16.00;
CROSS 33.52.72.13; Meteo 33.43.20.40; Auto 33.44.45.00;
Lockmaster 33.71.10.85; Police 33.42.00.17; Ⓗ 33.42.14.12;
Dr 33.42.33.21; Brit Consul 33.44.20.13.

FACILITIES
Marina (550 + 55 visitors) (☎ 33.42.24.44) FW, AC, C (25
ton), BH (16 ton), P and D, Access HW −2 to HW +3;
YC Croiseurs Côtiers de Carentan ☎ 33.42.40.42, Bar;
Hardy ☎ 33.42.02.87, ME, El, Sh, CH; **Itelec Nautic**
☎ 33.42.07.83, ME, El, Sh, CH; **Le Guen Hemidy
Marine** ☎ 33.42.26.55, Sh, CH; **G.A.M. Marine**
☎ 33.71.17.02, ME, BY, CH, El, **Town** Bar, Ⓑ, D, P; ✉,
⇌, R, V, ✈ (Cherbourg).
Ferry UK — Cherbourg—Portsmouth.

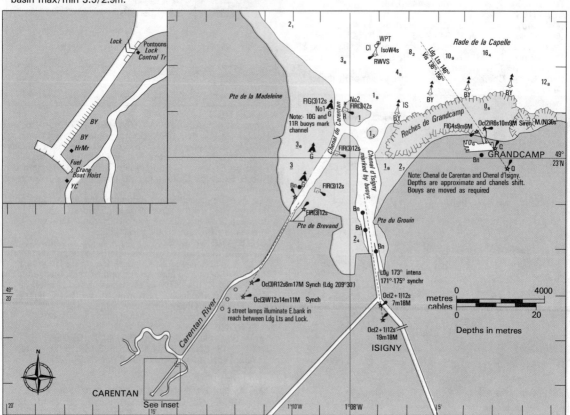

GRANDCAMP-MAISY   10-18-12
Calvados

CHARTS
Admiralty 2073; SHOM 7056; ECM 527; Stanford 1; Imray C32

TIDES
Dover −0220; ML Port-en-Bessin 4.2; Duration Port-en-Bessin 0520; Zone −0100

Standard Port LE HAVRE (→)

Times				Height (metres)			
HW		LW		MHWS	MHWN	MLWN	MLWS
0000	0500	0000	0700	7.9	6.6	3.0	1.2
1200	1700	1200	1900				

Differences PORT-en-BESSIN
−0045 −0040 −0040 −0045 −0.7 −0.6 −0.3 −0.1

RADIO TELEPHONE
VHF Ch 09.

TELEPHONE (31)
Hr Mr 31.22.63.16; Aff Mar 31.22.60.65; CROSS 33.52.72.13; SNSM 31.22.64.25; Meteo 31.74.48.11; Auto 31.75.14.14; Police 31.22.00.18; Dr 31.22.60.50; Brit Consul 35.42.27.47.

FACILITIES
Marina (268 + 25 visitors) ☎ 31.22.63.16, El, FW, BH (4 ton), Bar, V, AC; **Conin** ☎ 31.22.62.79, ME; **Galliot Marine** ☎ 31.22.61.95, CH; **Yachting 14** ☎ 31.22.67.02, ME, El, Ⓔ, Sh, CH, Gaz; **Town** Gaz, ✉; Ⓑ; ⇌ (Carentan); ✈ (Caen).
Ferry UK — Riva-Bella (Ouistreham)—Portsmouth. (May-Sept, also to Poole).

SHELTER
Access day and night but difficult in winds from NW to NE over force 6. Safe approach springs HW∓2, neaps HW∓1½. Wet basin, containing marina on W side, has gate which opens HW−2 to HW+2½. Visitors pontoon near gate. SW corner is very dirty.

NAVIGATION
Waypoint 49°25′.00N 01°04′.60W, 326°/146° from/to front Ldg Lt 146°, 2.0M. Large flat rocks, les Roches de Grandcamp, stretch for about 1½ M out from the harbour and dry about 1.5m. Entrance between HW∓2 is safe for most yachts.

LIGHTS AND MARKS
Line of three N cardinal buoys mark the seaward limit of Les Roches de Grandcamp, numbered 1, 3 and 5. Approach from between any of these. E pierhead Lt Oc(2) R 6s on a RW column. Ldg Lts 146°, both Q. E jetty due to be extended in 1988 as shown and Lt moved to the end.

PORT-EN-BESSIN   10-18-13
Calvados

CHARTS
Admiralty 2073; SHOM 7056, 5515; ECM 527; Stanford 1; Imray C32

TIDES
Dover −0215; ML 4.2; Duration 0520; Zone −0100

Standard Port LE HAVRE (→)

Times				Height (metres)			
HW		LW		MHWS	MHWN	MLWN	MLWS
0000	0500	0000	0700	7.9	6.6	3.0	1.2
1200	1700	1200	1900				

Differences PORT-EN-BESSIN
−0045 −0040 −0040 −0045 −0.7 −0.6 −0.3 −0.1

SHELTER
Good shelter although outer harbour dries completely. There is little room for yachts. Basins accessible from HW∓2. Yachtsmen must contact Hr Mr on arrival. Yachts waiting to enter, berth on Quai de L'Epi.

18

PORT-EN-BESSIN *continued*

NAVIGATION
Waypoint 49°22'.00N 00°44'.90W, 024°/204° from/to front Ldg Lt 204°, 1.1M. Anchoring prohibited in outer harbour and 1ca either side of 204° transit. Busy fishing port. Yachts are admitted for short stays (up to 24 hrs). Entry is difficult with strong winds from N and NE and may become impossible. Beware submerged jetty from end of E Wharf towards Mole Ouest marked by R Bn. Keep out of G sector of Mole Ouest Lt.

LIGHTS AND MARKS
Ldg Lts 204°. Front Oc (3) 12s 25m 10M; W pylon, G top; vis 069°-339°; Siren 20s (sounded over 90° each side of leading line, continuous in W sector, interrupted in E sector). Rear Oc (3) 12s 42m 11M; W and grey house; vis 114°-294°, synchronized with front; RC.
Entry signals: FR over FG, or R flag over G flag means basins closed. Bridge has FR Lt each side, and one in the middle, lit when bridge shut. Lock opens HW∓2. Bridge opens when lock first opens and before it shuts. Between, it opens on the hour for 5 mins.

RADIO TELEPHONE
VHF Ch 18 (HW∓2) for lock opening.

TELEPHONE (31)
Hr Mr 31.21.70.49; Aff Mar 31.21.71.52; CROSS 33.52.72.13; SNSM 31.22.49.44; ⌗ 31.21.71.09; Meteo 31.74.48.11; Auto 36.65.08.08; Lock 31.21.71.77; Police 31.21.70.10; Dr 31.21.74.26; Ⓗ 31.92.29.47; Brit Consul 35.42.27.47.

FACILITIES
EC: Open every day — including Sunday in summer; **Outer Harbour** Slip, L; **Bassin II** Slip, M, L, FW, AB, C (4 ton); **Ayello** ☎ 31.21.72.24, CH; **Hutrel** ☎ 31.21.72.36, CH; **M. Marie** ☎ 31.21.74.33 El, Ⓔ; **Digne Francoise** ☎ 31.21.72.16, ME; **LK Electronique** ☎ 31.21.93.79, Ⓔ; **Gaubert** ☎ 31.21.70.53, ME, El, Sh; **Nautic Port Bois** ☎ 31.21.17.01, Sh; **CRM** ☎ 31.21.70.41, Ⓔ; **Town** P, AB, V, Gaz, R, Bar. ✉; Ⓑ; ⇌ (bus to Bayeux); ✈ (Caen).
Ferry UK — Riva Bella (Ouistreham)—Portsmouth. (May-Sept, also to Poole).

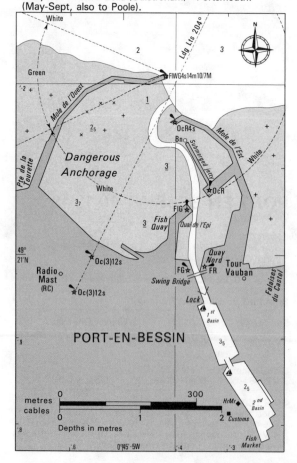

PORT-EN-BESSIN

COURSEULLES-SUR-MER
10-18-14
Calvados

CHARTS
Admiralty 1349, 2073, 1821; SHOM 5515, 5598, 6927; ECM 527, 528; Stanford 1; Imray C32

TIDES
−0300 Dover; ML 3.9; Duration No data; Zone −0100

Standard Port LE HAVRE (→)

Times				Height (metres)			
HW		LW		MHWS	MHWN	MLWN	MLWS
0000	0500	0000	0700	7.9	6.6	3.0	1.2
1200	1700	1200	1900				

Differences COURSEULLES-SUR-MER

−0030	No data	No data	−0020	−0.8	−1.0	−0.7	−0.3

COURSEULLES-SUR-MER

SHELTER
Good except in strong winds from NE through N to W. Best entry is at HW−1. Yachts enter basin (lock opens HW∓2) or go to marina in New Basin.

NAVIGATION
Waypoint 49°22'.50N 00°29'.50W, 313°/133° from/to Bernières-sur-Mer church Tr, 3.7M. Plateau du Calvados extends 2M offshore. Banks dry for ⅔M. RW buoy, Iso 4s, lies 1M N by W from entrance. To S of this beware rks awash at CD and sunken breakwater on W side extending 2 ca (370m) from entrance. When harbour entrance bears 198°, alter course to that bearing.

LIGHTS AND MARKS
Large crucifix at root of W pier is a conspic mark when entering. Day — two Ldg marks to seaward on this line. Crucifix in line with Chateau (conspic) 190°.

RADIO TELEPHONE
VHF Ch 09.

TELEPHONE (31)
Hr Mr 31.37.51.69; Lock Keeper 31.37.46.03; Aff Mar 31.37.46.19; CROSS 33.52.72.13; SNSM 31.37.45.24; ⌗

COURSEULLES-SUR-MER *continued*

West Quai, no ☎.; Meteo 31.74.48.11; Auto 31.75.14.14;
Police 31.37.46.75; Dr 31.37.45.24; Brit Consul
35.42.27.47.
FACILITIES
Marina ☎ 31.97.46.03, P, D, FW, ME, El, Sh; **Outer
Harbour** ☎ 31.37.46.03, M, FW, C (8 ton), AB; **Wet
Basin** Slip, P, FW, Sh, C (10 ton), CH, AB; **Chantier
Naval de la Seulles** ☎ 31.37.42.34 ME, El, Ⓔ, Sh, CH,
M, SM; **Chantiers Navals de la Côte de Nacre**
☎ 31.37.45.08, M, ME, El, Sh, CH; **Ste des Regates de
Courseulles** ☎ 31.37.47.42, Bar.
Town P, D, V, Gaz, R, Bar. ✉; Ⓑ; ⇌ (bus to Caen);
✈ (Caen).
Ferry UK — Riva-Bella (Ouistreham)—Portsmouth.
(May-Sept, also to Poole).

OUISTREHAM   10-18-15
Calvados

CHARTS
Admiralty 1349, 1821, 2613; SHOM 7055, 6928, 6927,
6614; ECM 526; Stanford 1; Imray C32
TIDES
Dover −0150; ML 4.4; Duration 0525; Zone −0100

Standard Port LE HAVRE (→)

Times				Height (metres)			
HW		LW		MHWS	MHWN	MLWN	MLWS
0000	0500	0000	0700	7.9	6.6	3.0	1.2
1200	1700	1200	1900				

Differences OUISTREHAM
−0020 −0010 −0005 −0010 −0.2 −0.2 −0.2 −0.2
DIVES-SUR-MER
−0055 No No −0115 −0.4 −0.5 −0.6 −0.3
     data data

SHELTER
Very good inside locks. Temporary berths on pontoons
outside, and moorings in R Orne. Enter canal by locks
each side of control tower. Yachts normally use E lock.
Locks open for departure HW−2 and HW+1¾; and for
entry HW−1½ and HW+2¼. From 15 June−15 Sep,
and at weekends and public holidays from 1 Apr−15 June
and 15 Sep−31 Oct, extra openings between 0700 and
2000 local time as follows: for departure at HW−3 and
HW+2¾, and for entry at HW−2½ and HW+3¼.
Marina (depth 3.5m) is 1 ca (185m) inside locks on E side
(Access HW∓3). Canal to Caen, 7.5 M, depth 10m to
2.5m, max speed 7 kts, overtaking prohibited. Good
marina at Caen. See 10.18.29.
NAVIGATION
Waypoint OC (safe water) buoy, Iso 4s, Whis, 49°19′.90N
00°14′.57W, 005°/185° from/to front Ldg Lt 185°, 2.7M.
Training walls run each side of entrance channel, marked
by beacons. Beware turbulence in locks. Passage of Caen
canal (four lifting bridges) is arranged at Ouistreham or
Caen.
LIGHTS AND MARKS
From Ouistreham buoy (RW, Iso 4s, 3M from Lt Ho)
follow Ldg Lts 185°. Main Lt Ho, conspic, W with R top,
Oc WR 4s. Traffic signals (full code − see 10.14.7) shown
from two panels on control tower between locks. The
main signals do not apply to yachts or fishing craft, which
must only enter lock when white light shows alongside
lowest light of signal panel referring to lock concerned.
RADIO TELEPHONE
Call: *Ouistreham Port* VHF Ch 12 16 68 (HW−2 to
HW+3). Call: *Caen Port* Ch 12 68; Ste des Regates Ch 09
(office hours).
TELEPHONE (31)
Hr Mr 31.97.14.43; Port de Plaisance/Ste des Regates
31.97.13.05; Aff Mar 31.97.18.65; CROSS 33.52.72.13;
SNSM 31.97.17.47; Lock Tower 31.97.14.43; Ferry
terminal 31.96.80.80; ⌗ 31.86.61.50; Meteo 31.74.48.11;
Auto 31.75.14.14; Police 31.97.13.15; Dr 31.97.18.45;
Brit Consul 35.42.27.47.
FACILITIES
Marina (600+65 visitors) ☎ 31.97.13.05, Slip, P, D, FW,
ME, El, Sh, CH, AC, BH (8 ton), Gas, Gaz, Kos, SM,
Bar; **Société des Régates de Caen-Ouistreham**
☎ 31.97.13.05, FW, ME, El, Sh, CH, V, Bar; **Nautl
Plaisance** ☎ 31.97.03.08, Sh, El, Ⓔ, ME, CH; **Serra
Marine** ☎ 31.97.03.60, ME, El, Ⓔ, CH, Sh, SHOM, SM;
Accastillage Diffusion ☎ 31.96.07.75, Ⓔ, ME, El, Sh,
CH, SHOM; **SNIP** ☎ 31.97.34.47, ME, El, Ⓔ, CH; **JPL
Marine** ☎ 31.96.29.92, ME, El, Sh; **Normandie Voile**
☎ 31.97.06.29, SM. **Town** V, Gaz, R, Bar. ✉; Ⓑ;
⇌ (bus to Caen); ✈ (Caen).
Ferry UK — Riva-Bella (Ouistreham)—Portsmouth.
(May-Sept, also to Poole).
CAEN — See 10.18.29.

DEAUVILLE/TROUVILLE
Calvados
10-18-16

CHARTS
Admiralty 1349, 2146, 2613; SHOM 5530, 6928; ECM 526;
Stanford 1; Imray C32
TIDES
Dover −0130; ML 4.5; Duration 0510; Zone −0100

Standard Port LE HAVRE (→)

Times				Height (metres)			
HW		LW		MHWS	MHWN	MLWN	MLWS
0000	0500	0000	0700	7.9	6.6	3.0	1.2
1200	1700	1200	1900				

Differences TROUVILLE
−0035 −0015 0000 −0010 −0.1 −0.2 −0.2 −0.1

SHELTER
Good shelter — entry to channel difficult in NW to N
winds above about force 6. Excellent marina and Yacht
Harbour but remainder of harbour dries. Yacht Harbour
gates open HW−2 to HW+2½.
NAVIGATION
Waypoint 49°23′.10N 00°03′.68E, 330°/150° from/to front
Ldg Lt 150°, 1.2M. About 2½ M from the harbour, on the
transit line, there is a wreck marked by a buoy. Do not
approach from E of N because of Banc de Trouville. SW
Trouville buoy, W cardinal, VQ(9) 10s, lies about 1M

18

DEAUVILLE/TROUVILLE *continued*

WNW of entrance. Access from seaward about HW∓2.

LIGHTS AND MARKS

The casino is conspic building on Trouville side. Ldg Lts 148° (both Oc R 4s synchronised). Lock signals 3 FR (vert) – closed, 3 FG (vert) – passage in one direction, 2G over 1W – passage allowed in both directions.

RADIO TELEPHONE

Deauville Yacht Harbour VHF Ch 11; Port Deauville Marina VHF Ch 09.

TELEPHONE (31)

Hr Mr Marina 31.98.30.01; Hr Mr Yacht Harbour 31.88.28.71; Aff Mar 31.88.36.21; SNSM 31.88.13.07; CROSS 33.52.72.13; ✠ 31.88.35.29; Meteo 31.88.84.22; Auto 31.88.84.22; Police 31.88.13.07; Dr 31.88.23.57; Ⓗ 31.88.14.00; Brit Consul 35.42.27.47.

FACILITIES

Port Deauville (Marina) (738+100 visitors) ☎ 31.98.30.01, Slip, D, AC, FW, ME, El, Sh, C (6 ton), BH (50 ton), CH, R, Bar; **Yacht Harbour** (320+80 visitors) ☎ 31.98.50.40, Slip, C (6 ton), D, FW, AC; Access HW∓2; **Top Marine** ☎ 31.88.65.55 SM, CH; **Chantier Naval** ☎ 31.88.05.75 Slip, Sh, ME, El; **Serra Deauville** ☎ 31.98.50.92 CH; **Bassin Morny** M, P, D, L, FW, ME, El, Sh, C (6 ton), AB; **Touques Nautisme** ☎ 31.88.45.00, Slip, ME, El, Sh, P, D, C (50 ton); **Deauville YC** ☎ 31.88.38.19, L, FW, C (5 ton), AB, CH, Bar; **Callac** ☎ 31.88.55.94, ME, El, CH; **Town** P, D, FW, CH, V, Gaz, R, Bar. ✉; Ⓑ; ➤; ✈ (Deauville).
Ferry UK — Le Havre—Portsmouth or Riva-Bella (Ouistreham)—Portsmouth. (May-Sept, also to Poole).

HONFLEUR 10-18-17
Calvados

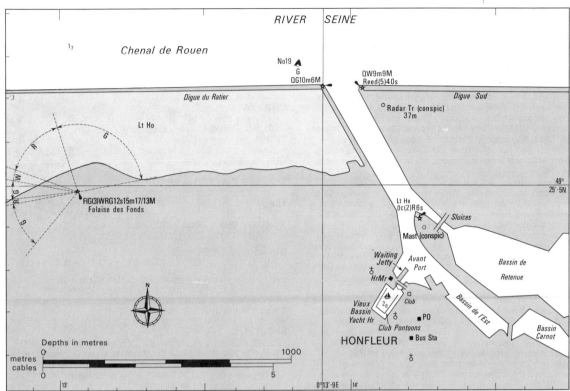

CHARTS
Admiralty 2146, 2994, 2613; SHOM 6796, 6683, 4937; ECM 1012; Stanford 1; Imray C31
TIDES
−0135 Dover; ML 4.6; Duration 0540; Zone −0100

Standard Port LE HAVRE (⟶)

Times				Height (metres)			
HW		LW		MHWS	MHWN	MLWN	MLWS
0000	0500	0000	0700	7.9	6.6	3.0	1.2
1200	1700	1200	1900				

Differences HONFLEUR
−0140 −0135 +0005 +0040 +0.2   +0.1   0.0   0.0
There is a stand of about 2 hours. Differences are for the beginning of the stand.

SHELTER
Shelter is very good indeed especially in the Vieux Bassin. Access HW∓1. Ask YC member when taking vacant spaces on pontoon. Visitors can use NW quay with no facilities. Larger yachts can lock into Bassin de l'Est; see Hr Mr.
NAVIGATION
Waypoint Ratier NW (stbd-hand) buoy, VQG, 49°26'.63N, 00°03'.41E, at entrance to Chenal de Rouen. Chenal de Rouen is well marked by buoys. Due to commercial shipping, yachtsmen should proceed HW∓3 between the Digue Nord, well marked by posts, and the port hand channel buoys. Entrance marked by conspic Radar tower. Access HW∓2½ but beware strong currents across entrance. Keep in mid channel approaching Avant Port. Bridge lifting & lock opening HW−1, HW, HW+1, HW+2 during day in high season and week-ends: out of season and at night HW−1, HW, HW+1. Make sure lock-keeper knows you are approaching.
LIGHTS AND MARKS
Falaise des Fonds Lt, ¾ M W of ent Fl (3) WRG 12s 15m, 17/13M, W square Tr vis G040°-080°, R080°-084°, G084°-100°, W100°-109° R109°-162°, G162°-260° E Mole QW 9m 9M; Y metal framework Tr with B top, Reed (5) 40s. West Mole QG 10m 6M; G framework Tr.

RADIO TELEPHONE
VHF Ch 68 **73** (H24). Other stations: Honfleur Radar Ch 16; **11** 13 71 73 (H24); Tancarville Ch 11 16 (H24). Lock Ch 18. Call: *Rouen Port Capitaincrie* Ch 16; 06 11 13 73 (H24); Call: *Rouen Port* Ch 11 13 73 74.
TELEPHONE (31)
Hr Mr 31.89.20.23; Lock Master 31.89.22.57; Aff Mar 31.89.20.67; CROSS 33.52.72.13; SNSM 31.89.06.02; ⌗ 31.89.12.13; Meteo 35.42.21.06; Auto 35.21.16.11; Police 31.89.21.24; Dr 31.89.07.40; Ⓗ 31.89.07.74; Brit Consul 35.42.27.47.
FACILITIES
Vieux Bassin Yacht Hr (20 visitors) ☎ 31.89.01.85, FW, C (16 ton), AB, AC; **Cercle Nautique d' Honfleur** ☎ 31.89.87.13, M; **Ateliers et Chantiers d'Honfleur** ☎ 31.89.13.71, Sh; **CRM** ☎ 31.89.05.17 Ⓔ; **Town** V, R, Bar, Gaz, ✉; Ⓑ; ⇌; ✈ (Deauville).
Ferry UK — Le Havre—Portsmouth.

RIVER SEINE 10-18-18

CHARTS
Admiralty 2146, 2994; SHOM 6796, 6683, 6117; Stanford 1; Imray C31
TIDES
Zone −0100

Standard Port LE HAVRE (⟶)

Times				Height (metres)			
HW		LW		MHWS	MHWN	MLWN	MLWS
0000	0500	0000	0700	7.9	6.6	3.0	1.2
1200	1700	1200	1900				

Differences TANCARVILLE*
−0105 −0100 +0105 +0140 0.0   0.0   +0.3   +1.0
QUILLEBOEUF*
−0045 −0050 +0120 +0200 0.0   +0.1   +0.5   +1.4
VATTEVILLE*
+0005 −0020 +0225 +0250 +0.1   0.0   +1.1   +2.4
CAUDEBEC*
+0020 −0015 +0230 +0300 −0.2   0.0   +1.2   +2.5

18

RIVER SEINE *continued*

ROUEN
+0440 +0415 +0525 +0525 −0.1   0.0   +1.9   +3.6
*HW differences refer to the beginning of the stand,
which can be up to 2½ to 3 hours.

The Seine is a beautiful river giving access to Paris and
central France, and to the Mediterranean via the canals
(see below). But there is constant traffic of *péniches*
(barges), and in the tidal section the strong stream and
the wash from ships make it dangerous to moor alongside
and uncomfortable to anchor. There are locks at
Amfreville (202km from Paris), Notre Dame de la Garenne
(161km), Mericourt (121km), Andresy (73km), Bougival
(49km), Le Chatou (44km) and Suresnes (17km). Above
Amfreville the current is about 1kt in summer, but more in
winter.

Masts can be unstepped at Le Havre (Société des
Régates) and Deauville. Yacht navigation is prohibited at
night, and anchorages are scarce. A good anchor light is
needed, and even with the mast lowered it is useful to
have a radar reflector and a VHF aerial.

Entrance is through the Chenal de Rouen, which is
dredged and buoyed but rough in a strong westerly wind
and ebb tide, or by the Canal de Tancarville (see 10.18.19
for details). The canal has two locks and nine bridges
which cause delay, and is best avoided unless sea
conditions are bad.

Care is needed, especially near the mouth where there
are shifting banks and often early morning fog. Between
Quilleboeuf (335km) and La Mailleraye (303km) the
mascaret (Seine bore) still runs at HWS when the river is
in flood. It is important to study the tides. The flood
stream starts progressively later as a boat proceeds
upriver. So even a 4-kn boat leaving the estuary at LW
can carry the flood for the 78M (123km) to Rouen (see
10.18.29). Coming down river on the ebb however a boat
will meet the flood: in a fast boat it is worth carrying on,
rather than anchoring for about four hours, because the
further downstream the sooner the ebb starts.

The most likely mooring places below Rouen are
Quilleboeuf, Villequier, Caudebec, Le Trait and Duclair. In
Rouen (a major port) yachts use the Bassin St Gervais,
some way from the city centre and rather squalid, but
there is also a marina on the north side of Ile Lacroix
above Pont Corneille. In the non-tidal section there are
alongside berths at Les Andelys, Vernon, Port Maria (near
Mantes) and Les Mureaux. In Paris the Touring Club de
France (Pont de la Concorde) is helpful and cheap, but
noisy and uncomfortable. Fuel is available alongside at
Rouen, Rolleboise, Conflans and Paris. There is a marina
near the Bastille.

For detailed information see *A Cruising Guide to the
Lower Seine* (Imray, Laurie, Norie and Wilson Ltd).

CANALS TO MEDITERRANEAN
The quickest route to the Mediterranean is Le Havre/Paris/

St Mammes/canal du Loing/canal du Briare/canal Latéral à
la Loire/canal du Centre/Saône/Rhône, a distance of
1319km (824 miles) with 182 locks. Maximum dimensions:
length 38.5m, beam 5.0m, draught 1.8m, air draught 3.5m.
Further details and list of chomages (stoppages) for current
year (available from March), can be obtained from French
Tourist Office, 178 Piccadilly, London, W1V 0AL.

LE HAVRE 10-18-19
Seine Maritime

CHARTS
Admiralty 2990, 2146; SHOM 6683, 6736, 6796; ECM 526,
1012; Stanford 1; Imray C31

TIDES
Dover −0120; ML La Roque 5.3 Le Havre 4.6; Duration
Le Havre 0543; Zone −0100

Standard Port LE HAVRE (→)

Times				Height (metres)			
HW		LW		MHWS	MHWN	MLWN	MLWS
0000	0500	0000	0700	7.9	6.6	3.0	1.2
1200	1700	1200	1900				

Differences LA ROQUE
−0120 −0124 +0036 +0120 +0.3   +0.2   +0.2   +0.9

NOTE: Le Havre is a Standard Port and the tidal
predictions for each day of the year are given below.
HW differences above refer to the beginning of the stand
which is about 2½ hours.

SHELTER
Excellent shelter in the marina. Visitors go to Pontoon O.
If this is full, the Bassin du Commerce can be used but
this can only be entered at HW when gates and three
bridges are opened. Advance request to the Hr Mr.
Harbour accessible at all tides.

NAVIGATION
Waypoint 49°31′.05N 00°04′.00W, 287°/107° from/to
front Ldg Lt 107°, 7M. Shingle banks, awash at LW, lie
to the N of approach channel. Keep in channel to avoid
lobster pots close each side. Beware boulders inside at the
base of Digue Nord. Anchoring is forbidden in the fairway
and over a large area to the N of the fairway. Crossing
the fairway the harbour side of buoys LH7 and LH8 is also
forbidden. Obey traffic signals given from end of Digue
Nord. Le Havre is a busy commercial port so yachts must
not obstruct shipping. The Canal de Tancarville runs
eastwards from Le Havre to the River Seine at Tancarville
(see 10.18.18). To enter the canal at Le Havre proceed
through the small craft lock (Écluse de la Citadelle) in the
NE corner of the Arrière Port, across Bassin de la Citadelle
and under a bridge into Bassin de l'Eure. Turn south, and
after 400m turn east into Bassin Bellot. At the far end
alter course to port under two bridges into Bassin
Vétillart. From here proceed straight through Garage de

FRANCE, NORTH COAST - LE HAVRE

LAT 49°29'N   LONG 0°07'E

TIMES AND HEIGHTS OF HIGH AND LOW WATERS

YEAR **1991**

TIME ZONE −0100
(French Standard Time)
Subtract 1 hour for GMT
For French Summer Time add
ONE hour in non-shaded areas

JANUARY

Day	Time	m	Time	m	Time	m	Time	m
1 TU	0535	1.4	1049	7.9	1808	1.0	2323	7.9
2 W	0631	1.3	1139	8.0	1901	0.9		
3 TH	0012	8.0	0721	1.2	1226	8.0	1949	0.9
4 F	0059	7.9	0807	1.3	1312	7.9	2032	1.1
5 SA	0144	7.7	0848	1.6	1355	7.7	2110	1.4
6 SU	0227	7.5	0926	1.9	1438	7.4	2147	1.9
7 M ☽	0310	7.2	1003	2.3	1522	7.0	2223	2.3
8 TU	0356	6.9	1043	2.7	1613	6.7	2305	2.8
9 W	0451	6.6	1133	3.0	1716	6.4		
10 TH	0000	3.1	0600	6.5	1241	3.2	1837	6.3
11 F	0117	3.3	0716	6.5	1402	3.1	1958	6.4
12 SA	0235	3.1	0821	6.7	1509	2.8	2056	6.6
13 SU	0335	2.8	0910	6.9	1603	2.5	2140	6.9
14 M	0425	2.5	0950	7.1	1649	2.1	2217	7.1
15 TU ●	0509	2.2	1026	7.3	1731	1.9	2251	7.3
16 W	0548	2.0	1100	7.5	1809	1.7	2325	7.4
17 TH	0624	1.8	1134	7.6	1844	1.5	2358	7.5
18 F	0659	1.7	1208	7.7	1918	1.4		
19 SA	0032	7.5	0733	1.7	1242	7.7	1952	1.4
20 SU	0107	7.5	0807	1.7	1318	7.6	2024	1.6
21 M	0143	7.4	0841	1.9	1356	7.5	2058	1.7
22 TU	0220	7.3	0916	2.1	1434	7.3	2132	2.0
23 W ☽	0259	7.1	0956	2.3	1517	7.1	2214	2.3
24 TH	0346	7.0	1045	2.6	1614	6.8	2310	2.6
25 F	0453	6.8	1151	2.8	1739	6.6		
26 SA	0026	2.8	0625	6.7	1321	2.8	1911	6.7
27 SU	0202	2.7	0746	6.9	1449	2.3	2028	7.0
28 M	0321	2.3	0854	7.3	1600	1.8	2132	7.4
29 TU	0429	1.8	0951	7.6	1706	1.3	2226	7.7
30 W ○	0532	1.4	1041	7.9	1804	1.0	2313	7.9
31 TH	0626	1.1	1127	8.0	1853	0.7	2357	8.0

FEBRUARY

Day	Time	m	Time	m	Time	m	Time	m
1 F	0711	1.0	1210	8.1	1934	0.7		
2 SA	0038	8.0	0749	1.1	1250	8.0	2010	0.9
3 SU	0117	7.8	0822	1.3	1328	7.8	2041	1.3
4 M	0153	7.6	0852	1.6	1404	7.5	2108	1.7
5 TU	0228	7.3	0920	2.1	1439	7.2	2134	2.2
6 W ☽	0303	7.0	0949	2.5	1517	6.8	2205	2.7
7 TH	0345	6.6	1029	3.0	1610	6.3	2251	3.2
8 F	0449	6.3	1128	3.4	1737	6.0		
9 SA	0004	3.6	0624	6.1	1302	3.5	1921	6.0
10 SU	0153	3.5	0749	6.2	1436	3.2	2032	6.3
11 M	0311	3.1	0847	6.6	1540	2.6	2119	6.7
12 TU	0407	2.6	0930	6.9	1631	2.2	2156	7.1
13 W	0453	2.1	1006	7.3	1715	1.8	2230	7.3
14 TH ●	0533	1.8	1041	7.5	1753	1.5	2304	7.5
15 F	0609	1.5	1115	7.7	1828	1.3	2337	7.6
16 SA	0643	1.4	1149	7.8	1901	1.1		
17 SU	0011	7.7	0717	1.3	1223	7.9	1934	1.1
18 M	0045	7.8	0750	1.3	1259	7.8	2007	1.2
19 TU	0120	7.7	0824	1.4	1336	7.7	2038	1.4
20 W	0156	7.5	0857	1.7	1414	7.4	2111	1.8
21 TH ☽	0232	7.3	0934	2.0	1456	7.1	2150	2.2
22 F	0317	7.0	1020	2.4	1554	6.7	2244	2.7
23 SA	0427	6.6	1126	2.8	1727	6.4		
24 SU	0005	3.0	0612	6.5	1303	2.8	1908	6.6
25 M	0151	2.9	0740	6.8	1440	2.4	2027	6.9
26 TU	0316	2.3	0849	7.2	1557	1.8	2126	7.4
27 W	0428	1.8	0942	7.5	1701	1.3	2213	7.7
28 TH ○	0526	1.3	1027	7.8	1753	0.9	2255	7.9

MARCH

Day	Time	m	Time	m	Time	m	Time	m
1 F	0612	1.0	1108	8.0	1834	0.7	2335	8.0
2 SA	0650	0.9	1147	8.0	1910	0.8		
3 SU	0012	7.9	0723	1.0	1224	8.0	1940	1.0
4 M	0046	7.8	0752	1.2	1259	7.8	2007	1.3
5 TU	0119	7.7	0818	1.5	1332	7.5	2031	1.7
6 W	0150	7.4	0842	1.9	1403	7.2	2053	2.2
7 TH	0219	7.1	0907	2.4	1435	6.8	2120	2.7
8 F ☽	0253	6.7	0941	2.9	1518	6.3	2201	3.2
9 SA	0345	6.2	1034	3.3	1636	5.9	2309	3.7
10 SU	0525	5.9	1202	3.6	1836	5.8		
11 M	0104	3.7	0708	6.0	1352	3.3	1954	6.2
12 TU	0237	3.2	0813	6.4	1505	2.7	2046	6.6
13 W	0336	2.6	0859	6.8	1559	2.2	2126	7.0
14 TH	0423	2.1	0937	7.2	1645	1.7	2201	7.4
15 F	0505	1.7	1013	7.6	1725	1.4	2236	7.6
16 SA ●	0543	1.4	1049	7.8	1802	1.1	2310	7.8
17 SU	0619	1.1	1125	7.9	1837	1.0	2346	7.9
18 M	0655	1.0	1201	8.0	1912	0.9		
19 TU	0021	7.9	0730	1.0	1239	7.9	1946	1.0
20 W	0058	7.8	0806	1.1	1319	7.7	2020	1.3
21 TH	0136	7.6	0841	1.4	1400	7.4	2054	1.8
22 F	0216	7.3	0919	1.9	1448	7.1	2135	2.3
23 SA ☽	0306	6.9	1007	2.3	1552	6.7	2233	2.8
24 SU	0423	6.6	1117	2.7	1730	6.4		
25 M	0001	3.1	0606	6.5	1259	2.7	1903	6.6
26 TU	0147	2.8	0730	6.7	1432	2.3	2016	7.0
27 W	0309	2.2	0835	7.1	1545	1.7	2109	7.4
28 TH	0415	1.7	0924	7.5	1644	1.3	2152	7.6
29 F	0506	1.3	1006	7.7	1729	1.1	2231	7.8
30 SA ○	0547	1.1	1045	7.8	1806	1.0	2308	7.8
31 SU	0621	1.1	1122	7.9	1838	1.0	2342	7.8

APRIL

Day	Time	m	Time	m	Time	m	Time	m
1 M	0652	1.1	1157	7.8	1908	1.2		
2 TU	0015	7.8	0721	1.3	1231	7.6	1935	1.5
3 W	0047	7.6	0747	1.5	1304	7.4	1959	1.8
4 TH	0118	7.4	0811	1.9	1336	7.1	2022	2.2
5 F	0147	7.1	0837	2.2	1408	6.7	2049	2.7
6 SA	0219	6.7	0909	2.7	1448	6.3	2127	3.1
7 SU	0306	6.3	0956	3.1	1551	6.0	2228	3.5
8 M	0423	5.9	1114	3.4	1742	5.9		
9 TU	0011	3.6	0614	6.0	1256	3.2	1903	6.2
10 W	0143	3.2	0725	6.3	1412	2.8	2001	6.6
11 TH	0247	2.7	0817	6.7	1510	2.2	2046	7.0
12 F	0339	2.1	0900	7.2	1601	1.8	2125	7.3
13 SA	0425	1.7	0940	7.5	1647	1.4	2203	7.6
14 SU ●	0509	1.4	1019	7.7	1729	1.2	2240	7.8
15 M	0551	1.1	1059	7.8	1809	1.0	2319	7.9
16 TU	0631	0.9	1139	7.9	1849	1.0	2358	7.9
17 W	0711	0.9	1222	7.9	1927	1.1		
18 TH	0039	7.8	0750	1.0	1306	7.7	2005	1.4
19 F	0121	7.6	0830	1.3	1352	7.4	2045	1.8
20 SA	0207	7.3	0912	1.7	1445	7.1	2131	2.3
21 SU ☽	0303	7.0	1005	2.2	1555	6.7	2235	2.7
22 M	0421	6.6	1118	2.5	1723	6.6		
23 TU	0003	2.8	0550	6.6	1249	2.6	1843	6.7
24 W	0130	2.6	0706	6.8	1408	2.2	1950	7.0
25 TH	0242	2.2	0809	7.0	1515	1.9	2043	7.3
26 F	0344	1.9	0859	7.3	1610	1.6	2126	7.5
27 SA	0434	1.6	0942	7.4	1655	1.5	2204	7.6
28 SU	0514	1.5	1021	7.5	1731	1.4	2240	7.7
29 M	0549	1.4	1058	7.6	1804	1.5	2314	7.7
30 TU	0621	1.4	1133	7.6	1836	1.5	2347	7.6

Chart Datum: 4.72 metres below Lallemand System (Mean Sea Level, Marseilles)

18

FRANCE, NORTH COAST - LE HAVRE

LAT 49°29′N   LONG 0°07′E

TIMES AND HEIGHTS OF HIGH AND LOW WATERS

YEAR **1991**

MAY

Day	TIME	m		Day	TIME	m
1 W	0652 / 1208 / 1905	1.4 / 7.4 / 1.7		16 TH	0655 / 1208 / 1914	0.9 / 7.8 / 1.2
2 TH	0020 / 0721 / 1242 / 1933	7.5 / 1.6 / 7.3 / 1.9		17 F	0026 / 0740 / 1257 / 1959	7.8 / 1.0 / 7.7 / 1.4
3 F	0053 / 0749 / 1316 / 2001	7.3 / 1.8 / 7.0 / 2.3		18 SA	0113 / 0826 / 1348 / 2045	7.7 / 1.2 / 7.5 / 1.7
4 SA	0124 / 0817 / 1350 / 2031	7.1 / 2.1 / 6.8 / 2.6		19 SU	0203 / 0915 / 1444 / 2137	7.4 / 1.5 / 7.2 / 2.1
5 SU	0200 / 0849 / 1430 / 2108	6.8 / 2.5 / 6.5 / 2.9		20 M	0300 / 1009 / 1548 / 2237	7.1 / 1.9 / 7.0 / 2.4
6 M	0244 / 0932 / 1522 / 2200	6.5 / 2.8 / 6.3 / 3.2		21 TU	0407 / 1112 / 1658 / 2345	6.9 / 2.1 / 6.8 / 2.5
7 TU ☾	0343 / 1034 / 1637 / 2319	6.3 / 3.0 / 6.2 / 3.3		22 W	0518 / 1220 / 1807	6.7 / 2.3 / 6.8
8 W	0504 / 1156 / 1802	6.2 / 3.0 / 6.3		23 TH ☽	0053 / 0628 / 1326 / 1912	2.5 / 6.8 / 2.3 / 6.9
9 TH	0040 / 0624 / 1310 / 1906	3.1 / 6.3 / 2.7 / 6.6		24 F	0158 / 0734 / 1428 / 2009	2.4 / 6.9 / 2.2 / 7.1
10 F	0147 / 0725 / 1412 / 1958	2.7 / 6.7 / 2.4 / 6.9		25 SA	0259 / 0830 / 1525 / 2056	2.2 / 7.0 / 2.1 / 7.2
11 SA	0246 / 0816 / 1510 / 2044	2.3 / 7.0 / 2.0 / 7.3		26 SU	0353 / 0918 / 1614 / 2138	2.0 / 7.1 / 2.0 / 7.4
12 SU	0341 / 0903 / 1604 / 2127	1.9 / 7.3 / 1.6 / 7.5		27 M	0438 / 1000 / 1655 / 2216	1.9 / 7.2 / 1.9 / 7.4
13 M	0433 / 0949 / 1654 / 2210	1.5 / 7.6 / 1.4 / 7.7		28 TU ○	0517 / 1038 / 1733 / 2251	1.7 / 7.3 / 1.9 / 7.5
14 TU ●	0522 / 1034 / 1743 / 2254	1.2 / 7.7 / 1.2 / 7.8		29 W	0554 / 1115 / 1809 / 2325	1.7 / 7.3 / 1.8 / 7.4
15 W	0609 / 1121 / 1829 / 2339	1.0 / 7.8 / 1.1 / 7.9		30 TH	0628 / 1150 / 1843	1.6 / 7.3 / 1.9
				31 F	0000 / 0701 / 1225 / 1915	7.4 / 1.7 / 7.2 / 2.0

JUNE

Day	TIME	m		Day	TIME	m
1 SA	0034 / 0733 / 1300 / 1947	7.3 / 1.8 / 7.1 / 2.2		16 SU	0105 / 0825 / 1341 / 2046	7.8 / 1.0 / 7.7 / 1.4
2 SU	0108 / 0804 / 1335 / 2020	7.2 / 2.0 / 7.0 / 2.4		17 M	0155 / 0913 / 1432 / 2133	7.6 / 1.2 / 7.5 / 1.7
3 M	0144 / 0838 / 1413 / 2056	7.0 / 2.2 / 6.8 / 2.6		18 TU	0246 / 1000 / 1524 / 2221	7.4 / 1.5 / 7.2 / 2.0
4 TU	0225 / 0916 / 1457 / 2140	6.8 / 2.4 / 6.7 / 2.8		19 W	0339 / 1047 / 1619 / 2311	7.1 / 1.9 / 7.0 / 2.3
5 W	0312 / 1003 / 1548 / 2235	6.7 / 2.5 / 6.6 / 2.9		20 TH	0437 / 1138 / 1718	6.8 / 2.3 / 6.8
6 TH	0408 / 1102 / 1650 / 2339 ☾	6.6 / 2.6 / 6.6 / 2.9		21 F ☽	0007 / 0541 / 1235 / 1823	2.5 / 6.7 / 2.5 / 6.8
7 F	0514 / 1207 / 1800	6.5 / 2.6 / 6.7		22 SA	0110 / 0652 / 1339 / 1929	2.6 / 6.6 / 2.6 / 6.8
8 SA	0046 / 0625 / 1314 / 1904	2.7 / 6.6 / 2.5 / 6.9		23 SU	0214 / 0801 / 1441 / 2027	2.6 / 6.7 / 2.6 / 6.9
9 SU	0154 / 0729 / 1422 / 2001	2.4 / 6.9 / 2.2 / 7.1		24 M	0313 / 0858 / 1537 / 2116	2.4 / 6.8 / 2.5 / 7.1
10 M	0300 / 0828 / 1526 / 2054	2.1 / 7.1 / 1.9 / 7.4		25 TU	0405 / 0944 / 1625 / 2157	2.2 / 7.0 / 2.3 / 7.2
11 TU	0401 / 0923 / 1625 / 2145	1.7 / 7.4 / 1.6 / 7.6		26 W	0450 / 1024 / 1709 / 2234	2.0 / 7.1 / 2.1 / 7.3
12 W ●	0458 / 1016 / 1720 / 2235	1.3 / 7.6 / 1.4 / 7.8		27 TH ○	0532 / 1059 / 1749 / 2308	1.8 / 7.2 / 2.0 / 7.4
13 TH	0552 / 1108 / 1814 / 2325	1.1 / 7.8 / 1.2 / 7.9		28 F	0610 / 1134 / 1827 / 2343	1.7 / 7.3 / 1.9 / 7.4
14 F	0645 / 1159 / 1906	0.9 / 7.8 / 1.2		29 SA	0646 / 1208 / 1902	1.7 / 7.3 / 1.9
15 SA	0015 / 0736 / 1250 / 1957	7.9 / 0.9 / 7.8 / 1.3		30 SU	0017 / 0720 / 1242 / 1935	7.4 / 1.6 / 7.3 / 1.9

JULY

Day	TIME	m		Day	TIME	m
1 M	0051 / 0753 / 1316 / 2009	7.4 / 1.7 / 7.2 / 2.0		16 TU	0137 / 0856 / 1408 / 2112	7.8 / 1.0 / 7.7 / 1.4
2 TU	0126 / 0826 / 1352 / 2043	7.3 / 1.8 / 7.2 / 2.1		17 W	0220 / 0934 / 1451 / 2150	7.6 / 1.4 / 7.4 / 1.8
3 W	0203 / 0900 / 1430 / 2119	7.2 / 2.0 / 7.0 / 2.3		18 TH	0303 / 1009 / 1535 / 2228	7.2 / 1.9 / 7.1 / 2.3
4 TH	0243 / 0937 / 1511 / 2201	6.7 / 2.2 / 6.9 / 2.5		19 F	0351 / 1048 / 1624 / 2314	6.9 / 2.4 / 6.8 / 2.7
5 F	0328 / 1020 / 1559 / 2251	6.9 / 2.4 / 6.8 / 2.6		20 SA	0449 / 1139 / 1727	6.5 / 2.8 / 6.6
6 SA	0421 / 1114 / 1658 / 2353	6.7 / 2.5 / 6.8 / 2.7		21 SU	0016 / 0606 / 1248 / 1846	3.0 / 6.3 / 3.1 / 6.5
7 SU	0530 / 1222 / 1813	6.7 / 2.6 / 6.8		22 M	0132 / 0735 / 1405 / 2001	3.0 / 6.3 / 3.1 / 6.6
8 M ☾	0108 / 0650 / 1343 / 1926	2.6 / 6.7 / 2.5 / 6.9		23 TU ☽	0242 / 0901 / 1510 / 2057	2.8 / 6.5 / 2.8 / 6.8
9 TU	0229 / 0803 / 1459 / 2031	2.3 / 6.9 / 2.2 / 7.2		24 W	0340 / 0929 / 1606 / 2140	2.5 / 6.8 / 2.5 / 7.1
10 W	0337 / 0908 / 1604 / 2130	1.8 / 7.3 / 1.8 / 7.5		25 TH	0431 / 1008 / 1653 / 2216	2.1 / 7.1 / 2.2 / 7.3
11 TH ●	0440 / 1006 / 1706 / 2224	1.4 / 7.6 / 1.5 / 7.8		26 F ○	0516 / 1042 / 1735 / 2250	1.9 / 7.2 / 2.0 / 7.4
12 F	0541 / 1059 / 1806 / 2316	1.1 / 7.8 / 1.2 / 7.9		27 SA	0556 / 1114 / 1813 / 2323	1.7 / 7.4 / 1.8 / 7.5
13 SA	0639 / 1150 / 1902	0.8 / 7.9 / 1.1		28 SU	0632 / 1147 / 1847 / 2356	1.5 / 7.4 / 1.7 / 7.6
14 SU	0005 / 0730 / 1238 / 1950	7.9 / 0.7 / 8.0 / 1.0		29 M	0705 / 1220 / 1920	1.4 / 7.5 / 1.6
15 M	0052 / 0815 / 1324 / 2033	8.0 / 0.7 / 7.9 / 1.2		30 TU	0030 / 0736 / 1253 / 1952	7.6 / 1.4 / 7.5 / 1.7
				31 W	0103 / 0808 / 1327 / 2024	7.6 / 1.5 / 7.4 / 1.8

AUGUST

Day	TIME	m		Day	TIME	m
1 TH	0139 / 0839 / 1402 / 2057	7.5 / 1.7 / 7.3 / 1.9		16 F	0227 / 0927 / 1451 / 2142	7.3 / 2.0 / 7.1 / 2.3
2 F	0216 / 0912 / 1439 / 2133	7.3 / 1.9 / 7.1 / 2.2		17 SA	0307 / 0957 / 1533 / 2220	6.9 / 2.6 / 6.8 / 2.8
3 SA	0256 / 0948 / 1520 / 2216	7.0 / 2.2 / 7.0 / 2.5		18 SU	0359 / 1040 / 1633 / 2318	6.4 / 3.1 / 6.4 / 3.2
4 SU	0345 / 1036 / 1615 / 2314	6.8 / 2.5 / 6.8 / 2.7		19 M	0520 / 1152 / 1802	6.0 / 3.5 / 6.2
5 M	0455 / 1144 / 1739	6.6 / 2.8 / 6.6		20 TU	0049 / 0706 / 1333 / 1933	3.4 / 6.0 / 3.5 / 6.3
6 TU	0036 / 0631 / 1318 / 1908	2.8 / 6.5 / 2.8 / 6.8		21 W	0215 / 0820 / 1449 / 2035	3.1 / 6.3 / 3.1 / 6.4
7 W ☾	0209 / 0753 / 1444 / 2021	2.6 / 6.8 / 2.4 / 7.1		22 TH	0318 / 0908 / 1546 / 2118	2.6 / 6.7 / 2.6 / 7.0
8 TH	0323 / 0901 / 1553 / 2122	1.9 / 7.3 / 1.9 / 7.5		23 F	0411 / 0944 / 1634 / 2153	2.2 / 7.1 / 2.2 / 7.3
9 F	0430 / 0958 / 1659 / 2215	1.4 / 7.6 / 1.5 / 7.8		24 SA	0456 / 1017 / 1716 / 2226	1.8 / 7.3 / 1.8 / 7.5
10 SA	0534 / 1048 / 1759 / 2302 ●	1.0 / 7.9 / 1.1 / 8.0		25 SU ○	0535 / 1049 / 1752 / 2259	1.5 / 7.5 / 1.6 / 7.7
11 SU	0628 / 1133 / 1849 / 2347	0.7 / 8.0 / 0.9 / 8.1		26 M	0610 / 1121 / 1825 / 2332	1.4 / 7.6 / 1.5 / 7.8
12 M	0714 / 1217 / 1931	0.6 / 8.1 / 0.9		27 TU	0642 / 1154 / 1857	1.3 / 7.7 / 1.4
13 TU	0030 / 0754 / 1258 / 2008	8.1 / 0.7 / 8.0 / 1.1		28 W	0005 / 0714 / 1227 / 1930	7.8 / 1.2 / 7.7 / 1.4
14 W	0111 / 0828 / 1337 / 2042	7.9 / 1.0 / 7.8 / 1.4		29 TH	0039 / 0745 / 1300 / 2002	7.8 / 1.3 / 7.6 / 1.5
15 TH	0149 / 0859 / 1414 / 2112	7.7 / 1.5 / 7.5 / 1.8		30 F	0115 / 0817 / 1335 / 2036	7.6 / 1.5 / 7.5 / 1.7
				31 SA	0152 / 0849 / 1411 / 2110	7.4 / 1.8 / 7.3 / 2.1

Chart Datum: 4.72 metres below Lallemand System (Mean Sea Level, Marseilles)

FRANCE, NORTH COAST - LE HAVRE

LAT 49°29'N LONG 0°07'E

TIMES AND HEIGHTS OF HIGH AND LOW WATERS

YEAR **1991**

TIME ZONE −0100
(French Standard Time)
Subtract 1 hour for GMT
For French Summer Time add
ONE hour in non-shaded areas

SEPTEMBER

Day	Time	m	Time	m	Time	m	Time	m
1 SU ☾	0233	7.1	0924	2.3	1453	7.0	2152	2.4
2 M	0325	6.7	1012	2.7	1552	6.7	2251	2.8
3 TU	0445	6.5	1124	3.0	1727	6.5		
4 W	0020	2.9	0628	6.5	1309	3.0	1901	6.7
5 TH	0201	2.5	0750	6.9	1437	2.5	2014	7.2
6 F	0316	1.9	0854	7.4	1547	1.9	2112	7.6
7 SA	0423	1.4	0945	7.7	1651	1.4	2200	7.9
8 SU ●	0521	1.0	1029	8.0	1743	1.1	2243	8.1
9 M	0609	0.7	1111	8.1	1827	0.9	2325	8.1
10 TU	0649	0.7	1151	8.1	1905	1.0		
11 W	0004	8.1	0724	0.9	1228	8.0	1938	1.1
12 TH	0042	7.9	0755	1.2	1304	7.8	2007	1.5
13 F	0118	7.6	0822	1.7	1338	7.5	2034	1.9
14 SA	0154	7.2	0846	2.2	1412	7.1	2101	2.4
15 SU ☽	0230	6.8	0913	2.7	1449	6.7	2134	2.9
16 M	0317	6.3	0953	3.3	1542	6.3	2226	3.3
17 TU	0436	6.0	1101	3.7	1716	6.0	2358	3.6
18 W	0625	5.9	1256	3.7	1853	6.1		
19 TH	0141	3.3	0743	6.2	1420	3.2	2000	6.5
20 F	0247	2.7	0834	6.7	1516	2.6	2045	6.9
21 SA	0339	2.2	0911	7.1	1603	2.2	2122	7.3
22 SU	0424	1.8	0945	7.4	1645	1.8	2156	7.6
23 M ○	0504	1.5	1018	7.6	1722	1.6	2230	7.8
24 TU	0540	1.3	1051	7.7	1757	1.4	2305	7.9
25 W	0614	1.2	1125	7.8	1831	1.3	2340	7.9
26 TH	0648	1.2	1159	7.8	1906	1.3		
27 F	0016	7.9	0722	1.3	1234	7.8	1942	1.4
28 SA	0055	7.7	0756	1.5	1312	7.6	2017	1.6
29 SU	0136	7.5	0831	1.9	1352	7.3	2054	2.0
30 M	0222	7.1	0909	2.3	1439	7.0	2138	2.4

OCTOBER

Day	Time	m	Time	m	Time	m	Time	m
1 TU ☾	0320	6.8	1001	2.8	1545	6.7	2241	2.8
2 W	0448	6.5	1120	3.1	1724	6.6		
3 TH	0017	2.8	0624	6.6	1307	2.9	1851	6.8
4 F	0154	2.4	0739	7.0	1429	2.4	1959	7.2
5 SA	0304	1.9	0837	7.4	1534	1.8	2054	7.6
6 SU	0405	1.4	0924	7.8	1631	1.4	2139	7.8
7 M ●	0457	1.1	1006	7.9	1719	1.2	2221	8.0
8 TU	0541	1.0	1045	8.0	1759	1.1	2301	8.0
9 W	0618	1.1	1123	8.0	1834	1.2	2339	7.9
10 TH	0651	1.3	1158	7.9	1906	1.3		
11 F	0015	7.8	0721	1.5	1232	7.7	1936	1.6
12 SA	0051	7.5	0749	1.9	1306	7.5	2003	1.9
13 SU	0126	7.2	0815	2.3	1339	7.1	2030	2.4
14 M	0202	6.8	0843	2.8	1414	6.8	2102	2.8
15 TU ☽	0244	6.4	0921	3.3	1501	6.4	2148	3.2
16 W	0349	6.1	1020	3.6	1618	6.1	2305	3.5
17 TH	0531	6.0	1101	3.7	1759	6.1		
18 F	0044	3.4	0648	6.2	1329	3.4	1909	6.4
19 SA	0157	2.9	0745	6.6	1430	2.8	2001	6.8
20 SU	0253	2.4	0834	7.0	1520	2.3	2043	7.2
21 M	0341	2.0	0907	7.4	1605	1.9	2122	7.5
22 TU	0425	1.7	0943	7.6	1646	1.6	2159	7.7
23 W ○	0505	1.5	1019	7.8	1726	1.4	2237	7.8
24 TH	0544	1.3	1056	7.9	1806	1.3	2316	7.9
25 F	0623	1.3	1133	7.9	1846	1.2	2356	7.9
26 SA	0702	1.4	1213	7.8	1925	1.3		
27 SU	0040	7.7	0741	1.6	1255	7.7	2005	1.5
28 M	0125	7.5	0820	1.9	1341	7.5	2046	1.9
29 TU	0216	7.2	0904	2.3	1433	7.2	2135	2.3
30 W ☾	0319	6.9	1001	2.7	1542	6.8	2241	2.6
31 TH	0443	6.7	1122	2.9	1710	6.7		

NOVEMBER

Day	Time	m	Time	m	Time	m	Time	m
1 F	0010	2.6	0604	6.8	1252	2.8	1827	6.8
2 SA	0133	2.4	0714	7.1	1406	2.4	1935	7.1
3 SU	0239	2.0	0812	7.4	1509	2.0	2031	7.4
4 M	0337	1.7	0900	7.6	1603	1.7	2118	7.6
5 TU	0427	1.5	0942	7.8	1649	1.5	2200	7.7
6 W ●	0509	1.5	1020	7.8	1729	1.5	2240	7.8
7 TH	0546	1.5	1057	7.8	1804	1.5	2317	7.7
8 F	0620	1.6	1132	7.8	1840	1.5	2354	7.6
9 SA	0652	1.8	1206	7.6	1909	1.7		
10 SU	0029	7.4	0723	2.0	1241	7.4	1940	1.9
11 M	0105	7.2	0753	2.4	1314	7.2	2009	2.3
12 TU	0141	6.9	0824	2.7	1349	6.9	2041	2.6
13 W	0219	6.6	0900	3.0	1430	6.6	2121	2.9
14 TH ☽	0307	6.4	0948	3.3	1525	6.4	2217	3.2
15 F	0416	6.3	1057	3.5	1641	6.2	2332	3.2
16 SA	0541	6.3	1215	3.4	1803	6.3		
17 SU	0046	3.1	0646	6.6	1325	3.1	1906	6.6
18 M	0152	2.7	0739	6.9	1426	2.7	1958	6.9
19 TU	0250	2.3	0825	7.2	1520	2.2	2044	7.3
20 W	0342	2.0	0907	7.5	1610	1.8	2128	7.5
21 TH ○	0430	1.7	0948	7.7	1658	1.5	2212	7.7
22 F	0517	1.5	1030	7.8	1744	1.3	2257	7.8
23 SA	0603	1.4	1113	7.9	1830	1.2	2342	7.9
24 SU	0648	1.4	1158	7.9	1915	1.2		
25 M	0030	7.8	0733	1.5	1245	7.8	2001	1.3
26 TU	0121	7.6	0819	1.8	1334	7.6	2048	1.6
27 W	0213	7.4	0909	2.1	1428	7.4	2139	1.9
28 TH ☾	0312	7.2	1004	2.4	1530	7.1	2237	2.2
29 F	0420	7.0	1108	2.6	1640	6.9	2343	2.4
30 SA	0529	6.9	1218	2.6	1751	6.8		

DECEMBER

Day	Time	m	Time	m	Time	m	Time	m
1 SU	0053	2.4	0637	7.0	1328	2.5	1900	6.9
2 M	0201	2.4	0740	7.1	1434	2.4	2004	7.1
3 TU	0302	2.2	0833	7.3	1531	2.1	2058	7.2
4 W	0355	2.1	0919	7.5	1620	2.0	2144	7.4
5 TH	0439	2.0	1001	7.6	1702	1.8	2225	7.5
6 F ●	0518	1.9	1038	7.6	1740	1.7	2303	7.5
7 SA	0555	1.9	1113	7.6	1816	1.7	2338	7.5
8 SU	0631	1.9	1147	7.6	1850	1.7		
9 M	0013	7.4	0705	2.0	1222	7.5	1924	1.8
10 TU	0047	7.3	0738	2.2	1255	7.3	1955	2.0
11 W	0121	7.1	0811	2.4	1329	7.2	2027	2.2
12 TH	0155	7.0	0844	2.6	1405	7.0	2101	2.5
13 F ☽	0234	6.8	0922	2.8	1447	6.8	2140	2.7
14 SA	0320	6.6	1008	3.0	1537	6.6	2230	2.9
15 SU	0416	6.6	1105	3.1	1638	6.5	2331	3.0
16 M	0526	6.6	1210	3.1	1753	6.5		
17 TU	0039	2.9	0637	6.7	1321	2.9	1905	6.7
18 W	0152	2.7	0738	7.0	1434	2.5	2007	7.0
19 TH	0301	2.3	0832	7.3	1537	2.1	2102	7.3
20 F	0401	2.0	0923	7.5	1634	1.6	2154	7.6
21 SA ○	0456	1.6	1012	7.8	1728	1.3	2244	7.8
22 SU	0549	1.4	1100	8.0	1820	1.0	2334	7.9
23 M	0642	1.3	1149	8.0	1911	0.9		
24 TU	0023	7.9	0732	1.3	1238	8.0	2000	0.9
25 W	0113	7.9	0820	1.4	1327	7.9	2047	1.1
26 TH	0202	7.7	0906	1.6	1416	7.6	2132	1.4
27 F	0252	7.5	0951	1.9	1506	7.3	2216	1.8
28 SA ☾	0345	7.2	1038	2.3	1601	7.0	2304	2.3
29 SU	0443	6.9	1132	2.6	1704	6.8		
30 M	0002	2.6	0548	6.8	1238	2.8	1818	6.6
31 TU	0112	2.8	0701	6.8	1351	2.8	1937	6.6

18

Chart Datum: 4.72 metres below Lallemand System (Mean Sea Level, Marseilles)

LE HAVRE *continued*

LE HAVRE

MEAN SPRING
AND NEAP CURVES

MEAN RANGES	
Springs 6·7m	——
Neaps 3·6m	- - -

Springs occur 2 days
after
New and Full Moon.

Graville, Bassin de Despujois, and across the north end of
Bassin de Lancement, which leads under two bridges into
Canal de Tancarville.

LIGHTS AND MARKS
Ldg Lts 107° both Dir FW 36/78m 25M; grey Trs, G tops;
intens 106°-108° (H24).

RADIO TELEPHONE
Call: *Havre Port* Sig Stn VHF Ch **12** 20 (or 2182 kHz).
Port Operations Ch 67 69 (H24). Marina Ch 09.
Other station: Havre-Antifer Ch 14 **67** 22 (H24).

TELEPHONE (35)
Hr Mr 35.22.72.72; Hr Mr Port de Plaisance 35.21.23.95;
Aff Mar 35.22.41.03; CROSS 33.52.72.13; SNSM
35.22.41.03; ✠ 35.41.33.51; Meteo 35.42.21.06;
Auto 35.21.16.11; Police 35.42.40.65; Dr 35.41.23.61;
Ⓗ 35.22.81.23; Brit Consul 35.42.27.47.

FACILITIES
Le Havre-Plaisance Marina (973 + 41 visitors)
☎ 35.21.23.95, Slip, AC, BH (16 ton), C (6 ton), CH, D,
P, El, FW, Gas, Gaz, R, ▢, V, Access H24; **Accastillage
Diffusion** ☎ 35.43.43.62, ME, Ⓔ, El, Sh, CH; **Manche
Yachting** ☎ 35.21.08.86, ME, CH; **Nautic Channel**
☎ 35.42.18.37, El, Sh, ME; **YC – Société des Regates
du Havre** ☎ 35.42.41.21, R, Bar; **Nautic-Service**
☎ 35.51.75.30 SHOM; **CRM** ☎ 35.26.61.53, Ⓔ; **Havre
Voiles** Tel. 35.42.58.15, SM; **Town** ME, El, CH, V, Gaz,
R, Bar. ✉; Ⓑ; ⇌; ✈.
Ferry UK – Portsmouth.

FÉCAMP   10-18-20
Seine Maritime

CHARTS
Admiralty 2612, 1352; SHOM 932, 6765; ECM 1012;
Stanford 1; Imray C31

TIDES
Dover −0100; ML 4.5; Duration 0550; Zone −0100

Standard Port DIEPPE (⟶)

Times				Height (metres)			
HW		LW		MHWS	MHWN	MLWN	MLWS
0100	0600	0100	0700	9.3	7.2	2.6	0.7
1300	1800	1300	1900				

Differences FÉCAMP

−0022	−0018	−0034	−0043	−1.4	−0.7	0.0	+0.1

ANTIFER

−0046	−0039	−0051	−0100	−1.3	−0.6	+0.4	+0.5

FECAMP *continued*

SHELTER
Excellent in basins but there is a scend in the Avant Port. Entry by boats of less than 1.2 m draught can be made at any tide and in most weathers. Even moderate W to NW winds make entrance and berthing in Avant Port (at marina-type pontoons) uncomfortable and a considerable surf runs off the entrance. Access best at HW+1. Yachts can lock into Berigny Basin (HW−2 to HW).

NAVIGATION
Waypoint 49°45'.90N 00°21'.00E, 265°/085° from/to Jetée Sud Lt, 0.58M. Beware the Charpentier Rks which run out from Pte Fagnet. Strong cross currents occur, depending on tides. Dredged channel subject to silting.

LIGHTS AND MARKS
Entrance can be identified by conspic church and signal station on Pte Fagnet, to the N.
Jetee Nord Fl (2) 10s 15m 16M; grey Tr, R top; Reed (2) 30s sounded HW−2½ to HW+2. Ldg Lts 085°. Front Jetée Sud, head, QG 14m 9M; vis 072°-217°. Rear QR. Normal entry signals on Sig mast show when dock gates of Bassin Bérigny and Bassin Freycinet open. (HW−2 to HW)

RADIO TELEPHONE
VHF Ch 12 16 (HW−2½ to HW+½). Yacht Hr Ch 09 (0800-2000 LT).

TELEPHONE (35)
Hr Mr (Marina) 35.28.13.58; Aff Mar 35.28.16.35; CROSS 21.87.21.87; SNSM 35.28.28.15; ⌗ 35.28.19.40; Meteo 35.42.21.06; Auto 35.21.16.11; Police 35.28.16.69; Ⓗ 35.28.05.13; Brit Consul 35.42.27.47.

FACILITIES
EC Monday (all day); **Marina (Avant Port)** (500+30 visitors) ☎ 35.28.11.25, D, L, FW, C (Mobile 36 ton); **Bassin Freycinet** Slip, FW, Sh; **Bassin Bérigny** Slip, M, D, L, FW, CH, AB; **Moré (Chantier)** ☎ 35.28.28.15, Slip, ME, El, Ⓔ, Sh, Gaz, C (30 ton), AC, CH; **Société des Régates de Fécamp** ☎ 35.28.08.44, L, FW, AB; **Société Houvenaghel Le Grand** ME, El, Sh; **Villetard** ☎ 35.28.30.34, M, ME, El, Sh, CH. **Town** P, D, V, Gaz, R, Bar. ⊠; Ⓑ; ⇌; ✈ (Le Havre).
Ferry UK — Le Havre—Portsmouth.
Dieppe—Newhaven.

▲ C pontoon

ST VALÉRY-EN-CAUX   10-18-21
Seine Maritime

CHARTS
Admiralty 2612; SHOM 6794; ECM 1012; Stanford 1; Imray C31

TIDES
Dover −0044; ML 4.9; Duration 0530; Zone −0100

Standard Port DIEPPE (→)

Times				Height (metres)			
HW		LW		MHWS	MHWN	MLWN	MLWS
0100	0600	0100	0700	9.3	7.2	2.6	0.7
1300	1800	1300	1900				

Differences ST VALÉRY-EN-CAUX

−0018	−0016	−0007	−0013	−0.4	−0.1	−0.1	+0.3

SHELTER
Good but outer harbour dries. Entry into outer harbour from HW−3. Marina access HW∓2. Bridge opens every half hour during the period, by day; at HW only at night.

NAVIGATION
Waypoint 49°53'.00N 00°42'.50E, 000°/180° from/to Jetée Ouest Lt, 0.50M. Entry is easy except in strong winds from E through N when seas break across entrance. Coast dries to approx 150 m off the pier heads. Inside the pier heads there are half-tide ramps to dampen the swell marked by posts each side. Shingle tends to build up against W wall.

LIGHTS AND MARKS
Harbour is difficult to identify between high chalk cliffs. Approaching from N or W the nuclear power station at Paluel is conspic 3 M W of entrance.
W pier head Lt Ho Oc (2+1) G 12s 13m 14M, E pier head light structure Fl (2)R 6s. Bu flag indicates sluicing (at about LW−1). Traffic signals are shown on both sides of the bridge/lock
G Lt — Vessels may enter but not leave
R Lt — Vessels may leave but not enter
R+G — Vessels may not enter or leave

RADIO TELEPHONE
VHF Ch 09.

18

ST VALÉRY-EN-CAUX *continued*

TELEPHONE
Hr Mr 35.97.01.30; Aff Mar 35.28.16.35; CROSS
21.87.21.87; SNSM 35.87.05.27; ⚓ 35.82.46.49; Meteo
35.80.11.44; Police 35.97.05.27; Dr 35.97.20.13;
Ⓗ 35.97.06.21; Brit Consul 35.42.27.47.

FACILITIES
EC Monday (all day); **Marina** (550 + some visitors)
☎ 35.97.01.30, AC, C (6 ton), V, CH, El, FW, Gaz, ME,
Sh, SM, Bar; **Nautic 76** ☎ 35.97.04.22, CH, ME, El, Sh,
M, Ⓔ, SM; **Prigent** ☎ 35.97.17.66, ME, El, Sh; **Club
Nautique Valeriquais** ☎ 35.97.10.88. **Town** P, D, FW,
CH, V, Gaz, R, Bar. ✉; Ⓑ; ⇌; ✈ (Dieppe).
Ferry UK   Dieppe   Newhaven.

DIEPPE   10-18-22
Seine Maritime

CHARTS
Admiralty 2147; SHOM 5927, 934; ECM 1011, 1012;
Stanford 1; Imray C31

TIDES
Dover −0035; ML 5.0; Duration 0535; Zone −0100

NOTE: Dieppe is a Standard Port. Tidal predictions for
each day of the year are given below.

SHELTER
Very good and the harbour can be entered at any state of
tide. Channel is exposed to winds from NW to NE, when
a heavy scend renders. Beware work in progress in the
Avant Port. Port de Plaisance is not comfortable for
yachts. The SW part is reserved for pleasure craft. Bassin
Duquesne is Yacht Basin.

NAVIGATION
Waypoint 49°56'.48N 01°04'.60E, 318°/138° from/to front
Ldg Lt 138°, 0.58M. Dieppe is a busy commercial and
fishing port and both entry and exit are forbidden during
shipping movements. Entry to harbour is simple and
yachts normally lie in SW corner of Avant Port at
pontoons and wait to pass through lock into Bassin
Duquesne. Access HW−2 to HW+1. The bridge opens
two or three times during each period. Beware strong
stream setting across entrance. Yachts are forbidden in
the Arriere Port.

LIGHTS AND MARKS
Ldg Lts in line at 138° (both QR).
W Jetty — Iso WG 4s 10m 12/8M W095°-164°,
                G 164°-095°
E Jetty — Oc (4) R 12s 19m 8M
Entry signals shown from Station at root of W jetty and
from station on W side of harbour, 2½ ca (480m) S of
former, (full code). Also repeated from repeating stations
at entrances to Bassin Duquesne, Arriere Port and Bassin
du Canada (simplified code). In low visibility a fog signal,
1 blast of 1 sec every 5 secs, is sounded from the head of
Jettée Ouest to indicate 'Entry Prohibited'.
International signals combined with: −
FG to right   — Ferry entering
FR to right   — Ferry leaving
FW to left   — Lock gates open
2 FR (hor) to right   — Dredger in channel.
Signals are repeated with flags from the sig stn on the
cliff top near church of Notre Dame de Bon-Secours.
Signals for Duquesne Basin: −
Bridge and lock gates to open − Sound 2 blasts
Vessels may enter but not leave − G Lt
Vessels may leave but not enter − R Lt
Request will not be met unless Flag P (W Lt at night) is
flying from pier head and dock.

RADIO TELEPHONE
Call: *Dieppe Port* VHF Ch **12** 16 (H24).

TELEPHONE (35)
Hr Mr 35.82.23.85; Hr Mr (Port de Plaisance) 35.84.32.99;
Aff Mar 35.82.59.40; CROSS 21.87.21.87;
SNSM 35.84.30.76; ⚓ 35.82.24.47; Meteo 35.80.11.44;
Auto 35.21.16.11; Police 35.82.04.35; Ⓗ 35.82.20.75;
Brit Consul 35.42.27.47.

FACILITIES
Quai Duquesne M, L, FW, C (by arrangement with
Hr Mr up to 30 ton), AB; **GAD-SA** ☎ 35.84.33.54 ME, El,
Sh, CH; **Cercle de la Voile de Dieppe** ☎ 35.84.32.99, P,
D, FW, C (3 ton), AB, R, Bar; **Thalassa** ☎ 35.82.16.08,
ME, El, Ⓔ, Sh, CH; **Plaisance** ☎ 35.84.34.95, CH. **Town**
P, D, FW, V, Gaz, R, Bar. ✉; Ⓑ; ⇌; ✈.
Ferry UK—Newhaven.

FRANCE, NORTH COAST - DIEPPE

LAT 49°56′N   LONG 1°05′E

TIMES AND HEIGHTS OF HIGH AND LOW WATERS

YEAR **1991**

TIME ZONE −0100
(French Standard Time)
Subtract 1 hour for GMT
For French Summer Time add
ONE hour in non-shaded areas

JANUARY

Day	Time	m	Time	m	Time	m	Time	m
1 TU	0628	0.9	1158	9.4	1855	0.7		
16 W	0001	8.3	0654	1.5	1219	8.7	1911	1.2
2 W	0024	9.2	0720	0.7	1250	9.5	1944	0.6
17 TH	0037	8.5	0728	1.3	1254	8.9	1943	1.1
3 TH	0115	9.2	0808	0.7	1338	9.5	2030	0.6
18 F	0110	8.6	0800	1.1	1327	8.9	2015	1.0
4 F	0200	9.1	0850	0.8	1423	9.3	2110	0.7
19 SA	0143	8.7	0831	1.1	1358	9.0	2046	1.0
5 SA	0243	8.9	0930	1.0	1503	9.1	2149	1.0
20 SU	0214	8.7	0901	1.1	1431	8.9	2116	1.0
6 SU	0322	8.6	1008	1.3	1543	8.7	2228	1.4
21 M	0247	8.6	0932	1.2	1503	8.7	2149	1.2
7 M	0404	8.1	1048	1.7	1625	8.1	2310	1.8
22 TU	0321	8.4	1006	1.4	1539	8.5	2224	1.4
8 TU	0448	7.6	1134	2.2	1714	7.6		
23 W	0358	8.1	1044	1.7	1620	8.1	2306	1.8
9 W	0001	2.4	0543	7.2	1230	2.6	1815	7.2
24 TH	0444	7.7	1132	2.0	1713	7.7		
10 TH	0105	2.8	0652	7.0	1344	2.8	1931	6.9
25 F	0003	2.2	0548	7.5	1238	2.3	1826	7.4
11 F	0223	2.9	0810	7.0	1503	2.8	2047	7.0
26 SA	0120	2.4	0711	7.4	1406	2.3	1956	7.4
12 SA	0340	2.7	0921	7.3	1613	2.5	2150	7.3
27 SU	0252	2.2	0840	7.7	1536	1.9	2121	7.8
13 SU	0443	2.4	1017	7.7	1710	2.1	2242	7.6
28 M	0417	1.7	0956	8.3	1653	1.4	2230	8.4
14 M	0535	2.1	1104	8.1	1757	1.7	2324	8.0
29 TU	0526	1.3	1100	8.9	1757	0.9	2327	8.9
15 TU	0617	1.7	1143	8.4	1836	1.4		
30 W	0623	0.9	1153	9.3	1848	0.6		
31 TH	0017	9.2	0711	0.6	1241	9.5	1933	0.4

FEBRUARY

Day	Time	m	Time	m	Time	m	Time	m
1 F	0102	9.3	0754	0.5	1323	9.6	2013	0.4
16 SA	0049	8.9	0738	0.8	1305	9.2	1954	0.7
2 SA	0142	9.3	0832	0.6	1401	9.5	2049	0.5
17 SU	0121	9.0	0809	0.7	1336	9.3	2025	0.6
3 SU	0219	9.1	0905	0.7	1437	9.2	2122	0.8
18 M	0152	9.1	0840	0.7	1408	9.2	2054	0.7
4 M	0253	8.8	0937	1.0	1509	8.8	2154	1.1
19 TU	0224	9.0	0910	0.8	1440	9.0	2125	0.9
5 TU	0325	8.4	1010	1.4	1543	8.2	2228	1.7
20 W	0256	8.7	0942	1.1	1513	8.7	2159	1.2
6 W	0401	7.7	1045	2.0	1620	7.6	2305	2.3
21 TH	0332	8.3	1018	1.4	1553	8.1	2240	1.7
7 TH	0442	7.1	1129	2.6	1710	6.8	2358	3.0
22 F	0416	7.8	1104	2.0	1644	7.5	2335	2.3
8 F	0542	6.6	1233	3.1	1823	6.3		
23 SA	0519	7.3	1212	2.4	1802	7.0		
9 SA	0119	3.4	0711	6.4	1409	3.2	2001	6.3
24 SU	0059	2.6	0653	7.1	1352	2.5	1948	7.0
10 SU	0258	3.2	0846	6.7	1542	2.9	2125	6.7
25 M	0246	2.4	0837	7.5	1534	1.9	2120	7.6
11 M	0419	2.4	0956	7.3	1648	2.3	2223	7.3
26 TU	0415	1.8	0955	8.2	1650	1.3	2226	8.3
12 TU	0515	2.2	1046	7.8	1738	1.8	2307	7.8
27 W	0520	1.2	1053	8.8	1748	0.9	2317	8.8
13 W	0559	1.7	1125	8.3	1818	1.3	2343	8.3
28 TH	0612	0.8	1140	9.3	1835	0.5		
14 TH	0635	1.3	1200	8.8	1852	1.0		
15 F	0017	8.7	0708	1.0	1234	9.0	1924	0.8

MARCH

Day	Time	m	Time	m	Time	m	Time	m
1 F	0001	9.2	0655	0.5	1222	9.5	1914	0.4
16 SA	0639	0.8	1204	9.1	1855	0.6		
2 SA	0042	9.3	0733	0.4	1300	9.6	1950	0.4
17 SU	0020	9.1	0711	0.6	1237	9.4	1927	0.5
3 SU	0117	9.3	0807	0.5	1335	9.5	2023	0.5
18 M	0053	9.3	0742	0.5	1310	9.4	1959	0.4
4 M	0151	9.2	0838	0.7	1406	9.2	2053	0.8
19 TU	0127	9.3	0815	0.5	1343	9.3	2032	0.6
5 TU	0222	8.9	0907	0.9	1437	8.8	2122	1.1
20 W	0200	9.2	0849	0.7	1418	9.1	2105	0.8
6 W	0252	8.4	0936	1.4	1506	8.2	2151	1.6
21 TH	0237	8.9	0923	1.0	1455	8.6	2142	1.2
7 TH	0322	7.8	1008	1.9	1540	7.5	2225	2.3
22 F	0315	8.4	1003	1.4	1538	8.0	2227	1.8
8 F	0359	7.2	1045	2.5	1621	6.7	2309	3.0
23 SA	0404	7.7	1054	2.0	1635	7.3	2327	2.4
9 SA	0449	6.5	1139	3.2	1724	6.1		
24 SU	0512	7.2	1208	2.4	1800	6.8		
10 SU	0020	3.5	0612	6.2	1311	3.4	1908	5.9
25 M	0058	2.6	0653	7.1	1352	2.3	1946	7.0
11 M	0209	3.4	0803	6.4	1500	3.0	2048	6.4
26 TU	0243	2.3	0833	7.6	1527	1.8	2110	7.6
12 TU	0341	2.8	0923	7.0	1614	2.4	2151	7.1
27 W	0403	1.6	0942	8.2	1634	1.3	2210	8.3
13 W	0442	2.2	1014	7.7	1705	1.7	2235	7.7
28 TH	0502	1.1	1034	8.8	1727	0.9	2257	8.8
14 TH	0527	1.6	1055	8.3	1746	1.2	2313	8.4
29 F	0550	0.8	1118	9.1	1810	0.6	2338	9.1
15 F	0604	1.1	1129	8.8	1821	0.9	2347	8.8
30 SA	0630	0.6	1156	9.3	1849	0.5		
31 SU	0015	9.2	0706	0.6	1233	9.3	1923	0.6

APRIL

Day	Time	m	Time	m	Time	m	Time	m
1 M	0049	9.2	0739	0.6	1306	9.2	1955	0.7
16 TU	0023	9.4	0715	0.5	1243	9.4	1934	0.5
2 TU	0122	9.1	0810	0.8	1337	9.0	2026	0.9
17 W	0102	9.4	0753	0.5	1322	9.3	2012	0.6
3 W	0154	8.8	0841	1.0	1409	8.6	2055	1.2
18 TH	0142	9.2	0833	0.7	1403	9.0	2052	0.9
4 TH	0224	8.4	0910	1.4	1440	8.0	2124	1.7
19 F	0224	8.9	0913	1.0	1446	8.5	2135	1.3
5 F	0255	7.9	0941	1.9	1512	7.5	2158	2.2
20 SA	0309	8.4	0958	1.4	1535	7.9	2225	1.8
6 SA	0331	7.3	1017	2.4	1552	6.8	2240	2.8
21 SU	0404	7.8	1054	1.9	1637	7.3	2329	2.2
7 SU	0417	6.7	1106	2.9	1648	6.2	2340	3.3
22 M	0515	7.5	1209	2.2	1759	7.1		
8 M	0528	6.3	1223	3.2	1817	6.0		
23 TU	0053	2.3	0645	7.5	1339	2.0	1930	7.3
9 TU	0113	3.3	0707	6.4	1402	2.9	1953	6.4
24 W	0222	2.0	0809	7.8	1501	1.7	2044	7.7
10 W	0245	2.8	0831	7.0	1522	2.4	2102	7.1
25 TH	0335	1.6	0913	8.2	1604	1.3	2141	8.2
11 TH	0351	2.2	0928	7.6	1618	1.7	2151	7.7
26 F	0432	1.3	1005	8.6	1656	1.1	2228	8.6
12 F	0441	1.5	1012	8.3	1702	1.2	2231	8.4
27 SA	0519	1.0	1049	8.8	1741	0.9	2309	8.8
13 SA	0522	1.1	1051	8.8	1741	0.9	2309	8.9
28 SU	0602	0.9	1128	8.9	1821	0.9	2347	8.9
14 SU	0601	0.8	1127	9.1	1820	0.6	2346	9.2
29 M	0640	0.9	1205	8.9	1857	0.9		
15 M	0639	0.6	1205	9.3	1857	0.5		
30 TU	0022	8.9	0714	0.9	1240	8.8	1931	1.0

18

Chart Datum: 4.89 metres below Lallemand System (Mean Sea Level, Marseilles)

FRANCE, NORTH COAST - DIEPPE

LAT 49°56′N   LONG 1°05′E

TIMES AND HEIGHTS OF HIGH AND LOW WATERS

YEAR **1991**

MAY

Day	Time	m		Day	Time	m
1 W	0057 / 0747 / 1314 / 2003	8.8 / 1.0 / 8.6 / 1.2		16 TH	0044 / 0738 / 1307 / 2000	9.3 / 0.6 / 9.2 / 0.7
2 TH	0131 / 0819 / 1347 / 2035	8.7 / 1.2 / 8.3 / 1.4		17 F	0131 / 0824 / 1355 / 2046	9.2 / 0.7 / 8.9 / 0.9
3 F	0203 / 0850 / 1420 / 2106	8.4 / 1.5 / 7.9 / 1.7		18 SA	0219 / 0909 / 1444 / 2133	9.0 / 0.9 / 8.6 / 1.2
4 SA	0237 / 0923 / 1454 / 2141	8.0 / 1.8 / 7.5 / 2.1		19 SU	0308 / 0957 / 1534 / 2224	8.6 / 1.2 / 8.1 / 1.5
5 SU	0313 / 1000 / 1533 / 2221	7.6 / 2.2 / 7.1 / 2.5		20 M	0402 / 1052 / 1632 / 2321	8.2 / 1.5 / 7.7 / 1.9
6 M	0357 / 1045 / 1624 / 2312	7.2 / 2.5 / 6.6 / 2.8		21 TU	0505 / 1155 / 1740	7.9 / 1.8 / 7.5
7 TU	0455 / 1145 / 1730	6.8 / 2.7 / 6.5		22 W	0030 / 0617 / 1307 / 1853	2.0 / 7.8 / 1.8 / 7.5
8 W	0021 / 0609 / 1300 / 1848	2.9 / 6.8 / 2.6 / 6.7		23 TH	0144 / 0730 / 1420 / 2004	1.9 / 7.8 / 1.8 / 7.6
9 TH	0139 / 0725 / 1416 / 1959	2.6 / 7.2 / 2.3 / 7.2		24 F	0253 / 0835 / 1525 / 2103	1.8 / 7.9 / 1.7 / 7.9
10 F	0249 / 0830 / 1518 / 2056	2.1 / 7.6 / 1.8 / 7.7		25 SA	0353 / 0930 / 1621 / 2155	1.6 / 8.1 / 1.5 / 8.2
11 SA	0345 / 0921 / 1610 / 2144	1.6 / 8.1 / 1.4 / 8.3		26 SU	0446 / 1018 / 1710 / 2241	1.4 / 8.3 / 1.4 / 8.4
12 SU	0434 / 1007 / 1658 / 2229	1.2 / 8.6 / 1.0 / 8.8		27 M	0534 / 1103 / 1755 / 2322	1.3 / 8.4 / 1.3 / 8.5
13 M	0522 / 1051 / 1745 / 2313	0.9 / 9.0 / 0.8 / 9.1		28 TU	0616 / 1142 / 1836	1.2 / 8.4 / 1.3
14 TU	0607 / 1135 / 1829 / 2357	0.7 / 9.2 / 0.7 / 9.3		29 W	0001 / 0654 / 1220 / 1912	8.6 / 1.2 / 8.4 / 1.3
15 W	0652 / 1220 / 1915	0.6 / 9.2 / 0.6		30 TH	0039 / 0729 / 1256 / 1946	8.6 / 1.2 / 8.4 / 1.4
				31 F	0114 / 0803 / 1331 / 2020	8.6 / 1.3 / 8.2 / 1.5

JUNE

Day	Time	m		Day	Time	m
1 SA	0148 / 0836 / 1405 / 2052	8.4 / 1.4 / 8.0 / 1.7		16 SU	0213 / 0904 / 1437 / 2127	9.2 / 0.8 / 8.8 / 1.0
2 SU	0223 / 0909 / 1440 / 2126	8.2 / 1.6 / 7.7 / 1.9		17 M	0301 / 0949 / 1524 / 2213	9.0 / 0.9 / 8.5 / 1.2
3 M	0258 / 0944 / 1517 / 2203	7.9 / 1.8 / 7.5 / 2.1		18 TU	0349 / 1036 / 1613 / 2300	8.7 / 1.2 / 8.1 / 1.5
4 TU	0337 / 1023 / 1559 / 2246	7.7 / 2.0 / 7.3 / 2.3		19 W	0439 / 1125 / 1707 / 2353	8.3 / 1.5 / 7.7 / 1.8
5 W	0423 / 1109 / 1648 / 2335	7.5 / 2.2 / 7.1 / 2.4		20 TH	0535 / 1223 / 1807	7.9 / 1.8 / 7.5
6 TH	0517 / 1204 / 1749	7.3 / 2.2 / 7.1		21 F	0055 / 0640 / 1328 / 1914	2.1 / 7.6 / 2.1 / 7.4
7 F	0036 / 0621 / 1309 / 1854	2.3 / 7.4 / 2.2 / 7.3		22 SA	0203 / 0748 / 1439 / 2022	2.2 / 7.5 / 2.2 / 7.5
8 SA	0143 / 0727 / 1416 / 1959	2.1 / 7.6 / 1.9 / 7.7		23 SU	0313 / 0853 / 1545 / 2123	2.1 / 7.5 / 2.1 / 7.6
9 SU	0249 / 0830 / 1519 / 2059	1.8 / 7.9 / 1.6 / 8.1		24 M	0414 / 0951 / 1643 / 2217	2.0 / 7.7 / 2.0 / 7.9
10 M	0349 / 0927 / 1619 / 2154	1.5 / 8.3 / 1.3 / 8.6		25 TU	0509 / 1042 / 1734 / 2304	1.7 / 7.8 / 1.8 / 8.1
11 TU	0447 / 1022 / 1715 / 2248	1.1 / 8.7 / 1.1 / 8.9		26 W	0557 / 1125 / 1818 / 2345	1.6 / 8.0 / 1.6 / 8.4
12 W	0544 / 1115 / 1810 / 2341	0.9 / 8.9 / 0.9 / 9.2		27 TH	0639 / 1205 / 1857	1.4 / 8.2 / 1.5
13 TH	0638 / 1207 / 1903	0.7 / 9.1 / 0.8		28 F	0023 / 0715 / 1242 / 1932	8.5 / 1.3 / 8.2 / 1.4
14 F	0034 / 0729 / 1259 / 1953	9.3 / 0.6 / 9.1 / 0.7		29 SA	0059 / 0749 / 1316 / 2006	8.6 / 1.3 / 8.3 / 1.4
15 SA	0125 / 0818 / 1350 / 2042	9.3 / 0.6 / 9.0 / 0.8		30 SU	0134 / 0822 / 1350 / 2038	8.6 / 1.3 / 8.2 / 1.4

JULY

Day	Time	m		Day	Time	m
1 M	0206 / 0853 / 1423 / 2109	8.5 / 1.3 / 8.2 / 1.5		16 TU	0244 / 0930 / 1503 / 2150	9.3 / 0.7 / 8.8 / 1.0
2 TU	0239 / 0925 / 1456 / 2142	8.4 / 1.4 / 8.0 / 1.6		17 W	0323 / 1005 / 1543 / 2229	8.9 / 1.0 / 8.4 / 1.3
3 W	0313 / 0959 / 1531 / 2217	8.2 / 1.5 / 7.8 / 1.7		18 TH	0405 / 1050 / 1626 / 2311	8.4 / 1.4 / 7.9 / 1.8
4 TH	0350 / 1036 / 1611 / 2256	8.0 / 1.7 / 7.7 / 1.9		19 F	0450 / 1135 / 1716	7.8 / 2.0 / 7.4
5 F	0434 / 1119 / 1659 / 2345	7.8 / 1.9 / 7.5 / 2.0		20 SA	0004 / 0546 / 1234 / 1821	2.3 / 7.3 / 2.5 / 7.0
6 SA	0526 / 1213 / 1757	7.6 / 2.1 / 7.4		21 SU	0111 / 0658 / 1350 / 1938	2.6 / 6.9 / 2.7 / 6.9
7 SU	0046 / 0631 / 1321 / 1907	2.1 / 7.5 / 2.1 / 7.5		22 M	0231 / 0818 / 1512 / 2055	2.7 / 6.9 / 2.7 / 7.1
8 M	0158 / 0745 / 1436 / 2022	2.0 / 7.6 / 2.0 / 7.8		23 TU	0348 / 0928 / 1621 / 2158	2.5 / 7.1 / 2.4 / 7.5
9 TU	0314 / 0857 / 1551 / 2131	1.8 / 7.9 / 1.7 / 8.2		24 W	0451 / 1024 / 1717 / 2248	2.1 / 7.5 / 2.1 / 7.9
10 W	0425 / 1004 / 1700 / 2234	1.4 / 8.3 / 1.3 / 8.7		25 TH	0541 / 1110 / 1803 / 2329	1.7 / 7.8 / 1.7 / 8.3
11 TH	0530 / 1105 / 1801 / 2333	1.0 / 8.7 / 1.0 / 9.1		26 F	0622 / 1149 / 1841	1.5 / 8.1 / 1.5
12 F	0629 / 1159 / 1856	0.7 / 9.0 / 0.7		27 SA	0007 / 0658 / 1228 / 1915	8.6 / 1.2 / 8.4 / 1.3
13 SA	0026 / 0721 / 1252 / 1945	9.4 / 0.5 / 9.2 / 0.6		28 SU	0041 / 0731 / 1258 / 1947	8.7 / 1.1 / 8.5 / 1.1
14 SU	0116 / 0809 / 1339 / 2030	9.5 / 0.4 / 9.2 / 0.6		29 M	0114 / 0803 / 1330 / 2018	8.8 / 1.0 / 8.6 / 1.1
15 M	0201 / 0851 / 1423 / 2111	9.5 / 0.5 / 9.1 / 0.7		30 TU	0145 / 0833 / 1400 / 2047	8.9 / 1.0 / 8.6 / 1.1
				31 W	0215 / 0902 / 1431 / 2116	8.8 / 1.0 / 8.5 / 1.2

AUGUST

Day	Time	m		Day	Time	m
1 TH	0247 / 0932 / 1503 / 2148	8.7 / 1.2 / 8.4 / 1.3		16 F	0328 / 1014 / 1547 / 2232	8.4 / 1.5 / 7.9 / 1.8
2 F	0320 / 1005 / 1538 / 2223	8.4 / 1.4 / 8.1 / 1.6		17 SA	0407 / 1053 / 1629 / 2316	7.7 / 2.2 / 7.3 / 2.5
3 SA	0358 / 1043 / 1619 / 2306	8.1 / 1.7 / 7.7 / 1.9		18 SU	0456 / 1144 / 1728	7.0 / 2.8 / 6.8
4 SU	0445 / 1133 / 1714	7.7 / 2.1 / 7.4		19 M	0019 / 0607 / 1301 / 1853	3.0 / 6.5 / 3.2 / 6.5
5 M	0004 / 0550 / 1241 / 1830	2.2 / 7.3 / 2.4 / 7.3		20 TU	0150 / 0743 / 1439 / 2027	3.1 / 6.4 / 3.2 / 6.8
6 TU	0125 / 0716 / 1411 / 2001	2.3 / 7.3 / 2.3 / 7.5		21 W	0323 / 0906 / 1559 / 2138	2.8 / 6.7 / 2.7 / 7.3
7 W	0256 / 0844 / 1539 / 2122	1.9 / 7.6 / 1.9 / 8.1		22 TH	0430 / 1005 / 1656 / 2228	2.3 / 7.3 / 2.2 / 7.8
8 TH	0418 / 0958 / 1653 / 2229	1.5 / 8.2 / 1.4 / 8.7		23 F	0519 / 1049 / 1741 / 2309	1.8 / 7.8 / 1.7 / 8.3
9 F	0525 / 1057 / 1753 / 2324	1.0 / 8.7 / 0.9 / 9.2		24 SA	0600 / 1126 / 1818 / 2343	1.4 / 8.2 / 1.3 / 8.7
10 SA	0621 / 1150 / 1845	0.6 / 9.1 / 0.6		25 SU	0635 / 1159 / 1851	1.1 / 8.6 / 1.1
11 SU	0014 / 0708 / 1237 / 1930	9.5 / 0.4 / 9.4 / 0.4		26 M	0016 / 0706 / 1232 / 1922	8.9 / 0.9 / 8.8 / 0.9
12 M	0059 / 0751 / 1320 / 2010	9.7 / 0.3 / 9.4 / 0.4		27 TU	0047 / 0737 / 1303 / 1951	9.1 / 0.8 / 9.0 / 0.8
13 TU	0140 / 0830 / 1359 / 2048	9.6 / 0.4 / 9.3 / 0.6		28 W	0118 / 0807 / 1334 / 2022	9.2 / 0.7 / 9.0 / 0.8
14 W	0217 / 0904 / 1436 / 2122	9.4 / 0.6 / 9.0 / 0.9		29 TH	0148 / 0836 / 1404 / 2050	9.1 / 0.8 / 8.9 / 0.9
15 TH	0253 / 0938 / 1510 / 2155	9.0 / 1.0 / 8.6 / 1.3		30 F	0220 / 0906 / 1437 / 2122	8.9 / 1.0 / 8.7 / 1.1
				31 SA	0253 / 0939 / 1511 / 2157	8.6 / 1.3 / 8.4 / 1.5

Chart Datum: 4.89 metres below Lallemand System (Mean Sea Level, Marseilles)

FRANCE, NORTH COAST - DIEPPE

LAT 49°56'N   LONG 1°05'E

TIMES AND HEIGHTS OF HIGH AND LOW WATERS

YEAR **1991**

TIMF ZONE **-0100**
(French Standard Time)
Subtract 1 hour for GMT
For French Summer Time add
ONE hour in non-shaded areas

SEPTEMBER

	TIME	m		TIME	m
1 SU ☾	0331 1017 1552 2240	8.1 1.7 7.9 1.9	**16** M	0415 1102 1643 2335	6.8 3.0 6.7 3.2
2 M	0418 1107 1649 2341	7.6 2.3 7.4 2.4	**17** TU	0521 1216 1808	6.3 3.5 6.4
3 TU	0528 1222 1814	7.1 2.6 7.2	**18** W	0106 0701 1359 1952	3.4 6.2 3.4 6.6
4 W	0112 0706 1405 1956	2.5 7.1 2.5 7.5	**19** TH	0246 0834 1526 2107	3.0 6.6 2.8 7.2
5 TH	0253 0841 1536 2119	2.1 7.6 1.9 8.2	**20** F	0358 0935 1624 2158	2.4 7.3 2.2 7.8
6 F	0413 0951 1645 2221	1.4 8.3 1.3 8.8	**21** SA	0447 1017 1707 2237	1.8 7.9 1.7 8.4
7 SA	0514 1046 1740 2311	0.9 8.9 0.8 9.3	**22** SU	0527 1054 1745 2312	1.4 8.4 1.3 8.8
8 SU ●	0605 1133 1827 2354	0.5 9.3 0.5 9.6	**23** M ○	0602 1127 1819 2344	1.0 8.8 1.0 9.1
9 M	0648 1215 1908	0.4 9.5 0.4	**24** TU	0636 1159 1851	0.8 9.1 0.8
10 TU	0036 0727 1254 1945	9.7 0.3 9.5 0.4	**25** W	0016 0707 1233 1923	9.3 0.7 9.2 0.7
11 W	0113 0803 1331 2020	9.6 0.4 9.3 0.6	**26** TH	0049 0738 1305 1954	9.4 0.6 9.3 0.7
12 TH	0148 0836 1405 2052	9.3 0.7 9.0 0.9	**27** F	0122 0811 1338 2027	9.3 0.7 9.2 0.8
13 F	0222 0908 1438 2123	8.9 1.1 8.6 1.3	**28** SA	0156 0844 1414 2102	9.1 1.0 8.9 1.1
14 SA	0255 0940 1512 2157	8.3 1.6 8.0 1.9	**29** SU	0233 0920 1453 2140	8.7 1.3 8.5 1.5
15 SU ☽	0331 1016 1551 2238	7.6 2.3 7.3 2.6	**30** M	0314 1002 1539 2228	8.1 1.8 7.9 2.0

OCTOBER

	TIME	m		TIME	m
1 TU ☾	0407 1058 1641 2335	7.5 2.4 7.4 2.5	**16** W	0442 1135 1722	6.4 3.4 6.6
2 W	0523 1220 1813	7.1 2.2 7.3	**17** TH	0017 0608 1304 1857	3.3 6.3 3.4 6.7
3 TH	0110 0704 1400 1952	2.4 7.2 2.4 7.7	**18** F	0150 0739 1431 2016	3.0 6.6 2.9 7.2
4 F	0246 0833 1525 2106	1.9 7.7 1.7 8.4	**19** SA	0305 0846 1535 2111	2.5 7.3 2.3 7.8
5 SA	0358 0936 1628 2202	2.4 8.4 1.2 8.9	**20** SU	0400 0934 1622 2154	1.9 7.9 1.7 8.3
6 SU	0454 1026 1718 2249	0.9 8.9 0.8 9.3	**21** M	0443 1013 1703 2232	1.4 8.8 1.3 8.8
7 M ●	0541 1110 1803 2329	0.7 9.2 0.6 9.5	**22** TU	0523 1050 1741 2309	1.1 8.9 1.0 9.1
8 TU ○	0623 1149 1842	0.5 9.3 0.6	**23** W	0600 1126 1818 2344	0.5 9.2 0.8 9.3
9 W	0009 0701 1227 1919	9.5 0.6 9.4 0.6	**24** TH	0637 1203 1855	0.7 9.3 0.7
10 TH	0045 0736 1303 1953	9.4 0.7 9.3 0.8	**25** F	0021 0713 1240 1932	9.4 0.7 9.4 0.7
11 F	0120 0809 1337 2026	9.1 0.9 9.0 1.1	**26** SA	0100 0751 1320 2010	9.3 0.8 9.3 0.8
12 SA	0154 0842 1410 2057	8.8 1.3 8.6 1.5	**27** SU	0140 0830 1400 2050	9.1 1.0 9.0 1.1
13 SU	0227 0914 1445 2130	8.2 1.8 8.1 2.0	**28** M	0223 0911 1446 2134	8.7 1.4 8.7 1.5
14 M	0302 0949 1522 2209	7.6 2.4 7.5 2.5	**29** TU	0309 0959 1536 2227	8.2 1.8 8.1 1.9
15 TU ☽	0344 1033 1610 2301	7.0 3.0 6.9 3.1	**30** W ☾	0407 1058 1641 2334	7.6 2.3 7.7 2.2
			31 TH	0521 1214 1805	7.3 2.4 7.7

NOVEMBER

	TIME	m		TIME	m
1 F	0058 0648 1341 1930	2.2 7.5 2.2 7.9	**16** SA	0039 0628 1317 1905	2.9 6.8 2.9 7.2
2 SA	0222 0807 1457 2040	1.8 7.9 1.7 8.4	**17** SU	0155 0739 1428 2010	2.6 7.2 2.5 7.6
3 SU	0330 0908 1559 2136	1.5 8.4 1.4 8.7	**18** M	0258 0838 1526 2103	2.2 7.7 2.0 8.1
4 M	0425 1000 1651 2223	1.2 8.8 1.1 9.0	**19** TU	0351 0926 1615 2149	1.7 8.3 1.5 8.6
5 TU	0514 1044 1736 2305	1.0 9.0 1.0 9.1	**20** W	0439 1011 1702 2233	1.3 8.7 1.2 8.9
6 W ●	0558 1125 1818 2344	0.9 9.1 0.9 9.1	**21** TH ○	0525 1054 1747 2316	1.1 9.1 0.9 9.1
7 TH	0638 1204 1856	0.9 9.1 0.9	**22** F	0609 1138 1831 2359	0.9 9.3 0.8 9.3
8 F	0022 0714 1241 1932	9.3 1.0 9.1 1.0	**23** SA	0654 1222 1916	0.8 9.4 0.7
9 SA	0059 0748 1316 2006	8.9 1.2 8.9 1.2	**24** SU	0045 0738 1308 2001	9.2 0.9 9.4 0.8
10 SU	0134 0823 1351 2039	8.6 1.5 8.6 1.5	**25** M	0132 0824 1355 2046	9.1 1.0 9.2 0.9
11 M	0208 0856 1425 2112	8.2 1.8 8.3 1.9	**26** TU	0219 0909 1443 2132	8.8 1.2 8.9 1.2
12 TU	0244 0929 1502 2149	7.7 2.2 7.8 2.3	**27** W	0307 0957 1533 2223	8.5 1.5 8.6 1.5
13 W	0322 1009 1545 2233	7.3 2.6 7.4 2.7	**28** TH ☾	0401 1050 1631 2319	8.0 1.8 8.3 1.7
14 TH ☽	0410 1059 1639 2329	6.9 3.0 7.1 2.9	**29** F	0503 1153 1737	7.8 2.0 8.0
15 F	0512 1203 1750	6.7 3.1 7.0	**30** SA	0027 0614 1304 1851	1.9 7.7 2.1 8.0

DECEMBER

	TIME	m		TIME	m
1 SU	0141 0728 1418 2002	1.9 7.8 2.0 8.1	**16** M	0037 0623 1311 1858	2.5 7.2 2.5 7.4
2 M	0252 0834 1524 2103	1.8 8.0 1.8 8.2	**17** TU	0147 0732 1421 2005	2.4 7.5 2.3 7.7
3 TU	0353 0930 1622 2157	1.7 8.3 1.6 8.4	**18** W	0254 0836 1526 2106	2.1 7.9 1.9 8.1
4 W	0448 1021 1713 2244	1.5 8.5 1.4 8.6	**19** TH	0357 0935 1627 2202	1.7 8.4 1.5 8.5
5 TH	0537 1107 1800 2327	1.4 8.7 1.3 8.6	**20** F	0455 1029 1723 2255	1.4 8.8 1.1 8.8
6 F ●	0620 1147 1840	1.4 8.8 1.2	**21** SA ○	0550 1120 1817 2346	1.1 9.1 0.8 9.1
7 SA	0007 0659 1225 1917	8.7 1.3 8.9 1.2	**22** SU	0642 1211 1907	0.9 9.4 0.7
8 SU	0044 0735 1302 1952	8.6 1.4 8.8 1.3	**23** M	0037 0731 1301 1955	9.2 0.7 9.5 0.6
9 M	0120 0809 1336 2026	8.5 1.5 8.7 1.4	**24** TU	0126 0818 1350 2041	9.2 0.7 9.5 0.6
10 TU	0154 0842 1410 2057	8.3 1.6 8.5 1.6	**25** W	0213 0903 1437 2124	9.1 0.8 9.3 0.8
11 W	0227 0914 1445 2130	8.0 1.8 8.2 1.8	**26** TH	0259 0946 1521 2208	8.9 1.0 9.0 1.0
12 TH	0302 0948 1521 2207	7.8 2.1 7.9 2.1	**27** F	0344 1031 1607 2254	8.6 1.3 8.7 1.4
13 F	0340 1026 1601 2247	7.5 2.3 7.7 2.3	**28** SA ☾	0433 1119 1700 2347	8.1 1.7 8.2 1.8
14 SA	0425 1110 1650 2337	7.3 2.5 7.5 2.5	**29** SU	0529 1217 1802	7.7 2.1 7.8
15 SU	0518 1206 1750	7.2 2.6 7.4	**30** M	0051 0636 1327 1914	2.2 7.5 2.3 7.5
			31 TU	0206 0752 1444 2028	2.4 7.5 2.4 7.5

Chart Datum: 4.89 metres below Lallemand System (Mean Sea Level, Marseilles)

18

DIEPPE *continued*

H.W.Hts.m.

DIEPPE

MEAN SPRING
AND NEAP CURVES

MEAN RANGES		
Springs	8·6m	———
Neaps	4·6m	- - -

Springs occur 2 days
after
New and Full Moon.

CHART DATUM

Factor

M.H.W.N.   M.H.W.S.

M.L.W.S.   M.L.W.N.

L.W.Hts.m.

L.W −4ʰ −3ʰ −2ʰ −1ʰ H.W +1ʰ +2ʰ +3ʰ +4ʰ +5ʰ +6ʰ L.W

LE TRÉPORT   10-18-23
Seine Maritime

CHARTS
Admiralty 1351, 2147; SHOM 5928, 934; ECM 1011;
Stanford 1; Imray C31
TIDES
Dover −0025; ML 5.0; Duration 0530; Zone −0100

Standard Port DIEPPE (←)

Times				Height (metres)			
HW		LW		MHWS	MHWN	MLWN	MLWS
0100	0600	0100	0700	9.3	7.2	2.6	0.7
1300	1800	1300	1900				

Differences LE TRÉPORT
+0001 +0005 +0005 +0011 +0.1   +0.2   −0.1   0.0

SHELTER
Shelter good but harbour dries. Access difficult in strong
on-shore winds. Entry channel dries — only usable from
HW∓1½. Wet basin opens from HW−1½ to HW. Signal
for opening of swing bridge — three blasts on passing
heads of jetties. Yachts lie on pontoons in NW corner of
Arrière Port.

NAVIGATION
Waypoint 50°04'.30N 01°21'.70E, 315°/135° from/to
entrance, 0.52M. Coast dries to approx 300m off the pier
heads. No navigational dangers. Entrance difficult in
strong winds: scend is caused in the Avant Port.
LIGHTS AND MARKS
Le Treport can be difficult to identify. "P" flag or W Lt
indicates entrance open. No Ldg Lts or marks.
Traffic signals shown from E jetty and entrance to
Arrière-Port.
RADIO TELEPHONE
Call: *Ovaro* VHF Ch 16; 12 (HW−2 to HW).
TELEPHONE (35)
Hr Mr 35.86.17.91; Aff Mar 35.86.08.88; CROSS
21.87.21.87; SNSM 35.86.33.71; ⌗ 35.86.15.34;
Meteo 21.05.13.55; Police 35.86.08.88; Dr 35.86.16.23;
Brit Consul 21.96.33.76.
FACILITIES
Outer Harbour M; **Arrière Port** AB, FW; **Chantier
Naval du Tréport** ☎ 35.86.12.33, ME, El, Sh, C, CH, M;
Yacht Club de la Bresle ☎ 35.86.19.93, C (3 ton), AB,
Bar; **Intermer Services** ☎ 35.50.26.42 ME, EL, Ⓔ, Sh,
CH; **Loisirs Yachting** ☎ 35.50.16.70, ME, CH, Ⓔ. **Town**
P, D, V, Gaz, R, Bar. ✉; Ⓑ; ⇌; ✈ (Dieppe).
Ferry UK — Dieppe—Newhaven.

LE TRÉPORT continued

ST VALÉRY-SUR-SOMME
Somme
10-18-24

CHARTS
Admiralty 2612; SHOM 3800; ECM 1011; Stanford 1; Imray C31
TIDES
Dover −0020; ML −; Duration −; Zone −0100

Standard Port DIEPPE (←)

Times				Height (metres)			
HW		LW		MHWS	MHWN	MLWN	MLWS
0100	0600	0100	0700	9.3	7.2	2.6	0.7
1300	1800	1300	1900				

Differences ST VALÉRY-SUR-SOMME
+0028 +0040   No data +0.7   +0.8   No data
LE HOURDEL and LE CROTOY
+0021 +0026   No data +0.7   +0.7   No data

SHELTER
The bay is open to W and can be dangerous in onshore winds over force 6.
The three harbours, St Valéry-sur-Somme, Le Crotoy and Le Hourdel, are very well protected. Yachts can
(1) dry out on hard sand or moor alongside at Le Hourdel
(2) go into marina at St Valéry (max. draught 2.5 m). Access HW∓2
(3) go into marina at Le Crotoy when tidal range at Dover exceeds 4.4 m (max. draught 1.6 m). See 10.18.29.
(4) go into Abbeville Canal at St. Valéry (max. draught 3.3 m). Entry by prior arrangement and in daylight only.
NAVIGATION
Waypoint 'ATSO' N cardinal buoy, VQ, 50°14'.00N 01°28'.50E, about 1M W of buoyed channel (shifts). The whole estuary dries up to 3 M seaward from Le Hourdel. The landfall buoy N cardinal VQ 'ATSO' should be closed and entrance commenced at HW−2. Departure at HW−1. Channels are constantly changing but buoys are moved as necessary. The sands build up in ridges offshore but inside Pt du Hourdel are generally flat except where the River Somme and minor streams scour their way to the sea. If range of tide exceeds 4.1 m Dover there is sufficient water over the sands inside Pt du Hourdel from HW−1 to HW+½ for vessels with less than 1.5 m draught. At all other times buoys marking the channels must be followed in strict sequence. There are fishing fleets based at all three harbours and small cargo vessels occasionally navigate to the commercial quay inside the lock to the Abbeville Canal.
LIGHTS AND MARKS
Lt Ho Cayeux-sur-Mer FlR 6s 32m 22M (off chartlet). Twenty-nine numbered buoys mark twisting channel up to Division Buoy YBY. Starboard hand green cone buoys (odd numbers) port hand red can buoys (even numbers). Buoys 9, 15 and 23 are lit. From division buoy, buoys C1 to C10 run N and E to Le Crotoy; buoys 39 to 50 S and SE to St Valery-sur-Somme.
LE HOURDEL Only landmark is Lt Ho Oc(3) WG 12s 19m. Channel unmarked. Follow St Valéry channel buoys until Lt Ho bears 270°, then head in.
ST VALERY-SUR-SOMME From Division Buoy, buoyed channel numbered up to 50. Starboard hand marks become beacons on submerged training wall the end of which is lit, Iso G 4s; then four Bns on end of groynes. Hut on lattice tower Iso G 4s marks beginning of tree lined promenade with port hand beacons marking submerged training wall.
W tower on beginning of Digue du Large Fl R 4s.
LE CROTOY — See 10.18.29.
RADIO TELEPHONE
VHF Ch 09 HW∓2.
TELEPHONE (22)
St Valery Hr Mr 22.26.91.64; Aff Mar 22.27.81.44; ⌗ 22.24.04.75; Lock (canal) 22.60.80.23; CROSS 21.87.21.87; Meteo 21.31.52.23; Police 22.60.82.08; Dr 22.26.92.25; Brit Consul 21.96.33.76.

18

ST VALÉRY-SUR-SOMME *continued*

FACILITIES
EC Monday. **Marina** (280+30 visitors) ☎ 22.26.91.64, C
(6 ton), Slip, R, ☐, Bar; **CNMF** ☎ 22.26.82.20, Sh, Ⓔ;
Latitude 50 ☎ 22.26.82.06, ME, El, CH, Ⓔ, charts;
Grandsaier ☎ 22.26.88.80, CH; **Valois** ☎ 22.60.81.36,
ME; **Town** P, D, CH, V, Gaz, R, Bar, ✉; Ⓑ;
≋ (Noyelles-sur-Mer); ✈ (Le Touquet).
Ferry UK — Boulogne—Dover/Folkestone.

Sh, SM; **Technical Composite** ☎ 21.05.62.97, BY.
Town P, D, V, Gaz, R, Bar. ✉; Ⓑ; ≋; ✈.
Ferry UK — Boulogne—Dover/Folkestone.

LE TOUQUET   10-18-25
Pas de Calais

CHARTS
Admiralty 2451; SHOM 6795; ECM 1011; Stanford 1, 9;
Imray C31

TIDES
Dover −0010; ML 4.8; Duration 0520; Zone −0100

Standard Port DIEPPE (←)

Times				Height (metres)			
HW		LW		MHWS	MHWN	MLWN	MLWS
0100	0600	0100	0700	9.3	7.2	2.6	0.7
1300	1800	1300	1900				

Differences LE TOUQUET

+0012		No data		−0.3	0.0	+0.2	+0.3

SHELTER
Good except in strong W winds. Yacht moorings, which
dry, are to stbd after passing Pt de Touquet. There are
plans to build a dam across the mouth of the R Canche,
with locks. Marina at Étaples — see 10.18.29.

NAVIGATION
Waypoint 50°35′.00N 01°31′.80E, 308°/128° from/to
Camiers Lt, 3.8M. Entrance is not easy — local pilots or
fishermen are available. Best entrance is at HW−1. In W
winds the sea breaks heavily a long way out and entry
should not be attempted. The channel is always changing
and buoys are moved accordingly. Beware stranded wreck
2M NW of Le Touquet-Paris Plage Lt Ho, marked by Lt
buoy.

LIGHTS AND MARKS
Good landmarks are the Terres de Tourmont, a conspic
range 175m high, visible for 25 miles. Le Touquet is at the
S end of this range. Entrance between Pt de Lornel and
Pt de Touquet. Pick up buoyed channel in R section of
Camiers Lt. Pt du Touquet light is Y tower, Brown band,
W & G top — Fl (2) 10s 54m 25M.

RADIO TELEPHONE
VHF Ch 21; 16.

TELEPHONE (21)
Hr Mr 21.05.12.77; Aff Mar Etaples 21.94.61.50; Meteo
21.05.13.55; ✇ 21.05.01.72; CROSS 21.87.21.87;
Police 21.94.60.17; Dr 21.05.14.42; Brit Consul
21.96.33.76.

FACILITIES
Cercle Nautique du Touquet ☎ 21.05.12.77, Slip, M, P,
ME, D, FW, C, CH, R, Bar; **Marina** (Etaples — see
10.18.29), AB, FW, P, D, AC; **Demoury** ☎ 21.84.51.76,

BOULOGNE-SUR-MER
Pas de Calais
10-18-26

CHARTS
Admiralty 1892, 438; SHOM 6436, 6682, 6795; ECM 1010,
1011; Stanford 1, 9; Imray C31, C8

TIDES
Dover 0000; ML 5.0; Duration 0515; Zone −0100

Standard Port DIEPPE (←)

Times				Height (metres)			
HW		LW		MHWS	MHWN	MLWN	MLWS
0100	0600	0100	0700	9.3	7.2	2.6	0.7
1300	1800	1300	1900				

Differences BOULOGNE

+0015	+0026	+0037	+0036	−0.4	0.0	+0.2	+0.4

SHELTER
Good except in strong NE winds. Turbulent water when R
Liane in spate. Entrance possible in most weathers and at
any state of tide. Yachts secure to pontoons in SW side
of tidal basin alongside Quai Chanzy. Max length 10 m
(over 10 m apply before arrival). Yacht berths tend to silt
up.

NAVIGATION
Waypoint 50°44′.50N 01°33′.00E, 270°/090° from/to
Digue Carnot Lt, 0.72M. Very busy commercial passenger
and fishing port. Respect warnings and instructions given
by harbour lights. There are no navigational dangers and
entrance is easily identified and is well marked. Beware
heavy wash from fishing boats. Also beware Digue Nord
which partially covers at HW. Keep W and S of N light
tower, Fl(2)R 6s.

LIGHTS AND MARKS
Ldg Lts 123° lead towards R Liane and marina. Besides
normal traffic signals, special signals apply as follows: —

*G	}	Movement suspended except for vessels with
W G	}	special permission to enter
R	}	
*G	}	Movement suspended except for vessels with
W R	}	special permission to leave inner and
R	}	outer harbour
*G	}	Movement suspended except for vessels with
W R	}	special permission to leave inner harbour
R R	}	

*Normal light signal prohibiting entry and departure.
Two Bu Lts (hor) mean sluicing from R Liane.

RADIO TELEPHONE
VHF Ch 12 16 (H24).

BOULOGNE continued

TELEPHONE (21)

Hr Mr 21.30.10.00; Hr Mr Plaisance 21.31.70.01; Harbour office 21.30.90.46; Aff Mar 21.30.53.23; CROSS 21.87.21.87; SNSM 21.31.42.58; ⌗ 21.30.14.24; Meteo 21.31.52.23; Auto 21.33.82.55; Police 21.31.75.17; Ⓗ 21.31.92.13; Brit Consul 21.30.25.11.

FACILITIES

Marina (350 + 50 visitors) ☎ 21.31.70.01, M, L, FW, C (1 ton); **Quai Gambetta** M, P*, D*, L, FW, AB, V, R, Bar; **Baude Electronique** ☎ 21.30.01.15, Ⓔ; **Opale Marine** ☎ 21.30.36.19, ME, El, Sh, M, CH, Divers; **Angelo** ☎ 21.31.37.61, CH; **Librairie Duminy** ☎ 21.30.06.75, SHOM; **YC Boulonnais** ☎ 21.31.80.67, C, Bar. **Town** P, D, FW, ME, El, Sh, CH, V, Gaz, R, Bar. ✉; Ⓑ; ⇌; ✈ (Le Touquet/Calais).
Ferry UK—Dover/Folkestone.
*Obtainable from Societé Maritime Carburante Liquide.

CALAIS 10-18-27
Pas de Calais

CHARTS

Admiralty 1892, 1352; SHOM 6474, 6651, 6681; ECM 1010; Stanford 1, 19; Imray C8

TIDES

Dover +0025; ML 4.1; Duration 0525; Zone −0100

Standard Port DIEPPE (←)

Times				Height (metres)			
HW		LW		MHWS	MHWN	MLWN	MLWS
0100	0600	0100	0700	9.3	7.2	2.5	0.7
1300	1800	1300	1900				

Differences CALAIS

+0043 +0057 +0105 +0054 −2.2 −1.3 −0.5 +0.2

SHELTER

Shelter is very good especially in the marina. Bar is dredged to 4.5m but is liable to build up in heavy weather. Entrance is difficult in strong NW to NE winds. Enter Bassin Carnot if headed for the French canals otherwise use Bassin de l'Ouest, the marina.

NAVIGATION

Waypoint 50°58'.50N 01°49'.90E, 298°/118° from/to Jetée Ouest Lt, 0.43M. Entrance is relatively easy but beware the Ridens de la Rade, about 1 M N of entrance, a sandbank which shoals in places to about 0.75m and seas break on it. Entrance is well marked but there is a great deal of shipping, including ferries, which can be hazardous. Yachts are required to enter/leave under power. It is forbidden to tack in entrance channel.

LIGHTS AND MARKS

From a point ¼M SE of CA 10 buoy, Fl(2) R 6s, the main Lt Ho, Fl(4) 15s, bearing 140° leads through entrance. Normal entry signals with following additions.

R Lt = indicates ferry leaving   movements
G Lt = ferry entering   prohibited
Lights on Tr of Gare Maritime are for car ferries and cargo vessels only. Yachts may not enter or leave when at least three Lts are on. They may follow a car ferry entering or leaving but must keep to the stbd side of the fairway. One R Lt denotes the presence of a dredger and does not mean movement is forbidden.

Bassin Carnot
Lock signals, gates open HW −1½ to HW +¾.
2 G Lt hor = entry from Arrière Port permitted.
2 R Lt hor = entry from Arrière Port prohibited.
1 G Lt   = entry from basin to Arrière Port permitted.
1 R Lt   = entry from basin to Arrière Port prohibited.
2 blasts = request permission to enter Bassin Carnot.
4 blasts = request permission to enter Bassin de l'Ouest.

Bassin de l'Ouest
Orange Lt = 10 mins before opening of lock.
Red Lt   = All movement prohibited.
Green Lt = Movement authorised.
Dock gates and bridge open HW −1½, HW and HW +½. (Sat and Sun HW −2 and HW +1).

CALAIS

CALAIS *continued*

RADIO TELEPHONE

VHF Ch 12 16 (H24). Hoverport Ch 20 (occas). Carnot
Lock Ch 12 (occas). Cap Gris Nez, Channel Navigation
Information Service (CNIS), call: *Gris Nez Traffic* Ch 16 **69**
79 (H24). Information broadcasts in English and French on
Ch 11, at H + 10, and also at H + 25 when visibility is less
than 2 M.

TELEPHONE (21)

Hr Mr 21.96.31.20; Aff Mar 21.34.52.70; Pilot (Quai de la
Gare Maritime) 21.96.40.18; CROSS 21.87.21.87; SNSM
21.96.40.18; Port de Plaisance 21.34.55.23;
⌗ 21.34.75.40; Meteo 21.31.52.23; Auto 21.33.82.55;
Polioo 21.96.74.17; Dr 21.96.31.20; Ⓗ 21.97.99.60;
Brit Consul 21.96.33.76.

FACILITIES

Marina (135 + 100 visitors) ☎ 21.34.55.23, D, FW, C
(6 ton), BH (3 ton), AC, CH, Gaz, R, ▢, Sh, SM, V, Bar;
Access HW − 1½ to HW + ½. **Bassin du Paradis** AB,
Grid; **YC de Calais** ☎ 21.34.55.23, M, P, Bar; **Ebaine**
☎ 21.34.69.01, CH, SM; **Godin Moteurs** ☎ 21.96.29.97,
ME; **Marinerie** ☎ 21.34.47.83, CH. **Nautic-Sport**
☎ 21.36.41.03 ME, CH; **Town** CH, V, Gaz, R, Bar. ✉;
Ⓑ; ⇌; ✈.
Ferry UK−Dover.

DUNKERQUE   10-18-28
Nord

CHARTS

Admiralty 1350, 323; SHOM 7057, 6651; ECM 1010;
Stanford 1, 19; Imray C30

TIDES

Dover +0050; ML 3.2; Duration 0530; Zone −0100

Standard Port DIEPPE (←)

Times				Height (metres)			
HW		LW		MHWS	MHWN	MLWN	MLWS
0100	0600	0100	0700	9.3	7.2	2.5	0.7
1300	1800	1300	1900				

Differences DUNKERQUE

+0059	+0122	+0121	+0108	−3.5	−2.4	−1.1	−0.1

SHELTER

Good shelter and harbour is available at all states of tide
and weather. Yachts must use E of harbour; all pleasure
craft are prohibited from entering W harbour. YC
pontoons are ¾ M down E side of harbour, or proceed
through Ecluse Trystram and under two opening bridges
to municipal marina in Bassin du Commerce.

DUNKERQUE *continued*

NAVIGATION

Waypoint Port Est 51°03'.90N 02°21'.00E, 355°/175° from/to Jetée Ouest Lt, 0.20M. From the W, fetch the Dunkerque Lanby 5M N of Calais, thence to DKA safe water pillar Lt Buoy, and then follow series of DW Lt buoys past Dunkerque Ouest to buoy DW 29, ½M WNW of ent. From the E, the series of E Lt buoys lead S of Banc Hills from the Nieuwpoort Bank W Cardinal Lt buoy. There is no bar. Strong currents reach about 3½ kn. This is a busy commercial port. Entrance is easy in most weathers, but fresh winds from NW to NE cause heavy seas at entrance to Avant Port and scend in harbour.

LIGHTS AND MARKS

Two sets of Ldg Lts (there are others in the Commercial Port):—

(1) Two Lts 179° (F Vi) giving entrance line between the E and W jetties. A second pair, with common rear, lead 185°.

(2) Two Lts in line at 137° (Oc(2) 6s) lead down to Port d'Echouage.

Normal entry signals with following additions, shown from head of Jetée Ouest

R ⎫
W ⎬ Prohibition does not apply to tugs,
R W ⎭ warships or fishing vessels

R R ⎫
W ⎬ Prohibition does not apply to
R ⎭ tankers or vessels with dangerous cargoes.

Lock signals (H24) are shown at Ecluse Watier and consist of three horizontal pairs disposed vertically. Middle pair refer to Ecluse Watier and lower pair to Ecluse Trystram:

2FG(hor) = lock open
2FR(hor) = lock closed

Lock signals at each lock:

2FG(hor) = lock ready
2FR(hor) = lock in use, no entry
FG FlG = enter and secure on side of flashing light
FW over = slack water, both gates open; enter lock.
2FG(hor)

RADIO TELEPHONE

VHF Ch 12 16 **73** (H24). Ecluse Trystram Ch 73.
YC Ch 09.

TELEPHONE (28)

Hr Mr 28.65.99.22; Port Control 28.29.70.70; Aff Mar 28.66.56.14; CROSS 21.87.21.87; SNSM 28.63.23.60; ⌗ 28.65.14.73; Meteo 28.66.45.25; Auto 28.63.44.44; Police 28.64.51.09; Ⓗ 28.66.70.01; Brit Consul 28.66.11.98.

FACILITIES

YC Mer du Nord Marina (250 ｜ 40 visitors) ☎ 28.66.79.90, Slip, D, P, FW, C (4½ ton), BH (15 ton), AC, ME, SM, R, Bar, Access H24. **Bassin du Commerce** ☎ 28.66.11.06, M, D, L, FW, CH, AB; **Port de Pêche** Slip, P, D, FW, ME, El, Sh, CH, V, R, Bar; **FMC** ☎ 28.59.32.32, SHOM; **Leroy Garage** ☎ 28.66.82.37, P, D; **Flandre-Chantier** ☎ 28.66.49.62, M, ME, El, Ⓔ, Sh, CH; **Norbert-Peche** ☎ 28.24.35.14, ME, El, Sh, CH; **Bleu Marine** ☎ 28.63.93.33 ME, El, Ⓔ, Sh, CH; **Marine Diffusion** ☎ 25.59.18.19 ME, El, Sh, M, CH; **Nord Marine** ☎ 28.66.98.75 ME, Ⓔ; **Town** P, D, V, Gaz, R, Bar. ✉; Ⓑ; ⇌, ✈ (Calais).
Ferry UK—Ramsgate/Dover.

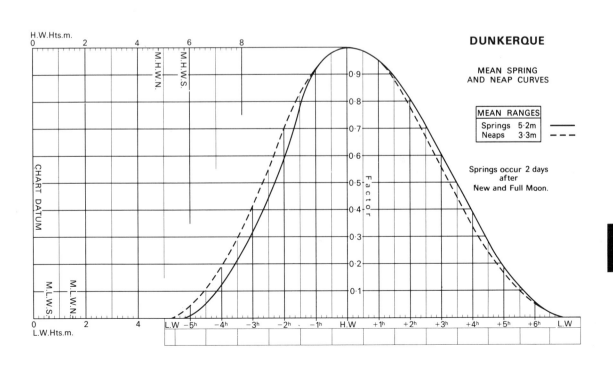

DUNKERQUE

MEAN SPRING AND NEAP CURVES

MEAN RANGES	
Springs 5·2m	——
Neaps 3·3m	- - -

Springs occur 2 days after New and Full Moon.

18

MINOR HARBOURS AND ANCHORAGES   10.18.29

ILES St MARCOUF, Manche, 49°30' N, 1°09' W, Zone −0100, Admty chart 2073; SHOM 847. For tides, see 10.18.11. There are two islands, Ile de Terre and to the N, Ile du Large. The former is a bird sanctuary, the latter has a small dinghy harbour on the W side. Anchor SW or SE of Ile du Large or SE or NE of the Ile de Terre. Both islands surrounded by drying rocks. Ile du Large Lt, VQ(3) 5s 18m 9M. Both islands are uninhabited and there are no facilities.

ISIGNY-SUR-MER, Calvados, 49°19' N, 1°06' W, Zone −0100, Admty chart 2073, SHOM 847. HW −0230 on Dover (GMT), −0025 on Le Havre (zone −0100). See 10.18.11. The channel is buoyed from the RWVS buoy NW of the Roches de Grandcamp to breakwaters (marked by Bns); best to start from outer buoy HW−2½. Where channel divides, take E leg up to Isigny. Ldg Lts 173° lead up between the breakwaters, front Oc(2+1) 12s 7m 18M, intens 171°-175°. Rear, 600m from front, Oc(2+1) 12s 19m 18M, intens 171°-175°, synchronised with front. Access difficult with strong NW winds. Berth on SW side ¼M N of town. Facilities: Hr Mr ☎ 31.22.00.40; Aff.Mar. ☎ 31.22.03.11. **Quay** D, FW, P, Slip; **Club Nautique d'Isigny** AB, C (2, 5, 7 ton) Bar, R; **Isigny Garage** ☎ 31.22.02.33. El, ME, Sh; **Miquelot Marine** ☎ 31.22.10.67 ME, El, Sh; **Town** ⒷBar, ✉, R, V.

CAEN, Calvados, 49°10' N, 0°19' W, Zone −0100, Admty chart 1349, SHOM 7055. HW depths sp 7.2m, np 5.8m. Proceed up Caen Canal from Ouistreham, 8M see 10.18.15. Report to lock control Tr at Ouistreham to pay and arrange. Speed limit 7 kn; passage only possible by day. Three bridges, at Bénouville (2½M from locks), Hérouville (5M) and Calix (6½M), each show G Lt when passage clear. Seaward bound vessels have right of way. Marina at Bassin St Pierre near city centre. VHF Ch 12 68. Facilities: Hr Mr ☎ 31.52.12.88. Aff Mar. ☎ 31.85.40.55. ⌗ ☎ 31.86.61.50; **Marina** (64 visitors) ☎ 31.93.74.47, P, D, ME, Sh, El, AB, FW; **Clinique du Bateau** ☎ 31.84.48.63 ME, El, Sh, SM, CH; **Quay** FW; **City** Ⓑ, Bar, Ⓗ, ✉, R, ⇌, V.

CABOURG, Calvados, 49°19' N, 0°07' W, Zone −0100, Admty charts 2146, 1892, SHOM 6928, 890, 6614. Tides for Dives-sur-Mer. See 10.18.15. HW −0135 on Dover (GMT), −0032 on Le Havre (zone −0100); HW height −0.4m on Le Havre; ML 4.1m. Shelter good but entrance rough in winds from NW to NE. Entrance Lt, between Dives and Houlgate, Oc(2+1) WRG 12s 6m 12/9M G124°-150°, W150°-157°, R157°-193°. Entrance buoys, R can and G conical are moved according to shifting channel. There is a landing place at Dives at Société des Régates de la Dive. Channel from Dives to Cabourg is buoyed and accessible approx HW∓2. Yachts can go alongside jetty in front of Cabourg YC. Facilities: Aff Mar 31.91.23.55; Harbour run by Cabourg YC ☎ 31.91.23.55, AB, Bar, M, Slip; **Cabourg Marine** ☎ 31.91.69.08, CH, ME, El, Sh, M, Ⓔ, BY; **Town** Bar, Ⓑ, ✉, R, V.

ROUEN, Seine Maritime, 49°29' N, 01°05' E, Zone −0100. Admty charts 2880, 2994; SHOM 6117. HW +0330 on Dover (GMT), +0430 on Le Havre (zone −0100); HW height −0.1m on Le Havre; ML 6.2m; Duration 0400. See 10.18.18 for Seine navigation. Yacht navigation forbidden from ½ hr after sunset to ½ hr before sunrise. Yachts use Bassin St Gervais, on N bank, berth SE side for mast removal or replacements (max stay 48 hrs); berth in La Halte de Plaisance de Rouen NE side of Ile Lacroix. VHF 11 13 73 74 call *Rouen Port Capitainerie*. Facilities: Hr Mr 35.88.81.55; Aff Mar 35.98.53.98; ⌗ 35.98.27.60; Meteo 35.80.11.44; **Bassin St Gervais** C (3 to 25 ton); FW; **La Halte de Plaisance de Rouen** (50) ☎ 35.88.00.00, FW, AC, Slip, C (4 ton); **Villetard** ☎ 35.88.00.00, ME, El, Sh, P, D, CH; **Rouen YC** ☎ 35.66.52.52; **Eponville Nautic** ☎ 35.72.28.24, ME, El, Ⓔ, Sh, CH.

LE CROTOY, Somme, 50°13' N, 1°37' E, Zone −0100, Admty chart 2612, SHOM 3800. HW −0020 on Dover (GMT), −0035 on Dieppe (zone −0100); HW height +0.7m on Dieppe. See 10.18.24. It is on the N side of R Somme estuary, which dries. Access when tidal range at Dover exceeds 4.4m. Max draught 1.6m. Follow buoyed channel for St Valery-sur-Somme until the Division Buoy YBY, from where Le Crotoy channel runs N and E marked by small R and G buoys numbered C1 to C10. Moor to the S side of S pontoon and check with YC. Access to non-tidal basin HW−1½ to HW+2. Le Crotoy Lt, Oc(2)R 6s 19m 9M, vis 285°-135°. Yacht harbour W side, Fl R 2s 4m 2M. E side Fl G 2s 4m 2M. Facilities: Hr Mr ☎ 22.27.81.59. ⌗ ☎ 22.27.50.36. **Quay** FW, C (3.5 ton); **YC Nautique de la Baie de Somme** ☎ 22.27.83.11, M, FW, Slip, Bar; **Marina Plaisance Baie de Somme** (280) ☎ 22.27.86.05, FW, CH, El, M, ME, Sh; **Nautique Côte d'Opale** ☎ 22.27.86.47 ME, El, Ⓔ, Sh, CH; **Town** Ⓑ, Bar, D, P, ✉, R, ⇌, V.

ÉTAPLES, Pas de Calais, 50°32' N, 1°38' E, Zone −0100, Admty chart 2451, SHOM 6795. HW 0000 on Dover (GMT), +0012 on Dieppe (zone −0100); HW height −0.3m on Dieppe; ML 4.8m; Duration 0520. See 10.18.25. Very good shelter but entry to R Canche should not be attempted in strong on-shore winds. Access HW∓2. Channel in river marked by posts between sunken training walls to Étaples, where shoal draft boats can lie afloat on pontoons at small marina just below the bridge. Alternatively yachts which can take the ground can dry out on sand opposite the YC at Le Touquet. Whole estuary dries. Camiers Lt Oc(2) WRG 6s 17m 9/6M. Facilities: Hr Mr ☎ 21.94.74.26; Aff Mar. ☎ 21.94.61.50. **Marina** (60+15 visitors), FW, AC; **Quay** C (3 ton), FW, Slip; **Centre Nautique YC** ☎ 21.94.74.26. Bar, Slip; **Agence Nautique du Nord** ☎ 21.94.26.55. CH, El, Ⓔ, M, ME, Sh; **ETS Lamour** ☎ 21.94.61.21, D; **Town** Ⓑ, Bar, D, P, ✉, R, ⇌, V.

GRAVELINES, Nord, 51°01' N, 2°06' E, Zone −0100, Admty chart 323, SHOM 6501, 6651. HW +0045 on Dover (GMT), +0100 on Dieppe (zone −0100); HW height −2.8m on Dieppe; ML 3.1m; Duration 0520. See 10.18.27. Good shelter but bar dries; entry should not be attempted in strong on-shore winds. Entrance between Grand Fort Philippe and Petit Fort Philippe. Beware strong tidal stream across ent to the E, at HW. Safest entry HW−1. Keep to W entering and to E when inside. Yachts may take the bottom or go into the yacht harbour to W of town, available HW∓1. Harbour dries but is soft mud. E Jetty Lt Fl(3)R 12s 5m 4M. W jetty Fl(2)WG 6s 14m 9/6M; vis W317°-327°, G078°-085°, W085°-244°. Facilities: Aff Mar. ☎ 28.23.06.12. **Bassin Vaubin** ☎ 28.23.06.12, C (1.5 ton to 15 ton); **Yacht Club Gravelines** ☎ 28.23.14.68 M, C (10 ton); **MER (Marine et Reparations)** ☎ 28.23.14.68. CH, El, M, ME, Sh; **Town** Ⓑ, Bar, D, P, ✉, R, ⇌, V.

AGENTS WANTED

Berwick-on-Tweed
Mallaig
Loch Sunart
Loch Aline
Fishguard
Kenmare River

Large number of French Ports

Rotterdam
Norderney
Dornumersiel
Langeoog
Wangerooge
Hooksiel
Bremerhaven

If you are interested in becoming our agent please write to the Editors and get your free copy annually. You do not have to be a resident in a port to be the agent but at least a fairly regular visitor.

VOLVO PENTA SERVICE

Sales and service centres in area 19
Names and addresses of Volvo Penta dealers in
this area are available from:

BELGIUM **Volvo Penta Belgium,** Wolvwelaan 9 B-1800 Vilvoorde Tel (02)
254-14-79, Telex 65249, Volvo BMB.
NETHERLANDS **Nebim Handelmaatschappij BV,** Postbus 195, 3640
Ad Mijdrecht Tel 02979-80111, Telex 15505 NEHANL.

Area 19

Belgium and the Netherlands
Nieuwpoort to Delfzijl

**VOLVO
PENTA**

19

10.19.3   AREA 19 TIDAL STREAMS

5 Hours before HW Dover (0420 after HW H van Holland)

4 Hours before HW Dover (0520 after HW H van Holland)

3 Hours before HW Dover (0605 before HW H van Holland)

2 Hours before HW Dover (0505 before HW H van Holland)

1 Hour before HW Dover (0405 before HW H van Holland)

HW Dover (0305 before HW H van Holland)

North-eastward 10.20.3   North-westward 10.4.3 10.5.3

1 Hour after HW Dover (0205 before HW H van Holland)

2 Hours after HW Dover (0105 before HW H van Holland)

3 Hours after HW Dover (0005 before HW H van Holland)

4 Hours after HW Dover (0055 after HW H van Holland)

5 Hours after HW Dover (0155 after HW H van Holland)

6 Hours after HW Dover (0255 after HW H van Holland)

19

10.19.4 LIGHTS, FOG SIGNALS AND WAYPOINTS

Abbreviations used below are given in 10.0.3. Principal lights are in **bold** print, places in CAPITALS, and light-vessels, light floats and Lanbys in *CAPITAL ITALICS*. Unless otherwise stated lights are white. m—elevation in metres; M—nominal range in n. miles. Fog signals are in *italics*. Useful waypoints are underlined use those on land with care. See 4.2.2.

BELGIUM AND NETHERLANDS

WEST HINDER LT V 51°23'.08N 02°26'.40E Fl(4) 30s 14m **17M**; R hull, 2 masts; RC; *Horn Mo(U) 30s.*
Oost-Dyck Lt Buoy 51°21'.55N 02°31'.20E QG; stbd-hand mark; *Whis* .
A-Zuid Lt Buoy 51°21'.50N 02°37'.00E Fl(3)G 10s; stbd- hand mark.
A-Noord Lt Buoy 51°23'.50N 02°37'.00E Fl(4)R 20s; port-hand mark.
Kwintebank Lt Buoy 51°21'.75N 02°43'.00E Q; N cardinal mark; *Whis.*
Middelkirkebank Lt Buoy 51°18'.25N 02°42'.80E FlG 5s; stbd-hand mark.
Middelkirkebank N Lt Buoy 51°20'.87N 02°46'.40E Q; N cardinal mark.
Akkaert SW Lt Buoy 51°22'.30N 02°46'.40E Q(9) 15s; W cardinal mark; *Whis* .
Midden Akkaert Lt Buoy 51°24'.23N 02°53'.50E VQ(3) 5s; E cardinal mark.
Goote Bank Lt Buoy 51°27'.00N 02°52'.70E Q(3) 10s; E cardinal mark; *Whis.*
Trapegeer Lt Buoy 51°08'.45N 02°34'.45E FlG 10s; stbd-hand mark; *Bell* .
Den Oever Wreck Lt Buoy 51°09'.20N 02°39'.50E Q; N cardinal mark.
Nieuwpoortbank Lt Buoy 51°10'.21N 02°36'.16E Q(9) 15s; W cardinal mark; *Whis.*
Weststroombank Lt Buoy 51°11'.39N 02°43'.15E Fl(4)R 20s; port-hand mark.

NIEUWPOORT.

East pier, near root Fl(2) R 14s 26m **21M**; R Tr, W bands.
E pier, head FR 11m 10M; W Tr; vis 025°-250°, 307°-347°; *Horn Mo(K) 30s.* West pier head FG 11m 9M; W Tr; vis 025°-250°, 284°-324°; RC; *Bell (2) 10s.*
Zuidstroombank Lt Buoy 51°12'.33N 02°47'.50E FlR 5s; port-hand mark.
Middelkirkebank S Lt Buoy 51°14'.78N 02°42'.00E Q(9)R 15s; port-hand mark.
Oostendebank West Lt Buoy 51°16'.25N 02°44'.85E Q(9) 15s; W cardinal mark; *Whis.*
Oostendebank Oost Lt Buoy 51°17'.36N 02°52'.00E Fl(4)R 20s; port-hand mark.
Nautica Ena Wreck Lt Buoy 51°18'.12N 02°52'.85E Q; N cardinal mark.
Wenduinebank West Lt Buoy 51°17'.30N 02°52'.87E Q(9) 15s; W cardinal mark; *Whis.*
Buitenstroombank Lt Buoy 51°15'.20N 02°51'.80E Q; N cardinal mark; *Whis.*
Binnenstroombank Lt Buoy 51°14'.50N 02°53'.73E Q(3) 10s; E cardinal mark.

OOSTENDE.

Oostende Fl(3) 10s 63m **27M**; W Tr; obsc 069°-071°; RC.
West pier head 51°14'.36N 02°55'.12E FG 12m 10M; W column; vis 057°-327°; *Bell (1) 4s.*
East pier head FR 13m 12M; W Tr; vis 333°-243°; *Horn Mo(OE) 30s.* QY Lt at signal mast when channel closed.

Ldg Lts 128°, both FR 4M on W framework Trs, R bands; v 051°-201°.
A1 Lt Buoy 51°21'.70N 02°58'.10E LFl 10s; safe water mar *Whis.*
Oostendebank Noord Lt Buoy 51°21'.25N 02°53'.00E Q; N cardinal mark; *Whis.*
A1 bis Lt Buoy 51°21'.70N 02°58'.10E LFl 10s; safe wate mark; *Whis.*
SW Wandelaar Lt Buoy 51°22'.00N 03°01'.00E Fl(4)R 20s port-hand mark.
Wenduine Bank N Lt Buoy 51°21'.50N 03°02'.70E QG; stbc hand mark.
Wenduine Bank E Lt Buoy 51°18'.85N 03°01'.70E QR; port hand mark.
A2 Lt Buoy 51°22'.50N 03°07'.05E Iso 8s; safe water mark *Whis.*

BLANKENBERGE.

Comte Jean Jetty Oc(2) 8s 30m **20M**; W Tr, B top; vis 065° 245°.
Ldg Lts 134° both FR 3M; R crosses on masts.
West mole head FG 14m 11M; W Tr; intens 065°-290°, unin tens 290°-335°.
East pier head FR 12m 11M; W Tr; vis 290°-245°; *Bell (2) 15s.*

ZEEBRUGGE APPROACHES.

Scheur 1 Lt Buoy 51°23'.18N 03°00'.15E FlG 5s; stbd-hand mark.
Scheur 2 Lt Buoy 51°23'.38N 02°58'.20E Fl(4)R 15s; port-hand mark
Scheur 3 Lt Buoy 51°24'.35N 03°02'.90E Q; N cardinal mark; *Whis.*
Scheur 5 Lt Buoy 51°23'.73N 03°05'.90E FlG 5s; stbd-hand mark.
Scheur-Zand Lt Buoy 51°23'.70N 03°07'.68E Q(3) 10s; E cardinal mark.
Zand Lt Buoy 51°22'.50N 03°10'.12E QG; stbd-hand mark.
Wielingen Zand Lt Buoy 51°22'.60N 03°10'.80E Q(9) 15s; W cardinal mark.
Bol van Heist Lt Buoy 51°23'.15N 03°12'.05E Q(6)LFlR 15s; port-hand mark.
MOW3 Tide Gauge 51°23'.45N 03°12'.00E Fl(5)Y 20s; special mark; *Whis*; Racon.

SCHEUR CHANNEL (continued).

HAAZ,
Droogte van Schooneveld 51°25'.50N 03°09'.00E Fl(4)Y 20s 12m 2M; measuring Bn with platform; Ra refl.
Scheur 7 Lt Buoy 51°24'.00N 03°10'.50E FlG 5s; stbd-hand mark.
Scheur 9 Lt Buoy 51°24'.45N 03°15'.05E QG; stbd-hand mark.
Scheur 12 Lt Buoy 51°24'.70N 03°18'.50E FlR 5s; port-hand mark.
Scheur- Wielingen Lt Buoy 51°24'.26N 03°18'.00E Q; N cardinal mark.

ZEEBRUGGE..

West breakwater Oc G 7s 31m 7M.
East breakwater Oc R 7s 31m 7M.
Heist, mole head Oc WR 15s 22m , **R18M**; grey Tr; vis W068°-145°, R145° 212°, W212° 296°; RC; *Horn (31) 90s.*
Ldg Lts 136°. Front and rear Oc 5s 8M.
Ldg Lts 154°. Front OcWR 6s 3M; vis W135°-160°, R160°-169°. Rear, 520m from front, Oc 6s 3M; vis 150°-162°, synchronised.
Ldg Lts 235°. Front QR 10m 5M; X on mast. Rear, 155m from front, QR 14m 5M; X on mast, synchronised.
Westhoofd, NE corner FG, NW corner FR.

WESTERSCHELDE
WIELINGEN CHANNEL.
Wielingen Lt Buoy 51°23'·00N 03°14'·10E Fl(3)G 15s; stbd-hand mark.
W1 Lt Buoy 51°23'·50N 03°18'·00E FlG 5s; stbd-hand mark.
W2 Lt Buoy 51°24'·64N 03°21'·58E Iso R 8s; port-hand mark.
W3 Lt Buoy 51°24'·03N 03°21'·58E Iso G 8s; stbd-hand mark.
W5 Lt Buoy 51°24'·33N 03°24'·48E Iso G 4s; stbd-hand mark.
W7 Lt Buoy 51°24'·65N 03°27'·30E Iso G 8s; stbd-hand mark.
W9 Lt Buoy 51°24'·97N 03°30'·13E Iso G 4s; stbd-hand mark.
W10 Lt Buoy 51°25'·80N 03°33'·00E QR; port-hand mark.
Wave observation post 51°22'·84N 03°22'·82E Fl(5)Y 20s.
Kruishoofd 51°23'·73N 03°28'·36E Iso WRG 8s 14m W8M, R6M, G5M; W square Tr, B post; vis R074°-091°, W091°-100°, G100°-118°, W118°-153°, R153°-179°, W179°-198°, G198°-205°, W205°-074°.
Nieuwe Sluis, on embankment 51°24'·49N 03°30'·33E Horn (3) 30s. 51°24'·48N 03°31'·38E Oc WRG 10s 27m W14M, R11M, G10M; B 8-sided Tr, W bands; vis R055°-084°, W084°-091°, G091°-132°, W132°-238°, G238°-244°, W244°-258°, G258°-264°, R264°-292°, W292°-055°.
Noorderhoofd Ldg Lts 149°, NW head of dyke. Front, 0·73M from rear Oc WRG 10s 18m W13M, R10M, G10M; R Tr, W band; vis R353°-008°, G008°-029°, W029°-169°.
Westkapelle, Common rear Fl 3s 48m **28M**; Tr, R top; obsc on certain brgs.
Zoutelande Ldg Lts 326°, Front 1·8M from rear FR 21m 12M; R square Tr; vis 321°-352°.
Molenhoofd 51°31'·61N 03°26'·07E Oc WRG 6s 9m; W mast R bands; vis R306°-328°, W328°-347°, R347°-008°, G008°-031°, W031°-035°, G035°-140°, W140°-169°, R169°-198°.
Kaapduinen, Ldg Lts 130°. Front 51°28'·5N 03°31'·0E Oc 5s 26m 13M; Y square Tr, R bands; vis 115°-145°. Rear 220m from front Oc 5s 36m 13M; Y square Tr, R bands; synchronised with front; vis 108°-152°.
Fort de Nolle 51°27'·00N 03°33'·20E Fl WRG 2·5s 11m W6M, R4M, G4M; W column, R bands; vis R293°-309°, W309°-333°, G333°-351°, R351°-013°, G013°-062°, R062°-086°, W086°-093°, G093°-110°, W110°-130°.

APPROACHES TO BRESKENS
Songa Lt Buoy 51°25'·34N 03°34'·78E QG; stbd-hand mark.
SS-VH Lt Buoy 51°24'·75N 03°34'·00E Q; N cardinal mark

BRESKENS FERRY HARBOUR
West mole head 51°24'·40N 03°33'·23E FG 8m 4M; B & W mast; in fog FY; Ra refl; Fog Det Lt..
East mole head FR 8m 5M; B & W mast; in fog FY.
BRESKENS
West mole head 51°24'·09N 03°34'·12E F WRG 6m; grey mast; vis vis R090°-128°, W128°-157°, R157°-172°, W172°-175°, G175°-296°, W296°-300°, R300°-008°, G008°-090°; in fog FY; Horn Mo(U) 30s.
East mole head FR 5m; Ra refl.

VLISSINGEN.
Ldg Lts 117°. Leugenaar causeway, front Oc R 5s 5m 7M; W&R pile; intens 108°-126°. Sardijngeul, rear 550m from front Oc WRG 5s 8m W12M, R9M, G8M; R triangle with W bands on R and W mast; synchronised; vis R245°-271°, G271°-285°, W285°-123°, R123°-147°.
Koopmanshaven, West mole root 51°26'·40N 03°34'·58E Iso WRG 3s 15m W12M, R10M, G9M; R pylon; vis R253°-270°, W270°-059°, G059°-071°, W071°-077°, R077°-101°, G101°-110°, W110°-114°.
East mole head FG 7m
Buitenhaven, East mole head FG 4M; grey mast on post; in fog FY.
Buitenhaven, West mole head 51°26'·44N 03°36'·12E Iso WRG 4s 10m 5M; B mast; vis W072°-021°, G021°-042°, W042°-056°, R056°-072°; traffic signals; Horn 15s.

Schone Waardin 51°26'·60N 0337'·95E Oc WRG 9s 10m W13M, R10M, G9M; R mast, W bands; vis R248°-260°, G260°-270°, W270°-282°, G282°-325°, W325°-341°, G341°-023°, W023°-024°, G024°-054°, R054°-066°, W066°-076°, G076°-094°, W094°-248°.

VLISSINGEN OOST
West mole head FR 8m 5M; W column; in fog FY; Horn (2) 20s.
East mole head FG 8m 4M; W column.
Ldg Lts 023°. Front Oc R 8s 7m 8M; G post. Rear 100m from front Oc R 8s 12m 8M; G mast; synchronised with front, both vis 015°-031°.

BORSSELE-NOORDNOL
Pier head 51°25'·55N 03°42'·80E Oc WRG 5s; 9m; R mast, W bands; vis R305°-331°, W331°-341°, G341°-000°, W000°-007°, R007°-023°, G023°-054°, W054°-057°, G057°-113°, W113°-128°, R128°-155°, W155°-305°.
FR on chimney 0·4M NNE.
Borssele, Total jetty, NW end 51°24'·85N 03°43'·61E Oc WR 10s; vis R135°-160°, W160°-135°.
Borssele-Everingen 51°24'·73N 03°44'·20E Iso WRG 4s 9m; W structure, R band; vis R021°-026°, G026°-080°, W080°-100°, R100°-137°, W137°-293°, R293°-308°, W308°-344°, G344°-357°, W357°-021°.

BRAAKMANHAVEN.
Ldg Lts 191°. Front 51°20'·3N 03°45'·8E Iso 4s 10m; B pile, W bands. Rear, 60m from front, Iso 4s 14m; B pile, W bands; synchronised with front, showing over harbour mouth.
Ldg Lts 211°, both Oc G 4s, synchronised, showing middle of turning basin.
West side 51°21'·0N 03°45'·9E FG; G pile, W bands; Ra refl.
East side 51°21'·1N 03°46'·3E FR; R mast, W bands; Ra refl, traffic signals.
Braakman 51°21'·03N 03°46'·31E Oc WRG 8s 7m W7M, R5M, G4M; B pedestal, W band; vis R116°-132°, W132°-140°, G140°-202°, W202°-116°.

TERNEUZEN.
Nieuw Neuzenpolder Ldg Lts 125°. Front Oc 5s 5m 13/9M; W column, B bands; intens 117°-133°. Rear 365m from front Oc 5s 16m 13/9M; B and W framework mast; synchronised with front, intens 117°-133°.
Dow Chemical jetty, 4 dolphins showing Fl 3s and Fl R 3s; Horn 15s.
Veer Haven, West jetty Oc WRG 5s 13m W9M, R7M, G6M; B and W framework Tr; vis R092°-115°, W115°-238°, G238°-248°, W248°-277°, R277°-309°, W309°-003°.
West mole head 51°20'·62N 03°49'·7E FG 6m.
East mole head FR 7m.

HOEDEKENSKERKE
De Val 51°25'·20N 03°55'·08E Iso WRG 2s 5m W8M, R5M, G4M; R Tr, W band; vis R008°-034°, W034°-201°, R201°-206°, W206°-209°, G209°-329°, W328°-008°.
HANSWEERT
West mole head 51°26'·45N 04°00'·50E Oc WRG 10s 9m W9M, R7M, G6M; R Tr, W band; vis R288°-310°, W310°-334°, G334°-356·5°, W356·5°-044°, R044°-061·5°, W061·5°-073°, G073°-089°, R089°-101·5°, G101·5°-109°, W109°-114·5°, R114·5°-127·5°W127·5°-288°; in fog F; Iso R 4s; SS(traffic).
East side, pier head FG 6m; greay column; in fog FY; Horn (4) 30s.

WALSOORDEN
Entrance South mole head 51°22'·96N 04°02'·18E FR 5m.

ZANDVLIET
Ldg Lts 118°. Front 51°20'·70N 04°16'·40E Oc WRG 5s 11m W9M, R7M, G6M; vis R shore-350°, W350°-017°, G017°-019°,

19

W019°-088°, G088°-109°, W109°-125°, R125°-shore. Rear, 200m from front, Oc 5s 18m 9M.

LILLO
Pier, SE end 58°18'·20N 04°17'·28E Oc WRG 10s 5m W9M, R7M, G6M; vis R shore-304°, W304°-322°, G322°-099°, W099°-148°, R148°-shore. **(TE 1989).**

ANTWERPEN
Imalso marina 51°13'·96N 04°23'·77E F ER 9m 3M; vis W shore-283°, R283°-shore.

OOSTERSCHELDE

OUTER APPROACHES.
Wave observation post VR 51 51°30'·35N 03°14'·53E Fl Y 5s
W Thornton Lt Buoy 51°31'·01N 02°51'·00E Iso 8s; safe water mark.
TB Lt Buoy 51°34'·45N 02°59'·15E Q; N cardinal mark.
Westpit Lt Buoy 51°33'·70N 03°10'·00E Iso 8s; safe water mark.
Rabsbank Lt Buoy 51°38'30N 03°10'·05E Iso 4s; safe water mark.
Middelbank Lt Buoy 51°40'·90N 03°18'·30E Iso 8s; safe water mark.
Schouwenbank Lt Buoy 51°45'·00N 03°14'·40E Mo(A) 8s; safe water mark; Racon.
Buitenbank Lt Buoy 51°51'·20N 03°25'·80E Iso 4s; safe water mark.

WESTGAT/OUDE ROOMPOT (selected marks).
WG1 Lt Buoy 51°38'·00N 03°26'·30E QG; stbd-hand mark.
WG Lt Buoy 51°38'·25N 03°28'·90E Q; N cardinal mark.
WG4 Lt Buoy 51°38'·62N 03°27'·80E Iso R 8s; port-hand mark.
Wave observation post OS11 51°38'·63N 03°28'·95E Fl Y 5s; Y pile.
WG7 Lt Buoy 51°39'·45N 03°32'·75E Iso G 4s; stbd-hand mark.
WG OR Lt Buoy 51°39'·75N 03°32'·60E VQ(6)LFl 10s; S cardinal mark.
OR2 Lt Buoy 51°39'·50N 03°33'·70E LFlR 8s; port-hand mark.
OR5 Lt Buoy 51°38'·55N 03°35'·50E QG; stbd- hand mark.
OR11 Lt Buoy 51°37'·00N°3 38.50E Iso G 2s; stbd- hand mark.
Roompotsluis Ldg Lts 073°. Front Oc G 5s. Rear, 280m from front, Oc G 5s; synchronised.
North breakwater head FR 6m; Horn(2) 30s.
South breakwater head FG 6m. Inner mole head QR.

COLIJNSPLAAT.
East jetty head 51°36'·25N 03°51'·15E FR 3m 3M; Horn.
West jetty head FG 5m 3M.
Zeeland Bridge. N and S passages marked by FY Lts, 14m.

KATS.
North jetty head FG 5m 5M.
South jetty head 51°34'·44N 03°53'·72E Oc WRG 8s 5m 5M; vis W344°-153°, R153°-165°, G165°-200°, W200°-214°, G214°-258°, W258°-260°, G260°-313°, W313°-331°.
VAN GOES.
South mole head 51°32'·34N 03°55'·95E FR.
North mole head FG.

WEMELDINGE.
West jetty head 51°31'·34N 04°00'·25E Oc WRG 5s 7m W9M, R7M, G6M; B mast, W band; vis R shore-116°, W116°-123°, G123°-151°, W151°-153°, R153°-262°, W262°-266°, R266°-shore; in fog Oc Y 4s; traffic signals.
East jetty head FR; Horn(4) 30s.

YERSEKE.
Ldg Lts 155° (through Schaar van Yerseke). Front Iso 4s 8m; in fog FY. Rear, 180m from front, Iso 4s 13m; synchronised; in fog 2FY. FG and FR mark mole heads.

BERGEN OP ZOOM.
Molenplaat Ldg Lts 119°, both Oc 5s.
Bergsche Diep Ldg Lts 065°. Front Iso 6s 6m; W daymark, B band. Rear, 100m from front, Oc 5s 9m; W daymark, B stripe.
Heodorushaven West mole head FR.
East mole head FG.
Ldg Lts 034° both Oc 5s; synchronised.
Lock Ldg Lts 057° both Iso G 6s; synchronised.

Tholensche Gat. Strijenham 51°31'·40N 04°08'·91E Oc WRG 5s 9m W8M, R5M, G5M; R square, W bands, on mast; vis W shore-298°, R298°-320°, W320°-052°, G052°-069°, W069°-085°, R085°-095°, W095°-shore.
Gorishoek'51°31'·57N 04°04'·68E Iso WRG 8s 7m W6M, R4M, G4M; R pedestal, W bands; vis R260°-278°, W278°-021°, G021°-025°, W025°- 071°, G071°-085°, W085°-103°, R103°-120°, W120°-260°.

STAVENISSE.
East mole head 51°35'·73N 04°00'·35E Oc WRG 5s 10m W12M, R9M, G8M; B pylon; W075°-090°, R090°-105·5°, W105·5°-108°, G108°-118·5°, W118·5°-124°, G124°-155°, W155°-158°, G158°-231°, W231°-238·5°, R238·5°-253°, W253°-350°.

ST ANNALAND.
Entrance, West side 51°36'·32N 04°06'·60E FG.
East side FR.

ZIJPE. ANNA JACOBAPOLDER
North mole head Iso G 4s.
St Philipsland, on dyke Oc WRG 4s 9m W8M, R5M, G4M; pylon on B round column; vis W051°-100°, R100°-144°, W144°-146°, G146°-173°.
Zijpsche Bout Oc WRG 10s 9m W12M, R9M, G8M; mast on R column; vis R208°-211°, W211°-025°, G025°-030°, W030°-040°, R040°-066°. Tramweghaven South mole Iso R 4s 7m; Gy Bn. North mole FG.
Stoofpolder Iso WRG 4s 10m W12M, R9M, G8M; B Tr, W bands; vis W147°-154°, R154°-226·5°, G226·5°-243°, W243°-253°, G253°-259°, W259°-263°, G263°-270°, R270°-283°, W283°-008°.
Hoek Van Ouwerkerk 51°36'·92N 03°58'·27E Iso WRG 6s; vis R268°-305°, W305°-313°, G313°-008°, W008°-011°, G011°-059°, W059°-065°, R065°-088°, W088°-098°, G098°-112°, R112°-125°, W125°-268°.

DE VAL.
Engelsche Vaarwater Ldg Lts 019°. Front 51°37'·74N 03°55'·60E Iso WRG 3s 7m W6M, R4M, G4M; R pedestal, W band; vis R290°-306°, W306°-317°, G317°-334°, W334°-336°, G336°-017°, W017°-026°, G026°-090°, R090°-108°, W108°-290°. Rear, 300m from front, Iso 3s 15m 6M; R square on W mast, R bands.

ZIERIKZEE.
West jetty head 51°37'·95N 03°53'·45E Oc WRG 6s 10m W6M, R4M, G4M; R pedestal, W band; vis G060°-107°, W107°-133°, R133°-156°, W156°-278°, R278°-304°, G304°-314°, W314°-331°, R331°-354°, W354°-060°.
West mole head FR.   East mole head FG.

FLAUWERSPOLDER.
West mole head 51°40'·70N 03°50'·86E Iso WRG 4s 7m W6M, R4M, G4M; W daymark, B band on pylon; vis R303°-344°, W344°-347°, G347°-083°, W083°-086°, G086°-103°, W103°-110°, R110°-128°, W128°-303°.

HAMMEN.
Schelphoek Ldg Lts 357°. Front, East mole head FG. Rear, 400m from front, Iso G 4s; vis 342°-012°.
East breakwater head 51°41'·28N 03°48'·79E Fl(2) 10s 8m.

BURGHSLUIS,
South mole head 51°40'·59N 03°45'·56E F WRG 9m W8M, R5M, G4M; mast on R column; vis W218°-230°, R230°-245°, W245°-253·5°, G253·5°-293°, W293°-000°, G000°-025·5°, W025·5°-032°, G032°-041°, R041°-070°, W070°-095°.

APPROACHES TO EUROPOORT
West Schouwen 51°42'·58N 03°41'·60E Fl(21) 15s 57m **30M**; grey Tr, R diagonal stripes on upper part.
Verklikker 51°43'·58N 03°42'·39E F WR 13m W9M, R7M; Tr with R lantern; vis R115°-127°, W127°-169°, R169°-175°, W175°-115°.
Wave observation posts. OS13 51°44'·00N 03°33'·40E FIY 5s; Y pile.
OS14 51°43'·30N 03°40'·60E FIY 5s; Y pile.
BG2 51°46'·10N 03°37'·20E FIY 5s; Y pile.
BG5 51°49'·50N 03°45'·70E FIY 5s; Y pile.
Ha10 51°51'·80N 03°51'·70E FIY 5s; Y pile.
Buitenbank Lt Buoy 51°51'·20N 03°25'·80E Iso 4s; safe water mark.

Westhoofd 51°48'·83N 03°51'·90E Fl(3) 15s 55m **30M**; R square Tr.
Kwade Hock 51°50'·3N 03°59'·1E Iso WRG 4s 8m W12M, R9M, G8M; B mast, W bands; vis W 235°-068°, R068°-088°, G088°-108°, W108°-111°, R111°-142°, W142°-228°, R228°-235°. FR on radio mast 4·2M NE.
Slijkgat SG Lt Buoy 51°52'·00N 03°51'·50E Iso 4s; safe water mark.
Hinder Lt Buoy 51°54'·60N 03°55'·50E Q(9) 15s; W cardinal mark.

HARINGVLIET.
Heliushaven, West jetty 51°49'·3N 04°07'·2E FR 7m 4M.
East jetty FG 7m 3M; *Horn (3) 20s.*

HELLEVOETSLUIS.
51 49'·2N 04°07'·7E Iso WRG 10s 16m W11M, R8M, G7M; W Tr, R cupola; vis G shore-275°, W275°-294°, R294°-316°, W316°-036°, G036°-058°, W058°-095°, R095°-shore.
West mole head FR 6m.
East mole head FG 6m; in fog FY.
Hoornsche Hoofden, watchhouse on dyke, 51°48'·3N 04°11'·0E Oc WRG 5s 7m W7M, R5M, G4M; vis W288°-297°, G297°-313°, W313°-325°, R325°-335°, G335°-345°, W345°-045°, G045°-055°, W055°-131°, R131°-shore.

MIDDELHARNIS.
West pier head F WRG 5m W8M, R5M, G4M; vis W144°-164°, R164°-176°, G176°-144°.
East pier head FR 5m 5M; in fog FY.
Nieuwendijk. Ldg Lts 303°. Front 51°45'·1N 04°19'·5E Iso WRG 6s 8m W9M, R7M, G6M; B framework Tr; vis G093°-100°, W100°-103°, R103°-113°, W113°-093°. Rear, 450m from front F 11m 9M; B framework Tr.

VOLKERAK.
Noorder Voorhaven. West mole head FG 6m 4M; R lantern on pedestal; in fog FY.

NOORD HINDER LTV 52°00'·15N 02° 51'·20E Fl(2) 10s 16m **27M**; R hull, W upperworks; RC; Racon; *Horn(2) 30s.*
Euro Platform 51°59'·9N 03°16'·6E Mo(U) 15s; W structure, R bands; helicopter platform; *Horn Mo(U) 30s.*
Goeree 51°55'·53N 03°40'·18E Fl(4) 20s 31m **28M**; R and W chequered Tr on platform; RC; helicopter platform; Racon; *Horn (4) 30s.*

Adriana Lt Buoy 51°56'·13N 03°50'·65E VQ(9) 10s; W cardinal mark.
Maas Center Lt Buoy 52°01'·18N 03°53'·57E Iso 4s; safe water mark; Racon.
Indusbank N Lt Buoy 52°02'·92N 04°03'·73E Q; N cardinal mark.

HOEK VAN HOLLAND.
Maasvlakte 51°58'·2N 04°00'·9E Fl(5) 20s 66m **28M**; B 8-sided Tr, Y bands.
Nieuwe Noorderdam, head 51°59'·71N 04°02'·92E FR 24m 10M; Y Tr, B bands; Helicopter platform; in fog Al Fl WR 6s, vis 278°-255°.
Nieuwe Zuiderdam, head 51°59'·19N 04°02'·58E FG 24m 10M; Y Tr, B bands; Helicopter platform; in fog Al Fl WG 6s, vis 330°-307°; *Horn 10s.*
Norderpier Oc R 10s 14m 6M. South pier Oc G 10s 14m 6M.
Maasmond Ldg Lts 112° for very deep draught vessels. **Front** 51°58'·9N 04°04'·9E Iso 4s 29m **21M**; W Tr, B bands; vis 101°-123°. **Rear**, 0.6M from front Iso 4s 46m **21M**; W Tr, B bands; synchronised with front. Ldg Lts 107° for other vessels. **Front** 51°58'·6N 04°07'·6E Iso R 6s 29m **18M**; R Tr, W bands; vis 100°-115°. **Rear** 450m from front Iso R 6s 43m **18M**; vis 100°-115°, synchronised.

EUROPOORT.
Calandkanaal Entrance Ldg Lts 116°. **Front** Oc G 6s 29m ; W Tr, R bands; vis 108°-124°, synchronised with **Rear** Lt 550m from front Oc G 6s 43m **16M**; W Tr, R bands; vis 108°-124°. R Lts on Chimney 1·63M SW.
Beerkanaal Ldg Lts 192°. Front Iso G 3s. Rear, 50m from front, Iso G 3s.
Rotterdamsche Waterweg, South side 20 G Lts 7M; B circle on groynes and dolphins.
North side 20 R Lts 5M; R circle on groynes and dolphins.

SCHEVENINGEN.
SCH Lt Buoy 52°07'·80N 04°14'·20E Iso 4s; safe water mark.
Scheveningen 52°06'·3N 04°16'·2E Fl(2) 10s 48m **29M**; brown Tr; vis 014°-244°.
Ldg Lts 156°. Front Iso 4s 17m 14M. Rear 100m from front Iso 4s 21m 14M; synchronised with front.
South mole head 52°06'·28N 04°15'·22E FG 11m 9M; B 6-sided Tr, Y bands, R lantern; *Horn (3) 30s.*
NE mole head FR 11m 9M; B 6-sided Tr, Y bands, R lantern.

Noordwijk-aan-Zee 52°15'·00N 04°26'·10E Oc(3) 20s 32m **18M**; W square Tr.
Survey platform 52°16'·4N 04°17'·9E FR and Mo(U) 15s; *Horn Mo(U) 20s.*

IJMUIDEN.
IJmuiden Lt Buoy 52°28'·70N 04°23'·93E Mo(A) 8s; safe water mark; Racon.
Ldg Lts 100°. **Front** F WR 30m **W16M**, R13M; dark R Tr; vis W050°-122°, R122°-145°, W145°-160°; RC. **Rear** 560m from front Fl 5s 52m **29M**; dark R Tr; vis 019°-199°.
South breakwater head 52°27'·86N 04°32'·00E FG 14m 10M; in fog Fl 3s, *Horn (2) 30s.*
North breakwater head FR 14m 10M. N pier head QR 11m 9M; vis 263°-096°; in fog FW.
South pier head QG 11m 9M; vis 096°-295°; in fog FW.

NORDZEE KANAL
Ø Km mark 52°27'·86N 04°35'·64E.
20 Km mark 52°25'·21N 04°51'·94E

AMSTERDAM
Yacht harbour 52°23'·02N 04°53'·77E F & FR.

19

IJMUIDEN TO TEXEL

Egmond-aan-Zee 52°37'.20N 04°37'.40E Iso WR 10s 36m **W18M**, R14M; W Tr; vis W010°-175°, R175°-188°. FR Lts on chimney 10·2M N.

ZEEGAT VAN TEXEL

TEXEL LT V. 52°47'.10N 04°06'.60E Fl(3+1) 20s 16m **26M**; R hull, W band; RC; Racon; *Horn (3) 30s*. During maintenance replaced by RW buoy Oc 10s; Racon.
H (Zuider Haaks) Lt Buoy 52°54'.70N 04°34'.84E VQ(6)LFl 10s; S cardinal mark.
MR (Middelrug) Lt Buoy 52°56'.80N 04°33'.90E Q(9) 15s; W cardinal mark.
NH (Noorder Haaks) Lt Buoy 53°00'.30N 04°35'.45E VQ; N cardinal mark.
Grote Kaap Oc WRG 10s 31m W11M, R8M, G8M; vis G041°-088°, W088°-094°, R094°-131°.
Schulpengat. Ldg Lts 026°. **Front** 53°00'.9N 04°44'.5E Iso 4s **18M**; vis 024°-028°. Rear, **Den Hoorn** 0·83M from front Oc 8s **18M**; church spire; vis 024°-028°.
Huisduinen 52°57'.20N 04°43'.37E F WR 27m W14M, R11M; square Tr; vis W070°-113°, R113°-158°, W158°-208°.
Kijkduin, Rear 52°57'.35N 04°43'.60E Fl(4) 20s 56m **30M**; brown Tr; vis except where obsc by dunes on Texel.
Ldg Lt 253° with Den Helder, Harssens Island (QG).

SCHULPENGAT.

SG Lt Buoy 52°52'.95N 04°38'.00E Mo(A) 8s; safe water mark.
S1 Lt Buoy 52°53'.74N 04°39'.25E Iso G 4s; stbd-hand mark.
S2 Lt Buoy 52°54'.05N 04°38'.20E Iso R 4s; port-hand mark.
S3 Lt Buoy 52°54'.60N 04°39'.80E Iso G 8s; stbd-hand mark.
S4 Lt Buoy 52°54'.70N 04°39'.30E Iso R 8s; port-hand mark.
S5 Lt Buoy 52°55'.40N 04°40'.30E Iso G 4s; stbd-hand mark.
S6 Lt Buoy 52°55'.50N 04°39'.95E Iso R 4s; port-hand mark.
S7 Lt Buoy 52°56'.20N 04°40'.80E Iso G 8s; stbd-hand mark.
S6A Lt Buoy 52°56'.55N 04°40'.50E QR; port-hand mark.
S8 Buoy 52°57'.10N 04°41'.14E (unlit); port-hand mark.
S9 Buoy 52°56'.90N 04°42'.15E (unlit); stbd-hand mark.
S10 Lt Buoy 52°57'.65N 04°41'.65E Iso R 8s; port-hand mark.
S11 Lt Buoy 52°57'.60N 04°43'.35E Iso G 4s; stbd-hand mark.

MOLENGAT.

MG Lt Buoy 53°03'.42N 04°39'.10E Mo(A) 8s; safe water mark.
MG1 Lt Buoy 53°01'.75N 04°41'.20E Iso G 8s; stbd-hand mark.
MG2 Lt Buoy 53°02'.30N 04°41'.42E Iso R 8s; port-hand mark.
MG2A Buoy 53°01'.75N 04°41'.57E (unlit); port-hand mark.
MG1A Buoy 53°01'.15N 04°41'.20E (unlit); stbd-hand mark.
MG4 Lt Buoy 53°01'.20N 04°41'.65E Iso R 4s; port-hand mark.
MG3 Buoy 53°00'.06N 04°41'.25E (unlit); stbd-hand mark.
MG6 Buoy 53°00'63N 04°41'.75E (unlit); port-hand mark.
MG5 Lt Buoy 53°00'.02N 04°41'.30E Iso G 4s; stbd-hand mark.
MG8 Lt Buoy 53°00'.00N 04°41'.85E Iso R 8s; port-hand mark.
MG7 Buoy 52°59'.60N 04°41'.74E (unlit); stbd-hand mark.
MG9 Lt Buoy 52°59'.20N 04°42'.30E Iso G 8s; stbd-hand mark.
MG10 Buoy 52°59'.52N 04°42'.50E (unlit); port-hand mark.
MG11 Buoy 52°58'.80N 04°42'.75E (unlit); stbd-hand mark.
MG 12 Buoy 52°59'.00N 04°43'.10E (unlit); port-hand mark.
S14/MG13 Lt Buoy 52°58'.40N 04°43'.30E VQ(3) 5s; E cardinal mark.
MG14 Lt Buoy 52°58'.50N 04°43'.68E Iso R 4s; port-hand mark.

MARSDIEP.
DEN HELDER,

Marinehaven, West breakwater head (Harssens Island) 52°58'.00N 04°46'.84E QG 12m 8M; *Horn 20s*.
MH6, East side of entrance, QR 9m 4M; R pile; Ra refl.
Entrance, West side, FIG 5s 9m 4M; vis 180°-067° (H24).
Entrance, East side, QR 9m 4M; (H24).

Ldg Lts 191°. Front Oc G 5s 15m 14M; B triangle on building; vis 161°-221°. Rear, 275m from front, Oc G 5s 25m 14M; triangle on building; vis 161°-247°, synchronised.

Schilbolsnol 53°00'.6N 04°45'.8E F WRG 27m **W15M**, R12M, G11M; G Tr; vis W338°-002°, G002°-035°, W035°-038° (leading sector for Schulpengat), R038°-051°, W051°-068°.

MOK

Mok 53°00'.25N 04°46'.85E Oc WRG 10s 10m W10M, R7M, G6M; vis R229°-317°, W317°-337°, G337°-112°.
Ldg Lts 284°30'. Front Iso 2s 7m 6M. Rear, 245m from front Iso 8s 10m 6M; both vis 224°-344°.

WADDENZEE

Malzwin KM/RA1 52°58'.6N 04°49'.2E Fl(5)Y 20s; post.
Malzwin M5 52°58'.3N 04°49'.9E Iso G 4s; G pile; Ra refl.
Wierbalg W3A 52°58'.1N 04°57'.1E QG; G pile.
Pile 01 52°57'.0N 05°00'.6E Iso G 8s; G pile.
Pile 05 52°56'.9N 05°01'.9E Iso G 4s; G pile.

DEN OEVER.

Ldg Lts 132°. Front and rear both Oc 10s 7M; vis 127°-137°.
Detached breakwater, North head, LFl R 10s.
Stevinsluizen, East wall, Iso WRG 5s 15m W10, R7, G7; vis G226°-231°, W231°-235°, R235°-290°, G290°-327°, W327°-335°, R335°-345°.
West wall, 80m from head, Iso WRG 2s; vis G195°-213°, W213°-227°, R227°-245°.

TEXELSTROOM.

T5/MH2 Lt Buoy 52°58'.38N 04°47'.80E Fl(2+1)G 12s; preferred channel to port.
T11/GvS2 Lt Buoy 52°59'.95N 04°49'.20E Fl(2+1)G 12s; preferred channel to port.
T17 Lt Buoy 53°01'.20N 04°51'50E Iso G 8s; stbd-hand mark.
T14 Lt Buoy 53°02'.27N 04°51'.50E Iso R 8s; port-hand mark.
Note: Buoys being renumbered.

OUDESCHILD.

South mole head 53°02'.37N 04°51'.26E FR 7m; *Horn(2) 30s* (sounded 0600-2300).
North mole head FG.
Oc 6s 7m Lt seen between FR and FG leads into harbour.
T23 Lt Buoy 53°03'.45N 04°55'.70E FlG 4s; stbd-hand mark.
DOOVE BALG.
D4 53°02'.7N 05°04'.1E Iso R 8s; R pile; Ra refl.
D3A/J2 53°02'.1N 05°07'.0E Fl(2+1)G 12s; G post, R band.
D14 53°02'.5N 05°09'.2E Iso R 4s; R pile; Ra refl.
D11 53°02'9N 05°12'.0E Iso G 8s; G pile; Ra refl.
KORNWERDERZAND.
West side, 53°04'.0N 05°17'.6E Iso R 4s 9m 4M; grey pedestal, R lantern; vis 049°-229°.
Buitenhaven, West mole head FG 9m 7M; *Horn Mo(N) 30s*.
East Mole head FR.
Spuihaven Noord, West mole head LFlG 10s 7m 7M.

BOONTJES/APPROACHES TO HARLINGEN.

BO11/K2/2 53°05'.0N 05°20'.3E Q; N cardinal mark.
BO28 53°07'.9N 05°22'.6E Iso R 8s; R pile.
BO34 53°08'.9N 05°23'.0E Iso R 2s; R pile.
BO39 53°10'.0N 05°23'.4E Iso G 4s; G pile.
BO40 53°10'.0N 05°23'.3E Iso R 4s; R pile.

TEXEL TO TERSCHELLING

Eierland, N point of Texel 53°10'.97N 04°51'.40E Fl(2) 10s 52m **29M**; R Tr; RC.
Tide gauge 53°11'.33N 04°48'05E Fl(5)Y 20s 5M.
Off Vlieland TSS. *VL Center Lanby* 53°27'.00N 04°40'.00E Fl 5s; Racon; *Horn(2) 30s*.
Oost Vlieland 53°17'.8N 05°03'.6E Iso 4s 53m **20M**; brown Tr; RC.

TERSCHELLING
VSM Lt Buoy 53°19'·05N 04°55'·73E Iso 4s; safe water mark.
TG Lt Buoy 53°24'·22N 05°02'·40E Q(9) 15s; W cardinal mark.
A Otto Lt Buoy 53°24'·68N 05°06'·50E VQ Fl(3); E cardinal mark.
VNG Lt Buoy 53°24'·87N 05°11'·82E Iso 4s; safe water mark.

APPROACH TO WADDENZEE.

ZUIDER STORTEMELK (selected marks
ZS-bank Lt Buoy 53°18'·85N 04°57'·95E VQ; N cardinal mark.
ZS1 Lt Buoy 53°18'·75N 04°59'·56E FIG 4s; stbd-hand mark.
ZS13/VS2 Lt Buoy 53°18'·80N 05°05'·93E Fl(2+1)G 12s; preferred channel to port.
ZS14 Lt Buoy 53°19'·00N 05°05'·55E LFIR 7s; port-hand mark.
ZS15 Lt Buoy 53°18'·97N 05°07'·10E LFIG 5s; stbd-hand mark.
ZS18 Lt Buoy 53°19'·36N 05°06'·95E LFIR 5s; port-hand mark.
WEST TERSCHELLING.
Brandaris Tr 53°21'·67N 05°12'·99E Fl 5s 55m **29M**; Y square Tr; vis except where obsc by dunes on Vlieland and Terschelling.
Ldg Lts 053°, West harbour mole head, front 53°21'·3N 05°13'·1E FR 5m W8M, R5M; R post, W bands, vis W049°-055°, R055°-252°, W252°-263°, R263°-049°; Horn 15s 3 **(TD 1989).** **Rear**, on dyke, 1·1M from front Iso 5s 14m **19M**; vis 045°-061°, intens 045°-052°.   East pier head FG 5m 4M.

VLIELAND
East mole head 53°17'·73N 05°05'·59E FG

WADDENZEE
VLIESTROOM (selected marks).
VL1 Lt Buoy 53°19'·00N 05°08'·80E QG; stbd-hand mark.
VL2/SG1 Lt Buoy 53°19'·30N 05°09'·80E Fl(2+1)R 12s; preferred channel to stbd.
VL5 Lt Buoy 53°18'·60N 05°09'·55E LFIG 8s; stbd-hand mark.
VL6 Lt Buoy 53°18'·60N 05°11'·00E LFIR 8s; port-hand mark.
VL9 Lt Buoy 53°17'·65N 05°10'·10E IsoG 4s; stbd-hand mark.
VL10/WM1 Lt Buoy 53°17'·20N 05°11'·26E VQ(9) 10s; W cardinal mark.
VL14 Lt Buoy 53°15'·90N 05°10'·72E LFIR 8s; port-hand mark.
VL15 Lt Buoy 53°16·05N 05°09'·80E LFIG 8s; stbd-hand mark.

APPROACH TO HARLINGEN

BLAUWE SLENK (selected marks).
BS1/IN2 Lt Buoy 53°14'·74N 05°10'·05E Fl(2+1)G 12s; preferred channel to port.
BS2 Lt Buoy 53°14.70N 05°10'·20E QR; port-hand mark.
BS3 Lt Buoy 53°14'·40N 05°10'·20E LFIG 5s; stbd-hand mark.
BS4 Lt Buoy 53°14'·50N 05°10'·40E LFIR 5s; port-hand mark.
BS7 Lt Buoy 53°13'·85N 05°11'·45E LFIG 8s; stbd-hand mark.
BS8 Lt Buoy 53°14'·05N 05°11'·54E LFIR 8s; port-hand mark.
BS11 Lt Buoy 53°13'·63N 05°13'·30E IsoG 4s; stbd-hand mark.

BS12 Lt Buoy 53°13'·80N 05°13'·30E IsoR 4s; port-hand mark.
BS19 Lt Buoy 53°13'·40N 05°17'·00E QG; stbd-hand mark.
BS20 Lt Buoy 53°13'·55N 05°17'·10E QR; port-hand mark.
BS27 Lt Buoy 53°11'·95N 05°18'·25E QG; stbd-hand mark.
BS28 Lt Buoy 53°12'·10N 05°18'·42E QR; port-hand mark.
BS31 Beacon 53°11'·60N 05°19'·70E LFIG 8s; G pile, stbd-hand mark.
BS32 Lt Buoy 53°11'·72N 05°19'·75E LFIR 8s; port-hand mark.
POLLENDAM.
Stbd-hand marks: P1 FIG 2s; P3 IsoG 4s; P5 FIG 2s.
Port-hand marks: P2 FIR 2s 7m; P4 IsoR 4s 7m; P6 FIR 2s 7m;
BS54 Beacon 53°10'·80N 05°23'·50E VQR; R pile, port-hand mark.
HARLINGEN.
Ldg Lts 112°. Front 53°10'·56N 05°24'·42E Iso 6s 8m 4M; vis 097°-127°; and FG 9m 7 Rear 500m from front Iso 6s 19m 13M; both on B masts, W bands; vis 104·5°-119·5° (H24).
North mole head 53°10'·57N 05°24'·42E Iso R 5s 8m 4M; R pedestal.
South mole head ; Horn(3) 30s.

TERSCHELLING TO AMELAND
TS Lt Buoy 53°28'·20N 05°21'·60E VQ; N cardinal mark.

AMELAND
Ameland, West end 53°27'·02N 05°37'·60E Fl(3) 15s 57m **30M**; brown Tr, W bands; RC.

NES
Nieue Veerdam Mole head 53°26'·02N 05°46'·53E Iso 6s 2m 8M

AMELAND TO SCHIERMONNICOOG

BR Lt Buoy 53°30'·75N 05°33'·60E Q Fl; N cardinal mark.
AM Lt Buoy 53°31'·00N 05°44'·80E VQ; N cardinal mark.
NAM 21 Lt Buoy 53°31'·18N 05°55'·50E Fl Y.
WRG Lt Buoy 53°32'·78N 06°01'·75E Q; N cardinal mark.
Schiermonnikoog 53°29'·20N 06°08'·90E Fl(4) 20s 43m **28M**; round Tr, dark R Tr. F WR 28m **W15M**, R12M; (same Tr) F WR **W15M** R12M; vis W210°-221°, R221°-230°.

SCHIERMONNIKOOG
Ferry pier head 53°28'·17N 06°12'·21E 2 Fl (5) Y 20s.

LAUWERSOOG
East mole head 53°24'·72N 06°12'·14E FR 4M.
West mole head FG 3M; in fog FY; Horn (2) 30s.

OOSTMAHORN
Entrance 53°23'·00N 06°09'·72E FG

ZOUTKAMP
Entrance (unlit) 53°20'·42N 06°17'·66E.

(For Die Ems see 10.20.4).

19

10.19.5   PASSAGE INFORMATION

CROSSING SOUTHERN NORTH SEA

From Crouch, Blackwater or Orwell the first stage is to make Long Sand Head Lt Buoy — from Crouch via Whitaker Chan and East Swin; from Blackwater via the Wallet and N of Gunfleet Bn to Wallet No 2 Lt Buoy; and from Orwell via Roughs Tower and Sunk Lt F. From Long Sand Head Lt Buoy proceed to Gallop Lt Buoy and thence to W Hinder Lt V, crossing traffic scheme at right angles. Care must be taken throughout with tidal streams, which may be setting across the yacht's track. The area is relatively shallow, and in bad weather seas are steep and short.

BELGIUM

Features of this coast (chart 1872) are the long shoals lying roughly parallel to it. Mostly the deeper, buoyed chans run within 3M of shore, where the outer shoals give some protection in strong onshore winds. Approaching from seaward it is essential to fix position from one of the many marks, so that the required chan is identified before shoal water is reached. Shipping is another hazard, but it helps to identify the main routes.

From the W, the natural entry to the buoyed chans is at Dunkerque Lanby: from the Thames, bound for Oostende (10.19.9) or the Schelde (10.19.14), identify W Hinder Lt V, or the N Hinder Lt V if bound from the N. For traffic schemes see Fig. 2(2). *North Sea Harbours and Pilotage* (Adlard Coles Ltd) is recommended for the coast of Belgium and of the Netherlands to Den Helder.

Off the Belgian coast the E-going stream begins at HW Vlissingen − 0320 (HW Dover − 0120), and the W-going at HW Vlissingen + 0240 (HW Dover + 0440), sp rates 2 kn. Mostly the streams run parallel with the coast. Nieuwpoort lies 8M from the French border. From the W (Dunkerque), approach through Passe de Zuydcoote (buoyed with least depth 3.3m) and West Diep. From ENE approach through Kleine Rede, the inner road off Oostende which carries a depth of 6m. There are other approaches through the channels and over the banks offshore, but they need care in bad weather.

Off Oostende the E-going stream begins at HW Vlissingen − 0245 (HW Dover − 0045), sp rate 2½ kn; the W-going stream begins at HW Vlissingen + 0245 (HW Dover + 0445), sp rate 1½ kn. So sailing E from Oostende, leave about HW Vlissingen − 0300 to catch the E-going stream. If bound for Blankenberge (10.19.10) it is only necessary to keep a mile or two offshore, but if heading E of Zeebrugge (10.19.11) it is advisable to clear the new harbour extension by a mile or more. The main route to Zeebrugge for commercial shipping is through Scheur (the deep water channel of the Westerschelde) as far as Scheur-Zand Lt Buoy, about 3M NW of harbour entrance. There is much commercial traffic, and yachts should keep clear (S of) the buoyed channel so far as possible. Beware strong tidal stream and possibly dangerous seas in approaches to Zeebrugge.

NETHERLANDS

The main approach chans to Westerschelde (chart 325) are Wielingen and Oostgat, but yachts are required to keep clear of these. Coming from Zeebrugge keep close to S side of estuary until past Breskens (10.19.12) when, if proceeding to Vlissingen (10.19.16), cross close W of buoy H-SS. From N, use Deurloo/Spleet chans to S side of estuary. The tide runs hard in the estuary, causing a bad sea in chans and overfalls on some banks in strong winds. Vessels under 20m must give way to larger craft; and yachts under 12m are requested to stay clear of main buoyed chan, and any buoyed chan between Walsoorden and Antwerpen (10.19.15) if navigation permits.

The final stages of the barrier across the Oosterschelde (chart 192) are now completed, and entry must be made through Roompotsluis in the S part of the barrage. Several banks (e.g. Schaar, Schouwenbank, Middelbank, Steenbank) lie in the W approaches to Oosterschelde, and the main channel runs through Westgat and Oude Roompot, which are well marked. Oude Roompot would also be used if approaching from the N.

Coming from the S, Oostgat runs close to the Walcheren shore. Westkapelle Lt Ho is conspic near the W end of Walcheren. There are two lesser Lts nearby — Molenhoofd ½M WSW and Noorderhoofd ¾M NNW. Having passed the latter the coast runs NE past Domburg but becomes shallower as Roompot is approached, so it is necessary to keep near the Roompot channel which here is marked by buoys (unlit). It is important to have updated information on the buoyage and the channels.

From here to Hoek van Holland (10.19.20) banks extend 7M W of Schouwen and WSW of Goeree. Shipping is very concentrated at the entrance to Europoort and Rotterdam (10.19.19). Traffic schemes must be noted and regulations for yachts (see 10.19.20) obeyed.

The coast N to Den Helder (10.19.25) is low, and not easily visible from seaward, like most of the Dutch coast. Conspic landmarks include Noordwijk aan Zee Lt, chys of steelworks N of IJmuiden, Egmond aan Zee Lt, and chys of nuclear power station 1½M NNE of Petten. For traffic schemes see Figs. 2(3)-2(5). 3M W of IJmuiden (10.19.22) the N-going stream begins at HW Hoek van Holland − 0120, and the S-going at HW Hoek van Holland + 0430, sp rates about 1½ kn. Off entrance to IJmuiden the stream turns about 1h earlier and is stronger, and in heavy weather there may be a dangerous sea.

FRISIAN ISLANDS (charts 2593, 3761)

N from Den Helder (10.19.25), and then running E for nearly 150M along the N coasts of Netherlands and Federal Republic of Germany, is the chain of Frisian Islands. The Dutch islands are in general larger and further offshore, but the great majority of Frisian Islands have similar characteristics — being low, long and narrow, with the major axis parallel to the coast.

Between the islands, narrow chans (zeegat in Dutch, seegat in German) give access to/from the North Sea. Most of these chans are shallow for at least part of their length, and in these shoal areas a dangerous sea builds up in strong winds between W and N on the outgoing (ebb) tide. In onshore winds there are occasions when safe entry is possible on the flood tide, but departure is dangerous.

The flood stream along this coast is E-going, so it starts to run in through the zeegaten progressively from W to E. Where the tide meets behind each island, as it flows in first at the W end and a little later at the E end, is formed a bank called a wad (Dutch) or watt (German). These banks between the islands and the coast are major obstacles to E/W progress inside the islands. The chans are narrow and winding, marked by buoys or by withies in the shallower parts, and they mostly dry — so that it is essential to time the tide correctly.

This is an area most suited to shallow-draught yachts, particularly with bilge keels or centreboards, that can take the ground easily. While the main zeegaten are described very briefly below, no attempt has been made to mention the many channels inside the islands. Reference should be made to *Frisian Pilot* (Stanford Maritime).

While British Admiralty charts are adequate for through passages, coastal navigation, and entry to the main ports, foreign charts are essential for any yacht exploring the cruising grounds along this coast or using the smaller harbours. In non-tidal waters chart datum usually refers to the level at which the water is kept. In the Netherlands this may be Kanaalpeil, which in turn is related to Normaal Amsterdams Peil (NAP), which is about Mean Sea Level (MSL). In the North Sea shoal waters are liable to change due to gales and tidal streams. Changes in sea level due to special meteorological conditions may also be encountered.

It should be realised that there are numerous wrecks and obstructions which lie offshore and in coastal areas. Some of these are marked, but many are not. The Texel traffic scheme extends NNE from the Texel Lt V — see Fig.2(5): the separation zone incorporates the Helder gas field. Some 20 – 30M N lie the Placid and Petroland fields with production platforms. For general notes on N Sea oil and gas installations see 10.5.5.

Zeegat van Texel (chart 191) lies between Den Helder and the island of Texel, and gives access to the Waddenzee, the tidal part of the former Zuider Zee. Haaksgronden shoals extend 5M seaward, with three chans: Schulpengat on S side, leading into Breewijd; Westgat through centre of shoals, where the stream sets across the chan but suitable for passage in good weather and in daylight; and Molengat near the Texel shore. Schulpengat is the main chan, and is well marked, buoys being prefixed with letter 'S'; but strong SW winds cause rough sea against the SW-going (ebb) stream which begins at HW Helgoland − 0330, while the NE-going (flood) stream begins at HW Helgoland + 0325, sp rates 1½ kn. In Molengat the NW-going (ebb) stream begins at HW Helgoland − 0145, and the SE-going (flood) stream at HW Helgoland + 0425, sp rates 1¼ kn. Molengat is marked by buoys prefixed by letters 'MG', but strong winds between W and N cause a bad sea, and in such conditions Schulpengat should be used.

E of Zeegat van Texel the flood stream runs in three main directions: to E and SE through Malzwin, Wierbalg and Den Oever (where there is a lock into IJsselmeer), NE along the Afsluitdijk, and then N towards Harlingen (10.19.26); to NE and E through Texelstroom, Doove Balg towards the Pollen flats; and to NE through Texelstroom, Scheurrak, Omdraai and Oude Vlie, where it meets the flood stream from Zeegat van Terschelling. The ebb stream runs the other way. The locks at Kornwerderzand, near NE end of Afsluitdijk, also give access to the IJsselmeer (10.19.24). For Oudeschild see 10.19.30.

Eierlandsche Gat, between Texel and Vlieland, is a dangerous unmarked chan, only used by fishermen.

Zeegat van Terschelling (chart 112) is the chan between Vlieland (10.19.27) and Terschelling, leading to the harbs of Oost Vlieland, West Terschelling (10.19.28) and Harlingen (10.19.26), and also to the locks at Kornwerderzand. Terschellinger Gronden are shallow banks extending more than 3M seaward; the main chan (buoyed) through them is Zuider Stortemelk passing close N of Vlieland. In this chan the buoys are prefixed by letters 'ZS', and the E-going (flood) stream begins at HW Helgland + 0325, while the W-going (ebb) stream begins at HW Helgoland − 0230, sp rates 2½ kn. Zuider Stortemelk leads into Vliesloot, and thence to Oost Vlieland where there is a yacht harbour, and on to Vliestroom. Vliestroom is a deep, well buoyed chan (buoy numbers prefixed by letters 'VL') which runs to about 4M until its junction with Blauwe Slenk and Inschot. The latter leads to Kornwerderzand and the IJsselmeer, while Blauwe Slenk runs SE to Harlingen. At the N end of Vliestroom, Schuitengat is a buoyed chan leading to West Terschelling.

Other chans through Terschellinger Gronden are, from W to E: Stortemelk, Thomas Smit Gat and Noordgat. The first two are unmarked, and are dangerous with an ebb tide and strong wind from W or N.

Zeegat van Ameland is the chan between Terschelling and Ameland, fronted by the sandbank of Bornrif extending 3M seaward. Westgat is the main entrance, with buoys prefixed by letters 'WG'. In Westgat the flood stream begins at HW Helgoland + 0425, and the ebb stream at HW Helgoland − 0150, sp rates 2 kn. The chan runs close to the Terschelling shore: a dangerous sea develops in strong onshore winds. For Ameland see 10.19.30.

Between Ameland and Schiermonnikoog (10.19.30) is Friesche Zeegat, with the main chan also called Westgat and buoys also marked 'WG'. In strong winds the sea breaks across the whole passage. Westgat leads SE through Wierumer Gronden, and then past Englesmanplaat (a prominent sandbank in mid-channel) into Zoutkamperlaag which is the main chan (marked by buoys prefixed 'Z') to Lauwersoog (10.19.30), where locks give access to the inland waterways.

Going E, the next main chan through the Is is Westerems (chart 3509), which runs SW of the German island of Borkum (10.20.9) and leads to Delfzijl (10.19.29) and Emden (10.20.23). Hubertgat, which runs S of the main Westerems chan, is more useful when bound to or from the W, but in both these chans there is a dangerous sea on the ebb stream in strong NW winds. The E-going (flood) stream begins at HW Helgoland + 0530, and the W-going (ebb) stream begins at HW Helgoland − 0030, sp rates 1½ kn.

10.19.6   DISTANCE TABLE

Approximate distances in nautical miles are by the most direct route while avoiding dangers and allowing for traffic separation schemes etc. Places in *italics* are in adjoining areas.

	1	2	3	4	5	6	7	8	9	10	11	12	13	14	15	16	17	18	19	20
1 *North Foreland*	1																			
2 *Dunkerque*	40	2																		
3 *Burnham-on-Crouch*	36	75	3																	
4 *Great Yarmouth*	77	101	76	4																
5 *Grimsby*	169	194	168	94	5															
6 Oostende	58	26	91	93	194	6														
7 Breskens	80	54	103	101	191	28	7													
8 Vlissingen	82	56	104	101	191	30	3	8												
9 Goeree Tower	91	73	108	83	169	51	40	40	9											
10 IJmuiden	137	119	151	102	182	97	86	86	46	10										
11 Amsterdam	150	132	164	115	195	110	99	99	59	13	11									
12 Den Helder	171	153	169	115	180	131	120	120	80	38	51	12								
13 West Terschelling	187	185	196	135	193	163	152	152	112	70	83	39	13							
14 Westerems Lt Buoy	226	224	235	174	232	202	191	191	151	109	122	78	47	14						
15 *Delzijl*	263	261	272	211	269	239	228	228	188	146	159	115	84	33	15					
16 *Norderney*	259	257	268	207	265	235	224	224	184	142	155	111	80	34	41	16				
17 *Wangerooge*	283	281	292	231	289	259	248	248	208	166	179	135	104	58	65	29	17			
18 *Wilhelmshaven*	307	305	316	255	313	283	272	272	232	190	203	159	128	82	89	53	27	18		
19 *Helgoland*	300	298	309	241	285	276	265	265	225	183	196	152	121	68	81	44	24	43	19	
20 *Brunsbüttel*	337	336	342	287	332	314	303	303	263	221	234	190	159	113	120	84	55	70	51	20

19

SPECIAL FACTORS AFFECTING BELGIUM AND THE NETHERLANDS   10-19-7

BELGIUM

TIME ZONE is −0100, which is allowed for in tidal predictions but no provision is made for daylight saving schemes which are indicated by the non-shaded areas on the tide tables (see 9.1.2).

SIGNALS International Port Traffic Signals (see colour plate 8) are shown at Nieuwpoort, Oostende and Zeebrugge. Small craft warnings (shown when wind from seaward is Force 4 or over) remain in force at Nieuwpoort, Oostende, Blankenberge and Zeebrugge as follows: −
By day: two black cones, points together
By night: blue flashing light.

CHARTS The chart most widely used is the 'Vlaamse Banken' issued by the Hydrografische Dienst der Kust. Admiralty, Stanford and Imray chart numbers are quoted.

PROVINCES In place of 'counties' in the UK, Provinces are given for Belgian ports.

MARINE RESCUE CO-ORDINATION CENTRES Sea Rescue Co-ordination Centre, Oostende, Tel. 70.10.00, 70.11.00, 70.77.01 or 70.77.02. Coast station, Oostende Radio Tel. 70.24.38.
In emergency Tel. 900, or call *Oostende Radio* VHF Ch 16. For medical advice call *Radiomédical Oostende* on Ch 16.

PUBLIC HOLIDAYS New Year's Day, Easter Monday, Labour Day (1 May), Ascension Day, Whit Monday, National Day (21 July), Feast of the Assumption (15 August), All Saints' Day (1 November), Armistice Day (11 November), King's Birthday or Fete de la Dynastie (15 November), Christmas Day.

TELEPHONE To call UK from Belgium, dial 00 (pause for new tone to be heard) 44. Then dial the full UK area code but omitting the prefix 0, followed by the number required. To call Belgium from UK, dial 010-32 followed by the code and number.

Emergencies Police − dial 101
Fire − dial 100

NOTE 1: Although the Hr Mr's tel no is given for Belgian ports, he is not the key figure for yachtsmen that he is in British ports. Berths and moorings are always administered by the local yacht clubs. British yachtsmen are very welcome in Belgian ports and YCs.
NOTE 2: Belgian harbour police are very strict about yachts using their engines entering harbour. If sails are used as well, display a black cone. Yachts may not navigate within 200m of shore (MLWS).
NOTE 3: Ports of entry are Nieuwpoort, Oostende and Zeebrugge.
NOTE 4: Further information can be obtained from The Belgian National Tourist Office, 38 Dover St., London, W1X 3RB, Tel. 071 499 5379.

NETHERLANDS

TIME ZONE is −0100, which is allowed for in tidal predictions but no provision is made for daylight saving schemes which are indicated by the non-shaded areas (see 9.1.2).

SIGNALS Traffic signals The standard French/Belgian system is not used in the Netherlands. Where possible the local system is given.
Sluicing signals In the Netherlands the following sluicing signals may be shown:
By day: A blue board, with the word 'SPUIEN' on it, often in addition to the night signal, of three red lights in a triangle, point up.
Visual storm signals Light signals only, shown day and night, in accordance with the International System (see 10.14.7) are shown at the following harbours: Vlissingen, Hoek van Holland, Amsterdam, IJmuiden, Den Helder, West Terschelling, Texel Lt V, Harlingen, Eierland, Ameland, Oostmahorn, Schiermonnikoog, Zoutkamp and Delfzijl.

Inland waterways
Bridge signals

Y −	You may pass under this arch
R each side −	Bridge closed (opens on request)
R one side G other side	Bridge about to open
G each side −	Bridge open
2 R (vert) 2 G (vert)	Bridge out of use
each side −	Bridge open but not in use (you may pass)

To request bridges to open sound 'long, short, long'.

Railway bridges
Opening times of railway bridges in the Netherlands are given in a leaflet 'Openingstijden Spoorwegbruggen' published annually by ANWB and available free (send A5 self addressed envelope with international reply coupon) from Aan de Chef der Hydrografie, Postbus 90704, 2509 LS 's-Gravenhage.

Buoyage
In certain inland waters, including the whole of the IJsselmeer, a buoyage system known as SIGNI is used. The main features are:
(1) Channel buoyage as for IALA (Region A).
(2) Supplementary port and starboard hand buoys may be red and white or green and white respectively.
(3) At division of channel, a spherical buoy with following characteristics:
  a. Channels of equal importance − red and green bands; topmark red and green sphere;
  b. Main channel to port − green above red; topmark green cone or green cone above a green sphere;
  c. Main channel to starboard − red above green; topmark red can or red can above a red sphere.
Offshore buoys are often marked with abbreviations of the banks or channels which they mark (e.g. ZS − Zuider Stortemelk). A separation buoy has the abbreviations of both channels meeting there.
Some channels are marked with perches, starboard hand bound, port hand unbound. On tidal flats (e.g. Friesland) where the direction of main flood stream is uncertain, bound perches are on the S side of a channel and unbound on the N side.
In minor channels the buoyage may be moved without notice to accommodate changes.

CHARTS Chart numbers are printed in the following order:− Admiralty; Zeekaarten (equivalent to Admiralty, issued by the Hydrographer, Royal Netherlands Navy and up-dated by Dutch Notices to Mariners); Dutch Yacht Charts (Kaarten voor Zeil en Motorjachten, also issued by the Hydrographer of the Royal Netherlands Navy. A new edition comes out each year in March and is updated in Dutch Notices to Mariners); the letters of the ANWB Waterkaarten are quoted, lettered from A in the north to O in the South; Stanford (where applicable); Imray (where applicable). Visiting yachts are required to carry the ANWB publication 'Almanak voor Watertoerisme'.

PROVINCES In place of 'counties' in the UK, Provinces are given for Netherlands ports.

MARINE RESCUE CO-ORDINATION CENTRES Coast station Scheveningen Radio Tel. 550.19104. In emergency call *Scheveningen Radio* VHF Ch 16. For medical advice call *Radiomédical Scheveningen* on Ch 16.

PUBLIC HOLIDAYS New Year's Day, Easter Monday, Queen's Birthday (30 April), Liberation Day (5 May), Ascension Day, Whit Monday, Christmas Day and Boxing Day.

TELEPHONE To call UK from the Netherlands, dial 09 (pause for new tone to be heard) 44. Then dial the full UK area code but omitting the prefix 0, followed by the number required.
To call the Netherlands from UK dial 010-31 followed by the area code and number.

Emergencies − Police dial 101; Ambulance and Fire 100.

CUSTOMS Main customs ports are Breskens, Vlissingen, Roompotsluis, Hoek van Holland, Scheveningen, IJmuiden, Den Helder, Harlingen, Oost Vlieland, West Terschelling, Lauwersoog and Delfzijl. No entry/customs facilities at Stellendam, Den Oever or Kornwonderzand.

Note Further information, including a useful publication 'Watersports Paradise' can be obtained from the Netherlands Board of Tourism, 25 Buckingham Gate, London, SW1E 6LD, Tel. (071) 630 0451. Royal Netherland Embassy, 12a Kensington Palace Gdns, London W8 4QU (071) 229 1594.

NIEUWPOORT (NIEUPORT)

West Flanders

10-19-8

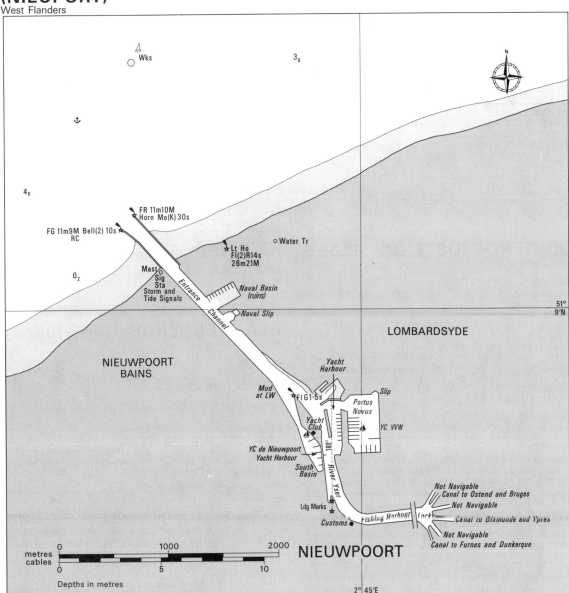

CHARTS
Admiralty 125, 1872; Belgian 101, D11; SHOM 6652;
Stanford 1, 19; Imray C30

TIDES
Dover +0105; ML 2.4; Duration 0515; Zone −0100

Standard Port VLISSINGEN (→)

Times				Height (metres)			
HW		LW		MHWS	MHWN	MLWN	MLWS
0300	0900	0400	1000	4.7	3.9	0.8	0.3
1500	2100	1600	2200				

Differences NIEUWPOORT
−0110 −0050 −0035 −0045 +0.6 +0.4 +0.4 +0.1

SHELTER
Shelter is good except for strong winds from the NW.
There are two yacht harbours, both with good shelter.
The YC of Nieuwpoort gets very full but there is always
ample room in the Portus Novus.

NAVIGATION
Waypoint 51°10'.00N 02°42'.00E, 308°/128° from/to
entrance, 0.90M. The bar is liable to silt up but there is
usually sufficient water for yachts. Entrance and channels
to both yacht harbours are dredged, although channel to
both yacht harbours can drop to about 2m. At springs
there is a strong stream across the entrance. The firing
range E of Nieuwpoort is not used mid-June to end of
September. At other times, contact range officer on
Ch 67.

LIGHTS AND MARKS
Lt Ho Fl(2)R 14s 26m 21M; R Tr, W bands. E pier, head
FR 11m 10M; W Tr; vis 025°-250°, 307°-347°; Horn
Mo(K) 30s. W pier, head FG 11m 9M; W Tr; vis
025°-250°, 284°-324°; Bell(2) 10s; RC. International Port
Traffic Signals from root of W pier, with addition of:
 ⚑ or Fl Bu Lt   Departure prohibited for craft
              under 6m length.

RADIO TELEPHONE
VHF Ch 09 19 16 (H24)

TELEPHONE (051 or 058)
Hr Mr 233000; CG 233045; Sea Rescue Helicopter
311714; ⌗ 233451; Duty Free Store 233433;
Police 233002; Ⓗ (Oostende) 707631; Dr 233089; Brit
Consul (02) 2179000.

19

NIEUWPOORT *continued*

FACILITIES
Koninklijke Yacht Club (400 + 80 visitors) ☎ 234413,
Slip, M, L, FW, C (10 ton), CH, AB, R, Bar, Gas, ME, El,
Sh, V, P, D, ☑, Access; H24 **Novus Portus** (1,900 + 500
visitors) ☎ 235232, Slip, FW, BH (30 ton), C (15 ton), AC,
CH, D, R, Bar; **YC Militair** ☎ 233433, M, L, FW, C (2
ton mobile), CH; **Belgian Boat Service** ☎ 234473, P, D,
L, ME, El, Sh, C (15 ton), Gaz, CH; **West Diep**
☎ 234061, ME, El, Sh, C (6 ton), SM, CH; **Ship Shop**
☎ 235032, L, ME, El, Sh, C (6 ton), CH.
Town P, D, V, R, Bar. ⊠; Ⓑ; ⇌; ✈ (Ostend).
Ferry UK — Ostend—Dover.
(Fuel can be bought on the harbour by arrangement).

OOSTENDE (OSTEND) 10-19-9
West Flanders

CHARTS
Admiralty 325, 125, 1872; SHOM 6652; Dutch Yacht Chart
1801; Stanford 1, 19; Imray C30
TIDES
Dover +0110; ML 2.4; Duration 0530; Zone −0100

Standard Port VLISSINGEN (→)

Times				Height (metres)			
HW		LW		MHWS	MHWN	MLWN	MLWS
0300	0900	0400	1000	4.7	3.9	0.8	0.3
1500	2100	1600	2200				

Differences OOSTENDE

−0055	−0040	−0030	−0045	+0.3	+0.3	+0.3	+0.1

SHELTER
Very good shelter especially in the Town and Mercator
Yacht Harbour (entered via the Montgomery Dock). Quiet
berths may be found further up harbour in the Voorhaven
by the VVW and Royal Oostende YCs.
NAVIGATION
Waypoint 51°15′.00N 02°53′.97E, 308°/128° from/to
entrance, 0.98M. Approaching Oostende beware crossing
the Stroombank and avoid altogether in rough weather;
then approach by channel inside the bank or through the
buoyed channel.
LIGHTS AND MARKS
Oostende Fl(3) 10s 63m 27M; W Tr; RC. W pier head FG
12m 10M: W Tr; vis 057°-327°; Bell(1) 4s. E pier head FR
13m 12M; W Tr; vis 333°-243°; Horn Mo(OE) 30s. Ldg Lts
128° both FR 12/18m 4M; both X on W pylons, R bands;
vis 051°-201°.
International Port Traffic Signals are shown from head of
E pier, with addition of following signals from S side of
entrance to Montgomery dock: –

    ⌀ or Fl Bu Lt   – Departure of craft under
                  6m length prohibited.

RADIO TELEPHONE
VHF Ch 09 16 67 (H24). Mercator Marina Ch 14 (H24).
TELEPHONE (059)
Hr Mr 705762; Life Saving Service 701100; Weather 991;
🚓 702009; Police 500925; Ⓗ 707637;
Brit Consul (02) 2179000.
FACILITIES
Mercator Yacht Harbour (450 + 50 visitors) ☎ 705762,
FW, AC, P, D, C, Slip; **North Sea YC** ☎ 702754, L, FW,
AB, R, Bar; **Royal YC of Oostende** (160 + 40 visitors)
☎ 321452, Slip, M, C (½ ton), L, V, FW, AB, R, Bar;
Montgomery Dock (70 + 50 visitors) YC, Bar, R, FW,
Slip; **Compas** ☎ 700057, ME, CH; **Maritime Bureau
Hindery CKT** ☎ 707261, ME, Sh, CH; **N end of Fishing
harbour** D; **North Sea Marine** ☎ 320688, ME, El, Sh,
SM; **Marina Yachting Centre** ☎ 320028, CH.
Town P and D (cans), CH, V, R, Bar. ⊠; Ⓑ; ⇌; ✈.
Ferry UK—Dover.

BLANKENBERGE 10-19-10
West Flanders

CHARTS
Admiralty 1872, 325; Dutch Yacht Chart 1801;
Stanford 1, 19; Imray C30
TIDES
Dover +0130; ML 2.5; Duration 0535; Zone −0100

Standard Port VLISSINGEN (→)

Times		Height (metres)			
HW	LW	MHWS	MHWN	MLWN	MLWS
All times	All times	4.7	3.9	0.8	0.3

Differences BLANKENBERGE

−0040	−0040	−0.3	−0.1	+0.3	+0.1

SHELTER
Good shelter in the basin in the town and in the yacht
harbour. There are also berths by the floating pontoons or
alongside the quay. Entrance channel between moles
subject to silting, but dredged continuously.
NAVIGATION
Waypoint Wenduine Bank N (stbd-hand) buoy, QG,
51°21′.55N 03°02′.67E, 317°/137° from/to entrance, 3.6M.
Entry should not be attempted when strong winds are
from the NW. Beware strong tides across entrance.
LIGHTS AND MARKS
Ldg Lts 134°, Front (Red X on column) FR 3M, Rear (Red
X on concrete post) FR, 3M, show the best water.
FS by Lt Ho shows
    ⌀ or Fl Bu Lt   – Departure of craft under 6m
                   length prohibited.
RADIO TELEPHONE
Private volunteer VHF service, Ch 08 (or relay via Ostend
or Zeebrugge).
TELEPHONE (050)
Hr Mr 411420; 🚓 Zeebrugge 544223; Police 411009;
Dr 333668; Ⓗ 413701; Brit Consul (02) 2179000.
FACILITIES
Marine Centre ☎ 413560, ME, El, Sh, C (15 ton), CH;
Agemex ☎ 414938, Slip, ME, El, Sh, C (5 ton), CH;
Yacht Harbour Slip, FW, C (10 ton); **Scarphout YC**
☎ 411420, Bar, R, M, C (2½ ton), D, P, CH, FW, L, Slip;
Wittervrongel Sails ☎ 411863, SM, CH; **N.V.
Internautic on Sea** ☎ 413178, Slip, P, D, L, ME, El, Sh,
C (22 ton), CH; **Marine Yachting Centre** ☎ 415712, CH;
YC Vrije Noordzeezeilers (VNZ) ☎ 429150, M, Bar, C (2
ton), FW, L; **YC VVW** ☎ 417536, Bar, M, D, P, FW, ☑,
Slip;. **Town** V, R, Gaz, Bar. ⊠; Ⓑ; ⇌; ✈ (Ostend).
Ferry UK — Zeebrugge—Dover/Hull/Felixstowe.

BLANKENBERGE *continued*

ZEEBRUGGE 10-19-11
West Flanders

CHARTS
Admiralty 325, 1872, 97; Zeekaart 1441; Dutch Yacht Chart 1801, 1803; Stanford 1, 19; Imray C30

TIDES
Dover +0110; ML 2.4; Duration 0535; Zone −0100

Standard Port VLISSINGEN (→)

Times				Height (metres)			
HW		LW		MHWS	MHWN	MLWN	MLWS
0300	0900	0400	1000	4.7	3.9	0.8	0.3
1500	2100	1600	2200				

Differences ZEEBRUGGE
| −0035 | −0015 | −0020 | −0035 | +0.1 | 0.0 | +0.3 | +0.1 |

SHELTER
Shelter in Zeebrugge is very good and harbour is always available. Zeebrugge is the port of Brugge (Zee Brugge) and the canal up to Brugge (or Bruges) is 6 M long. The yacht harbour is very well protected except in strong NE winds. New marina is projected.

NAVIGATION
Waypoint Scheur-Zand E cardinal buoy, Q(3) 10s, 51°23'.70N 03°07'.68E, 309°/129° from/to entrance, 3.1M. There are no hazards approaching the harbour mouth except harbour works which are still in progress (1989), marked by buoys. Beware strong currents in harbour approaches (up to 4 kn at HW − 1). Zeebrugge is the main fishing port of Belgium and is a ferry terminal, so keep clear of fishing boats and ferries. Call Harbour Control Ch 71 before entry.

LIGHTS AND MARKS
(1) Ldg Lts 136°. Oc 5s 8M, vis 131°-141° synchronised (H24).
(2) Ldg Lts 154°. Front Oc WR 6s. Rear Oc 6s synchronised (H24).
(3) Ldg Lts 235°. Both QR 5M, synchronised.
(4) Ldg Lts 220°, Front 2FW(vert) 30/22m. Rear FW 30m. Both W concrete columns, B bands.
(5) Ldg Lts 193°. Front 2FR(vert) 30/22m. Rear FR 29m. Both W concrete columns, R bands.
International Port Traffic Signals are shown at NE end of Leopold II Dam (old Zeebrugge mole). A QY Lt at S side of Visserhaven prohibits entry/departure to/from Visserhaven.

RADIO TELEPHONE
VHF Port Entrance and Port Control Ch 71 (H24).

TELEPHONE (050)
Hr Mr Bruges 544268; Hr Mr 543241; Port Control 546867; Lock Mr 543231; CG 545072; Sea Saving Service 544007; ⌗ 544223; Police 544148; Dr 544590; Ⓗ 320832; Brit Consul (02) 2179000.

FACILITIES
Yacht Harbour (100) ☎ 544903, Slip, Sh, CH, D, AB, R, Bar; Pontoon L, FW; Alberta (bar/restaurant of Royal Belgian SC) ☎ 544197, R, Bar; Royal Belgian SC ☎ 544903, M, AB; Brugge Marine ☎ 353375, ME, El; Hennion Luc Yachting ☎ 544829, CH.
Town P, D, FW, ME, El, Sh, CH, Gaz, V, R, Bar. ✉; Ⓑ; ⇌; Tram to Oostende; ✈ (Ostend).
Ferry UK—Dover/Hull/Folkestone.

BRESKENS 10-19-12
Zeeland

CHARTS
Admiralty 325; Zeekaart 1442, 1483; Dutch Yacht Chart 1801, 1803; Stanford 1,19; Imray C30

TIDES
Dover +0210; ML 2.5; Duration 0600; Zone −0100

Standard Port VLISSINGEN (→)

Times				Height (metres)			
HW		LW		MHWS	MHWN	MLWN	MLWS
0300	0900	0400	1000	4.7	3.9	0.8	0.3
1500	2100	1600	2200				

Differences BRESKENS
| −0005 | −0005 | −0002 | −0002 | +0.1 | 0.0 | 0.0 | 0.0 |

19

BRESKENS *continued*

SHELTER
Good shelter in all winds. The North finger of the marina is for visiting yachts. The marina is operated by Oostburg municipality. Anchor off Plaat van Breskens, not in harbour.

NAVIGATION
Waypoint SS-VH N cardinal buoy, Q, 51°24'.75N 03°34'.00E, 357°/177° from/to W breakwater Lt, 0.69M. Beware strong tides across the entrance. There is a shoal just to port after passing the entrance. Make sure the entrance is not confused with that of the ferry port 1000m WNW, where yachts are forbidden.

LIGHTS AND MARKS
West mole head F WRG 8m; vis R090°-128°, W128°-157°, R157°-172°, W172°-175°, G175°-296°, W296°-300°, R300°-008°, G008°-090°; Horn Mo(U) 30s. E mole head FR 5m. Nieuwe Sluis Lt Oc WRG 10s is 1.2M W of Ferry Hr.

RADIO TELEPHONE
VHF Ch 14.

TELEPHONE (01172)
Hr Mr 1902; ⌗ 2610; Police 3156; Dr 1566; Ⓗ (01170) 3355; Brit Consul (020) 764343.

FACILITIES
Marina ☎ 1902, FW, ▣; **YC Breskens** ☎ 3278, R, Bar; **Neil Pryde** ☎ 2101, SM; **C. Kosten** ☎ 1257, CH, D, Gaz, P, chart agent; **Standfast** ☎ 1797, BY, C (15 ton), El, ME, Sh, Slip; **Proctor** ☎ 1397 masts; **Jachtwerf Delta** ☎ 2440, BY, C (18 ton), El, ME, Sh; **M D Meeusen** ☎ 1996, Sh; **Tronik Shop** ☎ 3031, El, Ⓔ; **Town** V, R, Bar, ✉; Ⓑ; Gas, ⇌ (Flushing); ✈ (Ghent or Brussels). Ferry UK — Flushing—Sheerness.

TERNEUZEN   10-19-13
Zeeland

CHARTS
Admiralty 120; Zeekaart 1443; Dutch Yacht Chart 1803; Stanford 19; Imray C30

TIDES
Dover +0230; ML 2.6; Duration 0555; Zone −0100

Standard Port VLISSINGEN (→)

Times				Height (metres)			
HW		LW		MHWS	MHWN	MLWN	MLWS
0300	0900	0400	1000	4.7	3.9	0.8	0.3
1500	2100	1600	2200				

Differences TERNEUZEN

+0021	+0022	+0022	+0033	+0.3	+0.3	0.0	0.0

SHELTER
Very good except in strong NW winds. The Veerhaven is tidal and exposed to NE. Yachts can find shelter through the East Lock (Oostsluis); see Lockmaster for berth. Yachts are prohibited in West Lock (Westsluis) and Western Harbour.

NAVIGATION
Waypoint No 23A (stbd-hand) buoy, IsoG 4s, 51°21'.37N 03°45'.66E, 285°/105° from/to Veerhaven entrance, 2.6M. Westerschelde (see 10.19.14) is a mass of sand-banks but well marked. It is the waterway to Antwerpen and Ghent, very full of shipping and also of barges (which do not normally conform to the rules). The Ghent canal is 17M long with three bridges, minimum clearance 6.5m when closed; VHF Ch 11 is compulsory.

LIGHTS AND MARKS
For the Veerhaven, the water Tr to SE and the Oc WRG Lt on W mole are conspic. When entry prohibited, a R flag is shown at W mole head by day, or a second R Lt below FR on E mole by night.
Signals for Oostsluis: R Lts each side of lock — entry prohibited; G Lts each side — entry permitted.

RADIO TELEPHONE
Call: *Havendienst Terneuzen* VHF Ch 11 (H24). Information broadcasts every H + 00. For Terneuzen-Ghent canal call on Ch 11 and keep watch during transit. Contact Zelzate Bridge (call: *Uitkijk Zelzate*) direct on Ch 11, other bridges through Terneuzen. See also 10.19.14 for Schelde Information Service. Other stations: Ghent (call *Havendienst Ghent*) Ch 05 11 (H24); Antwerpen (call: *Antwerpen Havendienst*) Ch 18 (H24).

TELEPHONE (01150)
Hr Mr 96331; CG 13017 (H24); ⌗ 12377; Police 13017; Ⓗ 88000; Dr 12200; Brit Consul (020) 764343.

FACILITIES
Yacht harbour (120) ☎ 97089, Slip, ME, El, Sh, BH (15 ton), FW, AB; **de Honte YC** ☎ 17633, L, FW, ▣, AB; **Neuzen YC** ☎ 96331, M, L, FW, AB; **D. Hamelink** ☎ 97240, ME, El; **Vermeulen's Jachtwerf** (inside locks) ☎ 12716, P, D, L, FW, ME, El, C (40 ton), AB; **Pontoon** L, FW, AB (see Hr Mr); **Sluiskil** Sh; **Flodewijk Eprom Electronic** ☎ 30486 Ⓔ **A. Dam** ☎ 13774 Gaz. **Town** P, D, CH, V, R, Bar. ✉; Ⓑ; ⇌; ✈ (Ghent). Ferry UK — Flushing—Sheerness.

WESTERSCHELDE   10-19-14
Zeeland

CHARTS
Admiralty 120, 139, 325; Zeekaart 1443; Dutch Yacht Chart 1803; Stanford 19; Imray C30

TIDES
Dover +0200; ML (Hansweert) 2.7; Duration 0555; Zone −0100

Standard Port VLISSINGEN (→)

Times				Height (metres)			
HW		LW		MHWS	MHWN	MLWN	MLWS
0300	0900	0400	1000	4.7	3.9	0.8	0.3
1500	2100	1600	2200				

Differences WESTKAPELLE

−0024	−0014	−0012	−0023	−0.6	−0.5	−0.1	0.0

HANSWEERT

+0114	+0054	+0040	+0100	+0.5	+0.6	0.0	−0.1

BATH

+0126	+0117	+0117	+0144	+0.8	+0.9	0.0	0.0

WESTERSCHELDE *continued*

SHELTER
There are few harbours in the 38M from Terneuzen to Antwerpen. The following are possible for yachts:
HOEDEKENSKERKE — on N bank, disused ferry harbour (dries).
HANSWEERT — can be used temporarily, but it is the busy entrance to Zuid Beveland canal.
WALSOORDEN — on S bank with yacht harbour (Tijhaven, dries) on N side, and Diepe Haven on S side (depth 3m, but exposed to swell), both approached through same entrance.
ZANDVLIET — in Belgium, on N bank, is a commercial harbour; use only in emergency.
LILLO — customs post, for shallow-draught boats only.

NAVIGATION
Waypoints — see Breskens (10.19.12) and Terneuzen (10.19.13). Note traffic scheme off Vlissingen (see 10.19.5). The winding channel through the shifting banks is well marked, but full of commercial traffic. It is necessary to work the tide, which runs 2½ kn on average and more at springs. Yachts should keep at edge of main channel, and beware unpredictable actions of barges. Alternative channels must be used with caution, particularly going downstream on the ebb.

LIGHTS AND MARKS
The approaches to Westerschelde are well lit — on the S shore by Lt Trs at Kruishoofd and Nieuwe Sluis, and on the N shore at Westkapelle and Kaapduinen. Details of these and other important Lts are in 10.19.4. The main fairway is, for the most part, covered by the narrow white sectors of the various lights along the shore.

RADIO TELEPHONE
The following shore stations comprise the Schelde Information Service (all H24):
(1) Vlissingen.
A. Scheldemonding area, seaward of Kaapduinen and Kruishoofd Lts, call *Vlissingen Radio* VHF Ch 14.
B. Vlissingen area call *Post Vlissingen* Ch 21.
(2) Terneuzen area, call *Post Terneuzen* Ch **03** 14
(3) Hansweert area, call *Hansweert Radio* Ch 71
(4) Zandvliet area, call *Zandvliet Radio* Ch 12 14
Information broadcasts in Dutch and English every H + 05 on Ch 03 by Terneuzen; every H + 35 on Ch 12 by Zandvliet; Every H + 20 on Ch 71 by Hansweert and every H + 50 on Ch 14 by Vlissingen.
For other stations see harbour concerned.

FACILITIES
TERNEUZEN — see 10.19.13
HOEDEKENSKERKE (01193) — visitors berths, P, D, Gaz, FW; **W. Bek** ☎ 309 ME; **YC WV Hoedekenskerke** ☎ 259. **Town** ✉; Ⓑ; ⇌ (Goes); ✈ (Antwerpen)
HANSWEERT (01130) — visitors berths, ME, C (17 ton) R, P, D; **Ribbens** ☎ 1371 CH; **Scheepswerf Reimerswaal** ☎ 3021, BY. **Town** ✉; Ⓑ; ⇌ (Goes); ✈ (Antwerpen)
WALSOORDEN — visitors berths; **Havenmeester** ☎ 1235, P, D, Gaz; **De Klerk Scheepsbouw** ☎ 1614, BY. **Town** ✉; ⇌; ✈ (Antwerpen).

ANTWERPEN (ANTWERP)   10-19-15
Antwerpen

CHARTS
Admiralty 139; Stanford 19; Zeekaart 1443; Dutch Yacht Chart 1803;

TIDES
Dover +0334; ML 2.7; Duration 0605; Zone −0100

Standard Port VLISSINGEN (→)

Times				Height (metres)			
HW		LW		MHWS	MHWN	MLWN	MLWS
0300	0900	0400	1000	4.7	3.9	0.8	0.3
1500	2100	1600	2200				

Differences ANTWERPEN
| +0128 | +0116 | +0121 | +0144 | +1.1 | +0.9 | 0.0 | 0.0 |

SHELTER
Excellent in Imalso marina on W bank, 4ca (750m) SW of Kattendijksluis and ½M from city centre which can be reached through two tunnels. Access by lock HW∓1 (0600-2000). Lock closed in winter except by arrangement.

NAVIGATION
For Westerschelde see 10.19.12/13/14. On river bend before marina is a windmill, and G conical buoy Iso G 8s. Two unlit Y buoys N and S of lock can be used if entrance is closed.

LIGHTS AND MARKS
(marina signals)
R flag or R Lt	— Entrance prohibited
G flag or G Lt	— Departure prohibited
Bu cone/flag or Bu Lt	— Approach channel closed
B ball or FW Lt	— Depth over sill 2.5–3.0m
2 B balls or 2 FW Lts	— Depth over sill 3.0–3.5m
3 B balls or 3 FW Lts	— Depth over sill 3.5–3.8m

Yachts should make following Int Code signals:
UH — I wish to enter marina under power
UP — I have an emergency; request priority entry
Z — Request tug assistance for entry
P — I wish to leave harbour

RADIO TELEPHONE
Call: *Antwerpen Havendienst* VHF Ch 18 (H24). Imalso Marina, (call *Bolleke*) Ch 72.

TELEPHONE (03)
Marina Lock Keeper 2190895; ⌗ 2340840; Police 321840; Ⓗ 2177111.

FACILITIES
Imalso Marina ☎ 2190895, FW, P, D, R, V, Gaz, El, Sh, AC, C (1.5 ton), Slip; **Royal YC van België** ☎ 2192788 Bar, R, M, C (5 ton), D, P, CH, FW, L, Slip; **Kon. Liberty YC** ☎ 2191147; **Martin & Co** ☎ 7994, ACA; **Bogerd Navtec** ☎ 8476 ACA; **Landtmeters** ☎ 2333131; **City** All facilities including ✉; Ⓑ; ⇌; ✈;
Ferry UK — Flushing-Sheerness.

19

ANTWERPEN *continued*

VLISSINGEN (FLUSHING)

10-19-16

Zeeland

CHARTS
Admiralty 325, 120, 1872; Zeekaart 1442, 1443, 1533; Dutch Yacht Chart 1803; Stanford 19; Imray C30

TIDES
Dover +0200; ML 2.4; Duration 0555; Zone −0100

NOTE: Flushing is a Standard Port and the tidal predictions for each day of the year are given below.

SHELTER
Very good shelter, in both yacht harbours, one being near the entrance to the lock to Walcheren canal. The Old Harbour to the W has storm barrier (opens 1 Apr–1 Oct) leading to Michiel du Ruyter marina. Arrival restricted to 0800–2200 LT.

NAVIGATION
Waypoint H-SS N cardinal buoy, Q, 51°25'.97N 03°37'.54E, 125°/305° from/to Buitenhaven entrance, 0.95M. Approaching from the SW there are no dangers. Yachts are forbidden to sail in the main fairways. From Zeebrugge, keep S of Wielingen channel past Breskens, and cross to Flushing near buoy H-SS. From N use Deurloo/Spleet channels to S side of estuary, then as above. Heavy ocean-going traffic, often taking on or dropping pilots, off the town. In the harbour, frequent ferries berth at terminals near the locks and enter and leave at speed. See Westerschelde Traffic lanes Fig 2(3).

LIGHTS AND MARKS
The Lt Ho at the root of the W breakwater of Koopmanshaven is brown metal framework Tr, Iso WRG 3s 15m 12/9M.
Ldg Lts 117°. Front Leugenaar causeway, near head, OcR 5s 5m 7M. Rear Sardijngeul, 550m from front Oc WRG 5s 10m 12/8M, R Δ, W bands on R and W mast.
Entry signals from pier W side of Buitenhaven entrance:

R flag	or	Additional R Lt near R harbour Lt	Entry prohibited

R flag over G flag	or	Additional R and G Lt near R harbour Lt	Entry prohibited if over 6m draught

Two R Lts (vert) from lock indicate 'lock closed'.

RADIO TELEPHONE
Vlissingen Port Ch 21. Flushing – East Port Ch 09. Lock information Ch 22.
See also Westerschelde (10.19.14).

TELEPHONE (01184)
Hr Mr 68080; East Harbour Port Authority 68080; Buitenhaven Lock Keeper 12372; ⌗ 60000; Police 15050; Ⓗ 15000; Dr 12233; Brit Consul (020) 764343.

FACILITIES
Michiel de Ruyter (60 + 40 visitors) ☎ 14498 D, P, FW, AC, Bar, R, YC; **Jachthaven 'VVW Schelde'** (85 + 40 visitors) ☎ 65912 AC, Bar, C (10 ton), D, FW, R, Ⓞ, M, Slip, (Access H24); **Royal Schelde Repair Yard** Sh; **Bureau Kramer** ☎ 16364, ME, Sh; **Gerb van de Gruiter** ☎ 65961, SM; **F. J. Roovers Sport** ☎ 13361, Gaz; **Town** P, D, CH, V, R, Bar. ✉; Ⓑ; ⇌; ✈ (Antwerpen). Ferry UK–Sheerness.

TIME ZONE –0100
(Dutch Standard Time)
Subtract 1 hour for GMT
For Dutch Summer Time add
ONE hour in non-shaded areas

NETHERLANDS - VLISSINGEN (FLUSHING)

LAT 51°27'N   LONG 3°36'E

TIMES AND HEIGHTS OF HIGH AND LOW WATERS   YEAR 1991

JANUARY

#	TIME	m	#	TIME	m
1 TU	0146 / 0816 / 1406 / 2035	4.7 / 0.2 / 4.9 / 0.3	16 W	0218 / 0835 / 1438 / 2046	4.4 / 0.4 / 4.5 / 0.7
2 W	0236 / 0905 / 1455 / 2122	4.7 / 0.1 / 5.0 / 0.4	17 TH	0255 / 0915 / 1508 / 2120	4.5 / 0.3 / 4.6 / 0.6
3 TH	0322 / 0955 / 1543 / 2205	4.8 / 0.0 / 5.0 / 0.5	18 F	0325 / 0956 / 1541 / 2155	4.5 / 0.3 / 4.7 / 0.6
4 F	0407 / 1041 / 1630 / 2249	4.7 / 0.1 / 4.9 / 0.6	19 SA	0357 / 1030 / 1615 / 2229	4.6 / 0.2 / 4.6 / 0.6
5 SA	0456 / 1128 / 1718 / 2331	4.6 / 0.1 / 4.7 / 0.7	20 SU	0431 / 1108 / 1647 / 2306	4.5 / 0.2 / 4.6 / 0.7
6 SU	0542 / 1216 / 1811	4.5 / 0.2 / 4.5	21 M	0505 / 1146 / 1727 / 2346	4.5 / 0.3 / 4.5 / 0.7
7 M	0020 / 0636 / 1255 / (1906	0.8 / 4.3 / 0.4 / 4.3	22 TU	0546 / 1215 / 1807	4.4 / 0.3 / 4.4
8 TU	0108 / 0726 / 1345 / 2000	0.9 / 4.1 / 0.6 / 4.0	23 W	0026 / 0627 / 1306 /) 1901	0.7 / 4.3 / 0.4 / 4.3
9 W	0206 / 0819 / 1446 / 2105	1.0 / 3.9 / 0.8 / 3.8	24 TH	0116 / 0726 / 1358 / 2010	0.8 / 4.2 / 0.5 / 4.1
10 TH	0316 / 0936 / 1555 / 2226	1.1 / 3.7 / 0.9 / 3.7	25 F	0216 / 0835 / 1506 / 2126	0.9 / 4.0 / 0.6 / 4.0
11 F	0425 / 1045 / 1710 / 2330	1.1 / 3.7 / 1.0 / 3.8	26 SA	0336 / 0955 / 1620 / 2242	0.9 / 4.0 / 0.7 / 4.0
12 SA	0535 / 1155 / 1816	1.0 / 3.8 / 0.9	27 SU	0506 / 1740 / 2355	0.8 / 0.6 / 4.1
13 SU	0025 / 0635 / 1245 / 1856	3.9 / 0.8 / 4.0 / 0.8	28 M	0618 / 1216 / 1846	0.6 / 4.3 / 0.5
14 M	0109 / 0725 / 1329 / 1936	4.1 / 0.7 / 4.2 / 0.8	29 TU	0048 / 0718 / 1310 / 1938	4.3 / 0.3 / 4.6 / 0.4
15 TU	0145 / 0806 / 1408 / ● 2011	4.2 / 0.6 / 4.3 / 0.7	30 W	0136 / 0808 / 1357 / ○ 2026	4.5 / 0.1 / 4.8 / 0.4
			31 TH	0225 / 0857 / 1445 / 2105	4.7 / 0.0 / 4.9 / 0.4

FEBRUARY

#	TIME	m	#	TIME	m
1 F	0305 / 0942 / 1526 / 2150	4.8 / -0.1 / 4.9 / 0.4	16 SA	0301 / 0930 / 1516 / 2136	4.6 / 0.1 / 4.7 / 0.5
2 SA	0346 / 1025 / 1609 / 2225	4.8 / 0.0 / 4.9 / 0.5	17 SU	0332 / 1005 / 1549 / 2209	4.7 / 0.1 / 4.8 / 0.4
3 SU	0427 / 1101 / 1652 / 2306	4.8 / 0.1 / 4.7 / 0.5	18 M	0406 / 1042 / 1623 / 2249	4.7 / 0.1 / 4.7 / 0.5
4 M	0510 / 1139 / 1735 / 2346	4.7 / 0.2 / 4.5 / 0.6	19 TU	0439 / 1121 / 1701 / 2326	4.7 / 0.1 / 4.7 / 0.5
5 TU	0552 / 1218 / 1817	4.5 / 0.4 / 4.3	20 W	0516 / 1156 / 1742 / 2359	4.7 / 0.2 / 4.5 / 0.5
6 W	0026 / 0638 / 1255 / (1905	0.7 / 4.2 / 0.6 / 4.0	21 TH	0601 / 1236 / 1833)	4.5 / 0.3 / 4.3
7 TH	0105 / 0726 / 1350 / 1955	0.9 / 3.9 / 0.8 / 3.7	22 F	0055 / 0656 / 1330 / 1935	0.6 / 4.3 / 0.5 / 4.0
8 F	0226 / 0825 / 1454 / 2105	1.1 / 3.6 / 1.0 / 3.4	23 SA	0156 / 0816 / 1440 / 2059	0.7 / 4.0 / 0.7 / 3.8
9 SA	0346 / 0940 / 1626 / 2256	1.1 / 3.4 / 1.1 / 3.4	24 SU	0326 / 0940 / 1616 / 2224	0.8 / 3.9 / 0.8 / 3.7
10 SU	0506 / 1130 / 1736 / 2359	1.1 / 3.6 / 1.0 / 3.7	25 M	0456 / 1108 / 1736 / 2348	0.8 / 4.0 / 0.7 / 4.0
11 M	0615 / 1226 / 1830	0.9 / 3.9 / 0.9	26 TU	0616 / 1216 / 1840	0.5 / 4.3 / 0.5
12 TU	0049 / 0706 / 1315 / 1911	4.0 / 0.6 / 4.1 / 0.7	27 W	0045 / 0712 / 1308 / 1930	4.2 / 0.2 / 4.6 / 0.4
13 W	0130 / 0746 / 1346 / 1949	4.2 / 0.5 / 4.4 / 0.6	28 TH	0127 / 0800 / 1347 / ○ 2012	4.5 / 0.1 / 4.7 / 0.4
14 TH	0206 / 0820 / 1416 / ● 2026	4.4 / 0.4 / 4.5 / 0.6			
15 F	0232 / 0856 / 1448 / 2100	4.5 / 0.2 / 4.7 / 0.5			

MARCH

#	TIME	m	#	TIME	m
1 F	0207 / 0839 / 1427 / 2049	4.6 / 0.0 / 4.8 / 0.4	16 SA	0158 / 0826 / 1415 / ● 2036	4.5 / 0.1 / 4.7 / 0.4
2 SA	0246 / 0922 / 1506 / 2128	4.7 / -0.1 / 4.8 / 0.4	17 SU	0229 / 0859 / 1446 / 2108	4.7 / 0.1 / 4.8 / 0.3
3 SU	0326 / 1000 / 1545 / 2205	4.8 / 0.0 / 4.8 / 0.4	18 M	0303 / 0938 / 1523 / 2149	4.8 / 0.0 / 4.9 / 0.3
4 M	0400 / 1037 / 1622 / 2240	4.8 / 0.1 / 4.7 / 0.4	19 TU	0338 / 1016 / 1558 / 2225	4.9 / 0.0 / 4.8 / 0.3
5 TU	0438 / 1108 / 1659 / 2316	4.7 / 0.2 / 4.5 / 0.5	20 W	0415 / 1055 / 1638 / 2305	4.9 / 0.1 / 4.7 / 0.3
6 W	0516 / 1139 / 1737 / 2346	4.5 / 0.4 / 4.3 / 0.6	21 TH	0456 / 1136 / 1723 / 2346	4.8 / 0.1 / 4.5 / 0.3
7 TH	0552 / 1215 / 1816	4.3 / 0.6 / 4.0	22 F	0541 / 1215 / 1812	4.6 / 0.3 / 4.2
8 F	0014 / 0636 / 1255 / (1906	0.7 / 4.0 / 0.8 / 3.7	23 SA	0041 / 0635 / 1312 /) 1926	0.4 / 4.3 / 0.5 / 3.9
9 SA	0104 / 0736 / 1410 / 2005	0.9 / 3.6 / 1.1 / 3.4	24 SU	0145 / 0806 / 1425 / 2050	0.6 / 4.0 / 0.7 / 3.7
10 SU	0305 / 0855 / 1545 / 2150	1.1 / 3.4 / 1.2 / 3.2	25 M	0316 / 0932 / 1606 / 2219	0.7 / 3.9 / 0.8 / 3.7
11 M	0415 / 1057 / 1700 / 2331	1.0 / 3.4 / 1.0 / 3.5	26 TU	0456 / 1059 / 1736 / 2336	0.6 / 4.1 / 0.7 / 3.9
12 TU	0536 / 1156 / 1754	0.8 / 3.8 / 0.9	27 W	0606 / 1205 / 1829	0.4 / 4.3 / 0.5
13 W	0015 / 0636 / 1239 / 1850	3.9 / 0.6 / 4.1 / 0.7	28 TH	0028 / 0658 / 1251 / 1915	4.2 / 0.1 / 4.6 / 0.4
14 TH	0058 / 0715 / 1316 / 1925	4.2 / 0.4 / 4.4 / 0.6	29 F	0107 / 0739 / 1331 / 1951	4.4 / 0.0 / 4.7 / 0.4
15 F	0127 / 0749 / 1348 / 1955	4.4 / 0.3 / 4.6 / 0.5	30 SA	0146 / 0817 / 1405 / ○ 2028	4.6 / 0.0 / 4.7 / 0.3
			31 SU	0222 / 0856 / 1442 / 2103	4.7 / 0.1 / 4.7 / 0.3

APRIL

#	TIME	m	#	TIME	m
1 M	0258 / 0932 / 1519 / 2138	4.7 / 0.1 / 4.7 / 0.3	16 TU	0236 / 0910 / 1456 / 2126	4.9 / 0.0 / 4.9 / 0.2
2 TU	0336 / 1006 / 1555 / 2211	4.7 / 0.2 / 4.6 / 0.3	17 W	0315 / 0952 / 1535 / 2209	4.9 / 0.0 / 4.8 / 0.2
3 W	0412 / 1035 / 1632 / 2246	4.7 / 0.3 / 4.4 / 0.4	18 TH	0356 / 1032 / 1621 / 2252	4.9 / 0.1 / 4.7 / 0.2
4 TH	0445 / 1105 / 1705 / 2315	4.5 / 0.5 / 4.3 / 0.5	19 F	0439 / 1116 / 1708 / 2338	4.8 / 0.2 / 4.5 / 0.2
5 F	0521 / 1146 / 1739 / 2349	4.3 / 0.6 / 4.0 / 0.6	20 SA	0529 / 1206 / 1806	4.6 / 0.4 / 4.2
6 SA	0559 / 1216 / 1826	4.0 / 0.8 / 3.8	21 SU	0031 / 0635 / 1306 /) 1920	0.3 / 4.3 / 0.6 / 3.9
7 SU	0035 / 0656 / 1304 / (1926	0.8 / 3.7 / 1.1 / 3.5	22 M	0146 / 0800 / 1414 / 2040	0.4 / 4.1 / 0.7 / 3.8
8 M	0235 / 0816 / 1515 / 2046	0.9 / 3.5 / 1.1 / 3.3	23 TU	0316 / 0914 / 1550 / 2159	0.5 / 4.0 / 0.0 / 3.8
9 TU	0345 / 0943 / 1620 / 2236	0.9 / 3.5 / 1.0 / 3.4	24 W	0436 / 1046 / 1716 / 2309	0.4 / 4.2 / 0.7 / 4.0
10 W	0450 / 1116 / 1725 / 2335	0.8 / 3.8 / 0.9 / 3.8	25 TH	0546 / 1146 / 1810	0.3 / 4.4 / 0.5
11 TH	0549 / 1200 / 1810	0.6 / 4.1 / 0.7	26 F	0006 / 0635 / 1225 / 1856	4.2 / 0.2 / 4.5 / 0.5
12 F	0015 / 0635 / 1236 / 1850	4.1 / 0.4 / 4.4 / 0.5	27 SA	0046 / 0711 / 1307 / 1929	4.3 / 0.1 / 4.5 / 0.4
13 SA	0048 / 0715 / 1308 / 1926	4.3 / 0.2 / 4.6 / 0.4	28 SU	0126 / 0753 / 1345 / ○ 2006	4.4 / 0.2 / 4.5 / 0.4
14 SU	0126 / 0756 / 1343 / ● 2006	4.6 / 0.1 / 4.8 / 0.3	29 M	0158 / 0825 / 1421 / 2042	4.5 / 0.2 / 4.5 / 0.3
15 M	0158 / 0830 / 1419 / 2046	4.7 / 0.0 / 4.9 / 0.2	30 TU	0236 / 0902 / 1456 / 2115	4.6 / 0.3 / 4.5 / 0.3

Chart Datum: 2.50 metres below Normaal Amsterdams Peil

19

TIME ZONE −0100
(Dutch Standard Time)
Subtract 1 hour for GMT
For Dutch Summer Time add ONE hour in non-shaded areas

NETHERLANDS - VLISSINGEN (FLUSHING)

LAT 51°27′N   LONG 3°36′E

TIMES AND HEIGHTS OF HIGH AND LOW WATERS

YEAR **1991**

MAY

Day	TIME	m	Day	TIME	m
1 W	0311 0935 1531 2152	4.6 0.3 4.5 0.3	16 TH	0255 0933 1521 2153	5.0 0.1 4.8 0.1
2 TH	0345 1010 1607 2225	4.6 0.4 4.4 0.3	17 F	0341 1015 1608 2246	4.9 0.2 4.6 0.1
3 F	0420 1046 1642 2306	4.5 0.5 4.3 0.4	18 SA	0430 1102 1700 2336	4.8 0.3 4.4 0.1
4 SA	0459 1115 1718 2340	4.3 0.7 4.1 0.5	19 SU	0525 1156 1801	4.7 0.4 4.3
5 SU	0540 1144 1759	4.1 0.8 3.9	20 M	0036 0635 1255) 1905	0.1 4.5 0.6 4.1
6 M	0019 0630 1239 1856	0.6 3.9 1.0 3.7	21 TU	0145 0746 1359 2015	0.2 4.3 0.7 4.0
7 TU	0124 0740 1420 (2006	0.7 3.7 1.1 3.5	22 W	0246 0856 1515 2128	0.3 4.2 0.8 3.9
8 W	0301 0855 1535 2119	0.7 3.7 1.0 3.5	23 TH	0405 1005 1647 2235	0.3 4.2 0.7 4.0
9 TH	0406 1003 1630 2236	0.7 3.8 0.9 3.7	24 F	0516 1109 1740 2329	0.3 4.3 0.6 4.1
10 F	0500 1106 1726 2326	0.5 4.1 0.7 4.0	25 SA	0606 1206 1826	0.3 4.3 0.6
11 SA	0556 1151 1811	0.4 4.4 0.6	26 SU	0019 0650 1248 1906	4.2 0.3 4.4 0.5
12 SU	0010 0635 1232 1850	4.3 0.3 4.6 0.4	27 M	0101 0728 1328 1946	4.3 0.4 4.4 0.4
13 M	0051 0718 1316 1935	4.6 0.1 4.7 0.3	28 TU	0141 0806 1406 ○ 2020	4.4 0.4 4.4 0.4
14 TU	0130 0802 1356 ● 2020	4.8 0.1 4.8 0.2	29 W	0219 0836 1439 2055	4.4 0.5 4.4 0.3
15 W	0213 0846 1436 2106	4.9 0.0 4.8 0.1	30 TH	0255 0910 1516 2135	4.5 0.5 4.4 0.3
			31 F	0331 0945 1549 2216	4.5 0.5 4.4 0.3

JUNE

Day	TIME	m	Day	TIME	m
1 SA	0410 1026 1625 2256	4.4 0.6 4.3 0.3	16 SU	0422 1049 1655 2326	4.9 0.4 4.6 -0.1
2 SU	0445 1055 1701 2330	4.3 0.7 4.2 0.4	17 M	0519 1139 1746	4.8 0.5 4.5
3 M	0526 1136 1746	4.2 0.8 4.1	18 TU	0019 0618 1235 1841	0.0 4.6 0.6 4.3
4 TU	0010 0605 1220 1825	0.5 4.1 0.9 3.9	19 W	0116 0721 1330) 1946	0.1 4.5 0.7 4.2
5 W	0100 0659 1304 (1926	0.5 4.0 0.9 3.8	20 TH	0216 0815 1436 2045	0.2 4.3 0.8 4.0
6 TH	0155 0806 1426 2036	0.6 3.9 1.0 3.8	21 F	0315 0926 1545 2156	0.4 4.1 0.8 4.0
7 F	0255 0909 1535 2139	0.6 4.0 0.9 3.8	22 SA	0430 1036 1706 2255	0.5 4.1 0.8 4.0
8 SA	0400 1016 1625 2236	0.5 4.1 0.8 4.0	23 SU	0530 1135 1756 2355	0.6 4.1 0.7 4.1
9 SU	0455 1109 1726 2332	0.4 4.3 0.6 4.3	24 M	0620 1226 1846	0.6 4.1 0.6
10 M	0555 1202 1821	0.3 4.5 0.5	25 TU	0046 0706 1316 1926	4.1 0.6 4.2 0.5
11 TU	0021 0651 1249 1916	4.5 0.2 4.6 0.3	26 W	0128 0741 1351 2005	4.2 0.6 4.3 0.4
12 W	0108 0738 1336 ● 2006	4.7 0.2 4.7 0.2	27 TH	0209 0811 1428 ○ 2039	4.3 0.6 4.3 0.4
13 TH	0155 0826 1423 2056	4.9 0.2 4.7 0.0	28 F	0245 0850 1506 2119	4.4 0.6 4.4 0.3
14 F	0243 0915 1510 2145	4.9 0.2 4.7 0.0	29 SA	0319 0926 1537 2200	4.5 0.6 4.4 0.2
15 SA	0332 1002 1600 2236	4.9 0.3 4.7 -0.1	30 SU	0356 1005 1609 2240	4.5 0.6 4.4 0.2

JULY

Day	TIME	m	Day	TIME	m
1 M	0427 1040 1645 2320	4.5 0.6 4.4 0.3	16 TU	0455 1118 1719 2355	4.9 0.5 4.7 0.0
2 TU	0501 1118 1719 2349	4.4 0.7 4.4 0.3	17 W	0547 1206 1812	4.7 0.6 4.5
3 W	0539 1152 1756	4.3 0.8 4.2	18 TH	0039 0639 1244) 1901	0.2 4.5 0.7 4.3
4 TH	0030 0619 1236 1839	0.3 4.2 0.8 4.1	19 F	0130 0738 1345 2001	0.3 4.2 0.8 4.1
5 F	0116 0706 1326 (1935	0.4 4.1 0.8 4.0	20 SA	0219 0836 1445 2106	0.6 4.0 0.9 3.9
6 SA	0205 0820 1419 2045	0.5 4.1 0.8 4.0	21 SU	0336 0950 1605 2226	0.8 3.8 1.0 3.8
7 SU	0308 0925 1529 2155	0.5 4.1 0.8 4.0	22 M	0445 1105 1714 2335	0.9 3.8 0.9 3.9
8 M	0416 1036 1646 2302	0.5 4.2 0.7 4.2	23 TU	0545 1208 1819	0.8 3.9 0.7
9 TU	0526 1135 1759	0.5 4.3 0.6	24 W	0035 0640 1258 1916	4.0 0.8 4.1 0.6
10 W	0002 0626 1232 1856	4.4 0.4 4.5 0.4	25 TH	0126 0726 1340 1949	4.2 0.8 4.3 0.5
11 TH	0055 0726 1325 ● 1952	4.6 0.3 4.6 0.2	26 F	0200 0756 1411 ○ 2025	4.4 0.7 4.4 0.4
12 F	0146 0812 1413 2046	4.8 0.3 4.7 0.0	27 SA	0229 0832 1446 2106	4.5 0.6 4.5 0.3
13 SA	0233 0902 1500 2132	5.0 0.3 4.8 -0.1	28 SU	0301 0908 1515 2139	4.6 0.6 4.5 0.2
14 SU	0320 0948 1545 2221	5.0 0.3 4.8 -0.1	29 M	0330 0941 1548 2216	4.6 0.6 4.6 0.2
15 M	0409 1035 1635 2310	5.0 0.4 4.7 -0.1	30 TU	0406 1015 1619 2256	4.6 0.6 4.5 0.2
			31 W	0436 1056 1649 2328	4.6 0.6 4.5 0.3

AUGUST

Day	TIME	m	Day	TIME	m
1 TH	0507 1125 1726	4.5 0.7 4.4	16 F	0002 0558 1210 1818	0.3 4.4 0.7 4.4
2 F	0001 0546 1205 1802	0.3 4.5 0.7 4.4	17 SA	0039 0648 1256) 1905	0.5 4.2 0.7 4.1
3 SA	0036 0631 1246 (1856	0.4 4.3 0.7 4.3	18 SU	0124 0740 1406 2005	0.8 3.9 1.0 3.8
4 SU	0126 0736 1339 2000	0.5 4.2 0.8 4.1	19 M	0234 0844 1514 2146	1.0 3.6 1.1 3.6
5 M	0225 0848 1455 2120	0.6 4.0 0.9 4.0	20 TU	0353 1036 1646 2304	1.1 3.5 1.0 3.7
6 TU	0346 1005 1625 2235	0.7 4.0 0.8 4.1	21 W	0516 1146 1756	1.1 3.7 0.9
7 W	0506 1126 1746 2349	0.7 4.1 0.6 4.3	22 TH	0016 0616 1236 1850	4.0 0.9 4.0 0.7
8 TH	0616 1225 1850	0.6 4.3 0.4	23 F	0100 0659 1315 1929	4.2 0.8 4.3 0.5
9 F	0045 0712 1316 1945	4.6 0.4 4.5 0.2	24 SA	0135 0738 1349 2005	4.4 0.7 4.4 0.4
10 SA	0135 0759 1359 ● 2031	4.8 0.4 4.7 0.0	25 SU	0205 0810 1417 ○ 2040	4.6 0.6 4.6 0.3
11 SU	0219 0846 1443 2117	5.0 0.4 4.8 -0.1	26 M	0235 0841 1447 2111	4.7 0.6 4.7 0.2
12 M	0303 0930 1525 2201	5.0 0.4 4.9 -0.1	27 TU	0302 0918 1516 2146	4.8 0.6 4.7 0.2
13 TU	0345 1012 1606 2246	4.8 0.4 4.9 0.0	28 W	0333 0952 1548 2226	4.8 0.6 4.7 0.2
14 W	0428 1052 1651 2322	4.9 0.5 4.8 0.1	29 TH	0405 1026 1621 2255	4.8 0.6 4.7 0.3
15 TH	0516 1130 1736	4.7 0.6 4.6	30 F	0439 1100 1655 2332	4.7 0.6 4.7 0.3
			31 SA	0516 1135 1736	4.6 0.6 4.6

Chart Datum: 2.50 metres below Normaal Amsterdams Peil

NETHERLANDS - VLISSINGEN (FLUSHING)

LAT 51°27′N   LONG 3°36′E

TIMES AND HEIGHTS OF HIGH AND LOW WATERS   YEAR **1991**

TTMF ZONE **−0100**
(Dutch Standard Time)
Subtract 1 hour for GMT
For Dutch Summer Time add
ONE hour in non-shaded areas

SEPTEMBER

Day	TIME	m	Day	TIME	m
1 SU ☾	0011 / 0601 / 1220 / 1821	0.4 / 4.4 / 0.6 / 4.5	**16** M	0040 / 0645 / 1259 / 1915	1.0 / 3.8 / 1.0 / 3.8
2 M	0101 / 0655 / 1315 / 1926	0.5 / 4.2 / 0.8 / 4.2	**17** TU	0156 / 0746 / 1446 / 2040	1.2 / 3.5 / 1.2 / 3.5
3 TU	0206 / 0815 / 1435 / 2055	0.8 / 3.9 / 0.9 / 3.9	**18** W	0314 / 0930 / 1559 / 2236	1.3 / 3.3 / 1.1 / 3.5
4 W	0326 / 0946 / 1604 / 2225	0.9 / 3.8 / 0.9 / 4.0	**19** TH	0433 / 1110 / 1716 / 2339	1.2 / 3.6 / 0.9 / 3.9
5 TH	0456 / 1109 / 1735 / 2346	0.9 / 3.9 / 0.7 / 4.3	**20** F	0546 / 1205 / 1815	1.0 / 3.9 / 0.7
6 F	0610 / 1211 / 1842	0.7 / 4.3 / 0.4	**21** SA	0026 / 0635 / 1246 / 1906	4.2 / 0.8 / 4.2 / 0.5
7 SA	0037 / 0702 / 1259 / 1932	4.6 / 0.5 / 4.5 / 0.2	**22** SU	0105 / 0710 / 1315 / 1936	4.4 / 0.7 / 4.4 / 0.4
8 SU ●	0120 / 0748 / 1340 / 2015	4.8 / 0.5 / 4.7 / 0.0	**23** M O	0131 / 0739 / 1345 / 2008	4.6 / 0.7 / 4.6 / 0.3
9 M	0202 / 0825 / 1420 / 2057	4.9 / 0.4 / 4.8 / 0.0	**24** TU	0201 / 0811 / 1413 / 2039	4.8 / 0.6 / 4.7 / 0.3
10 TU	0242 / 0907 / 1458 / 2138	5.0 / 0.4 / 4.9 / 0.1	**25** W	0230 / 0848 / 1446 / 2116	4.9 / 0.5 / 4.8 / 0.2
11 W ·	0322 / 0945 / 1539 / 2216	4.9 / 0.5 / 4.9 / 0.2	**26** TH	0305 / 0926 / 1518 / 2152	4.9 / 0.5 / 4.9 / 0.3
12 TH	0400 / 1025 / 1619 / 2252	4.8 / 0.5 / 4.8 / 0.3	**27** F	0338 / 1002 / 1554 / 2228	4.9 / 0.5 / 4.8 / 0.3
13 F	0440 / 1100 / 1658 / 2325	4.6 / 0.6 / 4.7 / 0.5	**28** SA	0416 / 1041 / 1633 / 2309	4.8 / 0.5 / 4.9 / 0.4
14 SA	0521 / 1135 / 1737	4.4 / 0.7 / 4.4	**29** SU	0456 / 1118 / 1713 / 2346	4.7 / 0.5 / 4.8 / 0.5
15 SU ☽	0000 / 0602 / 1204 / 1819	0.7 / 4.1 / 0.8 / 4.1	**30** M	0541 / 1206 / 1805	4.4 / 0.6 / 4.5

OCTOBER

Day	TIME	m	Day	TIME	m
1 TU ☾	0041 / 0639 / 1305 / 1916	0.7 / 4.1 / 0.7 / 4.2	**16** W	0044 / 0706 / 1400 / 1956	1.3 / 3.6 / 1.1 / 3.6
2 W	0146 / 0806 / 1424 / 2050	0.9 / 3.8 / 0.9 / 4.0	**17** TH	0246 / 0816 / 1526 / 2114	1.4 / 3.4 / 1.1 / 3.5
3 TH	0315 / 0936 / 1606 / 2215	1.0 / 3.7 / 0.8 / 4.1	**18** F	0356 / 1016 / 1625 / 2249	1.3 / 3.5 / 1.0 / 3.8
4 F	0450 / 1056 / 1730 / 2336	1.0 / 3.9 / 0.6 / 4.3	**19** SA	0454 / 1116 / 1724 / 2346	1.1 / 3.8 / 0.8 / 4.1
5 SA	0554 / 1155 / 1830	0.8 / 4.2 / 0.4	**20** SU	0549 / 1159 / 1820	0.9 / 4.1 / 0.6
6 SU	0026 / 0645 / 1238 / 1916	4.6 / 0.6 / 4.5 / 0.2	**21** M	0026 / 0629 / 1235 / 1856	4.4 / 0.8 / 4.3 / 0.5
7 M ●	0106 / 0728 / 1319 / 1955	4.7 / 0.6 / 4.6 / 0.2	**22** TU	0056 / 0708 / 1306 / 1932	4.6 / 0.7 / 4.6 / 0.4
8 TU	0142 / 0805 / 1356 / 2033	4.8 / 0.5 / 4.8 / 0.2	**23** W O	0127 / 0742 / 1341 / 2009	4.6 / 0.6 / 4.7 / 0.3
9 W	0219 / 0846 / 1435 / 2110	4.8 / 0.5 / 4.8 / 0.3	**24** TH	0159 / 0821 / 1416 / 2045	4.9 / 0.5 / 4.9 / 0.3
10 TH	0256 / 0919 / 1516 / 2146	4.8 / 0.5 / 4.9 / 0.4	**25** F	0235 / 0901 / 1456 / 2126	4.9 / 0.5 / 5.0 / 0.3
11 F	0337 / 0958 / 1552 / 2220	4.7 / 0.5 / 4.8 / 0.5	**26** SA	0316 / 0940 / 1533 / 2205	4.9 / 0.4 / 5.0 / 0.3
12 SA	0416 / 1036 / 1629 / 2252	4.5 / 0.5 / 4.6 / 0.7	**27** SU	0356 / 1025 / 1613 / 2245	4.8 / 0.4 / 4.9 / 0.4
13 SU	0449 / 1106 / 1708 / 2326	4.4 / 0.7 / 4.4 / 0.9	**28** M	0442 / 1111 / 1659 / 2332	4.6 / 0.4 / 4.8 / 0.6
14 M	0528 / 1145 / 1751 / 2354	4.2 / 0.8 / 4.2 / 1.0	**29** TU	0531 / 1205 / 1758	4.4 / 0.5 / 4.5
15 TU ☽	0610 / 1206 / 1846	3.9 / 0.6 / 3.8	**30** W ☾	0028 / 0636 / 1306 / 1915	0.8 / 4.1 / 0.6 / 4.2
			31 TH	0136 / 0755 / 1426 / 2035	1.0 / 3.9 / 0.7 / 4.1

NOVEMBER

Day	TIME	m	Day	TIME	m
1 F	0255 / 0915 / 1550 / 2155	1.1 / 3.8 / 0.7 / 4.2	**16** SA	0306 / 0850 / 1536 / 2135	1.3 / 3.6 / 0.9 / 3.8
2 SA	0424 / 1029 / 1710 / 2310	1.0 / 4.0 / 0.6 / 4.3	**17** SU	0406 / 1006 / 1636 / 2246	1.2 / 3.7 / 0.8 / 4.0
3 SU	0540 / 1129 / 1811 / 2359	0.8 / 4.2 / 0.4 / 4.5	**18** M	0500 / 1106 / 1725 / 2336	1.1 / 4.0 / 0.7 / 4.3
4 M	0628 / 1215 / 1852	0.7 / 4.4 / 0.4	**19** TU	0546 / 1149 / 1816	0.9 / 4.2 / 0.6
5 TU	0040 / 0711 / 1255 / 1929	4.6 / 0.7 / 4.5 / 0.4	**20** W	0015 / 0631 / 1232 / 1856	4.5 / 0.8 / 4.5 / 0.5
6 W ●	0122 / 0746 / 1336 / 2008	4.6 / 0.6 / 4.6 / 0.4	**21** TH O	0056 / 0716 / 1313 / 1935	4.7 / 0.6 / 4.7 / 0.4
7 TH	0201 / 0822 / 1415 / 2042	4.6 / 0.5 / 4.7 / 0.5	**22** F	0136 / 0756 / 1351 / 2021	4.8 / 0.5 / 4.9 / 0.3
8 F	0237 / 0901 / 1455 / 2118	4.6 / 0.5 / 4.7 / 0.5	**23** SA	0216 / 0839 / 1434 / 2106	4.9 / 0.4 / 5.0 / 0.3
9 SA	0315 / 0936 / 1529 / 2152	4.6 / 0.5 / 4.7 / 0.6	**24** SU	0259 / 0928 / 1518 / 2148	4.8 / 0.3 / 5.0 / 0.4
10 SU	0351 / 1016 / 1607 / 2225	4.5 / 0.5 / 4.6 / 0.8	**25** M	0346 / 1016 / 1603 / 2236	4.7 / 0.3 / 4.9 / 0.5
11 M	0428 / 1045 / 1645 / 2300	4.4 / 0.6 / 4.4 / 0.9	**26** TU	0436 / 1105 / 1655 / 2322	4.6 / 0.3 / 4.8 / 0.6
12 TU	0505 / 1126 / 1725 / 2336	4.2 / 0.7 / 4.2 / 1.0	**27** W	0528 / 1200 / 1755	4.4 / 0.3 / 4.6
13 W	0545 / 1205 / 1816	4.0 / 0.8 / 4.0	**28** TH ☾	0015 / 0626 / 1300 / 1907	0.7 / 4.2 / 0.4 / 4.4
14 TH ☽	0015 / 0635 / 1304 / 1916	1.2 / 3.8 / 0.9 / 3.8	**29** F	0126 / 0735 / 1406 / 2016	0.9 / 4.1 / 0.5 / 4.3
15 F	0124 / 0735 / 1430 / 2026	1.3 / 3.7 / 1.0 / 3.7	**30** SA	0236 / 0846 / 1515 / 2126	1.0 / 4.0 / 0.6 / 4.2

DECEMBER

Day	TIME	m	Day	TIME	m
1 SU	0350 / 0951 / 1641 / 2235	1.0 / 4.0 / 0.6 / 4.2	**16** M	0234 / 0906 / 1526 / 2139	1.2 / 3.8 / 0.8 / 4.0
2 M	0511 / 1055 / 1741 / 2336	0.9 / 4.1 / 0.6 / 4.3	**17** TU	0356 / 1005 / 1631 / 2246	1.1 / 3.9 / 0.8 / 4.1
3 TU	0606 / 1148 / 1825	0.8 / 4.2 / 0.4	**18** W	0456 / 1105 / 1725 / 2337	1.0 / 4.1 / 0.7 / 4.3
4 W	0021 / 0646 / 1239 / 1908	4.3 / 0.8 / 4.3 / 0.6	**19** TH	0556 / 1200 / 1826	0.8 / 4.3 / 0.5
5 TH	0108 / 0726 / 1320 / 1945	4.4 / 0.7 / 4.4 / 0.6	**20** F	0030 / 0646 / 1247 / 1916	4.5 / 0.6 / 4.6 / 0.4
6 F ●	0147 / 0806 / 1400 / 2021	4.4 / 0.6 / 4.5 / 0.7	**21** SA O	0117 / 0741 / 1335 / 2002	4.6 / 0.4 / 4.8 / 0.4
7 SA	0226 / 0846 / 1441 / 2055	4.4 / 0.5 / 4.5 / 0.7	**22** SU	0202 / 0831 / 1420 / 2048	4.7 / 0.3 / 4.9 / 0.3
8 SU	0301 / 0920 / 1517 / 2130	4.3 / 0.5 / 4.6 / 0.7	**23** M	0248 / 0920 / 1508 / 2137	4.8 / 0.2 / 5.0 / 0.3
9 M	0338 / 1001 / 1555 / 2205	4.4 / 0.4 / 4.5 / 0.7	**24** TU	0335 / 1010 / 1556 / 2221	4.8 / 0.1 / 5.0 / 0.4
10 TU	0416 / 1041 / 1631 / 2240	4.4 / 0.5 / 4.5 / 0.8	**25** W	0423 / 1057 / 1646 / 2309	4.7 / 0.1 / 4.9 / 0.5
11 W	0445 / 1115 / 1709 / 2316	4.3 / 0.5 / 4.3 / 0.9	**26** TH	0516 / 1149 / 1737 / 2359	4.6 / 0.1 / 4.8 / 0.6
12 TH	0526 / 1150 / 1749 / 2355	4.2 / 0.6 / 4.2 / 1.0	**27** F	0610 / 1239 / 1842	4.5 / 0.2 / 4.6
13 F	0606 / 1224 / 1836	4.1 / 0.7 / 4.0	**28** SA ☾	0049 / 0706 / 1336 / 1946	0.8 / 4.3 / 0.3 / 4.4
14 SA ☽	0035 / 0656 / 1326 / 1936	1.1 / 3.9 / 0.8 / 3.9	**29** SU	0150 / 0808 / 1436 / 2045	0.9 / 4.1 / 0.5 / 4.1
15 SU	0129 / 0756 / 1426 / 2036	1.2 / 3.8 / 0.8 / 3.9	**30** M	0255 / 0909 / 1534 / 2158	1.0 / 4.0 / 0.7 / 4.0
			31 TU	0420 / 1026 / 1705 / 2305	1.0 / 3.9 / 0.8 / 4.0

Chart Datum: 2.50 metres below Normaal Amsterdams Peil

19

VLISSINGEN (FLUSHING) *continued*

VLISSINGEN (FLUSHING)

MEAN SPRING
AND NEAP CURVES

MEAN RANGES	
Springs	4·4m ———
Neaps	3·1m - - -

Springs occur 2 days
after
New and Full Moon.

OOSTERSCHELDE   10-19-17
Zeeland

CHARTS
Admiralty 110, 120, 192; Zeekaart 1448; Dutch Yacht
Charts 1805, 1807; Stanford 19; Imray C30
TIDES
Dover +0230; ML Sas van Goes 2.0;
　　　　　　　Zierikzee　　1.8
Duration Sas van Goes 0615;　Zone −0100
　　　Zierikzee　　0640

Standard Port VLISSINGEN (←)

Times				Height (metres)			
HW		LW		MHWS	MHWN	MLWN	MLWS
0300	0900	0400	1000	4.7	3.9	0.8	0.3
1500	2100	1600	2200				

Differences ROOMPOT

+0115	+0115	+0115	+0115	No data		No data	

WEMELDINGE

+0145	+0145	+0125	+0125	No data		No data	

LODIJKSE GAT

+0145	+0145	+0125	+0125	No data		No data	

SHELTER
Inside the barrier good shelter is found in several harbours
– for example Colijnsplaat and Zierikzee, which are both
west of Zeelandbrug (bridge connecting Noord Beveland
and Duiveland) and accessible at any tide. Veerse Meer is
a non-tidal waterway with mooring places for yachts:
access from Oosterschelde at Zandkreekdam lock, or
through Kanaal door Walcheren via Vlissingen and
Middelburg from Westerschelde. Access can be made via
Bergsediepsluis, near Tholen to the Schelde-Rijn Canal.
NAVIGATION
Waypoint WG1 (stbd-hand) buoy, QG, 51°38'.00N
03°26'.30E at entrance to Westgat/Oude Roompot
buoyed channel. Not advisable to enter in strong W to
NW winds, and only from HW−6 to HW+1½ Zierikzee.
There are several offshore banks, see 10.19.5. All vessels
must use the Roompotsluis (lock). The areas each side of
the barrier are very dangerous due to strong tidal streams
and many obstructions. Passage is prohibited west of
Roggenplaat. Zeelandbrug clearance 11.5m at centre of
arch in buoyed channels. Clearance is indicated on some

OOSTERSCHELDE *continued*

of bridge supports, in metres. Bascule bridge near N end lifts weekdays on at H and H + 30 0700–2130 LT (week-ends from 0900). Sundays — every hour, but not if wind in excess of Force 7.

LIGHTS AND MARKS
There are few prominent marks in the approaches. For principal lights and waypoints see 10.19.4. Roompot Marina Ldg Lts 070°30' both Oc G 5s Entrance, W side FG, E side FR; depth 5m.

RADIO TELEPHONE
Zeelandbrug VHF Ch 18. Roompotsluis Ch 18. Krammer Locks. Call *Krammersluizen* Ch 22 (H24). Wemeldinge Locks Ch 68. Zandreek lock. Sluis Katz Ch 18, Bruinisse lock Sluis Gevelingen Ch 20, Traffic control (Wemeldinge) (MUST be called if entering Wemeldinge or canal entrance) Central Post Scheepvaartdienst Ch 68.

There are numerous ports to visit and the following is a selection of the more important ones (working anti-clockwise, starting from the Roompotsluis).
ROOMPOT MARINA (150 + 80 visitors) ☎ (01115) 4225, AC, D, P, Slip, FW, Gas, Gaz, Kos, ⬡, R, V, Bar.
COLIJNSPLAAT Hr Mr ☎ 201; YC ☎ 806; Dr ☎ 304; **Marina WV Noord YC Beveland** AC, Slip, FW, berth N side of mole or W side of basin; **Tanker** (see YC) P, D; **De Koster** ME; **Town** V, R, Gaz, ✉; Ⓑ; ⇌ (Goes), ✈ (Antwerpen).
GOES The canal up to Goes starts at Sas van Goes where there is a marina; there are no facilities at Wilhelminadorp half way up the canal. At Goes Hr Mr ☎ 27257; Dr ☎ 27451; Ⓗ ☎ 27000; **Marina WV 'De Werf'** ☎ 16372, FW, C (3½ ton), P, D; **Beekman** ☎ 27383 ME, El, Sh; **Jachtwerf Goes** ☎ 23944, Slip; **Sporthuis Olympia** ☎ 16008, Gaz; **Delta** ☎ 27338, ⬡; **Sakko** ☎ 15100, P, D; **Town** V, R, ✉; Ⓑ; ⇌; ✈ (Antwerpen).
WEMELDINGE Hr Mr ☎ 1463; Dr ☎ 1438; Yachts pass through Westsluis locks and berth W side of Binnenhaven. **Florusse** ☎ 1253, ME, SM, AC, C (6.5 ton) ME; **Town** P, D, V, R, ✉; Ⓑ; ⇌ (Goes); ✈ (Antworpen).
YERSEKE Hr Mr ☎ 1726 (VHF Ch 09); Dr ☎ 1444; **Marina Prins Willem-Alexanderhaven** FW, P, D, C; **Prins Beatrixhaven** Slip, FW, P, D; **J. Zoetewey** ☎ 1390, Gaz, SM; **W. Bakker** ☎ 1521, ME; **Town** V, BY, R, ✉; Ⓑ; ⇌ (Kruiningen); ✈ (Antwerpen).

ST ANNALAND Dr ☎ 2400; **Marina** Hr Mr ☎ 2463, Slip, AC, FW; **YC** ☎ 2634, Bar, R; **J. Keur** ☎ 2454, P, D; **Jacht en Metaalbouw** ☎ 2282, Sh, El, CH, BY; **C. Bal** ☎ 2440, ME; **Town** Gaz, V, R, Ⓑ; ✉; ⇌ (Bergen op Zoom); ✈ (Antwerpen).
BRUINISSE Hr Mr ☎ 1444; Dr ☎ 1280 **Marina WV 'Bru'** ☎ 1506, FW, C (1.5 ton). Visserhaven (not for yachts). **Aquadelta** ☎ 1485, Slip, P, D, FW, ME, C, AC, ⬡; **J.D. de Korte** SM, Gaz; **Rowi** ☎ 2195, C, ME, Sh; **Town** V, R, Bar, ✉; Ⓑ; ⇌ (Roosendal or Rotterdam); ✈ (Rotterdam).
ZIERIKZEE Hr Mr ☎ 13151; Dr ☎ 12080; Ⓗ ☎ 16900. Yachts either go to Marina 't Luitje' or come into Havenkanaal before reaching Zierikzee or go up to Nieuwe Haven. 't Luitje' **Marina** ☎ 13403, FW, C (10 ton), AC, SM, CH.
NIEUWE HAVEN AB, FW; **W. Bouwman** ☎ 2966, P, D, Gaz, AC; **Town** V, R, ✉; Ⓑ; ⇌; ✈ (Rotterdam).
BURGHSLUIS Hr Mr ☎ 1302; **Marina** FW, C (1 ton), **Blom** ☎ 2020, ME, AC; Facilities at Burg-Haamstede P, D, Gaz, ✉; Ⓑ; ⇌; ✈ (Rotterdam)

TOWNS IN THE VEERSE MEER (non-tidal)
MIDDELBURG Dr ☎ 12637; Ⓗ ☎ 25555; **Marina WV 'Arne'** in the Dockhaven, ☎ 13852; **J. Boone** ☎ 29913, D, Gaz, FW; **Zeeuwse Motoren Revisie** ☎ 13242, SM; **Jachtwerf Jansen** ☎ 13925, AC, Slip; **Wassalon Miele** ☎ 13830, ⬡; **Town** V, R, Bar, ✉; Ⓑ; ⇌; ✈ (Antwerpen)
VEERE Dr ☎ 271; Yachts can berth in the Stadshaven or in the Buitenhaven. **Jachtwerf Veere** ☎ 551, Slip, P, D, Gaz, FW, ME, AC, C (3½ ton), BH (12 ton), ⬡; **Jachtclub Veere** ☎ 246, FW, M; **Jachthaven Oostwatering** ☎ 484, Slip, FW; **Town** V, R, Bar, ✉; Ⓑ; ⇌ (Middelburg); ✈ (Rotterdam).
KORTGENE **Delta Marina** ☎ (01108) 1315 C (16 ton), P, D, FW, AC, CH, El, ⬡, ME, R, S, V; **Town** V, R, Bar, ✉, Ⓑ, ⇌ (Goes), Air (Antwerp).

19

STELLENDAM
(HELLEVOETSLUIS)
Zuid Holland

10-19-18

CHARTS
Admiralty 2322; Zeekaart 1448; Dutch Yacht Chart: 1801; Stanford 19; Imray C30

TIDES
Dover +0300; Zone −0100

Standard Port VLISSINGEN (←)

Times				Height (metres)			
HW		LW		MHWS	MHWN	MLWN	MLWS
0300	0900	0400	1000	4.7	3.9	0.8	0.3
1500	2100	1600	2200				

Differences HARINGVLIETSLUIZEN

+0016	+0014	+0006	−0026	−1.8	−1.7	−0.5	0.0

NOTE: Double LWs occur — The rise after the first LW is called Agger — Predictions for Hoek van Holland are for the lower LW which is usually the second. Time differences for Secondary Ports referred to Hoek van Holland are approximate — Water levels on this coast are considerably affected by the weather. Strong NW gales can raise levels up to 3m.

SHELTER
There are pontoons exclusively for yachts in the Aqua Pesch Marina in the Outer Harbour. Dangerous to enter Slijkgat with strong NW to W winds. Once through the lock, shelter in fishing harbour just inside lock or at one of the three yacht harbours at Hellevoetsluis (4M), the Industriehaven, the old harbour to the W or in the Voorne canal.

NAVIGATION
Waypoint Slijkgat SG safe water buoy, Iso 4s, 51°52'.00N 03°51'.50E, 290°/110° from/to Kwade Hoek Lt, 5.0M. The N passage to the Stellendam Lock, the Gat van de Hawk is no longer buoyed. It is therefore advisable to take the Slijkgat passage along the Goeree Shore. This is well buoyed and lit but beware a shoal about 5 ca from the lock, marked by G conical buoys. Keep clear of dam during sluicing.

LIGHTS AND MARKS
Hellevoetsluis Lt Iso WRG 10s 16m 11/7M, W stone Tr, R cupola. G Shore-275°, W275°-294°, R294°-316°, W316°-036°, G036°-058°, W058°-095°, R096°-shore
Sluicing signals — 3 R Lts in triangle shown from pillar heads on dam. Danger area marked with small R buoys.

RADIO TELEPHONE
Call: *Goereesesluis* VHF Ch 20.

TELEPHONE (01879)
Hr Mr Stellendam 1000; Hellevoetsluis 30911; ✚ Rotterdam 298088 or Flushing 60000
Police 2444; Dr 1425; Dr Hellevoetsluis 12435; Brit Consul (020) 764343.

FACILITIES
STELLENDAM **Aqua Pesch Marina** ☎ 2600, Slip, P, D, FW, C (8 ton); **Het Dumppaleis** ☎ 1529 Gaz; **Town** V, R, Bar, ✉ (2½ km); ≷ (Hellevoetsluis); ✈ (Rotterdam).
HELLEVOETSLUIS **Het Groote Dok** ☎ 12166, P, D, L, El, Ⓔ, Gaz, FW, ME, CH, AB; **Helius Haven YC** ☎ 15868, P, D, FW, AB; **Voorne Canal YC** ☎ 12870, P, D, FW, AB; **Town** P, D, V, R, Bar, ✉; Ⓑ; ≷; ✈ (Rotterdam).
Ferry UK — Hook of Holland—Harwich or Rotterdam—Hull.
Note. Voorne canal is dammed 4½ M above entrance. An alternative port is Middelharnis, 4M upstream of Hellevoetsluis. Bound for Rotterdam, proceed by canals via Spui or Dordrecht.

ROTTERDAM   10-19-19
Zuid Holland

CHARTS
Admiralty 133, 132 1541; Zeekaart 1540/1/2;
Dutch Yacht Chart 1809; Stanford 19

TIDES
Dover +0510; ML 1.1; Duration 0440; Zone −0100

Standard Port VLISSINGEN (←)

Times				Height (metres)			
HW		LW		MHWS	MHWN	MLWN	MLWS
0300	0900	0400	1000	4.7	3.9	0.8	0.3
1500	2100	1600	2200				

Differences ROTTERDAM
+0202 +0156 +0313 +0400 −2.7   −2.2   −0.6   +0.1

NOTE: Double LWs occur — The rise after the first LW is
called the Agger — Predictions for Hoek van Holland are
for the lower LW which is usually the second. Time
differences for Secondary Ports referred to Hoek van
Holland are approximate — Water levels on this coast are
considerably affected by the weather. Strong NW gales
can raise levels by up to 3m.

SHELTER
Shelter is good in the various yacht harbours but in the
river there is always a very considerable sea and swell due
to constant heavy traffic (Rotterdam/Europoort is the
world's largest port complex). From Berghaven to
Rotterdam is about 19 M. All but local yachts are actively
discouraged from using the Nieuwe Maas.

NAVIGATION
See 10.19.20. There are no navigational dangers other
than the amount of heavy sea-going traffic. 7 M before
the centre of Rotterdam, the Oude Maas joins; from here
to Dordrecht, sailing is prohibited. Speed limit − 6 kn.

LIGHTS AND MARKS
Marks to locate Yacht Harbours:
(1) Where Oude Maas enters from S, on N bank by Delta
Hotel, between kilometre posts 1010-1011 entrance to
Vlaardingen YC.
(2) 2 M further up, just above the entrance to Wilhelmina
Haven at Schiedam is the Spuihaven.
(3) Parkhaven and the lock through to Coolhaven are
clearly marked on the N bank by the huge Euromast in
the park.
(4) The Royal Maas YC at the Veerhaven is less than
one M further up on the N bank. The Veerhaven is a
normal yacht harbour.

RADIO TELEPHONE
There is a comprehensive Traffic Management and
Information Service. See details under Hook of Holland.

TELEPHONE (010)
Hr Mr 137681; Local Rijn Pilot 659110;
Port Authority 894062; ⌗ 298088; Police 143144;
Ⓗ 112800; Brit Consul (020) 764343.

FACILITIES
Yacht Harbour ☎ 138514, Slip, M, P, D, L, FW, ME, El,
Sh, C, CH, AB, V, R, Bar; **Royal Maas YC** ☎ 137681, D,
L, FW, ME, El, Sh, CH, AB; **Schiedam YC** ☎ 267765, D,
L, FW, ME, El, Sh, CH, AB; **A.L. Valkhof** ☎ 131226, P,
D; **Watersport BV** ☎ 841937, ME; **Vlaardingen YC** M,
FW; **Observator** ☎ 130060, ACA; **Handelsmig**
☎ 181860, Gaz; **Town** all facilities. ✉; Ⓑ; ⇌; ✈.
Ferry UK — Hull.
Note: Special regulations apply to yachts in the Rhine.
These are given in a French booklet '*Service de la
Navigation du Rhin*' obtainable from 25 Rue de la Nuée
Bleu, 6700, Strasbourg.

19

HOEK VAN HOLLAND   10-19-20
(HOOK OF HOLLAND)
Zuid Holland

CHARTS
Admiralty 122, 132; Zeekaart 1540, 1349, 1350, 1449;
Dutch Yacht Chart 1809, 1801; Stanford 19; Imray C30, Y5
TIDES
Dover +0310; ML 1.1; Duration 0505; Zone −0100

Standard Port VLISSINGEN (←)

Times				Height (metres)			
HW		LW		MHWS	MHWN	MLWN	MLWS
0300	0900	0400	1000	4.7	3.9	0.8	0.3
1500	2100	1600	2200				

Differences HOEK VAN HOLLAND
+0033 +0038 +0118 +0107 −2.4   −2.1   −0.5   +0.1
MAASSLUIS
+0201 +0136 +0040 0000 −2.8   −2.2   −0.6   0.0

NOTE: Hook of Holland is a Standard Port and tidal
predictions for each day of the year are given below.
Double LWs occur — The rise after the first LW is called
The Agger — Predictions for Hoek van Holland are for the
lower LW which is usually the second. Time differences
for Secondary Ports referred to Hoek van Holland are
approximate — Water levels on this coast are considerably
affected by the weather. Strong NW gales can raise the
levels by up to 3m.

SHELTER
Entrance safe except in strong on-shore winds when
heavy seas develop. Berghaven harbour not open to
yachts. Better shelter at Maassluis, 10M up river.
NAVIGATION
Waypoints From S: MV-N N cardinal buoy, Q, 51°59'.65N
04°00'.30E, 288°/108° from/to Nieuwe Zuiderdam Lt,
1.5M. From N: Indusbank N cardinal buoy, Q, 52°02'.93N
04°03'.72E, 010°/190° from/to Nieuwe Noorderdam Lt,
3.2M. There are no real navigational dangers but care
should be taken of the strong tidal set across the
entrance. The river is a very busy waterway and the
stream of ocean-going and local shipping is constant. See
Maas Traffic Scheme Fig 2(4). Neither the Calandkanaal
nor the Beerkanaal may be used by pleasure craft. Yachts
crossing the Hook of Holland roadstead are recommended

to call Maas Entrance on Ch 03, reporting yacht's name,
position and course, and maintain watch on Ch 03.
Yachts should cross under power on a track close W of
line joining buoys MV (51°57'.5N, 3°58'.5E), MVN
(51°59'.7N, 4°00'.3E) and Indusbank N (52°03'.0N,
4°03'.7E).
LIGHTS AND MARKS
Maasvlakte Fl(5) 20s 66m 28M; B 8-sided Tr, Or bands; vis
340°-267° (H24). Nieuwe Noorderdam, head FR 24m 10M;
Or Tr, B bands, helicopter platform; in fog Al Fl WR 6s.
Nieuwe Zuiderdam, head FG 24m 10M; Or Tr, B bands,
helicopter platform; in fog Al Fl WG 6s; Horn 10s. Ldg Lts
107° (for Rotterdamsche Waterweg). Front Iso R 6s 29m
18M; R Tr, W bands; vis 100°-114° (H24). Rear Iso R 6s
43m 18M; R Tr, W bands, vis 100°-114° (H24),
synchronized with front.
Traffic signals from Pilot and Signal Station:
Visible to seaward

R R
W   } Entry to Rotterdamsche Waterweg prohibited
R R

Traffic signals from S side of Rotterdamsche Waterweg,
opposite Berghaven:
Visible from landward
R R
W   } Navigation to sea prohibited
R R

Patrol vessels show a Fl Bu Lt. If such vessels show a Fl
R Lt, it means 'Stop'.
RADIO TELEPHONE
A comprehensive Traffic Management and Information
Service operates in the Rotterdam waterway. Four Traffic
Centres are manned H24: Haven Coordinatie Centrum
(HCC) VHF Ch 11 14; Traffic Centre, Hoek van Holland
(TCH) Ch 13; Traffic Centre Botlek (VCB) Ch 13; Traffic
Centre Stad (VCS) Ch 13. The area is divided into sectors
as below; vessels should listen on the assigned frequency
and use it for messages unless otherwise directed.
Maas Approach Ch 01, TCH (Outer approaches to W
boundary of Precautionary Area); *Pilot Mass* Ch 02, TCH
(outer part of Precautionary Area); *Maas Entrance* Ch 03,
TCH (inner part of Precautionary Area); *Waterweg* Ch 65,
TCH (Nieuwe Waterweg to Kruitsteiger); *Europoort* Ch 66,
TCH (Calandkanaal); *Maassluis* Ch 80, VCB (kp 1023 to kp
1017); *Botlek* Ch 61, VCB (kp 1017 to kp 1011); *Eemhaven*
Ch 63, VCS (kp 1011 to kp 1007); *Waalhaven* Ch 60, VCS
(kp 1007 to kp 1003); *Massbruggen* Ch 81, VCS (kp 1003
to kp 998); *Brienenoord* Ch 21, VCS (kp 998 to kp 993).
Yachts should report to Maas Approach or Pilot Maas (or
to Maas Entrance if using the Inshore Traffic Zone) and
follow instructions. Information broadcasts by Maas
Approach and HCC on Ch 01. Weather on Ch 14 every
H+00.
Other stations: Oude Maas (call: *RHD Post Hartel*) Ch 10;
13. Botlekbrug Ch 13; Spijkenisserbrug Ch 18.
Dordrecht (call: *Post Dordrecht*) Ch 08 10 13 14 71 (H24).
TELEPHONE (01747)
Hr Mr Rotterdam 896911; Rotterdam Port Authority
894062; Pilot Hook of Holland 4840; CG 2579; ⌗ 2418;
Police 13444; Ⓗ Rotterdam 112800;
Brit Consul (020) 764343.
FACILITIES
Schoemeyer ☎ 3464, ME, Sh; **N.C. Ruygers** ☎ 2487.,
FW; **Maassluis** AB, BY, CH, El, ME, P, ✉; R, Sh, V, ⚡.
Town P, D, V, R, Bar. ✉; Ⓑ; ⚡; ✈ (Rotterdam).
Ferry UK−Harwich.

NETHERLANDS - HOEK VAN HOLLAND

LAT 51°59′N   LONG 4°07′E

TIMES AND HEIGHTS OF HIGH AND LOW WATERS   YEAR 1991

TIME ZONE −0100
(Dutch Standard Time)
Subtract 1 hour for GMT
For Dutch Summer Time add ONE hour in non-shaded areas

JANUARY

Day	DoW	Time	m	Time	m	Time	m	Time	m
1	TU	0217	2.0	0745	0.2	1434	2.2	2306	0.3
2	W	0308	2.0	0825	0.2	1525	2.3	2355	0.4
3	TH	0357	2.0	0915	0.1	1606	2.3		
4	F	0040	0.4	0439	2.0	1305	0.1	1656	2.3
5	SA	0124	0.4	0527	2.0	1400	0.0	1744	2.2
6	SU	0230	0.4	0613	2.0	1455	0.1	1838	2.1
7	M ☾	0326	0.4	0708	1.9	1244	0.1	1934	2.0
8	TU	0405	0.5	0753	1.8	1355	0.1	2035	1.9
9	W	0235	0.5	0853	1.7	1455	0.2	2144	1.8
10	TH	0345	0.4	1004	1.7	1615	0.3	2254	1.7
11	F	0455	0.4	1125	1.7	1737	0.3		
12	SA	0004	1.7	0555	0.4	1229	1.7	1837	0.4
13	SU	0104	1.8	0645	0.3	1313	1.8	1930	0.4
14	M	0143	1.8	0724	0.3	1404	1.9	2010	0.4
15	TU ●	0223	1.9	0810	0.3	1438	2.0	2050	0.4
16	W	0315	1.9	0824	0.2	1514	2.1	2150	0.4
17	TH	0333	2.0	0849	0.1	1544	2.1	2300	0.4
18	F	0403	2.0	0915	0.1	1614	2.1	2350	0.4
19	SA	0433	2.0	1235	0.1	1647	2.1		
20	SU	0045	0.4	0503	1.9	1025	0.1	1724	2.1
21	M	0115	0.4	0544	1.9	1059	0.1	1800	2.1
22	TU	0145	0.4	0618	1.9	1150	0.0	1845	2.0
23	W ☽	0207	0.4	0704	1.9	1235	0.0	1938	2.0
24	TH	0157	0.4	0805	1.9	1355	0.0	2044	1.9
25	F	0245	0.4	0914	1.8	1515	0.1	2159	1.8
26	SA	0400	0.4	1034	1.8	1635	0.2	2319	1.7
27	SU	0514	0.4	1145	1.8	1745	0.2		
28	M	0029	1.8	0604	0.3	1248	1.9	2100	0.3
29	TU	0124	1.8	0924	0.2	1337	2.1	2206	0.3
30	W ○	0214	1.9	1025	0.1	1424	2.2	2240	0.3
31	TH	0304	2.0	1116	0.1	1510	2.2	2335	0.3

FEBRUARY

Day	DoW	Time	m	Time	m	Time	m	Time	m
1	F	0344	2.0	1200	0.0	1555	2.2	2324	0.4
2	SA	0016	0.3	0425	2.0	1245	0.0	1635	2.2
3	SU	0115	0.3	0445	2.0	1335	0.0	1720	2.2
4	M	0155	0.3	0549	2.0	1425	0.0	1805	2.1
5	TU	0246	0.4	0628	2.0	1220	0.1	1854	1.9
6	W ☾	0110	0.4	0714	1.9	1315	0.1	1945	1.8
7	TH	0145	0.3	0804	1.8	1430	0.2	2034	1.6
8	F	0307	0.3	0903	1.6	1555	0.3	2144	1.5
9	SA	0424	0.3	1015	1.5	1705	0.3	2345	1.5
10	SU	0546	0.3	1159	1.6	1814	0.3		
11	M	0038	1.6	0624	0.2	1253	1.7	1910	0.3
12	TU	0135	1.7	0704	0.2	1344	1.9	2140	0.3
13	W	0215	1.8	0954	0.2	1413	2.0	2224	0.3
14	TH ●	0245	1.9	1030	0.1	1448	2.1	2227	0.4
15	F	0315	1.9	0819	0.1	1518	2.1	2250	0.4
16	SA	0338	2.0	0845	0.1	1547	2.2	2324	0.4
17	SU	0407	2.0	0915	0.0	1624	2.2		
18	M	0015	0.3	0445	2.0	0951	0.0	1656	2.1
19	TU	0045	0.3	0517	2.0	1036	0.0	1734	2.1
20	W	0130	0.3	0554	2.0	1120	−0.1	1818	2.0
21	TH ☽	0145	0.3	0637	2.0	1220	0.0	1908	1.9
22	F	0108	0.3	0735	1.9	1400	0.0	2015	1.8
23	SA	0230	0.3	0838	1.8	1504	0.1	2145	1.6
24	SU	0345	0.3	1015	1.7	1624	0.2	2309	1.5
25	M	0454	0.3	1133	1.8	1940	0.2		
26	TU	0035	1.6	0805	0.2	1244	1.9	2105	0.3
27	W	0124	1.7	0925	0.1	1335	2.0	2135	0.2
28	TH ○	0202	1.8	1015	0.1	1414	2.1	2220	0.3

MARCH

Day	DoW	Time	m	Time	m	Time	m	Time	m
1	F	0244	1.9	1056	0.0	1454	2.1	2306	0.3
2	SA	0320	2.0	1136	0.0	1531	2.2	2345	0.3
3	SU	0357	2.0	1214	0.0	1611	2.1		
4	M	0035	0.3	0435	2.1	1310	0.0	1655	2.1
5	TU	0126	0.3	0514	2.1	1355	0.0	1734	2.0
6	W	0205	0.3	0555	2.0	1407	0.1	1807	1.9
7	TH	0007	0.2	0634	1.9	1310	0.2	1855	1.7
8	F ☾	0055	0.2	0713	1.8	1400	0.2	1939	1.6
9	SA	0217	0.2	0825	1.6	1545	0.3	2044	1.4
10	SU	0404	0.2	0939	1.5	1644	0.3	2223	1.3
11	M	0510	0.2	1124	1.5	1735	0.3		
12	TU	0009	1.5	0559	0.1	1224	1.7	1850	0.3
13	W	0059	1.6	0654	0.1	1308	1.9	2107	0.2
14	TH	0133	1.7	0917	0.1	1344	2.0	2155	0.2
15	F	0204	1.8	1015	0.1	1414	2.1	2230	0.3
16	SA ●	0237	1.9	0745	0.1	1444	2.1	2237	0.3
17	SU	0305	2.0	0811	0.0	1520	2.2	2305	0.3
18	M	0337	2.0	0848	0.0	1555	2.2	2355	0.3
19	TU	0412	2.1	0925	0.0	1631	2.1	2146	0.3
20	W	0450	2.1	1010	0.0	1715	2.1	2225	0.2
21	TH	0530	2.1	1100	0.0	1757	2.0	2314	0.2
22	F	0617	2.0	1324	0.0	1844	1.8		
23	SA ☽	0100	0.2	0708	2.0	1354	0.1	1954	1.6
24	SU	0215	0.1	0835	1.8	1504	0.1	2135	1.5
25	M	0325	0.2	1015	1.7	1750	0.2	2304	1.5
26	TU	0434	0.2	1134	1.8	1925	0.2		
27	W	0013	1.6	0800	0.1	1234	1.9	2035	0.2
28	TH	0103	1.7	0854	0.0	1318	2.0	2124	0.2
29	F	0143	1.8	0944	0.0	1355	2.0	2155	0.3
30	SA ○	0224	1.9	1036	0.1	1435	2.0	2224	0.3
31	SU	0250	2.0	1105	0.1	1510	2.0	2315	0.3

APRIL

Day	DoW	Time	m	Time	m	Time	m	Time	m
1	M	0334	2.0	1156	0.1	1547	2.0	2355	0.2
2	TU	0407	2.0	1224	0.1	1627	2.0		
3	W	0050	0.2	0445	2.0	1315	0.1	1700	1.9
4	TH	0120	0.2	0518	2.0	1320	0.2	1734	1.8
5	F	0017	0.1	0559	1.9	1330	0.2	1814	1.7
6	SA	0027	0.1	0633	1.8	1400	0.2	1854	1.6
7	SU ☾	0130	0.1	0723	1.7	1520	0.3	1953	1.5
8	M	0335	0.1	0854	1.5	1625	0.3	2113	1.4
9	TU	0446	0.1	1023	1.5	1714	0.3	2254	1.4
10	W	0540	0.1	1134	1.7	1830	0.2		
11	TH	0015	1.5	0640	0.1	1228	1.8	2025	0.2
12	F	0043	1.7	0835	0.1	1304	2.0	2124	0.2
13	SA	0125	1.8	0945	0.1	1334	2.1	2215	0.2
14	SU ●	0155	1.9	0715	0.1	1414	2.1	2245	0.3
15	M	0234	2.0	0745	0.0	1448	2.2	2009	0.3
16	TU	0307	2.1	0821	0.0	1528	2.1	2046	0.2
17	W	0346	2.1	0906	0.0	1609	2.1	2126	0.2
18	TH	0427	2.2	0949	0.1	1655	2.0	2212	0.1
19	F	0511	2.2	1255	0.1	1740	1.9	2316	0.1
20	SA	0557	2.1	1315	0.1	1834	1.7		
21	SU ☽	0035	0.1	0658	2.0	1355	0.1	1954	1.6
22	M	0145	0.0	0823	1.8	1510	0.2	2125	1.5
23	TU	0255	0.1	0953	1.8	1745	0.2	2254	1.5
24	W	0605	0.1	1114	1.9	1917	0.1	2343	1.6
25	TH	0746	0.0	1204	1.9	2035	0.1		
26	F	0038	1.7	0834	0.0	1254	2.0	2055	0.2
27	SA	0117	1.8	0925	0.1	1334	2.0	2125	0.2
28	SU ○	0158	1.9	0950	0.1	1409	1.9	2204	0.2
29	M	0234	1.9	1024	0.2	1455	1.9	2237	0.2
30	TU	0307	2.0	1057	0.2	1528	1.9	2324	0.1

LOW WATERS – IMPORTANT NOTE. DOUBLE LOW WATERS OFTEN OCCUR. PREDICTIONS ARE FOR THE LOWER LOW WATER WHICH IS USUALLY THE SECOND.

Chart Datum: 1.03 metres below Normaal Amsterdams Peil

19

NETHERLANDS - HOEK VAN HOLLAND

LAT 51°59'N   LONG 4°07'E

TIMES AND HEIGHTS OF HIGH AND LOW WATERS

YEAR **1991**

TIME ZONE −0100
(Dutch Standard Time)
Subtract 1 hour for GMT
For Dutch Summer Time add
ONE hour in non-shaded areas

MAY

Day	TIME	m	Day	TIME	m
1 W	0345 / 1150 / 1604	2.0 / 0.2 / 1.9	16 TH	0326 / 0845 / 1555 / 2109	2.2 / 0.1 / 2.0 / 0.1
2 TH	0015 / 0420 / 1235 / 1638	0.1 / 2.0 / 0.2 / 1.8	17 F	0414 / 1240 / 1640 / 2205	2.2 / 0.2 / 1.9 / 0.1
3 F	0055 / 0459 / 1300 / 1707	0.1 / 2.0 / 0.2 / 1.8	18 SA	0457 / 1315 / 1730 / 2306	2.2 / 0.2 / 1.8 / 0.0
4 SA	0110 / 0534 / 1317 / 1744	0.0 / 1.9 / 0.2 / 1.7	19 SU	0555 / 1415 / 1833	2.1 / 0.2 / 1.7
5 SU	0047 / 0615 / 1400 / 1822	1.8 / 1.8 / 0.3 / 1.6	20 M	0005 / 0653 / 1515 / 1955	0.1 / 2.0 / 0.2 / 1.6
6 M	0100 / 0704 / 1454 / 1929	0.0 / 1.7 / 0.3 / 1.5	21 TU	0124 / 0825 / 1624 / 2054	0.0 / 1.9 / 0.2 / 1.6
7 TU	0325 / 0813 / 1555 / 2045	0.0 / 1.7 / 0.3 / 1.5	22 W	0224 / 0935 / 1734 / 2203	0.0 / 1.9 / 0.2 / 1.6
8 W	0426 / 0928 / 1644 / 2144	0.1 / 1.7 / 0.3 / 1.4	23 TH	0601 / 1045 / 1834 / 2315	0.0 / 1.9 / 0.2 / 1.6
9 TH	0515 / 1045 / 1747 / 2304	0.1 / 1.7 / 0.3 / 1.5	24 F	0654 / 1134 / 1944	0.0 / 1.9 / 0.2
10 F	0620 / 1139 / 1947 / 2359	0.1 / 1.9 / 0.2 / 1.7	25 SA	0004 / 0755 / 1228 / 2045	1.7 / 0.1 / 1.9 / 0.2
11 SA	0815 / 1224 / 2101	0.1 / 2.0 / 0.2	26 SU	0055 / 0847 / 1314 / 2125	1.8 / 0.1 / 1.9 / 0.2
12 SU	0045 / 0610 / 1300 / 2145	1.8 / 0.1 / 2.1 / 0.2	27 M	0134 / 0817 / 1354 / 1940	1.8 / 0.2 / 1.9 / 0.2
13 M	0124 / 0646 / 1344 / 1916	1.9 / 0.1 / 2.1 / 0.2	28 TU	0214 / 0827 / 1433 / 2020	1.9 / 0.3 / 1.8 / 0.1
14 TU	0204 / 0726 / 1425 / 1949	2.0 / 0.1 / 2.1 / 0.2	29 W	0255 / 0937 / 1514 / 2100	1.9 / 0.3 / 1.8 / 0.1
15 W	0244 / 0801 / 1608 / 2025	2.1 / 0.1 / 2.1 / 0.2	30 TH	0328 / 1050 / 1543 / 2340	2.0 / 0.3 / 1.8 / 0.1
			31 F	0405 / 1150 / 1625	2.0 / 0.3 / 1.8

JUNE

Day	TIME	m	Day	TIME	m
1 SA	0010 / 0444 / 1230 / 1653	0.0 / 2.0 / 0.3 / 1.8	16 SU	0447 / 1314 / 1724	2.2 / 0.2 / 1.8
2 SU	0055 / 0513 / 1315 / 1735	0.0 / 1.9 / 0.3 / 1.7	17 M	0151 / 0534 / 1415 / 1824	0.0 / 2.2 / 0.2 / 1.8
3 M	0130 / 0554 / 1350 / 1803	0.0 / 1.9 / 0.3 / 1.7	18 TU	0245 / 0644 / 1510 / 1925	0.0 / 2.1 / 0.3 / 1.8
4 TU	0204 / 0634 / 1424 / 1852	0.0 / 1.8 / 0.3 / 1.6	19 W	0045 / 0744 / 1615 / 2025	0.0 / 2.0 / 0.3 / 1.7
5 W	0105 / 0724 / 1520 / 2004	0.0 / 1.8 / 0.3 / 1.6	20 TH	0205 / 0843 / 1704 / 2124	0.0 / 1.9 / 0.3 / 1.7
6 TH	0154 / 0838 / 1610 / 2115	0.0 / 1.8 / 0.3 / 1.6	21 F	0304 / 1005 / 1755 / 2234	0.0 / 1.9 / 0.3 / 1.7
7 F	0255 / 0944 / 1700 / 2214	0.1 / 1.8 / 0.3 / 1.6	22 SA	0605 / 1104 / 1905 / 2328	0.1 / 1.8 / 0.3 / 1.7
8 SA	0344 / 1049 / 1747 / 2308	0.1 / 1.9 / 0.3 / 1.7	23 SU	0700 / 1205 / 1957	0.2 / 1.8 / 0.3
9 SU	0445 / 1145 / 1735	0.1 / 1.9 / 0.3	24 M	0024 / 0657 / 1253 / 2057	1.7 / 0.2 / 1.8 / 0.2
10 M	0007 / 0535 / 1230 / 1814	1.8 / 0.1 / 2.0 / 0.2	25 TU	0113 / 0704 / 1343 / 1924	1.8 / 0.3 / 1.8 / 0.2
11 TU	0054 / 0630 / 1321 / 1855	1.9 / 0.1 / 2.0 / 0.2	26 W	0215 / 0755 / 1423 / 1955	1.8 / 0.3 / 1.8 / 0.1
12 W	0140 / 0715 / 1406 / 1935	2.0 / 0.1 / 2.0 / 0.2	27 TH	0244 / 0835 / 1508 / 2040	1.9 / 0.4 / 1.8 / 0.1
13 TH	0226 / 0755 / 1455 / 2016	2.1 / 0.2 / 2.0 / 0.1	28 F	0318 / 0950 / 1533 / 2110	2.0 / 0.4 / 1.8 / 0.1
14 F	0315 / 1145 / 1541 / 2059	2.2 / 0.2 / 1.9 / 0.1	29 SA	0354 / 1057 / 1614 / 2124	2.0 / 0.4 / 1.9 / 0.0
15 SA	0400 / 1224 / 1635 / 2150	2.2 / 0.2 / 1.9 / 0.0	30 SU	0428 / 1200 / 1644	2.0 / 0.4 / 1.8

JULY

Day	TIME	m	Day	TIME	m
1 M	0035 / 0505 / 1235 / 1724	0.0 / 2.0 / 0.3 / 1.8	16 TU	0135 / 0519 / 1400 / 1757	0.0 / 2.2 / 0.3 / 1.9
2 TU	0104 / 0534 / 1325 / 1748	0.0 / 2.0 / 0.3 / 1.8	17 W	0230 / 0614 / 1454 / 1845	0.0 / 2.1 / 0.3 / 1.9
3 W	0144 / 0603 / 1416 / 1828	0.0 / 2.0 / 0.3 / 1.7	18 TH	0320 / 0703 / 1545 / 1939	0.0 / 2.0 / 0.4 / 1.9
4 TH	0004 / 0647 / 1440 / 1914	0.0 / 1.9 / 0.4 / 1.7	19 F	0115 / 0804 / 1415 / 2034	0.1 / 1.9 / 0.4 / 1.8
5 F	0104 / 0742 / 1456 / 2025	0.0 / 1.9 / 0.4 / 1.7	20 SA	0225 / 0909 / 1515 / 2139	0.1 / 1.8 / 0.4 / 1.7
6 SA	0204 / 0855 / 1520 / 2125	0.0 / 1.9 / 0.4 / 1.7	21 SU	0350 / 1029 / 1629 / 2254	0.2 / 1.7 / 0.3 / 1.7
7 SU	0316 / 0959 / 1605 / 2235	0.1 / 1.9 / 0.3 / 1.7	22 M	0454 / 1133 / 1734	0.3 / 1.7 / 0.3
8 M	0415 / 1105 / 1710 / 2335	0.1 / 1.9 / 0.3 / 1.8	23 TU	0004 / 0610 / 1245 / 1825	1.7 / 0.3 / 1.7 / 0.2
9 TU	0515 / 1209 / 1754	0.1 / 1.9 / 0.3	24 W	0103 / 0700 / 1334 / 1910	1.8 / 0.4 / 1.8 / 0.2
10 W	0035 / 0620 / 1304 / 1845	1.9 / 0.2 / 1.9 / 0.2	25 TH	0154 / 0735 / 1425 / 1935	1.9 / 0.4 / 1.8 / 0.2
11 TH	0127 / 0716 / 1354 / 1925	2.0 / 0.2 / 1.9 / 0.1	26 F	0223 / 0815 / 1459 / 2014	1.9 / 0.4 / 1.9 / 0.1
12 F	0214 / 1046 / 1445 / 2006	2.1 / 0.3 / 1.9 / 0.1	27 SA	0305 / 0858 / 1535 / 2034	2.0 / 0.4 / 1.9 / 0.1
13 SA	0300 / 1114 / 1530 / 2046	2.2 / 0.3 / 1.9 / 0.0	28 SU	0335 / 1030 / 1555 / 2059	2.1 / 0.4 / 1.9 / 0.1
14 SU	0344 / 1210 / 1617 / 2128	2.3 / 0.3 / 1.9 / 0.0	29 M	0404 / 1130 / 1624 / 2136	2.1 / 0.4 / 1.9 / 0.1
15 M	0435 / 1305 / 1704 / 2206	2.3 / 0.3 / 1.9 / 0.1	30 TU	0438 / 1214 / 1654 / 2206	2.1 / 0.4 / 1.9 / 0.1
			31 W	0504 / 1306 / 1725 / 2245	2.1 / 0.4 / 1.9 / 0.1

AUGUST

Day	TIME	m	Day	TIME	m
1 TH	0540 / 1346 / 1759 / 2314	2.1 / 0.4 / 1.9 / 0.0	16 F	0256 / 0628 / 1505 / 1855	0.1 / 2.0 / 0.4 / 2.0
2 F	0618 / 1404 / 1839	2.1 / 0.4 / 1.9	17 SA	0045 / 0719 / 1330 / 1945	0.2 / 1.9 / 0.4 / 1.9
3 SA	0003 / 0705 / 1316 / 1924	0.0 / 2.0 / 0.4 / 1.9	18 SU	0155 / 0814 / 1440 / 2044	0.2 / 1.7 / 0.4 / 1.7
4 SU	0120 / 0805 / 1435 / 2035	0.1 / 1.9 / 0.4 / 1.8	19 M	0315 / 0913 / 1604 / 2204	0.3 / 1.6 / 0.3 / 1.6
5 M	0235 / 0913 / 1524 / 2155	0.1 / 1.8 / 0.3 / 1.8	20 TU	0434 / 1104 / 1704 / 2338	0.4 / 1.5 / 0.3 / 1.7
6 TU	0354 / 1045 / 1644 / 2314	0.2 / 1.7 / 0.3 / 1.8	21 W	0544 / 1225 / 1755	0.4 / 1.6 / 0.2
7 W	0509 / 1155 / 1734	0.2 / 1.7 / 0.3	22 TH	0044 / 0635 / 1319 / 1844	1.8 / 0.4 / 1.8 / 0.2
8 TH	0025 / 0604 / 1254 / 1825	1.9 / 0.3 / 1.8 / 0.2	23 F	0128 / 0927 / 1354 / 1925	1.9 / 0.4 / 1.8 / 0.2
9 F	0114 / 0924 / 1348 / 1906	2.1 / 0.3 / 1.9 / 0.1	24 SA	0204 / 1025 / 1434 / 1944	2.0 / 0.4 / 1.9 / 0.2
10 SA	0204 / 1026 / 1434 / 1941	2.2 / 0.4 / 1.9 / 0.1	25 SU	0234 / 0830 / 1454 / 2005	2.1 / 0.5 / 2.0 / 0.2
11 SU	0244 / 1054 / 1515 / 2021	2.3 / 0.4 / 2.0 / 0.1	26 M	0305 / 0824 / 1524 / 2029	2.2 / 0.5 / 2.0 / 0.1
12 M	0330 / 1150 / 1558 / 2106	2.3 / 0.4 / 2.0 / 0.1	27 TU	0335 / 1104 / 1554 / 2100	2.2 / 0.5 / 2.0 / 0.1
13 TU	0411 / 1240 / 1637 / 2129	2.3 / 0.4 / 2.0 / 0.1	28 W	0407 / 1155 / 1624 / 2129	2.2 / 0.5 / 2.0 / 0.1
14 W	0115 / 0456 / 1335 / 1720	0.1 / 2.2 / 0.4 / 2.0	29 TH	0438 / 1235 / 1654 / 2205	2.2 / 0.4 / 2.0 / 0.1
15 TH	0215 / 0540 / 1414 / 1804	0.1 / 2.1 / 0.4 / 2.0	30 F	0511 / 1025 / 1727 / 2245	2.2 / 0.4 / 2.1 / 0.1
			31 SA	0555 / 1105 / 1806 / 2335	2.1 / 0.4 / 2.1 / 0.1

LOW WATERS – IMPORTANT NOTE. DOUBLE LOW WATERS OFTEN OCCUR. PREDICTIONS ARE FOR THE LOWER LOW WATER WHICH IS USUALLY THE SECOND.

Chart Datum: 1.03 metres below Normaal Amsterdams Peil

NETHERLANDS - HOEK VAN HOLLAND

LAT 51°59'N   LONG 4°07'E

TIMES AND HEIGHTS OF HIGH AND LOW WATERS — YEAR **1991**

TIME ZONE −0100
(Dutch Standard Time)
Subtract 1 hour for GMT
For Dutch Summer Time add ONE hour in non-shaded areas

SEPTEMBER

Day	TIME	m	Day	TIME	m
1 SU ☾	0637 / 1154 / 1855	2.1 / 0.3 / 2.0	**16** M	0130 / 0724 / 1325 / 2005	0.4 / 1.7 / 0.3 / 1.8
2 M	0045 / 0734 / 1340 / 2005	0.2 / 1.9 / 0.3 / 1.9	**17** TU	0304 / 0819 / 1535 / 2114	0.4 / 1.6 / 0.3 / 1.6
3 TU	0234 / 0844 / 1505 / 2124	0.2 / 1.7 / 0.3 / 1.8	**18** W	0414 / 0949 / 1655 / 2303	0.5 / 1.4 / 0.3 / 1.6
4 W	0344 / 1019 / 1614 / 2258	0.3 / 1.6 / 0.3 / 1.8	**19** TH	0519 / 1149 / 1740	0.5 / 1.5 / 0.3
5 TH	0510 / 1144 / 1714	0.4 / 1.6 / 0.3	**20** F	0014 / 0615 / 1245 / 1824	0.5 / 0.5 / 1.7 / 0.2
6 F	0015 / 0815 / 1243 / 2056	2.0 / 0.4 / 1.8 / 0.2	**21** SA	0053 / 0905 / 1335 / 1910	1.9 / 0.4 / 1.8 / 0.2
7 SA	0104 / 0905 / 1334 / 1841	2.1 / 0.4 / 1.9 / 0.2	**22** SU	0135 / 0950 / 1355 / 2150	2.1 / 0.4 / 1.9 / 0.3
8 SU ●	0144 / 0955 / 1415 / 1925	2.2 / 0.4 / 2.0 / 0.1	**23** M ○	0205 / 1030 / 1418 / 1929	2.1 / 0.5 / 2.0 / 0.2
9 M	0226 / 1025 / 1454 / 1957	2.3 / 0.5 / 2.0 / 0.1	**24** TU	0227 / 0754 / 1444 / 1955	2.2 / 0.5 / 2.1 / 0.2
10 TU	0308 / 1126 / 1531 / 2040	2.3 / 0.5 / 2.1 / 0.1	**25** W	0300 / 0819 / 1517 / 2030	2.3 / 0.5 / 2.1 / 0.2
11 W	0347 / 1216 / 1609 / 2119	2.2 / 0.5 / 2.1 / 0.2	**26** TH	0336 / 0856 / 1554 / 2101	2.3 / 0.5 / 2.2 / 0.1
12 TH	0430 / 1254 / 1650	2.2 / 0.4 / 2.1	**27** F	0410 / 0925 / 1628 / 2142	2.2 / 0.4 / 2.2 / 0.1
13 F	0135 / 0510 / 1335 / 1728	0.2 / 2.1 / 0.4 / 2.1	**28** SA	0448 / 1005 / 1705 / 2228	2.2 / 0.3 / 2.2 / 0.1
14 SA	0204 / 0550 / 1124 / 1808	0.3 / 2.0 / 0.4 / 2.0	**29** SU	0528 / 1050 / 1744 / 2314	2.1 / 0.3 / 2.2 / 0.2
15 SU ☽	0017 / 0635 / 1225 / 1854	0.3 / 1.9 / 0.4 / 1.9	**30** M	0615 / 1144 / 1835	2.0 / 0.3 / 2.1

OCTOBER

Day	TIME	m	Day	TIME	m
1 TU ☾	0130 / 0708 / 1324 / 1933	0.3 / 1.8 / 0.3 / 2.0	**16** W	0227 / 0734 / 1507 / 2035	0.5 / 1.6 / 0.3 / 1.7
2 W	0235 / 0834 / 1434 / 2119	0.3 / 1.6 / 0.3 / 1.8	**17** TH	0345 / 0849 / 1626 / 2159	0.5 / 1.5 / 0.3 / 1.6
3 TH	0340 / 1009 / 1544 / 2305	0.4 / 1.6 / 0.3 / 1.9	**18** F	0444 / 1026 / 1715 / 2329	0.5 / 1.5 / 0.3 / 1.8
4 F	0705 / 1145 / 1920	0.4 / 1.6 / 0.3	**19** SA	0600 / 1154 / 1804	0.5 / 1.6 / 0.3
5 SA	0004 / 0814 / 1234 / 2024	2.0 / 0.4 / 1.8 / 0.2	**20** SU	0015 / 0821 / 1239 / 2014	1.9 / 0.4 / 1.8 / 0.3
6 SU	0043 / 0855 / 1314 / 2114	2.1 / 0.4 / 1.9 / 0.2	**21** M	0054 / 0904 / 1308 / 2115	2.1 / 0.4 / 1.9 / 0.3
7 M ●	0127 / 0930 / 1354 / 1854	2.2 / 0.4 / 2.0 / 0.2	**22** TU	0124 / 0954 / 1344 / 1900	2.2 / 0.4 / 2.0 / 0.3
8 TU	0207 / 0955 / 1429 / 1940	2.2 / 0.5 / 2.1 / 0.2	**23** W ○	0155 / 0725 / 1415 / 1930	2.2 / 0.5 / 2.1 / 0.3
9 W	0246 / 1055 / 1507 / 2018	2.2 / 0.5 / 2.1 / 0.3	**24** TH	0231 / 0754 / 1448 / 2006	2.3 / 0.5 / 2.2 / 0.2
10 TH	0324 / 1145 / 1546 / 2059	2.2 / 0.4 / 2.2 / 0.3	**25** F	0308 / 0825 / 1526 / 2045	2.3 / 0.4 / 2.3 / 0.2
11 F	0407 / 1235 / 1624 / 2126	2.1 / 0.4 / 2.2 / 0.4	**26** SA	0349 / 0905 / 1606 / 2126	2.2 / 0.3 / 2.3 / 0.3
12 SA	0055 / 0444 / 1315 / 1704	0.3 / 2.2 / 0.4 / 2.2	**27** SU	0410 / 0945 / 1646 / 2208	2.2 / 0.3 / 2.3 / 0.3
13 SU ☽	0135 / 0525 / 1044 / 1745	0.4 / 2.0 / 0.3 / 2.1	**28** M	0515 / 1035 / 1735 / 2314	2.0 / 0.2 / 2.3 / 0.4
14 M	0048 / 0605 / 1154 / 1824	0.5 / 1.9 / 0.3 / 2.0	**29** TU	0605 / 1135 / 1824	1.9 / 0.2 / 2.1
15 TU	0110 / 0702 / 1245 / 1919	0.5 / 1.8 / 0.3 / 1.8	**30** W ☾	0115 / 0639 / 1254 / 1932	0.4 / 1.8 / 0.2 / 2.0
			31 TH	0224 / 0824 / 1415 / 2109	0.4 / 1.6 / 0.2 / 1.9

NOVEMBER

Day	TIME	m	Day	TIME	m
1 F	0525 / 0954 / 1515 / 2234	0.5 / 1.6 / 0.3 / 2.0	**16** SA	0414 / 0919 / 1655 / 2214	0.5 / 1.6 / 0.3 / 1.8
2 SA	0650 / 1103 / 1854 / 2344	0.4 / 1.7 / 0.2 / 2.0	**17** SU	0515 / 1034 / 1744 / 2325	0.5 / 1.6 / 0.3 / 1.9
3 SU	0805 / 1209 / 2004	0.4 / 1.8 / 0.2	**18** M	0717 / 1134 / 1934	0.5 / 1.7 / 0.3
4 M	0029 / 0835 / 1255 / 2054	2.1 / 0.4 / 1.9 / 0.2	**19** TU	0005 / 0824 / 1224 / 2046	2.0 / 0.4 / 1.9 / 0.3
5 TU	0115 / 0905 / 1334 / 2130	2.1 / 0.4 / 2.0 / 0.3	**20** W	0045 / 0935 / 1304 / 1824	2.1 / 0.4 / 2.0 / 0.3
6 W ●	0147 / 0935 / 1407 / 1925	2.1 / 0.5 / 2.0 / 0.3	**21** TH ○	0124 / 0659 / 1345 / 1905	2.2 / 0.4 / 2.1 / 0.3
7 TH	0227 / 1025 / 1448 / 2005	2.1 / 0.4 / 2.1 / 0.4	**22** F	0207 / 0735 / 1425 / 1945	2.2 / 0.3 / 2.2 / 0.3
8 F	0308 / 0829 / 1524 / 2317	2.1 / 0.4 / 2.1 / 0.4	**23** SA	0248 / 0809 / 1506 / 2025	2.2 / 0.3 / 2.3 / 0.3
9 SA	0344 / 1154 / 1604	2.0 / 0.3 / 2.2	**24** SU	0331 / 0856 / 1548 / 2115	2.2 / 0.3 / 2.3 / 0.3
10 SU	0010 / 0425 / 0945 / 1645	0.4 / 2.0 / 0.3 / 2.1	**25** M	0416 / 0936 / 1635 / 2205	2.1 / 0.2 / 2.3 / 0.4
11 M	0036 / 0458 / 1035 / 1718	0.5 / 1.9 / 0.2 / 2.1	**26** TU	0504 / 1025 / 1724	2.0 / 0.2 / 2.3
12 TU	0040 / 0534 / 1130 / 1758	0.5 / 1.9 / 0.2 / 2.0	**27** W	0127 / 0604 / 1123 / 1824	0.4 / 1.9 / 0.1 / 2.2
13 W	0107 / 0615 / 1214 / 1855	0.5 / 1.8 / 0.2 / 1.9	**28** TH	0217 / 0709 / 1234 / 1934	0.5 / 1.8 / 0.1 / 2.1
14 TH	0210 / 0715 / 1315 / 1944	0.5 / 1.7 / 0.2 / 1.8	**29** F ☽	0345 / 0825 / 1344 / 2044	0.5 / 1.7 / 0.2 / 1.9
15 F	0320 / 0803 / 1555 / 2054	0.5 / 1.6 / 0.3 / 1.8	**30** SA	0504 / 0925 / 1736 / 2154	0.5 / 1.7 / 0.2 / 2.0

DECEMBER

Day	TIME	m	Day	TIME	m
1 SU	0625 / 1035 / 1845 / 2309	0.4 / 1.7 / 0.2 / 2.0	**16** M	0430 / 0934 / 1514 / 2225	0.5 / 1.7 / 0.2 / 1.9
2 M	0735 / 1135 / 1940 / 2358	0.4 / 1.8 / 0.2 / 2.0	**17** TU	0520 / 1045 / 1614 / 2314	0.5 / 1.7 / 0.3 / 2.0
3 TU	0825 / 1225 / 2027	0.4 / 1.9 / 0.3	**18** W	0626 / 1138 / 1725	0.5 / 1.8 / 0.3
4 W	0054 / 0910 / 1310 / 2056	2.0 / 0.4 / 1.9 / 0.4	**19** TH	0011 / 0855 / 1230 / 1815	2.0 / 0.4 / 2.0 / 0.3
5 TH	0133 / 0940 / 1354 / 1950	2.0 / 0.4 / 2.0 / 0.4	**20** F	0104 / 0941 / 1320 / 1855	2.1 / 0.4 / 2.1 / 0.3
6 F ●	0217 / 0800 / 1434 / 2100	2.0 / 0.4 / 2.0 / 0.4	**21** SA ○	0146 / 0719 / 1406 / 1939	2.1 / 0.3 / 2.2 / 0.3
7 SA	0305 / 0840 / 1515 / 2150	2.0 / 0.3 / 2.1 / 0.5	**22** SU	0236 / 0754 / 1454 / 2019	2.1 / 0.3 / 2.3 / 0.4
8 SU	0333 / 0905 / 1547 / 2256	2.0 / 0.2 / 2.1 / 0.5	**23** M	0319 / 0835 / 1537	2.1 / 0.2 / 2.3
9 M	0415 / 0944 / 1628 / 2357	2.0 / 0.2 / 2.1 / 0.5	**24** TU	0005 / 0407 / 0926 / 1624	0.4 / 2.0 / 0.1 / 2.3
10 TU	0444 / 1024 / 1709	1.9 / 0.2 / 2.1	**25** W	0056 / 0454 / 1016 / 1714	0.4 / 2.0 / 0.1 / 2.3
11 W	0040 / 0518 / 1055 / 1745	0.5 / 1.9 / 0.1 / 2.0	**26** TH	0146 / 0554 / 1105 / 1808	0.4 / 2.0 / 0.1 / 2.2
12 TH	0110 / 0559 / 1145 / 1825	0.5 / 1.9 / 0.1 / 2.0	**27** F	0215 / 0644 / 1205 / 1908	0.4 / 1.9 / 0.1 / 2.1
13 F	0200 / 0645 / 1235 / 1908	0.5 / 1.8 / 0.2 / 1.9	**28** SA	0330 / 0745 / 1313 / 2015	0.5 / 1.9 / 0.1 / 1.9
14 SA	0230 / 0735 / 1330 / 2009	0.5 / 1.7 / 0.2 / 1.9	**29** SU	0445 / 0844 / 1424 / 2113	0.5 / 1.8 / 0.1 / 1.9
15 SU	0334 / 0845 / 1414 / 2115	0.5 / 1.7 / 0.2 / 1.9	**30** M	0540 / 0954 / 1529 / 2223	0.5 / 1.8 / 0.2 / 1.9
			31 TU	0625 / 1059 / 1844 / 2339	0.4 / 1.8 / 0.3 / 1.7

LOW WATERS – IMPORTANT NOTE. DOUBLE LOW WATERS OFTEN OCCUR. PREDICTIONS ARE FOR THE LOWER LOW WATER WHICH IS USUALLY THE SECOND.

Chart Datum: 1.03 metres below Normaal Amsterdams Peil

19

SCHEVENINGEN   10-19-21
Zuid Holland

CHARTS
Admiralty 122, 1406; Zeekaart 1035, 1349, 1350, 1449;
Dutch Yacht Chart 1801; Dutch Waterkaarts ANWB H/J;
Stanford 19; Imray Y5
TIDES
Dover +0320; ML No data; Duration 0445; Zone −0100

Standard Port VLISSINGEN (←)

Times				Height (metres)			
HW		LW		MHWS	MHWN	MLWN	MLWS
0300	0900	0400	1000	4.7	3.9	0.8	0.3
1500	2100	1600	2200				

Differences SCHEVENINGEN
+0105 +0102 +0226 +0246 −2.6 −2.2 −0.6 −0.1

NOTE: Double LWs occur — The rise after the first LW is
called The Agger — Predictions for Hoek van Holland are
for the lower LW which is usually the second. Time
differences for Secondary Ports referred to Hoek van
Holland are approximate — Water levels on this coast are
considerably affected by the weather. Strong NW gales
can raise levels by up to 3m, whereas strong E winds can
lower levels by 1m.

SHELTER
Entrance can be difficult in on-shore NW winds over force
6 but once in the Buitenhaven, shelter is good. The yacht
marina in the Second Harbour gives very good shelter.
Access H24.
NAVIGATION
Waypoint SCH safe water buoy, Iso 4s, 52°07'.80N
04°14'.20E, 336°/156° from/to entrance, 1.6M. Strong
tidal streams running NE/SW across the entrance can
cause problems. Strong winds from SW through NW to N
cause a scend in the outer harbour. Beware large ships
entering and leaving.
LIGHTS AND MARKS
Ldg Lts 156° to outer basin, 131° to inner basin.
Entry signals (from Semaphore Mast)
R over W Lts — Entry prohibited.
W over R Lts — Exit prohibited.
Fl Y Lt — entry difficult due to vessels leaving.
A QY Lt is shown by entrance to First Harbour (W side)
when vessels are entering or leaving port.
Tide signals:
G over W Lts — tide rising.
W over G Lts — tide falling.
R Lt   — less than 5m in entry channel.
RADIO TELEPHONE
Call: *Scheveningen Haven* VHF Ch 14 (H24).
Yachts must get permission from Traffic Centre before
entering.

TELEPHONE (070)
Hr Mr 527701, Marina Hr Mr 520017, Traffic Centre
(semaphore) 527721, Pilot Hook of Holland (01740) 38811,
⚓ ⚓ Scheveningen 514481, Police 104911, Dr. 455300,
Ambulance 222111, Brit Consul (020) 764343.
FACILITIES
Marina Scheveningen (223 + 100 visitors) ☎ 520017, AC,
Bar, C (15 ton), CH, D, El, FW, ME, R, ◯, Sh, SM;
Harbour Slip, FW, ME, Sh, C (60 ton), CH, R, Bar;
Hoogenraad & Kuyt, ME, El, Sh, CH; **Yachtclub
Scheveningen** ☎ 520308; **Vrolyk** ☎ 554957 SM; **E. Harri**
☎ 546292 Ⓔ, **Town** P, D, V, R, Bar. ✉; Ⓑ; ≉; ✈
(Rotterdam).
Ferry UK — Rotterdam—Hull;
         Hook of Holland—Harwich.

IJMUIDEN   10-19-22
Noord Holland

CHARTS
Admiralty 2322, 124; Zeekaart 1450, 1543, 1035, 1350;
Dutch Yacht Chart 1801; Stanford 19; Imray Y5
TIDES
Dover +0400; ML 1.1; Zone −0100

Standard Port VLISSINGEN (←)

Times				Height (metres)			
HW		LW		MHWS	MHWN	MLWN	MLWS
0300	0900	0400	1000	4.7	3.9	0.8	0.3
1500	2100	1600	2200				

Differences IJMUIDEN
+0145 +0143 +0304 +0321 −2.7 −2.2 −0.6 −0.1

NOTE: Water levels on this coast can be considerably
affected by the weather. Strong NW gales can raise the
levels by up to 3m.

SHELTER
Good shelter especially on the S quay on the canal side of
the small S locks. It is noteworthy that the canal level
may be above or below the sea level. Yachts can stay in
the Haringhaven for short periods but are not advised to
stay at the sea side of the locks longer than necessary.
There are marinas at IJmond (under lift bridge in
Zijkanaal, 6M from IJmuiden and at Nauerna 7M from
IJmuiden.
NAVIGATION
Waypoint IJmuiden Lt buoy, Mo(A) 8s, Racon,
52°28'.70N 04°23'.93E, 278°/098° from/to entrance, 5.0M.
Beware strong tidal streams across the harbour entrance
and heavy merchant traffic. Yachts normally use S lock.
LIGHTS AND MARKS
Ldg Lts 100° (front is the Lt Ho showing FWR 31m
16/13M, W050°-122°, R122°-145°, W145°-160°. RC,
storm, tidal & traffic signals; rear Fl 5s 53m 29M). Both
display a FW Lt by day. This line leads into the
Buitenhaven and the Zuider Buitenkanaal.
RADIO TELEPHONE
IJmuiden Port Operations Centre. (1) IJmuiden. Call
IJmuiden Port Control (or *IJmuiden Port Control Locks* for
direct contact with locks) Ch 09, in area from North Sea
to North Sea Locks. (2) Hembrug. Call IJmuiden Locks
Ch 11 in area North Sea locks to Hembrug. (3)
Amsterdam Ch 14, in area of Amsterdam port basins, E
and W of Hembrug. Harbour Radar. Traffic Centre
IJmuiden Ch 12 (W of IJmuiden Lt buoy) and IJmuiden
Port Control. (All H24).
Reports on visibility, when less than 1000m, every H + 00
on Ch 12 by Coastguard IJmuiden, every H + 30 on Ch 05
and 11 by IJmuiden, every H + 00 on Ch 14 by
Amsterdam.
Vessels in the roads area, the Buitenhaven and the
Noordzeekanaal should keep watch on the appropriate Ch,
and report to Port Operations Centre on departure from or
arrival in a port in Noordzeekanaal.
TELEPHONE (02550)
Hr Mr 19027; Traffic Centre IJmuiden (DGSM) 19027;
Pilot 19027; ⚓ 23309; Police 35035; Ⓗ 65100;
Brit Consul (020) 764343.
FACILITIES
IJmuiden YC ☎ 384457 AB, AC, Bar, BY, C (20 ton), ◯,
V, R, D; **Hermans** ☎ 12963, Gaz;
Town P, D, V, R, Bar. ✉; Ⓑ; ≉ (bus to Beverwijk);
✈ (Amsterdam).
Ferry UK — Hook of Holland—Harwich.

IJMUIDEN *continued*

AMSTERDAM   10-19-23
Noord Holland

CHARTS
Admiralty 124; Zeekaart 1543; Dutch Yacht Chart 1801, 1810; ANWB G, I

TIDES
Amsterdam is between the Noordzeekanaal and the IJsselmeer, both of which are non-tidal; Zone −0100.

SHELTER
Shelter is complete. There are several yacht harbours/marinas. The principal one is Sixhaven, on the N bank, NE of the railway station (conspic). Another is on the S bank, close NW of the Harbour Building (conspic), but beware of swell from passing ships. Amsterdam gives access to canals running to N and S and also, via the Oranjesluizen, to the IJsselmeer.

NAVIGATION
See 10.19.22. The transit of the Noordzeekanaal is straightforward, apart from the volume of commercial traffic. The speed limit for yachts is 9 kn. There is a slight set to the W during sluicing.

LIGHTS AND MARKS
Lights are shown along both banks of the canal at the entrances to branch canals and basins. The continuation E towards the Oranjesluizen and the Amsterdam-Rijn canal is marked by Lt buoys.

RADIO TELEPHONE
VHF Ch 14. See also 10.19.22.

TELEPHONE (020)
Port Control: 221201; ✇ 5867511; Police: 5599111; Dr: 6642111; Brit Consul: 764343.

FACILITIES
Sixhaven Marina (60 + some visitors) ☎ 370892, AC, Bar (weekends), FW; **L. J. Harri** ☎ 248052, ACA; **Jachthaven de Hoop** ☎ 718349, Gaz.
City: All facilities, Ⓑ; ✉; ⇌; ✈.
Ferry UK — Hook of Holland—Harwich.

IJSSELMEER   10-19-24

CHARTS
Admiralty 1408, 2593; Zeekaart 1351, 1454; Dutch Yacht Chart 1810
TIDES
IJsselmeer is non-tidal. Tides at lock at Kornwerderzand Dover −0230; Zone −0100.

Standard Port HELGOLAND (——➤)

Times				Height (metres)			
HW		LW		MHWS	MHWN	MLWN	MLWS
0200	0700	0200	0800	2.7	2.3	0.4	0.0
1400	1900	1400	2000				

Differences KORNWERDERZAND
−0200	−0305	−0250	−0210	−0.5	−0.5	0.0	+0.2

SHELTER
IJsselmeer is the name for the un-reclaimed part of the Zuiderzee. Shelter is excellent in the many marinas, some of which are listed below. It is divided into two parts, the SW part being called the Markerwaard (20M × 15M, 2 to 4.5m deep) divided from the rest by a dyke with two locks, Enkhuizen in the N and Houtribhaven in the S. The rest of the IJsselmeer is 30M × 20M.
NAVIGATION
Three entrances
(1) via IJmuiden and Noordzeekanaal.
(2) via Stevinsluizen (Den Oever) at the W end of the Afsluitdijk which operates during working hrs.
(3) via the Kornwerderzand lock at the E end of the Afsluitdijk which operates 24 hrs.
Yacht charts are essential to avoid shoals, traps, fishing areas, nets etc which are well marked on the charts. Strong winds get up very quickly and short seas are frequently encountered. Strong winds can raise water level on lee shore, or lower it on weather shore, by 1m or more. Most harbours have water level gauges which should be checked in bad weather. Speed restrictions: in buoyed channels 8.5kn; outside 4.8kn. Between sunset and 0800 4.8kn everywhere. The Signi buoyage system is in use (see 10.19.7).
RADIO TELEPHONES
The following channels are used
Oranjesluizen Ch 18; den Oeversluizen Ch 20; Kornwerder Zandsluizen Ch 18; Lemmer Ch 20; Enkhuizen Ch 22; Houtribsluizen Ch 20; Emergency Ch 16.

There are numerous ports to visit and the following is a selection of the more important: (working clockwise from the Waddenzee).
MAKKUM. Approx 2M SE of the Kornwerderzand breakwaters, there is a buoyed channel approx 2000m long from buoy MA7, Iso G4s. Ldg Lts FR and FG at 092° leading between breakwaters into Makkum harbour. Hr Mr ☎ 1450. **Vissershaven** ☎ 1450, AB, BY, ME, C, FW, P, D, SM, Gaz.
WORKUM, 2.5M, N of Hindeloopen, with buoyed channel leading to "It Soal" **Marina** ☎ 2927. Facilities: AB, BY, ME, C, FW, P, D, Gaz.
HINDELOOPEN has two marinas, one in town and one 180m to N. **Jachthaven Hindeloopen** (500) ☎ (05142) 1866 P, D, FW, AC, ▣, CH, R, Bar. Hr Mr ☎ 2009. **Old Harbour** D, P, FW, ME, El, Sh; **Jachthaven** ☎ 2009, P, D, FW, ME, El, Sh.
STAVOREN. Entrance between FR and FG on line 048° Iso 4s Dir Lt. Yacht berths S of entrance by Rly Stn in Buitenhaven. Stavoren has several marinas after passing lock. Lock entrance between FR and FG approx 1000m S of entrance to Buitenhaven. Hr Mr ☎ (05149) 1216. **Stavoren Marina** ☎ 1469, AB, BY, ME, C, FW, P, D, SM, Gaz.
LEMMER has some 14 marinas. Ldg Lts into Prinses Margrietkanaal both Iso 8s at 038°. Ldg Lts into town and marinas both Iso 8s at 083° and FG and Iso G 4s at 065°. **Gemeente Jachthaven** Hr Mr ☎ (05146) 3343. Tacozijl ☎ 2003, AB, BY, ME, C, FW, P, D, Gaz, SM.
URK Hr Ent ½M NE of Lt Ho FI 5s 27m 18M. Harbour ent FR & FG dir Ldg Lt Iso 4s. Harbour in four parts — yachts go into Nieuwe Haven or the Oosthaven (3.3 m). Hr Mr ☎ (05277) 1394. FW; **Westhaven** P, D, SM. **Oosthaven** ME, El, Sh, ⒺⒸH. Town EC Tuesday, V, R, ⒷⒷ, ✉.

KETELHAVEN From buoy WK1 IsoG 4s keep to buoyed channel. No Lts on marina ent. **Ketelmeer Marina** (200) FW, AC, R. Hr Mr (03210) 12271.
LELYSTAD has two marinas. **Houtribhaven** (560) ☎ (03200) 60198, D, CH, V, R, Bar, C; **Flevo Marina** (550) ☎ (03200) 21000 D, CH, V, R, C, M, Ⓔ, El. Both FR and FG on breakwaters. Hr Mr ☎ 21048. Facilities: AB, ME, C, FW, P, D, Gaz.
MUIDEN, home of the Royal Netherlands YC. Ldg Lts Q at 181° lead into Yacht Hr to W of entrance. **KNZ & RV Marina** (150) ☎ (02942) 1450 D, CH; **Stichting Jachthaven Muiden** (70) ☎ (02942) 1223 P.
MARKEN (picturesque show piece). Approach from N. Lt Ho (conspic), Oc 8s 16m 9M Hr Mr (02996) 1305.
MONNICKENDAM has three marinas with all facilities. Ldg Lts FR at 236°. Hr Mr ☎ (02995) 1616. Facilities: ME, C, FW, P, D, Gaz, AC, CH.
VOLENDAM; several yacht berths. Ldg Dir Lts FI 5s at 313°. Hr Mr ☎ (02993) 65590. Facilities: AB, ME, FW, C, P, D, Gaz, SM.
EDAM Enter keeping Iso W 8s between FG and FR at entrance. Narrow ent; beware commercial traffic. Yacht berth on N side or pass through lock to the Oorgat — at fork take S canal into Nieuwe Haven. Hr Mr ☎ (02993) 71092. Few facilities **T.D. Sails Oorgat** SM; **Ruud van Drunen** ME, el, Sh, **Town** V, R, Bar, ▣. Hr Mr (02993) 71092.
HOORN W harbour ent has Iso W4s 15m 10M and FR and FG. Yachts have four choices — **Stichting Jachthaven Hoorn** (700) ☎ (02993) 1757 FW, AC, ▣, CH, V, ME, El, Sh, C; Buitenhaven and lock FW, Gas, **Vluchthaven marina** run by WV Hoorn (100) ☎ (02290) 13540 FW; **Binnenhaven** through Buitenhaven and lock (always open) FW, Gaz. **Town** V, CH, ✉.
ENKHUIZEN. The Krabbersgat Ldg Lts Iso W4s at 039° and FR and FG at breakwaters gives access to the Krabbersgatock and also to the harbours of Enkhuizen. Call lock on Ch 22. Signals — RR = No entry; RG = Stand by; GG = enter. There are two marinas and the main harbour. **Compagniehaven** (500) Hr Mr (02280) 13353 P, D, FW, AC, CH; **Buyshaven** (195) ☎ (02280) 15660 FW, AC; **Town Harbour** ☎ (02280) 12444 FW. **Town** C, Slip, CH, SM, ME, El, Sh, Ⓑ, V, R, Bar.

ANDIJK. Has two marinas. But visitors use **Stichting Jachthaven Amdijk**. (600) ☎ (02289) 3075. Ent between FR and FG Lts on 015° ME, C, SM, Gaz, ⬚, D, CH,.
MEDEMBLIK. Entrance between FR and FG on line 232° Oc 5s Dir Lt. Visitors pass through Oosterhaven into Middenhaven ☎ (02274) 1686 CH, FW, ⬚; Fuel in Oosterhaven. **Stichting Jachthaven Medemblik** (150) ☎ (02274) 1861 FW, AC, ⬚, P, D, ME, El, Sh, C.

DEN HELDER 10-19-25
Noord Holland

CHARTS
Admiralty 2322, 191, 2593; Zeekaart 1454, 1546; Dutch Yacht Chart 1811, 1801; ANWB F; Imray Y5

TIDES
Dover −0430; ML 1.1; Duration No data; Zone −0100

Standard Port HELGOLAND (⟶)

Times				Height (metres)			
HW		LW		MHWS	MHWN	MLWN	MLWS
0200	0700	0200	0800	2.7	2.3	0.4	0.0
1400	1900	1400	2000				

Differences DEN HELDER							
−0350	−0500	−0515	−0425	−0.9	−0.8	0.0	+0.2
OUDESCHILD							
−0300	−0430	−0435	−0355	−0.9	−0.8	0.0	+0.2
DEN OEVER							
−0245	−0420	−0355	−0300	−0.8	−0.7	0.0	+0.2

SHELTER
There is good shelter in the Naval Harbour, the YC and yacht harbour being immediately to stbd on entering. Yachts can lock into the Koopvaarders Binnenhaven Yacht Harbour or the Den Helder Yacht Haven, in Westover.

NAVIGATION
Waypoint Schulpengat SG safe water buoy, Mo(A) 8s, 52°52'.95N 04°38'.00E (on leading line), 206.5°/026.5° from/to Kaap Hoofd, 6.0M.
There are two channels to the harbour entrance:—
(1) Molengat is good except in strong winds from NW when heavy breakers occur at this entrance.
(2) Schulpengat is well marked and well lit. Beware very strong tidal streams through the Marsdiep across the harbour entrance.
Note: the port mainly belongs to the Royal Netherlands Navy and, like the YC, is run by them. There is a large fishing fleet, and many coasters.

LIGHTS AND MARKS
Schulpengat Ldg Lts 026 30° on Texel. Front Iso 4s 18M. Rear Oc 8s 18M. Both vis 025°-028°.
Molengat Ldg Lts 141.7°. Front Iso 5s 13m 8M; vis 124°-157°. Rear, 650m from front, F 22m 8M; Tr on hosp; vis 124°-157°. Ldg Lts 191°. Front Oc G 5s 16m 14M; B triangle on building. Rear (synchronised) Oc G 5s 25m 14M; B triangle on B framework Tr.
Entry signals, shown from Harssens Harbour Office on W side of entrance:—

R   Entry to Marinehaven Willemsoord and
W   Rijkszeehaven Nieuwe Diep prohibited
R   without permission

Moormanbridge operates 7 days a week H24.
Kinsbergenbridge operates 0500-2300 Mon-Fri; 0700-1400 Sat. Burgemeester Vissersbrug operates H24. All bridges remain closed 0715-0810, 1200-1215, 1245-1300, Mon-Fri. Also 0830-0910 on Mon, 1545-1645 on Fri. All times LT.

RADIO TELEPHONE
VHF Ch 16; 14 (H24). Other stations: Den Oever Lock Ch 20. Kornwerderzand Locks Ch 18.
Koopvaardersschutsluis (Locks) Ch 22 (H24). Moorman Bridge Ch 18 (H24).

TELEPHONE (02230)
Hr Mr 52645 Hr Mr (Yacht Haven) 37444 CG 12732; Municipal Port Control 13955; Vessel Traffic Centre 52770, Naval Commander 56822; ⌗ 15182; Police 55700; Ⓗ 11414; Water Police 16767; Brit Consul (020) 764343.

Den Helder

FACILITIES
Yacht Harbours KMYC ☎ 56645, **MWY YC** (Binnenhaven) ☎ 17076, P (at garage), D, L, FW, AB; **YC WSOV** ☎ 52173; **YC HWN** ☎ 24422; **W. Visser & Son** ME, El, Sh, Floating dock; **Binnenhaven** ☎ 16641, L, FW, CH, AB, SM; **Yacht Haven** ☎ 37444, AB, ME, El, Sh, C, CH, Slip, FW, R, Bar; **W. Bakker** ☎ 17356, Gaz.
Town P, CH, V, R, Bar. ✉; Ⓑ; ⇌; ✈ (Amsterdam).
Ferry UK — Hook of Holland—Harwich.

19

HARLINGEN 10-19-26
Friesland

CHARTS
Admiralty 2593, 112; Zeekaart 1454, 1456; Dutch Yacht
Chart 1811; ANWB B; Imray Y5
TIDES
Dover −0210; ML 1.2; Duration 0520; Zone −0100

Standard Port HELGOLAND (→)

Times				Height (metres)			
HW		LW		MHWS	MHWN	MLWN	MLWS
0200	0700	0200	0800	2.7	2.3	0.4	0.0
1400	1900	1400	2000				

Differences HARLINGEN
−0145 −0245 −0155 −0115 −0.4 −0.4 −0.1 +0.2

SHELTER
Good shelter, but entrance can be rough at HW with
winds in W or SW. Coming in with flood, beware strong
current across entrance. Very good shelter in yacht
harbour in Noorderhaven and also inside the lock into the
Van Harinxma canal in the yacht harbour (immediately to
stbd on leaving the locks). There is limited room here and
only advisable if proceeding on to the lakes.
NAVIGATION
Waypoint BS1-IN2 buoy, GRG, Fl(2+1)G 10s, 53°14′.74N
05°10′.05E, at Blauwe Slenk/Inschot junction. Approach
via the Vliestroom and Blauwe Slenk, both buoyed and lit,
but channel is narrow for the last 2½ M. Beware the
Pollendam, marked with port and stbd beacons; when
covered, strong tidal stream sweeps across the Pollendam.
Hanerak, a second buoyed channel, runs about 600m S of
the Pollendam. At particularly high tides, the outer yacht
harbour may be closed off by flood gates from up to
HW−1½ to HW+1½.
LIGHTS AND MARKS
Ldg Lts 112° Front Iso 6s, rear Iso 6s. Entry signals for
locks in Nieuwe Voorhaven (at signal station)
2 FR (vert) = Arrival or departure of large vessel − all
other movement prohibited.
Bu Flag   = Sluicing, entry prohibited.
RADIO TELEPHONE
VHF Ch 11 (Mon 0000 to Sat 2200 LT).
VHF Ch 4 CG; VHF Ch 22 Harinxma Canal locks.
TELEPHONE (05178)
Hr Mr 13041; CG (Brandaris) (05620) 3100; Port Authority
3041; ⌗ 18750; Police 13333; Ⓗ 99999;
Brit Consul (020) 764343.
FACILITIES
EC Monday a.m.; **Noorderhaven Yacht Harbour**
☎ 15666, FW, El, CH, V, R, Bar,Ⓞ; **Yacht Harbour Van
Harinxma Canal** ☎ 16898, FW, Ⓞ, C (6 ton); **Het Anker
watersport** ☎ 14030, CH, El, E, Gaz, Diving and salvage;
Leeuwenbrug watersport ☎ 15666, El (by arrangement),
CH, ME (by arrangement); **Post, Zuiderhaven**, D, P;
Welgelegen Scheepsw ☎ 12744 (big ship firm) −
emergency only.
Town P, D, V, R, Bar. ✉; Ⓑ; ⇌; ✈ (Groningen).
Ferry UK — Hook of Holland−Harwich.

VLIELAND 10-19-27
WEST FRISIAN ISLANDS
Friesland

CHARTS
Admiralty 2593, 112; Zeekaart 1456;
Dutch Yacht Chart 1811; Imray Y5
TIDES
Dover −0300; Duration Rising 0600 Falling 0620;
Zone −0100

Standard Port HELGOLAND (→)

Times				Height (metres)			
HW		LW		MHWS	MHWN	MLWN	MLWS
0200	0700	0200	0800	2.7	2.3	0.4	0.0
1400	1900	1400	2000				

Differences VLIELAND−HAVEN
−0255 −0320 −0350 −0330 −0.4 −0.3 +0.1 +0.2

SHELTER
Shelter is good, but yacht harbour becomes very crowded
in high season. Anchorage about 1600m W of the harbour
is good except in S to SW winds, and it is near the
village. Yachts are forbidden to anchor in buoyed channel
or berth at pier ½M W of harbour.

NAVIGATION
Waypoint VSM safe water buoy, Iso 4s, 53°19′.08N
04°55′.74E, 274°/094° from/to ZS1 and ZS2 buoys at
Zuider Stortemelk entrance, 2.3M. Only safe approach is
through the Zuider Stortemelk which is deep and well
marked and lit. This leads to Vliesloot. There is an
alternative entrance from the S via Fransche Gaatje but it
is very much shallower and can even dry out at very LW.
LIGHTS AND MARKS
Ldg Lts 277°. Front FW 8M — Rear Oc W 10s.
Main Lt Ho Iso 4s 53m 20M; brown Tr, W lantern; RC.
Entry signals: R Flag or two R Lts on the pier indicates
harbour closed .
RADIO TELEPHONE
None.
TELEPHONE (05621)
Hr Mr 1563; Hr Mr (Yacht Hr) 1729; CG 1326; ⌗ 1522;
Police 1312; Dr 201307; Brit Consul (020) 764343.
FACILITIES
Yacht Harbour ☎ 1729, P, D, L, FW, AB; **Harbour** C
(12 ton); **North Shore W of Ferry Pier** M; **D.W. Floor**
☎ 1558 El, Ⓔ, **B. H. Iedema** ☎ 1336, Gaz; **C. D.
Hoogland** ☎ 1352, P, D; **Town** P, D, ME, El, CH, V, R,
Bar. ✉; Ⓑ; ⇌ (ferry to Harlingen); ✈ (Amsterdam).
Ferry UK — Hook of Holland−Harwich.

TERSCHELLING   10-19-28

WEST FRISIAN ISLANDS
Friesland

CHARTS
Admiralty 2593, 112; Zeekaart 1456;
Dutch Yacht Chart 1811; Imray Y5
TIDES
Dover −0300; ML 1.3; Duration No data; Zone −0100

Standard Port HELGOLAND (→)

Times				Height (metres)			
HW		LW		MHWS	MHWN	MLWN	MLWS
0200	0700	0200	0800	2.7	2.3	0.4	0.0
1400	1900	1400	2000				

Differences WEST TERSCHELLING
−0220 −0250 −0330 −0305 −0.4 −0.3 +0.1 +0.2

SHELTER
Good shelter especially in marina in N corner of harbour.
Very crowded in season. Yachts may go alongside near
Hr Mr's office.
NAVIGATION
See 10-19-27. Waypoint VL2-SG1 buoy, RGR, Fl(2+1)R
12s, 53°19′.30N 05°09′.80E, 225°/045° from/to front Ldg
Lt 053°, 2.9M. Entrance via the Schuitengat; the channel
is narrow and shifts but it is well buoyed.
The harbour has considerable commercial traffic.
LIGHTS AND MARKS
Ldg Lts 053°. Front (West mole) FR 5m 5M; R post, W
bands; vis W049°-055°, R055°-252°, W252°-263°,
R263°-049°; Horn 15s. Rear (on dyke 1.1M from front, off
chartlet) Iso 5s 14m 19M; metal mast, Y lantern; vis
045°-061° (intens 045°-052°).
RADIO TELEPHONE
None.
TELEPHONE (05620)
Hr Mr 2235; CG 2341; ⌗ Harlingen 5241; Police 2280;
Dr 2181; Brit Consul (020) 764343.

FACILITIES
EC Wednesday; **Marina − "Stichting Passantenhaven
Terschelling"** (500) ☎ 3337, Hr Mr, C, FW; **Harbour**
Slip, M, FW (in cans), ME, AB; **W. Bloem** ☎ 2076, ME;
L. G. Schiepstra ☎ 2694, ME; **C Bloem** ☎ 2178, SM;
Village P, D, FW, CH, V, R, Bar. ✉; Ⓑ
(W. Terschelling); ⇌ (ferry to Harlingen); ✈ (Groningen).
Ferry UK — Hook of Holland—Harwich.

DELFZIJL   10-19-29

Groningen

CHARTS
Admiralty 3510; Zeekaart 1555; Dutch Yacht Chart 1812;
Dutch ANWB A
TIDES
Dover −0025; ML 2.0; Duration 0605; Zone −0100

Standard Port HELGOLAND (→)

Times				Height (metres)			
HW		LW		MHWS	MHWN	MLWN	MLWS
0200	0700	0200	0800	2.7	2.3	0.4	0.0
1400	1900	1400	2000				

Differences DELFZIJL
+0020 −0005 −0035 +0005 +0.8 +0.9 +0.1 +0.2
EEMSHAVEN
−0025 −0045 −0115 −0035 +0.3 +0.4 +0.2 +0.2
LAUWERSOOG
−0130 −0150 −0230 −0225 +0.1 +0.2 +0.2 +0.2

SHELTER
Good shelter. Yacht harbour in Balkenhaven gives good
protection. Yachts can lock through into the Eemskanaal
and berth in Farmsumerhaven (1 day only) or at the end
of the old Eemskanaal near the obsolete lock, in new
yacht harbour.
NAVIGATION
Waypoint Hubertgat safe water buoy, Iso 8s, Whis,
53°34′.90N 06°14′.40E, 270°/090° from/to Borkum Kleiner
Lt, 15.5M. Westerems safe water buoy, Iso 4s, Racon,
53°37′.10N 06°19′.50E, 272°/092° from/to Nos 1 and 2
Westerems channel buoys, 1.9M. See also 10.20.8.
Channels in the Ems are well buoyed and lit. The entrance
is 3 M ESE of the town of Delfzijl. Beware strong tides
across the entrance, as these can be dangerous.
LIGHTS AND MARKS
Harbour entrance, FG on W arm and FR on E arm with
Horn 15s and FY (occasl). Ldg Lts 203°, Front QR No 2A,
W pedestal on dolphin; Rear FR. The channel from the
entrance has G Fl Lts to N and R Fl Lts to S.
Entry signals:—
2 R Flags or 2 R Lts —   All movement prohibited
                          except as directed by Hr Mr.

Sluicing signals:—
R Flag or 3 R Lts in triangle —Sluicing at Eemskanaal
                              Lock through gates.
Bu Flag or 3 R Lts in triangle—Sluicing at Eemskanaal
over G Lt   Lock through draining
                              sluices.
RADIO TELEPHONE
Call: *Port Office Delfzijl/Eemshaven* VHF Ch 14 (H24).
Traffic reports on Ch 14 every 10 min from H+00 when
visibility less than 500m. Locks (Eemskanaalsluizen) Ch 11
(Mon-Sat, H24). Die Ems (Ems Revier) Ch 18 20 21 (H24)
— information broadcasts in German every H+50 with
weather and tidal information, including storm warnings
for coastal waters between Die Ems and Die Weser.
Locks: Grosse Seeschleuse (call: *Emden Lock*) Ch 13 16
(H24). Nesserlander Seeschleuse (call: *Nesserland Lock*)
Ch 13 16 (H24). Leer Lock Ch 16 13 (0700-2300 LT).
Papenburg Lock Ch 16; 13 (H24).
Jann-Berghaus Bridge (call: *Leer Bridge*) Ch 15.
Friesen Bridge (call: *Weener Bridge*) Ch 15.
TELEPHONE (05960)
Hr Mr (Delfzijl Port Authorities) 14966; Neptunus Yacht Hr
Mr 15004; Sea locks 13293; CG (Police) 13831; ⌗ 15060;
Police 13394; Ⓗ 14944; Brit Consul (020) 764343.

DELFZIJL continued

⬥ See Yacht Hr Mr

FACILITIES

Neptunus Yacht Harbour ☎ 15004, D, Bar, M, L, FW;
Yacht Harbour 't Dok D, FW, AB; **Datema** ☎ 13810,
CH, ACA, chart agent; **P. Dinges** ☎ 15010, ME, El;
H. S. Hunfeld ☎ 13446, ME, El; **Ems Canal** L, FW, AB;
IJzerhandel Delken ☎ 30200, Gaz; **Motor Boat Club
Abel Tasman** ☎ 16560 Bar, M, D, FW, L, ▢, V;
Town P, D, V, R, Bar. ✉; Ⓑ; ⇌; ✈ (Groningen).
Ferry UK — Hook of Holland—Harwich.
Eemshaven—Immingham.

MINOR HARBOURS AND ANCHORAGES 10.19.30

WALSOORDEN Zeeland 51° 23′ N, 4° 2′ E. Zone −0100
Admty chart 120, Zeekart 1443. Dutch Yacht Chart 1803
HW +0300 on Dover (GMT), +0110 on Vlissingen (zone
−0100); HW height +0.7m on Vlissingen, ML 2.6m Ldg
Lts 220° both Oc W 3s. Hr ent marked with FG and FR.
Yacht basin dead ahead on entering harbour depth 2.3 to
3.4m. ☎ (01148) Hr Mr ☎ 1235 FW, Slip; **P Burm**
☎ 1504, Gas, P, D; **L Hemelaar** ☎ 1359 P, D;
Jachtwerf Moed en Trouw ☎ 1205 ME, El, **Town**, R,
Bar, ✉.

PAAL Zeeland 51° 21′ N, 4°7′ E Zone −0100 Admty Charts
120, 139 Zeekart 1443. Dutch Yacht Chart 1803; HW
+0310 on Dover (GMT), +0120 on Vlissingen (zone
−0100); HW height +0.8m on Vlissingen. ML 2.7m.
Yacht harbour entrance on W side at river mouth, marked
by withy. No lights. Harbour dries ☎ (01143) Hr Mr 346
Jachthaven AC, FW, **EPW Staal** ☎ 277 V, P, D, Gaz;
J J Verras ☎ 264 ME, El, R.

DOEL Antwerpen 51° 19′ N, 4° 16′ E Zone −0100 Admty
Chart 139, Zeekart 1443 Dutch Yacht Chart 1803 HW
+0310 on Dover (GMT); +0100 on Vlissingen (zone
−0100); HW height +0.7m Vlissingen Lt on N pierhead
Oc W5s ☎ (03) Hr Mr 7733072 **YC de Noord** ☎ 7733669
R, Bar, FW.

ELLEWOUTSDIJK Zeeland 51° 23′ N, 3° 49′ E. Zone
−0100. Admty Chart 120 Zeekart 1443 Dutch Yacht Chart
1803. HW +0230 on Dover (GMT), +0020 on Vlissingen
(zone −0100); HW height +0.3m on Vlissingen; ML2.6m.
Small harbour on the N bank. No lights. ☎ (01104) Hr Mr
☎ 248 FW, D. **YC Ellewontsdijk** ☎ 446. **M.P. de
Broekert** ☎ 302 Gaz.

OUDESCHILD, Texel, Noord Holland, 53°02′ N, 4°51′ E,
Zone −0100, Admty charts 191, 2593, Zeekaart 1546,
1454, Dutch Yacht 1811. HW −0355 on Dover (GMT),
−0425 on Helgoland (zone −0100); HW height −0.7m on
Helgoland; ML 1.1m; Duration 0625. On SE side of Texel,
Hr gives good shelter and has Yacht Harbour in the
Werkhaven, NNE of ent. Beware strong cross tides across
ent. Keep Ldg Lt, Oc 6s 14m between harbour entrance

Lts, FR and FG on course of 291°. VHF Ch 09,
0730 − 1500 LT. Facilities: ☎ (02220) Hr Mr ☎ 12710;
Marina ☎ 3608, AB, Bar, D, Dr, FW, M, R; **YC W. V.
Texel; Boom Shiprepairs** ☎ 12661, Sh, Dry dock.

NES, AMELAND, Friesland, 53°26′ N, 5°45′ E, Zone
−0100, Admty charts 2593, 1405, Zeekaart 1458, Dutch
Yacht 1811, 1812. HW −0055 on Dover (GMT), −0108
on Helgoland (zone −0100); HW height +0.4m on
Helgoland; ML 1.3m; Duration 0625. Harbour at Nes, mid
S of the island; no proper yacht hr but sheltered from all
but winds from E to S. Much of harbour dries but fin
keels sink into mud. Beware sandbanks in the Zeegat van
Ameland. Lt at W end of Ameland Fl(3) 15s 57m 30M,
RC. Nes Nieuwe Veerdam head Iso 6s 2m 8M. Facilities
are very limited; Gaz. Hr Mr (05191) 2304.

OOSTMAHORN, Friesland, 53°23′ N, 6°09′ E, Zone
−0100, Admty chart 3509, Zeekaarten 1458, Dutch Yacht
Chart 1812; non tidal. Harbour on W side of
Lauwersmeer; lock in from the Zoutkamperlaag to W of
Lauwersoog. Main harbour with FR and FG Lts at
entrance has yacht haven (2.5m to 3.4m). Approx 450m
to the SSE there is another yacht haven, the Voorm
Veerhaven (1.5m). Floating beacons with Y flags mark
fishing areas. Facilities: Hr Mr (05193) 1331; most normal
facilities in the Yacht Haven.

ZOUTKAMP, Friesland, 53°20′ N, 6°18′ E, Zone −0100.
Admty chart 3509, Zeekaarten 1458, Dutch Yacht Chart
1812; non tidal. Approach down the Zoutkamperril (3 to
4.5m); Approx 400m before the bridge, the yacht haven
'Hunzegat' (1.4 to 2.2m) is on the NE side. There is
another yacht haven, the Oude Binnenhaven (2m), further
SE. Pass through lock, Provinciale Sluis, and yacht haven
is immediately to NE. FW and FR Lts shown from lock.
Facilities: **Gruno BY** ☎ 2057, FW, Sh, C (20 ton), BH;
Oude-Binnenhaven AC, C, FW; **Hunzegat** ☎ 2588, AC,
FW, SC, Slip; **Town** BY, C, D, Dr, El, Gaz, ME, P, ✉,
R, Sh, SM, V.

LAUWERSOOG, Friesland, 53°25′ N, 6°12′ E, Zone −0100,
Admty chart 3509, Zeekaart 1458, Dutch Yacht 1812. HW
−0150 on Dover (GMT), −0120 on Helgoland (zone
−0100); HW height +0.5m on Helgoland; ML 1.3m. See
10.19.29. Good shelter in all conditions in inner harbour.
Outer harbour has swell in bad weather. Yachts lock into
inner harbour, the Lauwersmeer, 0400 − 2100 weekdays,
0400 − 1800 Saturdays, 0900 − 1000 and 1630 − 1830
Sundays LT. Yacht harbour to SE of lock; visitors
mooring on first pontoon. Lts, N of N jetty. W of
entrance FG 3M. E of entrance FR 4M. Locks, lead-in
jetty Iso 4s. VHF Ch 09 (Mon−0000−1700LT, Tue−Wed
0800−1700LT, Thur−Sat 0700−1500LT). Locks VHF CH 22
May−Sept: Mon−Fri 0700−2000LT, Sat 0700−1900LT,
Sun 0900−1200 & 1400−1830LT. Oct−Apr: Mon−Fri
0700−1800LT, Sat 0700−1700LT. Hr Mr ☎ (05193) 9023.
Lockmaster ☎ (05193) 9043. Facilities: Gaz, BY,
Pontoons AB, D, FW; **Near ferry terminal** P; **W end of
harbour**, Bar, R, V, YC.

SCHIERMONNIKOOG, Friesland, 53°28′ N, 6°12′ E, Zone
−0100. Admty chart 3761, 3509, Zeekaart 1458, Dutch
Yacht 1812 HW (Lauwersoog) −0150 on Dover (GMT),
−0120 on Helgoland (zone −0100); HW height +0.5m on
Helgoland. Entrance via Friesche Zeegat (Westgat),
buoyed but dangerous in bad weather due to the bar
across the harbour mouth. Gat van Schiermonnikoog
(buoyed) runs E from Zoutkamperlaag over bar (depth
variable). Groote Siege (marked) leads NE from a point
2.5M SSE of Lt Ho to the ferry pier. Access to Ferry Pier
at all states of tide, a natural sill keeping 1 to 1.5m in
harbour. Ent only 15m wide. Yachts may not go alongside
Ferrypier. About 1M before the pier there is a small yacht
harbour, entrance marked by perches. Access HW−2 to
HW+1. Picturesque, but very full in high season and also
expensive. Lights: near W end of island, Lt Ho Fl(4) 20s;
Ferry Pier head Lt, FW. Facilities: Hr Mr ☎ (05195) 544
(May-Sept), FW.

TERMUNTERZIJL Gronigen, 53°18′ N, 7°2′ E Zone
−0100Amty Chart 3369, Zeekart 1555 Dutch Yacht chart
1812 HW −0025 on Dover (GMT); +0015 on Helgoland;
HW height +0.8m on Helgoland. Entrance marked by
seven R and seven G bns. No lights. Yachts go to yacht
berths SW of entrance or to small pontoons to SE of
entrance. ☎ (05962) Hr Mr 2168 FW, AC, Bar, R.

VOLVO PENTA SERVICE

Sales and service centres in area 20
Names and addresses of Volvo Penta dealers in
this area are available from:

GERMANY BRD **Volvo Penta Deutschland GmbH,** Redderkoppel 5, Postfach
9013, D-2300 Kiel-17 Tel 0431 3948-0, Telex 292764.

Area 20

Federal Republic of Germany
Borkum to Danish border

VOLVO PENTA

20

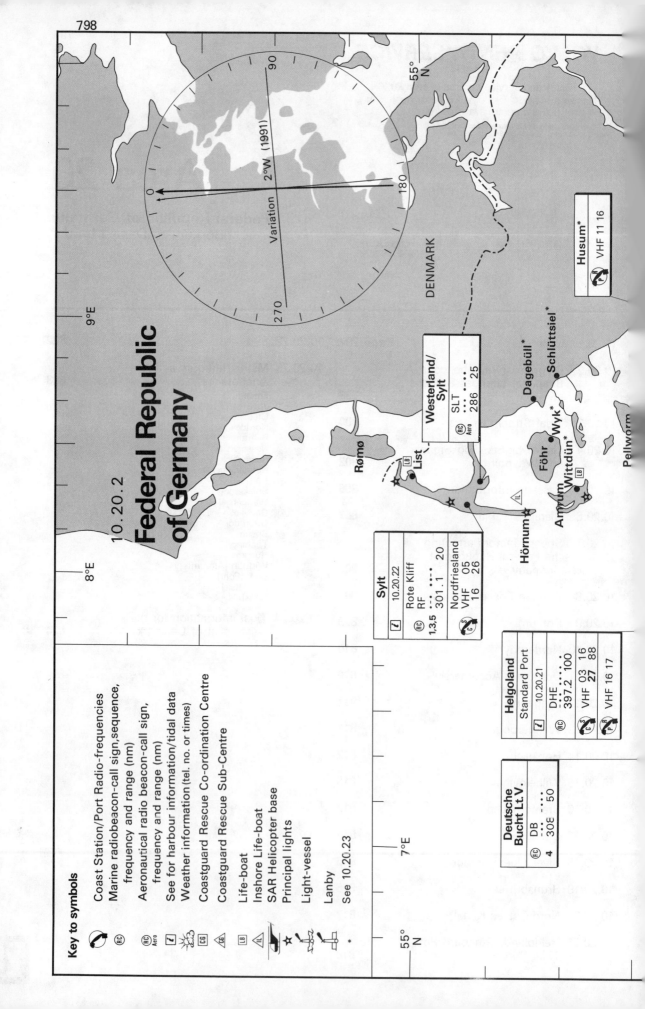

10.20.2

Federal Republic
of Germany

Key to symbols

	Coast Station/Port Radio-frequencies
ⓇⒸ	Marine radiobeacon-call sign,sequence, frequency and range (nm)
ⓇⒸ Aero	Aeronautical radio beacon-call sign, frequency and range (nm)
i	See for harbour information/tidal data
	Weather information (tel. no. or times)
ⒸⒼ	Coastguard Rescue Co-ordination Centre
⚠	Coastguard Rescue Sub-Centre
	Life-boat
ⓁⒷ	Inshore Life-boat
⚠	SAR Helicopter base
✦	Principal lights
	Light-vessel
	Lanby
*	See 10.20.23

Husum*

☎	VHF 11 16

Westerland/Sylt

ⓇⒸ Aero	SLT ··· ·-·· - 286 25

Sylt

i	10.20.22
ⓇⒸ	Rote Kliff RF 1,3,5 ··· ·-·· ·-·· 301.1 20
☎ ⒸⒼ	Nordfriesland VHF 05 16 26

Helgoland
Standard Port

i	10.20.21
ⓇⒸ	DHE -·· ···· 397.2 100
ⒸⒼ	VHF 03 16 27 88
☎	VHF 16 17

Deutsche Bucht Lt.V.

ⓇⒸ	DB -·· ···· 4 30E 50

DENMARK

Rømø

List ⓁⒷ

Hörnum ✦

Amrum ✦ ⓁⒷ

Föhr • Wyk*
Wittdün*

Dagebüll*

Schlüttsiel*

Pellwörm

Variation 2°W (1991)

90
180
270
O
55° N
9°E
8°E
7°E
55° N

10.20.3   AREA 20 TIDAL STREAMS

5 Hours before HW Dover (0440 before HW Helgoland)

4 Hours before HW Dover (0340 before HW Helgoland)

3 Hours before HW Dover (0240 before HW Helgoland)

2 Hours before HW Dover (0140 before HW Helgoland)

1 Hour before HW Dover (0040 before HW Helgoland)

HW Dover (0020 after HW Helgoland)

1 Hour after HW Dover (0120 after HW Helgoland)

2 Hours after HW Dover (0220 after HW Helgoland)

3 Hours after HW Dover (0320 after HW Helgoland)

4 Hours after HW Dover (0420 after HW Helgoland)

5 Hours after HW Dover (0520 after HW Helgoland)

6 Hours after HW Dover (0620 after HW Helgoland)

20

10.20.4 LIGHTS, FOG SIGNALS AND WAYPOINTS

Abbreviations used below are given in 10.0.3. Principal lights are in **bold print**, places in CAPITALS, and light vessels, light floats and Lanbys in *CAPITAL ITALICS*. Unless otherwise stated lights are white. m - elevation in metres; M - nominal range in n. miles. Fog signals are in *italics*. Useful waypoints are underlined use those on land with care. See 4.2.2.

FEDERAL REPUBLIC OF GERMANY

DIE EMS TO DIE JADE

LIMIT OF INSHORE TRAFFIC ZONE

DB1 Ems Lt Buoy 53°43'·35N 06°22'·40E IQ. G 13s; stbd-hand mark.

DB3 Lt Buoy 53°44'·65N 06°31'·20E Fl (2) G 9s; stbd-hand mark.

DB5 Lt Buoy 53°45'·69N 06°40'·10E Oc (3) G 12s; stbd-hand mark.

DB7 Lt Buoy 53°47'·35N 06°49'·75E Fl (2) G 9s; stbd-hand mark.

DB9 Lt Buoy 53°48'·45N 06°57'·80E Oc (3) G 12s; stbd-hand mark.

DB11 Lt Buoy 53°49'·72N 07°06'·60E Fl (2) G 9s; stbd-hand mark.

DB13 Lt Buoy 53°51'·00N 07°15'·50E Oc (3) G 12s; stbd-hand mark.

DB15 Lt Buoy 53°52'·20N 07°24'·35E Fl (2) G 9s; stbd-hand mark.

DB17 Lt Buoy 53°53'·47N 07°33'·22E Oc (3) G 12s; stbd-hand mark.

DB19 Jade 22 Lt Buoy 53°54'·70N 07°42'·20E IQ. G 13s; stbd-hand mark.

BORKUMRIFF LT BUOY 53°47'·50N 06°22'·13E Oc (3) 13s; Racon.

Westerems Lt Buoy 53°36'·98N 06°19'·40E Iso 4s; safe water mark; Racon (G).

Hubert Gat Lt Buoy 53°34'·90N 06°14'·32E Iso 8s; *Whis*; safe water mark.

Alte Ems 1/H 13A Buoy 53°34'·67N 06°37'·16E (unlit); stbd-hand mark.

INSHORE ROUTE EMS TO JADE

Riffgat Lt Buoy 53°38'·90N 06°27'·10E Iso 8s; safe water mark.

Oosterems Lt Buoy 53°42'·00N 06°36'·20E Iso 4s; *Whis*; safe water mark.

Juisterriff -N Lt Buoy 53°42'·90N 06°45'·80E Q; N cardinal.

Juist-N Lt Buoy 53°43'·90N 06°55'·50E VQ; N cardinal.

53°40'·95N 07°03'·50E Aero Fl 5s 14m (occas).

Schluchter Lt Buoy 53°44'·90N 07°05'·30E Iso 8s; safe water mark.

Dovetief Lt Buoy 53°45'·50N 07°11'·30E Iso 4s; safe water mark.

Platform 54°42'·1N 07°10'·0E Mo(U) 15s 24m 9M; R platform, Y stripes; *Horn Mo(U) 30s.*

Norderney N Lt Buoy 53°46'·15N 07°17'·22E Q; N cardinal.

Accumer Ee Lt Buoy 53°47'·10N 07°26'·65E Iso 8s; safe water mark; *Bell*; (frequently moved).

Otzumer Balje Lt Buoy 53°48'·13N 07°37'·23E Iso 4s; safe water mark (frequently moved).

Harle Lt Buoy 53°49'·28N 07°48'·00E Iso 8s; safe water mark.

DIE EMS

Borkum Grosser 53°35'·4N 06°39'·8E Fl (2) 12s 63m **24M**; brown Tr. F RWG 46m **W19M**, R15m, G15M; vis G107·4°-109°, W109°-111·2°, R111·2°-112·6°.

Borkum Kleiner 53°34'·78N 06°40'·08N FW 32m **30M**; R Tr, W bands; FW (intens) 089·9°-090·9° (Ldg sector for Hubertgat); Fl 3s; vis 088°-089·9°; Q (4) 10s; vis 090·9°-093°; RC; Iso Y 4s on tide gauge 420m SW.

BORKUM

Fischerbalje 53°33'·21N 06°43'·00E Oc (2) WRG 16s 1 **W16M**, R12M, G11M; W Tr, R top and lantern, on tripod; R260°-313°, G313°-014°, W014°-076·2°, (Ldg sector to Fischerbalje), R076·2°-112·5°, W112·5°-116°, R116°—119 W119·8°-125° (Ldg sector to Westerems), R125°-140°; F Det Lt.

Schutzhafen FR 8m 4M.

Binnen-Randzel 53°30'·20N 06°49'·95E F WRG 14m W7 R5M, G4M; B and grey framework Tr, W tank; vis W 318°-34 R345°-015·8°, W015·8-033·5°, R033·5°-077·3°, W077·3°-09 G098°-122°.

Campen 53°24'·39N 07°01'·00E F 62m **30M**; R framework 2 galleries, W central column, G cupola; vis 126·5°-127°. Fl (same Tr); vis 126°-127°. Fl (4) 15s (same Tr) vis 127·3°-127·8

ALTE EMS

No.15/H15/A2 Lt Buoy 53°34'·25N 06°38'·32E VQ; N cardin A2a Buoy 53°33'·49N 06°38'·78E (unlit); port-hand mark.

A3 Buoy 53°31'·76N 06°39'·80E (unlit); port-hand mark.

33/ Alte Ems No. 11 Buoy 53°28'·02N 06°50'·88E (unlit); stb hand mark.

EEMSHAVEN

West pier 53°27'·80N 06°50·15E FG 8m 3M; *Horn (2) 20s.*

DUKE GAT

No. 35 Lt Buoy 53°27'·13N 06°52'·90E Fl (2) G 9s; stbd-har mark.

No. 37 Lt Buoy 53°26'·00N 06°55'·00E QG; stbd-hand mark

No. 41 Lt Buoy 53°24'·32N 06°57'·20E Fl (2) G 9s; stbd-hand mark.

No. 45 Buoy 53°22'·05N 06°58'·57E (unlit); stbd-hand mark

No. 49 Lt Buoy 53°19'·99N 06°59'·75E Oc (2) G 9s; stbd-han mark.

KNOCK

K4 Lt Buoy 53°19'·87N 07°00'·82E QR; port-hand mark.

Knock 53°20'·37N 07°01'·50E F WRG 28m W12M, R9M G8M; grey Tr, four galleries, broad top, radar antenna; vis W270°-299°, R299-008°, G008°-023°, W023°-027°, R027° 039°, W039°-070°, R070°-116°, W116°-154°.

DELFZIJL entrance

Westerhoofd 53°19'·07N 07°00'·35E FG 3M; Ra Refl.

Oosterhoofd FR 3m; *Horn15s*; Ra Refl; In fog FY (occas).

Ldg Lts 203°. Rear 575m from front, FR. Common Front, No. 2A 53°18'·8N 07°00'·3E QR; W pedestal on dolphin; Ra Refl.

Ldg Lts 012°. Rear 500m fron front FR 6m; vis 087°-117°; Ra refl.

Zeehavenkannaal, North side (odd numbered posts); 2 QG; 3 Fl G 2s, 5 Fl G 5s; R refl.

Zeehavenkannaal, South side (even numbered posts); 1 Fl R 2s; 5 Fl R 5s; R refl.

East side entrance No. 21 (Marina entrance) Fl G 5s; W post on dolphin.

TERMUNTERZIJL

BW 15 Lt Buoy 53°18'·68N 07°02'·42E Fl G 4s; stbd-hand mark.

Wybelsum 53°20'·20N 07°06'·57E F WR 16m W6M, R5M; W framework Tr, R bands; radar antenna; vis W295°-320°, R320°-024°, W024°-049°; Fog Det Lt.

Logum Ldg Lts 075°. Front 53°20'·17N 07°08'·05E Oc (2) 12s 16m 12M; W mast, R bands. Rear, 630m from front, Oc (2) 12s 28m 12M; W mast, R bands; syncronised with front.

EMDEN

Ldg Lts 087°36'. Front 53°20'·07N 07°12'·15E Oc 5s 14m 14M; intens on Ldg line. Rear, 0·8M from front, Oc 5s 30m 14M; syncronised with front, intens on Ldg line.

Outer harbour, East pier head FG 7m 5M; Ra refl.

West pier head 53°20'·10N 07°10'·57E FR 10m 4M; Ra refl; *Horn Mo (ED) 30s.*

UIST
Training Wall, South end 53°39'·70N 06°59'·92E; pile;
S cardinal.
Juist 53°41'·9N 07°03'·5E Acro Fl 5s 14m.

NORDDEICH
West training wall, head 53°38'·7N 07°09'·0E FG 8m 4M; G
framework Tr, W lantern; vis 021°-327°.
East training wall, head FR 8m 4M; R & W triangle on R Tr; vis
327°-237°. Fog Lt.
Ldg Lts 144°. Front Iso WR 6s 6m W6M, R4M; B mast; vis
078°-122°, W122°-150°. Rear, 140m from front, Iso 6s 9m 6M;
B mast; synchronised with front.

NORDERNEY
Norderney 53°42'·6N 07°13'·8E Fl (3) 12s 59m **23M**; R 8 sided
Tr; unintens 067°-077° and 270°-280°.
Fish harbour Ldg Lts 274°30'. Front, West mole head 53°41'·9N
07°09'·9E Oc WR 4s 10m W7M, R4M; RW Tr; vis W062°-093°,
R093°-25·5°, W259·°-289·5°, R289·5°-062°. Rear. 460m from
front, Oc 4s 18m 7M; grey mast; synchronised with front.

BALTRUM
Baltrum groyne head 53°43'·3N 07°21'·7E Oc WRG 6s 7m
W6M, R4M, G3M; vis G 082·5°-098°, W098°-103°, R103°-
082·5°.

NESSMERSIEL
Mole, North head 53°41'·9N 07°21'·7E Oc 4s 6m 5M; G mast.

LANGEOOG
West mole head 53°43'·5N 07°30'·1E Oc WRG 6s 8m W7M,
R5M, G4M; R basket on R mast; vis G 064°-070°, W070°-074°,
R074°-326°, W326°-330°, G330°-335°, R335°-064°; *Horn Mo
(L) 30s (0730-1800LT).*

DORNUMER-ACCUMERSIEL
West breakwater head 53°41'·25N 07°29'·40E.

BENSERSIEL
West training wall head 53° 41'·62N 07°32'·95E.

NEUHARLINGERSIEL
Training wall head 53°43'·22N 07°42'·30E Oc 6s 6m 5M; G
mast.
Carolinensieler Balje. Leitdamm 53°44'·1N 07°50'·1E L Fl 8s
7m 6M; G mast.

HARLSIEL
Harleseil 53°42'·63N 07°48'·70E Iso R 4s 6m 7M.

SPIEKEROOG
Spiekeroog 53°45'·0N 07°41'·3E FR 6m 4M; R mast; vis 197°-
114°.

WANGEROOGE
Wangerooge, West end 53°47'·45N 07°51'·52E Fl R 5s 60m
23M; R Tr, 2 W bands; same Tr; F WRG 24m **W22M**, **W15M**,
R17M, R11M, **G18M**, G10M;vis R002°-011°, W011°-023°,
G023°-055°, W055°-060·5°, R060·5°-065·5°, W065·5°—71°,
G(18M) 137°-142·5°, W(22M) 142·5°-152°, Ldg sector, R (17M)
152°-157·5°; RC.

DEUTSCHE BUCHT LT F 54°10'·70N 07°26'·01E Oc (3) 15s
12m **17M**; R hull marked D-B; RC; Racon; *Horn Mo (DB) 30s.*
D-B Weser Lt Buoy 54°02'·42N 07°43'·05E Oc (3) R 12s; port-
hand mark; Racon.

DIE JADE
DB 19/Jade Lt Buoy 53°54'·74N 07°42'·10E IQ. G 13s; stbd-
hand mark
No. 1A Lt Buoy 53°52'·04N 07°45'·56E QG; stbd-hand mark.
No. 7 Lt Buoy 53°50'·30N 07°51'·24E Oc (3) G 12s; stbd-hand
mark.
No.11 Lt Buoy 53°49'·23N 07°55'·08E Fl G 4s; stbd-hand mark.
No.15/Blane Balje Lt Buoy 53°48'·13N 07°58'·88E IQ. G 13s;
stbd-hand mark.
No.19 Lt Buoy 53°47'·08N 08°01'·95E QG; stbd-hand mark.

No.23 Lt Buoy 53°45'·21N 08°02'·81E Oc (3) G 12s; stbd-hand
mark.
Mellumplate 53°46'·35N 08°05'·60E F 27m **24M**; R square Tr,
W band; vis 115 7° 116°; Ldg sector for outer part of
Wangerooger Fahrwasser. The following Lts are shown from
the same Tr over sectors indicated. Fl 4s **23M**; vis 113·7°-
114·9°. Fl (4) 15s; vis 116·9°-118·1°. Oc WRG 29m **W14M**,
R11M, G10M; vis R000°-006°, W006°-037·6°, G037·6°-113·7°,
R118·1°-168°, W168°-183·5°, R183·5°-212°, W212°-266°,
R266°-280°, W280°-000°. Mo(A) 7·5s; vis 114·9°-115·7° Ldg
sector. Mo(N) 7·5s; vis116°-116·9°; Ldg sector. Helicopter
platform.
Minsener Oog, Buhne A, North end 53°47'·30N 08°00'·45E F
WRG 16m W13M, R10M, G9M; square Tr; vis R050°-055°,
W055°-130°, G130°-138°, W138°-158°, R158°-176°, W176°-
268°, G268°-303°, W303°-050°.
Oldoog, Buhne C 53°45'·40N 08°01'·35E Oc WRG 4s 25m
W13M, R10M, G9M; B column, W bands, platform; visW153°-
180°, G180°-203°, W203°-232°, R232°-274°, W274°-033°; Fog
Det Lt.
Schillig 53°41'·8N 08°01'·7E Oc WR 6s 15m **W15M**, R12M; B
pylon, W band; vis W195·8°-221°, R221°-254·5°, W254·5°-
278·3°.
Hooksielplate Cross Lt 53°40'·20N 08°09'·00E Oc WRG 3s
25m W7M, R5M, G4M, W Tr, R bands; vis R345°-358·8°,
W358·8°-001·8°, G001·8°-012·4°, W012·4°-020·5°, R020·5°-
047·3°, W047·3°-061·9°, G061·9°-079·5°, W079·7°-092·5°,
R092·5°-110.5°; Fog Det Lt.
No. 31/Reede/West Siel 1 Lt Buoy 53°41'·59N 08°04'·50E Oc
(3) G 12s; stbd-hand mark.

WANGERSIEL
No.37/Hooksiel Lt Buoy 53°39'·38N 08°06'·63E Oc (2) G 9s;
stbd-hand mark.

HOOKSIEL
H3 Buoy 53°38'·68N 08°05'·42E (unlit); Stbd-hand mark.
Voslap Ldg Lts 164°35'. **Front** 53°37'·l9N 08°06'·88E Iso 6s
15m **24M**; R Tr, W bands, R lantern; R Refl; intens on Ldg line.
Rear, 2·35M from front Iso 6s 60m **27M**; W Tr, R bands. Same
structure, Cross light F RWG 20m W9M, R6M, G5M; vis
W200°-228°, G228°-248°, W248°-269°, R269°-310°.
Tossens. Ldg Lts 146°. **Front** 53°34'·56N 08°12'·42E Oc 6s
15m **20M**; B Tr, W stripes, R lantern. **Rear**, 2M from front, Oc
6s 51m **20M**; R Tr, W stripes, 3 galleries; Helicopter platform.

WILHELMSHAVEN
Eckwarden Ldg Lts 154°. **Front, Solthörner Watt** 53°32'·45N
08°13'·09E Iso WRG 3s 15m **W19M**, W12M, R9M, G8M; R Tr,
W bands; vis R346°-348°, W348°-028°, R028°-052°·; W (in-
tens) 052°-054° Ldg sector, G054°-067·5°, W067·5°-110°,
G110°-152·6°; W (intens) 152·6° across fairway, with unde-
fined limit on East side of Ldg line.
Rear, 1·27M from front, Iso 3s 41m **21M**; R Tr & lantern;
synchronised with front.
Neuer Vorhaven Ldg Lts 207°48'. Front Iso 4s 17m 11M; B
mast, R lantern. Rear, 180m from front, Iso 4s 23m 11M; Y
building; intens on Ldg line.
West mole head Oc G 6s 15m 4M.
East mole head Oc R 6s 5M.
Fluthaffen North mole head 53°30'·91N 08°09'·40E F WG 9m
W6M, G3M; G Tr; vis W216°-280°, W280°-010°, W010°-020°,
G020°-130°.
Flutmole head FR 6m 5M

DANGEST
Lock 53°26'·85N 08°06'·60E.

DIE WESER
Weser Lt Buoy 53°54'·25N 07°50'·00E Iso 5s 12m **17M**; safe
water mark; Racon.
Alte Weser 53°51'·85N 08°07'·72E F WRG 33m **W22M**,
R19M, **G17M**; R Tr, 2 W bands, B base, floodlit; vis W288°-

352°, R352°-003°, W003°-017°, Ldg sector for Alte Weser, G017°-045°, W045°-074°, G074°-118°, W118°-123°, Ldg sector for Alte Weser, R123°-140°, G140°-175°, W175°-183°, R183°-196°, W196°-238°; Fog Det Lt; RC; *Horn Mo (AL) 60s.*
Tegeler Plate, North end 53°47'·90N 08°11'·50E F WRG 21m **W27M**, **R17M**, **G16M**; R Tr, gallery, W lantern, R roof; vis W329°-340°, R340°-014°, W014°-100°, G100°-116°, R119°-123°, G123°-144°, R147°-264°; same structure, Oc 6s **21M**; vis 116°-119°; Ldg sector for Neue Weser; Ldg sector for Alte Weser 144°-147°.
Hohe Weg, NE part 53°42'·80N 08°14'·65E F WRG 29m **W19M**, **R16M**, **G15M**; R 8 sided Tr, 2 galleries, G lantern; vis W102°-138·5°, G138·5°-142·5°, W142·5°-145·5°, R145·5°-184°, W184°-278·5°; Fog Det Lt.
Robbennordsteert 53°42'·20N 08°20'·45E 11m W10M, R7M; R column on tripod; vis W324°-356°, R356°-089°, W089°-121°. Robbenplate Ldg Lts 122°18'. **Front**, Oc 15m **17M**; R tripod; intens on Ldg line. **Rear**, 0·54M from front, Oc 6s 37m **18M**; R Tr, 3 galleries, G lantern; vis 116°-125·5°; syncronised with front; Fog Det Lt.
Wremer loch Ldg Lts 140°48'. Front Iso WRG 15m W12M, R9M, G8M; vis R131°-139°, W139°-142·5°, R142·5°-183°, W183°-300°, G300°-303°. Rear, 0·57M from front, Iso 6s 31m 14M; synchronised with front; Ra refl.
Dwarsgat Ldg Lts 320°48'. Front Iso 6s 16m **15M**. **Rear** Iso 6s 35m **17M**; synchronised with front.
Langlütjen Ldg Lts 304°36'. Front Oc WRG 6s 15m W12M, R9M, G8M; B mast, B & W gallery; vis G141°-145°, W145°-211°, R299°-303°, W303°-306°, G306°-309°; Ra refl. Rear Oc 6s 35m **17M**; synchronised with front.
Imsum Ldg Lts 124°36'. Front Oc 6s 15m 13M; R tripod with gallery; **Rear**, 1·02M from front, Oc 6s 39m **16M**; synchronised with front.

BREMERHAVEN
Vorhafen North pier head 53°32'·19N 08°34'·57E FR 15m 5M; *Horn Mo (GG) 60s.*
South pier head 53°32'·14N 08°34'·57E FG 15m 5M.

BREMEN
Hasenbüren Sporthafen 53°07'·51N 08°40'·02E 2 FY (vert).

HELGOLAND
Restricted area Helgoland West Buoy 54°10'·65N 07°48'·25E (unlit); W cardinal.
Helgoland Lt Buoy 54°09'·00N 07°53'·55E Q(3) 10s; E cardinal; *Whis.*
Helgoland Lt Ho Fl 5s 82m **28M**; brown square Tr, B lantern, W balcony; RC;. FR on radio masts 180m SSE and 740m NNW. Cable Area Oc (3) WRG 8s 18m W6M, R4M, G4M; W mast, R bands; vis W179°-185°, R185°-190°, W190°-196°, W239°-244°, G244°-280°, W280°-285°.
Vorhafen. Ostmole, South elbow Oc WG 6s 5m W7M, G4M; G post; vis W203°-250°, G250°-109°; Fog Det Lt.
Ostmole head FG 7m 4M; vis 289°-180°; *Horn (3) 30s.*
Sudmole head Oc (2) R 12s 7m 4M; grey post, R lantern; vis 101°-334°.
Binnenhafen Ldg Lts 302°. West pier, Front Oc R 6s 8m 7M. **Rear**, 50m from front, Oc R 6s 10m 7M; synchronised with front.

DÜNE.
Ldg Lts 020°. Front Iso 4s 11m 8M; intens on Ldg line. Rear, 120m from front, Iso WRG 17M W11M, R10M, G10M; synchronsied with front; vis G010°-018·5°, W018·5°-021°, R210°-030°, G106°-125°, W125°-130°, R130°-144°.
Sellebrunn Lt Buoy 54°14'·43N 07°49'·83E Q(9) 15s; W cardinal; *Whis.*

DIE WESER TO DIE ELBE
Schlüsseltonne Lt Buoy 53°56'·28N 07°54'·85E Iso 8s; safe water mark.
Nordergründe-N Lt Buoy 53°57'·08N 08°00'·17W VQ; N cardinal.

Westertill-N Lt Buoy 53°58'·18N 08°06'·82E Q; N cardinal.
Scharnhörnriff-W Lt Buoy 53°58'·53N 08°08'·80E Q(9) 15s; W cardinal.
Scharnhörnriff-N Lt Buoy 53°58'·99N 08°11'·25E Q; N cardinal.

DIE ELBE
ELBE 1 LT FLOAT 54°00'·00N 08°06'·58E Iso 10s 12m **17M**; R hull and Lt Tr; RC; Racon; *Horn Mo(EL) 31s.*
No.1 Lt Buoy 53°59'·27N 08°13'·30E QG; stbd-hand mark.
No.5 Lt Buoy 53°59'·35N 08°19'·08E QG; stbd hand mark.
No.19 Lt Buoy 53°57'·83N 08°34'·48E QG; stbd hand mark.
No.25 Lt Buoy 53°56'·67N 08°38'·32W QG; stbd hand mark.
No.35 Lt Buoy 50°50'·73N 08°45'·80E Oc (2) G, stbd-hand mark
No.43 Lt Buoy 53°50'·27N 08°52'·30E Oc (2) G 9s; stbd-hand mark.
No.51 Lt Buoy 53°51'·07N 09°00'·22E QG; stbd-hand mark.
No.57 Lt Buoy 53°52'·55N 09°06'·38E QG stbd-hand mark.
Grosser Vogelsand 53°59'·78N 08°28'·68E Fl (3) 12s 39m **25M**; helicopter platform on R Tr, W bands; vis 085·1°-087·1°. Same Tr, Iso 3s **26M**; vis 087·1°-091·1°. Oc 6s **26M**; vis 091·1°-095·1°. Fl (4) 15s **19M**; vis 095·1°-101·9°. Fl (4) R 15s 12M; vis 101·9°-105·1°. Fl R 3s **15M**; vis 113°-270°. Oc (4) R 18s 9M; vis 322·5°-012°; Fog Det Lt; RC; *Horn Mo (VS) 30s.*
Neuwerk, South side 53°55'·0N 08°29'·8E L Fl (3) WRG 20s 39m **W16M**, R12M, G11M; vis G165·3°-215·3°, W215·3°-238·8°, R238·8°-321°, R343°-100°.

CUXHAVEN
Ldg Lts 151°12'. **Baumrönne**, front 1·55M from rear, Fl 3s 25m **17M**; W Tr, B band on gallery; vis 143·8°-149·2°. Same Tr, Iso 4s **17M**; vis 149·2°-154·2°. Fl (2) 9s **17M**; vis 154·2°-156·7°.
Altenbruch, Common rear, Iso 4s 58m **21M**; intens on Ldg line; synchronised with front. Same structure, Iso 8s 51m **22M**; synchronised with front. Crosslight Oc WR 44m W7M, R5M; vis 201·9°-232·8°, R232·8°-247·2°, W247·2°-254·6°.
Altenbruch Ldg Lts 261°. **Common front**, Iso 8s 19m **19M**; W Tr, B bands. Same structure, Iso WRG 8s W8M, R9M, G8M; vis G117·5°-124°, W124°-135°, R135°-140°. Rear, Wehldorf Iso 8s 31m 11M; W Tr, B bands; synchronised with front.
Balje Ldg Lts 130°48'. **Front** 53°51'·4N 09°02'·7E Iso WG 8s 24m **W17M**, **G15M**; W Tr, R bands; vis G shore-080·5°, W080·5°-shore. **Rear** 1·35M from front, Iso 8s 54m **21M**; W Tr, R bands; intens on Ldg line; synchronised with front. Same structure Oc WR 3s 24m **16M**; vis W180°-195°, R195°215°, W215°-223°.
Zweidorf 53°53'·5N 09°05'·7E Oc R 5s 9m 3M; R square on W pylon; vis 287°-107°.

BRUNSBÜTTEL
Ldg Lts 065°30'. Front **Schleuseninsel** Iso 3s 24m **16M; R Tr, W bands;** vis North of 063·3°. Same structure Fl 3s; vis South pg 063·5°. Rear **Industriegebiet**, 0·9M from front, Iso 3s 46m **21M**; R Tr, W bands; synchronised with front.
Alterhaven, North mole (Mole 4) head 53°53'·29N 09°07'·59E F WR (vert) 15m W10M, R8M; vis R275·5°-079°, W079°-084°.

NORD-OSTSEE KANAL (KIEL CANAL)
Rensburg
No. 2/Obereider 1 Lt Buoy 54°18'·95N 09°42'·71E Fl (2+1) R 15s; port-hand mark.

KIEL/HOLTENAU
Nordmole 54°21'·83N 10°09'·18E Oc (2) WR 9s 23m.

FRIEBURG
Entrance Bn (unlit) 53°50'·25N 09°18'·90E; stbd-hand mark.

GLUCKSTADT
North mole Oc WRG 6s 9m W8M R6M, G5M; W Tr with gallery; vis R330°-343°, W343°-346°, G346°145°, W145°-150°, R150°170°.
North pier head 53°47'·15N 09°24'·58E FR 5m 4M. (FG on South mole head).

STADE
Stadersand 53°37'·74N 09°31'·72E Iso 8s 20m 14M.

WEDEL
East entrance, East pier head 53°34'·30N 09°40'·87E FG.

HAMBURG

NESSKANAL
Entrance 53°32'·75N 09°50'·53E Oc (3) Y 12s 6m.

RÜSCHKANAL
Entrance 53°32'·63N 09°51'·10E FR 8m.

TEUFELSBRÜCK
Breakwater Head 53°32'·88N 09°52'·12E (unmarked).

INSHORE ROUTE ELBE TO SYLT
Süderpiep Lt Buoy 54°06'·55N 08°18'·85E Iso 8s; safe water mark.
Ausseneider Lt Buoy 54°14'·10N 08°18'·30E Iso 4s; safe water mark.
Mittelhever Lt Buoy 54°23'·10N 08°18'·15E Oc 4s; safe water mark; Whis.
Rütergat Lt Buoy 54°31'·00N 08°12'·05E Iso 8s; safe water mark.
Vortrapptief Lt Buoy 54°34'·95N 08°11'·30E Oc 4s; safe water mark.
Theeknobs West Lt Buoy 54°43'·52N 08°10'·00E Q(9) 15s; W cardinal.
Lister Tief Lt Buoy 55°05'·40N 08°16'·85E Iso 8s; safe water mark.

BÜSUM
Büsum 54°07'·65N 08°51'·55E Oc (2) WRG 16s 22m **W16M**, R14M, G13M; vis W248°-317°, R317°-024°, W024°-084°, G084°-091·5°, W091·5°-093·2° Ldg sector for Süder Piep, R093·5°-097°, W097°-148°.
West mole head Oc (3) R 12s 10m 4M; R Tr; FW Fog Det Lt.
East mole head Oc (3) G 12s 10m 4M; G Tr; vis 260°-168°.
Ldg Lts 355°. Front Iso 4s 9m 13M; B mast, W bands. Rear, 110m from front, Iso 4s 12m 13M; synchronised with front.

DIE EIDER
St Peter 54°17'·30N 08°39'·15E L Fl (2) WRG 15s 23m **W15M**, R13M, G11M; R Tr, B lantern; vis R271°-294°, W294°-325°, R325°-344°, W344°-035°, G035°-056·5°, W056·5°-068°, R068°-091°, W091°-113°, G113°-115°, W115°-116°, Ldg sector for Mittelhever, R116°-130°.
Eiderdamm Lock, North mole, West end Oc (2) R 12s 8m 5M; W Tr.
South mole, West end Oc G 6s 8m 5M: W Tr, grey top.

TÖNNING
West mole head FR 5m 4M; R column.
Quay FG 5m 4M; G column.

DIE HEVER
Westerheversand 54°22'·5N 08°38'·5E Oc (3) WR 15s 41m **W21M**, **R16M**; R Tr, W bands; vis W012·2°-089°, R089°-107°, W107°-155·5°, R155·5°-169°, W169°-206·5°, R206·5°-218·5°, W218·5°-233°, R233°-248°.

HUSUM
Husumer Al Outer Ldg Lts 106°30'. Front 54°28'·6N 09°00'·8E Iso R 8s 8m 5M; R mast, W bands; intens on Ldg line. Rear, 0·52M from front, Iso R 8s 17m 6M; Y mast; syncronised with front.
Inner Ldg Lts 090°. Front Iso G 8s 7m 3M; R mast, W bands; intens on Ldg line. Rear, 40m from front, Iso G 8s 9m 3M; intens on Ldg line; synchronised with front.

NORDSTRAND
Strucklahnungsh orn, West mole FG 5m 2M.

PELLWORM
Pellworm South side Ldg Lts 041°. **Front** Oc WR 5s 14m

W20M, W11M, R8M. Intens on Ldg line; vis W303·5°-313·5°, R313·5°-316·5°. **Rear**, 0·8M from front, Oc 5s 38m **20M**; R Tr, W band; synchronised with front. Same Tr as rear Lt, Cross Light Oc WR 5s 38m W14M, W9M, R11M, R6M., vis R(11M) 122·6°140°, W(14M) 140°-161·5°, R(11M) 161·5°-179·5°, W(14M) 179·5°-210·2°, R(6)M 255°-265·5°, W9M 265·5°-276°, R(6)M 276°-297°, W(9)M 297°-307°.

AMRUM
Amrum Hafen Ldg Lts 272°54'. Front 54°37'·9N 08°22'·9E Iso R 4s 11m 10M; W mast, R stripe; intens on Ldg Line. **Rear**, 0°9M fron front, Fl (3) 30s 63m **23M**; R Tr, W bands. Same structure Iso R 4s 33m **15M**.
Wriakhorn Cross light L Fl (2) WR 15s 26m W9M, R7M; vis W297·5°-319°, R319°-343°, W343°-014°, R014°-034°.
Nebel 54°38'·8N 08°21'·7E Oc WRG 5s 16m **W20M**, **R15M**; **G15M**; R Tr, W band; vis R255·5°-258·5°, W258·5°-260·5°, G260·5°-263·5°.
Norddorf 54°40'·3N 08°16'·6E Oc WRG 6s 22m **W15M**, R12M, G11M; W Tr, R lantern; vis W009-035°, G035-038°, Ldg sector, R040°-090°, W090°-156°, R156°-176·5°, W176·5-178·5°, G178·5°-188°, G(unintens) 188°-202°, W(partially obscured) 202°-230°.

LANGENESS
Nordmarsch 54°37'·6N 08°31'·8E F WRG 13m W14M, R11M, G10M; Dark Brown Tr; vis W268°-279°, R279°-311°, W311°350°, R350°-033°, W033°-045°, R045°-064°, W064°-123°, R123°-127°, W127°-218°.

OLAND
Near West point 54°40'·5N 08°41'·3E F WRG 12m W13M, R10M, G9M; R Tr; G086°-093°, W093°-160°, R160°-172°.

SCHLUTTSIEL
Harbour entrance 54°40'·9N 08°45'·0E (approx) (unlit).

FÖHR
Nieblum 54°41'·1N 08°29'·2E Oc (2) WRG 10s 11m **W19M**, **R15M, G15M**; R Tr, W band; vis G028°-031°, W031°-032·5°, R032·5°-035·5°.

DAGEBÜLL
53°43'·9N 08°41'·4E Iso WRG 8s 23m **W18M**, **R15M**, **G15M**; G mast; vis G042°-043°, W043°-044·5°, R044·5°-047°.
FW Lts shown on North and South mole head
Landemole 54°43'·9N 08°41'·3E Horn Mo(D) 30s; (sounded 0700-2200LT 1/4 - 30/9 & 0700-2000LT 1/10 - 31/3).

SYLT
Hörnum Ldg Lts 012°30'. Front 54°44'·8N 08°17'·4E Iso 8s 20m 14M; R Tr, W band; intens on Ldg line. **Rear** Iso 8s 45m **15M**; R Tr, W band; synchronised with front; intens on Ldg line.
Hörnum Fl (2) 9s 48m **20M**.
North pier head FG 6m 3M; vis 024°-260°.
Schutzmole head FR 6m 3M; mole floodlit.
Kampen, Rote Kliff 54°56'·87N 08°20'·50E Oc (4) WR 15s 62m **W20M**, 3R16M, W Tr, B band; vis W193°-260°, W(unintens) 260°-339°, W339°-165°, R165°-193°; RC.
Ellenbogen North end, List West 55°03'·25N 08°24'·19E Oc WRG 6s 19m W14M, R11M, G10M; W Tr, R lantern; vis R040°-133°, W133°-196°, R196°-210°, W210°-227°, R227°-266·4°, W266·4°-268°, G268°-285°, W285°-310°, W(unintens) 310°-040°.
North side, List ost Iso WRG 3s 13m W12M, R9M, G9M; W Tr, R band; vis W(unintens) 010·5°-098°, G098°-112°, W112°-114°, R114°-122°, W122°-262°, R262°-278°, W278°-296°, R296°-323·3°, W323·3°-324·5°, G324·5°-350°, W350°-010·5°.
List Land Oc WRG 3s 13m W12M, R9M, G8M; W mast, R band; vis W170°-203°, G203°-212°, W212°-215·5°, R215·5°-232·5°, W232·5°234°, G234°-243°, W243°-050°.
List Hafen, North mole head 55°01'·0N 08°26'·5E FG 5m 3M; G mast; vis 218°-038°.
South mole FR 5m 4M; R mast; vis 218°353°.

10.20.5   PASSAGE INFORMATION

DIE EMS TO DIE JADE (chart 3761)

The coastal route from the Hubertgat entrance of Die Ems to the Wangerooger Fahrwasser at the entrance to Die Jade (see below) is about 60 miles. The route leads along the Inshore Traffic Zone, S of the Terschellinger-Deutsche Bucht traffic scheme, the E-going lane of which is marked on its S side by stbd-hand buoys with the letters DB (DB1, DB3, DB5 etc). About 4M S of this line of buoys the landward side of the Inshore Traffic Zone is marked by buoys showing the approaches to the various zeegaten between the German Frisian Islands (see below). There are major Lts on Borkum, Norderney and Wangerooge. Near the traffic scheme the E-going stream begins at HW Helgoland 0500, and the W-going at HW Helgoland +0100, sp rates 1.2 kn. Inshore the stream is influenced by the flow through the zeegaten.

DIE EMS (charts 3509, 3510)

Die Ems forms the boundary between Netherlands and Germany, and is a major thoroughfare leading to ports such as Eemshaven, Delfzijl (10.19.29), Emden (10.20.23), Leer and Papenburg. Approach is made through Hubertgat or Westerems, which join W of Borkum. Both are well buoyed but can be dangerous with an ebb stream and a strong W or NW wind. The flood begins at HW Helgoland +0530, and the ebb at HW Helgoland −0030, sp rates 1½ kn.

From close SW of Borkum the chan divides into two — Randzel Gat to the N and Alte Ems running parallel to it to the S — as far as Eemshaven on the S bank. About 3M further on the chan again divides. Bocht van Watum is always varying so keep in main chan, Ostfriesisches Gatje, for Delfzijl (10.19.29) and beyond. Off Eemshaven the stream runs 2-3 kn.

Osterems is the E branch of the estuary of Die Ems, passing between Borkum and Memmert. It is not lit, but is a useful chan in daylight and good weather if bound to/from the E, although much shallower than Westerems. It also gives access to the Ley chan, leading to the harb of Greetsiel.

FRISIAN ISLANDS (chart 3761)

The German islands to the E of Die Ems have fewer facilities for yachtsmen than the Dutch islands to the W, and most of them are closer to the mainland. For general notes on the Frisian Islands see 10.19.5 and 10.20.8. For navigating inside the islands, in the so-called watt channels, it is essential to have the appropriate German charts and to understand the system of channel marking. Withies, unbound (with twigs pointing up) are used as port-hand markers, and withies which are bound (with twigs pointing down) as stbd-hand marks. Inshore of the islands the conventional direction of buoyage is always from west to east, even though this may conflict with the actual direction of the flood stream in places.

Borkum (10.20.9 and chart 3509) is the first of the German islands. It lies between Westerems and Osterems, with high dunes each end so that at a distance it looks like two separate islands. Round the W end of Borkum are unmarked groynes, some extending ¼ M offshore. Conspic landmarks include Grosse Beacon and Neue Beacon, a water Tr, Borkum Grosser Lt Ho, Borkum Kleiner Lt Ho, and a disused Lt Ho — all of which are near the W end of the island.

Memmert on the E side of Osterems is a bird sanctuary, and landing is prohibited. Juist (10.20.23) is the first of the chain of similar, long and narrow islands which lie in an E/W line between the estuaries of Die Ems and Die Jade. Most have groynes and sea defences on their W and NW sides. Their bare sand dunes are not easy to identify, and shoals extend seaward for 2M or more in places. The zeegaten between the islands vary in position and depth, and all of them are dangerous on the ebb tide — even in a moderate onshore wind. There are Nature Reserves (entry prohibited) inshore of Baltrum, Langeoog and the W end of Spiekeroog (chart 1875).

Norderneyer Seegat is a deep chan close W of Norderney, but there are dangerous shoals offshore, through which lead two shallow chans, Dovetief and Schluchter. Both are buoyed. The chans vary considerably and on occasions are silted up. Dovetief is the main chan, but Schluchter is more protected from the NE. Neither should be used in strong winds. Further inward Norderneyer Seegat leads round the W end of the island to Hafen von Norderney (10.20.10). Beware groynes and other obstructions along the shore.

SW of Norderney, Busetief leads in a general S direction to the tidal harb of Norddoioh (see 10.20.23), which can also be approached with sufficient rise of tide from Osterems through the Norddeich Wattfahrwasser with a depth of about 2m at HW. Busetief is deeper than Dovetief and Schluchter, and is marked by buoys and Lt buoys. The flood begins at HW Helgoland −0605, and the ebb at HW Helgoland −0040, sp rates 1 kn.

Baltrum (10.20.23) is an island about 2½ M long, very low in the E and only rising to dunes about 15m high in the W. With local knowledge and only in good weather it can be approached through Wichter Ee, a narrow chan obstructed by a bar between Norderney and Baltrum. There is a small pier alongside a groyne which extends about 2ca from the SW corner of Baltrum. The little harb dries, and is exposed to the S and SW. Continuing southwards from Wichter Ee is Nessmersiel Balje, with buoys on its W side prefixed by the letter 'N', leading to the sheltered harb of Nessmersiel (see 10.20.23).

Proceeding E, the next major chan through the islands is Acummer Ee between Baltrum and Langeoog. Shoals extend 2M to N, depths in chan vary considerably and it sometimes silts up. In onshore winds the sea breaks on the bar. Chan is marked by buoys prefixed with letter 'A', moved as necessary. Apart from Langeoog (10.20.12), Accumer Ee gives access to the mainland harbs of Dornumer-Accumersiel (10.20.11) and Bensersiel (10.20.23).

Westerbalje and Otzumer Balje are both buoyed and lead inward between Langeoog and Spiekeroog. Otzumer Balje is normally the deeper (0.7m-2.0m) but both chans may silt up and should be used only in good weather and on a rising tide.

Harle chan (buoys prefixed by letter 'H') leads W of Wangerooge (10.20.13), but beware Buhne H groyne which extends 7½ ca WSW from end of island to edge of fairway. Dove Harle (buoys prefixed by letter 'D') leads to the harb. In bad weather Harlesiel, 4M S on the mainland shore, is a more comfortable berth. See 10.20.23.

Blau Balje leads between the E end of Wangerooge and Minsener Oog. Although marked by buoys (lettered 'B' and moved as requisite) this chan is dangerous in N winds and there is a prohibited area (15 May – 31 Aug) S of the E end of Wangerooge for the protection of seals.

DIE JADE (charts 3368, 3369)

To the E of Wangerooge and Minsener Oog lie the estuaries of Die Jade and Die Weser. Die Jade is entered through the Wangerooger Fahrwasser (buoyed) and then leads SSE past Wangersiel and the yachting centre of Hooksiel (10.20.14) to Wilhelmshaven (10.20.15). S of Wilhelmshaven is a large but shallow area of water called Die Jadebusen, through which channels run to the small harbours of Dangastersiel (10.20.23) and Vareler Siel. Although not so dangerous as Die Elbe (see below), the outer parts of both Die Jade and Die Weser become very rough with wind against tide, and are dangerous on the ebb in strong NW winds.

DIE WESER (charts 3368, 3405, 3406, 3407)

Die Weser is an important waterway leading to the ports of Bremerhaven, Nordenham, Brake and Bremen which in turn connect with the inland waterways. From Bremen to Bremerhaven (10.20.16) the river is called Die Unterweser, and below Bremerhaven it is Die Aussenweser flowing into a wide estuary through which pass two main channels — Neue Weser and Alte Weser. The position and extent of sandbanks vary: on the W side they tend to be steep-to, but on the E side there are extensive shoals (e.g. Tegeler Plate).

Weser Lt Buoy marks the approach from NW to Neue Weser (the main fairway) and Alte Weser which are separated by Roter Sand and Roter Grund, marked by the disused Roter Sand Lt Tr (conspic). Both channels are well marked and they join about 3M S of Alte Weser Lt Tr (conspic). From this junction Hohewegrinne (buoyed) leads inward in a SE direction past Tegeler Plate Lt Tr (conspic) on the E side to the Fedderwarder Fahrwasser, which passes N of Hohe Weg Lt Tr (conspic). In Die Aussenweser the stream, which runs over 3 kn at sp, often sets towards the banks and the branch channels which pass through them.

Das Weser-Elbe Wattfahrwasser is a useful inshore passage between Die Weser and Die Elbe. It leads in a general NE direction from the Wurster Arm, part of the Weser which runs N of the N leitdamm, and keeps about 3M offshore. The normal yacht will take two tides to traverse it, but there are suitable anchs. Like other inshore passages behind the islands, it is well described in *Frisian Pilot* by Mark Brackenbury (Stanford Maritime).

DIE ELBE (charts 3262, 3266, 3268)

Yachts using the Elbe (see 10.20.18) are probably bound for the Nord-Ostee Kanal entrance at Brunsbüttel (10.20.19). Commercial traffic is very heavy. At Elbe 1 Lt F the E-going (flood) stream begins at HW Helgoland − 0500, and the W-going (ebb) stream at HW Helgoland + 0500, sp rates 2 kn. The stream runs harder N of Scharnhörn, up to 3½ kn on the ebb, when the Elbe estuary is dangerous in strong W or NW winds. From E end of traffic scheme the channel is well marked by buoys and Bn Trs.

DIE ELBE TO LISTER TIEF (charts 1875, 3767)

The W coast of Schleswig-Holstein is low and marshy, with extensive offshore banks which partly dry and on which are low offshore islands (Die Nordfriesischen Inseln). Between the banks and islands are many chans which change frequently. Süderpiep and Norderpiep are two chans (both buoyed, but the latter unlit) S of Die Eider, which join S of Blauort and lead to Büsum (10.20.23) and Meldorfer Hafen. Norderpiep has a bar (depth 3m) while Süderpiep does not and is preferable in W winds. Landmarks from seaward are Tertius Bn and Blauwortsand Bn, and a conspic silo at Büsum.

Die Eider is merged with much of its length with Der Nord-Ostsee Kanal, with which it connects at Gieselau. Below Tönning (10.20.23) it winds into an estuary, separated from Die Hever further N by the Eiderstedt Peninsula. About 5M below Tönning the estuary is closed by Eiderdamm — a storm barrage with a lock and sluices. The lock operates H24. Approaching from seaward, locate the Ausseneider Lt buoy, about 6M W of the buoyed entrance chan. St Peter Lt Ho is conspic on N shore. The entrance is rough in W winds, and dangerous in onshore gales.

Die Hever consists of several chans on the N side of Eiderstedt Peninsula, and S of the islands of Süderoogsand and Pellworm. Mittelhever is the most important of the three buoyed chans through the outer grounds, all of which meet SE of Süderoogsand before they separate once more into Heverstrom leading to Husum (10.20.23) and Noderhever which runs NE between Pellworm and Nordstrand into a number of watt channels. Schmaltief leads S of Amrun to Amrun Hafen, to Wyk on E side of Fohr, and to Dagebüll (see 10.20.23).

Sylt (10.20.22) is the largest of Die Nordfriesischen Inseln, and is some 20M from N to S. It has a straight coast facing the sea, and a peninsula on the E side connected to the mainland by Hindenburgerdamm. Vortrapptief is the chan inward between Amrum and Sylt, leading to Hörnum-Reede and Hafen von Hörnum. It has a depth of about 4m (subject to frequent change) and is marked by buoys and Lt buoys. The area should not be approached in strong W winds. The flood (ESE-going) stream begins at HW Helgoland − 0350, and the ebb (WNW-going) at HW Helgoland + 0110, sp rates 2½ kn.

Lister Tief, which marks the German-Danish border, leads between the N end of Sylt and Romo, and gives access to List Roadstead and Hafen von List as well as to Danish harbours. Lister Tief is well marked by buoys and Lt buoys, with a least depth over the bar of about 4m. After Süderpiep it is the safest chan on this coast, available for yachts seeking anch under the lee of Sylt in strong W winds (when however there will be a big swell over the bar on the ebb). Beware obstructions (ODAS) marked by Lt buoys, 18M WSW of List West Lt Ho.

10.20.6 DISTANCE TABLE

Approximate distances in nautical miles are by the most direct route while avoiding dangers and allowing for traffic separation schemes etc. Places in *italics* are in adjoining areas.

1 *North Foreland*	1																			
2 *Dunkerque*	40	2																		
3 *Burnham-on-Crouch*	36	75	3																	
4 *Grimsby*	169	194	168	4																
5 *Goeree Tower*	91	73	108	169	5															
6 *Den Helder*	171	153	169	180	80	6														
7 *Borkum*	243	241	252	249	168	95	7													
8 Norderney	259	257	268	265	184	111	31	8												
9 Wangerooge	283	281	292	289	208	135	55	29	9											
10 Bremerhaven	316	314	325	322	241	168	88	62	38	10										
11 Helgoland	300	298	309	285	225	152	67	44	24	44	11									
12 Brunsbüttel	337	335	347	332	263	190	110	84	55	78	51	12								
13 Holtenau	300	300	400	305	316	243	163	137	108	131	104	53	13							
14 Hamburg	374	372	384	369	300	189	104	81	61	81	88	37	90	14						
15 Husum	339	337	348	327	265	190	105	85	52	82	47	76	129	113	15					
16 Hörnum Lt (Sylt)	325	323	334	301	251	177	97	77	60	80	38	75	128	112	48	16				
17 *Esbjerg*	355	353	360	322	281	207	133	123	109	127	83	126	179	163	95	47	17			
18 *Thyboron*	393	390	400	348	329	256	200	186	178	201	154	196	249	233	163	120	90	18		
19 *Skagen*	501	499	507	442	437	364	305	291	283	306	259	301	—	338	268	225	195	104	19	
20 *Oksoy Lt (Norway)*	466	468	470	391	398	332	272	268	260	283	236	278	—	315	245	203	172	83	84	20

20

SPECIAL FACTORS AFFECTING THE FEDERAL REPUBLIC OF GERMANY 10-20-7

TIME ZONE is −0100, which is allowed for in the tidal predictions but no provision is made for daylight saving schemes which are indicated by the non-shaded areas on the tide tables (see 9.1.2).

SIGNALS Local port, tidal, distress and traffic signals are given where possible.

Light signals

R	R	— Passage or entry forbidden.
	R	— Be prepared to pass or enter.
W		Bridge closed or down; vessels
R	R	which can pass under the available clearance may proceed, but beware of oncoming traffic which have right of way.
W	W	Lift bridge will remain at first
R	R	step; vessels which can pass under the available vertical clearance may proceed.
G	G	Passage or entry permitted; oncoming traffic stopped.
W		Passage permitted, but beware of
G	G	oncoming traffic which may have right of way.
	R	Bridge, lock or flood barrage
	R	closed to navigation.
	R	— Exit from lock forbidden.
	G	— Exit from lock permitted.

Visual storm signals in accordance with the International System (see 10.14.7) are shown at: Borkum, Norderney, Norddeich, Accumersiel, Bensersiel, Bremerhaven, Brunsbüttel, Die Oste, Glückstadt, Stadersand, Hamburg, Büsum, Tönning, Husum, Wyk, List and Helgoland.

Lights In coastal waters particular use is made of light sectors. A leading sector (usually white, and often intensified) may be flanked by warning sectors to show the side on which the vessel has deviated. If to port — a red fixed light or a white group flashing light with an even number of flashes. If to starboard — a green fixed light or a white group flashing light with an odd number of flashes. Cross lights with red, white and green sectors may indicate the limits of roadsteads, turning points in channels etc.

Signals hoisted at masts

By day	By night	Meaning
Red cylinder	W	Reduce speed to minimize
	R	wash
	W	
Two black balls	R	
over cone point	R	Fairway obstructed
down	G	
Black ball over two cones points	R	
together (or red	G	Channel permanently closed
board with white	W	
band)		

When motoring always display motoring cone apex down.

CHARTS Where possible the Admiralty, Stanford, Imray and Dutch chart numbers are quoted. The German chart numbers are those of the charts issued by the Deutsches Hydrografisches Institut in Hamburg.

LANDS In place of the 'counties' in the UK, Lands are given.

MARINE RESCUE CO-ORDINATION CENTRES Coast station, Elbe Weser Radio ☎ (04721) 22066. Kiel Radio, ☎ (0431) 39011. Norddeich Radio, ☎ (04931) 1831.

PUBLIC HOLIDAYS New Year's Day, Good Friday, Easter Monday, Labour Day (1 May), Ascension Day, Whit Monday, Day of German Unity (17 June), Christmas Day and Boxing Day.

TELEPHONES To call UK from West Germany, dial 0044. Then dial the full UK area code, but omitting the prefix 0, followed by the number required.
To call Germany from UK, dial 010-49.
EMERGENCIES Police — dial 110
Fire, Ambulance — dial 112
Note: Two National Water Parks have been declared; one the Watten Sea area of Lower Saxony excluding the Jade and Weser rivers and the Ems-Dollard estuary; the other the west coast of Schleswig-Holstein. The rules for yachting in these areas have not yet been published other than a ban on leaving grounded boats unattended except in harbours. It is hoped that more detailed rules, due to be published by the Federal Ministry of Transport, will be available for the Supplements.
CUSTOMS Entry ports are Borkum, Norderney, Norddeich, Wilhelmshaven, Bremerhaven, Cuxhaven. Not Helgoland. Yachts passing through Kiel Canal without visiting Germany fly the third substitute pendant.
GAS Sometimes Calor gas bottles can be re-filled. German "Flussig" gas can be used with calor regulators.
CURRENCY 1 Deutch Mark = 100 Pfennigs
USEFUL ADDRESSES German Embassy, 23 Belgrave Sq, Chesham Place, London SW1X 8PX (Tel 071.235.5033). German National Tourist Office, 61 Conduit St, London W1 (Tel 071.734.2600).

GERMAN FRISIAN ISLANDS 10-20-8

The German Frisian Islands are a low lying chain of Islands off the north coast of Germany and make up a chain of Islands comprising the West Frisian Islands off the Netherlands, the East Frisian Islands off Germany and the North Frisian Islands off Schleswig-Holstein and Denmark. They lie between 3 and 20 miles off-shore and were, at one time, the north coast. The area between the islands and the present coastline which is now flooded by the sea is called the Watten. The German Frisian Islands run from the Ems estuary to the Jade Bay with two small islands in the Elbe estuary. The islands are known locally as the Ostfriesland and the inhabitants speak a patois known as Fries, a language with a close resemblance to English. The gaps between the islands are known as Seegats and the watersheds (where the tide meets having swept both ways round the island, usually about ⅓ the way from the E end of the S side) are known as Watts. Tidal streams are very slack over the watts but very strong in the Seegats. Deep water channels are buoyed but shallow channels are marked by withies (pricken in German). Withies the natural way up ⚲ are to be taken as port-hand lateral marks and withies inverted thus ⚲ are to be taken as starboard-hand lateral marks. As stated in 10.20.5, the conventional direction of buoyage is always from West to East inside the islands, so leave port-hand marks to the North whichever way the stream is flowing. With strong W or NW winds, the sea level rises over 0.25 m.

BORKUM (14 sq. miles), the largest, see 10.20.9

LUTJEHORN — bird sanctuary; landing prohibited.

MEMMERT, bird sanctuary; landing prohibited. Lt on stone Tr with G cupola, Oc (2) WRG 14s 15m 17/12 M.

JUIST (6½ sq. miles). No yacht harbour. See 10.20.23

NORDERNEY (10 sq. miles) Lt on R octagonal Tr, Fl (3) W 12s 59m 23M see 10.20.10

BALTRUM (3 sq. miles). Pretty island with small town and harbour at W end. See 10.20.23

LANGEOOG (7 sq. miles). See 10.20.12.

SPIEKEROOG (5 sq. miles). See 10.20.23.

WANGEROOGE (2 sq. miles). See 10.20.13.

MINSENER OOG Large Bn. Beware groynes and overfalls in strong NW winds

ALTE MELLUM Bird sanctuary; landing prohibited

SCHARNHÖRN (2 sq. miles) between Alte Mellum and Neu Werk; off charlet, in Elbe estuary. Uninhabited.

GROSSES KNECHTSAND between Alte Mellum and Neu Werk; Bird sanctuary; landing prohibited.

NEU WERK — off chartlet, in Elbe estuary. Only inhabited by Lifeboat Crew and Lighthouse men. Lt in square·brick Tr with B cupola LFl (3) WRG 20s 38m 18/12M. On W side there is a conspic W radar Tr and landing stage. Ferry to Cuxhaven.

BORKUM 10-20-9

EAST FRISIAN ISLANDS
Niedersachsen

CHARTS
Admiralty 3761, 3509; German D3012;
Dutch Yacht Chart 1812; ANWB A
TIDES
Dover −0105; ML 1.3; Duration 0610; Zone −0100

Standard Port HELGOLAND (→)

Times				Height (metres)			
HW		LW		MHWS	MHWN	MLWN	MLWS
0200	0700	0200	0800	2.7	2.3	0.4	0.0
1400	1900	1400	2000				

Differences BORKUM (FISCHERBALJE)

−0050	−0050	−0125	−0110	0.0	0.0	0.0	0.0

NORDDEICH HAFEN

−0010	−0020	−0040	−0025	+0.2	+0.2	+0.1	0.0

SHELTER
The shelter is reasonable in the Schutzhafen and it is available at all states of the tide. To the W there is a yacht harbour; access H24 with good shelter and facilities. There is another small harbour to the NE, the triangular Kleinbahnhafen (Light Railway Harbour) whose entrance is 65m wide. None give good protection in really bad weather, but the Yacht Harbour is best.
NAVIGATION
Waypoint Riffgat (safe water) buoy, Iso 8s, 53°38′.90N 06°27′.10E, 302°/122° from/to Fischerbalje Lt, 11M. See also 10.19.29. There are many groynes extending up to 2¾ ca (500 m) off shore. Approaching from any direction, pick up the Fischerbalje Lt at the end of the Leitdamm. Beware strong cross currents across the Fischerbalje channel. Speed limit in harbours 5 kn.
Note:— The S part of the island is a Nature Reserve. Borkum town is 7 km away.
LIGHTS AND MARKS
Landmarks — Water Tower, Grosse Beacon and 2 ca to the SW, Neve Beacon.
From the Fischerbalje to the channel up to the harbour is well buoyed.
Schutzhafen harbour ent shows FR on W and FG on E moles.
Fischerbalje Lt, Oc (2) WRG 16s 15m 16/11M, W Tr with R top and lantern on tripod; R256°-313°, G313°-014°, W014°-081°, R081°-109°, W109°-113°, R113°-120°, W120°-125° (Ldg Sector to Westerems), R125°-140°.
RADIO TELEPHONE
Hr Mr VHF Ch 16. See also Delfzijl, 10.19.29.
TELEPHONE (04922)
Hr Mr 2420; CG Borkum Kleiner Lt Tr; ☎ 2287; Police 3950; Ⓗ 813; Brit Consul (040) 446071.

20

FACILITIES

Yacht Harbour (30 + 170 visitors) ☎ 3880, AB, FW, Slip, D, R, Bar, AC, C (6 ton), V, R; **Kleinbahnhof** C (hand), AB; **F. Hellman** ☎ 2576, Gaz.

♦ — report to Hr Mr

Town P, ME, El, Gaz, V, R, Bar. ✉; Ⓑ; ⇌ (ferry to Emden); ✈ (services to Emden and Bremen). Ferry UK — Hamburg—Harwich.

NORDERNEY   10-20-10

EAST FRISIAN ISLANDS
Niedersachsen

CHARTS
Admiralty 3761; Dutch Yacht Chart 1812; German D3012
TIDES
Dover −0042; ML 1.4; Duration 0605; Zone −0100

Standard Port HELGOLAND (⟶)

Times				Height (metres)			
HW		LW		MHWS	MHWN	MLWN	MLWS
0200	0700	0200	0800	2.7	2.3	0.4	0.0
1400	1900	1400	2000				

Differences NORDERNEY (RIFFGAT)

−0025	−0030	−0055	−0040	+0.1	+0.1	+0.1	0.0

SHELTER
Good shelter and the harbour is always available. Yacht harbour is at the NE of the harbour, where yachts lie bow to pontoon, stern to posts.
NAVIGATION
Waypoint Schlu (safe water) buoy, Iso 8s, 53°44'.90N 07°05'.30E, 325°/145° from/to W point of Norderney, 3.0M. Entrance through the Dovetief (see 10.20.5) is well buoyed but the bar is dangerous in on-shore winds and seas break on it, especially on an ebb tide. Beware also that tidal streams run across the Dovetief and not up and down it. Beware merchant shipping. Harbour speed limit 3kn.
LIGHTS AND MARKS
Land marks — Norderney Light in centre of island — tall octagonal red brick tower, Fl (3) 12s 59m 23M. Water tower in town (conspic). Storm signal mast 4 ca NW of water tower.
Ldg Lts in line at 274°, synchronised.
RADIO TELEPHONE
None.
TELEPHONE (04932)
Hr Mr 793; CG 2293; ▦ 3386; Weather Emden 21458; Police 788; Ⓗ 477 & 416; Brit Consul (040) 446071.
FACILITIES
Segler-Verein (SVN) ☎ 2850, M, L, FW, C (10 ton), V, R; **W. Visser** ☎ 2207, CH, SM; **Dübbel & Jesse** ☎ 2928, Slip, ME, El, Sh; **Aral** ☎ 2913, P, D; **Shell** (in harbour) ☎ 2468, P; **Yacht Club** Bar; **A. Berghaus** ☎ 1689 Gaz; **Pontoon/Quay** P, D, FW;

Town V, R, Bar. ✉; Ⓑ; ⇌ (ferry to Norddeich); ✈ (services to Bremen).
Ferry UK — Hamburg—Harwich.

DORNUMER-ACCUMERSIEL   10-20-11

Niedersachsen

CHARTS
Admiralty 3761, 1875; German D3014, D89
TIDES
−0040 Dover; ML 1.4; Duration 0600; Zone −0100

DORNUMER-ACCUMERSIEL *continued*

Standard Port HELGOLAND (→)

Times				Height (metres)			
HW		LW		MHWS	MHWN	MLWN	MLWS
0200	0700	0200	0800	2.7	2.3	0.4	0.0
1400	1900	1400	2000				

Differences LANGEOOG OSTMOLE
+0005	+0005	−0030	−0020	+0.4	+0.4	+0.1	0.0

SHELTER
The marina provides complete shelter in all winds. Marina depth 3m, access HW∓4. Marina entrance is narrow; keep to W of channel on entering. Marina is fenced so obtain a key before leaving.

NAVIGATION
Approach through Accumer Ee (see 10.20.5 and 10.20.11) leading into Accumersieler Balje and to AB3 buoy, (stbd-hand), QG. From here keep four withies (downturned brooms) to stbd, clear of the Leitdamm. Note warnings on German chart D89.

LIGHTS AND MARKS
None.

RADIO TELEPHONE
None.

TELEPHONE (04933)
Hr Mr 1732; Deputy Hr Mr 441; ⌗ (04971) 7184; Lifeboat (04972) 247; Weather Emden 21458; Police 2218; Ⓗ 011502; Brit Consul (040) 446071.

FACILITIES
Dornumer Yacht Haven (250) All facilities and all pontoons removed out of season: FW, R, Slip, Gaz, D; **YC Dornumersiel** ☎ 622; **Rinjes** ☎ 712 ME, El, Sh; **Town** V, R, Bar, ✉, Ⓑ; ⇌ (Harlesiel); ✈ (Bremen or Hamburg).
Ferry UK — Hamburg—Harwich.

LANGEOOG   10-20-12

EAST FRISIAN ISLANDS
Niedersachsen

CHARTS
Admiralty 3761, 1875; Dutch Yacht Chart 1812; ANWB A; German D014

TIDES
Dover −0010; ML No data; Duration 0600; Zone −0100

Standard Port HELGOLAND (→)

Times				Height (metres)			
HW		LW		MHWS	MHWN	MLWN	MLWS
0200	0700	0200	0800	2.7	2.3	0.4	0.0
1400	1900	1400	2000				

Differences LANGEOOG OSTMOLE
+0005	+0005	−0030	−0020	+0.4	+0.4	+0.1	0.0

SPIEKEROOG REEDE
+0007	+0007	−0030	−0015	+0.4	+0.4	+0.1	0.0

SHELTER
At SW corner of the island, the harbour gives good shelter but it is open to the S. Sand dunes, 20m high, give considerable protection from winds.

NAVIGATION
Waypoint Accumer Ee (see 10.20.5) (safe water) buoy, Iso 8s, Bell, 53°46'.95N 07°25'.22E, 334°/154° from/to SW point of Langeoog, 5.3M. The E side of harbour dries and channel to yacht pontoons is marked by withies. Ice protectors extend about 40m E of E mole, awash at HW, marked by withies.

LIGHTS AND MARKS
Lt Bn on W pier Oc WRG 6s 8m 7/4M.
G064°-070°, W070°-074°, R074°-326°, W326°-330°, G330°-335°, R335°-064°, Horn Mo (L) 30s. (0730—1800 LT)
Landmarks:— Langeoog church, Esens church spire and Water Tower 2 ca WNW of Langeoog church.

RADIO TELEPHONE
None.

TELEPHONE (04971)
Hr Mr 301; Lifeboat CG 247; ⌗ 275; Weather Emden 21458; Police 810; Dr 589; Brit Consul (040) 446071.

FACILITIES
Langeoog Marina (70 + 130 visitors) ☎ 552, Slip, FW, C, (12 ton), El, Bar, R; **Segelverein Langeoog YC; Village** (1½ M) P, D, V, R, Gaz, Bar. ✉; Ⓑ; ⇌ (ferry to Norddeich); ✈ (services to Bremen).
Ferry UK — Hamburg—Harwich.
NOTE: Motor vehicles are prohibited on this island. Village is 1½ M away — go by foot, pony and trap or train. Train connects with ferries to Bensersiel.

WANGEROOGE   10-20-13

EAST FRISIAN ISLANDS
Niedersachsen

CHARTS
Admiralty 3368, 1875; German D2, D3011, D3014/5; Imray B B 70B

TIDES
E Wangerooge, Dover -0009, ML 1.9
W Wangerooge, Dover −0014, ML 1.5
Duration 0600; Zone −0100

Standard Port HELGOLAND (→)

Times		Height (metres)			
HW	LW	MHWS	MHWN	MLWN	MLWS
All Times	All Times	2.7	2.3	0.4	0.0

Differences WEST WANGEROOGE
+0003	−0019	+0.5	+0.4	+0.1	0.0

WANGEROOGE *continued*

SHELTER
Not good shelter except in N winds. Winds from all other directions make the harbour uncomfortable and, if strong, dangerous. Yachts lie against the E pier. In bad weather, yachts should make for Harlesiel, 4 M SSW.

NAVIGATION
Waypoint Harle (safe water) buoy, Iso 8s, 53°49'.25N 07°49'.00E, 321°/141° from/to Wangerooge Lt, 2.3M. From seaward the Harle channel (see 10.20.5) leads inward between Spiekeroog and Wangerooge: it varies in depth and position, and care is needed. Beware Buhne H groyne, extending 7½ ca (1390 m).
Yachts are forbidden to use the W jetty which is reserved for ferries. Beware protrusions on the E jetty.

LIGHTS AND MARKS
Wangerooge Lt Ho Fl R 5s 24m 23M; R Tr with two W bands. Also FWRG 24m 15/10M R002°-011°, W011°-023°, G023°-055°, W055°-060.5°, R060.5°-065.5°, W065.5°-071°, G137°-142°. W142°-152° Leading sector R152°-157.5° RC.

RADIO TELEPHONE
None.

TELEPHONE (04469)
Hr Mr 630; ⌗ 223; Weather Bremerhaven 72220; Police 205; Ambulance 588; Brit Consul (040) 446071.

FACILITIES
Wangerooge YC ☎ 364, FW, L, El, M; **Grunemann** ☎ 258, Gaz. **Village** El, V, R. ✉, R, P and D (cans), CH, ▣; Ⓑ; ⇌ (ferry to Harlesiel); ✈ (services to Bremen, Bremerhaven and Helgoland).
Ferry UK — Hamburg–Harwich.

HOOKSIEL 10-20-14
Niedersachsen

CHARTS
Admiralty 3369; German D3011, D7

TIDES
Dover +0034; ML 1.8; Duration 0605; Zone −0100

Standard Port HELGOLAND (→)

Times		Height (metres)			
HW	LW	MHWS	MHWN	MLWN	MLWS
All Times	All Times	2.7	2.3	0.4	0.0
Differences HOOKSIEL					
+0039	+0012	+1.0	+1.0	No data	

SHELTER
Yachts can lie alongside in the Vorhafen (approx 1m at MLWS) but it is very commercial and uncomfortable in E winds. Inside the lock there is complete shelter in a lake 2M long and approx 2.8m deep. Best berths for yachts are in Visitor Yacht Harbour at the far end, in the town. (Max draught 2m — bigger yachts go to YCs — see Lockmaster).

NAVIGATION
Waypoint No 35/Hooksiel 1 (stbd-hand) buoy, QG, 53°39'.43N, 08°05'.52E, 010°/190° from/to entrance, 0.80M. See also 10.20.15. Entrance is marked by H3 stbd-hand buoy, approx 1M W of main Innenjade channel. Approach to lock through Vorhafen, enclosed by two moles. Depth in channel 2.5m. Lock opens weekdays 0800-1900 (LT), Sundays 0900-2000 (LT), actual times on board at lock. Report to lock office. Secure well in lock. Beware tanker pier and restricted area to SE of entrance.

LIGHTS AND MARKS
Conspic chimneys of oil refinery 1.7M S of lock, which is in the W047°-062° sector of the Hooksielplate Cross Lt, Oc WRG 3s. There is a street lamp on the N mole and a pile with R dayglo paint on S mole. Ordinary traffic signals at lock.

RADIO TELEPHONE
VHF Ch 63.

TELEPHONE (04425)
Hr Mr 565; Lockmaster 430; ⌗ (0441) 42031; CG (0421) 5550555; Weather Bremerhaven 72220; Police Wilhelmshaven; Ⓗ (04421) 2080; Dr 1080; Brit Consul (040) 446071.

HOOKSIEL *continued*

FACILITIES
Visitors Yacht Hr (50) AC, FW, BH (25 ton), Slip, Bar;
Alter Hafen AB, FW, V, R, Bar; **Wilhelmshaven YC**
☎ 285; **Boot-Stove-North** Gaz; **Town** BY, SM, ME, El,
CH, P, D, Gaz, V, R, Bar, ⑧; ✉; ⇌ (Wilhelmshaven);
✈ (Wilhelmshaven or Bremen).
Ferry UK — Hamburg—Harwich.

WILHELMSHAVEN   10-20-15
Niedersachsen

CHARTS
Admiralty 3369; German D3011, D8
TIDES
Dover +0050; ML 2.0; Duration 0615; Zone −0100

Standard Port HELGOLAND (⟶)

Times		Height (metres)			
HW	LW	MHWS	MHWN	MLWN	MLWS
All Times	All Times	2.7	2.3	0.4	0.0

Differences WILHELMSHAVEN
+0109	+0034	+1.6	+1.5	+0.2	0.0

SHELTER
The yacht harbour, on E side of Ausrustungshafen inside
the locks is sheltered, but unattractive and remote. Locks
operate Mon-Fri: 0600-1830, Sat: 0630-1600, Sun and
holidays: 0800-1600 (all LT). The tidal yacht harbour in
Nassauhafen is better for a short stay.
NAVIGATION
Waypoint Die Jade. Wangerooge Fahrwasser No 3
(stbd-hand) buoy, QG, 53°52'.00N 07°45'.58E, 296°/116°
from/to Mellumplate Lt, 13M. The fairway is deep and
wide to Wilhelmshaven, a busy commercial port. The
Ems-Jade canal, 35M long, is usable by yachts with
lowering masts with max draught 1.7m. Min bridge
clearance 3.75m. There are six locks. Speed limit 4 kn.
LIGHTS AND MARKS
Die Jade is well marked and lit; for principal Lts see
10.20.4. Ldg Lts 208° into Neuer Vorhafen both Iso 4s.
Fluthafen N mole Oc WG (for sectors see chartlet);
S arm, head FR. Audio signals for bridge openings
(VHF Ch 11 09).
Kaiser Wilhelm — ···
Deich Bridge — —···
Ruestringer — —····

RADIO TELEPHONE
VHF Ch 11 16 (H24). Wilhelmshaven Lock Ch 13 16
(Mon-Fri: 0600-1830. Sat: 0630-1600. Sun and Public
Holidays: 0800-1600 LT). Other stations:
Die Jade (call: *Jade Revier*) Ch 20 63 (H24) gives
information broadcasts in German every H + 10.
TELEPHONE (04421)
Hr Mr 61552; Port Authority 26311; Lock 33404; ▦ 43136;
Weather Bremerhaven 72220; Police 43031;
Ⓗ 8011; Brit Consul (040) 446071.
FACILITIES
Nassauhafen Marina (28 + 100 visitors) ☎ 41439 Slip,
BY, ME, P, D, AC, Bar, FW, SM, R; **Wiking
Sportsboothafen** (30) ☎ 41301 AC, Bar, CH, El, FW,
Gaz, ME, R, SM, V; **Turbo-Technik** ☎ 44061, ME, El,
Sh; **Farymann** ☎ 23058, ME; **Hochsee YC Germania**
☎ 44121; **Ship-Shop** ☎ 26011 Gaz.
Town BY, SM, ME, CH, El, P, D, Gaz, V, ✉; ⑧; ⇌; ✈.
Ferry UK — Hamburg—Harwich.

BREMERHAVEN   10-20-16
Federal State of Bremen

CHARTS
Admiralty 3406; German D3011, D4
TIDES
Dover +0051; ML 2.0; Duration 0600; Zone −0100.

Standard Port HELGOLAND (⟶)

Times				Height (metres)			
HW		LW		MHWS	MHWN	MLWN	MLWS
0200	0800	0200	0800	2.7	2.3	0.4	0.0
1400	2000	1400	2000				

Differences BREMERHAVEN
+0136	+0144	+0119	+0129	+1.5	+1.4	+0.1	0.0

SHELTER
The fishing and yacht harbours are in the S-most basin,
entered through Vorhafen, close S of conspic Radar Tr
(112m). Yachts may go into R Geeste (uncomfortable in
SW-W winds) or to one of the three YC/marinas. The
Nordseeyachting Marina (NYC or Bremerhaven Marina) in
Fischereihafen II, 1.3M S of locks on W side (3m); the
Wassersportverein Wulsdorf Marina (WVW) 0.5M beyond;
the Weser Yacht Club Yacht Haven to E of Handelshafen.
There are also Yacht Harbours up the R Weser at
Nordenham, Rodenkirchen, Brake and at Elsfleth.
NAVIGATION
Waypoint Alte Weser. Schlüsseltonne (safe water) buoy,
Iso 8s, 53°56'.30N 07°54'.87E, 300°/120° from/to Alte
Weser Lt, 9M. For The Weser, see 10.20.5. R Weser is
very well marked. Beware large amounts of commercial
shipping and ferries using R Geeste. Leave R Weser at Lt
Buoy 61.
LIGHTS AND MARKS
Ldg Lts 151° lead down main channel (R Weser). Front
Oc 6s 17m 18M. Rear 0.68M from front, Oc 6s 45m 18M
synchronised. Vorhafen N mole head FR 15m 5M. To
enter Schleusenhafen sound Q and enter when G Lt is
shown.
RADIO TELEPHONE
Bremerhaven Port VHF Ch 12; 12 16 (H24). Bremerhaven
Weser Ch 14; **14** 16 (H24). Brake Lock Ch 10 (H24). The
Weser Radar Information Service broadcasts information
in German every H + 20 from Alte Weser Radar Ch 22,
Hohe Weg Radar I Ch 02, Hohe Weg Radar II Ch 02,
Robbenplate Radar I Ch 04, Robbenplate Radar II Ch 04
and Blexen Radar Ch 07; also from Bremen-Weser-Revier
at H + 30 on Ch 19 and by Hunte-Revier on Ch 17. Hunte
Bridge Ch 10 (daylight hours). Oslebshausen Lock,
Bremen, Ch 12. Bremen Port Ch 03 16; 03 14 16 (H24).
TELEPHONE (0471)
Hr Mr 481260; Bremerhaven Marina (NYC) 77555; Weser
YC Yacht Hafen 23531; Wassersportverein Wulsdorf
(WVW) 73268; Weather 72220; Fischereihafen Lock 4811;
Police 47011; Ⓗ 42028; Brit Consul (040) 446071.
FACILITIES
Bremerhaven Fischereihafen Hauptkanal (Weser YC)
☎ 23531 C, AC, FW, **Bremerhaven Fischereihafen 2**
☎ 73268 C, Slip, El, P, D, FW **Marina Bremerhaven**
☎ 77555 C, Slip, AC, FW; **Weser YC** ☎ 23531, R, Bar,
AB; **Yachting Club Wulsdorf** ☎ 23268, AB, FW, Slip;
W. G. Janssen ☎ 25095 Gaz. **Nordsee Yachting**
☎ 77555 **Town** all facilities, V, R, Bar, ✉; ⑧; ⇌; ✈.
Ferry UK — Hamburg—Harwich.

20

BREMERHAVEN *continued*

CUXHAVEN 10-20-17
Niedersachsen

CHARTS
Admiralty 3261; German D3010
TIDES
Dover +0103; ML 1.5; Duration 0535; Zone −0100

Standard Port HELGOLAND (→)

Times		Height (metres)			
HW	LW	MHWS	MHWN	MLWN	MLWS
All Times	All Times	2.7	2.3	0.4	0.0
Differences CUXHAVEN					
+0119	+0116	+0.6	+0.5	−0.1	−0.1
SCHARNHÖRN					
+0024	+0019	+0.7	+0.7	0.0	0.0

SHELTER
Good shelter both in the Alter Hafen and in the Yacht Harbours to the NW. Apply to Cuxhaven YC for moorings. Yachts over 20m may be allowed in Alter Fischereihafen.
NAVIGATION
Waypoint Elbe Lt buoy, Iso 10s, Horn, RC, Racon, 54°00'.00N 08°06'.6E, 271°/091° from/to Grosser Vogelsand Lt, 13M. Channel well marked by buoys and beacons, see 10.20.4 and 10.20.5. Tide is strong, up to 5 kn off Cuxhaven on the ebb. Much commercial shipping.
LIGHTS AND MARKS
Entrance to S Yacht Harbour is close NW of conspic radar Tr, and N of main Cuxhaven Lt Tr (dark R with copper cupola) FWR, Fl(4) 12s, Oc 6s and Fl(5) 12s (for sectors see chartlet).
Luminous tide signals (G by day, Y at night) from radar Tr. Top panel: chevron point up — tide rising; chevron point down — tide falling; horizontal line below chevron — level below CD. Lower panel: two figures show difference in decimetres between level and CD. S Yacht Harbour entrance, N side FWG, G108°-340°, W340°-108°. S side FWR, W056°-120°, R120°-272°, W272°-295°.

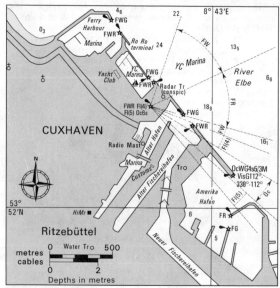

RADIO TELEPHONE
Cuxhaven Elbe. Call: *Cuxhaven Report (Radio)* VHF Ch 12 16; 12 14 16 (H24). Die Elbe information broadcasts in English and German every odd H+55 by *Revierzentrale Cuxhaven* simultaneously on Ch 19 18 05 21 and 03 for the East part of Deutsche Bucht. Cuxhaven Radar is part of Die Elbe Radar and Information Service which includes River Elbe Approach Ch 19, Neuwerk Radar 1 Ch 18, Neuwerk Radar 2 Ch 05, Belum Radar Ch 03.
TELEPHONE (04721)
Hr Mr 34111; CG 38011; Lifeboat 34622; Weather 36400; Port Authority 501450; ⌗ 21085; Brit Cruising Assn 35820; Police 37081; Ⓗ 181; Brit Consul (040) 446071.

FACILITIES

Cuxhaven YC Marina ☎ 34111 (summer only), Slip, M, L, FW, C, AB, R, Bar; **Cuxhavener Bootswerft** ☎ 22132, Slip, ME, El, Sh; **Glüsing** ☎ 24017, P, D, Gaz; **Ferry Harbour Marina** No tel, no visitors, no facilities; **Herbert Krause** ☎ 22197, CH, El; **Rauschenplath-Buchhandlung** ☎ 37137, chart agent;

Euromar ☎ 32929, CH; **Krause Wilhelmi** ☎ 22197, Ⓔ, El; **Cuxhaven SC** ☎ 35404, R, Bar; **B Hein** ☎ 24069, CH, SM; **Segler-Vereingung Cuxhaven** ☎ 34111; **Town** All facilities, R, V, Bar, ⊠; Ⓑ; ⇌; ✈ (Bremen, Hamburg, Hannover). Ferry UK — Hamburg—Harwich.

RIVER ELBE/ HAMBURG

10-20-18

Niedersachsen/Schleswig Holstein

CHARTS

Admiralty 3262, 3266, 3268; German D3010 Sheet 1 to 16, D46, D47, D48.

TIDES

Glückstadt	ML 1.2	Duration 0515	Zone −0100
Brunshausen	ML 1.1	Duration 0510	
Hamburg	ML 1.3	Duration 0435	
Bunthaus	ML 1.4	Duration 0435	

Standard Port HELGOLAND (→)

HW All Times	LW All Times	MHWS 2.7	MHWN 2.3	MLWN 0.4	MLWS 0.0
Differences GLÜCKSTADT					
+0322	+0329	+0.3	+0.3	−0.3	−0.1
STADERSAND					
+0359	+0413	+0.4	+0.4	−0.3	0.0
SCHULAU					
+0459	+0443	+0.6	+0.5	−0.3	−0.1
HAMBURG					
+0459	+0532	+0.8	+0.7	−0.4	−0.1
BUNTHAUS					
+0522	+0614	+0.6	+0.5	−0.4	0.0

The river is tidal up to Geesthacht, 24 M above Hamburg, and Hamburg is 78 M from the Elbe 1 Light Vessel. It is a very busy waterway and there are so many lights that at night it can be very confusing. Yachts should keep to starboard, preferably just outside the marked channel. The river is 13m deep all the way to Hamburg. Strong W winds can raise the level in the river by as much as 4m.

There are a number of places with good shelter and facilities but it is not a particularly salubrious yachting area. (Chart is D3010 and sheet numbers are shown below).

BRUNSBÜTTEL alter Hafen see 10.20.19. (Sheet 7).
ST. MARGARETHEN (Sheet 8). Depth HW 10m. No facilities.
FREIBURG (7 M above Brunsbüttel) on the SW bank. The river here is ½m wide. Small vessels can enter Freiburg harbour at HW and there is excellent shelter at Freiburg Reede. ML 2.2m. ☎ Hr Mr (04779) 8314. Facilities ME, El, Sh, C, FW, Slip, YC **Jugendheim** and **YC Klubheim** V, R, Bar. (Sheet 8).
STÖRLOCH/BORSFLETH Entrance approx 600 m above locks on E bank. ML 2.8m. Facilities. Hr Mr ☎ (04124) 71437 FW, YC. (Sheet 9).
STÖR/BEIDENFLETH MI 2.8m (Sheet 9). **Stör/Langes Rack YC**
GLÜCKSTADT, on the NE bank 2½ M up-stream from entrance to the Stör River. Good shelter both inner and outer harbours having min depth of 2.0 m. Hr Mr ☎ (04124) 2087; Customs ☎ (04124) 2171. YC, FW, C, D, V, R, ▢, Bar. (Sheet 9).
WISCHHAFEN Hr Mr ☎ (04770) 334; Customs (04770) 3014 FW, M, Slip, P, D, ML 2.7 m. (Sheet 9).
RUTHENSTROM ldg marks into harbour, two Bns with triangular topmarks on 197°. ML 2.6 m. Hr Mr ☎ (04143) 5282; C, Slip, FW, ME, El, Sh. (Sheet 10).
KRÜCKAUMÜNDUNG JACHTHAFEN ☎ (04121) 20945 Slip, FW. ML 2.7 m. Customs 20551. (Sheet 10).
PINNAUMÜNDUNG JACHTHAFEN Entrance via lock gate on N bank after passing through main locks. ML 2.5 m. Hr Mr ☎ (04101) 22447 Slip, M, FW, YC, C. (Sheet 10).
PINNAU-NEUENDEICH Marina 1½M up the Pinnau from main locks and another at approx. 2M. (Sheet 10).
ABBENFLETH Entrance maked by two Bns in line 221° with triangular topmarks. (Sheet 11).
HASELDORT Hafen. Hr Mr ☎ (04129) 268 Slip, FW, V, YC.

20

SCHWINGE -- BRUNSHAUSEN (04141) 3085
HÖRNE/WÖHRDEN ML 2.8m
STADE (04141) 101275 C, YC, V on SW
bank, 12M up-stream from Glückstadt. Access HW∓2.
Yachts lock into inner basin. Customs ☎ 3014.
(Sheet 11/12).
LÜHE Hafen in town of Lühe. (Sheet 12).

HAMBURG

A busy commercial port with several marinas. Visiting
yachts should stay in Wedel.
WEDEL on E bank, 12 M downstream from Hamburg,
Hamburger Yachthafen (1800) with 2 entrances (23 m
wide) marked by FR and FG Lts. Hr Mr (04103) 4438
(office), 5632 (Hr Mr east), 7751 (Hr Mr west); Customs
2688; Bar, BH (16 ton), BY, C, CH, D, El, Ⓔ, FW, ME,
P, SC, Sh, Slip, SM, **Bülow & Partner** (04103) 88492 Ⓔ,
El, ME, Sh;
BUKH (04103) 84402 ME, **Yachtelektrik Wedel** (04103)
87273 Ⓔ, El
Schulau, Ent marked by Oc (2) R and Oc (2) G Lts. Hr Mr
(04103) 2422, Slip, C, P, D, ME, El, Ch, SC (Sheet 12).
Neuenschleuse, opposite Wedel, FW, P, D (Sheet 13)
Mühlenberg (250), Slip, FW, SC (Sheet 13)
Teufelsbrück, small harbour, Bar, FW, SC (Sheet 13)
Rüschkanal, on S bank in Finkenwerder, C, CH, El, FW,
ME, Slip, Sh, SC new harbour with 4 SCs and nearby
resort area

RADIO TELEPHONE

Hamburg Port 14,17
Hamburg Elbe 12
Hamburg Radar 03, 05, 07, 19, 63, 80
Süderelbe Revier 13

TELEPHONE (040)

Met 3190 826/827, or (0)11509 for recorded message; Brit.
Consul 446071

FACILITIES

Subwaystation 'Rödingsmarkt' CH; **B. Schmeding**
☎ 353646 Gaz, **A.W. Niemeyer** ☎ 3614140 CH, **Möhrer**
☎ 366300 Ⓔ, El **City** all facilities ✉, Ⓑ, ⇌, ✈
Ferry UK. Hamburg – Harwich

BRUNSBÜTTEL   10-20-19
Schleswig-Holstein

CHARTS
Admiralty 2469, 3262; German D3010 Sheet 6

TIDES
Dover +0203; ML 1.4; Duration 0520; Zone −0100

Standard Port HELGOLAND (⟶)

Times		Height (metres)			
HW	LW	MHWS	MHWN	MLWN	MLWS
All Times	All Times	2.7	2.3	0.4	0.0
Differences BRUNSBÜTTEL					
+0221	+0234	+0.3	+0.3	−0.1	0.0

SHELTER
There is very good shelter in the yacht harbour on the N
bank, just inside the locks into the Kiel canal. There is
also good shelter in the yacht harbour outside the locks in
the Alter Hafen, available HW∓3.

NAVIGATION
For Die Elbe see 10.20.18 and 10.20.5. There are no
navigational dangers in the immediate approaches, but
commercial traffic is heavy. The stream sets strongly
across entrances to locks.

LIGHTS AND MARKS
Ldg Lts 065°, both Iso 3s 16M, synchronised.

RADIO TELEPHONE
Brunsbüttel Elbe. Call: *Brunsbüttel Report (Radio)* VHF
Ch 14 16; 11 **14** 16 (H24). Die Elbe information broadcasts
in English and German every odd H+05 by Revierzentrale
Brunsbüttel Ch 04 67 18 22 05 and 21 (see also Cuxhaven
10.20.17). Nord-Ostsee Kanal: Ports — Ostermoor
(Brunsbüttel to Burg) Ch 73 (H24), Breiholz (Breiholz to
Nübbel) Ch 73 (H24). Canal — Kiel Kanal I (Brunsbüttel
entrance and locks) Ch 13 (H24), Kiel Kanal II (Brunsbüttel
to Breiholz) Ch 02 (H24), Kiel Kanal III (Breiholz to
Holtenau) Ch 03 (H24). Kiel Kanal IV (Holtenau entrance
and locks) Ch 12 (H24). Information broadcasts by Kiel
Kanal II on Ch 02 at H+15, H+45 and by Kiel Kanal III
on Ch 03 at H+20, H+50. Vessels should monitor these
broadcasts and not call the station if this can be avoided.
Other stations: Oste Bridge Ch 16 69. Este Lock Ch 10 16.
Stör Bridge Ch 09 16. Stadersand Elbe. Call: *Stadersand
Report (Radio)* Ch 11 16; **11** 12 16 (H24). Hamburg Elbe
Port Ch **12** 16; 12 14 (H24). Hamburg Port. Call: *Hamburg
Report (Radio)* Ch 16; 06 13 **14** 73 (H24). Hamburg
Control Vessel Ch 14 16. Rethe Revier Ch 16 13 (Mon-Sat:
0600-2100 LT, Sun and Public Holidays on request).
Süderelbe Revier (at Kattwyk bridge) Ch 16 13 (H24).
Harburg Lock Ch 13 16 (H24). See also Cuxhaven
10.20.17.

TELEPHONE (04852)
Hr Mr 8011 ex 360; CG 8444; ⌗ 87241; Weather
Cuxhaven 36400; Police 1012; Ⓗ 601;
Brit Consul (040) 446071.

FACILITIES
Alter hafen ☎ 3107, Slip, BY, AC, C (20 ton), FW, R;
Kanal-Yachthafen ☎ 8011, FW, AC, ⌗, Bar; **P. Lützen**
☎ 51016, Gaz;
Town P, D, ME, El, Sh, V, R, Bar. ✉; Ⓑ; ⇌;
✈ (Hamburg).
Ferry UK — Hamburg–Harwich.

NORD-OSTSEE KANAL
(Kiel Canal)   10-20-20
Schleswig Holstein

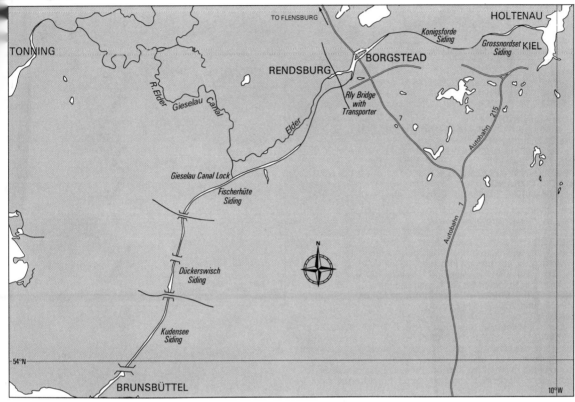

TONNING

TO FLENSBURG

HOLTENAU

Konigsforde Siding

Grossnordset Siding KIEL

RENDSBURG

BORGSTEAD

Rly Bridge with Transporter

R. Eider

Gieselau Canal

Elder

Autobahn 215

Autobahn 7

Gieselau Canal Lock

Fischerhüte Siding

Dückerswisch Siding

N

Kudensee Siding

— 54°N

BRUNSBÜTTEL

10°W

CHARTS
Admty 2469 German D 3010

Yachts are only permitted to use the Kiel Canal and the entrances thereto during the hours of daylight and in good visibility. This does not apply to craft proceeding to the yacht berths at Kiel-Holtenau, to the Inner Harbour at Brunsbüttel and the Old Harbour at Brunsbüttel.

Nord-Ostsee Kanal is 53.3M long (98.7 km) running from Brunsbüttel to Kiel-Holtenau. Width 103 to 162m on the surface, 44 to 90m on the bottom, with a depth of 11m. Kilometre marks start at Brunsbüttel; there are ten passing places (sidings or weichen) and seven bridges with 40m clearance. The speed limit is 8 kn. Sailing, except motor sailing is forbidden. Yachts must then display a B cone, apex down, or a B flag, cone shaped. Yachts should report before entering as follows: at Brunsbüttel through Kiel Kanal I on VHF Ch 13; at Holtenau through Kiel Kanal IV on VHF Ch 12.

Canal dues can be paid at either end of the canal at the 'Dues Office'.

Yachts purely in transit are not usually troubled by the Customs Authority and transiting yachts should fly the third substitute of the International Code.

Yachts are to regulate their transit so as to reach the intended berthing places during the day. These are:

1) Yacht Harbour at Kiel-Holtenau (km 0)
2) The Borgstedt Narrows (km 28.5)
3) The Ober Eider Lake (km 32.5)
4) Berthing place outside the Gieselau Canal Lock (km 58)
5) Berthing place at the jetty in Dückerswisch Siding (km 77)
6) Brunsbüttel (km 98.5)

Entrance Area: Signals shown from Canal Pilots House.
R — No entry

W
R — Prepare to enter

G — enter with pilot

W
G — enter without pilot
(yachts follow coasters flying Flag N)

Lock signals
R — No entry

W}
R} — Prepare to enter

G — enter with pilot; secure to middle wall

W}
G} — without pilot — enter; secure to middle wall

W}
W G} — with pilot enter and secure by W Lt

W — Yachts may enter

Other signals
In canal:—
   3FR (vert)   — all movement prohibited
   Other signals   — not relevant to yachts.
Other ports in the canal, Ostermoor Ch 73 (H24) and Breiholz Ch 73 (H24). The traffic signal of most concern to yachts is 3FR(vert) meaning 'STOP' and usually means the approach of a big ship. Yachts keep to starboard side. Speed limit in canal is 15 kilometres/hour; in the Gieselau Canal 10 and in the Achterwehr Shipping Canal 8 kilometres/hr.

The principal port along the canal is Rensburg, situated between kilometre posts 60 and 67. There are all facilities at Rensburg including dry docks and several shipyards. The Eider Canal connects Rensburg with Tonning (see 10.20.22). At the Baltic end of the canal is Kiel-Holtenau, a major port with all facilities. Here two pairs of locks lead into the Kieler Förde which is practically tideless and almost the same level as the canal.

20

HELGOLAND   10-20-21
Schleswig-Holstein

CHARTS
Admiralty 1875, 126; German D88,D3010,D3013/4

TIDES
Dover −0015; ML 1.4; Duration 0540; Zone −0100

Standard Port HELGOLAND (→)

Times				Height (metres)			
HW		LW		MHWS	MHWN	MLWN	MLWS
0100	0600	0100	0800	2.7	2.3	0.4	0.0
1300	1800	1300	2000				

Differences BÜSUM

+0051	+0051	+0014	+0014	+1.0	+0.8	+0.1	0.0

DAGEBULL

+0226	+0226	+0223	+0223	+0.5	+0.5	−0.1	0.0

HUSUM

+0210	+0158	+0120	+0205	+1.1	+1.1	+0.1	0.0

SUDEROOGSAND

+0108	+0108	+0101	+0101	+0.3	+0.4	+0.1	0.0

Helgoland is a Standard Port and tidal predictions for each day of the year are given below.

SHELTER
Good safe shelter in artificial harbour; yachts use the Vorhafen, or go through into the Südhafen.
NOTE 1. No customs clearance for entry into Germany. Customs in Helgoland is for passport control.
NOTE·2. It is forbidden to land from yachts on neighbouring Düne Island.

NAVIGATION
Waypoint Helgoland E cardinal buoy, Q(3) 10s, Whis, 54°09′.00N 07°53′.56E, 202°/022° from/to Düne front Ldg Lt, 2.1M. Beware the Hog Stean shoal, 4 ca (740 m) S of Sudmole head Lt. The S entrance is dangerous due to submerged rocks either side of channel. Beware lobster pots round Düne Is. Navigation is prohibited from 1 April to 12 July and from 1 Sept to 31 Dec in restricted areas. See Admty chart 3761.

LIGHTS AND MARKS
Helgoland Lt Ho, Fl 5s 82m 28M; brown sq Tr, B lantern, W balcony; RC.
Binnenhafen Ldg Lts 302°, both Oc R 6s, synchronised.

RADIO TELEPHONE
Helgoland Port Radio VHF Ch 16 17 (Mon-Sat: 0700-2100 LT): Coast Radio VHF Ch 03 16 27 88 (H24).
Information broadcasts in English and German every H+00 and H+30 on Ch 80 by Deutsche Bucht Revier (at Helgoland Lt Ho) for area within 26M of Helgoland.

TELEPHONE (04725)
Hr Mr 504; CG 210; ⌗ 304; Met (04725) 606; Police 607; Dr 7345; Ⓗ 8030; Brit Consul (040) 446071.

FACILITIES
Wasser Sport Club Helgolard ☎ 585 Bar, R, M, C (12 ton), D, P, CH, ME, El, Sh, FW, ▣, V; **Südhafen** ☎ 504, D, FW, ME, C (mobile 12 ton), CH, AB, V, R, Bar;
Binnenhafen ☎ 504, P, D, FW, ME, C (mobile 12 ton), CH, AB, V, R, Bar; **Vorhafen** L, AB; **Rickmers** ☎ 585, Gaz;
Town V, R, Bar. ✉; Ⓑ; ⇌ (ferry Cuxhaven or Hamburg); ✈ (services to Bremen or Hamburg).
Ferry UK — Hamburg—Harwich.

HELGOLAND
MEAN SPRING
AND NEAP CURVES

MEAN RANGES	
Springs 2·7m	——
Neaps 1·9m	- - -

Springs occur 3 days
after
New and Full Moon.

GERMANY - HELGOLAND

LAT 54°11′N   LONG 7°54′E

TIMES AND HEIGHTS OF HIGH AND LOW WATERS

YEAR **1991**

TIME ZONE **-0100**
(German Standard Time)
Subtract 1 hour for GMT
For German Summer Time add
ONE hour in non-shaded areas

JANUARY

	TIME	m		TIME	m
1 TU	0621 / 1159 / 1839	0.0 / 2.7 / 0.2	**16** W	0647 / 1221 / 1854	0.1 / 2.5 / 0.2
2 W	0016 / 0716 / 1250 / 1930	2.8 / -0.1 / 2.6 / 0.1	**17** TH	0033 / 0725 / 1258 / 1930	2.7 / 0.1 / 2.5 / 0.1
3 TH	0107 / 0809 / 1342 / 2020	2.9 / -0.2 / 2.6 / 0.1	**18** F	0109 / 0759 / 1333 / 2002	2.8 / 0.1 / 2.6 / 0.1
4 F	0157 / 0858 / 1431 / 2105	2.9 / -0.1 / 2.6 / 0.1	**19** SA	0142 / 0830 / 1404 / 2033	2.8 / 0.1 / 2.6 / 0.1
5 SA	0243 / 0941 / 1515 / 2145	3.0 / -0.1 / 2.6 / 0.2	**20** SU	0212 / 0900 / 1434 / 2105	2.9 / 0.1 / 2.5 / 0.1
6 SU	0324 / 1020 / 1556 / 2224	2.9 / 0.1 / 2.5 / 0.2	**21** M	0244 / 0935 / 1508 / 2141	2.8 / 0.1 / 2.5 / 0.1
7 M ☾	0405 / 1058 / 1638 / 2305	2.9 / 0.2 / 2.5 / 0.3	**22** TU	0321 / 1011 / 1547 / 2217	2.7 / 0.1 / 2.4 / 0.1
8 TU ☽	0450 / 1138 / 1723 / 2351	2.7 / 0.3 / 2.4 / 0.4	**23** W ☽	0401 / 1046 / 1625 / 2257	2.7 / 0.2 / 2.4 / 0.2
9 W	0541 / 1224 / 1815	2.6 / 0.4 / 2.3	**24** TH	0443 / 1125 / 1712 / 2350	2.6 / 0.3 / 2.4 / 0.3
10 TH	0048 / 0641 / 1324 / 1919	0.5 / 2.5 / 0.5 / 2.3	**25** F	0540 / 1225 / 1817	2.5 / 0.4 / 2.3
11 F	0159 / 0752 / 1435 / 2030	0.5 / 2.4 / 0.5 / 2.4	**26** SA	0105 / 0657 / 1346 / 1938	0.4 / 2.4 / 0.4 / 2.4
12 SA	0314 / 0904 / 1545 / 2136	0.5 / 2.4 / 0.5 / 2.5	**27** SU	0234 / 0825 / 1514 / 2101	0.3 / 2.4 / 0.3 / 2.5
13 SU	0422 / 1007 / 1644 / 2230	0.5 / 2.5 / 0.5 / 2.6	**28** M	0400 / 0947 / 1633 / 2215	0.2 / 2.4 / 0.2 / 2.6
14 M	0518 / 1100 / 1733 / 2315	0.3 / 2.5 / 0.4 / 2.7	**29** TU	0515 / 1057 / 1739 / 2317	-0.1 / 2.5 / 0.1 / 2.7
15 TU ●	0605 / 1143 / 1815 / 2356	0.2 / 2.5 / 0.3 / 2.7	**30** W ○	0618 / 1154 / 1834	-0.2 / 2.5 / -0.1
			31 TH	0008 / 0711 / 1242 / 1922	2.8 / -0.3 / 2.5 / -0.1

FEBRUARY

	TIME	m		TIME	m
1 F	0056 / 0758 / 1327 / 2007	2.8 / -0.3 / 2.5 / -0.2	**16** SA	0048 / 0740 / 1311 / 1946	2.7 / -0.2 / 2.5 / -0.2
2 SA	0142 / 0841 / 1410 / 2048	2.9 / -0.2 / 2.6 / -0.2	**17** SU	0119 / 0811 / 1341 / 2017	2.8 / -0.2 / 2.5 / -0.2
3 SU	0223 / 0919 / 1449 / 2124	2.9 / -0.2 / 2.6 / -0.1	**18** M	0150 / 0841 / 1411 / 2049	2.8 / -0.2 / 2.5 / -0.2
4 M	0259 / 0951 / 1523 / 2156	2.8 / -0.1 / 2.5 / -0.1	**19** TU	0223 / 0915 / 1444 / 2125	2.7 / -0.1 / 2.5 / -0.2
5 TU	0333 / 1021 / 1557 / 2228	2.7 / 0.1 / 2.5 / 0.1	**20** W	0301 / 0950 / 1522 / 2201	2.7 / -0.1 / 2.4 / -0.2
6 W ☾	0409 / 1050 / 1632 / 2303	2.6 / 0.1 / 2.4 / 0.2	**21** TH ☽	0340 / 1023 / 1559 / 2238	2.6 / -0.1 / 2.4 / -0.1
7 TH	0448 / 1124 / 1714 / 2348	2.5 / 0.3 / 2.3 / 0.3	**22** F	0422 / 1059 / 1643 / 2329	2.5 / 0.2 / 2.4 / 0.2
8 F	0540 / 1216 / 1813	2.4 / 0.5 / 2.2	**23** SA	0518 / 1158 / 1748	2.4 / 0.3 / 2.3
9 SA	0057 / 0652 / 1333 / 1931	0.4 / 2.3 / 0.5 / 2.2	**24** SU	0047 / 0638 / 1326 / 1916	0.2 / 2.2 / 0.3 / 2.3
10 SU	0225 / 0816 / 1500 / 2053	0.5 / 2.2 / 0.5 / 2.3	**25** M	0224 / 0814 / 1504 / 2048	0.2 / 2.2 / 0.3 / 2.4
11 M	0350 / 0936 / 1616 / 2201	0.4 / 2.2 / 0.4 / 2.4	**26** TU	0358 / 0942 / 1628 / 2207	-0.1 / 2.3 / 0.1 / 2.5
12 TU	0456 / 1037 / 1713 / 2253	0.2 / 2.3 / 0.3 / 2.5	**27** W	0512 / 1051 / 1732 / 2309	-0.2 / 2.4 / -0.1 / 2.6
13 W	0547 / 1124 / 1758 / 2335	0.1 / 2.4 / 0.1 / 2.6	**28** TH ○	0609 / 1144 / 1824 / 2357	-0.3 / 2.4 / -0.2 / 2.7
14 TH ●	0629 / 1203 / 1838	-0.1 / 2.4 / -0.1			
15 F	0014 / 0707 / 1238 / 1914	2.7 / -0.2 / 2.5 / -0.1			

MARCH

	TIME	m		TIME	m
1 F	0657 / 1227 / 1908	-0.3 / 2.5 / -0.2	**16** SA ●	0638 / 1208 / 1849	-0.3 / 2.5 / -0.2
2 SA	0040 / 0739 / 1305 / 1949	2.8 / -0.3 / 2.5 / -0.3	**17** SU	0019 / 0712 / 1240 / 1923	2.7 / -0.3 / 2.5 / -0.3
3 SU	0119 / 0816 / 1342 / 2025	2.8 / -0.3 / 2.5 / -0.3	**18** M	0052 / 0744 / 1312 / 1956	2.7 / -0.3 / 2.5 / -0.3
4 M	0156 / 0848 / 1416 / 2057	2.8 / -0.2 / 2.5 / -0.3	**19** TU	0126 / 0817 / 1345 / 2031	2.7 / -0.3 / 2.5 / -0.3
5 TU	0230 / 0917 / 1448 / 2126	2.7 / -0.1 / 2.5 / -0.2	**20** W	0203 / 0852 / 1421 / 2110	2.7 / -0.2 / 2.5 / -0.3
6 W	0302 / 0944 / 1518 / 2155	2.6 / 0.1 / 2.5 / -0.1	**21** TH	0243 / 0930 / 1501 / 2150	2.6 / -0.2 / 2.5 / -0.3
7 TH	0334 / 1009 / 1549 / 2225	2.5 / 0.2 / 2.4 / 0.1	**22** F	0326 / 1007 / 1542 / 2233	2.5 / -0.1 / 2.5 / -0.2
8 F ☾	0407 / 1037 / 1625 / 2304	2.4 / 0.3 / 2.3 / 0.2	**23** SA ☽	0414 / 1049 / 1630 / 2327	2.4 / 0.2 / 2.4 / -0.1
9 SA	0451 / 1122 / 1717	2.2 / 0.4 / 2.2	**24** SU	0514 / 1151 / 1738	2.3 / 0.3 / 2.4
10 SU	0006 / 0558 / 1236 / 1834	0.3 / 2.0 / 0.5 / 2.2	**25** M	0046 / 0635 / 1320 / 1907	0.1 / 2.1 / 0.3 / 2.4
11 M	0135 / 0727 / 1410 / 2004	0.4 / 2.0 / 0.4 / 2.4	**26** TU	0223 / 0809 / 1459 / 2040	0.1 / 2.1 / 0.2 / 2.4
12 TU	0309 / 0856 / 1538 / 2123	0.3 / 2.1 / 0.3 / 2.3	**27** W	0354 / 0934 / 1620 / 2156	-0.2 / 2.2 / 0.1 / 2.6
13 W	0424 / 1007 / 1644 / 2221	0.1 / 2.2 / 0.2 / 2.4	**28** TH	0501 / 1037 / 1718 / 2252	-0.3 / 2.3 / -0.1 / 2.6
14 TH	0517 / 1057 / 1732 / 2305	-0.1 / 2.3 / 0.1 / 2.6	**29** F	0549 / 1123 / 1804 / 2337	-0.3 / 2.4 / -0.2 / 2.7
15 F ○	0600 / 1135 / 1812 / 2344	-0.2 / 2.4 / -0.1 / 2.6	**30** SA ○	0632 / 1203 / 1846	-0.3 / 2.5 / -0.2
			31 SU	0017 / 0712 / 1239 / 1925	2.7 / -0.3 / 2.5 / -0.3

APRIL

	TIME	m		TIME	m
1 M	0055 / 0746 / 1312 / 1959	2.7 / -0.2 / 2.6 / -0.3	**16** TU	0023 / 0713 / 1243 / 1933	2.7 / -0.3 / 2.6 / -0.3
2 TU	0129 / 0816 / 1344 / 2029	2.7 / -0.1 / 2.6 / -0.2	**17** W	0103 / 0752 / 1322 / 2015	2.7 / -0.2 / 2.6 / -0.3
3 W	0202 / 0843 / 1416 / 2059	2.6 / -0.1 / 2.6 / -0.1	**18** TH	0146 / 0834 / 1404 / 2100	2.6 / -0.2 / 2.6 / -0.3
4 TH	0234 / 0910 / 1446 / 2129	2.6 / 0.1 / 2.6 / -0.1	**19** F	0232 / 0916 / 1447 / 2146	2.6 / -0.1 / 2.6 / -0.3
5 F	0306 / 0937 / 1516 / 2200	2.5 / 0.2 / 2.5 / 0.1	**20** SA	0320 / 0959 / 1534 / 2235	2.5 / -0.1 / 2.6 / -0.2
6 SA	0339 / 1005 / 1551 / 2236	2.3 / 0.2 / 2.4 / 0.1	**21** SU ☽	0413 / 1048 / 1628 / 2333	2.3 / 0.2 / 2.5 / -0.1
7 SU	0418 / 1045 / 1637 / 2329	2.1 / 0.3 / 2.3	**22** M	0516 / 1152 / 1737	2.2 / 0.3 / 2.5
8 M	0516 / 1150 / 1746	2.0 / 0.4 / 2.2	**23** TU	0048 / 0633 / 1314 / 1900	0.1 / 2.2 / 0.3 / 2.5
9 TU	0047 / 0638 / 1318 / 1911	0.3 / 2.0 / 0.4 / 2.2	**24** W	0215 / 0758 / 1444 / 2026	0.1 / 2.2 / 0.2 / 2.6
10 W	0218 / 0807 / 1449 / 2034	0.2 / 2.0 / 0.3 / 2.3	**25** TH	0336 / 0914 / 1559 / 2135	-0.1 / 2.3 / 0.1 / 2.6
11 TH	0337 / 0922 / 1600 / 2137	0.1 / 2.2 / 0.2 / 2.5	**26** F	0436 / 1010 / 1652 / 2225	-0.2 / 2.4 / -0.1 / 2.7
12 F	0434 / 1015 / 1652 / 2225	-0.1 / 2.3 / 0.1 / 2.6	**27** SA	0518 / 1052 / 1734 / 2309	-0.2 / 2.5 / -0.1 / 2.7
13 SA	0519 / 1056 / 1735 / 2306	-0.2 / 2.4 / -0.1 / 2.6	**28** SU ○	0558 / 1132 / 1818 / 2352	-0.2 / 2.5 / -0.1 / 2.7
14 SU ●	0559 / 1132 / 1816 / 2345	-0.3 / 2.5 / -0.2 / 2.7	**29** M	0639 / 1212 / 1859	-0.1 / 2.6 / -0.1
15 M	0637 / 1207 / 1854	-0.3 / 2.5 / -0.3	**30** TU	0031 / 0715 / 1246 / 1933	2.7 / -0.1 / 2.7 / -0.1

Chart Datum: 1.76 metres below Normal Null (German reference Level)

20

GERMANY - HELGOLAND

LAT 54°11'N   LONG 7°54'E

TIMES AND HEIGHTS OF HIGH AND LOW WATERS

YEAR **1991**

TIME ZONE -0100
(German Standard Time)
Subtract 1 hour for GMT
For German Summer Time add
ONE hour in non-shaded areas

MAY

Day	Time	m	Time	m	Time	m	Time	m
1 W	0105	2.7	0745	0.1	1317	2.7	2005	-0.1
2 TH	0130	2.6	0813	0.1	1349	2.7	2036	-0.1
3 F	0210	2.5	0843	0.1	1421	2.6	2109	-0.1
4 SA	0244	2.4	0913	0.2	1454	2.6	2142	0.1
5 SU	0319	2.3	0945	0.2	1529	2.5	2218	0.1
6 M	0358	2.2	1022	0.3	1612	2.5	2303	0.2
7 TU ☾	0447	2.2	1115	0.4	1708	2.4		
8 W	0005	0.3	0553	2.1	1228	0.4	1819	2.4
9 TH	0121	0.2	0711	2.1	1350	0.4	1935	2.4
10 F	0238	0.1	0824	2.2	1504	0.2	2042	2.5
11 SA	0340	-0.1	0923	2.3	1602	0.1	2137	2.6
12 SU	0430	-0.2	1011	2.5	1653	-0.1	2226	2.6
13 M	0517	-0.2	1054	2.6	1741	-0.1	2313	2.7
14 TU ●	0601	-0.2	1136	2.7	1827	-0.2	2358	2.7
15 W	0645	-0.2	1218	2.7	1913	-0.3		
16 TH	0045	2.7	0731	-0.2	1304	2.7	2003	-0.3
17 F	0135	2.6	0821	-0.2	1352	2.7	2055	-0.3
18 SA	0226	2.5	0909	-0.1	1440	2.7	2145	-0.3
19 SU	0316	2.5	0955	-0.1	1530	2.7	2236	-0.2
20 M ☽	0410	2.4	1046	0.1	1626	2.7	2332	-0.1
21 TU	0512	2.3	1146	0.3	1730	2.7		
22 W	0037	0.1	0619	2.3	1256	0.3	1842	2.7
23 TH	0149	0.1	0731	2.3	1412	0.3	1955	2.6
24 F	0259	0.1	0838	2.4	1522	0.2	2100	2.6
25 SA	0356	-0.1	0933	2.4	1616	0.1	2152	2.6
26 SU	0441	-0.1	1018	2.5	1702	0.1	2239	2.6
27 M	0523	0.1	1101	2.6	1748	0.1	2326	2.6
28 TU ○	0607	0.1	1144	2.7	1834	0.1		
29 W	0008	2.6	0647	0.2	1223	2.7	1912	0.1
30 TH	0044	2.6	0721	0.2	1256	2.8	1946	0.1
31 F	0118	2.6	0752	0.1	1329	2.7	2019	-0.1

JUNE

Day	Time	m	Time	m	Time	m	Time	m
1 SA	0152	2.5	0824	0.1	1403	2.7	2053	0.1
2 SU	0227	2.5	0856	0.2	1437	2.7	2126	0.1
3 M	0303	2.4	0929	0.2	1512	2.7	2203	0.1
4 TU ☽	0341	2.4	1006	0.2	1552	2.6	2243	0.2
5 W ☾	0423	2.3	1046	0.3	1637	2.6	2330	0.2
6 TH	0513	2.3	1144	0.4	1732	2.5		
7 F	0028	2.2	0614	2.2	1252	0.3	1837	2.5
8 SA	0134	0.1	0722	2.3	1403	0.3	1945	2.5
9 SU	0240	0.1	0826	2.4	1509	0.2	2049	2.6
10 M	0341	0.1	0925	2.5	1611	0.1	2150	2.7
11 TU	0438	0.1	1018	2.5	1710	0.1	2248	2.7
12 W ●	0534	-0.1	1112	2.7	1807	-0.1	2342	2.7
13 TH ○	0626	-0.1	1200	2.8	1901	-0.2		
14 F	0034	2.7	0719	-0.1	1252	2.8	1956	-0.3
15 SA	0127	2.6	0812	-0.2	1344	2.8	2050	-0.3
16 SU	0220	2.6	0902	-0.1	1435	2.9	2141	-0.3
17 M	0310	2.5	0948	-0.1	1523	2.9	2228	-0.2
18 TU	0359	2.5	1035	0.1	1614	2.8	2317	-0.1
19 W ☽	0452	2.4	1126	0.2	1709	2.8		
20 TH	0009	0.1	0549	2.4	1223	0.3	1808	2.7
21 F	0104	0.2	0647	2.4	1324	0.3	1910	2.6
22 SA	0205	0.2	0748	2.4	1431	0.3	2015	2.6
23 SU	0306	0.2	0849	2.5	1535	0.3	2116	2.6
24 M	0403	0.2	0945	2.6	1632	0.3	2212	2.6
25 TU	0454	0.3	1034	2.6	1725	0.2	2303	2.6
26 W	0541	0.3	1120	2.7	1813	0.1	2348	2.6
27 TH ○	0624	0.2	1202	2.7	1855	0.1		
28 F	0027	2.6	0702	0.1	1240	2.8	1931	0.1
29 SA	0102	2.5	0737	0.1	1315	2.8	2005	-0.1
30 SU	0138	2.5	0809	0.1	1349	2.8	2037	0.1

JULY

Day	Time	m	Time	m	Time	m	Time	m
1 M	0211	2.5	0841	0.1	1420	2.8	2109	0.1
2 TU	0244	2.5	0913	0.2	1453	2.8	2144	0.1
3 W	0319	2.5	0949	0.2	1530	2.8	2222	0.1
4 TH	0358	2.4	1027	0.2	1610	2.7	2300	0.1
5 F ☾	0438	2.4	1109	0.3	1653	2.6	2342	0.2
6 SA	0525	2.4	1201	0.3	1746	2.5		
7 SU	0036	0.2	0625	2.4	1308	0.3	1854	2.4
8 M	0145	0.3	0734	2.4	1424	0.3	2009	2.5
9 TU	0259	0.3	0847	2.5	1539	0.2	2123	2.6
10 W	0411	0.2	0955	2.6	1651	0.1	2231	2.6
11 TH ●	0518	0.1	1056	2.7	1756	-0.1	2332	2.6
12 F ○	0616	0.1	1151	2.8	1855	-0.2		
13 SA	0027	2.7	0710	-0.1	1243	2.9	1949	-0.3
14 SU	0118	2.6	0801	-0.2	1335	2.9	2040	-0.3
15 M	0208	2.6	0850	-0.2	1423	3.0	2127	-0.2
16 TU	0254	2.6	0933	-0.1	1507	3.0	2208	-0.2
17 W	0336	2.6	1013	0.1	1550	2.9	2248	0.1
18 TH ☽	0420	2.5	1055	0.1	1635	2.8	2328	0.2
19 F	0505	2.5	1139	0.2	1724	2.7		
20 SA	0010	0.3	0554	2.4	1229	0.3	1819	2.6
21 SU	0103	0.4	0652	2.4	1335	0.4	1925	2.5
22 M	0211	0.5	0801	2.4	1452	0.4	2038	2.4
23 TU	0324	0.4	0911	2.5	1605	0.4	2147	2.5
24 W	0429	0.4	1011	2.6	1706	0.3	2244	2.5
25 TH ●	0521	0.3	1100	2.7	1755	0.1	2331	2.5
26 F ○	0606	0.2	1143	2.7	1838	0.1		
27 SA	0010	2.5	0646	0.1	1222	2.7	1915	-0.1
28 SU	0046	2.7	0722	0.1	1258	2.8	1948	-0.1
29 M	0120	2.6	0754	0.1	1330	2.8	2018	-0.1
30 TU	0151	2.6	0823	0.1	1359	2.9	2047	0.1
31 W	0219	2.6	0853	0.1	1429	2.8	2119	0.1

AUGUST

Day	Time	m	Time	m	Time	m	Time	m
1 TH	0252	2.5	0928	0.1	1505	2.8	2156	0.1
2 F	0330	2.5	1005	0.1	1544	2.7	2231	0.1
3 SA ☾	0407	2.5	1040	0.2	1622	2.7	2304	0.2
4 SU	0446	2.5	1124	0.3	1710	2.6	2352	0.4
5 M	0541	2.4	1229	0.4	1818	2.5		
6 TU	0105	0.4	0656	2.4	1355	0.3	1943	2.4
7 W	0234	0.5	0821	2.5	1524	0.2	2109	2.5
8 TH	0358	0.3	0941	2.6	1644	0.1	2224	2.5
9 F	0509	0.2	1048	2.7	1750	-0.1	2326	2.6
10 SA ●	0608	0.1	1143	2.9	1846	-0.2		
11 SU ○	0018	2.7	0659	-0.1	1233	3.0	1936	-0.2
12 M	0104	2.7	0746	-0.1	1319	3.0	2021	-0.2
13 TU	0147	2.7	0830	-0.1	1403	3.0	2102	-0.2
14 W	0228	2.7	0909	-0.1	1442	2.9	2138	-0.1
15 TH	0306	2.6	0944	-0.1	1519	2.9	2211	0.1
16 F	0342	2.6	1019	0.1	1558	2.7	2243	0.3
17 SA ☽	0420	2.5	1055	0.2	1640	2.6	2317	0.4
18 SU	0502	2.5	1138	0.4	1729	2.5		
19 M	0004	0.6	0556	2.4	1241	0.5	1835	2.3
20 TU	0115	0.6	0710	2.4	1406	0.5	1958	2.3
21 W	0242	0.6	0834	2.4	1535	0.4	2119	2.3
22 TH	0402	0.5	0945	2.5	1645	0.3	2224	2.4
23 F	0501	0.4	1039	2.6	1734	0.2	2311	2.5
24 SA	0545	0.3	1120	2.7	1814	0.1	2349	2.5
25 SU ○	0624	0.2	1158	2.8	1851	-0.1		
26 M	0023	2.6	0659	0.1	1233	2.8	1923	-0.1
27 TU	0055	2.6	0731	0.1	1305	2.8	1952	-0.1
28 W	0124	2.6	0800	0.1	1334	2.9	2020	0.1
29 TH	0152	2.7	0830	0.1	1405	2.8	2051	0.1
30 F	0224	2.6	0905	0.1	1440	2.8	2127	0.2
31 SA	0301	2.6	0942	0.1	1519	2.7	2202	0.2

Chart Datum: 1.76 metres below Normal Null (German reference Level)

GERMANY - HELGOLAND

LAT 54°11′N   LONG 7°54′E

TIMES AND HEIGHTS OF HIGH AND LOW WATERS

YEAR **1991**

TIME ZONE -0100
(German Standard Time)
Subtract 1 hour for GMT
For German Summer Time add
ONE hour in non-shaded areas

SEPTEMBER

	TIME	m		TIME	m
1 SU ☾	0339 1019 1600 2237	2.6 0.2 2.6 0.3	**16** M	0417 1057 1646 2313	2.5 0.4 2.4 0.7
2 M	0419 1103 1650 2326	2.6 0.3 2.5 0.5	**17** TU	0508 1155 1748	2.4 0.6 2.2
3 TU	0516 1211 1801	2.5 0.4 2.4	**18** W	0021 0620 1318 1913	0.7 2.4 0.6 2.2
4 W	0045 0636 1344 1933	0.5 2.5 0.4 2.4	**19** TH	0152 0749 1451 2042	0.7 2.4 0.5 2.2
5 TH	0222 0810 1521 2105	0.5 2.5 0.2 2.4	**20** F	0323 0910 1610 2154	0.5 2.5 0.4 2.4
6 F	0352 0933 1640 2219	0.4 2.7 0.1 2.5	**21** SA	0430 1008 1702 2243	0.5 2.6 0.3 2.5
7 SA	0501 1039 1740 2315	0.2 2.8 -0.1 2.6	**22** SU	0515 1049 1741 2319	0.4 2.7 0.1 2.6
8 SU ●	0555 1131 1829	0.1 2.9 -0.1	**23** M ○	0553 1125 1816 2351	0.2 2.8 0.1 2.6
9 M	0001 0643 1216 1914	2.7 0.1 3.0 -0.1	**24** TU	0629 1201 1849	0.1 2.8 0.1
10 TU	0042 0726 1258 1954	2.7 -0.1 3.0 -0.1	**25** W	0022 0702 1234 1920	2.7 0.1 2.8 0.1
11 W	0121 0805 1337 2030	2.7 -0.1 3.0 0.1	**26** TH	0054 0735 1308 1951	2.7 0.1 2.8 0.2
12 TH	0158 0841 1414 2102	2.8 -0.1 2.9 0.2	**27** F	0125 0808 1343 2024	2.7 0.1 2.9 0.2
13 F	0233 0913 1449 2132	2.7 0.1 2.8 0.3	**28** SA	0159 0845 1421 2101	2.8 0.2 2.8 0.3
14 SA	0305 0944 1524 2200	2.7 0.2 2.7 0.4	**29** SU	0237 0925 1502 2140	2.7 0.2 2.7 0.3
15 SU ☽	0339 1017 1602 2231	2.6 0.3 2.5 0.5	**30** M	0318 1007 1548 2221	2.7 0.2 2.6 0.4

OCTOBER

	TIME	m		TIME	m
1 TU ☾	0404 1057 1644 2317	2.6 0.3 2.5 0.6	**16** W	0429 1116 1708 2334	2.5 0.6 2.2 0.8
2 W	0506 1208 1758	2.6 0.4 2.4	**17** TH	0534 1227 1824	2.4 0.7 2.2
3 TH	0037 0629 1340 1929	0.6 2.6 0.4 2.3	**18** F	0057 0656 1355 1950	0.8 2.4 0.6 2.2
4 F	0215 0803 1515 2059	0.6 2.6 0.3 2.4	**19** SA	0227 0818 1516 2106	0.7 2.5 0.5 2.4
5 SA	0343 0924 1629 2207	0.5 2.8 0.2 2.6	**20** SU	0340 0922 1614 2159	0.5 2.6 0.4 2.5
6 SU	0447 1024 1720 2256	0.3 2.9 0.1 2.6	**21** M	0432 1008 1656 2238	0.5 2.7 0.2 2.6
7 M ●	0534 1111 1741 2337	0.2 2.9 0.1 2.7	**22** TU	0513 1047 1734 2313	0.3 2.8 0.2 2.6
8 TU	0618 1154 1844	0.2 2.9 0.1	**23** W ○	0552 1125 1811 2348	0.2 2.8 0.2 2.7
9 W	0016 0700 1234 1923	2.8 0.1 2.9 0.2	**24** TH	0631 1204 1846	0.2 2.8 0.2
10 TH	0053 0737 1311 1956	2.8 0.2 2.9 0.3	**25** F	0024 0709 1243 1923	2.8 0.2 2.9 0.3
11 F	0128 0811 1348 2026	2.9 0.2 2.9 0.4	**26** SA	0102 0749 1325 2004	2.9 0.2 2.8 0.3
12 SA	0202 0832 1422 2056	2.9 0.3 2.8 0.4	**27** SU	0141 0832 1409 2045	2.9 0.2 2.8 0.3
13 SU	0234 0915 1456 2125	2.8 0.3 2.7 0.5	**28** M	0222 0916 1453 2127	2.9 0.2 2.7 0.4
14 M	0306 0948 1531 2155	2.7 0.4 2.5 0.5	**29** TU	0307 1003 1543 2214	2.8 0.2 2.6 0.4
15 TU ☽	0342 1026 1613 2235	2.6 0.3 2.3 0.6	**30** W ☾	0358 1057 1642 2313	2.7 0.3 2.5 0.6
			31 TH	0502 1206 1755	2.7 0.4 2.4

NOVEMBER

	TIME	m		TIME	m
1 F	0029 0622 1330 1918	0.7 2.7 0.5 2.4	**16** SA	0000 0559 1251 1847	0.8 2.5 0.6 2.3
2 SA	0158 0748 1455 2039	0.6 2.8 0.4 2.5	**17** SU	0119 0713 1406 2000	0.8 2.5 0.5 2.4
3 SU	0320 0903 1603 2142	0.5 2.8 0.3 2.6	**18** M	0235 0822 1512 2102	0.7 2.6 0.4 2.5
4 M	0421 1000 1650 2228	0.4 2.9 0.2 2.7	**19** TU	0337 0918 1604 2151	0.6 2.7 0.4 2.6
5 TU	0506 1045 1731 2309	0.4 2.9 0.3 2.7	**20** W	0428 1006 1650 2235	0.4 2.7 0.3 2.7
6 F ●	0550 1130 1813 2350	0.3 2.9 0.3 2.8	**21** TH ○	0515 1052 1735 2316	0.3 2.8 0.3 2.8
7 TH	0634 1212 1852	0.3 2.9 0.4	**22** F	0601 1138 1819 2358	0.3 2.8 0.3 2.9
8 F	0028 0713 1250 1926	2.9 0.3 2.9 0.5	**23** SA	0647 1224 1903	0.2 2.8 0.3
9 SA	0102 0747 1325 1956	2.9 0.3 2.8 0.5	**24** SU	0043 0736 1313 1952	2.9 0.2 2.8 0.3
10 SU	0136 0820 1359 2027	2.9 0.3 2.7 0.5	**25** M	0130 0826 1403 2038	2.9 0.1 2.7 0.3
11 M	0210 0853 1433 2058	2.9 0.4 2.6 0.5	**26** TU	0216 0914 1450 2122	2.9 0.1 2.7 0.3
12 TU	0243 0926 1508 2130	2.8 0.4 2.5 0.5	**27** W	0302 1001 1540 2209	2.9 0.2 2.6 0.4
13 W	0318 1002 1547 2206	2.7 0.4 2.4 0.6	**28** TH ☾	0353 1053 1636 2305	2.9 0.3 2.5 0.5
14 TH ☽	0400 1044 1634 2254	2.6 0.5 2.3 0.7	**29** F	0454 1154 1740	2.9 0.4 2.5
15 F	0452 1140 1734	2.6 0.6 2.3	**30** SA	0012 0603 1302 1850	0.6 2.8 0.5 2.5

DECEMBER

	TIME	m		TIME	m
1 SU	0126 0717 1415 2001	0.6 2.8 0.4 2.5	**16** M	0012 0606 1254 1849	0.7 2.5 0.5 2.3
2 M	0240 0827 1520 2104	0.5 2.7 0.4 2.5	**17** TU	0124 0716 1402 1957	0.6 2.5 0.5 2.4
3 TU	0344 0927 1614 2157	0.5 2.7 0.4 2.6	**18** W	0236 0824 1508 2100	0.6 2.6 0.4 2.6
4 W	0437 1019 1700 2243	0.4 2.8 0.4 2.7	**19** TH	0342 0926 1609 2158	0.5 2.7 0.4 2.7
5 TH	0525 1108 1745 2328	0.4 2.8 0.5 2.8	**20** F	0442 1025 1707 2250	0.4 2.7 0.3 2.8
6 F ●	0612 1153 1828	0.4 2.8 0.5	**21** SA ○	0540 1119 1800 2340	0.3 2.7 0.3 2.8
7 SA	0008 0654 1231 1903	2.9 0.4 2.8 0.5	**22** SU	0634 1211 1852	0.1 2.7 0.2
8 SU	0043 0730 1306 1935	2.9 0.3 2.7 0.4	**23** M	0030 0728 1303 1943	2.9 0.1 2.7 0.2
9 M	0117 0804 1341 2007	2.9 0.3 2.6 0.4	**24** TU	0122 0821 1356 2033	2.9 -0.1 2.7 0.2
10 TU	0152 0837 1416 2039	2.9 0.3 2.6 0.4	**25** W	0212 0910 1445 2118	3.0 -0.1 2.7 0.2
11 W	0225 0908 1449 2111	2.8 0.3 2.5 0.4	**26** TH	0257 0955 1531 2201	3.0 0.1 2.6 0.3
12 TH	0258 0941 1524 2144	2.8 0.4 2.5 0.5	**27** F	0342 1040 1619 2249	3.0 0.2 2.6 0.3
13 F	0334 1018 1602 2223	2.7 0.4 2.4 0.5	**28** SA ☾	0434 1129 1712 2342	2.9 0.3 2.5 0.4
14 SA	0416 1100 1647 2311	2.7 0.5 2.4 0.6	**29** SU	0530 1221 1808	2.8 0.4 2.5
15 SU	0506 1151 1743	2.6 0.5 2.3	**30** M	0041 0632 1321 1910	0.5 2.7 0.4 2.4
			31 TU	0149 0740 1428 2017	0.5 2.6 0.5 2.4

Chart Datum: 1.76 metres below Normal Null (German reference Level)

SYLT   10-20-22
Schleswig-Holstein

CHARTS
Admiralty 3767; German D107, D108, 3013 Sheet 4 (List)
TIDES
Dover +0110; ML 1.8; Duration 0540; Zone −0100

Standard Port HELGOLAND (⟵)

Times				Height (metres)			
HW		LW		MHWS	MHWN	MLWN	MLWS
0100	0600	0100	0800	2.7	2.3	0.4	0.0
1300	1800	1300	2000				

Differences LIST

+0248	+0248	+0206	+0206	−0.8	−0.6	−0.2	0.0

HÖRNUM

+0220	+0220	+0137	+0137	−0.5	−0.4	−0.2	0.0

AMRUM-HAFEN

+0137	+0137	+0129	+0129	+0.2	+0.2	0.0	0.0

The island of Sylt is about 20M long, has its capital
Westerland in the centre, Hornum in the S and List in the
N. It is connected to the mainland by the
Hindenburgdamm.

SHELTER
HÖRNUM Good in the small harbour, approx 370m × 90m,
protected by outer mole on the S side and by two inner
moles. Yachts secure on the N side. Good anchorage in
Hörnum Reede in W and N winds and in Hörnumtief in E
and S winds.
LIST The small harbour is sheltered except in NE to E
winds. Entrance is 25m wide and harbour 3m deep.

There are two other harbours; Rantum and Munkmarsch
which both dry; access HW∓3.

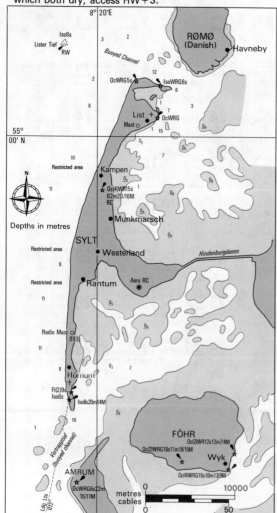

NAVIGATION
HÖRNUM Waypoint Westvortrapptief (safe water) buoy, Oc
4s, 54°35' N 08°11'.3E, 222°/042° from/to Norddorf Lt
(Amrum), 6.7M. Access through Vortrapptief buoyed
channel (see below) inside drying banks. In strong W
winds the sea breaks on off-lying banks and in the
channel. Keep mid-channel in harbour entrance,
approached from NE. Access at all tides. Large sections
of the area to landward of Sylt are nature reserves and
landing prohibited.
LIST Waypoint Lister Tief safe water buoy, Iso 8s,
55°05'.37N 08°16'.87E, 298°/118° from/to List West Lt,
4.7M. Lister Tief (see 10.20.5) is well marked. In strong W
or NW winds expect a big swell on the bar (depth 4m) on
the ebb, which sets on to Salzsand. NE quay is open
construction and not suitable for yachts. Channel buoys
through roadstead lead to harbour.Access at all tides, but
beware strong tidal streams across entrance.

LIGHTS AND MARKS
HÖRNUM Conspic radio mast 3M N of harbour. Follow
W041°-043° sector of Norddorf Lt (Oc WRG 6s) to line of
Hörnum Ldg Lts 012°, both Iso 8s. N pier head FG, vis
024°-260°, S pier head FR. Outer mole head FR (mole
floodlit).
LIST Kampen Lt, List West Lt, List Ost Lt and Romo
church are prominent. For Lts see 10.20.4. N mole head
FG, vis 218°-038°. S mole head FR, vis 218°-353°.

RADIO TELEPHONE
None.

TELEPHONE (04654)
HÖRNUM Hr Mr 1027, Dr 1016, Ⓗ (04651) 841.
LIST Hr Mr 374; Police 510 Ⓗ (04651) 841, ⌗ 413.

FACILITIES
HÖRNUM **Sylter YC** ☎ 274, AB, Bar, AC, FW, ▣; **Town**
V, R, Bar, ME, ✉; Ⓑ.
LIST **Harbour** SC, AB, FW, ⌗, C (3½ ton), Slip;
Village V, R, Bar, P and D (cans); Ferry to Römö
(Denmark).
WESTERLAND **HB Jensen** ☎ 7017, Gaz; CG 85199 Police
7047; **Town** V, R, Bar, P and D (cans), ⌗, ✉; Ⓑ; ⇌;
✈.

MINOR HARBOURS AND ANCHORAGES 10.20.23

EMDEN, Ostfriesland, 53°21′N, 7°12′E, Zone −0100. Admty chart 3510, German D91 3012 Sheet 4. HW +0022 on Dover (GMT), +0040 on Helgoland (zone −0100); HW height +0.8m on Helgoland; ML 1.9m. Ldg Lts 088°, both Oc 5s 12M, lead to Vorhafen entrance, marked by FR and FG Lts. Proceed up Aussenhafen to yacht harbour on E side before Nesserland Lock. Good shelter except in SW winds. If no room there, go through lock into inner harbour, and round to Jarssumer Hafen in SE corner of port. Locks operate 0600-2200 (0800-2000 Sundays) LT. Sound NV (−· ···−) for opening. Jarssumer Hafen is also approached through Grosse Seeschleuse (H24). Both lock-keepers on VHF Ch 13 (H24). Facilities: Hr Mr 29034 Weather 21458; Yacht Hafen ☎ 26020 FW; ⊞ ☎ 20371; all facilities in city (1M). Ferry to Borkum.

GREETSIEL Niedersachsen, 53°30′N, 7°06′E, Zone−0100 Admty charts 3509, 3761. German D89. HW −0040 on Dover (GMT), −0010 on Helgoland (zone−0100); ML2.6m. Watt channel marked by perches, leads 2M SE over flats of Leysand. Breakwater extends a mile NNW from coast to near Greetsiel Buoy. Harbour access HW+1½. Yachts berth in Yacht Hr on pontoons. Harbour dries. A canal connects Greetsiel to Emden. There are a few facilities. **Village** R, V, ⇌, ⊞ ☎ (04931) 2764. Hr Mr ☎ (04926) 760.

JUIST, Niedersachsen, 53°41′N, 7°00′E, Zone −0100. Admty chart 3509, German D90. HW −0105 on Dover (GMT), −0035 on Helgoland (zone −0100); HW height +0.1 on Helgoland (latter two readings taken at Memmert). Entrance through narrow channel running N in the centre of the S side of island, marked by withies to the W. To the W of these is the long (5 ca) landing pier. West Beacon, on Haakdünen at W end of island, Juist water tower (conspic) in centre and East Beacon, 1M from E end of island. Aero Lt Fl W 5s 14m (occas) at the airfield. There is no yacht harbour. Anchor a cable S of W part of town ½M E of Steamer Pier or at E end of island. Facilities: Hr Mr ☎ 724; ⊞ ☎ 351; Harbour FW, Slip, C; villages of Oosdorp, Westdorp and Loog in centre of island have limited facilities, V, R, Bar, Gaz. Train runs from Juist pier to Oosdorp. Ferry − Norddeich.

NORDDEICH, Niedersachsen, 53°37′N, 7°09′E, Zone −0100, Admty charts 3509, 3761, 1405, German D3014. HW −0030 on Dover (GMT), −0020 on Helgoland (zone −0100); HW height +0.2m on Helgoland. See 10.20.9. Very good shelter in harbour, reached by channel 50m wide, 2m deep and over 1M long between two training walls which cover at HW and are marked by stakes. Hr divided by central mole; yachts berth in West Hr. Lts on W training wall head FG 8m 4M, vis 021°−327°. On E training wall head FR 8m 4M, vis 327°−237°. Ldg Lts 144°, Front, Iso WR 6s 6m 6/4M, Rear, 140m from front, Iso W 6s 9m 6M synchronised. Ldg Lts 350°, Front Iso WR 3s 5m 6/4M, Rear, 95m from front, Iso W 3s 8m 6M. Ldg Lts 170°, Front Iso W 3s 12m 10M, Rear, 420m from front, Iso W 3s 23m 10M, synchronised. Facilities: Hr Mr ☎ 8060; **Fuel Stn** ☎ 2721; ⊞ ☎ 2735; **YC** ☎ 3560; **Fritz H. Venske** CH, German Chart Agent; **M. Wagner** Gaz; **Town** AB, ⑧, Bar, C (5 ton), D, Dr, FW, ✉, R, ⇌, Slip, V, Gaz. Ferry to Juist and Norderney.

BALTRUM, Niedersachsen, 53°43′N, 7°23′E, Zone −0100. Admty chart 3761, German D3012. HW −0040 on Dover (GMT), −0005 on Helgoland (zone −0100); HW height +0.4m on Helgoland (latter two readings taken at Langeoog Ostmole). Shelter is good except in SW winds. Without local knowledge, the approach via Wichter Ee Seegat is not recommended. Entrance channel marked by withies to be left approx 10m to the W. Harbour partly dries. Yacht moorings in the Bootshafen at the E end of harbour. Lt at the groyne head Oc WRG 6s 7m 6/3M G082.5°-098°, W098°-103°, R103°-082.5°. Facilities: Hr Mr ☎ (04939) 448; **Harbour** AB, FW: **Baltrumer Bootsclub YC; Village** (¼M NNE) V, R, Bar. There is no fuel. Ferry from Nessmersiel.

NESSMERSIEL, Niedersachsen, 53°41′N, 7°22′E, Zone −0100. Admty chart 3761, German D3012, D89; HW −0040 on Dover (GMT), −0020 on Helgoland (zone −0100); HW height −0.2m on Helgoland. Good shelter in all weathers. Approach down the Nessmersieler Balje, channel marked by stbd buoys and beacons leading to end of Leitdamm. End of Leitdamm has Bn, Oc W,

which, together with other unlit Bns mark the course of the Leitdamm on W; withies mark the E side of channel. Leitdamm covers at HW. Beyond ferry berth is a Yachthafen (1½M); secure to catamarans S of Ferry Quay. Harbour dries (2m at HW). Facilities: Hr Mr ☎ 2981; ⊞ ☎ 2735; **Nordsee Yachtclub Nessmersiel**; no supplies except FW: **Village** (1M to S) has limited facilities. Ferry to Baltrum.

BENSERSIEL, Niedersachsen, 53°41′N, 7°35′E, Zone −0100, Admty chart 1875, German D3012. HW −0024 on Dover (GMT), +0005 on Helgoland (zone −0100); HW height +0.4m on Helgoland. Very good shelter in the yacht harbour (dries). Entrance channel from Rute 1.5M between training walls with depth of 1.5m. Walls submerge at HW. Yacht Hr to SW just before harbour ent (2m). Yachts can also berth in the SW side of main hr. Lights: E training wall head Oc WRG 6s 6m 5/2M G110°−119°, W119°−121°, R121°−110°. W mole head FG, E mole head FR. Ldg Lts 138° Front Iso W 6s 7m 9M (intens on line), Rear, 167m from front, Iso W 6s 11m 9M, synchronised with front. Facilities: Hr Mr ☎ (04971) 2502, ⊞ ☎ (04421) 42031, Slip, C (8 ton), D (on E pier), FW, P (from garage); **Harle-Yachtbau** ☎ (04971) 1760, El, ME, Sh; **Kerkau** ☎ 2401, Gaz; **Town** ⑧, Bar, ✉, R, ⇌, V, Gaz. Ferry to Langeoog.

NEUHARLINGERSIEL, Niedersachsen, 53°42′N, 7°42′E, Zone −0100. Admty chart 1875, German D3012. HW 0000 on Dover (GMT), +0015 on Helgoland (zone −0100); HW height +0.5m on Helgoland. Approach channel well marked from Baklegde N end of Leitdamm, Oc 6s. Beware strong tidal streams across the entrance. Channel runs close E of Leitdamm which is marked by stakes with downturned brooms. It covers at HW. Yachts lie in NE corner of harbour; where there are numerous poles. Visitors berths very limited. Facilities: Hr Mr (04974) 289 **Quay** FW, D; **Village** V, R, Bar. Very picturesque place. Ferry to Spiekeroog (35 mins).

SPIEKEROOG, Niedersachsen, 53°45′N, 7°41′E, Zone −0100, Admty chart 3761, 1875, German D3015. HW −0008 on Dover (GMT), −0007 on Helgoland (zone −0100); HW height +0.5m on Helgoland; ML 1.3m; Duration 0555. See 10.20.12. Good shelter except in winds from S to SW when heavy swell builds up. Small harbour which dries. There is a harbour on S side of Spiekeroog used by ferries and yachts. Lt on rectangular structure FR 6m 4M, vis 197°−114°. There are no facilities except a 5 ton crane but the town can be reached by light railway. Hr Mr ☎ (04976) 217. Ferry from Nieuharlingersiel.

HARLESIEL , Niedersachsen, 53°43′N, 7°49′E; zone −0100. Admty chart 3369, 3368; German D3012. HW −0100 on Dover (GMT), −0005 on Helgoland (zone −0100) HW height +0.5m on Helgoland. Excellent shelter S of lock. Lock opens approx HW∓1. Yachts lie at pontoons to W by village or at BY to E after passing through lock on W side of 'pumping barrier'. River navigable up to Carolinensiel. Air and ferry to Wangerooge. Facilities: Hr Mr ☎ (04464) 472; ⊞ ≢ 249; **YC Harle** ☎ (04464) 1473; **Harbour** BY, C, V, R, Slip, P, D, FW **Town** El, ME, Gaz, ✉, V.

WANGERSIEL, Niedersachsen, (also known as Horumersiel) 53°41′N, 8°01′E, Zone −0100. Admty chart 3369, German D3011. HW −0100 on Dover (GMT), −0030 on Wilhelmshaven (zone −0100); HW height −0.6m on Wilhelmshaven; ML 3.3m. From buoy W3 (G conical) besom perches mark the N side of the channel t͟ the harbour. Best water 10 to 20m from perches. Dept͟ ent, 1.3m. Channel keeps shifting especially at H͟ Boats drawing 1.5m can cross the bar HW∓2½. N͟ harbour dries. Secure on N quay. In NW corner ͟ and FW. Facilities: Hr Mr ☎ 238. No fuel. At ͟ (¼M) V, R, Bar.

DANGAST, Niedersachsen, 53°27′N, 8°0͟ Admty chart 3369, German D3011. HW ͟ (GMT), −0007 on Helgoland (zone − ͟ Wilhelmshaven in the wide bay of ͟ mostly dries: the Hr dries. Ent vi͟ (0.5m at LWS) leading SW fro͟ NW side by stakes. There ar͟ Lt in the middle of Jadebu͟ before lock into Dangast͟ Very limited but usual f͟ seaside town of Dan͟

MINOR HARBOURS *continued*

OTTERNDORF , Niedersachsen, 53°49′ N, 8°54′ E, Zone −0100, Admty charts 3261, 3262; German D3010 Sheet 5. HW +0100 on Dover (GMT), +0120 on Helgoland (zone −0100); HW height +0.5 on Helgoland; ML 2.9m; Duration 0525. Channel from sea (0.6m) divides and yachts can take the W branch to Kutherhafen (0.9m) or go up the canal to E, pass through lock then turn sharp S, then W to yacht harbour. Entrance marked by the Buoy on N side. Ldg Lts 245° 30′, Front Iso W94s 23m 18/10M; W Tr, R bands, R conical roof; Vis G to S of 091° W to N or 091°; Rear Iso W4s 52 m 21 M; W Tr R bands, R conical roof. Lockmaster ☎ (04751) 2190. **Yacht harbour** ☎ 2213 C, AC, FW, Bar. **Town** (3km) ME, Gaz, V, PO. Hr Mr (04926) 760. The canal from Ottendorf goes to Bederkesa and Bremerhaven.

BÜSUM, Schleswig Holstein, 54°07′ N, 8°51′ E, Zone −0100, Admty charts 1875, 3767, German D105, 3013 Sheet 16. HW +0036 on Dover (GMT), +0051 on Helgoland (zone −0100); HW height +0.1m on Helgoland; ML 1.8m; Duration 0625. Very good shelter. Two fairways, Suderpiep and Norderpiep, marked by R and G buoys, each approx 17M, lead into the port. Beware strong tidal streams across ent and sudden winds over the moles. Yachts pass through lock at N of Vorhafen, turn to SE into Yacht harbour. Lock controlled by R and G Lts and manned H24. Signal for opening, one long blast on entering approach chan; two long blasts on reaching lock if not already open. VHF Ch 11 16; Call *Büsum Port*. Facilities: (04834) Hr Mr ☎ 2183; CG ☎ 2025; ⌗ ☎ 2376; Dr ☎ 2088; **Büsum YC** ☎ 2997; **Yacht harbour** AB, AC, El, FW, M, ME, C, P, D, ⊡**Town** CH, V, R, Bar, ✉, ⑧, ⇌, Ⓗ ✈ (Hamburg).

TÖNNING, Schleswig Holstein, 54°19′ N, 8°57′ E, Zone −0100; Admty chart 3767, German D104, D3013 Sheet 18. HW +0216 on Dover (GMT), +0246 on Helgoland (zone −0100); HW height +0.5m on Helgoland; ML 2.7m. Eiderdamm lock, 5M seawards, operates H24. R. Eider with the Gieselau Kanal connects Tonning with the Kiel Canal (see 10.20.20). VHF Ch 14 16; N mole Oc(2)R 12s, S mole Oc G 6s. Above the dam, Die Eider is tidal, depending on operation of sluices HW+3 to HW+ ½ (beware strong currents). Secure on S quay of middle section of harbour. If proceeding up river, bridge clearance 5.6m, opened on request Mon-Sat 0600 to sunset. Facilities: (04861) Hr Mr ☎ 1400; **Tönning YC** ☎ 754 (all welcome); Dr ☎ 389; Ⓗ ☎ 706; **Jetty** FW, P, D; **BY** C (5 ton), D, FW, Slip; **Hamkens** Gaz; **Town** Bar, ⑧,Ⓗ (☎ 706), ✉, R, ⇌, V.

HUSUM, Schleswig Holstein, 54°29′ N, 9°03′ E, Zone −0100. Admty chart 3767, German D105; 3013 Sheet 13. HW +0036 on Dover (GMT), +0205 on Helgoland (zone −0100), ML 1.9m; Duration 0555. See 10.20.21. Yachts can either anchor W of Rly bridge near YC on S bank or pass through bridge (clearance 5m when unopened) to Inner Harbour by SC Nordsee. Both dry. There is a sluice/lock 650m downstream from YC which is shut when level exceeds 0.3m over MHW. A R Lt is shown when closed. Beware the canal effect when passing big ships in the narrows. VHF call *Husum Port* on Ch 11. Traffic reports on Ch 11 every H +00 from HW −4 to ... 2, Outer Ldg Lts 106° both Iso R 8s, synchronised ... Lts 090° both Iso G ... Facilities: ..., in harbour. ... ☎ 65670; ...

[lower-left corner of page obscured/damaged — partial text]
... ost of ... s the YC ...orumersiel ... E, Zone −0100, ... +0055 on Dover ...100). S of ...adebusen, which ...Dangaster Aussentief ...tief, marked on ...h Stenkentief, other than Arngast ...sen, no lights on W side just ...Tief, access HW +2. Facilities: ...cilities can be found in the ...ast.
... −0100. Admty ... 7. HW ...nd (zone ...).22. Wittdün ...h on yacht ...oon, stern to ... quay 800m to ...s 2m. Ldg Lts ...stripe; intens ...4s 33m 15M ...is not advisable ...rked by withies ...own LFl(2) WR ...W343°-014°, ...294; ⌗ ☎ 2026, ...mrum YC

20

SCHLÜTTSIEL, Schleswig Holstein, 54°41′ N, 8°45′ E; Zone −0100. Admty charts 3760, 3767; German D107; 3013 sheets 7, 9. HW +0156 on Dover (GMT), +0026 on Helgoland (zone −0100). Approach between Langeness/Oland and Gröde-Appelland. Channel 2-3m deep, harbour 2m. Turn into harbour at buoy SCHL 20, proceed between groynes 300m long, ends marked by S and N cardinal beacons. Small harbour mainly used by ferries with no special places for yachts. Moor alongside north walls of the quay. In W winds a swell runs into the harbour. Beware warps across harbour from local boats. There are no lights. Facilities: there are very few facilities. Hr Mr ☎ 3301. **Dagebüll YC** ☎ 1463.

WYK, Island of Föhr, 54°42′ N, 8°35′ E, Zone −0100. Admty chart 3767, German D107; 3013 sheet 7. HW +0107 on Dover (GMT), +0137 on Helgoland (zone −0100); ML 2.8. Good yacht harbour to N of entrance, sheltered in all winds, or yachts can berth on E quay of Old Harbour. Yacht harbour (1.5m) Visitors go to seaward side of Pontoon 1. Access H24; Commercial harbour (4m). Lights − Oldenhorn (SE point of Föhr), R tower, Oc(4) WRG 15s 10m 13/9M; W208°-250°, R250°-281°, W281°-290°, G290°-333°, W333°-058°, R058°-080°. S mole head Oc(2) WR 12s 12m 7/4M; W220°-322°, R322°-220°. Facilities: (04681) Yacht harbour Hr Mr ☎ 3030; Commercial Hr Mr ☎ 2852; **YC** ☎ 1280; Dr ☎ 8998; ⌗ ☎ 2594; **Harbour road** (500m), CH, ⊡, P and D (cans); **Yacht Harbour** R, V. **W Quay** D.

DAGEBÜLL, Schleswig Holstein, 54°44′ N, 8°42′ E, Zone −0100. Admty chart 3767; German D107; 3013 Sheet 7. HW +0211 on Dover (GMT), +0026 on Helgoland (zone −0100) ML 2.9m. Small harbour mainly for ferries; there are no special yacht berths. Yachts berth on outer side of N mole. Iso WRG 8s 23m 18/15M; G042°-043°, W043°-044.5°, R044.5°-047° on G mast. Keep in W sector up to 1.3M from harbour. Ldg Lts 053°, Front Iso R 4s 7m 9M; R mast, W bands; vis 346°-121°. Rear, 50m from front, Iso R 4s 10m 9M; R mast, W bands; synchronised. FW Lts on N and S moles. Depth in basin 2.8m. Facilities: Hr Mr ☎ 233; Slip ☎ 209; **Village** R, V, P and D (cans); ⇌.

TIDAL INFORMATION FOR WEST COAST OF DENMARK   10-20-24

The following figures are average values and so are approximate and should be used with caution
Standard Port HELGOLAND (←)

Times				Height (metres)			
HW		LW		MHWS	MHWN	MLWN	MLWS
0300	0700	0100	0800	2.7	2.3	0.4	0.0
1500	1900	1300	2000				
Differences HOJER SLUICE							
+0247	+0322	No data		−0.3	−0.2	0.0	0.0
ROMO HAVN							
+0227	+0302	+0221	+0201	−0.8	−0.7	−0.1	0.0
GRADYB BAR							
+0137	+0152	No data		−1.2	−1.1	−0.1	0.0
ESBJERG							
+0307	+0307	+0221	+0221	−1.1	−0.9	−0.2	−0.1
BLAAVANDS HUK							
+0147	+0157	+0131	+0121	−0.9	−0.9	−0.1	0.0
TORSMINDE							
+0337	+0357	+0301	+0231	−1.8	−1.6	−0.3	0.0
THYBORON							
+0427	+0537	+0631	+0431	−2.3	−2.0	−0.3	0.0
HANSTHOLM							
+0407	+0647	+0601	+0351	−2.4	−2.0	−0.3	0.0
HIRTSHALS							
+0402	+0627	+0601	+0321	−2.4	−2.0	−0.3	0.0

Advertisers' Index

Enquiries about advertising in this book should be addressed to:

Communications Management International
Chiltern House
120 Eskdale Avenue
Chesham
Bucks
HP5 3BD

Late corrections

(up to and including Admiralty
Notices to Mariners, Weekly Edition No. 17/90).

Important navigational information in the body of the
Almanac is corrected up to Weekly Edition No.15/1990 of
Admiralty Notices to Mariners. For ease of reference each
correction is sequentially numbered, and the page number
is also given.

Chapter 4 - Radio Navigation Aids

1.41   RADIOBEACONS.
            No. A18 **Bournemouth/Hurn**. Frequency.
            DELETE: 394 kHz
            INSERT: 401·5 kHz.

2.41   RADIOBEACONS.
            No. A26 **Bembridge**. Frequency.
            DELETE: 276·5 kHz.
            INSERT: 274·5 kHz.

3.44   RADIOBEACONS.
            No. A54 **Ottringham**. Frequency.
            DELETE: 335 kHz.
            INSERT: 398·5 kHz.

4.64   RADAR BEACONS.
            No. 59 **Spurn Lt F**. Form of flash.
            DELETE: **S.**
            INSERT: **M.**

Chapter 10 - Harbour, Coastal & Tidal Information

Area 1 - South-West England

5.206   PLYMOUTH .
            CHARTLET.
            Inset, Drakes Island.
            DELETE: Radio Mast and R Lt.

Area 2 - Central Southern England

6..228   LIGHTS, FOG SIGNALS & WAYPOINTS.
            LH column.
            LYME REGIS.
            AMEND TO READ:
            Ldg Lts 296°. Front, at <u>inner pier head</u>
            50°43'·16N 02°56'·10W Oc WR 8s 6m W9M,
            R7M. Rear, 1·25ca from front, FG 8m 9M;
            both vis W106°-296°, R296°-106°.

Area 5 - North-East England

7.355   LIGHTS, FOG SIGNALS & WAYPOINTS.
            RH column.
            FARNE ISLANDS.
            DELETE: **29M.**
            INSERT: **24M.**

8.374   AMBLE
            RADIO TELEPHONE.
            DELETE: Ch 16 14.
            INSERT: Ch 16; 14.

Area 9 - South-West Scotland

9.465   LIGHTS, FOG SIGNALS & WAYPOINTS.
            RH column.
            GREAT CUMBRA.
            AMEND TO READ: GREAT CUMBRAE.

Area 10 - North-West England, Isle of Man and North Wales

10.495   WORKINGTON.
            RADIO TELEPHONE.
            VHF.
            AMEND TO READ: Ch 16; 11 14.

Area 11 - South Wales and Bristol Channel

11.514   AREA CHART.
            Barmouth block. Port Radio.
            DELETE: Ch 16; 12.
            INSERT: Ch **12** 16; 12.

12.524   PORTHMADOG.
            RADIO TELEPHONE.
            AMEND TO READ: Ch 16; 12 14 (0900-1700 LT).

Area 12 - South Ireland

13.553   LIGHTS, FOG SIGNALS & WAYPOINTS.
            WATERFORD.
            RH column,.
            Duncannon Ldg Lts 002°.
            DELETE: Present entry.
            INSERT: **Duncannon** Dir Lt 357°. Dir Oc WRG 4s'
            G8M, W11M, R8M; vis G353°-356·7°, W356·7°-
            357·2°, R357·2°-001°. Auxuliary Lt on same Tr,
            Oc WR 4s 13m 9/7M; vis R119°-149°, W149°-
            172°

Area 15 - South Brittany

14.647   LIGHTS, FOG SIGNALS & WAYPOINTS.
            LORIENT.
            RH column, lines 23 to 25 inc.
            DELETE: Present entry for Passe de la Citadelle
            Ldg Lts.
            INSERT: Île Saint-Michel, Passe de la Citadelle
            Ldg Lts 016°30'. **Front** Dir Oc(3)G 12 s 8m **16M**;
            W Tr. G top; intens 014·5°-017·5°;
            Rear, Dir Oc(3)G 12s 14m **16M**; W Tr, G top;
            syncronised with front; intens 014·5°-017·5°.
            Kerneval Ldg Lts 217°.
            AMEND TO READ: Kernevel Ldg Lts 217°. Front
            47°43'·08N 03°22'·23W Dir QR 10m 14M; R

square on R & W framework Tr; intens 215°-
219°. Rear, 290m from front, Dir QR 18m 14M;
W square, R top; syncronised with front; intens
215°-219°.

15.653   RIVER LOIRE/ST NAZAIRE.
          SHELTER.
          Line 4.
          DELETE: S end.
          INSERT: NE.

16.653   RIVER LOIRE/ST NAZAIRE.
          TELEPHONE.
          Hr Mr. **DELETE:** ☎ 40.22.08.46.
          INSERT: ☎ 40.00.45.20.

17.659   LORIENT.
          CHARTLET.
          Kernével Ldg Lts 217°. **AMEND TO READ:** Kernéval
          Ldg Lts 217°. Front, Dir QR 10m 14M. Rear,
          290m from front, Dir QR 18m 14M.

18.659   LORIENT.
          LIGHTS & MARKS.
          Item (6).
          AMEND TO READ: Kernével Ldg Lts 217°. Front, Dir
          QR 10m 14M; R square on R & W Tr; intens 215°-
          219°. Rear, 290m from front, Dir QR 18m 14M;
          W square, R top; syncronised with front; intens
          215°-219°.

Area 18 - North-East France

19.732   LIGHTS, FOG SIGNALS & WAYPOINTS.
          DUNQUERQUE LANBY
          DELETE: **25M.**
          INSERT: **20M.**

Area 20 - Federal Republic of Germany

20.803   LIGHTS, FOG SIGNALS & WAYPOINTS.
          RH column.
          DANGEST.
          AMEND TO READ: DANGAST.

Index

Explanation

Significant place names are shown in **bold** type without the definite article.

Abbreviations are entered under the full word and not the abbreviation.
For example, St Abb's comes under Saint and not St.

Page numbers in **bold** type indicate harbour and tidal information.

Page numbers in *italics* indicate tidal information only.

The prefix C before a page number indicates a Coast Radio Station.

The prefix L before a page number indicates an entry in the lists of Lights, Fog Signals and Waypoints.

The prefix R before a page number indicates a Radio Navigational Aid.

K

N

O

P

Q

R

W

Y

Z